2016

JANUARY
M	T	W	T	F	S	S
				1	2	3
4	5	6	7	8	9	10
11	12	13	14	15	16	17
18	19	20	21	22	23	24
25	26	27	28	29	30	31

FEBRUARY
M	T	W	T	F	S	S
1	2	3	4	5	6	7
8	9	10	11	12	13	14
15	16	17	18	19	20	21
22	23	24	25	26	27	28
29						

MARCH
M	T	W	T	F	S	S
	1	2	3	4	5	6
7	8	9	10	11	12	13
14	15	16	17	18	19	20
21	22	23	24	25	26	27
28	29	30	31			

APRIL
M	T	W	T	F	S	S
				1	2	3
4	5	6	7	8	9	10
11	12	13	14	15	16	17
18	19	20	21	22	23	24
25	26	27	28	29	30	

MAY
M	T	W	T	F	S	S
						1
2	3	4	5	6	7	8
9	10	11	12	13	14	15
16	17	18	19	20	21	22
23	24	25	26	27	28	29
30	31					

JUNE
M	T	W	T	F	S	S
		1	2	3	4	5
6	7	8	9	10	11	12
13	14	15	16	17	18	19
20	21	22	23	24	25	26
27	28	29	30			

JULY
M	T	W	T	F	S	S
				1	2	3
4	5	6	7	8	9	10
11	12	13	14	15	16	17
18	19	20	21	22	23	24
25	26	27	28	29	30	31

AUGUST
M	T	W	T	F	S	S
1	2	3	4	5	6	7
8	9	10	11	12	13	14
15	16	17	18	19	20	21
22	23	24	25	26	27	28
29	30	31				

SEPTEMBER
M	T	W	T	F	S	S
			1	2	3	4
5	6	7	8	9	10	11
12	13	14	15	16	17	18
19	20	21	22	23	24	25
26	27	28	29	30		

OCTOBER
M	T	W	T	F	S	S
					1	2
3	4	5	6	7	8	9
10	11	12	13	14	15	16
17	18	19	20	21	22	23
24	25	26	27	28	29	30
31						

NOVEMBER
M	T	W	T	F	S	S
	1	2	3	4	5	6
7	8	9	10	11	12	13
14	15	16	17	18	19	20
21	22	23	24	25	26	27
28	29	30				

DECEMBER
M	T	W	T	F	S	S
			1	2	3	4
5	6	7	8	9	10	11
12	13	14	15	16	17	18
19	20	21	22	23	24	25
26	27	28	29	30	31	

2017

JANUARY
M	T	W	T	F	S	S
						1
2	3	4	5	6	7	8
9	10	11	12	13	14	15
16	17	18	19	20	21	22
23	24	25	26	27	28	29
30	31					

FEBRUARY
M	T	W	T	F	S	S
		1	2	3	4	5
6	7	8	9	10	11	12
13	14	15	16	17	18	19
20	21	22	23	24	25	26
27	28					

MARCH
M	T	W	T	F	S	S
		1	2	3	4	5
6	7	8	9	10	11	12
13	14	15	16	17	18	19
20	21	22	23	24	25	26
27	28	29	30	31		

APRIL
M	T	W	T	F	S	S
					1	2
3	4	5	6	7	8	9
10	11	12	13	14	15	16
17	18	19	20	21	22	23
24	25	26	27	28	29	30

MAY
M	T	W	T	F	S	S
1	2	3	4	5	6	7
8	9	10	11	12	13	14
15	16	17	18	19	20	21
22	23	24	25	26	27	28
29	30	31				

JUNE
M	T	W	T	F	S	S
			1	2	3	4
5	6	7	8	9	10	11
12	13	14	15	16	17	18
19	20	21	22	23	24	25
26	27	28	29	30		

JULY
M	T	W	T	F	S	S
					1	2
3	4	5	6	7	8	9
10	11	12	13	14	15	16
17	18	19	20	21	22	23
24	25	26	27	28	29	30
31						

AUGUST
M	T	W	T	F	S	S
	1	2	3	4	5	6
7	8	9	10	11	12	13
14	15	16	17	18	19	20
21	22	23	24	25	26	27
28	29	30	31			

SEPTEMBER
M	T	W	T	F	S	S
				1	2	3
4	5	6	7	8	9	10
11	12	13	14	15	16	17
18	19	20	21	22	23	24
25	26	27	28	29	30	

OCTOBER
M	T	W	T	F	S	S
						1
2	3	4	5	6	7	8
9	10	11	12	13	14	15
16	17	18	19	20	21	22
23	24	25	26	27	28	29
30	31					

NOVEMBER
M	T	W	T	F	S	S
		1	2	3	4	5
6	7	8	9	10	11	12
13	14	15	16	17	18	19
20	21	22	23	24	25	26
27	28	29	30			

DECEMBER
M	T	W	T	F	S	S
				1	2	3
4	5	6	7	8	9	10
11	12	13	14	15	16	17
18	19	20	21	22	23	24
25	26	27	28	29	30	31

Court of Protection Practice 2016

Court of Protection Practice 2016

Published by Jordan Publishing, owned by LexisNexis
Regus Castlemead
Terrace Floor
Lower Castle Street
Bristol BS1 3AG

© Jordan Publishing 2016

All rights reserved. No part of this publication may be reproduced, stored in a retrieval system, or transmitted in any way or by any means, including photocopying or recording, without the written permission of the copyright holder, application for which should be addressed to the publisher.

British Library Cataloguing-in-Publication Data
A catalogue record for this book is available from the British Library.

ISSN 2040 2627

ISBN 978 1 78473 192 2

Whilst the publishers and the authors have taken every care in preparing the material included in this work, any statements made as to the legal or other implications of particular transactions are made in good faith purely for general guidance and cannot be regarded as a substitute for professional advice. Consequently, no liability can be accepted for loss or expense incurred as a result of relying in particular circumstances on statements made in this work.

Crown Copyright material is reproduced with kind permission of the Controller of Her Majesty's Stationery Office.

The kind permission of The Law Society to reproduce the Practice Notes of 8 December 2011: *Lasting Powers of Attorney* (© The Law Society 2011), 13 June 2013: *Financial Abuse* (© The Law Society 2013), 17 March 2014: *Mental Capacity: International Aspects* (© The Law Society 2014) and 2 July 2015: *Meeting the needs of vulnerable clients* (© The Law Society 2015) is also gratefully acknowledged.

This volume is typeset by Letterpart Ltd, Caterham on the Hill, Surrey CR3 5XL

PUBLISHER: Greg Woodgate LLB, LLM, Barrister

MAJOR WORKS MANAGER: Jonathan Cailes BA (Hons)

LEGAL EDITOR: Juliet Smith BA (Hons) Law

The Index is researched and compiled by Kim Harris

Printed in Great Britain by CPI William Clowes Ltd, Beccles, NR34 7TL

GENERAL EDITOR AND CONTRIBUTOR
Gordon R Ashton OBE
Retired District Judge and Nominated Judge of the Court of Protection

CONTRIBUTORS
District Judge Marc Marin
*Nominated Judge of the Court of Protection
The Family Court and the County Court at Barnet and First Avenue House*

Claire van Overdijk
*Barrister, No 5 Chambers
LLM teaching fellow, Faculty of Laws, University College London*

Alex Ruck Keene
*Barrister, 39 Essex Chambers
Honorary Research Lecturer at the University of Manchester
Visiting Research Fellow at the Dickson Poon School of Law, Kings College London*

Martin Terrell
Partner, Thomson Snell & Passmore

INTERNATIONAL CONTRIBUTORS
Richard Frimston
Partner, Russell-Cooke LLP

Adrian D Ward MBE
Consultant, TC Young LLP, Scotland

CASE SUMMARIES EDITOR
Annabel Lee
Barrister, 39 Essex Chambers

PAST CONTRIBUTORS
Penny Letts OBE
Policy Consultant, Editor of Elder Law Journal

Laurence Oates
Official Solicitor to the Supreme Court 1999–2006

Foreword by Sir James Munby, President of the Court of Protection

Court of Protection Practice goes from strength to strength, having worthily achieved in relation to the Court of Protection the same dominating position as its stable mate, *The Family Court Practice*, in relation to the Family Court.

In his Foreword to the First Edition, Sir Mark Potter P predicted that it would become an essential volume for those who work in or appear before the Court of Protection. He was of course correct, for *Court of Protection Practice* has indeed become essential for every judge and practitioner in the Court of Protection.

It was in Sir Mark's time as President that Charles J and Proudman J produced a report on the Court of Protection which, welcomed by everyone involved with the Court, spent far too long gathering dust. Now at last things are happening. An ad hoc Court of Protection Rules Committee, chaired by Charles J, the Vice President of the Court of Protection, is at work, with visible results.

2014 was dominated not just by the long-awaited decision of the Supreme Court in the *Cheshire West* case but also by the need to grapple with the procedural implications of that decision for the Court of Protection. The new 'streamlined' process for dealing with deprivation of liberty cases is now up and running, facilitated by the welcome recruitment from the Tribunals judiciary of additional judicial assistance for such cases.

2015 will, no doubt, see further change directed to improving the procedures of the Court of Protection. The ad hoc Court of Protection Rules Committee has much to do and is working as fast as possible.

For too long now, justified criticisms have been building up about the way in which the Court of Protection manages cases involving personal welfare, in particular in the heavier cases. Two things need to be done.

The first, long recommended by Charles J, is the regionalisation of such work, so that cases can be heard more locally, more quickly and, unless the case requires to be heard by a judge of the High Court, by the local judge best suited for the particular case.

The second is what has emerged as the pressing need to adopt in the Court of Protection in cases involving personal welfare the techniques which have proved so successful in the Family Court in cases involving children: the allocation of the case, wherever possible, to a single judge; and the robust and vigorous case management of the case by that judge in accordance with a timetable fixed by the judge at the outset and, in the light of the issues identified by the judge at a case management hearing, listed within days of the proceedings commencing. At the same time, and again in the same kind of way as has proved so successful in the Family Court, ways must be found to control the over-ready recourse to over-detailed and on occasions unduly prolix expert evidence. The effects in the Family Court have been striking, not least the astonishing reductions in the times such cases take before reaching finality. The same, I have no doubt, must and can be achieved in the Court of Protection.

All these ongoing developments have been expertly captured in the 2015 *Court of Protection Practice* as they will be, I am sure, in the future annual editions of this invaluable work.

Sir James Munby
President of the Court of Protection
January 2015

Foreword to the First Edition

Practitioners in the Court of Protection will be familiar both with the previous work of the authors, *Mental Capacity: The New Law*, and with the reputation of the authors as expert and experienced practitioners themselves.

The authors have developed their previous book into this practice volume with the objective of providing all who work in the Court of Protection with easily accessible guidance to the principles, law and practice to be followed when considering how to proceed in mental capacity cases.

The resulting *Court of Protection Practice* usefully brings together statutory materials and key forms, and case-law supporting practice and procedures in the Court of Protection, together with authoritative comment from the authors. It is laid out in a logical manner, easy to follow, and will be invaluable both to those who are already familiar with mental capacity work and those who are new to this area of the law.

The law is stated as at 1 February 2009, but the authors have also included a helpful chapter on the Deprivation of Liberty Safeguarding provisions which will come into effect in April 2009. It is likely that the law governing Mental Capacity issues will continue to develop apace; I therefore welcome the authors' intention to update at regular intervals what will surely prove to be an essential volume for those who work in or appear before the Court of Protection.

Mark Potter.

Sir Mark Potter
President of the Family Division and of the Court of Protection
December 2008

Foreword to the First Edition

Familiarisation Jurisdiction of Protection will be familiar both with the previous work of the authors, Newton Coombes, Day, Kew, and with the reputation of the authors as expert and experienced practitioners themselves.

The authors have developed their previous book into this practice volume with the objective of providing all who work in the Court of Protection with, as far as possible, guidance to the principles, law and procedure to be followed when continuing how to proceed in mental capacity cases.

The resulting Court of Protection Practice usefully brings together statutory materials and case law focus and case law supporting practice and procedure in the Court of Protection, together with authoritative comment from the authors. It is laid out in a logical manner, easy to follow, and will be invaluable both to those who are already familiar with mental capacity work and those who are new to this area of the law.

The law issued as at February 2009, but the authors have also included a helpful chapter on the Deprivation of Liberty Safeguarding provisions which will come into effect in April 2009. It is likely that the law governing Mental Capacity issues will continue to develop apace. Updates are welcome, the authors' intention to update regularly means that what will surely prove to be an essential volume for those who work in or appear before the Court of Protection.

Sir Mark Potter
President of the Family Division and of the Court of Protection
December 2008

Preface to the First Edition

Some 20 years ago the Law Society's Mental Health Sub-Committee drew attention to the legal vacuum in which people who lacked mental capacity were obliged to exist. This provoked the Law Commission to take the topic on board and, after several years of consultation, recommendations were made for a statutory mental incapacity jurisdiction. Different governments then pursued further consultation whilst lacking the will to introduce legislation, but pressures to do so became overwhelming with the introduction of community care policies, disability discrimination laws and ultimately human rights legislation. The Mental Capacity Act 2005 is the result, but a consequence of the changed climate is that it must meet higher standards than were expected when the need was first identified.

In addition to making provision for delegated decision-making and setting out the principles to be applied for assessment of capacity and a best interests approach, the Act establishes a new Court of Protection, with nominated judges and a regional presence. As a contributor on disability issues to Jordans' *The Family Court Practice* (the 'Red Book') and *Civil Court Service* (the 'Brown Book'), I perceived the need for a similar volume for those who practice in the new Court of Protection. So with the small team of 'experts' who wrote *Mental Capacity: The New Law*[1] as an introduction to this legislation, and joined by District Judge Marc Marin who sits in the Court of Protection at Archway, we have launched this further volume with the support of Jordans. In addition to the updated chapters from our previous work, it contains the Act, Regulations, Court Rules and Practice Directions (with our annotations where appropriate), together with the Code of Practice, Lasting Power of Attorney and Court Forms and some Procedural Guides. We hope that the *Court of Protection Practice 2009* will assist in the development and growth of this new jurisdiction and provide in a single handy volume all that those who work in or appear before the Court routinely need to accomplish their roles.

I wish to thank my co-authors for their dedicated contributions, each being highly experienced in the topics that they have covered. We have endeavoured to state the law as at 1 February 2009 whilst anticipating prospective changes coming into effect in April 2009. But this is an evolving area with new Lasting Power of Attorney forms, changes to the supervisory regime and a review of the working of the Rules all expected in 2009. It is hoped that, once this work is established, it will be updated at intervals so as to remain a reliable practice book, perhaps also identified by its colour!

Gordon R Ashton
Grange-over-Sands
December 2008

---

[1] G Ashton, P Letts, L Oates and M Terrell *Mental Capacity: The New Law*, New Law Series (Jordans, 2006).

Where we are now

First, I want to bang the drum I nearly always bang when I'm speaking about the Court of Protection and it is this: that one of the guiding principles looked at by the Rules Committee is that it is very important that the Court of Protection's tail does not wag the Court of Protection's dog. The tail is its contested jurisdiction. The dog is the uncontested property and affairs jurisdiction. It's the former, i e the contested jurisdiction, that attracts nearly all the attention in the public domain, but in terms of applications issued that is but a small part of the work of the Court of Protection. In broad terms, about 95% of the applications issued relate to property and affairs. About 93% of the property and affairs applications are truly non-contested and essential applications. Since its inception in 2007, the number of applications issued in the Court of Protection has increased year on year. It now receives 25,000, so if you can do your mental arithmetic we're talking in terms of about 22,000 uncontested property and affairs applications. The demographic of the population is likely to found continuing increases in this core and very important work.

The decision in *Cheshire West* has given rise to the prospect that the dog will get much bigger, or it now has a puppy which will now get much bigger. That is because there is a very significant number of non-contested applications to authorise a deprivation of liberty for somebody in supported living.

Regionalisation

At last I can say that this has started; for the past 3 years I have expressed the hope it will start soon. Fortunately I no longer have to repeat that hope.

The role of the lead judge in each region gives, to my mind, an excellent flavour of what it is hoped will be achieved from regionalisation. It is a staged process and this is important, a key to its success is the number of judge days that the Court of Protection will get for the year April 2016–17. So, key points concern budgets, allocation and funding and therefore the gathering of the information that the civil service require to make an effective bid for them. So I urge you to assist as far as you can in getting the required 'evidence base' for the relevant negotiations and decisions.

What has started is that the welfare work which is still being issued in London is being allocated and sent out to the regions essentially by postcode. It is going out electronically to the relevant region. The regions essentially replicate the old circuits and there is a hub in each region where the administration is based. We hope to be able at the same time to continue sending out property and affairs hearings as has been happening over the past 4 or 5 years.

The next proposed step is to send out more property and affairs applications to the regions, again on the basis of allocation, so rather than those in First Avenue House putting a file on the shelf for a district judge at that venue, they will put it on the computer for a judge in Liverpool or wherever it may be. That of course will not apply to the vast majority of those cases that are the uncontested ones, many of which are done by the nominated officers at the Court of Protection at First Avenue House.

To give you a flavour of what is hoped for and what is intended by regionalisation, I will give you some snippets from the description of the role of the lead judge in each region. He will be responsible for Court of Protection work in all the courts in that region but may be based at one main court. Importantly, it has now been recognised by HMCTS that that judge must have appropriate and adequate administrative support. Each hub now has what is thought to be an appropriate number of administrators. There will be delegation in all or many regions probably to a district judge who is experienced in Court of Protection work to act as the relevant gatekeeper. The lead judge will be responsible for making arrangements for the flexible transfer of judges between civil, family and Court of Protection work in their region. That is going to be one of the vital pieces of work.

So, hopefully, there will now be three participants in the bidding process for judge and court time – namely civil, family and Court of Protection rather than just the first two with the Court of Protection negotiating time on an ad hoc basis.

The lead judge will have to determine listing practices in accordance with the directions and guidance of the President and the Vice President. The lead judge will have to ensure that cases and applications of particular importance or sensitivity are heard by a judge who is specifically assigned to that case, ie once the judge gets it, the judge keeps it from beginning to end and gives appropriate case management. The lead judges are expected to hold regular meetings with the Operations Manager and the Delivery Manager under arrangements agreed with HMCTS; they are to agree deployment and sitting days, they are to chair user groups and they are to ensure effective arrangements are in place for the transfer of work between a regional hub and a local hearing venue.

The gatekeeper will allocate the work to a judge in the region based on the complexity and urgency of the case.

It is my hope that those roles of the lead judge and gatekeeper, together with administrative support and support of the relevant local judges, will make the Court of Protection more readily accessible throughout England and Wales. That is the core and important aim of regionalisation.

On a personal note, and far less important, I hope it proves that my predictive evidence before the House of Commons – that regionalisation is important and will work – was right!

The Ad Hoc Rules Committee

The Court of Protection does not have a standing Rules Committee, unlike the CPR and the FPR. This has advantages and of course it also has some disadvantages. It is important, I think, to remember and recognise that the Ad Hoc Rules Committee holds its deliberations in a public forum. So its minutes, such as they are, should be accessible to the public. Hence both its decisions as they go along and its recommendations are public documents. Whether you can find them or not, I have no idea but that is the underlying position.

The approach decided upon was to work in two tranches.

The timing of the first tranche was driven by the need to have appropriate appeal provisions in place to address the much wider pool of judges who can now sit in the Court of Protection. That amendment was introduced in an enormous rush into the Crime and Courts Act 2013. It is probably a good thing that this happened because if we had spotted at the time that we needed to have complicated provisions about appeals, the increased pool may well not have been provided. Those appeal changes have now been made. For the moment, I leave Rule 3A to one side and also piloting. But for example there is a change to Rule 4, which places duties on the parties in express terms to cooperate. In some cases, that may be wishful thinking, but we are not completely naïve and so we have also included a potential sanction in costs if they don't cooperate. Whether we will ever be able to enforce that, of course, is a different matter altogether but it is there.

The new rules will be addressing how else the Court can control behaviour in conducting proceedings and in the courtroom and there will be, or is planned to be, some further provision about civil restraint orders and possibly timing of how long somebody is allowed to give evidence/submissions etc. Also, importantly, by virtue of Rule 5, there is a duty placed on the Court to consider whether there should be a public hearing in every case and to consider what documents should be made public.

The earlier Ad Hoc Rules Committee, I think about 4 years before the last one, recommended the removal of the need for separate applications for permission; that is provided for in the new Rules. The need for permission in deprivation of liberty cases is removed. There have been changes to Part 13, which deals with what parties and others can tell people about the proceedings, ie the production of documents to other people such as an MP or researchers etc. There is also a freestanding provision that the Court can also make such disclosures. That is of course linked to the fact that the 'default position' in the Rules is that hearings are in private and the point that sadly, in my view anyway, the Court of Protection has generally proceeded on the basis that that default rule is to apply. Those of you who have appeared in my court will know that is not necessarily what you can expect to happen there. *Re NRA* for example was heard in public. I think I can say that generally my judgments have been public documents.

There are changes to the cost rules to make it clear that 'Jackson' does not apply in the Court of Protection.

The method of working of the Ad Hoc Committee has been to have a small drafting sub-committee or committees which met every Friday afternoon in my room. Sometimes, I provided the chocolate biscuits and sometimes they brought their own. By and large, that was very effective and I have to say that without the assistance of those volunteers this would not have been the case. The amount of time that they have spent working for the Committee has been extraordinary, exceptional and very helpful. Without that help, what has happened would not have happened.

Also, absent the support from the department, it would not have happened, because you do need your drafting lawyers. This was the problem with the first go at trying to get the Rules changed. At my request, I think, a departmental lawyer attended all of the meetings with a view that they would understand what they were meant to go away and draft. However, when the recommendations were sent, the departmental lawyer to put the recommendations into effect was no longer available. Everybody understands that there are problems with resources; we have been fortunate over the past year that we have had the support of a committed and expert departmental resource. It is a bridge too far to expect voluntary volunteers, or compulsory volunteers, ie judges, to sit down and draft rules.

Another important point in the first tranche of Rules is the introduction of the ability to pilot changes. It is intended that the second tranche will address issues that do, or may, require consultation or that can be piloted. It is hoped that the piloting will include (and indeed a recommendation by the Ad Hoc Committee has been made that it should include) public/private hearings and case management issues.

It is also likely that there will be a review of the default cost provisions in the Court of Protection. Whether that goes out to consultation or is piloted, time will tell.

So that is really where we are in the Ad Hoc Rules Committee. My understanding is that the relevant backup resources are there until the end of this financial year, so the hope is to get as much done as we can before then. We will also do what we can to get a fair share of the available resources for future periods.

Case management

Judge Marin has done an enormous amount of work on this for the Ad Hoc Rules Committee. He has been working with others in putting together a pilot on case management. I do not want to go into the details of it now but it has the approval of the full Ad Hoc Committee, not in terms of its detail but in terms of its general direction. It will come as no surprise to anybody who has read some of my judgments that I strongly support an underlying direction of travel which seeks to ensure that the parties identify the issues and that the parties recognise that they are involved in litigation and not in a best interests meeting and that, by the time you get to a court, a process of supporting P to make the relevant decision has been tried and failed. To my mind, this identifies an important part of the changes that are necessary in the culture and approach of many people who practise in the Court of Protection. And this is the key to making many of the improvements to which the case management pilot will be directed. I repeat, because it seems to me it needs repeating as often as possible, that when you are in a court, whether it be an inquisitorial court or an adversarial court, there is a need to identify the issues of fact and law that have to be addressed and resolved. It needs to be remembered and recognised that the Court of Protection makes its best interests decision on an evidential base. I had a go at trying to promote this in the old Practice Direction 13B. Sadly, that part of the Practice Direction is persistently not complied with. The proposed solution, unsurprisingly, will include better and more consistent case management which is aimed at eradicating such non-compliance. There is also in train management proposals to transfer a number of the cases that have previously been heard by High Court judges to other judges. Effective regionalisation will naturally be an important factor in bringing the planned improvements into effect. Without it there will simply not be the judicial resource to implement them.

Participation and representation of P

As I have said, in the NRA case and in an article in *Elder Law Journal*, and as it seems to me is obvious, the appropriate participation of P and the Court of Protection being properly informed about P are vital issues. They give rise to legal, welfare, financial resource and pragmatic issues. How they have been addressed, are being addressed and will be addressed is of essential importance to the Court of Protection and more importantly to the persons affected by the decisions made by the Court of Protection. Their resolution presents considerable difficulties. To my mind, it is important in this context to remember that by definition the Court of Protection simply does not have jurisdiction to make the relevant decision for P unless P does not have the capacity to do so him or herself with the appropriate support. So it follows that you have to bear that jurisdictional point in mind when you are working out what participation P should have in the proceedings.

To my mind, it also follows from that jurisdictional point that when you are making such a decision as a judge in the Court of Protection or indeed it seems to me when anyone is making a decision in reliance on the Mental Capacity Act and in particular Section 5, you should remember and recognise that you are making a decision for P, you are not supporting P to make the decision him or herself. Of course, that does not mean that P's wishes and feelings past and present are not relevant factors to be taken into account. Those feelings will have an important effect on which of the choices available you should select. For example, if P is making frequent and determined protests against being in a particular place that may well be a factor in favour of not placing P there because it simply won't work.

The weight you should give to the present feelings as opposed to the past wishes and feelings seems to me to be a value judgment. This of course brings into play what you have been told about the UN Convention on the Rights of People with Disabilities. It is discussed for example in the Law Commission Paper at paragraph 3.17 and onwards. I confess that I have not researched the views of the Commission very carefully on this but I remain puzzled as to how any supported decision-making process can work if it does not include something to cover cases when the relevant person simply cannot make a supported decision.

Leaving that to one side, it also seems to me that over-participation of P can lead to inappropriate and harmful pressures or confusion being imposed on P. Whereas of course under-participation of P can result in dissatisfaction, difficulties in giving effect to the order and the relevant information not being provided to the court. One process simple does not fit all.

Sadly, leaving DoLS to one side, the present position is that all too often the Court of Protection is faced with having to deal with a case at its early stages without P being a party or anyone speaking on P's behalf, for example, on an urgent (and often, as you will know in the long run, decisive) application on whether P should move from home to a care home.

One of the other changes in the first tranche of the Rules was that if the Court decides that P should be a party, that that order does not take effect until there is a litigation friend or an accredited legal representative appointed. At the moment there is no such thing as an accredited legal representative so it is a litigation friend or nothing.

Streamlined, proportionate and accessible procedures

I do not want to say much about *Re NRA* because I have received the next batch of five test cases. But I am not giving away any secrets if I say that I am looking forward to hearing what either Liz Eaton as a deponent or somebody else as a deponent on behalf of the Secretary of State says about the resources that are going to be provided in respect of the provision of a Rule 3A representative for P. In tranche one there was no such evidence. I wonder and hope that there will be some evidence in tranche two. If there is not appropriate support for a P who does not have family support on my approach in *NRA* there are problems relating to compliance with Article 5 and perhaps in particular Article 5.4.

Support is also clearly necessary and envisaged under the Care Act. It is not clear to me quite how that will be provided on a day-to-day basis or how, if at all, it can be used at a later stage to assist in Court of Protection proceedings. Although the proposals by the Law Commission may be some way off or may never see the light of day, it is clear that under their first two proposals the need for support on the ground before you get to a court is vital to their success.

I have also recently been involved in a series of appeals from the Mental Health Tribunal in which I have identified that the tests applicable by the Mental Health Tribunal, particularly those relating to protection of the public, are not ones which can easily, or in my view at all, be exercised by the Court of Protection. So, if applying the Mental Health Act tests, the First-Tier Tribunal concludes that someone should be discharged from hospital to the least restrictive available option at which, applying *Cheshire West*, P will be deprived of his or her liberty (which is likely to be the case, for example, when somebody has been convicted of offences of a sexual nature and in a number of situations when people are being discharged from hospital to a placement chosen by a guardian), there needs to be an accessible backup process from the Court of Protection to render that placement lawful. Such a process needs to be streamlined.

Will the Court of Protection get the benefit of help from the representative that P may well have had before the First-Tier Tribunal? That is an open question.

The Law Commission paper identifies and seeks views on whether essentially authorisation of deprivation of liberty should be given by the Court of Protection or by a Tribunal. Some of you may think it appropriate to respond to the Law Commission paper on this topic. If you do, I am going to take this opportunity to invite you to consider the following points on the basis of an assumption that the regionalisation of the Court of Protection works.

First, when considering whether the decision-making body should be a court or a tribunal, you need to consider the availability of hearing rooms in supported living and other settings. And so, health and safety issues.

Next the difference in the tests and the type of disputes that they give rise to in cases presently heard, for example, by a mental health tribunal and the Court of Protection, need to be considered and they trigger the following questions: Can there be one-stop shopping for all of the issues and cases? If not, how many shops do you need? Do you need a Mental Health Act test shop and a different Mental Capacity Act test shop or do those behind the counter whether they are called tribunal judges or Court of Protection judges change their hat and say

'Now I'm a Mental Health Act decision-maker and now I'm a Mental Capacity Act decision-maker'. If you need more than one shop, how do you transfer between the two shops?

In nearly all deprivation of liberty cases, the best interests test is determinative in the Court of Protection. As you all know, the consideration of the relevant care regime and care packages can introduce factual disputes and issues about, for example, improper behaviour by the family over contact. When you take such issues into account, the weight of the argument that the Mental Health Act Tribunals provide a quick, ready and easy solution is far less persuasive. Equally, an approach taken regularly in the Mental Health Act Tribunal that it is obviously in the best interests of the relevant patient that the detention should be tested is less persuasive.

There may well be a need for injunctive orders in some Court of Protection/DoLS cases. Can tribunals be given this jurisdiction to make injunctive orders? If they can, can they also have a contempt jurisdiction?

In some Court of Protection cases there is a need to resort to an administrative law challenge to the choices that are said by a public authority to be available. A district judge has the disadvantage that he cannot tell a local authority to 'put up or shut up' on a public law question. I can, because I can say 'I am now sitting in the Queen's Bench Division – I treat a judicial review as being before me'.

So, should the relevant tribunals be given an administrative law jurisdiction? I suspect that many in Whitehall would not be keen on that.

What about the inherent jurisdiction? In some of the cases it may be a very fine line as to whether or not P has capacity or is vulnerable. Again, if you can easily transform the court to one which has an inherent jurisdiction you can sort that out.

Finally, who will sit in this new court/tribunal? Is there a need for a doctor or a lay person as is the case in a number of tribunals?

In this context, it might be Batemanesque for me to say that I don't hold any real brief on whether the cases should be before the Court of Protection or a Tribunal. But it seems to me that the necessary judicial resource, whether called a tribunal or a court, will effectively be the same. And the real issues are the ones that I have just highlighted, and generalised argument founded on assertions that tribunals are quick, local, informal and get everything done at the speed of light and everybody is happy are seriously flawed. First, those assertions are not entirely true but secondly and importantly they would not necessarily transfer and apply if the cases were heard by a tribunal. Also, generalised argument based on assertions that courts are slower, more formal, less local and less accessible, and nobody really understands what is going on in them are not entirely true. Indeed, it may be that some court processes are much better suited to dealing with the wider issues that fall to be decided in applying the best interests test.

So I urge that the relevant issues concerning the choice between a court and a tribunal should not be generalised and that the points I have just highlighted are important.

Public/private hearings

The Ad Hoc Committee has approved a pilot. It is no secret that for a long time both I and the President have been supporters of public hearings with relevant anonymity injunctions. There is an obvious overlap with family cases and the debate that rages there. Also, there a number of differences between the issues that arise in the two jurisdictions.

Also, to my mind anyway, the family solution of allowing the newspapers in or accredited members of the media in as 'a public watchdog' without giving them any guidance as to what they can say in public when they go out is not particularly helpful.

I think experience tells us that the media do not attend family cases as a 'public watchdog'. Rather, they attend if they think there is something which they would like to write about.

If and when public hearings in the Court of Protection become more common, I am stating the obvious when I say that in large measure their continuation will depend upon responsible reporting in and by national and local media and upon how the internet is used by others.

We are all aware of the use of the internet to put things in the public domain about proceedings held both in public and in private. We are also aware that quite often the information that is so put in the public domain is not accurate. My own experience is that when faced with somebody who comes in and says this court is like the Star Chamber, it is a secret court and I am going to the newspapers, a response to the effect: 'by all means, we will have the newspapers here or you can talk to them but you do realise that, as soon as they walk outside the door or report what you say, the allegations that are being made against you will or may also go into the public domain' has the result that the attack and the threat are not pursued.

A wish for a private hearing reflects a natural reluctance to have assertions or findings about your behaviour or personal life published. However, balanced and fair reporting is likely to promote the public interest by informing the public of what is done and why and by improving the approach of all involved in the proceedings.

The Honourable Mr Justice Charles
Vice President of the Court of Protection
(An edited version of a lecture given on 13 October 2015)

Introduction

Last year in this Introduction I identified four significant challenges facing our mental capacity jurisdiction. Two relate to compliance with international Conventions and the other two affect the credibility of our Court of Protection. I now comment on the longer-term implications of these challenges.

European Convention on Human Rights

The Court has interpreted this Convention as requiring that care arrangements which deprive individuals of their liberty need a system of authorisation prescribed by law. This has become an expensive distraction from the business of providing good quality care best suited to the needs of the individual. It has proved to be fertile ground for lawyers but damages the credibility of the mental capacity jurisdiction in the eyes of disabled people and their carers. There remains uncertainty and disagreement as to what amounts to a deprivation of liberty and the care environments in which it must be authorised. Resources that should be devoted to the delivery of care are being diverted into reassuring lawyers (and the public if they are concerned) that incapacitated individuals are not being unnecessarily detained against their wishes even though they may not be capable of forming wishes or exercising their liberty. Their right not to be deprived of liberty becomes more important in law than any rights they may have to be provided with care and support, and the rights of involuntary family carers are subjugated to the freedom of the person cared for notwithstanding that their own freedom is impaired by the responsibility of caring. It is not clear where this is leading but it is hoped that the Law Commission will soon produce a workable solution so that the jurisdiction may continue to make inroads into society without this impediment.

These challenges have highlighted the question of how incapacitated persons should participate in proceedings. Making them a party and appointing a litigation friend to represent them is the usual procedure, but the position of an incapacitated person subject to Court of Protection proceedings differs from that of other incapacitated parties and mirrors that of children in proceedings that concern their future. Who can impartially fulfil the role of litigation friend? There are generally enough parties involved and with an inquisitorial approach and appropriate reports it is sufficient in most cases to resolve matters without seeking to appoint someone to speak on behalf of the incapacitated person. My approach as a nominated judge was to see the incapacitated person whenever possible and surely this is consistent with the principles of the 2005 Act. When we were writing the Rules, I was not successful in having this approach supported but there are signs almost a decade later that it is beginning to find favour. Of course, guidance would be needed as to the purpose and form of any such meeting but that is part of the evolution of the Court.

UN Convention on the Rights of Persons with Disabilities

Our jurisdiction was groundbreaking when it was first enacted and few if any could find fault in it. With the benefit of experience since then, new approaches to decision-making are now being promoted, even to the extent that decisions should not be delegated. The movement towards supported decision-making surely only relates to the stages before the individual is deemed to lack capacity and is relevant to how that state should be determined. Support should have been attempted before concluding that this stage has been reached, but thereafter the only options are delegated decision-making or uncertainty. Perhaps we should focus on the process and not be distracted by whether the decision has been 'delegated' or the use of the term 'supporter' as a replacement for 'decision-maker'. Support is the means of ascertaining the 'best interpretation' of the person's 'will and preference' and adopting this as the basis for decisions moves closer to the 'best interests' approach if we cease to relegate the 'wishes and feelings' to a contributory role so that they may be overridden by what a decision-maker thinks is best. The advantage of that approach is that there remain other criteria in the checklist on which to base a decision where it is simply not possible to discern a personal choice. It is not too late for the Court to revise the emphasis and pursue a more 'person-centred' approach. We have much to learn about the role of support in the decision-making process and in this way our jurisdiction will mature.

I remain of the view that our mental capacity jurisdiction is a reasonable adjustment that, far from discriminating against mentally disabled people, enables them to enjoy a lifestyle comparable with that of people without this impairment. But the 'diagnostic threshold' is an obstacle to the further development of this valuable jurisdiction for vulnerable adults and if it was removed or re-interpreted the inherent jurisdiction of the High Court which has no statutory basis would be largely superseded.

Access to justice

I was a member of the judiciary through a couple of decades when access to justice was the mantra and I used this to advocate access for disabled people. Now the emphasis seems to be on the denial of access through higher court fees, withdrawal of comprehensive legal aid and the closure of smaller courts. The concept of justice being delivered as a social service has been abandoned and the barriers to access to the courts are formidable. Could it be that we are moving back to the days when, in the absence of a mental capacity jurisdiction, people did whatever they could, lawful or otherwise, to resolve issues?

The virtual withdrawal of public funding creates a challenge for the nominated judges. This is counter-productive because applications take up more time and hearings become protracted. It has become necessary for courts generally to adjust their procedures to accommodate a preponderance of unrepresented parties. These parties generally desire a local outcome in a timely and economical manner under a procedure they can understand and without inflaming an already confrontational situation. An early directions hearing, possibly by telephone but ideally with the parties present, may result in considerable progress and the allocation to track approach in the Civil Procedure Rules 1998 has much to commend it. Inevitably, there are situations where the law needs to be clarified, but few cases in the Court of Protection set a precedent or require an adversarial hearing and an inquisitorial 'small claims' approach may be sufficient when lawyers are not involved. There is light at the end of this tunnel because an overhaul of the Rules to get cases resolved speedily and proportionately is now contemplated following a significant case management pilot.

This government's reluctance to allow courts to be utilised would be understandable if alternative dispute resolution procedures were readily available but we have not yet reached that stage for the Court of Protection. A contested hearing is the last resort, but the prospect frequently leads to a desire for conciliation or mediation and the Court should be given power to refer a case to the OPG for this purpose. The first Public Guardian did not see this as part of his role but fortunately that attitude has changed and a mediation scheme is now being tried. But there are limitations – the objective is to identify the 'best interests' of the incapacitated person and reaching agreement between members of a dysfunctional family vying for control may not achieve this.

The 'secret court'

Under a new initiative the Court of Protection is bowing to the demands of certain elements of the press that hearings should be in public. This will be for a trial period and is subject to restrictions on identifying the parties involved. It will be interesting to see where this leads. There is a perception that the press are only interested in publishing salacious stories and those about well known personalities but there are also concerns that the work of the Court is not well enough known. Perhaps a better public image will emerge from serious reporting of some of the more challenging cases or even routine ones. Quite apart from the press, my own concern based upon experience in the county court is that it is not the public who attend but the supporters of a party, which can be intimidating to the other party. If I were involved in a family dispute about the future of my elderly parent, I would not wish this to take place in a public arena and would question the motives of anyone who did.

Conclusion

Some of these sentiments may not find favour with the majority of those who rely on this book, but then I have lived the world of the lawyer/advocate and then the judge, and am now moving towards the viewpoint of the consumer. We must never overlook the fact that it is for the benefit of that person, not the lawyers, that this valuable jurisdiction exists. It is like an iceberg with most of the work taking place beneath the surface. Perhaps a better analogy would be a pyramid because the evolution taking place at the top in the appeal courts should not distract us from the beneficial social changes occurring at the bottom in the lives of mentally disabled people and their families. This is a gradual process: it may be a decade since the legislation was enacted but it is a quarter of a century since a small Law Society sub-committee persuaded the Law Commission to embark upon its consultation. That was ahead of the times because we did not then have an enlightened approach to persons with disabilities, there was no 'community care' and there was no legislation on human rights or equality. The climate has changed and is continuing to do so.

Introduction

Our contributors

As always I wish to thank our small team of contributors for their dedication and also James Beck from the Office of the Official Solicitor for continuing to support this work. We are indeed fortunate that one of our contributors is on secondment to the Law Commission to resolve the DoLS issue, another is taking a leading role in the case management pilot and a third has been appointed a consultant to the Council of Europe on a review of implementation of Ministerial Recommendation (2009)11 on *Principles Concerning Continuing Powers of Attorney and Advance Directives for Incapacity*. The comment in this work is therefore written by persons at the forefront of the development not only of our jurisdiction but of the evolution of the approach to decision-making across a wide range of jurisdictions throughout Europe and the free world.

With all these prospective changes, the 2017 issue of this volume is likely to look very different than the present one. We have endeavoured to state the law as at 1 December 2015 with some later additions. Constructive comment on the development of this volume would be welcome and should be sent to the publishers.

Gordon R Ashton OBE
Grange-over-Sands
January 2016

Contents

Calendars	Inside Front Cover
Foreword by Sir James Munby	vii
Foreword to the First Edition	ix
Preface to the First Edition	xi
Where we are now	xiii
Introduction	xxi
Table of Statutes	xxvii
Table of Statutory Instruments	xxxvii
Table of Cases	xlix
Table of Practice Directions	lxiii
Table of Codes of Practice	lxix
Table of EC and International Regulations	lxxi
List of Abbreviations	lxxiii
Part I: Narrative	1
Part II: Procedural Guides	527
Part III: Mental Capacity Act 2005	557
Part IV: Court of Protection Rules 2007 and Practice Directions	741
Part V: Other Statutory Instruments, Practice Directions and guidance	1081
Part VI: Codes of Practice	1511
Part VII: Forms	1847
Part VIII: Precedents	2183
Part IX: Case Summaries	2287
Part X: Scottish Legislation and Guidance	2335
Part XI: International Conventions and Recommendations	2445
Part XII: Directories	2551
Index	2583
Fixed Costs in the Court of Protection	Inside Back Cover

Contents

Foreword by Sir James Munby	vii
Foreword to the First Edition	ix
Preface to the First Edition	xi
Where we are now	xiii
Dedication	xxi
Table of Statutes	xxvii
Table of Statutory Instruments	xxxvii
Table of Cases	xliv
Table of Practice Directions	lxii
Table of Codes of Practice	lxv
Table of EC and International Regulations	lxxi
List of Abbreviations	lxxiii
Part I: Narrative	1
Part II: Procedural Guides	587
Part III: Mental Capacity Act 2005	727
Part IV: Court of Protection Rules 2007 and Practice Directions	747
Part V: Other Statutes, Instruments, Practice Directions and guidance	1081
Part VI: Codes of Practice	1511
Part VII: Forms	1841
Part VIII: Precedents	2115
Part IX: Case summaries	2227
Part X: Scottish Legislation and Guidance	2318
Part XI: International Conventions and Recommendations	2465
Part XII: Directories	2551
Index	2583
Fixed Costs in the Court of Protection	Inside Back Cover

Table of Statutes

References are to page numbers.

Administration of Estates Act 1925	453
Administration of Justice Act 1960	453
Administration of Justice Act 1982	446
Adoption and Children Act 2002	454
s 52	176
Adult Support and Protection (Scotland) Act 2007	23, 70
s 55	2342
s 56	2342
s 57(1)	2349
s 57(2)	2350
s 57(4)(b)	2351
s 57(5)	2353
s 57(6)	2353
s 57(7)	2354
s 57(8)	2354, 2355, 2356, 2357, 2358, 2359, 2360, 2361, 2362, 2363, 2364, 2365, 2366, 2367, 2368, 2369, 2370
s 57(9)	2411
s 59(1)	2384
s 59(2)	2384
s 59(3)	2385
s 60(1)	2387
s 60(2)	2388
s 60(3)	2389
s 60(4)	2390
s 60(5)	2391
s 60(6)	2392
s 60(7)	2394
s 60(8)	2398
s 60(9)	2399
s 60(10)	2400
s 60(11)	2401
s 60(12)	2402
s 60(13)	2403
s 60(14)	2403
s 60(15)	2404
s 60(16)	2406
s 60(17)	2426
s 61	2407
s 67	2344
s 77(1)	2344, 2372, 2373, 2411, 2417, 2422, 2426
s 77(2)	2378
Sch 1	
para 5(a)	2344
para 5(e)	2411
para 5(f)	2417
para 5(g)	2422
para 5(h)	2426
Sch 2	2378
Adult Support and Protection (Scotland) Act 2007—*continued*	
Sch 5	
para 5(b)	2372
para 5(c)	2373
Adults with Incapacity (Scotland) Act 2000	23, 57, 70, 77, 98, 99, 101, 108, 441, 2339
s 1	98
s 1(2)	110
s 1(3)	110
s 1(4)(b)	58
s 87(2)	58
Autism Act 2009	44
Care Standards Act 2000	43, 391, 1523, 1713
Pt 2	423, 432
Carers (Equal Opportunities) Act 2004	44
Carers (Recognition and Services) Act 1995	43
Carers and Disabled Children Act 2000	43
Charging Orders Act 1979	
s 5	870
Child Support Act 1991	453
Children Act 1989	25, 115, 116, 127, 176, 263, 280, 311, 312, 390, 417, 419, 585, 595, 1301, 1302, 1622, 1683, 1685, 1689, 1736, 2240
Pt V	1668
s 47	1668
Children and Young Persons Act 1933	
s 1	181, 182, 613
Chronically Sick and Disabled Persons Act 1970	43
Civil Evidence Act 1995	
s 11	407
Civil Partnership Act 2004	56, 57
s 1	56, 595
Community Care (Delayed Discharge, etc) Act 2003	43
Compulsory Purchase Act 1965	453
Constitutional Reform Act 2005	385
s 59(5)	737, 739, 1215
Sch 11	
para 1(2)	737, 739, 1188
Pt 1	
para 1(2)	1215
Consumer Credit Act 1974	453
Courts Act 2003	385
Courts and Legal Services Act 1990	
s 27	622
s 27(2)(c)	61

Courts and Legal Services Act
    1990—*continued*
  s 28 622
Crime and Courts Act 2013 819

Data Protection Act 1998 . . . . 28, 345, 1523,
        1725, 1726, 1728, 1729, 1737,
        1741
  s 7 . . . . 1725, 1727
Deregulation Act 2015
  s 19 737
  Sch 6
    para 20(4) 737
Disability Discrimination Act 1995 . 47, 59,
        453, 1094, 1523
Disabled Persons Act 1981 43
Disabled Persons (Services Consultation and
    Representation) Act 1986 43

Enduring Powers of Attorney Act 1985 . 62,
        73, 188, 189, 194, 227, 254, 256,
        451, 452, 453, 454, 629, 706,
        707, 1602, 1739
  s 1(1)(a) 188
  s 2(1)(a) 189
  s 4(1) 189, 193
  s 5 190
  s 6(4)(a) 190
  s 6(5) 190
  s 6(6) 252
  s 8 190
  s 8(2) 190
  s 8(2)(c) 274
  s 8(4) 190
  s 9 582
  s 9(3) 188
  s 10(1)(a) 73
  s 10(2) 73
  s 11(1) 221
  s 13 193
  s 48 194
  Sch 1
    para 2(1) 189, 227
    para 4(1) 190
Equality Act 2006 47
Equality Act 2010 . . . . 47, 48
  s 5 47
  s 6 47
  s 7 47
  s 8 47
  s 9 47
  s 10 47
  s 11 47
  s 12 47
  s 13 48
  s 15 . . . . 47, 49
  s 16 47
  s 19 49
  s 20 . . . . 49, 51
  s 21 50

Equality Act 2010—*continued*
  s 26 50
  s 27 50
  s 29 50
  ss 32–35 51
  ss 100–103 51
  Sch 1 47
Family Law Act 1996 57
Family Law (Scotland) Act 2006
  s 36 2355
Family Law Reform Act 1969 453
  s 8(1) 128, 1686
Fatal Accidents Act 1976 57
Fines and Recoveries Act 1833 453
Fraud Act 2006 1707

Health Act 1999 43
Health Act 2009 44
Health and Social Care Act 2001
  Pt 4 43
  s 60 1674
  s 61 1674
Health and Social Care Act 2008 44
Health and Social Care Act 2012 . 601, 627,
        674
Health and Social Care (Community Health
    and Standards) Act 2003
  s 148 391
Health and Social Services and Social
    Security Adjudications Act 1983 . . 43
Health Services and Public Health Act
    1968 43
Housing Act 1985 43
Housing Act 1996
  Pt VII 43
Human Fertilisation and Embryology Act
    1990 . . . . 175, 1522
Human Fertilisation and Embryology Act
    2008
  s 56 594
  s 65 . . . . 597, 2409, 2410
  Sch 6
    Pt 1
      para 40 594
  Sch 7
    para 18 . . . . 2409, 2410
    para 25 597
Human Rights Act 1998 . 46, 52, 55, 63, 129,
        397, 823, 1094, 1523, 1596,
        1726, 1740, 2332
  s 1 52
  s 2(1) 53
  s 3 53
  s 6 55
  s 7 55
  s 8(1) 54
  s 10 53
  s 19 52
  Sch 1 52

Human Tissue Act 2004	345, 1523, 1674, 1680, 1681, 1740
s 1(9)	1674, 1680
Human Tissue (Scotland) Act 2006	
s 57(2)	2350
s 57(3)	2394
Industrial and Provident Societies Act 1965	453
Inheritance Act 1984	
s 11(3)	290
s 142	290
Inheritance (Provisions for Family and Dependents) Act 1975	806
Insolvency Act 1986	453
Interpretation Act 1978	
s 7	712
Intestates' Estates Act 1952	453
Judicature (Northern Ireland) Act 1978	
s 28(1)	70
Land Registration etc (Scotland) Act 2012	
s 119	2385, 2390
Sch 5	
para 38(2)	2385
para 38(3)	2390
Law of Property Act 1925	453
s 22	207
s 204	390
Law of Property (Miscellaneous Provisions) Act 1989	
s 1	185, 241
Leasehold Reform Act 1967	453
Leasehold Reform, Housing and Urban Development Act 1993	453
Legal Services Act 2007	
s 210	737
Sch 23	737
Licensing Act 2003	454
Limitation Act 1980	
s 38	453
Local Authority Social Services Act 1970	453
s 1A	618
s 7	44, 1668
Local Government Act 1972	453
Lunacy Act 1890	62
Lunacy Regulation Act 1853	71
Lunacy Regulation Act 1862	71
Lunatics' Visitors Act 1833	71
Matrimonial Causes Act 1973	453
Medicines Act 1968	453
Mental Capacity Act 2005	23, 27, 28, 36, 40, 58, 78, 79, 91, 92, 93, 94, 95, 96, 97, 98, 105, 108, 109, 111, 114, 122, 125, 127, 128, 130, 140, 142, 148, 155, 160, 163, 167, 170, 178, 187, 189, 190, 193, 194, 195, 198, 199, 203,

Mental Capacity Act 2005—continued	204, 205, 208, 209, 210, 211, 212, 213, 215, 221, 226, 227, 234, 235, 241, 242, 245, 247, 251, 255, 256, 259, 260, 261, 262, 266, 268, 270, 280, 283, 309, 310, 311, 312, 313, 328, 345, 347, 349, 352, 385, 386, 387, 389, 395, 407, 428, 434, 439, 451, 455, 456, 458, 459, 536, 538, 551, 552, 564, 634, 757, 797, 871, 1086, 1087, 1092, 1094, 1302, 1515, 1518, 1521, 1523, 1685, 1690, 1747, 2189, 2199, 2205, 2209, 2210, 2216, 2227, 2237, 2240, 2244, 2262, 2263, 2264, 2266, 2268, 2280, 2299, 2300, 2302, 2325
Pt 1	547
s 1	79, 110, 144, 164, 195, 240, 262, 268, 365, 573, 575, 577, 616, 707, 757, 1524, 1590, 1605, 1613, 1621, 1624, 1632, 1658, 2190, 2193, 2200, 2269
ss 1–4	1086
s 1(1)–(6)	99
s 1(2)	101, 314, 550, 565, 1525
s 1(3)	102, 103, 146, 565, 569, 1526
s 1(4)	105, 565, 1528
s 1(5)	108, 142, 143, 144, 157, 209, 284, 286, 565, 571, 1529, 1562, 1577
s 1(6)	109, 162, 305, 565, 573, 1530
s 2	111, 180, 195, 293, 365, 460, 565, 567, 573, 575, 577, 583, 616, 633, 847, 1735, 1746, 2225, 2300
ss 2–5	312
s 2(1)	111, 117, 125, 242, 455, 460, 536, 549, 566, 1087, 1541, 1683, 1687, 1689
s 2(2)	566, 1542
s 2(3)	114, 145, 566, 569, 1542
s 2(4)	550, 566, 1543
s 2(5)	116, 566, 1684
s 2(6)	116, 566, 1684
s 3	111, 117, 180, 181, 365, 565, 566, 573, 575, 577, 616, 633, 1541, 1746, 2300
s 3(1)	117, 315, 537, 549, 1087, 1544, 2300, 2301, 2302
s 3(1)(a)	312, 567
s 3(1)(b)	567
s 3(1)(c)	122, 567, 568
s 3(1)(d)	118, 124, 212, 568
s 3(2)	119, 568, 1531, 1545
s 3(3)	121, 567, 1546
s 3(4)	119, 567, 1545
s 4	109, 142, 143, 144, 195, 196, 209, 240, 266, 268, 459, 565, 577, 584, 616, 634, 1098, 1530, 1563, 1565, 1578, 1605, 1613, 1633

Table of Statutes

Mental Capacity Act 2005—*continued*

s 4(1)	145, 566, 569, 1566
s 4(2)	145, 569
s 4(3)	146, 569, 1569
s 4(4)	147, 569, 1568
s 4(5)	148, 210, 570, 1571
s 4(6)	150, 334, 339, 570, 761, 1572
s 4(6)(a)	570, 1573
s 4(6)(b)	570
s 4(6)(c)	151, 570, 1575
s 4(7)	58, 155, 209, 213, 570, 1575, 1670
s 4(7)(b)	571
s 4(8)	126, 131, 157, 571
s 4(9)	157, 212, 571, 573, 613, 1577
s 4(10)	148, 570, 575, 579, 1644, 1742
s 4(11)	146, 569, 1568
s 4A	362, 574, 584, 693
s 4A(3)	571
s 4A(5)	571
s 4B	362, 574, 693
s 5	139, 158, 161, 162, 163, 164, 166, 170, 173, 174, 175, 176, 177, 209, 213, 347, 350, 417, 573, 574, 575, 596, 1573, 1581, 1583, 1584, 1586, 1587, 1588, 1589, 1590, 1592, 1593, 1596, 1597, 1599, 1644, 1645, 1683, 1684, 1687, 1688, 1692, 2198
s 5(1)	101, 126, 131, 275, 573, 613, 1552, 1584
s 5(1)(a)	164, 573, 1590
s 5(1)(b)	573
s 5(1)(b)(ii)	165, 573
s 5(2)	160, 573
s 5(3)	165, 573
s 5(4)	166, 573
s 6	166, 347, 350, 1586
s 6(1)	166, 574
s 6(2)	166, 574
s 6(3)	166, 574
s 6(3)(a)	1631
s 6(4)	166, 574, 1593, 1746
s 6(4)(b)	574
s 6(5)	169, 1586, 1596
s 6(6)	170, 174, 574, 576, 1598, 1600
s 6(6)(a)	209
s 6(7)	170, 575
s 7	171, 247, 1598
s 7(1)	172, 575
s 7(2)	171, 575, 1598
s 8	173, 174, 247, 576, 1599
s 8(1)(a)	173, 576
s 8(1)(b)	173, 576
s 8(2)	174
s 8(2)(a)	576
s 8(2)(b)	576
s 8(3)	174, 576
s 9	195, 270
ss 9–14	577, 593

Mental Capacity Act 2005—*continued*

s 9(1)	195, 199, 577, 1741
s 9(1)(a)	577
s 9(1)(b)	577
s 9(2)	241
s 9(2)(b)	242, 244, 247
s 9(2)(c)	272, 1686
s 9(3)	215
s 9(4)	577, 1605
s 9(4)(b)	198, 1614
s 10	221
s 10(1)	221
s 10(1)(b)	578
s 10(4)	221, 1604
s 10(4)–(7)	578
s 10(5)	578, 1604
s 10(6)	221
s 10(8)	1604
s 10(8)(b)	224, 578
s 11(1)–(5)	579
s 11(1)–(6)	577
s 11(3)	209
s 11(4)	209
s 11(4)(a)	1631
s 11(6)	209
s 11(7)	579
s 11(7)(a)	196, 209, 215, 244, 1607
s 11(7)(b)	210, 1607
s 11(7)(c)	208, 1608
s 11(8)	210, 579
s 11(8)(a)	339
s 11(8)(b)	339
s 12	198, 203, 205, 206, 285, 1611
s 12(2)	275, 283, 580, 1612
s 12(2)(b)	1611
s 12(3)	205
s 12(3)(b)	1611
s 12(4)	580
s 13	581
s 13(2)	581
s 13(3)	250
s 13(6)	187, 581
s 13(6)(a)–(d)	250, 578
s 13(6)(a)-(d)	222
s 13(6)(b)	250
s 13(6)(c)	581
s 13(8)	187
s 13(11)	581
s 15	271, 378, 458, 552, 1624, 1738, 2300
ss 15–16	379, 460, 590
ss 15–23	614
s 15(1)	133
s 16	262, 378, 379, 552, 590, 1626, 1652
ss 16–20	708
s 16(1)	133, 249
s 16(1)(b)	592
s 16(2)	1739
s 16(2)(a)	210, 571, 687
s 16(3)	110

Table of Statutes

Mental Capacity Act 2005—*continued*
- s 16(4)   110, 2198, 2310
- s 16A   362
- s 16A(1)   2304
- s 17   263, 271, 584, 1652
- s 17(1)(e)   1652
- s 17A   596
- s 18   247, 264, 271, 584
- s 18(1)   291
- s 18(1)(b)   296
- s 18(1)(c)   283
- s 18(1)(h)   283, 296, 306
- s 18(1)(i)   283, 296, 585
- s 18(1)(j)   1003
- s 18(2)   1686
- s 18(3)   116, 566, 586, 1301, 1683
- s 19   266, 584
- s 19(1)   1630
- s 19(1)(b)   587
- s 19(2)   220
- s 19(4)(c)   1630
- s 19(5)   587
- s 19(6)   587, 1633
- s 19(7)   267
- s 19(8)   267
- s 19(8)(b)   283
- s 19(9)   876
- s 19(9)(a)   1631
- s 19(13)   269
- s 20   267, 584, 585, 586, 1631
- s 20(1)   286
- s 20(3)   283, 285
- s 20(7)–(11)   268
- s 20(11)(a)   1631
- s 21   116, 263, 312, 390, 1622, 1689
- s 21A   378, 379, 589, 590, 2309
- s 21A(1)(a)   590
- s 21A(1)(b)   590
- s 21A(3)(b)   590
- s 21A(5)(b)   590
- s 22   251, 804, 1616
- s 22(1)(a)   591
- s 22(2)   247, 252, 271
- s 22(3)   250
- s 22(3)(a)   272
- s 22(3)(b)   232, 272, 591
- s 22(4)   251
- s 23   199, 207, 804, 1616
- s 23(1)   274
- s 23(2)   274
- s 23(3)   624
- s 23(3)(a)   277
- s 23(3)(a)–(c)   274
- s 23(3)(d)   275
- s 23(4)   203, 275, 592
- s 24   166, 573, 1574, 1638
- ss 24–26   213
- s 24(1)(a)   334
- s 24(2)   334
- s 24(3)   1645

Mental Capacity Act 2005—*continued*
- s 24(5)   334, 592
- s 25   166, 210, 573, 1638, 1647
- s 25(1)   1639
- s 25(2)   335
- s 25(2)(b)   209, 593
- s 25(3)   1647
- s 25(3), (4)   335
- s 25(4)   1648
- s 25(6)   213
- s 26   166, 573, 1638, 1650
- s 26(1)   594
- s 26(2)   336, 1593, 1651
- s 26(3)   336, 1651
- s 26(4)   336
- s 26(5)   594
- s 27   175, 187, 210, 577, 584, 1522, 2300
- ss 27–29   198, 1522
- s 27(1)(a)   595
- s 27(1)(b)   315, 418, 595
- s 27(1)(c)   595
- s 27(1)(d)   595
- s 27(1)(f)   595
- s 27(1)(g)   595
- s 27(2)   595
- s 28   175, 176, 210, 350, 577, 584, 1523, 1608, 1702
- s 28(1)   595
- s 28(1A)   176, 596
- s 28(1B)   177, 596
- s 29   175, 187, 211, 577, 584, 1523
- s 30   342, 343
- ss 30–33   1681, 1682
- s 30(1)   597, 598
- s 30(5)   597
- s 30(6)   597
- s 31   342, 343
- ss 31–34   597
- s 31(1)   598
- s 32   342, 343, 344, 1678, 1687
- s 32(3)   344, 599
- s 33   342, 343
- s 33(2)(b)   600
- s 34   342, 343, 344
- s 34(2)   600
- s 35   1741
- ss 35–41   163, 1654
- s 35(1)   601
- s 35(2)   601
- s 35(6)   1658, 1660
- s 35(6)(b)   1657
- s 36   329, 1741
- s 37   1664, 1668
- s 37(2)   603
- s 37(6)   603, 604
- s 37(7)   603, 604
- s 38   1668
- s 38(2)   604, 606
- s 38(6)   604
- s 38(7)   604

Mental Capacity Act 2005—*continued*

s 38(8)	604
s 39	1668
s 39(2)	605
s 39(3)	606
s 39A	607
s 39A(5)	606
s 39C(1)(b)	608
s 41(1)	610
s 42	93, 1515, 1516
s 42(1)	94
s 42(2)	94
s 42(3)	94, 611
s 42(4)	96, 611, 1524
s 42(5)	97, 611, 1524
s 43	98, 1515, 1516
s 43(1)	98
s 43(1)(a)	612
s 43(1)(b)	612
s 43(2)	98
s 43(2)(b)	612
s 43(3)	98, 612
s 43(4)	98, 612
s 43(5)	98, 612
s 44	179, 180, 181, 182, 184, 1619, 1683, 1685, 1704, 1711, 1740, 1746
s 44(1)(a)	179, 181, 613
s 44(1)(b)	179
s 44(1)(c)	179
s 44(2)	613
s 44(3)(b)	179
s 45	1621
ss 45–56	387
s 47(1)	390, 415, 616
s 47(3)	390
s 48	263, 391, 552, 565
s 48(a)	616
s 48(c)	616
s 49	287, 391, 408, 409, 431, 552, 761, 835, 836
s 49(2)	277, 625
s 49(5)	755, 1516
s 50	533, 535, 799, 1623
s 50(1)	799
s 50(1)(b)	209
s 50(1)(c)	276
s 50(2)	251, 799
s 50(3)	110
s 50(3)(b)	2199
s 50(3)(c)	2199
s 51	392, 755
s 51(3)	619
s 52	394, 619
s 53	414, 862, 1723
s 53(2)	620, 755
s 53(4)	620, 755
s 54	414
s 54(1)	621
s 55	412, 862

Mental Capacity Act 2005—*continued*

s 55(1)	622
s 55(5)	622
s 56	412
s 57	421, 595, 617, 1707, 1744
s 57(4), (5)	421
s 58	276, 277, 421, 595, 617
s 58(1)(c)	624
s 58(1)(d)	431, 624, 625, 1737
s 58(1)(e)	587
s 58(1)(f)	587, 624
s 58(1)(h)	276
s 58(3)(b)	624
s 58(3), (4)	422
s 58(4)	624
s 58(5), (6)	423
s 58A	596
s 59	1707
s 60	424
s 61	617, 1737
s 61(1)–(4)	429
s 61(5)	432
s 61(6)	432
s 62	148, 210, 570, 1522, 1523, 1639
s 64(1)	573, 578, 585, 587, 618, 1584
s 65(1)	755
s 66(1)(b)	706
s 66(4)	452
s 67(4)(b)	755
s47	832
Sch A1	352, 571, 607, 630, 679, 688, 693, 2308, 2309
para 14(1)	633
para 14(2)	633
para 16(1)	634, 664
para 16(5)	634
para 17	687
para 33(4)	639
para 42(2)(b)	641
para 47(1)	642
para 70(1)	648
para 70(2)	648
para 129(3)	648, 663
para 130(2)	664
para 130(5)	664
para 139	377
para 146	641
para 161	606
para 176	590, 635
para 177	590, 635
para 179	590, 635
paras 180–182	590
para 182(2)	377
Pt 1 (paras 1–4)	363
Pt 4	590
Pt 5	590
Pt 10	608, 609
Sch 1	185, 187, 215, 244, 577
para 1	578
para 1(2)	214, 680

Mental Capacity Act 2005—*continued*
　Sch 1—*continued*
　　para 1(3) 680
　　para 2(1) 233
　　para 2(1)(c) 227
　　para 2(1)(d) 239, 242
　　para 2(1)(e) 241
　　para 2(2)(a) 681
　　para 2(2)(b) 239
　　para 2(3) 681
　　para 3(1) 681
　　para 3(2) 271, 681
　　para 4(1)(a) 682
　　para 4(3) 246
　　para 6 247
　　para 7 248, 682
　　para 8 682
　　para 8(1) 248
　　para 8(2) 248
　　para 11(1) 215, 249, 684
　　para 11(2) 250, 684
　　para 11(3) 250
　　para 13(1) 250
　　para 13(1)(b) 685
　　para 13(2) 250
　　para 13(3) 250, 251
　　para 13(3)(b)(i) 685
　　para 13(3)(b)(ii) 685
　　para 13(4) 250
　　para 14(1)(b) 685
　　para 17(1) 686
　　para 18 252
　　para 18(b) 245
　　Pt 1 214
　Sch 1A 210, 366, 584, 679, 687, 693, 2247
　　para 2(a) 2307
　Sch 2 265, 586
　　para 5 265
　　para 6 265
　　para 7 265
　　para 8–9 266
　　para 13(4) 251
　Sch 3
　　para 19 704
　　para 20(2) 799
　　para 35 703
　　Pt 3 531
　Sch 4 185, 194, 254, 256, 451, 453, 531, 629, 706, 805, 1624, 1739
　　para 1 188, 189, 716
　　para 1(1) 451, 706, 707
　　para 1(1)(c) 707
　　para 1(2) 199, 247
　　para 2 706, 707
　　para 2(1) 189
　　para 2(3) 708, 716
　　para 2(9) 708, 805
　　para 2(10) 708
　　para 3(1) 199

Mental Capacity Act 2005—*continued*
　Sch 4—*continued*
　　para 3(2) 199, 283, 284, 286, 288
　　para 3(2)(a) 709
　　para 3(3) 199, 275, 283, 284, 286
　　para 4(1) 193, 709
　　para 4(2) 276
　　para 4(4) 709
　　para 4(5)(a), (b) 805
　　para 4(6) 708
　　para 4(8) 710
　　para 5 189
　　para 6 189, 227
　　para 7(2) 805
　　para 8 190
　　para 9 190
　　para 9(1) 199
　　para 9(e) 254
　　para 10(c) 805
　　para 13 805
　　para 13(3) 255
　　para 13(4) 190
　　para 13(9)(e) 273
　　para 14 421
　　para 15(1) 708
　　para 15(4) 714
　　para 16 582
　　para 16(2) 274, 805
　　para 16(2)(a) 190
　　para 16(2)(e) 190, 275
　　para 16(2)(f) 275
　　para 16(3) 805
　　para 16(4) 190, 805
　　para 16(4)(g) 591
　　para 16(6) 805
　　para 18(3) 188
　　para 20(1) 578
　　para 23 189
　　para 23(1) 193, 709, 719
　Sch 5 415, 452, 629
　　para 1(2)(a) 2197, 2265
　　para 5 755
　　para 12 755
　Sch 6 125, 566, 1549
　　para 20 1549
　Sch 7 256, 451, 453, 454
　　para 4(1) 451
　Sch 8 531
　Sch 9(2) 241
Mental Deficiency Act 1913 21, 36
Mental Health (Care and Treatment) (Scotland) Act 2003 23
　s 331 2371, 2411
　s 331(1) 2387
　s 331(2) 2345, 2347, 2378, 2413
　Sch 4
　　para 9 2371
　　para 9(4) 2387
　　para 9(5) 2411

Mental Health (Care and Treatment)
(Scotland) Act 2003—*continued*
Sch 5
    Pt 1   2345, 2347, 2371, 2378, 2387,
                 2411, 2413
Mental Health Act 1959   33, 62, 187
Mental Health Act 1983   24, 26, 33, 43, 62,
              176, 177, 187, 189, 331, 347,
              348, 349, 350, 351, 365, 366,
              452, 453, 454, 584, 604, 634,
              1086, 1088, 1519, 1523, 1558,
              1586, 1596, 1597, 1608, 1612,
              1638, 1665, 1667, 1668, 1685,
              1688, 1690, 1691, 1695, 1696,
              1697, 1703, 1719, 1733, 1735,
                   1743, 2304, 2306
    Pt 3   1693
    Pt 4   603, 1523, 1646, 1698, 1699, 1700, 1702
    Pt 7   629, 1086, 1089
    s 1(2)   26, 210, 347, 596, 633, 709, 1086
    s 1(2A)   633
    s 1(3)   26, 1086
    s 1(4)   633
    s 2   139, 1692, 1698
    ss 2–3   2306
    s 2(2)   348
    s 3   139, 1692, 1693, 1694, 1697, 1698
    s 3(2)   348
    s 4(4)(a)   1698
    s 5   1698
    s 7   1694
    s 12   375
    ss 17A–17G   176
    s 17A(5)   348
    s 17A(7)   177
    s 21   331
    s 25A   1696
    s 26   1693
    s 29   331
    s 35   1698
    s 37(4)   1698
    s 57   176, 1702
    s 58   176
    s 58A   176
    s 63   2304
    s 64B(3)(b)(ii)   177
    ss 93–111   1086
    s 93(4)   63
    s 94(1)   63
    s 94(2)   62
    s 99   2197, 2265
    s 103(7)   71
    s 103(8)   74
    s 117   331, 606, 1666, 1667, 1702
    s 129   72
    s 135   1558, 1698
    s 136   1698
    s 145   596

Mental Health Act 2007   92, 94, 176, 210,
              347, 348, 350, 352, 571, 709
    s 1(2)   596
    s 1(4)   719
    s 7   596
    s 27   596
    s 28(6)   176
    s 28(10)   176, 595
    s 32   596
    s 32(1), (2)   176
    s 35(4)   177, 595, 602
    s 35(5)   177, 595
    s 35(6)   602
    s 49   610
    s 50   169, 352, 362
    s 50(1)   571, 574, 579, 584, 588
    s 50(1), (2)   572
    s 50(2)   362, 571
    s 50(3)   362, 584
    s 50(4)(a)   574
    s 50(4)(b)   579
    s 50(4)(c)   588
    s 50(5)   630, 679
    s 50(6)   687, 693
    s 50(7)   94, 96, 589, 601, 604, 605, 606,
              607, 609, 610, 611, 619, 627, 628
    s 51   588
    s 55   269, 574, 579, 584, 588, 719
    Sch 1
        para 23(1)–(3)   719
    Sch 3
        para 3(5)   348
    Sch 7   352, 363, 630, 679
    Sch 8   352, 366, 687, 693
        para 2   378
    Sch 9
        para 1   94, 96, 589, 601, 604, 605,
              606, 607, 609, 610, 611, 619, 627, 628
        para 2   589
        para 3   601
        para 4(1)–(3)   604
        para 5(1)–(3)   605
        para 6   606, 607, 609
        paras 7(1)–(4)   610
        para 8(1)–(3)   611
        para 8(1), (2)   94
        para 8(3)   96
        para 9   619
        para 10(1)–(4)   627
        para 11   628
    Sch 11
        Pt 1   719
        Pt 10   269, 574, 579

National Assistance Act 1948   43
    s 49   453
National Health Service Act 1977   43
National Health Service Act 2006   44
    s 251   1674

National Health Service Act
   2006—*continued*
   s 252   1674
National Health Service (Consequential
   Provisions) Act 2006
   s 2   604
   Sch 1
     paras 277, 278   604
National Health Service (Wales) Act
   2006   44
National Health Service and Community
   Care Act 1990   41, 42, 43, 1523, 1656
   s 47   606, 1666
National Health Service Reform and Health
   Care Professions Act 2002
   Pt 1   43
New Zealand Protection of Personal and
   Property Rights Act 1988
   s 1(3)   105

Offences Against the Person Act 1861   179, 613

Personal Care at Home Act 2010   44
Police and Criminal Evidence Act 1984
   s 2   179, 613
Powers of Attorney Act 1971   185, 187
   s 1   185, 241
   s 3   714
   s 5   185, 582, 707, 716
   s 10   247
Prosecution of Offenders Act 1985   830
Public Interest Disclosure Act 1998   1714
Public Trustee Act 1906
   s 4(3)   578
Public Trustee and Administration of
   Funds Act 1986   453

Race Relations Act 1976   47
Regulation of Care (Scotland) Act 2001
   s 79   2371, 2373, 2375, 2409, 2413
   Sch 3
     para 23   2371
     para 23(3)   2373
     para 23(4)   2375
     para 23(5)   2409

Regulation of Care (Scotland) Act
   2001—*continued*
   Sch 3—*continued*
     para 23(6)   2413
Safeguarding Vulnerable Groups Act
   2006   44, 1658, 1712
Sale of Goods Act 1979   171, 453
   s 3(2)   575
   s 3(3)   171, 575
Senior Courts Act 1981
   s 1(1)   62
   s 9   390
   s 90   433
   s 144   72
Sex Discrimination Act 1975   47, 57
Sexual Offences Act 2003   595
Smoking, Health and Social Care (Scotland)
   Act 2005
   s 35(2)(a)(i)   2378
   s 35(3)   2378
   s 35(4)   2380
Social Security Administration Act
   1992   453
Statute de Prerogativa Regis, 17 Edw II
   (1339) St I cc 9, 10   31, 62
Suicide Act 1961
   s 2   626

Tribunals, Courts and Enforcement Act 2007
   Pt 1   348
Trustee Act 1925   33, 63, 453
   s 25   207
   s 36   207
   s 36(9)   1003
   s 54   1003
   s 68(1)   578, 587
Trusts of Land and Appointment of
   Trustees Act 1996   453
   s 20   1003

Variation of Trusts Act 1958   307, 453

Wills Act 1837   265, 581
   s 9   187, 265
   s 15   303
   s 20   187
Work and Families Act 2006   44

Table of Statutory Instruments

References are to page numbers.

A chronological list of statutory instruments referred to in this work appears at the end of the alphabetical list below.

Act of Sederunt (Ordinary Cause, Summary
    Application, Summary Cause and
    Small Claim Rules) Amendment
    (Miscellaneous) 2004, SSI 2004/
    197   2428
Act of Sederunt (Sheriff Court Rules)
    (Miscellaneous Amendments) (No 3)
    2013, SSI 2013/171   2429, 2430
Act of Sederunt (Summary Applications,
    Statutory Applications and
    Appeals etc Rules) 1999, SI 1999/
    929   2427
Act of Sederunt (Summary Applications,
    Statutory Applications and
    Appeals etc Rules) Amendment
    (Adult Support and Protection
    (Scotland) Act 2007) 2008, SSI 2008/
    111   2428, 2429, 2430, 2431
Act of Sederunt (Summary Applications,
    Statutory Applications and
    Appeals etc Rules) Amendment
    (Adults with Incapacity) 2001,
    SSI 2001/142   2428, 2429, 2430
Act of Sederunt (Summary Applications,
    Statutory Applications and
    Appeals etc. Rules) Amendment
    (International Protection of Adults)
    2003, SI 2003/556   2432, 2433, 2434
Act of Sederunt (Summary Applications,
    Statutory Applications and
    Appeals etc. Rules) Amendment (No
    3) (Adults with Incapacity) 2002,
    SSI 2002/146   2428, 2429, 2430,
    2431, 2432
Adult Support and Protection (Scotland) Act
    2007 (Commencement No 1,
    Transitional Provision and Savings)
    Order 2007, SSI 2007/334   2407
Adults with Incapacity (Electronic
    Communications) (Scotland)
    Order 2008, SSI 2008/380   2352
Adults with Incapacity (Management of
    Residents' Finances) (Scotland)
    Regulations 2005, SSI 2005/
    610   2371
Adults with Incapacity (Scotland) Act 2000
    (Commencement No 1) Order 2001,
    SSI 2001/81   2340, 2392
Allocation and Transfer of
    Proceedings Order 2008, SI 2008/
    2836   1320

Care Act 2014 and Children and
    Families Act 2014 (Consequential
    Amendments) Order 2015, SI 2015/
    914   605, 676
Civil Legal Aid (Financial Resources and
    Payment for Services)
    Regulations 2013, SI 2013/480
    r 5(1)(g)   379, 590
Civil Procedure Rules 1998, SI 1998/
    3132   26, 63, 64, 125, 187, 208, 395,
    396, 410, 412, 415, 454, 566,
    586, 756, 772, 829, 830, 868,
    869, 870, 1090, 1091
    r 2.7   1088
    r 3.1(7)   1102
    r 3.3   1097
    Pt 6   1095
    r 6.13   539, 1098
    r 6.13(2)   542
    r 6.13(4)   542
    r 6.13(6)   542
    r 6.25(2)   542
    r 6.25(3)   542
    r 6.25(5)   542
    Pt 8   544, 855, 1101
    r 12.10(a)(i)   543
    r 12.11(3)   543
    r 14.1(4)   543
    Pt 20   1091
    r 20.2(2)(a)   1094
    r 20.3(1)   539, 1091, 1094
    r 20.3(3)   543
    Pt 21   536, 846, 1086, 1094
    r 21.1   133, 538, 1091, 1557
    r 21.1(1)(b)   1087
    r 21.1(1)(c)   1086
    r 21.1(2)(a)   1086
    r 21.1(2)(d)   536, 1087
    r 21.1(2)(e)   545, 1087, 1103
    r 21.2   1097, 1098
    r 21.2(1)   537
    r 21.2(3)   1086
    r 21.2(5)   1086
    r 21.3   848, 1092
    r 21.3(2)   537, 1092
    r 21.3(3)   537, 1092
    r 21.3(4)   537, 1093
    r 21.4   1096, 1097
    rr 21.4–21.7   434

Civil Procedure Rules 1998, SI 1998/ 3132—continued

r 21.4(1)	1097
r 21.4(2)	538
r 21.4(3)	538, 539, 540, 541, 1092, 1094, 1096, 1097, 1098
r 21.4(3)(c)	1094, 1099
r 21.4(7)	540
r 21.5	539, 1096, 1098
r 21.5(3)	1096
r 21.5(4)(a)	539
r 21.5(4)(b)	539, 1096
r 21.6	537, 540, 1097, 1098
r 21.6(4)	540
r 21.6(5)	540
r 21.7	1094
r 21.7(1)(c)	1092
r 21.8	542
r 21.8(1)	542, 1097
r 21.8(2)	542, 1097
r 21.8(3)	542, 1097
r 21.8(4)	541, 1097
r 21.9(2)	541, 1092
r 21.9(3)	541, 1092, 1099
r 21.9(4)	541, 1099
r 21.9(5)	541, 1099
r 21.9(6)	547, 1099
r 21.9(6)(b)	1099
r 21.10	1092
r 21.10(1)	544
r 21.10(2)	544, 1101
r 21.11	545, 1092
r 21.11(1)(b)	545
r 21.11(2)	545
Pt 22	1092, 1107
r 22.1(5)	543, 1092
r 22.1(6)	543, 1092
r 30.7	545
r 31(2)	842
r 31(3)	845
r 31(4)	842
r 32.13(3)(e)	543
Pt 36	1100
r 39.2(3)(d)	543, 1102, 1103
Pt 44	305
Pt 45	1102
r 45.3(2)(c)(ii)	546
r 46.2	1095
r 46.4	546, 1101
Pt 47	305
r 47.3(1)(c)	546
Pt 48	305
r 52.13	864
Pt 67	855
Pt 70	869
Pt 71	869
Pt 72	870
Pt 73	870
Pt 75	1086
Pt 83	870

Civil Procedure Rules 1998, SI 1998/ 3132—continued

Pt 84	870
Civil Procedure (Amendment) Rules 2000, SI 2000/221	1180, 1182, 1183, 1184, 1185, 1186, 1187, 1188
Civil Procedure (Amendment No 4) Rules 2000, SI 2000/2092	1180
Civil Procedure (Amendment No 4) Rules 2001, SI 2001/2792	1209, 1210, 1211, 1212, 1213, 1214, 1215, 1216, 1217, 1218, 1219, 1220, 1221, 1222, 1223, 1224, 1225, 1226
Civil Procedure (Amendment No 5) Rules 2001, SI 2001/4015	1214, 1217
Civil Procedure (Amendment) Rules 2002, SI 2002/2058	1209
Civil Procedure (Amendment No 4) Rules 2003, SI 2003/2113	1189
Civil Procedure (Amendment No 5) Rules 2003, SI 2003/3361	1086, 1186, 1188
Civil Procedure (Amendment No 2) Rules 2004, SI 2004/2072	1185
Civil Procedure (Amendment No 4) Rules 2004, SI 2004/3419	1100
Civil Procedure (Amendment No 4) Rules 2005, SI 2005/3515	1180, 1182
Civil Procedure (Amendment) Rules 2006, SI 2006/1689	1182, 1183, 1226
Civil Procedure (Amendment No 3) Rules 2006, SI 2006/3435	1186
Civil Procedure (Amendment) Rules 2007, SI 2007/2204	1086, 1091, 1092, 1093, 1095, 1096, 1097, 1098, 1099, 1100, 1103, 1105, 1106, 1186
Civil Procedure (Amendment) Rules 2008, SI 2008/2178	1086, 1095, 1098, 1182
Civil Procedure (Amendment No 3) Rules 2008, SI 2008/3327	1211
Civil Procedure (Amendment) Rules 2009, SI 2009/2092	1188
Civil Procedure (Amendment No 2) Rules 2009, SI 2009/3390	1180, 1182, 1183, 1189, 1209, 1211, 1213, 1215, 1216, 1220, 1223, 1225, 1226
Civil Procedure (Amendment) Rules 2010, SI 2010/621	1100
Civil Procedure (Amendment No 2) Rules 2010, SI 2010/1953	1182, 1183
Civil Procedure (Amendment) Rules 2012, SI 2012/505	1213, 1215, 1220

Civil Procedure (Amendment No 2)
  Rules 2012, SI 2012/2208   1180,
      1182, 1187, 1213, 1214
Civil Procedure (Amendment) Rules 2013,
  SI 2013/262   1100, 1105, 1115,
      1116, 1117, 1118, 1119, 1120,
      1121, 1122, 1123, 1135, 1136,
      1137, 1138, 1139, 1140, 1141,
      1142, 1148, 1149, 1150, 1151,
      1152, 1153, 1154, 1155, 1156,
      1157, 1158, 1176, 1177, 1184
Civil Procedure (Amendment No 2)
  Rules 2013, SI 2013/515   1117
Civil Procedure (Amendment No 4)
  Rules 2013, SI 2013/1412   1187
Civil Procedure (Amendment No 7)
  Rules 2013, SI 2013/1974   1086,
      1105, 1120, 1138, 1139, 1155,
                                 1180
Civil Procedure (Amendment) Rules 2014,
  SI 2014/407   1086, 1115, 1139,
      1149, 1158, 1180, 1182, 1186,
      1187, 1189, 1209, 1210, 1211,
      1213, 1214, 1215, 1217, 1220,
      1227, 1229, 1230, 1231, 1233,
      1234, 1235, 1236, 1237, 1238,
      1239, 1240, 1241, 1242, 1243,
      1244, 1245, 1246, 1247, 1248,
      1249, 1250, 1251, 1253, 1254,
      1255, 1256, 1257, 1258, 1259,
      1260, 1261, 1262
Civil Procedure (Amendment No 2)
  Rules 2014, SI 2014/482   1251, 1252
Civil Procedure (Amendment No 4)
  Rules 2014, SI 2014/867   1229
Civil Procedure (Amendment No 6)
  Rules 2014, SI 2014/2044   1182,
      1183, 1184, 1187, 1231, 1234
Civil Procedure (Amendment No 8)
  Rules 2014, SI 2014/3299   1105,
      1120, 1157, 1186
Civil Procedure (Amendment No 2)
  Rules 2015, SI 2015/670   1136, 1142
Civil Procedure (Amendment No 4)
  Rules 2015, SI 2015/1569   1150
Companies (Tables A to F)
  Regulations 1985, SI 1985/805
  Table A, art 71   186
Costs in Criminal Cases (General)
  Regulations 1986, SI 1986/1335   830
Court Funds Rules 2011, SI 2011/1734   546
Court of Proptection Rules 2007, SI 2007/
  1744
  Pt 5
  r 25(2)(m)   782
Court of Protection (Amendment)
  Rules 2009, SI 2009/582   378, 770,
                                  816
Court of Protection (Amendment)
  Rules 2011, SI 2011/2753   771

Court of Protection (Amendment)
  Rules 2015, SI 2015/548   755, 760,
      762, 763, 770, 772, 773, 774,
      775, 780, 786, 789, 790, 791,
      792, 793, 794, 796, 797, 798,
      800, 801, 802, 803, 804, 805,
      808, 811, 814, 815, 817, 819,
      820, 821, 824, 827, 837, 845,
      846, 848, 849, 850, 851, 852,
      853, 854, 857, 858, 860, 861,
      862, 863, 864, 865, 866, 867, 869
Court of Protection (Enduring Power of
  Attorney) Rules 2001, SI 2001/
  825   393, 756
  r 15(1)   190
Court of Protection Fees (Amendment)
  Order 2009, SI 2009/513   621, 1267,
                                 1268
Court of Protection Fees Order 2007,
  SI 2007/1745   414, 621, 1265
Court of Protection Rules 2001, SI 2001/
  824   63, 64, 392, 393, 756
  r 8   64
  Pt 10A   378
  r 11   438
  r 13   438
  r 29   74
Court of Protection Rules 2007, SI 2007/
  1744   140, 255, 256, 259, 275, 276,
      392, 393, 395, 396, 398, 399,
      402, 404, 405, 407, 408, 411,
      412, 414, 415, 434, 618, 619,
      703, 794, 1094, 2229, 2238, 2262
  Pt 2   2226
  r 3   798
  r 3(3)   819
  r 3(3)(b)   757, 794
  r 5   757
  r 5(2)   819
  r 5(2)(a)   841
  r 5(2)(b)(ii)   794, 808
  r 5(2)(g)   838
  r 25   757
  Pt 3
  r 6   836, 847, 871
  Pt 4   398, 2225
  r 10   802
  r 10(3)(a)   770
  r 11(2)   775
  r 13   808
  r 14   839
  r 15   802
  r 15(4)   776
  r 16   802
  r 16(b)   777
  r 17   802
  r 17(1)   777
  r 18   803
  r 19   777
  r 20(6)   777

Court of Protection Rules 2007, SI 2007/1744—continued

Pt 5
r 25(2)(h)	826
r 25(7)	838
r 27	2199, 2232
r 5	534

Pt 6
r 31(5)	784
r 37	798
r 6	396

Pt 7 400, 401, 794, 878, 2226
r 40(2)	794
r 41(1)(c)	795
r 42(2)	796
r 42(4)	795
r 43(4)	796
r 49	794
r 7	396

Pt 8 533, 535, 553, 619, 801, 2225
rr 50–53	794
rr 50–60	619
r 51(2)(b)	532
r 51(4)	808
r 54	803
r 8	396

Pt 9 398, 401, 533, 535, 553, 2225, 2226
rr 62–64	533, 535
r 64	532
rr 66–70	806
r 68(4)	531, 534
r 69	534, 794
r 69(4)	531
r 70	534, 803
r 70(3)	534
r 71	806
r 72	531, 534
r 72(5)	808
r 72(6)	808
r 73	808, 2226
r 73(1)(b)	808
r 73(2)	819
r 73(4)	794, 809
r 74	757, 794

Pt 10 398, 403, 535, 555, 795, 808, 826, 868, 2225

Pt 11	817
r 11	434
rr 11–14	398

Pt 12
r 84	534
r 84(3)	819
r 85	534, 2226
r 85(2)(a)	835
r 85(c)	794
r 86	781
r 87	2225
r 89	862, 877, 2199, 2232

Pt 13 2227
r 90	777, 823, 825, 826

Court of Protection Rules 2007, SI 2007/1744—continued

Pt 13—continued
r 90(1)	825
r 90(2)	822
r 91	823, 825, 826
r 92	823, 825, 826
r 13	434

Pt 14 407, 2226
r 97	808
r 99	828
r 99(1)	808
r 100	808
r 107	842
r 116	834
r 117	835

Pt 15 409, 836, 837, 2226
r 123(2)(d)	838
r 125(7)	839
r 126	839
r 130	837
r 15	398

Pt 16 410, 2226
rr 16–19	399

Pt 17 411, 2225, 2226
r 140	850
r 140(1)	847, 849
r 141(4)	848
r 141(6)	848
r 142(3)(a)	849
r 144(1)	847
r 148	820

Pt 18
r 152(2)(b)	856

Pt 19 305, 622
rr 155–168	622
r 156	758, 1002
r 157	758, 773
r 159	857
r 159(2)(e)	758
r 167	1002
r 168	1002

Pt 20 553, 620, 862
rr 169–182	620
r 20	399
r 21	399

Pt 22 415, 862

Pt 23 416
r 202	2197
r 23	398
r 24	398
r 25	534
rr 25–28	396
rr 29–39	399
rr 40–49	400
r 42	400
r 49(2)	434
r 51	296
r 52	296
r 54	409, 533

Court of Protection Rules 2007, SI 2007/
1744—continued
rr 55–56	553
r 56	553
r 57	553
r 59	534
rr 61–76	401
rr 62–64	553
r 63(c)(iii)	299
r 64(a)	409
r 65	533, 553
r 66	533, 554
r 67	434
r 68	434
r 69	554
r 70	554
rr 77–82	403
r 83	398
r 84	533
rr 84–89	404
r 89	414, 553
rr 90–93	405
rr 94–118	407
rr 119–131	409
rr 132–139	410
rr 140–149	411
rr 150–154	411
rr 155–168	412
r 156	305
r 159	305
rr 183–194	415
rr 195–199	415
rr 200–202	416

Courts and Tribunals Fee
Remissions Order 2013, SI 2013/
2302 1265, 1267, 1268, 1276
Courts and Tribunals Fees (Miscellaneous Amendments) Order 2014,
SI 2014/590 1276
Crime and Courts Act 2013 (Family Court: Consequential Provision) (No 2) Order 2014, SI 2014/879 1182, 1186

Employment Equality (Age)
Regulations 2006, SI 2006/1031 47
Enduring Powers of Attorney Act 1985 (Commencement Order) 1986,
SI 1986/125 188
European Communities (Quality System for Blood Establishments)
Regulations 2006, SI 2006/562 597
European Qualifications (Health and Social Care Professions) Regulations 2007,
SI 2007/3101 597

Family Procedure Rules 2010, SI 2010/
2955 586, 772
Pt IX 595
r 21.1(1) 842

Family Procedure Rules 2010, SI 2010/
2955—continued
r 21.1(3)(a)	842
r17.4	775

Family Procedure (Amendment) Rules 2011,
SI 2011/1328 1343
Financial Services and Markets Act 2000 (Consequential Amendments and Repeals) Order 2001, SI 2001/
3649 2417

Health and Social Care Act 2008 (Commencement No.16, Transitory and Transitional Provisions) Order 2010, SI 2010/807 1320
Health and Social Care Act 2008 (Consequential Amendments No 2) Order 2010, SI 2010/813 601, 604, 617, 624, 625, 664, 673, 674
Health and Social Care Act 2012 (Consequential Provision – Social Workers) Order 2012, SI 2012/
1479 1280
Health and Social Care Act 2012 (Consequential Provision—Social Workers) Order 2012, SI 2012/
1479 1333, 1335
Health Service (Control of Patient Information) Regulations 2002,
SI 2002/1438 1674

Insolvency Rules 1986, SI 1986/1925 454

Lasting Powers of Attorney, Enduring Powers of Attorney and Public Guardian (Amendment)
Regulations 2007, SI 2007/2161 624, 710, 719, 1284
Lasting Powers of Attorney, Enduring Powers of Attorney and Public Guardian (Amendment)
Regulations 2009, SI 2009/1884 214, 624, 680, 710, 719, 1286, 1291, 2045
Lasting Powers of Attorney, Enduring Powers of Attorney and Public Guardian (Amendment)
Regulations 2010, SI 2010/
1063 1288, 1293, 1298, 1300
Lasting Powers of Attorney, Enduring Powers of Attorney and Public Guardian (Amendment)
Regulations 2013, SI 2013/506 1283, 1284, 1285, 1292, 1293
Lasting Powers of Attorney, Enduring Powers of Attorney and Public Guardian (Amendment)
Regulations 2015, SI 2015/899 1278, 1279, 1281, 1282, 1284, 1298, 1299, 1300

Lasting Powers of Attorney, Enduring
Powers of Attorney and Public
Guardian Regulations 2007, SI 2007/
1253   194, 214, 255, 256, 422, 624,
680, 710, 719, 756, 1278, 2045
reg 5   214
reg 6   681
reg 8(1)   236
reg 8(3)   237
reg 9(1)   241
reg 9(5)   239
reg 10   247, 532
reg 11   532
reg 12   532, 682
reg 13   532
reg 14(2)   532
reg 14(4)   532
reg 15(3)   532
reg 17   532
reg 17(5)   249
reg 21   245, 252, 581, 686
reg 23   531
reg 24   531
reg 26   531
reg 33   876
reg 43   423
reg 46   624
reg 47   624
Sch 2   247, 532, 682, 683
Sch 3   532
Sch 4   682, 683
Sch 5   249, 685
Sch 7   190, 531, 711
Sch 8   709
Lay Representatives (Right of Audience)
Order 1999, SI 1999/1225   61
Legal Aid, Sentencing and Punishment of
Offenders Act 2012 (Consequential,
Transitional and Saving Provisions)
Regulations 2013, SI 2013/534   770,
855
Lord Chancellor (Transfer of Functions and
Supplementary Provisions) (No 2)
Order 2006, SI 2006/1016   588, 614,
615, 619, 620, 628

Medicines (Advisory Bodies) (No 2)
Regulations 2005, SI 2005/2754   597
Medicines for Human Use (Clinical Trials)
Amendment (No 2)
Regulations 2006, SI 2006/2984   597,
2382
Medicines for Human Use (Clinical Trials)
Amendment Regulations 2006,
SI 2006/1928   597
Medicines for Human Use (Clinical Trials)
Regulations 2004, SI 2004/1031   341,
342, 343, 344, 1672, 1674, 1681,
2382

Medicines (Marketing Authorisations and
Miscellaneous Amendments)
Regulations 2004, SI 2004/3224   597
Medicines (Marketing Authorisations Etc)
Amendment Regulations 2005,
SI 2005/2759   597
Mental Capacity Act 2005 (Appropriate
Body) (England) Regulations 2006,
SI 2006/2810   597, 1675
Mental Capacity Act 2005 (Appropriate
Body) (Wales) Regulations 2007,
SI 2007/833   597
Mental Capacity Act 2005 (Commencement
No 1) (Amendment) Order 2006,
SI 2006/3473   630
Mental Capacity Act 2005 (Commencement
No 1) (England and Wales)
Order 2007, SI 2007/563   630
Mental Capacity Act 2005 (Commencement
No 1) Order 2006, SI 2006/2814   630
Mental Capacity Act 2005 (Commencement
No 2) Order 2007, SI 2007/1897   630
Mental Capacity Act 2005 (Commencement)
(Wales) Order 2007, SI 2007/
856   630
Mental Capacity Act 2005 (Independent
Mental Capacity Advocates)
(Expansion of Roles)
Regulations 2006, SI 2006/2883   610,
1655
Mental Capacity Act 2005 (Independent
Mental Capacity Advocates)
(General) Regulations 2006, SI 2006/
1832   329, 601, 602, 1655
reg 4(2)   603
Mental Capacity Act 2005 (Independent
Mental Capacity Advocates) (Wales)
Regulations 2007, SI 2007/852   601,
602, 610, 1655
Mental Capacity Act 2005 (Loss of Capacity
During Research Project) (England)
Regulations 2007, SI 2007/679   344,
600, 1681
Mental Capacity Act 2005 (Loss of Capacity
During Research Project) (Wales)
Regulations 2007, SI 2007/837   600
Mental Capacity Act 2005 (Transfer of
Proceedings) Order 2007, SI 2007/
1899   312, 390, 589, 1300
art 2   1303
art 2(2)   116
art 2(3)   1301
art 2(3)(a)   1301
art 2(3)(b)   1302
art 2(3)(c)   1302
art 2(3)(d)   1302
art 3(2)   116
art 3(3)(c)   116

Mental Capacity Act 2005 (Transitional and
  Consequential Provisions)
  Order 2007, SI 2007/1898 454, 1303
  Sch 1 454
Mental Capacity (Deprivation of Liberty:
  Appointment of Relevant
  Person's Representative)
  (Amendment) Regulations 2008,
  SI 2008/2368 374, 377, 641, 667
Mental Capacity (Deprivation of Liberty:
  Appointment of Relevant
  Person's Representative)
  Regulations 2008, SI 2008/1315 374,
    377, 641, 666, 1327
  Pt 1 667
  reg 3 377
  reg 4 377
  reg 5 377, 609
  reg 6 377
  reg 7 377
  reg 8 377
  reg 9 377
  reg 10 377, 667
  reg 12 668
  regs 12–14 377
  reg 13 608, 668
  reg 14 608, 668
  reg 15 377, 669
Mental Capacity (Deprivation of Liberty:
  Appointment of Relevant
  Person's Representative) (Wales)
  Regulations 2009, SI 2009/266 (W
  29) 601, 638, 641
  reg 15 668
Mental Capacity (Deprivation of Liberty:
  Assessments, Standard
  Authorisations and Disputes about
  Residence) (Wales) Regulations 2009,
  SI 2009/783 648, 663
Mental Capacity (Deprivation of Liberty:
  Monitoring and Reporting; and
  Assessments – Amendment)
  Regulations 2009, SI 2009/827 648,
    663, 664, 671, 1334, 1340
Mental Capacity (Deprivation of Liberty:
  Standard Authorisations,
  Assessments and Ordinary
  Residence) Regulations 2008,
  SI 2008/1858 648
  Pt 2 664
  Pt 3 664
  reg 2 664
  reg 3 375
  reg 4 376
  reg 5 376
  reg 6 376
  reg 7 376
  reg 8 376
  reg 9 376
  reg 10 376
  reg 11 376

Mental Capacity (Deprivation of Liberty:
  Standard Authorisations,
  Assessments and Ordinary
  Residence) Regulations 2008,
  SI 2008/1858—continued
  reg 12 376
  reg 13 376
  reg 14 376
  reg 15 376
  reg 16 376, 638
Mental Health Act 2007 (Commencement
  No 7 and Transitional Provisions)
  Order 2008, SI 2008/1900 595
Mental Health Act 2007 (Commencement
  No 10 and Transitional Provisions)
  Order 2009, SI 2009/139 (C.9) 630,
    679
Mental Health and Mental Capacity
  (Advocacy) Amendment (England)
  Regulations 2009, SI 2009/2376 601,
    1264
Mental Health (Care and Treatment)
  (Scotland) Act 2003 (Modification of
  Enactments) Order 2005, SI 2005/
  465 2372, 2373, 2395, 2400, 2401,
    2411
Mental Health (Care and Treatment)
  (Scotland) Act 2003 (Modification of
  Subordinate Legislation) Order 2005,
  SSI 2005/445 2428, 2429, 2433
Mental Health Review Tribunal Rules 1983,
  SI 1983/942 454
Motor Vehicles (Tests) Regulations 1981,
  SI 1981/1694 454

National Savings Bank Regulations 1972,
  SI 1972/764 454
National Savings Stock
  Register Regulations 1976, SI 1976/
  2012 454
National Treatment Agency (Abolition) and
  the Health and Social Care Act 2012
  (Consequential, Transitional and
  Saving Provisions) Order 2013,
  SI 2013/235 1339
Non-contentious Probate Rules 1987,
  SI 1987/2024 454

Pharmacists and Pharmacy
  Technicians Order 2007, SI 2007/
  289 597
Premium Savings Bond Regulations 1972,
  SI 1972/765 454
Public Bodies (Joint Working) (Scotland)
  Act 2014 (Consequential
  Modifications and Saving)
  Order 2015, SI 2015/157 2344, 2345
Public Guardian (Fees, etc) (Amendment)
  Regulations 2007, SI 2007/2616 423,
    624, 1324

Public Guardian (Fees, etc) (Amendment)
    Regulations 2009, SI 2009/514   624,
                                     1321
Public Guardian (Fees, etc) (Amendment)
    Regulations 2010, SI 2010/
    1062   1325, 1326
Public Guardian (Fees, etc) (Amendment)
    Regulations 2013, SI 2013/
    1748   1325, 1326
Public Guardian (Fees, etc)
    Regulations 2007, SI 2007/2051   246,
            423, 624, 710, 711, 719, 1300,
                  1321, 1323, 1324, 1326
Public Guardian (Fees, etc.) (Amendment)
    Regulations 2011, SI 2011/
    2189   1322, 1323, 1324, 1325
Public Services Reform (Scotland) Act 2010
    (Consequential Modifications)
    Order 2011, SSI 2011/211   2371,
                               2373, 2413

Road Vehicles (Construction and Use)
    Regulations 1986, SI 1986/1078   454

Savings Certificates Regulations 1991,
    SI 1991/1031   454

Tribunals, Courts and Enforcement Act 2007
    (Consequential Amendments)
    Order 2012, SI 2012/2404   578, 581,
                   627, 686, 708, 715, 719

Welfare Reform (Consequential
    Amendments) (Scotland) (No 2)
    Regulations 2013, SI 2013/137   2372,
                                     2373

Chronological List of Statutory Instruments

1972 National Savings Bank
Regulations 1972, SI 1972/764
Premium Savings Bond
Regulations 1972, SI 1972/765
1976 National Savings Stock
Register Regulations 1976, SI 1976/2012
1981 Motor Vehicles (Tests)
Regulations 1981, SI 1981/1694
1983 Mental Health Review Tribunal
Rules 1983, SI 1983/942
1985 Companies (Tables A to F)
Regulations 1985, SI 1985/805
1986 Enduring Powers of Attorney Act 1985 (Commencement Order) 1986, SI 1986/125
Road Vehicles (Construction and Use) Regulations 1986, SI 1986/1078
Costs in Criminal Cases (General) Regulations 1986, SI 1986/1335
Insolvency Rules 1986, SI 1986/1925
1987 Non-contentious Probate Rules 1987, SI 1987/2024
1991 Savings Certificates Regulations 1991, SI 1991/1031
1998 Civil Procedure Rules 1998, SI 1998/3132
1999 Act of Sederunt (Summary Applications, Statutory Applications and Appeals etc Rules) 1999, SI 1999/929
Lay Representatives (Right of Audience) Order 1999, SI 1999/1225
2000 Civil Procedure (Amendment) Rules 2000, SI 2000/221
Civil Procedure (Amendment No 4) Rules 2000, SI 2000/2092
2001 Adults with Incapacity (Scotland) Act 2000 (Commencement No 1) Order 2001, SSI 2001/81
Act of Sederunt (Summary Applications, Statutory Applications and Appeals etc Rules) Amendment (Adults with Incapacity) 2001, SSI 2001/142
Court of Protection Rules 2001, SI 2001/824
Court of Protection (Enduring Power of Attorney) Rules 2001, SI 2001/825
Civil Procedure (Amendment No 4) Rules 2001, SI 2001/2792
Financial Services and Markets Act 2000 (Consequential Amendments and Repeals) Order 2001, SI 2001/3649
Civil Procedure (Amendment No 5) Rules 2001, SI 2001/4015
2002 Act of Sederunt (Summary Applications, Statutory Applications and Appeals etc. Rules) Amendment (No 3) (Adults with Incapacity) 2002, SSI 2002/146
Health Service (Control of Patient Information) Regulations 2002, SI 2002/1438
Civil Procedure (Amendment) Rules 2002, SI 2002/2058
2003 Act of Sederunt (Summary Applications, Statutory Applications and Appeals etc. Rules) Amendment (International Protection of Adults) 2003, SI 2003/556
Civil Procedure (Amendment No 4) Rules 2003, SI 2003/2113
Civil Procedure (Amendment No 5) Rules 2003, SI 2003/3361
2004 Act of Sederunt (Ordinary Cause, Summary Application, Summary Cause and Small Claim Rules) Amendment (Miscellaneous) 2004, SSI 2004/197
Medicines for Human Use (Clinical Trials) Regulations 2004, SI 2004/1031
Civil Procedure (Amendment No 2) Rules 2004, SI 2004/2072
Medicines (Marketing Authorisations and Miscellaneous Amendments) Regulations 2004, SI 2004/3224
Civil Procedure (Amendment No 4) Rules 2004, SI 2004/3419
2005 Mental Health (Care and Treatment) (Scotland) Act 2003 (Modification of Subordinate Legislation) Order 2005, SSI 2005/445
Mental Health (Care and Treatment) (Scotland) Act 2003 (Modification of Enactments) Order 2005, SI 2005/465
Adults with Incapacity (Management of Residents' Finances) (Scotland) Regulations 2005, SSI 2005/610
Medicines (Advisory Bodies) (No 2) Regulations 2005, SI 2005/2754
Medicines (Marketing

Authorisations Etc) Amendment Regulations 2005, SI 2005/2759
Civil Procedure (Amendment No 4) Rules 2005, SI 2005/3515

2006 European Communities (Quality System for Blood Establishments) Regulations 2006, SI 2006/562
Lord Chancellor (Transfer of Functions and Supplementary Provisions) (No 2) Order 2006, SI 2006/1016
Employment Equality (Age) Regulations 2006, SI 2006/1031
Civil Procedure (Amendment) Rules 2006, SI 2006/1689
Mental Capacity Act 2005 (Independent Mental Capacity Advocates) (General) Regulations 2006, SI 2006/1832
Medicines for Human Use (Clinical Trials) Amendment Regulations 2006, SI 2006/1928
Mental Capacity Act 2005 (Appropriate Body) (England) Regulations 2006, SI 2006/2810
Mental Capacity Act 2005 (Commencement No 1) Order 2006, SI 2006/2814
Mental Capacity Act 2005 (Independent Mental Capacity Advocates) (Expansion of Roles) Regulations 2006, SI 2006/2883
Medicines for Human Use (Clinical Trials) Amendment (No 2) Regulations 2006, SI 2006/2984
Civil Procedure (Amendment No 3) Rules 2006, SI 2006/3435
Mental Capacity Act 2005 (Commencement No 1) (Amendment) Order 2006, SI 2006/3473

2007 Pharmacists and Pharmacy Technicians Order 2007, SI 2007/289
Adult Support and Protection (Scotland) Act 2007 (Commencement No 1, Transitional Provision and Savings) Order 2007, SSI 2007/334
Mental Capacity Act 2005 (Commencement No 1) (England and Wales) Order 2007, SI 2007/563
Mental Capacity Act 2005 (Loss of Capacity During Research Project) (England) Regulations 2007, SI 2007/679
Mental Capacity Act 2005 (Appropriate Body) (Wales) Regulations 2007, SI 2007/833
Mental Capacity Act 2005 (Loss of Capacity During Research Project) (Wales) Regulations 2007, SI 2007/837
Mental Capacity Act 2005 (Independent Mental Capacity Advocates) (Wales) Regulations 2007, SI 2007/852
Mental Capacity Act 2005 (Commencement) (Wales) Order 2007, SI 2007/856
Lasting Powers of Attorney, Enduring Powers of Attorney and Public Guardian Regulations 2007, SI 2007/1253
Court of Proptection Rules 2007, SI 2007/1744
Court of Protection Rules 2007, SI 2007/1744
Court of Protection Fees Order 2007, SI 2007/1745
Mental Capacity Act 2005 (Commencement No 2) Order 2007, SI 2007/1897
Mental Capacity Act 2005 (Transitional and Consequential Provisions) Order 2007, SI 2007/1898
Mental Capacity Act 2005 (Transfer of Proceedings) Order 2007, SI 2007/1899
Public Guardian (Fees, etc) Regulations 2007, SI 2007/2051
Lasting Powers of Attorney, Enduring Powers of Attorney and Public Guardian (Amendment) Regulations 2007, SI 2007/2161
Civil Procedure (Amendment) Rules 2007, SI 2007/2204
Public Guardian (Fees, etc) (Amendment) Regulations 2007, SI 2007/2616
European Qualifications (Health and Social Care Professions) Regulations 2007, SI 2007/3101

2008 Act of Sederunt (Summary Applications, Statutory Applications and Appeals etc Rules) Amendment (Adult Support and Protection (Scotland) Act 2007) 2008, SSI 2008/111
Adults with Incapacity (Electronic Communications) (Scotland) Order 2008, SSI 2008/380
Mental Capacity (Deprivation of Liberty: Appointment of Relevant Person's Representative) Regulations 2008, SI 2008/1315
Mental Capacity (Deprivation of Liberty: Standard Authorisations, Assessments and Ordinary Residence) Regulations 2008, SI 2008/1858

Table of Statutory Instruments

　　Mental Health Act 2007
　　　(Commencement No 7 and
　　　Transitional Provisions)
　　　Order 2008, SI 2008/1900
　　Civil Procedure (Amendment)
　　　Rules 2008, SI 2008/2178
　　Mental Capacity (Deprivation of
　　　Liberty: Appointment of
　　　Relevant Person's Representative)
　　　(Amendment) Regulations 2008,
　　　SI 2008/2368
　　Allocation and Transfer of
　　　Proceedings Order 2008, SI 2008/
　　　2836
　　Civil Procedure (Amendment No 3)
　　　Rules 2008, SI 2008/3327
2009　Mental Health Act 2007
　　　(Commencement No 10 and
　　　Transitional Provisions)
　　　Order 2009, SI 2009/139 (C.9)
　　Mental Capacity (Deprivation of
　　　Liberty: Appointment of
　　　Relevant Person's Representative)
　　　(Wales) Regulations 2009, SI
　　　2009/266 (W 29)
　　Court of Protection
　　　Fees (Amendment) Order 2009,
　　　SI 2009/513
　　Public Guardian (Fees, etc)
　　　(Amendment) Regulations 2009,
　　　SI 2009/514
　　Court of Protection (Amendment)
　　　Rules 2009, SI 2009/582
　　Mental Capacity (Deprivation of
　　　Liberty: Assessments, Standard
　　　Authorisations and
　　　Disputes about Residence)
　　　(Wales) Regulations 2009, SI
　　　2009/783
　　Mental Capacity (Deprivation of
　　　Liberty: Monitoring and
　　　Reporting; and Assessments –
　　　Amendment) Regulations 2009,
　　　SI 2009/827
　　Lasting Powers of Attorney,
　　　Enduring Powers of Attorney
　　　and Public Guardian
　　　(Amendment) Regulations 2009,
　　　SI 2009/1884
　　Civil Procedure (Amendment)
　　　Rules 2009, SI 2009/2092
　　Mental Health and Mental
　　　Capacity (Advocacy)
　　　Amendment (England)
　　　Regulations 2009, SI 2009/2376
　　Civil Procedure (Amendment No 2)
　　　Rules 2009, SI 2009/3390
2010　Civil Procedure (Amendment)
　　　Rules 2010, SI 2010/621
　　Health and Social Care Act 2008
　　　(Commencement No.16,
　　　Transitory and Transitional
　　　Provisions) Order 2010, SI 2010/
　　　807
　　Health and Social Care Act 2008
　　　(Consequential Amendments No
　　　2) Order 2010, SI 2010/813
　　Public Guardian (Fees, etc)
　　　(Amendment) Regulations 2010,
　　　SI 2010/1062
　　Lasting Powers of Attorney,
　　　Enduring Powers of Attorney
　　　and Public Guardian
　　　(Amendment) Regulations 2010,
　　　SI 2010/1063
　　Civil Procedure (Amendment No 2)
　　　Rules 2010, SI 2010/1953
　　Family Procedure Rules 2010, SI
　　　2010/2955
2011　Public Services Reform (Scotland)
　　　Act 2010 (Consequential
　　　Modifications) Order 2011, SSI
　　　2011/211
　　Family Procedure (Amendment)
　　　Rules 2011, SI 2011/1328
　　Court Funds Rules 2011, SI 2011/
　　　1734
　　Public Guardian (Fees, etc.)
　　　(Amendment) Regulations 2011,
　　　SI 2011/2189
　　Court of Protection (Amendment)
　　　Rules 2011, SI 2011/2753
2012　Civil Procedure (Amendment)
　　　Rules 2012, SI 2012/505
　　Health and Social Care Act 2012
　　　(Consequential Provision – Social
　　　Workers) Order 2012, SI 2012/
　　　1479
　　Health and Social Care Act 2012
　　　(Consequential Provision—Social
　　　Workers) Order 2012, SI 2012/
　　　1479
　　Civil Procedure (Amendment No 2)
　　　Rules 2012, SI 2012/2208
　　Tribunals, Courts and Enforcement
　　　Act 2007 (Consequential
　　　Amendments) Order 2012, SI
　　　2012/2404
2013　Welfare Reform (Consequential
　　　Amendments) (Scotland) (No 2)
　　　Regulations 2013, SI 2013/137
　　Act of Sederunt (Sheriff Court
　　　Rules)
　　　(Miscellaneous Amendments)
　　　(No 3) 2013, SSI 2013/171
　　National Treatment Agency
　　　(Abolition) and the Health and
　　　Social Care Act 2012
　　　(Consequential, Transitional and
　　　Saving Provisions) Order 2013, SI
　　　2013/235
　　Civil Procedure (Amendment)
　　　Rules 2013, SI 2013/262
　　Civil Legal Aid (Financial

Resources and Payment for Services) Regulations 2013, SI 2013/480
Lasting Powers of Attorney, Enduring Powers of Attorney and Public Guardian (Amendment) Regulations 2013, SI 2013/506
Civil Procedure (Amendment No 2) Rules 2013, SI 2013/515
Legal Aid, Sentencing and Punishment of Offenders Act 2012 (Consequential, Transitional and Saving Provisions) Regulations 2013, SI 2013/534
Civil Procedure (Amendment No 4) Rules 2013, SI 2013/1412
Public Guardian (Fees, etc) (Amendment) Regulations 2013, SI 2013/1748
Civil Procedure (Amendment No 7) Rules 2013, SI 2013/1974
Courts and Tribunals Fee Remissions Order 2013, SI 2013/2302

2014 Civil Procedure (Amendment) Rules 2014, SI 2014/407
Civil Procedure (Amendment No 2) Rules 2014, SI 2014/482
Courts and Tribunals Fees (Miscellaneous Amendments) Order 2014, SI 2014/590
Civil Procedure (Amendment No 4) Rules 2014, SI 2014/867
Crime and Courts Act 2013 (Family Court: Consequential Provision) (No 2) Order 2014, SI 2014/879
Civil Procedure (Amendment No 6) Rules 2014, SI 2014/2044
Civil Procedure (Amendment No 8) Rules 2014, SI 2014/3299

2015 Public Bodies (Joint Working) (Scotland) Act 2014 (Consequential Modifications and Saving) Order 2015, SI 2015/157
Court of Protection (Amendment) Rules 2015, SI 2015/548
Civil Procedure (Amendment No 2) Rules 2015, SI 2015/670
Lasting Powers of Attorney, Enduring Powers of Attorney and Public Guardian (Amendment) Regulations 2015, SI 2015/899
Care Act 2014 and Children and Families Act 2014 (Consequential Amendments) Order 2015, SI 2015/914
Civil Procedure (Amendment No 4) Rules 2015, SI 2015/1569

Table of Cases

References are to page numbers.

From April 2014, there has been a dedicated case reference to all reported Court of Protection cases in the following style: [2015] EWCOP 50. This has been applied retrospectively by BAILII, although the old citation will still find the case and has been retained in this volume.

(1) Northamptonshire Healthcare NHS Foundation Trust and (2) Northampton
    and Nene CCG v ML (By His Litigation Friend the Official Solicitor),
    EL and BL [2014] EWCOP 2, [2014] COPLR 439   2307

A (Conjoined Twins: Medical Treatment) (No 2), Re [2001] 1 FLR 267, CA   851, 1098, 1102
A (Male Sterilisation), Re [2000] 1 FLR 549, CA   151, 310, 311, 1530, 1575, 1579, 1625
A and B (Court of Protection: Delay and Costs) [2014] EWCOP 48, [2015]
    COPLR 1   404, 757, 767, 1032, 2323
A and C (Equality and Human Rights Commission Intervening), Re [2010]
    EWHC 978 (Fam), [2010] COPLR Con Vol 10   162, 573, 2305
A County Council v DP, RS, BB (by the Children's Guardian) [2005] EWHC
    1593 (Fam), [2005] 2 FLR 1031   764
A County Council v MB, JB and A Residential Home [2010] EWHC 2508
    (COP), [2010] COPLR Con Vol 65   2309
A Healthcare NHS Trust v P (By His Litigation Friend the Official Solicitor)
    and Q [2015] EWCOP 15 (Fam), [2015] COPLR 147   824, 2320
A Hospital v SW and A PCT [2007] EWHC 425 (Fam)   439
A Local Authority v (1) MA (2) NA and (3) SA [2005] EWHC 2942, [2006] 1
    FLR 867   456
A Local Authority v A [2004] Fam 96, [2004] 1 FLR 541   311
A Local Authority v AK & Ors [2012] EWHC B29 (COP), [2013] COPLR 163   119, 121,
                                                                                   567, 2303
A Local Authority v B, F and G [2014] EWHC B18 (COP)   781, 871
A Local Authority v DL [2011] EWHC 1022 (Fam), [2011] COPLR Con Vol
    101   1478
A Local Authority v E and Others [2012] EWHC 1639 (COP), [2012] COPLR
    441   123, 325, 336, 337, 570, 2316
A Local Authority v ED [2013] EWHC 3069 (COP)   757
A Local Authority v FG and Others (No 1) [2011] EWHC 3932 (COP), [2012]
    COPLR 473   861
A Local Authority v H [2012] EWHC 49 (COP), [2012] COPLR 305   315
A Local Authority v K and Others [2013] EWHC 242 (COP), [2013] COPLR
    194   319, 806, 825, 919, 2317
A Local Authority v M (By His Litigation Friend the Official Solicitor), E and
    A [2014] EWCOP 33, [2015] COPLR 6   764, 2322
A Local Authority v Mrs A and Mr A [2010] EWHC 1549 (Fam), [2011] Fam
    61, [2010] COPLR Con Vol 138   120, 568, 2301
A Local Authority v PB and P (By his Litigation Friend the Official Solicitor)
    [2011] EWHC 2675 (COP), [2012] COPLR 1   444, 762, 763, 765, 2308
A Local Authority v PB and P [2011] EWHC 502 (COP), [2011] COPLR Con
    Vol 166   781, 2322
A Local Authority v S [2012] EWHC 1442 (Fam), [2012] 1 WLR 3098, [2013]
    1 FLR 1429   839
A Local Authority v TZ (By his Litigation Friend, the Official Solicitor) [2013]
    EWHC 2322 (COP), [2013] COPLR 477   315, 317, 444, 2302
A Local Authority v TZ (No 2) [2014] EWCOP 97   445
A Local Health Board v AB [2015] EWCOP 31   459
A NHS Foundation Trust v Ms X (By Her Litigation Friend, the Official
    Solicitor) [2014] EWCOP 35, [2015] COPLR 11   337

xlix

Table of Cases

A NHS Trust v P [2013] EWHC 50 (COP), [2013] COPLR 405   319
A PCT v LDV [2013] EWHC 272 (Fam), [2013] COPLR 204   352
A Primary Care Trust v LDV [2013] EWHC 272 (Fam), [2013] COPLR 204   365, 367, 369, 633
A v A Health Authority [2002] EWHC 18 (Fam), [2002] Fam 213, [2002] 1 FLR 845   463
A v A Local Authority, A Care Home Manager and S [2011] EWHC 727 (COP), [2011] COPLR Con Vol 190   759, 2308
A, B & C v X & Z (unreported, 30 July 2012)   242
A, B and C v X, Y and Z [2012] EWHC 2400 (COP), [2013] COPLR 1   111, 121, 136, 294, 314, 444, 566, 768, 2303
A, Re; D v B Case No 11661992 [2009] COPLR Con Vol 1   155, 570, 2331
AB v LCC (A Local Authority) and the Care Manager of BCH [2011] EWHC 3151 (COP), [2012] COPLR 314   374, 378, 439, 590, 765, 846, 2321
AB, Re [2014] COPLR 381   446, 788, 794, 806
ACCG & Anor v MN & Anor [2013] EWHC 3859 (COP), [2014] COPLR 11   476
Adrian Douglas Ward, Applicant, 2014 SLT (Sh Ct) 15   521
AG, Re [2015] EWCOP 78   764
AH (Costs), Re; AH and Others v Hertfordshire Partnership NHS Foundation Trust [2011] EWHC 3524 (COP), [2012] COPLR 327   2323
AH v (1) Hertfordshire Partnership NHS Foundation Trust and (2) Ealing Primary Care trust [2011] EWHC 276 (COP), [2011] COPLR Con Vol 195   444
Aintree University Hospitals NHS Foundation Trust v James & Ors [2013] UKSC 67, [2014] AC 591, [2013] COPLR 492   149, 150, 154, 156, 322, 325, 339, 340, 445, 866, 2317, 2331
Airedale NHS Trust v Bland [1993] AC 789, [1993] 1 FLR 1026, HL   32, 310, 323, 1625
Airey v Ireland (Application No 6289/73) [1979] ECHR 6289/73, (1979) 2 EHRR 305   359
AJ (By Her Litigation Friend the Official Solicitor) v A Local Authority [2015] EWCOP 5, [2015] COPLR 167   163, 377, 2308
AK (gift application), Re [2014] EWHC B11 (COP)   446
AK (Medical Treatment: Consent), Re [2001] 1 FLR 129   119, 125, 568, 1547
AKP, Re (CoP Case No: 10185666, Preston County Court, 1 November 2007)   468
Albon v Naza Motor Trading Sdn Bhd [2007] EWHC 2613 (Ch), [2008] 1 WLR 2380   759
Ali v Caton & Anor [2013] EWHC 1730 (QB)   132
AM v South London & Maudsley NHS Foundation Trust & Secretary of State for Health [2013] UKUT 365 (AAC), [2013] COPLR 510   362, 364, 366, 367, 370, 630, 632, 634, 636, 688, 2307
An English Local Authority v SW and Others [2014] EWCOP 43, [2015] COPLR 29   2315
An NHS Foundation trust v VT and A [2013] EWHC 826 (Fam)   445
An NHS Trust and B PCT v DU and Others [2009] EWHC 3504 (Fam), [2009] COPLR Con Vol 210   2328
An NHS Trust v (1) K (2) Another Foundation Trust [2012] EWHC 2922 (COP), [2012] COPLR 694   319
An NHS Trust v D [2012] EWHC 885 (COP), [2012] COPLR 493   336
An NHS Trust v DE & Ors [2013] EWHC 2562 (Fam), [2013] COPLR 531   156, 319, 440, 445
An NHS Trust v DJ and Others [2012] EWHC 3524 (COP)   445
An NHS Trust v Dr A [2013] EWHC 2442 (COP), [2013] COPLR 605   327, 347, 362, 368, 369, 445, 457, 459, 687, 688
An NHS Trust v S [2003] EWHC 365 (Fam)   1568
Application by Public Guardian for Directions (Glasgow Sheriff Court, 30 June 2010)   501
Application by the Public Guardian re DC (Glasgow Sheriff Court, 14 August 2012)   507, 512
Application for guardianship in respect of NW, 2014 SLT (Sh Ct) 83   508, 510
Application in respect of S, 2013 SLT (Sh Ct) 65   511

Artico v Italy A/37 (1980) 3 EHRR 1 56
AS and DS, Re (2004) Case No 2120091/2 140
AS, Re [2013] COPLR 29 2311
Ashingdale v UK [1985] ECHR 8225/78, (1985) 7 EHRR 528 352
Aster Healthcare Ltd v Estate of Mr Shafi [2014] EWHC 77 (QB), [2014]
   COPLR 397 172
AVS v NHS Foundation Trust [2010] EWHC 2746 (COP), [2010] COPLR Con
   Vol 237 210, 763, 827

B (A Local Authority) v RM, MM and AM [2010] EWHC 3802 (Fam), [2010]
   COPLR Con Vol 247 116, 312, 566
B (Consent to Treatment: Capacity), Re [2002] EWHC 429 (Fam), [2002] 1
   FLR 1090 61, 311, 1652
B (Court of Protection: Notice of Proceedings), Re [1987] 1 WLR 552, [1987]
   2 FLR 155, ChD 300, 806
B Children, Re [2008] UKHL 35, [2009] AC 11, [2008] 2 FLR 141 764
B v H, 2014 SLT (Sh Ct) 160 510
B, Applicant, 2005 SLT (Sh Ct) 95 521
Bailey v Warren [2006] EWCA Civ 51 132, 1090, 1101
Baker Tilly (A Firm) v Makar [2013] EWHC 759 (QB), [2013] COPLR 245   131, 139, 850,
   1473, 2299
Baker, Re (an order of the Senior Judge made on 12 November 2010) 205
Banks v Goodfellow (1870) LR 5 QB 549 125, 295, 566, 1469, 1549
Barnsley Metropolitan Borough Council v GS and Others [2014] EWCOP 46,
   [2015] COPLR 51 2306
BC v PBA and Others [2011] EWHC 2580 (Fam), [2011] COPLR Con Vol
   1095 96
Beaney (deceased), Re [1978] 1 WLR 770, ChD 125, 193, 1549
Beaney, Re [1978] 2 All ER 595 1470
Beatham v Carlisle Hospitals NHS Trust (1999) *The Times*, May 20, QBD 1102, 1103
Begum, Re (an order of the Senior Judge made on 24 April 2008) 217
Bird v Luckie (1850) 8 Hare 301 105, 565
Birkin v Wing (1890) 63 LT 80 133
BJ (Incapacitated Adult), Re [2009] EWHC 3310 (Fam), [2010] 1 FLR 1373 369
BJ, Re [2008] EWHC 1097 (Fam), [2008] 2 FLR 1295; *sub nom* Re GJ
   (Incapacitated Adults); *sub nom* Salford City Council v GJ, NJ and BJ
   (by their Litigation Friends) 347, 363
Black v Yates [1992] QB 526 1101
Blankley v Central Manchester and Manchester Children's University
   Hospitals NHS Trust [2015] EWCA Civ 18, [2015] 1 WLR 4307 1473
Bloom, Re (an order of the Senior Judge made on 16 March 2012) 203, 204, 218
BM, Re; JB v AG[2014] EWCOP B20 154
Bostridge v Oxleas NHS Foundation Trust [2015] EWCA Civ 79 476
Bouette v Rose [2000] Ch 662 292
Boughton v Knight (1873) LR 3 PD 64 125, 1549
Bradbury and Others v Paterson and Others [2014] EWHC 3992 (QB), [2015]
   COPLR 425 849, 850
Bratt, Re (an order made by the Senior Judge on 14 September 2009) 222
Bray v Pearce (unreported, 6 March 2014) 126
Britton v Britton's Curator Bonis 1992 SCLR 947 497
Broomleigh Housing Association Ltd v Okonkwo [2010] EWCA Civ 1113 1509
Buckenham v Dickinson [1997] CLY 661 134
Buckley, Re: The Public Guardian v C [2013] EWCOP 2965, [2013] COPLR
   39 186, 204, 254, 285, 287, 2325

C (2009) 23 Sept, Kilmarnock Sh Ct 493
C (Adult: Refusal of Treatment), Re [1994] 1 WLR 290, [1994] 1 FLR 31 349, 1088
C (By his Litigation Friend the Official Solicitor v Blackburn with Darwen BC
   & Ors [2011] EWHC 3321 (COP), [2012] COPLR 350 2306

li

C (Care Proceedings: Parents with Disabilities), Re [2014] EWCA Civ 128,
  [2014] 1 WLR 2495, [2015] 1 FLR 521 767
C (Mental Patient: Contact), Re [1993] 1 FLR 940 310
C (Power of Attorney), Re [2000] 2 FLR 1, CA 274
C (Spinster and Mental Patient), Re [1992] 1 FLR 51 293
C (Withdrawal of Treatment: Vegetative State), Re [2010] EWHC 3448 (COP),
  [2010] COPLR Con Vol 257 149
C v A Local Authority [2011] EWHC 1539, [2011] COPLR Con Vol 972 109
C v Blackburn with Darwen Borough Council [2011] EWHC 3321 (COP),
  [2012] COPLR 350 .... 689, 691
C v C (Court of Protection: Disclosure) [2014] EWHC 131 (COP), [2014] 1
  WLR 2731, [2014] COPLR 351 137
C, Applicant (2013) 2 April, Airdrie Sh Ct 513
Cameron (deceased), Re; Phillips v Cameron [1999] Ch 386 .... 188, 203, 288
Cathcart, Re [1893] 1 Ch 466, CA 66
Cattermole v Prisk [2006] 1 FLR 693, ChD 134
CC v KK and STCC [2012] EWHC 2136 (COP), [2012] COPLR 627   107, 119, 132, 162,
                                                        378, 565, 568, 573, 590, 2301
Chan U Seek v Alvis Vehicles Ltd and Guardian Newspapers [2004] EWHC
  3092 (Ch), [2005] 1 WLR 2965 777
Chaudhry v Prabhakar [1989] 1 WLR 29, CA 186
Cheshire West and Chester Council v P [2011] EWHC 1330 (Fam), [2011]
  COPLR Con Vol 273 .... 354, 379, 444, 477, 859, 1753
Cheshire West and Chester Council v P (No 2) [2011] EWCA Civ 1333, [2012]
  COPLR 76 862
CIBC Mortgages plc v Pitt [1994] 1 AC 200, [1994] 1 FLR 17, HL 31
City of Edinburgh Council v D 2010 GWD 33-711 520
City of Sunderland v MM (by her litigation friend, the Official Solicitor), RS,
  SB, MP and SA [2009] COPLR Con Vol 881 476
City of Westminster v IC and KC and NN 5 [2008] EWCA Civ 198, [2009]
  Fam 11, [2008] 2 FLR 267 458
Clarke, Re (an order of the Senior Judge made on 18 November 2009) 216
Clarkson v Gilbert [2000] 2 FLR 839, CA 61, 622
Clauss v Pir [1988] 1 Ch 267 187
Coles v Perfect [2013] EWHC 1955 (QB) 1101
Commissioner of Police for the Metropolis v ZH [2013] EWCA Civ 69, [2013]
  1 WLR 3021, [2013] COPLR 332 .... 157, 167, 571, 573, 574
Crossley v Crossley [2007] EWCA Civ 1491, [2008] 1 FLR 1467 144
CYC v PC and NC [2012] COPLR 670 .... 112, 200, 202, 313

D (A Child), Re [2014] EWFC 39, [2015] 1 FLR 531 839
D (Costs), Re [2012] EWHC 886 (COP), [2012] COPLR 499 .... 439, 849, 2324
D (J), Re [1982] Ch 237 .... 151, 264, 292, 296
D (Statutory Will), Re [2010] EWHC 2159 (Ch), [2012] Ch 57, [2010] COPLR
  Con Vol 302 265
D Borough Council v AB [2011] EWHC 101 (COP), [2011] COPLR Con Vol
  313 .... 315, 444
D County Council v LS [2010] EWHC 1544 (Fam), [2012] Fam 36, [2010]
  COPLR Con Vol 331 444
D v An NHS Trust (Medical Treatment: Consent: Termination) [2003] EWHC
  2793 (Fam), [2004] 1 FLR 1110 .... 319, 320, 1625
D v R (Deputy of S) and S [2010] EWHC 3748 (CoP) 133
D, Re [2010] EWHC 2535 (COP) 444
D, Re [2012] EWHC 885 (COP), [2012] COPLR 493 339
D, Re; VAC v JAD [2010] EWHC 2159 (COP), [2012] Ch 57, [2010] COPLR
  Con Vol 302 .... 292, 293
Davey (Deceased), Re [1981] 1 WLR 164, ChD 292, 806
Davies, Re (an order of the Senior Judge made on 5 July 2010) 216
DCC v KH (2009) CoP Case No 11729380 363
DD v Lithuania (Application No 13469/06) (2012) ECHR 254 355

DD v Lithuania [2007] ECHR 27527/03, (2007) 46 EHRR 431   352
DE (Child under Care Order: Injunction under Human Rights Act 1998), Re
    [2014] EWFC 6, [2015] Fam 145, [2015] 1 FLR 1001   1482
De Maroussem v Commissioner of Income Tax [2004] UKPC 43, [2004] 1
    WLR 2865   181
Derbyshire CC v AC, EC and LC [2014] EWCOP 38   317
DH NHS Foundation Trust v PS [2010] EWHC 1217 (Fam), [2010] COPLR
    Con Vol 346   169, 319, 574
Dian AO v Davis Frankel and Mead [2004] EWHC 2662 (Comm), [2005] 1
    WLR 2951   777
Dietz v Lennin Chemicals Ltd [1969] 1 AC 170   1101
DL v A Local Authority and Others [2012] EWCA Civ 253, [2013] Fam 1,
    [2012] COPLR 504   455, 456, 460, 1477, 2313
DM v Doncaster Metropolitan Borough Council [2011] EWHC 3652 (Admin),
    [2012] COPLR 362   630, 2304
DN v Northumberland Tyne and Wear NHS Foundation Trust [2011] UKUT
    327 (AAC)   369, 687, 689
DP (Revocation of Lasting Power of Attorney), Re [2014] COPLR 188   2327
DP, Re; The Public Guardian v JM [2014] EWCOP 7   758, 824
Drew v Nunn (1879) 4 QBD 661, CA   187
Drinkall v Whitwood [2003] EWCA Civ 1547, [2004] 1 WLR 462   1101
Druce, Re (an order of the Senior Judge dated 31 May 2011)   223
DT, Re; the Public Guardian and IT and others [2015] EWCOP 10, [2015]
    COPLR 225   201, 203
Dunhill (A Protected Party By Her Litigation Friend Tasker) v Burgin (Nos 1
    and 2) [2014] UKSC 18, [2014] 1 WLR 933, [2014] COPLR 199   848, 1093, 1101,
    1470, 1471, 1480
Dunnett v Railtrack PLC [2002] EWCA Civ 303   766
Durham County Council v Dunn [2002] EWCA Civ 1654   844

E & K v SB & JB [2012] EWHC 4161 (COP)   873
E (An Alleged Patient), Re [2004] EWHC 2808 (Fam), [2005] Fam 326, [2005]
    1 FLR 965; sub nom Sheffield City Council v E and S   125, 566, 1470, 1549
E (By her litigation friend the Official Solicitor) v Channel Four;
    News International Ltd and St Helens Borough Council [2005] EWHC
    1144 (Fam), [2005] 2 FLR 913   310
E (Enduring Power of Attorney), Re [2001] Ch 364, [2000] 1 FLR 882, sub
    nom Re E; X v Y   221
E (Mental Health Patient), Re [1985] 1 WLR 245, CA   843
E, Re; X v Y [2001] Ch 364, [2000] 1 FLR 882; sub nom Re E (Enduring
    Power of Attorney), Re   221
Eeeles v Cobham Hire Services Ltd [2009] EWCA Civ 204, [2010] 1 WLR 409   475
EG v RS, JS and BEN PCT [2010] EWHC 3073 (COP), [2010] COPLR Con
    Vol 350   2311
Enfield LBC v SA, FA and KA [2010] EWHC 196 (Admin), [2010] COPLR
    Con Vol 362   766, 773, 827, 843
Engel & Ors v The Netherlands (Application nos 5100/71, 5101/71, 5102/71,
    5354/72, 5370/72) (1976) 1 EHRR 647   356
Essex County Council v RF [2015] EWCOP 1   476

F (A Child), Re [2014] EWCA Civ 789   765
F (Mental Capacity: Interim Jurisdiction), Re [2009] EWHC B30 (Fam), [2010]
    2 FLR 28   263
F (Mental Patient: Sterilisation), Re [1990] 2 AC 1, [1989] 2 FLR 376, HL   32, 158, 199,
    310, 1581
F v S 2012 SLT (Sh Ct) 189   493, 500
F, Re Case No 11649371 [2009] EWHC B30 (Fam), [2009] COPLR Con Vol
    390   102, 391, 565, 616, 2321
Fischer v Diffley [2013] EWHC 4567 (Ch), [2014] COPLR 212   126
Folks v Faizey [2006] EWCA Civ 381   1090
Forrest, Re (a decision of the Senior Judge made on 2 March 2012)   218

liii

FP v GM and A Health Board [2011] EWHC 2778 (COP) 146, 151, 570
G (Adult) (Costs), Re [2014] EWCOP 5, [2014] COPLR 432 773, 858, 2324
G (Adult), Re; London Borough of Redbridge v G, C and F [2014] EWCOP
 1361, [2014] COPLR 416 810, 2320
G (An Adult) (By Her Litigation Friend the Official Solicitor) (Costs), Re
 [2015] EWCA Civ 446, [2015] COPLR 438 857, 858, 862
G (An Adult) (By Her Litigation Friend The Official Solicitor) (Costs), Re
 [2015] EWCA Civ 446, [2015] COPLR 438 2324
G (TJ), Re [2010] EWHC 3005 (COP), [2010] COPLR Con Vol 403 152
G (TJ), Re [2010] EWHC 3005 (CoP), [2010] COPLR Con Vol 403 201
G (TJ), Re [2010] EWHC 3005 (COP), [2010] COPLR Con Vol 403 570, 2330
G v E [2010] EWCA Civ 822, [2012] Fam 78, [2010] COPLR Con Vol 431 352, 589, 799,
 859, 2308, 2310
G v E [2010] EWHC 2512 (COP), [2010] COPLR Con Vol 470 164, 266, 326, 573
G v E and Others [2010] EWHC 2042 (COP), [2010] COPLR Con Vol 499 259
G v E, A Local Authority and F [2010] EWHC 621 (Fam), [2010] COPLR Con
 Vol 510 259, 389, 759
G v G [2007] EWCA Civ 680, [2007] 2 FLR 1127; *sub nom* Greensill v
 Greensill 871
G v West Lothian Council 2014 GWD 40-730 505
G, Applicant, 2009 SLT (Sh Ct) 122 521
G, Re [2004] EWHC 2222 (Fam) 314
GC and Anor, Re [2008] EWHC 3402 (Fam), [2008] COPLR Con Vol 422 2331
Gillick v West Norfolk and Wisbech Area Health Authority and the DHSS
 [1986] 1 AC 112, [1986] 1 FLR 224, HL; *sub nom* Gillick v West
 Norfolk and Wisbech Area Health Authority and Another 127, 128, 848, 1686
GJ (Incapacitated Adults), Re [2008] EWHC 1097 (Fam), [2008] 2 FLR 1295;
 sub nom Salford City Council v GJ, NJ and BJ (by their Litigation
 Friends); *sub nom* Re BJ 347, 363
GJ v (1) The Foundation Trust (2) The PCT and (3) The Secretary of State
 for Health [2009] EWHC 2972 (Fam), [2010] Fam 70, [2009] COPLR
 Con Vol 567 362, 363, 366, 634, 687, 2306
Gladys Meek, Re; Jones v Parkin and Others [2014] EWCOP 1, [2014] COPLR
 535 2320
GM, Re [2013] COPLR 290 206, 286, 2311
Goodwin, Re (an order of the Senior Judge made on 17 June 2013) 218
Gorjat v Gorjat [2010] EWHC 1537 (Ch) 121
Gray v Haig (1855) 20 Beav 219 186
Great Ormond Street Hospital v Pauline Rushie (unreported, 19 April 2000) 134
Great Stuart Trustees Ltd v Public Guardian, [2015] SC 379, [2014] CSIH 114,
 2015 SLT 115 502, 510
Great Western Hospitals NHS Foundation Trust v AA, BB, CC, DD [2014]
 EWHC 132 (Fam), [2014] 2 FLR 1209 445
Greensill v Greensill [2007] EWCA Civ 680, [2007] 2 FLR 1127; *sub nom* G v
 G 871
Gregory v Turner [2003] EWCA Civ 183, [2003] 1 WLR 1149 187, 208, 360, 1094
GS, Re (CoP Case No: 11582024, Preston County Court, 10 July 2008) 141, 467
Guardian News and Media Ltd, Re [2010] UKSC 1, [2010] 2 AC 697 767
Guzzardi v Italy (1980) 3 EHRR 333, ECHR 352, 353

H (2008) 6 May, Dunoon Sh Ct 493
H (A Minor and Incapacitated Person), Re; Baker v H and the Official
 Solicitor [2009] COPLR Con Vol 606 876
H (Minors) (Sexual Abuse: Standard of Proof), Re [1996] AC 563, [1996] 1
 FLR 80, HL 566
H, Applicant, 2007 SLT (Sh Ct) 5 493, 517
H, Kilmarnock Sheriff Court, 27 January 2010 507
H, Re; Baker v H & Anor Case No 11461874 [2009] COPLR Con Vol 606 2312
H-L (Expert Evidence: Test for Permission), Re [2013] EWCA Civ 655, [2013]
 2 FLR 1434 1033

HA, Re [2012] EWHC 1068 (COP), [2012] COPLR 534 363
Hale v Tanner [2000] 1 WLR 2377, [2000] 2 FLR 879, CA 872
Hammerton v Hammerton [2007] EWCA Civ 248, [2007] 2 FLR 1133 871
Harbin v Masterman [1896] 1 Ch 351, CA 438, 551, 1090
Harcourt, Re [2013] COPLR 69 186, 198, 254, 2327
Hawes v Burgess [2013] EWCA Civ 74 133, 134
HE v A Hospital NHS Trust [2003] EWHC 1017 (Fam), [2003] 2 FLR 408 310, 333, 335
Health Service Executive of Ireland v PA and Others [2015] EWCOP 38,
 [2015] COPLR 447 2315
Heart of England NHS Fundation Trust v JB [2014] EWHC 342 (COP) 445
Henry v Hammond [1913] 2 KB 515 186
Hill v Fellowes Solicitors LLP [2011] EWHC 61 (QB) 131
Hillingdon LBC v Neary [2011] EWHC 413 (COP), [2012] 1 WLR 287, [2011]
 COPLR Con Vol 677 327, 364, 444, 826, 859, 2319
HL v The United Kingdom (Application No 45508/99) [2004] 1 FLR 1019,
 ECHR 169, 177, 210, 351, 352, 353, 355, 1596, 1597, 1703, 1757, 1763, 1770, 1840
HM (A child), Re [2012] WTLR 281 1104
HM v Switzerland [2002] ECHR 39187/98, (2002) 38 EHRR 314 352
HMF (Mental Patient: Will), Re [1976] Ch 33 292, 809
Hoff v Atherton [2004] EWCA Civ 1554 134
Hughes, Re (1999) *The Times*, 8 January 304
Hussain & Qutb v Bank of Scotland [2012] EWCA Civ 264 1093
HW, Re (2005) Case No 2122208 140

IM v (1) LM (By Her Litigation Friend the Official Solicitor) (2) AB (3)
 Liverpool City Council [2014] EWCA Civ 37, [2015] Fam 61, [2014]
 COPLR 246 316, 317, 444, 2302
Imperial Loan Company v Stone [1892] 1 QB 599, CA 171, 575
Independent News Media Ltd v A (By the Official Solicitor) [2009] EWHC
 2858, [2009] COPLR Con Vol 702 825
Independent News Media v A [2010] EWCA Civ 343, [2010] 1 WLR 2262,
 [2010] COPLR Con Vol 686 327, 2318
IRC v Duke of Westminster [1936] AC 1 293
Izzo v Phillip Ross & Co [2002] BPIR 310, ChD 61

J (A Minor) (Medical Treatment) [1993] Fam 15, [1992] 2 FLR 165, CA 311
J (A Minor) (Wardship: Medical Treatment), Re [1991] Fam 33, [1991] 1 FLR
 366, CA 323
J (Enduring Power of Attorney), Re [2009] EWHC 436 (Ch), [2010] 1 WLR
 210, [2009] COPLR Con Vol 753 224
J Council v GU, J Partnership NHS Foundation Trust, Care Quality
 Commission, X Limited [2012] EWHC 3531 (COP), [2013] COPLR 83 2332
J, Re [2011] COPLR Con Vol 716 2327
JE (Jamaica) v SSHD [2014] EWCA Civ 192 859, 862
JE v DE and Surrey County Council [2006] EWHC 3459 (Fam), [2007] 2 FLR
 1150 358
JG (A Child) v The Legal Services Commission [2013] EWHC 804 (Admin),
 [2013] 2 FLR 1174 839
JIH v News Group Newspapers [2011] EWCA Civ 42, [2011] 1 WLR 1645 1507
JMcA's Application [2013] NIQB 77 689, 691
JO v GO (Re PO) [2013] EWHC 3932 (COP), [2014] Fam 197, [2014] COPLR
 62 572, 573, 706, 2314
Joan Treadwell, Deceased, Re; Public Guardian v Lutz [2013] EWHC 2409
 (COP), [2013] COPLR 587 2311
JS v KB and MP (Property and Affairs Deputy for DB) [2014] EWHC 483
 (COP), [2014] COPLR 275 762, 859, 2324
JSC BTA Bank v Mukhtar Ablyazon [2013] EWHC 1979 (Comm) 871

K and H (Children), Re [2015] EWCA Civ 543 839
K and H (Children: Unrepresented Father: Cross-Examination of Child), Re
 [2015] EWFC 1, [2015] 2 FLR 802 839

lv

K v LBX & Ors [2012] EWCA Civ 79, [2012] COPLR 411   145, 146, 445, 569
K v LBX and Ors [2012] EWCA Civ 79, [2012] COPLR 411   2329, 2332
Kędzior v Poland (Application No 45026/07) [2012] ECHR 1809   352, 355, 372, 639
K, Re; Re F [1988] Ch 310, [1988] 2 FLR 15   242, 1088
KA, Re (unreported)   319
KC and Anor v City of Westminster Social and Community Services Department and Anor [2008] EWCA Civ 198, [2009] Fam 11, [2008] 2 FLR 267   32
KC v Poland [2014] ECHR 1322   365, 366, 372
KD and LD v Havering London Borough Council [2009] COPLR Con Vol 770   757, 782
KD v A Borough Council, the Department of Health and Others [2015] UKUT 251 (AAC), [2015] COPLR 486   2307
Kenward v Adams (1975) *The Times*, November 29   133, 1471, 1557
Key v Key [2010] EWHC 408 (Ch), [2010] 1 WLR 2020   134
Kicks v Leigh [2014] EWHC 3926 (Ch)   1469
Kittle, Re (a judgment of the Senior Judge given on 1 December 2009)   218

L (A Child), Re [2013] EWCA Civ 1557   758, 866
Law Hospital NHS Trust v Lord Advocate [1996] SC 301, [1996] 2 FLR 407   496
LB Hillingdon v Neary & Ors [2011] EWHC 1377 (COP), [2011] COPLR Con Vol 632   146, 162, 573
LB Hillingdon v Neary & Ors [2011] EWHC 1377 (COP), [2011] COPLR Con Vol 677   373
LB Hillingdon v PS and CS [2014] EWCOP 55   799
LB Tower Hamlets v TB [2014] EWCOP 53, [2015] COPLR 87   316
LBB v JM, BK and CM Case No 1155000T [2010] COPLR Con Vol 779   2322
LBL v PB and P [2011] EWHC 2675 (COP), [2012] COPLR 1   363, 364
LBL v RYJ and VJ [2010] EWHC 2665 (COP), [2010] COPLR Con Vol 795   32, 118, 119, 567, 2313
LBL v RYJ and VJ [2010] EWHC 2665 (Fam), [2010] COPLR Con Vol 795   312, 456, 461
Leather v Kirby [1965] 1 WLR 1489, HL   1104
Leigh v Michelin Tyre plc [2003] EWCA (Civ) 1766, [2004] 1 WLR 46   1127
LG v DK [2011] EWHC 2453 (COP), [2012] COPLR 80   445
Ligaya Nursing v R [2012] EWCA Crim 2521   181, 183
Lilly Icos Ltd v Pfizer (No 2) [2002] EWCA Civ 2, [2002] 1 WLR 2253   777
Lindsay v Wood [2006] EWHC 2895 (QB)   1089, 1090
London Borough of Enfield v SA [2010] EWHC 196 (Admin), [2010] COPLR Con Vol 362   407, 2318
London Borough of Havering v LD and KD [2010] EWHC 3876 (COP), [2010] COPLR Con Vol 809   109, 565, 2310
London Borough of Lewisham v Malcolm [2008] UKHL 43, [2008] 1 AC 1399   49
London Borough of Redbridge v G, C and F [2014] EWHC 485 (COP), [2014] COPLR 292   405, 445, 760, 820
London Borough of Tower Hamlets v TB (By Her Litigation Friend the Official Solicitor) [2014] EWCOP 53, [2015] COPLR 87   2302
Loughlin v Singh & Ors [2013] EWHC 1641 (QB), [2013] COPLR 371   123, 468, 567
Lumba v Secretary of State for the Home Department, [2011] UKSC 12, [2012] 1 AC 245   477

M (Best Interests: Deprivation of Liberty), Re [2013] EWHC 3456 (COP), [2014] COPLR 35   151, 760, 2331
M, Applicant, 2007 SLT (Sh Ct) 24   510, 521
M, ITW v Z & Ors, Re [2009] EWHC 2525 (Fam), [2011] 1 WLR 344, [2009] COPLR Con Vol 828   144, 146, 153, 156, 264, 570, 2329
M, Re [2011] EWHC 3590 (COP), [2012] COPLR 430   688, 2315
M, Re; N v O and P [2013] COPLR 91   2311
Manchester City Council v G, E (by his Litigation Friend the Official Solicitor) and F [2011] EWCA Civ 939, [2012] COPLR 95   2323
MASM v MMAM (By Her Litigation Friend the Official Solicitor) and Others [2015] EWCOP 3, [2015] COPLR 239   2318

Masterman-Lister v Brutton & Co and Jewell & Home Counties Dairies [2002]
    EWCA Civ 1889, [2003] 1 WLR 1511   24, 125, 132, 133, 208, 548, 1088, 1089,
                1090, 1091, 1093, 1095, 1096, 1101, 1445, 1470, 1480, 1549, 1557
MB (Medical Treatment), Re [1997] 2 FLR 426, CA   122, 311, 567, 1087, 1088, 1530, 1546
MB, Re [2010] EWHC 2508 (COP), [2010] COPLR Con Vol 65   371, 372, 375, 646, 652,
                                                                                                                                653
McDowall's Executors v Inland Revenue Commissioners [2003] UKSC
    SPC00382, [2004] STC (SCD) 22   189, 509, 510
MIG and MEG, Re [2010] EWHC 785 (Fam), [2010] COPLR Con Vol 850   354
Mihailovs v Latvia (Application No 35939/10) (2013) ECHR 65   355
Miles v The Public Guardian; Beattie v The Public Guardian [2015] EWHC
    2960 (Ch), [2015] COPLR 676   2326
Miles, Re; The Public Guardian v Miles and Others [2014] EWCOP 40, [2015]
    COPLR 107   223
Millburn-Snell v Evans [2011] EWCA Civ 577, [2012] 1 WLR 41   1093
Mitchell v Alasia [2005] EWHC 11 (QB)   1089
MM (An Adult), Re; Local Authority X v MM and KM [2007] EWHC 2003
    (Fam), [2009] 1 FLR 443   126, 151, 153, 154, 315
MN (Adult), Re [2015] EWCA Civ 411, [2015] COPLR 505   327, 470, 476, 2332
MN, Re [2010] EWHC 1926 (Fam), [2010] COPLR Con Vol 893   2314
MN, Re [2015] EWCA Civ 411, [2015] COPLR 505   463
MOD (Deprivation of Liberty), Re [2015] EWCOP 47   761, 816
Montgomery v Lanarkshire Health Board [2015] UKSC 11, [2015] 1 AC 1430   131
Moore, Re (an order of the Senior Judge made on 26 October 2010)   216, 221
Morris, Petitioner 1986, Ct of Sess (IH)   497
Morton, Minuter for Directions (Edinburgh Sheriff Court, 21 July 2010)   501
MRJ (Reconsideration of an order), Re [2014] EWHC B15 (COP)   822
Muldoon, Applicant, 2005 SCLR 611   494

National Westminster Bank v Morgan [1985] 1 AC 686, HL   31
NCC v PB and TB [2014] EWCOP 14, [2015] COPLR 118   113, 457, 2314
Newcastle City Council v PV and Criminal Injuries Compensation Authority
    [2015] EWCOP 22, [2015] COPLR 265   472, 475
Newcastle-upon-Tyne Hospitals Foundation Trust v LM [2014] EWHC 454
    (COP)   321
NHS Trust & Ors v FG [2014] EWCOP 30, [2015] 1 WLR 1984, [2014]
    COPLR 598   320
NHS Trust A v H [2001] 2 FLR 501   323
NHS Trust and B Trust v DU, AO, EB and AU [2009] EWHC 3504 Fam,
    [2009] COPLR Con Vol 210   858
NHS Trust v Dr A [2013] EWHC 2442 (COP), [2013] COPLR 605   2304, 2313
Nielson v Denmark (1988) 11 EHRR 175, ECHR   352
NK v (1) VW (By her Litigation Friend the Official Solicitor) (2) LCC (3) JW
    and (4) WW [2012] COPLR 105   2321
North Ayrshire Council v JM 2004 SCLR 956, Sh Ct   494
North Somerset Council v LW and Others [2014] EWCOP 3   320, 762, 764, 859
Northamptonshire Healthcare NHS Foundation Trust and Others v ML and
    Others [2014] EWCOP 2   367
Nottinghamshire Healthcare NHS Trust v RC [2014] EWCOP 1136   445
Nottinghamshire Healthcare NHS Trust v RC [2014] EWCOP 1317, [2014]
    COPLR 468   176, 321, 337, 445, 2316
NRA and Others, Re [2015] EWCOP 59, [2015] COPLR 690   761, 816, 846, 847, 848, 2309
NT v FS and Others [2013] EWHC 684 (COP), [2013] COPLR 313   2326

O v P [2015] EWHC 935 (Fam)   456
OL, Re: Public Guardian and DA, YS and ES [2015] EWCOP 41   186
Oldham MBC v GW and PW [2007] EWHC 136 (Fam), [2007] 2 FLR 597   107, 163

P (Abortion), Re [2013] EWHC 50 (COP), [2013] COPLR 405   2329

Table of Cases

P (By His Litigation Friend the Official Solicitor) v Cheshire West and
    Chester Council and Another; P and Q (By Their Litigation Friend the
    Official Solicitor) v Surrey County Council [2014] UKSC 19, [2014] AC
    896, [2014] COPLR 313   2305
P (Placement Orders: Parental Consent), Re [2008] EWCA Civ 535, [2008] 2
    FLR 625   1033
P (Vulnerable Adults: Deputies), Re [2010] EWHC 1592 (Fam), [2010]
    COPLR Con Vol 922   2310
P and Q (by their litigation friend the Official Solicitor) v Surrey Council
    [2014] UKSC 19, [2014] AC 896, [2014] COPLR 313   353
P and Q [2011] EWCA Civ 90, [2011] COPLR Con Vol 931   362
P and Q v Surrey County Council [2011] EWCA Civ 190, [2012] Fam 170,
    [2011] COPLR Con Vol 931   352, 354, 444, 1753
P v Cheshire West and Chester Council [2014] UKSC 19, [2014] AC 896,
    [2014] COPLR 313   280, 353, 356, 357, 364, 380, 381, 383, 388, 416, 444, 782, 816
P v Independent Print Ltd & Ors [2011] EWCA Civ 756, [2012] COPLR 110   444, 826, 2319
P v United Kingdom (2002) 12 EHRR 619   758
P, Re [2009] EWHC 163 (Ch), [2010] Ch 33, [2009] COPLR Con Vol 906   151, 154, 201, 264, 298, 2330
P, Re [2010] EWHC 1592 (Fam), [2010] COPLR Con Vol 922   266, 267, 2310
PC and Anor v City of York Council [2013] EWCA Civ 478, [2014] Fam 10,
    [2013] COPLR 409   107, 112, 113, 120, 313, 445, 565, 566, 1468, 2300
PC, Re: the Public Guardian v AC and JC [2014] EWCOP 41   186, 205
PCT v P, AH & The Local Authority [2009] EW Misc 10 (EWCOP), [2011] 1
    FLR 287   567
PD, Re; Health Service Executive of Ireland v CNWL [2015] EWCOP 48,
    [2015] COPLR 544   2316
Peters v East Midlands Strategic Health Authority [2009] EWCA Civ 145,
    [2010] QB 48   473, 474
Petition by PW and AW, Court of Session, 18 December 2013   519
PH v A Local Authority and Others [2011] EWHC 1704 (Fam), [2012] COPLR
    128   2301
PO, Re [2013] EWHC 3932 (COP), [2014] Fam 197, [2014] COPLR 62   165, 327
Press Association v Newcastle-Upon-Tyne Hospitals Foundation Trust [2014]
    EWCOP 6, [2014] COPLR 502   823
Pretty v UK (Application No 2346/02) [2002] 2 FLR 45, ECHR   323, 333
Primary Care Trust v XB [2012] EWHC 1390 (Fam), [2012] COPLR 577   445
PS (Incapacitated or Vulnerable Adult), Re [2007] EWHC 623 (Fam), [2007] 2
    FLR 1083; sub nom Sunderland City Council v P; sub nom Sunderland
    City Council v PS   32, 347
PS v LP [2013] EWHC 1106 (COP)   150, 153, 570
Public Guardian v Boff [2013] COPLR 653   2326
Public Guardian, Applicant, 2011 SLT (Sh Ct) 66   512

Q v Q; Re B (A Child); Re C (A Child) [2014] EWFC 31, [2015] 1 WLR 2040,
    [2015] 1 FLR 324   839

R (A Minor) (Wardship: Consent to Medical Treatment), Re [1992] Fam 11,
    [1992] 1 FLR 190, CA   127
R (Burke) v General Medical Council and Others [2005] EWCA Civ 1003,
    [2006] QB 273, [2005] 2 FLR 1223; [2004] EWHC 1879 (Admin),
    [2005] QB 424, [2004] 2 FLR 1121   213, 311, 323, 324, 332, 333, 435
R (C) v A Local Authority [2011] EWHC 1539 (Admin), [2011] COPLR Con
    Vol 972   2304
R (C) v Sevenoaks Youth Court [2009] EWHC 3088 (Admin)   1467
R (Chatting) v Viridian Housing [2012] EWHC 3595 (Admin), [2013] COPLR
    108   465
R (DO) v LBH [2012] EWHC 4044 (Admin)   465
R (Enduring Power of Attorney), Re [1990] Ch 647, [1991] 1 FLR 128   207
R (KM) v Cambridgeshire County Council, National Autistic Society and
    others intervening [2012] UKSC 23   466

R (on the application of Hussain) v Birmingham City Council [2002] EWHC
  949 (Admin)   1094
R (on the application of Sessay) v South London and Maudsley NHS
  Foundation Trust [2011] EWHC 2617 (QB). [2012] QB 760   167
R (OP) v SS Justice, Cheltenham MC, and CPS (Just for Kids Law intervening)
  [2014] EWHC 1944 (Admin)   1467
R (R, E, J and K by their Litigation Friend, the Official Solicitor) v
  Cafcass [2011] EWHC 1774 (Admin), [2011] 2 FLR 1206   846
R (S) v Plymouth City Council and C [2002] EWCA Civ 388, [2002] 1 WLR
  2583, [2002] 1 FLR 1177   28, 137, 156, 1557
R (T) v Legal Aid Agency [2013] EWHC 960 (Admin), [2013] 2 FLR 1315   839
R (Von Brandenburg) v East London and City NHS Trust [2003] UKHL 58,
  [2004] 2 AC 280   363
R (W) v LB Croydon [2011] EWHC 696 (Admin)   156, 570
R v A Local Authority and Ors [2011] EWHC 1539, [2011] COPLR Con Vol
  972   444
R v Bournewood Community and Mental Health NHS Trust ex p L [1999] AC
  458, [1998] 2 FLR 550, HL   210, 351
R v C [2009] UKHL 42, [2009] 1 WLR 1786   315, 444, 595
R v Collins and Ashworth Hospital Authority ex parte Brady [2001] 58 BMLR
  173   122, 567, 1546
R v Dunn [2010] EWCA Crim 2935   180, 181, 613
R v Holmes (1979) 1 Cr App R (S) 233   181, 613
R v Hopkins; R v Priest [2011] EWCA Crim 1513   181, 182, 613
R v Humberside and Scunthorpe Coroner, ex parte Jamieson [1995] QB 1   181, 613
R v Misra & Anor [2004] EWCA Crim 2375   183
R v Newington (1990) 91 Cr App R 247   181, 613, 1711
R v North Yorkshire CC, ex p Hargreaves (1994) 26 BMLR 121   44
R v Patel [2013] EWCA Crim 965   182, 613
R v Rimmington: R v Goldstein [2005] UKHL 63, [2006] 1 AC 459   183
R v Sheppard [1981] AC 394, HL   181, 613
R, Re [2003] WTLR 1051   304
RB (By His Litigation Friend the Official Solicitor) v Brighton and Hove City
  Council [2014] EWCA Civ 561, [2014] COPLR 629   2329
RC (Deceased), Re [2010] COPLR Con Vol 1022   2323
RC v CC (By Her Litigation Friend the Official Solicitor) and X Local
  Authority [2014] EWHC 131 (COP), [2014] 1 WLR 2731, [2014]
  COPLR 35   359
RC v CC and X Local Authority [2013] EWHC 1424 (COP), [2013] COPLR
  431   445, 844, 2318
Reeves, Re (CoP Case No: 99328848, 5 January 2011)   471, 474, 475
RGB v Cwm Taf Health Board and Others [2013] EWHC B23 (COP), [2014]
  COPLR 83   150, 339, 2331
RGS (No 3), Re [2014] EWHC B12 (COP)   444
RGS, Re [2012] EWHC 4162 (COP)   139
Richmond v Richmond (1914) 111 LT 273   133
RK v (1) BCC (2) YB (3) AK [2011] EWCA Civ 1305, [2012] Fam 170,
  [2012] COPLR 146   365, 444, 595
Rochdale Metropolitan Borough Council v KW & Ors (Rev 1) [2015] EWCOP
  13   862
Rochdale Metropolitan Borough Council v KW, PK and MW [2014] EWCOP
  45   862
Rodman, Re; Long v Rodman and Others [2012] EWHC 347 (Ch), [2012]
  COPLR 433   2312
Roult (by his mother and litigation friend) v North West Strategic Health
  Authority [2009] EWCA Civ 444, [2010] 1 WLR 487   1102
Royal Bank of Scotland v Etridge (No 2) [2001] UKHL 44, [2002] 2 AC 773,
  [2001] 2 FLR 1364   31, 1527
RP and Others v UK (Application No 38245/08) [2013] 1 FLR 744   360
RP v Nottingham City Council and the Official Solicitor (Mental Capacity of
  Parent) [2008] EWCA Civ 462, [2008] 2 FLR 1516   846, 1089, 1467

RP v United Kingdom (2008) ECHR 1124 — 846
RS, Re [2015] EWCOP 56 — 836
RT v LT and A Local Authority [2010] EWHC 1910 (Fam), [2010] COPLR Con Vol 1061 — 118, 2300

S (A Child) (Identification: Restrictions on Publication), Re [2004] UKHL 47, [2005] 1 AC 593, [2005] 1 FLR 591 — 825
S (Adult Patient: Jurisdiction), Re [1995] Fam 26, [1995] 1 FLR 302 — 32
S (Adult Patient: Sterilisation), Re [2001] Fam 15, [2000] 2 FLR 389, CA; *sub nom* Re S (Sterilisation: Patient's Best Interests) — 142, 310, 311, 1530
S (Hospital Patient: Court's Jurisdiction), Re [1996] Fam 1, [1995] 1 FLR 1075; [1995] Fam 26, [1995] 1 FLR 302 — 32
S (Sterilisation: Patient's Best Interests), Re [2001] Fam 15, [2000] 2 FLR 389, CA; *sub nom* Re S (Adult Patient: Sterilisation) — 142, 310, 1530
S (Vulnerable Adult), Re [2007] 2 FLR 1095 — 463, 464
S and S (Protected Persons), Re [2008] COPLR Con Vol 1074 — 147, 154, 200, 569, 767, 822, 2329
S, D v R and S, Re [2010] EWHC 2405 (COP), [2010] COPLR Con Vol 1112 — 106, 120, 133, 134, 567, 2301, 2303
S, Re; D v R (The Deputy of S) and S (Costs) [2010] EWHC 3748 (COP), [2012] COPLR 154 — 859
SA (Vulnerable Adult With Capacity: Marriage), Re [2005] EWHC 2942 (Fam), [2006] 1 FLR 867 — 104, 311, 460
Salford City Council v GJ, NJ and BJ (by their Litigation Friends) [2008] EWHC 1097 (Fam), [2008] 2 FLR 1295; *sub nom* Re GJ (Incapacitated Adults); *sub nom* Re BJ — 347, 363
Sandwell and West Birmingham Hospitals NHS Trust v CD and Others [2014] EWCOP 23, [2014] COPLR 650 — 321, 437, 801
Sandwell Metropolitan Borough Council v RG & Ors [2013] EWHC 2373 (COP), [2013] COPLR 643 — 444, 459, 2328
Saulle v Nouvet [2007] EWHC 2902 (QB) — 125, 141, 467, 566, 1089, 1100
SB (A patient: Capacity to consent to termination), Re [2013] EWHC 1417 (COP), [2013] COPLR 445 — 102, 106, 118, 445
SB, Re (unreported, 19 October 2010) — 319
SBC v and PBA and Others [2011] EWHC 2580 (Fam), [2011] COPLR Con Vol 1095 — 2310
SC v BS and A Local Authority [2012] COPLR 567 — 133, 837, 2300
SC v London Borough of Hackney [2010] EWHC B29 (COP) — 859
Scammell and Scammell v Farmer [2008] EWHC 1100 (Ch) — 126, 134
Secretary of State for Justice v RB [2011] EWCA Civ 1608, [2012] 1 WLR 3 — 367, 689
Sharma and Judkins v Hunters [2011] EWHC 2546 (COP), [2012] COPLR 166 — 862, 2325
Sheffield City Council v E and S [2004] EWHC 2808 (Fam), [2005] Fam 326, [2005] 1 FLR 965; *sub nom* Re E (An Alleged Patient) — 125, 566, 1549, 2303
Shtukaturov v Russia, Application no 44009/05, 27 June 2008, ECHR — 79
Simms v Simms; A v A (a child) [2002] EWHC 2734 (Fam), [2003] Fam 83, [2003] 1 FLR 879 — 341
Simpson (Deceased), Re, Schaniel v Simpson (1977) 121 SJ 224 — 134
SK (By his litigation friend the Official Solicitor), Re [2012] EWHC 1990 (COP), [2012] COPLR 712 — 809, 810, 1100, 2321
SK (Impact of Best Interests Decision on Queen's Bench Proceedings), Re [2013] COPLR 458 — 470, 758
SK, Re [2012] EWHC 1990, [2012] COPLR 712 — 468, 469, 470
SM v HM (by the Official Solicitor as her Litigation Friend) [2012] COPLR 187 — 307, 472, 473, 2312
SMBC v WMP and Others Cases No 11915104/11915369/11915093 [2011] COPLR Con Vol 1177 — 766, 841, 2322
Smith, Re [2014] EWHC 3926 (Ch), [2015] COPLR 284 — 126
Spurling v Broadhurst [2012] EWHC 2883 (Ch) — 1094
St George's Healthcare NHS Trust v S [1999] Fam 26, [1998] 2 FLR 728, CA — 148, 310
Stanev v Bulgaria (2012) 55 EHRR 22 — 352, 355, 366, 639
Stankov v Bulgaria (Application No 25820/07, decision of 17 March 2015) — 352

Table of Cases

Storck v Germany [2005] ECHR 61603/00, (2005) 43 EHRR 96	352
Sunderland City Council v PS [2007] EWHC 623 (Fam), [2007] 2 FLR 1083; *sub nom* Sunderland City Council v P; *sub nom* Re PS (Incapacitated or Vulnerable Adult)	32, 347
Swain v Hillman [2001] 1 All ER 91, CA	865
Sykes, Re (an order of the Senior Judge made on 9 July 2009)	217
T (A Minor) (Wardship: Medical Treatment), Re [1997] 1 WLR 242, [1997] 1 FLR 502, CA	310
T (Adult: Refusal of Treatment), Re [1993] Fam 95, [1992] 2 FLR 458, CA	1527
T, Applicant, 2005 SLT (Sh Ct) 97	521
TF v PJ [2014] EWHC 1840 (Admin)	781
TG (A Child), Re [2013] EWCA Civ 5, [2013] 1 FLR 1250	768, 839
The Commissioner of Police of the Metropolis v ZH [2013] EWCA Civ 69, [2013] 1 WLR 3021, [2013] COPLR 332	2328
The Local Authority v Mrs D and Mr D [2013] EWCOP B34	444
The Mental Health Trust/The Acute Trust & The Council v DD and BC (No 1) [2014] EWCOP 11, [2015] 1 FLR 1430	96, 444
The Mental Health Trust/The Acute Trust & The Council v DD and BC (No 2) [2014] EWCOP 13	444
The NHS Trust v L & Ors [2012] EWHC 2741 (COP), [2013] COPLR 139	325
The PCT v P, AH & The Local Authority [2009] EW Misc 10 (COP), [2009] COPLR Con Vol 956	122, 2330
The Press Association v Newcastle upon Tyne Hospitals Foundation Trust [2014] EWCOP 6, [2014] COPLR 502	2320
Turner v Turner [2012] CSOH 41	521
UF, Re [2013] EWHC 4289 (COP), [2014] COPLR 93	379, 589, 646, 2309
United Lincolnshire Hospital Trust v N [2014] EWCOP 16, [2014] COPLR 660	324, 325, 340, 592, 594
V (Declaration against Parents), Re [1995] 2 FLR 1003	32
V Hackett v CPS [2011] EWHC 1170 (Admin)	104
V v R [2011] EWHC 822 (QB)	567
VA and others v Hertfordshire Partnership NHS Foundation Trust and others [2011] EWHC 3524 (COP), [2012] COPLR 327	763
VAC v JAD & Others [2010] EWHC 2159 (Ch), [2012] Ch 57, [2010] COPLR Con Vol 302	2326
W (A Child), Re; Re H (Children) [2013] EWCA Civ 1177	762
W (By her Litigation Friend B) v (1) M (By her Litigation Friend the Official Solicitor) (2) S and (3) A NHS Primary Care Trust [2011] EWHC 2443 (Fam), [2012] 1 WLR 1653, [2012] COPLR 222	124, 149, 214, 319, 322, 324, 325, 339, 445, 570, 592, 594, 2317
W (EEM), Re [1971] Ch 123	31
W (Enduring Power of Attorney), Re [2001] Ch 609, [2001] 1 FLR 832, CA; [2000] Ch 343, [1999] 2 FLR 1163	193, 206, 238, 243, 252
W (Power of Attorney), Re [2000] Ch 343, [1999] 2 FLR 1163	206
W City Council v Mrs L (By Her Litigation Friend PC) (Deprivation of Liberty: Own Home) [2015] EWCOP 20, [2015] COPLR 337	2305
W PCT v TB (an adult by her litigation friend the Official Solicitor) [2009] EWHC 1737 (Fam), [2010] 1 WLR 2662, [2009] COPLR Con Vol 1193	362, 366, 634, 687
W v Egdell [1990] Ch 359	28, 137, 1557
W v M and S (Reporting Restriction Order) [2011] EWHC 1197 (COP), [2012] 1 WLR 287, [2011] COPLR Con Vol 1205	444, 826, 2319
W v UK Series A No 121, (1987) 10 EHRR 29	55
Walker v Dadmin [2014] All ER (D) 258	1469
Walker, Re [2014] EWHC 71 (Ch), [2015] COPLR 348	126
WCC v GS, RS and JS [2011] EWHC 2244 (COP)	764
Webb Resolutions Ltd v JT Ltd [2013] EWHC 509 (TCC)	767

West Lothian Council in respect of LY, Livingston Sheriff Court, 30 May 2014   508
Weyell, Re (an order of the senior Judge made on 2 December 2010)   217
Wheatley, Re (an order of the Senior Judge dated 31 January 2011)   204
White v Fell (1987) 12 November (unreported)   1089
White v White [1999] Fam 304, [1998] 2 FLR 310   144
White v White [2001] 1 AC 596, [2000] 2 FLR 981   144
Whiting, Re [2013] EWHC B27 (Fam), [2014] COPLR 107   871, 872
Wigan Council v M and others (Veracity Assessment) [2015] EWFC 8   837
Winterwerp v The Netherlands [1979] ECHR 4   457
WLW, Re [1972] Ch 456   74, 843
Wychavon District Council v EM (HB) [2012] UKUT 12 (AAC)   172, 575

X (Court of Protection Practice), Re [2015] EWCA Civ 599, [2015] COPLR
      582   457, 761, 816
X and Ors (Deprivation of Liberty), Re [2014] EWCOP 25, [2015] 1 WLR
      2454, [2014] COPLR 674   280, 359, 360, 378, 416, 440, 442, 457, 761, 816, 940
X and others (Deprivation of Liberty) (No 2), Re [2014] EWCOP 37   280, 410, 416, 761,
    816, 940
X City Council v MB, NB and MAB [2006] EWHC 168 (Fam), [2006] 2 FLR
      968   315, 2303
X Primary Care Trust v XB [2012] EWHC 1390 (Fam), [2012] COPLR 577   337, 2316
X v United Kingdom (Application No 7215/75), decision of 5 November 1981)   457
X, Y and Z, Re [2014] EWHC 87 (COP), [2014] COPLR 364   152, 2325
XCC v AA and Others [2012] EWHC 2183 (COP), [2012] COPLR 730   311, 327, 458, 459,
    767, 2314
XZ, Re; XZ v The Public Guardian [2015] EWCOP 35, [2015] COPLR 630   2327

Y (Mental Incapacity: Bone Marrow Transplant), Re [1997] Fam 110, [1996] 2
      FLR 787; *sub nom* Re Y (Mental Patient: Bone Marrow Donation)   151, 341, 1575,
    1625
Y (Mental Patient: Bone Marrow Donation), Re [1997] Fam 110, [1996] 2 FLR
      787; *sub nom* Re Y (Mental Incapacity: Bone Marrow Transplant)   151, 341, 1575,
    1625
YA (F) v A Local Authority [2010] EWHC 2770 (COP), [2011] 1 WLR 1505,
      [2010] COPLR Con Vol 1226   444, 476, 2332
YA v Central and NW London NHS Trust and Others [2015] UKUT 37 (AAC)   854
YLA v PM and Another [2013] EWHC 4020 (COP), [2014] COPLR 114   2300
YLA v PM and MZ [2013] EWHC 3622 (Fam)   444
Yonge v Toynbee [1910] 1 KB 215, CA   187, 1095
YW v Office of the Public Guardian (Peterhead Sheriff Court, 25 June 2010)   501

ZH v Commissioner of Police for the Metropolis [2012] EWHC 604 (Admin),
      [2012] COPLR 588   167, 574

Table of Practice Directions

References are to page numbers.

2010
    Public Guardian Practice Note No 1 of 2010 (Deputies and Attorneys
        Release of Visit Reports) 1390
    Public Guardian Practice Note No 2 of 2010 (Deputies and Attorneys
        The Independent Safeguarding Authority) 1393

2011
    Law Society Practice Note of 8 December 2011 (Lasting Powers of
        Attorney) 1420
    Public Guardian Practice Note No 1 of 2011 (Court of Protection Costs
        The Public Guardian and Costs in Court of Protection Proceedings) 1396
    Public Guardian Practice Note No 2 of 2011 (Updating Public Guardian
        Registers
        Notification of Death) 1399

2012
    Practice Direction of 24 March 2012 (Citation of Authorities) 1484
    Public Guardian Practice Note No 1 of 2012 (Deputy Final Reports
        Requesting the LPA, EPA Final Report pursuant to Regulation 40 of the
        LPA, EPA and Public Guardian Regulations 2007) 1403
    Public Guardian Practice Note No 2 of 2012 (Gifts
        Deputies and EPA/LPA Attorneys) 1407
    Public Guardian Practice Note No 3 of 2012 (Surety Bonds
        Statement of Surety Bonds Expectations of the Public Guardian) 1415

2013
    Law Society Practice Note of 13 June 2013 (Financial Abuse) 1440

2014
    Guidance Note
        Acting as a litigation friend in the Court of Protection 1490
    Law Society Practice Note of 17 March 2014 (Mental Capacity
        International Aspects) 1456
    Practice Guidance of 16 January 2014 (Transparency in the Court of
        Protection – Publication of Judgments) 1486

2015
    Law Society Practice Note of 2 July 2015 (Meeting the Needs of Vulnerable
        Clients) 1462
    Practice Direction of 26 March (Committal for Contempt of Court – Open
        Court) 871, 872, 1505
    Practice Guidance of 24 June (Committal for Contempt of Court – Open
        Court) 871, 1505

2016
    Public Guardian Practice Note No 1 of 2016 (Public Authority Deputyship
        Responsibilities) 1418, 1508
    Public Guardian Practice Note No 2 of 2016 (Public Guardian Practice Note
        No 2 of 2016
        OPG's Approach to Solicitor Client Accounts) 1419

Civil Procedure Rules 1998, SI 1998/3132
    Practice Direction 2B – Allocation of Cases to Levels of Judiciary
        para 5.1(a) 544
    Practice Direction 12 – Default Judgment
        para 2.3(1) 543
        para 4.2 543

Civil Procedure Rules 1998, SI 1998/3132—*continued*
  Practice Direction 21 – Children and Protected Parties   1086, 1091, 1095, 1096, 1099,
                                                           1100, 1103, 1105, 1107
    para 1.1   538
    para 2.1   1092, 1094
    para 2.2   539
    para 2.2(2)(e)   1094
    para 2.3   1091
    para 2.3(4)   1094
    para 2.4   1091
    paras 3.1–3.4   540
    para 3.4   541, 1097
    para 4.5   541
    para 4.6   541
    para 4.7   541
    paras 5.1–5.6   544
    para 5.5   547
    para 5.6   1101, 1103
    para 6.5   1101, 1103
    paras 8–12   1103
    para 8.1–8.3   546
    paras 8.1–8.4   545
    paras 8.1(2)   545
    para 8.2(3)   545
    paras 9.1–9.8   545
    paras 10.1–10.7   545, 546
    para 10.2   1104
    para 10.2(2)   546
    para 13   545
    para 13.3   546
  Practice Direction 22 – Statements of Truth
    para 3.1(1)   543
    para 3.7   543
  Practice Direction 23 – Applications
    para 6   2231
  Practice Direction 39 – Miscellaneous provisions relating to hearings
    para 1.4A   1102
    para 1.6   543, 1102
  Practice Direction 41 – Provisional Damages   1102
  Practice Direction 44 – General Rules About Costs   1123
  Practice Direction 46 – Costs Special Cases   1142
  Practice Direction 47 – Procedure for Detailed Assessment of Costs and
      Default Provisions   1158
  Practice Direction 48 – Part 2 of The Legal Aid, Sentencing And
      Punishment Of Offenders Act 2012 Relating To Civil Litigation
      Funding And Costs
    Transitional Provision And Exceptions   1178
  Practice Direction 52A – Appeals: General Provisions   1189
  Practice Direction 52C – Appeals to the Court of Appeal   1197
Court of Protection Rules 2007
  Practice Direction – Case Management Pilot   1033
  Practice Direction – Deprivation of Liberty Applications   378, 816
  Practice Direction – Section 49 Reports Pilot   1073
  Practice Direction – Transparency Pilot   822, 964, 1028
  Practice Direction 4A – Court Documents   398
    para 7   770, 774
    para 7(c)   770, 774
  Practice Direction 4B – Statements of Truth   398, 405, 775
    paras 7–16   775
    para 16   775

Table of Practice Directions

Court of Protection Rules 2007—*continued*
   Practice Direction 4B – Statements of Truth—*continued*
      paras 17–20   775
   Practice Direction 6A – Service   399, 793
      paras 1–8   785
      para 3   795
      paras 4–8   767
      para 5(a)   785
      para 13   784
      para 15   785
      para 17   788
   Practice Direction 7A – Notifying P   400
   Practice Direction 8A – Permission   619, 799
   Practice Direction 9A – The Application form   294, 401, 532, 533, 535
      paras 2–8   802
      paras 9–12   803
      para 14   803
   Practice Direction 9B – Notification of other persons that an application
      form has been issued   300, 401, 533, 806
      para 6   806
      para 7   805, 806
      para 9   806
      para 10   806
      para 11   806
   Practice Direction 9C – Responding to an application   401
      para 3   808
      para 4   808
      para 6–13   808
      para 14   808
   Practice Direction 9D – Application by currently appointed Deputies,
      Attorneys, and Donees in relation to P's property and affairs   533
   Practice Direction 9D – Applications by currently appointed Deputies,
      Attorneys, and Donees in relation to P's property and affairs   276, 283, 290, 291,
             307, 401, 806
      paras 4, 5   802
      para 8   802
   Practice Direction 9E – Applications relating to serious medical treatment   401, 535, 806, 819
      paras 11, 12   781
      paras 13–15   819
   Practice Direction 9F – Applications relating to statutory wills, codicils,
      settlements and other dealings with P's property   295, 297, 298, 299, 301, 401, 806
      paras 2–4   802
      para 6   802
   Practice Direction 9G – Applications to appoint or discharge a trustee   401
      paras 2, 3   802
      para 5   802
      paras 8, 9   802
   Practice Direction 9H – Applications relating to the registration of Enduring
      Powers of Attorney   401, 806, 878
      para 2   802
      paras 6–8   802
      paras 6–10   531
   Practice Direction 10A – Applications within proceedings   403, 535, 811
      para 4   812
      para 7   812
      para 9   813
      para 10   813
      para 11   813
      para 13   813

Table of Practice Directions

Court of Protection Rules 2007—*continued*
    Practice Direction 10A – Applications within proceedings—*continued*
        paras 18–20   767, 781
        paras 18–21   811
        para 21   781
        paras 22, 23   811
    Practice Direction 10AA – Deprivation of Liberty Applications   936
    Practice Direction 10B – Urgent and interim applications   403, 535, 811, 815
        para 5   815
        para 6   815
        para 7   767, 815
        para 9   815
        para 11   815
        para 12   767
        para 16   815
    Practice Direction 11A – Human Rights   398, 817
        para 9   817
    Practice Direction 12A – Court's jurisdiction to be exercised by Certain
        Judges   404
        paras 2, 3   781, 819
        para 3(b)   817
    Practice Direction 12B – Process for disputing the Court's jurisdiction   404, 820
    Practice Direction 13A – Hearings (including reporting restrictions)   948
        para 6   826
        paras 7, 8   823
        para 27   826
        para 29   826
        Pt 2   826
    Practice Direction 13B – Court bundles   958
    Practice Direction 14A – Written evidence   407
        Annex   767
        Annex 2   781, 828
        paras 1–19   829
        paras 20–31   829
        para 21   767
        para 32   829
        paras 33–45   829
        paras 33–50   808
        para 35   829
        para 42   829
        para 54   831
    Practice Direction 14B – Depositions   407, 408, 831, 834
    Practice Direction 14C – Fee for examiners of the Court   407, 832
    Practice Direction 14D – Witness summons   407, 830
        para 9   830
    Practice Direction 14E – Section 49 reports   407, 408, 835, 2226
        Annex   836
        paras 11–16   836
    Practice Direction 15A – expert evidence   409
        para 1   837, 841
        paras 2–7   838
        paras 3, 4   837
        paras 8–12   841
    Practice Direction 17A – Litigation friend   411, 846, 854
    Practice Direction 18A – Change of solicitor   411, 855
    Practice Direction 19A – Costs in the Court of Protection   412, 622, 857
    Practice Direction 19B – Fixed costs in the Court of Protection   412, 1002
    Practice Direction 20A – Appeals   620, 862, 863, 1006
    Practice Direction 20B – Allocation of Appeals   863, 864, 1012

Court of Protection Rules 2007—*continued*
Practice Direction 21A – Contempt of Court 415, 868
　paras 4–6 871
　para 9 871
Practice Direction 22A – Transitional provisions 415
Practice Direction 22B – Transitory provisions 415
Practice Direction 22C – Appeals against decisions made under Pt 7 of
　MHA 1983 or the EPA 1985 which are brought on
　or after commencement 415
Practice Direction 23A – Request for directions where notice of objection
　prevents the Public Guardian from registering an Enduring Power of
　Attorney 416, 877
Practice Direction 23B – Where P ceases to lack capacity or dies 416, 878, 2197

Family Procedure Rules 2010, SI 2010/2955
Practice Direction 6B – Service out of the Jurisdiction 1345
Practice Direction 6C – Disclosure of Addresses by Government
　Departments 13 February 1989 1368

Practice Note (Official Solicitor: Medical and Welfare Decisions for Adults who Lack
　Capacity) [2001] 2 FLR 158 434
Practice Note: Family Division: Incapacitated Adults (2002) *The Times*, 4 January 434
Practice Note: PVS Cases [2001] 2 FLR 155 434
President's Direction 'Applications Relating to Serious Medical Treatment' 318

Table of Codes of Practice

References are to page numbers.

Code of Practice to supplement the main Mental Capacity Act 2005 – Deprivation of Liberty Safeguards 2008   94, 611
Code of Practice under the Mental Capacity Act 2005   91, 93, 94, 95, 96, 97, 101, 125, 127, 129, 194, 196, 266, 565, 611, 2190, 2193, 2200, 2269
    Ch 3   104, 565, 569
    Ch 9   337
    Ch 11   342, 343
    Ch 16   137
    para 2   611
    para 2.5   101
    para 4.20   121
    para 4.24   125
    para 4.45   126, 573
    para 5.11   131
    para 5.28   147
    para 5.31   211
    para 5.38   570
    para 5.47   152
    para 5.51   156
    para 6.5   161, 573
    paras 6.7–6.19   162
    para 6.18   163
    paras 6.49–6.53   169
    para 6.58   575
    para 9.19   337
    para 9.51   340
    para 12.13   128

Table of EC and International Regulations

References are to page numbers.

Convention on the International Protection
    of Adults 2000   626, 697, 706, 2449
    Art 4   705
    Art 7   699
    Art 8   699
    Art 12   700
    Arts 28–36   704
    Art 33   703, 704
    Art 38   705
Council of Europe Committee of Ministers Recommendation No R (99) 4 of the Committee of Ministers to Member States on Principles Concerning the Legal Protection of Incapable Adults   2507
Council of Europe Convention on Human Rights and Biomedicine   343

European Convention on Human Rights   52, 53, 55, 59, 77, 210, 323, 1090, 1738, 1740
    Art 2   52
    Art 3   52
    Art 5   52
    Art 5(1)   169, 209, 269, 351, 574, 1596

European Convention on Human Rights—*continued*
    Art 5(4)   351
    Art 6   52, 55, 823
    Art 6(1)   1102
    Art 8   28, 53, 79, 825, 1726
    Art 10   50, 825
    Art 14   46, 53
    First Protocol
        Art 2   53
European Union Directive on Good Clinical Practice in Clinical Trials, Directive 2001/20/EC   341

Helsinki Declaration 1964   343

Recommendation CM/REC(2009)11 of the Committee of Ministers to Member States on Principles Concerning Continuing Powers of Attorney and Advance Directives for Incapacity and its Explanatory Memorandum   2515

UN Convention on the Rights of Persons with Disabilities   2463

List of Abbreviations

Statutes

AWI(S)A 2000	Adults with Incapacity (Scotland) Act 2000
CPA 2004	Civil Partnership Act 2004
DDA 1995	Disability Discrimination Act 1995
EPAA 1985	Enduring Powers of Attorney Act 1985
HRA 1998	Human Rights Act 1998
MCA 2005	Mental Capacity Act 2005
MHA 1983/2007	Mental Health Act 1983/2007
SGA 1979	Sale of Goods Act 1979

Statutory instruments

2007 Regs	Lasting Powers of Attorney, Enduring Powers of Attorney and Public Guardian Regulations 2007
COPR 2001/2007	Court of Protection Rules 2001/2007
CPR	Civil Procedure Rules 1998
FPR	Family Procedure Rules 2010

International Conventions

ECHR	European Convention on Human Rights and Fundamental Freedoms 1950

General

ADR	Alternative dispute resolution
ANH	Nutrition and hydration supplied by artificial means
CAFCASS	Children and Family Court Advisory and Support Service
CLS	Community Legal Service
Convention rights	ECHR rights
CTO	Community treatment order
DCA	Department for Constitutional Affairs
DHSS	Department of Health and Social Security
DSS	Department of Social Security
DWP	Department for Work and Pensions
ECT	Electro-convulsive therapy
EPA	Enduring power of attorney
FDR	Financial dispute resolution
GMC	General Medical Council
IMCA	Independent mental capacity advocate
JAC	Judicial Appointments Commission
JCHR	Joint Committee on Human Rights
JSB	Judicial Studies Board
LPA	Lasting power of attorney
MCIP	Mental Capacity Implementation Programme
MHRT	Mental health review tribunal
NHS	National Health Service

List of Abbreviations

OPG	Office of the Public Guardian
PGO	(Old) Public Guardianship Office
PTO	Public Trust Office
PVS	persistent vegetative state
SDD	Social services departments of local authorities
section 5 act	Act which may be carried out with protection from liability under MCA 2005, s 5
SFE	Solicitors for the Elderly Limited

PART I

Narrative

PART I

Narrative

PART I: Narrative

Contents

CHAPTER 1
Background 21

Preliminary	21
Overview	21
Issues	21
Capacity	21
Decision-making	22
Communication	22
Conclusion	23
Legal competence	23
Tests of mental capacity	24
Assessment of mental capacity	24
Incapacitated people	25
Decision-making	26
Delegated decision-making	26
Decision-makers	26
Best interests	27
A special jurisdiction	27
Confidentiality	28
Undue influence	29
Assisted decision-making	29
The legal position	30
Legal background	31
Historical	31
Parens patriae	31
The declaratory jurisdiction	31
Terminology	32
Incapacity	33
Legislation	33
Mental Health Acts	33
Enduring Powers of Attorney Act 1985	33
The new climate	34
The social climate	34
General	34
Community care	34
Discrimination	34
Attitudes to disability	35
Terminology	36
Attitudes of minority ethnic communities	37
Role of the law	38
Support	38
Protection	39

Empowerment	39
Problems	39
Role of lawyers	40
Who is the client?	40
The legal climate	40
General	40
Legal publishing	41
Elderly client practices	41
Community Care	41
Background	41
Reports	42
Legislation	42
Circulars and directions	44
The Care Act 2014	44
Equality and discrimination	46
Background	46
Equality Act 2010	47
Prohibited conduct	48
Direct discrimination	48
Discrimination arising from disability	48
Indirect discrimination	49
Duty to make adjustments	49
Harassment	50
Victimisation	50
Implications of conduct	50
Premises	51
Associations	51
Human Rights Act 1998	52
The Convention	52
The legislation	52
Interpretation	53
Remedies	54
New concepts	54
Application to the Court of Protection and Public Guardian	55
Comment	55
Civil Partnership Act 2004	56
Background	56
The legislation	56
Same sex marriage	57
Incapacity issues	57
Access to justice	58
Background	58
A change of culture	58
Discrimination	59
Unrepresented parties	59
Disadvantages	60
Personal assistance	60
Physical and sensory impairments	61
Hearings	61

Interpreters	62
The (former) Court of Protection	**62**
Origins of the jurisdiction	62
Practice and procedure	63
General	63
Applications	63
Short orders	64
Service	64
Evidence	64
Hearings	64
Conduct	64
Reviews and appeals	65
Fees and costs	65
Court fees	65
Legal costs	65
Venue	66
Background	66
Regional hearings	67
An evaluation of the Court of Protection	67
Court Rules	68
Contested hearings	68
Other hearings	68
The Public Guardianship Office	**69**
Background	69
Other jurisdictions	70
Scotland	70
Northern Ireland	70
Ireland	71
The Lord Chancellor's Visitors	**71**
Historical	71
Medical Visitors	72
General Visitors	73
Enduring powers of attorney	73
Confidentiality of reports	74
The Official Solicitor	**74**
Background	74
Creation of the OSPT	74
Law reform	**75**
Origins	75
The Law Commission	75
Consultation	75
Report	76
The Government's response	77
'Who Decides?'	77
'Making decisions'	77
Legislation	77
Adults with Incapacity (Scotland) Act 2000	77

PART 1

5

Mental Incapacity Bill	78
Mental Capacity Act 2005	78
Human rights compatibility	79
An initial assessment of the MCA 2005	79
The *ad hoc* Rules Committee	82
House of Lords Select Committee Report	83
The Government response	84
A New Ad Hoc Rules Committee	84
UN Convention on the Rights of Persons with Disabilities	84
Background	84
The diagnostic threshold	86
Best interests	86
The functional test	86
Substituted decision-making	87
Individuals who cannot be supported	87
A view of the future	88

CHAPTER 2
The Mental Capacity Jurisdiction

	91
Introduction	91
Part 1: Overview	91
Key elements	91
General	91
Essential provisions	92
The public bodies	93
The Code of Practice	93
Application	94
Legal effect	95
Sanctions for non-compliance	97
Creation and revision	98
Part 2: Principles and concepts	98
The principles	98
Background	98
The statement of principles	99
Presumption of capacity	100
Law Commission proposals	101
The legislation	101
The Code of Practice	101
Practicable steps to help decision-making	102
Law Commission proposals	102
The legislation	103
The Code of Practice	104
Unwise decisions	105
The legislation	105
Law Commission proposals	105
Evidence before the Joint Committee	106

Best interests	107
The Law Commission proposals	107
The Joint Committee's view	108
The legislation	108
Less restrictive alternative	109
The Law Commission proposals	109
The legislation	109
The Scottish approach	110
Relevance to the Court of Protection	110
Defining lack of capacity	110
The functional approach	110
People who lack capacity	111
The two-stage test of capacity	112
A diagnostic threshold	114
Principle of 'equal consideration'	114
Qualifying age	115
Inability to make decisions	117
Understand the information relevant to the decision	118
Retain the information	121
Use or weigh the information	122
Unable to communicate	124
Common law tests of capacity	125
Reasonable belief of lack of capacity	126
Competence and capacity: children and young people	127
Children under 16: '*Gillick* competence'	127
Young people aged 16 or 17: Capacity or competence?	128
The assessment of capacity	129
Background	129
When should capacity be assessed?	130
Who should assess capacity?	130
The need for formal assessment	132
Legal or professional requirements	133
The 'Golden Rule'	133
Other expert assessments	135
How capacity is assessed	135
Confidentiality	136
Refusal to be assessed	138
Recording assessments of capacity	139
Professional records	139
Formal reports or certificates of capacity	140
Assessments by solicitors	140
Assessments for civil courts	141
Determining best interests	142
Background	142
The best interests checklist	143
Principle of equal consideration	145
All relevant circumstances	145
Regaining capacity	146
Permitting and encouraging participation	147

Life-sustaining treatment	148
The person's wishes and feelings, beliefs and values	150
The weight to be given to P's wishes and feelings	152
The views of other people	155
Duty to apply the best interests principle	157
Reasonable belief	157
Part 3: General powers and duties	**158**
Acts in connection with care or treatment – background	158
The problem	158
The Law Commission proposal	158
The general authority	159
The views of the Joint Committee	159
Acts in connection with care or treatment – the legislation	160
Protection from liability	160
Section 5 acts	161
Serious acts relating to medical treatment or welfare	161
Who can act in connection with care or treatment?	164
No protection in cases of negligence	165
Effect on advance decisions to refuse treatment	166
Limitations on permitted acts	166
Restraint	166
Deprivation of liberty	168
Decisions of donees or deputies	170
Paying for goods, services and other expenditure	170
Background	170
The legislation	171
Responsibility to pay for necessary goods and services	172
Expenditure	173
Excluded decisions	174
Background	174
The legislation	175
Family relationships etc	175
Mental Health Act matters	176
Voting rights	178
Ill-treatment or neglect	178
Background	178
Criminal offence	179
Scope of the offence	179
Person who lacks capacity	180
Ill-treatment	181
Wilful neglect	181
Courts and Criminal Justice Act 2015	183

CHAPTER 3
Lasting Powers of Attorney

	185
Background	185
Powers of attorney	185
Limitations	186

The incapable donor	187
Statutory powers of attorney	188
Enduring powers of attorney	188
Success of enduring powers	190
Problems with enduring powers	191
Abolition of enduring powers	194
Lasting Powers of Attorney	194
Nature of lasting power of attorney	195
Character of lasting power of attorney	195
Problems in practice with 'presumption of capacity'	197
Scope of lasting power of attorney	198
Property and affairs	199
Acting in the best interests of the donor	200
Power to maintain others	202
Limited power to make gifts	205
The donor as trustee	207
The donor as a litigant	207
Welfare matters	208
Limits on welfare matters	209
Alternatives to welfare lasting powers of attorney	213
Form of lasting power of attorney	214
Who can give a lasting power of attorney?	214
Prescribed forms	214
Use of different prescribed forms	214
Defective forms	215
Content of LPA	219
Section 1 – The donor's details	220
Section 2 – Choice of attorney	220
Section 3 – More than one attorney	221
Section 4 – Replacement attorneys	222
Section 5 – Limiting when attorneys can make decisions (property and affairs)	225
Section 5 – Life-sustaining treatment (welfare LPA)	226
Section 6 – Named persons to be notified or told	226
Section 7 – Preferences and instructions	229
Welfare instructions	231
Preferences (guidance)	232
Section 8 – Prescribed information	233
Section 9 – Execution by donor	234
Section 10 – The certificate provider's statement	234
Section 11 – The attorney's statement	239
Creation of lasting power of attorney	240
A lasting power of attorney is created in two stages	240
The first stage: completing Sections 1 to 11	241
Capacity to create a power	242

PART I

The second stage: registration 244
  The requirement of registration 244
    Problems with capacity not being relevant to registration 244
    Problems with early registration 245
    Procedure for registration – Sections 12 to 15 246
    Status of attorney prior to registration 247
    Notices 247
      Service of notices 248
      Dispensing with notice 248
    Completion of registration 249
  Objections to registration 249
    The role of the Public Guardian 249
      Objections made to the Public Guardian 250
    The role of the Court of Protection 251
      Whether the requirements for the creation of the power have been met 252
      Whether the power has been revoked 252
      That fraud or undue pressure was used to induce the donor to create the power 253
      That the donee has behaved, is behaving or proposes to behave in a way that contravenes his or her authority or contrary to the donor's best interests 253
    Procedure 255

Enduring powers of attorney 256
  The future of existing powers 256

CHAPTER 4
Powers of the Court

Preliminary 259

Declarations 260
  Background 260
  General powers of the Court 261
    Declarations as to capacity 261
    Declarations as to medical treatment 262

Making decisions and appointing deputies 262
  Powers of the Court 262
  Making decisions 263
    General 263
    Children 263
    Personal welfare 263
    Property and affairs 264
      Wills 264
      Settlements 265
      Miscellaneous 266
  Deputies 266
    Appointment 266
      Who may be appointed? 267

Control of the deputy	267
Powers	267
Conditional on lack of capacity	268
Powers that cannot be given	268
Medical treatment	268
Conflict with an attorney	268
Restraint	268
Revocation of appointment	269
How will the Court exercise these powers?	269
The court's approach	269
What happened to receiverships?	270
The past regime	270
The present regime	270

Control of lasting powers of attorney	270
Court's powers to intervene	270
General	270
Specific powers	271
Creation and revocation	271
Capacity	272
Registration	272
Meaning and effect of the power	274
Directions to the attorney	274
Rendering accounts etc	274
Relieving the attorney of liability	275
Gifts	275
Applying to the Court	275
The role of the Public Guardian	276

Challenges faced by the Court	277
Overview	277
Property and affairs	278
Personal welfare	278
Health care	278
Personal care	279

The future	280

CHAPTER 5
Gifts, Statutory Wills and Settlements

Preliminary	283
The statutory framework	283

Gifts not requiring the Court's authority	284
Enduring powers of attorney	284
Lasting powers of attorney	285
Deputy appointed by the Court	285
Value of gifts not requiring the Court's authority	286
Maintenance not requiring the Court's authority	288

Gifts requiring the court's approval 289
  Application required 289
  Gifts using the 'short procedure' 290

Statutory wills 291
  Background 291
  The testator 293
  Medical evidence 294
  The applicant 296
  The application 297
  Respondents and persons who must be notified of an application 299
  Subsequent procedure and final hearing 301
  Execution of a statutory will 303

Urgent applications 304
  Costs 305

Settlements 306
  When necessary 306
  Procedure 307

CHAPTER 6
Health Care and Welfare, IMCAs, Advance Decisions and Research 309

Preliminary 309

The pre-existing common law 309
  Medical treatment 309
  Welfare 310
  Injunctive relief 311
  Capacity 311

The position under the Mental Capacity Act 2005 311
  General 311
    The issue-specific nature of capacity in the health and welfare context 312
    Fluctuating capacity 313
    Capacity to consent to sexual relations 315

Practice and procedure 317
  Serious medical treatment cases 318
    Definition 318
    When should serious medical treatment cases be brought to Court? 318
    Allocation, urgency and case management 320
    Best interests in medical treatment cases: life sustaining treatment 322
  Health and welfare cases 326

Independent mental capacity advocates 328
  Establishment 328
    Appointment, functions and role 329

The duty to instruct	330
NHS bodies	330
Local authorities	331
Expansion of role	331
Powers of the IMCA	331
Comment	331
Advance decisions	332
Preliminary: the position at common law	332
The starting point: the principle of adult autonomy	332
Refusal of treatment	332
The relationship with suicide	333
Requests for treatment	333
Advance decisions under the Mental Capacity Act 2005	334
Recognition	334
Advance refusals of treatment	334
Advance requests for treatment and care arrangements	334
Applicability	335
Life-sustaining treatment	335
Effect	336
Doubt or disagreement	336
The Code of Practice	337
A cautionary tale: *X Primary Care Trust v XB*	337
Comment: striking a balance	339
The alternative of a lasting power of attorney	339
Decisions by health care professionals	339
Medical research	340
Common law position	340
The regulation of research	340
General principles	340
Clinical Trials Regulations	341
Research authorised by the Mental Capacity Act 2005	342
Background	342
Application of the Act	343
Pre-condition to authorisation	343
Pre-conditions relating to the individual	343
Comment	344

CHAPTER 7
Deprivation of Liberty Safeguards 347

Background	347
The Mental Health Act 1983, as amended by the Mental Health Act 2007	347
Powers of admission, detention and treatment	347
Review and appeals	348
Purpose	349

Comparisons 349
   Differences 349
   Overlaps 350

The Deprivation of liberty safeguards 350
   The 'Bournewood Gap' 350
   The decisions of the domestic courts 351
   European Court of Human Rights 351

The MCA solution 352
   Meaning of deprivation of liberty 352
   Court of Protection powers 362
   Deprivation of liberty in a hospital or care home 363
   The authorisation procedure 365
   The age requirement 365
   The mental health requirement 365
   The mental capacity requirement 365
   The best interests requirement 366
   The eligibility requirement 366
   The no refusals requirement 369

Standard authorisations 370
   Urgent authorisations 374
   The Standard Authorisations, Assessments and Ordinary
      Residence Regulations 375
   The Appointment of Relevant Person's Representative Regulations 377

Review by the Court of Protection 378

Monitoring 379

Statistics 380

Comment 381

CHAPTER 8
Court Practice and Procedure 385

Preliminary 385
   Role of the Lord Chancellor 385
   Judiciary 386
   Rules and Practice Directions 386

Status of the Court of Protection 387
   Preliminary 387
   The Court 387
      Name and venue 387
      Administration 387
      Forms 387
   Judges 388
      Regional judges 389
      Allocation of cases 389
      Transfer of cases 390

Powers	390
General	390
Interim orders and directions	391
Reports	391
The Court Rules	392
Court of Protection Rules 2007 (COPR 2007)	392
Practice Directions	394
Practice Guidance	394
Interface with other rules	395
The overriding objective	395
General	395
Duties of the Court and parties	395
Interpretation	396
Case management powers	396
General	396
Security for costs	397
Court's own initiative	397
Human rights	397
Practice and procedure	398
Court documents	398
Statements of truth	398
Personal details	398
Access to documents	399
Service of documents	399
Who serves?	399
How is service effected?	399
Notifying the incapacitated person	400
Permission to apply	400
Who may apply?	400
Starting proceedings	401
Initial steps	401
Responding to an application	401
Parties	402
Applications within proceedings	403
Applications without notice	403
Interim remedies	403
Dealing with applications	404
Directions	404
Allocation	405
Disputing the Court's jurisdiction	405
Hearing the incapacitated person	405
Reconsideration	405
Hearings	405
Types of case	406
Evidence	407
Admissions	407
Witnesses' evidence	407
Depositions	408

Reports	408
Experts	409
Disclosure	410
Inspection	410
Litigation friends and representatives	410
Representation	411
Costs	412
The general rule	412
Assessment	413
Fees	413
Appeals	414
Permission to appeal	414
Enforcement	415
Transitional provisions	415
Miscellaneous provisions	416
Practical points	416
The workload	416
Volume of cases	416
Cases under the court's jurisdiction	416
Integration with other courts	418
Judicial support	418
Dual jurisdiction	419

CHAPTER 9
The Public Guardian and Supporting Services — 421

Introduction	421
The Public Guardian	421
Office of the Public Guardian	421
Functions	421
Powers	423
Fees	423
Annual Report	424
The Office of the Public Guardian Board	424
Panel of Deputies	424
Challenges ahead	425
Public Guardian's role	425
Dispute resolution	425
Investigating abuse	426
Use of technology	426
Partnerships	427
Funding	427
Relationship with the Court of Protection	427
Transforming the services of the OPG	428
Court of Protection Visitors	428
Background	428

The new regime	429
Appointment	429
General Visitors	429
Special Visitors	430
Reports by Visitors	431
Powers	432
The changed climate	432
Association of Independent Visitors	432
The Official Solicitor	433
Status and function	433
The present office	433
Acceptance policy	435
The incapacity work of the Official Solicitor	436
Giving advice	436
Representing adults who lack capacity	436
Assisting the civil and family courts	438
Role in the Court of Protection	438
Adult personal welfare declarations including serious medical treatment	440
Other jurisdictions	441
Scotland	441
Northern Ireland	441
Ireland	441
Current and future issues	442
Court Funds Office	446
Background	446
Court Funds Rules 2011	447
Investments on behalf of protected beneficiaries	447
Contacting the CFO	448
Independent Mental Capacity Advocate Service	449
Advocates	449
IMCAs	449
Who can be an IMCA?	450
How do IMCAs challenge a decision?	450

CHAPTER 10
Miscellaneous 451

Enduring powers – transitional (Mental Capacity Act 2005, Sch 4)	451
Transitional provisions (Mental Capacity Act 2005, Sch 5)	452
Mental Health Act 1983, Part VII	452
Enduring Powers of Attorney Act 1985	453
Consequential amendments and repeals (Mental Capacity Act 2005, Sch 6)	453

CHAPTER 11
The Margins of the MCA 455

Preliminary 455

The inherent jurisdiction 455
  Background 455
  Vulnerable adults 456
  Incapacitated adults 458
  Adults lacking capacity for a reason outside MCA 2005 460
  Statutory reform 461

Overlap with judicial review 462
  The approach of the Court of Protection 462
  The approach of the Administrative Court 464

Overlap with personal injury proceedings 466
  Overview 466
  Assessment of capacity 467
  Best interests 470
  Management of monies received by P in civil proceedings 471
  Double recovery and the Court of Protection 473

The European Convention on Human Rights 475

CHAPTER 12
International Protection of Adults 479

Introduction 479

Private International Law 479

Cross-border issues and mental capacity 480

Hague 35 481

Mental Capacity Act 2005, Schedule 3 483

Jurisdiction and habitual residence 485
  Re MN: 486
  Re O: 487
  Re SW: 488

Applicable law 488

Recognition and enforcement 489

Protective measures 489

Within the United Kingdom 489

The position in Non-Convention Countries 490

CHAPTER 13
Scotland 493
  Background 493
    Scots law 494

The Scottish courts	495
Development of adult incapacity law prior to 2000	497
Particular characteristics of Scots law	498
Literature	498
Adults with Incapacity (Scotland) Act 2000	499
General	499
Jurisdiction and roles	499
The Courts	500
The Sheriff Court	500
The Court of Session	502
Other functions under the Act	502
Public Guardian	502
Mental Welfare Commission	503
Local authorities	503
Other Incapacity Act roles	504
Limitation of liability	504
Ill treatment and wilful neglect	504
The principles	504
Definitions of adult, incapable and incapacity	506
Powers of Attorney (Part 2)	508
Terminology	508
Overview	508
Underlying law, the POA document	510
Formalities	510
Revocation and termination	512
POA's executed before 2 April 2001	512
Non-Scottish Powers of Attorney	513
Powers of the sheriff	513
Accounts and funds (Part 3)	514
Joint accounts	514
'Access to funds'	514
Procedure	515
Transition from guardianship	515
Part 3 scheme inapplicable or inappropriate	516
Management of residents' finances (Part 4)	516
Medical treatment and research (Part 5)	517
Guardianship and intervention orders (Part 6)	517
Intervention orders	518
Guardianship	519
Deprivation of Liberty	520
Provisions applicable to guardians and non-Scottish equivalents	520
Wills and related matters	521
Ademption	521
Measures outwith the Incapacity Act	521

PART I

CHAPTER 14
Northern Ireland 523
Existing law 523
Mental Capacity Bill 523

CHAPTER 15
Ireland 525
Existing law 525
Legislation 525
Comment 526

Chapter 1

Background

PRELIMINARY

Overview

Issues

1.1 The *Concise Oxford Dictionary* defines a decision as 'a conclusion or resolution reached after consideration', and we all assume that fellow citizens are able to make their own decisions. Those who cannot do so depend upon the support of others and are vulnerable to abuse or neglect. A civilised society must make provision for such people in its laws, but this assumes that they can be properly identified.

Capacity

1.2 The assessment of capacity is not an easy matter for society. To deprive people who are capable of making their own decisions of the right to do so would be an abuse,[1] yet failure to recognise lack of capacity results in continuing vulnerability. It is possible to stigmatise a person as lacking capacity for a variety of reasons and our history provides many examples of this.[2] Is the objective to protect the individual or society? Is it to afford power to one section of society over another by categorising some people as being unable to make decisions? We accept that children may be denied capacity, especially during their formative years, but the age at which capacity becomes recognised by the law has progressively reduced during recent years. It is only within the past century that all people in our society have been recognised as equals, and this means that some objective justification must exist before personal capacity is denied to an adult. That justification is generally to be found in the diagnosis of some form of mental impairment.

1.3 Legal incompetence is thus to be found when there is lack of capacity due to a mental disability. It may arise for a variety of reasons and may be merely temporary or may be a permanent condition. The lack of capacity may be partial or total. Insofar as an individual does have capacity, any decisions that are made should be recognised and an 'all or nothing' approach should not be adopted. Some decisions require little thought and

---

[1] It would also be a breach of the human rights of the individual if not justified and a proportionate response.
[2] Women, felons and lunatics have all at some time been treated as incompetent. The Mental Deficiency Act 1913 extended to 'moral imbeciles' and thus unmarried mothers could be deprived of their liberty.

may be identified from a mere assent or even body language. Others require knowledge and understanding and need to be communicated in a reasoned manner.

Decision-making

1.4 When lack of capacity is temporary it may be possible to defer decisions until capacity is restored. But if it is of lasting duration or permanent, or if an urgent decision otherwise needs to be made, there must be some legally recognised procedure whereby necessary decisions can be made by some other person or body. The decision-maker must be identified so that any decision that is made will be recognised by others.

1.5 There are different types of decision that we all make. We have to manage our financial affairs, and those who enter into transactions with us must be satisfied that these are enforceable and not likely to be set aside due to lack of competence on our part or lack of authority on the part of the person who transacts them for us. Decisions about medical treatment may also need to be made and should not simply be left to doctors, especially if they could have a serious effect upon the rest of our lives. Many personal welfare decisions are trivial, but some may have implications for other persons and lead to disputes within families.[3] Each of these three types of decision-making needs to come within any jurisdiction afforded by the law.

1.6 If personal choices are to be made for us then there must be a recognised basis on which this should be done. Is the decision-maker free to make whatever decisions he or she thinks best, which might be subjective and influenced by personal interests, or is an objective basis to be adopted? What might that basis be? There seems to be general acceptance that the paternalistic approach adopted in respect of children is not appropriate for an adult.

1.7 It is not acceptable for one person to assume dominion over another without the facility for this to be questioned and it is a function of the law to provide this facility. Although various procedures may be devised to resolve disputes, as a last resort it is the courts that are usually relied upon to undertake this task. They need to be legally empowered to do so, but it is not only disputes that may need to be referred to the courts: where there is uncertainty as to what may be done or what would be lawful, the courts are usually expected to determine this.

Communication

1.8 There is no magic about decision-making: it merely means making a choice, but this does require the ability to identify the range of possible choices and the implications of each. It also requires the ability to

---

[3] Compare decisions about what to wear and what to eat with decisions about where to live or with whom.

communicate the choice once this has been made. Communication is a two-way process: it is as important to ensure that the person understands what is being said to them as that their attempts to respond are understood. Impairment of communication does not necessarily indicate lack of mental capacity and, where there is doubt, a medical report may establish the capacity of the individual.

1.9 If we are to empower people we must not rely solely upon normal methods of communication, but should explore and adopt any method that will achieve effective communication.[4] This may involve using available aids or an interpreter where this will assist. If verbal dialogue is not possible, written notes or sign language may facilitate communication. A simple response to questions, such as movement of a finger, may be found reliable but in that event questions must be phrased so as to facilitate a range of responses.

Conclusion

1.10 These are the fundamental issues that should be addressed by any legal system, and other countries including Germany, the provinces in Canada and the states of the USA, Australia and New Zealand have through their legislation over the years developed adult guardianship laws. The Mental Capacity Act 2005 was an early attempt to remedy this shortcoming in England and Wales and contained some innovative features.[5] A slightly different approach had already been adopted in Scotland.[6]

Legal competence

1.11 The law assumes that an adult has the capacity to make and the ability to communicate personal decisions so there is a vacuum if someone is not able to do this. Concerns may also arise as to whether an individual is competent to make a particular decision or acquiesce in the decisions of others, even though he or she purports to do so. In a legal context we are assessing whether any choice would be recognised by the law.

1.12 When talking about competence we are considering the ability to understand, make a choice and then make this clear to others, even though assistance may be needed to carry the choice into effect. It follows that neither age nor physical or sensory impairment should by itself affect competence. Lack of legal competence may arise through mental incapacity, an inability to communicate or a combination of the two, but every effort should be made to overcome communication difficulties.

---

[4] The phrase 'locked in syndrome' is used to describe a person who can reason and make decisions but is unable to communicate.
[5] The implementation date was 1 October 2007 for England and Wales and it could be adopted in Northern Ireland by regulations (although it has not been).
[6] Adults with Incapacity (Scotland) Act 2000; Mental Health (Care and Treatment) (Scotland) Act 2003; and Adult Support and Protection (Scotland) Act 2007.

Tests of mental capacity

1.13 Although the term 'mental incapacity' conveys a fairly consistent impression to most people it does not have a precise meaning. It would be convenient if there were a universal definition, so that we could readily identify those members of society who are eligible for special treatment, but this could never be the case because very few people are incapable in all things. Legal tests of capacity must vary according to the circumstances.

1.14 In some situations, specific tests have been developed by case-law so textbooks are able to identify testamentary capacity and the capacity required to sign an enduring power of attorney, enter into a marriage or make a gift. The classic definition of a 'patient'[7] which was found in the Mental Health Act 1983 and the various court rules was not interpreted by the appeal courts until the turn of the century.[8] Otherwise general principles must be relied upon, and these are now based upon function rather than the status of the person making the decision or the outcome of decisions. Furthermore, it is the individual's understanding rather than judgment that is relevant – we are all entitled to make unwise decisions.

Assessment of mental capacity

1.15 Doubts about capacity may arise for several reasons but these should not be confused with tests of capacity. Thus the status of the individual (such as being elderly and living in a nursing home), the outcome of a decision (viewed by others as illogical) or the appearance or behaviour of the individual may cause capacity to be questioned. Yet it is not unusual for outward appearances to create a false impression of incapacity and, conversely, the absence of any of these indications does not mean that the individual is capable. In all these situations a proper assessment should be made according to appropriate criteria.

1.16 One of the difficulties is that the various professionals who may be involved approach the question of capacity from different standpoints so often reach different conclusions. In case of dispute, capacity is a question of fact for the Court to decide on the balance of probabilities with a presumption of capacity. The opinions of professionals will be admitted as 'expert' evidence but considered alongside factual evidence from those who know the individual and will only be persuasive if the experts have been given all relevant information and applied the appropriate legal test.

1.17 The medical profession tends to be concerned with diagnosis and prognosis rather than the severity and implications of mental disability. The doctor may well be able to identify the cause of the disability and indicate its likely future consequences, but what is in issue to the lawyer is the effect

---

[7] 'Incapable by reason of mental disorder of managing and administering his property and affairs.'
[8] *Masterman-Lister v Brutton & Co and Jewell & anor* [2002] EWCA Civ 1889.

on the individual at this moment in time.⁹ Care workers classify people according to their degree of independence, which involves consideration of levels of competence in performing skills such as eating, dressing, communication and social skills. These skills may be affected by mental or physical causes and also enhanced by a learnt behaviour pattern. An assessment based upon a medical diagnosis is of little use to the care worker other than to explain the reason for the present impairment and indicate whether improvement or deterioration is to be expected. The carer may become concerned as to the vulnerability of the person cared for and the entitlement of others to take decisions on that person's behalf but vulnerability does not by itself signal a lack of capacity.

1.18 The lawyer wishes to establish whether the individual is capable of making a reasoned and informed decision, although there may be a need to assess the degree of dependence, for example, when considering what financial provision should be made for the individual. There can be no universally applied test because the capacity required will depend upon the nature of the decision to be made, but the medical diagnosis will be largely irrelevant except insofar as it points to the degree of capacity that may be anticipated and the carer's view may be helpful but will not be based on any particular legal test. Thus the lawyer may need to consult the doctor and carer (or social worker) but their views merely form part of the evidence when considering the question of legal capacity. Having gathered this evidence the lawyer is in the best position to form a considered view as to legal capacity or to refer the issue to a court for determination.

Incapacitated people

1.19 Children are adequately catered for under the law of England and Wales.¹⁰ Those adults who may lack capacity fall into four main groups. The largest group comprises elderly people who are deprived of their capacity by senile dementia but have previously been able to manage their own affairs. At the other extreme are those with learning disabilities which may be so severe that they have never been able to enjoy personal autonomy. In between are those who encounter a period of mental illness or have an acquired brain injury rendering them incapable of making decisions that others should recognise. The situation is made more complicated by the fact that for some capacity may fluctuate and in every instance there is the potential for partial capacity.

---

[9] The Law Society and the British Medical Association have produced guidance in a book entitled *Assessment of Mental Capacity: A Practical Guide for Doctors and Lawyers* (Law Society Publishing, 4th edn, 2015).

[10] The Children Act 1989 contains the necessary powers for intervention by the courts and the High Court wardship jurisdiction remains.

Decision-making

1.20 Decisions fall into three broad categories: financial, personal welfare and health care. When an adult is incapable of making decisions special procedures should be available for these to be taken on his or her behalf if that is appropriate. This raises the questions of when decision-making powers should be delegated, who should then be empowered to take the decisions and the basis on which they should be taken.

Delegated decision-making

1.21 Although under general legal principles a specific decision may be held to be invalid due to lack of competence this may be merely a 'one-off' situation[11] and something more is needed if decision-making powers are to be delegated. This criteria – which makes clear that there is an ongoing problem that needs to be addressed – is known as the 'diagnostic threshold'. It was previously the existence of a 'mental disorder' which caused the lack of capacity.

1.22 'Mental disorder' was defined in the Mental Health Act 1983 as: 'mental illness, arrested or incomplete development of mind, psychopathic disorder and any other disorder or disability of mind' but did not include the effect of alcohol or drugs.[12] This definition is extremely wide but provided a useful screening process because merely being eccentric should not be a basis for being deprived of one's rights. However, it was widely used in other contexts so was not ideal.

Decision-makers

1.23 There have in the past been various persons who might represent the interests of a mentally disabled individual to a greater or lesser extent. These included:[13]

- appointee for state benefits;
- receiver appointed by the former Court of Protection for financial affairs;
- attorney under an enduring power for financial affairs;
- trustees for financial affairs;
- litigation friend for civil proceedings;[14] or family proceedings;[15]
- next friend or guardian ad litem for family proceedings (now litigation friend);
- personal advocate – used in practice but not recognised in law.

---

[11] The individual may be under the influence of alcohol or drugs at the time.
[12] Mental Health Act 1983, s 1(2) and (3).
[13] This list applies to England and Wales. A different list could be produced for Scotland.
[14] Civil Procedure Rules 1998, SI 1998/3132, Part 21.
[15] Family Procedure Rules 2010, SI 2010/2955, Part 15.

Most of these roles still exist, but despite the length of this list the authority of such representatives extended to very few ordinary decisions for the individual and there were large gaps where no one had any power to make such decisions.

1.24 In a climate where many marriages end in separation or divorce and 'living together relationships' have become almost the norm, it would no longer be acceptable for a spouse or designated blood relative to be given special status by the law as decision-maker. Preserving personal autonomy requires that the incapacitated individual has the opportunity to make the choice of decision-maker in advance (if then capable) and to influence that choice even after losing mental capacity to the extent that wishes can be ascertained. Introducing such flexibility creates its own problems but there must be a procedure whereby the appointment of a nominee can be challenged on established principles.

Best interests

1.25 There has been much debate about the basis on which delegated decisions are to be made. Should this be what the decision-maker thinks best or what the incapacitated individual would have decided had he or she been capable? The former is too paternalistic for contemporary society whereas the latter is not feasible for those who have never been able to express their own wishes. The concept of best interests has emerged, which is an attempt to combine respect for the wishes of the individual with the views of others in a climate of minimum intervention. But what exactly does this mean in practice?

A *special jurisdiction*

1.26 There is an increasing number of adults who lack mental capacity and have property or financial affairs that need to be dealt with. This is partly because the population is living longer with greater home ownership, and partly because more brain-damaged children survive – some with substantial damages awards. Former procedures allowed these affairs to be dealt with but there was a vacuum in our law for other forms of decision-making.

1.27 It was a nonsense that financial management should control personal welfare: none of us run our own lives in that way. We each decide what we wish to do and how we wish to conduct our lives and then temper this according to what we can afford. It was also unacceptable that uncertainty prevailed on issues such as where the individual should live, with whom he or she should have contact and what medical treatment should be given. It was inevitable that sooner or later legislation would have to be introduced to tackle this issue. The Mental Capacity Act 2005 now superimposes a procedure for decision-making on our existing law.

1.28 It has to be acknowledged that any jurisdiction whose role is to address the needs of 'adults with incapacity'[16] has little relevance to the work of most lawyers and, apart from an occasional high-profile case, is of little interest to the public at large. But to anyone who encounters a decline in the mental capacity of a loved one, and to the professionals involved, the manner in which issues that arise are addressed is seen as a test of the integrity of the legal system. No one can afford to ignore reform in this area, because this is not a 'them and us' situation. Any of us may encounter a period when we lack capacity whether temporary, progressive or permanent, especially as we grow older. We and our loved ones then depend on the new jurisdiction established by the Mental Capacity Act 2005.

1.29 The new jurisdiction must also set standards for others to follow in the field of disability. Disabled people must be assured of equal access to justice and that the discrimination they still encounter in society will not be reproduced within the system of justice. This applies to the legal principles that are applied, the procedures that are followed, the facilities available and the attitudes of those involved. There will be many lessons to be learnt by the Public Guardian and the new Court of Protection, but hopefully these will be well learned and thereafter permeate throughout the legal system.[17]

Confidentiality

1.30 Doctors, lawyers, social workers and professional persons generally owe a duty of confidentiality to their patients or clients, which means that personal information should only be revealed to others with the consent of the patient or client.[18] This duty is not absolute and may be overridden where there is a stronger public interest in disclosure.[19] Where the individual lacks the mental capacity to consent to (or refuse) disclosure, it may be desirable to permit disclosure in certain circumstances. This has been expressed as follows:[20]

> 'C's interest in protecting the confidentiality of personal information about himself must not be underestimated. It is all too easy for professionals and parents to regard ... incapacitated adults as having no independent interests of their own: as objects rather than subjects. But we are not concerned here with the publication of information to the whole wide world. There is a clear distinction between disclosure to the media with a view to publication to all and sundry and disclosure in confidence to those with a proper interests in having the information in question.'

---

[16] This is the terminology now creeping into use, based on the title to the Scottish legislation, but it is questionable. It may be thought that referring to those who 'lack capacity' is demeaning and to be discouraged, but it is illogical to refer to someone as being with something that they are without.
[17] Guidance to judges is available from the Judicial College (formerly JSB) in the *Equal Treatment Bench Book*, which can be accessed at: www.judiciary.gov.uk/publications-and-reports/judicial-college/Pre+2011/equal-treatment-bench-book.
[18] This may be imposed by codes of professional conduct or by the law, e g Data Protection Act 1998 or European Convention on Human Rights, Art 8.
[19] *W v Egdell* [1990] Ch 359, at 419.
[20] *R (S) v Plymouth City Council and C* [2002] EWCA Civ 388, [2002] 1 FLR 1177, per Hale LJ.

1.31 During an assessment as to mental capacity it is essential that information is shared by the professionals involved. The individual's consent to this should be obtained wherever possible, but in the absence of this relevant disclosure may be permitted. However, this does not extend to confidential information about the individual unrelated to the assessment. Disclosure will be based on a need-to-know and the overall test is the best interests of the individual.

1.32 Similar principles must apply in a family context. Parents may choose not to reveal their financial affairs to their children and the situation does not change simply because a parent ceases to be mentally capable. This can cause suspicion when one of the children is appointed to deal with those affairs, but the duty of confidentiality will apply to such child whether acting as attorney or deputy (formerly receiver) appointed by the Court of Protection. In appropriate circumstances that Court may direct that some disclosure do take place (eg, of financial affairs) to dispel suspicion.

Undue influence

Assisted decision-making

1.33 One of the problems when dealing with individuals who are frail or of borderline mental capacity is undue influence. Some adults prefer to have many of their decisions made by others and tests of capacity encourage the acceptance of support from others even though this may amount to influence.[21] But there may be cause for concern if an individual is too easily influenced or becomes too much under the influence of another person. Also, understanding of relevant factors may be corrupted by the manner and selectivity in which information is provided. A person who is constantly given incomplete or even incorrect information is likely to make choices that they would not otherwise have made. The ability to make a choice may also be affected by threats, perceived or actual. Thus a decision which appears to have been competently made could be the outcome of at best a limited perception of the choices available or at worst fear of the consequences of making a different decision.

1.34 This problem is magnified by the fact that those seeking to challenge a decision may themselves be seeking to exert an influence over the individual. All too often these situations of conflict develop from a power struggle between otherwise concerned relatives with the vulnerable person becoming a pawn in the game. A tendency by this person to agree with the party who presently has their audience either because of a short-term desire for peace or the strength of that party's personality merely provides evidence which fuels the problem. Experience in the Court of Protection demonstrates that many of the disputes arise from the abuse of power or desire of another individual for control over the vulnerable individual.

---

[21] The real problem is likely to become undue influence of those whose capacity is impaired but not lacking. To what extent should one decide that an individual lacks capacity because they have become too susceptible to the influence of others?

1.35 Perhaps of more concern is the situation where undue influence is not recognised and financial or emotional abuse is taking place. An individual who needs assistance from others before making significant personal decisions is vulnerable. There is a tendency to delegate decisions to others who demonstrate a willingness to take them over, and when those others are influenced by personal gain or improper motives there is likely to be abuse. The courts are prepared to set aside transactions adverse to an individual when these are the result of undue influence, but these matters can be expensive to litigate and the interaction between improper influence and mental capacity has yet to be fully developed.

The legal position

1.36 People may not be saved from their own foolishness but will be protected from being victimised by other people. The common law developed a principle of duress but equity supplemented this by enabling gifts and other transactions to be set aside if procured by undue influence or if they are otherwise unconscionable. The manner in which the intention to enter into the transaction was secured may be investigated and if produced by unacceptable means, the law will not permit the transaction to stand. There are thus three situations where transactions may be set aside:

- where duress or undue influence has been expressly used for the purpose of achieving a gift or benefit – the burden of proof is on the party alleging this;
- where undue influence is presumed – the burden is then on the other party to justify the transaction; and
- where a contract of an improvident nature has been made by a poor and ignorant person acting without independent advice, and the other party cannot show that it was fair and reasonable – this is a fall-back remedy for unconscionable conduct.

1.37 The law has appeared to approach the issue of undue influence according to the specific relationship between the parties but the question is whether one party has placed sufficient trust and confidence in the other, rather than whether the relationship between the parties is of a particular type.[22] However, a presumption may arise in two ways:

(1) *The type of relationship*: where there is a recognised relationship in which one party acquires influence over another who is vulnerable (eg client and solicitor, patient and doctor, beneficiary and trustee). There is then an irrebuttable presumption of influence and it is not necessary to establish that the relationship was based upon trust and confidence. If it appears that this influence has been inappropriately exercised then the party with influence must prove that this was not the case.

(2) *The evidential presumption*: where there is evidence that the relationship was based on trust and confidence in relation to the

---

[22] GH Treitel *The Law of Contract* (Sweet & Maxwell, 10th edn, 1999), at pp 380–381.

management of the complainant's financial affairs, coupled with a transaction giving rise to suspicions which must be addressed. There may then be a rebuttable presumption of undue influence and it is for the other party to produce evidence to counter the inference which otherwise should be drawn.

1.38 There are thus two prerequisites to the burden of proof shifting to the other party. First, that trust and confidence was placed in the other party, or that party was in a position of dominance or control. Secondly, that the transaction is not readily explicable by the relationship of the parties. The mere existence of influence is not enough, but it is not essential that the transaction should be disadvantageous to the pressurised or influenced person, either in financial terms or in any other way.[23] However, questions of undue influence will not usually arise where the transaction is innocuous.[24]

Legal background

Historical

Parens patriae

1.39 Until 1959, the High Court and its predecessors had jurisdiction over the lives of incompetent adults pursuant to the rights of the Crown, known as the Royal Prerogative or parens patriae jurisdiction which was given statutory recognition in 1339.[25] In practice this meant state involvement in the financial affairs of the mentally incapacitated citizen and there was no equivalent of the modern welfare state or social services. The Mental Health Act 1959 abolished the delegation of the Royal Prerogative in respect of adults and established a completely statutory jurisdiction but, although this was not realised at the time, it deprived the courts of jurisdiction over personal welfare and health care decisions other than in the context of treatment for mental disorder. This became apparent after it was held that the statutory jurisdiction of the Court of Protection only extended to financial affairs.[26]

The declaratory jurisdiction

1.40 Nevertheless, the High Court found it necessary to facilitate decisions in extreme cases for incompetent adults (ie, where the individual lacked capacity) and did so by making *declarations* as to best interests, relying on its inherent jurisdiction. This was initially in respect of serious health care

---

[23] The label 'manifest disadvantage' adopted by Lord Scarman in *National Westminster Bank v Morgan* [1985] AC 686, HL can give rise to misunderstanding and should no longer be adopted – see the judgment of Lord Nicholls in *Bank of Scotland plc v Etridge (No 2)* [2001] UKHL 44, [2001] 2 FLR 1364.
[24] *CIBC Mortgages plc v Pitt* [1994] 1 FLR 17, HL.
[25] Statute de Prerogativa Regis, 17 Edw II (1339) St I cc 9, 10. The earliest reference is to be found in a semi-official tract known as the *De Praerogativa Regis* ('On the King's Prerogative') dating from the reign of Edward 1 (1272–1307).
[26] *Re W (EEM)* [1971] Ch 123.

decisions[27] but subsequently this remedy was extended to personal welfare decisions. In 1995, Mrs Justice Hale not only applied the procedure to a personal welfare decision[28] but also backed it up with an injunction and this was upheld by the Court of Appeal.[29] In that same year the High Court held that the Court had jurisdiction to grant a declaration that a child with cerebral palsy and learning difficulties was upon attaining majority entitled to choose where to live and with whom to associate, and to restrain the parents by injunction from interfering.[30] However, it should be noted that the making of a declaration or an injunction is a discretionary remedy and this procedure is inordinately expensive and scarcely available for everyday situations even though these do arise.

1.41 More recently the High Court has extended this power beyond incompetent adults to those who were vulnerable for other reasons. Thus it has been stated:[31]

> '... there is no doubt that the court has jurisdiction to grant whatever relief in declaratory form is necessary to safeguard and promote the vulnerable adult's welfare and interests.'

and subsequently:[32]

> '... the inherent jurisdiction remains alive, in appropriate cases, to meet circumstances unmet by the scope of the legislation'

So, the inherent jurisdiction continues notwithstanding that the Mental Capacity Act 2005 now provides a statutory decision-making jurisdiction for those who lack capacity according to the criteria specified in the Act.[33]

Terminology

1.42 Even if there was no need for decisions to be made on behalf of those who lacked capacity, it was necessary for the courts to decide whether decisions could be made by the individual or whether those purported to have been made were effective. There was confusion in the legal terms found in statutes and law reports well into the twentieth century which pointed to a general condition but did not assist in determining the specific implications. Undefined and stigmatising phrases such as 'of unsound

---

[27] This power was first recognised by the House of Lords in *Re F (Mental Patient: Sterilisation)* [1989] 2 FLR 376 and confirmed in *Airedale NHS Trust v Bland* [1993] 1 FLR 1026, HL. See generally Chapter 5.
[28] *Re S (Adult Patient: Jurisdiction)* [1995] 1 FLR 302. An injunction was granted to stop the wife of an elderly, infirm man taking him abroad out of the care of his mistress.
[29] *Re S (Hospital Patient: Court's Jurisdiction)* [1995] 1 FLR 1075; [1995] 1 FLR 302.
[30] *Re V (Declaration against Parents)* [1995] 2 FLR 1003, Johnson J.
[31] *Re PS* [2007] EWHC 623 (Fam), [2007] 2 FLR 1083, Munby J, at [13].
[32] *KC and Anor v City of Westminster Social and Community Services Department and Anor* [2008] EWCA Civ 198, [2008] 2 FLR 267, Roderic Wood J, at [56].
[33] For a contrary view see Macur J in *LBL v RYJ and VJ* [2010] EWHC 2665 (COP), [2010] COPLR Con Vol 795: 'I reject what appears to have been the initial contention of this local authority that the inherent jurisdiction of the court may be used in the case of a capacitous adult to impose a decision upon him/her whether as to welfare or finance ... the relevant case law establishes the ability of the court, via its inherent jurisdiction, to facilitate the process of unencumbered decision-making by those who they have determined have capacity free of external pressure or physical restraint in making those decisions.' But, see now Chapter 11.

mind',[34] 'mentally defective' and 'mentally disordered' were sometimes used with little attempt to define or assess the implications in any particular case. These terms reflected the period when used rather than the interpretation that should now be placed on the words chosen.

Incapacity

1.43 Lawyers too frequently failed to distinguish mental illness, mental handicap (now known as learning disability) and brain injury or to realise that although any of these conditions may result in lack of mental capacity they did not inevitably do so. Their approach tended to concentrate upon the nature of the condition rather than its effect on the individual. Unless a status test applied lawyers relied on doctors to assess capacity and little guidance was given as to the specific test to be applied. An 'all or nothing' approach tended to be adopted rather than asking whether the individual was capable of making the particular decision in question. Thus there were people who were without doubt capable and those who clearly lacked capacity, but between these extremes was a grey area for the most part avoided by lawyers.

Legislation

Mental Health Acts

1.44 The Lunacy Act 1890 gave various powers to the Office of the Master in Lunacy (which was not renamed the Court of Protection until 1947) and these were the basis of the provisions contained in the Mental Health Act 1983, Part VII.[35] This former Court of Protection had powers over the property and affairs of an individual who was 'incapable, by reason of mental disorder, of managing and administering his property and affairs' but this was interpreted as relating to financial affairs only. Usually someone would be appointed as a *receiver* to handle those affairs under the supervision of the Court, but a *short order* was available for small or straightforward cases.

Enduring Powers of Attorney Act 1985

1.45 Demand for a less expensive and simpler procedure of choice[36] coupled with the inability of the Court of Protection to cope with the financial affairs of all mentally incapacitated persons resulted in recommendations by the Law Commission in 1983[37] and the passing of the Enduring Powers of Attorney Act 1985. This overcame the problem with

---

[34] This phrase is defined in the Trustee Act 1925 as 'incapable from infirmity of mind of managing his own affairs'. Typical of the 1925 property legislation this has stood the test of time.
[35] These largely re-enact the Mental Health Act 1959, Part VIII.
[36] Ie the choice of the person whose affairs are to be dealt with.
[37] *The Incapacitated Principal*, Law Com No 122, Cmnd 8977 (HMSO, 1983).

ordinary powers of attorney that they were revoked by the subsequent mental incapacity of the donor[38] under normal agency principles. Some formality was introduced into the documentation and an application had to be made to the Public Guardianship Office for the power to be registered with the Court of Protection upon the donor becoming mentally incapable but there was no supervision although the Court had power to intervene.

1.46 Enduring powers have proved to be a great success but they have their limitations (only financial decisions can be dealt with in this way) and leave considerable scope for financial abuse. In terms of numbers they far surpassed receivership orders. The development of enduring powers into lasting powers dealing with a wider range of decision-making is considered in Chapter 3, but enduring powers that existed in October 2007 when the new jurisdiction was introduced remain valid under the former principles.

THE NEW CLIMATE

The social climate

General

1.47 There is now a new social and legal climate that emphasises personal autonomy, favours community care and disapproves of discrimination in any form. It should not be overlooked that those who lack mental capacity frequently have other physical or mental impairments as well, so the combined implications of mental and physical disabilities have to be considered.

Community care

1.48 New community care policies were introduced in 1993. There are many facets to community care, but of particular relevance to disabled people are the requirement for their needs to be assessed, the duty placed upon the social services departments of local authorities (subject to available funding) to ensure that these needs are met rather than expecting the individual to cope with whatever services are available and the move away from institutional care to care in the community. The consequence is that people with disabilities are more visible in society and both they and their family/carers have greater expectations as to how they will be treated. Their rights are increasingly being recognised and enforced, by others if not by themselves.

Discrimination

1.49 Discrimination is not always intentional. It may be due to pure ignorance or mere thoughtlessness (ie treating people in an insensitive way) but stereotyping and prejudice also give rise to discrimination. Unwitting or

---

[38] Ie the person who granted the power.

unconscious prejudice – demonstrating prejudice without realising it – is difficult to tackle. Ignorance of the cultures, beliefs and disadvantages of others encourages prejudices and these are best dispelled by greater awareness. For people with disabilities it is not just a question of avoiding these forms of discrimination because any special needs also have to be addressed. Providing equal treatment may involve different treatment so as to ensure equal opportunity.

1.50 Discrimination takes many forms: it may be actual or perceived and it may be direct or indirect. *Direct* discrimination occurs where a person is treated less favourably on grounds of race, colour, religion, gender, ethnic or national origin or disability than others would be in similar circumstance. *Indirect* discrimination occurs where a requirement is applied equally to all groups, but has a disproportionate effect on the members of one group because a considerably smaller number of members of that group can comply with it.

1.51 Discrimination may also be found in an entire organisation through its processes, attitudes and behaviour.[39] A culture of prejudice may have grown up within an organisation which is seen as acceptable by those involved and results in unquestioning behaviour that disadvantages a section of the community.[40] If this arises in the legal system or in any environment it should be addressed in an appropriate way.

1.52 Discrimination in any form is now disapproved of as it means being treated unfairly or denied opportunities. It should be avoided even if not intended. Indirect discrimination should not be tolerated unless it can be objectively justified by a legitimate aim and the means of achieving that aim are appropriate and necessary. Even if there is no discrimination, every effort should be made to avoid the perception that there has been.

Attitudes to disability

1.53 Attitudes to disability in general have also changed in three significant respects:
(1) We have moved away from the medical model of disability which concentrates on the limitations of the individual to a social model which identifies the barriers created in society. Thus lack of access to a building is not seen as being due to the fact that the individual is a wheelchair user but rather that the building has been constructed with steps but no ramp. In other words, don't blame the individual but blame the way society is structured. It is the barriers that should be removed (or not put there in the first place) rather than the individual that should be given special treatment.

---

[39] This was one of the conclusions of *The Stephen Lawrence Inquiry – Report by Sir William Macpherson*, Cmnd 4264-1 (1999). 'Institutional racism' was identified in the police force.
[40] Eg failure to provide assistance to wheelchair users or to communicate in a friendly manner with people from ethnic minorities.

(2) Stereotyping has been recognised as the most significant form of discrimination that affects people with disabilities. This is exhibited in the unjustified assumption that people who meet particular criteria will behave in a particular way. In other words, we must be careful not to apply labels to people, often unconsciously, and then make assumptions based thereon. People who have a specific condition should not all be assumed to have the same limitations or approach to life – they should be treated as 'people first' rather than identified by their perceived disability.

(3) There is a greater awareness of mental health problems and arguably less social stigma involved although it is still prevalent in certain sections of the community.[41] There are many myths about people with mental health problems, in particular that they are dangerous and violent, can't work and are incapable of making their own decisions. Contrary to popular belief, mental health problems are not rare and unusual. However, there remains a tension, reflected in the debate about reform of the Mental Health Act, between the need to protect society and the best interests of the individual. Society and politicians, fuelled by the media, still tend to be obsessed with those few cases where the individual has become a public danger when in the vast majority of cases any risk is purely to the individual.

Terminology

1.54 How we refer to people is important. Use of inappropriate terms can cause great offence to the individual and also demonstrates prejudicial attitudes towards disabled people. Also, if we attach labels to people there is a danger that we then use these, however inadvertently, to take away their rights by making assumptions that are not in fact justified. Comparisons should never be made with 'normal'[42] and we should avoid referring to 'the disabled' or 'the handicapped' as if these are a class of person.[43] Terminology that suggests a value judgment should also be avoided.[44] One of the difficulties is that defined medical or legal terms have over the years tended to become used in a derogatory manner[45] and then new neutral terms have to be found. Thus 'mental handicap' has been replaced by 'learning disability' and efforts are being made to find a new term for 'mentally ill'.[46]

---

[41] Stigma arises from negative stereotypes associated with the symptoms or diagnosis of mental health problems.
[42] Instead refer to non-disabled or able bodied.
[43] These terms are grammatically incorrect! Similarly 'the blind' or 'the deaf' – instead use 'people with impaired sight' or 'people with impaired hearing'.
[44] Eg referring to someone as 'a victim of ...', 'suffering from ...', 'afflicted by ...' or 'wheelchair bound'.
[45] Eg the terms *idiot*, *imbecile*, *lunatic*, *cretin*, *moron*, all of which have appeared in earlier legislation or medical textbooks. The Mental Deficiency Act 1913 used the defined terms 'idiot' and 'imbecile'.
[46] MIND, the national organisation, tends to use 'people who experience mental distress' or 'people with mental health problems' but at one time the expression 'mentally challenged' was advocated.

1.55 Use of appropriate terminology is not just political correctness but is also an attitude of mind: we should recognise the person rather than any disability. Organisations such as People First[47] prefer that we state 'people with disabilities' for this reason. More recently the Disability Rights Commission opted for 'disabled people' because this emphasises that the individual is disabled by society (the social model of disability).[48]

Attitudes of minority ethnic communities

1.56 It has become apparent that some minority ethnic communities have a distrust of mental health authorities, try to deal with problems within the family and viewed the former Public Guardianship Office as 'interfering'. It is essential that our new mental capacity jurisdiction reaches out to such communities and recognises cultural norms. The problems that are faced may be illustrated by reference to two communities.

1.57 Asian communities in the UK have tended to be young, with the men mainly working and in consequence controlling the finances. This is changing as they move into the second and third generation, and as members become older more are presenting with senile dementia. There is a stigma associated with mental health problems which tend to be concealed with a consequent delay in accessing services. Many unwritten transactions take place within the community so incapacity issues are not being faced up to. There is a need to raise awareness of the legal position because families react with disbelief when told that they have no authority over the finances of an incapacitated member.

1.58 The Jewish community ranges across a religious spectrum from liberal to ultra-orthodox and increased numbers come from a range of racial groups, mainly Asian and African. They generally live in urban areas situated around local and regional centres close to religious, education and cultural venues. Some are assimilated into the general community but others lead segregated lives. Parents tend to request the continuation of a Jewish life and value base for their children, of whom they have high expectations. Jews have a different experience, both historically and culturally, from the mainstream population. They would define themselves as an ethnic minority and carry a shared past and present experience of persecution and discrimination.

National statistics tend to show a higher than average incidence of mental health problems in the Jewish community, especially in students and young people. This is coupled with a lack of knowledge and awareness of mental health issues and a feeling of stigma within families who have difficulty in accepting problems. In consequence these are often concealed and not regularly acknowledged as a Jewish issue. There are a large number of

---

[47] There are many People First Groups – see www.peoplefirstltd.com
[48] The Disability Rights Commission has now become part of the Equality and Human Rights Commission. The website is www.equalityhumanrights.com.

Jewish social care agencies and care tends to be segregated in the Jewish community with culturally specific services – kosher food, prayer facilities and religious activities.

Role of the law

1.59 People with disabilities are vulnerable to neglect, abuse and exploitation and may need support, protection and empowerment.

Support

1.60 There have traditionally been three sources of support, all regulated by the law:

(1) DWP – the Department for Work and Pensions,[49] which through the *Benefits Agency* provided state benefits, generally on a weekly basis. These may be contributory, non-contributory[50] or a means-tested top-up to ensure that everybody has a minimum income to meet their requirements.[51] The Benefits Agency has since been replaced by *Job Centre Plus* (for adults of working age), the *Disability and Carers Service* (for disability-related benefits) and the *Pensions Service* (for people over pension age);

(2) SSD – the social services departments of local authorities,[52] which are responsible for providing or arranging community care services and services for disabled persons. These must generally be paid for, subject to a means test;

(3) NHS – the National Health Service which, largely now through NHS Trusts, provides free hospital and nursing care and general medical services.[53]

1.61 The respective roles of these providers are changing and overlapping, with social services applying means tests which may take away state benefit yet now providing cash to pay for services, whilst state benefits are withdrawn from those in 'hospital'.[54] In some areas, Care Trusts provide both health and social care services, particularly mental health and learning disability services and care for older people.

---

[49] Formerly known as the Department of Social Security (DSS), and previously the Department of Health and Social Security (DHSS).
[50] For example, disability benefits. Contributory benefits are generally for earnings replacement, eg, retirement pension and incapacity benefit.
[51] Often referred to as 'welfare benefits'.
[52] Not all local authorities have such departments and reference is often now made to 'local authorities with social services responsibilities'.
[53] Older readers will remember the DHSS, when health and social security came within the same government department.
[54] The definition of 'hospital' for benefits purposes is wider than the generally recognised meaning.

Protection

1.62 The law must also ensure protection and has done so by providing a representative in the form of an *appropriate adult* for police interviews and a *statutory guardian* or *nearest relative* for Mental Health Act functions. The authorities should investigate and intervene where there is a suspicion of abuse but their powers are limited at present when compared with those under the Children Act 1989 and there is no duty to act – which means that often they do not do so despite conflict or perceived abuse. Some local authorities have set up adult protection procedures under the *No Secrets* guidance.[55]

Empowerment

1.63 Empowerment means enabling individuals to take decisions for which they are competent. There must be a proper assessment of capacity and any communication difficulties should be overcome. A suitable person should be empowered to take decisions for individuals who are not competent. At present we have a number of potential representatives but coverage is not comprehensive.

Problems

1.64 There have been four significant problems in the provision of services and in our present law and procedures:
(1) A lack of adequate public funding to cover the needs of disabled people and a lack of ring-fencing of the funds that could be available.
(2) Buck-passing between the DWP, local authorities and health authorities with the disabled individual becoming a pawn in the funding game, and money that could have been expended on unquestionable needs being wasted on the argument over which funder must provide. Many appeal decisions have sought to define responsibilities but to some extent the problem has been alleviated by the introduction of joint commissioning of services by health and social services.
(3) The delicate balance between protection and empowerment, because protection involves taking away the personal autonomy it is desired to preserve. This dilemma is frequently encountered when dealing with vulnerable persons and is especially apparent when seeking to identify the best interests of an incapacitated individual.
(4) No adequate legally authorised representative in many situations because of the piecemeal nature of our legal system, in particular the lack of procedures for personal and medical decision-making.

---

[55] Department of Health and Home Office 'No secrets: guidance on developing and implementing multi-agency policies and procedures to protect vulnerable adults from abuse', 20 March 2000. Available on the website at www.dh.gov.uk.

The new jurisdiction introduced by the Mental Capacity Act 2005 has addressed the third and fourth of these problems and assists family and carers to address the second, but will not assist where there is inadequate funding for care needs.

Role of lawyers

1.65 Lawyers have developed considerable skills in negotiating on behalf of, and promoting the rights of, individuals who for one reason or another are at a disadvantage in looking after their own interests. The lawyer can also act as a whistle-blower to draw attention to situations where the rights of a vulnerable person are being overlooked or abuse is taking place.

Who is the client?

1.66 It is essential for any adviser in these situations to start by identifying the client. The identity of the client does not change just because of communication difficulties or even lack of capacity. Undue reliance should not be placed on relatives or carers in identifying the wishes of the client especially where these persons may be affected by the outcome of any decision. Any potential conflicts of interest should be identified at an early stage and if appropriate independent legal advice recommended either for the would-be client or for the relatives or carers.

1.67 A solicitor receiving instructions from a third party on behalf of an individual who is or may become mentally incapacitated should at all times remember that this individual is the client, not the third party. This is so even if the third party has legal authority to represent the individual, whether as deputy appointed by the Court of Protection, attorney acting under a registered enduring power of attorney or donee of a lasting power of attorney. The third party is merely an agent with a duty to act in the best interests of the incapacitated principal, and any solicitor who accepts instructions shares this duty even if it brings them into conflict with the agent through whom they receive instructions.

The legal climate
General

1.68 Driven by these social forces the legal climate has changed too over the past decade. Lawyers and the courts are having to cope with the needs of infirm elderly and disabled people. Some practitioners concentrate upon this aspect of legal practice and have developed considerable expertise. There have also been significant legislative initiatives which provide the basis for the growth of legal activity and a wide range of new outcomes from the courts.

Legal publishing

1.69 A new approach to legal publishing and the practice of the law was also developing. In July 1992 *Mental Handicap and the Law*[56] was published with the aim of addressing the needs of people with learning disabilities and their families and carers. This was followed by further books by the same author relating to elderly people[57] which represented a radical new approach to the law based on the needs of client groups rather than the coverage of legal topics as hitherto favoured by practitioners, authors and academics.

Elderly client practices

1.70 With the encouragement of the Law Society, solicitors have developed 'elderly client practices' providing a full range of services targeting the needs of older clients that go beyond the traditional wills, tax planning and enduring powers of attorney.[58] These developments have resulted in a wider range of legal services being available to the public thereby increasing expectations and creating a greater awareness of the weaknesses of our existing legal system in regard to incapacitated people.

Community Care

Background

1.71 Care in the community is not a new concept. For many it had been the reality for years, but meant living alone or being cared for by family with little support from the state in an indifferent society. The need became apparent to reduce institutional care and provide alternative services in a community setting, and increasing pressure from concerned people and organisations to recognise the rights and freedoms of people who need care or support found expression in policies which have become known as *community care*.

1.72 It was also recognised that this meant more than just the provision of a home in the community for former hospital patients: a whole range of support and services had to be provided for all persons needing care, including those already living in their own family homes. The emphasis should be upon enabling them to remain in their own homes or otherwise in the community when they, their family and friends could no longer cope without support. In the absence of a suitable range of services the only alternative had been long-term care in a residential home or hospital.

---

[56] G Ashton and AD Ward *Mental Handicap and the Law* (Sweet & Maxwell, 1992).
[57] C Bielanska and M Terrell (general eds), G Ashton (consultant ed) *The Elderly Client Handbook* (The Law Society, 1994; 4th edn, 2010); G Ashton *Elderly People and the Law* (1995; 2nd edn Jordan Publishing, 2014 by G Ashton and C Bielanska). Further books have followed by other authors.
[58] First advocated by this author at the Annual Conference of the Law Society in 1992. A new professional body, Solicitors for the Elderly Limited (SFE), now has 1,500 members, runs conferences and has a website at www.solicitorsfortheelderly.com.

Reports

1.73 In 1986 the Audit Commission carried out a review of community-based care services and identified many problems which needed to be tackled. Resources, staffing and training were all directed towards the more institutional forms of care, organisation was fragmented and there was a lack of effective joint working and planning between the different agencies involved in the provision of services. The Commission regarded community care as providing clients with a full range of services, and a wide range of options; bringing services to people, rather than people to services; the adjustment of services to meet the needs of people, rather than the adjustment of people to meet the needs of services.[59]

1.74 A further review, *Community Care: Agenda for Action*, was published in 1988.[60] It acknowledged the need to promote 'the provision of services to individuals, developed from a multi-disciplinary assessment of their needs and made with proper participation of the individuals concerned, their families and other carers'. This was followed in 1989 by the publication of a White Paper *Caring for People: Community Care in the Next Decade and Beyond* in which it was stated:

> 'Community care means providing the services and support which people who are affected by problems of ageing, mental illness, mental handicap or physical or sensory disability need to be able to live as independently as possible in their own homes, or in homely settings in the community.'

1.75 Since the introduction of the new community care policies further changes have been implemented within social services and the NHS.[61] There have been many consultation papers and policy initiatives reflecting the need for fundamental change in the provision and funding of services. It has been recognised that people want greater control and choice over the services and support they receive and this has led to the introduction of direct payments and personal budgets. Following consultation two Green Papers were published: *Shaping the Future of Care Together* (Cm7673) and *Paying for Care in Wales*, identifying the need to provide early intervention or prevention services to avoid the need for more intensive care.[62]

Legislation

1.76 Although the legislation seen as introducing community care policies and procedures is the National Health Service and Community Care Act 1990, this devoted only nine sections[63] to the topic in England. The Act did not create new rights to new services, and although it imposed a new

---

[59] Audit Commission Report *Making a Reality of Community Care* (1986).
[60] Report to the Secretary of State for Social Services by Sir Roy Griffiths (the *Griffiths Report*).
[61] See in particular the White Paper *Modernising Social Services* 1998, *The NHS Plan* (Cmd 4818-I) July 2000 and subsequent reports.
[62] The DoH White Paper *Building the National Care Service* (Cm7854) 2010 promoted joined up services with a national and portable needs assessment.
[63] See National Health Service and Community Care Act 1990, Part III.

duty upon local authorities to assess anyone who appeared to them to need a community care service which they may provide, it relied heavily on the following earlier legislation some of which had existed for many years:
- National Assistance Act 1948, Part III;
- Health Services and Public Health Act 1968;
- Chronically Sick and Disabled Persons Act 1970;
- Housing Act 1985;
- National Health Service Act 1977;
- Disabled Persons Act 1981;
- Mental Health Act 1983;
- Health and Social Services and Social Security Adjudications Act 1983;[64] and
- Disabled Persons (Services Consultation and Representation) Act 1986.

1.77 The 1990 Act extended the role of local authorities in the provision of residential accommodation and welfare services, enabling them to make agency arrangements with other organisations and persons whilst restricting their powers to provide accommodation. It amended the provisions as to charges for residential accommodation and other community care services and dealt with recovery of such charges. Local authorities were required following consultation with health and housing authorities to prepare and publish a community care plan. They had to assess the care needs of any person who might appear to them to require community care services and decide what services needed to be provided. Disabled individuals were given a right to an assessment. Further provisions dealt with the inspection of certain premises used for community care services, access to information and the transfer of staff from health authorities to local authorities. Finally, local authorities had to provide a complaints procedure and comply with directions from the Secretary of State in carrying out their social services functions failing which default powers became available.

1.78 Further legislation followed and this proved a prolific area for litigation with many appeal cases contributing to the implementation of the policy:[65]
- Carers (Recognition and Services) Act 1995;
- Housing Act 1996 Part VII (replacing the 1985 Act);
- Health Act 1999;
- Carers and Disabled Children Act 2000;
- Care Standards Act 2000 (to be replaced);
- Health and Social Care Act 2001, Part 4;
- National Health Service Reform and Health Care Professions Act 2002 Part 1;
- Community Care (Delayed Discharge, etc.) Act 2003;

---

64   Known as the HASSASSA Act.
65   For a useful introduction to this complex area see C Bielanska and M Terrell (general eds), GR Ashton (consultant ed) *The Elderly Client Handbook* (The Law Society, 1994; 4th edn, 2010).

- Carers (Equal Opportunities) Act 2004;
- National Health Service Act 2006;
- National Health Service (Wales) Act 2006;
- Work and Families Act 2006;
- Safeguarding Vulnerable Groups Act 2006;
- Health and Social Care Act 2008;
- Autism Act 2009;
- Health Act 2009;
- Personal Care at Home Act 2010.

Circulars and directions

1.79 The legislation was supplemented by government guidance and circulars, and by directions issued by the Secretary of State. A local authority may only be obliged to take account of advice contained in circulars and having done so may not be under a duty to comply,[66] though where an appeal to the Secretary of State is provided for it may be expected that he or she will follow his or her own advice. The policy documents of a local authority (including its community care plan) should reflect any directions and guidance in circulars and these are likely to be quoted in court proceedings and could form the basis for a legal challenge of an authority's action or inaction. The Secretary of State was empowered to issue directions to local authorities in regard to the exercise of their social services functions, and these had to be observed with the sanction being the use of default powers.

The Care Act 2014

1.80 Following a Law Commission report[67] and the Dilnot Report[68] the Government set out its vision to reform the care and support system in a White Paper, 'Caring for our future: reforming care and support'.[69] This resulted in the Care Act 2014 which consolidates the current piecemeal legislation described above into a unified adult social care statute. The Act has been described as 'the most significant reform of care and support in more than 60 years, putting people and their carers in control of their care and support'[70] but limitations on local authority funding are such that considerable time may elapse before it has a significant impact.

---

[66] Local Authority Social Services Act 1970, s 7. In this respect there may be a difference between general guidance and a direction, but the other view is that guidance is instruction that must be followed – see *R v North Yorkshire CC, ex p Hargreaves* (1994) 26 BMLR 121.
[67] Adult Social Care Law Com No 326 (10 May 2011).
[68] Fairer Care Funding: July 2011, Commission on Funding of Care and Support.
[69] Cm 8378 (July 2012).
[70] See People First available at www.peoplefirstinfo.org.uk/money-and-legal/care-act-2014/the-care-act-an-overview.aspx).

1.81 The Act makes provision:
- to reform the law relating to care and support for adults and the law relating to support for carers;
- about safeguarding adults from abuse or neglect;
- about integrating care and support with health services;
- about care standards;
- to establish Health Education England and a Health Research Authority.

The primary legislation sets out the duties imposed and powers conferred on local authorities, avoiding the need to use directions and approvals, and regulations are to provide the detail. The first parts of the Act came into effect in April 2015 and the remaining changes (including a 'cap' on care costs) were due to come into force in April 2016 but the Government has announced that they are to be delayed until April 2020.

1.82 The Act establishes core responsibilities to help guide decision-making under the legislation and promote a consistent application of the legislation. The duty to undertake a community care assessment is triggered where a person appears to the local authority to have social care needs that can be met by the provision of community care services (including a direct payment in lieu of services) and where a local authority has a legal power to provide or arrange for the provision of community care services (or a direct payment) to the person. The duty to undertake a carer's assessment applies to all carers who are providing or intend to provide care to another person, not just those providing a substantial amount of care on a regular basis. There is no definition of a disabled person or service user as the right to assessment and services will be based on a person's needs for support.[71]

1.83 The local authority must produce a care plan for people who have assessed eligible needs and Regulations are to set out the form and content that the care plan should take. Services will be portable by the introduction of an enhanced duty to co-operate when service users move areas coupled with a national portable needs assessment and national eligibility criteria.

A national and consistent framework for charging for all services has been introduced and authorities will be obliged to offer deferred payment agreements.

1.84 The local authority is under a general duty whenever it exercises a social care function to promote the adult's 'well-being' which includes personal dignity, physical and mental health, emotional well-being, personal relationships, protection from abuse and neglect, and control by the individual over day-to-day life (including over care and support).[72] In doing

---

[71] There is no need to request an assessment.
[72] Care Act 2014, s 1(3).

so the local authority must have regard to the following matters which resemble the 'best interests' criteria in the Mental Capacity Act 2005:[73]

1. the importance of beginning with the assumption that the individual is best-placed to judge the individual's well-being;
2. the individual's views, wishes, feelings and beliefs;
3. the importance of preventing or delaying the development of needs for care and support or needs for support and the importance of reducing needs of either kind that already exist;
4. the need to ensure that decisions about the individual are made having regard to all the individual's circumstances (and are not based only on the individual's age or appearance or any condition of the individual's or aspect of the individual's behaviour which might lead others to make unjustified assumptions about the individual's well-being);
5. the importance of the individual participating as fully as possible in decisions relating to the exercise of the function concerned and being provided with the information and support necessary to enable the individual to participate;
6. the importance of achieving a balance between the individual's well-being and that of any friends or relatives who are involved in caring for the individual;
7. the need to protect people from abuse and neglect;
8. the need to ensure that any restriction on the individual's rights or freedom of action that is involved in the exercise of the function is kept to the minimum necessary for achieving the purpose for which the function is being exercised.

Equality and discrimination

Background

1.85 People with impaired capacity are particularly susceptible to discrimination on account of their age or disabilities. During recent years certain forms of discrimination have been made unlawful and statutory remedies provided for a breach, more recently fuelled by European Directives. Standards have been set in these areas and enforced through the courts and tribunals. Failure to comply could lead to an expensive lesson but, whilst a few test cases achieved a high profile, discrimination remained rife in society without effective sanction. Article 14 of the European Convention on Human Rights, now part of UK law,[74] is particularly relevant because it provides:

> 'Prohibition of discrimination: the enjoyment of the rights and freedoms set forth in this Convention shall be secured without discrimination on any ground such as sex, race, colour, language, religion, political or other opinion, national or social origin, association with a national minority, property, birth or other status.'

---

[73] Care Act 2014, s 1(3).
[74] Under the Human Rights Act 1998.

This provision is not, however, freestanding and has to be joined to other Articles.

1.86 Until recently we had a plethora of inconsistent yet overlapping legislation dealing with substantive law on discrimination.[75] The Equality Act 2006 established from October 2007 a new *Equality and Human Rights Commission* (EHRC)[76] which merged the three existing commissions.[77] The EHRC can tackle prejudice based on race, gender and sexual orientation and disability as well as human rights, and has wide powers to enforce legislation.

In February 2005, the Government set up the Discrimination Law Review to address long-term concerns about inconsistencies in the current discrimination law framework, and this was followed by consultation[78] and further papers.

Equality Act 2010

1.87 The outcome is this Act whose purpose is to harmonise discrimination law and strengthen the law to support progress on equality. It brings together and re-states all the existing anti-discrimination legislation and a number of other related provisions and most provisions were brought into effect from October 2010. It also extends the categories by identifying the following 'protected characteristics':

- age (section 5)
- disability (sections 6 and 15, and Schedule 1)
- gender reassignment (sections 7 and 16)
- marriage and civil partnership (section 8)
- race (section 9)
- religion or belief (section 10)
- sex (ie gender) (section 11)
- sexual orientation (section 12)

1.88 The definitions are similar to those that applied before,[79] but the application of disability discrimination is brought into line with the other categories. The Act also strengthens the law in a number of areas by:

- placing a new duty on certain public bodies to consider socio-economic disadvantage when making strategic decisions about how to exercise their functions;

---

[75] Sex Discrimination Act 1975, Race Relations Act 1976, Disability Discrimination Act 1995 and Employment Equality (Age) Regulations 2006.
[76] The website is: www.equalityhumanrights.com.
[77] Equal Opportunities Commission, Commission for Racial Equality and Disability Rights Commission.
[78] *A Framework for Fairness – Proposals for a Single Equality Bill for Great Britain* – a consultation paper, June 2007.
[79] The definition of a disabled person is complex but extends to mental impairments and includes an adult who lacks capacity.

- extending the circumstances in which a person is protected against discrimination, harassment or victimisation because of a protected characteristic;
- making it unlawful to discriminate against, harass or victimise a person when (a) providing a service (which includes the provision of goods or facilities), (b) exercising a public function or (c) disposing of (for example, by selling or letting) or managing premises;
- making it unlawful for associations (for example, private clubs) to discriminate against, harass or victimise members, associates or guests.
- requiring taxis, other private hire vehicles, public service vehicles (such as buses) and rail vehicles to be accessible to disabled people and to allow them to travel in reasonable comfort.

1.89 The Act creates a duty on listed public bodies when carrying out their functions and on other persons when carrying out public functions to have due regard to the need to:

- eliminate conduct which the Act prohibits;
- advance equality of opportunity between persons who share a relevant protected characteristic and those who do not; and
- foster good relations between people who share a relevant protected characteristic and people who do not.

Prohibited conduct

1.90 Several forms of conduct are now defined for the purpose of prohibition. Enforcement continues to be through the County Courts (in relation to services and public functions) and employment tribunals (in relation to work and related areas, and equal pay).

Direct discrimination

1.91 This occurs where the reason for a person being treated less favourably than another is a protected characteristic.[80] This definition is broad enough to cover cases where the treatment is because of the victim's association with someone who has that characteristic (for example, is disabled). For age, different treatment that is justified as a proportionate means of meeting a legitimate aim is not direct discrimination. In relation to disability it is not discrimination to treat a disabled person more favourably than a person who is not disabled.

Discrimination arising from disability

1.87 It is discrimination to treat a disabled person unfavourably not because of the person's disability itself but because of something arising

---

[80] Equality Act 2010, s 13. Thus excluding old people would be discrimination.

from, or in consequence of, his or her disability.[81] The perpetrator must know, or reasonably be expected to know, of the disability, and it is possible to justify such treatment if it can be shown to be a proportionate means of achieving a legitimate aim.[82]

Indirect discrimination

1.92 This would occur when a policy which applies in the same way for everybody has an effect which particularly disadvantages people with a protected characteristic.[83] Where a particular group is disadvantaged in this way, a person in that group is indirectly discriminated against if he or she is put at that disadvantage, unless the person applying the policy can justify it. Indirect discrimination can also occur when a policy would put a person at a disadvantage if it were applied and thus acts as a deterrent.[84]

The treatment of the claimant must be compared with that of an actual or a hypothetical person – the comparator – who does not share the same protected characteristic as the claimant but who is (or is assumed to be) in not materially different circumstances from the claimant.

Duty to make adjustments

1.93 Section 20 defines what is meant by the duty to make reasonable adjustments to the 'provision, criterion or practice' whereby things are done.[85] The duty comprises three requirements which apply where a disabled person is placed at a substantial disadvantage in comparison to non-disabled people:

- the first covers changing the way things are done (such as changing a practice);
- the second covers making changes to the built environment (such as providing access to a building); and
- the third covers providing auxiliary aids and services (such as providing special computer software or providing a different service).

For the second requirement, taking steps to avoid the disadvantage would include removing or altering the physical feature where it would be reasonable to do so. For the first and third a reasonable step might include providing information in an accessible format). Except where the Act states otherwise, it would never be reasonable for a person bound by the duty to pass on the costs of complying with it to an individual disabled person.

---

[81] Equality Act 2010, s 15. This would cover the need to have a guide dog.
[82] This is a new provision designed to overcome the problem caused by *London Borough of Lewisham v Malcolm* [2008] UKHL 43 explained above.
[83] Equality Act 2010, s 19. This would cover the need to have a guide dog.
[84] The extension of indirect discrimination to disability is new, coming after consultation following *London Borough of Lewisham v Malcolm* [2008] UKHL 43.
[85] This replaces with some changes provisions in the Disability Discrimination Acts.

1.94 A failure to comply with any one of the reasonable adjustment requirements amounts to discrimination against a disabled person to whom the duty is owed.[86]

Harassment

1.95 There are three types of harassment, but the one which applies to disability and age involves unwanted conduct which is related to the characteristic and has the purpose or effect of creating an intimidating, hostile, degrading humiliating or offensive environment for the complainant or violating the complainant's dignity.[87] There may be a need to balance the right of freedom of expression (as set out in Article 10 of the European Convention on Human Rights) against the right not to be offended in deciding whether a person has been harassed.

Victimisation

1.96 Victimisation takes place where one person treats another badly because he or she in good faith has done a 'protected act' or is suspected of having done so or intending to do so.[88] This might include taking or supporting any action taken in relation to any alleged breach of the Act. Only an individual can bring a claim for victimisation and a person is not protected from victimisation where he or she maliciously makes or supports an untrue complaint.

Implications of conduct

1.97 Previous legislation provided some protection from discrimination, harassment and victimisation in the provision of services and the exercise of public functions. However, the protection was not uniform for the different protected characteristics. For example, there was no protection for discrimination on account of age, either in the provision of services or in the exercise of public functions. Section 29 replaces the provisions in previous legislation and extends protection so that it is generally uniform across all the protected characteristics.

It is unlawful to discriminate against or harass a person because of a protected characteristic, or victimise someone when providing services (which includes goods and facilities). The person is protected both when requesting a service and during the course of being provided with a service. It is also unlawful to discriminate against, harass or victimise a person when exercising a public function which does not involve the provision of a service. Examples of such public functions include law enforcement and

---

[86] Equality Act 2010, s 21. This replaces comparable provisions in the Disability Discrimination Acts.
[87] Equality Act 2010, s 26.
[88] Equality Act 2010, s 27. This is not really a form of discrimination.

revenue raising and collection. Public functions which involve the provision of a service, for example, medical treatment on the NHS, are covered by the provisions dealing with services. This section also imposes the section 20 duty to make reasonable adjustments in relation to providing services and exercising public functions.

Premises

1.98 There is protection from discrimination in the disposal and management of premises across all the protected characteristics with the exception of age and marriage and civil partnership, although other provisions may be relied on where they apply.[89] It is unlawful for a person who has the authority to dispose of premises (for example, by selling, letting or subletting a property) to discriminate against or victimise someone else in a number of ways including by offering the premises to them on less favourable terms; by not letting or selling the premises to them or by treating them less favourably. It is also unlawful for a person whose permission is needed to dispose of premises to discriminate against or victimise someone else by withholding that permission.

It is unlawful for a person who manages premises to discriminate against or victimise someone who occupies the property in the way he or she allows the person to use a benefit or facility associated with the property, by evicting the person or by otherwise treating the person unfavourably.

Associations

1.99 It is unlawful for an association to discriminate against, harass or victimise an existing or potential member, or an associate. This means that an association cannot refuse membership to a potential member or grant it on less favourable terms because of a protected characteristic. It does not, however, prevent associations restricting their membership to people who share a protected characteristic.[90] It is also unlawful to discriminate against, harass or victimise existing or potential guests. In particular, an association cannot refuse to invite a person as a guest because of a particular characteristic or invite that person on certain conditions which the association would not apply to other would-be guests. There is also a duty to make reasonable adjustments for disabled members and guests.

1.100 The courts are not exempted from these provisions: they provide legal services and may be in breach of this legislation if they do not take into account the needs of disabled people.[91] The Office of the Public Guardian and the Court of Protection must be fully conversant with these provisions both as regards the manner in which they deal with disabled people and the

---

[89] Equality Act 2010, ss 32–35. Similar protection was available in the previous legislation.
[90] Equality Act 2010, ss 100–103. Similar protection was available in the previous legislation.
[91] HM Courts Service has already found itself having to admit liability in a claim involving access to the courts for a hearing impaired person.

expectations that they have for incapacitated persons when dealing with their financial, social welfare and health care decisions.

Human Rights Act 1998

The Convention

1.101 The European Convention on Human Rights[92] (ECHR) is a treaty of the Council of Europe.[93] It was signed in 1950 and ratified by the UK in 1951, which means that under international law the UK became obliged to abide by its terms, although the right of individual petition was only afforded in 1966. But this did not mean that Convention rights could be relied upon in proceedings in our courts. The treaty has subsequently been amended by Protocols which are either mandatory or optional, the latter only binding states that choose to ratify them.

The legislation

1.102 The long title to the Human Rights Act 1998 (HRA 1998) states that it is 'to give further effect to' the Convention rights and it was said to be 'bringing rights home' on the basis that individuals within the UK would be enabled to rely on their rights in their home courts,[94] although the right to bring a case in Strasbourg is not prevented. The Act is a compromise, representing an attempt to incorporate the ECHR into our law whilst still recognising the traditions of the common law and the sovereignty of Parliament. Every new Bill must, when introduced, be supported by a *statement of compatibility* by the Minister responsible.[95]

1.103 Only certain of the rights contained in the ECHR have been designated as 'Convention rights' for the purpose of HRA 1998,[96] but those omitted must no doubt be 'taken into account'. Those of particular relevance in the present context are:

- Article 2 – the right to life, which has implications for the health services and especially decisions as to whether to treat those who would otherwise die.
- Article 3 – the prohibition of inhuman or degrading treatment, which is of particular relevance to the abuse and neglect of vulnerable people.
- Article 5 – the protection of liberty, which may affect detention in a care home or hospital.
- Article 6 – the right to a fair trial, which concerns participation and ensuring an independent and impartial tribunal.

---

[92] The full title is *Convention for the Protection of Human Rights and Fundamental Freedoms*.
[93] This is a separate organisation from the European Union and now comprises more than 40 member states. For further information see www.coe.int.
[94] See the White Paper *Bringing Rights Home*, Cm 3782 (1997).
[95] HRA 1998, s 19.
[96] HRA 1998, s 1. The text of these Articles is set out in HRA 1998, Sch 1.

- Article 8 – respect for private and family life, home and correspondence, which extends to bodily integrity, access to information, confidentiality and sexual relations.
- First Protocol, Art 2 – protection of property, which has implications for ownership, access to and control of property.

Some of these are 'absolute' in the sense that they do not include any qualification or allow for any derogation[97] by a ratifying country and others are qualified by some limitation or restriction.[98] Non-discrimination operates within all other rights pursuant to Art 14.[99]

Interpretation

1.104 The courts must interpret our primary and secondary legislation 'so far as it is possible to do so' in a way which is not incompatible with the ECHR whilst not having power to overrule any such legislation.[100] Where this cannot be done a *declaration of incompatibility* may be made[101] and it then becomes a matter for Parliament (which has a fast-track procedure for remedying the incompatibility[102]), although in the meanwhile the legislation must still be applied.[103] So legislation must henceforth be interpreted so as to give effect, if possible, to Convention rights.

1.105 It has been stated that an Act must receive a 'generous and purposive' interpretation to ensure that Convention rights are effective rather than illusory. Techniques may include 'reading down' (choosing between two possible interpretations and opting for the narrower) and 'reading in' (inserting words to make the statute compatible). Strasbourg jurisprudence must be 'taken into account' by our courts and tribunals,[104] which means that decisions of the European Court of Human Rights now become part of our case-law.

1.106 The European Court has recognised that the obligations of states under the ECHR are not limited to refraining from interfering with individual human rights. There is a positive obligation to ensure that one person's rights are protected from violation by another person and this has led to five duties being imposed on states in relation to Convention rights:

---

[97] An exceptional limitation imposed by the ratifying country on a particular right in specified circumstances. It must be in accordance with the law, directed to a 'particular purpose' and 'necessary in a democratic society'.

[98] This relates to some existing law of the country concerned which is not to be affected.

[99] A breach of another Convention right does not need to be established, but the circumstances must fall within the ambit of an ECHR provision.

[100] HRA 1998, s 3.

[101] HRA 1998, s 4. This power is restricted to the High Court, Court of Appeal and House of Lords and the Crown is entitled to make representations.

[102] HRA 1998, s 10. This procedure will also be appropriate when a finding of the European Court in proceedings against the UK renders a provision incompatible.

[103] If subordinate legislation (eg a statutory instrument) is incompatible with Convention rights, and the incompatibility is not required by primary legislation, either the courts will find ways of interpreting it so as to be compatible or will set it aside.

[104] HRA 1998, s 2(1).

(1) to have a legal framework providing effective protection;
(2) to prevent breaches;
(3) to provide information and advice;
(4) to respond to breaches; and
(5) to provide resources to individuals to prevent breaches.

Remedies

1.107 When a Convention right is found to have been breached (or is about to be breached) the Court may grant such relief or remedy, or make such order, within its powers as it considers 'just and appropriate'.[105] The Act does not give additional powers and the normal routes of an appeal or judicial review apply. There can be no claim for damages in respect of a judicial act done in good faith except in the case of a breach of liberty.

New concepts

1.108 It follows that each branch of government (legislature, executive and judicial) is responsible for giving effect to Convention rights when exercising public powers. However, various concepts apply in the interpretation and application of Convention rights which will not be familiar to lawyers brought up on the common law and statute law:

(1) Not only can proceedings be brought against a public authority in relation to Convention rights (the 'vertical' effect), but as the courts are public authorities they must apply Convention rights when adjudicating on proceedings between private individuals (the 'horizontal' effect). So litigants can argue their human rights in the courts and these must be respected.
(2) To some extent the European Court adopts a hands-off approach to the way that individual countries apply Convention rights, although this 'margin of appreciation' has no application to national courts. This reflects the fact that those courts are in a better position to assess the needs and standards of their own society and the national authorities should be deferred to (especially in moral matters and social policy) as long as the whole process is fair and the outcome is true to the Convention.
(3) Where a state interferes with a Convention right, the means ('the limitation') must be balanced against the end ('the permitted purpose') and shown to be necessary. There must be a reasonable relationship between the goal pursued and the means employed. This follows from the fact that any limitation on a Convention right must be in accordance with law and 'necessary in a democratic society',[106] and has become the principle of 'proportionality'.

---

[105] HRA 1998, s 8(1).
[106] A 'democratic society' means a society which is pluralistic and tolerant. The interests of minorities and individuals must be carefully considered.

(4) A 'principle of legality' is derived from the use by the ECHR of the phrases 'in accordance with the law' and 'prescribed by law' and the use of the word 'lawful'. It has been stated to mean:[107]
   (a) the legal basis for any restriction on Convention rights must be identified and established by the domestic law;
   (b) that law must be accessible and not interpreted according to unpublished criteria; and
   (c) the law must be clear to those affected by it so that they can understand it, although it may allow some discretion as long as the limits are clear.

Application to the Court of Protection and Public Guardian

1.109 Not only must the courts apply Convention rights but rather than giving individuals personal rights HRA 1998 imposes a new statutory duty on 'public authorities' not to act in contravention thereof. This term is not defined but a function based test is to be applied. Courts and tribunals are expressly included, as is 'any person certain of whose functions are functions of a public nature' which would include the Public Guardian. It is 'unlawful for a public authority to act in a way which is incompatible with a Convention right'[108] and even a failure to act would be construed as non-compliance. An individual who claims that a public authority has acted in an incompatible way may bring proceedings against that authority either directly or within the context of other proceedings.[109]

1.110 Where the public body determining the civil rights or obligations is not a court or tribunal[110] a two-limbed test is applied: either that body must comply with the right to a fair hearing under ECHR, Art 6 or there must be a right of appeal or review from that body to a court or tribunal which fully complies. The previous right to apply for judicial review is not sufficient because the Administrative Court cannot make findings of fact.[111]

Comment

1.111 People who lack capacity do not lose their human rights, but the rights of others must also be respected. In delivering its services the new jurisdiction must not overlook the human rights of anyone, but there will be many situations when there is a conflict between the rights of those involved, whether it be the incapacitated individual, family members or others. An appropriate balance must then be achieved.

---

[107] K Starmer *European Human Rights Law* (Legal Action Group, 1999), at paragraph 4.29.
[108] HRA 1998, s 6.
[109] HRA 1998, s 7.
[110] For example, a local housing authority, a health authority, social services and probably the Public Guardian.
[111] *W v UK* (1987) 10 EHRR 29, at [82].

1.112 The ECHR is a living instrument so, unlike the common law where previous decisions of higher courts create precedents, it must be interpreted in accordance with present-day conditions. This means that what was decided yesterday may be decided differently tomorrow, although this may be a whole generation later. The difficulty lies in determining what the contemporary standards are which merit protection. However, the ECHR is intended to guarantee rights that are practical and effective rather than theoretical and illusory.[112]

Civil Partnership Act 2004

Background

1.113 This legislation reflects more liberal social attitudes. It has become widely accepted that it is both logically and morally indefensible to prevent homosexual couples from access to formal recognition of their relationships and to the 'next of kin' rights and the tax, pension and other advantages that flow from marriage. Encouraging stability in relationships, whether heterosexual or homosexual, should involve the same sorts of protections as come with marriage, and the Civil Partnership Act 2004 (CPA 2004) addresses these issues in considerable detail.

The legislation

1.114 CPA 2004[113] introduces greater recognition for same-sex relationships in England and Wales, Scotland and Northern Ireland by an option of registration as 'civil partners'. A 'civil partnership' is defined as:[114]

> '... a relationship between two people of the same sex ... which is formed when they register as civil partners of each other ...'

It ends only on death, dissolution or annulment. Heterosexual couples are specifically excluded because they have the option of marriage. The general approach is to make detailed provision for the formation and ending of civil partnerships, and for the consequences that flow from them. It deals with these matters by treating civil partners in very much the same way as married couples.

1.115 To create a civil partnership a specific document is required, signed in the presence of each other and of a civil partnership registrar and two witnesses. No religious service is to be used during the registration formalities, and it cannot take place on religious premises. A couple cannot register if one is already married or a civil partner of someone else, nor if either is under 16 or within prohibited degrees of relationship.

---

[112] *Artico v Italy* A/37 (1980) 3 EHRR 1.
[113] It has 196 sections arranged in 8 Parts and there are 22 Schedules.
[114] CPA 2004, s 1.

Background

1.116 The provisions for court proceedings to end partnerships[115] and as to children and finances in most cases mirror existing provisions for married couples. In the case of disputes about property either civil partner may apply to the County Court, and the Court may make such order with respect to the property as it thinks fit, including an order for sale. Contributions to property improvement if substantial and in money or money's worth are recognised.

1.117 Other amendments align civil partners with married persons, for example, in certain parts of the law relating to housing and tenancies, in domestic violence proceedings[116] and under the Fatal Accidents Act 1976. Interpretation of statutory references to step-relationships (eg stepson, stepmother etc), and the terms 'in-law' (eg brother-in-law and daughter-in-law) are amended to apply in civil partnerships. There are amendments to the sex discrimination, social security, child support and tax credits legislation. Civil partners will have an insurable interest in each other. Implementation involves significant changes in many areas, for example, in court rules, the registration service, training and guidance for employers. CPA 2004 not address the problems in the legal treatment of those cohabitating without registration by marriage or by civil partnership.

Same sex marriage

1.118 More recent legislation enables a civil same sex marriage for those who desire more than civil partnership.[117]

Incapacity issues

1.119 Civil partnership is not merely a matter of contract but affects status and creates a completely new legal relationship. Clearly this has implications for a mental capacity jurisdiction. The civil partner must be recognised to the same extent as a spouse when decisions are to be made, whether relating to financial matters, personal welfare or health care. Comparable duties and responsibilities may also arise on the part of the civil partner.

1.120 The civil partner must also be afforded the same status as a spouse as regards participation in any of the procedures. This is not as radical as it may seem, because the new social attitudes have already resulted in domestic partners being involved in many situations, and this has included same-sex partners even in the absence of a civil partnership. To this extent there has been a move away from relationships of blood and marriage to de facto relationships. The Adults with Incapacity (Scotland) Act 2000 provided 'next of kin' rights to same-sex partners by including them within the

---

[113] Including nullity, presumption of death and separation orders.
[116] Under Family Law Act 1996, Part IV.
[117] Marriage (Same Sex Couples) Act 2013.

definition of nearest relative whose views must be taken into account,[118] and the equivalent provision under the Mental Capacity Act 2005 includes 'anyone engaged in caring for the person or interested in his welfare' as well as 'anyone named by the person as someone to be consulted on the matter in question or matters of that kind'.[119]

Access to justice

Background

1.121 Any court that seeks to protect and empower those who have mental impairments must set a good example to other courts and tribunals in ensuring equal access to justice, and the establishment of a new Court of Protection was an opportunity to get things right from the start.[120]

A change of culture

1.122 There has been a change of culture in the civil and family courts during the past two decades. Proceedings not only have to be fair, but also have to be seen as fair and it is the view of the public that is relevant rather than that of lawyers. No longer are litigants expected to cope with the court process and denied access to justice if unable to do so. There is an expectation, in a diverse and multi-cultural society, that judges will ensure that there is effective communication with all manner of persons and take into account their personal attributes and beliefs. This is the art of *Judgecraft* on which judges receive training through the Judicial College (formerly the Judicial Studies Board (JSB)).

1.123 An Equal Treatment Advisory Committee of the JSB[121] ensured that all training courses included this topic and produced an *Equal Treatment Bench Book* which is supplied to all judges including tribunal judges.[122] This identifies potential problem areas, offers information and guidance, and then concentrates upon the following areas of particular concern:

(1) minority ethnic communities;
(2) belief systems (different religions);
(3) gender issues;
(4) disability;
(5) children; and
(6) sexual orientation.

---

[118] Adults with Incapacity (Scotland) Act 2000, ss 1(4)(b) and 87(2).
[119] Mental Capacity Act 2005, s 4(7).
[120] The Mental Capacity Bill team set the standard for the Department for Constitutional Affairs by producing various documents in easy read format for their stakeholders with learning difficulties prior to Royal Assent. It also worked closely with the Disability Rights Commission and various representative disability groups.
[121] The author of this chapter was a member of that Committee.
[122] This is available on the Judicial College website: www.judiciary.gov.uk/publications/equal-treatment-bench-book.

The issues of unrepresented parties and social exclusion are also addressed. Equal access to justice is not assured if people are too frightened to attend a hearing or unable to cope when they get there.

Discrimination

1.124 There must be no discrimination in the delivery of legal services. A person who cannot cope with the facilities and procedures of the courts and the administration is as entitled to justice as those who have no such difficulty. It is fundamental to the delivery of justice that those involved are able to appear before and communicate with the relevant court or tribunal. It is equally important that judges understand what those who appear before them are endeavouring to say and that they in turn understand what the judge and any advocates are saying and have an adequate opportunity to consider this. Any misunderstanding may impair justice and it is not sufficient to say that this is the failing of the individual who must take the consequences – it is the responsibility of the court to ensure that communication is effective.

1.125 A further development is that those who appear before the courts are no longer expected to cope with whatever facilities happen to be available. The special needs of those with disabilities must be addressed in an effective way both by the administration in regard to the facilities made available and by the judge in the manner in which hearings are conducted. All courts and tribunals must comply with the Equality Act 2010 (formerly the Disability Discrimination Act 1995) and also ensure that the human rights of those who become involved in the justice system are respected.[123]

1.126 It follows that courts and tribunals must be accessible to those who appear before them. This is not merely a question of access to the building or the provision of disabled facilities within the courtroom, but also of proximity and the recent closure of many of the smaller courts makes it difficult for people in those areas to attend a hearing. A judge may, of course, hold a hearing or part of a hearing other than in the normal courtroom.

Unrepresented parties

1.127 Some litigants seek to represent themselves rather than instruct a lawyer[124] and everybody of full age and capacity is entitled to do so. This may be because they cannot afford a solicitor, distrust lawyers or believe that they will be better at putting their case across.

---

[123] Before the European Convention on Human Rights became enforceable it was the principles of 'natural justice' that were invoked.
[124] Traditionally known as 'litigants in person'.

Disadvantages

1.128 Those who do exercise this right find that they are operating in an alien environment because the courts have not traditionally been receptive to their needs:[125]

> 'All too often the litigant in person is regarded as a problem for judges and for the court system rather than a person for whom the system of civil justice exists.'

They are likely to experience feelings of fear, ignorance, anger, frustration and bewilderment. Their cases will tend to dominate their thoughts and they will feel at a disadvantage. The aim of the judge should be to ensure that the parties leave with the sense that they have been listened to and have had a fair hearing – whatever the outcome.

1.129 Disadvantages stem from a lack of knowledge of the law and court procedure. For many their perception of the court environment will based on what they have seen on the television and in films. They:

- are likely to be unfamiliar with the language and specialist vocabulary of legal proceedings;
- have little knowledge of the procedures involved and find it difficult to apply the rules even if they do read them;
- tend to lack objectivity and emotional distance from their case;
- may not be skilled in advocacy and are unlikely to be able to undertake cross-examination or to test the evidence of an opponent;
- may be confused about the presentation of evidence; and
- are unlikely to understand the relevance of law and regulations to their own problem, or to know how to challenge a decision that they believe to be wrong.

1.130 The aim must be to ensure that unrepresented parties understand what is going on and what is expected of them at all stages of the proceedings. The Court is therefore under an obligation to ensure that:

(1) the process is (or has been) explained to them in a manner that they can understand;
(2) they have access to appropriate information through books or websites;
(3) they are informed about what is expected of them in ample time for them to comply; and
(4) wherever possible they are given sufficient time according to their needs.

Personal assistance

1.131 A litigant who cannot arrange legal representation may request that someone be permitted to 'quietly assist' at the hearing (the role of the *McKenzie friend*). The Court can refuse this and will do so if the friend is

---

[125] Lord Woolf *Access to Justice*: Interim Report (June 1995).

unsuitable.[126] Such assistance is less likely to be needed at a hearing in the Court of Protection because a more informal approach is adopted and the judge is more likely to provide explanations and assistance.

1.132 Alternatively the litigant may request that someone speak for him or her (known as a *lay representative*). There is no right of audience but the Court has a discretion to allow such representation and it may be in the interests of justice to do so.[127] The litigant should normally justify the request and be present in court when personal interests are involved.[128] The doubt about the status of an attorney under a power of attorney has recently been resolved – there is still no right of audience.[129]

Physical and sensory impairments

Hearings

1.133 When it is known that a party or witness has a physical impairment, arrangements should be made for any hearing to take place where there are appropriate facilities.[130] These may extend beyond wheelchair access to the existence of disabled toilets and the loop system for those with hearing impairments. Ideally every regional venue of the Court of Protection will have suitable facilities but if these are inadequate for a particular hearing consideration should be given to conducting the hearing at a more suitable venue. When necessary justice should be taken to those who are unable to come to the Court and the examination of a witness or even part of a hearing may take place elsewhere, for example, in a residential care home or mental hospital. A video link may assist where an infirm party cannot travel far.[131]

1.134 It may be appropriate to arrange hearings at particular times, keep them shorter or take more frequent breaks. Allowance should be made for the need to attend a toilet, take medication or otherwise recover concentration. This may result in a longer time estimate for the hearing.

---

[126] The 'friend' may be seeking to provide general advocacy services or pursuing a separate agenda the pursuit of which is not in the best interests of the litigant.

[127] Advocacy rights may be granted under the Courts and Legal Services Act 1990, s 27(2)(c) – see also Civil Procedure Rules 1998, SI 1998/3132, PD 27, paragraph 3.2; Lay Representatives (Right of Audience) Order 1999, SI 1999/1225.

[128] *Clarkson v Gilbert & Ors* [2000] 2 FLR 839, CA; *Izzo v Phillip Ross & Co* [2002] BPIR 310.

[129] If this is an enduring power of attorney inquiry should be made as to whether it has been registered with the Public Guardianship Office, because if it has the litigant may be a protected party who needs a litigation friend.

[130] Some guidance is available at www.justice.gov.uk/courts.

[131] The President of the Family Division adopted both these procedures in *Re R* [2002] EWHC 429 (Fam), [2002] 1 FLR 1090 when she attended at the hospital and then continued by video-link.

Interpreters

1.135 Interpreters[132] are provided for a party or witness who does not speak the language of the Court or has a hearing impairment, and the Court must arrange one if the party cannot. Other communication difficulties may need to be addressed in a similar manner.[133] The interpreter should not be simply a relative or friend but needs to be independent and fully conversant with the individual's preferred method of communication. A witness will only need an interpreter whilst giving evidence but a party may need one before, during and after the hearing. The interpreter should be provided with breaks at regular intervals.

THE (FORMER) COURT OF PROTECTION

Origins of the jurisdiction

1.136 The former Court of Protection existed to protect and manage the property and financial affairs of people in England and Wales (known as 'patients') who were incapable, by reason of mental disorder, of managing and administering their own affairs.[134] The origins of state involvement in the financial affairs of the mentally incapacitated citizen go back a long way.[135] Until 1960 the jurisdiction 'in Lunacy' was in part statutory and in part dependent on the inherent jurisdiction of the Court derived from the Royal Prerogative which is often referred to as the parens patriae jurisdiction. Under the Lunacy Act 1890 the jurisdiction relating to the administration and management of patients' affairs was assigned to a Master in Lunacy, who operated under different titles[136] until 1947 when the term Court of Protection was established. The Mental Health Act 1959, Part VIII re-established the Court of Protection and its continuing existence was confirmed by the Mental Health Act 1983, Part VII. Further jurisdiction was conferred on the Court by the Enduring Powers of Attorney Act 1985.

1.137 This was not a court as such but an office of the Supreme Court of Judicature (as it then was),[137] although in practice this was of little significance and some High Court judges were nominated to conduct its work. Headed by the Master and situated in London, much of the work was delegated to nominated officers appointed by the Lord Chancellor. The three senior ones adopted the courtesy title of Assistant Master and were given

---

[132] The HMCTS website provides information as to the facilities available at particular courts – www.justice.gov.uk/courts.
[133] The special measures directions introduced by the Youth Justice and Criminal Evidence Act 1999, Part II to assist vulnerable and intimidated witnesses to give evidence in criminal proceedings refer to communicators rather than just language interpreters. These include the use of *intermediaries* and *communication aids*.
[134] Mental Health Act 1983, s 94(2).
[135] The earliest reference is to be found in a semi-official tract known as the *De Praerogativa Regis* ('On the King's Prerogative') dating from the reign of Edward 1 (1272–1307).
[136] Initially the 'Office of the Master in Lunacy' but this was changed to the 'Management and Administration Department' in 1934 (note the abbreviation MAD).
[137] Supreme Court Act 1981, s 1(1) – now the Senior Courts Act 1981.

more authority including the conduct of hearings.[138] The Public Guardianship Office provided administrative support for the Court and had a staff of several hundred, including those in the Judicial Support Unit who processed formal applications and appeals.

Practice and procedure

General

1.138 The procedure of the Court was governed by the Court of Protection Rules 2001 (COPR 2001),[139] which were briefly compared with the Civil Procedure Rules 1998 (CPR).[140] Instead of a statement of objectives they started with an Interpretation clause in which reference was made to the Supreme Court Act 1981 for the meaning of expressions used: a 'direction' meant a direction or authority given under the seal of the Court and an 'order' included a certificate, direction or authority of the Court under the official seal of the Court. A 'patient' was a person who was alleged to be or who the Court had reason to believe might be 'incapable by reason of mental disorder of managing and administering his property and affairs'.

1.139 Any function of the Court could be exercised by a nominated judge of the High Court, the Master or (to the extent authorised) a nominated officer and this might, except where COPR 2001 provided otherwise, be:

(1) without an appointment for a hearing;
(2) by the Court of its own motion or at the instance or on the application of a person concerned;
(3) whether or not proceedings have been commenced with respect to the patient.

COPR 2001 then dealt with applications and hearings.

Applications

1.140 Provision was made as to the form of applications, but apart from those for the first appointment of a receiver there was considerable informality and a letter might be sufficient. Hearings were notified by letter and might be dispensed with where it was considered that the application could properly be dealt with without one. Special rules dealt with applications under the Trustee Act 1925, for settlement or a gift of a patient's property and for the execution of a will for a patient.

---

[138] Mental Health Act 1983, ss 93(4) and 94(1). It is questionable whether and to what extent judicial powers should have been delegated in this way following the Human Rights Act 1998.

[139] SI 2001/824. This update to the existing Rules was required following the demise of the Public Trust Office and the creation of the Public Guardianship Office from 1 April 2001. The authority for the rules was to be found in Mental Health Act 1983, s 106.

[140] SI 1998/3132.

Short orders

1.141 COPR 2001, r 8 provided that where the property of the patient did not exceed a specified value[141] or it was otherwise considered appropriate, the Court might instead of appointing a receiver make a short order or direction which authorised some suitable person to deal with the patient's property or affairs in the manner specified. This power came to be used increasingly where it was felt that intrusive supervision was not necessary. Not only might small estates be dealt with in this summary way but, for example, a tenancy could be authorised.

Service

1.142 COPR 2001 specified the persons who should be given notice, who included 'such other persons who appear to the Court to be interested as the Court may specify'. The mode of service was prescribed and far from antiquated, being personal service, first class post or document exchange and even fax or 'other electronic means'. Service on a solicitor and substituted service were provided for, and service on a person under a disability was to be on the parent or guardian (for a minor) and the receiver, registered attorney or 'person with whom he resides or in whose care he is' (for a patient).

Evidence

1.143 Except where COPR 2001 otherwise provided evidence was by affidavit.[142] However, the Court might accept such oral or written evidence as it considered sufficient even if not on oath. Persons who gave written evidence could be ordered by the Court to attend and the oath might then be administered. Any such evidence could be used in other proceedings in the Court relating to the same patient and, if authorised by the Court, in proceedings in other specified courts.

Hearings

Conduct

1.144 Where appropriate the Master referred matters to a High Court judge who might refer any question back to the Master for inquiry and report.[143] Applications were heard in chambers (ie in private) unless, in the case of an application before a judge, the judge otherwise directed.[144] The Master and Assistant Masters had their own private hearing rooms. The Court decided who attended any part of a hearing, although obviously certain persons

---

[141] Latterly £16,000.
[142] COPR 2001 did not introduce the concept of a statement containing a certificate of truth that now applies under the CPR.
[143] This mirrors the procedure in Chancery and insolvency proceedings in the High Court.
[144] This inevitably means a High Court judge.

needed to attend although they might be excluded for part of a hearing. A witness summons could be issued to require a person to attend and give oral evidence or produce any document.

1.145 The Court had wide powers to require persons having conduct of proceedings to explain delay or other causes of dissatisfaction and to make orders for expediting proceedings. It could direct any person to make an application or carry out directions and even appoint the Official Solicitor (with his or her consent) to act as solicitor for a patient. There was also a valuable power to require a patient to attend at a specified time and place for examination by the Master, a Visitor or any medical practitioner.

Reviews and appeals

1.146 Where a decision was made without an attended hearing, any aggrieved person could apply to have the decision reviewed and if still not satisfied apply for an attended hearing. Appeals from decisions made at attended hearing were heard by High Court judges of the Chancery or Family Division.

Fees and costs
Court fees

1.147 The Court charged fees which were usually paid out of the estate of the patient, or by the donor in the case of a registered enduring power of attorney. A policy of full costs recovery applied and the fees were intended to reflect the actual cost of the service provided. There was power to remit or postpone the payment of the whole or part of any fee on grounds of hardship.

Legal costs

1.148 All costs incurred in relation to proceedings were at the discretion of the Court, which could order them to be paid out of the estate of the patient (or donor in the case of an enduring power of attorney), or by an applicant, objector or any other person attending or taking part in the proceedings. Unlike proceedings in the civil courts, costs did not automatically follow the event and the Court had an unlimited discretion to make whatever order it considered that the justice of the case required. In exercising its discretion the Court had regard to all the circumstances of the case, including the relationship between the parties, their conduct, their respective means and the amount of costs involved.

1.149 Where an application was made in good faith, supported by medical evidence, in the best interests of the donor and without any personal motive, the applicant was generally awarded his or her costs, even if unsuccessful. However, in cases where the Court considered an objection or application to have been made in bad faith, frivolous, malicious, vexatious or motivated by self-interest, it might order the applicant or objector to pay some or all of the costs. Similarly, where a person placed him- or herself in a hostile position to the donor, or where his or her conduct resulted in the costs of the proceedings being more expensive than they might otherwise have been, the Court might consider it appropriate to penalise him or her as to costs.[145]

1.150 There was a range of procedures available to approve the costs including fixed costs, agreed costs and assessment of costs. The costs actually charged by solicitors had to be approved by the Court before being paid from the funds of a patient and although summary assessment was not allowed the Court sometimes ordered the patient to pay a fixed contribution towards the costs of a party.

Venue

Background

1.151 Although in the early days inquisitions took place throughout the country and involved local people who knew the alleged patient, since its creation the Court of Protection sat in London despite having a jurisdiction extending to England and Wales. Following an extensive consultation[146] the Law Commission proposed that a reconstituted Court of Protection with jurisdiction over incapacity matters should have a regional presence, with designated judges throughout the country dealing with hearings locally. After further consultation the Lord Chancellor published the Government's proposals in October 1999 in the Report *Making Decisions* and these included a new Court of Protection with a regional presence. It thus became current policy to make the Court of Protection more accessible to the public by providing it with a regional presence.

1.152 The Court of Protection was not readily accessible to those in the North of England and other parts of the country. The cost to parties of travelling to and staying in London for a hearing was prohibitive and represented a denial of justice to those involved. In addition, solicitors in the provinces were discouraged from gaining 'hands-on' experience of the work of the Court by attending hearings and therefore less able to give well-informed advice to their clients. Concerns were also expressed that the Master was the only human rights-compliant judge of the Court, as the Assistant Masters did not have a judicial appointment.[147] In consequence it was proposed that even before the implementation of a new mental incapacity jurisdiction a few district judges based at carefully selected locations (e g one on each circuit) should be appointed as Deputy Masters to hear locally cases that were referred to them by the Master.[148]

---

[145] *Re Cathcart* [1893] 1 Ch 466.
[146] This is outlined below. The proposal of a tribunal for some types of case was rejected.
[147] The term Assistant Master was a courtesy title and they were in reality legally qualified civil servants in the Department of Constitutional Affairs who were 'nominated officers' under the Mental Health Act 1983, s 93(4).
[148] Supreme Court Act 1981, s 91 permitted the Lord Chancellor to appoint deputy judges if he

Regional hearings

1.153 On 1 October 2001 District Judge Ashton was appointed a part-time Deputy Master of the Court of Protection to hear any case where it was more convenient for the parties to attend at Preston in Lancashire. Thereafter the 'Northern Court of Protection' operated as a 'satellite' of the central Court in London and on certain days in each month hearings took place at Preston Combined Court Centre. These were generally contested hearings (mainly disputes over enduring powers of attorney and the choice of receiver) and fund management hearings for large damages awards, but also hearings of applications for gifts, statutory wills and to be discharged from the jurisdiction due to recovery. This link with the civil and family courts led to the cross-fertilisation of ideas and resulted in more local practitioners becoming familiar with the work of this specialised but nonetheless essential jurisdiction. Based on experience at Preston the Court of Protection in London then introduced the recording of hearings, telephone conferences and attendance by video link.

1.154 The selection of venues and judges is crucial to the success of a regionalised Court of Protection. Having a centralised administration with satellite courts raises many problems. To a large extent these were tackled in the Preston pilot and workable solutions devised. Communication by e-mail proved effective and the main problems proved to be access to the case file, uncertainty amongst parties and solicitors as to where to send documents and delay in receiving documents sent at a late stage to the Public Guardianship Office. There was a lack of administrative support because HM Courts Service staff had no involvement with the Public Guardianship Office. Experience showed that these difficulties could be overcome.

An evaluation of the Court of Protection

1.155 The former Court of Protection was the Cinderella of the judicial system, underfunded, unrecognised and only appreciated by those who knew it well. This has changed with generic judges becoming involved, a regional structure and the acquisition of jurisdiction for declarations previously dealt with by the High Court. There is more inter-dependence between the civil and family courts and the Court of Protection now it is no longer restricted to financial affairs.

1.156 How different is the Court of Protection from other courts? Which functions are truly judicial? How many judges should be nominated to the Court and where should they be deployed? On what basis should the different levels of the judiciary be allocated cases? What procedural rules are appropriate? How should hearings be conducted and what human rights issues arise? To what extent and in what manner should judgments be reported? What right should individuals have to disclosure of information

---

considered that it was expedient to do so in order to facilitate the disposal of the business of the court. This has now been renamed the Senior Courts Act 1981.

held about them by the Court? What should be the relationship between the new Court of Protection and the Public Guardian? To what extent may the legal profession become involved and who funds the non-money cases? When should cases be publicly funded? These are all questions that had to be faced when the new Court of Protection was set up.

Court Rules

1.157 It will be seen from the above outline that COPR 2001 provided only the most basic structure for the conduct of applications and hearings, and much was left to the discretion of the Master, Deputy Master or Assistant Master dealing with the case. The lack of guidance to practitioners or the parties themselves as to the submission of applications and preparation for or conduct of hearings coupled with no requirement for active case management might be seen as an obstacle to justice. However, the issues that have to be tackled are very different from those in the civil courts, although a parallel may be drawn with proceedings relating to the welfare of children. Whilst a paternalistic approach is acceptable when considering the best interests of children, it must be avoided for adults. A Court of Protection is concerned to identify and safeguard the best interests of incapacitated adults rather than to impose what other persons think is best for them, and will be influenced more by the previous lifestyle and any expressed wishes of the individual. However, the former Court only had power to do this through the management and administration of the individual's property and financial affairs.

Contested hearings

1.158 It is only when there is disagreement or conflict resulting in the need for an attended hearing that more prescriptive Rules are required to regulate the conduct of the parties involved. Under the former regime this might arise in the following situations, namely where:

(1) there was uncertainty as to whether an individual was a patient within the jurisdiction of the Court and this had to be resolved;
(2) there was a dispute as to who should be appointed to act as receiver;
(3) there was an unresolved challenge to the registration of an enduring power of attorney;
(4) a receiver or registered attorney was not satisfied with the extent of any authority given or restriction imposed;
(5) family, carers or other persons concerned with the welfare of the patient were in dispute; or
(6) an application was made for a statutory will, gift or settlement.

Other hearings

1.159 Attended hearings were also required for the setting of broad policy where substantial compensation had been awarded for brain injury, typically following a clinical negligence claim. The family, who may have been the carers to date and contemplate the continued provision of a care environment, would be anxious to have authoritative guidance as to how they should handle the funding. There might be an enhancement in their own standard of living and judicial approval assuaged any feeling of guilt in a context where earning capacity was otherwise impaired.

1.160 These hearings or 'attendances' were generally friendly and constructive. The Master would look to the heads of loss in the civil claim as pointers to what should be considered but would not seek to impose these on the family. It was more appropriate to concentrate upon what was achievable with the personal and financial resources available whilst keeping an eye on the future when intensive family care may no longer be available. Headings that were discussed included:

(1) the provision of a suitable home and modifications to meet disability needs;
(2) transport (usually a personal vehicle which can accommodate any disability needs);
(3) the monthly personal and household budget;
(4) care provision and funding;
(5) holidays;
(6) disability aids and appliances (including computers); and
(7) the retention by the parents or family carers of a personal stake in the housing market where the shared home is purchased by the patient.

Investment policy then had to be determined for the contingency fund available after the provision of a home, although in some cases there would be an index-linked tax-free annuity for the life of the patient from a structured settlement. This type of support is less frequent under the new jurisdiction because there is more delegation to the deputies appointed by the Court, but it could still be provided.

THE PUBLIC GUARDIANSHIP OFFICE

Background[149]

1.161 The former Court of Protection depended heavily upon the support that it received from its administrative arm, the Public Guardianship Office[150], whose responsibilities extended across the whole of England and Wales.[151] That office supported the court in the same way that HM Courts and Tribunals Service now supports all other courts, but that was only a small part of its functions. The administration also provided services to promote the financial and social well-being of clients who were not able to manage their financial affairs because of mental incapacity (known as 'patients').

---

[149] The evolution of the Public Guardianship Office from the former Public Trust Office is more fully described in the 2012 and previous volumes of this work.
[150] Previously the Public Trust Office.
[151] Separate arrangements existed for Scotland and Northern Ireland.

1.162 Support was provided for the families and advisers of the incapable person after someone had applied to the Court of Protection to manage that person's financial affairs. When the Court had considered the application, it appointed a Receiver, to manage and administer the person's financial affairs whilst they were unable to do so themselves. The administration thus assisted and supported the Receiver in completing his or her duties and worked with the Receiver to promote the best interests of the patient (the 'Protection function').

1.163 Sometimes the administration would act as Receiver through a designated official (the 'Receivership function'). This occurred only as a last resort when the Court of Protection could find no one else willing or suitable to become the Receiver. The staff would then be involved on a daily basis in the client's financial and legal affairs. As a result, the administrative arm developed and maintained very close working relationships with its clients, their families, carers and any other people or organisations involved in their welfare.

Other jurisdictions

1.164 There was a difference of approach to the need for and the services provided by a Public Guardian in the separate jurisdictions of the UK and Ireland.

Scotland

1.165 The Adults with Incapacity (Scotland) Act 2000 introduced a new jurisdiction for Scotland. This established with effect from 2 April 2001 a Public Guardian based in Falkirk with supervisory and support functions. She has published a useful range of forms, precedents and guidance notes.[152] There is also a Mental Welfare Commission which was established in 1960 and has been given additional functions under the Act. A two-year review of the operation of this legislation was commissioned by the Scottish Executive in 2002 and the Report, *Learning from Experience*, was published in the Autumn of 2004. In broad terms the Adults with Incapacity (Scotland) Act 2000 was considered to be meeting its central aims, but there was concern about lack of publicity and knowledge as to how it may benefit incapacitated adults and their carers. This Report resulted in amendments to the Act by the Adult Support and Protection (Scotland) Act 2007. The jurisdiction in Scotland is outlined in Chapter 12.

Northern Ireland

1.166 There is at present no equivalent of a Public Guardian in Northern Ireland. All jurisdiction relating to incapacitated persons is vested in the High Court by virtue of s 28(1) of the Judicature (Northern Ireland)

---

[152] These are available on the website: www.publicguardian-scotland.gov.uk.

Act 1978 and carried out by the Office of Care and Protection, which is a part of the Family Division of the Court. Judicial responsibility lies with the Family Judge (or another Judge assigned by the Lord Chief Justice) and with the Master (Care and Protection). An assessment is presently being made of future needs and the additional functions which might be assigned to a Public Guardian. There is concern about a single organisation being both regulator and provider and a desire to relinquish last resort work. An advocacy service would be welcomed with a cadre of advocates to take on legal representation unless the Official Solicitor was engaged for this. The availability of funding is a crucial issue.

Ireland

1.167 There is no equivalent of the Public Guardian in the Republic of Ireland and any intervention by the courts is based on the Wardship jurisdiction exercised by the President of the High Court, who has Medical Visitors at his disposal. There is a need for modernising legislation and it is likely that a comprehensive new jurisdiction will be introduced in the foreseeable future. The Office of the General Solicitor for Minors and Wards of Court assists the court.

THE LORD CHANCELLOR'S VISITORS

Historical

1.168 The office of Visitor dates from the Lunatics' Visitors Act 1833, which authorised the Lord Chancellor to appoint two physicians and a barrister to visit patients at least once a year – more often, if necessary – and to superintend, inspect and report on their care and treatment.[153] Under the Lunacy Regulation Act 1853 the Masters in Lunacy became ex officio Visitors.[154] The first Visitors were paid an annual salary, but only worked part-time and were allowed to remain in private practice. The Lunacy Regulation Act 1862 required them to visit on a full-time basis and increased their salary to compensate. Consequently, the post became both lucrative and prestigious and attracted some of the leading psychiatrists of the day.

1.169 Until 1981 all visits to Court of Protection patients were carried out by the Medical and Legal Visitors. The majority of these visits required a combination of social work, public relations and plain common sense, and did not warrant the expense of being made by an eminent psychiatrist or leading counsel. So, with effect from 1 October 1981, the Lord Chancellor created a panel of lay General Visitors, membership of which was initially

---

[153] 3 & 4 Will IV, c 36. The Act also introduced a system of percentage, whereby patients were required to pay a percentage of their clear annual income to the court, in order to fund the Visitors' salaries. This is the origin of the present fee structure in the Court of Protection.

[154] This provision could be found in the Mental Health Act 1983, s 103(7). The Master occasionally visited patients in their own home.

drawn from the welfare officers in his own department.[155] The Medical Visitors and Legal Visitors subsequently ceased to be full-time employees of the Lord Chancellor's Department, and made their visits on an ad hoc basis. In March 2000 there were six General Visitors, each covering a particular region of England and Wales.

1.170 If the Court considered that a patient should be visited for any reason, it sent one of the Lord Chancellor's Visitors and there was a strategy to ensure that visits were carried out in the most suitable cases. The visits were usually carried out at the patient's place of residence, but the Visitors did not have automatic rights of entry and inspection, although anyone who obstructed a visit might commit an offence.[156]

Medical Visitors

1.171 A Medical Visitor had to be a 'registered medical practitioner who appears to the Lord Chancellor to have special knowledge and experience of cases of mental disorder'.[157] There were six and between them they conducted about one hundred visits each year. They were all senior consultant psychiatrists, mostly retired or semi-retired, and some also sat as medical members of Mental Health Review Tribunals. Each Medical Visitor covered a particular region of England and Wales, roughly approximating to the former court Circuits, but there were reserve Visitors who could be called upon when necessary

1.172 The reports by Medical Visitors addressed the particular issues they had been asked to investigate. Their principal function was to assess an individual's:

- capacity to manage and administer their property and financial affairs, either on entry into the jurisdiction or exit from it;
- capacity to create or revoke an enduring power of attorney, which nearly always requires a retrospective assessment; and
- testamentary capacity.

1.173 These visits were only commissioned where other medical evidence was conflicting, unsatisfactory or non-existent. The Medical Visitors also reported on a variety of other matters which the Court might wish to consider before taking action, for example, a patient's life expectancy, which might be helpful for setting an investment strategy, or deciding whether an intended lifetime gift was likely to be effective for inheritance tax purposes. Occasionally a medical visit was abortive because the patient either refused to admit the Visitor into his or her home or was no longer available. Nevertheless, even though a visit was abortive, it might still be possible for the Court to accept jurisdiction on the basis of the Visitor's examination of the patient's medical records alone. The Court had an emergency

---

[155] Supreme Court Act 1981, s 144 (now renamed the Senior Courts Act 1981).
[156] Mental Health Act 1983, s 129. This was also a contempt of court.
[157] MHA 1983, s 102(3)(a).

jurisdiction which enabled it to intervene if it had *reason to believe* that a person may be incapable, by reason of mental disorder, of managing and administering his or her property and affairs, and it was of the opinion that it was *necessary* to make immediate provision in respect of that person's affairs.[158]

General Visitors

1.174 The General Visitors regarded themselves as 'the eyes and the ears of the court, and the voice of the patient'. The purpose of their visits was to enable the Court and the PGO to assess whether a patient's needs were being properly addressed and to alert them to any action needed to bring about improvements. Their reports might cover, for example, how money had actually been expended; the patient's or donor's present wishes and feelings, so far as they were ascertainable, as to who should manage their property and financial affairs during their incapacity; whether a proposed course of action was likely to be in a patient's best interests; the suitability of a patient's accommodation; whether a patient required residential care or specialist nursing care.

1.175 Additionally, the Visitors could show patients, receivers and carers that the Court and the PGO were interested in their welfare and ready to discuss any particular difficulties or concerns. In most cases they represented the only face-to-face contact a patient or receiver had with the authorities. Occasionally, a General Visitor was asked to carry out a special visit when a particular problem arose. For example:

- where the relationship between a patient and his or her receiver, carers or family was strained or appeared to have broken down completely;
- where a receiver was behaving in a manner or proposing a course of action which the Court had reason to believe might not be in the patient's best interests; or
- to assist in resolving some particular difficulty with the Court or the PGO, for example, expenditure, accounts or investment strategy.

Enduring powers of attorney

1.176 Although there was provision[159] for the donors of enduring powers of attorney to be visited, in practice they were never visited by the General Visitors.[160] This was principally because the philosophy underlying the Enduring Powers of Attorney Act 1985 was that there should be minimal public intervention in the operation of the enduring powers of attorney scheme.

---

[158] MHA 1983, s 98.
[159] Enduring Powers of Attorney Act 1985, s 10(1)(a) and (2).
[160] The donor of an enduring power of attorney might be visited by a Medical Visitors when there was a conflict of evidence as to whether the donor had the capacity to create or revoke an enduring power, or whether an application to register the power was premature.

Confidentiality of reports

1.177 Visitors' reports were confidential: their contents could not be disclosed to anyone unless authorised by the Court of Protection.[161] However, the Court might in its discretion allow the report, or part of it, to be disclosed and in that event there was provision for written questions to be submitted. The General Visitors were reluctant to have their reports routinely disclosed because this could inhibit their comments, but one way round this was for them to include an addendum with confidential comments which would not be disclosed. Some cases, though not all, held that the principles of natural justice must prevail over the Court of Protection's paternalistic jurisdiction.[162]

THE OFFICIAL SOLICITOR

Background

1.178 The state has for many centuries recognised the need for representation of an incapacitated person when a benevolent relative or friend cannot be found to act on his or her behalf. This function was undertaken on behalf of the Crown as parens patriae in various ways. The development of the functions of the Official Solicitor's office date back to the eighteenth century. The office of the Official Solicitor to the Supreme Court of Judicature was created by an Order of the Lord Chancellor on 6 November 1875 under the power given to him by the Supreme Court of Judicature Act 1873, s 84 to appoint officers to serve the Supreme Court generally. The Official Solicitor has been a civil servant since 1919. It was not until 1981 that this became a statutory office and was renamed the Official Solicitor to the Supreme Court (now the Official Solicitor to the Senior Courts).

Creation of the OSPT

1.179 The distinct office of the Public Trustee was created under the Public Trustee Act 1906. Since then trustee services have become more readily available in the private sector so the Public Trustee has tended to become a trustee of last resort. In the early 1980s the Court of Protection was relocated within the Public Trustee Office, which later became known as the Public Trust Office. Subsequently the Public Trustee was given the additional responsibilities of acting as receiver of last resort, performing judicial functions as authorised by the Court of Protection Rules and dealing with the registration of enduring powers of attorney.

---

[161] MHA 1983, s 103(8). Any unauthorised disclosure is an offence. This goes further than the rules in relation to reports by CAFCASS (Children and Family Court Advisory and Support Service) Reporters in children cases which may only be disclosed to the parties and their legal advisers.
[162] *Re WLW* [1972] Ch 456, Goff J.

1.180 The offices of the Official Solicitor and the Public Trustee were co-located from 1 April 2001 when the trust division of the PTO was abolished and some of the Official Solicitor's work was transferred to CAFCASS. The joint office of the Official Solicitor and Public Trustee is known as the OSPT. The OSPT is an 'arm's length body' which exists to support the work of the Official Solicitor and Public Trustee. The two office holders continue to have separate corporate functions and the Public Trustee is not involved in mental capacity issues.

LAW REFORM

Origins

1.181 During the 1980s it became apparent that the law and procedures in England and Wales failed to address in a comprehensive manner the problems raised by those who were incompetent in the sense that they could not make their own decisions. The courts did not have adequate powers to fill the vacuum and such legislation as there had been was piecemeal and not based upon an underlying philosophy. Comprehensive reform became essential. This was first highlighted in a paper produced by the Law Society in 1989[163] which was followed by a conference when the speakers included Professor Brenda Hoggett who had recently been appointed as a Law Commissioner.[164]

The Law Commission

1.182 Prompted by this initiative the Law Commission of England and Wales embarked upon a consideration of the whole question of decision-making and mental incapacity.[165] Serious deficiencies were identified during a protracted consultation and it became clear that reform was badly needed.[166]

Consultation

1.183 The first consultation paper in March 1991[167] provided an invaluable overview of the present state of the law and its procedures. It recognised that the existing law was inadequate to cope with the range of decisions that needed to be made on behalf of mentally incapable people but that the issue was large and complex. Further consultation followed.

---

[163] *Decision-making and Mental Incapacity: A Discussion Document*: Memorandum by the Law Society's Mental Health Sub-Committee, January 1989.
[164] *Decision-making and Mental Incapacity*, The Law Society, 5 May 1989.
[165] A similar review was undertaken by the Law Commission of Scotland.
[166] Professor Brenda Hoggett, the Law Commissioner responsible, later became Mrs Justice Hale and rapidly progressed through the Court of Appeal to become the first lady to sit in the House of Lords (now the Supreme Court). In these capacities she has had the opportunity to shape the law in accordance with her previous thinking.
[167] *Mentally Incapacitated Adults and Decision-Making: An Overview*, Law Com No 119.

1.184 The second consultation paper in December 1992[168] dealt with private law aspects and proposed procedures whereby decisions relating to the personal care and financial affairs of incapacitated people could be made. A third consultation paper in March 1993[169] explored legal procedures whereby substitute decisions about medical treatment could be authorised at an appropriate level. The fourth consultation paper in April 1993[170] considered the powers of public authorities and was expanded to cover vulnerable as well as mentally incapacitated people.

Report

1.185 The Law Commission published its final Report in March 1995[171] with the almost unanimous support of charities and others concerned with the welfare of mentally incapacitated people. This set out comprehensive recommendations and included a draft Mental Incapacity Bill. It was recommended that there should be a single comprehensive piece of legislation[172] to make new provision for people who lack mental capacity. This should provide a coherent statutory scheme to which recourse could be had when any decision (whether personal, medical or financial) needed to be made for a person aged 16 or over who lacked capacity. Two concepts were identified as being fundamental to any new decision-making jurisdiction, namely capacity and best interests.[173]

1.186 The proposals included:

(1) a general authority to act reasonably;
(2) living wills to be given statutory authority subject to safeguards;
(3) the appointment of someone to take treatment decisions;
(4) independent supervision of certain medical and research procedures;
(5) 'continuing power of attorney' which could extend to a donor's personal welfare, health care and property and affairs;
(6) decision-making by the Court and power to make declarations and one-off orders or appoint a manager with substitute decision-making powers;
(7) a new Court of Protection with a central registry in London and regional hearing centres;
(8) a code of practice; and
(9) public law protection of vulnerable adults.[174]

---

[168] *Mentally Incapacitated Adults and Decision-Making: A New Jurisdiction*, Law Com No 128.
[169] *Mentally Incapacitated Adults and Decision-Making: Medical Treatment and Research*, Law Com No 129.
[170] *Mentally Incapacitated and Other Vulnerable Adults: Public Law Protection*, Law Com No 130.
[171] *Mental Incapacity*, Law Com No 231.
[172] This would move these problems away from the Mental Health Act 1983 and facilitate a different approach to the needs of incapacitated persons from that of mental health professionals.
[173] These concepts have been further developed in the Mental Capacity Act 2005.
[174] These proposals, which went beyond the initial Law Commission brief, have not been adopted.

The Government's response

1.187 The Government announced that it did not intend to proceed with legislation 'in its present form' but would undertake further consultation on the Report. That consultation did not materialise until October 1997 when the new Lord Chancellor, Lord Irvine of Lairg, announced that he intended to issue a consultation paper seeking views on the Report.

'Who Decides?'

1.188 In December 1997, the Lord Chancellor's consultation document *Who Decides? Making Decisions on Behalf of Mentally Incapacitated Adults*[175] was published with a relatively short period for consultation. This was in addition to an ambitious programme of law reform which included a Human Rights Bill to give effect to the ECHR in the UK and the continuance of civil justice reforms following Lord Woolf's Report *Access to Justice*.

1.189 This Green Paper was structured to follow the Law Commission's Report *Mental Incapacity*. The Government accepted that there was a clear need for law reform in this area and contemplated that there would be codes of practice dealing with specific areas. Whilst emphasising that there would be no move towards euthanasia (which is illegal) the Government supported many of the Law Commission's recommendations and expressed the wish to consult further on how they might best be implemented and those that might be controversial.[176] Inevitably the issue of resources arose.

'Making decisions'

1.190 In October 1999, the Government's proposals were published in the Report *Making Decisions*. Much, but not all, of the Law Commission's recommendations survived.[177] The Lord Chancellor announced in November 1999 that there would be legislation 'when Parliamentary time allows' but much of the detail had still to be worked out. In the meanwhile some of the recommendations of the Law Commission were already finding their way into our law through decisions of the courts.

Legislation

Adults with Incapacity (Scotland) Act 2000

1.191 Scotland achieved legislation first. The Adults with Incapacity (Scotland) Act 2000, which followed recommendations of the Scottish Law Commission[178] and was widely welcomed as a significant and much-needed

---

[175] Cm 3803, issued by the Lord Chancellor's Department.
[176] These included advance statements about health care and non-therapeutic research.
[177] In particular the proposals for public law protection have not been followed up.
[178] *Report on Incapable Adults*, Scot Law Com No 151 (July 1995).

reform of the law, received Royal Assent on 16 May 2000 and came into force in stages.[179] It protects the rights and interests of adults in Scotland who are incapable of managing their own affairs, acknowledged to be one of the most vulnerable groups in society. There are regulations under the Act and codes of practice which provide guidance on the legislation itself and offer further practical information for those people and organisations that have functions given to them by the Act.

1.192 A number of different agencies are involved in supervising those who take decisions on behalf of the adult:

(1) the Public Guardian has a supervisory role and keeps registers of attorneys, people who can access an adult's funds, guardians and intervention orders;
(2) local authorities look after the welfare of adults who lack capacity; and
(3) the Mental Welfare Commission protects the interests of adults who lack capacity as a result of mental disorder.

Mental Incapacity Bill

1.193 On 27 June 2003, the Government published a draft Mental Incapacity Bill which was then scrutinised by a joint committee of both Houses of Parliament which published its response in November 2003.[180] The Government commented on some of those recommendations.[181] The title was to be changed to the *Mental Capacity Bill* and it was considered that draft *Codes of Practice* should be available before the Bill was passed. The joint committee considered that priority should be given to the Bill so that account could be taken of its provisions when framing new mental health legislation.

Mental Capacity Act 2005

1.194 A Bill, duly called the Mental Capacity Bill and incorporating the desired changes to the draft Bill, was introduced in Parliament in June 2004. This Bill (as amended) was finally passed in April 2005 and extends to England and Wales only. It was intended to come into force on 1 April 2007 but this date was postponed to 1 October 2007 due to delays in the implementation process. The Mental Capacity Act 2005 (MCA 2005) does

---

[179] Available at www.opsi.gov.uk/legislation/scotland/s-acts.htm and also accessible through the Office of Public Sector Information website: www.opsi.gov.uk. Information about implementation, which is updated at intervals, is to be found on the Scottish Executive website: www.scotland.gov.uk.
[180] *Report of the Joint Committee on the Draft Mental Incapacity Bill*, HL Papers 189-1 and 189-II, HC 1083-1 and 1083-II) (TSO, 2003), vols I and II.
[181] *The Government's Response to the Scrutiny Committee's Report on the draft Mental Incapacity Bill*, Cm 6121 (TSO, 2004).

not provide all the answers but laid down the principles, creates a statutory framework and authorises rules, practice directions and codes of practice to be made.

Human rights compatibility

1.195 Explanatory notes[182] prepared by the Department for Constitutional Affairs and the Department of Health state that MCA 2005 meets the state's positive obligation under ECHR, Art 8 to ensure respect for private life.

1.196 The European Court of Human Rights has made it clear that there must be adequate involvement of the individual in the court process. A person of unsound mind must be allowed to be heard either in person or, where necessary, through some form of representation. He will play a double role in the proceedings: as an interested party, and, at the same time, the main object of the court's examination. Participation is therefore necessary not only to enable him to present his own case, but also to allow the judge to form a personal opinion about mental capacity. In one case it was held that despite the applicant's mental illness he had been a relatively autonomous person. In such circumstances it was indispensable for the judge to have at least a brief visual contact with the applicant, and preferably to question him. The decision of the judge to decide the case on the basis of documentary evidence, without seeing or hearing the applicant, was unreasonable and in breach of the principle of adversarial proceedings enshrined in Article 6.[183]

1.197 This analysis concentrates upon the rights of the incapacitated person. Procedures for decisions to be made on behalf of such persons may also have an impact upon the human rights of other persons, and especially members of the family. Experience of the former Court of Protection shows that there may be strong sibling rivalry for control over the financial affairs of a parent and that the person in control of the finances, although not legally empowered to make personal welfare decisions, has a strong influence over such decisions. This may impact upon the human rights of other members of the family to respect for family life. The new jurisdiction is better able to tackle these issues but must do so in a way that is human rights compliant for all concerned.

An initial assessment of the MCA 2005

1.198 At last there was in England and Wales a statutory jurisdiction for decision-making in respect of mentally incapacitated adults. The need for this had been clearly demonstrated and the legislation was overdue, but would it fill the vacuum in our legal system? The general principles contained in MCA 2005, s 1 were relatively innovative so far as UK legislation was concerned and were much praised. However, there followed

---

[182] These do not form part of MCA 2005 and have not been endorsed by Parliament.
[183] *Shtukaturov v Russia*, Application no 44009/05, 27 June 2008.

complaints that the system is 'a legal and bureaucratic minefield' and that 'a secret court is seizing the assets of thousands of elderly and mentally impaired people and turning control of their lives over to the State – against the wishes of their relatives'.[184]

1.199 Of key importance are the statutory formulae for assessing a lack of capacity and determining best interests. The MCA 2005 set a benchmark against which people with a mental impairment are to be assessed and interventions must be justified. This should apply beyond the specialist jurisdiction of the Court of Protection and be adopted by all courts and tribunals when they encounter people with impaired capacity. There is the potential for the specialist judges to sit in a dual jurisdiction but the benchmark should become second nature to all professionals working in this field. There was also a developing awareness of the need to identify incapacity as a discrete area of law divorced from provisions that deal with the treatment of those who are mentally ill.

1.200 The new procedures to implement decision-making over a wider range of content are intended to empower those members of our families and society who lack capacity, but must also ensure that they are protected from abuse. This is a delicate balance and where that balance should be struck depends upon one's viewpoint and how one interprets the statistics. It should not be assumed that everyone is satisfied with the present balance.[185] There is a range of diversity within mental incapacity and a 'one size fits all' approach cannot be adopted. There is a world of difference between the needs of a wealthy senior citizen who develops Alzheimer's, an autistic young person dependent on means-tested benefits and a brain-injured individual who has recovered compensation of several million pounds. There is also a difference between the incapacitated adult with dedicated family carers and the similarly incapacitated adult who has been abandoned by family.

1.201 Those working in this field are concerned about vulnerability, but this does not feature in the test of mental capacity. In a decision of the Court of Appeal it was stated:[186]

> '... the courts have ample powers to protect those who are vulnerable to exploitation from being exploited; it is unnecessary to deny them the opportunity to take their own decisions if they are not being exploited. It is not the task of the courts to prevent those who have the mental capacity to make rational decisions from making decisions which others may regard as rash or irresponsible.'

Many practitioners working in this field would question the suggestion that the courts have ample powers to protect those who are vulnerable. However,

---

[184] *The Mail on Sunday* (25 October 2009). The editorial commented that the system assumed individuals to have suspect motives and treated them as potential thieves, and that this tendency should be reversed.

[185] The Law Society paper of 1989 was concerned about protection and the Law Commission proposals were perhaps the high point of empowerment. The consultation appeared to swing back towards protection but the emphasis in MCA 2005 appears to be empowerment.

[186] Chadwick LJ in *Masterman-Lister v Brutton & Co and Jewell & anor* [2002] EWCA Civ 1889. It is not clear what those 'ample powers' actually were.

where vulnerability is perceived it becomes appropriate to inquire why this should be so and a thorough investigation may reveal that the underlying cause is a mental impairment. Although there may be sufficient understanding, resulting personal qualities such as impulsiveness, recklessness and being easily manipulated may mean that there is an inability to make and implement decisions based on that understanding.

1.202 The procedures need to be publicly known and accessible. There is a role for the Office of the Public Guardian in this respect, but that role should extend to resolving uncertainties where these exist and assisting in facilitating the resolution of disputes as to best interests. We now have a specialist Court charged with the responsibility of interpreting the statutory criteria and exercising the new jurisdiction, but although empowering a new court to make all types of decisions or to authorise other persons to do so is a *sine qua non*, delivering that which is needed depends upon those called upon to implement the new jurisdiction at all levels. Where will these people come from and how will they be trained? The success or failure of this much needed initiative depends on the guidance that is produced and the availability of professionals who are familiar with the new law and procedures.

1.203 Within the framework established by MCA 2005 there is the prospect of a ground-breaking improvement in the lives of those who have the misfortune to be unable to structure these for themselves. Whether that improvement actually takes place may depend upon those involved adopting a pragmatic approach rather than becoming rule-bound. The following questions were raised initially and would only be answered as the new jurisdiction reached maturity:

- Is a decision-specific assessment of capacity viable?
- Does a test based on understanding protect those who are mentally unstable or vulnerable to influence?
- Does the 'best interest' approach involving the need to consult create too much opportunity for disputes?
- Does a 'best interest' test for the incapacitated person infringe the human rights of others?
- Will the Court be accessible and affordable to those who need it?
- Will the Court become a battleground between families/carers and social services/health authorities?
- Will the Court resolve disputes or address best interests?
- Will the new jurisdiction achieve the right balance between empowerment and protection?
- Is the new jurisdiction too complex and theoretical?
- Will HRA 1998, which made the new jurisdiction inevitable, now render it illusory?

1.204 A decade later the most serious issues facing the Court of Protection have proved to be:
- providing safeguards against unlawful deprivation of liberty to comply with HRA 1998;

- public access to hearings;
- whether the incapacitated person should be joined as a party to proceedings and if so the need for a litigation friend;
- access to justice in view of the virtual absence of Legal Aid and the high court fees involved;
- coping with the volume of applications, including the prospect of further regionalization;
- compliance with the *United Nations Convention on the Rights of Persons with Disabilities*.

These topics are considered where appropriate in this volume.

The *ad hoc* Rules Committee

1.205 In response to public criticisms and concerns expressed by practitioners an *ad hoc* Rules Committee was set up early in 2010 to consider what improvements could be made. The following recommendations were made, but these have not been implemented although some administrative changes have been made:[187]

1. The procedure and practice of the court should reflect the differences in the nature of the following categories of its work, namely (a) non-contentious property and affairs applications, (b) contentious property and affairs applications and (c) health and welfare applications.
2. This change should be implemented by (a) the introduction of new forms, and (b) relevant changes in the rules and practice directions.
3. The distinction between serving and notifying people who are or may be interested in making representations to the court should be preserved. But it should be better explained and some amendments to the present provisions relating to this process should be made.
4. The present position relating to the notification and participation of P should be retained (with some minor amendments).
5. Strictly defined and limited non-contentious property and affairs applications should be dealt with by court officers (eg, applications for a property and affairs deputy by local authorities and in respect of small estates that do not include defined types of property). The provisions will also have to provide for an automatic right to refer any such decision to a judge and internal monitoring and review by the judges.
6. Separate applications for permission should be abandoned and the application for permission should be incorporated into the main application form.
7. The detailed and minor changes set out in Annex 1 [to the Report] should be considered. It is recognised that on a detailed

---

[187] The full Report is available at: www.judiciary.gov.uk/publications-and-reports/reports/family/court-of-protection.

consideration some may be rejected and others added and this recommendation and annex is included to assist those who are performing that detailed exercise.

8. Issues as to whether and when the court should sit in public or permit its proceedings to be made public should be dealt with by the courts through decisions rather than any rule change.

9. The proposed new forms prepared by members of this committee should be 'tested' with a range of potential users before they are finalised and the relevant rules and practice directions are altered.

10. A Committee should be established to review and make recommendations relating to the procedure and practice of the Court of Protection.

House of Lords Select Committee Report

1.206 On 13 March 2014 after a mammoth evidence gathering exercise the House of Lords Committee appointed to consider the MCA 2005 provided a damning report upon its implementation.[188] The Committee was unanimous in its overall finding that the MCA 2005 is important – indeed visionary – legislation, with the potential to transform lives. However, they were equally clear that the Act is not working well, because people do not know about the Act and, where they do know about it, they do not understand it:

> '... [f]or many who are expected to comply with the Act it appears to be an optional add-on, far from being central to their working lives. The evidence presented to us concerns the health and social care sectors principally. In those sectors the prevailing cultures of paternalism (in health) and risk-aversion (in social care) have prevented the Act from becoming widely known or embedded. The empowering ethos has not been delivered. The rights conferred by the Act have not been widely realised. The duties imposed by the Act are not widely followed.'

In regard to the Deprivation of Liberty (DOLS) regime the conclusion was that:

> '... [t]he provisions are poorly drafted, overly complex and bear no relationship to the language and ethos of the Mental Capacity Act. The safeguards are not well understood and are poorly implemented. Evidence suggested that thousands, if not tens of thousands, of individuals are being deprived of their liberty without the protection of the law, and therefore without the safeguards which Parliament intended. Worse still, far from being used to protect individuals and their rights, they are sometimes used to oppress individuals, and to force upon them decisions made by others without reference to the wishes and feelings of the person concerned. Even if implementation could be improved, the legislation itself is flawed.'

1.207 The main recommendations to ensure effective implementation of the Act are:

(1) Overall responsibility for the Act be given to an independent body whose task will be to oversee, monitor and drive forward implementation;

---

[188] www.publications.parliament.uk/pa/ld201314/ldselect/ldmentalcap/139/13902.htm.

(2) The DOLS regime be ripped up and the Government goes back to the drawing board to draft replacement provisions that are easy to understand and implement, and in keeping with the style and ethos of the Mental Capacity Act;
(3) The Government works with regulators and the medical Royal Colleges to ensure the Act is given a higher profile in training, standard setting and inspections;
(4) The Government increases the staff resources at the Court of Protection to speed up handling of non-controversial cases;
(5) The Government reconsiders the provision of non-means tested legal aid to those who lack capacity, especially in cases of deprivation of liberty;
(6) Local authorities use their discretionary powers to appoint Independent Mental Capacity Advocates more widely than is currently the case;
(7) The Government addresses the poor levels of awareness and understanding of Lasting Powers of Attorney and advance decisions to refuse treatment among professionals in the health and social care sectors;
(8) The Government review the criminal law provision for ill-treatment or neglect of a person lacking capacity to ensure that it is fit for purpose.

The Government response

1.208 In its response[189] *Valuing every voice, respecting every right: Making the case for the Mental Capacity Act* the Government agreed with the Committee's overall finding and set out a system-wide programme of work over the coming year and beyond that should realise a real improvement in implementation of the Act.[190]

A New Ad Hoc Rules Committee

1.209 Another Rules Committee was then formed to consider further and possibly more extensive changes to the Court of Protection Rules 2007 and an initial batch of rule changes took place in 2015. More are expected.

UN Convention on the Rights of Persons with Disabilities

Background

1.210 The *United Nations Convention on the Rights of Persons with Disabilities* (CRPD) was adopted by the UN General Assembly in 2006, came into force internationally in 2008, was ratified by the UK in 2009, and

---

[189] See www.gov.uk/government/publications/mental-capacity-act-government-response-to-the-house-of-lords-select-committee-report.
[190] The Government has now requested the Law Commission to consider the entire DOLs regime.

by the EU (on behalf of all member states) in 2010. The CRPD does not have the force of law in UK courts, but in ratifying the Convention the UK committed itself to revising domestic legislation as necessary to conform with CRPD standards. The *UN Committee on the Rights of Persons with Disabilities* (the Committee) was then established to implement the Convention and review compliance by signatory nations. In signing the CRPD's Optional Protocol, the UK agreed to have its domestic law and practice reviewed regularly by the Committee and the first such review is awaited although significant concerns are being raised[191] about the 'diagnostic threshold', substituted decision-making on a 'best interests' basis and the potential for discrimination against disabled persons due to differential treatment.

1.211 Of particular concern is Article 12 – 'Equal recognition before the law' which provides:
1. States Parties reaffirm that persons with disabilities have the right to recognition everywhere as persons before the law.
2. States Parties shall recognise that persons with disabilities enjoy legal capacity on an equal basis with others in all aspects of life.
3. States Parties shall take appropriate measures to provide access by persons with disabilities to the support they may require in exercising their legal capacity.
4. States Parties shall ensure that all measures that relate to the exercise of legal capacity provide for appropriate and effective safeguards to prevent abuse in accordance with international human rights law. Such safeguards shall ensure that measures relating to the exercise of legal capacity respect the rights, will and preferences of the person, are free of conflict of interest and undue influence, are proportional and tailored to the person's circumstances, apply for the shortest time possible and are subject to regular review by a competent, independent and impartial authority or judicial body. The safeguards shall be proportional to the degree to which such measures affect the person's rights and interests.
5. Subject to the provisions of this article, States Parties shall take all appropriate and effective measures to ensure the equal right of persons with disabilities to own or inherit property, to control their own financial affairs and to have equal access to bank loans, mortgages and other forms of financial credit, and shall ensure that persons with disabilities are not arbitrarily deprived of their property.

The right to legal capacity on an equal basis was thus identified as a subsidiary to the right to equal recognition before the law. It encompasses both a 'static' element (the right to be a person before the law and a holder of rights) and an 'active' element' (the right to be a legal agent whose decisions are respected and validated by the law).

---

[191] An interesting *Discussion Paper* on the CRPD is available on the website of ThirtyNine Essex Street at: www.39essex.com/newsletters.

The diagnostic threshold

1.212 The MCA 2005 adopts a 'functional test' of decision-making ability but also includes a second requirement. In order for an individual to be deemed lacking in mental capacity, the lack of decision-making ability must be because of 'an impairment of, or a disturbance in the functioning of the mind or brain'. It is this second component of the definition that has come to be known as the 'diagnostic threshold'. It is suggested that the diagnostic threshold constitutes a form of indirect discrimination against persons with disabilities because they are far more likely than are the general population to comply with this test. The functional tests then amount to indirect discrimination because many people without disabilities might fail if they were subjected to them, but only people with disabilities are required to take them and experience the consequences of failing them.

1.213 Differential treatment does not of itself constitute unlawful discrimination, but the Committee calls into question any system that denies legal capacity on the basis of disability or impairment or is indirectly discriminatory against people with disability. The Committee's aim is to ensure that legal capacity is de-coupled from prejudicial perceptions of an individual's 'mental capacity', and that regardless of an individual's level of decision-making skills, she or he is still respected as a person before the law and a legal agent. If intervention in legal decision-making does occur, it must be based on factors that all individuals could be subject to, not merely people who have a cognitive disability or are perceived as lacking decision-making skills.

Best interests

1.214 The CRPD requires states parties to ensure that legal principles and practices affecting the legal capacity of persons with disabilities are devised so as to provide safeguards that ensure 'respect for the rights, will and preferences' of disabled persons. Under the MCA 2005 the best interests decision-maker is only required to 'consider, so far as is reasonably ascertainable, the person's past and present wishes and feelings ... [and] the beliefs and values that would be likely to influence his decision if he had capacity' and an objective approach is adopted to the decision that in some cases override the wishes of the individual. The Committee considers that this pays insufficient 'respect' to the rights, will and preferences of the individual.

The functional test

1.215 The Act provides that 'A person is not to be treated as unable to make a decision unless all practicable steps to help him to do so have been taken without success' but there is little guidance as to what form this support should take, or who has the legal obligation to provide it. Compliance with the CRPD requires at the very least that this 'support principle' within the MCA 2005 be strengthened and developed.

The Committee provides guidance for States on the development of support for the exercise of legal capacity but does not provide a comprehensive list of examples of good practice so as to allow States to develop their own culturally and jurisdictionally specific practices. The MCA 2005 approach to support may not comply with the CRPD's approach in four key respects. The purpose is to help the person to exercise their legal capacity, rather than to pass a functional test of capacity, so support must be available regardless of mental capacity. The Committee's model of support is consensual: support cannot be imposed against a person's will, and 'must be based on the will and preference of the person, not on what is perceived as being in his or her objective best interests'. The requirement is for 'Legal recognition of the support person(s) formally chosen by a person' to 'be available and accessible', but the MCA 2005 affords no means for a person to designate a chosen and trusted individual to be recognised by others as their supporter.

Substituted decision-making

1.216 Although some of these failings could be resolved by adjusting the present law and practice, it is suggested that the MCA 2005 suffers from non-remediable forms of non-compliance with the CRPD. The Committee has stated that support systems for the exercise of legal capacity must replace regimes of substituted decision-making that deny legal capacity. There are problems in this approach. How do you distinguish support from influence and when does this become undue? The supporter may become the effective decision-maker, because a decision can be influenced by the provision of selective information. What if the person providing support is motivated by self-interest? There are dangers in treating a decision as that of the individual when in reality it has been dictated by the 'supporter'.

1.217 The Committee defined what constitutes a 'substituted decision-making regime' and the MCA 2005 meets all three elements of that definition. The provision for 'declarations of incapacity' and voiding a person's past or future decisions in the relevant area, meet the first element: the removal of legal capacity. The second element is also met because the Act allows for the appointment of a deputy, potentially against the will of the person concerned. In addition, once a person is found to 'lack capacity', a substitute decision-maker is empowered to make a best interest decision. Where a person objects to an 'informal' decision-maker making substitute decisions under the 'general defence' provided by section 5 this would also meet this second element, as informal decision-makers are empowered to make decisions whether or not the person wishes them to do so. Finally, the last element is met because 'best interests' decisions are made on the basis of 'objective' criteria, rather than the person's own will and preference.

Individuals who cannot be supported

1.218 There are cases where the individual cannot communicate or their will and preference is unclear, conflicting or impracticable and where there is concern of undue influence by another individual. It is contended that the CRPD addresses these situations but on the basis that there are clear distinctions with existing substitute decision-making systems by:

(1) using 'will and preference' as the guiding model as opposed to 'best interest,'
(2) not denying legal capacity to individuals with disabilities on a different basis, and
(3) not imposing outside decision-makers against the will of the individual.

1.219 Under the CRPD model, where significant attempts to provide support have failed, an outside decision-maker can make a decision on the individual's behalf in accordance with the 'best interpretation' of her or his will and preference, taking into account past expressed preferences, where available, knowledge gained from family and friends and any other evidence that is available. In this situation, the individual must be closely consulted to discover who she or he would like to appoint as a representative decision-maker. If she or he is communicating but not clearly expressing who she or he would like to make a decision on her or his behalf, then a decision-maker could be appointed, but again, could only make decisions that were in accordance with the best interpretation of her or his will and preference.

A view of the future

1.220 The MCA 2005 adopts a three-stage approach to decision-making:

(1) people with capacity make their own decisions – that fulfils their legal capacity;
(2) people with impaired capacity are required to be supported in making decisions, and will not be treated as lacking capacity unless and until all appropriate support has been tried – that enhances their legal capacity;
(3) people who lack mental capacity have decisions made for them in their best interests. By definition they could not make decisions of their own even with support and this is the process whereby the law implements legal capacity.

It may be that a re-interpretation of the Act would be sufficient to resolve most of the potential conflicts with the CRPD. Placing more emphasis on support as a pre-requisite to a finding of lack of mental capacity and as a preliminary to determining best interests would be a starting point, coupled with a recognition that the matters expressed in s 4(6) of the MCA 2005 represent the will and preference of the individual and must be adopted if ascertainable. However, a more specific shift from an objective to a subjective approach may be required and that would require legislation.

1.221 It then appears that the MCA 2005 definition of capacity is not wide enough, thereby requiring the inherent jurisdiction to fill a newly recognised vacuum, namely adults who 'are incapacitated by external forces – whatever they may be – outside their control from reaching a decision'. Is the retention of a diagnostic threshold an outdated approach inherited from the previous jurisdiction when this was the existence of a 'mental disorder'? Should the diagnostic threshold perhaps become: 'unable to make a decision due to an impairment of or disturbance in the decision-making process through internal or external factors beyond the control of the individual'? This change may not be necessary. The new definition now refers to both the mind and the brain, so have we continued to adopt too medical an approach? Might the impairment or disturbance of the mind be a consequence not only of internal factors but also external forces such as fear, oppression or overwhelming cultural pressures? That would bring some, if not all, of the cases now being dealt with under the inherent jurisdiction within the ambit of the Court of Protection – it is a shame to create a specialised court to deal with vulnerable adults and then have to supplement it elsewhere. This interpretation may also satisfy the concerns about direct discrimination against disabled people.

1.222 We were ahead of the game with the Mental Capacity Act 2005 but are perhaps now at a turning point where there is the opportunity to interpret the legislation in a manner that diminishes the need to rely upon the inherent jurisdiction and ensures that it complies with current international expectations. If we do not take advantage of this we may cease to be a leading jurisdiction in this field.[192]

---

[192] The reader may wish to look at the development of new legislation in Northern Ireland and Ireland – see chapters later in Part I of this work.

Chapter 2

The Mental Capacity Jurisdiction

INTRODUCTION

2.1 The Mental Capacity Act 2005 (MCA 2005) was intended to establish a comprehensive statutory framework setting out how decisions should be made by and on behalf of adults whose capacity to make specific decisions is in doubt. It also clarifies what actions can be taken by others involved in the care or medical treatment of people lacking capacity to consent. The framework provides a hierarchy of processes, extending from informal day-to-day care and treatment, to decision-making requiring formal powers and ultimately to court decisions and judgments. The full range of processes was intended to govern the circumstances in which necessary acts of caring can be carried out, and necessary decisions taken, on behalf of those lacking capacity to consent to such acts or make their own decisions. Some decisions affecting vulnerable or incapacitated people may not fall clearly within the remit of MCA 2005 – those cases 'at the margins' of the MCA are dealt with in Chapter 11.

2.2 This chapter is in three parts:
- Part 1 gives a brief overview of the jurisdiction created by MCA 2005 and discusses the role and status of the Code of Practice which provides statutory guidance on its operation.
- Part 2 looks in detail at the guiding statutory principles that underpin MCA 2005's key messages and govern how the Act should be interpreted and implemented. The two fundamental concepts – capacity and best interests, which form the basis of the statutory framework – are discussed and their definitions explained.
- Part 3 looks at the provisions in MCA 2005 which permit actions to be taken in relation to the care and treatment of people lacking capacity to consent to those actions. Some types of decisions are excluded from the Act's provisions and these are explored. Finally, an explanation is given of the criminal offence created under the Act to deal with cases of ill-treatment or wilful neglect of people lacking capacity to protect themselves from such abuse.

PART 1: OVERVIEW

Key elements

General

2.3 MCA 2005 sets out a comprehensive integrated jurisdiction for the making of personal welfare decisions, health care decisions and financial decisions on behalf of people who may lack capacity to make specific decisions for themselves. The Act's starting point is to enshrine in statute the presumption at common law that an adult has full legal capacity unless it is established that he or she does not. It also includes provisions to ensure that people are given all appropriate help and support to enable them to make their own decisions or to maximise their participation in the decision-making process.

2.4 MCA 2005 also enshrines in statute best practice and former common law principles concerning people who lack capacity and those who take decisions on their behalf. The statutory framework is based on two fundamental concepts:[1] lack of capacity and best interests. For those who lack capacity to make particular decisions, the Act provides a range of processes, extending from informal arrangements to court-based powers, to govern the circumstances in which necessary decisions can be taken on their behalf and in their best interests.

Essential provisions

2.5 The essential provisions of MCA 2005 are intended to:
- set out five guiding principles to underpin the Act's fundamental concepts and to govern its implementation and operation;
- define people who lack decision-making capacity;
- set out a single clear test for assessing whether a person lacks capacity to take a particular decision at a particular time;
- establish a single criterion (best interests) for carrying out acts or taking decisions on behalf of people who lack capacity to consent to such acts or take those specific decisions for themselves;
- clarify the law when acts in connection with the care or treatment of people lacking capacity to consent are carried out in their best interests, without formal procedures or judicial intervention, but with clear restrictions on the use of restraint and, in particular, acts resulting in deprivation of liberty;[2]
- extend the provisions for making powers of attorney which outlast capacity (lasting powers of attorney (LPA)) covering health and welfare decisions as well as financial affairs, with improved safeguards against abuse and exploitation;
- provide for a decision to be made, or a decision-maker (deputy) to be appointed, by a specialist Court of Protection;
- make statutory rules, with clear safeguards, for the making of advance decisions to refuse medical treatment;

---

[1] A full discussion of the meaning of these concepts is set out in the Law Commission Report, *Mental Incapacity*, Law Com No 231 (HMSO, 1995), Part III. See also Part 2 of this chapter below.

[2] MCA 2005 amended by the Mental Health Act 2007 to provide procedural safeguards in cases where someone lacking capacity may be deprived of their liberty in their best interests – see Chapter 7.

- set out specific parameters for research involving, or in relation to, people lacking capacity to consent to their involvement;
- provide for the appointment of independent mental capacity advocates (IMCAs) to support people with no one to speak for them who lack capacity to make important decisions about serious medical treatment and changes of accommodation, and in some circumstances to support those lacking capacity who are involved in safeguarding adults procedures; and
- provide statutory guidance, in the form of a code (or codes) of practice, setting good practice standards for the guidance of people using the Act's provisions.

The public bodies

2.6 MCA 2005 also created two public bodies to support and implement the statutory framework:

(1) a superior court of record, the Court of Protection, with jurisdiction relating to the whole of MCA 2005 and its own procedures and nominated judges; and
(2) a Public Guardian, whose office is the registering authority for LPAs and deputies, with responsibility to supervise deputies and respond to any concerns raised about donees or deputies.

The Code of Practice

2.7 It has long been recognised that complex legislation of this sort requires an accompanying code (or codes) of practice for the guidance of practitioners using MCA 2005 and those affected by its provisions, and also to assist with interpretation and implementation of the Act.[3] Provision for such statutory guidance is made in the Act.[4] Following parliamentary pre-legislative scrutiny of the Draft Mental Incapacity Bill in 2003, the Joint Scrutiny Committee specifically recommended that the Bill should not be introduced into Parliament unless it could be considered alongside a draft code of practice.[5]

2.8 Following Royal Assent of MCA 2005, a revised version of the draft Code was issued for formal public consultation during 2006. It was further revised in the light of responses to the consultation and the final version was laid before Parliament in February 2007. The Code of Practice[6] was formally issued in April 2007 and came fully into effect on 1 October 2007 as the statutory guidance for the entire MCA 2005 as originally enacted. A

---

[3] Law Com No 231, at para 2.53 (see **2.4**, footnote).
[4] MCA 2005, s 42.
[5] *Report of the Joint Committee on the Draft Mental Incapacity Bill, Vol 1*, HL 189-1, HC 1083-1 (TSO, 2003), at paragraph 229.
[6] Mental Capacity Act 2005: Code of Practice (TSO, 2007). The Code is reproduced in Part VI of this book.

supplement to the Code[7] has since been issued separately to deal with the deprivation of liberty provisions inserted into MCA 2005 by the Mental Health Act 2007, which came into effect in April 2009 (see Chapter 7).

Application

The Lord Chancellor is required to prepare and issue one or more codes of practice and MCA 2005 specified the particular issues, as well as particular categories of people, that guidance in the Code(s) must address.[8] These are:

- persons involved in assessing capacity;
- persons acting in connection with the care or treatment of a person lacking capacity;
- donees of LPAs;
- deputies appointed by the Court of Protection;
- persons carrying out research involving people lacking capacity;
- independent mental capacity advocates (IMCAs);
- persons involved in using the deprivation of liberty procedures;
- representatives appointed for people deprived of their liberty;
- the provisions in the Act covering advance decisions to refuse treatment;
- any other matters concerned with the Act as the Lord Chancellor thinks fit.

2.10 The Government originally decided to issue one Code of Practice (sometimes referred to as the main Code) to include guidance on the whole of the MCA jurisdiction. However, the deprivation of liberty provisions subsequently inserted into MCA 2005 (which came into effect in 2009) are dealt with in a separate supplement.[9] The main Code is intended to give practical guidance and examples to illustrate the provisions of MCA 2005, rather than imposing any new legal or formal requirements. It was originally intended that the Code would be revised as and when required[10] but this has not as yet happened. The Lord Chancellor may delegate the preparation or revision of the whole or any part of the Code as he considers expedient.[11]

2.11 Responsibility for the dissemination of the Code of Practice passed from the Ministry of Justice (MoJ) (formerly the Department for Constitutional Affairs, which published the Code) to the Office of the Public Guardian (OPG) although policy responsibility, including any updating, returned to the MoJ in 2011. Apart from the Code appearing on the Ministry

---

[7] Mental Capacity Act 2005: Deprivation of Liberty Safeguards – Code of Practice to supplement the main Mental Capacity Act 2005 Code of Practice (TSO, 2008). Also reproduced in Part VI of this book.
[8] MCA 2005, s 42(1), as amended by the Mental Health Act 2007, s 50(7), Sch 9, Part 1, paras 1, 8(1), (2).
[9] Mental Capacity Act 2005: Deprivation of Liberty Safeguards – Code of Practice to supplement the main Mental Capacity Act 2005 Code of Practice (TSO, 2008).
[10] MCA 2005, s 42(2).
[11] MCA 2005, s 42(3).

of Justice website,[12] it appears that little effort has been made to promote the Code or to make sure that the people required by MCA 2005 to 'have regard' to it have it drawn to their attention.

2.12 In June 2013, the House of Lords established a Select Committee to 'consider and report on the Mental Capacity Act 2005'.[13] Perhaps surprisingly, the Code of Practice was the subject of remarkably little discussion before or by the Committee in its report.[14] The Government in its response,[15] *Valuing every voice, respecting every right: Making the case for the Mental Capacity Act,* stated its belief that the Code still represents a valuable and respected source of guidance for professionals. The Coalition Government committed itself to 'determining whether amendments or additions to the Code would be valuable;' as at the point of writing, no further steps have been taken in this regard.[16] It also ruled out carrying out major revisions to the deprivation of liberty supplement until the Law Commission reported upon reforms relating to deprivation of liberty in summer 2017 (now the end of 2016), although the supplement is now significantly out of step with the case-law developments discussed in Chapter 7.[17] The Law Commission's consultation upon reform of the law relating to deprivation of liberty noted that it would be essential in establishing a new scheme for the legislation to be accompanied by a code of practice, and that, the introduction of new legislation would be an opportunity to review the main Mental Capacity Act Code of Practice more generally.[18]

Legal effect

2.13 The Code of Practice is statutory guidance in that MCA 2005 imposes a duty on certain people to 'have regard to any relevant Code' when acting in

---

[12] See www.justice.gov.uk/protecting-the-vulnerable/mental-capacity-act. Perhaps tellingly, that webpage is now, itself, archived. The Code of Practice can now be found (together with other key documents relating to MCA 2005 and other useful materials) on the MCA Directory maintained by the Social Care Institute for Excellence available at www.scie.org.uk/mca-directory.
[13] See www.parliament.uk/business/committees/committees-a-z/lords-select/mental-capacity-act-2005.
[14] See HL Paper 139 (TSO, 2014): www.publications.parliament.uk/pa/ld201314/ldselect/ldmentalcap/139/13902.htm.
[15] See www.gov.uk/government/publications/mental-capacity-act-government-response-to-the-house-of-lords-select-committee-report, at paras 5.6–5.8.
[16] Paragraph 7.31.
[17] The Department of Health commissioned guidance from the Law Society to assist front-line professionals in identifying when deprivations of liberty may be occurring; this guidance, published in April 2015 and discussed in chapter 7, may be regarded as an informal update to the Deprivation of Liberty Code of Practice, but does not have the same status and legal effect as that Code. That guidance, available at www.lawsociety.org.uk/support-services/advice/articles/deprivation-of-liberty/ must, itself, be read subject to further case-law developments.
[18] Law Commission Consultation Paper No 222 *Mental Capacity and Deprivation of Liberty: A Consultation Paper* (TSO, 2015), at [2.43].

relation to a person lacking capacity.[19] The specified people are those acting in one or more of the following ways:

(1) as a donee of a LPA;
(2) as a deputy appointed by the Court;
(3) as a person carrying out research under the Act;
(4) as an IMCA;
(5) in exercising the procedures authorising deprivation of liberty;
(6) as a representative of someone deprived of their liberty;
(7) in a professional capacity; and/or
(8) for remuneration.

In the context of considering the threshold test for the appointment of a deputy in *SBC v PBA and Others*,[20] Roderic Wood J held that the Court should look at the 'unvarnished words' of the MCA 2005. There was no additional requirement to be derived from the Code of Practice, although the Court may take account of the guidance in the Code in coming to its conclusions. He set out the following reasons for this interpretation (at [67]):

'(i) the words of the statute are the essential provisions laid down by Parliament;
(ii) whatever its genesis and weight, the Code of Practice is indeed only guidance;
(iii) there is a reasonable expectation in the Code that its provisions should be followed;
(iv) departure from it, if undertaken, should require careful explanation;
(v) ... [the Code] remains essentially guidance – however weighty and significant – and is not the source of the relevant power which is to be found only in the statutory provision.'[21]

2.14 The statutory duty to have regard to the Code therefore applies to those exercising formal powers or duties under MCA 2005, and to professionals (including lawyers, health and social care professionals) and others acting for remuneration (such as paid carers). The position of informal carers, such as family members, was considered by the Joint Committee on the Draft Bill:[22]

'The position is different with regard to guidance issued to assist non-professional or informal decision-makers, such as family members and unpaid carers acting under the general authority. It is essential that family members and carers carrying out such responsibilities are provided with appropriate guidance and assistance, both to promote good practice and also to impress upon them the seriousness of their actions and the need to be accountable for them. However, we accept that it would be inappropriate to impose on them a strict requirement to act in accordance with the codes of practice.'

---

[19] MCA 2005, s 42(4), as amended by the Mental Health Act 2007, s 50(7), Sch 9, Part 1, paras 1, 8(3).
[20] [2011] EWHC 2580 (Fam), [2011] COPLR Con Vol 1095.
[21] See also *The Mental Health Trust & Ors v DD & Anor* [2014] EWCOP 11, [2015] 1 FLR 1430, at [156].
[22] *Report of the Joint Committee on the Draft Mental Incapacity Bill, Vol 1*, HL 189-1, HC 1083-1 (TSO, 2003), at para 232.

Sanctions for non-compliance

2.15 MCA 2005 provides that a provision of a code of practice, or a failure to comply with the guidance set out in a code, can be taken into account by a court or tribunal where it appears relevant to a question arising in any criminal or civil proceedings.[23] There is no liability for breach of the Code itself, but compliance or non-compliance may be an element in deciding the issue of liability for breach of some other statutory or common law duty. For example, the need to have regard to the Code is highly likely to be relevant to a question of whether someone has acted or behaved in a way which is contrary to the best interests of a person lacking capacity. Breach of the Code might also be relevant to an action in negligence or to a criminal prosecution (including, potentially, to a prosecution under the care worker and care provider offences created by ss 20 and 21 of the Criminal Justice and Courts Act 2015 respectively (see further **2.226–2.228**).

2.16 This applies not only to those categories of people who have a duty to have regard to the Code of Practice, but also to those who are not under a duty. This is because informal carers still have an obligation to act in accordance with the principles of MCA 2005 and in the best interests of a person lacking capacity.[24] The provision therefore remains applicable where any such person is facing civil or criminal proceedings and the court or tribunal considers the Code to be relevant.

2.17 As no arrangements have been made to monitor compliance with the Code of Practice (or indeed the Act more generally),[25] it is next to impossible to gauge how it is being used in practice. An on-line survey of health and social care practitioners conducted in 2010–11 as part of research into *'Making Best Interests Decisions'* commissioned by the Department of Health found that only 16.2 per cent of participants had used the Code of Practice as a source of information and guidance in relation to the particular decision described in the survey.[26] The Care Quality Commission as part of its strategy for 2013–16 has placed increased emphasis upon monitoring compliance with MCA 2005 as part of its assessment of regulated providers,[27] and it is to be expected – or at least hoped – that this increased focus will see a commensurately increased awareness of the Code. Other professionals (such as lawyers) must monitor their own compliance with the Code.

---

[23] MCA 2005, s 42(5).
[24] See Part 2 at **2.19**ff below.
[25] A point made with some force in the House of Lords Select Committee's report: www.parliament.uk/business/committees/committees-a-z/lords-select/mental-capacity-act-2005 at paragraphs 35–36. By way of comparison, the Secretary of State for Health delegated to the Mental Health Act Commission (which in April 2009 became part of the Care Quality Commission) responsibility to monitor compliance with the Code of Practice to the Mental Health Act 1983 and to advise Ministers of any changes to the Code which the Commission feels might be appropriate.
[26] V Williams et al, *Making Best Interests Decisions: People and Processes*, (Mental Health Foundation, 2012), p 111.
[27] *Raising Standards, Putting People First*, available at www.cqc.org.uk/public/about-us/our-performance-and-plans/our-strategy-and-business-plan.

Creation and revision

2.18 MCA 2005 sets out the procedures required for the preparation or revision of the Code(s) and for parliamentary approval.[28] In particular, there must be formal consultation with anyone whom the Lord Chancellor considers appropriate before a Code is prepared or revised.[29] Since health and social care responsibilities are devolved in relation to Wales, the National Assembly for Wales must specifically be consulted and involved in the preparation of the Codes.

A draft of the Code(s) must be laid before Parliament.[30] The Code takes effect after 40 days unless, within that time, either House has resolved not to approve it (known as the 'negative resolution' procedure).[31]

The Lord Chancellor is allowed considerable flexibility in arranging for the Codes to be produced in the most appropriate format and for bringing the guidance to the attention of everyone who needs to know about it.[32] It had been suggested that separate Codes should be produced for different types of decisions or aimed at different decision-makers, but this suggestion was not taken up. The prospects for revisions to the main Code and/or the DoLS supplement are discussed at **2.13** above.

PART 2: PRINCIPLES AND CONCEPTS

The principles

Background

2.19 Much of the evidence submitted to the Joint Committee undertaking pre-legislative scrutiny of the Draft Mental Incapacity Bill was concerned with the principles said to underlie the provisions of the Bill. In particular, commentators stressed the need for a clear statement of those principles to be set out on the face of the legislation.[33] Comparisons were made with s 1 of the Adults with Incapacity (Scotland) Act 2000 (AWI(S)A 2000), which sets out five general principles to govern all 'interventions' in the affairs of an adult taken under or in pursuance of AWI(S)A 2000.[34]

2.20 It is important to note that while some of the specific provisions of AWI(S)A 2000 and the MCA 2005 are similar, there are significant differences in the underlying intentions and operation of both pieces of legislation as well as in the respective jurisdictions. Both are based on the recommendations of the respective Law Commissions, each of which

---

[28] MCA 2005, s 43.
[29] MCA 2005, s 43(1).
[30] MCA 2005, s 43(2).
[31] The 40-day period is defined in MCA 2005, s 43(4)–(5).
[32] MCA 2005, s 43(3).
[33] See in particular the evidence submitted by the Making Decisions Alliance, *Joint Committee Report*, Vol II, HL 198-II, HC 1083-II (TSO, 2003), at Ev 85.
[34] AWI(S)A 2000, s 1.

adopted a different approach as a result of their separate consultation exercises. There are also differences in drafting styles.

2.21 The Joint Committee examined these differences in approach, and was persuaded that the statement of principles in AWI(S)A 2000 provided not only necessary protection for people with impaired capacity and a framework for ensuring that appropriate action is taken in individual cases, but also that the specified principles were extremely helpful in pointing the way to solutions in difficult or uncertain situations. In conclusion, the Joint Committee commented:[35]

> '... we were struck by the absence of a specific statement of principles on the face of the Bill as an initial point of reference, as had been done in the Scottish Act. Although the principles of the draft Bill may be discernible to lawyers from the opening clauses of the draft Bill, they may not be so obvious to the majority of non-legal persons who will have to deal with the Bill in practice.'

Given the approaches adopted by the judiciary in the respective jurisdictions, it is questionable whether, in practice, the differences between the Scottish and English legislation are as great as might appear from these statements.[36]

The statement of principles

2.22 The Joint Committee's strong recommendations[37] that a statement of principles be incorporated on the face of MCA 2005 were accepted by the Government. MCA 2005, s 1 sets out five guiding principles designed to emphasise the underlying ethos of the Act, which is not only to protect people who lack capacity to make specific decisions, but also to maximise their ability to participate in decision-making. This section provides as follows:

> '(1) The following principles apply for the purposes of this Act.
> (2) A person must be assumed to have capacity unless it is established that he lacks capacity.
> (3) A person is not to be treated as unable to make a decision unless all practicable steps to help him to do so have been taken without success.
> (4) A person is not to be treated as unable to make a decision merely because he makes an unwise decision.
> (5) An act done, or decision made, under this Act for or on behalf of a person who lacks capacity must be done, or made, in his best interests.
> (6) Before the act is done, or the decision is made, regard must be had to whether the purpose for which it is needed can be as effectively achieved in a way that is less restrictive of the person's rights and freedom of action.'

---

[35] *Report of the Joint Committee on the Draft Mental Incapacity Bill, Vol 1*, HL 189-1, HC 1083-1 (TSO, 2003), at para 39.
[36] See Adrian D Ward 'Abolition of guardianship? "Best interests" versus "best interpretation"' (2015) SLT 150.
[37] Ibid, Recommendations 4 and 5.

2.23 In his ministerial statement announcing the publication of the Mental Capacity Bill and its introduction into Parliament, David Lammy, the then Parliamentary Under Secretary of State for Constitutional Affairs said:[38]

> 'The overriding aim of the Bill is to improve the lives of vulnerable adults, their carers, families and professionals. It provides a statutory framework for decision making for people who lack capacity, making clear who can take decisions, in which situations and how they should go about this.
>
> The Bill is based on clearly defined principles. Its starting point is that everyone has the right to make his or her own decisions, and must be assumed to have capacity to do so unless it is proved otherwise. No-one should be labelled as incapable – each decision should be considered individually and everyone should be helped to make or contribute to making decisions about their lives. The Bill sets out clear guidelines for, and limits on, other people's role in decision making.'

2.24 The statement of principles was warmly welcomed, not only by voluntary and professional organisations involved with people who lack capacity,[39] but also by MPs and Peers commenting on the principles during the parliamentary debates. In particular, during the Bill's second reading in the House of Lords, the Lord Bishop of Worcester said:[40]

> 'The result is not just a Bill with important protections for vulnerable people; Clause 1 contains a statement about a vision of humanity and how humanity is to be regarded. I hope children in generations to come will study that as one of the clearest and most eloquent expressions of what we think a human being is and how a human being is to be treated ...
>
> I believe that [the Bill] states what is fundamentally right. In the course of Committee we shall no doubt improve and tighten some of the wording, but we shall never take away the powerful and eloquent statement in Clause 1. That should underlie our treatment of one another in all circumstances and for all purposes.'

2.25 The principles underpinning the Act were strongly endorsed in evidence given to and in the report produced by the House of Lords Select Committee appointed to consider MCA 2005.[41] The following paragraphs consider the origins of each of the key principles and their operation in practice. It is impossible to understate how important it is for all concerned with the Act to start their application and use of the legislation by considering and complying with the principles.

Presumption of capacity

2.26 Practitioners will have been familiar with the presumption, at common law, that an adult has full legal capacity unless it is established that he or she does not. If a question of capacity comes before a court, the burden

---

[38] *Hansard*, HC Deb, vol 422 ser 6, col 67WS (18 June 2004).
[39] See e g Making Decisions Alliance *Briefing for 2nd Reading debate in House of Commons* (11 October 2004), at pp 7–9.
[40] *Hansard*, HL Deb, vol 668, ser 5, cols 53–54, 55 (10 January 2005).
[41] HL Paper 139 (TSO, 2014), available at www.publications.parliament.uk/pa/ld201314/ldselect/ldmentalcap/139/13902.htm at paragraph 12.

of proof is generally on the person who is seeking to establish a lack of capacity and the matter is decided according to the usual civil standard, the balance of probabilities.

Law Commission proposals

2.27 Taking account of responses to consultation and in keeping with its proposal to establish a single comprehensive jurisdiction, the Law Commission recommended that the new statutory provisions should expressly include and re-state both the common law principle of presumption of capacity and the relevant standard of proof.[42]

The legislation

2.28 The Joint Committee also supported the principle of presumption of capacity and recommended that this principle should be given primacy of place in the legislation:[43]

> 'This is because it better reflects the positive nature of the Bill's purpose and will increase confidence in the operation of this legislation.'

The presumption of capacity therefore appears in MCA 2005, s 1(2) as the first principle relating to the Act.

The Code of Practice

2.29 The Code of Practice stresses that the starting point for assessing someone's capacity to make a particular decision is always the assumption that the individual does have capacity:[44]

> 'Some people may need help to be able to make a decision or to communicate their decision. However, this does not necessarily mean that they cannot make that decision – unless there is proof that they do lack capacity to do so.'

2.30 Capacity must then be judged in relation to the particular decision at the time that decision needs to be made, and the presumption of capacity may only be rebutted if there is acceptable evidence that the person is incapable of making the decision in question. In relation to most decisions in connection with the person's care and treatment, a 'reasonable belief' that the person lacks capacity is sufficient, so long as reasonable steps have been taken to establish this.[45]

2.31 Where the question of capacity is to be decided in proceedings before the Court of Protection, it has been held that the threshold for engagement of the court's powers (under MCA 2005, s 48) is lower than that of evidence

---

[42] Law Com No 231, at para 3.2 (see **2.4**, footnote). In Scotland, the presumption of capacity is established under common law and is not re-stated in AWI(S)A 2000.
[43] *Report of the Joint Committee on the Draft Mental Incapacity Bill, Vol 1*, HL 189-1, HC 1083-1 (TSO, 2003), at para 66 67.
[44] Mental Capacity Act 2005: Code of Practice, at paragraph 2.5.
[45] MCA 2005, s 5(1). See **2.87–2.90**.

sufficient in itself to rebut the presumption of capacity. The proper test in such circumstances is whether there is evidence giving good cause for concern that the person may lack capacity in some relevant regard.[46] The operation of this threshold test was clearly illustrated in the decision in *Re SB*,[47] involving a woman with a history of bipolar disorder who wished to terminate her pregnancy at the 23rd week of its term, having previously shown signs of wanting to keep the baby. Permission was given for the NHS Trust treating her to apply to the Court of Protection for a determination of SB's capacity to make this decision since there was cause for concern that deterioration in her mental state had caused her to change her mind. Despite expert evidence to the contrary, Holman J found her to have capacity to make the decision herself:[48]

> '... even if aspects of the decision making are influenced by paranoid thoughts in relation to her husband and her mother, she is nevertheless able to describe, and genuinely holds, a range of rational reasons for her decision. When I say rational, I do not necessarily say they are good reasons, nor do I indicate whether I agree with her decision, for section 1(4) of the Act expressly provides that someone is not to be treated as unable to make a decision simply because it is an unwise decision. It seems to me that this lady has made, and has maintained for an appreciable period of time, a decision. It may be that aspects of her reasons may be skewed by paranoia. There are other reasons which she has and which she has expressed. My own opinion is that it would be a total affront to the autonomy of this patient to conclude that she lacks capacity to the level required to make this decision. It is of course a profound and grave decision, but it does not necessarily involve complex issues. It is a decision that she has made and maintains; and she has defended and justified her decision against challenge. It is a decision which she has the capacity to reach. So for those reasons I conclude that it has not been established that she lacks capacity to make decisions about her desired termination, and I will either make a declaration to that effect or dismiss these proceedings.'

Practicable steps to help decision-making

2.32 The second of MCA 2005's key principles[49] clarifies that a person should not be treated as unable to make a decision until everything practicable has been done to help the person make his or her own decision. All practicable steps to enable decision-making must first be shown to be unsuccessful before the person can be assessed as lacking capacity.

Law Commission proposals

2.33 The Law Commission had originally proposed that it would only be necessary for 'reasonable attempts' to be made to understand a person who has difficulty in communicating a decision.[50] However, many respondents to

---

[46] *Re F* [2009] EWHC B30 (Fam), [COPLR] Con Vol 390.
[47] *Re SB (A patient: Capacity to consent to termination)* [2013] EWHC 1417 (COP), [2013] COPLR 445.
[48] Ibid at paragraph 44.
[49] MCA 2005, s 1(3).
[50] *Mentally Incapacitated Adults and Decision-Making: A New Jurisdiction*, Law Com Consultation Paper No 128 (HMSO, 1993), at para 3.41.

the consultation paper made the point that the reference to 'reasonable attempts' was too weak and, for people who are not simply unconscious, 'strenuous steps must be taken to assist and facilitate communication before any finding of incapacity is made'.[51] Other respondents stressed the need for help and support to maximise a person's potential to make their own decisions, not just those with communication difficulties.

The legislation

2.34 This requirement has now been translated into MCA 2005's guiding principles in s 1(3). Although the requirement is contained in the guiding principles, it is perhaps of note that s 1(3) represents the sole reference to support in the MCA 2005. The contrast to the Mental Capacity Bill under consideration in Northern Ireland[52] in this regard is noteworthy; that legislation which – in some regards – is very similar to MCA 2005, includes an entire clause (4) relating to support. Further, 'serious interventions' require a formal assessment of capacity where the assessor must specifically document what help and support has been given to enable P to make a decision (clause 13).

2.35 Perhaps because the Act contains no further reference to the need for support, the principle enshrined in s 1(3) can all too often be overlooked. It is striking, for instance, how rarely cases before the Court of Protection involve consideration of providing support to the person said to lack capacity to take the decision(s) in question: conversely, it is also striking how in the rare cases where judges have taken active measures to ensure compliance with s 1(3), findings of incapacity have been avoided. A particularly good example of this is *An NHS Trust v DE & Ors*,[53] in which it became clear during the course of what was intended to be the final hearing that a clinical psychologist, who knew the man in question well, considered that he might be able to attain capacity to enter into sexual relations in time if the right sort of direct work was done with him; the court therefore adjourned proceedings for such work to take place, which had the result that it was able in due course to conclude that he had acquired such capacity.

2.36 In addition, since the UK has formally ratified the United Nations Convention on the Rights of Persons with Disabilities (CRPD), Article 12 of which calls on state parties to recognise the right of people with disabilities to 'enjoy legal capacity on an equal basis with others in all aspects of life', the need to maximise individual autonomy and promote supported decision-making would be minimum requirements in ensuring the law is CRPD compliant. For a further discussion of the requirements of the CRPD in this regard see **1.218–1.230**. It is also of note that the Law Commission in its consultation on reform of the law relating to deprivation of liberty has

---

[51] Law Com No 231, at para 3.21 (see **2.4**, footnote).
[52] For a discussion of the earlier draft Bill and its contrasts with MCA 2005, see Alex Ruck Keene and Catherine Taggart, 'A brave new (fused) world? The draft Northern Irish Mental Capacity Bill' *Elder Law Journal*, Jordan Publishing, [2014] Eld LJ 395.
[53] [2013] EWHC 2562 (Fam), [2013] COPLR 531.

provisionally proposed amending the Act so as to introduce a formal legal process in which a person (known as a 'supporter') is appointed to assist with decision-making. This step is proposed with a view to moving towards compliance with the CRPD. One key part of their task would be to ensure that, in accordance with s 1(3), all practical steps have been taken to help the person make a decision.[54]

2.37 In the interim and prior to any statutory amendments, there are a number of ways in which people can be given help and support to enable them to make their own decisions, and these will vary depending on the decision to be made, the timescale for making the decision and the individual circumstances of the person wishing to make it. The practicable steps to be taken might include using specific communication strategies, providing information in an accessible form or treating an underlying medical condition to enable the person to regain capacity. However, those taking practicable steps to help someone make a decision must be careful to avoid subjecting the person to pressure or undue influence, possibly based on their own beliefs or their family or cultural obligations.[55]

The Code of Practice

2.38 The main Code of Practice devotes a whole chapter to provide guidance and prompt consideration of a range of practicable steps which may assist decision-making, although the relevance of the various factors will vary depending on each particular situation.[56] As a minimum, the following steps should be considered:

(1) Try to minimise anxiety or stress by making the person feel at ease. Choose the best location where the client feels most comfortable and the time of day when the client is most alert.

(2) If the person's capacity is likely to improve, wait until it has improved (unless the decision is urgent). If the cause of the incapacity can be treated, it may be possible to delay the decision until treatment has taken place.

(3) If there are communication or language problems, consider using a speech and language therapist or interpreter, or consult family members on the best methods of communication.

(4) Be aware of any cultural, ethnic or religious factors which may have a bearing on the person's way of thinking, behaviour or communication.

(5) Consider whether or not a friend or family member should be present to help reduce anxiety. But in some cases the presence of others may be intrusive.

---

[54] Law Commission Consultation Paper No 222, *Mental Capacity and Deprivation of Liberty: A Consultation Paper* (TSO, 2015) at [12.13].

[55] Undue influence can affect both those with or without capacity. See for example, *Re SA (Vulnerable Adult with Capacity: Marriage)* [2005] EWHC 2942, [2006] 1 FLR 867. For consideration of the law relating to undue influence, see *V Hackett v CPS* [2011] EWHC 1170 (Admin).

[56] Mental Capacity Act 2005: Code of Practice, chapter 3.

Unwise decisions

The legislation

2.39 The third principle underlying the Act, set out in MCA 2005, s 1(4), confirms that a person should not be treated as lacking capacity merely because he or she makes a decision that others consider to be unwise. The intention here is to reflect the nature of human decision-making. Different people will make different decisions because they give greater weight to some factors than to others, taking account of their own values and preferences. Some people are keen to express their own individuality or may be more willing to take risks than others. The diagnostic threshold requiring evidence of some mental impairment or disturbance[57] will to some extent ensure that the capacity of those who are merely eccentric is not challenged unnecessarily. However, people who have mental disabilities which could affect their decision-making capacity should not be expected to make 'better' or 'wiser' decisions than anyone else. What matters is the ability to make a decision – not the outcome.

Law Commission proposals

2.40 Originally, the Law Commission had suggested that it was unnecessary to make such provision in MCA 2005. The right to make unwise decisions has been part of the common law since at least 1850.[58] In a consultation paper the Law Commission argued:[59]

> 'If it is feared that a function test along these lines is not strong enough, interference in the lives of the merely deviant or eccentric could be expressly excluded. New Zealand law (Protection of Personal and Property Rights Act 1988, s 1(3)) provides that the fact that the client "has made or is intending to make any decision that a person exercising ordinary prudence would not have made or would not make is not in itself sufficient ground for the exercise of its jurisdiction by the court." A similar safeguard is proposed by the Scottish Law Commission, with a stipulation that "the fact that the person has acted or intends to act in a way an ordinary prudent person would not should not by itself be evidence of lack of capacity" (Discussion Paper No 94, para 4.40). We, however, doubt the need for any such stipulation, in the light of the definition we have proposed, which clearly directs an assessor to the decision-making process, rather than its outcome. We invite views on this.'

2.41 The views received by the Law Commission were strongly in favour of explicit provision being made in the legislation:[60]

> 'Those we consulted, however, overwhelmingly urged upon us the importance of making such an express stipulation. This would recognise that the "outcome" approach to capacity has been rejected, while recognising that it is almost certainly in daily use. We recommend that a person should not be regarded as unable to make a decision by reason of mental disability merely because he or she makes a decision which would not be made by a person of ordinary prudence.'

---

[57] See **2.60–2.61**.
[58] *Bird v Luckie* (1850) 8 Hare 301.
[59] *Mentally Incapacitated Adults and Decision-Making: A New Jurisdiction*, Law Com No 128, at para 3.25.
[60] Law Com No 231, at para 3.19 (see **2.4**, footnote).

Evidence before the Joint Committee

2.42 During pre-legislative scrutiny of the draft Bill, the Joint Committee received evidence from some witnesses expressing concern that a person with apparent capacity may be able to make repeatedly unwise decisions that put him or her at risk or result in preventable suffering or disadvantage.[61] Particular concerns were raised by Denzil Lush, then Master of the Court of Protection (now Senior Judge of the Court of Protection), who drew attention to the distinction between decision-specific capacity and more general ongoing incapacity. He gave examples of cases where people had made unwise decisions, each of which they appeared capable of making, but where they in fact lacked an overall awareness or understanding of the implications of those decisions.[62] Senior Judge Lush explained his concerns as follows:[63]

> 'Even though they may be suffering from a condition that restricts their ability to govern their life and make independent choices, so long as they have the basic ability to consider the options and make choices, we must not intervene against their will. By intervening against their will, even for their own good, we show less respect for them than if we had allowed them to go ahead and make a mistake. This lack of inter-personal respect is potentially a more serious infringement of their rights and freedoms than allowing them to make an unwise decision.'

2.43 Some caution may therefore need to be applied in operating this principle in practice. Although as a general rule, capacity should be assessed in relation to each particular decision or specific issue, there may be circumstances where a person has an ongoing condition which affects his or her capacity to make a range of interrelated or sequential decisions. One decision on its own may make sense but the combination of decisions may raise doubts as to the person's capacity or at least prompt the need for a proper assessment. The Code of Practice suggests that further investigation (such as a formal assessment of capacity) may be needed if somebody:[64]

> '... repeatedly makes unwise decisions that put them at significant risk of harm or exploitation; or makes a particular unwise decision that is obviously irrational or out of character.'

For example, in *D v R (Deputy of S) v S*, having confirmed a person's right to act in an unwise, capricious or even spiteful manner, Henderson J said:[65]

> 'The significance of section 1(4) must not, however, be exaggerated. The fact that a decision is unwise or foolish may not, without more, be treated as conclusive, but it remains in my judgment a relevant consideration for the court to take into account in considering whether the criteria of inability to make a decision for oneself in

---

[61] *Report of the Joint Committee on the Draft Mental Incapacity Bill*, Vol 1, HL 189-1, HC 1083-1 (TSO, 2003), at paras 72, 78.
[62] *Evidence for the Law Society of Scotland*, Joint Committee Report, Vol II, HL 198-II, HC 1083-II (TSO, 2003), at Ev 184, Q495–Q496.
[63] Denzil Lush 'The Mental Capacity Act and the new Court of Protection' (2005) *Journal of Mental Health Law* 12, at p 34.
[64] Mental Capacity Act 2005: Code of Practice, at paragraph 2.11.
[65] [2010] EWHC 2405 (COP) at [40]. A different approach was taken in the case of *Re SB* [2013] EWHC 1417 (COP), [2013] COPLR 445 where Holman J reached the conclusion that SB, a woman with bipolar disorder, had capacity to decide to terminate her pregnancy, despite her previously expressed wish of wanting to have the baby – see **2.31** above.

section 3(1) are satisfied. This will particularly be the case where there is a marked contrast between the unwise nature of the impugned decision and the person's former attitude to the conduct of his affairs at a time when his capacity was not in question.'

2.44 But equally, an unwise decision should not, by itself, be sufficient to indicate lack of capacity. For example, in *CC v KK and STCC*, Baker J concluded, against all the expert evidence, that KK had capacity to decide where to live, even though the local authority and the experts believed her decision to return to her bungalow was unwise:[66]

> 'There is, I perceive, a danger that professionals, including judges, may objectively conflate a capacity assessment with a best interests analysis and conclude that the person under review should attach greater weight to the physical security and comfort of a residential home and less importance to the emotional security and comfort that the person derives from being in their own home. I remind myself again of the danger of the "protection imperative" identified by Ryder J in Oldham MBC v GW and PW [2007] EWHC 136 (Fam). These considerations underpin the cardinal rule, enshrined in statute, that a person is not to be treated as unable to make a decision merely because she makes what is perceived as being an unwise one.'

In *PC and Anor v City of York Council*, concerning the capacity of a woman with learning disabilities to decide to resume cohabitation with her husband on his release from prison having been convicted of serious sexual offences, the Court of Appeal recognised that:[67]

> '... the court's jurisdiction is not founded upon professional concern as to the 'outcome' of an individual's decision. There may be many women who are seen to be in relationships with men regarded by professionals as predatory sexual offenders. The Court of Protection does not have jurisdiction to act to "protect" these women if they do not lack the mental capacity to decide whether or not to be, or continue to be, in such a relationship. The individual's decision may be said to be "against the better judgment" of the woman concerned, but the point is that, unless they lack mental capacity to make that judgment, it is against their better judgment. It is a judgment that they are entitled to make. The statute respects their autonomy so to decide and the Court of Protection has no jurisdiction to intervene.
>
> ... there is a space between an unwise decision and one which an individual does not have the mental capacity to take and ... it is important to respect that space, and to ensure that it is preserved, for it is within that space that an individual's autonomy operates.'

Best interests

The Law Commission proposals

2.45 In seeking to establish a clear legal framework for making decisions with, or on behalf of people who lack capacity, the Law Commission proposed a single criterion to govern all decision-making:[68]

> 'Although decisions are to be taken by a variety of people with varying degrees of formality, a single criterion to govern any substitute decision can be established.

---

[66] *CC v KK and STCC* [2012] EWHC 2136 (COP), [2012] COPLR 627, at [65].
[67] *PC and Anor v City of York Council* [2013] EWCA Civ 478, [2013] COPLR 409 at [53]–[54] per McFarlane LJ.
[68] Law Com No 231, at paras 3.24–3.25 (see **2.4**, footnote).

'Whatever the answer to the question "who decides?", there should only be one answer to the subsequent question "on what basis?".

We explained in our overview paper that two criteria for making substitute decisions for another adult have been developed in the literature in this field: "best interests", on the one hand, and "substituted judgment", on the other. In Consultation Paper No 128 we argued that the two were not in fact mutually exclusive and we provisionally favoured a "best interests" criterion which would contain a strong element of "substituted judgment". It had been widely accepted by respondents to the overview paper that, where a person has never had capacity, there is no viable alternative to the "best interests" criterion. We were pleased to find that our arguments in favour of a "best interests" criterion found favour with almost all our respondents, with the Law Society emphasising that the criterion as defined in the consultation papers was in fact "an excellent compromise" between the best interests and substituted judgment approaches. We recommend that anything done for, and any decision made on behalf of a person without capacity should be done or made in the best interests of that person.'

2.46 It is notable that the Scottish Law Commission took a different approach in formulating proposals which led to AWI(S)A 2000:[69]

'We consider that "best interests" by itself is too vague and would require to be supplemented by further factors which have to be taken into account. We also consider that "best interests" does not give due weight to the views of the adult, particularly to wishes and feeling which he or she had expressed while capable of doing so. The concept of best interests was developed in the context of child law where a child's level of understanding may not be high and will usually have been lower in the past. Incapable adults such as those who are mentally ill, head injured or suffering from dementia at the time when a decision has to be made in connection with them, will have possessed full mental powers before their present incapacity. We think it is wrong to equate such adults with children and for that reason would avoid extending child law concepts to them. Accordingly, the general principles [of AWI(S)A 2000] are framed without express reference to best interests.'

The Joint Committee's view

2.47 The Joint Committee on the draft Bill compared the two approaches and came down in favour of including the concept of best interests within the Act's key principles:[70]

'We heard evidence that the concept of best interests has been usefully developed by the courts and that its inclusion in statute would assist in promoting awareness and good practice, thereby ensuring some consistency in approach.'

The legislation

2.48 MCA 2005, s 1(5) establishes in statute the former common law principle that any act done, or any decision made, under MCA 2005 for or on behalf of a person who lacks capacity must be done, or made, in that person's best interests. This establishes 'best interests' as the single criterion

---

[69] *Report on Incapable Adults*, Scot Law Com No 151 (Scottish Executive, 1995) paragraph 2.50.
[70] *Report of the Joint Committee on the Draft Mental Incapacity Bill, Vol 1*, HL 189-1, HC 1083-1 (TSO, 2003), at para 82.

to govern all decision making affecting people who lack capacity to make their own decisions. Further details on the meaning and determination of best interests are set out in the Act.[71] Whether the concept of 'best interests' is one that is – in and of itself – a concept that is fundamentally incompatible with the CRPD is a topic of increasingly hot debate: see in this regard the discussion at **1.218–1.230**.

Less restrictive alternative

The Law Commission proposals

2.49 The Law Commission originally proposed that the 'least restrictive alternative' principle should be included in the new legislation as one of the factors to be taken into account in determining the best interests of a person who lacks capacity.[72] The Commission considered that the principle had been developed over many years by experts in the field so as to become widely recognised and accepted.[73] The Draft Mental Incapacity Bill therefore included this principle in the proposed statutory checklist for best interests.[74]

The legislation

2.50 However, in response to the Joint Committee's recommendation[75] the Government agreed to incorporate in MCA 2005, s 1(6) the principle that, where possible, a *less* restrictive option should be chosen (rather than the *least* restrictive alternative). This became the fifth key principle to guide the use of MCA 2005 generally, rather than just one factor in the best interests checklist.

2.51 Before any action is taken, or any decision is made under MCA 2005 in relation to a person lacking capacity, the person taking the action or making the decision must consider whether it is possible to act or decide in a way that is less restrictive of the person's rights and freedom of action. Where there is more than one course of action or a choice of decisions to be made, all possible options or alternatives should be explored (including whether there is a need for any action or decision at all) in order to consider which option would be less restrictive or intrusive. However, other options need only be considered so long as the desired purpose of the action or decision can still be achieved. In any event, the option chosen must be in the person's best interests, which may not in fact be the least restrictive.[76]

---

[71] MCA 2005, s 4, and see **2.122–2.153**.
[72] Law Com No 231, paras 3.28, 3.37 (see **2.4**, footnote).
[73] For a discussion of the origins and development of the principle of least restrictive alternative, see Denzil Lush 'The Mental Capacity Act and the new Court of Protection' (2005) *Journal of Mental Health Law* 12, at pp 37–38.
[74] Draft Mental Incapacity Bill, Cm 5859-I (TSO, 2003) cl 4(2)(e).
[75] *Report of the Joint Committee on the Draft Mental Incapacity Bill, Vol 1*, HL 189-1, HC 1083-1 (TSO, 2003), at para 44.
[76] Confirmed by Ryder J in *C v A Local Authority* [2011] EWHC 1539, [2011] COPLR Con

The Scottish approach

2.52 This formulation differs from the principles set out in AWI(S)A 2000, which starts with a specific 'no intervention' provision[77] – that there shall be no intervention in the affairs of an adult unless the intervention will benefit the adult and that such benefit cannot reasonably be achieved in any other way. This is then followed by the 'least restrictive option' principle.[78] The Joint Committee considered this approach, but took the view that the less restrictive alternative principle would involve decision-makers in having to consider whether any intervention at all was in fact necessary.[79]

Relevance to the Court of Protection

2.53 Although the Court of Protection is subject to the principles set out in MCA 2005, s 1,[80] including best interests and the less restrictive alternative, specific provision is made to limit the scope of any intervention where court proceedings are contemplated with the intention of ensuring that a less restrictive or interventionist approach is adopted. MCA 2005 requires the Court, in deciding whether to grant permission for an application to it (where permission is required), to consider the reasons for the application, the benefit to the person lacking capacity and whether the benefit can be achieved in any other way.[81] In addition, the Act imposes an obligation on the Court to make a single order in preference to appointing a deputy, and where the appointment of a deputy is considered necessary, that the powers conferred on the deputy should be as limited in scope and duration as possible.[82]

Defining lack of capacity

The functional approach

2.54 Before MCA 2005 came into effect, the lack of a clear statutory definition of capacity (or lack of capacity) caused confusion and difficulty for all concerned, not least for professionals called on to assess someone's decision-making capacity. There were also significant differences in approach between legal and medical or psychological concepts of capacity.[83] Case-law offered a number of tests of capacity depending on the

---

Vol 972 at paragraph 61. In other words, 'The "best interests" principle takes priority': *London Borough of Havering v LD & KD* [2010] EWHC 3876 (COP), [2010] COPLR Con Vol 809, at [9].

[77] AWI(S)A 2000, s 1(2).
[78] AWI(S)A 2000, s 1(3).
[79] *Report of the Joint Committee on the Draft Mental Incapacity Bill, Vol 1*, HL 189-1, HC 1083-1 (TSO, 2003), at para 96.
[80] MCA 2005, s 16(3).
[81] MCA 2005, s 50(3).
[82] MCA 2005, s 16(4).
[83] The Law Society and British Medical Association attempted to address this problem by providing guidance in *Assessment of Mental Capacity: A Practical Guide for Doctors and Lawyers* (BMA, 1995; Law Society Publishing, 4th edn, 2015).

type of decision in issue.[84] The Law Commission recommended that, in order to provide certainty and clarity in using the new jurisdiction, a single statutory definition of capacity should be adopted.[85] Therefore, having set out the key principles governing its operation, MCA 2005 goes on to define the people affected by its provisions.

2.55 MCA 2005, s 2 sets out the definition of a person who lacks capacity. MCA 2005, s 3 sets out the test for assessing whether a person is unable to make a decision and therefore lacks capacity. By applying these together, MCA 2005 adopts a functional approach to defining capacity, requiring capacity to be assessed in relation to each particular decision at the time the decision needs to be made, and not the person's ability to make decisions generally. This means that individuals should not be labelled 'incapable' simply on the basis that they have been diagnosed with a particular condition, or because of any preconceived ideas or assumptions about their abilities due, for example, to their age, appearance or behaviour. Rather, it must be shown that they lack capacity for each specific decision, or type of decision, at the time the particular decision needs to be made. In *A, B and C v X and Z*, an important case demonstrating the approach taken by the court in determining capacity, Hedley J was required to decide whether X had capacity to (a) marry; (b) make a will; (c) revoke or grant an enduring or lasting power of attorney; (d) manage his property and affairs; (d) litigate; and (e) decide with whom to have contact (although the last issue was not currently for the court to decide). He stressed from the outset 'Each of those questions requires an answer, but each must be considered individually'.[86]

The following paragraphs consider in turn each element of the Act's definition and test of capacity.

People who lack capacity

2.56 MCA 2005, s 2(1) sets out the definition of a person who lacks capacity as follows:

> 'For the purposes of this Act, a person lacks capacity in relation to a matter if at the material time he is unable to make a decision for himself in relation to the matter because of an impairment of, or a disturbance in the functioning of, the mind or brain.'

Capacity is therefore both decision-specific and time-specific. The inability to make the particular decision in question must be *because of* 'an impairment of, or a disturbance in the functioning of, the mind or brain' (ie a mental disability or disorder) and the causal link (that the impairment or disturbance directly causes the inability to make the decision) must be

---

[84] See **2.85–2.86**.
[85] Law Com No 231, para 3.7 (see **2.4**, footnote).
[86] *A, B and C v X, Y and Z* [2012] EWHC 2400 (COP), [2013] COPLR 1, at [1]. Note: permission was granted to A, B and C to appeal the decision in relation to X's capacity to marry, but the appeal lapsed when X subsequently died.

clearly demonstrated.[87] It does not matter whether the impairment or disturbance is permanent or temporary.[88] A person can lack capacity to make a decision even if the loss of capacity is partial or temporary or if his or her capacity fluctuates. In particular, a person may lack capacity in relation to one matter but not in relation to others.

2.57 There has been considerable legal debate, particularly in cases concerning capacity to marry or to consent to sexual relations as to whether the test of capacity is act-specific or person-specific (for further discussion, see Chapter 6). The Court of Appeal has now clarified that, unless the common law and/or the MCA 2005 expressly state otherwise, capacity is to be assessed in relation to the specific decision. It will depend on the character of the particular decision as to whether the information relevant to that decision relates to an act, to a particular person or to a specific set of circumstances:[89]

> 'The determination of capacity under MCA 2005, Part 1 is decision specific. Some decisions, for example agreeing to marry or consenting to divorce, are status or act specific. Some other decisions, for example whether P should have contact with a particular individual, may be person specific. But all decisions, whatever their nature, fall to be evaluated within the straightforward and clear structure of MCA 2005, ss 1 to 3 which requires the court to have regard to 'a matter' requiring 'a decision'. There is neither need nor justification for the plain words of the statute to be embellished. I do not agree with the Official Solicitor's submission[90] that absurd consequences flow from a failure to adopt either an act-specific or a person-specific approach to each category of decision that may fall for consideration. To the contrary, I endorse Mr Hallin's argument to the effect that removing the specific factual context from some decisions leaves nothing for the evaluation of capacity to bite upon. The MCA 2005 itself makes a distinction between some decisions (set out in s 27) which as a category are exempt from the court's welfare jurisdiction once the relevant incapacity is established (for example consent to marriage, sexual relations or divorce) and other decisions (set out in s 17) which are intended, for example, to relate to a 'specified person' or specific medical treatments.'

The two-stage test of capacity

2.58 In applying the test for capacity set out in ss 2–3 of the MCA 2005 to determine whether an individual has capacity to make a particular decision, the Code of Practice advises that a two-stage procedure must be applied:[91]

(1) it must be established that there is an impairment of, or disturbance in the functioning of, the person's mind or brain; and

---

[87] This point was strongly made by the Court of Appeal in *PC & Anor v City of York Council* [2013] EWCA Civ 478, [2013] COPLR 409, as described in **2.59** below.
[88] MCA 2005, s 2(2).
[89] *PC & Anor v City of York Council* [2013] EWCA Civ 479, [2013] COPLR 409, at [35] per McFarlane LJ, approving the approach adopted by Hedley J in *CYC v PC and NC* [2012] COPLR 670, at [19].
[90] For an explanation of the Official Solicitor's submission in this case, see Alastair Pitblado, 'The decision of the Court of Appeal in *PC & NC v City of York*', *Elder Law Journal*, Jordan Publishing, [2013] Eld LJ 361.
[91] Mental Capacity Act 2005: Code of Practice, pp 44–45.

(2) it must be established that the impairment or disturbance is sufficient to render the person unable to make that particular decision at the relevant time.

2.59 This approach to assessing capacity was based on the Law Commission's conclusion that considering first whether the 'diagnostic threshold' was met (see below) would serve to protect the autonomy of people who merely make unusual or unwise decisions. If there is no indication of impairment or disturbance in the mind or brain, the individual should be presumed to have capacity and his or her ability to make decisions should not be questioned. However, in *PC & Anor v City of York Council* the Court of Appeal appeared to hold that the test should be applied in the sequence set out in s 2(1), that is focussing first on the functional aspect of whether the person concerned is unable to make the decision in question, and if so, whether that inability is *because of* an impairment or disturbance:[92]

> 'There is, however, a danger in structuring the decision by looking to s 2(1) primarily as requiring a finding of mental impairment and nothing more and in considering s 2(1) first before then going on to look at s 3(1) as requiring a finding of inability to make a decision. The danger is that the strength of the causative nexus between mental impairment and inability to decide is watered down. That sequence – "mental impairment" and then "inability to make a decision"- is the reverse of that in s 2(1) – "unable to make a decision ... **because of** an impairment of, or a disturbance in the functioning of, the mind or brain' [emphasis added]. The danger in using s 2(1) simply to collect the mental health element is that the key words "because of" in s 2(1) may lose their prominence and be replaced by words such as those deployed by Hedley J: 'referable to' or 'significantly relates to.'

Although the passage cited above would appear to suggest that the Court of Appeal suggested that it was necessary to reverse the order in which the two limbs of the test are applied, there has been some considerable debate about this and Parker J in *NCC v PB and TB*[93] expressed the view that it had not. It may be, we suggest, that the question is more one of focus – in some settings (for instance the psychiatric hospital setting) the functional aspect will be more important; in some settings (for instance the community setting) the diagnostic element will be more important.

In all cases, however, the 'causative nexus' is crucial. Indeed, it is sufficiently important that it may – in practice – be prudent to proceed on the basis that there is a three-stage test. In other words, in all cases (and whether the diagnostic aspect is considered before the functional aspect or vice versa), the final question must always be whether there is a sufficient causative link between the identified impairment or disturbance and the identified functional inability to take the decision in question. It is undoubtedly the case that any *pro forma* capacity assessment tool that does not include such a question runs the risk of leading the assessor into error.

---

[92] *PC & Anor v City of York Council* [2013] EWCA Civ 479, [2013] COPLR 409 at paragraph 58 per McFarlane LJ.
[93] [2014] EWCOP 14, [2015] COPLR 118.

A diagnostic threshold

2.60 During its consultation processes, the Law Commission considered the finely balanced arguments for and against having a diagnostic threshold, requiring a 'mental disability' to be established before someone is deemed to lack capacity.[94] The Commission concluded that a diagnostic 'hurdle' would serve a useful gate-keeping function, to ensure that decision-making rights are not taken over prematurely or unnecessarily and to make the test of capacity stringent enough *not* to catch large numbers of people who make unusual or unwise decisions. It was felt that the protection offered by a diagnostic threshold outweighs any risk of prejudice or stigma affecting those who need help with decision-making.[95]

2.61 Instead of using the term 'mental disability', MCA 2005, s 2(1) refers to 'an impairment of, or a disturbance in the functioning of, the mind or brain'. This covers a wide range of conditions. For example, people taken to casualty requiring treatment for a physical disorder who are incapacitated in the short term through alcohol or drug misuse, delirium or following head injury may need urgent attention which cannot wait until their capacity has been restored. People in such situations are entitled to the protections and safeguards offered by the Act in the same way as those found to lack the capacity to make specific financial, health or welfare decisions as a result, for example, of mental illness, dementia, learning disabilities or the long-term effects of brain damage.[96] Although there was a deliberate attempt not to use the language of disability in MCA 2005, it does however appear increasingly likely that the existence of a diagnostic threshold, thereby creating a link between legal capacity and mental capacity, brings the law into conflict with the CRPD: see further **1.218–1.230**.

Principle of 'equal consideration'

2.62 During the Bill's Report stage in the House of Lords, an amendment was passed to make it clear that lack of capacity cannot be established merely by reference to a person's age or appearance, or any condition or aspect of his or her behaviour which might lead others to make unjustified assumptions about the person's capacity.[97] This amendment was originally proposed by the Making Decisions Alliance[98] as a 'principle of non-discrimination and equal consideration' which the Alliance sought to

---

[94] The arguments are set out in *Mentally Incapacitated Adults and Decision-Making: A New Jurisdiction*, Law Com No 128, at paras 3.10–3.14.
[95] Law Com No 231, at para 3.8 (see **2.4**, footnote).
[96] For a discussion on medical conditions which may impact on capacity, see BMA/Law Society *Assessment of Mental Capacity: A Practical Guide for Doctors and Lawyers* (Law Society Publishing, 4th edn, 2015).
[97] MCA 2005, s 2(3).
[98] A coalition of around 40 charities that campaigned for MCA 2005.

have included in MCA 2005's statement of principles, in order to ensure that people with impaired capacity are treated no less favourably than people with capacity:[99]

> 'Our concerns stem from evidence, anecdotal and otherwise, that prejudices and attitudes about the quality of life of a person with serious learning disabilities, mental health problem or a head injury or other condition that leads to loss of capacity can get in the way of supporting that person and how they are, what they want and what they need.'

2.63 While the Government was sympathetic to these concerns, the drafting of a broad 'equal consideration' principle proved unworkable. Instead the Government put forward two amendments, one relating to the definition of capacity and the second concerning best interests determinations[100] in order to:[101]

> '... reinforce the belief, shared across the House, that no-one should be assumed to lack capacity, excluded from decision-making, discriminated against or given substandard care and treatment simply, for example, as a result of disability.'

2.64 Section 2(3) of MCA 2005 therefore ensures that individuals should not be labelled 'incapable' because of their age or appearance, or because of any preconceived ideas or prejudicial assumptions about their abilities due to their particular condition or behaviour. The reference to 'condition' covers a range of factors, including both mental or physical disabilities, age-related illness and temporary conditions such as drunkenness. 'Appearance' is also deliberately broad, covering all aspects of physical appearance, visible medical problems or disfiguring scars, disabilities, skin colour, religious dress or simply being unkempt or dishevelled. 'Behaviour' relates to ways of behaving that might seem unusual or odd to others, such as failing to make eye contact, talking to oneself or laughing inappropriately.

Qualifying age

2.65 It had originally been the intention that the jurisdiction created by the new statutory framework should apply only to *adults* who lack capacity, leaving disputes about the care and welfare of children and young people to be resolved under the Children Act 1989. However, the Law Commission commented that a number of the statutory provisions in the Children Act 1989 do not apply to 16–18 year olds or only in 'exceptional' circumstances. The Law Commission concluded that:[102]

> 'If continuing substitute decision-making arrangements are needed for someone aged 16 or 17, this is likely to be because the young person lacks mental capacity and not because he or she is under the age of legal majority.'

---

[99] Making Decisions Alliance *House of Lords Briefing*, Second Reading (10 January 2005), at p 3.
[100] See **2.130–2.131**.
[101] *Hansard*, HL Deb, vol 670, ser 5, col 1318 (15 March 2005).
[102] Law Com No 231, at para 2.52 (see **2.4**, footnote).

2.66 It followed that the provisions of the MCA 2005, rather than the Children Act 1989, should apply in those circumstances for young people aged 16 or 17, and not just where there is no one available to exercise parental responsibility. For example, there may be circumstances where it is in the young person's best interests for someone other than a person with parental responsibility to be appointed as deputy to make financial or property decisions. Or it may be appropriate for the Court of Protection to make personal decisions, for example, where the young person should live, or medical treatment decisions concerning a young person lacking capacity where it is considered that those with parental responsibility are not acting in the young person's best interests. It was suggested that the resultant overlap would pose no great problems in practice.

2.67 MCA 2005, s 2(5) therefore makes it clear that the powers exercisable under MCA 2005 apply in general only to people lacking capacity who are aged 16 years or over. However, as was the case under the previous law, MCA 2005's powers to deal with property and financial affairs might be exercised in relation to a child whose disabilities will cause a lack of capacity to manage those affairs to continue into adulthood.[103]

2.68 In cases where legal proceedings are required to resolve disputes or make legally effective arrangements for someone aged 16 or 17, the Law Commission pointed out that it would not make sense to require two sets of legal proceedings to be conducted within a short period of time where the problems arising from the young person's incapacity are likely to continue after the age of 18. MCA 2005, therefore, makes provision for transfer from the Court of Protection to the family courts, and vice versa.[104] The choice of court will depend on what is 'just and convenient' in the particular circumstances of the case.[105] In particular, in considering whether to transfer a case from a court having jurisdiction under the Children Act 1989 to the Court of Protection, the court must consider:[106]

> 'The extent to which any order made as respects a person who lacks capacity is likely to continue to have effect when that person reaches 18.'

2.69 The court should also take into account any other matters it considers relevant.[107] Some helpful guidance on what matters may often be relevant in such cases has been given by Hedley J in *B (A Local Authority) v RM, MM, and AM*:[108]

> 'One, is the child over 16? Otherwise of course, there is no power. Two, does the child manifestly lack capacity in respect of the principal decisions which are to be made in the Children Act proceedings? Three, are the disabilities which give rise to lack of capacity lifelong or at least long-term? Four, can the decisions which arise in respect of the child's welfare all be taken and all issues resolved during the child's

---

[103] MCA 2005, ss 2(6) and 18(3).
[104] MCA 2005, s 21.
[105] Mental Capacity Act 2005 (Transfer of Proceedings) Order 2007, SI 2007/1899, arts 2(2) and 3(2).
[106] Ibid, art 3(3)(c).
[107] Ibid, art 3(3)(d).
[108] [2010] EWHC 3802 (Fam) at [28], [2010] COPLR Con Vol 247 at paragraph 28.

minority? Five, does the Court of Protection have powers or procedures more appropriate to the resolution of outstanding issues than are available under the Children Act? Six, can the child's welfare needs be fully met by the exercise of Court of Protection powers? These provisional thoughts are intended to put some flesh on to the provisions of Article 3(3); no doubt, other issues will arise in other cases. The essential thrust, however, is whether looking at the individual needs of the specific young person, it can be said that their welfare will be better safeguarded within the Court of Protection than it would be under the Children Act.'

In that case, Hedley J concluded that the case should be transferred to the Court of Protection for the following reasons:[109]

'A) I think that there should be a Court determination as to U [residential placement] and the need for AM to stay there. B) I think the Court door should remain open during those delicate planning stages and potentially difficult decisions over the placement, even if the Court does not actively intervene in that process unless it is specifically invited so to do. C) I am far from satisfied that these matters will be resolved by the time of AM's 18th birthday. D) Her disabilities and acute care needs are lifelong. E) Declarations in the Court of Protection avoid all the negative consequences as I see them of making of a care order whilst at the same time, setting the necessary framework within which AM's needs can be addressed. F) Her lack of capacity on all relevant issues for decision is manifest. It follows, that I propose pursuant to Article 3(4)(a) to transfer on my own initiative having as required given my reasons for so doing. Accordingly, I propose to reconstitute as the Court of Protection and it would be quite unnecessary in these circumstances to have a separate hearing in the Court of Protection, because all the evidence and all the issues are before me and I am myself a judge of the Court of Protection. Therefore, I propose to restrict myself to considering how what I have said in this judgment, can properly be given effect to by an order of the Court of Protection.'

The different concepts of 'competence' in relation to children under 16 years and 'capacity' applying to young people aged 16–17 are considered further below.[110]

Inability to make decisions

2.70 MCA 2005, s 2(1)[111] requires it to be shown that the person is unable to make the decision in question because of an impairment of, or disturbance in the functioning of, the person's mind or brain. The impairment or disturbance must be shown to cause the person to be unable to make that decision at the relevant time. MCA 2005, s 3 sets out the test for assessing whether a person is unable to make a decision for him or herself. This is a 'functional' test, focusing on the personal ability of the individual concerned to make a particular decision and the processes followed by the person in arriving at the decision – not on the outcome. A person is unable to make a decision if he or she is unable:[112]

'(a) to understand the information relevant to the decision,
(b) to retain that information,
(c) to use or weigh that information as part of the process of making the decision, or

---

[109] Ibid, at paragraph 30.
[110] See **2.91–2.94**.
[111] See **2.56 ff**.
[112] MCA 2005, s 3(1).

(d) to communicate his decision (whether by talking, using sign language or any other means).'

If someone cannot undertake any one of these four aspects of the decision-making process, then he or she is unable to make the decision.[113] The fourth criterion in MCA 2005, s 3(1)(d) relates only to a residual category of people who are totally unable to communicate.[114]

Some guidance as to the interpretation of the functional test was given by Macur J (as she then was) in *LBL v RYJ*:[115]

'I read section 3 to convey, amongst other detail, that it is envisaged that it may be necessary to use a variety of means to communicate relevant information, that it is not always necessary for a person to comprehend all peripheral detail and that it is recognised that different individuals may give different weight to different factors.'

2.71 In *Re SB (A patient: Capacity to consent to termination)*, Holman J appeared to consider the question of being 'unable' to make a decision separately in relation to its ordinary meaning (whether SB had in fact made a decision) and its legal meaning by reference to MCA 2005, s 3 (whether she could understand, use or weigh the relevant information etc.):[116]

'Where I very respectfully differ from, and disagree with, the engaged psychiatrists is as to, what I might call, the level of the bar as to capacity. The relevant question under section 2 is whether she is "unable" to make a decision. There is absolutely no doubt whatsoever that this lady has, many weeks ago, made a decision. She persists in it, and she very, very strongly urges it upon me today. So there is no doubt that she has a capacity to "make" a decision and she has made one.'

While the judge went on to consider the clinical evidence in relation to s 3(1)(a)-(c) (at [39]), the evidence of SB herself was influential on the court's judgment that she had capacity to make the decision:[117]

'...even if aspects of the decision making are influenced by paranoid thoughts in relation to her husband and her mother, she is nevertheless able to describe, and genuinely holds, a range of rational reasons for her decision ... It may be that aspects of her reasons may be skewed by paranoia. There are other reasons which she has and which she has expressed. My own opinion is that it would be a total affront to the autonomy of this patient to conclude that she lacks capacity to the level required to make this decision. It is of course a profound and grave decision, but it does not necessarily involve complex issues.'

Understand the information relevant to the decision

2.72 Information relevant to the decision includes the particular nature of the decision in question, the purpose for which the decision is needed and

---

[113] *RT v LT and A Local Authority* [2010] EWHC 1910 (Fam), [2010] COPLR Con Vol 1061 at [40].
[114] See **2.83–2.84**.
[115] [2010] EWHC 2665 (COP), [2010] COPLR Con Vol 795, at [24].
[116] *Re SB* [2013] EWHC 1417 (COP), [2013] COPLR 445, at [38].
[117] Ibid, (at [44]).

the likely effects of making the decision. It must also include the reasonably foreseeable consequences of deciding one way or another or of making no decision at all.[118]

2.73 Following lobbying by the Making Decisions Alliance, amendments were made to the Bill in both Houses of Parliament to require communication support, as is *appropriate* to meet individual needs, to be provided to help people with impaired capacity to express their views and, wherever possible, to make their own decisions.[119] As a result, MCA 2005[120] requires every effort to be made to provide an explanation of information relevant to the decision in question in a way that is appropriate to the circumstances of the person concerned and using the most effective means of communication (such as simple language, visual aids or any other means) to assist their understanding. Cursory or inadequate explanations are not acceptable unless the situation is urgent.

2.74 The threshold of understanding is quite low, requiring an ability to understand an explanation of what is proposed and any possible consequences given in broad terms and simple language – the 'salient details' but not necessarily 'all peripheral details'.[121] This approach is consistent with the desire to enable people to take as many decisions as possible for themselves, while also ensuring that the more serious the consequences of any decision, the greater the degree of understanding required. However, in an important case relating to the assessment of capacity *CC v KK and STCC,* Baker J criticised what he called the 'blank canvas' approach where the person being assessed was given little information about the choices she was being asked to make:[122]

> 'The person under evaluation must be presented with detailed options so that their capacity to weigh up those options can be fairly assessed. I find that the local authority has not identified a complete package of support that would or might be available should KK return home, and that this has undermined the experts' assessment of her capacity. The statute requires that, before a person can be treated as lacking capacity to make a decision, it must be shown that all practicable steps have been taken to help her to do so. As the Code of Practice makes clear, each person whose capacity is under scrutiny must be given 'relevant information' including 'what the likely consequences of a decision would be (the possible effects of deciding one way or another)'. That requires a detailed analysis of the effects of the decision either way, which in turn necessitates identifying the best ways in which option would be supported. In order to understand the likely consequences of deciding to re *A Local Authority v AK and Others*[123] turn home, KK should be given full details of the care package that would or might be available.'

---

[118] MCA 2005, s 3(4).
[119] See eg *Re AK (Medical Treatment: Consent)* [2001] 1 FLR 129, where strenuous efforts were made to communicate with someone able only to move one eyelid.
[120] MCA 2005, s 3(2).
[121] *LBL v RYJ* [2010] EWHC 2665 (COP), [2010] COPLR Con Vol 795, at [24] and [58].
[122] [2012] EWHC 2136 (COP), [2012] COPLR 627 at [68].
[123] *A Local Authority v AK & Ors* [2012] EWHC B29 (COP), [2013] COPLR 163 at [51].

2.75 Identifying what is the specific decision in question, and the information relevant to the decision, is not always straightforward.[124] For example, in *Re S: D v R (Deputy of S) and S*,[125] in the context of assessing whether S had capacity to continue litigation commenced in his name by his property and affairs deputy, his daughter, to set aside gifts he had made to Mrs D, Henderson J commented[126]:

> 'At a superficial level, the nature of the decision may be simply stated ... it is whether to discontinue, or to continue to prosecute, the Chancery proceedings. But that decision cannot be taken, it seems to me, without at least a basic understanding of the nature of the claim, of the legal issues involved, and of the circumstances which have given rise to the claim. It would be an over-simplification to say that the claim is just a claim to set aside or reverse the gifts which Mr S made to Mrs D, because in the ordinary way a gift is irrevocable once it has been made and perfected by delivery or transfer of the relevant assets. If a gift is to be set aside or recovered, some vitiating factor such as fraud, misrepresentation or undue influence has to be established; and if the donor is to decide whether or not to pursue a claim, he needs to understand, at least in general terms, the nature of the vitiating factor upon which he may be able to rely, and to weigh up the arguments for and against pursuing the claim. Provided that the donor is equipped with this information, and provided that he understands it and takes it into account in reaching his decision, it will not matter if his decision is an imprudent one, or one which would fail to satisfy the 'best interests' test in section 4. But if the donor is unable to assimilate, retain and evaluate the relevant information, he lacks the capacity to make the decision, however clearly he may articulate it.'

In this case, the decision was held to be 'a complex one which requires a good deal of detailed information and self-awareness'.[127]

2.76 Similarly, it may not always be easy to identify the 'reasonably foreseeable consequences' of deciding one way or another or making no decision at all, particularly in relation to a personal welfare decision. In *A Local Authority v Mrs A*, concerning the capacity of a woman to make decisions about contraceptive treatment, the local authority argued that 'the reasonably foreseeable consequences' included the ability to understand and envisage what would actually be involved in caring for and committing to a child, but this argument was rejected by the court:[128]

> 'Although in theory the "reasonably foreseeable consequences" of not taking contraception involve possible conception, a birth and the parenting of a child, there should be some limit in practice on what needs to be envisaged, if only for public policy reasons. I accept the submission that it is unrealistic to require consideration of a woman's ability to foresee the realities of parenthood, or to expect her to be able to envisage the fact-specific demands of caring for a particular child not yet conceived (let alone born) with unpredictable levels of third-party support. I do not

---

[124] In *PC and Anor v City of York Council* [2013] EWCA Civ 478, [2013] COPLR 409, the Court of Appeal endorsed the approach taken by Hedley J at first instance in 'the fixing of attention upon the actual decision in hand', 'to articulate the question actually under discussion in the case and apply the statutory capacity test to that decision' which includes identifying the information relevant to the decision – see paragraphs 13, 31, 35 and 56.
[125] *Re S: D v R (Deputy of S) and S* [2010] EWHC 2405 (COP), [2010] COPLR Con Vol 1112.
[126] Ibid, at [43].
[127] Ibid, at [144].
[128] *A Local Authority v Mrs A* [2010] EWHC 1549 COP, [2010] COPLR Con Vol 138 at [63]. Further consideration of the issues involved in capacity to consent to sexual relations is given in Chapter 6.

think such matters *are* reasonably foreseeable: or, to borrow an expression from elsewhere, I think they are too remote from the medical issue of contraception. To apply the wider test would be to "set the bar too high" and would risk a move away from personal autonomy in the direction of social engineering. Further, if one were to admit of a requirement to be able to foresee things beyond a child's birth, then drawing a line on into the child's life would be nigh impossible.'

However, in financial transactions dealing with significant amounts of money, the reasonably foreseeable consequences may be more clearly identified.[129] Useful guidance as to the assessment of capacity to make financial decisions was commissioned by the Department of Health in 2014 and is now available online.[130]

Retain the information

2.77 The ability to retain information for a short period only should not automatically disqualify the person from making the decision.[131] The person must be able to retain the information for long enough to make a choice or take an effective decision and the length of time will therefore depend on what is necessary for the decision in question. The Code of Practice suggests that items such as notebooks, photographs, videos and voice recorders could be used to assist retention and recording of information.[132]

2.78 It has been suggested that MCA 2005's failure to define for how long the information must be retained may cause confusion for those seeking to assess a person's capacity, particularly, for example, a person suffering from dementia or other condition affecting his or her short-term memory. In *A Local Authority v AK & Ors*, a case concerning capacity to marry of a person whose brain injuries caused him to have severe memory problems, Bodey J commented:[133]

> 'The reference to the retention of information for 'a short period' in s3(3) of the Act cannot seriously be interpreted to mean, in the context of the lifetime commitment of marriage, for so short a period as AK is able to recall whether he is married at all, or reliably (when he does remember) to whom.'

However, in *A, B and C v X and Z*, in making 'qualified' declarations regarding X's capacity to make a will and to create an LPA, the court has suggested a way forward in cases of borderline or fluctuating capacity where the ability to retain information may be in doubt. In weighing up the evidence demonstrating X's understanding and retention of the information relevant to these decisions as compared with medical evidence of a dramatic decline in his memory and executive functions, Hedley J concluded:[134]

---

[129] See for example, *Gorjat v Gorjat* [2010] EWHC 1537 (Ch)
[130] See www.empowermentmatters.co.uk/Wordpress/wp-content/uploads/2014/09/Assessing-Capacity-Financial-Decisions-Guidance-Final.pdf.
[131] MCA 2005, s 3(3).
[132] Mental Capacity Act 2005: Code of Practice, at paragraph 4.20.
[133] *A Local Authority v AK & Ors* [2012] EWHC B29 (COP), [2013] COPLR 163, at [51].
[134] *A, B and C v X, Y and Z* [2012] EWHC 2400 (COP), [2013] COPLR 1, at [37]. Hedley J reached a similar conclusion in relation to X's capacity to make an LPA (at [38]). Note: permission was granted to A, B and C to appeal this decision, but the appeal lapsed when X subsequently died.

'... that I cannot make a general declaration that X lacks testamentary capacity, but that needs to be strongly qualified. There will undoubtedly be times when he does lack testamentary capacity. There will be many times when he does not do so. The times when he does lack such capacity are likely to become more frequent. It follows that, in my judgment, any will now made by X, if unaccompanied by contemporary medical evidence asserting capacity, may be seriously open to challenge.'

A similar 'qualified' declaration was made concerning X's capacity to make an LPA.

Use or weigh the information

2.79 Prior to MCA 2005 coming into effect, a number of cases came before the courts where the person concerned had the ability to understand information but where the effects of a mental health problem or disability prevented him or her from using that information in the decision-making process.[135] The Law Commission gave examples of certain compulsive conditions (such as anorexia) which cause people, who are quite able to absorb information, to make decisions which are inevitable (eg not to eat) regardless of the information and their understanding of it. To reflect these concerns, the Law Commission originally proposed that in order to have capacity, a person must be able to make a 'true choice'.[136] However, in its final report, the Commission recognised that:[137]

> 'Common to all these cases is the fact that the person's eventual decision is divorced from his or her ability to understand the relevant information. Emphasising that the person must be able to use the information which he or she has successfully understood in the decision-making process deflects the complications of asking whether a person needs to "appreciate" information as well as understand it. A decision based on a compulsion, the overpowering will of a third party or any other inability to act on relevant information as a result of mental disability is not a decision made by a person with decision-making capacity.'

2.80 The courts further defined the process as the ability to weigh all relevant information in the balance as part of the process of making a decision and then to use the information in order to arrive at a decision. MCA 2005, s 3(1)(c) translates this former common law provision into statute. The focus of this element of the test is on the personal ability of the individual concerned to make a particular decision (such as the ability to weigh up any risks involved) and the processes followed by the person in arriving at the decision, and not on the outcome.

2.81 Further guidance on applying this element of the capacity test was given in *The PCT v P, AH & The Local Authority* where Hedley J, noting – correctly – that it is the most difficult aspect of the test to apply, described it as 'the capacity actually to engage in the decision-making process itself and to be able to see the various parts of the argument and to relate the one to

---

[135] See eg *Re MB* [1997] 2 FLR 426, CA; *R v Collins and Ashworth Hospital Authority ex parte Brady* [2000] 58 BMLR 173.
[136] *Mentally Incapacitated Adults and Decision-Making: A New Jurisdiction*, Law Com No 128, at paras 3.31–3.35.
[137] Law Com No 231, at para 3.17 (see **2.4**, footnote).

another'.[138] In assessing P's capacity to make a range of decisions concerning his care, residence and medical treatment, the judge concluded that, in addition to his disabilities, P's relationship with his adoptive mother hindered his ability to 'use or weigh' information which conflicted in any way with his mother's views:[139]

> 'The reasons that I am persuaded that he lacks that capacity are the cumulative force of the following: (a) his epilepsy and its impact on his functioning, (b) his learning disability which is at the lower end of mild, (c) the enmeshed relationship that he has with AH [his adoptive mother] which severely restricts his perspective in terms of being able to think about his future, (d) his inability, frequently articulated by him to those who have interviewed him, to visualise any prospect of having a different view to his mother on any subject that matters and his inability to understand what the other aspects of the argument may be in relation to his expressed wishes simply to return and live undisturbed with his mother. Finally, I have regard to that which has emerged more recently ... namely some disparity between his words on the one hand and his actions and attitudes in his dealings with staff on the other ...
>
> No one of those matters by themselves would justify a finding of disability, but the cumulative effect of all of them is to satisfy me beyond a peradventure that at the present time he wants capacity to deal with the matters to which I have related.'

2.82 The provision of advice and support, or even some degree of constraint (for example, to overcome impulsivity) may be appropriate ways to enable someone to weigh up information and understand the consequences of any actions they might or might not take, and thus have capacity to make some types of decisions, such as capacity to litigate when assisted by family members and professional advisers.[140] However, in cases where the issue of capacity is finely balanced, it may be difficult to establish the extent to which the person can 'use or weigh' information in order to act on the advice given or understand when assistance was needed. In *Loughlin v Singh*,[141] a case concerning the assessment of damages in a personal injury claim of a young man who sustained brain injuries in a traffic accident, Parker J took account of a range of evidence, relying in particular on the evidence of one expert witness that, while the claimant may be able to respond to prompting or make a decision in a 'laboratory setting', he would be 'vulnerable in an unpredicted and unmanaged environment' and therefore lacked capacity to 'respond in an appropriate manner' in the real world.

2.83 In the case of *A Local Authority v E and Others*,[142] E, a 32-year-old woman suffered from severe anorexia and other adverse health conditions, had gone to great lengths to demonstrate her ability to use or weigh information and hence her capacity to make an advance decision to the

---

[138] *The PCT v P, AH & The Local Authority* [2009] EW Misc 10 (COP), [2009] COPLR Con Vol 956 at [35].
[139] Ibid, at [37]–[38].
[140] See for example, *V v R* [2011] EWHC 822 (QB).
[141] *Loughlin v Singh* [2013] EWHC 1641 (QB), [2013] COPLR 371 at [36] and [51]. This case is discussed in more detail in Chapter 11.
[142] [2012] EWHC 1639 (COP), [2012] COPLR 441. To the extent that Peter Jackson J appeared to imply that the presumption of capacity was displaced in such cases, it is suggested that this was incorrect; rather, it is suggested that the correct approach is that raising a prima facie case that the decision was made without capacity shifts the burden to the person seeking to uphold the original decision. See also Chapter 6, at **6.35** and **6.63**.

effect that she wished to be allowed to die rather than be force fed. At the time of the hearing, E was near death, refusing food and taking only small amounts of water, and Peter Jackson J was satisfied that E then lacked capacity to consent to or refuse treatment (at paragraph 49):

> '... there is strong evidence that E's obsessive fear of weight gain makes her incapable of weighing the advantages and disadvantages of eating in any meaningful way. For E, the compulsion to prevent calories entering her system has become the card that trumps all others. The need not to gain weight overpowers all other thoughts.'

But at the earlier time of making the advance decisions, E had been eating and had even put on some weight. The judge acknowledged that people with severe anorexia may be in a 'Catch 22 situation', that deciding not to eat is seen as proof of lack of capacity to decide at all. Nevertheless, on the balance of probabilities the judge concluded that E did not have capacity when she signed either of the two advance decisions she had made, saying (at paragraph 65):

> 'Against such an alerting background, a full, reasoned and contemporaneous assessment evidencing mental capacity to make such a momentous decision would in my view be necessary. No such assessment occurred in E's case and I think it at best doubtful that a thorough investigation at the time would have reached the conclusion that she had capacity.'

Unable to communicate

2.84 The final criterion which would indicate an inability to make a decision is the fact that the person is *unable to communicate the decision* by any possible means.[143] There are obvious situations, such as unconsciousness, which would result in a person being unable to communicate a decision. Other types of cases may include people in a vegetative state[144] (previously referred to as a persistent or permanent vegetative state), a minimally conscious state or with the condition sometimes known as 'locked-in syndrome'. The Law Commission intended this to be very much a residual category affecting a minority of people:[145]

> 'This test will have no relevance if the person is known to be incapable of deciding (even if also unable to communicate) but will be available if the assessor does not know, one way or the other, whether the person is capable of deciding or not.'

Strenuous efforts must first be made to assist and facilitate communication before any finding of incapacity is made. Communication by simple muscle movements, such as blinking an eye or squeezing a hand, to indicate 'yes' or 'no', can be sufficient to indicate that the person has the ability to

---

[143] MCA 2005, s 3(1)(d).
[144] For elaboration as to the different diagnoses of vegetative state and minimally conscious state, see *W v M and S, and a NHS Primary Care Trust* [2011] EWHC 2443 (Fam), [2012] COPLR 222. See also the POST (Parliamentary Office of Science and Technology) Note on Vegetative and Minimally Conscious States published in March 2015, available at http://www.parliament.uk/briefing-papers/post-pn-489/vegetative-and-minimally-conscious-states.
[145] Law Com No 231, at para 3.20 (see **2.4**, footnote).

communicate and therefore may have capacity.[146] The Code of Practice recommends that in cases of this sort, the involvement of speech and language therapists or professionals with specialist skills in verbal and non-verbal communication may be required to assist in the assessment.[147]

Common law tests of capacity

2.85 The definition and two-stage test of capacity set out in MCA 2005 are expressed to apply 'for the purposes of this Act'[148] and MCA 2005, Sch 6 makes consequential amendments to existing statutes, inserting the new statutory definition. There are also several *common law* tests of capacity set out in case-law before MCA 2005 came into effect.[149] Examples given in the Code of Practice are as follows:

- capacity to make a will;[150]
- capacity to enter into marriage;[151]
- capacity to make a gift;[152]
- contractual capacity;[153] and
- capacity to litigate.[154]

2.86 MCA 2005's definition of capacity is intended to build on, rather than contradict, the terms of pre-existing common law tests.[155] The Code of Practice suggests that, as cases come before the Court, judges may adopt the statutory definition if they see fit and use it to develop common law rules in particular cases.[156]

- For example, the High Court has confirmed that the correct approach is to apply the MCA test for capacity in deciding whether a person has capacity to conduct litigation in proceedings to which the Civil Procedure Rules apply,[157] since those Rules were subsequently amended to conform with changes brought about by MCA 2005.
- In relation to testamentary capacity, in respect of wills made before MCA 2005 came into effect on October 2007, it is clear the

---

[146] *Re AK (Adult Patient) (Medical Treatment: Consent)* [2001] 1 FLR 129.
[147] Mental Capacity Act 2005: Code of Practice, at paragraph 4.24.
[148] MCA 2005, s 2(1).
[149] Details of the relevant common law tests of capacity can be found in *Assessment of Mental Capacity: A Practical Guide for Doctors and Lawyers* (Law Society Publishing, 4th edn, 2015).
[150] *Banks v Goodfellow* (1870) LR 5 QB 549.
[151] *Sheffield City Council v E and S* [2004] EWHC 2808 (Fam), [2005] 1 FLR 965.
[152] *Re Beaney (deceased)* [1978] 1 WLR 770.
[153] *Boughton v Knight* (1873) LR 3 PD 64.
[154] *Masterman-Lister v Brutton & Co and Jewell & anor* [2002] EWCA Civ 1889.
[155] Law Com No 231, at para 3.23 (see **2.4**, footnote).
[156] Mental Capacity Act 2005: Code of Practice at paragraph 4.33
[157] See *Saulle v Nouvet* [2007] EWHC 2902 (QB) for an early decision under the new jurisdiction on capacity to litigate in regard to a brain-injured claimant. See also Chapter 11 for further discussion of the assessment of capacity of those 'at the margins of the MCA 2005', in particular the overlap with personal injury proceedings and consideration as to whether P is a 'protected party' (ie lacking capacity to litigate) and/or a 'protected beneficiary' (ie lacking capacity to manage any money recovered).

question of capacity should be based on the common law test, without reference to the Act.[158] There have been conflicting conclusions as regards wills made before MCA 2005 came into force, and the question remains one that is ripe for consideration by the superior courts.[159]

It may, over time, be that the common law tests that continue to survive will assimilate more and more of the features of the statutory test under MCA 2005.[160]

Reasonable belief of lack of capacity

2.87 In most day-to-day decisions or actions involved in caring for someone, it will not be appropriate or necessary to carry out a formal assessment of the person's capacity. Indeed many informal carers or others exercising powers under MCA 2005 will not be equipped to carry out a detailed assessment. Rather, it is sufficient that they 'reasonably believe' that the person lacks capacity to make the decision or consent to the action in question,[161] but, if challenged, they must be able to point to objective reasons to justify why they hold that belief.

2.88 This is based on the Law Commission's explanation that:[162]

'It would be out of step with our aims of policy, and with the views of the vast majority of the respondents to our overview paper, to have any general system of certifying people as "incapacitated" and then identifying a substitute decision-maker for them, regardless of whether there is any real need for one. In the absence of certifications or authorisations, persons acting informally can only be expected to have reasonable grounds to believe that (1) the other person lacks capacity in relation to the matter in hand and (2) they are acting in the best interests of that person.'

2.89 Reasonable steps must be taken to establish the person's lack of capacity to make a particular decision. Responses to the consultation on the draft Code of Practice requested additional guidance on what might be considered 'reasonable'. The Code confirms that:[163]

'... the steps that are accepted as "reasonable" will depend on individual circumstances and the urgency of the decision. Professionals who are qualified in their particular field are normally expected to undertake a fuller assessment,

---

[158] *Scammell and Scammell v Farmer* [2008] EWHC 1100 (Ch).
[159] *Fischer v Diffley* [2013] EWHC 4567 (Ch), [2014] COPLR 212 and *Bray v Pearce* (unreported, 6 March 2014) suggested that MCA 2005 should be applied; to contrary effect is *Re Walker* [2014] EWHC 71 (Ch), [2015] COPLR 348. In the context of gifts, see *Re Smith* [2014] EWHC 3926 (Ch), [2015] COPLR 284. For a discussion of some of the issues in this area, see Martyn Frost et al *Testamentary Capacity: Law, Practice and Medicine* (Oxford University Press, 2015), Chapter 2 and Alex Ruck Keene and Annabel Lee, 'Testamentary Capacity' *Elder Law Journal*, Jordan Publishing [2013] Eld LJ 272.
[160] See for example, *MM (An Adult), Re; Local Authority X v MM and KM* [2007] EWHC 2003 (Fam), [2009] 1 FLR 443.
[161] MCA 2005, ss 4(8) and 5(1).
[162] Law Com No 231, at para 4.5 (see **2.4**, footnote).
[163] Mental Capacity Act 2005: Code of Practice, at paragraph 4.45.

reflecting their higher degree of knowledge and experience, than family members or other carers who have no formal qualifications.'

2.90 It goes on to suggest a number of steps that may be helpful in establishing a 'reasonable belief' of lack of capacity:

- Start by assuming the person has capacity to make the specific decision. Is there anything to prove otherwise?
- Does the person have a previous diagnosis of disability or mental disorder? Does that condition now affect their capacity to make this decision? If there has been no previous diagnosis, it may be best to get a medical opinion.
- Make every effort to communicate with the person to explain what is happening.
- Make every effort to try to help the person make the decision in question.
- See if there is a way to explain or present information about the decision in a way that makes it easier to understand. If the person has a choice, do they have information about all the options?
- Can the decision be delayed to take time to help the person make the decision, or to give the person time to regain the capacity to make the decision for themselves?
- Does the person understand what decision they need to make and why they need to make it?
- Can they understand information about the decision? Can they retain it, use it and weigh it to make the decision?
- Be aware that the fact that a person agrees with you or assents to what is proposed does not necessarily mean that they have capacity to make the decision.'

Competence and capacity: children and young people

Children under 16: 'Gillick competence'

2.91 MCA 2005 generally applies only to people aged 16 years and over.[164] Where welfare or healthcare decisions are required of a child aged under 16, any disputes may be resolved by the family courts under the Children Act 1989. In such cases, the common law test of *Gillick* competence applies:[165] whether the child has sufficient maturity and intelligence to understand the nature and implications of the proposed treatment.[166] *Gillick*-competence is a developmental concept and will not be lost or acquired on a day-to-day or week-by-week basis.[167] The understanding required for different treatments or decisions may vary, depending on the nature of the decision in question.

---

[164] See **2.65–2.69**.
[165] For a thought-provoking suggestion that MCA 2005 should apply also to those under 16, see McFarlane LJ, 'Mental Capacity: One Standard for All Ages' *Family Law* Jordan Publishing [2011] Fam Law 479.
[166] *Gillick v West Norfolk and Wisbech Area Health Authority and the DHSS* [1986] 1 FLR 224, HL.
[167] *Re R (A Minor) (Wardship: Consent to medical treatment)* [1992] 1 FLR 190 at 200.

Young people aged 16 or 17: Capacity or competence?

2.92 The main provisions of MCA 2005 apply to adults, which includes young people aged 16 years or over. The starting point for assessing whether a young person aged 16 or 17 has capacity to make a specific decision is therefore the test of capacity in MCA 2005, having regard to the MCA principles. However, there may be circumstances where 16-17 year olds who are unable to make a decision for themselves will not be covered by the provisions of MCA 2005. A young person may be unable to make a decision either:

- because of an impairment of, or disturbance in the functioning of, their mind or brain (they lack capacity within the meaning of the MCA); or
- for reasons of immaturity (due to the person's age, they are unable to make the decision in question).

2.93 Young people aged 16 and 17 are presumed to have capacity in relation to any surgical, dental or medical treatment.[168] If a young person suffers from an impairment of, or a disturbance in the functioning of, the mind or brain which may affect their ability to make a particular healthcare decision, an assessment of capacity under MCA 2005 will be required, notwithstanding the presumption that the young person has capacity. However, if there is no such impairment or disturbance, MCA 2005 will not apply if it can be established that the young person's inability to make a decision is because:

- they do not have the maturity to understand fully what is involved in making the decision (ie they lack *Gillick* competence); or
- the lack of maturity means that they feel unable to make the decision for themselves (for example, where particularly complex or risky treatment is proposed, they may be overwhelmed by the implications of the decision).[169]

2.94 In cases where MCA 2005 applies, decisions about a young person's care or treatment may be made under the provisions of the MCA in the person's best interests (see below and Chapter 6), without the need to obtain parental consent, although those with parental responsibility for the young person should generally be consulted.[170]

---

[168] Family Law Reform Act 1969, s 8(1).
[169] Mental Capacity Act 2005: Code of Practice, at paragraph 12.13. Specific guidance on assessing the ability of children and young people to make treatment decisions is given in National Institute for Mental Health in England (2009) *The Legal Aspects of the Care and Treatment of Children and Young People with Mental Disorder: A guide for professionals* (National Mental Health Development Unit), Chapter 2 (available online at www.nmhdu.org.uk).
[170] MCA 2005, s 4(7)(b).

The assessment of capacity

Background

2.95 By making a judgment on an individual's decision-making capacity, anyone with authority over that person can deprive him or her of civil rights and liberties enjoyed by most adults and now safeguarded by the Human Rights Act 1998. Alternatively, such a judgment could permit a person lacking capacity to do something, or carry on doing something, whereby serious prejudice could result, either putting that person at risk or causing harm or inconvenience to others. However, the House of Lords Select Committee in its post-legislative scrutiny of MCA 2005 emphasised that misplaced reliance upon the presumption of capacity can be just as pernicious as proceeding to make decisions on a best interests basis where no proper assessment of capacity has been carried out.[171] A further complicating factor is that the very process of assessing a person's capacity can be seen as demeaning by the individual concerned, because (rightly) it can be seen as expressing doubt that the person is, in fact, capable of making their own decisions. This is particularly so where a person is subjected to repeated capacity assessments. Balancing these various factors mean that professionals must always be clear why they are, or are not, carrying out a capacity assessment in circumstances where one might on its face be called for, and document any decision carefully.

2.96 The Joint Committee on the Draft Mental Incapacity Bill received evidence from a number of organisations expressing concern that the Bill made no specific provisions for the assessment of capacity, despite the far-reaching implications of the outcome of assessment.[172] These concerns were discussed during the Bill's Committee stage in the House of Lords, when Lord Carter put forward a probing amendment, seeking to impose a statutory duty on public bodies to carry out a formal assessment of a person's capacity where it may be relevant in the context of any assessment of needs or the provision of services to meet those needs. The Minister responded:[173]

> 'This is important – I recognise that – but I am not sure that is something I want to see covered in primary legislation. The purpose of the Bill is to set out the broad principles and absolutes ... to be followed, but we cannot lay out on the face of the Bill the practical detail of how professionals should operate ... The details of the assessment procedure must be a matter for professional judgement in relation to the case, with support from the code of practice in training and guidance.'

2.97 Guidance as to the assessment of capacity is given in the Code of Practice. Professional guidance for doctors and lawyers in particular on the assessment of mental capacity has been issued jointly by the BMA and the

---

[171] HL Paper 139 (TSO, 2014) at paragraphs 104 and 105 available at www.publications.parliament.uk/pa/ld201314/ldselect/ldmentalcap/139/13902.htm.
[172] *Report of the Joint Committee on the Draft Mental Incapacity Bill, Vol 1*, HL 189-1, HC 1083-1 (TSO, 2003), at para 242.
[173] *Hansard*, HL Deb, vol 668, ser 5, col 1230 (25 January 2005).

Law Society.[174] Attention is also drawn to the article by Dr Steven Luttrell, Consultant Geriatrician, 'Impact of Dementia and Other Conditions Affecting Capacity'[175] which includes some guidance on good practice in the assessment of capacity.

When should capacity be assessed?

2.98 According to the principles of MCA 2005, the starting point should be the presumption of capacity. Doubts as to a person's capacity may arise for a number of reasons, either because of the person's behaviour or circumstances, or through concerns raised by someone else, but any concerns must be considered specifically in relation to the particular decision which needs to be made. Where doubts are raised about a person's decision-making abilities, the following questions should first be considered:

(1) Does the person have all the relevant information needed to make the decision in question? If there is a choice, has information been given on any alternatives?
(2) Could the information be explained or presented in a way that is easier for the person to understand?
(3) Are there particular times of day when the person's understanding is better, or particular locations where they may feel more at ease? Can the decision be put off until the circumstances are right for the person concerned?
(4) Can anyone else help or support the person to make a choice or express a view, such as an advocate or someone to assist communication?

2.99 If all these steps have been taken without success in helping the person make a decision, an assessment of their capacity to make the decision in question should be made.

Who should assess capacity?

2.100 In keeping with the functional approach, the question of who assesses an individual's capacity will depend on the particular decision to be made, but will in general be the person who needs the decision to be made. For most day-to-day decisions in connection with the person's care or treatment, the carer most directly involved with the person at the time the decision has to be made assesses his or her capacity to make the decision in question. Carers acting informally are not expected to be experts in assessing capacity, but they must be able to show they have reasonable grounds for believing that the person lacks capacity to make the decision or

---

[174] BMA/Law Society *Assessment of Mental Capacity: A Practical Guide for Doctors and Lawyers* (Law Society Publishing, 4th edn, 2015).
[175] Steven Luttrell, 'Impact of Dementia and Other Conditions Affecting Capacity' in *Elder Law Journal*, Jordan Publishing [2011] Eld LJ 403.

do the act in question, at that particular time.[176] Formal processes are rarely required unless the assessment is challenged, for example, by the person whose capacity is being assessed or by another family member. In such circumstances, the assessor must be able to point to objective reasons as to why they believe the person lacks capacity to make the decision in question.

2.101 Where consent to medical treatment or examination is required, the doctor or healthcare professional proposing the treatment must decide whether the patient has capacity to consent and should record the assessment process and findings in the person's medical notes.[177] Where a legal transaction is involved, such as making a will or a power of attorney, the solicitor handling the transaction must be satisfied that their client has the capacity to give them the necessary instructions. This may require the solicitor to assess whether the client has the required capacity to satisfy the relevant legal test, perhaps assisted by an opinion from a doctor.[178] The position is less clear where the decision relates to the provision of social care services – the assessment of capacity may be carried out by a social worker or care manager, depending on the particular circumstances. The Code of Practice advises:[179]

> 'There are also times when a joint decision might be made by a number of people. For example, when a care plan for a person who lacks capacity to make relevant decisions is being put together, different healthcare or social care staff might be involved in making decisions or recommendations about the person's care package. Sometimes these decisions will be made by a team of healthcare or social care staff as a whole. At other times, the decision will be made by a specific individual within the team.'

2.102 The more serious the decision, the more formal the assessment of capacity may need to be, but whoever assesses capacity must be prepared to justify their findings. Ultimately, if a person's capacity to do something is disputed, it is a question for the court to decide.[180] Cases referred to the Court of Protection will require formal evidence of the assessment of capacity, either to enable the court to make a declaration as to whether the person has or lacks capacity to make a specific decision or to confirm that

---

[176] MCA 2005, ss 4(8) and 5(1). See **2.87–2.90** above.
[177] Doctors must in this regard have in mind the heightened requirements as to the information to be provided to all patients (whether or not it is thought that they may lack capacity) imposed upon them following the judgment of the Supreme Court in *Montgomery v Lanarkshire Health Board* [2015] UKSC 11.
[178] In *Hill v Fellowes Solicitors LLP* [2011] EWHC 61 (QB), the court confirmed (at paragraph 77): 'there is plainly no duty upon solicitors in general to obtain medical evidence on every occasion upon which they are instructed by an elderly client just in case they lack capacity. Such a requirement would be insulting and unnecessary.' In the contentious probate case of *Hawes v Burgess* [2013] EWCA Civ 74, it was held that (at paragraph 60): 'the courts should not too readily upset, on grounds of lack of mental capacity, a will that has been drafted by an experienced independent lawyer.' However, see also **2.106** and **2.120** below, for a discussion on when a medical opinion should be obtained and pitfalls to be avoided when solicitors undertake capacity assessments.
[179] Mental Capacity Act 2005: Code of Practice, para 5.11
[180] In *Baker Tilly v Makar* [2013] EWHC 759 (QB), [2013] COPLR 245 it was held that the absence of medical evidence cannot be a bar to the court making a finding of lack of capacity, but in such cases the court must be cautious before concluding that the presumption of capacity had been rebutted.

the court has jurisdiction to deal with the matter in question.[181] While such evidence will usually be provided by a registered medical practitioner or psychiatrist, other professionals are now recognised as having the ability to provide such evidence.[182] Other types of evidence may also be relevant to the court in considering someone's capacity.[183] In *CC v KK and STCC* the court received both written and oral evidence from KK, an 82-year-old woman alleged to lack capacity, which helped Baker J to conclude, against all the expert evidence, that she had capacity to decide where to live:[184]

> 'I remind myself that the court must be careful when weighing up the evidence of someone in KK's position against expert opinion evidence. Nonetheless, I found her to be clear and articulate. She betrayed relatively few signs of the dementia which, I accept, afflicts her. Furthermore, I agree ... that she demonstrated an understanding of and insight into her care needs and the reality of life if she returned home. ... I found her to be broadly realistic as to her physical limitations. My conclusion on this point is that, whilst KK may have underestimated or minimised some of her needs, she did not do so to an extent that suggests that she lacks capacity to weigh up information.'

The need for formal assessment

2.103 For certain more complex or serious decisions, a formal assessment of capacity may be required, sometimes involving different professionals. Doctors are generally regarded as experts in the assessment of capacity,[185] and in many cases all that may be needed is an opinion from the person's GP or family doctor. Where the person has been diagnosed with a particular condition or disorder, it may be more appropriate to seek an opinion from a specialist, such as a consultant psychiatrist or psychologist who has extensive clinical experience of the disorder and is familiar with caring for patients with that condition. In some cases, a multi-disciplinary approach is best, using the skills and expertise of different professionals. A professional opinion may help to justify a finding about capacity, but the decision as to whether someone has or lacks capacity must be taken by the potential decision-maker, and not the professional who is merely there to advise.[186]

2.104 Doctors or other experts should never express an opinion without first conducting a proper assessment of the person's capacity to make the decision in question and applying the appropriate test of capacity. Solicitors

---

[181] See Chapters 4 and 6.
[182] Court of Protection Rules 2007 (SI 2007/1744 (L.12)), r 64(c). The Court of Protection Form COP3 'Assessment of Capacity', was revised in 2013 to this effect, making clear that, for instance, social workers can provide the necessary evidence upon capacity for purposes of making an application to the Court.
[183] In *Masterman-Lister v Brutton & Co and Jewell & anor* [2002] EWCA Civ 1889, the court gave detailed consideration to diaries, letters and computer documents; in *Saulle v Nouvet* [2007] EWHC 2902 (QB), the court took into account evidence from family members as well as home videos.
[184] *CC v KK and STCC* [2012] EWHC 2136 (COP), [2012] COPLR 627 at paragraph 64.
[185] In *Ali v Caton & Anor* [2013] EWHC 1730 (QB), Stuart-Smith J acknowledged (at [296]) that 'other experts tended to defer to the neuropsychologists' but he did not accept that other experts were unable to provide assistance on the issue of capacity.
[186] *Bailey v Warren* [2006] EWCA Civ 51, at [87].

requesting a professional opinion should send full letters of instruction, setting out details of the decision in question, the requisite test of capacity[187] and how this should be applied in relation to the client's particular circumstances.[188] However, a doctor's opinion may not necessarily be given greater weight than other relevant evidence, such as the views of a solicitor where capacity to undertake a legal transaction is involved.[189]

Legal or professional requirements

2.105 In some cases it is a requirement of the law, or good professional practice, that a formal assessment of capacity be carried out. These include the following situations:

(1) where a doctor or other expert witness certifies a legal document (such as a will) signed by someone whose capacity could be challenged (the so-called 'golden rule' established in *Kenward v Adams*[190] – see below);
(2) to establish that a particular person requires the assistance of the Official Solicitor or other litigation friend in civil proceedings;[191]
(3) to establish that a particular person comes within the jurisdiction of the Court of Protection;[192]
(4) where the Court is required to determine a person's capacity to make a particular decision;[193] and
(5) if there may be legal consequences of a finding of capacity (eg in the settlement of damages following a claim for personal injury) (see **2.121** below and Chapter 11 for further details).

The 'Golden Rule'

2.106 There are particular circumstances where the courts have strongly advised that a doctor should witness a person's signature on a legal document such as a will, thereby providing medical evidence as to the person's capacity. In *Kenward v Adams* Templeman J set out what he called

---

[187] In *SC v BS and Anor* [2012] COPLR 567 the opinion of an expert in autism was discounted in Court of Protection proceedings as he was unfamiliar with the MCA test of capacity, referring instead in his report to 'unfitness to plead'.
[188] Sample letters have been provided in BMA/Law Society *Assessment of Mental Capacity: A Practical Guide for Doctors and Lawyers* (Law Society Publishing, 4th edn, 2015) and Denzil Lush et al *Elderly Clients: A Precedent Manual* (Jordan Publishing, 4th edn, 2013). In *D v R (Deputy of S) and S* [2010] EWHC 2405 (COP), [2010] COPLR Con Vol 1112, Henderson J made a number of critical comments about the expert evidence, and in particular the inadequate instructions given to the expert asked by D to report on S's capacity (at for example paragraphs 109 and 147), subsequently resulting in an award of costs against D and her advisers – see *D v R (Deputy of S) and S* [2010] EWHC 3748 (CoP) at paragraphs 29–30.
[189] *Richmond v Richmond* (1914) 111 LT 273; *Birkin v Wing* (1890) 63 LT 80; *Hawes v Burgess* [2013] EWCA Civ 74.
[190] (1975) *The Times*, November 29.
[191] Civil Procedure Rules 1998, SI 1998/3132, r 21.1.
[192] MCA 2005, ss 15(1), 16(1). See Form COP3 – *Assessment of Capacity* reproduced in Part VII of this book.
[193] *Masterman-Lister v Brutton & Co and Jewell & anor* [2002] EWCA Civ 1889, at [54].

'the golden if tactless rule' that, where a will has been drawn up for an elderly person or for someone who is seriously ill, it should be witnessed or approved by a medical practitioner, who should make a formal assessment of capacity and fully record the examination and findings. The need to observe this 'golden rule' was restated in subsequent cases,[194] albeit balanced with acknowledgement that failure to observe the 'golden rule' would not necessarily invalidate the will.[195] More recently in *Key v Key*, the 'golden rule' was again reinforced and the solicitor involved strongly criticised for failing to follow it:[196]

> '[The solicitor's] failure to comply with what has come to be well known in the profession as the Golden Rule has greatly increased the difficulties to which this dispute has given rise and aggravated the depths of mistrust into which his client's children have subsequently fallen ...
>
> Compliance with the Golden Rule does not, of course, operate as a touchstone of the validity of a will, nor does non-compliance demonstrate its invalidity. Its purpose, as has repeatedly been emphasised, is to assist in the avoidance of disputes, or at least in the minimisation of their scope. As the expert evidence in the present case confirms, persons with failing or impaired mental faculties may, for perfectly understandable reasons, seek to conceal what they regard as their embarrassing shortcomings from persons with whom they deal, so that a friend or professional person such as a solicitor may fail to detect defects in mental capacity which would be or become apparent to a trained and experienced medical examiner, to whom a proper description of the legal test for testamentary capacity had first been provided.'

2.107 Some commentators have argued that attempted compliance with the so-called 'golden rule' can in fact cause more practical problems than non-compliance, because of the practical difficulties, consequent delay and increased costs that may be involved in obtaining an in-depth specialist assessment of capacity before accepting instructions even for a straightforward will or gift.[197] As noted above, the courts have also not always been consistent as to their approach to the rule, and, in the case of dispute, have shown a preference for the contemporaneous of the solicitor in question over retrospective evidence from a medical expert as to capacity, as demonstrated by the Court of Appeal in the contentious probate case of *Hawes v Burgess*, where Mummery LJ said:[198]

> 'If, as here, an experienced lawyer has been instructed and has formed the opinion from a meeting or meetings that the testatrix understands what she is doing, the will so drafted and executed should only be set aside on the clearest evidence of lack of mental capacity. The court should be cautious about acting on the basis of evidence

---

[194] The advice to observe the 'golden rule' was repeated in *Re Simpson (Deceased), Schaniel v Simpson* (1977) 121 SJ 224; *Buckenham v Dickinson* [1997] CLY 661; and more forcefully in *Great Ormond Street Hospital v Pauline Rushie* (unreported) 19 April 2000, in which the solicitor was strongly criticised for failing to follow the 'golden rule'.
[195] *Buckenham v Dickinson* [1997] CLY 661; *Hoff v Atherton* [2004] EWCA Civ 1554; *Cattermole v Prisk* [2006] 1 FLR 693. The 'golden rule' was also considered in some detail in *Scammell and Scammell v Farmer* [2008] EWHC 1100 (Ch), at [117]–[123].
[196] *Key v Key* [2010] EWHC 408 (Ch), at [6] and [8].
[197] See for example, Martyn Frost et al, *Testamentary Capacity: Law, Practice and Medicine* (Oxford University Press, 2015), at paragraphs 6.13–6.21. See also *Re S* [2010] EWHC 2405 (COP), [2010] COPLR Con Vol 1112 for an illustration of the costs and complexity that may be involved.
[198] *Hawes v Burgess* [2013] EWCA Civ 74, [2013] WTLR 453 at [60].

of lack of capacity given by a medical expert after the event, particularly when that expert has neither met nor medically examined the testatrix, and particularly in circumstances when that expert accepts that the testatrix understood that she was making a will and also understood the extent of her property.'

Ultimately, it is perhaps best to see the so-called 'golden rule' as an aspect on the duty on the draftsman taking the client's instructions to be satisfied as to the person's capacity and understanding of the decision in question, and to keep a proper record and attendance notes of the steps taken and the evidence on which they base their conclusions.[199]

Other expert assessments

2.108 In other cases, a judgment will need to be made as to whether the particular circumstances make it appropriate or necessary to seek a formal assessment of capacity by obtaining a professional opinion from a doctor or other expert. The Code of Practice suggests that any of the following factors might indicate the need for a professional to be involved in the assessment:[200]

- the decision that needs to be made is complicated or has serious consequences;
- an assessor concludes a person lacks capacity, and the person challenges the finding;
- family members, carers and/or professionals disagree about a person's capacity;
- there is a conflict of interest between the assessor and the person being assessed;
- the person being assessed is expressing different views to different people – they may be trying to please everyone or telling people what they think they want to hear;
- somebody might challenge the person's capacity to make the decision – either at the time of the decision or later (eg a family member might challenge a will after a person has died on the basis that the person lacked capacity when they made the will);
- somebody has been accused of abusing a vulnerable adult who may lack capacity to make decisions that protect them;
- a person repeatedly makes decisions that put them at risk or could result in suffering or damage.

How capacity is assessed

2.109 Where there are doubts about capacity, it is important that people are assessed when they are at their highest level of functioning because this is the only realistic way of determining what they may or may not be capable of doing. Many of the practicable steps which can be taken to enable a

---

[199] See the discussion in Frost et al *Testamentary Capacity: Law, Practice and Medicine* (Oxford University Press, 2015), at paragraphs 6.13–6.120.
[200] Mental Capacity Act 2005: Code of Practice, at paragraph 4.53.

person to make his or her own decisions[201] may also be helpful in creating the best environment for capacity to be assessed. Once this has been done, the test of capacity set out in MCA 2005, ss 1-3[202] must then be applied, to determine whether the person is unable to make a decision *because of* an impairment of, or a disturbance in the functioning of, the mind or brain.

2.110 In many cases, it may be obvious whether there is any impairment or disturbance which could affect the person's ability to make a decision. For example, there may have been a previous diagnosis of an ongoing mental illness or learning disability, or recognisable symptoms to indicate the recurrence of illness or the disabling effects of a head injury. However, in other cases, such as dementia, the onset of debilitating illness is gradual and the point at which capacity is affected is hard to define. During the period when capacity is borderline, a medical opinion may be required. It should be noted that this is both to allow appropriate decision-making by others as at the point of assessment (if the individual is considered to lack capacity) and to prevent retrospective challenges to the decisions of the individual (where the individual is considered to have capacity at the time, but their decisions are questioned later).[203]

2.111 People should not be considered 'incapable' simply on the basis that they have a particular diagnosis or condition. Rather, the impairment of, or disturbance in the functioning of, the person's mind or brain must be shown to cause the person to be unable to make a decision at the time the decision needs to be made.[204] The following questions must be considered:

(1) Does the person have a general understanding of what the decision is and why he or she is being asked to make it?
(2) Does the person have a general understanding of the consequences of making, or not making, this decision?
(3) Is the person able to understand and weigh up the information relevant to the decision as part of the process of arriving at it?

In borderline cases, or where there is any element of doubt, the person doing the assessment must be able to show that it is more likely than not that the answer to the above questions is 'No'.

Confidentiality

2.112 Carrying out an assessment of capacity requires the sharing of information about the personal circumstances of the person being assessed. Yet doctors, lawyers and other professionals are bound by a duty of confidentiality towards their clients, imposed through their professional

---

[201] Mental Capacity Act 2005: Code of Practice, chapter 3. See **2.36–2.39** above.
[202] See **2.58–2.59** above.
[203] See in this regard *A, B and C v X and Z* [2012] EWHC 2400 (COP), [2013] COPLR 1.
[204] The way in which different conditions and disabilities may impact on an individual's decision-making abilities, and hence their capacity, is discussed in the article by Steven Luttrell 'Impact of Dementia and Other Conditions Affecting Capacity' in *Elder Law Journal*, Jordan Publishing [2011] Eld LJ 403.

ethical codes and reinforced by law.[205] As a general principle, personal information may only be disclosed with the client's consent, even to close relatives. However, there are circumstances when disclosure is necessary in the absence of consent.[206]

2.113 In relation to people who lack capacity to consent to (or refuse) disclosure, a balance must be struck between the public and private interests in maintaining confidentiality and the public and private interest in permitting, and occasionally requiring, disclosure for certain purposes. Some guidance has been offered in the case of *S v Plymouth City Council and C*, which established:[207]

> '... a clear distinction between disclosure to the media with a view to publication to all and sundry and disclosure in confidence to those with a proper interest in having the information in question.'

A similar balancing act must be carried out by professionals seeking or undertaking assessments of capacity. It is essential that information concerning the person being assessed which is directly relevant to the decision in question is made available to ensure that an accurate and focused assessment can take place. Every effort must first be made to obtain the person's consent to disclosure by providing a full explanation as to why this is necessary and the risks and consequences involved. If the person is unable to consent, relevant disclosure – that is the minimum necessary to achieve the objective of assessing capacity – may be permitted where this is in the person's best interests.[208] However, this does not mean that everyone has to know everything.

2.114 When matters come to court, the position is somewhat different, in light of the demands of open justice – in other words that parties to proceedings should be entitled to see all material relevant to the determination by the court of the application before it. In *C v C (Court of Protection: Disclosure)*,[209] Sir James Munby P considered whether an unredacted psychological report and social worker statements should be disclosed to a birth mother who sought the reintroduction of indirect contact with her adopted 20-year-old daughter who lacked capacity to consent, either to the requested contact or to disclosure of the reports. Applying principles derived from cases involving children, Sir James Munby P held that the test for denying disclosure was one of strict necessity, requiring consideration of the following points:

- The court should first consider whether disclosure of the material would involve a real possibility of significant harm to the child.

---

[205] In particular, solicitors must comply with *The Solicitors' Code of Conduct 2011* (Solicitors Regulation Authority, SRA Handbook, 2011), O (4.1).
[206] *W v Egdell and others* [1990] Ch 359, at [848].
[207] [2002] EWCA Civ 388, [2002] 1 FLR 1167, at [49].
[208] Further guidance is given in the Code of Practice, Chapter 16, and the specific considerations relating to confidentiality in the medical setting can be found in Chapters 13 and 16 of BMA/Law Society *Assessment of Mental Capacity: A Practical Guide for Doctors and Lawyers* (Law Society Publishing, 4th edn, 2015).
[209] [2014] EWHC 131 (COP), [2014] COPLR 351.

- If it would, the court should next consider whether the overall interests of the child would benefit from non-disclosure, weighing on the one hand the interest of the child in having the material properly tested, and on the other both the magnitude of the risk that harm will occur and the gravity of the harm if it does occur.
- If the court is satisfied that the interests of the child point towards non-disclosure, the next and final step is for the court to weigh that consideration, and its strength in the circumstances of the case, against the interest of the parent or other party in having an opportunity to see and respond to the material. In the latter regard the court should take into account the importance of the material to the issues in the case.

He noted, further, that consideration should always be given to the fact that disclosure is never a binary exercise, and a proper evaluation and weighing of the various interests may lead to the conclusion that (i) there should be disclosure but (ii) the disclosure needs to be subject to safeguards such as limits to the use that may be made of the documents, in particular so as to limit the release into the public domain of intensely personal information about third parties. Further, the position initially arrived at is never set in stone and that it may be appropriate to proceed one step at a time. In a conclusion that may we suggest be tested further in a suitable case, Sir James Munby P also endorsed the potential limitation of disclosure to a party's legal representatives, albeit that he noted there were obviously practical difficulties to such an approach, chief amongst them being the requirement that such disclosure cannot take place without the consent of the lawyers to whom the disclosure is to be made; and they may find themselves, for reasons they may be unable to communicate to the court, unable to give such consent. Moreover, as the President noted, the lawyers cannot consent unless satisfied that they can do so without damage to their client's interests.

Refusal to be assessed

2.115 There may be circumstances in which a person whose capacity is in doubt refuses to undergo an assessment of capacity or refuses to be examined by a doctor. It will usually be possible to persuade someone to agree to an assessment if the consequences of refusal are carefully explained. For example, it should be explained to people wishing to make a will that the will could be challenged and held to be invalid after their death, while evidence of their capacity to make a will would prevent this from happening.

2.116 If the person lacks capacity to consent to or refuse assessment, it will normally be possible for an assessment to proceed so long as the person is compliant and this is considered to be in the person's best interests. In many situations, a 'reasonable belief' of lack of capacity will be sufficient.[210]

---

[210] See **2.87–2.90** above.

However, where a formal formal assessment is needed, no one can be forced to undergo an assessment of capacity in the face of an outright refusal.[211] For example, entry to a person's home cannot be forced and a refusal to open the door to the doctor may be the end of the matter. Where there are serious concerns about the person's mental health, an assessment under mental health legislation may be warranted, but only so long as the statutory grounds are fulfilled.[212] If there are proper grounds to believe that the person's refusal to undergo the assessment is due to the influence of a third party, then it may be possible to invoke the inherent jurisdiction of the High Court (see **11.3**) to seek injunctions requiring that third party to allow access to the person. Note, finally, that it may in some cases be necessary for a court to take steps to circumvent a refusal by an individual to undergo an assessment of capacity to litigate so that appropriate steps can be taken to appoint a litigation friend.[213]

Recording assessments of capacity

2.117 The majority of decisions made on behalf of people lacking capacity will be informal day-to-day decisions and, as such, those caring for them on a daily basis will be able to assess their capacity and carry out acts in connection with their care and treatment in accordance with MCA 2005, s 5.[214] No formal assessment procedures or recorded documentation will be required. However, if the carer's assessment is challenged, they must be able to point to the steps they have taken to establish the person's capacity to make the decision in question and the grounds which justified a reasonable belief of lack of capacity.[215]

Professional records

2.118 Where professionals are involved, it is a matter of good practice that a proper assessment of capacity is made and the findings recorded in the relevant professional records. This includes, for example:

(1) an assessment of a patient's capacity to consent to medical treatment made by the doctor proposing the treatment and recorded in the patient's clinical notes;

---

[211] See for example *Baker Tilley v Makar* [2013] EWHC 759 (QB), [2013] COPLR 245, in which the court held that a Costs Judge was wrong to conclude that M lacked capacity to litigate on the basis of a single incident even though she had refused to undergo a capacity assessment or allow access to her medical records.

[212] Mental Health Act 1983, ss 2, 3. A refusal to be assessed is in no way sufficient grounds for assessment under the Mental Health Act 1983.

[213] In *Re RGS* [2012] EWHC 4162 (COP), for instance, the court found itself able to reach conclusions as to the capacity of P's son to conduct the litigation on the basis of evidence before the court from professional witness and the son's own account, even though the son declined to undertake a formal medical assessment. Obiter comments in *Bennett v Compass Group* [2002] EWCA Civ 642, [2002] CP Rep 58 could also be read as suggesting that a court might be able to go so far (in an exceptional case) as making an order requiring a GP or hospital to disclose medical records without the consent of the person in question.

[214] See **2.158–2.173** below.

[215] See **2.87–2.90** above.

(2) an assessment of a client's capacity to instruct a solicitor to carry out a legal transaction (where necessary supported by a medical opinion) made by the solicitor and recorded in a clear attendance note on the client's file; and
(3) an assessment of a person's capacity to consent to or agree the provision of services should be made as part of the care planning processes for health or social care needs and should be recorded in the relevant documentation.

Formal reports or certificates of capacity

2.119 In some cases, a more detailed report or certificate will be required, for example:
(1) for use in court or other legal proceedings;
(2) as required by regulations made under MCA 2005;
(3) as required by the Court of Protection Rules.

Assessments by solicitors

2.120 Two cases in the former Court of Protection highlight the pitfalls for solicitors concerning capacity assessments when asked by an expectant attorney to take instructions for the preparation of an EPA from a donor. In his first judgment Deputy Master Ashton stated:[216]

'The assessment of an experienced solicitor must be taken very seriously by the Court provided that adequate enquiry has been made and all appropriate information obtained. In this case the solicitor's assessment does not stand up to scrutiny for the following reasons:

1. the interview note is brief and the solicitor was only able to give evidence as to what she would have done because she could not remember;
2. the interview lasted 30 minutes which included getting to know the new clients, explaining the wisdom of signing enduring powers of attorney, making a choice of attorney, considering any limitations or conditions, preparing and going through the documentation (which would be a slow process as [the donor] was hard of hearing) and arranging for the safe custody of the documents. There was thus little time for an effective mental health assessment;
3. despite the age of the client there is no indication that enquiry was made as to [his] mental health or a letter sought from [his] own GP. The solicitor was not informed of mental health problems and did not suspect these because of the demeanour of the client who was being 'led' by the daughter. Had the solicitor been more circumspect and insisted on the most basic enquiry, or insisted upon a second interview at a later date with the client on his own, the true position would almost certainly have emerged.'

In the subsequent case the Deputy Master stated:[217]

'... the solicitor did not carry out a proper assessment of mental capacity of the client (the Donor) for the following reasons:

---
[216] *Re AS and DS* (2004) Case No 2120091/2.
[217] *Re HW* (2005) Case No 2122208.

1. instructions were taken from the daughter and son-in-law who wished to be appointed as attorneys and there was no independent corroboration of any of the information that they provided (eg. as to the existence of other members of the family or the nature of the task involved);
2. the interview was conducted on the basis of explanations by the solicitor of the particular document involved, with remarkably little communication by the client other than apparent nods of assent. There should have been an initial 'getting to know the client' discussion at which he was encouraged to do most of the talking, with a few questions designed to test his knowledge and the depth of his understanding;
3. there was no preliminary assessment of capacity as such – the understanding of the client was perceived rather than tested. There was merely a basic interview lasting half-an-hour which appears to have progressed on the assumption that there was capacity. This assumption was based upon the client's responses as the interview progressed to the explanations being given whereas these may merely have been manifestations of a learnt behaviour pattern;
4. despite the fact that the intended donor was elderly and in hospital no prior approach was made to the medical staff as to his diagnosis and present condition. This would have revealed that he had advanced Alzheimer's dementia and was under the care of a psychiatrist who considered that he did not have capacity to sign any documents.
5. I find that the half hour interview would not (and did not) reveal the true state of understanding of the client. It was not searching at all and relied solely upon the impression gained by a solicitor with little experience in this area whilst explaining a legal document.'

Assessments for civil courts

2.121 Uncertainty sometimes arises during high value personal injury claims as to whether a brain damaged claimant is a protected party (CPR, r 21.1(d)) and, if so, also a protected beneficiary (CPR, r 21.1(e)) (see Chapter 11 for further details). Consideration was given to the approach to these issues and the implications of the MCA in *Saulle v Nouvet*.[218] The Court of Protection can assist, as illustrated by the following judgment:[219]

'This is an application to the new Court of Protection for a declaration pursuant to the Mental Capacity Act 2005, section 15 as to [P]'s capacity:
a) to conduct his civil claim (which is now well advanced); and
b) to manage his property and affairs (which will include damages of up to £400,000).

If he lacks capacity to do the former a litigation friend will need to be appointed for him in the civil proceedings although this would normally be any deputy already appointed. If he lacks capacity to do the latter his financial affairs will come under the jurisdiction of this Court and a financial deputy will need to be appointed for him. The calculation of compensation in the personal injury proceedings may in consequence be affected by the need to appoint such a deputy.

... [The decision in *Saulle v Nouvet*] identifies a weakness of dealing with the issue of capacity in the civil court. That court can make a definitive decision as to capacity to litigate but it cannot make a decision as to capacity to manage financial affairs that will be binding on the Court of Protection. Conversely, the Court of Protection has a statutory power to make declarations as to capacity which may

---

[218] [2007] EWHC 2902 (QB), Andrew Edis QC sitting as a deputy judge.
[219] *Re GS* – CoP Case No11582024, 10 July 2008, DJ Ashton.

relate to both litigation and management of financial affairs and any such declarations are likely to be followed by a civil court. In substantial personal injury claims where the quantum of damages may be affected by the involvement of the Court of Protection there are therefore advantages in the civil court referring both issues of capacity to the Court of Protection for determination. However, where the amount of money involved would not normally trigger the intervention of the Court of Protection it is proportionate and desirable for the civil court to adjudicate on both aspects of capacity (ie to decide whether the litigant is a protected party and if so then whether he or she is also a protected beneficiary).'

Determining best interests

Background

2.122 Before MCA 2005 came into effect, the principle of acting in the best interests of a person who lacks capacity had become well established in the common law and the concept had been developed by the courts in cases relating to incapacitated adults, mainly those concerned with the provision of medical treatment.[220] MCA 2005, s 1(5) enshrines this principle in statute as the overriding principle that must guide all actions done for, or all decisions made on behalf of, someone lacking capacity.[221] MCA 2005, s 4 goes on to describe, for the purposes of this Act, the steps that must be taken in determining what is in a person's best interests.

2.123 Given the wide range of decisions and acts covered by this legislation and the varied circumstances of the people affected by its provisions, the concept of best interests is not defined in MCA 2005. In considering the need for a definition, the Law Commission acknowledged that:[222]

'... no statutory guidance could offer an exhaustive account of what is in a person's best interests, the intention being that the individual person and his or her individual circumstances should always determine the result.'

2.124 Instead, the Law Commission recommended that statute should set out a checklist of common factors which should always be taken into account. It also set out some important considerations as to how a statutory checklist should be framed:[223]

'First, a checklist must not unduly burden any decision-maker or encourage unnecessary intervention; secondly it must not be applied too rigidly and should leave room for all considerations relevant to the particular case; thirdly, it should be confined to major points, so that it can adapt to changing views and attitudes.'

2.125 The Joint Committee on the Draft Mental Incapacity Bill agreed with this approach:[224]

---

[220] See eg *Re A (Male Sterilisation)* [2000] 1 FLR 549; *Re S (Sterilisation: Patient's Best Interests)* [2000] 2 FLR 389.
[221] See **2.45–2.48** above.
[222] Law Com No 231, at para 3.26 (see **2.4**, footnote).
[223] Ibid, at paragraph 3.28.
[224] *Report of the Joint Committee on the Draft Mental Incapacity Bill, Vol 1*, HL 189-1, HC 1083-1 (TSO, 2003), at para 85.

'We agree that no list of "best interest" factors can ever be comprehensive or applicable in all situations. We therefore endorse the approach recommended by the Law Commission that a checklist of common factors to be considered in all cases should be set out in statute. However, it should be made clearer in the Bill that in addition to these common factors, all other matters relevant to the incapacitated individual and the decision in question must also be considered.'

Both as a result of recommendations made by the Joint Committee and amendments made during the parliamentary process, the best interests checklist contained in MCA 2005, s 4 was extended and made more prescriptive in relation to certain types of decisions, in particular, those involving end-of-life decisions. The specific requirements for determining best interests are considered in detail in the following paragraphs.

The best interests checklist

2.126 Under MCA 2005, a person's capacity to make the decision or take the action in question must first be assessed. MCA 2005, s 4 only comes into play once it has been established (or there are reasonable grounds for believing) that the person lacks capacity to make the decision in question and needs someone else to decide or act on his or her behalf. It then sets out a checklist of factors which must be considered in deciding what is in a person's best interests aimed at identifying those issues most relevant to the individual who lacks capacity (as opposed to the decision-maker or any other persons). The particular factors in the checklist can be broadly summarised as follows:

- equal consideration and non-discrimination;
- considering all relevant circumstances;
- regaining capacity;
- permitting and encouraging participation;
- special considerations for life-sustaining treatment;
- the person's wishes and feelings, beliefs and values;
- the views of other people.

Not all the factors in the checklist will be relevant to all types of decisions or actions, but they must still be considered if only to be disregarded as irrelevant to that particular situation. It is also important always to be clear before applying the checklist whether the decision to be taken is actually a best interests decision for purposes of MCA, s 1(5). The fact that a person may lack capacity to take decisions (for instance regarding their care arrangements) does not mean that every decision taken in relation to them – in particular by public bodies discharging their statutory obligations – is a best interests decision. This is discussed further at **11.19–11.24**, but a sensible rule of thumb is always to ask whether the decision in question is one that the individual in question could take for themselves if they had capacity. If so, then the best interests checklist will need to be applied by whoever is to take the decision on their behalf.[225] If not, then it is more

---

[225] The precise identity of the decision-maker is – deliberately – not set out in MCA 2005. See further **2.174** and the discussion of MCA 2005, s 5.

likely than not that MCA 2005, s 1(5) and the best interests checklist in MCA 2005, s 4 will have no application.

2.127 The serious nature of this task of determining best interests was recognised by the Joint Committee:[226]

'We acknowledge that consideration of best interests requires flexibility, by allowing and encouraging the person [lacking capacity] to be involved to the fullest possible extent but also enabling the decision-maker to take account of a variety of circumstances, views and attitudes which may have a bearing on the decision in question. This flexibility is particularly important in cases of partial or fluctuating capacity. Determining best interests is a judgement, requiring consideration of what will often be conflicting or competing concerns, while seeking to achieve a consensus approach to decision-making.'

2.128 There is an increasing discussion as to the extent to which there is (or should be) a hierarchy in the checklist. The Law Commission had suggested that the best interests test should be modified by a requirement that the substitute decision-maker first goes through an exercise in substituted judgment.[227] However, this suggestion was not adopted and, on the face of MCA, s 1(4), no one of the factors identified therein is to take priority. This reflected a deliberate policy decision that 'a prioritisation of the factors would unnecessarily fetter their operation in the many and varied circumstances in which they might fall to be applied'.[228] This approach was carried through into the Code of Practice accompanying the MCA.In *Re M, ITW v Z*, applying the statutory scheme under MCA 2005, ss 1 and 4, Munby J (as he then was), held that there was no hierarchy, and summarised three points derived from experience in other jurisdictions:[229]

'(i) The first is that the statute lays down no hierarchy as between the various factors which have to be borne in mind, beyond the overarching principle that what is determinative is the judicial evaluation of what is in P's "best interests".

(ii) The second is that the weight to be attached to the various factors will, inevitably, differ depending upon the individual circumstances of the particular case. A feature or factor which in one case may carry great, possibly even preponderant, weight may in another, superficially similar, case carry much less, or even very little, weight.

(iii) The third, following on from the others, is that there may, in the particular case, be one or more features or factors which, as Thorpe LJ has frequently put it, are of "magnetic importance" in influencing or even determining the outcome: see, for example, *Crossley v Crossley*,[230] at para [15] (contrasting "the peripheral factors in the case" with the "factor of magnetic importance") and *White v White*[231] where at page 314 he said "Although there is no ranking of the criteria to be found in the statute, there is as it were a magnetism that draws the individual case to attach to one, two, or several factors as having decisive

---

[226] Ibid, at paragraph 89.
[227] See Mental Incapacitated Adults and Decision-Making: A New Jurisdiction, Law Com No 128 (HMSO, 1993), 2.4.
[228] Government Response to the Joint Scrutiny Committee's Report on the Draft Mental Incapacity Bill (February 2004) Cm 6121. See further in this regard also Alex Ruck Keene and Cressida Auckland, 'More Presumptions, Please: Wishes, Feelings and Best Interests Decision-Making' Elder Law Journal, Jordan Publishing [2015] Eld LJ 293.
[229] *Re M, ITW v Z & Ors* [2009] EWHC 2525 (Fam), [2009] COPLR Con Vol 828, at [32].
[230] *Crossley v Crossley* [2007] EWCA Civ 1491, [2008] 1 FLR 1467.
[231] [1998] 2 FLR 310 (affirmed, [2000] 2 FLR 981).

influence on its determination." Now that was said in the context of section 25 of the Matrimonial Causes Act 1973 but the principle, as it seems to me, is of more general application.'

2.129 However, and as discussed further in this regard at **2.148–2.149**, the case-law does not all speak with one voice as regards the status of P's wishes and feelings, and it may well also be that MCA 2005, s 4 is, itself, amended in due course to reflect the challenge of the CRPD. It should also be noted that while 'the right to private and family life' confirmed by ECHR Article 8 will always be a relevant factor in determining a person's best interests, it should not be 'the starting point' or given priority over other relevant factors, not least because 'there may well be a conflict between the incapacitated person's right to family life and that person's right to private life'.[232]

Principle of equal consideration

2.130 Similar to the 'equal consideration' requirement imposed as an amendment to the definition of people who lack capacity,[233] MCA 2005, s 4(1) begins with a clear statement that a determination of someone's best interests must not be based merely on the person's age or appearance, or any condition or aspect of his or her behaviour which might lead others to make unjustified assumptions about the person's best interests. As in MCA 2005, s 2(3), the reference here to 'condition' covers a range of factors, including both mental or physical disabilities and age-related illness as well as temporary conditions, such as drunkenness. 'Appearance' is also deliberately broad, covering all aspects of physical appearance, visible medical problems or disfiguring scars, disabilities, skin colour, religious dress and so on. 'Behaviour' relates to ways of behaving that might seem unusual or odd to others, such as failing to make eye contact or laughing inappropriately.

2.131 This is intended to ensure that people with impaired capacity are treated no less favourably than people with capacity. Thus, decisions about best interests must not be based on any preconceived ideas or negative assumptions, for example, about the value or quality of life experienced by older people or people with mental or physical disabilities who now lack capacity to make decisions for themselves.

All relevant circumstances

2.132 A determination of a person's best interests involves identifying those issues most relevant to the individual who lacks capacity in the context of the decision in question. The statutory checklist sets out the minimum necessary considerations but all other matters relevant in the particular situation must also be taken into account. MCA 2005, s 4(2) therefore

---

[232] *K v LBX & Ors* [2012] EWCA Civ 79, [2012] COPLR 411 at paragraph 30.
[233] See **2.62–2.64** above.

requires the person making the determination to consider 'all the relevant circumstances' as well as following the steps set out in the checklist. In *Re M, ITW v Z,* Munby J (as he then was) gave the following example:[234]

> '... the use of the words "engaged in caring" in section 4(7)(b), which would seem to connote only someone who is currently caring and to exclude someone whose caring has come to an end, does not mean that the views of a past carer are irrelevant. The effect of section 4(7)(b) may be to limit the decision-maker's duty to consult to current carers, but the views of a past carer if known are nonetheless part of the circumstances which have to be taken into account under section 4(2).'

2.133 It is recognised that the person making the determination may not be in a position to make exhaustive inquiries to investigate every issue which may have some relevance to the incapacitated person or the decision in question. Therefore relevant circumstances are defined in MCA 2005 as those:[235]

(a) of which the person making the determination is aware; and
(b) which it would be reasonable to regard as relevant.

For example, in decisions about the living arrangements of a person who lacks capacity to decide where to live, the courts have confirmed that 'the right to private and family life' under ECHR Article 8 will always be a relevant factor in determining the person's best interests.[236]

Regaining capacity

2.134 Following further consultation on the checklist suggested by the Law Commission for the determination of best interests, the Government proposed an additional factor – whether the person is likely to regain capacity.[237] One of MCA 2005's key principles is that before a person is found to be incapable of making a decision, all practicable steps must be taken to help the person make that decision.[238]

2.135 In keeping with this approach, when looking at best interests, it is important to consider whether the individual concerned is likely to have capacity to make that particular decision in the future and, if so, when that is likely to be.[239] It may be possible to put off the decision until the person can make it him or herself. This delay may allow further time for additional steps to be taken to restore the person's capacity or to provide support and assistance which would enable the person to make the decision.

---

[234] *Re M, ITW v Z & Ors* [2009] EWHC 2525 (Fam), [2009] COPLR Con Vol 828, at [36].
[235] MCA 2005, s 4(11).
[236] *LB Hillingdon v Neary & Ors* [2011] EWHC 1377, [2011] COPLR Con Vol 632, at [24]; *FP v GM and A Health Board* [2011] EWHC 2778 (COP), at [20]; *K v LBX & Ors* [2012] EWCA Civ 79, [2012] COPLR 411, at [52] per Black LJ.
[237] Lord Chancellor's Department *Making Decisions*, Cm 4465 (TSO, 1999), at paragraph 1.12.
[238] MCA 2005, s 1(3). See **2.32–2.38** above.
[239] MCA 2005, s 4(3).

2.136 The Code of Practice suggests some factors which may indicate that a person may regain capacity:[240]

- '• the cause of the lack of capacity can be treated, either by medication or some other form of treatment or therapy;
- • the lack of capacity is likely to decrease in time (for example, where it is caused by the effects of medication or alcohol, or following a sudden shock);
- • a person with learning disabilities may learn new skills or be subject to new experiences which increase their understanding and ability to make certain decisions;
- • the person may have a condition which causes capacity to come and go (such as some forms of mental illness) so it may be possible to arrange for the decision to be made during a time when they do have capacity;
- • a person previously unable to communicate may learn a new form of communication.'

Permitting and encouraging participation

2.137 MCA 2005, s 4(4) requires that, even where a person does not have capacity to make an effective decision, he or she should be both permitted and encouraged to participate, or to improve his or her ability to participate as fully as possible, in the decision-making process or in relation to any act done for him or her. It will always be important to consult the person on the particular act or decision to be made and to try to seek their views, not only to encourage the development of decision-making skills, but also as an important contribution in determining best interests. The practicable steps to enable decision-making will also be relevant here.[241] The importance of involving the person in the decision-making process has been reinforced by the Court of Protection (*Re S and S (Protected Persons); C v V*.[242] In *Wye Valley NHS Trust v Mr B*,[243] a case concerned with whether a man lacking the material decision-making capacity should have a life-saving medical procedure imposed upon him against his strongly expressed wishes, Peter Jackson J emphasised that the principle applies equally when the judge is to be the decision-maker:

> Lastly, I refer to the principle at s 4(4) that so far as is reasonably practicable, the person must be permitted and encouraged to participate as fully as possible in any decision affecting him. In this case, given the momentous consequences of the decision either way, I did not feel able to reach a conclusion without meeting Mr B myself. There were two excellent recent reports of discussions with him, but there is no substitute for a face-to-face meeting where the patient would like it to happen. The advantages can be considerable, and proved so in this case. In the first place, I obtained a deeper understanding of Mr B's personality and view of the world, supplementing and illuminating the earlier reports. Secondly, Mr B seemed glad to have the opportunity to get his point of view across. To whatever small degree, the meeting may have helped him to understand something of the process and to make sense of whatever decision was then made. Thirdly, the nurses were pleased that Mr B was going to have the fullest opportunity to get his point across. A case like

---

[240] Mental Capacity Act 2005: Code of Practice, at paragraph 5.28.
[241] See **2.33–2.38** above.
[242] [2008] COPLR Con Vol 1074, at [54]–[55].
[243] [2015] EWCOP 60, [2015] COPLR forthcoming, the extract being from [18].

this is difficult for the nursing staff in particular and I hope that the fact that Mr B has been as fully involved as possible will make it easier for them to care for him at what will undoubtedly be a difficult time.

It is strongly suggested that the approach adopted by Peter Jackson J is one that can and should be adopted more generally by judges determining other cases with significant consequences for the person concerned.

Life-sustaining treatment

2.138 A specific best interests factor relates to decisions concerning the provision (or withdrawal) of life-sustaining treatment, which is defined as treatment which a person providing health care regards as necessary to sustain life, usually the life of a person lacking capacity to consent to that treatment.[244] MCA 2005, s 4(5) clarifies that in determining whether the treatment is in the best interests of someone who lacks capacity to consent to it, the person making the determination must not be motivated by a desire to bring about the individual's death.

2.139 A great deal of the debate in both Houses of Parliament concerned life and death decisions affecting people who lack capacity to make those decisions for themselves. In order to provide clarity and reassurance on these very difficult issues, the Government agreed to a number of amendments introducing specific statements in the legislation. In particular, MCA 2005, s 62 confirms that the Act does not have the effect of authorising or permitting unlawful killing (including euthanasia) or assisted suicide. Secondly, in relation to decisions about whether the provision or continuance of life-sustaining treatment would be in a person's best interests, MCA 2005, s 4(5) clarifies that the decision-maker must not be motivated by a desire to bring about the person's death.

2.140 This particular factor was introduced as an amendment in the House of Lords after an undertaking was given in correspondence between the Lord Chancellor and the Roman Catholic Archbishop of Cardiff, Peter Smith, that MCA 2005 would make this point absolutely clear. Commenting on a situation where no advance decision has been made about whether treatment should be continued or refused, the Lord Chancellor said:[245]

> 'The decision about whether to continue to give life-sustaining treatment will then fall to be taken by the doctor, acting with an attorney who has relevant powers ... In some cases a decision ... will still be taken by the court. The Bill preserves the jurisdiction exercised in the Tony Bland case and restates the principles applied in that case. These are very difficult decisions, even for a court. In making them the decision-maker must act in the best interests of the patient. Above all, he must make an objective assessment. The decision cannot simply be the personal value

---

[244] MCA 2005, s 4(10). In parliamentary debate, it was also clarified that 'in the case of a pregnant woman we want to ensure that the life of the baby, not only the life of the mother, must be considered': *Hansard*, HL Deb, vol 668, ser 5, col 1184 (25 January 2005). However, an unborn child does not have an independent set of interests to be weighed against the mother's best interests (*St George's Healthcare NHS Trust v S* [1998] 2 FLR 728).

[245] *Hansard*, HL Deb, vol 668, ser 5, cols 14–15 (10 January 2005).

judgement of the decision-maker – the decision-maker cannot say "If I were in the patient's position, I would want to die" – nor can it be motivated by the desire to bring about the death of the patient.'

2.141 Any decision about life-sustaining treatment for a person lacking capacity will take as its starting point the assumption that it is in the person's best interests for life to continue. This was confirmed by the Court of Protection in *W v M*, where Baker J held:[246]

> 'The factor which does carry substantial weight, in my judgment, is the preservation of life. Although not an absolute rule, the law regards the preservation of life as a fundamental principle. As another judge has said: "there is a very strong presumption in favour of taking all steps which will prolong life and, save in exceptional circumstances, or where the person is dying, the best interests of the patient will normally require such steps to be taken".'

However, there will be some cases, for example, in the final stages of terminal illness or for some patients in a vegetative state,[247] where treatment is futile, overly burdensome or intolerable for the patient or where there is no prospect of recovery, where it may be in the best interests of the patient to withdraw or withhold treatment or to give palliative care that might incidentally shorten life.[248] All the factors in the best interests checklist must be considered, but the person determining best interests must not be motivated in any way by the desire to bring about the person's death.[249]

---

[246] *W v M & Ors* [2011] EWHC 2443 (Fam), [2012] COPLR 222, at [7]. The strong presumption in favour of preserving life can 'tip the balance' despite the person's known wishes to die: *A Local Authority v E* [2012] EWHC 1639 (COP), [2012] COPLR 441 at paragraph 140. See, however, the decision in *United Lincolnshire Hospitals NHS Trust v N* [2014] EWCOP 16, [2014] COPLR 660 for a different approach where the known wishes of a patient in an MCS were given significant weight in declaring that it was not in her best interests for PEG feeding to be re-introduced where (whether by reflex or otherwise) she consistently pulled out her feeding tube.

[247] It has been confirmed that the court also has jurisdiction to hear applications for the withdrawal of artificial nutrition and hydration (ANH) from a patient in a minimally conscious state: *W v M & Ors*, ibid. In his judgment, Baker J made some observations (at paragraphs 256–261), which have been approved by the President of the Court of Protection, designed to assist in future applications for the withdrawal of ANH from a person in a vegetative state or minimally conscious state.

[248] Mental Capacity Act 2005: Code of Practice, paragraphs 5.31–5.33. See for example *Re C (Withdrawal of Treatment: Vegetative State)* [2010] EWHC 3448 (COP), [2010] COPLR Con Vol 257. See also Chapter 6 for further details concerning best interests in relation to the provision or withdrawal of life-sustaining treatment, including discussion of the Supreme Court's decision in *Aintree University NHS Hospitals Trust v James* [2013] UKSC 67, [2013] COPLR 492.

[249] In *Aintree University NHS Hospitals Trust v James* [2013] UKSC 67, [2013] COPLR 492, the Supreme Court held that 'decision-makers must look at [the patient's] welfare in the widest sense, not just medical but social and psychological' and then set out the various factors that must be considered (at [39]). The British Medical Association has published specific guidance on the provision or withdrawal of life-sustaining treatment (*Withholding and withdrawing life-prolonging medical treatment: Guidance for decision making*, BMA, 3rd edn, 2007). The General Medical Council has also issued guidance for doctors (*Treatment and care towards the end of life: good practice in decision making*, GMC, 2010).

The person's wishes and feelings, beliefs and values

2.142 A particularly important element of the best interests checklist is the consideration, so far as these can be ascertained, of:

'(a) the person's past and present wishes and feelings (and in particular, any relevant written statements made by him when he had capacity),
(b) the beliefs and values that would be likely to influence his decision if he had capacity, and
(c) the other factors that he would be likely to consider if he were able to do so.'

This places the focus firmly on the person lacking capacity, taking into account the issues most important to him or her and what he or she would have wanted to achieve and in the words of the Supreme Court in *Aintree University Hospitals NHS Foundation Trust v James*[250] requiring the decision-maker: 'to consider matters from the patient's point of view'. It also reflects the need to make every effort to find out whether the person has expressed any relevant views in the past, whether verbally, in writing or through behaviour or habits, as well as trying to seek his or her current views.

2.143 The reference to written statements was included as a Government amendment in the House of Lords in response to lobbying by the Making Decisions Alliance and other stakeholder organisations. Those organisations had requested that advance statements, particularly those expressing wishes about medical treatment, should be given some form of statutory recognition and should specifically be taken into account in determining a person's best interests. The Minister for Constitutional Affairs, Baroness Ashton, confirmed:[251]

'... the purpose of this amendment is to clarify that if someone with capacity has written down their wishes and feelings in respect of a matter, including positive preferences, those must be explicitly taken into account in a best interests determination.

Patients do not have a right to demand and receive treatment, so advance requests cannot have the same legal effect as advance decisions to refuse treatment. However, the amendment makes clear that preferences about any aspect of a person's life, including treatment, should be respected and taken into account ... The more specific and well thought out the statement, the more likely it will be persuasive in determining best interests.'

An example of such a case is *PS v LP*,[252] concerning whether LP should have contact with her husband and family whom she had left to live with her lover, shortly before suffering a cerebral aneurism which robbed her of capacity to make her own decision. HHJ Cardinal considered that LP's clear expression of her wishes not to have any contact with her family, which she had set out in a hand-written will and a signed 'letter of wishes', was a

---

[250] [2013] UKSC 67, [2013] COPLR 492, at [45].
[251] *Hansard*, HL Deb, vol 670, ser 5, cols 1441–1442 (17 March 2005).
[252] *PS v LP* [2013] EWHC 1106 (COP). See also *RGB v Cwm Taf Health Board* [2013] EWHC B23 (COP), [2014] COPLR 83 (advance statement by wife as to contact with her estranged husband determinative of question of whether it was in her best interests for them to have contact in a care facility).

magnetic factor in the case. After weighing all the relevant matters, he concluded that it was not in the best interests of LP to see her family unless there was a change in LP's situation at some point in the future.

2.144 The Draft Mental Incapacity Bill published in 2003 made no mention of the person's 'beliefs and values' but this was added to the Bill in response to a recommendation of the Joint Committee:[253]

'The Medical Ethics Alliance suggested to us that the factor involving the need to consider the incapacitated person's "past and present wishes and feelings" should also contain reference to that person's values. Others suggested that specific reference should be made to social, psychological, cultural, spiritual and religious issues. It is anticipated that the need to consider a wide range of issues, in particular religious and cultural concerns, will be spelt out in the Code of Practice. We seek reassurance that the form of words used in the Bill will require a person's values to be given due weight.'

2.145 The reference to factors the person 'would be likely to consider' if able to do so provides a '"substituted judgment' element of the best interests checklist, as previously reflected in case-law in relation to the powers exercised by the previous Court of Protection to make a statutory will, where:[254]

'... subject to all due allowances ... the court must seek to make the will which the actual patient, acting reasonably, would have made if notionally restored to full mental capacity, memory and foresight.'

2.146 MCA 2005, s 4(6)(c) extends this notion as a factor to consider for all decisions or actions, whether or not the person concerned ever had capacity in relation to the matter in question. Prior to implementation of MCA 2005, the courts had held that the possible wider benefits to a person lacking capacity, arising for example from emotional support from close relationships, are important factors which the person would be likely to consider if able to do so, and are therefore relevant in determining the person's own best interests.[255] The Court of Protection has since upheld the significance of the 'emotional dimension' of the best interests analysis:[256]

'There is of course more to human life than [physical care needs], there is fundamentally the emotional dimension, the importance of relationships, the importance of a sense of belonging in the place in which you are living, and the sense of belonging to a specific group in respect of which you are a particularly important person.'

Or in the words of Munby J (as he then was) 'What good is it making someone safer if it merely makes them miserable?'[257] For a further, very powerful, example of the application of this principle, see *Re M (Best Interests: Deprivation of Liberty)*.[258]

---

[253] Report of the Joint Committee on the Draft Mental Incapacity Bill, Vol 1, HL 189-1, HC 1083-1 (TSO, 2003), at para 90.
[254] *Re D (J)* [1982] Ch 237, at [43].
[255] See eg *Re Y (Mental Incapacity: Bone marrow transplant)* [1996] 2 FLR 787; *Re A (Male Sterilisation)* [2000] 1 FLR 549.
[256] *FP v GM and A Health Board* [2011] EWHC 2778 (COP), at [21].
[257] *X v MM & KM* [2007] EWHC 2003 (Fam), [2009] 1 FLR 443, at [120].
[258] [2013] EWHC 3456 (COP), [2014] COPLR 35.

2.147 The Code of Practice suggests that such emotional factors might include altruistic motives, such as 'the effect of the decision on other people, obligations to dependants or the duties of a responsible citizen'.[259] In the case of *Re G (TJ)*, Morgan J considered whether it was in Mrs G's best interests to continue to pay a regular sum for the maintenance of her adult daughter. In considering the difference between substituted judgment and best interests, he reviewed the relevant cases (summarised below) and reached the following conclusions:[260]

> 'The best interests test involves identifying a number of relevant factors. The actual wishes of P can be a relevant factor: section 4(6)(a) says so. The beliefs and values which would be likely to influence P's decision, if he had capacity to make the relevant decision, are a relevant factor: section 4(6)(b) says so. The other factors which P would be likely to consider, if he had the capacity to consider them, are a relevant factor: section 4(6)(c) says so. Accordingly, the balance sheet of factors which P would draw up, if he had capacity to make the decision, is a relevant factor for the court's decision. Further, in most cases the court will be able to determine what decision it is likely that P would have made, if he had capacity. In such a case, in my judgment, P's balance sheet of factors and P's likely decision can be taken into account by the court. This involves an element of substituted judgment being taken into account, together with anything else which is relevant. However, it is absolutely clear that the ultimate test for the court is the test of best interests and not the test of substituted judgment. Nonetheless, the substituted judgment can be relevant and is not excluded from consideration. As Hoffmann LJ said in the *Bland* case, the substituted judgment can be subsumed within the concept of best interests. That appeared to be the view of the Law Commission also.
>
> Further, the word 'interest' in the best interests test does not confine the court to considering the self interest of P. The actual wishes of P, which are altruistic and not in any way, directly or indirectly self-interested, can be a relevant factor. Further, the wishes which P would have formed, if P had capacity, which may be altruistic wishes, can be a relevant factor. It is not necessary to establish that P would have been aware of the fact that P's wishes were carried into effect. Respect for P's wishes, actual or putative, can be a relevant factor even where P has no awareness of, and no reaction to, the fact that such wishes are being respected.'

The weight to be given to P's wishes and feelings

2.148 It is clear that a conclusion that a person lacks decision-making capacity is not an 'off-switch' for his rights and freedoms. In *Wye Valley NHS Trust v Mr B*,[261] a submission was made that the views expressed by a person lacking capacity were in principle entitled to less weight than those of a person with capacity. Peter Jackson J roundly rejected this submission, noting that it was:

> 'true only to the limited extent that the views of a capacitous person are by definition decisive in relation to any treatment that is being offered to him so that the question of best interests does not arise. However, once incapacity is established so that a best

---

[259] Mental Capacity Act 2005: Code of Practice, at paragraph 5.47.
[260] *Re G (TJ)* [2010] EWHC 3005 (COP), [2010] COPLR Con Vol 403, at [55]–[56]. *Re X, Y and Z* [2014] EWHC 87 (COP), [2014] COPLR 364 (in P's best interests for funds awarded her in compensation for personal injuries to be used to provide care to her children).
[261] *Wye Valley NHS Trust v Mr B* [2015] EWCOP 60, [2015] COPLR forthcoming at [10]–[11]. It is somewhat astonishing that such a submission could have been advanced in 2015, some eight years after the coming into force of the Act.

interests decision must be made, there is no theoretical limit to the weight or lack of weight that should be given to the person's wishes and feelings, beliefs and values. In some cases, the conclusion will be that little weight or no weight can be given; in others, very significant weight will be due.

11. This is not an academic issue, but a necessary protection for the rights of people with disabilities. As the Act and the European Convention make clear, a conclusion that a person lacks decision-making capacity is not an 'off-switch' for his rights and freedoms. To state the obvious, the wishes and feelings, beliefs and values of people with a mental disability are as important to them as they are to anyone else, and may even be more important. It would therefore be wrong in principle to apply any automatic discount to their point of view.'

If it is clear that, as a matter of principle, an automatic discount should not be applied to the wishes, feelings, beliefs and values of those lacking the material decision-making capacity, there is still something of a debate as to whether to give particular weight to P's wishes and feelings in the application of MCA 2005, s 4[262] and the case-law reveals something of a split. At one end of the spectrum is the decision of Munby J (as he then was) in *Re M, ITW v Z and others,* a statutory will application in a case in which an elderly woman had been the victim of financial abuse by a neighbour. When considering the weight and importance to be attached to the person's (P's) wishes and feelings, he made the following observations:[263]

'i) First, P's wishes and feelings will always be a significant factor to which the court must pay close regard: see *Re MM; Local Authority X v MM (by the Official Solicitor) and KM* [2007] EWHC 2003 (Fam), [2009] 1 FLR 443, at paras [121]–[124].

ii) Secondly, the weight to be attached to P's wishes and feelings will always be case-specific and fact-specific. In some cases, in some situations, they may carry much, even, on occasions, preponderant, weight. In other cases, in other situations, and even where the circumstances may have some superficial similarity, they may carry very little weight. One cannot, as it were, attribute any particular *a priori* weight or importance to P's wishes and feelings; it all depends, it must depend, upon the individual circumstances of the particular case. And even if one is dealing with a particular individual, the weight to be attached to their wishes and feelings must depend upon the particular context; in relation to one topic P's wishes and feelings may carry great weight whilst at the same time carrying much less weight in relation to another topic. Just as the test of incapacity under the 2005 Act is, as under the common law, 'issue specific', so in a similar way the weight to be attached to P's wishes and feelings will likewise be issue specific.

iii) Thirdly, in considering the weight and importance to be attached to P's wishes and feelings the court must of course, and as required by section 4(2) of the 2005 Act, have regard to *all* the relevant circumstances. In this context the relevant circumstances will include, though I emphasise that they are by no means limited to, such matters as:

(a)

---

[262] See for a discussion of some of these issues Alex Ruck Keene and Cressida Auckland, 'More Presumptions, Please: Wishes, Feelings and Best Interests Decision-Making' *Elder Law Journal,* Jordan Publishing, [2015] Eld LJ 293. The relevant paragraphs (5.37–5.48) in the Mental Capacity Act 2005 Code of Practice remain of importance but need to be read in light of the developing body of case-law.

[263] *Re M, ITW v Z & Ors* [2009] EWHC 2525 (Fam), [2009] COPLR Con Vol 828, at [35]. See also *PS v LP* [2013] EWHC 1106 (COP).

the degree of P's incapacity, for the nearer to the borderline the more weight must in principle be attached to P's wishes and feelings: *Re MM; Local Authority X v MM (by the Official Solicitor) and KM*,[264] at para [124];

(b) the strength and consistency of the views being expressed by P;

(c) the possible impact on P of knowledge that her wishes and feelings are not being given effect to: see again *Re MM; Local Authority X v MM (by the Official Solicitor) and KM*,[265] at para [124];

(d) the extent to which P's wishes and feelings are, or are not, rational, sensible, responsible and pragmatically capable of sensible implementation in the particular circumstances; and

(e) crucially, the extent to which P's wishes and feelings, if given effect to, can properly be accommodated within the court's overall assessment of what is in her best interests.'

2.149 To contrary effect could be seen to be the judgment in *Re S and S (Protected Persons); C v V* when HHJ Hazel Marshall QC held that there is a presumption in favour of implementing the person's wishes unless they are irrational, impractical, or irresponsible (with reference to resources), or there is a sufficiently countervailing consideration.[266] Further, it is entirely possible to read the decision of the Supreme Court, given by Lady Hale in *Aintree University Hospitals NHS Foundation Trust v James*[267] as suggesting that the individual's wishes and feelings (where it is possible reliably to identify them) as having an especial status.[268] It is perhaps not surprising that Lady Hale expressed this view, given her previous role at the Law Commission in developing what ultimately became the Mental Capacity Act: as noted at **2.128**, the Law Commission had sought to ensure that there was an element of substituted judgment within the overall best interests test, an element that can only be achieved where proper steps are taken to obtain and respect the person's wishes and feelings. Senior Judge Lush has also noted, in placing weight upon the views expressed by P in the form of a will, that '[a]lthough it has been said that there is no hierarchy of factors in the checklist in section 4 of the Mental Capacity Act, I attach weight to EO's views, because section 4(6)(a) refers "in particular"' (my emphasis) to "any relevant written statement made by him when he had capacity."'[269] Further, as discussed at **1.218–1.230**, it would seem that construing the Act so as to allow particular weight to be placed upon the

---

[264] [2007] EWHC 2003 (Fam), [2009] 1 FLR 443.
[265] Ibid.
[266] [2008] EWHC B16 (Fam), [2008] COPLR Con Vol 1074 at paragraphs 57–58, 87. In the later case of *Re P*, in the context of a statutory will application, Lewison J complimented HHJ Marshall QC for considering the MCA 2005 'in a most impressive and sensitive judgment', the broad thrust of which he agreed with, but he thought she 'may have slightly overstated the importance to be given to P's wishes' and he preferred 'not to speak in terms of presumptions': *Re P* [2009] EWHC 163 (Ch), [2009] COPLR Con Vol 906, at [40] and [41]. Senior Judge Lush has recently referred to HHJ Marshall's approach in approving terms in – unusually – dismissing the application of the Public Guardian to revoke and cancel the registration of an EPA, in part on the basis of the wishes and feelings expressed by the adult in question: *Re DT* [2015] EWCOP 10 at [44]–[46].
[267] *Aintree University Hospitals NHS Foundation Trust v James* [2013] UKSC 67, [2013] COPLR 492.
[268] See paragraph 45 in particular.
[269] *Re BM; JB v AG* [2014] EWCOP B20, at [58].

individual's wishes and feelings is likely to be necessary as a step towards achieving compliance with the CRPD (as well as the right to autonomy enshrined in Article 8 of the ECHR[270]). Responding, in particular, to the challenge of the CRPD, but also to evidence that the wishes and feelings of the person lacking capacity are not routinely prioritised in best interests decision-making, and instead 'clinical judgments or resource-led decision-making predominate,'[271] the Law Commission has provisionally proposed that MCA 2005, s 4 should be amended to establish that decision-makers should begin with the assumption that the person's past and present wishes and feelings should be determinative of the best interests decision.[272] Whether or not the MCA is amended in precisely this fashion,[273] it is suggested that both practical experience and the shifts in the domestic and international legal landscape since MCA was enacted mean that an amendment along these lines is very likely to be necessary in due course.

The views of other people

2.150 For the first time, MCA 2005 ensured that carers, family members and other relevant people are consulted on decisions affecting the person lacking capacity to make those decisions for themselves. People who must be consulted include anyone previously named by the person who now lacks capacity as someone they would wish to be consulted, carers and anyone interested in the person's welfare, donees and deputies.[274] Any person who is determining the best interests of someone lacking capacity is required to take into account the views of these key people, but only if it is 'practicable and appropriate' to consult them. Further, the Senior Judge of the Court of Protection has held that where consultation is likely to be unduly onerous, contentious, futile or serve no useful purpose, it is not 'practicable or appropriate'.[275]

---

[270] A right that a person does not lose upon losing decision-making capacity: *Re E* [2012] EWHC 1639 (COP), [2012] COPLR 441 at paragraph 124.

[271] Law Commission Consultation Paper No 222 *Mental Capacity and Deprivation of Liberty: A Consultation Paper* (TSO, 2015) at paragraph 12.36, citing the House of Lords Post-Legislative Scrutiny Select Committee (HL 139) at paragraph 90; the Law Commission also cites the Department of Health Green Paper on the care and treatment provided to those with learning disabilities, autism and mental health: No Voice Unheard, No Right Ignored – A Consultation for People with Learning Disabilities, Autism and Mental Health Conditions (2015) Cm 9007, pp 13, 33–34.

[272] Law Commission Consultation Paper No 222 *Mental Capacity and Deprivation of Liberty: A Consultation Paper* (TSO, 2015).

[273] Peter Jackson J cast 'respectful' doubt upon this suggestion in *Wye Valley NHS Trust v Mr B* [2015] EWCOP 60, [2015] COPLR forthcoming at [17], on the basis that it would not lead to greater certainty but a debate about whether there was good reason to depart from the assumption. However, it is equally respectfully submitted that his conclusion that all is required to protect the rights of the individuals in question is the proper application of MCA 2005 as it stands is one that is questionable in light of the matters set out here and in the Law Commission's Consultation Paper.

[274] MCA 2005, s 4(7).

[275] *Re A; D v B* [2009] COPLR Con Vol 1.

2.151 The Code of Practice suggests:[276]

> 'Decision-makers must show they have thought carefully about who to speak to. If it is practical and appropriate to speak to the above people, they must do so and must take their views into account. They must be able to explain why they did not speak to a particular person – it is good practice to have a clear record of their reasons.'

Consultation with all relevant people must be 'undertaken at a time when proposals are still formative, with sufficient reasons for proposals ... and adequate time to allow intelligent consideration and response to be given'[277] and taken into account in making the decision.

2.152 The consultation is limited to two matters – first, what those people consider to be in the person's best interests on the matter in question and, secondly, whether they can provide any information on the wishes, feelings, values or beliefs of the person lacking capacity. The latter is arguably of more importance that the former.[278] If, prior to losing capacity, the person concerned has nominated someone whom he or she would like to be consulted, the named person is more likely to have that information. People who are close to the person lacking capacity, such as relatives, partners and other carers, may also be able to assist with communication or interpret signs which give an indication of the person's present wishes and feelings. In *Re M, ITW v Z* Munby J suggested that in determining best interests, it may be appropriate to consult with former carers and to take into account oral statements made to them by the person who lacks capacity.[279]

2.153 The requirement for consultation must be balanced against the right to confidentiality of the person lacking capacity. That right should be protected so that consultation only takes place where relevant and with people whom it is appropriate to consult. For example, it is unlikely to be appropriate to consult anyone whom the person had previously indicated should not be involved. However, there may be occasions where it is in the person's best interests for specific information to be disclosed, or where the public interest in disclosure may override the person's private interest in maintaining confidentiality.[280] If professionals are involved in the determination of best interests, they will also need to comply with their own duties of confidentiality in accordance with their professional codes of conduct.

---

[276] Mental Capacity Act 2005: Code of Practice, at paragraph 5.51.
[277] *R (W) v LB Croydon* [2011] EWHC 696 (Admin), at [39].
[278] See in this regard *Aintree University Hospitals NHS Foundation Trust v James* [2013] UKSC 67, [2013] COPLR 492, at 39 per Lady Hale: the decision-maker 'must consult others who are looking after him or interested in his welfare, in particular for their view of what his attitude would be.' In *An NHS Trust v DE & Ors* [2013] EWHC 2562 (Fam), [2013] COPLR 531, concerning whether it was in the best interests of an incapacitated learning disabled young man to have a vasectomy as a method of contraception, while it was clearly appropriate to consult DE's parents, it appears that their own feelings of distress caused by his unexpected fathering of a child and their views of the disruption that a further pregnancy would cause, were given undue weight.
[279] *Re M, ITW v Z and Ors* [2009] EWHC 2525 (Fam), [2009] COPLR Con Vol 828, at [36].
[280] *R (S) v Plymouth City Council and C* [2002] EWCA Civ 388, [2002] 1 FLR 1177, at [49]. See **2.112–2.114**.

Duty to apply the best interests principle

2.154 The principle set out in MCA 2005, s 1(5) confirms that any act done, or any decision made, on behalf of a person lacking capacity must be done in his or her best interests. MCA 2005, s 4(8) confirms that the best interests principle, and the duties to be carried out in determining best interests, also apply in certain circumstances where the person concerned may not in fact lack capacity in relation to the act or decision in question. This applies in relation to any powers which:

(1) are exercisable under a lasting power of attorney;
(2) are exercisable by a person under MCA 2005 where he or she 'reasonably believes' that another person lacks capacity.

Reasonable belief

2.155 The second situation reflects the position that in most day-to-day decisions or actions involved in caring for someone, it will not be appropriate or necessary to carry out a formal assessment of the person's capacity. Rather, it is sufficient for there to be a 'reasonable belief' that the person lacks capacity to make the decision or consent to the action in question.[281]

2.156 Similarly, MCA 2005, s 4(9) confirms that, in cases where the Court is not involved, carers (both professionals and family members) and others who are acting informally can only be expected to have reasonable grounds for believing that what they are doing or deciding is in the best interests of the person concerned, but they must still, so far as possible, apply the best interests checklist and therefore be able to point to objective reasons to justify why they hold that belief.[282]

2.157 MCA 2005, s 4(9) also applies to donees and deputies appointed to make welfare or financial decisions, as well as to those carrying out acts in connection with the care and treatment of a person lacking capacity. In deciding what is 'reasonable' in any particular case, higher expectations are likely to be placed on those appointed to act under formal powers and those acting in a professional capacity than on family members and friends who are caring for a person lacking capacity without any formal authority.

---

[281] See **2.87–2.90** above.
[282] In *Commissioner of Police for the Metropolis v ZH* [2013] EWCA Civ 69, [2013] COPLR 332, the Court of Appeal upheld the decision at first instance that the police had failed to provide objective evidence to demonstrate that the actions they had taken in forcibly removing ZH from a swimming pool were in ZH's best interests. See **2.177** below for further discussion on this case.

PART 3: GENERAL POWERS AND DUTIES

Acts in connection with care or treatment – background

The problem

2.158 Until MCA 2005 came into effect, legislation has been silent about what actions could lawfully be taken by carers in looking after the day-to-day personal or health care needs of people who lack capacity to consent to those actions. These actions may include helping individuals to wash, dress and attend to their personal hygiene, feeding them, taking them out for walks and leisure activities, taking them to the doctor or dentist or providing necessary treatment.

2.159 In consequence, doctors, dentists and other health care professionals were hesitant about carrying out examinations, treatment or nursing care on patients unable to consent to those medical procedures. In the absence of any clear statutory provision, it was left to the courts to establish the former common law 'principle of necessity', setting out the circumstances in which actions and decisions could lawfully be taken on behalf of adults who lack capacity.[283]

2.160 The courts confirmed that where the principle of necessity applied (ie that it was necessary to act in relation to the well-being of a person lacking capacity to consent), and the action taken was reasonable and in the person's best interests, that action which would otherwise amount to a civil wrong, or even a crime (eg of battery or assault) would in fact be lawful. The principle of necessity is *not* equivalent to having consent but may constitute a defence if an action is subsequently challenged.

2.161 Such actions might involve touching or interfering with the person's bodily integrity, or using or interfering with the person's property or possessions. In such cases, the lack of capacity of the people concerned means that they cannot give their informed consent and therefore the proposed actions, if they were to take place, could potentially be unlawful unless the principle of necessity applied.

The Law Commission proposal

2.162 The Law Commission acknowledged that within the new jurisdiction it proposed, there should remain scope for caring actions to take place, and for some informal decision-making 'without certifications, documentation or judicial determinations'.[284] However, the Commission recognised that the common law 'principle of necessity' was not widely understood and there was therefore a need to clarify the confused state of the law governing such actions:[285]

---

[283] *Re F (Mental Patient: Sterilisation)* [1989] 2 FLR 376, at [75].
[284] Law Com No 231, at para 4.1 (see **2.4**, footnote).
[285] Ibid, at paragraph 4.2.

'We suggested in our consultation papers that there was a strong case for clarifying in statute the circumstances in which decisions can be taken for people who lack capacity, but without anyone having to apply for formal authorisation. We did not envisage this as conferring any new power on anyone, but rather as a clarification of the uncertain "necessity" principle. Respondents gave an enthusiastic welcome to our provisional proposals. There was very broad agreement that a statutory provision would be invaluable in dispelling doubt and confusion and setting firm and appropriate limits to informal action.'

The general authority

2.163 The Law Commission proposed a new statutory authority, which it called the 'general authority to act reasonably', to codify in statute what had become practice under common law and to clarify the 'principle of necessity'. It was intended that the general authority would provide legal authorisation for acts connected with the personal welfare or health care of a person lacking capacity to consent if it is reasonable in the particular circumstances for the act to be done by the person who does it. The legal authorisation would apply to different people acting at different times, so long as it was appropriate for them to do the act in question and they were acting reasonably and in the best interests of the person lacking capacity.

The views of the Joint Committee

2.164 However, the clauses in the Draft Mental Incapacity Bill making provision for the 'general authority'[286] caused significant concerns and confusion to a number of witnesses giving evidence to the Joint Committee on the Bill:[287]

'A number of the concerns which have been brought to our attention seem to be premised on a misunderstanding of the general authority as it is set out in the draft Bill. The extent of the misunderstandings apparent in the evidence we have received suggests that the drafting of this provision is not sufficiently clear. Many interested parties appear to be under the erroneous impression that the general authority would be assumed by a single individual who would then take all decisions on behalf of an incapacitated individual. In fact the general authority is for the relevant person, in the context of a specific decision or action, at a particular point in time, so long as it is reasonable for that person to act. Others have suggested that the general authority may be used by carers to justify taking decisions for which they would otherwise need formal authorisation. In fact the general authority is not intended to convey any new powers on anyone but rather to clarify the uncertain principle of "necessity".

We have come to the conclusion that the term "general authority" itself has contributed to the misinterpretations apparent within the evidence we have received. The word "authority" implies an imposition of decision making upon an incapacitated individual rather than an enabling process designed to enact decisions taken in their best interests. This may have contributed to perceptions of the general authority as likely to promote "over-paternalistic attitudes" towards incapacitated

---

[286] Draft Mental Incapacity Bill, cls 6–7.
[287] *Report of the Joint Committee on the Draft Mental Incapacity Bill, Vol 1*, HL 189-1, HC 1083-1 (TSO, 2003), at para 109–110.

individuals. We are convinced that semantic issues are important in affecting public perceptions of the draft Bill as well as in determining legal interpretations of the provisions it contains.'

2.165 The Joint Committee recommended radical redrafting to clarify the legislative intent of the 'general authority' and the use of alternative terminology to avoid its misleading connotations. The Government's response was to recast the provisions to allow for a limitation of liability for people who need to act in connection with the care or treatment of a person lacking capacity to consent. Offering protection from liability is intended to enable caring actions to take place in the absence of consent, but also to make clear that anyone acting unreasonably, negligently or not in the person's best interests would forfeit that protection.

Acts in connection with care or treatment – the legislation

Protection from liability

2.166 MCA 2005, s 5 makes provision to allow carers (both informal carers, such as family members, and paid carers) and health and social care professionals to carry out certain acts in connection with the personal care, health care or treatment of a person lacking capacity to consent to those acts. These provisions are intended to give legal backing, in the form of protection from liability, for actions which are essential for the personal welfare or health of people lacking capacity to consent to having things done to or for them. Such actions can be performed as if the person concerned had capacity and had given consent.[288] There is no need to obtain any formal powers or authority to act.

2.167 In introducing the Bill into the House of Commons, the Under Secretary of State for Constitutional Affairs, David Lammy explained:[289]

> 'Clause 5, entitled "Acts in connection with care and treatment", is an important clarification of the law surrounding what someone can do to or for a person lacking mental capacity who is unable to give consent. The current law is based on the poorly understood and obscure "doctrine of necessity". Hon. Members will know of constituents who are worried and uncertain about what they are allowed to do, because they do not understand the law. For example, a nurse may want to restrain someone who is having an epileptic fit. Someone caring for an elderly patient at home may need to help them to use the toilet. Someone whose daughter suffers from bipolar disease may want to go to her house to cook for her and to help her to eat because she is in too much distress.
>
> It is not right that people in such situations should have to rely on what seems to them to be an outdated and obscure legal concept. Clause 5 explains what they can do. It provides that one is protected from liability when the person cannot consent, provided that one takes reasonable steps to establish whether that person lacks mental capacity in relation to the matter in question, that one reasonably believes that the person lacks capacity in relation to the matter, and that what one does is in the person's best interests.'

---

[288] MCA 2005, s 5(2).
[289] *Hansard*, HC Deb, vol 425, ser 6, col 29 (11 October 2004).

Section 5 acts

2.168 The types of acts which may be carried out with protection from liability under MCA 2005, s 5 (sometimes referred to as 'section 5 acts') are those carried out *in connection with the care or treatment* of a person who is believed to lack capacity in relation to the matter in question, at the time the act needs to be carried out. The Code of Practice provides examples (but not an exhaustive list) as follows:[290]

'Personal care

- helping with washing, dressing or personal hygiene
- helping with eating and drinking
- helping with communication
- helping with mobility (moving around)
- helping someone take part in education, social or leisure activities
- going into a person's home to drop off shopping or to see if they are alright
- doing the shopping or buying necessary goods with the person's money
- arranging household services (for example, arranging repairs or maintenance for gas and electricity supplies)
- providing services that help around the home (such as homecare or meals on wheels)
- undertaking actions related to community care services (for example, day care, residential accommodation or nursing care)
- helping someone to move home (including moving property and clearing the former home)

Healthcare and treatment

- carrying out diagnostic examinations and tests (to identify an illness, condition or other problem)
- providing professional medical, dental and similar treatment
- giving medication
- taking someone to hospital for assessment or treatment
- providing nursing care (whether in hospital or in the community)
- carrying out any other necessary medical procedures (for example, taking a blood sample) or therapies (for example, physiotherapy or chiropody)
- providing care in an emergency.'

As a general rule, a 'section 5 act' is one where consent (either explicit or implied) would normally be required from a person of full capacity for the particular act to be carried out. Only acts or arrangements involving minimum legal formality are covered, since more formal legal transactions (particularly those requiring written documentation) would require more than the person's 'consent'.

Serious acts relating to medical treatment or welfare

2.169 In a briefing on the Mental Capacity Bill, the Making Decisions Alliance expressed concern that the scope of MCA 2005, s 5 'remains unclear and is too wide'. It argued that the legislation should:[291]

---

[290] Mental Capacity Act 2005: Code of Practice, at paragraph 6.5.
[291] Making Decisions Alliance *Mental Capacity Bill: Briefing for 2nd Reading* (11 October 2004).

'... establish a clear hierarchy of safeguards which reflect the seriousness of the action taken and the consequences for that individual. The MDA recommends that some actions taken under section 5 require additional safeguards to counter against its inappropriate use. For example, we think it is important that a person has the support of an independent advocate when moving home which would involve a change of carer. Similarly, we think that there should be an independent second medical opinion, in relation to serious medical treatment.'

2.170 The Government recognised that some acts in connection with care or treatment may cause major life changes with significant consequences for the person concerned, particularly those involving a change of residence (eg into a care home or nursing home) or major decisions about serious medical treatment. The Code of Practice, therefore, gives detailed guidance aimed at ensuring that the decision in question is made in accordance with the principles of MCA 2005 and is in the person's best interests.[292] The best interests checklist must therefore be carefully applied and particular consideration must be given to whether there is any other choice that would be less restrictive of the person's rights and freedom of action (under MCA 2005, s 1(6)). The Act itself also imposes some limitations on the scope of MCA 2005, s 5, described below.[293]

2.171 If a proposed move to a hospital or care home would have the effect of depriving the person of their liberty, the protection afforded by section 5 will not be available.[294] Instead, authorisation for the deprivation of liberty will be required using the deprivation of liberty safeguards (DOLS) (see Chapter 7) or by order of the Court of Protection. In *Re A and C (Equality and Human Rights Commission Intervening)*, Munby LJ gave guidance to local authorities as to the exercise of their powers in respect of the welfare of adults lacking capacity to consent. He stressed that:[295]

'People in the situation of A and C, together with their carers, look to the State – to a local authority – for the support, the assistance and the provision of the services to which the law, giving effect to the underlying principles of the Welfare State, entitles them. They do not seek to be "controlled" by the State or by the local authority. And it is not for the State in the guise of a local authority to seek to exercise such control. The State, the local authority, is the servant of those in need of its support and assistance, not their master.'

He warned against the 'mindset' of some local authorities seeking to exercise control, citing examples of the removal of incapacitated adults from the care of their relatives into residential accommodation, without the sanction of the court and, therefore in some cases, without any legal authority. Further criticism of a local authority abusing its powers was given in *LB Hillingdon v Neary & Ors*,[296] in which Peter Jackson J set out some guidance on the responsibilities of public authorities and when matters should be referred to the court for a decision regarding residence. In *CC v*

---

[292] Mental Capacity Act 2005: Code of Practice, at paragraphs 6.7–6.19.
[293] See **2.178**ff.
[294] See **2.185–2.189** below and Chapter 7.
[295] [2010] EWHC 978 (Fam), [2010] COPLR Con Vol 10, at [52].
[296] [2011] EWHC 1377, [2011] COPLR Con Vol 632, at [33].

KK and STCC, Baker J reminded himself of the danger of the 'protection imperative' identified by Ryder J in *Oldham MBC v GW and PW,* whereby:[297]

'... professionals, including judges, may objectively conflate a capacity assessment with a best interests analysis and conclude that the person under review should attach greater weight to the physical security and comfort of a residential home and less importance to the emotional security and comfort that the person derives from being in their own home.'

The importance of ensuring that steps that give rise to a deprivation of liberty are not taken in the purported best interests of the individual without due consideration was emphasised by Baker J in *AJ (Deprivation of Liberty Safeguards) v A Local Authority,*[298] discussed further in Chapter 7.

2.172 In relation to serious medical treatment, the Code of Practice confirms that the previous case-law requirement to seek a declaration from the Court in cases where particularly serious forms of medical treatment are proposed, is unaffected by MCA 2005.[299] The Court of Protection Rules, supplemented by Practice Directions, make provision for the allocation of cases involving serious medical treatment; either the President of the Court of Protection or a judge of the High Court (sitting in the Court of Protection) must hear any application for withdrawal or withholding of life-sustaining treatment from patients in a vegetative or minimally conscious state, the proposed non-therapeutic sterilisation of a person lacking capacity or other cases involving an ethical dilemma in an untested area.[300] Other cases involving serious medical treatment, especially where there is any doubt as to where the person's best interests may lie, may well require a decision of the Court of Protection to put the lawfulness of the actions of the treating clinicians beyond doubt. These issues are discussed further in Chapter 6 (see in particular **6.30–6.36**).

2.173 An additional safeguard is provided where serious medical treatment or a change of residence is proposed for a person lacking capacity, but where the person concerned has no family or friends available to be consulted or to speak up on his or her behalf. In such cases, MCA 2005 makes provision for an independent mental capacity advocate (IMCA) to be appointed to support and represent the person.[301] In these and any other cases where there is a doubt or dispute about whether a particular section 5 act is in the person's best interests, and the matter cannot be resolved through negotiation or other means of dispute resolution, the Court of Protection has ultimate jurisdiction to resolve the matter.

---

[297] [2012] EWHC 2136 (COP), [2012] COPLR 627, at [65].
[298] [2015] EWCOP 5, [2015] COPLR 167.
[299] Mental Capacity Act 2005: Code of Practice, at paragraph 6.18. See also Chapter 6.
[300] Court of Protection Rules 2007, SI 2007/1744, r 86, supplemented by Practice Direction 9E *Applications relating to Serious Medical Treatment* and Practice Direction 12A *Court's Jurisdiction to be exercised by Certain Judges.*
[301] MCA 2005, ss 35–41. See Chapter 6.

Who can act in connection with care or treatment?

2.174 There is no intention that MCA 2005, s 5 applies to a single identifiable person involved in the care or treatment of a person lacking capacity, nor does it convey any powers on anyone to make substitute decisions or to give consent on behalf of the person lacking capacity. The intention is to allow carers, health and social care professionals to do whatever is necessary to safeguard and promote the welfare and health of individuals who lack capacity to consent, so long as it is appropriate for the particular carer or professional to take the action in question and the act is in the best interests of the incapacitated person. Some guidance on the limits of MCA 2005, s 5 was given by Baker J in *G v E*:[302]

> 'The Act and Code are ... constructed on the basis that the vast majority of decisions concerning incapacitated adults are taken informally and collaboratively by individuals or groups of people consulting and working together. It is emphatically not part of the scheme underpinning the Act that there should be one individual who as a matter of course is given a special legal status to make decisions about incapacitated persons. Experience has shown that working together is the best policy to ensure that incapacitated adults such as E receive the highest quality of care. This case is an example of what can go wrong when people do not work together. Where there is disagreement about the appropriate care and treatment, (which cannot be resolved by the methods suggested in Chapter 15 [of the Code]) or the issue is a matter of particular gravity or difficulty, the Act and Code provide that the issue should usually be determined by the court. The complexity and/or seriousness of such issues are likely to require a forensic process and formal adjudication by an experienced tribunal.'

2.175 Before doing anything, the person wishing to take action in connection with the care or treatment of another person must take 'reasonable steps' to establish whether the person concerned has capacity in relation to the matter in question.[303] This does not necessarily require a formal assessment of capacity, although professional practice may require this, for example, in respect of medical treatment. In any event, steps must be taken to look for objective reasons which would justify a reasonable belief of lack of capacity.[304] If it is found that the person has capacity, his or her consent to the action will be required to provide protection from liability.

2.176 Anyone proposing to carry out an act under MCA 2005, s 5 must also take account of the MCA 2005's key principles set out in s 1.[305] This includes starting with the presumption of capacity and taking all practicable steps to enable the person to express a view about the proposed action. If it is believed the person lacks capacity, the 'less restrictive alternative' principle requires consideration of whether the act is needed at all and if so, whether the purpose for which the act is needed can be achieved in a way less restrictive of the person's future choices or would allow him or her the most freedom.

---

[302] [2010] EWHC 2512 (COP), [2010] COPLR Con Vol 470, at [57].
[303] MCA 2005, s 5(1)(a).
[304] See **2.87–2.90** above.
[305] See **2.19–2.53** above.

In addition, the person wishing to act must 'reasonably believe' that what they are doing is in the best interests of the person lacking capacity.[306] Again, they must be able to point to objective reasons to justify that belief. They must be able to show that they have taken account of all relevant circumstances, including those set out in the best interests checklist.[307] If their judgment of best interests is challenged, they will be protected if they can show that it was reasonable in all the circumstances of that particular case for them to have arrived at that judgment. Where professionals are involved, their professional skills and levels of competence will be taken into account in determining what would be considered 'reasonable'.

2.177 As recognised by the Court of Appeal in *Commissioner of Police for the Metropolis v ZH*, '[a]striking feature of the statutory defence (provided by MCA 2005, s 5) is the extent to which it is pervaded by the concepts of reasonableness, practicality and appropriateness'.[308] The Court of Appeal upheld the decision of Sir Robert Nelson at first instance that the police had not taken appropriate steps or been able to point to objective reasons that they were acting in ZH's best interests, nor had they considered a less restrictive approach, when they had forcibly removed ZH, a severely autistic 16 year old who suffered from epilepsy, from a swimming pool and subsequently restrained him. Lord Dyson commented:[309]

> '... the MCA does not impose impossible demands on those who do acts in connection with the care or treatment of others. It requires no more than what is reasonable, practicable and appropriate. What that entails depends on all the circumstances of the case. As the judge recognised, what is reasonable, practicable and appropriate where there is time to reflect and take measured action may be quite different in an emergency or what is reasonably believed to be an emergency.'

No protection in cases of negligence

2.178 Professionals and other carers may have duties of care which, if breached, give rise to liability in the tort of negligence. Consent is not a defence to a claim of negligence. Similarly in relation to people who lack capacity to consent, MCA 2005, s 5(3) clarifies that protection from liability does not extend to situations where the person taking the action has acted negligently, whether in carrying out the act or by failing to act in breach of duty. Therefore, there is no protection excluding a person's civil liability for any loss or damage, or his or her criminal liability, resulting from his or her negligence in carrying out or failing to do an act.

---

[306] MCA 2005, s 5(1)(b)(ii).
[307] See **2.122–2.153** above.
[308] *Commissioner of Police for the Metropolis v ZH* [2013] EWCA Civ 69, [2013] COPLR 332, at [40] per Lord Dyson.
[309] Ibid at paragraph 49. This approach was endorsed by Sir James Munby P in *Re PO* [2013] EWHC 3932 (COP), [2014] COPLR 62, in which the President reaffirmed the doctrine of necessity, and held that there is (at [18]): 'nothing in the 2005 Act to displace this approach'.

Effect on advance decisions to refuse treatment

2.179 In cases where an advance decision to refuse treatment is known to exist, is clear and unambiguous and is valid and applicable in the circumstances which have arisen, any health professionals who knowingly provide treatment contrary to the terms of the advance decision may be liable to legal action for battery or assault, or for breach of the patient's human rights.[310] The provisions of MCA 2005, s 5 do not provide protection from liability in these circumstances, since s 5(4) specifically excludes the operation of advance decisions to refuse treatment.

Limitations on permitted acts

2.180 MCA 2005, s 6 imposes two important limitations on the acts which can be carried out with protection from liability under s 5. The first relates to acts intended to restrain a person who lacks capacity and the second to situations where the act might conflict with a decision made by a donee of a lasting power of attorney or a deputy appointed by the Court.

Restraint

2.181 As a general rule, any act that is intended to restrain a person lacking capacity will not attract protection from liability[311] and any carer or professional using restraint could be liable to legal action and will be personally accountable for their actions. In particular, no protection from liability is offered to people who use or threaten violence in order to carry out any action in connection with the care or treatment of a person lacking capacity or to force that person to comply with the carers' actions. However, the practicalities of caring for and providing protection for people who are unable to protect themselves are also recognised. MCA 2005 therefore permits the use of some form of restraint or physical intervention in limited circumstances in order to protect the person from harm.[312]

2.182 An individual restrains a person lacking capacity if he or she (a) uses, or threatens to use, force to secure the doing of an act which the person resists or (b) restricts that person's liberty of movement, whether or not there is resistance.[313] Restraint may take many forms. It may be verbal or physical and may vary from shouting at someone, to holding them down, to locking them in a room. It may also include the prescribing of a sedative or other chemical restraint which restricts liberty of movement.

2.183 MCA 2005 permits restraint to be used *only* where two conditions are satisfied:[314]

---

[310] MCA 2005, ss 24–26. See also Chapter 6.
[311] MCA 2005, s 6(1).
[312] MCA 2005, s 6(2).
[313] MCA 2005, s 6(4).
[314] MCA 2005, s 6(2) and (3).

(1) the person using it must reasonably believe that it is necessary to do the act in order to prevent harm to the person lacking capacity; and
(2) the restraint used must be a proportionate response both to the likelihood of the person suffering harm and the seriousness of that harm.

MCA 2005 does not define 'harm', since this will vary according to individual circumstances. The restraining act must be 'necessary' to avert harm – not simply to enable the carer or professional to do something more quickly or easily. Similarly, what is likely to be a 'proportionate response' to harm, both in scale and nature, will depend on the seriousness of the particular circumstances and the desired outcome. However, where there are objective reasons for believing that restraint is necessary to prevent the person from coming to any harm, only the minimum necessary force or intervention may be used and for the shortest possible duration.

2.184 In *R (on the application of Sessay) v South London and Maudsley NHS Foundation Trust*, the court confirmed that MCA 2005, s 6 did not extend to giving the police powers to remove someone lacking capacity to consent to hospital or other place of safety and endorsed the following statement which had been agreed by the parties:[315]

> 'Sections 135 and 136 of the Mental Health Act 1983 are the exclusive powers available to police officers to remove persons who appear to be mentally disordered to a place of safety. Sections 5 and 6 of the Mental Capacity Act 2005 do not confer on police officers authority to remove persons to hospital or other places of safety for the purposes set out in sections 135 and 136 of the Mental Health Act 1983.'

This decision was applied in the case of *ZH v Commissioner of Police for the Metropolis* where the court gave detailed consideration to the provisions of s 6 of the MCA 2005 in the context of awarding damages against the police as a result of their actions in forcibly removing a young man with severe autism and learning disabilities from a swimming pool and subsequently restraining him, without having first consulted his carers, informed themselves of the nature of his disabilities or considered any less restrictive options. In that case, Sir Robert Nelson concluded that it was not necessary for the police officers to know the relevant sections of MCA 2005, or indeed to know about the Act itself, but rather:[316]

> 'What they must reasonably believe at the material time are the facts which determine the applicability of the Mental Capacity Act. Thus, at the material time they need to believe that the Claimant lacked capacity to deal with and make decisions about his safety at the swimming pool, that when they carried out the acts that they did, they believed that the Claimant so lacked capacity, and that they believed that it was in the Claimant's best interests for them to act as they did. A belief that the situation created a need for them to act in order to protect the Claimant's safety and prevent him from severely injuring himself would in my judgment be sufficient to satisfy the Act, provided of course that the belief was reasonable under sections 5 and 6 and a proportionate response under section 6 of the

---

[315] [2011] EWHC 2617 (QB). [2012] QB 760 at paragraph 4.
[316] [2012] EWHC 604 (QD), [2012] COPLR 588, at [40]. Sir Robert Nelson's judgment was upheld in its entirety by the Court of Appeal in *Commissioner of Police for the Metropolis v ZH* [2013] EWCA Civ 69, [2013] COPLR 332 – see also para **2.177** above.

Act. It is also necessary for the Police to have considered whether there might be a less restrictive way of dealing with the matter under section 1(6) and, if practicable and appropriate to consult the carers, to take into account their views. These are not only matters which they must have in mind when they carry out the acts of touching, grabbing or restraint but are matters which they must have had regard to before carrying out such acts.'

Deprivation of liberty

2.185 The provisions of s 6 (as originally drafted) attracted some criticism from the Joint Committee on Human Rights (JCHR) in two of its reports on the human rights implications of the Mental Capacity Bill.[317] The Committee was concerned that use of these provisions could lead to deprivations of liberty which are not compatible with Art 5(1) of the European Convention on Human Rights, and in particular could lead to involuntary placement in hospital of a person lacking capacity and thereby deprive them of the procedural safeguards available if they had been detained under Mental Health Act powers:[318]

> 'Although clauses 5 and 6 contain important safeguards against the inappropriate use of restraint ... the combined effect of the two clauses appears to be to authorise (in the sense of protect against liability for) the use of force or the threat of force to overcome an incapacitated person's resistance in certain circumstances, or restrict their liberty of movement, in order to avert a risk of harm. For example, the power in clause 5 could be used to secure the admission into hospital of a person lacking capacity who is resisting such admission, where the person using or threatening force reasonably believes that the person lacks capacity in relation to his treatment, that it is in his best interests for him to be admitted to hospital for treatment and that it is necessary to admit the person in order to prevent harm to himself.
>
> We have written to the minister asking why the Government has not adopted the recommendation of the Joint Committee [on the Draft Mental Incapacity Bill] that the use or threat of force or other restriction of liberty of movement be expressly confined to emergency situations. Without such an express limitation on the face of the Bill, it appears to us that these provisions are likely to lead to deprivations of liberty which are not compatible with Article 5(1) ECHR, because they do not satisfy the Winterwerp requirements that deprivations of liberty be based on objective medical expertise and are necessary in the sense of being the least restrictive alternative. The Bill as drafted therefore does not appear to contain sufficient safeguards against arbitrary deprivation of liberty.'

2.186 The response from the Under Secretary of State, Baroness Ashton, confirmed that: 'It has never been the Government's policy that acts in connection with care and treatment in clause 5 might amount to a deprivation of liberty.'[319] The Government therefore moved a series of amendments in the House of Lords to address the Committee's concerns:[320]

> 'The committee wanted the Bill to confirm expressly that actions amounting to deprivation of liberty do not fall within the definition of "restraint" used in the Bill.

---

[317] JCHR, Twenty-third Report of Session 2003–04 *Scrutiny of Bills: Final Progress Report*, HL Paper 210, HC 1282, Part 2; JCHR, Fourth Report of Session 2004–05 *Scrutiny: First Progress Report*, HL Paper 26, HC 224, Part 4.
[318] JCHR, Twenty-third Report of Session 2003–04, at paras 2.22–2.23. See also Chapter 7.
[319] JCHR, Fourth Report of Session 2004–05, Appendix 4, at paragraph 11.
[320] *Hansard*, HL Deb, vol 670, ser 5, col 1468 (17 March 2005).

The amendments achieve this ... This means that no-one acting in connection with care or treatment under Clause 5, nor an attorney or deputy, may deprive a person who lacks capacity of his liberty. "Restraint" includes only restrictions of liberty.'

2.187 One amendment introduced by the Government (previously MCA 2005, s 6(5), now repealed) expressly confirmed that someone carrying out an act under MCA 2005, s 5 will do more than 'merely restrain' a person lacking capacity if he or she deprives that person of liberty within the meaning of Art 5(1). This applied not only to public authorities covered by the Human Rights Act 1998 but to anyone carrying out acts in connection with care or treatment under s 5. Subsequent amendments to the Act introducing the 'deprivation of liberty safeguards' (DOLS) made these provisions redundant, but confirm that specific authorisation is required to deprive someone of their liberty. These amendments have now been recognised as failing to meet their desired purpose, and the Law Commission has been charged with preparing draft legislation to put in place a proper framework for the authorisation of deprivation of liberty in this context (see further Chapter 7).[321]

2.188 There is clearly a fine line to be drawn between *restriction* of liberty, permitted under the definition of restraint, and *deprivation* of liberty under Art 5(1).[322] This was considered by the European Court of Human Rights in *HL v The United Kingdom* (the so-called *Bournewood* case) which said:[323]

> '... in order to determine whether there has been a deprivation of liberty, the starting point must be the specific situation of the individual concerned and account must be taken of a whole range of factors arising in the particular case such as the type, duration, effects and manner of implementation of the measure in question. The distinction between a deprivation of, and restriction upon, liberty is merely one of degree or intensity and not one of nature or substance ...
>
> ... the Court considers the key factor in the present case to be that the health care professionals treating and managing the applicant exercised complete and effective control over his care and movements ...'

2.189 The judgment in this case was delivered at a very late stage in the parliamentary passage of the Mental Capacity Bill. It identified serious deficiencies (known as the '*Bournewood* gap') in that the law provided insufficient safeguards against unlawful deprivation of liberty of people lacking capacity to consent. The Government promised further safeguards, which have now been introduced into MCA 2005 by the Mental Health Act 2007 (MHA 2007). MHA 2007, s 50 repealed MCA 2005, s 6(5) and substituted complex provisions and procedures allowing for the lawful deprivation of liberty of a person with mental disorder who lacks capacity to consent, where that is in the person's best interests.[324] The interface between

---

[321] Law Commission Consultation Paper No 222 *Mental Capacity and Deprivation of Liberty: A Consultation Paper* (TSO, 2015).
[322] Some guidance is given in the Mental Capacity Act 2005: Code of Practice, at paras 6.49–6.53.
[323] *HL v The United Kingdom* (Application No 45508/99) [2004] 1 FLR 1019, ECHR, at [89] and [91].
[324] These provisions and procedures were implemented in April 2009 accompanied by guidance in a supplement to the Code of Practice.

MCA 2005 and mental health legislation, and the Deprivation of Liberty Safeguards introduced in response to the European Court judgment, are considered in more detail in Chapter 7. The Law Commission is to produce draft legislation to reform the (distinctly unsatisfactory) law in this area by the end of 2016.[325]

Decisions of donees or deputies

2.190 The provisions of MCA 2005, s 5 provide protection from liability to carers and professionals in circumstances where no formal decision-making powers are required. However, where formal powers already exist, for example, under a lasting power of attorney or through an order made by the Court of Protection, these formal decision-making powers will take precedence. Thus, MCA 2005, s 6(6) confirms that the provisions of s 5 do not authorise a person to do an act which conflicts with a decision made by a donee of a lasting power of attorney previously granted by the person lacking capacity, or by a deputy appointed by the Court, so long as the donee or deputy is acting within the scope of their authority. Anyone acting contrary to a decision of a donee or deputy will not have protection from liability.

2.191 In cases of dispute, for example, when carers or health professionals feel that a donee or deputy is acting outside the scope of his or her authority, or contrary to the incapacitated person's best interests, an application may be made for permission to apply to the Court of Protection to resolve the matter. Where the dispute involves serious health care decisions, MCA 2005, s 6(7) clarifies that life-sustaining treatment, or treatment necessary to prevent a serious deterioration in the person's condition, can be given pending a ruling from the Court.[326]

Paying for goods, services and other expenditure

Background

2.192 Before implementation of MCA 2005, the law already made provision for the enforceability of contracts, including contracts to purchase goods, which were made 'with' a person who lacked capacity or whose mental capacity was in doubt. In such cases, the courts have had to balance two important policy considerations. One is a duty to protect those who are incapable of looking after themselves, and the other is to ensure that other people are not prejudiced by the actions of persons who lack capacity to contract but who appear to have full capacity. So, people without contractual capacity are bound by the terms of a contract they have entered into, even if it was unfair, unless it can be shown that the other party to the contract was

---

[325] Its provisional proposals can be found in Law Commission Consultation Paper No 222 *Mental Capacity and Deprivation of Liberty: A Consultation Paper* (TSO, 2015).
[326] Issues around life-sustaining treatment are dealt with in Chapter 6.

aware of their lack of capacity or should have been aware of this.[327] If the other party knows, or must be taken to have known, of the lack of capacity the contract is voidable.

2.193 The Sale of Goods Act 1979 (SGA 1979) modified this rule when applied to contracts for 'necessaries'. A person without mental capacity who agrees to pay for goods which are necessaries is legally obliged to pay a reasonable price for them. Although SGA 1979 applies to goods, similar common law rules were believed to apply to essential services.

The legislation

2.194 These rules are now brought together and given statutory force under MCA 2005, s 7. This clarifies that the obligation to pay a reasonable price applies to both the supply of necessary goods and the provision of necessary services to a person without capacity to contract for them, and it is the person who lacks capacity who must pay.

2.195 The definition of 'necessary' set out in MCA 2005, s 7(2) is based on that in SGA 1979,[328] meaning goods and services which are suitable to the person's condition in life (ie his or her place in society, rather than any mental or physical condition) and his or her actual requirements at the time of sale and delivery (eg ordinary drink, food and clothing or the provision of domiciliary or residential care services).

2.196 During parliamentary debate of these provisions, Lord Goodhart put forward some probing amendments to try to protect people with impaired capacity from entering into contracts which may be disadvantageous to them, for example, through abusive doorstep selling:[329]

> 'These amendments have been proposed by the CAB [Citizens Advice Bureau] which is concerned with the number of cases in which businesses have entered into contracts with people who lack capacity, and those contracts were unduly disadvantageous to those people. At present under English law, though not under the law of Scotland, a contract entered into by a person lacking capacity can be set aside only if the other party to that contract was aware of the incapacity. The CAB amendment alters this, and it wants to apply to England the rule in Scotland which is that a contract can be set aside on grounds of incapacity even if the other party was not aware of the incapacity.'

The amendments were resisted by the Government on the ground that they may have unintended consequences, either by disempowering people with impaired capacity with whom traders may be reluctant to contract, or by allowing the possibility of abuse by people claiming incapacity in order to avoid being bound by a contract. However, the Minister committed the Government to further work during implementation of the Act to ensure that

---

[327] *Imperial Loan Company v Stone* [1892] 1 QB 599.
[328] SGA 1979, s 3(3).
[329] *Hansard*, HL Deb, vol 668, ser 5, col 1396 (27 January 2005). See also HL Deb, vol 670, ser 5, cols 1469–1472 (17 March 2005).

'policy development ... on consumer strategy, credit and indebtedness is sensitive to the needs of consumers who lack capacity'.[330]

Responsibility to pay for necessary goods and services

2.197 MCA 2005 confirms that the legal responsibility for paying for necessary goods and services lies with the person for whom they are supplied even though that person lacks the capacity to contract for them.[331] The obligation is to pay 'a reasonable price' for them[332] so this provision cannot be used to enforce a contract which involves gross overcharging for goods or services. In the case of *Wychavon District Council v EM (HB)*[333] concerning entitlement to Housing Benefit of a woman with profound physical and mental disabilities who lacked capacity to enter into a tenancy agreement, the Upper Tribunal overturned its previous decision that Housing Benefit was not payable because there was no valid tenancy agreement. When the provisions of s 7 of the MCA 2005 were brought to the attention of Judge Mark, he reconsidered his original decision. He expressed some doubt as to whether 'services' in s 7 of the MCA 2005 is wide enough to cover the provision of accommodation, but even if it was not, the common law doctrine of necessities would apply, obliging the claimant to pay for the necessary accommodation with the assistance of Housing Benefit. He held (at paragraph 30):

> 'Neither section 7 nor the common law imposed on her any liability under the terms of any putative tenancy agreement, whether for rent or under any repairing or other covenants. So far as long term decisions are concerned, it is clear that suitable accommodation is a necessary at common law, and I see no reason why, so long as it being provided, either accommodation or any other necessary should be excluded from either the common law requirements or those of the 2005 Act, whichever is applicable.'

It was suggested that matters such as a tenancy ought to be dealt with through the Court of Protection and that was eventually done in this case.[334] Judge Mark took a pragmatic view that during the course of an application to the Court of Protection, a person lacking capacity ought not to be left

---

[330] *Hansard*, HL Deb, vol 670, ser 5, col 1472 (17 March 2005). The Office of Fair Trading has issued guidance for creditors on granting credit to people who may lack capacity to make informed borrowing decisions: *Mental Capacity: OFT guidance for creditors* (OFT, September 2011), available online at: http://webarchive.nationalarchives.gov.uk/20140402142426/http://www.oft.gov.uk/about-the-oft/legal-powers/legal/cca/mental-capacity-guidance.

[331] See also in this regard, and for a discussion of s 7 more generally, *Aster Healthcare* [2014] EWHC 77 (QB), [2014] COPLR 397, upheld on appeal ([2014] EWCA Civ 1350).

[332] MCA 2005, s 7(1).

[333] [2012] UKUT 12 (AAC).

[334] The Court of Protection has issued guidance on 'Applications to the Court of Protection in relation to tenancy agreements' (February 2012), available online at: www.mentalhealthlaw.co.uk/File:COP_guidance_on_tenancy_agreements_February_2012.pdf.

without necessaries (including accommodation), which, as the judge pointed out, will only be supplied if there is confidence that they will be paid for.[335]

2.198 Where the person also lacks the capacity to arrange for payment to be made, the carer who has arranged for the provision of goods and services necessary for the person's care or treatment may also have to arrange settlement of the bill. The Law Commission described the problem as follows:[336]

> 'We are not here concerned with ways in which a person may gain access to another person's income or assets. Where assets are held by a bank or other institution, specific authority will certainly be required before they can be transferred to anyone other than the legal owner. We are concerned, rather, with the situation where a carer arranges for something which will cost money to be done for a person without capacity. Family members often arrange for milk to be delivered, or for a hairdresser, gardener or chiropodist to call. More costly arrangements might be roof repairs, or for an excursion or holiday. In many cases it may be reasonable for a family member to arrange such matters, if it is done in the best interests of the person without capacity. Such actions could therefore fall within the confines of the general authority to provide for the person's welfare and care recommended above. Who, however, is to pay the provider of the goods or services supplied?'

2.199 Where it is appropriate for carers to arrange such matters, and so long as the arrangements made are in the best interests of the person lacking capacity, the carers' actions are therefore likely to be considered 'acts in connection with care or treatment' under MCA 2005, s 5, providing them with some protection from liability if their actions were to be challenged. However, some further arrangements may need to be made to meet the costs involved or to pay the provider of the goods or services supplied.

Expenditure

2.200 In such cases where necessary goods or services must be paid for, provision is made under MCA 2005, s 8 to meet the expenditure involved. This may be done in any one of three ways, described in the Code of Practice as follows (with footnotes added):[337]

- 'If neither the carer nor the person who lacks capacity can produce the necessary funds, the carer may promise that the person who lacks capacity will pay.[338] A supplier may not be happy with this, or the carer may be worried they may be held responsible for any debt. In such cases the carer must follow the formal steps ... below.
- If the person who lacks capacity has cash, the carer may use that money to pay for goods or services[339] (for example, to pay the milkman or the hairdresser).

---

[335] Note that, for s 7 to be applicable, the supplier of the necessaries must intend to impose a liability upon the individual lacking capacity: see the first instance decision in *Aster Healthcare* at [50]–[59].
[336] Law Com No 231, at para 4.7 (see **2.4**, footnote).
[337] Mental Capacity Act 2005: Code of Practice, at paragraph 6.61
[338] 'The carer may pledge the credit of the person who lacks capacity': MCA 2005, s 8(1)(a).
[339] MCA 2005, s 8(1)(b).

- The carer may choose to pay for the goods or services with their own money. The person who lacks capacity must pay them back.[340] This may involve using cash in the person's possession or running up an IOU. (This is not appropriate for paid care workers, whose contracts might stop them handling their clients' money.) The carer must follow formal steps to get money held in a bank or building society account.'

2.201 The intention of these provisions is to make it possible for ordinary but necessary goods and services to be provided for people who lack the capacity to organise and pay for them, but without requiring carers to invoke expensive and time-consuming court proceedings to obtain authority to do so. However, MCA 2005, s 8 does not give any authorisation to a carer to gain access to the incapacitated person's income or assets or to sell the person's property. A distinction is drawn between the use of available cash already in the possession of the person lacking capacity, on the one hand, and the removal of money from a bank account or selling valuable items of property, on the other. Where a carer has promised that the person lacking capacity will pay for the goods or services supplied (ie has pledged the person's credit), formal authority may then need to be obtained before that promise can be put into effect. Similarly, formal arrangements may need to be made before a carer can be reimbursed if a large amount of expenditure is involved.

2.202 Some carers (such as family members) may already have such formal authority, for example, under an enduring or lasting power of attorney, as a deputy appointed by the Court of Protection or as a social security 'appointee' (although the precise scope of authority of such an appointee is not absolutely clear). MCA 2005, s 8(3) makes clear that these arrangements are not affected or changed by the above provisions allowing carers to arrange and pay for necessary goods and services on behalf of a person lacking capacity to make their own arrangements. However, as confirmed by s 6(6), an informal carer cannot make arrangements for goods or services to be provided for someone lacking capacity if this conflicts with a decision made by a donee or deputy acting within the scope of their authority.

Excluded decisions
Background

2.203 The Law Commission recognised the need to place some restrictions on carers and others acting under its proposed 'general authority' (now section 5 acts) without the need to apply for formal powers:[341]

'One benefit of setting out a clear general authority in statute is that the statute can then specify which matters fall outside the scope of that general authority. The general law already provides that certain acts can only be effected by a person acting for himself or herself. Examples would be entering into marriage or casting a vote in a public election. For the avoidance of doubt, our draft Bill lists certain matters

---

[340] MCA 2005, s 8(2).
[341] Law Com No 231, at para 4.29 (see **2.4**, footnote).

which must be done by a person acting for him or herself ... In many areas, however, it is at present quite unclear whether action may be lawfully taken on behalf of a person without capacity. If no-one is sure what can lawfully be done, then no-one can be sure what must and must not be done.'

The legislation

2.204 MCA 2005 therefore seeks to make clear what can and cannot be done by someone else in relation to a person lacking capacity. There are certain acts which cannot be done and certain decisions which can never be made on behalf of a person who lacks capacity to consent to those actions or to make those decisions for him or herself, either because they are so personal to the individual concerned or because they are governed by other legislation. In ,ss 27–29, the Act lists those specific decisions which are excluded and cannot be made under MCA 2005, whether by a carer or professional acting under MCA 2005, s 5, a donee under a lasting power of attorney, a deputy or by the Court of Protection itself.

Family relationships etc

2.205 MCA 2005, s 27 excludes the following decisions on family relationships from being taken on behalf of a person lacking capacity to make the decision:

'(a) consenting to marriage or civil partnership,
(b) consenting to have sexual relationships,
(c) consenting to a decree of divorce being granted on the basis of two years' separation,
(d) consenting to a dissolution order being made in relation to a civil partnership on the basis of two years' separation,
(e) consenting to a child's being placed for adoption by an adoption agency,
(f) consenting to the making of an adoption order,
(g) discharging parental responsibilities in matters not relating to a child's property,
(h) giving a consent under the Human Fertilisation and Embryology Act 1990.'

However, the Court of Protection retains the power to make declarations under MCA 2005, s 15 with regard to the person's capacity to consent to the matters set out above.[342]

2.206 Where a person lacking capacity becomes involved in divorce or dissolution proceedings on any basis other than 2 years' separation, or where someone loses capacity during the course of such proceedings, a litigation friend will be appointed under the Family Procedure Rules 2010 to give instructions and otherwise act on their behalf in relation to the proceedings.[343] Where a decision needs to be made about placing a child for adoption, if the birth parent lacks capacity to consent to an adoption order,

---

[342] See **2.56ff** above. See also Chapter 6 for consideration of the test of capacity to consent to sexual relations.
[343] Family Procedure Rules 2010, SI 2010/2955, Part 15.

the rules relating to dispensing with consent in adoption legislation apply.[344] Matters concerned with the discharging of parental responsibilities not related to a child's property are dealt with under the Children Act 1989.

Mental Health Act matters

2.207 MCA 2005, s 28 states that the Act's decision-making powers cannot be used to give or to consent to treatment for mental disorder if the treatment is regulated by the Mental Health Act (MHA) 1983, Part 4. The purpose of Part 4 is to clarify the extent to which treatment for mental disorder can be imposed on detained patients in hospital and to provide specific statutory safeguards concerning the provision of treatment without consent.[345] Section 28 ensures that where a person lacking capacity to consent to treatment is detained in hospital under the long term provisions of MHA 1983, the powers available under MHA 1983, Part 4 would 'trump' the decision-making powers under MCA 2005 in relation to treatment for mental disorder.

2.208 This means that the safeguards and procedures of MHA 1983 (as amended by MHA 2007) relating to treatment for the person's mental disorder cannot be avoided by reference to MCA 2005, s 5 or by the consent or refusal of treatment by a donee or deputy. However, depending on the scope of their authority, a welfare attorney or deputy may apply to a mental health tribunal, or to the hospital managers, for the patient's discharge where the patient lacks capacity to make the application. For all other decisions affecting that person, the principles and provisions of MCA 2005 would apply. Moreover, the existence of a valid advance decision to refuse medical treatment (as to which, see further Chapter 6) must be taken into account when considering whether to impose forced treatment under the provisions of Part 4 and has been said to 'weigh most heavily in the scales' upon an application for a declaration that a decision <u>not</u> to impose such treatment was lawful where the consequences were potentially life-threatening.[346]

2.209 Provisions in the Mental Health Act 2007 amended MCA 2005, s 28 to take account of the new provisions in the amended MHA 1983 relating to the use of electro-convulsive therapy (ECT)[347] and those introducing compulsory community treatment orders (CTOs – also referred to as supervised community treatment) for patients previously detained in hospital who are now living in the community, but who continue to need treatment for their mental disorder.[348] The new MHA 1983, s 28(1A)[349]

---

[344] Adoption and Children Act 2002, s 52.
[345] MHA 1983, ss 57–58.
[346] *Nottinghamshire Healthcare NHS Trust v RC* [2014] EWCOP 1317, [2014] COPLR 468, at [30] (whether blood transfusion – falling within the scope of the compulsory treatment provisions of MHA 1983, s 63 – should be imposed upon a self-harming capacitous patient refusing such transfusion).
[347] MHA 1983, s 58A, inserted by MHA 2007, s 28(6).
[348] MHA 1983, ss 17A–17G, inserted by MHA 2007, s 32(1), (2).
[349] Inserted by MHA 2007, s 28(10).

removes the exclusion in relation to patients aged 16–17 years who lack capacity to consent to ECT, thus allowing ECT to be given to informal patients aged 16-17 under MCA 2005, s 5 rather than under the amended provisions of MHA 1983, where such patients lack capacity to consent, so long as the treatment is in their best interests, it is being given in circumstances that do not amount to a deprivation of their liberty and a Second Opinion Appointed Doctor considers ECT to be appropriate. Where a patient subject to a CTO (known as a 'community patient'[350]) is being treated under Part 4A of the amended 1983 Act, MCA 2005, s 28(1B) [351] prohibits that treatment being given under s 5, so that powers under the 1983 Act must be used. However, MHA 1983, Part 4A provides authority for attorneys or deputies with relevant powers to consent to treatment on behalf of a community patient.[352]

2.210 During the two pre-legislative scrutiny exercises carried out – on the draft Mental Incapacity Bill in 2003 and on the draft Mental Health Bill in 2004–05, both Joint Committees expressed concern about the interrelation between the two pieces of legislation and the potential for overlap and confusion between them.[353] These concerns were also raised frequently during the parliamentary debates on the Mental Capacity Bill. Of particular concern were the need to:

(1) provide appropriate safeguards in relation to the treatment of adults lacking capacity who are compliant with their care and treatment as required by the European Court judgment in *HL v The United Kingdom*;[354] and
(2) ensure that health professionals are clear about which law should be used to provide treatment for serious mental disorder for those lacking capacity to consent.

Several years after the amendments to both Acts were introduced, the interface between them is still causing considerable problems for practitioners and for both courts and tribunals,[355] and the Law Commission has provisionally proposed significant changes to the law in this area so as to seek to eliminate the overlap insofar as possible.[356] These matters are considered further in Chapter 7.

---

[350] MHA 1983, s 17A(7).
[351] Inserted by MHA 2007, s 35(4), (5).
[352] MHA 1983, s 64B(3)(b)(ii).
[353] Joint Committee on the Draft Mental Incapacity Bill, Vol I, HL Paper 189-I, HC 1083-I, chapter 12; Joint Committee on the Draft Mental Health Bill, Vol I, HL Paper 79-I, HC 95-I, chapter 4.
[354] *HL v The United Kingdom* (Application No 45508/99) [2004] 1 FLR 1019, ECHR. MCA 2005 was amended by MHA 2007 to introduce the Deprivation of Liberty Safeguards (DOLS) which have been widely criticised as unworkable and 'not fit for purpose' – see Chapter 7.
[355] See for example, *An NHS Trust v Dr A* [2013] EWHC 2442 (COP), [2013] COPLR 605; *AM v South London & Maudsley NHS Foundation Trust & Secretary of State for Health* [2013] UKUT 0365 (AAC), [2013] COPLR 510.
[356] Law Commission Consultation Paper No 222 *Mental Capacity and Deprivation of Liberty: A Consultation Paper* (TSO, 2015), Chapter 10.

Voting rights

2.211 The final category of excluded decisions concerns voting rights. MCA 2005, s 29 confirms that no one can make a decision on voting or cast a vote at an election or a referendum on behalf of a person lacking capacity to vote (for example through a proxy, or where acting as a deputy or donee of a Lasting Power of Attorney). A proxy vote can only be cast on behalf of a person who has capacity to nominate someone as their proxy voter. The precise test for capacity to appoint a proxy has yet to be established. It is very important to understand that since the coming into force of the Electoral Administration Act 2006, s 73, a person's mental health problems or learning disabilities cannot, by themselves, constitute a ground to disqualify them from voting. There is therefore, in law, no test of 'mental capacity to vote.' A person registered on the relevant electoral roll cannot be refused a ballot paper, or in other words be excluded from voting, on the grounds of mental incapacity.

Ill-treatment or neglect

Background

2.212 MCA 2005 created a number of ways in which someone can acquire powers over another person who lacks some decision-making capacity. For this reason the Law Commission concluded that:[357]

> 'It is right that a person with such powers should be subject to criminal sanction for ill-treating or wilfully neglecting the other person concerned.'

2.213 The Government was not at first 'persuaded that the creation of a new offence would be the best way of tackling abuse'.[358] However, a number of high-profile cases concerning abuse and ill-treatment of vulnerable people resulted in such an offence being included in the Draft Mental Incapacity Bill. This proposed the creation of an offence of ill-treatment or neglect with a maximum penalty of two years' imprisonment.[359]

2.214 The original impetus for the creation of a specific offence was the *Longcare* case, in which more than 50 adults with learning difficulties were abused at two care homes in South Buckinghamshire between 1983 and 1993. Despite the severity of abuse (which included rape, assault, over-sedation, starvation and neglect over a period of 10 years) existing law meant those responsible only received light sentences. The *Independent Longcare Inquiry*, the report of which was published in 1998,[360] recommended that the Government introduce a new, arrestable offence of harming or exploiting a vulnerable adult, with a maximum penalty of 10 years in prison. Lack of action in implementing any changes led to a

---

[357] Law Com No 231, at para 4.38 (see **2.4**, footnote).
[358] Lord Chancellor's Department *Making Decisions*, Cm 4465 (1999), at paragraph 1.37.
[359] Draft Mental Incapacity Bill, cl 31.
[360] Tom Burgner *Independent Longcare Inquiry* (Buckingham County Council, 1998).

campaign called 'Justice for Survivors' launched in 2003 by the journal *Disability Now* and supported by leading disability organisations and charities.

Criminal offence

2.215 MCA 2005, s 44 addressed some of these concerns by creating a specific criminal offence of ill-treatment or wilful neglect of a person who lacks, or is believed to lack, capacity by any person involved in caring for that person or in a position of trust or power over the person. The penalty will vary according to the seriousness of the offence, ranging from a fine to a term of imprisonment, but the maximum penalty has been increased to 5 years' imprisonment.[361] This has the effect of making it an 'arrestable offence' under the Police and Criminal Evidence Act 1984, s 2. It also reflects the potential severity of the crime, with sentences in parallel with those for serious assaults on individuals, including the offences of inflicting grievous bodily harm and assault occasioning actual bodily harm under the Offences Against the Person Act 1861, which both carry maximum sentences of 5 years. For example, after acts of neglect and abuse at Winterbourne View private hospital were uncovered by BBC Panorama, subsequent prosecutions under MCA 2005, s 44 resulted in 6 out of 11 care workers being given sentences ranging from 6 months to 2 years imprisonment and the other five were given suspended sentences.[362]

Scope of the offence

2.216 The criminal offence has a wide application to 'anyone who has the care of' a person who lacks, or is reasonably believed to lack, capacity.[363] This includes not only family carers, but also health and social care staff in hospital or care homes (including the owner or manager of the care home) or those providing domiciliary care. It also applies to donees of a lasting power of attorney or attorneys of an enduring power of attorney previously made by the person now lacking capacity[364] and to any deputy appointed by the Court of Protection for that person.[365] No lower age limit is specified, so the offence also applies to the ill-treatment or wilful neglect of children under 16 whose lack of capacity is caused by an impairment of, or disturbance in the functioning of, the mind or brain, not solely by the immaturity of youth.

2.217 During the parliamentary stages, amendments were put aimed at extending the application of the new offence to appointees, appointed by the

---

[361] MCA 2005, s 44(3)(b).
[362] BBC News at: www.bbc.co.uk/news/uk-england-bristol-20092894.
[363] MCA 2005, s 44(1)(a). The section does not specify which particular decision the person lacks capacity to make – see **2.219–2.220** on its interpretation by the courts. See also Neil Allen, 'Criminal Care: ill-treatment and wilful neglect', *Elder Law Journal*, Jordan Publishing [2012] Eld LJ 71-75, for further consideration of this point and on who should be prosecuted.
[364] MCA 2005, s 44(1)(b).
[365] MCA 2005, s 44(1)(c).

Department for Work and Pensions (DWP) to collect and manage social security benefits on behalf of claimants unable to do so for themselves. The Minister clarified that:[366]

'... it is clear that noble Lords are still concerned that because DWP appointees are handling only financial matters they might not be considered as having "care of the person" and, as such, would fall outside the scope of the offence. Again, we made clear during the Report stage in the other place that, in the majority of cases, the appointee will have care of the person and will therefore be covered by the offence.'

2.218 The Minister also confirmed that DWP officials were considering ways of introducing more effective monitoring of appointees. In 2011, the DWP carried out an equality impact assessment on the Government's intention to introduce an 'appointee review system', both to meet the requirements of the Equality Act 2010 and to satisfy Article 12.4 of the UN Convention on the Rights of Persons with Disabilities (CRPD).[367] When ratifying the CRPD, the UK Government entered a reservation stating that the UK was actively working towards introducing a proportionate system of review for appointees, but no date has yet been set for implementing the review system to enable the Government to lift the reservation.

Person who lacks capacity

2.219 In *R v Dunn*,[368] the court considered the meaning of 'a person who lacks capacity' since this is not defined further within MCA 2005, s 44. Dunn had been convicted of four counts of ill-treating a person without capacity contrary to MCA 2005, s 44 against three victims at the residential care home of which she was manageress. The judge in the Crown Court had directed that 'a person without capacity' meant a person unable to make decisions for himself because of a disturbance or impairment of function of the mind or brain, that a diagnosis of dementia was not enough, that 'impairment' could be permanent or temporary, that capacity was presumed unless disproved on the balance of probabilities, and that this direction applied to all three victims. The defendant appealed on the basis that the direction on 'a person without capacity' was inadequate, failed to focus on the capacity of each victim to make a decision at the relevant time, and failed to identify the questions required by MCA 2005, s 3. The appeal was dismissed on the following grounds:[369]

'(1) The legislation, including MCA 2005 s 2, was convoluted and did not appropriately define the elements of the offence (including 'matter' and 'disturbance or impairment').

(2) Lack of capacity had to be decided on the balance of probabilities.

(3) There was a disconnect between MCA 2005, s 44 (referring to 'persons without capacity') and the elaborate definition sections (MCA 2005, ss 2 and 3), but it was open for the jury to conclude that the decisions regarding care (the 'matter') had been made because the victims lacked capacity.

---

[366] *Hansard*, HL Deb, vol 669, ser 5, col 746 (8 February 2005).
[367] Department for Work and Pensions, Appointee Review: Integrated equality impact assessment, (September 2011), available at www.dwp.gov.uk/docs/appointee-review.pdf.
[368] *R v Dunn* [2010] EWCA Crim 2935.
[369] Ibid, at [22]–[23]. Based on the summary at [2010] All ER (D) 250 (Nov).

(4) It was unnecessary for the judge to complicate matters by referring to MCA 2005 s 3, and the conviction was safe.'

2.220 This matter was considered again by the Court of Appeal in the case of *R v Hopkins; R v Priest* where the court observed:[370]

'Unconstrained by authority, this court would be minded to accept the submission made on behalf of the appellants that Section 44 (1) (a), read together with Section 2 (1) of the Mental Capacity Act 2005, is so vague that it fails the test of sufficient certainty at common law and under Article 7.1, ECHR. However this court has made a decision upon Section 44 of the Act which binds this court.'

The judgment then quotes at length from *R v Dunn*, confirming (at paragraph 43) that 'the matter in respect of which capacity was required to be lacking for the purposes of Section 44 was the person's ability to make decisions concerning his or her own care.' This approach was followed in the Court of Appeal cases culminating in *Ligaya Nursing v R*.[371]

Ill-treatment

2.221 A single act is sufficient to show ill-treatment.[372] For a conviction of ill-treatment, it is necessary to show deliberate conduct by the accused which could properly be described as ill-treatment, whether or not it had caused or was likely to cause harm. The accused must either realise that he or she is inexcusably ill-treating the other person or be reckless as to whether he or she is doing so.[373]

Wilful neglect

2.222 Ill-treatment and neglect are separate offences.[374] Neglect relates to a failure to provide nourishment, fluid, shelter, warmth or medical attention to a dependant person.[375] The meaning of 'wilful neglect' may vary according to the circumstances, but is generally taken to mean that there has been an intentional or deliberate omission that the person in question knows s/he has a duty to do.[376] In the context of the offence of wilfully neglecting a child in a manner likely to cause unnecessary suffering or injury to health (under the Children and Young Persons Act (CYPA) 1933, s 1), it has been held that neglect cannot be described as *wilful* unless the person:[377]

- either had directed his or her mind to whether there was some risk (although it might fall far short of a probability) that the child's health might suffer from the neglect, and had made a conscious decision to refrain from acting; or

---

[370] [2011] EWCA Crim 1513, at [40].
[371] [2012] EWCA Crim 2521.
[372] *R v Holmes* [1979] Crim LR 52.
[373] *R v Newington* (1990) 91 Cr App R 247.
[374] *R v Newington* (1990) 91 Cr App R 247.
[375] *R v Humberside and Scunthorpe Coroner, ex parte Jamieson* [1995] QB 1.
[376] De *Maroussem v Commissioner of Income Tax* [2004] UKPC 43.
[377] *R v Sheppard* [1981] AC 394, HL.

- had so refrained because he or she did not care whether the child might be at risk or not.

2.223 However, by contrast to the offence under CYPA 1933, s 1 which specifies acting 'in a manner likely to cause unnecessary suffering or injury to health', s 44 makes no such reference. In *R v Patel*,[378] concerning a conviction for wilful neglect of a nurse who failed to carry out cardiopulmonary resuscitation (CPR) on an elderly resident in a nursing home, the nurse appealed on the ground that judge had wrongly directed the jury that neglect could be established even if it was unlikely that the appellant's inaction caused any adverse consequence. The Court of Appeal held the the *actus reus* of the offence under MCA 2005, s 44 is complete if the nurse (or a medical practitioner) neglects to do an act which should be done in the treatment of the patient. The Court also noted the clear distinction between the offence of neglect under MCA 2005, s 44 and the (much more serious) offence of gross negligence manslaughter, where causation would be an issue.

The nurse also contended that the judge had failed to direct the jury properly about the meaning of 'wilful', objecting in particular to his direction that if the appellant acted out of stress or panic that would not constitute a defence. The Court of Appeal held that:[379]

> '... neglect is wilful if a nurse or medical practitioner knows that it is necessary to administer a piece of treatment and deliberately decides not to carry out that treatment, which is within their power but which they cannot face performing ... if the appellant was acting at a time of stress, that would be a matter which the judge could take into account at the time of sentence.'

2.224 In *R v Hopkins*, the Court of Appeal confirmed that 'Neglect may be an instant or a continuing phase. We note that section 44 does not require proof of any particular harm or proof of the risk of any particular harm.'[380] That case related to the prosecution of the owner and manager of a care home concerning a number of incidents of 'systematic incompetence' and substandard care of residents. However, the Court was critical of the trial judge's inadequate direction to the jury as to the law relating to wilful neglect, and in particular, his lack of explanation of *R v Sheppard*, suggesting that a short, unambiguous statement of the law and a 'written route to verdict' was needed to assist the jury:[381]

> 'By way of example, returning to count 1 which alleged wilful neglect of [a resident], the prosecution relied on several alleged failings. The jury needed to ask in respect of each one (1) are we sure lack of care is proved?; (2) if so, are we sure that it amounted to neglect?; (3) if so, are we sure either (i) that the defendant knew of the lack of care and deliberately or recklessly neglected to act, or (ii) that the defendant was unaware of the lack of care and deliberately or recklessly closed her mind to the obvious? We do not suggest that this is the form of question required in every case. But in this case the appellants were persons whose primary responsibility was

---

[378] *R v Patel* [2013] EWCA Crim 965, at [34].
[379] Ibid, at [42].
[380] *R v Hopkins; R v Priest* [2011] EWCA Crim 1513, at [49].
[381] Ibid, at [57]–[60].

supervision and management rather than hands-on care. The issue whether or not either or both of them was aware of the failing was a principal fact about which the jury required direction or, in the alternative, if unaware of that failing, whether the jury were sure that it was the consequence of a deliberate or reckless closing of the eyes to the obvious. The judge did not explain the concept of wilful neglect as it applied to each defendant in the circumstances of her role in the care plan. Neither did he relate the requirement for wilful neglect to any of the failings which, it was alleged, applied to any particular count.'

In this case, the verdicts were considered unsafe and the appeals against conviction were allowed, although the care home had since been closed down.

2.225 In *Ligaya Nursing v R*, the Court of Appeal acknowledged the difficulties involved in cases of alleged wilful neglect, in that evidence purporting to establish wilful neglect was often 'elusive'. However, the Court set out some key principles in relation to such cases:[382]

> 'The purpose of s 44 of the Act is clear. Those who are in need of care are entitled to protection against ill-treatment or wilful neglect. The question whether they have been so neglected must be examined in the context of the statutory provisions which provide that, to the greatest extent possible, their autonomy should be respected. The evidential difficulties which may arise when this offence is charged do not make it legally uncertain within the principles in *Mirsa* [2005] 1 Cr App R 328 and *R v Rimmington: R v Goldstein* [2006] 1 AC 459. On analysis, the offence created by s 44 is not vague. It makes it an offence for an individual responsible for the care of someone who lacks the capacity to care for himself to ill-treat or wilfully to neglect that person. Those in care who still enjoy some level of capacity for making their own decisions are entitled to be protected from wilful neglect which impacts on the areas of their lives over which they lack capacity. However s 44 did not create an absolute offence. Therefore, actions or omissions, or a combination of both, which reflect or are believed to reflect the protected autonomy of the individual needing care do not constitute wilful neglect. Within these clear principles, the issue in an individual prosecution is fact specific.'

Courts and Criminal Justice Act 2015

2.226 With respect to incidents occurring on or after 13 April 2015, the provisions of the Courts and Criminal Justice Act 2015 have made it an offence (under s 20) for an individual who has the care of another individual by virtue of being a care worker to ill-treat or wilfully to neglect that individual. A 'care worker' is an individual who, as paid work, provides health care for an adult or a child (with certain exceptions), or social care for an adult. Significantly, a care worker also includes those with managerial responsibility and directors (of equivalents) of organisations providing such care.

2.227 There is also a separate offence (under s 21) relating to care providers. A care provider will commit this offence where:

---

[382] [2012] EWCA Crim 2521, at [18].

- an individual who has the care of another individual by virtue of being part of the care provider's arrangements ill-treats or wilfully neglects that individual,
- the care provider's activities are managed or organised in a way which amounts to a gross breach of a relevant duty of care owed by the care provider to the individual who is ill-treated or neglected, and
- in the absence of the breach, the ill-treatment or wilful neglect would not have occurred or would have been less likely to occur.

It should perhaps be noted in relation that this offence is not relevant to service users who are receiving direct payments.

2.228 It is likely that that use will be made wherever possible of two new offences, which do not depend upon the capacity (or otherwise) of the individual to whom care is being provided. However, the offence under MCA 2005, s 44 will remain of importance to cover instances of ill-treatment or wilful neglect by family members or others falling outside the category of paid care workers or care providers. In the circumstances, it is to be regretted that the opportunity was not taken in this Bill also to revisit MCA 2005, s 44 and the flawed approach adopted there to capacity.

Chapter 3

Lasting Powers of Attorney

BACKGROUND

Powers of attorney

3.1 A power of attorney is simply a formal arrangement, undertaken by deed, whereby one person ('the donor') entrusts to another person ('the attorney' or 'the donee') authority to act in his or her name and on his or her behalf. A power of attorney is a form of agency which has been recognised at common law and used for centuries to enable the affairs of the donor (the principal) to be conducted on his or her behalf by an attorney (the agent) while the donor is away on business, overseas or physically unwell.

3.2 Common law principles of agency apply to powers of attorney, although the law relating to powers of attorney has been developed by statute, beginning with the Powers of Attorney Act 1971.[1] This short statute confirmed that a power of attorney must be made by deed[2] and provided for the protection of the attorney and a third person where they act in good faith without knowledge of revocation of the power.[3]

3.3 Notwithstanding the introduction of statutory rules governing their operation, common law principles concerning the creation, operation and revocation continue to apply, and in particular the principle that a power of attorney is revoked by the supervening incapacity of the donor. The rationale behind this principle is quite straightforward. An act carried out by an attorney is treated in law as an act carried out by the donor. The attorney can only do what the donor can give authority for him or her to do and if the donor lacks capacity then the donor cannot give that authority. The attorney and any third party dealing with the attorney can therefore assume, in the absence of any evidence to the contrary, that the donor is able to know and approve of what is being done on his or her behalf. The only exception to this cardinal rule is where the power of attorney is made in a prescribed statutory form. The Mental Capacity Act 2005 (MCA 2005), Sch 1 (Lasting Powers of Attorney) or Sch 4 (Enduring Powers of Attorney) provide for the powers made in a prescribed form to continue notwithstanding the supervening incapacity of the donor.

---

[1] This implemented the recommendations of the Law Commission's report *Powers of Attorney (1970)* Law Com No 30 (HMSO, 1970).
[2] Law of Property (Miscellaneous Provisions) Act 1989, s 1.
[3] Powers of Attorney Act 1971, ss 1 and 5.

Limitations

3.4 Any power of attorney has to be understood in the context of the common law principles of agency and their limitations, which underpin the further statutory obligations imposed by MCA 2005. A power of attorney confers rights on the attorney as well as responsibilities. And while an attorney may, if authorised, do anything that can lawfully be done by the donor, this is not an open-ended right to deal with the donor's property as the attorney wishes.[4] In particular:

- an attorney owes a fiduciary duty to the donor and cannot act so as to benefit him or herself or any other person to the detriment of the donor or the donor's estate.[5] The attorney must act in good faith, keep accounts and disclose any conflict of interest;[6]
- an attorney contracts in the name of the donor and while not personally liable under the contract, any property acquired or money held as attorney should be kept in the donor's name and must be kept separate from the attorney's own estate;[7]
- an attorney owes a duty of skill and care commensurate with the degree of expertise offered by him or her and whether he or she is acting gratuitously or for reward;[8]
- an attorney owes a duty of confidentiality to the donor and cannot disclose information unless authorised or to the extent required by the agency. This duty survives the operation of the power;
- an attorney cannot generally delegate his or her authority to another person;[9]
- an attorney is chosen to exercise personal skill and cannot appoint a successor in the same way as a trustee can appoint a new or replacement trustee;

---

[4] The relevance of the common law principles to the role of an attorney under a modern LPA was eloquently restated by Senior Judge Lush in the case of *Re Harcourt: the Public Guardian v A* [2013] COPLR 69.

[5] The Code of Practice issued under MCA 2005 defines an attorney's fiduciary duty as follows: 'A fiduciary duty means attorneys must not take advantage of their position. Nor should they put themselves in a position where their personal interests conflict with their duties. They must also not allow any other influences to affect the way in which they act as an attorney. Decisions should always benefit the donor, and not the attorney. Attorneys must not profit or get any personal benefit from their position, apart from receiving gifts where the Act allows it, whether or not it is at the donor's expense' (7.60).

[6] An attorney must be prepared to produce accounts or depending on the size and nature of the estate, financial records. See *Gray v Haig* (1855) 20 Beav 219.

[7] If the attorney holds property of the donor then he or she holds it as trustee. See *Henry v Hammond* [1913] 2 KB 515. For a recent case where an attorney was criticised for intermingling his own money with that of the donor, see the decisions of Senior Judge Lush in *Re PC: the Public Guardian v AC and JC* [2014] EWCOP 41 and *Re OL: Public Guardian and DA, YS and ES* [2015] EWCOP 41.

[8] See e g *Chaudhry v Prabhakar* [1989] 1 WLR 29. See also the decision of Senior Judge Lush in *Re Buckley: The Public Guardian v C* [2013] EWCOP 2965, [2013] COPLR 39.

[9] Delegation may be permitted if authorised by the instrument or by statute, if it is purely administrative, it is usual practice in the business of the donor or the attorney or if it is due to necessity. For example, directors of a company may delegate powers to an attorney or agent who may in turn delegate all or any of his or her powers (Art 71 of Table A).

- a power of attorney may be revoked by the donor by a deed or other act inconsistent with the continued operation of the power, which must include the giving of notice to the attorney;[10]
- the authority of the attorney is revoked by the death, incapacity or bankruptcy of the attorney;[11]
- the attorney may disclaim the power at any time;
- the attorney may only do such things as may lawfully be done by an attorney. Thus an attorney cannot perform an act which can only be performed personally, such as swearing an affidavit[12] or executing a will.[13] Neither can an attorney perform an act arising by virtue of the donor's office[14] or which is of a personal nature;[15]
- Rules of Court do not permit an attorney, in that role, to conduct legal proceedings in the name of the donor;[16] and
- a power of attorney is revoked by the incapacity of the donor.[17]

The incapable donor

3.5 It is the last limitation that has been regarded as having the largest impact for most people. A power of attorney made using common law principles or under the Powers of Attorney Act 1971 was adequate for businessmen or families going abroad leaving a relative or solicitor to manage their property. It would also help where a donor was physically unable to manage his or her affairs.[18] However, it was of no assistance in the increasingly frequent cases where a person had become incapable and had property and affairs that required administration. There were only three ways of responding to that situation. Either the person's affairs were neglected, were dealt with under a potentially invalid power of attorney or the Court of Protection would appoint a receiver to manage that person's property and affairs.[19]

3.6 The traditional power of the Court to appoint a receiver was reviewed by the Law Commission in its report *The Incapacitated Principal* (1983).[20]

---

[10] Thus the creation of a new power does not operate to revoke an earlier one, in contrast to a will under the Wills Act 1837, s 20.

[11] In respect of lasting powers of attorney, see MCA 2005, s 13(6). A welfare lasting power of attorney is not, however, revoked by the bankruptcy of the donee: s 13(8).

[12] *Clauss v Pir* [1988] 1 Ch 267.

[13] Wills Act 1837, s 9.

[14] For example, the attorney of a judge cannot pass a sentence nor the attorney of a bishop ordain a priest.

[15] Thus an attorney cannot e g sit an exam, drive a car, marry or vote on behalf of the donor. These last two circumstances are specifically excluded from the scope of an attorney's authority under a lasting power of attorney by MCA 2005, ss 27 and 29.

[16] See *Gregory v Turner* [2003] EWCA Civ 183. The appointment of a litigation friend for a 'protected party' is dealt with by the Civil Procedure Rules 1998, SI 1998/3132, Part 21.

[17] See *Drew v Nunn* (1879) 4 QBD 661, CA; *Yonge v Toynbee* [1910] 1 KB 215, CA.

[18] Such powers of attorney can still be made and are often used for those specific situations; especially if a power of attorney needs to be used immediately and there would otherwise be a delay in completing a Lasting Power of Attorney.

[19] First under the Mental Health Act 1959 and then under the Mental Health Act 1983. Under MCA 2005, the Court has power to appoint a deputy.

[20] Law Com No 122.

This drew attention to the fact that the slow and bureaucratic procedures of the Court of Protection and the Public Trust Office (which administered the property and affairs of persons under the Court's jurisdiction) might not be necessary or appropriate in every situation where an incapable person's property and affairs needed to be administered. Surely if a person could plan ahead and choose who would administer their property and affairs in the event of their incapacity, that person should be allowed to do just that without having to undergo a formal judicial process. In such cases a loving spouse or mature and sensible children could look after the affairs of the incapable person without having to go to the expense and indignity of accounting for their conduct. It was also assumed that the existing judicial and administrative framework would not be able to cope with the increasing demands placed upon it by an ageing population.

Statutory powers of attorney

Enduring powers of attorney

3.7 In response to the Law Commission report *The Incapacitated Principal*, Parliament enacted the Enduring Powers of Attorney Act 1985 (EPAA 1985) which came into force on 10 March 1986.[21] This created a new type of power of attorney, known as an enduring power of attorney (EPA), which would function in the same way as a conventional power of attorney but which, subject to a basic registration process, would continue or 'endure' beyond the onset of incapacity.[22] So long as that formality was complied with, a third party dealing with the attorney could assume that the attorney had a valid form of authority from the donor.[23] Although EPAs have since 1 October 2007 been superseded by new Lasting Powers of Attorney (LPAs) created under the MCA 2005, EPAs created before that date remain valid and need to be understood in their own terms.[24] Furthermore, LPAs cannot be fully understood without reference to this earlier history.

3.8 An attorney acting under an EPA would still be subject to the laws and principles governing the relationship between the donor and the attorney, except in so far as they were altered by statute. Thus an attorney acting under an EPA would be able to make gifts or provide for the needs of someone the donor might be expected to provide for.[25] For example, a husband looking after an incapable wife would be able to make gifts at Christmas to grandchildren on behalf of their grandmother and an attorney could use the donor's estate to maintain a disabled child or pay a grandchild's school fees.[26]

---

[21] Enduring Powers of Attorney Act 1985 (Commencement Order) 1986, SI 1986/125.
[22] EPAA 1985, s 1(1)(a); MCA 2005, Sch 4, para 1.
[23] EPAA 1985, s 9(3); MCA 2005, Sch 4, para 18(3).
[24] See 3.17 below.
[25] EPAA 1985, s 3(4), (5); MCA 2005, Sch 4, paras 2, 3. The donor of an EPA could restrict this additional power but could not extend it.
[26] *Re Cameron* [1999] Ch 386.

3.9 EPAA 1985 further provided a number of safeguards for the protection of donors of EPAs and placed the EPA jurisdiction under the authority of the Court of Protection. However, such safeguards were the result of a compromise between two competing objectives: on the one hand, individuals should be able to entrust their affairs to someone with as little interference from the state as possible; on the other, the vulnerable would need protection from the unscrupulous as well as the inefficient. Any system of protection would also have to be simple to operate, cost effective and largely self-financing.

3.10 The result of this tension was a simple system of protection which would operate on two levels. On the first level, there would be an administrative process of registration which would involve the donor and his or her next of kin being notified of an intention to register the EPA and therefore having an opportunity to object. The onus would be on the donor and his or her family to alert the Court of Protection in the event of misuse. On the second level, the civil law would apply to acts carried out by an attorney who was acting beyond the scope of his or her authority, particularly if the donor were incapable and the power was not registered. Acts carried out by an attorney would be invalid and provide the donor or his or her estate with a form of redress.[27]

3.11 The level of protection offered by an EPA, reflecting two opposing ideals, represented an imperfect compromise.[28] EPAA 1985 (which is largely incorporated in MCA 2005, Sch 4 insofar as existing EPAs are concerned, and which governs the operation of EPAs made prior to 1 October 2007) would provide the following safeguards:

- The power of attorney must be in a prescribed form[29] and must be executed by the donor and attorney.
- The prescribed form contains a brief explanation of the nature and effect of the power.
- The attorney or attorneys must undertake a process of official validation or registration when they believe that the donor is or is becoming mentally incapable of managing their property and affairs.[30] The EPA is registered by the Public Guardian, the registration providing a degree of protection for the donor and for third parties dealing with the attorney.
- Before applying for registration the attorney or attorneys must notify the donor of their intention and also at least three relatives in a prescribed order of classes of relatives.[31] All the members of a

---

[27] Although a Scottish case and not directly involving EPAs, this principle was applied in *McDowall's Executors v IRC* [2003] UKSC SPC00382, [2004] STC (SCD) 22. Ironically the beneficiary of this case was not the donor's estate but the Inland Revenue.
[28] Problems with the EPA jurisdiction are considered in more detail at **3.15**.
[29] EPAA 1985, s 2(1)(a); MCA 2005, Sch 4, para 2(1).
[30] EPAA 1985, s 4(1); MCA 2005, Sch 4, paras 4(1) and 23. Notwithstanding the implementation of MCA 2005, the Mental Health Act 1983 definition of 'mental disorder' is preserved in relation to existing EPAs.
[31] EPAA 1985, Sch 1, para 2(1); MCA 2005, Sch 4, paras 5 and 6.

- class must be notified, even if there are more than three persons, so that if a donor has one child, one sibling and six grandchildren all eight relatives must be notified.
- The donor must be given notice personally of the intention to register.[32]
- Any notices must be in a prescribed form and provide the recipient with details of the applicant and the grounds on which an objection can be made.[33]
- Any person notified of an application to register an EPA, and any other person at any other time (with the leave of the Court), may apply to the Court to refuse registration or to revoke the EPA.
- The Court shall refuse to register a power or cancel the registration of a power if satisfied that the donor has revoked the power, the donor remains capable, the donor has died or become bankrupt, that fraud or undue influence was used to create the power or 'having regard to all the circumstances and in particular the attorney's relationship or connection with the donor, the attorney is unsuitable to be the donor's attorney'.[34]
- If no valid notice of objection is received within five weeks of the last notice being given, the EPA is registered.[35]
- The Court of Protection has powers to intervene generally on behalf of the incapable or potentially incapable donor of the EPA. Thus the Court may exercise its powers to determine whether the EPA is effective,[36] and give directions as to the management of the donor's affairs and the rendering of accounts or the making of gifts.[37] In addition the Court retains its powers under MCA 2005 to intervene in the affairs of a person who lacks capacity so that there is an overlap between the two jurisdictions.

Success of enduring powers

3.12 That the EPA responded to a legal and social need is evident from the substantial number of EPAs in place. Because EPAs were often made for use prior to the onset of incapacity or as an insurance against incapacity, there remains no reliable method of knowing how many EPAs have been created. Those that can be measured are those which been registered with the Court of Protection or Public Guardian and the number of registrations has increased steadily each year since the first such powers were registered in 1986. In 2004, 16,314 EPAs were registered.[38] Even though no new EPAs

---

[32] EPAA 1985, Sch 1, para 4(1) and Court of Protection (Enduring Power of Attorney) Rules 2001, SI 2001/825, r 15(1); MCA 2005, Sch 4, para 8.
[33] The current notices are set out in the Lasting Powers of Attorney, Enduring Powers of Attorney and Public Guardian Regulations 2007, SI 2007/1253, Sch 7.
[34] EPAA 1985, ss 6(5) and 8(4); MCA 2005, Sch 4, paras 9 and 16(4).
[35] EPAA 1985, s 6(4)(a); MCA 2005, Sch 4, para 13(4).
[36] EPAA 1985, ss 5 and 8; MCA 2005, Sch 4, para 16(2)(a).
[37] EPAA 1985, s 8(2); MCA 2005, Sch 4, para 16(2)(e).
[38] National Audit Office *Protecting and promoting the financial affairs of people who lose capacity*, HC 27 (Session 2005–6). Under MCA 2005, the Public Guardian is the registration authority for EPAs: see Sch 1.

could be made from October 2007, the number of registrations has remained relatively stable, although modest when compared to the large number of LPAs being registered. As time goes on their number will diminish. In 2009/2010 over 20,000 applications to register an EPA were received by the Public Guardian.[39] In 2010/2011, 19,000 applications were made. In 2012/2013 there were 18,000 applications and 16,000 applications in 2013/2014.[40]

3.13 While the number of registered EPAs has increased, the number of incapable persons whose affairs are subject to the traditional jurisdiction of the Court of Protection has also continued to increase, to around 50,000. Thus, without the introduction of EPAs (and their successors, LPAs), it would not have been possible for the existing judicial and administrative system to manage without a significant increase in resources.

3.14 There is no doubt that EPAs have, by the measure of their popularity alone, proved useful. They were seen as simple documents and therefore inexpensive to create. Forms could be obtained from stationers and on-line. The registration process was – and remains – easy to operate, with registration forms available from the Public Guardian and a one-off fee of £110 payable on an application for registration.[41]

Problems with enduring powers

3.15 Despite the widespread acceptance and use of EPAs, the EPA jurisdiction had several clear drawbacks. It is important not to lose sight of these. Not only so these still exist with EPAs which are still valid but they also have also influenced the new legislation relating to LPAs. Furthermore the benefits and failings of LPAs can be measured against them. The main drawbacks of the EPA jurisdiction can be summarised as follows

- An EPA relates only to the property and affairs of the donor. The attorney therefore has no authority over the personal welfare of the incapable donor, covering matters such as where the donor should live, what care he or she should receive or whether a particular treatment can be given or withheld. This is despite the fact that an attorney acting in the best interests of the incapable donor needs to take account of the welfare of the donor. The donor's estate cannot, in practice, be dealt with in isolation from the actual needs of the donor.

---

[39] The number of registrations contrasts with the much higher number of LPAs registered. It is however impossible to compare with LPAs, which are generally registered while the donor has capacity; EPAs by their nature remain unregistered while the donor has capacity.
[40] Annual Report of the Office of the Public Guardian 2012/2013, HC345 and Annual Report of the Office of the Public Guardian 2013/2014, HC334. In this last period, there were 295,000 applications to register LPAs, an increase of 22% on the previous year's figure of 242,000 applications.
[41] Public Guardian (Fees, etc) Regulations 2007, SI 2007/2051 as amended by the Public Guardian (Fees, etc) (Amendment) Regulations 2013, SI 2013/1748. The prescribed fee was increased from £120 to £130 from 1 October 2011, and reduced to £110 from 1 October 2013.

- The EPA jurisdiction rests on the principle that the donor's autonomy and right to choose the person to manage his or her affairs needs to be respected, so that the attorney can operate with as little official intervention as possible. This delays and limits such intervention, which is to protect the incapable person who is by the nature of his or her situation vulnerable and at risk from abuse. The Senior Judge of the Court of Protection had estimated that financial abuse took place in about 10–15% of cases.[42] This substantial proportion included not just cases of actual fraud but also cases of misuse where, for instance, an attorney was acting beyond the scope of his or her authority, and may have been overly optimistic in view of the extent to which unregistered EPAs were often used beyond the onset of incapacity.[43]
- That fraud or misuse takes place so extensively is due to the very limited degree of official supervision provided. There is no means of knowing that a particular EPA is being used, let alone that it is being used correctly. The Court of Protection relies on misuse being notified to it, but this in turn presupposes that an attorney who registers an EPA correctly notifies relatives and they in turn file an objection with the Court of Protection. In one case the manager of a nursing home was attorney for several residents and systematically defrauded them of their savings over a couple of years. The residents had no relatives and, in any event, the EPAs were not registered. An improper benefit claim brought the fraud to light. Although the Court of Protection revoked the EPA, the civil and criminal laws offered little recompense for the victims. Recovery of the stolen assets was impossible as these had been dissipated and a criminal prosecution was made difficult by the fact that the witnesses could not give evidence for themselves.[44] The failure of the system to protect vulnerable adults was recognised officially in 1999 by the Quinquennial Review of the then Public Trust Office:[45]

> 'An EPA bestows virtually unfettered control of someone's finances once it is brought into force. While its objective (to put someone's financial affairs into the hands of an individual they have pre-selected, rather than surrendering to the Court of Protection) fits entirely with the objective of keeping the state out of family affairs unless there is no alternative, if an

---

[42] This bold assertion was first made by Denzil Lush in 'Taking Liberties: Enduring Powers of Attorney and financial abuse' (1998) *Solicitors Journal*, 11 September, at p 808 but has been restated by Denzil Lush in *Cretney & Lush on Enduring Powers of Attorney* (Jordan Publishing, 5th edn, 2001) at p 133 and see also oral evidence given by Master Lush to the Joint Committee on the Draft Mental Incapacity Bill, HL Paper 189-11, HC 1083-11, at p 188.

[43] This may be less of an issue today as the EPAs still in existence and which are now being registered were prepared some years ago and have remained dormant, and only activated by the attorneys as the requirement to use them and therefore register them has arisen.

[44] In this tragic example, although the Crown prosecuted the former manager, it accepted an admission of liability in respect of only certain counts where the victims were capable of giving evidence. Where the victims were incapable or had subsequently died, there was no conviction in their individual cases, making civil recovery very difficult to pursue.

[45] Ann Chant CB *The Public Trust Office of the Lord Chancellor's Department: A Quinquennial Review* (November 1999), at paragraph 47.

EPA goes wrong the results can be catastrophic for the person concerned. Although comparatively rare, there are plenty of instances where the system has been deliberately or accidentally abused and getting the position rectified through the Court is a long and difficult process ...'

- In view of these difficulties, the choice of attorney is crucial to the success or failure of a person's EPA. Unfortunately, many EPAs are made long before they are needed and the donor is unable to foresee changes in his or her circumstances that might otherwise have led him or her to choose a different attorney. The knowledge of the donor and the advice received at the time the EPA was made are therefore of utmost importance. However, the prescribed form of EPA was easy to obtain and complete and offered little effective protection. The form only required a signature by the donor and one witness whereupon it is presumed to have been validly executed.[46] There is furthermore no requirement that the donor has any form of legal or independent advice or that there be any assessment of the donor's capacity to create the power. Thus the ability to misuse the EPA is instituted quite easily at the time the form is created.

- EPAs have proved a victim of their own success. They were designed to be simple to complete and the forms could be obtained from stationers or from the internet. Many solicitors prepared EPAs for a nominal cost, often in connection with another matter such as a will. The problem, however, was that many such EPAs were prepared too quickly, without proper care, and without proper thought being given to problems that might arise in the future. A carefully prepared EPA would take account of family dynamics, the donor's capacity, conditions and restrictions available to the donor and the nature of his or her estate: in too many cases advice on such matters was not available.[47]

- An attorney is required to register an EPA once he or she 'has reason to believe that the donor is or is becoming mentally incapable'.[48] Therefore once the EPA has been registered, it appears to anyone dealing with the attorney that the donor is mentally incapable and thereby incapable, by reason of mental disorder, of managing and administering his or her property and affairs.[49] The presumption arises therefore that once the EPA is registered, the donor is unable to manage or administer the full extent of his or her property and affairs. This sits uneasily with the principle, now enshrined in MCA 2005, that capacity is function specific and that a person may have capacity or lack capacity in respect of different functions.[50] Thus a donor could be prevented from making decisions in respect of which he or she had capacity. For example, a

---

[46] *Re W (Enduring Power of Attorney)* [2001] 1 FLR 832.
[47] The Law Society published detailed Guidance in 1995 (revised in 1995) on EPAs and while this was very detailed and encouraged best practice among solicitors, it was not always followed and of course not all EPAs were professionally prepared.
[48] EPAA 1985, s 4(1). Notwithstanding the implementation of MCA 2005, this is still the case for existing EPAs; see MCA 2005, Sch 4, para 4(1).
[49] EPAA 1985, s 13. This is now set out in MCA 2005, Sch 4, para 23(1).
[50] *Re Beaney* (deceased) [1978] 1 WLR 770 and see generally Chapter 2.

donor might be able to manage small amounts of money or collect his pension, but his bank or pension administrator would assume, from the fact that the EPA had been registered, that he could not and would therefore deny him any rights whatsoever over his own estate.

Abolition of enduring powers

3.16 The Law Commission considered these inherent failings in the EPA jurisdiction in the context of a review of the law relating to mental incapacity in its report *Mental Incapacity* (1995).[51] This review of the law, considered in more detail in Chapter 1, led to the passing of MCA 2005 in April 2005 which came into force on 1 October 2007.

3.17 Although no new EPAs may be made after 1 October 2007, all existing EPAs made prior to that date, even though not registered, continue to remain effective. The Law Commission had proposed converting all existing EPAs to new-style powers of attorney. However, EPAs have been made in good faith to comply with a different statutory framework and for many of those powers there is no means for the persons who made them to change them. Therefore instead of cancelling or converting existing EPAs into new lasting powers of attorney (LPAs), MCA 2005 provides for existing EPAs to continue to operate under the same legal basis as they were created, but within the framework of the new 2005 Act. MCA 2005 does, however, impose one further set of obligations on an attorney making decisions for a donor who lacks capacity. The attorney must act in the donor's best interests within the meaning of MCA 2005, s 4 and must also comply with the statutory Code of Practice.[52]

3.18 The provisions of the new Act relating to existing EPAs are contained in MCA 2005, Sch 4. Apart from a few small changes, Sch 4 incorporates the provisions of EPAA 1985 into the new Act.[53]

Lasting Powers of Attorney

3.19 MCA 2005 provides expressly for the revocation of the EPAA 1985,[54] and for the creation of a new type of Lasting Power of Attorney (LPA).[55]

3.20 LPAs and MCA 2005 jurisdiction cannot, however, be comprehended without reference to EPAs:

---

[51] Law Com No 231 (see **2.4**, footnote).
[52] MCA 2005, s 1(4). The 'best interests' requirements are dealt with at **2.127–2.157** and the Code of Practice is dealt with at **2.7–2.22**.
[53] Forms and procedures are dealt with by provisions issued under MCA 2005, such as the Lasting Powers of Attorney, Enduring Powers of Attorney and Public Guardian Regulations 2007, SI 2007/1253.
[54] MCA 2005, s 66(1)(b).
[55] MCA 2005, s 9.

- EPAs made before MCA 2005 came into force will continue to operate in accordance with the same legal principles as existed as when they were made, although within the framework of the 2005 Act.[56] Thus different procedures as well as laws will operate side by side for many years to come.
- The Public Guardian and the Court of Protection will be responsible for administering the two sets of procedures and laws.
- A LPA, like an EPA, is a statutory form of power of attorney that builds on existing common law and statutory principles. Thus decisions of the courts affecting EPAs as well as practical and professional experience gained in their use will have a bearing on the use and understanding of LPAs.
- Attorneys acting under LPAs and EPAs are, where the donor lacks capacity, bound by the same requirements to act in the donor's best interests under MCA 2005, s 4.
- The principle requirement of the LPA is to address problems inherent in the EPA jurisdiction. It therefore needs to be measured against that standard.

NATURE OF LASTING POWER OF ATTORNEY

Character of lasting power of attorney

3.21 A LPA is defined by MCA 2005, s 9 as 'a power of attorney' under which one party (the donor) confers on another (the donee) authority to make certain decisions.[57] A LPA is therefore at heart 'a power of attorney' so that the principles governing the relationship in law between principal and agent apply to it. As with the EPA, the scope of such a power is both restricted and extended by statute.

3.22 Under a LPA the donor may confer authority on the attorney to make decisions, including decisions in circumstances where the donor no longer has capacity in relation to all or any of:

- the donor's personal welfare or specified matters concerning the donor's personal welfare; and
- the donor's property and affairs or specified matters concerning the donor's property and affairs.[58]

3.23 The essential character of the LPA is that it respects the presumption contained in MCA 2005, ss 1 and 2, that a person must be assumed to have capacity unless it can be established that he or she lacks capacity and that capacity is only relative to the matter and at the time that capacity needs to

---

[56] See **3.132**.
[57] MCA 2005 generally refers to a 'donee' in the context of LPAs and an 'attorney' in the context of EPAs. The author has used the term 'attorney' as a generic term that applies to a person to whom authority has been delegated under a power of attorney, whether it be an ordinary, enduring or lasting power.
[58] MCA 2005, s 9(1).

be determined. The LPA of itself is silent as to the capacity of the donor.[59] The LPA therefore must work in tandem with the ability of the donor to make decisions in person over a range or spectrum of matters for which decisions might be made. At one end of the spectrum, the donor continues to make all decisions in person, with the attorney having no role to play (waiting in the background to be called upon to act); further along the spectrum, the donee carries out specific functions such as the sale of a property and the investment of the proceeds. The donor may or may not have capacity to make these decisions in person. At the other end of the spectrum, the attorney makes all the decisions which can be made by an attorney.

3.24 A LPA therefore functions at several different levels, applying different principles according to the circumstances in which the power is being operated. Thus:
- the LPA operates, in respect of property and affairs, as an ordinary power of attorney so that the attorney acts with the implied knowledge and approval of the donor;
- the LPA operates, in respect of property and affairs, in relation to matters which the donor lacks capacity to determine for him or herself;
- in respect of welfare decisions, the LPA only operates where the donor lacks capacity to make decisions; and
- where the attorney makes decisions on behalf of the donor which the donor lacks capacity to make, the attorney must also act in the donor's best interests, applying the criteria laid down in MCA 2005, s 4 as well as the Code of Practice.

3.25 This holistic approach to the requirements of the donor obviates the need for an attorney to register the LPA specifically on the onset of incapacity. Although registration might be delayed until that point is reached, the lalack ck of capacity of itself does not trigger the registration process required to complete or validate the power. The existence of a completed LPA thereby avoids a presumption, as is the case with an EPA, that the donor is incapable of managing the full extent of his or her property and affairs.[60] Thus to any third party dealing with the property and affairs of the donor are concerned, the state of mind of the donor is irrelevant and the donor is not labelled or stigmatised as being incapable.

3.26 This approach is not followed where the power relates to welfare matters. Although the LPA can be registered at any time irrespective of the capacity of the donor, when the LPA comes to be used, it can only be used where the donor lacks capacity to make the decision in question.[61] For obvious reasons, the capable donor's right to make decisions over his or her

---

[59] By contrast with EPAs whose registration is triggered by a defined medical state which therefore creates a presumption that the donor lacks capacity (see **3.15**).
[60] This follows the recommendation of the Law Commission, see Law Com No 231 (see **3.16**), at para 7.31.
[61] MCA 2005, s 11(7)(a).

own welfare takes precedence over another person's judgment, and in practice a doctor or carer will obtain consent or refusal to treatment from the donor in person so long as the donor has capacity. Only if the donor clearly lacks capacity does the LPA come into play.

Problems in practice with 'presumption of capacity'

3.27 While it is obviously sensible to allow people autonomy over their own affairs to the extent possible without making presumptions about a lack of capacity, this can cause practical difficulties. Any third party dealing with the attorney acting under a LPA is not 'on notice' that the donor lacks capacity. This may cause problems if there are conflicting instructions or the LPA is being used fraudulently. It may, for instance, be possible for the attorney to arrange the sale of the donor's property against the donor's wishes. Will anyone check with the donor that the donor wants the property sold? Or take the case of a donor who makes regular withdrawals from his account to pay a friendly tradesman, even though there is a LPA in place and registered with the bank. In both cases the status of the LPA does not of itself provide any greater degree of protection for either party than an ordinary power of attorney.

3.28 The protection afforded by the LPA is in the making and registration of the power. Once those steps have been taken and the LPA is in place, there is no further formal protection for the donor. The status of the LPA and the statutory presumption of capacity may well make it easier for the confused and the vulnerable to make mistakes which will be harder to detect in practice. Although LPAs may be drafted to ensure that they will only operate on the onset of incapacity (in the same way as an EPA), this does not appear to be common in practice (although the new prescribed forms introduced on 1 July 2015 now include this as an option).[62] Where a LPA is restricted in this way, the donor ends up reversing the statutory presumption in favour of capacity intended by Parliament to benefit the donor. Restrictions also cause their own difficulties in terms of drafting, evidence and defining the actual trigger for registration.[63] Should for instance the LPA be used if the donor is physically incapable but mentally capable? Should it be used if the donor needs the attorneys to act (In relation to property and affairs) while he has capacity? What sort of medical evidence should be presented and to whom, before the LPA can be used. Should registration be delayed until the condition has been satisfied? There is then a danger in delaying registration until a triggering condition has arisen, as the registration process takes time and the LPA may need to be used at short

---

[62] See the Lasting Powers of Attorney, Enduring Powers of Attorney and Public Guardian (Amendment) Regulations 2015, SI 2015/1899. See further **3.77**. Problems caused by the policy of early registration are considered in more detail at **3.117**.
[63] The Law Society Practice Note of 8 December 2011 discourages such a condition, pointing out that: '… as a registered property and financial affairs LPA can be used while the donor retains capacity, restrictions that attempt to limit the attorney's power to use the LPA while the donor still has capacity are difficult to draft'.

notice.[64] Experience suggests that most LPAs are drafted on the basis that there should be flexibility to make decisions for the donor when they need to be taken and the donees should be trusted to act accordingly.

Scope of lasting power of attorney

3.29 The scope of the attorney's authority is very extensive. Principles concerning powers of attorney tend to be drafted in quite wide terms, and then refined or limited for particular situations. For example, an attorney may do anything that may lawfully be done by the donor. There are then things an attorney cannot do, such as make gifts or receive a benefit. But there are cases in which a benefit may be received. A LPA may consist of a web of interconnected powers and limitations, as well as interventions, involving one or more of the following:

(1) *The donor*. The donor may limit the authority of the attorney so that the power relates only to specified matters or operates in certain circumstances.[65] For example, a power may provide that it only relates to property and affairs or that it will only operate if the donor becomes incapable. Limitations in the form of the power are considered in more detail at **3.76**.

(2) *Common law*. There are certain personal acts that cannot be delegated to an attorney and an attorney cannot act to benefit him or herself or delegate his or her authority. These and other restrictions, including duties imposed on the attorney by law, such as a duty of care and a fiduciary duty not to benefit from the role, are considered in more detail at **3.4**.[66]

(3) *Statute*. MCA 2005 includes some crucial extensions to these restrictions. Subject to the formalities of the Act being complied with, a LPA is not revoked by the lack of capacity of the donor and in certain circumstances a power can be used to make gifts, delegate trustee functions and make decisions concerning personal welfare matters. MCA 2005 also sets out limits on the scope of the 2005 Act itself and limits on the attorney's authority.[67] For instance an attorney's power to make gifts is defined by MCA 2005, s 12.[68]

(4) *The Court*. The Court of Protection has powers to intervene in the operation of the power. The Court can cancel the power in favour of an attorney, attach conditions to the power or provide the attorney with authority to make a decision which is beyond the scope of the

---

[64] The prescribed period which must expire before the Public Guardian can register an LPA where there are no objections is 6 weeks (Lasting Powers of Attorney, Enduring Powers of Attorney and Public Guardian Regulations 2007, SI 2007/1253, reg 12).
[65] MCA 2005, s 9(4)(b) and see **3.77**.
[66] See also the recent case of *Re Harcourt: the Public Guardian v A* [2013] COPLR 69 for an illustration of the application of common law principles to a modern LPA. The fiduciary role of the attorney of an attorney (or deputy) is robustly stated in the Code of Practice at paragraph 7.60.
[67] MCA 2005, ss 27–29.
[68] See **3.37–3.43** below.

attorney's authority within the LPA.[69] The Court can also make decisions of its own concerning the property and affairs and welfare of the donor.[70]

Property and affairs

3.30 MCA 2005 does not define in any detail the extent or scope of an attorney's powers over a person's property and affairs. MCA 2005, s 9(1) describes a LPA as 'a power of attorney' which confers authority on a donee to make decisions about 'all or any of' the donor's property and affairs or specified matters concerning the donor's property and affairs. What is peculiar to a LPA (as opposed to an ordinary power of attorney) is that the LPA includes authority to make such decisions in circumstances where the donor no longer has capacity.

3.31 The wording used for the attorney's authority under a LPA is similar, if not as clearly defined as it is under an EPA. Under an EPA, where a donor has conferred general authority, the power 'operates to confer, subject to the restriction [relating to the making of gifts] ... and to any conditions or restrictions contained in the instrument, authority to do on behalf of the donor anything which the donor can lawfully do by an attorney'.[71] Thus the EPA refers back to common law principles. MCA 2005, Sch 4, para 1(2) also provides a useful reminder of an attorney's limited but essential authority to 'maintain the donor or prevent loss to his estate' which can operate when an application for registration has been made and the power has not been registered. The attorney acting under an EPA also has authority to make gifts and provide for the needs of any other person if the donor might be expected to provide for that person's needs.[72]

3.32 Nevertheless, a LPA is a power of attorney and must also be understood in terms of the common law relationship between principal and agent. MCA 2005, s 9(1) defines the scope of the attorney's authority in expansive terms, referring to 'all or any' of the donor's property and affairs.' As there is a clear distinction between separate LPAs created for personal welfare and for property and affairs, the latter can only be understood in terms of 'business matters, legal transactions and other dealings of a similar kind.'[73] The attorney has a fiduciary duty to act as the donor's agent and secure the proper management of the donor's estate, for the benefit of the donor.[74] MCA 2005 however takes the attorney into a new area of responsibility, requiring the attorney to make decisions where the donor

---

[69] MCA 2005, s 23. As to the role of the Court of Protection in making decisions concerning LPAs, see **3.138** et seq.
[70] MCA 2005, ss 15–17.
[71] MCA 2005, Sch 4, para 3(1).
[72] MCA 2005, Sch 4, para 3(2) and (3). Curiously, the specific reference to a power to provide for another person's needs is not repeated in the provisions of the MCA 2005 dealing with LPAs. See **3.35** below.
[73] *Re F (Mental Patient: Sterilisation)* [1989] 2 FLR 376, at [554] per Lord Brandon.
[74] The attorney's common law duties are summarised at 3.4 above.

lacks capacity, and which must be in accordance with the best interests criteria of the Act.[75] The attorney must therefore take into account matters such as the donor's past and present wishes and feelings, beliefs and values, the views of anyone specified as a person to be consulted or caring for the donor or interested in the welfare of the donor as well as the other factors the donor would be likely to consider if he or she had capacity.

Acting in the best interests of the donor

3.33 The importance of the application of 'best interests' to the attorney's role is more than a restatement of the common law duty of an agent to act in the best interests of his or her principal. Neither is the attorney necessarily doing what the donor would have done and making a substituted decision on his behalf. The attorney must act in the best interests of the donor, taking account of a whole range of factors, only one of which might be the actual or likely wishes of the donor.

3.34 The extended test of best interests requires an attorney to possess an appropriate understanding of the character and circumstances of the donor. It may though be difficult to reconcile this with an objective responsibility towards the donor's estate. For example, a donor may have been determined to live in his own home, notwithstanding a worrying degree of self-neglect.[76] Or a donor may have been profligate or lived beyond his means, without an appreciation of his limited resources. The donor may have chosen to make unwise decisions with his lifestyle, property and investments. An attorney may however have to make a tactful compromise between these personal circumstances and his or her responsibilities to the estate (and its preservation for the long-term benefit of the donor). There is often an inherent tension between making the decision which the donor would make (the substituted judgment test) and the decision which is financially prudent or morally correct (the objective test). In trying to make the decision which the donor would make, if capable, the attorney may have to assume that the donor could appreciate his predicament as one of the 'other factors he would be likely to consider if he were able to do so'. This dilemma was addressed by Her Honour Judge Marshall QC in the case of *Re S and S*.[77] Although this case related to the wishes of a donor of an EPA (that the attorneys should act jointly and if they could not act jointly a professional deputy should be appointed), the judge explained that the donor's wishes should where possible have priority over other considerations. Although the donor's wishes in this case could be adhered to, they are not by themselves binding. They are a factor that must be

---

[75] MCA 2005, s 4(7) and also s 9(4).
[76] A person acting in a fiduciary role should not replicate the unwise decision which would have been made by the principal. See *Re P* [2009] EWHC 163 (Ch), [2009] COPLR Con Vol 906 (para 42) and in the context of an attorney acting under a LPA see *Re Buckley: The Public Guardian v C* [2013] EWCOP 2965, [2013] COPLR 39. In exceptional circumstances, it may be in a person's best interests to have an unwise unwise decision made by a court, see the decision of Hedley J in *CYC v PC and NC* [2012] COPLR 670.
[77] [2008] COPLR Con Vol 1074.

considered, and one to which a great deal of weight must be given. But they remain just one of several factors in the balancing act that the attorney must perform when acting in the donor's best interests. As the judge pointed out (at [57] and [58]):[78]

> '... where P can and does express a wish or view which is not irrational (in the sense of being a wish which a person with full capacity might reasonably have), is not impracticable as far as its physical implementation is concerned, and is not irresponsible having regard to the extent of P's resources (ie whether a responsible person of full capacity who had such resources might reasonably consider it worth using the necessary resources to implement his wish) then that situation carries great weight, and effectively gives rise to a presumption in favour of implementing those wishes, unless there is some potential sufficiently detrimental effect for P of doing so which outweighs this.
>
> That might be some extraneous consequence, or some other unforeseen, unknown or unappreciated factor. Whether this further consideration actually should justify overriding P's wishes might then be tested by asking whether, had he known of this further consideration, it appears (from what is known of P) that he would have changed his wishes. It might be further tested by asking whether the seriousness of this countervailing factor in terms of detriment to P is such that it must outweigh the detriment to an adult of having one's wishes overruled, and the sense of impotence, and the frustration and anger, which living with that awareness (insofar as P appreciates it) will cause to P. Given the policy of the Act to empower people to make their own decisions wherever possible, justification for overruling P and "saving him from himself" must, in my judgment be strong and cogent. Otherwise, taking a different course from that which P wishes would be likely to infringe the statutory direction in s 1(6) of the Act, that one must achieve any desired objective by the route which least restricts P's own rights and freedom of actions.'

Where there is a conflict between different objectives, it is important that an attorney should not be exposed to liability. It must be remembered that an attorney under a property and affairs LPA is also acting in a fiduciary role and has been appointed to act on that basis. It is not the role of the attorney to speculate with the donor's assets or determine alone how or where the donor should be cared for. This point was emphasised in the case of *Re Buckley, the Public Guardian v C*, where the attorney's justification for making an unusual investment (in a reptile breeding business) was that she was doing what the donor would have wanted. Senior Judge Lush was keen to dismiss this approach:[79]

'Managing your own money is one thing. Managing someone else's money is an entirely different matter. People who have the capacity to manage their own financial affairs are generally not accountable to anyone and don't need to keep accounts or records of their income and expenditure. They can do whatever they like with their money, and this includes doing nothing at all. They can stash their cash under the mattress, if they wish and, of course,

---

[78] This approach was followed in the High Court decisions of Lewison J in the case of *Re P* [2009] EWHC 163 (Ch), [2009] COPLR Con Vol 906 and Morgan J in the case of *Re G (TJ)* [2010] EWHC 3005 (CoP), [2010] COPLR Con Vol 403. It has been applied more recently in similar circumstances, in respecting the donor's wishes concerning who should manage his estate, in the case of *Re DI; the Public Guardian and IT and others* [2015] EWCOP 10, [2015] COPLR 225.
[79] [2013] EWCOP 2965, [2013] COPLR 39.

they are entitled to make unwise decisions. None of these options are open to an attorney acting for an incapacitated donor, partly because of their fiduciary obligations and partly because an attorney is required to act in the donor's best interests. The Mental Capacity Act 2005, section 1(5), states that, "an act done, or decision made, under this Act for or on behalf of a person who lacks capacity must be done, or made, in his best interests."'

Thus not only does the attorney have a fiduciary duty to the donor's estate, exercising this responsibility correctly is also on the best interests of the donor. In practice, it may still be difficult to reconcile the attorney's wishes and doing what the donor would have wanted. Sometimes this can be resolved with tact and good judgment. There may be a range of options, one of which may be close to the donor's wishes. For example a donor may wish to be generous and make gifts to his children. The attorney can give effect to the sentiment, but the amounts that can be given are limited.[80] Sometimes, there will be a degree of uncertainty or risk that may need to be justified in terms of the donor's best interests. For example, the donor's estate may not be able to manage the cost of a desired level of care. So long as the attorney is not being extravagant or reckless, possibly a degree of has to be accepted to preserve the donor's quality of life. The question for the attorney is: can I do what the donor is expecting me to do, within an acceptable level of risk? If this dilemma still cannot be resolved, then the objective best interests of the donor should prevail. If there is any prospect of the attorney acting beyond the scope of the authority conferred by the donor, or the attorney may be inclined to make an unwise decision, then an application should be made to the Court of Protection.[81]

Power to maintain others

3.35 It is a basic fiduciary duty of an attorney to use the property under his or her control for the benefit of the donor, and not to benefit in person or to benefit a third party. However, the donor may have commitments to other dependents or objects which need to continue beyond the onset of incapacity, and which therefore the donor cannot authorise in person. This difficulty was recognised by the Law Commission in its report *Mental Incapacity* which recommended that attorneys should have a limited authority to maintain others, subject to any express restriction specified by the donor.[82] Thus the attorney acting under a registered EPA 'may so act in relation to himself or in relation to any other person if the donor might be expected to provide for his or that person's needs respectively; and ... may do whatever the donor might be expected to do to meet those needs'.[83] This power provides some very useful flexibility in practice, especially where a

---

[80] See 3.37 below.
[81] For an example of a case in which the Court of Protection authorised the making of an unwise decision, see the decision of Hedley, J in *CYC v PC and NC* [2012] COPLR 670.
[82] Law Com No 122, paras 4.23 to 4.30.
[83] MCA 2005, Sch 4, para 3(2); formerly covered by EPAA 1985, s 3(4).

donor has a pre-existing commitment to maintain a spouse or disabled child.[84] This power is distinct from the power to make gifts, which is dealt with at **3.37** below.

3.36 By contrast with the EPA framework, where LPAs are concerned, MCA 2005 makes no reference to the maintenance of another party. In the absence of such an express power, a benefit to the attorney or a third party, is inconsistent with the attorney's fiduciary duty the donor.

In its report *Mental Incapacity* the Law Commission took the view that the power to act in a donor's 'best interests' was more flexible and wider than the power of an attorney at common law, because:[85]

> '... it requires the attorney to consider the wishes and feelings of the donor and the factors he or she would have taken into account, the attorney would in appropriate cases be quite able to meet another person's needs (including the attorney's own needs) or make seasonal or charitable gifts, while still acting within the best interests duty.'

However, this rather sweeping assumption is implicitly contradicted by MCA 2005, s 12, which expressly prohibits an attorney from making gifts, except to the limited extent permitted:

> 'Where a lasting power of attorney confers authority to make decisions about P's property and affairs, it does not authorise a done ... to dispose of the donor's property by making gifts except to the extent permitted by subsection (2).'

This is further emphasised by s 23(4), which provides that any gifts not within the scope of that section must be authorised by the Court of Protection. A benefit to another person of necessity involves a disposition of property and the making of a gift, irrespective of the desirability or necessity of the act. For Inheritance Tax purposes, there is no distinction between maintenance and gifts, which are invariably classed as transfers of value.[86] If the attorney had such wide powers on a wide interpretation of the attorney's ability to act in the donor's best interests, then there would be no need for an express provision dealing solely with gifts and then to a clearly limited extent only.[87] There is no corresponding provision addressing maintenance. While it can be argued that a distinction should be made between the provision of maintenance and the making of a gift, there must be some uncertainty as to whether the attorney can – or the extent to which the attorney should – benefit another person without the sanction of the Court of Protection.[88] The Court takes this approach, but will make a pragmatic exception for a spouse, civil partner or child under the age of 18.[89]

---

[84] The extent of the EPAA 1985 power was illustrated in the case of *Re Cameron (deceased); Phillips v Cameron* [1999] Ch 386. In the more recent case of *Re DT; the Public Guardian and IT and others* [2015] EWCOP 10, [2015] COPLR 225 the attorneys were acting within their authority is using the donor's pension to maintain the donor.
[85] Law Com No 231, at para 7.11.
[86] Inheritance Tax Act 1984, s 3 (although s 11 allows a limited exception for maintenance for a spouse. Civil partner or child who is under the age of 18 or in full time education.
[87] MCA 2005, s 12 and see **3.37–3.43**. The draft Bill prepared by the Law Commission made no reference to gifts or to maintenance, perhaps assuming that all such gifts could be permitted so long as they were within the donor's best interests.
[88] It might be argued that maintenance in return for consideration such as the care of the donor

The clear wishes of the donor expressed on the face of the LPA cannot provide assistance, although they may serve as evidence of the donor's wishes. In a case where the donor of a LPA purported to extend the attorney's authority to 'continue to make contributions to my grandchildren's' Child Trust Funds and any other saving/pension plans that I fund for their benefit' the Court severed the provision from the instrument.[90] Guidance that 'I hereby express the wish that my Attorneys will continue to pay my contribution to the school fees of my granddaughters, A and B, as per my previous pattern of contributions' was likewise severed.[91] However, the Court has accepted a provision which authorised the attorney to maintain the donor's wife. This was however accepted on the basis that the attorney was simply carrying out the donor's legal obligation to maintain his spouse and not because of an express or implied power in MCA 2005.[92]

Where the attorney is also the person whom the donor might be expected to provide for there is a further conflict of interest which the attorney, as a fiduciary, cannot resolve in that role. In the case of *Re Buckley:* the *Public Guardian v C*, Senior Judge Lush stated emphatically that (subject to a sensible *de minimis* exception), any gift that exceeds the scope of the attorney's authority under s 23 as well as loans to the attorney or attorney's family or any other transaction involving a conflict of interest must be approved by the Court of Protection.[93]

---

is not the same as a gift. But unless the recipient is actually providing care whose value can be measured, there is bound to be some uncertainty as to what is bounty and what is value. The Court has accepted that the maintenance of a spouse is a legal obligation which an attorney may – or indeed, must – implement (see *Re Bloom*, referred to below). However, unless such an exception exists, an attorney would be acting appropriately in referring such a matter to the Court of Protection.

[89] See guidance 'Avoiding Invalid Provisions in a Lasting Power of Attorney' published on the Government website under www.gov.uk/government/publications/lasting-power-of-attorney-avoid-invalid-provisions. The wording here seems to reflect the wording used by Inheritance Tax Act 1984, s 11 although without reference to a child in full time education. This may be an unlikely situation where most LPAs are made by older people and the Court of Protection decisions on this point involve a donor and a donor's spouse.

[90] See the decision in the case of *Re Wheatley* (an order of the Senior Judge dated 31 January 2011). The decision is no longer reported on the Ministry of Justice website, but is referred to in the guidance on severing invalid provisions (see note above). For severance of provisions in an LPA see **3.62**.

[91] See the decision in *Re Forrest* (an order of the Senior Judge made on 2 March 2012).

[92] See the decision in *Re Bloom* (an order of the Senior Judge made on 16 March 2012). The LPA included the following direction: 'I direct my attorneys to use such of my capital and income as they shall at their discretion deem necessary to make provision for my wife's maintenance and benefit.' The Court severed the reference to 'benefit' but allowed the reference to 'maintenance' to remain in place. The Court also confirmed its understanding that the attorney's authority to maintain the donor's spouse rested on the donor's own common law duties to his wife. This approach was queried in the later case of *Re Strange* (an order of the senior judge made on 21 May 2012). Even if there is no common law obligation of one spouse to maintain the other, other statutes impose maintenance obligations. For example a donor's estate can be required to provide for the maintenance of a spouse under the Inheritance (Provision for Family and Dependants) Act 1975.

[93] *Re Buckley: The Public Guardian v C* [2013] EWCOP 2965, [2013] COPLR 39.

Limited power to make gifts

3.37 MCA 2005, s 12 restates the principle that an attorney cannot make gifts, but allows gifts to be made in certain limited circumstances. The donor can limit this authority, but cannot extend it.[94] Subject to any limitation contained in the power, the donee may make gifts:[95]

'(a) on customary occasions to persons (including himself) who are related to or connected with the donor, or
(b) to any charity to whom the donor made or might have been expected to make gifts,

if the value of each such gift is not unreasonable having regard to all the circumstances and, in particular, the size of the donor's estate.'

3.38 MCA 2005 therefore imposes four basic conditions on an attorney before a gift can be made:

(1) there must be no restriction in the power itself which prevents the gift from being made;
(2) the gift must be made on a 'customary occasion';
(3) an individual must be related to or connected with the donor, while a charity must be one which has benefited or might be expected to benefit from the donor; and
(4) the value of any gift must not be unreasonable having regard to all the circumstances and especially to the value of the donor's estate.

3.39 'Customary occasion' is defined by MCA 2005, to allow for all types of family, seasonal or religious events which justify the making of a gift, as:[96]

'(a) the occasion or anniversary of a birth, a marriage or the formation of a civil partnership, or
(b) any other occasion on which presents are customarily given within families or among friends or associates.'

3.40 The attorney cannot therefore make a gift at a time that is not a 'customary occasion' such as the beginning or end of a tax year, or to make gifts of surplus income at the end of a tax year.[97] For the attorney to make a valid gift as part of a tax-planning exercise, it must also be of a 'customary occasion'. An attorney who wishes to make a series of small gifts to the donor's children and grandchildren cannot therefore make simultaneous payments on 6 April. The payments would need to be made on each birthday, or may be made at the same time at Christmas.

---

[94] See the decision in the case of *Re Baker* (an order of the Senior Judge made on 12 November 2010). An LPA included the following provision: 'I authorise my Attorneys to make gifts from my assets on such terms and conditions as they think fit, for the purposes of inheritance tax planning, including but not restricted to the making of gifts in line with the annual lifetime gift allowance' On the application of the Public Guardian the provision was severed on the grounds that it contravened section 12 of the MCA 2005.
[95] MCA 2005, s 12(2).
[96] MCA 2005, s 12(3).
[97] See the case of *Re PC: the Public Guardian v AC and JC* [2014] EWCOP 41, where a LPA was revoked due to excessive gifts made by attorneys, ostensibly to mitigate Inheritance Tax.

3.41 Although any gift made by an attorney on behalf of a donor should be in the donor's best interests, MCA 2005, s 12 contains an express provision that where the gift is to a charity, the charity must be one 'to whom the donor made or might have been expected to make gifts'. This would, for instance, allow an attorney to continue an established pattern of giving, for example, maintaining standing orders to charities. This power is therefore meant to be used to continue existing arrangements or to reflect past associations and interests of the donor, rather than to reflect new wishes and interests.

3.42 consideration of the donor's best interests is consistent with the attorney's responsibilities to act prudently in relation to the donor's estate. A donor who had in the past been very generous may now have a commitment to funding long term care costs. The sale of the donor's property may mean that gifts are now affordable. These are factors that the donor would consider if he had capacity. The gift must in any event comply with MCA 2005, s 12 and be reasonable 'having regard to all the circumstances and, in particular, the size of the donor's estate'. The attorney cannot avoid a fiduciary duty to the estate and could not make a gift which the donor could not afford to make. It is for the attorney to exercise his or her judgment in measuring the appropriate value of a gift. There is no fixed limit as to what is reasonable or not. Different recipients may have greater or lesser needs or be more or less deserving of a gift. A wealthy donor may be able to afford a gift of several thousand pounds, although a gift of £20,000 was treated as beyond the scope of an attorney's authority under an EPA.[98] A donor with limited capital and in receipt of benefits may, by contrast, only be able to afford a gift of a few pounds. In any event, an attorney acting under an LPA should have regard to the guidance given by Senior Judge Lush in the case of *Re GM* [2013] COPLR 290. Although this judgment referred to the conduct of a deputy, the deputy's authority in this case – as in most cases – reflects the statutory wording used to define an attorney's attorney. The judge stated that gifts beyond a *de minimis* level should not be made without the express authority of the Court. The *de minimis* exception could be construed as covering use of the annual IHT exemption of £3,000 and use of the annual small gifts exemption of £250 per person, up to a maximum of, say, ten people where P has a life expectancy of less than five years, has an estate in excess of the IHT nil rate band, the gifts are affordable by P and there is no evidence that P would be opposed to gifts of this magnitude. Gifts which are potentially exempt transfers or which are made from surplus income to avoid Inheritance Tax should only be made on the authority of the Court.

---

[98] See *Re W (Enduring Power of Attorney)* [2001] 1 FLR 832 and in particular the comments of the judge at first instance, Julian Sher QC [1999] 2 FLR 1163 at pp 1168–1170. At the time of the hearing, and allowing for three gifts of £20,000 each to the three children of the donor, the estate was worth approximately £260,000. Apart from the value of the gifts, they were made following the sale of a property. The facts that the donor had the resources and that the gifts would potentially reduce liability to inheritance tax ensured that the gifts were sufficient to render them beyond the scope of the attorney's authority.

3.43 Where there is any doubt about the attorney's authority to make the gift or it is clear that a proposed gift exceeds the attorney's authority under the LPA, the Court of Protection can authorise the gift under MCA 2005, s 23, which deals with the Court's powers in relation to the operation of LPAs. Under this power, the Court can authorise the making of gifts which are not permitted by s 12(2). The Court cannot, however, ignore an express limitation in the power itself. This section would not allow the Court to ignore an express restriction relating to the making of gifts[99] In this situation, the attorney or any other person who may apply, may request the Court to authorise a gift under MCA 2005, s 18(1)(b).[100] However, the Court would be required to have regard to the restriction in the LPA which would stand as a 'relevant written statement' in determining the donor's best interests.[101]

The donor as trustee

3.44 A LPA confers the same rights as an EPA in favour of an attorney who is a trustee of land. An attorney acting under a LPA has no power to act as a trustee unless the power complies with the Trustee Act 1925, s 25 or the provisions of the Trustee Act 1925, s 36 apply. This latter provision saves most domestic situations where a property is owned by husband and wife under a trust for land. One of the owners, who is also a trustee for land becomes incapable. To fulfil the 'two trustee' rule, the attorney of the incapable trustee – acting under a registered power[102] – can appoint a new trustee to act on the sale and give a valid receipt for capital monies.[103] An appointment of a new trustee in place of the donor by the donee of a LPA may however have to be accompanied by medical evidence of the lack of capacity as the fact of registration is not evidence that the trustee lacks capacity to exercise his functions as a trustee for the purposes of the Law of Property Act 1925, s 22.

The donor as a litigant

3.45 A person's right or standing to conduct proceedings is governed by the relevant Rules of Court in which those proceedings take place. Civil

---

[99] See *Re R (Enduring Power of Attorney)* [1991] 1 FLR 128 where the EPA contained an express restriction that the attorney could not make gifts to friends or relatives. The position should not be different where an LPA is in issue. This does not prevent a person applying to the Court of Protection for an order for a gift under MCA 2005, s18(1)(b). Although the Court is not bound by a restriction on the face of the LPA, this would be a factor that the Court would have to take into account.

[100] Unless the LPA expressly prevents the making of gifts, the attorney has a choice between ss 23(4) and 18(1)(b). There are therefore two similar provisions that can be used. This may be due to the fact that EPAA 1985 provided authority for the Court to authorise gifts by attorneys (which is now contained in MCA 2005, Sch 4 para 16(e)) so that attorneys would have their own legislative framework.

[101] MCA 2005, s 4(6)(a).

[102] 'Registered power' is defined as an 'Enduring Power of Attorney or Lasting Power of Attorney registered under the Mental Capacity Act 2005' (Trustee Act 1925, s 36(6C)).

[103] Trustee Act 1925, s 36(6A).

proceedings in the High Court and County Court are governed by the Civil Procedure Rules 1998 (CPR).[104] The issue of whether a person has capacity to conduct or settle proceedings is the very matter for which capacity is required. A person may therefore have capacity to issue and then settle proceedings even though he or she might otherwise be unable to administer his or her property and affairs.[105] CPR Part 21 therefore distinguishes between the person conducting proceedings who is the 'protected party' and the person who is in receipt of a damages award who is the 'protected beneficiary'.

3.46 The litigation friend can be appointed to act by the Court of Protection[106] but if the Court of Protection is not involved in the affairs of the person who lacks capacity, a suitable representative can nominate him or herself as litigation friend. The litigation friend must be someone capable of acting in the protected party's best interests with no conflict of interest in the matter and whose role is limited to the proceedings in question.

3.47 An attorney acting under a LPA has no standing as an attorney to bring or defend proceedings on behalf of the donor who lacks capacity.[107] There is no reference in the CPR to an attorney. There is therefore no change to the established procedure whereby if the donor lacks capacity, the attorney – if he or she wishes to act in the proceedings – must demonstrate his or her suitability to act as a litigation friend or obtain the express authority of the Court of Protection to conduct the proceedings.[108]

Welfare matters

3.48 The donor of a personal welfare LPA may authorise the attorney to make decisions on behalf of the donor about his or her personal welfare or specified matters concerning personal welfare. This appears at first sight an extensive power to make vitally important decisions such as where and how the donor shall live and to give or refuse consent to treatment.[109] In certain circumstances, the attorney's authority may even extend to giving or refusing consent to life-sustaining treatment.

3.49 The principle application of this authority is to enable those providing health care or treatment for a person who lacks capacity to obtain consent to what they propose to do in that person's best interests. A doctor performing a

---

[104] SI 1998/3132.
[105] *Masterman-Lister v Jewell* [2002] EWHC 417 (QB); on appeal *Masterman-Lister v Brutton & Co and Jewell & anor* [2002] EWCA Civ 1889.
[106] MCA 2005, s 18(1)(k).
[107] The Law Commission's draft Bill proposed giving the attorney power over 'all matters relating to the donor's property or affairs, including the conduct of legal proceedings' (clause 16(1) of the draft Bill set out as Appendix A to Law Com No 231 (see **3.16**)). There is no corresponding reference in MCA 2005.
[108] See *Gregory v Turner* [2003] EWCA Civ 183. Although this case concerned an action conducted by an attorney acting under an EPA, the principle will be the same where a LPA is concerned.
[109] MCA 2005, s 11(7)(c).

hip replacement or a dentist fitting a denture can be assured of having formal consent to an invasive treatment rather than having to rely on his or her own judgment about the necessity of the treatment and whether it is covered by MCA 2005, s 5.[110] A LPA also gives an attorney certain rights, in particular:

- a person or body determining whether a proposed act is in the best interests of the incapable person must take into account the views of, and if possible consult, the donee of the LPA (MCA 2005, s 4(7));
- an act performed in connection with 'care or treatment' under MCA 2005, s 5 is not authorised by that section if it conflicts with a decision of an attorney acting within the scope of his or her power (MCA 2005, s 6(6)(a));
- a LPA made after an advance decision conferring authority in respect of treatment to which the advance decision relates takes precedence over the refusal of consent contained in the advance decision (MCA 2005, s 25(2)(b)); and
- the attorney may apply to the Court of Protection for the exercise of any of its powers under MCA 2005 without seeking prior permission (MCA 2005, s 50(1)(b)).

Limits on welfare matters

3.50 The scope of an attorney's authority in welfare matters is more limited than may at first be apparent. The principal limitations are as follows:

- A ny act performed by an attorney must be in accordance with the donor's best interests (MCA 2005, ss 1(5) and 4)).
- There is no power to make decisions if the donor has capacity to make decisions for him or herself (MCA 2005, s 11(7)(a)). The fact that there is a valid registered LPA in place does not of itself authorise the person treating the donor to take instructions directly from the attorney. The carer or clinician must also be satisfied that the donor lacks capacity.
- A LPA does not authorise the attorney to restrain the donor unless the attorney reasonably believes that it is necessary to prevent harm to the donor and the act of restraint is a proportionate response to the likelihood of the donor suffering harm and the seriousness of that harm (MCA 2005, s 11(3) and (4)).
- Any restraint of the donor cannot deprive the donor of his or her liberty within the meaning of Art 5(1) of the European Convention on Human Rights (MCA 2005, s 11(6))). This may be at odds with the power to restrain the donor which by its nature deprives the donor of his or her liberty. In the light of the Bournewood case, it is likely that the power to 'restrain' under MCA 2005 will be interpreted narrowly, for use in emergencies or as a very temporary

---

[110] Acts in connection with care or treatment are dealt with at **2.158ff**.

measure.[111] A longer-term detention of a person who cannot consent to it or detention for the purposes of treatment, must either be authorised by the Court of Protection under MCA 2005, s 16(2)(a) or by one of the bodies empowered by MCA 2005, Sch 1A using the Deprivation of Liberty Safeguards.[112]

- The donor's authority to consent to care or treatment is subject to a valid and applicable advance decision made after the LPA.[113]
- The attorney only has authority to give or refuse consent to life-sustaining treatment if this is expressly allowed by the LPA and this authority is furthermore subject to any restrictions or conditions in the power.[114] This power of 'life and death' is considered in more detail below, but is in its turn subject to two further safeguards:
  - a person considering whether a life-sustaining treatment is in a person's best interests must not be motivated by a desire to bring about that person's death;[115] and
  - the declaration in MCA 2005, s 62 that the existing law relating to murder or manslaughter is not affected by anything contained in MCA 2005.
- An attorney acting under a welfare LPA cannot compel the carrying out of a particular treatment or decision. An attorney may give or refuse consent to treatment, but if a doctor is unwilling to carry out a treatment, the attorney cannot force another person to make a decision which he or she believes is contrary to the donor's best interests.[116]
- MCA 2005 confers no authority on any person or body to make decisions in respect of:
  - family relations, including consent to a marriage or civil partnership, sexual relations, divorce (based on 2 years' separation) and parental responsibilities relating to a child's welfare;[117]
  - MCA 2005 matters, where medical treatment is required for mental disorder as defined by the Mental Health Act 1983;[118] and

---

[111] *HL v United Kingdom* (2004) 40 EHRR 761 (the Strasbourg proceedings arising out of the decision of the House of Lords in *R v Bournewood Community and Mental Health NHS Trust ex p L* [1998] 2 FLR 550).

[112] For a more detailed consideration of the powers of restraint in MCA 2005 in the light of the European Convention on Human Rights, see Chapter 6. The Act has been considerably amended by the Mental Health Act 2007, which introduced new safeguards dealing with the deprivation of liberty.

[113] MCA 2005, ss 11(7)(b) and 25(7).

[114] MCA 2005, s 11(8).

[115] MCA 2005, s 4(5). This was a late amendment to the Mental Capacity Bill, first referred to in a letter from the Lord Chancellor to Archbishop Smith on 14 December 2004 and subsequently incorporated in an amendment introduced in the House of Lords by Baroness Ashton of Upholland.

[116] See *AVS v a NHS Foundation Trust* [2011] EWCA Civ 7, [2011] COPLR Con Vol 219.

[117] MCA 2005, s 27.

[118] MCA 2005, s 28 and see also Mental Health Act 1983, s 1(2), which defines 'mental disorder' as 'mental illness, arrested or incomplete development of mind, psychopathic disorder and any other disorder or disability of mind'.

– voting rights where the election is for any public office or at a referendum.[119]

3.51 It is unclear therefore how useful or widespread welfare LPAs have become since MCA 2005 came into force. The majority of LPAs appear to be restricted to property and affairs.[120] Even where welfare LPAs are made, they are not necessarily used in practice. They are made at a time when the donor has capacity and to bring peace of mind, even if they do not need to be used. Even when they do need to be used, it is not necessarily the case that a lay attorney must make a complex welfare decision. It may be that beyond giving the donor peace of mind, they ensure that a person named by the donor has authority to act as a 'consultee' or advocate at a time when the donor lacks capacity, thus someone who can speak for the donor when the donor can no longer speak for him or herself. Experience of the operation of the new LPA forms indicates that they are of limited popularity or applicability where personal welfare matters are concerned. The length and complexity of the statutory forms acts as a deterrent to all but the most determined of donors. Many donors appreciate the usefulness of a property and affairs LPA and can contemplate the circumstances in which the LPA will be used. It is harder to anticipate the circumstances in which a personal welfare LPA will be needed unless the donor is suffering a long running condition and is concerned about the making of day to day decisions. Even then, the clearly expressed wishes of the potential donor should inform a decision maker acting at a time when capacity is lacking, so that there are alternative ways of addressing these concerns.[121]

3.52 The provisions of MCA 2005 relating to LPAs and life-sustaining treatment are both confusing and controversial.[122] How, for instance, is the authority of an attorney to refuse consent to 'life-sustaining treatment' reconciled with the requirement that 'best interests' cannot include a desire to bring about the death of the donor? These provisions of the Act appear mutually inconsistent, but the Act does clearly allow the donor to authorise the attorney to make these decisions on his or her behalf. The only way of giving effect to this requirement is to ensure that a decision to withhold treatment can be made on the basis that it is unduly burdensome or futile and it is not in the best interests of the donor to continue treatment. The motive of the attorney is to relieve pain and suffering and not primarily or exclusively to bring about the death of the donor.[123]

---

[119] MCA 2005, s 29. The Act makes no reference to voting as a member of any other association such as a political party or unincorporated association.
[120] The Office of the Public Guardian Annual Report does not distinguish between property and affairs LPAs and welfare LPAs. It is thought that approximately 90 per cent of all LPAs are property and affairs LPAs. This is supported by anecdotal and practical experience. Furthermore, many welfare LPAs are made as a form of insurance, without necessarily being used.
[121] See **3.55** below.
[122] An article in the *Daily Mail* of 8 December 2004 by Melanie Philips, headed 'A barbaric Bill that would destroy the value of life', was not untypical of some of the press coverage of the Bill at the time of its passage in the House of Commons.
[123] See Mental Capacity Act 2005: Code of Practice, at paragraph 5.31.

3.53 The problem remains therefore that LPAs may be easy to abuse.[124] The attorney may well end up as sole arbiter of whether a refusal of a treatment is in the donor's 'best interests'. This gives rise to several potential problems:

- MCA 2005 does not address the fundamental question of who is making the decision. The attorney is still exercising his or her judgment as to what is in the donor's best interests;[125]
- doctors and other carers may find that the permission of an attorney to withdraw life-sustaining treatment avoids the inconvenience of a more detailed or independent assessment of the donor's best wishes;
- the fiduciary character of a power of attorney is more difficult to apply to a power which relates to welfare. Many attorneys will have an obvious conflict of interest as potential beneficiaries of the donor's estate. While an attorney (who is a beneficiary) should not benefit from his or her dealings with the property and affairs of the donor, there is no equivalent safeguard to dealings with the welfare of the donor;
- a person may be deemed to lack capacity because he or she is unable to communicate a decision;[126]
- an attorney acting in respect of a donor's welfare will generally be a relative or friend, and is unlikely to be a professional person with a professional duty of care. It is unclear therefore what skill or judgment a lay attorney may be expected to exercise in making welfare decisions;
- an attorney acting in the best interests of the donor must take account of the views of anyone caring for the donor, so may be expected to act on medical advice where this is appropriate. But a decision to treat or not to treat can only be informed by medical advice – the actual decision remains with the attorney. The attorney makes what he or she believes to be the right decision and is protected by MCA 2005 so long as the attorney 'reasonably believes that what he does or decides is in the best interests of the person concerned'.[127]

3.54 Although LPAs will be of use to some people in some circumstances, these concerns and the extent of the attorney's powers will need to be addressed carefully by donors when executing LPAs. The drafting and execution of LPAs will therefore be a relatively painstaking process, involving clear professional advice from solicitors and doctors. This will affect the costs involved and either deter potential donors from making LPAs or encourage the making of such powers without proper advice or assistance.

---

[124] The scope for abuse in the creation of LPAs is considered at **3.84**.
[125] Much of the controversy around this question is based on the assumption that the attorney will bring about the death of the donor when the donor might not have wished that outcome. But the reverse scenario might also cause concern, where the attorney refuses consent to the withdrawal of treatment which prolongs the life of a donor who has no desire to go on living.
[126] MCA 2005, s 3(1)(d).
[127] MCA 2005, s 4(9).

Alternatives to welfare lasting powers of attorney

3.55 While there are situations in which LPAs are necessary and useful, many people who might benefit from their provision will be put off by the length and complexity of the forms. If they seek professional assistance, they may be further deterred by the costs involved. They may therefore consider whether a LPA is really necessary and whether their objectives can be achieved in other ways:

- MCA 2005, s 5 provides a defence for a person who carries out an act in connection with the care or treatment of a person lacking capacity so long as the act carried out is in that person's best interests. Most day to day acts of care and treatment of persons who lack capacity are carried out by carers and doctors without the permission of an attorney or deputy or order of the Court of Protection, relying on this provision.
- Any determination of P's best interests requires the person making the determination to take into account the views of 'anyone named as someone to be consulted' as well as the views of anyone engaged in caring for P or interested in his or her welfare.[128] Many people worry that when they lack capacity their loved ones will have no rights and that they will be abandoned to painful and pointless treatment. Although in practice it would be unethical for a physician to treat a patient lacking capacity without consulting the views of family and carers and MCA 2005 gives carers rights to be consulted.[129] However, such rights are not binding or prescriptive and are may be just one of many factors to be taken into account.
- MCA 2005 gives statutory recognition to an advance refusal of treatment.[130] The difference between an advance refusal and a LPA is that the former represents the decision of the person made at a time when he or she has capacity for use when he or she subsequently lacks capacity; the LPA, by contrast, requires the attorney to make the decision at the relevant time. While the LPA has the benefit of being a flexible document, an advance directive is easier to complete. So long as it is clear in its purpose, there is no prescribed form. Only an advance refusal of life-sustaining treatment must be in writing and witnessed.[131] It may well be that many individuals who are primarily concerned at being over-treated will find that a simple advance refusal of treatment will meet those concerns.
- While an advance decision may appear overly inflexible or prescriptive, a person may also provide a 'relevant written statement' which must be considered by anyone making a decision on behalf of such person while lacking capacity. This might not

---

[128] MCA 2005, s 4(7).
[129] See eg the General Medical Council Guidelines considered in the case of *R (on the application of Burke) v General Medical Council* [2005] EWCA Civ 1003, [2005] 2 FLR 1223.
[130] MCA 2005, ss 24–26.
[131] MCA 2005, s 25(6).

necessarily be an advance directive. For instance, a statement expressing a wish not to be resuscitated or kept alive in certain circumstances might not be too vague to be applicable or not signed and witnessed and thus not valid. However, many people will be satisfied knowing that their wishes will be taken into account but that there will be some flexibility to take account of other considerations.[132]

FORM OF LASTING POWER OF ATTORNEY

Who can give a lasting power of attorney?

3.56 Any person who has reached the age of 18 and who has capacity to do so, may grant a LPA.[133] For a LPA to be effective, it must be made in a prescribed form and in a prescribed manner, must comply with certain requirements as to the appointment of an attorney and must be registered.

Prescribed forms

3.57 No instrument can be effective as a LPA unless it is in the prescribed form.[134] The principle of using a standard statutory form is the same that applied to an EPA made prior to 1 October 2007. However, the 2007 Regulations provide for two different prescribed forms depending on whether the power relates to personal welfare or property and affairs. The forms that accompanied the MCA 2005 have been revised and replaced with new forms introduced on 1 October 2009 and 1 July 2015. The current forms are prescribed by the Lasting Powers of Attorney, Enduring Powers of Attorney and Public Guardian (Amendment) Regulations 2015.[135]

Use of different prescribed forms

3.58 Because different powers may be given for different purposes, there are two prescribed forms, one for personal welfare matters and one for property and affairs.[136]

3.59 The same donor may therefore give two LPAs dealing respectively with personal welfare matters and property and affairs respectively.

---

[132] See for example the consideration given to the wishes expressed by M in the case of *W v M & S* [2011] EWHC 2443 (Fam), [2012] COPLR 222. For a more detailed account of advance decisions and their relevance see Chapter 5.
[133] For capacity to grant a LPA, see **3.109–3.110**.
[134] MCA 2005, Sch 1, Part 1.
[135] SI 2015/899. The 2015 Regulations amend the 2007 Regulations, SI 2007/1253. The original prescribed forms issued under the 2007 Regulations could be used until 1 April 2011. New forms were introduced on 1 October 2009 by the Lasting Powers of Attorney, Enduring Powers of Attorney and Public Guardian (Amendment) Regulations 2009, SI 2009/1884. These remain valid until 31 December 2015.
[136] Although MCA 2005, Sch 1, Part 1, para 1(2) allows for an instrument dealing with *both* welfare matters and property and affairs, a hybrid form has not been prescribed. The measure requiring the prescribed forms is contained in the Lasting Powers of Attorney, Enduring Powers of Attorney and Public Guardian Regulations 2007, SI 2007/1253, reg 5.

Different considerations apply to the requirements and content of each power, different attorneys may be appointed for different purposes and the powers may be registered at different times. For instance, a donor may want a solicitor to act as an attorney in respect of property and affairs but a relative to act in respect of personal welfare matters. The former power can also be used at any time after it has been registered and without reference to the capacity of the donor; a power dealing with personal welfare matters only extends to making decisions in circumstances where the donor lacks capacity.[137] The LPAs may also be made at different times. A donor may create a LPA when he or she has capacity and requires assistance and then makes a welfare power later to anticipate medical treatment. The donor may already have made an EPA and now requires a separate welfare LPA.

Defective forms

3.60 At first sight, MCA 2005 appears unequivocal about a LPA being in the prescribed form. Thus s 9(3) clearly states that an instrument which does not comply with the relevant sections 'confers no authority'. When it comes to registration, Sch 1, para 11(1) states that the Public Guardian must not register an instrument (unless directed to do so by the Court) if it appears to him that the instrument is not made in accordance with Sch 1. The role of the Public Guardian is to register the instrument and act as the gatekeeper or guardian of the system. Registration confers formal validity on the power. It is therefore vital for the integrity of the system that a defective form is not registered and therefore the Public Guardian is obliged to refuse registration of a defective instrument, 'if it appears to the Public Guardian' that the instrument has not been made in accordance with schedule 1 of the Act.[138]

On receipt of an application to register an instrument that is potentially defective, the Public Guardian has a limited number of options. He may:

- Reject the application and return the papers to the applicant. The applicant may then either correct the LPA or apply to the Court of Protection to exercise its powers relating to the validity of the LPA.
- The Public Guardian has a limited power to register a LPA if there is a minor error or 'slip'. Sch 1, para 3(1) 'if an instrument differs in an immaterial respect in form or mode of expression from the prescribed form, it is to be treated by the Public Guardian as sufficient in point of form and expression.[139]
- Apply to the Court to exercise its powers. Under Sch 1, para 11(2) the Public Guardian must refer to the Court an instrument which contains a provision which prevents it from operating as an LPA, for

---

[137] MCA 2005, s 11(7)(a).
[138] MCA 2005, Sch 1, para 11(1).
[139] This might be used where there is a clerical error where the content or meaning in the power can be readily inferred from other evidence. For example, an inconsistency in an address, a crossing out and correction or a box has been ticked incorrectly or not ticked. For example, the pre 2009 forms required a certificate provider to tick the box marked 'I am 18 or over'. Where the certificate provider also states his qualification as a consultant psychiatrist or solicitor, ticking this box might be considered immaterial.

the Court to sever the provision. If it appears to the Public Guardian that the LPA may be valid but there is a doubt for instance over the capacity of the donor, then the Public Guardian will refer it to the Court.

3.61 The Court of Protection has a number of powers under MCA 2005 to determine questions relating to the validity or form of a LPA:

- Under s 23(1) the Court may 'determine any question as to the meaning or effect of a lasting power of attorney or an instrument purporting to create one.'
- Under Sch 1, para 3(2) the Court may 'declare that an instrument which is not in the prescribed form is to be treated as if it were, if it is satisfied that the persons executing the instrument intended it to create a lasting power of attorney.'
- Under s 23(1) and Sch 1, para 11(4) the Court may sever a provision from an instrument which prevents it operating as a valid LPA.

3.62 The interaction of the Public Guardian's responsibility to register an LPA and the Court's authority to determine the validity of the power, whether by a declaration or severance of a provision which would otherwise invalidate the power is illustrated by a number of cases reported by way of short summaries on the website of the Public Guardian. Many of these cases relate to restrictions or conditions that are inconsistent either with the status of an attorney or the appointment of more than one attorney. For example:

- In the case of *Re Davies* (an order of the Senior Judge made on 5 July 2010), the donor appointed two attorneys, A and B, to act jointly and severally. He then imposed the following restriction: 'If in the unlikely event of A and B not being wholly in agreement, B is to defer to the wishes of A.' On the application of the Public Guardian the Court severed the restriction as being incompatible with a joint and several appointment.
- In the case of *Re Clarke* (an order of the Senior Judge made on 18 November 2009) the donor appointed three attorneys, A (his wife), B, and C, to be his attorneys. They were appointed to act jointly in some matters and jointly and severally in others. He then stated that the attorneys were to act independently for transactions not exceeding £5,000 'but together in respect of all other decisions subject to my wife A's opinion prevailing in the event that my attorneys are not unanimous in any decision involving property or expenditure exceeding £5,000'. On the application of the Public Guardian, the words 'subject to my wife A's opinion ...' onwards were severed on the ground that they purported to allow one of the three attorneys to act independently in relation to matters that had been specified as subject to the joint decision making powers of the attorneys.
- In the case of *Re Moore* (an order of the Senior Judge made on 26 October 2010) the donor appointed three attorneys to act jointly. She then imposed the following restriction: 'At least two attorneys

to act on any transactions'. On the application of the Public Guardian the Court severed the restriction as being incompatible with a joint appointment.
- In the case of *Re Weyell* (an order of the senior Judge made on 2 December 2010) the donor appointed three attorneys, A, B and C, to act jointly for some decisions and jointly and severally for others. He then imposed the following restrictions:

  '(a) Two out of three of my attorneys must act jointly in relation to any transaction with a value in excess of £5,000 and my attorneys may act jointly and severally in relation to everything else.

  (b) I direct that when acting jointly and severally where possible my attorneys are to act in the following order of priority: firstly A, then B and then C.'

On the application of the Public Guardian the first restriction was severed as being incompatible with the joint aspect of the appointment. As to the second restriction, the Public Guardian submitted that a direction that attorneys appointed to act jointly and severally must act in an order of priority would normally be regarded as incompatible with a joint and several appointment, the addition of the words 'where possible' made the direction in effect a statement of wishes only. The Court accepted this submission and did not sever the second restriction.

- In the case of *Re Sykes* (an order of the Senior Judge made on 9 July 2009), the donor of a property and affairs LPA imposed a restriction stating that no gifts of any of her assets should be made other than 'annual or monthly gifts already being made by me at the date of my signing this LPA by regular bank standing orders or direct debits'. On the application of the Public Guardian the Court severed this restriction on the ground that the gifts envisaged by the donor exceeded the attorney's authority to make gifts as set out in MCA 2005, s 12.[140]
- In the case of *Re Begum* (an order of the Senior Judge made on 24 April 2008), the Court directed the severance from a Property and Affairs LPA instrument of the following clauses, on the ground that they were ineffective as part of an LPA:

  (a) 'All decisions about the use or disposal of my property and financial resources must be driven by what my Personal Welfare Lasting Power of Attorney(s) believe will support my long term interests.

  (b) Any decisions affecting assets (individually or together) worth more than £5,000 at any one time must be discussed and agreed with Dr X.

  (c) In the event of there being any disagreement between my Personal Welfare Lasting Power of Attorney(s) and/or Dr X this should be resolved by these parties appointing an independent advocate to adjudicate.'

---

[140] The clearly defined and limited authority of a donor to make gifts is dealt with at **3.37** above.

- In the case of *Re Kittle* (a judgment of the Senior Judge given on 1 December 2009), the Court was asked to consider whether a first cousin was prevented from acting as a certificate provider. Regulation 8(3) of the LPA, EPA and PG Regulations 2007 sets out categories of persons who cannot act in this role, who include 'a family member' of the donor or of the attorney (or of the owner, director, manager or employee of any care home in which the donor is living when the instrument is executed). The Public Guardian declined to register the instrument on the ground that a first cousin was a family member of the donor. The Court ruled that a first cousin is not a family member, and so the LPA was valid.
- In *Re Forrest* (a decision of the Senior Judge made on 2 March 2012) in *Re Bloom* (an order of the Senior Judge made on 16 March 2012) the Court of Protection severed respectively guidance and a special condition concerning an attorney's power to provide for the maintenance or benefit of another person, which was outside the scope of MCA 2005, s 12.[141]
- In the case of *Re Goodwin* (an order of the Senior Judge made on 17 June 2013) the donor appointed three attorneys and two replacements. Regarding the replacements, she directed that if one ceased to act the other could act alone, and added: 'She should also make every effort to find one or two replacement attorneys to take over her responsibilities in the event of her own death, or if she no longer has the mental capacity to carry on, so that there is a continuing 'Lasting Power of Attorney' in place during the donor's lifetime.' On the application of the Public Guardian this provision was severed on the ground that section MCA 2005, s 10(8)(a) invalidates any provision in an LPA giving an attorney power to appoint a substitute or successor.

3.63 It is not, however, always for the Court to remedy a failing on the part of the donor or a solicitor and there is a limit as to how far the Court will go in assisting a party in these circumstances. It is likely that the circumstances will determine the outcome. There will for instance be cases where the donor no longer has capacity and there is no possibility of a new LPA being prepared. In general, the Public Guardian and the Court will assist where possible, especially where the LPA was prepared without professional support or there is a disproportionate burden on the parties to complete a new LPA. In the case of Re Nazran, the certificate provider had not completed the first two boxes in Part B of the instrument to confirm that he was acting independently of the donor, was not ineligible to provide a certificate, and was aged 18 or over.[142] The Public Guardian refused to register the instrument. As the donor was suffering a wasting illness and

---

[141] These cases are dealt with in more detail at **3.36** above in the context of an attorney's authority to make gifts under the MCA 2005.
[142] An order of the Senior Judge made on 27 June 2008. This case related to a LPA made using the 2007 prescribed form. This sort of problem is unlikely to occur where the prescribed form is used, as there are fewer fields or boxes for a certificate provider to complete and therefore less scope for errors being made on the face of the document.

could not make a new LPA, the attorneys applied to the Court for a declaration that the instrument was a valid LPA or, alternatively, that the instrument was to be treated as valid under MCA 2005, Sch 1, para 3(2). The Court, in the exercise of its discretion under Sch 1, para 3(2), declared that the instrument was to be treated as if it were an LPA and registered accordingly.

Content of LPA

3.64 The current prescribed forms are up to 24 pages long with continuation sheets and the application to register the power (which is part of the prescribed form) and at first sight somewhat daunting.[143] Large parts of the LPA form consists of boxes and fields which may or may not be relevant. A lot of space is taken up by guidance which makes it difficult to distinguish essential details, options and the core provisions of a power of attorney. The wording which distinguishes the form as a power of attorney is almost concealed at section 9 on page 10, amidst the guidance for the donor and the witness to sign. Where there is insufficient space in the form, then supplementary pages need to be added. The 2007 and 2009 forms (the latter of which remain valid to 31 December 2015) could be broken down into their component parts, which reflected the sequence in which they would be completed:

- The Prescribed Information – set out in pages 1–2, which the donor, certificate provider(s) and any attorney(s) are required to read or have read or have read to them;
- Part A – the Donor's Declaration – setting out the powers granted by the donor;
- Part B – the Certificate Provider's Declaration; and
- Part C – the Attorney's Declaration.

The current forms are not so clearly divided and are set out in fifteen sections as follows:

- Section 1 – Donor's details;
- Section 2 – Attorneys' details. There are spaces for up to four attorneys; if further attorneys are to be appointed, a continuation sheet is required;
- Section 3 – Showing how the attorneys are appointed, whether jointly or jointly and severally or jointly for some purposes and jointly and severally for others;
- Section 4 – Replacement attorneys' details. There are spaces for two replacement attorneys; if further replacement attorneys are to be appointed, a continuation sheet is required; a continuation sheet is also required if the power is to specify when or how then may act;
- Section 5 – the property and affairs form allows the donor to specify when the attorneys can make decisions, thus whether the power can

---

[143] As prescribed by the Lasting Powers of Attorney, Enduring Powers of Attorney and Public Guardian (Amendment) Regulations 2015, SI 2015/899.

be utilised immediately or on the onset of incapacity; the personal welfare power allows the donor to select whether the attorneys can give or refuse consent to life sustaining treatment;
- Section 6 – Showing the names of persons to be notified;
- Section 7 – Preferences and instructions. There is limited space only for preference and instructions and a continuation sheet for this part of the form may be added;
- Section 8 – the Prescribed Information – now headed 'Everyone signing the LPA must read this information';
- Section 9 – Execution by donor;
- Section 10 – certificate of capacity;
- Section 11 – Execution by attorneys or replacement attorneys. The prescribed form incorporates four pages, one for each attorney; more forms can be added if necessary;
- Section 12 – Details of person making application to register the instrument;[144]
- Section 13 – Correspondent's details (where the registered instrument should be returned to)
- Section 14 – Payment details for the application fee; and
- Section 15 – Declaration by person applying to register the instrument.

Section 1 – The donor's details

3.65 The prescribed form provides space for the donor to write or print his or her name and address and date of birth. The benefit of the new form is that the donor's details are shown on the very first page of the form, making it easier to use in practice (earlier versions showed the prescribed information at the front of the form, so the user would have to find the third page to identify the donor).

Section 2 – Choice of attorney

3.66 A donor may appoint any person or, in the case of a power relating to property and affairs, a trust corporation, to act as his or her attorney. Apart from where a trust corporation is appointed, the appointment of an attorney is personal and an attorney cannot be appointed by reference to an office or title.[145]

---

[144] It is assumed that the instrument will be registered as part of the same process and therefore dealt with at the same time. Thus early registration of the LPA is to be encouraged.

[145] The Law Commission assumed that an officeholder could be appointed under existing law (Law Com No 231 (see **3.16**), at para 7.21) but recommended a specific provision authorising an attorney to be described as 'the holder for the time being or a specified office or position'. This provision was not included in MCA 2005, and contrasts with the power of the Court to appoint 'the holder for the time being or a specified office or position' as a deputy (MCA 2005, s 19(2)).

3.67 Where an individual is appointed then he or she must have reached 18 and must not be a bankrupt.[146] If the attorney subsequently becomes bankrupt, then his or her appointment as an attorney is terminated.

3.68 Clearly the choice of attorney is essential to the effective operation of a LPA. And because a LPA may be made many years before it is used, the donor may need some insurance against the risk of an attorney becoming unable to act due to death, divorce, bankruptcy, incapacity or disclaimer. MCA 2005 therefore allows the donor to appoint two or more attorneys and also allows for the appointment of replacement attorneys.

Section 3 – More than one attorney

3.69 MCA 2005, s 10(4) allows the donor to appoint more than one attorney provided that the attorneys are appointed to act 'jointly' or 'jointly and severally'. The Act uses the terms 'jointly' or 'jointly and severally' whereas the 2007 forms use the terms 'together' or 'together and separately'. The current forms use the statutory terminology. Section 10 also permits attorneys to be appointed jointly in respect of some matters and jointly and severally in respect of others. Thus a donor is able to appoint attorneys to act jointly and severally in respect of his or her investments but require them to act jointly where a major decision was required, for instance, to sell the donor's home or, in a welfare power, to withhold consent to life-sustaining treatment.[147] If it is unclear whether attorneys are appointed jointly or jointly and severally, the appointment is construed in favour of their being appointed jointly.[148]

3.70 A joint appointment of attorneys clearly provides a greater degree of protection, as the attorneys must act unanimously in any act carried out under the power. For example, a contract for a care home or even a cheque drawn on the donor's bank account must be signed by both attorneys. The disadvantages are that the LPA may be cumbersome to operate in practice and that the LPA is terminated if the appointment of any one attorney fails.[149] These difficulties inherent in a joint appointment can be remedied by limiting the scope of the joint appointment to certain decisions or by

---

[146] MCA 2005, s 10(1).
[147] Care needs to be taken to prevent rendering a joint and several appointment ineffective. See for instance the decision of the Senior Judge in the case of *Re P (an order of the Senior Judge made on 9 June 2009)* where the donor appointed three attorneys to act jointly and severally, and imposed the following restriction: 'I require that two attorneys must act at any one time so that no attorney may act alone.' On the application of the Public Guardian the Court severed the restriction on the ground that it was ineffective as part of an LPA. The requirement for a majority or quorum was ineffective as being neither a joint appointment nor a jointly and several appointment for the purposes of section (10)(4). See the Ministry of Justice website. See also the case of *Re Moore* described at **3.62** above.
[148] This avoids the problem created by EPAA 1985, s 11(1), where an EPA had to appoint attorneys either jointly or jointly and severally to be valid as an EPA. An instrument that was unclear might therefore be defective. See also *Re E (enduring power of attorney)* [2000] 1 FLR 882, sub nom *Re E, X v Y*
[149] MCA 2005, s 10(6).

appointing a replacement attorney to act on the failure of the joint appointment. Where these issues are addressed, careful drafting is required.

3.71 Where two or more attorneys are appointed *jointly and severally*, each attorney may act independently of the other. Most LPAs which appoint more than one attorney to deal with a person's property and affairs provide for the attorneys being appointed jointly and severally. It is simply more practical for attorneys to work separately, either with a clear division of responsibility between them or on the understanding that one will take a lead role and another will act as a spare or default attorney. However, any potential conflict or discord between the attorneys will make the power extremely difficult to operate in practice. Care must be taken to address the issue of how they are to act at the time the instrument is made, rather than leave matters to wishful thinking. If the authority of one attorney to act independently of another is limited, there is a danger that the 'joint and several' nature of the appointment will be fatally compromised.[150] Where one of the attorneys is a professional attorney, it will also be important for the donor to define the extent to which the professional attorney is expected to be actively involved in the administration of the donor's affairs or the supervision of the other attorney.

Section 4 – Replacement attorneys

3.72 The top of Section 4 contains the words: 'this section is optional, but we recommend you consider it. Replacement attorneys are a backup in case one of your original attorneys can't make decisions for you any more'. The appointment of a replacement attorney is often desirable, especially as attorneys are often appointed several years before they may need to act. Attorneys cannot appoint their own successors in the same way that trustees can.[151] This preserves the distinction between an attorney and a trustee in that the attorney is the agent of the donor and is appointed personally in his or her own right.[152] MCA 2005 provides expressly for the appointment of a replacement attorney, so that a new attorney, who has also been chosen by the donor, may replace the old attorneys, but only on the failure of the earlier appointment on one of the grounds specified in s 13(6)(a)–(d).[153] Thus if the appointment of the first attorney should fail on the disclaimer, death, divorce, bankruptcy or incapacity of that attorney, a new attorney is appointed, within the same instrument, to act in that event. The replacement

---

[150] For instance in the case of *Re Bratt* (an order made by the Senior Judge on 14 September 2009) the donor appointed two attorneys, A and B, to act jointly and severally, and directed that 'B is only to act as attorney in the event of A being physically or mentally incapable of acting in this capacity'. On the application of the Public Guardian this provision was severed as being inconsistent with a joint and several appointment. See also the cases referred to at **3.62** above.
[151] MCA 2005, s 10(8)(a).
[152] A trust by contrast is a distinct legal entity that may need to be administered for much longer and the trustees owe their primary duty to the beneficiaries.
[153] There was no equivalent provision in the Enduring Powers of Attorney Act 1985. A donor could achieve the same result by creating more than one EPA, with the later being conditional on the failure of the first. See **3.74** below.

attorney is only appointed on the failure of the prior appointment on one of the specified grounds. If, for example, the first appointed attorney is removed by the Court for failure to act in the donor's best interests, then the condition that allows the replacement attorney to act is not satisfied.

3.73 A replacement attorney will often be appointed to cover the failure of a joint appointment of attorneys. Where joint attorneys are appointed there will be an obvious concern that the appointment of all the attorneys will fail if the appointment of just one will fail. However this can also give rise to some unintended consequences. For example, a donor may appoint his children A and B to act jointly. Aware of the risk of a joint appointment, the donor takes advantage of the prescribed form to appoint his solicitor C as a replacement attorney. If A dies or becomes bankrupt, then the appointment of both A and B fails and C will then be appointed as sole attorney.[154] Care therefore needs to be taken in drafting as, in this scenario, the donor may well have preferred to have C act with B. The donor therefore needs to appoint three replacement attorneys. On the basis that he could not know which of his children might become unable to act, he would have to re-appoint A, B and C as replacement attorneys, jointly and severally. It is not however straightforward re-appointing the same persons in different capacities within the same instrument. In the case of *Re Miles*, Senior Judge Lush severed a clause re-appointing attorneys, as the prescribed form did not provide a page for specifying how those attorneys would act, and recommended that a separate conditional LPA should be made. However, this case was based on the 2009 forms.[155] The new forms provide at the end of Section 4 a tick-box and link to a continuation sheet to show 'how replacement attorneys step in and act.' Continuation Sheet 2 then has a tick-box for use where it is to be used in conjunction with Section 4. This can be used to confirm that the replacement attorneys are appointed to act jointly and severally. It can also be used to replace one attorney. For example if the donor appoints A and B jointly and severally, the donor can also appoint C as a replacement for A and D as a replacement for B.

3.74 While it makes sense for a donor to cover as many eventualities as possible within the same instrument, this can give rise to another unexpected complication, whereby the donor does not receive all the protection afforded by the registration process. The practice with EPAs and which was recommended for LPAs by Senior Judge Lush in the case of re Miles, had been for a donor to create separate instruments, with the replacement power taking effect on the failure of the first. In this way, if the first power failed, the attorneys under the second or replacement power would apply to register

---

[154] See the case of *Re Druce* (an order of the Senior Judge dated 31 May 2011) where the donor made LPAs appointing A and B as her attorneys, to act jointly, and C and D to be her replacement attorneys. She then imposed the following restriction: 'Both C and D should jointly replace the first attorney who needs replacing so that on the first replacement there will be three acting attorneys. No further replacements will be needed.' On the application of the Public Guardian the court severed the restriction as being incompatible with the principle that the survivor of joint attorneys cannot act.

[155] [2014] EWCOP 40, [2015] COPLR 107. The case illustrates how complicated LPAs can become when planning for different eventualities.

that instrument. As the new power of attorney could only take effect on the failure of the first, evidence of its failure would need to be produced to register the new EPA and once it was registered, no further explanation would be needed. The protection afforded by the registration process would come into play, even if the first EPA had been registered previously. It was, however, cumbersome to prepare two instruments for use in situations that might not arise and the practice arose of appointing successor attorneys within the same instrument.[156] This would, after all, only reflect the practice used in will drafting. However, as EPAs were usually made long before they would be used, it was anticipated that registration would be effected just once by the first attorney. It was never established what would happen if the EPA was registered by the first attorney who died or became unable to act, leaving the successor attorney appointed on the face of the instrument.[157]

3.75 MCA 2005, s 10(8)(b) provides for a replacement attorney being appointed in the same instrument. In most such cases the first attorney will accept the appointment. The attorney (or donor) sends out the notices in the usual way and the named persons are satisfied that the attorney is acting in the donor's best interests.[158] Form LPA3 is given to the named persons, but this only shows the names of the original attorneys. Subsequently the authority of the first attorney is terminated. The replacement attorney has already been appointed, but no new registration is required. Although the Public Guardian must be notified, no one else is notified of the existence of a different attorney who unlike the first attorney may be wholly unsuitable for the role.[159] The named person will have no knowledge that a replacement attorney has been appointed, let alone of that attorney's identity. A further difficulty may arise if there is a delay in registration, as the replacement. In many cases, the replacement attorney is also someone who will be concerned for the best interests of the donor. A donor may, for instance, appoint one child as an attorney in the first instance and another child as a replacement attorney. The second child cannot be a named person and is not given notice by the Public Guardian and may be unaware that the instrument is being registered.[160] In contrast, a co-attorney who did not join in making the application for the purposes of the notification requirements is automatically notified.[161]

---

[156] The practice was shown in *Elderly Clients: A Precedent Manual* (Jordan Publishing, 2005) edited by the Master (now Senior Judge) of the Court of Protection, Denzil Lush, and is based on a simple application of existing legal principles. See also Law Com No 231 (see **3.16**), at para 114. This approach was approved in the decision of Lewison J in the case of *Re J (Enduring Power of Attorney)* [2009] EWHC 436 (Ch), [2009] COPLR Con Vol 753.

[157] Take the case of a donor who appointed A as his attorney and B as his replacement attorney; on losing capacity, A applied to register the EPA. Some time later, A dies. Presumably B step into his shoes and carry out the functions of an attorney. B should then notify the Public Guardian so that the EPA is noted with the death of A.

[158] The continued role and effectiveness of persons named as persons to be notified are considered at **3.82ff**.

[159] It is of course open to a donor to create two LPAs with separate appointments, the second taking effect on the failure of the first. But, given the complexity of the forms, it is unlikely that many donors will realistically complete two LPAs to deal with their property and affairs.

[160] This also contrasts with the principle applied in the registration of EPAs where a class of relatives is notified, and a replacement attorney would be notified if within the prescribed

Section 5 – Limiting when attorneys can make decisions (property and affairs)

3.76 Whereas a welfare LPA can only operate when the donor lacks capacity, a property and affairs LPA is capable of being used at any time as soon as it has been registered. As has been mentioned, this can give rise to problems, especially when combined with a policy which encourages early registration.[162] Many donors wish to remain in control of their affairs for as long as possible and will be concerned that their LPAs may be used prematurely. The new prescribed form for a property and affairs LPA introduced on 1 July 2015 incorporates a provision that expressly deals with this concern. This is set out at Section 5 where the donor is asked: 'When do you want your attorneys to make decisions?' and is then provided with a choice of two options, each with its own tick-box. The first allows the LPA to be used as soon as it has been registered, thus while the donor still has capacity; the second allows the LPA only to be used when the donor lacks capacity.

3.77 It may appear sensible to encourage donors to consider when their LPAs might be used. However, such a provision may also create hostages to fortune. Therefore while donors are encouraged to consider this option, they are also discouraged from exercising it! The second option, to make use of the LPA conditional on a lack of capacity, is followed by the words 'Be careful – this can make your LPA a lot less useful. Your attorneys might be asked to prove you do not have mental capacity each time they try to use this LPA.' Clearly use of the second option is impractical. Any third party relying on the LPA, such as a bank or building society, will need evidence of the donor's lack of mental capacity to address the decision in issue. Different tests of capacity may be required for different decisions. Furthermore, the use of such a policy sits uncomfortably with the ethos of the property and affairs LPA which is to avoid questions of capacity, so that use of the LPA does not label the donor as incapable and prevent the donor from making decisions which he or she retains capacity to make. The main benefit of this new provision is to force the donor to address the issue of when the LPA should be used. However, the tick-boxes provided only allow for two choices. For such a provision to work, careful consideration needs to be given to how this will work in practice. For instance how will a lack of capacity be proved when the attorney comes to operate the LPA? More detailed instructions need to be set out elsewhere in the form, at Section 7. At which point, consideration should also be given to whether the attorneys are trustworthy and can be relied upon to act at the right time. There may also be simpler and less restrictive ways of using the LPA such as leaving the original with a solicitor who can only release the document if satisfied that it needs to be used, or delaying registration.

---

class. See MCA 2005, Sch 4, Part 3, para 6(2). The inclusion of named persons and the problems associated with their role is dealt with in more detail at **3.82**ff.
[161] MCA 2005, Sch 1, para 8(2).
[162] See **3.28**.

Section 5 – Life-sustaining treatment (welfare LPA)

3.78 The authority of an attorney under a welfare LPA does not extend to 'giving or refusing of consent to the carrying out or continuation of life-sustaining treatment' unless the instrument so permits.[163] MCA 2005 does therefore contain a default provision so that a LPA should not deal with issues of life-sustaining treatment unless this is positively specified. The prescribed form departs from this presumption by setting out two choices and requiring the donor to specify one of them, which is contained in Section 5 of the welfare LPA. Thus the donor must sign the box beside Option A or Option B specifying as follows:

A   I want to give my attorney(s) authority to give or refuse consent to life-sustaining treatment;

B   I **do not** want to give my attorney(s) authority to give or refuse consent to life-sustaining treatment.

3.79 As a further safeguard and to prevent the donor signing the wrong box in error, the signature beside the chosen box must be signed in the presence of a witness, who must sign and complete the boxes at the foot of the same page. The form does not specify who can witness this statement. The guidance notes on the form merely state that 'the witness must not be an attorney or replacement attorney appointed under this LPA, and must be aged 18 or over.'[164]

Section 6 – Named persons to be notified or told

3.80 LPAs, in the same way as EPAs, are designed as a simple and accessible means of providing a legal basis for future decision-making on behalf of a person who lacks capacity. By exercising a choice over the attorney, the donor of a power of attorney obviates the need for a formal court-based process or official supervision. This does not, however, mean that there is no protection available to a donor and there are in effect three levels of protection:

- the creation of the power of attorney;
- the notification of specified persons on registration; and
- the registration process which allows time for objections to be made by the donor and the persons notified, as well as allowing the registration authority to ensure that the documentation is all correct.

3.81 MCA 2005 improved the protection provided at the first of these levels, as a LPA requires a certificate of capacity from an independent person who can confirm that the donor understands the scope and purpose of the power. However, at the second of these levels, the notification procedure has been reduced in importance. On registration of an EPA, the attorney

---

[163] MCA 2005, s 11(8).
[164] The declaration concerning life-sustaining treatment is in effect a separate advance statement within the LPA and complies with MCA 2005, s 25(5) and (6).

must notify prescribed members of a class of relatives.[165] By contrast, the donor of a LPA may specify in the instrument the names of one of more persons to be notified of an application to register the LPA. This follows on from the principle that the donor should be free to make his or her own choice of persons to be notified. That principle is taken a stage further, as the donor is also free to specify that there should be no such persons to be notified.[166] Prior to new prescribed forms being introduced on 1 July 2015, the only limit on the donor's freedom of choice was that a named person could not be a donee of the power (including a replacement donee), that there were a maximum of five named persons and that if there were no named persons, then two certificates of capacity must be provided.[167] The new prescribed forms introduced on 1 July 2015 provides space for persons to be notified, but only as an option. This satisfies the literal wording of MCA 2005 which allows the donor to state 'that there are no persons whom he wishes to be notified of any such application.'

3.82 The right of the donor to choose or not choose persons to be notified of the application to register the LPA differs significantly from the requirements of EPAA 1985, which requires prescribed members of a class of relatives to be notified. This has proved controversial, but embodies a recommendation of the Law Commission,[168] which was critical of the statutory list of notifiable relatives which:

> '... makes no acknowledgement that close and important relationships may exist outside of legal marriage and blood ties. It conflicts with the autonomy principle to require, regardless of the donor's wishes, that certain relatives must be notified of a private arrangement to govern future decision making.'

3.83 This approach was actively supported by the Government in the long legislative process that led to the passing of MCA 2005. In the Report Stage of the Bill in the House of Lords, the Minister of State, Baroness Ashton provided the following justification:[169]

> 'I said that families are different. I did not say that they were not very important. I simply said that families are not what they used to be. We have lots of different kinds of families. People have many strong relationships – for example, half-siblings, step-children, and different situations within families ...
>
> I am also very clear that this provision is about the donor making a choice. Ultimately, the donor should say who they would like to have notified. It could be a relative, but there may not be any relatives around or the donor may be estranged from his or her family – so there would be little point in notifying a relative. Just because someone is related does not necessarily mean that he will care anything for the donor. He may even have his own selfish motives for showing an interest in trying to object to the donor's chosen attorney.

---

[165] EPAA 1985, Sch 1, Part 1, para 2(1). The same provisions apply to EPAs registered after 1 October 2007: MCA 2005, Sch 4, Part 3, para 6. Safeguards in the EPA jurisdiction are considered at **3.11**.
[166] MCA 2005, Sch 1, Part 1, para 2(1)(c).
[167] MCA 2005, Sch 1, Part 1, para 2(2)(b). The certificate of capacity is considered in more detail at **3.90ff**.
[168] Law Com No 231 (see **3.16**), at para 7.37.
[169] *Hansard*, HL Deb, vol 670, ser 5, col 1316 (15 March 2005).

So the Bill provides freedom of choice, but it does not lose sight of protection. My noble friend has made it clear that he is worried about the coercion or pressure that could be put on someone to give a decision-making power to a person through a lasting power of attorney.

That is why the Bill provides that all applications to register a lasting power of attorney must be accompanied by a certificate from a person of prescribed description that, in his opinion, the donor understands what he is doing and that no fraud or undue pressure is being used to induce the donor to create that lasting power of attorney. It goes one step further than that. Where there is no named person, regulations may require two certificates of that kind to be provided. This is the balance that I feel we have struck within the Bill: freedom and protection working in tandem.'

3.84 The obligation to give notice of an intention to register the power is therefore a key safeguard against abuse. But the then Government's approach was political as much as functional, as concerned with reflecting its particular view of society as protecting the donor. However well-intentioned was this approach, it assumed that the competent donor putting his or her affairs in order is acting with a complete understanding of all the relevant factors and will choose sensibly those persons who might actually be in a position to protect his or her interests in the event of abuse or a future change in circumstances. The benefit inherent in a prescribed list of relatives is lost. Disputes concerning EPAs often come to light when relatives are notified. Sometimes relatives will conduct their own disputes with each other at the expense of the donor, but there are also many cases where the attorney was in a position of trust and confidence at the time the power was made. The attorney may have abused that position of trust to influence a power of attorney in his or her favour; but there are other more innocent but equally difficult cases where at the time the power was made, the choice of attorney seemed sensible. The trusted friend may subsequently have had financial difficulties or have fallen out with the donor; or the favourite nephew may have moved away and become less helpful. Problems may arise with second marriages where the spouse may be appointed to act as an attorney without any notice being given to the donor's children. When preparing a LPA a donor will be under the influence of the circumstances that exist at that time and the persons named will reflect that. By choosing who should be notified or indeed by not notifying anyone, the creation of the LPA can be a purely private act, limited to the persons involved in the process. While it may be good practice for a donor to let other relatives, friends or professional advisers know of the LPA, there is absolutely no requirement for this to be the case.

3.85 In practice therefore the act of notifying named persons has added very little value to the registration system. In the absence of any notification of a party who is not connected to the LPA, the registration process does not provide any greater degree of protection. This contrasts with the EPA and the registration requirements that have been carried into MCA 2005, Sch, para 6 which apply if there is no person capable of being notified. In this case, the Public Guardian cannot register the EPA and 'must undertake such inquiries as he thinks appropriate in all the circumstances.' While such inquiries may be a formality, at least there is some sort of delay that requires an enquiry to be made.

Section 7 – Preferences and instructions

3.86 The authority of an attorney is not only subject to the limitations imposed by MCA 2005 but also any conditions or restrictions specified in the instrument.[170] In view of the wide-ranging scope of a LPA, the donor needs to consider very carefully how the LPA can be 'tailored' to meet his or her requirements and provide the right level of compromise between function and protection. Although the forms are designed with plenty of space for donors to insert their own conditions, there is a danger that instructions made without proper advice will prove unworkable in practice.[171]

INSTRUCTIONS

3.87 Special instructions that a donor might add, in respect of property and affairs, to the prescribed form include:

- A right to remuneration by a professional attorney. An attorney acts as a fiduciary role and should not benefit from his or her so acting without the consent of the donor. It is therefore advisable for this to be expressly provided for in the instrument.
- Authority for the delegation of investment powers to a professional fund manager. An attorney cannot generally delegate his or her functions except where he or she cannot be expected to attend to them personally.[172]
- Requiring the attorney to keep accounts or to render an account to a co-attorney or to a third party such as another member of the family, a solicitor or accountant. Although an attorney has a common law duty to keep accounts, this is not always followed in practice. The Court of Protection has authority to require an attorney to deliver an account, but it is unlikely that this authority will be widely exercised.[173] Many of the disputes that arise around EPAs and LPAs have been caused by a lack of awareness of what an attorney is

---

[170] MCA 2005, s 9(4)(b).
[171] Although the forms are intended for completion without professional help, not every donor will be able to deal with this unaided. The Guidance Notes LP12 provides some assistance, and a long list of useful precedents, but not every donor will work through the 48 pages of notes to find the right advice and even this concludes: 'we are not able to provide you with wording for restrictions or conditions. In any particular situation, you may want to seek further advice from a legal or financial professional such as a solicitor or accountant' (at p 38).
[172] The Guidance Notes provide some useful precedents, but not for this case. The notes state, somewhat unhelpfully: 'The only circumstances in which you must write an instruction is in a financial LPA if you have investments managed by a bank and you want that to continue. Contact the Office of the Public Guardian (OPG) or a legal adviser if you want advice on the wording.'
[173] MCA 2005, s 23(3)(a).

doing: a duty or power to disclose information and/or account to another party or to an independent professional often provides an adequate degree of reassurance in such cases.[174]
- Authorising disclosure of personal financial information. An attorney owes a duty of confidentiality and may have concerns about providing other family members with information about the donor's estate. A careful donor should consider whether, when and to what extent information should be disclosed. Family arguments may often be avoided if attorneys are authorised (and therefore encouraged) to disclose information to other family members.
- Restricting the operation of the LPA to use in specified circumstances. The LPA can be used – subject to registration – at any time by the attorney. Many donors will be unhappy with going through the formalities and expense of registration when the power only needs to be used for a limited time or purpose. They may also be unhappy with the prospect of the LPA being used while they still have capacity. Section 5 allows a donor to specify that the LPA can only be used when he or she lacks capacity. This may need clarification as to what evidence should be produced. Although this is allowed by Section 5 and is referred to in the guidance notes, such a condition does contradict the spirit of a property and affairs LPA which is that the LPA itself is neutral as to the donor's capacity.[175]
- Restricting the power to make gifts under MCA 2005, s 12 by setting a maximum amount for gifts or prohibiting the making of gifts without the consent of the Court or a third party.
- Restricting the amount of capital which can be applied or limiting the value of transactions that may be entered into by the attorney.
- Giving authority to the attorney to receive the donor's Will (or a copy). An attorney may need to refer to a Will when dealing with the property and affairs of a donor who lacks capacity sometime after the LPA has been created. The Will remains a privileged document and should not ordinarily be disclosed by a person holding the Will without the express consent of the donor (which may be in the LPA or by the Court of Protection).[176]

---

[174] See for instance the case of Public Guardian and CS and PL [2015] EWCOP 30 where the lack of co-operation between the attorneys made it impossible for the LPA to function.

[175] The current guidance states (at page 30): 'If you have opted (in section 5 of the LPA form) for your attorneys to act under your financial LPA only if you've lost mental capacity, you might add instructions about how your mental capacity should be assessed. For example, you might write: 'This lasting power of attorney only applies if a doctor confirms in writing that I don't have the capacity to make decisions about my finances.' Such provisions can create their own difficulties. For an example of the complications such a clause can create, see the case of *Re XZ; XZ v the Public Guardian* [2015] EWCOP 35. See also **3.28** above.

[176] See the Law Society Practice Note of 8 December 2011 at paragraph 11.5. It should be noted that while the attorney may be authorised to inspect or retain the donor's Will, there is some uncertainty as to whether this can compel a third party to act on this. If this might be a concern, then the donor should separately authorise the third party to release this information in specified circumstances.

- Restricting the scope of the LPA so that it does not apply to a particular asset, for instance, that it should not apply to the sale of the family home.

Great care needs to be taken in drafting instructions, as there is a danger in making the power unworkable in practice or even invalidating it. Curiously the 2015 prescribed forms refer to instructions rather than conditions. There is a danger of taking this too literally and making an instruction overly prescriptive and undermine the attorney's ability to exercise his or her own skill and judgment or end up requiring the attorney to do something that is contrary to his or her authority. An attorney cannot for example be authorised to make gifts that go beyond what is permitted by MCA 2005, section 12 or to maintain another person. It may appear safer to refer to conditions and therefore specify when the LPA cannot be used, thus the attorneys have the authority available to them as attorneys, except where there is restricted. But this also gives rise to problems where for instance conditions are attached that require attorneys appointed jointly and severally to act together and therefore jointly. Furthermore, conditions may be unworkable in practice. For instance, a LPA may give effect to the sensibilities of an elderly donor who is determined to stay in his own home and restrict the power accordingly. The attorney then finds he or she lacks authority to sell the property when inevitably the donor needs to go into a care home. Likewise, a condition that prevents use while the donor has capacity, may prevent the LPA being used when it is needed if the donor becomes physically incapable, but still has capacity It may be far safer and more useful to address these concerns of the donor in the form of preferences, whether recorded in the LPA or separately (see **3.79** below).

Welfare instructions

3.88 Where the welfare of the donor is concerned, the same restrictions as to when and with what evidence the LPA is created may be applicable. A welfare LPA is perhaps a more personal and subjective instrument than its financial counterpart. It may need careful consideration and discussions with the attorneys, family members, carers and doctors. The donor may need to address a particular set of circumstances the LPA is required to address, such as a terminal illness. The donor may have strong views as to how he or she should be treated and whether or not the LPA extends to the giving or refusing of consent to life-sustaining treatment. Special conditions might include:
- restricting the right to 'give or refuse consent to life-sustaining treatment' so that the attorney may only give such consent (and not refuse consent);
- qualifying the right to refuse consent to life-sustaining treatment so that it does not include the right to refuse artificial nutrition and hydration or that such a decision should be subject to the consent of other relatives or medical experts.

The guidance notes provide the following examples of instructions that might be used this this type of LPA:

> 'My attorneys must not decide I am to move into residential care unless, in my doctor's opinion, I can no longer live independently.'
>
> 'My attorneys must not consent to any medical treatment involving blood products, as this is against my religion.'
>
> 'My attorneys must ensure I am given only vegetarian food.'

Preferences (guidance)

3.89 The prescribed forms also contain space for the donor to set out preferences or guidance for the attorney. A LPA should if possible provide an attorney with discretion and autonomy, in that trust and confidence are at the heart of the appointment. It goes against the nature of the relationship between donor and attorney to be overly prescriptive. However, attorneys may well benefit from a record of the donor's wishes and concerns. While these may not be binding in the same way as express instructions, the attorney will be obliged to take them into account as a relevant written statement in determining the donor's best interests. The importance of written preferences or guidance should not be underestimated as it can be used to allow other parties to be involved and provide a remedy where there are concerns about the conduct of an attorney. For instance a donor may record as guidance his wish that his attorneys should consult with his other children over certain decisions or obtain professional advice when taking certain decisions; a failure to do so would not invalidate their decisions. It would however give the other children the ability to apply to the Court of Protection on the grounds that the attorney is failing to act in the best interests of the donor under s 22(3)(b) of the MCA 2005. Preferences need not be contained in the instrument itself and could be set out in a separate letter or memorandum, as this will have to be considered in any assessment of the donor's best interests. The guidance provided by the Public Guardian sets out the following examples of preferences:

> 'I prefer to live within five miles of my sister.'
>
> 'I'd like to be prescribed generic medicines where they are available.'
>
> 'I would like to take exercise at least three times a week whenever I am physically able to do so. Whether or not I am mobile, I would like to spend time outdoors at least once a day.'
>
> 'I'd like my pets to live with me for as long as possible – if I go into a care home, I'd like to take them with me.'
>
> 'I'd like to have regular haircuts, manicures and pedicures.'
>
> (for a health and welfare LPA)
>
> 'I like to reinvest all interest from each year's investments into next year's ISA allowance.'
>
> 'I would like to maintain a minimum balance of £1,000 in my current account.'
>
> 'I prefer to invest in ethical funds.'
>
> 'I'd like my attorneys to consult my doctor if they think I don't have the mental capacity to make decisions about my house.'

'I would like to donate £100 each year to Age UK.'
(for a Property and financial affairs LPA)

Section 8 – Prescribed information

3.90 For a LPA to comply with MCA 2005, Sch 1, para 2(1) the instrument must include 'prescribed information about the purpose of the instrument and the effect of a lasting power of attorney.' This is set out at Section 8 so that it follows the previous sections which set out the details of the parties and the terms of the attorney's appointment (the 2007 and 2009 prescribed forms showed this information at the beginning of the form on the basis that it would be read before the donor commenced preparing the form).[177] The prescribed information is to be read by the donor, as well as any attorney, and contains the following essential information:

'Everyone signing the LPA must read this information

In sections 9 to 11, you, the certificate provider, all your attorneys and your replacement attorneys must sign this lasting power of attorney to form a legal agreement between you (a deed).

By signing this lasting power of attorney, you (the donor) are appointing people (attorneys) to make decisions for you.

LPAs are governed by the Mental Capacity Act 2005 (MCA), regulations made under it and the MCA Code of Practice. Attorneys must have regard to these documents. The Code of Practice is available from www.gov.uk/opg/mca-code or from The Stationery Office.

Your attorneys must follow the principles of the Mental Capacity Act:

1. Your attorneys must assume that you can make your own decisions unless it is established that you cannot do so.
2. Your attorneys must help you to make as many of your own decisions as you can. They must take all practical steps to help you to make a decision. They can only treat you as unable to make a decision if they have not succeeded in helping you make a decision through those steps.
3. Your attorneys must not treat you as unable to make a decision simply because you make an unwise decision.
4. Your attorneys must act and make decisions in your best interests when you are unable to make a decision.
5. Before your attorneys make a decision or act for you, they must consider whether they can make the decision or act in a way that is less restrictive of your rights and freedom but still achieves the purpose.

Your attorneys must always act in your best interests. This is explained in the Application guide, part A8, and defined in the MCA Code of Practice.

Before this LPA can be used:

- it must be registered by the Office of the Public Guardian (OPG)
- it may be limited to when you don't have mental capacity, according to your choice in section 5

---

[177] Rule 9(3) of the Lasting Powers of Attorney, Enduring Powers of Attorney and Public Guardian Regulations 2007, SI 2007/1253 as amended implies that the donor must first read the prescribed information and then complete Sections 1 to 7 – even though it follows on in Section 8. Thus the punctilious donor should first read Section 8 and then go back to Section 1.

Cancelling your LPA: You can cancel this LPA at any time, as long as you have mental capacity to do so. It doesn't matter if the LPA has been registered or not. For more information, see the Guide, part D.

Your will and your LPA: Your attorneys cannot use this LPA to change your will. This LPA will expire when you die. Your attorneys must then send the registered LPA, any certified copies and a copy of your death certificate to the Office of the Public Guardian.'

Section 9 – Execution by donor

3.91 Once the donor has read the prescribed information, the donor executes the instrument as a deed, therefore in the presence of a witness. the donor may not witness any signature required for the power and an attorney may not witness any signature required for the power apart from that of another attorney.

This part of the form also confirms the core legal structure of the power of attorney. Thus for the property and affairs LPA the donor confirms as follows: 'I appoint and give my attorneys authority to make decisions about my property and financial affairs, including when I cannot act for myself because I lack mental capacity, subject to the terms of this LPA and to the provisions of the Mental Capacity Act 2005.' For the welfare LPA the declaration is similar, save that it explicitly states that the LPA only applies if the donor lacks capacity: ' I appoint and give my attorneys authority to make decisions about my health and welfare, when I cannot act for myself because I lack mental capacity, subject to the terms of this LPA and to the provisions of the Mental Capacity Act 2005.

If the donor is unable to sign in person, then the form can be signed on behalf of the donor by another signatory, provided there are two independent witnesses.[178] If the LPA is being executed in this way then Continuation Sheet 3 must be used.

Section 10 – The certificate provider's statement

3.92 One of the principal objections to EPAs was that they were completed too readily, without the extent of the donor's capacity being addressed. The presumption would then arise that the EPA had been validly executed and as it might be several years before the problem came to light, there was no contemporaneous evidence to address the issue one way or the other. To address this particular problem and to add a further safeguard, the LPA must also contain a certificate of capacity. This added level of protection is all the more important where the LPA relates to welfare decisions, which may include decisions concerning life-sustaining treatment.

---

[178] Lasting Powers of Attorney, Enduring Powers of Attorney and Public Guardian Regulations 2007, SI 2007/1253, reg 9(7).

3.93 The LPA instrument therefore requires a certificate to be given by a person of a prescribed description, who is not a donee of the power, stating that in his or her opinion, at the time the donor executes the instrument:[179]

(a) the donor understands the purpose of the instrument and the scope of the authority given under it;
(b) no fraud or undue pressure is being used to induce the donor to create a LPA; and
(c) there is nothing else which would prevent a LPA from being created.[180]

3.94 The certificate provider's statement constitutes Section 10 of the prescribed form, and must be completed after Sections 1 to 7 and 9 have been completed. There is set no time-limit in which the certificate must be completed, although the instrument cannot be registered until it has been completed. Clearly, the longer the gap between execution and the giving of the certificate, the harder it is for the certificate provider to be able to certify the facts required by MCA 2005. All that the legislation actually requires is that the certificate of capacity is completed 'as soon as reasonably practicable' after the preceding steps (the execution of the instrument) have been carried out.[181] However, it can be argued that any gap between the two events makes it impossible for the certificate to be given, as the certificate provider is addressing a prior event of which he or she had no actual knowledge. To address this difficulty, the certificate provider should if at all possible be a witness to the LPA or be present when the LPA is executed.

3.95 The prescribed forms do not prevent the witness to the donor's signature also completing the certificate of capacity. This may therefore reflect standard practice among solicitors, where the LPA is professionally prepared. Any professional who has prepared a LPA for a client and can witness the client's solicitor should also be satisfied that the client can give instructions and is able to understand the contents of the instrument.[182] If the solicitor is unsure of the client's capacity then another professional may be asked to give a certificate of capacity. This should complement the solicitor's understanding of the client's capacity, and is not a substitute for the solicitor's own judgment. Where a solicitor obtains advice as to capacity it is essential that the person giving the advice understands the relevant tests of capacity and that the solicitor is therefore able to rely on that advice.

3.96 The certificate of capacity is an important safeguard provided by MCA 2005; but it is not intended to be so onerous that it deters potential donors from making LPAs. To encourage completion of LPAs, the certificate

---

[179] Capacity to create a LPA is considered in more detail at **3.109** below.
[180] MCA 2005, Sch 1, Part 1, para 2(1)(e).
[181] Lasting Powers of Attorney, Enduring Powers of Attorney and Public Guardian Regulations 2007, SI 2007/1253, reg 9(4).
[182] This was common when solicitors prepared EPAs for clients, although the problem was that many EPAs were created too quickly without sufficient attention to the donor's capacity. See further **3.15**.

can be given by a wide class of persons, who need not necessarily be professionally qualified. A certificate may therefore be given by:[183]

'(a) someone the donor has known personally for two years;
[OR]
(b) someone who because of their relevant professional skills and expertise, considers themselves able to provide the certificate.'

3.97 The 2007 and 2009 prescribed forms required the certificate provider to specify whether he or she was acting in a personal or a professional capacity and then provide some evidence to support this. There is no requirement for the lay certificate provider to show any particular level of expertise or experience. The Regulations refer to 'a person chosen by the donor as being someone who has known him personally for the period of at least two years which ends immediately before the date on which that person signs the LPA certificate'.[184] There is no way of showing or indeed requiring the certificate provider to show that he or she understands the concept of capacity in the light of MCA 2005 as well as the nature and effect of the form. The onus is on the donor to choose – and the Regulations deliberately use the words 'chosen by the donor' – a suitable certificate provider who can if called upon to do so, show that he understood what he was doing and more importantly, that he understood what the donor was doing at the relevant time.

3.98 There is no prescriptive definition of who can be a professional certificate provider. The Regulations refer to:

'... a person chosen by the donor who, on account of his professional skills and expertise, reasonably considers that he is competent to make the judgments necessary to certify the matters set out in paragraph (2)(1)(e) of Schedule 1 to the Act.'

As with choosing a lay certificate provider, the onus is on the donor to choose a suitable certificate provider but it also rests on the certificate provider to consider that he or she is competent. As to who may or may not be competent, the Regulations merely provide the following examples of persons who can act as certificate providers, namely:[185]

- a registered health care professional;
- a barrister, solicitor or advocate called or admitted in any part of the United Kingdom;
- a registered social worker; or
- an independent mental capacity advocate.

3.99 This list is not exhaustive, and the defined skills are provided as examples only. Although the Regulations refer to the 'professional skills' of the certificate provider, the prescribed form requires the certificate provider

---

[183] Lasting Powers of Attorney, Enduring Powers of Attorney and Public Guardian Regulations 2007, SI 2007/1253, reg 8(1).
[184] Lasting Powers of Attorney, Enduring Powers of Attorney and Public Guardian Regulations 2007, SI 2007/1253, reg 8(1).
[185] Lasting Powers of Attorney, Enduring Powers of Attorney and Public Guardian Regulations 2007, SI 2007/1253, reg 8(2).

to complete two tests. He must state his profession and then state his particular skills. Clearly a certificate provider acting in a professional capacity must have a profession; it must also be a relevant profession. A solicitor may for instance be a professional person but may specialise in commercial litigation and have no experience of assessing capacity and understanding the nature and effect of the LPA. A solicitor experienced in this area of law should state this in the box in provided for the certificate provider to place this information on record.[186]

3.100 There are, however, some persons who cannot provide a certificate.[187] A certificate provider must be over 18.[188] A donee of a power – including a replacement donee as well as the donee of another LPA or EPA given by the same donor – cannot be a certificate provider. A certificate provider must be acting 'independently' and must not be a relative of the donor or the attorney, a business partner or paid employee, or anyone involved in the care home in which the donor lives.[189] This may cause difficulties where the donor wishes to appoint a professional attorney. A donor appointing a professional attorney will not be able to have the certificate given by a partner or employee of the attorney's firm. The donor will need to find someone else to complete the certificate or else take it to a doctor or another solicitor. By contrast, however, the certificate provider can be an employer of the donee. There is also nothing to prevent a named person or the witness to the donor's signature being a certificate provider.[190]

3.101 A professional certificate provider will furthermore need to consider carefully matter such as:[191]

- the identity of the client and the extent of the instructions or retainer;[192]
- whether the donor(s) should provide proof of their identity;
- the time that has passed between execution of the instrument and the certificate of capacity;

---

[186] The prescribed form refers to a consultant specializing in geriatric care as an example of the particular skills of a professional certificate provider.
[187] Lasting Powers of Attorney, Enduring Powers of Attorney and Public Guardian Regulations 2007, SI 2007/1253, reg 8(3).
[188] The forms prescribed by the 2007 Regulations contained a box requiring the certificate provider to confirm that he or she was over 18. The 2009 forms require the certificate provider to sign the declaration 'I confirm that I act independently of the attorneys and of the donor and I am aged 18 or over.'
[189] In the case of *Re Kittle* referred to at **3.62** above and reported on the Ministry of Justice website, it was held that a first cousin was not a 'relative' for the purposes of preventing a person from acting as a certificate provider.
[190] It may in fact be good practice for a doctor or solicitor who knows the donor sufficiently well to give a certificate of capacity and also to act as a named person, especially if the donor has few close friends or relatives.
[191] It is unclear what responsibility or duty a non-professional person has in giving a certificate of capacity. However, there is no doubt that a professional person will have a greater responsibility and this will be reflected in the fee he or she will be obliged to charge, thereby making it more likely that LPAs will not be certified appropriately.
[192] A solicitor who prepares a LPA for a client needs to be satisfied that on the balance of probabilities the client has the mental capacity to make a LPA (see the Law Society's Practice Note of 8 December 2011 at paragraph 4).

- whether the contents of the instrument give rise to any queries or concerns;
- whether, if he or she is not medically qualified, medical advice is required;
- whether, if he or she is not legally qualified, legal advice is required;
- what records should be kept and for how long; and
- that if the power is given by one spouse (or civil partner) to the other, the donor in each case must be interviewed separately.

3.102 Notwithstanding these considerations, the three tests set out in MCA 2005, Sch 1, para 1(e) are ostensibly quite limited. It should quickly be established that there is no fraud or undue pressure and that there is nothing else to prevent the instrument taking effect as a LPA. It is the first of the statutory requirements – that 'the donor understands the purpose of the instrument and the scope of the authority given under it' – that in practice requires the greatest degree of attention. But the certificate provider is not primarily concerned with the content of the instrument or the wisdom or lack of wisdom in the decisions being made by the donor, or even the capacity of the donor to make his own decisions. All the Act requires is an assessment that the donor understands the purpose of the instrument – that it is a power of attorney, who the attorneys are and when they may act and the scope of the power – that it extends to property and affairs or welfare matters.[193] Clearly the certificate provider should be alert to a lack of understanding of the proposed LPA, but neither is he or she conducting a separate examination on the subject, or expecting the donor to go through the same set of instructions twice.

3.103 The certificate of capacity is intended to provide an important safeguard, to protect the donor from undue influence of abuse and also to avoid subsequent doubts about the validity of the power. This will therefore reinforce the presumption that already exists in the due execution of an EPA, that a LPA which has been properly executed and contains such a certificate is a valid power.[194] A certificate of capacity will, to most persons dealing with the LPA, serve as a badge of authenticity that will make it that much harder to query or object to the power, although this is less prominent on the 2015 forms which do not provide any space for the certificate provider to set out his or her qualifications, whether acting in a personal capacity or a professional capacity. This will widen the scope for abuse where a certificate of capacity is procured fraudulently or without proper consideration for the importance of the subject matter. Only when the validity of the LPA or the

---

[193] The donor must show that he or she understands the 'purpose' and 'scope' of the instrument. Most definitions of capacity to perform a legal act refer to 'nature' and 'effect' and it is arguable that the former requires a lesser degree of understanding. See the decision of the Senior Judge of the Court of Protection in the case of *Re Collis* (27 October 2010) reported on the website of the Ministry of Justice under the heading 'other orders of interest made by the Court of Protection since 1 October 2007'.

[194] *Re W (Enduring Power of Attorney)* [2001] 1 FLR 832.

conduct of the attorneys is queried and addressed by the Court of Protection will it become obvious that the certificate of capacity is only as good as the person giving the certificate.

3.104 In the event that the donor does not require any person to be notified of registration of the instrument, the instrument must contain two such certificates.[195] The prescribed forms therefore have space for two certificates to be given.

Section 11 – The attorney's statement

3.105 The final section of the form is the Attorney's Statement, which must be completed after the Donor and the Certificate Provider have completed their respective sections of the form.[196] As with the prescribed form of EPA, the prescribed form must also contain a statement by the attorney that he or she is prepared to take on the role of attorney and understands his or her obligations. Although often completed as a mere addendum to the main part of the document, it serves as a useful reminder of the attorney's core duties and a solicitor preparing a LPA should emphasise to the attorney that by signing this part of the form, these obligations are imposed on the attorney. Thus to act as an attorney under a LPA (for property and affairs), each attorney must make a statement in the following terms:[197]

- I am aged 18 or over
- I have read this lasting power of attorney (LPA) including section 8 'Your legal rights and responsibilities', or I have had it read to me
- I have a duty to act based on the principles of the Mental Capacity Act 2005 and to have regard to the Mental Capacity Act Code of Practice
- I must make decisions and act in the best interests of the donor
- I must take into account any instructions or preferences set out in this LPA
- I can make decisions and act only when this LPA has been registered and at the time indicated in section 5 of this LPA.'

Curiously the 2015 forms omit the following wording from the attorney's declaration which was contained on the 2007 and 2009 forms:[198]

- I can spend money to make gifts but only to charities or on customary occasions and for reasonable amounts [property and affairs power only]
- I have a duty to keep accounts and financial records and produce them to the Office of the Public Guardian and/or the Court of Protection on request [property and affairs power only]'

---

[195] MCA 2005, Sch 1, Part 1, para 2(2)(b). The space for two certificates adds to the length and complexity of the form. There can be no demand for two certificates as it is hardly a hindrance to name at least one person to be notified on registration, especially as the persons named can be complete strangers.
[196] Lasting Powers of Attorney, Enduring Powers of Attorney and Public Guardian Regulations 2007, SI 2007/1253, reg 9(5).
[197] MCA 2005, Sch 1, Part 1, para 2(1)(d) which requires a statement that the donee 'has read the prescribed information or a prescribed part of it (or has had it read to him), and understands the duties imposed on a donee of a lasting power of attorney under sections 1 (the principles) and 4 (best interests).'
[198] This wording does however appear in the form for use by a trust corporation.

3.106 The same form is used for a replacement attorney and should be completed in the same way, although clearly the replacement attorney is also endorsing the words on the form: 'I understand that I have the authority to act under this LPA only after an original attorney's appointment is terminated. I must notify the Public Guardian if this happens.' As we have seen, it is easy for the appointment of a replacement attorney to be overlooked on registration and subsequently when he is called upon to act.[199] Therefore in the event of a triggering event arising – namely the disclaimer, death, divorce, bankruptcy or incapacity of the first attorney – the replacement attorney will notify the Public Guardian and return the original LPA to the Public Guardian. This serves two important purposes:

- The Public Guardian has notice of an event that has occurred which not only triggers the appointment of the replacement attorney but which also allows him to update his records.
- The original LPA can be endorsed so that the replacement attorney can produce this (or a certified copy) of his authority to act.

3.107 Under a welfare LPA the attorney's statement is modified to make it clear that the attorney understands that he or she can only act where the power has been registered and the donor lacks mental capacity.

3.108 MCA 2005 refers to the duties imposed on an attorney under ss 1 (the principles) and 4 (best interests) in the same way as they are imposed on any person or body who makes decisions which another person lacks capacity to make. This is however a minimum requirement, as the attorney may well have other duties. A donee of a property and affairs LPA for instance, has other common law or fiduciary obligations when dealing with property and affairs.[200] A professional attorney or an attorney who has been appointed on account of a particular expertise is likely to have a higher duty of care. The sensible aim of the forms is to ensure that an attorney makes a positive commitment to carry out his or her legal obligations (and provides a measure against which performance can be judged in the future) and no attorney should undertake the role without careful consideration. Nevertheless, it is likely that many attorneys will sign a form without thinking too carefully about what they are signing, but at least there is a record of what they should be thinking about when signing the forms.

CREATION OF LASTING POWER OF ATTORNEY

A lasting power of attorney is created in two stages

3.109 A power of attorney intended to be a LPA for the purposes of MCA 2005 must be made in two stages for it to be valid as a LPA: the drawing up and execution of the instrument followed by its formal registration by the Public Guardian. The terminology can cause some confusion. Until both stages have been completed, a properly completed and

---

[199] See **3.72**.
[200] See **3.4**.

duly executed instrument has no legal effect.[201] A completed document headed 'Lasting Power of Attorney' is not therefore a LPA until both stages have been completed. Until that has been done, the document is a worthless piece of paper, of no legal effect whatsoever. MCA 2005, s 9(2) describes the unregistered form somewhat clumsily as 'an instrument conferring authority of the kind mentioned in subsection (1)'; thereafter it is referred to as an instrument 'intended to create a lasting power of attorney' or, more commonly, simply as an 'instrument'.

THE FIRST STAGE: COMPLETING SECTIONS 1 TO 11

3.110 The first stage is the completion and execution of the prescribed form. This involves a number of steps, which may or may not be taken at some distance in time from each other, although the Regulations assume that each step will be taken 'as soon as reasonably practicable' after the previous step.[202] The steps must however be taken in the correct sequence.[203] Thus:

(1) The donor reads the prescribed information.
(2) The donor completes the provisions of the instrument that pertain to him or her (Sections 1 to 10) and executes the instrument, by signing Section 9 in the presence of a witness.[204] Although MCA 2005 refers to the time when the donor 'executes the instrument' there is no mention in the Act to execution as a deed.[205] A power of attorney, however, is regarded as a deed and a LPA complies with the Law of Property (Miscellaneous Provisions) Act 1989, s 1.[206] The original prescribed forms introduced by the 2007 Regulations made no reference to the document being a deed; this is now made clear in the 2009 and 2015 forms.
(3) A welfare LPA also requires Section 5, dealing with life-sustaining treatment, to be completed and that page must therefore be signed separately in the presence of a witness.
(4) The Certificate of Capacity (Section 10) is signed by a person of a prescribed description confirming that in his or her opinion, at the time the donor executes the instrument:[207]
  '(i) the donor understands the purpose of the instrument and the scope of the authority conferred under it,
  (ii) no fraud or undue pressure is being used to induce the donor to create a lasting power of attorney, and
  (iii) there is nothing else which would prevent a lasting power of attorney from being created by the instrument.'

---

[201] MCA 2005, s 9(2).
[202] Lasting Powers of Attorney, Enduring Powers of Attorney and Public Guardian Regulations 2007, SI 2007/1253, reg 9(1).
[203] This is a simple trap for the unwary. It is not unusual for donors and donees (especially if they are a close family) to complete their parts first and then organise a certificate of capacity. If the forms are completed in the wrong order, an application for registration will be rejected.
[204] Lasting Powers of Attorney, Enduring Powers of Attorney and Public Guardian Regulations 2007, SI 2007/1253, reg 9(9).
[205] MCA 2005, s 9(2)(c).
[206] Powers of Attorney Act 1971, s 1.
[207] MCA 2005, Sch 1, para 2(1)(e). The Certificate of Capacity is dealt with at **3.89**ff.

(5) A statement (Part C) is made by the donee or by each donee to the effect that he or she:[208]
> '(i) I have read the prescribed information (the section called 'information you must read on page 2), and
> (ii) I understand the role and responsibilities under this lasting power of attorney ...'

3.111 Only when all these steps have been completed can the instrument be registered by the Public Guardian. It is this second stage which 'creates' the power in its registration with the Public Guardian and until the instrument is actually registered, it is ineffective as a power of attorney.[209] The registration procedure is described in more detail below.

Capacity to create a power

3.112 A person's capacity to execute a LPA is specific to that matter at the material time.[210] Although MCA 2005 sets out a framework for assessing capacity, and expects a certificate provider to certify that the donor 'understands the purpose of the instrument and the scope of the authority conferred under it', existing case-law will assist in determining questions concerning capacity to grant a LPA.

3.113 The principle that capacity to create an EPA required its own test which was distinct from that of managing property and affairs was considered in the case of *Re K, Re F*.[211] Registration of an EPA was objected to on the grounds that the power had been made immediately before an application was made for its registration – on the basis that the donor lacked capacity to manage her property and affairs. Hoffman J confirmed the validity of the power, it being a specific legal act at the time it was made and therefore distinct from the donor's ability to manage or not manage her property and affairs. He set out four basic requirements as to what the donor should understand:[212]

> '... first, if such be the terms of the power, that the attorney will be able to assume complete authority over the donor's affairs; second, if such be the terms of the power, that the attorney will in general be able to do anything with the donor's property which the donor could have done; third, that the authority will continue if the donor should be or become mentally incapable; fourth, that if he should be or become mentally incapable, the power will be irrevocable without confirmation by the court.'

3.114 The test of capacity to create an EPA will be different for an LPA made under MCA 2005. In the case of *Re Collis* Senior Judge Lush suggested the following modifications to the tests set out in *Re K, Re F*:[213]

---

[208] MCA 2005, Sch 1, para 2(1)(d). See **3.102** above for the complete declaration.
[209] MCA 2005, s 9(2)(b).
[210] MCA 2005, s 2(1).
[211] [1988] 2 FLR 15.
[212] [1988] 2 FLR 15, at p 20.
[213] Reported on the website of the Ministry of Justice. See also **3.99**. Capacity to create a LPA was also considered briefly by Hedley J in the case of *A, B & C v X & Z* (a judgment of given on 30 July 2012).

- the donor would need to understand that the LPA cannot be used until it is registered by the Public Guardian.
- the donor would need to understand that the attorney under an LPA for personal welfare can only make decisions that the donor is contemporaneously incapable of making.
- unlike an EPA, the donor can revoke an LPA at any time when he or she has the capacity to do so without the court having to confirm the revocation.
- the authority conferred by an LPA, unlike an EPA, is subject to the provisions of the Mental Capacity Act 2005 and, in particular, sections 1 (the principles) and section 4 (best interests).

The last requirement sets a high threshold for the donor, as it requires an understanding of information that is beyond the scope of the form or merely summarised in the form. Thus the donor needs some understanding of the basis on which the attorneys must act if the donor lacks capacity. There are also matters that are specific to the LPA such as the choice of attorneys or the restrictions and guidance contained in the instrument. The donor must also understand the consequences of deciding one way or another, or failing to make the decision.[214] In the context of an LPA this might include the consequences of not appointing a particular person as an attorney or not including guidance as well as the consequences of not making an LPA. There is no doubt that the complexity of the form and the registration process, the options available to the donor and additional information the donor needs to understand set a high threshold for capacity.

3.115 As with an EPA, a properly executed LPA will create a presumption of due execution. The certificate of capacity alone places a very strong burden on anyone objecting to registration on the grounds that the power is invalid. The Public Guardian furthermore has a positive duty to register a LPA unless he receives a valid objection to registration within the prescribed period or an objection is made to the Court.[215] The Court can only revoke the power if it is satisfied that one of the limited grounds allowed by MCA 2005 has been established.[216] Thus, unless the Court is satisfied that the ground for revocation has been established, it cannot prevent the LPA from being registered. This approach is the same applied by the Court of Protection in the context of registration of EPAs.[217] The evidential burden is weighted against the objector, which in practice makes it very difficult for the Court to revoke an EPA on the grounds of its invalidity. Unless there is clear and compelling evidence that the donor lacked capacity at the time of execution or that there was fraud or undue influence, the Court must register the EPA. An even greater burden of proof will apply on anyone seeking to challenge the validity of the LPA.

---

[214] MCA 2005, s 3(4).
[215] MCA 2005, Sch 1, Part 2, para 5.
[216] MCA 2005, s 22(3).
[217] *Re W (Enduring Power of Attorney)* [2001] 1 FLR 832.

THE SECOND STAGE: REGISTRATION

The requirement of registration

3.116 A LPA is not effective as a power of attorney unless and until it is registered with the Public Guardian in accordance with MCA 2005, Sch 1.[218] The aim of the Act is to encourage early registration of LPAs, so that the process of validation and supervision is started as soon as the power is used. However, a welfare power – which has in any event already been registered – can only operate in respect of those decisions which the donor lacks capacity to make.[219]

3.117 An attorney operating a welfare power must therefore pass two separate thresholds before he or she can make a decision: the first is that the power must be registered; the second is that the donor lacks capacity. Any clinician or other person treating or caring for a person and seeking to take instructions from the attorney must likewise ensure that the two thresholds are passed, checking that there is a registered LPA in place and also verifying that the donor lacks capacity.

3.118 Unless it has been restricted, a property and affairs LPA is by contrast more straightforward as it can operate notwithstanding the capacity of the donor. This has three practical benefits:

(1) It avoids misuse of the power where the attorney continues to act notwithstanding the revocation of the power on the incapacity of the donor. As often happens with EPAs the power is used by an attorney where it should be registered with the result that the donor's interests are not protected and the attorney (even though he or she may be acting in good faith) is acting beyond the scope of his or her authority.

(2) The attorney is not required to conduct a medical assessment of the donor's capacity. He or she does not need to take responsibility for or undergo the awkwardness of asserting that the donor is mentally incapable.

(3) No other person is entitled to make an assessment based on the fact, that by virtue of registration, the donor is incapable of managing all his or her property and affairs. Thus the fact of registration does not give rise to a presumption of incapacity.

Problems with capacity not being relevant to registration

3.119 While the benefits of avoiding the issue of capacity on registration of a LPA are self-evident, there are also several disadvantages. A third party dealing directly with the donor of the LPA cannot make any assumption as to the donor's lack of capacity, but must make his or her own assessment of the donor's capacity at the relevant time. While this respects the integrity of the donor, the third party's position is less clear. A bank, for example, cannot

---

[218] MCA 2005, s 9(2)(b).
[219] MCA 2005, s 11(7)(a).

rely on the fact of registration to prevent the donor from using his or her account, where, for instance, there are large or frequent withdrawals from the account. Likewise a solicitor selling a property on the authority of the attorney of a LPA cannot assume that the donor is incapable and the property is being sold to pay for nursing care. The donor therefore may have less protection against financial abuse than the donor of an EPA.

Problems with early registration

3.120 Although the aim of MCA 2005 is to encourage early registration of LPAs, it should not be assumed that all donors and attorneys will follow this in practice. A capable donor may well feel stigmatised by the fact of registration but is more likely to resent the expense and inconvenience of registration as well as the perception that this restricts his or her freedom. Of course the donor can revoke the LPA but he or she must still go through the process of having the registration cancelled. There is no prescribed form or procedure for a donor who has revoked a LPA to cancel registration. A donor who has capacity or who recovered capacity and wishes to revoke the LPA needs to provide the Public Guardian with sufficient evidence to cancel the registration.[220] This may cause not only inconvenience, expense, embarrassment or family discord, but also force the donor to demonstrate to the Public Guardian that he or she is capable of revoking the power. Moreover if the revocation is contested or the donor's evidence of revocation is contested, then the matter must be referred to the Court of Protection for determination.[221]

3.121 Following the implementation of the MCA 2005, the practice appears to be for instruments to be registered even though there is no intention to use them.[222]. The donor and the attorneys have the benefit of knowing that the LPA has been properly completed and any disputes can be addressed early on while the donor is still capable of being consulted.

3.122 Early registration can also cause practical problems where the LPA is registered long in advance of its use. The donor's circumstances may have changed and the protection afforded by registration is no longer available. Furthermore, once the LPA is registered it can be used; not every donor will want it to be used but an attorney who is insensitive or dishonest can still operate the LPA unless and until the donor takes active steps to revoke the LPA. A donor may include a special condition limiting registration of operation to a time when capacity is lacking, but this creates its own problems in drafting as well as in timing as a restriction may delay

---

[220] Lasting Powers of Attorney, Enduring Powers of Attorney and Public Guardian Regulations 2007, SI 2007/1253, reg 21.
[221] MCA 2005, Sch 1, para 18(b).
[222] This does perhaps explain why applications for registration, which amounted to 7,500 in September 2008 was higher than expected (Bridget Prentice MP, addressing the Public Guardian Board General Meeting, 7 October 2008). This is more than double the level predicted and may account in part for some of the administrative problems faced by the Public Guardian in the early period the new regime.

registration at the time it is needed. However, if registration is delayed, the benefits of early registration are also lost.[223]

Procedure for registration – Sections 12 to 15

3.123 The procedure for registration of a LPA is relatively straightforward, and should not therefore deter attorneys from taking on their responsibilities to register and act under the LPA. This is facilitated and encouraged by incorporating the application for registration in the body of the form. In contrast to the procedure for registration of an EPA, the application may be made by the donor as well as by the attorney.

3.124 Application to register a LPA can be made by the donor or donee or by one of two or more donees appointed to act jointly and severally. Where the attorneys are appointed jointly and the attorneys rather than the donor make the application, then all the attorneys must make the application. Application must be made using Sections 12 to 15 of the prescribed forms. These are short and self-explanatory and contain sufficient information about the donor, the donee or donees and service of notices to enable the Public Guardian to deal with the registration process. The applicant for registration will also need to submit the original LPA and the prescribed fee of £110.[224]

3.125 Where the donor has created separate LPAs in respect of property and affairs and welfare matters, then they will need to be registered separately. It will often be the case that different attorneys are appointed for different purposes or the powers need to be registered at different times. There is therefore no obvious mechanism for registering the two powers by the same process. An attorney registering welfare and financial powers for his elderly parents will therefore have to make four applications and pay four separate fees each of £130. It is therefore possible that a separate fee for each process may deter attorneys from registering LPAs – especially welfare powers – until the last moment.[225]

---

[223] The role of notified persons and the problems of early registration are also considered at **3.87**.

[224] MCA 2005, Sch 1, para 4(3). The actual fees prescribed are set out in the Public Guardian (Fees, etc) Regulations 2007, SI 2007/2051, as amended by the Public Guardian (Fees, etc) (Amendment) Regulations 2013, SI 2013/1748.

[225] The unintended consequence may prove positive: a welfare LPA is only intended as a 'last resort' and may well not need to be registered. Many donors whose property and affairs are dealt with by an attorney will carry on being cared for informally without the need for intervention by an attorney. Thus a welfare power will not be registered as a matter of course on incapacity, but may be held back until there is a dispute or contentious treatment that requires the authority of an attorney to resolve. This should not, however, be used to overlook the risk of the power being needed urgently and its use is delayed by registration.

Status of attorney prior to registration

3.126 A LPA has no legal effect until it is registered.[226] As the document is not a power of attorney, there is no legal basis on which an attorney can act or the Court of Protection can assist. MCA 2005 does not therefore provide any interim or limited authority for the attorney to act after the application has been made but before the power has been registered.[227] Where a donor has become incapable of carrying out an act for which authority is urgently required by the donee, the donee has no ability to act under the LPA, even though an application to register the power has been made.

3.127 This omission from MCA 2005 may cause difficulties for an attorney who needs to administer the donor's affairs while the power is being registered. It may be that a short delay will not prejudice the donor's interests, but the situation is more complicated if registration is delayed for perhaps several months while there is a dispute over the validity of the power or the conduct of the attorney. If the attorney requires authority in this period, he or she must either apply to the Court for a specific order under MCA 2005, s 18 or rely on the provisions of MCA 2005, ss 7 and 8. Thus an attorney who needs to access the donor's bank account to pay for nursing home fees must either apply to the Court of Protection for an order, or spend his or her own money and be reimbursed by the donor subsequently.[228]

3.128 Where the donee wishes to resolve any queries concerning the validity of the power, he or she can apply to the Court of Protection for a determination under MCA 2005, s 22(2).

Notices

3.129 The person applying to register the LPA (who may be the donor or the donee) must notify any person named in the LPA for that purpose of his or her intention to register the power.[229] Notification is made in the prescribed form LPA3.[230]

3.130 The applicant is only obliged to notify the persons named in the LPA for that purpose of his or her intention to register the power. There is no requirement for one attorney where there is more than one attorney to notify the other attorney(s). The Public Guardian is responsible for notifying:

---

[226] MCA 2005, s 9(2)(b).
[227] Compare the provisions of MCA 2005, Sch 4, para 1(2). An EPA is already a power of attorney when it is made.
[228] It has therefore been suggested by some practitioners that a donor who does not want his or her LPA used immediately should also complete a simple power of attorney in accordance with the Powers of Attorney Act 1971, s 10 to operate while the donor has capacity and before the LPA is registered.
[229] MCA 2005, Sch 1, para 6. The rationale for notifying only named persons is dealt with at **3.84–3.85**. There is no requirement for the donee to notify any close relatives or persons involved in the care and welfare of the donor unless they have been actually named by the donor for this purpose.
[230] Lasting Powers of Attorney, Enduring Powers of Attorney and Public Guardian Regulations 2007, SI 2007/1253, reg 10 and Sch 2 (as amended by SI 2015/899..

- the donee or donees where the application is made by the donor, using form LPA003A;[231]
- the donor where the application is made by the donee or donees, using form LPA003B;[232] and
- a donee where two or more donees have been appointed jointly and severally and who has not applied to register the power (using form LPA003A).[233]

Service of notices

3.131 MCA 2005, Sch 1 refers to the applicant having to 'notify' a person; the Lasting Powers of Attorney, Enduring Powers of Attorney and Public Guardian Regulations 2007, regs 10 and 13 refer to notices being 'given'. Even form LPA003A and LPA003B must be 'given' by the Public Guardian. There is, however, no reference in the legislation to the mode of service of documents.[234] Form LPA3 refers to the form being 'received' by the recipient, but makes no reference to how it has come to be received. Likewise the guidance from the Public Guardian refers to notices being sent.[235]

Dispensing with notice

3.132 Only the Court can direct that service of a notice on a named person be dispensed with.[236] However, the Court must first be satisfied that no useful purpose would be served by giving notice. There is no corresponding power for the Court to dispense with the requirement for the Public Guardian to notify the donor.

3.133 There is no provision in MCA 2005 or regulations which allows the person who is applying to register the LPA to dispense with the service of notice without reference to the Court. This is an unlikely event given that most LPAs are registered at the time they are drawn up and notified persons are chosen as people who can be readily notified at the time, if indeed they are notified at all. The 2015 forms no longer make notification a requirement so it will become unusual for anyone to receive formal notice in this way. However, in the unlikely event that notification was required and the named person ccould located, has died or is incapable, the Court must first agree to notice being dispensed with before the application to register

---

[231] MCA 2005, Sch 1, para 7.
[232] MCA 2005, Sch 1, para 8(1).
[233] MCA 2005, Sch 1, para 8(2).
[234] Compare the Court of Protection (Enduring Power of Attorney) Rules 2001, SI 2001/825, rr 15 and 16 which applied to the registration of EPAs prior to 1 October 2007. A notice of intention to register an EPA must also be served personally on the donor: Lasting Powers of Attorney, Enduring Powers of Attorney and Public Guardian Regulations 2007, SI 2007/1253, reg 23(3). It is difficult to see how the sending of a form by post to a donor will provide a greater degree of protection.
[235] 'Guidance for people who want to register a lasting power of attorney' at page 4.
[236] MCA 2005, Sch 1, para 10.

the power is made.[237] If that is the approach of the Court, and a formal application needs to be made to dispense with notice (with a fee payable), then it is likely that many applicants in such cases will simply send the notice to the address on the form. They can claim to have 'notified' the named persons at their last known address.

Completion of registration

3.134 Unless there is a valid objection to registration of the LPA, the Public Guardian must register the power at the end of the prescribed period.[238] There is therefore a positive duty on the Public Guardian to register the power unless there is a defect in the power or a valid objection is received.

3.135 Once the LPA is registered, the Public Guardian must notify the donor and attorney(s) of the fact of registration in form LPA004.[239] While the original LPA will be endorsed with details of the registration and returned to the applicant or his or her solicitor, MCA 2005, s 16(1) provides authority for office copies to be conclusive evidence of the fact of registration and the contents of the power.

Objections to registration

The role of the Public Guardian

3.136 The registration authority is the Public Guardian who must register the LPA unless:

- it appears to the Public Guardian that the LPA is not a valid power, in which case the power cannot be registered unless directed by the Court;[240]
- the Court of Protection has already appointed a deputy and it appears to the Public Guardian that the powers conferred on the deputy would conflict with the powers conferred on the attorney, in which case the power cannot be registered unless directed by the Court;[241]

---

[237] In contrast to the donee of an EPA who does not need to notify a relative if his or her name or address is not known to the attorney and cannot reasonably be ascertained or the attorney believes that the relative is aged under 18 or mentally incapable (EPAA 1985, Sch 1, para 2(2)).

[238] MCA 2005, Sch 1, para 5. The Lasting Powers of Attorney, Enduring Powers of Attorney and Public Guardian Regulations 2007, SI 2007/1253, reg 12 specifies a period of 4 weeks, from the date of the last notice given to a person required to be notified (the prescribed period was reduced from 6 weeks to 4 weeks from 1 April 2013 by the Lasting Powers of Attorney, Enduring Powers of Attorney and Public Guardian (Amendment) Regulations 2013, SI 2013/506).

[239] Lasting Powers of Attorney, Enduring Powers of Attorney and Public Guardian Regulations 2007, SI 2007/1253, reg 17(5) and Sch 5.

[240] MCA 2005, Sch 1, para 11(1). For example, where the power was made using the incorrect form or there was a technical defect in the form which prevented it from operating as a valid LPA.

[241] MCA 2005, Sch 1, para 12.

- it appears to the Public Guardian that there is a provision in the instrument which would be ineffective as part of a LPA or which would prevent the power from operating as a LPA, in which case the power must be referred to the Court for determination;[242]
- the Public Guardian receives a notice of objection from the donee or named person on one of the specified grounds and it appears to the Public Guardian that the ground for making the objection is satisfied, in which case the Public Guardian must not register the power unless directed by the Court;[243] or
- the Court of Protection receives a notice of objection from the donee or named person on one of the prescribed grounds, in which case the Public Guardian must not register the power unless directed by the Court.[244]

Objections made to the Public Guardian

3.137 The Public Guardian's authority to refuse registration of the LPA is limited to cases where there is a defect of form in the power, which is either apparent from the facts or which is brought to the Public Guardian's attention by a named person who is objecting to registration of the power. Although MCA 2005 provides for the Public Guardian to be notified by means of an objection, it would be more appropriate to describe this process as a technical or procedural notice. The notice form given to a named person (LPA3) or by the Public Guardian to a co-attorney who is not applying to register the LPA (LPA003A) refer to these grounds as the 'factual grounds'.

3.138 An objection to proposed registration on one of the 'factual' grounds can only be made to the Public Guardian by the donor, an attorney or named person, before the expiry of the period of 3 weeks beginning with the date on which the notice is given.[245] An attorney or named person must file their objection with the Public Guardian using form LPA007. The 'factual' or specified grounds on which a named person or a donee (where the application is made by the donor or the other donee) can 'object' in this way are limited to the following cases:[246]

- insofar as the LPA relates to the property and affairs of the donor, the bankruptcy of the donor or the donee or, where the donee is a trust corporation, its winding up or dissolution;

---

[242] MCA 2005, Sch 1, para 11(2) and (3).
[243] MCA 2005, Sch 1, para 13(1) and (2). These are the narrow or factual grounds defined in s 13(3) and (6)(a)–(d) on which the Public Guardian can refuse to register the power without reference to the Court. See **3.134**.
[244] MCA 2005, Sch 1, para 13(3) and (4). This part of the Act refers to prescribed grounds and these are not defined. It can be assumed that these are the wider or substantive grounds defined in s 22(3) whereby the Court can direct that the power is not to be registered or revoke the power.
[245] Lasting Powers of Attorney, Enduring Powers of Attorney and Public Guardian Regulations 2007, SI 2007/1253, reg 14. The prescribed period was reduced from 5 weeks from 1 April 2013 by the Lasting Powers of Attorney, Enduring Powers of Attorney and Public Guardian (Amendment) Regulations 2013, SI 2013/506.
[246] MCA 2005, s 13(3) and (6)(a) to (d).

- the LPA has been disclaimed by the attorney;
- the death of the attorney;
- the dissolution or annulment of the donor's marriage or civil partnership between the donor and the donee (unless the power excludes revocation in these circumstances); or
- the attorney lacks capacity.

3.139 On receipt of an objection on the factual grounds, the Public Guardian will simply stop the registration process. It is then for the applicant to accept the situation or apply to the Court of Protection to consider the matter and require the Public Guardian to register the power. The onus here is very much on the person applying for registration to take further steps to proceed with the application.[247]

3.140 If the donor objects to registration, he or she simply gives notice to the Public Guardian in form LPA006. The Public Guardian must refuse to register the LPA unless the Court of Protection is satisfied that the donor lacks capacity to object to the registration.[248] However, it would be unlikely for the Public Guardian to refer the case immediately to the Court of Protection and it will be for the attorneys – if they wish – to persist with their application and refer the matter to the Court.

The role of the Court of Protection

3.141 Where a donee or a named person receives a notice of registration and objects on one of the 'prescribed grounds' the Public Guardian cannot register the LPA until directed to do so by the Court.[249] The 'prescribed grounds' on which a person can object to registration are not defined by MCA 2005 but mirror the substantive grounds on which the Court can revoke a power under MCA 2005, s 22.

3.142 The Court's powers are not limited to the period of registration, but can be exercised at any time after a person has executed a power or a power has been registered as a LPA. However, an objection to registration made after the power has been registered will require a formal application to the Court.[250]

3.143 The Court may in such cases either refuse to register the LPA or, if the donor lacks capacity, revoke the LPA.[251] MCA 2005 does not, however, allow the Court to revoke the LPA if the donor retains capacity, although registration can be refused or cancelled. Thus if the power has already been

---

[247] MCA 2005, Sch 1, para 13 (2).
[248] MCA 2005, Sch 1, para 14.
[249] MCA 2005, Sch 1, para 13(3) and (4).
[250] COPR 2007, r67. Permission is not required where the applications concerns 'a lasting power of attorney which is, or purports to be created under the Act.' MCA 2005, s 50(2) and COPR 2007, r 51(2)(b). See further **3.154** below.
[251] MCA 2005, s 22(4). The power to refuse registration or revoke the power is without prejudice to the Court's powers to give directions under s 22.

registered where the donor has capacity and the Court is satisfied that undue pressure was used to create the power, it appears that the Court cannot interfere with the donor's choice of attorney.

Whether the requirements for the creation of the power have been met

3.144 The Court can determine any question relating to whether or not any of the requirements for creating or revoking a lasting power have been met.[252] This power covers not just the formal requirements of completing and executing the power, but also covers the ability or capacity of the donor to grant the power.

3.145 Although the Court may determine any question relating to the validity of the power, where an application to register is made, the Public Guardian is obliged to register the power unless one of the grounds for objection exists. This is consistent with EPAA 1985, which imposes a positive obligation to register an EPA unless a valid ground for objection is established to the satisfaction of the Court, thereby placing the evidential burden of proof on the objector.[253] The Court will assume that a LPA which has been correctly executed and which contains a certificate of capacity has been validly executed and that alone will place a strong burden of proof on the objector seeking to establish that the donor lacked capacity.

Whether the power has been revoked

3.146 The Court may determine any question relating to whether the power has been revoked or otherwise come to an end.[254] This power enables the Court to determine whether the power has been revoked by the donor. The donor must not only demonstrate capacity to revoke the instrument, but must also communicate to the donee an intention to revoke the power. If the Court determines the power has been revoked, it will direct the Public Guardian to cancel registration of the power.

3.147 The role of the Court to determine such matters is in addition to a separate power of the Public Guardian to cancel registration if he receives notice of revocation and is satisfied 'that the donor has taken such steps as are necessary in law to revoke it'.[255]

---

[252] MCA 2005, s 22(2).
[253] EPAA 1985, s 6(6) and see *Re W (Enduring Power of Attorney)* [2001] 1 FLR 832.
[254] MCA 2005, Sch 1, para 18.
[255] Lasting Powers of Attorney, Enduring Powers of Attorney and Public Guardian Regulations 2007, SI 2007/1253, reg 21. This does appear to confer on the Public Guardian a judicial discretion to consider evidence and either cancel or refuse to cancel registration of the LPA.

That fraud or undue pressure was used to induce the donor to create the power

3.148 If the use of fraud is alleged, the objection will be considered very carefully with the Court expecting all available evidence to be placed before it. Although the Court of Protection has wide powers to summon witnesses and cross-examine them, it is not an appropriate venue for a detailed investigation into an alleged fraud. If the LPA has been used improperly to commit a fraud then the police should be notified and the Court may revoke the power. If fraud is alleged, this usually comes to light when the LPA is being used fraudulently. At that point, the manner in which the LPA was made may be academic. The grounds for revocation are established by the conduct of the donee, who is clearly acting contrary to the donor's best interests. Revocation on these grounds is considered below at **3.147**.

3.149 Similar considerations arise where 'undue pressure' is alleged. Pressure may be brought which is not 'undue pressure', for instance, where an elderly client is regularly advised by a solicitor or concerned relative that he or she should make a power of attorney. 'Undue pressure' is a matter of degree and requires a subjective assessment of whether the pressure was extreme or disproportionate to the extent that the donor could not have executed the power of his or her own free will.

That the donee has behaved, is behaving or proposes to behave in a way that contravenes his or her authority or contrary to the donor's best interests

3.150 The Court's power to intervene in the absence of fraud or undue influence being used to procure the LPA, is limited to two grounds only:

(1) the donee has behaved, is behaving or proposes to behave in a way that contravenes his or her authority; or
(2) the donee has behaved, is behaving or proposes to behave in a way that is not or would not be in the donor's best interests.

3.151 These two grounds represent a limitation in the Court's powers to intervene in the conduct of an attorney. The first ground, where the attorney contravenes his or her authority, can only cover acts which are illegal or in breach of the attorney's fiduciary duty to the donor. Thus they are acts which are actionable in their own right and for which there would be a civil or criminal remedy. For instance, an attorney who causes loss to the donor's estate may be liable to remedy the loss and an attorney who uses the donor's funds for his own benefit or ill-treats the donor may be guilty of a criminal offence.[256]

---

[256] A dramatic instance of financial abuse was reported in the Daily Mail on 6 October 2013 and concerned a donee who used a LPA to steal £471,000 from an elderly relative, most of which was spent on clothes.

3.152 It is the second of these two grounds that may be problematic in practice. The difficulty for the Court is that the Court must impose its own view of what is in the donor's 'best interests' when there is no objective measure of a person's best interests. If the attorney takes account of the factors and consults with the persons referred to in MCA 2005, s 4, then he or she has complied with the requirements of MCA 2005 if he or she 'reasonably believes that what he does or decides is in the best interests of the person concerned'. There has been some uncertainty as to how the Court will measure the attorney's belief against attorney's statutory and fiduciary duties. The Court has recently taken a robust approach to this issue and applying an objective standard to the attorney's duties. Where an attorney has failed to account for funds under her control in breach of her fiduciary duties to the donor, the Court had no hesitation in finding that her conduct was not in the donor's best interests.[257] Where the attorney used the donor's property to invest in her own business, despite a reasonable belief that she was doing what the donor would have wanted, the Senior Judge had no hesitation in finding that the clear breach of a fiduciary duty was contrary to the donor's best interests and revoking the LPA.[258]

3.153 A person challenging a LPA on this ground also has to cross a high evidential threshold in showing that an action (let alone a proposed action) is contrary to a person's 'best interests'. Unless there is a clear act of negligence or breach of fiduciary duty on the part of the attorney, such cases are likely to centre around a different and subjective views of 'best interests.' For instance an allegation that the attorney is acting contrary to the donor's best interests in paying for an inferior care home or paying too much for a care may involve the Court being asked to make a welfare decision on a matter such as where the donor should live rather than on the operation of the LPA.

3.154 By contrast with EPAA 1985 and MCA 2005, Sch 4, the Court may refuse to register an enduring power or cancel such a power if satisfied that:[259]

> '... having regard to all the circumstances and in particular the attorney's relationship to or connection with the donor, the attorney is unsuitable to be the donor's attorney.'

3.155 The 'unsuitability' ground ostensibly gives the Court more discretion to intervene in cases where it might be difficult to prove, on the balance of probabilities, that an act or proposed act is not in a person's best interests. There are cases where an attorney is unsuitable despite ostensibly acting in the donor's best interests. For example:

---

[257] See *Re Harcourt: the Public Guardian v A* [2013] COPLR 69, which involved a failure to account on the part of the attorney acting under an LPA. Senior Judge Lush held that the donor was entitled to expect 'that her property and financial affairs should be managed competently, honestly and for her benefit' (paragraph 60). By failing to pay care costs on time, account for her actions or co-operate with an investigation by the Public Guardian, the donee was not acting in the donor's best interests and the LPA was revoked.
[258] See *Re Buckley: The Public Guardian v C* [2013] EWCOP 2965, [2013] COPLR 39.
[259] MCA 2005, Sch 4, Part 4, para 9(e).

- two attorneys are in conflict and both claim to be acting in the donor's best interests;
- the attorney's financial dealings with the donor's estate give rise to a potential conflict of interest or require further investigation, even though there is no evidence or it is very difficult to prove any actual wrongdoing.
- the attorney may act diligently in connection with the donor's estate but refuses to discuss the donor's welfare with close relatives who have an interest in this.

3.156 The reason for changing the basis on which the Court of Protection can intervene is that the Court's powers should be consistent with MCA 2005 generally and applied in the context of the attorney's duty to act in the best interests of the donor.[260] However, an attorney who may otherwise be unsuitable by reason of his conduct is unlikely, on a close examination of the circumstances, to be acting in the donor's best interests. The MCA 2005 simply requires a careful assessment of the facts and a review of the 'best interests' criteria rather than using 'unsuitability' as a catch-all ground on which an attorney can be removed.

Procedure

3.157 The process for objection is not defined by MCA 2005. The separate roles of the Public Guardian as the registration authority and the Court of Protection as the judicial authority cause some confusion and the procedure for dealing with objections and further proceedings falls between the Lasting Powers of Attorney, Enduring Powers of Attorney and Public Guardian Regulations 2007[261] and the Court of Protection Rules 2007.[262] A person who has been notified of an application and who wishes to object on one of the substantive grounds therefore has quite an arduous responsibility. It is not possible for a concerned relative to write to the Public Guardian setting out his or her concerns. Not only must a formal application be made to the Court of Protection, but the Public Guardian must also be notified so that the application for registration is suspended.[263] The objector must, within the prescribed period of 3 weeks (beginning with the date on which the notice is given):

- file a formal application for objection in form COP7 with the Court of Protection; and
- notify the Public Guardian in form LPA008.

3.158 Form COP7 serves as the formal application to the Court of Protection (instead of form COP1). This form is issued by the Court and must be served on the donor and attorneys as soon as practicable and in any

---

[260] This follows the recommendation of the Law Commission: see Law Com No 231 (at **3.16**), at para 7.58.
[261] SI 2007/1253.
[262] SI 2007/1744.
[263] MCA 2005, Sch 4, Part 2, para 13(3).

event within 21 days of issue. Each application form must be accompanied by a form for acknowledging service (COP5) and a certificate of service (COP20) must be filed with the Court within 7 days of service.

3.159 A person who is not a person named for notification and who wishes to object to registration of the LPA or who if the LPA has already been registered wishes to apply to have power cancelled must apply directly to the Court of Protection in form COP1, paying an application fee and using the procedure under the Court of Protection Rules, Part 9. Applications to the Court of Protection and its procedures are dealt with in more detail in Chapter 4. An attorney also has standing to make applications to the Court of Protection where the donor lacks capacity and will use the same procedures as any other person who has standing to make an application. These are also dealt with in Chapter 4.

ENDURING POWERS OF ATTORNEY
The future of existing powers

3.160 MCA 2005 repeals EPAA 1985 and provides for a new type of power of attorney, the LPA. No new EPAs can therefore be created.[264] There will, however, remain in place countless numbers of EPAs.[265] There is no reliable record of how many EPAs have been made and what proportion of them should be registered or might in future need to be registered on the grounds that the donor lacks capacity. Those EPAs which are registrable as well as the thousands which have already been registered cannot be replaced by new powers of attorney. Not only does the donor lack capacity to grant a new power, but it would be contrary to public policy to require donors – who have in good faith provided for the management of their property and affairs in the event of incapacity – to go to the effort and expense of making new powers of attorney. Neither was it considered appropriate to alter the terms on which a person was appointed to act.[266] MCA 2005 therefore addresses the status of those EPAs, registered and unregistered, made before its commencement. These transitional provisions are considered in Chapter 9.[267] The procedure for registering EPAs is set out in the Lasting Powers of Attorney, Enduring Powers of Attorney and Public Guardian Regulations 2007[268] and the prescribed forms set out in the Schedules thereto.

3.161 EPAs are dealt with in more detail above and a detailed account of the rules and principles applicable to their operation is beyond the scope of

---

[264] MCA 2005, Sch 7.
[265] There is no reliable record of how many EPAs have actually been created. Probably tens if not hundreds of thousands have been created as 'insurance policies' and remain in deed boxes and solicitors' offices across the country.
[266] The Law Commission had proposed that unregistered EPAs could be converted to new-style powers of attorney, but that the expectations of donors should continue to be met. See Law Com No 231 (at **3.16**), at para 7.59.
[267] See MCA 2005, Sch 4.
[268] SI 2007/1253.

this work.[269] However, practitioners will need to be able to advise on and administer two distinct types of statutory power of attorney and apply different principles and procedures to each one. Debate over whether one is better than the other will no doubt continue, until a new form of power of attorney is introduced that replaces them both. In the meantime, the inevitable result is the complexity of comprehending two different jurisdictions and two procedures applicable to persons in similar circumstances. Given the difficulties faced by the Court of Protection and Public Guardianship Office in operating one jurisdiction, it must be hoped that the new Court of Protection and Public Guardian will fare better than its predecessor in the operation of two jurisdictions.

---

[269] See **3.7–3.18**. The topic is covered in greater and better detail in *Cretney & Lush on Lasting and Enduring Powers of Attorney* (Jordan Publishing, 6th edn, 2009) which will remain the definitive work on the subject. See also *Heywood & Massey: Court of Protection Practice* (Sweet & Maxwell). The same law and procedure will apply to existing EPAs, only different statutory provisions will apply to their operation.

this.ward.[20] However, practitioners will need to be able to advise on and administer two distinct types of enduring powers of attorney and apply different principles and procedures to each one. Debate over whether one is better than the other will no doubt continue, until a new form or power of attorney is introduced that replaces them both. In the meantime, the inevitable result is the complexity of comprehending two different instruments and two procedures, applicable to persons in similar circumstances. Given the difficulties faced by the Court of Protection and Public Guardianship Office in operating one jurisdiction, it must be hoped that the new Court of Protection and Public Guardian will fare better than its predecessor in the operation of two jurisdictions.

---

[20] See s.s. 9–23. The point is even more apparent and acute when it is realised that Cretney and Lush on Lasting Powers of Attorney (Jordan Publishing, 6th edn, 2009), which will supplant the hitherto work on the subject. See the two Heywood & Massey, Court of Protection Practice Sweet & Maxwell). The same law and procedure will apply to existing EPAs, yet different enabling provisions will apply to their operation.

Chapter 4

Powers of the Court

PRELIMINARY

4.1 The Mental Capacity Act 2005 (MCA 2005) only sets out the basic powers of the new Court of Protection and one must look at the Court of Protection Rules 2007[1] and Practice Directions to see how these are to be implemented. In addition to explaining the Court's jurisdiction an attempt is made here to address some of the issues that must be faced. The manner in which the Court conducts its business is dealt with in Chapter 8.

4.2 A helpful summary of the Court's approach to the exercise of its powers is to be found in *G v E and Others*.[2] The following extracts from the judgment of Mr Justice Baker are worth setting out as an introduction to this Chapter:

> '(i) The vast majority of decisions about incapacitated adults are taken by carers and others without any formal general authority. That was the position prior to the passing of the MCA under the principle of necessity ... In passing the MCA, Parliament ultimately rejected the Law Commission's proposal of a statutory general authority and opted for the same approach as under the previous law by creating in section 5 a statutory defence to protect all persons who carry out acts in connection with the care or treatment of an incapacitated adult, provided they reasonably believe that it will be in that person's best interests for the act to be done. Crucially, however, all persons who provide such care and treatment are expected to look to the Code ...
>
> (ii) The Act and Code are therefore constructed on the basis that the vast majority of decisions concerning incapacitated adults are taken informally and collaboratively by individuals or groups of people consulting and working together. It is emphatically not part of the scheme underpinning the Act that there should be one individual who as a matter of course is given a special legal status to make decisions about incapacitated persons.
>
> (iii) it will usually be the case that decisions about complex and serious issues are taken by a court rather than any individual. In certain cases, as explained in paragraphs 8.38 and 8.39 of the Code, it will be more appropriate to appoint a deputy or deputies to make these decisions. But because it is important that such decisions should wherever possible be taken collaboratively and informally, the appointments must be as limited in scope and duration as is reasonably practicable in the circumstances. ... the appointment of deputies is likely to be more common for property and affairs than for personal welfare.
>
> (iv) It is axiomatic that the family is the cornerstone of our society and a person who lacks capacity should wherever possible be cared for by members of his natural family, provided that such a course is in his best interests and assuming

---

[1] SI 2007/1744.
[2] [2010] EWHC 2042 (COP), [2010] COPLR Con Vol 499. An earlier judgment on an emergency application in this case was reported as *G v E and Others* [2010] EWHC 621 (Fam), [2010] COPLR Con Vol 510.

that they are able and willing to take on what is often an enormous and challenging task. That does not, however, justify the appointment of family members as deputies simply because they are able and willing to serve in that capacity.'

4.3 Applying this approach to the facts of the particular case Baker J. stated:

'(v) ... the application for the appointment of F and G as personal welfare deputies is, in my judgment, misconceived. The routine decisions concerning E's day-to-day care, including decisions about holidays and respite care can be taken by F as his carer. Decisions about his education should be taken collaboratively by F, G, his teacher, and other relevant professionals. Decisions about possible medical treatment should be taken by his treating clinicians, who will doubtless consult both F and G and others as appropriate. If there is any disagreement about any of these matters, an application can be made to the Court of Protection. Decisions about who should look after E in the event that F is no longer able to do so should equally be considered (when the need arises) in a collaborative way and only referred to the court for endorsement if required or if there is any disagreement. That is an issue for the very long term and it would be wholly inappropriate to appoint a deputy or deputies now to make that decision ...

(vi) I am also unpersuaded that the appointment of deputies for property and affairs is justified at this point. Currently, E's income consists of state benefits alone and his savings are less than one thousand pounds. ... the management of his independent budget ... do not justify the appointment of a financial deputy. I recognise that an appointment of a deputy for property and affairs would become appropriate were E to acquire assets of a size that required the sort of management decisions described in section 18. That might occur, for example, were he to be awarded a significant sum of damages as a result of his forthcoming claim ...'

DECLARATIONS

Background

4.4 In regard to serious medical treatment and welfare decisions the High Court found it necessary to make declarations as to both capacity and then best interests when there was uncertainty or dispute over these issues in relation to an individual.[3] The High Court then enforced these declarations when necessary. The court had to do this under its inherent powers because the courts did not have power to make decisions on behalf of those who lacked capacity.

4.5 However, the MCA 2005 filled the legal vacuum in the law which was left to the inherent jurisdiction of the High Court and instead allowed the court to make a wide range of orders and decisions relating to P. Nevertheless, the inherent jurisdiction still remains for vulnerable adults who do not lack capacity and who therefore fall outside the scope of the MCA 2005.

---

[3] For the case-law and a further explanation reference should be made to Chapter 5.

4.6 Traditionally, the civil and family courts struggled when doubt was raised as to the mental capacity of a party because generic judges had little experience in this area. However, the increase of awareness of the MCA 2005 and more judges being nominated to hear Court of Protection cases especially in the Regional Courts, judges faced with issues of capacity are either able to address the issues in the case themselves or they have colleagues nearby who can do so.

General powers of the Court

4.7 The new Court of Protection may make declarations as to:
(1) whether a person has or lacks capacity to make a decision specified in the declaration;
(2) whether a person has or lacks capacity to make decisions on such matters as are described in the declaration;
(3) the lawfulness or otherwise of any act done, or yet to be done, in relation to that person.

In this respect an 'act' includes an omission and a course of conduct.[4] There is a clear distinction here, which has always applied at common law, between a declaration as to capacity and a declaration as to the lawfulness of an act. But one follows from the other – if the person does not lack capacity it will not be appropriate for the Court to make a declaration as to the lawfulness of an act. What is lawful will generally be what is in the best interests of the individual applying the statutory criteria.

Declarations as to capacity

4.8 The previous jurisdiction under the Mental Health Acts required the former Court of Protection to make an initial decision as to whether the individual was a patient and thus within its jurisdiction. That decision was seldom reconsidered thereafter and usually a receiver would be appointed to manage the patient's property and financial affairs under fairly close supervision unless there was so little involved that a short order could be made delegating everything to a suitable person without continuing supervision. The emphasis was thus on protection.

4.9 Under the MCA 2005's jurisdiction there is a need to reassess capacity in regard to different decisions and at different times. The emphasis is on empowerment, with protection when necessary. This power to make declarations as to capacity in regard to a particular decision or range of decisions is of considerable importance. In every case the Court will need to make a decision about capacity before it exercises its jurisdiction although it may not need to make a declaration in each instance.[5]

---

[4] MCA 2005, s 15.
[5] Refer to **4.12** for an elaboration of this.

4.10 As the judges of the Court of Protection either sit full-time in the Court at the Central Registry in London or are nominated from amongst circuit and district judges and sit on a regional basis, it has become possible for them to be treated as specialists in capacity issues. Colleagues may refer to the regional judges for guidance or even transfer cases to them when difficult issues as to capacity arise. This may be helpful not only for case management but also for substantive decisions. There is the potential for these judges not only to make declarations as to capacity in the Court of Protection (which may be treated as binding within particular proceedings in another court) but also to sit in a dual jurisdiction.

Declarations as to medical treatment

4.11 The Code of Practice provides that certain types of medical decision should be brought before the Court.[6] Although the Court may actually make decisions concerning medical treatment under its new statutory powers, it is likely that in serious or developing situations a declaration as to the lawfulness of treatment will be preferred because this delegates to the medical profession the decision as to whether treatment is appropriate in the circumstances.

4.12 For situations where the treatment will definitely be provided if it is authorised (e g non-therapeutic dental treatment or cosmetic surgery for a learning disabled adult) there is no reason why the Court should not exercise its power to make the treatment decision.

MAKING DECISIONS AND APPOINTING DEPUTIES

Powers of the Court

4.13 If a person ('P') lacks capacity in relation to a matter or matters concerning his or her personal welfare, or his or her property and affairs, the Court is given certain powers, but these are subject to the provisions of MCA 2005 and, in particular, to s 1 (the principles) and s 4 (best interests).[7] In these situations the Court may:[8]

(1) by making an order, make the decision or decisions on P's behalf in relation to the matter or matters; or
(2) appoint a person (a 'deputy') to make decisions on P's behalf in relation to the matter or matters.

An order of the Court may be varied or discharged by a subsequent order.

4.14 It is a pre-requisite of the jurisdiction of the Court that the person to whom the proceedings relate (now referred to as 'P') lacks capacity. In an early case a held that since the Act laid down that mental capacity was to be presumed, there was no jurisdiction to make an order for directions unless

---

[6] See paras 8.18–8.24 of the Code.
[7] These are dealt with in Chapter 2.
[8] MCA 2005, s 16.

and until this presumption was rebutted.[9] This therefore raised issues of the correct test to be applied for the Court to assume jurisdiction under s 48 of the MCA, to make 'Interim orders and directions'. On appeal it was held that the 'gateway' test for the engagement of the Court's powers under s 48 must be lower than that of evidence sufficient, in itself, to rebut the presumption of capacity. It was held that the proper test for the engagement of s 48 in the first instance is whether there is evidence giving good cause for concern that P may lack capacity in some relevant regard. Once that is raised as a serious possibility, the court then moves on to the second stage to decide what action, if any, it is in P's best interests to take before a final determination of his capacity can be made.

Making decisions

General

4.15 Instead of making the decision in question the Court may decide to appoint a deputy with powers to make decisions both now and in the future. The appointment of deputies is dealt with below.[10]

Children

4.16 Some flexibility has been provided in regard to people under the age of 18 years. The Lord Chancellor may by order make provision as to the transfer of proceedings relating to a person under 18, in such circumstances as are specified in the order:

(1) from the Court of Protection to a court having jurisdiction under the Children Act 1989; or
(2) from a court having jurisdiction under that Act to the Court of Protection.[11]

Personal welfare

4.17 The powers as respects P's personal welfare extend in particular to:[12]

(1) deciding where P is to live;
(2) deciding what contact, if any, P is to have with any specified persons;
(3) making an order prohibiting a named person from having contact with P;
(4) giving or refusing consent to the carrying out or continuation of a treatment by a person providing health care for P; and
(5) giving a direction that a person responsible for P's health care allows a different person to take over that responsibility,

---

[9] *Re F (Mental Capacity: Interim Jurisdiction)* [2009] EWHC B30 (Fam), [2010] 2 FLR 28.
[10] See **4.25** *et seq*.
[11] MCA 2005, s 21. See the Mental Capacity Act 2005 (Transfer of Proceedings) Order 2007, SI 2007/1899.
[12] MCA 2005, s 17.

but this is subject to the restrictions on deputies set out at **4.25**ff.

Property and affairs

4.18 he powers as respects P's property and affairs extend in particular to:[13]

(1) the control and management of P's property;
(2) the sale, exchange, charging, gift or other disposition of P's property;
(3) the acquisition of property in P's name or on P's behalf;
(4) the carrying on, on P's behalf, of any profession, trade or business;
(5) the taking of a decision which will have the effect of dissolving a partnership of which P is a member;
(6) the carrying out of any contract entered into by P;
(7) the discharge of P's debts and of any of P's obligations, whether legally enforceable or not;
(8) the settlement of any of P's property, whether for P's benefit or for the benefit of others;
(9) the execution for P of a will;
(10) the exercise of any power (including a power to consent) vested in P whether beneficially or as trustee or otherwise; and
(11) the conduct of legal proceedings in P's name or on P's behalf.

4.19 The powers as respects matters relating to P's property and affairs may be exercised even though P has not reached 16, if the Court considers it likely that P will still lack capacity to make decisions in respect of that matter when he or she reaches 18. Once again restrictions apply to deputies as set out at **4.25**ff.

Wills

4.20 The Court can thus, if P is an adult, make an order or give directions requiring or authorising a person (the 'authorised person') to execute a will on behalf of P. The restrictions prevent this being done by a deputy or if P has not reached 18.[14] However, the approach of the Court to the terms of the will has changed. It is no longer a question of seeking to make the will that the testator would have made if acting reasonably on competent legal advice and notionally restored to full mental capacity, memory and foresight.[15] The Court must now act in the best interests of the testator in accordance with the statutory formula, and this will include consideration of how the testator would be remembered after his death.[16] It seems that the best interests

---

[13] MCA 2005, s 18.
[14] It has been held that the approach is the best interests of the testator, which is different from the enquiry as to what the testator 'might be expected to have done' under the former jurisdiction – see *Re P* [2009] EWHC 163 (Ch), [2009] COPLR Con Vol 906.
[15] The test expounded by Megarry J in *Re D (J)* [1982] Ch 237.
[16] *Re P* [2009] EWHC 163 (Ch), [2009] COPLR Con Vol 906, Lewison J; *Re M* [2009] EWHC 2525 (Fam), [2009] COPLR Con Vol 828, Munby J.

approach may justify the Court authorising a statutory will when there is doubt as to the validity of the last will due to concerns as to testamentary capacity or undue influence.[17]

4.21 There are further provisions in respect of wills in MCA 2005, Sch 2. The will may make any provision (whether by disposing of property or exercising a power or otherwise) which could be made by a will executed by P if he or she had capacity to make it. The will must:

(1) state that it is signed by P acting by the authorised person;
(2) be signed by the authorised person with the name of P and his or her own name in the presence of two or more witnesses present at the same time;
(3) be attested and subscribed by those witnesses in the presence of the authorised person; and
(4) be sealed with the official seal of the Court.

4.22 If a will has been so executed the Wills Act 1837 has effect in relation to the will as if it were signed by P by his or her own hand, except that the Wills Act 1837, s 9 (requirements as to signing and attestation) does not apply, and in the subsequent provisions of the Act any reference to execution in the manner required by the previous provisions is to be read as a reference to execution as stated above.

4.23 The will then has the same effect for all purposes as if P had had the capacity to make a valid will, and the will had been executed by him or her in the manner required by the Wills Act 1837. But this does not apply in relation to the will insofar as:

(1) it disposes of immovable property outside England and Wales; or
(2) it relates to any other property or matter if, when the will is executed, P is domiciled outside England and Wales, and under the law of P's domicile, any question of his or her testamentary capacity would fall to be determined in accordance with the law of a place outside England and Wales.

Settlements

4.24 Special provisions in regard to settlements are also to be found in MCA 2005, Sch 2. The Court may make vesting or other orders as required, and may vary or revoke a settlement in certain circumstances. The Court may also order that investments be vested in a suitable curator outside England and Wales.[18] This provision is sometimes used to facilitate personal personal injury settlements in the case of brain injury awards, thereby by-passing the statutory procedures for the management of financial affairs where there is a lack of capacity. Such settlements were common under the former regime, but now need to be justified because the primary jurisdiction

---

[17] *Re D (Statutory Will)* [2010] EWHC 2159 (Ch), [2010] COPLR Con Vol 302, HHJ Hodge QC sitting as a nominated Judge.
[18] MCA 2005, Sch 2, paras 5, 6 and 7.

is that of the Court of Protection. Supervision and intervention is more difficult in the cases of a settlement and would involve expensive Chancery proceedings, whereas the decisions of a deputy can readily be examined by the Court of Protection and the Public Guardian and costs are more closely monitored.

Miscellaneous

4.25 Further provisions enable the Court to preserve the interests of others (eg under a will or in intestacy) in property disposed of on behalf of the person lacking capacity. This might involve transferring the interest to a replacement property. There can also be a charge imposed for P's benefit on property that has been improved at P's expense.[19]

Deputies

Appointment

4.26 As stated above, instead of making decisions itself the Court may appoint a person (a 'deputy') to make decisions on P's behalf in relation to matters concerning P's personal welfare, or P's property and affairs, or both.[20] A deputy is to be treated as P's agent in relation to anything done or decided by the deputy within the scope of his or her appointment and in accordance with MCA 2005.

4.27 When deciding whether it is in P's best interests to appoint a deputy, the Court must have regard (in addition to the matters mentioned in MCA 2005, s 4[21]) to the principles that:

(1) a decision by the Court is to be preferred to the appointment of a deputy to make a decision; and
(2) the powers conferred on a deputy should be as limited in scope and duration as is reasonably practicable in the circumstances.

The Code of Practice gives examples of decisions that it may be appropriate for the Court to make[22] and also of situations where it may be appropriate to appoint a welfare deputy.[23]

4.28 The Court may make such further orders or give such directions, and confer on a deputy such powers or impose on him or her such duties, as it thinks necessary or expedient for giving effect to, or otherwise in connection with, an order or appointment made by it. The Court may make the order,

---

[19] MCA 2005, Sch 2, paras 8 and 9.
[20] MCA 2005, s 19.
[21] This defines the concept of best interests – see generally Chapter 2.
[22] See paragraphs 8.27–8.28 of the Code.
[23] See paragraphs 8.38–8.39 of the Code. For different views as to whether a personal welfare deputy should be appointed see *Re P* [2010] EWHC 1592 (Fam), [2010] COPLR Con Vol 922, Hedley J, and *G v E* [2010] EWHC 2512 (COP), [2010] COPLR Con Vol 470, Baker J.

give the directions or make the appointment on such terms as it considers are in P's best interests, even though no application is before the Court for an order, directions or an appointment on those terms.

Who may be appointed?

4.29 A deputy appointed by the Court must be an individual who has reached 18, but for powers in relation to property and affairs the deputy could be a trust corporation. A person may not be appointed as a deputy without his or her consent, but the Court may appoint an individual by appointing the holder for the time being of a specified office or position.

4.30 The Court may appoint two or more deputies to act jointly, jointly and severally, or jointly in respect of some matters and jointly and severally in respect of others. The Court may also appoint one or more other persons to succeed the existing deputy or deputies in such circumstances, or on the happening of such events, as may be specified by the Court and for such period as may be so specified.[24]

Control of the deputy

4.31 The Court may require a deputy:

(1) to give to the Public Guardian such security as the Court thinks fit for the due discharge of his or her functions; and
(2) to submit to the Public Guardian such reports at such times or at such intervals as the Court may direct.

4.32 The levels of supervision by the Public Guardian are considered in Chapter 9.

Powers

4.33 The Court may confer on a deputy powers to take possession or control of all or any specified part of P's property and to exercise all or any specified powers in respect of it, including such powers of investment as the Court may determine.[25]

4.34 The deputy is entitled to be reimbursed out of P's property for his or her reasonable expenses in discharging his or her functions and, if the Court so directs when appointing him or her, to remuneration out of P's property.[26]

4.35 There are various restrictions on the powers of deputies appointed by the Court and indeed of the powers that the Court may give to deputies[27] and

---

[24] For guidance as to the appointment of family members see *Re P* [2010] EWHC 1592 (Fam), [2010] COPLR Con Vol 922, Hedley J.
[25] MCA 2005, s 19(8).
[26] MCA 2005, s 19(7).
[27] See MCA 2005, s 20.

these are dealt with under the following headings. The authority conferred on a deputy is always subject to the provisions of MCA 2005 and, in particular, s 1 (the principles) and s 4 (best interests).[28]

Conditional on lack of capacity

4.36 A deputy does not have power to make a decision on behalf of P in relation to a matter if he or she knows or has reasonable grounds for believing that P has capacity in relation to the matter.

Powers that cannot be given

4.37 A deputy may not be given power:
   (1) to prohibit a named person from having contact with P;
   (2) to direct a person responsible for P's health care to allow a different person to take over that responsibility;
   (3) with respect to the settlement of any of P's property, whether for P's benefit or for the benefit of others;
   (4) with respect to the execution for P of a will; or
   (5) with respect to the exercise of any power (including a power to consent) vested in P whether beneficially or as trustee or otherwise.

Medical treatment

4.38 A deputy may not refuse consent to the carrying out or continuation of life-sustaining treatment in relation to P.

Conflict with an attorney

4.39 A deputy may not be given power to make a decision on behalf of P which is inconsistent with a decision made, within the scope of his or her authority and in accordance with MCA 2005, by the donee of a lasting power of attorney granted by P (or, if there is more than one donee, by any of them).

Restraint

4.40 A deputy may not do an act that is intended to restrain P unless the following four conditions are satisfied:[29]
   (1) in doing the act, the deputy is acting within the scope of an authority expressly conferred on him or her by the Court;
   (2) P lacks, or the deputy reasonably believes that P lacks, capacity in relation to the matter in question;

---

[28] These are dealt with in Chapter 2.
[29] MCA 2005, s 20(7)–(11).

(3) the deputy reasonably believes that it is necessary to do the act in order to prevent harm to P; and
(4) the act is a proportionate response to the likelihood of P's suffering harm, or the seriousness of that harm.

4.41 A deputy will be treated as having restrained P if he or she uses, or threatens to use, force to secure the doing of an act which P resists, or restricts P's liberty of movement, whether or not P resists, or if he or she authorises another person to do any of those things. But a deputy does more than merely restrain P if he or she deprives P of his or her liberty within the meaning of Art 5(1) of the European Convention on Human Rights (whether or not the deputy is a public authority).[30]

Revocation of appointment

4.42 The Court may revoke the appointment of a deputy or vary the powers conferred on him or her if it is satisfied that the deputy:

(1) has behaved, or is behaving, in a way that contravenes the authority conferred on him or her by the Court or is not in P's best interests; or
(2) proposes to behave in a way that would contravene that authority or would not be in P's best interests.

How will the Court exercise these powers?
The court's approach

4.43 The Court has a wide range of options for decision-making on behalf of the incapacitated person ('P'). It may make supervised or non-supervised single orders, or may appoint a deputy to make all decisions or a specified range of decisions in regard to personal welfare matters and/or financial affairs. The Court has a duty to take into account P's best interests as now defined but also to act in a way that is least restrictive of P's rights and freedom of action.

4.44 There is also a desire to deal with matters so that they do not need to be repeatedly referred back to the Court although there are some cases where this is necessary such as where deprivation of P's liberty is in issue and review of arrangements is appropriate. Often, however, a one-off decision will suffice on one of many issues the court has to deal with; perhaps about the grant of a tenancy or minor medical treatment for a person with learning disabilities

4.45 The bulk of the work of the court relates to P's financial affairs and the judiciary have devised a lot of standard orders which are available to the

---

[30] MCA 2005, s 19(13). This provision has been repealed by the Mental Health Act 2007, s 55, Sch 11, Pt 10 upon the introduction of the deprivation of liberty safeguards.

profession in various publications and online in the hope that its approach can be understood and to generally assist practitioners.

What happened to receiverships?

The past regime

4.46 Unless a short order was appropriate, the standard outcome had been to appoint a receiver who administered the financial affairs of the patient under the supervision of the Court. This was costly and bureaucratic, and although control over day-to-day finances might be delegated to the patient there was a reluctance by receivers to allow this in case they were later criticised.

The present regime

4.47 Existing receivers have been replaced by a deputy, but with wider delegated powers. The Court may also be inclined, especially in the case of professional deputies, to give them powers similar to those exercisable by donees under lasting powers of attorney dealing with financial affairs. There is a greater willingness in some cases to approve settlements rather than retain funds, although the statutory jurisdiction of the Court of Protection is often preferred for substantial brain injury awards.

4.48 A key criteria will be whether the continued involvement of the Office of the Public Guardian provides added value. This may depend upon an assessment of the family and other persons involved and of the risks involved in permitting more delegation. To some extent this risk can be minimised by requiring insurance bonds to be in place. The levels of supervision by the Public Guardian are considered in Chapter 9.

4.49 The approach to investment of funds has also changed, with the deputy being expected to seek advice from an independent financial adviser, and the special account which for many years has provided a high interest return but now provides interest below market rates may ultimately cease to be a viable option.

CONTROL OF LASTING POWERS OF ATTORNEY

Court's powers to intervene

General

4.50 Lasting powers of attorney (LPAs) introduced by MCA 2005, s 9 are dealt with in more detail in Chapter 3. Until the registration of a LPA is revoked by a donor with capacity or by the Court on any of the specified grounds, the attorney (in MCA 2005 referred to as 'the donee') can continue to act with all the powers of an attorney subject to any restrictions and conditions contained in the power.[31] The Court, however, retains the following powers which are exercisable at any time, not just to revoke or cancel the power or attach conditions to the donee's conduct, but also to guide the donee or provide authority where the donee requires this to carry out his or her duties under the power.[32]

4.51 All these powers which are specific to the operation of LPAs are in addition to the Court's general powers which are exercisable in respect of any matter in which a person lacks capacity, whether or not the donee has authority to act in respect of the same matter. Thus the Court has power to make a declaration of capacity under MCA 2005, s 15, decisions in respect of personal welfare under s 17 and decisions concerning a person's property and affairs under s 18.

4.52 In most cases, the Court will be required to exercise its powers where these are needed to supplement the donee's powers under the LPA. For example, if the power is restricted to property and affairs the donee may apply to the Court of Protection for a decision concerning medical treatment or personal welfare. A LPA furthermore does not authorise the donee to make a will or settlement. Equally the Court may need to supplement the powers of an attorney under a registered enduring power of attorney.

4.53 Conflicts between the authority of the Court and the authority of the donee should be rare. If the donee has authority to carry out an act under the LPA then there is no need for the Court to intervene unless there are grounds for overruling the donee, for instance, if the donee is acting contrary to the best interests of the donor. There may also be cases where the donee simply requires the assistance of the Court to confirm that a proposed act may be carried out.

Specific powers
Creation and revocation

4.54 The Court may determine any question relating to whether the requirements for the creation of the power have been met or the power has been revoked or come to an end.[33] There is concern that although there is a prescribed form which must be adopted, the Public Guardian is to ignore an immaterial difference and the Court:[34]

> '... may declare that an instrument which is not in the prescribed form is to be treated as if it were, if it is satisfied that the persons executing the instrument intended it to create a lasting power of attorney.'

4.55 There is always a fear that the Office of the Public Guardian and the Court will be faced with numerous applications to permit registration of

---

[31] See generally Chapter 3.
[32] These matters are considered in greater detail in Chapter 3.
[33] MCA 2005, s 22(2).
[34] MCA 2005, Sch 1, Part 1, para 3(2).

otherwise defective forms. A relaxed response would encourage a sloppy approach to these important documents, whereas refusal to register will generally result in an application for the appointment of a deputy.

4.56 Unless a hearing is needed these applications are dealt with 'on paper' by a judge at the Central Registry rather than sent to regional judges.[35] Whilst the view may be taken that in the absence of objections it is preferable to empower the donor by registering the power, how will the intention of the donor be known? Defective forms are most likely to arise where there has been no proper professional advice and these are the very situations where lack of capacity or undue pressure tends to arise. To some extent the certificate of capacity on the form provides a safeguard, but at this stage this will merely be a signature on the form. The absence of such a certificate would be a fatal defect and the Court may adopt a policy of requiring further information from the maker of the certificate before accepting a defective form.

Capacity

4.57 The Court's power to determine any question relating to whether the requirements for the creation of the power have been met extends to whether the donor had the capacity to execute it.[36] Lack of capacity at the time of execution is often alleged in dysfunctional family cases, but the onus is on an objector to establish this and it is difficult to do so retrospectively in the absence of contemporary medical evidence. The objectors must therefore turn to one of the grounds on which registration of the power may be refused.

Registration

4.58 The Court may refuse registration or revoke an otherwise valid lasting power if satisfied that:

(1) fraud or undue pressure was used to induce the donor to create the power;[37] or
(2) the donee (or, if more than one, any of them) has behaved, is behaving or proposes to behave in a way that contravenes his or her authority or is not in the donor's best interests.[38]

4.59 If there is more than one donee the Court may revoke the power so far as it relates to any of them thus allowing it to be registered as regards

---

[35] Significant decisions are reported on the Justice website – commence a search at www.justice.gov.uk/guidance/protecting-the-vulnerable/mental-capacity-act/orders-made-by-the-court-of-protection/index.htm.
[36] MCA 2005, s 9(2)(c).
[37] MCA 2005, s 22(3)(a).
[38] MCA 2005, s 22(3)(b). The criteria for refusing to register or revoking an enduring power of attorney are slightly different – see Chapter 3.

another.[39] Presumably if fraud or undue pressure is established the whole power must fail (although MCA 2005 appears to provide otherwise), but it is not clear whether the Court is empowered to remove one misbehaving donee under a joint power (as distinct from a joint and several power).[40]

4.60 The approach to fraud or undue pressure is unlikely to differ from that previously adopted in relation to enduring powers of attorney. Fraud does not require further comment, but in the case of dysfunctional families (and even where a solicitor has been involved) there is generally an objection on the basis of undue pressure in the execution of the power. There can be no objection to mere influence – it is undue pressure that is objectionable, but the boundaries may be difficult to define.[41]

4.61 The new certificate of capacity on the LPA form should assist in these cases as the makers of these certificates can be asked to attend a hearing to give evidence as to the manner in which they have formed their opinion that the donor understood the purpose of the instrument and the scope of the authority given under it, and that execution was not induced by fraud or undue pressure.[42] 63

In the dysfunctional family cases it will generally also be necessary for the Court to decide whether one or more of the attorneys has behaved, is behaving or intends to behave in a way that contravenes his or her authority or is not in the donor's best interests.[43]

4.62 Even if such a finding is made there will be a discretion on the part of the Court to overlook the behaviour, taking into account all the circumstances. This differs from the equivalent ground under enduring powers of attorney, which is (and remains for those powers yet to be registered):[44]

> '... that, having regard to all the circumstances and in particular the attorney's relationship to or connection with the donor, the attorney is unsuitable to be the donor's attorney.'

4.63 A test based on behaviour is very different from one based upon suitability and this can provoke the need for the court to make findings of fact. If past behaviour is relied upon and the donor knew about this when the LPA was executed, it may be difficult to argue that such behaviour, or the propensity for such behaviour in the future, is not in the donor's best interests. This approach demonstrates a move away from a paternalistic approach towards empowerment of the donor, whose choice of donee must

---

[39] MCA 2005, s 22(5).
[40] Reference should be made to MCA 2005, s 10(6) in this context.
[41] There may be no difference between 'undue pressure' as now defined and the previous term 'undue influence' in respect of which there is considerable case-law.
[42] The limited extent to which solicitors who have acted in the preparation of enduring powers of attorney are presently called to give evidence in support of the power does not provide an encouraging precedent.
[43] See MCA 2005, s 22(3)(b) and also Sch 1, Part 3.
[44] See MCA 2005, Sch 4, Part 4, para 13(9)(e).

be respected. It will shift the emphasis when objections are raised from suitability of the donees to the validity of the power and the presumption of validity may dictate the outcome in many cases. There will be cases where, despite genuine concerns as to the manner in which an LPA was procured and the intentions of the donee, family members cannot establish an objection to registration.

Meaning and effect of the power

4.64 The Court may determine any question as to the meaning or the effect of the LPA (or an instrument purporting to create a LPA). The Court may therefore clarify any uncertainty as to the form of the power or the scope of the donee's authority.[45]

Directions to the attorney

4.65 The Court may, if the donor lacks capacity, give directions with respect to decisions the donee has authority to make or give any consent or authorisation to act which the donee would have to obtain from a mentally capable donor.[46] Thus a donee who is unsure about whether he or she has authority to act can obtain prior approval from the Court before acting. A donee who might otherwise need to obtain the consent of the donor to a proposed act, where, for instance, he or she may benefit from the act or the act is subject to the express agreement of the donor, can also obtain the prior approval of the Court.

Rendering accounts etc

4.66 The Court may, if the donor lacks capacity, give directions to the donee with respect to the rendering of accounts or production of records, require the donee to supply information or produce documents,[47] and give directions with regard to remuneration or expenses.[48] These are useful powers and mirror those for enduring powers of attorney.[49]

4.67 In some cases the Court may authorise the production of accounts, whether to the Court or to a third party,,[50] and the power can be useful to dispel mistrust and suspicion within families in regard to financial management. An objection to registration may be withdrawn if the Court is prepared to require basic financial disclosure to an objector whose intervention might be justifiable, and the power must then be registered.

---

[45] MCA 2005, s 23(1).
[46] MCA 2005, s 23(2).
[47] For example, the deeds to a property or a testamentary document where it is a confidential document.
[48] MCA 2005, s 23(3)(a), (b) and (c).
[49] Cf Enduring Powers of Attorney Act 1985, s 8(2)(c), now reproduced in MCA 2005, Sch 4, para 16(2).
[50] *Re C (Power of Attorney)* [2000] 2 FLR 1 provides one example of an account being required.

This is sometimes viewed as preferable to revocation of an enduring power and the imposition of a professional receiver under the former jurisdiction and a similar approach is likely to be adopted towards the appointment of a deputy as an alternative to registration of a lasting power. There is a difficult balance to be achieved between maintaining confidentiality in regard to the donor's financial affairs, which should not automatically be disclosed to family members on the onset of mental incapacity, and avoiding the suspicion and mistrust that arises when a financial manager is unduly secretive, especially when all involved are potential beneficiaries of the donor's estate.

Relieving the attorney of liability

4.68 The Court has power, if the donor lacks capacity, to relieve the donee wholly or partly from any liability which he or she has or may have incurred on account of a breach of his or her duties as attorney.[51] Although this power is included in MCA 2005 with those set out under the above heading it is fundamentally different in nature, being retrospective in nature. Where financial shortcomings are involved it may be difficult to find that relief for the attorney is in the best interests of the donor. Where a liability has been incurred to a third party, which could presumably be for breach of contract or negligence, relieving the attorney of liability would presumably involve requiring the donor to provide an indemnity because this provision is not intended to take away the rights of third parties. Nevertheless, this provision enables the Court to provide relief where the donor would have so done if capable.

Gifts

4.69 The Court may authorise the making of any gift which is beyond the scope of the donor's limited authority under MCA 2005, s 12(2).[52]

Applying to the Court

4.70 Following creation by registration, any person who wishes to apply to the Court to invoke its powers dealing with the validity and operation of a LPA must apply directly to the Court in form COP1. A donee or other party who wishes to apply for an order for a gift or authority for any decision not within the scope of the donee's authority must use the same formal procedure. The formalities of an application are governed by Court of Protection Rules 2007[53] made pursuant to MCA 2005, s 51(1), as supplemented by Practice Directions.

---

[51] MCA 2005, s 23(3)(d). For enduring powers see MCA 2005, Sch 4, para 16(2)(f).
[52] MCA 2005, s 23(4). For enduring powers see MCA 2005, Sch 4, paras 3(3) and 16(2)(e).
[53] SI 2007/1744.

4.71 A donor or donee under a LPA does not require permission from the Court to make an application for the exercise of any of its powers.[54] Neither does MCA 2005 appear to prevent the Court from exercising its powers of its own volition, for instance, in response to a report made to it by the Public Guardian or a Visitor. Although permission may be required for another person to make an application to the Court, this does not apply in respect of disputes about enduring or lasting powers of attorney.[55]

4.72 Instead of applying to the Court directly a concerned relative or other body may make a complaint to the Public Guardian about the conduct of the donee and then leave the Public Guardian to make inquiries or take action directly or through the Court of Protection.[56]

4.73 If the applicant knows or has reasonable grounds for believing that the donor lacks capacity, then the procedure for notifying P under the Court of Protection Rules 2007, Part 7 applies to the donor. Any person making such an application must proceed on the basis that the Court has no existing record of the case and cannot assume that P lacks capacity. Clearly the fact that the LPA is operational does not in any way indicate that the donor lacks capacity. Each application must stand alone and be justified on its own merits and with its own evidence, including medical evidence. Only in very straightforward cases covered by Practice Direction 9D is this procedural burden relaxed.

The role of the Public Guardian

4.74 The role of the Public Guardian has been considered in more detail in Chapter 9 in the context of his or her principle role of registering LPAs. The Public Guardian is also responsible for registering enduring powers of attorney (EPAs) created before the coming into force of MCA 2005.[57] However, the Public Guardian has a distinct legal personality as well as an important administrative role, dealing with most routine applications to the Court of Protection.[58]

4.75 Where LPAs are concerned, the Public Guardian is the main administrative focus for all applications and inquiries, whether contentious or non-contentious. Thus the Public Guardian will be able to determine whether applications need to be forwarded to the Court or can be addressed through correspondence by the Public Guardian.

4.76 The Public Guardian therefore has the following statutory functions:[59]

(1) establishing and maintaining registers of LPAs and EPAs;

---

[54] MCA 2005, s 50(1)(c).
[55] See Court of Protection Rules 2007, SI 2007/1744, Part 8 and in particular r 51.
[56] MCA 2005, s 58(1)(h).
[57] MCA 2005, Sch 4, para 4(2). See Chapter 8.
[58] The powers and responsibilities of the Public Guardian are considered in more detail in Chapter 7.
[59] MCA 2005, s 58.

(2) directing Court of Protection Visitors to visit the donee of a LPA and making reports on such matters as the Public Guardian may direct;
(3) receiving reports from donees of LPAs;[60]
(4) reporting to the Court of Protection on such matters as the Court requires; and
(5) dealing with representations (including complaints) about the way in which a donee is exercising his or her powers.

4.77 The Secretary of State may by regulations confer other functions in connection with MCA 2005 upon the Public Guardian or make provision in connection with the discharge of his functions.[61] It is clear that the Public Guardian's role is being developed beyond the scope of the former Public Guardianship Office, so that through his office he can take a more proactive role in monitoring the operation of LPAs. In view of the likely volume of transactions it is unlikely that there will be much scope for routine investigation, but where there are complaints or concerns are expressed about the conduct of a donee (or an attorney), the Public Guardian will be able to respond and make inquiries. In most cases a call for a report from a public body such as the Public Guardian and some discrete correspondence or negotiation may be sufficient to address the particular concern. In other cases the Public Guardian will be expected to advise and involve the Court to ensure that action is taken.

CHALLENGES FACED BY THE COURT

Overview

4.78 People who lack mental capacity fall into four broad groups:
(1) The largest group comprises elderly people who are deprived of capacity due to senile dementia, a condition that tends to be irreversible. They have enjoyed personal autonomy in the past and may have a personal income and savings that require management, but are no longer able to conduct their own lives.
(2) People with learning disabilities[62] form the second distinct group. They may never have matured to the stage where they can live a totally independent and self-supporting life, and in consequence do not have significant savings or income unless they have come into an inheritance.
(3) Some people are deprived of mental capacity for a period or periods of their lives due to a mental illness which might be treatable. They will need to be supported and protected when the illness is acute but at other times can make their own decisions and may be financially successful.

---

[60] The Public Guardian receives the report but only the Court can direct a report: see MCA 2005, ss 23(3)(a) and 49(2).
[61] MCA 2005, s 58.
[62] In an educational context referred to as 'learning difficulties' and previously known as 'mental handicap'.

(4) The fourth group comprises people who have had an acquired brain injury which affects their ability to make decisions. This is seldom treatable and may be linked with physical disabilities. Large sums of compensation may need to be managed to finance a comprehensive care plan.

4.79 Each of these groups presents different challenges as regards both financial and care management, and some people overlap these groups. Those working in this jurisdiction must be sensitive to this diversity and there can be no standard approach.

4.80 The old Court of Protection was only concerned with financial management, but the Court now has to contend with a mixture of financial and welfare issues and the myriad issues this brings through its doors.

Property and affairs

4.81 The management of financial affairs is not a new concept for a Court of Protection and statutory criteria have been imposed, and in particular a 'best interests' approach In human terms, however, the Court still adjudicates on struggles for control, whether this be the appointment of a donee or a deputy, to approve gifts and wills and to make policy decisions in regard to large damages awards. The change is the availability of a wider range of possible outcomes and the requirement for minimum intervention.

Personal welfare

4.82 However, some may say the court's real test is in the making of personal welfare decisions, especially when the need for these arises through conflict within families or between families, carers and professionals. A simple decision may have wider implications. The issue is always the best interests of the incapacitated individual, but the process whereby this is addressed may differ according to whether the Court is required to resolve a dispute or an uncertainty. The Official Solicitor will generally be involved to represent the incapacitated individual although public funding issues and a heavy workload can stand in the way of his involvement in some cases leaving P without representation and hence a voice in the proceedings. This in turn has led to amendments to the court rules which are discussed in Chapter 8.

Health care

4.83 The Family Division of the High Court was accustomed to identifying best interests in regard to serious medical treatment, often in controversial and high-profile situations. Little change following the transfer of this work to the new Court of Protection and the same judges are nominated to hear these cases, but instead of doing so under the inherent jurisdiction they do so under a statutory framework. Again, the challenge for the Family Division is more one of resources with an ever increasing workload generally.

4.84 Applications relating to less serious medical treatment and health care issues that do not need to be dealt with by High Court judges will tend to be resolved in the same way as other personal welfare issues, although expert medical evidence will be required. These applications do not necessarily result from disputes but may arise due to uncertainty, such as a proposal for non-therapeutic dental treatment or cosmetic surgery.

Personal care

4.85 The issues arising under this heading encompass the full range of decisions, from where to live and with whom to have contact down to holiday arrangements, mode of dress and choice of diet. Any issue that parents cannot agree in respect of their adult child with severe learning disabilities or siblings cannot agree in respect of their parent with senile dementia has the potential to be referred to the Court. Professional carers may also wish to validate their plans for vulnerable individuals, such as participation in adventure holidays that carry some degree of risk.

4.86 'Adult contact' disputes are becoming more common and previously could only be resolved in the High Court at disproportionate expense, but the seniority of that court discouraged the type of application that is now the norm for the Court of Protection. Hearings in these cases now are usually before a nominated district judge who spends much of his or her time deciding such issues in respect of children and is best placed to hear such cases.

4.87 These cases cannot all be treated as litigation to be resolved on an adversarial basis. In some instances findings of fact are required, but otherwise the hearing will be more of an inquiry with input from family, friends, carers and professionals – and, of course, the incapacitated person to the extent that a contribution is meaningful. The parties may seek to bring issues before the Court yet fail to address the best interests of this person. In such cases it may be appropriate for the incapacitated person to be made a party with a litigation friend and a legal representative (unless one professional such as the Official Solicitor can act in both capacities) or for the Court to obtain a report from a Visitor to ascertain the situation on the ground.[63]

4.88 Applications for 'adult care orders' are also becoming frequent where a child with learning disabilities has been placed in care under the Children Act 1989 and is approaching legal majority. The local authority may

---

[63] Such representation may be required in any event so as not to infringe the human rights of the incapacitated person, but the manner in which the proceedings are conducted must be proportionate to the matters in issue and funding may not be available for independent legal representation. See Court of Protection Rules 2007, SI 2007/1744, r 73, which gives the Court discretion as to whether the incapacitated person is made a party.

consider it necessary to continue to prevent or restrict a relationship with the parents and an application to the Court of Protection is then required. This may coincide with a transfer of responsibility from child services to adult services with a different approach from the social workers involved. The best interests approach under the MCA 2005 differs from the more paternalistic 'welfare of the child' approach under the Children Act 1989.

4.89 A new and perhaps unwanted challenge presented itself to the court in 2014 in the form of deprivation of liberty cases. Following the decision in *P v Cheshire West and Chester Council* [2014] UKSC 19, [2014] COPLR 313, the definition of deprivation of liberty was held to be wider than was previously thought. Consequently, it was appreciated that the Court would face a flood of applications in the tens of thousands seeking approval of arrangements that fell within the Supreme Court's definition of deprivation of liberty. This prompted the President of the Court of Protection to formulate a streamlined procedure to allow cases where there was no challenge to the deprivation of liberty to pass through the court speedily to receive approval. This exercise is recorded in two judgments in *Re X and others (Deprivation of Liberty)* [2014] EWCOP 25, [2014] COPLR 674 and [2014] EWCOP 37.

However, certain aspects of the decision were appealed. This brought about the surprising result that the Court of Appeal felt they had no jurisdiction to determine the appeal although at the same time, they opined that their view was that P should be a party in cases involving deprivation of liberty.[64] This observation threw the court into crisis because its implications were huge in terms of the resources available to the court and the Official Solicitor to deal with so many cases where P was a party and where funding might not be available in every case. This brought about a number of cases being referred to the Vice President for decisions on vital points raised although his decision still left some matters unresolved. There are therefore likely to be further test cases and meanwhile, the streamlined procedure limps along.[65]

THE FUTURE

4.90 In 2014, the House of Lords Select Committee on the Mental Capacity Act published its first report and the Government replied. The report made a large number of recommendations including that the overall responsibility for implementation of the Mental Capacity Act be given to a single independent body. The report stated that this would not remove ultimate accountability for its successful implementation from Ministers, but it would locate within a single independent body the responsibility for oversight, co-ordination and monitoring of implementation activity across sectors, which is currently lacking. This new responsibility could be located within a new or existing body. The new independent body would make an annual report to Parliament on the progress of its activities.

---

[64] *Re X (Court of Protection Practice)* [2015] EWCA Civ 599.
[65] See *Re MOD (Deprivation of Liberty)* [2015] EWCOP 47 and *Re NRA* [2015] EWCOP 59.

The report also addressed the need for more awareness of the MCA and LPAs; the role of IMCAs; the need for consideration of the deprivation of liberty safeguard provisions; the provision of legal aid; the need to increase resources at the Court of Protection and the need for changes to the rules. This latter recommendation brought about the setting up of the Ad Hoc Rules Committee in 2014.

4.91 In the first quarter of 2015, the Ad Hoc Rules Committee completed its first tranche of reforms to the rules and by 1 July 2015, all these changes were in place. These changes are discussed in Chapter 8. Work on the second tranche of changes is in progress. In November 2015, a draft pilot on transparency was published and it is anticipated that in the early part of 2016, further changes will be made.

Chapter 5

Gifts, Statutory Wills and Settlements

PRELIMINARY

The statutory framework

5.1 The statutory framework set out in MCA 2005 extends beyond just making decisions for the direct benefit of the incapable person. Decisions that a person lacks capacity to make in person and that may need to be made include the making of gifts or other provisions for the benefit of another person. Where such decisions are delegated to an attorney or deputy, they are permitted by MCA 2005 as an exception to the common law principle that a fiduciary cannot dispose of property for the benefit of a third party, let alone for his or her own benefit. MCA 2005 enshrines this principle and makes it clear that no such decisions can be made unless they are permitted by the Court (whether by the Court directly or delegated to a deputy) or by the Act itself.

Decisions that can be made for the benefit of another party and that are permitted by MCA 2005 fall into the following categories:

- Small gifts and the provision of maintenance that may be made by an attorney acting under an Enduring Power of Attorney (MCA 2005, Sch 4, paras 3(2) and 3(3));
- Small gifts that may be made by an attorney acting under a Lasting Power of Attorney (MCA 2005, s 12(2));
- Small gifts and the provision of maintenance that may be made by a deputy within the scope of the authority conferred on the deputy (MCA 2005, s 19(8)(b));
- Gifts (and the provision of maintenance) that may only be permitted by express order of the Court (MCA 2005, s 18(1)(c) and that fall within the scope of Practice Direction 9D);[1]
- Gifts (and the provision of maintenance) that may only be permitted by express order of the Court (MCA 2005, s 18(1)(c) and that fall outside the scope of Practice Direction 9D);
- The making of a settlement or will for a person that may only be permitted by express order of the Court (MCA 2005, ss 18(1)(h), 18(1)(i), 20(3)).

---

[1] The Court of Protection also has power under MCA 2005, Sch 4 para 16(2)(e), in respect of a registered EPA to 'authorise the attorney to act so as to benefit himself or other persons than the donor otherwise than in accordance with paragraph 3(2) and (3). In practice, an attorney would be expected to use s 18 of the Act.

GIFTS NOT REQUIRING THE COURT'S AUTHORITY
Enduring powers of attorney

5.2 MCA 2005, Sch 4, paras 3(2) and 3(3) allow an attorney to benefit another person (or the attorney directly) but only in certain circumstances. These provide as follows:

'(2) Subject to any conditions or restrictions contained in the instrument, an attorney under an enduring power, whether general or limited, may (without obtaining any consent) act under the power so as to benefit himself or other persons than the donor to the following extent but no further –
   (a) he may so act in relation to himself or in relation to any other person if the donor might be expected to provide for his or that person's needs respectively, and,
   (b) he may do whatever the donor might be expected to do to meet those needs.
(3) Without prejudice to sub-paragraph (2) but subject to any conditions or restrictions contained in the instrument, an attorney under an enduring power, whether general or limited, may (without obtaining any consent) dispose of the property of the donor by way of gift to the following extent but no further –
   (a) he may make gifts of a seasonal nature or at a time, or on an anniversary, of a birth, a marriage or the formation of a civil partnership, to persons (including himself) who are related to or connected with the donor, and,
   (b) he may make gifts to any charity to whom the donor made or might be expected to make gifts,
   provided that the value of each such gift is not unreasonable having regard to all the circumstances and in particular the size of the donor's estate.'

5.3 The provisions of MCA 2005 relating to gifts made by an attorney acting under an EPA do not distinguish between a donor who has capacity and a donor who lacks capacity. Clearly, an attorney would be acting contrary to his authority if he acted contrary to the wishes of the capable donor. If the donor lacks capacity, then any decision made by the attorney must be made in the donor's best interests under MCA 2005, s 1(5). The authority of the attorney is further limited by Sch 4, paras 3(2) and 3(3):

- The power is subject to any conditions or restrictions in the instrument. While the donor cannot extend these powers, the donor may have limited these powers by an express condition or restriction.
- The provision for the maintenance or benefit for the attorney or other person is limited to doing what the donor 'might be expected to do' to meet that person's needs. Thus there must be a 'need' that is being addressed. This power cannot be used as a way of making a gift by other means. The attorney must also aim to do what the donor might be expected to do, thus exercising a substituted judgment. There is also a sense that the attorney is carrying out a moral obligation, doing something that the particular donor is expected to do. Thus a husband may be expected to provide for his wife.
- Gifts can only be made to persons who are related to or connected to the donor. This is not defined more closely, but there must be a relationship or some connection between donor and donee.

- Gifts must be of a seasonal or anniversary nature or made on a special occasion such as a wedding. Thus gifts may be made on a birthday, wedding anniversary or at Christmas. Gifts cannot be made arbitrarily or by reference to a tax period.
- Gifts to a charity must be to a charity where there is a record of past donation or which the donor might be expected to provide for. The attorney cannot indulge a generous whim or choose a charity that is supported by the attorney.
- The value of each gift must not be unreasonable having regard to all the circumstances and in particular the size of the donor's estate.

5.4 Where the attorney acting under an EPA wishes to make a gift that is outside the scope of his or her authority, whether because of an express limitation in the power of because it goes beyond what is permitted by MCA 2005, then a formal application must be made to the Court.

Lasting powers of attorney

5.5 The authority of an attorney to make gifts while acting under a LPA is dealt with in more detail at **3.35–3.43**. The attorney has limited authority to make gifts under MCA 2005, s 12 and, as with an EPA, any gifts that exceed this authority must be approved by the Court.[2] However, there is no express authority conferred on the attorney to maintain a person whom the donor may be expected to provide for, as there is for an attorney acting under an EPA. In these cases, the approval of the Court should be sought unless there is a contractual or other obligation that is enforceable in a court of law against the donor. For example, the donor's spouse who is financially dependent on the donor would have a claim for financial provision against the donor.

Deputy appointed by the Court

5.6 When appointing a deputy, the Court of Protection can confer on the deputy powers to 'exercise all or any specified powers in respect of [all or any part of P's property] including such powers of investment as the court may determine'. The Court has a very wide discretion to confer powers on a deputy, so long as these are not the powers that are reserved to the Court under MCA 2005, s 20(3). In practice, the Court will, in the majority of orders appointing a deputy, provide authority to make gifts in the following terms:

> 'The deputy may (without obtaining any further authority from the court) dispose of [P]'s money or property by way of gift to any charity to which he/she made or might have been expected to make gifts and on customary occasions to persons who are related to or connected with him/her, provided that the value of each such gift is not unreasonable having regard to all the circumstances and, in particular, the size of his/her estate.'

---

[2] See *Re Buckley: The Public Guardian v C* [2013] EWCOP 2965, [2013] COPLR 39, at [43].

5.7 The Court will also use its powers to allow a deputy authority to provide maintenance. Most orders appointing a deputy include the following provisions:

> 'The deputy may make provision for the needs of anyone who is related or connected with [P], if he/she provided for or might be expected to provide for that person's needs, by doing whatever he/she did or might reasonably be expected to do to meet those needs.'

The wording used in such orders is derived from the wording used in MCA 2005, Sch 4, paras 3(2) and 3(3) regarding the authority of an attorney under an EPA.[3]

The provisions relating to maintenance and gifts to charity require a degree of substituted judgment. The deputy must aim to stand in P's shoes and either continue what P has been doing or do what P might have been expected to do. There is no such proviso in relation to the making of gifts. Such gifts can only be made on customary occasions and the value of each gift must be reasonable. Clearly such gifts must also be made in the best interests of P.

The deputy's authority is exercised subject to MCA 2005, s 1(5) that any act done on behalf of a person who lacks capacity must be done in that person's best interests. The deputy is further constrained by the proviso in s 20(1) that no decision can be made on behalf of P if the deputy knows or has reasonable grounds for believing that the person has capacity to make the decision in person.

Value of gifts not requiring the Court's authority

5.8 The statutory wording used for EPAs and LPAs and the authority conferred on a deputy are intentionally vague where maintenance and gifts are concerned. This is because each person's circumstances are different and some discretion or judgment has to be allowed to the individual attorney or deputy to act appropriately. In most cases it is self-evident what can or cannot be done. For a pensioner about to go into care whose estate is no more than a few thousand pounds, a gift of £100 to a child at Christmas may be unreasonable; for a millionaire with a private pension, a gift of several thousand pounds that utilises the annual Inheritance Tax allowance may be quite reasonable.

Guidance on what constitutes a reasonable gift was provided by the Court of Protection in *Re GM* [2013] COPLR 290. The 'gifts' made by the deputies purportedly in accordance with their authority were so excessive that they were set aside by the Court. The estate of GM had been worth approximately £500,000 (£300,000 had been bequeathed to her by her only daughter who had died intestate). Following their appointment as deputies, MJ and JM took it upon themselves to interpret their authority, which included the usual provision for the making of small gifts and maintenance,

---

[3] This in turn uses the wording first set out in the Enduring Powers of Attorney Act 1985, s 3.

to make gifts to themselves and their families, as well as charities. These did not come to light until a routine meeting with a Court of Protection Visitor, who (according to the judgment) had 'recommended that the applicants apply to the court for the retrospective approval of the money they had given away on GM's behalf'. A report prepared by the Public Guardian under MCA 2005, s 49 disclosed gifts of £231,259 (of which £57,532 were to charitable organisations) and expenses of £46,552. Gifts included a Rolex watch valued at £18,275 and a ring valued at £16,500. Expenses for each of the deputies included a car and computer equipment. Obviously the purported gifts were excessive and were in large part set aside. But what gifts should have been made or could have been made, without being considered excessive? In a very helpful judgment, the Senior Judge laid down some very helpful guidelines (at [85]):

> 'The wording of the order appointing deputies for property and affairs envisages a threshold, albeit an imprecise one, beyond which any gifting by them could be regarded as unreasonable. For convenience, I shall call it the "reasonableness threshold".'

The reasonableness threshold differs from case to case depending on the individual circumstances. In *Re Buckley: The Public Guardian v C* [2013] EWCOP 2965, [2013] COPLR 39, at paragraph [43], I said that:

> '... subject to a sensible de minimis exception, where the potential infringement is so minor that it would be disproportionate to make a formal application to the court, an application must be made to the court for an order under section 23 of the Mental Capacity Act 2005 in any of the following cases:
>
> (a) gifts that exceed the limited scope of the authority conferred on attorneys by section 12 of the Mental Capacity Act ...'

Re Buckley involved an LPA but the same principle would apply to a deputyship, where the wording of the order appointing the deputies is virtually identical to that in s 12 of the Mental Capacity Act 2005.

Being both proportionate and pragmatic, and to prevent the court from being overwhelmed with applications, with which it does not have the resources to cope, this de minimis exception can be construed as covering the annual IHT exemption of £3,000 and the annual small gifts exemption of £250 per person, up to a maximum of, say, 10 people in the following circumstances:

(a) where P has a life expectancy of less than 5 years;
(b) their estate exceeds the nil rate band for Inheritance Tax (IHT) purposes, currently £325,000;
(c) the gifts are affordable having regard to P's care costs and will not adversely affect P's standard of care and quality of life, and
(d) there is no evidence that P would be opposed to gifts of this magnitude being made on their behalf.

The *de minimis* exception referred to in the preceding paragraph does not apply to potentially exempt transfers, or to the use of the normal expenditure out of income exemption, where the authorisation of the court is required under ss 18(1)(b) and 23(4) of, and para 16(2)(e) of Sch 4 to, the Mental Capacity Act 2005.

The guidance given in the case of *GM* should apply equally to cases involving enduring and lasting powers of attorney, and this case has been referred to as well in Chapter 3 where gifts by attorneys acting under LPAs are considered in more detail in their own context.[4]

Maintenance not requiring the Court's authority

5.9 It is not uncommon for a person who lacks capacity to have commitments to maintain another person. The most obvious example is that of the elderly husband who has historically been the main bread-winner with a pension that has been used to support himself and his wife in their retirement. On losing capacity and perhaps requiring full-time nursing care for himself, his deputy or attorney may continue to maintain his wife who continues to live in the family home. There are many other examples of a person lacking capacity also being or becoming responsible for maintaining another person. For example:

- a parent may be maintaining an adult child who is disabled;
- a parent may have been helping an adult child with living costs;
- a grandparent has been helping an adult child with family costs or paying school fees;[5]
- a disabled child has received a personal injury settlement which is used to acquire a property which is also lived in by the child's parents who are also caring for the child. The parents have no other employment.

An attorney acting under an EPA may, as mentioned above, authority under MCA 2005, Sch 4, para 3(2), to act in relation to any other person (including himself) if the donor might be expected to provide for his or that person's needs respectively, and may do whatever the donor might be expected to do to meet those needs. There is no equivalent provision conferred on the donee of a LPA, although the Court of Protection has allowed some leeway where there is a legal obligation to provide maintenance (see **3.36** above). Where a deputy is appointed, then the deputy is in effect exercising a power conferred on the deputy by the Court. The Court has a very wide discretion to confer such powers and, as mentioned at **5.7** above, these powers will usually include authority to maintain someone who has been maintained by P or whom P might be expected to maintain.

5.10 As with the making of gifts, there is no clear guidance as to when provision should be made and as to what level of provision should be provided. Clearly, there is a public policy to ensure that decisions that are necessary and often moral should be taken by those involved in implementing them and without putting unnecessary strain on themselves or

---

[4] By suggesting that gifts should be measured by reference to the Inheritance Tax allowances, the court has taken a more restrictive approach to the making of gifts. By comparison, in the 2000 case of *Re W*, the judge did not consider gifts of £20,000 to each of three children to be unreasonable. See **3.42** and the footnote.
[5] See the EPA case of *Re Cameron (deceased), Phillips v Cameron* [1999] Ch 38.

on the court system. Often the sums in issue may be considerable, for instance where a personal injury award is maintaining a family in a property and covers property running costs, food, holidays and transport. The fact that there is conflict of interest is not of itself a barrier to this authority being exercised. For example, it is not uncommon for a deputy or attorney to be living in P's property. The deputy, or the attorney acting under an Enduring Power of Attorney, must act in P's best interests and apply common sense. A careful consideration of the relevant factors should lead to a satisfactory decision; if it might not or if there is any doubt of conflict, then an application should be made to the Court.

Factors that a deputy may need to take into account:

- The wishes and feelings of P, to the extent that these can be ascertained;
- The nature of the relationship, for example a husband who has looked after his wife for many years or the parents of a disabled child who are totally dependent on the child's personal injury award;
- The extent to which the maintenance is affordable (whether relative to the value of the estate or any budget set by the Court) as well as in the context of P's own wishes and feelings;
- Whether the maintenance confers a benefit on P, whether material or personal;
- Whether there is a conflict of interest. The deputy, or attorney, may be the beneficiary of the maintenance. This may be necessary and affordable, but care needs to be taken in measuring the level of maintenance being provided. A deputy in this position may consult with P (if P is able to assist) and other relatives, or obtain professional advice.

GIFTS REQUIRING THE COURT'S APPROVAL

Application required

5.11 Where the value of the proposed gift falls beyond the scope of the attorney's or deputy's authority, then an application must be made to the Court of Protection. The procedure is the same for any formal application and the generic steps to be taken are dealt with in more detail in Chapter 7. Thus, the application may be made by the attorney or deputy or by a person who is a beneficiary under a will or intestacy or who may be a person 'for whom P might be expected to provide if he had capacity to do so'.[6] Persons adversely affected may need to be served with the application as respondents (unless the 'short procedure' applies, see **5.13** below). The Court will have to consider the application judicially, thus taking account of evidence of P's capacity and best interests and then making the order sought. The similar procedure involving an application for a statutory will is described at **5.30** below.

---

[6] COPR 2007, rr 51(2)(a), r 52(4).

5.12 A gift authorised by the Court may not necessarily be by a reference to a fixed sum being given to a particular person. A 'gift' in this context is any disposition that creates a transfer of value from P's estate to another's estate during P's lifetime or that confers a benefit on another party to P's detriment.[7] The maintenance of another person is technically a gift where it represents a transfer from P's estate to another's estate, although this may not necessarily be a transfer of value for Inheritance Tax purposes.[8] An application may need to be made to the Court of Protection where the gift is:

- A chattel – a valuable picture or item of jewellery may not be the sort of gift that is made on customary occasions;
- The making of gifts for Inheritance Tax planning, for example to use the annual exemptions outside of customary occasions, or to make gifts out of surplus income;
- To be made pursuant to a general power or authority to make gifts into the future (for example, a power to make gifts out of surplus income may be exercised over several years, likewise a commitment to pay care home fees or school fees may involve significant expenditure over many years);
- To provide for the maintenance of a relative or someone whom P might be expected to provide for, where the amounts involved are significant or controversial;
- The variation of an entitlement under a will or intestacy, so as to comply with Inheritance Act 1984, s 142;
- The making of a loan on favourable terms or a loan to the deputy or attorney or a member of his or her family; or
- The sale of property to the deputy or attorney or a member of his or her family.

Gifts using the 'short procedure'

5.13 In the context of making gifts, one of the problems caused by MCA 2005 is that in formal terms a gift must be either one which can be made by an deputy or attorney under his or her own authority or one which must be authorised by the Court of Protection. In the latter case, it will involve the Court's jurisdiction and all the effort (and expense) of a formal application. However, in practice there is a vast difference between on the one hand a major tax planning exercise involving several hundred thousand pounds and on the other hand, a gift of a few thousand pounds which is not made on a customary occasion.

It is recognised in practice that not all applications require the same amount of time, effort and expense. Practice Direction 9D therefore provides a

---

[7] The creation of a settlement may also constitute a 'gift' and transfer of value, and similar principles apply in measuring P's best interests. However, the statutory authority for creating a settlement is contained in MCA 2005, s 18(1)(h). See also **5.62** below.

[8] Inheritance Tax Act 1984, s 11(3): 'A disposition is not a transfer of value if it is made in favour of a dependent relative of the person making the disposition and is a reasonable provision for his care or maintenance.'

simplified or short procedure for routine and simple applications by existing deputies and as attorneys. This sets out a list of cases where the 'short procedure' would be appropriate. The cases involving a gift, include:

- applications for regular payments from P's assets to the deputy in respect of remuneration;
- applications seeking minor variations only as to the expenses that can be paid from P's estate;
- applications in relation to the sale of property owned by P, where the sale is non-contentious;
- applications to make a gift or loan from P's assets, provided that the sum in question is not disproportionately large when compared with the size of P's estate as a whole;

5.14 Paragraphs 6 and 7 of the Practice Direction go on to specify the following situations where (in the context of making gifts) the short procedure is not appropriate:

- where the sum in question is disproportionately large when compared with the size of P's estate as a whole;
- the application is likely to be contested;
- the application concerns large sums of money when compared with the size of P's estate

5.15 An application within the scope of Practice Direction 9D still requires a formal application. However, there is no requirement to file medical evidence or give notice to P or any other person unless specifically directed to do so by the Court. The applicant should not, however, assume that the Court has any information about the case and should, therefore, provide the Court with some up-to-date background information about P's estate, P's physical condition and any other recent decisions made by P or on P's behalf. As a matter of good practice, the Court should, therefore, be provided with an up-to-date form COP1A and recent medical evidence, especially where the case involves a power of attorney (as registration will not have involved obtaining formal medical evidence).

STATUTORY WILLS[9]
Background

5.16 A statutory will is the term commonly used where a will is made on behalf of a *person who lacks capacity to make a will*[10] pursuant to an order of the Court of Protection under MCA 2005, s 18(1). The making of a will is one of the most distinctive and important decisions that can be made for a person who lacks capacity. This decision is, however, one that cannot be delegated to a deputy; it is expressly reserved to the Court of Protection, so

---

[9] The commentary relating to statutory wills has been adapted from the commentary by the same author in *Elderly Clients: A Precedent Manual* (Jordan Publishing 2013).
[10] MCA 2005, s 2(1) defines such a person who lacks capacity in relation to a matter if at the material time he is unable to make a decision for himself in relation to the matter because of an impairment of, or a disturbance in the functioning of, the mind or brain.

that no will can be made without a formal application and consideration by a judge.[11] A will made in this way is no different to a will made by an adult testator who has testamentary capacity, save that it cannot apply to immovable property outside England and Wales.[12]

5.17 The statutory will jurisdiction is an unusual one and around 400 such applications are made each year. A will is a powerful expression of a person's autonomy. A person has a right to make a will or not to make a will, and this should not be interfered with lightly. However, there are cases where a carefully made will cannot foresee future events or the making of a will is put off and good intentions are cut off by incapacity. There are also cases where a person has never had an opportunity to make a will or the consequences of an intestacy would be unjust or even harmful. Examples of when a statutory will should be considered include situations where:

- there has been a major change in a person's status or circumstances such as a marriage, which has the effect of revoking any earlier will[13], or an inheritance or personal injury award, which has the effect of altering the nature of the estate;[14]
- a legacy in an existing will adeems, for example where a property that is a specific gift in a will is sold to pay for care home fees;[15]
- there has been a major change in the personal circumstances of the beneficiaries, or any major change in P's relationship with them;[16]
- the effects of an existing will or intestacy might prejudice the interests of a beneficiary, for example where the beneficiary is a child or someone who is also disabled and where their interests can be better protected within a trust;
- there are concerns over the validity of an existing will. While a statutory will application cannot be used to conduct an examination into the validity of an earlier act, a new will might avoid future conflict and allow beneficiaries and claimants to resolve their differences in the context of P's best interests;[17]

---

[11] MCA 2005, s 20(3)(b). Practice Direction 9A expressly limits the authority of nominated officers acting under r 7A of the Court of Protection Rules 2007 to the making of certain decisions, which do not include the making of a will.
[12] MCA 2005, Sch 2, paras (3) and (4).
[13] As in *Re Davey (Deceased)* [1981] 1 WLR 164. See the summary of this case below. When making a new will in a person's best interests, the fact of a marriage and its consequences in terms of an intestacy are 'other factors' that P would be likely to consider for the purposes of MCA 2005, s 4(6)(c).
[14] Such as where a parent is left alone to care for a severely disabled child; under an intestacy, both parents will inherit in equal measure even where one parent has played little or no part in the child's life. While the parent who is a dependant may have a claim following death, see *Bouette v Rose* [2000] Ch 662, the parent must live with uncertainty and the prospect of litigation throughout the child's lifetime.
[15] As in *Re D (J)* [1982] Ch 237. See the summary of this case below.
[16] As in *Re HMF* [1976] Ch 33, where the patient began to take a renewed interest in her two nephews with whom she had previously lost contact. See the summary of this case below.
[17] See *Re D; VAC v JAD* [2010] EWHC 2159 (COP), [2010] COPLR Con Vol 302. See the summary of this case below.

- an existing will, or an intestacy, fails to make provision for a person or organisation for whom a person 'might be expected to provide' if he had capacity;[18]
- there are substantial legacies that cannot now be satisfied because P's financial circumstances have been diminished through care fees;
- there is a tax planning advantage to a new will. The right of everyone 'if he can, to arrange his affairs so that the tax attaching under the appropriate Acts is less than it otherwise would be'[19] is not confined to those who are capable of arranging their affairs in the most tax-efficient manner. One of the principal reasons for creating the statutory will jurisdiction in the first place was to facilitate tax planning, even though such an exercise is not directly for P's benefit but for the greater advantage of P's beneficiaries.[20] This does not, however, allow P's interests to be prejudiced and taken advantage of; a tax advantage for beneficiaries must be in P's best interests in the same way as any other increased benefit created by a new will.
- there is actual or potential financial abuse, and there is a possibility that a new will may have been executed in suspicious circumstances. While it is not for the Court to determine the validity of an existing will, it may be in P's best interests to make a new statutory will that resolves any potential uncertainty over the provisions of a will.[21]

The testator

5.18 The Court of Protection can only order the execution of a statutory will on behalf of a person ('P') who is:
- aged 18 or over;[22]
- lacks capacity to make a will. Under MCA 2005, s 2: 'a person lacks capacity in relation to a matter [the making of a will] if at the material time he is unable to make a decision for himself in relation to the matter because of an impairment of, or a disturbance in the functioning of, the mind or brain'; and
- there is property in England and Wales capable of being disposed of by a will.[23]

---

[18] As in *Re C (Spinster and Mental Patient)* [1992] 1 FLR 51. See the summary of this case below. Although MCA 2005 does not refer to persons for whom P 'might be expected to provide', the interests or claims of such persons are a legitimate consideration of P's best interests.
[19] *IRC v Duke of Westminster* [1936] AC 1, per Lord Tomlin.
[20] Christopher Sherrin, *op cit*.
[21] See *Re D, VAC v JAD* [2010] EWHC 2159 (COP), [2010] COPLR Con Vol 302.
[22] MCA 2005, s 18(2), The court can, however, order the settlement of property belonging to a person who is a minor; s 18(3). It may therefore be advisable to consider an application for a revocable lifetime settlement for a minor who is unlikely to reach the age of 18 and where an intestacy might cause an unjust result.
[23] MCA 2005, Sch 2, para 4(4). If the testator is domiciled outside of England and Wales then property in England and Wales may be disposed of by a statutory will if the law of the testator's domicile permits this.

The court can also order the execution of a statutory will on behalf of the donor of an enduring power of attorney, or lasting power of attorney provided that he or she satisfies the above criteria.[24]

Medical evidence

5.19 A person's capacity to make any decision under MCA 2005 is function-specific. Capacity to make a will must, therefore, be assessed on its own terms and in the context of the individual testator's circumstances. The requirements of testamentary capacity will differ from other decisions or functions under MCA 2005. Capacity to manage and administer property and affairs require a different level of understanding. Even if a person lacks capacity to manage property and affairs and a deputy has been appointed or a registered EPA or LPA is in place, the same person may be perfectly capable of making a valid will.[25] Thus, the Court cannot approve a will for a person unless it has up-to-date primary medical evidence addressing that person's lack of capacity to make a will.

5.20 Medical evidence must be provided in form COP3 to comply with Practice Direction 9A. The making of a will for someone who lacks capacity represents a significant assumption of power over an individual's autonomy. It is therefore essential to provide the Court with the reassurance that it can make this decision on behalf of another person. Form COP3 is, therefore, designed to address the nature of the decision being made, the medical diagnosis and the inability to make the decision in question. Thus the form is set out in two parts: the first part is for the applicant to complete and sets out the nature of the application and explains the decision that the Court is being asked to make; the second part is for 'the practitioner' to complete and addresses the question of capacity to make that decision.

5.21 Form COP3 need not necessarily be completed by a medical practitioner, although it must be given by someone professionally qualified and able to give expert evidence on this subject. The guidance notes state that the form may be given by:

> '... a registered medical practitioner, psychologist or psychiatrist who has examined and assessed the capacity of the person to whom the application relates. In some circumstances it might be appropriate for a registered therapist, such as a speech therapist or occupational therapist, to complete the form.'

5.22 If P has a particular disability, for instance one that prevents communication (which is evidence of an inability to make a decision), then the applicant may consider submitting a separate COP3 from a speech therapist or linguistic psychologist who can address this aspect of capacity. In practice, where P's capacity is complex, it is likely that the application will be accompanied by medical reports addressing capacity – or even specific aspects of capacity – in detail.

---

[24] MCA 2005, s 16(1).
[25] See *A, B and C v X, Y and Z* [2012] EWHC 2400 (COP), [2013] COPLR 1.

5.23 The quality of the medical evidence given to the Court rests on the medical expert having a clear understanding of how the legal test of capacity is to be applied to the circumstances of the individual concerned. There is little point asking a doctor whether a patient has testamentary capacity or not, without the doctor knowing the requirements for capacity and, therefore, the information that is relevant to the decision. It is also important that the right practitioner is asked to complete the certificate. A busy GP or hospital doctor may not have the time or the necessary skills to deal with this adequately, and it is not unusual to request an assessment from a consultant psychiatrist or geriatrician or a neuropsychologist especially where capacity is borderline.

5.24 In the context of a will, the 'information relevant to the decision' includes:[26]

- the nature and effect of a will;
- the extent of the assets being disposed of;
- the claims to which P ought to give effect (which encompasses anyone whose interest under an existing will is reduced); and
- the consequences of deciding one way or the other or failing to make a decision (which would include understanding what would happen if no will were made).[27]

5.25 A medical practitioner who is asked to complete Form COP3 needs, therefore, to have some background information about P's property and affairs. He or she will also need some information about P's existing testamentary history and current intentions, if these can be ascertained.[28] It is probably unnecessary to disclose a copy of a current will, but a practitioner should be informed that for instance P is currently intestate or that there is a will in place that provides for a particular person and why it appears to be in P's best interests to alter those provisions.

5.26 Practice Direction 9F also asks for evidence in the application of 'an up to date report of P's present medical condition, life expectancy, likelihood of requiring increased expenditure in the foreseeable future, and testamentary capacity'. This information is not expressly requested in Form COP3 and the practitioner completing the form should be asked to provide this information while completing the certificate. The space for general comments (box 7.9) in the form can be used for this purpose.[29]

---

[26] The statutory test of testamentary capacity is consistent with the approach set out by Cockburn CJ in *Banks v Goodfellow* (1870) LR 5 QB 549, at 565.
[27] MCA 2005, s 3(4).
[28] The disclosure of confidential information about a person's property and affairs as well as family dynamics raises an ethical dilemma. Ideally, the consent of the P should be obtained whenever P is capable of giving consent. On the question of confidentiality generally, see Solicitors Regulation Authority's Solicitor's Code of Conduct s 4.05(a).
[29] If the case is particularly complicated then this information may be given in a separate witness statement.

The applicant

5.27 Section 50 of MCA 2005 sets out the general rule that permission is required to make an application to the Court of Protection, which is followed by a number of exemptions. Thus permission is not required if the application is made by:

- P;
- if P is under 18, anyone with parental responsibility;
- the donor or donee of an LPA to which the application relates;
- a deputy appointed by the Court for a person to whom the application relates;
- a person named in an existing order of the Court, if the application relates to the order; or
- a person permitted to make an application under the Court of Protection Rules 2007.

5.28 Rule 51 of the Court of Protection Rules 2007, provides further exemptions to the general rule. Permission is not required if the application:

- is made by the Official Solicitor;
- is made by the Public Guardian;
- concerns an LPA which is, or purports to be, created under the Act;
- concerns an instrument which is, or purports to be, an EPA;
- is made within existing proceedings in accordance with Part 10;
- where a person files an acknowledgment of service or notification, for any order proposed that is different from that sought by the applicant; or
- concerns P's property and affairs, unless the application is of a kind specified in r 52.

5.29 Rule 52 goes on to state that permission is in fact required in any application seeking the exercise of the Court's jurisdictions under s 18(1)(b) (the making of a gift of P's property), s 18(1)(h) (settlement of property) or s 18(1)(i) (execution of a will) of the Act, but then is not required, if it is made by a person:

- who has made an application for the appointment of a deputy for which permission has been granted but which has not yet been determined;
- who, under any known will of P or under his intestacy, may become entitled to any property of P or any interest in it;
- who is an attorney appointed under an EPA that has been registered in accordance with the Act or the regulations referred to in Sch 4 to the Act;
- who is a donee of an LPA that has been registered in accordance with the Act; or
- for whom P might be expected to provide if he had capacity to do so.[30]

---

[30] For example, a beneficiary under an existing will whose legacy has adeemed: see *Re D (J)* [1982] Ch 237, summarised below.

Gifts, Statutory Wills and Settlements

The aim of these provisions is simply to ensure that applications are only made by people with a genuine interest in the application. Any other person would have to make a separate application to the Court for permission to make an application, using form COP2.

The application

5.30 The following documents should be sent to: the Court of Protection, PO Box 70185, First Avenue House, 42–49 High Holborn, LONDON WC1A 9JA or DX 160013 Kingsway 7:

- general form of application (Form COP1) in duplicate;
- if the applicant needs permission, COP2;
- medical certificate (Form COP3);
- a statement of truth in support of the application, plus exhibits; and
- a cheque for £400, being the application fee, payable to 'HMCTS'.[31]

5.31 To assist an applicant in setting out the evidence required, Practice Direction 9F specifies the information required by the Court in support of an application. Paragraph 6 provides as follows:

'In addition to the application form COP1 (and its annexes) and any information or documents required to be provided by the Rules or another practice direction, the following information must be provided (in the form of a witness statement, attaching documents as exhibits where necessary) for any application to which this practice direction applies:

(a) where the application is for the execution of a statutory will or codicil, a copy of the draft will or codicil, plus one copy;
(b) a copy of any existing will or codicil;
(c) any consents to act by proposed executors;
(d) details of P's family, preferably in the form of a family tree, including details of the full name and date of birth of each person included in the family tree;
(e) a schedule showing details of P's current assets, with up to date valuations;
(f) a schedule showing the estimated net yearly income and spending of P;
(g) a statement showing P's needs, both current and future estimates, and his general circumstances;
(h) if P is living in National Health Service accommodation, information on whether he may be discharged to local authority accommodation, to other fee-paying accommodation or to his own home;
(i) if the applicant considers it relevant, full details of the resources of any proposed beneficiary, and details of any likely changes if the application is successful;
(j) details of any capital gains tax, inheritance tax or income tax which may be chargeable in respect of the subject matter of the application;
(k) an explanation of the effect, if any, that the proposed changes will have on P's circumstances, preferably in the form of a "before and after" schedule of assets and income;
(l) if appropriate, a statement of whether any land would be affected by the proposed will or settlement and if so, details of its location and title number, if applicable;

---

[31] A further fee of £500 is payable on an attended hearing.

(m) where the application is for a settlement of property or for the variation of an existing settlement or trust, a draft of the proposed deed, plus one copy;
(n) a copy of any registered enduring power of attorney or lasting power of attorney;
(o) confirmation that P is a resident of England or Wales; and
(p) an up to date report of P's present medical condition, life expectancy, likelihood of requiring increased expenditure in the foreseeable future, and testamentary capacity.'

5.32 The Practice Direction sets out the essential background to the application. The application also needs to show why the proposed will is P's best interests and this needs to be explained in the applicant's witness statement.[32] Where possible, additional evidence should be enclosed with the application. For example, close friends or relatives may provide evidence of P's past and present wishes and feelings, beliefs and values. The applicant should try to take into account the views of anyone engaged in caring for P or interested in P's welfare. Nevertheless, it is always important to distinguish evidence as to P's best interests from argument or speculation, which can all too easily over-complicate a statutory will application. The application may also need to be accompanied by expert reports dealing with capacity, care needs or finances.

5.33 Although an application should be as complete as possible, it is also likely that not all the evidence will be available to the applicant. There may be other evidence that is not produced until respondents file their own evidence, whether supporting or opposing the application. The applicant may not have access to evidence such as an earlier will, medical records, a solicitors' file or private correspondence.[33]

5.34 Where the applicant or other party needs the court to take further action unilaterally to assist the application, a separate or application notice (form COP9) should be filed with the Court at the earliest opportunity. This may be necessary for instance where:

- the application is urgent and needs to be expedited;
- the applicant does not have access to confidential documents or information;
- the applicant is unsure who should be a respondent owing to the number of the respondents or if they cannot be traced. Respondents may themselves be under a disability and require the appointment of a litigation friend;
- considerable costs need to be incurred in tracing or serving respondents. An elderly testator may have no immediate relatives and the beneficiaries on the intestacy may be the issue of the parents' next of kin, where contact was lost several decades previously. A genealogist may need to be instructed, and if the costs

---

[32] See for example *Re P* [2009] EWHC 163 (Ch), [2009] COPLR Con Vol 906 and the other cases summarised below for examples of wills made in a the best interests of P.
[33] The Official Solicitor plays an invaluable role in identifying where further evidence might be needed. It is also common for Official Solicitor staff to visit P.

are likely to be high or more than an applicant can afford, an application should be made to authorise the research and the expenditure from P's estate;[34]
- further evidence to assist in determining P's best interests and cannot provide this, an application notice (form COP9) should be filed with the Court at the earliest opportunity.

5.35 The application notice should be accompanied by any evidence required to explain the proposed decision. For example, a request to expedite the application should be accompanied by medical evidence and a request for a will or file from a solicitor should be accompanied by a letter from the solicitor confirming that this information is in the firm's custody. A person required to act in accordance with a proposed order such as a solicitor holding confidential records (who is not a party to the main application) should be named as a respondent in the application notice.

Respondents and persons who must be notified of an application

5.36 On receipt of the papers, the Court will ensure that they are in order and allocate a case number. The application form is then issued, which is the point at which proceedings are started.[35] The issued application form is returned to the applicant who is responsible for serving a copy on any named respondent, together with copies of any documents filed with the application and a form for acknowledging service (COP5).[36] Service must be affected within 21 days of the application form being issued and the applicant must file a certificate of service (form COP20B) within 7 days.[37]

5.37 It is the responsibility of the applicant to identify and name in the application form any respondents and persons to be notified. The Court of Protection Rules and Practice Directions distinguish between the two categories of person. Rule 63(c)(iii) describes a respondent as 'any person (other than P) whom the applicant reasonably believes to have an interest which means that he ought to be heard in relation to the application'. Practice Direction 9F explains that in the context of a statutory will application, the following must be named as a respondent:

(a) any beneficiary under an existing will or codicil who is likely to be materially or adversely affected by the application;
(b) any beneficiary under a proposed will or codicil who is likely to be materially or adversely affected by the application; and
(c) any prospective beneficiary under P's intestacy where P has no existing will.

---

[34] While the costs will generally be recoverable from P's estate, this should not be taken for granted, especially if the application is unsuccessful or the costs disproportionately high. A lay applicant or solicitor's office account may also struggle to fund the considerable costs that may be involved.
[35] Court of Protection Rules 2007, r 62(1).
[36] Court of Protection Rules 2007, r 66(1).
[37] Court of Protection Rules 2007, r 66(2). Practice Direction 6A provides for service by fax, electronic means or by post.

5.38 The reference to someone who is 'materially or adversely' affected covers two types of people. It is often assumed that a statutory will application only affects someone who stands to receive less under the new will than under an existing will or intestacy. However, someone 'materially' affected is also someone who stands to receive more under the proposed will as well as someone who stands to receive the same. That person has a material interest in the outcome and may wish to submit further evidence as to P's best interests. Likewise, a person who may inherit on a contingency may also be said to have a material interest in the outcome, especially if the original beneficiary is elderly and likely to predecease P. Generally, the Court will interpret these requirements strictly, as a person with a legitimate interest in the outcome should be able to respond.[38] Unfortunately, the Practice Direction provides no threshold as to whether any particular interest might be *de minimis*. In practice, the Court will generally overlook the interests of legatees or proposed legatees where the legacies are small in themselves or relative to the value of the estate, and do not affect the substantive provisions of the will.[39]

5.39 Practice Direction 9B identifies other people who should be notified of an application. The main distinction is that a person notified does not have a material interest in the outcome; he or she does not, therefore, receive all the documents filed with the application but only a short summary of the application (form COP15) and a form for acknowledgement of service (COP5). The onus is then on the notified person to apply to be a party to the application. The role of notified persons is usually considered when making an application to appoint a deputy (where there are no respondents who have a material interest in the outcome). Nevertheless, the status of notified persons should not be overlooked on a statutory will application. In most cases there will be an overlap between the two in that a respondent will also comply with the description of family members to be notified in Practice Direction 9B. However, this is not always going to be the case. For example where the beneficiaries under an existing will or proposed statutory will are charities or friends, and P has relatives, then at least three relatives (or all the members of the appropriate class of relatives) should be notified of the application.

5.40 The Court of Protection Rules do not assume that P will be a party, and P should not be named as a respondent in the application.[40] It is up to the Court to decide whether P should be joined as a party.[41] The person most directly connected with the outcome is of course, P, and therefore Practice

---

[38] See *Re B (Court of Protection: notice of proceedings)* [1987] 2 FLR 155. In one case dealt with by Brian Bacon of Thomson Snell & Passmore, where P was intestate, the applicant identified 77 residuary beneficiaries, all of whom were respondents to the application. The parties included over 30 of the residuary beneficiaries who responded as well as six proposed charities, a legatee, the applicant and the Official Solicitor.

[39] There is no reason why a proposed legatee should not be notified of the application and therefore informed of what is being proposed. It would then be for the proposed legatee to apply to be a party if he or she felt that the proposed legacy was inappropriate.

[40] Court of Protection Rules 2007, r 73(4).

[41] Court of Protection Rules 2007, r 73(2).

Direction 9F requires the Court to consider at the earliest opportunity whether P should be joined as a party to the proceedings and, if he is so joined, whether the Official Solicitor should be invited to act as a litigation friend, or whether some other person should be appointed as a litigation friend.[42] In most cases involving a statutory will, P will be joined as a party and the Official Solicitor asked to act as litigation friend.[43] Where P is joined as a party, the application form and other papers must be served on the litigation friend. P does not need to be notified in person.[44]

Subsequent procedure and final hearing

5.41 Once the Court has issued an application, it must then consider how to deal with it.[45] On a statutory will application, the current practice is to issue initial or case management directions at an early stage and then return these to the applicant together with the issued application form. This will allow the Court to address any missing evidence, confirm the appointment of P as a party and direct service on the respondents, including the Official Solicitor (subject to his agreement to act as a litigation friend). The Court may also set a date for a hearing. Depending on the complexity of this case, this may be a directions hearing (which may be a telephone hearing) or a final hearing. This hearing date may be adjourned if more time is needed or disposed of if the case can be agreed on the papers.

5.42 The timeframe set by the Court will allow for the respondents and P to be served with the application papers and to respond to the application. Any respondent or notified person who wishes to be a party to the application must file an acknowledgement of service (form COP5) within 21 days of being served with the application.[46] A respondent is automatically a party if he files an acknowledgement of service.[47] A person notified is only a respondent if he files an acknowledgement of service and the Court agrees to make such person a party.[48]

5.43 The requirement to respond to an application within 21 days may be unduly harsh especially if the application is complicated and the respondent needs time to consider the application, take legal advice and prepare evidence in response. In view of the timeframe laid down in the Court of Protection Rules, unless the time for service has already been extended by

---

[42] At paragraph 10. The Official Solicitor is usually invited to act as litigation friend, but this is not necessarily done in every case. Where a professional deputy has no personal interest in the case then it may be possible for the deputy to act as litigation friend.
[43] If case is straightforward, for instance if it simply involves a codicil to change executors, then it may be possible to avoid joining P as a party. In almost every case, P is joined as a party and the Official Solicitor is appointed as litigation friend. If the Official Solicitor has a conflict of interest (for instance the Official Solicitor is already acting for P's spouse) then another solicitor will be appointed to take on this role.
[44] Court of Protection Rules 2007, r 40(2).
[45] Court of Protection Rules 2007, r 84(1).
[46] Court of Protection Rules 2007, r 72(2).
[47] Court of Protection Rules 2007, r 73(1)(b).
[48] Court of Protection Rules 2007, r 72(8).

the initial directions order, a respondent who needs more time to file evidence should file an acknowledgement of service (form COP5) within the time limit as well as a request for an extension of time to file further evidence.[49]

5.44 The period of time before a hearing takes place allows the parties to exchange evidence and deal with additional information that may not have been supplied in the application. The Official Solicitor will also need time to review the application, any responses filed and where possible, meet P.[50] To save the time and expense of an attended hearing, the parties are expected to attempt to settle the papers or, where agreement cannot be reached, to establish the level of consensus that can be achieved. Negotiations may be conducted through the Official Solicitor who may act as a lead party in applying to the Court for further directions or with the terms of a proposed agreement. If there is an agreement and this is supported by the Official Solicitor as P's litigation friend, the Court may make a final order on the papers, without an attended hearing.

5.45 If the case is complex and likely to proceed to an attended hearing, the directions order may require an applicant to file and serve complete trial bundles and the parties to circulate skeleton arguments.

5.46 Where the application proceeds to a hearing, this will be before a judge. Most cases are heard before a district judge or the Senior Judge (at First Avenue House); however, depending on the complexity of the case (especially if extensive cross-examination is required or the case must deal with an important point of legal principle), a hearing may be referred to a circuit judge or puisne judge.[51] An attended hearing imposes a considerable burden on all the parties, especially the applicant, to ensure that all the evidence is available to the parties and the judge, in the form of an agreed bundle. Unless the Court has directed otherwise, an agreed bundle must be prepared by the applicant and served on the parties at least 5 days before the hearing and lodged with the Court at least 3 days before the hearing. Skeleton arguments must be lodged with the Court by at least 11 am on the day before the hearing.[52]

5.47 Parties will be expected to attend in good time before the time listed for a hearing and it is not uncommon for discussions to take place at the courtroom door in a final attempt to limit the issues between the parties. A judge will expect the parties to have used their best efforts to reduce the scope of disagreement as far as possible and concentrate the Court's time only on those matters that remain in issue. No further evidence can be

---

[49] This should be included in form COP5.
[50] Even if P lacks capacity to provide any insight into his or her present wishes, it is useful for P's representative to establish that this is the case and observe P's natural environment. Seeing how P is cared for and talking to carers may also help complete a picture of P's character and circumstances.
[51] Practice Direction 13A.
[52] Practice Direction 13B.

produced without the Court's permission.⁵³ Any evidence already given in writing stands as a witness's final evidence, although a witness may be cross-examined on his evidence. Parties or their representatives will also be allowed to make submissions on the legal principles the Court is being asked to resolve.

5.48 Unless judgment is reserved or the hearing is adjourned, the judge will make the order at the hearing that will authorise the applicant or some other person to execute the statutory will in the form approved by the Court. Usually, the judge will agree the terms of the statutory will and direct the applicant or the Official Solicitor to file an agreed final draft. A draft will approved by the judge will be referred to in the final order.

5.49 Whether or not the order is made at the hearing, it will also provide for the costs of the applicant, the Official Solicitor and any other party who was legally represented to be assessed and paid from P's estate and for the safe custody of the will.

Execution of a statutory will

5.50 After the order has been made, it will be drawn up, sealed and entered. Sealed copies will be sent to all the parties to the application. However, the order is effective immediately it is made. In an emergency, a statutory will can be engrossed and executed immediately after the order has been made by the judge and before the order has been drawn up and sealed.

5.51 It is the responsibility of the applicant to engross the will that has been approved by the judge. The will is expressed to be signed by P acting by the *authorised person* (usually the applicant or the deputy):

- signed by the authorised person with the name of P, and with his or her own name, in the presence of two or more witnesses present at the same time;
- attested and subscribed by those witnesses in the presence of the authorised person; and
- sealed with the official seal of the Court of Protection.

5.52 As the authorised person is signing the statutory will on behalf of P and is not a witness as such, he or she will not be barred from benefiting under the will by virtue of the Wills Act 1837, s 15 (gifts to an attesting witness, or to the spouse or civil partner of an attesting witness, to be void). In all other respects, a statutory will is to be treated in the same way as a will made by P in accordance with the Wills Act 1837. Therefore, no beneficiary named in the statutory will, nor a spouse or civil partner of such a beneficiary may act as a witness.⁵⁴ The statutory will also serves to revoke all earlier wills and is revoked in the event of P's marriage.

---

53 Court of Protection Rules 2007, r 96(4).
54 MCA 2005, Sch 2, para 4(2) states that: 'The Wills Act 1837 has effect in relation to the will as if it were signed by P in his own hand, except that [s 9 of that Act shall not apply].'

5.53 Once a statutory will has been executed, the applicant must send the original and two copies of the will to the court for sealing. The court will seal the original document and return this to the applicant or the applicant's solicitor for safe custody.[55] The will is effective on being executed; the requirement that it be sealed is confirmation that the will has been executed under MCA 2005.[56]

URGENT APPLICATIONS

5.54 The average time-span between lodging an application and a final hearing is about 5 months and can be longer if there are any extensions of time to obtain further evidence or comply with other directions. If, however, there is evidence that P is critically ill and may die before the hearing date, an application notice may be filed requesting an expedited hearing. However, this must be accompanied by medical evidence that directly addresses P's illness and life expectancy. The applicant must also explain to the Court why the application could not have been made earlier and whether anyone will be prejudiced by the application being dealt with urgently. Any other respondent as well as the Official Solicitor should be notified as soon as possible and provided with any evidence that has already been lodged, even if the application has not yet been issued. The Court should also be provided with a draft will.

5.55 The Court will aim to be as helpful as it can and in extreme cases the application may be heard by telephone within a matter of days. The judge may authorise the applicant's solicitor or the Official Solicitor to execute the statutory will so that this can be done immediately after the order has been made.

5.56 The Court does not favour urgent applications because they have a tendency to be weighted procedurally in favour of the applicant. An order made without proper notice to an affected party would breach Art 6 of the European Convention on Human Rights – the right to a fair trial. In *Re R* [2003] WTLR 1051, Ferris J declined to approve a statutory will for a patient (under the Mental Health Act 1983) as the emergency did not allow the Court enough time to consider the application fully, especially in view of the 'procedural prejudice' suffered by the adversely affected party. In this case, the applicant had delayed making the application and therefore any adverse consequences of the delay would fall on the applicant. It is important that where there are concerns about P's health and life-expectancy, no time is lost in making the application and giving as much notice as possible to the other parties.

---

[55] It is no longer the practice of the Court to require a receipt and undertaking for the original will. Once it has been returned for safe custody, it is the responsibility of the custodian to hold the document safely to the order of P. Thus the Will should not be released without the further order of the Court of Protection during P's lifetime and for as long as P lacks capacity.

[56] *Re Hughes* (1999) *The Times*, 8 January.

5.57 Where time is limited and there is any risk of prejudice to P or another party, the Court will proceed with great care. It will also have regard to the principle in MCA 2005, s 1(6) that the decision should be the least restrictive of P's rights and freedom of action. Therefore, if the Court does approve an 'emergency will', this should depart as narrowly as possible from the provisions of an existing will or intestacy. The Court will often approve a holding or temporary will that deals with administrative matters such as the appointment of professional executors, which may make a great difference to the efficient winding up of P's estate. The will might also deal with matters that are unlikely to be uncontroversial. Small legacies could for instance be included to acknowledge a moral debt and that are unlikely to affect the substantive provisions of the existing intestacy. If the will is likely to be complicated or involve parties who have not yet been identified or given adequate time to respond, the Court may approve a discretionary will. The Court would, however, need to be persuaded that such a will did not represent an abdication of its powers but a decision that can be properly made in P's best interests. There would have to be some record of the basis on which trustees might be expected to exercise their discretionary powers; for instance, that they should provide for the needs of a dependent but otherwise follow an existing intestacy.[57]

Costs[58]

5.58 Costs incurred in any proceedings are governed by Pt 19 of the Court of Protection Rules in addition to Pts 44, 47 and 48 of the Civil Procedure Rules 1998. Court of Protection Rules, r 156 sets out the following general rule:

> 'Where the proceedings concern P's property and affairs the general rule is that the costs of the proceedings or of that part of the proceedings that concerns P's property and affairs, shall be paid by P or charged to his estate.'

5.59 As a statutory will relates to P's property and affairs, the Court will usually follow the general rule. The general rule is not inflexible and can be avoided by the Court. Rule 159 provides the Court with power to depart from the general rule 'if the circumstances so justify'. The Court must have regard to all the circumstances, including the conduct of the parties, whether a party has succeeded on part of his case, even if he has not been wholly successful; and the role of any public body involved in the proceedings. Rule 159(2) defines conduct of the parties as including:

(a) conduct before, as well as during, the proceedings;
(b) whether it was reasonable for a party to raise, pursue or contest a particular issue;
(c) the manner in which a party has made or responded to an application or a particular issue; and

---

[57] Although the Court cannot approve a letter of wishes for P, a record of P's likely wishes setting out the understanding between the parties as to how the discretionary powers should be applied, could be recorded on the face of the will.
[58] See, generally, Court of Protection Rules 2007, rr 155–168.

(d) whether a party who has succeeded in his application or response to an application, in whole or in part, exaggerated any matter contained in his application or response.

5.60 To depart from the general rule does, therefore, involve an allocation of blame that the Court generally tries to avoid. In many statutory will cases, the Court will look to a solution that respects the *bona fides* of the parties. Where the parties have made genuine attempts to compromise and present P's best interests fairly, there are no winners or losers. The right will has been made in P's best interests. To deprive a party of costs or to award costs against a party involves a finding of blame. This will involve further argument, with parties making further representations and having a right to be heard (especially if the order was made without a hearing). It is often taken for granted that in property and affairs cases costs are payable from the estate as a matter of course. However, exceptions to the general rule do arise from time to time and can be illustrated by the following examples:

- An application was made by for a deed of variation redirecting the estate of P's deceased husband to his son (P's stepson). The stepson was a party to the proceedings and the main beneficiary of the variation that was approved by the Court. He was ordered to pay half of the applicant's costs in the proceedings.
- In a statutory will application, one party produced a home-made will, which she claimed was P's last will and which should be upheld by the Court. The Court would not make a finding on the validity of this earlier will, but the party had caused delays in producing the will and was evasive and inconsistent in cross-examination. No order for costs was made in favour of that party.
- In a lengthy statutory will hearing before the High Court, it was argued by the successful applicant that the respondent had needlessly asked for a second day's hearing. No further material evidence was disclosed on the second day. The respondent's costs were limited to the first day of the hearing only.

5.61 The final order will provide authority for a party to recover costs from P's estate. A solicitor will, however, still have to submit these costs for detailed assessment in the same way as any other costs that are payable from P's estate that are not covered by fixed costs.

SETTLEMENTS

When necessary

5.62 The Court of Protection may approve a settlement under MCA 2005, 18(1)(h). The approval of a settlement, as with a statutory will, is a decision reserved specifically to the Court. These are not common procedures and generally a settlement will involve a benefit for another party. They may be appropriate in the following circumstances:

- where a direct gift to an individual is inappropriate but a transfer of property from P's estate should still be made, for example where the proposed beneficiary is a minor or has special needs;
- where P is a beneficiary under an existing will or settlement and P does not require an absolute interest or interest in possession that will be charged to inheritance tax on P's death. Rather than complete a deed of variation giving P's interest to another beneficiary absolutely, it may be appropriate to create a new settlement on discretionary trusts that include P as a discretionary beneficiary.
- where P is a recipient of a substantial damages award or other sum of money and it can be shown to the Court of Protection that it is in P's best interests for such money to be more effectively managed within a trust than through a deputyship. For instance, parents may prefer the flexibility of a private trust as a means of maintaining a severely disabled child, especially where the award is limited and their involvement may help reduce the costs of administering the estate while allowing some professional input from a professional trustee (see the detailed judgment of Hazel Marshall QC in *SM v HM* [2012] COPLR 187.
- where P is a beneficiary of an existing settlement that needs to be varied. If the beneficiaries of the settlement are not all of full age then the matter must also be dealt with under the Variation of Trusts Act 1958.

Procedure

5.63 An application for the approval of a settlement must be dealt with as a formal application to the Court of Protection in Form COP1. The application is similar to an application for a statutory will and is covered by Practice Direction 9D in the same way (see **5.30** above).

Chapter 6

Health Care and Welfare, IMCAs, Advance Decisions and Research[1]

PRELIMINARY

6.1 A number of issues can arise under the Mental Capacity Act 2005 (MCA 2005) in regard to welfare and health care. For example, as to health care, first, what medical treatment should be provided for an adult who cannot make choices; secondly, how can the adult before losing capacity influence decisions about subsequent treatment; thirdly, to what extent should medical research be permitted; and, fourthly, whether the adult should make a donation of their body tissues or organs? Similar issues as the first two can arise in relation to such a person's more general welfare, for example, where they should live or with whom they should have contact. The welfare issue may be linked to a health care issue, but may be quite separate. Whilst questions of health care and welfare in relation to an incapacitated adult are fully integrated into the statutory framework provided by the MCA 2005, the pre-existing common law remains relevant to an understanding of these provisions as they apply in relation to these issues, and a brief overview is therefore provided at the outset of this chapter.

THE PRE-EXISTING COMMON LAW

Medical treatment

6.2 The starting point at common law was that any 'invasive' or 'intrusive' medical treatment constituted an unlawful act unless authorised by statute, done under the doctrine of necessity (see below) or with the consent of the person concerned.[2] A competent adult had an unfettered right at common law to refuse medical treatment; conversely an 'incompetent'[3] adult could not consent to treatment, nor did the common law recognise the ability of anyone else to give consent on their behalf.

6.3 From an early time, however, the common law allowed the High Court to make medical treatment decisions for children and for adults without the

---

[1] The first edition of this work contained significantly more material regarding the position under the common law. This has, however, been pruned in light of the passage of time since the enactment of the MCA 2005. The contribution of James Beck from the Official Solicitor's office to the material under this heading is gratefully acknowledged.
[2] Such consent being capable of being provided by an adult parent on behalf of a child, or by a child over the age of 16: Family Law Reform Act 1969, s 8.
[3] This term was the consistent term used prior to the enactment of MCA 2005; whilst it would not now be used, for clarity's sake, it is retained in this part of the chapter.

mental capacity to decide for themselves. Originally the judges of the High Court exercised the Crown's prerogative power as parens patriae. This power still exists in relation to children. Although it was excluded in relation to adults by the enactment of a succession of Mental Health Acts, the practical effect of this was limited by the dramatic development in the last decade of the 20th century of the declaratory jurisdiction of the High Court. Starting in 1990 with *Re F (Mental Patient: Sterilisation)*,[4] a series of decisions established clearly that the High Court retained an inherent jurisdiction to make declarations as to what was lawful as being in the best interests of an incompetent adult.

6.4 Substantially prior to 2007, therefore, it had become one of the many roles of the Family Division of the High Court of Justice in England and Wales to decide whether medical procedures should or should not be carried out on an adult who was unable to consent to the treatment in question. Such cases tended to divide into three main types, namely where medical opinion was that:

- A particular course of treatment would save life, for example, a blood transfusion or a Caesarean section;[5]
- A particular procedure should be carried out to enhance the patient's quality of life or prevent physical or mental deterioration, for example, a liver transplant or sterilisation;[6]
- Life-prolonging treatment should either be withheld or withdrawn to allow the patient to die with dignity.[7]

Welfare

6.5 Parallel to the development of the inherent jurisdiction in the medical realm, the High Court developed a similar declaratory jurisdiction in respect of decisions regarding the welfare of incompetent adults.[8] Indeed, prior to the enactment of MCA 2005, one High Court judge had already commented:[9]

> '... we have come a long way since the decision in *In Re F*. The courts have created and now exercise what is, in substance and reality, a jurisdiction in relation to incompetent adults which is for all practical purposes indistinguishable from its well-established *parens patriae* or wardship jurisdiction in relation to children.'

---

[4] [1989] 2 FLR 376.
[5] *HE v A Hospital NHS Trust* [2003] EWHC 1017 (Fam), [2003] 2 FLR 408 (blood transfusion); *St George's Healthcare NHS Trust v S* [1998] 2 FLR 728 (Caesarean section).
[6] *Re T (A Minor) (Wardship: Medical Treatment)* [1997] 1 FLR 502 (kidney transplant); *Re A (Male Sterilisation)* [2000] 1 FLR 549; and eg *Re S (Adult Patient: Sterilisation)* [2000] 2 FLR 389.
[7] *Airedale NHS Trust v Bland* [1993] 1 FLR 1026.
[8] See eg *Re F (Mental Patient: Sterilisation)* [1989] 2 FLR 376; *Re C (Mental Patient: Contact)* [1993] 1 FLR 940; *Re F (Adult: Court's Jurisdiction)* [2000] Fam 38; and *A v A Health Authority, Re J (a child), R (on the application of S) v Secretary of State for the Home Department* [2002] Fam 213.
[9] *E (By her litigation friend the Official Solicitor) v Channel Four; News International Ltd and St Helens Borough Council* [2005] 2 FLR 913, at [55], per Munby J as he then was.

Injunctive relief

6.6 Prior to the enactment of MCA 2005, there was a distinction in principle between the adult jurisdiction to declare what is lawful and the power under the Children Act 1989 to make orders in children's cases. But this became more apparent than real as it was established that injunctive relief (where permissible) in support of a declaration could be granted.[10] However, the principle remained that doctors could not be compelled personally to undertake a treatment they did not, in their clinical judgment, wish to provide; in some circumstances, though, the NHS Trust responsible for the treatment might be required to transfer the patient to the care of other doctors who would treat as the patient wanted or in his or her best interests.[11]

Capacity

6.7 As set out further in Chapter 2 above, the common law test of capacity was specific to the decision in question. In the medical context, for instance, it depended on whether the patient fully understood the nature of the proposed intervention, the reasons and the consequences of submitting or not submitting to it, and could weigh these in the balance and reach and communicate a decision.[12]

6.8 Prior to the enactment of MCA 2005, the Courts had developed a clear principle that it was necessary to attempt to reach an objective view of what was in the best interests of the incompetent adult in the light of all the relevant circumstances and evidence available to it. In medical cases, this went considerably further than medical considerations, to embrace emotional and all other welfare issues. In a seminal judgment in *Re A (Male Sterilisation)*, Lord Justice Thorpe held that the Court should draw up a checklist of the actual benefits and disadvantages and the potential gains and losses, including physical and psychological risks and consequences, and should reach a balanced conclusion as to what is right from the point of view of the individual concerned.[13]

THE POSITION UNDER THE MENTAL CAPACITY ACT 2005

General

6.9 Adult cases relating to a health care or welfare issue concerning someone who cannot choose for him or herself are dealt with by the Court of Protection under the jurisdiction granted it by MCA 2005.[14] No power

---

[10] See eg *A Local Authority v A* [2004] 1 FLR 541; and *Re SA (Vulnerable Adult With Capacity: Marriage)* [2005] EWHC 2942 (Fam), [2006] 1 FLR 867.
[11] *Re J (A Minor) (Child in Care: Medical Treatment)* [1992] 2 FLR 165; *Re B (Consent to Treatment: Capacity)* [2002] 1 FLR 1090; and *R (Burke) v GMC and Others* [2004] EWHC 1879 (Admin), [2004] 2 FLR 1121, at [180]–[194], per Munby J.
[12] *Re MB (Medical Treatment)* [1997] 2 FLR 426.
[13] *Re A (Male Sterilisation)* [2000] 1 FLR 549.
[14] See Chapter 2. In some cases, where the remedy sought is not within the repertoire of

under the Act may be exercised in relation to a child under 16, whose personal welfare is exclusively covered by the Children Act 1989. Cases concerning children of 16 or 17 may be started under either jurisdiction, and there is power for the Court to transfer a case to whichever jurisdiction in the particular circumstances is more appropriate.[15]

6.10 The general provisions of MCA 2005 relating to capacity, inability to make decisions, best interests and acts in connection with care or treatment apply to medical treatment and welfare issues as to all other areas. They are dealt with in detail in Chapters 1 and 2; for present purposes, space is devoted to three topics which have revealed themselves to be of particular importance (and difficulty) in the health and welfare context: (1) the issue-specific nature of capacity; (2) the problem of fluctuating capacity; and (3) the question of capacity to consent to sexual relations.

The issue-specific nature of capacity in the health and welfare context

6.11 In the health and welfare context, it is of particular importance to identify with precision the issue the person is said to lack the capacity to decide, and also to identify what information is relevant to consideration of that issue for purposes of s 3(1)(a) of the MCA 2005.[16] The basis of the approach to be taken, and the reason why it is so important, was succinctly set out by Hedley J thus:

> '... what the statute requires is the fixing of attention upon the actual decision in hand. It is the capacity to take a specific decision, or a decision of a specific nature, with which the Act is concerned. Sometimes that will most certainly be generic. Can this person make any decision as to residence or contact or care by reason of, for example, their dementia? Or does this person have any capacity to consent to sexual relations by reason of an impairment of mind which appears to withdraw all the usual restraints that are in place? Such generic assessments will often be necessary in order to devise effective protective measures for the benefit of the protected person, but it will not always be so. There will be cases, for example, in relation to medical treatment where attention is centred not only on a specific treatment or action but on the specific circumstances prevailing at the time of the person whose decision making capacity is in question. The hysteric resisting treatment in the course of delivering a child is an example from my own experience. Accordingly, I see no

---

remedies afforded by MCA 2005, relief may nonetheless be granted by way of the parallel exercise by the High Court of its inherent jurisdiction: see *XCC v AA and Others* [2012] EWHC 2183 (COP), [2012] COPLR 730.

[15] Mental Capacity Act 2005 (Transfer of Proceedings) Order 2007, SI 2007/1899 made under MCA 2005, s 21. In relation to a child aged 16 or 17, the Children Act 1989 should in general only be invoked if the matter is capable of resolution prior to the child's 18th birthday. Guidance as to when proceedings in respect of 16 and 17 year olds should be brought in the Court of Protection was given by Hedley J in *B (A Local Authority) v RM, MM, and AM* [2010] EWHC 3802 (Fam), [2010] COPLR Con Vol 247, the most important questions being whether the matters in respect of which relief is sought are likely to be long-lasting and extend beyond the child's majority. It should also be noted that s 31(2) of the Children's Act 1989 prevents a care or supervision order being made if a child has already reached the age of 17 or if married has reached the age of 16.

[16] In *LBL v RYJ* [2010] EWHC 2665 (Fam), [2010] COPLR Con Vol 795, Mrs Justice Macur referred to the necessity that 'the person under review must comprehend and weigh the salient details relevant to the decision to be made' (emphasis added).

reason why in the construction of the statute in any particular case the question of capacity should not arise in relation to an individual or in relation to specific decision making relating to a specific person. In my judgment, given the presumption of capacity in section 1(2) this may indeed be very necessary to prevent the powers of the Court of Protection, which can be both invasive and draconian, being defined or exercised more widely than is strictly necessary in each particular case.'[17]

By way of further example, the contention is frequently advanced that 'X lacks the capacity to make decisions regarding her care needs.' Framed too widely, especially in the context of a person who is close to the threshold of having such capacity, proceeding on the basis could deprive the person in question of important autonomy over day-to-day 'micro' decisions about specific care being provided to them. Drawing the question too narrowly, conversely, could prevent appropriate consideration being given to whether the person fully understands (for instance) that they are only able to remain at home given the continuation of a specific care package.

Fluctuating capacity

6.12 Experience has shown that particular problems can arise where a person has fluctuating capacity to make decisions regarding medical treatment and/or their welfare needs. An example is a 'needle phobic' case where the adult understands and retains the relevant information to make a capacitous decision (and may give consent in advance) but whose ability to weigh in the balance is impaired when confronted with the sight of the needle which caused them to withdraw their consent. In practice (and as set out below), serious medical treatment cases are restricted to judges from the Family Division of the High Court[18] and where necessary such a judge will choose to sit in a dual jurisdiction; they have also shown themselves willing to be robust in their interpretation of their mandate under MCA 2005 so as to ensure that whenever the person in question's capacity has decreased sufficiently they are brought within the protective scope of the Act. By way of one example within the author's experience, the Court has been prepared to make 'contingent' declarations (on an interim basis) as to the circumstances under which a person would lack the capacity to make decisions as to medical treatment, and as to what would be in their best interests in such circumstances.[19]

---

[17] *CYC v PC and NC* [2012] COPLR 670 at [19]. These dicta were approved on appeal by the Court of Appeal sub nom *PC & Anor v City of York Council* [2013] EWCA Civ 478, [2013] COPLR 409, at [35] per McFarlane LJ, although the Court of Appeal allowed the decision on the facts of the particular case.

[18] All Queen's Bench Division judges are now nominated, but it is suggested that it would be unlikely were such a judge to be allocated a serious medical treatment case (save in the event of dire emergency).

[19] A decision of McFarlane J (as he then was) in March 2009. The circumstances of this case were very unusual, it being held by the Court that the individual in question suffered from a particularly acute form of PTSD which would be triggered by certain clearly identifiable events linked to the prospect of hospital admission and would render her incapable of taking decisions as to whether she required such admission in the event of medical emergency. It is therefore a limited foundation upon which to build a general statement of principle, but it is submitted that the decision was one that was entirely sound in law.

6.13 Under the common law, the Courts had shown themselves on at least one occasion to be creative in their approach to be taken to fluctuating capacity in welfare cases. In the pre-MCA case of *Re G*[20], Bennett J made declarations as to the best interests of the person concerned in circumstances where, essentially as a result of the prior protective measures that had been put in place by the Court, she had at the time of the final hearing regained the capacity to make the relevant decisions. Bennett J concluded that it would be a:

> '... sad failure were the law to determine that I had no jurisdiction to investigate and if necessary make declarations as to G's best interests to ensure that the continuing protection of the court put in place with effect from 11 March 2004 is not summarily withdrawn simply because she has now regained her mental capacity in respect of the matters referred to, given the likely consequences to G if the court withdrew its protection'[21]

He therefore held that, on a proper analysis, G did not have the relevant capacity, such that he retained jurisdiction to make declarations as to her best interests and grant injunctions to give effect to those declarations. The approach taken in *Re G* does not at first blush sit easily with the presumption of capacity enshrined ins 1(2) of the MCA 2005; it is also the case that (as the Code of Practice recognises[22]) it necessary always to ensure that care is taken to identify whether the person in question is under a temporary disability which may lift (especially with the taking of appropriate steps by a person responsible for their care). However, it is suggested that the result reached in *Re G* can continue to be justified in appropriate cases where it is sufficiently clear that it is only because of the imposition of a sufficient protective framework on the part of the Court that the person in question has regained (or can retain) the relevant capacity. On a proper analysis, though, the route to the result may well now be by way of the exercise by the High Court of its residual inherent jurisdiction to protect vulnerable adults who fall outside the scope of the MCA 2005 (as to which see Chapter 11 below), but this is an untested area of the law, upon which judicial clarification will be required.

Fluctuating capacity is particularly problematic if an individual is likely to lose capacity frequently over a given period of time for relatively short periods. It raises serious practicalities in terms of capacity to conduct proceedings or to handle property and affairs. One view taken is that in such cases a 'longitudal' view must be taken of capacity' and the individual must be assessed as being capable of maintaining their recovery over a sustained period of time to make it practicable for a litigation friend of property and affairs deputy to be discharged. There is no clear case law on this point but Hedley J made comments supportive of such a position in his judgment in *A, B and C v X, Y*[23] and Bennett J in *Re G (An Adult) (Mental Capacity: Court's Jurisdiction).*[24]

---

[20] [2004] EWHC 2222 (Fam).
[21] At [103].
[22] Paragraphs 4.26–427.
[23] [2012] EWHC 2400 (COP).
[24] [2004] EWHC 2222 (Fam).

Capacity to consent to sexual relations

6.14 The question of the appropriate test to apply when determining whether a person has capacity to consent to sexual relations has been one of the most vexed issues before the Courts since the enactment of MCA 2005. A detailed study of the principles and issues involved is outside the scope of this work,[25] but for those involved in applications before the Court, it is vital to have in mind a number of considerations, set down below.

6.15 Section 27(1)(b) of the MCA 2005 provides expressly that nothing in the Act permits any person to consent on behalf of any other person to have sexual relations. Unlike many other questions regarding P's capacity, questions of capacity to consent to sexual relations are ones that (in principle) afford of a binary 'yes'/'no' answer, with no consequent ability on the part of a decision-maker to go on to consider whether it is in P's best interests to have sexual relations.

6.16 Perhaps the thorniest question is whether capacity to consent to sexual relations is act-specific or person (or situation)-specific: in other words, is the relevant information for purposes of s 3(1) solely information relevant to the proposed act (and its consequences), or does the information also include information about the proposed sexual partner? Prior to the enactment of MCA 2005, it had been established by Munby J (as he then was) that the question was act-specific.[26] However, the law was then thrown into doubt by the powerful dicta of Baroness Hale in *R v C*[27] (with which the balance of the House associated themselves), in which she made it clear her view that it was:

> '… difficult to think of an activity which is more person- and situation-specific than sexual relations. One does not consent to sex in general. One consents to this act of sex with this person at this time and in this place.'

6.17 A number of attempts were made by first instance judges to reconcile the incompatible views of Munby J and Baroness Hale.[28] Mostyn J in *D Borough Council v AB*[29] and Hedley J in *A Local Authority v H*,[30] essentially abandoned any attempt so to do. In *D Borough Council*, Mostyn J concluded[31] that the capacity to consent to sex remained act-specific and required an understanding and awareness of: (a) the mechanics of the act;

---

[25] See, for a discussion of the issues involved which is now slightly out of date as regards the law, but remains of assistance, *Assessment of Mental Capacity: A Practical Guide for Doctors and Lawyers* (Law Society Publishing, 4th edn, 2015).
[26] *X City Council v MB, NB and MAB* [2006] EWHC 168 (Fam), [2006] 2 FLR 968 and *Local Authority X v MM and KM* [2007] EWHC 2003 (Fam), [2009] 1 FLR 443.
[27] [2009] UKHL 42. The case concerned the criminal provisions contained in the Sexual Offences Act 2003, rather than the common law (or MCA 2005) test for capacity to consent.
[28] The most comprehensive attempt was that of Roderic Wood J in *D County Council v LS* [2010] EWHC 1544 (Fam), [2010] COPLR Con Vol 331.
[29] [2011] EWHC 101 (COP), [2011] COPLR Con Vol 313.
[30] [2012] EWHC 49 (COP), [2012] COPLR 305. A further decision *A Local Authority v TZ* [2013] EWHC 2322 (COP), [2013] COPLR 477 was handed down whilst this work was at the proofing stage. It is to similar effect as the decisions in *D Borough Council v AB* and *A Local Authority v H*.
[31] At [42].

(b) that there are health risks involved, particularly the acquisition of sexually transmitted and sexually transmissible infections; and (c) that sex between a man and a woman may result in the woman becoming pregnant. In *A Local Authority v H*, Hedley J identified the same factors, but also (of his own motion) considered whether capacity also needed 'in some way to reflect or encompass the moral and emotional aspect of human sexual relationships'.[32] He concluded with relative ease that the moral aspect played no specific role in the test, but had more difficulty with the emotional aspect. Hedley J recognised that it remained 'an important, some might argue the most important, component [and that] certainly it is the source of the greatest damage when sexual relations are abused'; however, acknowledging the difficulty inherent in articulating the component into a workable test, he concluded that one could do no more than ask the question whether 'the person whose capacity is in question understand[s] that they do have a choice and that they can refuse'.[33]

6.18 The matter came before the Court of Appeal in *IM v LM & Ors*[34] in November 2013. In this judgment, the Court of Appeal reconciled the apparent clash between the approaches of Munby J and of Baroness Hale by noting that the criminal law bites only retrospectively, to ask whether particular conduct, in particular circumstances, and with the knowledge or understanding of the particular participants, contravened the law; the civil law, by contrast, requires prospective assessment in light of the particular circumstances of the affected individual. The Court of Appeal therefore found that 'the fact that a person either does or does not consent to sexual activity with a particular person at a fixed point in time, or does or does not have capacity to give such consent, does not mean that it is impossible, or legally impermissible, for a court assessing capacity to make a general evaluation which is not tied down to a particular partner, time and place.' (emphasis in original). Indeed, it went on:

> '... it would be totally unworkable for a local authority or the Court of Protection to conduct an assessment every time an individual over whom there was doubt about his or her capacity to consent to sexual relations showed signs of immediate interest in experiencing a sexual encounter with another person. On a pragmatic basis, if for no other reason, capacity to consent to future sexual relations can only be assessed on a general and non-specific basis.'[35]

6.19 The Court of Appeal, further, emphasised that: 'The requirement for a practical limit on what needs to be envisaged as "reasonably foreseeable consequences" [of the sexual act in question] derives not just from pragmatism but from the imperative that the notional decision-making process attributed to the protected person with regard to consent to sexual

---

[32] At [24].
[33] At [26]; this approach was also endorsed by Mostyn J in *LB Tower Hamlets v TB* [2014] EWCOP 53, [2015] COPLR 87 who stated that he had been persuaded that the more nuanced approach adopted by Hedley J in *A Local Authority v H* was to be preferred to the approach that he himself had adopted in *D Borough Council v AB*, and that this more nuanced approach aligned the civil and criminal law.
[34] [2014] EWCA Civ 37, [2014] COPLR 246.
[35] *IM* at [77] per Sir Brian Leveson giving the judgment of the Court.

relations should not become divorced from the actual decision-making process carried out in that regard on a daily basis by persons of full capacity. That process, as Ms Richards [on behalf of the Official Solicitor] observes, is largely visceral rather than cerebral, owing more to instinct and emotion than to analysis.' In holding that the ability to use and weigh information is unlikely to loom large in the evaluation of capacity to consent to sexual relations, the Court of Appeal emphasised that 'the information typically, and we stress typically, regarded by persons of full capacity as relevant to the decision whether to consent to sexual relations is relatively limited. The temptation to expand that field of information in an attempt to simulate more widely informed decision-making is likely to lead to ... both paternalism and a derogation from personal autonomy.'[36]

In light of this judgment the focus in the area of capacity to consent to sexual relations is now on the question of whether the person has capacity to decide on contact with a particular person.[37] It is also noteworthy that concern has been expressed with regards to the outcome of the Court of Appeal's decision, particularly in *Derbyshire CC v AC, EC and LC*[38] where Cobb J stated:

> 'I have not heard detailed argument on this aspect of the case, as the parties were not in disagreement about it; but I must record my small misgivings about the conclusion reached. The distinguished line of judges sitting in the jurisdictions of the Family Division and Court of Protection who have opined on the question of what "relevant information" should inform the test of capacity in this vexed area have not sought to include within the scope of information the understanding of "P" that she (or he) may at any time change her (or his) mind about consenting to sexual relations. Hedley J. considered that it would be legitimate to ask the question whether "the person whose capacity is in question understand[s]that they do have a choice and that they can refuse." The evidence in this case reveals that AC may not always fully understand that she does have a choice, and/or that she can change her mind in relation to consent to sex; given the extent to which she has been exploited this gives me considerable anxiety. However, on the established test as it stands the professional consensus (with which I do not feel I should disagree) is that the criteria (summarised above) are established in relation to this issue at this time. Accordingly, I conclude that AC currently has capacity in this regard although, given the fluctuating nature of her capacity in this respect, I urge those who have continued responsibility for AC to keep this issue under careful review.'

PRACTICE AND PROCEDURE

6.20 The practice and procedure of the Court of Protection generally is dealt with in detail in Chapter 8. This section limits itself to considerations specific to welfare and medical treatment cases. As was recognised by the work of the Rules Review Committee established by the then-President,[39] these considerations are not always the same as those prevailing in property and affairs cases. Notwithstanding the fact that the Court of Protection is a

---

[36] *IM* at [80] and [82].
[37] *A Local Authority v TZ (No 2)* [2014] EWHC 973 (COP).
[38] [2014] EWCOP 38, at [36].
[39] See the Press Release issued by the Judicial Communications Office on 29 July 2010 available at www.judiciary.gov.uk/media/media-releases/2010/news-release-2210.

unified jurisdiction, it is likely that the trend will be towards an increasing recognition of the different case-management approaches that are required to the different categories of case.

Serious medical treatment cases

Definition

6.21 The President's Practice Direction 'Applications Relating to Serious Medical Treatment'[40] makes special provision for these cases. 'Serious medical treatment' is defined for this purpose as treatment which involves providing, withdrawing or withholding treatment in circumstances where:

- (If a single treatment is proposed) there is a fine balance between its benefits and burdens and risks;
- (If there is a choice) a decision as to which treatment is finely balanced; or
- The treatment, procedure or investigation would be likely to involve serious consequences for the patient.

6.22 The Practice Direction first spells out that there are certain decisions which should be regarded as serious medical treatment decisions and should be brought to the Court. It also gives examples of other decisions which should be considered serious medical treatment (see also **6.24** below).[41] It provides that in these cases the person bringing the application will always be a party to the proceedings, as will a respondent named in the application form who files an acknowledgment of service, and the organisation providing clinical or caring services should usually be named as a respondent (if not the applicant). Whether or not 'P' is to be joined as a party is to be determined at the first directions hearing (as is the question of who should be appointed as that person's litigation friend: the Official Solicitor or some other person). In practice, however, the increasing trend (at least where time allows) is that such questions – along with any questions of permission – are determined on paper by the Court in advance of that hearing. It is unlikely that P would not be joined as a party except in out of hours emergency cases where a decision is immediately required and which cannot await the appointment of a litigation friend.

When should serious medical treatment cases be brought to Court?

6.23 The Practice Direction in large part reflects the position that had been reached at common law as to when a serious medical treatment decision should be decided by the Court. The first category concerns decisions to

---

[40] Practice Direction 9E.
[41] As at the date of writing, there remains outstanding a proposal (from the Rules Review Committee referred to in the footnote to **6.20**) that this Practice Direction be amended so as to make it clear that serious medical treatment can encompass treatment which is not in and of itself serious, but where the consequence of administering/not administering it would be serious. The current President of the Court of Protection has indicated his intention to press ahead with implementing in full the recommendations of the Committee.

withhold or withdraw artificial nutrition and hydration ('ANH').[42] This covers people in a Persistent Vegetative State or a Minimally Conscious State. Prior to the enactment of MCA 2005, it had been established[43] that, as a matter of good practice, all cases where it was proposed to withdraw ANH from a patient in Persistent Vegetative State should go to court. This was partly a reflection of the importance of the decision for the individual and also provides a reassurance to the public as to how these decisions are taken. This is now buttressed by the Practice Direction, which also covers withholding or withdrawal of ANH in cases where a person is in a Minimally Conscious State.[44]

6.24 The second category of case set out in the Practice Direction is organ or bone marrow donation by a person who lacks capacity to consent. The third is non-therapeutic sterilisation (whether of a woman or a man by way of a vasectomy).[45] Other examples of 'serious medical treatment' given in the Practice Direction which should be taken to the Court of Protection are:

- Certain termination of pregnancy cases, where there is a dispute over capacity or the patient may regain capacity during her pregnancy, any lack of unanimity, where the procedures under the Abortion Act 1967, s 1 have not been followed, where the patient or members of her immediate family have opposed a termination, or where there are other exceptional circumstances (including that this may be the patient's last chance to bear a child, following Coleridge J's decision in *D v An NHS Trust (Medical Treatment: Consent)* cited at **6.25** below);
- Other medical treatment for the purpose of a donation to someone else[46];
- Treatment which requires a degree of force to restrain the person concerned;[47]

---

[42] In all such cases reference should now be made to the guidelines issued by the Royal College of Physicians in December 2013 on 'Prolonged disorders of consciousness', available at: www.rcplondon.ac.uk/prolonged-disorders-consciousness-national-clinical-guidelines.
[43] See *Airedale NHS Trust v Bland* [1993] 1 FLR 1026.
[44] That such matters must be brought before the Court of Protection was reaffirmed in *W (by her Litigation Friend) v (1) M (by her Litigation Friend the Official Solicitor) (2) S and (3) A NHS Primary Care Trust* [2011] EWHC 2443 (Fam), [2012] COPLR 222 at paragraph 257, per Baker J (in observations specifically endorsed by the President). It is a moot point as to whether section 2 of the Royal College of Physicians 2013 Guidelines comply with the observations of Baker J at paragraph 259 of his judgment as to the formal testing required before a diagnosis can safely be reached for the purposes of withdrawing ANH from patients in a vegetative or minimally conscious state.
[45] See in this regard *A Local Authority v K and Others* [2013] EWHC 242 (COP), [2013] COPLR 194 (female sterilisation) and *An NHS Trust v DE & Ors* [2013] EWHC 2562 (Fam), [2013] COPLR 531 (male sterilisation).
[46] Hedley J in *A NHS Trust v P* [2013] EWHC 50 (COP), [2013] COPLR 405 recommended that the case be explicit. It is referred to as guidance in all serious medical treatment cases concerning the termination of pregnancies.
[47] Examples of the levels of restraint that have been permitted by the Court of Protection include covert sedation and the use of force if required to transport P to hospital for purposes of undergoing surgery (*DH NHS Foundation Trust v PS* [2010] EWHC 1217 (Fam), [2010] COPLR Con Vol 346); restraining P for 18 hours a day for 5 days to ensure she received an intravenous immunosuppressant drug (*Re SB, 19 October 2010, Hogg J*); and restraining P for 3 hours every fortnight for 6 months (*Re KA*). The latter two cases were only reported by

- Treatment which is experimental or innovative; and
- Cases involving an ethical dilemma in an untested area.[48]

6.25 These situations apart, there may be other procedures or treatments which can be regarded as serious medical treatment (because of the circumstances and consequences) and which, if so, may be brought to court. Where the decision as to the appropriate treatment is finely balanced either as to its benefit or the choice of treatment, testing whether it is in the best interests of the person concerned through Court of Protection proceedings may well be appropriate. The general principle is that the Court's jurisdiction should be invoked whenever there is a serious justiciable issue requiring a decision by a court:

> 'In cases of controversy and cases involving momentous and irrevocable decisions, the courts have treated as justiciable any genuine question as to what the best interests of a patient require or justify.'[49]

Specific and detailed guidance as to when and how applications should made where a treating Trust is concerned that pregnant woman lacks, or may lack, the capacity to take decisions about her antenatal, perinatal and post natal care as a result of an impairment of, or a disturbance in, the functioning of her mind or brain resulting from a diagnosed psychiatric illness is set out by Keehan J in *NHS Trust & Ors v FG*.[50] It may be the case that this important guidance will feed through into a revision of Practice Direction 9E in due course, both in terms of the circumstances under which applications should be brought and in terms of the procedure that should be adopted.

Allocation, urgency and case management

6.26 The Practice Direction makes provision for the allocation of serious medical treatment cases. Where the application relates to the lawfulness of withholding or withdrawing ANH from a person in a Persistent Vegetative State or a Minimally Conscious State or it is a case involving an ethical dilemma in an untested area then the whole proceedings (including the permission stage) must be conducted by the President or a judge nominated by the President. All other serious medical treatment cases or cases in which a declaration of incompatibility is sought pursuant to the Human Rights Act 1998, s 4 must be conducted by the President, the Chancellor or a High Court judge (nominated to sit as a Court of Protection judge). However, there have been instances of High Court judges subsequently transferring

---

way of press reports. In *An NHS Trust v (1) K (2) Another Foundation Trust* [2012] EWHC 2922 (COP), [2012] COPLR 694, Holman J authorised the use of mild sedation so as to render P more likely to be compliant in advance of an operation, but declined to authorise physical restraint because of the risks that it would pose to P.

[48] A pre-MCA example of this case was the authorisation of the use of an unlicensed treatment for a patient suffering from CJD: *Simms v An NHS Trust* [2002] EWHC 2734 (Fam).

[49] Coleridge J in *D v An NHS Trust (Medical Treatment: Consent)* [2003] EWHC 2793 (Fam), [2004] 1 FLR 1110. See also *North Somerset Council v LW & Others* [2014] EWCOP 3 where an adverse costs order was made where the NHS trust failed to make an application to the Court of Protection.

[50] [2014] EWCOP 30, [2015] 1 WLR 1984, [2014] COPLR 598.

such cases for determination by circuit and district judges sitting as nominated judges of the Court of Protection.[51] Whether the Practice Direction covers a case is a matter for the Senior Judge of the Court of Protection or a judge nominated by him or her. In practice, this has meant that applications lodged at the Court which have not been made on an urgent basis are referred to a district judge to make a decision as to allocation (for urgent cases see **6.27**). In a case requiring to be allocated to a High Court Judge which is not urgent (in the sense that P's life or health is not at immediate risk) but which nonetheless needs a speedy process (such as where P needs to be given treatment for cancer and any significant delay is likely to prejudicial), it is advisable before issue to alert the Court's Listing and Appeals team to the application and the need for it to be processed and issued quickly.

6.27 The practice to be followed in urgent cases is set out in Practice Direction 10B. The Practice Direction suggests that for urgent applications brought during office hours contact should be made with the Court of Protection. However, in serious medical treatment cases the practice which has developed is to go direct to the Clerk of the Rules of the High Court Family Division to seek an urgent hearing before the first available Family Division judge and giving an undertaking to issue the proceedings at the Court of Protection within the next working day.[52] That judge will determine the allocation of the case. When it is not possible to apply within court hours contact should be made with the security officer at the Royal Courts of Justice, who will invariably refer the matter to the Family Division High Court judge covering urgent out-of-hours business. It should be noted that the Official Solicitor does not operate an out-of-hours service. Where an application is brought out of normal court hours the court will normally strive to make the most limited order possible until such point as the matter can be brought back with P legally represented (invariably through the appointment of the Official Solicitor as litigation friend). This will also generally be the case where the urgency of the application means that the litigation friend is unable to attend.[53] However, where a decision needs to be made without even the shortest delay, the court will make a decision on the spot without the assistance of the Official Solicitor.[54]

---

[51] For example if the High Court judge took the view that the case did not meet the criteria for serious medical treatment.

[52] Difficulties have been encountered when listing a return date for the application after the urgent hearing has occurred as the Clerk of the Rules usually requires a case number, which is not always issued immediately. It may be advisable to phone the listings office at the Court of Protection to ensure that they are aware of the urgency of the application and the need for it to be promptly issued. It is worth noting that the Clerk of the Rules office has clerks with specific responsibility for dealing with Court of Protection cases who can be very helpful to speak to in urgent cases.

[53] See, for example, *Nottinghamshire Healthcare NHS Trust v RC* [2014] EWCOP 1317, [2014] COPLR 468.

[54] See *Newcastle-upon-Tyne Hospitals Foundation Trust v LM* [2014] EWHC 454 (COP). See also guidance given by Theis J in *Sandwell and West Birmingham Hospitals NHS Trust v CD & Others* [2014] EWCOP 23.

6.28 In *Aintree University NHS Hospitals Trust v James*,[55] the Supreme Court confirmed in relation to the timing of applications relating to the withholding of life-sustaining treatment that if clinicians bring an application too early, there is a risk that the court may be unable to say that when the treatments are needed that they will not be in the best interests of the patient. Unfortunately, the Supreme Court did not provide further assistance as to precisely when such applications should be brought, but did emphasise that it is necessary to be precise in the framing of the declarations sought.

6.29 Case management in serious medical treatment cases is subtly different to that of other less serious health and welfare cases, in that (1) the presumption is that P will be joined as the party; (2) that the Official Solicitor will invariably be appointed to act as P's litigation friend;[56] and (3) the presumption is that the application will be heard in public, with suitable restrictions to be imposed in respect of the publication of information about the proceedings.[57] The President of the Family Division issued in January 2014 guidance upon the publication of judgments in cases before the Court of Protection, which preserves and extends the position in relation to such medical treatment cases, and suggests that, where a judge authorises publication of a judgment: public authorities and expert witnesses should be named in the judgment approved for publication, unless there are compelling reasons why they should not be so named; (ii) the person who is the subject of proceedings in the Court of Protection and other members of their family should not normally be named in the judgment approved for publication unless the judge otherwise orders; (iii) anonymity in the judgment as published should not normally extend beyond protecting the privacy of the adults who are the subject of the proceedings and other members of their families, unless there are compelling reasons to do so.

Best interests in medical treatment cases: life sustaining treatment

6.30 Whilst space precludes a detailed consideration of the specific evidential matters that arise in the context of serious medical treatment cases,[58] one matter that does call for particular attention in the determination of P's best interests is MCA 2005 s 4(5), which specifically relates to life-sustaining treatment and provides that:

---

[55] [2013] UKSC 67, [2013] COPLR 492.
[56] The Official Solicitor in serious medical treatment cases will consent to act even if there are potential alternative litigation friends as he does not apply 'the last resort' criteria which form part of his acceptance criteria in other personal welfare cases. In serious medical treatment cases he might more accurately be described as the litigation friend of 'first resort'.
[57] Practice Direction 9E; for a discussion of the principles underpinning the making of reporting restrictions in such cases, see *W (by her Litigation Friend, B) v M, S, an NHS PCT and Times Newspapers Ltd* [2011] EWHC 1197 (COP), [2011] Con Vol 1206. The former judgment provides very helpful guidance as to the form of order which can be sought in high profile cases, preventing the door stepping of P's family and other press intrusion which may be distressing to them or which may directly impact on P.
[58] Detailed consideration of the specific issues that arise in serious medical treatment cases can be found in Johnston et al, *Medical Treatment: Decisions and the Law* (Bloomsbury, 2010).

'Where the determination relates to life-sustaining treatment *[the decision-maker]* must not, in considering whether the treatment is in the best interests of the person concerned, be motivated by a desire to bring about his death.'[59]

Given the importance accorded by both Houses of Parliament during the Parliamentary Debates on the MCA 2005 to issues related to withholding or withdrawing life-sustaining treatment, a short commentary drawing some of the threads together is appropriate. Two of the leading cases (both pre-dating MCA 2005) are *Bland* and *Burke*.[60]

6.31 In *Bland* the House of Lords decided that, where there is no continuing duty on doctors to sustain life through medical treatment, including the provision of ANH, because of the futility of doing so in the case of a patient in Persistent Vegetative State, it would be lawful to withhold or withdraw that treatment. It has subsequently been held that this decision is compatible with the incorporation of the European Convention on Human Rights in our law[61] and the decision has been re-affirmed in *Pretty v UK (Application No 2346/02)*.[62] It is the basis for the distinction in this jurisprudence between omissions and positive acts causing death.

6.32 The *Burke* case was a judicial review concerning the lawfulness of guidelines issued by the General Medical Council (GMC)[63] and was brought by a competent adult who feared that the guidance would not adequately protect him from doctors' withholding or withdrawing ANH at a time when, as a result of his wasting disease, he would need it to be kept alive. The case provided the opportunity, taken by Munby J (as he then was), for a judgment covering a number of important issues, although the Court of Appeal in its judgment, allowing the GMC's appeal and setting aside the declarations made at first instance, approached the case very more narrowly. The Court of Appeal recognised that, whilst the duty to keep a patient alive by administering ANH or other life-prolonging treatment is not absolute, the only exceptions are either where a competent patient refuses to receive it or where it is not considered to be in the best interests of an incompetent patient artificially to be kept alive. This latter circumstance covers patients in Persistent Vegetative State and where the patient's continued life involves an extreme degree of pain, discomfort or indignity and he or she has not shown a wish to be kept alive.[64]

---

[59] Section 62 further provides that nothing in MCA 2005 is to be taken as affecting the law relating to murder, manslaughter or assisted suicide.
[60] *Airedale NHS Trust v Bland* [1993] 1 FLR 1026; *R (Burke) v General Medical Council and Others* [2004] EWHC 1879 (Admin), [2004] 2 FLR 1121; [2005] EWCA Civ 1003, [2005] 2 FLR 1223.
[61] *NHS Trust A v H* [2001] 2 FLR 501.
[62] [2002] 2 FLR 45.
[63] *Withholding and Withdrawing Life-prolonging Treatments: Good Practice in Decision-making* (August 2002). With effect from 1 July 2010, this guidance was replaced by *Treatment and care towards the end of life: good practice in decision making*, which expressly incorporates reference to *Burke* and is available at: www.gmc-uk.org/End_of_life.pdf_32486688.pdf.
[64] This issue also arises in severely damaged baby cases: see e g *Re J (a Minor)(Wardship: Medical Treatment)* [1991] Fam 33.

6.33 In relation to Mr Burke's own situation, the Court of Appeal robustly declared:[65]

> 'Indeed, it seems to us that for a doctor deliberately to interrupt life-prolonging treatment in the face of a competent patient's expressed wish to be kept alive, with the intention of thereby terminating the patient's life, would leave the doctor with no answer to a charge of murder.'

and:[66]

> 'Where life depends upon the continued provision of ANH there can be no question of the supply of ANH not being clinically indicated unless a clinical decision has been taken that the life in question should come to an end. That is not a decision that can lawfully be taken in the case of a competent patient who expresses the wish to remain alive.'

6.34 That the MCA 2005 has not fundamentally altered the position reached at the common law in respect of the withdrawal or withholding of life-sustaining treatment was put beyond doubt in *W v M and S and A NHS Primary Care Trust*.[67] This decision is of significance not just for its comprehensive review of the domestic (and Strasbourg) jurisprudence, but also because it concerned – for the first time – an application for the withdrawal of ANH from a patient in a Minimally Conscious State.[68]

6.35 A final consideration is the tension that can sometimes arise between what may appear to have been the past wishes of the person and what might now appear objectively to be in their best interests. This tension (discussed further in Chapter 2) can be particularly stark in the context of life-sustaining treatment, and was the subject of detailed judicial scrutiny in the *W v M* case outlined above. In this case, the incapacitated adult had made no formal advance decision[69] as to medical treatment, but had expressed views to relatives about the matter in conversations prior to their suffering the viral infection which led to their loss of capacity. However, whilst acknowledging the accuracy of M's views relayed by her relatives, Baker J concluded that:

> 'Given the importance of the sanctity of life, and the fatal consequences of withdrawing treatment, and the absence of an advance decision that complied with the requirements previously specified by the common law and now under statute, it would be in my judgment be wrong to attach significant weight to those statements made prior to her collapse.'[70]

---

[65] *R (Burke) v General Medical Council and Others* [2005] EWCA Civ 1003, [2005] 2 FLR 1223, at [297].
[66] Ibid, at [301].
[67] [2011] EWHC 2443 (Fam), [2012] COPLR 222.
[68] A detailed discussion of this case lies outside the remit of this book; suffice it to say for these purposes that Baker J held (contrary to the submissions of the Official Solicitor) that the 'conventional' balance sheet approach applies to the withdrawal of ANH in such circumstances, and hence that as a matter of logic there are circumstances under which the person's best interests would be satisfied by its withdrawal. Applying the balance sheet, Baker J concluded that it was not in M's best interests for ANH to be withdrawn. See also the decision of Pauffley J in *United Lincolnshire Hospital Trust v N* [2014] EWCOP 16, [2014] COPLR 660 discussed in paragraph **6.36** below.
[69] Advance decisions are discussed further at **6.53**ff below.
[70] At [230].

The decision was perhaps even more finely balanced in the case of *A Local Authority v E and Others*.[71] In this case, discussed further at **6.65** below, Peter Jackson J had to consider the case of young woman, E, who was suffering from severe anorexia nervosa and who wished to refuse all food and drink. In circumstances where: (1) in consequence of her severe anorexia nervosa E 'above all [did] not want to eat or be fed;' and (2) she had sought twice – unsuccessfully – to make advance decisions refusing life-sustaining treatment, Peter Jackson J noted that the case 'raised for the first time in my experience[72] the real possibility of life-sustaining treatment not being in the best interests of a person who, while lacking capacity, is fully aware of her situation'. In particular given the high respect that had to be afforded to the view of E, an intelligent and articulate adult, he found that the competing factors were almost exactly in equilibrium; but he ultimately found the balance 'tip[ped] slowly but unmistakably in the direction of life-preserving treatment'. In the end, the presumption in favour of the preservation of life was not displaced.[73]

6.36 In *Aintree University NHS Hospitals Trust v James*[74] the Supreme Court held that:

> 'The purpose of the best interests test is to consider matters from the patient's point of view. That is not to say that his wishes must prevail, any more than those of a fully capable patient must prevail. We cannot always have what we want. Nor will it always be possible to ascertain what an incapable patient's wishes are. Even if it is possible to determine what his views were in the past, they might well have changed in the light of the stresses and strains of his current predicament. In this case, the highest it could be put was, as counsel had agreed, that "It was likely that Mr James would want treatment up to the point where it became hopeless". But insofar as it is possible to ascertain the patient's wishes and feelings, his beliefs and values or the things which were important to him, it is those which should be taken into account because they are a component in making the choice which is right for him as an individual human being.'

However, the balance has tipped further away from protective decision making as a result of the decision of Pauffley J in *United Lincolnshire Hospital Trust v N* [2014] EWCOP 16 in which the Court went further than any case before involving a protected party in a minimally conscious state by declaring that it was not in N's best interests for the Trust to make any further attempts to establish and maintain a method for providing N with artificial nutrition.

N's case is distinguishable from the *W v M* case on the facts; in particular, M's case was about withdrawal of ANH rather than sanctioning the decision not to keep offering ANH. Further, the facts demonstrate that M did not manifest the same resistance as N to the provision of ANH. However, legally, both were held to be in the same position of minimal consciousness

---

[71] [2012] EWHC 1639 (COP), [2012] COPLR 441.
[72] And, indeed to the author's knowledge.
[73] To contrasting effect, see the decision of Eleanor King J in case concerning a young woman, L, who also suffered from anorexia nervosa: *The NHS Trust v L & Ors* [2012] EWHC 2741 (COP), [2013] COPLR 139.
[74] [2013] UKSC 67, [2013] COPLR 492, at [45] per Baroness Hale.

and, importantly, Pauffley J did not, as she could have done, seek to ascribe to N wishes and feelings based on her actions. Rather she focused on N's earlier expression (recounted by N's adult daughter) that she would not like to continue life in a reduced capacity in the event of a road traffic accident. Even though N's comments were of a similar level of generality to those expressed by M, and the views expressed by the families of the two women as to what they would have wished were materially identical, it seems that in N's case they were given very significant weight, but in M's case they were not.

St George's Healthcare NHS Trust v P &Q[75] is a recent case providing an interesting illustration of the impact on end-of-life decision making following Aintree. It emphasises the importance of viewing matters through the eyes of the patient with regard to the evaluation of whether the treatment is either overly burdensome and whether it would result in even a severely compromised quality of life which the patient would nonetheless regard as worthwhile. In this context respecting P's wish to be kept alive in any state, can mean just as much as respecting another P's wish not to be kept alive.[76]

Health and welfare cases

6.37 Outside the category of serious medical treatment cases addressed, in most instances it will be perfectly proper to proceed upon the basis of the authority given by MCA 2005, s 6.[77] It must be a decision to be taken in the circumstances of an individual case whether the protection of seeking a decision from the Court should be obtained. Similarly, more general welfare decisions may be taken in the best interests of the person concerned without going to court. This point was strongly emphasised by Baker J in *G v E*,[78] where (in the context of refusing an application for a welfare deputy to be appointed) he emphasised that:

---

[75] [2015] EWCOP 42 (Newton J); this case is also worthy of mention because of Newton J's criticism of the Trust for having brought the application relatively shortly after patient suffered the hypoxic brain injury, and before a Sensory Modality Assessment and Rehabilitation Technique ('SMART') assessment had been carried out. See also *CWM Taf University v M* [2015] EWHC 2533 (Fam) (Newton J).

[76] See also *Wye Valley NHS Trust v Mr B* [2015] EWCOP 60 (COP) (Jackson J), a case where the NHS Trust applied for permission to amputate the foot of a 73-year-old man lacking capacity in order to save his life. The man opposed the operation in the strongest terms and his religious beliefs were an intrinsic part of him. Jackson J refused to grant the application holding that it was not in his best interests for the operation to be enforced. It was held that the fact that a person lacked a decision-making capacity was not an 'off-switch' for their rights and freedoms. The man opposed the operation in the strongest terms and his religious beliefs were an intrinsic part of him.

[77] See also Chapter 2 of this work.

[78] [2010] EWHC 2512 (COP) (Fam), [2010] COPLR Con Vol 470. NB, this was not the same *G v E* judgment as the more well-known one addressing questions of deprivation of liberty, discussed in Chapter 7.

'The Act and Code are ... constructed on the basis that the vast majority of decisions concerning incapacitated adults are taken informally and collaboratively by individuals or groups of people consulting and working together.'[79]

However, there may be a dispute which cannot be resolved by any other means, for example, between a close family member and the local authority's social services or between family members or between treating clinicians and/or other professionals involved in a person's care, as to what those best interests are: 'Ultimately, if all other attempts to resolve the dispute have failed, the court might need to decide what is in the person's best interests.'[80]

6.38 When any health and welfare cases need to be taken to the Court (and, if required, permission is granted) the Court decides who is to hear the case and gives directions as to the procedure to be followed. It determines who the parties are to be, and in particular whether the person concerned is to be made a party and, if so, who the litigation friend is to be, or whether it can reach a decision on the basis of the information made available to it (as well, potentially, as a report from the Public Guardian or Visitor or social or health services under MCA 2005, s 49). It also considers such matters as permission to obtain independent expert evidence, obtaining disclosure from third parties (e.g., medical records, social services' files, care home records, financial documents) and the filing of statements. Whilst Rule 90(1) of the Court of Protection Rules 2007 provides that 'the general rule is that a hearing should be held in private,'[81] the Court is also increasingly likely to consider whether to allow the case to proceed in public (subject to appropriate reporting restrictions): the President of the Court of Protection, Sir James Munby, recently indicating that he considers to be 'compelling' the arguments in favour of allowing accredited journalists to attend hearings unless proper grounds for excluding them can be established on narrowly defined grounds.[82] Where there is a possibility that the Court will wish to consider the grant of relief that does not lie within the repertoire of remedies that are afforded it by MCA 2005, consideration will also be given to whether the matter should be transferred to be heard before a High Court judge so that they can (in parallel) grant relief under the inherent jurisdiction.[83]

6.39 The Court of Appeal in *MN (Adult)* [2015] EWCA Civ 411, [2015] COPLR 505 provided important guidance on the approach the Court of Protection should adopt when a care provider is unwilling to provide, or to

---

[79] See also *Re PO* [2013] EWHC 3932 (COP), [2014] COPLR 62, at [26] per Sir James Munby P.
[80] Code of Practice, paragraph 5.68. Note akin to that which was promulgated in relation to proceedings under the inherent jurisdiction ([2006] 2 FLR 373, attaching to it the Practice Note from the Official Solicitor: "Declaratory Proceedings: Medical and Welfare Decisions for Adults who Lack Capacity.") The central themes of that guidance remain as pertinent today as they did in 2006.
[81] See also *Independent News Media v A* [2010] EWCA Civ 343, [2010] COPLR Con Vol 686.
[82] Sir James Munby P, 'The Court of Protection – the Way Forward?' (2013) ELJ 221. See also *Hillingdon LBC v Neary* [2011] EWHC 413 (COP), [2011] COPLR Con Vol 677.
[83] See *XCC v AA and Others* [2012] EWHC 2183 (COP), [2012] COPLR 730, *An NHS Trust v Dr A* [2013] EWHC 2442 (COP), [2013] COPLR 605.

fund, the care sought, whether by the patient or by the patient's family. In particular, it was held that the Court of Protection, like the family court and the Family Division, can explore the care plan being put forward by a public authority and, where appropriate, require the authority to go away and think again. However, the Court of Protection cannot compel a public authority to agree to a care plan which the authority is unwilling to implement. In support of this the Court of Appeal stated that it is not the proper function of the Court of Protection to embark upon a factual inquiry into some abstract issue the answer to which cannot affect the outcome of the proceedings before it. Nor is it a proper function of the Court of Protection (nor of the family court of the Family Division) to embark upon a factual inquiry designed to create a platform or springboard for possible future proceedings in the Administrative Court. Such an exercise runs the risk of confusing the very different perspectives and principles which govern the exercise by the Court of Protection of its functions and those which govern the exercise by the public authority of its functions, and also runs the risk of exposing the public authority to impermissible pressure.

INDEPENDENT MENTAL CAPACITY ADVOCATES

Establishment

6.40 MCA 2005 imposes a duty on the Secretary of State (in practice the Secretary of State for Health) in England and the Welsh Assembly in Wales to make arrangements to enable independent mental capacity advocates (IMCAs) to be available to represent and support incapacitated persons in circumstances defined in the Act.[84] These arrangements must be designed to achieve the laudable principle that:[85]

> '... a person to whom a proposed act or decision relates should, so far as practicable, be represented and supported by a person who is independent of any person who will be responsible for the act or decision.'

6.41 This adopts the conclusion of the Joint Parliamentary Committee scrutinising the draft Bill which was accepted by the Government that:[86]

> 'We are convinced that independent advocacy services play an essential role in assisting people with capacity problems to make and communicate decisions; helping them to enforce their rights and guard against unwarranted intrusion into their lives; providing a focus on the views and wishes of an incapacitated person in the determination of their best interests; providing additional safeguards against abuse and exploitation; and assisting in the resolution of disputes.'

6.42 MCA 2005 empowers the Secretary of State (or Welsh Assembly) to discharge this duty by making Regulations providing for the circumstances and conditions under which such an advocate may act and as to his or her

---

[84] MCA 2005, s 36.
[85] MCA 2005, s 35(4).
[86] Joint Committee on the Draft Mental Incapacity Bill, Session 2002–2003, HL 189-1, HC 1083, paragraph 297.

appointment. This he has done (in England) in the Mental Capacity Act 2005 (Independent Mental Capacity Advocates) (General) Regulations 2006.[87]

Appointment, functions and role

6.43 The IMCA service is locally based (commissioned by the relevant local authority). The qualifying conditions for a person to be an IMCA are that he or she is (or belongs to a class of persons) approved by the local authority, and that he or she has appropriate experience or training, is a person of integrity and good character and is able to act independently of any person who instructs him or her.

6.44 The Regulations provide for the functions of such advocates and the steps to be taken for the purposes of:[88]
- providing support so the person whom he or she has been instructed to represent may participate as fully as possible in any relevant decision;
- obtaining and evaluating relevant information;
- ascertaining what the person's wishes and feelings would be likely to be and the beliefs and values likely to influence that person;
- ascertaining what alternative courses of action are available; and
- obtaining a further medical opinion.

6.45 The IMCA's functions are to:
(1) verify that the instructions were issued by an authorised person;
(2) to the extent it is practicable and appropriate, interview the patient and examine relevant health, social services or care home records;
(3) to the extent practicable and appropriate, consult the professional carers and other persons in a position to comment on the patient's wishes, feelings, beliefs or values;
(4) take all practicable steps to obtain information about the patient, or the proposed act or decision;
(5) evaluate all the information he or she has obtained so as to ascertain the extent of the support provided to enable the patient to participate in the decision and what the patient's wishes and feelings would likely be and the beliefs and values likely to influence the patient, what alternative courses of action are available and where medical treatment is proposed whether the patient would benefit from a further medical opinion; and
(6) prepare a report for the person who instructed him or her, to include such submissions as he or she considers appropriate.

---
[87] SI 2006/1832.
[88] MCA 2005, s 36.

An IMCA who has been instructed also has power to challenge the decision taken as if he or she were someone engaged in caring for the patient or interested in the patient's welfare.

The duty to instruct

NHS bodies

6.46 An NHS body is under a duty to instruct such an advocate and to take into account any information given or submissions made by that advocate before providing 'serious medical treatment' (as defined in the Regulations in a similar way to that subsequently adopted in the President's Practice Direction as described at **6.21**ff) when there is no one else for the provider of the treatment to discuss it with.[89] This will occur when there is neither a person in the specified list[90] who can speak for the person – namely, a person nominated by the person, an attorney under a lasting power of attorney or pre-existing enduring power of attorney, or a deputy – nor a non-professional carer or friend whom it is appropriate to consult.[91] If the treatment has to be provided as a matter of urgency it may be provided even though no advocate has been instructed.

6.47 A similar duty arises where it is proposed that an incapacitated person should be accommodated in long-stay accommodation in a hospital or care home, or should transfer to another hospital or care home, where this accommodation is provided or arranged by the NHS.[92] If the accommodation is to last more than 28 days in a hospital or 8 weeks in a care home an advocate is to be instructed when there is no other person to discuss it with. The role of the advocate is again to support and represent the person concerned and any information and submissions from the advocate must be taken into account. This does not apply if the accommodation arises as a result of an obligation under the Mental Health Act 1983 nor when it is being arranged as a matter of urgency.[93]

---

[89] Not being treatment regulated by the Mental Health Act 1983, Part 4: MCA 2005, s 37.
[90] This is set out in MCA 2005, s 40.
[91] Paragraph 10.69 of the Code of Practice refers to IMCAs being available to people who have no family or friends who are available and appropriate to support or represent them. There is currently no case law on what factors would prevent a family member or friend from being an "appropriate adult". Clearly concerns as to such a person having a conflict of interest or mental health problems would seem a reasonable basis to exclude their involvement as an appropriate adult but – for instance – would the fact that such a person may hold strong religious views sufficient to deem them to be not appropriate. The author has been informed of cases where IMCAs have been appointed where there are dissenting family members who simply have strong moral objections to the proposed provision or withholding of treatment. The IMCA should only accept appointment where satisfied that that person is not appropriate. The author is further aware of a recent case where the IMCA declined to report where she considered the husband of P was an appropriate adult for the NHS Trust to consult in a serious medical treatment case.
[92] MCA 2005, s 38.
[93] Provision is made to ensure that an advocate is involved in relation to people whose residence is initially intended to be less than the 28 days or 8 weeks if the period is later extended beyond the applicable period (MCA 2005, s 38(4)).

Local authorities

6.48 Matching provisions are made in respect of, and a duty imposed, on a local authority in relation to long-stay accommodation arranged by that authority.[94] These apply to residential accommodation provided in accordance with the National Assistance Act 1948, s 21 or 29 or following discharge under the Mental Health Act 1983, s 117. The accommodation may be in a care home, nursing home, ordinary or sheltered housing, housing association or other registered social housing, or in private sector housing provided by a local authority or in hostel accommodation. Similar exceptions are made where the person concerned is required to live in the accommodation in question under the Mental Health Act 1983 or in relation to urgent placements.[95]

Expansion of role

6.49 Separate Regulations were made in 2006[96] expanding the role, adjusting the obligation to make arrangements and prescribing different circumstances in which an advocate may be instructed to act. In consequence, an NHS body or local authority may instruct an IMCA (if satisfied it would be beneficial to the person to be so represented) when reviewing accommodation arrangements or proposing to take protective measures to minimise the risk of abuse or neglect.

Powers of the IMCA

6.50 An IMCA may, for the purpose of enabling him or her to carry out his or her functions:

- interview in private the person he or she has been instructed to represent; and
- examine and take copies of any health record, social services record or care home record which the person holding the record considers may be relevant to the advocate's investigation.[97]

Comment

6.51 IMCAs are a valuable part of the machinery provided by MCA 2005.[98] Their primary role is to support someone where there are no family members or friends (except where protective measures are being considered) – particular examples include older people with dementia who have lost contact with all friends and family, or people with severe learning

---

[94] MCA 2005, s 39.
[95] MCA 2005, s 39(3) and (4).
[96] These are the Mental Capacity Act 2005 (Independent Mental Capacity Advocates) (Expansion of Role) Regulations 2006 SI 2006/2883.
[97] MCA 2005, s 35(6).
[98] See, for instance John Williams, Sarah Wydell and Alan Clarke, 'Protecting Older Victims of Abuse: the Role of the Independent Mental Capacity Advocate' [2013] Eld LJ 167

disabilities or long-term mental health problems who have been in residential institutions for long periods and lack outside contacts.

6.52 The House of Lords Select Committee appointed to consider and report upon MCA 2005 took extensive oral evidence upon the operation of the IMCA service,[99] it also specifically called for evidence upon the safeguards. In its report published in March 2014[100] the Committee recommended that consistency of the service be ensured through national standards and mandatory training in the MCA 2005 and the IMCA Role. The Committee further recommended that local authorities use their discretionary powers to appoint IMCAs more widely than is currently the case and that the Government consider the establishment of a form of self-referral for IMCA services to prevent the damaging delay that occurred in the *Neary* case. The Government has accepted these recommendations in its response to the Committee report.[101]

ADVANCE DECISIONS
Preliminary: the position at common law

6.53 Advance decisions play so significant part in the framework established by MCA 2005 for making of medical decisions that they merit separate consideration, starting with a brief tour d'horizon of the position that had been reached at common law prior to the enactment of the Act.

The starting point: the principle of adult autonomy

6.54 Whether as Munby J (as he then was) analysed it in *Burke*[102] that the adult is the arbiter of his or her own best interests or it is purely a matter of adult autonomy irrespective of best interests, the court has no basis or jurisdiction to investigate a competent adult's best interests. The principle of adult autonomy is determinative.

Refusal of treatment

6.55 At common law, it was clear that advance refusals[103] to consent to particular treatments were an aspect of a competent adult's autonomy. An advance refusal of medical treatment was required to be given binding effect if, but only if:

---

[99] See www.parliament.uk/business/committees/committees-a-z/lords-select/mental-capacity-act-2005.
[100] 'Mental Capacity Act 2005: post-legislative scrutiny' (13 March 2014) at paras 164–178.
[101] 'Valuing every voice, respecting every right: Making the case for the Mental Capacity Act' (June 2014) at paragraphs 6.38–6.44.
[102] *R (Burke) v General Medical Council and Others* [2004] EWHC 1879 (Admin), [2004] 2 FLR 1121.
[103] Documents setting out wishes as to medical treatment were initially described as 'living wills'.

(1) made at a time when the adult had capacity to make a decision of such a nature;
(2) intended to apply when that person was incapable;
(3) it related to the circumstances which had arisen;
(4) the maker understood the nature and consequences of his or her decision; and
(5) there was no undue influence or coercion by a third party.

6.56 No particular form was needed, and such a refusal could be revoked in any way or as a result of a change in relevant circumstances. The courts had to be satisfied that the advance refusal remained valid and applicable to the particular circumstances; it there was doubt, that doubt was to be resolved in favour of the preservation of life and the best interests test applied.[104] The greatest difficulty in practice was whether from the drafting of an advance directive it could be clearly inferred that such a refusal was intended to apply in the circumstances which had arisen; and it was clear that there was not always consistency of practice amongst medical professionals in their interpretation of the application of the facts to the directive before them.

The relationship with suicide

6.57 Well prior to 2007, it was settled law that whilst no one had the right to ask for and be given Well prior to 2007, it was settled law that whilst no one had the right to ask for and be given treatment which constituted a positive act (such as the administration of an excessive dose of diamorphine) to assist in their suicide, they could refuse the provision or continuation of life-sustaining treatment such as ANH even when the inevitable consequence was death.[105]

Requests for treatment

6.58 An advance directive could request rather than seek to refuse treatment. There was (and is) at common law no general right for a person to require, either at the time or in an advance decision, that a particular form of medical treatment be given. This was reaffirmed in robust terms by the Court of Appeal in its judgment in *Burke*.[106]

---

[104] *HE v A Hospital NHS Trust* [2003] EWHC 1017 (Fam), [2003] 2 FLR 408.
[105] Reaffirmed in *Pretty v UK (Application No 2346/02)* [2002] 2 FLR 45, ECHR. In deciding whether effect must be given to an advance refusal of life-sustaining treatment it is not necessary to inquire into the motives of the person making it. The Catholic Bishops Conference of England and Wales submitted to the Court of Appeal in *Burke* that adult autonomy is limited by an inability to refuse treatment motivated by a suicidal intent. It is suggested that this was not established in existing case-law as at that point, and remains the case at present.
[106] *R (Burke) v General Medical Council and Others* [2005] EWCA Civ 1003, [2005] 2 FLR 1223.

ADVANCE DECISIONS UNDER THE MENTAL CAPACITY ACT 2005

Recognition

6.59 MCA 2005, ss 24–26 give statutory recognition to, and govern the applicability and effect of, advance decisions to refuse specified treatments made by an adult when they have capacity to consent to or refuse medical treatment which are to have effect when the adult loses that capacity. A number of conditions are laid down which must be met before such a decision is to be valid and applicable. These replicate the common law position in a number of respects in relation to refusals of treatment, and in some modify it by providing additional safeguards as indicated below.

Advance refusals of treatment

6.60 These provisions of MCA 2005 in their terms only apply to advance refusals of specified treatments. It is necessary to specify the treatment which is to be refused, although this does not have to be done in medical language and can be expressed in layman's terms.[107] The circumstances in which the refusal is to apply may also be specified. Such a decision may be subsequently withdrawn or altered when the maker of the decision has capacity to do so. This need not be in writing unless the altered decision is a decision to refuse life-sustaining treatment.[108]

Advance requests for treatment and care arrangements

6.61 Advance requests for treatment are dealt with differently under MCA 2005. They are treated as a relevant written statement which, if made when the person had capacity, must be considered by the decision-maker in determining best interests.[109] They cannot be determinative if, taking into account all relevant factors, that treatment would not in P's best interests.[110] This would also apply to an advance statement relating to care arrangements, for instance as to where P would wish to live or with whom they would wish to have contact, statements which find no express place in the scheme of MCA 2005 but which can be useful tools for individuals who either have fluctuating capacity or are aware that their capacity is likely to diminish over time, but who wish to have some say in arrangements to be made for them when they lack capacity.

---

[107] MCA 2005, s 24(1)(a) and (2).
[108] MCA 2005, s 24(5).
[109] MCA 2005, s 4(6).
[110] However, there may be situations where the P considers the life that such treatment might allow him to live to be worthwhile, in which case it may mean that such treatment is in his best interests; See *St George's Healthcare NHS Trust v P & Anor* [2015] EWCOP 42.

6.62 To have the effect prescribed in MCA 2005 an advance decision to refuse a treatment must have been made by a person after he or she has reached the age of 18 and at a time when he or she had capacity to do so. It loses its validity if:[111]

- the person has withdrawn the decision (by any means) at a time when he or she had capacity to do so;
- he or she has created a lasting power of attorney after the decision was made in which he or she gives the donee of the power the authority to give or refuse consent to the treatment in question; or
- he or she has since the decision was made acted inconsistently with that being his or her fixed intention.[112]

Applicability

6.63 An advance decision is not applicable if:[113]

- at the time the provision of the treatment is in question the person has the capacity to give or refuse consent to it;
- the treatment falls outside the treatment specified in the decision;
- any circumstances specified in the decision are absent; or
- there are reasonable grounds for believing that circumstances exist which the maker of the advance decision did not anticipate at the time of its making and which would have affected his or her decision had he or she anticipated them.

Life-sustaining treatment

6.64 In addition to these conditions, there are statutory conditions for the applicability of advance decisions refusing life-sustaining treatment. These are that:[114]

- the decision includes a statement by the maker that it is to apply to the life-sustaining treatment even if his or her life is at risk;
- the decision is in writing; and
- it is signed by or under the direction and in the presence of its maker and that signature is made or acknowledged in the presence of a witness who signs or acknowledges his or her signature in the presence of the maker of the decision. Peter Jackson J confirmed in

---

[111] MCA 2005, s 25(2).
[112] See *HE v A Hospital NHS Trust* [2003] EWHC 1017 (Fam), [2003] 2 FLR 408 as a good example (a previous Jehovah's Witness who had become betrothed to a Muslim and was professing she would live by the principles of that faith). This was a pre-MCA 2005 case but it is suggested that the same outcome would prevail under the Act.
[113] MCA 2005, s 25(3) and (4).
[114] MCA 2005, s 25(5) and (6). The first and third of the requirements do not apply in the case of an advance decision made prior to 1 October 2007 where P has at all stages subsequent to that point lacked capacity to make a new advance decision. See article 5 of the Mental Capacity Act 2005 (Transitional and Consequential Provisions) Order 2007/1898. A pre-October 2007 decision must be in written form in order for it to be applicable in such situations.

An NHS Trust v D that the absence of a witness rendered invalid an advance decision refusing life-sustaining treatment.[115]

Effect

6.65 A valid and applicable advance decision has effect as if the maker had made it, and had the capacity to make it, at the time the question arises whether the treatment specified in it should be carried out or continued. In *A Local Authority v E and Others*[116], Peter Jackson J held that for 'an advance decision relating to life-sustaining treatment to be valid and applicable, there should be clear evidence establishing on the balance of probability that the maker had capacity at the relevant time. Where the evidence of capacity is doubtful or equivocal it is not appropriate to uphold the decision.'[117]

6.66 If the person providing treatment withholds or withdraws the treatment when he or she reasonably believes that an advance decision refusing the treatment exists which is valid and applicable to the treatment, he or she is protected from legal liability in doing so.[118] Conversely, a person does not incur liability for carrying out or continuing treatment unless or until he or she is satisfied that an advance decision exists which is valid and applicable to the treatment.[119]

Doubt or disagreement

6.67 If there is any doubt or disagreement over whether an advance decision exists, is valid or is applicable to a treatment, an application can be made to the Court of Protection for it to make a declaration.[120] By way of example, in an unreported case in 2009 where P's family claimed that a valid written advanced decision was given to paramedics during air ambulance evacuation and subsequently lost, the court heard oral evidence and made a finding that a valid and applicable advance decision existed refusing the use of blood or blood products in P's treatment. While a decision is being sought, those treating the person concerned are entitled to take nothing in the advance decision as preventing them providing life-sustaining treatment or doing any act they reasonably believe to be necessary to prevent a serious deterioration in that person's condition.[121] The importance of bringing matters relating to the validity of an advance decision to Court as quickly as possible has recently been emphasised in the

---

[115] [2012] EWHC 885 (COP), [2012] COPLR 493. It is not entirely clear whether Peter Jackson J was also of the view that the advance decision failed to comply with the requirement in MCA, s 25(5)(a) that it was to apply even if life was at risk. On the facts of the case, however, Peter Jackson J was able to conclude that withdrawal of treatment from D (who was in a permanent vegetative state) was in his best interests.
[116] [2012] EWHC 1639 (COP), [2012] COPLR 441.
[117] At [56]. See also **6.35** above.
[118] MCA 2005, s 26(3).
[119] MCA 2005, s 26(2).
[120] MCA 2005, s 26(4).
[121] MCA 2005, s 26(5).

cases of *A Local Authority v E and Others* (discussed above at **6.35** and **6.64**) and *X Primary Care Trust v XB* (discussed further below at **6.69**).

The Code of Practice

6.68 Chapter 9 of the Code of Practice contains valuable guidance and suggestions for best practice in this area, and has been the subject of specific judicial endorsement.[122] In particular, Chapter 9 suggests that, whilst there is no set form for written advance decisions, it is helpful to include the following information:[123]

- full details of its maker, including date of birth, home address and any distinguishing features (so that eg an unconscious person might be identified);
- the name and address of general practitioner and whether they have a copy;
- a statement that the document should be used if the maker lacks capacity to make treatment decisions;
- a clear statement of the decision, the treatment to be refused and the circumstances in which the decision will apply;
- the date the document was written (or reviewed); and
- the person's signature (or that of the person signing in their presence on their behalf) and the signature of a witness (if there is one).

6.69 In addition, if the decision relates to life-sustaining treatment, it must contain a clear statement that the decision is intended to apply even if the treatment in question is necessary to sustain life (and there must be a witness to the signature).

A cautionary tale: *X Primary Care Trust v XB*

6.70 The danger of using pro forma advance decisions was graphically illustrated by the case of *X Primary Care Trust v XB*,[124] the first reported case in which the Court of Protection was asked to make a declaration under the provisions of MCA 2005, s 26(4). As it also stands as a cautionary tale in a number of other respects, the case merits more than a passing mention.

6.71 XB, who suffered from Motor Neurone Disease, sought to make an advance decision that he wished life-sustaining treatment to be withdrawn as at the point when he was no longer able to communicate his needs or have control over his decisions as to his care and management. As he was unable

---

[122] *X Primary Care Trust v XB* [2012] EWHC 1390 (Fam), [2012] COPLR 577, Theis J endorsing (at paragraph 34) the guidance at paragraphs 9.10–9.23 of the Code of Practice as to what should be included.
[123] Code of Practice, paragraph 9.19. See also *Nottinghamshire Healthcare NHS Trust v RC* [2014] EWCOP 1317, [2014] COPLR 468 and *A NHS Foundation Trust v Ms X (By Her Litigation Friend, the Official Solicitor)* [2014] EWCOP 35, [2015] COPLR 11 as recent and interesting illustrations of the court's consideration of the validity of advanced decisions.
[124] [2012] EWHC 1390 (Fam), [2012] COPLR 577.

to write (or indeed to communicate other than moving his eyes) at the material time, it was necessary for the advance decision to be completed on his behalf. The advance decision was recorded on a form downloaded from the internet. The form included a box to enter a date upon which it was to be reviewed; it also included a box to enter a date against the cryptic entry 'valid until.'

6.72 Doubt having arisen as to the circumstances under which XB had made the advance decision and in particular, as to whether he given his express consent by moving his eyes, the Primary Care Trust investigated and ultimately brought the matter before the Court of Protection. However, as it had taken over a month to investigate the circumstances, the matter did not come before the Court until days before the 'valid until' date upon the form. XB's condition had by that stage progressed to the point where he lacked the capacity to communicate (and hence, prima facie, the decision would be applicable). The Court had to decide in very short order[125] whether the advance decision had been properly made and (if so) whether the words 'valid until' in fact meant what on their face they did. If the decision was properly made but the words meant what they appeared to mean, then XB – who was no longer in a position to make a fresh advance decision but was still conscious and alert – would have been in the position where; (1) his original decision would have expired and those near to him could no longer lawfully act upon it; (2) in light of the case-law upon withdrawal of life-sustaining treatment,[126] his wishes as contained in the original decision could not have been determinative of the question, and there would there therefore have been a very real prospect that the Court would have found that withdrawal was not in XB's best interests; and (3) XB would have been aware that his wishes as contained in the decision were not being acted upon in precisely the circumstances in which he sought them to be honoured.

6.73 Fortuitously (if that is the correct word in such a situation), Theis J was able to find upon the facts before her that the 'valid until' date had been entered by one of the professionals attending XB at the point at which the advance decision had been made without discussing it with him and without XB's consent, such XB had not intended to time-limit his advance decision. Evidence having been received which allayed the earlier concerns as to the circumstances under which the decision had been made, Theis J was therefore able therefore to make a declaration that the advance decision had properly been made and was not time-limited. Unsurprisingly, Theis J emphasised for the future that (1) in the event that an issue is raised as to the circumstances in which an advance decision has been made, this should be investigated as a matter of urgency by the relevant statutory body; and (2) organisations producing pro forma documents might wish to look again at the merits of including a 'valid until' date.

---

[125] The matter first came before the Court on a Friday; a two-day hearing was concluded by close of play on the Tuesday (the 'valid until' date being the Wednesday).
[126] See **6.35** above.

Comment: striking a balance

6.74 The statutory provisions on advance decisions are designed to strike a balance between, on the one hand, recognition of a competent adult's autonomy and, on the other, the fears expressed during the parliamentary debates on the Bill[127] that a person could be locked into an advance refusal he or she would wish to change but can no longer do so. The main way in which they have sought to strike this balance has been by placing a particular emphasis (in the case of life-sustaining treatment) upon the advance refusal taking the form specified by statute; the serious consequences of failure to comply with these requirements have been emphasised by the Courts in decisions handed down since the enactment of the Act.[128]

The alternative of a lasting power of attorney

6.75 It is a matter of individual choice whether a person wishes to plan in advance for possible future lack of capacity by indicating a refusal of specified treatments. An alternative is to create a lasting power of attorney with the authority for the person chosen as donee to take health care decisions. If it is intended that the attorney should have the power to refuse life-sustaining treatment, this power must be expressly granted in the instrument (and the grant witnessed); a box to this effect appears in the prescribed form.[129] The power would also be subject to any conditions or restrictions in the instrument.[130]

Decisions by health care professionals

6.76 In the absence of either an advance decision or a lasting power of attorney, decisions will be taken by the health care professionals in the person's best interests.[131] A written statement which does not amount to an advance decision will be taken into account,[132] but it will depend on the facts of the case at the time what the overall best interests are. Where

---

[127] See eg, *Hansard*, HC Deb, vol 425, ser 6, cols 37–102 (11 October 2004); *Hansard*, HC Official Report, SC A (Mental Capacity Bill), 28 October 2004, vol 1, HL Paper 79-1, HC Paper 95-1; and *Hansard*, HL Deb, vol 668, ser 5, cols 11–26 and 42–106 (10 January 2005), 1396–1432 and 1443–1512 (27 January 2005), vol 670, cols 1276–1324 (15 March 2005) and vol 671, cols 412–459 (24 March 2005).
[128] *W v M and S and A NHS Primary Care Trust* [2011] EWHC 2443 (Fam), [2012] COPLR 222 and *Re D* [2012] EWHC 885 (COP), [2012] COPLR 493. See also the discussion at **6.35** above.
[129] MCA 2005, s 11(8)(a).
[130] MCA 2005, s 11(8)(b).
[131] In the context of decisions made at the end of life, reference should be made to the decision of the Supreme Court in *Aintree University NHS Hospitals Trust v James*, See above, **6.36**.
[132] See, by analogy, *RGB v Cwm Taf Health Board* [2013] EWHC B23 (COP), [2014] COPLR 83 (advance statement made by wife regarding contact with husband). MCA 2005, s 4(6).

life-sustaining treatment is in question, significant weight may be attached to views even if they are expressed in a form which does not comply with the statutory requirements.[133]

6.77 Those taking treatment decisions when faced with an advance refusal of the treatment will need to take a view on the validity and applicability of the decision. For example, they will need to make an assumption as to the person's capacity at the time the decision was made (to which the statutory presumption of capacity will apply). In most instances there may be no doubt. The formalities around making an advance decision refusing life-sustaining treatment may make it easier to make this assumption in such a case. In some instances, however, where it is thought possible that the advance decision may be challenged in the future and there may be some doubt as to capacity, it may be helpful for the maker to obtain evidence confirming his or her capacity at the time.

6.78 Of greater difficulty may be (now as under the common law) whether the maker of the decision really had in mind the circumstances which have arisen and intended it to apply in those circumstances; or whether relevant circumstances have changed (eg the prospect of a new cure) so as to invalidate the decision. As the Code of Practice states, particular care will need to be taken for advance decisions which do not appear to have been reviewed or updated for some time.[134]

MEDICAL RESEARCH

Common law position

The regulation of research

6.79 It is beyond the scope of this chapter to delve deeply into the different types of research – for example, therapeutic, non-therapeutic and observational – and the volume of current learning on what is or is not permissible in accordance with modern ethical principles. There is in place a system of Local Research Ethics Committees and Multi-Centre Research Ethics Committees to regulate research carried out in an NHS body. This came into existence to relate to research involving patients who are fully informed and freely give their consent.

General principles

6.80 As a general principle it can be stated that medical research which involves some invasion of bodily integrity on a person who is not able to consent to it is not permissible under the existing common law, as it cannot be justified under the doctrine of necessity. A court might declare therapeutic research lawful if done in that person's best interests, although

---

[133] See *Aintree University NHS Hospitals Trust v James* and *United Lincolnshire Hospital Trust v N* and the discussion at **6.34–6.36** above.
[134] Code of Practice, paragraph 9.51.

this has not been tested in court and often the point of research is not to benefit the particular individual but others who might in the future be suffering from a similar condition.

6.81 The closest the common law came to recognising benefits to others as a factor in the best interests equation arose in the cases in which the taking of samples from one sibling for the potential benefit of another were authorised as benefiting the child, or incapacitated adult, to contribute to the family's welfare in this way.[135] This is not a precedent justifying research. Nor is the decision in *Simms v Simms; A v A (a child)*[136] in which experimental and innovative treatment was authorised to victims of vCJD (Variant Creutzfeldt-Jakob disease), not by way of research, but as medical treatment in their best interests as in the circumstances being the only hope for them in slowing down the decline in their condition.

Clinical Trials Regulations

6.82 Therapeutic research in the form of clinical trials on medicinal products for human use is now authorised and regulated under and in accordance with the Medicines for Human Use (Clinical Trials) Regulations 2004[137] made under the authority given by the European Union Directive on Good Clinical Practice in Clinical Trials.[138] The Regulations govern such trials in relation to both those who can provide informed consent and those who cannot.

6.83 The general principles underlying these Regulations are that:

- the clinical trial must have the approval of the relevant ethics committee and be authorised by the appropriate minister as licensing authority;
- the anticipated therapeutic and public health benefits must justify the risks; and
- informed consent must be given (which must be written, signed and dated) after an interview with a member of the investigating team.[139]

---

[135] *Re Y (Mental Patient: Bone Marrow Donation)* [1996] 2 FLR 787.
[136] [2002] EWHC 2734 (Fam), [2003] 1 FLR 879.
[137] SI 2004/1031. These Regulations came into force on 1 May 2004 and have been subsequently amended on numerous occasions.
[138] Directive 2001/20/EC. The Regulations now also incorporate the requirements of Directive 2005/28/EC setting down (inter alia) principles and detailed guidelines for good clinical practice as regards investigational medicinal products for human use.
[139] There is an exception in the case of urgency where treatment is being or is about to be provided for an incapacitated adult as a matter of urgency, and it is also necessary to take action for the purposes of the clinical trial as a matter of urgency but it is not reasonably practicable to obtain such informed consent; in such instances, the action required for the purposes of the clinical trial can be carried out if it is in accordance with a procedure approved by an Ethics Committee (or by an appeal panel considering an appeal against an unfavourable decision of an Ethics Committee): Schedule 1 to the Regulations, paragraphs 6 and 7.

6.84 The involvement of an adult who lacks capacity to consent requires the informed consent of his or her 'legal representative' and is subject to the following additional conditions:

- the research is essential to validate data obtained in clinical trials on persons able to give consent and relates directly to a life-threatening or debilitating clinical condition from which the incapacitated adult suffers; and
- the trial has the potential to produce a benefit to the patient which outweighs the potential risks.

6.85 For the purposes of the Regulations, an incapacitated participant's legal representative is either:

(1) a person close to the patient (a 'personal legal representative'); or, where no one can act in that capacity,
(2) someone such as the doctor responsible for the care of the patient or other person nominated by the health care provider, being someone not involved in the conduct of the trial (a 'professional legal representative').

6.86 The legal representative may withdraw the subject from the trial at any time.[140] If an adult prior to the onset of incapacity has refused to give his or her consent, he or she cannot be included as a subject.

Research authorised by the Mental Capacity Act 2005

Background

6.87 The draft Mental Incapacity Bill presented to Parliament in June 2003 did not contain any provisions on research. The Joint Scrutiny Committee on this Bill, in response to evidence it received from the British Medical Association, the Royal College of Psychiatrists, the British Psychological Society and The Law Society, concluded that if properly regulated research involving people who may lack capacity was not possible then treatment for incapacitating disorders would not be developed. It recommended, therefore, that clauses should be included to enable strictly controlled medical research to explore the causes and consequences of mental incapacity and to develop effective treatment for such conditions. It further recommended that these clauses should set out the key principles governing such research and the protections against exploitation or harm.[141]

6.88 As a result, provisions were included in the Mental Capacity Bill as presented to Parliament, and these were refined through various amendments made during the course of the Bill's consideration. They now form MCA 2005, ss 30–34.[142]

---

[140] Subject to the 'urgency' exemption set out at **6.83** (footnote).
[141] See recommendations 81–88, HL Paper 189-1 HC Paper 1083-1 (Session 2002–03).
[142] See Chapter 11 of the Code of Practice for a general explanation of and guide to these provisions.

Application of the Act

6.89 The provisions of ss 30–34 apply to any intrusive research carried out on, or in relation to, a person who lacks capacity to consent to it other than a clinical trial subject to the Medicines for Human Use (Clinical Trials) Regulations 2004 (because they already make provision for trials involving participants who lack capacity). They are based upon long-standing international standards such as those laid down by the World Medical Association (originally in the Helsinki Declaration in 1964 and updated since) and in the Council of Europe Convention on Human Rights and Biomedicine.

Pre-condition to authorisation

6.90 The pre-condition to the authorisation of research under these provisions is that a committee established to advise on the ethics of intrusive research in relation to people who lack capacity to consent to it and recognised for this purpose by the Secretary of State for Health (in relation to research in England) or the Welsh Assembly (in relation to Wales) has approved the research project.[143]

6.91 That approval can only be given in relation to a person who lacks capacity to consent if:[144]

- the research is connected with the person's impairing condition or its treatment;
- there are reasonable grounds for believing that research of comparable effectiveness cannot be carried out if the project is confined to persons who can consent;
- the research has the potential to benefit the person without imposing a disproportionate burden or it is intended to provide knowledge of the causes or treatment of, or the care of persons affected by, the same or a similar condition;
- in the case of research which falls only in the latter category, there are reasonable grounds for believing that the risk to the individual in taking part is negligible and anything done to that person will not interfere with his or her freedom of action or privacy in any way or be unduly invasive or restrictive; and
- there are arrangements in place to ensure the particular conditions (referred to below) will be met.

Pre-conditions relating to the individual

6.92 Before a person who lacks capacity to consent can take part in an approved research project, particular conditions relating to his or her participation must be met.

---

[143] MCA 2005, s 30.
[144] MCA 2005, s 31.

6.93 These conditions relate first to the requirement for a researcher to consult a carer (someone not professionally interested in the person's welfare) or, if a carer who is prepared to be consulted cannot be identified, a person not connected with the research project whom, in accordance with guidance to be issued by the Secretary of State (or the Welsh Assembly), the researcher has nominated as the person prepared to be consulted (eg a general practitioner or specialist engaged in the person's treatment).[145]

6.94 The regime established here is the equivalent of that provided for under the Clinical Trials Regulations outlined above. It includes provision for the consultee advising that the person concerned would not have wanted to take part, in which event that person is not to be included, or if already taking part, must be withdrawn. It also includes provision relating to treatment being provided as a matter of urgency and carrying on necessary research associated with that treatment.

6.95 Secondly, additional safeguards are provided that:
- nothing may be done in the course of the research to which the person appears to object (except where what is being done is intended to protect the person or reduce his or her pain or discomfort) or would be contrary to any known advance decision of that person or current statement of wishes;
- the person's interests must be assumed to outweigh those of science and society; and
- if the person lacking capacity indicates in any way that he or she wishes to be withdrawn he or she must be withdrawn, as he or she must be if any of the conditions for the approval of the research project cease to be met (although any treatment being given to which the research is associated may continue if there is a significant risk to health if discontinued).[146]

6.96 Regulations have been made (by the Secretary of State and the Welsh Assembly) covering the continuation of a research project in relation to a person who had consented to take part in it before these provisions were brought into force and who loses capacity to consent to continuing to take part in it before the conclusion of the project.[147]

Comment

6.97 These provisions, which have yet to be the subject of any decisions (either reported, or, to the best of the author's knowledge, unreported), cover the whole range of research activities which would require a person's

---

[145] MCA 2005, s 32. The Secretary of State and Welsh Ministers have, in accordance with MCA 2005 s 32(3), issued 'Guidance on nominating a consultee for research involving adults who lack capacity to consent' (February 2008).
[146] MCA 2005, s 33.
[147] See Mental Capacity Act 2005 (Loss of Capacity During Research Project) (England) Regulations 2007, SI 2007/679 and Mental Capacity Act 2005 (Loss of Capacity during Research Project) (Wales) Regulations, SI 2007/837, both made under MCA 2005, s 34.

consent if that person had capacity, which includes research involving them, their tissue or their data.[148] The provisions strike a careful balance between allowing intrusive procedures when not necessarily of direct benefit to that person and facilitating research into an impairing condition. They are also designed to cater for situations where the research is but one aspect of the clinical or professional care of the person who lacks capacity (which will be governed by the best interests test).

---

[148] Research on anonymised medical data or tissue may be possible outside the terms of MCA 2005, although subject to controls under the Data Protection Act 1998 or the Human Tissue Act 2004 respectively.

Chapter 7

Deprivation of Liberty Safeguards

BACKGROUND

7.1 With effect from 1 April 2009, the Mental Capacity Act 2005 (MCA 2005) was substantively amended by the Mental Health Act 2007 (MHA 2007) to provide mechanisms for authorising, subject to safeguards, the deprivation of liberty of a person who cannot consent when that is necessary in their best interests for their care or treatment.[1] The Mental Health Act 1983 (MHA 1983), as amended by the MHA 2007, contains its own compulsory powers for the detention, assessment or treatment of patients for their mental disorder. Whilst it is beyond the scope of this book to set out any detailed description or analysis of the mental health legislation, there are some interesting parallels and comparisons with the MCA 2005, particularly in relation to some health care issues discussed in Chapter 6. These set the scene and provide the context for a more detailed explanation of the deprivation of liberty safeguards.

THE MENTAL HEALTH ACT 1983, AS AMENDED BY THE MENTAL HEALTH ACT 2007

Powers of admission, detention and treatment

7.2 The MHA 1983, as amended by the MHA 2007, is principally concerned with the admission of patients to hospital for assessment and treatment for their mental disorder. However, the MHA 2007 extended powers of compulsion by introducing compulsory community treatment orders (also referred to as supervised community treatment) for patients previously detained in hospital who are now living in the community, but who continue to need treatment for their mental disorder. Mental disorder is defined as any disorder or disability of the mind (MHA 1983, s 1(2), as amended by MHA 2007). MHA 1983 enables compulsory powers of detention and treatment to be used when the statutory conditions for 'sectioning' the patient are met. In the case of admission for assessment, the

---

[1] Prior to that date under the MCA 2005 as originally enacted a person acting in connection with the care or treatment in the best interests of an incapacitated person could restrain that person if it was to prevent harm to that person and was a proportionate response but could not deprive them of their liberty (ss 5 and 6 – see Chapter 2). The High Court could make an order under its inherent jurisdiction which had the effect of depriving the person concerned of their liberty putting in place as many safeguards as practicable, including provision for review (see *Re PS (Incapacitated or Vulnerable Adult)* [2007] EWHC 623 (Fam), [2007] 2 FLR 1083 and *Salford City Council v GJ, NJ and BJ (by their litigation friends)* [2008] EWHC 1097 (Fam), [2008] 2 FLR 1295). That the inherent jurisdiction to grant such an order survives in an appropriate situation was confirmed by Baker J in *An NHS Trust v Dr A* [2013] EWHC 2442 (COP), [2013] COPLR 605, discussed further at **7.55** below.

patient must be suffering from mental disorder of a nature or degree which warrants the detention of the patient in a hospital for assessment, and:[2]

'... he ought to be so detained in the interests of his own health or safety or with a view to the protection of other persons.'

7.3 In the case of admission for treatment, the grounds need to be established that:[3]

'(a) he is suffering from mental disorder of a nature or degree which makes it appropriate for him to receive medical treatment in a hospital; and

...

(c) it is necessary for the health or safety of the patient or for the protection of other persons that he should receive such treatment and it cannot be provided unless he is detained under this section; and

(d) appropriate medical treatment is available for him.'

7.4 The relevant criteria for community treatment orders are that:[4]

'(a) the patient is suffering from mental disorder of a nature or degree which makes it appropriate for him to receive medical treatment;

(b) it is necessary for his health or safety or for the protection of other persons that he should receive such treatment;

(c) subject to his being liable to be recalled as mentioned in para (d) below, such treatment can be provided without his continuing to be detained in a hospital;

(d) it is necessary that the responsible clinician should be able to exercise the power ... to recall the patient to hospital; and

(e) appropriate medical treatment is available for him.'

7.5 MHA 1983 sets out the conditions and procedures for use of these powers. These include that the application for admission (either for assessment or treatment) must be made on the recommendation in the prescribed form of two registered medical practitioners. The Act also provides for patients to be received into guardianship, giving the appointed guardian (usually a local authority) the power to require a patient in the community to reside at a specified place and attend for treatment. The 2007 Act broadened the powers of the guardian by introducing a new power to take and convey a person subject to guardianship to their required place of residence (MHA 2007, Sch 3, para 3(5)).

Review and appeals

7.6 MHA 1983 then provides the procedures for review and appeals to the Health, Education and Social Care Chamber of the First-tier Tribunal (prior to 3 November 2008 the independent mental health review tribunals (MHRT)) in relation to the use, or continued use, of the compulsory powers.[5] The MHRT for Wales remains as a separate devolved tribunal. There is a right of appeal on a point of law from both tribunals to the Upper Tribunal.

---

[2] MHA 1983, s 2(2).
[3] MHA 1983, s 3(2), as amended by MHA 2007.
[4] MHA 1983, s 17A(5), as amended by MHA 2007.
[5] Tribunals, Courts and Enforcement Act 2007, Part 1.

Purpose

7.7 The purpose of MHA 1983 is to provide the statutory framework for the compulsory care and treatment of people for their mental disorder when they are unable or unwilling to consent to that care and treatment, and when it is necessary for that care and treatment to be given to protect themselves or others from harm.

7.8 The key point for the exercise of these powers is the inability or unwillingness of the patient who suffers from a mental disorder to consent to the relevant care and treatment. This encompasses people who, notwithstanding their mental disorder, have capacity to do so – and it is entirely possible for someone detained under the MHA 1983 to have capacity in relation to a treatment decision.[6] Inability to consent will also include people who do not have capacity, but the question whether an individual patient has or does not have decision-making capacity is not the key determinant of whether the powers conferred by MHA 1983 should be used.

COMPARISONS

7.9 The Mental Capacity Act 2005 (MCA 2005) is based wholly on a capacity test. Its provisions have no application to people who have the capacity to make their own decisions. Some who lack capacity will not come within the definition of those for whom compulsory powers under MHA 1983 can be exercised. People with learning difficulties, for example, who may thereby not be able to give their consent to treatment, will not generally be subject to the compulsory powers of MHA 1983, unless they are also abnormally aggressive or seriously irresponsible. Other examples are people in a persistent vegetative state or anyone suffering from 'locked-in' syndrome, which prevents them from communicating, persons with brain injuries or temporarily unconscious, drunk or under the influence of drugs.

Differences

7.10 It can be seen that the differences between these two approaches are that:
 (1) MCA 2005 relates to a person's functioning – incapacity to make a particular decision – whereas MHA 1983 relates to a person's status, as someone diagnosed as having a mental disorder within the meaning of the Act and subject to its powers;
 (2) MCA 2005 covers all decision-making, whereas MHA 1983 is, to a very large degree, limited to decisions about care in hospital and medical treatment for mental disorder;

---

[6] See, for a clear pre-MCA 2005 example, *Re C (Adult: Refusal of Treatment)* [1994] 1 FLR 31.

(3) MHA 1983 authorises detention, but this was specifically excluded under MCA 2005 as originally enacted;[7] and
(4) MCA 2005 specifically excludes[8] anyone giving a patient medical treatment for mental disorder, or consenting to a patient being given medical treatment for mental disorder, if the patient is, at the relevant time, already detained and subject to the compulsory treatment provisions of MHA 1983, Part 4.

Overlaps

7.11 There are areas of overlap. For example:
(1) people who are detained in hospital under MHA 1983 and who also lack capacity to make financial decisions may be subject to the provisions of MCA 2005 when it comes to the taking of such decisions; and, equally,
(2) an elderly person, for example, with Alzheimer's disease, whose day-to-day life is managed in accordance with the provisions of MCA 2005, may be made subject to MHA 1983 if it is no longer possible to care for such a person at home and he or she requires treatment for the mental disorder and is resisting being admitted to hospital.

THE DEPRIVATION OF LIBERTY SAFEGUARDS

The 'Bournewood Gap'

7.12 The great majority of people with a mental disorder are not treated under the MHA 1983. That Act specifically provides that nothing in that Act is to be treated as preventing the informal admission of a patient requiring treatment for mental disorder to any hospital or registered establishment.[9] Moreover, there are those people being treated or living in hospitals or care homes who suffer from a mental disorder but are not there to be treated for their mental disorder and are not within scope of the MHA 1983. They may not have resisted nor objected to their admission nor to their continued stay in the hospital or care home. This does not give rise to any issue of particular concern when they have capacity and it is their choice. However, it can be seen that questions can arise as to how such patients should be dealt with who may be compliant but who do not have the capacity to reach their own decisions about what is happening to them. This is particularly the case so far as they are deprived of their liberty.[10] That there were no safeguards in

---

[7] See MCA 2005, s 6, which provides the conditions under which a person may 'restrain' a person whilst remaining within the protection given by s 5, but this protection is not available if there is a deprivation of liberty. The provisions introduced into MCA 2005 by MHA 2007 allow deprivation of liberty in specific circumstances – see **7.17ff**.
[8] See MCA 2005, s 28.
[9] MHA 1983, s 131.
[10] This is not a new problem. The Mental Health Act Commission, established to keep under review the care and treatment of patients detained under MHA 1983, identified in its *First Biennial Report (1983–1985)* (HMSO, 1985) the lack of safeguards for 'de facto' detained patients.

relation to the deprivation of their liberty was characterised as 'the Bournewood gap'. The 'Bournewood gap' takes its name from, and achieved prominence as a result of, the decision of the European Court of Human Rights in *HL v UK*.[11]

The decisions of the domestic courts

7.13 Mr HL, an autistic man, was readmitted to the Bournewood Hospital after a period in the community with paid carers, but the decision was taken not to section him under MHA 1983 as he had not resisted admission. The ensuing dispute between the carers and the hospital over his care and treatment was first litigated in judicial review proceedings in the domestic courts. The carers lost at first instance and ultimately in the House of Lords, in the latter case essentially on the ground that the circumstances were covered by the common law doctrine of necessity. This reversed the decision of the Court of Appeal, which had upheld their claim that Mr HL had been unlawfully detained.[12]

European Court of Human Rights

7.14 The case was then taken to the European Court of Human Rights. The unanimous decision was:

(1) that Mr HL had been deprived of his liberty contrary to Art 5(1) of the European Convention on Human Rights (ECHR);
(2) that detention was arbitrary and not in accordance with a procedure prescribed by law; and
(3) the procedures available to Mr HL did not comply with the requirements of Art 5(4) as there was no procedure under which he could seek a merits review of whether the conditions for his detention remained applicable.

7.15 The specific criticisms the European Court made, and the contrast it drew between the safeguards available to a person detained under MHA 1983 and an informal patient in Mr HL's position, related to the lack of any formal procedures as to:

- who could authorise an admission;
- the reasons needing to be given for that admission (whether it was for treatment or assessment);
- the need for continuing clinical assessment and review; and
- who could represent the patient and be able to seek a review in an independent tribunal as to the lawfulness of the continued detention.

---

[11] Application no 45508/99, judgment on the merits given on 5 October 2004 [2004] 1 FLR 1019.
[12] *R v Bournewood Community and Mental Health NHS Trust ex parte L* [1998] 2 FLR 550, CA.

7.16 The discussion in the court related to the position under the inherent jurisdiction as it was at the time these events occurred (1997). The enactment of MCA 2005, notably the creation of the Independent Mental Capacity Advocacy Service, dealt with some of the points raised. However, the decision in the case came too late for the Government to deal with it fully in MCA 2005 as enacted and it was recognised that it did not fill the gap. Following a period of consultation, the Government brought forward a new scheme enacted in the MHA 2007, amending MCA 2005 so that it can be lawful to deprive a compliant patient of their liberty other than through activating the MHA 1983 powers if the conditions of the scheme are met.

THE MCA SOLUTION

7.17 MHA 2007, s 50 and Schs 7 and 8 amended MCA 2005 so as to render it lawful to deprive a person of their liberty either if it is a consequence of giving effect to an order of the Court of Protection on a personal welfare matter or, if the deprivation of liberty is in a hospital or care home, if a standard or urgent authorisation (under the provisions of MCA 2005, Sch A1) is in force.[13] The Court of Appeal confirmed in *G v E*[14] that the scheme enacted by these amendments is both compliant with Article 5(1) of the ECHR and plugs the 'Bournewood Gap.'

Meaning of deprivation of liberty

7.18 For the purposes of these provisions deprivation of liberty is defined as having the same meaning as in Art 5(1) of the ECHR.[15] The starting principles are clearly established in the Strasbourg jurisprudence:

- There are three elements necessary for there to be a deprivation of liberty falling within the scope of Art 5(1): an objective element of a person's confinement in a particular restricted space for a non-negligible length of time;[16] a subjective element, namely that the person has not validly consented to the confinement in question;[17] and that the deprivation of liberty must be imputable to the State.[18]

---

[13] The amendments came into force on 1 April 2009 (The Mental Health Act 2007 (Commencement No 10 and Transitional Provisions) Order 2009, SI 2009/139.

[14] [2010] EWCA Civ 822, [2010] COPLR Con Vol 431.

[15] Section 64(5) MCA 2005. The ECHR cases relating to deprivation of liberty in the context with which we are concerned can be divided into two parts. The 'canon' is made up of *Guzzardi v Italy* (1980) 3 EHRR 333; *Ashingdale v UK* [1985] ECHR 8225/78; *Nielson v Denmark* (1988) 11 EHRR 175; *HM v Switzerland* [2002] ECHR 39187/98; *HL v UK* (2004) 40 EHRR 761; and *Storck v Germany* [2005] ECHR 61603/00. There was then something of a pause, before a recent flurry of activity in Strasbourg resulting in resulting in *Stanev v Bulgaria* (2012) 55 EHRR 22; *DD v Lithuania* [2007] ECHR 27527/03; *Austin v United Kingdom* (2012) 55 EHRR 14; *Kędzior v Poland* [2012] ECHR 1809; and more recently in *Stankov v Bulgaria* (Application No 25820/07, decision of 17 March 2015). For a detailed discussion of the recent Strasbourg jurisprudence, see the paper by Alex Ruck Keene entitled 'Tying ourselves into (Gordian) knots?' available from: www.39essex.com/resources/article_listing.php?id=748.

[16] *Storck v Germany* [2005] ECHR 61603/00, at [74].

[17] Ibid, at [74]. There is some suggestion in the recent Strasbourg jurisprudence that it may in

- The difference between restricting a person and depriving them of their liberty is one of degree or intensity rather than of nature or substance.[19]
- In order to determine whether there is a deprivation of liberty there must be an assessment of the specific factors in each case, such as the type, duration, effects and manner of implementation of the measure in question and its impact on the person.[20]
- Not all restrictions on a person's liberty will constitute a deprivation of liberty.[21]

7.19 While the DOLS Code of Practice provides guidance on identifying a deprivation of liberty,[22] the domestic courts have struggled to identify principles by which it may be determined where restrictions have crossed the line to amounting to deprivation of a person's liberty.[23] However, the Supreme Court's landmark decision in the linked appeals of *P (by his litigation friend the Official Solicitor) v Cheshire West and Cheshire Council and Another* [2014] UKSC 19, [2014] COPLR 313 and *P and Q (by their litigation friend the Official Solicitor) v Surrey Council* [2014] UKSC 19, [2014] COPLR 313 clarifies the meaning of deprivation of liberty. The decision concerned the living arrangements of three disabled people: P, MIG and MEG.

7.20 P, a man with cerebral palsy and Down's Syndrome, lived in a staffed bungalow with other residents near his home and had one-to-one support to enable him to leave the house frequently for activities and visits. He needed

---

some circumstances be possible for 'substituted' consent to be given: *Stanev v Bulgaria*, at [130]. However, the recent decision of *Stankov v Bulgaria* confirmed that, in asking whether a person has the capacity to consent to their confinement for social care purposes, the same approach is to be taken as in relation to placement for psychiatric treatment purposes. Thus, the consent of a person (and their ability to understand the consequences of this) can only be considered valid if determined through a fair procedure in which all necessary information concerning the placement and the proposed treatment is provided (paragraph 90). This is in essence consistent with the approach suggested by Baker J in *A PCT v LDV* [2013] EWHC 272 (Fam), [2013] COPLR 204.
[18] Ibid, at [89].
[19] *Guzzardi v Italy* (1980) 3 EHRR 333, at [92].
[20] *HL v UK* (2004) 40 EHRR 761 at [89].
[21] *Guzzardi v Italy* (1980) 3 EHRR 333, at [92].
[22] See Chapter 2; in addition to the DOLS Code of Practice, practical guidance on the law on deprivation of liberty for lawyers and health and social care professionals has recently (April 2015) been published by The Law Society: www.lawsociety.org.uk/support-services/advice/articles/deprivation-of-liberty/
[23] One consequence of this is the wide variation in the use of authorisations under Schedule A1 of the MCA 2005. In significant part in reaction to widespread criticism of the way in which the amendments to MCA 2005 to bring in the DOLS safeguards were drafted, on 1 October 2014 the Scottish Law Commission published a Report on Adults with Incapacity including a draft Bill (Scot Law Com No 240). The Commission recommends that the Adults with Incapacity (Scotland) Act 2000 should be amended to include a legal process to authorise measures preventing an adult from going out of a hospital and a more detailed legal process for the scrutiny of significant restriction of liberty of an adult in a care home or other placement in the community. Further, the Act should also be amended to provide for a right to apply to the sheriff court for release of an adult who may lack capacity from unlawful detention in certain care settings. The report can be found at www.scotlawcom.gov.uk/law-reform-projects/adults-with-incapacity.

24 hour care including prompting with activities of daily living including hygiene and continence. Intervention was sometimes required when he exhibited challenging behaviour. He wore a 'bodysuit' and required invasive interventions including 'fingersweep' to the mouth to stop him ingesting harmful substances. Baker J held that these arrangements did deprive him of his liberty but that it was in P's best interests for them to continue.[24] The Court of Appeal substituted a declaration that the arrangements did not involve a deprivation of liberty, after comparing his circumstances with another person of the same age and disabilities as P.[25]

7.21 MIG and MEG (otherwise known as P and Q) were sisters who became the subject of care proceedings in 2007 when they were respectively 16 and 15. Both suffered from learning disabilities. MIG was placed with a foster mother to whom she was devoted and went to a further education unit daily. She never attempted to leave the foster home by herself but would have been restrained from doing so had she tried. MEG was moved from foster care to a residential home for learning disabled adolescents with complex needs. She sometimes required physical restraint and received tranquillising medication. When the care proceedings were transferred to the Court of Protection, Parker J held that these living arrangements were in the sisters' best interests and did not amount to a deprivation of liberty.[26] This finding was upheld by the Court of Appeal.[27]

7.22 The Supreme Court unanimously overruled the Court of Appeal in P and overruled the Court of Appeal in MIG and MEG's case by a majority of 4 to 3. The ultimate question before the Supreme Court was summarised by Lady Hale at paragraph 33:

> 'The first and most fundamental question is whether the concept of physical liberty protected by article 5 is the same for everyone, regardless of whether or not they are mentally or physically disabled.'

Lady Hale had no hesitation in holding that it was:

> '45. [I]t is axiomatic that people with disabilities, both mental and physical, have the same human rights as the rest of the human race. It may be that those rights have sometimes to be limited or restricted because of their disabilities, but the starting point should be the same as that for everyone else. This flows inexorably from the universal character of human rights, founded on the inherent dignity of all human beings, and is confirmed in the United Nations Convention on the Rights of Persons with Disabilities. Far from disability entitling the state to deny such people human rights: rather it places upon the state (and upon others) the duty to make reasonable accommodation to cater for the special needs of those with disabilities.
> 46. Those rights include the right to physical liberty, which is guaranteed by article 5 of the European Convention. This is not a right to do or to go where

---

[24] *Cheshire West and Chester Council v P* [2011] EWHC 1330 (Fam), [2011] COPLR Con Vol 273.
[25] *Cheshire West and Chester Council v P* [2011] EWCA Civ 1257, [2012] COPLR 37; Munby LJ, who delivered the lead judgment, adopted the "relative normality" approach, considering that P was not deprived of his liberty because his life was no more restricted than that which anyone with his disabilities and difficulties might be expected to lead.
[26] *Re MIG and MEG* [2010] EWHC 785 (Fam), [2010] COPLR Con Vol 850.
[27] *Re P and Q* [2011] EWCA Civ 190, [2011] COPLR Con Vol 931.

one pleases. It is a more focussed right, not to be deprived of that physical liberty. But, as it seems to me, what it means to be deprived of liberty must be the same for everyone, whether or not they have physical or mental disabilities. If it would be a deprivation of my liberty to be obliged to live in a particular place, subject to constant monitoring and control, only allowed out with close supervision, and unable to move away without permission even if such an opportunity became available, then it must also be a deprivation of the liberty of a disabled person. The fact that my living arrangements are comfortable, and indeed make my life as enjoyable as it could possibly be, should make no difference. A gilded cage is still a cage.'

Lord Kerr, who agreed with Lady Hale and Lord Neuberger, noted at paragraph 76 that:

'Liberty means the state or condition of being free from external constraint. It is predominantly an objective state. It does not depend on one's disposition to exploit one's freedom. Nor is it diminished by one's lack of capacity.'

7.23 Lady Hale analysed the European Court of Human Rights case law in this area[28] and identified the twin ingredients of a deprivation of liberty where there is no valid consent to the living arrangements as:

(a) the person is not free to leave; and
(b) under continuous supervision and control.

This is identified as the 'acid test' for whether or not a person is deprived of their liberty to avoid the minute examination of the living arrangements of each mentally incapacitated person for whom the state makes arrangements which might otherwise be required.

At paragraph 50, Lady Hale also identified as irrelevant factors:

- P's compliance or lack of objections;
- the relative normality of the placement; and
- the reasons/purpose behind the placement.

7.24 Applying this test to the facts of these cases, the majority held that all three appellants were deprived of their liberty. Lords Hodge, Carnwath and Clarke dissented in MIG and MEG's case, taking the view that the sisters were not deprived of their liberty.

7.25 The Supreme Court's decision effectively restores the classical interpretation of what constitutes a deprivation of liberty and reiterates that deprivation of liberty safeguards also apply to locations other than hospitals and care homes. There is now an acid test as set out by Lady Hale. Further, at paragraph 63, Lord Neuberger considered the essential ingredients of a deprivation of liberty to be 'continuous supervision and control and lack of freedom to leave' as well as 'the area and period of confinement'. At paragraph 78 Lord Kerr said that the duration of the restriction was paramount.

---

[28] *HL v UK* (2004) 40 EHRR 761, *Stanev v Bulgaria* (2012) 55 FHRR 696, *DD v Lithuania* (Application No 13469/06) (2012) ECHR 254, *Kędzior v Poland* [2012] ECHR 1809, *Mihailovs v Latvia* (Application No 35939/10) (2013) ECHR 65.

7.26 While the judgment sets out what factors are irrelevant when applying the acid test, no further guidance is given as to the parameters of this test and, for example, when supervision does not amount to control and when supervision and control are not complete or continuous. Nor is there analysis of what it means to be 'free to leave' or how to determine the area and period of confinement. Until these issues are further tested before the courts it would appear that the best guidance currently available on these issues is way in which the Supreme Court applied the acid test to the P and MIG and MEG.

7.27 It is also apparent that the concepts of relative normality and a disabled comparator are no longer applicable. The concept of relative normality originates from ECHR jurisprudence[29] and was embraced in the P & Q proceedings. The more controversial concept of disabled normality originated in the *Cheshire West* proceedings.[30]

7.28 As regards the role of a comparator in determining whether there is a deprivation of liberty, their Lordships expressed differing views. Lady Hale did not consider that comparing the lives of MIG and MEG with the ordinary lives that young people of their ages might live to answer the question and was of the view that the relative normality of the placement (whatever the comparison made) is not relevant (paragraph 50). At paragraph 46 Lady Hale went on to suggest that an appropriate comparator ought to be herself: 'if it would be a deprivation of my liberty ... then it must also be a deprivation of liberty of a disabled person'.

7.29 At paragraph 80 Lords Carnwath and Hodge recognised that the comparator should in principle be a person with unimpaired health and capacity. Lord Kerr on the other hand considered that it was necessary to compare the person's age and 'station in life'. Thus, for MIG and MEG the relevant comparator was 'a teenager of the same age and familial background as them'. Lord Clarke, by contrast, expressly endorsed the approach of Parker J, which was to consider the sisters' lives as dictated by their own cognitive limitations.

7.30 In this context, Lady Hale has recently commented on what she considered the case had decided:

> 'We all held that the man had been deprived of his liberty, but three members of the court held that the sisters had not been deprived of their liberty, while the majority held that they had. The acid test was whether they were under the complete control and supervision of the staff and not free to leave. Their situation had to be compared, not with the situation of someone with their disabilities, but with the situation of an ordinary, normal person of their age. This is because the right to liberty is the same for everyone. The whole point about human rights is their universal quality, based as

---

[29] *Engel & Ors v The Netherlands* (Application nos 5100/71, 5101/71, 5102/71, 5354/72, 5370/72) (1976) 1 EHRR 647.
[30] However, none of the parties in the appeals to the Supreme Court supported a disabled comparator test.

they are upon the ringing declaration in article 1 of the Universal Declaration of Human Rights, that "All human beings are born free and equal in dignity and rights".'[31]

7.31 Finally, P's objection or lack of objection is now irrelevant as the right to liberty is deemed to be too important for a person to lose the benefit of protection because he may have given himself up to detention. This is a departure from both domestic and Strasbourg jurisprudence, which has often referred to the relevance of the person's objections and the 'effect' of the measure as a relevant criteria to be taken into account.

7.32 As an illustration of the difficulties this area of law continue to present for practitioners and the judiciary, reference is made to a decision handed down by Mostyn J on 18 November 2014 in the case of *Rochdale MBC v KW* [2014] EWCOP 45 in which Mostyn J essentially attempted to take on the Supreme Court in *Cheshire West* and demanded that it 'reconsider' the application of Article 5 ECHR in the context of deprivation of liberty at home. Although Mostyn J's judgment has since been successfully appealed to the Court of Appeal (see further below), the facts of this case are worthy of mention. The case concerned a 52 year old woman who has cognitive and mental health problems, epilepsy and physical disability as a result of a subarachnoid haemorrhage sustained during a medical operation many years previously. At the time that the matter came before Mostyn J, she was cared for in her own home with a package of 24-hour care funded jointly by Rochdale MBC and the local CCG. Both the local authority and KW (by her litigation friend) agreed that the decision of the majority in *Cheshire West* compelled the conclusion that KW was deprived of her liberty. However, Mostyn J decided to the contrary, holding at paragraph 7 that he:

> '[found] it impossible to conceive that the best interests arrangement for Katherine, in her own home, provided by an independent contractor, but devised and paid for by Rochdale and CCG, amounts to a deprivation of liberty within Article 5. If her family had money and had devised and paid for the very same arrangement this could not be a situation of deprivation of liberty. But because they are devised and paid for by organs of the state they are said so to be, and the whole panoply of authorisation and review required by Article 5 (and its explications) is brought into play. In my opinion this is arbitrary, arguably irrational, and a league away from the intentions of the framers of the Convention.'

7.33 In order to reach this conclusion, Mostyn J embarked upon his own analysis of the meaning of Article 5 and of the concept of liberty, holding that the first question he had to ask was what the concept of 'liberty' was for KW. In doing so he considered what J S Mill had to say on the subject. He considered it "inconceivable" that Mill would have found that the provision of care to KW in her own home involved an encroachment on her liberty and that he would have taken the same view of each the of three cases that were before the Supreme Court in *Cheshire West*.

---

[31] See www.supremecourt.uk/docs/speech-141031.pdf for the speech made by Lady Hale at the Lord Rodger Memorial Lecture on 31 October 2014.

7.34 Somewhat controversially, Mostyn J considered that 'freedom to leave' in the objective test of confinement did not mean 'wandering out of the front door' but leaving in the sense of permanently removing oneself to live where and with whom one likes.[32] Further, the conception of freedom relied upon by Mostyn J is fundamentally predicated upon a concept of liberty that is dependent upon a person's ability to exercise that right, either themselves or by another. He considered that a person who is severely physically disabled, and therefore house-bound, could not be considered to be deprived of their liberty. Such a conception is extremely difficult to square with the conclusion of Lady Hale (with whom Lord Kerr agreed) that liberty must mean the same for all, regardless of whether they are mentally or physically disabled.

7.35 The Court of Appeal allowed KW's appeal against Mostyn's decision by endorsing a consent order without a hearing. This led to a further decision by Mostyn J where he held that the Court of Appeal procedurally erred in permitting the appeal by consent without delivering a judgment as the question of whether or not KW was deprived of her liberty required judicial determination.[33] A further appeal was made to the Court of Appeal who disagreed with Mostyn J on the procedural issues and referred to the unfortunate history of this litigation, which had led to considerable unnecessary costs to the public purse, and that it was Mostyn J's 'tenacious adherence to his jurisprudential analysis leading to the conclusion that *Cheshire West* was wrongly decided that has been the root of this'. For this reason it was ordered that the review of KW's deprivation of liberty should be conducted by a different judge. It is therefore clear that Mostyn J's conclusions as to what 'freedom to leave' means now ought to be treated with an abundance of caution.

7.36 *W City Council v Mrs L*[34] is the second reported case that has sought to distance its factual circumstances from *Cheshire West*. It concerned Mrs L, a 93-year old lady with Alzheimer's dementia, and whether she was deprived of her liberty in her own home, where care and safety arrangements had been set up for her between her adult daughters and the Local Authority. Bodey J distinguished Mrs L's case from *Cheshire West* by finding that, while she was not free to leave her home, she was not under such continuous supervision and control as to mean that the arrangements in place constitute a deprivation of liberty. Further, even if she was deprived of her liberty, it was not imputable to the State. Bodey J held that, given the shared arrangement was set up by agreement with a caring and pro-active

---

[32] See paragraph 20, which relies upon the dicta of Munby J in *JE v DE and Surrey County Council* [2006] EWHC 3459 (Fam), [2007] 2 FLR 1150, at [115] per Munby J, which Mostyn J considered to have been 'implicitly approved' in the Supreme Court at paragraph 40. In the speech noted at **7.28** (footnote), Lady Hale, explaining the decision, noted that P, MIG and MEG 'were under the complete control of the people looking after them and were certainly not free to go, either for a short time or to go and live somewhere else' (emphasis added). It is therefore far from clear that Mosytn J's definition of freedom to leave is the same as that of the majority.
[33] Rochdale MBC v KW [2015] EWCOP 13.
[34] [2015] EWCOP 20.

family, the responsibility of the State is diluted by the strong role which the family has played and continues to play in caring for Mrs L.

7.37 There can be no doubt that one of the practical implications of the judgment of the Supreme Court is a significant increase in deprivation of liberty applications to the Court of Protection. In *Re X and Others (Deprivation of Liberty)* [2014] EWCOP 25, [2014] COPLR 674, the President of the Court of Protection devised a streamlined process to seek to enable the court to deal with deprivation of liberty cases in a timely, just, fair and ECHR-compatible way.[35] The streamlined process[36] is based on the following principles:

- Deprivation of liberty authorisations must be judicial and not administrative.
- There are circumstances in which an authorisation for the deprivation of someone's liberty can be determined on the papers, but there must still be an unimpeded right to request a speedy review.
- The 'triggers' for deciding whether an oral hearing is necessary include whether P is objecting to the deprivation of liberty, whether there is any dispute around the care arrangements and whether there is any dispute around whether the patient lacks capacity to decide where to live.
- Evidence in support of an application for a deprivation of liberty authorisation must include professional medical opinion but should be 'succinct and focussed' and the evidence and supporting material should not ordinarily exceed 50 pages.
- There is no requirement that P be joined as a party to deprivation of liberty proceedings. P should always be given the opportunity to be joined if he wishes and, whether joined as a party or not, must be given the support necessary to express views about the application and to participate in the proceedings to the extent that they wish.[37] Typically P will also need some form of representation, which should be professional though not necessarily always legal.

---

[35] Permission was sought by three of the parties to appeal certain aspects of this judgment, including the President's conclusion that P did not need to be a party in all cases. Judgment from the Court of Appeal was handed down on 16 June 2015: *Re X (Court of Protection Practice)* [2015] EWCA Civ 599 (see below).

[36] A new process came into effect on 17 November 2014 on a pilot basis to implement the judgments.

[37] The President used the analogy of wardship proceedings, where wards do not always have to be a party. Drawing on his conclusions in *RC v CC (By Her Litigation Friend the Official Solicitor) and X Local Authority* [2014] EWHC 131 (COP), [2014] COPLR 351, namely that the principles of disclosure in the family division also applied in the COP, and the essentially welfare-based nature of COP proceedings, he concluded that there is no distinction to be drawn between the need to join P in a COP case and the need to join a child who is a ward. Further, the President noted P's entitlement to the safeguards of Article 5(4) and the UNCRPD, and concluded that Article 6 requires that P be able to participate in the proceedings in such a way as to enable P to present his case 'properly and satisfactorily': see *Airey v Ireland* (Application No 6289/73) [1979] ECHR 6289/73, at [24].

- P can participate and be represented in proceedings in the Court of Protection without being a party and if P is participating other than as a party there is no need for a litigation friend. Therefore, P could be represented without one.
- If P is a party, then there is no reason in principle why the rules cannot be amended to allow P to act without a litigation friend.[38] However, at present rule 141(1) requires P, if a party, to have a litigation friend. The President indicated that this is a matter that requires consideration by the ad hoc Rules Committee convened to review the Court of Protection Rules
- A litigation friend does not need to act through a solicitor to conduct litigation, but requires the permission of the court to act as an advocate on behalf of P.[39]
- Reviews should be annually unless otherwise required. They must be judicial and may take place on the papers, whether or not there has been an earlier oral hearing, raising the possibility of a process where there is no hearing at all and where P would not have the benefit of legal aid which requires an oral hearing.
- 'Bulk' deprivation of liberty applications are unlawful. Each application must be individual so that it can be considered separately and on its own merits.

7.38 A new process came into effect on 17 November 2014 (on a pilot basis) to implement the streamlined procedure set out by the President of the Court of Protection in *Re X and Others (Deprivation of Liberty)* [2014] EWCOP 25, [2014] COPLR 674,[40] which seeks to enable the court to deal with deprivation of liberty cases in a timely, just, fair and ECHR-compatible way. This is founded on a new form,[41] which is accompanied by a new Practice Direction.[42] A model form of order has also been made available which will be made – on the papers – if all the necessary criteria are satisfied.[43]

---

[38] The President noted that the requirement to have a litigation friend is compliant with, but not mandated by, the ECHR: *RP and Others v UK (Application No 38245/08)* [2013] 1 FLR 744. The ECHR requirement is to ensure that P's interests are properly represented and that does not, of itself, require the appointment of a litigation friend.
[39] *Gregory v Turner* [2003] EWCA Civ 183.
[40] Her Majesty's Courts and Tribunal Service have indicated that they intend to review the process once it has been up and running for a while, and would be grateful for any feedback on how it works in practice. Comments can be emailed to the DoL Team: COPDOLS/S16@hmcts.gsi.gov.uk.
[41] COP DOL 10.
[42] Practice Direction A: Deprivation of Liberty Applications. Part 1 addresses the procedure to be followed in applications to the court for orders under s 21A of the Mental Capacity Act 2005 relating to a standard or urgent authorisation under Schedule A1 of that Act to deprive a person of his or her liberty; or proceedings (for example, relating to costs or appeals) connected with or consequent upon such applications. Part 2 addresses the procedure to be followed in applications under s 16(2)(a) of that Act to authorise deprivation of liberty under s 4A(3) and (4) pursuant to a streamlined procedure. Part 3 makes provision common to applications under both Parts 1 and 2.
[43] Broadly speaking, this will be the case where all the factors point to the situation being a 'state' deprivation of liberty that is incontrovertibly in P's best interests requiring authorisation because they are unable to give the requisite consent.

7.39 The future of this process is unclear following the judgment of the Court of Appeal in *Re X (Court of Protection Practice)* handed down on 16 June 2015 where all three members of the Court of Appeal decided that the President's rulings were, for technical reasons, a procedural nullity and therefore of no effect. They also expressed the obiter view that, in any event, the President had erred in finding that P did not need to be joined as a party in all cases involving a deprivation of liberty. On the contrary, each of the judges of the Court of Appeal considered (obiter) that P did need to be a party, with all the procedural consequences that flowed from this.

7.40 In an attempt to deal with the fall out following the Court of Appeal's decision in *Re X*, in *Re NRA & Ors*[44] Mr Justice Charles, the Vice President of the Family Division, reached the following key conclusions:

(1) The streamlined *Re X* procedure should be reintroduced, subject to a number of improvements aimed at drawing more information from social services authorities at the outset.
(2) Family members, in particular family members that have been devoted to caring for P for years, are generally to be trusted by the Court as capable of advocating for P's best interests.
(3) In the large number of cases in which there is every reason to trust the judgment of family members, P need not therefore be joined as a party to proceedings. To do so would add no value and would, on the contrary, cause some detriment.
(4) In practice it may be preferable for family members to be formally appointed as representatives under the new COPR 3A, because in that capacity the Court can exercise a degree of direction over them, they have a formal status, and there is an identified person who is responsible for ensuring future compliance.
(5) Where there was no suitable family member to consult, rather than falling back on joining P as a party, the Court should fill the deficit itself by taking on a more inquisitorial role, principally though the increased use of s.49 reports and witness summonses.

7.41 Charles J further held that the Court of Appeal in *Re X* had failed to properly appreciate that, first, joining P as a party in all cases was unworkable in practice and so did not provide the practical and effective procedural safeguard sought and, second, that welfare cases in the Court of Protection were to be distinguished from all other deprivation of liberty in important respects.[45] Finally, Charles J agreed that the current Re X forms direct the minds of their authors to the key issues and that they can provide all of the required information to demonstrate that the care package satisfies the determinative test and no more information is needed. However, at

---

[44] [2015] EWCOP 59.
[45] Firstly, the determinative issue in a welfare case is not whether P should be deprived of their liberty, but whether a particular arrangement is the least restrictive option in their best interests; secondly, as such arrangements are necessarily in P's best interests, they differ qualitatively from, for example, imprisonment following criminal conviction or detention under the Mental Health Act 1983; and thirdly, the issues in the Court of Protection are more investigatory than adversarial.

paragraphs 224–226 he recommended a number of improvements to the forms. It is presently unclear what procedures (and the timing of the necessary amendments to the DOL 10 form) are to be implemented by the Court of Protection to reflect the judgment of Charles J. Further, a judgment from Charles J is expected in the near future providing guidance in relation to what should happen when there is no one suitable to act as a Rule 3A representative among family members.

Court of Protection powers

7.42 Under MCA 2005, s 4A (inserted by MHA 2007, s 50) the Court of Protection has the power by making an order under MCA 2005, s 16(2)(a) to make the decision which has the effect of lawfully depriving a person of their liberty.[46] It cannot, however, do so if the patient is ineligible to be deprived of their liberty under that Act as amended by MHA 2007 because they are or should be detained under the Mental Health Act powers.[47] A person may lawfully deprive someone of their liberty whilst a decision is sought from the Court if there is a question about whether that person may be lawfully deprived of their liberty and the deprivation is necessary to enable life-sustaining treatment to be given or any treatment believed necessary to prevent a serious deterioration in their condition.[48]

7.43 Where the Court of Protection has been seised of a matter concerning the welfare of an individual,[49] the questions can sometimes arise: (1) as to whether that individual is deprived of their liberty; and (2) how such deprivation of liberty is to be authorised thereafter. As regards the first question, the Court will either have to endorse an agreed position that the person is or is not deprived of their liberty or, failing such agreement, determine[50] that issue. As regards the second question, the answer will depend upon whether the person is detained in hospital or care home (and hence they are within the scope of Schedule A1 to MCA 2005). If they are not, then it is suggested that the Court will have to retain the case on an ongoing basis so that it can oversee the regular reviews that are necessary to

---

[46] There is an interesting debate as to the precise effect of the decision, and whether such decision amounts to the giving of consent by the Court on the part of the person. This was largely an academic debate until recently, but may now assume more relevance in light of the possibility that 'substituted' consent could nullify what would otherwise be a deprivation of liberty (see **7.18** (footnote)). There is also an interesting, if largely academic, debate as to whether the Court can also authorise a deprivation of liberty by way of a declaration under s 15 of the MCA 2005. Given the wording of s 4A, it is suggested that the route of a decision under s 16(2)(a) is to be preferred.

[47] MCA 2005, s 16A, as inserted by MHA 2007, s 50(3); and see *W PCT v TB (an adult by her litigation friend the Official Solicitor)* [2009] EWHC 1737 (Fam), [2009] COPLR Con Vol 1193, *GJ v The Foundation Trust* [2009] EWHC 2972 (Fam), [2009] COPLR Con Vol 567 and *AM v South London & Maudsley NHS Foundation Trust & Secretary of State for Health* [2013] UKUT 0365 (AAC), [2013] COPLR 510. See also **7.55** below for a discussion of *An NHS Trust v Dr A* [2013] EWHC 2442 (COP), [2013] COPLR 605.

[48] MCA 2005, s 4B, as inserted by MHA 2007, s 50(2).

[49] Other than by way of an application under MCA 2005, 21A.

[50] The cases would suggest that such should be done by way of a declaration under s 15 MCA of the 2005, as occurred (for instance) in *P and Q* [2011] EWCA Civ 90, [2011] COPLR Con Vol 931.

satisfy the requirements of Article 5 of the ECHR.[51] If the person is within the scope of Schedule A1, then it is suggested that the appropriate course of action is for the Court to authorise (by way of a s 16(2)(a) decision) the deprivation of liberty for a limited period of time to enable the grant of a standard authorisation by the relevant supervisory authority.[52] The Court, it is suggested, should then relinquish its supervisory jurisdiction in favour of the regime established by Parliament.[53]

Deprivation of liberty in a hospital or care home

7.44 The managing authority of a hospital or care home is able lawfully to deprive a patient or resident of their liberty if they are detained for the purpose of being given care or treatment and a standard or urgent authorisation is in force which relates to the relevant person and to the hospital or care home in which they are detained. In this event the managing authority is put in the same position as if the resident had capacity to consent and had consented to their detention (no liability is incurred for the deprivation of liberty but there is no protection for any negligence).[54] The authorisation also extends to cover (1) any deprivation of liberty that occurs during transport of P to and from contact sessions;[55] and (2) the ability of the managing authority to return P to the establishment at which he resides upon any outing from there.[56] It is suggested that it cannot cover any deprivation of liberty which may occur during the course of P's initial journey to the hospital or care home mentioned in the authorisation (and hence a separate authorisation from the Court will be required[57]). The

---

[51] See in this regard *P and Q*, at [4]. The Court of Appeal, following *Salford City Council v GJ, NJ and BJ (by their litigation friends)* [2008] EWHC 1097 (Fam), [2008] 2 FLR 1295, considered that the review would be at least annual and would require independent representation of the detained person; Wilson LJ considered (paragraph 4) that such reviews could be on paper unless requested otherwise.

[52] But what then happens (as the author has experience of happening) if the best interests assessor determines that the person in question is not deprived of their liberty? It is suggested that, akin to the position that prevails in relation to the decisions of the First Tier Tribunal (Mental Health), namely that clinicians or other professionals involved in the care of an individual can only proceed in a way incompatible with that decision if they reasonably and in good faith consider that they have information, unknown to the Court, which put a significantly different complexion on the case: see *R (Von Brandenburg) v East London and City NHS Trust* [2003] UKHL 58. Otherwise, the proper course of action would be for the public authority to seek to appeal the determination of the Court that there is a deprivation of liberty.

[53] The proposition that if the DOLS regime applies, or would apply if there is a deprivation of liberty, it should be used in preference to authorisation and review by the Court has been endorsed by Charles J: *LBL v PB and P* [2011] EWHC 2675 (COP), [2012] COPLR 1 at paragraph 64(iii); see also *Re HA* [2012] EWHC 1068 (COP), [2012] COPLR 534 at paragraph 8, where he noted that the DOLS regime had 'checks and balances that generally should be preferred to review by the court'.

[54] MCA 2005, Sch A1, Part 1, inserted by MHA 2007, Sch 7.

[55] *DCC v KH* (2009) CoP Case No 11729380.

[56] Unreported decision of Mostyn J of June 2010 brought to the author's attention by the Official Solicitor's office.

[57] See paragraph 2.15 of the Deprivation of Liberty Safeguards Code of Practice, although it is not the author's experience that deprivations of liberty in the initial transport are necessarily as exceptional as the Code of Practice envisages. The judgment of Charles J in *GJ v The*

authorisation under these procedures does not extend to the treatment to which the patient cannot consent, to which MCA 2005, s 5 will continue to apply.

7.45 In *Hillingdon London Borough Council v Neary*[58] Peter Jackson J made it very clear that it is unlawful for a public authority to use the procedure provided for under Sch A1 to foreclose a genuine dispute about where it is in the incapacitated adult's best interests to reside. In setting out the purpose of authorisations under Sch A1, he commented as follows:

> 'Significant welfare issues that cannot be resolved by discussion should be placed before the Court of Protection, where decisions can be taken as a matter of urgency where necessary. The DOL scheme is an important safeguard against arbitrary detention. Where stringent conditions are met, it allows a managing authority to deprive a person of liberty at a particular place. It is not to be used by a local authority as a means of getting its own way on the question of whether it is in the person's best interests to be in the place at all. Using the DOL regime in that way turns the spirit of the Mental Capacity Act 2005 on its head, with a code designed to protect the liberty of vulnerable people being used instead as an instrument of confinement. In this case, far from being a safeguard, the way in which the DOL process was used masked the real deprivation of liberty, which was the refusal to allow Steven to go home.'[59]

7.46 In similar vein, in *LBL v PB and P*,[60] a decision handed down before that of the Supreme Court in *Cheshire West* (and therefore to be read subject to that decision), Charles J expressed the strong view that debates about whether circumstances amounted to a deprivation of liberty could all too easily lead to a loss of focus about the real question, namely whether the placement and care arrangements were in P's best interests and subjected him or her to the least possible restrictions. He expressed the view that in such circumstances, it would frequently be appropriate to put in place a standard authorisation on an essentially precautionary basis, ie by resolving any doubt as to whether there was a deprivation of liberty in favour of there being such a deprivation. Charles J reached a similar conclusion, albeit in a different context, in his subsequent decision in *AM v South London & Maudsley NHS Foundation Trust & Secretary of State for Health*,[61] in which he confirmed that the DOLS regime 'applies when there may be a deprivation of liberty in the sense that [the regime] applies when it appears that judged objectively there is a risk that cannot sensibly be ignored that the relevant circumstances amount to a deprivation of liberty.'[62]

Foundation Trust [2009] EWHC 2972 (Fam), [2009] COPLR Con Vol 567 supports the proposition that an authorisation cannot cover transport: see paragraph 75.
[58] [2011] EWHC 1377 (COP), [2011] COPLR Con Vol 632.
[59] At [33].
[60] [2011] EWHC 2675 (COP), [2012] COPLR 1.
[61] [2013] UKUT 365 (AAC) [2013] COPLR 510. See further **7.54** below.
[62] At [59].

The authorisation procedure

7.47 The authorisation procedure usually begins with a request by the managing authority (generally the managers of a hospital or care home where the person is, or may be, deprived of their liberty) to the supervisory body (see **7.61**). Before a standard authorisation can be obtained, the supervisory body arranges for assessments to be carried out to determine whether the following requirements are met in relation to the detained resident.[63]

The age requirement

7.48 The person must be 18 or over. Note in this regard that a parent cannot authorise restrictions upon the liberty of their child which amount to a deprivation of that child's liberty;[64] if such restrictions amount to a deprivation of liberty, authorisation must be obtained other than under the provisions of Schedule A1.

The mental health requirement

7.49 The person must be suffering from a mental disorder within the meaning of MHA 1983, as amended (which includes for these purposes a learning disability whether or not associated with abnormally aggressive or seriously irresponsible conduct). The importance in this context of ensuring that there is evidence of a mental disorder which is both current and given on the basis of objective medical expertise (and that such evidence is periodically reviewed) has recently been emphasised by the European Court of Human Rights in *KC v Poland*.[65]

The mental capacity requirement

7.50 The person must lack capacity in relation to the question whether or not they should be accommodated in the hospital or care home for the purpose of being given the care or treatment concerned. This question must be assessed in accordance with MCA 2005, ss 1–3, and the question is the same whether consideration is being given for purposes of an authorisation or a court order.[66]

---

[63] MCA 2005, Sch A1, Part 3; the DoLS forms applicable to the authorisation procedure were reviewed and published in 2015, and are available at http://www.adass.org.uk/mental-health-Drugs-and-Alcohol/key-documents/New-DoLS-Forms/
[64] *RK v BCC & Ors* [2011] EWCA Civ 1305, [2012] COPLR 146.
[65] [2014] ECHR 1322.
[66] *A Primary Care Trust v LDV* [2013] EWHC 272 (Fam), [2013] COPLR 204 at paragraph 29 per Baker J.

The best interests requirement

7.51 It must be in the person's best interests to be a detained resident and the deprivation of liberty must be necessary to prevent harm and be a proportionate response to the likelihood and seriousness of that harm. In this context, the European Court of Human Rights has emphasised that detention in a care home is 'such a serious measure that it is only justified where other, less severe measures have been considered to be insufficient to safeguard the individual or public interest which might require the person concerned be detained.'[67]

The eligibility requirement

7.52 A person is ineligible if already subject to MHA 1983 through being:
- detained in hospital under MHA 1983 powers or meeting the criteria for detention and objecting to being detained in the hospital or to some or all of the treatment (ie in those circumstances MHA 1983 powers should be used if the person is to be detained);[68]
- on leave of absence or subject to guardianship, a community treatment regime or conditional discharge and subject to a measure which would be inconsistent with an authorisation if granted; or
- on leave of absence or subject to a community treatment regime or conditional discharge and the authorisation if granted would be for deprivation of liberty in a hospital for the purpose of treatment for mental disorder.[69]

7.53 The presence of the eligibility requirement gives rise to the question of whether MHA 1983 is intended to have primacy over MCA 2005 (or vice versa). In *GJ v The Foundation Trust*[70], Charles J expressed the view that MHA 1983 had primacy over MCA 2005 in the following terms:[71]

> '45. In my judgment, the deeming provisions alone,[72] and together with that view on assessments, are strong pointers in favour of the conclusions that (1) the Mental Health Act 1983 is to have primacy when it applies, and (2) the medical practitioners referred to in sections 2 and 3 of the 1983 Act cannot pick and choose between the two statutory regimes as they think fit having regard to general considerations (eg the preservation or promotion of a therapeutic relationship with P) that they consider render one regime preferable to the other.'

---

[67] See *Stanev v Bulgaria* (2012) 55 EHRR 22, at [143]. See also *KC v Poland* [2014] ECHR 1322.

[68] This was considered by Roderic Wood J in *W PCT v TB (an adult by her litigation friend the Official Solicitor)* [2009] EWHC 1737 (Fam), [2009] COPLR Con Vol 1193 and by Charles J in *GJ v The Foundation Trust* [2009] EWHC 2972 (Fam), [2009] COPLR Con Vol 567 and *AM v South London & Maudsley NHS Foundation Trust & Secretary of State for Health* [2013] UKUT 365 (AAC), [2013] COPLR 510.

[69] The details of 'Persons ineligible' are set out in MCA 2005, Sch 1A, as inserted by MHA 2007, Sch 8. A person ineligible to be deprived of their liberty by virtue of the operation of Sch 1A cannot be deprived of their liberty by way of the procedure contained in Sch A1 or by way of a court order under s 16 (see s 16A(1)).

[70] [2009] EWHC 2972 (Fam), [2009] COPLR Con Vol 567.

[71] At [45].

[72] In MCA 2005, Sch 1A, paragraph 12.

7.54 However, in *A AM v South London & Maudsley NHS Foundation Trust & Secretary of State for Health*,[73] Charles J, sitting as the Chamber President of the Upper Tribunal (Administrative Appeals Chamber), revisited his earlier decision.[74] He confirmed[75] that (1) general propositions in respect of issues that arise concerning the interrelationship between MHA 1983 and MCA 2005 are 'dangerous;' and (2) his references to 'primacy' in his earlier decision were made in and should be confined to the position where the person was within the scope of MHA 1983. Whilst strictly of persuasive effect only before the Court of Protection,[76] it is suggested that that this decision, reached after full argument and by the judge in charge of the Court of Protection, should carry significant weight before that latter court.

7.55 The decision in *AM* is also of importance for the confirmation given by Charles J as to the approach that should be adopted by decision-makers responsible for determining whether a person who requires assessment or treatment as an in-patient in a psychiatric hospital in circumstances amounting to a deprivation of liberty should be detained under the provisions of MHA 1983 or whether the provisions of MCA 2005, Sch A1 should be used.[77] He set out three questions that such decision-makers need to ask:

(1) does the person have capacity to consent to admission as an informal patient?[78]
(2) might the hospital be able to rely upon the provisions of MCA 2005 lawfully to assess or treat the person (most importantly, would the person be compliant with the arrangements, as a non-compliant patient who is within the scope of MHA 1983 can only be detained under the provisions of that Act)?
(3) if there is a choice between reliance on MHA 1983 and MHA 2005, Sch A1, which is the least restrictive way of best achieving the proposed assessment or treatment?

Charles J emphasised[79] that the answer to the last of these questions of necessity requires the exercise of a value judgment and a consideration of all

---

[73] [2013] UKUT 365 (AAC), [2013] COPLR 510.
[74] In light of a decision of Upper Tribunal Judge Jacobs in *DN v Northumberland Tyne & Wear NHS Foundation Trust* [2011] UKUT 327 (AAC), and a letter provided by the Department of Health in that case setting out the policy intentions behind MCA 2005, Sch 1A.
[75] At [78].
[76] See, by analogy, *Secretary of State for Justice v RB* [2010] UKUT 454 (AAC). Weight was placed upon the decision in *Northamptonshire Healthcare NHS Foundation Trust and Others v ML and Others* [2014] EWCOP 2, although Hayden J then – rather curiously – held that MHA 1983 was 'magnetic north' in cases falling within Case E.
[77] Charles J's judgment encompassed situations other than those amounting to a deprivation of liberty, but for present purposes the discussion is limited to those which either do or are likely to amount to such a deprivation.
[78] As to which, see also *A Primary Care Trust v LDV* [2013] EWHC 272 (Fam) [2013] COPLR 204.
[79] At [72]–[74].

the circumstances, including the actual availability of the MCA 2005 regime and a comparison of its impact, if it were used, with the impact of detention under MHA 1983.

7.56 If further proof were needed that the DOLS provisions are unwieldy and capable of producing potentially absurd results, in *An NHS Trust v Dr A*[80] Baker J has recently identified a further lacuna in the statutory schemes provided for by MHA 1983 and MCA 2005. That lacuna arose where a person unable to make decisions about their medical needs and subject to detention under MHA 1983 is to be treated in a way outwith the treatment provided under that Act for his mental disorder and that treatment involves a deprivation of liberty. Such a person would be ineligible to be deprived of their liberty (whether by way of a standard authorisation or by way of a court order).[81] If the treatment could not properly be said to be treatment falling within the compulsory provisions of MHA 1983 s63, then the MHA 1983 would not afford a route to authorise the administration of such treatment and any ancillary deprivation of liberty:

> 'To take a stark example: if someone detained under section 3 is suffering from gangrene so as to require an amputation in his best interests and objects to that operation, so that it could only be carried by depriving him of his liberty, that process could not prima facie be carried out either under the MHA or under the MCA. This difficulty potentially opens a gap every bit as troublesome as that identified in the Bournewood case itself.'[82]

7.57 In the case before Baker J, it was clear (a) that the adult lacked the capacity to decide whether to consent to forcible feeding; (b) that such forcible feeding would involve a deprivation of their liberty; (c) that it was in the adult's best interests; but that (d) the forcible feeding could not be said to be medical treatment for the mental disorder from which he suffered so as to fall within the provisions of MCA s63. After an exhaustive analysis of the statutory provisions and the authorities, Baker J held that he could not read into the prohibition in MCA 2005 s16A(1) against welfare orders being made depriving ineligible adults of their liberty the words 'save where such provision is necessary to uphold the person's right to life under Article 2 of the European Convention on Human Rights,' but that he could authorise forcible feeding and the ancillary deprivation of liberty by way of the exercise of the inherent jurisdiction.[83] The inherent jurisdiction of the High Court is discussed further in Chapter 11.

7.58 Another potential lacuna that falls to be resolved is where the eligibility assessor considers that the adult is within scope of MHA 1983 (and therefore ineligible to be deprived of their liberty by way of MCA 2005), but where either the relevant doctors are not willing to make the statutory recommendations for admission under MHA 1983 or, as anecdotally appears not to be uncommon, the Approved Mental Health

---

[80] [2013] EWHC 2442 (COP), [2013] COPLR 605.
[81] Ie they would be within Case A of MCA 2005, Sch Al. See also **7.52** above.
[82] Paragraph 67.
[83] Paragraph 96.

Professional ('AMHP') is not willing to make the application for admission. If such a stand-off cannot be resolved, then it is suggested that steps be taken as a matter of some urgency to bring the matter to the court so that the deprivation of the person's liberty can be authorised.[84] It is further suggested that:

- the Court of Protection is the ultimate arbiter of whether a person is or is not eligible to be deprived of their liberty under MCA 2005;
- the Court of Protection cannot, however, dictate to either clinicians or AMHPs how they are to discharge their duties under MHA 1983, such that, especially if the bar to application is the unwillingness of an AMHP to make an application for admission, it may be necessary to consider whether that unwillingness amounts to a public law error capable of being challenged by way of judicial review proceedings;
- pending the resolution of the question of eligibility and the taking of appropriate steps to authorise the deprivation of liberty under either MHA 1983 or MCA 2005, and by way of analogy with *An NHS Trust v Dr A*, the High Court can properly authorise the deprivation of liberty by way of the exercise of the inherent jurisdiction if satisfied that (a) the individual in question suffers from a mental disorder; and (b) it is in their best interests to be deprived of their liberty for purposes of receiving care and treatment at the relevant facility. Appropriate mechanisms would need to be put in place so as to allow the court to review the deprivation of liberty.[85]

7.59 Finally in this regard, it should be noted that it is possible for an authorisation to be granted under Schedule A1 in respect of a person currently detained under MHA 1983 in anticipation of the person's discharge so that suitable arrangements are in place upon their arrival; in other words, merely because a person is, in fact, detained under MHA 1983 does not necessarily mean that they are therefore to be considered ineligible for a future authorisation under Schedule A1.[86]

The no refusals requirement

7.60 There must not be a valid and effective advance advance decision by the detained resident refusing the treatment in question, nor a valid refusal of the proposed care or treatment by a deputy or donee of a lasting power of attorney (LPA) within the scope of their authority.

---

[84] As happened in *A Primary Care Trust v LDV* [2013] EWHC 272 (Fam), [2013] COPLR 204, in which the matters considered in this paragraph fell for determination. Matters then evolved in such a way that the issue fell away, although it is clear that they will need to be determined sooner rather than later.

[85] *An NHS Trust v Dr A* at paragraph 94, citing Munby J (as he then was) in *Re BJ (Incapacitated Adult)* [2009] EWHC 3310 (Fam), [2010] 1 FLR 1373.

[86] *DN v Northumberland Tyne & Wear NHS Foundation Trust* [2011] UKUT 327 (AAC). In this regard, note also that Paragraph 12(3) of Schedule 1A directs the attention of the decision-maker to the circumstances which are expected to apply at the time the authorisation is expected to come into effect.

STANDARD AUTHORISATIONS

7.61 A standard authorisation is an authorisation given by the supervisory body after it has been requested to do so and once the procedure set out below has been followed.[87] With effect from 1 April 2013, and as a result of amendments made by the Health and Social Care Act 2012 to reflect the abolition of Primary Care Trusts in England and Wales,[88] the supervisory body is:

- in the case of a care home in England or Wales, the local authority where the person is ordinarily resident or where the care home is situated; or
- in the case of a hospital in England, the local authority for the area in which the person is ordinary resident;
- in the case of a hospital in Wales, the National Assembly for Wales or the local health board if the care is commissioned by it (this also applies if the hospital is in England but the care is commissioned by the National Assembly for Wales or a local health board);
- in the case of a hospital in England where the person is not ordinarily resident in England or Wales or their ordinary residence cannot be determined, the local authority for the area where the hospital is situated.

The Department of Health afforded limited additional funding to local authorities to support them in the extension of their statutory role, emphasising in so doing that:

'... [h]ospitals will remain responsible as managing authorities for compliance with the DOLS legislation, for understanding DOLS and knowing when and how to make referrals. Hospitals remain responsible for ensuring that all staff in hospitals are Mental Capacity Act (MCA) compliant. Clinical Commissioning Groups (CCGs) will oversee these responsibilities; and be responsible for training and MCA compliance. All CCGs must have a named MCA lead and MCA policies to support their responsibilities.'[89]

7.62 The managing authority must request a standard authorisation if it is accommodating a detained resident who appears to meet all the qualifying requirements or is likely to do so within the next 28 days or if it will be so accommodating or detaining the person up to 28 days in advance of its doing so. In *AM v South London & Maudsley NHS Foundation Trust & Secretary of State for Health*,[90] Charles J considered the meaning of the

---

[87] See generally MCA 2005, Sch A1, Part 4. Provisions relating to the suspension of a standard authorisation are in Part 6, a change in supervisory responsibility in Part 7, review in Part 8 and generally relating to assessments in Part 9. Part 10 provides for the relevant person's representative and Part 11 for the role of independent mental capacity advocates.

[88] The material amendments being contained in the Health and Social Care Act 2012, Sch 5, paragraph 136(3).

[89] See www.dh.gov.uk/health/files/2012/09/Deprivation-of-Liberty-Safeguards_Funding-Fact-Sheet-for-2013-14.pdf, page 4.

[90] [2013] UKUT 365 (AAC) [2013] COPLR 510. See also *AJ (Deprivation of Liberty Safeguards) v A Local Authority* [2015] EWCOP 5, [2015] COPLR 167 (Baker J) where it was emphasised at [113] that 'the scheme of the DOLS is that, in the vast majority of cases, it should be possible to plan in advance so that a standard authorisation can be obtained

phrase 'likely – at some time within the next 28 days – to be a detained resident' in Sch 1A, para 24(2) and (3), and agreed with the Secretary of State's submission that 'the DOLS regime applies when there may be a deprivation of liberty in the sense that [the regime] applies when it appears that judged objectively there is a risk that cannot sensibly be ignored that the relevant circumstances amount to a deprivation of liberty.' The relevant managing authority must also make a request if there is, or is to be, a change in the place of detention.

7.63 An authorisation cannot be given unless assessments have been commissioned by the supervisory body which conclude that all the qualifying requirements are met. Regulations[91] specify who can carry out assessments, covering the need for more than one assessor, the professional skills, training and competence required and independence from decisions about providing or commissioning care to the person concerned and the timeframe within which the assessments must be completed. The mental health and best interests assessments must be carried out by different assessors. It is the responsibility of the supervisory body to appoint eligible and suitable assessors. Anyone carrying out assessments (other than the age assessment) must have undergone specific training.

7.64 The best interests assessor must first decide whether a deprivation of liberty is occurring or is likely to occur. The assessment must take account of any relevant needs assessment or care plan, and of the opinion of the mental health assessor on the impact of the proposed course of action on the person's mental health. The assessor must consult the managing authority and take into account the views of anyone named by the person, anyone engaged in caring for the person or interested in their welfare, any donee of a LPA granted by the person or deputy appointed by the Court. If the person does not have anyone to speak for them who is not paid to provide care an independent mental capacity advocate (IMCA) must be appointed to support and represent them during the assessment process.

7.65 In determining whether a deprivation of liberty is justified as being in the person's best interests, it is suggested that the best interests assessor is carrying out a public law function and their decision would be open to challenge upon standard public law principles. By way of example, in *Re MB*[92], a best interests assessor had concluded that the best interests requirement was not met in the case of an elderly lady in a residential home, even though there was no practical alternative accommodation for her to go

---

before the deprivation of liberty begins. It is only in exceptional cases, where the need for the deprivation of liberty is so urgent that it is in the best interests of the person for it to begin while the application is being considered, that a standard authorisation need not be sought before the deprivation begins.' See also **7.54–7.55** above.

[91] The Mental Capacity (Deprivation of Liberty: Standard Authorisations, Assessments and Ordinary Residence) Regulations 2008, SI 2008/1858, as amended by SI 2009/827.

[92] [2010] EWHC 2508 (COP), [2010] COPLR Con Vol 65.

to. Charles J found, however, that the assessor's reasoning was flawed because she did not compare and contrast viable and practically available alternative placements.

7.66 The best interests assessor is required to record the name and address of every interested person consulted (as they will be entitled to information about the outcome). If that assessor concludes that deprivation of liberty is not in the person's best interests but becomes aware that they are already being deprived of their liberty, the assessor must draw this to the attention of the supervisory body. If the assessment recommends authorisation the assessor must state the maximum authorisation period, which may not be for more than a year.[93] The assessor may also recommend conditions to be attached to the authorisation. Whilst not expressly stated in Sch A1, it would appear that the only conditions which can be imposed are those over the implementation of which the relevant managing authority has a degree of control.[94] The best interests assessor must also identify someone to recommend for appointment as representative of the person being deprived of their liberty.

7.67 If existing equivalent assessments have been carried out within the past year they may be used if the supervisory body is satisfied there is no reason that they may no longer be accurate.[95] If any of the assessments conclude that the person does not meet the criteria the supervisory body must turn down the request for authorisation and inform all persons with an interest. If all the assessments recommend it, the supervisory body must give the authorisation and:

- set the period of the authorisation, which may not be longer than the maximum period identified in the best interests assessment;
- issue the authorisation in writing, stating the period for which it is valid, the purpose for which it is given and the reason why each qualifying requirement is met;
- if appropriate, attach conditions;

---

[93] The period starting either at the exact time on the day when it was granted or on any later time specified in the document giving the authorisation: *Re MB* [2010] EWHC 2508 (COP), [2010] COPLR Con Vol 65, at [45]. The maximum period that can be included in the authorisation should be calculated by including the whole of the day on which the authorisation is given (or expressed to start) and on the basis that it ends at the end of the last day: paragraph 47.

[94] This flows from the wording of Sch A1, paragraph 53(3), which has the effect that conditions cannot be imposed which are directed solely against third parties (for instance, by way of providing that other statutory bodies should undertake assessments). In practice, this can significantly limit the utility of conditions, although where a supervisory body takes the view that a deprivation of liberty can only be authorised subject to a condition falling outside the scope of paragraph 53, such is a clear indication that the supervisory body should be taking appropriate steps to obtain an authorisation from the Court of Protection by way of an order under MCA, s 17.

[95] It is suggested that particular caution must be exercised to ensure that the mental health assessment is subject to periodic review in light of the decision of the European Court of Human Rights in *Kędzior v Poland* (Application No 45026/07) [2012] ECHR 1809 and the emphasis placed by the Court in the decision upon the importance of there being evidence of a mental disorder which is both current and given on the basis of objective medical expertise. See also in this regard *KC v Poland* [2014] ECHR 1322.

- appoint someone to act as the person's representative during the term of the authorisation;
- provide a copy of the authorisation to the managing authority, the person being deprived of their liberty and their representative, any IMCA who has been involved and any other interested person consulted by the best interests assessor (in due course notifying them when the authorisation ceases to be in force); and
- keep written records.

7.68 In *LB Hillingdon v Neary & Ors*[96] Peter Jackson J emphasised the importance of the role of the supervisory authority thus:

> 'The granting of DOL standard authorisations is a matter for the local authority in its role as a supervisory body. The responsibilities of a supervisory body, correctly understood, require it to scrutinise the assessment it receives with independence and a degree of care that is appropriate to the seriousness of the decision and to the circumstances of the individual case that are or should be known to it. Where, as here, a supervisory body grants authorisations on the basis of perfunctory scrutiny of superficial best interests assessments, it cannot expect the authorisations to be legally valid.'[97]

Expanding upon this later in his judgment, Peter Jackson J held as follows:

> '174. Although the framework of the Act requires the supervising body to commission a number of paper assessments before granting a standard authorisation, the best interests assessment is anything but a routine piece of paperwork. Properly viewed, it should be seen as a cornerstone of the protection that the DOL safeguards offer to people facing deprivation of liberty if they are to be effective as safeguards at all.
> 175. The corollary of this, in my view, is that the supervisory body that receives the best interests assessment must actively supervise the process by scrutinising the assessment with independence and with a degree of care that is appropriate to the seriousness of the decision and the circumstances of the individual case that are or should be known to it.
> 177. Paragraph 50 provides that a supervisory body must give a standard authorisation if all assessments are positive. This obligation must be read in the light of the overall scheme of the schedule, which cannot be to require the supervisory body to grant an authorisation where it is not or should not be satisfied that the best interests assessment is a thorough piece of work that adequately analyses the four necessary conditions.
> 177. In support, I refer to the fact that the supervisory body has control over the terms of the authorisation in relation to its length and any conditions that should be attached. It does not have to follow the recommendations of the best interests assessor on those issues. It would not be possible for the supervisory body to make decisions of this kind rationally without having a sufficient knowledge base about the circumstances of the person affected. In all cases, it is open to the supervisory body to go back to the best interests assessor for discussion or for further enquiries to be made.'

7.69 If the supervisory body knows or ought to know that a best interests assessment is inadequate, it is not obliged to follow the recommendation.

---

[96] [2011] EWHC 1377 (COP), [2011] COPLR Con Vol 677.
[97] At [3].

'On the contrary it is obliged to take all necessary steps to remedy the inadequacy, and if necessary bring the deprivation of liberty to an end, including by conducting a review under Part 8 or by applying to the court.'[98]

7.70 If an authorisation is granted the supervisory body must appoint a person to be the detained resident's representative,[99] this being someone who the supervisory body considers will maintain contact with the resident and support and represent them in relation to the authorisation, including requesting review or appealing to the Court of Protection on their behalf. The representative has a right of access to the Court (any person other than the detained resident would require the permission of the Court to bring a case).[100] The managing authority in acting on the authorisation must:

- ensure that any conditions are complied with;
- take all practicable steps to ensure that the detained resident understands the effect of the authorisation, their right of appeal to the Court of Protection and their right to request a review;
- give the same information to the person's representative; and
- keep the person's case under consideration and request a review if necessary.

7.71 The supervisory body may review a standard authorisation at any time and must do so if requested by the detained resident, their representative or the managing authority. The managing authority must request a review if it appears that there has been a change in the person's circumstances. The relevant person or their representative may make a request at any time. The supervisory body must decide whether any of the qualifying requirements appear to be reviewable and, if so, commission review assessments. A review may lead to the authorisation being terminated, a change in the recorded reasons or a change in the conditions attached to the authorisation. When the review is complete the supervisory body must inform the managing authority, the relevant person and their representative of the outcome.

7.72 A managing authority may apply for a further authorisation to begin when an authorisation expires. In this event, the full assessment process is repeated.

Urgent authorisations

7.73 Urgent authorisations[101] may be given by the managing authority of a care home or hospital to provide a lawful basis for a deprivation of liberty

---

[98] Ibid, at [80].
[99] See the Mental Capacity (Deprivation of Liberty: Appointment of Relevant Person's Representative) Regulations 2008 (SI 2008/1315), as amended by SI 2008/2368.
[100] In *AB v LCC (A Local Authority) and the Care Manager of BCH* [2011] EWHC 3151 (COP), [2012] COPLR 314, Mostyn J reviewed the role of the RPR in bringing proceedings to the Court of Protection, and emphasised that, prima facie, there is no reason why an RPR cannot act as litigation friend for P in proceedings under MCA 2005, s 21A.
[101] MCA 2005, Sch A1, Part 5.

whilst a standard authorisation is being obtained when it is urgently required and the qualifying requirements appear to be met. The managing authority must record the urgent authorisation in writing, giving its reasons for giving the authorisation. The managing authority is to take all practicable steps (verbally and in writing) to ensure the person understands the effect of the authorisation and their right of appeal to the Court of Protection and to notify any IMCA who has been involved.

7.74 An urgent authorisation takes effect at the exact time that it was given on a particular day.[102] It can only last for a maximum of 7 days,[103] unless extended for up to a further 7 days by the supervisory body if there are exceptional reasons why it has not been possible to decide on a request for standard authorisation and it is essential that the detention continues. Absent such exceptional circumstances, an urgent authorisation can only be extended by a standard authorisation or a court order. In any event, it is only possible for one urgent authorisation to be given in respect of any one period of deprivation of liberty.[104]

The Standard Authorisations, Assessments and Ordinary Residence Regulations

7.75 The Mental Capacity (Deprivation of Liberty: Standard Authorisations, Assessments and Ordinary Residence) Regulations 2008[105] fill out the detail of obtaining standard authorisations and who the assessors are to be.

7.76 The eligibility requirements for people who are to carry out the assessments are that:

- all assessors are adequately insured[106] and the supervisory body (primary care trust or local authority) is satisfied that they have suitable skills and have undergone a Criminal Record Bureau check (reg 3);
- mental health assessments can only be carried out by medical practitioners who have been approved under MHA 1983, s 12[107] or

---

[102] *Re MB* [2010] EWHC 2508 (COP), [2010] COPLR Con Vol 65, at [35].
[103] Calculated by including the whole of the day upon which the authorisation was granted. The maximum period for which the authorisation can run extends to the end of the relevant day upon which the authorisation expires: *Re MB*, at [43]. The same goes for the calculation of any extended period: at [41].
[104] Ibid at [59]–[77], construing paragraph 77 of Sch A1. Charles J also indicated that, where the best interests assessor upon an application for a standard authorisation following an urgent authorisation reaches the view that the best interests requirement was no longer met, it could in some circumstances nonetheless still be in the person's best interests for them to be subject to a short further period of deprivation of liberty pending changes to arrangements and/or the assistance of the Court. Such a period could only be authorised by the grant of a standard authorisation, rather than the grant of a second urgent authorisation.
[105] SI 2008/1858, as subsequently amended.
[106] This has been amended by SI 2009/827 to include assessors covered by an indemnity arrangement.
[107] Medical practitioners eligible to recommend the admission of a patient to hospital under MHA 1983.

are registered medical practitioners who have at least 3 years' post-registration experience in the diagnosis or treatment of mental disorder and have completed the relevant training[108] (reg 4);
- best interests assessments can only be carried out by mental health practitioners approved under MHA 1983, s 114(1)[109] or certain health practitioners (nurses, occupational therapists or psychologists) with the relevant skills and specialism, or social workers, all of whom must have had at least 2 years' post-registration experience, and have completed the required training (reg 5);
- mental capacity assessments can only be carried out by people who are eligible to carry out a mental health or best interests assessment (reg 6);
- eligibility assessments can only be carried out by medical practitioners approved under MHA 1983, s 12 and eligible to carry out a mental health assessment or an approved mental health professional eligible to carry out a best interests assessment (reg 7); and
- age assessments and no refusals assessments can only be carried out by people who are eligible to carry out a best interests assessment (regs 8 and 9)).

7.77 The Regulations provide some limitations on who a supervisory body may select as assessors (even if otherwise eligible) by preventing the selection of:
- a person who is a relative of the relevant person or a person or relative of someone who has a financial interest in that person's care (regs 10 and 11); and
- a person to carry out a best interests assessment who is involved in the care of the person to be assessed or who is employed by the supervisory body where the managing authority and supervisory body are the same (reg 12).

7.78 All assessments for a standard authorisation are to be completed within 21 days or where an urgent authorisation is in force during the period of that authorisation (reg 13) and assessments to decide whether or not there is an unauthorised deprivation of liberty within 7 days (reg 14). When the eligibility and best interests assessors are not the same person the former may require the latter to provide any relevant information as to eligibility they have (reg 15).

7.79 Regulation 16 specifies the information to be provided in a request for a standard authorisation (the text of this regulation is reproduced in Part IV of this book). The Regulations also provide the mechanism for resolving a

---

[108] A Mental Health Assessors training programme made available by the Royal College of Psychiatrists.
[109] Approved mental health professionals appointed under MHA 1983 by a local social services authority.

dispute over which local authority is the supervisory body where there is a question as to the relevant person's ordinary residence).[110]

The Appointment of Relevant Person's Representative Regulations

7.80 MCA 2005, Sch A1, para 139 requires that the supervisory body appoints a representative, selected for that purpose, to represent a person in respect of whom a standard authorisation has been issued. That representative is to maintain contact and to support and represent the person in matters relating to their deprivation of liberty. The Mental Capacity (Deprivation of Liberty: Appointment of Relevant Person's Representative) Regulations 2008[111] provide for the selection and appointment of representatives by:

- detailing the eligibility requirements for appointment as a representative (reg 3);
- enabling the best interests assessor to determine whether the relevant person has capacity to select a person to be their representative (reg 4);
- enabling the relevant person to select a family member, friend or carer to be their representative where they have capacity to make that decision (reg 5);
- enabling a donee of a LPA (granting welfare powers) or a deputy appointed by the Court of Protection to select themselves or a family member, friend or carer to be the representative where the scope of their authority permits it (reg 6);
- requiring the best interests assessor to confirm the eligibility of the person selected by the relevant person or donee or deputy, and if so to recommend that appointment but if not to invite a further selection (reg 7);
- where no selection has been made by the relevant person, donee or deputy, enabling the best interests assessor to select a relevant person's family member, friend or carer (reg 8);
- enabling the supervisory body to select and pay for a person in a professional capacity to be a representative (regs 9 and 15); and
- requiring that the process of appointing a representative begins as soon as a best interests assessor is selected upon a request for a standard authorisation or as soon as an existing representative's appointment is about to terminate (reg 10).

7.81 The formalities of appointment and termination of appointment of a representative are detailed in regulations 12–14.

---

[110] MCA 2005, Sch A1, paragraph 182(2).
[111] SI 2008/1315, as amended by SI 2008/2368; for a fuller discussion on the interpretation of these regulations see *AJ (Deprivation of Liberty Safeguards)* [2015] EWCOP 5, [2015] COPLR 167 (Baker J) at [52]–[91].

REVIEW BY THE COURT OF PROTECTION

7.82 A person who has been deprived of their liberty or their representative may apply to the Court of Protection for a review of the lawfulness of their detention.[112] Where a standard authorisation has been given, the Court of Protection may determine any question relating to:

(1) whether the person meets any of the qualifying requirements;
(2) the period for which the standard authorisation is to be in force;
(3) the purpose for which it has been given; or
(4) the conditions subject to which it has been given,

and may make an order terminating or varying the authorisation, or requiring the supervisory body to do so. A new process came into effect on 17 November 2014 on a pilot basis to implement the streamlined process set out by the President of the Court of Protection in *Re X and Others (Deprivation of Liberty)* [2014] EWCOP 25, [2014] COPLR 674. However, the future of this process is uncertain following the Court of Appeal's judgment in *Re X* (see **7.39**).

7.83 Where an urgent authorisation has been given, the Court may determine:

(1) whether the urgent authorisation should have been given;
(2) the period during which the urgent authorisation is to be in force; or
(3) the purpose for which it is given,

and may make an order terminating or varying the authorisation, or requiring the managing authority to do so.

7.84 Once an application is made to the Court under MCA 2005, s 21A, the Court's powers are not confined simply to determining that question. Once its jurisdiction is invoked, the court has a discretionary power under MCA 2005, s 15 to make declarations as to (a) whether a person has or lacks capacity to make a decision specified in the declaration; (b) whether a person has or lacks capacity to make decisions on such matters as are described in the declaration, and (c) the lawfulness or otherwise of any act done, or yet to be done, in relation to that person. Where P lacks capacity, the court has wide powers under MCA 2005, s 16 to make decisions on P's behalf in relation to matters concerning his personal welfare or property or affairs.[113]

---

[112] MCA 2005, s 21A, as inserted by MHA 2007, Sch 8, paragraph 2. See also Court of Protection (Amendment) Rules 2009 (SI 2009/582) which inserted Part 10A to the Court of Protection Rules 2007. In *AB v LCC (A Local Authority) and the Care Manager of BCH* [2011] EWHC 3151 (COP), [2012] COPLR 314, Mostyn J reviewed the role of the RPR in bringing proceedings to the Court of Protection, and emphasised that, prima facie, there is no reason why an RPR cannot act as litigation friend for P in proceedings under MCA 2005, s 21A. An RPR may therefore bring a case as an applicant in his own name, or as litigation friend for P. This is consistent with the findings of the President of the Court of Protection in *Re X and Others (Deprivation of Liberty)*.

[113] See *CC v KK and STCC* [2012] EWHC 2136 (COP), [2012] COPLR 627, at [16] per Baker J.

7.85 In *Re UF*,[114] Charles J expressed the view that, where an application is made under MCA 2005, s 21A, the Court can either: (1) take control of the matter itself and grant interim relief and authorisations under MCA 2005, ss 15–16; or (2) reach effectively the same result under s 21A, by continuing in force the relevant authorisation, or otherwise bringing about the result that a standard authorisation is in existence.[115] Charles J held that the Court has the power 'to vary an existing standard authorisation by extending (or shortening) it and that if and when it exercises that power it would normally be sensible for the court to give consideration to whether it should then exercise its powers under subsections (6) and (7) or give directions concerning its future exercise of those powers,' but doubted that the Court would have the power to extend a standard authorisation beyond the possible maximum period of one year. In the judgment he also recorded[116] concessions by the Ministry of Justice and the Legal Aid Agency that, despite the wording of Regulation 5(1)(g) of the Civil Legal Aid (Financial Resources and Payment for Services) Regulations 2013 to apparently contrary effect, the 'taking control' by the Court of the authorisation of a deprivation of liberty by the making of orders under MCA 2005, s 16 and the consequent coming to an end of any existing standard authorisation would not be regarded as a contrivance giving rise to the removal of non-means-tested public funding.

7.86 In approaching questions relating to the deprivation of P's liberty (including as to whether P is deprived of his liberty at all), it would appear that the Court of Protection is engaged in an inquisitorial process, such that questions of burdens of proof do not arise.[117] When making orders under MCA 2005, s 21A, the Court may also consider a person's liability for any act done in connection with the standard or urgent authorisation before its variation or termination, including making an order excluding a person from liability.

MONITORING

7.87 The operation of these provisions is monitored and is reported on by the Care Quality Commission.[118] To this end, both hospitals and care homes must notify the Commission about any application to deprive a person of their liberty and about the outcome of that application.[119] The Commission has now published five reports, the most recent covering the period 2013–14.[120]

---

[114] [2013] EWHC 4289 (COP), [2014] COPLR 93.
[115] Ibid, at [33].
[116] Ibid, at [32].
[117] See *Cheshire West and Chester Council v P* [2011] EWHC 1330 (Fam), [2011] COPLR Con Vol 273, at [45] per Baker J.
[118] See the Mental Capacity (Deprivation of Liberty: Monitoring and Reporting; and Assessments – Amendment) Regulations 2009 (SI 2009/827).
[119] Regulations 18(1) and (4A) of the Care Quality Commission (Registration) Regulations 2009 (SI 2009/3112). This obligation applies both to an application for a standard authorisation and for an application to the Court of Protection for an order under MCA 2005, s 16(2)(a).
[120] Available at: www.cqc.org.uk/content/deprivation-liberty-safeguards-201314

STATISTICS

7.88 Prior to the decision of the Supreme Court in *Cheshire West*, the rate of increase in applications has started to slow: 11,890 were made in the year to 31 March 2013 as opposed to 11,380 for the year to 30 June 2012.[121] More than half of applications completed in 2012/3 resulted in an authorisation being granted,[122] continuing a trend from previous years that remains well above the Department of Health's expectation that less than a quarter of applications would result in an authorisation being granted.[123]

7.89 However, this landscape is subject to significant change: during the first full year since the decision in *Cheshire West* There were 137,540 DoLS applications received by councils, the most since the safeguards were introduced in 2009. This is a tenfold increase from 2013–14.[124] There were 52,125 granted applications in 2014-15, 83% of all completed applications. This the highest percentage granted since the deprivation of liberty safeguards were introduced.[125]

7.90 The effect of the acid test identified by the Supreme Court in *Cheshire West* is that many 'ordinary' placements may amount to a deprivation of liberty. This has far-reaching implications. According to the Alzheimer's Society,[126] there are 200,000 people with dementia in care homes in England and Wales. In addition, between 2012 and 2013 there were over 28,000 people aged 18–64 with learning disability in care and nursing homes. It would seem that all of those unable to give valid consent are now likely to be deprived, necessitating a deprivation of liberty authorisation. The impact also extends to hospitals, supported living and shared lives schemes. All disabled and vulnerable adults lacking the relevant capacity who receive care or support funded by, or arranged by, a public body may now need to be reviewed to see if the acid test satisfied. Further, foster carers, children in local authority care, and family members receiving support from health or social services may now be acting unlawfully unless the procedural and substantive safeguards in Article 5 are met. Only time

---

[121] Health and Social Care Information Centre: Mental Capacity Act 2005, Deprivation of Liberty Safeguards Assessments, England: 2012–13, Annual report, available at www.hscic.gov.uk/article/3401/Mental-Health-Use-of-Deprivation-of-Liberty-Safeguards-continues-to-rise.

[122] Ibid, showing that 55 per cent of applications resulted in an authorisation being granted; where an application was not granted, this was in 80 per cent of cases because the supervisory body considered that the best interests requirement had not been met.

[123] See https://catalogue.ic.nhs.uk/publications/mental-health/legislation/m-c-a-2005-dep-lib-saf-ass-eng-2011-12/m-c-a-2005-dep-lib-saf-ass-eng-2011-12-rep.pdf at pp.4 and 9, citing the Department of Health's Impact Assessment of the Mental Capacity Act 2005 Deprivation of Liberty Safeguards to accompany the Code of Practice and regulations, now available at webarchive.nationalarchives.gov.uk/20130107105354/http://www.dh.gov.uk/en/Publicationsandstatistics/Publications/PublicationsLegislation/DH_084982. That impact assessment also predicted that applications would fall at a constant rate between 2009/10 and 2015/16.

[124] Health and Social Care Information Centre: Mental Capacity Act (2005) Deprivation of Liberty Safeguards (England) Annual Report 2014-15 http://www.hscic.gov.uk/catalogue/PUB18577/dols-eng-1415-rep.pdf

[125] Between 2010 and 2014 between 55% and 60% of applications were granted.

[126] See www.alzheimers.org.uk.

will tell how the statistics will pan out post *Cheshire West* and whether the recent streamlined process implemented by the Court of Protection will be effective in managing the significantly increased workload.

COMMENT

7.91 There is rising groundswell of opinion that the deprivation of liberty safeguards have not achieved the (laudable) aims for which they were introduced. In its post-legislative scrutiny of MHA 2007 published in August 2013,[127] the House of Commons Health Select Committee considered the deprivation of liberty safeguards, and found them profoundly wanting. Evidence was received from (inter alia) the Department of Health, the Care Quality Commission and the Mental Health Alliance, and the Committee concluded thus:

> '106. The Committee found the evidence it received about the effective application of deprivation of liberty safeguards (DOLS) for people suffering from mental incapacity profoundly depressing and complacent. The Department itself described the variation as "extreme". People who suffer from lack of mental capacity are among the most vulnerable members of society and they are entitled to expect that their rights are properly and effectively protected. The fact is that despite fine words in legislation they are currently widely exposed to abuse because the controls which are supposed to protect them are woefully inadequate.
>
> 107. Against this background, the Committee recommends that the Department should initiate an urgent review of the implementation of DOLS for people suffering from mental incapacity and calls for this review to be presented to Parliament, within twelve months, together with an action plan to deliver early improvement.'

7.92 The House of Lords Select Committee appointed to consider and report upon MCA 2005 took extensive oral evidence upon the operation of the DOLS safeguards,[128] the tenor of which was largely to the effect that the safeguards were complex and unwieldy and of questionable effectiveness in discharging the purpose for which they were enacted. In its final report,[129] the Select Committee pulled no punches:

> 'The intention behind the safeguards – to provide protection in law for individuals who were being deprived of their liberty for reasons of their own safety – was understood and supported by our witnesses. But the legislative provisions and their operation in practice are the subject of extensive and wideranging criticism. The provisions are poorly drafted, overly complex and bear no relationship to the language and ethos of the Mental Capacity Act. The safeguards are not well understood and are poorly implemented. Evidence suggested that thousands, if not tens of thousands, of individuals are being deprived of their liberty without the protection of the law, and therefore without the safeguards which Parliament intended. Worse still, far from being used to protect individuals and their rights, they are sometimes used to oppress individuals, and to force upon them decisions made by others without reference to the wishes and feelings of the person concerned.
>
> The only appropriate recommendation in the face of such criticism is to start again. We therefore recommend a comprehensive review of the Deprivation of

---

[127] See www.publications.parliament.uk/pa/cm201314/cmselect/cmhealth/584/584.pdf.
[128] See www.parliament.uk/business/committees/committees-a-z/lords-select/mental-capacity-act-2005.
[129] See www.publications.parliament.uk/pa/ld201314/ldselect/ldmentalcap/139/139.pdf.

Liberty Safeguards with a view to replacing them with provisions that are compatible in style and ethos to the rest of the Mental Capacity Act.'[130]

7.93 No immediate legislative change is forthcoming. However, on 7 July 2015 the Law Commission's consultation paper on deprivation of liberty was published.[131] The consultation paper considers how the law should regulate deprivations of liberty and proposes that the deprivation of liberty safeguards should be replaced by a new system called "protective care". It also proposes that there should be a new code of practice, and that the existing MCA 2005 Code of Practice should also be reviewed.

7.94 The Law Commission's consultation paper highlights the main problems of the deprivation of liberty safeguards as follows:

- The concept of deprivation of liberty is poorly understood and the safeguards fail to take sufficient account of the person's article 8 rights to family life.
- The safeguards are seen as incompatible with the style and empowering ethos of the MCA 2005.
- Tensions arise between local authority commissioning and safeguarding functions, and their role as supervisory body under the safeguards.
- The safeguards apply only to hospitals and care homes, and not to other care settings such as supported living and shared lives accommodation.
- The safeguards impose a single approach irrespective of setting. Thus, deprivations of liberty in an intensive care hospital ward are dealt with in the same way administratively as they would in a long-stay care home.
- There is a lack of oversight and effective safeguards.
- The statutory provisions are seen as tortuous, complex, extensive and overly bureaucratic.
- The safeguards use Ill-suited and inadequate terminology: terms such as 'deprivation of liberty safeguards' are widely criticised as cumbersome and Orwellian.
- The safeguards were designed to provide a comprehensive set of safeguards for a relatively small number of cases. They were not intended to deal with the numbers of cases that have been apparent post *Cheshire West*.

7.95 In the interim, the system is under huge pressure, both as regards the need to authorise deprivations of liberty under Sch A1 in respect of those who satisfy the 'acid test', and to bring applications to the Court of Protection for those deprivations of liberty taking place outside care homes and hospitals. There is a real risk that, under this pressure, we will lose sight of the reason why questions of deprivation of liberty is so important in this

---

[130] Ibid, summary, page 7, emphasis in the original.
[131] Law Commission, Mental Capacity and Deprivation of Liberty: A Consultation Paper (2015), CP No 222; the consultation is open until 2 November 2015 and the Law Commission's final report with its recommendations and a draft Bill is expected in 2016.

context. It is not so that boxes can be ticked and forms completed. Rather, it is because those who are deprived of their liberty for purposes of providing care and treatment – and who lack capacity to consent to such deprivation– are, by definition, intensely vulnerable. They need, as Lady Hale was at pains to emphasise in *Cheshire West*, regular independent scrutiny of the arrangements made for them to ensure that they are in their best interests.[132]

7.96 We can certainly legitimately ask the question whether looking at matters through the prism of Article 5 ECHR is the best way in which to achieve this policy aim; at the very least, all can probably agree that the debates of the past few years as to what constitutes a deprivation of liberty have not been of the slightest assistance to those most affected. The Law Commission's final report with its recommendations and a draft Bill are therefore eagerly awaited in 2016 in the hope that numerous difficulties with the present system can be remedied for the benefit of some of the most vulnerable individuals in our society.

---

[132] *Cheshire West*, at [57].

Chapter 8

Court Practice and Procedure

PRELIMINARY

Role of the Lord Chancellor

8.1 In the Mental Capacity Act 2005 (MCA 2005) and hence the paragraphs that follow, references are made to the Lord Chancellor, who was given various powers. These references must be interpreted in the light of the constitutional reforms that overlapped with the Act before Parliament, so an overview of the impact of those reforms is needed.[1]

8.2 In June 2003, abolition of the office of Lord Chancellor was announced as part of a suite of constitutional reforms which also included the establishment of an independent Judicial Appointments Commission and a new Supreme Court. The overall aim of these reforms was to put the relationship between the executive, legislature and judiciary on a modern footing, respecting the separation of powers between the three. On 26 January 2004 the Government announced proposals which included the transfer of the Lord Chancellor's judiciary-related functions, and these were effected within the reforms by the Constitutional Reform Act 2005.[2]

8.3 Following concerns expressed by the judiciary a Concordat was established between the Lord Chancellor and the Lord Chief Justice.[3] So far as is relevant to the new mental capacity jurisdiction the roles become as follows. The Lord Chancellor is:

- under a duty to ensure that there is an efficient and effective system to support the carrying on of the business of the courts in England and Wales, as set out in the Courts Act 2003, Part 1;[4]
- accountable to Parliament for the overall efficiency and effectiveness of the administration of the court system, including the proper use of public resources voted by Parliament;

---

[1] The consequential amendments have been made by statutory instrument under the Constitutional Reform Act 2005.
[2] The title Lord Chancellor was to be abolished in favour of Secretary of State for Constitutional Affairs but the Bill was amended to retain that title although the role and functions of the office are substantively recast.
[3] The Concordat is 'an essential tool for protecting the independence of the judiciary, as a blueprint governing the relations between the judiciary and the government for the long-term and as providing a much-needed, non-contentious way of appointing and disciplining the judiciary', per Lord Woolf CJ.
[4] This includes the provision and allocation of resources which include financial, material and human resources.

- responsible for ensuring that the public interest is served in decisions taken on matters affecting the judiciary in relation to the administration of justice; and
- responsible for supporting the judiciary in enabling them to fulfil their functions for dispensing justice.

8.4 The Lord Chief Justice is responsible for ensuring that appropriate structures are in place to ensure the well-being of and training and provision of guidance for the judiciary, and for the deployment of individual members of the judiciary and the allocation of work within the courts.

8.5 The Lord Chancellor, in consultation with the Lord Chief Justice, is responsible for the efficient and effective administration of the court system including setting the framework for the organisation of the courts system (such as geographical and functional jurisdictional boundaries). This includes determining the number of judges required for each jurisdiction and region and the number required at each level of the judiciary; also the provision of the courts, their location and sitting times and consequent administrative staffing to meet the expected business requirement.

Judiciary

8.6 The majority of judicial appointments fall within the remit of the Judicial Appointments Commission (JAC). The Lord Chief Justice is responsible, after consulting the Lord Chancellor, for determining which individual judge should be assigned to which court and the authorisation of individual members of the judiciary to sit in particular levels of court. Also for deciding the level of judge appropriate to hear particular classes of case (including the issuing of Practice Directions in that regard) and the nominations of judges to particular posts including those that provide judicial leadership not formal promotion.

8.7 The Lord Chief Justice is responsible for the provision and sponsorship of judicial training within the resources provided by the Lord Chancellor, but responsibility for assessing the need for and providing training of professional judicial office-holders remains with the Judicial College (formerly the Judicial Studies Board).

Rules and Practice Directions

8.8 In general, functions relating to the allowing of procedural Rules of Court remain with the Lord Chancellor. The making of such rules and Practice Directions will rest with the relevant rule committees where such a committee exists, and otherwise will be exercised by the Lord Chief Justice, with the concurrence of the Lord Chancellor.[5]

---

[5] MCA 2005 makes no provision for a Rules Committee.

STATUS OF THE COURT OF PROTECTION
Preliminary
8.9 MCA 2005, Part 2, comprising ss 45–56, deals with the creation of the new Court of Protection and its powers.

The Court
Name and venue
8.10 MCA 2005 created a new superior court of record[6] with an official seal known as the Court of Protection and the former office of the Supreme Court (as it was then known) called the Court of Protection ceased to exist. The functions of the new Court are described in Chapter 4.

8.11 The Court has a central office and registry at a place appointed by the Lord Chancellor. This was originally at Archway Tower, Junction Road, London N19. In January 2012, the court moved to the Thomas Moore Buildings at the Royal Courts of Justice and in December 2013 the court moved again to its present home at First Avenue House where it joined what was then known as the Principal Registry of the Family Division and what is now called the Central Family Court. The Court of Protection remains separate and retains its individual identity and staff. The court may also sit at any place in England and Wales, on any day and at any time and a number of courts have been designated as regional courts.

Administration
8.12 The court is managed by HM Courts and Tribunals Service. Prior to 2009, the Office of the Public Guardian managed the court and was also responsible for its funding. This arrangement was not good. The OPG had never been responsible for a court and this created difficulties and it was also felt that as the Public Guardian is a common litigant in the Court of Protection, it was not appropriate that he should also be running and funding the court. It was therefore against this background that HMCTS (or rather its predecessor HM Courts Service) took over the running of the court.

Forms
8.13 The forms used by the former Court of Protection were reviewed and rewritten so as to be fit for purpose and align with other court forms. As might be expected of a court of this nature, the applications and acknowledgment of service forms inquire whether the party needs any special assistance or facilities at an attended hearing. This information should be volunteered in advance for any other person who attends a hearing.

---

[6] Thus able to establish precedent unlike the former Court.

There has been criticism of the court's forms as requests for the same information are repeated on some forms and they can be awkward to complete. Work was therefore undertaken to address the criticisms and this led in July 2015 to some of the main forms being amended to make them easier for court users.

Judges

8.14 MCA 2005 also provides that, subject to the Court of Protection rules, the jurisdiction of the new Court shall be exercisable by a number of judges nominated for that purpose by the Lord Chancellor.[7] The judges who may be nominated are the President of the Family Division, the Chancellor of the Chancery Division,[8] puisne judges of the High Court,[9] circuit judges and district judges. There was originally no provision for part time judges such as Recorders, deputy district judges or tribunal judges to sit in the Court of Protection. This denied the court the important resource of judges who could sit in place of full time judges on annual or sick leave, a pool of potential future appointees to the court and crucially extra judicial resources when needed to cope with the ever increasing work load. This issue was finally resolved by the Crime and Courts Act 2013 which allowed a large number of full time and part time judges from across the judicial spectrum to sit in the court. Indeed, these provisions proved to be vital recently. After the decision of the Supreme Court in *P v Cheshire West and Chester Council*[10] it became clear that the court would not be able to deal with the high volume of applications to authorise deprivation of liberty. These provisions have allowed the court to nominate judges from tribunals to assist with these cases. Although the authiorsation procedure has encountered legal difficulties, nonetheless the fact remains that this was the the first time there has been judicial cross fertilisation.

8.15 In October 2007 the Lord Chancellor appointed the then President of the Family Division, Sir Mark Potter, as President of the Court of Protection. On his retirement, Sir Nicholas Wall took over until December 2012, to be followed by the present incumbent Sir James Munby. The Vice-President is Mr Justice Charles who was appointed in December 2013.[11]

The former Master of the old Court of Protection, Denzil Lush, was appointed to be Senior Judge.

In addition, all judges of the Family and Chancery Divisions were originally nominated as judges of the Court of Protection although now, only certain Chancery Division judges are nominated. In 2011, the President nominated

---

[7] The references in this and the following paragraph to the Lord Chancellor may be interpreted as being to the Lord Chief Justice after consulting the Lord Chancellor – see **8.1**ff.
[8] The Senior Judge of the Chancery Division whose title was previously the Vice-Chancellor.
[9] This is no longer reserved to judges of the Family or Chancery Division although no judges of the Queen's Bench Division have yet been nominated.
[10] [2014] UKSC 19, [2014] COPLR 313.
[11] MCA 2005, s 46.

all judges of the Queen's Bench Division but it is understood that they are only used as a resource when other High Court Judges are unavailable.

In the High Court, it is the Family Division that really shoulders the bulk of the responsibility for Court of Protection work. At one point, it was said that approximately 10 per cent of the Family Division's work derives from the Court of Protection which led one judge to complain that urgent attention needed to be given to increasing the resources of the Family Division to accommodate this work.[12] This level of work is only increasing.

There are five full time district judges at the main registry at First Avenue House and one district judge who sits part time in the court, spending the rest of his time in the Family and County Courts. They are regularly joined by district judges who sit in the regional courts who wish to gain experience by sitting at the main registry and who are a valuable resource to ensure cases can be properly processed.

In 2011, a decision was taken to appoint Mr Justice Charles as Judge in Charge of the Court of Protection. Now that he is Vice President of the court, that position is really redundant as the Vice President carries out the same role which is effectively to lead the court and ensure it runs smoothly.

Regional judges

8.16 District judges and circuit judges specialising in chancery or family work have been nominated to sit in the Court on a regional basis.[13]

One of the advantages of regionalisation is that more provincial solicitors and barristers will appear before the 'local' Court of Protection and thereby gain experience with which they may better advise their clients.

In fact, regionalisation is taking on a more prominent role with designated centres or hubs being created which will be responsible for Court of Protection work in that area. Each region has a lead judge whose role is to ensure that gatekeeping procedures are put in place to ensure cases are sent to the most appropriate judge and court. The lead judge also has to ensure that nominated judges have sufficient time to hear Court of Protection cases. The hope is that ultimately, court users will be able to issue certain types of proceedings in the regional court.

Allocation of cases

8.17 MCA 2005 provides for three levels of the judiciary to be nominated to sit in the Court, thus following the practice in the civil and family courts where the Rules and Practice Directions allocate cases between these

---

[12] See *G v E* [2010] EWHC 621 (Fam), [2010] COPLR Con Vol 510, at [4] and [5] per Baker J.
[13] In Scotland the new jurisdiction was given to every Sheriff but this has not proved to be ideal because some have little experience or interest in the jurisdiction.

levels.[14] The rules as recently amended refer to judges as being in tiers so Tier 1 are district judges and first tier tribunal judges, Tier 2 are circuit judges and upper tribunal judges and Tier 3 are High Court Judges.

However, the reality is that the majority of the court's work is undertaken by district judges. Serious medical treatment decisions are heard by High Court judges, though sitting in the Court of Protection rather than as Family Division judges. Other personal welfare decisions are allocated to district judges who will either hear the case or send it to a circuit judge or High Court Judge if that is more appropriate. Financial management decisions tend to be heard at first instance by district judges although appeals from them lie to circuit judges.

Transfer of cases

8.18 In the case of a mentally incapacitated person under the age of 18 years the Lord Chancellor may by order make provision as to transfer of proceedings from the Court of Protection to a court with jurisdiction under the Children Act 1989, or vice versa.[15]

Powers

General

8.19 The Court has in connection with its jurisdiction the same powers, rights, privileges and authority as the High Court.[16] It must be emphasised that the powers may only be exercised within the Court's jurisdiction, so although it may resolve disputes or uncertainty concerning the personal welfare, health care or financial management of the mentally incapacitated person, the Court has no jurisdiction to resolve disputes between that person and other persons. Similarly it has no power to order a local authority to provide a particular care plan or to resolve a dispute between two authorities as to responsibility based upon ordinary residence. In such instances the Court of Protection may need to authorise the conduct of proceedings in another court which has the appropriate jurisdiction.

8.20 Office copies of orders made, directions given or other instruments issued by the Court and sealed with its official seal are admissible in all legal proceedings as evidence of the originals without further proof.[17]

---

[14] Circuit judges (unlike district judges) do not sit in the High Court unless specifically authorised to do so on a case-by-case basis under Senior Courts Act 1981 (formerly Supreme Court Act 1981), s 9.
[15] MCA 2005, s 21. See the Mental Capacity Act 2005 (Transfer of Proceedings) Order 2007, SI 2007/1899.
[16] MCA 2005, s 47(1). The Law of Property Act 1925, s 204 (orders of High Court conclusive in favour of purchasers) will apply in relation to orders and directions of the court as it applies to orders of the High Court.
[17] MCA 2005, s 47(3).

Interim orders and directions

8.21 The Court may, pending the determination of an application to it in relation to a person, make an order or give directions in respect of any matter if:[18]

(1) there is reason to believe that this person lacks capacity in relation to the matter;
(2) the matter is one to which its powers under MCA 2005 extend; and
(3) it is in the person's best interests to make the order, or give the directions, without delay.

The proper test for the involvement of the Court in the first instance is whether there is evidence giving good cause for concern that P may lack capacity in some relevant regard. Once that is raised as a serious possibility, the Court then moves on to the second stage to decide what action, if any, it is in P's best interests to take before a final determination of his capacity can be made.[19]

Reports

8.22 The Court may, where in proceedings brought in respect of a person it is considering a question relating to that person:[20]

(1) require a report to be made to it by the Public Guardian or by a Court of Protection Visitor; or
(2) require a local authority, or an NHS body,[21] to arrange for a report to be made by one of its officers or employees, or such other person as the authority, or the NHS body, considers appropriate.

8.23 The report must deal with such matters relating to the person, and be made in writing or orally, as the Court may direct.[22]

8.24 When preparing a report the Public Guardian or a Court of Protection Visitor[23] may, at all reasonable times, examine and take copies of any health record, any record of or held by, a local authority and compiled in connection with a social services function, and any record held by a person registered under the Care Standards Act 2000, Part 2 so far as the record relates to the person. When making a visit the Public Guardian or a Court of Protection Visitor may interview the person in private.

---

[18] MCA 2005, s 48.
[19] *Re F (Interim Declarations)* [2009] COPLR Con Vol 390, HHJ Hazel Marshall QC.
[20] MCA 2005, s 49.
[21] As defined in the Health and Social Care (Community Health and Standards) Act 2003, s 148.
[22] Court of Protection Rules may specify matters which, unless the court directs otherwise, must also be dealt with in the report.
[23] The status and role of the Public Guardian and the Visitors is considered in Chapter 8.

8.25 A Special Visitor when making a visit may, if the Court so directs, carry out in private a medical, psychiatric or psychological examination of the person's capacity and condition.

THE COURT RULES
Court of Protection Rules 2007[24] (COPR 2007)

8.26 The Lord Chancellor is empowered to make Rules of Court with respect to the practice and procedure of the Court,[25] and these may, in particular, make provision:

(1) as to the manner and form in which proceedings are to be commenced;

(2) as to the persons entitled to be notified of, and be made parties to, the proceedings;

(3) for the allocation, in such circumstances as may be specified, of any specified description of proceedings to a specified judge or to specified descriptions of judges;

(4) for the exercise of the jurisdiction of the Court, in such circumstances as may be specified, by its officers or other staff;

(5) for enabling the Court to appoint a suitable person (who may, with his consent, be the Official Solicitor) to act in the name of, or on behalf of, or to represent the person to whom the proceedings relate;

(6) for enabling an application to the Court to be disposed of without a hearing;

(7) for enabling the Court to proceed with, or with any part of, a hearing in the absence of the person to whom the proceedings relate;

(8) for enabling or requiring the proceedings or any part of them to be conducted in private and for enabling the Court to determine who is to be admitted when the Court sits in private and to exclude specified persons when it sits in public;

(9) as to what may be received as evidence (whether or not admissible apart from the rules) and the manner in which it is to be presented; and

(10) for the enforcement of orders made and directions given in the proceedings.

COPR 2007 may, instead of providing for any matter, refer to provision made by directions.

8.27 The Court of Protection Rules 2001[26] and their predecessors were brief and left much to judicial discretion. This may have been useful in a jurisdiction of where the objective was to address the best interests of the

---

[24] SI 2007/1744.
[25] MCA 2005, s 51. The reference to the Lord Chancellor should be interpreted as being to the Lord Chief Justice with the concurrence of the Lord Chancellor. There is no provision for a Rules Committee.
[26] SI 2001/824.

incapacitated person rather than personal disputes between members of their families, carers and other concerned persons. But it was not easy for practitioners to know how they should prepare or conduct their cases.

8.28 An Informal Rules Group was set up to consider the content of the first Rules of the new Court of Protection and these were made on 24 June 2007 and came into force on 1 October 2007.[27]

8.29 In December 2009, an Ad Hoc and informal rules committee was set up with a view to seeing how the rules worked and whether change was necessary. The committee held a number of meetings and published a report which recommended many changes in July 2010. Although the President of the Court of Protection accepted the committee's proposals, save for one exception, nothing was done to implement the recommendations.

8.30 The exception was a new rule 7A which allows authorised court officers to undertake certain work.

However, the rule went beyond the intention of the rules committee which was to allow court officers to only undertake a very limited scope of work. The Practice Direction for this rule reveals a far greater scope of work being devolved on the authorised court officer than was ever imagined.

The Senior Judge monitored the situation for the first six months and thereafter, the scheme seems to have worked well in practice with the authorised court officers readily referring cases to a judge if they have a query and feel the case is better handled at a higher level.

In March 2014, the House of Lords Select Committee on the MCA 2005 published its report and this lead to another Ad Hoc Rules Committee being set up in July 2014.

The Committee reported on the first tranche of its work in early 2015 and amendments were proposed to the rules which were accepted by the Lord Chancellor and the President of the Court of Protection. Some rules took effect in April 2015, others in July 2015.

The first tranche of amendments were designed to remedy problems in the working of the rules. In particular, many time limits were shortened to hasten the pace of cases. The most significant amendment was rule 3A which is dedicated to considering P's participation in proceedings.

The Committee then set about the second tranche of its work. This really amounts to a consideration of all the rules. So far, a transparency pilot has been published which provides for many hearings to be in public. The pilot

---

[27] The COPR 2007, SI 2007/1744. The 2001 Rules were revoked along with the Court of Protection (Enduring Powers of Attorney) Rules 2001, SI 2001/825.

started in January 2016. Work is still being undertaken on many other aspects of the rules and it is expected that the fruits of the Committee work will be published by mid-2016.

Practice Directions

8.31 The President of the Court of Protection may, with the concurrence of the Lord Chancellor, give directions as to the practice and procedure of the Court. No such directions may be given by anyone else without the approval of the President and the Lord Chancellor, but this does not prevent the President from giving directions which contain guidance as to law or making judicial decisions.[28] Thus, the rules are supplemented by a large number of practice directions which fill out the rules.

One recent amendment to the rules is rule 9A. This allows a practice direction to be made to operate a pilot scheme for a specified period and in respect of certain parts of the country. Furthermore, a practice direction may now modify or disapply a rule. This rule has already been used by the publishing in November 2015 of a transparency pilot. It will be interesting to see how else this rule is used. Of course, the main advantage of a pilot is that it can be monitored and amendments made to the proposed rule before it is formally incorporated into the rules in its own right.

Practice Guidance

8.32 In May and June 2013, the President issued two Practice Guidance documents relating to contempt of court applications. This marked the start of the practice of Practice Guidance documents being issued. These have now been superceeded by new Practice Guidance documents relating to contempt issued in March and June 2015.

In July 2013, a draft Practice Guidance was issued on the subject of transparency and reporting of judgments of the court which was introduced formally in May 2014. One positive effect of this is that a large number of decisions of the Senior Judge on property and affairs cases are now available on the Bailli website which some practitioners feel has helped them to understand the court's approach to a variety of issues.

However, given the provisions in rule 9A for pilot schemes to be introduced, it might be felt that Practice Guidance documents have no place. Time will only tell if this is the case or not.

---

[28] MCA 2005, s 52. The references to the Lord Chancellor may be interpreted as being to the Lord Chief Justice though with the concurrence of the Lord Chancellor.

Interface with other rules

8.33 Provision is made in the rules to apply the CPR or the Family Procedure Rules 2010 including their practice directions[29]. This gives the court flexibility to incorporate other rules into Court of Protection proceedings if they will assist.

The overriding objective

General

8.34 COPR 2007 commence in Part 2 with a statement of the 'overriding objective', borrowed from the original Civil Procedure Rules 1998[30] (CPR) in which context it has proved extremely successful.

The objective is to enable the Court to deal with cases justly, having regard to the principles contained in MCA 2005, and the Court will seek to give effect to the overriding objective when it exercises any power or interprets any rule or Practice Direction. The present version of the CPR, however, talks about the need to deal with a case at proportionate cost. This part of the CPR has not been incorporated into the COPR 2007 although given concerns about costs in Court of Protection proceedings, it would not be surprising if such a provision were incorporated into the COPR 2007.

8.35 Dealing with a case justly includes, so far as is practicable, ensuring that it is dealt with expeditiously and fairly, that the parties are on an equal footing and that the incapacitated person's interests and position are properly considered. Also dealing with the case in ways which are proportionate to the nature, importance and complexity of the issues, saving expense and allotting to it an appropriate share of the Court's resources, while taking account of the need to allot resources to other cases.

Duties of the Court and parties

8.36 The Court is expected to further the overriding objective by actively managing cases, which means encouraging the parties to co-operate with each other in the conduct of the proceedings. It should identify the issues at an early stage, including who should be parties, decide the way in which P will participate and then decide which issues need a full investigation and hearing and which do not, and the procedure to be followed. In the process the Court will decide the order in which issues are to be resolved and fix timetables or otherwise control the progress of the case. The parties are required to help the Court to further the overriding objective.

8.37 The parties will be encouraged to use an alternative dispute resolution procedure when appropriate. The Court will also consider whether the likely benefits of taking a particular step justify the cost, deal with as many aspects

---

[29] COPR 2007, r 9
[30] SI 1998/3132.

of the case as it can on the same occasion and where possible without the parties needing to attend. All of this involves giving directions to ensure that the case proceeds quickly and efficiently and making use of technology.

The court must now also consider whether a hearing should be held in public and if any document should be made public.

An important amendment to the rules is rule 3A. This rule obliges the court to consider how P can participate in the proceedings. Until now, the court only had to ensure that P's interests and position were considered but now, right at the very start of the proceedings, the Court has to tackle the issue of how P is involved in a case.

The rule allows for P to be a party as well as not being a party. It also creates two new roles, that of an accredited legal representative and a representative, The former will be chosen from a panel which has yet to be set up and approved), the latter can be anyone such as a family member, a friend or IMCA.

Rule 4 has also been completely amended to require the parties not only to help the court further the overriding objective but to co-operate with each other, adhere to timetables set by the court and to comply with all rules, orders and directions. The rule also contains a warning that if without reasonable excuse, a party fails to satisfy the requirements of rule 4, the court may depart from the general costs rule under rule 159.

Interpretation

8.38 COPR 2007, Part 3 contains an interpretation clause and also makes provision for computation of time. In order to fill any gaps the CPR (and Practice Directions) are to be applied with any necessary modifications.[31]

Case management powers

General

8.39 COPR 2007, Part 5[32] deals with the Court's general powers of case management. The Court may take any step or give any direction for the purpose of managing the case and furthering the overriding objective, and in particular:

(1) extend or shorten the time for compliance with any rule, Practice Direction, or court order or direction (even if an application is made out of the time);
(2) adjourn or bring forward a hearing;
(3) require the incapacitated person or a party (including the legal representative or litigation friend) to attend Court;

---

[31] COPR 2007, rr 6–8.
[32] COPR 2007, rr 25–28.

(4) hold a hearing and receive evidence by telephone or any other method of direct oral communication;
(5) stay any proceedings or judgment generally or until a specified date or event;
(6) consolidate proceedings;
(7) hear two or more applications on the same occasion;
(8) direct a separate hearing of any issue;
(9) decide the order in which issues are to be heard;
(10) exclude an issue from consideration;
(11) dismiss or give judgment on an application after a preliminary decision; and
(12) direct a party to file and serve an estimate of costs.

8.40 The Court will take into account whether or not a party has complied with any rule or Practice Direction.

Security for costs

8.41 The rules have been amended to incorporate[33] new rules which specifically allow an application for security for costs to be made if the court is satisfied that having regard to all the cirucmstances of the case, it is just to make the order and certain conditions are satisfied.

Court's own initiative

8.42 The Court may make (or vary or revoke) any order, even if a party has not sought that order, dispense with the requirement of any rule and generally exercise its powers on its own initiative without hearing the parties. But if it proposes to make an order on its own initiative it may give the parties and any person it thinks fit an opportunity to make representations and, where it does so, it will specify the time by which, and the manner in which, the representations must be made. If the Court proposes to hold a hearing it will give the parties and any other person likely to be affected by the order at least 3 days' notice.

8.43 An error of procedure will not invalidate any step taken unless the Court so orders and the Court may waive the error or require it to be remedied or make such other order as appears just.

Human rights

8.44 A party who seeks to rely upon any provision of or right arising under the Human Rights Act 1998 or who seeks a remedy available under that Act must inform the Court in the manner set out in the relevant Practice Direction specifying the Convention right which it is alleged has been infringed and details of the alleged infringement, and the remedy sought and

---

[33] COPR 2007, rr 81A to 81D

whether this includes a declaration of incompatibility.[34] The Court may not make a declaration of incompatibility unless 21 days' notice, or such other period of notice as the Court directs, has been given to the Crown, and a minister or other permitted person will then be joined as a party on filing an application.[35]

PRACTICE AND PROCEDURE

Court documents

8.45 COPR 2007, Part 4 deals with Court documents.[36] The documents used in proceedings include application forms application notices and other documents referred to in Practice Directions. An application form is used to commence proceedings, and an application notice will relate to an application within existing proceedings.[37] The usual slip rule enables the Court to correct any clerical mistakes in an order or direction or any error arising in an order or direction from any accidental slip or omission, but an endorsement shall show that this has been done.[38]

Statements of truth

8.46 When submitted by a party such documents, and also witness statements, may need to be verified by a 'statement of truth', which is the modern form of oath. This is a statement that the party putting forward the document (or litigation friend on that person's behalf) believes that the facts stated therein are true. The statement must be signed by the party or litigation friend (or legal representative on such person's behalf) or the witness. If this is not done the document may not be relied upon without the Court's permission, and it would be contempt of court to make a false statement.[39] A position statement does not need to be verified by a statement of truth.[40]

Personal details

8.47 Where a party does not wish to reveal a home address or telephone number, or other personal details, those particulars must be provided to the Court but will not be revealed to any other person unless the Court so directs. Nevertheless a party must provide an address for service within the jurisdiction.[41]

---

[34] Ie under the Human Rights Act 1998, s 4.
[35] COPR 2007, Part 11, r 83. A Practice Direction (PD 11A) deals with this.
[36] A Practice Direction (PD 4A) deals with Court Documents.
[37] COPR 2007, Pts 9 and 10 respectively.
[38] COPR 2007, rr 23–24.
[39] COPR 2007, rr 11–14. A Practice Direction (PD 4B) deals with Statements of Truth.
[40] COPR 2007, r 11A.
[41] COPR 2007, r 15.

Access to documents

8.48 Unless the Court orders otherwise, a party may inspect or obtain a copy of any filed document and any communication with the Court in the proceedings. A non-party may generally inspect or obtain a copy of a judgment or order given or made in public, and the Court may authorise further disclosure (with or without editing). There are restrictions on the use of such documents in other proceedings.[42] Further provisions deal with the Public Guardian's access to Court documents.[43]

Service of documents

8.49 COPR 2007, Part 6[44] makes general provision for service which includes both the service of documents and notifying the issue of an application form, but other rules may make different provision or the Court may order otherwise. The rules have also been amended to include provisions for service out of the jurisdiction[45]

Who serves?

8.50 An order or judgment, an acknowledgment of service or notification and a notice of hearing (other than for committal) will generally be served by the Court. Any other document is to be served by the party seeking to rely upon it, except where the Court directs or a rule or Practice Direction provides otherwise.

How is service effected?

8.51 Several methods of service are allowed. Unless a solicitor is acting the document may be delivered to the person personally or his or her last known home address. It may also be sent to that address by first class post (or by an alternative method of service which provides for delivery on the next working day). Otherwise documents will be served on a solicitor who has stated that he or she is authorised to accept service unless personal service is required. COPR 2007 confirms when a document is deemed to have been served, deals with service out of the jurisdiction and makes provision for a certificate of service (or non-service).

8.52 The Court may direct that service be effected by another method (including substituted service) where there is good reason for this and will then specify the method of service and the date when the document will be deemed to be served. It may also dispense with service. Special provision is made for service of documents on children and protected parties (which will

---

[42] COPR 2007, rr 16–19.
[43] COPR 2007, rr 20–21.
[44] COPR 2007, rr 29–39. A Practice Direction (PD 6A) deals with Service of Documents.
[45] COPR 2007, rr 39 to 39H.

include the incapacitated person to whom the proceedings relate), the aim being to reach a responsible person who will arrange representation for the child protected party.

Notifying the incapacitated person

8.53 Clearly the person alleged to be incapacitated and thereby the subject of the proceedings should be notified of the steps being taken and given an opportunity to intervene or contribute, unless clearly unable to do so. Even then it may be that this person should be notified in case someone in close contact needs to know and thereby have an opportunity to become involved. Part 7 of the COPR 2007 which makes appropriate provision to achieve this aim.[46] If the incapacitated person is made a party (see below) other provisions then apply.

8.54 Notification must be given when an application form has been issued or withdrawn, of the date of any hearing to dispose of the application and on the appointment of a litigation friend, accredited legal representative or representative.[47] This will be done by the applicant or his or her agent, or such other person as the Court directs, and appropriate explanations must be given.[48] Final orders and appeals are similarly dealt with, and the Court may direct notification on other occasions. The manner of notification is prescribed in COPR 2007 and provision made for a certificate of notification to be filed, although the Court may dispense with or vary any of these requirements.

Permission to apply

Who may apply?

8.55 It has in the past been found necessary to control those who may bring applications to the Court of Protection. The rules as originally drafted sought to ensure that genuine applications were not be discouraged but that a screening process was in place to prevent those who seek to interfere without justification from causing inconvenience and expense to others. However, the rules governing permission have been amended to allow far more applications to be made without the requirement of permission being granted such as applications involving deprivation of liberty. The rules also now provide that the application for permission is made when making the application.[49]

---

[46] COPR 2007, rr 40–49. A Practice Direction (PD 7A) deals with Notifying P.
[47] COPR 2007, rr 41A and 3A
[48] These are specified in COPR 2007, r 42.
[49] COPR 2007, r 54.

Starting proceedings

Initial steps

8.56 COPR 2007, Part 9[50] and its Practice Directions[51] cover the procedure for starting new proceedings. The appropriate forms must be used and may need to be varied, but not so as to omit any information or guidance which the form gives to the intended recipient. Proceedings are started when the Court issues an application form at the request of the applicant but this will not be done until any required permission is granted. The date will be entered on the application form by the Court. The rules and Practice Directions prescribe the information to be contained in the form and the documents to be filed with it.[52]

8.57 Within 14 days of issue the applicant must serve a copy of the application form on the named respondents, together with copies of any filed documents and a form for acknowledging service. A certificate of service must then be filed within 7 days. Specific requirements are then specified in respect of applications relating to lasting and enduring powers of attorney.

8.58 As stated above, the incapacitated person must be notified in accordance with COPR 2007, Part 7 that an application form has been issued, unless the requirement to do so has been dispensed with. The applicant must also within 14 days of issue notify the persons specified in the relevant Practice Direction of the application whether it relates to property and affairs or personal welfare, or to both, and the orders sought. A form for acknowledging service should be attached and a certificate of service must then be filed within seven days of service.

Responding to an application

8.59 A person who is served with or notified of an application form and wishes to take part in proceedings must within 14 days file an acknowledgment of service or notification providing an address for service within the jurisdiction and stating the interest in the proceedings and whether he or she wishes to be joined as a party. The Court then serves this on the applicant and on anyone else who has filed an acknowledgment. The acknowledgment or notification must also state whether the person consents to or opposes the application, and if so the grounds for doing so, and if a different order is sought what that order is. A witness statement should in those events accompany the form containing any evidence upon which the

---

[50] COPR 2007, rr 61–76.
[51] In particular they cover the Application Form (PD 9A), Notifying other Persons (PD 9B), Responding to an Application (PD 9C), Applications by Deputies, Attorneys and Donees relating to Property and Affairs (PD 9D), Applications relating to Serious Medical Treatment (PD 9E), Applications relating to Statutory Wills and Gifts (PD 9F), Applications relating to Trustees (PD 9G) and Applications relating to Registration of Enduring Powers of Attorney (PD 9H).
[52] PD 9A contains a Table setting out the documents that must be filed.

person intends to rely. The Court will then consider whether to join this person as a party and make any appropriate order.

Parties

8.60 The Court addresses the best interests of vulnerable incapacitated individuals so will not be concerned to resolve disputes between members of the family which may have continued for years and resurface in the context of a struggle for control over the incapacitated member and his affairs.

This has implications as to who is, or may be, party to the proceedings. In this respect the Court differs from the civil courts whose purpose is to resolve disputes between parties who select themselves. The approach is more akin to the family courts when addressing the best interests of children. In reality the Court is often called upon to make a decision following an application by a party and will only do so after giving other persons with a relevant interest the opportunity to state their case. Treating these persons as parties introduces an unnecessarily adversarial approach to the hearing, yet those persons may expect this.

8.61 The court now has an obligation to consider P's involvement in the proceedings and whether P should be joined as a party or represented in some other way.[53]

The new r 3A introduces an accredited legal representative. This is defined in rule 6 as a legal representative authorised pursuant to a scheme of accreditation approved by the President to represent persons meeting the definition of P in the COPR 2007. So far, no scheme has been made or approved. The rule comes into effect in July 2015 and it remains to be seen how use of this rule will develop. If the court is minded to appoint an accredited legal representative, that person must consent and P does not have to be a party to the proceedings.

However, it is hoped that the r 3A(2)(c) representative will be useful. This could enable P to play a part in proceedings without being a party but having a family member, friend, IMCA or some other appropriate person to represent his interests to the court.

With the ever increasing workload of the Official Solicitor and the lack of legal aid, it is hoped that these alternative representatives will be of use in court proceedings.

8.62 Any person with sufficient interest may apply to be joined as a party and this is done by filing an application notice within the proceedings which will state the applicant's full name and address, his or her interest in the proceedings and the further information required when responding to an application including, where appropriate, a statement in support. The Court

---

[53] See 8.38 and COPR 2007, r 3A

will serve this on all parties make an order joining the person if it decides to do so. A person who wishes to be removed as a party must apply for an order to that effect.

Applications within proceedings

8.63 The procedure in COPR 2007, Part 10 is used for these applications.[54] The Court may grant an interim remedy before an application form has been issued only if the matter is urgent or it is otherwise necessary to do so in the interests of justice. The applicant must file an application notice with the evidence upon which he relies (unless such evidence has already been filed) unless any rule or Practice Direction permits an application without or the Court dispenses with the requirement. If the applicant makes an application without giving notice, the evidence in support must state why notice has not been given.

8.64 An application notice must state the order or direction that the applicant is seeking, the brief grounds relied on and such other information as may be required by any rule or a Practice Direction. The Court will issue the application notice and, if there is to be a hearing, give notice of the date to the applicant. The applicant must within 21 days serve a copy of the application notice together with the notice of hearing and evidence relied upon on anyone named as a respondent (if not otherwise a party to the proceedings), every party and any other person that the Court may direct. The applicant must then file a certificate of service within 7 days.

Applications without notice

8.65 Where the Court has dealt with an application made without notice and made an order, whether granting or dismissing the application, the applicant must, as soon as practicable or within such period as the Court may direct, serve a copy of the application notice, the court's order and any evidence filed with the application on the respondent, the parties and any other peron as the court may direct.[55] A person affected by the order may ask for it to be reconsidered.[56]

Interim remedies

8.66 The Court may grant an interim injunction, declaration or any other interim order it considers appropriate. Unless the Court orders otherwise, a person on whom a new application is served or who is given notice of such an application may not apply for an interim remedy before filing an acknowledgment of service or notification.

---

[54] COPR 2007, rr 77–82. Practice Directions deal with such applications (PD 10A) and also Urgent and Interim Applications (PD 10B).
[55] COPR 2007, r 81
[56] COPR 2007, r 89

Dealing with applications

8.67 COPR 2007, Part 12[57] explains how the Court deals with applications. As soon as practicable after any application has been issued the Court considers how to deal with it and may do so at a hearing or without a hearing. In considering whether it is necessary to hold a hearing, the Court has regard to:

(1) the nature of the proceedings and the orders sought;
(2) whether the application is opposed by a person who appears to the Court to have an interest in matters relating to the incapacitated person's best interests;
(3) whether the application involves a substantial dispute of fact;
(4) the complexity of the facts and the law;
(5) any wider public interest in the proceedings;
(6) the circumstances of the incapacitated person and of any party, in particular, as to whether their rights would be adequately protected if a hearing were not held;
(7) whether the parties agree that the Court should dispose of the application without a hearing; and
(8) any other matter specified in the relevant Practice Direction.

8.68 Where the Court considers that a hearing is necessary, it gives notice of the date to the parties and any other person it directs and will state what is to be dealt with at the hearing, including whether the matter is to be disposed of at that hearing.

Directions

8.69 The Court may give directions in writing or set a date for a directions hearing and do anything else required by a Practice Direction. The rule sets out a long list of things the Court might do, including requiring a report, joining or removing parties, and setting a timetable (eg for disclosure of documents and witness statements). In fact the Court may give directions at any time on its own initiative or on the application of a party.

8.70 The Court will always be concerned to approach a case in a way that ensure that it is heard as quickly as possible and having regard to proportionality. Thus, it will carefully scrutinise requests for expert evidence, limit disclosure only to the documents required and impose a timetable. As stated above, the Ad Hoc Rules Committee is looking at the whole case management process and it is likely that changes will be made to achieve these aims especially as there have been examples of cases where the costs have been wholly disproportionate to the issues in dispute.[58]

---

[57] COPR 2007, rr 84–89. Practice Directions deal with the exercise of the jurisdiction by certain judges (PD 12A) and the procedure for disputing the Court's jurisdiction (PD 12B).
[58] See *A and B (Court of Protection: Delay and Costs)* [2014] EWCOP 48, [2015] COPLR 1.

Allocation

8.71 The Court will also consider whether the application is of a type that must under a Practice Direction be dealt with by a particular level of judge and generally who is the best judge to hear a case.

Disputing the Court's jurisdiction

8.72 A person who wishes to dispute the Court's jurisdiction or argue that the Court should not exercise its jurisdiction may apply to the Court at any time for an appropriate order. The appropriate form should be used and the application must be supported by evidence. The consequence may be the setting aside of the original application, the discharge of any order made and a stay of the proceedings.

Hearing the incapacitated person

8.73 It has already been noted that the new r 3A obliges the court to consider how to involve P in a case. Outside whether P should be a party or not, however, the court will readily agree if appropriate to hear P or to allow P to observe the proceedings[59] or take part in some other meaningful way by allowing P to address the court or write a letter to the judge.

Reconsideration

8.74 Where the Court makes an order without a hearing or without notice to any person who is affected by it, that order must contain a statement of the right to apply for a reconsideration. A party or person affected by the order (including the incapacitated person) may then apply, within 21 days of service or such other period as the Court may direct, for reconsideration of the order. The Court will reconsider the order without a hearing or arrange a hearing for this purpose, and may affirm, set aside or vary the order. Any judge of the Court may do this, including the judge who made the first decision, but any further challenge must be by appeal.

Hearings

8.75 The Court is anxious not to exclude any person with a legitimate interest but also conscious that personal information concerning the incapacitated individual is to be discussed and there should not be any unnecessary intrusion into this person's right to privacy. COPR 2007, Pt 13[60] deals with hearings, which are to be in private unless the Court orders otherwise for the whole or part of the hearing, in which event it may exclude any person, or class of persons, from attending. A private hearing is a

---

[59] See, for example, *London Borough of Redbridge v G, C and F* [2014] EWHC 485 (COP), [2014] COPLR 292.
[60] COPR 2007, rr 90–93. A Practice Direction (PD 4B) deals with the privacy of hearings and reporting restrictions.

hearing which only the parties, their legal representatives, the incapacitated person, any litigation friend and court officers are entitled to attend, but the judge may authorise other persons to attend or exclude any person from attending in whole or in part.

8.76 The Court may also impose restrictions on the publication of any information or the identity of any party (including the incapacitated person even if not a party), witness or other person. Conversely, the Court may make an order authorising the publication of information. Such orders may be made only where it appears to the Court that there is good reason for doing so.

8.77 How formal should hearings be? Options include the formality of a courtroom trial, the relative informality of a chambers hearing or around the table conference. The proceedings are now recorded so transcripts can be obtained where appropriate.[61] Telephone conferences and video links may be utilised as part of the hearing process.[62] Should evidence be taken on oath? Should the public be admitted and how far should the existing rules on publishing case reports be extended? These issues are now the subject of debate and it is likely that further changes will occur.

Types of case

8.78 One of the challenges faced by the court is how to approach the different types of cases. A judge can be confronted with heavily contested personal welfare cases involving medical or ethical issues that require careful deliberation, disputes between public authorities and families about P's care and residence or about financial management and investment of P's property and money and who is to be responsible for financial management. Cases can involve the difficult issue of deprivation of liberty and disputes surrounding Enduring and Lasting Powers of Attorney.

Moreover, some cases raise public law issues which overlap with the Administrative Court and others may interface with other jurisdictions such as personal injury claims.

All this challenges the court to ensure the right judge hears the case and to ensure that the case is properly managed.

---

[61] This also protects the judge from allegations of inappropriate behaviour by a disaffected party.
[62] There should be consistency so these facilities need to be available at all regional hearing centres.

Evidence

8.79 COPR 2007, Part 14[63] and several Practice Directions deal with the delivery of evidence. In contrast to the regimes for civil and family proceedings, which have express statutory provisions concerning the admissibility of hearsay evidence, neither the MCA 2005 nor the COPR 2007 directly refer to hearsay evidence. Nevertheless, it has been held that proceedings in the Court of Protection fall within the wide definition of 'civil proceedings' under the Civil Evidence Act 1995, s 11 and hearsay evidence will be admissible in accordance with the provisions of that Act.[64]

Admissions

8.80 A party may admit the truth of the whole or part of another party's case by giving notice in writing, and the Court may allow a party to amend or withdraw an admission.

Witnesses' evidence

8.81 The Court may control the evidence by giving directions as to the issues on which it is required, the nature of the evidence and the way in which the evidence is to be placed before the Court. In so doing it may exclude evidence that would otherwise be admissible, allow or limit cross-examination and admit such evidence, whether written or oral, as it thinks fit. The court may admit such evidence, whether written or oral as it thinks fit[65] and admit, accept and act upon such information, whether oral or written from P as the court considers sufficient whether or not it would be admissible in a court of law apart from under the COPR 2007[66]. The Court may allow a witness to give evidence through a video link or by other communication technology.

8.82 A witness statement is a written statement of the evidence which that person would be allowed to give orally, and it must contain a statement of truth and be in proper form.[67] A party may not rely upon written evidence unless it has been duly filed, or this is expressly permitted by the Rules or a Practice Direction or the Court gives permission. The Court will give directions about the service of witness statements including the order in which they are to be served. A witness giving oral evidence at the final hearing may, if there is good reason for this and the Court permits, amplify

---

[63] COPR 2007, rr 94–118. The Practice Directions deal with Written Evidence (PD 14A), Depositions (PD 14B), Fees for Examiners (PD 14C), Witness Summons (PD 14D) and Section 49 Reports (PD 14E).
[64] See the decision of McFarlane J in *London Borough of Enfield v SA* [2010] EWHC 196 (Admin), [2010] COPLR Con Vol 362.
[65] COPR 2007, r 95
[66] COPR 2007, r 95(e)
[67] In some instances an affidavit may be required. A witness summary may be permitted to be served where for some reason the statement is going to be late.

his or her witness statement and give evidence in relation to new matters which have arisen since the witness statement was made.

8.83 The Court may allow or direct any party to issue a witness summons requiring the person named in it to attend before the Court and give oral evidence or produce any document to the Court. Provision is made in COPR 2007 for applications of this nature. Where a party has access to information which is not reasonably available to the other party, the Court may direct that party to prepare and file a document recording the information.

Depositions

8.84 A party may apply for an order for a person (the 'deponent') to be examined on oath before a judge or other person nominated by the Court prior to the hearing. Documents may be ordered to be produced at such examination. Provision is made in COPR 2007 for applications of this nature. The resulting deposition may be put in evidence at a hearing unless the Court orders otherwise. There are further provisions concerned with taking evidence outside the jurisdiction.[68]

Reports

8.85 Where the Court orders a report pursuant to MCA 2005, s 49, it is the duty of the person who is required to make the report to help the Court on the matters within his or her expertise. COPR 2007 spells out further the duty of this person to:

(1) contact or seek to interview such persons as he or she thinks appropriate or as the Court directs;
(2) ascertain what the incapacitated person's wishes and feelings are, and the beliefs and values that would be likely to influence him or her if he or she had the capacity to make a decision in relation to the matter to which the application relates;
(3) describe the incapacitated person's circumstances; and
(4) address such other matters as are required in a Practice Direction or as the Court may direct.

8.86 The Court may, on the application of any party, permit written questions to be put to the maker of the report and send a copy of the replies to the parties and to such other persons as the Court may direct. Unless the Court directs otherwise, the maker of the report may examine and take copies of any document in the Court records.[69]

---

[68] See generally PD 14B.
[69] See generally PD 14E.

Experts

8.87 COPR 2007, Part 15[70] deals with expert evidence. In this context an expert is one who has been instructed other than pursuant to MCA 2005, s 49 to give or prepare evidence for the purpose of proceedings. No person may file expert evidence unless the Court or a Practice Direction permits, or if it is filed with the permission or application form[71] and is evidence that the incapacitated person is a person who lacks capacity to make a decision in relation to the matter to which the application relates or as to his or her best interests. An applicant may only rely upon such evidence to the extent and for the purposes that the Court allows.

8.88 Expert evidence is generally given in a written report. It is the duty of the expert to help the Court on the matters within his or her expertise, and expert evidence will be restricted to that which is reasonably required (a lower threshold than the requirement of necessity in family proceedings) to resolve the proceedings. When a party applies for directions as to expert evidence he or she must identify the field and, where practicable, the expert and also provide any other material information about the expert with a draft letter of instruction. The Court when giving directions will confirm such matters and also deal with service of the report on the parties and on persons.

8.89 In a simple or non-controversial situation a single expert may be allowed or appointed. Where each party instructs their own expert there may be a direction for these experts to communicate with one another and produce a joint statement of issues on which they are agreed and issues on which they disagree, with reasons. There are also provisions for 'single joint experts' who will be instructed by the parties jointly. An expert may request directions from the Court to clarify his or her function, and the Court may allow the parties to put written questions to an expert on his or her report. Where a party has disclosed an expert's report, any party may use this as evidence at any hearing in the proceedings.

8.90 The expert's report must state the substance of all material instructions, whether written or oral, on the basis of which it was written and conclude with a statement that the expert understands his or her duty to the Court and has complied with that duty. Unless the Court otherwise directs, and subject to any final costs order, the instructing party is responsible for the payment of the expert's fees and expenses, including the cost of answering questions put by any other party.

---

[70] COPR 2007, rr 119–131. A Practice Direction (PD 15A) deals with Expert Evidence.
[71] COPR 2007, r 64(a) requires the applicant to file any evidence upon which he or she wishes to rely with the application form and r 54 requires certain documents to be filed with the application for permission form.

Disclosure

8.91 Disclosure of documents means stating that documents exist or have existed, and is dealt with in COPR 2007, Part 16.[72] A party's duty to disclose documents by producing a list is limited to documents which are or have been in his or her control.[73] The list must indicate separately the documents in respect of which the party claims a right or duty to withhold inspection and those that are no longer in his or her control, stating what has happened to them. There is a need to balance the incapacitated persons right to privacy against the need for adequate disclosure to enable best interests to be addressed. For example, in property and affairs applications the Court must consider whether it is necessary to disclose the contents of the last Will.

8.92 The Court may either on its own initiative or on the application of a party make an order to give general or specific disclosure. Any party to whom the order applies is under a continuing duty to provide such disclosure until the proceedings are concluded. General disclosure relates not only to documents that are to be relied upon but also to those that adversely affect the party's own case, or adversely affect or support another party's case. Specific disclosure relates to specified documents or classes of documents and may include carrying out a search to the extent stated in the order. There is no equivalent to the provision in the Civil Procedure Rules 1998 for pre-action disclosure.

Inspection

8.93 A party has a right to inspect any document disclosed to him or her except where it is no longer in the control of the party who disclosed it, or the party disclosing the document has a right or duty to withhold inspection of it. An opportunity must be given for inspection and a copy of the document may be requested on payment of reasonable copying costs. A timetable is usually laid down for this process. Where documents are withheld the party wishing to inspect may apply to the Court to decide whether this should be upheld. A party may not without the permission of the Court rely upon any document which he or she fails to disclose or in respect of which he or she fails to permit inspection.

Litigation friends and representatives

8.94 A party will normally need a litigation friend to conduct the proceedings on his or her behalf if he or she is a child[74] or a 'protected party' (ie lacks capacity to conduct the proceedings) although in *Re X and Others (Deprivation of Liberty) (No 2)*[75] the court stated that there is no

---

[72] COPR 2007, rr 132–139.
[73] This means that he or she has or has had physical possession of them or the right to inspect or take copies of them.
[74] The Court may allow a child to proceed without a litigation friend if of sufficient understanding.
[75] [2014] EWCOP 37.

fundamental principle of law that dictates that P must have a litigation friend. It is simply that court rules demand it. COPR 2007, Part 17[76] and a Practice Direction make detailed provision for this. A person may act as a litigation friend if he or she satisfies two conditions, namely he or she can fairly and competently conduct proceedings on behalf of the incapacitated party and he or she has no interests adverse to those of that person.

8.95 The incapacitated person, if made a party, may also need a litigation friend but this will generally be the Official Solicitor because the persons who might otherwise provide such support are likely to be parties themselves or have an adverse interest. In other words, a person who should really be a party may not hijack the incapacitated person's case.

8.96 The Court has full control over the appointment and removal of litigation friends. It may make an order appointing the Official Solicitor or some other person to act as a litigation friend either on its own initiative or on the application of any person, but only with the consent of the person to be appointed. A deputy with the power to conduct legal proceedings on the protected party's behalf is entitled to be the litigation friend of that party, but otherwise if no one has been appointed by the Court, a person who wishes to act as a litigation friend must file a certificate of suitability and serve this on the child or protected party. The certificate states that he or she satisfies the above two conditions.

8.97 Specific provision is made for the situation where the appointment of a litigation friend comes to an end and where the incapacitated person who is the subject of proceedings ceases to lack capacity.

Consequent upon the introduction of the r 3A representative, the rules have been amended in Part 17 to address the appointment of the representative. The court must be satisfied that the representative can fairly and competently discharge his or her functions on behalf of P[77]. The court now has power to direct a person may not act as a representative[78].

Representation

8.98 The procedure to be followed when there is a change of solicitor is dealt with in COPR 2007, Part 18.[79] A notice of the change must be filed with the Court and served on all other parties, and the new address for service must be stated. A solicitor may apply for an order declaring that he or she has ceased to be the solicitor acting for a party.

---

[76] COPR 2007, rr 140–149 and Practice Direction PD 17A. Part 17 was completely amended on 1 July 2015.
[77] COPR 2007, r 147
[78] COPR 2007, r 148B
[79] COPR 2007, rr 150–154. A Practice Direction (PD 18A) deals with Change of Solicitor.

Costs

8.99 TThe he costs of and incidental to all proceedings are in the Court's discretion but the MCA 2005 requires the Rules to make detailed provision for regulating those costs.[80] The Court has full power to determine by whom and to what extent the costs of any proceedings are to be paid, and to disallow costs or order the legal or other representatives[81] concerned to meet the whole or part of any wasted costs. 'Wasted costs' means any costs incurred by a party:

(1) as a result of any improper, unreasonable or negligent act or omission on the part of any legal or other representative or any employee of such a representative; or

(2) which, in the light of any such act or omission occurring after they were incurred, the Court considers it is unreasonable to expect that party to pay.

This enables unreasonable conduct by representatives to be controlled by costs sanctions.

8.100 COPR 2007 may make provision:[82]

(1) as to the way in which, and funds from which, fees and costs are to be paid;

(2) for charging fees and costs upon the estate of the person to whom the proceedings relate; and

(3) for the payment of fees and costs within a specified time of the death of the person to whom the proceedings relate or the conclusion of the proceedings.

8.101 A charge on the estate of a person created by this provision does not cause any interest of the person in any property to fail or determine or to be prevented from recommencing.

8.102 COPR 2007, Part 19[83] and a Practice Direction deal with costs and incorporate much of the regime for assessment of the CPR which is accordingly reproduced in Part IV of this volume (including the Practice Direction on costs).

The general rule

8.103 Where the proceedings concern the incapacitated person's property and affairs, the general rule is that the costs of the proceedings or of that part of the proceedings that concerns his or her property and affairs shall be paid by him or her or charged to his or her estate. Where the proceedings concern

---

[80] MCA 2005, s 55.
[81] This expression means any person exercising a right of audience or right to conduct litigation on behalf of a party to proceedings.
[82] MCA 2005, s 56.
[83] COPR 2007, rr 155–168. The Practice Directions deal with costs generally (PD 19A) and Fixed Costs (PD 19B).

the incapacitated person's personal welfare, the general rule is that there will be no order as to the costs of the proceedings or of that part of the proceedings that concerns his or her personal welfare. Where the proceedings concern both property and affairs and personal welfare, the Court, insofar as practicable, will apportion the costs as between the respective issues.

8.104 The Court may depart from the general rule if the circumstances so justify, and in deciding whether departure is justified the Court will have regard to all the circumstances, including the conduct of the parties, whether a party has succeeded on part of his or her case, even if he or she has not been wholly successful, and the role of any public body involved in the proceedings. The conduct of the parties includes conduct before, as well as during, the proceedings and whether it was reasonable for a party to raise, pursue or contest a particular issue. Also the manner in which a party has made or responded to an application or a particular issue, and whether a party who has succeeded in his or her application or response to an application, in whole or in part, exaggerated any matter contained in his or her application or response. Costs can even be awarded against non-parties but appropriate procedures must be followed.

Assessment

8.105 The Court may order fixed costs or the payment of a contribution to the costs. It may also where appropriate carry out a summary assessment of the costs, but where the Court orders costs to be assessed by way of detailed assessment, this takes place in the High Court. Where the Court orders that a deputy, donee or attorney is entitled to remuneration out of the incapacitated person's estate for discharging his or her functions, the Court may make such order as it thinks fit, including an order that he or she be paid a fixed amount, he or she be paid at a specified rate or the amount of the remuneration shall be determined in accordance with the schedule of fees set out in the relevant Practice Direction. Alternatively, the Court may order a detailed assessment of such remuneration by a costs officer.

Fees

8.106 It has been Government policy that the existing Court of Protection like the other courts be self-funding, raising its income from court fees, although some subsidy is necessary for those who cannot afford the fees. Such subsidy is likely to be enhanced and increased for the new enlarged jurisdiction because many applications relate to situations where there is no money available or involved.

8.107 The Lord Chancellor may with the consent of the Treasury by order prescribe fees payable in respect of anything dealt with by the Court.[84] Such order may (and does) contain provision as to scales or rates of fees, exemptions from and reductions in fees and remission of fees in whole or in part.[85] Before making an order the Lord Chancellor must consult the President and Vice-President and the Senior Judge of the Court of Protection. Such steps as are reasonably practicable must then be taken to bring information about fees to the attention of persons likely to have to pay them. The fees will be recoverable summarily as a civil debt.

Appeals

8.108 MCA 2005 provides some flexibility as to how appeals may be dealt with.[86] COPR 2007, Part 20[87] makes detailed provision for appeals. Judges are defined by reference to tiers. Tier 1 comprises district judges and certain first tier tribunal judges, Tier 2 comprises the Senior Judge, circuit judges and Upper Tribunal Judges and Tier 3 are High Court Judges. Appeal is normally to the next tier of judge.

8.109 The Court may deal with an appeal or any part of an appeal at a hearing or without a hearing, having regard to the same matters as on reconsideration of orders made without a hearing or without notice to a person.[88] An appeal will generally be limited to a review of the decision of the first instance judge although there is some discretion. The appeal judge has all the powers of the first instance judge whose decision is being appealed and may affirm, set aside or vary any order made by the first instance judge, refer any issue to that judge for determination or order a new hearing as well as making a costs order. But authorisation is not limited to cases concerning medical treatment and may extend to decisions which would have the effect of depriving a person who lacked capacity to consent of their liberty.

Permission to appeal

8.110 COPR 2007 provides that permission is required to appeal against a decision of the Court (other than an order for committal to prison) and prescribes how this is obtained, the requirements to be satisfied and the considerations to be taken into account. An application for permission to appeal may be made by an 'appellant's notice' or a 'respondent's notice' to the first instance judge or the appeal judge, and where it is refused by the

---

[84] MCA 2005, s 54. Following the constitutional reforms this remains the responsibility of the Lord Chancellor.
[85] See Court of Protection Fees Order 2007, SI 2007/1745.
[86] MCA 2005, s 53.
[87] COPR 2007, rr 169–182. A Practice Direction (PD 20A) deals with Appeals.
[88] See COPR 2007, r 89.

first instance judge, a further application for permission may be made to a specified higher judge. There are time-limits but these may be varied on application.

8.111 Permission to appeal will be granted only where the Court considers that the appeal would have a real prospect of success, or there is some other compelling reason why the appeal should be heard. Where a higher judge of the Court makes a decision on an appeal, no appeal may be made to the Court of Appeal from that decision unless the Court of Appeal considers that the appeal would raise an important point of principle or practice, or there is some other compelling reason for the Court of Appeal to hear it.

Enforcement

8.112 The Court's powers of enforcement are much more extensive than may at first appear. The Court has in connection with its jurisdiction the same powers, rights, privileges and authority as the High Court,[89] which means that it may fine or commit to prison for contempt, grant injunctions, summons witnesses and order production of evidence. COPR 2007, Part 21 makes further provision,[90] while the relevant Practice Direction (PD21A) and Practice Guidance notes deals with Contempt of Court. Applications for enforcement may be made and the CPR relating to third party debt orders and charging orders apply. The rules have now been amended to ensure that the enforcement provisions incorporate the latest version of the CPR which was extensively amended recently.

8.113 The Court may direct that a penal notice is to be attached to any order warning the person on whom the copy of the order is served that disobeying the order would be a contempt of court punishable by imprisonment or a fine. An application relating to the committal of a person for contempt of court can be made to a judge (which includes a district judge) by filing an application notice, stating the grounds of the application, and must be supported by an affidavit made in accordance with the relevant Practice Direction. COPR 2007 makes further provision. In addition the Court may make an order for committal on its own initiative against a person guilty of contempt of court, which may include misbehaviour in the face of the Court.

Transitional provisions

8.114 These are to be found in COPR 2007, Part 22.[91] They include the transition from receiver to deputy and the nomination of officers to deal with such matters thereby implementing MCA 2005, Sch 5, Part 1.

---

[89] MCA 2005, s 47(1).
[90] COPR 2007, rr 183–194.
[91] COPR 2007, rr 195–199. Practice Directions deal with Transitional Provisions (PD 22A), Transitory Provisions (PD 22B) and Certain Specified Appeals (PD 22C).

Miscellaneous provisions

8.115 Provision is made in COPR 2007, Part 23[92] for the giving of security by deputies, references to the Court by the Public Guardian following objections to the registration of an enduring power of attorney and disposal of property where an incapacitated person ceases to lack capacity. Practice Directions deal with certain objections to the registration of enduring powers of attorney (PD23A) and the procedure where 'P' ceases to lack capacity or dies (PD23B).

PRACTICAL POINTS

The workload

Volume of cases

8.116 With a wide range of cases relating not only to financial management but also to social welfare and health care – in fact the entire range of personal decision-making for adults who lack capacity, the consequence is an ever increasing volume of cases for the Court of Protection to cope with which shows no sign of abatement. The withdrawal of legal aid in family work and a general downturn in the economy means that more solicitors and barristers are looking to the Court of Protection as a source of work which is to be encouraged.

The court also faced a major challenge (if not its biggest administrative challenge) following the decision in *P v Cheshire West and Chester Council*[93] and the need for more types of situations involving deprivation of liberty to be authorised by the court. After the case, there was a fear that thousands of applications would be made. This prompted the President to convene a hearing to consider the best process to manage such cases (see *Re X and Others (Deprivation of Liberty)*[94] and *Re X (Deprivation of Liberty) (No 2)*.[95] As a result, a streamlined *Re X* procedure was developed. However, the Court of Appeal in strong obiter dicta disagreed with the President's view on whether P should be joined. This again, threw matters into chaos. This provoked a further decision in *Re NRA*[96] where it was held that P did not always have to be a party. Nevertheless, the *Re X* procedure is still undergoing amendment following this decision and other situations that need to be catered for.

Cases under the court's jurisdiction

8.117 The following are examples of situations that the court can encounter and illustrate the need for local dispute resolution by a nominated district or circuit judge as to the best interests of the person lacking capacity.

---

[92] COPR 2007, rr 200–202.
[93] [2014] UKSC 19, [2014] COPLR 313.
[94] [2014] EWCOP 25.
[95] [2014] EWCOP 37.
[96] [2015] EWCOP 59.

- *Residential care dispute* – Dispute between a son and daughter who live some distance apart as to which residential care or nursing home their mother should move to. She has Alzheimer's disease and is incapable of participating in the decision but has adequate funds to meet the fees.
- *Contact disputes* – There may be a preliminary issue as to whether the adults in the following examples have capacity to decide whom they wish to have contact with. The Court may wish to decide this first and only proceed to an intrusive best interests inquiry if capacity to make the decision is lacking.
  (a) A daughter from an Asian background has married outside her ethnic origins and adopted a way of life that results in her being cut off by her family. She still wishes to visit her learning disabled brother but the family prevent this.
  (b) Older parents with a learning disabled son became involved in a bitter divorce which results in father being excluded from the matrimonial home where mother continues to care for this son. A daughter who has sided with father is then denied access to her brother.
- *Adult care dispute* – A child with learning disabilities has been placed in care under the Children Act 1989 and the social workers involved are concerned about the role of the parents upon the child attaining majority.[97]
- *Adult protection issues* – Social services respond to allegations of abuse by moving a senile elderly person into a care home and restricting access by family carers who then challenge this intervention.[98]
- *Activities* – A charity providing outdoor adventure holidays for adults with learning disabilities wishes to take an individual on a mountaineering course but mother (who may be over-protective) thinks it is too dangerous and objects. Care workers and a personal advocate support this opportunity for personal development. The charity seeks reassurance that this is in the best interests of the individual so that it would only be vulnerable to legal proceedings if negligent (and not irrespective of fault in the event of an accident).[99]
- *Education* – Father wants his 19-year-old son with severe learning disabilities to attend a residential training college and has arranged funding. Mother prefers him to live with her but has made no arrangements for his daytime activities. The local authority has offered a place at the local training centre and is very concerned that mother will not allow him to attend. A local nominated judge could see the parties, consider welfare reports and make a decision (if an attempt at mediation did not result in the deadlock being resolved).

---

[97] Such cases have become quite common.
[98] Ideally the local authority should initiate proceedings to justify its intervention but there have been cases where the family members have had to apply to the Court.
[99] This type of activity may well be covered under MCA 2005, s 5 and not require Court of Protection authority.

- *Minor medical decisions* – Parents wish to arrange for their 23-year-old daughter with Down's syndrome to have some dental treatment which will improve her appearance but is not otherwise necessary. She appears to want this treatment but there is doubt as to whether she can legally consent so the dentist is unwilling to proceed, perhaps because there is some element of risk. A local nominated judge could resolve this.
- *Sexual relationships* – Care workers are concerned as to whether a resident with learning disabilities being supported in a group living arrangement is competent to enter into a sexual relationship with another resident. They seek a declaration from the Court.[100]

Integration with other courts

Judicial support

8.118 Historically there has been little liaison between the former Court of Protection and the civil or family courts, although there were occasions when one must refer to the other. Now that there are generic judges spread throughout the country nominated to sit in the new Court of Protection there is proving to be more integration of an informal nature, with judicial colleagues seeking support and guidance on capacity issues and cases raising issues that require Court of Protection input. Cases with a capacity element may be transferred to, or listed before, the local nominated judge because of their additional expertise. For example:

- *Financial remedies* – Following a divorce between an elderly couple financial claims are made which include the future of the former matrimonial home. At a financial dispute resolution hearing the husband makes proposals under which the wife may remain in the home for life. The lawyers involved agree that these proposals are more beneficial to the wife than she is likely to achieve at a contested hearing. She cannot grasp the implications and refuses to accept. The district judge is in a dilemma because if she persists in refusing the offer she is in danger of paying all the costs and losing the home. The judge questions whether she lacks mental capacity and should be treated as a 'protected party' with a 'next friend' appointed to conduct the proceedings on her behalf (often the Official Solicitor), but she refuses to be medically examined. A nominated judge to whom the case is transferred could tackle all the issues and resolve them locally with minimum delay and expense.
- *Possession* – A landlord or mortgagee brings a possession claim for non-payment of sums due and the elderly tenant or mortgagor attends but appears confused and unable to cope. Doubts arise as to mental capacity and the judge is in great difficulty knowing how to proceed. If this defendant is a protected party a litigation friend must be appointed but a separate application would have to be made

---

[100] The Court does not have power to consent on a person's behalf to a sexual relationship: MCA 2005, s 27(1)(b).

to the Court of Protection for the appointment of a deputy. The case could be referred to a nominated judge who could deal with the capacity issue, the need for practical support and the merits of the possession claim all in the same series of hearings, invoking the jurisdiction of the Court of Protection if necessary.
- *Contract* – A local shopkeeper sues a customer with learning disabilities who has been placed 'in the community' for non-payment of bills for normal provisions. Support from social services (who set up this living arrangement) has evaporated with everyone passing the buck. A district judge dealing with the matter as a 'small claim' in the County Court will be in difficulty, but could pass the case to a nominated judge who would have the powers (under a dual jurisdiction if necessary) and experience to deal with it.

Dual jurisdiction

8.119 There are situations where it might be helpful for a nominated judge to sit in a dual capacity, namely in the Court of Protection and also the civil or family court. The following examples illustrate both the need for local dispute resolution and an overlap with the existing role of the civil or family courts:

(1) Following a divorce between elderly parents there is a dispute as to which parent is to continue to care for their 40-year-old mentally disabled child and the future of the matrimonial home may depend on this. *A nominated district judge could simultaneously deal with the care issue under the new jurisdiction and the ancillary relief claims in the County Court, these being interdependent.*[101]

(2) There is a dispute between parents relating to contact by father with their two children, the older of whom has learning disabilities but is by now an adult. *An application in the County Court under the Children Act 1989 relating to the younger child could be linked with an application to the Court of Protection in respect of the older child and heard together by a nominated district judge.*

(3) Older parents with a learning disabled adult son became involved in a bitter divorce which results in father being excluded from the matrimonial home where mother continues to care for the son. A daughter who has sided with father is then denied access to her brother and seeks to establish that it is in his best interests to see her on a regular basis. *A nominated district judge could resolve the issue under the new jurisdiction in the context of the divorce proceedings thereby having an overview of the whole family situation.*

(4) A local authority has made a decision about the placement of an incapacitated adult, and it may be necessary, if that decision is to be

---

[101] If the child had not yet attained majority the residence and ancillary relief claims would have been amalgamated in the County Court.

challenged, to proceed both by way of proceedings for judicial review and a best interests claim under the new Court of Protection jurisdiction. *A nominated High Court judge could deal with both matters together.*

8.120 If a case requires transfer in whole or part to the Court of Protection, if a judge is also nominated to sit in the Court of Protection, he can reconstitute himself as a Court of Protection judge and make appropriate orders to bring the case within that court. He may also dispense with the need to make an application. Some judges prefer an application to be made although the overriding objective would suggest that the most economical and expeditious method of transfer of a case should be adopted especially when the same judge will continue to hear it. If a case is being transferred by a judge who is not nominated to sit in the Court of Protection, he can order that the case is transferred and the court file will be sent to the Court of Protection's main registry in the normal way of transfer of any case. On arrival, a judge will give appropriate directions.

Chapter 9

The Public Guardian and Supporting Services

INTRODUCTION

9.1 The mental capacity jurisdiction, and in particular the Court of Protection, is supported by a range of statutory and other bodies, and other professional individuals. This Chapter considers the nature of such resources and their purpose or role.

THE PUBLIC GUARDIAN[1]

9.2 The Mental Capacity Act 2005[2] (MCA 2005) established a new a statutory office-holder appointed by the Lord Chancellor[3] and known as the Public Guardian.

Office of the Public Guardian[4]

9.3 The Lord Chancellor[5] may, after consulting the Public Guardian, provide him with such officers and staff, or enter into such contracts with other persons for the provision (by them or their subcontractors) of officers, staff or services, as the Lord Chancellor thinks necessary for the proper discharge of the Public Guardian's functions. Any functions of the Public Guardian may, to the extent authorised by him or her, be performed by any of his officers. So the Office of the Public Guardian ('OPG'), an agency of the Ministry of Justice, is itself recognised by and funded under the authority of Parliament.[6]

Functions

9.4 The Public Guardian has the following basic functions:[7]

(1) establishing and maintaining a register of lasting powers of attorney;[8]

---

[1] See www.justice.gov.uk/about/opg. For the background to this Office see Chapter 1 at paragraph 1.162.1.
[2] MCA 2005, s 57.
[3] For the meaning in this context see Chapter 7 at **7.1**ff.
[4] The assistance of Joan Goulbourn from the Office of the Public Guardian with the material under this heading is gratefully acknowledged.
[5] For the meaning in this context see Chapter 7 at **7.1**ff.
[6] MCA 2005, s 57(4), (5).
[7] MCA 2005, s 58.
[8] He must also continue the Register of enduring powers of attorney: MCA 2005, Sch 4, Pt 4, paragraph 14.

(2) establishing and maintaining a register of orders appointing deputies;
(3) supervising deputies appointed by the Court;
(4) directing a Court of Protection Visitor to visit (i) a donee of a lasting power of attorney, (ii) a deputy appointed by the Court, or (iii) the person granting the power of attorney or for whom the deputy is appointed, and to make a report to the Public Guardian on such matters as he or she may direct;
(5) receiving security which the Court requires a person to give for the discharge of his or her functions;
(6) receiving reports from donees of lasting powers of attorney and deputies appointed by the Court;
(7) reporting to the Court on such matters relating to proceedings under MCA 2005 as the Court requires;
(8) dealing with representations (including complaints) about the way in which a donee of a lasting power of attorney or a deputy appointed by the Court is exercising his or her powers;
(9) publishing, in any manner the Public Guardian thinks appropriate, any information he or she thinks appropriate about the discharge of his or her functions.

9.5 These functions thus fall into three categories: registration, supervision and investigation. With the exception of the first one they may be discharged in co-operation with any other person who has functions in relation to the care or treatment of the incapacitated person. The Public Guardian works closely with organisations such as local authorities, care providers and NHS Trusts, and can request information from them under this provision. The Lord Chancellor[9] may by regulations make provision conferring on the Public Guardian other functions in connection with MCA 2005 or in connection with the discharge by the Public Guardian of his or her functions. In particular, regulations may make provision as to:[10]

- the giving of security by deputies appointed by the Court and the enforcement and discharge of security so given;
- the fees which may be charged by the Public Guardian;
- the way in which, and funds from which, such fees are to be paid;
- exemptions from and reductions in such fees;
- remission of such fees in whole or in part;
- the making of reports to the Public Guardian by deputies appointed by the Court and others who are directed by the Court to carry out any transaction for a person who lacks capacity.

This provides considerable scope for development of the operation and services of the OPG as experience is gained under the new jurisdiction. In particular it is hoped that the Public Guardian will be able to address some of the abuse that takes place by attorneys and others.

---

[9] For the meaning in this context see Chapter 7 at **7.1**ff.
[10] MCA 2005, s 58(3) and (4). See Lasting Powers of Attorney, Enduring Powers of Attorney and Public Guardian Regulations 2007, SI 2007/1253.

9.6 The OPG may be contacted at:

Office of the Public Guardian

PO Box 16185

Birmingham B2 2WH

DX 744240 Birmingham 79

Tel: 0300 456 0300 (Phone lines are open Monday–Friday 9am–5pm (Except Wednesday 10am–5pm))

Fax: 0870 739 5780

Textphone: 0115 934 2778

Powers

9.7 For the purpose of enabling him to carry out his functions, the Public Guardian may, at all reasonable times, examine and take copies of any health record, any record of (or held by) a local authority and compiled in connection with a social services function and any record held by a person registered under the Care Standards Act 2000, Part 2 so far as the record relates to the client. He (or his officers) may also for that purpose interview the incapacitated person in private.[11] The Public Guardian is empowered to apply to the Court of Protection in connection with his functions under the Act in such circumstances as he considers it necessary or appropriate to do so.[12]

Fees

9.8 Annual fees are charged for the supervision of deputies payable annually in arrears on 31 March.[13] Following a Consultation in February 2011, the OPG fee regime has been changed. With effect from 1 October 2011, one flat fee of £320 is being charged under Type I, Type IIa and II supervision and there is a one-off fee of £100 on the appointment.[14] The fees are revised at intervals and are to be found on the OPG website.[15] There is a fee of £35 for Type III supervision. Each case will be reviewed regularly and the type of supervision allocated may change as circumstances change. Supervision fees will be calculated on a pro-rata basis if:

- there has been more than one type of supervision applied in a one-year period; or
- supervision has been in place for less than one year; or
- the person lacking capacity or the deputy dies. (Fees are payable up to the date of death).

---

[11] MCA 2005, s 58(5) and (6).
[12] 2007 Regs, reg 43.
[13] Public Guardian (Fees etc) Regulations 2007, SI 2007/2051 and Public Guardian (Fees etc) (Amendment) Regulations 2007, SI 2007/2616.
[14] Previously £800 for Type I and £350 (£175 at lower rate) for Type II. There was no fee for Type III supervision.
[15] See www.gov.uk/government/organisations/office-of-the-public-guardian.

Fees are also charged for the registration of enduring powers of attorney and lasting powers of attorney. In certain circumstances fee exemption or remission may apply.[16]

Annual Report

9.9 The Public Guardian must make an annual report to the Lord Chancellor[17] about the discharge of his or her functions.[18]

The Office of the Public Guardian Board

9.10 The Office of the Public Guardian Board provides strategic leadership on the broad direction for the agency and supports the delivery of the aims and objectives agreed within the Business Plan. It consists of executive and non-executive board members. The Board operates within Ministry of Justice/OPG governance and its members take decisions collectively and not as representatives of any business area or interest.

Panel of Deputies

9.11 OPG maintains a panel of deputies for use by the court in 'last resort' cases; that is, cases where there is no one else willing, suitable, or able to act as deputy. As part of the terms of membership a panel deputy must agree to accept any appointment as deputy at the request of the Court of Protection unless they have a valid reason not to do so. The panel appointed in April 2011 was comprised mainly of solicitors who have deputyship experience and relevant specialist skills. Currently most deputies are family members but the panel is a useful facility especially where there are continuing disputes within the family or there is no one suitable to accept appointment. Panel deputies are generally only appointed for property and affairs because they charge professional fees. Many local authorities also provide deputyship services but on the basis of fixed costs and these services are therefore subsidised.

9.12 In an attempt to widen the pool of potential deputies the Public Guardian launched a consultation in late 2011 on the appointment of not-for-profit organisations as deputies which it has used to inform the recruitment for the refreshment of the panel for 2015. A greater representation of different organisation types on the panel increases the options available to the court ensuring that the most appropriate deputy can be appointed in each case. For example, in straightforward cases it may be more appropriate for the person's affairs to be managed by a deputy who is not a solicitor and whose charges would therefore be lower, or the person

---

16 Refer to www.gov.uk/government/publications/deputy-fees-remission-or-exemption.
17 For the meaning in this context see Chapter 7 at **7.1**ff.
18 MCA 2005, s 60. The Annual Reports and Accounts are available at: www.justice.gov.uk/publications/corporate-reports/office-of-the-public-guardian.

who lacks capacity may benefit from having a deputy who can provide advocacy and support services as part of their package of services.

Challenges ahead

9.13 The OPG is fundamentally different in status and functions from its predecessor, the PGO, despite a similarity of name. It has a statutory existence with supervisory and regulatory functions.[19] It is hoped that the Public Guardian (through his or her senior staff to whom he or she can delegate his or her powers) will act fearlessly and independently, becoming a mediator and problem-solver as well as performing administrative functions and investigating abuse.

Public Guardian's role

9.14 The Public Guardian has three distinct roles: administrative, supervisory and policy-making. He or she must:

(1) be a supporter of incapacitated persons and their families and carers;
(2) be a supporter of good attorneys and deputies;
(3) provide guidance on, and as part of the investigation process monitor standards in decision-making for vulnerable adults that everyone is expected to follow;
(4) establish procedures for investigating allegations of abuse; and
(5) work with local authorities and other agencies who have an interest in safeguarding vulnerable adults, such as the Police, Care Quality Commission, Care and Social Services Inspectorate Wales, and regulators such as the Solicitors Regulation Authority.

The new OPG places emphasis on promoting the concept of the assumption of capacity and being dedicated to ensure that appointed decision makers only become involved in decisions when necessary and always act in the best interests of the client. Partnerships must be developed with social services and health authorities and agencies and also those charitable organisations working in this area.

Dispute resolution

9.15 OPG is looking at ways in which it can establish its own dispute resolution procedures. It must not be overlooked that the objective is to address the best interests of the incapacitated individual rather than resolve disputes between other persons, especially when these persons are not addressing this individual's welfare. In the case of many dysfunctional families the issue becomes control over rather than the welfare of the vulnerable member and involving an outsider may be the appropriate

---

[19] It also provided the administrative arm of the Court of Protection until this function was transferred to HM Courts Service (now HM Courts and Tribunals Service) on 1 April 2009.

solution. A pilot mediation scheme is running until April 2015, following which OPG will evaluate the results and merits of continuing such a scheme.

Investigating abuse

9.16 An Investigations Unit was established at the PGO and lessons were learnt as to how such a unit may best function. The OPG has drawn on this experience. Internal procedures for referring cases have been developed and other procedures agreed for external referrals. A protocol has been agreed by the OPG with local authorities on how to work with them to safeguard vulnerable adults. Publicity is necessary if this is to function effectively and a dedicated helpline is in place, together with a programme for raising awareness. Cases may be referred by safeguarding staff in local authorities and OPG has consulted with the Association of Directors of Social Services on a Working Protocol. Referrals may now extend beyond financial abuse and include other forms of abuse. If OPG does not have the jurisdiction to investigate a case it will ensure that the person raising the concern is signposted to the relevant authority or OPG may contact the relevant authority itself. In some instances a new deputy will be appointed following an application to the Court and instructed to take appropriate action. The Public Guardian can also apply to the Court for an attorney to be removed from acting under an LPA. If this still leaves other attorneys then the LPA will remain in force. If it means that there are no longer any attorneys or replacement attorneys then an application will be made to court to appoint a deputy.

The Public Guardian's jurisdiction is to investigate representations and complaints about the way in which an attorney of LPA or a deputy appointed by the Court is exercising his powers.[20] As LPAs can be registered before the donor loses capacity, the Public Guardian is obliged to consider representations about the actions of an LPA donee even if the donor has capacity. However, the practice adopted is to firstly investigate the donor's capacity and ability to address the concerns himself, and the Public Guardian will generally only take forward a full investigation if the donor lacks capacity or is otherwise unable to address the concerns.

Use of technology

9.17 OPG is developing its use of technology as one of MoJ's 'digital exemplars' which form part of the Government's digital by default strategy. In September 2014, OPG published its first digital strategy outlining its programme of transformation up to 2018 and its plans to be a digital by default agency by 2015. In May 2014 a digital service was launched to aid the process of completing the LPA forms. The forms can be completed

---

[20] Under MCA, s 58(1)(h). This is extended to attorneys acting under a registered EPA by Reg 48 of the LPA, EPA and PG Regs.

without the need to enter details multiple times and embedded help and guidance helps users avoid common administrative errors.

Partnerships

9.18 OPG is proactive in developing partnerships. These include working with voluntary and third sector organisations, the legal sector, the Financial Ombudsman, the Financial Conduct Authority, the British Banking Association and individual banks and utility companies. It also works closely with other government departments and agencies including the Department for Work and Pensions, the Department of Health, HM Revenue and Customs, the police and the Criminal Records Bureau.

Funding

9.19 Separate fees are now charged for the work of OPG as distinct from the Court of Protection (as they are now statutorily separate bodies). OPG has a regime of fees in place which ensure that 100 per cent of the costs of the organisation (other than remissions and exemptions) are met from the fees paid. There is a remissions and exemptions policy in place to ensure that those with lower incomes are not eligible to pay fees. At times, OPG has looked to increase its fees to cover the cost of transformation but the fee for registering an LPA is currently lower than it has been at any time since OPG came into being.

Relationship with the Court of Protection

9.20 The Court of Protection deals with disputes that require a hearing and may be the ultimate decision-maker when matters cannot be resolved by the Public Guardian. The Court also retains a considerable volume of paper-based decision-making which is to some extent delegated to nominated officers with any challenges being referred to the nominated district judges. Recourse to the Court for the resolution of disputes should be regarded as a last resort. The extent to which the Public Guardian may ultimately act on his own initiative will be dictated by decisions of the Court of Protection on references and appeals, and no doubt by the High Court in the event of judicial reviews. But OPG will have a more authoritative role than the former PGO as it is a separate statutorily defined body.

9.21 This enhanced role for the Public Guardian leads to a change in the relationship with the Court of Protection. It was questioned whether, if the OPG was to act independently from the Court of Protection, it should also administer the Court in the same way as HM Courts Service administered the civil and criminal courts. There was a need to demonstrate the distinction between administrative and judicial functions and to maintain judicial independence, yet there were significant advantages in maintaining a link between the Court and the OPG. Master Lush had identified a need to 'disentangle the close relationship that exists between the Court of

Protection and the PGO in a way that achieves a proper distinction between the two organisations, whilst retaining the positive aspects of the present close working arrangements' but the former Chief Executive of the PGO had concerns as to how that close relationship might be maintained.

9.22 The list of functions conferred by MCA 2005 does not expressly include the PGO's previous function of processing originating applications to the Court of Protection. Initially there were two separate administrations, in separate offices within Archway but both under the control of the Public Guardian, with the Court having its own staff. The concern that the Public Guardian, who may be a party to court proceedings and appeal orders of the judges, also administered the Court has now been resolved. During 2009 the administration of the Court was transferred to HM Courts Service (now HM Courts and Tribunals Service) and much of the work of the OPG has been moved to Birmingham and Nottingham.[21]

Transforming the services of the OPG

9.23 In August 2014 OPG published a consultation 'Transforming the services of the Office of the Public Guardian: enabling Digital by Default'. The consultation paper considered the next phase of the OPG transformation programme, as well as exploring some of the future changes that OPG may seek to make within the next few years. The consultation included proposed improvements to the design of the paper forms for creating a LPA, fees for a new combined form, access to the OPG registers and changes to the supervision of court appointed deputies.

9.24 It also considered the bigger picture and proposals for future changes, in line with MoJ's Transforming Justice agenda and the Government's commitment for more public services to be digital by default. Initial proposals for the delivery of a fully digital method of creating and registering LPAs were outlined which would require primary legislation in the future. The proposals were designed to ensure that OPG is able to deal effectively with future volumes across all areas of its business and deliver services that are more effective, less costly and more responsive for its users. The response to the consultation was published in August 2014.

COURT OF PROTECTION VISITORS

Background

9.25 For the history of the role of the Lord Chancellor's Visitors and the proposals for reform prior to the MCA 2005 reference should be made to Chapter 1 at paragraph 1.188 *et seq*.

---

[21] The postal address is now Office of the Public Guardian, PO Box 16185, Birmingham B2 2WH (DX 744240 Birmingham 79.

The new regime

Appointment

9.26 For the purpose of the new jurisdiction there are two panels of Court of Protection Visitors[22] appointed by the Lord Chancellor:[23] a panel of Special Visitors and a panel of General Visitors.[24] They are appointed to carry out visits and produce reports in much the same way as previously although the brief may be wider. There is not seen to be the need for a Legal Visitor under the new regime. It is the OPG practice to recruit by open competition rather than private invitation. Visitors are appointed for such term and subject to such conditions, and may be paid such remuneration and allowances, as the Lord Chancellor may determine. The OPG administers the panel of visitors but the Court can draw on this as a resource.

General Visitors

9.27 A General Visitor need not have a medical qualification. Many have social work, welfare or experience in mental capacity backgrounds but more recently there has been recruitment from new areas such as local authority finance teams and those with legal and medical experience. It is unlikely that outsourcing to bodies such as other government agencies, local authorities or NHS organisations would be adopted because this would lack the transparent independence of the Visitors Service. In some cases the Court needs a report because of conflict between family and such bodies. There is a statutory power to request reports from these bodies when that is thought appropriate, but in most instances the judges will seek a report from their own reporting service just as they turn to CAFCASS in children cases. Outsourcing to the not-for-profit sector may not be desirable because consistent training might not be available and uniform standards would be difficult to impose and enforce. It is essential for the Public Guardian to maintain his or her own independent 'eyes and ears' and for this facility to be available to the Court. Mental capacity issues represent a discrete area where a body of experience needs to be developed, and the role of the Visitors is so important that a specialist service needs to be established and maintained.

9.28 There is now a core of a small number of General Visitors employed by the OPG supported by casuals. The employed full-timers are based at home and operate on a regional basis. In order to maintain a sufficient reserve of visiting services a panel of self-employed casual General Visitors are retained who can be commissioned to prepare reports. An employment basis for the General Visitors may be preferred because this allows for more central control and frees the way for more training, the provision of standard facilities (including laptop computers with appropriate pro formas) and

---

[22] This title replaces 'Lord Chancellor's Visitors'.
[23] All references to the Lord Chancellor should be read in the light of the constitutional reforms – see Chapter 7 at **7.1ff**.
[24] MCA 2005, s 61(1)–(4).

access to networked or secure e-mail communication. But this must not be at the expense of a loss of independence. The Visitors may be accountable to the Public Guardian as employees but are accountable to the Court when delivering reports requested directly by the Court. They may be required to attend hearings to give evidence and in that respect are vulnerable to cross-examination. So their approach to the reporting process and any constraints placed upon them will become apparent.

9.29 A high proportion of the visiting carried out for the OPG is still done by the enlarged body of self-employed visitors supplementing the small employed group. This has enabled the Public Guardian to guarantee a rapid response if necessary but also to deploy some very experienced or more specialist Visitors within the wider group for particular visits. Reporting timescales have been greatly shortened to only six weeks or less from the time of visits being commissioned, and the Public Guardian can also get a visit done the same day if need be.

Frequency of visiting, including the decision whether there will be a visit at all, is now tied to supervision levels (from 1 to 3) allocated after the order is received from the Court. Only Type 1 cases are routinely visited and repeat visited. Type 2A has been introduced as an intermediate level for new lay deputies largely but also to address other short term situations and these also generally receive a visit. Prior to implementation and this 'risk based' approach to supervision and visiting, the OPG had aimed to have some level of visiting to almost all its clients although it never fully achieved this. Many clients will now not be visited at all in this model but they should have been assessed first as low risk/'light touch'.

9.30 The OPG no longer directs all its visiting to the client – in many cases the Visitor is instructed to interview the deputy only, or to ensure that the deputy is seen as well as the client. OPG operates a system of 'assurance visits' to professional deputies and local authorities, who are visited to discuss several clients at the same time, following a visit to a sample of their clients. There is a new emphasis on regulation and ensuring that principles of the Act and the Code of Practice are complied with, for example that clients are seen by the deputy or their representative and that as far as possible efforts are made to consult with them.

Special Visitors

9.31 A Special Visitor must be a registered medical practitioner (or appear to the Lord Chancellor to have other suitable qualifications or training), and must also appear to the Lord Chancellor to have special knowledge of and experience in cases of impairment of or disturbance in the functioning of the mind or brain. This is the main distinction between the Special and General Visitors. The scale of remuneration is also different and the method of recruitment may differ as these are specialist appointments, but fundamentally the funding mechanism and the process of recruitment is the same with both groups of visitors. A small number of suitably experienced psychiatrists (or in some instances psychologists) are appointed on a consultancy basis and called upon when the need arises.

9.32 The role of the Special Visitors is largely restricted to reporting in two areas. First, they are by reason of their qualification and experience well placed to provide reports expressing an opinion on capacity. Secondly, they are able to assist in cases where there are communication difficulties and to report on the wishes and feelings of the incapacitated individual when others have difficulty in doing so. It may be that, other than in these two respects, the Court will not seek a report from a Special Visitor in health and welfare cases because where guidance is needed that will be the role of experts' evidence. The use of Special Visitors in serious medical treatment involving the withholding and withdrawal of treatment is likely to be exceptional. It would appear that there is potential for Special Visitors to be used more widely, particularly in cases where there are problems funding independent experts. They have been used relatively frequently in personal welfare cases to deal with issues relating to P's capacity, such as where a number of parties are unrepresented and there is no local authority involvement (eg, a dispute amongst family members as to residence and contact) and where perhaps P has not been joined as a party due to problems over funding his or her legal representation.

Reports by Visitors

9.33 Under MCA 2005 the Court of Protection may require a report to be made to it by a Visitor, in writing or orally, on such matters as may be specified.[25] The Public Guardian may also direct a Visitor to visit a donee of a lasting power of attorney, a deputy or the incapacitated person and make a report on such matters as may be directed.[26] The jurisdiction now extends to personal welfare and health care decisions affecting mentally incapacitated adults, in addition to the former jurisdiction over their property and financial affairs. Accordingly, the Visitors may now be required to report on matters relating to where a patient should live and whether a decision should be made to withhold or withdraw medical treatment.

9.34 The demand for reports is unlikely to reduce from the previous level for financial affairs, and to this are now added health and welfare reports of a more specific nature. There may of course be an overlap. However, the Official Solicitor is appointed to represent the incapacitated person in many personal welfare cases and a report is unlikely to be required then from a General Visitor. Where there is an issue as to mental capacity and the evidence from medical experts is felt by the Court to be insufficient, a report from a Special Visitor who has reviewed the existing evidence is often a process of great value.

---

[25] MCA 2005, s 49.
[26] MCA 2005, s 58(1)(d).

Powers

9.35 For the purpose of carrying out their functions in relation to a person who lacks capacity, Court of Protection Visitors may, at all reasonable times, examine and take copies of:

(1) any health record;
(2) any record of, or held by, a local authority and compiled in connection with a social services function; and
(3) any record held by a person registered under the Care Standards Act 2000, Part 2 so far as the record relates to the person who lacks capacity.

They may also for that purpose interview the person who lacks capacity in private.[27]

The changed climate

9.36 I It has been recognised that changes are required in the relationship between the Public Guardian and the new panels of Visitors compared with that of the PGO, which dealt with the former Visitors as self-employed contractors. There is a need to ensure that Visitors are adequately protected financially and legally, with health and safety checks (especially in respect of lone visits), public liability insurance, and clearly defined job roles, skills sets and person specifications. The Public Guardian has established increased levels of accountability in terms of quality standards, reporting timescales, professional updating and training.

Association of Independent Visitors

9.37 After October 2007 clients of the Court were no longer certain to receive a periodic visit from a Court of Protection Visitor or their successors. Some solicitors and local authorities regretted the loss of the useful independent monitoring and advice this gave them about their clients. They saw the need to commission such visits themselves to fill this gap and to address Mental Capacity Act issues and the good practice requirements enshrined in the Code of Practice. One new resource which can assist in this area is the *Association of Independent Visitors* which was set up by a group of experienced former and current Court Visitors following the implementation of the Act. Its members emphasise that their private work is, as the name suggests, completely independent of the OPG or the Court.[28]

---

[27] MCA 2005, s 61(5)–(6).
[28] They can be contacted via their website www.aivuk.org.uk which enables the enquirer to find the visitor covering every area of the country according to postcode.

THE OFFICIAL SOLICITOR[29]

Status and function

9.38 The Official Solicitor to the Senior Courts is an independent statutory officer holder appointed by the Lord Chancellor under the Senior Courts Act 1981, s 90.[30] His main function is to represent parties to proceedings who are without capacity, deceased or unascertained when no other suitable person or agency is able and willing to do so. The purpose is to prevent a possible denial of justice and safeguard the welfare, property or status of the party. Such proceedings may be in the family proceedings court, County Court, High Court or Court of Protection.

9.39 The Official Solicitor can as at 1 January 2014 be contacted at:

Victory House
30–34 Kingsway
London WC2B 6EX
DX 141423 Bloomsbury[31]
Tel: 020 3681 2751 (Health & Welfare); 020 3681 2758 (Property & Affairs)[32]
Fax: 020 3681 2762
E-mail: enquiries@offsol.gsi.gov.uk (general enquiries)
E-mail: OS_Healthcare_&_@offsol.gsi.gov.uk (healthcare and welfare referrals)
Website: www.gov.uk/government/organisations/official-solicitor-and-public-trustee

The present office

9.40 The joint office of the Official Solicitor and Public Trustee is known as the OSPT. The OSPT is an 'arm's length body' of the Ministry of Justice which exists to support the work of the Official Solicitor and Public Trustee.[33] The two office holders continue to have separate corporate functions and the Public Trustee is not involved in mental capacity issues. Functionally the Official Solicitor is part of the judicial system of England and Wales (that is, excluding Scotland and Northern Ireland), while the Public Trustee is a separate and independent statutory body. The office is currently administered as part of the Ministry of Justice. At the time of writing the Official Solicitor to the Senior Courts is Alastair Pitblado and the Public Trustee is Eddie Bloomfield.

---

[29] The extensive contribution of James Beck from the Official Solicitor's office to the material under this heading is gratefully acknowledged.

[30] Following the creation of a new Supreme Court to replace the House of Lords as the ultimate appeal court, from October 2009 his title changed from Official Solicitor to the Supreme Court. Constitutional Reform Act 2005, Sch 11, paragraph 26. The Supreme Court Act 1981 was also renamed the Senior Courts Act 1981.

[31] Official Solicitor's office moved in August 2013 from 81 Chancery Lane, London WC2A 1DD.

[32] There is no single enquiry number for the Office. Telephone numbers for enquiries concerning Civil Litigation and family proceedings please consult the website.

[33] For the background to the Office see Chapter 1.

9.41 For the financial year 2015–16, the office has an agreed compliment equivalent to 136 full time staff.[34] All the staff are civil servants who specialise in different areas of work. As at September 2015, the Official Solicitor employed 25 lawyers (including part time and agency) amongst his staff. About 40 of his other staff are caseworkers who are not employed as lawyers but who are responsible for managing litigation friend cases on behalf of the Official Solicitor. Their primary role is to discharge the Official Solicitor's duties as litigation friend in the cases they manage, which will usually involve the appointment of an external firm of solicitors to act for the incapacitated party, ensuring that funding arrangements are in place to pay those solicitors and providing instructions to them for the duration of the proceedings. The non-lawyer caseworkers in the office have access to in-house legal advice where appropriate and sometimes conduct litigation themselves under the direct supervision of a lawyer.

During the financial year 2014–15 the Official Solicitor had 1,278 cases referred to him in proceedings in the Court of Protection with 623 relating to property and affairs and 655 relating to healthcare and welfare (of which 46 related to potential serious medical treatment).[35]

9.42 Both the Official Solicitor and the Public Trustee have such powers and perform such duties as may be conferred on them by statute and by Rules of Court, and, in the case of the Official Solicitor, also at common law. The Official Solicitor's role in court proceedings is Official recognised by the Court Rules,[36] and the Court of Protection Rules 2007[37] and Practice Directions make specific provision for his involvement[38]. By way of guidance he issued Practice Notes dealing with medical and welfare decisions for incapacitated adults,[39] including sterilisation[40] and persistent vegetative state (PVS) cases.[41] These are no longer of direct application following the implementation of the MCA 2005 but a Practice Note relating to the Official Solicitor's Appointment in Family Proceedings and Proceedings under the Inherent Jurisdiction in relation to Adults was issued in March 2013 which will be applicable in some adult welfare cases which fall outside the MCA 2005.[42]

---

[34] This information has been provided with the approval of the Official Solicitor from the internal records of the OSPT.
[35] This information has been provided with the approval of the Official Solicitor from the internal records of the OSPT.
[36] See the Civil Procedure Rules 1998, SI 1998/3132, PD 21, para 3.4 and the Family Procedure Rules 2010, SI 2010/2955, r 15.4(4), 15.5(6) and r 15.6(1)(b) and PD15A, paras 4.4–4.5.
[37] SI 2007/1744, see r 51 (a) (i), r 142 (1)(c), r 14(91)(a) and 6163.
[38] PD9E, para 8 and para14(b) in respect of serious medical treatment applications, PD9F, para10 in respect of applications relating to statutory wills, codicils, settlements and other dealings with P's property and PD17A para 4(c) in respect of the appointment of a litigation friend.
[39] Practice Note: *Medical and Welfare Decisions for Adults* [2001] 2 FLR 158 and Practice Note: *Family Division: Incapacitated Adults* (2002) *The Times*, 4 January.
[40] Practice Note: *Sterilisation Cases* [2001] 2 FLR 155.
[41] Practice Note: *PVS Cases* [2001] 2 FLR 155.
[42] This replaces the Practice Note dated 2 April 2001.

Acceptance policy

9.43 The Official Solicitor usually requires three criteria[43] to be met before he will accept appointment as litigation friend:
- there must be evidence (or a finding by the court) that the party (or intended party)
- lacks capacity to conduct the proceedings
- there is no one else suitable and willing to act as litigation friend
- that there is security for the costs which the Official Solicitor will incur in providing legal representation for the incapacitated party or the case falls in one of the classes in which, exceptionally, the Official Solicitor funds the costs of litigation out of his budget, in accordance with long standing practice. In practice this means that either the incapacitated party will be eligible for legal aid, or have the means to pay for such costs out of income and/or capital or there is some third party willing to agree to pay such costs. The category of cases that Official Solicitor is likely to fund in part or in whole from his budget is usually limited to cases where he agrees to act as advocate to the court, or where he is joined in a case as an interested party (usually one of wide pubic importance such as in *Burke*) or cases in the Court of Protection concerning serious medical treatment (where half his costs are met from his own and the remaining half is usally paid by the NHS body or bodies or local authority which brought, or should have brought, the proceedings).

9.44 It is important to note that whilst the Official Solicitor usually only acts as litigation friend of last resort that there are two significant exceptions:
(a) in Court of Protection property and affairs cases referred to in PD9F it has been long established practice for the Official Solicitor to act as both litigation friend and solicitor on record; and
(b) In serious medical treatment cases the Official Solicitor does not apply the same acceptance criteria and will invariably accept appointment provided he is invited to act by the Court or, prior to any invitation from the Court, the applicant NHS or other public body confirms that it will pay half his costs of representing P and provides evidence that P lacks litigation capacity. In practice, the Official Solicitor may be more accurately described as the litigation friend of first resort rather than of last resort in serious medical treatment cases.

9.45 Once appointed as litigation friend the Official Solicitor will decide whether the solicitor's role is handled in-house or external solicitors are to be instructed. In practice external solicitors are instructed in almost all cases except those in the Court of Protection which concern property and affairs or serious medical treatment and some divorce main suit cases (but rarely

---

[43] See Official Solicitor's Note dated 21 February 2012 'Court of Protection: Acceptance of Appointment as Litigation Friend', which is available on the Justice website.

financial proceedings). The Official Solicitor operates to a fixed budget and has to consider how his costs in litigation to which he may become a party are to be funded. Depending on the circumstances, this may be out of the incapacitated party's own estate[44]; where external solicitors are used their costs may be met through legal aid where available; or he can seek an undertaking as to costs, or an order for all or some of his costs, from another party to the litigation.[45]

The incapacity work of the Official Solicitor

Giving advice

9.46 Inquiries are frequently made by the judiciary and members of the legal profession, IMCAs, members of the medical profession, managers of care homes and social workers. It is important to note that the advisory role is necessarily limited to the role of the Official Solicitor in respect of the proceedings and not to the law generally. Members of the general public are usually encouraged to obtain the advice of their own solicitor, or perhaps consult their local Citizens Advice Bureau.

Representing adults who lack capacity

9.47 An order of the Court, appointing the Official Solicitor to act as litigation friend in a civil court case for a person who lacks capacity, will either be made with his prior consent or will only take effect if his consent is obtained. The Official Solicitor needs to be satisfied that that there is no suitable alternative person who is willing to act as litigation friend and that there is a satisfactory funding arrangement available to meet his charges and expenses of providing legal representation for the incapacitated person before agreeing to act.

9.48 It may be desirable that the Official Solicitor be consulted about a proposed application which seeks his involvement in any proceedings before a court in England and Wales (this is particularly the case with regard to serious medical treatment cases and other cases involving urgent

---

[44] The Official Solicitor's current policy in Court of Protection personal welfare cases is that he will generally not accept appointment where the incapacitated party has insufficient liquid capital to pay a realistic lump sum on account of the costs to any solicitors to be instructed by him on behalf of that party (unless there is a strong prospect that an incapacitated party would become eligible for legal aid where their liquid capital takes them slightly over the eligibility level and is likely to be used in initial legal costs). However, in the exceptional circumstances arising following the judgement by the Court of Appeal *Re X (Court of Protection Practice)* [2015] EWCA Civ 599, the Official Solicitor did consent to act in cases concerning the review of court authorised deprivation of liberty orders provided P could fund a lump sum of £2,500 see *NRA & Ors, Re* [2015] EWCOP 59 at [77].

[45] Undertakings are quite frequently used in civil proceedings where the claimant requires the defendant to be represented in order to proceed with the litigation, such as in possession claims. They are also sometimes used in Court of Protection personal welfare cases where a local authority urgently requires P to be represented in the proceedings but the Official Solicitor has not yet been able to conclude his enquiries in respect of the funding of the costs of P's legal representation.

applications).[46] In proceedings before the Court of Protection, particularly with regard to personal welfare applications, the Official Solicitor will have to first establish that his acceptance criteria are met. The time required by the Official Solicitor to carry out such financial enquiries should not be underestimated, particularly if the incapacitated party's financial circumstances are complicated or where a relative or partner is managing those finances and are obstructive.[47] Where a public body such as a local authority is bringing proceedings the Official Solicitor will encourage the public body concerned to carry out its own enquiries as to the availability of an alternative litigation fund and as to the incapacitated party's financial resources. It is now the Official Solicitor's practice where his appointment as litigation friend is sought to request that the Court makes directions which will allow his staff (and the staff of any public body acting as applicant) to obtain financial information from third parties and public bodies about the incapacitated party and allow for that party's costs to be obtained from legal aid where eligible.[48] The Official Solicitor's staff may provide precedent draft orders to facilitate his involvement and to expedite acceptance of appointment where this is appropriate.

9.49 Failure to provide any obtainable financial and personal information about the incapacitated party (such as their National Insurance Number) may result in avoidable delay. Where it is established that the incapacitated party is required to fund the costs of legal representation from his/her own financial resources, it is likely that the Official Solicitor will require a further detailed order to be made which will facilitate the payment of the costs of legal representation, including a payment on account of costs and provision for the payment of interim bills and disbursements. This is particularly likely if the incapacitated party does not have a financial deputy or an attorney who could make such payments. The need for a further order may cause further delay as the Official Solicitor will not usually consent to act until fully satisfied over the funding arrangements and a case will not even be placed on his waiting list for acceptance until this criterion is satisfied.

9.50 The Official Solicitor will, if necessary act for two (and potentially more) incapacitated parties in the same court proceedings. In such cases special arrangements are put in place to prevent any conflict of interest and to preserve confidentiality of communications between the litigation friend case manager and the instructed solicitors and counsel. Accordingly each incapacitated party has a separate case manager and supervising line manager at the office and separate external solicitors will be retained to act on behalf of each party. A strict conflict of interest information barrier is

---

[46] See PD9E, Para 8 and *Sandwell and West Birmingham Hospitals NHS Trust v CD & Others* [2014] EWCOP 23, [2014] COPLR 650, at [39] per Theis J.
[47] For example, as at 25 February 2013 the Official Solicitor had 68 Court of Protection personal welfare cases which were being investigated by his staff to establish whether they met his criteria for acceptance – see Official Solicitor's letter to the 39 Essex Street Chambers Court of Protection Newsletter dated 25 February 2013.
[48] Orders relating to third party disclosure should be drawn as separate orders so as to avoid giving private and confidential information about P's proceedings to such third parties – Ibid.

maintained to prevent privileged information being disclosed within the office to the staff responsible for the case management of the other incapacitated party or parties. Before accepting appointment for a second or further incapacitated party the Official Solicitor may seek the Court's approval of these arrangements.

The Official Solicitor is unable to act as solicitor to individual members of the general public as though he were a solicitor in private practice, nor will he respond to inquiries from individuals who are seeking free legal advice for their own benefit.

Assisting the civil and family courts

9.51 The Official Solicitor may also be called on to give confidential advice to judges and invited to instruct counsel to appear before a judge to assist the court as advocate to the court, or to investigate any matter on which the court needs a special report.[49] This has happened where for instance the court has difficulties in ascertaining the mental capacity of a party to proceedings before the court. A special report might also be requested by the court from the Official Solicitor when the judge feels he or she needs help to ascertain facts or information relevant to the case which would not otherwise be made available to the court. In adult welfare cases this tends to occur with cases brought under the inherent jurisdiction regarding a 'vulnerable adults' where there is uncertainty as to capacity or as to whether a party's will is being overborne by undue influence or duress. In such cases the Official Solicitor will usually seek payment of all his costs from any public body which may be seeking such a report. It is probably a contempt of court to interfere with an investigation by the Official Solicitor.

Role in the Court of Protection

9.52 The Official Solicitor may bring an application without the permission of the Court. Subject to his consent, the Official Solicitor may be appointed to act as litigation friend for an incapacitated party (whether P or a Protected Party) in any proceedings.[50] He is often invited to act as litigation friend for the incapacitated subject of the application or a protected party or child in property and affairs applications for authority to execute statutory wills or to make gifts or other dispositions. This work is undertaken in-house and costs tend to be paid from the funds of the incapacitated party in accordance with the general rule as to costs. Similarly, in serious medical treatment cases the Official Solicitor usually acts in-house both as litigation friend and solicitor. However, in such cases the Official Solicitor does not seek to fund his costs either from public funding or from the incapacitated party's own estate. Instead the current practice is that he seeks half his costs from the NHS body or other public body seeking

---

[49] Known as a *Harbin v Masterman* inquiry [1896] 1 Ch 351.
[50] Court of Protection Rules 2001, rr 11 and 13.

the Court's decision and funds the balance from his own budget.[51] In most personal welfare proceedings in the Court of Protection the Official Solicitor will retain an external firm of solicitors to act for the incapacitated party and the proceedings will be funded by legal aid or from the incapacitated party's own financial resources.

9.53 Due to the rise in Court of Protection healthcare and welfare cases the Official Solicitor operated from early 2012 until October 2013 a waiting list in relation to his acceptance of invitations to act in personal welfare cases under the MCA 2005. Although there continues to be a high volume of cases and the resources of the Official Solicitor remain limited by public spending restraints, it is currently the Official Solicitor's practice to allocate immediately to his case managers those cases which meet his criteria for acceptance.

9.54 In cases involving a challenge to a DOLS authorisation under s 21A of the MCA 2005, the Official Solicitor will, where the Relevant Person's Representative (RPR) is the Applicant, write to the RPR to check whether s/he will remain the Applicant and that P does not need to be made a party. Where the RPR is not the Applicant and P has already been joined as a party, the Official Solicitor will also write to the RPR to establish if the RPR is willing and able to act as P's litigation friend.[52]

9.55 The Official Solicitor currently has two separate teams at his office which undertake work in respect of the Court of Protection:
1. The *Court of Protection Property and Affairs Team* which acts both as litigation friend and solicitor principally in applications for statutory Wills and gifts and other proceedings referred to in PD9F, is led by a Senior Lawyer who is also one of three Deputy Official Solicitors. The Senior Lawyer is supported by a further 6.5 lawyers.
2. The *Healthcare and Welfare Division* which undertakes all work in relation to personal welfare applications is led by a Senior Lawyer who is also one of the three Deputy Official Solicitors. The Senior Lawyer is supported by a a further 5.5 lawyers and a team of paralegal case managers who undertake the litigation friend role on behalf of the Official Solicitor. The team is supported to a limited extent by 3 lawyers in the office who principally undertake family law cases (often in relation to Court of Protection applications where there are related family proceedings such as care proceedings involving P's children, forced marriage or where P was previously the subject of Children Act orders).

---

[51] Most recently approved by Peter Jackson J in Re D (Costs) [2012] EWHC 886 (COP), [2012] COPLR 499 which followed judgment of the former President, Sir Mark Potter, in *A Hospital v SW and A PCT* [2007] EWHC 425 (Fam). See generally Chapter 5.
[52] See *AB v LCC (A Local Authority)* [2011] EWHC 3151 (COP), [2012] COPLR 314 in which Mostyn J approved of the appointment of a RPR as litigation friend in such cases. A transcript of the judgment is available on BAILII.

Adult personal welfare declarations including serious medical treatment

9.56 The Official Solicitor is invariably appointed as litigation friend of P whenever there are serious medical treatment cases in the Court unless an urgent out of hours decision[53] is made which does not require any further hearing or exceptionally where there is an alternative litigation friend already acting (this might occur where an application has been brought by P through such an alternative litigation friend)[54] The most common cases concerning serious medical treatment in which the Official Solicitor acts have been those involving the use of significant restraint including sedation, the withholding of life-sustaining treatment, the refusal by P of proposed treatment such as amputations or caesarian sections, disputes concerning DNAR notices, the termination of pregnancy, those where there is uncertainty as to capacity. Other cases less commonly handled are those concerning donation of organs or bone marrow and sterilisation (both male[55] and female) and the validity, applicability or existence of advanced decisions. The Official Solicitor is also often appointed to act as litigation friend in other personal welfare cases. These commonly involve disputes either within families or between families and local authorities or NHS bodies. They invariably relate to disputes concerning capacity, residence, contact and or care provision. Some are challenges to authorisations made under the DOLS. Others are brought by local authorities and NHS bodies to enable P to be deprived of their liberty in locations not covered by DOLS (such as supported living tenancies or foster home placements).[56]

9.57 Where the Official Solicitor is appointed to act, he will wish to play a full role in the proceedings and to have an opportunity to properly investigate the case. The Official Solicitor will often wish to instruct, on a sole or joint basis, one or more experts to advise on capacity and/or best interests or seek s.49 reports from local authorities and NHS bodies. When drafting directions orders prior to the Official Solicitor accepting appointment, care should be taken to ensure that as far as possible the timetable for his involvement is realistic and allows sufficient time for investigations, including the selection and instruction of independent experts.[57]

---

[53] The Official Solicitor has not provided an out of hours service with lawyers on duty to cover such applications since 15 December 2011.

[54] In a number of cases the Official Solicitor has taken over the role of litigation friend where it has been determined that the alternative litigation friend should not continue to act.

[55] See *An NHS Trust v DE & Ors* [2013] EWHC 2562 (Fam), [2013] COPLR 531 for the first decision made in respect of a male sterilisation under MCA 2005.

[56] The number of these deprivation of liberty cases falling outside DOLS which require a litigation friend may fall significantly following the judgment of Charles J in NRA & Ors, Re [2015] WLR(D) 394 [2015] EWCOP 59..

[57] Neither the Official Solicitor nor his staff are social care or mental health experts and that they rely on the use of such experts to obtain expert evidence independent from that provided by any local authority or NHS body which may be a party to the proceedings.

Other jurisdictions

9.58 Although there should be a clear definition of the range of services to be provided by the Official Solicitor, there is a diversity of services available in the jurisdictions of the UK and Ireland.

Scotland

9.59 There is no equivalent of the Official Solicitor in Scotland and the Office of the Public Guardian has no recourse to a professional legal service other than in response to its own departmental administrative requirements. However, in a case where the incapacitated party had been moved to Scotland it was possible through liaison with the relevant Scottish local authority to obtain a mirror order from the local Sheriff's Court under the Adults with Incapacity (Scotland) Act 2000 to confirm and implement an earlier decision of the Court of Protection relating to residence and contact.

Northern Ireland

9.60 Northern Ireland also has an Official Solicitor with a similar role to that of the Official Solicitor to the Senior Courts in England and Wales. The contact details are:

Official Solicitor's Office
Royal Courts of Justice
Chichester Street
Belfast
BT1 3JF
Tel: 028 9072 5940
Fax: 028 9023 1759

Ireland

9.61 The equivalent of the Official Solicitor in the Republic of Ireland is the Office of the General Solicitor for Minors and Wards of Court situated in Dublin. Its origins lie in Chancery practice but it was brought within the public service in 1969. There is no equivalent of the Public Guardian. The General Solicitor may assist the High Court to arrange medical examinations, act as guardian ad litem of a Ward (or a minor) and act as a Committee of the Estate (or of the Person) of last resort. In many ways this latter role appears similar to that of a social worker but with a legal or administrative bias and legal services may be provided.

Office of the General Solicitor for Minors and Wards of Court
2nd Floor
15/24 Phoenix Street North
Smithfield
Dublin 7
Phone: +353 (0) 1 888 6231
Fax: +353 (0) 1 872 2681
Email: GenSol@courts.ie
For more information see: www.courts.ie

Current and future issues[58]

9.62 Funding of litigation in the Court of Protection has been an ongoing challenge for the Official Solicitor since the inception of the MCA 2005. Increasing numbers of incapacitated parties are ineligible for legal aid but often lack significant capital other than the equity in their homes. Whilst it is technically possible to fund litigation by way of charging such property this has not proven to be a practical solution due to the staff resources required to secure such funding and the fact that there is inevitably a long delay in recovering the expenditure on legal representation from an incapacitated party's property and a degree of risk over recovery (in that a charge cannot be registered until the case has concluded and P's legal costs have been agreed or assessed by the Senior Courts Costs Office). As such the Official Solicitor will rarely, if ever, agree to fund cases by way of deferred charge on the incapacitated party's estate. Where there is a lack of liquid capital the Official Solicitor has in some cases agreed to act only where a public body, such as a local authority, has undertaken to pay his legal costs (with the provision that the public body is then authorised to recoup these costs from the incapacitated party's estate at the conclusion of the case). There will inevitably also be cases where although a protected party is ineligible for legal aid they have no realistic means of paying for their costs due to the fact that their ineligibility arises from having income only marginally above qualifying levels. In such cases the Official Solicitor is again unlikely to be willing to consent to act as it will not comply with the funding criterion relating to his acceptance of appointment.[59] These funding problems have increased following the implementation on 1 April 2013 of the changes introduced by the Legal Aid, Sentencing and Punishment of Offenders Act 2012 in April 2013. Legal Aid reforms have also presented problems in the conduct of cases themselves particularly around the instruction of independent experts.[60]

---

[58] The material under this heading has been contributed by James Beck from the Official Solicitor's Office.

[59] In his judgment in *NRA & Ors* [2015] Charles J noted that family members might be appointed as s 3A representatives instead of joining P and appointing a litigation friend. This may perhaps prove to be the only option where there are no realistic means to pay for P's legal representation.

[60] See Transforming Legal Aid: Developing a more credible and effective system. Ministry of Justice Consultation Paper CP14/2013 – Response of the Official Solicitor 04.6.2013.

9.63 The number of personal welfare cases has grown at a considerable pace from implementation of the MCA in October 2007. As at 1 April 2008 there were only 42 cases. This rose to 216 as at 1 April 2009 and 368 cases as at 1 April 2010. During the last financial year 2014/15 the number of referrals had risen to a new peak of 655 cases. To put this in some context, during 2012 and 2013 the healthcare and welfare team on average received 26 new case referrals per month. In 2014 the monthly average had risen to 50 and during 2015 (to end October) the monthly average has been 73. Given demographic trends and the increasing awareness of the Mental Capacity Act 2005 amongst the general public the volume of new cases was always likely rise. One additional and significant factor was the Supreme Court decision in (1) *P v Cheshire West and Chester Council and another*; (2) *P and Q v Surrey County Council* which hugely increased the number of incapacitated people requiring DOLS authorisations or Court authorised deprivations of liberty and which inevitably gave rise to additional personal welfare cases.[61]

The resource implications of providing P with legal representation in these cases has been a driving force for some significant changes in the rules and practice and procedure and case law relating to P's involvement in personal welfare cases. The NRA judgment and the new Rule 3A introduced by the Court of Protection (amendment) Rules 2015 are likely to reduce the number of cases where P is joined as party and therefore in need of a litigation friend. Further, the anticipated creation of a panel of accredited legal representatives, as envisaged by the 2015 amendments, will offer an alternative to appointing a litigation friend where P is joined a party.[62] As such the number of new personal welfare referrals to the Official Solicitor may start to drop as these changes take effect. Given the current economic climate and the reductions in public spending, the Official Solicitor is likely, in any event, to continue to face significant challenges in the delivery of his office's services.

The Official Solicitor has been particularly involved in several important areas of litigation in recent years concerning the Mental Capacity Act 2005 before the Court of Protection and the High Court. These related to the following areas:

- Cases concerned with whether P was being deprived of his liberty for the purposes of Article 5 of the European Convention on Human Rights. This is of importance not only to those detained under DOLS but also those in placements not covered by DOLS, such as

---

[61] The number of cases may now fall significantly following the President's guidance in *Re X and others (Deprivation of Liberty)* [2014] EWCOP 25 (7 August 2014).
[62] See 39 Essex Street Chambers Newsletter November 2016: Issue 60 Court of protection Practice and Procedure see article 'A step towards Rule 3A accredited legal representatives' which advises that applications were being received for the appointment of assessors for the Mental Health (Welfare) accreditation.

- supported tenancies and foster home placements. It has included restraint beyond the limits permitted by the Mental Health Act 1983.[63]
- Cases concerning whether P needed to be joined as a party in all cases concerning deprivations of liberty and if not, what Article 5-compliant procedural safeguards were required.[64]
- The duties of local authorities as supervisory bodies under the DOLS scheme to ensure compliance with Article 5 (4) ECHR.[65]
- Cases concerning capacity to consent to sexual relations, particularly in the light of Baroness Hale's comments in *R v C* [2009] 1 WLR 1786.[66]
- Cases concerning capacity to marry.[67]
- Cases concerning the power of the Court to review the decisions made by local authorities in the allocation of their resources on best interests grounds.[68]
- The power of the Court to award damages under the Human Rights Act 1998.[69]
- Media access to private Court proceedings and restrictions on media reporting of open court proceedings which concerned the countervailing rights to protection and privacy under Article 8 of those lacking mental capacity.[70]
- The limits upon the levels of restraint which can be justified in providing medical treatment to a person lacking capacity.[71]

---

[63] Which have included *R v A Local Authority and Ors* [2011] EWHC 1539, [2011] COPLR Con Vol 972; *London Borough of Hillingdon v Steven Neary* [2011] EWHC 413 (COP), [2011] COPLR Con Vol 677; *P (otherwise known as MIG) and Q (otherwise known as MEG) v (1) Surrey County Council (2) CA (3) LA and Equality and Human Rights Commission, intervener* [2011] EWCA Civ 190, [2011] COPLR Con Vol 931; *Cheshire West and Chester Council v P* [2011] EWCA Civ 1257, [2012] COPLR 37; *RK v (1) BCC (2) YB and (3) AK* [2011] EWCA Civ 1305, [2012] COPLR 146; *(1) P v Cheshire West and Chester Council and another*; (2) *P and Q v Surrey County Council* [2014] UKSC 19, [2014] COPLR 313.

[64] Re: X [2014] EWCOP 25; [2015] 1 WLR 2454, Re: X (Court of Protection Procedure) [2015] EWCA Civ 599 and Re NRA and Ors [2015] EWCOP 59.

[65] AJ (deprivation of Liberty Safeguards) [2015] EWCOP 5.

[66] *D County Council v LS* [2010] EWHC 1544 (Fam), [2010] COPLR Con Vol 331; *D Borough Council v AB* [2011] EWHC 101 (COP), COPLR Con Vol 313; *A Local Authority v TZ* [2013] EWHC 2322 (COP), [2013] COPLR 477; *IM v LM and Others* [2014] EWCA Civ 37, [2014] COPLR 246; Re A Local Authority V TZ No.2 [2014] EWHC 973 (COP).

[67] *A, B and C v X, Y and Z* [2012] EWHC 2400 (COP), [2013] COPLR 1 in respect of which an appeal to the Court of Appeal was due to be heard in 2013 but 'P' died after permission had been granted. *Sandwell Metropolitan Borough Council v RG & Ors* [2013] EWHC 2373 (COP), [2013] COPLR 643; *YLA v PM and MZ* [2013] EWHC 3622 (Fam).

[68] *AH v (1) Hertfordshire Partnership NHS Foundation Trust and (2) Ealing Primary Care trust* [2011] EWHC 276 (COP), [2011] COPLR Con Vol 195 and *A Local Authority v PB and P* [2011] EWHC 2675 (COP), [2012] COPLR 1.

[69] *YA (F) v A Local Authority (2) YA(M) (3) A NHS trust and (4) A Primary Care Trust* [2010] EWHC 2770 (Fam), [2010] COPLR Con Vol 1226; *The Local Authority v Mrs D and Mr D* [2013] EWCOP B34.

[70] *P v Independent Print Ltd* [2011] EWCA Civ 756, [2012] COPLR 110; *W v M* [2011] EWHC 1197 (COP), 2011] COPLR Con Vol 1205; *Re RGS (No 3)* [2014] EWHC B12 (COP).

[71] *Re D* [2010] EWHC 2535 (COP); *The Mental Health Trust/The Acute Trust & The Council v DD and BC (No 1 and No 2)* [2014] EWCOP 11, [2015] 1 FLR 1430; [2014] EWCOP 13.

- Whether it can ever be lawful and in the best interests of a person in the minimally conscious state to have artificial nutrition and hydration withdrawn or withheld if they are not in the dying process.[72]
- Whether an advanced decision was lawful and applicable.[73]
- Whether the placement of a DNAR notice is in the best interests of a person and other cases concerning the withholding or withdrawal of intensive care and other life sustaining treatment.[74]
- ECHR Article 8 – right to family and right to privacy and its applicability in respect of an incapacitated person's bests interests regarding care and residence.[75]
- Whether the taking of a DNA sample for the purposes of a Statutory Will notice is in the best interests of P.[76]
- Whether it can be in the best interests of a man to be sterilised.[77]
- The correct test for capacity to cohabit with a spouse.[78]
- The correct test for capacity to make decision about contact to others.[79]
- Whether it was appropriate to withhold disclosure of statements and and un-redacted reports.[80]
- Whether P has capacity to consent to the requisite medical treatment.[81]
- Whether treatment is futile and should be withdrawn or withheld.[82]
- The importance of P's wishes and feelings in determining P's best interests.[83]
- The interface between the Mental Capacity Act and Inherent Jurisdiction.[84]

---

[72] *W v M and Ors* [2011] EWHC 2443 (Fam), [2012] COPLR 222 and *United Lincolnshire Hospital Trust v N* [2014] EWCOP 16.

[73] *Primary Care Trust v XB* [2012] EWHC 1390 (Fam), [2012] COPLR 577; *Nottinghamshire Healthcare NHS Trust v RC* [2014] EWCOP 1136 (9 April 2014) and *Nottinghamshire Healthcare NHS Trust v RC* [2014] EWCOP 1317, [2014] COPLR 468 (1 May 2014).

[74] *Aintree University Hospitals NHS Foundation Trust v DJ* [2013] EWCA Civ 65, [2013] COPLR 217 (the Official Solicitor was not involved in the subsequent appeal to the Supreme Court). *A NHS Hospital Trust v M and K* [2013] EWHC 2402; *An NHS Foundation trust v VT and A* [2013] EWHC 826 (Fam).

[75] *K v LBX & Ors* [2012] EWCA Civ 79, [2012] COPLR 411.

[76] *LG v DK* [2011] EWHC 2453 (COP), [2012] COPLR 80.

[77] *An NHS Trust v DE & Ors* [2013] EWHC 2562 (Fam), [2013] COPLR 531.

[78] *PC and NC v City of York* [2013] EWCA Civ 478, [2013] COPLR 409.

[79] Ibid and *A Local Authority v TZ (No 2)* [2014] EWCOP 973 (1 April 2014).

[80] *RC v CC and X Local Authority* [2013] EWHC 1424 (COP), [2013] COPLR 431.

[81] *Heart of England NHS Fundation Trust v JB* [2014] EWHC 342 (COP) – amputation; *Re SB (A patient: Capacity to consent to termination)* [2013] EWHC 1417 (COP), [2013] COPLR 445. – termination of pregnacy.

[82] Aintree University Hospitals NHS Foundation Trust v James & Ors [2013] PTSR D22, [2013] 4 All ER 67, [2013] EWCA Civ 65, [2013] Med LR 110, (2013) 131 BMLR 124 (but not the subsequent appeal to the Supreme Court). St George's Healthcare NHS Trust and P v Q [2015] EWCOP 42.

[83] Wye Valley NHS Trust v Mr B [2015] EWCOP 60.

[84] *An NHS Trust v Dr A* [2013] EWHC 2442 (COP), [2013] COPLR 605; *Great Western Hospitals NHS Foundation Trust v AA, BB, CC, DD* [2014] EWHC 132 (Fam), [2014] 2 FLR 1209; *London Borough of Redbridge v G, C and F* [2014] EWHC 485 (COP), [2014]

- The basis for dispensing with service in statutory will cases.[85]
- Providing inter vivos gifts to parents.[86]
- The role of the Court of Protection in relation to managing CICA awards on behalf of recipients who lack capacity.[87]
- The use of P's funds to pay school fees in the context of mutual dependency.[88]

COURT FUNDS OFFICE

Background

9.64 The Court Funds Office provides investment and banking administration services for clients whose money is held under the control of the civil courts of England and Wales, including the Court of Protection (CoP). The practice of holding funds 'in-court' on behalf of litigants goes back several hundred years but an Act of Parliament was passed in 1726, creating the post now known as the Accountant General of the Senior Courts and giving him responsibility for safeguarding funds in court.

9.65 Under the Administration of Justice Act 1982 (AJA), the Court Funds Office, which operates as an arm's length body of the Ministry of Justice, is responsible for administering £3.7bn (£3.5bn in cash and £0.2bn in securities) held in court on behalf of over 140,000 clients. The money held by Court Funds Office originates primarily from three sources:[89]

(1) Damages awarded to children represented by litigation friends as a result of civil legal action and held on their behalf until majority (18 years of age);
(2) Damages awarded to adults represented by litigation friends as a result of civil legal action and held on their behalf because they are 'protected beneficiaries' and the amount does not justify an application to the Court of Protection;
(3) Assets belonging to people who lack the capacity to manage their own financial affairs where the Court of Protection has appointed a deputy to manage their affairs.

A 'protected beneficiary' is as a party who lacks capacity to conduct proceedings who also lacks capacity to manage and control any money recovered by him or on his behalf or for his benefit in the proceedings.[90]

COPLR 292; *London Borough of Redbridge v G & Ors (No 2)* [2014] EWCOP 959; *Nottinghamshire Healthcare NHS Trust v RC* [2014] EWCOP 1136 and [2014] EWCOP 1317, [2014] COPLR 468.
[85] *Re AB* [2014] COPLR 381.
[86] *Re AK (gift application)* [2014] EWHC B11 (COP).
[87] *Newcastle City Council v PV and Criminal Injuries Compensation Authority* [2015] EWCOP 22
[88] *David Ross v A* [2015] EWCOP 46.
[89] Only the second and third sources are considered here.
[90] Civil Procedure Rules 1998, r 21.1(2)(e).

The Mental Capacity Act 2005 now provides greater choice for the deputy and only some Court of Protection clients have to keep money at the Court Funds Office.

Court Funds Rules 2011

9.66 The Court Funds Office has been working in partnership with National Savings & Investments (NS&I) to modernise the service it provides to clients. The Court Funds Rules 2011 came into force on 3 October 2011.[91] They govern the manner in which the Accountant General may accept funds into, hold and pay funds out of court. The new Rules were introduced to make the procedures clearer, less confusing and more user friendly. They restate, clarify and modernise the former Rules rather than alter their substantive effect.

9.67 Part 1 of the new Rules contains provisions for interpreting the Rules and also prescribes the courts to which the Rules apply. Part 2 sets out which documents are required to deposit funds in court and how funds may be deposited. Part 3 deals with investment options for a fund in court, who may make investment decisions and when investments may be made. Part 4 deals with payment out of a fund in court, including which documents are required for payment out and the circumstances in which a fund can be released where the person entitled to the fund has died. Part 5 deals with unclaimed funds. Part 6 contains miscellaneous provisions including how to obtain information about a fund in court.

Investments on behalf of protected beneficiaries

9.68 The Accountant General may only invest money in a common investment fund if it amounts to £10,000 or more and it is held on behalf of a person lacking capacity who a court, deputy or investment manager has reason to believe will require the investment to be held for 5 years or more.[92]

9.69 The Court Funds Office has introduced a new investment framework on behalf of protected beneficiaries where the sum to be invested is more than £10,000 but less than £30,000. In these cases, following the hearing of an application for the approval of a settlement or compromise, the judge completes form CFO 320PB[93] and indicates which investment policy is to apply from one of the following four options:

- Capital growth only – where no income is likely to be required from the fund for over 10 years;
- Capital growth and income – where some income is likely to be required from the fund within 5 to 10 years;

---

[91] Replacing the Court Funds Rules 1987.
[92] Court Funds Rules 2011, r 14(2).
[93] Form CFO 320PB is available via: www.justice.gov.uk/global/forms/cfo.htm.

- Maximum income – where income is likely to be required from the fund within 5 years;
- Place all funds on special - where there is less than £10,000 to invest, the funds are likely to be invested for less than 5 years, there is a specific request not to invest or the protected beneficiary is 80 years of age or more.

Court staff then complete form CFO 212 and on receipt the Court Funds Office apply the investment framework set out in the following table:[94]

Capital growth only	65%
Capital growth and income	50%
Maximum income	Special
Place all funds on special	Special

The percentage figure represents investment in the Equity Index Tracker Fund.

9.70 An annual review is undertaken of all cases where funds have been invested in the Equity Index Tracker Fund to ensure that the percentage split between the equity and cash components remains appropriate.

An application must be made to the Court of Protection for the appointment of a deputy where the award is £30,000 or more, unless a deputy or attorney has already been appointed as required by the relevant Practice Direction.[95]

Contacting the CFO

9.71 The CFO has for many years been based at Kingsway, London but from 5 December 2011 moved to:

Court Funds Office, Glasgow, G58 1AB
DX: 501757 Cowglen
Email: enquiries@cfo.gsi.gov.uk
Tel: 0845 223 8500
Fax: 0141 636 4398

---

[94] Where the court has not selected an investment policy the money will be placed to the special account.
[95] Civil Procedure Rules 1998, PD 21, para 10.2.

INDEPENDENT MENTAL CAPACITY ADVOCATE SERVICE

Advocates

9.72 Advocacy involves helping people to express their views and wishes, access information and services, explore choices and options, and secure their rights. In some situations an advocate may need to represent another person's interests. This is called non-instructed advocacy, and is used when a person is unable to communicate their views.

An advocate is someone who supports a person so that their views are heard and their rights are upheld especially when decisions are being made about their life. An advocate will support a person to speak up for themselves or, in some situations, will speak on a person's behalf. Advocates are independent: they are not connected to the carers or services that are involved in supporting the person.

IMCAs

9.73 Independent Mental Capacity Advocates (IMCAs) provide a new type of statutory advocacy introduced by the MCA 2005.[96] Some people who lack capacity have a right to receive support from an IMCA and responsible bodies, the NHS and local authorities all have a duty to make sure that IMCAs are available to represent them.[97] IMCA services are provided by organisations that are independent from those authorities.[98]

The majority of service users who access the IMCA service are people with learning disabilities, older people with dementia, people who have an acquired brain injury or people with mental health problems. If the person is unable to communicate their views and wishes relating to the decision to be made, an advocate uses non-instructed advocacy.

> 'Non-instructed advocacy is taking affirmative action with or on behalf of a person who is unable to give a clear indication of their views or wishes in a specific situation. The non-instructed advocate seeks to uphold the person's rights; ensure fair and equal treatment and access to services; and make certain that decisions are taken with due consideration for their unique preferences and perspectives.' (Action for Advocacy, 2006.)

---

[96] See MCA 2005, ss 35–36 and The Mental Capacity Act 2005 (Independent Mental Capacity Advocates) (General) Regulations 2006. The DH and OPG produced a booklet called Making decisions: The Independent Mental Capacity Advocate (IMCA) service [OPG606], which can be downloaded at: www.dh.gov.uk/prod_consum_dh/groups/dh_digitalassets/documents/digitalasset/dh_095893.pdf.
[97] For an explanation of the appointment, functions and role of IMCAs and the duty to instruct them refer to Ch. 5 at paragraph 5.42 et seq.
[98] Local authorities have commissioned IMCA services in England and local health boards have commissioned them in Wales.

The advocate goes to meetings on the person's behalf and actively probes the process by which service providers reach a decision and causes them to think about why they are making the specific decision and to justify the actions proposed.

Who can be an IMCA?

9.74 Individual IMCAs must have relevant experience and receive IMCA training. They must have integrity and a good character[99] and be able to act independently.

How do IMCAs challenge a decision?

9.75 The IMCA may initially use informal methods to challenge decisions and ask for a meeting with the decision-maker to explain any concerns and request a review of the decision. Where there are serious concerns about the decision made, an IMCA may decide to use formal methods to challenge the decision. These include using the relevant complaints procedure, approaching the Official Solicitor and referring the case to the Court of Protection. They may also seek legal advice on the incapacitated person's behalf and consider applying for a judicial review.

---

[99] They must have enhanced checks with the Criminal Records Bureau that show no areas of concern.

Chapter 10

Miscellaneous

ENDURING POWERS – TRANSITIONAL (MENTAL CAPACITY ACT 2005, SCH 4)

10.1 The Mental Capacity Act 2005 (MCA 2005) repealed the Enduring Powers of Attorney Act 1985 (EPAA 1985) so no new enduring powers of attorney (EPAs) can now be created.[1] There remain in place countless numbers of EPAs, some already registered but perhaps the majority unregistered and held in deed boxes and solicitors' offices across the country as 'insurance policies' in case of future incapacity. The registered EPAs cannot be replaced by new lasting powers of attorney (LPAs) because the donors will invariably lack capacity to grant a new power. Although it may be prudent for those who have already executed an enduring power to replace this with a new lasting power, many simply will not do so and it would be contrary to public policy to require donors – who have in good faith provided for the management of their property and affairs in the event of incapacity – to go to the effort and expense of making new LPAs. The status of these EPAs, registered and unregistered, has therefore been addressed.

10.2 MCA 2005, Sch 4 provides for the recognition and operation of EPAs made before the commencement of the Act. Although EPAA 1985 is repealed, all EPAs made prior to the commencement of MCA 2005 remain effective and operate as EPAs. The provisions of Sch 4 replicate the provisions of EPAA 1985. MCA 2005 therefore confirms that an EPA is a power of attorney, which has been executed in the prescribed form and which is not revoked on the onset of incapacity provided it is registered with the Public Guardian.[2] The attorney must, as soon as is practicable, make an application to register the EPA if he or she has reason to believe that the donor is or is becoming mentally incapable.[3] The attorney must, furthermore, notify a prescribed class of relatives before applying to register the LPA.

10.3 EPAs are dealt with in more detail in Chapter 3 and a detailed account of the rules and principles applicable to their operation is beyond the scope

---

[1] MCA 2005, Sch 7.
[2] This preserves, for existing EPAs, a 'diagnostic threshold' which has to be attained before the power can be registered and as a result, a presumption that the donor is incapable of managing his or her property and affairs. MCA 2005, s 1 does not therefore apply (MCA 2005, Sch 4, para 1(1)).
[3] MCA 2005, Sch 7, Part 2, para 4(1). MCA 2005, Sch 7, Part 8 defines 'mentally incapable' in the context of the management of the donor's property and affairs.

of this work.[4] However, practitioners will need to be able to advise on and administer two distinct types of statutory power of attorney and apply different principles and procedures to each one. There will no doubt be endless debate over whether one is better than the other, but the inevitable result will be the complexity of two different jurisdictions applicable to persons in identical circumstances.

TRANSITIONAL PROVISIONS (MENTAL CAPACITY ACT 2005, SCH 5)

10.4 MCA 2005, Sch 5[5] deals with transitional provisions and savings in two Parts. Part 1 covers the repeal of the Mental Health Act 1983, Part VII (which established the jurisdiction of the previous Court of Protection) and Part 2 covers the repeal of EPAA 1985 (which established EPAs).

Mental Health Act 1983, Part VII

10.5 A receiver under the former regime is in effect converted into a deputy under the new jurisdiction from its commencement but with the same functions as he or she had as receiver. Application may be made to the Court to end the appointment, to make a decision not authorised or for the Court to exercise its powers. Any existing order or appointment, direction or authority will continue to have effect despite the repeal of the Mental Health Act 1983, Part VII.

10.6 Any pending application for the exercise of a power under the Mental Health Act 1983, Part VII was treated, insofar as a corresponding power is exercisable, as an application for the exercise of that power.[6] An appeal which had not been determined continued to be dealt with under the former regime. All fees and other payments which, having become due, had not been paid were to be paid to the new Court of Protection after the commencement day.

10.7 The records of the former Court of Protection are to be treated as records of the new Court of Protection and the Public Guardian for the purpose of exercising any of his or her functions has access thereto. The new Court of Protection Rules may provide that former receivers must continue to render accounts.

---

[4] The topic is covered in greater and better detail in *Cretney & Lush on Enduring Powers of Attorney* (Jordan Publishing, 5th edn, 2001), which will remain the definitive work on the subject. The same law and procedure will apply to existing EPAs, only different statutory provisions will apply to their operation.
[5] MCA 2005, s 66(4).
[6] An application for the appointment of a receiver will be treated as an application for the appointment of a deputy.

Enduring Powers of Attorney Act 1985

10.8 Any order or determination made, or other thing done, under EPAA 1985 continues to have effect under the new jurisdiction from its commencement and insofar as it could have been done under MCA 2005, Sch 4[7] is so treated. Any instrument registered under EPAA 1985 is to be treated as having been registered by the Public Guardian under Sch 4.

10.9 Any pending application for the exercise of a power under EPAA 1985 was treated, insofar as a corresponding power was exercisable under MCA 2005, Sch 4, as an application for the exercise of that power. Special provisions apply to powers given by trustees. An appeal which had not been determined continued to be dealt with under the former regime.

CONSEQUENTIAL AMENDMENTS AND REPEALS (MENTAL CAPACITY ACT 2005, SCH 6)

10.10 It is inevitable that there is a long list of minor and consequential amendments to earlier legislation and these are to be found in MCA 2005, Sch 6. They date from the Fines and Recoveries Act 1833 and include amendments to the following legislation:

- Trustee Act 1925;
- Law of Property Act 1925;
- Administration of Estates Act 1925;
- National Assistance Act 1948, s 49;
- Intestates' Estates Act 1952;
- Variation of Trusts Act 1958;
- Administration of Justice Act 1960;
- Industrial and Provident Societies Act 1965;
- Compulsory Purchase Act 1965;
- Leasehold Reform Act 1967;
- Medicines Act 1968;
- Family Law Reform Act 1969;
- Local Authority Social Services Act 1970;
- Local Government Act 1972;
- Matrimonial Causes Act 1973;
- Consumer Credit Act 1974;
- Sale of Goods Act 1979;
- Limitation Act 1980, s 38;
- Mental Health Act 1983;
- Insolvency Act 1986;
- Public Trustee and Administration of Funds Act 1986;
- Child Support Act 1991;
- Social Security Administration Act 1992;
- Leasehold Reform, Housing and Urban Development Act 1993;
- Disability Discrimination Act 1995;
- Trusts of Land and Appointment of Trustees Act 1996;

---

[7] See above.

- Adoption and Children Act 2002; and
- Licensing Act 2003.

10.11 In addition, specific repeals of earlier legislation are to be found in MCA 2005, Sch 7. The following wholesale repeals are noteworthy:
- Mental Health Act 1983, Part VII; and
- Enduring Powers of Attorney Act 1985.

10.12 With effect from 1 October 2009 numerous amendments were made by the Mental Capacity Act 2005 (Transitional and Consequential Provisions) Order 2007[8] to various Statutory Instruments. These are set out in Schedule 1 and include such diverse regulations and court rules as:
- National Savings Bank Regulations 1972;
- Premium Savings Bond Regulations 1972;
- National Savings Stock Register Regulations 1976;
- Motor Vehicles (Tests) Regulations 1981;
- Mental Health Review Tribunal Rules 1983;
- Road Vehicles (Construction and Use) Regulations 1986;
- Insolvency Rules 1986;
- Non-contentious Probate Rules 1987;
- Savings Certificates Regulations 1991.

In the present context the most significant amendment is that to the Insolvency Rules 1986 whereby the new definition of 'lacks capacity' is adopted for incapacitated persons. Similar changes were made by amendments to the Civil Procedure Rules 1998 and the Family Procedure Rules 2010.

---

[8] SI 2007/1898.

Chapter 11

The Margins of the MCA[1]

PRELIMINARY

11.1 In this chapter, we highlight four areas at the fringes of the jurisdiction of the Court which are of particular significance to practitioners:
- the inherent jurisdiction of the High Court;
- the overlap with judicial review;
- the overlap with civil proceedings; and
- the jurisdiction of the Court of Protection to grant declarations and award damages for breaches of the European Convention on Human Rights.

In each case, a health warning should be given. The precise boundaries and interrelationship between the Court of Protection and other courts are not fixed by statute; they are therefore subject to evolution and what is set out below of necessity therefore represents a snapshot as at the time of writing.

THE INHERENT JURISDICTION

Background

11.2 It is now clear that the inherent jurisdiction of the High Court has survived the implementation of MCA 2005 so as to remain of relevance in two distinct ways when considering the position of adults requiring the protection of the courts:
- To protect <u>vulnerable</u> persons who require such protection but do not fall within the categories of incapacitated persons covered by MCA 2005. A number of cases determined since the enactment of MCA 2005 had suggested that this was so, but the matter was put definitively beyond doubt in *DL v A Local Authority and Others*,[2] at least insofar as it concerns those who require protection from the baleful influence of third parties;
- To enable a High Court judge, exercising the inherent jurisdiction, to afford protection to <u>incapacitated</u> adults where the remedy sought does not fall within the remedies provided for in MCA 2005.

Both of these are discussed in turn. At **11.10**ff is discussed a third potential way in which the inherent jurisdiction has survived, namely to afford

---

[1] Parts of this chapter first appeared in Alex Ruck Keene '*The Inherent Jurisdiction: Where are we now?*' (2013) Eld LJ 88; it also draws upon case summaries included in the 39 Essex Chambers Mental Capacity Law newsletter (available at www.copcasesonline.com).
[2] [2012] EWCA Civ 253, [2012] COPLR 504.

protection in the case of an adult unable to take a decision for themselves but who does not suffer from an impairment of or disturbance in the functioning of the mind such as to fall within MCA 2005, s 2(1).

Vulnerable adults

11.3 The precise scope of the High Court's powers under the inherent jurisdiction in respect of those who are not considered to lack capacity within the meaning of MCA 2005 but who require its protection against third parties has still to be finally tested, but it is suggested that the following points are uncontroversial:

- The jurisdiction can only be exercised by High Court judges (most usually of the Family Division) sitting in their capacity as such, rather than as judges of the Court of Protection. The Court of Protection only has jurisdiction over those who lack capacity within the meaning of MCA 2005, and the powers exercised over the capacitous but vulnerable are therefore powers of the High Court;
- For these purposes, 'vulnerable' adults includes those who, even if not incapacitated by mental disorder or mental illness, are, or are reasonably believed to be, either (i) under constraint or (ii) subject to coercion or undue influence or (iii) for some other reason deprived of the capacity to make the relevant decision, or disabled from making a free choice, or incapacitated or disabled from giving or expressing a real and genuine consent.[3]
- The test for engaging the inherent jurisdiction of the High Court is whether the proposed intervention is necessary and proportionate;[4]
- The High Court will in the first instance seek to exercise the inherent jurisdiction so as to facilitate the process of unencumbered decision-making by the adult, rather than taking the decision for or on behalf of the adult;[5]
- However, the inherent jurisdiction of the High Court is not limited solely to affording a vulnerable adult a temporary 'safe space' within which to make a decision free from any alleged source of undue influence.[6] The High Court could therefore impose long-term injunctive relief to protect the vulnerable adult (for instance, by

---

[3] Per Munby J (as he then was) in *A Local Authority v (1) MA (2) NA and (3) SA* [2005] EWHC 2942, [2006] 1 FLR 867, at [77], the seminal case in which the jurisdiction of the High Court was identified. To this end the term 'vulnerable adult' retains a specific meaning even if in the context of safeguarding and the Care Act 2014 the term is no longer one that has currency.

[4] *DL v A Local Authority and Others* [2012] EWCA Civ 253, [2012] COPLR 504, at [66] (per McFarlane LJ) and [76] (per Davis LJ).

[5] See in this regard, in particular, *LBL v RYJ and VJ* [2010] EWHC 2665 *(COP)*, [2010] COPLR Con Vol 795 and the dicta of Macur J in that case as to the 'facilitative, rather than dictatorial, approach of the court' to the exercise of the inherent jurisdiction in the case of vulnerable adults, her dicta being expressly endorsed by the Court of Appeal in *DL v A Local Authority and Others* [2012] EWCA Civ 253, [2012] COPLR 504, at [67], per McFarlane LJ.

[6] *DL v A Local Authority and Others* [2012] EWCA Civ 253, [2012] COPLR 504, at [68] per McFarlane LJ. For an example of the type of relief that may be granted, see the decision of Baker J in *O v P* [2015] EWHC 935 (Fam).

making orders without limit of time prohibiting third parties from taking steps to remove the adult from the jurisdiction).

11.4 A difficult question which has yet definitively to be answered is whether the High Court in the exercise of its inherent jurisdiction in respect of a vulnerable adult can grant relief which goes further than that aimed against third parties. For instance, could the High Court require that the adult be removed from the environment in which they are subject to coercion? In the author's experience, the courts have sought vigorously to explore all steps short of this, and have fought shy of granting such relief. In very significant part, this is because whilst it is conceptually easy to formulate effective relief against a third party or parties so as to protect the vulnerable adult, it is much less easy to formulate relief directed against the vulnerable adult in such a way that it does not become dictatorial rather than facilitative. However, it is suggested that in a sufficiently extreme case the High Court could properly take the view that the welfare of the vulnerable adult required their removal.[7] It is suggested that this could only ever be justified where it could be shown all other protective measures had failed and where there was a realistic possibility that the removal would put the adult in a position to make a free choice about the matter or matters in respect of which it was considered that their will was being overborne. This, though, is subject to the caveat that steps amounting to a deprivation of liberty can only be taken where one of the bases for such deprivation contained in Article 5(1) of the ECHR is made out; the most obvious being where the adult suffers from a 'mental disorder' so as to come within the scope of Article 5(1)(e) of the ECHR.[8] In *NCC v PB and TB*,[9] Parker J expressed the view – obiter – that the inherent jurisdiction extended so as to allow a vulnerable adult to be deprived of their liberty in circumstances where they strongly objected to such a course of action. It is respectfully suggested that these obiter observations should be approached with caution, especially the analysis of the interaction between the inherent jurisdiction and Art 5(1)(e).[10]

---

[7] A comparison with the position in relation to Scotland is instructive: the interested reader is directed to the paper by Alex Ruck Keene available at http://www.39essex.com/inherent-jurisdiction-note/, which considers the extent to which the High Court could or should model the relief that it grants under the inherent jurisdiction upon the relief available under the Adult Support and Protection Act 2007.

[8] That the High Court can grant relief under the inherent jurisdiction which involves the deprivation of liberty of an adult suffering from a mental disorder was confirmed in *An NHS Trust v Dr A* [2013] EWHC 2442 (COP), [2013] COPLR 605. It may not be necessary to have medical evidence of such a disorder in advance in a true emergency: *Winterwerp v The Netherlands* [1979] ECHR 4, at [39] and *X v United Kingdom (Application No 7215/75*, decision of 5 November 1981) at [41] and [45]), but evidence of such disorder must be obtained as soon as practicable.

[9] [2014] EWCOP 14, [2015] COPLR 118.

[10] Whilst 'P' in the case before Parker J had a recognised psychiatric condition, it is suggested that it is very far from obvious how such a condition could be said to be such as to warrant detention applying the strict criteria set down in *Winterwerp* ([1979] ECHR 4). Further, Parker J's statement that 'deprivation of liberty is specifically authorised under the 2005 Act in cases of incapacity without reference to unsoundness of mind' (para 118) is not easy to square with the conclusion of the President in *Re X & Ors (Deprivation of Liberty)* [2014] EWCOP 25, [2014] COPLR 674 that an application for judicial authorisation of a

Incapacitated adults

11.5 In *XCC v AA & Anor*,[11] Parker J emphasised a point which (although made by the Court of Appeal early in the life of MCA 2005) has sometimes been overlooked, namely that there remains the possibility that the High Court can grant relief under the inherent jurisdiction in respect of a person who is incapacitated within the meaning of MCA 2005, but where such relief does not lie within the gift of the Court of Protection under the powers granted it by MCA 2005. The decision of Parker J is also of some importance – and potentially no little difficulty – as regards how the High Court will exercise the inherent jurisdiction in such circumstances.

11.6 In *XCC*, Parker J was concerned with the question of whether she had power under MCA 2005 to make a declaration that a marriage entered into in and recognised as valid in Bangladesh was to be recognised under the law of England and Wales in circumstances where P had lacked the capacity to marry. She held that the repertoire of declarations available to the Court of Protection in MCA 2005, s 15 expressly circumscribed and limited the power of the Court under that Act and did not extend to the making of such a 'non-recognition declaration.' She did not therefore have the power, as a Court of Protection judge, to make such a declaration.[12] Importantly, however, she went on to hold that:

> 'The protection or intervention of the inherent jurisdiction of the High Court is available to those lacking capacity within the meaning of the MCA 2005 as it is to capacitous but vulnerable adults who have had their will overborne, and on the same basis, where the remedy sought does not fall within the repertoire of remedies provided for in the MCA 2005. It would be unjustifiable and discriminatory not to grant the same relief to incapacitated adults who cannot consent as to capacitous adults whose will has been overborne.'[13]

There being a lacuna in the law, in the form of the absence of a power under MCA 2005 to make a non-recognition declaration, Parker J held that she had the jurisdiction – as a High Court judge – to make such a declaration under the inherent jurisdiction.

11.7 In reaching this conclusion, Parker J noted that she considered the Court of Appeal decision in *City of Westminster v IC and KC and NN*[14] to be binding authority for the proposition that she had jurisdiction to make such a declaration under the inherent jurisdiction. This may be doubted, because the question of why the Court of Appeal felt it had to proceed under the inherent jurisdiction when making such a declaration had not been

---

deprivation of liberty requires evidence not just of lack of capacity to consent to the care arrangements but also of unsoundness of mind (see paras 14 and 35(v)). Although the Court of Appeal held that the President had not, in fact, made any binding decision in this case ([2015] EWCA Civ 599, [2015] COPLR 582), no party challenged these obiter remarks, nor did the Court of Appeal cast any doubt upon them.

[11] [2012] EWHC 2183 (COP), [2012] COPLR 730.
[12] At [48].
[13] At [54].
[14] [2008] EWCA Civ 198, [2008] 2 FLR 267.

considered by that court.[15] In any event, however, the decision in *XCC* would seem to put the question of whether it was necessary to use the inherent jurisdiction beyond doubt.

11.8 Finally in this regard, it should also be noted that Parker J proceeded in *XCC* on the basis that, in considering whether to grant a non-recognition declaration, the court was not confined to making a decision dictated only by considerations as to best interests, whether those set out in MCA 2005, s 4 or more general welfare considerations.[16] She therefore found that she was entitled to take into account public policy considerations and – specifically – that the marriage had been arranged for the purpose of engineering the entry of P's spouse into this country so as to allow him to work here. This is in very clear contrast to the position that prevails under MCA 2005: see *Sandwell Metropolitan Borough Council v RG & Ors*,[17] in which Holman J declined to declare (under MCA 2005) that it was in P's best interests that steps be taken to annul a marriage which was voidable as he had not had capacity to enter into it. He considered *XCC*, but noted that there was – for purposes of decisions being made under MCA 2005 – no place for policy considerations.

11.9 It is important to note, however, that where 'policy' considerations are not in issue, the court is likely to proceed <u>as if</u> it were conducting a best interests analysis governed by MCA 2005, s 5. In *An NHS Trust v Dr A*,[18] Baker J held that force-feeding and the ancillary deprivation of liberty required to bring about such feeding was in the best interests of the incapacitated adult in question, but that it could not be authorised save under the inherent jurisdiction because (a) the adult was detained under the Mental Health Act 1983 and therefore ineligible to be deprived of his liberty under MCA 2005,[19] but (b) force-feeding could not properly be considered to be medical treatment for a mental disorder which could be compulsorily administered under the provisions of the MHA 1983. Baker J, following Parker J in *XCC*, identified that there was a lacuna, and deployed the provisions of the inherent jurisdiction so as to authorise the treatment and the ancillary deprivation of the adult's liberty.[20]

---

[15] The earlier case is also somewhat curious in that Wall LJ appeared (at paragraphs 54–55) to entertain the possibility that there was no power under MCA 2005 to take steps to prevent an incapacitated adult being removed from the jurisdiction. Thorpe LJ proceeded on the basis that there was such a power, contained in MCA 2005, s 17(1)(a) (paragraph 13). Hallett LJ agreed with both judgments without explaining which analysis she preferred. The author would respectfully suggest that the approach of Thorpe LJ is to be preferred, and indeed has been in (unreported) cases in which the Court of Protection has made 'non-removal' orders so to ensure that 'P' remains at an identified location in England and Wales.

[16] *XCC v AA and Others* [2012] EWHC 2183 (COP), [2012] COPLR 730, at [56].

[17] [2013] EWHC 2373 (COP), [2013] COPLR 643.

[18] *An NHS Trust v Dr A* [2013] EWHC 2442 (COP), [2013] COPLR 605.

[19] By virtue of Schedule 1A, paras 1 and 2 to and section 16A of MCA 2005. See also Chapter 7.

[20] A similar approach was adopted in *A Local Health Board v AB* [2015] EWCOP 31. Note, however, that the parties and the court appear to have proceeded on a misunderstanding in this case as to the proper operation of Schedule 1A, and – as Mostyn J made clear in *An NHS Trust v A* [2015] EWCOP 71 and *Re CD* [2015] EWCOP 74 – this decision was wrong, and this was not a case in which recourse to the inherent jurisdiction was required.

Adults lacking capacity for a reason outside MCA 2005

11.10 It is important to remember that there are those who lack the capacity to take decisions but for a reason which does not satisfy the diagnostic threshold set down in MCA 2005, s 2, and whose lack of capacity does not depend upon the overbearing influence of a third party. They are likely to be relatively few in number, but a possible example of such a person (drawn from an unreported case in the author's experience) might be someone born deaf and deprived of access to signing throughout their childhood. Such a combination can lead to language deprivation, resulting in concrete thinking, limited theory of mind and poor problem solving. Whilst fundamentally impacting upon a person's ability to make choices, it is not necessarily the case that such a combination of difficulties (flowing from the consequences of physical disability combined with the deleterious circumstances of the individual's childhood) would satisfy the diagnostic criteria contained in MCA, s 2(1). This category of person was not discussed by the Court of Appeal in *DL*.[21] However, the definition given by Munby J in *Re SA*[22] of the 'vulnerable' included those 'for some other reason... incapacitated or disabled from giving or expressing a real and genuine consent.'

11.11 The definition given by Munby J of the 'vulnerable' in *Re SA*[23] was expressly endorsed by the Court of Appeal in *DL*.[24] It is further suggested that it is wide enough to capture the category under discussion and, indeed, logic would dictate that if they do not fall to be considered by reference to the MCA 2005, they either fall to be protected by reference to the inherent jurisdiction or fall not to be protected at all. The tenor of both *DL* and *XCC* is very firmly that the Courts can and should be flexible and creative in deploying the inherent jurisdiction, so long as its deployment is not inconsistent with the MCA 2005. Taking this approach would not, it is suggested, be incompatible with the MCA 2005, and it is therefore suggested that such persons would fall – in an appropriate case – to benefit from the protection of the High Court by the exercise of the inherent jurisdiction even if their inability to make a choice does not arise because they are subject at the material time to the baleful influence of a third party.

11.12 In such a case, a very real question would arise as to whether the High Court should exercise its inherent jurisdiction as if it were exercising its powers under MCA 2005, ss 15-16. It is suggested that there is no logical objection in principle to such an approach. Indeed, in such a case, limiting the grant of relief to injunctive relief against third parties would not necessarily serve any purpose, not least as there may well be no third party involved at all.

---

21 [2012] EWCA Civ 253, [2012] COPLR 504. See also **11.3–4**.
22 [2005] EWHC 2942 (Fam), [2006] 1 FLR 867.
23 Ibid.
24 [2012] EWCA Civ 253, [2012] COPLR 504, at [56].

11.13 It is likely, though, that in the event that the High Court is considering the exercise of its inherent jurisdiction in the circumstances outlined in the paragraphs above:

- The High Court will take very considerable care to reassure itself that the person is not, in fact, materially incapacitated within the meaning of ss 2–3 of the MCA 2005;[25]
- The High Court will be likely to wish to limit itself in the first place to the grant of relief designed – if possible – to improve the adult's autonomy in decision-making. In other words, the High Court will – and should – be slow to use the inherent jurisdiction in this regard as a simple fall-back in the event that the public authority in question is unable to make good an application founded upon the MCA 2005.[26]
- The High Court can only grant relief which involves a deprivation of the adult's liberty if they suffer a mental disorder so as to bring them within Article 5(1)(e) of the ECHR.[27]

11.14 It is further suggested that, if the High Court were to be exercising the inherent jurisdiction in such a case, it should proceed as if it were bound by the principles contained in (in particular) s 4 of the MCA 2005. In other words, it should not adopt the approach taken by Parker J in *XCC* (above, **11.5**). That approach could in any event be distinguished because Parker J there was not exercising the inherent jurisdiction to take a decision on behalf of the adult before her; rather, she was using it to grant a declaration which lay outside the suite of remedies that were provided for in MCA 2005.

Statutory reform

11.15 Responding both to the Law Commission's report upon Adult Social Care[28] and the report of the Dilnot Commission,[29] the Coalition Government enacted the Care Act 2014 to modernise the entirety of adult social services

---

[25] In *LBL v RYJ and VJ* [2010] EWHC 2665 *(COP)*, [2010] COPLR Con Vol 795, for instance, Macur J noted that '[i]f I were to have found that [RYJ's] vulnerability was exceptional/greater by reason of her limited intellectual functioning and age, these factors would need to have been considered in reaching my decision concerning capacity. If she is unable to withstand external pressure of "normal/everyday" degree, whether emotional or physical, it seems to me that it would necessarily inform the answer to the question posed at section 3(1)(c) of the Act' (paragraph 64). In the case discussed at **11.10** above for instance, a further report produced by a psychiatrist (as opposed to a psychologist) identified a material impairment which satisfied the diagnostic criteria under MCA 2005, s 2(1).

[26] A course of action Macur J deprecated in *LBL*. This case can be distinguished from the situation under consideration here because it was common ground that RYJ satisfied the diagnostic criteria in s 2(1); we are concerned here with the position where the individual's material inability to take the decision in question stems from a situation where they do not so satisfy the criteria.

[27] See **11.4** and the footnotes.

[28] Available at: http://lawcommission.justice.gov.uk/publications/1460.htm.

[29] Available at: www.dilnotcommission.dh.gov.uk/

law in England. The Act started to come in force in April 2015 and impacts upon the issues under discussion in this section in two ways.[30]

11.16 First, the Care Act repealed s 47 of the National Assistance Act 1948, which gave a notional power to local authorities to remove someone from his or her home in certain circumstances. It had been very rarely used, in large part because of concerns as to its compatibility with Art 5(1)(e) of the ECHR.[31]

11.17 Second, the Care Act imposes, for the first time, a statutory duty upon authorities to make enquiries where there is a safeguarding concern in respect of an adult in its area who satisfies a number of criteria.[32] In such a case, the local authority 'must make (or cause to be made) whatever enquiries it thinks necessary to enable it to decide whether any action should be taken (whether under [the Act] or otherwise]) and, if so, what and by whom.'[33] The Department of Health had previously consulted upon whether there should be a new power of entry enacted to support this duty, enabling the local authority to speak to someone with mental capacity who they think could be at risk of abuse or neglect, in order to ascertain that they are making their decisions freely. Equivalent powers exist in Scotland in the Adult Support and Protection (Scotland) Act 2007[34] and (with effect from 1 April 2016) in Wales.[35] To the considerable consternation of many groups such as Action on Elder Abuse, the Department declined to include such a power in the Bill. This means that recourse is likely to be required regularly to the inherent jurisdiction to enable local authorities to discharge their statutory safeguarding functions.

OVERLAP WITH JUDICIAL REVIEW

The approach of the Court of Protection

11.19 The procedure described in the main body of this work works well when the public body responsible for the wellbeing of the person concerned (whether in a medical context or in the context of their welfare more generally) either brings proceedings to seek a decision from the court or is a party to the proceedings and is willing to abide by the result. However, there may be cases in which the public body has already taken a decision and the question then arises how that decision can appropriately be challenged.

---

[30] The equivalent for legislation for Wales is contained in the Social Services and Well-being (Wales) Act 2014, which will come into force on 1 April 2016 ('the 2014 Act').
[31] Section 47 of the 1948 Act is removed, for Wales, by section 129 of the 2014 Act.
[32] Namely (1) that they have needs for care and support (whether or not the authority is meeting any of those needs); (2) is experiencing, or is at risk of, abuse or neglect; and (2) as a result of those needs is unable to protect himself or herself against the abuse or neglect or the risk of it. The equivalent duty in Wales are found in s 129 of the 2014 Act.
[33] Section 42.
[34] Section 7. The Scottish powers, in fact, extend significantly further: for a discussion of the powers and their use, see Michael Preston-Shoot and Sally Cornish, 'Paternalism or proportionality? Experiences and outcomes of the Adult Support and Protection (Scotland) Act 2007,' *The Journal of Adult Protection*, Emerald Publishing, [2014] JAP 5.
[35] Section 127 of the 2014 Act.

Alternatively, the public body may decide in the currency of Court of Protection proceedings that it does not wish to put before the Court a particular option for consideration. For instance, a local authority may contend that a placement to which P has been moved in discharge of its community care functions sufficiently meets their needs that they are not prepared to incur the substantially greater expenditure that may be required to allow them to move home. The question that then arises is as to the extent the Court of Protection is able to compel a public authority to discharge its statutory functions in a certain way or to make a specific funding decision. Put another way, how and when will parallel public law proceedings be required in such situations?

11.20 Cases decided prior to the enactment of MCA 2005 suggested that, in the event of an impasse of the nature described above, it would be necessary to proceed by way of judicial review in order to challenge the decision of the public authority.[36] In May 2015, the Court of Appeal confirmed in *Re MN*[37] that this remains the position. Sir James Munby P, giving the sole reasoned judgment of the court, held that:

> '80. The function of the Court of Protection is to take, on behalf of adults who lack capacity, the decisions which, if they had capacity, they would take themselves. The Court of Protection has no more power, just because it is acting on behalf of an adult who lacks capacity, to obtain resources or facilities from a third party, whether a private individual or a public authority, than the adult if he had capacity would be able to obtain himself. [...] The Court of Protection is thus confined to choosing between available options, including those which there is good reason to believe will be forthcoming in the foreseeable future.
>
> 81. The Court of Protection, like the family court and the Family Division, can explore the care plan being put forward by a public authority and, where appropriate, require the authority to go away and think again. Rigorous probing, searching questions and persuasion are permissible; pressure is not. And in the final analysis the Court of Protection cannot compel a public authority to agree to a care plan which the authority is unwilling to implement. I agree with the point Eleanor King J made in her judgment (para 57):
>
> > "In my judgment, such discussions and judicial encouragement for flexibility and negotiation in respect of a care package are actively to be encouraged. Such negotiations are however a far cry from the court embarking on a 'best interests' trial with a view to determining whether or not an option which has been said by care provider (in the exercise of their statutory duties) not to be available, is nevertheless in the patient's best interest."'

The Court of Appeal in *Re MN* also upheld the approach of the judge below in respect of the application of HRA 1998. Eleanor King J had held that, exceptionally, and where a properly pleaded case is raised under HRA 1998, s 7(1)(b), the court must consider a hypothetical option for purposes of determining whether a public authority has acted in a way that is disproportionate and incompatible with a Convention right. This will, however, be very much the exception rather than the norm.

---

[36] See, in particular, *A v A Health Authority* [2002] EWHC 18 (Fam), [2002] 1 FLR 845 and *Re S (Vulnerable Adult)* [2007] 2 FLR 1095.
[37] [2015] EWCA Civ 411, [2015] COPLR 505.

11.21 The following procedural matters arise in consequence:

- It is necessary to grapple early and clearly with whether the case in question is one in which this thorny issue arises. It may well be the case that the public authority, for good reason, may well not wish to commit itself to a stark statement that 'option A is not available' so as to allow room for discussion and the maintenance of a working relationship. However, if the reality is that it is not, it is likely to be better for this to be established sooner rather than later;
- Before deciding whether to issue parallel proceedings, the parties should consider whether the public authority has genuinely put one option before the Court to the exclusion of all others or has simply indicated its preference. If it is a question of preference, parallel public law proceedings may not be required – it may suffice to seek a direction from the Court that the public authority offers an alternative;
- If there is a disagreement between the parties as to how P's best interests should be met, the party/parties advancing a contrary position to that of the public authority should adduce their own evidence as to how those interests can properly be met;
- Where the decision under challenge is clearly one in which the public authority has exercised its discretion in such a way as expressly (or by necessary implication) to seek to balance P's interests against the funding implications for others, then it is more likely than not that the proper forum to such a challenge will be in the Administrative Court. The public law challenge should be expedited such that the Court of Protection's best interests analysis can be conducted in light of the available options on the ground (see, by analogy: *Re S (Vulnerable Adult)*[38]);
- As in the earlier cases determined in relation to children and vulnerable adults, there can frequently be room for creative negotiation between the parties and between (in a loose sense) the parties and the Court even if the result can, on occasion, be a stand-off which affords of no proper resolution save a public law challenge;
- If a party does intend to rely upon the provisions of the ECHR to seek to persuade the court to adopt a specific approach to the decision(s) that fall to be taken in respect of P, this must be pleaded in detail at the earliest possible stage. The position where a party wishes to raise a claim for declarations and/or damages for a breach of rights under the ECHR is addressed at **11.50** below.

The approach of the Administrative Court

11.22 The Administrative Court will be astute to ensure that cases that should properly be determined within the four walls of the Court of

---

[38] [2007] 2 FLR 1095.

Protection remain there. In *R (DO) v LBH*,[39] permission was refused to the sister of 'P' in concurrent Court of Protection proceedings to bring judicial review applications against decisions of the local authority which had the effect of removing her from caring for her brother and making decisions as to his care arrangements. HHJ Jarman QC (sitting as a Deputy High Court Judge) noted[40] that such questions were ones which the Court of Protection with its expertise was particularly suited to deal with and that judicial review was only a remedy of last resort which should only be deployed where (for instance) an application or appeal within Court of Protection proceedings was not available.

11.23 Of even greater importance is the decision in *R (Chatting) v Viridian Housing*,[41] in which the Court was asked to consider a contention that the local authority had erred by not making reference to the Claimant's best interests when deciding as to arrangements made for her accommodation under the National Assistance Act 1948. Rejecting that submission, Nicholas Paines QC (sitting as a Deputy High Court Judge) noted (it is suggested entirely accurately) that:

> '99 ... Plainly they would have erred in law if they had regarded Miss Chatting's best interests as an irrelevance, because they would have been in breach of their duty under section 21(2) of the 1948 Act to have regard for her welfare. But the fact that Miss Chatting is mentally incapacitated does not import the test of "what is in her best interests?" as the yardstick by which all care decisions are to be made.
>
> 100 Section 1(5) of the Act applies to "an act done, or decision made ... for or on behalf of a person who lacks capacity". Its decision-making criteria and procedures are designed to be a substitute for the lack of independent capacity of the person to act or take decisions for him or herself. They come into play in circumstances where a person with capacity would take, or participate in the taking of, a decision. In deciding not to press for the registration of Miss Chatting's flat as a residential home for one person and in deciding (as they appear to have done) to agree to a novation of their section 26 arrangements for Miss Chatting so as to substitute Gold Care for Viridian, Wandsworth Borough Council were taking decisions that fell to them to take, with due regard for her welfare. They could rationally conclude that the decisions were compatible with her welfare. They did not as a matter of law require Miss Chatting's assent to these decisions; no decision, or participation in a decision was involved on her part.'

The approach adopted by the Deputy Judge was specifically endorsed by the Court of Appeal in *Re MN*.[42]

11.24 In light of the decision in *Chatting*, it is suggested that practitioners would be well-advised to proceed on the basis that the Administrative Court in deciding whether a public body has discharged the obligations imposed upon it by the relevant community care legislation in respect of an incapacitated adult will therefore:

---

[39] [2012] EWHC 4044 (Admin), available on the www.mentalhealthlaw.co.uk website.
[40] At [18]–[19].
[41] [2012] EWHC 3595 (Admin), [2013] COPLR 108.
[42] See para 11.20.

- proceed by reference to that legislation (and any obligations imposed, for instance, by the Human Rights Act 1998), rather than by asking itself whether the decision is in the incapacitated adult's best interests; and
- be very cautious before reading into any consultation requirements imposed (for instance) by the Care Act 2014 any additional obligations imposed by MCA 2005.

11.25 It is, though, important to note that the Administrative Court is likely to adopt an 'intense' standard of review of public law decisions taken in respect of those without capacity to take material decisions. This is not because of their lack of capacity per se, but because their lack of such capacity is likely to indicate their vulnerability. In such cases, following *R(KM) v Cambridgeshire County Council, National Autistic Society and others intervening*,[43] it is likely that the Administrative Court will consider that the impact of the decision upon the service user is sufficiently profound as to call for a high intensity of review.

OVERLAP WITH PERSONAL INJURY PROCEEDINGS

Overview

11.26 Prior to the introduction of MCA 2005, there was a very close link between the Court of Protection and personal injury litigants in that the Court's approval was required in cases involving settlements out of court on behalf of incapacitated claimants. That approval is no longer required, and the automatic link therefore largely severed. However, there remain an important number of areas in which coordination will be required between the Court of Protection and the civil courts as regards personal injury claimants. Four main areas give rise to points of sufficient importance to practitioners to warrant coverage in this chapter:

- The assessment of P's capacity in civil proceedings, both to litigate and to manage and control any money received;
- The approach to assessment of P's needs in personal injury proceedings contrasted to assessment of P's best interests in proceedings before the Court of Protection;
- The approach that the Court of Protection will take to approving proposals for the management of any monies recovered by P by way of compensation;
- The approach taken by the Court of Protection to steps in the civil proceedings aimed at preventing double recovery.[44]

---

[43] [2012] UKSC 23, at [36] per Lord Wilson SCJ (with whom Lords Phillips, Walker, Brown, Kerr and Dyson SCJJ agreed).
[44] The contribution of Simon Edwards of 39 Essex Chambers to material under this heading is gratefully acknowledged.

Assessment of capacity

11.27 It is not unusual for an issue to arise in civil proceedings as to whether P (the claimant) is a protected party (i.e. lacking capacity to conduct the proceedings[45]) or a protected beneficiary (i.e. lacking capacity to managing and control any money recovered[46]). The former is important because if the claimant is a protected party any proceedings conducted without a litigation friend will be invalid. The latter is important because an additional head of damages will arise if the damages have to be administered by a deputy appointed by the Court of Protection (see further **11.41** below).

11.28 In *Saulle v Nouvet*,[47] Andrew Edis QC, sitting as a deputy High Court judge, confirmed that the High Court was required for purposes of civil proceedings to consider the question of whether P is either a protected party or a protected beneficiary by applying the test set down in MCA 2005.[48] Whilst in that case the Court resolved for itself the questions of the Claimant's status for purposes of the CPR, in some circumstances it is suggested that it will be appropriate for the questions of P's capacity to litigate and/or to manage his financial affairs to be transferred to the Court of Protection. As identified by District Judge Ashton:[49]

> [The decision in *Saulle v Nouvet*] identifies a weakness of dealing with the issue of capacity in the civil court. That court can make a definitive decision as to capacity to litigate but it cannot make a decision as to capacity to manage financial affairs that will be binding on the Court of Protection. Conversely, the Court of Protection has a statutory power to make declarations as to capacity which may relate to both litigation and management of financial affairs and any such declarations are likely to be followed by a civil court. In substantial personal injury claims where the quantum of damages may be affected by the involvement of the Court of Protection there are therefore advantages in the civil court referring both issues of capacity to the Court of Protection for determination. However, where the amount of money involved would not normally trigger the intervention of the Court of Protection it is proportionate and desirable for the civil court to adjudicate on both aspects of capacity (i e to decide whether the litigant is a protected party and if so then whether he or she is also a protected beneficiary).'

11.29 Transferring questions of capacity to the Court of Protection will bring its own problems, not least because it may well take longer to convene a hearing than it would in the Queen's Bench Division. However, if questions of P's capacity to litigate and/or to manage his financial affairs are transferred to the Court of Protection, it is suggested that it would be appropriate for the defendant to the civil proceedings to participate in the proceedings before the Court of Protection, if for no other reason that this will facilitate the introduction of all the medical evidence from the civil

---

[45] Civil Procedure Rules 1998 (CPR), r 21.1(2)(d).
[46] CPR, r 21.1(2)(e).
[47] [2007] EWHC 2902 (QB).
[48] Although he made it clear that this because he was required to do so by virtue of the CPR, the MCA 2005 strictly only establishing the definition of capacity for purposes of that Act, and not regulating the conduct of any court other than the Court of Protection. See, in particular, paragraph 21.
[49] *Re GS* (CoP Case No: 11582024, Preston County Court, 10 July 2008).

proceedings. It is suggested that as a discrete issue in the civil proceedings has been delegated for decision to the Court of Protection the defendant to those proceedings would have a sufficient interest to satisfy r 75 of the Court of Protection Rules 2007, and their joinder would be desirable for purposes of r 73 (and thus the position would be different to that contemplated by Bodey J in *Re SK* discussed at **11.35**ff below).[50]

11.30 Difficult issues can, though, arise where the question of capacity to manage property and affairs is properly before both the Court of Protection and a court considering a civil claim. Whilst District Judge Ashton in *GS* noted that declarations as to capacity made by the Court of Protection are likely to be followed by the civil court, that this will not necessarily be the case can be seen from the decision in *Loughlin v Singh & Ors*.[51] This case represents something of a cautionary tale, so merits consideration in a little detail.

11.31 Mr Loughlin, the claimant in personal injury proceedings, had already had a deputy appointed to manage his property and affairs. That deputy had been appointed upon the application of the Court of Protection department of the solicitors instructed on his behalf in the personal injury proceedings. The defendant to the personal injury proceedings contended that, in fact, the claimant had the capacity to manage his property and affairs, and for the purposes of the personal injury proceedings, Kenneth Parker J therefore embarked upon a full-fledged determination of the question with the assistance of expert evidence called by both parties. In the civil proceedings, it emerged that the claimant's solicitors' Court of Protection department had in fact had evidence that he had capacity to manage his property and affairs, but had not put this evidence before the District Judge when making the application for the appointment of a deputy, relying instead upon evidence subsequently commissioned (independently) by the same firm's litigation department. That evidence was, itself, unsatisfactory because the expert providing it had initially considered that the claimant had had capacity, but then changed his mind without apparent good reason. However, only the later of the expert's reports was put before the Court of Protection, and it was on the basis of that report that it appears that the District Judge made the appointment upon the papers.

11.32 Whilst Kenneth Parker J found, on a fine balance, that the claimant had at all material times lacked capacity to manage his property and affairs, such that the appointment of the deputy had, in fact, been appropriate, he was, understandably, highly critical of the approach adopted by the claimant's solicitors,[52] noting that this was a case in which all available

---

[50] A defendant was joined for these purposes by District Judge Ashton in *Re AKP* (CoP Case No: 10185666, Preston County Court, 1 November 2007), although to the extent that the Court took into account that the defendant had a financial interest in the outcome, that must now be read subject to the dicta of Bodey J in *Re SK*.
[51] [2013] EWHC 1641 (QB), [2013] COPLR 371.
[52] His criticisms are contained in a separate annex to the judgment explaining, inter alia, why he was unable to place any weight upon the evidence of the claimant's expert who had changed his mind.

medical evidence relating to the question of capacity should have been disclosed to the Court of Protection. Kenneth Parker J made it clear that he considered that:

> '... the lamentable failures that occurred here, and the invidious position in which the judge in the Court of Protection was unwittingly placed, must never be repeated. The issue of capacity is of very great importance, and all involved must ensure that the Court of Protection has all the material which, on proper reflection, is necessary for a just and accurate decision.'[53]

Kenneth Parker J held that, had all the medical evidence in the possession of the claimant's solicitors been put before the Court of Protection at the time of applying for the appointment of a deputy, it would then have been 'almost certain' that the District Judge considering the application would have insisted on an oral hearing. He further noted that the possibility could not be ruled out that the court might have found at that hearing that the claimant had capacity, a finding which 'although not unreasonable, would have been incorrect.'

11.33 Most likely because of the curious and unsatisfactory way in which the Court of Protection had appointed the deputy, Kenneth Parker J did not anywhere ask himself the question of whether the defendant was entitled to put in issue before him the question of whether the claimant had capacity to make decisions as to the management of his property and affairs. On one view, it might be said that to do so amounted to a collateral attack upon the decision of the Court of Protection, and the proper course of action would have been for the defendant to seek to take steps before the Court of Protection to put the evidence disclosed in the civil proceedings before the Court of Protection and invite it to take appropriate steps to revisit its decision. On the other hand, it could also be said that (as per, for instance *Re SK*[54]) the two courts were considering the question of the claimant's capacity for two different purposes,[55] and that the civil court was entitled to reach a different conclusion upon the totality of the evidence as it stood before it. On balance, it is suggested that there is no necessary bar upon the issue of capacity being determined in both jurisdictions, although whichever court is the later in time to consider the matter should be astute to give clear reasons as to why it is conducting a separate investigation. It is likely, though, that this procedural question will ultimately have to be the subject of judicial determination.

11.34 Finally, it should be noted that a claimant may already, for entirely unrelated reasons, be subject to the jurisdiction of the Court of Protection, and in that event will (very likely) be a protected beneficiary and (almost inevitably) a protected party for purposes of civil proceedings. However, because capacity is decision specific, it is possible to contemplate a claimant with very substantial property and affairs who is a protected beneficiary for

---

[53] Paragraph 15 of the Annex.
[54] See **11.38** below.
[55] Before the Queen's Bench Division, the issue was whether the Claimant was entitled to recover for the past and future costs associated with the fact that his property and affairs had been (and were for the future to be) managed by a professional deputy.

purposes of personal injury proceedings yet not a protected party for the purposes of a simple claim dealt with under the small claims procedure.

Best interests

11.35 An examination of the way in which the civil courts determine damages in cases where P lacks capacity to determine questions of care and residence is outside the scope of this work.[56] The approach that the Court of Protection should take has, however, been the subject of detailed consideration by Bodey J and therefore merits standalone discussion in this chapter.

11.36 In *Re SK*,[57] Bodey J was confronted with a complicated factual matrix. In essence, there was on foot a personal injury claim concerning a man who had sustained a brain injury in a road traffic accident for which a bus company had been liable. The bus company wished to participate in Court of Protection proceedings brought subsequently (but before the personal injury proceedings had been concluded), in which the question of where SK should reside and what level of rehabilitation he required was in issue.[58]

11.37 In his decision upon the defendant bus company's application to intervene in the Court of Protection proceedings, Bodey J confirmed that the Court of Protection is unable to take a judicial review approach, such that where the only candidates for funding are statutory authorities, the Court is 'largely restricted' to the options advanced by the statutory authorities.[59] However, where another source of potential funding is available (in SK's case, a judgment against an insured tortfeasor), Bodey J made it clear that he considered that the Court of Protection should be able to make a decision between all options where there is a reasonable prospect of funding being secured from an accessible funding source.

11.38 Bodey J recognised the pragmatic attraction to having one hearing to determine the question of where SK should live and with what level of rehabilitation. However, Bodey J ultimately decided that this pragmatic attraction could not outweigh the fact that:

> '... the underlying issue in the two sets of proceedings, however similar, is not the same. The jurisdiction of the Court of Protection is as to best interests and that of the

---

[56] The reader is directed in this regard, inter alia, to *McGregor on Damages* (19th Edition, Sweet & Maxwell), paras 38.183–38.194. See also **11.45–11.49** below for a discussion of the specific issues which arise as regards the avoidance of double recovery in such cases.
[57] *Re SK* [2012] EWHC 1990, [2012] COPLR 712.
[58] SK's brother, who acted as his litigation friend in the personal injury proceedings, also wished to be joined to the Court of Protection proceedings. His application was ultimately less contentious and is not discussed further here.
[59] Paragraph 20. See also the second judgment in the proceedings, [2013] COPLR 458, at [11]–[12]. SK was endorsed by the Court of Appeal in *Re MN*: see **11.19**ff.

Queen's Bench is compensatory. The tests to be applied, although very similar ('best interests' as against 'reasonable needs') are not the same.'[60]

In the circumstances, he considered that a defendant who had not been a party to Court of Protection proceedings would not be bound at a hearing as to quantum in the damages proceedings by any Court of Protection declaration as to that person's best interests; by the same token, the judge hearing the damages claim would not be bound to follow any such declaration, but would rather decide the issue according to the applicable principles relating to the assessment of damages. The bus company's particular interests would therefore be heard and protected according to law in a different forum, namely the personal injury proceedings.

11.39 Separately, Bodey J also held that a defendant to personal injury proceedings brought by P would unlikely to be a person with a sufficient interest in Court of Protection proceedings concerning P's residence to fall within r 75 of the Court of Protection Rules, as any interest they would have would be a commercial one as opposed to an interest in the ascertainment of P's best interests.[61] Finally, Bodey J emphasised that, wherever possible, P should be represented by the same litigation friend in both civil and Court of Protection proceedings so as to ensure that differently held opinions are not reached as to where their interests may lie in the different proceedings.

11.40 Whilst the facts of *SK* are unusual,[62] it stands as a reminder that proceedings before the Court of Protection have a special character and proceed upon a particular basis the focus of which is – and is legitimately – different to proceedings before other courts. Conversely, it stands also as a reminder that the position of P in proceedings before other courts will be considered primarily by reference to the principles applied in those courts to the tasks assigned them, rather than by reference to the fact that P does not have capacity to take the relevant decisions.

Management of monies received by P in civil proceedings

11.41 Where a person lacks capacity to manage property and affairs, it is usually the case that the Court of Protection will appoint a deputy. In some cases, however, there is an argument that a person's estate can be dealt with

---

[60] At [37]. A similar theme was developed by Senior Judge Lush in the case of *Re Reeves* discussed at **11.48** below (*Re Reeves* not being cited to Bodey J).

[61] At [41]. He also found that, on the facts of the case, joining the defendant would not satisfy the requirement in r.73 that such addition would be desirable for the purpose of dealing with the application in the Court of Protection. See **11.27ff** for a discussion of the different position that may pertain if the sole issue the Court of Protection is asked to determine is P's capacity to litigate and/or manage his property and affairs.

[62] In part because, for reasons which need not detain us here, it was not possible for SK's brother to act as his litigation friend in the Court of Protection proceedings. It would be very rare for the Official Solicitor to act as litigation friend in personal injury proceedings, so the normal course of events in the case of parallel proceedings would be for the litigation friend in such proceedings to act as litigation friend in the Court of Protection proceedings. It should perhaps be noted that an appeal against the decision at Bodey J was launched and the single judge (Munby LJ) gave permission. At the last minute, though, the appeal was withdrawn.

more effectively through the creation of a trust. Trusts are often created for claimants in personal injury cases to protect an award from being treated as capital when assessing entitlement to means-tested benefits.[63] Prior to the introduction of MCA 2005, such trusts were often created by the Court of Protection for persons who lacked capacity, often on the grounds that a trust would be cheaper and more flexible to administer compared to a receivership. Clear guidance was given by HHJ Marshall QC in *Re HM*[64] as to the approach that the 'new' Court of Protection is likely to take to such an application.

11.42 *Re HM* originated in an application for a personal injury award to be placed in trust. Liability was limited on causation and therefore there was only partial recovery. It was contended by the applicant that a trust with HM's mother and a solicitor acting as trustees would be cheaper in the long run, and thus would be in the best interests of HM. The application was refused by District Judge Ashton. The matter was put for reconsideration to HHJ Marshall QC so that a 'guiding judgment' could be obtained.[65]

11.43 HHJ Marshall QC concluded that, whilst every application had to be considered on its merits, the facts of the case before her would allow a trust to be created. She identified three factors 'without which [she] would not have been prepared to authorise the creation of the relevant settlement,'[66] namely:

- The administration of a trust, on the evidence before her, would be cheaper than a deputyship (there would for instance be no security bond premium or Public Guardian supervision fee);
- HM's mother was 'a competent, forceful, well-educated and responsible person'[67] and her presence as a trustee would provide a means of monitoring legal costs (in the absence of the procedure for detailed assessment required by a deputy); and
- The proposed professional trustee had agreed that his firm's costs would be limited to the guideline rates that would be allowed on detailed assessment.

It should also be noted that it was of particular importance in the case before HHJ Marshall QC that the degree of benefit to HM which could be achieved by only a modest saving in costs was significant, because she had under-recovered in her damages claim. In other words, although the saving was a slight one in monetary terms, it was (in context) a very valuable one.

---

[63] In *Newcastle City Council v PV and Criminal Injuries Compensation Authority* [2015] EWCOP 22, [2015] COPLR 265, Senior Judge Lush held that, where the Criminal Injuries Compensation Authority ('CICA') makes it a condition of an award that there is a trust, then the Court of Protection, where the applicant lacks capacity so to do, should set up the trust and an application must be made to the Court of Protection for an order under MCA 2005 s 18(1)(h). Aspects of his decision are under appeal at the time of writing.
[64] *SM v HM (by the Official Solicitor as her Litigation Friend)* [2012] COPLR 187.
[65] At [2].
[66] At [172].
[67] At [169].

The case does not therefore represent authority for the proposition (which may have had held sway under the old regime) that any little saving can justify the endorsement of a trust.

11.44 In light of the decision in *Re HM*, it should not be assumed that an application for a trust to be created will automatically be endorsed. A party proposing a trust must complete a detailed analysis of the costs and benefits of a trust compared to a deputyship and show that the former will be materially more cost effective without prejudicing the safety of the trust assets. Evidence will also need to be produced of the professional trustee's charges and commitment to a charging policy as well as to the lay trustee's competence. The Official Solicitor will also need to be instructed. In the circumstances, therefore, the process of obtaining authorisation for the creation of a trust is now significantly riskier, and more expensive, than it was prior to the introduction of MCA 2005, and it is even more important that applications are prepared with care.

Double recovery and the Court of Protection

11.45 The civil courts have grappled for some time with finding a principled basis upon which to assess damages for personal injury where the claimant's care needs resulting from the injury are such that they could properly look to the state for those needs to be met. In such circumstances, the civil courts have been particularly astute to identify ways in which to ensure that there is no element of double recovery – ie that the claimant recovers damages from the tortfeasor on the basis that those damages will go towards their care costs, but that then all or part of the costs of care are, in fact, ultimately met by the state. That gives rise to particular complications where the claimant lacks the capacity to manage his property and affairs (and/or take decisions about his health and welfare), and therefore gives rise to the question of what – if any – role the Court of Protection is required to play.

11.46 In *Peters v East Midlands Strategic Health Authority*,[68] an action for damages for personal injury, the Court of Appeal accepted an undertaking from the Deputy appointed to manage P's property and affairs that she would (inter alia) seek from the Court of Protection (a) a limit on the authority whereby no application for public funding of the claimant's care under National Assistance Act 1948, s 21 could be made without further order, direction or authority from the Court of Protection and (b) provision for the defendants to be notified of any application to obtain authority to apply for public finding of the claimant's care under s 21 and be given the opportunity to make representations in relation thereto. The Court of Appeal held that this was:

> '... an effective way of dealing with the risk of double recovery in cases where the affairs of the claimant are being administered by the Court of Protection. It places the control over the Deputy's ability to make an application for the provision of a

---

[68] [2009] EWCA Civ 145.

claimant's care and accommodation at public expense in the hands of a court. If a Deputy wishes to apply for public provision even where damages have been awarded on the basis that no public provision will be sought, the requirement that the defendant is to be notified of any such application will enable a defendant who wishes to do so to seek to persuade that the Court of Protection should not allow the application to be made because it is unnecessary and contrary to the intendment of the assessment of damages. The court accordingly accepts the undertaking that has been offered.'[69]

11.47 The decision in *Peters* and, in particular, the approach that deputies should take in consequence, was the subject of detailed consideration by Senior Judge Lush in *Re Reeves*.[70] In that case, the local authority which was prima facie liable to contribute towards the costs of Mr Reeves' care at a rehabilitation unit wrote to his Deputy, noting that he had been awarded a personal injury award on the basis that he would be paying for future care himself, and formally requesting (on the basis of *Peters*), that the Deputy apply to the Court of Protection for authority to make a request of St Helen's Council to provide public funding for future care. The Deputy did so. Senior Judge Lush found, however, that the application was misconceived, not least in seeking to apply the *Peters* decision retrospectively to a personal injury claim resolved some six years prior to *Peters*.

11.48 Senior Judge Lush noted that Mr Reeves' Deputy had a duty to act in his best interests, including 'claiming all state benefits to which Mr Reeves may entitled and, if appropriate to do so, applying to a local authority under the National Assistance Act 1948.' He found that, in most cases, the order appointing a Deputy would give sufficient general authority to them to allow them to apply for social security benefits and to a local authority for a care needs assessment without having to obtain specific authorisation; indeed, Senior Judge Lush considered that it was implicit in the judgment in *Peters* that the Deputy had such authority – the purpose of the undertaking given in Peters was therefore to remove this authority from the Deputy and give it to the Court. Senior Judge Lush considered that the *Peters* undertaking was specific to that case, and noted that no such undertaking had been given in Mr Reeves' case; further 'there is no obligation upon the Court of Protection to adjudicate as between the claimant and defendant, or the claimant and local authority on the issue of double recovery.' Senior Judge Lush continued:

> 'Notwithstanding the undertaking that was approved in Peters and other undertakings of a similar nature, I am of the view that the Court of Protection is no longer really the appropriate forum to adjudicate on matters of this kind. Its primary function is to act in the best interests of a protected beneficiary and, even though it would strive to be impartial, there may be a perception of bias for this reason. Furthermore, the close links which the court had with personal injury litigants generally were effectively severed when the Mental Capacity Act 2005 came into force on 1 October 2007, and the court's approval was no longer required in cases involving settlements out of

---

[69] At [65].
[70] *Re Reeves* (CoP Case No: 99328848, 5 January 2011). The decision in *Peters* and its consequences has also been the subject of critical commentary by Robert Glancy QC: 'Reverse Indemnities – whether and when to give them,' (2012) Journal of Personal Injury Law 3, 54–159.

court on behalf of incapacitated claimants.[71] Additionally, the court no longer supervises deputies: that is one of the functions of the Office of the Public Guardian.

In the absence of any order of the Court of Protection restricting the authority of a claimant's deputy from applying for public funding of the claimant's care under section 21 of the National Assistance Act, the correct procedure would seem to be for the deputy to apply to the local authority and, if he is dissatisfied with the response he receives, to consider the merits of an application for judicial review.'

11.49 There is perhaps something of a tension between the approach adopted by the Court of Appeal in *Peters* and that of Senior Judge Lush in *Re Reeves*; the former clearly envisaged the Court of Protection playing a potentially important role in preventing double recovery, the latter had considerable reservations as to whether this is appropriate. It is suggested that (at least as regards the duties imposed upon deputies, which were not specifically addressed by the Court of Appeal in *Peters*) the approach of Senior Judge Lush is to be preferred, and that deputies should always be astute to ensure that monies received by P by way of compensation for personal injuries should be maximised by seeking such assistance from the state as is properly open to them.

THE EUROPEAN CONVENTION ON HUMAN RIGHTS

11.50 Almost every application brought under MCA 2005 will involve consideration of the rights under the European Convention on Human Rights ('ECHR') of the person without capacity and, very often, of his or her family members. Further, the Court of Protection is required itself to act compatibly with the Convention by Human Rights Act 1998, ss 6(1) and 6(3). We are concerned here not with the duty to have regard to those rights for purposes of making the substantive decisions relating to P (see **11.20**ff), but with the situation where the suggestion is that those rights have been breached in some way by a public authority and declarations and/or damages are sought to reflect that breach.[72] The rights most likely to have been breached (at least in applications concerning P's health and welfare) are those arising under Article 5(1) (the right to liberty) and Article 8(1) (the right to respect for private and family life).

---

[71] Whilst Senior Judge Lush did not cite it, the case of *Eeeles v Cobham Hire Services Ltd* [2009] EWCA Civ 204, [2010] 1 WLR 409 emphasises this point. In giving guidance as to the proper approach to the award of interim payments in personal injury proceedings, the Court of Appeal emphasised that the judge need have no regard to what a claimant intends to do with money awarded him, that being a matter (in the case of a claimant unable to manage his property and affairs) for the Court of Protection. At paragraph 45, the Court of Appeal noted by way of example, 'where the request is for money to buy a house, [the judge] must be satisfied that there is a real need for accommodation now (as opposed to after the trial) and that the amount of money requested is reasonable. He does not need to decide whether the particular house proposed is suitable; that is a matter for the Court of Protection.' Senior Judge Lush confirmed in *Newcastle City Council v PV and Criminal Injuries Compensation Authority* [2015] EWCOP 22, [2015] COPLR 265 that the approval of the Court of Protection is not required for awards made by the Criminal Injuries Compensation Authority to be accepted by an individual lacking capacity in the material domains. The decision in *PV* was under appeal at the time of writing; this aspect of the decision is not understood to be challenged.

[72] And that the public authority in so doing has acted contrary to s 6 of the Human Rights Act 1998.

11.51 It was for some considerable period of time after October 2007 unclear whether in such a situation the Court of Protection had the power to grant relief by way of a declaration or damages, or whether it was necessary for the affected person to bring a standalone action under s 7 of the Human Rights Act 1998. However, in *YA (F) v A Local Authority & Ors*[73], Charles J concluded that the Court of Protection has jurisdiction:

- To make declarations as to breaches of the ECHR rights of P himself;
- To make declarations as to breaches of the ECHR rights of a person other than P who can claim to be a victim of such a breach (in the case before him, P's mother), where those breaches are said to arise out of acts done in relation to P;[74] and
- To grant damages under s 8(1) of the Human Rights Act 1998 to reflect either category of breach (subject to the statutory caveat in s 8(3) that such damages must be necessary to afford the person affected just satisfaction.

11.52 The judgment is a complex one, and Charles J acknowledged that his conclusions were 'possibly against the instinct of a number of lawyers dealing with a welfare jurisdiction'[75], a tacit acknowledgment that others may differ. Until an appellate court provides a binding decision, the position is therefore not entirely free from doubt. However, the approach adopted by Charles J accords with both the language and purpose of MCA 2005, together with the wider policy goal of minimising the need that would otherwise arise for parallel proceedings. Further, there is a now an increasing body of first instance decisions from the Court of Protection providing (most commonly by endorsing consent orders) for declarations and/or damages in respect of breaches of the ECHR.[76] That body of decisions represents the tip of an iceberg of unreported cases in which claims have been settled.

11.53 An interesting issue which has yet to be subject of judicial determination is as to whether the conventional rules as to the burden of proof in relation to claims raising Convention rights apply when such claims

---

[73] [2010] EWHC 2770 (COP), [2011] 1 WLR 1505, [2010] COPLR Con Vol 1226.
[74] The same approach was taken subsequently (albeit without reference to this case) by HHJ Moir in *City of Sunderland v MM (by her litigation friend, the Official Solicitor), RS, SB, MP and SA* [2009] COPLR Con Vol 881.
[75] At [45]. This case was not cited to Eleanor King J in *ACCG & Anor v MN & Anor* [2013] EWHC 3859 (COP), [2014] COPLR 11, but she independently reached the conclusion that Court of Protection could consider claims based upon HRA 1998, s 7(1)(b) brought within the currency of welfare proceedings, a position endorsed by the Court of Appeal in *Re MN*: see **11.20** above.
[76] Summarised in *Essex County Council v RF* [2015] EWCOP 1. This has no precedent value, being the decision of a District Judge, but contains a helpful summary of the case-law and also an indication of a 'tariff' of damages for an unlawful deprivation of liberty of between £3,000 and £4,000 per month where the individual would not have been detained had the public authority in question acted lawfully. Where the public authority can show the proper application of MCA 2005 would have led inevitably to the detention of the individual, only nominal damages are likely to flow: see, by analogy, *Bostridge v Oxleas NHS Foundation Trust* [2015] EWCA Civ 79.

are brought in the Court of Protection. In *Cheshire West and Chester Council v P*,[77] Baker J rejected a contention that it was for the individual contending that they were deprived of their liberty to establish that fact; rather, he found that, as the processes of the Court of Protection were essentially inquisitorial rather than adversarial, 'the question of whether or not the circumstances as a whole amount to a deprivation of liberty is not one which falls to be determined by application of a burden or standard of proof.'[78] This would suggest that the Court of Protection would approach other situations engaging Convention rights on the same inquisitorial basis.

11.54 However, claims under the HRA conventionally require the victim to prove that they have suffered a breach of their Convention rights (the burden then lying upon the State to establish that any interference with the right in question was justified).[79] Moreover, in *Lumba v Secretary of State for the Home Department*,[80] Lord Dyson made it clear that the same approach applied in the context of domestic false imprisonment claims.[81] It does not appear that *Lumba* was cited to Baker J in *Cheshire West*.

11.55 The tension between these two approaches (and the possibility that two different Courts would take different evidential approaches to the question – for instance – of whether P has been deprived of his liberty depending upon where he brought his claim) has yet to be resolved. The author would respectfully suggest that – at least where the Court of Protection is being asked to determine whether a breach of a Convention right has taken place for purposes of establishing a claim for declarations and/or damages – the better approach is the conventional one applicable to Convention cases, such that the burden of proof lies with the person making the assertion to establish a breach (subject to the person resisting the assertion establishing that any interference with P's Convention right was justified).

---

[77] [2011] EWHC 1330 (Fam), [2011] COPLR Con Vol 273. This part of his judgment was not appealed or the subject of any consideration by the Court of Appeal upon appeal and therefore stands unchallenged.
[78] At [52].
[79] See Clayton & Tomlinson (eds), *The Law of Human Rights* (2nd Edn, OUP 2009), paragraph 6.187.
[80] [2011] UKSC 12.
[81] At [53].

are brought before the Court of Protection. In *Chewings-Ven* and *Chewings County v R T Baker*,¹ Baker J appeared to pronounce that it was for the individual contending him they were deprived of their liberty to establish that fact, rather he found that, as the processes of the Court of Protection were reasonably inquisitorial rather than adversarial, the question of whether or not the circumstances as a whole amount to a deprivation of liberty is not one which falls to be determined by reference to a burden or standard of proof.¹⁵⁴ This would suggest that the Court of Protection would approach other situations engaging Convention rights on the same inquisitorial basis.

11.54 However, claims under the HRA conventionally require the victim to prove that they have suffered a breach of their Convention right. The burden lying upon the State to establish that any interference with the right in question was justified.¹⁵⁵ Moreover, in *Lumba v Secretary of State for the Home Department*,¹⁵⁶ Lord Dyson made it clear that the same approach applies in the context of domestic false imprisonment claims.¹⁵⁷ It does not appear that *Lumba* was cited to Baker J in *Chewing West*.

11.55 The tension between these two approaches (and the possibility that two different Courts would take different evidential approaches to the question — for instance — of whether P has been deprived of his liberty depending upon where he brought his claim) has yet to be resolved. The author would respectfully suggest that — at least where the Court of Protection is being asked to determine whether a breach of a Convention right has taken place for purposes of establishing a claim for declaration and/or damages — the better approach is the conventional one applicable to Convention cases such that the burden of proof lies with the person making the assertion to establish a breach (subject to the person resisting the assertion establishing that any interference with P's Convention rights was justified).

---

¹⁵³ [2013] EWHC 1320 (Fam); [2013] COPLR Con Vol 273. This particular judgment was not appealed or the subject of any consideration by the Court of Appeal upon appeal and therefore stands undisturbed.

¹⁵⁴ At [58].

¹⁵⁵ See Clayton & Tomlinson (eds), *The Law of Human Rights* (2nd edn, OUP, 2009), paragraph 6.197.

¹⁵⁶ [2011] UKSC 12.

¹⁵⁷ At [65].

Chapter 12

International Protection of Adults

INTRODUCTION

12.1 The lengthening of the human life span and the corresponding rise in the incidence of illnesses related to old age, such as Alzheimer's disease, have in recent years become heightened at the international level as a result of the increasing ease of international travel. In a world which is globally interlinked, it is now not unusual for people to have assets situated in another jurisdiction, or to encounter healthcare or other personal welfare issues when abroad, or go to another state for particular healthcare treatment. The same issues arise with particular frequency between the different jurisdictions of the UK. These natural movements in population have made practitioners and in particular notaries more concerned to have at their disposal private international law rules that are well defined. Each state has, or fails to have (as the case may be), its own mental capacity jurisdiction which may be applicable or overlap in the particular circumstances and it is an understanding of how these laws co-exist in the field of private international law that guides practitioners through these difficult issues.

12.2 Previous chapters deal with the mental capacity jurisdiction in England and Wales, but all too often knowledge of this law and procedure is not sufficient. This Chapter addresses the legal framework concerning the international protection of adults who lack capacity and issues that arise in this context from the perspective of the MCA 2005.

PRIVATE INTERNATIONAL LAW

12.3
> 'Private international law is that part of law which comes into play when the issue before the court is so closely connected with a foreign system of law as to necessitate recourse to that system'[1]

Private international law deals primarily with the application of laws in space and time. The local jurisdiction at a particular time is sovereign and can define as it wishes, and place a boundary at that or any other time as it thinks appropriate. Unlike garden fences, the boundaries created by separate jurisdictions are rarely co-terminous, and can be in different places at different times. Each jurisdiction has its own separate and distinct private international law rules which do not necessarily mesh with that of another state.

---
[1] See Cheshire, North and Fawcett (eds), *Private International Law* (14th Edn, OUP 2008).

12.4 It is common in all private international law to consider separately issues of:
(1) Jurisdiction – which court has jurisdiction to make orders in relation to a vulnerable adult's personal welfare, health and medical treatment, and/or property and affairs and how extensive is that jurisdiction?
(2) Applicable Law – if they do, which state's laws will be applied?
(3) Recognition and Enforcement – Will the courts of a state recognise and enforce an order of the courts of a different state and, if so, will it apply local conditions of implementation? Equally, will the courts of a state accept and enforce a private mandate intended to have effect after the onset of mental incapacity, if it is valid in another state?[2]

12.5 English private international law in the area of capacity of adults has in the past been very uncertain. Mental capacity is really a particular requirement for many separate and different legal acts, each with their own test and different connecting factor. Other jurisdictions have completely different private international law rules. Many jurisdictions with law based on a civil code hold that issues to do with questions of capacity are governed by the personal law of the person. This is often governed by the law of either nationality or by domicile in a civil law sense rather than habitual residence.[3]

CROSS-BORDER ISSUES AND MENTAL CAPACITY

12.6 Cross-border issues arise whenever someone holds assets in more than one jurisdiction, encounters capacity issues whilst living or present in another jurisdiction or has a factor, such as domicile, habitual residence or nationality linking them with another jurisdiction. It is increasingly common for people to have such connections.

12.7 In any case with a cross-border element, it will be necessary to consider questions such as which court has jurisdiction over the person, which state's laws will be applied, and whether orders made in one state will be recognised by the authorities of a different state. Equally applicable is the question of whether there exists any form of private mandate intended to have effect upon incapacity and whether this will be effective in another state.

---

[2] For example, will an Enduring or Lasting Power of Attorney that is valid in England also be valid and accepted in another state? Will the appointment of a Deputy be recognised?

[3] Previous editions of this book include completed questionnaires from various states across the globe setting out the way their legal system deals with adults who lack capacity to which the reader is referred for details on the law in these jurisdictions: Albania, Australia (NSW), Australia (Queensland), Australia (Victoria), Austria, Belgium, Bulgaria, Canada (Alberta), Canada (Manitoba), Canada (Nova Scotia), Canada (Ontario), Canada (Saskatchewan), Croatia, Denmark, Finland, France, Germany, Greece, Hong Kong, Hungary, Iceland, Italy, Japan, Netherlands, Norway, Portugal, Serbia, Singapore, Slovenia, Spain, Switzerland, Tunisia, USA (Florida) ad USA (Oregon).

12.8 Examples of cross border issues that arise in the context of property and affairs are:
  (1) Whether an Enduring or Lasting Power of Attorney or the appointment of a Deputy by the Court of Protection will be recognised in another jurisdiction; or whether a foreign private mandate or foreign protective measure will be recognised by the Court of Protection.
  (2) Dealings in relation to assets owned by an incapacitated adult habitually resident in England and Wales but located in another jurisdiction; or dealings in relation to an incapacitated adult habitually resident abroad who has assets located in England and Wales.
  (3) The making of a statutory will for an individual habitually resident in England and Wales with movable and immovable property located in another state.

12.9 Examples of cross border issues that arise in the context of health and welfare are:
  (1) Care arrangements for an incapacitated adult who is to move, or has moved, from England and Wales to another state, and the impact of such a move on the adult's habitual residence.
  (2) Urgent care arrangements for an incapacitated adult habitually resident in another jurisdiction but present in England and Wales.
  (3) Whether a Lasting Power of Attorney or the appointment of a Deputy by the Court of Protection will be recognised in another state; or whether a foreign advance directive or foreign protective measure will be recognised by the Court of Protection.
  (4) Orders seeking the return to England and Wales of an incapacitated adult wrongfully removed from the jurisdiction.

HAGUE 35

12.10 The Hague Conference on Private International Law seeks to establish international agreements to reduce conflicts of law and to lay down rules to determine jurisdiction and related matters. Under its auspices the Hague Convention on the International Protection of Adults ('Hague 35') was concluded on 13 January 2000.

12.11 The underlying principle of Hague 35 is to improve the protection in international situations of adults who, by reason of an impairment or insufficiency in their personal faculties, are not able to safeguard their own interests. Part of the background to Hague 35 was the fact that a number of jurisdictions had, or were in the course of, reforming their domestic law in this area. This enabled guidance to be proffered in relation to international problems faced by jurisdictions that had recently legislated and those states that yet to legislate.

12.12 Hague 35 entered into force on 1 January 2009. It has, to date, been ratified by eight states: Austria, Czech Republic, Estonia, Finland, France,

Germany, Switzerland and the UK (in respect of Scotland only).[4] Hague 35 does not deal with the PIL of all capacity issues but solely with the jurisdiction, applicable law and recognition and enforcement of protective measures and with the applicable law of particular anticipatory powers of representation granted by an adult.

12.13 Cyprus, Greece, Ireland, Italy, Luxembourg, the Netherlands, Poland and the UK (in respect of England & Wales) have all signed but not yet ratified. It is understood that the UK Ministry of Justice is committed to ratifying Hague 35 as soon as practicable and is actively working towards this although no set time frame has been set down in this respect. It is anticipated that Monaco, Ireland and Northern Ireland may ratify during 2016. Portugal is also likely to accede shortly and Italy is also now working towards ratification. On a broader level, the EU Parliament Resolution of 18 December 2008[5] called on the EU Commission to assess the option of the accession of the Community as a whole to Hague 35, and the EU Commission Action Plan of April 2010 implementing the Stockholm Programme[6] referred to the desirability of EU Member states acceding to Hague 35.

12.14 Hague 35 does not deal with the private international law of all capacity issues but solely with the jurisdiction, applicable law and recognition and enforcement of protective measures and with the applicable law of particular anticipatory powers of representation granted by an adult. It applies to 'the protection in international situations of adults who, by reason of an impairment or insufficiency of their personal faculties, are not in a position to protect their interests'.[7] An adult is defined as a person who has reached the age of 18 years; however, Hague 35 also applies to measures of protection taken in respect of an adult who had not reached the age of 18 years at the time the measures were taken.[8]

12.15 The objectives of Hague 35 are set out in Article 1(2):
'a) to determine the State whose authorities have jurisdiction to take measures directed to the protection of the person or property of the adult;
b) to determine which law is to be applied by such authorities in exercising their jurisdiction;
c) to determine the law applicable to representation of the adult;
d) to provide for the recognition and enforcement of such measures of protection in all Contracting States;
e) to establish such co-operation between the authorities of the Contracting States as may be necessary in order to achieve the purposes of this Convention.'

---

[4] The UK made use of the federal states clause in Hague 35 in order to ratify it for only one part of its territory. As Hague 35 allows the distinction between territories with separate systems of law within a state, the UK was able to ratify in respect of Scotland only.
[5] See www.europarl.europa.eu/sides/getDoc.do?type=TA&reference=P6-TA-2008-0638&format=XML&language=EN#top.
[6] COM(2010) 171.
[7] Article 1(1).
[8] Article 2.

12.16 Hague 35 recognises the difficulties posed in a situation where an individual has made advance arrangements with regard to how he wishes his affairs to be dealt with in the event that he loses capacity and the importance of being able to ascertain whether these arrangements will be recognised in other jurisdictions (and, if so, to what extent). It also contains provisions concerning co-operation between Contracting States designed to enhance the protection of incapacitated adults. The system of co-operation, which is flexible and enables use of existing channels, encompasses, among other things, information exchange, the facilitation of agreed solutions in contested cases, and the location of missing adults. Further, Contracting States must designate a Central Authority to discharge the duties which are imposed by Hague 35, which primarily relate to facilitating effective communication between Contracting States and mutual assistance.

12.17 Some examples of the type of situation Hague 35 is intended to address are set out in the outline of the convention prepared by the Hague Conference on Private International Law:[9]

> '1. A Scotsman has been living in Argentina since his retirement 10 years ago. He owns property in Scotland and Argentina. He now suffers from age-related dementia and is not capable of managing his affairs. The property needs to be sold to provide funds for the care of the man living in Argentina. He has a son living in Scotland. Some years ago, the man granted his son extensive powers of attorney to be exercised in the event of any incapacitating illness certified by a Scottish medical practitioner. If the Convention were in force between the countries, the powers of attorney would be recognised in Argentina and the son could act on the man's behalf to make the necessary arrangements to manage his father's affairs. The powers of representation would be exercised in accordance with the law in Argentina.
>
> 2. A man with Japanese nationality dies in Japan. He is survived by a 40 year old daughter who is living in Canada, and who has both Canadian and Japanese nationality. She suffers from schizophrenia and has been placed under a protective regime in Canada. If the Convention were in force in between the countries, the jurisdiction lies with the Canadian courts to make decisions related to the protection of her interests, as she is habitually resident in Canada. The Convention would ensure that the powers of her guardian in Canada would also be recognised in Japan and other Convention States. The guardian in Canada would be issued with a certificate outlining his or her powers of representation and would be able to act in Japan on the daughter's behalf in relation to the succession of her father's estate.'

MENTAL CAPACITY ACT 2005, SCHEDULE 3

12.18 The UK has not yet ratified Hague 35 in respect of England and Wales, but by making provision for it in Schedule 3 of the Mental Capacity Act 2005[10] the UK gives effect to Hague 35 internally in relation to England and Wales, so far as it can.[11] Thus the territory of England and Wales is regarded as a proto-Hague 35 state since it deals with matters as if it has ratified Hague 35 and will also extend its application to the recognition and enforcement of protective measures from other Non-Contracting States.

---

[9] See www.hcch.net/upload/outline35e.pdf.
[10] See MCA 2005, s 63 and Sch 3.
[11] The provisions of the Schedule are intended to be compatible with the Adults with Incapacity (Scotland) Act 2000, Sch 3, which gave effect to the Hague 35 in Scotland.

However, as a matter of international law the UK (in so far as England and Wales is concerned) is not recognised as a Contracting State of Hague 35 until full ratification takes place.

12.19 Schedule 3 is implemented into the domestic law of England and Wales by the Mental Capacity Act 2005 (Commencement No.2) Order 2007.[12] However, Para 35 of Schedule 3 excepts the application of some provisions.[13] Some experts express the view that this meant that the excepted sections only had effect when Hague 35 comes into force in England and Wales. Others believe that since Hague 35 has come into force in other jurisdictions, the excepted sections are now in force in England and Wales.[14] Subject to this, Schedule 3 provides private international law rules to govern jurisdictional issues within the United Kingdom between Scotland and England and Wales and Northern Ireland. It also provides private international law rules for England and Wales with all other jurisdictions, and is not limited to those rules in relation to jurisdictions that have ratified Hague 35. In any event, unless or until the UK Government ratifies the Convention in relation to England and Wales, there cannot be full reciprocity in these countries – the UK Government has not yet, for example, designated the Central Authority for England and Wales under Hague 35, which means that Article 38 certificates[15] cannot yet be produced and a transfer of jurisdiction cannot be made under Articles 7 and 8 of Hague 35.[16]

12.20 Schedule 3 to the MCA 2005 extends Hague 35 in two ways. Firstly, Hague 35 applies to adults over the age of 18 whereas the MCA 2005 applies to persons over the age of 16 (other than children to whom either the Hague Protection of Children Convention XXXIV or Brussels II bis apply[17]). Secondly, Hague 35 only applies to adults who, by reason of an impairment or insufficiency of their personal faculties, are not in a position to protect their interests, whilst the MCA 2005 also applies to the donors of powers of attorney even if not impaired or insufficient.

12.21 Schedule 3 does not apply in all circumstances. The exclusions contained in Article 4 of Hague 35 are specifically referred to in paragraph 33 of Schedule 3:

---

[12] SI 2007/1897
[13] These excepted provisions are predicted on England and Wales being a Contracting State of Hague 35 and in a position to undertake reciprocal arrangements with other Contracting States as regards the transfer of jurisdiction and international co-operation.
[14] The former view is supported in the judgment of Sir James Munby in *Re PO* [2013] EWHC 3932 (COP) at [9].
[15] Article 38 of Hague 35 provides for the authorities of a Contracting State where a measure of protection has been taken or a power of representation confirmed to issue to the person entrusted with the protection of the adult's person or property a certificate indicating the capacity in which that person is entitled to act and the powers conferred (see Paragraph 30 of Schedule 3).
[16] See paragraph 8 of Schedule 3.
[17] Regulations 1(2) and 17 of The Parental Responsibility and Measures for the Protection of Children (International Obligations) (England and Wales and Northern Ireland) Regulations 2010.

'Nothing in this Schedule applies [therefore also excluding the effect of the provisions of para.13 which extends Hague 35 to all Lasting Powers], and no provision made under para.32 is to apply, to any matter to which the Convention, as a result of art.4, does not apply.'

The exclusions contained in Article 4 are:
(a) maintenance obligations;
(b) the formation, annulment and dissolution of marriage or any similar relationship, as well as legal separation;
(c) property regimes in respect of marriage or any similar relationship;
(d) trusts or succession;
(e) social security;
(f) public measures of a general nature in matters of health;
(g) measures taken in respect of a person as a result of penal offences committed by that person;
(h) decisions on the right of asylum and on immigration;
(i) measures directed solely to public safety.

12.22 In relation to any capacity or other legal issue arising under Schedule 3, the first questions should always be:
(1) Does the issue fall within the scope of Schedule 3?
(2) Do the courts of England and Wales have jurisdiction?
(3) If so, which law will they apply? Will it be that of England and Wales or another state?
(4) if not, where does jurisdiction lie and what is the relevant law?

JURISDICTION AND HABITUAL RESIDENCE

12.23 In place of the traditional connecting factor of domicile, Hague 35 and Schedule 3 now use habitual residence as the relevant connecting factor. Thus Schedule 3 paragraph 7(1) gives the Court jurisdiction to exercise its powers in respect of:

(1) an adult habitually resident in England and Wales;[18]
(2) an adult's property in England and Wales;
(3) an adult present in England and Wales or who has property there, if the matter is urgent;
(4) an adult present in England and Wales, if a protective measure which is temporary and limited in its effect to England and Wales is proposed in relation to him.

12.24 In addition, paragraph 7(2) and 8 of Schedule 3 states that the Court may also have jurisdiction in relation to:

(1) the worldwide property and the person of an adult present in England and Wales whose habitual residence cannot be ascertained, is a refugee, or has been displaced as a result of disturbance in the country of his habitual residence;

---

[18] In relation to the adult and his worldwide property.

(2) a British citizen and his worldwide property, who has a closer connection with England and Wales than with Scotland or Northern Ireland, and Article 7 of the Convention has, in relation to the matter concerned, been complied with;[19]
(3) a person and his worldwide property, for whom the jurisdiction of habitual residence is available and the UK Minister of Justice agrees that the matter is better dealt with in England as the state of nationality, of former residence or where property is situated, and Article 8 of the Convention has, in relation to the matter concerned, been complied with.[20]

12.25 The concept of habitual residence is expressly not defined in Hague 35, being a term 'which, despite the important legal consequences attaching to it, should remain a factual concept.'[21] and there is otherwise no universal definition of the term. It is therefore for individual national courts to provide the local interpretation. It has been pointed out that the advantages of habitual residence as a connecting factor as being that it is generally easier to establish than domicile because it is less dependent on the intention of the person concerned and is a simpler concept overall.[22]

12.26 The Explanatory Report to Hague 35 provides only limited assistance in understanding the meaning of habitual residence in the context of adult incapacity.[23] The cases of *Re MN (Recognition and Enforcement of Foreign Protective Measures)*,[24] in *Re O (Court of Protection: Jurisdiction)*[25] and *An English Local Authority v SW*[26] provide helpful guidance on the approach to be taken by the courts in England and Wales.

Re MN:

12.27 This was the first reported England and Wales decision relating to cross border capacity issues, since the advent of Schedule 3. The proceedings related to an elderly lady, MN, who has habitually resident in California and had been removed from there to Canada and thereafter to England in circumstances said to involve a breach of the terms of an Advance Health Care Directive signed by her. After the removal, the Californian court made various orders including directing the return of MN

---

[19] See paragraph 8 of Schedule 3, although it is unlikely that this provision will enter into force until the UK ratifies Hague 35 in respect of England and Wales.
[20] Ibid.
[21] Explanatory Report on Hague 35, paragraph 49.
[22] Law Commission, Private International Law: Law of Domicile (Law Com No 168, 1987)
[23] See for example the commentary to Articles 5(2) and 6(2) of Hague 35, which suggest that the acquisition of a new habitual residence can be instantaneous in certain circumstances whereas in others it may be appropriate to allow for a reasonable waiting time in order to ensure that previous habitual residence, itself well established, has definitively been lost.
[24] [2010] COPLR Con Vol 893 (CP).
[25] [2014] Fam 197 (CP).
[26] [2014] EWCOP 43.

to California. The matter was brought before Hedley J who was asked to consider whether MN's habitual residence had changed to England and Wales. He held that:

> '22. ... the question of authority to remove is the key in this case to the question of habitual residence. Habitual residence is an undefined term and in English authorities it is regarded as a question of fact to be determined in the individual circumstances of the case. It is well recognised in English law that the removal of a child from one jurisdiction to another by one parent without the consent of the other is wrongful and is not effective to change habitual residence — see, e.g. *Re PJ (Abduction, Habitual Residence: Consent)* [2009] EWCA Civ 588, [2010] 1 WLR 1237, [2009] 2 FLR 1051. It seems to me that the wrongful removal (in this case without authority under the Directive whether because Part 3 is not engaged or the decision was not made in good faith) of an incapacitated adult should have the same consequence and should leave the courts of the country from which she was taken free to take protective measures. Thus in this case were the removal 'wrongful', I would hold that MN was habitually resident in California at the date of [the Californian] orders.
>
> 23. If, however the removal were a proper and lawful exercise of authority under the Directive, different considerations arise. The position in April 2010 was that MN had been living with her niece in England and Wales on the basis that the niece was providing her with a permanent home. There is no evidence other than that MN is content and well cared for there and indeed may lose or even have lost any clear recollection of living on her own in California. In those circumstances it seems to me most probable that MN will have become habitually resident in England and Wales and this court will be required to accept and exercise a full welfare jurisdiction under the Act pursuant to paragraph 7(1)(a) of Schedule 3. Hence my view that authority to remove is the key consideration.'

Re O:

12.28 This case concerned the move of a woman, PO, from England to Scotland, the move having taken place at the instigation of three of her children and strongly objected to by the fourth. A key question before Sir James Munby P, was whether PO was habitually resident in England and Wales, or whether her habitual residence had changed to Scotland. Sir James Munby P endorsed paragraphs 22 and 23 of *MN* and further held that habitual residence can in principle be lost and another habitual residence acquired on the same day;[27] in the case of an incapacitated adult habitual residence can in principle be lost and another habitual residence acquired without the need for any court order or other formal process (such as the appointment of a deputy or attorney to make decisions on behalf of the adult);[28] and habitual residence will not change if the removal has been wrongful, for example in the circumstances in *Re MN* or where there has been a breach of a court order, such as in the case of *Re HM (Vulnerable Adult: Abduction)* [2010] 2 FLR 1057 (Fam Div), which concerned the removal of an incapacitated adult from England to Israel.

---

[27] See paragraph 17 of *Re O* with reference to the decision of the Supreme Court in *A v A and another (Children: Habitual Residence) (Reunite International Child Abduction Centre and others intervening)* [2014] AC 1 and paragraph 50 of the Lagarde Report.

[28] *Re O*, paragraph 18.

Re SW:

12.29 In this case Moylan J. gave judgment on the habitual residence of a Scottish woman placed by the Scottish statutory authorities in a rehabilitation placement in England. SW was born and lived in Scotland. She had an accident in 2006 and was moved to England under a compulsory order in 2009. She was then moved to her current home in England in a sheltered flat in 2010. She lacked the capacity to decide where to live although she was able to express wishes and feelings in relation to her present and future accommodation. Her placement was open ended and she had been present in England for approximately 5 years by the time the question of her habitual residence was determined by the Court of Protection. The Scottish and English Local Authorities argued that SW was still habitually resident in Scotland. The court held that the definition of habitual residence under Schedule 3 should be kept free of analytical constructs and should be the same as other private law family law instruments including Brussels II bis, and that this approach was consistent with the Lagarde Report. Moylan J was not persuaded that the determinative question was the degree of integration of SW in England. Rather, he considered that there were a wide range of factors which would affect the court's ability to establish a person's state of mind and in the circumstances decided that SW was habitually resident in England notwithstanding the fact that SW's residence had been determined by compulsory order and had been governed by the relevant authorities, and that SW had expressed a dislike of her residence and her wish to move somewhere else.

APPLICABLE LAW

12.30 The relevant rules relating to applicable law are set out in Schedule 3, Part 3, which are largely based on those set out in Chapter III of Hague 35. This provides a general rule that each court is to apply its own law unless it considers that there is a substantial connection with another state, in which case it may apply the internal law of that other state.[29] *Renvoi* is excluded and it is the internal law of that other state that will be applied.

12.31 In relation to 'Lasting Powers'[30] the law applicable is:
(1) that of the state of the donor's habitual residence
(2) that of a state of which he is a national, or in which he has formerly been habitually resident or in which he has property (but only in respect of that property), if the donor specifies that law in writing,[31] (even if that applicable law does not itself accept such powers).

Clearly there can be problems here if the applicable law is that of another state which does not accept such a power or it was created in English form, when it should have been created in the form of another state.

---

[29] MCA 2005, Schedule 3, para 11.
[30] Defined as Lasting Powers of Attorney, Enduring Powers of Attorney and other powers having a like effect.
[31] MCA 2005, Schedule 3, para 13.

RECOGNITION AND ENFORCEMENT

12.32 England and Wales will now recognise protective measures[32] taken in another state provided that the relevant adult is habitually resident in that other state.[33] Once Hague 35 is ratified in respect of England and Wales, a protective measure taken in another Contracting State will be recognised if it was taken on any of the grounds set out for jurisdiction under chapter II of Hague 35.[34] Recognition can be refused on limited grounds if the English Court finds that:

(1) the case in which the measure was taken was not urgent and the adult was not given an opportunity to be heard and the omission was in breach of the rules of natural justice; or
(2) recognition would be contrary to public policy; or
(3) the measure would be inconsistent with a mandatory provision in England and Wales; or
(4) the measure is inconsistent with a protective measure in England and Wales; or[35]
(5) Article 33 has not been complied with in relation to cross-border placement.[36]

There are provisions under paras 20 and 22 for interested persons to apply to the Court for a declaration as to whether a protective measure taken under the law of another state is to be recognised or enforced.

PROTECTIVE MEASURES

12.33 Protective measures have a very wide definition both under Hague 35 and under para 5.1 of Schedule 3 and may also include an order for a Statutory Will, subject to the special rules of Schedule 2, but do not extend to Lasting Powers of Attorney.

WITHIN THE UNITED KINGDOM

12.34 Schedule 3 applies these private international law rules to dealings with Scotland and Northern Ireland in the same way as to other states. An order of the Court of Protection will therefore be recognised in Scotland pursuant to Schedule 3, paragraph 7 of the Adults with Incapacity (Scotland) Act 2000[37] unless a Scottish guardian has been appointed with relevant powers

---

[32] Defined by MCA 2005, Schedule 3, para 5.
[33] MCA 2005, Schedule 3, para 19(1) and *Re MN* [2010] EWHC 1926 (Fam).
[34] MCA 2005, Schedule 3, para 19(2).
[35] MCA 2005, Schedule 3, para 19(3) & (4).
[36] MCA 2005, Schedule 3, para 19(5).
[37] Schedule 3, paragraph 7 provides that any measure taken under the law of a country other than Scotland for the personal welfare or the protection of property of an adult with incapacity shall be recognised by the law of Scotland if the jurisdiction of the authority of the other country was based on the adult's habitual residence there; or the UK and the other country were, when the measure was taken, parties to Hague 35 and the jurisdiction of the authority of the other country was based on a ground of jurisdiction provided for in Hague 35; see further Chapter 13.

The position in Northern Ireland is somewhat more complex until it too introduces private international law rules similar to the Convention.

THE POSITION IN NON-CONVENTION COUNTRIES

12.35 Although the Court of Protection may have jurisdiction pursuant to Schedule 3, traditionally it would not make an order directly affecting property in another state if such an order would not be recognised in that other state or if it would infringe another court's jurisdiction. If Hague 35 does not apply there are no universal rules if a person who lacks capacity is resident in a non-Convention State or has assets which are situated in such a state. Many states do, however, have authorities for the management of the property and affairs of people who lack capacity, similar to those in the UK.

12.36 In the same way that the Court of Protection will take jurisdiction in relation to assets in England and Wales belonging to a person resident in another state, the courts of other states may recognise the authority of their counterparts. This is consistent with the principles of many private international laws which provide that the capacity of a person is determined by the person's personal law. Some jurisdictions may therefore apply similar principles to those contained in Hague 35.

12.37 In the case of a person lacking capacity who is habitually resident in England and Wales and has assets in another state, the requirements of that state will be different in each case and an agent in that state will need to be instructed. Many states will require a formal application to the local court. The possible requirements may include:

(1) a sealed and certified copy of the order appointing the deputy and also authorising the action in the other state, plus an explanation of the deputy's authority to act and the arrangements made for the protection of the property and affairs in England and Wales;
(2) a sealed and certified copy of the relevant enduring, lasting, durable or continuing power of attorney[38];
(3) details of the assets for which authority is required and whether they are movable or immovable;
(4) confirmation that no person has been appointed to administer those assets in the state where they are situated.

The court in the other state is likely either to confirm the deputy's authority, provide the deputy with authority to act or appoint a local guardian with authority to remit assets back to the deputy or the Court of Protection. In the event of dispute, the assets are likely to be retained in the other state until the dispute is resolved.

12.38 It remains difficult to determine jurisdiction and ascertain the relevant law in non-Convention countries and yet with increased tourism

---

[38] This has been problematic, since there was no mechanism for the OPG to produce such a copy, but it is understood that this issue is currently being addressed.

and home ownership abroad (especially for retired people) capacity issues arise quite frequently. An attempt has been made in the previous annual volumes of *Court of Protection Practice* (Jordan Publishing) to lead a pathway through this jungle by reproducing the responses to Questionnaires completed for many other jurisdictions.[39]

---

[39] The most comprehensive analysis of the law in this area is to be found in Frimston, Ruck Keene, van Overdijk and Ward *The International Protection of Adults* (OUP, 2015) ISBN 978-0-19-872725-5.

and home ownership abroad (especially for named people) cannot, as noted, arise little frequently. An attempt has been made in the previous annual volumes of Prefernot Property (Jordan Publishing) to lead a pathway through this tangle by reproducing the responses to Questionnaires completed for many other jurisdictions.

Chapter 13

Scotland

Background

13.1 Legal practice reflects the society which it serves. Estimates by the Alliance which campaigned for passage of the Adults with Incapacity (Scotland) Act 2000, and referred to during the parliamentary proceedings, indicated that at any one time an estimated 100,000 Scots have impairments of capacity of potential significance in law. More recent estimates, taken cumulatively, would suggest a figure well above that. Modern private client practice accordingly encompasses a significant amount of adult incapacity work. Inevitably, that work can involve significant links outside Scotland, reflecting the multiplicity of connections between Scottish society and the present and past countries of the Commonwealth, the United States of America, Europe and elsewhere; and above all the other jurisdictions of the British Isles.

13.2 Inward and outward mobility is traditional. Many well-established Scottish families have interests elsewhere. An interim order in Scottish guardianship proceedings allowed spouse's consent to be given to the sale of property in Italy.[1] Modern travel and communications now counteract many of the previous consequences of distance. The attorney in London can in most practical ways be close to her elderly aunt in Edinburgh. The only son in California, whose job takes him worldwide, visited his father in Scotland with sufficient regularity to satisfy statutory criteria for appointment as his guardian.[2]

13.3 Also new is the mobility of people with impairments of capacity, sometimes to access specialist provision, sometimes to follow or return to their families or for similar reasons of convenience; and sometimes moved by others for questionable motives. An elderly lady returned to her native Northern Ireland for nursing home care: a Scottish guardian was appointed to deal with her property in Scotland.[3] Another lady, subject to an order and proceedings in France, went to Scotland and a day after her arrival there purported to grant a Scottish POA.[4]

13.4 The relevant private international law of England and Wales, including from that perspective the Hague Convention on the International

---

[1] *C*, 23 Sept, 2009, Kilmarnock Sh Ct.
[2] *H*, 6 May, 2008, Dunoon Sh Ct.
[3] *H, Applicant*, 2007 SLT (Sh Ct) 5.
[4] *F v S* 2012 SLT (Sh Ct) 189.

Protection of Adults, is described in Chapter 12. This chapter outlines salient points of Scots law from the viewpoint of practitioners and others in England and Wales and should be read in conjunction with the legislation, court rules and guidance set out in Part X.

13.5 Be warned at the outset that Scots law is different. It is different in its fundamentals and structures. This chapter does not contain full descriptions, and is referenced only selectively, in the more recent experience leading to the introduction of modern incapacity provision, and in the content of that provision. Do not assume that similar terminology has the same meaning, or that relevant provisions of Scots law can be understood simply by translating terminology. Where concepts are substantially the same, terminology sometimes differs to indicate Englishness or Scottishness, such as 'social services' in England and 'social work' in Scotland – hence the Social Work (Scotland) Act 1968 ('SW(S)A 1968'); a 'substitute attorney' is the same as a 'replacement attorney'; and the Judicial Institute fulfils the same function as the Judicial Studies Board, to give a few random examples. However, each jurisdiction has its own Public Guardian without any differentiation in titles, and surprisingly only the Scottish Public Guardian – though established first – makes clear (on her website and email addresses, for example) which one she is.

Scots law

13.6 Scots law is based on Roman law,[5] emphasising principles rather than precedents, and thus in its fundamentals is akin to European rather than Anglo-American systems. While foreign law lacks legitimacy as a formal source of law, Roman law is always potentially or actually Scots law. The influence of English law has been so great that Scots law is now often described as a hybrid system. However, the development of Scottish adult incapacity law continues to be driven mainly by the application of principles, hence the central importance of the principles stated in s 1 of Adults with Incapacity (Scotland) Act 2000[6] as exemplified by the development, without any express statutory provision, of a power to make and alter Wills,[7] and the methodology adopted by the courts in resolving matters of fundamental importance.[8]

13.7 From 1707 to 2000 Scotland lacked its own separate legislature. The perpetual tendency for the needs of vulnerable people to slip down the order of priorities was compounded by the failure of the UK Parliament to meet the needs of law reform in Scotland. For many Scots lawyers, the establishment by the Scotland Act 1998 of a devolved Scottish Parliament

---

[5] For a review of the modern influence of Roman law, see Cairns and du Plessis 'Ten years of Roman Law in Scottish Courts' 2008 SLT News 191: 'while foreign law lacks legitimacy as a formal source of law, Roman law is always potentially or actually Scots law'.
[6] See **13.36**.
[7] See **13.87**.
[8] See for example *Muldoon, Applicant*, 2005 SLT (Sh Ct) 52; 2005 SCLR 611; 2005 GWD 5–57; and *North Ayrshire Council v JM*, 2004 SCLR 956, Sh Ct.

was valued more as a means to address a serious backlog of essential law reform, rather than for any nationalistic or party political significance. 'Parliament' refers to the UK Parliament at Westminster, 'the Parliament' to the Scottish Parliament at Holyrood. The legislative competence of the Scottish Parliament is limited to matters devolved to it by the Scotland Act. At time of writing, following the rejection of independence for Scotland in a referendum on 18th September 2014, devolution of further matters is proposed. Legislation incompatible with ECHR is ultra vires. Acts of the pre-1707 Parliament of Scotland are designated APS (Act of the Parliament of Scotland) and those of 'the Parliament' asp (Acts of the Scottish Parliament). Note the distinction between SI (Statutory Instrument, which includes Instruments of solely Scottish application made under Westminster legislation) and SSI (Scottish Statutory Instrument, made under legislation of the Scottish Parliament).

13.8 Within its first decade the Parliament comprehensively reformed land tenure and related matters in Scotland. Even before that, as its first and highest priority, it produced the Adults with Incapacity (Scotland) Act 2000 ('AWI(S)A 2000'). Legislation to cover the three overlapping areas of adult incapacity, mental health and vulnerable adults continued with the Mental Health (Care and Treatment) (Scotland) Act 2003 ('MH(CT)(S)A 2003') and the Adult Support and Protection (Scotland) Act 2007 ('ASP(S)A 2007'), both of which included amendments to AWI(S)A 2000, in the latter case following review of experience of the working of AWI(S)A 2000 as originally enacted. AWI(S)A 2000 has also been amended by the Regulation of Care (Scotland) Act 2001, the Smoking, Health and Social Care (Scotland) Act 2005 and various SI's and SSI's. See **13.20** for proposals for further amendment.[9] In October 2014 the Scottish Law Commission published its conclusions and recommendations following further review, concentrating on issues of deprivation of liberty. The Public Guardian[10] has initiated debate on the need for review of guardianship procedures.[11] The scope of the Essex Autonomy Project, which reviewed the compliance of MCA 2005 with the UN Convention on the Rights of Persons with Disabilities, has been extended to cover Scotland (and Northern Ireland), and that "three jurisdictions" project continues at time of writing.

The Scottish courts

13.9 In civil matters Scotland has two tiers of courts of first instance, the Court of Session, which sits only in Edinburgh, and the Sheriff Court. Lords Ordinary sit singly in the Outer House of the Court of Session. Appeal lies from them to the Inner House, which usually sits in divisions comprising at

---

[9] See Scottish Law Commission Report No 240 on Adults with Incapacity (October 2014).
[10] In this chapter 'the Public Guardian' refers to Scotland's Public Guardian except where otherwise indicated.
[11] Both the Public Guardian and the Mental Welfare Commission have proposed systems of graded guardianship; see paper on Graded Guardianship on the Public Guardian's website (**13.30**) and comments thereon on the website of the Law Society of Scotland www.lawscot.org.uk.

least three judges, though a larger court may be convened for matters of particular importance. In a few matters the Inner House hears cases at first instance, examples being exercise of the nobile officium, which is an inherent jurisdiction to address matters not previously provided for in Scots law, and the parens patriae jurisdiction. Although that jurisdiction was invoked in *Morris, Petitioner*, 1986, the Inner House declared that future applications for appointment of tutors could be presented in the Outer House, and in *Law Hospital NHS Trust v Lord Advocate*[12], the Inner House declared similarly in relation to applications to authorise withdrawal of treatment. Appeal lies from the Inner House to the Supreme Court (previously the House of Lords).

13.10 Sheriffs frequently hear cases of substantial value and great importance. There is no general upper financial limit to their civil jurisdiction. They now have exclusive competence in cases of a value up to £100,000.[13] Relatively few matters are excluded from their jurisdiction. There are six Sheriffdoms, each led by a Sheriff Principal. Apart from Glasgow, the Sheriffdoms are divided into Sheriff Court Districts, each with its own Sheriff Court of which there are 39 altogether, five of them on islands. Courthouses range from small buildings in locations such as Lochmaddy to massive ones in the main cities. With a few exceptions, up until recently the first level of appeal has been to the Sheriff Principal of that Sheriffdom, thence to the Inner House of the Court of Session, and thence to the Supreme Court (formerly House of Lords). Sheriffs have been bound by precedents set by their own Sheriff Principal, but not by those of other Sheriffs Principal or other Sheriffs. Sheriffs Principal are not bound by the precedents of their own predecessors. All are bound by precedents set by the Inner House of the Court of Session and the Supreme Court.

13.11 The Courts Reform (Scotland) Act 2014 introduced (with effect from January 2016 in civil matters) a single Scotland-wide Sheriff Appeal Court, in which Sheriffs Principal and Appeal Sheriffs sit, and which may sit anywhere in Scotland. Further appeal is still to the Court of Session, but only with permission of the Sheriff Appeal Court, which failing the Court of Session, and only where the case raises an important point of principle or there is another compelling reason for such further appeal. It also introduced two tiers at first instance, of Sheriffs and Summary Sheriffs; designation of specialisms to which particular Sheriffs would be assigned; and appointment of all-Scotland specialist Sheriffs.

13.12 Scotland has no Court of Protection, or equivalent separate court, nor an Official Solicitor (though since 2007 the Public Guardian may now initiate or enter proceedings as described in **13.30**).[14] Much information is available at www.scotcourts.gov.uk. For decisions under AWI(S)A 2000 go to 'Library', then 'Court Judgments', then 'Sheriff Courts Search' and

---

12 1996 SC 301; 1996 SLT 848; [1996] 2 FLR 407; (1998) 39 BMLR 166; [1996] Fam Law 670, IH.
13 Courts Reform (Scotland) Act 2014, s 39.
14 AWI(S)A 2000, s 6(2)(da).

search for 'Adults with Incapacity'. The Mental Health Tribunal for Scotland was established by MH(CT)(S)A 2003, s 21 and has jurisdiction under that Act, but not in incapacity matters. At time of writing it is understood that consideration is being given to utilising the reforms described in **13.11** to introduce shrieval specialisation in the adult incapacity jurisdiction.

Development of adult incapacity law prior to 2000

13.13 Fifteen years prior to AWI(S)A 2000 it was generally believed (though not universally accepted) that Powers of Attorney ceased to have effect upon the incapacity of the granter. Prior to AWI(S)A 2000 the only general form of financial management for adults lacking relevant capacity was to appoint a curator bonis, whereupon the adult was deprived of all management capacity, even to decide and manage matters of which the adult was in fact capable; and the only available form of welfare guardianship was Mental Health Act guardianship, with fixed and limited powers, which, under the Mental Health (Scotland) Act 1984, were similar to those under Mental Health Act 1983.

13.14 To the demand for Powers of Attorney that would indisputably be operable following the granter's incapacity, Westminster responded simplistically in the Law Reform (Miscellaneous Provisions) (Scotland) Act 1990, s 71, under which – for a decade – Powers of Attorney automatically remained in force in the event of subsequent incapacity of the granter, unless the document explicitly provided otherwise. Scotland thus experienced continuing Powers of Attorney with no effective regulation or control. The majority met a clear need and worked well, due to the sense and integrity of appointed attorneys rather than anything in relevant legislation; but inevitably there were many horror stories, such as the hospital patient who purportedly granted three Powers of Attorney in rapid succession to three different relatives; large numbers of Powers of Attorney granted by residents in a care home to the proprietor and operated dubiously; and so forth. Powers of Attorney granted during that decade remain valid, but become subject to many of the provisions of AWI(S)A 2000.

13.15 The most positive progress was achieved by going back to the tutors to adults originating in Roman law, reviving first the tutor-dative[15] and then the tutor-at-law.[16] Tutors-dative, as revived, were appointed as guardians with specific welfare powers, tailored to need in each individual case, and usually for a limited period. Joint appointments were permitted, and common. Tutors-dative were also appointed for limited purposes in relation to property and financial affairs, such as approving and executing a deed of family arrangement (for example, to establish a family discretionary trust following the death of a parent). Tutors-at-law had plenary financial and welfare powers, and were generally appointed to displace a curator bonis. In

---

[15] *Morris, Petitioner*, 1986; see Ward 'Revival of Tutors-Dative' 1987 SLT News 69.
[16] *Britton v Britton's curator bonis*, 1992 SCLR 947.

Britton (see footnote),the first modern case, the curator bonis was a professional who had never met his ward and allowed her an income – from a substantial award of damages – less than if she had been dependent solely upon state benefits.

13.16 As noted in **13.9**, in 1996 a test case established procedure for dealing with applications under the *parens patriae* jurisdiction to deal with proposed discontinuance of treatment in cases of persistent vegetative state.

Particular characteristics of Scots law

13.17 In addition to experience of the developments in the years leading up to AWI(S)A 2000, described in the previous section, two well-established characteristics of Scots law, unchanged by AWI(S)A 2000, are relevant to the understanding of Scottish incapacity law. Firstly, in Scotland if an adult lacks adequate capacity for a particular act or transaction, it will be void, regardless of whether any other party was at the time aware of the incapacity. With a few exceptions such as purchase of 'necessaries', the position in law is the same as if the purported act or transaction had not taken place. Secondly, for most practical purposes adulthood in Scotland begins at 16. For example, it has always been possible, without parental consent, to marry at 16. Some special provisions apply to young people aged 16-18, but for adult incapacity legislation to commence at 16 fits easily with other statutes such as the Age of Legal Capacity (Scotland) Act 1991. In cross-border and international matters this does not fit so easily with commencement of adulthood at 18 under the Hague Convention on the International Protection of Adults 2000.[17] This issue is addressed in Chapter 12 of Frimston et al *International Protection of Adults*, OUP, 2015. A guardianship application may be lodged up to three months prior to the young person's 16th birthday, but the guardianship comes into force no earlier than that birthday (s 79A).

Literature

13.18 On adult incapacity law in Scotland, see Ward *Adult Incapacity* (2003) and *Adults with Incapacity Legislation* (2008), which updates *Adult Incapacity* and contains the updated text of AWI(S)A 2000. Together, the two volumes reproduce all relevant Statutory Instruments. See also Chapter 12 (by Ward) in Frimston et al *International Protection of Adults* (2015). On mental health law, see Franks and Cobb *Mental Health (Care and Treatment) (Scotland) Act 2003* – the text of the Act with annotations. On ASP(S)A 2007 and related topics, see Patrick and Smith *Adult Protection and the Law in Scotland* (2010). For a wider-ranging text on relevant subjects, see Patrick *Mental Health, Incapacity and the Law in*

---

[17] Converse issues will arise if a state where the age of majority is higher than 18 should ratify the Convention.

Scotland (2006).[18] On private international law issues see *International Protection of Adults* (see **12.38**, footnote). Several Codes of Practice have been issued under AWI(S)A 2000. For useful websites see **13.12** and **13.30**.

Adults with Incapacity (Scotland) Act 2000
General

13.19 AWI(S)A 2000 (set out in Part X; also referred to as 'the Act' in this section) is a co-ordinated and integrated, but non-exclusive, code of provision for adults with incapacity in Scotland. The topics covered differ from those in MCA 2005. As noted above, adults are persons over 16. During the law reform process, 'Incapable Adults' was used, but only as a working title. The title eventually adopted was a contraction of 'adults with impairments of capacity'. In practice, 'the adult' has been almost universally adopted to refer to the person whose capacity is, or may be, impaired.

13.20 The Act follows a similar overall pattern to several reformed jurisdictions. Gateway definitions of adult and incapacity give access to the Act's provisions. Guided by principles, procedures enable solutions to be selected from a flexible range of possibilities, and tailored to individual need. Implementation of those solutions is also guided by principles, and is subject (generally but not always) to supervision, accountability and re-assessment. AWI(S)A 2000 has been amended on various occasions, as narrated in **13.8**. Further amendment is to be expected following upon the Scottish Law Commission Report mentioned in **13.84**, and the process of engagement with the UN Committee on the Rights of Persons with Disabilities regarding compliance with the Convention of that name.

Jurisdiction and roles

13.21 Practitioners in England and Wales may choose not to instruct a city solicitor in a matter in which Lerwick Sheriff Court has jurisdiction; nor to instruct a Stornoway solicitor when the Court of Session in Edinburgh has jurisdiction; nor to instruct any Scottish solicitor where the judicial and administrative authorities of some other country have jurisdiction, or more appropriately have jurisdiction; and they may choose to attend themselves to matters dealt with by the Public Guardian upon submission of appropriate forms, without court process.

13.22 The jurisdiction and private international law provisions of AWI(S)A 2000 are set out in Sch 3, based on the Hague Convention on the International Protection of Adults of 13 January 2000. For description and discussion of them see Frimston et al *International Protection of Adults*, OUP, 2015 (in particular Chapter 12, by Ward). The Convention applies

---

[18] At time of writing, updated editions of *Adult Protection and the Law in Scotland* and *Mental Health, Incapacity and the Law in Scotland* were expected to be published in December 2015.

among jurisdictions in respect of which it has been ratified, currently Scotland, Austria, Czech Republic, Estonia, Finland, France, Germany and Switzerland. As explained in **12.18–12.22** it also, to an extent, in effect applies as between Scotland and England and Wales, by virtue of MCA 2005, Sch 3, notwithstanding that the Convention has not yet been ratified in respect of England and Wales. The Central Authority for Scotland under the Hague Convention is the Scottish Government's Constitution, Law and Courts Directorate, EU and International Law Branch, Civil Law Division, The Scottish Government, 2 West, St Andrew's House, Regent Road, Edinburgh EH1 3DG, Tel: 0131 244 2417. On registration of international measures, see **13.23** below, last sentence.

The Courts

The Sheriff Court

13.23 The main jurisdiction under AWI(S)A 2000 rests with the Sheriff Court, and allocation to Sheriffdom is governed by similar rules to those in the Convention. Accordingly, the Sheriff having jurisdiction is the Sheriff in whose Sheriffdom:

(a) the adult is habitually resident;[19]
(b) relevant property is situated;
(c) the adult, or property belonging to the adult, is present in urgent cases where the adult is not habitually resident in Scotland;
(d) the adult is present, when the intervention sought is temporary and its effect limited to Scotland; and
(e) the adult is present, where the Sheriff considers it necessary in the adult's interests to take the proposed measure immediately.[20]

The Sheriff has jurisdiction to vary or recall intervention and guardianship orders[21] made by that Sheriff if no Contracting State under the Convention (other than the United Kingdom) has jurisdiction and either:

(a) no other court or authority has jurisdiction; or
(b) another court or authority has jurisdiction but (i) it would be unreasonable to expect an applicant to invoke that jurisdiction or (ii) that court or authority has declined to exercise jurisdiction.[22]

The sheriff also has jurisdiction to determine applications to register international measures, the register itself being maintained by the Public Guardian.[23]

---

[19] A change of habitual residence is not immediately effected by removal of an adult lacking relevant capacity from one jurisdiction to another – see *F v S*, referred to in **13.3** (footnote 27).
[20] AWI(S)A 2000, Sch 3, paras 2(1) and (3).
[21] See **13.86**.
[22] AWI(S)A 2000, Sch 3, para 2(2).
[23] See chapter XXIV 'International Protection of Adults' of the Act of Sederunt (Summary Applications, Statutory Applications and Appeals etc. Rules) 1999, as amended (set out in Part X).

13.24 Note that the qualification 'other than the United Kingdom' means that recall or variation will be by the French courts where they have jurisdiction, but not automatically by the English courts even after ratification in respect of England. If the Scottish courts have jurisdiction, but no particular Sheriffdom is identified by the relevant rules, the fall-back Sheriff is the Sheriff at Edinburgh.

13.25 The Sheriff has jurisdiction to grant intervention and guardianship orders, to give directions to persons exercising functions under the Act,[24] to hear appeals against decisions as to incapacity and appeals against any decision under the Act as to the medical treatment of an adult[25] (but not under the procedure described at **13.75**), and a wide range of remits and appeals under the Act. Unlike the position in England and Wales, the Act does not provide for stand-alone declaratory powers, but the powers to give directions and to determine appeals against decisions as to incapacity may in some cases have similar effect. For the sheriff's powers in relation to Powers of Attorney, including non-Scottish Powers of Attorney, see **13.64**; and for powers in relation to non-Scottish equivalents of guardians see **13.86**.

13.26 'Which forum?' was a major issue during the law reform process. The Law Society of Scotland recommended that the primary jurisdiction should rest with the Sheriff Court, but that individual Sheriffs should be designated to deal with adult incapacity matters. That suggestion was adopted by the Scottish Law Commission in the draft Bill annexed to its *Report on Incapable Adults*.[26] Sadly, that proposal was not included in the Act, with inconsistent and uncoordinated results. In Glasgow and Edinburgh Sheriff Courts the designated sheriff concept has been informally adopted. Many of the leading judgments which have developed this jurisdiction are those of Sheriff John Baird at Glasgow, who retired in April 2015. In many other Sheriff Courts, several Sheriffs exercise this jurisdiction in a consistent and appropriate way. Overall, however, there is often a lack of the case management which such a jurisdiction requires and there are inconsistencies which would have been less likely with designated sheriffs. In difficult cases where there is a possible choice of jurisdiction, it might be wise to seek advice about the particular Sheriff Court.[27] See **13.12** as to the possible introduction of shrieval specialisation in the adult incapacity jurisdiction under the provisions of the Courts Reform (Scotland) Act 2014.

---

[24] Under AWI(S)A 2000, s 3(3): for examples see: *Application by Public Guardian for Directions* (Glasgow Sh. Ct. 30 June 2010), *Morton, Minuter for Directions* (Edinburgh Sh. Ct. 21 July 2010) and, as an ancillary matter, *Y W v Office of the Public Guardian* (Peterhead Sh. Ct. 25 June 2010).
[25] With further appeal to the Court of Session, bypassing the Sheriff Principal.
[26] Report No 151, published September 1995.
[27] Also disappointing is the reluctance of the Sheriff Court Rules Council to address the requirements and consequences of this jurisdiction adequately.

The Court of Session

13.27 The role of the Court of Session as the first court to which a matter under the Act may be taken is limited to certain medical matters. See **13.66**. By agreement of parties, and subject to certain qualifying requirements, a special case may be taken to the Court of Session, which is available in incapacity matters and has been done at least once.[28]

Other functions under the Act

Public Guardian[29]

13.28 Scotland has its own entirely separate Public Guardian. In this chapter 'the Public Guardian' refers to Scotland's Public Guardian except where otherwise indicated. The Office of the Public Guardian has extensive registration functions (including notification of registration), administers the scheme of Access to Funds (see **13.76**ff), supervises guardians and appointees under intervention orders with financial powers, has investigative powers in relation to property and financial matters, and other powers and functions; but does not act as guardian, or have any other management functions, for any individual adults.

13.29 The Public Guardian's investigative functions include investigating, in relation to property and financial matters, complaints against continuing attorneys and non-Scottish equivalents, against guardians and non-Scottish equivalents, against appointees under intervention orders, and concerning the Access to Funds provisions of Part 3 of the Act. Certificates issued by the Public Guardian are conclusive evidence of their contents. They include certificates of registration of continuing and welfare Powers of Attorney ((CPA's) and (WPA's) respectively), various certificates under the Access to Funds scheme, and certificates of appointment under intervention and guardianship orders.

13.30 The Public Guardian has statutory duties to provide information and advice in property and financial matters, on request, to guardians, appointees under intervention orders, continuing attorneys and withdrawers under the Access to Funds scheme; and will generally provide helpful advice and guidance in response to reasonable requests from others, though the considerable information available on the Public Guardian's website should be checked before making an enquiry. The Public Guardian must investigate where she becomes aware of circumstances in which the property or financial affairs of an adult seem to be at risk. The Public Guardian may initiate or enter 'any proceedings before a court' where she considers that necessary to safeguard the property or financial affairs of an adult who lacks relevant capacity. Fees chargeable by the Public Guardian

---

[28] See *Great Stuart Trustees Ltd v Public Guardian*, [2015] SC 379, [2014] CSIH 114: see **13.55** below.
[29] AWI(S)A 2000, ss 6 and 7.

are prescribed by regulations and have been increased substantially.[30] Much useful information is available on her website (www.publicguardian-scotland.gov.uk) and the links which it provides.

Mental Welfare Commission[31]

13.31 The Mental Welfare Commission for Scotland exercises independent protective functions in relation to the rights, welfare and interests of adults with mental disorders in Scotland, including those with impairments of capacity. Many of the Commission's functions and powers are contained in MH(CT)(S)A 2003. Under AWI(S)A 2000 the Commission's functions include providing information and advice in personal welfare matters to guardians, welfare attorneys and appointees under intervention orders; and investigating complaints where either a local authority has failed to investigate, or the Commission is not satisfied with a local authority investigation. The Commission's investigative functions include investigating, in relation to personal welfare matters, complaints against welfare attorneys and non-Scottish equivalents, guardians and non-Scottish equivalents, and appointees under intervention orders. Important examples include the 'JL Report' referred to in **13.46** (footnote) and the 'D Report',[32] referred to in **13.43** and **13.56**.

Local authorities[33]

13.32 The functions of local authorities under the Act include supervising guardians in relation to welfare functions, investigating circumstances where the personal welfare of an adult appears to be at risk, and initiating applications for intervention or guardianship orders (in both personal welfare and property and financial matters) where this appears to be required and no-one else is taking action. The local authority supervises welfare guardians; supervises persons authorised under intervention orders and welfare attorneys where that has been ordered by the court; and has a duty to provide information and advice in welfare matters, when asked, to all of the foregoing.

---

[30] See Ward 'Out of the wrong pocket' 2008 JLSS 9.
[31] AWI(S)A 2000, s 9.
[32] The Commission's report on 'An investigation into the response by statutory services and professionals to concerns raised in respect of Mr and Mrs D' (published 13 February, 2012).
[33] AWI(S)A 2000, ss 10, 53(3) and 57(2).

Other Incapacity Act roles

13.33 The Act confers significant roles on an adult's primary carer[34] and nearest relative.[35] Others with roles include any named person[36] and any person providing independent advocacy services.[37]

Limitation of liability

13.34 The Act exempts certain persons exercising roles under the Act from liability for any breach of any duty of care or fiduciary duty owed to the adult. The exemption applies only if the person has acted reasonably and in good faith, and in accordance with the Act's general principles (see **13.36**), or has failed to act and the failure was reasonable and in good faith, and in accordance with the general principles. The persons protected by this provision are guardians, including non-Scottish equivalents, continuing and welfare attorneys and non-Scottish equivalents, appointees under intervention orders, withdrawers under the Access to Funds scheme, and managers of establishments acting under Part 4 of the Act.[38]

Ill treatment and wilful neglect

13.35 It is an offence under the Act for any person exercising powers under the Act in relation to an adult's personal welfare to ill-treat or wilfully neglect that adult. The maximum penalties are two years' imprisonment or a fine, or both.[39]

The principles

13.36 The Act commences with a statement of principles[40] which have proved to be invaluable, and which have been subject to minor consequential amendment but no calls for significant alteration. This Scottish experience led to the strong recommendation, described in Chapter 2, that legislation for England and Wales should likewise be governed by general principles. Scotland rejected a 'best interests' test for the reasons explained by the Scottish Law Commission in the passage quoted at **2.46**. The Scottish principles, with brief comments in ensuing paragraphs, are as follows:

> '1.(1) The principles set out in subss (2) and (4) shall be given effect to in relation to any intervention in the affairs of an adult under or in pursuance of this Act, including any order made in or for the purpose of any proceedings under this Act for or in connection with an adult.

---

[34] AWI(S)A 2000, s 87(1).
[35] MH(CT)(S)A 2003, s 254; AWI(S)A 2000, s 4.
[36] MH(CT)(S)A 2003, s 329.
[37] AWI(S)A 2000, s 3(5A) and (5B); MH(CT)(S)A 2003, s 259(1).
[38] AWI(S)A 2000, s 82.
[39] AWI(S)A 2000, s 83.
[40] AWI(S)A 2000, s 1(1)–(5).

(2) There shall be no intervention in the affairs of an adult unless the person responsible for authorising or effecting the intervention is satisfied that the intervention will benefit the adult and that such benefit cannot reasonably be achieved without the intervention.

(3) Where it is determined that an intervention as mentioned in subs(1) is to be made, such intervention shall be the least restrictive option in relation to the freedom of the adult, consistent with the purpose of the intervention.

(4) In determining if an intervention is to be made and, if so, what intervention is to be made, account shall be taken of–

    (a) the present and past wishes and feelings of the adult so far as they can be ascertained by any means of communication, whether human or by mechanical aid (whether of an interpretative nature or otherwise) appropriate to the adult;

    (b) the views of the nearest relative, named person and the primary carer of the adult, in so far as it is reasonable and practicable to do so;

    (c) the views of –
        (i) any guardian, continuing attorney or welfare attorney of the adult who has powers relating to the proposed intervention; and
        (ii) any person whom the sheriff has directed to be consulted,
in so far as it is reasonable and practicable to do so; and

    (d) the views of any other person appearing to the person responsible for authorising or effecting the intervention to have an interest in the welfare of the adult or in the proposed intervention, where these views have been made known to the person responsible, in so far as it is reasonable and practicable to do so.

(5) Any guardian, continuing attorney, welfare attorney or manager of an establishment exercising functions under this Act or under any order of the sheriff in relation to an adult shall, in so far as it is reasonable and practicable to do so, encourage the adult to exercise whatever skills he has concerning his property, financial affairs or personal welfare, as the case may be, and to develop new such skills.'

13.37 In AWI(S)A 2000 'intervention' has a wide meaning, and encompasses a decision not to do something. It may mean an intervention affecting a second adult in the course of proceedings initiated in relation to another.[41]

13.38 In s 1(2) 'benefit' can include anything which the adult would have done if capable, including something gratuitous, such as making gifts or participating in non-therapeutic medical research – both of which are expressly provided for in the Act.[42] In *G v West Lothian Council*,[43] Sheriff Principal Stephen controversially offered the novel proposition that the benefit principle was 'the essential principle' which should be addressed before consideration is given to the other principles. That would appear to

---

[41] See Ward "Two 'adults' in one incapacity case? – thoughts for Scotland from an English deprivation of liberty decision", 2013 SLT (News) 239–242.
[42] AWI(S)A 2000, ss 66 and 51 respectively.
[43] 2014, GWD 40-730 (see also case commentary by Eccles and Watson at 2015 SLT (News) 35).

equate 'benefit' with a 'best interests test' notwithstanding that the latter approach was expressly rejected for the purposes of AWI(S)A 2000 – see quotation at **2.46**. That approach would also appear to be inconsistent with the obligations undertaken by the United Kingdom under the UN Convention on the Rights of Persons with Disabilities. For criticism of the Sheriff Principal's approach, see Ward "Abolition of Guardianship? 'Best interests' versus 'best interpretation'", 2015 SLT (News) 150.[44]

13.39 Section 1(3) requires not the simplest or cheapest option, nor even – without qualification – the least restrictive option, but 'the least restrictive option in relation to the freedom of the adult, consisting with the purpose of the intervention'. The exercise of quasi-guardianship powers without assessment, judicial procedure or procedure subject to judicial control, or appropriate supervision and accountability, can never be the least restrictive option under this definition.

13.40 Section 1(4)(a), unlike the following provisions of s 1(4), is not limited to 'in so far as it is reasonable and practicable to do so'. The obligation is unqualified. The sheriff (only) must take account of the adult's wishes and feelings so far as expressed by a person providing independent advocacy services.[45]

13.41 Section 1(4)(c)(i) includes similar appointments under the law of any country, but in the case of guardianship only if the guardianship is recognised by the Law of Scotland.[46]

Definitions of adult, incapable and incapacity

13.42 These definitions are contained in s 1(6), which is in the following terms:

'(6) For the purposes of this Act, and unless the context otherwise requires –

"adult" means a person who has attained the age of 16 years;
"incapable" means incapable of –
(a) acting; or
(b) making decisions; or
(c) communicating decisions; or
(d) understanding decisions; or
(e) retaining the memory of decisions,
as mentioned in any provision of this Act, by reason of mental disorder[47] or of inability to communicate because of physical disability; but a person shall not fall within this definition by reason only of a lack or deficiency in a faculty of communication if that lack or deficiency can be made good by human or mechanical aid (whether of an interpretative nature or otherwise); and

---

[44] See also Mental Capacity Law Newsletter, April 2015, Scotland section, page 9.
[45] AWI(S)A 2000, s 3(5A).
[46] AWI(S)A 2000, s 1(7).
[47] See **13.48**.

"incapacity" shall be construed accordingly.'

13.43 The initial words of s 1(6) mean that the above definition does not necessarily apply for other purposes, where other tests of incapacity may apply. This element of 'acting' in (a) broadens the scope of the definition significantly beyond decision-making, and includes (for example) acting to assert and safeguard the adult's own rights and interests; acting in accordance with decisions otherwise competently made; and acting to resist undue influence – see the 'D Report' referred to in **13.31**. Element (e) is usually interpreted as meaning memory to a degree, and for a duration, appropriate to the matter in question. As with s 1(4)(a) (see **13.36** and **13.40**), the requirement to facilitate communication is not subject to the qualification 'in so far as it is reasonable and practicable to do so'. Compliance with the UN Convention on the Rights of Persons with Disabilities is likely to require extension of this important exception to require provision of any necessary support where that will enable competent decision-making; though robust safeguards against undue influence will be necessary.

13.44 In modern Scottish usage, and in accordance with the above definition, 'incapacity' is the noun from 'incapable', referring to factual impairments of the ability to act or decide with legal effect. It does not refer to the consequences of any process of 'incapacitation', which is unknown in Scots law, nor to any outmoded (in Scotland) usages of 'legal capacity' to refer to elements of legal personality, rights and status, which all Scottish adults have regardless of any intellectual disabilities.[48]

13.45 On the one hand, capacity is function-specific. For example, AWI(S)(A) 2000, s 57(1) expressly recognises and provides that an adult may be capable of himself making application for appointment of a guardian to deal with matters of which that same adult is incapable.[49]

13.46 On the other hand, a broad rather than narrow view is taken in assessing capacity for a particular purpose. In *Application by the Public Guardian re DC*, Glasgow Sheriff Court, August 14, 2012 (a decision upheld on appeal by the Sheriff Principal on December 06, 2012), an adult's decision to revoke a Power of Attorney might on a narrow view have been considered competent, but his mental disorder – as to which he lacked any insight – prevented him from comprehending that his purpose, which was to return home to the care of his wife from the care home in which his attorney had placed him, was a practical impossibility which if attempted would have had dire consequences. The sheriff held that the adult lacked capacity to make a valid revocation, and directed the Public Guardian not to register it. Whether that same adult was in consequence unlawfully deprived of his

---

[48] There is potential confusion, in relation to Scots law, in the terminology of Article 12 of the UN Convention on the Rights of Persons with Disabilities, which uses 'legal capacity' in a much wider sense, and even more so in the terminology of the pronouncements of the UN Committee on the Rights of Persons with Disabilities.
[49] Such an application was granted in *H*, Kilmarnock Sheriff Court, 27 January 2010.

liberty was an issue in subsequent separate proceedings before the Court of Session in which interim liberation was ordered (that action was settled without final determination by the Court). Clear and consistently repeated articulation of a decision does not necessarily mean that it was competent.[50]

13.47 On whether an adult could be capable of decisions about use of contraception but not about having sexual relations, and related issues, see *Application for directions by West Lothian Council in respect of LY*, Livingston Sheriff Court, 30 May 2014 (judgment on scotcourts website).

13.48 The relevant definition of mental disorder is contained in s 328 of MH(CT)(S)A 2003, and is as follows:

> '(1) Subject to subs (2) below, in this Act "mental disorder" means any – (a) mental illness; (b) personality disorder; or (c) learning disability, however caused or manifested; and cognate expressions shall be construed accordingly.
>
> (2) A person is not mentally disordered by reason only of any of the following – (a) sexual orientation; (b) sexual deviancy; (c) transsexualism; (d) transvestism; (e) dependence on, or use of, alcohol or drugs; (f) behaviour that causes, or is likely to cause, harassment, alarm or distress to any other person; (g) acting as no prudent person would act.'

At time of writing there is debate as to whether this 'diagnostic threshold' is compatible with the UN Convention on the Rights of Persons with Disabilities.

Powers of Attorney (Part 2)

Terminology

13.49 Continuing and welfare Powers of Attorney are governed principally by the s 1 principles, and by Part 2, of AWI(S)A 2000. A continuing Power of Attorney ('CPA') is a Power of Attorney ('POA') in respect of the financial and property affairs of the granter (not 'donor') capable of operation after loss of relevant capacity. A welfare Power of Attorney ('WPA') confers powers in relation to personal welfare, which term includes healthcare matters, operable during relevant incapacity.

Overview

13.50 No POA other than a CPA or WPA granted in accordance with the Act's provisions, and registered by the Public Guardian, may be operated after loss of relevant capacity of the granter. Careful compliance with the Act's provisions is essential: see *Application for guardianship in respect of NW*, referred to in **13.55**. A human rights based system of incapacity law emphasises the importance of autonomy and self-determination, and thus encourages the granting of such POA's while granters have the capacity to

---

[50] Scottish Law Commission Report 'Left alone – the end of life support and treatment of Mr JL', 8th July 2014

do so, or by people with some impairments of capacity who are nevertheless capable of granting POA's.[51] In Scotland large, and increasing, numbers of such POA's have been granted.[52] Granting of such POA's has become as much recommended, as a matter of prudence, as making a Will, and for reasons including speedier transfer of hospital patients ready for discharge was promoted in an advertising campaign which commenced in 2013 and continued in 2014 and 2015.[53] On the cross-border status of Powers of Attorney see **13.62**.

13.51 Procedural requirements contain necessary safeguards but avoid such difficulty and complexity as might be a deterrent to prospective granters or attorneys. Under the principles of autonomy and self-determination, it is for the granter to decide whom to appoint, with what powers, when the POA should be registered, and in what circumstances the powers which are conferred may be exercised. However, welfare powers may only be exercised during relevant incapacity (or while the attorney reasonably believes that there is relevant incapacity), and a welfare attorney may not place the granter in hospital for treatment of a mental disorder against the granter's will, consent on behalf of the granter to forms of treatment specified by regulations, or take other specified steps generally in relation to healthcare matters.[54] These are minimum statutory limitations. The granter may – and often will – further limit the powers conferred, and further limit the circumstances in which they may be operated (such as by requiring written medical certification as a prerequisite for operation).

13.52 The competence of authorising a deprivation of liberty in a WPA was an issue before the Court of Session (in a case brought by the adult, *DC*, see **13.46**), even although that is not among the statutory exclusions. That case settled and the point was not determined. However, anything contrary to the presumed purpose of a WPA would, as with a CPA,[55] require explicit provision even if competent. In *McDowall's Executors v IRC* [2004] STC (SCD) 22 it was held that making gifts was contrary to the presumed purpose of conserving the granter's estate, and therefore required explicit power. It would probably be held that the presumed purpose of a WPA would include safeguarding the granter's liberty.

---

[51] See Council of Europe Recommendation on Principles concerning Powers of Attorney and Advance Directives for Incapacity and relative explanatory memorandum R (2009) 11. At time of writing it is anticipated that a review of implementation of R(2009)11 will form part of the Council of Europe's programme of work for 2016/2017.

[52] Rising every year from 5,592 registrations in the first year after Part 2 came into force to 55,527 in the year to 31 March 2015.

[53] 'Begin the Conversation', promoted by Glasgow City Council, NHS Greater Glasgow and Clyde, and TC Young LLP, Solicitors.

[54] See AWI(S)A 2000, s 16(6).

[55] In *McDowall's Executors v IRC* [2003] UKSC SPC00382, [2004] STC (SCD) 22 it was held that making gifts was contrary to the presumed purpose of conserving the granter's estate, and therefore required explicit power.

Underlying law, the POA document

13.53 As in England and Wales the general law of POA's applies, subject only to the particular provisions of AWI(S)A 2000 if the POA is to be operable following loss of relevant capacity. A basic rule, applicable also to CPA's and WPA's, is that the attorney has no powers other than those conferred in the document. None are implied. No standard form is provided by or under the Act. A common form of POA document will contain a general power to do everything which may be competently done by such an attorney, followed by a list – often a long list – of specific powers conferred without prejudice to the general power. Some POA documents contain only specific powers, and no general power: in these cases the specific powers are strictly construed, and may be held not to have covered actions actually taken by the attorney.[56]

Formalities

13.54 This and the following paragraphs **13.55–13.59** apply only to CPA's and WPA's granted on or after 2 April 2001.[57] For POA's granted before that date, see **13.61**. CPA's and WPA's must be in writing and subscribed by the granter. They need not be witnessed, but usually are, such witnessing making them 'self-proving'. They must expressly state the granter's intention that they shall be a CPA or WPA (or both). Where a CPA is to be exerciseable only during relevant incapacity of the granter, the document must state that the granter has considered how such incapacity is to be determined, and all WPA's must contain such a statement. Curiously, the granter must state that he has considered this, but is not expressly required to include the outcome of such consideration! This requirement was introduced by ASP(S)A 2007 and accordingly is not reflected in the styles offered in Ward *Adult Incapacity* (see **13.18**).

13.55 In *Application for guardianship in respect of NW*, 2014 SLT (Sh Ct) 83, Sheriff Baird held that a CPA did not comply with the requirements described in either of the preceding sentences, and in consequence was invalid. The document was in accordance with a bank's standard form, which in turn was similar to a 'sample' which appeared on the Public Guardian's website until removed following issue of Sheriff Baird's decision. In *B v H*, 2014 SLT (Sh Ct) 160, Sheriff Murray, upon the facts of that case, came to the opposite conclusion to Sheriff Baird in *NW* regarding a not dissimilar power of attorney document, but commented: 'I do not dispute that the deed could have been better drafted'. Sheriff Murray took into account extraneous evidence of the granter's intentions including as to whether the document should indeed be a CPA and WPA. In *Great Stuart Trustees Limited v Public Guardian*, 2015, SLT 115, a Special Case decided by an Extra Division of the Inner House of the Court of Session, the validity of yet another similar power of attorney document was considered. The

---

[56] See *McDowall's Executors* above and *M, Applicant* 2007 SLT (Sh Ct) 24; 2006 GWD 19–418.
[57] When Part 3 of AWI(S)A 2000 was brought into force.

court rejected the reasoning of Sheriff Baird and preferred that of Sheriff Murray. The Scottish Parliament had chosen not to prescribe any particular form of document. No particular form of words was accordingly essential, provided that the granter's intention was clear. In *Application in respect of S*, 2013 SLT (Sh Ct) 65, Sheriff Baird held that a POA document was not fit for purpose. In both that case and *NW* he granted guardianship orders. There is no reason for concern about the validity of a carefully drawn CPA or WPA, but as Scots law does not provide prescribed forms granters may well opt to engage appropriate professional expertise in drafting such documents.

13.56 The document must incorporate a certificate in prescribed form by a practising solicitor (which means a practising Scottish solicitor), practising advocate or registered medical practitioner. The certificate confirms that:

(a) the certifier has interviewed the granter immediately before the granter subscribed the POA,

(b) the certifier is satisfied that the granter understood the nature and extent of the POA document, either from the certifier's own knowledge of the granter or because the certifier has consulted a person, named in the certificate, who has knowledge of the granter, and

(c) the certifier has no reason to believe that the granter is acting under undue influence or that the granting of the POA is otherwise vitiated.

For a case where neither the solicitor who prepared POA's, nor the medical practitioner who certified them, identified pernicious undue influence which had grave consequences for the granters, see the "D Report" referred to in **13.31**. In implementation of one of the recommendations in that Report, the Law Society of Scotland issued two sets of professional guidance, and continues to update guidance in the light of experience. See 'Guidance on Continuing and Welfare Powers of Attorney' and 'Vulnerable Clients Guidance', both set out in Part X.

13.57 CPA's and WPA's may only be operated after registration. The form of application for registration is prescribed, and is available from the Public Guardian's website.[58] If they are registered before loss of relevant capacity, there is no provision for further registration upon loss of relevant capacity. However, the granter may state in the document a prerequisite for registration, such as medical certification of loss of capacity, though in practice it appears that relatively few granters do so, probably because of fear that it would then be too late to rectify if some defect caused the Public Guardian to refuse to register. The POA document should be checked for prerequisites for operation, as opposed to prerequisites for registration.

13.58 If a CPA or WPA is produced for use in England and Wales, it is essential to see a certificate of registration (or official copy thereof) and either an official copy of the POA document issued by the Public Guardian;

---

[58] See **13.30**.

or a copy certified in accordance with the Powers of Attorney Act 1971; or an official extract registered copy of the document registered in the Books of Council and Session which, in accordance with s 4 of the Evidence and Powers of Attorney Act 1940, is evidence of the contents thereof 'in any part of the United Kingdom, without further proof'.

13.59 If the POA document has not been registered with the Public Guardian, it is not (yet) operable, regardless of what it may say, and even if it has been registered the attorney may only exercise powers conferred by the document, and may only exercise those powers subject to any provisions in the document as to the circumstances in which they may be exercised.

Revocation and termination

13.60 The formalities for revocation are similar to those for granting, and include similar certification and registration of a revocation notice. No liability is incurred by persons acting in good faith in ignorance of the revocation. However, in matters of any significance it is prudent to check with the Office of the Public Guardian that the POA has not been revoked, and that no other termination of the POA or of the attorney's authority has been registered. Where the Public Guardian receives *prima facie* credible representations that a purported revocation, or a revocation coupled with a fresh POA, presented to her for registration may be invalid, it is her practice to seek directions under s 3(3) from the sheriff with primary jurisdiction as to whether she should register.[59]

POA's executed before 2 April 2001

13.61 Doubts remain as to whether any Scottish POA executed before 1 January 1991 may be operated following the granter's loss of capacity. See **13.13**. It would be wise to take Scottish advice before acting in reliance on such a POA if the granter lacks relevant capacity. In the case of Scottish POA's granted from 1 January 1991 to 1 April 2001, the position is the opposite, as explained in **13.14**. Unless the document specifies that it shall not be operable during the granter's incapacity, it may be relied upon (subject to its actual terms, and except in welfare matters) without enquiry as to whether the granter still has capacity or not. The formalities described in **13.54** do not apply, though the same rules of interpretation do apply. Under the transitional provisions of AWI(S)A 2000 such POA's are however now described as CPA's or WPA's or both, and several of the provisions of AWI(S)A 2000, including the powers of the sheriff described in **13.64**, apply to them. Commonly, what will be presented will be an official extract from the Books of Council and Session of the POA document (see **13.58**).

---

[59] The sheriff directed the Public Guardian not to register in *Public Guardian, Applicant*, 2011 SLT (Sh Ct) 66 and in *Application by Public Guardian re DC*: see **13.46**.

Non-Scottish Powers of Attorney

13.62 Subject to the next paragraph, the law governing the existence, extent, modification and extinction of CPA's, WPA's and non-Scottish equivalents is the law of the habitual residence of the granter at time of granting, unless the granter specified in writing the law of a jurisdiction in which the granter had previously been habitually resident; or the law of the jurisdiction where property is situated, but only as regards that property; or, in the case of a non-British granter, the law of the state of the granter's nationality. Where a non-Scottish POA or equivalent is exercised in Scotland, the manner of exercise is governed by Scots law. A transaction entered in Scotland between an attorney or equivalent and a third party is not challengeable on the grounds that the attorney was not entitled to enter it by the law of some other country, unless the third party knew or ought to have known that the attorney's entitlement to act was governed by the law of that other country.[60] In *C, Applicant*,[61] it was held that an English Enduring Power of Attorney had automatic recognition in Scotland under AWI(S)A 2000 and had the same effect as a Scottish CPA. As an interim measure pending resolution of the unacceptable uncertainty regarding POAs in both directions between England and Scotland, the Public Guardian offers a non-statutory certificate which may be downloaded from her website (see **13.30**) in the following terms:

> 'I, Sandra McDonald, Public Guardian for Scotland, hereby advise that interpretation of Scottish legislation suggests a non-Scottish Power of Attorney is automatically valid in Scotland. There is no provision for having a non-Scottish Power of Attorney endorsed for use in Scotland; this action being unnecessary.'

13.63 The provisions described in **13.62** are subject to the powers of the sheriff described in **13.64**. Also, they do not displace any enactment or rule of law which has mandatory effect for the protection of an adult with incapacity in Scotland, whatever law would otherwise be applicable; and no provision of the law of any country other than Scotland may be applied so as to produce a result manifestly contrary to public policy.

Powers of the sheriff

13.64 The powers of the sheriff described in this paragraph may be exercised under AWI(S)A 2000, s 20 in relation to CPA's, WPA's and non-Scottish equivalents. The law applicable to exercise of these powers is Scots law, but the sheriff must to the extent possible take into account the law which governs the POA under the rules described in **13.62**.[62] The sheriff's powers may be exercised upon application by anyone claiming an interest in the property, financial affairs or personal welfare of the granter. The prerequisites for granting an order under s 20 are that the sheriff is satisfied that the granter is incapable in relation to relevant matters and that the order is necessary to safeguard or promote the granter's interests in those

---

[60] AWI(S)A 2000, Sch 3, para 4.
[61] Airdrie Sheriff Court, 2 April 2013, unreported.
[62] AWI(S)A 2000, Sch 3, para 3(3).

matters. Under CPA's, the sheriff may order supervision by the Public Guardian, and/or may order the attorney to submit accounts for any specified period for audit by the Public Guardian. In relation to WPA's, the sheriff may order supervision by the local authority, and/or may order the welfare attorney to give a report to the sheriff as to the manner in which the attorney has exercised the attorney's powers during any specified period. In relation to both CPA's and WPA's, the sheriff may revoke any of the powers granted by the CPA or WPA, or may revoke the appointment of an attorney. Where there are joint attorneys, the sheriff may thus revoke the appointment of one of them. Revocation may be appealed, but the other orders under s 20 are final. Orders under s 20 are subject to provisions for registration with, and intimation by, the Public Guardian. The sheriff's powers under s 20 are in addition to the sheriff's general powers, including the power to give directions described in **13.25**.

Accounts and funds (Part 3)

Joint accounts

13.65 AWI(S)A 2000, s 32 is the only provision of Part 3 of the Act which has remained unaltered since original enactment. It effected the simple but important reform that where one holder of a joint account loses relevant capacity, any other joint holder may continue to operate the account, unless the terms of the account provide otherwise or the court has barred the joint holder from operating it. Many accounts are now operated under this provision, which often renders any other intervention unnecessary.

'Access to funds'

13.66 The remainder of Part 3, replaced in its entirety with effect from 1 April 2008,[63] provides a scheme of limited financial guardianship under the jurisdiction of the Public Guardian rather than the sheriff (except where the Public Guardian refers a Part 3 application to the sheriff for determination[64]). Where applicable, Part 3 administration must be utilised rather than financial guardianship under Part 6.[65] Under the core provisions of Part 3, 'authority to intromit' is given to a 'withdrawer' who opens an operating account called the 'designated account', which receives funds of the adult held by 'fundholders', and from which the withdrawer makes payments for the adult's benefit[66] in accordance with a budget approved by the Public Guardian. 'Intromit' covers dealing with funds, mainly receiving, paying out or investing them.

---

[63] The original Part 3 was the only Part of the Act which was not a success, and under-utilised. Usage has almost doubled since it was replaced: rising to a peak of 491 in the year to 31 March 2012, then dwindling; compared with 195 and 197 in the two preceding years.
[64] AWI(S)A 2000, s 27F.
[65] AWI(S)A 2000, s 58(1)(b).
[66] See AWI(S)A 2000, s 24A for the purposes for which the withdrawer may intromit with the adult's funds.

13.67 The scheme allows for individual or joint withdrawers, reserve (ie replacement) withdrawers, and organisations as withdrawers.[67] The scheme is operated by various types of application on prescribed forms to the Public Guardian,[68] who issues certificates of authority. Preliminary application may be made to obtain information from fundholders about the adult's assets, and to authorise release of information by the fundholder for that purpose. Authority may be obtained to open an 'adult's current account' to receive the adult's income to 'feed' the withdrawer's 'designated account', if the adult does not have an existing account suitable for that purpose.

13.68 Authority may also be obtained to open an 'adult's second account', normally a savings-type account to hold surplus funds at a better rate of interest than the current account.[69] Other possibilities include authority to transfer funds between different accounts in the adult's name, to terminate existing standing orders and direct debits, to close existing accounts, and to authorise payment of lump sums in addition to the regular budgeted expenditure. The budget may be amended.

Procedure

13.69 Applications for authority to provide information about the adult's funds, to open accounts, and to intromit with the adult's funds must be accompanied by a medical certificate of incapacity in prescribed form by any medical practitioner. All or any of these applications may be made on a single combined form with a single medical certificate. Those applications, and also applications to add a joint withdrawer, except where the applicant is an organisation rather than one or more individuals, must also be countersigned by someone who has known the adult for at least a year,[70] and who confirms that he or she believes (a) that the information in the application form is true; and (b) that the applicant is a fit and proper person to intromit with the adult's funds. Intimation (notification) requirements are dealt with by the Public Guardian upon receipt of the application.[71] Where there are joint withdrawers, or a withdrawer and a reserve, a countersignatory's certificate is required for each. Authority to intromit is usually granted for three years, but the Public Guardian may reduce or extend the period of validity of the withdrawal certificate.

Transition from guardianship

13.70 The procedural requirements are simplified for transition to Part 3 administration from financial guardianship under Part 6. If the Part 3

---

[67] Organisations cannot be financial guardians under Part 6.
[68] The various forms are designated ATF (Access to Funds), which may be downloaded from the Public Guardian's website: see **13.30**.
[69] That at least was the intention, before interest rates plummeted.
[70] See AWI(S)A 2000, s 27A(1)(b) for persons not permitted to countersign.
[71] See AWI(S)A 2000, s 27C.

applicant is the financial guardian, countersignature is not required. The Public Guardian has discretion to dispense with the requirement for a medical certificate.

Part 3 scheme inapplicable or inappropriate

13.71 An application may not be made under Part 3 where, in relation to the funds in question, a guardian or continuing attorney has powers, or an intervention order has been granted. Circumstances in which Part 3 administration is inappropriate include 'where the adult has financial assets of a complex nature, for example, stocks and shares, investment bonds, etc. to be managed';[72] where heritable property[73] requires to be dealt with, or where a tenancy is to be given up; where a claim for compensation or other remedies require to be pursued, or there is other litigation; where a business is to be dealt with; and where tax-planning arrangements are contemplated.

Management of residents' finances (Part 4)

13.72 Part 4 of AWI(S)A 2000 provides a procedure for the management of the finances of an adult resident in an 'authorised establishment' by the managers of that establishment. Authorised establishments are NHS hospitals, for which the supervisory body for the purposes of Part 4 is the relevant health board, and independent hospitals, care homes and other services registered with the Care Inspectorate, for which the Inspectorate is the supervisory body. The procedure requires consideration of options by the managers of the establishment, medical examination, issue of a medical certificate of incapacity, and various intimation and notification requirements.

13.73 The consent of the supervisory body is required to manage funds in excess of £10,000. Subject to limitations, the managers may for the resident's benefit claim, receive, hold and spend funds, may hold moveable[74] property, and may dispose of moveable property (but only up to a cumulative value of £100 except with consent of the supervisory body). The supervisory body may authorise a named manager to withdraw funds from an existing account of the resident. An establishment registered with the Care Inspectorate may opt out of the Part 4 scheme, and the supervisory body may revoke the power of a particular establishment to operate the scheme. The Part 4 scheme is not available when relevant powers are in force under a CPA, or a guardianship or intervention order.

---

[72] Access to Funds Revised Code of Practice.
[73] Land and buildings.
[74] Property which is not land or buildings.

Medical treatment and research (Part 5)

13.74 Medical treatment, with some limited exceptions, may be authorised by a certificate of incapacity by a medical practitioner, dental practitioner, ophthalmic optician or registered nurse.[75] Certificates may be issued for up to three years where incapacity is unlikely to improve because of severe or profound learning disability, dementia or a severe neurological disorder. Otherwise the maximum duration is one year. Authorisation is limited to treatment to preserve life or prevent serious deterioration when the certifier is aware of a pending application for a guardianship or intervention order with relevant powers.

13.75 The certification procedure may be followed when an appointee under a WPA, guardianship order or intervention order has relevant powers, but treatment is only authorised if the appointee consents or by reference of disagreement to a practitioner nominated by the Mental Welfare Commission, subject to appeal to the Court of Session. Some other disputes about medical treatment may also be appealed to the Court of Session; otherwise they may be appealed to the sheriff, and thence, with leave of the sheriff, to the Court of Session.

13.76 Persons with impaired capacity may also be treated on grounds of necessity; and they may be treated under relevant provisions of MH(CT)(S)A 2003. There is statutory provision for advance statements in MH(CT)(S)A 2003, but not in AWI(S)A 2000, nor is there statutory provision for withholding and withdrawing treatment.[76]

Guardianship and intervention orders (Part 6)

13.77 A guardian is the approximate equivalent of a deputy in England and Wales. Guardianship orders have increased in each successive year since Part 6 came into force, from 288 in 2002/03 to 2,534 in 2014/15. Intervention orders have risen in most years, to 340 or more in each of the three years to 2014/15. The procedure for both guardianship and intervention orders is substantially the same. They are granted by the sheriff upon an application supported by three reports, two of them medical reports. One medical report must be produced by a 'relevant medical practitioner', usually a practitioner approved by a (Scottish) health board as having special experience in the diagnosis and treatment of mental disorder, though where the adult is not present in Scotland the term covers a medical practitioner with similar qualifications and experience who has consulted the Mental Welfare Commission about the report.[77] The other medical report may be provided by any medical practitioner, who need not be a Scottish medical practitioner.[78] The third report is provided by a mental health officer (a specialised social worker) where the powers sought are or include welfare

---

[75] Regulations may specify other categories of certifiers.
[76] Still regulated under the *nobile officium*: see **13.9**.
[77] Other categories of 'relevant medical practitioners' may be specified by regulations.
[78] *H, Applicant*, 2007 SLT (Sh Ct) 5; 2006 GWD 21-447.

powers,[79] and by a 'person who has sufficient knowledge' where only property and financial powers are sought.

13.78 Procedure includes requirements for intimation (giving notice in accordance with relevant procedural requirements) and a hearing. For details of these and other procedural requirements, see the rules set out in Part X. The sheriff may only dispense with intimation to the adult if satisfied that this would be likely to pose a serious risk to the adult's health. Where property and financial powers are given, the sheriff may order that caution[80] be obtained or other security given. Once the order has been made and any requirement for caution met, the Public Guardian issues a certificate of appointment. The certificate is the document which should be inspected to ascertain details of the appointment, including the powers conferred. Where the order confers powers in relation to heritable property,[81] it must be recorded or registered in the appropriate property register.[82] The local authority must apply for an order if it appears to be necessary and no-one else is applying or likely to apply.

13.79 Until 2009 some guardians had no certificate of appointment, because they were originally appointed as curators bonis, tutors-dative or tutors-at-law under previous law and became guardians under the transitional provisions of AWI(S)A 2000. All such appointments still in force have now been renewed under the Act. The deadline for lodgement of renewal applications – for appointments otherwise still in force – was 5 October 2009. There could however be a small number of remaining transitional guardians originally appointed to children who have still not yet reached age 18.

Intervention orders

13.80 An intervention order may either authorise action specified in the order, or authorise a person to take action or make decisions as may be specified. The order may cover a single act such as signing a document, or a series of acts and decisions, such as giving up the lease of the adult's home and arranging all aspects of a transition to residential care. With limited exceptions, an intervention order can authorise anything which the adult, if capable, could have done in relation to the adult's personal welfare and/or property and financial affairs. An intervention order is the appropriate

---

[79] Section 57(4) requires that the third report be prepared within 21 days of notice to the chief social work officer from the applicant of intention to make an application under Part 6, but substantial delays are common. The increase in applications noted above has far exceeded any increase in numbers of mental health officers.
[80] Pronounced 'kay-shun', a guarantee bond covering loss through default which the appointee fails to make good.
[81] Land and buildings.
[82] The Land Register of Scotland, or for properties not yet registered in the Land Register, the General Register of Sasines.

(though not the only) way to pursue or defend civil proceedings on behalf of an adult with impaired capacity, unless ongoing guardianship powers are likely to be required.

13.81 A guardianship order may not be granted where an intervention order will suffice, and the sheriff may grant an intervention order where guardianship has been applied for (but not vice versa). However, there is no rigid dividing line. Generally, an intervention order will be preferred for a self-limiting matter or series of matters, and guardianship where ongoing management may be required. However, while an intervention order was previously preferred for transactions such as selling a house when the proceeds were to be managed under Part 3, guardianship may now be preferred in such cases because the simplified transition to Part 3 administration described in **13.70** applies only to guardianship, and not to intervention orders.

Guardianship

13.82 Guardianship may be plenary or partial. The categories of powers which may be conferred are set out in s 64(1) as follows:

'(a) power to deal with such particular matters in relation to the property, financial affairs or personal welfare of the adult as may be specified in the order;

(b) power to deal with all aspects of the personal welfare of the adult, or with such aspects as may be specified in the order;

(c) power to pursue or defend an action of declarator of nullity of marriage, or of divorce or separation in the name of the adult;

(d) power to manage the property or financial affairs of the adult, or such parts of them as may be specified in the order;

(e) power to authorise the adult to carry out such transactions or categories of transactions as the guardian may specify.'

Unless otherwise ordered by the sheriff, the guardian is the adult's legal representative within the scope of the powers conferred. See s 64(2) for matters excluded from a guardian's powers. For a case where guardianship powers were sought to make decisions about engagement in sexual relations, see *LY*, **13.47**. The status of consent on behalf of a patient by a guardian for the purposes of MH(CT)(S)A 2003 is unclear in statute and was addressed in *Petition by PW and AW*, Court of Session, 18 December 2013.

13.83 The sheriff may appoint an individual guardian, joint guardians (guardians jointly exercising the same powers), dual guardians (such as one guardian exercising welfare powers and another exercising financial powers, though the term 'dual guardian' is not used in the Act), one or more substitute (ie replacement) guardians, permutations of the foregoing, and the chief social work officer as welfare guardian. No other office holder may be appointed as such, nor may any trust, corporation or other entity. Financial guardians are under the supervision of the Public Guardian, to whom they must normally submit an inventory of estate and management plan following appointment, and annual accounts thereafter. Welfare guardians are supervised by local authorities.

Deprivation of Liberty

13.84 There are no specific provisions for deprivation of liberty cases, but the Scottish Law Commission has made proposals, including for a new Part 5A in AWI(S)A 2000, in that regard in Report No 240 on Adults with Incapacity (October 2014).[83] It is generally considered that an order of a sheriff under AWI(S)A 2000, s 70 ordering compliance with a guardian's decision (see **13.86**) could authorise a deprivation of liberty. That procedure is not available to attorneys or appointees under an intervention order.

Provisions applicable to guardians and non-Scottish equivalents

13.85 The provisions of Part 6 described in this paragraph apply both to Scottish guardians and to non-Scottish equivalents. Guardians and equivalents with welfare powers may exercise their powers whether or not the adult is in Scotland at the time.[84] Guardians and equivalents are personally liable under any transaction which they enter outwith the scope of their authority; and when they act without disclosing that they do so as guardians, they are also personally liable but (if not otherwise in breach of the Act) are entitled to be reimbursed from the adult's estate.[85]

13.86 Guardians and equivalents with welfare powers may obtain an order from the sheriff in the event of non-compliance with their decisions: orders can ordain the adult to comply; authorise a constable to enter premises, apprehend and remove the adult to a place specified by the guardian (or equivalent); and order compliance in the event of a person other than the adult failing to comply with a decision which 'that person might reasonably be expected to comply with'.[86] The sheriff has powers, upon application, to replace or remove a guardian or equivalent, or to recall a guardianship order or equivalent.[87] Guardianship and equivalent orders cease on the adult's death, though there is protection for persons acting in good faith and unaware of the adult's death.[88]

---

[83] See https://s3-eu-west-1.amazonaws.com/tcylandingpages/AWI/AWI+-+Proposed+Law+Reform+-+2014.pdf for a description of the provisions proposed in that Report.
[84] AWI(S)A 2000, s 67(3).
[85] AWI(S)A 2000, s 67(4).
[86] AWI(S)A 2000, s 70.
[87] AWI(S)A 2000, s 71, which contains the criteria for recall, considered in *City of Edinburgh Council v D* 2010 GWD 33-711.
[88] AWI(S)A 2000, s 77.

Wills and related matters

13.87 Scots law has always lacked any specific statutory procedure for making a Will for an incapable adult. However, a line of precedents has applied the s 1 principles in appropriate cases to confirm the competence of using intervention orders, and guardianship orders, to renounce inheritance rights, execute a codicil amending an existing Will, or execute a new Will.[89] In *Application by Adrian Douglas Ward*, 2014 SLT (Sh Ct) 15, the Sheriff Principal of North Strathclyde upheld an appeal against a refusal by a Sheriff at first instance to authorise execution of a Will but, despite the mandatory requirement of AWI(S)A 2000 in terms of s 1(1) to determine any decision under that Act by reference to the s 1 principles, controversially declined to do so and held that evidence of competent testamentary intention was required 'in such a case'. Those words may have been intended to limit that aspect of the decision to the situation in that case that the evidence indicated that the adult's incapacity included an inability actually to commit to implementation of a decision, the implication being that aspects of the decision-making process were severable and could be competent in isolation.

Ademption

13.88 If a testator bequeaths an asset by Will but subsequently disposes of it, the bequest is adeemed, that is to say treated as revoked. Questions arise as to whether a disposal by an attorney, guardian or appointee under an intervention order is ademptive. Whereas in England this depends upon whether the disposal was authorised, in Scotland the test is necessity; so that if an attorney has no option but to sell an asset to pay for accommodation and care costs, a bequest of an asset is adeemed. The reason for that outcome is that if the adult had been capable, the adult would likewise have had no option but to sell and adeem. This rule was confirmed in *Turner v Turner*,[90] the sale of a house 'was a prudent act of administration but not a necessary act in the relevant sense', therefore a bequest of the house was not adeemed. That case arose after the death of the testator. Having made that finding, the judge proceeded to determine what provision should be made in favour of the legatee in place of the house which was no longer part of the deceased's estate. Where this issue arises during the testator's lifetime, but after loss of relevant capacity, it can be addressed by procedure under Part 6 of AWI(S)A 2000.[91]

Measures outwith the Incapacity Act

13.89 While Scottish law of trusts is distinct from that of England and Wales, trusts are frequently used in relation to incapacity in similar ways.

---

[89] *B, Applicant*, 2005 SLT (Sh Ct) 95; *T, Applicant*, 2005 SLT (Sh Ct) 97; *M, Applicant*, 2007 SLT (Sh Ct) 24; *G, Applicant*, 2009 SLT (Sh Ct) 122.
[90] [2012] CSOH 41.
[91] In *T, Applicant*, 2005 SLT (Sh Ct) 97, the sheriff authorised execution of a codicil replacing a bequest of a house with a legacy equal to the net proceeds of sale of the house.

Rules for administration of state benefits, vaccine damage payments and criminal injuries compensation payments are similar. Provisions for administration of sums awarded by the courts exist but have not been properly updated since the passing of AWI(S)A 2000. There is no Scottish equivalent to s 5 of MCA 2005, but the principle of necessity remains available to authorise some interventions.

Chapter 14

Northern Ireland

EXISTING LAW

14.1 The Mental Capacity Act 2005 was not introduced into Northern Ireland and the law relating to adults without capacity has continued to be governed by the Mental Health (Northern Ireland) Order 1986 (SI 1986/595). Part Vlll deals with the property and affairs of a person ('the patient') who is 'incapable, by reason of mental disorder, of managing and administering his property and affairs'. This is similar to the previous law in England and Wales found in Part VII of the Mental Health Act 1983, save that its powers have been exercised by the Office of Care and Protection, part of the Northern Ireland Courts and Tribunals Service.

The Office of Care and Protection
Room 2.2A, Second Floor
Royal Courts of Justice
Chichester Street
Belfast
BT1 3JF
Telephone (028) 9072 4733
Fax (028) 9032 2782
www.courtsni.gov.uk

14.2 A person appointed in Northern Ireland to make decisions in respect of a patient's property and affairs is a Controller. The Enduring Powers of Attorney (Northern Ireland) Order 1987 [SI 1987 No. 1627 (N.I. 16)] still subsists, so that Northern Ireland Enduring Powers of Attorney remain valid and can still be made. The legal vacuum in regard to personal welfare decisions has not yet been addressed.

MENTAL CAPACITY BILL

14.3 The review of Northern Irish legislation has lagged behind that in Scotland and England and Wales. The Bamford Review, published in November 2007,[1] suggested a new comprehensive legislative model. A Mental Capacity Bill has now been published which places greater emphasis on the need to support people to exercise their capacity to make decisions where they can. If, on the other hand, it is established that a person lacks capacity to make a specific decision at a particular time, the Bill provides

---

[1] The Bamford Review of Mental health and Learning Disability (Northern Ireland): A Comprehensive Legal Framework (2007); www.dhsspsni.gov.uk/sites/default/files/publications/dhssps/legal-issue-comprehensive-framework.pdf.

alternative decision making mechanisms. This approach goes part way to meeting the expectations of the UN Committee on the Rights of Persons with Disabilities in regard to supported decision-making.

14.4 The Bill is currently at committee stage with the publication of a report expected by the end of January 2016. The Bill is expected to be passed by the Northern Ireland Assembly during 2016. Until then, Northern Irish private international law remains similar to that of England and Wales before the Mental Capacity Act 2005.[2] It is intended that relevant legislative provisions will appear in Part X in future editions.

---

[2] The draft Mental Capacity Bill is available as part of the consultation on: www.dhsspsni.gov.uk/mental_capacity_bill_consultation_paper.pdf.

Chapter 15

Ireland

EXISTING LAW

15.1 Until very recently, there was no mental capacity legislation in Ireland and an all or nothing status approach involving a Ward of Court procedure has continued to be utilised.[1] This was inherited from the inherent jurisdiction of the High Court in England and Wales derived from the Royal prerogative notwithstanding that Ireland became a Republic. Agency arrangements under social welfare legislation are available but other agencies cease if the principal becomes mentally incapable, and trusts have been used as a means of advance financial planning for older people. However, enduring powers of attorney have been introduced similar to those that formerly applied in England and Wales.

15.2 However, Ireland has pursued significant law reform in recent years, which has culminated in the Assisted Decision-Making (Capacity) Bill 2015, which was signed into law on 30 December 2015.

LEGISLATION

15.3 The Explanatory Memorandum to the Assisted Decision-Making (Capacity) Bill 2013 states:

> 'The purpose of the Bill is to reform the law and to provide a modern statutory framework that supports decision-making by adults and enables them to retain the greatest amount of autonomy possible in situations where they lack or may shortly lack capacity.
>
> The Bill changes the existing law on capacity, shifting from the current all or nothing status approach to a flexible functional one, whereby capacity is assessed on an issue- and time-specific basis. The Bill replaces the Wards of Court system with a modern statutory framework to assist persons in exercising their decision-making capacity.
>
> The Bill provides a statutory framework enabling formal agreements to be made by persons who consider that their capacity is in question, or may shortly be in question, to appoint a trusted person to act as their decision-making assistant to assist them in making decisions or as a co-decision-maker who will make decisions jointly with them.
>
> The Bill also provides for the making of applications to court in respect of persons whose capacity may be in question to seek a declaration as to whether those persons lack capacity and for the making of consequent orders approving co-decision-making agreements or appointing decision-making representatives.
>
> The Bill provides for protection from liability for informal decision-makers in relation to personal welfare and healthcare decisions made on behalf of a person with

---

[1] Lunacy Regulation (Ireland) Act 1871.

impaired capacity where such decisions are necessary and where no formal decision-making arrangements are in place. It modernises the law relating to enduring powers of attorney.

The Bill also provides for the establishment of a new statutory office, the Office of the Public Guardian. The Office of the Public Guardian will supervise decision-making assistants, co-decision- makers, decision-making representatives and persons holding enduring powers of attorney.

Reform of the law on decision-making capacity is one of the actions required to enable the State to ratify the United Nations Convention on the Rights of Persons with Disabilities.

The Bill gives effect in the State to the Hague Convention on the International Protection of Adults.'

COMMENT

15.4 On first reading this appears to replicate the approach and objectives of the Mental Capacity Act 2005, but closer examination reveals a desire to comply with the latest thinking emerging through the UN Convention on the Rights of Persons with Disabilities. The reference to decision-making assistants, co-decision-makers and decision-making representatives reflects the desire to adopt a supported decision-making approach as distinct from substitute decision-making on basis of best interests, which the UN Committee on the Rights of Persons with Disabilities recommends be rejected. Only time will prove whether this approach is feasible in practice and does not create more opportunity for abuse.

PART II

Procedural Guides

PART II: Procedural Guides

Contents

Procedural Guide 1: Application to Register an Enduring Power of Attorney   531

Procedural Guide 2: Application to Register a Lasting Power of Attorney   532

Procedural Guide 3: Application for Appointment of a Deputy Relating to Property and Financial Affairs   533

Procedural Guide 4: Applications Relating to Personal Welfare   535

Procedural Guide 5: Proceedings in the High Court or a County Court Involving a Protected Party   536

Procedural Guide 6: Resolving doubt about capacity under the Civil Procedure Rules 1998   547

Procedural Guide 7: Application for a Statutory Will or Codicil   553

PROCEDURAL GUIDE 1: APPLICATION TO REGISTER AN ENDURING POWER OF ATTORNEY

The procedure for registering an enduring power of attorney is as follows.

(1) Notice of registration to be given – the legislation sets out to whom notice is given	MCA 2005, Sch 3, Part 3 2007 Regs, reg 23 and Sch 7	Form EP1PG
(2) Registration	MCA 2005, Sch 8	Form EP2PG
	2007 Regs, reg 24	Original or certified copy of the enduring power of attorney; Fee (see Form OPG506 for fees details and exemptions); no evidence of capacity is required
(3) If no objections are received, registration is completed with a target time of 35 days	MCA 2005, Sch 4	
(4) Objections		
(a) Objections must be made within 5 weeks on specified grounds	MCA 2005, Sch 4	
(b) The objection is made by application to the Court supported by evidence	MCA 2005, Sch 4. COPR 2007, Practice Direction H, Part 9, paras 6–10	Form COP8 or COP1 if the person objecting was not entitled to notice of registration; Form COP24; No fee
(c) The application and Form COP5 must be served on the donor/attorney within 14 days	2007 Regs, reg 26, Practice Direction 9H, para 9A.	
(d) Duties of Public Guardian	COPR 2007, r 68(4)	
(e) Certificate of service to be filed within 7 days of service	COPR 2007, r 69(4)	Form COP20
(f) Acknowledgment of service to be filed in 14 days	COPR 2007, r 72	Form COP5
(g) Court gives directions or makes an order		

PART II

PROCEDURAL GUIDE 2: APPLICATION TO REGISTER A LASTING POWER OF ATTORNEY

The procedure in regard to application to register a lasting power of attorney is as follows.

(1) Notice of registration	2007 Regs, reg 10 and Sch 2	Form LPA001
(2) Application to register	2007 Regs, reg 11 and Sch 3	Form LPA002
		The lasting power of attorney
		Fee
(3) OPG sends notice of receipt	2007 Regs, reg 13	Form LPA003A/003B
(4) OPG registers after 6 weeks	2007 Regs, regs 12 and 17	Form LPA004
(5) Objections		
(a) An objection should be made within 5 weeks: objections can be made to the Public Guardian on factual grounds or to the Court on prescribed grounds	2007 Regs, regs 14(2) and 15(3)	
(b) If an objection is made to the Public Guardian, he or she will give notification if the ground is established	2007 Regs, reg 14(4)	
(c) If the objection is made to the Court, an application is required (no permission is needed) and evidence must be filed	COPR 2007, rr 51(2)(b) and 64 and Part 9, Practice Direction A	Form COP7; Form COP24
		No fee is payable
		If the person objecting is not a person who received Form LPA001 the application is made on Form COP1

PROCEDURAL GUIDE 3: APPLICATION FOR APPOINTMENT OF A DEPUTY RELATING TO PROPERTY AND FINANCIAL AFFAIRS

The procedure in regard to application for appointment of a deputy relating to property and financial affairs is as follows.

(1) Is permission needed?	MCA 2005, s 50; COPR 2007, Part 8	
(2) The substantive application should be filed at the same time as permission is sought	COPR 2007, Part 9 Practice Direction A; COPR 2007, rr 62–64 and Practice Directions A, B and D; COPR 2007, r 54 provides that the applicant must apply for permission when making an application.	Form COP1 (application form) and an information form COP1A; Form COP3 (assessment of capacity form); Form COP4 (deputy's declaration form); Copy enduring power of attorney or lasting power of attorney if applicable; Court fee
(3) As soon as practicable after an application form is filed, the court must issue it	COPR 2007, r 65	
(4) As soon as practicable after the application is issued, the court will consider the application and any application for permission	COPR 2007, r 84	
(5) As soon as practicable and in any event within 14 days from which the application form is issued, the applicant must serve the application	COPR 2007, r 66	

	COPR 2007, r 59 provides that the court must serve the order granting or refusing permission and any directions given in the case. The court will exercise its case management powers if appropriate (COPR 2007, rr 5 and 25)	If a hearing is fixed, a person notified of the hearing must file Form COP5 within 14 days The Court will give the applicant: Form COP5 (acknowledgement of service) Form COP14 (notice of proceedings to P) Form COP14A (guidance notes for Form COP14) Form COP15 (notice that an application has been issued) Form COP15A (guidance notes for Form COP15) Form COP20 (certificate of service and notification)
(6) Notify P of the application (NB: P may not be a party and hence not a respondent)	COPR 2007, r 69	P is served with Forms COP14 and COP5
Notify any other persons of the application.	COPR 2007, r 70	Forms COP15 and COP5
(7) Within 7 days of service and notification, the applicant must file a certificate of service	COPR 2007, rr 68(4) and 70(3)	Form COP20
(8) Any person who is served or notified of an application and who wishes to take part in the proceedings must file an acknowledgement of service within 14 days	COPR 2007, r 72	Form COP5
(9) Consideration of application by the Court. The Court will order a hearing, give directions or make a final order without a hearing	COPR 2007, rr 84 and 85	

PROCEDURAL GUIDE 4: APPLICATIONS RELATING TO PERSONAL WELFARE

The procedure in regard to applications relating to personal welfare is as follows.

(1) Is permission required?	MCA 2005, s 50; COPR 2007, Part 8	
(2) The substantive application should be filed at the same time as permission is sought	COPR 2007 Part 9, Practice Direction A (what is filed when seeking permission); COPR 2007, rr 62–64 and Practice Directions A and E (if appropriate); COPR 2007, r 54 provides that the applicant must apply for permission when making an application	Form COP1 (application form); Form COP1B and information form COP1B; Form COP3 (assessment of capacity); Form COP4 (deputy's declaration form); Copy of enduring power of attorney or lasting power of attorney (if appropriate); Court fee
(3)–(9) Steps from seeking permission to the final hearing	See Procedural Guide 3: Application for Appointment of a Deputy Relating to Property and Financial Affairs	
(10) Miscellaneous points		
(a) Urgent applications	If an urgent hearing is required, an urgent application should be filed as soon as possible: see COPR 2007, Part 10 and Practice Directions A and B	Form COP9 and evidence in support and, if appropriate, a disc with a draft order
(b) Serious medical treatment applications	COPR 2007 Part 9, Practice Direction E sets out the Court's approach	

PROCEDURAL GUIDE 5: PROCEEDINGS IN THE HIGH COURT OR A COUNTY COURT INVOLVING A PROTECTED PARTY

Legal background

The Civil Procedural Rules 1998 Part 21 contains special provisions which apply to proceedings involving protected parties (as defined). These are supplemented by a Practice Direction. Unless the Court orders otherwise it is necessary for a protected party to be represented by a litigation friend.

Any proceedings commenced or conducted in breach of this requirement will be a nullity (unless the Court otherwise orders) and a solicitor who purports to act on the record for a protected party without a litigation friend may become personally liable for the costs of opposing parties.

Under the 2007 amendment to the CPR the old term 'patient' was replaced by the new term 'protected party' and a new definition applies. This became necessary because of the implementation on 1 October 2007 of the Mental Capacity Act 2005.[1]

[1] The assistance of District Judge Anson in updating Procedural Guides 5 and 6 is acknowledged.

Procedure

The procedure in regard to 'protected parties' is as follows.

Who is a protected party?	A party, or an intended party, who lacks capacity (within the meaning of MCA 2005) to conduct the proceedings	CPR, r 21.1(2)(d)
Who 'lacks capacity'?	A person lacks capacity in relation to a matter if at the material time he or she is unable to make a decision for him or herself in relation to the matter because of an impairment of, or a disturbance in the functioning of, the mind or brain	MCA 2005, s 2(1)
When is a person unable to make a decision for him or herself?	If unable to: • understand the information relevant to the decision; • retain that information;	

	• use or weigh that information as part of the process of making the decision; or	
	• communicate his or her decision (whether by talking, using sign language or any other means)	MCA 2005, s 3(1)
Requirement for a litigation friend	A *protected party* must have a litigation friend to conduct proceedings on his or her behalf	CPR, r 21.2(1)
When must a litigation friend be appointed?	A person may not, without permission of the Court:	
	• make an application against a protected party before proceedings have started; or	
	• take any step in proceedings except:	
	• issuing and serving a claim form; or	
	• applying for the appointment of a litigation friend under CPR, r 21.6,	
	until the protected party has a litigation friend	CPR, r 21.3(2)
	If a party becomes a protected party during proceedings, no party may take any step in the proceedings without the permission of the Court until the protected party has a litigation friend	CPR, r 21.3(3)
	Any step taken before a protected party has a litigation friend shall be of no effect, unless the Court otherwise orders	CPR, r 21.3(4)

How do you decide if a party is a protected party?	As to assessment of mental capacity see generally the notes to CPR, r 21.1 In case of uncertainty, application should be made to the Court to resolve this	
Title to proceedings	The name of a protected party should be followed by '(a protected party by … his litigation friend)'	PD21, para 1.1
Who is appointed (without a court order)?	A deputy appointed by the Court of Protection under MCA 2005 with power to conduct proceedings on the protected party's behalf is entitled to be the litigation friend of the protected party in any proceedings to which his or her power extends	CPR, r 21.4(2)
	If nobody has been appointed by the Court (or appointed as a deputy as above) a person may act as a litigation friend if he or she: • can fairly and competently conduct proceedings on behalf of the protected party; and • has no interest adverse to that of the protected party; • (claim or counterclaim) undertakes to pay any costs which the protected party may be ordered to pay.	CPR, r 21.4(3)
Appointment without a court order	(If the Court has not appointed one) a person wishing to act as a litigation friend must:	

	• (if empowered by the Court of Protection) file an official copy of the order conferring the power;	
	• (otherwise) file a certificate of suitability:	
	• claimant) when making the claim;	
	• (defendant) when first taking a step in the proceedings	CPR, r 21.5
Certificate of suitability of litigation friend	States that the proposed litigation friend:	
	• consents to act;	
	• believes the person to be a protected party (with reasons and medical evidence);	
	• can fairly and competently conduct proceedings on behalf of the person;	
	• has no adverse interest; and	
	• (claimant) undertakes to pay any costs which the claimant may be ordered to pay in the proceedings	
	A counterclaim is treated like a claim for the purpose of the costs undertaking	Form N235; CPR, rr r 20.3(1) and 21.4(3); PD21, para 2.2
Service of certificate of suitability	The litigation friend must:	
	• serve the certificate of suitability on every person on whom the claim form should be served; and	CPR, r 21.5(4)(a)
	• file a certificate of service when he or she files the certificate of suitability	CPR, rr 6.13 and 21.5(4)(b)
Certificate of service	States required details of method of service	CPR, rr 6.17 and 6.29

Application for appointment by the Court	An application for an order appointing a litigation friend may be made by: • a person who wishes to be the litigation friend; or • a party The claimant must apply where: • a person makes a claim against a protected party; • the protected party has no litigation friend; and • either (i) someone who is not entitled files a defence or (ii) the claimant wishes to take some step in the proceedings	CPR, r 21.6; PD21, paras 3.1–3.4
	An application must be supported by evidence and the Court must be satisfied that the person appointed is 'suitable'	CPR, rr 21.4(3); 21.6(4); 21.6(5)
Change of litigation friend	The Court may: • direct that a person may not act as a litigation friend; • terminate the appointment; and • appoint a new litigation friend in substitution for an existing one	
	An application for an order must be supported by evidence and the Court may not appoint a litigation friend unless satisfied that the person is suitable	CPR, r 21.4(3) and r 21.7
Who is appointed by the Court?	On an application the Court may appoint: • the person proposed; or	

	• any other person who complies with the conditions in CPR, r 21.4(3)	CPR, r 21.8(4)
Appointment of the Official Solicitor	The Official Solicitor may be appointed as litigation friend provided: • he or she consents; and • provision is made for payment of his or her costs	PD21, para 3.4
Appointment ceasing – protected party	When a protected party acquires capacity, the litigation friend's appointment continues until ended by a court order:	CPR, r 21.9(2)
	application may be made by former protected party, litigation friend or a party; and	CPR, r 21.9(3); PD21, para 4.5
	the application must be supported by evidence	PD21, para 4.6
	The protected party must file and serve a notice: • that the appointment has ceased; • giving his or her address for service; and • stating whether or not he or she intends to carry on the proceedings	CPR, r 21.9(4); PD21, para 4.7
	If he or she does not do so within 28 days the Court may, on application, strike out any claim or defence brought by the protected party	CPR, r 21.9(5)
Service of claim form – protected party	Service of the claim form is upon: • the attorney under a registered enduring power of attorney; • the donee of a lasting power of attorney;	

	• the deputy appointed by the Court of Protection; or	
	• (if none) an adult with whom the protected party resides or in whose care he or she is	CPR, r 6.13(2)
Service of claim form – general	The court may by order:	
	• permit the claim form to be served on the ... protected party, or on a person other than as specified;	CPR, r 6.13(4)
	• treat a document as if it had been properly served although it has been served on someone other than as specified.	CPR, r 6.13(6)
Service generally	Once a litigation friend has been appointed, service will be upon him or her as if the litigation friend was the party	CPR, r 6.25(2)
	The Court may by order:	
	• permit a document to be served on the protected party, or on a person other than as specified;	CPR, r 6.25(3)
	• treat a document as if it had been properly served although it has been served on someone other than as specified	CPR, r 6.25(5)
Service of application relating to a litigation friend	An application for an order appointing or changing a litigation friend must be served on:	CPR, r 21.8
	• every person on whom the claim form should be served; and	CPR, r 21.8(1)
	• (if appointing) the protected party unless the Court otherwise orders; or	CPR, r 21.8(2)
	• (if changing) the existing and proposed litigation friend	CPR, r 21.8(3)

Statement of truth	Where a statement of truth is required the litigation friend or his or her legal representative signs this to verify that the litigation friend believes the facts stated in the document are true	CPR, r 22.1(5)–(6); PD22, paras 3.1(1) and 3.7
Default judgment	A claimant may only obtain a default judgment against a protected party:	
	• on an application supported by evidence that he or she is entitled to the judgment claimed;	CPR, r 12.10(a)(i); PD12, para 2.3(1)
	• after appointment of a litigation friend	CPR, r 12.11(3); PD12, para 4.2
	A counterclaim is treated like a claim.	CPR, r 20.3(3)
Judgment on an admission	There are restrictions on obtaining a judgment by or against a protected party based on an admission.	CPR, r 14.1(4)
Hearing	A hearing may be in private if this is necessary to protect the interests of a protected party:	CPR, r 39.2(3)(d)
	• eg 'approval of a compromise or settlement, or application for payment of money out of court to such party'	PD39, para 1.6
Availability of witness statements	The Court may at a trial make a direction that a witness statement which stands as evidence in chief is not open to inspection due to the need to protect the interests of a protected party	CPR, r 32.13(3)(e)

Compromise or settlement	Where a claim or counterclaim is made: • by or on behalf of a protected party; or • against a protected party, no settlement, compromise or payment and no acceptance of money paid into Court shall be valid, so far as it relates to such claim, without Court approval	CPR, r 21.10(1)
	Where before proceedings in which such a claim is made are begun: • an agreement is reached for the settlement of the claim; • and the sole purpose of proceedings is to obtain the approval of the Court to a settlement or compromise the claim must be made using the CPR Part 8 procedure and include a request to the Court for approval	CPR, r 21.10(2); PD21, paras 5.1–5.6; Form N292
	If in the Chancery Division, it will be heard by the judge, rather than the master or district judge, if the amount involved exceeds £100,000	CPR, PD2B, para 5.1(a)
Interim payments	The approval of the Court must be obtained before making a voluntary interim payment to a protected party	CPR, r 21.10(1)
Acceptance of offers and payments into court	An offer or payment may only be accepted on behalf of a protected party with the permission of the Court.	CPR, r 21.10(1)

	In such cases a payment out of court requires a court order	CPR, r 21.11(1)(b)
Who is a protected beneficiary?	A protected party who lacks capacity to manage and control any money recovered by him or her or on his or her behalf or for his or her benefit in the proceedings	CPR, r 21.1(2)(e)
Control of money recovered	Where in any proceedings: • money is recovered on behalf of or for the benefit of a protected party; or • money paid into court is accepted by or on behalf of a protected party, the Court will first consider whether the protected party is a protected beneficiary, and subject thereto:	
	• the money is dealt with under directions of the Court and not otherwise	CPR, r 21.11; PD21, paras 8.1–8.4
	These may provide that the money shall be wholly or partly paid into court and:	CPR, r 21.11(2)
	• invested; or	
	• otherwise dealt with (eg paid to or for the benefit of the protected beneficiary); or	PD21, para 8.1(2); paras 9.1–9.8; and paras 10.1–10.7;
	• transferred to another court or County Court hearing centre if more convenient	CPR, r 30.7; PD21, para 8.2(3)
Payment out of funds in court held for protected beneficiaries	Applications are to a master or district judge (a hearing may not be required): • for payment out to (or for the benefit of) a protected beneficiary;	PD21, para 13

	• to vary an investment strategy	
	Funds in court are held in the Court Funds Office and there are procedures for the payment in and out of monies	Court Funds Rules 2011
	Where a fund is less than £50,000 it may be held in court for a protected beneficiary if involvement of the Court of Protection would not otherwise be necessary	PD21, para 10.2(2)
	Small funds may be paid out to a responsible adult in the court's discretion	PD21, para 8.1-8.3
Deputy for a protected beneficiary	If the fund is over £50,000 it will usually be necessary for the Court of Protection to appoint a financial deputy for the estate of a protected beneficiary:	PD21, paras 10.1–10.7
	• money of a protected beneficiary will be transferred;	Forms N292; CFO 200
	• applications for payment out of funds are to the Court of Protection	PD21, para 13.3
Costs	Costs payable to the solicitor for a protected party must be approved by the Court	CPR, r 46.4
	Neither:	
	• the fast-track costs provision; nor	CPR, r 45.3(2)(c)(ii)
	• the power of a court officer to assess costs (unless under CPR, r 46.4)	CPR, r 47.3(1)(c)
	apply to a hearing for the Court's approval of a settlement or compromise of a claim by a protected party	

	The liability of a litigation friend for costs continues until:	
	• the appointment ceases; and	
	• the former protected party serves notice on the other parties; or	
	the litigation friend serves notice.	CPR, r 21.9(6); PD21, para 5.5
Forms	Certificate of suitability of litigation friend: Form N235	
	Order approving terms of a settlement or compromise (includes transfer of fund to Court of Protection): Form N292	
Court fees	No additional fee is prescribed	

PROCEDURAL GUIDE 6: RESOLVING DOUBT ABOUT CAPACITY UNDER THE CIVIL PROCEDURE RULES 1998

Issue

A problem arises when there is a significant doubt as to whether a party lacks capacity because the proceedings should not continue until this doubt has been resolved. There is no simple solution but this Procedural Guide sets out some of the options available to the parties and the court.

Procedure

The procedure in regard to 'protected parties' is as follows.

The Procedural Problem		
Why is 'capacity' relevant?	Special provisions apply to parties who lack capacity – **See generally PG5**	Rule 21 & PD21; MCA 2005, Part 1

What aspects of capacity are relevant?	Capacity: • ... to conduct the proceedings • ... to manage and control any monies recovered	See generally Rule 21 & PD21
What are the implications?	A party who lacks capacity to conduct the proceedings is a protected party	Rule 21.1(2)(d)
	A party who lacks capacity to manage and control any monies recovered is a *protected beneficiary*	Rule 21.1(2)(e)
What are the consequences?	A *protected party* will normally require a *litigation friend* to be appointed	Rule 21.2(1)
	A *protected beneficiary* will not be permitted to receive money	Rule 21.11(3)
Who may raise doubts as to the capacity of a party?	The solicitors to the party, another party or the court	Rule 3.3
	The court should investigate question of capacity whenever there is reason to suppose it may be absent	*Masterman-Lister* case [2002] EWCA Civ 1889
What should be done when doubts are raised?	The doubts must be resolved and any proceedings stayed until this has been done	Rule 21.3(2),(3); Rule 21.3(4)
What discretion does the court have?	The court may allow steps to be taken before the appointment of a litigation friend	Rule 21.3(2),(3)
How will the court exercise that discretion?	The court may allow steps to be taken which are needed at that stage provided that these will not prejudice the party who may lack capacity	

Procedural Guide 6: Resolving doubt about capacity

What if proceedings continue and a party is later found to lack capacity?	Any step taken before a protected party has a litigation friend has no effect *unless the court orders otherwise*	Rule 21.3(4)
When will the court order otherwise?	The court may waive the procedural irregularity and give consequential directions if this will not prejudice the party who lacked capacity and there has been no abuse of process	
How will the court know if there has been prejudice?	A litigation friend will have been appointed and can make submissions	

Resolving Doubt as to Capacity

What help do the CPR provide?	The Rules assume that it is known whether a party lacks capacity so any doubt must be addressed as an issue in the proceedings	Rule 1.1(2)(a); Rule 3.1(2)
What is required?	• Expert evidence • Factual evidence	
The expert evidence	Medical evidence as to *an impairment of, or a disturbance in the functioning of, the mind or brain* [the diagnostic threshold].	MCA 2005, s 2(1)
The factual evidence	Evidence of expert and lay witnesses as to whether the party is *unable to make a decision in the matter for himself* according to the statutory criteria	MCA 2005, s 3(1)
Are both types of evidence required?	In practice the medical evidence may extend to ability to make and communicate decisions – in which event unless challenged it will be all that is required	

PART II

What is the standard of proof?	There is a presumption of capacity but lack of capacity may be proved on the balance of probability	MCA 2005, ss 1(2) and 2(4)
Claimant	Where significant doubt arises the court will expect the party to produce evidence to dispel that doubt	
	Claim may be stayed until claimant submits to a medical examination	
Defendant	The court will expect the claimant to produce evidence if the defendant does not respond	
What if a Defendant will not Co-operate? *The following options may be available to the claimant*		
Certificate	A suitable adult may be prepared to complete the *Certificate of suitability of litigation friend* which states a belief that the person is a protected party	Form N235
Evidence	Medical evidence may already exist which establishes the diagnostic threshold	
	Evidence of conduct may be available (eg as to how the party has responded to the claim) – this may in itself create doubts as to capacity	

Procedural Guide 6: Resolving doubt about capacity

Lack of medical evidence	The court has no power to force the defendant to submit to a medical examination	
	A default order would not be appropriate because an actual finding of lack of capacity is required	
	In the absence of medical evidence a court should be cautious before concluding that capacity is lacking	*Baker Tilly v Makar* [2013] EWHC 759 (QB)
Involve social services?	A recital in a court order that there is an appearance of need for community care services coupled with a request for an indication as to whether such assessment has been or will be carried out may produce information. A social worker may be invited to attend the next directions hearing.	NHS and Community Care Act 1990, s 47
Official Solicitor	Cannot act for party in the absence of a finding of lack of capacity	*Harbin v Masterman* [1896] 1 Ch 351, CA
	The court can direct Official Solicitor to make inquiries and report	
Court of Protection	*See below*	
Who will be the Litigation Friend? *The following options may be available for a defendant*		
Person already involved	• *Attorney* (under registered enduring or lasting power) • *Deputy* appointed by Court of Protection • *Appointee* for social security benefits	Rule 21.4(2); MCA 2005

PART II

551

PART II   COURT OF PROTECTION PRACTICE 2016

Concerned person	Relative, partner, friend, carer or personal advocate	Rule 21.4(3)
Solicitor to party	Not appropriate – conflict of roles	
Official Solicitor	Litigation friend of last resort if consents. Will require provision for costs	
Involving the Court of Protection		
What can this Court do?	• Make declaration as to capacity • Make decisions on behalf of a person who lacks capacity • Appoint a deputy to do so Nominate a person to conduct proceedings	MCA 2005, ss 15, 16
Why involve this Court?	• Resolve capacity issues • Find someone to be litigation friend • Clarify whether the Court of Protection needs to be involved with any damages recovered	MCA 2005
Advantages	• Expertise in this area • Power to give directions even before finding of incapacity • Additional powers to obtain reports	MCA 2005, ss 48, 49
What reports can be obtained?	• Local authority (eg. social services) • NHS body (clinical commissioning group or Trust) • Court of Protection general visitor • Court of Protection special visitor • Public Guardian	MCA 2005, s 49

552

| Disadvantages | • Cost and delay |
| | • Someone must apply to this Court (but that may become necessary anyway) |

PROCEDURAL GUIDE 7: APPLICATION FOR A STATUTORY WILL OR CODICIL
Procedure

The procedure for statutory will or codicil applications is as follows.

(1) Is permission needed?	MCA 2005, s 50; COPR 2007, Pt 8	Form COP2 should be filed with the application
(2) The substantive application should be filed at the same time as permission is sought	COPR 2007, Pt 9, Practice Direction F; COPR 2007, rr 62–64 and Practice Directions 9A, B and D	Form COP1 (application form); Form COP1A (Annex A being supporting information required); Form COP3 (assessment of capacity form); COP24 addressing and exhibiting all relevant matters set out in PD9F, paragraph 6; Court fee
(3) Within 14 days, the Court will deal with the application for permission if this is required. The Court will either grant permission, refuse the application without a hearing or fix a hearing. If a hearing is fixed, the Court will give directions to notify any person of the hearing	COPR 2007, rr 55 and 56; COPR 2007, r 89 will apply where permission is refused without a hearing; COPR 2007, Pt 20 deals with an appeal following a hearing; COPR 2007, r 56 and Practice Direction A, para 8 deal with notification of persons of a permission hearing; COPR 2007, r 57 deals with acknowledgement of the permission application	If a hearing is fixed, a person notified of the hearing must file Form COP5 within 21 days
(4) If permission is given for the application, the Court will issue the application	COPR 2007, r 65	The Court will give the applicant:

PART II
COURT OF PROTECTION PRACTICE 2016

		Form COP5 (acknowledgement of service)
		Form COP14 (notice of proceedings to P)
		Form COP14A (guidance notes for Form COP14)
		Form COP15 (notice that an application has been issued)
		Form COP15A (guidance notes for Form COP15)
		Form COP20 (certificate of service and notification)
(5) Serve application form and accompanying documents on respondent(s) within 21 days. Respondents must include: (a) any beneficiary under an existing will or codicil who is likely to be materially or adversely affected by the application; (b) any beneficiary under a proposed will or codicil who is likely to be materially or adversely affected by the application; and (c) any prospective beneficiary under P's intestacy where P has no existing will	COPR 2007, r 66; Practice Direction 9F (paragraph 9)	Forms COP1, COP1A and any other accompanying documents to that form, COP24, COP5 and COP15
(6) Notify P of the application (NB: P may not be a party and hence not a respondent)	COPR 2007, r 69	P is served with Forms COP14 and COP5
Notify any other persons of the application	COPR 2007, r 70	Forms COP15 and COP5
(7)-(9) Steps from service to the final hearing	See Procedural Guide 3: Application for Appointment of a Deputy Relating to Property and Financial Affairs	

(10) Miscellaneous points:

(a) Urgent applications for a 'holding' will	If an urgent hearing is required, an urgent application should be filed as soon as possible; see COPR 2007, Pt 10 and Practice Directions A and B	Form COP9 and evidence in support and, if appropriate, a disc with a draft order
(b) Execution of a statutory will	If a statutory will or codicil is made it must be executed in accordance with para 3(2) of Sch 2 of the MCA 2005	Once the statutory will has been executed the applicant must send the original and two copies of the will to the Court for sealing. The Court will seal the original and the copy and return both to the applicant (PD9F, paras 11 and 12)

PART III

Mental Capacity Act 2005

PART III

Mental Capacity Act 2005

PART III: Mental Capacity Act 2005

Contents

Mental Capacity Act 2005   561

Mental Capacity Act 2005

ARRANGEMENT OF SECTIONS

PART 1
PERSONS WHO LACK CAPACITY

Section		Page
	The principles	
1	The principles	564
	Preliminary	
2	People who lack capacity	565
3	Inability to make decisions	567
4	Best interests	568
4A	Restriction on deprivation of liberty	571
4B	Deprivation of liberty necessary for life-sustaining treatment etc	572
5	Acts in connection with care or treatment	572
6	Section 5 acts: limitations	573
7	Payment for necessary goods and services	575
8	Expenditure	575
	Lasting powers of attorney	
9	Lasting powers of attorney	576
10	Appointment of donees	577
11	Lasting powers of attorney: restrictions	578
12	Scope of lasting powers of attorney: gifts	579
13	Revocation of lasting powers of attorney etc	580
14	Protection of donee and others if no power created or power revoked	581
	General powers of the court and appointment of deputies	
15	Power to make declarations	582
16	Powers to make decisions and appoint deputies: general	583
16A	Section 16 powers: Mental Health Act patients etc	584
17	Section 16 powers: personal welfare	584
18	Section 16 powers: property and affairs	585
19	Appointment of deputies	586
20	Restrictions on deputies	587
21	Transfer of proceedings relating to people under 18	588
	Powers of the court in relation to Schedule A1	
21A	Powers of court in relation to Schedule A1	589
	Powers of the court in relation to lasting powers of attorney	
22	Powers of court in relation to validity of lasting powers of attorney	590
23	Powers of court in relation to operation of lasting powers of attorney	591
	Advance decisions to refuse treatment	
24	Advance decisions to refuse treatment: general	592
25	Validity and applicability of advance decisions	593
26	Effect of advance decisions	593
	Excluded decisions	
27	Family relationships etc	594
28	Mental Health Act matters	595

29	Voting rights	596

Research

30	Research	596
31	Requirements for approval	597
32	Consulting carers etc	598
33	Additional safeguards	599
34	Loss of capacity during research project	600

Independent mental capacity advocate service

35	Appointment of independent mental capacity advocates	600
36	Functions of independent mental capacity advocates	602
37	Provision of serious medical treatment by NHS body	602
38	Provision of accommodation by NHS body	603
39	Provision of accommodation by local authority	604
39A	Person becomes subject to Schedule A1	606
39B	Section 39A: supplementary provision	606
39C	Person unrepresented whilst subject to Schedule A1	607
39D	Person subject to Schedule A1 without paid representative	608
39E	Limitation on duty to instruct advocate under section 39D	609
40	Exceptions	609
41	Power to adjust role of independent mental capacity advocate	610

Miscellaneous and supplementary

42	Codes of practice	610
43	Codes of practice: procedure	612
44	Ill-treatment or neglect	612

PART 2
THE COURT OF PROTECTION AND THE PUBLIC GUARDIAN

The Court of Protection

45	The Court of Protection	614
46	The judges of the Court of Protection	614

Supplementary powers

47	General powers and effect of orders etc	616
48	Interim orders and directions	616
49	Power to call for reports	617

Practice and procedure

50	Applications to the Court of Protection	618
51	Court of Protection Rules	619
52	Practice directions	620
53	Rights of appeal	620

Fees and costs

54	Fees	621
55	Costs	621
56	Fees and costs: supplementary	622

The Public Guardian

57	The Public Guardian	622
58	Functions of the Public Guardian	623
60	Annual report	624

Mental Capacity Act 2005

Court of Protection Visitors
61 Court of Protection Visitors — 625

PART 3
MISCELLANEOUS AND GENERAL

Declaratory provision
62 Scope of the Act — 626

Private international law
63 International protection of adults — 626

General
64 Interpretation — 626
65 Rules, regulations and orders — 627
66 Existing receivers and enduring powers of attorney etc — 628
67 Minor and consequential amendments and repeals — 629
68 Commencement and extent — 629
69 Short title — 630

SCHEDULES

Schedule A1 – Hospital and Care Home Residents: Deprivation of Liberty — 630
  Part 1 – Authorisation to Deprive Residents of Liberty etc — 630
  Part 2 – Interpretation: Main Terms — 631
  Part 3 – The Qualifying Requirements — 632
  Part 4 – Standard Authorisations — 635
  Part 5 – Urgent Authorisations — 649
  Part 6 – Eligibility Requirement not Met: Suspension of Standard Authorisation — 653
  Part 7 – Standard Authorisations: Change in Supervisory Responsibility — 655
  Part 8 – Standard Authorisations: Review — 655
  Part 9 – Assessments under this Schedule — 662
  Part 10 – Relevant Person's Representative — 666
  Part 11 – IMCAs — 669
  Part 12 – Miscellaneous — 671
  Part 13 – Interpretation — 673
Schedule 1 – Lasting Powers of Attorney: Formalities — 680
  Part 1 – Making instruments — 680
  Part 2 – Registration — 682
  Part 3 – Cancellation of registration and notification of severance — 686
  Part 4 – Records of alterations in registered powers — 686
Schedule 1A – Persons Ineligible to be Deprived of Liberty by this Act — 687
  Part 1 – Ineligible Persons — 687
  Part 2 – Interpretation — 690
Schedule 2 – Property and Affairs: Supplementary Provisions — 693
Schedule 3 – International Protection of Adults — 697
  Part 1 – Preliminary — 697
  Part 2 – Jurisdiction of competent authority — 699
  Part 3 – Applicable law — 700
  Part 4 – Recognition and enforcement — 702
  Part 5 – Co-operation — 704
  Part 6 – General — 704
Schedule 4 – Provisions Applying to Existing Enduring Powers of Attorney — 706
  Part 1 – Enduring powers of attorney — 706

Part 2 – Action on actual or impending incapacity of donor	709
Part 3 – Notification prior to registration	710
Part 4 – Registration	712
Part 5 – Legal position after registration	714
Part 6 – Protection of attorney and third parties	716
Part 7 – Joint and joint and several attorneys	717
Part 8 – Interpretation	719
Schedule 5 – Transitional Provisions and Savings	719
Part 1 – Repeal of Part 7 of the Mental Health Act 1983	719
Part 2 – Repeal of the Enduring Powers of Attorney Act 1985	722
Schedule 6 – Minor and Consequential Amendments	724
Schedule 7 – Repeals	737

An Act to make new provision relating to persons who lack capacity; to establish a superior court of record called the Court of Protection in place of the office of the Supreme Court called by that name; to make provision in connection with the Convention on the International Protection of Adults signed at the Hague on 13th January 2000; and for connected purposes.

[7 April 2005]

BE IT ENACTED by the Queen's most Excellent Majesty, by and with the advice and consent of the Lords Spiritual and Temporal, and Commons, in this present Parliament assembled, and by the authority of the same, as follows:–

PART 1
PERSONS WHO LACK CAPACITY

The principles

1 The principles

(1) The following principles apply for the purposes of this Act.

(2) A person must be assumed to have capacity unless it is established that he lacks capacity.

(3) A person is not to be treated as unable to make a decision unless all practicable steps to help him to do so have been taken without success.

(4) A person is not to be treated as unable to make a decision merely because he makes an unwise decision.

(5) An act done, or decision made, under this Act for or on behalf of a person who lacks capacity must be done, or made, in his best interests.

(6) Before the act is done, or the decision is made, regard must be had to whether the purpose for which it is needed can be as effectively achieved in a way that is less restrictive of the person's rights and freedom of action.

Scope of provision—This section sets out the principles on which the Mental Capacity Act 2005 (MCA 2005) is based. A clear statement of principles was recommended by the Joint Scrutiny Committee on the Draft Mental Incapacity Bill as 'an initial point of reference' to underpin the Act and guide its interpretation and operation. Anyone using the provisions of MCA 2005 is required to act in accordance with the principles, which serve as 'benchmarks' for decision-makers. The common law origins of each of the five principles and their operation in practice are described in Part I, Chapter 2 of this work. The importance of the principles was reiterated by the House of Lords Select Committee conducting post-legislative scrutiny of MCA 2005: HL Paper 139 (TSO, 2014), opening summary and Chapter 3.

'assumed to have capacity' (s 1(2))—This principle is more generally known as the presumption of capacity – the starting point when assessing someone's capacity to make a particular decision. The presumption is rebuttable if it is established that the person concerned lacks the capacity to make the decision in question at the relevant time, using the test of capacity set out in ss 2–3. Where capacity is in doubt, a lower threshold is required for engagement of the powers of the Court of Protection under MCA2005, s 48 (*Re F* [2009] EWHC B30 (Fam), [2010] 2 FLR 28, at [44]).

'unable to make a decision' (s 1(3))—As defined in s 3.

'all practicable steps' (s 1(3))—The term 'practicable' is interpreted in the MCA 2005 Code of Practice as 'practical and appropriate', depending on 'personal circumstances, the kind of decision that has to be made and the time available to make the decision'. Resource constraints may also be relevant. Chapter 3 of the Code suggests a range of practicable steps to help someone make a decision for themselves. A distinction must be drawn between providing appropriate support and using excessive persuasion or 'undue influence'.

'an unwise decision' (s 1(4))—Based on the common law principle that the law does not insist that a person behaves 'in such a manner as to deserve approbation from the prudent, the wise or the good' (*Bird v Luckie* (1850) 8 Hare 301). When someone's capacity is being assessed, it is the ability to make the decision (not necessarily a sensible or wise decision) that is under scrutiny, not the outcome (see for example, *CC v KK and STCC* [2012] EWHC 2136 (COP), [2012] COPLR 627 at [65] and *PC and Anor v City of York Council* [2013] EWCA Civ 478, [2013] COPLR 409 at [53]-[54] per McFarlane LJ).

'best interests' (s 1(5))—This principle establishes 'best interests' as the criterion to govern all actions done for, and all decisions made on behalf of, someone who lacks capacity to make those decisions for themselves. The term 'best interests' is not defined in MCA 2005, but s 4 expands on the determination of best interests.

'regard must be had' (s 1(6))—While 'regard must be had' to the principle of acting in a less restrictive way, the 'best interests' principle takes priority – the option which is in the person's best interests must be chosen, which may not necessarily be the least restrictive alternative. In other words, 'the "best interests" principle takes priority': *London Borough of Havering v LD & KD* [2010] EWHC 3876 (COP), [2010] COPLR Con Vol 809, at [9].

'the purpose for which it is needed' (s 1(6))—Other options need only be considered so long as the desired purpose of the action or decision can still be achieved.

'less restrictive' (s 1(6))—But not necessarily the least restrictive alternative (see above).

Preliminary

2 People who lack capacity

(1) For the purposes of this Act, a person lacks capacity in relation to a matter if at the material time he is unable to make a decision for himself in relation to the matter because of an impairment of, or a disturbance in the functioning of, the mind or brain.

(2) It does not matter whether the impairment or disturbance is permanent or temporary.

(3) A lack of capacity cannot be established merely by reference to –

(a) a person's age or appearance, or
(b) a condition of his, or an aspect of his behaviour, which might lead others to make unjustified assumptions about his capacity.

(4) In proceedings under this Act or any other enactment, any question whether a person lacks capacity within the meaning of this Act must be decided on the balance of probabilities.

(5) No power which a person ('D') may exercise under this Act –
   (a) in relation to a person who lacks capacity, or
   (b) where D reasonably thinks that a person lacks capacity,
is exercisable in relation to a person under 16.

(6) Subsection (5) is subject to section 18(3).

Scope of provision—This section sets out the Act's definition of a person who lacks capacity to make a decision. Section 3 sets out the test for assessing whether a person is unable to make a decision and therefore lacks capacity (see below). By applying these together, the Act adopts a functional approach to defining capacity, requiring capacity to be assessed in relation to a specific decision rather than the ability to make decisions generally. The definition and test of capacity are described in Part I, Chapter 2 of this work.

'For the purposes of this Act' (s 2(1))—The definition applies 'For the purposes of this Act'. Schedule 6 makes consequential amendments to existing statutes in order to ensure that the definition is used in relation to other proceedings. Common law definitions of capacity (such as capacity to make a will (*Banks v Goodfellow* (1870) LR 5 QB 549) or to enter into marriage (*Sheffield City Council v E and S* [2004] EWHC 2808 (Fam), [2005] 1 FLR 965)) are not affected. In relation to testamentary capacity, in respect of wills made before MCA 2005 came into effect on October 2007, it is clear the question of capacity should be based on the common law test, without reference to the Act. There have been conflicting conclusions as regards wills made before MCA 2005 came into force: see *Fischer v Diffley* [2013] EWHC 4567 (Ch) and *Bray v Pearce* (unreported, 6 March 2014) suggested that MCA 2005 should be applied; to contrary effect is *Re Walker* [2014] EWHC 71 (Ch), [2015] COPLR 348. In *Saulle v Nouvet* [2007] EWHC 2902 (QB) it was confirmed that the MCA test of capacity should be used to assess litigation capacity in proceedings to which the Civil Procedure Rules apply.

'unable to make a decision' (s 2(1))—As defined in s 3. In *PC and Anor v City of York Council* [2013] EWCA Civ 478 the Court of Appeal held that the test of capacity should be applied in the sequence set out in s 2(1), that is focussing first on the functional aspect of whether the person concerned is unable to make the decision in question, and if so, whether that inability is because of an impairment or disturbance: at [58] per McFarlane LJ.

'in relation to a matter' (s 2(1))—This confirms that capacity is decision-specific. See *A, B and C v X and Z* [2013] COPLR 1 at [1] and *PC and Anor v City of York Council* [2013] EWCA Civ 478, [2013] COPLR 409, at [35] per McFarlane LJ.

at the material time' (s 2(1))—This confirms that capacity is time-specific.

'because of an impairment of, or a disturbance in the functioning of, the mind or brain' (s 2(1))—This sets a 'diagnostic threshold' for a lack of capacity to be established. If a person fails the diagnostic test, there can be no finding of lack of capacity under the Act. The diagnostic threshold covers a wide range of conditions and disorders, whether temporary or permanent (s 2(2)). See the Annex to Part I, Chapter 2 of this work for a medical view of the impact of various conditions affecting capacity.

Equal consideration or non-discrimination—(s 2(3))—During parliamentary debates on the Bill, attempts were made to introduce some form of 'non-discrimination' or 'equal consideration' principle into the legislation. The Government's response was to insert s 2(3), aimed at preventing unjustified assumptions being made about a person's mental capacity. A similar provision was introduced in s 4(1) relating to the determination of best interests.

'balance of probabilities' (s 2(4))—That a lack of capacity is 'more likely than not' (*Re H (Minors) (Sexual Abuse—Standard of Proof)* [1996] 1 FLR 80, at p 586).

'a person under 16' (s 2(5)–(6))—The powers under this Act apply in general only to people lacking capacity who are aged 16 years or over. However, as was the case under the previous law, the Act's powers to deal with property and financial affairs might be exercised in relation to a child whose disabilities will cause a lack of capacity to manage those affairs to continue into adulthood (see s 18(3)). In cases where legal proceedings are required, MCA 2005, s 21 provides for transfer from the Court of Protection to the family courts and vice versa – see also *B (A Local Authority) v*

RM, MM and AM [2010] EWHC 3802 (Fam), [2010] COPLR Con Vol 247. The different concepts of 'competence' in relation to children under 16 years and 'capacity' applying to young people aged 16–17 are discussed in Chapter 2 of Part I of this work.

3 Inability to make decisions

(1) For the purposes of section 2, a person is unable to make a decision for himself if he is unable –

    (a) to understand the information relevant to the decision,
    (b) to retain that information,
    (c) to use or weigh that information as part of the process of making the decision, or
    (d) to communicate his decision (whether by talking, using sign language or any other means).

(2) A person is not to be regarded as unable to understand the information relevant to a decision if he is able to understand an explanation of it given to him in a way that is appropriate to his circumstances (using simple language, visual aids or any other means).

(3) The fact that a person is able to retain the information relevant to a decision for a short period only does not prevent him from being regarded as able to make the decision.

(4) The information relevant to a decision includes information about the reasonably foreseeable consequences of –

    (a) deciding one way or another, or
    (b) failing to make the decision.

Scope of provision—This section sets out the test for determining whether a person is unable to make a particular decision and therefore lacks capacity for the purposes of this Act (see s 2). This is a 'functional' test, focusing on the ability of the person concerned to make a particular decision and the processes followed by the person in arriving at the decision – not on the outcome.

'information relevant to the decision' (s 3(1)(a))—Includes the particular nature of the decision in question, the purpose for which the decision is needed and the likely effects of making the decision. It also includes the reasonably foreseeable consequences of deciding one way or another or of making no decision at all (s 3(4)). Identifying what is the specific decision in question, and the information relevant to the decision, is not always straightforward – see for example *Re S: D v R (Deputy of S) and S* [2010] EWHC 2405 (COP), [2010] COPLR Con Vol 1112. The person must be able to understand the 'salient details' but not necessarily 'all peripheral details' (*LBL v RYJ* [2010] EWHC 2665 (COP), [2010] COPLR Con Vol 795, at [24] and [58]).

'retain the information' (s 3(1)(b))—For long enough to make an effective decision, depending on what is necessary for the decision in question (see for example, in relation to capacity to consent to marriage *A Local Authority v AK & Ors* [2012] EWHC B29 (COP), [2013] COPLR 163, at [51]). The ability to retain information for a short period only will not automatically disqualify the person from making the decision (s 3(3)).

'use or weigh that information' (s 3(1)(c))—Understanding the information is not sufficient – the person must be able to use the information as part of the process of making a decision. The courts have defined the process as the ability to weigh all relevant information in the balance and then use the information in order to arrive at a decision (*Re MB* [1997] 2 FLR 426; *R v Collins and Ashworth Hospital Authority ex parte Brady* [2001] 58 BMLR 173). Further guidance on applying this element of the capacity test is given in *The PCT v P, AH & The Local Authority* [2009] EW Misc 10 (FWCOP), [2011] 1 FLR 287. The provision of advice and support, or even some degree of constraint, is permissible to assist in this process – see for example, *V v R* [2011] EWHC 822 (QB) so long as the person knows when to seek assistance and can act on the advice given (*Loughlin v Singh* [2013] EWHC 1641 (QB), [2013] COPLR 371, at [36] and [51]).

'[unable to] communicate his decision' (s 3(1)(d))—By any possible means. This residual category will affect a minority of people where 'the assessor does not know, one way or the other, whether the person is capable of deciding or not' (Law Com No 231, at para 3.20). Communicating by blinking one eye can be sufficient to indicate capacity (*Re AK (Adult Patient) (Medical Treatment—Consent)* [2001] 1 FLR 129).

'explanation ... appropriate to his circumstances' (s 3(2))—Appropriate to the particular circumstances of the person concerned, using the most effective means of communication ('simple language, visual aids or any other means') to assist his or her understanding and to enable the person to use the information as required by s 3(1)(c). In *CC v KK and STCC* [2012] EWHC 2136 (COP) (at [68]) Baker J criticized what he called the 'blank canvas' approach where the person being assessed was given little information about the choices she was being asked to make.

'reasonably foreseeable consequences' (s 3(4))—see *A Local Authority v Mrs A* [2010] EWHC 1549, [2010] COPLR Con Vol 138 for an example of the court's interpretation of the reasonably foreseeable consequences of making a personal welfare decision (in this case concerning consent to contraceptive treatment).

4 Best interests

(1) In determining for the purposes of this Act what is in a person's best interests, the person making the determination must not make it merely on the basis of –

(a) the person's age or appearance, or
(b) a condition of his, or an aspect of his behaviour, which might lead others to make unjustified assumptions about what might be in his best interests.

(2) The person making the determination must consider all the relevant circumstances and, in particular, take the following steps.

(3) He must consider –

(a) whether it is likely that the person will at some time have capacity in relation to the matter in question, and
(b) if it appears likely that he will, when that is likely to be.

(4) He must, so far as reasonably practicable, permit and encourage the person to participate, or to improve his ability to participate, as fully as possible in any act done for him and any decision affecting him.

(5) Where the determination relates to life-sustaining treatment he must not, in considering whether the treatment is in the best interests of the person concerned, be motivated by a desire to bring about his death.

(6) He must consider, so far as is reasonably ascertainable –

(a) the person's past and present wishes and feelings (and, in particular, any relevant written statement made by him when he had capacity),
(b) the beliefs and values that would be likely to influence his decision if he had capacity, and
(c) the other factors that he would be likely to consider if he were able to do so.

(7) He must take into account, if it is practicable and appropriate to consult them, the views of –

(a) anyone named by the person as someone to be consulted on the matter in question or on matters of that kind,
(b) anyone engaged in caring for the person or interested in his welfare,
(c) any donee of a lasting power of attorney granted by the person, and
(d) any deputy appointed for the person by the court,

as to what would be in the person's best interests and, in particular, as to the matters mentioned in subsection (6).

(8) The duties imposed by subsections (1) to (7) also apply in relation to the exercise of any powers which –

(a) are exercisable under a lasting power of attorney, or
(b) are exercisable by a person under this Act where he reasonably believes that another person lacks capacity.

(9) In the case of an act done, or a decision made, by a person other than the court, there is sufficient compliance with this section if (having complied with the requirements of subsections (1) to (7)) he reasonably believes that what he does or decides is in the best interests of the person concerned.

(10) 'Life-sustaining treatment' means treatment which in the view of a person providing health care for the person concerned is necessary to sustain life.

(11) 'Relevant circumstances' are those –

(a) of which the person making the determination is aware, and
(b) which it would be reasonable to regard as relevant.

Scope of provision—This section sets out a checklist of factors that must be always considered when determining whether a decision made on behalf of a person lacking capacity to make that decision for themselves, or an act carried out in connection with the person's care or treatment, is in that person's best interests. There is no statutory definition of best interests, since this will depend on the particular act or decision in question and the individual circumstances of the person concerned. The processes involved in determining best interests are described in Chapter 2 of Part I of this work. 'The purpose of the best interests test is to consider matters from the [person]'s point of view': *Aintree University Hospitals NHS Foundation Trust v James* at [45] per Lady Hale.

Equal consideration or non-discrimination (s 4(1))—See also s 2(3) above. This is to ensure that determinations of best interests are not based on preconceived ideas or negative assumptions, for example, about the value or quality of life experienced by older people or people with mental or physical disabilities who now lack capacity to make specific decisions for themselves.

'all relevant circumstances' (s 4(2))—The statutory checklist sets out the minimum necessary considerations but all other matters relevant in the particular situation must also be taken into account. Relevant circumstances are defined in s 4(11). While 'the right to private and family life' confirmed by ECHR Article 8 will always be a relevant factor in determining a person's best interests, it should not be 'the starting point' or given priority over other relevant factors (*K v LBX & Ors* [2012] EWCA Civ 79, [2012] COPLR 411, at [30]).

'in particular, take the following steps' s 4(2))—Not all the factors in the checklist will be relevant to all types of decisions or actions, but they must still be considered if only to be disregarded as irrelevant to that particular situation. The extent to which there is, or should be, a hierarchy as between the factors is discussed at **2.128**

Regaining capacity (s 4(3))—If the individual concerned is likely to regain capacity to make that particular decision in the future, it may be possible to delay the decision until the person can make it him or herself, if that is in the person's best interests. Clearly, urgent decisions should not be delayed.

'so far as reasonably practicable, permit and encourage the person to participate' (s 4(4))—This complements the principle in s 1(3). The guidance in Chapter 3 of the Code of Practice suggests a range of steps, particularly help with communication, which may permit and encourage someone lacking capacity to be involved and to participate as fully as possible in decision-making. What is 'reasonably practicable' will depend on the particular circumstances. The importance of involving the person in the decision-making process has been reinforced by the Court of Protection (*Re S and S (Protected Persons); C v V Cases No 11475121 & 11475138* [2008] COPLR Con Vol 1074, at [54]–[55]); the principle applies equally when the judge is to be the decision-maker: *Wye Valley NHS Trust v Mr B* [2015] EWCOP 60 at [18].

'life-sustaining treatment' (s 4(5))—Defined in s 4(10).

'not be motivated by a desire to bring about his death' (s 4(5))—A great deal of the debate in both Houses of Parliament concerned life and death decisions affecting people who lack capacity to make those decisions for themselves. In order to provide clarity and reassurance on these very difficult issues, the Government agreed to a number of amendments introducing specific statements in the legislation (see also s 62). This provision does not change the law, but it puts beyond doubt that the decision-maker's motivation must be the objective determination of the person's best interests, not a desire to bring about the person's death, when the decision relates to the provision, withholding or withdrawal of life-sustaining treatment. 'Although not an absolute rule, the law regards the preservation of life as a fundamental principle': *W v M & Ors* [2011] EWHC 2443 (Fam), [2012] COPLR 222, at [7]. The strong presumption in favour of preserving life can 'tip the balance' despite the person's known wishes to die: *A Local Authority v E and Others* [2012] EWHC 1639 (COP), [2012] COPLR 441, at [140].

'reasonably ascertainable' (s 4(6))—Whether expressed orally, in writing or through behaviour, or reported by family members or others who know (or knew) the person concerned – see also s 4(7). This factor in the best interests checklist places the focus firmly on the person lacking capacity, taking into account the issues most important to him or her. However, the person's views will not automatically determine the outcome.

'past and present wishes and feelings' (s 4(6)(a))—'The wishes and feelings, beliefs and values of people with a mental disability are as important to them as they are to anyone else, and may even be more important. It would therefore be wrong in principle to apply any automatic discount to their point of view [on the basis that they lack capacity to take the decision in question]': *Wye Valley NHS Trust v Mr B* [2015] EWCOP 60 at [11]. As discussed at **2.148–2.149**, the case-law does not speak with one voice as to whether it is necessary to give particular weight to P's wishes and feelings in the application of MCA 2005. Note that past and present wishes may conflict (MCA 2005, Code of Practice, para 5.38).

'relevant written statements' (s 4(6)(a))—Including any written expressions of wishes or preferences about medical treatment. 'The more specific and well thought out the statement, the more likely it will be persuasive in determining best interests' (*Hansard*, HL Deb, vol 670, ser 5, cols 1441–1442 (17 March 2005)). See for example *PS v LP* [2013] *EWHC 1106* (COP). The Senior Judge of the Court of Protection has noted, in placing weight upon the views expressed by P in the form of a will, that '[a]lthough it has been said that there is no hierarchy of factors in the checklist in section 4 of the Mental Capacity Act, I attach weight to EO's views, because section 4(6)(a) refers 'in particular" (my emphasis) to "any relevant written statement made by him when he had capacity."' *Re BM; JB v AG* [2014] EWCOP B20 at [58].

'beliefs and values' (s 4(6)(b))—Including any social or psychological factors, political affiliations, cultural background, spiritual and religious beliefs, subscriptions to charitable causes or known past behaviour.

'other factors' (s 4(6)(c))—Such as emotional ties, family obligations, altruistic motives or concern for others. 'The actual wishes of P, which are altruistic and not in any way, directly or indirectly self-interested, can be a relevant factor' (*Re G (TJ)* [2010] EWHC 3005 (COP), [2010] COPLR Con Vol 403, at [56]). The 'emotional dimension, the importance of relationships, the importance of a sense of belonging' are relevant factors: *FP v GM and A Health Board* [2011] EWHC 2778 (COP) at [21].

'if it is practicable and appropriate to consult them' (s 4(7))—This ensures that carers, family members and other relevant people are consulted (in an appropriate and timely fashion – see *R (W) v LB Croydon* [2011] EWHC 696 (Admin)) on decisions affecting the person lacking capacity to make those decisions for themselves, but only if it is 'practicable and appropriate' to do so, depending on the particular circumstances. It may be appropriate to consult with former carers and to take into account oral statements made to them by the person who lacks capacity (*Re M (ITW v Z)* [2009] EWHC 2525 (Fam), [2009] COPLR Con Vol 828, at [36]).The Senior Judge of the Court of Protection has held that where consultation is likely to be unduly onerous, contentious, futile or serve no useful purpose, it is not 'practicable or appropriate' (*Re Allen* [2009] (CoP No 11661992) (unreported)). The requirement for consultation must be balanced against the right to confidentiality of the person lacking capacity. The views of those consulted will not necessarily determine the outcome – the weight given to them will depend on their relationship and amount of contact with the person concerned and the extent of their knowledge of the matter in question. The purpose of consultation is designed, in particular, to allow the decision-maker to obtain the view of those consulted of what the person's attitude would be in relation to the decision in question: *Aintree University Hospitals NHS Foundation Trust v James* at [39] per Lady Hale.

'interested in his welfare' (s 4(7)(b))—The nature of and motivation for the interest will be relevant in deciding whether to consult persons in this category.

'The duties imposed' (s 4(8))—The principle set out in s 1(5) confirms that any act done, or any decision made, on behalf of a person lacking capacity must be done in his or her best interests. Section 4(8) confirms that the best interests principle, and the duties to be carried out in determining best interests, also apply in the specified circumstances where the person concerned may not in fact lack capacity in relation to the act or decision in question.

'reasonably believes' (s 4(9))—This is an objective test – the decision-maker must, so far as possible, apply the best interests checklist and therefore be able to point to objective reasons to justify why they 'reasonably believe' that what they are doing or deciding is in the person's best interests (see for example *Commissioner of Police for the Metropolis v ZH* [2013] EWCA Civ 69, [2013] COPLR 332, where the Court of Appeal upheld the decision at first instance that the police had failed to provide objective evidence to demonstrate that the actions they had taken in forcibly removing ZH from a swimming pool and subsequently restraining him were in ZH's best interests). In considering what is 'reasonable' in any particular case, higher expectations are likely to be placed on those appointed to act under formal powers (attorneys and deputies) and those acting in a professional capacity than on family members and friends who are caring for a person lacking capacity without any formal authority.

4A Restriction on deprivation of liberty

(1) This Act does not authorise any person ('D') to deprive any other person ('P') of his liberty.

(2) But that is subject to –

    (a)   the following provisions of this section, and
    (b)   section 4B.

(3) D may deprive P of his liberty if, by doing so, D is giving effect to a relevant decision of the court.

(4) A relevant decision of the court is a decision made by an order under section 16(2)(a) in relation to a matter concerning P's personal welfare.

(5) D may deprive P of his liberty if the deprivation is authorised by Schedule A1 (hospital and care home residents: deprivation of liberty).

Amendment—Section inserted by the Mental Health Act 2007, s 50(1), (2).

Scope of provision—This section is part of the Deprivation of Liberty safeguards enacted in the Mental Health Act 2007 (MHA 2007) and brought into force on 1 April 2009. The safeguards are explained in Part I, Chapter 6 of this work.

'Deprive any other person of his liberty'—See discussion in Part I, Chapter 6 of this work.

'Relevant decision of the court' (s 4A(3))—The Court of Protection may by making an order under s 16(2)(a) decide on P's behalf that in their best interests they should be treated or accommodated in such a way that they are deprived of their liberty (subject to any conditions contained in the order).

'Authorised by Schedule A1' (s 4A(5))—This Schedule sets out the procedures to be followed, assessments to be made and safeguards to be in place for a managing authority of a hospital or care home to obtain authorisation from a primary care trust (or in Wales, Welsh ministers) or local authority to deprive a person in its care of their liberty.

4B Deprivation of liberty necessary for life-sustaining treatment etc

(1) If the following conditions are met, D is authorised to deprive P of his liberty while a decision as respects any relevant issue is sought from the court.

(2) The first condition is that there is a question about whether D is authorised to deprive P of his liberty under section 4A.

(3) The second condition is that the deprivation of liberty –

    (a) is wholly or partly for the purpose of –
        (i) giving P life-sustaining treatment, or
        (ii) doing any vital act, or
    (b) consists wholly or partly of –
        (i) giving P life-sustaining treatment, or
        (ii) doing any vital act.

(4) The third condition is that the deprivation of liberty is necessary in order to –

    (a) give the life-sustaining treatment, or
    (b) do the vital act.

(5) A vital act is any act which the person doing it reasonably believes to be necessary to prevent a serious deterioration in P's condition.

Amendments—Inserted by Mental Health Act 2007, s 50(1), (2).

Scope of provision—This section makes clear that, if the conditions are met, a person may be deprived of his liberty to save his life or prevent a serious deterioration in his condition whilst a decision is sought from the Court of Protection on any question as to whether he may lawfully be deprived of his liberty.

5 Acts in connection with care or treatment

(1) If a person ('D') does an act in connection with the care or treatment of another person ('P'), the act is one to which this section applies if –

    (a) before doing the act, D takes reasonable steps to establish whether P lacks capacity in relation to the matter in question, and
    (b) when doing the act, D reasonably believes –
        (i) that P lacks capacity in relation to the matter, and
        (ii) that it will be in P's best interests for the act to be done.

(2) D does not incur any liability in relation to the act that he would not have incurred if P –

    (a) had had capacity to consent in relation to the matter, and
    (b) had consented to D's doing the act.

(3) Nothing in this section excludes a person's civil liability for loss or damage, or his criminal liability, resulting from his negligence in doing the act.

(4) Nothing in this section affects the operation of sections 24 to 26 (advance decisions to refuse treatment).

Scope of provision—This section provides protection from liability for anyone involved in providing care or treatment for a person who lacks capacity to consent to such care or treatment, provided they are acting in the person's best interests and without negligence. In this way, the Act clarifies in statute the former common law 'doctrine of necessity' as confirmed by Sir James Munby P in *JO v GO & Ors* [2013] EWHC 3932 (COP), [2014] COPLR 62 at [18]), setting out the circumstances in which caring actions and decisions can lawfully be taken on behalf of adults who lack capacity to consent to them. 'A striking feature of the statutory defence [provided by MCA

2005, s 5] is the extent to which it is pervaded by the concepts of reasonableness, practicality and appropriateness': *Commissioner of Police for the Metropolis v ZH* [2013] EWCA Civ 69, [2013] COPLR 332, at [40] per Lord Dyson.

'a person ('D')' (s 5(1))—The Act does not define who may act – it depends on what is reasonable and appropriate for the act in question. The provision therefore refers to anyone carrying out such an act and may relate to several people at any given time with no-one having any 'special legal status' or power to act (*G v E* [2010] EWHC 2512 (COP), [2010] COPLR Con Vol 470, at [57]). It may also include a person who instructs another to act. Munby LJ has given guidance to local authorities as to the exercise of their powers in respect of the welfare of adults lacking capacity to consent, stressing that 'the local authority, is the servant of those in need of its support and assistance, not their master' (*Re A and C (Equality and Human Rights Commission Intervening)* [2010] EWHC 978 (Fam), [2010] COPLR Con Vol 10, at [52]). For further guidance on the responsibilities of public authorities, see *LB Hillingdon v Neary & Ors* [2011] EWHC 1377, [2011] COPLR Con Vol 632, at [33]. In *CC v KK and STCC* [2012] EWHC 2136 (COP), [2012] COPLR 627 (at [65]), Baker J warned of the danger of the 'protection imperative', whereby professionals 'may objectively conflate a capacity assessment with a best interests analysis' and attach greater weight to physical safety over emotional security.

'in connection with the care or treatment of another person ('P')' (s 5 (1))—The Act does not define 'care' or 'treatment' other than to clarify that treatment includes 'a diagnostic or other procedure' (s 64(1)). The Code of Practice provides a non-exhaustive list of examples (para 6.5) of such acts which would otherwise require consent.

'reasonable steps to establish whether P lacks capacity' (s 5(1)(a))—applying the definition and test of capacity in ss 2–3, in accordance with the principles in s 1. What is 'reasonable' will depend on the particular circumstances. This does not necessarily require a formal assessment of capacity, although professional practice may require this (e g in relation to capacity to consent to medical treatment). The Code of Practice suggests some reasonable steps to provide objective evidence of lack of capacity (para 4.45).

'reasonably believes' (s 5(1)(b))—This is an objective test. See also s 4(9).

'best interests' (s 5(1)(b)(ii))—determined by following the checklist set out in s 4 and the 'less restrictive' principle in s 1(6). For comments on the interaction between s 4 (best interests) and s 5, see *Commissioner of Police for the Metropolis v ZH* [2013] EWCA Civ 69, [2013] COPLR 332 and *JO v GO & Ors* [2013] EWHC 3932 (COP), [2014] COPLR 62.

'D does not incur any liability' (s 5(2))—Such acts can be performed as if the person concerned had capacity and had given consent. There is no need to obtain any formal powers or authority to act.

'negligence' (s 5(3))—Consent is not a defence to a claim of negligence. Similarly in relation to people who lack capacity to consent, this clarifies that protection from liability does not extend to situations where D has acted negligently, whether in carrying out the act or by failing to act in breach of duty.

'advance decisions to refuse treatment' (s 5(4))—A valid and applicable advance decision is not affected by s 5 which gives no protection from liability if the advance decision is not followed (see ss 24–26).

6 Section 5 acts: limitations

(1) If D does an act that is intended to restrain P, it is not an act to which section 5 applies unless two further conditions are satisfied.

(2) The first condition is that D reasonably believes that it is necessary to do the act in order to prevent harm to P.

(3) The second is that the act is a proportionate response to –

    (a) the likelihood of P's suffering harm, and
    (b) the seriousness of that harm.

(4) For the purposes of this section D restrains P if he –
   (a) uses, or threatens to use, force to secure the doing of an act which P resists, or
   (b) restricts P's liberty of movement, whether or not P resists.

(5) ...

(6) Section 5 does not authorise a person to do an act which conflicts with a decision made, within the scope of his authority and in accordance with this Part, by –
   (a) a donee of a lasting power of attorney granted by P, or
   (b) a deputy appointed for P by the court.

(7) But nothing in subsection (6) stops a person –
   (a) providing life-sustaining treatment, or
   (b) doing any act which he reasonably believes to be necessary to prevent a serious deterioration in P's condition,

while a decision as respects any relevant issue is sought from the court.

Amendments—Subsection (5) repealed by the Mental Health Act 2007, ss 50(1), (4)(a), 55, Sch 11, Pt 10. See Part I, Chapter 6 of this work for a description of the Deprivation of Liberty Safeguards, which made this subsection redundant.

Scope of provision—This section imposes two important limitations on the acts which can be carried out with protection from liability under s 5. The first relates to acts intended to restrain a person who lacks capacity and the second to situations where the act might conflict with a decision made by a donee of a lasting power of attorney or a deputy appointed by the court.

'restrain' (s 6(1))—Restraint is defined in s 6(4) and can take many forms. Restraint may be verbal or physical and may vary from shouting at someone, to holding them down, using mechanical devices such as seat belts or cot sides, to locking them in a room. It may also include the prescribing of a sedative or other chemical restraint which restricts liberty of movement. See for example *DH NHS Foundation Trust v PS* [2010] EWHC 1217 (Fam), [2010] COPLR Con Vol 346.

'necessary to do the act in order to prevent harm to P' (s 6(2))—The Act does not define 'harm', since this will vary according to individual circumstances. It is not confined to physical harm. The restraining act must be 'necessary' to avert harm – not simply to enable the carer or professional to do something more quickly or easily.

'a proportionate response' (s 6(3))—What is likely to be a 'proportionate response' to the likelihood and seriousness of harm, both in scale and nature, will depend on the particular circumstances and the desired outcome. Where there are objective reasons for believing that restraint is necessary to prevent the person from coming to any harm, only the minimum necessary force or intervention may be used and for the shortest possible duration. In *ZH v Commissioner of Police for the Metropolis* [2012] EWHC 604 (Admin), [2012] COPLR 588, the court gave detailed consideration to s 6 of the MCA 2005 when awarding damages against the police for forcibly removing and restraining a young man with severe autism and learning disabilities, without having first consulted his carers, informed themselves of the nature of his disabilities or considered any less restrictive options. The decision was upheld in its entirety by the Court of Appeal: *Commissioner of Police for the Metropolis v ZH* [2013] EWCA Civ 69, [2013] COPLR 332.

'restricts P's liberty of movement' (s 6(4)(b))—But not where such restrictions on movement amount to a deprivation of liberty under the European Convention on Human Rights (ECHR), Art 5(1). This is dealt with in ss 4A–4B.

Decisions of donees or deputies (s 6(6))—This section confirms that the provisions of s 5 do not authorise a person to do any act which conflicts with a decision made by a donee of a lasting power of attorney previously granted by the person lacking capacity, or by a deputy appointed by the Court, so long as the donee or deputy is acting within the scope of their authority. The formal decision-making powers provided by the Act therefore take precedence. In cases of dispute, an application may be made for permission to apply to the Court of Protection to resolve the matter.

'life sustaining treatment' (s 6(7))—Defined in s 4(10). Life-sustaining treatment, or treatment necessary to prevent a serious deterioration in the person's condition, can be given pending a ruling from the court.

7 Payment for necessary goods and services

(1) If necessary goods or services are supplied to a person who lacks capacity to contract for the supply, he must pay a reasonable price for them.

(2) 'Necessary' means suitable to a person's condition in life and to his actual requirements at the time when the goods or services are supplied.

Scope of provision—This section combines the provision under the Sale of Goods Act 1979, s 3(2) concerning the enforceability of a contract to provide necessary goods with the matching common law rule about necessary services. It clarifies that the obligation to pay a reasonable price applies to both the supply of necessary goods and the provision of necessary services to a person without capacity to contract for them, and it is the person who lacks capacity who must pay.

'necessary' (s 7(1))—Defined in s 7(2), based on the definition set out in the Sale of Goods Act 1979, s 3(3). In *Wychavon District Council v EM (HB)* [2012] UKUT 12 (AAC) the Upper Tribunal expressed some doubt as to whether 'services' in s 7 of the MCA 2005 is wide enough to cover the provision of accommodation, but even if it was not, the common law doctrine of necessities would apply. See also in this regard, and for a discussion of s 7 more generally, *Aster Healthcare* [2014] EWHC 77 (QB), upheld on appeal ([2014] EWCA Civ 1350).

'lacks capacity to contract for the supply' (s 7(1))—Applying the definition and test of capacity in ss 2–3, in accordance with the principles in s 1. The person is bound by the terms of the contract, even if it was unfair, unless it can be shown that the other party to the contract was aware of the person's lack of capacity or should have been aware of this (*Imperial Loan Company v Stone* [1892] 1 QB 599). If the other party knows, or must be taken to have known of the lack of capacity, the contract is voidable.

'he must pay' (s 7(1))—The legal responsibility for paying for necessary goods and services lies with the person for whom they are supplied even though that person lacks the capacity to contract for them. Where the person also lacks the capacity to arrange for payment to be made, the carer who has arranged for the supply of goods or services (as an act in connection with care or treatment carried out under s 5) may also arrange settlement of the bill. The carer will have protection from liability so long as the provision of goods or services was in the person's best interests.

'reasonable price' (s 7(1))—The obligation is to pay 'a reasonable price' so this provision cannot be used to enforce a contract which involves gross overcharging for goods or services.

'condition in life' (s 7(2))—This refers to the person's living conditions and place in society, rather than any mental or physical condition. 'The aim is to make sure that people can enjoy a similar standard of living and way of life to those they had before lacking capacity' (Code of Practice, para 6.58).

'actual requirements' (s 7(2))—Goods are not necessary if the person already has an adequate supply.

8 Expenditure

(1) If an act to which section 5 applies involves expenditure, it is lawful for D –

    (a)   to pledge P's credit for the purpose of the expenditure, and
    (b)   to apply money in P's possession for meeting the expenditure.

(2) If the expenditure is borne for P by D, it is lawful for D –

(a) to reimburse himself out of money in P's possession, or
(b) to be otherwise indemnified by P.

(3) Subsections (1) and (2) do not affect any power under which (apart from those subsections) a person –

(a) has lawful control of P's money or other property, and
(b) has power to spend money for P's benefit.

Scope of provision—Under this section, arrangements may be made to meet the expenditure involved in cases where necessary goods or services must be paid for. The intention is to make it possible for ordinary but necessary goods and services to be provided for people who lack the capacity to arrange and pay for them, but without requiring formal authority to meet any expenditure involved. However, s 8 does not authorise access to the incapacitated person's income or assets or to sell the person's property.

'to pledge P's credit' (s 8(1)(a))—If neither the carer (D) who arranged the supply of goods or services nor the person who lacks capacity (P) can produce the necessary funds, D may promise that P will pay.

'money in P's possession' (s 8(1)(b) and (2)(a))—A distinction is drawn between the use of available cash in the possession of the person lacking capacity, which can be used to pay for goods or services (s 8(1)(b)) or to repay D (s 8(2)(a)), and the removal of money from a bank account or selling valuable items of property, which is not permitted without formal authority (s 8(3)).

'to be otherwise indemnified by P' (s 8(2)(b))—Formal arrangements may need to be made (such as registering a relevant power of attorney or applying to the Court of Protection) before D can be reimbursed.

'any power' (s 8(3))—Someone may already have formal authority to deal with the person's property or financial affairs, for example, under an enduring or lasting power of attorney, as a deputy appointed by the Court of Protection or as a social security 'appointee'. Section 8(3) makes clear that these arrangements are not affected or changed by the above provisions. D cannot make arrangements for goods or services to be provided for P if this conflicts with a decision made by a donee or deputy (s 6(6)).

Lasting powers of attorney

9 Lasting powers of attorney

(1) A lasting power of attorney is a power of attorney under which the donor ('P') confers on the donee (or donees) authority to make decisions about all or any of the following –

(a) P's personal welfare or specified matters concerning P's personal welfare, and
(b) P's property and affairs or specified matters concerning P's property and affairs,

and which includes authority to make such decisions in circumstances where P no longer has capacity.

(2) A lasting power of attorney is not created unless –

(a) section 10 is complied with,
(b) an instrument conferring authority of the kind mentioned in subsection (1) is made and registered in accordance with Schedule 1, and
(c) at the time when P executes the instrument, P has reached 18 and has capacity to execute it.

(3) An instrument which –

(a) purports to create a lasting power of attorney, but
(b) does not comply with this section, section 10 or Schedule 1,

confers no authority.

(4) The authority conferred by a lasting power of attorney is subject to –

(a) the provisions of this Act and, in particular, sections 1 (the principles) and 4 (best interests), and
(b) any conditions or restrictions specified in the instrument.

Scope of provision—Sections 9–14 introduce the legal framework for lasting powers of attorney, whereby one person, the donor, can confer authority on a donee by a power of attorney to make decisions. The formalities for making a lasting power of attorney, which includes the registration process, are dealt with at Sch 1.

'power of attorney' (s 9(1))—It cannot be emphasised enough that a lasting power of attorney is a power of attorney and therefore the common law principles governing the relationship between a principal and his or her agent apply to a lasting power of attorney. See Part I, para **3.4**.

'donee (or donees)' (s 9(1))—The Act uses the term donee to define the attorney acting under a lasting power of attorney. This distinguishes the donee of a lasting power of attorney from an attorney acting under an enduring power of attorney where the term 'attorney' is used.

'specified matters' (s 9(1)(a) and (b))—Sections 2 and 3 define capacity in relation to a particular decision at a particular time. A donor of a power of attorney may therefore delegate specific decisions to an attorney as well as a more general authority to make decisions in relation to more broadly defined matters such as property and affairs or welfare.

'personal welfare' (s 9(1)(a))—This term is not defined by the Act. It does include giving or refusing consent to the carrying out or continuation of a treatment by a person providing health care for P. It can be interpreted in its widest sense and by reference to what it does not include. Thus it excludes acts of restraint unless authorised by the Act (s 11(1)–(6)), acts outside the scope of the Act (ss 27–29) and the giving or refusing of consent to life-sustaining treatment unless expressly authorised in the power.

'property and affairs' (s 9(1)(b))—This term is likewise not defined but can be construed in its literal sense. See Part I, para **3.30**.

'and which includes authority to make such decisions in circumstances where P lacks capacity' (s 9(1))—A lasting power of attorney can be used in respect of property and affairs where P has capacity; it can therefore also be used where P lacks capacity.

'is subject to' (s 9(4))—The authority conferred on the donee of a power is subject to the provisions of the Act and in particular the principles contained in s 1 and the best interests criteria in s 4, as well as any conditions or restrictions contained in the instrument. The power cannot therefore be expanded, only restricted.

10 Appointment of donees

(1) A donee of a lasting power of attorney must be –

(a) an individual who has reached 18, or
(b) if the power relates only to P's property and affairs, either such an individual or a trust corporation.

(2) An individual who is bankrupt or is a person in relation to whom a debt relieve order is made may not be appointed as donee of a lasting power of attorney in relation to P's property and affairs.

(3) Subsections (4) to (7) apply in relation to an instrument under which two or more persons are to act as donees of a lasting power of attorney.

(4) The instrument may appoint them to act –

    (a) jointly,
    (b) jointly and severally, or
    (c) jointly in respect of some matters and jointly and severally in respect of others.

(5) To the extent to which it does not specify whether they are to act jointly or jointly and severally, the instrument is to be assumed to appoint them to act jointly.

(6) If they are to act jointly, a failure, as respects one of them, to comply with the requirements of subsection (1) or (2) or Part 1 or 2 of Schedule 1 prevents a lasting power of attorney from being created.

(7) If they are to act jointly and severally, a failure, as respects one of them, to comply with the requirements of subsection (1) or (2) or Part 1 or 2 of Schedule 1 –

    (a) prevents the appointment taking effect in his case, but
    (b) does not prevent a lasting power of attorney from being created in the case of the other or others.

(8) An instrument used to create a lasting power of attorney –

    (a) cannot give the donee (or, if more than one, any of them) power to appoint a substitute or successor, but
    (b) may itself appoint a person to replace the donee (or, if more than one, any of them) on the occurrence of an event mentioned in section 13(6)(a) to (d) which has the effect of terminating the donee's appointment.

Amendment—SI 2012/2404.

Scope of provision—Who can be a donee of a lasting power of attorney.

'trust corporation' (s 10(1)(b))—A trust corporation cannot therefore act as a welfare attorney. The term is defined by s 64(1), which imports the definition supplied by the Trustee Act 1925, s 68(1): 'the Public Trustee or a corporation either appointed by the court in any particular case to be a trustee, or entitled by rules made under subsection (3) of section four of the Public Trustee Act 1906, to act as custodian trustee'.

'jointly and severally' (s 10(4)–(7))—The prescribed forms issued pursuant to Sch 1, para 1 alter the terminology and refer to two or more attorneys being appointed together and independently.

'the instrument is to be assumed to appoint them to act jointly' (s 10(5))—The prescribed forms provide for a clear choice in the way an attorney is appointed, but if this is not exercised or the appointment of more than one attorney is incompatible with a joint and several appointment then there is a presumption in favour of a joint appointment. This is to avoid such a clause making the appointment invalid which may have arisen where the appointment of attorneys under an enduring power of attorney was unclear. See Sch 4, para 20(1).

'a person to replace the donee' (s 10(8)(b))—While a donee cannot him or herself appoint a successor, the donor may appoint a replacement attorney. However, the replacement attorney can only be appointed on the occurrence of one of the events mentioned in s 13(6)(a)–(d), ie disclaimer, death, bankruptcy, dissolution of a marriage or incapacity. A donee whose authority is terminated, for instance, by an order of the Court of Protection, cannot be replaced under this provision.

11 Lasting powers of attorney: restrictions

(1) A lasting power of attorney does not authorise the donee (or, if more than one, any of them) to do an act that is intended to restrain P, unless three conditions are satisfied.

(2) The first condition is that P lacks, or the donee reasonably believes that P lacks, capacity in relation to the matter in question.

(3) The second is that the donee reasonably believes that it is necessary to do the act in order to prevent harm to P.

(4) The third is that the act is a proportionate response to –
  (a) the likelihood of P's suffering harm, and
  (b) the seriousness of that harm.

(5) For the purposes of this section, the donee restrains P if he –
  (a) uses, or threatens to use, force to secure the doing of an act which P resists, or
  (b) restricts P's liberty of movement, whether or not P resists,

or if he authorises another person to do any of those things.

(6) ...

(7) Where a lasting power of attorney authorises the donee (or, if more than one, any of them) to make decisions about P's personal welfare, the authority –
  (a) does not extend to making such decisions in circumstances other than those where P lacks, or the donee reasonably believes that P lacks, capacity,
  (b) is subject to sections 24 to 26 (advance decisions to refuse treatment), and
  (c) extends to giving or refusing consent to the carrying out or continuation of a treatment by a person providing health care for P.

(8) But subsection (7)(c) –
  (a) does not authorise the giving or refusing of consent to the carrying out or continuation of life-sustaining treatment, unless the instrument contains express provision to that effect, and
  (b) is subject to any conditions or restrictions in the instrument.

Amendment—Subsection (6) repealed by the Mental Health Act 2007, ss 50(1), (4)(b), 55, Sch 11, Pt 10.

Scope of provision—Section 11(1)–(5) deal with a welfare attorney's limited authority to restrain the donor. Section 11(7) establishes the vital principle that a welfare power can only be used to make decisions which the donor lacks capacity to make and s 11(8) allows a welfare lasting power of attorney to extend to the giving or refusing of consent to life-sustaining treatment so long as an express provision to that effect is contained in the power.

'life-sustaining treatment' (s 11(8))—Section 4(10) defines this as 'treatment which in the view of a person providing health care for the person concerned is necessary to sustain life'.

12 Scope of lasting powers of attorney: gifts

(1) Where a lasting power of attorney confers authority to make decisions about P's property and affairs, it does not authorise a donee (or, if more than one, any of them) to dispose of the donor's property by making gifts except to the extent permitted by subsection (2).

(2) The donee may make gifts –
  (a) on customary occasions to persons (including himself) who are related to or connected with the donor, or
  (b) to any charity to whom the donor made or might have been expected to make gifts,

if the value of each such gift is not unreasonable having regard to all the circumstances and, in particular, the size of the donor's estate.

(3) 'Customary occasion' means –

(a) the occasion or anniversary of a birth, a marriage or the formation of a civil partnership, or

(b) any other occasion on which presents are customarily given within families or among friends or associates.

(4) Subsection (2) is subject to any conditions or restrictions in the instrument.

Scope of provision—This section allows a donee of a financial power to act to benefit him or herself or others to the extent permitted by the Act. This is to escape the normal rule that a donee of a power of attorney cannot act to benefit him or herself. The power to benefit him or herself or others must, however, be within the scope of this section. There is no authority within this section to maintain another person whom the donor might be expected to provide for. A donee who wishes to make a provision or gift not within the scope of this section must apply to the Court of Protection.

'the value of each such gift is not unreasonable having regard to all the circumstances and in particular, the size of the donor's estate' (s 12(2))—There is no limit or even guidance to what is reasonable. An attorney must use his or her judgment, balancing prudence with an assessment of the donor's best interests.

'subject to any conditions or restrictions in the instrument' (s 12(4))—A donor of a power of attorney can only act to restrict this power; he or she cannot expand it. See Part I, para **3.37**.

13 Revocation of lasting powers of attorney etc

(1) This section applies if –

(a) P has executed an instrument with a view to creating a lasting power of attorney, or

(b) a lasting power of attorney is registered as having been conferred by P,

and in this section references to revoking the power include revoking the instrument.

(2) P may, at any time when he has capacity to do so, revoke the power.

(3) P's bankruptcy, or the making of a debt relief order (under Part 7A of the Insolvency Act 1986) in respect of P revokes the power so far as it relates to P's property and affairs.

(4) But where P is bankrupt merely because an interim bankruptcy restrictions order has effect in respect of him or where P is subject to an interim debt relief restrictions order (under Schedule 4ZB of the Insolvency Act 1986), the power is suspended, so far as it relates to P's property and affairs, for so long as the order has effect.

(5) The occurrence in relation to a donee of an event mentioned in subsection (6) –

(a) terminates his appointment, and

(b) except in the cases given in subsection (7), revokes the power.

(6) The events are –

(a) the disclaimer of the appointment by the donee in accordance with such requirements as may be prescribed for the purposes of this section in regulations made by the Lord Chancellor,

(b) subject to subsections (8) and (9), the death or bankruptcy of the donee or the making of a debt relief order (under Part 7A of the Insolvency Act 1986) in respect of the donee or, if the donee is a trust corporation, its winding-up or dissolution,

(c) subject to subsection (11), the dissolution or annulment of a marriage or civil partnership between the donor and the donee,
(d) the lack of capacity of the donee.

(7) The cases are –
(a) the donee is replaced under the terms of the instrument,
(b) he is one of two or more persons appointed to act as donees jointly and severally in respect of any matter and, after the event, there is at least one remaining donee.

(8) The bankruptcy of a donee or the making of a debt relief order (under Part 7A of the Insolvency Act 1986) in respect of a donee does not terminate his appointment, or revoke the power, in so far as his authority relates to P's personal welfare.

(9) Where the donee is bankrupt merely because an interim bankruptcy restrictions order has effect in respect of him or where the donee is subject to an interim debt relief restrictions order (under Schedule 4ZB of the Insolvency Act 1986), his appointment and the power are suspended, so far as they relate to P's property and affairs, for so long as the order has effect.

(10) Where the donee is one of two or more appointed to act jointly and severally under the power in respect of any matter, the reference in subsection (9) to the suspension of the power is to its suspension in so far as it relates to that donee.

(11) The dissolution or annulment of a marriage or civil partnership does not terminate the appointment of a donee, or revoke the power, if the instrument provided that it was not to do so.

Amendment—SI 2012/2404.

Scope of provision—Section 13 sets out the common law principle for revocation of a lasting power of attorney and expands the circumstances in which automatic revocation takes place. Revocation of the power does not of itself lead to cancellation of registration – that is subject to a separate process. For instance, the Lasting Power of Attorney, Enduring Power of Attorney and Public Guardian Regulations 2007, SI 2007/1253, reg 21 requires the Public Guardian to cancel registration of a power if he or she is satisfied that it has been properly revoked.

'revoke' (s 13(2))—There is no definition of revocation and common law principles apply to an act of revocation and the Act's principles will apply to whether the donor has capacity to revoke the power. There is, however, no formal process for revocation to lead to cancellation of registration. See Part I, para **3.117**.

'events' (s 13(6))—These events automatically terminate the appointment of the donee. If there is no replacement donee, then the power is revoked. However, cancellation of the registration still requires an application to the Public Guardian.

'the dissolution or annulment of a marriage or civil partnership' (s 13(6)(c))—This is an extension of the common law principle, which does not revoke an appointment on such an event. An enduring power of attorney, for instance, is not revoked on the divorce of the donee from the donor. This is a concept borrowed from the Wills Act 1837, which provides for the failure of the appointment of an executor or a gift in favour of a divorced spouse. Section 13(11) does, however, make such revocation subject to a contrary intention in the instrument appointing the donee.

14 Protection of donee and others if no power created or power revoked

(1) Subsections (2) and (3) apply if –
(a) an instrument has been registered under Schedule 1 as a lasting power of attorney, but

(b) a lasting power of attorney was not created,

whether or not the registration has been cancelled at the time of the act or transaction in question.

(2) A donee who acts in purported exercise of the power does not incur any liability (to P or any other person) because of the non-existence of the power unless at the time of acting he –

(a) knows that a lasting power of attorney was not created, or
(b) is aware of circumstances which, if a lasting power of attorney had been created, would have terminated his authority to act as a donee.

(3) Any transaction between the donee and another person is, in favour of that person, as valid as if the power had been in existence, unless at the time of the transaction that person has knowledge of a matter referred to in subsection (2).

(4) If the interest of a purchaser depends on whether a transaction between the donee and the other person was valid by virtue of subsection (3), it is conclusively presumed in favour of the purchaser that the transaction was valid if –

(a) the transaction was completed within 12 months of the date on which the instrument was registered, or
(b) the other person makes a statutory declaration, before or within 3 months after the completion of the purchase, that he had no reason at the time of the transaction to doubt that the donee had authority to dispose of the property which was the subject of the transaction.

(5) In its application to a lasting power of attorney which relates to matters in addition to P's property and affairs, section 5 of the Powers of Attorney Act 1971 (protection where power is revoked) has effect as if references to revocation included the cessation of the power in relation to P's property and affairs.

(6) Where two or more donees are appointed under a lasting power of attorney, this section applies as if references to the donee were to all or any of them.

Scope of provision—This repeats similar provisions in the Powers of Attorney Act 1971, s 5 and the Enduring Powers of Attorney Act 1985, s 9 (now MCA 2005, Sch 4, para 16) to protect an attorney and a third party dealing in good faith without knowledge of the non-existence of the power at the relevant time.

General powers of the court and appointment of deputies

15 Power to make declarations

(1) The court may make declarations as to –

(a) whether a person has or lacks capacity to make a decision specified in the declaration;
(b) whether a person has or lacks capacity to make decisions on such matters as are described in the declaration;
(c) the lawfulness or otherwise of any act done, or yet to be done, in relation to that person.

(2) 'Act' includes an omission and a course of conduct.

Scope of provision—This section confers on the Court the discretionary power to make declarations of the nature stated. This includes the initial decision as to whether there is a lack of capacity which will trigger the remaining jurisdiction of the Court. This new statutory jurisdiction largely replaces the former inherent jurisdiction previously assumed by the Family Division of the High Court to make declarations in respect of mentally incapacitated adults in regard to medical treatment and personal welfare.

Further explanation—This topic is covered in Part I, Chapter 4 of this work.

'**Lacks capacity**'—For the purposes of the Act this is defined in s 2.

16 Powers to make decisions and appoint deputies: general

(1) This section applies if a person ('P') lacks capacity in relation to a matter or matters concerning –

    (a) P's personal welfare, or
    (b) P's property and affairs.

(2) The court may –

    (a) by making an order, make the decision or decisions on P's behalf in relation to the matter or matters, or
    (b) appoint a person (a 'deputy') to make decisions on P's behalf in relation to the matter or matters.

(3) The powers of the court under this section are subject to the provisions of this Act and, in particular, to sections 1 (the principles) and 4 (best interests).

(4) When deciding whether it is in P's best interests to appoint a deputy, the court must have regard (in addition to the matters mentioned in section 4) to the principles that –

    (a) a decision by the court is to be preferred to the appointment of a deputy to make a decision, and
    (b) the powers conferred on a deputy should be as limited in scope and duration as is reasonably practicable in the circumstances.

(5) The court may make such further orders or give such directions, and confer on a deputy such powers or impose on him such duties, as it thinks necessary or expedient for giving effect to, or otherwise in connection with, an order or appointment made by it under subsection (2).

(6) Without prejudice to section 4, the court may make the order, give the directions or make the appointment on such terms as it considers are in P's best interests, even though no application is before the court for an order, directions or an appointment on those terms.

(7) An order of the court may be varied or discharged by a subsequent order.

(8) The court may, in particular, revoke the appointment of a deputy or vary the powers conferred on him if it is satisfied that the deputy –

    (a) has behaved, or is behaving, in a way that contravenes the authority conferred on him by the court or is not in P's best interests, or
    (b) proposes to behave in a way that would contravene that authority or would not be in P's best interests.

Scope of provision—This section confers on the Court the power to make decisions on behalf of an incapacitated adult or to appoint a deputy in respect of personal welfare or financial affairs. It also confirms the principles that must be applied, and a decision of the Court is to be preferred. The power may be exercised of the Court's own initiative and does not depend upon the specific application being made. Any order may be varied or discharged subsequently.

Further explanation—This topic is covered in Part I, Chapter 4 of this work.

'decisions'—The Court or the deputy may only make the decisions that P could have made and may not, for example, dictate what care provision is to be made for P.

'best interests'—See s 4 and Part I, Chapter 2 of this work.

'personal welfare'—Includes health care (s 17). For the extent of the power see s 17.

'property and affairs'—For examples of the powers that are generally exercised see s 18.

Excluded decisions—For decisions that may not be made see ss 27–29. For decisions that may not be made by a deputy see s 20.

'deputy'—See ss 19–20.

16A Section 16 powers: Mental Health Act patients etc

(1) If a person is ineligible to be deprived of liberty by this Act, the court may not include in a welfare order provision which authorises the person to be deprived of his liberty.

(2) If –

(a) a welfare order includes provision which authorises a person to be deprived of his liberty, and
(b) that person becomes ineligible to be deprived of liberty by this Act,
the provision ceases to have effect for as long as the person remains ineligible.

(3) Nothing in subsection (2) affects the power of the court under section 16(7) to vary or discharge the welfare order.

(4) For the purposes of this section –

(a) Schedule 1A applies for determining whether or not P is ineligible to be deprived of liberty by this Act;
(b) 'welfare order' means an order under section 16(2)(a).

Amendment—Section inserted by the Mental Health Act 2007, s 50(1), (3).

Scope of provision—As part of the Deprivation of Liberty safeguards implemented on 1 April 2009, this section secures that a person ineligible to be deprived of their liberty under this Act because they may be made subject to the compulsory powers for treatment of their mental disorder under the Mental Health Act 1983 (MHA 1983) (as amended) cannot be deprived of their liberty by a welfare order made by the Court of Protection. See s 4A above for the power of the Court to make a welfare order which deprives someone of their liberty. See Sch 1A for when someone is ineligible to be deprived of their liberty by this Act.

17 Section 16 powers: personal welfare

(1) The powers under section 16 as respects P's personal welfare extend in particular to –

(a) deciding where P is to live;
(b) deciding what contact, if any, P is to have with any specified persons;
(c) making an order prohibiting a named person from having contact with P;
(d) giving or refusing consent to the carrying out or continuation of a treatment by a person providing health care for P;

(e) giving a direction that a person responsible for P's health care allow a different person to take over that responsibility.

(2) Subsection (1) is subject to section 20 (restrictions on deputies).

Scope of provision—This section helpfully identifies the typical decisions that may be made in respect of personal welfare, but the powers of the Court are not restricted to these.

'consent to … treatment'—The Court does not have power to order that treatment shall be carried out.

Age—These powers only apply in respect of persons aged at least 16 years. Between ages 16 and 18 they overlap powers under the Children Act 1989.

Deputies—The powers of deputies are restricted under s 20.

18 Section 16 powers: property and affairs

(1) The powers under section 16 as respects P's property and affairs extend in particular to –

(a) the control and management of P's property;
(b) the sale, exchange, charging, gift or other disposition of P's property;
(c) the acquisition of property in P's name or on P's behalf;
(d) the carrying on, on P's behalf, of any profession, trade or business;
(e) the taking of a decision which will have the effect of dissolving a partnership of which P is a member;
(f) the carrying out of any contract entered into by P;
(g) the discharge of P's debts and of any of P's obligations, whether legally enforceable or not;
(h) the settlement of any of P's property, whether for P's benefit or for the benefit of others;
(i) the execution for P of a will;
(j) the exercise of any power (including a power to consent) vested in P whether beneficially or as trustee or otherwise;
(k) the conduct of legal proceedings in P's name or on P's behalf.

(2) No will may be made under subsection (1)(i) at a time when P has not reached 18.

(3) The powers under section 16 as respects any other matter relating to P's property and affairs may be exercised even though P has not reached 16, if the court considers it likely that P will still lack capacity to make decisions in respect of that matter when he reaches 18.

(4) Schedule 2 supplements the provisions of this section.

(5) Section 16(7) (variation and discharge of court orders) is subject to paragraph 6 of Schedule 2.

(6) Subsection (1) is subject to section 20 (restrictions on deputies).

Scope of provision—This section helpfully identifies the typical decisions that may be made in respect of property and affairs, and follows the powers of the former Court of Protection.

'property'—Includes any thing in action and any interest in real or personal property (s 64(1)).

'execution … of a will' (s 18(1)(i))—This refers to the so-called 'statutory will' which can be authorised by the Court (and was also within the powers of the former Court of Protection). This includes a codicil (s 64(1)).

'**conduct of legal proceedings**'—For civil proceedings see Civil Procedure Rules 1998, SI 1998/3132, Part 21 and for family proceedings see Family Procedure Rules 2010, SI 2010/2955, Part 15.

Gift or settlement—This power may be exercised to enable an attorney to make a gift or settlement which is beyond the authority of a lasting or enduring power of attorney.

Age—These powers generally only apply in respect of persons aged at least 16 years, but may be exercised where the Court is satisfied that the individual will lack capacity on attaining majority (s 18(3)). Typically this would be a child with a substantial damages award following a serious brain injury. However, a will may not be made for a person under the age of 18.

Deputies—The powers of deputies are restricted under s 20.

Schedule 2—This deals in particular with wills, vesting orders, variation of settlements and the preservation of interests in property disposed of on behalf of persons lacking capacity.

19 Appointment of deputies

(1) A deputy appointed by the court must be –

    (a) an individual who has reached 18, or
    (b) as respects powers in relation to property and affairs, an individual who has reached 18 or a trust corporation.

(2) The court may appoint an individual by appointing the holder for the time being of a specified office or position.

(3) A person may not be appointed as a deputy without his consent.

(4) The court may appoint two or more deputies to act –

    (a) jointly,
    (b) jointly and severally, or
    (c) jointly in respect of some matters and jointly and severally in respect of others.

(5) When appointing a deputy or deputies, the court may at the same time appoint one or more other persons to succeed the existing deputy or those deputies –

    (a) in such circumstances, or on the happening of such events, as may be specified by the court;
    (b) for such period as may be so specified.

(6) A deputy is to be treated as P's agent in relation to anything done or decided by him within the scope of his appointment and in accordance with this Part.

(7) The deputy is entitled –

    (a) to be reimbursed out of P's property for his reasonable expenses in discharging his functions, and
    (b) if the court so directs when appointing him, to remuneration out of P's property for discharging them.

(8) The court may confer on a deputy powers to –

    (a) take possession or control of all or any specified part of P's property;
    (b) exercise all or any specified powers in respect of it, including such powers of investment as the court may determine.

(9) The court may require a deputy –

(a) to give to the Public Guardian such security as the court thinks fit for the due discharge of his functions, and
(b) to submit to the Public Guardian such reports at such times or at such intervals as the court may direct.

Scope of provision—This section regulates the appointment of a deputy by the Court for an adult who lacks capacity. Such appointment will generally be made where property and affairs need to be managed, but is less likely in respect of personal welfare decisions that can be made by the Court on a one-off basis. Different deputies may be appointed for different functions.

Age—A deputy must be at least 18 years old.

Trust corporation (s 19(1)(b))—May be a deputy in regard to property and affairs but not personal welfare. But the holder for the time being of a specified office or position may be appointed. Trust corporation has the meaning given in the Trustee Act 1925, s 68(1) (s 64(1)).

Number—There is no restriction on the number of deputies that may be appointed for an incapacitated individual but in practice a single appointment is likely to be made for each type of decision unless there are circumstances justifying a joint appointment.

Succession (s 19(5))—This provision helpfully allows the Court to appoint successors whose powers arise in specified circumstances (e g on the death of the primary deputy).

Status (s 19(6))—The Act makes it clear that a deputy acts as agent rather than trustee.

Expenses—The deputy may be reimbursed for expenses and also charge remuneration when so authorised by the Court, but this depends upon the incapacitated person having financial resources and many personal welfare deputies will have to carry out their duties at their own expense.

Security (s 58(1)(e))—This is generally only required from a deputy for property and affairs. It is ordered by the Court and dealt with through the Office of the Public Guardian.

Reports (s 58(1)(f))—It is part of the functions of the Public Guardian to receive reports from deputies.

20 Restrictions on deputies

(1) A deputy does not have power to make a decision on behalf of P in relation to a matter if he knows or has reasonable grounds for believing that P has capacity in relation to the matter.

(2) Nothing in section 16(5) or 17 permits a deputy to be given power –

(a) to prohibit a named person from having contact with P;
(b) to direct a person responsible for P's health care to allow a different person to take over that responsibility.

(3) A deputy may not be given powers with respect to –

(a) the settlement of any of P's property, whether for P's benefit or for the benefit of others,
(b) the execution for P of a will, or
(c) the exercise of any power (including a power to consent) vested in P whether beneficially or as trustee or otherwise.

(4) A deputy may not be given power to make a decision on behalf of P which is inconsistent with a decision made, within the scope of his authority and in accordance with this Act, by the donee of a lasting power of attorney granted by P (or, if there is more than one donee, by any of them).

(5) A deputy may not refuse consent to the carrying out or continuation of life-sustaining treatment in relation to P.

(6) The authority conferred on a deputy is subject to the provisions of this Act and, in particular, sections 1 (the principles) and 4 (best interests).

(7) A deputy may not do an act that is intended to restrain P unless four conditions are satisfied.

(8) The first condition is that, in doing the act, the deputy is acting within the scope of an authority expressly conferred on him by the court.

(9) The second is that P lacks, or the deputy reasonably believes that P lacks, capacity in relation to the matter in question.

(10) The third is that the deputy reasonably believes that it is necessary to do the act in order to prevent harm to P.

(11) The fourth is that the act is a proportionate response to –
   (a) the likelihood of P's suffering harm, and
   (b) the seriousness of that harm.

(12) For the purposes of this section, a deputy restrains P if he –
   (a) uses, or threatens to use, force to secure the doing of an act which P resists, or
   (b) restricts P's liberty of movement, whether or not P resists,

or if he authorises another person to do any of those things.

(13) ...

Amendment—Mental Health Act 2007, ss 50(1), (4)(c), 51, 55, Sch 11, Pt 10.

Scope of provision—This section confirms the underlying principle that decisions may only be made for adults who are unable to make those decisions for themselves, and identifies a range of decisions that the Court cannot delegate to deputies but must make itself. It then imposes restrictions on the exercise of a deputy's powers.

Lasting power of attorney—A valid decision of a donee may not be overridden by a deputy.

Restraint—Four conditions precedent apply to the exercise of any powers of restraint by a deputy. These are required to make the Act human rights compliant.

Deprivation of liberty—See generally Part I, Chapter 6 of this work.

21 Transfer of proceedings relating to people under 18

(1) The Lord Chief Justice, with the concurrence of the Lord Chancellor, may by order make provision as to the transfer of proceedings relating to a person under 18, in such circumstances as are specified in the order –
   (a) from the Court of Protection to a court having jurisdiction under the Children Act 1989, or
   (b) from a court having jurisdiction under that Act to the Court of Protection.

(2) The Lord Chief Justice may nominate any of the following to exercise his functions under this section –
   (a) the President of the Court of Protection;
   (b) a judicial office holder (as defined in section 109(4) of the Constitutional Reform Act 2005).

Amendments—SI 2006/1016.

Provision—Mental Capacity Act 2005 (Transfer of Proceedings) Order 2007, SI 2007/1899.

Powers of the court in relation to Schedule A1

Amendments—Heading inserted by Mental Health Act 2007, s 50(7), Sch 9, Pt 1, paras 1, 2.

21A Powers of court in relation to Schedule A1

(1) This section applies if either of the following has been given under Schedule A1 –

    (a) a standard authorisation;
    (b) an urgent authorisation.

(2) Where a standard authorisation has been given, the court may determine any question relating to any of the following matters –

    (a) whether the relevant person meets one or more of the qualifying requirements;
    (b) the period during which the standard authorisation is to be in force;
    (c) the purpose for which the standard authorisation is given;
    (d) the conditions subject to which the standard authorisation is given.

(3) If the court determines any question under subsection (2), the court may make an order –

    (a) varying or terminating the standard authorisation, or
    (b) directing the supervisory body to vary or terminate the standard authorisation.

(4) Where an urgent authorisation has been given, the court may determine any question relating to any of the following matters –

    (a) whether the urgent authorisation should have been given;
    (b) the period during which the urgent authorisation is to be in force;
    (c) the purpose for which the urgent authorisation is given.

(5) Where the court determines any question under subsection (4), the court may make an order—

    (a) varying or terminating the urgent authorisation, or
    (b) directing the managing authority of the relevant hospital or care home to vary or terminate the urgent authorisation.

(6) Where the court makes an order under subsection (3) or (5), the court may make an order about a person's liability for any act done in connection with the standard or urgent authorisation before its variation or termination.

(7) An order under subsection (6) may, in particular, exclude a person from liability.

Amendments—Inserted by Mental Health Act 2007, s 50(7), Sch 9, Pt 1, paras 1, 2.

Scope of provision—As part of the Deprivation of Liberty safeguards, this section ensures compliance with Art 5(4) of the ECHR by giving the Court of Protection jurisdiction to review the lawfulness of the detention of anyone for whom authorisation has been granted to provide care or treatment in conditions which amount to a deprivation of their liberty. The Court of Appeal in *G v E* [2010] EWCA Civ 822, [2010] COPLR Con Vol 431 confirmed that the scheme implemented by this section and Sch A1 is compatible with Art 5 of the ECHR. In *Re UF* [2013] EWHC 4289 (COP), [2014] COPLR 93, Charles J expressed the view that, where an application is made under MCA 2005, s 21A, the Court can either (1) take control of the matter itself and grant interim relief and authorisations under MCA 2005, ss 15–16; or (2) reach effectively the same result under s 21A, by continuing in force the relevant authorisation, or otherwise bringing about the result that a standard authorisation is in existence. Charles J held that the Court has the power 'to vary an existing standard authorisation by extending (or shortening) it and that if and when it exercises that power it would normally be sensible for the court to give consideration to whether it should then exercise its powers under sub-sections (6) and (7) or give directions concerning its future exercise of those powers,' but doubted that the Court would have the power to extend a standard authorisation beyond the possible maximum period of one year. In the judgment Charles J also recorded concessions by the Ministry of Justice and the Legal Aid Agency that, despite the wording of Regulation 5(1)(g) of the Civil Legal Aid (Financial Resources and Payment for Services) Regulations 2013 to apparently contrary effect, the 'taking control' by the Court of the authorisation of a deprivation of liberty by the making of orders under MCA 2005, s 16 and the consequent coming to an end of any existing standard authorisation would not be regarded as a contrivance giving rise to the removal of non-means-tested public funding (see further **8.105–107**). Where P lacks the relevant decision-making capacity, once its jurisdiction has been invoked under MCA 2005, s 21A, the court has wide powers under MCA 2005, s 16 to make decisions on P's behalf in relation to matters concerning his personal welfare or property or affairs: *CC v KK and STCC* [2012] EWHC 2136 (COP), [2012] COPLR 627 at para [16] per Baker J. In *AB v LCC (A Local Authority) and the Care Manager of BCH* [2011] EWHC 3151 (COP), [2012] COPLR 314, Mostyn J indicated that Parliament had made it clear that relevant persons' representatives should play a central role in challenges under s 21A of the MCA 2005 (inter alia as they did not require permission to bring applications under s 21A), and exhorted consideration being given to paid RPRs acting as applicant (and as P's litigation friend). See also **7.80** and **9.45–9.75**.

'**Standard authorisation**' (s 21A(1)(a))—An authorisation given under Part 4 of Sch A1 authorising deprivation of liberty for a period of up to 12 months. The procedures and qualifying requirements for a standard authorisation are described in Part I, Chapter 6 of this work.

'**Urgent authorisation**' (s 21A(1)(b))—An authorisation given under Part 5 of Sch A1 authorising deprivation of liberty in urgent circumstances for up to 7 days (renewable for a further 7 days) while a standard authorisation is obtained. The procedures to obtain an urgent authorisation are described in Part I, Chapter 6 of this work.

'**supervisory body**' (s 21A(3)(b))—See definitions at Sch A1, paras 180–182.

'**managing authority**' (s 21A(5)(b))—See definitions at Sch A1, paras 176,177 and 179.

Powers of the court in relation to lasting powers of attorney

22 Powers of court in relation to validity of lasting powers of attorney

(1) This section and section 23 apply if –

    (a) a person ('P') has executed or purported to execute an instrument with a view to creating a lasting power of attorney, or

    (b) an instrument has been registered as a lasting power of attorney conferred by P.

(2) The court may determine any question relating to –

    (a) whether one or more of the requirements for the creation of a lasting power of attorney have been met;

    (b) whether the power has been revoked or has otherwise come to an end.

(3) Subsection (4) applies if the court is satisfied –

    (a) that fraud or undue pressure was used to induce P –

        (i) to execute an instrument for the purpose of creating a lasting power of attorney, or

        (ii) to create a lasting power of attorney, or

(b) that the donee (or, if more than one, any of them) of a lasting power of attorney –
    (i) has behaved, or is behaving, in a way that contravenes his authority or is not in P's best interests, or
    (ii) proposes to behave in a way that would contravene his authority or would not be in P's best interests.

(4) The court may –
    (a) direct that an instrument purporting to create the lasting power of attorney is not to be registered, or
    (b) if P lacks capacity to do so, revoke the instrument or the lasting power of attorney.

(5) If there is more than one donee, the court may under subsection (4)(b) revoke the instrument or the lasting power of attorney so far as it relates to any of them.

(6) 'Donee' includes an intended donee.

Scope of provision—The Court of Protection has jurisdiction for determining issues concerning the validity of a lasting power of attorney (as opposed to a formal defect which the Public Guardian can deal with).

'contravenes his authority or is not in P's best interests' (s 22(3)(b))—The Court may revoke the power if satisfied that the donee has behaved or proposes to behave in such a way. At the time of publication, no case has yet been brought before the Court on these grounds. An application to revoke a lasting power of attorney on such grounds requires a high standard of proof and this contrasts with the more flexible grounds of 'unsuitability' that apply to enduring powers of attorney – see Sch 4, para 16(4)(g).

'purported to execute an instrument' (s 22(1)(a))—The Court's powers are also exercisable before the instrument is registered, and before it is actually a lasting power of attorney.

23 Powers of court in relation to operation of lasting powers of attorney

(1) The court may determine any question as to the meaning or effect of a lasting power of attorney or an instrument purporting to create one.

(2) The court may –
    (a) give directions with respect to decisions –
        (i) which the donee of a lasting power of attorney has authority to make, and
        (ii) which P lacks capacity to make;
    (b) give any consent or authorisation to act which the donee would have to obtain from P if P had capacity to give it.

(3) The court may, if P lacks capacity to do so –
    (a) give directions to the donee with respect to the rendering by him of reports or accounts and the production of records kept by him for that purpose;
    (b) require the donee to supply information or produce documents or things in his possession as donee;
    (c) give directions with respect to the remuneration or expenses of the donee;
    (d) relieve the donee wholly or partly from any liability which he has or may have incurred on account of a breach of his duties as donee.

(4) The court may authorise the making of gifts which are not within section 12(2) (permitted gifts).

(5) Where two or more donees are appointed under a lasting power of attorney, this section applies as if references to the donee were to all or any of them.

Scope of provision—It is for the Court to provide authority for the attorney to carry out certain acts that are otherwise beyond the scope of his or her authority, or to require the attorney to carry out a particular act.

'the Court may authorise the making of gifts' (s 23(4))—The Court may authorise the attorney to make gifts on an application by the attorney. This is without prejudice to the Court's powers to authorise the making of gifts under s 16(1)(b).

Advance decisions to refuse treatment

24 Advance decisions to refuse treatment: general

(1) 'Advance decision' means a decision made by a person ('P'), after he has reached 18 and when he has capacity to do so, that if –

    (a) at a later time and in such circumstances as he may specify, a specified treatment is proposed to be carried out or continued by a person providing health care for him, and

    (b) at that time he lacks capacity to consent to the carrying out or continuation of the treatment,

the specified treatment is not to be carried out or continued.

(2) For the purposes of subsection (1)(a), a decision may be regarded as specifying a treatment or circumstances even though expressed in layman's terms.

(3) P may withdraw or alter an advance decision at any time when he has capacity to do so.

(4) A withdrawal (including a partial withdrawal) need not be in writing.

(5) An alteration of an advance decision need not be in writing (unless section 25(5) applies in relation to the decision resulting from the alteration).

Scope of provision—This and the following two sections provide the statutory framework within which advance decisions refusing specified medical treatment are to be given effect. They are discussed in Part I, Chapter 6 of this work. In *W v M* [2011] EWHC 2443 (Fam), [2012] COPLR 222, a case concerning withdrawal of treatment from a person in a minimally conscious state, where the individual concerned had not made any statement complying with the provisions of ss 24–25 (and had lost the relevant capacity substantially prior to the coming into force of MCA 2005), Baker J emphasised that that the importance of the preservation of life meant that only limited weight could be placed on statements made by M to her family regarding her wishes as to life-sustaining treatment. However, see the recent decision of Pauffley J in *United Lincolnshire Hospital Trust v N* [2014] EWCOP 16, [2014] COPLR 660 in which the Court went further than any case before involving a protected party in a minimally conscious state by declaring that it was not in N's best interests for the Trust to make any further attempts to establish and maintain a method for providing N with artificial nutrition. The facts were somewhat similar to *W v M* in that N had not made a statement complying with ss 24–25, her comments were of a similar level of generality to those expressed by M, and the views expressed by the families of the two women as to what they would have wished were materially identical. However, in N's case they were given very significant weight, but in M's case they were not. See **6.36** for further discussion of these cases.

'An alteration of an advance decision' (s 24(5))—Needs only be in writing if the effect of the alteration is a decision to refuse a life-sustaining treatment even though life is at risk.

25 Validity and applicability of advance decisions

(1) An advance decision does not affect the liability which a person may incur for carrying out or continuing a treatment in relation to P unless the decision is at the material time –

   (a) valid, and
   (b) applicable to the treatment.

(2) An advance decision is not valid if P –

   (a) has withdrawn the decision at a time when he had capacity to do so,
   (b) has, under a lasting power of attorney created after the advance decision was made, conferred authority on the donee (or, if more than one, any of them) to give or refuse consent to the treatment to which the advance decision relates, or
   (c) has done anything else clearly inconsistent with the advance decision remaining his fixed decision.

(3) An advance decision is not applicable to the treatment in question if at the material time P has capacity to give or refuse consent to it.

(4) An advance decision is not applicable to the treatment in question if –

   (a) that treatment is not the treatment specified in the advance decision,
   (b) any circumstances specified in the advance decision are absent, or
   (c) there are reasonable grounds for believing that circumstances exist which P did not anticipate at the time of the advance decision and which would have affected his decision had he anticipated them.

(5) An advance decision is not applicable to life-sustaining treatment unless –

   (a) the decision is verified by a statement by P to the effect that it is to apply to that treatment even if life is at risk, and
   (b) the decision and statement comply with subsection (6).

(6) A decision or statement complies with this subsection only if –

   (a) it is in writing,
   (b) it is signed by P or by another person in P's presence and by P's direction,
   (c) the signature is made or acknowledged by P in the presence of a witness, and
   (d) the witness signs it, or acknowledges his signature, in P's presence.

(7) The existence of any lasting power of attorney other than one of a description mentioned in subsection (2)(b) does not prevent the advance decision from being regarded as valid and applicable.

'Under a lasting power of attorney' (s 25(2)(b))—See ss 9–14.

26 Effect of advance decisions

(1) If P has made an advance decision which is –

   (a) valid, and
   (b) applicable to a treatment,

the decision has effect as if he had made it, and had had capacity to make it, at the time when the question arises whether the treatment should be carried out or continued.

(2) A person does not incur liability for carrying out or continuing the treatment unless, at the time, he is satisfied that an advance decision exists which is valid and applicable to the treatment.

(3) A person does not incur liability for the consequences of withholding or withdrawing a treatment from P if, at the time, he reasonably believes that an advance decision exists which is valid and applicable to the treatment.

(4) The court may make a declaration as to whether an advance decision –

  (a) exists;
  (b) is valid;
  (c) is applicable to a treatment.

(5) Nothing in an apparent advance decision stops a person –

  (a) providing life-sustaining treatment, or
  (b) doing any act he reasonably believes to be necessary to prevent a serious deterioration in P's condition,

while a decision as respects any relevant issue is sought from the court.

'**Has effect ...**' (s 26(1))—A valid and applicable advance refusal of treatment is to be respected as a binding decision by the person concerned. See the note to s 24 above as to the cases of *W v M* and *United Lincolnshire Hospital Trust v N*.

'**Any relevant issue**' (s 26(5))—Examples are whether an advance decision has been made, whether it is valid and applicable as applying to the specified treatment or whether it has been revoked or the maker has acted inconsistently with this being his or her fixed intent.

Excluded decisions

27 Family relationships etc

(1) Nothing in this Act permits a decision on any of the following matters to be made on behalf of a person –

  (a) consenting to marriage or a civil partnership,
  (b) consenting to have sexual relations,
  (c) consenting to a decree of divorce being granted on the basis of two years' separation,
  (d) consenting to a dissolution order being made in relation to a civil partnership on the basis of two years' separation,
  (e) consenting to a child's being placed for adoption by an adoption agency,
  (f) consenting to the making of an adoption order,
  (g) discharging parental responsibilities in matters not relating to a child's property,
  (h) giving a consent under the Human Fertilisation and Embryology Act 1990,
  (i) giving a consent under the Human Fertilisation and Embryology Act 2008.

(2) 'Adoption order' means –

  (a) an adoption order within the meaning of the Adoption and Children Act 2002 (including a future adoption order), and
  (b) an order under section 84 of that Act (parental responsibility prior to adoption abroad).

Amendment—Paragraph (1)(i) inserted by Human Fertilisation and Embryology Act 2008, s 56, Sch 6, Pt 1, para 40.

Scope of provision—There are certain acts and decisions which can never be made under the Act on behalf of a person who lacks capacity to make such decisions for themselves, either because they are so personal to the individual concerned or because they are governed by other legislation. This section excludes specified decisions on family relationships from being taken on behalf of a person lacking capacity to make the decision in question. The Court of Protection retains the power to make declarations under MCA 2005, s 15 with regard to the person's capacity to consent to such matters.

'civil partnership' (s 27(1)(a))—As defined in the Civil Partnership Act 2004, s 1.

'sexual relations' (s 27(1)(b))—While the Act does not permit anyone to consent to sexual relations on behalf of a person lacking capacity to consent, this does not prevent action being taken under the common law to protect a vulnerable person from abuse or exploitation or under the criminal law (Sexual Offences Act 2003) if a sexual offence has been committed (see *R v C* [2009] UKHL 42).

'decree of divorce' (s 27(1)(c)); **'dissolution order'** (s 27(1)(d))—Where a person lacking capacity becomes involved in divorce or dissolution proceedings on any basis other than 2 years' separation, or where someone loses capacity during the course of such proceedings, a litigation friend will be appointed under the Family Procedure Rules 2010, SI 2010/2955, Part IX to give instructions and otherwise act on their behalf in relation to the proceedings.

'adoption order' (s 27(1)(f))—Defined in s 27(2).

'parental responsibilities' (s 27(1)(g))—Matters concerned with the discharging of parental responsibilities not related to a child's property are dealt with under the Children Act 1989. In the discharge of such responsibilities a person cannot consent to a state of affairs amounting to a deprivation of their child's liberty: *RK v (1) BCC (2) YB (3) AK* [2011] EWCA Civ 1305, [2012] COPLR 146.

28 Mental Health Act matters

(1) Nothing in this Act authorises anyone –

  (a) to give a patient medical treatment for mental disorder, or

  (b) to consent to a patient's being given medical treatment for mental disorder,

if, at the time when it is proposed to treat the patient, his treatment is regulated by Part 4 of the Mental Health Act.

(1A) Subsection (1) does not apply in relation to any form of treatment to which section 58A of that Act (electro-convulsive therapy, etc) applies if the patient comes within subsection (7) of that section (informal patient under 18 who cannot give consent).

(1B) Section 5 does not apply to an act to which section 64B of the Mental Health Act applies (treatment of community patients not recalled to hospital).

(2) 'Medical treatment', 'mental disorder' and 'patient' have the same meaning as in that Act.

Amendments—Subsections (1A) and (1B) inserted by the Mental Health Act 2007, s 28(10), s 35(4), (5): SI 2008/1900.

Scope of provision—This confirms that the Act's decision-making powers cannot be used to give or to consent to treatment for mental disorder if the treatment is regulated by MHA 1983, Part 4. The powers available under Part 4 take precedence over the decision-making powers under MCA 2005 in relation to treatment for mental disorder of detained patients.

'regulated by Part 4 of the Mental Health Act' (s 28(1))—The purpose of Part 4 is to clarify the extent to which treatment for mental disorder can be imposed on detained patients in hospital and to provide specific statutory safeguards concerning the provision of treatment without consent (MHA 1983, ss 57–58).

'electro-convulsive therapy' (s 28(1A))—New requirements for patients to consent to ECT are set out in MHA 1983, s 58A (inserted by MHA 2007, s 27). Section 28(1A) allows patients aged 16-17 who lack capacity to consent to ECT to be treated under MCA 2005, s 5, rather than using MHA powers, so long as the treatment is in their best interests, does not amount to a deprivation of their liberty and a Second Opinion Appointed Doctor considers ECT to be appropriate.

'community patients' (s 28(1B))—Means patients being treated compulsorily under a community treatment order made under MHA 1983, s 17A (inserted by MHA 2007, s 32). Section 28(1B) prohibits such patients being treated under s 5, requiring MHA powers to be used instead.

'Medical treatment'—Includes nursing and also psychological intervention and specialist mental health habilitation, rehabilitation and care; and is to be construed as a reference to medical treatment the purpose of which is to alleviate, or prevent a worsening of, the disorder or one or more of its symptoms or manifestations (MHA 1983, s 145, as amended by MHA 2007, s 7).

'Mental disorder'—Means any disorder or disability of the mind (MHA 1983, s 1(2), as amended and simplified by MHA 2007, s 1(2)).

'Patient'—Means a person suffering or appearing to be suffering from mental disorder (MHA 1983, s 145).

29 Voting rights

(1) Nothing in this Act permits a decision on voting at an election for any public office, or at a referendum, to be made on behalf of a person.

(2) 'Referendum' has the same meaning as in section 101 of the Political Parties, Elections and Referendums Act 2000.

Scope of provision—This confirms that no one can make a decision on voting or cast a vote at an election or a referendum on behalf of a person lacking capacity to vote.

Research

30 Research

(1) Intrusive research carried out on, or in relation to, a person who lacks capacity to consent to it is unlawful unless it is carried out –

  (a) as part of a research project which is for the time being approved by the appropriate body for the purposes of this Act in accordance with section 31, and
  (b) in accordance with sections 32 and 33.

(2) Research is intrusive if it is of a kind that would be unlawful if it was carried out –

  (a) on or in relation to a person who had capacity to consent to it, but
  (b) without his consent.

(3) A clinical trial which is subject to the provisions of clinical trials regulations is not to be treated as research for the purposes of this section.

(3A) Research is not intrusive to the extent that it consists of the use of a person's human cells to bring about the creation in vitro of an embryo or human admixed embryo, or the subsequent storage or use of an embryo or human admixed embryo so created.

(3B) Expressions used in subsection (3A) and in Schedule 3 to the Human Fertilisation and Embryology Act 1990 (consents to use or storage of gametes, embryos or human admixed embryos etc.) have the same meaning in that subsection as in that Schedule.

(4) 'Appropriate body', in relation to a research project, means the person, committee or other body specified in regulations made by the appropriate authority as the appropriate body in relation to a project of the kind in question.

(5) 'Clinical trials regulations' means –
   (a) the Medicines for Human Use (Clinical Trials) Regulations 2004 and any other regulations replacing those regulations or amending them, and
   (b) any other regulations relating to clinical trials and designated by the Secretary of State as clinical trials regulations for the purposes of this section.

(6) In this section, section 32 and section 34, 'appropriate authority' means –
   (a) in relation to the carrying out of research in England, the Secretary of State, and
   (b) in relation to the carrying out of research in Wales, the National Assembly for Wales.

Amendment—Subsections (3A) and (3B) inserted by Human Fertilisation and Embryology Act 2008, s 65, Sch 7, para 25.

Scope of provision—This section, ss 31–34 and the Regulations and Guidance referred to in the notes provide the legal framework within which beneficial research in relation to impairing conditions may be carried out on someone who is unable to consent, subject to the safeguards provided. These provisions are discussed in Part I, Chapter 6 of this work.

'Appropriate body' (s 30(1))—Prescribed in the Mental Capacity Act 2005 (Appropriate Body) (England) Regulations 2006, SI 2006/2810 as a committee established to advise on, or on matters which include, the ethics of intrusive research in relation to people who lack capacity to consent to it and recognised for that purpose by the Secretary of State. For Wales, see the equivalent 2007 Regulations approved by the Minister for Health and Social Services (SI 2007/833 (W 71)).

'Clinical trials regulations' (s 30(5))—See SI 2004/3224, SI 2005/2754, SI 2005/2759, SI 2006/562, SI 2006/1928, SI 2006/2984, SI 2007/289, SI 2007/3101, SI 2008/192, SI 2008/941, SI 2009/389, SI 2009/1164, SI 2010/231, SI 2010/504, SI 2010/551, SI 2010/1882, SI 2011/2531, 2011/2581, SI 2012/134, SI 2012/504, SI 2012/1479, SI 2012/1641, SI 2012/1916, SI 2013/235, SI 2013/532 for amendments to the Medicines for Human Use (Clinical Trials) Regulations 2004.

'Secretary of State' (s 30(6))—For England the appropriate authority is the Secretary of State for Health.

31 Requirements for approval

(1) The appropriate body may not approve a research project for the purposes of this Act unless satisfied that the following requirements will be met in relation to research carried out as part of the project on, or in relation to, a person who lacks capacity to consent to taking part in the project ('P').

(2) The research must be connected with –
   (a) an impairing condition affecting P, or
   (b) its treatment.

(3) 'Impairing condition' means a condition which is (or may be) attributable to, or which causes or contributes to (or may cause or contribute to), the impairment of, or disturbance in the functioning of, the mind or brain.

(4) There must be reasonable grounds for believing that research of comparable effectiveness cannot be carried out if the project has to be confined to, or relate only to, persons who have capacity to consent to taking part in it.

(5) The research must –

- (a) have the potential to benefit P without imposing on P a burden that is disproportionate to the potential benefit to P, or
- (b) be intended to provide knowledge of the causes or treatment of, or of the care of persons affected by, the same or a similar condition.

(6) If the research falls within paragraph (b) of subsection (5) but not within paragraph (a), there must be reasonable grounds for believing –

- (a) that the risk to P from taking part in the project is likely to be negligible, and
- (b) that anything done to, or in relation to, P will not –
    - (i) interfere with P's freedom of action or privacy in a significant way, or
    - (ii) be unduly invasive or restrictive.

(7) There must be reasonable arrangements in place for ensuring that the requirements of sections 32 and 33 will be met.

Scope of provision—This section sets out the primary requirements which must be met before a research project which includes research on a person who cannot consent can be approved.

'Appropriate body' (s 31(1))—See note to s 30(1).

32 Consulting carers etc

(1) This section applies if a person ('R') –

- (a) is conducting an approved research project, and
- (b) wishes to carry out research, as part of the project, on or in relation to a person ('P') who lacks capacity to consent to taking part in the project.

(2) R must take reasonable steps to identify a person who –

- (a) otherwise than in a professional capacity or for remuneration, is engaged in caring for P or is interested in P's welfare, and
- (b) is prepared to be consulted by R under this section.

(3) If R is unable to identify such a person he must, in accordance with guidance issued by the appropriate authority, nominate a person who –

- (a) is prepared to be consulted by R under this section, but
- (b) has no connection with the project.

(4) R must provide the person identified under subsection (2), or nominated under subsection (3), with information about the project and ask him –

- (a) for advice as to whether P should take part in the project, and
- (b) what, in his opinion, P's wishes and feelings about taking part in the project would be likely to be if P had capacity in relation to the matter.

(5) If, at any time, the person consulted advises R that in his opinion P's wishes and feelings would be likely to lead him to decline to take part in the project (or to wish to withdraw from it) if he had capacity in relation to the matter, R must ensure –

(a) if P is not already taking part in the project, that he does not take part in it;
(b) if P is taking part in the project, that he is withdrawn from it.

(6) But subsection (5)(b) does not require treatment that P has been receiving as part of the project to be discontinued if R has reasonable grounds for believing that there would be a significant risk to P's health if it were discontinued.

(7) The fact that a person is the donee of a lasting power of attorney given by P, or is P's deputy, does not prevent him from being the person consulted under this section.

(8) Subsection (9) applies if treatment is being, or is about to be, provided for P as a matter of urgency and R considers that, having regard to the nature of the research and of the particular circumstances of the case –

(a) it is also necessary to take action for the purposes of the research as a matter of urgency, but
(b) it is not reasonably practicable to consult under the previous provisions of this section.

(9) R may take the action if –

(a) he has the agreement of a registered medical practitioner who is not involved in the organisation or conduct of the research project, or
(b) where it is not reasonably practicable in the time available to obtain that agreement, he acts in accordance with a procedure approved by the appropriate body at the time when the research project was approved under section 31.

(10) But R may not continue to act in reliance on subsection (9) if he has reasonable grounds for believing that it is no longer necessary to take the action as a matter of urgency.

'**In accordance with guidance issued by the appropriate authority**' (s 32(3))—Guidance has been issued by the Department of Health in partnership with the Welsh Assembly Government in February 2008 (see www.dh.gov.uk/publications).

33 Additional safeguards

(1) This section applies in relation to a person who is taking part in an approved research project even though he lacks capacity to consent to taking part.

(2) Nothing may be done to, or in relation to, him in the course of the research –

(a) to which he appears to object (whether by showing signs of resistance or otherwise) except where what is being done is intended to protect him from harm or to reduce or prevent pain or discomfort, or
(b) which would be contrary to –
  (i) an advance decision of his which has effect, or
  (ii) any other form of statement made by him and not subsequently withdrawn,

of which R is aware.

(3) The interests of the person must be assumed to outweigh those of science and society.

(4) If he indicates (in any way) that he wishes to be withdrawn from the project he must be withdrawn without delay.

(5) P must be withdrawn from the project, without delay, if at any time the person conducting the research has reasonable grounds for believing that one or more of the requirements set out in section 31(2) to (7) is no longer met in relation to research being carried out on, or in relation to, P.

(6) But neither subsection (4) nor subsection (5) requires treatment that P has been receiving as part of the project to be discontinued if R has reasonable grounds for believing that there would be a significant risk to P's health if it were discontinued.

'An advance decision ... which has effect' (s 33(2)(b))—See ss 24–26.

34 Loss of capacity during research project

(1) This section applies where a person ('P') –

(a) has consented to take part in a research project begun before the commencement of section 30, but
(b) before the conclusion of the project, loses capacity to consent to continue to take part in it.

(2) The appropriate authority may by regulations provide that, despite P's loss of capacity, research of a prescribed kind may be carried out on, or in relation to, P if –

(a) the project satisfies prescribed requirements,
(b) any information or material relating to P which is used in the research is of a prescribed description and was obtained before P's loss of capacity, and
(c) the person conducting the project takes in relation to P such steps as may be prescribed for the purpose of protecting him.

(3) The regulations may, in particular, –

(a) make provision about when, for the purposes of the regulations, a project is to be treated as having begun;
(b) include provision similar to any made by section 31, 32 or 33.

'**Regulations**' (s 34(2))—See the Mental Capacity Act 2005 (Loss of Capacity during Research Project) (England) Regulations 2007, SI 2007/679 and equivalent Welsh Regulations (SI 2007/837 (W 72)).

Independent mental capacity advocate service

35 Appointment of independent mental capacity advocates

(1) The responsible authority must make such arrangements as it considers reasonable to enable persons ('independent mental capacity advocates') to be available to represent and support persons to whom acts or decisions proposed under sections 37, 38 and 39 relate or persons who fall within section 39A, 39C or 39D.

(2) The appropriate authority may make regulations as to the appointment of independent mental capacity advocates.

(3) The regulations may, in particular, provide –

(a) that a person may act as an independent mental capacity advocate only in such circumstances, or only subject to such conditions, as may be prescribed;

(b) for the appointment of a person as an independent mental capacity advocate to be subject to approval in accordance with the regulations.

(4) In making arrangements under subsection (1), the responsible authority must have regard to the principle that a person to whom a proposed act or decision relates should, so far as practicable, be represented and supported by a person who is independent of any person who will be responsible for the act or decision.

(5) The arrangements may include provision for payments to be made to, or in relation to, persons carrying out functions in accordance with the arrangements.

(6) For the purpose of enabling him to carry out his functions, an independent mental capacity advocate –

(a) may interview in private the person whom he has been instructed to represent, and
(b) may, at all reasonable times, examine and take copies of –
 (i) any health record,
 (ii) any record of, or held by, a local authority and compiled in connection with a social services function, and
 (iii) any record held by a person registered under Part 2 of the Care Standards Act 2000 [or Chapter 2 of Part I of the Health and Social Care Act 2008],

which the person holding the record considers may be relevant to the independent mental capacity advocate's investigation.

(6A) In subsections (1) and (4), 'the responsible authority' means –

(a) in relation to the provision of the services of independent mental capacity advocates in the area of a local authority in England, that local authority, and
(b) in relation to the provision of the services of independent mental capacity advocates in Wales, the Welsh Ministers.

(6B) In subsection (6A)(a), 'local authority' has the meaning given in section 64(1) except that it does not include the council of a county or county borough in Wales.

(7) In this section, section 36 and section 37, 'the appropriate authority' means –

(a) in relation to the provision of the services of independent mental capacity advocates in England, the Secretary of State, and
(b) in relation to the provision of the services of independent mental capacity advocates in Wales, the National Assembly for Wales.

Amendment—Mental Health Act 2007, s 50(7), Sch 9, Pt 1, paras 1, 3; SI 2010/813; Health and Social Care Act 2012.

Scope of provision—The Secretary of State for Health in England and National Assembly for Wales have discharged their duty to make arrangements (s 35(1)) to make available independent mental capacity advocates through the provision of local funding, circulars and the Regulations referred to in the notes to this and the following sections (see http://webarchive.nationalarchives.gov.uk/+/www.dh.gov.uk/en/SocialCare/Deliveringadultsocialcare/MentalCapacity/IMCA/index.htm). IMCAs are a locally contracted service and there are a large number of different providers in different parts of the country. See further chapter 6 in Part I of this work.

'Regulations' (s 35(2))—For England see the Mental Capacity Act 2005 (Independent Mental Capacity Advocates) (General) Regulations 2006, SI 2006/1832 as amended by the Mental Health and Mental Capacity (Advocacy) Amendment (England) Regulations 2009, SI 2009/2376 and for Wales the Mental Capacity Act 2005 (Independent Mental Capacity Advocates) (Wales) Regulations 2007, SI 2007/852 (W 77) and the Mental Capacity (Deprivation of Liberty: Appointment of Relevant Person's Representative) (Wales) Regulations 2009, SI 2009/266 (W 29).

36 Functions of independent mental capacity advocates

(1) The appropriate authority may make regulations as to the functions of independent mental capacity advocates.

(2) The regulations may, in particular, make provision requiring an advocate to take such steps as may be prescribed for the purpose of –

  (a) providing support to the person whom he has been instructed to represent ('P') so that P may participate as fully as possible in any relevant decision;
  (b) obtaining and evaluating relevant information;
  (c) ascertaining what P's wishes and feelings would be likely to be, and the beliefs and values that would be likely to influence P, if he had capacity;
  (d) ascertaining what alternative courses of action are available in relation to P;
  (e) obtaining a further medical opinion where treatment is proposed and the advocate thinks that one should be obtained.

(3) The regulations may also make provision as to circumstances in which the advocate may challenge, or provide assistance for the purpose of challenging, any relevant decision.

'**Regulations**'—See the Mental Capacity Act 2005 (Independent Mental Capacity Advocates) (General) Regulations 2006, SI 2006/1832 and for Wales SI 2007/852 (W 77).

37 Provision of serious medical treatment by NHS body

(1) This section applies if an NHS body –

  (a) is proposing to provide, or secure the provision of, serious medical treatment for a person ('P') who lacks capacity to consent to the treatment, and
  (b) is satisfied that there is no person, other than one engaged in providing care or treatment for P in a professional capacity or for remuneration, whom it would be appropriate to consult in determining what would be in P's best interests.

(2) But this section does not apply if P's treatment is regulated by Part 4 or 4A of the Mental Health Act.

(3) Before the treatment is provided, the NHS body must instruct an independent mental capacity advocate to represent P.

(4) If the treatment needs to be provided as a matter of urgency, it may be provided even though the NHS body has not been able to comply with subsection (3).

(5) The NHS body must, in providing or securing the provision of treatment for P, take into account any information given, or submissions made, by the independent mental capacity advocate.

(6) 'Serious medical treatment' means treatment which involves providing, withholding or withdrawing treatment of a kind prescribed by regulations made by the appropriate authority.

(7) 'NHS body' has such meaning as may be prescribed by regulations made for the purposes of this section by –

  (a) the Secretary of State, in relation to bodies in England, or
  (b) the National Assembly for Wales, in relation to bodies in Wales.

Amendments—Mental Health Act 2007, s 35(4), (6).

'**Regulated by Part 4 or 4A of the Mental Health Act**' (s 37(2))—Where a person is being treated under Mental Health Act powers and that treatment is regulated by Part 4, which lays down the extent to which treatment for mental disorder can be imposed on detained patients in hospital under MHA 1983 and the safeguards available concerning the provision of treatment without consent, or by Part 4A, which regulates the treatment of community patients in the community, an IMCA is not required in relation to that treatment.

'**Prescribed by regulations**' (s 37(6) and (7))—'Serious medical treatment' for the purposes of this section is treatment which involves providing, withdrawing or withholding treatment in circumstances where (a) in a case where a single treatment is being proposed, there is a fine balance between its benefits to the patient and the burdens and risks it is likely to entail for him or her, (b) in a case where there is a choice of treatments, a decision as to which one to use is finely balanced, or (c) what is proposed would be likely to involve serious consequences for the patient (Mental Capacity Act 2005 (Independent Mental Capacity Advocates) (General) Regulations 2006, SI 2006/1832, reg 4(2)), as amended by National Treatment Agency (Abolition) and the Health and Social Care Act 2012 (Consequential, Transitional and Saving Provisions) Order SI 2013/235. The meaning of NHS Body in England is (a)an NHS foundation trust, (b) a clinical commissioning group, (c) the NHS Commissioning Board; (d) a local authority acting in the exercise of public health functions within the meaning of the National Health Service 2006, (e) an NHS trust or (e) a care trust. In Wales the meaning is (a) a local health board, (b) an NHS trust all or most of whose hospitals, establishments and facilities are situated in Wales or (c) a Special Health Authority performing functions only or mainly in respect of Wales (reg 3 of the respective Regulations).

38 Provision of accommodation by NHS body

(1) This section applies if an NHS body proposes to make arrangements –

  (a) for the provision of accommodation in a hospital or care home for a person ('P') who lacks capacity to agree to the arrangements, or
  (b) for a change in P's accommodation to another hospital or care home,

and is satisfied that there is no person, other than one engaged in providing care or treatment for P in a professional capacity or for remuneration, whom it would be appropriate for it to consult in determining what would be in P's best interests.

(2) But this section does not apply if P is accommodated as a result of an obligation imposed on him under the Mental Health Act.

(2A) And this section does not apply if –

  (a) an independent mental capacity advocate must be appointed under section 39A or 39C (whether or not by the NHS body) to represent P, and
  (b) the hospital or care home in which P is to be accommodated under the arrangements referred to in this section is the relevant hospital or care home under the authorisation referred to in that section.

(3) Before making the arrangements, the NHS body must instruct an independent mental capacity advocate to represent P unless it is satisfied that –

  (a) the accommodation is likely to be provided for a continuous period which is less than the applicable period, or
  (b) the arrangements need to be made as a matter of urgency.

(4) If the NHS body –

  (a) did not instruct an independent mental capacity advocate to represent P before making the arrangements because it was satisfied that subsection (3)(a) or (b) applied, but
  (b) subsequently has reason to believe that the accommodation is likely to be provided for a continuous period

(i) beginning with the day on which accommodation was first provided in accordance with the arrangements, and
(ii) ending on or after the expiry of the applicable period,

it must instruct an independent mental capacity advocate to represent P.

(5) The NHS body must, in deciding what arrangements to make for P, take into account any information given, or submissions made, by the independent mental capacity advocate.

(6) 'Care home' has the meaning given in section 3 of the Care Standards Act 2000.

(7) 'Hospital' means –
   (a) in relation to England, a hospital as defined by section 275 of the National Health Service Act 2006; and
   (b) in relation to Wales, a health service hospital as defined by section 206 of the National Health Service (Wales) Act 2006 or an independent hospital as defined by section 2 of the Care Standards Act 2000.

(8) 'NHS body' has such meaning as may be prescribed by regulations made for the purposes of this section by –
   (a) the Secretary of State, in relation to bodies in England, or
   (b) the National Assembly for Wales, in relation to bodies in Wales.

(9) 'Applicable period' means –
   (a) in relation to accommodation in a hospital, 28 days, and
   (b) in relation to accommodation in a care home, 8 weeks.

(10) For the purposes of subsection (1), a person appointed under Part 10 of Schedule A1 to be P's representative is not, by virtue of that appointment, engaged in providing care or treatment for P in a professional capacity or for remuneration.

Amendments—National Health Service (Consequential Provisions) Act 2006, s 2, Sch 1, paras 277, 278; Mental Health Act 2007, s 50(7), Sch 9, Pt 1, paras 1, 4(1), (2), (3); SI 2010/813.

'Obligation imposed under the Mental Health Act' (s 38(2))—Where the person concerned is to be detained in hospital or otherwise required to live in particular accommodation under the compulsory powers in MHA 1983 an IMCA is not required.

'Care home' (s 38(6))—This covers any care home, not being a hospital, independent clinic or a children's home, which provides accommodation together with nursing or personal care.

'Hospital' (s 38(7))—This covers (a) any NHS hospital in which treatment is provided and (b) any non-NHS hospital the main purpose of which is to provide treatment or palliative care or treatment or nursing care for persons liable to be detained under the Mental Health Act.

'Regulations prescribing NHS body' (s 38(8))—See note to s 37(6) and (7).

39 Provision of accommodation by local authority

(1) This section applies if a local authority propose to make arrangements –
   (a) for the provision of residential accommodation for a person ('P') who lacks capacity to agree to the arrangements, or
   (b) for a change in P's residential accommodation,

and are satisfied that there is no person, other than one engaged in providing care or treatment for P in a professional capacity or for remuneration, whom it would be appropriate for them to consult in determining what would be in P's best interests.

(1A) But this section applies only if –

(a) in the case of a local authority in England, subsection (1B) applies;
(b) in the case of a local authority in Wales, subsection (2) applies.

(1B) This subsection applies if the accommodation is to be provided in accordance with –

(a) Part 1 of the Care Act 2014, or
(b) section 117 of the Mental Health Act.

(2) This subsection applies if the accommodation is to be provided in accordance with –

(a) section 21 or 29 of the National Assistance Act 1948, or
(b) section 117 of the Mental Health Act,

as the result of a decision taken by the local authority under section 47 of the National Health Service and Community Care Act 1990.

(3) This section does not apply if P is accommodated as a result of an obligation imposed on him under the Mental Health Act.

(3A) And this section does not apply if –

(a) an independent mental capacity advocate must be appointed under section 39A or 39C (whether or not by the local authority) to represent P, and
(b) the place in which P is to be accommodated under the arrangements referred to in this section is the relevant hospital or care home under the authorisation referred to in that section.

(4) Before making the arrangements, the local authority must instruct an independent mental capacity advocate to represent P unless they are satisfied that –

(a) the accommodation is likely to be provided for a continuous period of less than 8 weeks, or
(b) the arrangements need to be made as a matter of urgency.

(5) If the local authority –

(a) did not instruct an independent mental capacity advocate to represent P before making the arrangements because they were satisfied that subsection (4)(a) or (b) applied, but
(b) subsequently have reason to believe that the accommodation is likely to be provided for a continuous period that will end 8 weeks or more after the day on which accommodation was first provided in accordance with the arrangements,

they must instruct an independent mental capacity advocate to represent P.

(6) The local authority must, in deciding what arrangements to make for P, take into account any information given, or submissions made, by the independent mental capacity advocate.

(7) For the purposes of subsection (1), a person appointed under Part 10 of Schedule A1 to be P's representative is not, by virtue of that appointment, engaged in providing care or treatment for P in a professional capacity or for remuneration.

Amendments—Mental Health Act 2007, s 50(7), Sch 9, Pt 1, paras 1, 5(1), (2), (3); SI 2015/914.

'**If the accommodation is to be provided in accordance with ...**' (s 39(2))—This may be accommodation in a care home, nursing home, ordinary and sheltered housing, housing association or other registered social housing, or in private sector housing provided by a local authority, or in hostel accommodation; and it includes people accommodated following discharge under MHA 1983, s 117. It applies where following a care needs assessment under the National Health Service and Community Care Act 1990, s 47 the local authority decides that the person's needs call for the provision of any such services.

'**Obligation imposed under the Mental Health Act**' (s 39(3))—See note to s 38(2).

39A Person becomes subject to Schedule A1

(1) This section applies if –

(a) a person ('P') becomes subject to Schedule A1, and
(b) the managing authority of the relevant hospital or care home are satisfied that there is no person, other than one engaged in providing care or treatment for P in a professional capacity or for remuneration, whom it would be appropriate to consult in determining what would be in P's best interests.

(2) The managing authority must notify the supervisory body that this section applies.

(3) The supervisory body must instruct an independent mental capacity advocate to represent P.

(4) Schedule A1 makes provision about the role of an independent mental capacity advocate appointed under this section.

(5) This section is subject to paragraph 161 of Schedule A1.

(6) For the purposes of subsection (1), a person appointed under Part 10 of Schedule A1 to be P's representative is not, by virtue of that appointment, engaged in providing care or treatment for P in a professional capacity or for remuneration.

Amendment—Inserted by Mental Health Act 2007, s 50(7), Sch 9, Pt 1, paras 1, 6.

Effect of provision—The effect of this section, part of the Deprivation of Liberty safeguards, is that when in any of the circumstances set out in the following section, an authorisation is sought by the managing authority of a hospital or care home to deprive a patient or resident of their liberty and there are no family, friends or non-professional carers to support that person, an independent mental capacity advocate (IMCA) must be instructed by the supervising primary care trust (or in Wales, the National Assembly or local health board) or local authority.

'**Subject to paragraph 161 of Schedule A1**' (s 39A(5))—An IMCA under this section does not retain the full powers of an IMCA after a representative for that person has been appointed under Sch A1, Part 10 once a standard authorisation has been given.

39B Section 39A: supplementary provision

(1) This section applies for the purposes of section 39A.

(2) P becomes subject to Schedule A1 in any of the following cases.

(3) The first case is where an urgent authorisation is given in relation to P under paragraph 76(2) of Schedule A1 (urgent authorisation given before request made for standard authorisation).

(4) The second case is where the following conditions are met.

(5) The first condition is that a request is made under Schedule A1 for a standard authorisation to be given in relation to P ('the requested authorisation').

(6) The second condition is that no urgent authorisation was given under paragraph 76(2) of Schedule A1 before that request was made.

(7) The third condition is that the requested authorisation will not be in force on or before, or immediately after, the expiry of an existing standard authorisation.

(8) The expiry of a standard authorisation is the date when the authorisation is expected to cease to be in force.

(9) The third case is where, under paragraph 69 of Schedule A1, the supervisory body select a person to carry out an assessment of whether or not the relevant person is a detained resident.

Amendments—Inserted by Mental Health Act 2007, s 50(7), Sch 9, Pt 1, paras 1, 6.

Effect of provision—See s 39A.

'Urgent authorisation/standard authorisation/assessment of whether or not a detained resident'—See notes to Sch A1.

39C Person unrepresented whilst subject to Schedule A1

(1) This section applies if –
   (a) an authorisation under Schedule A1 is in force in relation to a person ('P'),
   (b) the appointment of a person as P's representative ends in accordance with regulations made under Part 10 of Schedule A1, and
   (c) the managing authority of the relevant hospital or care home are satisfied that there is no person, other than one engaged in providing care or treatment for P in a professional capacity or for remuneration, whom it would be appropriate to consult in determining what would be in P's best interests.

(2) The managing authority must notify the supervisory body that this section applies.

(3) The supervisory body must instruct an independent mental capacity advocate to represent P.

(4) Paragraph 159 of Schedule A1 makes provision about the role of an independent mental capacity advocate appointed under this section.

(5) The appointment of an independent mental capacity advocate under this section ends when a new appointment of a person as P's representative is made in accordance with Part 10 of Schedule A1.

(6) For the purposes of subsection (1), a person appointed under Part 10 of Schedule A1 to be P's representative is not, by virtue of that appointment, engaged in providing care or treatment for P in a professional capacity or for remuneration.

Amendments—Inserted by Mental Health Act 2007, s 50(7), Sch 9, Pt 1, paras 1, 6.

Scope of provision—This section provides for an IMCA to be appointed to represent the person who is being deprived of their liberty while an authorisation is in force, during gaps in the appointment of a representative for the person (e g when a new representative is being sought) and there is no one other than a paid or professional carer who it is appropriate to consult about the person's best interests.

'The appointment of a person as P's representative ends in accordance with regulations made under Part 10 of Schedule A1' (s 39C(1)(b))—See the Mental Capacity (Deprivation of Liberty—Appointment of Relevant Person's Representative) Regulations 2008, SI 2008/1315, regs 13 and 14.

39D Person subject to Schedule A1 without paid representative

(1) This section applies if –

(a) an authorisation under Schedule A1 is in force in relation to a person ('P'),
(b) P has a representative ('R') appointed under Part 10 of Schedule A1, and
(c) R is not being paid under regulations under Part 10 of Schedule A1 for acting as P's representative.

(2) The supervisory body must instruct an independent mental capacity advocate to represent P in any of the following cases.

(3) The first case is where P makes a request to the supervisory body to instruct an advocate.

(4) The second case is where R makes a request to the supervisory body to instruct an advocate.

(5) The third case is where the supervisory body have reason to believe one or more of the following –

(a) that, without the help of an advocate, P and R would be unable to exercise one or both of the relevant rights;
(b) that P and R have each failed to exercise a relevant right when it would have been reasonable to exercise it;
(c) that P and R are each unlikely to exercise a relevant right when it would be reasonable to exercise it.

(6) The duty in subsection (2) is subject to section 39E.

(7) If an advocate is appointed under this section, the advocate is, in particular, to take such steps as are practicable to help P and R to understand the following matters –

(a) the effect of the authorisation;
(b) the purpose of the authorisation;
(c) the duration of the authorisation;
(d) any conditions to which the authorisation is subject;
(e) the reasons why each assessor who carried out an assessment in connection with the request for the authorisation, or in connection with a review of the authorisation, decided that P met the qualifying requirement in question;
(f) the relevant rights;
(g) how to exercise the relevant rights.

(8) The advocate is, in particular, to take such steps as are practicable to help P or R –

(a) to exercise the right to apply to court, if it appears to the advocate that P or R wishes to exercise that right, or
(b) to exercise the right of review, if it appears to the advocate that P or R wishes to exercise that right.

(9) If the advocate helps P or R to exercise the right of review –

(a) the advocate may make submissions to the supervisory body on the question of whether a qualifying requirement is reviewable;

(b) the advocate may give information, or make submissions, to any assessor carrying out a review assessment.

(10) In this section –

'relevant rights' means –
(a) the right to apply to court, and
(b) the right of review;

'right to apply to court' means the right to make an application to the court to exercise its jurisdiction under section 21A;

'right of review' means the right under Part 8 of Schedule A1 to request a review.

Amendments—Iinserted by Mental Health Act 2007, s 50(7), Sch 9, Pt 1, paras 1, 6.

Scope of provision—Under this section, the supervisory body must instruct an IMCA if requested to do so by the person deprived of their liberty or their unpaid representative, in order to assist them to exercise their rights either to request a review or to apply to the Court of Protection for determination of any matter relating to the authorisation to deprive the person of their liberty. The supervisory body may also appoint an IMCA if this will help to ensure that the person's rights are protected.

'Is not being paid under Regulations under Part 10 of Schedule A1'—Under the Mental Capacity (Deprivation of Liberty—Appointment of Relevant Person's Representative) Regulations 2008, SI 2008/1315, reg 5 where a supervisory body selects the representative it may pay that representative.

39E Limitation on duty to instruct advocate under section 39D

(1) This section applies if an advocate is already representing P in accordance with an instruction under section 39D.

(2) Section 39D(2) does not require another advocate to be instructed, unless the following conditions are met.

(3) The first condition is that the existing advocate was instructed –

(a) because of a request by R, or
(b) because the supervisory body had reason to believe one or more of the things in section 39D(5).

(4) The second condition is that the other advocate would be instructed because of a request by P.

Amendments—Inserted by Mental Health Act 2007, s 50(7), Sch 9, Pt 1, paras 1, 6.

40 Exceptions

(1) The duty imposed by section 37(3), 38(3) or (4), 39(4) or (5), 39A(3), 39C(3) or 39D(2)] does not apply where there is –

(a) a person nominated by P (in whatever manner) as a person to be consulted on matters to which that duty relates,
(b) a donee of a lasting power of attorney created by P who is authorised to make decisions in relation to those matters, or
(c) a deputy appointed by the court for P with power to make decisions in relation to those matters.]

(2) A person appointed under Part 10 of Schedule A1 to be P's representative is not, by virtue of that appointment, a person nominated by P as a person to be consulted in matters to which a duty mentioned in subsection (1) relates.

Amendments—Substituted by Mental Health Act 2007, s 49; amended by Mental Health Act 2007, s 50(7), Sch 9, Pt 1, paras 1, 7(1)–(4).

41 Power to adjust role of independent mental capacity advocate

(1) The appropriate authority may make regulations –

   (a) expanding the role of independent mental capacity advocates in relation to persons who lack capacity, and
   (b) adjusting the obligation to make arrangements imposed by section 35.

(2) The regulations may, in particular –

   (a) prescribe circumstances (different to those set out in sections 37, 38 and 39) in which an independent mental capacity advocate must, or circumstances in which one may, be instructed by a person of a prescribed description to represent a person who lacks capacity, and
   (b) include provision similar to any made by section 37, 38, 39 or 40.

(3) 'Appropriate authority' has the same meaning as in section 35.

'Regulations' (s 41(1))—This power has been exercised in England in the Mental Capacity Act 2005 (Independent Mental Capacity Advocates) (Expansion of Role) Regulations 2006, SI 2006/2883 and in Wales in SI 2007/852 (W 77).

Miscellaneous and supplementary

42 Codes of practice

(1) The Lord Chancellor must prepare and issue one or more codes of practice –

   (a) for the guidance of persons assessing whether a person has capacity in relation to any matter,
   (b) for the guidance of persons acting in connection with the care or treatment of another person (see section 5),
   (c) for the guidance of donees of lasting powers of attorney,
   (d) for the guidance of deputies appointed by the court,
   (e) for the guidance of persons carrying out research in reliance on any provision made by or under this Act (and otherwise with respect to sections 30 to 34),
   (f) for the guidance of independent mental capacity advocates,
   (fa) for the guidance of persons exercising functions under Schedule A1,
   (fb) for the guidance of representatives appointed under Part 10 of Schedule A1,
   (g) with respect to the provisions of sections 24 to 26 (advance decisions and apparent advance decisions), and
   (h) with respect to such other matters concerned with this Act as he thinks fit.

(2) The Lord Chancellor may from time to time revise a code.

(3) The Lord Chancellor may delegate the preparation or revision of the whole or any part of a code so far as he considers expedient.

(4) It is the duty of a person to have regard to any relevant code if he is acting in relation to a person who lacks capacity and is doing so in one or more of the following ways –

(a) as the donee of a lasting power of attorney,
(b) as a deputy appointed by the court,
(c) as a person carrying out research in reliance on any provision made by or under this Act (see sections 30 to 34),
(d) as an independent mental capacity advocate,
(da) in the exercise of functions under Schedule A1,
(db) as a representative appointed under Part 10 of Schedule A1,
(e) in a professional capacity,
(f) for remuneration.

(5) If it appears to a court or tribunal conducting any criminal or civil proceedings that –

(a) a provision of a code, or
(b) a failure to comply with a code,

is relevant to a question arising in the proceedings, the provision or failure must be taken into account in deciding the question.

(6) A code under subsection (1)(d) may contain separate guidance for deputies appointed by virtue of paragraph 1(2) of Schedule 5 (functions of deputy conferred on receiver appointed under the Mental Health Act).

(7) In this section and in section 43, 'code' means a code prepared or revised under this section.

Amendments—Paragraphs in square brackets inserted by the Mental Health Act 2007, s 50(7), Sch 9, Pt 1, paras 1, 8(1)–(3).

Scope of provision—This makes provision for the Lord Chancellor to prepare and issue a statutory Code (or Codes) of Practice for the guidance of practitioners using the Act and those affected by its provisions, and also to assist with interpretation and implementation of the Act. The Government decided to issue one main Code of Practice to include guidance on the whole of the MCA 2005 as enacted. A supplement to main Code has since been issued, dealing with the Deprivation of Liberty Safeguards which came into effect on 1 April 2009. The main Code and supplement are reproduced in Part V of this book.

'delegate the preparation or revision' (s 42(3))—Policy responsibility for the Code of Practice, including any revision, remains with the Ministry of Justice (formerly the Department for Constitutional Affairs, which published the Code) in conjunction with the Department of Health for those chapters dealing with health and social care decisions (including the supplement dealing with the deprivation of liberty safeguards). The Office of the Public Guardian (OPG) assists with dissemination of the Code.

'have regard to' (s 42(4))—The statutory duty to 'have regard to' the Code applies to those exercising formal powers or duties under the Act, and to professionals and others acting for remuneration. Family members or informal carers not under such a duty 'should follow the guidance in the Code so far as they are aware of it' (Code of Practice, p 2).

'a court or tribunal conducting any criminal or civil proceedings' (s 42(5))—There is no liability for breach of the Code itself, but compliance or non-compliance may be an element in deciding the issue of liability for breach of some other statutory or common law duty. This applies not only to those categories of people who have a duty to have regard to the Code of Practice, but also to others involved in legal proceedings, since they may also have an obligation to act in accordance with the principles of the Act and in the best interests of a person lacking capacity.

43 Codes of practice: procedure

(1) Before preparing or revising a code, the Lord Chancellor must consult –

  (a) the National Assembly for Wales, and
  (b) such other persons as he considers appropriate.

(2) The Lord Chancellor may not issue a code unless –

  (a) a draft of the code has been laid by him before both Houses of Parliament, and
  (b) the 40 day period has elapsed without either House resolving not to approve the draft.

(3) The Lord Chancellor must arrange for any code that he has issued to be published in such a way as he considers appropriate for bringing it to the attention of persons likely to be concerned with its provisions.

(4) '40 day period', in relation to the draft of a proposed code, means –

  (a) if the draft is laid before one House on a day later than the day on which it is laid before the other House, the period of 40 days beginning with the later of the two days;
  (b) in any other case, the period of 40 days beginning with the day on which it is laid before each House.

(5) In calculating the period of 40 days, no account is to be taken of any period during which Parliament is dissolved or prorogued or during which both Houses are adjourned for more than 4 days.

Scope of provision—This section sets out the procedures required for the preparation or revision of the Code(s) and for parliamentary approval.

'National Assembly for Wales' (s 43(1)(a))—Since health and social care responsibilities are devolved in relation to Wales, the National Assembly for Wales must specifically be consulted and involved in the preparation of the Codes.

'such other persons' (s 43(1)(b))—There must be formal consultation with anyone whom the Lord Chancellor considers appropriate before a Code is prepared or revised.

'resolving not to approve the draft' (s 43(2)(b))—The Code takes effect after the 40-day period (as defined in s 43(4)–(5)) unless, within that time, either House has resolved not to approve it (known as the 'negative resolution' procedure).

'published in such a way as he considers appropriate' (s 43(3))—The Lord Chancellor is allowed considerable flexibility in arranging for the Codes to be produced in the most appropriate format and for bringing the guidance to the attention of everyone who needs to know about it.

44 Ill-treatment or neglect

(1) Subsection (2) applies if a person ('D') –

  (a) has the care of a person ('P') who lacks, or whom D reasonably believes to lack, capacity,
  (b) is the donee of a lasting power of attorney, or an enduring power of attorney (within the meaning of Schedule 4), created by P, or
  (c) is a deputy appointed by the court for P.

(2) D is guilty of an offence if he ill-treats or wilfully neglects P.

(3) A person guilty of an offence under this section is liable –

(a) on summary conviction, to imprisonment for a term not exceeding 12 months or a fine not exceeding the statutory maximum or both;
(b) on conviction on indictment, to imprisonment for a term not exceeding 5 years or a fine or both.

Scope of provision—This section creates new criminal offences of ill-treatment or wilful neglect of a person lacking capacity, carrying penalties on conviction ranging from a fine to a term of imprisonment of up to 5 years. Ill-treatment and neglect are separate offences (*R v Newington* (1990) Cr App R 247, CA). No lower age limit is specified, so the offence will also apply to the ill-treatment or wilful neglect of children under 16 whose lack of capacity is caused by an impairment of, or disturbance in the functioning of, the mind or brain, not solely by the immaturity of youth.

'has the care of a person ('P')' (s 44(1)(a))—This includes not only family carers, but also health and social care staff in hospitals or care homes (including in some circumstances the owner or manager of a care home) or those providing domiciliary care.

'who lacks ... capacity' (s 44(1)(a)—Section 44 provides no further guidance on the particular decision (or decisions) P lacks capacity to make, so there is a 'disconnect between MCA 2005, s 44 (referring to 'persons without capacity') and the elaborate definition sections (MCA 2005, ss 2 and 3)' (*R v Dunn* [2010] EWCA Crim 2935); confirmed in *R v Hopkins; R v Priest* [2011] EWCA Crim 1513). In this case of ill-treatment of residents by the manageress of a care home, it was held that it was open for the jury to conclude that the decisions regarding care (the 'matter') had been made because the victims lacked capacity, and there was no need to complicate matters by referring to MCA 2005, s 3.

'reasonably believes' (s 44(1)(a))—This is an objective test. See also ss 4(9) and 5(1).

'ill-treats' (s 44(2))—A single act is sufficient to show ill-treatment (*R v Holmes* (1979) 1 Cr App R (S) 233). For a conviction of ill-treatment, it is necessary to show deliberate conduct by the accused which could properly be described as ill-treatment, whether or not it had caused or was likely to cause harm. The accused must either realise that he or she is inexcusably ill-treating the other person or be reckless as to whether he or she is doing so (*R v Newington* (1990) Cr App R 247).

'wilfully neglects' (s 44(2))—Neglect relates to a failure to provide nourishment, fluid, shelter, warmth or medical attention to a dependant person (*R v Humberside and Scunthorpe Coroner, ex parte Jamieson* [1995] QB 1). In the context of the offence of wilfully neglecting a child (Children and Young Persons Act 1933, s 1), it has been held that neglect cannot be described as *wilful* unless the person either had directed his or her mind to whether there was some risk (although it might fall far short of a probability) that the child's health might suffer from the neglect and had made a conscious decision to refrain from acting, or had so refrained because he or she did not care whether the child might be at risk or not (*R v Sheppard* [1981] AC 394, HL). By contrast, the Court of Appeal has held that the *actus reus* of the offence of wilful neglect under s 44 is complete if a nurse (or medical practitioner) neglects to do an act which should be done in the treatment of the patient, whether or not acting at a time of stress: *R v Patel* [2013] EWCA Crim 965, at [34] and [42]. The Court also noted the clear distinction between the offence of neglect under MCA 2005, s 44 and the (much more serious) offence of gross negligence manslaughter, where causation would be an issue. A jury will need careful directions on the law relating to willful neglect – see *R v Hopkins; R v Priest* [2011] EWCA Crim 1513.

'imprisonment for a term not exceeding 5 years' (s 44(3)(b))—This has the effect of making it an 'arrestable offence' under the Police and Criminal Evidence Act 1984, s 2. It also reflects the potential severity of the crime, with sentences in parallel with those for serious assaults on individuals, including the offences of inflicting grievous bodily harm and assault occasioning actual bodily harm under the Offences Against the Person Act 1861, which both carry maximum sentences of 5 years' imprisonment.

PART 2
THE COURT OF PROTECTION AND THE PUBLIC GUARDIAN

The Court of Protection

45 The Court of Protection

(1) There is to be a superior court of record known as the Court of Protection.

(2) The court is to have an official seal.

(3) The court may sit at any place in England and Wales, on any day and at any time.

(4) The court is to have a central office and registry at a place appointed by the Lord Chancellor, after consulting the Lord Chief Justice.

(5) The Lord Chancellor may, after consulting the Lord Chief Justice, designate as additional registries of the court any district registry of the High Court and any county court office.

(5A) The Lord Chief Justice may nominate any of the following to exercise his functions under this section –

    (a) the President of the Court of Protection;

    (b) a judicial office holder (as defined in section 109(4) of the Constitutional Reform Act 2005).

(6) The office of the Supreme Court called the Court of Protection ceases to exist.

Amendments—SI 2006/1016.

Scope of provision—This section establishes the new Court of Protection which effectively replaces the former court of that name. This is not simply 'new wine in an old bottle' – it is an 'entirely new vintage' with a different status and structure and its own Rules.

Further explanation—This topic is covered in Part I, Chapter 8 of this work.

Central office and registry—The main registry is at First Avenue House, 42–49 High Holborn, London WC1V 6NP. Previously, it was at Archway Tower, London N19 and the Royal Courts of Justice.

'The court may sit …'—There are a number of regional courts who hear Court of Protection cases in addition to civil and family work. These courts receive work from the main registry where cases must be issued.

Lord Chancellor—For consideration of the relative powers of the Lord Chancellor and the Lord Chief Justice (who in practice delegates his functions to the President of the Court) see Part I, Chapter 8 of this work.

Powers—For the powers of the Court see ss 15–23.

Administration—The Court of Protection is part of the Royal Courts of Justice Group within Her Majesty's Courts and Tribunals Service. The Court of Protection administration is responsible for processing all applications made to the court.

46 The judges of the Court of Protection

(1) Subject to Court of Protection Rules under section 51(2)(d), the jurisdiction of the court is exercisable by a judge nominated for that purpose by –

    (a) the Lord Chief Justice, or

(b) where nominated by the Lord Chief Justice to act on his behalf under this subsection –
   (i) the President of the Court of Protection; or
   (ii) a judicial office holder (as defined in section 109(4) of the Constitutional Reform Act 2005).

(2) To be nominated, a judge must be –
   (a) the President of the Family Division,
   (b) the Chancellor of the High Court,
   (c) a puisne judge of the High Court,
   (d) a circuit judge,
   (e) a district judge,
   (f) a District Judge (Magistrates' Courts).
   (g) a judge of the First-tier Tribunal, or of the Upper Tribunal, by virtue of appointment under paragraph 1(1) of Schedule 2 or 3 to the Tribunals, Courts and Enforcement Act 2007,
   (h) a transferred-in judge of the First-tier Tribunal or of the Upper Tribunal (see section 31(2) of that Act),
   (i) a deputy judge of the Upper Tribunal (whether under paragraph 7 of Schedule 3 to, or section 31(2) of, that Act).
   (j) the Chamber President, or Deputy Chamber President, of a chamber of the First-tier Tribunal or of a chamber of the Upper Tribunal,
   (k) the Judge Advocate General,
   (l) a Recorder,
   (m) the holder of an office listed in the first column of the table in section 89(3C) of the Senior Courts Act 1981 (senior High Court Masters etc),
   (n) a holder of an office listed in column 1 of Part 2 of Schedule 2 to that Act (High Court Masters etc),
   (o) a deputy district judge appointed under section 102 of that Act or under section 8 of the County Courts Act 1984,
   (p) a member of a panel of Employment Judges established for England and Wales or for Scotland,
   (q) a person appointed under section 30(1)(a) or (b) of the Courts-Martial (Appeals) Act 1951 (assistants to the Judge Advocate General),
   (r) a deputy judge of the High Court,
   (s) the Senior President of Tribunals,
   (t) an ordinary judge of the Court of Appeal (including the vice-president, if any, of either division of that court),
   (u) the President of the Queen's Bench Division,
   (v) the Master of the Rolls, or
   (w) the Lord Chief Justice.

(3) The Lord Chief Justice, after consulting the Lord Chancellor, must –
   (a) appoint one of the judges nominated by virtue of subsection (2)(a) to (c) to be President of the Court of Protection, and
   (b) appoint another of those judges to be Vice-President of the Court of Protection.

(4) The Lord Chief Justice, after consulting the Lord Chancellor, must appoint one of the judges nominated by virtue of subsection (2)(d) to (q) to be Senior Judge of the Court of Protection, having such administrative functions in relation to the court as the Lord Chancellor, after consulting the Lord Chief Justice, may direct.

Amendments—SI 2006/1016; Crime and Courts Act 2013, s 21(4), Sch 14, Pt 3.

PART III   COURT OF PROTECTION PRACTICE 2016

Scope of provision—This section has been substantially amended by Part 3, Schedule 14 of the Crime and Courts Act 2013 which expands the catagories of judge who may be nominated to sit in the Court of Protection. See chapter 8, paras 8.14–8.19.

'President'—Presently the President of the Family Division of the High Court (Sir James Munby).

'Vice-President'—Presently the Mr Justice Charles.

'Senior Judge'—Presently Denzil Lush, the former Master of the old Court of Protection.

The nominated judges—There is a complement of five district judges sitting at the main registry. A large number of district and circuit judges have been nominated to sit on a regional basis. All Family Division and Chancery Division High Court judges are nominated, and Queen's Bench Division judges are nominated to sit although normally only in an emergency. To assist with deprivation of liberty cases, a number of tribunal judges were also nominated only for such cases.

Supplementary powers

47 General powers and effect of orders etc

(1) The court has in connection with its jurisdiction the same powers, rights, privileges and authority as the High Court.

(2) Section 204 of the Law of Property Act 1925 (orders of High Court conclusive in favour of purchasers) applies in relation to orders and directions of the court as it applies to orders of the High Court.

(3) Office copies of orders made, directions given or other instruments issued by the court and sealed with its official seal are admissible in all legal proceedings as evidence of the originals without any further proof.

Scope of provision—This section confirms the powers of the nominated judges when sitting in the Court of Protection and how their orders may be proven in other courts and situations.

'the same powers … as the High Court' (s 47(1))—This provision, which can easily be overlooked, is extremely important. It vests in judges of the Court of Protection when sitting in that jurisdiction all the powers, rights, privileges and authority of a judge sitting in the High Court. This will include the power to grant injunctions and enforcement powers, including the power to commit for contempt. Equally, any order will have the same status as an order made in the High Court.

48 Interim orders and directions

The court may, pending the determination of an application to it in relation to a person ('P'), make an order or give directions in respect of any matter if –

   (a) there is reason to believe that P lacks capacity in relation to the matter,
   (b) the matter is one to which its powers under this Act extend, and
   (c) it is in P's best interests to make the order, or give the directions, without delay.

Scope of provision—This section enables the Court, following an application, to exercise its powers on an interim basis if satisfied that this is in P's best interests provided that the Court has reason to believe that P lacks capacity in relation to the matter. A finding of lack of capacity on the part of P will not be required. The Court must nevertheless apply the general principle in MCA 2005, s 1. See *Re F* [2009] COPLR Con Vol 390.

'lacks capacity' (s 48(a))—See ss 2–3, and Part I, Chapter 2 of this work.

'Best interests' (s 48(c))—See s 4 and Part I, Chapter 2 of this work.

49 Power to call for reports

(1) This section applies where, in proceedings brought in respect of a person ('P') under Part 1, the court is considering a question relating to P.

(2) The court may require a report to be made to it by the Public Guardian or by a Court of Protection Visitor.

(3) The court may require a local authority, or an NHS body, to arrange for a report to be made –

    (a) by one of its officers or employees, or
    (b) by such other person (other than the Public Guardian or a Court of Protection Visitor) as the authority, or the NHS body, considers appropriate.

(4) The report must deal with such matters relating to P as the court may direct.

(5) Court of Protection Rules may specify matters which, unless the court directs otherwise, must also be dealt with in the report.

(6) The report may be made in writing or orally, as the court may direct.

(7) In complying with a requirement, the Public Guardian or a Court of Protection Visitor may, at all reasonable times, examine and take copies of –

    (a) any health record,
    (b) any record of, or held by, a local authority and compiled in connection with a social services function, and
    (c) any record held by a person registered under Part 2 of the Care Standards Act 2000 or Chapter 2 of Part 1 of the Health and Social Care Act 2008,

so far as the record relates to P.

(8) If the Public Guardian or a Court of Protection Visitor is making a visit in the course of complying with a requirement, he may interview P in private.

(9) If a Court of Protection Visitor who is a Special Visitor is making a visit in the course of complying with a requirement, he may if the court so directs carry out in private a medical, psychiatric or psychological examination of P's capacity and condition.

(10) 'NHS body' has the meaning given in section 148 of the Health and Social Care (Community Health and Standards) Act 2003.

(11) 'Requirement' means a requirement imposed under subsection (2) or (3).

Amendments—SI 2010/813.

Scope of provision—The Court may, in the exercise of its jurisdiction, obtain independent reports from several sources and this section sets out the authority for this.

'Report'—The Court decides which of the bodies specified shall provide the report, but a local authority or an NHS body may delegate the task (though not to the Public Guardian or by a Court of Protection Visitor).

Fees—There is no provision for fees to be charged for any report requested by the Court.

'Public Guardian'—See ss 57–58 and Part I, Chapter 8 of this work.

'Court of Protection Visitor'—See s 61 and Part I, Chapter 8 of this work.

'**Court of Protection Rules**'—See Court of Protection Rules 2007, SI 2007/1744, reproduced in Part IV of this book. Rules 117 and 118 implement this provision and are supplemented by Practice Direction E (PD14E) which includes precedent clauses for an order.

'**local authority, or an NHS body**'—This will typically be a social services department or NHS Trust.

'**in writing or orally**'—A report in writing will usually be produced but the Court can require the individual producing the report to give evidence at a hearing and this is likely in cases of urgency.

'**Special Visitor**'—This will be a medical visitor, usually a consultant psychiatrist, who is asked to report (inter alia) on capacity issues.

'**social services function**'—Defined in s 64(1) as having the meaning given in the Local Authority Social Services Act 1970, s 1A.

'**local authority**'—According to s 64(1) means:

(a) the council of a county in England in which there are no district councils;
(b) the council of a district in England;
(c) the council of a county or county borough in Wales;
(d) the council of a London borough;
(e) the Common Council of the City of London; or
(f) the Council of the Isles of Scilly.

'**NHS body**'—The statutory reference extends to a primary care trust, a strategic health authority, an NHS trust and an NHS foundation trust. Also in Wales a local health board and a special health authority.

Practice and procedure

50 Applications to the Court of Protection

(1) No permission is required for an application to the court for the exercise of any of its powers under this Act –

(a) by a person who lacks, or is alleged to lack, capacity,
(b) if such a person has not reached 18, by anyone with parental responsibility for him,
(c) by the donor or a donee of a lasting power of attorney to which the application relates,
(d) by a deputy appointed by the court for a person to whom the application relates, or
(e) by a person named in an existing order of the court, if the application relates to the order.

(1A) Nor is permission required for an application to the court under section 21A by the relevant per-son's representative.

(2) But, subject to Court of Protection Rules and to paragraph 20(2) of Schedule 3 (declarations relating to private international law), permission is required for any other application to the court.

(3) In deciding whether to grant permission the court must, in particular, have regard to –

(a) the applicant's connection with the person to whom the application relates,
(b) the reasons for the application,
(c) the benefit to the person to whom the application relates of a proposed order or directions, and
(d) whether the benefit can be achieved in any other way.

(4) 'Parental responsibility' has the same meaning as in the Children Act 1989.

Amendments—Mental Health Act 2007, s 50(7), Sch 9, Pt 1, paras 1, 9.

Scope of provision—Certain categories of person are entitled to apply to the Court, but others need permission and the Court in considering whether to grant such permission must have regard to specified factors.

Court of Protection Rules—Permission to apply is dealt with in Part 8 (rr 50–60) and Practice Direction 8A.

51 Court of Protection Rules

(1) Rules of court with respect to the practice and procedure of the court (to be called 'Court of Protection Rules') may be made in accordance with Part 1 of Schedule 1 to the Constitutional Reform Act 2005.

(2) Court of Protection Rules may, in particular, make provision –

(a) as to the manner and form in which proceedings are to be commenced;
(b) as to the persons entitled to be notified of, and be made parties to, the proceedings;
(c) for the allocation, in such circumstances as may be specified, of any specified description of proceedings to a specified judge or to specified descriptions of judges;
(d) for the exercise of the jurisdiction of the court, in such circumstances as may be specified, by its officers or other staff;
(e) for enabling the court to appoint a suitable person (who may, with his consent, be the Official Solicitor) to act in the name of, or on behalf of, or to represent the person to whom the proceedings relate;
(f) for enabling an application to the court to be disposed of without a hearing;
(g) for enabling the court to proceed with, or with any part of, a hearing in the absence of the person to whom the proceedings relate;
(h) for enabling or requiring the proceedings or any part of them to be conducted in private and for enabling the court to determine who is to be admitted when the court sits in private and to exclude specified persons when it sits in public;
(i) as to what may be received as evidence (whether or not admissible apart from the rules) and the manner in which it is to be presented;
(j) for the enforcement of orders made and directions given in the proceedings.

(3) Court of Protection Rules may, instead of providing for any matter, refer to provision made or to be made about that matter by directions.

(4) Court of Protection Rules may make different provision for different areas.

Amendments—SI 2006/1016.

Scope of provision—This section authorises the court rules and identifies some of the matters that should be dealt with in those rules.

'Court of Protection Rules'—See Court of Protection Rules 2007, SI 2007/1744, reproduced in Part IV of this book.

'directions' (s 51(3))—This refers to the Practice Directions authorised by s 52.

52 Practice directions

(1) Directions as to the practice and procedure of the court may be given in accordance with Part 1 of Schedule 2 to the Constitutional Reform Act 2005.

(2) Practice directions given otherwise than under subsection (1) may not be given without the approval of –

(a) the Lord Chancellor, and
(b) the Lord Chief Justice.

(3) The Lord Chief Justice may nominate any of the following to exercise his functions under this section –

(a) the President of the Court of Protection;
(b) a judicial office holder (as defined in section 109(4) of the Constitutional Reform Act 2005).

Amendments—Substituted by SI 2006/1016.

Scope of provision—This section enables Practice Directions (sometimes referred to as 'PDs') to be formulated for the guidance of the Court and practitioners (and those who appear before the Court). The current Practice Directions are reproduced in Part IV of this work.

53 Rights of appeal

(1) Subject to the provisions of this section, an appeal lies to the Court of Appeal from any decision of the court.

(2) Court of Protection Rules may provide that, where a decision of the court is made by a specified description of person, an appeal from the decision lies to a specified description of judge of the court and not to the Court of Appeal.

(3) *(repealed)*

(4) Court of Protection Rules may make provision –

(a) that, in such cases as may be specified, an appeal from a decision of the court may not be made without permission;
(b) as to the person or persons entitled to grant permission to appeal;
(c) as to any requirements to be satisfied before permission is granted;
(d) that where a judge of the court makes a decision on an appeal, no appeal may be made to the Court of Appeal from that decision unless the Court of Appeal considers that –
   (i) the appeal would raise an important point of principle or practice, or
   (ii) there is some other compelling reason for the Court of Appeal to hear it;
(e) as to any considerations to be taken into account in relation to granting or refusing permission to appeal.

Amendments—Criminal Justice and Courts Act 2015, s 62(1)–(4).

Scope of provision—This section authorises the Court of Protection Rules to make provision for appeals from first instance decisions, with a default provision that appeals lie to the Court of Appeal.

'Court of Protection Rules' (s 53(2) and (4))—See Court of Protection Rules 2007, SI 2007/1744, Part 20 (rr 169–182) and Practice Direction 20A.

Fees and costs

54 Fees

(1) The Lord Chancellor may with the consent of the Treasury by order prescribe fees payable in respect of anything dealt with by the court.

(2) An order under this section may in particular contain provision as to –

   (a) scales or rates of fees;
   (b) exemptions from and reductions in fees;
   (c) remission of fees in whole or in part.

(3) Before making an order under this section, the Lord Chancellor must consult –

   (a) the President of the Court of Protection,
   (b) the Vice-President of the Court of Protection, and
   (c) the Senior Judge of the Court of Protection.

(4) The Lord Chancellor must take such steps as are reasonably practicable to bring information about fees to the attention of persons likely to have to pay them.

(5) Fees payable under this section are recoverable summarily as a civil debt.

Scope of provision—This section enables fees to be prescribed (and recovered) for applications to the Court. The principle of full cost recovery applies to the Court but some subsidy from central government is inevitable in respect of those who are fees exempt or for whom a waiver is applied.

'prescribe fees' (s 54(1))—See Court of Protection Fees Order 2007, SI 2007/1745, as amended by Court of Protection Fees (Amendment) Order 2009, SI 2009/513. Current guidance is available through the Directgov website (search on this site for Court of Protection).

55 Costs

(1) Subject to Court of Protection Rules, the costs of and incidental to all proceedings in the court are in its discretion.

(2) The rules may in particular make provision for regulating matters relating to the costs of those proceedings, including prescribing scales of costs to be paid to legal or other representatives.

(3) The court has full power to determine by whom and to what extent the costs are to be paid.

(4) The court may, in any proceedings –

   (a) disallow, or
   (b) order the legal or other representatives concerned to meet,

the whole of any wasted costs or such part of them as may be determined in accordance with the rules.

(5) 'Legal or other representative', in relation to a party to proceedings, means any person exercising a right of audience or right to conduct litigation on his behalf.

(6) 'Wasted costs' means any costs incurred by a party –

   (a) as a result of any improper, unreasonable or negligent act or omission on the part of any legal or other representative or any employee of such a representative, or
   (b) which, in the light of any such act or omission occurring after they were incurred, the court considers it is unreasonable to expect that party to pay.

Scope of provision—This section establishes the basic principle that the costs of and incidental to all proceedings are in the discretion of the Court and allows the rules to make provision for regulating the costs.

'**Court of Protection Rules**' (s 55(1))—See Court of Protection Rules 2007, SI 2007/1744, Part 19 (rr 155–168) and Practice Direction 19A.

'**right of audience**' (s 55(5))—General rights of audience are granted to duly qualified barristers or solicitors and a party may be represented at a trial or hearing in the courts by a person with these advocacy rights. Fellows of the Institute of Legal Executives and the Association of Law Costs Draftsmen also have limited advocacy rights. Employees of solicitors may appear at hearings 'in private'. The Court has a discretionary power to grant an unqualified person a right of audience in relation to particular proceedings before that court. See the Courts and Legal Services Act 1990, ss 27–28. The term 'lay representative' relates to a person who does not possess advocacy rights and may not even be a lawyer, but to whom the Court grants a right of audience on behalf of a party in relation to the proceedings before that Court. The party must apply at the outset of a hearing if he or she wishes an unqualified individual to be granted a right of audience – *Clarkson v Gilbert* [2000] 2 FLR 839, CA.

Decisions of the Court—See the case summaries in Part IX of this work.

56 Fees and costs: supplementary

(1) Court of Protection Rules may make provision –

   (a) as to the way in which, and funds from which, fees and costs are to be paid;
   (b) for charging fees and costs upon the estate of the person to whom the proceedings relate;
   (c) for the payment of fees and costs within a specified time of the death of the person to whom the proceedings relate or the conclusion of the proceedings.

(2) A charge on the estate of a person created by virtue of subsection (1)(b) does not cause any interest of the person in any property to fail or determine or to be prevented from recommencing.

'**Court of Protection Rules**' (s 56(1))—See Court of Protection Rules 2007, SI 2007/1744, Part 19 (rr 155–168) and Practice Direction 19A.

The Public Guardian

57 The Public Guardian

(1) For the purposes of this Act, there is to be an officer, to be known as the Public Guardian.

(2) The Public Guardian is to be appointed by the Lord Chancellor.

(3) There is to be paid to the Public Guardian out of money provided by Parliament such salary as the Lord Chancellor may determine.

(4) The Lord Chancellor may, after consulting the Public Guardian –

   (a) provide him with such officers and staff, or
   (b) enter into such contracts with other persons for the provision (by them or their sub-contractors) of officers, staff or services,

as the Lord Chancellor thinks necessary for the proper discharge of the Public Guardian's functions.

(5) Any functions of the Public Guardian may, to the extent authorised by him, be performed by any of his officers.

Scope of provision—This section establishes a new a statutory office-holder known as the Public Guardian, with officers and staff to whom the functions of the office may be delegated. Hence the 'Office of the Public Guardian' which effectively replaces the former 'Public Guardianship Office'.

Further explanation—This topic is covered in Part I, Chapter 8 of this work.

58 Functions of the Public Guardian

(1) The Public Guardian has the following functions –
- (a) establishing and maintaining a register of lasting powers of attorney,
- (b) establishing and maintaining a register of orders appointing deputies,
- (c) supervising deputies appointed by the court,
- (d) directing a Court of Protection Visitor to visit –
  - (i) a donee of a lasting power of attorney,
  - (ii) a deputy appointed by the court, or
  - (iii) the person granting the power of attorney or for whom the deputy is appointed ('P'),

  and to make a report to the Public Guardian on such matters as he may direct,
- (e) receiving security which the court requires a person to give for the discharge of his functions,
- (f) receiving reports from donees of lasting powers of attorney and deputies appointed by the court,
- (g) reporting to the court on such matters relating to proceedings under this Act as the court requires,
- (h) dealing with representations (including complaints) about the way in which a donee of a lasting power of attorney or a deputy appointed by the court is exercising his powers,
- (i) publishing, in any manner the Public Guardian thinks appropriate, any information he thinks appropriate about the discharge of his functions.

(2) The functions conferred by subsection (1)(c) and (h) may be discharged in co-operation with any other person who has functions in relation to the care or treatment of P.

(3) The Lord Chancellor may by regulations make provision –
- (a) conferring on the Public Guardian other functions in connection with this Act;
- (b) in connection with the discharge by the Public Guardian of his functions.

(4) Regulations made under subsection (3)(b) may in particular make provision as to –
- (a) the giving of security by deputies appointed by the court and the enforcement and discharge of security so given;
- (b) the fees which may be charged by the Public Guardian;
- (c) the way in which, and funds from which, such fees are to be paid;
- (d) exemptions from and reductions in such fees;
- (e) remission of such fees in whole or in part;
- (f) the making of reports to the Public Guardian by deputies appointed by the court and others who are directed by the court to carry out any transaction for a person who lacks capacity.

(5) For the purpose of enabling him to carry out his functions, the Public Guardian may, at all reasonable times, examine and take copies of –
   (a) any health record,
   (b) any record of, or held by, a local authority and compiled in connection with a social services function, and
   (c) any record held by a person registered under Part 2 of the Care Standards Act 2000 or Chapter 2 of Part 1 of the Health and Social Care Act 2008,

so far as the record relates to P.

(6) The Public Guardian may also for that purpose interview P in private.

Amendments—SI 2010/813.

Scope of provision—This section defines the basic functions and powers of the Public Guardian but more may be added by regulations made by the Lord Chancellor.

Further explanation—This topic is covered in Part I, Chapter 8 of this work.

'supervising deputies' (s 58(1)(c))—The Public Guardian's power or duty to 'supervise' extends only to deputies appointed by the Court. The Public Guardian has further powers in respect of donees of lasting powers of attorney or attorneys under enduring powers of attorney under the Lasting Power of Attorney, Enduring Power of Attorney and Public Guardian Regulations 2007, SI 2007/1253, regs 46 and 47.

'directing a Court of Protection Visitor' (s 58(1)(d))—The Public Guardian may direct a visit if it is in connection with an investigation or report that the Public Guardian has been directed to carry out by the Court.

'Report' (s 58(1)(d))—The Public Guardian may require a report by a Court of Protection Visitor independently of the Court of Protection.

'receiving reports' (s 58(1)(f))—The Public Guardian may receive reports, but it is for the Court to order that a report be made to the Public Guardian – see s 23(3).

'Regulations' (s 58(3)(b))—See the Lasting Power of Attorney, Enduring Power of Attorney and Public Guardian Regulations 2007, SI 2007/1253; Lasting Powers of Attorney, Enduring Powers of Attorney and Public Guardian (Amendment) Regulations 2007, SI 2007/2161 and Lasting Powers of Attorney, Enduring Powers of Attorney and Public Guardian (Amendment) Regulations 2009, SI 2009/1884.

'Regulations' (s 58(4))—Public Guardian (Fees, etc) Regulations 2007, SI 2007/2051; Public Guardian (Fees, etc) (Amendment) Regulations 2007, SI 2007/2616; and Public Guardian (Fees, etc) (Amendment) Regulations 2009, SI 2009/514.

59 (*repealed*)

60 Annual report

(1) The Public Guardian must make an annual report to the Lord Chancellor about the discharge of his functions.

(2) The Lord Chancellor must, within one month of receiving the report, lay a copy of it before Parliament.

Scope of provision—This section requires the Public Guardian to make an annual report.

Annual report—The annual reports and business plans of the Office of the Public Guardian are available through the website: www.justice.gov.uk/publications/corporate-reports/office-of-the-public-guardian

Court of Protection Visitors

61 Court of Protection Visitors

(1) A Court of Protection Visitor is a person who is appointed by the Lord Chancellor to –

(a) a panel of Special Visitors, or
(b) a panel of General Visitors.

(2) A person is not qualified to be a Special Visitor unless he –

(a) is a registered medical practitioner or appears to the Lord Chancellor to have other suitable qualifications or training, and
(b) appears to the Lord Chancellor to have special knowledge of and experience in cases of impairment of or disturbance in the functioning of the mind or brain.

(3) A General Visitor need not have a medical qualification.

(4) A Court of Protection Visitor –

(a) may be appointed for such term and subject to such conditions, and
(b) may be paid such remuneration and allowances,

as the Lord Chancellor may determine.

(5) For the purpose of carrying out his functions under this Act in relation to a person who lacks capacity ('P'), a Court of Protection Visitor may, at all reasonable times, examine and take copies of –

(a) any health record,
(b) any record of, or held by, a local authority and compiled in connection with a social services function, and
(c) any record held by a person registered under Part 2 of the Care Standards Act 2000 or Chapter 2 of Part 1 of the Health and Social Care Act 2008,

so far as the record relates to P.

(6) A Court of Protection Visitor may also for that purpose interview P in private.

Amendments—SI 2010/813.

Scope of provision—The former Lord Chancellor's Visitors are recreated as Court of Protection Visitors though with some variation.

Further explanation—This topic is covered in Part I, Chapter 8 of this work.

'Special Visitor'—This will be a medical visitor, usually a consultant psychiatrist, who is asked to report (inter alia) on capacity issues.

Reports—The Visitors may be required to prepare reports for the Court of Protection (s 49(2)) or the Public Guardian (s 58(1)(d)).

PART 3
MISCELLANEOUS AND GENERAL

Declaratory provision

62 Scope of the Act

For the avoidance of doubt, it is hereby declared that nothing in this Act is to be taken to affect the law relating to murder or manslaughter or the operation of section 2 of the Suicide Act 1961 (assisting suicide).

'section 2 of the Suicide Act 1961'—It is an offence to aid, abet, counsel or procure the suicide, or attempted suicide, of another, but no prosecution may be brought without the consent of the Director of Public Prosecutions.

Private international law

63 International protection of adults

Schedule 3 –

    (a) gives effect in England and Wales to the Convention on the International Protection of Adults signed at the Hague on 13 January 2000 (Cm. 5881) (in so far as this Act does not otherwise do so), and

    (b) makes related provision as to the private international law of England and Wales.

Convention on the International Protection of Adults—Under the auspices of the Hague Conference on Private International Law (which aims to establish international agreements to reduce conflicts of law and to lay down rules to determine jurisdiction and related matters) this Convention (No 35) was concluded on 13 January 2000. It came into force on 1 January 2009. So far eight countries have ratified – the UK (in relation to Scotland), Austria, the Czech Republic, Estonia, Finland, France, Germany and Switzerland. For a full text see www.hcch.net.

General

64 Interpretation

(1) In this Act –

    'the 1985 Act' means the Enduring Powers of Attorney Act 1985,
    'advance decision' has the meaning given in section 24(1),
    'authorisation under Schedule A1' means either –
        (a) a standard authorisation under that Schedule, or
        (b) an urgent authorisation under that Schedule;
    'the court' means the Court of Protection established by section 45,
    'Court of Protection Rules' has the meaning given in section 51(1),
    'Court of Protection Visitor' has the meaning given in section 61,
    'deputy' has the meaning given in section 16(2)(b),
    'enactment' includes a provision of subordinate legislation (within the meaning of the Interpretation Act 1978),
    'health record' has the meaning given in section 68 of the Data Protection Act 1998 (as read with section 69 of that Act),
    'the Human Rights Convention' has the same meaning as 'the Convention' in the Human Rights Act 1998,
    'independent mental capacity advocate' has the meaning given in section 35(1),
    'lasting power of attorney' has the meaning given in section 9,

'life-sustaining treatment' has the meaning given in section 4(10),
'local authority', except in section 35(6A)(a) and Schedule A1, means –
  (a) the council of a county in England in which there are no district councils,
  (b) the council of a district in England,
  (c) the council of a county or county borough in Wales,
  (d) the council of a London borough,
  (e) the Common Council of the City of London, or
  (f) the Council of the Isles of Scilly,
'Mental Health Act' means the Mental Health Act 1983,
'prescribed', in relation to regulations made under this Act, means prescribed by those regulations,
'property' includes anything in action and any interest in real or personal property,
'public authority' has the same meaning as in the Human Rights Act 1998,
'Public Guardian' has the meaning given in section 57,
'purchaser' and 'purchase' have the meaning given in section 205(1) of the Law of Property Act 1925,
'social services function' has the meaning given in section 1A of the Local Authority Social Services Act 1970,
'treatment' includes a diagnostic or other procedure,
'trust corporation' has the meaning given in section 68(1) of the Trustee Act 1925, and
'will' includes codicil.

(2) In this Act, references to making decisions, in relation to a donee of a lasting power of attorney or a deputy appointed by the court, include, where appropriate, acting on decisions made.

(3) In this Act, references to the bankruptcy of an individual include a case where a bankruptcy restrictions order under the Insolvency Act 1986 has effect in respect of him.

(3A) In this Act references to a debt relief order (under Part 7A of the Insolvency Act 1986) being made in relation to an individual include a case where a debt relief restrictions order under the Insolvency Act 1986 has effect in respect of him.

(4) 'Bankruptcy restrictions order' includes an interim bankruptcy restrictions order.

(4A) 'Debt relief restrictions order' includes an interim debt relief restrictions order.

(5) In this Act, references to deprivation of a person's liberty have the same meaning as in Article 5(1) of the Human Rights Convention.

(6) For the purposes of such references, it does not matter whether a person is deprived of his liberty by a public authority or not.

Amendments—Mental Health Act 2007, s 50(7), Sch 9, Pt 1, paras 1, 10(1)–(4); Health and Social Care Act 2012; SI 2012/2404.

Scope of provision—This section provides an interpretation of some of the terms used in the Act.

65 Rules, regulations and orders

(1) Any power to make rules, regulations or orders under this Act[, other than the power in section 21] –

  (a) is exercisable by statutory instrument;

(b) includes power to make supplementary, incidental, consequential, transitional or saving provision;
(c) includes power to make different provision for different cases.

(2) Any statutory instrument containing rules, regulations or orders made by the Lord Chancellor or the Secretary of State under this Act, other than –

(a) regulations under section 34 (loss of capacity during research project),
(b) regulations under section 41 (adjusting role of independent mental capacity advocacy service),
(c) regulations under paragraph 32(1)(b) of Schedule 3 (private international law relating to the protection of adults),
(d) an order of the kind mentioned in section 67(6) (consequential amendments of primary legislation), or
(e) an order under section 68 (commencement),

is subject to annulment in pursuance of a resolution of either House of Parliament.

(3) A statutory instrument containing an Order in Council under paragraph 31 of Schedule 3 (provision to give further effect to Hague Convention) is subject to annulment in pursuance of a resolution of either House of Parliament.

(4) A statutory instrument containing regulations made by the Secretary of State under section 34 or 41 or by the Lord Chancellor under paragraph 32(1)(b) of Schedule 3 may not be made unless a draft has been laid before and approved by resolution of each House of Parliament.

(4A) Subsection (2) does not apply to a statutory instrument containing regulations made by the Secretary of State under Schedule A1.

(4B) If such a statutory instrument contains regulations under paragraph 42(2)(b), 129, 162 or 164 of Schedule A1 (whether or not it also contains other regulations), the instrument may not be made unless a draft has been laid before and approved by resolution of each House of Parliament.

(4C) Subject to that, such a statutory instrument is subject to annulment in pursuance of a resolution of either House of Parliament.

(5) An order under section 21 –

(a) may include supplementary, incidental, consequential, transitional or saving provision;
(b) may make different provision for different cases;
(c) is to be made in the form of a statutory instrument to which the Statutory Instruments Act 1946 applies as if the order were made by a Minister of the Crown; and
(d) is subject to annulment in pursuance of a resolution of either House of Parliament.

Amendments—SI 2006/1016. Subsections (4A)–(4C) inserted by the Mental Health Act 2007, s 50(7), Sch 9, Pt 1, paras 1, 11.

66 Existing receivers and enduring powers of attorney etc

(1) The following provisions cease to have effect –

(a) Part 7 of the Mental Health Act,
(b) the Enduring Powers of Attorney Act 1985.

(2) No enduring power of attorney within the meaning of the 1985 Act is to be created after the commencement of subsection (1)(b).

(3) Schedule 4 has effect in place of the 1985 Act in relation to any enduring power of attorney created before the commencement of subsection (1)(b).

(4) Schedule 5 contains transitional provisions and savings in relation to Part 7 of the Mental Health Act and the 1985 Act.

Scope of provision—The former jurisdiction in regard to the financial affairs of 'patients' under MHA 1983, Part 7 has been replaced by MCA 2005 subject to transitional provisions in Sch 5, and the Enduring Powers of Attorney Act 1985 has ceased to have effect save that its provisions have in effect been repeated in Sch 4 to the MCA 2005 in respect of those powers executed before 1 October 2007.

67 Minor and consequential amendments and repeals

(1) Schedule 6 contains minor and consequential amendments.

(2) Schedule 7 contains repeals.

(3) The Lord Chancellor may by order make supplementary, incidental, consequential, transitional or saving provision for the purposes of, in consequence of, or for giving full effect to a provision of this Act.

(4) An order under subsection (3) may, in particular –

(a) provide for a provision of this Act which comes into force before another provision of this Act has come into force to have effect, until the other provision has come into force, with specified modifications;
(b) amend, repeal or revoke an enactment, other than one contained in an Act or Measure passed in a Session after the one in which this Act is passed.

(5) The amendments that may be made under subsection (4)(b) are in addition to those made by or under any other provision of this Act.

(6) An order under subsection (3) which amends or repeals a provision of an Act or Measure may not be made unless a draft has been laid before and approved by resolution of each House of Parliament.

68 Commencement and extent

(1) This Act, other than sections 30 to 41, comes into force in accordance with provision made by order by the Lord Chancellor.

(2) Sections 30 to 41 come into force in accordance with provision made by order by –

(a) the Secretary of State, in relation to England, and
(b) the National Assembly for Wales, in relation to Wales.

(3) An order under this section may appoint different days for different provisions and different purposes.

(4) Subject to subsections (5) and (6), this Act extends to England and Wales only.

(5) The following provisions extend to the United Kingdom –

(a) paragraph 16(1) of Schedule 1 (evidence of instruments and of registration of lasting powers of attorney),

(b) paragraph 15(3) of Schedule 4 (evidence of instruments and of registration of enduring powers of attorney).

(6) Subject to any provision made in Schedule 6, the amendments and repeals made by Schedules 6 and 7 have the same extent as the enactments to which they relate.

Scope of provision—Most of the provisions of the original Act came into effect for England and Wales on 1 October 2007 though some were implemented earlier.

Orders—Mental Capacity Act 2005 (Commencement No 1) Order 2006, SI 2006/2814 (as amended by SI 2006/3473); Mental Capacity Act 2005 (Commencement No 1)(England and Wales) Order 2007, SI 2007/563; Mental Capacity Act 2005 (Commencement) (Wales) Order 2007, SI 2007/856; and Mental Capacity Act 2005 (Commencement No 2) Order 2007, SI 2007/1897.

69 Short title

This Act may be cited as the Mental Capacity Act 2005.

SCHEDULES

SCHEDULE A1
HOSPITAL AND CARE HOME RESIDENTS: DEPRIVATION OF LIBERTY

PART 1
AUTHORISATION TO DEPRIVE RESIDENTS OF LIBERTY ETC

Application of Part

1 (1) This Part applies if the following conditions are met.

(2) The first condition is that a person ('P') is detained in a hospital or care home – for the purpose of being given care or treatment – in circumstances which amount to deprivation of the person's liberty.

(3) The second condition is that a standard or urgent authorisation is in force.

(4) The third condition is that the standard or urgent authorisation relates –

(a) to P, and
(b) to the hospital or care home in which P is detained.

Amendments—Schedule A1 inserted by Mental Health Act 2007, s 50(5), Sch 7. This schedule below and related provisions above, which amend the Act to provide deprivation of liberty safeguards, were commenced on 1 April 2009 (the Mental Health Act 2007 (Commencement No 10 and Transitional Provisions) Order 2009, SI 2009/139 (C.9)). The nature and effect of the deprivation of liberty safeguards are discussed in Part I, Chapter 7 of this work. Schedule A1 does not give a power to public authorities to accommodate individuals, let alone impose an obligation upon them to do so; rather it serves solely to authorise any deprivation of their liberty arising from the fact of their accommodation by a public body: *DM v Doncaster Metropolitan Borough Council* [2011] EWHC 3652 (Admin), [2012] COPLR 362. In *AM v South London & Maudsley NHS Foundation Trust & Secretary of State for Health* [2013] UKUT 365 (AAC), [2013] COPLR 510, Charles J held (para 59) that the regime set out in this Schedule 'applies when there may be a deprivation of liberty in the sense that [the regime] applies when it appears that judged objectively there is a risk that cannot sensibly be ignored that the relevant circumstances amount to a deprivation of liberty.'

Note—With effect from 1 April 2013, when Primary Care Trusts were abolished in England, Sch A1 was amended so as to provide that local authorities perform the functions of supervisory body in respect of all authorisations of deprivations of liberty in England falling within the scope of MCA 2005, ie in both care homes and hospitals. See further paras 180–182 below.

Authorisation to deprive P of liberty

2 The managing authority of the hospital or care home may deprive P of his liberty by detaining him as mentioned in paragraph 1(2).

'Deprive P of his liberty'—See discussion at paragraphs **7.18–7.40** in Part I of this work. By virtue of MCA, s 64(5) (and whatever the position by strict reference to Article 5 of the European Convention on Human Rights), it is irrelevant whether the hospital or care home is private or state-run or the placement is arranged privately or by public authorities.

No liability for acts done for purpose of depriving P of liberty

3 (1) This paragraph applies to any act which a person ('D') does for the purpose of detaining P as mentioned in paragraph 1(2).

(2) D does not incur any liability in relation to the act that he would not have incurred if P –

    (a) had had capacity to consent in relation to D's doing the act, and
    (b) had consented to D's doing the act.

No protection for negligent acts etc

4 (1) Paragraphs 2 and 3 do not exclude a person's civil liability for loss or damage, or his criminal liability, resulting from his negligence in doing any thing.

(2) Paragraphs 2 and 3 do not authorise a person to do anything otherwise than for the purpose of the standard or urgent authorisation that is in force.

(3) In a case where a standard authorisation is in force, paragraphs 2 and 3 do not authorise a person to do anything which does not comply with the conditions (if any) included in the authorisation.

PART 2
INTERPRETATION: MAIN TERMS

Introduction

5 This Part applies for the purposes of this Schedule.

Detained resident

6 'Detained resident' means a person detained in a hospital or care home – for the purpose of being given care or treatment – in circumstances which amount to deprivation of the person's liberty.

'Deprivation of the person's liberty'—See discussion at paragraphs **7.18–7.40** in Part I of this work. By virtue of MCA, s 64(5) (and whatever the position by strict reference to Article 5 of the European Convention on Human Rights), it is irrelevant whether the hospital or care home is private or state-run or the placement is arranged privately or by public authorities. In *AM v South London & Maudsley NHS Foundation Trust & Secretary of State for Health* [2013] UKUT 365 (AAC), [2013] COPLR 510, Charles J held (para 59) that the regime set out in this Schedule 'applies when there may be a deprivation of liberty in the sense that [the regime] applies when it appears that judged objectively there is a risk that cannot sensibly be ignored that the relevant circumstances amount to a deprivation of liberty.'

Relevant person etc

7 In relation to a person who is, or is to be, a detained resident –

'relevant person' means the person in question;
'relevant hospital or care home' means the hospital or care home in question;
'relevant care or treatment' means the care or treatment in question.

Authorisations

8 'Standard authorisation' means an authorisation given under Part 4.

9 'Urgent authorisation' means an authorisation given under Part 5.

10 'Authorisation under this Schedule' means either of the following –

(a) a standard authorisation;
(b) an urgent authorisation.

11 (1) The purpose of a standard authorisation is the purpose which is stated in the authorisation in accordance with paragraph 55(1)(d).

(2) The purpose of an urgent authorisation is the purpose which is stated in the authorisation in accordance with paragraph 80(d).

PART 3
THE QUALIFYING REQUIREMENTS

The qualifying requirements

12 (1) These are the qualifying requirements referred to in this Schedule –

(a) the age requirement;
(b) the mental health requirement;
(c) the mental capacity requirement;
(d) the best interests requirement;
(e) the eligibility requirement;
(f) the no refusals requirement.

(2) Any question of whether a person who is, or is to be, a detained resident meets the qualifying requirements is to be determined in accordance with this Part.

(3) In a case where –

(a) the question of whether a person meets a particular qualifying requirement arises in relation to the giving of a standard authorisation, and
(b) any circumstances relevant to determining that question are expected to

change between the time when the determination is made and the time when the authorisation is expected to come into force,

those circumstances are to be taken into account as they are expected to be at the later time.

The age requirement

13 The relevant person meets the age requirement if he has reached 18.

The mental health requirement

14 (1) The relevant person meets the mental health requirement if he is suffering from mental disorder (within the meaning of the Mental Health Act, but disregarding any exclusion for persons with learning disability).

(2) An exclusion for persons with learning disability is any provision of the Mental Health Act which provides for a person with learning disability not to be regarded as suffering from mental disorder for one or more purposes of that Act.

'**mental disorder**' (para 14(1))—Defined as 'any disorder or disability of the mind' (MHA 1983 (as amended), s 1(2)).

'**learning disability**' (para 14(1))—Defined as 'a state of arrested or incomplete development of the mind which includes significant impairment of intelligence and social functioning' (MHA 1983 (as amended), s 1(4)).

'**exclusion for persons with learning disability**' (para 14(2))—Under MHA 1983, a person with learning disability is not to be regarded as suffering from mental disorder unless that disability 'is associated with abnormally aggressive or seriously irresponsible conduct' (MHA 1983 (as amended), s 1(2A)). This exclusion should be disregarded for the purpose of applying the deprivation of liberty safeguards.

The mental capacity requirement

15 The relevant person meets the mental capacity requirement if he lacks capacity in relation to the question whether or not he should be accommodated in the relevant hospital or care home for the purpose of being given the relevant care or treatment.

'**lacks capacity**'—Defined in MCA 2005, ss 2–3. The question is the same whether consideration is being given for purposes of an authorisation or a court order: *A Primary Care Trust v LDV* [2013] EWHC 272 (Fam), [2013] COPLR 204, at [29]. per Baker J.

The best interests requirement

16 (1) The relevant person meets the best interests requirement if all of the following conditions are met.

(2) The first condition is that the relevant person is, or is to be, a detained resident.

(3) The second condition is that it is in the best interests of the relevant person for him to be a detained resident.

(4) The third condition is that, in order to prevent harm to the relevant person, it is necessary for him to be a detained resident.

(5) The fourth condition is that it is a proportionate response to –

(a) the likelihood of the relevant person suffering harm, and
(b) the seriousness of that harm,

for him to be a detained resident.

'**best interests**' (para 16(1))—Defined in MCA 2005, s 4. See Part I, Chapter 2 of this work.

'**harm**' (para 16(5))—For a discussion on the meaning of 'harm' Part I, Chapter 2 of this work.

The eligibility requirement

17 (1) The relevant person meets the eligibility requirement unless he is ineligible to be deprived of liberty by this Act.

(2) Schedule 1A applies for the purpose of determining whether or not P is ineligible to be deprived of liberty by this Act.

'**eligibility**' (para 17(1))—The eligibility requirement and the interface between MCA 2005 and MHA 1983 were considered by Roderic Wood J in *W PCT v TB (an adult by her litigation friend the Official Solicitor)* [2009] EWHC 1737 (Fam), [2009] COPLR Con Vol 1193 and by Charles J in *GJ v The Foundation Trust* [2009] EWHC 2972 (Fam), [2009] COPLR Con Vol 567 and *AM v South London & Maudsley NHS Foundation Trust & Secretary of State for Health* [2013] UKUT 365 (AAC), [2013] COPLR 510.

The no refusals requirement

18 The relevant person meets the no refusals requirement unless there is a refusal within the meaning of paragraph 19 or 20.

19 (1) There is a refusal if these conditions are met –

(a) the relevant person has made an advance decision;
(b) the advance decision is valid;
(c) the advance decision is applicable to some or all of the relevant treatment.

(2) Expressions used in this paragraph and any of sections 24, 25 or 26 have the same meaning in this paragraph as in that section.

'**advance decision**'—See Part I, Chapter 6 of this work.

20 (1) There is a refusal if it would be in conflict with a valid decision of a donee or deputy for the relevant person to be accommodated in the relevant hospital or care home for the purpose of receiving some or all of the relevant care or treatment –

(a) in circumstances which amount to deprivation of the person's liberty, or
(b) at all.

(2) A donee is a donee of a lasting power of attorney granted by the relevant person.

(3) A decision of a donee or deputy is valid if it is made –

(a) within the scope of his authority as donee or deputy, and
(b) in accordance with Part 1 of this Act.

'**donee of a lasting power of attorney**'—See Part I, Chapter 3 of this work.

'**deputy**'—See Part I, Chapter 4 of this work.

PART 4
STANDARD AUTHORISATIONS

Supervisory body to give authorisation

21 Only the supervisory body may give a standard authorisation.

'the supervisory body'—See definitions at paras 180–182 of this Schedule. With effect from 1 April 2013, when Primary Care Trusts were abolished in England, Sch A1 was amended so as to provide that local authorities perform the functions of supervisory body in respect of all authorisations of deprivations of liberty in England falling within the scope of MCA 2005,i.e. in both care homes and hospitals. See further paras 180-182 below.

22 The supervisory body may not give a standard authorisation unless –

  (a) the managing authority of the relevant hospital or care home have requested it, or
  (b) paragraph 71 applies (right of third party to require consideration of whether authorisation needed).

'the managing authority'—See definitions at paras 176,177 and 179 of this Schedule.

23

The managing authority may not make a request for a standard authorisation unless –

  (a) they are required to do so by paragraph 24 (as read with paragraphs 27 to 29),
  (b) they are required to do so by paragraph 25 (as read with paragraph 28), or
  (c) they are permitted to do so by paragraph 30.

Duty to request authorisation: basic cases

24 (1) The managing authority must request a standard authorisation in any of the following cases.

(2) The first case is where it appears to the managing authority that the relevant person –

  (a) is not yet accommodated in the relevant hospital or care home,
  (b) is likely – at some time within the next 28 days – to be a detained resident in the relevant hospital or care home, and
  (c) is likely –
    (i) at that time, or
    (ii) at some later time within the next 28 days,
    to meet all of the qualifying requirements.

(3) The second case is where it appears to the managing authority that the relevant person –

  (a) is already accommodated in the relevant hospital or care home,
  (b) is likely – at some time within the next 28 days – to be a detained resident in the relevant hospital or care home, and
  (c) is likely –
    (i) at that time, or
    (ii) at some later time within the next 28 days,

to meet all of the qualifying requirements.

(4) The third case is where it appears to the managing authority that the relevant person –

(a) is a detained resident in the relevant hospital or care home, and
(b) meets all of the qualifying requirements, or is likely to do so at some time within the next 28 days.

(5) This paragraph is subject to paragraphs 27 to 29.

'likely – at some time within the next 28 days – to be a detained resident'—See definitions at paras 176,177 and 179 of this Schedule. In *AM v South London & Maudsley NHS Foundation Trust & Secretary of State for Health* [2013] UKUT 365 (AAC), [2013] COPLR 510, Charles J considered the meaning of the phrase 'likely – at some time within the next 28 days – to be a detained resident in Sch 1A, para 24(2) and (3), and (at para 59) agreed with the Secretary of State's submission that 'the DOLS regime applies when there may be a deprivation of liberty in the sense that [the regime] applies when it appears that judged objectively there is a risk that cannot sensibly be ignored that the relevant circumstances amount to a deprivation of liberty.'

Duty to request authorisation: change in place of detention

25 (1) The relevant managing authority must request a standard authorisation if it appears to them that these conditions are met.

(2) The first condition is that a standard authorisation –

(a) has been given, and
(b) has not ceased to be in force.

(3) The second condition is that there is, or is to be, a change in the place of detention.

(4) This paragraph is subject to paragraph 28.

26 (1) This paragraph applies for the purposes of paragraph 25.

(2) There is a change in the place of detention if the relevant person –

(a) ceases to be a detained resident in the stated hospital or care home, and
(b) becomes a detained resident in a different hospital or care home ('the new hospital or care home').

(3) The stated hospital or care home is the hospital or care home to which the standard authorisation relates.

(4) The relevant managing authority are the managing authority of the new hospital or care home.

Other authority for detention: request for authorisation

27 (1) This paragraph applies if, by virtue of section 4A(3), a decision of the court authorises the relevant person to be a detained resident.

(2) Paragraph 24 does not require a request for a standard authorisation to be made in relation to that detention unless these conditions are met.

(3) The first condition is that the standard authorisation would be in force at a time immediately after the expiry of the other authority.

(4) The second condition is that the standard authorisation would not be in force at any time on or before the expiry of the other authority.

(5) The third condition is that it would, in the managing authority's view, be unreasonable to delay making the request until a time nearer the expiry of the other authority.

(6) In this paragraph –
 (a) the other authority is –
  (i) the decision mentioned in sub-paragraph (1), or
  (ii) any further decision of the court which, by virtue of section 4A(3), authorises, or is expected to authorise, the relevant person to be a detained resident;
 (b) the expiry of the other authority is the time when the other authority is expected to cease to authorise the relevant person to be a detained resident.

Request refused: no further request unless change of circumstances

28 (1) This paragraph applies if –
 (a) a managing authority request a standard authorisation under paragraph 24 or 25, and
 (b) the supervisory body are prohibited by paragraph 50(2) from giving the authorisation.

(2) Paragraph 24 or 25 does not require that managing authority to make a new request for a standard authorisation unless it appears to the managing authority that –
 (a) there has been a change in the relevant person's case, and
 (b) because of that change, the supervisory body are likely to give a standard authorisation if requested.

Authorisation given: request for further authorisation

29 (1) This paragraph applies if a standard authorisation –
 (a) has been given in relation to the detention of the relevant person, and
 (b) that authorisation ('the existing authorisation') has not ceased to be in force.

(2) Paragraph 24 does not require a new request for a standard authorisation ('the new authorisation') to be made unless these conditions are met.

(3) The first condition is that the new authorisation would be in force at a time immediately after the expiry of the existing authorisation.

(4) The second condition is that the new authorisation would not be in force at any time on or before the expiry of the existing authorisation.

(5) The third condition is that it would, in the managing authority's view, be unreasonable to delay making the request until a time nearer the expiry of the existing authorisation.

(6) The expiry of the existing authorisation is the time when it is expected to cease to be in force.

Power to request authorisation

30 (1) This paragraph applies if –

    (a) a standard authorisation has been given in relation to the detention of the relevant person,

    (b) that authorisation ('the existing authorisation') has not ceased to be in force,

    (c) the requirement under paragraph 24 to make a request for a new standard authorisation does not apply, because of paragraph 29, and

    (d) a review of the existing authorisation has been requested, or is being carried out, in accordance with Part 8.

(2) The managing authority may request a new standard authorisation which would be in force on or before the expiry of the existing authorisation; but only if it would also be in force immediately after that expiry.

(3) The expiry of the existing authorisation is the time when it is expected to cease to be in force.

(4) Further provision relating to cases where a request is made under this paragraph can be found in –

    (a) paragraph 62 (effect of decision about request), and

    (b) paragraph 124 (effect of request on Part 8 review).

Information included in request

31 A request for a standard authorisation must include the information (if any) required by regulations.

'information ... required by regulations'—See the Mental Capacity (Deprivation of Liberty—Standard Authorisations, Assessments and Ordinary Residence) Regulations 2008, SI 2008/1858, reg 16 (text reproduced in Part V of this work) (and in relation to Wales, see SI 2009/266).

Records of requests

32 (1) The managing authority of a hospital or care home must keep a written record of –

    (a) each request that they make for a standard authorisation, and

    (b) the reasons for making each request.

(2) A supervisory body must keep a written record of each request for a standard authorisation that is made to them.

Relevant person must be assessed

33 (1) This paragraph applies if the supervisory body are requested to give a standard authorisation.

(2) The supervisory body must secure that all of these assessments are carried out in relation to the relevant person –

    (a) an age assessment;

    (b) a mental health assessment;

(c) a mental capacity assessment;
(d) a best interests assessment;
(e) an eligibility assessment;
(f) a no refusals assessment.

(3) The person who carries out any such assessment is referred to as the assessor.

(4) Regulations may be made about the period (or periods) within which assessors must carry out assessments.

(5) This paragraph is subject to paragraphs 49 and 133.

'**Regulations**' (para 33(4))—See the Mental Capacity (Deprivation of Liberty—Standard Authorisations, Assessments and Ordinary Residence) Regulations 2008, SI 2008/1858, regs 13 and 14 (text reproduced in Part V of this work).

Age assessment

34 An age assessment is an assessment of whether the relevant person meets the age requirement.

Mental health assessment

35 A mental health assessment is an assessment of whether the relevant person meets the mental health requirement.

'**mental health assessment**'—The importance in this context of ensuring that there is evidence of a mental disorder which is both current and given on the basis of objective medical expertise (and that such evidence is periodically reviewed) was emphasised by the European Court of Human Rights in *Kędzior* v Poland (Application No 45026/07) [2012] ECHR 1809, at [67] and [69].

36 When carrying out a mental health assessment, the assessor must also –
  (a) consider how (if at all) the relevant person's mental health is likely to be affected by his being a detained resident, and
  (b) notify the best interests assessor of his conclusions.

Mental capacity assessment

37 A mental capacity assessment is an assessment of whether the relevant person meets the mental capacity requirement.

Best interests assessment

38 A best interests assessment is an assessment of whether the relevant person meets the best interests requirement.

'**best interests assessment**'—The Grand Chamber of the European Court of Human Rights has emphasised that detention in a care home is 'such a serious measure that it is only justified where other, less severe measures have been considered to be insufficient to safeguard the individual or public interest which might require the person concerned be detained.' *Stanev v Bulgaria* (2012) 55 EHRR 22, at [143].

39 (1) In carrying out a best interests assessment, the assessor must comply with the duties in sub-paragraphs (2) and (3).

(2) The assessor must consult the managing authority of the relevant hospital or care home.

(3) The assessor must have regard to all of the following –

(a) the conclusions which the mental health assessor has notified to the best interests assessor in accordance with paragraph 36(b);
(b) any relevant needs assessment;
(c) any relevant care plan.

(4) A relevant needs assessment is an assessment of the relevant person's needs which –

(a) was carried out in connection with the relevant person being accommodated in the relevant hospital or care home, and
(b) was carried out by or on behalf of –
   (i) the managing authority of the relevant hospital or care home, or
   (ii) the supervisory body.

(5) A relevant care plan is a care plan which –

(a) sets out how the relevant person's needs are to be met whilst he is accommodated in the relevant hospital or care home, and
(b) was drawn up by or on behalf of –
   (i) the managing authority of the relevant hospital or care home, or
   (ii) the supervisory body.

(6) The managing authority must give the assessor a copy of –

(a) any relevant needs assessment carried out by them or on their behalf, or
(b) any relevant care plan drawn up by them or on their behalf.

(7) The supervisory body must give the assessor a copy of –

(a) any relevant needs assessment carried out by them or on their behalf, or
(b) any relevant care plan drawn up by them or on their behalf.

(8) The duties in sub-paragraphs (2) and (3) do not affect any other duty to consult or to take the views of others into account.

40 (1) This paragraph applies whatever conclusion the best interests assessment comes to.

(2) The assessor must state in the best interests assessment the name and address of every interested person whom he has consulted in carrying out the assessment.

41 Paragraphs 42 and 43 apply if the best interests assessment comes to the conclusion that the relevant person meets the best interests requirement.

42 (1) The assessor must state in the assessment the maximum authorisation period.

(2) The maximum authorisation period is the shorter of these periods –

(a) the period which, in the assessor's opinion, would be the appropriate maximum period for the relevant person to be a detained resident under the standard authorisation that has been requested;

(b) 1 year, or such shorter period as may be prescribed in regulations.

(3) Regulations under sub-paragraph (2)(b) –
- (a) need not provide for a shorter period to apply in relation to all standard authorisations;
- (b) may provide for different periods to apply in relation to different kinds of standard authorisations.

(4) Before making regulations under sub-paragraph (2)(b) the Secretary of State must consult all of the following –
- (a) each body required by regulations under paragraph 162 to monitor and report on the operation of this Schedule in relation to England;
- (b) such other persons as the Secretary of State considers it appropriate to consult.

(5) Before making regulations under sub-paragraph (2)(b) the National Assembly for Wales must consult all of the following –
- (a) each person or body directed under paragraph 163(2) to carry out any function of the Assembly of monitoring and reporting on the operation of this Schedule in relation to Wales;
- (b) such other persons as the Assembly considers it appropriate to consult.

'prescribed in regulations' (para 42(2)(b))—The power has not yet been exercised.

43 The assessor may include in the assessment recommendations about conditions to which the standard authorisation is, or is not, to be subject in accordance with paragraph 53.

44 (1) This paragraph applies if the best interests assessment comes to the conclusion that the relevant person does not meet the best interests requirement.

(2) If, on the basis of the information taken into account in carrying out the assessment, it appears to the assessor that there is an unauthorised deprivation of liberty, he must include a statement to that effect in the assessment.

(3) There is an unauthorised deprivation of liberty if the managing authority of the relevant hospital or care home are already depriving the relevant person of his liberty without authority of the kind mentioned in section 4A.

45 The duties with which the best interests assessor must comply are subject to the provision included in appointment regulations under Part 10 (in particular, provision made under paragraph 146).

'appointment regulations'—Mental Capacity (Deprivation of Liberty—Appointment of Relevant Person's Representative) Regulations 2008, SI 2008/1315 (as amended by SI 2008/2368) (text reproduced in Part V of this work). For Wales, see the Mental Capacity (Deprivation of Liberty: Appointment of Relevant Person's Representative) (Wales) Regulations 2009, SI 2009/266. No provision has as yet been made under para 146.

Eligibility assessment

46 An eligibility assessment is an assessment of whether the relevant person meets the eligibility requirement.

47 (1) Regulations may –

(a) require an eligibility assessor to request a best interests assessor to provide relevant eligibility information, and

(b) require the best interests assessor, if such a request is made, to provide such relevant eligibility information as he may have.

(2) In this paragraph –

'best interests assessor' means any person who is carrying out, or has carried out, a best interests assessment in relation to the relevant person;

'eligibility assessor' means a person carrying out an eligibility assessment in relation to the relevant person;

'relevant eligibility information' is information relevant to assessing whether or not the relevant person is ineligible by virtue of paragraph 5 of Schedule 1A.

'Regulations may' (para 47(1))—See the Mental Capacity (Deprivation of Liberty—Standard Authorisations, Assessments and Ordinary Residence) Regulations 2008, SI 2008/1858, reg 15 (text reproduced in Part V of this work).

No refusals assessment

48 A no refusals assessment is an assessment of whether the relevant person meets the no refusals requirement.

Equivalent assessment already carried out

49 (1) The supervisory body are not required by paragraph 33 to secure that a particular kind of assessment ('the required assessment') is carried out in relation to the relevant person if the following conditions are met.

(2) The first condition is that the supervisory body have a written copy of an assessment of the relevant person ('the existing assessment') that has already been carried out.

(3) The second condition is that the existing assessment complies with all requirements under this Schedule with which the required assessment would have to comply (if it were carried out).

(4) The third condition is that the existing assessment was carried out within the previous 12 months; but this condition need not be met if the required assessment is an age assessment.

(5) The fourth condition is that the supervisory body are satisfied that there is no reason why the existing assessment may no longer be accurate.

(6) If the required assessment is a best interests assessment, in satisfying themselves as mentioned in sub-paragraph (5), the supervisory body must take into account any information given, or submissions made, by –

(a) the relevant person's representative,
(b) any section 39C IMCA, or
(c) any section 39D IMCA.

(7) It does not matter whether the existing assessment was carried out in connection with a request for a standard authorisation or for some other purpose.

(8) If, because of this paragraph, the supervisory body are not required by paragraph 33 to secure that the required assessment is carried out, the existing assessment is to be treated for the purposes of this Schedule –

  (a) as an assessment of the same kind as the required assessment, and
  (b) as having been carried out under paragraph 33 in connection with the request for the standard authorisation.

Duty to give authorisation

50 (1) The supervisory body must give a standard authorisation if –

  (a) all assessments are positive, and
  (b) the supervisory body have written copies of all those assessments.

(2) The supervisory body must not give a standard authorisation except in accordance with sub-paragraph (1).

(3) All assessments are positive if each assessment carried out under paragraph 33 has come to the conclusion that the relevant person meets the qualifying requirement to which the assessment relates.

Terms of authorisation

51 (1) If the supervisory body are required to give a standard authorisation, they must decide the period during which the authorisation is to be in force.

(2) That period must not exceed the maximum authorisation period stated in the best interests assessment.

52 A standard authorisation may provide for the authorisation to come into force at a time after it is given.

53 (1) A standard authorisation may be given subject to conditions.

(2) Before deciding whether to give the authorisation subject to conditions, the supervisory body must have regard to any recommendations in the best interests assessment about such conditions.

(3) The managing authority of the relevant hospital or care home must ensure that any conditions are complied with.

'**Conditions**' (para 53(1))—It is suggested that the wording of para 53(3) is such that the only conditions which can be imposed are those over the implementation of which the managing authority has a degree of control. A managing authority could not otherwise be expected to be able to comply with the duty to ensure that they are complied with. In other words, conditions cannot be imposed which are directed solely against third parties (for instance, by way of providing that other statutory bodies should undertake assessments). In practice, this can significantly limit the utility of conditions, although where a supervisory body takes the view that a deprivation of liberty can only be authorised subject to a condition falling outside the scope of para 53, such is a clear indication that the supervisory body should be taking appropriate steps to obtain an authorisation from the Court of Protection by way of an order under MCA 2005, s 16.

'**managing authority**' (para 53(3))—See paras 176–179 below. In respect of a care home, this is a specific individual required to be registered by the relevant provisions of the English or Welsh legislation.

Form of authorisation

54 A standard authorisation must be in writing.

55 (1) A standard authorisation must state the following things –

    (a) the name of the relevant person;
    (b) the name of the relevant hospital or care home;
    (c) the period during which the authorisation is to be in force;
    (d) the purpose for which the authorisation is given;
    (e) any conditions subject to which the authorisation is given;
    (f) the reason why each qualifying requirement is met.

(2) The statement of the reason why the eligibility requirement is met must be framed by reference to the cases in the table in paragraph 2 of Schedule 1A.

56 (1) If the name of the relevant hospital or care home changes, the standard authorisation is to be read as if it stated the current name of the hospital or care home.

(2) But sub-paragraph (1) is subject to any provision relating to the change of name which is made in any enactment or in any instrument made under an enactment.

Duty to give information about decision

57 (1) This paragraph applies if –

    (a) a request is made for a standard authorisation, and
    (b) the supervisory body are required by paragraph 50(1) to give the standard authorisation.

(2) The supervisory body must give a copy of the authorisation to each of the following –

    (a) the relevant person's representative;
    (b) the managing authority of the relevant hospital or care home;
    (c) the relevant person;
    (d) any section 39A IMCA;
    (e) every interested person consulted by the best interests assessor.

(3) The supervisory body must comply with this paragraph as soon as practicable after they give the standard authorisation.

58 (1) This paragraph applies if –

    (a) a request is made for a standard authorisation, and
    (b) the supervisory body are prohibited by paragraph 50(2) from giving the standard authorisation.

(2) The supervisory body must give notice, stating that they are prohibited from giving the authorisation, to each of the following –

    (a) the managing authority of the relevant hospital or care home;
    (b) the relevant person;
    (c) any section 39A IMCA;
    (d) every interested person consulted by the best interests assessor.

(3) The supervisory body must comply with this paragraph as soon as practicable after it becomes apparent to them that they are prohibited from giving the authorisation.

Duty to give information about effect of authorisation

59 (1) This paragraph applies if a standard authorisation is given.

(2) The managing authority of the relevant hospital or care home must take such steps as are practicable to ensure that the relevant person understands all of the following –

    (a) the effect of the authorisation;
    (b) the right to make an application to the court to exercise its jurisdiction under section 21A;
    (c) the right under Part 8 to request a review;
    (d) the right to have a section 39D IMCA appointed;
    (e) how to have a section 39D IMCA appointed.

(3) Those steps must be taken as soon as is practicable after the authorisation is given.

(4) Those steps must include the giving of appropriate information both orally and in writing.

(5) Any written information given to the relevant person must also be given by the managing authority to the relevant person's representative.

(6) They must give the information to the representative as soon as is practicable after it is given to the relevant person.

(7) Sub-paragraph (8) applies if the managing authority is notified that a section 39D IMCA has been appointed.

(8) As soon as is practicable after being notified, the managing authority must give the section 39D IMCA a copy of the written information given in accordance with sub-paragraph (4).

Records of authorisations

60 A supervisory body must keep a written record of all of the following information –

    (a) the standard authorisations that they have given;
    (b) the requests for standard authorisations in response to which they have not given an authorisation;
    (c) in relation to each standard authorisation given: the matters stated in the authorisation in accordance with paragraph 55.

Variation of an authorisation

61 (1) A standard authorisation may not be varied except in accordance with Part 7 or 8.

(2) This paragraph does not affect the powers of the Court of Protection or of any other court.

Effect of decision about request made under paragraph 25 or 30

62 (1) This paragraph applies where the managing authority request a new standard authorisation under either of the following –

(a) paragraph 25 (change in place of detention);
(b) paragraph 30 (existing authorisation subject to review).

(2) If the supervisory body are required by paragraph 50(1) to give the new authorisation, the existing authorisation terminates at the time when the new authorisation comes into force.

(3) If the supervisory body are prohibited by paragraph 50(2) from giving the new authorisation, there is no effect on the existing authorisation's continuation in force.

When an authorisation is in force

63 (1) A standard authorisation comes into force when it is given.

(2) But if the authorisation provides for it to come into force at a later time, it comes into force at that time.

'**Comes into force when it is given**' (para 63(1)—this means the exact time on the day when it is given: *Re MB* [2010] EWHC 2508 (COP), [2010] COPLR Con Vol 65 at paragraph 45, per Charles J.

64 (1) A standard authorisation ceases to be in force at the end of the period stated in the authorisation in accordance with paragraph 55(1)(c).

(2) But if the authorisation terminates before then in accordance with paragraph 62(2) or any other provision of this Schedule, it ceases to be in force when the termination takes effect.

(3) This paragraph does not affect the powers of the Court of Protection or of any other court.

'**Ceases to be in force**' (para 64(1)]—In *Re UF* [2013] EWHC 4289 (COP), [2014] COPLR 93, Charles J held that the Court has the power 'to vary an existing standard authorisation by extending (or shortening) it and that if and when it exercises that power it would normally be sensible for the court to give consideration to whether it should then exercise its powers under ss (6) and (7) or give directions concerning its future exercise of those powers,' but doubted that the Court would have the power to extend a standard authorisation beyond the possible maximum period of one year

65 (1) This paragraph applies if a standard authorisation ceases to be in force.

(2) The supervisory body must give notice that the authorisation has ceased to be in force.

(3) The supervisory body must give that notice to all of the following –

(a) the managing authority of the relevant hospital or care home;
(b) the relevant person;
(c) the relevant person's representative;
(d) every interested person consulted by the best interests assessor.

(4) The supervisory body must give that notice as soon as practicable after the authorisation ceases to be in force.

Mental Capacity Act 2005 **Sch A1**

When a request for a standard authorisation is 'disposed of'

66 A request for a standard authorisation is to be regarded for the purposes of this Schedule as disposed of if the supervisory body have given –

(a) a copy of the authorisation in accordance with paragraph 57, or
(b) notice in accordance with paragraph 58.

Right of third party to require consideration of whether authorisation needed

67 For the purposes of paragraphs 68 to 73 there is an unauthorised deprivation of liberty if –

(a) a person is already a detained resident in a hospital or care home, and
(b) the detention of the person is not authorised as mentioned in section 4A.

68 (1) If the following conditions are met, an eligible person may request the supervisory body to decide whether or not there is an unauthorised deprivation of liberty.

(2) The first condition is that the eligible person has notified the managing authority of the relevant hospital or care home that it appears to the eligible person that there is an unauthorised deprivation of liberty.

(3) The second condition is that the eligible person has asked the managing authority to request a standard authorisation in relation to the detention of the relevant person.

(4) The third condition is that the managing authority has not requested a standard authorisation within a reasonable period after the eligible person asks it to do so.

(5) In this paragraph 'eligible person' means any person other than the managing authority of the relevant hospital or care home.

69 (1) This paragraph applies if an eligible person requests the supervisory body to decide whether or not there is an unauthorised deprivation of liberty.

(2) The supervisory body must select and appoint a person to carry out an assessment of whether or not the relevant person is a detained resident.

(3) But the supervisory body need not select and appoint a person to carry out such an assessment in either of these cases.

(4) The first case is where it appears to the supervisory body that the request by the eligible person is frivolous or vexatious.

(5) The second case is where it appears to the supervisory body that –

(a) the question of whether or not there is an unauthorised deprivation of liberty has already been decided, and
(b) since that decision, there has been no change of circumstances which would merit the question being decided again.

(6) The supervisory body must not select and appoint a person to carry out an assessment under this paragraph unless it appears to the supervisory body that the person would be –

(a) suitable to carry out a best interests assessment (if one were obtained in connection with a request for a standard authorisation relating to the relevant person), and
(b) eligible to carry out such a best interests assessment.

(7) The supervisory body must notify the persons specified in sub-paragraph (8) –

(a) that the supervisory body have been requested to decide whether or not there is an unauthorised deprivation of liberty;
(b) of their decision whether or not to select and appoint a person to carry out an assessment under this paragraph;
(c) if their decision is to select and appoint a person, of the person appointed.

(8) The persons referred to in sub-paragraph (7) are –

(a) the eligible person who made the request under paragraph 68;
(b) the person to whom the request relates;
(c) the managing authority of the relevant hospital or care home;
(d) any section 39A IMCA.

70 (1) Regulations may be made about the period within which an assessment under paragraph 69 must be carried out.

(2) Regulations made under paragraph 129(3) apply in relation to the selection and appointment of a person under paragraph 69 as they apply to the selection of a person under paragraph 129 to carry out a best interests assessment.

(3) The following provisions apply to an assessment under paragraph 69 as they apply to an assessment carried out in connection with a request for a standard authorisation –

(a) paragraph 131 (examination and copying of records);
(b) paragraph 132 (representations);
(c) paragraphs 134 and 135(1) and (2) (duty to keep records and give copies).

(4) The copies of the assessment which the supervisory body are required to give under paragraph 135(2) must be given as soon as practicable after the supervisory body are themselves given a copy of the assessment.

'**Regulations**' (para 70(1))—See the Mental Capacity (Deprivation of Liberty—Standard Authorisations, Assessments and Ordinary Residence) Regulations 2008, SI 2008/1858, reg 14 (text reproduced in Part V of this work).

'**Regulations made under paragraph 129(3)**' (para 70(2))—Namely the Mental Capacity (Deprivation of Liberty—Standard Authorisations, Assessments and Ordinary Residence) Regulations 2008, SI 2008/1858, as amended by Mental Capacity (Deprivation of Liberty: Monitoring and Reporting; and Assessments – Amendment) Regulations 2009, SI 2009/827. For Wales, the relevant regulations are Mental Capacity (Deprivation of Liberty: Assessments, Standard Authorisations and Disputes about Residence) (Wales) Regulations 2009, SI 2009/783.

71 (1) This paragraph applies if –

(a) the supervisory body obtain an assessment under paragraph 69,
(b) the assessment comes to the conclusion that the relevant person is a detained resident, and
(c) it appears to the supervisory body that the detention of the person is not authorised as mentioned in section 4A.

(2) This Schedule (including Part 5) applies as if the managing authority of the relevant hospital or care home had, in accordance with Part 4, requested the supervisory body to give a standard authorisation in relation to the relevant person.

(3) The managing authority of the relevant hospital or care home must supply the supervisory body with the information (if any) which the managing authority would, by virtue of paragraph 31, have had to include in a request for a standard authorisation.

(4) The supervisory body must notify the persons specified in paragraph 69(8) –

    (a) of the outcome of the assessment obtained under paragraph 69, and
    (b) that this Schedule applies as mentioned in sub-paragraph (2).

72 (1) This paragraph applies if –

    (a) the supervisory body obtain an assessment under paragraph 69, and
    (b) the assessment comes to the conclusion that the relevant person is not a detained resident.

(2) The supervisory body must notify the persons specified in paragraph 69(8) of the outcome of the assessment.

73 (1) This paragraph applies if –

    (a) the supervisory body obtain an assessment under paragraph 69,
    (b) the assessment comes to the conclusion that the relevant person is a detained resident, and
    (c) it appears to the supervisory body that the detention of the person is authorised as mentioned in section 4A.

(2) The supervisory body must notify the persons specified in paragraph 69(8) –

    (a) of the outcome of the assessment, and
    (b) that it appears to the supervisory body that the detention is authorised.

PART 5
URGENT AUTHORISATIONS

Managing authority to give authorisation

74 Only the managing authority of the relevant hospital or care home may give an urgent authorisation.

75 The managing authority may give an urgent authorisation only if they are required to do so by paragraph 76 (as read with paragraph 77).

Duty to give authorisation

76 (1) The managing authority must give an urgent authorisation in either of the following cases.

(2) The first case is where –

    (a) the managing authority are required to make a request under paragraph 24 or 25 for a standard authorisation, and

(b) they believe that the need for the relevant person to be a detained resident is so urgent that it is appropriate for the detention to begin before they make the request.

(3) The second case is where –

(a) the managing authority have made a request under paragraph 24 or 25 for a standard authorisation, and
(b) they believe that the need for the relevant person to be a detained resident is so urgent that it is appropriate for the detention to begin before the request is disposed of.

(4) References in this paragraph to the detention of the relevant person are references to the detention to which paragraph 24 or 25 relates.

(5) This paragraph is subject to paragraph 77.

77 (1) This paragraph applies where the managing authority have given an urgent authorisation ('the original authorisation') in connection with a case where a person is, or is to be, a detained resident ('the existing detention').

(2) No new urgent authorisation is to be given under paragraph 76 in connection with the existing detention.

(3) But the managing authority may request the supervisory body to extend the duration of the original authorisation.

(4) Only one request under sub-paragraph (3) may be made in relation to the original authorisation.

(5) Paragraphs 84 to 86 apply to any request made under sub-paragraph (3).

Terms of authorisation

78 (1) If the managing authority decide to give an urgent authorisation, they must decide the period during which the authorisation is to be in force.

(2) That period must not exceed 7 days.

Form of authorisation

79 An urgent authorisation must be in writing.

80 An urgent authorisation must state the following things –

(a) the name of the relevant person;
(b) the name of the relevant hospital or care home;
(c) the period during which the authorisation is to be in force;
(d) the purpose for which the authorisation is given.

81 (1) If the name of the relevant hospital or care home changes, the urgent authorisation is to be read as if it stated the current name of the hospital or care home.

(2) But sub-paragraph (1) is subject to any provision relating to the change of name which is made in any enactment or in any instrument made under an enactment.

Duty to keep records and give copies

82 (1) This paragraph applies if an urgent authorisation is given.

(2) The managing authority must keep a written record of why they have given the urgent authorisation.

(3) As soon as practicable after giving the authorisation, the managing authority must give a copy of the authorisation to all of the following –

- (a) the relevant person;
- (b) any section 39A IMCA.

Duty to give information about authorisation

83 (1) This paragraph applies if an urgent authorisation is given.

(2) The managing authority of the relevant hospital or care home must take such steps as are practicable to ensure that the relevant person understands all of the following –

- (a) the effect of the authorisation;
- (b) the right to make an application to the court to exercise its jurisdiction under section 21A.

(3) Those steps must be taken as soon as is practicable after the authorisation is given.

(4) Those steps must include the giving of appropriate information both orally and in writing.

Request for extension of duration

84 (1) This paragraph applies if the managing authority make a request under paragraph 77 for the supervisory body to extend the duration of the original authorisation.

(2) The managing authority must keep a written record of why they have made the request.

(3) The managing authority must give the relevant person notice that they have made the request.

(4) The supervisory body may extend the duration of the original authorisation if it appears to them that –

- (a) the managing authority have made the required request for a standard authorisation,
- (b) there are exceptional reasons why it has not yet been possible for that request to be disposed of, and
- (c) it is essential for the existing detention to continue until the request is disposed of.

(5) The supervisory body must keep a written record that the request has been made to them.

(6) In this paragraph and paragraphs 85 and 86 –

- (a) 'original authorisation' and 'existing detention' have the same meaning as in paragraph 77;

(b) the required request for a standard authorisation is the request that is referred to in paragraph 76(2) or (3).

85 (1) This paragraph applies if, under paragraph 84, the supervisory body decide to extend the duration of the original authorisation.

(2) The supervisory body must decide the period of the extension.

(3) That period must not exceed 7 days.

(4) The supervisory body must give the managing authority notice stating the period of the extension.

(5) The managing authority must then vary the original authorisation so that it states the extended duration.

(6) Paragraphs 82(3) and 83 apply (with the necessary modifications) to the variation of the original authorisation as they apply to the giving of an urgent authorisation.

(7) The supervisory body must keep a written record of –

    (a) the outcome of the request, and
    (b) the period of the extension.

'**must not exceed 7 days**' (para 85(3))—The calculation of the maximum period of 7 days for an urgent authorisation and any extension of an urgent authorisation should be calculated by including the whole of the day on which the urgent authorisation was actually given: *Re MB* [2010] EWHC 2508 (COP), [2010] COPLR Con Vol 65, at [41], per Charles J. In calculating whether an urgent authorisation or its extension exceeds the maximum period allowed, the period ends at the end of the last day: *Re MB,* at [43].

86 (1) This paragraph applies if, under paragraph 84, the supervisory body decide not to extend the duration of the original authorisation.

(2) The supervisory body must give the managing authority notice stating –

    (a) the decision, and
    (b) their reasons for making it.

(3) The managing authority must give a copy of that notice to all of the following –

    (a) the relevant person;
    (b) any section 39A IMCA.

(4) The supervisory body must keep a written record of the outcome of the request.

No variation

87 (1) An urgent authorisation may not be varied except in accordance with paragraph 85.

(2) This paragraph does not affect the powers of the Court of Protection or of any other court.

When an authorisation is in force

88 An urgent authorisation comes into force when it is given.

'**Comes into force when it is given**'—This means the exact time on the day when it is given: *Re MB* [2010] EWHC 2508 (COP), [2010] COPLR Con Vol 65, at [35], per Charles J. The calculation of the maximum period of 7 days for an urgent authorisation and any extension of an urgent authorisation should be calculated by including the whole of the day on which the urgent authorisation was actually given: *Re MB*, at [41].

89 (1) An urgent authorisation ceases to be in force at the end of the period stated in the authorisation in accordance with paragraph 80(c) (subject to any variation in accordance with paragraph 85).

(2) But if the required request is disposed of before the end of that period, the urgent authorisation ceases to be in force as follows.

(3) If the supervisory body are required by paragraph 50(1) to give the requested authorisation, the urgent authorisation ceases to be in force when the requested authorisation comes into force.

(4) If the supervisory body are prohibited by paragraph 50(2) from giving the requested authorisation, the urgent authorisation ceases to be in force when the managing authority receive notice under paragraph 58.

(5) In this paragraph –

'required request' means the request referred to in paragraph 76(2) or (3);
'requested authorisation' means the standard authorisation to which the required request relates.

(6) This paragraph does not affect the powers of the Court of Protection or of any other court.

90 (1) This paragraph applies if an urgent authorisation ceases to be in force.

(2) The supervisory body must give notice that the authorisation has ceased to be in force.

(3) The supervisory body must give that notice to all of the following –

(a) the relevant person;
(b) any section 39A IMCA.

(4) The supervisory body must give that notice as soon as practicable after the authorisation ceases to be in force.

PART 6
ELIGIBILITY REQUIREMENT NOT MET: SUSPENSION OF STANDARD AUTHORISATION

91 (1) This Part applies if the following conditions are met.

(2) The first condition is that a standard authorisation –

(a) has been given, and
(b) has not ceased to be in force.

(3) The second condition is that the managing authority of the relevant hospital or care home are satisfied that the relevant person has ceased to meet the eligibility requirement.

(4) But this Part does not apply if the relevant person is ineligible by virtue of paragraph 5 of Schedule 1A (in which case see Part 8).

PART III COURT OF PROTECTION PRACTICE 2016

92 The managing authority of the relevant hospital or care home must give the supervisory body notice that the relevant person has ceased to meet the eligibility requirement.

93 (1) This paragraph applies if the managing authority give the supervisory body notice under paragraph 92.

(2) The standard authorisation is suspended from the time when the notice is given.

(3) The supervisory body must give notice that the standard authorisation has been suspended to the following persons –

   (a) the relevant person;
   (b) the relevant person's representative;
   (c) the managing authority of the relevant hospital or care home.

94 (1) This paragraph applies if, whilst the standard authorisation is suspended, the managing authority are satisfied that the relevant person meets the eligibility requirement again.

(2) The managing authority must give the supervisory body notice that the relevant person meets the eligibility requirement again.

95 (1) This paragraph applies if the managing authority give the supervisory body notice under paragraph 94.

(2) The standard authorisation ceases to be suspended from the time when the notice is given.

(3) The supervisory body must give notice that the standard authorisation has ceased to be suspended to the following persons –

   (a) the relevant person;
   (b) the relevant person's representative;
   (c) any section 39D IMCA;
   (d) the managing authority of the relevant hospital or care home.

(4) The supervisory body must give notice under this paragraph as soon as practicable after they are given notice under paragraph 94.

96 (1) This paragraph applies if no notice is given under paragraph 94 before the end of the relevant 28 day period.

(2) The standard authorisation ceases to have effect at the end of the relevant 28 day period.

(3) The relevant 28 day period is the period of 28 days beginning with the day on which the standard authorisation is suspended under paragraph 93.

97 The effect of suspending the standard authorisation is that Part 1 ceases to apply for as long as the authorisation is suspended.

PART 7
STANDARD AUTHORISATIONS: CHANGE IN SUPERVISORY RESPONSIBILITY

Application of this Part

98 (1) This Part applies if these conditions are met.

(2) The first condition is that a standard authorisation –

    (a) has been given, and

    (b) has not ceased to be in force.

(3) The second condition is that there is a change in supervisory responsibility.

(4) The third condition is that there is not a change in the place of detention (within the meaning of paragraph 25).

99 For the purposes of this Part there is a change in supervisory responsibility if –

    (a) one body ('the old supervisory body') have ceased to be supervisory body in relation to the standard authorisation, and

    (b) a different body ('the new supervisory body') have become supervisory body in relation to the standard authorisation.

Effect of change in supervisory responsibility

100 (1) The new supervisory body becomes the supervisory body in relation to the authorisation.

(2) Anything done by or in relation to the old supervisory body in connection with the authorisation has effect, so far as is necessary for continuing its effect after the change, as if done by or in relation to the new supervisory body.

(3) Anything which relates to the authorisation and which is in the process of being done by or in relation to the old supervisory body at the time of the change may be continued by or in relation to the new supervisory body.

(4) But –

    (a) the old supervisory body do not, by virtue of this paragraph, cease to be liable for anything done by them in connection with the authorisation before the change; and

    (b) the new supervisory body do not, by virtue of this paragraph, become liable for any such thing.

PART 8
STANDARD AUTHORISATIONS: REVIEW

Application of this Part

101 (1) This Part applies if a standard authorisation –

    (a) has been given, and

    (b) has not ceased to be in force.

(2) Paragraphs 102 to 122 are subject to paragraphs 123 to 125.

Review by supervisory body

102 (1) The supervisory body may at any time carry out a review of the standard authorisation in accordance with this Part.

(2) The supervisory body must carry out such a review if they are requested to do so by an eligible person.

(3) Each of the following is an eligible person –

(a) the relevant person;
(b) the relevant person's representative;
(c) the managing authority of the relevant hospital or care home.

Request for review

103 (1) An eligible person may, at any time, request the supervisory body to carry out a review of the standard authorisation in accordance with this Part.

(2) The managing authority of the relevant hospital or care home must make such a request if one or more of the qualifying requirements appear to them to be reviewable.

Grounds for review

104 (1) Paragraphs 105 to 107 set out the grounds on which the qualifying requirements are reviewable.

(2) A qualifying requirement is not reviewable on any other ground.

Non-qualification ground

105 (1) Any of the following qualifying requirements is reviewable on the ground that the relevant person does not meet the requirement –

(a) the age requirement;
(b) the mental health requirement;
(c) the mental capacity requirement;
(d) the best interests requirement;
(e) the no refusals requirement.

(2) The eligibility requirement is reviewable on the ground that the relevant person is ineligible by virtue of paragraph 5 of Schedule 1A.

(3) The ground in sub-paragraph (1) and the ground in sub-paragraph (2) are referred to as the non-qualification ground.

Change of reason ground

106 (1) Any of the following qualifying requirements is reviewable on the ground set out in sub-paragraph (2) –

(a) the mental health requirement;
(b) the mental capacity requirement;
(c) the best interests requirement;

(d) the eligibility requirement;
(e) the no refusals requirement.

(2) The ground is that the reason why the relevant person meets the requirement is not the reason stated in the standard authorisation.

(3) This ground is referred to as the change of reason ground.

Variation of conditions ground

107 (1) The best interests requirement is reviewable on the ground that –
  (a) there has been a change in the relevant person's case, and
  (b) because of that change, it would be appropriate to vary the conditions to which the standard authorisation is subject.

(2) This ground is referred to as the variation of conditions ground.

(3) A reference to varying the conditions to which the standard authorisation is subject is a reference to –
  (a) amendment of an existing condition,
  (b) omission of an existing condition, or
  (c) inclusion of a new condition (whether or not there are already any existing conditions).

Notice that review to be carried out

108 (1) If the supervisory body are to carry out a review of the standard authorisation, they must give notice of the review to the following persons –
  (a) the relevant person;
  (b) the relevant person's representative;
  (c) the managing authority of the relevant hospital or care home.

(2) The supervisory body must give the notice –
  (a) before they begin the review, or
  (b) if that is not practicable, as soon as practicable after they have begun it.

(3) This paragraph does not require the supervisory body to give notice to any person who has requested the review.

Starting a review

109 To start a review of the standard authorisation, the supervisory body must decide which, if any, of the qualifying requirements appear to be reviewable.

No reviewable qualifying requirements

110 (1) This paragraph applies if no qualifying requirements appear to be reviewable.

(2) This Part does not require the supervisory body to take any action in respect of the standard authorisation.

One or more reviewable qualifying requirements

111 (1) This paragraph applies if one or more qualifying requirements appear to be reviewable.

(2) The supervisory body must secure that a separate review assessment is carried out in relation to each qualifying requirement which appears to be reviewable.

(3) But sub-paragraph (2) does not require the supervisory body to secure that a best interests review assessment is carried out in a case where the best interests requirement appears to the supervisory body to be non-assessable.

(4) The best interests requirement is non-assessable if –

(a) the requirement is reviewable only on the variation of conditions ground, and
(b) the change in the relevant person's case is not significant.

(5) In making any decision whether the change in the relevant person's case is significant, regard must be had to –

(a) the nature of the change, and
(b) the period that the change is likely to last for.

Review assessments

112 (1) A review assessment is an assessment of whether the relevant person meets a qualifying requirement.

(2) In relation to a review assessment –

(a) a negative conclusion is a conclusion that the relevant person does not meet the qualifying requirement to which the assessment relates;
(b) a positive conclusion is a conclusion that the relevant person meets the qualifying requirement to which the assessment relates.

(3) An age review assessment is a review assessment carried out in relation to the age requirement.

(4) A mental health review assessment is a review assessment carried out in relation to the mental health requirement.

(5) A mental capacity review assessment is a review assessment carried out in relation to the mental capacity requirement.

(6) A best interests review assessment is a review assessment carried out in relation to the best interests requirement.

(7) An eligibility review assessment is a review assessment carried out in relation to the eligibility requirement.

(8) A no refusals review assessment is a review assessment carried out in relation to the no refusals requirement.

113 (1) In carrying out a review assessment, the assessor must comply with any duties which would be imposed upon him under Part 4 if the assessment were being carried out in connection with a request for a standard authorisation.

(2) But in the case of a best interests review assessment, paragraphs 43 and 44 do not apply.

(3) Instead of what is required by paragraph 43, the best interests review assessment must include recommendations about whether – and, if so, how – it would be appropriate to vary the conditions to which the standard authorisation is subject.

Best interests requirement reviewable but non-assessable

114 (1) This paragraph applies in a case where –

(a) the best interests requirement appears to be reviewable, but
(b) in accordance with paragraph 111(3), the supervisory body are not required to secure that a best interests review assessment is carried out.

(2) The supervisory body may vary the conditions to which the standard authorisation is subject in such ways (if any) as the supervisory body think are appropriate in the circumstances.

Best interests review assessment positive

115 (1) This paragraph applies in a case where –

(a) a best interests review assessment is carried out, and
(b) the assessment comes to a positive conclusion.

(2) The supervisory body must decide the following questions –

(a) whether or not the best interests requirement is reviewable on the change of reason ground;
(b) whether or not the best interests requirement is reviewable on the variation of conditions ground;
(c) if so, whether or not the change in the person's case is significant.

(3) If the supervisory body decide that the best interests requirement is reviewable on the change of reason ground, they must vary the standard authorisation so that it states the reason why the relevant person now meets that requirement.

(4) If the supervisory body decide that –

(a) the best interests requirement is reviewable on the variation of conditions ground, and
(b) the change in the relevant person's case is not significant,

they may vary the conditions to which the standard authorisation is subject in such ways (if any) as they think are appropriate in the circumstances.

(5) If the supervisory body decide that –

(a) the best interests requirement is reviewable on the variation of conditions ground, and
(b) the change in the relevant person's case is significant,

they must vary the conditions to which the standard authorisation is subject in such ways as they think are appropriate in the circumstances.

(6) If the supervisory body decide that the best interests requirement is not reviewable on –

(a) the change of reason ground, or
(b) the variation of conditions ground,

this Part does not require the supervisory body to take any action in respect of the standard authorisation so far as the best interests requirement relates to it.

Mental health, mental capacity, eligibility or no refusals review assessment positive

116 (1) This paragraph applies if the following conditions are met.

(2) The first condition is that one or more of the following are carried out –

    (a) a mental health review assessment;
    (b) a mental capacity review assessment;
    (c) an eligibility review assessment;
    (d) a no refusals review assessment.

(3) The second condition is that each assessment carried out comes to a positive conclusion.

(4) The supervisory body must decide whether or not each of the assessed qualifying requirements is reviewable on the change of reason ground.

(5) If the supervisory body decide that any of the assessed qualifying requirements is reviewable on the change of reason ground, they must vary the standard authorisation so that it states the reason why the relevant person now meets the requirement or requirements in question.

(6) If the supervisory body decide that none of the assessed qualifying requirements are reviewable on the change of reason ground, this Part does not require the supervisory body to take any action in respect of the standard authorisation so far as those requirements relate to it.

(7) An assessed qualifying requirement is a qualifying requirement in relation to which a review assessment is carried out.

One or more review assessments negative

117 (1) This paragraph applies if one or more of the review assessments carried out comes to a negative conclusion.

(2) The supervisory body must terminate the standard authorisation with immediate effect.

Completion of a review

118 (1) The review of the standard authorisation is complete in any of the following cases.

(2) The first case is where paragraph 110 applies.

(3) The second case is where –

    (a) paragraph 111 applies, and
    (b) paragraph 117 requires the supervisory body to terminate the standard authorisation.

(4) In such a case, the supervisory body need not comply with any of the other provisions of paragraphs 114 to 116 which would be applicable to the review (were it not for this sub-paragraph).

(5) The third case is where –
   (a) paragraph 111 applies,
   (b) paragraph 117 does not require the supervisory body to terminate the standard authorisation, and
   (c) the supervisory body comply with all of the provisions of paragraphs 114 to 116 (so far as they are applicable to the review).

Variations under this Part

119 Any variation of the standard authorisation made under this Part must be in writing.

Notice of outcome of review

120 (1) When the review of the standard authorisation is complete, the supervisory body must give notice to all of the following –
   (a) the managing authority of the relevant hospital or care home;
   (b) the relevant person;
   (c) the relevant person's representative;
   (d) any section 39D IMCA.

(2) That notice must state –
   (a) the outcome of the review, and
   (b) what variation (if any) has been made to the authorisation under this Part.

Records

121 A supervisory body must keep a written record of the following information –
   (a) each request for a review that is made to them;
   (b) the outcome of each request;
   (c) each review which they carry out;
   (d) the outcome of each review which they carry out;
   (e) any variation of an authorisation made in consequence of a review.

Relationship between review and suspension under Part 6

122 (1) This paragraph applies if a standard authorisation is suspended in accordance with Part 6.

(2) No review may be requested under this Part whilst the standard authorisation is suspended.

(3) If a review has already been requested, or is being carried out, when the standard authorisation is suspended, no steps are to be taken in connection with that review whilst the authorisation is suspended.

Relationship between review and request for new authorisation

123 (1) This paragraph applies if, in accordance with paragraph 24 (as read with paragraph 29), the managing authority of the relevant hospital or care home make a request for a new standard authorisation which would be in force after the expiry of the existing authorisation.

(2) No review may be requested under this Part until the request for the new standard authorisation has been disposed of.

(3) If a review has already been requested, or is being carried out, when the new standard authorisation is requested, no steps are to be taken in connection with that review until the request for the new standard authorisation has been disposed of.

124 (1) This paragraph applies if –
   (a) a review under this Part has been requested, or is being carried out, and
   (b) the managing authority of the relevant hospital or care home make a request under paragraph 30 for a new standard authorisation which would be in force on or before, and after, the expiry of the existing authorisation.

(2) No steps are to be taken in connection with the review under this Part until the request for the new standard authorisation has been disposed of.

125 In paragraphs 123 and 124 –
   (a) the existing authorisation is the authorisation referred to in paragraph 101;
   (b) the expiry of the existing authorisation is the time when it is expected to cease to be in force.

PART 9
ASSESSMENTS UNDER THIS SCHEDULE

Introduction

126 This Part contains provision about assessments under this Schedule.

127 An assessment under this Schedule is either of the following –
   (a) an assessment carried out in connection with a request for a standard authorisation under Part 4;
   (b) a review assessment carried out in connection with a review of a standard authorisation under Part 8.

128 In this Part, in relation to an assessment under this Schedule –
   'assessor' means the person carrying out the assessment;
   'relevant procedure' means –
   (a) the request for the standard authorisation, or
   (b) the review of the standard authorisation;
   'supervisory body' means the supervisory body responsible for securing that the assessment is carried out.

Supervisory body to select assessor

129 (1) It is for the supervisory body to select a person to carry out an assessment under this Schedule.

(2) The supervisory body must not select a person to carry out an assessment unless the person –

    (a) appears to the supervisory body to be suitable to carry out the assessment (having regard, in particular, to the type of assessment and the person to be assessed), and

    (b) is eligible to carry out the assessment.

(3) Regulations may make provision about the selection, and eligibility, of persons to carry out assessments under this Schedule.

(4) Sub-paragraphs (5) and (6) apply if two or more assessments are to be obtained for the purposes of the relevant procedure.

(5) In a case where the assessments to be obtained include a mental health assessment and a best interests assessment, the supervisory body must not select the same person to carry out both assessments.

(6) Except as prohibited by sub-paragraph (5), the supervisory body may select the same person to carry out any number of the assessments which the person appears to be suitable, and is eligible, to carry out.

'**Regulations**' (para 129(3))—See the Mental Capacity (Deprivation of Liberty—Standard Authorisations, Assessments and Ordinary Residence) Regulations 2008, SI 2008/1858 (text reproduced in Part V of this work), as amended by the Mental Capacity (Deprivation of Liberty: Monitoring and Reporting; and Assessments – Amendment) Regulations 2009, SI 2009/827 and for Wales the Mental Capacity (Deprivation of Liberty: Assessments, Standard Authorisations and Disputes about Residence) (Wales) Regulations 2009, SI 2009/783.

130 (1) This paragraph applies to regulations under paragraph 129(3).

(2) The regulations may make provision relating to a person's –

    (a) qualifications,
    (b) skills,
    (c) training,
    (d) experience,
    (e) relationship to, or connection with, the relevant person or any other person,
    (f) involvement in the care or treatment of the relevant person,
    (g) connection with the supervisory body, or
    (h) connection with the relevant hospital or care home, or with any other establishment or undertaking.

(3) The provision that the regulations may make in relation to a person's training may provide for particular training to be specified by the appropriate authority otherwise than in the regulations.

(4) In sub-paragraph (3) the 'appropriate authority' means –

    (a) in relation to England: the Secretary of State;
    (b) in relation to Wales: the National Assembly for Wales.

(5) The regulations may make provision requiring a person to be insured in respect of liabilities that may arise in connection with the carrying out of an assessment.

(6) In relation to cases where two or more assessments are to be obtained for the purposes of the relevant procedure, the regulations may limit the number, kind or combination of assessments which a particular person is eligible to carry out.

(7) Sub-paragraphs (2) to (6) do not limit the generality of the provision that may be made in the regulations.

'The regulations may' (para 130(2))—See the Mental Capacity (Deprivation of Liberty—Standard Authorisations, Assessments and Ordinary Residence) Regulations 2008, SI 2008/1858, Parts 2 and 3, as amended by SI 2009/827 (text reproduced in Part V of this work).

'The regulations may' (para 130(5))—This is provided for in the Mental Capacity (Deprivation of Liberty—Standard Authorisations, Assessments and Ordinary Residence) Regulations 2008, SI 2008/1858, reg 2 (the text of which is reproduced in Part V of this book).

'the regulations may' (para 130(6))—See the Mental Capacity (Deprivation of Liberty – Standard Authorisations, Assessments and Ordinary Residence) Regulations 2008, SI 2008/1858, Part 2, as amended by SI 2009/827 (text reproduced in Part V of this work).

Examination and copying of records

131 An assessor may, at all reasonable times, examine and take copies of –

(a) any health record,
(b) any record of, or held by, a local authority and compiled in accordance with a social services function, and
(c) any record held by a person registered under Part 2 of the Care Standards Act 2000 or Chapter 2 of Part 1 of the Health and Social Care Act 2008,

which the assessor considers may be relevant to the assessment which is being carried out.

Amendments—Words in subsection (c) inserted by SI 2010/813.

Representations

132 In carrying out an assessment under this Schedule, the assessor must take into account any information given, or submissions made, by any of the following –

(a) the relevant person's representative;
(b) any section 39A IMCA;
(c) any section 39C IMCA;
(d) any section 39D IMCA.

Assessments to stop if any comes to negative conclusion

133 (1) This paragraph applies if an assessment under this Schedule comes to the conclusion that the relevant person does not meet one of the qualifying requirements.

(2) This Schedule does not require the supervisory body to secure that any other assessments under this Schedule are carried out in relation to the relevant procedure.

(3) The supervisory body must give notice to any assessor who is carrying out another assessment in connection with the relevant procedure that they are to cease carrying out that assessment.

(4) If an assessor receives such notice, this Schedule does not require the assessor to continue carrying out that assessment.

Duty to keep records and give copies

134 (1) This paragraph applies if an assessor has carried out an assessment under this Schedule (whatever conclusions the assessment has come to).

(2) The assessor must keep a written record of the assessment.

(3) As soon as practicable after carrying out the assessment, the assessor must give copies of the assessment to the supervisory body.

135 (1) This paragraph applies to the supervisory body if they are given a copy of an assessment under this Schedule.

(2) The supervisory body must give copies of the assessment to all of the following –

- (a) the managing authority of the relevant hospital or care home;
- (b) the relevant person;
- (c) any section 39A IMCA;
- (d) the relevant person's representative.

(3) If –

- (a) the assessment is obtained in relation to a request for a standard authorisation, and
- (b) the supervisory body are required by paragraph 50(1) to give the standard authorisation,

the supervisory body must give the copies of the assessment when they give copies of the authorisation in accordance with paragraph 57.

(4) If –

- (a) the assessment is obtained in relation to a request for a standard authorisation, and
- (b) the supervisory body are prohibited by paragraph 50(2) from giving the standard authorisation,

the supervisory body must give the copies of the assessment when they give notice in accordance with paragraph 58.

(5) If the assessment is obtained in connection with the review of a standard authorisation, the supervisory body must give the copies of the assessment when they give notice in accordance with paragraph 120.

136 (1) This paragraph applies to the supervisory body if –

- (a) they are given a copy of a best interests assessment, and
- (b) the assessment includes, in accordance with paragraph 44(2), a statement that it appears to the assessor that there is an unauthorised deprivation of liberty.

(2) The supervisory body must notify all of the persons listed in sub-paragraph (3) that the assessment includes such a statement.

(3) Those persons are –

(a) the managing authority of the relevant hospital or care home;
(b) the relevant person;
(c) any section 39A IMCA;
(d) any interested person consulted by the best interests assessor.

(4) The supervisory body must comply with this paragraph when (or at some time before) they comply with paragraph 135.

PART 10
RELEVANT PERSON'S REPRESENTATIVE

The representative

137 In this Schedule the relevant person's representative is the person appointed as such in accordance with this Part.

138 (1) Regulations may make provision about the selection and appointment of representatives.

(2) In this Part such regulations are referred to as 'appointment regulations'.

'appointment regulations'—See the Mental Capacity (Deprivation of Liberty – Appointment of Relevant Person's Representative) Regulations 2008, SI 2008/1315 (as amended by SI 2008/2368) (the text of which is reproduced in Part V of this book).

Supervisory body to appoint representative

139 (1) The supervisory body must appoint a person to be the relevant person's representative as soon as practicable after a standard authorisation is given.

(2) The supervisory body must appoint a person to be the relevant person's representative if a vacancy arises whilst a standard authorisation is in force.

(3) Where a vacancy arises, the appointment under sub-paragraph (2) is to be made as soon as practicable after the supervisory body becomes aware of the vacancy.

140 (1) The selection of a person for appointment under paragraph 139 must not be made unless it appears to the person making the selection that the prospective representative would, if appointed –

(a) maintain contact with the relevant person,
(b) represent the relevant person in matters relating to or connected with this Schedule, and
(c) support the relevant person in matters relating to or connected with this Schedule.

141 (1) Any appointment of a representative for a relevant person is in addition to, and does not affect, any appointment of a donee or deputy.

(2) The functions of any representative are in addition to, and do not affect –

(a) the authority of any donee,
(b) the powers of any deputy, or
(c) any powers of the court.

Appointment regulations

142 Appointment regulations may provide that the procedure for appointing a representative may begin at any time after a request for a standard authorisation is made (including a time before the request has been disposed of).

'**Appointment regulations may**'—See the Mental Capacity (Deprivation of Liberty – Appointment of Relevant Person's Representative) Regulations 2008, SI 2008/1315, reg 10 (the text of which is reproduced in Part V of this book).

143 (1) Appointment regulations may make provision about who is to select a person for appointment as a representative.

(2) But regulations under this paragraph may only provide for the following to make a selection –

- (a) the relevant person, if he has capacity in relation to the question of which person should be his representative;
- (b) a donee of a lasting power of attorney granted by the relevant person, if it is within the scope of his authority to select a person;
- (c) a deputy, if it is within the scope of his authority to select a person;
- (d) a best interests assessor;
- (e) the supervisory body.

(3) Regulations under this paragraph may provide that a selection by the relevant person, a donee or a deputy is subject to approval by a best interests assessor or the supervisory body.

(4) Regulations under this paragraph may provide that, if more than one selection is necessary in connection with the appointment of a particular representative –

- (a) the same person may make more than one selection;
- (b) different persons may make different selections.

(5) For the purposes of this paragraph a best interests assessor is a person carrying out a best interests assessment in connection with the standard authorisation in question (including the giving of that authorisation).

'**Appointment regulations may**'—See the Mental Capacity (Deprivation of Liberty – Appointment of Relevant Person's Representative) Regulations 2008, SI 2008/1315, Part 1 (as amended by SI 2008/2368) (the text of which is reproduced in Part V of this book).

144 (1) Appointment regulations may make provision about who may, or may not, be –

- (a) selected for appointment as a representative, or
- (b) appointed as a representative.

(2) Regulations under this paragraph may relate to any of the following matters –

- (a) a person's age;
- (b) a person's suitability;
- (c) a person's independence;
- (d) a person's willingness;
- (e) a person's qualifications.

'**Appointment regulations may**'—See the Mental Capacity (Deprivation of Liberty – Appointment of Relevant Person's Representative) Regulations 2008, SI 2008/1315 (as amended by SI 2008/2368) (the text of which is reproduced in Part V of this book).

145 Appointment regulations may make provision about the formalities of appointing a person as a representative.

'**Appointment regulations may**'—See the Mental Capacity (Deprivation of Liberty—Appointment of Relevant Person's Representative) Regulations 2008, SI 2008/1315, reg 12 (the text of which is reproduced in Part V of this book).

146 In a case where a best interests assessor is to select a person to be appointed as a representative, appointment regulations may provide for the variation of the assessor's duties in relation to the assessment which he is carrying out.

'**Regulations may**'—This power has not yet been exercised.

Monitoring of representatives

147

Regulations may make provision requiring the managing authority of the relevant hospital or care home to –

    (a) monitor, and
    (b) report to the supervisory body on,

the extent to which a representative is maintaining contact with the relevant person.

'**Regulations may**'—For Wales, the Mental Capacity (Deprivation of Liberty: Appointment of Relevant Person's Representative) (Wales) Regulations 2009, SI 2009/266, reg 15.

Termination

148 Regulations may make provision about the circumstances in which the appointment of a person as the relevant person's representative ends or may be ended.

'**Regulations may**'—See the Mental Capacity (Deprivation of Liberty – Appointment of Relevant Person's Representative) Regulations 2008, SI 2008/1315, reg 13 (the text of which is reproduced in Part V of this book).

149 Regulations may make provision about the formalities of ending the appointment of a person as a representative.

'**Regulations may**'—See the Mental Capacity (Deprivation of Liberty – Appointment of Relevant Person's Representative) Regulations 2008, SI 2008/1315, reg 14 (the text of which is reproduced in Part V of this book).

Suspension of representative's functions

150 (1) Regulations may make provision about the circumstances in which functions exercisable by, or in relation to, the relevant person's representative (whether under this Schedule or not) may be –

    (a) suspended, and
    (b) if suspended, revived.

(2) The regulations may make provision about the formalities for giving effect to the suspension or revival of a function.

(3) The regulations may make provision about the effect of the suspension or revival of a function.

'**Regulations may**'—This power has not yet been exercised.

Payment of representative

151 Regulations may make provision for payments to be made to, or in relation to, persons exercising functions as the relevant person's representative.

'**Regulations may**'—See the Mental Capacity (Deprivation of Liberty – Appointment of Relevant Person's Representative) Regulations 2008, SI 2008/1315, reg 15 (the text of which is reproduced in Part V of this book), under which a supervisory body may pay a representative when selected by that body.

Regulations under this Part

152 The provisions of this Part which specify provision that may be made in regulations under this Part do not affect the generality of the power to make such regulations.

Effect of appointment of section 39C IMCA

153 Paragraphs 159 and 160 make provision about the exercise of functions by, or towards, the relevant person's representative during periods when –

  (a) no person is appointed as the relevant person's representative, but
  (b) a person is appointed as a section 39C IMCA.

PART 11
IMCAS

Application of Part

154 This Part applies for the purposes of this Schedule.

The IMCAs

155 A section 39A IMCA is an independent mental capacity advocate appointed under section 39A.

156 A section 39C IMCA is an independent mental capacity advocate appointed under section 39C.

157 A section 39D IMCA is an independent mental capacity advocate appointed under section 39D.

158 An IMCA is a section 39A IMCA or a section 39C IMCA or a section 39D IMCA.

Section 39C IMCA: functions

159 (1) This paragraph applies if, and for as long as, there is a section 39C IMCA.

(2) In the application of the relevant provisions, references to the relevant person's representative are to be read as references to the section 39C IMCA.

(3) But sub-paragraph (2) does not apply to any function under the relevant provisions for as long as the function is suspended in accordance with provision made under Part 10.

(4) In this paragraph and paragraph 160 the relevant provisions are –

   (a) paragraph 102(3)(b) (request for review under Part 8);
   (b) paragraph 108(1)(b) (notice of review under Part 8);
   (c) paragraph 120(1)(c) (notice of outcome of review under Part 8).

160 (1) This paragraph applies if –

   (a) a person is appointed as the relevant person's representative, and
   (b) a person accordingly ceases to hold an appointment as a section 39C IMCA.

(2) Where a function under a relevant provision has been exercised by, or towards, the section 39C IMCA, there is no requirement for that function to be exercised again by, or towards, the relevant person's representative.

Section 39A IMCA: restriction of functions

161 (1) This paragraph applies if –

   (a) there is a section 39A IMCA, and
   (b) a person is appointed under Part 10 to be the relevant person's representative (whether or not that person, or any person subsequently appointed, is currently the relevant person's representative).

(2) The duties imposed on, and the powers exercisable by, the section 39A IMCA do not apply.

(3) The duties imposed on, and the powers exercisable by, any other person do not apply, so far as they fall to be performed or exercised towards the section 39A IMCA.

(4) But sub-paragraph (2) does not apply to any power of challenge exercisable by the section 39A IMCA.

(5) And sub-paragraph (3) does not apply to any duty or power of any other person so far as it relates to any power of challenge exercisable by the section 39A IMCA.

(6) Before exercising any power of challenge, the section 39A IMCA must take the views of the relevant person's representative into account.

(7) A power of challenge is a power to make an application to the court to exercise its jurisdiction under section 21A in connection with the giving of the standard authorisation.

PART 12
MISCELLANEOUS

Monitoring of operation of Schedule

162 (1) Regulations may make provision for, and in connection with, requiring one or more prescribed bodies to monitor, and report on, the operation of this Schedule in relation to England.

(2) The regulations may, in particular, give a prescribed body authority to do one or more of the following things –

(a) to visit hospitals and care homes;
(b) to visit and interview persons accommodated in hospitals and care homes;
(c) to require the production of, and to inspect, records relating to the care or treatment of persons.

(3) 'Prescribed' means prescribed in regulations under this paragraph.

'**Regulations may**'—See the Mental Capacity (Deprivation of Liberty: Monitoring and Reporting; and Assessments – Amendment) Regulations 2009, SI 2009/827.

163 (1) Regulations may make provision for, and in connection with, enabling the National Assembly for Wales to monitor, and report on, the operation of this Schedule in relation to Wales.

(2) The National Assembly may direct one or more persons or bodies to carry out the Assembly's functions under regulations under this paragraph.

'**Regulations may**'—This power has not yet been exercised.

Disclosure of information

164 (1) Regulations may require either or both of the following to disclose prescribed information to prescribed bodies –

(a) supervisory bodies;
(b) managing authorities of hospitals or care homes.

(2) 'Prescribed' means prescribed in regulations under this paragraph.

(3) Regulations under this paragraph may only prescribe information relating to matters with which this Schedule is concerned.

'**Regulations may**'—This power has not yet been exercised.

Directions by National Assembly in relation to supervisory functions

165 (1) The National Assembly for Wales may direct a Local Health Board to exercise in relation to its area any supervisory functions which are specified in the direction.

(2) Directions under this paragraph must not preclude the National Assembly from exercising the functions specified in the directions.

(3) In this paragraph 'supervisory functions' means functions which the National Assembly have as supervisory body, so far as they are exercisable in relation to hospitals (whether NHS or independent hospitals, and whether in Wales or England).

166 (1) This paragraph applies where, under paragraph 165, a Local Health Board ('the specified LHB') is directed to exercise supervisory functions ('delegated functions').

(2) The National Assembly for Wales may give directions to the specified LHB about the Board's exercise of delegated functions.

(3) The National Assembly may give directions for any delegated functions to be exercised, on behalf of the specified LHB, by a committee, sub-committee or officer of that Board.

(4) The National Assembly may give directions providing for any delegated functions to be exercised by the specified LHB jointly with one or more other Local Health Boards.

(5) Where, under sub-paragraph (4), delegated functions are exercisable jointly, the National Assembly may give directions providing for the functions to be exercised, on behalf of the Local Health Boards in question, by a joint committee or joint sub-committee.

167 (1) Directions under paragraph 165 must be given in regulations.

(2) Directions under paragraph 166 may be given –

(a) in regulations, or
(b) by instrument in writing.

168 The power under paragraph 165 or paragraph 166 to give directions includes power to vary or revoke directions given under that paragraph.

Notices

169 Any notice under this Schedule must be in writing.

Regulations

170 (1) This paragraph applies to all regulations under this Schedule, except regulations under paragraph 162, 163, 167 or 183.

(2) It is for the Secretary of State to make such regulations in relation to authorisations under this Schedule which relate to hospitals and care homes situated in England.

(3) It is for the National Assembly for Wales to make such regulations in relation to authorisations under this Schedule which relate to hospitals and care homes situated in Wales.

171 It is for the Secretary of State to make regulations under paragraph 162.

172 It is for the National Assembly for Wales to make regulations under paragraph 163 or 167.

173 (1) This paragraph applies to regulations under paragraph 183.

(2) It is for the Secretary of State to make such regulations in relation to cases where a question as to the ordinary residence of a person is to be determined by the Secretary of State.

(3) It is for the National Assembly for Wales to make such regulations in relation to cases where a question as to the ordinary residence of a person is to be determined by the National Assembly.

PART 13
INTERPRETATION

Introduction

174 This Part applies for the purposes of this Schedule.

Hospitals and their managing authorities

175 (1) 'Hospital' means –

  (a) an NHS hospital, or
  (b) an independent hospital.

(2) 'NHS hospital' means –

  (a) a health service hospital as defined by section 275 of the National Health Service Act 2006 or section 206 of the National Health Service (Wales) Act 2006, or
  (b) a hospital as defined by section 206 of the National Health Service (Wales) Act 2006 vested in a Local Health Board.

(3) 'Independent hospital' –

  (a) in relation to England, means a hospital as defined by section 275 of the National Health Service Act 2006 that is not an NHS hospital; and
  (b) in relation to Wales, means a hospital as defined by section 2 of the Care Standards Act 2000 that is not an NHS hospital.

Amendments—SI 2010/813.

176 (1) 'Managing authority', in relation to an NHS hospital, means –

  (a) if the hospital –
      (i) is vested in the appropriate national authority for the purposes of its functions under the National Health Service Act 2006 or of the National Health Service (Wales) Act 2006, or
      (ii) consists of any accommodation provided by a local authority and used as a hospital by or on behalf of the appropriate national authority under either of those Acts,
      The Local Health Board or Special Health Authority responsible for the administration of the hospital;

(aa) in relation to England, if the hospital falls within paragraph (a)(i) or (ii) and no Special Health Authority has responsibility for its administration, the Secretary of State;
(b) if the hospital is vested in a National Health Service trust or NHS foundation trust, that trust;
(c) if the hospital is vested in a Local Health Board, that Board.

(2) For this purpose the appropriate national authority is –
(a) in relation to England: the Secretary of State;
(b) in relation to Wales: the National Assembly for Wales;
(c) in relation to England and Wales: the Secretary of State and the National Assembly acting jointly.

Amendments—Health and Social Care Act 2012.

177 'Managing authority', in relation to an independent hospital, means –
(a) in relation to England, the person registered, or required to be registered, under Chapter 2 of Part 1 of the Health and Social Care Act 2008 in respect of regulated activities (within the meaning of that Part) carried on in the hospital, and
(b) in relation to Wales, the person registered, or required to be registered, under Part 2 of the Care Standards Act 2000 in respect of the hospital.

Amendments—SI 2010/813.

Care homes and their managing authorities

178 'Care home' has the meaning given by section 3 of the Care Standards Act 2000.

179 'Managing authority, in relation to a care home, means –
(a) in relation to England, the person registered, or required to be registered, under Chapter 2 of Part 1 of the Health and Social Care Act 2008 in respect of the provision of residential accommodation, together with nursing or personal care, in the care home, and
(b) in relation to Wales, the person registered, or required to be registered, under Part 2 of the Care Standards Act 2000 in respect of the care home.

Amendments—SI 2010/813.

Supervisory bodies: hospitals

180 (1) The identity of the supervisory body is determined under this paragraph in cases where the relevant hospital is situated in England.

(2) If the relevant person is ordinarily resident in the area of a local authority in England, the supervisory body are that local authority.

(3) If the relevant person is not ordinarily resident in England and the National Assembly for Wales or a Local Health Board commission the relevant care or treatment, the National Assembly are the supervisory body.

(4) In any other case, the supervisory body is the local authority for the area in which the relevant hospital is situated.

(4A) 'Local authority' means –

    (a) the council of a county;
    (b) the council of a district for which there is no county council;
    (c) the council of a London borough;
    (d) the Common Council of the City of London;
    (e) the Council of the Isles of Scilly.

(5) If a hospital is situated in the areas of two (or more) local authorities, it is to be regarded for the purposes of sub-paragraph (4) as situated in whichever of the areas the greater (or greatest) part of the hospital is situated.

Amendments—Health and Social Care Act 2012, Sch 5, para 136(3).

'ordinarily resident' (para 180(2))—See para 183.

181 (1) The identity of the supervisory body is determined under this paragraph in cases where the relevant hospital is situated in Wales.

(2) The National Assembly for Wales are the supervisory body.

(3) But if the relevant person is ordinarily resident in the area of a local authority in England, the supervisory body are that local authority.

(4) 'Local authority' means –

    (a) the council of a county;
    (b) the council of a district for which there is no county council;
    (c) the council of a London borough;
    (d) the Common Council of the City of London;
    (e) the Council of the Isles of Scilly.

Amendments—Health and Social Care Act 2012, Sch 5, para 136(3).

Supervisory bodies: care homes

182 (1) The identity of the supervisory body is determined under this paragraph in cases where the relevant care home is situated in England or in Wales.

(2) The supervisory body are the local authority for the area in which the relevant person is ordinarily resident.

(3) But if the relevant person is not ordinarily resident in the area of a local authority, the supervisory body are the local authority for the area in which the care home is situated.

(4) In relation to England 'local authority' means –

    (a) the council of a county;
    (b) the council of a district for which there is no county council;
    (c) the council of a London borough;
    (d) the Common Council of the City of London;
    (e) the Council of the Isles of Scilly.

(5) In relation to Wales 'local authority' means the council of a county or county borough.

(6) If a care home is situated in the areas of two (or more) local authorities, it is to be regarded for the purposes of sub-paragraph (3) as situated in whichever of the areas the greater (or greatest) part of the care home is situated.

Supervisory bodies: determination of place of ordinary residence

183 (1) Subsections (5) and (6) of section 24 of the National Assistance Act 1948 (deemed place of ordinary residence) apply to any determination of where a person is ordinarily resident for the purposes of paragraphs 180, 181 and 182 as those subsections apply to such a determination for the purposes specified in those subsections.

(2) In the application of section 24(6) of the 1948 Act by virtue of subparagraph (1) to any determination of where a person is ordinarily resident for the purposes of paragraph 182, section 24(6) is to be read as if it referred to a hospital vested in a Local Health Board as well as to hospitals vested in the Secretary of State and the other bodies mentioned in section 24(6).

(2A) Section 39(1), (2) and (4) to (6) of the Care Act 2014 and paragraphs 1(1), 2(1) and 8 of Schedule 1 to that Act apply to any determination of where a person is ordinarily resident for the purposes of paragraphs 180, 181 and 182 as they apply for the purposes of Part 1 of that Act.

(3) Any question arising as to the ordinary residence of a person is to be determined by the Secretary of State or by the National Assembly for Wales.

(4) The Secretary of State and the National Assembly must make and publish arrangements for determining which cases are to be dealt with by the Secretary of State and which are to be dealt with by the National Assembly.

(5) Those arrangements may include provision for the Secretary of State and the National Assembly to agree, in relation to any question that has arisen, which of them is to deal with the case.

(6) Regulations may make provision about arrangements that are to have effect before, upon, or after the determination of any question as to the ordinary residence of a person.

(7) The regulations may, in particular, authorise or require a local authority to do any or all of the following things –

(a) to act as supervisory body even though it may wish to dispute that it is the supervisory body;
(b) to become the supervisory body in place of another local authority;
(c) to recover from another local authority expenditure incurred in exercising functions as the supervisory body.

Amendments—Health and Social Care Act 2012, Sch 5, para 136(3); SI 2015/914.

'**Regulations may**' (para 183(6))—See the Mental Capacity (Deprivation of Liberty – Standard Authorisations, Assessments and Ordinary Residence) Regulations 2008, SI 2008/1858, Part 6, as amended by SI 2009/827 (the text of which is reproduced in Part V of this book).

Same body managing authority and supervisory body

184 (1) This paragraph applies if, in connection with a particular person's detention as a resident in a hospital or care home, the same body are both –

(a) the managing authority of the relevant hospital or care home, and
(b) the supervisory body.

(2) The fact that a single body are acting in both capacities does not prevent the body from carrying out functions under this Schedule in each capacity.

(3) But, in such a case, this Schedule has effect subject to any modifications contained in regulations that may be made for this purpose.

Interested persons

185 Each of the following is an interested person –

(a) the relevant person's spouse or civil partner;
(b) where the relevant person and another person are not married to each other, nor in a civil partnership with each other, but are living together as if they were a married couple: that other person;
(d) the relevant person's children and step-children;
(e) the relevant person's parents and step-parents;
(f) the relevant person's brothers and sisters, half-brothers and half-sisters, and stepbrothers and stepsisters;
(g) the relevant person's grandparents;
(h) a deputy appointed for the relevant person by the court;
(i) a donee of a lasting power of attorney granted by the relevant person.

Amendments—SI 2014/560.

186 (1) An interested person consulted by the best interests assessor is any person whose name is stated in the relevant best interests assessment in accordance with paragraph 40 (interested persons whom the assessor consulted in carrying out the assessment).

(2) The relevant best interests assessment is the most recent best interests assessment carried out in connection with the standard authorisation in question (whether the assessment was carried out under Part 4 or Part 8).

187 Where this Schedule imposes on a person a duty towards an interested person, the duty does not apply if the person on whom the duty is imposed –

(a) is not aware of the interested person's identity or of a way of contacting him, and
(b) cannot reasonably ascertain it.

188 The following table contains an index of provisions defining or otherwise explaining expressions used in this Schedule –

age assessment	paragraph 34
age requirement	paragraph 13
age review assessment	paragraph 112(3)
appointment regulations	paragraph 138
assessment under this Schedule	paragraph 127
assessor (except in Part 8)	paragraph 33
assessor (in Part 8)	paragraphs 33 and 128

authorisation under this Schedule	paragraph 10
best interests (determination of)	section 4
best interests assessment	paragraph 38
best interests requirement	paragraph 16
best interests review assessment	paragraph 112(6)
care home	paragraph 178
change of reason ground	paragraph 106
complete (in relation to a review of a standard authorisation)	paragraph 118
deprivation of a person's liberty	section 64(5) and (6)
deputy	section 16(2)(b)
detained resident	paragraph 6
disposed of (in relation to a request for a standard authorisation)	paragraph 66
eligibility assessment	paragraph 46
eligibility requirement	paragraph 17
eligibility review assessment	paragraph 112(7)
eligible person (in relation to paragraphs 68 to 73)	paragraph 68
eligible person (in relation to Part 8)	paragraph 102(3)
expiry (in relation to an existing authorisation)	paragraph 125(b)
existing authorisation (in Part 8)	paragraph 125(a)
hospital	paragraph 175
IMCA	paragraph 158
in force (in relation to a standard authorisation)	paragraphs 63 and 64
in force (in relation to an urgent authorisation)	paragraphs 88 and 89
ineligible (in relation to the eligibility requirement)	Schedule 1A
interested person	paragraph 185
interested person consulted by the best interests assessor	paragraph 186
lack of capacity	section 2
lasting power of attorney	section 9
managing authority (in relation to a care home)	paragraph 179
managing authority (in relation to a hospital)	paragraph 176 or 177
maximum authorisation period	paragraph 42
mental capacity assessment	paragraph 37
mental capacity requirement	paragraph 15
mental capacity review assessment	paragraph 112(5)
mental health assessment	paragraph 35

mental health requirement	paragraph 14
mental health review assessment	paragraph 112(4)
negative conclusion	paragraph 112(2)(a)
new supervisory body	paragraph 99(b)
no refusals assessment	paragraph 48
no refusals requirement	paragraph 18
no refusals review assessment	paragraph 112(8)
non-qualification ground	paragraph 105
old supervisory body	paragraph 99(a)
positive conclusion	paragraph 112(2)(b)
purpose of a standard authorisation	paragraph 11(1)
purpose of an urgent authorisation	paragraph 11(2)
qualifying requirements	paragraph 12
refusal (for the purposes of the no refusals requirement)	paragraphs 19 and 20
relevant care or treatment	paragraph 7
relevant hospital or care home	paragraph 7
relevant managing authority	paragraph 26(4)
relevant person	paragraph 7
relevant person's representative	paragraph 137
relevant procedure	paragraph 128
review assessment	paragraph 112(1)
reviewable	paragraph 104
section 39A IMCA	paragraph 155
section 39C IMCA	paragraph 156
section 39D IMCA	paragraph 157
standard authorisation	paragraph 8
supervisory body (except in Part 8)	paragraph 180, 181 or 182
supervisory body (in Part 8)	paragraph 128 and paragraph 180, 181 or 182
unauthorised deprivation of liberty (in relation to paragraphs 68 to 73)	paragraph 67
urgent authorisation	paragraph 9
variation of conditions ground	paragraph 107]

Amendment—Schedule inserted by the Mental Health Act 2007, s 50(5), Sch 7. The MCA 2005, Schs A1 and 1A and related provisions above, which amend the Act to provide deprivation of liberty safeguards, commenced on 1 April 2009 (the Mental Health Act 2007 (Commencement No 10 and Transitional Provisions) Order 2009, SI 2009/139 (C.9)). The nature and effect of the deprivation of liberty safeguards are discussed in Part I, Chapter 7 of this work.

SCHEDULE 1
LASTING POWERS OF ATTORNEY: FORMALITIES

Section 9

PART 1
MAKING INSTRUMENTS

General requirements as to making instruments

1 (1) An instrument is not made in accordance with this Schedule unless –

   (a) it is in the prescribed form,
   (b) it complies with paragraph 2, and
   (c) any prescribed requirements in connection with its execution are satisfied.

(2) Regulations may make different provision according to whether –

   (a) the instrument relates to personal welfare or to property and affairs (or to both);
   (b) only one or more than one donee is to be appointed (and if more than one, whether jointly or jointly and severally).

(3) In this Schedule –

   (a) 'prescribed' means prescribed by regulations, and
   (b) 'regulations' means regulations made for the purposes of this Schedule by the Lord Chancellor.

'Regulations' (paras 1(2) and (3))—See Lasting Power of Attorney, Enduring Power of Attorney and Public Guardian Regulations 2007, SI 2007/1253; Lasting Powers of Attorney, Enduring Powers of Attorney and Public Guardian (Amendment) Regulations 2009, SI 2009/1884.

Requirements as to content of instruments

2 (1) The instrument must include –

   (a) the prescribed information about the purpose of the instrument and the effect of a lasting power of attorney,
   (b) a statement by the donor to the effect that he –
      (i) has read the prescribed information or a prescribed part of it (or has had it read to him), and
      (ii) intends the authority conferred under the instrument to include authority to make decisions on his behalf in circumstances where he no longer has capacity,
   (c) a statement by the donor –
      (i) naming a person or persons whom the donor wishes to be notified of any application for the registration of the instrument, or
      (ii) stating that there are no persons whom he wishes to be notified of any such application,
   (d) a statement by the donee (or, if more than one, each of them) to the effect that he –
      (i) has read the prescribed information or a prescribed part of it (or has had it read to him), and
      (ii) understands the duties imposed on a donee of a lasting power of attorney under sections 1 (the principles) and 4 (best interests), and

(e) a certificate by a person of a prescribed description that, in his opinion, at the time when the donor executes the instrument –
   (i) the donor understands the purpose of the instrument and the scope of the authority conferred under it,
   (ii) no fraud or undue pressure is being used to induce the donor to create a lasting power of attorney, and
   (iii) there is nothing else which would prevent a lasting power of attorney from being created by the instrument.

(2) Regulations may –
   (a) prescribe a maximum number of named persons;
   (b) provide that, where the instrument includes a statement under sub-paragraph (1)(c)(ii), two persons of a prescribed description must each give a certificate under sub-paragraph (1)(e).

(3) The persons who may be named persons do not include a person who is appointed as donee under the instrument.

(4) In this Schedule, 'named person' means a person named under sub-paragraph (1)(c).

(5) A certificate under sub-paragraph (1)(e) –
   (a) must be made in the prescribed form, and
   (b) must include any prescribed information.

(6) The certificate may not be given by a person appointed as donee under the instrument.

'maximum number' (para 2(2)(a))—There is a maximum of five named persons – see the Lasting Power of Attorney, Enduring Power of Attorney and Public Guardian Regulations 2007, SI 2007/1253, reg 6.

'named persons' (para 2(2)(a))—The donor must refer to named individuals, rather than to a class of persons or a description. The status of the named persons is determined by reference to when the instrument is executed, not the application for registration.

'a donee' (para 2(3))—This includes a replacement donee.

Failure to comply with prescribed form

3 (1) If an instrument differs in an immaterial respect in form or mode of expression from the prescribed form, it is to be treated by the Public Guardian as sufficient in point of form and expression.

(2) The court may declare that an instrument which is not in the prescribed form is to be treated as if it were, if it is satisfied that the persons executing the instrument intended it to create a lasting power of attorney.

'treated by the Public Guardian' (para 3(1))—The Public Guardian has the sole discretion of determining whether the difference is immaterial or not. There is no redress against a decision of the Public Guardian other than by way of an application to the Court of Protection for a declaration under para 3(2).

PART 2
REGISTRATION

Applications and procedure for registration

4 (1) An application to the Public Guardian for the registration of an instrument intended to create a lasting power of attorney –

   (a) must be made in the prescribed form, and
   (b) must include any prescribed information.

(2) The application may be made –

   (a) by the donor,
   (b) by the donee or donees, or
   (c) if the instrument appoints two or more donees to act jointly and severally in respect of any matter, by any of the donees.

(3) The application must be accompanied by –

   (a) the instrument, and
   (b) any fee provided for under section 58(4)(b).

(4) A person who, in an application for registration, makes a statement which he knows to be false in a material particular is guilty of an offence and is liable –

   (a) on summary conviction, to imprisonment for a term not exceeding 12 months or a fine not exceeding the statutory maximum or both;
   (b) on conviction on indictment, to imprisonment for a term not exceeding 2 years or a fine or both.

'**prescribed form**' (para 4(1)(a))—Form LPA001 – Lasting Power of Attorney, Enduring Power of Attorney and Public Guardian Regulations 2007, SI 2007/1253, Sch 2.

5 Subject to paragraphs 11 to 14, the Public Guardian must register the instrument as a lasting power of attorney at the end of the prescribed period.

'**the Public Guardian must**'—There is a positive obligation on the Public Guardian to register the instrument unless there is a defect in the form or process or there is an objection.

'**prescribed period**'—The period of 6 weeks beginning with the date on which the Public Guardian gave out the last notice under para 7 or 8 – Lasting Power of Attorney, Enduring Power of Attorney and Public Guardian Regulations 2007, SI 2007/1253, reg 12.

Notification requirements

6 (1) A donor about to make an application under paragraph 4(2)(a) must notify any named persons that he is about to do so.

(2) The donee (or donees) about to make an application under paragraph 4(2)(b) or (c) must notify any named persons that he is (or they are) about to do so.

7 As soon as is practicable after receiving an application by the donor under paragraph 4(2)(a), the Public Guardian must notify the donee (or donees) that the application has been received.

'**the Public Guardian must notify**'—The Public Guardian can provide notice by post using Form LPA003A – Lasting Power of Attorney, Enduring Power of Attorney and Public Guardian Regulations 2007, SI 2007/1253, Sch 4.

8 (1) As soon as is practicable after receiving an application by a donee (or donees) under paragraph 4(2)(b), the Public Guardian must notify the donor that the application has been received.

(2) As soon as is practicable after receiving an application by a donee under paragraph 4(2)(c), the Public Guardian must notify –

(a) the donor, and
(b) the donee or donees who did not join in making the application,

that the application has been received.

'**the Public Guardian must notify the donor**'—The Public Guardian can provide notice by post using Form LPA003B – Lasting Power of Attorney, Enduring Power of Attorney and Public Guardian Regulations 2007, SI 2007/1253, Sch 4.

9 (1) A notice under paragraph 6 must be made in the prescribed form.

(2) A notice under paragraph 6, 7 or 8 must include such information, if any, as may be prescribed.

'**prescribed form**'—Form LPA001 – Lasting Power of Attorney, Enduring Power of Attorney and Public Guardian Regulations 2007, SI 2007/1253, Sch 2.

Power to dispense with notification requirements

10 The court may –

(a) on the application of the donor, dispense with the requirement to notify under paragraph 6(1), or
(b) on the application of the donee or donees concerned, dispense with the requirement to notify under paragraph 6(2),

if satisfied that no useful purpose would be served by giving the notice.

'**The court may ... on an application by**'—Only the Court (ie not the Public Guardian) can dispense with notice, pursuant to a formal application being made.

Instrument not made properly or containing ineffective provision

11 (1) If it appears to the Public Guardian that an instrument accompanying an application under paragraph 4 is not made in accordance with this Schedule, he must not register the instrument unless the court directs him to do so.

(2) Sub-paragraph (3) applies if it appears to the Public Guardian that the instrument contains a provision which –

(a) would be ineffective as part of a lasting power of attorney, or
(b) would prevent the instrument from operating as a valid lasting power of attorney.

(3) The Public Guardian –

(a) must apply to the court for it to determine the matter under section 23(1), and
(b) pending the determination by the court, must not register the instrument.

(4) Sub-paragraph (5) applies if the court determines under section 23(1) (whether or not on an application by the Public Guardian) that the instrument contains a provision which –

(a) would be ineffective as part of a lasting power of attorney, or
(b) would prevent the instrument from operating as a valid lasting power of attorney.

(5) The court must –

(a) notify the Public Guardian that it has severed the provision, or
(b) direct him not to register the instrument.

(6) Where the court notifies the Public Guardian that it has severed a provision, he must register the instrument with a note to that effect attached to it.

'**If it appears to the Public Guardian**' (para 11(1))—A failure to complete the form correctly may mean that it has not been completed in accordance with the Schedule. The Public Guardian has discretion as to whether or not he or she should refuse registration and there is no redress against this decision except by an application to the Court of Protection to direct the Public Guardian to register the instrument.

'**if it appears to the Public Guardian**' (para 11(2))—This provision covers a situation where the instrument contains a provision such as a condition or restriction which prevents the instrument from operating as lasting power. The Public Guardian must then apply to the Court of Protection for the provision to be severed.

Deputy already appointed

12 (1) Sub-paragraph (2) applies if it appears to the Public Guardian that –

(a) there is a deputy appointed by the court for the donor, and
(b) the powers conferred on the deputy would, if the instrument were registered, to any extent conflict with the powers conferred on the attorney.

(2) The Public Guardian must not register the instrument unless the court directs him to do so.

Objection by donee or named person

13 (1) Sub-paragraph (2) applies if a donee or a named person –

(a) receives a notice under paragraph 6, 7 or 8 of an application for the registration of an instrument, and
(b) before the end of the prescribed period, gives notice to the Public Guardian of an objection to the registration on the ground that an event mentioned in section 13(3) or (6)(a) to (d) has occurred which has revoked the instrument.

(2) If the Public Guardian is satisfied that the ground for making the objection is established, he must not register the instrument unless the court, on the application of the person applying for the registration –

(a) is satisfied that the ground is not established, and
(b) directs the Public Guardian to register the instrument.

(3) Sub-paragraph (4) applies if a donee or a named person –

(a) receives a notice under paragraph 6, 7 or 8 of an application for the registration of an instrument, and

(b) before the end of the prescribed period –
   (i) makes an application to the court objecting to the registration on a prescribed ground, and
   (ii) notifies the Public Guardian of the application.

(4) The Public Guardian must not register the instrument unless the court directs him to do so.

'**gives notice to**' (para 13(1)(b))—Using Form LPA007.

'**makes an application to the court**' (para 13(3)(b)(i))—Using Form COP7.

'**notifies the Public Guardian**' (para 13(3)(b)(ii))—Using Form LPA008.

Objection by donor

14 (1) This paragraph applies if the donor –
   (a) receives a notice under paragraph 8 of an application for the registration of an instrument, and
   (b) before the end of the prescribed period, gives notice to the Public Guardian of an objection to the registration.

(2) The Public Guardian must not register the instrument unless the court, on the application of the donee or, if more than one, any of them –
   (a) is satisfied that the donor lacks capacity to object to the registration, and
   (b) directs the Public Guardian to register the instrument.

'**gives notice**' (para 14(1)(b))—Using Form LPA006.

Notification of registration

15 Where an instrument is registered under this Schedule, the Public Guardian must give notice of the fact in the prescribed form to –
   (a) the donor, and
   (b) the donee or, if more than one, each of them.

'**the Public Guardian must give notice**'—Form LPA004 set out in the Lasting Power of Attorney, Enduring Power of Attorney and Public Guardian Regulations 2007, SI 2007/1253, Sch 5.

Evidence of registration

16 (1) A document purporting to be an office copy of an instrument registered under this Schedule is, in any part of the United Kingdom, evidence of –
   (a) the contents of the instrument, and
   (b) the fact that it has been registered.

(2) Sub-paragraph (1) is without prejudice to –
   (a) section 3 of the Powers of Attorney Act 1971 (proof by certified copy), and
   (b) any other method of proof authorised by law.

PART 3
CANCELLATION OF REGISTRATION AND NOTIFICATION OF SEVERANCE

17 (1) The Public Guardian must cancel the registration of an instrument as a lasting power of attorney on being satisfied that the power has been revoked –

(a) as a result of the donor's bankruptcy or a debt relief order (under Part 7A of the Insolvency Act 1986) having been made in respect of the donor, or
(b) on the occurrence of an event mentioned in section 13(6)(a) to (d).

(2) If the Public Guardian cancels the registration of an instrument he must notify –

(a) the donor, and
(b) the donee or, if more than one, each of them.

Amendment—SI 2012/2404.

'**cancel the registration**' (para 17(1))—This power is expanded by the Lasting Power of Attorney, Enduring Power of Attorney and Public Guardian Regulations 2007, SI 2007/1253, reg 21, which covers revocation by the donor.

18 The court must direct the Public Guardian to cancel the registration of an instrument as a lasting power of attorney if it –

(a) determines under section 22(2)(a) that a requirement for creating the power was not met,
(b) determines under section 22(2)(b) that the power has been revoked or has otherwise come to an end, or
(c) revokes the power under section 22(4)(b) (fraud etc).

19 (1) Sub-paragraph (2) applies if the court determines under section 23(1) that a lasting power of attorney contains a provision which –

(a) is ineffective as part of a lasting power of attorney, or
(b) prevents the instrument from operating as a valid lasting power of attorney.

(2) The court must –

(a) notify the Public Guardian that it has severed the provision, or
(b) direct him to cancel the registration of the instrument as a lasting power of attorney.

20 On the cancellation of the registration of an instrument, the instrument and any office copies of it must be delivered up to the Public Guardian to be cancelled.

PART 4
RECORDS OF ALTERATIONS IN REGISTERED POWERS

Partial revocation or suspension of power as a result of bankruptcy

21 If in the case of a registered instrument it appears to the Public Guardian that under section 13 a lasting power of attorney is revoked, or suspended, in relation to the donor's property and affairs (but not in relation to other matters), the Public Guardian must attach to the instrument a note to that effect.

Termination of appointment of donee which does not revoke power

22 If in the case of a registered instrument it appears to the Public Guardian that an event has occurred –

(a) which has terminated the appointment of the donee, but
(b) which has not revoked the instrument,

the Public Guardian must attach to the instrument a note to that effect.

Replacement of donee

23 If in the case of a registered instrument it appears to the Public Guardian that the donee has been replaced under the terms of the instrument the Public Guardian must attach to the instrument a note to that effect.

Severance of ineffective provisions

24 If in the case of a registered instrument the court notifies the Public Guardian under paragraph 19(2)(a) that it has severed a provision of the instrument, the Public Guardian must attach to it a note to that effect.

Notification of alterations

25 If the Public Guardian attaches a note to an instrument under paragraph 21, 22, 23 or 24 he must give notice of the note to the donee or donees of the power (or, as the case may be, to the other donee or donees of the power).

SCHEDULE 1A
PERSONS INELIGIBLE TO BE DEPRIVED OF LIBERTY BY THIS ACT

PART 1
INELIGIBLE PERSONS

Application

1 This Schedule applies for the purposes of –

(a) section 16A, and
(b) paragraph 17 of Schedule A1.

Amendment—Schedule 1A inserted by MHA 2007, s 50(6), Sch 8.

Scope of the Schedule—Schedule 1A sets out who is ineligible to be lawfully deprived of their liberty under the provisions of MCA 2005 either through a welfare order made under MCA 2005, s 16(2)(a) or a standard authorisation pursuant to MCA 2005, Sch A1, para 17. For a discussion of the issues involved, see *W PCT v TB (an adult by her litigation friend the Official Solicitor)* [2009] EWHC 1737 (Fam), [2009] COPLR Con Vol 1193, *GJ v The Foundation Trust* [2009] EWHC 2972 (Fam), [2009] COPLR Con Vol 567 and *An NHS Trust v Dr A* [2013] EWHC 2442 (COP), [2013] COPLR 605. In *DN v Northumberland Tyne and Wear NHS Foundation Trust* [2011] UKUT 327 (AAC), the view of the Department of Health was recorded – and accepted – to the effect that neither the MHA 1983 nor the MCA 2005 take primacy, save in the circumstances specifically covered by the provisions of case E below. The letter submitted to the Tribunal by the Department of Health and recorded in the judgment provides a useful summary of the provisions of and policy underlying Sch A1. In *AM v South London & Maudsley NHS Foundation Trust & Secretary of State for Health* [2013] UKUT 365 (AAC), [2013] COPLR 510, Charles J revisited his earlier decision in *GJ* and confirmed that general propositions in respect of issues that arise concerning the interrelationship between MHA 1983 and MCA 2005 are 'dangerous;' and (2) his references to 'primacy' in his earlier decision were made in and should be confined to the position where the person was with the scope of MHA 1983. Note also that a person whom it is intended will be detained in England and Wales pursuant to a protective measure taken in a foreign jurisdiction which is recognised and declared to be enforceable pursuant to the provisions of Schedule 3 to MCA 2005 is not ineligible to be deprived of their liberty by virtue of Schedule 1A: *Re M* [2011] EWHC 3590 (COP), [2012] COPLR 430.

In *An NHS Trust v Dr A* [2013] EWHC 2442 (COP), [2013] COPLR 605, Baker J identified a lacuna in the statutory schemes provided for by the Mental Health Act 1983 ('MHA 1983') and MCA 2005, namely where a person unable to make decisions about their medical needs subject to detention under MHA 1983 is to be treated in a way outwith the treatment provided under that Act for his mental disorder and that treatment involves a deprivation of liberty: in the case before him, force-feeding for purposes other than the treatment of a mental disorder. Such a person would be ineligible to be deprived of their liberty (whether by way of a standard authorisation or by way of a court order) because they would be within case A; if the treatment could not properly be said to be treatment falling within the compulsory provisions of MHA 1983, s 63, then the MHA 1983 would not afford a route to authorise the administration of such treatment and any ancillary deprivation of liberty. After an exhaustive analysis of the statutory provisions and the authorities, Baker J held, though, that he could authorise the treatment and the deprivation of liberty by way of the exercise of the inherent jurisdiction. See also chapter 7 in Part I of this work.

Determining ineligibility

2 A person ('P') is ineligible to be deprived of liberty by this Act ('ineligible') if –

(a) P falls within one of the cases set out in the second column of the following table, and

(b) the corresponding entry in the third column of the table – or the provision, or one of the provisions, referred to in that entry – provides that he is ineligible.

	Status of P	Determination of ineligibility
Case A	P is (a) subject to the hospital treatment regime, and (b) detained in a hospital under that regime.	P is ineligible.
Case B	P is – (a) subject to the hospital treatment regime, but (b) not detained in a hospital under that regime.	See paragraphs 3 and 4.
Case C	P is subject to the community treatment regime.	See paragraphs 3 and 4.

| Case D | P is subject to the guardianship regime. | See paragraphs 3 and 5. |
| Case E | P is – (a) within the scope of the Mental Health Act, but (b) not subject to any of the mental health regimes. | See paragraph 5. |

Case E—In *DN v Northumberland Tyne and Wear NHS Foundation Trust* [2011] UKUT 327 (AAC), the Upper Tribunal held that a person without capacity to decide where they wished to live could be discharged from the compulsory provisions of the MHA 1983 to a care regime which would amount to a deprivation of their liberty, where such regime could and would be authorised by way of a standard authorisation. By contrast, in *Secretary of State for Justice v RB* [2011] EWCA Civ 1608, the Court of Appeal held that the First-Tier Tribunal (Mental Health) could not grant a conditional discharge to a person with the requisite capacity where the conditions in which they would be required to reside amounted to a deprivation of liberty. It is something of an irony that the person with capacity to decide where they wish to live may therefore find it more difficult to be discharged from the provisions of MHA 1983 than a person without capacity.

Authorised course of action not in accordance with regime

3 (1) This paragraph applies in cases B, C and D in the table in paragraph 2.

(2) P is ineligible if the authorised course of action is not in accordance with a requirement which the relevant regime imposes.

(3) That includes any requirement as to where P is, or is not, to reside.

(4) The relevant regime is the mental health regime to which P is subject.

'any requirement as to where P is, or is not, to reside' (s 3(1)(3))—While a guardianship order would prevent the authorisation of the deprivation of a person's liberty at a place other than that identified in the order, the order does not, itself, provide authorisation for any deprivation of liberty that may occur as a result of the care arrangements established at the place that the person is required to live under the terms of that order: *C v Blackburn with Darwen Borough Council* [2011] EWHC 3321 (COP). Peter Jackson J also expressed the view that, where there is are genuinely contested issues about the place of residence of a resisting incapacitated person, they should not be determined either under the guardianship regime or by means of a standard authorisation under the DOLS regime, but rather by way of a decision of the Court of Protection under s 16. The views expressed by Peter Jackson J as to both matters are strictly obiter, but it is suggested that they are plainly correct. In *JMcA's Application* [2013] NIQB 77, a Northern Irish case, Treacy J held that the equivalent provisions in the Northern Irish legislation, giving the power to the guardian to require the person to reside at a specified location, did not give authority to the guardian to detain or deprive the patient of his liberty.

Treatment for mental disorder in a hospital

4 (1) This paragraph applies in cases B and C in the table in paragraph 2.

(2) P is ineligible if the relevant care or treatment consists in whole or in part of medical treatment for mental disorder in a hospital.

PART III

P objects to being a mental health patient etc

5 (1) This paragraph applies in cases D and E in the table in paragraph 2.

(2) P is ineligible if the following conditions are met.

(3) The first condition is that the relevant instrument authorises P to be a mental health patient.

(4) The second condition is that P objects –
   (a) to being a mental health patient, or
   (b) to being given some or all of the mental health treatment.

(5) The third condition is that a donee or deputy has not made a valid decision to consent to each matter to which P objects.

(6) In determining whether or not P objects to something, regard must be had to all the circumstances (so far as they are reasonably ascertainable), including the following –
   (a) P's behaviour;
   (b) P's wishes and feelings;
   (c) P's views, beliefs and values.

(7) But regard is to be had to circumstances from the past only so far as it is still appropriate to have regard to them.

PART 2
INTERPRETATION

Application

6 This Part applies for the purposes of this Schedule.

Mental health regimes

7 The mental health regimes are –
   (a) the hospital treatment regime,
   (b) the community treatment regime, and
   (c) the guardianship regime.

Hospital treatment regime

8 (1) P is subject to the hospital treatment regime if he is subject to –
   (a) a hospital treatment obligation under the relevant enactment, or
   (b) an obligation under another England and Wales enactment which has the same effect as a hospital treatment obligation.

(2) But where P is subject to any such obligation, he is to be regarded as not subject to the hospital treatment regime during any period when he is subject to the community treatment regime.

(3) A hospital treatment obligation is an application, order or direction of a kind listed in the first column of the following table.

(4) In relation to a hospital treatment obligation, the relevant enactment is the enactment in the Mental Health Act which is referred to in the corresponding entry in the second column of the following table.

Hospital treatment obligation	Relevant enactment
Application for admission for assessment	Section 2
Application for admission for assessment	Section 4
Application for admission for treatment	Section 3
Order for remand to hospital	Section 35
Order for remand to hospital	Section 36
Hospital order	Section 37
Interim hospital order	Section 38
Order for detention in hospital	Section 44
Hospital direction	Section 45A
Transfer direction	Section 47
Transfer direction	Section 48
Hospital order	Section 51

Community treatment regime

9 P is subject to the community treatment regime if he is subject to –

(a) a community treatment order under section 17A of the Mental Health Act, or
(b) an obligation under another England and Wales enactment which has the same effect as a community treatment order.

Guardianship regime

10 P is subject to the guardianship regime if he is subject to –

(a) a guardianship application under section 7 of the Mental Health Act,
(b) a guardianship order under section 37 of the Mental Health Act, or
(c) an obligation under another England and Wales enactment which has the same effect as a guardianship application or guardianship order.

Guardianship—Whilst a guardianship order would prevent the authorisation of the deprivation of a person's liberty at a place other than that identified in the order (see para 3(3) above), the order does not, itself, provide authorisation for any deprivation of liberty that may occur as a result of the care arrangements established at the place that the person is required to live under the terms of that order: *C v Blackburn* with Darwen Borough Council [2011] EWHC 3321 (COP), [2012] COPLR 350. The view expressed by Peter Jackson J was strictly obiter, but it is suggested that it is plainly correct, and was in any event prefigured by Paragraph 13.16 of the Code of Practice, to same effect. In *JMcA's Application* [2013] NIQB 77, a Northern Irish case, Treacy J held that the equivalent provisions in the Northern Irish legislation, giving the power to the guardian to require the person to reside at a specified location, did not give authority to the guardian to detain or deprive the patient of his liberty.

England and Wales enactments

11 (1) An England and Wales enactment is an enactment which extends to England and Wales (whether or not it also extends elsewhere).

(2) It does not matter if the enactment is in the Mental Health Act or not.

P within scope of Mental Health Act

12 (1) P is within the scope of the Mental Health Act if –

 (a) an application in respect of P could be made under section 2 or 3 of the Mental Health Act, and
 (b) P could be detained in a hospital in pursuance of such an application, were one made.

(2) The following provisions of this paragraph apply when determining whether an application in respect of P could be made under section 2 or 3 of the Mental Health Act.

(3) If the grounds in section 2(2) of the Mental Health Act are met in P's case, it is to be assumed that the recommendations referred to in section 2(3) of that Act have been given.

(4) If the grounds in section 3(2) of the Mental Health Act are met in P's case, it is to be assumed that the recommendations referred to in section 3(3) of that Act have been given.

(5) In determining whether the ground in section 3(2)(c) of the Mental Health Act is met in P's case, it is to be assumed that the treatment referred to in section 3(2)(c) cannot be provided under this Act.

Authorised course of action, relevant care or treatment & relevant instrument

13 In a case where this Schedule applies for the purposes of section 16A –

 'authorised course of action' means any course of action amounting to deprivation of liberty which the order under section 16(2)(a) authorises;
 'relevant care or treatment' means any care or treatment which –
 (a) comprises, or forms part of, the authorised course of action, or
 (b) is to be given in connection with the authorised course of action;
 'relevant instrument' means the order under section 16(2)(a).

14 In a case where this Schedule applies for the purposes of paragraph 17 of Schedule A1 –

 'authorised course of action' means the accommodation of the relevant person in the relevant hospital or care home for the purpose of being given the relevant care or treatment;
 'relevant care or treatment' has the same meaning as in Schedule A1;
 'relevant instrument' means the standard authorisation under Schedule A1.

15 (1) This paragraph applies where the question whether a person is ineligible to be deprived of liberty by this Act is relevant to either of these decisions –

 (a) whether or not to include particular provision ('the proposed provision') in an order under section 16(2)(a);

(b) whether or not to give a standard authorisation under Schedule A1.

(2) A reference in this Schedule to the authorised course of action or the relevant care or treatment is to be read as a reference to that thing as it would be if –

(a) the proposed provision were included in the order, or
(b) the standard authorisation were given.

(3) A reference in this Schedule to the relevant instrument is to be read as follows –

(a) where the relevant instrument is an order under section 16(2)(a): as a reference to the order as it would be if the proposed provision were included in it;
(b) where the relevant instrument is a standard authorisation: as a reference to the standard authorisation as it would be if it were given.

Expressions used in paragraph 5

16 (1) These expressions have the meanings given –

'donee' means a donee of a lasting power of attorney granted by P;
'mental health patient' means a person accommodated in a hospital for the purpose of being given medical treatment for mental disorder;
'mental health treatment' means the medical treatment for mental disorder referred to in the definition of 'mental health patient'.

(2) A decision of a donee or deputy is valid if it is made –

(a) within the scope of his authority as donee or deputy, and
(b) in accordance with Part 1 of this Act.

Expressions with same meaning as in Mental Health Act

17 (1) 'Hospital' has the same meaning as in Part 2 of the Mental Health Act.

(2) 'Medical treatment' has the same meaning as in the Mental Health Act.

(3) 'Mental disorder' has the same meaning as in Schedule A1 (see paragraph 14).]

Amendments—Schedule inserted by the Mental Health Act 2007, s 50(6), Sch 8. MCA 2005, Schs A1 and 1A and related provisions above (ss 4A–4B), which provide Deprivation of Liberty Safeguards under MCA 2005, were commenced on 1 April 2009. They are outlined in Part I, Chapter 6 of this book.

SCHEDULE 2
PROPERTY AND AFFAIRS: SUPPLEMENTARY PROVISIONS

Section 18(4)

Wills: general

1 Paragraphs 2 to 4 apply in relation to the execution of a will, by virtue of section 18, on behalf of P.

Provision that may be made in will

2 The will may make any provision (whether by disposing of property or exercising a power or otherwise) which could be made by a will executed by P if he had capacity to make it.

Wills: requirements relating to execution

3 (1) Sub-paragraph (2) applies if under section 16 the court makes an order or gives directions requiring or authorising a person ('the authorised person') to execute a will on behalf of P.

(2) Any will executed in pursuance of the order or direction –

(a) must state that it is signed by P acting by the authorised person,
(b) must be signed by the authorised person with the name of P and his own name, in the presence of two or more witnesses present at the same time,
(c) must be attested and subscribed by those witnesses in the presence of the authorised person, and
(d) must be sealed with the official seal of the court.

Wills: effect of execution

4 (1) This paragraph applies where a will is executed in accordance with paragraph 3.

(2) The Wills Act 1837 has effect in relation to the will as if it were signed by P by his own hand, except that –

(a) section 9 of the 1837 Act (requirements as to signing and attestation) does not apply, and
(b) in the subsequent provisions of the 1837 Act any reference to execution in the manner required by the previous provisions is to be read as a reference to execution in accordance with paragraph 3.

(3) The will has the same effect for all purposes as if –

(a) P had had the capacity to make a valid will, and
(b) the will had been executed by him in the manner required by the 1837 Act.

(4) But sub-paragraph (3) does not have effect in relation to the will –

(a) in so far as it disposes of immovable property outside England and Wales, or
(b) in so far as it relates to any other property or matter if, when the will is executed –
(i) P is domiciled outside England and Wales, and
(ii) the condition in sub-paragraph (5) is met.

(5) The condition is that, under the law of P's domicile, any question of his testamentary capacity would fall to be determined in accordance with the law of a place outside England and Wales.

Vesting orders ancillary to settlement etc

5 (1) If provision is made by virtue of section 18 for –

(a) the settlement of any property of P, or
(b) the exercise of a power vested in him of appointing trustees or retiring from a trust,

the court may also make as respects the property settled or the trust property such consequential vesting or other orders as the case may require.

(2) The power under sub-paragraph (1) includes, in the case of the exercise of such a power, any order which could have been made in such a case under Part 4 of the Trustee Act 1925.

Variation of settlements

6 (1) If a settlement has been made by virtue of section 18, the court may by order vary or revoke the settlement if –

(a) the settlement makes provision for its variation or revocation,
(b) the court is satisfied that a material fact was not disclosed when the settlement was made, or
(c) the court is satisfied that there has been a substantial change of circumstances.

(2) Any such order may give such consequential directions as the court thinks fit.

Vesting of stock in curator appointed outside England and Wales

7 (1) Sub-paragraph (2) applies if the court is satisfied –

(a) that under the law prevailing in a place outside England and Wales a person ('M') has been appointed to exercise powers in respect of the property or affairs of P on the ground (however formulated) that P lacks capacity to make decisions with respect to the management and administration of his property and affairs, and
(b) that, having regard to the nature of the appointment and to the circumstances of the case, it is expedient that the court should exercise its powers under this paragraph.

(2) The court may direct –

(a) any stocks standing in the name of P, or
(b) the right to receive dividends from the stocks,

to be transferred into M's name or otherwise dealt with as required by M, and may give such directions as the court thinks fit for dealing with accrued dividends from the stocks.

(3) 'Stocks' includes –

(a) shares, and
(b) any funds, annuity or security transferable in the books kept by any body corporate or unincorporated company or society or by an instrument of transfer either alone or accompanied by other formalities,

and 'dividends' is to be construed accordingly.

Preservation of interests in property disposed of on behalf of person lacking capacity

8 (1) Sub-paragraphs (2) and (3) apply if –
   (a) P's property has been disposed of by virtue of section 18,
   (b) under P's will or intestacy, or by a gift perfected or nomination taking effect on his death, any other person would have taken an interest in the property but for the disposal, and
   (c) on P's death, any property belonging to P's estate represents the property disposed of.

(2) The person takes the same interest, if and so far as circumstances allow, in the property representing the property disposed of.

(3) If the property disposed of was real property, any property representing it is to be treated, so long as it remains part of P's estate, as if it were real property.

(4) The court may direct that, on a disposal of P's property –
   (a) which is made by virtue of section 18, and
   (b) which would apart from this paragraph result in the conversion of personal property into real property,

property representing the property disposed of is to be treated, so long as it remains P's property or forms part of P's estate, as if it were personal property.

(5) References in sub-paragraphs (1) to (4) to the disposal of property are to –
   (a) the sale, exchange, charging of or other dealing (otherwise than by will) with property other than money;
   (b) the removal of property from one place to another;
   (c) the application of money in acquiring property;
   (d) the transfer of money from one account to another;

and references to property representing property disposed of are to be construed accordingly and as including the result of successive disposals.

(6) The court may give such directions as appear to it necessary or expedient for the purpose of facilitating the operation of sub-paragraphs (1) to (3), including the carrying of money to a separate account and the transfer of property other than money.

9 (1) Sub-paragraph (2) applies if the court has ordered or directed the expenditure of money –
   (a) for carrying out permanent improvements on any of P's property, or
   (b) otherwise for the permanent benefit of any of P's property.

(2) The court may order that –
   (a) the whole of the money expended or to be expended, or
   (b) any part of it,

is to be a charge on the property either without interest or with interest at a specified rate.

(3) An order under sub-paragraph (2) may provide for excluding or restricting the operation of paragraph 8(1) to (3).

(4) A charge under sub-paragraph (2) may be made in favour of such person as may be just and, in particular, where the money charged is paid out of P's general estate, may be made in favour of a person as trustee for P.

(5) No charge under sub-paragraph (2) may confer any right of sale or foreclosure during P's lifetime.

Powers as patron of benefice

10 (1) Any functions which P has as patron of a benefice may be discharged only by a person ('R') appointed by the court.

(2) R must be an individual capable of appointment under section 8(1)(b) of the 1986 Measure (which provides for an individual able to make a declaration of communicant status, a clerk in Holy Orders, etc to be appointed to discharge a registered patron's functions).

(3) The 1986 Measure applies to R as it applies to an individual appointed by the registered patron of the benefice under section 8(1)(b) or (3) of that Measure to discharge his functions as patron.

(4) 'The 1986 Measure' means the Patronage (Benefices) Measure 1986 (No 3).

SCHEDULE 3
INTERNATIONAL PROTECTION OF ADULTS

Section 63

PART 1
PRELIMINARY

Introduction

1 This Part applies for the purposes of this Schedule.

The Convention

2 (1) 'Convention' means the Convention referred to in section 63.

(2) 'Convention country' means a country in which the Convention is in force.

(3) A reference to an Article or Chapter is to an Article or Chapter of the Convention.

(4) An expression which appears in this Schedule and in the Convention is to be construed in accordance with the Convention.

'Convention'—This is the Convention on the International Protection of Adults concluded at the Hague on 13 January 2000 (No 35) (see www.hcch.net). It came into force on 1 January 2009.

'Convention country'—The Convention countries are currently the UK (in relation to Scotland), Estonia (with effect from 1 November 2011), Finland, France, Germany and Switzerland.

Countries, territories and nationals

3 (1) 'Country' includes a territory which has its own system of law.

(2) Where a country has more than one territory with its own system of law, a reference to the country, in relation to one of its nationals, is to the territory with which the national has the closer, or the closest, connection.

Adults with incapacity

4 (1) 'Adult' means (subject to sub-paragraph (2) a person who –

  (a) as a result of an impairment or insufficiency of his personal faculties, cannot protect his interests, and
  (b) has reached 16.

(2) But 'adult' does not include a child to whom either of the following applies –

  (a) the Convention on Jurisdiction, Applicable Law, Recognition, Enforcement and Co-Operation in respect of Parental Responsibility and Measures for the Protection of Children that was signed at The Hague on 19 October 1996;
  (b) Council Regulation (EC) No. 2201/2003 concerning jurisdiction and the recognition and enforcement of judgments in matrimonial matters and the matters of parental responsibility.

Amendment—Amended by SI 2010/1898.

'Adult'—This contrasts with the Convention which is limited to persons who have reached 18.

Protective measures

5 (1) 'Protective measure' means a measure directed to the protection of the person or property of an adult; and it may deal in particular with any of the following –

  (a) the determination of incapacity and the institution of a protective regime,
  (b) placing the adult under the protection of an appropriate authority,
  (c) guardianship, curatorship or any corresponding system,
  (d) the designation and functions of a person having charge of the adult's person or property, or representing or otherwise helping him,
  (e) placing the adult in a place where protection can be provided,
  (f) administering, conserving or disposing of the adult's property,
  (g) authorising a specific intervention for the protection of the person or property of the adult.

(2) Where a measure of like effect to a protective measure has been taken in relation to a person before he reaches 16, this Schedule applies to the measure in so far as it has effect in relation to him once he has reached 16.

Central Authority

6 (1) Any function under the Convention of a Central Authority is exercisable in England and Wales by the Lord Chancellor.

(2) A communication may be sent to the Central Authority in relation to England and Wales by sending it to the Lord Chancellor.

'**Central Authority in relation to England and Wales**'—No authority has yet been designated.

PART 2
JURISDICTION OF COMPETENT AUTHORITY

Scope of jurisdiction

7 (1) The court may exercise its functions under this Act (in so far as it cannot otherwise do so) in relation to –

(a) an adult habitually resident in England and Wales,
(b) an adult's property in England and Wales,
(c) an adult present in England and Wales or who has property there, if the matter is urgent, or
(d) an adult present in England and Wales, if a protective measure which is temporary and limited in its effect to England and Wales is proposed in relation to him.

(2) An adult present in England and Wales is to be treated for the purposes of this paragraph as habitually resident there if –

(a) his habitual residence cannot be ascertained,
(b) he is a refugee, or
(c) he has been displaced as a result of disturbance in the country of his habitual residence.

8 (1) The court may also exercise its functions under this Act (in so far as it cannot otherwise do so) in relation to an adult if sub-paragraph (2) or (3) applies in relation to him.

(2) This sub-paragraph applies in relation to an adult if –

(a) he is a British citizen,
(b) he has a closer connection with England and Wales than with Scotland or Northern Ireland, and
(c) Article 7 has, in relation to the matter concerned, been complied with.

(3) This sub-paragraph applies in relation to an adult if the Lord Chancellor, having consulted such persons as he considers appropriate, agrees to a request under Article 8 in relation to the adult.

'**Article 7 has ... been complied with**'—Under this Article if it is considered that the state of nationality is in a better position to assess the interests of one of its nationals habitually resident elsewhere (or if habitual residence cannot be established elsewhere) it is to advise the authorities of the state of habitual residence (or presence) before assuming jurisdiction to take protective measures, and shall not do so if that state has either taken or declined to take protective measures.

'**a request under Article 8**'—The authorities of the state of habitual residence (or presence where habitual residence cannot be established) may request the authorities of another state with which the person has a connection (which includes the state of nationality) to take protective measures.

Exercise of jurisdiction

9 (1) This paragraph applies where jurisdiction is exercisable under this Schedule in connection with a matter which involves a Convention country other than England and Wales.

(2) Any Article on which the jurisdiction is based applies in relation to the matter in so far as it involves the other country (and the court must, accordingly, comply with any duty conferred on it as a result).

(3) Article 12 also applies, so far as its provisions allow, in relation to the matter in so far as it involves the other country.

'**Article 12 applies**'—Under this Article once a state with jurisdiction under the Convention has taken protective measures they remain in force even if the circumstances on which the jurisdiction was taken have changed (eg a change of habitual residence) unless the authorities of a state which has jurisdiction have modified, replaced or terminated them.

10 A reference in this Schedule to the exercise of jurisdiction under this Schedule is to the exercise of functions under this Act as a result of this Part of this Schedule.

PART 3
APPLICABLE LAW

Applicable law

11 In exercising jurisdiction under this Schedule, the court may, if it thinks that the matter has a substantial connection with a country other than England and Wales, apply the law of that other country.

12 Where a protective measure is taken in one country but implemented in another, the conditions of implementation are governed by the law of the other country.

Lasting powers of attorney, etc

13 (1) If the donor of a lasting power is habitually resident in England and Wales at the time of granting the power, the law applicable to the existence, extent, modification or extinction of the power is –

 (a) the law of England and Wales, or
 (b) if he specifies in writing the law of a connected country for the purpose, that law.

(2) If he is habitually resident in another country at that time, but England and Wales is a connected country, the law applicable in that respect is –

 (a) the law of the other country, or
 (b) if he specifies in writing the law of England and Wales for the purpose, that law.

(3) A country is connected, in relation to the donor, if it is a country –

 (a) of which he is a national,
 (b) in which he was habitually resident, or
 (c) in which he has property.

(4) Where this paragraph applies as a result of sub-paragraph (3)(c), it applies only in relation to the property which the donor has in the connected country.

(5) The law applicable to the manner of the exercise of a lasting power is the law of the country where it is exercised.

(6) In this Part of this Schedule, 'lasting power' means –

   (a) a lasting power of attorney (see section 9),
   (b) an enduring power of attorney within the meaning of Schedule 4, or
   (c) any other power of like effect.

14 (1) Where a lasting power is not exercised in a manner sufficient to guarantee the protection of the person or property of the donor, the court, in exercising jurisdiction under this Schedule, may disapply or modify the power.

(2) Where, in accordance with this Part of this Schedule, the law applicable to the power is, in one or more respects, that of a country other than England and Wales, the court must, so far as possible, have regard to the law of the other country in that respect (or those respects).

'**Donor**'—It should be noted that the provisions of paragraph 14 are not limited to Adults as in the Convention. These provisions unlike the remainder of Sch 3 do therefore apply whether or not the Donor has an impairment or insufficiency of personal faculties.

15 Regulations may provide for Schedule 1 (lasting powers of attorney: formalities) to apply with modifications in relation to a lasting power which comes within paragraph 13(6)(c) above.

'**Regulations**'—No specific Regulations relating to this Schedule have yet been made.

Protection of third parties

16 (1) This paragraph applies where a person (a 'representative') in purported exercise of an authority to act on behalf of an adult enters into a transaction with a third party.

(2) The validity of the transaction may not be questioned in proceedings, nor may the third party be held liable, merely because –

   (a) where the representative and third party are in England and Wales when entering into the transaction, sub-paragraph (3) applies;
   (b) where they are in another country at that time, sub-paragraph (4) applies.

(3) This sub-paragraph applies if –

   (a) the law applicable to the authority in one or more respects is, as a result of this Schedule, the law of a country other than England and Wales, and
   (b) the representative is not entitled to exercise the authority in that respect (or those respects) under the law of that other country.

(4) This sub-paragraph applies if –

   (a) the law applicable to the authority in one or more respects is, as a result of this Part of this Schedule, the law of England and Wales, and
   (b) the representative is not entitled to exercise the authority in that respect (or those respects) under that law.

(5) This paragraph does not apply if the third party knew or ought to have known that the applicable law was –

    (a)   in a case within sub-paragraph (3), the law of the other country;
    (b)   in a case within sub-paragraph (4), the law of England and Wales.

Mandatory rules

17 Where the court is entitled to exercise jurisdiction under this Schedule, the mandatory provisions of the law of England and Wales apply, regardless of any system of law which would otherwise apply in relation to the matter.

Public policy

18 Nothing in this Part of this Schedule requires or enables the application in England and Wales of a provision of the law of another country if its application would be manifestly contrary to public policy.

'Public Policy'—The judgment in *Re MN* [2010] EWHC 1926 concludes that the best interests test and other principles of s 1 are not matters of public policy.

PART 4
RECOGNITION AND ENFORCEMENT

Recognition

19 (1) A protective measure taken in relation to an adult under the law of a country other than England and Wales is to be recognised in England and Wales if it was taken on the ground that the adult is habitually resident in the other country.

(2) A protective measure taken in relation to an adult under the law of a Convention country other than England and Wales is to be recognised in England and Wales if it was taken on a ground mentioned in Chapter 2 (jurisdiction).

(3) But the court may disapply this paragraph in relation to a measure if it thinks that –

    (a)   the case in which the measure was taken was not urgent,
    (b)   the adult was not given an opportunity to be heard, and
    (c)   that omission amounted to a breach of natural justice.

(4) It may also disapply this paragraph in relation to a measure if it thinks that –

    (a)   recognition of the measure would be manifestly contrary to public policy,
    (b)   the measure would be inconsistent with a mandatory provision of the law of England and Wales, or
    (c)   the measure is inconsistent with one subsequently taken, or recognised, in England and Wales in relation to the adult.

(5) And the court may disapply this paragraph in relation to a measure taken under the law of a Convention country in a matter to which Article 33 applies, if the court thinks that that Article has not been complied with in connection with that matter.

'Mandatory provision'—The judgment in *Re MN* [2010] EWHC 1926 concludes that the best interests test and other principles of s1 are not mandatory provisions.

'**Article 33**'—Under this Article it is possible for the authorities in one contracting state to place someone in an establishment in another contracting state. The authorities in the requesting state must first consult the authorities in that contracting state and may not make the placement if that state has indicated opposition within a reasonable time. See note to Sch 3, para 35.

20 (1) An interested person may apply to the court for a declaration as to whether a protective measure taken under the law of a country other than England and Wales is to be recognised in England and Wales.

(2) No permission is required for an application to the court under this paragraph.

21 For the purposes of paragraphs 19 and 20, any finding of fact relied on when the measure was taken is conclusive.

Enforcement

22 (1) An interested person may apply to the court for a declaration as to whether a protective measure taken under the law of, and enforceable in, a country other than England and Wales is enforceable, or to be registered, in England and Wales in accordance with Court of Protection Rules.

(2) The court must make the declaration if –

  (a) the measure comes within sub-paragraph (1) or (2) of paragraph 19, and
  (b) the paragraph is not disapplied in relation to it as a result of sub-paragraph (3), (4) or (5).

(3) A measure to which a declaration under this paragraph relates is enforceable in England and Wales as if it were a measure of like effect taken by the court.

Measures taken in relation to those aged under 16

23 (1) This paragraph applies where –

  (a) provision giving effect to, or otherwise deriving from, the Convention in a country other than England and Wales applies in relation to a person who has not reached 16, and
  (b) a measure is taken in relation to that person in reliance on that provision.

(2) This Part of this Schedule applies in relation to that measure as it applies in relation to a protective measure taken in relation to an adult under the law of a Convention country other than England and Wales.

Supplementary

24 The court may not review the merits of a measure taken outside England and Wales except to establish whether the measure complies with this Schedule in so far as it is, as a result of this Schedule, required to do so.

25 Court of Protection Rules may make provision about an application under paragraph 20 or 22.

'**Court of Protection Rules**'—No special provisions have been made in the Court of Protection Rules 2007, SI 2007/1744.

PART 5
CO-OPERATION

Proposal for cross-border placement

26 (1) This paragraph applies where a public authority proposes to place an adult in an establishment in a Convention country other than England and Wales.

(2) The public authority must consult an appropriate authority in that other country about the proposed placement and, for that purpose, must send it –

   (a) a report on the adult, and
   (b) a statement of its reasons for the proposed placement.

(3) If the appropriate authority in the other country opposes the proposed placement within a reasonable time, the public authority may not proceed with it.

27 A proposal received by a public authority under Article 33 in relation to an adult is to proceed unless the authority opposes it within a reasonable time.

'*Article 33*'—See note under Sch 3, para 19.

Adult in danger etc

28 (1) This paragraph applies if a public authority is told that an adult –

   (a) who is in serious danger, and
   (b) in relation to whom the public authority has taken, or is considering taking, protective measures,

is, or has become resident, in a Convention country other than England and Wales.

(2) The public authority must tell an appropriate authority in that other country about –

   (a) the danger, and
   (b) the measures taken or under consideration.

29 A public authority may not request from, or send to, an appropriate authority in a Convention country information in accordance with Chapter 5 (co-operation) in relation to an adult if it thinks that doing so –

   (a) would be likely to endanger the adult or his property, or
   (b) would amount to a serious threat to the liberty or life of a member of the adult's family.

'*Chapter 5*'—See text of Convention (Arts 28–36) for the duties placed under the Convention of co-operation between contracting states to achieve the purposes of the Convention.

PART 6
GENERAL

Certificates

30 A certificate given under Article 38 by an authority in a Convention country other than England and Wales is, unless the contrary is shown, proof of the matters contained in it.

'**Article 38**'—This Article provides for the authorities of a contracting state where a measure of protection has been taken or a power of representation confirmed to issue to the person entrusted with the protection of the adult's person or property a certificate indicating the capacity in which that person is entitled to act and the powers conferred. Sadly Article 38 Certificates are not currently available in England and Wales.

Powers to make further provision as to private international law

31 Her Majesty may by Order in Council confer on the Lord Chancellor, the court or another public authority functions for enabling the Convention to be given effect in England and Wales.

'**Order in Council**'—No Order has yet been made.

32 (1) Regulations may make provision –

(a) giving further effect to the Convention, or
(b) otherwise about the private international law of England and Wales in relation to the protection of adults.

(2) The regulations may –

(a) confer functions on the court or another public authority;
(b) amend this Schedule;
(c) provide for this Schedule to apply with specified modifications;
(d) make provision about countries other than Convention countries.

'**Regulations**'—No Regulations have yet been made.

Exceptions

33 Nothing in this Schedule applies, and no provision made under paragraph 32 is to apply, to any matter to which the Convention, as a result of Article 4, does not apply.

'**Article 4**'—Article 4 sets out a list of matters to which the Convention does not apply, namely maintenance obligations, formation, annulment or dissolution of marriage (or similar relationship), property regimes in respect of marriage, trusts or succession, social security, public health measures, criminal sanctions, asylum or immigration or public safety. This is an extremely complex area of the law. Professor Lagarde's report is a helpful resource in understanding some of these complexities.

Regulations and orders

34 A reference in this Schedule to regulations or an order (other than an Order in Council) is to regulations or an order made for the purposes of this Schedule by the Lord Chancellor.

Commencement

35 The following provisions of this Schedule have effect only if the Convention is in force in accordance with Article 57 –

(a) paragraph 8,
(b) paragraph 9,

(c) paragraph 19(2) and (5),
(d) Part 5,
(e) paragraph 30.

If the Convention is in force in accordance with Article 57—The Convention came into force on 1 January 2009, however the view that these provisions will not have effect until the Convention is ratified for England & Wales is supported in the judgment of Sir James Munby in *JO v GO & Ors* [2013] EWHC 3932 (COP), [2014] COPLR 62, at [9].

Scope of provision—Accordingly it is thought that these provisions cannot currently be used in a case arising in England or Wales with a Scottish or other Convention country element.

SCHEDULE 4
PROVISIONS APPLYING TO EXISTING ENDURING POWERS OF ATTORNEY

Section 66(3)

PART 1
ENDURING POWERS OF ATTORNEY

Enduring power of attorney to survive mental incapacity of donor

1 (1) Where an individual has created a power of attorney which is an enduring power within the meaning of this Schedule –

(a) the power is not revoked by any subsequent mental incapacity of his,
(b) upon such incapacity supervening, the donee of the power may not do anything under the authority of the power except as provided by sub-paragraph (2) unless or until the instrument creating the power is registered under paragraph 13, and
(c) if and so long as paragraph (b) operates to suspend the donee's authority to act under the power, section 5 of the Powers of Attorney Act 1971 (protection of donee and third persons), so far as applicable, applies as if the power had been revoked by the donor's mental incapacity,

and, accordingly, section 1 of this Act does not apply.

(2) Despite sub-paragraph (1)(b), where the attorney has made an application for registration of the instrument then, until it is registered, the attorney may take action under the power –

(a) to maintain the donor or prevent loss to his estate, or
(b) to maintain himself or other persons in so far as paragraph 3(2) permits him to do so.

(3) Where the attorney purports to act as provided by sub-paragraph (2) then, in favour of a person who deals with him without knowledge that the attorney is acting otherwise than in accordance with sub-paragraph (2)(a) or (b), the transaction between them is as valid as if the attorney were acting in accordance with sub-paragraph (2)(a) or (b).

Scope of provision—Schedule 4 incorporates the provisions of the Enduring Powers of Attorney Act 1985, which is repealed by s 66(1)(b) so that the same provisions apply to instruments made in accordance with that Act, but within the framework of the MCA 2005.

'enduring power of attorney' (para 1(1))—That is an enduring power of attorney as defined by para 2 of this Schedule and made prior to 1 October 2007.

'**an enduring power within the meaning of this Schedule**' (para 1(1))—That is an enduring power of attorney created under the Enduring Powers of Attorney Act 1985 prior to 1 October 2007 (and see Sch 4, para 2). This Schedule sets out the regime to apply to enduring powers of attorney made before this date in replacement of the provisions of the 1985 Act.

'**section 5 of the Powers of Attorney Act 1971**' (para 1(1)(c))—Provides that a donee who acts in pursuance of a power when it has been revoked shall not incur any liability by reason of the revocation if not aware of the revocation; and that a transaction with a third party dealing with the donee without knowledge of the revocation shall be as valid as if the power had been in existence. It also provides a mechanism for a purchaser to establish conclusive proof that he or she was unaware of a revocation.

'**section 1 of this Act does not apply**' (para 1(1))—That is the principles which otherwise apply for the purposes of the Act, such as in relation to lasting powers of attorney.

Characteristics of an enduring power of attorney

2 (1) Subject to sub-paragraphs (5) and (6) and paragraph 20, a power of attorney is an enduring power within the meaning of this Schedule if the instrument which creates the power –

  (a) is in the prescribed form,
  (b) was executed in the prescribed manner by the donor and the attorney, and
  (c) incorporated at the time of execution by the donor the prescribed explanatory information.

(2) In this paragraph, 'prescribed' means prescribed by such of the following regulations as applied when the instrument was executed –

  (a) the Enduring Powers of Attorney (Prescribed Form) Regulations 1986,
  (b) the Enduring Powers of Attorney (Prescribed Form) Regulations 1987,
  (c) the Enduring Powers of Attorney (Prescribed Form) Regulations 1990,
  (d) the Enduring Powers of Attorney (Welsh Language Prescribed Form) Regulations 2000.

(3) An instrument in the prescribed form purporting to have been executed in the prescribed manner is to be taken, in the absence of evidence to the contrary, to be a document which incorporated at the time of execution by the donor the prescribed explanatory information.

(4) If an instrument differs in an immaterial respect in form or mode of expression from the prescribed form it is to be treated as sufficient in point of form and expression.

(5) A power of attorney cannot be an enduring power unless, when he executes the instrument creating it, the attorney is –

  (a) an individual who has reached 18 and is not bankrupt or is not subject to a debt relief order (under Part 7A of the Insolvency Act 1986), or
  (b) a trust corporation.

(6) A power of attorney which gives the attorney a right to appoint a substitute or successor cannot be an enduring power.

(7) An enduring power is revoked by the bankruptcy of the donor or attorney [or the making of a debt relief order (under Part 7A of the Insolvency Act 1986) in respect of the donor or attorney].

(8) But where the donor or attorney is bankrupt merely because an interim bankruptcy restrictions order has effect in respect of him or where the donor or attorney is subject to an interim debt relief restrictions order, the power is suspended for so long as the order has effect.

(9) An enduring power is revoked if the court –

   (a) exercises a power under sections 16 to 20 in relation to the donor, and
   (b) directs that the enduring power is to be revoked.

(10) No disclaimer of an enduring power, whether by deed or otherwise, is valid unless and until the attorney gives notice of it to the donor or, where paragraph 4(6) or 15(1) applies, to the Public Guardian.

Amendments—SI 2012/2404.

'**the prescribed explanatory information**' (para 2(3))—Namely the explanatory information as prescribed in whichever of the above regulations apply.

'**a power under sections 16 to 20**' (para 2(9))—That is the Court makes a decision for the incapacitated person or appoints a deputy.

'**where paragraph 4(6) or 15(1) applies**' (para 2(10))—That is once the attorney has reason to believe that the donor is or is becoming mentally incapable or after the power has been registered.

Scope of authority etc of attorney under enduring power

3 (1) If the instrument which creates an enduring power of attorney is expressed to confer general authority on the attorney, the instrument operates to confer, subject to –

   (a) the restriction imposed by sub-paragraph (3), and
   (b) any conditions or restrictions contained in the instrument,

authority to do on behalf of the donor anything which the donor could lawfully do by an attorney at the time when the donor executed the instrument.

(2) Subject to any conditions or restrictions contained in the instrument, an attorney under an enduring power, whether general or limited, may (without obtaining any consent) act under the power so as to benefit himself or other persons than the donor to the following extent but no further –

   (a) he may so act in relation to himself or in relation to any other person if the donor might be expected to provide for his or that person's needs respectively, and
   (b) he may do whatever the donor might be expected to do to meet those needs.

(3) Without prejudice to sub-paragraph (2) but subject to any conditions or restrictions contained in the instrument, an attorney under an enduring power, whether general or limited, may (without obtaining any consent) dispose of the property of the donor by way of gift to the following extent but no further –

   (a) he may make gifts of a seasonal nature or at a time, or on an anniversary, of a birth, a marriage or the formation of a civil partnership, to persons (including himself) who are related to or connected with the donor, and
   (b) he may make gifts to any charity to whom the donor made or might be expected to make gifts,

provided that the value of each such gift is not unreasonable having regard to all the circumstances and in particular the size of the donor's estate.

'**provide for ... that person's needs**' (para 3(2)(a))—In contrast to the donee of a lasting power of attorney, an attorney acting under an enduring power of attorney has an express power to provide for the needs of the attorney or a third party that the donor might be expected to provide for. See Part I, Chapter 3 of this work.

PART 2
ACTION ON ACTUAL OR IMPENDING INCAPACITY OF DONOR

Duties of attorney in event of actual or impending incapacity of donor

4 (1) Sub-paragraphs (2) to (6) apply if the attorney under an enduring power has reason to believe that the donor is or is becoming mentally incapable.

(2) The attorney must, as soon as practicable, make an application to the Public Guardian for the registration of the instrument creating the power.

(3) Before making an application for registration the attorney must comply with the provisions as to notice set out in Part 3 of this Schedule.

(4) An application for registration –

  (a) must be made in the prescribed form, and
  (b) must contain such statements as may be prescribed.

(5) The attorney –

  (a) may, before making an application for the registration of the instrument, refer to the court for its determination any question as to the validity of the power, and
  (b) must comply with any direction given to him by the court on that determination.

(6) No disclaimer of the power is valid unless and until the attorney gives notice of it to the Public Guardian; and the Public Guardian must notify the donor if he receives a notice under this sub-paragraph.

(7) A person who, in an application for registration, makes a statement which he knows to be false in a material particular is guilty of an offence and is liable –

  (a) on summary conviction, to imprisonment for a term not exceeding 12 months or a fine not exceeding the statutory maximum or both;
  (b) on conviction on indictment, to imprisonment for a term not exceeding 2 years or a fine or both.

(8) In this paragraph, 'prescribed' means prescribed by regulations made for the purposes of this Schedule by the Lord Chancellor.

'**mentally incapable**' (para 4(1))—Defined by para 23(1) as meaning 'in relation to any person, that he is incapable by reason of mental disorder ... of managing and administering his property and affairs and "mentally capable" and "mental capacity" are to be construed accordingly'. The definition of 'mental disorder' is still supplied by MHA 1983, s 1(2) (for these purposes without amendment by MHA 2007) as meaning 'mental illness, arrested or incomplete development of mind, psychopathic disorder and any other disorder or disability of mind'.

'**prescribed form/statements as may be prescribed**' (para 4(4))—See the Lasting Powers of Attorney, Enduring Powers of Attorney and Public Guardian Regulations 2007, SI 2007/1253, Sch 8.

'**prescribed by regulations**' (para 4(8))—See the Lasting Powers of Attorney, Enduring Powers of Attorney and Public Guardian Regulations 2007, SI 2007/1253, as amended by the Public Guardian (Fees, etc) Regulations 2007, SI 2007/2051; the Lasting Powers of Attorney, Enduring Powers of Attorney and Public Guardian (Amendment) Regulations 2007, SI 2007/2161 and the Lasting Powers of Attorney, Enduring Powers of Attorney and Public Guardian (Amendment) Regulations 2009, SI 2009/1884.

PART 3
NOTIFICATION PRIOR TO REGISTRATION

Duty to give notice to relatives

5 Subject to paragraph 7, before making an application for registration the attorney must give notice of his intention to do so to all those persons (if any) who are entitled to receive notice by virtue of paragraph 6.

6 (1) Subject to sub-paragraphs (2) to (4), persons of the following classes ('relatives') are entitled to receive notice under paragraph 5 –

    (a)   the donor's spouse or civil partner,
    (b)   the donor's children,
    (c)   the donor's parents,
    (d)   the donor's brothers and sisters, whether of the whole or half blood,
    (e)   the widow, widower or surviving civil partner of a child of the donor,
    (f)   the donor's grandchildren,
    (g)   the children of the donor's brothers and sisters of the whole blood,
    (h)   the children of the donor's brothers and sisters of the half blood,
    (i)   the donor's uncles and aunts of the whole blood,
    (j)   the children of the donor's uncles and aunts of the whole blood.

(2) A person is not entitled to receive notice under paragraph 5 if –

    (a)   his name or address is not known to the attorney and cannot be reasonably ascertained by him, or
    (b)   the attorney has reason to believe that he has not reached 18 or is mentally incapable.

(3) Except where sub-paragraph (4) applies –

    (a)   no more than 3 persons are entitled to receive notice under paragraph 5, and
    (b)   in determining the persons who are so entitled, persons falling within the class in sub-paragraph (1)(a) are to be preferred to persons falling within the class in sub-paragraph (1)(b), those falling within the class in sub-paragraph (1)(b) are to be preferred to those falling within the class in sub-paragraph (1)(c), and so on.

(4) Despite the limit of 3 specified in sub-paragraph (3), where –

    (a)   there is more than one person falling within any of classes (a) to (j) of sub-paragraph (1), and
    (b)   at least one of those persons would be entitled to receive notice under paragraph 5,

then, subject to sub-paragraph (2), all the persons falling within that class are entitled to receive notice under paragraph 5.

7 (1) An attorney is not required to give notice under paragraph 5 –

(a) to himself, or
(b) to any other attorney under the power who is joining in making the application,

even though he or, as the case may be, the other attorney is entitled to receive notice by virtue of paragraph 6.

(2) In the case of any person who is entitled to receive notice by virtue of paragraph 6, the attorney, before applying for registration, may make an application to the court to be dispensed from the requirement to give him notice; and the court must grant the application if it is satisfied –

(a) that it would be undesirable or impracticable for the attorney to give him notice, or
(b) that no useful purpose is likely to be served by giving him notice.

Duty to give notice to donor

8 (1) Subject to sub-paragraph (2), before making an application for registration the attorney must give notice of his intention to do so to the donor.

(2) Paragraph 7(2) applies in relation to the donor as it applies in relation to a person who is entitled to receive notice under paragraph 5.

Contents of notices

9 A notice to relatives under this Part of this Schedule must –

(a) be in the prescribed form,
(b) state that the attorney proposes to make an application to the Public Guardian for the registration of the instrument creating the enduring power in question,
(c) inform the person to whom it is given of his right to object to the registration under paragraph 13(4), and
(d) specify, as the grounds on which an objection to registration may be made, the grounds set out in paragraph 13(9).

'notice ... in the prescribed form'—See the Lasting Powers of Attorney, Enduring Powers of Attorney and Public Guardian Regulations 2007, SI 2007/1253, Sch 7, as amended by the Public Guardian (Fees, etc) Regulations 2007, SI 2007/2051.

10 A notice to the donor under this Part of this Schedule –

(a) must be in the prescribed form,
(b) must contain the statement mentioned in paragraph 9(b), and
(c) must inform the donor that, while the instrument remains registered, any revocation of the power by him will be ineffective unless and until the revocation is confirmed by the court.

'notice ... in the prescribed form'—See the Lasting Powers of Attorney, Enduring Powers of Attorney and Public Guardian Regulations 2007, SI 2007/1253, Sch 7, as amended by the Public Guardian (Fees, etc) Regulations 2007, SI 2007/2051.

Duty to give notice to other attorneys

11 (1) Subject to sub-paragraph (2), before making an application for registration an attorney under a joint and several power must give notice of his intention to do so to any other attorney under the power who is not joining in making the application; and paragraphs 7(2) and 9 apply in relation to attorneys entitled to receive notice by virtue of this paragraph as they apply in relation to persons entitled to receive notice by virtue of paragraph 6.

(2) An attorney is not entitled to receive notice by virtue of this paragraph if –

(a) his address is not known to the applying attorney and cannot reasonably be ascertained by him, or

(b) the applying attorney has reason to believe that he has not reached 18 or is mentally incapable.

Supplementary

12 Despite section 7 of the Interpretation Act 1978 (construction of references to service by post), for the purposes of this Part of this Schedule a notice given by post is to be regarded as given on the date on which it was posted.

'Despite section 7 of the Interpretation Act 1978'—That is the default position that a document served by post is deemed to have been effected at the time at which it would be delivered in the ordinary course of post is disapplied.

PART 4
REGISTRATION

Registration of instrument creating power

13 (1) If an application is made in accordance with paragraph 4(3) and (4) the Public Guardian must, subject to the provisions of this paragraph, register the instrument to which the application relates.

(2) If it appears to the Public Guardian that –

(a) there is a deputy appointed for the donor of the power created by the instrument, and

(b) the powers conferred on the deputy would, if the instrument were registered, to any extent conflict with the powers conferred on the attorney,

the Public Guardian must not register the instrument except in accordance with the court's directions.

(3) The court may, on the application of the attorney, direct the Public Guardian to register an instrument even though notice has not been given as required by paragraph 4(3) and Part 3 of this Schedule to a person entitled to receive it, if the court is satisfied –

(a) that it was undesirable or impracticable for the attorney to give notice to that person, or

(b) that no useful purpose is likely to be served by giving him notice.

(4) Sub-paragraph (5) applies if, before the end of the period of 5 weeks beginning with the date (or the latest date) on which the attorney gave notice under paragraph 5 of an application for registration, the Public Guardian receives a valid notice of objection to the registration from a person entitled to notice of the application.

(5) The Public Guardian must not register the instrument except in accordance with the court's directions.

(6) Sub-paragraph (7) applies if, in the case of an application for registration –

(a) it appears from the application that there is no one to whom notice has been given under paragraph 5, or
(b) the Public Guardian has reason to believe that appropriate inquiries might bring to light evidence on which he could be satisfied that one of the grounds of objection set out in sub-paragraph (9) was established.

(7) The Public Guardian –

(a) must not register the instrument, and
(b) must undertake such inquiries as he thinks appropriate in all the circumstances.

(8) If, having complied with sub-paragraph (7)(b), the Public Guardian is satisfied that one of the grounds of objection set out in sub-paragraph (9) is established –

(a) the attorney may apply to the court for directions, and
(b) the Public Guardian must not register the instrument except in accordance with the court's directions.

(9) A notice of objection under this paragraph is valid if made on one or more of the following grounds –

(a) that the power purported to have been created by the instrument was not valid as an enduring power of attorney,
(b) that the power created by the instrument no longer subsists,
(c) that the application is premature because the donor is not yet becoming mentally incapable,
(d) that fraud or undue pressure was used to induce the donor to create the power,
(e) that, having regard to all the circumstances and in particular the attorney's relationship to or connection with the donor, the attorney is unsuitable to be the donor's attorney.

(10) If any of those grounds is established to the satisfaction of the court it must direct the Public Guardian not to register the instrument, but if not so satisfied it must direct its registration.

(11) If the court directs the Public Guardian not to register an instrument because it is satisfied that the ground in sub-paragraph (9)(d) or (e) is established, it must by order revoke the power created by the instrument.

(12) If the court directs the Public Guardian not to register an instrument because it is satisfied that any ground in sub-paragraph (9) except that in paragraph (c) is established, the instrument must be delivered up to be cancelled unless the court otherwise directs.

Register of enduring powers

14 The Public Guardian has the function of establishing and maintaining a register of enduring powers for the purposes of this Schedule.

PART 5
LEGAL POSITION AFTER REGISTRATION

Effect and proof of registration

15 (1) The effect of the registration of an instrument under paragraph 13 is that –

(a) no revocation of the power by the donor is valid unless and until the court confirms the revocation under paragraph 16(3);
(b) no disclaimer of the power is valid unless and until the attorney gives notice of it to the Public Guardian;
(c) the donor may not extend or restrict the scope of the authority conferred by the instrument and no instruction or consent given by him after registration, in the case of a consent, confers any right and, in the case of an instruction, imposes or confers any obligation or right on or creates any liability of the attorney or other persons having notice of the instruction or consent.

(2) Sub-paragraph (1) applies for so long as the instrument is registered under paragraph 13 whether or not the donor is for the time being mentally incapable.

(3) A document purporting to be an office copy of an instrument registered under this Schedule is, in any part of the United Kingdom, evidence of –

(a) the contents of the instrument, and
(b) the fact that it has been so registered.

(4) Sub-paragraph (3) is without prejudice to section 3 of the Powers of Attorney Act 1971 (proof by certified copies) and to any other method of proof authorised by law.

'section 3 of the Powers of Attorney Act 1971' (para 15(4))—Provides that that the contents of an instrument creating a power of attorney may be proved by means of a copy which is certified by the donor, a solicitor, notary public or stockbroker that it is a true and complete copy of the original.

Functions of court with regard to registered power

16 (1) Where an instrument has been registered under paragraph 13, the court has the following functions with respect to the power and the donor of and the attorney appointed to act under the power.

(2) The court may –

(a) determine any question as to the meaning or effect of the instrument;
(b) give directions with respect to –
  (i) the management or disposal by the attorney of the property and affairs of the donor;
  (ii) the rendering of accounts by the attorney and the production of the records kept by him for the purpose;
  (iii) the remuneration or expenses of the attorney whether or not in default of or in accordance with any provision made by the instrument, including directions for the repayment of excessive or the payment of additional remuneration;
(c) require the attorney to supply information or produce documents or things in his possession as attorney;
(d) give any consent or authorisation to act which the attorney would have to obtain from a mentally capable donor;
(e) authorise the attorney to act so as to benefit himself or other persons than

the donor otherwise than in accordance with paragraph 3(2) and (3) (but subject to any conditions or restrictions contained in the instrument);

(f) relieve the attorney wholly or partly from any liability which he has or may have incurred on account of a breach of his duties as attorney.

(3) On application made for the purpose by or on behalf of the donor, the court must confirm the revocation of the power if satisfied that the donor –

(a) has done whatever is necessary in law to effect an express revocation of the power, and
(b) was mentally capable of revoking a power of attorney when he did so (whether or not he is so when the court considers the application).

(4) The court must direct the Public Guardian to cancel the registration of an instrument registered under paragraph 13 in any of the following circumstances –

(a) on confirming the revocation of the power under sub-paragraph (3),
(b) on directing under paragraph 2(9)(b) that the power is to be revoked,
(c) on being satisfied that the donor is and is likely to remain mentally capable,
(d) on being satisfied that the power has expired or has been revoked by the mental incapacity of the attorney,
(e) on being satisfied that the power was not a valid and subsisting enduring power when registration was effected,
(f) on being satisfied that fraud or undue pressure was used to induce the donor to create the power,
(g) on being satisfied that, having regard to all the circumstances and in particular the attorney's relationship to or connection with the donor, the attorney is unsuitable to be the donor's attorney.

(5) If the court directs the Public Guardian to cancel the registration of an instrument on being satisfied of the matters specified in sub-paragraph (4)(f) or (g) it must by order revoke the power created by the instrument.

(6) If the court directs the cancellation of the registration of an instrument under sub-paragraph (4) except paragraph (c) the instrument must be delivered up to the Public Guardian to be cancelled, unless the court otherwise directs.

Cancellation of registration by Public Guardian

17 The Public Guardian must cancel the registration of an instrument creating an enduring power of attorney –

(a) on receipt of a disclaimer signed by the attorney;
(b) if satisfied that the power has been revoked by the death or bankruptcy of the donor or attorney or the making of a debt relief order (under Part 7A of the Insolvency Act 1986) in respect of the donor or attorney or, if the attorney is a body corporate, by its winding up or dissolution;
(c) on receipt of notification from the court that the court has revoked the power;
(d) on confirmation from the court that the donor has revoked the power.

Amendments—SI 2012/2404.

PART 6
PROTECTION OF ATTORNEY AND THIRD PARTIES

Protection of attorney and third persons where power is invalid or revoked

18 (1) Sub-paragraphs (2) and (3) apply where an instrument which did not create a valid power of attorney has been registered under paragraph 13 (whether or not the registration has been cancelled at the time of the act or transaction in question).

(2) An attorney who acts in pursuance of the power does not incur any liability (either to the donor or to any other person) because of the non-existence of the power unless at the time of acting he knows –

   (a) that the instrument did not create a valid enduring power,
   (b) that an event has occurred which, if the instrument had created a valid enduring power, would have had the effect of revoking the power, or
   (c) that, if the instrument had created a valid enduring power, the power would have expired before that time.

(3) Any transaction between the attorney and another person is, in favour of that person, as valid as if the power had then been in existence, unless at the time of the transaction that person has knowledge of any of the matters mentioned in sub-paragraph (2).

(4) If the interest of a purchaser depends on whether a transaction between the attorney and another person was valid by virtue of sub-paragraph (3), it is conclusively presumed in favour of the purchaser that the transaction was valid if –

   (a) the transaction between that person and the attorney was completed within 12 months of the date on which the instrument was registered, or
   (b) that person makes a statutory declaration, before or within 3 months after the completion of the purchase, that he had no reason at the time of the transaction to doubt that the attorney had authority to dispose of the property which was the subject of the transaction.

(5) For the purposes of section 5 of the Powers of Attorney Act 1971 (protection where power is revoked) in its application to an enduring power the revocation of which by the donor is by virtue of paragraph 15 invalid unless and until confirmed by the court under paragraph 16 –

   (a) knowledge of the confirmation of the revocation is knowledge of the revocation of the power, but
   (b) knowledge of the unconfirmed revocation is not.

'**section 5 of the Powers of Attorney Act 1971**' (para 18(5))—See note to Sch 4, para 1.

Further protection of attorney and third persons

19 (1) If –

   (a) an instrument framed in a form prescribed as mentioned in paragraph 2(2) creates a power which is not a valid enduring power, and
   (b) the power is revoked by the mental incapacity of the donor,

sub-paragraphs (2) and (3) apply, whether or not the instrument has been registered.

(2) An attorney who acts in pursuance of the power does not, by reason of the revocation, incur any liability (either to the donor or to any other person) unless at the time of acting he knows –

(a) that the instrument did not create a valid enduring power, and
(b) that the donor has become mentally incapable.

(3) Any transaction between the attorney and another person is, in favour of that person, as valid as if the power had then been in existence, unless at the time of the transaction that person knows –

(a) that the instrument did not create a valid enduring power, and
(b) that the donor has become mentally incapable.

(4) Paragraph 18(4) applies for the purpose of determining whether a transaction was valid by virtue of sub-paragraph (3) as it applies for the purpose or determining whether a transaction was valid by virtue of paragraph 18(3).

PART 7
JOINT AND JOINT AND SEVERAL ATTORNEYS

Application to joint and joint and several attorneys

20 (1) An instrument which appoints more than one person to be an attorney cannot create an enduring power unless the attorneys are appointed to act –

(a) jointly, or
(b) jointly and severally.

(2) This Schedule, in its application to joint attorneys, applies to them collectively as it applies to a single attorney but subject to the modifications specified in paragraph 21.

(3) This Schedule, in its application to joint and several attorneys, applies with the modifications specified in sub-paragraphs (4) to (7) and in paragraph 22.

(4) A failure, as respects any one attorney, to comply with the requirements for the creation of enduring powers –

(a) prevents the instrument from creating such a power in his case, but
(b) does not affect its efficacy for that purpose as respects the other or others or its efficacy in his case for the purpose of creating a power of attorney which is not an enduring power.

(5) If one or more but not both or all the attorneys makes or joins in making an application for registration of the instrument –

(a) an attorney who is not an applicant as well as one who is may act pending the registration of the instrument as provided in paragraph 1(2),
(b) notice of the application must also be given under Part 3 of this Schedule to the other attorney or attorneys, and
(c) objection may validly be taken to the registration on a ground relating to an attorney or to the power of an attorney who is not an applicant as well as to one or the power of one who is an applicant.

(6) The Public Guardian is not precluded by paragraph 13(5) or (8) from registering an instrument and the court must not direct him not to do so under paragraph 13(10) if an enduring power subsists as respects some attorney who is not affected by the ground or grounds of the objection in question; and where the Public Guardian registers an instrument in that case, he must make against the registration an entry in the prescribed form.

(7) Sub-paragraph (6) does not preclude the court from revoking a power in so far as it confers a power on any other attorney in respect of whom the ground in

paragraph 13(9)(d) or (e) is established; and where any ground in paragraph 13(9) affecting any other attorney is established the court must direct the Public Guardian to make against the registration an entry in the prescribed form.

(8) In sub-paragraph (4), 'the requirements for the creation of enduring powers' means the provisions of –

(a) paragraph 2 other than sub-paragraphs (8) and (9), and
(b) the regulations mentioned in paragraph 2.

Joint attorneys

21 (1) In paragraph 2(5), the reference to the time when the attorney executes the instrument is to be read as a reference to the time when the second or last attorney executes the instrument.

(2) In paragraph 2(6) to (8), the reference to the attorney is to be read as a reference to any attorney under the power.

(3) Paragraph 13 has effect as if the ground of objection to the registration of the instrument specified in sub-paragraph (9)(e) applied to any attorney under the power.

(4) In paragraph 16(2), references to the attorney are to be read as including references to any attorney under the power.

(5) In paragraph 16(4), references to the attorney are to be read as including references to any attorney under the power.

(6) In paragraph 17, references to the attorney are to be read as including references to any attorney under the power.

Joint and several attorneys

22 (1) In paragraph 2(7), the reference to the bankruptcy of the attorney is to be read as a reference to the bankruptcy of the last remaining attorney under the power; and the bankruptcy of any other attorney under the power causes that person to cease to be an attorney under the power.

(1A) In paragraph 2(7), the reference to the making of a debt relief order (under Part 7A of the Insolvency Act 1986) in respect of the attorney is to be read as a reference to the making of a debt relief order in respect of the last remaining attorney under the power; and the making of a debt relief order in respect of any other attorney under the power causes that person to cease to be an attorney under the power.

(2) In paragraph 2(8), the reference to the suspension of the power is to be read as a reference to its suspension in so far as it relates to the attorney in respect of whom the interim bankruptcy restrictions order has effect.

(2A) In paragraph 2(8), the reference to the suspension of the power is to be read as a reference to its suspension in so far as it relates to the attorney in respect of whom the interim debt relief restrictions order has effect.

(3) The restriction upon disclaimer imposed by paragraph 4(6) applies only to those attorneys who have reason to believe that the donor is or is becoming mentally incapable.

Amendments—SI 2012/2404.

PART 8
INTERPRETATION

23 (1) In this Schedule –

'enduring power' is to be construed in accordance with paragraph 2,
'mentally incapable' or 'mental incapacity', except where it refers to revocation at common law, means in relation to any person, that he is incapable by reason of mental disorder ... of managing and administering his property and affairs and 'mentally capable' and 'mental capacity' are to be construed accordingly,
'notice' means notice in writing, and
'prescribed', except for the purposes of paragraph 2, means prescribed by regulations made for the purposes of this Schedule by the Lord Chancellor.

(1A) In sub-paragraph (1), 'mental disorder' has the same meaning as in the Mental Health Act but disregarding the amendments made to that Act by the Mental Health Act 2007.

(2) Any question arising under or for the purposes of this Schedule as to what the donor of the power might at any time be expected to do is to be determined by assuming that he had full mental capacity at the time but otherwise by reference to the circumstances existing at that time.

Amendments—Mental Health Act 2007, ss 1(4), 55, Sch 1, Pt 2, para 23(1)-(3), Sch 11, Pt 1.

'prescribed by regulations' (para 23(1))—See the Lasting Powers of Attorney, Enduring Powers of Attorney and Public Guardian Regulations 2007, SI 2007/1253, as amended by the Public Guardian (Fees, etc) Regulations 2007, SI 2007/2051; the Lasting Powers of Attorney, Enduring Powers of Attorney and Public Guardian (Amendment) Regulations 2007, SI 2007/2161; and the Lasting Powers of Attorney, Enduring Powers of Attorney and Public Guardian (Amendment) Regulations 2009, SI 2009/1884.

SCHEDULE 5
TRANSITIONAL PROVISIONS AND SAVINGS

Section 66(4)

PART 1
REPEAL OF PART 7 OF THE MENTAL HEALTH ACT 1983
Existing receivers

1 (1) This paragraph applies where, immediately before the commencement day, there is a receiver ('R') for a person ('P') appointed under section 99 of the Mental Health Act.

(2) On and after that day –

(a) this Act applies as if R were a deputy appointed for P by the court, but with the functions that R had as receiver immediately before that day, and
(b) a reference in any other enactment to a deputy appointed by the court includes a person appointed as a deputy as a result of paragraph (a).

(3) On any application to it by R, the court may end R's appointment as P's deputy.

(4) Where, as a result of section 20(1), R may not make a decision on behalf of P in relation to a relevant matter, R must apply to the court.

(5) If, on the application, the court is satisfied that P is capable of managing his property and affairs in relation to the relevant matter –

(a) it must make an order ending R's appointment as P's deputy in relation to that matter, but
(b) it may, in relation to any other matter, exercise in relation to P any of the powers which it has under sections 15 to 19.

(6) If it is not satisfied, the court may exercise in relation to P any of the powers which it has under sections 15 to 19.

(7) R's appointment as P's deputy ceases to have effect if P dies.

(8) 'Relevant matter' means a matter in relation to which, immediately before the commencement day, R was authorised to act as P's receiver.

(9) In sub-paragraph (1), the reference to a receiver appointed under section 99 of the Mental Health Act includes a reference to a person who by virtue of Schedule 5 to that Act was deemed to be a receiver appointed under that section.

Orders, appointments etc

2 (1) Any order or appointment made, direction or authority given or other thing done which has, or by virtue of Schedule 5 to the Mental Health Act was deemed to have, effect under Part 7 of the Act immediately before the commencement day is to continue to have effect despite the repeal of Part 7.

(2) In so far as any such order, appointment, direction, authority or thing could have been made, given or done under sections 15 to 20 if those sections had then been in force –

(a) it is to be treated as made, given or done under those sections, and
(b) the powers of variation and discharge conferred by section 16(7) apply accordingly.

(3) Sub-paragraph (1) –

(a) does not apply to nominations under section 93(1) or (4) of the Mental Health Act, and
(b) as respects receivers, has effect subject to paragraph 1.

(4) This Act does not affect the operation of section 109 of the Mental Health Act (effect and proof of orders etc) in relation to orders made and directions given under Part 7 of that Act.

(5) This paragraph is without prejudice to section 16 of the Interpretation Act 1978 (general savings on repeal).

Pending proceedings

3 (1) Any application for the exercise of a power under Part 7 of the Mental Health Act which is pending immediately before the commencement day is to be treated, in so far as a corresponding power is exercisable under sections 16 to 20, as an application for the exercise of that power.

(2) For the purposes of sub-paragraph (1) an application for the appointment of a receiver is to be treated as an application for the appointment of a deputy.

Appeals

4 (1) Part 7 of the Mental Health Act and the rules made under it are to continue to apply to any appeal brought by virtue of section 105 of that Act which has not been determined before the commencement day.

(2) If in the case of an appeal brought by virtue of section 105(1) (appeal to nominated judge) the judge nominated under section 93 of the Mental Health Act has begun to hear the appeal, he is to continue to do so but otherwise it is to be heard by a puisne judge of the High Court nominated under section 46.

Fees

5 All fees and other payments which, having become due, have not been paid to the former Court of Protection before the commencement day, are to be paid to the new Court of Protection.

Court records

6 (1) The records of the former Court of Protection are to be treated, on and after the commencement day, as records of the new Court of Protection and are to be dealt with accordingly under the Public Records Act 1958.

(2) On and after the commencement day, the Public Guardian is, for the purpose of exercising any of his functions, to be given such access as he may require to such of the records mentioned in sub-paragraph (1) as relate to the appointment of receivers under section 99 of the Mental Health Act.

Existing charges

7 This Act does not affect the operation in relation to a charge created before the commencement day of –

(a) so much of section 101(6) of the Mental Health Act as precludes a charge created under section 101(5) from conferring a right of sale or foreclosure during the lifetime of the patient, or
(b) section 106(6) of the Mental Health Act (charge created by virtue of section 106(5) not to cause interest to fail etc).

Preservation of interests on disposal of property

8 Paragraph 8(1) of Schedule 2 applies in relation to any disposal of property (within the meaning of that provision) by a person living on 1 November 1960, being a disposal effected under the Lunacy Act 1890 as it applies in relation to the disposal of property effected under sections 16 to 20.

Accounts

9 Court of Protection Rules may provide that, in a case where paragraph 1 applies, R is to have a duty to render accounts –

(a) while he is receiver;
(b) after he is discharged.

Interpretation

10 In this Part of this Schedule –

(a) 'the commencement day' means the day on which section 66(1)(a) (repeal of Part 7 of the Mental Health Act) comes into force,
(b) 'the former Court of Protection' means the office abolished by section 45, and
(c) 'the new Court of Protection' means the court established by that section.

PART 2
REPEAL OF THE ENDURING POWERS OF ATTORNEY ACT 1985

Orders, determinations, etc

11 (1) Any order or determination made, or other thing done, under the 1985 Act which has effect immediately before the commencement day continues to have effect despite the repeal of that Act.

(2) In so far as any such order, determination or thing could have been made or done under Schedule 4 if it had then been in force –

(a) it is to be treated as made or done under that Schedule, and
(b) the powers of variation and discharge exercisable by the court apply accordingly.

(3) Any instrument registered under the 1985 Act is to be treated as having been registered by the Public Guardian under Schedule 4.

(4) This paragraph is without prejudice to section 16 of the Interpretation Act 1978 (general savings on repeal).

Pending proceedings

12 (1) An application for the exercise of a power under the 1985 Act which is pending immediately before the commencement day is to be treated, in so far as a corresponding power is exercisable under Schedule 4, as an application for the exercise of that power.

(2) For the purposes of sub-paragraph (1) –

(a) a pending application under section 4(2) of the 1985 Act for the registration of an instrument is to be treated as an application to the Public Guardian under paragraph 4 of Schedule 4 and any notice given in connection with that application under Schedule 1 to the 1985 Act is to be treated as given under Part 3 of Schedule 4,
(b) a notice of objection to the registration of an instrument is to be treated as a notice of objection under paragraph 13 of Schedule 4, and

(c) pending proceedings under section 5 of the 1985 Act are to be treated as proceedings on an application for the exercise by the court of a power which would become exercisable in relation to an instrument under paragraph 16(2) of Schedule 4 on its registration.

Appeals

13 (1) The 1985 Act and, so far as relevant, the provisions of Part 7 of the Mental Health Act and the rules made under it as applied by section 10 of the 1985 Act are to continue to have effect in relation to any appeal brought by virtue of section 10(1)(c) of the 1985 Act which has not been determined before the commencement day.

(2) If, in the case of an appeal brought by virtue of section 105(1) of the Mental Health Act as applied by section 10(1)(c) of the 1985 Act (appeal to nominated judge), the judge nominated under section 93 of the Mental Health Act has begun to hear the appeal, he is to continue to do so but otherwise the appeal is to be heard by a puisne judge of the High Court nominated under section 46.

Exercise of powers of donor as trustee

14 (1) Section 2(8) of the 1985 Act (which prevents a power of attorney under section 25 of the Trustee Act 1925 as enacted from being an enduring power) is to continue to apply to any enduring power –

(a) created before 1st March 2000, and
(b) having effect immediately before the commencement day.

(2) Section 3(3) of the 1985 Act (which entitles the donee of an enduring power to exercise the donor's powers as trustee) is to continue to apply to any enduring power to which, as a result of the provision mentioned in sub-paragraph (3), it applies immediately before the commencement day.

(3) The provision is section 4(3)(a) of the Trustee Delegation Act 1999 (which provides for section 3(3) of the 1985 Act to cease to apply to an enduring power when its registration is cancelled, if it was registered in response to an application made before 1 March 2001).

(4) Even though section 4 of the 1999 Act is repealed by this Act, that section is to continue to apply in relation to an enduring power –

(a) to which section 3(3) of the 1985 Act applies as a result of sub-paragraph (2), or
(b) to which, immediately before the repeal of section 4 of the 1999 Act, section 1 of that Act applies as a result of section 4 of it.

(5) The reference in section 1(9) of the 1999 Act to section 4(6) of that Act is to be read with sub-paragraphs (2) to (4).

Interpretation

15 In this Part of this Schedule, 'the commencement day' means the day on which section 66(1)(b) (repeal of the 1985 Act) comes into force.

SCHEDULE 6
MINOR AND CONSEQUENTIAL AMENDMENTS

Section 67(1)

Fines and Recoveries Act 1833

1 (1) The Fines and Recoveries Act 1833 is amended as follows.

(2) In section 33 (case where protector of settlement lacks capacity to act), for the words from 'shall be incapable' to 'is incapable as aforesaid' substitute 'lacks capacity (within the meaning of the Mental Capacity Act 2005) to manage his property and affairs, the Court of Protection is to take his place as protector of the settlement while he lacks capacity'.

(3) In sections 48 and 49 (mental health jurisdiction), for each reference to the judge having jurisdiction under Part 7 of the Mental Health Act substitute a reference to the Court of Protection.

Improvement of Land Act 1864

2 In section 68 of the Improvement of Land Act 1864 (apportionment of rentcharges) –

   (a) for ', curator, or receiver of' substitute 'or curator of, or a deputy with powers in relation to property and affairs appointed by the Court of Protection for,', and
   (b) for 'or patient within the meaning of Part VII of the Mental Health Act 1983' substitute 'person who lacks capacity (within the meaning of the Mental Capacity Act 2005) to receive the notice'.

Trustee Act 1925

3 (1) The Trustee Act 1925 is amended as follows.

(2) In section 36 (appointment of new trustee) –

   (a) in subsection (6C), for the words from 'a power of attorney' to the end, substitute 'an enduring power of attorney or lasting power of attorney registered under the Mental Capacity Act 2005', and
   (b) in subsection (9) –
       (i) for the words from 'is incapable' to 'exercising' substitute 'lacks capacity to exercise', and
       (ii) for the words from 'the authority' to the end substitute 'the Court of Protection'.

(3) In section 41(1) (power of court to appoint new trustee) for the words from 'is incapable' to 'exercising' substitute 'lacks capacity to exercise'.

(4) In section 54 (mental health jurisdiction) –

   (a) for subsection (1) substitute –

   '(1) Subject to subsection (2), the Court of Protection may not make an order, or give a direction or authority, in relation to a person who lacks capacity to exercise his functions as trustee, if the High Court may make an order to that effect under this Act.',

(b) in subsection (2) –
   (i) for the words from the beginning to 'of a receiver' substitute 'Where a person lacks capacity to exercise his functions as a trustee and a deputy is appointed for him by the Court of Protection or an application for the appointment of a deputy',
   (ii) for 'the said authority', in each place, substitute 'the Court of Protection', and
   (iii) for 'the patient', in each place, substitute 'the person concerned', and
(c) omit subsection (3).

(5) In section 55 (order made on particular allegation to be conclusive evidence of it) –

(a) for the words from 'Part VII' to 'Northern Ireland' substitute 'sections 15 to 20 of the Mental Capacity Act 2005 or any corresponding provisions having effect in Northern Ireland', and
(b) for paragraph (a) substitute –
   '(a) that a trustee or mortgagee lacks capacity in relation to the matter in question;'.

(6) In section 68 (definitions), at the end add –

'(3) Any reference in this Act to a person who lacks capacity in relation to a matter is to a person –

(a) who lacks capacity within the meaning of the Mental Capacity Act 2005 in relation to that matter, or
(b) in respect of whom the powers conferred by section 48 of that Act are exercisable and have been exercised in relation to that matter.'.

Law of Property Act 1925

4 (1) The Law of Property Act 1925 is amended as follows.

(2) In section 22 (conveyances on behalf of persons who lack capacity) –

(a) in subsection (1) –
   (i) for the words from 'in a person suffering' to 'is acting' substitute ', either solely or jointly with any other person or persons, in a person lacking capacity (within the meaning of the Mental Capacity Act 2005) to convey or create a legal estate, a deputy appointed for him by the Court of Protection or (if no deputy is appointed', and
   (ii) for 'the authority having jurisdiction under Part VII of the Mental Health Act 1983' substitute 'the Court of Protection',
(b) in subsection (2), for 'is incapable, by reason of mental disorder, of exercising' substitute 'lacks capacity (within the meaning of that Act) to exercise', and
(c) in subsection (3), for the words from 'an enduring power' to the end substitute 'an enduring power of attorney or lasting power of attorney (within the meaning of the 2005 Act) is entitled to act for the trustee who lacks capacity in relation to the dealing.'.

(3) In section 205(1) (interpretation), omit paragraph (xiii).

Administration of Estates Act 1925

5 (1) The Administration of Estates Act 1925 is amended as follows.

(2) In section 41(1) (powers of personal representatives to appropriate), in the proviso –

(a) in paragraph (ii) –
  (i) for the words from 'is incapable' to 'the consent' substitute 'lacks capacity (within the meaning of the Mental Capacity Act 2005) to give the consent, it', and
  (ii) for 'or receiver' substitute 'or a person appointed as deputy for him by the Court of Protection', and
(b) in paragraph (iv), for 'no receiver is acting for a person suffering from mental disorder' substitute 'no deputy is appointed for a person who lacks capacity to consent'.

(3) Omit section 55(1)(viii) (definitions of 'person of unsound mind' and 'defective').

National Assistance Act 1948

6 In section 49 of the National Assistance Act 1948 (expenses of council officers acting for persons who lack capacity) –

(a) for the words from 'applies' to 'affairs of a patient' substitute 'applies for appointment by the Court of Protection as a deputy', and
(b) for 'such functions' substitute 'his functions as deputy'.

USA Veterans' Pensions (Administration) Act 1949

7 In section 1 of the USA Veterans' Pensions (Administration) Act 1949 (administration of pensions) –

(a) in subsection (4), omit the words from 'or for whom' to '1983', and
(b) after subsection (4), insert –

'(4A) An agreement under subsection (1) is not to be made in relation to a person who lacks capacity (within the meaning of the Mental Capacity Act 2005) for the purposes of this Act if –

(a) there is a donee of an enduring power of attorney or lasting power of attorney (within the meaning of the 2005 Act), or a deputy appointed for the person by the Court of Protection, and
(b) the donee or deputy has power in relation to the person for the purposes of this Act.

(4B) The proviso at the end of subsection (4) also applies in relation to subsection (4A).'.

Intestates' Estates Act 1952

8 In Schedule 2 to the Intestates' Estates Act 1952 (rights of surviving spouse or civil partner in relation to home), for paragraph 6(1) substitute –

'(1) Where the surviving spouse or civil partner lacks capacity (within the meaning of the Mental Capacity Act 2005) to make a requirement or give a consent under this Schedule, the requirement or consent may be made or given by a deputy appointed by the Court of Protection with power in that respect or, if no deputy has that power, by that court.'.

Variation of Trusts Act 1958

9 In section 1 of the Variation of Trusts Act 1958 (jurisdiction of courts to vary trusts) –

(a) in subsection (3), for the words from 'shall be determined' to the end substitute 'who lacks capacity (within the meaning of the Mental Capacity Act 2005) to give his assent is to be determined by the Court of Protection', and

(b) in subsection (6), for the words from 'the powers' to the end substitute 'the powers of the Court of Protection'.

Administration of Justice Act 1960

10 In section 12(1)(b) of the Administration of Justice Act 1960 (contempt of court to publish information about proceedings in private relating to persons with incapacity) for the words from 'under Part VIII' to 'that Act' substitute 'under the Mental Capacity Act 2005, or under any provision of the Mental Health Act 1983'.

11 (*Repealed*)

Compulsory Purchase Act 1965

12 In Schedule 1 to the Compulsory Purchase Act 1965 (persons without power to sell their interests), for paragraph 1(2)(b) substitute –

'(b) do not have effect in relation to a person who lacks capacity (within the meaning of the Mental Capacity Act 2005) for the purposes of this Act if –

(i) there is a donee of an enduring power of attorney or lasting power of attorney (within the meaning of the 2005 Act), or a deputy appointed for the person by the Court of Protection, and

(ii) the donee or deputy has power in relation to the person for the purposes of this Act.'.

Leasehold Reform Act 1967

13 (1) For section 26(2) of the Leasehold Reform Act 1967 (landlord lacking capacity) substitute –

'(2) Where a landlord lacks capacity (within the meaning of the Mental Capacity Act 2005) to exercise his functions as a landlord, those functions are to be exercised –

(a) by a donee of an enduring power of attorney or lasting power of attorney (within the meaning of the 2005 Act), or a deputy appointed for him by the Court of Protection, with power to exercise those functions, or

    (b)   if no donee or deputy has that power, by a person authorised in that respect by that court.'.

(2) That amendment does not affect any proceedings pending at the commencement of this paragraph in which a receiver or a person authorised under Part 7 of the Mental Health Act is acting on behalf of the landlord.

Medicines Act 1968

14 In section 72 of the Medicines Act 1968 (pharmacist lacking capacity) –

(a) in subsection (1)(c), for the words from 'a receiver' to '1959' substitute 'he becomes a person who lacks capacity (within the meaning of the Mental Capacity Act 2005) to carry on the business',
(b) after subsection (1) insert –

'(1A) In subsection (1)(c), the reference to a person who lacks capacity to carry on the business is to a person –

    (a)   in respect of whom there is a donee of an enduring power of attorney or lasting power of attorney (within the meaning of the Mental Capacity Act 2005), or
    (b)   for whom a deputy is appointed by the Court of Protection,

and in relation to whom the donee or deputy has power for the purposes of this Act.',

(c) in subsection (3)(d) –
    (i)   for 'receiver' substitute 'deputy', and
    (ii) after 'guardian' insert 'or from the date of registration of the instrument appointing the donee', and
(d) in subsection (4)(c), for 'receiver' substitute 'donee, deputy'.

Family Law Reform Act 1969

15 For section 21(4) of the Family Law Reform Act 1969 (consent required for taking of bodily sample from person lacking capacity), substitute –

'(4) A bodily sample may be taken from a person who lacks capacity (within the meaning of the Mental Capacity Act 2005) to give his consent, if consent is given by the court giving the direction under section 20 or by –

    (a)   a donee of an enduring power of attorney or lasting power of attorney (within the meaning of that Act), or
    (b)   a deputy appointed, or any other person authorised, by the Court of Protection,

with power in that respect.'.

Local Authority Social Services Act 1970

16 (1) Schedule 1 to the Local Authority Social Services Act 1970 (enactments conferring functions assigned to social services committee) is amended as follows.

(2) In the entry for section 49 of the National Assistance Act 1948 (expenses of local authority officer appointed for person who lacks capacity) for 'receiver' substitute 'deputy'.

(3) At the end, insert –

'Mental Capacity
Act 2005

Section 39   Instructing independent mental capacity advocate before providing accommodation for person lacking capacity.

Section 49   Reports in proceedings.'.

Courts Act 1971

17 In Part 1A of Schedule 2 to the Courts Act 1971 (office-holders eligible for appointment as circuit judges), omit the reference to a Master of the Court of Protection.

Local Government Act 1972

18 (1) Omit section 118 of the Local Government Act 1972 (payment of pension etc where recipient lacks capacity).

(2) Sub-paragraph (3) applies where, before the commencement of this paragraph, a local authority has, in respect of a person referred to in that section as 'the patient', made payments under that section –

(a) to an institution or person having the care of the patient, or
(b) in accordance with subsection (1)(a) or (b) of that section.

(3) The local authority may, in respect of the patient, continue to make payments under that section to that institution or person, or in accordance with subsection (1)(a) or (b) of that section, despite the repeal made by sub-paragraph (1).

Matrimonial Causes Act 1973

19 In section 40 of the Matrimonial Causes Act 1973 (payments to person who lacks capacity) (which becomes subsection (1)) –

(a) for the words from 'is incapable' to 'affairs' substitute '('P') lacks capacity (within the meaning of the Mental Capacity Act 2005) in relation to the provisions of the order',
(b) for 'that person under Part VIII of that Act' substitute 'P under that Act',
(c) for the words from 'such persons' to the end substitute 'such person ('D') as it may direct', and
(d) at the end insert –
'(2) In carrying out any functions of his in relation to an order made under subsection (1), D must act in P's best interests (within the meaning of that Act).'.

Juries Act 1974

20 In Schedule 1 to the Juries Act 1974 (disqualification for jury service), for paragraph 3 substitute –

'3 A person who lacks capacity, within the meaning of the Mental Capacity Act 2005, to serve as a juror.'.

Consumer Credit Act 1974

21 For section 37(1)(c) of the Consumer Credit Act 1974 (termination of consumer credit licence if holder lacks capacity) substitute –

> '(c) becomes a person who lacks capacity (within the meaning of the Mental Capacity Act 2005) to carry on the activities covered by the licence.'.

Solicitors Act 1974

22 (1) The Solicitors Act 1974 is amended as follows.

(2) *(repealed)*

(3) In section 62(4) (contentious business agreements made by clients) for paragraphs (c) and (d) substitute –

> '(c) as a deputy for him appointed by the Court of Protection with powers in relation to his property and affairs, or
> (d) as another person authorised under that Act to act on his behalf.'.

(4) In paragraph 1(1) of Schedule 1 (circumstances in which Law Society may intervene in solicitor's practice), for paragraph (f) substitute –

> '(f) a solicitor lacks capacity (within the meaning of the Mental Capacity Act 2005) to act as a solicitor and powers under sections 15 to 20 or section 48 of that Act are exercisable in relation to him;'.

Local Government (Miscellaneous Provisions) Act 1976

23 In section 31 of the Local Government (Miscellaneous Provisions) Act 1976 (the title to which becomes 'Indemnities for local authority officers appointed as deputies or administrators'), for the words from 'as a receiver' to '1959' substitute 'as a deputy for a person by the Court of Protection'.

Sale of Goods Act 1979

24 In section 3(2) of the Sale of Goods Act 1979 (capacity to buy and sell) the words 'mental incapacity or' cease to have effect in England and Wales.

Limitation Act 1980

25 In section 38 of the Limitation Act 1980 (interpretation) substitute –

(a) in subsection (2) for 'of unsound mind' substitute 'lacks capacity (within the meaning of the Mental Capacity Act 2005) to conduct legal proceedings', and
(b) omit subsections (3) and (4).

Public Passenger Vehicles Act 1981

26 In section 57(2)(c) of the Public Passenger Vehicles Act 1981 (termination of public service vehicle licence if holder lacks capacity) for the words from 'becomes a patient' to 'or' substitute 'becomes a person who lacks capacity (within the meaning of the Mental Capacity Act 2005) to use a vehicle under the licence, or'.

Judicial Pensions Act 1981

27 In Schedule 1 to the Judicial Pensions Act 1981 (pensions of Supreme Court officers, etc), in paragraph 1, omit the reference to a Master of the Court of Protection except in the case of a person holding that office immediately before the commencement of this paragraph or who had previously retired from that office or died.

Senior Courts Act 1981

28 In Schedule 2 to the Senior Courts Act 1981 (qualifications for appointment to office in Supreme Court), omit paragraph 11 (Master of the Court of Protection).

Mental Health Act 1983

29 (1) The Mental Health Act is amended as follows.

(2) In section 134(3) (cases where correspondence of detained patients may not be withheld) for paragraph (b) substitute –

'(b) any judge or officer of the Court of Protection, any of the Court of Protection Visitors or any person asked by that Court for a report under section 49 of the Mental Capacity Act 2005 concerning the patient;'.

(3) In section 139 (protection for acts done in pursuance of 1983 Act), in subsection (1), omit from 'or in, or in pursuance' to 'Part VII of this Act,'.

(4) Section 142 (payment of pension etc where recipient lacks capacity) ceases to have effect in England and Wales.

(5) Sub-paragraph (6) applies where, before the commencement of sub-paragraph (4), an authority has, in respect of a person referred to in that section as 'the patient', made payments under that section –

(a) to an institution or person having the care of the patient, or
(b) in accordance with subsection (2)(a) or (b) of that section.

(6) The authority may, in respect of the patient, continue to make payments under that section to that institution or person, or in accordance with subsection (2)(a) or (b) of that section, despite the amendment made by sub-paragraph (4).

(7) In section 145(1) (interpretation), in the definition of 'patient', omit '(except in Part VII of this Act)'.

(8) In section 146 (provisions having effect in Scotland), omit from '104(4)' to 'section),'.

(9) In section 147 (provisions having effect in Northern Ireland), omit from '104(4)' to 'section),'.

Administration of Justice Act 1985

30 In section 18(3) of the Administration of Justice Act 1985 (licensed conveyancer who lacks capacity), for the words from 'that person' to the end substitute 'he becomes a person who lacks capacity (within the meaning of the Mental Capacity Act 2005) to practise as a licensed conveyancer.'.

Insolvency Act 1986

31 (1) The Insolvency Act 1986 is amended as follows.

(2) *(repealed)*

(3) In section 390 (people not qualified to be insolvency practitioners), in subsection (4) –

    (a) omit the 'or' immediately after paragraph (b),
    (b) in paragraph (c), omit 'Part VII of the Mental Health Act 1983 or', and
    (c) after that paragraph, insert ', or
    (d) he lacks capacity (within the meaning of the Mental Capacity Act 2005) to act as an insolvency practitioner.'.

Building Societies Act 1986

32 In section 102D(9) of the Building Societies Act 1986 (references to a person holding an account on trust for another) –

    (a) in paragraph (a), for 'Part VII of the Mental Health Act 1983' substitute 'the Mental Capacity Act 2005', and
    (b) for paragraph (b) substitute –
        '(b) to an attorney holding an account for another person under –
            (i) an enduring power of attorney or lasting power of attorney registered under the Mental Capacity Act 2005, or
            (ii) an enduring power registered under the Enduring Powers of Attorney (Northern Ireland) Order 1987;'.

Public Trustee and Administration of Funds Act 1986

33 In section 3 of the Public Trustee and Administration of Funds Act 1986 (functions of the Public Trustee) –

    (a) for subsections (1) to (5) substitute –

    '(1) The Public Trustee may exercise the functions of a deputy appointed by the Court of Protection.',

    (b) in subsection (6), for 'the 1906 Act' substitute 'the Public Trustee Act 1906', and
    (c) omit subsection (7).

Patronage (Benefices) Measure 1986 (No 3)

34 (1) The Patronage (Benefices) Measure 1986 (No 3) is amended as follows.

(2) In section 5 (rights of patronage exercisable otherwise than by registered patron), after subsection (3) insert –

'(3A) The reference in subsection (3) to a power of attorney does not include an enduring power of attorney or lasting power of attorney (within the meaning of the Mental Capacity Act 2005).'

(3) In section 9 (information to be sent to designated officer when benefice becomes vacant), after subsection (5) insert –

'(5A) Subsections (5B) and (5C) apply where the functions of a registered patron are, as a result of paragraph 10 of Schedule 2 to the Mental Capacity Act 2005 (patron's loss of capacity to discharge functions), to be discharged by an individual appointed by the Court of Protection.

(5B) If the individual is a clerk in Holy Orders, subsection (5) applies to him as it applies to the registered patron.

(5C) If the individual is not a clerk in Holy Orders, subsection (1) (other than paragraph (b)) applies to him as it applies to the registered patron.'

Courts and Legal Services Act 1990

35 (1) The Courts and Legal Services Act 1990 is amended as follows.

(2) In Schedule 11 (judges etc barred from legal practice), for the reference to a Master of the Court of Protection substitute a reference to each of the following –

(a) Senior Judge of the Court of Protection,
(b) President of the Court of Protection,
(c) Vice-President of the Court of Protection.

(3) In paragraph 5(3) of Schedule 14 (exercise of powers of intervention in registered foreign lawyer's practice), for paragraph (f) substitute –

'(f) he lacks capacity (within the meaning of the Mental Capacity Act 2005) to act as a registered foreign lawyer and powers under sections 15 to 20 or section 48 are exercisable in relation to him;'.

Child Support Act 1991

36 In section 50 of the Child Support Act 1991 (unauthorised disclosure of information) –

(a) in subsection (8) –
  (i) immediately after paragraph (a), insert 'or',
  (ii) omit paragraphs (b) and (d) and the 'or' immediately after paragraph (c), and
  (iii) for ', receiver, custodian or appointee' substitute 'or custodian', and
(b) after that subsection, insert –

'(9) Where the person to whom the information relates lacks capacity (within the meaning of the Mental Capacity Act 2005) to consent to its disclosure, the appropriate person is –

(a) a donee of an enduring power of attorney or lasting power of attorney (within the meaning of that Act), or
(b) a deputy appointed for him, or any other person authorised, by the Court of Protection,

with power in that respect.'.

Social Security Administration Act 1992

37 In section 123 of the Social Security Administration Act 1992 (unauthorised disclosure of information) –

(a) in subsection (10), omit –
   (i) in paragraph (b), 'a receiver appointed under section 99 of the Mental Health Act 1983 or',
   (ii) in paragraph (d)(i), 'sub-paragraph (a) of rule 41(1) of the Court of Protection Rules 1984 or',
   (iii) in paragraph (d)(ii), 'a receiver ad interim appointed under sub-paragraph (b) of the said rule 41(1) or', and
   (iv) 'receiver,', and
(b) after that subsection, insert –

'(11) Where the person to whom the information relates lacks capacity (within the meaning of the Mental Capacity Act 2005) to consent to its disclosure, the appropriate person is –

(a) a donee of an enduring power of attorney or lasting power of attorney (within the meaning of that Act), or
(b) a deputy appointed for him, or any other person authorised, by the Court of Protection,

with power in that respect.'.

Judicial Pensions and Retirement Act 1993

38 (1) The Judicial Pensions and Retirement Act 1993 is amended as follows.

(2) In Schedule 1 (qualifying judicial offices), in Part 2, under the cross-heading 'Court officers', omit the reference to a Master of the Court of Protection except in the case of a person holding that office immediately before the commencement of this sub-paragraph or who had previously retired from that office or died.

(3) In Schedule 5 (retirement: the relevant offices), omit the entries relating to the Master and Deputy or temporary Master of the Court of Protection, except in the case of a person holding any of those offices immediately before the commencement of this sub-paragraph.

(4) In Schedule 7 (retirement: transitional provisions), omit paragraph 5(5)(i)(g) except in the case of a person holding office as a deputy or temporary Master of the Court of Protection immediately before the commencement of this sub-paragraph.

Leasehold Reform, Housing and Urban Development Act 1993

39 (1) For paragraph 4 of Schedule 2 to the Leasehold Reform, Housing and Urban Development Act 1993 (landlord under a disability), substitute –

'4 (1) This paragraph applies where a Chapter I or Chapter II landlord lacks capacity (within the meaning of the Mental Capacity Act 2005) to exercise his functions as a landlord.

(2) For the purposes of the Chapter concerned, the landlord's place is to be taken –

- (a) by a donee of an enduring power of attorney or lasting power of attorney (within the meaning of the 2005 Act), or a deputy appointed for him by the Court of Protection, with power to exercise those functions, or
- (b) if no deputy or donee has that power, by a person authorised in that respect by that court.'.

(2) That amendment does not affect any proceedings pending at the commencement of this paragraph in which a receiver or a person authorised under Part 7 of the Mental Health Act 1983 is acting on behalf of the landlord.

Goods Vehicles (Licensing of Operators) Act 1995

40 (1) The Goods Vehicles (Licensing of Operators) Act 1995 is amended as follows.

(2) In section 16(5) (termination of licence), for 'he becomes a patient within the meaning of Part VII of the Mental Health Act 1983' substitute 'he becomes a person who lacks capacity (within the meaning of the Mental Capacity Act 2005) to use a vehicle under the licence'.

(3) In section 48 (licence not to be transferable, etc) –

- (a) in subsection (2) –
  - (i) for 'or become a patient within the meaning of Part VII of the Mental Health Act 1983' substitute ', or become a person who lacks capacity (within the meaning of the Mental Capacity Act 2005) to use a vehicle under the licence,', and
  - (ii) in paragraph (a), for 'became a patient' substitute 'became a person who lacked capacity in that respect', and
- (b) in subsection (5), for 'a patient within the meaning of Part VII of the Mental Health Act 1983' substitute 'a person lacking capacity'.

Disability Discrimination Act 1995

41 In section 20(7) of the Disability Discrimination Act 1995 (regulations to disapply provisions about incapacity), in paragraph (b), for 'Part VII of the Mental Health Act 1983' substitute 'the Mental Capacity Act 2005'.

Trusts of Land and Appointment of Trustees Act 1996

42 (1) The Trusts of Land and Appointment of Trustees Act 1996 is amended as follows.

(2) In section 9 (delegation by trustees), in subsection (6), for the words from 'an enduring power' to the end substitute 'an enduring power of attorney or lasting power of attorney within the meaning of the Mental Capacity Act 2005'.

(3) In section 20 (the title to which becomes 'Appointment of substitute for trustee who lacks capacity') –

(a) in subsection (1)(a), for 'is incapable by reason of mental disorder of exercising' substitute 'lacks capacity (within the meaning of the Mental Capacity Act 2005) to exercise', and
(b) in subsection (2) –
  (i) for paragraph (a) substitute –
    '(a) a deputy appointed for the trustee by the Court of Protection,',
  (ii) in paragraph (b), for the words from 'a power of attorney' to the end substitute 'an enduring power of attorney or lasting power of attorney registered under the Mental Capacity Act 2005', and
  (iii) in paragraph (c), for the words from 'the authority' to the end substitute 'the Court of Protection'.

Human Rights Act 1998

43 In section 4(5) of the Human Rights Act 1998 (courts which may make declarations of incompatibility), after paragraph (e) insert –

'(f) the Court of Protection, in any matter being dealt with by the President of the Family Division, the Vice-Chancellor or a puisne judge of the High Court.'

Access to Justice Act 1999

44 In paragraph 1 of Schedule 2 to the Access to Justice Act 1999 (services excluded from the Community Legal Service), after paragraph (e) insert –

'(ea) the creation of lasting powers of attorney under the Mental Capacity Act 2005,
(eb) the making of advance decisions under that Act,'.

Adoption and Children Act 2002

45 In section 52(1)(a) of the Adoption and Children Act 2002 (parental consent to adoption), for 'is incapable of giving consent' substitute 'lacks capacity (within the meaning of the Mental Capacity Act 2005) to give consent'.

Licensing Act 2003

46 (1) The Licensing Act 2003 is amended as follows.

(2) In section 27(1) (lapse of premises licence), for paragraph (b) substitute –

'(b) becomes a person who lacks capacity (within the meaning of the Mental Capacity Act 2005) to hold the licence,'.

(3) In section 47 (interim authority notice in relation to premises licence) –

(a) in subsection (5), for paragraph (b) substitute –
  '(b) the former holder lacks capacity (within the meaning of the Mental Capacity Act 2005) to hold the licence and that person acts for him under an enduring power of attorney or lasting power of attorney

registered under that Act,', and
(b) in subsection (10), omit the definition of 'mentally incapable'.

Courts Act 2003

47 (1) The Courts Act 2003 is amended as follows.

(2) In section 1(1) (the courts in relation to which the Lord Chancellor must discharge his general duty), after paragraph (a) insert –

'(aa) the Court of Protection,'.

(3) In section 64(2) (judicial titles which the Lord Chancellor may by order alter) –
  (a) omit the reference to a Master of the Court of Protection, and
  (b) at the appropriate place insert a reference to each of the following –
    (i) Senior Judge of the Court of Protection,
    (ii) President of the Court of Protection,
    (iii) Vice-president of the Court of Protection.

Amendments—Legal Services Act 2007, s 210, Sch 23; Constitutional Reform Act 2005, s 59(5), Sch 11, Pt 1, para 1(2); Deregulation Act 2015, s 19, Sch 6, para 20(4).

SCHEDULE 7
REPEALS

Section 67(2)

Short title and chapter	Extent of repeal
Trustee Act 1925	Section 54(3).
Law of Property Act 1925	Section 205(1)(xiii).
Administration of Estates Act 1925	Section 55(1)(viii)
U.S.A. Veterans' Pensions (Administration) Act 1949	In section 1(4), the words from 'or for whom' to '1983'.
Mental Health Act 1959	In Schedule 7, in Part 1, the entries relating to – section 33 of the Fines and Recoveries Act 1833, section 68 of the Improvement of Land Act 1864, section 55 of the Trustee Act 1925, section 205(1) of the Law of Property Act 1925, section 49 of the National Assistance Act 1948, and section 1 of the Variation of Trusts Act 1958.
Courts Act 1971	In Schedule 2, in Part 1A, the words 'Master of the Court of Protection'.

Short title and chapter	Extent of repeal
Local Government Act 1972	Section 118.
Limitation Act 1980	Section 38(3) and (4).
Senior Courts Act 1981	In Schedule 2, in Part 2, paragraph 11.
Mental Health Act 1983	Part 7. In section 139(1) the words from 'or in, or in pursuance' to 'Part VII of this Act,'. In section 145(1), in the definition of 'patient' the words '(except in Part VII of this Act)'. In sections 146 and 147 the words from '104(4)' to 'section),'. Schedule 3. In Schedule 4, paragraphs 1, 2, 4, 5, 7, 9, 14, 20, 22, 25, 32, 38, 55 and 56. In Schedule 5, paragraphs 26, 43, 44 and 45.
Enduring Powers of Attorney Act 1985	The whole Act.
Insolvency Act 1986	In section 389A(3) – the 'or' immediately after paragraph (b), and in paragraph (c), the words 'Part VII of the Mental Health Act 1983 or'. In section 390(4) – the 'or' immediately after paragraph (b), and in paragraph (c), the words 'Part VII of the Mental Health Act 1983 or'.
Public Trustee and Administration of Funds Act 1986	Section 2. Section 3(7).
Child Support Act 1991	In section 50(8) – paragraphs (b) and (d), and the 'or' immediately after paragraph (c).
Social Security Administration Act 1992	In section 123(10) – in paragraph (b), 'a receiver appointed under section 99 of the Mental Health Act 1983 or', in paragraph (d)(i), 'sub-paragraph (a) of rule 41(1) of the Court of Protection Rules Act 1984 or', in paragraph (d)(ii), 'a receiver ad interim appointed under sub-paragraph (b) of the said rule 41(1) or', and 'receiver,'.

Short title and chapter	Extent of repeal
Trustee Delegation Act 1999	Section 4.
	Section 6.
	In section 7(3), the words 'in accordance with section 4 above'.
Care Standards Act 2000	In Schedule 4, paragraph 8.
Licensing Act 2003	In section 47(10), the definition of 'mentally incapable'.
Courts Act 2003	In section 64(2), the words 'Master of the Court of Protection'.

Amendments—Constitutional Reform Act 2005, s 59(5), Sch 11, Pt 1, para 1(2).

Short title and chapter	Extent of repeal
Trustee Delegation Act 1999	Section 7. Section 4. In section 7(3), the words 'in accordance with section 4 above'.
Care Standards Act 2000	In Schedule 4, paragraph 8.
Licensing Act 2003	In section 172(8), the definition of 'mentally incapable'.
Courts Act 2003	In section 64(2), the words 'Master of the Court of Protection'.

Amendment—Constitutional Reform Act 2005, s 59(5), Sch 11, Pt 1, para 1(2).

PART IV

Court of Protection Rules 2007 and Practice Directions

PART IV: Court of Protection Rules 2007 and Practice Directions

Contents

Court of Protection Rules 2007	747
Practice Direction 2A – Participation of P	879
Authorised Court Officers	881
Practice Direction 3A – Authorised Court Officers	881
Practice Direction 3B – Levels of Judiciary	883
Practice Direction 3C – Application of the Civil Procedure Rules 1998 and the Family Procedure Rules 2010	885
General Provisions	886
Practice Direction 4A – Court documents	886
Practice Direction 4B – Statements of truth	888
Service of Documents	891
Practice Direction 6A – Service	891
Practice Direction 6B – Service out of the Jurisdiction	894
Notifying P	905
Practice Direction 7A – Notifying P	905
Permission	907
Practice Direction 8A – Permission	907
How to start proceedings	908
Practice Direction 9A – The application form	908
Practice Direction 9B – Notification of other persons that an application form has been issued	912
Practice Direction 9C – Responding to an application	914
Practice Direction 9D – Applications by currently appointed deputies, attorneys and donees in relation to P's property and affairs	916
Practice Direction 9E – Applications relating to serious medical treatment	919
Practice Direction 9F – Applications relating to statutory wills, codicils, settlements and other dealings with P's property	923
Practice Direction 9G – Applications to appoint or discharge a trustee	926
Practice Direction 9H – Applications relating to the registration of enduring powers of attorney	928

Applications within proceedings	930
Practice Direction 10A – Applications within proceedings	930
Practice Direction 10B – Urgent and interim applications	933
Deprivation of Liberty	936
Practice Direction 10AA – Deprivation of Liberty Applications	936
Human Rights	945
Practice Direction 11A – Human Rights Act 1998	945
Dealing with Applications	946
Practice Direction 12A – Court's jurisdiction to be exercised by certain judges	946
Practice Direction 12B – Procedure for disputing the court's jurisdiction	947
Hearings	948
Practice Direction 13A – Hearings (Including Reporting Restrictions)	948
Practice Direction 13B – Court bundles	958
Practice Direction – Transparency Pilot	964
Admissions, Evidence and Depositions	966
Practice Direction 14A – Written evidence	966
Practice Direction 14B – Depositions	976
Practice Direction 14C – Fees for examiners of the court	981
Practice Direction 14D – Witness summons	983
Practice Direction 14E – Section 49 reports	984
Experts	988
Practice Direction 15A – Expert evidence	988
Litigation friend	990
Practice Direction 17A – Litigation friend	990
Practice Direction 17B – Representatives	993
Change of Solicitor	994
Practice Direction 18A – Change of solicitor	994
Practice Direction 19A – Costs	995
Fixed Costs	997
Practice Direction 19B – Fixed costs in the Court of Protection	997
Solicitors' and other professionals' fixed costs	1002
Practice Direction 19B – Fixed costs in the Court of Protection	1002
Appeals	1006
Practice Direction 20A – Appeals	1006
Practice Direction 20B – Allocation of Appeals	1012

Enforcement	1015
Practice Direction 21A – Contempt of court	1015
Transitory and transitional provisions	1017
Practice Direction 22A – Transitional provisions	1017
Practice Direction 22B – Transitory provisions	1019
Practice Direction 22C – Appeals against decisions made under Part 7 of the Mental Health Act 1983 or under the Enduring Powers of Attorney Act 1985 which are brought on or after commencement	1022
Miscellaneous	1024
Practice Direction 23A – Request for directions where notice of objection prevents public guardian from registering enduring power of attorney	1024
Practice Direction 23B – Where P ceases to lack capacity or dies	1026
Pilot Schemes	1028
Practice Direction – Transparency Pilot	1028
Practice Direction – Case Management Pilot	1030
Practice Direction – Section 49 Reports Pilot	1073

Court of Protection Rules 2007, SI 2007/1744

ARRANGEMENT OF RULES

PART 1
PRELIMINARY

Rule		Page
1	Title and commencement	755
2	Revocations	755

PART 2
THE OVERRIDING OBJECTIVE

3	The overriding objective	756
3A	Participation of P	759
4	The duty of the parties	762
5	Court's duty to manage cases	763

PART 3
INTERPRETATION AND GENERAL PROVISIONS

6	Interpretation	768
7	Court officers	770
7A		770
8	Computation of time	772
9	Application of Civil Procedure Rules and Family Procedure Rules	772
9A	Pilot schemes	773

PART 4
COURT DOCUMENTS

10	Documents used in court proceedings	773
11	Documents required to be verified by a statement of truth	774
11A	Position statement not required to be verified by statement of truth	775
12	Failure to verify a document	775
13	Failure to verify a witness statement	775
14	False statements	776
15	Personal details	776
16	Supply of documents to a party from court records	776
17	Supply of documents to a non-party from court records	777
18	Subsequent use of court documents	778
19	Editing information in court documents	778
20	Public Guardian to be supplied with court documents relevant to supervision of deputies	778
21	Provision of court order to Public Guardian	779
22	Amendment of application	779
23	Clerical mistakes or slips	779
24	Endorsement of amendment	779

PART 5
GENERAL CASE MANAGEMENT POWERS

25	The court's general powers of case management	779
26	Court's power to dispense with requirement of any rule	782
27	Exercise of powers on the court's own initiative	782
28	General power of the court to rectify matters where there has been an error of procedure	783

PART 6
SERVICE OF DOCUMENTS

Service generally

29	Scope	783
30	Who is to serve	783
31	Methods of service	784
32	Service of documents on children and protected parties	785
33	Service of documents on P if he becomes a party	786
34	Substituted service	786
35	Deemed service	787
36	Certificate of service	787
37	Certificate of non-service	788
38	Power of court to dispense with service	788

Service out of the jurisdiction

39	Scope and interpretation	788
39A	Service of application form and other documents out of the jurisdiction	789
39B	Period for acknowledging service or responding to application where application is served out of the jurisdiction	789
39C	Method of service – general provisions	790
39D	Service in accordance with the Service Regulation	790
39E	Service through foreign governments, judicial authorities and British Consular authorities	791
39F	Procedure where service is to be through foreign governments, judicial authorities and British Consular authorities	791
39G	Translation of application form or other document	792
39H	Undertaking to be responsible for expenses of the Foreign and Commonwealth Office	793

PART 7
NOTIFYING P

General requirement to notify P

40	General	793
41	Who is to notify P	794
41A	Notifying P of appointment of a litigation friend, etc	794

Circumstances in which P must be notified

42	Application forms	794
43	Appeals	795
44	Final orders	796
45	Other matters	796

Manner of notification, and accompanying documents

46	Manner of notification	797
47	Acknowledgment of notification	797
48	Certificate of notification	798
49	Dispensing with requirement to notify, etc	798

PART 8
PERMISSION

50	General	798
51	Where the court's permission is not required	799
53	Permission – supplementary	800
54	Application for permission	800
59	Service of an order giving or refusing permission	800
60	Appeal against a permission decision following a hearing	800

PART 9
HOW TO START PROCEEDINGS

Initial steps

61	General	801
62	When proceedings are started	801
63	Contents of the application form	801
64	Documents to be filed with the application form	802
65	What the court will do when an application form is filed	803

Steps following issue of application form

66	Applicant to serve the application form on named respondents	803
67	Applications relating to lasting powers of attorney	804
68	Applications relating to enduring powers of attorney	804
69	Applicant to notify P of an application	805
70	Applicant to notify other persons of an application	805
71	Requirements for certain applications	806

Responding to an application

72	Responding to an application	807

The parties to the proceedings

73	Parties to the proceedings	808
74	Persons to be bound as if parties	809
75	Application to be joined as a party	810
76	Applications for removal as a party to proceedings	810

PART 10
APPLICATIONS WITHIN PROCEEDINGS

77	Types of applications for which the Part 10 procedure may be used	811
78	Application notice to be filed	811
79	What an application notice must include	812
80	Service of an application notice	812
81	Applications without notice	813
81A	Security for costs	813
81B	Conditions to be satisfied	814
81C	Security for costs other than from the applicant	814
81D	Security for costs of an appeal	815

Interim Remedies

82	Orders for interim remedies	815

PART 10A
DEPRIVATION OF LIBERTY

82A	816

PART 11
HUMAN RIGHTS

83	General	816

PART 12
DEALING WITH APPLICATIONS

84	Dealing with the application	817
85	Directions	818

Allocation of proceedings
86 Court's jurisdiction in certain kinds of case to be exercised by certain judges ... 819

Disputing the jurisdiction of the court
87 Procedure for disputing the court's jurisdiction ... 819
87A Permission required to withdraw proceedings ... 820

Participation in hearings
88 Participation in hearings ... 820

Reconsideration of court orders
89 Orders made without a hearing or without notice to any person ... 821

PART 13
HEARINGS

Private hearings
90 General rule – hearing to be in private ... 822
91 Court's general power to authorise publication of information about proceedings ... 823

Power to order a public hearing
92 Court's power to order that a hearing be held in public ... 824

Supplementary
93 Supplementary provisions relating to public or private hearings ... 825

PART 14
ADMISSIONS, EVIDENCE AND DEPOSITIONS

Admissions
94 Making an admission ... 827

Evidence
95 Power of court to control evidence ... 827
96 Evidence of witnesses – general rule ... 827
97 Written evidence – general rule ... 828
98 Evidence by video link or other means ... 828
99 Service of witness statements for use at final hearing ... 828
100 Form of witness statement ... 829
101 Witness summaries ... 829
102 Affidavit evidence ... 829
103 Form of affidavit ... 829
104 Affidavit made outside the jurisdiction ... 830
105 Notarial acts and instruments ... 830
106 Summoning of witnesses ... 830
107 Power of court to direct a party to provide information ... 831

Depositions
108 Evidence by deposition ... 831
109 Conduct of examination ... 831
110 Fees and expenses of examiners of the court ... 832
111 Examiners of the court ... 832
112 Enforcing attendance of a witness ... 832
113 Use of deposition at a hearing ... 833

Taking evidence outside the jurisdiction

114	Interpretation	833
115	Where a person to be examined is in another Regulation State	833
116	Where a person to be examined is out of the jurisdiction – letter of request	834

Section 49 reports

117	Reports under section 49 of the Act	835
118	Written questions to person making a report under section 49	836

PART 15
EXPERTS

119	References to expert	836
120	Restriction on filing an expert's report	837
121	Duty to restrict expert evidence	837
122	Experts – overriding duty to the court	838
123	Court's power to restrict expert evidence	838
124	General requirement for expert evidence to be given in a written report	839
125	Written questions to experts	839
126	Contents of expert's report	840
127	Use by one party of expert's report disclosed by another	841
128	Discussions between experts	841
129	Expert's right to ask court for directions	841
130	Court's power to direct that evidence is to be given by a single joint expert	841
131	Instructions to a single joint expert	842

PART 16
DISCLOSURE

132	Meaning of disclosure	842
133	General or specific disclosure	843
134	Procedure for general or specific disclosure	844
135	Ongoing duty of disclosure	844
136	Right to inspect documents	844
137	Inspection and copying of documents	845
138	Claim to withhold inspection or disclosure of document	845
139	Consequence of failure to disclose documents or permit inspection	845

PART 17
LITIGATION FRIENDS AND RULE 3A REPRESENTATIVES

Section 1
Litigation friends

140	Who may act as a litigation friend	846
141	Requirement for a litigation friend	847
142	Litigation friend without a court order	848
143	Litigation friend by court order	849
144	Court's power to prevent a person from acting as a litigation friend or to bring an end to an appointment of a person as a litigation friend or to appoint another one	850
145	Appointment of litigation friend by court order – supplementary	851
145A	Procedure where appointment of a litigation friend comes to an end for a child	851
146	Practice direction in relation to litigation friends	852

Section 2
Rule 3A representatives

146A	Interpretation	852
147	Who may act as a rule 3A representative for P	852
148	Rule 3A representative by court order	852
148A	Application by rule 3A representative or by P for directions	853
148B	Court's power to prevent a person from acting as a rule 3A representative or to bring an end to an appointment of a person as a rule 3A representative or appoint another one	853
148C	Appointment of rule 3A representative by court order – supplementary	854
149	Practice direction in relation to rule 3A representatives	854

PART 18
CHANGE OF SOLICITOR

150	Change of solicitor	854
151	Legally aided persons	855
152	Order that a solicitor has ceased to act	855
153	Removal of solicitor who has ceased to act on application of another party	856
154	Practice direction relating to change of solicitor	856

PART 19
COSTS

155	Interpretation	856
156	Property and affairs – the general rule	857
157	Personal welfare – the general rule	858
158	Apportioning costs – the general rule	858
159	Departing from the general rule	858
160	Rules about costs in the Civil Procedure Rules to apply	859
161	Detailed assessment of costs	860
162	Employment of a solicitor by two or more persons	860
163	Costs of the Official Solicitor	861
164	Procedure for assessing costs	861
165	Costs following P's death	861
166	Costs orders in favour of or against non-parties	861
167	Remuneration of a deputy, donee or attorney	862
168	Practice Direction as to costs	862

PART 20
APPEALS

169	Scope of this Part	862
170	Interpretation	863
171	Dealing with appeals	863
171A	Destination of appeals	863
171B	Permission to appeal – appeals to the Court of Appeal	864
172	Permission to appeal – other cases	864
172A	Appeal against an order for committal to prison	865
173	Matters to be taken into account when considering an application for permission	865
174	Power to treat application for permission to appeal as application for reconsideration under rule 89	866
175	Appellant's notice	866
176	Respondent's notice	866
177	Variation of time	867
178	Power of appeal judge on appeal	867
179	Determination of appeals	868

PART 21
ENFORCEMENT

183	Enforcement methods – general	868
184	Application of the Civil Procedure Rules 1998 and RSC Orders	869

Orders for committal

185	Contempt of court – generally	870
186	Application for order of committal	871
187	Oral evidence	871
188	Hearing for committal order	872
189	Power to suspend execution of committal order	873
190	Warrant for arrest	873
191	Discharge of person committed	873
192	Penal notices	873
193	Saving for other powers	873
194	Power of court to commit on its own initiative	874

PART 22
TRANSITORY AND TRANSITIONAL PROVISIONS

195	Transitory provision: applications by former receivers	874
196	Transitory provision: dealing with applications under rule 195	874
197	Appeal against a decision of a nominated officer	875
198	Application of Rules to proceedings within paragraphs 3 and 12 of Schedule 5 to the Act	875
199	Practice direction	875

PART 23
MISCELLANEOUS

200	Order or directions requiring a person to give security for discharge of functions	875
201	Objections to registration of an enduring power of attorney: request for directions	877
202	Disposal of property where P ceases to lack capacity	878

Practice Direction 2A – Participation of P	879
Practice Direction 3A – Authorised Court Officers	881
Practice Direction 3B – Levels of Judiciary	883
Practice Direction 3C – Application of the Civil Procedure Rules 1998 and the Family Procedure Rules 2010	885
Practice Direction 4A – Court documents	886
Practice Direction 4B – Statements of truth	888
Practice Direction 6A – Service	891
Practice Direction 6B – Service out of the Jurisdiction	894
Practice Direction 7A – Notifying P	905
Practice Direction 8A – Permission	907
Practice Direction 9A – The application form	908
Practice Direction 9B – Notification of other persons that an application form has been issued	912
Practice Direction 9C – Responding to an application	914

PART IV
COURT OF PROTECTION PRACTICE 2016

Practice Direction 9D – Applications by currently appointed deputies, attorneys and donees in relation to P's property and affairs — 916

Practice Direction 9E – Applications relating to serious medical treatment — 919

Practice Direction 9F – Applications relating to statutory wills, codicils, settlements and other dealings with P's property — 923

Practice Direction 9G – Applications to appoint or discharge a trustee — 926

Practice Direction 9H – Applications relating to the registration of enduring powers of attorney — 928

Practice Direction 10A – Applications within proceedings — 930

Practice Direction 10B – Urgent and interim applications — 933

Practice Direction 10AA – Deprivation of Liberty Applications — 936

Practice Direction 11A – Human Rights Act 1998 — 945

Practice Direction 12A – Court's jurisdiction to be exercised by certain judges — 946

Practice Direction 12B – Procedure for disputing the court's jurisdiction — 947

Practice Direction 13A – Hearings (Including Reporting Restrictions) — 948

Practice Direction 13B – Court bundles — 958

Practice Direction – Transparency Pilot — 964

Practice Direction 14A – Written evidence — 966

Practice Direction 14B – Depositions — 976

Practice Direction 14C – Fees for examiners of the court — 981

Practice Direction 14D – Witness summons — 983

Practice Direction 14E – Section 49 reports — 984

Practice Direction 15A – Expert evidence — 988

Practice Direction 17A – Litigation friend — 990

Practice Direction 17B – Representatives — 993

Practice Direction 18A – Change of solicitor — 994

Practice Direction 19A – Costs — 995

Practice Direction 19B – Fixed costs in the Court of Protection — 997

Practice Direction 19B – Fixed costs in the Court of Protection — 1002

Practice Direction 20A – Appeals — 1006

Practice Direction 20B – Allocation of Appeals — 1012

Practice Direction 21A – Contempt of court — 1015

Practice Direction 22A – Transitional provisions — 1017

Practice Direction 22B – Transitory provisions — 1019

Practice Direction 22C – Appeals against decisions made under Part 7 of the Mental Health Act 1983 or under the Enduring Powers of Attorney Act 1985 which are brought on or after commencement — 1022

Practice Direction 23A – Request for directions where notice of objection
prevents public guardian from registering enduring power of attorney   1024

Practice Direction 23B – Where P ceases to lack capacity or dies   1026

Practice Direction – Transparency Pilot   1028

Practice Direction – Case Management Pilot   1030

Practice Direction – Section 49 Reports Pilot   1073

PART 1
PRELIMINARY

1 Title and commencement

These Rules may be cited as the Court of Protection Rules 2007 and come into force on 1 October 2007.

Authority—The authority to make the rules is derived from the Mental Capacity Act 2005 (MCA 2005), ss 49(5), 51, 53(2) and (4), 65(1) and 67(4)(b).

Jurisdiction—The jurisdiction of the Court of Protection and hence of the rules is limited to England and Wales. The rules are made by the Lord Chief Justice who can appoint a nominee with the agreement of the Lord Chancellor. The President of the Family Division was therefore appointed President of the Court of Protection and authorised to make these rules.

Commencement—The rules came into force on 1 October 2007, although the original rules have been amended, the most recent being in 2015 with further amendments likely to come into force in 2016.

MCA 2005—MCA 2005, Sch 5, paras 5 and 12 also contain provisions in respect of pending proceedings.

Future changes—In 2009, an Ad Hoc Rules Committee (the '2010 Rules Committee') was set up by the then President of the Family Division. Its stated aim was to 'review the Court of Protection Rules 2007 which govern practice and procedure in the Court of Protection' and 'to produce recommendations for new rules or amendments to existing rules, and supporting practice directions and forms, which set out a fair and efficient procedure in rules which are both simple and simply expressed'.

The Committee presented its final report in July 2010 and its recommendations were accepted by the President of the Family Division. However, apart from the introduction of rule 7A, none of its recommendations were acted upon.

In March 2014, the House of Lords Committee on the Mental Capacity Act 2005 published a report on the working of the Act. The report also examined the work of the Court of Protection. Paragraph 211 recommended:

> '... that the Government consider as a matter of urgency the updating of the Rules of the Court, as recommended by the ad hoc Rules Committee and, as necessary, in light of subsequent changes.'

The Ad Hoc Rules Committee was therefore reconvened and produced a first report in early 2015 on what it referred to as its first tranche of amendments. These are found in the Court of Protection (Amendment) Rules 2015 and came into force partly in April 2015 with the remainder in July 2015. Since that report, the Committee has been working on tranche two. The Committee has recommended a pilot scheme on transparency, which commenced in January 2016. Further amendments and pilot schemes are expected to be announced. It is likely that by 2017, the Rules may be completely updated to ensure that cases proceed swiftly and at proportionate cost.

2 Revocations

The following rules are revoked –

(a) the Court of Protection Rules 2001; and
(b) the Court of Protection (Enduring Powers of Attorney) Rules 2001.

Rule 2(a)—The Court of Protection Rules 2001, SI 2001/824 are replaced by these rules, which have been amended since they came into force in 2007.

Policy aim—The stated policy aim of the new rules was described as providing a human-rights compliant process equally appropriate for cases relating to property and financial affairs which were heard in the 'old' Court of Protection and the personal welfare cases heard under the inherent jurisdiction of the High Court and which were governed by the Civil Procedure Rules 1998 (CPR), SI 1998/3132. The new rules were supposed seek to synthesise the previous regimes in the High Court and the old Court of Protection into one new set of rules able to cope with the new Court of Protection and its wide and extended jurisdiction.

The old Court of Protection was a more informal office of the Supreme Court. During the consultation process leading to the implementation of the rules, concerns were expressed by some that these rules would bring with them a loss of informality, ease of use, accessibility and speed that court users enjoyed with the old Court. However, a stated objective of the rules is to ensure that there is a greater understanding of procedures and to lend clarity to the court process.

Thus, the previous practice of making applications by informal letter or even by telephone to the Court was replaced by the need for a formal application when an order of the court was required. The rules also impose specific time-limits and requirements to give effect to the need for a proper process. Directions are given in all cases and hearings tend to be largely formal.

One aim of the rules was to ensure there was judicial scrutiny of all matters and the use of civil servants known as nominated officers to deal with routine matters was abolished.

On implementation of the MCA 2005, the clear challenge for the Court was to ensure that cases progressed in a way appropriate for each particular case but at the same time to ensure that procedural rules did not frustrate the real aims of the Court and the legislation that created it. This has not been an easy task. The court has seen a steady increase in its work which shows no signs of abating, perhaps a sign of society in general.

What therefore resulted was the introduction in 2011 of rule 7A, which allowed authorised court officers who are civil servants to deal with a large variety of straight forward applications. However, the Ad Hoc Rules Committee is looking at the rules and the court forms and is gradually reforming where needed. In April and July 2015, certain rules were amended, which are highlighted in the commentary, and further rule reform is imminent. In July 2015, new forms replaced some of the more unwieldly forms. It is likely that by 2017, the rules will be completely updated to ensure they allow the court to process its work in a way that assists litigants.

Rule 2(b)—The Court of Protection (Enduring Powers of Attorney) Rules 2001, SI 2001/825 are replaced by the Lasting Powers of Attorney, Enduring Powers of Attorney and Public Guardian Regulations 2007, SI 2007/1253.

Scope—As the title suggests, these regulations deal with lasting powers of attorney, enduring powers of attorney and the functions of the Public Guardian. The Schedules to the regulations set out draft forms referred to in the Regulations.

PART 2
THE OVERRIDING OBJECTIVE

3 The overriding objective

(1) These Rules have the overriding objective of enabling the court to deal with a case justly, having regard to the principles contained in the Act.

(2) The court will seek to give effect to the overriding objective when it –

    (a) exercises any power under these Rules; or
    (b) interprets any rule or practice direction.

(3) Dealing with a case justly includes, so far as is practicable –

    (a) ensuring that it is dealt with expeditiously and fairly;
    (b) ensuring that P's interests and position are properly considered;

(c) dealing with the case in ways which are proportionate to the nature, importance and complexity of the issues;
(d) ensuring that the parties are on an equal footing;
(e) saving expense; and
(f) allotting to it an appropriate share of the court's resources, while taking account of the need to allot resources to other cases.

Rule 3(1)—The overriding objective of the rules is placed at the beginning to emphasise its importance and the need to support this objective when considering any matter under the other rules. The overriding objective, however, is not a new concept. Its genesis is in the CPR from where it has been imported with slight variations into the Family Procedure Rules 2010, SI 2010/2955 and the Criminal Procedure Rules 2005, SI 2005/384. The overriding objective compels the court to deal with a case justly. These rules derive from MCA 2005 and the concept of dealing with a case justly must therefore be read in the context of the statutory principles set out at MCA 2005, s 1. In particular, one of the principles is that any act or decision must be in P's best interests. Accordingly, r 3(1) provides that regard must be had to the statutory principles.

Rule 3(3): 'Justly'—Dealing with a case justly may require the court to balance the litigation interests of a party against P's interests which may be different but which must be considered under r 3(3)(b). In such a situation, the court will take a balance sheet approach and reach a conclusion based on the overall interests of justice.

Rule 3(3)(a): 'Expeditiously'—The work of the court reveals a difference in the definition of dealing with a case expeditiously. An application for a statutory will where P's death is imminent may require a final hearing in a matter of hours; some serious personal welfare application involving medical treatment may require almost immediate decisions; P may suffer loss if his deputy is not given permission to sell or purchase a property within a few days. In each case therefore, the court needs to assess the nature of the application, the need to act quickly and how best to allocate the courts resources.

However, the reality is that in almost all cases, it will be in P's best interests for the Court to progress a case quickly. For example, the inability to buy necessities for P from his funds whilst an application for the appointment for a property and affairs deputy progresses is very important to P and his family or the decision where P is to live.

Dealing with a case expeditiously and fairly does not ordinarily allow the court to take a summary approach to the determination of a dispute or an issue and Article 6 ECHR rights could be compromised: see *KD and LD v Havering London Borough Council* [2009] COPLR Con Vol 770.

What is expected of the court is that it will properly manage a case by setting a timetable and dates for all steps to be taken so that the case proceeds to a conclusion speedily.

Rule 3(3)(b): 'P's interests and position are considered'—Rule 73(4) provides that unless the court orders otherwise, P is not a respondent in proceedings although through r 74, P will be bound by the court's decision. However, r 73 must be read with rule 3A, which was introduced in July 2015 and is designed to ensure that P's participation is considered in every case. See also PD2A, which deals with P's participation.

Rule 3(3)(c): 'Proportionate to the nature, importance and complexity of the issues'—The Court's work is diverse and what is proportionate in one case may not be so in another. The court must, therefore, ensure that it ascertains at the earliest possible stage the issues in a case and then decides what is needed to determine those issues. Proportionality also means that costs must not be allowed to escalate (see, for example, *Cases A and B (Court of Protection: Delay and Costs)* [2014] EWCOP 48, [2015] COPLR 1 and *A Local Authority v ED* [2013] EWHC 3069 (COP), where Roderick Wood J referred to the 'inordinate' amount of paperwork and the 'astonishing' costs involved of £138,000 for the local authority: £130,000 for the Official Solicitor and £82,000 for the parents). This rule should also be read with r 5 (the court's duty to manage cases) and r 25 (the court's case management powers).

When making final orders, proportionality still needs to be considered. For example, when appointing a deputy, the Court should consider how wide the order should be drawn and balance the supervisory role of the Court against the freedom of a deputy or P's family to act on their own initiative on a day-to-day basis without having to constantly refer back to the Court. Consideration should therefore be given to whether the deputy should have permission to purchase property without reference to the court or to carry out certain works. In personal welfare cases, the court should consider a paper review rather than an attended hearing and whether the court needs to maintain any supervisory role. Where the court has agreed a care plan, consideration should be given as to whether the case needs any further court input.

Proportionality also extends to the presentation of a case. In A Local Authority v FG and Others (No 1) 2012 COPLR 473, Hedley J refused to consider another first instance decision 'to avoid a multiplicity of first instance judgments being cited as a matter of course in these cases' saying that 'debates in proceedings about saying the same thing in many different ways does not seem to me helpful.

In *Re SK (Impact of Best Interests Decision on Queen's Bench Proceedings)* [2013] COPLR 458, Bodey J considered whether P's brother who was his litigation friend in personal injury proceedings should be joined as a party in Court of Protection proceedings relating to P's welfare. Despite the proceedings having similar issues, Bodey J noted that they were different in that a best interests test was used in the Court of Protection whereas the Queen's Bench Division proceedings were compensatory. In the Court of Protection proceedings, the brother also argued that the court should not make a final order relating to P's residence as P may need to move in 1 or 2 years' time and if the proceedings were ended, this could prevent P's personal injury proceedings being settled or allow the claimant in the personal injury proceedings to make a Part 36 CPR 1998 offer based on its interpretation of the Court of Protection order. Making a final order in the Court of Protection might place the brother as litigation friend in a risky position with regard to a decision whether or not to accept that offer. However, Bodey J felt that a case should only be kept alive if there was an actual dispute which required determination and not simply to monitor P's circumstances.

'**nature**'—The case load of the Court of Protection is the most diverse of any of our courts. Personal welfare cases can cover serious medical treatment, safeguarding and issues about vulnerability, limitations on P's freedom not only in terms of where P lives or with whom P has contact but also in terms of actions being done to P without his consent. Property and affairs cases can cover statutory wills, financial abuse enquiries instigated by the Public Guardian or others, contested family disputes concerning deputies and attorneys and applications to utilise P's funds for specific purposes. Consideration of the nature of a dispute will require the court to examine legal and social issues that arise and to judge whether the case is merely the outgrowth of a family dispute or whether serious issues of public importance arise.

'**Importance**'—The Court has to be aware that its decision will affect P, a person who has no capacity and who may be personally removed from the decision-making process by dint of his medical condition. The decision may also have a lifetime effect on P and his family. Furthermore, reputations of family members may be at stake (see for example *Re DP; The Public Guardian v JM* [2014] EWCOP 7 as well as family relationships with P, P's safety and security and P's funds and their use.

'**Complexity**'—This follows on from the comments made in respect of the nature of a dispute. Cases vary and the Court should adapt to each case's needs.

Rule 3(3)(d): 'Equal footing'—This refers to the parties only and P may not be a party. However, P's best interests still need to be considered.

With the lack of public funding, issues are likely to arise more often with litigants in person such as granting adjournments to allow them further time to comply with orders to prepare for a final hearing or where they are no longer represented and need further time to prepare for a hearing. See *P v United Kingdom* (2002) 12 EHRR 619, *Re L (A Child)* [2013] EWCA Civ 1557, where Article 6 of the ECHR was considered and an adjournment allowed and *Re GB* 7 February 2013, unreported (Court of Appeal) where refusal to adjourn was not considered to be a breach of Article 6. Although *Re L* and *Re GB* were decisions in family cases, similar facts and considerations could arise in Court of Protection cases. In all cases, P's best interests must be considered. This may present a dilemma to the court. Whilst a litigant in person may genuinely need time to prepare for a hearing, P's best interests may dictate that the hearing should go on in some cases. Each case will turn on its own facts and will require a balancing exercise by the court.

Rule 3(3)(e): 'Saving expense'—Every case-management decision should take into account the cost of the step ordered by the Court. The Court must therefore ensure that disclosure is limited to documents that serve the case, unnecessary experts are not instructed and where possible, a joint expert should be used. Rule 159(2)(e) allows the court to depart from the normal costs orders in rr 156 and 157 if a party fails to comply with a court order. Courts should not be slow to use this provision, if anything to emphasise that failure to comply with court orders causes delay and increases costs.

Saving expense also extends to final orders where the court should consider if it imposes the potential for unnecessary costs being incurred. For example, an order appointing a property and affairs deputy should give the deputy sufficiently wide powers to avoid further applications having to be made. A common example is where a professional deputy has to apply to the court for permission to sell a property. Some personal welfare cases need a review of arrangements ordered by the court and again, the court should consider if a paper review can be undertaken with the provision for an attended hearing if necessary rather than simply fixing a date for a review hearing and incurring costs. Indeed, in cases where a local authority has to implement a care plan for P, as in children's proceedings, perhaps the court should allow the local authority to implement its court approved plan in some cases without a court review.

In *A v A Local Authority, A Care Home Manager and S* [2011] EWHC 727 (COP), [2011] COPLR Con Vol 190, a report was required on P's capacity. To save costs, Wall P ordered a Visitor's report rather than an expert's report on the basis that this was consistent with the overriding objective.

Rule 3(3)(f): 'Court's resources'—Within the context of civil and family rules, this provision is often used to justify a conclusion that the court will not allow any more court time to be spent on a particular application or case. See *Albon v Naza Motor Trading* [2007] EWHC 2613 (Ch) where Lightman J refused to adjourn a trial where a party had failed to act justly, reasonably and in accordance with the court's directions which could equally be applied in the Court of Protection.

See also *G v E, A Local Authority and F* [2010] EWHC 621 (Fam), [2010] COPLR Con Vol 510 where Baker J set out at paragraphs 4 and 5 of his judgment the effect of Court of Protection on the work of the Family Division and concluded that '… urgent attention needs to be given to increasing the resources of the Family Division to deal with these difficult and urgent cases'. Although this was said 5 years ago, the Court's resources are still precious and with the work of the Court increasing yearly, the imperative to have regard to the Court's resources is still present.

In the Court of Protection, reference to the Court's resources may also include considering whether a hearing should take place in an old age home, whether a case merits hearing before a High Court judge or whether the case can be dealt with on paper.

The issue of the court's resources may also influence the court's approach to repeat applications by an obsessive or difficult family member who keeps trying to raise the same issue or who seeks to derail a case when it appears that the outcome may be unfavourable to his or her position.

Lack of funding—See the commentary to r 123(6).

Vulnerable persons—In the Court of Protection, the typical vulnerability will be an old person with physical disabilities or health conditions. However, there can also be younger people whose vulnerability comes about through mental health issues or disorders and learning difficulties. Whatever the vulnerability, the Court must be alive to it and react properly.

By definition, P is a vulnerable person, although his need for assistance may be mitigated because he is represented by a litigation friend or r 3A representative. However, this alone does not absolve the court from ensuring that if P is participating by giving evidence, addressing the court or just observing the proceedings, his situation must be taken into account.

As well as P, others involved in a case may be vulnerable people; for example, P's relatives or other interested parties who simply by age require extra assistance and facilities to participate.

In some cases, there is a troublesome relative who has issues of his own which make his conduct in proceedings at times unacceptable. Sometimes, those people clearly have borderline mental health issues of their own. In such cases, the court needs to consider how the participation of such a person can be consistent with the overriding objective and how to ensure that the court's resources and costs are not wasted.

3A Participation of P

(1) The court shall in each case, on its own initiative or on the application of any person, consider whether it should make one or more of the directions in paragraph (2), having regard to –

    (a)   the nature and extent of the information before the court;
    (b)   the issues raised in the case;
    (c)   whether a matter is contentious; and

(d) whether P has been notified in accordance with the provisions of Part 7 and what, if anything, P has said or done in response to such notification.

(2) The directions are that –

(a) P should be joined as a party;
(b) P's participation should be secured by the appointment of an accredited legal representative to represent P in the proceedings and to discharge such other functions as the court may direct;
(c) P's participation should be secured by the appointment of a representative whose function shall be to provide the court with information as to the matters set out in section 4(6) of the Act and to discharge such other functions as the court may direct;
(d) P should have the opportunity to address (directly or indirectly) the judge determining the application and, if so directed, the circumstances in which that should occur;
(e) P's interests and position can properly be secured without any direction under sub-paragraphs (a) to (d) being made or by the making of an alternative direction meeting the overriding objective.

(3) Any appointment or directions made pursuant to paragraph (2)(b) to (e) may be made for such period or periods as the court thinks fit.

(4) Unless P has capacity to conduct the proceedings, an order joining P as a party shall only take effect –

(a) on the appointment of a litigation friend on P's behalf; or
(b) if the court so directs, on or after the appointment of an accredited legal representative.

(5) If the court has directed that P should be joined as a party but such joinder does not occur because no litigation friend or accredited legal representative is appointed, the court shall record in a judgment or order –

(a) the fact that no such appointment was made; and
(b) the reasons given for that appointment not being made.

(6) A practice direction may make additional or supplementary provision in respect of any of the matters set out in this rule.

(The appointment of litigation friends, accredited legal representatives and representatives under paragraph (2)(c) is dealt with under Part 17.)

('Accredited legal representative' is defined in rule 6.)

Amendments—Inserted by SI 2015/548.

This rule, and PD2A which accompanies it, was introduced in July 2015. One of the most important issues in the Court of Protection is P's participation in a case and ensuring that P's voice is heard.

The rules do not make P a party automatically, which makes sense given the diverse nature of the court's work. In a routine application for appointment of a property and affairs deputy, P is almost never a party and the court will make its order based on the evidence filed. At the other end of the spectrum, in serious personal welfare cases it would be unthinkable for P not to be a party. However, there are cases in the middle ground where the decision regarding P's involvement is open for consideration.

Traditionally, pursuant to the court's case management powers in r 5, the court would decide P's involvement and participation in a case as one of a number of case management decisions that had to be made. This revealed varying approaches and attitudes to P's participation. Thus, in *London Borough of Redbridge v G, C and F* [2014] EWHC 485 (COP), [2014] COPLR 292, P sat in court 'displaying dignity and determination to get her views across'. Some judges made a point of visiting P to ensure that P felt included (see for example *Re M (Best Interests: Deprivation of Liberty)*

[2013] EWHC 3456 (COP), [2014] COPLR 35). However good this was, it was not based on any formal footing that delineated P's role in a case. It is therefore against this background that the Ad Hoc Rules Committee introduced this rule.

The rule is a standalone requirement for the court to consider P's position, which is done deliberately to emphasise the importance of deciding P's role in proceedings. The need for the rule is explained in PD2A, which was introduced with the new rule.

The rule offers various alternatives. The first in r 3A(2)(a) is to join P as a party and he will have a litigation friend. If P is a party, although he will be represented, it still does not absolve the court from considering P's personal involvement in a case. At the earliest possible opportunity, therefore, the court should consider if P wants to address the court, meet the judge, attend and listen to hearings or be visited by the judge.

The second alternative set out in r 3A(2)(b) is that P is represented by the appointment of an accredited legal representative. This is defined by r 6 as a person accredited pursuant to a scheme of accreditation approved by the President to represent persons meeting the definition of P in proceedings. At present, though, no such scheme exists and this option is not available. It may be with time that such a scheme will be set up but there is nothing in place at present.

The third alternative in r 3(A)(2)(c) is that a representative is appointed to provide the court with information of matters set out in MCA 2005, s 4(6). This could cover matters such as P's past and present wishes and his beliefs and value systems. The representative can also be directed by the court to carry out other functions. In some cases, this could be useful if the court needs information about a particular issue and the representative can obtain it rather than instructing an expert.

The fourth alternative in r 3(A)(2)(d) is for P to address the court. Although there is nothing to stop P from addressing the court if another alternative is chosen, this rule emphasises that P's participation by addressing the court may of itself be a sufficient means of appropriate participation. This can be done directly by P coming to court or the court going to P or indirectly such as by videolink, a DVD being played to the court or by some other written communication.

The fifth alternative in r 3(A)(2)(e) is that none of the options under this rule are utilised on the basis that P's participation is secured. This might come about because there is a Visitor's report that sets out P's position or where the court has sufficient information on the papers filed in the case and there is no added value in P taking any further role. P's health alone may justify an order under this alternative.

Following on from the obligation under r 3A to consider P's position, the rules impose obligations to secure P's involvement. Thus, P must be notified of any directions made under this rule (r 41A) and of any decision apart from a case management decision that relates to him and be given a copy of the order (rr 44(1) and 44(3)).

It should be noted that P's joinder as a party only takes effect on the appointment of a litigation friend (r 3A(4)).

The appointment of a representative or accredited legal representative can be for such period as the court thinks fit (r 3A(3)). This might be useful when the court requires a specific piece of information and a representative can be appointed to obtain the information and thereafter the appointment will come to an end.

Although not in r 3A, it should not be overlooked that P's participation in the widest sense could be achieved in some cases through a MCA 2005, s 49 Visitor's report, although great care should be taken to ensure that such reports do not substitute the need in a case for expert evidence such as that of an independent social worker.

However, the future of this rule is by no means certain as the issue regarding P's participation continues to be scrutinised.

One of the recent challenges for the court has been in deprivation of liberty cases. The commentary to Pt 10A of the rules sets out the issue that flows from the discussion of whether P should be joined as a party to such a case. Munby P in *Re X and Others (Deprivation of Liberty)* [2014] EWCOP 25 and R*Re X and others (Deprivation of Liberty) No 2* [2014] EWCOP 37 said that P should always be given the opportunity to be joined if he wishes and whether joined as a party or not, P should be given the support necessary to express views about the application and to participate in proceedings to the extent that they wish but, ultimately, there was no need to join P. However, in what are regarded as strong obiter dicta, the Court of Appeal disagreed and suggested that P should always be a party (*Re X (Court of Protection Practice)* [2015] EWCA Civ 599, [2015] COPLR 582). Almost immediately, this caused problems in that the Official Solicitor intimated that he could not act for P in many cases, thus creating a situation whereby P could consequently not be a party. The magnitude of the problem was highlighted in *Re MOD (Deprivation of Liberty)* [2015] EWCOP 47 and produced a decision from the Vice President Charles J in *Re NRA* [2015] EWCOP 59 saying that P did not have to be joined as a party. If anything, this all demonstrates the frailty of this issue.

See also r 88, which allows the court to hear P on any question, and r 95, which is the court's duty to control evidence.

4 The duty of the parties

(1) The parties are required to help the court to further the overriding objective.

(2) Without prejudice to the generality of paragraph (1), each party is required to –
   (a) co-operate with the other parties and with the court in identifying and narrowing the issues that need to be determined by the court, and the timetable for that determination;
   (b) adhere to the timetable set by these Rules and by the court;
   (c) comply with all directions and orders of the court;
   (d) be full and frank in the disclosure of information and evidence to the court (including any disclosure ordered under Part 16);
   (e) co-operate with the other parties in all aspects of the conduct of the proceedings, including in the preparation of bundles.

(3) If the court determines that any party has failed without reasonable excuse to satisfy the requirements of this rule, it may under rule 159 depart from the general rules about costs in so far as they apply to that party.

(Rule 133(2) deals with the requirements of general disclosure.)

Amendments—Substituted by SI 2015/548.

Scope—This rule was completely amended in July 2015 to spell out the duties of parties in a case. Whereas the original rule contained a mere requirement to help achieve the overriding objective, it was clear that this was insufficient. Accordingly, the rule has now been redrafted to set out exactly what is expected. The rule should also be read together with r 159(2)(e), which allows the court to depart from the normal costs rules when there has been a failure to comply with a rule, practice direction or court order.

Cooperation—In *A Local Authority v PB and P* [2011] EWHC 502 (COP), [2011] COPLR Con Vol 166, Charles J set out general guidance for the preparation of welfare cases and in particular the need for the parties to identify the real issues in a case. Despite this guidance, it was routinely ignored. The guidance is now a rule.

Adherence to the timetable and compliance with orders—See *Re W (A Child); Re H (Children)* [2013] EWCA Civ 1177, a family case where the President of the Family Division roundly criticised practitioners who approached court orders as if they were just an aspiration. He said:

'The court is entitled to expect – and from now on family courts will demand – strict compliance with all such orders. Non-compliance with orders should be expected to have and will usually have a consequence.

Let me spell it out. An order that something is to be done by 4pm on Friday, is an order to do that thing by 4pm on Friday, not by 4.21pm on Friday let alone by 3.01pm the following Monday or sometime later the following week. A person who finds himself unable to comply timeously with his obligations under an order should apply for an extension of time before the time for compliance has expired. It is simply not acceptable to put forward as an explanation for non-compliance with an order the burden of other work. If the time allowed for compliance with an order turns out to be inadequate, the remedy is either to apply to the court for an extension of time or to pass the task to someone else who has available the time in which to do it.'

This rule emphasises this approach in the Court of Protection. See also *North Somerset Council v LW and others* [2014] EWCOP 3, where Keehan J made a costs order against a NHS Trust where it failed to attend court and also failed to properly deal with matters.

Parties who embark on fruitless litigation may also find themselves subject to a costs order (*JS v KB and MP (Property and Affairs Deputy for DB)* [2014] EWHC 483 (COP), [2014] COPLR 275).

5 Court's duty to manage cases

(1) The court will further the overriding objective by actively managing cases.

(2) Active case management includes –
   (a) encouraging the parties to co-operate with each other in the conduct of the proceedings;
   (b) identifying at an early stage –
       (i) the issues; and
       (ii) who should be a party to the proceedings;
   (c) deciding promptly –
       (i) which issues need a full investigation and hearing and which do not; and
       (ii) the procedure to be followed in the case;
   (d) deciding the order in which issues are to be resolved;
   (e) encouraging the parties to use an alternative dispute resolution procedure if the court considers that appropriate;
   (f) fixing timetables or otherwise controlling the progress of the case;
   (g) considering whether the likely benefits of taking a particular step justify the cost of taking it;
   (h) dealing with as many aspects of the case as the court can on the same occasion;
   (i) dealing with the case without the parties needing to attend at court;
   (j) making use of technology;
   (k) giving directions to ensure that the case proceeds quickly and efficiently;
   (l) considering whether any hearing should be held in public; and
   (m) considering whether any document relating to proceedings should be a public document and, if so, whether and to what extent it should be redacted.

   (Rules 91 to 93 make provision about the court's powers to authorise publication of information about proceedings and to order that a hearing be held in public.)

Amendments—SI 2015/548.

Rule 5(1)—All case files are seen by a judge who will make appropriate orders or directions in every case (see r 89 and the rules concerning reconsideration of orders).

In some cases, the court's involvement may simply be the giving of directions on paper or at a single hearing. Other cases may require a number of directions or case management hearings to allow the court to monitor events and to make appropriate directions to progress the case to a final hearing.

See *AVS v NHS Foundation Trust* [2010] EWHC 2746 (COP), [2010] COPLR Con Vol 237 where at a directions hearing Wall P said that 'I regard such appointments [as] being of the utmost importance in proceedings of any kind'.

PD13B contains the requirements for court bundles. Paragraph 4.2 sets out the documents that should be available for directions or interim hearings. It is suggested that even where the practice direction does not apply, at the very least, a a position statement should be filed. See *A Local Authority v PB and P* [2011] EWHC 502 (COP), [2011] COPLR Con Vol 166 at [41] generally for the expected approach to hearings set out by Charles J. Failure to comply with PD13B could result in breach of r 4 and provoke a costs order under r 159(2)(e).

Rule 5(2)(a)—It is not so much encouragement now to cooperate but rather reminding the parties of their obligations under the amended r 4 to cooperate and the likely costs consequences if they do not.

In *VA and others v Hertfordshire Partnership Foundation Trust and others* [2011] EWHC 3524 (COP), [2012] COPLR 327, Peter Jackson J considered litigation conduct in his judgment which addressed the issue of costs after complicated proceedings. He departed from the no costs rule in personal welfare cases and said:

'... The conclusion I have reached in this case represents a partial departure from the general rule that there should be no order for costs. It is a case where there has been no bad faith or flagrant misconduct, but there has been substandard practice and a failure by the public bodies to recognise the weakness of their own cases and the strength of the cases against them. In such circumstances, they cannot invoke rule 157 at the expense of others.'

Similarly, in *North Somerset Council v LW and others* [2014] EWCOP 3 Keehan J ordered a party to pay costs as a result of their failure to address issues in the case.

Rule 5(2)(b)(i)—The judge will read the court file, ascertain the issues and give appropriate directions. If the issues are not clear, the judge may seek clarification on paper or arrange a directions hearing.

The Court is alive to the fact that some cases are an expression of family tensions and disagreements that can go back many years. It will therefore wish to ascertain whether or not there are genuine issues to be tried. A directions hearing will enable the court to achieve this aim.

Fact finding hearings—In some cases, the court may need to decide if a fact finding hearing is necessary. This can arise where allegations are made against a party which can affect the outcome of the case.

Munby P stated in *Re AG* [2015] EWCOP 78 that 'the task of a judge sitting in the Court of Protection is to concentrate on the issues that really need to be resolved rather than addressing every conceivable legal or factual issue'.

The case also refers to a decision of McFarlane J (as he then was) in *A County Council v DP, RS, BB (by the Children's Guardian)* [2005] EWHC 1593 (Fam), [2005] 2 FLR 1031, where the court set out factors to be borne in mind when deciding whether or not to conduct a fact finding hearing in a children's case. There seems to be no reason why this case cannot be used as a guideline in the Court of Protection.

The factors were:

1   The interests of the child (which in the Court of Protection would be in interests of P)
2   The time the investigation would take
3   The likely cost to public funds
4   The evidential result
5   The necessity or otherwise of the investigation
6   The relevance of the potential result of the investigation to the future plans for the child (which in the Court of Protection would be P)
7   The impact of any fact finding process upon the other parties
8   The prospects of a fair trial of the issue
9   The justice of the case.

For an example of the approach to a fact-finding hearing taken by a district judge, see *WCC v GS,RS and JS* [2011] EWHC 2244 (COP) w.

In cases where a fact finding hearing is required, Baker J sets out guidance in *A Local Authority v M by his litigation friend the Official Solicitor, E and A* [2014] EWCOP 33, [2015] COPLR 6 as follows:

1   The burden of proof lies with the local authority who bring the proceedings and who must identify the findings they invite the court to make.
2   The burden of proof is on the balance of probabilities (*Re B Children* [2008] UKHL 35, [2008] 2 FLR 141).
3   Findings of fact must be based on evidence.
4   Findings of fact must take account of all the evidence and consider each piece of evidence in the context of all the other evidence.
5   Whilst appropriate attention must be paid to the opinion of medical experts, those opinions need to be considered in the context of all the other evidence. Then roles of the expert and the court are distinct. It is the court that is in the position to weigh up expert evidence against the other evidence.
6   In assessing expert evidence which involves a multi-disciplinary analysis of the medical information conducted by a group of specialists each bringing their own expertise to bear on the problem, one important consideration is that the court must be careful to ensure that each expert keeps within the bounds of their own expertise and defers where appropriate to the expertise of others.
7   The evidence of parents is of the utmost importance. It is essential that the court forms a clear assessment of their credibility and reliability.
8   It is not uncommon for witnesses to tell lies and the court must bear in mind that a witness

may lie for many reasons such as shame, misplaced loyalty, panic, fear and stress. The fact a witness has lied about some matters does not mean that he has lied about everything.

Identifying issues—This rule should now be read with the amended r (2)(a).

Careful consideration should also be given to the decision of Charles J in *A Local Authority v PB and P* [2011] EWHC 502 (COP), [2011] COPLR Con Vol 166. This case deals with the approach that is expected in respect of the preparation and presentation of personal welfare cases. Although the decision is aimed at Court of Protection cases heard in the Family Division, the judgment should apply equally to cases heard in the main registry of the court and in the regional courts before all tiers of judges and in other divisions of the High Court where property and affairs cases can be heard (in practice the Chancery Division although judges of the Queen's Bench Division have also been nominated for Court of Protection work).

Some basic principles emerge from the judgment:

1. Where it is clear from initial witness evidence that there are hotly disputed issues which affect issues the court needs to determine, it is incumbent on litigants to identify the facts they will seek to prove to support their case
2. At each stage of a case, parties should consider the legal and factual issues that arise or are likely to arise
3. A case should not reach a final hearing without there having been a hearing to identify the legal issues which arise and any fact finding process that is required
4. The parties should serve a document which sets out alternative care options for P if relevant, facts that require a finding and facts which are agreed and what relief is sought in the proceedings.

Jurisdiction—Issues relating to jurisdiction should be addressed at the outset of proceedings: *Re F (A Child)* [2014] EWCA Civ 789.

Rule 5(2)(b)(ii)—The first consideration should be P's role and rr 3A and 73(4).

When considering who should be a party, reference should be made to r 73. Rule 73(2) provides that the court may order a person to be joined as a party if it is desireable to do so. However, when making this decision, the court must consider proportionality and the overriding objective. The court may also look further than those intimately involved in a dispute. It may consider that notice of the proceedings be given to a local authority, the Public Guardian, a NHS Trust or some other public body with a view to ultimately joining them as a party.

Where there are a number of relatives who wish to take part in a welfare case, it may be sensible to nominate one to represent the views of the family in a case where the family is united in its position.

In some cases, it may be desirable to allow only a person or public body to intervene in the proceedings. This may arise because that person wants to play a lesser role or contribute to part only of a case or the court feels that full party status may not be desirable, especially as that would give the right to see all documents in a case. Costs considerations may play a part. In some personal welfare cases, for example, a NHS Trust may wish to hold a watching brief to protect its interests or to offer assistance to the court on a particular issue.

If P is joined, he will require a litigation friend who is normally the Official Solicitor. This arises because there is very often no-one else who can act for P. See however the comments of Mostyn J in *AB v CC A Local Authority* [2011] EWHC 3151 (COP), [2012] COPLR 314 where he suggests that other alternatives to the Official Solicitor should be considered. It is difficult in practice, however, to see how far this decision will affect the invariable appointment of the Official Solicitor in many cases. In personal welfare cases, relatives of P may lack independence and may hold views that have provoked the need for a determination of an issue by the court and in a statutory will application where relatives or those closely connected with P can also be beneficiaries under a will, there is a lack of a pool of potential litigation friends hence the involvement of the Official Solicitor.

Rule 5(2)(c)(i)—This rule again falls to be considered with rr 4(2)(a) and 5(2)(b) where the parties and ultimately the court need to clarify the issues and decide pursuant to this rule how they are to be tried. In family disputes, the court will be careful to ensure that it does not allow a case to become a vehicle to allow disgruntled family members or others to litigate about issues that are not relevant to the case.

See also comments about case preparation and fact finding hearings under rule 5(2)(b)(i) above.

Rule 5(2)(c)(ii)—The diverse nature of the court's work means that the approach in cases will vary. Many applications may require simple directions for the parties simply to file evidence and for a hearing date to be allocated. Others may require more involved directions. The Court will need to ascertain what is best for each case.

For example, where objections to registration of an enduring power of attorney are received from a family member, the Court may simply order the attorney and the family member to file evidence so the case can proceed to a final hearing quickly. However, if the issues raised are more complicated, the court may need to consider the need for expert evidence and if capacity is an issue, the need for a preliminary hearing. Some cases may require the involvement of the Official Solicitor to represent P.

Rule 5(2)(d)—If, for example, among the many issues in a case, there is a question about P's capacity, the Court should deal with this issue first. Indeed, if P is found not to lack capacity, the court will have no jurisdiction. This may then require the case to be transferred to the Family Division of the High Court to invoke the inherent jurisdiction in respect of a vulnerable person. See *SMBC v WMP* [2011] COPLR Con Vol 1177 for an example of a case where the court needed to consider first whether the threshold for Court of Protection intervention had been met and where capacity was in question.

Rule 5(2)(e)—Litigants in any forum are expected to try to resolve their disputes and litigation is regarded as a last resort. Failure to engage in alternative dispute resolution (ADR) or mediation can result in unfavourable costs orders being made (see for example *Dunnett v Railtrack PLC* [2002] EWCA Civ 303).

Some argue that mediation in the Court of Protection is different to mediation in civil disputes because in a civil dispute, the dispute concerns the two parties who attend mediation. However, in the Court of Protection, the dispute concerns P and the mediation would be between two parties who differ about what they see as being in P's best interests. It follows that the result of mediation is a compromise of those parties' views, which may itself not be in P's best interests. It is suggested that the answer to this concern is that ultimately, the court would have to approve the outcome of mediation and approval by the court would endorse the mediated agreement as being in P's best interests. It could be argued that this is no different to a dispute between parents about an issue regarding their children when the court approves their agreement if it feels that the child's welfare interests are accommodated by the agreement. There is also no reason why parties should not attend mediation prior to court proceedings as the attendance alone must be in P's best interests as it will save costs and be evidence of the parties working together to serve P's best interests. The court is likely to expect parties to do their best to resolve issues anyway, which is consistent with the obligations in r 4 and mediation should be a part of this process if possible.

Rule 5(2)(f)—The Court should fix a timetable up to trial in most cases. The timetable will set out the steps to be taken by the parties and the dates for compliance. Those dates must be obeyed.

Some judge impose self-reporting orders in more serious cases in terms that if a party fails to comply with an order, that party must inform the Court so that the judge may give further directions to keep the case on track for its trial date. Indeed, failure to comply with an order is almost certainly not going to be in P's best interests.

The need to control the progress of a case must include where possible the need for judicial continuity. In cases in the main registry of the Court of Protection and in regional courts, judges can reserve a case to themselves to ensure that they follow the case through. However, in cases before a High Court Judge, this may present difficulties.

In *Enfield LBC v SA, FA and KA* [2010] EWHC 196 (Admin), [2010] COPLR Con Vol 362, McFarlane J commented that: '... it is difficult to determine any difference between a case in the Court of Protection and public law child protection proceedings where there is a split hearing ...' and where the same judge should hear all hearings. In this case, the order setting up a fact finding hearing and also a best interests hearing did not state that the two hearings should be before the same judge and they were therefore listed before two High Court Judges. As the case could not come back before McFarlane J in an appropriate timescale, the best interests hearing had to continue before another judge.

There have been suggestions that Court of Protection litigation should be subject to a similar regime to proceedings in the Family Court. For example, cases should be concluded in a fixed period similar to the 26-week limit in care proceedings and a decision should be final without review hearings. Although it is tempting to transpose Family Court ideals into the Court of Protection, it should be recognised that by their nature, Court of Protection proceedings are not the same as children's cases. The court may be involved with the life of P for decades; reviews of arrangements then become vital especially if P is deprived of his liberty. More detailed assessments of P and gathering of information too may be required thus making a 26-week deadline impossible and not in P's best interests. See also Peter Jackson J's comments in *A and B (Court of Protection: Delay and Costs)* [2014] EWCOP 48, [2015] COPLR 1.

Rule 5(2)(i)—Most of the Court's applications are dealt with on paper as they are non-contentious, for example an application to appoint a deputy. However, even in a contentious case, the court may choose to deal with an application on paper.

> 'The processes in the Court of Protection are intended to give the court wide flexibility to reach a decision quickly, conveniently and cost effectively where it can, whilst preserving a proper opportunity for those affected by its orders to have their views taken into account in full argument if necessary. To that end, on receiving an application, the court can make a decision on the papers, or direct a full hearing, or make any order as to how the application can best be dealt with. This will often lead to a speedy decision made solely on paper which everyone is content to accept, but any party still has the right to ask for a reconsideration'. (Per HHJ Marshall QC in *Re S and S (Protected Persons)* [2008] COPLR Con Vol 1074.)

See r 89 and the right to seek reconsideration of an order.

Rule 5(2)(j)—Part 14, Practice Direction A, para 21 and Practice Direction A, Annex 2 refer to video conferencing. Part 10, Practice Direction B, para 7 requires a disk containing a draft order when an urgent application is made. Part 10, Practice Direction A, paras 18–20 and Practice Direction B, para 12 deal with telephone hearings. Part 6, Practice Direction A, paras 4–8 deal with service by electronic means.

Rule 5(2)(k)—This may include shortening time for service of documents and taking other steps to ensure that the next or final hearing is not delayed. To achieve this objective, r 26 gives the court unparalleled flexibility.

Rule 5(2)(l) and (m)—These rules were introduced in July 2015 as part of the court's progress towards greater transparency. However, the effect of the rule is changed now that it is proposed to start a pilot scheme to open the court to the public in many hearings (see the commentary to r 90).

Disability—In *Re C (Care Proceedings: Parents with Disabilities)* [2014] EWCA Civ 128, [2015] 1 FLR 521 inadequate provision of interpretation support in the form of a sign language interpreter and a Deaf Relay Interpreter for a mother who had a low level of cognitive function and a degree of speech and hearing impediment lead to an appeal being allowed. The Court of Appeal held that the first instance court had failed to meet the disability needs of the parties. Although a family case, it illustrates the importance of fairness in proceedings and there seems no reason why this should not apply equally to cases in the Court of Protection.

See also the commentary under r 3 about vulnerable persons.

Drawing of orders—Orders following hearings should be drafted as soon as possible and should reflect what the court ordered. *Webb Resolutions Ltd v JT Ltd* [2013] EWHC 509 (TCC) is an example as to what could happen when orders are not properly drafted. In *Webb* the Claimant's solicitors were ordered to pay the Defendant's costs when a draft order following a hearing ignored what the court ordered but instead contained what the Claimant preferred.

The Inherent Jurisdiction—See *XCC v AA and Others* [2012] EWHC 2183 (COP), [2012] COPLR 730 where Parker J states that once a matter is before the Court of Protection, the High Court may make orders of its own motion particularly if such orders are ancillary to or in support of orders made on application to the Court of Protection.

Link with the Family Jurisdiction—There may be cases where a case started in the family court raises issues which belong in the Court of Protection. Consideration to be given to one judge hearing the case and specific issues being transferred to the Court of Protection for determination by the same judge at one hearing dealing with all matters.

Headings of Orders—In J Council v GU and Others [2013] EWHC 3531 (COP)) Mostyn J said that:

> '… In the memorable words of Lord Rodger of Earlsferry in *Re Guardian News and Media Ltd* [2010] 2 AC 697 at para 1 the case has become an 'alphabet soup'. There is absolutely no reason for this, although for some mysterious reason, which I cannot work out, it has become standard practice. Not only is it very confusing to any reader but it dehumanises the participants …'

General—If possible, judicial continuity should be encouraged (see *A, B and C v X, Y and Z* [2012] EWHC 2400 (COP), [2013] COPLR 1 per Hedley J). The advantages of having the same judge preside over all hearings are obvious both in terms of costs savings and the overall management of a case. If the same judge cannot preside over the final hearing, then at least one judge should deal with all pre-trial hearings and case management.

Pre-trial review—In some cases, it may also be useful to hold a pre-trial review. This approach was endorsed by Hedley J in *A, B and C v X, Y and Z*.

General practice—It is also worthwhile to note to comments of Munby P in *Re TG (A Child)* [2013] EWCA Civ 5, [2013] 1 FLR 1250). Although a decision in care proceedings brought under the Children Act 1989, it touches on important areas of case management such as the instruction of experts and the role of the appellate court when considering case management decisions. It is suggested that the general approach in the judgment applies equally in the Court of Protection. One point made by the court that is worthy of consideration is the observation about the need for the attendance of every party when a number of parties take the same point which could be made to the court by just one of them.

PART 3
INTERPRETATION AND GENERAL PROVISIONS

6 Interpretation

In these Rules –

'the Act' means the Mental Capacity Act 2005;

'accredited legal representative' means a legal representative authorised pursuant to a scheme of accreditation approved by the President to represent persons meeting the definition of 'P' in this rule in proceedings before the court;

'applicant' means a person who makes, or who seeks permission to make, an application to the court;

'application form' means the document that is to be used to begin proceedings in accordance with Part 9 of these Rules or any other provision of these Rules or the practice directions which requires the use of an application form;

'application notice' means the document that is to be used to make an application in accordance with Part 10 of these Rules or any other provision of these Rules or the practice directions which requires the use of an application notice;

'attorney' means the person appointed as such by an enduring power of attorney created, or purporting to have been created, in accordance with the regulations mentioned in paragraph 2 of Schedule 4 to the Act;

'business day' means a day other than –
   (a) a Saturday, Sunday, Christmas Day or Good Friday; or
   (b) a bank holiday in England and Wales, under the Banking and Financial Dealings Act 1971;

'child' means a person under 18;

'court' means the Court of Protection;

'deputy' means a deputy appointed under the Act;

'donee' means the donee of a lasting power of attorney;

'donor' means the donor of a lasting power of attorney, except where this expression is used in rule 68 or 201(5) (where it means the donor of an enduring power of attorney);

'enduring power of attorney' means an instrument created in accordance with such of the regulations mentioned in paragraph 2 of Schedule 4 to the Act as applied when it was executed;

'filing' in relation to a document means delivering it, by post or otherwise, to the court office;

'hearing' includes a hearing conducted by telephone, video link, or any other method permitted or directed by the court;'judge' means a judge nominated to be a judge of the court under the Act;
'judge' means a judge nominated to be a judge of the court under the Act;
'lasting power of attorney' has the meaning given in section 9 of the Act;
'legal representative' means a –
   (a) barrister,
   (b) solicitor,
   (c) solicitor's employee,
   (d) manager of a body recognised under section 9 of the Administration of Justice Act 1985, or
   (e) person who, for the purposes of the Legal Services Act 2007, is an authorised person in relation to an activity which constitutes the conduct of litigation (within the meaning of that Act),
who has been instructed to act for a party in relation to any application;
'legally aided person' means a person to whom civil legal services (within the meaning of the Legal Aid, Sentencing and Punishment of Offenders Act 2012) have been made available under arrangements made for the purposes of Part 1 of that Act);
'order' includes a declaration made by the court;
'P' means
   (a) any person (other than a protected party) who lacks or, so far as consistent with the context, is alleged to lack capacity to make a decision or decisions in relation to any matter that is the subject of an application to the court; and
   (b) a relevant person as defined by paragraph 7 of Schedule A1 to the Act,
and references to a person who lacks capacity are to be construed in accordance with the Act;
'party' is to be construed in accordance with rule 73;
'personal welfare' is to be construed in accordance with section 17 of the Act;
'President' and 'Vice-President' refer to those judges appointed as such under section 46(3)(a) and (b) of the Act;
'property and affairs' is to be construed in accordance with section 18 of the Act;
'protected party' means a party or an intended party (other than P or a child) who lacks capacity to conduct the proceedings;
'representative' means a person appointed under rule 3A(2)(c), except where the context otherwise requires;
'respondent' means a person who is named as a respondent in the application form or notice, as the case may be;
'Senior Judge' means the judge who has been nominated to be Senior Judge under section 46(4) of the Act, and references in these Rules to a circuit judge include the Senior Judge;
'Tier 1 Judge' means any judge nominated to act as a judge of the Court of Protection under section 46 of the Act who is neither a Tier 2 Judge nor a Tier 3 Judge;
'Tier 2 Judge' means –
   (a) the Senior Judge; and
   (b) such other judges nominated to act as a judge of the Court of Protection under section 46 of the Act as may be set out in the relevant practice direction;
'Tier 3 Judge' means –
   (a) the President;
   (b) the Vice-President; and

(c) such other judges nominated to act as a judge of the Court of Protection under section 46 of the Act as may be set out in the relevant practice direction;

'Visitor' means a person appointed as such by the Lord Chancellor under section 61 of the Act.

Amendment—SI 2009/582; SI 2013/534; SI 2015/548.

'**Accredited legal representative**'—The accredited legal representative was introduced by r 3A(2)(b). So far, no scheme has been approved.

'**Child**'—Section 18(3) of the Act allows the court to appoint a deputy for P where P is under 18 years so a person can be both a child and P.

'**Filing**'—Reference to is made to delivering a document by 'post or otherwise' to the Court office. Rule 10(3)(a) permits filing by fax and para 7 of Practice Direction A to Part 4 sets out the requirements for filing by fax. In particular, para 7(c) provides that the document is only considered filed when delivered by the Court's fax machine regardless of the time that is shown to have been transmitted from the party's machine. There is no provision for e-mail filing.

Hearing—The definition has now been amended to include the recommendation of the 2010 Rules Committee to include hearings by telephone and videolink.

'**Judge**'—The MCA 2005 was originally enacted to provide that only a High Court, Circuit or District Judge could be nominated to sit in the Court of Protection. This meant that part-time judicial office holders such as Recorders and Deputy District Judges could not sit in the court and a Circuit Judge could not be given permission to hear cases that could only be heard by a High Court Judge unlike in other jurisdictions. The provisions of Part 3 to Schedule 14 of the Crime and Courts Act 2003 remedied this lacuna and amend the MCA 2005 to allow a larger number of judicial office holders (including tribunal judges) to be nominated to hear Court of Protection cases. The Act received Royal Assent in April 2013 and is now in force. In the *Re X* procedure cases under r 82A, tribunal judges were nominated and trained to deal with these cases. For this reason, judges were divided into tiers that reflect their seniority. For example, an Upper Tribunal Judge would come within Tier 2 being on the same level as a Circuit Judge.

'**Senior Judge**'—The present incumbent is Senior Judge Denzil Lush, who sits at the main registry of the court at First Avenue House.

7 Court officers

(1) Where these Rules permit or require the court to perform an act of a purely formal or administrative character, that act may be performed by a court officer.

(2) A requirement that a court officer carry out any act at the request of any person is subject to the payment of any fee required by a fees order for the carrying out of that act.

Rule 7(1)—Court officers include those authorised to carry out certain work pursuant to r 7A.

7A (1) The Senior Judge or the President may authorise a court officer to exercise the jurisdiction of the court in such circumstances as set out in the relevant practice direction.

(2) A court officer who has been authorised under paragraph (1) –

    (a) must refer to a judge any application, proceedings or any question arising in any application or proceedings which ought, in the officer's opinion, to be considered by a judge;

    (b) may not deal with any application or proceedings or any question arising in any application or proceedings by way of a hearing; and

(c) may not deal with an application for the reconsideration of an order made by that court officer or another court officer.

Amendment—This rule was introduced by the Court of Protection (Amendment) Rules 2011 (SI 2011/2753) and took effect on 12 December 2011.

Practice Direction—The rule should be read together with Practice Direction 3A, which sets out how the rule works in practice.

It is clear from the Practice Direction that the authorised court officer has far more jurisdiction than was recommend by the 2010 Rules Committee and there is no provision for monitoring of the scheme set up by this rule although it is not suggested that this system has not worked well.

Scope of provision—The Rules Committee recommended that 'strictly defined and limited non-contentious property and affairs applications' should be dealt with by court officers with an automatic right to refer any decision taken by the court officer to a judge. This recommendation was based on the reasoning that many issues placed before the court were administrative or straightforward and undisputed and by allowing the work to be undertaken by a court officer, delays would be reduced and the judges would have more time to deal with contentious or more serious applications.

The authorised court officers cannot undertake the following:

EPA and LPA applications

— All applications relating to an LPA or EPA;
— Personal; welfare applications;
— All applications relating to the court's personal welfare jurisdiction, including where part of the application relates to property and affairs (including hybrid applications);
— Applications for the appointment of a personal welfare deputy (including hybrid applications);
— Applications under Part 10A of the Rules Deprivation of Liberty safeguards (DoLS).

Property and affairs applications

— Applications to remove a deputy where concerns have been raised about the actions of the deputy;
— Contentious applications where someone served or notified of an application opposes the application by filing a COP5;
— Where P owns real property outside of the jurisdiction;
— Where the majority of P's property is held outside the jurisdiction;
— Where P the proposed deputy resides or intends to reside outside the jurisdiction;
— Financial dealings between P and the deputy or relatives of P which potentially give rise to a conflict of interest, for example where a relative wishes to purchase P's property;
— Where P is in receipt of a damages award over £1 million and the proposed deputy is a family member;
— Where the proposed deputy is an undischarged bankrupt or is subject to an IVA (individual voluntary arrangement);
— Application to be joined as a party to proceedings including COP5s;
— Applications for the settlement of P's property whether for P's benefit or for the benefit of others;
— Applications for a statutory will or codicil;
— Applications to vary the terms of a trust or will in which P has an interest;
— Applications to manage a business or partnership belonging to P or in which P has an interest;
— Applications to start, continue or defend litigation on behalf of P;
— Applications relating to the enforcement or recognition of protective measures taken outside England and Wales ('Hague convention cases');
— Applications for a report under section 49 of the MCA;
— Applications to take a copy document or inspect the court file where the request is made by someone who is not a party to existing or previous proceedings;
— Where the proposed deputy may be unsuitable for appointment by answering yes to questions in section 3 of COP4 Deputy's declaration.

Other

— All applications by the Public Guardian;
— Applications to reconsider an order under rule 89;

— Appeals against any decision of the court.

During the first 3 months of its operation, requests for reconsideration of an authorised court officer's decision were considered by the Senior Judge. Thereafter, all judges deal with reconsiderations. In practice, authorised court officers will refer to a judge cases that raise novel or difficult legal points, where there are substantial assets, where the papers show that the matter is not straightforward or where a hearing is necessary.

8 Computation of time

(1) This rule shows how to calculate any period of time which is specified –

    (a) by these Rules;
    (b) by a practice direction; or
    (c) in an order or direction of the court.

(2) A period of time expressed as a number of days must be computed as clear days.

(3) In this rule 'clear days' means that in computing the number of days –

    (a) the day on which the period begins; and
    (b) if the end of the period is defined by reference to an event, the day on which that event occurs,

are not included.

(4) Where the specified period is 7 days or less, and would include a day which is not a business day, that day does not count.

(5) When the specified period for doing any act at the court office ends on a day on which the office is closed, that act will be done in time if done on the next day on which the court office is open.

Court times—The court office closes at 4 pm.

'In an order or direction of the court' (Rule 8(1)(c))—In certain urgent matters, there may be a need to abridge time and adapt the effect of this rule.

9 Application of Civil Procedure Rules and Family Procedure Rules

(1) In any case not expressly provided for by these Rules or the practice directions made under them, the court may apply either the Civil Procedure Rules 1998 or the Family Procedure Rules 2010 (including in either case the practice directions made under them) with any necessary modifications, in so far as is necessary to further the overriding objective.

(2) A reference in these Rules to the Civil Procedure Rules 1998 or to the Family Procedure Rules 2010 is to the version of those rules in force at the date specified for the purpose of that reference in the relevant practice direction.

Amendment—Substituted by SI 2015/548.

Application of CPR and FPR—This rule was amended in July 2015 to allow for application of both the CPR and the FPR if desired. The provision is not mandatory. The Court *may* apply them with any modifications. Before doing so, the court will not only consider the overriding objective but also whether it is in P's best interests, which will include any extra costs incurred by the application of these rules.

The main reason for this rule was to give flexibility and to allow the court to adopt rules that may serve a case better. For example, in a personal welfare case, parts of the FPR relating to experts might be appropriate to incorporate. However, the powers in rr 26 and 25(2)(m) should give the court sufficient flexibility to avoid use of this provision.

Rule 9(2)—This part of the rule was introduced in July 2015 to remedy the situation that arose whereby the provisions in these rules concerning costs and enforcement referred to rules in the CPR that had themselves been amended. This meant that the Court of Protection Rules were almost meaningless. To avoid the situation happening again, this rule provides that references to the CPR and FPR are to the latest version of those rules. Clearly, it will be for the practitioner to ensure that this rule does not need to be modified by an order in a particular case, for example, if the costs rules in the CPR were to undergo further change or where the parties wishes to preserve the application of provisions in an older version of the CPR or FPR.

See also *Enfield LBC v SA, FA and KA* [2010] EWHC 196 (Admin), [2010] COPLR Con Vol 362, which considers rules of evidence in the CPR and the approach to Court of Protection cases.

In *Re G (Adult) (Costs)* [2014] EWCOP 5, [2014] COPLR 432 a local authority and the Official Solicitor sought an order for costs against ANL (a media outlet) that was refused permission to become a party to the case. One of the arguments was that r 9 incorporated the CPR to allow the court to follow the CPR rule that the loser of an application to be added as a party had to pay the other parties' costs. Munby P disagreed saying that this was a personal welfare case and the costs regime in r 157 therefore applied and not the CPR.

9A Pilot schemes

(1) Practice directions may make provision for the operation of pilot schemes for assessing the use of new practices and procedures in connection with proceedings –

    (a) for specified periods; and
    (b) in relation to proceedings –
        (i) in specified parts of the country; or
        (ii) relating to specified types of application.

(2) Practice directions may modify or disapply any provision of these Rules during the operation of such pilot schemes.

Amendments—Inserted by SI 2015/548.

Pilot schemes—It is anticipated that the Ad Hoc Rules Committee will use this rule, which was introduced in July 2015, to allow changes first to be piloted so that a proper evaluation can be undertaken of any proposed rule. Normally, any rule change is implemented through a statutory instrument, which takes longer to implement and longer to change, whereas a pilot scheme can be introduced quickly and for that matter abandoned quickly if the scheme does not work. This rule, therefore, give flexibility to try out new ways of working.

In November 2015, a pilot regarding transparency was published, which started in January 2016, whereby the provisions of Pt 13 are amended for the duration of the pilot to provide that the default position in certain proceedings will be that the hearings are in public. It is also anticipated that a further pilot will be introduced relating to case management.

PART 4
COURT DOCUMENTS

10 Documents used in court proceedings

(1) The court will seal or otherwise authenticate with the stamp of the court the following documents on issue –

    (a) …
    (b) an application form;
    (c) an application notice;
    (d) an order; and
    (e) any other document which a rule or practice direction requires to be sealed or stamped.

(2) Where these Rules or any practice direction require a document to be signed, that requirement is satisfied if the signature is printed by computer or other mechanical means.

(3) A practice direction may make provision for documents to be filed or sent to the court by –

    (a)   facsimile; or
    (b)   other means.

Amendments—SI 2015/548.

Rule 10(1)—The absence of a seal will mean that the document is not prima facie valid.

Rule 10(3)(a)—Practice Direction 4A, para 7 deals with filing documents at court by fax. Paragraph 7(c) provides that a document sent by fax is not considered delivered until it is delivered to the Court's fax machine. The fact that the sender has a record of its transmission is irrelevant.

Rule 10(3)(b)—There are no facilities to file by e-mail, although it is anticipated that e-filing may be introduced during 2016. Provisions for e-filing are contained in PD5B of CPR 1998.

11 Documents required to be verified by a statement of truth

(1) The following documents must be verified by a statement of truth –

    (a)   an application form, an application notice, an appellant's notice or a respondent's notice, where the applicant seeks to rely upon matters set out in the document as evidence;
    (b)   a witness statement;
    (c)   a certificate of –
        (i)   service or non-service; or
        (ii)   notification or non-notification;
    (d)   a deputy's declaration; and
    (e)   any other document required by a rule or practice direction to be so verified.

(2) Subject to paragraph (3), a statement of truth is a statement that –

    (a)   the party putting forward the document;
    (b)   in the case of a witness statement, the maker of the witness statement; or
    (c)   in the case of a certificate referred to in paragraph (1)(c), the person who signs the certificate,

believes that the facts stated in the document being verified are true.

(3) If a party is conducting proceedings with a litigation friend, the statement of truth in –

    (a)   ...
    (b)   an application form; or
    (c)   an application notice;
    (d)   an appellant's notice or a respondent's notice

is a statement that the litigation friend believes the facts stated in the document being verified are true.

(4) The statement of truth must be signed –

    (a)   in the case of an application form, an application notice, an appellant's notice or a respondent's notice –
        (i)   by the party or litigation friend; or

(ii) by the legal representative on behalf of the party or litigation friend; and
(b) in the case of a witness statement, by the maker of the statement.

(5) A statement of truth which is not contained in the document which it verifies must clearly identify that document.

(6) A statement of truth in an application form, an application notice, an appellant's notice or a respondent's notice may be made by –

(a) a person who is not a party; or
(b) two or more parties jointly,

where this is permitted by a relevant practice direction.

Amendments—SI 2015/548.

Rule 11(1)—Practice Direction 4B sets out the form and requirements of the statement of truth. The purpose of the statement of truth is set out at r 11(2).

Rule 11(4)—Paragraphs 7–16 of Practice Direction B explain who may sign the statement of truth.
A legal representative who signs the statement of truth should have regard to para 16 of Practice Direction B, which sets out the basis upon which he or she is able to sign.
Paragraphs 17–20 set out the procedure to follow where the person who should sign the statement of truth cannot read or sign the document.

11A Position statement not required to be verified by statement of truth

Nothing in these Rules requires a position statement to be verified by a statement of truth.

Amendments—Inserted by SI 2015/548. This amendment to the rules was introduced in July 2015 as some thought that position statements fell within r 11.

12 Failure to verify a document

If an application form, an application notice, an appellant's notice or a respondent's notice is not verified by a statement of truth, the applicant (or respondent as the case may be) may not rely upon the document as evidence of any of the matters set out in it unless the court permits.

Note—Although the document cannot be relied upon as evidence, the rule does not state that the document itself becomes ineffective. The court could strike out the document using its case management powers, although this would be a serious step and the court would need to consider if it were in P's best interests.

13 Failure to verify a witness statement

If a witness statement is not verified by a statement of truth, it shall not be admissible in evidence unless the court permits.

Note—When considering whether or not to allow a party to rely on a statement, the court is making a case management decision. It will therefore need to consider P's best interests, the overriding objective, proportionality, the effect of any failure to have regard to a duty imposed by r 4 and the court's obligation to control evidence contained in r 95.
The parallel provision in the FPR in r 17.4 provides only that the court may direct that the statement is not admissible in evidence, unlike this rule, which precludes reliance without the court's

permission. The emphasis in r 12 seems to be on ensuring compliance in the first place and in default, it is for the court exercising its case management powers, to decide whether the evidence should be allowed to be admitted. Rule 12 therefore gives the court more control than the FPR allows.

14 False statements

(1) Proceedings for contempt of court may be brought against a person if he makes, or causes to be made, a false statement in a document verified by a statement of truth without an honest belief in its truth.

(2) Proceedings under this rule may be brought only –

    (a) by the Attorney General; or
    (b) with the permission of the court.

15 Personal details

(1) Where a party does not wish to reveal –

    (a) his home address or telephone number;
    (b) P's home address or telephone number;
    (c) the name of the person with whom P is living (if that person is not the applicant); or
    (d) the address or telephone number of his place of business, or the place of business of any of the persons mentioned in sub-paragraphs (b) or (c),

he must provide those particulars to the court.

(2) Where paragraph (1) applies, the particulars given will not be revealed to any person unless the court so directs.

(3) Where a party changes his home address during the course of the proceedings, he must give notice of the change to the court.

(4) Where a party does not reveal his home address, he must nonetheless provide an address for service which must be within the jurisdiction of the court.

Rule 15(4)—Although a party may not wish to reveal his personal details, r 15(4) provides that an address for service must be provided.

Rule 15(2)—When considering whether to reveal an address, the Court will consider why the request for confidentiality is made, for example if there are safeguarding concerns. If a person wishes to play a full role in the proceedings and confidentiality will impede the fair conduct of those proceedings, the court may decline to allow confidentiality.

16 Supply of documents to a party from court records

Unless the court orders otherwise, a party to proceedings may inspect or obtain from the records of the court a copy of –

    (a) any document filed by a party to the proceedings; or
    (b) any communication in the proceedings between the court and –
        (i) a party to the proceedings; or
        (ii) another person.

'Unless the court orders otherwise'—For example, because it is not in P's best interests or where P or a party's rights of privacy would be compromised.

'**Document**'—This may include transcripts of hearings or of a judgment, skeleton arguments and opening and closing submissions. It does not include letters as r 16(b) refers to communications.

17 Supply of documents to a non-party from court records

(1) Subject to rules 20 and 92(2), a person who is not a party to proceedings may inspect or obtain from the court records a copy of any judgment or order given or made in public.

(2) The court may, on an application made to it, authorise a person who is not a party to proceedings to –

(a) inspect any other documents in the court records; or
(b) obtain a copy of any such documents, or extracts from such documents.

(3) A person making an application for an authorisation under paragraph (2) must do so in accordance with Part 10.

(4) Before giving an authorisation under paragraph (2), the court will consider whether any document is to be provided on an edited basis.

'**Court records**' (r 17(1))—Whereas each case at the Court of Protection has its own file, some files opened before 1 October 2007 may contain Court and Public Guardian documents; for example, court orders and correspondence relating to court proceedings together with Receiver's accounts and correspondence between the Receiver and the Public Guardian. This occurred because the Public Guardian was responsible for the old Court of Protection and the two offices worked together in many ways. The court would therefore need to ensure that if a document were disclosed, it is properly a court document or record.

'**Given or made in public**'—Given that r 90 provides that proceedings are held in private, the opportunity to use r 17(1) may be limited, although with the proposed transparency pilot scheme, which will create more open hearings, there is greater likelihood of use of this provision being utilised.

'**any other documents**'—This could include skeleton arguments, position statements or experts reports.

'**extracts**' (r 17(2))—Any order permitting disclosure would have to set out exactly what part of a document is to be extracted and disclosed.

'**edited basis**' (r 17(4))—See rules 19 and 20(6) which allow a document to be edited prior to service or disclosure.

When considering an application under this rule, there are some authorities decided under the CPR that may provide some principles:

- The applicant should identify what document he or she requires as far as possible (per Moore-Bick J in *Dian v Davis Frankel and Mead* [2004] EWHC 2662 (Comm)).
- An application should be made promptly (*Chan U Seek v Alvis Vehicles Ltd and Guardian Newspapers* [2004] EWHC 3092 (Ch)).
- An application by a newspaper for disclosure in an 'old and stale case' may be refused (per Parker J in *Chan*).
- What end is disclosure intended to serve (per Moore-Bick J in *Dian*).
- Where an applicant wanted disclosure of documents that would help it in related litigation, despite there being a private and evidence interest as opposed to a public interest, disclosure was granted (see *Dian*).
- Although a newspaper's motive in seeking disclosure went beyond its stated desire to prepare an accurate report of the case disclosure was still given (see *Chan*).
- The fact that only the judge read the document may not bar disclosure (*Chan* and *Dian*).
- The 'press are just part of the public' (per Parker J in *Chan*).
- A transcript may not be part of the records of the court (*Chan*).
- Disclosure may be refused where there are strong considerations of commercial confidentiality (*Lilly Icos Ltd v Pfizer (No 2)* [2002] EWCA Civ 2).

18 Subsequent use of court documents

(1) Where a document has been filed or disclosed, a party to whom it was provided may use the document only for the purpose of the proceedings in which it was filed or disclosed, except where –

(a) the document has been read to or by the court or referred to at a public hearing; or
(b) the court otherwise permits.

(2) Paragraph (1)(a) is subject to any order of the court made under rule 92(2).

19 Editing information in court documents

(1) A party may apply to the court for an order that a specified part of a document is to be edited prior to the document's service or disclosure.

(2) An order under paragraph (1) may be made at any time.

(3) Where the court makes an order under this rule any subsequent use of that document in the proceedings shall be of the document as edited, unless the court directs otherwise.

(4) An application under this rule must be made in accordance with Part 10.

20 Public Guardian to be supplied with court documents relevant to supervision of deputies

(1) This rule applies in any case where the court makes an order –

(a) appointing a person to act as a deputy; or
(b) varying an order under which a deputy has been appointed.

(2) Subject to paragraphs (3) and (6), the Public Guardian is entitled to be supplied with a copy of qualifying documents if he reasonably considers that it is necessary for him to have regard to them in connection with the discharge of his functions under section 58 of the Act in relation to the supervision of deputies.

(3) The court may direct that the right to be supplied with documents under paragraph (2) does not apply in relation to such one or more documents, or descriptions of documents, as the court may specify.

(4) A direction under paragraph (3) or (6) may be given –

(a) either on the court's own initiative or on an application made to it; and
(b) either –
    (i) at the same time as the court makes the order which appoints the deputy, or which varies it; or
    (ii) subsequently.

(5) 'Qualifying documents' means documents which –

(a) are filed in court in connection with the proceedings in which the court makes the order referred to in paragraph (1); and
(b) are relevant to –
    (i) the decision to appoint the deputy;
    (ii) any powers conferred on him;
    (iii) any duties imposed on him; or

(iv) any other terms applying to those powers and duties which are contained in the order.

(6) The court may direct that any document is to be provided to the Public Guardian on an edited basis.

21 Provision of court order to Public Guardian

Any order of the court requiring the Public Guardian to do something, or not to do something, will be served by the court on the Public Guardian as soon as practicable and in any event not later than 7 days after the order was made.

Note—This rule only covers a situation where the court's order is directed to the Public Guardian. However, there may be cases where it is sensible to allow the Public Guardian to see an order made by the court.

22 Amendment of application

(1) The court may allow or direct an applicant, at any stage of the proceedings, to amend his application form or notice.

(2) The amendment may be effected by making in writing the necessary alterations to the application form or notice, but if the amendments are so numerous or of such a nature or length that written alteration would make it difficult or inconvenient to read, a fresh document amended as allowed or directed may be issued.

23 Clerical mistakes or slips

The court may at any time correct any clerical mistakes in an order or direction or any error arising in an order or direction from any accidental slip or omission.

The slip rule—This provision adopts what is commonly known as the slip rule.

24 Endorsement of amendment

Where an application form or notice, order or direction has been amended under this Part, a note shall be placed on it showing the date on which it was amended and the alteration shall be sealed.

PART 5
GENERAL CASE MANAGEMENT POWERS

25 The court's general powers of case management

(1) The list of powers in this rule is in addition to any powers given to the court by any other rule or practice direction or by any other enactment or any powers it may otherwise have.

(2) The court may –
   (a) extend or shorten the time for compliance with any rule, practice direction, or court order or direction (even if an application for extension is made after the time for compliance has expired);
   (b) adjourn or bring forward a hearing;

(c) require P, a party, a party's legal representative or litigation friend, to attend court;
(d) hold a hearing and receive evidence by telephone or any other method of direct oral communication;
(e) stay the whole or part of any proceedings or judgment either generally or until a specified date or event;
(f) consolidate proceedings;
(g) hear two or more applications on the same occasion;
(h) direct a separate hearing of any issue;
(i) decide the order in which issues are to be heard;
(j) exclude an issue from consideration;
(k) dismiss or give judgment on an application after a decision is made on a preliminary basis;
(l) direct any party to file and serve an estimate of costs; and
(m) take any step or give any direction for the purpose of managing the case and furthering the overriding objective.

(3) A judge to whom a matter is allocated may, if he considers that the matter is one which ought properly to be dealt with by another judge, transfer the matter to such a judge.

(4) Where the court gives directions it may take into account whether or not a party has complied with any rule or practice direction.

(5) The court may make any order it considers appropriate even if a party has not sought that order.

(6) A power of the court under these Rules to make an order includes a power to vary or revoke the order;

(7) *(revoked)*

Amendments—SI 2015/548.

Scope of rule—In the past year, the structure of the Court has changed due to the regionalisation programme. The main registry at First Avenue House remains and the Senior Judge sits there, together with a number of district judges. However, once the regionalisation programme reaches its conclusion in 2016, it is anticipated that contentious cases will be issued at a regional centre, where the case will be passed to a judge who will manage the case. If that is not achieved, the case will be issued in the main registry and then transferred to a regional judge. This means that the local centre will take charge of case management. Non-contentious work will remain at the main registry although with time, this too may change.

Whatever the final position with regionalisation, the reality will be that cases will be managed by a judge who will consider the issues and give appropriate directions. The court will consider P's position and whether he should be a party pursuant to r 3A and the matters referred to in r 5.

Rule 25(2)(a)—This provision was especially important prior to recent changes to the Rules because many time limits were 21 days, which caused delay. These are now changed to 14 days, although this rule allows the court to make other provisions. Cases where this may be necessary are those involving serious medical treatment and a statutory will application where time is of the essence.

Rule 25(2)(b)—Adjournments should only be granted when they are in P's best interests. Failure by the parties to comply with directions should not be a reason for an adjournment; rather the court should refocus the case.

Bringing forward a hearing may be necessary where, for example, in an application for a statutory will the Court is informed that P's health has deteriorated such that P may not live until the hearing date.

Rule 25(2)(c)—See r 3A regarding P's participation.

As well as considering attendance at a hearing, the court should consider if it can dispense with attendance at a hearing. For example, whether the Official Solicitor needs to attend a directions hearing and if he can present his position in writing. See paragraph 7 of the President's Guidance dated December 2010.

Rule 25(2)(d): 'telephone'—See Part 10, Practice Direction A, paras 18–20 which deal with telephone hearings. A telephone hearing is very useful in the context of the work of the Court of Protection. Many applications are dealt with on paper and if the papers are not clear on a point, the judge may arrange for a telephone hearing to take place on short notice to allow the issue to be clarified and the matter finalised.

'other method of direct oral communication' (r 25(2)(d))—See Part 10, Practice Direction A, para 21 and Part 14, Practice Direction A, Annex 2 which deal with video conferencing.

Rule 25(2)(e)—When ordering a stay, the court must ensure that it is in P's best interests and that any delay to the final outcome of a case is not contrary to P's interests.

Rule 25(2)(f)—For example, an application by a sibling to have contact with P and an application by a local authority authorising a deprivation of liberty.

Rule 25(2)(h)—Common examples of the need for a separate hearing are where there is a need to determine if P lacks capacity or not and a fact finding hearing. These hearings would be prior to the substantive hearing of an application.

Rule 25(2)(j)—In some cases, family members use litigation as an excuse to vent anger about family issues and disputes that date back many years. The court should be astute to avoid this and ensure that orders set out the specific issues that are to be determined and to direct that witness statements address only those issues.

Rule 25(2)(m): 'any direction ... and furthering the overriding objective'—This rule gives the court almost unlimited power to ensure a case is managed properly. It could include a costs capping order, for example.

Rule 25(3)—Part 9, Practice Direction E, paras 11 and 12 contain guidelines for serious medical cases which should be heard by a High Court judge.

Rule 86 and Part 12, Practice Direction A, paras 2 and 3 also deal with allocation of certain cases to the President and others to a High Court judge.

Transfer of a case may include transfer to a regional court near P or the parties.

Rule 25(4)—See *A Local Authority v B, F and G* [2014] EWHC B18 (COP) and the application in Court of Protection proceedings of a Hadkinson order. Although this is used in contempt proceedings, some of the general considerations may be relevant under this rule. However, when considering conduct of a party, the court has to ensure that P's best interests are not compromised which may mitigate the ability to apply some sanctions.

Rule 25(6)—Mostyn J held in a family case *TF v PJ* [2014] EWHC 1840 (Admin) that under r 4.1(6) of the Family Procedure Rules 2010 which is identical to this provision, varying or revoking an order did not apply only to a procedural or case management order but also to a final order although this was limited to cases where there had been non-disclosure or a significant change of circumstances.

Rule 25(7)—This provision was revoked in July 2015. It incorporated the CPR's provisions for security of costs which are now contained in r 81A (see below).

See also the comments about case management under rule 5 and *A Local Authority v PB and P* [2011] EWHC 502 (COP), [2011] COPLR Con Vol 166, a decision of the Vice President Charles J and its guidance in respect of practice and procedure in personal welfare cases.

26 Court's power to dispense with requirement of any rule

In addition to its general powers and the powers listed in rule 25, the court may dispense with the requirement of any rule.

Scope of rule—This rule gives immense power to the court especially if taken together with r 25(2)(m). The CPR and FPR have no similar provision. It could be argued that the existence of such a rule goes against the purpose of having procedural rules which is to define the court process, to allow litigants to understand the path they must follow and to apply the same procedure to all court users. However, taken together with the overriding objective and the need to always act in P's best interests, the effect of the rule is to give the court flexibility in its approach and allow it to act in P's best interests.

27 Exercise of powers on the court's own initiative

(1) Except where these Rules or some other enactment make different provision, the court may exercise its powers on its own initiative.

(2) The court may make an order on its own initiative without hearing the parties or giving them the opportunity to make representations.

(3) Where the court proposes to make an order on its own initiative it may give the parties and any person it thinks fit an opportunity to make representations and, where it does so, it will specify the time by which, and the manner in which, the representations must be made.

(4) Where the court proposes –

   (a)   to make an order on its own initiative; and
   (b)   to hold a hearing to decide whether to make the order,

it will give the parties and may give any other person it thinks likely to be affected by the order at least 3 days' notice of the hearing.

Note—See *KD and LD v Havering London Borough Council* [2009] COPLR Con Vol 770 where it was stated that the power in this rule to deal with issues summarily and without the parties present should be used carefully and 'with a modicum of restraint'. The court must also have regard to the overriding objective and the need to deal with a case justly.

This rule gives no power to the court to grant summary judgment to a party. Unlike the CPR, there is no summary judgment provision in these rules which makes sense. This rule simply allows the court to make orders on its own initiative which means without the need for an application or some other process to start before the court can act.

A summary judgment process normally arises when the court forms a view that a case should be ended before a full trial either because there is no reasonable prospect of success on an issue or where there is good reason for the court to reach the conclusion that the case should end at an early stage. Such a process can have no place in the Court of Protection Rules; unlike civil proceedings where two parties oppose each other, Court of Protection proceedings have the additional layer of P (whether or not as a party).P's best interests need to be considered fully before any decision is made and a summary determination of best interests is not provided for in the MCA. Furthermore, the United Nations Convention on the Rights of Persons With Disabilities provide for the full and effective participation of P in proceedings (see para 45 of Lady Hale's judgment in *P v Cheshire West and Chester Council* [2014] UKSC 19, [2014] COPLR 313, which recognised those rights). Of course, there may be cases where the court uses its case management powers to bring determination of an issue to an end but this will only be done where all the information is before the court and not through a speculative summary process.

28 General power of the court to rectify matters where there has been an error of procedure

Where there has been an error of procedure, such as a failure to comply with a rule or practice direction –

(a) the error does not invalidate any step taken in the proceedings unless the court so orders; and

(b) the court may waive the error or require it to be remedied or may make such other order as appears to the court to be just.

PART 6
SERVICE OF DOCUMENTS

Service generally

29 Scope

(1) Subject to paragraph (2), the rules in this Part apply to –

(a) the service of documents; and

(b) to the requirement under rule 70 for a person to be notified of the issue of an application form,

and references to 'serve', 'service', 'notice' and 'notify', and kindred expressions shall be construed accordingly.

(2) The rules in this Part do not apply where –

(a) any other enactment, a rule in another Part or a practice direction makes different provision; or

(b) the court directs otherwise.

30 Who is to serve

(1) The general rule is that the following documents will be served by the court –

(a) an order or judgment of the court;

(b) an acknowledgment of service or notification; and

(c) except where the application is for an order for committal, a notice of hearing.

(2) Any other document is to be served by the party seeking to rely upon it, except where –

(a) a rule or practice direction provides otherwise; or

(b) the court directs otherwise.

(3) Where the court is to serve a document –

(a) it is for the court to decide which of the methods of service specified in rule 31 is to be used; and

(b) if the document is being served on behalf of a party, that party must provide sufficient copies.

Note—Proposals for reform: The 2010 Rules Committee considered the rules of service and notification. It stated that it was:

'... clear that many people do not understand the difference between these concepts and the purpose of the present provisions, and that they introduce confusion and annoyance and the potential for turning a non-contentious application into one that is disputed.'

The 2010 Rules Committee made a number of recommendations to Parts 6 and 7 including:

1. PD 6A should be amended to allow for service on a legal representative qualified to practice in England and Wales but working elsewhere in the EU (see EU Services Directive 2006/123/EC)
2. Guidance should be incorporated into a practice direction to set out how an applicant should give notice prior to proceedings including if appropriate obtaining consents to file with an application. This would allow an application that is non-contentious and unopposed to be filed with all necessary notifications and consents such that it could proceed to the making of a final order without any delay
3. The time limits in the various rules needed to be changed. This recommendation is set against the criticism that delay in a routine application occurs naturally by dint of time limits imposed in the rules.

So far, only time limits have been changed by amendments made in 2015, although the present Ad Hoc Rules Committee may well revisit these provisions.

'**It is for the court to decide ...**' (r 30(3)(a))—Practice Direction 6A, para 13 provides that service by the Court will normally be by first class post although there is nothing to stop the Court using the document exchange or some other means of service if it wishes.

31 Methods of service

(1) A document may be served by any of the methods specified in this rule.

(2) Where it is not known whether a solicitor is acting on behalf of a person, the document may be served by –

- (a) delivering it to the person personally;
- (b) delivering it at his home address or last known home address; or
- (c) sending it to that address, or last known address, by first class post (or by an alternative method of service which provides for delivery on the next working day).

(3) Where a solicitor –

- (a) is authorised to accept service on behalf of a person; and
- (b) has informed the person serving the document in writing that he is so authorised,

the document must be served on the solicitor, unless personal service is required by an enactment, rule, practice direction or court order.

(4) Where it appears to the court that there is a good reason to authorise service by a method other than those specified in paragraphs (2) or (3), the court may direct that service is effected by that method.

(5) A direction that service is effected by an alternative method must specify –

- (a) the method of service; and
- (b) the date when the document will be deemed to be served.

(6) A practice direction may set out how documents are to be served by document exchange, electronic communication or other means.

Rule 31(3) 'unless personal service is required'—Good practice would suggest that the solicitor is told about any service direct on his or her client and provided with a copy of any relevant order unless this would not be appropriate.

Rule 31(4)—This rule and r 31(5) deal with service by an alternative method.

The procedure to follow when making the application is set out at Practice Direction 15A, para 15. The application must be made on Form COP9. This means that even if the application is made at the outset of proceedings on filing COP1, Form COP9 should still be used for this application. The witness statement in support of the application is on Form COP24.

An order under this rule could therefore allow service on P through the manager of a residential home or for oral service by a relative or solicitor explaining the application personally to P.

Rule 31(6)—Practice Direction 6A, paras 1–8 contain rules about electronic service and service by document exchange.

Paragraph 5(a) sets out conditions to allow service by electronic means.

32 Service of documents on children and protected parties

(1) The following table shows the person on whom a document must be served if it is a document which would otherwise be served on –

  (a) a child; or
  (b) a protected party.

Type of document	Nature of party	Person to be served
Application form	Child	A person who has parental responsibility for the child within the meaning of the Children Act 1989; or
		if there is no such person, a person with whom the child resides or in whose care the child is.
Application form	Protected party	The person who is authorised to conduct the proceedings in the protected party's name or on his behalf; or
		a person who is a duly appointed attorney, donee or deputy of the protected party; or
		if there is no such person, a person with whom the protected party lives or in whose care the latter is.
Application for an order appointing a litigation friend, where a child or protected party has no litigation friend	Child or protected party	See rule 145 (appointment of litigation friend by court order – supplementary).
Any other document	Child or protected party	The litigation friend or other duly authorised person who is conducting the proceedings on behalf of the child or protected party.

(2) The court may make an order for service on a child or a protected party by permitting the document to be served on some person other than the person specified in the table set out in paragraph (1) above (which may include service on the child or the protected party).

(3) An application for an order under paragraph (2) may be made without notice.

(4) The court may order that, although a document has been served on someone other than the person specified in the table, the document is to be treated as if it had been properly served.

(5) This rule does not apply in relation to the service of documents upon a child in any case where the court has made an order under rule 141(4) permitting the child to conduct proceedings without a litigation friend.

Rule 32(2)—The application should be made on Form COP9. Although the Practice Direction is silent as to the procedure to follow, it is suggested that a witness statement in Form COP24 should accompany the application explaining why the order is required.

33 Service of documents on P if he becomes a party

(1) If P becomes a party to the proceedings, all documents to be served on him must be served on his litigation friend as directed by the court on P's behalf.

(2) The court may make an order for service on P by permitting the document to be served on some person other than the person specified in paragraph (1) above (which may include service on P).

(3) An application for an order under paragraph (2) may be made without notice.

(4) The court may order that, although a document has been served on someone other than a person specified in paragraph (1), the document is to be treated as if it had been properly served.

(5) This rule does not apply in relation to the service of documents upon P in any case where the court has made an order under rule 144(1)(b) (power of court to bring to an end the appointment of a litigation friend).

> (Rule 41A requires P to be notified where a direction has been made under rule 3A, and of the appointment of a litigation friend, accredited legal representative or representative.)

Amendments—SI 2015/548.

Rule 33(1)—A person duly authorised to conduct proceedings would include the Official Solicitor.

Rule 33(2)—This would cover service on a care worker or the manager of a care home if appropriate or anyone else whom the Court felt should be involved. Before allowing any document to be served personally on P, however, the Court should exercise care as P could be caused unnecessary distress.

34 Substituted service

Where it appears to the court that it is impracticable for any reason to serve a document in accordance with any of the methods provided under rule 31, the court may make an order for substituted service of the document by taking such steps as the court may direct to bring it to the notice of the person to be served.

Scope of rule—Substituted service of a document could include an order that it is served on the manager of a care home for him or her to serve on P.

35 Deemed service

(1) A document which is served in accordance with these Rules or any relevant practice direction shall be deemed to be served on the day shown in the following table –

Method of service	Deemed day of service
First class post (or other service for next-day delivery)	The second day after it was posted.
Document exchange	The second day after it was left at the document exchange.
Delivering the document to a permitted address	The day after it was delivered to that address.
Fax	If it is transmitted on a business day before 4 p.m., on that day; or
	in any other case, on the business day after the day on which it is transmitted.
Other electronic means	The second day after the day on which it is transmitted.

(2) If a document is served personally –

   (a) after 5 p.m., on a business day; or
   (b) at any time on a Saturday, Sunday or a Bank Holiday,

it will be treated as being served on the next business day.

36 Certificate of service

(1) Where a rule, practice direction or court order requires a certificate of service for the document, the certificate must state the details set out in the following table –

Method of service	Details to be certified
First class post (or any other service for next-day delivery)	Date of posting.
Personal service	Date of personal service.
Document exchange	Date when the document was left at the document exchange.
Delivery of document to permitted address	Date when the document was delivered to that address.
Fax	Date of transmission.
Other electronic means	Date of transmission and the means used.
Alternative method permitted by the court	As required by the court.

(2) The certificate must be filed within 7 days after service of the document to which it relates.

Form—The certificate of service is Form COP20. The Rules Committee has recommended that the form be changed to allow service of a number of people to be included on one shorter form as opposed to the present requirement of filing one long form for each person served.

37 Certificate of non-service

(1) Where an applicant or other person is unable to serve any document under these Rules or as directed by the court, he must file a certificate of non-service stating the reasons why service has not been effected.

(2) The certificate of non-service must be filed within 7 days of the latest date on which service should have been effected.

Form—The certificate of non-service is Form COP20.

38 Power of court to dispense with service

(1) The court may dispense with any requirement to serve a document.

(2) An application for an order to dispense with service may be made without notice.

Practice Direction—Practice Direction 6A, para 17 provides that the application should be made on Form COP9. Although not mandatory, it may be prudent in some cases to file a witness statement in Form COP24 explaining why the order is required.

In *Re AB* [2014] COPLR 381 a district judge held that in general, permission to dispense with service or notification should only be made in exceptional circumstances where there are compelling reasons for doing so. Otherwise, the interests of justice will not be served and the court will not be seen to be acting fairly towards all parties. Relevant considerations may include the conduct of the respondent, the value of the financial benefit to the respondent and whether the cost to P's estate or the parties or the delay caused in concluding the application is disproportionate relative to the value of the respondents of the benefit they will lose by the proposed final order.

This case concerned a statutory will and it is suggested that in other applications, the court may apply a more general approach by looking at the facts and weighing P's best interests and the overriding objective rather than applying a strict test. Within the general approach will be a consideration of the matters set out in Re AB.

Service out of the jurisdiction

39 Scope and interpretation

(1) This rule and rules 39A to 39H make provision about –

    (a) service of application forms and other documents out of the jurisdiction; and

    (b) the procedure for service.

(2) In this rule and rules 39A to 39H –

    'application form' includes an application notice;
    'Commonwealth State' means a State listed in Schedule 3 to the British Nationality Act 1981;
    'jurisdiction' means, unless the context otherwise requires, England and Wales and any part of the territorial waters of the United Kingdom adjoining England and Wales;
    'Member State' means a Member State of the European Union;

'the Service Convention' means the Convention on the service abroad of judicial and extra-judicial documents in civil or commercial matters signed at the Hague on November 15, 1965;

'Service Convention country' means a country, not being a Member State, which is a party to the Service Convention; and

'the Service Regulation' means Regulation (EC) No 1393/2007 of the European Parliament and of the Council of 13 November 2007 on the service in the Member States of judicial and extra-judicial documents in civil and commercial matters (service of documents) and repealing Council Regulation (EC) No 1348/2000(2).

(3) In rules 39A to 39H, a reference to service by a party includes service by a person who is not a party where service by such a person is required under these Rules.

Amendments—Substituted by SI 2015/548.

Scope of rule—The provisions for service out of the jurisdiction in the Family Procedure Rules 2010 is contained in rules 6.40 to 6.48 and Practice Directions 6B and 6C which are reproduced in Section V of this work.

39A Service of application form and other documents out of the jurisdiction

(1) Subject to paragraph (2), any document to be served for the purposes of these Rules may be served out of the jurisdiction without the permission of the court.

(2) An application form may not be served out of the jurisdiction unless the court has power to determine the application to which it relates under the Act.

Amendments—Inserted by SI 2015/548.

39B Period for acknowledging service or responding to application where application is served out of the jurisdiction

(1) This rule applies where, under these Rules, a party is required to file –

    (a)   an acknowledgment of service; or

    (b)   an answer to an application,

and sets out the time period for doing so where the application is served out of the jurisdiction.

(2) Where the applicant serves an application on a respondent in –

    (a)   Scotland or Northern Ireland; or

    (b)   a Member State or Service Convention country within Europe,

the period for filing an acknowledgment of service or an answer to an application is 21 days after service of the application.

(3) Where the applicant serves an application on a respondent in a Service Convention country outside Europe, the period for filing an acknowledgment of service or an answer to an application is 31 days after service of the application.

(4) Where the applicant serves an application on a respondent in a country not referred to in paragraphs (2) and (3), the period for filing an acknowledgment of service or an answer to an application is set out in Practice Direction 6B.

Amendments—Inserted by SI 2015/548.

39C Method of service – general provisions

(1) This rule contains general provisions about the method of service of an application form or other document on a party out of the jurisdiction.

Where service is to be effected on a party in Scotland or Northern Ireland

(2) Where a party serves an application form or other document on a party in Scotland or Northern Ireland, it must be served by a method permitted by this Part.

Where service is to be effected out of the United Kingdom

(3) Where an application form or other document is to be served on a person out of the United Kingdom, it may be served by any method –

    (a) provided for by –
        (i) rule 39D (service in accordance with the Service Regulation); or
        (ii) rule 39E (service through foreign governments, judicial authorities and British Consular authorities); or
    (b) permitted by the law of the country in which it is to be served.

(4) Nothing in paragraph (3) or in any court order authorises or requires any person to do anything which is contrary to the law of the country where the application form or other document is to be served.

Amendments—Inserted by SI 2015/548.

39D Service in accordance with the Service Regulation

(1) This rule applies where an application form or other document is to be served on a person out of the United Kingdom in accordance with the Service Regulation.

(2) The person wishing to serve must file –

    (a) the application form or other document;
    (b) any translation; and
    (c) any other documents required by the Service Regulation.

(3) When the person wishing to serve files the documents referred to in paragraph (2), the court officer must –

    (a) seal, or otherwise authenticate with the stamp of the court, the copy of the application form; and
    (b) forward the documents to the Senior Master of the Queen's Bench Division.

(4) In addition to the documents referred to in paragraph (2), the person wishing to serve may, if of the view that this would assist in ensuring effective service, file a photograph of the person to be served.

    (The Service Regulation is annexed to Practice Direction 6B.)

    (Rule 39E makes provision for service on a person in a Service Convention country.)

Amendments—Inserted by SI 2015/548.

39E Service through foreign governments, judicial authorities and British Consular authorities

(1) Where an application form or other document is to be served on a person in a Service Convention country, it may be served –

- (a) through the authority designated under the Service Convention in respect of that country; or
- (b) if the law of that country permits, through –
  - (i) the judicial authorities of that country; or
  - (ii) a British Consular authority in that country.

(2) Where an application form or other document is to be served on a person in a country which is not a Service Convention country, it may be served, if the law of that country so permits, through –

- (a) the government of that country, where that government is willing to serve it; or
- (b) a British Consular authority in that country.

(3) Where an application form or other document is to be served in –

- (a) any Commonwealth State which is not a Service Convention country;
- (b) the Isle of Man or the Channel Islands; or
- (c) any British Overseas Territory,

the methods of service permitted by paragraphs (1)(b) and (2) are not available and the person wishing to serve, or that person's agent, must effect service direct unless Practice Direction 6B provides otherwise.

(4) This rule does not apply where service is to be effected in accordance with the Service Regulation.

(Rule 39D makes provision for service on a party in a Member State in accordance with the Service Regulation.)

(A list of British Overseas Territories is reproduced in Practice Direction 6B.)

Amendments—Inserted by SI 2015/548.

39F Procedure where service is to be through foreign governments, judicial authorities and British Consular authorities

(1) This rule applies where an application form or other document is to be served under rule 39E(1) or (2).

(2) Where this rule applies, the person wishing to serve must file –

- (a) a request for service of the application form or other document, by specifying one or more of the methods in rule 39E(1) or (2);
- (b) a copy of the application form or other document;
- (c) any other documents or copies of documents required by Practice Direction 6B; and
- (d) any translation required under rule 39G.

(3) When the person wishing to serve files the documents specified in paragraph (2), the court officer must –

(a) seal, or otherwise authenticate with the stamp of the court, the copy of the application form; and
(b) forward the documents to the Senior Master of the Queen's Bench Division.

(4) The Senior Master shall send documents forwarded under this rule –

(a) where the application form or other document is being served through the authority designated under the Service Convention, to that authority; or
(b) in any other case, to the Foreign and Commonwealth Office with a request that it arranges for the application form or other document to be served.

(5) An official certificate which –

(a) states that the method requested under paragraph (2)(a) has been performed and the date of such performance;
(b) states, where more than one method is requested under paragraph (2)(a), which method was used; and
(c) is made by –
 (i) a British Consular authority in the country where the method requested under paragraph (2)(a) was performed;
 (ii) the government or judicial authorities in that country; or
 (iii) the authority designated in respect of that country under the Service Convention,

is evidence of the facts stated in the certificate.

(6) A document purporting to be an official certificate under paragraph (5) is to be treated as such a certificate unless it is proved not to be.

Amendments—Inserted by SI 2015/548.

39G Translation of application form or other document

(1) Except where paragraphs (4) and (5) apply, every copy of the application form or other document filed under rule 39E (service through foreign governments, judicial authorities and British Consular authorities) must be accompanied by a translation of the application form or other document.

(2) The translation must be –

(a) in the official language of the country in which it is to be served; or
(b) if there is more than one official language of that country, in any official language which is appropriate to the place in the country where the application form or other document is to be served.

(3) Every translation filed under this rule must be accompanied by a statement by the person making it that it is a correct translation, and the statement must include that person's name, address and qualifications for making the translation.

(4) The applicant is not required to file a translation of the application form or other document filed under rule 39E where it is to be served in a country of which English is an official language.

(5) The applicant is not required to file a translation of the application form or other document filed under rule 39E where –

(a) the person on whom the document is to be served is able to read and understand English; and
(b) service of the document is to be effected directly on that person.

(This rule does not apply to service in accordance with the Service Regulation, which contains its own provisions about the translation of documents.)

Amendments—Inserted by SI 2015/548.

39H Undertaking to be responsible for expenses of the Foreign and Commonwealth Office

Every request for service under rule 39F (procedure where service is to be through foreign governments, judicial authorities, etc) must contain an undertaking by the person making the request –

(a) to be responsible for all expenses incurred by the Foreign and Commonwealth Office or foreign judicial authority; and .
(b) to pay those expenses to the Foreign and Commonwealth Office or foreign judicial authority on being informed of the amount.

Amendments—Inserted by SI 2015/548.

PART 7
NOTIFYING P

General requirement to notify P

40 General

(1) Subject to paragraphs (2) and (3), the rules in this Part apply where P is to be given notice of any matter or document, or is to be provided with any document, either under the Rules or in accordance with an order or direction of the court.

(2) Except where rule 41A applies, if P becomes a party, the rules in this Part do not apply and service is to be effected in accordance with Part 6 or as directed by the court.

(3) In any case the court may, either on its own initiative or on application, direct that P must not be notified of any matter or document, or provided with any document, whether in accordance with this Part or at all.

(4) Subject to paragraph (5), where P is a child –

(a) if the person to be notified under this rule is a person with parental responsibility for the child within the meaning of the Children Act 1989 or, if there is no such person, a person with whom the child resides or in whose care the child is;
(b) all references to 'P' in this Part, except that in paragraph (2), are to be read as referring to the person notified in accordance with sub-paragraph (a).

(5) Paragraph (4) does not apply, and there is no requirement to notify P, where the person referred to in paragraph (4)(a) has already been served or notified of the relevant matter in accordance with another rule or practice direction.

Amendments—SI 2015/548.

Scope of rule—This rule sets out a general obligation to notify P of any matter or document. It is supplemented by Practice Direction A. See the commentary under r 30 regarding recommendations for change to this rule made by the 2010 Rules Committee.

It should be noted that unlike r 32, there is no provision for service on a person who has parental responsibility under the Children Act 1989 where P is a child.

Rule 69 specifically provides that P must be notified in accordance with COPR 2007, Part 7 unless this requirement has been dispensed with under r 49 or where P is a party and P will be served in accordance with Part 6 (r 40(2)).

Rule 74 provides that P will be bound by any order made or directions given by the court in the same way that a party is bound.

For consideration as to whether it is appropriate for P to be a party to proceedings, see rr 3(3)(b), 5 (2)(b)(ii), 50–53, 73(4) and 85(c).

Rule 40(2)—Part 6 sets out the manner in which proceedings are served.

Rule 40(3)—For example, if notification will harm or distress P in some way. If at the outset of a case, it is believed that notice will harm P in any way, the medical practitioner who completes the assessment of capacity form (COP3) should include this information which should be brought to the Court's attention. See the commentary under rule 38 regarding the decision in *Re AB* [2014] COPLR 381 where a district judge set out guidelines to follow when considering dispensing with service and notification of P.

'**Except where rule 41A applies**'—Rule 41A provides for notification on P where a direction under r 3A is made for the appointment of a litigation friend, accredited legal representative or representative.

'**parental responsibility**'—Section 3 of the Children Act 1989 defines this as meaning 'all the rights, duties, powers, responsibilities and authority which by law a parent of a child has in relation to the child and his property'.

'**a person with whom the child resides or in whose care the child is**'—This could include relatives, foster carers and a local authority with a care order.

41 Who is to notify P

(1) Where P is to be notified under this Part, notification must be effected by –

    (a) the applicant;
    (b) the appellant (where the matter relates to an appeal);
    (c) an agent duly appointed by the applicant or the appellant; or
    (d) such other person as the court may direct.

(2) The person within paragraph (1) is referred to in this Part as 'the person effecting notification'.

'**an agent**' (r 41(1)(c))—This could include a doctor, care worker, social worker or a member of P's family. The question of notifying P is a delicate matter and the applicant must give careful consideration as to how this should be done.

41A Notifying P of appointment of a litigation friend, etc

P must be notified –

    (a) where a direction has been made under rule 3A; and
    (b) of the appointment of a litigation friend, accredited legal representative or representative on P's behalf.

Amendments—Inserted by SI 2015/548.

Circumstances in which P must be notified

42 Application forms

(1) P must be notified-

(a) that an application form has been issued by the court;
(b) that an application form has been withdrawn; and
(c) of the date on which a hearing is to be held in relation to the matter, where that hearing is for disposing of the application.

(2) Where P is to be notified that an application form has been issued, the person effecting notification must explain to P –

(a) who the applicant is;
(b) that the application raises the question of whether P lacks capacity in relation to a matter or matters, and what that means;
(c) what will happen if the court makes the order or direction that has been applied for; and
(d) where the application contains a proposal for the appointment of a person to make decisions on P's behalf in relation to the matter to which the application relates, details of who that person is.

(3) Where P is to be notified that an application form has been withdrawn, the person effecting notification must explain to P –

(a) that the application form has been withdrawn; and
(b) the consequences of that withdrawal.

(4) The person effecting notification must also inform P that he may seek advice and assistance in relation to any matter of which he is notified.

Rule 42(1)(a)—Practice Direction A, para 3 provides that an application does not include an application notice that is made under Part 10, being an application made in the course of proceedings. However, P may be notified if the applicant believes this is appropriate. The language of para (3) suggests that notice is not given before the application notice is issued but only once it is issued.

Rule 42(2)—If an agent is instructed to effect service in accordance with r 41(1)(c), the agent should be informed as to the requirements of this rule so that notice is properly given. The agent should be aware that in many cases, P will not have any understanding as to what is being said but the rule's requirements still apply. Rule 42(4) states that P should be told that he or she may take advice. The obvious criticism of this rule is that it is an onerous and/or unnecessary task to explain something to a person who may have no ability to understand the information at all. It can also be distressing for family members to comply with this requirement. Nonetheless, it is only in extreme cases that the court might consider a waiver of the notification requirement. An example could be where P would become very ill by knowing about the proceedings. If this is the case, any application to dispense with notification should contain evidence to substantiate the position. See also the commentary on rr 43 and 46.

43 Appeals

(1) P must be notified –

(a) that an appellant's notice has been issued by the court;
(b) that an appellant's notice has been withdrawn; and
(c) of the date on which a hearing is to be held in relation to the matter, where that hearing is for disposing of the appellant's notice.

(2) Where P is to be notified that an appellant's notice has been issued, the person effecting notification must explain to P –

(a) who the appellant is;
(b) the issues raised by the appeal; and
(c) what will happen if the court makes the order or direction that has been applied for.

(3) Where P is to be notified that an appellant's notice has been withdrawn, the person effecting notification must explain to P –

    (a) that the appellant's notice has been withdrawn; and
    (b) the consequences of that withdrawal.

(4) The person effecting notification must also inform P that he may seek advice and assistance in relation to any matter of which he is notified.

Rule 43(2)—Care must be taken as with r 42(2) that the person giving notice is aware of the requirements of this rule and of r 43(4).

The 2010 Rules Committee recognised that rr 42 and 43 are difficult to comply with when P has no ability to comprehend information. Instead of dispensing with notice, it suggested that the person who effects service should instead comment on the extent to which P appeared to comprehend information and this should be included in the information given in the certificate filed in accordance with r 48. So far, however, the Ad Hoc Rules Committee established in 2014 has not taken this matter further.

44 Final orders

(1) P must be notified of any decision of the court relating to P except for a case management decision.

(2) Where P is notified in accordance with this rule, the person effecting notification must explain to P the effect of the decision.

(3) The person effecting notification must also inform P that P may seek advice and assistance in relation to any matter of which P is notified.

(4) The person effecting notification must also provide P with a copy of any order relating to a decision of which P must be notified in accordance with paragraph (1).

Amendments—SI 2015/548.

'except for a case management decision'—The exception would be where a case management order also contains a declaration or other order that will affect P but which is not a case management order.

'any decision of the court'—The heading of this rule is wrong. The original rule prior to its amendment in July 2015 was that only a final order had to be notified to P. This has now been amended to any non-case management decision of the court that would include an interim order. In many cases, interim orders are made which are significant to P such as the appointment of an interim deputy to manage P's finances or an order that P may be moved from his home for a short period of time for a given purpose. The rule clearly suggests that such orders must be notified to P.

'the effect of the decision'—The manner in which an explanation is given requires thought. Consideration should be given to the need to involve carers, an IMCA, an intermediary, social worker or other professional in helping to communicate the decision. This can be crucial if the order being communicated is significant, for example where P's liberty will be restricted or where P is to live somewhere else. In more complex cases, consideration will need to be given to the effect on P of continual notification of orders. Such matters should be raised with the court at the earliest opportunity if there is likely to be a problem.

See also r 46.

45 Other matters

(1) This rule applies where the court directs that P is to be notified of any other matter.

(2) The person effecting notification must explain to P such matters as may be directed by the court.

(3) The person effecting notification must also inform P that he may seek advice and assistance in relation to any matter of which he is notified.

Note—See the commentary on rr 42 and 44, which apply here.

Manner of notification, and accompanying documents

46 Manner of notification

(1) Where P is to be notified under this Part, the person effecting notification must provide P with, or arrange for P to be provided with, the information specified in rules 41A to 45 in a way that is appropriate to P's circumstances (for example, using simple language, visual aids or any other appropriate means).

(2) The information referred to in paragraph (1) must be provided to P personally.

(3) P must be provided with the information mentioned in paragraph (1) as soon as practicable and in any event within 14 days of the date on which –

    (a) the application form or appellant's notice was issued or withdrawn;
    (b) the decision was made;
    (c) the person effecting notification received the notice of hearing from the court and in any event no later than 14 days before the date specified in the notice of the hearing; and
    (d) the order referred to in rule 44(4) was served upon the person who is required to effect notification of P under that rule,

as the case may be.

(4) Where the provisions of rule 40(4) apply, paragraphs (1) and (2) of this rule do not apply and the person effecting notification may provide information and documents of which P must be notified to the person to be notified under rule 40(4), by any method by which service of documents would be permitted under rule 31.

Amendments—SI 2015/548.

Scope of rule—In many cases, P will not be able to understand anything and the requirement of this rule may be discharged by simply telling P about the application or order in very simple terms.
    A letter is unlikely to be acceptable as P may not understand its contents.
    Every effort should be made to inform P in a way that he or she will understand. The rule gives examples such as using simple language or visual aids. It should also not be forgotten that MCA 2005 allows the Court to determine that P lacks capacity for one matter but not for another.
    For example, P may not be able to look after his or her intricate financial affairs but may have capacity to understand basic matters. P is therefore entitled to know about any application or order and for that information to be imparted to him or her in a way which he or she will understand.
    The manner of notification should be considered as soon as possible so that immediately it is required, P can be notified in a considered way.
    Notification is given on Form COP14. Form COP14A gives guidance on how to complete Form COP14.

Note—See the commentary also on rr 42 and 44.

47 Acknowledgment of notification

When P is notified that an application form or an appellant's notice has been issued, he must also be provided with a form for acknowledging notification.

Scope of rule—The acknowledgement is Form COP5. Very often P will be unable to do anything with the form. When the certificate of notification (Form COP20A) is returned to the Court, good practice suggests that the Court is informed in an accompanying letter that it is unlikely that P will return the acknowledgement. For example, it could be noted that 'I left the acknowledgement on P's bedside table but as he had no understanding of what was happening, I believe that he will do nothing with it'.

48 Certificate of notification

(1) The person effecting notification must, within 7 days beginning with the date on which notification in accordance with this Part was given, file a certificate of notification which certifies –

(a) the date on which, and how, P was notified; and
(b) that P was notified in accordance with this Part.

(2) Subject to paragraph (3), the person effecting notification in accordance with this Part must in the certificate required by paragraph (1) describe the steps taken to enable P to understand, and the extent to which P appears to have understood, the information.

(3) Where the provisions of rule 40(4) apply, paragraph (2) does not apply.

Amendments—Substituted by SI 2015/548.

Scope of rule—The certificate is Form COP20A. If notification has not been possible, r 37 provides that COP20 must be filed within 7 days of the latest date on which service should have been effected. It should be noted that until COP20 is filed, the Court often cannot take any further step in an application. It is very common for this step to be overlooked, which causes unnecessary delay.

49 Dispensing with requirement to notify, etc

(1) The applicant, the appellant or other person directed by the court to effect notification may apply to the court seeking an order –

(a) dispensing with the requirement to comply with the provisions in this Part; or
(b) requiring some other person to comply with the provisions in this Part.

(2) An application under this rule must be made in accordance with Part 10.

Scope of rule—The application is made on COP9. Practice Direction 7A, para 9 gives examples where an application may be appropriate, such as where P is in a persistent vegetative state or where notification will cause significant and disproportionate distress.

The Court will consider if dispensing with notification is in P's best interests and consistent with the overriding objective contained in r 3 which compels the Court to consider P's interests and position. However, the court does set a high threshold before it will dispense with service of an application.

See the commentary to r 38 and the reference to the decision in Re AB [2014 COPLR 381].

PART 8
PERMISSION

50 General

Subject to these Rules and to section 50(1) of, and paragraph 20 of Schedule 3 to, the Act, the applicant must apply for permission to start proceedings under the Act.

(Section 50(1) of the Act specifies persons who do not need to apply for permission. Paragraph 20 of Schedule 3 to the Act specifies an application for which permission is not needed.)

Scope of rule—This rule deals with the requirement to seek permission before making an application. It is supplemented by Practice Direction A.

MCA 2005, s 50 sets out when permission is required.

MCA 2005, s 50(1) provides that permission is not required for an application by:

(a) a person who lacks capacity;
(b) a person who has parental responsibility for a person who lacks capacity who is under 18 years;
(c) the donor of a lasting power of attorney to which the application relates;
(d) a deputy appointed by the court for a person to whom the application relates; or
(e) a person named in an existing order of the court if the application relates to that order.

MCA 2005, Sch 3, para 20(2) provides that permission is not required when an interested person applies to the Court for a declaration as to whether a protective measure taken under the law of a country outside England and Wales is to be recognised in England and Wales.

MCA 2005, s 50(2) also allows the Court's rules to expand the above categories.

The rules relating to permission were amended in July 2015. In summary, the changes are:

1. A separate permission form (COP2) is no longer required.
2. Rule 84(1)(A) requires the court to consider if permission is required when dealing with an application.
3. Permission is not required in a property and affairs case.
4. Permission is not required where the court's authorisation of a deprivation of liberty is sought.

The changes to the permission rules reflect these changes.

In NK v VW and others (2010 but reported at 2012 COPLR 105) Macur J held that when deciding whether to grant permission the court must in particular have regard to (a) the applicant's connection with the person to whom the application relates; (b) the reasons for the application; (c) the benefit to the person to whom the application relates or the proposed order or directions, and (d) whether the benefit can be achieved in any other way.

See also *LB Hillingdon v PS and CS* [2014] EWCOP 55 on the granting of permission in a personal welfare application.

Following the decision of Baker J in *G v E (Deputyship and Litigation Friend)* [2010] EWHC 2512 (COP), [2010] COPLR Con Vol 470, many applications for appointment as a personal welfare deputy were dismissed on the basis that the court held that it makes personal welfare decisions if all other options have failed and a deputy appointment should be limited in scope and duration as is reasonably practical in the circumstances. It followed that an order giving a deputy general personal welfare powers was not suitable in most situations. However, it is suggested that this approach has moved on and the appointment of personal welfare deputies should not be restricted in the way suggested *G v E*. There are many cases where for example, a parent cares for P but the parent would be better served in his or her dealings with social services or the medical professional if s/he were a personal welfare deputy as in practice, that would force the decision maker to include the parent or other carer in the decision making process.

51 Where the court's permission is not required

The permission of the court is not required –

(a) where an application is made by –
   (i) the Official Solicitor; or
   (ii) the Public Guardian;
(b) where the application concerns –
   (i) P's property and affairs;
   (ii) a lasting power of attorney which is, or purports to be, created under the Act; or
   (iii) an instrument which is, or purports to be, an enduring power of attorney;

(c) where an application is made under section 21A of the Act;
(d) where an application is made for an order under section 16(2)(a) of the Act, which is to be relied on to authorise the deprivation of P's liberty pursuant to section 4A(3) of the Act;
(e) where an application is made in accordance with Part 10;
(f) where a person files an acknowledgment of service or notification in accordance with this Part or Part 9, for any order proposed that is different from that sought by the applicant; or
(g) in any other case specified for this purpose in a practice direction.

Amendments—Substituted by SI 2015/548.

52 (*revoked*)

53 Permission – supplementary

(1) (*revoked*)

(2) Where part of the application concerns a matter which requires permission, and part of it does not, permission need only be sought for that part of it which requires permission.

Amendments—SI 2015/548.

54 Application for permission

Where permission is required, the applicant must apply for permission when making an application.

> (Rule 84(1A) explains how the court will deal with an application for permission.)

Amendments—Substituted by SI 2015/548.

55–58 (*revoked*)

59 Service of an order giving or refusing permission

The court must serve –
(a) the order granting or refusing permission;
(b) if refusing permission without a hearing, the reasons for its decision in summary form; and
(c) any directions,

on the applicant and on any other person served with or notified of the application form.

Amendments—SI 2015/548.

60 Appeal against a permission decision following a hearing

Where the court grants or refuses permission following a hearing, any appeal against the permission decision shall be dealt with in accordance with Part 20 (appeals).

(Rule 89 deals with reconsideration of orders and decisions made without a hearing or without notice to any person who is affected by such order or decision.)

Amendments—SI 2015/548.

PART 9
HOW TO START PROCEEDINGS

Initial steps

61 General

(1) Applications to the court to start proceedings shall be made in accordance with this Part and, as applicable, Part 8 and the relevant practice directions.

(2) The appropriate forms must be used in the cases to which they apply, with such variations as the case requires, but not so as to omit any information or guidance which any form gives to the intended recipient.

(3) (*revoked*)

Amendments—SI 2015/548.

Rule 61(1)—Part 8 sets out the procedure where permission is required to commence an application.

Rule 61(2)—New forms were introduced in July 2015. The basic form for most applications is COP1. There are also accompanying forms that provide extra information called Annex forms. Annex A is used to give supporting information for property and affairs applications; Annex B is for personal welfare applications; Annex C for applications concerning statutory wills, codicils, settlements, deeds of variation and gifts; Annex D for applications to appoint or discharge a trustee; Annex E for applications by an existing deputy or attorney; Annex F for applications concerning the validity or operation of an EPA or LPA.

The forms for objecting to registration of an LPA are LPA006, LPA007 and LPA008. Objection to registration of an EPA is on form EPA3PG.

Out-of-hours medical treatment applications—In *Sandwell and West Birmingham Hospitals NHS Trust v CD and Others* [2014] EWCOP 23, [2014] COPLR 650, Theis J set out guidelines to be followed in out-of-hours medical treatment cases. These included: making suitable and sensitive arrangements for the parents to participate in the hearing (joining a hearing in the waiting room in the hospital was not appropriate); alerting the Official Solicitor with sufficient time to get a direction from the court for him to be invited to act for P; the court is there to assist in applications and the urgent applications judge and so the Clerk of the Rules should be alerted at the earliest opportunity; a Word version of the draft order should be available so amendments can be made promptly; the statement in support should have information regarding the history or quality of P's life. Identical considerations apply in applications under the inherent jurisdiction.

62 When proceedings are started

(1) The general rule is that proceedings are started when the court issues an application form at the request of the applicant.

(2) An application form is issued on the date entered on the application form by the court.

63 Contents of the application form

The application form must –

(a) state the matter which the applicant wants the court to decide;
(b) state the order which the applicant is seeking;
(c) name –
  (i) the applicant;
  (ii) P;
  (iii) as a respondent, any person (other than P) whom the applicant reasonably believes to have an interest which means that he ought to be heard in relation to the application (as opposed to being notified of it in accordance with rule 70); and
  (iv) any person whom the applicant intends to notify in accordance with rule 70; and
(d) if the applicant is applying in a representative capacity, state what that capacity is.

Rule 63(c)(iii)—See for example PD9F paragraph 9. This rule also needs to be read in conjunction with PD9A paragraph 2 which repeats the rule and PD9B.

64 Documents to be filed with the application form

When an applicant files his application form with the court, he must also file –
(a) in accordance with the relevant practice direction, any evidence upon which he intends to rely;
(b) ...
(c) an assessment of capacity form, where this is required by the relevant practice direction;
(d) any other documents referred to in the application form; and
(e) such other information and material as may be set out in a practice direction.

Amendments—SI 2015/548.

The application form—Care is required to ensure that the correct forms are filed at Court when making an application and also that the forms are completed properly. Much time can be lost by using an obsolete form as it will be rejected by the court or not providing full information.

Evidence—This should be in Form COP24.

Contents of the application form—Rule 63 sets out the basic requirements of the contents of the application form. Rule 64 sets out the documents that must be filed with the application form.

Practice Direction A, paras 2–8 contain further requirements as to the contents of the application form.

Certain applications also have their own specific requirements:

(1) Practice Direction 9D deals with certain applications by deputies, attorneys or donors which are listed at paras 4 and 5. Paragraph 8 deals with the contents of the application form.
(2) Practice Direction 9F deals with applications relating to statutory wills and codicils, settlements and other dealings with P's property which are listed at paras 2–4. Paragraph 6 sets out the information that must be given when an application is made.
(3) Practice Direction 9G deals with applications to appoint or discharge a trustee as listed at paras 2 and 3. Paragraphs 5, 8 and 9 set out the required information when an application is made.
(4) Practice Direction 9H deals with applications relating to the registration of an enduring power of attorney as listed at para 2. Paragraphs 6–8 deal with the form of application.

The following rules are also connected:

(1) Rule 10 provides that the Court must seal the application form.
(2) Rule 15 contains provisions where a party does not wish to reveal personal details.
(3) The provisions of rr 16 and 17 which allow others to seek copies of court documents.

(4) Rule 18 restricts the use of documents filed at Court outside of the proceedings.

An application relating to deprivation of liberty is governed by its own rules and practice direction: see Part 10A and the DOLS practice direction. This sets out the requirements for such an application.

What is filed at Court—Practice Direction A, paras 9–12 set out what has to be filed with the application form.

Procedural Guides 1–4 set out which documents are filed when making an application which will vary depending on the application.

Assessment of capacity form—This is Form COP3, although in some cases a medical report may suffice. This is common in applications that follow a personal injury or clinical negligence action where those proceedings produce medical evidence that is not out of date. There should not be an objection, therefore, to the use of that material provided to address the issue of capacity specific to the application being made.

If it is not possible to file the assessment of capacity form (COP3), Practice Direction A, para 14 provides that a witness statement must be filed with the application explaining why it has not been possible to obtain an assessment of capacity, what attempts have been made to obtain the assessment and why the applicant knows or believes that P lacks capacity.

Care should be taken to ensure that COP3 is completed be an appropriate person. In some cases, issues of capacity are complex and only an appropriate medical practitioner should sign the form. Where a social worker is used, his qualifications to assess capacity should be stated. Given that a finding that P lacks capacity will disenfranchise P in proceedings, the court will be concerned that the capacity evidence is the best possible.

Rule 63(c)(iii)—See the commentary on r 70 regarding notification.

See also r 54 and its commentary.

65 What the court will do when an application form is filed

As soon as practicable after an application form is filed the court must issue it and do anything else that may be set out in a practice direction.

Amendments—Substituted by SI 2015/548.

Issue of application—Rule 65 provides that the court must issue an application form when it is received. In practice, this means that once issued, the application is placed before a judge to address the issue of permission rather than permission being considered first and only then the application being issued as occurred prior to the amendment to this rule in July 2015.

Steps following issue of application form

66 Applicant to serve the application form on named respondents

(1) As soon as practicable and in any event within 14 days of the date on which the application form was issued, the applicant must serve a copy of the application form on any person who is named as a respondent in the application form, together with copies of any documents filed in accordance with rule 64 and a form for acknowledging service.

(2) The applicant must file a certificate of service within 7 days beginning with the date on which the documents were served.

Amendments—SI 2015/548.

Rule 66(1)—The time limit under this rule was changed in July 2015 to 14 days together with similar changes in other rules. It was felt by the Ad Hoc Rules Committee that the standard time of 21 days to carry out basic steps was the cause of delay to applications.

Rule 66(2)—The certificate of service is Form COP20.

67 Applications relating to lasting powers of attorney

(1) Where the application concerns the powers of the court under section 22 or 23 of the Act (powers of the court in relation to the validity and operation of lasting powers of attorney) the applicant must serve a copy of the application form, together with copies of any documents filed in accordance with rule 64 and a form for acknowledging service –

    (a) unless the applicant is the donor or donee of the lasting power of attorney ('the power'), on the donor and every donee of the power;
    (b) if he is the donor, on every donee of the power; and
    (c) if he is a donee, on the donor and any other donee of the power,

but only if the above-mentioned persons have not been served or notified under any other rule.

(2) Where the application is solely in respect of an objection to the registration of a power, the requirements of rules 66 and 70 do not apply to an application made under this rule by –

    (a) a donee of the power; or
    (b) a person named in a statement made by the donor of the power in accordance with paragraph 2(1)(c)(i) of Schedule 1 to the Act.

(3) The applicant must comply with paragraph (1) as soon as practicable and in any event within 14 days of date on which the application form was issued.

(4) The applicant must file a certificate of service within 7 days beginning with the date on which the documents were served.

(5) Where the applicant knows or has reasonable grounds to believe that the donor of the power lacks capacity to make a decision in relation to any matter that is the subject of the application, he must notify the donor in accordance with Part 7.

Amendments—SI 2015/548.

Rule 67(1)—This rule contains specific provisions for service of the application when it relates to a lasting power of attorney.

MCA 2005, ss 22 and 23 allow the Court to determine questions relating to lasting powers of attorney.

Rule 67(4)—Form COP20.

68 Applications relating to enduring powers of attorney

(1) Where the application concerns the powers of the court under paragraphs 2(9), 4(5)(a) and (b), 7(2), 10(c), 13, or 16(2), (3), (4) and (6) of Schedule 4 to the Act, the applicant must serve a copy of the application form, together with copies of any documents filed in accordance with rule 64 and a form for acknowledging service –

    (a) unless the applicant is the donor or attorney under the enduring power of attorney ('the power'), on the donor and every attorney of the power;
    (b) if he is the donor, on every attorney under the power; or
    (c) if he is an attorney, on the donor and any other attorney under the power,

but only if the above-mentioned persons have not been served or notified under any other rule.

(2) Where the application is solely in respect of an objection to the registration of a power, the requirements of rules 66 and 70 do not apply to an application made under this rule by –

    (a)   an attorney under the power; or
    (b)   a person listed in paragraph 6(1) of Schedule 4 to the Act.

(3) The applicant must comply with paragraph (1) as soon as practicable and in any event within 14 days of the date on which the application form was issued.

(4) The applicant must file a certificate of service within 7 days beginning with the date on which the documents were served.

(5) Where the applicant knows or has reasonable grounds to believe that the donor of the power lacks capacity to make a decision in relation to any matter that is the subject of the application, he must notify the donor in accordance with Part 7.

Amendments—SI 2015/548.

Rule 68(1)—This rule applies to specific paragraphs in MCA 2005, Sch 4, namely:

  (1) para 2(9): revocation of an enduring power of attorney;
  (2) para 4(5)(a) and (b): referral to the Court any question as to the validity of the power;
  (3) para 7(2): application to dispense with notice of registration;
  (4) para 10(c): provisions relating to notice of registration to the donor;
  (5) para 13: registration by the Public Guardian and the Court's powers; and
  (6) para 16(2), (3), (4) and (6): determining questions relating to the enduring power of attorney and cancelling registration.

Rule 68(3)—The time limit has been reduced by amendment from 21 days to 14 days.

Rule 68(4)—Form COP20.

69 Applicant to notify P of an application

P must be notified in accordance with Part 7 that an application form has been issued, unless the requirement to do so has been dispensed with under rule 49.

70 Applicant to notify other persons of an application

(1) As soon as practicable and in any event within 14 days of the date on which the application form was issued, the applicant must notify the persons specified in the relevant practice direction –

    (a)   that an application form has been issued;
    (b)   whether it relates to the exercise of the court's jurisdiction in relation to P's property and affairs, or his personal welfare, or to both; and
    (c)   of the order or orders sought.

(2) Notification of the issue of the application form must be accompanied by a form for acknowledging notification.

(3) The applicant must file a certificate of notification within 7 days beginning with the date on which notification was given.

Amendments—SI 2015/548.

Rule 70(1)—Practice Direction B deals with notification. Notice is given by Form COP15. Notification should be given to:

  (1) The respondent to the application.

(2) At least three people who have an interest in being notified.
(3) Members of P's family who are likely to have an interest (see in particular para 7 of the Practice Direction).
(4) Other persons set out in the Practice Direction, for example, an NHS Trust responsible for P's care (see para 10 of the Practice Direction).

The Practice Direction Contains a presumption of notification (see paras 7 and 10) although para 6 sets out circumstances when the presumption may be displaced.

In cases where the applicant contends that notification should not be given, paras 9 and 11 provide that the application form must contain evidence to explain why the person or body is not notified.

'**As soon as practicable**'—The 14 days period in r 70(1) was introduced in July 2015, although in some cases the Court may need to direct that notification takes place in an even shorter period.

Although not binding, there are some decisions under the old rules which may assist.

In *Re B (Court of Protection: Notice of Proceedings)* [1987] 2 FLR 155 Millett J (as he then was) considered an application by a Receiver for guidance as to who should be notified of an application.

The Receiver was concerned that certain relatives would indulge in what Millett J described as 'mutual mud-slinging and exacerbate the existing family divisions' such that the Receiver believed that notification of proceedings should be dispensed with to avoid bitterness and hostility. Millett J referred to this 'as the price which has to be paid if a dispute is to be resolved by judicial means'. He refused to dispense with notification on this ground alone.

Re Davey (Deceased) [1981] 1 WLR 164 concerned an application for a statutory will. P was 92 years old and in poor health. Unbeknown to P's family, P had recently married an employee of the care home where she resided. The marriage revoked an earlier will of P. The deputy master dispensed with notice of the application to P's husband and made an order in the same terms as the will that had been revoked by P's marriage. He did so on the basis that due to P's health and age, the matter was urgent; if P died before the court made a final order it would not be possible to challenge the validity of the will and the estate would devolve on intestacy to the husband; the marriage was suspicious and if P died, the husband could still challenge the will under the Inheritance (Provisions for Family and Dependents) Act 1975. Fox J upheld the deputy master's decision. Indeed, P died a few days after execution of the statutory will.

See also *Re AB* [2014] COPLR 381 and the commentary in rr 38 and 40.

Rule 70(2)—See Form COP5.

Rule 70(3)—See Form COP20.

71 Requirements for certain applications

A practice direction may make additional or different provision in relation to specified applications.

Scope of rules—Rules 66–70 essentially deal with service and notification of applications by the applicant to others.

Rule 71 allows a Practice Direction to make 'additional or different provision in relation to specified applications'. Since the court will often require more specific information to enable it to properly consider certain applications, this rule allows for a practice direction to ensure that particular documents or information are filed at the start of a case. Thus, Practice Directions 9D to 9H set out specific requirements for certain named applications. See also the Practice Direction for deprivation of liberty applications at Part 10A.

In *A Local Authority v K and Others* [2013] EWHC 242 (COP), [2013] COPLR 194, Cobb J emphasised the need for a referral to the Court of Protection in a case of non-therapeutic sterilisation as quickly as possible. The judgment also highlights steps to be taken by reference to PD 9E. The following points are of note:

1. The decision of someone who lacks capacity to consent in such a case of non-therapeutic sterilisation is a question involving 'serious medical treatment'.
2. The issue should be 'brought to the court' as provided for at paragraph 5 of Practice Direction 9E
3. The proposed applicant should discuss the application with the Official Solicitor's department before the application is made: such cases should be addressed to a family and medical litigation lawyer at the Office of the Official Solicitor

4. The organisation that will provide clinical or caring services to P should normally be named as a respondent
5. At the first hearing, the court will decide whether P should be joined as a party; whether the Official Solicitor should be invited to act as litigation friend or some other person; identify anyone else who has been notified of the proceedings and who has filed an acknowledgment of service and applied to be joined as a party and set a timetable for the proceedings.
6. The hearing will generally be in public although the court will make a reporting restriction order.

Responding to an application

72 Responding to an application

(1) A person who is served with or notified of an application form and who wishes to take part in proceedings must file an acknowledgment of service or notification in accordance with this rule.

(2) The acknowledgment of service or notification must be filed not more than 14 days after the application form was served or notification of the application was given.

(3) The court will serve the acknowledgment of service or notification on the applicant and on any other person who has filed such an acknowledgment.

(4) The acknowledgment of service or notification must –

(a) state whether the person acknowledging service or notification consents to the application;
(b) state whether he opposes the application and, if so, set out the grounds for doing so;
(c) state whether he seeks a different order from that set out in the application form and, if so, set out what that order is;
(d) provide an address for service, which must be within the jurisdiction of the court; and
(e) be signed by him or his legal representative.

(5) Subject to rules 120 and 123 (restriction on filing an expert's report and court's power to restrict expert evidence), unless the court directs otherwise, where a person who has been served in accordance with rule 66, 67 or 68 opposes the application or seeks a different order, that person must within 28 days of such service file a witness statement containing any evidence upon which that person intends to rely.

(6) In addition to complying with the other requirements of this rule, an acknowledgment of notification filed by a person notified of the application in accordance with rule 67(5), 68(5), 69 or 70 must –

(a) indicate whether the person wishes to be joined as a party to the proceedings; and
(b) state the person's interest in the proceedings.

(7) Subject to rules 120 and 123 (restriction on filing an expert's report and court's power to restrict expert evidence), unless the court directs otherwise, where a person has been notified in accordance with rule 67(5), 68(5), 69, 70, that person must within 28 days of such service file a witness statement containing any evidence of his interest in the proceedings and, if he opposes the application or seeks a different order, any evidence upon which he intends to rely.

(8) The court will consider whether to join a person mentioned in paragraph (6) as a party to the proceedings and, if it decides to do so, will make an order to that effect.

(9) Where a person who is notified in accordance with rule 67(5), 68(5), 69 or 70 complies with the requirements of this rule, he need not comply with the requirements of rule 75 (application to be joined as a party).

(10) *(revoked)*

(11) A practice direction may make provision about responding to applications.

Amendments—SI 2015/548.

Rule 72(1)—Acknowledgement is on Form COP5.
The effect of filing COP5 is that if the person served was named as a respondent, he or she becomes a party (r 73(1)(b) and Practice Direction 9C, para 3).
If COP5 is filed to acknowledge notification, this can be considered as an application to be a party (r 72(6) and Practice Direction 9C, para 4).
If a person is not served with or notified of an application, he or she must apply to be a party by making an application under Part 10.
Practice Direction 9C contains rules at paras 6–13 about signing Form COP5 and the address for service on the form.
If the name of the person served or notified is incorrect, this should be noted on Form COP5. For example, if John Smith is referred to as John Brown, the form should state 'John Smith described as John Brown' (Practice Direction 9C, para 14).
The acknowledgment cannot be amended without a formal application under Part 10 seeking the Court's permission to do so.

Rule 72(2): 'not more than 14 days'—This suggests that if someone wishes to file COP 5 after the expiration of 21 days, an application on COP9 is required and the court will need to make a specific order. The 14 days period was introduced by amendment to the rules in July 2015.

Rule 72(3)—Even though the person is not a party, by filing COP 5 he would be entitled to see COP 5's filed by others whether or not they are parties.

'seeks a different order' (r 72(4)(c))—Rule 51(4) provides that permission is not required if a different order is required.

'witness statement' (r 72(5))—This rule follows the general rule in r 97.
Rule 99(1) states that a witness statement is a written statement which contains the evidence which the person would be allowed to give orally.
It must contain a statement of truth (r 100). Without one, r 13 provides that it is not admissible in evidence unless the Court permits.
Part 14, Practice Direction 14A, paras 33–50 set out the main requirements of a witness statement.

Rule 72(7)—See the comments on r 72(5) concerning witness statements.

Rule 72(8)—Rule 5(2)(b)(ii) contains the obligation of the Court when managing a case to consider who should be a party. See also the commentary to r 73. It is assumed that this rule does not apply to a person covered by r 73(1).

Rule 72(11)—This is the basis for Practice Direction C.

The parties to the proceedings

73 Parties to the proceedings

(1) Unless the court otherwise directs, the parties to any proceedings are –

    (a) the applicant; and
    (b) any person who is named as a respondent in the application form and who files an acknowledgment of service in respect of the application form.

(2) The court may order a person to be joined as a party if it considers that it is desirable to do so for the purpose of dealing with the application.

(3) The court may at any time direct that any person who is a party to the proceedings is to be removed as a party.

(4) Unless the court orders otherwise, P shall not be named as a respondent to any proceedings.

(5) A party to the proceedings is bound by any order or direction of the court made in the course of those proceedings.

Rule 73(1)—This would appear to be an automatic consequence of filing COP5. See also rule 72(8) and rule 78(3).

Rule 73(2)—The Court will consider whether P is joined as a party. The effect of r 73(4) is that P is not named as a respondent unless the Court permits.

Rule 73(2) and (4)—The rules provide that P is not automatically a party. However, there has been considerable debate about whether P should automatically be a party. This rule should be read in conjunction with r 3A, which obliges the court to consider P's position. See the commentary there.

For people other than P, in the context of a statutory will case decided under pre-MCA law, in *Re HMF* [1976] Ch 33 Goulding J offered some guidance on the question of who should be a respondent, namely:

(1) consideration should be given to the best interests of P;
(2) the Court should consider what course will enable the Court to exercise its jurisdiction properly;
(3) where an application is made for a statutory will, it is better for the legatees under a previous will to be brought before the Court rather than be represented by the Attorney-General;
(4) the need to maintain confidentiality of P's affairs must cede to the necessity of the Court to act fairly in exercising its powers;
(5) the fact that individual charities joined as parties may result in a process of bargaining or unseemly contention was not a factor to justify the Attorney-General representing the charities who were legatees under a previous will of P; and
(6) there may be cases of emergency where the Court would feel that it ought to proceed without any representation of a previous interest at all.

See *Re SK (By his litigation friend the Official Solicitor)* [2012] EWHC 1990 (COP), [2012] COPLR 712, which is discussed in the commentary to rr 75(1) and 3(3)(a).

In personal welfare cases, key members of P's family may also have such a direct interest in the case that they should be joined as a party. Some argue that they could simply be given permission to intervene; however, the lack of party status could inhibit the grant of legal aid and restrict the documents they can access in the case.

74 Persons to be bound as if parties

(1) The persons mentioned in paragraph (2) shall be bound by any order made or directions given by the court in the same way that a party to the proceedings is so bound.

(2) The persons referred to in paragraph (1) are –

(a) P; and
(b) any person who has been served with or notified of an application form in accordance with these Rules.

Rule 74(2)—The effect of this rule is that if a person is notified of an application but not joined as a party, he or she will be bound by the Court's order.

75 Application to be joined as a party

(1) Any person with sufficient interest may apply to the court to be joined as a party to the proceedings.

(2) An application to be joined as a party must be made by filing an application notice in accordance with Part 10 which must –

- (a) state the full name and address of the person seeking to be joined as a party to the proceedings;
- (b) state his interest in the proceedings;
- (c) state whether he consents to the application;
- (d) state whether he opposes the application and, if so, set out the grounds for doing so;
- (e) state whether he proposes that an order different from that set out in the application form should be made and, if so, set out what that order is;
- (f) provide an address for service, which must be within the jurisdiction of the court; and
- (g) be signed by him or his legal representative.

(3) Subject to rules 120 and 123 (restriction on filing an expert's report and court's power to restrict expert evidence), an application to be joined must be accompanied by –

- (a) a witness statement containing evidence of his interest in the proceedings and, if he proposes that an order different from that set out in the application form should be made, the evidence on which he intends to rely; and
- (b) a sufficient number of copies of the application notice to enable service of the application on every other party to the proceedings.

(4) The court will serve the application notice and any accompanying documents on all parties to the proceedings.

(5) The court will consider whether to join a person applying under this rule as a party to the proceedings and, if it decides to do so, will make an order to that effect.

'**with sufficient interest**' (r 75 (1))—In *Re SK (By his litigation friend the Official Solicitor)* [2012] EWHC 1990 (COP), [2012] COPLR 712 Bodey J held that sufficient interest should be interpreted to mean 'a sufficient interest in the proceedings' as distinct from some commercial interest of the applicant's own.

'An applicant for joinder who or which does not have a an interest in the ascertainment of the incapacitated person's best interests is unlikely to be a person with sufficient interest. The clear import of the wording in r 73(2) is that the joinder of such an applicant would be to enable the court better to deal with the substantive application. The word "desirable" necessarily imports a judicial decision as regards balancing the pros and cons of the particular joinder sought in the particular circumstances of the case'.

The decision in *Re SK* was approved by Munby P in *Re G (Adult); London Borough of Redbridge v G and others* [2014] EWCOP 1361, [2014] COPLR 416 where an application by the media to be joined was referred to as 'misconceived' on the basis that they were no more than an 'officious bystander'.

76 Applications for removal as a party to proceedings

A person who wishes to be removed as a party to the proceedings must apply to the court for an order to that effect in accordance with Part 10.

PART 10
APPLICATIONS WITHIN PROCEEDINGS

77 Types of applications for which the Part 10 procedure may be used

(1) The Part 10 procedure is the procedure set out in this Part.

(2) The Part 10 procedure may be used if the application is made by any person –

   (a) in the course of existing proceedings; or
   (b) as provided for in a rule or practice direction.

(3) The court may grant an interim remedy before an application form has been issued only if –

   (a) the matter is urgent; or
   (b) it is otherwise necessary to do so in the interests of justice.

(4) An application made during the course of existing proceedings includes an application made during appeal proceedings.

(5) Where the application seeks solely to withdraw an existing application –

   (a) the applicant must file a written request for permission setting out succinctly the reasons for the request;
   (b) the request must be in an application notice;
   (c) the court may permit an application to be made orally at a hearing or in such alternative written form as it thinks fit.

(6) Where the court deals with a written request under paragraph (5) without a hearing, rule 89 applies to any order so made.

(Rule 87A requires the court's permission to withdraw proceedings.)

Amendments—SI 2015/548.

Scope of rule—This rule deals with applications made to the Court. It is supplemented by Practice Directions A and B.

Practice Directions—Practice Direction A deals with applications made within proceedings. Practice Direction B deals with urgent applications.

Application—An application can be by telephone or by video conference (Practice Direction A, paras 18–21).

Consent—If a consent order is filed for approval, the parties must ensure the Court has all the necessary material to allow it to approve the order. Consent to an order may be by letter. If a hearing is to be vacated as a consequence of the consent order, the Court should be informed as soon as the matter is compromised (Practice Direction A, paras 22 and 23).

Rule 77(5) and (6)—This is a new requirement introduced in July 2015 through r 87A. The court's approach to an application to withdraw should be based on whether it is in P's best interests to allow the application rather than the wishes of the others, especially if P is not a party.

78 Application notice to be filed

(1) Subject to paragraph (5), the applicant must file an application notice to make an application under this Part.

(2) The applicant must, when he files the application notice, file the evidence upon which he relies (unless such evidence has already been filed).

(3) The court will issue the application notice and, if there is to be a hearing, give notice of the date on which the matter is to be heard by the court.

(4) Notice under paragraph (3) must be given to –
   (a) the applicant;
   (b) anyone who is named as a respondent in the application notice (if not otherwise a party to the proceedings);
   (c) every party to the proceedings; and
   (d) any other person, as the court may direct.

(5) An applicant may make an application under this Part without filing an application notice if –
   (a) this is permitted by any rule or practice direction; or
   (b) the court dispenses with the requirement for an application notice.

(6) If the applicant makes an application without giving notice, the evidence in support of the application must state why notice has not been given.

Rule 78(1)—The application is made on Form COP9.

Rule 78(2)—The evidence should be filed using Form COP24.

Rule 78(3)—If no hearing date is listed, the court will not notify the parties and the applicant must serve the application: see r 80.

Rule 78(5)(b)—For example, an application is made during the course of a hearing or by letter and the Court treats the letter as a formal application.

79 What an application notice must include

An application notice must state –
   (a) what order or direction the applicant is seeking;
   (b) briefly, the grounds on which the applicant is seeking the order or direction; and
   (c) such other information as may be required by any rule or a practice direction.

Practice Direction—Practice Direction 10A sets out further requirements of the application notice.
   If the order required is unusually long or complex, a disk containing the draft order should be made available to the Court. The practitioner is also expected to ensure that the disk will be compatible with the Court's software (Practice Direction 10A, para 4).
   The evidence in support of the application must set out all the facts on which the applicant relies and of which the Court should be made aware (Practice Direction 10A, para 7).

80 Service of an application notice

(1) Subject to paragraphs (4) and (5), the applicant must serve a copy of the application notice on –
   (a) anyone who is named as a respondent in the application notice (if not otherwise a party to the proceedings);
   (b) every party to the proceedings; and
   (c) any other person, as the court may direct,

as soon as practicable and in any event within 21 days of the date on which it was issued.

(2) The application notice must be accompanied by a copy of the evidence filed in support.

(3) The applicant must file a certificate of service within 7 days beginning with the date on which the documents were served.

(4) This rule does not require a copy of evidence to be served on a person upon whom it has already been served, but the applicant must in such a case give to that person notice of the evidence upon which he intends to rely.

(5) An application may be made without serving a copy of the application notice if this is permitted by –

    (a) a rule;
    (b) a practice direction; or
    (c) the court.

Rule 80(1)—Practice Direction 10A, para 9 sets out the circumstances where an application may be made without service of the application notice.

The evidence in support of the application must say why service was not effected (Practice Direction 10A, para 10).

However, the Court retains the overall discretion to decide if service should be effected or not (see Practice Direction 10A, para 11).

Rule 80(3)—Form COP20.

81 Applications without notice

(1) This rule applies where the court has dealt with an application which was made without notice having been given to any person.

(2) Where the court makes an order, whether granting or dismissing the application, the applicant must, as soon as practicable or within such period as the court may direct, serve the documents mentioned in paragraph (3) on –

    (a) anyone named as a respondent in the application notice (if not otherwise a party to the proceedings);
    (b) every party to the proceedings; and
    (c) any other person, as the court may direct.

(3) The documents referred to in paragraph (2) are –

    (a) a copy of the application notice;
    (b) the court's order; and
    (c) any evidence filed in support of the application.

(Rule 89 provides for reconsideration of orders made without a hearing or without notice to a person.)

Rule 81(1)—The requirements for notice being given of an application are contained in Practice Direction 10A, para 13.

There is no requirement to file a certificate of service in Form COP20.

81A Security for costs

(1) A respondent to any application may apply for security for the respondent's costs of the proceedings.

(2) An application for security for costs must be supported by written evidence.

(3) Where the court makes an order for security for costs, it must –

 (a) determine the amount of security; and
 (b) direct –
  (i) the manner in which; and
  (ii) the time within which,

the security must be given.

Amendments—Inserted by SI 2015/548.

81B Conditions to be satisfied

(1) The court may make an order for security for costs under rule 81A –

 (a) if it is satisfied, having regard to all the circumstances of the case, that it is just to make such an order; and
 (b) if –
  (i) one or more of the conditions in paragraph (2) applies; or
  (ii) an enactment permits the court to require security for costs.

(2) The conditions are –

 (a) the applicant is –
  (i) resident out of the jurisdiction; but
  (ii) not resident in a Brussels Contracting State, a State bound by the Lugano Convention or a Regulation State, as defined in section 1(3) of the Civil Jurisdiction and Judgments Act 1982;
 (b) the applicant is a company or other body (whether incorporated inside or outside Great Britain) and there is reason to believe that it will be unable to pay the respondent's costs if ordered to do so;
 (c) the applicant has changed address since proceedings were commenced with a view to avoiding the consequences of the litigation;
 (d) the applicant failed to give an address, or gave an incorrect address, in the application form commencing the proceedings;
 (e) the applicant is acting as a nominal applicant and there is reason to believe that the applicant will be unable to pay the respondent's costs if ordered to do so;
 (f) the applicant has taken steps in relation to the applicant's assets that would make it difficult to enforce an order for costs against the applicant.

Amendments—Inserted by SI 2015/548.

81C Security for costs other than from the applicant

(1) The respondent may seek an order against a person other than the applicant, and the court may make an order for security for costs against that person, if –

 (a) it is satisfied, having regard to all the circumstances of the case, that it is just to make such an order; and
 (b) one or more of the conditions in paragraph (2) applies.

(2) The conditions are that the person –

 (a) has assigned the right to the substantive matter to the applicant with a view to avoiding the possibility of a costs order being made against the person; or

(b) has contributed or agreed to contribute to the applicant's costs in return for a share of any money or property which the applicant may recover or be awarded in the proceedings; and

is a person against whom a costs order may be made.

(Rule 166 makes provision about costs orders against non-parties.)

Amendments—Inserted by SI 2015/548.

81D Security for costs of an appeal

(1) The court may order security for costs of an appeal against –

(a) an appellant;
(b) a respondent who also appeals,

on the same grounds as it may order security for costs against an applicant under rule 81A.

(2) The court may also make an order under paragraph (1) where the appellant or the respondent who also appeals is a limited company and there is reason to believe it will be unable to pay the costs of the other parties to the appeal should its appeal be unsuccessful.

Amendments—Inserted by SI 2015/548.

Note—It is likely that an application for security for costs will be rare in the Court of Protection. They are modelled on the CPR. Similar provisions have also been incorporated into the FPR.

However, some situations may justify an application under these provisions; for example, an applicant in a personal welfare application who disputes the position taken by P's family and the local authority and brings an application that is clearly misconceived or likely to fail.

Interim Remedies

82 Orders for interim remedies

(1) The court may grant the following interim remedies –

(a) an interim injunction;
(b) an interim declaration; or
(c) any other interim order it considers appropriate.

(2) Unless the court orders otherwise, a person on whom an application form is served under Part 9, or who is given notice of such an application, may not apply for an interim remedy before he has filed an acknowledgment of service or notification in accordance with Part 9.

(3) This rule does not limit any other power of the court to grant interim relief.

Practice Direction—Practice Direction 10B amplifies this rule. The following should be noted:

(1) The respondent should be informed unless justice would be defeated by so doing (para 5).
(2) A further hearing will be ordered to fully consider the matter (para 6).
(3) If the order sought is unusually long or complex, a disk should be provided for the Court's use (para 7).
(4) In exceptional cases, an oral application may be made without issue of an application notice (para 9).
(5) An urgent hearing may be by telephone (para 11).

An injunction may be varied by another judge (para 16).

PART 10A
DEPRIVATION OF LIBERTY

82A The practice direction to this Part sets out procedure governing –

(a) applications to the court for orders relating to the deprivation, or proposed deprivation, of liberty of P; and
(b) proceedings (for example, relating to costs or appeals) connected with or consequent upon such applications.

Amendment—Part 10A inserted by Court of Protection (Amendment) Rules 2009, SI 2009/582.

'Practice Direction'—This rule is supplemented by Practice Direction 10AA, which deals with deprivation of liberty applications. It is divided into two parts. Part 1 is for applications under s 21A, which have their own forms and procedure, and Part 2 is for applications under s 16(2) and what is known as the streamlined procedure.

Following the decision in *P v Cheshire West and Chester Council* [2014] UKSC 19, [2014] COPLR 313, it was clear that a new streamlined deprivation of liberty procedure needed to be introduced to the court. A hearing was convened by the President of the Court of Protection to discuss issues concerned with a new scheme. This resulted in two decisions of Munby P, namely *Re X and others (Deprivation of Liberty)* 2014 EWCOP 25, [2014] COPLR 674 *and Re X and others (Deprivation of Liberty) (Number 2)* [2014] EWCOP 37. What then followed was a new Practice Direction 10AA, which dealt with deprivation of liberty and which also sets out a new streamlined procedure to cater for certain cases. The new procedure came into force in November 2014.

Meanwhile, aspects of the decisions in *Re X* were appealed to the Court of Appeal. The Court of Appeal's decision in *Re X (Court of Protection Practice)* [2015] EWCA Civ 599, [2015] COPLR 582 came as a surprise because the Court decided that it had no jurisdiction to entertain an appeal from the decisions made by Munby P in *Re X*. However, they indicated, in what were regarded as strong obiter remarks, that their view was that P should be a party in such proceedings.

The Court of Appeal's decision, therefore, derailed the *Re X* procedure that was set up under this rule because a feature of it was that P was not a party. Rule 3A had been introduced in April 2015 but that was not considered by the Court of Appeal so the question then arose as to whether the view of the Court of Appeal about P's involvement in a case could still be met by P not being a party given the provisions of r 3A. The issues that arose are set out in *Re MOD (Deprivation of Liberty)* [2015] EWCOP 47, where the court referred the issue of P's involvement in the *Re X* procedure to the Vice-President for consideration. The decision of Charles J in *Re NRA and Others* [2015] EWCOP 59, [2015] COPLR 690 deals with the various issues, although there is still further litigation in other cases before Charles J.

The position now is that following *Re NRA*, steps are being taken to amend the *Re X* application form and this work is ongoing. The *Re X* procedure is therefore still in a state of flux.

PART 11
HUMAN RIGHTS

83 General

(1) A party who seeks to rely upon any provision of or right arising under the Human Rights Act 1998 ('the 1998 Act') or who seeks a remedy available under that Act must inform the court in the manner set out in the relevant practice direction specifying –

(a) the Convention right (within the meaning of the 1998 Act) which it is alleged has been infringed and details of the alleged infringement; and
(b) the remedy sought and whether this includes a declaration of incompatibility under section 4 of the 1998 Act.

(2) The court may not make a declaration of incompatibility unless 21 days' notice, or such other period of notice as the court directs, has been given to the Crown.

(3) Where notice has been given to the Crown, a Minister or other person permitted by the 1998 Act will be joined as a party on filing an application in accordance with rule 75 (application to be joined as a party).

'**Practice Direction**'—This rule is supplemented by Practice Direction 11A.
A claim under Part 11 will be heard by a High Court judge, the Chancellor or the President of the Family Division (Practice Direction A, para 9 and Part 12, Practice Direction A, para 3(b)).
In practice, if such a claim is issued, a resident judge at the Court of Protection will immediately transfer the case to a High Court judge who will give directions and deal with the case thereafter.

Rule 83(1)—Practice Direction A provides that the claim is made on:

(1) COP1 if it is part of an application;
(2) COP5 if the claim is made in response to an application;
(3) COP9 if the claim is made during the course of proceedings;
(4) COP35 or COP36 if raised on an appeal.

PART 12
DEALING WITH APPLICATIONS

84 Dealing with the application

(1) As soon as practicable after any application has been issued the court shall consider how to deal with it.

(1A) Where permission to start proceedings is required, and whether or not it has been applied for, the court's consideration under paragraph (1) shall include whether to grant or refuse permission without a hearing, or to direct a hearing to consider whether permission should be granted.

(2) The court may deal with an application or any part of an application at a hearing or without a hearing.

(3) In considering whether it is necessary to hold a hearing, the court shall, as appropriate, have regard to –

(a) the nature of the proceedings and the orders sought;
(b) whether the application is opposed by a person who appears to the court to have an interest in matters relating to P's best interests;
(c) whether the application involves a substantial dispute of fact;
(d) the complexity of the facts and the law;
(e) any wider public interest in the proceedings;
(f) the circumstances of P and of any party, in particular as to whether their rights would be adequately protected if a hearing were not held;
(g) whether the parties agree that the court should dispose of the application without a hearing; and
(h) any other matter specified in the relevant practice direction.

(4) Where the court considers that a hearing is necessary, it will –

(a) give notice of the hearing date to the parties and to any other person it directs; and
(b) state what is to be dealt with at the hearing, including whether the matter is to be disposed of at that hearing.

(5) Where the court decides that it can deal with the matter without a hearing it will do so and serve a copy of its order on the parties and on any other person it directs.

Amendments—SI 2015/548.

Rule 84(1)—The application will be placed before a judge who will consider what directions or orders should be made. Sometimes, the application may not be given to the judge until time for notification or service has elapsed and Form COP20 is filed or time for acknowledging service has expired, on the basis that prior to these stages in the proceedings, no step can be taken. Given the volume of work being processed at the court, if an application needs to be processed quickly for good reason, the practitioner should inform the court by letter of the need for expedition or consider arranging a short hearing for the judge to deal with matters.

'As soon as practicable'—This is not defined anywhere.

Rule 84(1A)—This rule was introduced in July 2015 when the Rules were amended to dispense with the need for a separate form seeking permission. Now, an application is issued and given to a judge who will decide whether or not to grant permission.

Rule 84(2)—The Court's practice is to aim to deal with an application solely on paper unless a hearing is necessary.

Rule 84(3)—For the court's approach on these matters, see the commentary on rr 3, 5 and 25.

85 Directions

(1) The court may –

  (a) give directions in writing; or
  (b) set a date for a directions hearing; and
  (c) do anything else that may be set out in a practice direction.

(2) When giving directions, the court may do any of the following –

  (a) require a report under section 49 of the Act and give directions as to any such report;
  (b) give directions as to any requirements contained in these Rules or a practice direction for the giving of notification to any person or for that person to do anything in response to a notification;
  (c), (d) …
  (e) if the court considers that any other person or persons should be a party to the proceedings, give directions joining them as a party;
  (f) if the court considers that any party to the proceedings should not be a party, give directions for that person's removal as a party;
  (g) give directions for the management of the case and set a timetable for the steps to be taken between the giving of directions and the hearing;
  (h) subject to rule 86, give directions as to the type of judge who is to hear the case;
  (i) give directions as to whether the proceedings or any part of them are to be heard in public, or as to whether any particular person should be permitted to attend the hearing, or as to whether any publication of the proceedings is to be permitted;
  (j) give directions as to the disclosure of documents, service of witness statements and any expert evidence;
  (k) give directions as to the attendance of witnesses and as to whether, and the extent to which, cross-examination will be permitted at any hearing; and
  (l) give such other directions as the court thinks fit.

(3) The court may give directions at any time –

  (a) on its own initiative; or
  (b) on the application of a party.

(4) Subject to paragraphs (5) and (6) and unless these Rules or a practice direction provide otherwise or the court directs otherwise, the time specified by a rule or by the court for a person to do any act may be varied by the written agreement of the parties.

(5) A party must apply to the court if he wishes to vary –

(a) the date the court has fixed for the final hearing; or
(b) the period within which the final hearing is to take place.

(6) The time specified by a rule or practice direction or by the court may not be varied by the parties if the variation would make it necessary to vary the date the court has fixed for any hearing or the period within which the final hearing is to take place.

(Participation of P in proceedings is addressed in rule 3A (participation of P) and Part 17 (litigation friends and rule 3A representatives).)

Amendments—SI 2015/548.

Rule 85(1)—When deciding whether to order a hearing, the Court will consider the matters in r 84(3) together with rr 3(3) and 5(2).

In respect of a matter involving serious medical treatment, Part 9, Practice Direction 9E, para 13 anticipates that there will be a first directions hearing. Paragraphs 14 and 15 set out the matters that will be considered.

Rule 85(2)(c)—See the commentary to r 73(2).

Allocation of proceedings

86 Court's jurisdiction in certain kinds of case to be exercised by certain judges

(1) A practice direction made under this rule may specify certain categories of case to be dealt with by a specific judge or a specific class of judges.

(2) Applications in any matter other than those specified in the practice direction referred to in paragraph (1) may be dealt with by any judge.

Amendments—Substituted by SI 2015/548.

Note—This rule was completely amended in July 2015 to reflect the fact that more classes of judge can now be nominated to sit in the Court of Protection as a result of the Crime and Courts Act 2013.

'Practice Direction'—This rule is supplemented by Practice Direction 12A, which provides that certain applications must be heard by certain judges. Reference should also be made to Practice Direction 9E.

Disputing the jurisdiction of the court

87 Procedure for disputing the court's jurisdiction

(1) A person who wishes to –

(a) dispute the court's jurisdiction to hear an application; or
(b) argue that the court should not exercise its jurisdiction,

may apply to the court at any time for an order declaring that it has no such jurisdiction or should not exercise any jurisdiction that it may have.

(2) An application under this rule must be –

(a) made by using the form specified in the relevant practice direction; and
(b) supported by evidence.

(3) An order containing a declaration that the court has no jurisdiction or will not exercise its jurisdiction may also make further provision, including –

(a) setting aside the application;
(b) discharging any order made;
(c) staying the proceedings;
(d) discharging any litigation friend, accredited legal representative or representative.

Amendments—SI 2015/548.

'Practice Direction'—This rule is supplemented by Practice Direction 12B. The application is made in accordance with Part 9 on Form COP9 or on the acknowledgement in Form COP5. This rule should also be read with r 148 which applies where P ceases to lack capacity. Strangely, Part 12, Practice Direction 12B deals with such an application which should be made on Form COP9 and be supported by evidence.

87A Permission required to withdraw proceedings

(1) Proceedings may only be withdrawn with the permission of the court.

(2) An application to withdraw proceedings must be made in accordance with Part 10.

Amendments—Inserted by SI 2015/548.

Rule 77(5) and (6)—This is a new requirement introduced in July 2015. The Court's approach to an application to withdraw should be based on whether it is in P's best interests to allow the application rather than the wishes of the others, especially if P is not a party.

Participation in hearings

88 Participation in hearings

(1) The court may hear P on the question of whether or not an order should be made, whether or not he is a party to the proceedings.

(2) The court may proceed with a hearing in the absence of P if it considers that it would be appropriate to do so.

(3) A person other than P who is served with or notified of the application may only take part in a hearing if –

(a) he files an acknowledgment in accordance with the Rules and is made a party to the proceedings; or
(b) the court permits.

(Rule 3A deals with participation of P.)

Amendments—SI 2015/548.

Rule 88(1)—See *London Borough of Redbridge v G, C and F* [2014] EWHC 485 (COP), [2014] COPLR 292 where Russell J provided for P to be present throughout the hearing.

The introduction of r 3A means that the role of P in the proceedings must be considered in every case.

Reconsideration of court orders

89 Orders made without a hearing or without notice to any person

(1) This rule applies where the court makes an order –

    (a) without a hearing; or

    (b) without notice to any person who is affected by it.

(2) Where this rule applies –

    (a) P;

    (b) any party to the proceedings; or

    (c) any other person affected by the order,

may apply to the court for reconsideration of the order made.

(3) An application under paragraph (2) must be made –

    (a) within 21 days of the order being served or such other period as the court may direct; and

    (b) in accordance with Part 10.

(4) The court will –

    (a) reconsider the order without directing a hearing; or

    (b) fix a date for the matter to be heard, and notify all parties to the proceedings and such other persons as the court may direct, of that date.

(5) Where an application is made in accordance with this rule, the court may affirm, set aside or vary any order made.

(6) An order made by a court officer authorised under rule 7A may be reconsidered by any judge.

(6A) An order made by a Tier 1 Judge may be reconsidered by any judge.

(6B) An order made by a Tier 2 Judge may be reconsidered by any Tier 2 Judge or by a Tier 3 Judge.

(6C) An order made by a Tier 3 Judge may be reconsidered by any Tier 3 Judge.

(6D) In any case to which paragraphs (6A) to (6C) apply the reconsideration may be carried out by the judge who made the order being reconsidered.

(7) No application may be made seeking a reconsideration of –

    (a) an order that has been made under paragraph (5); or

    (b) an order granting or refusing permission to appeal.

(8) An appeal against an order made under paragraph (5) may be made in accordance with Part 20 (appeals).

(9) Any order made without a hearing or without notice to any person, other than one made under paragraph (5) or one granting or refusing permission to appeal, must contain a statement of the right to apply for a reconsideration of the decision in accordance with this rule.

(10) An application made under this rule may include a request that the court reconsider the matter at a hearing.

    (Rule 7A(2)(c) provides that a court officer authorised under that rule may not deal with an application for the reconsideration of an order made by that court officer or another court officer.)

Amendments—SI 2015/548.

Note—The purpose of a reconsideration is set out in *Re S and S (Protected Persons)* [2008] COPLR Con Vol 1074. It is not an appeal. The court wishes to reach decisions quickly, conveniently and cost effectively whilst allowing a person affected by its decision to have his views fully taken into account. Dealing with a matter on paper will lead to a speedy decision but a party may ask for that decision to be reconsidered.

On a reconsideration, the court will look at the matter afresh and not on the basis of whether there is a justifiable attack on the order.

This decision was approved by Senior Judge Lush in *Re MRJ (Reconsideration of an order)* [2014] EWHC B15 (COP).

Rules 6-6D clearly set out who can reconsider an order. The rule is clear that the judge who made the order does not have to deal with the reconsideration.

PART 13
HEARINGS

Private hearings

90 General rule – hearing to be in private

(1) The general rule is that a hearing is to be held in private.

(2) A private hearing is a hearing which only the following persons are entitled to attend –

(a) the parties;
(b) P (whether or not a party);
(c) any person acting in the proceedings as a litigation friend;
(d) any legal representative of a person specified in any of sub-paragraphs (a) to (c); and
(e) any court officer.

(3) In relation to a private hearing, the court may make an order –

(a) authorising any person, or class of persons, to attend the hearing or a part of it; or
(b) excluding any person, or class of persons, from attending the hearing or a part of it.

Introduction—On 12 July 2013, the President of the Court of Protection issued a paper called: 'Transparency in the Family Courts and the Court of Protection'. This document started the debate about transparency in the Court of Protection. The intention of the document was to 'bring about an immediate and significant change in practice in relation to the publication of judgments ... in order to improve public understanding of the court process and confidence in the court system'.

On 16 January 2014, formal Guidance was issued that imposed a mandatory requirement that certain judgments of circuit judges and High Court judges be published.

This has led to more public awareness of the court's work. Furthermore, many practitioners have found judgments of the Senior Judge that deal with property and affairs matters to be very useful. District judges have also been encouraged to report their decisions to allow the public to gain a greater awareness of the Court's daily work.

The Ad Hoc Rules Committee considered this issue and, in November 2015, a transparency pilot scheme to be implemented through r 9A was published that began in January 2016 (see the Practice Direction set out after PD13B).

The effect of this pilot is that the default position will be that most hearings will be in public, subject to an order being made restricting the publication of details of the case. A draft order has also been published. However, until the pilot starts, Pt 13 will continue to apply. Openness is now the starting position and unless the pilot scheme fails for whatever reasons, it seems likely that it will be made permanent.

Rule 90(1)—A hearing will be in private. Rule 90(2) sets out who may attend.

Prior to the implementation of this rule, there was some debate as to whether the hearing should be in public or private, some favouring more openness. However, the rules committee finally settled on a presumption that a hearing will be in private unless it is ordered otherwise.

A private hearing prima facie does not contravene the European Convention for the Protection of Human Rights and Fundamental Freedoms 1950, Art 6, which is incorporated into law through the Human Rights Act 1998 (see *R v Bow County Court ex parte*).

For some years, however, the debate about transparency has continued and the pilot referred to above, if successful, is likely to be implemented and the rules changed accordingly.

Publication of information about proceedings in private could amount to contempt of court. Thus, without permission, there can be no lawful publication of information about a case (see Practice Direction A, paras 7 and 8).

Rules 90, 91 and 92 allow the Court to order to displace the rule of privacy.

Rule 90(3)(a) and (b)—For example, the press, certain relatives or interested groups.

Post-death of P anonymity—*Press Association v Newcastle-Upon-Tyne Hospitals Foundation Trust* [2014] EWCOP 6, [2014] COPLR 502 considers the court's jurisdiction to restrict reporting after P's death of information gathered during proceedings in P's lifetime. Peter Jackson J upheld the general principle that P's death means that P no longer has any need for the special protection afforded by anonymity to the extent that it conveys that, at least in the eyes of the law, a dead person cannot be affected by what is said about them. However, this does not mean that protection required in life is automatically lost on death. There are a number of considerations that may make it necessary and proportionate to continue to uphold after death the privacy that existed in lifetime. Two of these are medical confidentiality, where the death of the patient does not entitle the doctor to publish her medical records and the interests of justice, which require that people should not be deterred from approaching the court out of fear that any privacy will automatically lapse on death. He also said that there is a need to treat the rights of those who are subject to public and private hearings with consistency. The COP Rules must be read conformably with the court's obligations under the Human Rights Act 1998.

Bundles—See the practice direction PD13B on court bundles.

91 Court's general power to authorise publication of information about proceedings

(1) For the purposes of the law relating to contempt of court, information relating to proceedings held in private (whether or not contained in a document filed with the court) may be communicated in accordance with paragraph (2) or (2A).

(2) The court may make an order authorising –

  (a) the publication or communication of such information or material relating to the proceedings as it may specify; or
  (b) the publication of the text or a summary of the whole or part of a judgment or order made by the court.

(2A) Subject to any direction of the court, information referred to in paragraph (1) may be communicated in accordance with Practice Direction 13A.

(3) Where the court makes an order under paragraph (2) it may do so on such terms as it thinks fit, and in particular may –

  (a) impose restrictions on the publication of the identity of –
    (i) any party;
    (ii) P (whether or not a party);
    (iii) any witness; or
    (iv) any other person;
  (b) prohibit the publication of any information that may lead to any such person being identified;

(c) prohibit the further publication of any information relating to the proceedings from such date as the court may specify; or

(d) impose such other restrictions on the publication of information relating to the proceedings as the court may specify.

(4) The court may on its own initiative or upon request authorise communication –

(a) for the purposes set out in Practice Direction 13A; or
(b) for such other purposes as it considers appropriate,

of information held by it.

Amendments—SI 2015/548.

Scope of rule—The rule was amended in July 2015 to bring the rule into line with the Family Court and communication of information about proceedings. PD13B has been amended and paras 33–38 should be read together with this rule.

Anonymity—In *Re DP; The Public Guardian v JM* [2014] EWCOP 7, the media applied for an order permitting the identification of JM who was found at an earlier hearing to have not acted in P's best interests such that the court revoked a power of attorney granted to him. Munby P held that it is not the role of the court to exercise editorial control over the media and if JM was treated unfairly by the media, he had his remedies elsewhere. Comment and criticism may be ill-informed and based on misunderstanding or misrepresentation of the facts but the fear of criticism, however unjustified, is not of itself a justification for prior restraint by injunction. The court would ultimately balance the rights of the parties.

Reporting Restriction Order—See *A Healthcare NHS Trust v P (By His Litigation Friend the Official Solicitor) and Q* [2015] EWCOP 15 (Fam), [2015] COPLR 147, where it was held that P's identity could be revealed to the Injunctions Alert Service, although it would be a breach of confidence to publish P's identity prior to the court's determination of the application for reporting restrictions.

Power to order a public hearing

92 Court's power to order that a hearing be held in public

(1) The court may make an order –

(a) for a hearing to be held in public;
(b) for a part of a hearing to be held in public; or
(c) excluding any person, or class of persons, from attending a public hearing or a part of it.

(2) Where the court makes an order under paragraph (1), it may in the same order or by a subsequent order –

(a) impose restrictions on the publication of the identity of –
  (i) any party;
  (ii) P (whether or not a party);
  (iii) any witness; or
  (iv) any other person;
(b) prohibit the publication of any information that may lead to any such person being identified;
(c) prohibit the further publication of any information relating to the proceedings from such date as the court may specify; or
(d) impose such other restrictions on the publication of information relating to the proceedings as the court may specify.

Scope of rule—This rule allows waiver of the rule that a hearing must be in private. It also allows the court to restrict the publication of information in respect of a case heard in public.

In *A Local Authority v K and Others* [2013] EWHC 242 (COP), [2013] COPLR 194 in a case involving considering of non-therapeutic sterilisation of P, Cobb J stated that such a hearing would generally be in public given the nature of the application although the court would ordinarily make an order pursuant to r 92 to impose restrictions in relation to the publication of information about the proceedings. Cobb J held that such proceedings came under the heading of serious medical treatment which leaves open the suggestion that other categories of case under this heading are also likely to be heard in public.

Supplementary

93 Supplementary provisions relating to public or private hearings

(1) An order under rule 90, 91 or 92 may be made –

 (a) only where it appears to the court that there is good reason for making the order;
 (b) at any time; and
 (c) either on the court's own initiative or on an application made by any person in accordance with Part 10.

(2) A practice direction may make further provision in connection with –

 (a) private hearings;
 (b) public hearings; or
 (c) the publication of information about any proceedings.

Scope of rule—This rule sets out the test for determining an application under rr 90, 91 and 92.

Rule 93(1)(a) provides that there has to be a good reason for making the order.

In *Independent News and Media Limited v A* [2009] EWHC 2858, [2009] COPLR Con Vol 702, Hedley J considered this rule in connection with an application by the media under r 91. He held that the court needs to adopt a two-stage approach. The first stage is to consider whether 'good reason' can be established. He described this as a gatekeeping test and 'necessarily of a somewhat summary nature'. If no good reason can be found, that is the end of the matter. If good reason is found, this will not automatically entitle an applicant to an order. Instead, it obligates the court to undertake the exercise applied in *Re S (A Child) (Identification: Restrictions on Publication)* [2004] UKHL 47, [2005] 1 FLR 591.

In *Re S*, Lord Steyn considered the interplay between Arts 8 and 10 of the European Convention on Human Rights and set out four propositions.

The first is that neither article has precedence over the other. Second, where the values under the two articles are in conflict, an 'intense focus' on the comparative importance of the specific rights being claimed in the individual case is necessary. Third, the justification for interfering with or restricting each right must be taken into account. Fourth, the proportionality test must be applied to each. Lord Steyn called this the ultimate balancing test.

As there is no statutory commentary on the meaning of 'good reason', Hedley J held that it should be given its ordinary meaning. He also stated that 'real weight' had to be given to r 90(1) and the general rule that matters were dealt with in private and 'real value' must be given to the concept of good reason before the court acts otherwise than in accordance with the general rule.

In this case, Hedley J held that the applicant media organisations had demonstrated good reason; first, all of the issues in the case were within the public domain and the issues they addressed were readily apparent; second, the court was equipped with powers to preserve privacy whilst addressing the issues in the case and third, the court's decision would have major implications for the future welfare of A and it was in the public interest that there should be understanding of the jurisdiction and powers of the court and how they are exercised. Accordingly, Hedley J allowed the media to attend the proceedings but in all other respects, the proceedings would remain private. He also allowed some reporting of the case.

Hedley J's decision was appealed ([2010] EWCA Civ 343) and save for the issue of when Article 10 of the European Convention of Human Rights was engaged, the decision was upheld.

With regard to 'good reason' in r 93, the Court of Appeal said that '… We do not propose to rewrite the words 'good reason'. They mean what, taken together, they say …' They also said that even when good reason appears, there may be better reason to refuse authorization of publicity. The Court of Appeal also endorsed the two stage approach to be undertaken before making an order. First, whether there is good reason and if so, whether the requisite balancing exercise justified the making of the order. When considering the issues raised by rr 90, 91 and 92, the following additional matters may also be relevant:

(1) The need to prevent disclosure of private and confidential information relating to P or others.
(2) Whether information relating to the mental or physical condition of P should be in the public domain.
(3) The effect of publicity on P's family and others connected with P.
(4) The effect and any distress suffered by P, his or her family or those connected with P due to a public hearing.
(5) The inability of P to respond to public debate or media comment due to his or her lack of capacity.
(6) Any loss of dignity to P.
(7) The effect of publicity on any medical or care team, residential unit or service.
(8) Whether the public interest be satisfied by anonymised court reporting of any judgment or of the proceedings
(9) Whether the need for a public hearing will cause delay to the proceedings
(10) Whether the matter or issue is already in the public domain.

When considering an application, the aim should be to protect P rather than to confer anonymity on other individuals and organisations (Practice Direction 13A, para 27). See *Cheshire West & Chester Council v P and M* [2011] EWHC 1330 (Fam), [2011] COPLR Con Vol 273 where Baker J held that the public interest in holding public authorities accountable for the actions of their employees amounted to a good reason for publishing the judgment in an anonymised format but authorising the name of the local authority to be published.

An order may include restrictions on identifying specified family members, carers, doctors or organisations where the absence of such a restriction is likely to prejudice their ability to care for P or where their identification might lead to identifying P and defeat the purpose of the order.

See *W v M and S (Reporting Restriction Order)* [2011] EWHC 1197 (COP), [2011] COPLR Con Vol 1205 where Baker J held that neither Article 8 nor Article 10 of the European Convention of Human Rights had automatic precedence over the other and a balancing exercise had to be undertaken between the competing rights when consider reporting restrictions.

In *Hillingdon LBC v Neary* [2011] EWHC 413 (COP), [2011] COPLR Con Vol 677, Peter Jackson J referred to the cumulative effect of (a) the genuine public interest in the work of the court being understood (b) the allegation that the rights of P and his father had been seriously prejudiced for a prolonged period by the local authority and (c) the considerable prior public airing of the issues in the case including the naming of the parties established a good reason to exercise the court's power to allow publication.

The ability of the media to participate in Court of Protection cases need not be limited to cases involving extraordinary individuals; when considering whether good reason had been shown, the question was not whether the individual was exceptional but whether the issue was one of genuine public interest (see *Hillingdon LBC v Neary*).

An application under rr 90, 91 or 92 must be made on Form COP9 using the Part 10 procedure.

Rule 25(2)(h) allows the Court to deal with an application under this rule as a discrete issue and Part 13, Practice Direction 13A, para 6 calls on the Court to consider doing so. Delay in deciding the substantive issue in a case may call upon the court to consider not dealing with a media application as a discrete issue.

The order should last for no longer than is necessary to achieve the purpose for which it was made. However, in some cases, it may need to last until P's death or even a later date (see Practice Direction A, para 29).

See *P v Independent Print Ltd and Others* [2011] EWCA Civ 756, [2012] COPLR 110: it is not for the Court of Appeal to give guidance on how urgent media applications should be managed at an early stage in the Court of Protection. It is for the President and judges of the Family Division to establish proper practice and the best way to cope with unexpected applications made under rules 90 to 93.

Practice Direction—Practice Direction 13A, Part 2 sets out the circumstances where notice may need to be given to the national media and the procedural route to follow.

PART 14
ADMISSIONS, EVIDENCE AND DEPOSITIONS

Admissions

94 Making an admission

(1) Without prejudice to the ability to make an admission in any other way, a party may admit the truth of the whole or part of another party's case by giving notice in writing.

(2) The court may allow a party to amend or withdraw an admission.

Evidence

95 Power of court to control evidence

The court may –
  (a) control the evidence by giving directions as to –
    (i) the issues on which it requires evidence;
    (ii) the nature of the evidence which it requires to decide those issues; and
    (iii) the way in which the evidence is to be placed before the court;
  (b) use its power under this rule to exclude evidence that would otherwise be admissible;
  (c) allow or limit cross-examination;
  (d) admit such evidence, whether written or oral, as it thinks fit; and
  (e) admit, accept and act upon such information, whether oral or written, from P, any protected party or any person who lacks competence to give evidence, as the court considers sufficient, although not given on oath and whether or not it would be admissible in a court of law apart from this rule.

Amendments—SI 2015/548.

Note—The importance of this rule cannot be overstated. In order to ensure that cases are dealt with in a proportionate and cost-effective manner, the court must control the evidence. This means that it needs to consider what evidence is necessary in a case and only allow that evidence. Unlike the CPR, which places civil claims into tracks that reflect the value, difficulty or seriousness of a case, these Rules do not have such a system and instead depend on the court in each case taking a robust view of what evidence is needed to justly and fairly dispose of the case. The lack of a tracking system makes sense given the diverse nature of the Court's work.

Rule 95(e)—This rule was implemented in July 2015 and includes the situation dealt with under a previous version of the rules in *Enfield LBC v SA, FA and KA* [2010] EWHC 196 (Admin), [2010] COPLR Con Vol 362 where it was held that rule 95(d) allowed the Court to admit hearsay evidence that originated from a person who was not competent as a witness and which would otherwise be inadmissible under section 5 of the Civil Evidence Act 1995.

See also *AVS v NHS Foundation Trust* [2010] EWHC 2746 (COP), [2010] COPLR Con Vol 237, which gives an insight into the court's approach under this rule.

96 Evidence of witnesses – general rule

(1) The general rule is that any fact which needs to be proved by evidence of a witness is to be proved –
  (a) where there is a final hearing, by their oral evidence; or
  (b) at any other hearing, or if there is no hearing, by their evidence in writing.

(2) Where a witness is called to give oral evidence under paragraph (1)(a), his witness statement shall stand as his evidence in chief unless the court directs otherwise.

(3) A witness giving oral evidence at the final hearing may, if the court permits –
  (a) amplify his witness statement; and
  (b) give evidence in relation to new matters which have arisen since the witness statement was made.

(4) The court may so permit only if it considers that there is good reason not to confine the evidence of the witness to the contents of his witness statement.

(5) This rule is subject to –
  (a) any provision to the contrary in these Rules or elsewhere; or
  (b) any order or direction of the court.

Rule 96(4)—A good reason will include consideration of P's best interests and the overriding objective. In some cases, evidence from family members outside what is in their statement may help the court gain a greater understanding of their position or that of P. Each case will depend on its own facts and circumstances.

97 Written evidence – general rule

A party may not rely upon written evidence unless –
  (a) it has been filed in accordance with these Rules or a practice direction;
  (b) it is expressly permitted by these Rules or a practice direction; or
  (c) the court gives permission.

Rule 97(c)—Rule 99 provides that the Court will order when witness statements have to be filed for the final hearing of a case. However, if a party wants to adduce further evidence, it will require permission under this rule.

When considering whether to give permission, the Court will consider P's best interests, the overriding objective and the general interests of justice. In all cases, the Court will need to have full information to allow it to reach a fair decision. It is not uncommon for practitioners to assume that the Court will accede to the request to adduce late evidence as a matter of course. This is not correct. The absence of proper reasons may result in evidence not being admitted.

P's interests will also include considering the costs consequences of any delay or adjournment to a hearing.

98 Evidence by video link or other means

The court may allow a witness to give evidence through a video link or by other communication technology.

'Practice Direction'—Practice Direction A, Annex 2 sets out rules for video conferences.

99 Service of witness statements for use at final hearing

(1) A witness statement is a written statement which contains the evidence which that person would be allowed to give orally.

(2) The court will give directions about the service of any witness statement that a party intends to rely upon at the final hearing.

(3) The court may give directions as to the order in which witness statements are to be served.

(Rules 11 and 100 require witness statements to be verified by a statement of truth.)

100 Form of witness statement

A witness statement must contain a statement of truth and comply with the requirements set out in the relevant practice direction.

'Practice Direction'—Practice Direction 14A, paras 33–45 set out the format of the witness statement.
The witness statement must be included in or attached to Form COP24 which is the witness statement designed for use in the Court of Protection.
The statement should be in the witness's own words and should ideally follow the chronological sequence of the events or matters dealt with, and each paragraph should be confined to a distinct portion of the subject (Practice Direction 14A, paras 35 and 42). This requirement is taken from the CPR.
An exhibit should be verified and identified by the witness and remain separate from the witness statement.

101 Witness summaries

(1) A party who wishes to file a witness statement for use at final hearing, but is unable to do so, may apply, without notice, to be permitted to file a witness summary instead.

(2) A witness summary is a summary of –

(a) the evidence, if known, which would otherwise be included in a witness statement; or
(b) if the evidence is not known, the matters about which the party filing the witness summary proposes to question the witness.

(3) Unless the court directs otherwise, a witness summary must include the name and address of the intended witness.

(4) Unless the court directs otherwise, a witness summary must be filed within the period in which a witness statement would have had to be filed.

(5) Where a party files a witness summary, so far as practicable, rules 96(3)(a) (amplifying witness statements) and 99 (service of witness statements for use at a final hearing) shall apply to the summary.

102 Affidavit evidence

Evidence must be given by affidavit instead of or in addition to a witness statement if this is required by the court, a provision contained in any rule, a practice direction or any other enactment.

103 Form of affidavit

An affidavit must comply with the requirements set out in the relevant practice direction.

'Practice Direction'—Practice Direction 14A, paras 1–19 contain the rules relating to the format of affidavits and other general matters. Paragraphs 20–31 set out the rules relating to exhibits. Paragraph 32 allows an affirmation instead of an affidavit.

104 Affidavit made outside the jurisdiction

A person may make an affidavit outside the jurisdiction in accordance with –

(a) this Part; or
(b) the law of the place where he makes the affidavit.

105 Notarial acts and instruments

A notarial act or instrument may, without further proof, be received in evidence as duly authenticated in accordance with the requirements of law unless the contrary is proved.

106 Summoning of witnesses

(1) The court may allow or direct any party to issue a witness summons requiring the person named in it to attend before the court and give oral evidence or produce any document to the court.

(2) An application by a party for the issue of a witness summons may be made by filing an application notice which includes –

(a) the name and address of the applicant and of his solicitor, if any;
(b) the name, address and occupation of the proposed witness;
(c) particulars of any document which the proposed witness is to be required to produce; and
(d) the grounds on which the application is made.

(3) The general rule is that a witness summons is binding if it is served at least 7 days before the date on which the witness is required to attend before the court, and the requirements of paragraph (6) have been complied with.

(4) The court may direct that a witness summons shall be binding although it will be served less than 7 days before the date on which the witness is required to attend before the court.

(5) Unless the court directs otherwise, a witness summons is to be served by the person making the application.

(6) At the time of service the witness must be offered or paid –

(a) a sum reasonably sufficient to cover his expenses in travelling to and from the court; and
(b) such sum by way of compensation for loss of time as may be specified in the relevant practice direction.

(7) The court may order that the witness is to be paid such general costs as it considers appropriate.

Rule 106(2)—Practice Direction 14D sets out the rules relating to witness summonses.
The application for a witness summons will be made on Form COP9 and Part 10 will apply.

Rule 106(6)—The sum paid is calculated by reference to the sums payable to witnesses attending the Crown Court which is the same basis as payment under the CPR (Practice Direction 14D, para 9). The sums payable are fixed pursuant to the Prosecution of Offenders Act 1985 and the Costs in Criminal Cases (General) Regulations 1986, SI 1986/1335. The amount for an ordinary witness (as opposed to an expert or professional witness) for a period not exceeding 4 hours is £29.75 and exceeding 4 hours is £59.50. Subsistence allowance starts at £2.25 for a period not exceeding 5 hours.

107 Power of court to direct a party to provide information

(1) Where a party has access to information which is not reasonably available to the other party, the court may direct that party to prepare and file a document recording the information.

(2) The court will give directions about serving a copy of that document on the other parties.

'Practice Direction'—This rule is supplemented by Practice Direction 14A, para 54.

Depositions

108 Evidence by deposition

(1) A party may apply for an order for a person to be examined before the hearing takes place.

(2) A person from whom evidence is to be obtained following an order under this rule is referred to as a 'deponent' and the evidence is referred to as a 'deposition'.

(3) An order under this rule shall be for a deponent to be examined on oath before –

(a) a circuit judge or a district judge, whether or not nominated as a judge of the court;
(b) an examiner of the court; or
(c) such other person as the court appoints.

(4) The order may require the production of any document which the court considers is necessary for the purposes of the examination.

(5) The order will state the date, time and place of the examination.

(6) At the time of service of the order, the deponent must be offered or paid –

(a) a sum reasonably sufficient to cover his expenses in travelling to and from the place of examination; and
(b) such sum by way of compensation for loss of time as may be specified in the relevant practice direction.

(7) Where the court makes an order for a deposition to be taken, it may also order the party who obtained the order to file a witness statement or witness summary in relation to the evidence to be given by the person to be examined.

Rule 108(1)—Practice Direction 14B contains further rules about depositions. The application is made on Form COP9 and may be made without notice.

109 Conduct of examination

(1) Subject to any directions contained in the order for examination, the examination must be conducted in the same way as if the witness were giving evidence at a final hearing.

(2) If all the parties are present, the examiner may conduct the examination of a person not named in the order for examination if all the parties and the person to be examined consent.

(3) The examiner must ensure that the evidence given by the witness is recorded in full.

(4) The examiner must send a copy of the deposition –

    (a) to the person who obtained the order for the examination of the witness; and
    (b) to the court.

(5) The court will give directions as to the service of a copy of the deposition on the other parties.

110 Fees and expenses of examiners of the court

(1) An examiner of the court may charge a fee for the examination and he need not send the deposition to the court until the fee is paid, unless the court directs otherwise.

(2) The examiner's fees and expenses must be paid by the party who obtained the order for examination.

(3) If the fees and expenses due to an examiner are not paid within a reasonable time, he may report that fact to the court.

(4) The court may order the party who obtained the order for examination to deposit in the court office a specified sum in respect of the examiner's fees and, where it does so, the examiner will not be asked to act until the sum has been deposited.

(5) An order under this rule does not affect any decision as to the person who is ultimately to bear the costs of the examination.

'Practice Direction'—Practice Direction C supplements this rule.

Rule 110(3) contains a provision for the examiner to report non-payment of his fee to the court. It is assumed that the court would then make an order that the fee be paid and if this were not obeyed, it could be treated as a contempt of court. Alternatively, the court might order that if not paid, judgment could be entered in the County or High Court for the sum claimed. It is unlikely that the Court of Protection itself has power to grant a judgment as its power comes from MCA 2005 and although s 47 grants it the same powers as the High Court, it states that those powers are 'in connection with its jurisdiction' only.

111 Examiners of the court

(1) The Lord Chancellor shall appoint persons to be examiners of the court.

(2) The persons appointed shall be barristers or solicitor-advocates who have been practising for a period of not less than 3 years.

(3) The Lord Chancellor may revoke an appointment at any time.

(4) In addition to appointing persons in accordance with this rule, examiners appointed under rule 34.15 of the Civil Procedure Rules 1998 may act as examiners in the court.

112 Enforcing attendance of a witness

(1) If a person served with an order to attend before an examiner –

    (a) fails to attend; or
    (b) refuses to be sworn for the purpose of the examination or to answer any lawful question or produce any document at the examination,

a certificate of his failure or refusal, signed by the examiner, must be filed by the party requiring the deposition.

(2) On the certificate being filed, the party requiring the deposition may apply to the court for an order requiring that person to attend or to be sworn or to answer any question or produce any document, as the case may be.

(3) An application for an order under this rule may be made without notice.

(4) The court may order the person against whom an order is sought or made under this rule to pay any costs resulting from his failure or refusal.

113 Use of deposition at a hearing

(1) A deposition ordered under rule 108, 115 or 116 may be put in evidence at a hearing unless the court orders otherwise.

(2) A party intending to put a deposition in evidence at a hearing must file notice of his intention to do so on the court and serve the notice on every other party.

(3) Unless the court directs otherwise, he must file the notice at least 14 days before the day fixed for the hearing.

(4) The court may require a deponent to attend the hearing and give evidence orally.

Taking evidence outside the jurisdiction

114 Interpretation

In this Section –

 (a) 'Regulation State' has the same meaning as 'Member State' in the Taking of Evidence Regulation, that is all Member States except Denmark; and
 (b) 'the Taking of Evidence Regulation' means Council Regulation (EC) No. 1206/2001 of 28 May 2001 on co-operation between the courts of Member States in the taking of evidence in civil and commercial matters.

115 Where a person to be examined is in another Regulation State

(1) This rule applies where a party wishes to take a deposition from a person who is –

 (a) outside the jurisdiction; and
 (b) in a Regulation State.

(2) The court may order the issue of the request to a designated court ('the requested court') in the Regulation State in which the proposed deponent is.

(3) If the court makes an order for the issue of a request, the party who sought the order must file –

 (a) a draft Form A as set out in the annex to the Taking of Evidence Regulation (request for the taking of evidence);
 (b) except where paragraph (4) applies, a translation of the form;
 (c) an undertaking to be responsible for the costs sought by the requested court in relation to –
  (i) fees paid to experts and interpreters; and

(ii) where requested by that party, the use of special procedure or communications technology; and

(d) an undertaking to be responsible for the court's expenses.

(4) There is no need to file a translation if –

(a) English is one of the official languages of the Regulation State where the examination is to take place; or
(b) the Regulation State has indicated, in accordance with the Taking of Evidence Regulation, that English is a language which it will accept.

(5) Where article 17 of the Taking of Evidence Regulation (direct taking of evidence by the requested court) allows evidence to be taken directly in another Regulation State, the court may make an order for the submission of a request in accordance with that article.

(6) If the court makes an order for the submission of a request under paragraph (5), the party who sought the order must file –

(a) draft Form I as set out in the annex to the Taking of Evidence Regulation (request for direct taking of evidence);
(b) except where paragraph (4) applies, a translation of the form; and
(c) an undertaking to be responsible for the requested court's expenses.

'**Practice Direction**'—Practice Direction 14B contains further rules relevant to this rule and r 116.

'**Form**'—An application is made on Form COP9.

116 Where a person to be examined is out of the jurisdiction – letter of request

(1) This rule applies where a party wishes to take a deposition from a person who is –

(a) out of the jurisdiction; and
(b) not in a Regulation State within the meaning of rule 114.

(2) The court may order the issue of a letter of request to the judicial authorities of the country in which the proposed deponent is.

(3) A letter of request is a request to a judicial authority to take the evidence of that person, or arrange for it to be taken.

(4) If the government of a country permits a person appointed by the court to examine a person in that country, the court may make an order appointing a special examiner for that purpose.

(5) A person may be examined under this rule on oath or affirmation in accordance with any procedure permitted in the country in which the examination is to take place.

(6) If the court makes an order for the issue of a letter of request, the party who sought the order must file –

(a) the following documents and, except where paragraph (7) applies, a translation of them –
  (i) a draft letter of request;
  (ii) a statement of the issues relevant to the proceedings; and
  (iii) a list of questions or the subject matter of questions to be put to the person to be examined; and

(b) an undertaking to be responsible for the Secretary of State's expenses.

(7) There is no need to file a translation if –
  (a) English is one of the official languages of the country where the examination is to take place; or
  (b) a practice direction has specified that country is a country where no translation is necessary.

Section 49 reports

117 Reports under section 49 of the Act

(1) This rule applies where the court requires a report to be made to it under section 49 of the Act.

(2) It is the duty of the person who is required to make the report to help the court on the matters within his expertise.

(3) Unless the court directs otherwise, the person making the report must –
  (a) contact or seek to interview such persons as he thinks appropriate or as the court directs;
  (b) to the extent that it is practicable and appropriate to do so, ascertain what P's wishes and feelings are, and the beliefs and values that would be likely to influence P if he had the capacity to make a decision in relation to the matter to which the application relates;
  (c) describe P's circumstances; and
  (d) address such other matters as are required in a practice direction or as the court may direct.

(4) The court will send a copy of the report to the parties and to such persons as the court may direct.

(5) Subject to paragraphs (6) and (7), the person who is required to make the report may examine and take copies of any document in the court records.

(6) The court may direct that the right to inspect documents under this rule does not apply in relation to such documents, or descriptions of documents, as the court may specify.

(7) The court may direct that any information is to be provided to the maker of the report on an edited basis.

Scope of rule—MCA 2005, s 49 allows the Court to call for reports.
Rule 117 will apply where a request for a report has been made pursuant to MCA 2005, s 49. Practice Direction E supplements this rule.
When giving directions in a case, r 85(2)(a) allows the Court to order a report.
In deciding whether to order a report, the following may be useful to have in mind:

(1) Where there is no particular legal or factual dispute, it is not appropriate to order a report.
(2) Where P requires a high level of protection, it may be preferable for P to be joined as a party and legally represented instead of ordering a report.
(3) An impartial report may be welcome for cases between (1) and (2) above to assist the Court in reaching a decision or to help the Court to solve a particular issue.
(4) The appropriateness of a stranger interviewing P.
(5) Consideration should be given to proportionality.
(6) The author of a report should be properly trained and qualified to carry out the task. For example, to asses a person who lacks capacity and who has serious communication difficulties requires an appropriately trained assessor.

(7) It should not always follow that P should pay for the report whether or not he or she is a party.
(8) The cost of a report should be proportionate.

'Practice Direction'—Practice Direction 14E, paras 11–16 set out the contents of a report. The Practice Direction also sets out what steps to take to notify the person or body making the report. The Annex to Practice Direction E contains a draft order which can be adapted in each case.

If a report is ordered and the author of the report is required to attend court, the court will need to address who is to pay for the costs of attendance.

In *Re RS* [2015] EWCOP 56, a district judge ordered a s 49 report from an NHS Trust. The Trust raised a number of objections, including that they had no clinical involvement with P; such a report was not a joint instruction and there was room for dispute if it were not agreed; the Trust's consultants were not court experts; the Trust had no involvement in the proceedings; the preparation of the report placed a significant and disproportionate burden on the Trust; clinics would be cancelled to make time to prepare the report; locum cover would not be compensated. The court rejected these arguments.

118 Written questions to person making a report under section 49

(1) Where a report is made under section 49 the court may, on the application of any party, permit written questions relevant to the issues before the court to be put to the person by whom the report was made.

(2) The questions sought to be put to the maker of the report shall be submitted to the court, and the court may put them to the maker of the report with such amendments (if any) as it thinks fit and the maker of the report shall give his replies in writing to the questions so put.

(3) The court will send a copy of the replies given by the maker of the report under this rule to the parties and to such other persons as the court may direct.

PART 15
EXPERTS

119 References to expert

A reference to an expert in this Part –
    (a) is to an expert who has been instructed to give or prepare evidence for the purpose of court proceedings; but
    (b) does not include any person instructed to make a report under section 49 of the Act.

General—The Ad Hoc Rules Committee is considering this Part of the Rules carefully. It is clear that many cases are delayed or incur disproportionate costs due to the involvement of experts. The situation is similar to the problems experienced in the Family Court. It is therefore likely that these rules will be brought more into line with the FPR.

The most likely change is to the test to decide if an expert should be instructed. Currently, r 121 has a low threshold of whether the expert evidence is reasonably required. It is likely that this will be changed to the 'necessary' test used in the FPR, necessary being defined as something that is an imperative and something the court cannot do without.

The court is also likely to encourage the use of MCA 2005, s 49 as a source of obtaining expert evidence, although this is not without its problems (see *Re RS* [2015] EWCOP 56).

It is hoped that if the rules do change, there will be a proper structure to ensure that letters of instruction to experts, the scope of the work to be undertaken by the expert and the costs of the expert will be matters that the court scrutinises carefully.

Meaning of expert—An expert itself is not defined in the rules either in Part 15 or in r 6.

During the consultation process before the Rules were made, it was suggested that no distinction should be made between a heath care professional (such as a doctor) acting as an expert and that of carers or family who are close to P. However, this idea is not reflected in the rules.

Those close to P cannot be independent or unbiased which is a requirement for an expert acting within Part 15 (see Practice Direction 15A, paras 3 and 4). Family members too cannot be said to have expertise within the meaning of this Part. Thus, the expert in these rules is to be understood in the traditional sense only.

120 Restriction on filing an expert's report

(1) No person may file expert evidence unless the court or a practice direction permits, or if it is filed with the application form and is evidence –

   (a) that P is a person who lacks capacity to make a decision or decisions in relation to the matter or matters to which the application relates;
   (b) as to P's best interests; or
   (c) that is required by any rule or practice direction to be filed with the application form.

(2) An applicant may only rely upon any expert evidence so filed in support of the application form to the extent and for the purposes that the court allows.

(Rule 64(a) requires the applicant to file any evidence upon which he wishes to rely with the application form.)

Amendments—SI 2015/548.

Rule 120(1)—After the filing of the application form, no expert evidence may be filed without permission of the Court (Practice Direction 15A, para 1) or pursuant to a Practice Direction.

121 Duty to restrict expert evidence

Expert evidence shall be restricted to that which is reasonably required to resolve the proceedings.

General—See the commentary under r 119.

'Practice Direction'—Practice Direction 15A, para 1 supposes that expert evidence will be given by a single joint expert. Rule 130 gives the Court power to order a joint expert. The Practice Direction makes it clear that the aim of this Part of the rules is to limit the use of expert evidence to that which is reasonably required (Practice Direction A, para 1).

Expert evidence—The Court will consider what added value expert evidence will give to the case. If expert evidence is allowed, it should be restricted to what is reasonably required to resolve the proceedings.

Reference should also be made to the President's guidance note dated December 2010 wherein it is made clear that it will be rare for the court to sanction the instruction of more than one expert. The guidance also warns the expert not to analyse or summarise the evidence and to be brief (see paragraphs 8 and 9).

See *SC v BS and A Local Authority* [2012] COPLR 567, which addresses the issue of instructing the correct expert.

In *Wigan Council v M and others (Veracity Assessment)* [2015] EWFC 8, Peter Jackson J in this family case held that as a matter of law, there was no bar on the admission of expert evidence about whether evidence of a witness could be relied on, although such cases would be rare. In this case, two children alleged they had been sexually abused by their stepfather, who applied for a veracity assessment of the children's ability to give evidence. To this end, he instructed a clinical psychologist. It is suggested that this case has relevance to the Court of Protection.

122 Experts – overriding duty to the court

It is the duty of the expert to help the court on the matters within his expertise.

Practice Direction—Practice Direction 15A, paras 2–7 set out the general duties of an expert. For example, that the expert be objective and independent.

If a matter is beyond his or her expertise, the expert should say so (Practice Direction 15A, para 6(a)). When applying for an expert, the court should be shown evidence that the proposed expert has the necessary qualifications and experience to undertake the work.

The duty of the expert is to help the Court; this duty overrides any obligation to the person from whom the expert has received instructions or by whom he or she is paid.

123 Court's power to restrict expert evidence

(1) Subject to rule 120, no party may file or adduce expert evidence unless the court or a practice direction permits.

(2) When a party applies for a direction under this rule he must –

 (a) identify the field in respect of which he wishes to rely upon expert evidence;
 (b) where practicable, identify the expert in that field upon whose evidence he wishes to rely;
 (c) provide any other material information about the expert; and
 (d) provide a draft letter of instruction to the expert.

(3) Where a direction is given under this rule, the court shall specify the field or fields in respect of which the expert evidence is to be provided.

(4) The court may specify the person who is to provide the evidence referred to in paragraph (3).

(5) Where a direction is given under this rule for a party to call an expert or put in evidence an expert's report, the court shall give directions for the service of the report on the parties and on such other persons as the court may direct.

(6) The court may limit the amount of the expert's fees and expenses that the party who wishes to rely upon the expert may recover from any other party.

Rule 123(2)—The Court should be given the fullest possible information. It is not acceptable to simply say that, for example, a psychiatrist is required.
 The Court should be told the following:

(1) Why the expert evidence is required.
(2) Whether all parties agree that an expert is required and, if not, why there is disagreement.
(3) Whether a joint expert is appropriate.
(4) The name of the proposed expert and confirmation that he can accept the instruction.
(5) The expert's qualifications.
(6) The reason the expert is suitable.
(7) How much the expert will charge by reference to his hourly rate and the likely total charge for the work.
(8) Who is to pay initially for the report (but see r 125(7)).
(9) When the report can be served.
(10) Whether P needs to be seen or examined.
(11) Whether any order for disclosure is required to allow the expert to properly complete his or her report.

The Court will also have regard to the overriding objective: in particular, the need to deal with a case justly. See also r 5(2)(g).

A draft letter of instruction to the expert should also be available for the Court to consider (see r 123(2)(d)).

In serious cases where an urgent hearing is being convened and where time is of the essence, it may be necessary to arrange for an expert to be on standby to deal with matters arising from the hearing.

Issues often arisen with public funding being granted for the instruction of experts. See *JG (A Child) v The Legal Services Commission* [2013] EWHC 804 (Admin), [2013] 2 FLR 1174) where Ryder J (as he then was) found that in the ordinary course, where a single joint expert is instructed the parties should bear the cost equally; the court may not make a different order from that which would normally be made just because a party has legal aid; where a court makes an order that a legally aided party pays a certain cost, the Legal Aid Agency has the power to refuse to provide funds for those costs as long as the refusal is not irrational or otherwise unlawful in the public law sense.

See also *R (T) v Legal Aid Agency* [2013] EWHC 960 (Admin), [2013] 2 FLR 1315: this case was a successful challenge to the Legal Aid Agency's refusal to authorise the cost of expert evidence. The decision gives guidance on applications for expert evidence where legal aid is involved. It refers to guidance given in family cases by Wall P in *A Local Authority v S* [2012] EWHC 1442 (Fam)).

It would seem sensible to ensure that any order allowing expert evidence gives reasons why it has been allowed and any other information the Legal Aid Agency might find useful.

The decision in *Re TG (A Child)* [2013] EWCA Civ 5, [2013] 1 FLR 1250 is also relevant. Although a family case, the judgment of Munby P deals with expert evidence and the court's approach. Although the threshold for permission in a family case is that the expert's instruction must be necessary as opposed to the test in the Court of Protection Rules of whether it is reasonably required, the case is still relevant if only for the sensible guidance it provides and even more so if these Rules are changed and brought into line with the FPR (see r 119 commentary).

See also r 125(7) which deals with the costs of an expert's report.

Inability to fund experts: Due to the lack of legal aid and the increase generally in the courts of litigants in person, the court may well find itself in a situation where an expert is required in a case but the parties cannot afford the expert. In the Family Court, this problem has already manifested itself. In *Q v Q; Re B (A Child); Re C (A Child)* [2014] EWFC 31, [2015] 1 FLR 324 Munby P concluded that where no other source of funding was available, the cost of experts had to be funded by HMCTS. See also *Re D (A Child)* [2014] EWFC 39, [2015] 1 FLR 531 where the lack of legal representation in the absence of legal aid and the issue of who pays for it in order to have a fair hearing was considered by Munby P. In *Re K and H (Children: Unrepresented Father: Cross-Examination of Child)* [2015] EWFC 1, [2015] 2 FLR 802, HHJ Bellamy sitting in the Family Division decided that HMCTS should fund an advocate to cross-examine a child in a fact-finding hearing. On appeal, the Court of Appeal said that the approach taken by the judge (which was itself taken from *Q v Q*, referred to above) was unlawful. The Lord Chancellor could not be asked to fund representation outside the legal aid scheme by any other means, which included ordering HMCTS to pay the costs (*Re K and H (Children)* [2015] EWCA Civ 543). Although these are family cases, a similar problem could arise in the Court of Protection. The only difference is that if a case is contested, it is likely that P would be represented through the Official Solicitor, who the court could trust to carry out a dispassionate enquiry through cross-examination. However, this is not the ideal solution to a problem that seems to have no answer.

124 General requirement for expert evidence to be given in a written report

Expert evidence is to be given in a written report unless the court directs otherwise.

Scope of rule—The purpose of this rule is to ensure that an expert attends only when it is necessary and in the interests of justice.

Content of the report—Rule 126 deals with the content of the report.

Rule 14—The expert should also be told about r 14, which sets out the consequences of making a false statement.

125 Written questions to experts

(1) A party may put written questions to –

(a) an expert instructed by another party; or
(b) a single joint expert appointed under rule 130,

about a report prepared by such person.

(2) Written questions under paragraph (1) –

(a) may be put once only;
(b) must be put within 28 days beginning with the date on which the expert's report was served; and
(c) must be for the purpose only of clarification of the report.

(3) Paragraph (2) does not apply in any case where –

(a) the court permits it to be done on a further occasion;
(b) the other party or parties agree; or
(c) any practice direction provides otherwise.

(4) An expert's answers to questions put in accordance with paragraph (1) shall be treated as part of the expert's report.

(5) Paragraph (6) applies where –

(a) a party has put a written question to an expert instructed by another party in accordance with this rule; and
(b) the expert does not answer that question.

(6) The court may make one or both of the following orders in relation to the party who instructed the expert –

(a) that the party may not rely upon the evidence of that expert; or
(b) that the party may not recover the fees and expenses of that expert, or part of them, from any other party.

(7) Unless the court otherwise directs, and subject to any final costs order that may be made, the instructing party is responsible for the payment of the expert's fees and expenses, including the expert's costs of answering questions put by any other party.

Rule 125(7)—This rule lays down a general principle that the party who instructs an expert is responsible for payment of the expert's fees, which include the cost of answering questions put by the other party. It must follow that where a joint expert is instructed, the parties initially pay an equal contribution to the cost. However, the Court may make another order for payment of the expert's costs both initially and after a final hearing.

126 Contents of expert's report

(1) The court may give directions as to the matters to be covered in an expert's report.

(2) An expert's report must comply with the requirements set out in the relevant practice direction.

(3) At the end of an expert's report there must be a statement that –

(a) the expert understands his duty to the court; and
(b) he has complied with that duty.

(4) The expert's report must state the substance of all material instructions, whether written or oral, on the basis of which the report was written.

(5) The instructions to the expert shall not be privileged against disclosure.

Form and content of the report—The expected form and content of the report are set out at Practice Direction 15A, paras 8–12.

127 Use by one party of expert's report disclosed by another

Where a party has disclosed an expert's report, any party may use that expert's report as evidence at any hearing in the proceedings.

128 Discussions between experts

(1) The court may, at any stage, direct a discussion between experts for the purpose of requiring the experts to –

    (a) identify and discuss the expert issues in the proceedings; and
    (b) where possible, reach an agreed opinion on those issues.

(2) The court may specify the issues which the experts must discuss.

(3) The court may direct that following a discussion between the experts they must prepare a statement for the court showing –

    (a) those issues on which they agree; and
    (b) those issues on which they disagree and a summary of their reasons for disagreeing.

(4) Unless the court otherwise directs, the content of the discussions between experts may be referred to at any hearing or at any stage in the proceedings.

Scope of rule—This rule furthers the overriding objective: see r 5(2)(a).

129 Expert's right to ask court for directions

(1) An expert may file a written request for directions to assist him in carrying out his function as an expert.

(2) An expert must, unless the court directs otherwise, provide a copy of any proposed request for directions under paragraph (1) –

    (a) to the party instructing him, at least 7 days before he files the request; and
    (b) to all other parties, at least 4 days before he files it.

(3) The court, when it gives directions, may also direct that a party be served with a copy of the directions.

Practice Direction—Practice Direction 15A, para 1 states that where possible a single expert is appropriate. However, there may be cases where the Court would be assisted by having two expert views on a matter to allow the Court to become acquainted with a range of views.

Note—In *SMBC v WMP* [2011] COPLR Con Vol 1177 His Honour Judge Cardinal held that as a matter of good practice, an expert should seek clarifications and raise questions under this rule rather than complete a report that refers to lacunae in the information before him.

130 Court's power to direct that evidence is to be given by a single joint expert

(1) Where two or more parties wish to submit expert evidence on a particular issue, the court may direct that the evidence on that issue is to be given by one expert only.

(2) The parties wishing to submit the expert evidence are called 'the instructing parties'.

(3) Where the instructing parties cannot agree who should be the expert, the court may –

    (a) select the expert from a list prepared or identified by the instructing parties; or
    (b) direct the manner by which the expert is to be selected.

131 Instructions to a single joint expert

(1) Where the court gives a direction under rule 130 for a single joint expert to be used, each party may give instructions to the expert.

(2) Unless the court otherwise directs, when an instructing party gives instructions to the expert he must, at the same time, send a copy of the instructions to the other instructing parties.

(3) The court may give directions about –

    (a) the payment of the expert's fees and expenses; and
    (b) any inspection, examination or experiments which the expert wishes to carry out.

(4) The court may, before an expert is instructed, limit the amount that can be paid by way of fees and expenses to the expert.

(5) Unless the court otherwise directs, and subject to any final costs order that may be made, the instructing parties are jointly and severally liable for the payment of the expert's fees and expenses.

PART 16
DISCLOSURE

132 Meaning of disclosure

A party discloses a document by stating that the document exists or has existed.

Scope of rule—This rule deals with disclosure. There is no Practice Direction. The provisions are based on the CPR 1998.

When considering disclosure, it is useful to have in mind r 107, which provides that where a party has access to information which is not reasonably available to the other party, the Court may direct that party to prepare and file a document recording the information.

Disclosure is a process whereby a party states that he knows that a document exists or has existed: it is not a duty to produce the document (CPR, r 31(2) and FPR, r 21.1(1)).

Certain documents may be immune from disclosure due to issues of confidentiality and privilege. In cases where disclosure may cause harm to P, the court will need to decide if the document is disclosed fully or in a redacted form. For this purpose, harm includes a risk to P's health or general well-being.

Unlike the CPR, document is not defined in the rules. It is defined in the CPR and FPR as 'anything in which information of any description is recorded' (CPR, r 31(4) and FPR, r 21.1(3)(a)).

It is submitted that a document within the context of these rules should be given the widest possible interpretation to include not only paper documents but also electronic documents, disks and audio tapes.

When dealing with any issue relating to disclosure, it should not be overlooked that the Court will always have P's best interests in mind as well as proportionality.

133 General or specific disclosure

(1) The court may either on its own initiative or on the application of a party make an order to give general or specific disclosure.

(2) General disclosure requires a party to disclose –
   (a) the documents on which he relies; and
   (b) the documents which –
      (i) adversely affect his own case;
      (ii) adversely affect another party's case; or
      (iii) support another party's case.

(3) An order for specific disclosure is an order that a party must do one or more of the following things –
   (a) disclose documents or classes of documents specified in the order;
   (b) carry out a search to the extent stated in the order; or
   (c) disclose any document located as a result of that search.

(4) A party's duty to disclose documents is limited to documents which are or have been in his control.

(5) For the purpose of paragraph (4) a party has or has had a document in his control if –
   (a) it is or was in his physical possession;
   (b) he has or has had possession of it; or
   (c) he has or has had a right to inspect or take copies of it.

Rule 133(2)—Sometimes a document may attract legal professional privilege. There are two categories of document: the first are communications which are privileged in all circumstances whether or not litigation is involved. This category would include letters between a solicitor and client or counsel. The second category comprise those which are privileged only if they came into existence in contemplation of litigation. If such correspondence or other documents are relevant to a dispute, care should be taken when dealing with disclosure and careful consideration given as to whether privilege needs to be waived.

Rule 133(3)—The following principles have been extracted from case-law under the old rules of the Court of Protection although they may be of use:

(1) Disclosure could be given of a confidential report to the Court by the Lord Chancellor's Visitor unless it is against the best interests of P (*Re WLW* [1972] Ch 456).
(2) On an application by P for release of papers held by the Official Solicitor in litigation relating to P, the Court of Appeal in *Re E (Mental Health Patient)* [1985] 1 WLR 245 held:
   (a) the paramount consideration was the interest and benefit of P;
   (b) the Official Solicitor may have access to confidential papers to which an ordinary litigation friend may not have access and it is important to preserve the confidence of those who gave information; and
   (c) the cases where the Court should exercise its discretion to withhold disclosure of a confidential report or other confidential documents from a party or parent must be rare and where the Court is fully satisfied judicially that real harm to the patient must ensue from disclosure.

In *Enfield LBC v SA, FA and KA* [2010] EWHC 196 (Admin), [2010] COPLR Con Vol 362, McFarlane J noted that unlike the rules in family proceedings, the Court of Protection Rules did not impose a duty of full and frank disclosure. He saw no justification for a difference of this degree between the family court and the Court of Protection in the context of a fact finding case. He held that the court would be justified in making a specific disclosure order under this rule requiring the parties to give full and frank disclosure of all relevant material.

134 Procedure for general or specific disclosure

(1) This rule applies where the court makes an order under rule 133 to give general or specific disclosure.

(2) Each party must make, and serve on every other party, a list of documents to be disclosed.

(3) A copy of each list must be filed within 7 days of the date on which it is served.

(4) The list must identify the documents in a convenient order and manner and as concisely as possible.

(5) The list must indicate –

   (a) the documents in respect of which the party claims a right or duty to withhold inspection (see rule 138); and
   (b) the documents that are no longer in his control, stating what has happened to them.

Denying disclosure—In *RC v CC and X Local Authority* [2013] EWHC 1424 (COP), [2013] COPLR 431, P sought indirect contact with her adopted child. An issue arose as to whether an unredacted psychological report and social work evidence should be disclosed to P. The local authority opposed disclosure as it would reveal the whereabouts of P's child and other information. The circuit judge adopted the approach that denial of disclosure should be only where strictly necessary, adopted the test set out in *Durham County Council v Dunn* [2002] EWCA Civ 1654 and refused to allow disclosure of the full report. One interesting criticism of this decision is that Counsel for P alone was allowed to see the social work evidence. This caused the difficulty of placing Counsel in a position where he cannot discuss or disclose evidence to his client, P. The decision was appealed and heard by Munby P at [2014] EWHC 131 (COP). The judgment clarifies that the principles relating to withholding of disclosure in COP proceedings is identical to those in relation to children.

135 Ongoing duty of disclosure

(1) Where the court makes an order to give general or specific disclosure under rule 133, any party to whom the order applies is under a continuing duty to provide such disclosure as is required by the order until the proceedings are concluded.

(2) If a document to which the duty of disclosure imposed by paragraph (1) extends comes to a party's notice at any time during the proceedings, he must immediately notify every other party.

136 Right to inspect documents

(1) A party to whom a document has been disclosed has a right to inspect any document disclosed to him except where –

   (a) the document is no longer in the control of the party who disclosed it; or
   (b) the party disclosing the document has a right or duty to withhold inspection of it.

(2) The right to inspect disclosed documents extends to any document mentioned in –

   (a) a document filed or served in the course of the proceedings by any other party; or
   (b) correspondence sent by any other party.

Scope of rule—This provision is taken from CPR, r 31(3) with one omission. The CPR allow a party to not give disclosure where that party believes it is disproportionate to the issues in the case. This provision is not included in this rule presumably because this would not be in P's interests.

137 Inspection and copying of documents

(1) Where a party has a right to inspect a document, he –

　(a)　must give the party who disclosed the document written notice of his wish to inspect it; and
　(b)　may request a copy of the document.

(2) Not more than 14 days after the date on which the party who disclosed the document received the notice under paragraph (1)(a), he must permit inspection of the document at a convenient place and time.

(3) Where a party has requested a copy of the document, the party who disclosed the document must supply him with a copy not more than 14 days after the date on which he received the request.

(4) For the purposes of paragraph (2), the party who disclosed the document must give reasonable notice of the time and place for inspection.

(5) For the purposes of paragraph (3), the party requesting a copy of the document is responsible for the payment of reasonable copying costs, subject to any final costs order that may be made.

138 Claim to withhold inspection or disclosure of document

(1) A party who wishes to claim that he has a right or duty to withhold inspection of a document, or part of a document, must state in writing –

　(a)　that he has such a right or duty; and
　(b)　the grounds on which he claims that right or duty.

(2) The statement must be made in the list in which the document is disclosed (see rule 134(2)).

(3) A party may, by filing an application notice in accordance with Part 10, apply to the court to decide whether the claim made under paragraph (1) should be upheld.

139 Consequence of failure to disclose documents or permit inspection

A party may not rely upon any document which he fails to disclose or in respect of which he fails to permit inspection unless the court permits.

PART 17
LITIGATION FRIENDS AND RULE 3A REPRESENTATIVES

Amendments—Part substituted by SI 2015/548.

Section 1
Litigation friends

Amendments—Section title inserted by SI 2015/548.

140 Who may act as a litigation friend

(1) A person may act as a litigation friend on behalf of a person mentioned in paragraph (2) if that person –

(a) can fairly and competently conduct proceedings on behalf of that person; and
(b) has no interests adverse to those of that person.

(2) The persons for whom a litigation friend may act are –

(a) P;
(b) a child;
(c) a protected party.

Amendments—Substituted by SI 2015/548.

Practice Direction—See the Practice Direction – Litigation friend (PD 17A).

Background—Rules of Court generally make special provision for parties who are not capable of conducting their own litigation (e g Civil Procedure Rules 1998 Part 21; Family Procedure Rules 2010, Parts 15 and 16). There are two categories, namely children and those who lack mental capacity (now termed 'protected party' but previously 'patient'). They must have a representative known as a 'litigation friend' (previously a 'next friend' or 'guardian ad litem' in family proceedings). The model used in civil and family proceedings was translated across to the Court of Protection; as it applies to P, it is questionable whether, in fact, it is appropriate, or whether the better model would not have been that adopted in relation to the representation of children in public law family law proceedings, where there is a clear recognition that the interests of the child may require (broadly) the appointment of their own legal representative to advocate on their behalf (and, where the child is competent, upon instructions) and a guardian to advise the court as to where the child's interests lie: see *R (R, E, J and K by their Litigation Friend, the Official Solicitor) v Cafcass* [2011] EWHC 1774 (Admin), [2011] 2 FLR 1206, at [38].

Litigation friend—This is the person who acts as representative for a child or protected party (or for 'P' in the Court of Protection). There is a difference between the role of the litigation friend and a solicitor and for this reason a solicitor will not usually be appointed as a litigation friend, although a litigation friend may instruct a solicitor. A lay litigation friend can conduct proceedings (and address the court) without a solicitor: *Re NRA and Others* [2015] EWCOP 59, [2015] COPLR 690.

Suitability—This rule makes it clear that a litigation friend must fairly and competently conduct the proceedings for the party and have no adverse interest. The litigation friend should not have any personal involvement in the proceedings, but see **Persons for whom a litigation friend may act**, below. There is also the duty under MCA 2005 to act in the 'best interests' of the protected party/P: *AB v CC A Local Authority* [2011] EWHC 3151 (COP), [2012] COPLR 314. In *Re NRA and Others* [2015] EWCOP 59, [2015] COPLR 690, Charles J recognised that 'by applying the best interests test the litigation friend may have to control all aspects of the proceedings and, in doing so, may have to take a position that is contrary to, or does not fully accord with, the expressed wishes and feelings of a P'. It suggested that, as a matter of principle, such an approach is very difficult to square with the requirements of ECHR, Arts 6 and 8 (as well as Arts 12 and 13 of the Convention on the Rights of Persons with Disabilities is questionable). It is further suggested that *RP v Nottingham City Council & Official Solicitor* [2008] EWCA Civ 462, [2008] 2 FLR 1516 (subsequently upheld by the ECHR: *RP v United Kingdom* (2008) ECHR 1124), upon which reliance is regularly placed by the Courts, in fact provides only a very limited analogy because it concerned the representation of the mother in care proceedings, not the subject of those proceedings). It is suggested in such circumstances that the Court should consider very carefully whether an amicus should not be appointed to perform the function of advancing an independent assessment as to where P's best interests lie, leaving the litigation friend free to advance a positive case upon the basis of P's wishes and feelings.

Persons for whom a litigation friend may act—There has never been any doubt that a family member or friend can act as litigation friend for a child or protected party. The decision in *Re NRA and Others* [2015] EWCOP 59, [2015] COPLR 690 represented a distinct shift in practice in the Court of Protection. Not least because the Official Solicitor, who has traditionally acted as litigation friend for P (when P is joined to proceedings) is significantly overstretched, Charles J re-examined the extent to which it is appropriate for a family member or friend to act as litigation friend for P. He made clear that a family member or friend can (and indeed should) be appointed as a litigation friend if they can perform the functions of a litigation friend and so in a balanced way consider and properly promote P's best interests: *Re NRA* (above).

'P'—Means 'any person (other than a protected party) who lacks or, so far as consistent with the context, is alleged to lack capacity to make a decision or decisions in relation to any matter that is the subject of an application to the court and references to a person who lacks capacity are to be construed in accordance with the Act' (r 6). Thus P is the person to whom the proceedings relate.

'child'—This refers to 'a person under 18' rather than a child of a party.

'protected party'—Means 'a party or an intended party (other than P or a child) who lacks capacity to conduct the proceedings' (r 6). Lack of capacity is defined in MCA 2005, s 2. For a fuller explanation see the annotations to CPR 1998, Pt 21 in this volume.

Status of litigation friend—As the appointment is to 'conduct proceedings on behalf of' the child or protected party, any act which in the ordinary conduct of any proceedings is required or authorised to be done by a party shall or may be done by the litigation friend. Unless the litigation friend is also a deputy appointed by the Court of Protection or an attorney under a lasting or registered enduring power of attorney, he or she will have no status in regard to the affairs of the protected party outside the proceedings in which he or she is appointed.

Need for a solicitor—There is no requirement in the Rules for a solicitor to act on behalf of a child or protected party whose proceedings are being conducted by a litigation friend. A lay litigation friend can conduct proceedings (and address the court) without a solicitor: *Re NRA and Others* [2015] EWCOP 59, [2015] COPLR 690. Nevertheless, in a complex or high value case the Court may consider that the litigation friend who acts without a solicitor is not 'suitable' within r 140(1) and appoint someone else under r 144(1).

141 Requirement for a litigation friend

(1) (1) This rule does not apply to P (whether P is an adult or a child).

(2) A protected party (if a party to the proceedings) must have a litigation friend.

(3) A child (if a party to the proceedings) must have a litigation friend to conduct those proceedings on that child's behalf unless the court makes an order under paragraph (4).

(4) The court may make an order permitting a child to conduct proceedings without a litigation friend.

(5) An application for an order under paragraph (4) –

    (a)   may be made by the child;
    (b)   if the child already has a litigation friend, must be made on notice to the litigation friend; and
    (c)   if the child has no litigation friend, may be made without notice.

(6) Where –

    (a)   the court has made an order under paragraph (4); and

(b) it subsequently appears to the court that it is desirable for a litigation friend to conduct the proceedings on behalf of the child,

the court may appoint a person to the child's litigation friend.

Amendments—Substituted by SI 2015/548.

Scope of rule—The general principle is that a child or protected party may only conduct proceedings by a litigation friend.

'child'—An all or nothing approach to age is no longer adopted (*Gillick v West Norfolk & Wisbech Area Health Authority* [1986] 1 FLR 224, HL). There is provision for a child to act personally even before attaining 18, but approval of the court is required (r 141(4)) and may subsequently be withdrawn (r 141(6)). The Court will only authorise a child to conduct proceedings when satisfied that the child has the required capacity (ie is of sufficient maturity and understanding). It is both prudent and good practice for the litigation friend to consult the child once the child is able to make a meaningful contribution, and particularly as the child approaches 18 since on attaining that age the appointment of the litigation friend ceases and the child (now an adult) may take over conduct of the proceedings.

Exceptions—Unlike the CPR (r 21.3), the Court is not given an express discretion to permit specified steps to be taken before a litigation friend is appointed or retrospectively to approve any steps that have been taken without such appointment, but there is no specific provision that a step taken in the absence of a litigation friend for a party is of no effect so the Court probably retains a discretion. This point was considered in passing in *Re NRA and Others* [2015] EWCOP 59, [2015] COPLR 690 (by reference to the approach adopted to CPR 1998, r 21.3 in *Dunhill (A Protected Party By Her Litigation Friend Tasker) v Burgin (Nos 1 and 2)* [2014] UKSC 18, [2014] COPLR 199), but Charles J did not make a definitive determination: at [86].

142 Litigation friend without a court order

(1) This rule does not apply –

    (a) in relation to P;
    (b) where the court has appointed a person under rule 143 or 144; or .
    (c) where the Official Solicitor is to act as a litigation friend.

(2) A deputy with the power to conduct legal proceedings in the name of a protected party or on the protected party's behalf is entitled to be a litigation friend of the protected party in any proceedings to which the deputy's power relates.

(3) If no-one has been appointed by the court or, in the case of a protected party, there is no deputy with the power to conduct proceedings, a person who wishes to act as a litigation friend must –

    (a) file a certificate of suitability stating that they satisfy the conditions in rule 140(1); and
    (b) serve the certificate of suitability on –
        (i) the person on whom an application form is to be served in accordance with rule 32 (service on children and protected parties); and
        (ii) every other person who is a party to the proceedings.

(4) If the person referred to in paragraph (2) wishes to act as a litigation friend for the protected party, that person must file and serve on the persons mentioned in paragraph (3)(b) a copy of the court order which appointed that person.

Amendments—Substituted by SI 2015/548.

Scope of rule—This rule sets out the procedural steps for the appointment of a litigation friend otherwise than by a court order. It will be relied upon in most cases. A deputy already authorised to conduct proceedings in the name of the protected party will be entitled to act in that capacity. If there is no such deputy an appointment can be made upon the appropriate documents being filed by the person desiring to be appointed a litigation friend.

Exceptions—This provision does not apply if the appointment is for P or it is to be of the Official Solicitor or if the Court has already made other provision.

'certificate of suitability' (r 142(3)(a))—This document confirms that the person to be appointed meets the criteria whereby a person may be regarded as suitable for appointment as litigation friend (r 140(1)). The certificate does not include an undertaking as to costs (unlike proceedings in the civil courts). It is not required where the person is a deputy authorised by the Court of Protection to conduct the proceedings.

Deputy appointed by the Court of Protection—An official copy of the order of the Court of Protection, which confers his or her power to act, must be filed and served.

Service—The certificate of suitability must be served on the child or person alleged to lack capacity (thus providing an opportunity for objections) and also on the other parties.

143 Litigation friend by court order

(1) The court may make an order appointing –

　(a)　the Official Solicitor; or
　(b)　some other person,

to act as a litigation friend for a protected party, a child or P.

(2) The court may make an order under paragraph (1) –

　(a)　either on its own initiative or on the application of any person; but
　(b)　only with the consent of the person to be appointed.

(3) An application for an order under paragraph (1) must be supported by evidence.

(4) The court may not appoint a litigation friend under this rule unless it is satisfied that the person to be appointed satisfies the conditions in rule 140(1).

(5) The court may at any stage of the proceedings give directions as to the appointment of a litigation friend.

> (Rule 3A requires the court to consider how P should participate in the proceedings, which may be by way of being made a party and the appointment of a litigation friend under this Part.)

Amendments—Substituted by SI 2015/548.

Litigation friend for P—This rule must be read with r 3A(4), which provides that, unless P has the capacity to conduct the proceedings, an order joining P as a party shall only take effect on the appointment of a litigation friend on P's behalf or (if the court so directs) on or after the appointment of an accredited legal representative (as to which see r 6). Note that, at time of writing, no scheme has been established to enable accreditation of such legal representatives.

Official Solicitor—Not least because of the limits upon his resources, the Official Solicitor operates strict acceptance criteria. He will only accept an appointment where: (a) no other suitable and willing person can be identified to act as litigation friend; and (b) he is either given suitable security for the costs of any external solicitors he retains to act for P; or (c) where he acts as solicitor as well as litigation friend, security for those costs. He will also require evidence that P lacks capacity the conduct the proceedings. The Official Solicitor cannot be compelled to act absent suitable funding: see, by analogy, *Bradbury and Others v Paterson and Others* [2014] EWHC 3992 (QB), [2015] COPLR 425. In serious medical treatment cases, the Official Solicitor's acceptance criteria are modified, because he does not require that there is no other suitable person who could act. In *Re D (Costs)* [2012] EWHC 886 (COP), [2012] COPLR 499, the earlier pre-MCA 2005 practice for funding the Official Solicitor in such cases was endorsed: i e the relevant NHS body will therefore be expected to meet half of those costs, with the balance being met by the Official Solicitor out of his own budget. The Official Solicitor may be contacted at Victory House, 30–34 Kingsway, London WC2B 6EX, tel: 020 3681 2751, fax: 020 3681 2762.

'on its own initiative'—The Court does not have to await an application and can proceed to make an appointment of its own initiative. This may occur where the need for a litigation friend is first identified at a hearing.

Consent—A person will not be appointed without their consent. That consent must be continuing: see, by analogy, *Bradbury and Others v Paterson and Others* [2014] EWHC 3992 (QB), [2015] COPLR 425.

Evidence—This will be in the form of a medical report (or certificate) or a witness statement, and possibly both. The Court will need to make a relevant finding of lack of capacity and should be very slow to make such a finding absent medical evidence: see, by analogy, *Baker Tilly (A Firm) v Makar* [2013] EWHC 759 (QB), [2013] COPLR 245.

Directions—Where the Court does not have the evidence on the basis of which to make a decision it will give directions as to how matters are to proceed.

144 Court's power to prevent a person from acting as a litigation friend or to bring an end to an appointment of a person as a litigation friend or to appoint another one

(1) (1) The court may either on its own initiative or on the application of any person –

(a) direct that a person may not act as a litigation friend;
(b) bring to an end a litigation friend's appointment; or
(c) appoint a new litigation friend in place of an existing one.

(2) If an application for an order under paragraph (1) is based on the conduct of the litigation friend, it must be supported by evidence.

(3) The court may not appoint a litigation friend under this rule unless it is satisfied that the person to be appointed satisfies the conditions in rule 140(1).

(4) The appointment of a litigation friend continues until brought to an end by court order.

> (Rule 87 applies if P has capacity in relation to the matter or matters to which the application relates.)

Amendments—Substituted by SI 2015/548.

Scope of rule—This rule addresses a number of separate situations. The first is where a protected party or P either regains or contends that (unrecognised) they always had capacity to conduct the proceedings. Such an application does not need to be supported by evidence, thereby removing the anomaly in the Rules that existed previously which required P, in essence, to prove that they had litigation capacity: all P has to do now is to make an application and the Court will then decide whether evidence is required. The second is where a litigation friend is considered to be acting in an improper fashion, in which case evidence of their improper conduct is required. The third is where the litigation friend wishes to be discharged from their appointment (for instance, in the case of the Official Solicitor, because he is no longer in receipt of suitable security for his legal costs: see, by analogy*Bradbury and Others v Paterson and Others* [2014] EWHC 3992 (QB), [2015] COPLR 425). In that case, evidence is not, strictly, required, but it is suggested that a clear explanation of why the litigation friend wishes to be discharged should be given in the application. The Court may also, of its own motion, prevent a person from being a litigation friend or replace a litigation friend during the course of proceedings, whether or not appointed by an order. See **'Suitability'** in r 140. Any dispute as to who should be the litigation friend would be dealt with under this provision. See also r 141 in relation to the position where a child seeks an order that they be permitted to conduct proceedings themselves (an application that can be brought at any stage). If P had (or has regained) subject-matter capacity, application should be made under r 87.

Evidence—Where the application is brought on the basis of the conduct of the litigation friend, clear evidence of that conduct will be required. The rules express no limit on the power to terminate the appointment and if the litigation friend manifestly acts contrary to the interests of a child, protected party or P, the Court will remove him or her, even though neither his or her good faith nor his or her diligence is in issue (*Re A (Conjoined Twins: Medical Treatment) (No 2)* [2001] 1 FLR 267, CA). See also **Suitability** under r 140.

145 Appointment of litigation friend by court order – supplementary

The applicant must serve a copy of an application for an order under rule 143 or 144 on –

(a) the person on whom an application form is to be served in accordance with rule 32 (service on children and protected parties);
(b) every other person who is a party to the proceedings;
(c) any person who is the litigation friend, or who is purporting to act as the litigation friend, when the application is made; and
(d) unless that person is the applicant, the person who it is proposed should be the litigation friend,

as soon as practicable and in any event within 14 days of the date on which the application was issued.

Amendments—Substituted by SI 2015/548.

Scope of rule—This rule makes provision for the service of applications for the appointment or removal of a litigation friend. Essentially, everyone involved or with a relevant interest must be notified. This includes the child or person alleged to lack capacity.

145A Procedure where appointment of a litigation friend comes to an end for a child

When a child reaches 18, provided the child is neither –

(a) P; nor
(b) a protected party,

the litigation friend's appointment ends and the child must serve notice on every other party –

(i) stating that the child has reached full age;
(ii) stating that the appointment of the litigation friend has ended; and
(iii) providing an address for service.

Amendments—Inserted by SI 2015/548.

Scope of rule—Prior to 1 July 2015, the old r 146 dealt compendiously with the ending of an appointment for a child and a protected party. Recognising that the two raise different issues, the one (in the majority of cases) relating solely to the age of the child and the other to the question of whether the individual has capacity to conduct the proceedings, the rules have now been split out. Rule 145A now addresses solely the question of children who attain their majority but who are not also protected parties. A P or a protected party who wishes to act without a litigation friend, either on the basis that they have regained litigation capacity or had it (unrecognised) all along, is to make (or have an application made in their regard) under r 144; if P had (or has regained) subject-matter capacity, the application is to be made under r 87.

Child—When a child (who is not also a protected party) attains majority, the appointment ceases but the child must serve notice on the other parties to this effect stating his or her address for service.

146 Practice direction in relation to litigation friends

A practice direction may make additional or supplementary provision in relation to litigation friends.

Amendments—Substituted by SI 2015/548.

Section 2
Rule 3A representatives

Amendments—Section title inserted by SI 2015/548.

146A Interpretation

In this Section, references to 'rule 3A representatives' are references to both accredited legal representatives and representatives.

('Accredited legal representative' and 'representative' are defined in rule 6.)

Amendments—Inserted by SI 2015/548.

Scope of rule—See r 3A, which this rule and rr 147–149 amplify.

147 Who may act as a rule 3A representative for P

A person may act as an accredited legal representative, or a representative, for P, if that person can fairly and competently discharge his or her functions on behalf of P.

Amendments—Substituted by SI 2015/548.

Scope of rule—This rule (to be read with r 3A) amplifies the requirements in relation to those who may act as accredited legal representatives (ALR) or representatives (under r 3A(b)). Note that, at time of writing, no scheme has been established to enable accreditation of legal representatives.

Suitability—Note that, deliberately, the requirement that in r 140(1)(b) that applies in relation to a litigation friend that they have no interest adverse to P (or the protected party) is not replicated in relation to r 3A representatives, essentially because both are discharging duties at the behest of, and under the oversight of, the Court.

148 Rule 3A representative by court order

(1) The court may make an order appointing a person to act as a representative, or an accredited legal representative, for P.

(2) The court may make an order under paragraph (1) –

(a) either of its own initiative or on the application of any person; but
(b) only with the consent of the person to be appointed.

(3) The court may not appoint a representative or an accredited legal representative under this rule unless it is satisfied that the person to be appointed satisfies the conditions in rule 147.

(4) The court may at any stage of the proceedings give directions as to the terms of appointment of a representative or an accredited legal representative.

(Rule 3A requires the court to consider how P should participate in the proceedings, which may be by way of the appointment of a representative or accredited legal representative under this Part.)

Amendments—Substituted by SI 2015/548.

Scope of rule—This rule mirrors r 143 and the discussion there is equally relevant in this context (with the one difference that, as per r 147, the conditions for appointment of a r 3A representative are different to those applying to a litigation friend).

148A Application by rule 3A representative or by P for directions

A representative, an accredited legal representative or P may, at any time and without giving notice to the other parties, apply to the court for directions relating to the performance, terms of appointment or continuation of the appointment of the representative or accredited legal representative.

Amendments—Inserted by SI 2015/548.

Scope of rule—This rule is designed to reflect that r 3A representatives are appointed for limited and specific purposes and that either category may consider that the issues are such that they require specific directions and/or – for instance – that an ALR may consider that the case is now such that it requires a litigation friend to be appointed instead.

148B Court's power to prevent a person from acting as a rule 3A representative or to bring an end to an appointment of a person as a rule 3A representative or appoint another one

(1) The court may, either of its own initiative or on the application of any person –

(a) direct that a person may not act as a representative or accredited legal representative;

(b) bring to an end a representative's or accredited legal representative's appointment;

(c) appoint a new representative or accredited legal representative in place of an existing one; or

(d) vary the terms of a representative's or accredited legal representative's appointment.

(2) If an application for an order under paragraph (1) is based on the conduct of the representative or accredited legal representative, it must be supported by evidence.

(3) The court may not appoint a representative or accredited legal representative under this rule unless it is satisfied that the person to be appointed satisfies the conditions in rule 147.

(4) The appointment of a representative or accredited legal representative continues until brought to an end by court order.

(5) The court must bring to an end the appointment of a representative or an accredited legal representative if P has capacity to appoint such a representative and does not wish the appointment by the court to continue.

Amendments—Inserted by SI 2015/548.

Scope of rule—This rule mirrors r 144, providing the powers to the Court (of its own motion, or upon application) to bring to an end a r 3A representative's appointment, appoint a replacement or vary the terms of their appointment.

Capacity to appoint a representative—The test for appointment of a capacity to appoint a representative has not been defined. The Court would apply MCA 2005, s 2, analogies are likely to be drawn with the approach adopted to the question of whether an applicant before the Mental Health Tribunal (MHRT in Wales) has the capacity to instruct their own representative: see *YA v Central and NW London NHS Trust and Others* [2015] UKUT 37 (AAC).

148C Appointment of rule 3A representative by court order – supplementary

The applicant must serve a copy of an application for an order under rule 148 or rule 148B on –

  (a) the person on whom an application form is to be served in accordance with rule 32 (service on children and protected parties);
  (b) every other person who is a party to the proceedings;
  (c) any person who is the representative, or accredited legal representative, purporting to act as such representative, when the application is made; and
  (d) unless that person is the applicant, the person who it is proposed should be the representative or accredited legal representative,

as soon as practicable and in any event within 14 days of the date on which the application was issued.

Amendments—Inserted by SI 2015/548.

Scope of rule—This rule mirrors r 145, setting out the steps that must be taken to notify other relevant persons of applications made either for the appointment of a r 3A representative, a direction that a person not act as a r 3A representative, the termination/substitution of a r 3A representative or the variation of their term of appointment.

149 Practice direction in relation to rule 3A representatives

A practice direction may make additional or supplementary provision in relation to representatives or accredited legal representatives.

Amendments—Substituted by SI 2015/548.

Practice Direction—This rule provides the authority for the Practice Direction – Litigation friend (PD 17A). It is strange that the rule allows the Practice Direction to make different provision because in the event of conflict between the Rules and a Practice Direction the former normally take precedence.

PART 18
CHANGE OF SOLICITOR

150 Change of solicitor

(1) This rule applies where a party to proceedings –

  (a) for whom a solicitor is acting wants to change his solicitor or act in person; or
  (b) after having conducted the proceedings in person, appoints a solicitor to act on his behalf (except where the solicitor is appointed only to act as an advocate for a hearing).

(2) The party proposing the change must –

  (a) file a notice of the change with the court; and

(b) serve the notice of the change on every other party to the proceedings and, if there is one, on the solicitor who will cease to act.

(3) The notice must state the party's address for service.

(4) The notice filed at court must state that it has been served as required by paragraph (2)(b).

(5) Where there is a solicitor who will cease to act, he will continue to be considered the party's solicitor unless and until –

    (a) the notice is filed and served in accordance with paragraphs (2), (3) and (4); or

    (b) the court makes an order under rule 152 and the order is served in accordance with that rule.

Scope of rule—This rule sets out the procedure where there is a change of solicitor. It is supplemented by Practice Direction 18A.

For the sake of completeness, reference should be made to Part 67 of the CPR. This deals with proceedings against solicitors where an order is sought for the solicitor to deliver a bill or cash account, where there are issues concerning solicitors' remuneration and matters arising from an intervention in a solicitors' practice. Such proceedings would need to be brought as Part 8 CPR proceedings and not in the Court of Protection.

Rule 150(2)(a)—Form COP30 should be used.

151 Legally aided persons

(1) Where the certificate of any person ('A') who is a legally aided person is revoked or withdrawn –

    (a) the solicitor who acted for A will cease to be the solicitor acting in the case as soon as his retainer is determined under regulation 24 or 41 of the Civil Legal Aid (Procedure) Regulations 2012; and

    (b) if A wishes to continue and appoints a solicitor to act on his behalf, rule 150(2), (3) and (4) will apply as if A had previously conducted the application in person.

(2) In this rule, 'certificate' means a certificate issued under the Civil Legal Aid (Procedure) Regulations 2012.

Amendments—SI 2013/534.

152 Order that a solicitor has ceased to act

(1) A solicitor may apply for an order declaring that he has ceased to be the solicitor acting for a party.

(2) Where an application is made under this rule –

    (a) the solicitor must serve the application notice on the party for whom the solicitor is acting, unless the court directs otherwise; and

    (b) the application must be supported by evidence.

(3) Where the court makes an order that a solicitor has ceased to act, the solicitor must –

    (a) serve a copy of the order on every other party to the proceedings; and

    (b) file a certificate of service.

Rule 152(1)—The application is made on Form COP9 and should be supported by evidence (r 152(2)(b)).

Rule 152(3)(b)—The certificate of service is Form COP20.

153 Removal of solicitor who has ceased to act on application of another party

(1) Where –
  (a) a solicitor who has acted for a party –
    (i) has died;
    (ii) has become bankrupt;
    (iii) has ceased to practice; or
    (iv) cannot be found; and
  (b) the party has not served a notice of a change of solicitor or notice of intention to act in person as required by rule 150,

any other party may apply for an order declaring that the solicitor has ceased to be the solicitor acting for the other party in the case.

(2) Where an application is made under this rule, the applicant must serve the application on the party to whose solicitor the application relates, unless the court directs otherwise.

(3) Where the court makes an order under this rule –
  (a) the court will give directions about serving a copy of the order on every other party to the proceedings; and
  (b) where the order is served by a party, that party must file a certificate of service.

154 Practice direction relating to change of solicitor

A practice direction may make additional or different provision in relation to change of solicitor.

PART 19
COSTS

155 Interpretation

(1) In this Part –
  'authorised court officer' means any officer of the Senior Courts Costs Office whom the Lord Chancellor has authorised to assess costs;
  'costs' include fees, charges, disbursements, expenses, remuneration and any reimbursement allowed to a litigant in person;
  'costs judge' means a taxing Master of the Senior Courts;
  'costs officer' means a costs judge or an authorised court officer;
  'detailed assessment' means the procedure by which the amount of costs or remuneration is decided by a costs officer in accordance with Part 47 of the Civil Procedure Rules 1998 (which are applied to proceedings under these Rules, with modifications, by rule 160);
  'fixed costs' are to be construed in accordance with the relevant practice direction;

'fund' includes any estate or property held for the benefit of any person or class of persons, and any fund to which a trustee or personal representative is entitled in that capacity;
'paying party' means a party liable to pay costs;
'pro bono representation' means representation provided free of charge;
'receiving party' means a party entitled to be paid costs;
'summary assessment' means the procedure by which the court, when making an order about costs, orders payment of a sum of money instead of fixed costs or detailed assessment.

(2) The costs to which the rules in this Part apply include –

   (a) where the costs may be assessed by the court, costs payable by a client to their legal representative; and

   (b) costs which are payable by one party to another party under the terms of a contract, where the court makes an order for an assessment of those costs.

(3) Where advocacy or litigation services are provided to a client under a conditional fee agreement, costs are recoverable under this Part notwithstanding that the client is liable to pay his legal representative's fees and expenses only to the extent that sums are recovered in respect of the proceedings, whether by way of costs or otherwise.

(4) In paragraph (3), the reference to a conditional fee agreement means an agreement enforceable under section 58 of the Courts and Legal Services Act 1990.

Amendments—SI 2015/548.

Scope of rule—This Part of the Rules deals with costs and has undergone substantial change following changes to the CPR. The amendments to the costs rules and PD19A commenced in July 2015. See the commentary to r 160. The rules are supplemented by PD19A.

From the perspective of the Court of Protection, though, the issue of costs is being considered by the Ad Hoc Rules Committee and it is likely that further changes may come about. This is a timely review.

In property and affairs cases, the normal rule is that P's estate pays the costs. However, questions arise from this approach. For example, is it correct that siblings who fight together should have an indemnity from P in every case? Should the court have an obligation to consider costs in every case to avoid injustice to P? Such an approach may be preferable to using r 159.

In personal welfare cases, is the no-costs rule being abused by parties who are litigating without a real just cause and would doing away with the no-costs rule force litigants to concentrate their minds more on settlement, co-operation and avoiding unnecessary litigation?

Some argue that r 159 is the remedy for misbehaving litigants and therefore amendment to the general costs rules should not be allowed. However, it cannot be overlooked that r 159 is there to allow a departure from the normal rules, which suggests a higher threshold than the court having to decide how costs are paid in each case.

Appealing costs orders: *Re G (An Adult) (By Her Litigation Friend the Official Solicitor) (Costs)* [2015] EWCA Civ 446, [2015] COPLR 438 highlights the difficulty of appealing a costs order. Lord Justice Ryder noted that "an appeal against the exercise of by a judge of his discretion faces a high hurdle". The Court of Appeal will only interfere if the judge exceeds the generous ambit of his discretion.

156 Property and affairs – the general rule

Where the proceedings concern P's property and affairs the general rule is that the costs of the proceedings or of that part of the proceedings that concerns P's property and affairs, shall be paid by P or charged to his estate.

Scope of rule—This rule lays down a general presumption. However, r 159 allows the Court to depart from the general presumption.

157 Personal welfare – the general rule

Where the proceedings concern P's personal welfare the general rule is that there will be no order as to the costs of the proceedings or of that part of the proceedings that concerns P's personal welfare.

Scope of rule—This rule reflects a presumption that each party will pay its own costs. Hedley J in *A NHS Trust and B Trust v DU, AO, EB and AU* [2009] EWHC 3504 (Fam), [2009] COPLR Con Vol 210 referred to this as 'the conventional approach'. One advantage of such a presumption is that some cases may settle at an early stage due to the fear of financing a long case.

In *Re G (Adult) (Costs)* [2014] EWCOP 5,[2014] COPLR 432 , an application was made by the Associated Newspapers Limited ('ANL') to be joined to the proceedings. The application was dismissed. The local authority and the Official Solicitor sought an order for costs against ANL. One of the arguments before the court was that the joinder application was not in respect of the 'part of the proceedings that concerns P's personal welfare' and therefore the default position was that rule 9 would apply incorporating the CPR costs rules whose general principle was that costs follow the event. Munby P rejected this saying that the application was made in the personal welfare proceedings and rule 157 applied. He then applied rule 159 to consider departing from the no costs principle and did so on the facts of that case. The decision was upheld by the Court of Appeal: [2015] EWCA Civ 446, [2015] COPLR 438.

158 Apportioning costs – the general rule

Where the proceedings concern both property and affairs and personal welfare the court, insofar as practicable, will apportion the costs as between the respective issues.

159 Departing from the general rule

(1) The court may depart from rules 156 to 158 if the circumstances so justify, and in deciding whether departure is justified the court will have regard to all the circumstances, including –

   (a) the conduct of the parties;
   (b) whether a party has succeeded on part of his case, even if he has not been wholly successful; and
   (c) the role of any public body involved in the proceedings.

(2) The conduct of the parties includes –

   (a) conduct before, as well as during, the proceedings;
   (b) whether it was reasonable for a party to raise, pursue or contest a particular issue;
   (c) the manner in which a party has made or responded to an application or a particular issue;
   (d) whether a party who has succeeded in his application or response to an application, in whole or in part, exaggerated any matter contained in his application or response; and
   (e) any failure by a party to comply with a rule, practice direction or court order.

(3) Without prejudice to rules 156 to 158 and the foregoing provisions of this rule, the court may permit a party to recover their fixed costs in accordance with the relevant practice direction.

Amendments—SI 2015/548.

Rule 159(2)(e)—This rule was introduced in July 2015. A breach of the obligations in r 4 would enable the court to utilise this rule to make an adverse costs order.

Note—In *SC v London Borough of Hackney* [2010] EWHC B29 (COP) Senior Judge Lush suggested that departure from the usual costs rules would normally only apply where a party had acted in bad faith. He also said that a warning should be given to a party that the court was likely to make a costs order against him. However, this decision was overruled in *AH and others v Hertfordshire Partnership NHS Foundation Trust and others* [2011] EWHC 3524 (COP)) a decision of Peter Jackson J.

Peter Jackson J considered various cases which were suggested to be authority on costs and concluded that:

'... they do not purport to give guidance over and above the words of the Rules themselves – had such guidance been needed the Court of Appeal would no doubt have given it in *Manchester v G*. Instead, the decisions give useful examples of the manner in which the court has exercised its powers'.

Peter Jackson J also said that where there is a general rule from which the court can depart where the circumstances justify, it adds nothing to say that a case must be exceptional or atypical for costs to be ordered. Each application for costs must be considered on its own merit or lack of merit with the clear appreciation that there must be a good reason before the court will contemplate departure from the general rule.

It would also seem from this case that where there is bad faith or flagrant misconduct, an order for indemnity costs may be appropriate.

See also *G v E* [2010] EWHC 3385 (Fam), [2010] COPLR Con Vol 454, a decision of Baker J on costs where he stated that local authorities and other public bodies could not be excluded from liability to pay costs in appropriate cases and the rules about costs must be applied fairly to all litigants.

See too *Hillingdon LBC v Neary* [2011] EWHC 413 (COP), [2011] COPLR Con Vol 677 and *JS v KB and MP (Property and Affairs Deputy for DB)* [2014] EWHC 483 (COP), [2014] COPLR 275 where Cobb J said that reported cases were all 'essentially, no more or less than illustrations of the rules' and where he departed from r 156.

In *Cheshire West and Cheshire Council v P* [2011] EWCA Civ 1257, [2012] COPLR 37, Munby LJ stated that on an appeal from the Court of Protection, the Court of Protection Rules will not apply on costs; instead the relevant CPR 1998 will apply and r 157 was therefore irrelevant.

In respect of the costs of an appeal, consideration should be given to rule 52.9A of the CPR which allows the court to order that the appeal costs are limited to the extent specified by the court. See *JE (Jamaica) v SSHD* [2014] EWCA Civ 192.

Relevance of old law—*Re S; D v R (The Deputy of S) and S (Costs)* [2010] EWHC 3748 (COP), [2012] COPLR 154: some assistance can be obtained from old cases but caution is needed and the assistance is only limited (per Henderson J).

Departure from costs rules—See *North Somerset Council v LW and Others* [2014] EWCOP 3 where there had been unacceptable delays, a failure to plan and a poor response to court orders.

160 Rules about costs in the Civil Procedure Rules to apply

(1) Subject to the provisions of these Rules, Parts 44, 46 and 47 of the Civil Procedure Rules 1998 ('the 1998 Rules') apply with the modifications in this rule and such other modifications as may be appropriate, to costs incurred in relation to proceedings under these Rules as they apply to costs incurred in relation to proceedings in the High Court.

(2) Rules 3.12 to 3.18 of the 1998 Rules and Practice Direction 3E supporting those Rules do not apply in relation to proceedings under these Rules.

(3) The provisions of Part 47 of the 1998 Rules apply with the modifications in this rule and such other modifications as may be appropriate, to a detailed assessment of the remuneration of a deputy under these Rules as they apply to a detailed assessment of costs in proceedings to which the 1998 Rules apply.

(4) Where the definitions in Part 44 (referred to in Parts 44, 46 and 47) of the 1998 Rules are different from the definitions in rule 155 of these Rules, the latter definitions prevail.

(5) Rules 44.2(1) to (5), 44.5, 44.6, 44.9 and 44.13 to 44.18 of the 1998 Rules do not apply.

(6) For rule 46.1(1) of the 1998 Rules there is substituted –

'(1) This paragraph applies where a person applies for an order for specific disclosure before the commencement of proceedings.'.

(7) Rules 46.2, 46.5 and 46.10 to 46.14 of the 1998 Rules do not apply.

(8) In rule 47.3(1)(c) of the 1998 Rules, the words 'unless the costs are being assessed under rule 46.4 (costs where money is payable to a child or protected party)' are omitted.

(9) In rule 47.3(2) of the 1998 Rules, the words 'or a District Judge' are omitted.

(10) Rule 47.4(3) and (4) of the 1998 Rules do not apply.

(11) Rules 47.9(4), 47.10 and 47.11 of the 1998 Rules do not apply where the costs are to be paid by P or charged to P's estate.

Amendments—Substituted by SI 2015/548.

The costs issue— In January 2010, Lord Justice Jackson published his final report in his fundamental review of the rules and principles governing the costs of civil litigation. This resulted in the costs rules in the CPR being substantially amended in 2013. This caused a problem. Rule 160 incorporated parts of the CPR costs rules subject to various modifications set out in the rule and PD19A. However, rule 160 was not amended in 2013, which meant that its provisions were almost meaningless as they referred to rules that no longer existed. This was remedied by amendments to the rule and PD19A in July 2015.

Rule 160 applies various provisions of the CPR costs rules into these rules.

161 Detailed assessment of costs

(1) Where the court orders costs to be assessed by way of detailed assessment, the detailed assessment proceedings shall take place in the High Court.

(2) A fee is payable in respect of the detailed assessment of costs and on an appeal against a decision made in a detailed assessment of costs.

(3) Where a detailed assessment of costs has taken place, the amount payable by P is the amount which the court certifies as payable.

Assessment—The assessment will be carried out at the Senior Courts Costs Office.

162 Employment of a solicitor by two or more persons

Where two or more persons having the same interest in relation to a matter act in relation to the proceedings by separate legal representatives, they shall not be permitted more than one set of costs of the representation unless and to the extent that the court certifies that the circumstances justify separate representation.

163 Costs of the Official Solicitor

Any costs incurred by the Official Solicitor in relation to proceedings under these Rules or in carrying out any directions given by the court and not provided for by remuneration under rule 167 shall be paid by such persons or out of such funds as the court may direct.

Medical Treatment Cases—Prior to the MCA 2005, when NHS bodies brought applications for withdrawal of treatment, the starting point was that they paid 50 per cent of Official Solicitors' costs. *A Local Authority v FG and Others (No 1)* [2011] EWHC 3932 (COP), [2012] COPLR 473 considered whether this continued under the present rules. Peter Jackson J accepted that to exercise discretion in this way displaced the general rule in cases in which the Official Solicitor acts, but the pragmatic basis for this compromise: '... is as strong as it ever was. To disturb long-standing practice would introduce uncertainty into every case, and foster costs arguments between public bodies. It would make it very difficult for public bodies to budget in individual cases and for the Official Solicitor to budget generally.'

164 Procedure for assessing costs

Where the court orders a party, or P, to pay costs to another party it may either –

 (a) make a summary assessment of the costs; or
 (b) order a detailed assessment of the costs by a costs officer,

unless any rule, practice direction or other enactment provides otherwise.

Rule 164(a)—A statement of costs should be filed before a hearing which is listed for up to one day. However, it has to be recognised that some matters may incur substantial costs even though they take one day to be heard and a detailed assessment may be more appropriate.

165 Costs following P's death

An order or direction that costs incurred during P's lifetime be paid out of or charged on his estate may be made within 6 years after P's death.

Note—This is an example of the Court of Protection having jurisdiction after P dies.

166 Costs orders in favour of or against non-parties

(1) Where the court is considering whether to make a costs order in favour of or against a person who is not a party to proceedings, that person must be –

 (a) added as a party to the proceedings for the purposes of costs only;
 (aa) served with such documents as the court may direct; and
 (b) given a reasonable opportunity to attend any hearing at which the court will consider the matter further.

(2) This rule does not apply where the court is considering whether to make an order against the Lord Chancellor in proceedings in which the Lord Chancellor has provided legal aid to a party to the proceedings.

Amendments—SI 2015/548.

167 Remuneration of a deputy, donee or attorney

(1) Where the court orders that a deputy, donee or attorney is entitled to remuneration out of P's estate for discharging his functions as such, the court may make such order as it thinks fit, including an order that –

(a) he be paid a fixed amount;
(b) he be paid at a specified rate; or
(c) the amount of the remuneration shall be determined in accordance with the schedule of fees set out in the relevant practice direction.

(2) Any amount permitted by the court under paragraph (1) shall constitute a debt due from P's estate.

(3) The court may order a detailed assessment of the remuneration by a costs officer, in accordance with rule 164(b).

Practice Direction—See Practice Direction 19B and fixed costs.

168 Practice Direction as to costs

A practice direction may make further provision in respect of costs in proceedings.

Practice Direction—See Practice Direction 19B, which deals with fixed costs in the Court of Protection. See also PD19A.

Wasted costs orders—MCA 2005, s 55 gives the court jurisdiction to make a wasted costs order against a 'legal or other representative'. See *Sharma and Judkins v Hunters* [2011] EWHC 2546 (COP), [2012] COPLR 166. The procedure for wasted costs orders is the same as in the High Court.

PART 20
APPEALS

169 Scope of this Part

This Part applies to an appeal against any decision of the court.

Amendments—Substituted by SI 2015/548.

Scope of part—MCA 2005, s 53 allows the rules to provide a mechanism for appeals. MCA 2005 also allows the rules to consider whether permission to appeal is required or not. Part 20 sets out these rules. It is supplemented by Practice Direction 20A.

Reference should also be made to r 89 which contains provision for the Court to reconsider orders made without a hearing or without notice to any person.

The rule was amended in July 2015 to reflect the fact that the transitional provisions in Pt 22 are defunct. The rule, therefore, refers to dealing with an appeal against any decision.

Court of Appeal appeals—The Court of Protection Rules 2007 do not apply to hearings in the Court of Appeal: see *Cheshire West and Chester Council v P (No 2)* [2011] EWCA Civ 1333, [2012] COPLR 76.

Costs of appeal—In respect of the costs of an appeal, see the commentary to r 159 and the reference there to CPR, r 52.9A. See also *JE (Jamaica) v SSHD* [2014] EWHC Civ 192. An application under r 52.9A of the CPR should be made as soon as practicable.

Leapfrog appeal—In *Rochdale Metropolitan Borough Council v KW, PK and MW* [2014] EWCOP 45 Mostyn J held that a High Court Judge sitting in the Court of Protection can grant a leapfrog certificate to allow the decision to be reviewed directly by the Supreme Court (although in the event, the matter was heard by the Court of Appeal and it is unlikely that this procedure is appropriate). See also the sequel to this case in [2015] EWCOP 13 and in *Re G (An Adult) (By Her Litigation Friend* *the Official Solicitor) (Costs)* [2015] EWCA Civ 446, [2015] COPLR 438. However, PD20B does allow an appeal from a Tier-1 judge to be heard by a Tier-3 judge if the criteria set out in the PD are met.

170 Interpretation

(1) In the following provisions of this Part –
- (a) 'appeal judge' means a judge of the court to whom an appeal is made;
- (b) 'first instance judge' means the judge of the court from whose decision an appeal is brought;
- (c) 'appellant' means the person who brings or seeks to bring an appeal;
- (d) 'respondent' means –
  - (i) a person other than the appellant who was a party to the proceedings before the first instance judge and who is affected by the appeal; or
  - (ii) a person who is permitted or directed by the first instance judge or the appeal judge to be a party to the appeal; and
- (e) 'a second appeal' means an appeal from a decision of a judge of the court which was itself made on appeal from a judge of the court.

(2) In this Part, where the expression 'permission' is used it means 'permission to appeal' unless otherwise stated.

Amendments—SI 2015/548.

Note—The appeal rules were amended in July 2015 and are supplemented by two practice directions, PD20A and PD20B. PD20A deals with general matters relating to appeals and PD20B deals with allocation of appeals.

171 Dealing with appeals

(1) The court may deal with an appeal or any part of an appeal at a hearing or without a hearing.

(2) In considering whether it is necessary to hold a hearing, the court shall have regard to the matters set out in rule 84(3).

(3) Any person bound by an order of the court by virtue of rule 74 (persons to be bound as if parties) may seek permission under this Part.

(4) All parties to an appeal must comply with any relevant practice direction.

(5) Where permission is required, it is to be granted or refused in accordance with this Part.

> (Rule 89 provides for reconsideration of orders made without a hearing or without notice to a person.)

Amendments—SI 2015/548.

171A Destination of appeals

(1) An appeal from a decision of a judge of the court shall lie to the Court of Appeal in the following cases –
- (a) where it is an appeal from a decision of a Tier 3 Judge; or
- (b) where it is a second appeal.

(2) Subject to paragraph (1) and to any alternative provision made by the relevant practice direction –

(a) where the first instance judge was a Tier 1 Judge, any appeal shall be heard by a Tier 2 Judge;
(b) where the first instance judge was a Tier 2 Judge, any appeal shall be heard by a Tier 3 Judge.

(3) No appeal may be made against a decision of a court officer authorised under rule 7A.

(A decision of a court officer authorised under rule 7A can be reconsidered by a judge under rule 89.)

Amendments—Inserted by SI 2015/548.

Note—See PD20B, which sets out circumstances when an appeal from a Tier-1 judge's decision can be heard by a Tier-3 judge.

171B Permission to appeal – appeals to the Court of Appeal

(1) Subject to rule 172A, an appeal to the Court of Appeal against a decision of a judge of the court may not be made without permission.

(2) Where an appeal to the Court of Appeal is made from a decision of a Tier 3 Judge, permission may be granted by the first instance judge or by the Court of Appeal, unless the appeal is a second appeal.

(3) Where an appeal to the Court of Appeal is a second appeal, permission may only be granted by the Court of Appeal.

(4) No appeal shall lie against –

(a) the granting or refusal of permission under this rule; or
(b) an order allowing an extension of time for appealing from an order.

(The procedure for an appeal from a decision of a judge of the court to the Court of Appeal, including requirements for permission, is governed by the Civil Procedure Rules 1998.)

Amendments—Inserted by SI 2015/548.

Appeals to the Court of Appeal—Such appeals are governed by the CPR. In the case of a second appeal, the Court of Appeal will not give permission unless it considers that the appeal would raise an important point of principle or practice or that there is some other compelling reason for the Court of Appeal to hear it (CPR, r 52.13, set out in Part V).

172 Permission to appeal – other cases

(1) Subject to rules 171B and 172A, an appeal against a decision of the court may not be made without permission.

(2) An application for permission to appeal may be made to –

(a) the first instance judge; or .
(b) another judge who satisfies the relevant condition in paragraph (4) or (5).

(3) Where an application for permission is refused by the first instance judge, a further application for permission may be made to a judge who satisfies the relevant condition in paragraph (4) or (5).

(4) Where the decision sought to be appealed is a decision of a Tier 1 Judge, permission may also be granted or refused by –

(a) a Tier 2 Judge; or
(b) a Tier 3 Judge.

(5) Where the decision sought to be appealed is a decision of a Tier 2 Judge, permission may also be granted or refused by a Tier 3 Judge.

(6) Subject to paragraph (7) and except where another rule or a practice direction provides otherwise, where a judge who satisfies the relevant condition in paragraph (4) or (5), without a hearing, refuses permission to appeal against the decision of the first instance judge, the person seeking permission may request the decision to be reconsidered at a hearing.

(7) Where a Tier 3 Judge or the Senior Judge refuses permission to appeal without a hearing and considers that the application is totally without merit, that judge may order that the person seeking permission may not request the decision to be reconsidered at a hearing.

(8) Subject to paragraph (6), no appeal shall lie against –

(a) the granting or refusal of permission under this rule; or
(b) an order allowing an extension of time for appealing from an order.

Amendments—Substituted by SI 2015/548.

Rule 172(1)—During the consultation process prior to implementation of these rules, it was suggested that permission should not be required for cases involving serious medical decisions. This was not adopted and there seems now to be no need for such a provision.

Rule 172(7)—This is a new power following amendment to the rules in April 2015.

172A Appeal against an order for committal to prison

Permission is not required to appeal against an order for committal to prison.

Amendments—Inserted by SI 2015/548.

173 Matters to be taken into account when considering an application for permission

(1) Permission to appeal shall be granted only where –

(a) the court considers that the appeal would have a real prospect of success; or
(b) there is some other compelling reason why the appeal should be heard.

(2) An order giving permission may –

(a) limit the issues to be heard; and
(b) be made subject to conditions.

(3) Paragraphs (1) and (2) do not apply to second appeals.

Amendments—SI 2015/548.

'reasonable prospect of success'—See *Swain v Hillman* [2001] 1 All ER 91 where the Court of Appeal said that this phrase was self-explanatory.

'compelling reason'—In serious medical cases, this could be the fact that the consequences of the decision would be irreversible for P or that it could lead to P's death.

See *Re L (A Child)* [2013] EWCA Civ 1557: Black LJ noted that 'the assessment of witnesses, including expert witnesses, is very much a matter for the judge who conducts the hearing'. Although a children's case, it would seem relevant to the Court of Protection.

See also *Aintree v James* [2013] UKSC 67, [2013] COPLR 492 where Lady Hale remarked that 'if the judge has correctly directed himself as to the law... an appellate court can only interfere with his decision if satisfied that it was wrong.'

174 Power to treat application for permission to appeal as application for reconsideration under rule 89

(1) Where a person seeking permission to appeal a decision would be entitled to seek reconsideration of that decision under rule 89 (or would have been so entitled had the application been made within 21 days of the date of that decision) –

(a) a practice direction may provide; or
(b) the court may direct,

that an application for permission shall be treated as an application for reconsideration under rule 89.

(2) In any case where paragraph (1) applies, the decision in question shall be reconsidered in accordance with the provisions of rule 89.

Amendments—Substituted by SI 2015/548.

Scope—This provision was introduced in April 2015. Reconsideration can still take place even though the 21-day period normally imposed for it has passed.

175 Appellant's notice

(1) Where the appellant seeks permission a judge other than the first instance judge, it must be requested in the appellant's notice.

(2) The appellant must file an appellant's notice at the court within –

(a) such period as may be directed or specified in the order of the first instance judge; or
(b) where that judge makes no such direction or order, 21 days after the date of the decision being appealed.

(3) The court will issue the appellant's notice and unless it orders otherwise, the appellant must serve the appellant's notice on each respondent and on such other persons as the court may direct, as soon as practicable and in any event within 21 days of the date on which it was issued.

(4) The appellant must file a certificate of service within 7 days beginning with the date on which he served the appellant's notice.

Amendments—SI 2015/548.

Rule 175(1)—The appellant's notice is Form COP35.

Rule 175(4)—The certificate of service is Form COP20.

176 Respondent's notice

(1) A respondent who –

(a) is seeking permission from a judge other than the first instance judge; or

(b) wishes to ask the appeal judge to uphold the order of the first instance judge for reasons different from or additional to those given by the first instance judge,

must file a respondent's notice.

(2) Where the respondent seeks permission from a judge other than the first instance judge, permission must be requested in the respondent's notice.

(3) A respondent's notice must be filed within –
  (a) such period as may be directed by the first instance judge; or
  (b) where the first instance judge makes no such direction, 21 days beginning with the date referred to in paragraph (4).

(4) The date is the soonest of –
  (a) the date on which the respondent is served with the appellant's notice where –
     (i) permission was given by the first instance judge; or
     (ii) permission is not required;
  (b) the date on which the respondent is served with notification that a judge other than the first instance judge has given the appellant permission; or
  (c) the date on which the respondent is served with the notification that the application for permission and the appeal itself are to be heard together.

(5) The court will issue a respondent's notice and, unless it orders otherwise, the respondent must serve the respondent's notice on the appellant, any other respondent and on such other parties as the court may direct, as soon as practicable and in any event within 21 days of the date on which it was issued.

(6) The respondent must file a certificate of service within 7 days beginning with the date on which the copy of the respondent's notice was served.

Amendments—SI 2015/548.

Forms—The respondent's notice is Form COP36. Skeleton arguments should be on Form COP37.

177 Variation of time

(1) (*revoked*)

(2) The parties may not agree to extend any date or time limit for or in respect of an appeal set by –
  (a) these Rules;
  (b) the relevant practice direction; or
  (c) an order of the appeal judge or the first instance judge.

Amendments—SI 2015/548.

178 Power of appeal judge on appeal

(1) In relation to an appeal, an appeal judge has all the powers of the first instance judge whose decision is being appealed.

(2) In particular, the appeal judge has the power to –
  (a) affirm, set aside or vary any order made by the first instance judge;
  (b) refer any claim or issue to that judge for determination;

(c) order a new hearing;
(d) make a costs order.

(3) The appeal judge may exercise his powers in relation to the whole or part of an order made by the first instance judge.

179 Determination of appeals

(1) An appeal will be limited to a review of the decision of the first instance judge unless –

(a) a practice direction makes different provision for a particular category of appeal; or
(b) the appeal judge considers that in the circumstances of the appeal it would be in the interests of justice to hold a re-hearing.

(2) Unless he orders otherwise, the appeal judge will not receive –

(a) oral evidence; or
(b) evidence that was not before the first instance judge.

(3) The appeal judge will allow an appeal where the decision of the first instance judge was –

(a) wrong; or
(b) unjust, because of a serious procedural or other irregularity in the proceedings before the first instance judge.

(4) The appeal judge may draw any inference of fact that he considers justified on the evidence.

(5) At the hearing of the appeal a party may not rely upon a matter not contained in his appellant's or respondent's notice unless the appeal judge gives permission.

180–182 (*revoked*)

PART 21
ENFORCEMENT

183 Enforcement methods – general

(1) The rules in this Part make provision for the enforcement of judgments and orders.

(2) The relevant practice direction may set out methods of enforcing judgments or orders.

(3) An application for an order for enforcement may be made on application by any person in accordance with Part 10.

Scope of rule—This rule deals with enforcement. It is supplemented by Practice Direction 21A.

Rule 183(3)—This rule provides that an application for enforcement is made in accordance with Part 10. The application is therefore made on Form COP9.
  This presents a problem. In the civil courts, applications for orders to obtain information, third party debt orders and charging orders have their own dedicated application forms. This is because the application forms follow the relevant Practice Direction in the CPR which prescribes the information that has to be included on an application form.

Where an application is made in the Court of Protection, only Form COP9 is used. This form is a general application form. Accordingly, the practitioner must ensure that all the information required by the CPR for a particular method of enforcement is included in COP9. The alternative is to attach the appropriate civil court application form to COP9. This way, nothing will have been omitted. Furthermore, if the enforcement application is transferred to the High Court or the county court, it will avoid the problem of being asked to complete a proper application form there, which will only delay the process.

The civil court application forms are:

- Order to question an individual debtor: N316.
- Order to question an officer of a company or other corporation: N316A.
- Third Party Debt Orders: N349.
- Charging Orders: N379.

It is suggested that it may be better to simply ask the Court of Protection to transfer the enforcement application to the High Court or the County Court as they are better used to processing these applications and this will avoid delay.

184 Application of the Civil Procedure Rules 1998 and RSC Orders

The following provisions apply, as far as they are relevant and with such modifications as may be necessary, to the enforcement of orders made in proceedings under these Rules –

(a) Parts 70 (General Rules about Enforcement of Judgments and Orders), 71 (Orders to Obtain Information from Judgment Debtors), 72 (Third Party Debt Orders), 73 (Charging Orders, Stop Orders and Stop Notices), 83 (Writs and Warrants – General Provisions) and 84 (Enforcement by Taking Control of Goods) of the Civil Procedure Rules 1998.

(b) …

Amendments—SI 2015/548.

Scope of rule—This rule incorporates provisions of the CPR, which deal with enforcement of judgments, and was amended in July 2015 to take account of amendments to the CPR.

CPR Part 70—This rule contains general rules about enforcement.

It allows a judgment creditor to use any method of enforcement or even more than one method of enforcement. It allows transfer of a High Court case to the county court for enforcement purposes.

CPR Part 70 has a Practice Direction which supplements the rule.

CPR Part 71—This rule sets out the procedure for obtaining an order to obtain information from a judgment debtor.

The judgment creditor may wish to ascertain the full extent of the judgment debtor's assets, liabilities, income and expenditure and other information. He or she may therefore apply to the Court for an order that the judgment debtor attend the court on a specified day.

The purpose of this rule is to enable the judgment creditor to enforce a judgment or order which he or she will be able to do effectively if he or she has knowledge of the judgment debtor's financial position.

The Practice Direction to CPR Part 71 contains a sample of the form that the judgment debtor will complete when he or she attends court. However, there is nothing to stop the judgment creditor from asking further questions.

Normally, the examination is carried out by a court officer. The court officer will ask the judgment debtor to complete the form. On occasion, the judgment creditor will attend to put questions to the judgment debtor. If the judgment debtor refuses to answer questions, a judge (or master in the High Court) can rule on whether the question should be answered. In complicated cases, a judge is often asked by the judgment creditor to preside over the questioning.

If the judgment debtor fails to attend court, a committal order can be made and if he or she still fails to attend, a warrant can be issued by a judge for him or her to be arrested and brought to court.

It is suggested that if such a procedure is invoked following a judgment in the Court of Protection, the case should be transferred either to the High Court or the county court for enforcement. This is more sensible as those courts regularly deal with these matters.

The Practice Direction to CPR Part 71 sets out the information that must be included in the application form.

CPR Part 72—This rule allows the court to make a third party debt order. Prior to the CPR, this process used to be known as obtaining a garnishee order.

This rule allows the court to make an order requiring a third party to pay the judgment creditor a specified sum.

The application is made without notice to the judgment debtor. Assuming the application form contains the correct information and the debt is one that can be attached, an interim third party debt order will be made. This is served on the judgment debtor and the third party. The court will also list a date for the hearing when it will consider making the order final. Pending the final order, the third party will not release the attached funds to the judgment debtor.

There is a considerable body of case-law concerning what is and what is not an attachable debt and reference should be made to this before making the application.

The rules also contain provisions to allow a debtor who will suffer hardship by the order applying to the court for an order to release funds from his or her account.

CPR Part 73—This rule allows a judgment creditor to apply for a charging order which is an equitable mortgage over land or other property such as shares. It is a discretionary order.

The normal application has to contain specific information as provided for in the Practice Direction which supplements this rule. If a charging order over land is sought, up-to-date official copies of the entry at HM Land Registry should be attached to the application as proof that the judgment debtor owns the property.

The application is considered without notice by a judge on paper. An interim charging order is then granted if the application is approved. The interest created by the interim order can be immediately registered at HM Land Registry. The interim order will also contain a hearing date for the final hearing when the Court will determine if the interim order should be made final. Once a final order is granted, that is the end of the application. If the judgment creditor wants to obtain an order for sale of the property, this requires new proceedings in the civil courts. If the application is by a deputy, permission of the Court of Protection will be required.

This rule also allows the Court to make a stop order and stop notice to effectively stop certain steps in relation to securities and funds. The Charging Orders Act 1979, s 5 sets out the scope of the Court's power. Unlike charging orders, there is no specified application notice in the civil courts and Form COP9 will not present any problem.

CPR Parts 83 and 84—These provisions replace Orders 45, 46 and 47 of the Rules of the Supreme Court 1965, which dealt with writs of fi fa and warrants of execution. The CPR were amended to remove reference to these rules are replace them with CPR Pts 83 and 84 and these rules were amended in July 2015 to match the CPR.

The changes come from Part 3 of the Tribunals, Courts and Enforcement Act 2007, the Taking Control of Goods Regulations 2013 (SI 2013/1894), the Taking Control of Goods (Fees) Regulations 2014 (SI 1041/1), the Certification of Enforcement Agents Regulations 2014 (SI 2014/421) and the Civil Procedure (Amendment) Rules 2014 (SI 2014/407).

Part 83 deals with writs and warrants; Part 84 deals with enforcement by taking control of goods; and Part 85 deals with claims on controlled and executed goods. These rules are reproduced in Part V of this work for your reference. The terminology is also different. Writs of fi fa and warrants of execution are replaced with a writ or warrant of control. National standards of good practice also exist so a creditor should act proportionately taking into account the debtor's circumstances and not issue a warrant knowing that the debtor is not at an address.

Orders for committal

185 Contempt of court – generally

An application relating to the committal of a person for contempt of court shall be made to a judge and the power to punish for contempt may be exercised by an order of committal.

General—The rules which apply to proceedings for contempt of court are governed by PD21A (Contempt of Court). There is also a Practice Direction made by the Lord Chief Justice dated 26 March 2015 that applies to committal proceedings in civil and family proceedings as well as the

Court of Protection. This provides for a general rule of an open hearing for committal proceedings and the PD sets out the procedures to be followed. A further Practice Guidance was issued on 24 June 2015 to answer questions that arose from the 26 March 2015 guidance (both are set out in Part V).

Definition of a judge—Judge is defined by r 6 as a judge nominated to be a judge of the Court of Protection under MCA 2005. In *Re Whiting* [2013] EWHC B27 (Fam), [2014] COPLR 107 Hayden J seems to question the need for a committal application to be transferred to a High Court Judge because use of the Tipstaff might be required. Section 47(1) of the MCA 2005 gives all judges in the Court of Protection the same powers as a High Court Judge which would include a committal application. It is suggested that thought should be given to whether it is necessary therefore to transfer a case having regard to the overriding objective. If the Tipstaff is likely to be required, a transfer may be unavoidable.

In *A Local Authority v B, F and G* [2014] EWHC B18 (COP), the court was invited to make a Hadkinson order. This is an order preventing any application to the court by a person who is in contempt of court until he has purged himself of his contempt (see *Hadkinson v Hadkinson* [1952], p 285, per Denning MR). The circuit judge held that it was open to make a Hadkinson order in the Court of Protection.

The test for the making of a *Hadkinson* order is set out in *JSC BTA Bank v Mukhtar Ablyazov* [2013] EWHC 1979 (Comm). Popplewell J held that the issue is:

'... whether, taking into account all the circumstances of the case, it is in the interests of justice not to hear the contemnor. Refusing to hear a contemnor is a step that the court will only take where the contempt itself impedes the course of justice. What is meant by impeding the course of justice in this context... means making it more difficult for the court to ascertain the truth or to enforce the orders which it may make.'

It remains to be seen whether the application of a best interests test reduces a Hadkinson order to rare cases or not.

186 Application for order of committal

(1) An application for an order of committal must be made by filing an application notice, stating the grounds of the application, and must be supported by an affidavit made in accordance with the relevant practice direction.

(2) Subject to paragraph (3), the application notice, a copy of the affidavit in support thereof and notice of the date of the hearing of the application must be served personally on the person sought to be committed.

(3) Without prejudice to its powers under Part 6, the court may dispense with service under this rule if it thinks it just to do so.

Rule 186(1)—The application is made on Form COP9. The contents of the affidavit are set out at Practice Direction 21A, paras 4, 5 and 6.

187 Oral evidence

If on the hearing of the application the person sought to be committed expresses a wish to give oral evidence on his own behalf, he shall be entitled to do so.

Legal advice—The person should also be given an opportunity to obtain legal advice if he or she is not legally represented at the hearing. (See *Hammerton v Hammerton* [2007] EWCA Civ 248, [2007] 2 FLR 1133 and *Greensill v Greensill* [2007] EWCA Civ 680.)

Practice Direction 21A, para 9 clearly contemplates the situation where at the first hearing the Court cannot proceed for whatever reason.

188 Hearing for committal order

(1) Except where the court permits, no grounds shall be relied upon at the hearing except the grounds set out in the application notice.

(2) Notwithstanding rule 90(1) (general rule – hearing to be in private), when determining an application for committal the court will hold the hearing in public unless it directs otherwise.

(3) If the court hearing an application in private decides that a person has committed a contempt of court, it shall state publicly –

  (a) the name of that person;
  (b) in general terms the nature of the contempt in respect of which the order of committal is being made; and
  (c) any punishment imposed.

(4) If the person sought to be committed does not attend the hearing, the court may fix a date and time for the person to be brought before the court.

The hearing—See the Practice Direction on Committal for Contempt of Court dated 27 March 2015 (set out in Part V), which provides that, save for exceptional circumstances, a committal shall be held in public. It also provides for the manner in which the outcome of the hearing is published. This rule should therefore be read together with the Practice Direction.

The background to this Practice Direction arises from the case of *SCC v LM and others* [2013] EWHC 1137 (COP) and *Stoke City Council v Maddocks* [2012] EWHC B31 (COP), which prompted two Practice Guidance notes in 2013, which have now been superseded by this Practice Direction.

Standard of proof—The standard of proof is that a breach must be proved beyond reasonable doubt and the breach must normally be wilful and deliberate.

The nature of Court of Protection proceedings should be considered when approaching the imposition of a punishment for contempt.

Proceedings in the Court of Protection are varied: some cases may be identical or similar to regular civil proceedings, others may be more like family cases. The Court will therefore have to approach punishment with care and consideration of the various authorities (see e g *Hale v Tanner* [2000] 2 FLR 879).

The Court should also have in mind that the objective of committal is to mark disapproval of the breach of its order and to secure compliance.

It is also suggested that the effect on P or P's family of committal proceedings and any punishment imposed should be considered.

In *Re Whiting* [2013] EWHC B27 (Fam), [2014] COPLR 107 Hayden J made a number of comments on committal applications, namely:

1. That the procedure has an essentially criminal law complexion and contempt must therefore be proved to the criminal standard. The burden of proof rests on the applicant.
2. Contempt of court involves a deliberate contumelious disobedience to the court
3. It is not enough to suspect recalcitrance; it must be proved
4. Committal is not an automatic consequence of contempt though the options before the court are limited. Those options may include doing nothing, adjourning the application, levying a fine, sequester assets or making orders under the Mental Health Act.
5. The objective of the application is dual: to punish for the breach and to ensure future compliance.
6. An application should be brought expeditiously whilst primary evidence is available and the incidents are fresh in the mind of the relevant parties. In the Court of Protection, this was very important as there may be reliance on a vulnerable witness and where capacity might have to be assessed.
7. Injunction orders must be clear, unambivalent and drafted with care.
8. Breaches must be particularised with care so the contemnor knows exactly what is said against him so he can defend himself.

Procedure—In *Re Whiting* (above) Hayden J emphasised the need for lawyers and social workers to work together to ensure a committal application was properly prepared

189 Power to suspend execution of committal order

(1) A judge who has made an order of committal may direct that the execution of the order of committal shall be suspended for such period or on such terms and conditions as may be specified.

(2) Where an order is suspended under paragraph (1), the applicant for the order of committal must, unless the court otherwise directs, serve on the person against whom it was made a notice informing him of the making and terms of the direction under that paragraph.

190 Warrant for arrest

A warrant for the arrest of a person against whom an order of committal has been made shall not, without further order of the court, be enforced more than 2 years after the date on which the warrant is issued.

191 Discharge of person committed

(1) The court may, on the application of any person committed to prison for contempt of court, discharge him.

(2) Where a person has been committed for failing to comply with a judgment or order requiring him to deliver any thing to some other person or to deposit it in court or elsewhere, and a writ of sequestration has also been issued to enforce that judgment or order, then, if the thing is in the custody or power of the person committed, the commissioners appointed by the writ of sequestration may take possession of it as if it were the property of that person and, without prejudice to the generality of paragraph (1), the court may discharge the person committed and may give such directions for dealing with the thing taken by the commissioners as it thinks fit.

192 Penal notices

(1) The court may direct that a penal notice is to be attached to any order warning the person on whom the copy of the order is served that disobeying the order would be a contempt of court punishable by imprisonment or a fine.

(2) Unless the court gives a direction under paragraph (1), a penal notice may not be attached to any order.

(3) A penal notice is to be in the following terms: 'You must obey this order. If you do not, you may be sent to prison for contempt of court.'.

Note—See *E & K v SB & JB* [2012] EWHC 4161 (COP) for an example of a penal notice being used in a health and welfare case to enforce contact orders.

193 Saving for other powers

The rules in this Part do not limit the power of the court to make an order requiring a person guilty of contempt to pay a fine or give security for his good behaviour and those rules, so far as applicable, shall apply in relation to an application for such an order as they apply in relation to an application for an order of committal.

194 Power of court to commit on its own initiative

The preceding provisions of these Rules shall not be taken as affecting the power of the court to make an order for committal on its own initiative against a person guilty of contempt of court.

PART 22
TRANSITORY AND TRANSITIONAL PROVISIONS

195 Transitory provision: applications by former receivers

(1) This rule and rule 196 –

    (a) apply in any case where a person becomes a deputy by virtue of paragraph 1(2) of Schedule 5 to the Act; but

    (b) shall cease to have effect at the end of the period specified in the relevant practice direction.

(2) The deputy may make an application to the court in connection with –

    (a) any decision in connection with the day-to-day management of P's property and affairs; or

    (b) any supplementary decision which is necessary to give full effect to any order made, or directions given, before 1 October 2007 under Part 7 of the Mental Health Act 1983.

(3) Decisions within paragraph (2) include those that may be specified in the relevant practice direction.

(4) An application –

    (a) may relate only to a particular decision or decisions to be made on P's behalf;

    (b) must specify details of the decision or decisions to be made; and

    (c) must be made using the application form set out in the relevant practice direction.

Scope of rule—The provisions of Pt 22 are now defunct given the passing of time.

196 Transitory provision: dealing with applications under rule 195

(1) The court may, in determining an application under rule 195, treat the application as if it were an application to vary the functions of the deputy which is made in accordance with the relevant practice direction made under rule 71, and dispose of it accordingly.

(2) In any other case, an application under rule 195 may be determined by an order made or directions given by –

    (a) the court; or

    (b) a person nominated under paragraph (3).

(3) The Senior Judge or the President may nominate an officer or officers of the court for the purpose of determining applications under rule 195.

(4) Where an officer has been nominated under paragraph (3) to determine an application, he may refer to a judge any proceedings or any question arising in any proceedings which ought, in the officer's opinion, to be considered by a judge.

197 Appeal against a decision of a nominated officer

(1) This rule applies in relation to decisions made under rules 195 and 196 by a nominated officer.

(2) An appeal from a decision to which this rule applies lies to a judge of the court nominated by virtue of section 46(2)(e) of the Act.

(3) No permission is required for an appeal under paragraph (2).

(4) A judge determining an appeal under paragraph (2) has all the powers that an appeal judge on appeal has by virtue of rule 178.

(5) An appeal from a decision made under paragraph (2) ('a second appeal') lies to a judge of the court nominated by virtue of section 46(2)(d) of the Act.

(6) A second appeal may be made from a decision of a nominated officer, and a judge to whom such an appeal is made may, if he considers the matter is one which ought to be heard by a judge of the court nominated by virtue of section 46(2)(a) to (c), transfer the matter to such a judge.

(7) An appeal from a decision made on a second appeal lies to the Court of Appeal.

198 Application of Rules to proceedings within paragraphs 3 and 12 of Schedule 5 to the Act

(1) In this rule, 'pending proceedings' means proceedings on an application within paragraph 3 or 12 of Schedule 5 to the Act.

(2) A practice direction shall make provision for the extent to which these Rules shall apply to pending proceedings.

199 Practice direction

A practice direction may make additional or different provision in relation to transitory and transitional matters.

PART 23
MISCELLANEOUS

200 Order or directions requiring a person to give security for discharge of functions

(1) This rule applies where the court makes an order or gives a direction –

  (a) conferring functions on any person (whether as deputy or otherwise); and
  (b) requiring him to give security for the discharge of those functions.

(2) The person on whom functions are conferred must give the security before he undertakes to discharge his functions, unless the court permits it to be given subsequently.

(3) Paragraphs (4) to (6) apply where the security is required to be given before any action can be taken.

(4) Subject to paragraph (5), the security must be given in accordance with the requirements of regulation 33(2)(a) of the Public Guardian Regulations (which

makes provision about the giving of security by means of a bond that is endorsed by an authorised insurance company or deposit-taker).

(5) The court may impose such other requirements in relation to the giving of the security as it considers appropriate (whether in addition to, or instead of, those specified in paragraph (4)).

(6) In specifying the date from which the order or directions referred to in paragraph (1) are to take effect, the court will have regard to the need to postpone that date for such reasonable period as would enable the Public Guardian to be satisfied that –

(a) if paragraph (4) applies, the requirements of regulation 34 of the Public Guardian Regulations have been met in relation to the security; and
(b) any other requirements imposed by the court under paragraph (5) have been met.

(7) 'The Public Guardian Regulations' means the Lasting Powers of Attorney, Enduring Powers of Attorney and Public Guardian Regulations 2007.

The giving of security (r 200)—Section 19(9) of the MCA 2005 provides that the court may require a deputy to provide such security as the court thinks fit for the discharge of his functions. Rule 200 contains details as to the time and manner of the giving of security. It is almost inevitable that a property and affairs deputy will be asked by the court to give security unless the deputy is a local authority.

The usual means of giving security is by way of a bond endorsed by an authorised insurance company or deposit taker although security can be provided in some other manner: see reg 33 of the Lasting Powers of Attorney, Enduring Powers of Attorney and Public Guardian Regulations 2007.

The amount of the security is decided by a judge when the order appointing the deputy is made. The decision is a judicial decision and not a mechanical one based on a formula or percentage of P's assets.

In *Re H (A Minor and Incapacitated Person); Baker v H and the Official Solicitor* [2009] COPLR Con Vol 606, HHJ Marshall QC provides helpful guidance on how the court should approach fixing the level of security. She emphasised that the purpose of the security is to protect P and his resources from the consequences of negligence or default. The court should therefore consider the real and realistic degree of the risk to P. If the cost of obtaining security imposes an unreasonable burden on P's estate, it may be possible to mitigate this by reconsidering the terms of the deputyship order and restricting the assets under the deputy's control.

However, the court concluded that 'the whole issue of the appropriate level of security must therefore be considered in the round, if possible together with any aspects of the deputyship order which can sensibly be tailored to minimise the risks whilst not causing serious practical disadvantages.'

The judge did suggest some factors to have in mind when fixing a security, namely:

(1) The value and vulnerability of the assets which are under the control of the deputy.
(2) How long it might be before a default or loss is discovered.
(3) The availability and extent of any other remedy or resource available to P in the event of a default or loss.
(4) P's immediate needs in the event of a default or loss.
(5) The cost to P of ordering security and the possibilities and cost of increasing his protection in any other way.
(6) The gravity of the consequences of loss or default for P in his circumstances.
(7) The status, experience and record of the particular deputy.

A particular problem can arise with a solicitor deputy. He may argue (as was the case in *Baker*) that the combination of his professional indemnity insurance and experience as a deputy acting for others should obviate the need for a security.

When confronting this problem, the court should have in mind the following:

(1) The amount of experience of the solicitor deputy.
(2) The level of the solicitor's indemnity cover.
(3) The fact that a claim under the solicitor's policy will be based on alleged negligence of the deputy and the insurers will need to evaluate the claim and settlement may take a long time as opposed to a claim under a security which will provoke an immediate payment.

(4) Whether a delay due to a claim under the solicitor's indemnity insurance is in P's best interests having regard to the nature of P's funds and P's needs.
(5) Whether there should be some level of cover calculated by reference to P's annual expenditure as opposed to the total value of P's assets.

To ensure that the court fixes the security at a sensible level, when submitting an application to appoint a deputy the practitioner would be well advised to file a short note addressing the issue and providing as much information as possible to allow the court to arrive at a fair conclusion on the issue of security.

It is open to a deputy nevertheless to object to the level of security by seeking a reconsideration under r 89.

201 Objections to registration of an enduring power of attorney: request for directions

(1) This rule applies in any case where –

(a) the Public Guardian (having received a notice of objection to the registration of an instrument creating an enduring power of attorney) is prevented by paragraph 13(5) of Schedule 4 to the Act from registering the instrument except in accordance with the court's directions; and

(b) on or before the relevant day, no application for the court to give such directions has been made under Part 9 (how to start proceedings).

(2) In paragraph (1)(b) the relevant day is the later of –

(a) the final day of the period specified in paragraph 13(4) of Schedule 4 to the Act; or

(b) the final day of the period of 14 days beginning with the date on which the Public Guardian receives the notice of objection.

(3) The Public Guardian may seek the court's directions about registering the instrument by filing a request in accordance with the relevant practice direction.

(4) As soon as practicable and in any event within 21 days of the date on which the request was made, the court will notify –

(a) the person (or persons) who gave the notice of objection; and
(b) the attorney or, if more than one, each of them.

(5) As soon as practicable and in any event within 21 days of the date on which the request is filed, the Public Guardian must notify the donor of the power that the request has been so filed.

(6) The notice under paragraph (4) must –

(a) state that the Public Guardian has requested the court's directions about registration;

(b) state that the court will give directions in response to the request unless an application under Part 9 is made to it before the end of the period of 21 days commencing with the date on which the notice is issued; and

(c) set out the steps required to make such an application.

(7) 'Notice of objection' means a notice of objection which is made in accordance with paragraph 13(4) of Schedule 4 to the Act.

Scope of rule—This rule is supplemented by Practice Direction 23A. The rule deals with the situation where the Public Guardian has received an objection to registration of an enduring power of attorney but no application has been made to the Court. The Public Guardian may apply to the Court for directions.

The application by the Public Guardian is made on Form COP17. The Public Guardian will also notify the donor in accordance with Part 7 that he or she has applied for directions.

Once Form COP17 has been filed, the Court will give notice that an application has been made to the person who gave notice of the objection and to the attorneys under the enduring power of attorney.

Any person who wishes to participate in the proceedings has to file Form COP8 and comply with the requirements of Part 9, Practice Direction H.

If no application is received, the Court will proceed to deal with the matter.

It is likely that the Court will order that unless any application is made to object to registration of the enduring power of attorney within a given period of time, the enduring power of attorney can be registered.

202 Disposal of property where P ceases to lack capacity

(1) This rule applies where P ceases to lack capacity.

(2) In this rule, 'relevant property' means any property belonging to P and forming part of his estate, and which –

   (a) remains under the control of anyone appointed by order of the court; or
   (b) is held under the direction of the court.

(3) The court may at any time make an order for any relevant property to be transferred to P, or at P's direction, provided that it is satisfied that P has the capacity to make decisions in relation to that property.

(4) An application for an order under this rule is to be made in accordance with Part 10.

Practice Direction—Practice Direction 23B supplements this rule.

Procedure—Where P ceases to lack capacity, the application is brought using the procedure under Part 10 and therefore Form COP9 will be used.

If P has died, Form COP9 should be used when applying for any final directions hearing. The Public Guardian will require a final report from the deputy. Any security bond will not be discharged until the Court is satisfied that the Public Guardian does not require a final report or that he or she is satisfied with the final report.

Practice Direction 2A – Participation of P

This Practice Direction supplements Part 2 of the Court of Protection Rules 2007

1 Developments in the case law both of the European Court of Human Rights and domestic courts have highlighted the importance of ensuring that P takes an appropriate part in the proceedings and the court is properly informed about P; and the difficulties of securing this in a way which is proportionate to the issues involved and the nature of the decisions which need to be taken and avoids excessive delay and cost.

2 To this end, rule 3A makes provision to –

   (a) ensure that in every case the question of what is required to ensure that P's "voice" is properly before the court is addressed; and
   (b) provide flexibility allowing for a range of different methods to achieve this,

with the purpose of ensuring that the court is in a position to make a properly informed decision at all relevant stages of a case.

3 The great majority of cases in terms of numbers before the Court of Protection relate to non-contentious matters concerning property and affairs, where there is a need to preserve P's resources and experience has shown that they can be dealt with on paper and without joining P as a party or appointing anyone to represent P. This is covered by Rule 3A(2)(e) which provides that none of the listed directions need be made.

4 Other cases, involving a range of issues relating to both property and affairs and personal welfare do or may call for a higher level of participation by or on behalf of P at one or more stages of the case.

5 Rule 3A accordingly requires the court in every case to consider whether it should make one, or more, of a number of possible directions for securing P's participation. These directions cover a range from the joining of P as a party securing P's participation by the appointment of an accredited legal representative; securing P's participation by the appointment of a representative; securing P's participation by giving P the opportunity to address the judge directly or indirectly; and securing P's participation in some other way which meets the overriding objective.

6 In considering whether it should make any of these directions, and if so which of them, the court is required to have regard to a range of factors to determine the participation and representation needed. In this way the court is both required and enabled to tailor the provision it directs for P's participation and representation to the circumstances of the individual case.

7 If the court concludes that P lacks capacity to conduct the proceedings and the circumstances require that P should be joined as a party, the order joining P as a party shall only take effect on the appointment of a litigation friend or, if the court so directs, on or after the appointment of an accredited legal representative. This enables steps to be taken and orders to be made before P becomes a party. During that period P's participation can be secured and the court can seek relevant information in any of the ways set out Rule 3A(2)(b) to (e).

8 Provisions relating to the appointment of a litigation friend and Rule 3A representatives (namely an accredited legal representative appointed pursuant to Rule 3A(2)(b) and a representative appointed pursuant to Rule 3A(2)(c)) are contained in Part 17. Rule 3A representatives can only be appointed with their consent.

9 An accredited legal representative is defined in Rule 6. When such representatives exist one can be appointed whether or not P is joined as a party and this may be of assistance if urgent orders are needed, particularly if they are likely to have an impact on the final orders (e.g. an urgent order relating to residence).

10 When P lacks capacity to conduct the proceedings and is made a party an accredited legal representative is not intended as a substitute for a litigation friend, but as an alternative in a suitable case (or in the early stages of the case).

11 When P lacks capacity to conduct the proceedings and an order that he is to be a party is made factors relevant to the choice between appointing a litigation friend and an accredited legal representative to represent him as a party will include –

- Whether there will be a need for expert or other evidence to be obtained and filed, or other material gathered, on P's behalf;
- The nature and complexity of the case;
- The likely range of issues.

12 In other cases their nature and complexity, the issues raised or likely to be raised in them and the stage they have reached could mean that the assistance of an accredited legal representative is not required or is inappropriate and that P's participation is best secured and the court will be properly informed by the appointment of a representative under Rule 3A(2)(c) (who could be a friend, an IMCA, an advocate appointed under the Care Act 2014, a family member or anyone with relevant knowledge) or by directions being made under Rule 3A(d) or (e).

13 A Rule 3A representative must be able to discharge his or her functions fairly and competently It is possible that a Rule 3A representative may be in, or find himself or herself in, a personal or professional position in which he or she cannot properly represent P, provide the court with information about P or carry out other functions directed by the court. In such a case, Section 2 of Part 17 allows for the court to vary the terms of the appointment with a view to resolving the difficulty, or to discharge the appointment altogether (in which case the court will consider afresh whether it should make one or more of the directions in paragraph (2) of Rule 3A).

Authorised Court Officers

Practice Direction 3A – Authorised Court Officers

This practice direction supplements Part 3 of the Court of Protection Rules 2007

General

1.1. Rule 7A enables a practice direction to specify the circumstances in which an authorised court officer is able to exercise the jurisdiction of the court.

1.2. A court officer is so authorised by the Senior Judge or the President pursuant to rule 7A(1).

Applications that may be dealt with by authorised court officers

2.1. Subject to paragraphs 2.2, 3 and 4.2 an authorised court officer may deal with any of the following applications:

(a) applications to appoint a deputy for property and affairs;
(b) applications to vary the powers of a deputy appointed for property and affairs under an existing order;
(c) applications to discharge a deputy for property and affairs and appoint a replacement deputy;
(d) applications to appoint and discharge a trustee;
(e) applications to sell or purchase real property on behalf of P;
(f) applications to vary the security in relation to a deputy for property and affairs;
(g) applications to discharge the security when the appointment of a deputy for property and affairs comes to an end;
(h) applications for the release of funds for the maintenance of P, or P's property, or to discharge any debts incurred by P;
(i) applications to sell or otherwise deal with P's investments;
(j) applications for authority to apply for a grant of probate or representation for the use and benefit of P;
(k) applications to let and manage property belonging to P;
(l) applications for a detailed assessment of costs;
(m) applications to obtain a copy of P's will;
(n) applications to inspect or obtain copy documents from the records of the court; and
(o) applications which relate to one or more of the preceding paragraphs and which a judge has directed should be dealt with by an authorised court officer.

2.2. An authorised court officer may not conduct a hearing and must refer to a judge any application or any question arising in any application which is contentious or which, in the opinion of the officer:

(a) is complex;
(b) requires a hearing; or
(c) for any other reason ought to be considered by a judge.

Case management powers of authorised court officers

3. Authorised court officers may only exercise the following case management powers when dealing with any of the applications listed at paragraph 2.1:

   (a) extend or shorten the time for compliance with any rule, practice direction, or court order or direction pursuant to rule 25(2)(a) (even if an application for extension is made after the time for compliance has expired);
   (b) take any step or give any direction for the purpose of managing the case and furthering the overriding objective pursuant to rule 25(2)(m);
   (c) make any order they consider appropriate pursuant to rule 25(5) even if a party has not sought that order; and
   (d) vary or revoke an order pursuant to rule 25(6).

Reconsideration of decisions of authorised court officers

4.1. P, any party to the proceedings or any other person affected by an order made by an authorised court officer may apply to the court, pursuant to rule 89, to have the order reconsidered by a judge.

4.2. An authorised court officer may not in any circumstances deal with an application for reconsideration of an order made by him or made by another authorised court officer.

Appeals against decisions of authorised court officers

5.1 No appeal lies against a decision of an authorised court officer. If P, any party, or any other person affected by an order of an authorised court officer is dissatisfied with a decision made by that officer they should apply for it to be reconsidered by a judge pursuant to rule 89 and to paragraph 4 of this Practice Direction.

Practice Direction 3B – Levels of Judiciary

This Practice Direction supplements Part 3 of the Court of Protection Rules 2007

General

1.1 Rule 6 makes provision for a practice direction to set out which of the judges who have been nominated to act as a judge of the Court of Protection under section 46 of the Act are to be Tier 2 Judges and Tier 3 Judges.

1.2 A judge who has been nominated to act as a judge of the Court of Protection under section 46 of the Act and who is neither a Tier 2 Judge nor a Tier 3 Judge is a

Tier 1 Judge.

1.3 Rule 89 makes provision as to which judges of the Court of Protection may reconsider decisions made by Tier 1 Judges, Tier 2 Judges and Tier 3 Judges.

1.4 Part 20 makes provision as to the destination of appeals from Tier 1 Judges, Tier 2 Judges and Tier 3 Judges.

Tier 2 Judges

2 The following judges are Tier 2 Judges for the purposes of the Court of Protection Rules 2007:

 (a) The Senior Judge
 (b) a judge who has been nominated to act as a judge of the Court of Protection under section 46 of the Act by virtue of holding one of the following offices:
  (i) a circuit judge;
  (ii) a recorder
  (iii) a judge of the Upper Tribunal, by virtue of appointment under paragraph 1(1) of Schedule 3 to the Tribunals, Courts and Enforcement Act 2007,
  (iv) a transferred-in judge of the Upper Tribunal (see section 31(2) of the Tribunals, Courts and Enforcement Act 2007),
  (v) a deputy judge of the Upper Tribunal (whether under paragraph 7 of Schedule 3 to, or section 31(2) of, the Tribunals, Courts and Enforcement Act 2007),
  (vi) the Judge Advocate General,
  (vii) a person appointed under section 30(1)(a) or (b) of the Courts-Martial (Appeals) Act 1951 (assistants to the Judge Advocate General),
  (viii) the Chamber President, or Deputy Chamber President, of a chamber of the First-tier Tribunal or of a chamber of the Upper Tribunal.

Tier 3 Judges

3 The following judges are Tier 3 Judges for the purposes of the Court of Protection Rules 2007:

 (a) The President
 (b) The Vice-President
 (c) a judge who has been nominated to act as a judge of the Court of Protection under section 46 of the Act by virtue of holding one of the following offices:

(i) The President of the Family Division
(ii) The Chancellor
(iii) The President of the Queen's Bench Division
(iv) The Master of the Rolls
(v) The Lord Chief Justice
(vi) The Senior President of Tribunals
(vii) a puisne judge of the High Court
(viii) a deputy judge of the High Court
(ix) an ordinary judge of the Court of Appeal (including the vice-president, if any, of either division of that court).

Practice Direction 3C – Application of the Civil Procedure Rules 1998 and the Family Procedure Rules 2010

This Practice Direction supplements Part 3 of the Court of Protection Rules 2007

1 Rule 9(2) allows a practice direction to specify the date at which the relevant versions of the Civil Procedure Rules 1998 and the Family Procedure Rules 2010 were in force for the purposes of references to either body of those Rules in the Court of Protection Rules 2007.

2 A reference in these Rules to the Civil Procedure Rules 1998 is to that version of those Rules in force on the 6th April 2015.

3 A reference in these Rules to the Family Procedure Rules 2010 is to that version of those Rules in force on the 6th April 2015.

General Provisions

Practice Direction 4A – Court documents

This practice direction supplements Part 4 of the Court of Protection Rules 2007

Signature of documents by mechanical means

1. Where, under rule 10(2), a replica signature is printed electronically or by other mechanical means on any document, the name of the person whose signature is printed must also be printed so that the person may be identified.

Form of documents

2. Documents drafted by a legal representative should bear his signature and if they are drafted by a legal representative as a member or employee of a firm, they should state the capacity in which he is signing, and the name of the firm by which he is employed.

3. Every document prepared by a party for filing or use at the court must:

   (a) unless the nature of the document renders it impracticable, be on A4 paper of durable quality having a margin not less than 3.5 centimetres wide;
   (b) be fully legible and should normally be typed;
   (c) where possible be bound securely in a manner which would not hamper filing;
   (d) have the pages numbered consecutively;
   (e) be divided into numbered paragraphs; and
   (f) have all numbers, including dates, expressed as figures.

4. A document which is a copy produced by a colour photostat machine or other similar device may be filed at the court office provided that the coloured date seal of the court is not reproduced on the copy.

Documents for filing at court

5. The date on which a document was filed at court must be recorded on the document. This may be done with a seal or a receipt stamp.

6. Particulars of the date of delivery at a court office of any document for filing and the title of the proceedings in which the document is filed shall be entered in court records, on the court file, or on a computer kept in the court office for that purpose. Except where a document has been delivered at the court office through the post, the time of delivery should also be recorded.

Filing by facsimile

7. In relation to the filing of documents by facsimile ('fax'):

   (a) subject to subparagraphs (h) and (i), a party may file a document at court by sending it by fax;
   (b) where a party files a document by fax, he must not send a hard copy in addition;
   (c) a party filing a document by fax should be aware that the document is not

filed at court until it is delivered by the court's fax machine, regardless of the time that is shown to have been transmitted from the party's machine;
(d) the time of delivery of the faxed document will be recorded on it in accordance with paragraph 6;
(e) it remains the responsibility of the party to ensure that the document is delivered to the court in time;
(f) if a fax is delivered after 4pm, it will be treated as filed on the next day the court office is open;
(g) if a fax relates to a hearing, the date and time of the hearing should be prominently displayed;
(h) fax should not be used to send letters or documents of a routine or non-urgent nature;
(i) fax should not be used, except in an unavoidable emergency, to deliver:
  (i) a document which attracts a fee;
  (ii) a document relating to a hearing less than 2 hours ahead of that hearing; or
  (iii) skeleton arguments;
(j) where paragraph 7(i)(i) applies, the fax should give an explanation for the emergency and include an undertaking that the fee or money has been dispatched that day by post or will be paid at the court office counter the following business day; and
(k) where the court has several fax machines, each allocated to an individual section, fax messages should only be sent to the machine of the section for which the message is intended.

Editing information from court documents

8. An application made pursuant to rule 19 for an order that a specified part of a document is to be edited must be made in accordance with the Part 10 procedure, using a COP9 application notice.

9. The person making the application must provide the court with a draft copy of the document which is sought to be edited, with the part or parts which are sought to be deleted clearly marked.

Copies

10. Unless:

(a) a rule or practice direction provides otherwise; or
(b) the court directs otherwise,

when a document is to be filed at the court, the person filing the document must provide the original and one copy of the document.

Practice Direction 4B – Statements of truth

This practice direction supplements Part 4 of the Court of Protection Rules 2007

General

1. Rule 11 makes provision for certain documents to be verified by a statement of truth. These documents are specified in rule 11(1).

Form of the statement of truth

2. The form of the statement of truth verifying an application form is as follows:

> '[I believe] [The applicant believes] that the facts stated in this application form and its annex(es) are true.'[1]

3. The form of the statement of truth verifying a document for court proceedings is as follows:

> '[I believe] [The (applicant or as may be) believes] that the facts stated in this [name of document being verified] [and attachments] are true.'

4. The form of the statement of truth verifying a witness statement is as follows:

> 'I believe that the facts stated in this witness statement are true.'

5. The form of the statement of truth verifying an expert's report or a report prepared pursuant to section 49 of the Act is as follows:

> 'I confirm that insofar as the facts stated in my report are within my own knowledge I have made clear which they are and I believe them to be true and that the opinions expressed represent my true and complete professional opinion.'

6. Where the statement of truth is contained in a separate document, the document being verified should be identified in the statement of truth by including in the statement of truth:

   (a) the name of the person to whom the proceedings relate (P) (unless an order to the contrary pursuant to rule 19 has been made);
   (b) the case number as entered on the application form, if available;
   (c) the date the application form was issued, if available; and
   (d) the title of the document being verified.

Who may sign the statement of truth

7. A statement of truth verifying a witness statement must be signed by the witness.

8. A statement of truth verifying an expert's report must be signed by the expert.

9. A statement of truth verifying a report prepared pursuant to section 49 of the Act must be signed by the person who prepared the report.

10. The individual who signs a statement of truth must print his name clearly beneath his signature.

---

[1] Rule 11(3) provides that where a party is conducting proceedings with a litigation friend, a statement of truth in a permission form, an application form or application notice is a statement that the litigation friend believes the facts stated in the document being verified are true.

11. Where a document is to be verified on behalf of a company or other corporation the statement of truth must be signed by a person holding a senior position in the company or corporation. That person must state the office or position he holds.

12. For the purposes of paragraph 11, each of the following persons is a person holding a senior position:

   (a) in respect of a registered company or corporation, a director, the treasurer, secretary, chief executive, manager or other officer of the company or corporation; and
   (b) in respect of a corporation which is not registered, in addition to those persons set out in (a), the mayor, chairman, president, town clerk or similar officer of the corporation.

13. Where the document is to be verified on behalf of a partnership, those who may sign the statement of truth are:

   (a) any of the partners; and
   (b) a person having the control or management of the partnership business.

14. Where a party is legally represented, the legal representative may sign the statement of truth on behalf of the client. The statement signed by the legal representative will refer to the client's belief, not the belief of the legal representative. In signing he must state the capacity in which he signs and the name of his firm where appropriate.

15. A legal representative who signs a statement of truth must sign in his own name and not that of his firm or employer.

16. Where a legal representative has signed a statement of truth, his signature will be taken by the court as his statement:

   (a) that the client on whose behalf he has signed had authorised him to do so;
   (b) that before signing he had explained to the client that in signing the statement of truth he would be confirming the client's belief that the facts stated in the document were true; and
   (c) that before signing he had informed the client of the possible consequences to the client if it should subsequently appear that the client did not have an honest belief in the truth of those facts.

   (Rule 14 sets out the consequences of verifying a document containing a false statement without an honest belief in its truth.)

Persons unable to read or sign documents to be verified by a statement of truth

17. Where a document containing a statement of truth is to be signed by a person who is unable to read or sign the document, it must contain a certificate made by an authorised person.

18. An authorised person is a person able to administer oaths and take affidavits but need not be independent of the parties or their representatives.

19. The authorised person must certify:

   (a) that the document has been read to the person signing it;
   (b) that the person appeared to understand it and approved its content as accurate;
   (c) that the declaration of truth has been read to that person;

(d) that the person appeared to understand the declaration and the consequences of making a false declaration (see rule 14); and
(e) that the person signed or made his mark in the presence of the authorised person.

Form of certificate of authorised person

20. 'I certify that I [name and address of authorised person] have read over the contents of this document and the declaration of truth to the person signing the document [if there are exhibits, add 'and explained the nature and effect of the exhibits referred to in it'] who appeared to understand (a) the document and approved its content as accurate and (b) the declaration of truth and the consequences of making a false declaration, and made his mark in my presence.'

Service of Documents

Practice Direction 6A – Service

This practice direction supplements Part 6 of the Court of Protection Rules 2007

Service by document exchange

1. Rule 31(6) allows documents to be served by document exchange in accordance with a practice direction.

2. Service by document exchange (DX) may take place only where:
   (a) the party's address for service includes a numbered box at a DX; or
   (b) the writing paper of the party who is to be served or of his legal representative sets out the DX box number; and
   (c) the party or his legal representative has not indicated in writing that he is unwilling to accept service by DX.

3. Service by DX is effected by leaving the document addressed to the numbered box:
   (a) at the DX of the party who is to be served; or
   (b) at a DX which sends documents to the party's DX every business day.

Service by electronic means

4. Rule 31(6) allows documents to be served by electronic means in accordance with a practice direction.

5. Subject to the provisions of paragraph 7 below, where a document is to be served by electronic means:
   (a) the party who is to be served or his legal representative must have previously expressly indicated in writing to the party serving:
      (i) that he is willing to accept service by electronic means, and
      (ii) the fax number, e-mail address, or electronic identification to which it should be sent; and
   (b) the following shall be taken as sufficient written identification for the purposes of the preceding paragraph:
      (i) a fax number set out on the writing paper of the legal representative of the party who is to be served, or
      (ii) a fax number, e-mail address or electronic identification set out on an application form or a response to an application filed with the court.

6. Where a party seeks to serve a document by electronic means he should first seek to clarify with the party who is to be served whether there are any limitations to the recipient's agreement to accept service by such means, including in relation to the format in which documents are to be sent and the maximum size of attachments that may be received.

7. An address for service given by a party must be within the jurisdiction and any fax number must be at the address for service. Where an email address or electronic identification is given in conjunction with an address for service, the email address or electronic identification will be deemed to be at the address for service.

8. Where a document is served by electronic means, the party serving the document need not in addition send a hard copy by post or document exchange.

Service on business partners

9. A document which is served by leaving it with a person at the principal or last known place of business of the partnership, must at the same time have served with it a notice as to whether the person is being served:

   (a)   as a partner;
   (b)   as a person having control or management of the partnership business; or
   (c)   as both.

Service on a company or other corporation

10. Personal service on a registered company or corporation in accordance with rule 31 is effected by leaving a document with a person holding a senior position in the company or corporation.

11. Each of the following persons is a person holding a senior position:

   (a)   in respect of a registered company or corporation, a director, the treasurer, secretary, chief executive, manager or other officer of the company or corporation; and
   (b)   in respect of a corporation which is not registered, in addition to those persons set out in (a), the mayor, chairman, president, town clerk or similar officer of the corporation.

Change of address

12. A party or his legal representative who changes his address for service shall give notice in writing of the change as soon as it has taken place to the court and every other party.

Service by the court

13. Where the court effects service of a document, the method will normally be by first class post.

14. Where the court effects service of an acknowledgment of service, the court will also serve or deliver a copy of any notice of funding that has been filed provided:

   (a)   it was filed at the same time as the acknowledgment of service; and
   (b)   copies were provided for service.

Applications for service by an alternative method

15. An application for an order for service by an alternative method pursuant to rule 31(4) must be made by filing a COP9 application notice in accordance with Part 10, and supported by a witness statement containing evidence which states:

   (a)   the reason an order for an alternative method of service is sought;
   (b)   what steps have been taken to serve by other permitted means; and
   (c)   the alternative method of service that is proposed, and the reason/s why it is believed that service by such a method will come to the notice of the person to be served.

Certificate of service or non-service

16. Where a certificate of service or non-service is required to be filed, Form COP20A should be used.

Application to dispense with service

17. An application for an order to dispense with service pursuant to rule 38 should be made by filing a COP9 application notice in accordance with Part 10.

Practice Direction 6B – Service out of the Jurisdiction

This Practice Direction supplements Part 6 of the Court of Protection Rules 2007

Scope of this Practice Direction

1.1 This Practice Direction supplements rules 39 to 39H (service out of the jurisdiction) of Part 6.

Documents to be filed under rule 39F(2)(c)

2.1 A party must provide the following documents for each party to be served out of the jurisdiction –

(1) a copy of the application form and any other relevant documents;
(2) a duplicate of the application form, copies of any documents accompanying the application and copies of any other relevant documents;
(3) forms for responding to the application; and
(4) any translation required under rule 39G in duplicate.

2.2 Some countries require legalisation of the document to be served and some require a formal letter of request which must be signed by the Senior Master. Any queries on this should be addressed to the Foreign Process Section (Room E02) at the Royal Courts of Justice.

Service in a Commonwealth State or British overseas territory

3.1 The judicial authorities of certain Commonwealth States which are not a party to the Hague Convention require service to be in accordance with rule 39E(1)(b)(i) and not 39E(3). A list of such countries can be obtained from the Foreign Process Section (Room E02) at the Royal Courts of Justice.

3.2 The list of British overseas territories is contained in Schedule 6 to the British Nationality Act 1981. For ease of reference, these are –

(a) Anguilla;
(b) Bermuda;
(c) British Antarctic Territory;
(d) British Indian Ocean Territory;
(e) British Virgin Islands;
(f) Cayman Islands;
(g) Falkland Islands;
(h) Gibraltar;
(i) Montserrat;
(j) Pitcairn, Henderson, Ducie and Oeno;
(k) St Helena and Dependencies;
(l) South Georgia and the South Sandwich Islands;
(m) Sovereign Base Areas of Akrotiri and Dhekelia; and
(n) Turks and Caicos Islands.

Practice Direction 6B – Service out of the Jurisdiction **PD6B**

Period for responding to an application

4.1 Where rule 39B(4) applies, the periods within which the respondent must file an acknowledgment of service or an answer to the application is the number of days listed in the Table after service of the application.

4.2 Where an application is served out of the jurisdiction any statement as to the period for responding to the application contained in any of the forms required by the Court of Protection Rules to accompany the application must specify the period prescribed under rule 39B.

Period for responding to a document other than an application

5.1 Where a document other than an application is served out of the jurisdiction, the period for responding is 7 days less than the number of days listed in the Table.

Further information

5.2 Further information concerning service out of the jurisdiction can be obtained from the Foreign Process Section, Room E02, Royal Courts of Justice, Strand, London WC2A 2LL (telephone 020 7947 6691).

Place or country	number of days
Afghanistan	23
Albania	25
Algeria	22
Andorra	21
Angola	22
Anguilla	31
Antigua and Barbuda	23
Antilles (Netherlands)	31
Argentina	22
Armenia	21
Ascension Island	31
Australia	25
Austria	21
Azerbaijan	22
Azores	23
Bahamas	22

Place or country	number of days
Bahrain	22
Balearic Islands	21
Bangladesh	23
Barbados	23
Belarus	21
Belgium	21
Belize	23
Benin	25
Bermuda	31
Bhutan	28
Bolivia	23
Bosnia and Herzegovina	21
Botswana	23
Brazil	22
British Virgin Islands	31
Brunei	25
Bulgaria	23
Burkina Faso	23
Burma	23
Burundi	22
Cambodia	28
Cameroon	22
Canada	22
Canary Islands	22
Cape Verde	25
Caroline Islands	31
Cayman Islands	31

Place or country	number of days
Central African Republic	25
Chad	25
Chile	22
China	24
China (Hong Kong)	31
China (Macau)	31
China (Taiwan)	23
China (Tibet)	34
Christmas Island	27
Cocos (Keeling) Islands	41
Colombia	22
Comoros	23
Congo (formerly Congo Brazzaville or French Congo)	25
Congo (Democratic Republic)	25
Corsica	21
Costa Rica	23
Croatia	21
Cuba	24
Cyprus	31
Czech Republic	21
Denmark	21
Djibouti	22
Dominica	23
Dominican Republic	23
East Timor	25
Ecuador	22

Place or country	number of days
Egypt	22
El Salvador	25
Equatorial Guinea	23
Eritrea	22
Estonia	21
Ethiopia	22
Falkland Islands and Dependencies	31
Faroe Islands	31
Fiji	23
Finland	24
France	21
French Guyana	31
French Polynesia	31
French West Indies	31
Gabon	25
Gambia	22
Georgia	21
Germany	21
Ghana	22
Gibraltar	31
Greece	21
Greenland	31
Grenada	24
Guatemala	24
Guernsey	21
Guinea	22
Guinea-Bissau	22

Place or country	number of days
Guyana	22
Haiti	23
Holland (Netherlands)	21
Honduras	24
Hungary	22
Iceland	22
India	23
Indonesia	22
Iran	22
Iraq	22
Ireland (Republic of)	21
Ireland (Northern)	21
Isle of Man	21
Israel	22
Italy	21
Ivory Coast	22
Jamaica	22
Japan	23
Jersey	21
Jordan	23
Kazakhstan	21
Kenya	22
Kiribati	23
Korea (North)	28
Korea (South)	24
Kosovo	21
Kuwait	22

Place or country	number of days
Kyrgyzstan	21
Laos	30
Latvia	21
Lebanon	22
Lesotho	23
Liberia	22
Libya	21
Liechtenstein	21
Lithuania	21
Luxembourg	21
Macedonia	21
Madagascar	23
Madeira	31
Malawi	23
Malaysia	24
Maldives	26
Mali	25
Malta	21
Mariana Islands	26
Marshall Islands	32
Mauritania	23
Mauritius	22
Mexico	23
Micronesia	23
Moldova	21
Monaco	21
Mongolia	24

Place or country	number of days
Montenegro	21
Montserrat	31
Morocco	22
Mozambique	23
Namibia	23
Nauru	36
Nepal	23
Netherlands	21
Nevis	24
New Caledonia	31
New Zealand	26
New Zealand Island Territories	50
Nicaragua	24
Niger (Republic of)	25
Nigeria	22
Norfolk Island	31
Norway	21
Oman (Sultanate of)	22
Pakistan	23
Palau	23
Panama	26
Papua New Guinea	26
Paraguay	22
Peru	22
Philippines	23
Pitcairn, Henderson, Ducie and Oeno Islands	31

Place or country	number of days
Poland	21
Portugal	21
Portuguese Timor	31
Puerto Rico	23
Qatar	23
Reunion	31
Romania	22
Russia	21
Rwanda	23
Sabah	23
St. Helena	31
St. Kitts and Nevis	24
St. Lucia	24
St. Pierre and Miquelon	31
St. Vincent and the Grenadines	24
Samoa (U.S.A. Territory) (See also Western Samoa)	30
San Marino	21
Sao Tome and Principe	25
Sarawak	28
Saudi Arabia	24
Scotland	21
Senegal	22
Serbia	21
Seychelles	22
Sierra Leone	22
Singapore	22

Practice Direction 6B – Service out of the Jurisdiction **PD6B**

Place or country	number of days
Slovakia	21
Slovenia	21
Society Islands (French Polynesia)	31
Solomon Islands	29
Somalia	22
South Africa	22
South Georgia (Falkland Island Dependencies)	31
South Orkneys	21
South Shetlands	21
Spain	21
Spanish Territories of North Africa	31
Sri Lanka	23
Sudan	22
Surinam	22
Swaziland	22
Sweden	21
Switzerland	21
Syria	23
Tajikistan	21
Tanzania	22
Thailand	23
Togo	22
Tonga	30
Trinidad and Tobago	23
Tristan Da Cunha	31
Tunisia	22

Place or country	number of days
Turkey	21
Turkmenistan	21
Turks & Caicos Islands	31
Tuvalu	23
Uganda	22
Ukraine	21
United Arab Emirates	22
United States of America	22
Uruguay	22
Uzbekistan	21
Vanuatu	29
Vatican City State	21
Venezuela	22
Vietnam	28
Virgin Islands – U.S.A	24
Wake Island	25
Western Samoa	34
Yemen (Republic of)	30
Zaire	25
Zambia	23
Zimbabwe	22

ANNEX (SERVICE REGULATION)

****

Notifying P

Practice Direction 7A – Notifying P

This practice direction supplements Part 7 of the Court of Protection Rules 2007

General

1. Part 7 sets out the procedure to be followed where P is to be given notice of any matter or document, or provided with any document.[2] Where P becomes a party, Part 7 does not apply (except for rule 41A) and service is to be effected in accordance with Part 6 or as directed by the court.[3]

When P must be notified

2. P must be notified of the things specified in rules 41A to 45, unless the court directs otherwise. P must, therefore, be notified:

   (a) that an application form has been issued by the court or withdrawn;[4]
   (b) that an appellant's notice has been issued by the court or withdrawn;[5]
   (c) that the court has made a decision relating to him or her (other than a case management decision);[6]
   (ca) of a direction under rule 3A and of the appointment of a litigation friend, accredited legal representative, or representative on his or her behalf; and
   (d) of any other matter as the court may direct.[7]

When P may be notified of an application notice

3. The applicant is not required to, but may notify P of an application notice that is issued in accordance with Part 10. This should be done if the applicant considers it appropriate to do so, and must be done if the court makes a direction to that effect.

4. Where P is to be notified of an application notice, unless the court directs otherwise, the person notifying P must explain to him:

   (a) who the applicant is;
   (b) what the application is about;
   (c) what will happen if the court makes the order or direction that has been applied for; and
   (d) that P may seek advice and assistance in relation to any matter of which he is notified.

5. The person effecting notification must provide P with the information referred to in paragraph 4 in the manner set out in rule 46, and must comply with rules 47 and 48.

---

[2] Rule 40.
[3] Rule 40(2).
[4] Rule 42.
[5] Rule 43.
[6] Rule 44.
[7] Rule 45.

How and of what P is to be notified

6. Rule 46 sets out the manner in which P is to be notified, and rules 41A to 45 set out the matters of which P is to be notified. Rule 47 provides that P must be provided with a COP5 form for acknowledging notification. P must also be provided with a COP14 form which explains the matter for which notification is being provided.

Certificates of notification and non-notification

7. Rule 48 requires the person notifying P to file a certificate within 7 days of providing notification. Where a person fails to notify P (or is unable to do so), he must file a certificate of non-notification.[8] Certificates of notification, or non-notification (as appropriate), must be filed using forms COP20A and COP20B.

Dispensing with notification

8. The person required to notify P may apply to the court for an order either:

    (a) dispensing with the requirement to notify P; or
    (b) requiring some other person to effect the notification,[9]

using a COP9 application notice in accordance with Part 10.

9. Such an application would be appropriate where, for example, P is in a permanent vegetative state or a minimally conscious state; or where notification by the applicant is likely to cause significant and disproportionate distress to P.

---

[8] Rule 37.
[9] Rule 49.

Permission

Practice Direction 8A – Permission

This practice direction supplements Part 8 of the Court of Protection Rules 2007

Where permission is required

1. An applicant must apply for permission to start proceedings under the Act, unless either section 50 of, paragraph 20(2) of Schedule 3 to, the Act or rule 51 applies. The applicant must apply for permission when making the application, in accordance with rule 54.

2. If part of the application is a matter for which permission is required and part of it is not, permission must be sought for the part that requires it.[10]

3. In such circumstances, the applicant may file a single application form seeking both orders.

4–7. ...

Notice of permission application

8. Where the court decides to hold a hearing in order to make a decision as to permission, it will notify the parties and such other persons it requires to be notified under rule 84(4)(a).[11]

9. ...

---

[10] Rule 53(2).
[11] See r 56.

How to start proceedings

Practice Direction 9A – The application form

This practice direction supplements Part 9 of the Court of Protection Rules 2007

The application form

1. To begin proceedings, the applicant must file an application form using Form COP1.

2. The application form must:
   (a) state the matter which the applicant wants the court to decide;
   (b) state the order which the applicant is seeking;
   (c) name (unless an order to the contrary pursuant to rule 19 has been made):
      (i) the applicant,
      (ii) P,
      (iii) as a respondent, any person (other than P) whom the applicant reasonably believes to have an interest which means that he ought to be heard in relation to the application (as opposed to being notified of it), and
      (iv) any person whom the applicant intends to notify in accordance with rule 70; and
   (d) if the applicant is applying in a representative capacity, state what that capacity is.[12]

3. The application form must include (unless an order to the contrary pursuant to rule 19 has been made):
   (a) an address at which the applicant resides or carries on business;
   (b) an address at which P resides or carries on business;
   (c) an address at which each person named as a respondent to the proceedings resides or carries on business, and details of how each respondent is connected to P; and
   (d) an address at which any person (other than P) whom the applicant intends to notify of the application resides or carries on business, and details of how each person is connected to P.

4. Paragraph 3 applies even though a solicitor or litigation friend has agreed, as the case may be, to accept service.

5. The application form must be headed with the name of the person to whom the application relates (unless an order to the contrary pursuant to rule 19 has been made).

Statement of truth

6. Rule 11 requires an application form to be verified by a statement of truth where the applicant seeks to rely on matters set out in it as evidence.

7. The form of the statement of truth is as follows:

---

[12] Rule 63.

'[I believe] [The applicant believes] that the facts stated in this application form and its annex(es) are true.'

8. Attention is drawn to rule 14 which sets out the consequences of verifying an application form containing a false statement without an honest belief in its truth.

(Practice Direction B accompanying Part 4 sets out more detailed requirements for statements of truth.)

Documents to be filed with the application form

9. The application form must be supported by evidence set out in either:

(a) a witness statement; or
(b) the application form provided it is verified by a statement of truth.

10. A witness statement must be verified by a statement of truth in the following terms:

'I believe that the facts stated in this witness statement are true.'

11. The evidence must set out the facts on which the applicant relies, and all material facts known to the applicant of which the court should be made aware.

12. The documents or instruments, as the case may be, specified in the table below must be filed with the court along with the application form, unless this is impractical or the court has directed otherwise.

Type of document or instrument	When document is to be filed
Assessment of capacity form (COP3)	All applications except those concerning the court's powers under section 22 or 23 of, Schedule 4 of the Act, or applications made under practice direction 9D
Annex A Supporting information for property and affairs applications (COP1A)	Where an order relating to P's property and affairs is sought.
Annex B Supporting information for personal welfare applications (COP1B)	Where an order relating to P's personal welfare is sought.
Deputy's declaration (COP4)	Where the application is for the appointment of a deputy.
Annex C supporting information for statutory will, codicil, gift(s), deed of variation or settlement of property (COP1C)	Where an order relating to a statutory will, codicil, gift(s), deed of variation or settlement of property is sought
Annex D Supporting information for applications to appoint or discharge a trustee (COP1D)	Where an order relating to the appointment or discharge of a trustee is sought.

PART IV   COURT OF PROTECTION PRACTICE 2016

Type of document or instrument	When document is to be filed
Annex E Supporting information for an application by an existing deputy or attorney (COP1E)	Where the application is made by a person appointed deputy, an attorney under a registered enduring power of attorney or a donee of a registered lasting power of attorney; and the application relates to the applicant's powers and duties as deputy, attorney or donee in connection with P's property and affairs.
Annex F Supporting information relating to the validity or operation of an enduring power of attorney or lasting power of attorney (COP1F)	Where an relating to the validity or operation of an enduring power of attorney or lasting power of attorney order is sought.
Lasting power of attorney or enduring power of attorney	Where the application concerns the court's power under section 22 or 23 of, or Schedule 4 to, the Act (where available).
Order appointing a deputy	Where the application relates to or is made by a deputy.
Order appointing a litigation friend	Where the application is made by, or where the application relates to the appointment of, a litigation friend.
Order of the Court of Protection	Where the application relates to the order.
Order of another court (and where the judgment is not in English, a translation of it into English: (i) certified by a notary public or other qualified person; or (ii) accompanied by written evidence confirming that the translation is accurate).	Where the application relates to an order made by another court.

13. Rule 10 and Practice Direction A accompanying Part 4 set out how documents are to be filed at court.

14. If the applicant is unable to complete an assessment of capacity form (as may be the case, for example, where P does not reside with the applicant and the applicant is unable to take P to a doctor, or where P refuses to undergo the assessment), the applicant should file a witness statement with the application form explaining:

   (a) why he has not been able to obtain an assessment of capacity;
   (b) what attempts (if any) he has made to obtain an assessment of capacity; and
   (c) why he knows or believes that P lacks capacity to make a decision or decisions in relation to any matter that is subject of the proposed application.

Practice Direction 9A – The application form **PD9A**

Start of proceedings

15. The date on which the application form was received by the court will be recorded by a date stamp either on the application form held on the court file or on the letter that accompanied the application form when it was received by the court.

16. Any enquiry as to the date on which the court received an application form should be directed to a court officer.

Practice Direction 9B – Notification of other persons that an application form has been issued

This practice direction supplements Part 9 of the Court of Protection Rules 2007

General

1. Rule 70 requires the applicant to notify certain persons of the application in accordance with the relevant practice direction.[13]

Who is to be notified

2. The persons who should be notified will vary according to the nature of the application.

3. A person who has been named as respondent in the application form should not also be notified. Any reference in this practice direction to a person to be notified does not apply where the person has already been named as a respondent.

4. The applicant must seek to identify at least three persons who are likely to have an interest in being notified that an application form has been issued. The applicant should notify them:

  (a) that an application form has been issued;
  (b) whether it relates to the exercise of the court's jurisdiction in relation to P's property and affairs, or his personal welfare, or both; and
  (c) of the order or orders sought.

5. Members of P's close family are, by virtue of their relationship to P, likely to have an interest in being notified that an application has been made to the court concerning P. It should be presumed, for example that a spouse or civil partner, any other partner, parents and children are likely to have an interest in the application.

6. This presumption may be displaced where the applicant is aware of circumstances which reasonably indicate that P's family should not be notified, but that others should be notified instead. For example, where the applicant knows that the relative in question has had little or no involvement in P's life and has shown no inclination to do so, he may reasonably conclude that that relative need not be notified. In some cases, P may be closer to persons who are not relatives and if so, it will be appropriate to notify them instead of family members.

7. The following list of people is ordered according to the presumed closeness in terms of relationship to P. They should be notified in descending order (as appropriate to P's circumstances):

  (a) spouse or civil partner;
  (b) person who is not a spouse or a civil partner but who has been living with P as if they were;
  (c) parent or guardian;
  (d) child;
  (e) brother or sister;
  (f) grandparent or grandchild;
  (g) aunt or uncle;

---

[13] See r 67(2) for certain applications relating to lasting powers of attorney, and r 68(2) for certain applications relating to enduring powers of attorney, which do not require notification to be given in accordance with this practice direction.

(h) child of a person falling within subparagraph (e);
(i) step-parent; and
(j) half-brother or half-sister.

(If any of the people to be notified are children or protected parties, see rule 32.)

8. Where the applicant decides that a person listed in one of the categories in paragraph 7 ought to be notified, and there are other persons in that category (eg P has four siblings), the applicant should notify all persons falling within that category unless there is a good reason not to do so. For example, it may be a good reason not to notify every person in the category if one or more of them has had little or no involvement in P's life and has shown no inclination to do so.

9. Where the applicant chooses not to notify a person listed in paragraph 7 because the presumption has been displaced (see paragraphs 6 and 8 above) the evidence in support of the application form must also set out why that person was not notified.

10. In addition to the list in paragraph 7, the following persons must be notified where appropriate:

(a) where P is under 18, any person with parental responsibility for P within the meaning of the Children Act 1989;
(b) any legal or natural person who is likely to be affected by the outcome of any application. For example, where there is an organisation (including an NHS body) responsible for P's care (and the application is made by another person) the organisation should be notified where the application relates to the provision to, or withdrawal from, P of medical or other treatment or accommodation;
(c) any deputy appointed by the court, an attorney appointed under an enduring power of attorney or a donee of a lasting power of attorney (where that person has power to make decisions on behalf of P in regard to a matter to which the application relates). For example, where the application relates to P's property, and a deputy has been appointed to make decisions in relation to P's property, the deputy should be notified; and
(d) any other person not already mentioned whom the applicant reasonably considers has an interest in being notified that an application form has been issued. For example, P may have a close friend with an interest in being notified because he provides care to P on an informal basis.

11. Where the applicant chooses not to notify a person listed in paragraph 10 the evidence in support of the application form must also set out why that person was not notified.

Method of notification

12. Notification must be provided using a COP15 form.

13. The provisions of Part 6 and Practice Direction A accompanying Part 6 apply similarly to notification as they do to service.[14]

---

[14] See r 29(1).

Practice Direction 9C – Responding to an application

This practice direction supplements Part 9 of the Court of Protection Rules 2007

General

1. Rule 72(11) enables a practice direction to make provision about responding to applications. Rule 72 sets out the procedure to be followed where a person who has been served with or notified of an application form wishes to become, or apply to become, a party to proceedings.

2. Rule 75 sets out the procedure to be followed where a person who has not been served with or notified of an application form in accordance with rules 66 to 70 wishes to apply to become a party to proceedings.

Responding to the application

Persons served with an application

3. Where a person is served with an application form pursuant to rule 66, 67 or 68 he must, if he wishes to be a party to the proceedings, file an acknowledgment of service using Form COP5 in accordance with rule 72. By doing this, he becomes a party.[15]

Persons notified of an application

4. Where a person has been notified of an application pursuant to rule 67(5), 68(5), 69 or 70, he must, if he wishes to be a party to the proceedings, apply to the court to be joined as a party by filing an acknowledgment of notification using Form COP5 in accordance with rule 72.

Persons not served with or notified of an application

5. Where a person was not served with or notified of an application form, he must, if he wishes to be a party to the proceedings, apply to the court to be joined as a party, by filing an application to be joined using Form COP10 in accordance with rule 75.

Signing the acknowledgment

6. An acknowledgment must be signed by the person acknowledging service or notification, or by his legal representative or litigation friend.

7. Where the respondent is a company or other corporation, a person holding a senior position in the company or corporation may sign the acknowledgment on the respondent's behalf, but must state the position he holds.

8. Each of the following persons is a person holding a senior position:

 (a) in respect of a registered company or corporation, a director, the treasurer, secretary, chief executive, manager or other officer of the company or corporation; and

---

[15] Rule 73(1)(b).

(b) in respect of a corporation which is not a registered company, in addition to those persons set out at (a), the mayor, chairman, president, town clerk or similar officer of the corporation.

9. Where the respondent is a partnership, the acknowledgment may be signed by:
   (a) any of the partners; or
   (b) a person having the control or management of the partnership business.

10. The name of the person acknowledging service or notification should be set out in full on the acknowledgment.

11. If two or more persons acknowledge service or notification of an application through the same legal representative at the same time, only one acknowledgment of service need be used.

Address for service

12. The acknowledgment must include an address for the service of documents, which must be within the jurisdiction of the court.

13. When the person acknowledging service or notification is represented by a legal representative, and the legal representative has signed the acknowledgment, the address must be the legal representative's business address.

Corrections and amendments to the acknowledgment

14. Where the name of the person acknowledging service or notification has been set out incorrectly on the application form, it should be correctly set out in the acknowledgment followed by the words 'described as' and the incorrect name.

15. An acknowledgment of service or notification may be amended only with the permission of the court.

16. An application under paragraph 15 must be made by filing a COP9 application notice in accordance with Part 10 and supported by evidence.

Practice Direction 9D – Applications by currently appointed deputies, attorneys and donees in relation to P's property and affairs

This practice direction supplements Part 9 of the Court of Protection Rules 2007

General

1. Rule 71 enables a practice direction to make additional or different provision in relation to specified applications.

Applications to which this Practice Direction applies

2. This Practice Direction applies to applications:

   (a) which are made by a person who is appointed to act as a deputy for P, or by an attorney under a registered enduring power of attorney or a donee of a registered lasting power of attorney;
   (b) which relate to the applicant's powers and duties as a deputy, attorney or donee, in connection with making decisions as to P's property and affairs;
   (c) where the applicant reasonably considers that the order sought is not likely to be significant to P's estate or to any other of P's interests; and
   (d) where the applicant knows, or reasonably believes, that there are unlikely to be any objections to the application he proposes to make.

3. Applications may only be made using the procedure in this practice direction if the deputy, attorney or donee does not have the authority to make the decision or decisions in question.

Applications by deputies which may be suitable for the procedure set out in this practice direction

4. Examples of applications by deputies that may be suitable for the procedure in this practice direction include, but are not limited to:

   (a) applications for regular payments from P's assets to the deputy in respect of remuneration;
   (b) applications seeking minor variations only as to the expenses that can be paid from P's estate;
   (c) applications to change an accounting period;
   (d) applications to set or change the time by which an annual account may be submitted;
   (e) applications in relation to the sale of property owned by P, where the sale is non-contentious;
   (f) applications for authority to disclose information as to P's assets, state of health or other circumstances;
   (g) applications to make a gift or loan from P's assets, provided that the sum in question is not disproportionately large when compared to the size of P's estate as a whole;
   (h) applications to sell or otherwise deal with P's investments, provided that the sum in question is not disproportionately large when compared to the size of P's estate as a whole;
   (i) applications for the receipt or discharge of a sum due to or by P;

(j) applications for authority to apply for a grant of probate or representation, where P would be the person entitled to the grant but for his lack of capacity;
(k) applications relating to the lease or grant of a tenancy in relation to property owned by P;
(l) applications for release of funds to repair or improve P's property;
(m) applications to sell P's furniture or effects;
(n) applications for release of capital to meet expenses required for the care of P;
(o) applications to arrange an overdraft or bank loan on P's behalf;
(p) applications to open a bank account on behalf of P or for the purpose of the deputyship at a private bank, a bank that is not located in England and Wales, or at a bank which has unusual conditions attached to the operation of the account; and
(q) applications for the variation of an order for security made pursuant to rule 200.[16]

Applications by attorneys or donees which may be suitable for the procedure set out in this practice direction

5. Examples of applications by attorneys or donees that may be suitable for the procedure in this practice direction include, but are not limited to –
   (a) applications for regular payments from P's assets to the attorney or donee in respect of remuneration;
   (b) applications to make a gift from P's assets, provided that the sum in question is not disproportionately large when compared to the size of P's estate as a whole;
   (c) applications to authorise a sale of P's property to the attorney or donee, or a family member of P, the attorney or donee, at proper market value, and provided that the market value of the property in question is not disproportionately large when compared to the size of P's estate as a whole;
   (d) applications for authority to obtain a copy of P's will;
   (e) applications for the approval of equity releases; and
   (f) applications for orders for sale pursuant to paragraphs 8 and 9 of Schedule 2 to the Act.

Applications which are not suitable for the procedure set out in this practice direction

6. Examples of applications which are not suitable for the procedure in this practice direction include, but are not limited to:
   (a) applications for the removal of a deputy;
   (b) applications seeking authorisation to commence, continue or defend litigation on behalf of P;
   (c) applications for the settlement of P's property, whether for P's benefit or for the benefit of others;
   (d) applications to vary the terms of a trust or estate in which P has an interest;
   (e) applications for a statutory will or codicil; and

---

[16] Notwithstanding para 9 of this practice direction, the Public Guardian must be notified of such an application.

(f) applications to operate or cease to operate a business belonging to P, or to dissolve a partnership of which P is a member.

7. An application which is likely to be contested, or which involves large sums of money (when compared to the size of P's estate as a whole) is not suitable for the procedure set out in this practice direction.

Procedure for applications to which this Practice Direction applies

8. Applications must be made by filing a COP1 application form, together with any evidence in support of the application. However, Annexes A and B to the application form (COP1A and COP1B) are not required to be filed, nor is an assessment of capacity form.

9. Notwithstanding rules 66 to 70, applications to which this Practice Direction applies may be made, in the first instance, without serving the application form on anyone and without notifying anyone that the application has been made.

10. The court may decide, upon considering the application, that other persons ought to be notified of the application and given the opportunity to respond. In such a case, the court will give directions as to who should be served with or notified of the application and the manner in which they are to be served or notified, as the case may be.

11. The court may deal with the application without a hearing and will give directions as to who should be served with any order that it makes.

Right of reconsideration

12. Where the application is determined without notice having been given to any person or without a hearing, P, any party or any person affected by the order may apply to the court, within 21 days of having been served with the court's order, to have the order reconsidered.[17] An application to have an order reconsidered must be made by filing a COP9 application notice in accordance with Part 10.

---

[17] Rule 89 sets out the procedure for applications for reconsideration.

Practice Direction 9E – Applications relating to serious medical treatment

This practice direction supplements Part 9 of the Court of Protection Rules 2007

General

1. Rule 71 enables a practice direction to make additional or different provision in relation to specified applications.

Note—See the commentary to r 71 and in particular the comments of Cobb J in *A Local Authority v K and Others* [2013] EWHC 242 (COP), [2013] COPLR 194 cited there.

Applications to which this Practice Direction applies

2. This practice direction sets out the procedure to be followed where the application concerns serious medical treatment in relation to P.

Meaning of 'serious medical treatment' in relation to the Rules and this practice direction

3. Serious medical treatment means treatment which involves providing, withdrawing or withholding treatment in circumstances where:

 (a) in a case where a single treatment is being proposed, there is a fine balance between its benefits to P and the burdens and risks it is likely to entail for him;
 (b) in a case where there is a choice of treatments, a decision as to which one to use is finely balanced; or
 (c) the treatment, procedure or investigation proposed would be likely to involve serious consequences for P.

4. 'Serious consequences' are those which could have a serious impact on P, either from the effects of the treatment, procedure or investigation itself or its wider implications. This may include treatments, procedures or investigations which:

 (a) cause, or may cause, serious and prolonged pain, distress or side effects;
 (b) have potentially major consequences for P; or
 (c) have a serious impact on P's future life choices.

Matters which should be brought to the court

5. Cases involving any of the following decisions should be regarded as serious medical treatment for the purpose of the Rules and this practice direction, and should be brought to the court:

 (a) decisions about the proposed withholding or withdrawal of artificial nutrition and hydration from a person in a permanent vegetative state or a minimally conscious state;
 (b) cases involving organ or bone marrow donation by a person who lacks capacity to consent; and
 (c) cases involving non-therapeutic sterilisation of a person who lacks capacity to consent.

6. Examples of serious medical treatment may include:

(a) certain terminations of pregnancy in relation to a person who lacks capacity to consent to such a procedure;
(b) a medical procedure performed on a person who lacks capacity to consent to it, where the procedure is for the purpose of a donation to another person;
(c) a medical procedure or treatment to be carried out on a person who lacks capacity to consent to it, where that procedure or treatment must be carried out using a degree of force to restrain the person concerned;
(d) an experimental or innovative treatment for the benefit of a person who lacks capacity to consent to such treatment; and
(e) a case involving an ethical dilemma in an untested area.

7. There may be other procedures or treatments not contained in the list in paragraphs 5 and 6 above which can be regarded as serious medical treatment. Whether or not a procedure is regarded as serious medical treatment will depend on the circumstances and the consequences for the patient.

Consultation with the Official Solicitor

8. Members of the Official Solicitor's staff are prepared to discuss applications in relation to serious medical treatment before an application is made. Any enquiries about adult medical and welfare cases should be addressed to a senior healthcare lawyer at the Office of the Official Solicitor, Victory House, 30 to 34 Kingsway, London WC2B 6EX, telephone 020 3681 2751, fax 020 3681 2762, email: enquiries@offsol.gsi.gov.uk.

Note—In fact, this position is now known as the Healthcare and Welfare Lawyer at the Official Solicitor.

Parties to proceedings

9. The person bringing the application will always be a party to proceedings, as will a respondent named in the application form who files an acknowledgment of service.[18] In cases involving issues as to serious medical treatment, an organisation which is, or will be, responsible for providing clinical or caring services to P should usually be named as a respondent in the application form (where it is not already the applicant in the proceedings).

(Practice Direction B accompanying Part 9 sets out the persons who are to be notified that an application form has been issued.)

10. The court will consider whether anyone not already a party should be joined as a party to the proceedings. Other persons with sufficient interest may apply to be joined as parties to the proceedings[19] and the court has a duty to identify at as early a stage as possible who the parties to the proceedings should be.[20]

Allocation of the case

11. Where an application is made to the court in relation to:

---
[18] Rule 73(1).
[19] Rule 75.
[20] Rule 5(2)(b)(ii).

(a) the lawfulness of withholding or withdrawing artificial nutrition and hydration from a person in a permanent vegetative state, or a minimally conscious state; or
(b) a case involving an ethical dilemma in an untested area,

the proceedings (including permission, the giving of any directions, and any hearing) must be conducted by the President of the Court of Protection or by another judge nominated by the President.

12. Where an application is made to the court in relation to serious medical treatment (other than that outlined in paragraph 11) the proceedings (including permission, the giving of any directions, and any hearing) must be conducted by a judge of the court who has been nominated as such by virtue of section 46(2)(a) to (c) of the Act (ie the President of the Family Division, the Chancellor or a puisne judge of the High Court).

Matters to be considered at the first directions hearing

13. Unless the matter is one which needs to be disposed of urgently, the court will list it for a first directions hearing.

(Practice Direction B accompanying Part 10 sets out the procedure to be followed for urgent applications.)

14. The court may give such directions as it considers appropriate. If the court has not already done so, it should in particular consider whether to do any or all of the following at the first directions hearing:

(a) decide whether P should be joined as party to the proceedings, and give directions to that effect;
(b) if P is to be joined as a party to the proceedings, decide whether the Official Solicitor should be invited to act as a litigation friend or whether some other person should be appointed as a litigation friend;
(c) identify anyone else who has been notified of the proceedings and who has filed an acknowledgment and applied to be joined as a party to proceedings, and consider that application; and
(d) set a timetable for the proceedings including, where possible, a date for the final hearing.

15. The court should also consider whether to give any of the other directions listed in rule 85(2).

16. The court will ordinarily make an order pursuant to rule 92 that any hearing shall be held in public, with restrictions to be imposed in relation to publication of information about the proceedings.

Declarations

17. Where a declaration is needed, the order sought should be in the following or similar terms:

- That P lacks capacity to make a decision in relation to the (proposed medical treatment or procedure).
  Eg 'That P lacks capacity to make a decision in relation to sterilisation by vasectomy'; and
- That, having regard to the best interests of P, it is lawful for the (proposed medical treatment or procedure) to be carried out by (proposed healthcare provider).

18. Where the application is for the withdrawal of life-sustaining treatment, the order sought should be in the following or similar terms:

- That P lacks capacity to consent to continued life-sustaining treatment measures (and specify what these are); and
- That, having regard to the best interests of P, it is lawful for (name of healthcare provider) to withdraw the life-sustaining treatment from P.

Practice Direction 9F – Applications relating to statutory wills, codicils, settlements and other dealings with P's property

This practice direction supplements Part 9 of the Court of Protection Rules 2007

General

1. Rule 71 enables a practice direction to make additional or different provision in relation to specified applications.

Applications to which this Practice Direction applies

2. This practice direction makes provision for applications that relate to:

   (a) the execution of a will or codicil of P;
   (b) the settlement of any of P's property; and
   (c) the sale, exchange, charging, gift or other disposition of P's property.

3. A deputy may not be given powers with respect to:

   (a) the settlement of any of P's property;
   (b) the execution of a will of P; or
   (c) the exercise of any power (including a power to consent) vested in P whether beneficially or as a trustee or otherwise.[21]

4. Hence, an application must be made to the court for a decision in relation to such matters. This practice direction is concerned with matters mentioned at paragraphs 3(a) and (b) above. Practice direction G accompanying Part 9 contains provisions as to applications falling with paragraph 3(c).

Permission to make applications to the court

5. Section 50(1) of, paragraph 20(2) to Schedule 3 to, the Act and rule 51 set out the circumstances in which permission is or is not required to make an application to the court for the exercise of any of its powers under the Act.

Information to be provided with application form

6. In addition to the application Form COP1 (and its annexes) and any information or documents required to be provided by the Rules or another practice direction, the following information must be provided (in the form of a witness statement, attaching documents as exhibits where necessary) for any application to which this Practice Direction applies:

   (a) where the application is for the execution of a statutory will or codicil, a copy of the draft will or codicil,[22] plus one copy;
   (b) a copy of any existing will or codicil;
   (c) any consents to act by proposed executors;
   (d) details of P's family, preferably in the form of a family tree, including details of the full name and date of birth of each person included in the family tree;

---

[21] Section 20(3) of the Act.
[22] The Annex to this practice direction contains an example of a will.

(e) a schedule showing details of P's current assets, with up to date valuations;
(f) a schedule showing the estimated net yearly income and spending of P;
(g) a statement showing P's needs, both current and future estimates, and his general circumstances;
(h) if P is living in National Health Service accommodation, information on whether he may be discharged to local authority accommodation, to other fee-paying accommodation or to his own home;
(i) if the applicant considers it relevant, full details of the resources of any proposed beneficiary, and details of any likely changes if the application is successful;
(j) details of any capital gains tax, inheritance tax or income tax which may be chargeable in respect of the subject matter of the application;
(k) an explanation of the effect, if any, that the proposed changes will have on P's circumstances, preferably in the form of a 'before and after' schedule of assets and income;
(l) if appropriate, a statement of whether any land would be affected by the proposed will or settlement and if so, details of its location and title number, if applicable;
(m) where the application is for a settlement of property or for the variation of an existing settlement or trust, a draft of the proposed deed, plus one copy;
(n) a copy of any registered enduring power of attorney or lasting power of attorney;
(o) confirmation that P is a resident of England or Wales; and
(p) an up to date report of P's present medical condition, life expectancy, likelihood of requiring increased expenditure in the foreseeable future, and testamentary capacity.

7. The court may direct that other material is to be filed by the applicant, and if it does, the information will be set out in the form of a witness statement.

8. If any of the information mentioned above has been provided already (e g by way of inclusion in an annex to the application form) it need not be provided again.

Respondents and persons who must be notified of an application

9. The applicant must name as a respondent:

(a) any beneficiary under an existing will or codicil who is likely to be materially or adversely affected by the application;
(b) any beneficiary under a proposed will or codicil who is likely to be materially or adversely affected by the application; and
(c) any prospective beneficiary under P's intestacy where P has no existing will.

(Practice Direction B accompanying Part 9 sets out the procedure for notifying others of an application.)

10. The court will consider at the earliest opportunity whether P should be joined as a party to the proceedings and, if he is so joined, the court will consider whether the Official Solicitor should be invited to act as a litigation friend, or whether some other person should be appointed as a litigation friend.

Procedure on execution of a will

11. Once a will of P has been executed, the applicant must send the original and two copies of the will to the court for sealing.

12. The court shall seal the original and the copy and return both documents to the applicant.

(Paragraph 3(2) of Schedule 2 to the Mental Capacity Act 2005 sets out the requirements for execution of a will on behalf of P, where the will is executed pursuant to an order or direction of the court.)

ANNEX

Example form of statutory will

(This only shows the manner in which the authorised person makes the will and executes the same.)

This is the last will of me AB [the person who lacks capacity] of _____ acting by CD the person authorised in that behalf by an order dated the _____ day of _____ 20____ made under the Mental Capacity Act 2005.

I revoke all my former wills and codicils and declare this to be my last will.

1. I appoint EF and GH to be executors and trustees of this my will.

2. I give _____

In witness of which this will is signed by me AB acting by CD under the order mentioned above on (date).

SIGNED by the said AB
[the person who lacks capacity]

by the said CD [authorised person]

and by the said CD with   AB [person who lacks capacity
his (or her) own name   CD [authorised person]
pursuant to the said order
in our presence and
attested by us in the
presence of the said CD

[Name and addresses of witness]

Sealed with the official seal of the Court of Protection the _____ day of _____ 20____

Practice Direction 9G – Applications to appoint or discharge a trustee

This practice direction supplements Part 9 of the Court of Protection Rules 2007

General

1. Rule 71 enables a practice direction to make additional or different provision in relation to specified applications.

Applications to which this Practice Direction applies

2. This practice direction makes provision for applications:
    (a) for the exercise of any power (including a power to consent) vested in P whether as a trustee or otherwise (section 18(1)(j) of the Act);
    (b) under section 36(9) of the Trustee Act 1925 for leave to appoint a new trustee in place of P;
    (c) under section 54 of the Trustee Act 1925 as to the court's jurisdiction;
    (d) under section 20 of the Trusts of Land and Appointment of Trustees Act 1996; or
    (e) for the court's approval of the appointment of a trustee in accordance with the terms of a trust.

3. A deputy may not be appointed to exercise any power vested in P, whether as a trustee or otherwise.[23] Hence, an application must be made to the court for the court to make such a decision.

Permission to make applications to the court

4. Section 50(1) of, paragraph 20(2) to Schedule 3 to, the Act and rule 51 set out the circumstances in which permission is or is not required to make an application to the court for the exercise of any of its powers under the Act.

Information to be provided with the application form

5. In addition to the application Form COP1 (and its annexes) and any information or documents required to be provided by the Rules or another practice direction, the following information must be provided (in the form of a witness statement, attaching documents as exhibits where necessary) for any application to which this Practice Direction applies:
    (a) a copy of the existing trust document;
    (b) where relevant, a copy of any original conveyance, transfer, lease, assignment, settlement trust or will trust;
    (c) the names and addresses of any present trustees and details of any beneficial interest they have in the trust property. If the present trustees are not the original trustees, an explanation should be provided as to how they became trustees and copies of any deeds of appointment and retirement should be provided;
    (d) the full name, address and date of birth of any person proposed to replace P as a trustee, and details of his relationship to P;

---

[23] Section 20(3) of the Act prevents a deputy being given power to exercise such powers on behalf of P.

(e) confirmation that the trust is not under an order for administration in the Chancery Division;
(f) if there is only one continuing trustee, the applicant must confirm that both the trustee and the proposed new trustee have not made an enduring power of attorney or a lasting power of attorney in favour of the other party;
(g) if an enduring power of attorney or a lasting power of attorney has been executed by a continuing trustee, a certified copy of that document must be provided. If the power has not been registered, the applicant must confirm that the trustee is still capable of carrying out his duties as a trustee;
(h) the full name and address of any person who has an interest in any trust property as the beneficiary of a will, and whether any of them are children or persons who lack capacity;
(i) if the proposed new trustee is not a solicitor or a trust corporation (for example, a bank) and has not been appointed as a deputy for the trustee lacking capacity, the applicant must provide a witness statement from a person independent of the applicant, who has no interest in the trust property, attesting to the applicant's fitness to be appointed as trustee;
(j) if the application relates to a transfer of assets in a will trust or similar settlement into the names of new trustees, accurate details of the trust assets must be provided (including full details of any stocks and shares held);
(k) a copy of any notice of severance and evidence of service;
(l) a copy of the will and grant of probate to the deceased's estate (where relevant);
(m) confirmation of all relevant consents; and
(n) a copy of a signed trustee's special undertaking.

6. The court may direct that other material is to be filed by the applicant, and if it does, the information will be set out in the form of a witness statement.

7. If any of the information mentioned above has been provided already (eg by way of inclusion in an annex to the application form) it need not be provided again.

Additional information to be provided where the application relates to real property

8. In addition to the information specified in paragraph 5 above, where the application relates to real property, the information specified in paragraph 9 below must be provided. The information will be set out in the form of a witness statement.

9. The information which must be provided is:
    (a) the address of the property concerned, and whether it is freehold or leasehold;
    (b) the title number of the property and a copy of its entry in the Land Registry (if registered land). If the land is unregistered, the applicant should inform the court accordingly; and
    (c) if the property is leasehold the applicant should advise the court as to whether he has a licence or consent to the assignment, and provide a copy of the same (or advise if a licence or consent is not necessary and the reason why it is not needed).

10. If any of the information mentioned above has been provided already (eg by way of inclusion in an annex to the application form) it need not be provided again.

Practice Direction 9H – Applications relating to the registration of enduring powers of attorney

This practice direction supplements Part 9 of the Court of Protection Rules 2007

General

1. Rule 71 enables a practice direction to make additional or different provision in relation to specified applications.

Applications to which this Practice Direction applies

2. This Practice Direction applies where:
    (a) an application has been made to the Public Guardian to register an instrument creating an enduring power of attorney; and
    (b) the Public Guardian has received a notice of objection to registration which prevents him from registering the instrument except in accordance with the court's directions.

Objections to registration

3. A notice of objection will prevent the Public Guardian from registering the instrument if the objection is made on one of the following grounds:[24]
    (a) that the power purported to have been created by the instrument was not valid as an enduring power of attorney;
    (b) that the power created by the instrument no longer subsists;
    (c) that the application is premature because the donor is not yet becoming mentally incapable;
    (d) that fraud or undue pressure was used to induce the donor to create the power; or
    (e) that, having regard to all the circumstances and in particular the attorney's relationship to or connection with the donor, the attorney is unsuitable to be the donor's attorney.

4. This practice direction sets out the procedure to be followed by a person entitled to be given notice of the application to register the instrument who wishes to apply to the court for:
    (a) directions that the instrument should be registered; or
    (b) directions that the instrument should not be registered.

5. The persons who are entitled to receive notice of an application are the donor, certain of his relatives and any attorneys under the enduring power who are not making the application for registration.[25]

Procedure for applications to which this Practice Direction applies

6. An application must be made using Form COP8.

---

[24] The grounds are set out in para 13(9) of Sch 4 to the Act. The Public Guardian is prevented from registering the instrument by para 13(4) and (5) of that Schedule.
[25] Paragraphs 5 to 11 of Sch 4 to the Act set out who is entitled to receive notice.

Practice Direction 9H – Applications relating to the registration of enduring powers of attorney **PD9H**

(Practice Direction B accompanying Part 4 sets out more detailed requirements for statements of truth.)

7. The application form must state:
   (a) what directions the applicant is seeking; and
   (b) if the applicant objects to registration, the grounds on which he does so; or
   (c) if the applicant is seeking registration, his reasons for doing so.

8. The application form must be supported by evidence set out in either:
   (a) a witness statement; or
   (b) if it is verified by a statement of truth, the application form.

9. As soon as practicable and in any event within 14 days of the application form being issued, the applicant must serve a copy of the application form, together with an acknowledgment of service using Form COP5:
   (a) unless the applicant is the donor or an attorney, on the donor of the power and every attorney under the power;
   (b) if he is the donor, on every attorney under the power; or
   (c) if he is an attorney, on the donor and any other attorney under the power.

10. Where the applicant knows or has reasonable grounds to believe that the donor of the power lacks capacity to make a decision in relation to any matter that is the subject of the application, he must notify the donor of the application in accordance with Part 7.

929

Applications within proceedings

Practice Direction 10A – Applications within proceedings

This practice direction supplements Part 10 of the Court of Protection Rules 2007

Application notice

1. Rule 77 provides that an applicant may use the Part 10 procedure if the application is made:

   (a) in the course of existing proceedings; or
   (b) as provided for in a rule or relevant practice direction.

2. An application under Part 10 must be made by filing an application notice using Form COP9.

3. An application notice must, in addition to the matters set out in rule 79, be signed and include (unless an order to the contrary pursuant to rule 19 has been made):

   (a) the name of the person to whom the application relates (P);
   (b) the case number (if available);
   (c) the full name of the applicant;
   (d) where the applicant is not already a party, his address; and
   (e) a draft of the order sought.

4. If the order sought is unusually long or complex, a disk containing the draft order sought should be made available to the court in a format compatible with the word processing software used by the court. (Queries in relation to software should be directed to a court officer.)

5. The application notice must be supported by evidence set out in either:

   (a) a witness statement; or
   (b) the application notice provided that it is verified by a statement of truth.

6. For the purposes of rules 90 to 92, a statement of truth in an application notice may be made by a person who is not a party.[26]

7. The evidence must set out the facts on which the applicant relies for the application, and all material facts known to the applicant of which the court should be made aware.

8. A copy of the application notice and evidence in support must be served by the person making the application as soon as practicable and in any event within 14 days of the application notice being issued.

9. An application may be made without service of an application notice only:

   (a) where there is exceptional urgency;
   (b) where the overriding objective is best furthered by doing so;
   (c) by consent of all parties;
   (d) with the permission of the court; or
   (e) where a rule or other practice direction permits.

---

[26] See r 11(6)(a).

(Practice Direction B accompanying Part 10 sets out more detailed requirements for urgent applications.)

10. Where an application is made without service on the respondent, the evidence in support of the application must also set out why service was not effected.

11. The court may decide, upon considering the application, that other persons ought to be served with or notified of it and have the opportunity of responding. In such a case, the court will give directions as to who should be served with or notified of the application.

12. On receipt of an application notice, the court will issue the application notice and, if there is to be a hearing, give notice of the date on which the matter is to be heard by the court.

13. Notice will be given to:
    (a) the applicant;
    (b) anyone who is named as a respondent in the application notice (if not otherwise a party to the proceedings);
    (c) every other party to the proceedings; and
    (d) any other person, as the court may direct.

14. Any directions given by the court may specify the form that the evidence is to take and when it is to be served.

15. Applications should wherever possible be made so that they can be considered at a directions hearing or other hearing for which a date has already been fixed or for which a date is about to be fixed.

16. Where a date for a hearing has been fixed and a party wishes to make an application at that hearing but does not have sufficient time to file an application notice, he should inform the court (if possible in writing) and, if possible, the other parties as soon as he can of the nature of the application and the reason for it. He should then make the application orally at the hearing.

Type of case may be indicated in the application notice

17. The applicant may indicated in the application notice that the application:
    (a) is urgent;
    (b) should be dealt with by a particular judge or level of judge within the court;
    (c) requires a hearing; or
    (d) any combination of the above.

Telephone hearings

18. The court may direct that an application or part of an application will be dealt with by a telephone hearing.

19. The applicant should indicate in his application notice if he seeks a direction pursuant to paragraph 17. Where he has not done so but nevertheless wishes to seek such a direction the request should be made as early as possible.

20. A direction under paragraph 17 will not normally be given unless every party entitled to be given notice of the application and to be heard at the hearing has consented to the direction.

Video conferencing

21. Where the parties to a matter wish to use video conferencing facilities, and those facilities are available, they should apply to the court for such a direction.

(Practice Direction A accompanying Part 14 contains guidance on the use of video conferencing.)

Consent orders

22. The parties to an application for a consent order must ensure that they provide the court with any material it needs to be satisfied that it is appropriate to make the order. Subject to any rule or practice direction, a letter signed by all parties will generally be acceptable for this purpose.

23. Where an order has been agreed in relation to an application for which a hearing date has been fixed, the parties must inform the court immediately.

Practice Direction 10B – Urgent and interim applications

This practice direction supplements Part 10 of the Court of Protection Rules 2007

Urgent applications and applications without notice

1. These fall into two categories:

    (a) applications where an application form has already been issued; and
    (b) applications where an application form has not yet been issued,

and, in both cases, where notice of the application has not been given to the respondent(s).

2. Wherever possible, urgent applications should be made within court hours. These applications will normally be dealt with at court but cases of extreme urgency may be dealt with by telephone. Telephone contact may be made with the court during business hours on 0300 456 4600.

3. When it is not possible to apply within court hours, contact should be made with the security office at the Royal Courts of Justice on 020 7947 6000. The security officer should be informed of the nature of the case.

4. In some cases, urgent applications arise because applications to the court have not been pursued sufficiently promptly. This is undesirable, and should be avoided. A judge who has concerns that the facility for urgent applications may have been abused may require the applicant or the applicant's representative to attend at a subsequent hearing to provide an explanation for the delay.

Applications without notice

5. The applicant should take steps to advise the respondent(s) by telephone or in writing of the application, unless justice would be defeated if notice were given.

6. If an order is made without notice to any other party, the order will ordinarily contain:

    (a) an undertaking by the applicant to the court to serve the application notice, evidence in support and any order made on the respondent and any other person the court may direct as soon as practicable or as ordered by the court; and
    (b) a return date for a further hearing at which the other parties can be present.

Applications where an application form has already been issued

7. An application notice using Form COP9, evidence in support and a draft order should be filed with the court in advance of the hearing wherever possible. If the order sought is unusually long or complex, a disk containing the draft order sought should be made available to the court in a format compatible with the word processing software used by the court. (Queries in relation to software should be directed to a court officer.)

(Practice Direction A accompanying Part 10 sets out more detailed requirements in relation to an application notice.)

8. If an application is made before the application notice has been filed, a draft order should be provided at the hearing, and the application notice and evidence in support must be filed with the court on the next working day or as ordered by the court.

Applications made before the issue of an application form

9. Where the exceptional urgency of the matter requires, an application may be started without filing an application form if the court allows it (but where time permits an application should be made in writing). In such a case, an application may be made to the court orally. The court will require an undertaking that the application form in the terms of the oral application be filed on the next working day, or as required by the court.

10. An order made before the issue of the application form should state in the title after the names of the applicant and the respondent, 'the Applicant and Respondent in an Intended Application'.

Applications made by telephone

11. Where it is not possible to file an application form or notice, applications can be made by telephone in accordance with the contact details set out in paragraphs 2 and 3 of this practice direction.

Hearings conducted by telephone

12. When a hearing is to take place by telephone, if practical it should be conducted by tape-recorded conference call, and arranged (and paid for in the first instance) by the applicant. All parties and the judge should be informed that the call is being recorded by the service provider. The applicant should order a transcript of the hearing from the service provider.

Type of case may be indicated in the application notice

13. The applicant may indicate in the application notice that the application:

    (a)   is urgent;
    (b)   should be dealt with by a particular judge or level of judge within the court;
    (c)   requires a hearing; or
    (d)   any combination of the above.

Urgent cases in relation to serious medical treatment

14. Practice Direction E accompanying Part 9 sets out the procedure in relation to applications relating to serious medical treatment. Practice Direction A accompanying Part 12 sets out the manner in which those cases are to be allocated.

Interim injunction applications

15. Rule 82 enables the court to grant an interim injunction.

16. Any judge of the court may vary or discharge an interim injunction granted by any judge of the court.

17. Any order for an interim injunction must set out clearly what the respondent or any other person must or must not do. The order may contain an undertaking by the

applicant to pay any damages which the respondent(s) sustains which the court considers the applicant should pay.

Deprivation of Liberty

Practice Direction 10AA – Deprivation of Liberty Applications

This practice direction supplements Part 10A of the Court of Protection Rules 2007

Introduction

1. This Practice Direction is in three parts. Part 1 addresses the procedure to be followed in applications to the court for orders under section 21A of the Mental Capacity Act 2005 relating to a standard or urgent authorisation under Schedule A1 of that Act to deprive a person of his or her liberty; or proceedings (for example, relating to costs or appeals) connected with or consequent upon such applications. Part 2 addresses the procedure to be followed in applications under s 16(2)(a) of that Act to authorise deprivation of liberty under section 4A(3) and (4) pursuant to a streamlined procedure. Part 3 makes provision common to applications under both Parts 1 and 2.

PART 1
APPLICATIONS UNDER SECTION 21A RELATING TO A STANDARD OR URGENT AUTHORISATION UNDER SCHEDULE A1

2. This Part sets out the procedure to be followed in applications to the court for orders under section 21A of the Mental Capacity Act 2005 relating to a standard or urgent authorisation under Schedule A1 of that Act to deprive a person of his or her liberty. By their nature, such applications are of special urgency and therefore will be dealt with by the court according to the special procedure described here. Other applications may, while not being DoL applications within the meaning of the term explained above, raise issues relating to deprivation of liberty and require similarly urgent attention; and while the special DoL procedure will not apply to such applications, they should be raised with the DoL team at the earliest possible stage so that they can be handled appropriately. The key features of the special DoL procedure are:

(a) special DoL court forms ensure that DoL court papers stand out as such and receive special handling by the court office;

(b) the application is placed before a judge of the court as soon as possible – if necessary, before issue of the application – for judicial directions to be given as to the steps to be taken in the application, and who is to take each step and by when;

(c) the usual Court of Protection Rules (for example, as to method and timing of service of the application) will apply only so far as consistent with the judicial directions given for the particular case;

(d) a dedicated team in the court office ('the DoL team') will deal with DoL applications at all stages, including liaison with would-be applicants/other parties;

(e) the progress of each DoL case will be monitored by a judge assigned to that case, assisted by the DoL team.

Before issuing an application

3. Potential applicants should contact the DoL team at the earliest possible stage before issuing a DoL application. Where this is not possible, the applicant should liaise with the DoL team at the same time as, or as soon as possible after, lodging the application. The DoL team can be contacted by telephone in the first instance and by fax.

4. The information that the DoL team needs, with as much advance warning as possible, is (1) that a DoL application is to be made; (2) how urgent the application is (i.e., by when should the Court's decision, or interim decision, on the merits be given); and (3) when the Court will receive the application papers. In extremely urgent cases, the DoL team can arrange for a telephone application to be made to the judge for directions and/or an interim order even before the application has been issued. Further brief details should be given which may include:

(a) the parties' details
(b) where the parties live
(c) the issue to be decided
(d) the date of urgent or standard authorisation
(e) the date of effective detention
(f) the parties' legal representatives
(g) any family members or others who are involved
(h) whether there have been any other court proceedings involving the parties and if so, where.

5. Contact details for the DoL team are:

PO Box 70185
First Avenue House
42–49 High Holborn
London
WC1A 9 JA
DX: 160013 Kingsway 7
Enquiries: 0300 456 4600

6. The public counter is open between 9.30 a.m. to 4.30 p.m. on working days. The DoL team can receive telephone calls and faxes between 9.00 a.m. and 5.00 pm. Faxes transmitted after 4.30 p.m. will be dealt with the next working day.

7. When in an emergency it is necessary to make a telephone application to a judge outside normal court hours, the security office at the Royal Courts of Justice should be contacted on 020 7947 6000. The security officer should be informed of the nature of the case. In the Family Division, the out-of-hours application procedure involves the judge being contacted through a Family Division duty officer, and the RCJ security officer will need to contact the duty officer and not the judge's clerk or the judge.

8. Intending applicants/other parties may find it helpful to refer to:

(a) the Code of Practice Deprivation of Liberty Safeguards (June 2008), ISBN 978-0113228157, supplementing the main Mental Capacity Act 2005 Code of Practice: in particular Chapter 10, What is the Court of Protection and who can apply to it?; and
(b) the judgment of Mr Justice Munby in *Salford City Council v. GJ, NJ and BJ (Incapacitated Adults)* [2008] EWHC 1097 (Fam), [2008] 2 FLR 1295. Although this case was decided before the coming into force of the DoL

amendments to the Mental Capacity Act 2005, it sets out helpful guidance on the appropriate court procedures for cases relating to the deprivation of liberty of adults.

9. The DoL team will be pleased to explain the court's procedures for handling DoL cases. Please note that the team (as with all court staff) is not permitted to give advice on matters of law. Please do not contact the DoL team unless your inquiry concerns a deprivation of liberty question (whether relating to a potential application, or a case which is already lodged with the Court).

DoL court forms

10. The special DoL court forms are as follows:
    (a) DLA: Deprivation of Liberty Application Form: to be used for all DoL applications;
    (b) DLB: Deprivation of Liberty Request for Urgent Consideration: this short form allows applicants to set out the reasons why the case is urgent, the timetable they wish the case to follow, and any interim relief sought. A draft of any order sought should be attached. Ideally, the DLB (plus any draft order) should be placed at the top of the draft application and both issued and served together;
    (c) DLD: Deprivation of Liberty Certificate of Service/non-service and Certificate of notification/non-notification;
    (d) DLE: Deprivation of Liberty Acknowledgement of service/notification.

These forms can be obtained from the Court of Protection office or downloaded from the court's website http://hmctsformfinder.justice.gov.uk/HMCTS/GetForms.do?court_forms_category=court_of_protection.

11. To ensure that papers relating to DoL applications are promptly directed to the DoL team at the court, it is essential that the appropriate DoL court forms are used.

12. The DoL court forms should be used for, and only for, DoL applications. If in such a case it is anticipated that other issues may arise, the DoL forms should identify and describe briefly those issues and any relief which may be sought in respect of them: sections 3.5 and 5 of form DLA, the Deprivation of Liberty Application Form, offer an opportunity to do this. 'Other issues' are perhaps most likely to arise in the event that the court decides the DoL application in the applicant's favour. In such a case, if the applicant has already identified the 'other issues' in his/her form DLA, the court will be able to address these, either by dealing with them immediately or by giving directions for their future handling.

13. Accordingly, unless the court expressly directs, applicants should not issue a second and separate application (using the standard court forms) relating to any 'other issues'.

14. Where an application seeks relief concerning a deprivation of P's liberty other than under section 21A in respect of a standard or urgent authorisation (for example, where the application is for an order under section 16(2)(a)), the dedicated DoL court forms should not be used. Rather the standard court forms should be used for such an application, but it should be made clear on them that relief relating to a deprivation of P's liberty is being sought, and the proposed applicant should contact the DoL team to discuss handling at the earliest possible stage before issuing the application.

How to issue a DoL application

15. To issue a DoL application, the following forms should be filed at court:
    (a) form DLA
    (b) form DLB (plus draft order)
    (c) the appropriate court fee.

Where a draft order is lodged with the court, it would be helpful – although not compulsory – if an electronic version of the order could also be lodged on disc, if possible.

16. In cases of extreme emergency or where it is not possible to attend at the court office, for example during weekends, the court will expect an applicant to undertake to file form DLA and to pay the court fee unless an exemption applies.

Inviting the court to make judicial directions for the handling of the application

17. The following is a sample list of possible issues which the court is likely to wish to consider in judicial directions in a DoL case. It is intended as a prompt, not as a definitive list of the issues that may need to be covered:

    (a) upon whom, by when and how service of the application should be effected;
    (b) dispensing with acknowledgement of service of the application or allowing a short period of time for so doing, which in some cases may amount to a few hours only;
    (c) whether further lay or expert evidence should be obtained;
    (d) whether P/the detained person should be a party and represented by the Official Solicitor and whether any other person should be a party;
    (e) whether any family members should be formally notified of the application and of any hearing and joined as parties;
    (f) fixing a date for a First Hearing and giving a time estimate;
    (g) fixing a trial window for any final hearing and giving a time estimate;
    (h) the level of judge appropriate to hear the case;
    (i) whether the case is such that it should be immediately transferred to the High Court for a High Court Judge to give directions;
    (j) provision for a bundle for the judge at the First Hearing.

18. If you are an applicant without legal representation, and you are not sure exactly what directions you should ask for, you may prefer simply to invite the judge to make appropriate directions in light of the nature and urgency of the case as you have explained it on the DLB form. In exceptionally urgent cases, there may not be time to formulate draft directions: the court will understand if applicants in such cases (whether or not legally represented) simply ask the judge for appropriate directions.

After issue of the application

19. The DoL team will immediately take steps to ensure that the application is placed before a judge nominated to hear Court of Protection cases and DoL applications. Out of hours, at weekends and on public holidays, the application will be placed before the judge who is most immediately available.

20. As soon as the court office is put on notice of a DoL application, the DoL team will notify a judge to put the judge on stand-by to deal with the application. The judge will consider the application on the papers and make a first order.

Steps after the judge's first order

21. The DoL team will:
    (a) action every point in the judge's note or instruction;
    (b) refer any query that arises to the judge immediately or, if not available, to another judge;
    (c) make all arrangements for any transfer of the case to another court and/or for a hearing.

22. The applicant or his/her legal representative should follow all steps in the judge's order and:
    (a) form DLD should be filed with the court if appropriate; and
    (b) form DLE should be included in any documents served unless ordered otherwise.

The First Hearing

23. The First Hearing will be listed for the court to fix a date for any subsequent hearing(s), give directions and/or to make an interim or final order if appropriate. The court will make such orders and give such directions as are appropriate in the case.

24. The court will aim to have the First Hearing before a judge of every DoL application within 5 working days of the date of issue of the application.

25. Applicants can indicate on the DLB form if they think that the application needs to be considered within a shorter timetable, and set out proposals for such a timetable. On the first paper consideration the court will consider when the First Hearing should be listed.

26. If time allows and no specific direction has been made by the court, an indexed and paginated bundle should be prepared for the judge and any skeleton arguments and draft orders given to the court as soon as they are available. A copy of the index should be provided to all parties and, where another party appears in person, a copy of the bundle should be provided.

PART 2
APPLICATIONS UNDER SECTION 16(2)(A) FOR AN ORDER AUTHORISING DEPRIVATION OF LIBERTY UNDER SECTION 4A(3) AND (4) PURSUANT TO A STREAMLINED PROCEDURE

27. This Part sets out the procedure to be followed in applications to the court under section 16(2)(a) to authorise deprivation of liberty under section 4A(3) of the Act pursuant to a streamlined procedure and applies only to such applications. Reference should be made generally to the decision of the Supreme Court in *P (by his litigation friend the Official Solicitor) v Cheshire West and Chester Council and another; P and Q (by their litigation friend the Official Solicitor) v Surrey County Council* [2014] UKSC 19, and in relation to the procedure in these cases, to the judgments of the President of the Court of *Protection in Re X and Others (Deprivation of Liberty)* [2014] EWCOP 25 and in *Re X and Others (Deprivation of Liberty) (Number 2)* [2014] EWCOP 37.

Making the application

28. To bring proceedings, the applicant must file an application using form COPDOL 10, verified by a statement of truth and accompanied by all attachments and evidence required by that form and its annexes.

29. The application form and accompanying annexes and attachments are specifically designed to ensure that the applicant provides the court with essential information and evidence as to the proposed measures, on the basis of which the court may adjudicate as to the appropriateness of authorising a deprivation of liberty, and in particular to identify whether a case is suitable for consideration without an oral hearing. The use of the form and its annexes is mandatory and they must be provided fully completed and verified by the required statements of truth.

30. The applicant must ensure that the evidence in the application form, accompanying annexes and attachments is succinct and focussed.

31. A separate application must be made for every individual for whom the applicant requests an authorisation of deprivation of liberty. However, where there are matters in relation to which the facts are identical for a number of individuals, such as common care arrangements, the applicant may, in addition to addressing the specific issues relating to each individual, attach a generic statement dealing with the common care arrangements or other matters common to those individuals.

Deponent

32. The applicant must consider carefully who should complete the form and each annex with regard to the nature of the evidence required by each. There is no requirement that the same individual should complete and verify by statement of truth the form and each annex and indeed it might be inappropriate for this to be the case, where different people are best placed to provide evidence on different matters.

Applicant's duty of full and frank disclosure

33. The applicant has a duty of full and frank disclosure to the court of all facts and matters that may have an impact on the court's decision whether to authorise the deprivation of liberty. The applicant should therefore scrutinise the circumstances of the case and clearly identify in the evidence in support (in Annex A to form COPDOL 10) factors –

   (a) needing particular judicial scrutiny;
   (b) suggesting that the arrangements in relation to which authorisation is sought may not in fact be in the best interests of the person the application is about, or the least restrictive option; or
   (c) otherwise tending to indicate that the order should not be made.

Pursuant to this duty, the applicant should also identify those persons, not consulted by the applicant, who are in the same category under paragraph 39 as persons with whom the applicant has consulted. Those persons must be listed in Annex B to form COPDOL 10 together with an explanation in that Annex of why they have not been consulted.

Draft order

34. The application must be accompanied by a draft of the order which the applicant seeks, including the duration of the authorisation sought, appropriate directions for review, and liberty to apply for its reconsideration.

Consultation with the person the application is about

35. Consultation with the person the application is about must take place before the application form is lodged with the court. The applicant must arrange for that person to be informed of the following matters –

   (a) that the applicant is making an application to court;
   (b) that the application is to consider whether the person lacks capacity to make decisions in relation to his or her residence and care, and whether to authorise a deprivation of their liberty in connection with the arrangements set out in the care plan;
   (c) what the proposed arrangements under the order sought are;
   (d) that the person is entitled to express his or her views, wishes and feelings in relation to the proposed arrangements and the application, and that the person undertaking the consultation will ensure that these are communicated to the court;
   (e) that the person is entitled to seek to take part in the proceedings by being joined as a party or otherwise, what that means, and that the person undertaking the consultation will ensure that any such request is communicated to the court;
   (f) that the person undertaking the consultation can help him or her to obtain advice and assistance if he or she does not agree with the proposed arrangements in the application.

36. The person undertaking the consultation must complete Annex C to form COPDOL 10.

37. The applicant must confirm that the person the application is about has been supported and assisted to express his or her views, wishes and feelings in relation to the application and the arrangements proposed in it, and encouraged to take part in the proceedings to the extent that he or she wishes, in accordance with section 4(4) of the Act.

Consultation with other persons regarding the making of the application

38. The consultation required by paragraph 39 below must take place before the application is lodged with the court.

39. The applicant must ensure that the following people are consulted about the intention to make the application –

   (a) any donee of a lasting power of attorney granted by the person;
   (b) any deputy appointed for the person by the court;

together with, if possible, at least three people in the following categories –

   (c) anyone named by the person the application is about as someone to be consulted on the matters raised by the application; and
   (d) anyone engaged in caring for the person or interested in his or her welfare.

40. When consulting such people, the applicant must inform them of the following matters –

   (a) that the applicant is making an application to court;
   (b) that the application is to consider whether the person the application is about lacks capacity to make decisions in relation to his or her residence and care and whether he or she should be deprived of liberty in connection with the arrangements set out in the care plan;

(c) what the proposed arrangements under the order are; and
(d) that the applicant is under an obligation to inform the person the application is about of the matters listed in paragraph 35 above, unless in the circumstances it is inappropriate for the applicant to give that person such information.

Dispensing with notification or service of the application form

41. Provided that the court is satisfied as to the adequacy of consultation with the person the application is about in accordance with paragraphs 35 to 37, and with other persons with whom consultation should take place in accordance with paragraphs 38 to 40, the court may dispense with notification of the issue of the application under rules 42, 69 and 70.

Court fees

42. An application fee is payable for all applications, and if the court decides to hold a hearing before making a decision, a hearing fee will be payable.

43. If an application is received without a fee it will be treated as incomplete and returned.

44. ...

Applications suitable for the streamlined procedure

45. As soon as practicable after receipt the court officers will consider the suitability of the application to be the subject of paper determination, or to be considered at an oral hearing.

46. All applications considered suitable for the streamlined procedure will be referred to a judge for consideration without an oral hearing, as soon as practicable after receipt.

Applications not suitable for the streamlined procedure

47. If the judge considers that the application is not suitable for the streamlined process, case management directions shall be given.

Applicant to supply a copy of the order to each person consulted

48. The applicant must provide all persons consulted, including the person the application is about, with a copy of the order made pursuant to the streamlined procedure granting or refusing the authorisation of the deprivation of liberty.

Review of the authorisation

49. An application for a review of the authorisation of the deprivation of liberty must be made in accordance with the terms of the order.

PART 3
PROVISIONS COMMON TO APPLICATIONS UNDER PART 1 AND PART 2

Hearing in private

50. Part 13 of the Court of Protection Rules 2007 provides at rule 90, as supplemented by Practice Direction A to Part 13, that the general rule is that a hearing is held in private. Rule 92 allows the court to order that a hearing be in public if the criteria in rule 93 apply.

Costs

51. The general rule, in rule 157 of the Court of Protection Rules 2007, is that in a health and welfare case there will be no order as to costs of the proceedings. The general rule applies to DoL applications.

Appeals

52. Part 20 of the Court of Protection Rules 2007 applies to appeals. Permission is required to appeal (rules 171B and 172) and this will only be granted where the court considers that the appeal would have a real prospect of success or there is some other compelling reason why the appeal should be heard (rule173).

53. ...

Human Rights

Practice Direction 11A – Human Rights Act 1998

This practice direction supplements Part 11 of the Court of Protection Rules 2007

Procedure for making claim

1. A claim made pursuant to rule 83 in relation to the Human Rights Act 1998 ('the 1998 Act') should be included in the application form using Form COP1. If the claim forms part of a response by a person served with or notified of the application, it should be included in the acknowledgment of service using Form COP5.

2. If the claim in relation to the 1998 Act is made during the course of proceedings, it should be made by filing an application notice using Form COP9.

3. If the claim is raised in an appeal, the claim should be filed with the appellant's or the respondent's notice as appropriate, using Form COP35 or COP36.

Notice to the Crown

4. Where notice is served on the Crown in accordance with rule 83(2), notice of the claim must be served by the person making the claim on the person named in the list published under section 17 of the Crown Proceedings Act 1947.

5. The notice must be in the form directed by the court and will normally include the directions given by the court. The notice must also be served by the person making the claim on all the parties. The applicant must provide the Crown with a copy of the document in which the claim in relation to the 1998 Act is raised (for example, the application form).

6. The court may ask the parties to assist in the preparation of the notice.

Joining of the Crown

7. Unless the court orders otherwise, the Minister or other person permitted by the 1998 Act to be joined as a party must, if he wishes to be joined, file an application to be joined using Form COP10. (Section 5(2) of the 1998 Act entitles the Crown to be joined to proceedings where the court is considering whether to make a declaration of incompatibility, provided notice is given in accordance with rules of court. The Minister or other person will be regarded as having sufficient interest for the purpose of rule 75(1).)

8. Where the Minister has nominated a person to be joined as a party (as permitted by section 5(2)(a) of the 1998 Act) that person must (unless the court orders otherwise) file an application to be joined using Form COP10, which must also be accompanied by the Minister's written nomination.

> (Paragraph 3(b) of Practice Direction 12A deals with allocation of an application for a declaration of incompatibility under section 4 of the Human Rights Act 1998.)

9. …

Dealing with Applications

Practice Direction 12A – Court's jurisdiction to be exercised by certain judges

This practice direction supplements Part 12 of the Court of Protection Rules 2007

General

1. Rule 86 allows a practice direction to specify that certain categories of case must be dealt with by a specific judge or a specific class of judges.

Cases to be heard by the President or the President's nominee

2. Where an application is made to the court in relation to:
   (a) the lawfulness of withholding or withdrawing artificial nutrition and hydration from a person in a permanent vegetative state, or a minimally conscious state; or
   (b) a case involving an ethical dilemma in an untested area,

the proceedings (including permission, the giving of any directions, and any hearing) must be conducted by the President of the Court of Protection or by another judge nominated by the President.

Cases concerning serious medical treatment or declarations of incompatibility pursuant to section 4 of the Human Rights Act 1998

3 (a) Where an application is made to the court in relation to serious medical treatment (other than that outlined in paragraph 2), the proceedings must be conducted by a tier 3 judge;
   (b) Where an application is made to the court pursuant to rule 83, in which a declaration of incompatibility pursuant to section 4 of the Human Rights Act 1998 is sought, the proceedings (including permission, the giving of any directions, and any hearing) must be conducted by a judge of the court who has been nominated as such by virtue of section 46(2)(a) to (c) of the Act (i.e. the President of the Family Division, the Chancellor or a puisne judge of the High Court).

Court's general discretion as to allocation

4. The Senior Judge or his nominee may determine whether a matter is one to which this Practice Direction applies.

5. The judge to whom a matter is allocated in accordance with this practice direction may determine that the matter is one which may properly be heard by a judge of the court other than one nominated by virtue of section 46(2)(a) to (c) of the Act; and he may reallocate the matter accordingly.

Applications relating to serious medical treatment

6. Applications which relate to serious medical treatment should also be conducted in accordance with Practice Direction E accompanying Part 9 of the Rules.

Practice Direction 12B – Procedure for disputing the court's jurisdiction

This practice direction supplements Part 12 of the Court of Protection Rules 2007

Disputing the jurisdiction of the court – generally

1. A person who wishes to:

    (a)   dispute the court's jurisdiction to hear an application; or

    (b)   argue that the court should not exercise such jurisdiction as it may have,

may apply to the court for an order to that effect.[27]

2. ...

3. Where a person who has been served with or notified of an application form wishes to dispute the court's jurisdiction, he must state this in the acknowledgment of service or notification (as the case may be), using Form COP5 filed in accordance with rule 72.

4. In any other case (with the exception of those cases provided for in paragraphs 5 to 7), a person who wishes to dispute the court's jurisdiction must do so by filing an application notice using Form COP9 in accordance with Part 10.

Disputing the jurisdiction of the court – where P has or regains capacity

5. Where P has or regains capacity in relation to the matter or matters to which the application relates, an application may be made to the court for the proceedings to come to an end.[28]

6. Applications in such circumstances may only be made by the following persons:

    (a)   P;

    (b)   his litigation friend; or

    (c)   any other person who is a party to the proceedings.[29]

7. The application must be made by filing an application notice using Form COP9 in accordance with Part 10. The application must be served on all other parties to the proceedings.[30]

8. ...

---

[27]   Rule 87.
[28]   Rule 148.
[29]   Rule 148(3).
[30]   See r 148(4).

Hearings

Practice Direction 13A – Hearings (Including Reporting Restrictions)

This Practice Direction supplements Part 13 of the Court of Protection Rules 2007

General

1 Hearings before the court will generally be in private but the court may order that the whole or part of any hearing is to be held in public. The court also has power to:
 (a) authorise the publication of information about a private hearing;
 (b) authorise persons to attend a private hearing;
 (c) exclude persons from attending either a private or public hearing; or
 (d) restrict or prohibit the publication of information about a private or public hearing.

2 Part 1 of this practice direction applies to any application for an order under rules 90 to 92.

3 Part 2 of the practice direction makes additional provision in relation to orders founded on Convention rights which would restrict the publication of information.

(Section 1 of the Human Rights Act 1998 defines "the Convention rights".)

PART 1

Applications under rules 90, 91 or 92

4 An application for an order under rule 90, 91 or 92 must be commenced by filing an application notice form using COP9 in accordance with Part 10.

5 For the purposes of rules 90 to 92, a statement of truth in an application notice may be made by a person who is not a party.

6 For an application commenced under rules 90, 91 or 92, the court should consider whether to direct that the application should be dealt with as a discrete issue.

PART 2

Powers of the court to impose reporting restrictions

Court sitting in private

7 Section 12(1) of the Administration of Justice Act 1960 provides that, in any proceedings brought under the Mental Capacity Act 2005 before a court which is sitting in private, publication of information about the proceedings will generally be contempt of court. However, rule 91(1) makes it clear that there will be no contempt where the court has authorised the publication of the information under rule 91 or the publication is authorised in accordance with Part 3 of this Practice Direction. Where the court makes an order authorising publication, it may (at the same time or subsequently) restrict or prohibit the publication of information relating to a person's identity. Such restrictions may be imposed either on an application made by any person (usually a party to the proceedings) or of the court's own initiative.

8 The general rule is that hearings will be in private and that there can be no lawful publication of information unless the court has authorised it or the publication is authorised in accordance with Part 3 of this Practice Direction. Where reporting restrictions are imposed as part of the order authorising publication, they will simply set out what can be published and there will be no need to comply with the requirements as to notice which are set out in Part 2 of this practice direction. But if the restrictions are subsequent to the order authorising publication, then the requirements of Part 2 should be complied with.

Court sitting in public

9 Where a hearing is to be held in public as a result of a court order under rule 92, the court may restrict or prohibit the publication of information about the proceedings. Such restrictions may be imposed either on an application made by any person (usually a party to the proceedings) or of the court's own initiative.

Notification in relation to reporting restrictions

10 In connection with the imposition of reporting restrictions, attention is drawn to section 12(2) of the Human Rights Act 1998. This means that where an application has been made for an order restricting the exercise of the right to freedom of expression, the order must not be made where the person against whom the application is made is neither present nor represented unless the court is satisfied –

(a) that the applicant has taken all practicable steps to notify the respondent; or
(b) that there are compelling reasons why the respondent should not be notified.

11 The need to ensure that P's Convention rights are protected may be at issue when the court is considering whether to make an order that a public hearing should be held. Part 2 of this practice direction should therefore be complied with where the court is considering making an order under rule 92(2) of its own initiative.

12 In summary, the requirements to notify in accordance with the requirements of Part 2 of this practice direction will apply in any case where –

(a) the court has made an order for the publication of information about proceedings which are conducted in private and, after the order has been made:
  (i) an application founded on P's Convention rights is made to the court for an order under rule 91(3) which would impose restrictions (or further restrictions) on the information that may be published, or
  (ii) of its own initiative, the court is considering whether to impose such restrictions on the basis of P's Convention rights; or
(b) the court has already made an order for a hearing to be held in public and:
  (i) an application founded on Convention rights is made to the court for an order under rule 92(2) which would impose restrictions (or further restrictions) on the information that may be published, or
  (ii) of its own initiative, the court is considering whether to vary or impose further such restrictions.

Notice of reporting restrictions to be given to national news media

13 Notice of the possibility that reporting restrictions may be imposed can be effected via the Press Association's CopyDirect service, to which national newspapers and broadcasters subscribe as a means of receiving notice of such

applications. Such service should be the norm. The court retains the power to make orders without notice (whether in response to an application or of its own initiative) but such cases will be exceptional.

14 CopyDirect will be responsible for notifying the individual media organisations. Where the order would affect the world at large this is sufficient service for the purposes of advance notice. The website: http://www.medialawyer.press.net/courtapplications gives details of the organisations represented and instructions for service of the application.

Notice of an application to be given by applicant

15 A person who has made an application founded on Convention rights should give advance notice of the application to the national media via the Press Association's CopyDirect service. He should first telephone CopyDirect (tel. no 0870 837 6429). Unless an order pursuant to rule 19 has been made, a copy of the following documents should be sent either by fax (fax no 0870 830 6949) or to the e-mail address provided by CopyDirect –

(a) the application form or application notice seeking the restriction order;
(b) the witness statement filed in support;
(c) any legal submissions in support; and
(d) an explanatory note setting out the nature of the proceedings in the form set out in the Annex to this practice direction.

16 It is helpful if applications are accompanied by an explanatory note from which persons served can readily understand the nature of the case (though care should be taken that the information does not breach any rule or order of the court in relation to the use or publication of information). In any case where notice of an application has not been given, the explanatory note should explain why.

17 Unless there is a particular reason not to do so, copies of all the documents referred to above should be served. If there is a reason for not serving some or all of the documents (or parts of them), the applicant should ensure sufficient detail is given to enable the media to make an informed decision as to whether it wishes to attend a hearing or be legally represented.

18 The CopyDirect service does not extend to local or regional media or magazines. If service of the application on any specific organisation or person not covered is required, it should be effected directly.

19 The court may dispense with any of the requirements set out in paragraphs 15 to 18.

Notice of own-initiative order to be given by court

20 In any case where the court gives advance notice of an own-initiative order to the national media, it will send such of the information listed in paragraph 15 as it considers necessary.

Responding to a notice

21 Where a media organisation or any other person has been notified of an application or own-initiative order, they may decide that they wish to participate in any hearing to determine whether reporting restrictions should be imposed. In order to take part, the person must file an acknowledgment of service ("the

acknowledgment") using form COP5 within 14 days beginning with the date on which the notice of the reporting restrictions was given to him by CopyDirect.

22 The acknowledgment must be filed in accordance with rule 75.

23 A person who has filed an acknowledgment will not become a party to the substantive proceedings (ie. the proceedings in relation to which an application form was filed) except to such extent (if any) as the court may direct.

The hearing

24 Any application or own-initiative order which invokes Convention rights will involve a balancing of rights under Article 8 (right to respect for private and family life) and Article 10 (freedom of expression). There is no automatic precedence as between these Articles, and both are subject to qualification where (among other considerations) the rights of others are engaged.

25 In the case of an application, section 12(4) of the Human Rights Act 1998 requires the court to have particular regard to the importance of freedom of expression. It must also have regard to the extent to which material has or is about to become available to the public, the extent of the public interest in such material being published and the terms of any relevant privacy code (such as the Editor's Code of Practice enforced by the Independent Press Standards Organisation).

26 The same approach will be taken where the court is considering an own-initiative order imposing reporting restrictions.

Scope of order

Persons protected

27 The aim should be to protect P rather than to confer anonymity on other individuals or organisations. However, the order may include restrictions on identifying or approaching specified family members, carers, doctors or organisations or other persons as the court directs in cases where the absence of such restriction is likely to prejudice their ability to care for P, or where identification of such persons might lead to identification of P and defeat the purpose of the order. In cases where the court receives expert evidence the identity of the experts (as opposed to treating clinicians) is not normally subject to restriction, unless evidence in support is provided for such a restriction.

Information already in the public domain

28 Orders will not usually be made prohibiting publication of material which is already in the public domain, other than in exceptional cases.

Duration of order

29 Orders should last for no longer than is necessary to achieve the purpose for which they are made. The order may need to last until P's death. In some cases a later date may be necessary, for example to maintain the anonymity of doctors or carers after the death of a patient.

PART 3
COMMUNICATION OF INFORMATION RELATING TO PROCEEDINGS HELD IN PRIVATE

Introduction

30 Rule 91 deals with the communication of information (whether or not contained in a document filed with the court) relating to proceedings in the Court of Protection which are held in private.

31 Subject to any direction of the court, information may be communicated for the purposes of the law relating to contempt in accordance with paragraphs 33 to 37.

32 Nothing in this Part of this Practice Direction permits the communication to the public at large or any section of the public of any information relating to the proceedings.

Communication of information – general

33 Information may be communicated where the communication is to –

(a) a party;
(b) the legal representative of a party;
(c) an accredited legal representative or a representative within the meaning of rule 3A;
(d) a professional legal adviser;
(e) the Director of Legal Aid Casework;
(f) an expert whose instruction by a party has been authorised by the court for the purposes of the proceedings;
(g) any person instructed to make a report under section 49 of the Mental Capacity Act 2005;
(h) the Official Solicitor (prior to the Official Solicitor becoming a litigation friend);
(i) the Public Guardian.

Communication of information for purposes connected with the proceedings

34

(1) A party or the legal representative of a party, on behalf of and upon the instructions of that party, may communicate information relating to the proceedings to any person where necessary to enable that party –

(a) by confidential discussion, to obtain support, advice or assistance in the conduct of the proceedings;
(b) to engage in mediation or other forms of non-court dispute resolution;
(c) to make and pursue a complaint against a person or body concerned in the proceedings; or
(d) to make and pursue a complaint regarding the law, policy or procedure relating to proceedings in the Court of Protection.

(2) Where information is communicated to any person in accordance with sub-paragraph (1)(a), no further communication by that person is permitted.

(3) When information relating to the proceedings is communicated to any person in accordance with sub-paragraphs (1)(b),(c) or (d) –

Practice Direction 13A – Hearings (Including Reporting Restrictions) **PD13A**

(a) the recipient may communicate that information to a further recipient, provided that –
  (i) the party who initially communicated the information consents to that further communication; and
  (ii) the further communication is made only for the purpose or purposes for which the party made the initial communication; and
(b) the information may be successively communicated to and by further recipients on as many occasions as may be necessary to fulfil the purpose for which the information was initially communicated, provided that on each such occasion the conditions in sub-paragraph (a) are met.

Communication of information by a party etc. for other purposes

35 A person specified in the first column of the following table may communicate to a person listed in the second column such information as is specified in the third column for the purpose or purposes specified in the fourth column –

A party	A lay adviser, a McKenzie Friend, or a person arranging or providing pro bono legal services	Any information relating to the proceedings	To enable the party to obtain advice or assistance in relation to the proceedings
A party	A health care professional or a person or body providing counselling services for persons lacking capacity or their families		To enable the party or a member of the party's family to obtain health care or counselling
A party	The European Court of Human Rights		For the purpose of making an application to the European Court of Human Rights
A party, any person lawfully in receipt of information or a court officer	A person or body conducting an approved research project		For the purpose of an approved research project
A legal representative or a professional legal adviser, and the Public Guardian	A person or body responsible for investigating or determining complaints in relation to legal representatives or professional legal advisers		For the purposes of the investigation or determination of a complaint in relation to a legal representative or a professional legal adviser

PART IV

953

A party	A lay adviser, a McKenzie Friend, or a person arranging or providing pro bono legal services	Any information relating to the proceedings	To enable the party to obtain advice or assistance in relation to the proceedings
A legal representative or a professional legal adviser	A person or body assessing quality assurance systems		To enable the legal representative or professional legal adviser to obtain a quality assurance assessment
A legal representative or a professional legal adviser	An accreditation body	Any information relating to the proceedings providing that it does not, or is not likely to, identify any person involved in the proceedings	To enable the legal representative or professional legal adviser to obtain accreditation
A party, or the Public Guardian	A police officer	The text or summary of the whole or part of a judgment given in the proceedings	For the purpose of a criminal investigation
A party or any person lawfully in receipt of information	A member of the Crown Prosecution Service		To enable the Crown Prosecution Service to discharge its functions under any enactment

Communication to and by Ministers of the Crown and Welsh Ministers

36 A person specified in the first column of the following table may communicate to a person listed in the second column such information as is specified in the third column for the purpose or purposes specified in the fourth column –

A party or any person lawfully in receipt of information relating to the proceedings	A Minister of the Crown with responsibility for a government department engaged, or potentially engaged, in an application before the European Court of Human Rights relating to the proceedings	Any information relating to the proceedings of which he or she is in lawful possession	To provide the department with information relevant, or potentially relevant, to the proceedings before the European Court of Human Rights
A Minister of the Crown	The European Court of Human Rights		For the purpose of engagement in an application before the European Court of Human Rights relating to the proceedings
A Minister of the Crown	Lawyers advising or representing the United Kingdom in an application before the European Court of Human Rights relating to the proceedings		For the purpose of receiving advice or for effective representation in relation to the application before the European Court of Human Rights
A Minister of the Crown or a Welsh Minister	Another Minister, or Ministers, of the Crown or a Welsh Minister		For the purpose of notification, discussion and the giving or receiving of advice regarding issues raised by the information in which the relevant departments have, or may have, an interest

37

(1) This paragraph applies to communications made in accordance with paragraphs 35 and 36 and the reference in this paragraph to 'the table' means the table in the relevant paragraph.

(2) A person in the second column of the table may only communicate information relating to the proceedings received from a person in the first column for the purpose or purposes –

(a) for which he or she received that information;

(b) of professional development or training, providing that any communication does not, or is not likely to, identify any person involved in the proceedings without that person's consent; or
(c) of fulfilling a statutory process.

38 In this Practice Direction –

'accreditation body' means –
(a) The Law Society, or
(b) the Lord Chancellor in exercise of the Lord Chancellor's functions in relation to legal aid;

'approved research project' means a project of research –
(a) approved in writing by a Secretary of State after consultation with the President of the Court of Protection, or
(b) approved in writing by the President of the Court of Protection.

'body assessing quality assurance systems' includes –
(a) The Law Society,
(b) the Lord Chancellor in exercise of the Lord Chancellor's functions in relation to legal aid, or
(c) The General Council of the Bar;

'body or person responsible for investigating or determining complaints in relation to legal representatives or professional legal advisers' means –
(a) The Law Society,
(b) The General Council of the Bar,
(c) The Institute of Legal Executives,
(d) The Legal Services Ombudsman; or
(e) The Office of Legal Complaints.

'criminal investigation' means an investigation conducted by police officers with a view to it being ascertained –
(a) whether a person should be charged with an offence, or
(b) whether a person charged with an offence is guilty of it;

'health care professional' means –
(a) a registered medical practitioner,
(b) a registered nurse or midwife, or
(c) a clinical psychologist.

'lay adviser' means a non-professional person who gives lay advice on behalf of an organisation in the lay advice sector;

'McKenzie Friend' means any person permitted by the court to sit beside an unrepresented litigant in court to assist that litigant by prompting, taking notes and giving advice.

ANNEX

Application for a Reporting Restriction Order

EXPLANATORY NOTE

1 AB is in a permanent vegetative state. An application has been made by the NHS Hospital Trust responsible for his care for the Court of Protection to make a decision on the question of withdrawing artificial nutrition and hydration. This course is supported by AB's family.

2 On [date] the application will be heard by the Court of Protection [in public].

3 A Reporting Restriction Order has been [made/applied for] to protect AB's right to confidentiality in respect of his medical treatment. This does not restrict publication of information or discussion about the treatment of patients in a

permanent vegetative state, provided that such publication is not likely to lead to the identification of AB, those caring for him, the NHS Trust concerned or the establishment at which he is being cared for.

Practice Direction 13B – Court bundles

This practice direction supplements Part 13 of the Court of Protection Rules 2007

Introduction

1 This practice direction is issued to achieve consistency in the preparation of court bundles in the Court of Protection.

Application of the practice direction

2.1 Except as specified in paragraph 2.4, and subject to a direction under paragraph 2.5 or specific directions given in any particular case, this Practice Direction applies to all hearings in the Court of Protection:

 (a) before the President of the Family Division, the Chancellor or a puisne judge of the High Court;
 (b) relating in whole or in part to personal welfare, health or deprivation of liberty that are listed for a hearing of one hour or more before a judge other than a judge specified at sub-paragraph (a);
 (c) relating solely to property and affairs that are listed before a judge other than a judge specified at sub-paragraph (a) for:
  (i) a final hearing; or
  (ii) an interim hearing of one hour or more.

2.2 'Hearings' includes all appearances before a judge whether with or without notice to other parties and whether for directions or for substantive relief.

2.3 This Practice Direction applies whether a bundle is being lodged for the first time or is being re-lodged for a further hearing.

2.4 This practice direction does not apply to the hearing of any urgent application if and to the extent that it is impractical to comply with it.

2.5 The President may, after such consultation as is appropriate, direct that this practice direction will apply to such other hearings as he may specify irrespective of the length of hearing.

Responsibility for the preparation of the bundle

3.1 A bundle for the use of the court at the hearing must be provided by the party in the position of applicant at the hearing (or, if there are cross-applications, by the party whose application was first in time) or, if that person is a litigant in person, then (and subject to any direction by the court) by the first listed respondent who is not a litigant in person or P.

3.2 Where the first named respondent is P and he or she is represented by the Official Solicitor, the responsibility for preparing the bundle will fall to the next named respondent who is represented.

3.3 The party preparing the bundle must paginate it. If possible the contents of the bundle must be agreed by all parties.

Contents of the bundle

4.1 The bundle must contain copies of all documents relevant to the hearing, in chronological order from the front of the bundle, paginated (either in separate sections or sequentially), indexed and divided into separate sections as follows:

(a) preliminary documents (see paragraphs 4.2 to 4.7);
(b) any other case management documents required by any other practice direction;
(c) a time estimate (see paragraph 10.1);
(d) applications and orders including all Court of Protection forms filed with the application;
(e) any registered enduring or lasting power of attorney,
(f) any urgent or standard authorisation given under Schedule A1 of the Mental Capacity Act 2005
(g) statements and affidavits (which must state on the top right corner of the front page the date when it was signed or sworn);
(h) care plans (where appropriate);
(i) experts' reports and other reports; and
(j) other documents, divided into further sections as may be appropriate.

Preliminary Documents for Directions and Interim Hearings

4.2 At the start of the bundle there must be inserted a document or documents prepared by each party ('the preliminary documents for a directions or interim hearing') which should set out (either within the preliminary documents themselves or by cross-reference to what is set out in another document that is in, or is to be put in the bundle):

(a) a case summary;
(b) the issues for determination at the hearing;
(d) an outline of the likely factual and legal issues at the trial of the case;
(e) the relief sought at the hearing; and
(f) a list of essential reading.

4.3 Where appropriate, the preliminary documents for a directions or interim hearing should include:

(a) a description of relevant family members and other persons who may be affected by or interested in the relief sought;
(b) a particularised account of the issues in the case;
(c) the legal propositions relied on, and in particular whether it is asserted that any issue is not governed by the Mental Capacity Act 2005;
(d) any directions sought concerning the identification and determination of the facts that are agreed, the facts the court will be invited to find and the factors it will be invited to take into account based on such agreed facts or findings of facts;
(e) any directions sought concerning the alternatives the court will be invited to consider in determining what is in P's best interests;
(f) any directions sought relating to expert evidence;
(g) any other directions sought; and
(h) a skeleton argument.

Preliminary Documents for Fact Finding Hearings

4.4 At the start of the bundle there must be inserted a document or documents prepared by each party ('the preliminary documents for a fact finding hearing') which should set out (either within the preliminary documents themselves, or by crossreference to what is set out in another document that is in, or is to be put in the bundle):

(a) the findings of fact that the court is being asked to make; and

(b) cross references to the evidence relied on to found those findings.

4.5 Where appropriate, the preliminary documents for a fact finding hearing should include:

(a) a chronology;
(b) a skeleton argument; and
(c) a description of relevant family members and other persons who may be affected by or interested in the relief sought.

Preliminary Documents for Final Hearings

4.6 At the start of the bundle there must be inserted a document or documents prepared by each party ('the preliminary documents for a final hearing') which should set out (either within the preliminary documents themselves, or by cross-reference to what is set out in another document that is in, or is to be put in the bundle):

(a) the relief sought;
(b) a skeleton argument.

4.7 Where appropriate, the preliminary documents for a final hearing should include:

(a) a chronology;
(b) the findings of fact that the court is being invited to make and the factors based on such findings or agreed facts that the court is being invited to take into account;
(c) an appropriately particularised description of the alternatives the court is being invited to consider; and
(d) a description of relevant family members and other persons who may be affected by or interested in the relief sought.

4.8 Each of the preliminary documents must state on the front page immediately below the heading the date when it was prepared and the date of the hearing for which it was prepared.

4.9 All case summaries, chronologies and skeleton arguments contained in the preliminary documents must be cross-referenced to the relevant pages of the bundle.

4.10 Where the nature of the hearing is such that a complete bundle of all documents is unnecessary, the bundle (which need not be repaginated) may comprise only those documents necessary for the hearing, but

(a) the preliminary documents must state that the bundle is limited or incomplete; and
(b) the bundle must if reasonably practicable be in a form agreed by all parties.

4.9 Where the bundle is re-lodged in accordance with paragraph 9.2, before it is re-lodged:

(a) the bundle must be updated as appropriate; and
(b) all superseded documents must be removed from the bundle.

Format of the bundle

5.1 The bundle must be contained in one or more A4 size ring binders or lever arch files (each lever arch file being limited to 350 pages).

5.2 All ring binders and lever arch files must have clearly marked on the front and the spine:

   (a)   the title and number of the case;
   (b)   the court where the case has been listed;
   (c)   the hearing date and time;
   (d)   if known, the name of the judge hearing the case; and
   (e)   where there is more than one ring binder or lever arch file, a distinguishing letter (A, B, C etc.) or number and confirmation of the total number of binders or files (1 of 3 etc.).

Timetable for preparing and lodging the bundle

6.1 The party preparing the bundle must, whether or not the bundle has been agreed, provide a paginated index and, when practicable, paginated copies of updating material to all other parties not less than 5 working days before the hearing.

6.2 Where counsel is to be instructed at any hearing, a paginated bundle must (if not already in counsel's possession) be delivered to counsel by the person instructing that counsel not less than 4 working days before the hearing.

6.3 The bundle (with the exception of the preliminary documents, if and insofar as they are not then available) must be lodged with the court not less than 3 working days before the hearing, or at such other time as may be specified by the judge.

6.4 The preliminary documents (and where appropriate any documents referred to therein that are not in the bundle) must be lodged with the court no later than 11 am on the day before the hearing and, where the hearing is before a judge of the High Court and the name of the judge is known, must at the same time be sent by email to the judge's clerk.

Lodging the bundle

7.1 The bundle must be lodged at the appropriate office as detailed at paragraph 7.2 If the bundle is lodged in the wrong place the judge may:

   (a)   treat the bundle as having not been lodged; and
   (b)   take the steps referred to in paragraph 12.

7.2 Unless the judge has given some other direction as to where the bundle in any particular case is to be lodged (for example a direction that the bundle is to be lodged with the judge's clerk) the bundle must be lodged:

   (a)   for hearings before a judge of the Family Division, in the office of the Clerk of the Rules, 1st Mezzanine, Queen's Building, Royal Courts of Justice, Strand, London WC2A 2LL (DX 44450 Strand);
   (b)   for hearings before a judge of the Chancery Division, in the office of the Chancery Judges' Listing Officer, Room WG 4, Royal Courts of Justice, Strand, London WC2A 2LL (DX 44450 Strand);
   (c)   for hearings at the central registry of the Court of Protection in the office of the Listing & Appeals team, Court of Protection, PO Box 70185, First Avenue House, 42 to 49 High Holborn, London WC1A 9 JA (DX 160013 Kingsway 7);
   (d)   for hearings in the Central Family Court at First Avenue House, at the List Office counter, 3rd floor, First Avenue House, 42/49 High Holborn, London, WC1V 6NP (DX 160010 Kingsway); and
   (e)   for hearings at any other court, including regional courts where a Court of Protection judge is sitting, at such place as may be designated and in

PART IV   COURT OF PROTECTION PRACTICE 2016

default of any such designation, at the court office or Court of Protection section of the court where the hearing is to take place.

7.3 Any bundle sent to the court by post, DX or courier must be clearly addressed to the appropriate office and must show the date and place of the hearing on the outside of any packaging as well as on the bundle itself. It must in particular expressly and prominently state that it relates to Court of Protection business.

Lodging the bundle – additional requirements for cases being heard at the Central Family Court or before a judge of the High Court at the RCJ

8.1 In the case of hearings at the Central Family Court or before a High Court judge at the RCJ, parties must:

(a) if the bundle or preliminary and other documents are delivered personally, ensure that they obtain a receipt from the clerk accepting it or them; and

(b) if the bundle or preliminary and other documents are sent by post or DX, ensure that they obtain proof of posting or despatch.

8.2 The receipt (or proof of posting or despatch, as the case may be) must be brought to court on the day of the hearing and must be produced to the court if requested. If the receipt (or proof of posting or despatch) cannot be produced to the court the judge may:

(a) treat the bundle as having not been lodged; and

(b) take the steps referred to in paragraph 12.

8.3 For hearings at the RCJ before a judge of the High Court:

(a) bundles or preliminary and other documents delivered after 11 am on the day before the hearing will not be accepted by the Clerk of the Rules or Chancery Judges' Listing Officer and must be delivered directly to the clerk of the judge hearing the case;

(b) upon learning before which judge a hearing is to take place, the clerk to counsel, or other advocate, representing the party responsible for the bundle must, no later than 3 pm the day before the hearing, telephone the clerk of the judge hearing the case to ascertain whether the judge has received the bundle (including the preliminary and other documents), and, if not, must organise prompt delivery.

Removing and re-lodging the bundle

9.1 Following completion of the hearing the party responsible for the bundle must retrieve it from the court immediately or, if that is not practicable, must collect it from the court within five working days. Bundles which are not collected within the stipulated time may be destroyed.

9.2 The bundle must be re-lodged for the next (and for any further hearings of whatever type) in accordance with the provisions of this Practice Direction and in a form, which complies with paragraphs 5.1 and 5.2.

Time estimates

10.1 In every case a time estimate for the hearing must be prepared which must so far as practicable be agreed by all parties and must:

(a) specify separately:

       (i) the time estimated to be required for judicial pre-reading;
       (ii) the time required for hearing all evidence and submissions; and
       (iii) the time estimated to be required for preparing and delivering judgment; and
  (b) be prepared on the basis that before they give evidence all witnesses will have read all relevant filed statements and reports.

10.2 Once a case has been listed, any change in time estimates must be notified immediately by telephone (and then immediately confirmed in writing):

  (a) in the case of hearings in the RCJ, to the Clerk of the Rules or the Chancery Judges' Listing Officer as appropriate;
  (b) in the case of hearings in the central Registry of the Court of Protection, to the Diary Manager in the Listing & Appeals team at the Court of Protection, RCJ;
  (c) in the case of hearings in the Central Family Court at First Avenue House, to the List Officer at First Avenue House; and
  (d) in the case of hearings elsewhere, to the relevant listing officer.

Taking cases out of the list

11 As soon as it becomes known that a hearing will no longer be effective, whether as a result of the parties reaching agreement or for any other reason, the parties or their representatives must immediately notify the court by telephone and by letter. The letter, which must wherever possible be a joint letter sent on behalf of all parties with their signatures applied or appended, must include:

  (a) a short background summary of the case;
  (b) the written consent of each party who consents and, where a party does not consent, details of the steps which have been taken to obtain that party's consent and, where known, an explanation of why that consent has not been given;
  (c) a draft of the order being sought; and
  (d) enough information to enable the court to decide:
       (i) whether to take the case out of the list; and
       (ii) whether to make the proposed order.

Penalties for failure to comply with this practice direction

12 Failure to comply with any part of this practice direction may result in the judge removing the case from the list or putting the case further back in the list and may also result in a 'wasted costs' order in accordance with CPR Part 46.8 or some other adverse costs order.

Practice Direction – Transparency Pilot

This Practice Direction supplements Part 13 of the Court of Protection Rules 2007

1 General

1.1 This Practice Direction is made under rule 9A[1] of the Court of Protection Rules 2007 ('CoPR'). It provides for a pilot scheme for the holding of hearings to be in public pursuant to orders under rule 92[2] with a standard order for restrictions on reporting to ensure the anonymity of P and, where appropriate, other persons.

> 1 Renumbered as rule 2.6 where the practice direction *Practice Direction – Case Management Pilot* ('the Case Management pilot') applies.
> 2 Renumbered as rule 4.3 where the Case Management pilot applies.

1.2 Where the provisions of this Practice Direction conflict with the provisions of Part 13 of the CoPR or Practice Direction 13A[3], this Practice Direction shall take precedence.

> 3 Renumbered respectively as Part 4 and Practice Direction 4A where the Case Management Pilot applies.

1.3 The pilot scheme is to –

(a) operate from 29 January 2016 to 31 July 2016;
(b) apply to hearings in all proceedings except applications relating to serious medical treatment (for which Practice Direction 9E makes specific provision) and applications for a committal order (for which rule 188 makes specific provision); and
(c) apply to hearings which the court has, on or after 29 January 2016, directed to take place (but not hearings taking place after that date pursuant to a direction before that date).

2 General rule – standard order under rule 92(1)(a) and (2)[4]

> 4 Rule 92 is renumbered as rule 4.3 where the Case Management pilot applies.

2.1 Where the pilot scheme applies, the court will ordinarily –

(a) make an order under rule 92(1)(a) that any attended hearing shall be in public; and
(b) in the same order, impose restrictions under rule 92(2) in relation to the publication of information about the proceedings.

2.2 An 'attended hearing', except where a practice direction provides otherwise, means a hearing where one or more of the parties to the proceedings have been invited to attend the court for the determination of the application.

2.3 An order pursuant to paragraph 2.1 will ordinarily be in the terms of the standard order set out in the Annex to this Practice Direction.

2.4 The court may decide not to make an order pursuant to paragraph 2.1 if it appears to the court that there is good reason for not making the order, but will consider whether it would be appropriate instead to make an order (under rule 92(1)(b) or (c)) –

(a) for a part only of the hearing to be held in public; or
(b) excluding any persons, or class of persons from the hearing, or from such part of the hearing as is held in public.

2.5 (1) In deciding whether there is good reason not to make an order pursuant to

paragraph 2.1 and whether to make an order pursuant to paragraph 2.4 instead, the court will have regard in particular to –
(a) the need to protect P or another person involved in the proceedings;
(b) the nature of the evidence in the proceedings;
(c) whether earlier hearings in the proceedings have taken place in private;
(d) whether the court location where the hearing will be held has facilities appropriate to allowing general public access to the hearing, and whether it would be practicable or proportionate to move to another location or hearing room;
(e) whether there is any risk of disruption to the hearing if there is general public access to it;
(f) whether, if there is good reason for not allowing general public access, there also exists good reason to deny access to duly accredited representatives of news gathering and reporting organisations.
(2) In sub-paragraph (1)(f), 'duly accredited' refers to accreditation in accordance with any administrative scheme for the time being approved for the purposes of this pilot by the Lord Chancellor.

2.6 Where the court makes an order pursuant to paragraph 2.1 or 2.4 that an attended hearing or part of it is to be in public, the court will grant, to any person who would have been entitled under the Legal Services Act 2007 to exercise rights of audience at that hearing if such an order had not been made and the hearing was held in private (and who is not otherwise entitled to exercise such rights), the equivalent rights of audience at that attended hearing and any further hearing, unless the court is satisfied that there is good reason not to do so.

****

Note—The Standard Order is set out in Part VIII.

Admissions, Evidence and Depositions

Practice Direction 14A – Written evidence

This practice direction supplements Part 14 of the Court of Protection Rules 2007

Affidavits

Deponent

1. A deponent is a person who gives evidence by affidavit or affirmation.

Heading

2. The affidavit should be headed with the title of the proceedings, including the case number (if known) and the full name of the person to whom the proceedings relate (unless an order to the contrary pursuant to rule 19 has been made).

3. At the top right hand corner of the first page (and on the back-sheet) there should be clearly written:

   (a) the party on whose behalf it is made (unless an order to the contrary pursuant to rule 19 has been made);
   (b) the initials and surname of the deponent;
   (c) the number of the affidavit in relation to that deponent; and
   (d) the date sworn.

Body of affidavit

4. The affidavit must, if practicable, be in the deponent's own words. It should be expressed in the first person, and the deponent should:

   (a) commence 'I (full name) of (address) state on oath …';
   (b) if giving evidence in his professional, business or other occupational capacity, give the address at which he works in (a) above, the position he holds and the name of his firm or employer;
   (c) give his occupation or, if he has none, his description; and
   (d) state if he is a party to the proceedings or employed by a party to the proceedings.

5. An affidavit must indicate:

   (a) which of the statements in it are made from the deponent's own knowledge and which are matters of information or belief; and
   (b) the source for any matters of information or belief.

6. Where a deponent:

   (a) refers to an exhibit or exhibits, he should state 'there is now produced and shown to me marked '…' the (*description of exhibit*)'; and
   (b) makes more than one affidavit (to which there are exhibits) in the same proceedings, the numbering of the exhibits should run consecutively throughout and not start again with each affidavit.

Jurat

7. The jurat of an affidavit is a statement set out at the end of the document which authenticates the affidavit.

8. It must:

   (a) be signed by all deponents;
   (b) be completed and signed by the person before whom the affidavit was sworn whose name and qualifications must be printed beneath his signature;
   (c) contain the full address of the person before whom the affidavit was sworn; and
   (d) follow immediately on from the text and not be put on a separate page.

Format of affidavits

9. An affidavit should:

   (a) be produced on durable quality A4 paper with a 3.5 centimetre margin;
   (b) be fully legible and should normally be typed on one side of the paper only;
   (c) where possible, be bound securely in a manner which would not hamper filing;
   (d) have the pages numbered consecutively as a separate document;
   (e) be divided into numbered paragraphs; and
   (f) have all numbers, including dates, expressed in figures.

10. It is usually convenient for an affidavit to follow the chronological sequence of events or matters dealt with. Each paragraph of an affidavit should as far as possible be confined to a distinct portion of the subject.

11. An affidavit must be included in, or attached to, a COP25 form.

Inability of deponent to read or sign affidavit

12. Where an affidavit is sworn by a person who is unable to read or sign it, the person before whom the affidavit is sworn must certify in the jurat that:

    (a) he read the affidavit to the deponent;
    (b) the deponent appeared to understand it; and
    (c) the deponent signed, or made his mark, in his presence.

13. If that certificate is not included in the jurat, the affidavit may not be used in evidence unless the court is satisfied that it was read to the deponent and that he appeared to understand it. Two versions of the form of the jurat with the certificate are set out in Annex 1 to this practice direction.

Alterations to affidavits

14. Any alteration to an affidavit must be initialled by both the deponent and the person before whom the affidavit was sworn.

15. An affidavit which contains an alteration that has not been initialled may be filed or used in evidence only with the permission of the court.

Who may administer oaths

16. Only the following may administer oaths:

(a) Commissioners for Oaths;[31]
(b) practising solicitors;[32]
(c) other persons specified by statute;[33]
(d) certain officials of the Senior Courts;[34]
(e) a circuit judge or district judge;[35]
(f) any justice of the peace;[36] and
(g) certain officials of the County Court appointed for the purpose.[37]

17. An affidavit must be sworn before a person independent of the parties or their representatives.

Filing of affidavits

18. If the court directs that an affidavit is to be filed, it must be filed in the court office.

19. Where an affidavit is in a foreign language:

(a) the party wishing to rely on it:
   (i) must have it translated, and
   (ii) must file the foreign language affidavit with the court; and
(b) the translator must make and file with the court an affidavit verifying the translation and exhibiting both the translation and a copy of the foreign language affidavit.

Exhibits

Manner of exhibiting documents

20. A document used in conjunction with an affidavit should be:

(a) produced to and verified by the deponent, and remain separate from the affidavit; and
(b) identified by a declaration of the person before whom the affidavit was sworn.

21. The declaration should be headed with the name of the proceedings in the same way as the affidavit.

22. The first page of each exhibit should be marked:

(a) as in paragraph 3 above; and
(b) with the exhibit mark referred to in the affidavit.

Letters

23. Copies of individual letters should be collected together and exhibited in a bundle or bundles. The letters should be arranged in chronological order with the earliest at the top, and firmly secured.

---

[31] Commissioner for Oaths Act 1889 and 1891.
[32] Section 81 of the Solicitors Act 1974.
[33] Section 65 of the Administration of Justice Act 1985; s 113 of the Courts and Legal Services Act 1990 and the Commissioners for Oaths (Prescribed Bodies) Regulations 1994 and 1995.
[34] Section 2 of the Commissioners for Oaths Act 1889.
[35] Section 58 of the County Courts Act 1984.
[36] Section 58 as above.
[37] Section 58 as above.

24. When a bundle of correspondence is exhibited it should be arranged and secured as above and numbered consecutively.

Other documents

25. Photocopies instead of original documents may be exhibited provided the originals are made available for inspection by other parties before the hearing and by the judge at the hearing.

26. Court documents must not be exhibited (official copies of such documents prove themselves).

Exhibits other than documents

27. Items other than documents should be clearly marked with an exhibit number or letter in such a manner that the mark cannot become detached from the exhibit.

28. Small items may be placed in a container and the container appropriately marked.

General provisions

29. Where an exhibit contains more than one document:

    (a) the bundle should not be stapled but should be securely fastened in a way that does not hinder the reading of the documents; and
    (b) the pages should be numbered consecutively at the bottom centre.

30. Every page of an exhibit should be clearly legible. Typed copies of illegible documents should be included, paginated with 'a' etc numbers.

31. Where on account of their bulk the service of copies of exhibits on the other parties would be difficult or impracticable, the directions of the court should be sought as to the arrangements for bringing the exhibits to the attention of the other parties and as to their custody pending the final hearing.

Affirmations

32. All provisions in this or any other practice direction relating to affidavits apply to affirmations with the following exceptions:

    (a) the deponent should commence 'I (*name*) of (*address*) do solemnly and sincerely affirm ...'; and
    (b) in the jurat the word 'sworn' is replaced by the word 'affirmed'.

Witness statements

Heading

33. The witness statements should be headed with the title of the proceedings; including the case number (if known) and the full name of the person to whom the proceedings relate (unless an order to the contrary pursuant to rule 19 has been made).

34. At the top right hand corner of the first page there should be clearly written:

    (a) the party on whose behalf it is made (unless an order to the contrary pursuant to rule 19 has been made);

(b) the initials and surname of the witness;
   (c) the number of the statement in relation to that witness; and
   (d) the date the statement was made.

Body of witness statement

35. The witness statement must, if practicable, be in the intended witness's own words. The statement should be expressed in the first person and should also state:
   (a) his place of residence or, if he is making the statement in his professional, business or other occupational capacity, the address at which he works, the position he holds and the name of his firm or employer;
   (b) his occupation, or if he has none, his description; and
   (c) if he is a party to the proceedings or employed by a party to the proceedings.

36. A witness statement must indicate:
   (a) which of the statements in it are made from the witness's own knowledge and which are matters of information or belief; and
   (b) the source for any matters of information or belief.

37. An exhibit used in conjunction with a witness statement should be verified and identified by the witness and remain separate from the witness statement.

38. Where a witness refers to an exhibit or exhibits, he should state: 'I refer to the (*description of exhibit*) marked "…".

39. The provisions of paragraphs 22 to 31 apply similarly to witness statements as they do to affidavits, where appropriate.

40. Where a witness makes more than one witness statement to which there are exhibits, the numbering of the exhibits should run consecutively throughout and not start again with each witness statement.

Format of witness statement

41. A witness statement should adhere to the format specified in paragraph 9 for affidavits.

42. It is usually convenient for a witness statement to follow the chronological sequence of the events or matters dealt with and each paragraph of a witness statement should, as far as possible, be confined to a distinct portion of the subject.

43. A witness statement must be included in, or attached to, a COP24 form.

Statement of truth

44. A witness statement is the equivalent of oral evidence which the witness would, if called, give in evidence. It must be verified by a statement of truth in the following terms:

   'I believe that the facts stated in this witness statement are true.'

(Practice Direction B accompanying Part 4 sets out more detailed requirements for statements of truth.)

45. Attention is drawn to rule 14 which sets out the consequences of verifying a witness statement containing a false statement without an honest belief in its truth.

Alterations to witness statements

46. Any alteration to a witness statement must be initialled by the person making the statement or by the authorised person where appropriate.

47. A witness statement which contains an alteration that has not been initialled may only be used in evidence with the permission of the court.

Filing of witness statements

48. Where a witness statement is in a foreign language:
    (a) the party wishing to rely on it must:
        (i) have it translated, and
        (ii) file the foreign language witness statement with the court; and
    (b) the translator must make and file with the court an affidavit verifying the translation and exhibiting both the translation and a copy of the foreign language witness statement.

Defects in affidavits, witness statements and exhibits

49. Where:
    (a) an affidavit;
    (b) a witness statement; or
    (c) an exhibit to either an affidavit or a witness statement,

does not comply with Part 14 or this practice direction in relation to its form, the court may refuse to admit it as evidence and may refuse to allow the costs arising from its preparation.

50. However, the court may allow a person to file a defective affidavit or witness statement or to use a defective exhibit.

Agreed bundles for hearings

51. The court may give directions requiring the parties to use their best endeavours to agree a bundle or bundles of documents for use at any hearing.

52. All documents contained in bundles which have been agreed for use at a hearing shall be admissible at that hearing as evidence of their contents, unless –
    (a) the court orders otherwise; or
    (b) a party gives written notice of objection to the admissibility of particular documents.

Evidence by video link

53. Guidance on the use of video conferencing is set out at Annex 2 to this practice direction.

Information

54. The court may direct a party with access to information which is not reasonably available to another party to serve on that other party a document which records the

information.[38] The document served must include sufficient details of all the facts, tests, experiments and assumptions which underlie any part of the information to enable the party on whom it is served to make, or to obtain, a proper interpretation of the information and an assessment of its significance.

ANNEX 1

Certificate to be used where a deponent to an affidavit is unable to read or sign it

Sworn at ...this ...day of ... Before me, I having first read over the contents of this affidavit to the deponent [if there are exhibits, add 'and explained the nature and effect of the exhibits referred to in it'] who appeared to understand it and approved its contents as accurate, and made his mark on the affidavit in my presence.

Or (after, *Before me*) the witness to the mark of the deponent having first sworn that he had read over etc. (*as above*) and that he saw him make his mark on the affidavit. (*Witness must sign*).

Certificate to be used where a deponent to an affirmation is unable to read or sign it

Affirmed at ...this ...day of ... Before me, I having first read over the contents of this affirmation to the deponent [if there are exhibits, add 'and explained the nature and effect of the exhibits referred to in it'] who appeared to understand it and approved its content as accurate, and made his mark on the affirmation in my presence.

Or (after, *Before me*) the witness to the mark of the deponent having been first sworn that he had read over etc (*as above*) and that he saw him make his mark on the affirmation. (*Witness must sign*).

ANNEX 2

Guidance on the use of video conferencing

1. This guidance is for the use of video conferencing (VC) to provide evidence in the Court of Protection. It is in part based upon the VC guidance contained in the practice direction that supplements Part 32 of the Civil Procedure Rules.

2. Rule 98 of the Court of Protection Rules provides that the court may allow a witness to give evidence through a video link or by other means. It is, however, inevitably not as ideal as having the witness physically present in court. Its convenience should not therefore be allowed to dictate its use. Consideration should be given in each case as to whether its use is likely to be beneficial to the efficient, fair and economic disposal of the proceedings.

3. For VC purposes, the location at which the judge sits is referred to as the 'local site'. The local site may be either a courtroom with VC equipment either permanently or temporarily installed, or another venue such as a studio or conference room set-up for VC. The other site or sites to and from which transmission is made are referred to as 'the remote site'.

---

[38] Rule 107.

Preliminary arrangements

4. The court's permission is required for any part of any proceedings to be dealt with by means of VC Before seeking a direction, the applicant should notify the appropriate court officer of the intention to seek it, and should enquire as to the availability of the court's VC equipment for the duration of the proposed VC. The application for a direction should be made to the court by filing a COP9 application notice in accordance with the Part 10 procedure.

5. If a witness at a remote site is to give evidence by an interpreter, consideration should be given at this stage as to whether the interpreter should be at the local site or the remote site.

6. Where the VC process is to be used to take evidence from a person in a foreign jurisdiction, the parties should consider whether that is permissible under local law.

7. If a VC direction is given, arrangements for the transmission will then need to be made. The court will ordinarily direct that the party seeking permission to use VC is to be responsible for this. That party is hereafter referred to as 'the VC arranging party'.

VC arranging party's responsibilities

8. The VC arranging party must contact the appropriate court officer and make arrangements for the VC transmission.

9. The court has established procedures with Her Majesty's Court and Tribunal Service that enables the witness's nearest local court with VC facilities to be used as the remote site. The VC arranging party must advise the court whether the party wishes to make use of local court facilities for the remote site.

10. If the party is unable to make use of local court VC facilities, then the VC arranging party is responsible for arranging an alternative remote site. This may consist of a solicitor's office or a commercial VC facility, and in some circumstances may require portable VC equipment to be brought to the witness. Details of the remote site, and of the equipment to be used, together with all necessary contact names and telephone numbers, will have to be provided to the court.

11. The VC arranging party must arrange for recording equipment to be provided by the court so that the evidence can be recorded. A court officer will normally be present to operate the recording equipment when the local site is a courtroom. The equipment should be set up and tested before the VC transmission.

12. In rare instances, it may be necessary for the local site to be somewhere other than the courtroom (or other VC facility onsite at the court). If this is the case, the VC arranging party should ensure:

    (a)   that arrangements are made, if practicable, for the royal coat of arms to be placed above the judge's seat at the alternate venue;
    (b)   that the number of microphones is adequate for the speakers;
    (c)   that the panning of the camera for the practitioners' table encompasses all legal representatives so that the viewer can see everyone seated there; and
    (d)   that a court officer is present to operate the recording equipment.

Court of Protection responsibilities

13. If the VC arranging party has advised that the party wishes to utilise local court facilities for the remote site, a court officer will contact the nearest local court (with VC facilities) to the witness and:

(a) agree and book a mutually convenient date and time for the attendance;
(b) advise the local court as to the number and details of those parties attending to give evidence by VC;
(c) confirm with the local court the reporting arrangements for the parties attending to give their evidence; and
(d) advise the parties by letter of the date, time and arrangements for attending the designated local court to give their evidence by VC.

14. Provided the local site is to be the courtroom (or other VC facility on-site at the court), a court officer will also:

(a) set-up the courtroom for the VC;
(b) establish the VC link with the remote site at the date and time that has been booked; and
(c) be available in order to deal with any technical problems during the transmission should they develop.

Local court responsibilities

15. The local court will advise the court staff (London or regional court as applicable) of the number to be called to establish the VC link with the remote site. Where the local court is utilising a third party networked VC service (such as the *Martin Dawes* service utilised by the closed nation-wide prison network), it will be responsible for arranging a bridging link for the date and time agreed.

16. The local court will make arrangements to meet the witness on their arrival at the court, escort them to the room where they are to give evidence by VC, switch on the VC equipment and ensure a link is established with the local site.

The hearing

17. Those involved with VC need to be aware that due to varying technology standards, there may be delays between the receipt of the picture and that of the accompanying sound. If due allowance is not made for this, there may be a tendency to 'speak over' the witness, whose voice will continue to be heard for a short period after he or she appears on the screen to have finished speaking.

18. Picture quality may also vary, and is generally enhanced if those appearing on VC monitors keep their movements to a minimum.

19. It is recommended that the practitioners and witness should arrive at their respective VC sites about 20 minutes prior to the scheduled commencement of the transmission.

20. Consideration will need to be given in advance to any documents to which the witness is likely to be referred. The parties should endeavour to agree on this. It will usually be most convenient for a bundle of the copy documents to be prepared in advance, which the VC arranging party should then send to the remote site.

21. Additional documents are sometimes quite properly introduced during the course of a witness's evidence. To cater for this, the VC arranging party should ensure that equipment is available to enable documents to be transmitted between sites during the course of the VC transmission. The procedure for conducting the transmission will be determined by the judge. The judge will also determine who is to control the cameras.

22. At the beginning of the transmission, the judge may wish to give directions as to the seating arrangements at the remote site so that those present are visible at the local site during the taking of the evidence.

23. The examination of the witness at the remote site should then follow as closely as possible the practice adopted when a witness is in the courtroom. During examination, cross-examination and re-examination, the witness must be able to see the legal representative asking the question and also any other person (whether another legal representative or the judge) making any statements in regard to the witness's evidence. It will in practice be most convenient if everyone remains seated throughout the transmission.

Practice Direction 14B – Depositions

This practice direction supplements Part 14 of the Court of Protection Rules 2007

Depositions to be taken in England and Wales

1. A party may apply for an order for a person to be examined on oath before:

    (a) a judge;
    (b) an examiner of the court; or
    (c) such other person as the court may appoint.[39]

2. The party who obtains an order for the examination of a deponent before an examiner of the court must:

    (a) apply to the court for the allocation of an examiner;
    (b) when allocated, provide the examiner with copies of all documents in the proceedings necessary to inform the examiner of the issues; and
    (c) pay the deponent a sum to cover his travelling expenses to and from the examination and compensation for his loss of time.

3. In ensuring that the deponent's evidence is recorded in full, the court or the examiner may permit it to be recorded in full on audiotape or videotape, but the deposition must always be recorded in writing by the examiner or by a competent shorthand writer or stenographer.

4. If the deposition is not recorded word for word, it must contain, as nearly as may be, the statement of the deponent. The examiner may record word for word any particular questions or answers which appear to him to have special importance.

5. If a deponent objects to answering any question or where any objection is taken to any question, the examiner must:

    (a) record in the deposition or a document attached to it:
        (i) the question,
        (ii) the nature of and grounds for the objection, and
        (iii) any answer given; and
    (b) give his opinion as to the validity of the objection and must record it in the deposition or a document attached to it.

6. Documents and exhibits must:

    (a) have an identifying number or letter marked on them by the examiner; and
    (b) be preserved by the party or his legal representative who obtained the order for the examination, or as the court or the examiner may direct.

7. The examiner may put any question to the deponent as to:

    (a) the meaning of any of his answers; or
    (b) any matter arising in the course of the examination.

8. Where a deponent:

    (a) fails to attend the examination; or
    (b) refuses to:
        (i) be sworn, or
        (ii) answer any lawful question, or
        (iii) produce any document,

---

[39] Rule 108.

the examiner will sign a certificate of such failure or refusal and may include in his certificate any comment as to the conduct of the deponent or of any person attending the examination.

9. The party who obtained the order for the examination must file the certificate with the court and may apply for an order that the deponent attend for examination or such other order as he considers appropriate.[40] The application must be made by filing a COP9 application notice, and may be made without notice.

10. The court will make such order on the application as it thinks fit including an order for the deponent to pay any costs resulting from his failure or refusal.

11. A deponent who wilfully refuses to obey an order made against him under Part 14 may be proceeded against for contempt of court.[41]

12. A deposition must:
   (a) be signed by the examiner;
   (b) have any amendments to it initialled by the examiner and the deponent; and
   (c) be endorsed by the examiner with:
      (i) a statement of the time occupied by the examination, and
      (ii) a record of any refusal by the deponent to sign the deposition and of his reasons for not doing so, and
      (iii) be sent by the examiner to the court where the proceedings are taking place for filing on the court file.

13. Rule 110 deals with the fees and expenses of the examiner.

Travelling expenses and compensation for loss of time

14. When a deponent is served with an order for examination he must be offered a sum to cover his travelling expenses to and from the examination and compensation for his loss of time.[42]

15. The sum referred to in paragraph 14 is to be based on the sums payable to witnesses attending the Crown Court.[43]

Depositions to be taken abroad for use as evidence in proceedings before courts in England and Wales (where the Taking of Evidence Regulation does not apply)

16. Where a party wishes to take a deposition from a person outside the jurisdiction, the court may order the issue of a letter of request to the judicial authorities of the country in which the proposed deponent is.[44]

17. An application for an order referred to in paragraph 16 should be made by filing a COP9 application notice in accordance with Part 10. The documents which a party applying for an order for the issue of a letter of request must file with his application notice are set out in rule 116.

18. In addition, the party applying for the order must file a draft order.

---

[40] Rule 112.
[41] Rules 185–194.
[42] Rule 108(6).
[43] These sums are fixed pursuant to the Prosecution of Offenders Act 1985 and the Costs in Criminal Cases (General) Regulations 1986.
[44] Rule 116.

19. The application will be dealt with by the Senior Judge or his nominee who will, if appropriate, sign the letter of request.

20. If parties are in doubt as to whether a translation under rule 116(7) is required, they should seek guidance from the court office.

21. A special examiner appointed under rule 116(4) may be the British Consul or the Consul-General or his deputy in the country where the evidence is to be taken if:

    (a)   there is in respect of that country a Civil Procedure Convention providing for the taking of evidence in that country for the assistance of proceedings in the High Court or other court in this country; or

    (b)   with the consent of the Secretary of State.

22. The provisions of paragraphs 1 to 12 above apply to the depositions referred to in paragraphs 16 to 22.

Taking of evidence between EU Member States

Taking of Evidence Regulation

23. Where evidence is to be taken:

    (a)   from a person in another Member State of the European Union for use as evidence in proceedings before courts in England and Wales; or

    (b)   from a person in England and Wales for use as evidence in proceedings before a court in another Member State,

Council Regulation (EC) No 1206/2001 of 28 May 2001 on co-operation between the courts of the Member States in the taking of evidence in civil or commercial matters ('the Taking of Evidence Regulation') applies.

24. The website link to the Taking of Evidence Regulation is annexed to this Practice Direction as Annex B.

25. The Taking of Evidence Regulation does not apply to Denmark. In relation to Denmark, therefore, rule 116 will continue to apply.

(Article 21(1) of the Taking of Evidence Regulation provides that the Regulation prevails over other provisions contained in bilateral or multilateral agreements or arrangements concluded by the Member States and in particular the Hague Convention of 1 March 1954 on Civil Procedure and the Hague Convention of 18 March 1970 on the Taking of Evidence Abroad in Civil or Commercial Matters.)

Meaning of 'designated court'

26. In accordance with the Taking of Evidence Regulation, each Regulation State has prepared a list of courts competent to take evidence in accordance with the Regulation indicating the territorial and, where appropriate, special jurisdiction of those courts.

27. Where rule 115 refers to a 'designated court' in relation to another Regulation State, the reference is to the court, referred to in the list of competent courts of that State, which is appropriate to the application in hand.

Evidence to be taken in another Regulation State for use in England and Wales

28. Where a person wishes to take a deposition from a person in another Regulation State, the court where the proceedings are taking place may order the issue of a request as is prescribed as Form A in the Taking of Evidence Regulation.

29. An application to the court for an order under rule 115 should be made by filing a COP9 application notice in accordance with Part 10.

30. Rule 115 provides that the party applying for the order must file a draft form of request in the prescribed form. Where completion of the form requires attachments or documents to accompany the form, these must also be filed.

31. If the court grants an order under rule 115, it will send the form of request directly to the designated court.

32. Where the taking of evidence requires the use of an expert, the designated court may require a deposit in advance towards the costs of that expert. Subject to any final order in relation to costs, the party who obtained the order is responsible for the payment of any such deposit which should be deposited with the court for onward transmission. Under the provisions of the Taking of Evidence Regulation, the designated court is not required to execute the request until such payment is received.

33. Article 17 permits the court where proceedings are taking place to take evidence directly from a deponent in another Regulation State if the conditions of the article are satisfied. Direct taking of evidence can only take place if evidence is given voluntarily without the need for coercive measures. Rule 115 provides for the court to make an order for the submission of a request to take evidence directly. The form of request is Form I annexed to the Taking of Evidence Regulation and rule 115 makes provision for a draft of this form to be filed by the party seeking the order. An application for an order under rule 115 should be by filing a COP9 application notice in accordance with Part 10.

ANNEX A

Draft letter of request (where the Taking of Evidence Regulation does not apply)

To the Competent Judicial Authority of   in   the   of

I [*name*] Senior Judge of the Court of Protection of England and Wales respectfully request the assistance of your court with regard to the following matters.

1. An application is now pending in the   Court of Protection in England and Wales entitled as follows [*set out full title and case number*] in which [*name*] of [*address*] is the applicant and [*name*] of [*address*] is the respondent.

2. The names and addresses of the representatives or agents of [*set out names and addresses of representatives of the parties*].

3. The application by the applicant is for:
    (a) [set out the nature of the application]
    (b) [the order sought, and]
    (c) [a summary of the facts.]

4. It is necessary for the purposes of justice and for the due determination of the matter in dispute between the parties that you cause the following witnesses, who are resident within your jurisdiction, to be examined. The names and addresses of the witnesses are as follows: [*set out names and addresses of witnesses*]

5. The witnesses should be examined on oath or if that is not possible within your laws or is impossible of performance by reason of the internal practice and procedure of your court or by reason of practical difficulties, they should be examined in accordance with whatever procedure your laws provide for in these matters.

6. Either

The witness should be examined in accordance with the list of questions annexed hereto.

Or

The witness should be examined regarding [*set out full details of evidence sought*].

N.B. Where the witness is required to produce documents, these should be clearly identified.

7. I would ask that you cause me, or the agents of the parties (if appointed), to be informed of the date and place where the examination is to take place.

8. Finally, I request that you will cause the evidence of the said witness to be reduced into writing and all documents produced on such examinations to be duly marked for identification and that you will further be pleased to authenticate such examinations by the seal of your court or in such other way as is in accordance with your procedure and return the written evidence and documents produced to me addressed as follows:

> The SeniorJudge,
> Court of Protection,
> First Avenue House,
> 42—49 High Holborn,
> London WC1V 6NP
> (DX 160013 Kingsway)

ANNEX B

Council Regulation (EC) NO 1206/2001

This regulation can be found on the EU legislation website at http://eur-lex.europa.eu.

Practice Direction 14C – Fees for examiners of the court

This practice direction supplements Part 14 of the Court of Protection Rules 2007

General

1. This practice direction sets out:
    (a) how to calculate the fees an examiner of the court ('an examiner') may charge; and
    (b) the expenses he may recover.

(Rule 108 provides that the court may make an order for evidence to be obtained by the examination of a witness before an examiner.)

2. Subject to any final order or direction of the court in relation to costs, the party who obtained the order for the examination must pay the fees and expenses of the examiner.

(Rule 110 permits an examiner to charge a fee for the examination and contains other provisions about his fees and expenses, and rule 111 provides who may be appointed as an examiner.)

The examination fee

3. An examiner may charge an hourly rate for each hour (or part of an hour) that he is engaged in examining the witness.

4. The hourly rate is to be calculated by reference to the formula set out in paragraph 6.

5. The examination fee will be the hourly rate multiplied by the number of hours the examination has taken. That is:

Examination fee = hourly rate x number of hours.

How to calculate the hourly rate – the formula

6. Divide the amount of the minimum annual salary of a post within Group 7 of the judicial salary structure as designated by the Review Body on Senior Salaries,[45] by 220 to give 'x'; and then divide 'x' by **6** to give **the hourly rate**.

That is:

$$\frac{\text{Minimum annual salary}}{220} = x$$

$$\frac{x}{6} = \text{hourly rate}$$

---

[45] The Report of the Review Body on Senior Salaries is published annually by the Stationery Office.

Single fee chargeable on making the appointment for examination

7. An examiner is also entitled to charge a single fee of twice the hourly rate (calculated in accordance with paragraph 6 above) as 'the appointment fee' when the appointment for the examination is made.

8. The examiner is entitled to retain the appointment fee where the witness fails to attend on the date and time arranged.

9. Where the examiner fails to attend on the date and time arranged he may not charge a further appointment fee for arranging a subsequent appointment.

(The examiner need not send the deposition to the court until his fees are paid, unless the court directs otherwise – see rule 110(1).)

Examiner's expenses

10. An examiner is also entitled to recover the following expenses –
    (a) all reasonable travelling expenses;
    (b) any other expenses reasonably incurred; and
    (c) subject to paragraph 11, any reasonable charge for the room where the examination takes place.

11. No expenses may be recovered under sub-paragraph 10(c) if the examination takes place at the examiner's usual business address.

(If the examiner's fees and expenses are not paid within a reasonable time he may report the fact to the court – see rule 110(3).)

Practice Direction 14D – Witness summons

This practice direction supplements Part 14 of the Court of Protection Rules 2007

Issue of a witness summons

1. Rule 106 makes provision as to the taking out of a witness summons.

2. A witness summons may require a witness to:

    (a) attend court to give evidence;
    (b) produce documents to the court; or
    (c) both (a) and (b),

on either a date fixed for a hearing or such date as the court may direct.

3. An application for a witness summons should be made by filing a COP9 application notice in accordance with the Part 10 procedure.

4. In the event the court grants the application, the witness summons will be prepared by the court.

5. A mistake in the name or address of a person named in the witness summons may be corrected if the summons has not been served.

6. If the mistake is a result of an error in the original application notice, an application to correct the mistake should be made by filing a further COP9 application notice in accordance with the Part 10 procedure. The application notice should set out the corrections that need to be made to the witness summons.

7. If the mistake is a result of a clerical mistake, the person taking out the summons should write to the court advising them of the mistake and seeking an amendment under rule 23 (clerical mistakes or slips).

8. The corrected summons must be re-sealed by the court and marked 'Amended and Re-sealed'.

Travelling expenses and compensation for loss of time

9. When a witness is served with a witness summons he must be offered a sum to cover his travelling expenses to and from the court and compensation for his loss of time.[46]

10. The sum referred to in paragraph 9 is to be based on the sums payable to witnesses attending the Crown Court.[47]

11. In addition, the witness must be paid such general or other costs as the court may allow.[48]

---

[46] Rule 106(6)(a) and (b).
[47] These sums are fixed pursuant to the Prosecution of Offenders Act 1985 and the Costs in Criminal Cases (General) Regulations 1986.
[48] Rule 106(7).

Practice Direction 14E – Section 49 reports

This practice direction supplements Part 14 of the Court of Protection Rules 2007

General

1. Attention is drawn to:

   (a) section 49 of the Act – which makes provision for the court to require a report dealing with such matters relating to P as the court may direct;

   (b) rule 85(2)(a) – which provides that the court, when giving directions, may require a section 49 report and give directions about any such report;

   (c) rule 117 – which sets out the duties of a person required to prepare a section 49 report and specifies to whom the report may be sent; and

   (d) rule 118 – which makes provision for the court to permit written questions to be put to a person who has made a section 49 report.

The court's direction for a report

2. The Annex to this Practice Direction Contains the form of an order requiring a report under section 49 of the Act and the forms of directions relating to the report. When requiring a section 49 report, the court will as far as possible base its order and directions on those forms.

Reports by Public Guardian or a Court of Protection Visitor

3. Where a report is to be prepared by either the Public Guardian or a Court of Protection Visitor,[49] a copy of the order and the directions will be sent to the Public Guardian.

4. In the case of a report which is to be made by a Court of Protection Visitor, the Public Guardian must ensure that:

   (a) a person is nominated from the panel of General Visitors or the panel of Special Visitors, as appropriate; and

   (b) the court is notified of his name and contact details as soon as practicable.

5. The nomination of a Court of Protection Visitor should be made before the end of the period of 7 days beginning with the date on which the Public Guardian received a copy of the order.

Reports under arrangements made by a local authority or an NHS body

6. Where a report is to be prepared under arrangements made by a local authority or an NHS body,[50] a copy of the order and the directions will be sent to a senior officer of that authority or body. That person must ensure that:

   (a) an appropriate person is nominated to make the report; and

   (b) the court is notified of his name and contact details as soon as practicable.

7. The nomination should be made before the end of the period of 7 days beginning with the date on which the senior office of that local authority or NHS body received a copy of the order.

---

[49] See s 49(2) of the Act.
[50] See s 49(3) of the Act.

Access to information

8. The court will generally provide to the person who is to produce a report:

    (a) a copy of the application form and any annexes to it;
    (b) the name and contact details of P;
    (c) the name and contact details of the parties; and
    (d) the name and contact details of any legal representative of a person specified in (b) or (c).

9. The court order requiring the report, the directions relating to it and the information described in paragraph 8 will generally be sent by first class mail or by facsimile. If the circumstances warrant a different form of communication, the documents and information will also be sent by first class mail or by facsimile at the first available opportunity.

10. Section 49(7) of the Act sets out other documents relating to P which the Public Guardian or a Court of Protection Visitor may examine or of which he may take copies for the purpose of making the report.

The contents of the report

11. The person required to prepare a section 49 report must:

    (a) prepare it having regard to the provisions of rule 117;
    (b) produce it in the manner specified in this practice direction (subject to any directions given by the court); and
    (c) produce it in accordance with the timetable set out in the court's directions.

12. The report should contain four main sections. These are:

    (a) the details of the person who prepared the report;
    (b) the details of P;
    (c) the matters and material considered in preparing the report; and
    (d) the conclusions reached.

13. In the first section (details of the person who prepared the report), the report should:

    (a) state the full name of the person who prepared the report;
    (b) state whether he was appointed under section 49(2) or (3) of the Act;
    (c) state whether he is:
        (i) the Public Guardian,
        (ii) a General Visitor,
        (iii) a Special Visitor,
        (iv) an officer, employee or other person nominated by a local authority, or
        (v) an officer, employee or other person nominated by an NHS body;
    (d) state his occupation or employment (for example, social worker employed by a local authority or general practitioner in private practice); and
    (e) list his qualifications and experience.

14. In the second section (P's details), the report should (unless an order to the contrary pursuant to rule 19 has been made):

    (a) state P's full name, date of birth and present place of residence;
    (b) state P's nationality, racial origin, cultural background and religious persuasion (if appropriate);
    (c) identify P's immediate family (specifying their relationship to P and contact details);

(d) identify any other person who has a significant role in P's life (for example, a close friend or a carer) specifying their role and contact details; and
(e) give a summary of P's medical history.

15. In the third section (matters and material considered), the report should:
    (a) list any interview conducted with P (specifying time and place);[51]
    (b) list any interview conducted with one or more persons other than P (specifying time and place);[52]
    (c) state:
        (i) whether any examination of P was conducted by a Special Visitor under section 49(9) of the Act, and
        (ii) the name and qualifications of any person who assisted with any such examination;
    (d) give a summary of any key events in P's life which appear to have a direct bearing on the matters to be dealt with in the report;
    (e) set out the details of any of the following material which was relied on in the preparation of the report:
        (i) any literature or other material,
        (ii) any records obtained under section 49(7) of the Act;
    (f) set out the details of facts and opinions relied on in the preparation of the report (ensuring that there is a clear distinction between the two);
    (g) where there is a range of opinion on an issue addressed in the report:
        (i) summarise the range of opinion,
        (ii) state the views held by the person who prepared the report and give reasons for them, and
        (iii) if those views are qualified in any way, state the nature of the qualification; and
    (h) indicate which of the facts are within the knowledge of the person who prepared the report.

16. In the fourth section (conclusions), the report should:
    (a) identify any issues or questions which were specified in the directions given by the court as being matters in which the court had a particular interest;
    (b) address clearly such issues or questions;
    (c) state clearly all conclusions reached by the person who prepared the report;
    (d) state clearly the recommendations made by the person who prepared the report; and
    (e) contain a statement of truth in the following terms:
        'I confirm that insofar as the facts stated in my report are within my own knowledge I have made clear which they are, and I believe them to be true, and that the opinions I have expressed represent my true and complete professional opinion.'

---

[51] The person preparing the report should ensure that he keeps any notes made during the interview with P, so that the notes are available for production to the court if necessary.
[52] The person preparing the report should ensure that he keeps any notes made during the interview with an person other than P, so that the notes are available for production to the court if necessary.

ANNEX
Order for section 49 report
Requirement for section 49 report
1. That in relation to case number [*insert case number*] a report is required under section 49 of the Mental Capacity Act 2005 in relation to [*insert name of P*].

Person required to prepare the report
2. The report must be prepared by [the Public Guardian] [a Court of Protection Visitor who is a General Visitor] [a Court of Protection Visitor who is a Special Visitor] [a person nominated by a local authority] [a person nominated by an NHS body].

3. [In the case of a report to be prepared by a Special Visitor, the Visitor may carry out in private a [medical] [psychiatric] [psychological] examination of P's capacity or condition].

Producing the report
4. [The report must be made to the court in writing]. [The report must be made orally to the court].

5. The report must be produced on or before [*insert date*].

6. [Where the report is made in writing, it must be delivered to the court by [first class post] [facsimile] [.   ]]

Content of report
7. Subject to any directions given under the next paragraph, the report must contain all the material required by relevant Practice Direction and be prepared in the form there specified.

8. The report need not address the following:

9. The court is particularly interested in the following issues or questions and these must also be addressed in the report:

Persons to whom report is likely to be disclosed
10. At the time of ordering the report, it is the court's intention to disclose it under rule [117(4)] to [the parties only] [the parties and   ]

Other directions
11. [   ].

Experts

Practice Direction 15A – Expert evidence

This practice direction supplements Part 15 of the Court of Protection Rules 2007

General

1. Part 15 is intended to limit the use of expert evidence to that which is reasonably required. In addition, where possible, matters requiring expert evidence should be dealt with by a single expert. After a permission form or an application form is issued, no person may file expert evidence unless the court or a practice direction permits.[53]

Expert evidence – general requirements

2. It is the duty of an expert to help the court on matters within his own expertise.[54]

3. Expert evidence should be the independent product of the expert uninfluenced by the pressures of the proceedings.

4. An expert should assist the court by providing objective, unbiased opinion on matters within his expertise, and should not assume the role of an advocate.

5. An expert should consider all material facts, including those which might detract from his opinion.

6. An expert should make it clear:

　(a)　when a question or issue falls outside his expertise; and
　(b)　when he is not able to reach a definite opinion, for example because he has insufficient information.

7. If, after producing a report, an expert changes his view on any material matter, such change of view should be communicated to all the parties without delay, and when appropriate to the court.

Form and content of expert's report

8. An expert's report should be addressed to the court and not to the party from whom the expert has received his instructions.

9. An expert's report must:

　(a)　give details of the expert's qualifications;
　(b)　give details of any literature or other material which the expert has relied on in making the report;
　(c)　contain a statement setting out the substance of all facts and instructions given to the expert which are material to the opinions expressed in the report or upon which those opinions are based (or annex the instructions insofar as they are in writing);
　(d)　make clear which of the facts stated in the report are within the expert's own knowledge;

---

[53]　Rule 120.
[54]　Rule 122.

(e) say who carried out any examination, measurement, test or experiment which the expert has used for the report, give the qualifications of that person, and say whether or not the test or experiment has been carried out under the expert's supervision;
(f) where there is a range of opinion on the matters dealt with in the report–
  (i) summarise the range of opinion, and
  (ii) give reasons for his own opinion;
(g) contain a summary of the conclusions reached;
(h) if the expert is not able to give his opinion without qualification, state the qualification; and
(i) contain a statement that the expert understands his duty to the court, and has complied and will continue to comply with that duty.

10. An expert's report must be verified by a statement of truth as well as containing the statements required in paragraph 9(h) and (i) above.

11. The form of the statement of truth is as follows:

'I confirm that insofar as the facts stated in my report are within my own knowledge I have made clear which they are and I believe them to be true and that the opinions I have expressed represent my true and complete professional opinion.'

12. Attention is drawn to rule 14 which sets out the consequences of verifying a document containing a false statement without an honest belief in its truth.

(Practice Direction B accompanying Part 4 sets out more detailed requirements for statements of truth.)

Questions to experts

13. Questions asked for the purpose of clarifying the expert's report should be put, in writing, to the expert not later than 28 days after service of the expert's report.[55]

14. Where a party sends a written question or questions direct to an expert, a copy of the questions should, at the same time, be sent to the other party or parties.

Orders

15. Where an order requires an act to be done by an expert, or otherwise affects an expert, the party instructing that expert must serve a copy of the order on the expert instructed by him. In the case of a jointly instructed expert, the applicant must serve the order.

---

[55] Rule 125.

Litigation friend

Practice Direction 17A – Litigation friend

This practice direction supplements Part 17 of the Court of Protection Rules 2007

General

1. Section 1 of Part 17 contains rules about the appointment of a litigation friend to conduct proceedings on behalf of P, a child, or a protected party.[56] This practice direction is made under rule 146 and provides guidance in relation to the appointment and removal of a litigation friend pursuant to Part 17.

2. Rule 140 provides that a litigation friend may be appointed for:

   (a) P;
   (b) a child; or
   (c) a protected party.

3. Where:

   (a) P has a litigation friend, P should be referred to in the proceedings as 'P (by A.B., his litigation friend)';
   (b) the protected party has a litigation friend, he should be referred to in the proceedings as 'E.F. (by A.B., his litigation friend)';
   (c) a child has a litigation friend, the child should be referred to in the proceedings as 'C.D. (a child by A.B., his litigation friend)'; and
   (d) a child is conducting proceedings on his own behalf, the child should be referred to in the proceedings as 'A.B. (a child)'.

Litigation friend without a court order

4. Rule 142 makes provision for the appointment of a litigation friend without a court order. The rule does not apply:

   (a) in relation to P;
   (b) where the court has appointed a litigation friend; or
   (c) where the Official Solicitor is to act as litigation friend.

Deputy as a litigation friend

5. Rule 142(2) provides that where there is a deputy appointed with power to conduct legal proceedings in the name of the protected party or on the protected party's behalf, that deputy is entitled to be a litigation friend of the protected party in any proceedings to which the deputy's power relates. To be a litigation friend the deputy must file and serve a copy of the court order which appointed him on:

   (a) every person on whom an application form in relation to a protected party must be served in accordance with rule 32; and
   (b) every other person who is a party to the proceedings.

---

[56] 'Protected party' means a party, or an intended party (other than P or a child) who lacks capacity to conduct the proceedings.

Litigation friend where there is no deputy

6. A person who wishes to become a litigation friend without a court order pursuant to rule 142 must file a certificate of suitability using Form COP22.

7. In addition to the matters listed in rule 140(1), the certificate of suitability referred to in rule 142(3) which the litigation friend files must also:

    (a) state that he consents to act;
    (b) state that he knows or believes that the child or the protected party lacks capacity to conduct the proceedings himself; and
    (c) state the grounds of his belief and, if his belief is based upon medical opinion, or the opinion of another suitably qualified expert, attach any relevant document to the certificate.

8. The certificate of suitability must contain a statement of truth.

9. The litigation friend must serve the certificate of suitability on:

    (a) every person on whom an application form must be served in accordance with rule 32; and
    (b) every other person who is a party to the proceedings.

10. The litigation friend is not required to serve the document referred to in paragraph 7(c) when he serves a certificate of suitability under paragraph 9 (unless the court directs otherwise).

11. The litigation friend must file the certificate of suitability together with a certificate of service of it when he first takes a step in the proceedings.

Litigation friend by court order

12. Rule 143 sets out when and how the court may appoint a litigation friend, either on application or on its own initiative.

13. An application for an order appointing a litigation friend must be made by filing a COP9 application notice in accordance with the Part 10 procedure. The application must be supported by evidence, as required by rule 143(3).

14. The evidence in support must satisfy the court that the proposed litigation friend:

    (a) consents to act;
    (b) can fairly and competently conduct proceedings on behalf of P, the child, or the protected party; and
    (c) has no interest adverse to that of P, the child, or the protected party.

Change of litigation friend and prevention of person acting as litigation friend

15. Rule 144(1) provides that the court may, on application or on its own initiative:

    (a) direct that a person may not act as a litigation friend;
    (b) bring to an end a litigation friend's appointment; or
    (c) appoint a new litigation friend in place of an existing one.

16. An application made pursuant to rule 144 should be made by filing a COP9 application notice in accordance with the Part 10 procedure.

Procedure where the need for a litigation friend has come to an end

17. Rule 145A makes provision for where the need for a litigation friend comes to an end during proceedings, for a child who is not P nor a protected party.

18. Where a child having reached full age files a notice under rule 145A and the notice states that the child intends to carry on with or continue to participate in the proceedings he shall subsequently be described in the proceedings as:

'A.B. (formerly a child but now of full age).'

Practice Direction 17B – Representatives

This Practice Direction supplements Part 17 of the Court of Protection Rules 2007

1 Section 2 of Part 17 contains rules about the appointment of an accredited legal representative or a representative for P. This Practice Direction is made under rule 149 and provides guidance on the appointment and removal of an accredited legal representative or a representative pursuant to Part 17.

2 Rule 147 provides that an accredited legal representative or representative may be appointed for P.

3 An application for –

(a) the appointment of an accredited legal representative, or a representative pursuant to rule 148;
(b) directions pursuant to rule 148A; or
(c) for an order under rule 148B

should be made by filing an application in form COP 9 under the procedure in Part 10.

4 In respect of an application pursuant to rule 148, or for the substitution of an accredited legal representative or a representative in place of an existing one pursuant to rule 148B, the evidence in support must satisfy the court that the conditions in rule 147 are met.

Change of Solicitor

Practice Direction 18A – Change of solicitor

This practice direction supplements Part 18 of the Court of Protection Rules 2007

General

1. Part 18 contains rules about a change of solicitor. This practice direction is made under rule 154 and specifies the forms and procedures to be used in relation to a change of solicitor in specified circumstances.

Where COP30 form should be used

2. A COP30 form should be used where a party to proceedings:
    (a) for whom a solicitor is acting, wishes to change his solicitor, or intends to act in person; or
    (b) having conducted the proceedings in person, appoints a solicitor to act on his behalf (this requirement does not apply where a solicitor is appointed only to act as an advocate for a hearing).

Where COP9 form should be used

3. A COP9 form should be used where:
    (a) a solicitor applies for an order declaring that he has ceased to be the solicitor acting for a party; or
    (b) another party applies for an order declaring that the solicitor has ceased to be the solicitor acting for another party in the proceedings.

Practice Direction 19A – Costs

This Practice Direction supplements Part 19 of the Court of Protection Rules 2007

Changes to costs rules—See commentary to rule 155 above regarding possible changes to costs rules.

Modifications to the Civil Procedure Rules 1998

1 The Practice Directions which supplement Parts 44 to 48 of the Civil Procedure Rules 1998 ("CPR Practice Directions 44 to 48") apply, insofar as those Parts apply to proceedings in the Court of Protection, with such modifications as are appropriate together with the modifications specified in this practice direction.

Provisions which do not apply

2 The following provisions of CPR Practice Directions 44 to 48 do not apply –
   (a) in CPR Practice Direction 44: paragraphs 3.1–3.7, 4.1, 7.1–7.3, 9.2(a), 9.3, 9.4, 9.9, 9.10 and 12.1–12.7;
   (b) the whole of CPR Practice Direction 45;
   (c) in CPR Practice Direction 46: paragraphs 1.1–2.1 and 7.1–9.12;
   (d) in CPR Practice Direction 47: paragraphs 4.1–4.3;
   (e) in CPR Practice Direction 48: paragraphs 2.1–4.2.

Modifications of provisions which do apply

3 In paragraph 9.5(4) of CPR Practice Direction 44, the words "any party against whom an order for payment of those costs is intended to be sought" are replaced with "all parties to the proceedings and any other person that the court may direct."

4 In paragraphs 5.4 and 5.9 of CPR Practice Direction 46 and paragraphs 3.3, 9.2, 15 and 16.6 of CPR Practice Direction 47, the words "Part 23" are removed and replaced with "Part 10 (Applications within proceedings)".

5 In paragraph 1.2 of CPR Practice Direction 47, the words "or the parties may agree in writing" are removed.

6 Paragraphs 1.3 1.4, 3.2, 3.3, 10.5(a) 11.1, 11.3, 16.11(a), 20.4 and 20.6 of CPR Practice Direction 47 are to be read as if the references in those paragraphs to a district judge were removed.

7 In paragraph 6.1 of CPR Practice Direction 47, the words "(rule 2.11)" and "(rule 3.1(2)(a))" are omitted.

8 Paragraph 8.1 of CPR Practice Direction 47 is replaced with the following: "A party may apply to the appropriate officer for an order to shorten or extend the time for service of points of dispute".

9 In paragraph 10.3 of CPR Practice Direction 47, the words "Rules 40.3" to "default costs certificate" are replaced with the words "rule 30 of the Court of Protection Rules 2007, which applies to the service of court orders".

10 In paragraph 11.1 of CPR Practice Direction 47, the words "A court officer" are replaced with "An authorised court officer".

11 In rule 11.3 of CPR Practice Direction 47, the following words are removed: "rule 3.1(3) (which enables the court when making an order to make it subject to conditions) and to".

12 References in CPR Practice Directions 44 to 48 to "claimant" and "defendant" shall be read, in proceedings to which this Practice Direction applies, as references to "applicant" and "respondent" respectively.

Other provisions

13 The Senior Courts Costs Office Guide of October 2013 gives practical information and guidance on dealing with costs, and contains, in Section 23 of the Guide, provision relating specifically to Court of Protection cases. Regard should accordingly be had to Section 23 and to those matters of good practice, guidance and procedure referred to in the Guide as are directly applicable to costs arising under Court of Protection Rules.

14 The appropriate venue for detailed assessment of costs proceedings is the Senior Court Costs Office, Thomas More Building, Royal Courts of Justice, Strand, London WC2A 2LL (DX 44454 (Strand)). Details of how to contact the Senior Courts Costs Office are provided in Section 1 (Introduction) of the Senior Courts Costs Office Guide of October 2013.

Practice Direction 19B – Fixed costs in the Court of Protection **PD19B**

		An amount not exceeding
	(b) for the second and subsequent years:	£1,185 (plus VAT)
	Where the net assets* of P are below £16,000, the professional deputy for property and affairs may take an annual management fee not exceeding 4.5% of P's net assets* on the anniversary of the court order appointing the professional as deputy.	
Category IV	Where the court appoints a professional deputy for personal welfare, the deputy may take an annual management fee not exceeding 2.5% of P's net assets* on the anniversary of the court order appointing the professional as deputy for personal up to a maximum of £500.	
Category V	Preparation and lodgement of the annual report or annual account to the Public Guardian	£235 (plus VAT)
Category VI	Preparation of an HMRC income tax return on behalf of P	£235 (plus VAT)

10. The categories of remuneration, above will apply as follows:

- Category III and IV to all annual management fees for anniversaries falling on or after 1 February 2011.
- Category V to reports or accounts lodged on or after 1 February 2011.
- Category VI to all HMRC returns made on or after 1 February 2011.

11. In cases where fixed costs are not appropriate, professionals may, if preferred, apply to the Supreme Court Costs Office for a detailed assessment of costs. However, this does not apply if P's net assets are below are £16,000 where the option for detailed assessment will only arise if the court makes a specific order for detailed assessment in relation to an estate with net assets of a value of less than £16,000.

12. Where the period for which an annual management fee claimed is less than one year, for example where the deputyship comes to an end before the anniversary of appointment, then the amount claimed must be the same proportion of the applicable fee as the period bears to one year.

Conveyancing costs

13. Where a deputy or other person authorised by the court is selling or purchasing a property on behalf of P, the following fixed rates will apply except where the sale or purchase is by trustees in which case, the costs should be agreed with the trustees:

Category VII	A value element of 0.15% of the consideration with a minimum sum of £350 and a maximum sum of £1,500, plus disbursements.

14. Category VII applies to any conveyancing transaction where contracts are exchanged on or after 1 February 2011.

Remuneration of public authority deputies

15. The following fixed rates of remuneration will apply where the court appoints a holder of an office in a public authority to act as deputy:

		An amount not exceeding
Category I	Work up to and including the date upon which the court makes an order appointing a deputy for property and affairs.	£670
Category II	Annual management fee where the court appoints a local authority deputy for property and affairs, payable on the anniversary of the court order	
	(a) for the first year:	£700
	(b) for the second and subsequent years:	£585
	(c) Where the net assets* of P are below £16,000, the local authority deputy for property and affairs may take an annual management fee not exceeding 3% of P's net assets on the anniversary of the court order appointing the local authority as deputy	

Practice Direction 19B – Fixed costs in the Court of Protection **PD19B**

		An amount not exceeding
	(d) Where the court appoints a local authority deputy for personal welfare, the local authority may take an annual management fee not exceeding 2.5% of P's net assets* on the anniversary of the court order appointing the local authority as deputy for personal welfare up to a maximum of £500.	
Category III	Annual property management fee to include work involved in preparing property for sale, instructing agents, conveyancers, etc or the ongoing maintenance of property including management and letting of a rental property.	£270
Category IV	Preparation and lodgement of an annual report or account to the Public Guardian	£195

16. The categories of remuneration, above will apply as follows:
- Category I to all orders appointing a deputy for property and affairs made on or after 1 February 2011.
- Category II to all annual management fees for anniversaries falling on or after 1 February 2011.
- Category III on the anniversary of appointment as deputy where the anniversary falls on or after 1 February 2011; or upon completion of the sale of a property, where the transaction was concluded on or after 1 February 2011.
- Category V to reports or accounts lodged on or after 1 February 2011.

17. Where the period for which the annual management fee ends before an anniversary, for example where the deputyship comes to an end before the anniversary of appointment, then the amount claimed must be the same proportion of the applicable fee as the period bears to one year.

Solicitors' and other professionals' fixed costs

Practice Direction 19B – Fixed costs in the Court of Protection

Important note—This Practice Direction has been superseded by a new PD19B (reproduced above), however, the rates in this previous version will apply to costs incurred prior to 1 February 2011 so it is reproduced here in italics.

This practice direction supplements Part 19 of the Court of Protection Rules 2007 (PD19B)

- *Solicitors' costs in court proceedings*
- *Remuneration of solicitors appointed as deputy for P*
- *Remuneration of public authority deputies*

General

1. This practice direction sets out the fixed costs that may be claimed by solicitors and public authorities acting in Court of Protection proceedings and the fixed amounts of remuneration that may be claimed by solicitors and office holders in public authorities appointed to act as a deputy for P. Rule 167 enables a practice direction to set out a schedule of fees to determine the amount of remuneration payable to deputies.

Rule 168 enables a practice direction to make provision in respect of costs in proceedings.

2. This Practice Direction applies where the period covered by the category of fixed costs or remuneration ends on or after 1 May 2009. The Practice Direction supersedes the earlier Practice Directions and Practice Notes relating to fixed costs issued by the Court of Protection. However solicitors and office holders in public authorities should continue to claim the rates applicable in the previous Practice Directions and Practice Notes, where the period covered by the category of fixed costs or remuneration ended before 1 May 2009.

When does this Practice Direction apply?

3. Rule 156 provides that, where the proceedings concern P's property and affairs, the general rule is that costs of the proceedings shall be paid by P or charged to his estate. The provisions of this Practice Direction apply where the solicitor or deputy is entitled to be paid costs out of P's estate. They do not apply where the court order provides for one party to receive costs from another.

Claims by solicitors – generally

4. The court order or direction will state whether fixed costs or remuneration applies, or whether there is to be a detailed assessment by a costs officer. Where a court order or direction provides for a detailed assessment of costs, solicitors may elect to take fixed costs or remuneration in lieu of a detailed assessment.

Solicitors' costs in court proceedings

5. The fixed costs are as follows:

Category I

Work up to and including the date upon which the court makes an order appointing a deputy for property and affairs.

Amount £825 (plus VAT)

Category II

Applications under sections 36(9) or 54 of the Trustee Act 1925 or section 20 of the Trusts of Land and Appointment of Trustees Act 1996 for the appointment of a new trustee in the place of 'P' and applications under section 18(1)(j) of the Mental Capacity Act 2005 for authority to exercise any power vested in P, whether beneficially, or as trustee, or otherwise.

Amount £370 (plus VAT)

6. The categories of fixed costs above will apply as follows:

- Category I to all orders appointing a deputy for property and affairs made on or after 1 May 2009.
- Category II to all applications for the appointment of a new trustee made on or after 1 May 2009.

Remuneration of solicitors appointed as deputy for P

7. The following fixed rates of remuneration will apply where the court appoints a solicitor to act as deputy:

Category III

Annual management fee where the court appoints a professional deputy for property and affairs, payable on the anniversary of the court order

(a) For the first year: Amount £1,440 (plus VAT)
(b) For the second and subsequent years: Amount £1,140 (plus VAT)
 Provided that, where the net assets of P are below £16,000, the professional deputy for property and affairs may take an annual management fee not exceeding 4.5% of P's net assets on the anniversary of the court order appointing the professional as deputy.

Category IV

Where the court appoints a professional deputy for health and welfare, the deputy may take an annual management fee not exceeding 2.5% of P's net assets on the anniversary of the court order appointing the professional as deputy for health and welfare up to a maximum of £500.

Category V

Preparation and lodgement of the annual report or annual account to the Public Guardian.

Amount £225 (plus VAT)

Category VI

Preparation of an HMRC income tax return on behalf of P.

Amount £225 (plus VAT)

8. The categories of remuneration, above will apply as follows:

- Category III and IV to all annual management fees for anniversaries falling on or after 1 April 2009.
- Category V to reports or accounts lodged on or after 1 May 2009.
- Category VI to all HMRC returns made on or after 1 May 2009.

9. Where the period for which an annual management fee claimed is less than one year, for example where the deputyship comes to an end before the anniversary of appointment, then the amount claimed must be the same proportion of the applicable fee as the period bears to one year.

Remuneration of public authority deputies

10. Where an office holder in a public authority is appointed to act as deputy for P, he may claim the following fixed costs:

Category I

Work up to and including the date upon which the court makes an order appointing a deputy for property and affairs.

Amount £645 (plus VAT)

Category II

Annual management fee where the court appoints a local authority deputy for property and affairs, payable on the anniversary of the court order:

(a) for the first year: Amount £670 (plus VAT)
(b) for the second and subsequent years: Amount £565 (plus VAT)
(c) Provided that, where the net assets of P are below £16,000, the local authority deputy for property and affairs may take an annual management fee not exceeding 3% of P's net assets on the anniversary of the court order appointing the local authority as deputy
(d) Where the court appoints a local authority deputy for health and welfare, the local authority may take an annual management fee not exceeding 2.5% of P's net assets on the anniversary of the court order appointing the local authority as deputy for health and welfare up to a maximum of £500.

Category III

Annual property management fee to include work involved in preparing property for sale, instructing agents, conveyancers, etc or the ongoing maintenance of property including management and letting of a rental property.

Amount £260 (plus VAT)

Category IV

Preparation and lodgement of an annual report or account to the Public Guardian

Amount £185 (plus VAT)

11. The categories of remuneration, above will apply as follows:
- Category I to all orders appointing a deputy for property and affairs made on or after 1 May 2009.
- Category II to all annual management fees for anniversaries falling on or after 1 May 2009.
- Category III on the anniversary of appointment as deputy where the anniversary falls on or after 1 May 2009; or upon completion of the sale of a property, where the transaction was concluded on or after 1 May 2009.
- Category V to reports or accounts lodged on or after 1 May 2009.

12. Where the period for which the annual management fee ends before an anniversary, for example where the deputyship comes to an end before the anniversary of appointment, then the amount claimed must be the same proportion of the applicable fee as the period bears to one year.

This Practice Direction is made by the President with the agreement of the Lord Chancellor, and will come into effect on 1 May 2009.

Sir Mark Potter
President

Appeals

Practice Direction 20A – Appeals

This practice direction supplements Part 20 of the Court of Protection Rules 2007

1. This Practice Direction applies to appeal proceedings within the Court of Protection pursuant to Part 20 (except where Part 22 makes different provision). Where an appeal lies to the Court of Appeal, the Civil Procedure Rules 1998 apply to such an appeal.

Permission

2. Rules 171B, 172 and 173 set out the procedure for seeking the court's permission to appeal.

3. Unless the appeal is against an order of committal to prison, the court's permission is required to appeal. An application for permission may be made either to the judge at the hearing at which the decision being appealed was made (the first instance judge), or to an appeal judge.[57]

APPELLANT

Appellant's Notice

4. Rule 175 sets out the procedure and time limits for filing and serving an appellant's notice. This is summarised in the following table:

Permission given by the first instance judge	Permission not given by a first instance judge	Permission not needed
Appellant's notice to be filed within the time directed by the first instance judge; OR Where no time directed, within 21 days of the decision being appealed/ permission decision.	Appellant's notice including application for permission to be filed within 21 days of the decision being appealed.	Appellant's notice to be filed within 21 days of the decision being appealed.
Appellant's notice to be served on all respondents as soon as practicable, and no later than 21 days after it is issued.	Appellant's notice to be served on all respondents as soon as practicable, and no later than 21 days after it is issued.	Appellant's notice to be served on all respondents as soon as practicable, and no later than 21 days after it is issued.

---

[57] But see r 182, which sets out certain requirements in relation to second appeals.

5. Where the first instance judge announces his decision and reserves the reasons for his judgment until a later date, he should, in the exercise of his powers under rule 175(2)(a), fix a period for filing the appellant's notice that takes this into account.

6. Except where the appeal judge orders otherwise, a sealed copy of the appellant's notice must be served on all respondents in accordance with the time limits prescribed by rule 175(3). At this time the appellant should also serve a skeleton argument on all respondents if permission was granted by the first instance judge.

7. The appellant must, within 7 days beginning on the date on which the copy of the appellant's notice was served, file a certificate of service in relation to service of the appellant's notice.[58]

> (Part 6 sets out the rules relating to service and Part 7 sets out the rules relating to notification of P, including the requirement to notify P that an appellant's notice has been issued by the court.)

Extension of time for filing appellant's notice

8. Where the time for filing an appellant's notice has expired, the appellant must:
    (a) file an appellant's notice; and
    (b) include in that appellant's notice an application for an extension of time.

9. The appellant's notice should state the reason(s) for the delay and the steps taken prior to the application being made.

10. Where the appellant's notice includes an application for an extension of time and permission to appeal has been given or is not required, the respondent has the right to be heard on that application.

Documents to be filed and served with appellant's notice

11. The appellant must file the following documents with his appellant's notice:
    (a) one additional copy of the appellant's notice for the court;
    (b) one copy of his skeleton argument;
    (c) a sealed copy of the order being appealed;
    (d) a copy of any order giving or refusing permission to appeal, together with a copy of the judge's reasons for allowing or refusing permission to appeal;
    (e) any witness statements or affidavits in support of any application included in the appellant's notice;
    (f) the application form and any application notice or response (where relevant to the subject of the appeal);
    (g) any other documents which the appellant reasonably considers necessary to enable the court to reach its decision on the hearing of the application or appeal;
    (h) a suitable record of the judgment of the first instance judge; and
    (i) such other documents as the court may direct.

12. Where it is not possible to file all of the above documents with the appellant's notice, the appellant must indicate which documents have not yet been filed and the reasons why they are not currently available. The appellant must then provide a reasonable estimate of when the missing document or documents can be filed and file and serve them as soon as reasonably practicable.

---

[58] Rule 175(4).

13. Notice of an application to be made to the court for a remedy incidental to the appeal (eg an interim remedy under rule 82) may be included in the appellant's notice, or in an application notice using Form COP9 (which is to be attached to the appellant's notice).

14. The appellant should consider what other information the court will need. This may include a list of persons who feature in the case or glossaries of technical terms. A chronology of relevant events will be necessary in most appeals.

15. The information set out in paragraph 11 must be served on each respondent when the appellant's notice is served.

Skeleton arguments

16. The appellant's notice must, subject to paragraph 17, be accompanied by a skeleton argument using, or attached to, a skeleton argument COP37 form.

17. Where the appellant is unable to provide a skeleton argument to accompany the appellant's notice it must be filed and served on all respondents within 21 days of filing the notice.

18. A skeleton argument must contain a numbered list of the points which the party wishes to make. These should both define and confine the areas of controversy. Each point should be stated as concisely as the nature of the case allows.

19. A numbered point must be followed by a reference to any document on which the appellant wishes to rely.

20. A skeleton argument must state, in respect of each authority cited:
    (a) the proposition of law that the authority demonstrates; and
    (b) the parts of the authority (identified by page or paragraph references) that support the proposition.

21. If more than one authority is cited in support of a given proposition, the skeleton argument must briefly state the reason for taking that course. This statement should not materially add to the length of the skeleton argument but should be sufficient to demonstrate, in the context of the argument:
    (a) the relevance of the authority or authorities to that argument; and
    (b) that the citation is necessary for a proper presentation of that argument.

Suitable record of the judgment

22. Where the judgment to be appealed has been officially recorded by the court, an approved transcript of that record should accompany the appellant's notice. Photocopies will not be accepted for this purpose. However, where there is no officially recorded judgment, the following will be acceptable:

Written judgments

23. Where the judgment was given in writing, a copy of that judgment endorsed with the judge's signature.

Note of judgment

24. When the judgment was not officially recorded or given in writing, a note of the judgment (agreed between the appellant's and respondent's advocates) should be submitted for approval to the first instance judge. If the parties cannot agree on a

single note of the judgment, both versions should be provided to that judge with an explanatory letter. For the purpose of an application for permission to appeal the note need not be approved by the respondent or the first instance judge.

Advocates' notes of judgments where appellant is unrepresented

25. When the appellant was unrepresented before the first instance judge it is the duty of any advocate for the respondent to make his note of the judgment promptly available, free of charge, to the appellant where there is no officially recorded judgment or if the court so directs. Where the appellant was represented before the first instance judge, it is the duty of his own former advocate to make his note available in these circumstances. The appellant should submit the note of the judgment to the appeal judge.

Transcripts or notes of evidence

26. When the evidence is relevant to the appeal an official transcript of the relevant evidence must be obtained. Transcripts or notes of evidence are generally not needed for the purpose of determining an application for permission to appeal.

27. If evidence relevant to the appeal was not officially recorded, a typed version of the judge's notes of evidence must be obtained.

28. Where the first instance judge or the appeal judge is satisfied that:

   (a) an unrepresented appellant; or
   (b) an appellant whose legal representation is provided free of charge to the appellant and who is not in receipt of civil Legal Aid,

is in such poor financial circumstances that the cost of a transcript would be an excessive burden the court may certify that the cost of obtaining one official transcript should be borne at public expense.

29. In the case of a request for an official transcript of evidence or proceedings to be paid for at public expense, the court must also be satisfied that there are reasonable grounds for appeal. Whenever possible a request for a transcript at public expense should be made to the first instance judge when asking for permission to appeal.

RESPONDENT

30. A person who has been named as a respondent in appeal proceedings and who wishes only to request that the appeal judge upholds the judgment or order of the first instance judge, whether for the reasons given by the first instance judge or otherwise, does not make an appeal and does not therefore require permission to appeal in accordance with rules 171B and 172.

31. A person who has been named as a respondent in appeal proceedings, and who also wishes to seek permission to appeal must do so in accordance with rules 171B and 172.

32. Unless the court otherwise directs, a respondent need not take any action when served with an appellant's notice until such time as notification is given to him that permission to appeal has been granted (unless paragraph 31 applies).

Respondent's notice

33. A respondent who wishes to appeal or who wishes to ask the appeal judge to uphold the order of the first instance judge for reasons different from or additional to those given by the first instance judge must file a respondent's notice.

34. If the respondent does not file a respondent's notice, he will not be entitled, except with the permission of the court, to rely on any reasons for upholding the decision which are different from or additional to those relied on by the first instance judge.

35. Rule 176 sets out the procedure and time limits for filing and serving a respondent's notice.

36. Where the first instance judge announces his decision and reserves the reasons for his judgment until a later date, he should, in the exercise of his powers under rule 176(3)(a) fix a period for filing the respondent's notice that takes this into account.

37. Except where the appeal judge orders otherwise, a sealed copy of the respondent's notice must be served on all parties to the appeal proceedings in accordance with the time limits prescribed by rule 176(5), along with any other material required to be served in accordance with paragraphs 40 to 43 below.

38. The respondent must, within 7 days beginning with the date on which the copy of the respondent's notice was served, file a certificate of service in relation to service of the respondent's notice.

(Part 6 sets out the rules relating to service.)

39. Paragraphs 8 to 10 apply in respect of a respondent's notice as they apply to an appellant's notice.

Documents to be filed and served with respondent's notice

40. The respondent must file the following documents with his respondent's notice:
    (a) one additional copy of the respondent's notice for the court;
    (b) one copy of his skeleton argument;
    (c) a sealed copy of the order being appealed;
    (d) a copy of any order giving or refusing permission to appeal, together with a copy of the judge's reasons for allowing or refusing permission to appeal; and
    (e) any witness statements or affidavits in support of any application included in the respondent's notice.
    (f) any other documents which the respondent reasonably considers necessary to enable the court to reach its decision on the hearing of the application or appeal; and
    (g) such other documents as the court may direct.

41. A respondent may include an application for a remedy incidental to the appeal as set out in paragraph 13.

42. The respondent should consider what other information the appeal judge will need. This may include a list of persons who feature in the case or glossaries of technical terms. A chronology of relevant events will be necessary in most appeals.

43. The information set out in paragraph 40 must be served on the appellant and any other respondent when the respondent's notice is served.

Skeleton argument

44. The respondent must file and serve a skeleton argument in all cases where he proposes to address arguments to the court.

45. The respondent's notice must, subject to paragraph 46, be accompanied by a skeleton argument using, or attached to, a skeleton argument COP37 form.

46. Where the respondent is unable to provide a skeleton argument to accompany the respondent's notice it must be filed and served on all respondents within 21 days of filing the notice.

47. A respondent who does not file a respondent's notice but who files a skeleton argument must file and serve that skeleton argument at least 7 days before the appeal hearing.

48. A respondent's skeleton argument must conform to the requirements at paragraphs 18 to 21 with any necessary modifications. It should, where appropriate, answer the arguments set out in the appellant's skeleton argument.

49. Where a respondent's skeleton argument is not served with the respondent's notice, the respondent must serve his skeleton argument on all parties to the proceedings at the same time as he files it at the court, and must file a certificate of service.

APPEAL HEARING

50. The court will send the parties notification of the date of the hearing of the appeal, together with any other directions given by the court.

Practice Direction 20B – Allocation of Appeals

This Practice Direction supplements Part 20 of the Court of Protection Rules 2007

General

1.1 Rule 171A provides for a practice direction to set out the destination of appeals from decisions of judges of the Court of Protection.

1.2 Rule 6 and Practice Direction 3B set out which judges of the Court of Protection are Tier 1 Judges, Tier 2 Judges and Tier 3 Judges.

Appeals to the Court of Appeal

2.1 Rule 171A(1) provides that an appeal from a judge of the Court of Protection lies to the Court of Appeal where:

(1) the appeal is from a decision of a Tier 3 Judge; or
(2) where the appeal is from a decision which was itself made on appeal ("a second appeal").

Other Appeals

3.1 Rule 171A(2) provides that the general rule in relation to other appeals is that:

(1) an appeal from a decision of a Tier 1 Judge lies to a Tier 2 Judge; and
(2) an appeal from a decision of a Tier 2 Judge lies to a Tier 3 Judge.

3.2 Notwithstanding rule 171A(2), an appeal from a Tier 1 Judge may be heard by a Tier 3 Judge where:

(1) the Tier 1 Judge whose decision is being appealed; or
(2) a Tier 2 Judge; or
(3) a Tier 3 Judge

has directed that the appeal should be heard by a Tier 3 Judge. The judge making a direction under this paragraph need not be:

    (a) the same judge who grants permission to appeal; or
    (b) the judge who hears the appeal.

3.3 A direction under paragraph 3.2 may only be made if:

(1) the appeal would raise an important point of principle or practice; or
(2) there is some other compelling reason for a Tier 3 Judge to hear the appeal.

3.4 No appeal shall lie against a refusal by a judge to make a direction under paragraph 3.2.

Tables

4.1 The following tables set out the destination of appeals from decisions of judges of the Court of Protection

Practice Direction 20B – Allocation of Appeals **PD20B**

Table 1 Appeals from a decision of a Tier 1 Judge

Appeal lies to	In the following circumstances	Permission to appeal may be granted by
Tier 2 Judge	This is the usual destination for appeals from a Tier 1 Judge	(1) The Tier 1 Judge whose decision is being appealed (2) A Tier 2 Judge (3) A Tier 3 Judge
Tier 3 Judge	It is certified by a judge listed in column 3 that (a) the appeal would raise an important point of principle or practice; or (b) there is some other compelling reason for a Tier 3 Judge to hear the appeal	(1) The Tier 1 Judge whose decision is being appealed (2) A Tier 2 Judge (3) A Tier 3 Judge

Table 2 Appeals from a decision of a Tier 2 Judge

Appeal lies to	In the following circumstances	Permission to appeal may be granted by
Tier 3 Judge	This is the usual destination for appeals from a Tier 2 Judge (other than second appeals)	(1) The Tier 2 Judge whose decision is being appealed (2) A Tier 3 Judge
Court of Appeal	The appeal is a second appeal.	The Court of Appeal

Table 3 Appeals from a decision of a Tier 3 Judge

Appeal lies to	In the following circumstances	Permission to appeal may be granted by
Court of Appeal	This is the usual destination for appeals from a Tier 3 Judge (other than second appeals)	(1) The Tier 3 Judge whose decision is being appealed (2) The Court of Appeal

PART IV

Appeal lies to	In the following circumstances	Permission to appeal may be granted by
Court of Appeal	The appeal is a second appeal.	The Court of Appeal

Enforcement

Practice Direction 21A – Contempt of court

This practice direction supplements Part 21 of the Court of Protection Rules 2007

General

1. This Practice Direction applies to any application for an order for committal of a person to prison for contempt of court ('the committal application').

Applications for committal after permission granted or where permission not needed

2. An application for an order of committal must be commenced by filing a COP9 application notice in accordance with Part 21.

3. The applicant must file the original and one copy of the application notice, together with the original and one copy of the affidavit that is required by rule 186(1).

4. The affidavit must contain:

   (a) the name and description of the person making the application;
   (b) the name, address and description of the person sought to be committed;
   (c) the grounds on which committal is sought;
   (d) a description of each alleged act of contempt, identifying:
       (i) each act separately and numerically, and
       (ii) if known, the date of each act; and
   (e) any additional information required by paragraphs 5 and 6.

5. Where the allegation of contempt relates to prior proceedings before the court, the affidavit must also state:

   (a) the case number of those prior proceedings;
   (b) the date of the proceedings; and
   (c) the name of P.

6. The affidavit must also set out in full any order, judgment or undertaking which it is alleged has been disobeyed or broken by the person sought to be committed. This will apply where the allegation of contempt is made on the grounds that:

   (a) a person is required by a judgment or order to do an act, and has refused or neglected to do it within the time fixed by the judgment or order or any subsequent order;
   (b) a person has disobeyed a judgment or order requiring him to abstain from doing an act; or
   (c) a person has breached the terms of an undertaking which he gave to the court.

   (Practice Direction A accompanying Part 14 sets out further details in relation to affidavits.)

Hearing of application

7. When filing the application notice, the applicant must obtain from the court a date for the hearing of the committal application.

8. The court may at any time give case management directions (including directions for the service of evidence by the person sought to be committed and evidence in reply by the applicant) or may hold a directions hearing.

9. The court may on the hearing date:
   (a) give case management directions with a view to a hearing of the committal application on a future date; or
   (b) if the committal application is ready to be heard, proceed forthwith to hear it.

10. Where the person sought to be committed gives oral evidence at the hearing (in accordance with rule 187), he may be cross-examined.

Note—For the Committal for Contempt of Court Practice Guidance dated 3 May 2013 and the Committal for Contempt of Court Practice Guidance dated 4 June 2013 see Part V of this work.

Transitory and transitional provisions

Practice Direction 22A – Transitional provisions

This practice direction supplements Part 22 of the Court of Protection Rules

Introductory

1. In this practice direction:

 (a) 'commencement' means 1 October 2007;
 (b) 'pending proceedings' means proceedings on an application within paragraph 3 or 12 of Schedule 5 to the Act; and
 (c) 'the Previous Rules' means the Court of Protection Rules 2001,[59] as in force immediately before commencement.

Applications received after commencement

2. If an application under the Previous Rules is received at the court on or after commencement, it will be returned.

Applications received before commencement

3. The general presumption will be that:

 (a) any step in pending proceedings which is to be taken on or after commencement is to be taken under the Rules; and
 (b) pending proceedings are to be decided having regard to the Rules.

4. However, the general presumption is subject to:

 (a) any contrary provision in paragraphs 5 to 8 of this practice direction; and
 (b) any directions given by the court (including directions which disapply one or more of those paragraphs).

5. Any step already taken in the proceedings before commencement in accordance with the Previous Rules will remain valid on or after commencement.

6. A party to the proceedings will not normally be required to take any action that would amount to taking that step again under the Rules. For example, if evidence has been given in accordance with Part 5 of the Previous Rules, a person will not normally be required to comply with the requirements in Part 14 of the Rules (admissions, evidence and depositions).

7. Any question as to whether permission is required for the making of the application which commenced the pending proceedings will normally be determined in accordance with the Previous Rules.

8. If after commencement a party to the proceedings has served a document, or given notification, in accordance with:

 (a) Part 4 of the Previous Rules (which makes provisions as to service of documents and giving of notice); or

---

[59] SI 2001/824.

(b) rule 10(4) of the Enduring Powers of Attorney Rules 2001 (notifications in connection with certain applications relating to enduring powers of attorney),[60]

the court may treat that as valid service or notification. If it does, it will give directions as to the extent to which it is appropriate to disapply rules 66 to 70 of the Rules or to modify the application of the Rules to the proceedings.

Case management

9. Part 2 of the Rules (the overriding objective) will apply to all pending proceedings and a court officer may at any time refer the proceedings to a judge so that case management decisions can be made about the proceedings and the conduct of any hearing.

10. A judge may at any time direct how the Rules are to apply to the proceedings.

Orders made before commencement

11. Where a court order has been made before commencement under the Previous Rules, the order must still be complied with on or after commencement.

Costs

12. Any assessment of costs that takes place on or after commencement will be in accordance with Part 19 of the Rules.

---

[60] SI 2001/825.

Practice Direction 22B – Transitory provisions

This practice direction supplements Part 22 of the Court of Protection Rules 2007

Applications to which this Practice Direction applies

1. Rules 195 and 196 make provision for an application by a person who becomes a deputy by virtue of paragraph 1(2) of Schedule 5 to the Act, ie a receiver appointed under the Mental Health Act 1983 at the time of commencement (referred to in this Practice Direction as 'a deputy').

2. Rules 195 and 196 and the provisions of this practice direction will cease to have effect on 30 June 2008. On and after 30 June 2008, a deputy who wishes to apply to the court for an order must use the procedure under either Part 9 or Part 10 of the Rules, as appropriate.

Applications which may be suitable for the procedure set out in this practice direction

3. Examples of applications that may be suitable for the procedure set out in this practice direction include, but are not limited to:

  (a) applications for regular payments from P's assets to the deputy in respect of remuneration;
  (b) applications seeking minor variations only to the expenses that can be paid from P's estate;
  (c) applications for the receipt or discharge of a sum due to or by P as a result of an entitlement in or obligation to an estate;
  (d) applications for release of funds to repair or improve P's property;
  (e) applications to sell P's furniture and effects;
  (f) applications for the release of capital to meet expenses required for the care of P;
  (g) applications for authority to access P's funds on P's behalf;
  (h) applications for directions with regard to the management of P's investments (including any held at the Court Funds Office);
  (i) applications to approve the sale price of a property, where the sale has previously been authorised;
  (j) applications to approve the purchase of a property, where the purchase has previously been authorised; and
  (k) applications for authority to manage and let a property belonging to P.

4. Applications listed in paragraph 3 above may be heard by an officer nominated by the Senior Judge or the President pursuant to rule 196.

Applications which must be dealt with by a judge

5. Examples of applications which are not suitable for the procedure set out in this practice direction include, but are not limited to:

  (a) applications to appoint a new deputy, or to discharge an existing deputy;
  (b) applications seeking authorisation to commence, continue or defend litigation on behalf of P;
  (c) applications for the settlement of P's property, whether for P's benefit or the benefit of others;
  (d) applications to vary the terms of a trust in which P has an interest;
  (e) applications for a statutory will or codicil;

(f) applications to operate or to cease to operate a business belonging to P, or to dissolve a partnership of which P is a member;
(g) applications for authority to purchase or sell real property;
(h) applications to make a gift or loan from P's assets;
(i) applications to end proceedings or discharge court orders, where it is alleged that P has ceased to lack capacity;
(j) applications to set, vary or dispense with security in relation to a deputy;
(k) applications to change an accounting period;
(l) applications to set or change the time by which an annual account may be submitted;
(m) applications in relation to the sale of property owned by P;
(n) applications for authority to disclose information as to P's assets, state of health or other circumstances;
(o) applications to sell or otherwise deal with P's investments;
(p) applications for authority to apply for a grant of probate or representation, where P would be the person entitled to the grant but for his lack of capacity;
(q) applications relating to the lease or grant of a tenancy in relation to a property owned by P;
(r) applications to arrange an overdraft on the bank account operated for the purpose of the deputyship; and
(s) applications to open a bank account on behalf of P or for the purpose of the deputyship at a private bank, a bank that is not located in England and Wales, or at a bank which has unusual conditions attached to the operation of the account.

6. An application which is likely to be contested, or which involves large sums of money (when compared with the size of P's estate as a whole) is not suitable for the procedure set out in this practice direction.

Procedure to be followed

7. Applications to which the procedure in this Practice Direction applies may be made by filing a COP9 application notice, together with any evidence in support of the application.

8. The application may be made without serving an application notice on anyone and without notifying anyone that the application has been made.

How applications will be dealt with under the transitory procedure

9. Subject to paragraph 10, the nominated officer will deal with an application made in accordance with this practice direction without a hearing.

10. The nominated officer may decide, upon considering the application, that other persons ought to be informed of the application and given the opportunity to respond. In such a case, the nominated officer will refer the application to a judge.

11. The nominated officer will give directions as to who is to be served with any order that he makes.

12. Following a nominated officer's decision, the nominated officer will refer the matter to a judge, who will consider what (if any) further orders may be required to ensure that the deputy is on the same footing as a person who became a deputy by virtue of section 19 of the Act.

Practice Direction 22B – Transitory provisions **PD22B**

Reconsideration of and appeals against decisions of nominated officers

13. Where the application is determined without a hearing or without notice having been given to anyone, P, any party to the proceedings or any person affected by the order may apply to the court, within 21 days of having been served with the court's order, to have the order reconsidered.[61] An application to have an order reconsidered must be made by filing a COP9 application notice in accordance with Part 10.

14. Rule 197 sets out the appeal route in relation to decisions of nominated officers.

---

[61] Rule 89.

Practice Direction 22C – Appeals against decisions made under Part 7 of the Mental Health Act 1983 or under the Enduring Powers of Attorney Act 1985 which are brought on or after commencement

This practice direction supplements Part 22 of the Court of Protection Rules 2007

General

1. Rule 199 enables a practice direction to be made in relation to transitory and transitional matters.

2. This practice direction sets out the procedure to be followed in relation to appeals against decisions made under Part 7 of the Mental Health Act 1983 ('the 1983 Act') or under the Enduring Powers of Attorney Act 1985 ('the 1985 Act'), which are brought on or after commencement of the Mental Capacity Act 2005 ('the 2005 Act').

3. Appeals to which this Practice Direction applies are to be dealt with in accordance with Part 20 (appeals), unless this practice direction makes different provision.[62]

Appeals against decisions made by nominated officers

4. Where the appeal is from a first instance decision of an officer nominated by virtue of section 93(4) of the 1983 Act, the appeal will be heard by a district judge nominated to exercise the jurisdiction of the court under section 46(2)(e) of the 2005 Act.

5. Where the appeal is from a decision of a district judge made under paragraph 4 above, it will be heard by a circuit judge nominated to exercise the jurisdiction of the court under section 46(2)(d) of the 2005 Act.

6. The Court of Appeal will hear an appeal against a decision of a circuit judge made under paragraph 5 above. Rule 182(2) and (3) apply to such an appeal.

Appeals by decisions of the Master of the former Court of Protection

7. An appeal from a decision of the Master of the Court of Protection[63] will be heard by a judge of the court nominated by virtue of section 46(2)(a) to (c) of the 2005 Act (ie the President, the Chancellor, or a puisne judge of the High Court).

8. Where the appeal is from a decision that was made under paragraph 7 above, it must be dealt with in accordance with rule 181 (appeals against decisions of a puisne judge of the High Court etc).

---

[62] See r 169.
[63] The judicial officer appointed by the Lord Chancellor under s 89 of the Supreme Court Act 1981.

Appeals made under Part 7 of the 1983 Act or under the 1985 Act pending at the time of commencement

9. This practice direction does not apply to appeals made under Part 7 of the 1983 Act or under the 1985 Act which are pending on 1 October 2007.

10. Paragraph 4(1) of Schedule 5 to the 2005 Act provides that an appeal brought by virtue of section 105 of the 1983 Act and which has not been determined before the commencement day, shall be determined in accordance with Part 7 of the 1983 Act and the rules made under it.

11. Where an appeal has been brought by virtue of section 10(1)(c) of the 1985 Act and has not been determined before the commencement day, the provisions of the 1985 Act, Part 7 of the 1983 Act (so far as they are relevant) and the rules made under that Part as applied by section 10 of the 1985 Act, shall continue to apply to such an appeal.[64]

12. If the appeal has been brought under section 105(1) of the 1983 Act, or by virtue of section 10(1)(c) of the 1985 Act, and the judge nominated under section 93 of the 1983 Act has begun to hear the appeal, he will continue to do so; otherwise, the appeal is to be heard by a puisne judge of the High Court nominated under section 46 of the 2005 Act.[65]

---

[64] Paragraph 13(1) of Sch 5 to the 2005 Act.
[65] Paragraph 4(2) and para 13(2) of Sch 5 to the 2005 Act.

Miscellaneous

Practice Direction 23A – Request for directions where notice of objection prevents public guardian from registering enduring power of attorney

This practice direction supplements Part 23 of the Court of Protection Rules 2007

1. Rule 201 provides for the Public Guardian to request the court's directions where a notice of objection prevents him from registering an instrument creating an enduring power of attorney. This practice direction makes provision about such requests.

(Practice direction H accompanying Part 9 deals with applications made by persons other than the Public Guardian who are seeking the court's directions about registration.)

2. Time limits apply before the Public Guardian can request directions.[66] These are measured from the date (or the latest date) on which the attorney gave notice[67] to the donor's relatives of the attorney's intention to make an application for the registration of the instrument creating the enduring power. The Public Guardian cannot request directions until 5 weeks have expired beginning with the date of notification.

3. However, this period is extended if it would otherwise expire less than 14 days after the Public Guardian receives the notice of objection which prevents him from registering the instrument. In this case, the Public Guardian may not request directions from the court until the end of the 14 day period which begins with the date on which he received the notice of objection.

4. The request for directions must be made using Form COP17. The Public Guardian must file the form and any document he considers may assist the court to give directions about the registration of the instrument.

5. The Public Guardian will notify the donor in accordance with Part 7 that he has made a request within 21 days of the date on which he makes it. However, the Public Guardian is not required to serve the request on any other person or otherwise to notify them that a request has been made. He will participate in the proceedings only if the court requests him to do so.

6. As soon as practicable after a request has been filed, notice of that fact[68] will be given by a court officer to:

    (a) the person (or persons) who gave the notice of objection; and
    (b) the attorney under the enduring power or, if more than one, each of them.

7. If any person wishes to participate in the proceedings, he then has 21 days to file an application using Form COP8. The application must be made in accordance with the detailed requirements for applications relating to the registration of enduring powers of attorney, which are set out in practice direction H accompanying Part 9. If

---

[66] These time limits are imposed by r 201(1)(b) and (2).
[67] See para 5 of Sch 4 to the Act.
[68] Rule 200(6) sets out what the notice must contain.

Practice Direction 23A – Request for directions where notice of objection prevents public guardian from registering enduring power of attorney **PD23A**

no such application is received, the court will proceed to consider the matter in response to the Public Guardian's request and will give directions to the Public Guardian.

Practice Direction 23B – Where P ceases to lack capacity or dies

This practice direction supplements Part 23 of the Court of Protection Rules 2007

General

1. An order of the Court of Protection will continue until it is discharged or, if made for a specified period, will cease to have effect when that period comes to an end.

2. Where P ceases to lack capacity or dies, steps may need to be taken to finalise the court's involvement in P's affairs.

Application to end proceedings

3. Where P ceases to lack capacity in relation to the matter or matters to which the proceedings relate, an application may be made by any of the following people to the court to end the proceedings and discharge any orders made in respect of that person:[69]

   (a) P;
   (b) his litigation friend; or
   (c) any other person who is a party to the proceedings.

4. An application under rule 202 should be made by filing a COP9 application notice in accordance with the Part 10 procedure, together with any evidence in support of the application. The application should in particular be supported by evidence that P no longer lacks capacity to make decisions in relation to the matter or matters to which the proceedings relate.

Applications where proceedings have concluded

5. Where P ceases to lack capacity after proceedings have concluded, an application may be made to the court to discharge any orders made (including an order appointing a deputy or an order in relation to a security bond) by filing a COP9 application notice in accordance with the Part 10 procedure, together with any evidence in support of the application. The application notice should set out details of the order or orders the applicant seeks to have discharged, and should in particular be supported by evidence that P no longer lacks capacity to make decisions in relation to the matter or matters to which the proceedings relate.

6. If the Court Funds Office is holding funds or assets on behalf of P, it will require an order of the court to the effect that P no longer lacks capacity to make decisions with regard to the use and disposition of those funds or assets before any funds or assets can be transferred to him.

Procedure to be followed when P dies

7. An application for any final directions needed following P's death (including to discharge an order appointing a deputy or to discharge a security bond) should be made by filing a COP9 application notice in accordance with the Part 10 procedure. An application should attach the original or a certified copy of P's death certificate.

---

[69] Rule 148.

Practice Direction 23B – Where P ceases to lack capacity or dies **PD23B**

8. Any security bond taken out by the deputy will remain in force until the end of the period of 2 years commencing with the date of P's death, or until it is discharged by the court.[70]

9. The Public Guardian may require a deputy to submit a final report upon P's death.[71] Before it will discharge a security bond, the court must be satisfied that the Public Guardian either:

(a) does not require a final report; or
(b) is satisfied with the final report provided by the deputy.

Personal representatives and administrators

10. Where there are solicitor's costs outstanding which would be due from P's estate, the personal representative or administrator may agree any of these costs without an order from the court. If these costs cannot be agreed, the personal representative, administrator or the solicitor may apply to the court for costs to be assessed,[72] using a COP9 application notice in accordance with the Part 10 procedure.

11. If there are funds or other assets held in the Court Funds Office on behalf of P, P's personal representative or administrator will need to contact the Court Funds Office directly regarding those funds.

---

[70] Regulation 37 of the Lasting Powers of Attorney, Enduring Powers of Attorney and Public Guardian Regulations 2007.
[71] Regulation 4C of the Lasting Powers of Attorney, Enduring Powers of Attorney and Public Guardian Regulations 2007.
[72] Rule 166 provides that an order or directions that costs incurred during P's lifetime be paid out of or charged on his estate may be made within 6 years after P's death.

Pilot Schemes

Practice Direction – Transparency Pilot

This Practice Direction supplements Part 13 of the Court of Protection Rules 2007

1 General

1.1 This Practice Direction is made under rule 9A[1] of the Court of Protection Rules 2007 ('CoPR'). It provides for a pilot scheme for the holding of hearings to be in public pursuant to orders under rule 92[2] with a standard order for restrictions on reporting to ensure the anonymity of P and, where appropriate, other persons.

  1 Renumbered as rule 2.6 where the practice direction *Practice Direction – Case Management Pilot* ('the Case Management pilot') applies.
  2 Renumbered as rule 4.3 where the Case Management pilot applies.

1.2 Where the provisions of this Practice Direction conflict with the provisions of Part 13 of the CoPR or Practice Direction 13A[3], this Practice Direction shall take precedence.

  3 Renumbered respectively as Part 4 and Practice Direction 4A where the Case Management Pilot applies.

1.3 The pilot scheme is to –

  (a) operate from 29 January 2016 to 31 July 2016;
  (b) apply to hearings in all proceedings except applications relating to serious medical treatment (for which Practice Direction 9E makes specific provision) and applications for a committal order (for which rule 188 makes specific provision); and
  (c) apply to hearings which the court has, on or after 29 January 2016, directed to take place (but not hearings taking place after that date pursuant to a direction before that date).

2 General rule – standard order under rule 92(1)(a) and (2)[4]

  4 Rule 92 is renumbered as rule 4.3 where the Case Management pilot applies.

2.1 Where the pilot scheme applies, the court will ordinarily –

  (a) make an order under rule 92(1)(a) that any attended hearing shall be in public; and
  (b) in the same order, impose restrictions under rule 92(2) in relation to the publication of information about the proceedings.

2.2 An 'attended hearing', except where a practice direction provides otherwise, means a hearing where one or more of the parties to the proceedings have been invited to attend the court for the determination of the application.

2.3 An order pursuant to paragraph 2.1 will ordinarily be in the terms of the standard order set out in the Annex to this Practice Direction.

2.4 The court may decide not to make an order pursuant to paragraph 2.1 if it appears to the court that there is good reason for not making the order, but will consider whether it would be appropriate instead to make an order (under rule 92(1)(b) or (c)) –

  (a) for a part only of the hearing to be held in public; or

(b) excluding any persons, or class of persons from the hearing, or from such part of the hearing as is held in public.

2.5 (1) In deciding whether there is good reason not to make an order pursuant to paragraph 2.1 and whether to make an order pursuant to paragraph 2.4 instead, the court will have regard in particular to –
    (a) the need to protect P or another person involved in the proceedings;
    (b) the nature of the evidence in the proceedings;
    (c) whether earlier hearings in the proceedings have taken place in private;
    (d) whether the court location where the hearing will be held has facilities appropriate to allowing general public access to the hearing, and whether it would be practicable or proportionate to move to another location or hearing room;
    (e) whether there is any risk of disruption to the hearing if there is general public access to it;
    (f) whether, if there is good reason for not allowing general public access, there also exists good reason to deny access to duly accredited representatives of news gathering and reporting organisations.
(2) In sub-paragraph (1)(f), 'duly accredited' refers to accreditation in accordance with any administrative scheme for the time being approved for the purposes of this pilot by the Lord Chancellor.

2.6 Where the court makes an order pursuant to paragraph 2.1 or 2.4 that an attended hearing or part of it is to be in public, the court will grant, to any person who would have been entitled under the Legal Services Act 2007 to exercise rights of audience at that hearing if such an order had not been made and the hearing was held in private (and who is not otherwise entitled to exercise such rights), the equivalent rights of audience at that attended hearing and any further hearing, unless the court is satisfied that there is good reason not to do so.

****

Note—The Standard Order is set out in Part VIII.

Practice Direction – Case Management Pilot

Note—This pilot Practice Direction is published in draft format for information only; it will not be signed or come into force until June 2016. Further amendments may be made to the pilot Practice Direction during that time. The final pilot Practice Direction will be available on the Courts and Tribunals Judiciary website when the pilot commences.

Introduction

The case management pilot introduces a new scheme of management of Court of Protection cases.

The pilot was published on 2 March 2016 and is scheduled to run for about 12 months. The expected commencement date is June 2016. During the pilot, it will be ascertained whether the scheme contained in the pilot is workable and whether it can be improved in any way. If successful, the pilot should eventually be incorporated into new rules.

The pilot was published in advance of the commencement date to allow practitioners and court users to prepare for the new regime. The announcement that accompanied the publication of the pilot stated that it:

'will place an obligation on applicants to provide improved analysis of the issues at the start of a case, allowing for more robust case management decisions to be taken at the outset and all issues to be identified at the earliest opportunity in proceedings. It will also seek to encourage early resolution of cases, to reduce the number and length of hearings required in contested cases and to promote judicial continuity…'

The announcement also made it clear that the version published on 2 March 2016 (reproduced below) may contain amendments when finally published. This is presumably to allow for any observations made in the period prior to publication.

Accordingly, this commentary provides a basic outline of the new scheme and highlights new concepts that the pilot introduces. It is based on the version published on 2 March 2016.

Authority for the Pilot

The authority for introducing a pilot scheme derives from COPR 2007, r 9A, which allows a Practice Direction to make provision for the operation of a pilot scheme.

Where to find the new scheme of case management

The pilot brings about a radical change in the way cases are managed. The new structure is found completely in the pilot documentation. The Practice Direction sets out the structural changes to case management that the pilot introduces and the working of the new scheme. To give effect to the changes made by the pilot, COPR 2007 has been amended.

The Ad Hoc Rules Committee of the Court of Protection were concerned that the case management rules should be grouped together in one place in the rules. This would allow judges and court users to find the whole range of the court's powers in one place. Thus, the pilot at Annex A has what are referred to as Pilot Parts 1 to 5, which are the consolidated rules that supplement the pilot.

Annex B1 and Annex B2 contain changes to the rules that govern experts in COPR 2007, Pt 15. The pilot helpfully includes a completely amended version of Pt 15 incorporating the amendments to avoid confusion.

The purpose of Annex C and Annex D is explained below.

Any case managed under the pilot scheme will rely solely on the rules and practice as set out in the pilot.

What is not included

Paragraph 3.1 of the Practice Direction contains a list of cases that are not included in the pilot. These include uncontested applications, applications for statutory wills and gifts, serious medical treatment cases and certain deprivation of liberty applications. All other cases are potentially within the pilot.

How the scheme works

In the pilot scheme, cases will be allocated to one of three tracks, which are called pathways. There are three potential pathways. The personal welfare pathway is for cases where the sole issues to be decided concern P's personal welfare. The property and affairs pathway is for cases where the sole issues to be decided concern P's property and affairs. Where a case has elements of both personal welfare and property and affairs matters, the Mixed Welfare and Property Pathway will apply.

The pathways are just that; each one sets a path for a case to follow from issue to the very end of the case. Each stage of a case's journey has steps that are set out in the pathway. The aim of each step is to ensure that a case is properly prepared and can end as soon as possible whether by final

Practice Direction – Case Management Pilot **PD**

hearing or settlement. It should also be noted that the end of the case does not just mean the final hearing but also covers any enforcement steps that are required when the pilot will still apply.

The Personal Welfare Pathway

The Personal Welfare Pathway has six stages.

The first stage is the pre-issue stage. The Practice Direction sets out the steps that an applicant must take before issuing proceedings. There are additional steps for urgent matters. These steps include identifying all potential respondents and explaining to those notified the nature of the proceedings.

The second stage is when the proceedings are issued. The Practice Direction sets out the documents that have to be filed and other requirements. This includes the applicant giving a clear explanation of why an order is sought, an explanation of the nature of the dispute, the names of the people involved and key documents such as a support plan for P and evidence that key individuals have been consulted. In urgent cases, an explanation of why the case is urgent must be given.

The third stage is that when the case is issued and all papers are filed at court, the court's active management duties will immediately start.

The case papers will be placed before a judge who will list a case management conference normally within 28 days before the correct level of judge for that case.

Directions will be given to ensure that the case management hearing is used properly. The court will also consider other matters such as whether to order an advocates meeting and directing who should act as litigation friend.

If a case is urgent and needs to be transferred to the High Court, this will be immediately identified and the case will be transferred.

The fourth stage is the case management conference. The Practice Direction expects the court to carry out a number of tasks that are listed, such as recording the issues in disputes, considering how P will be involved in the case, giving directions, setting a timetable for the proceedings and determining if a further best interests meeting is necessary.

One novel feature concerns expert evidence. Paragraph 4.5(m) of the Practice Direction obliges the court to consider whether a section 49 report or the use of a representative could achieve a better result than an expert.

The fifth stage is the Final Management Hearing. The purpose of this hearing is to enable the court to determine if the case can be resolved and if not, to ensure that everything is ready to enable to final hearing to be fully effective. An advocates meeting must take place, which again is to ensure that outstanding issues can be highlighted and addressed. The court can also use this hearing to explore whether settlement of all or part of the issues is possible.

The sixth stage is the final hearing. In particular, rules are set out to ensure that bundles for the hearing are properly prepared.

The Property and Affairs Pathway

This pathway has four stages because it starts at a later point in the case than the Personal Welfare Pathway.

The reason, as explained in the Practice Direction, is that many property and affairs applications start life with the intent that they are non-contentious and only later become contentious when someone served with the application opposes it.

For example, someone might apply to be a deputy believing no-one opposes the application. However, a relative files an acknowledgment of service indicating opposition to the application. At that point, the first stage of the pathway will be engaged.

The first stage is when it is recognised that the case is contested when Form COP 5 is filed, which indicates opposition to the application. The COP5 will be served on the applicant by the court.

The case will then proceed to the second stage, which is when the case is placed before a judge at the main registry. The case will formally be allocated to the property and affairs pathway.

The court will also list the case for a Dispute Resolution Hearing or transfer the case to a regional court for this hearing to be listed.

The only other order made at this point will be for the respondent to file a summary of reasons for the opposition to the application or for seeking a different order. It should be noted that the requirement is for a summary as opposed to full evidence and material in support.

The third stage is the Dispute Resolution Hearing. This will normally be listed before a district judge. The aim of the hearing is to determine if the case can be resolved and avoid unnecessary litigation. To achieve this aim, the parties are expected to approach the hearing 'openly and without reserve' and the court will give a view on the likely outcome of the proceedings.

It is expected that the hearing will be similar to Financial Dispute Resolution hearings in financial remedy proceedings in the Family Court where judges openly give the parties a full and frank view of the case and the likely outcome and where the judge will try and narrow the gap between the parties' respective positions in the hope that a settlement will be achieved. The expectation is that the Dispute Resolution Hearing will bring about settlement of a large number of cases.

If the case is not settled at the dispute resolution hearing, directions will be given to allow the case to proceed to a final hearing before a different judge, as the first cannot continue having given a view of the case.

For urgent applications allocated to this pathway, the Practice Direction requires specific information to be included in an application such as an explanation of why the case is urgent.

The fourth stage is the final hearing.

The Mixed Welfare and Property Pathway

Some cases may have elements of both pathways. For example, a case where a decision is needed to decide where P is to live and who is to manage P's finances in the face of family conflict.

In such a case, the court on issue will decide which pathway is the most appropriate and allocate the case to one pathway or it may give directions that will draw from relevant elements of both pathways. This will allow the court to ensure that the best possible directions are given to the case.

Furthermore, when issuing such a case, the applicant must also consider which pathway is most suitable and provide the court with the appropriate documentation relevant to that pathway.

In the above example of a dispute concerning where P lives and the management of his financial affairs, the information required on issuing in the personal welfare pathway would have to be provided as this is a core element of the dispute.

The Pilot Rules

The overriding objective and the parties' duties—Part 1 of the Pilot Rules contains the overriding objective. This has been amended in a number of significant ways.

Pilot Rule 1.1 gives a new definition to the overriding objective as dealing with a case justly 'and at proportionate cost'.

This clearly has in mind the criticisms of high levels of costs is some cases such as in *Re A and B (Court of Protection: Delay and Costs)* [2014] EWCOP 48, [2015] COPLR 1.

Dealing with a case justly and at proportionate cost by virtue of Pilot Rule 1.1(3) now applies when considering the enforcement of compliance with rules, Practice Directions and orders.

The Pilot Rules also set out duties to further the overriding objective.

The first duty (Pilot Rule 1.3) is on the court, which must 'actively' manage cases. This duty is not a one-off duty on issue of a case but on every occasion when a court file is referred to a judge, every hearing, at all stages of a final hearing and when enforcement is considered.

The rule also defines active case management. Allocation to the correct pathway and the appropriate judge is included, as is judicial continuity. There is also a duty to avoid delay and 'keeping costs down'.

Although it might be argued that these steps are already taken, this is not always the case and by emphasising the scope of the court's management duty, the need to manage a case properly is highlighted.

However, not only do the rules impose duties on the court but on others involved in the court process.

The parties have to ask the court to manage a case further if new circumstances arise or an existing direction does not deal with a matter; they must identify before issue if the case is within the scope of a pathway and comply with its requirements (Pilot Rule 1.4(2)(a) and (b)).

Legal representatives also have duties, which are contained in Pilot Rule 1.5. They must help the court to further the overriding objective and comply with rules, Practice Directions and orders, follow the case pathway and address whether the case can be swiftly resolved.

The final duty in the rules is on unrepresented litigants and is set out in Pilot Rule 1.6. They, too, must help the court further the overriding objective by engaging with the court process, presenting their case fairly, seeking the court's direction if an issue or dispute arises and seeking early resolution of any dispute where practicable.

Managing the case—Pilot Part 3 sets out the court's case management powers. Most of the rules are drawn together from COPR 2007 to become one unit as already explained.

The section is entitled 'Managing the Case', which emphasises that managing a case is a continuous obligation that exists throughout the life of a case; it is not just a passing phase when the court on one or two occasions gives case management directions, nor does it end at the final hearing but also extends to enforcement matters.

The court is obliged to have regard to a fact that a party is unrepresented and adopt such procedure as it considers appropriate (Pilot Rule 3.2).

This section also includes the rules allowing for the allocation of cases to case pathways.

Other pilot rules—The other sections in the Pilot Rules are Pilot Part 2, which deals with interpretation and general provisions; Pilot Part 4, which covers hearings and is supplemented by the Transparency Pilot, which commenced in January 2016; and Pilot Part 5, which deals with court documents.

Experts—Annex B1 to the Practice Direction modifies the rules for expert evidence. Helpfully, COPR 2007, Pt 15, as modified by Annex B1, is attached as Annex B2 so the expert rules can be read as a whole with the new amendments.

The most significant change (using the modified Pt 15) is r 121, which provides that permission to rely on expert evidence will be given only if it is necessary.

In *Re H-L (Expert Evidence: Test for Permission)* [2013] 2 FLR 1434, a family case, Munby P defined 'necessary' as follows within the context of expert evidence in family proceedings:

'The short answer is that "necessary" means necessary. It is, after all, an ordinary English word. It is a familiar expression nowadays in family law, not least because of the central role it plays, for example, in Article 8 of the European Convention and the wider Strasbourg jurisprudence. If elaboration is required, what precisely does it mean? That was a question considered, albeit in a rather different context, in *Re P (Placement Orders, Parental Consent)* [2008] EWCA Civ 535… This court said it "has a meaning lying somewhere between 'indispensable' on the one hand and 'useful', 'reasonable' or 'desirable' on the other hand", having "the connotation of the imperative, what is demanded rather than what is merely optional or reasonable or desirable."'

This definition is intended to apply to r 121.

Rule 123 sets out the information required when applying for an expert, which again is modelled on the Family Procedure Rules.

Annex C and Annex D—Annex C to the Practice Direction contains a useful table that shows where a pilot rule is contained in COPR 2007. Annex D does the same for Practice Directions.

Part 1 – General

1.1 This Practice Direction is made under rule 9A of the Court of Protection Rules 2007 ('CoPR'). It provides for a pilot scheme for the management of cases within which cases to which the pilot applies, and which are not excepted cases, are allocated to one of three case management pathways.

1.2 Where the provisions of this Practice Direction conflict with the provisions of the CoPR and the practice directions supporting the CoPR, this Practice Direction shall take precedence.

1.3 The pilot scheme is to –

(a) operate from [DATE A] to [DATE B];
(b) apply to all proceedings which are started (in accordance with rule 62) on or after [DATE A].

(Rule 62 provides that proceedings are started when the court issues an application form at the request of the applicant.)

1.4 Where the pilot scheme applies –

(a) the CoPR will apply with the modifications set out in Part 2 of this Practice Direction and the annexes to it; and
(b) the relevant practice directions will apply with corresponding modifications as set out in Part 2 of this Practice Direction and the annexes to it.

1.5 In applying this Practice Direction and the CoPR and practice directions as modified by it, the parties must have regard to any guidance issued in relation to allocation of Court of Protection cases to High Court Judges.

Part 2 – Modifications

2.1 Where this pilot applies –

(a) Parts 1 to 5 and 13, and rules 84, 85 and 86 in Part 12 (but not the practice directions supplementing them), are disapplied;
(b) Pilot Parts 1–5 as set out in Annex A to this Practice Direction (which contains modified versions of those Parts in a new arrangement) will apply in their place, together with the practice directions supplementing the disapplied rules (renumbered as appropriate to supplement Pilot Parts 1–5); and
(c) rule 72(5) and (7) will not apply where a case is allocated to a case management pathway.

2.2 In addition, Part 15 will apply with the modifications set out in Annex B1 to this Practice Direction. Annex B2 to this Practice Direction contains Pilot Part 15 as so modified.

2.3 References in the remainder of the CoPR to the disapplied rules are amended to refer to the modified rules which apply in their place, as set out in Annex C to this Practice Direction.

2.4 The practice directions supporting the disapplied rules are renumbered so as to relate to the modified rules which apply in place of the disapplied rules, and references in those and other practice directions to the modified rules and renumbered practice directions are amended accordingly, as set out in Annex D to this Practice Direction.

Part 3 – Scope of the case management pathways

3.1 Rule 3.9 (as it appears in Pilot Part 3 of the CoPR in Annex A to this Practice Direction) provides for each case which is started in the CoP to be allocated to one of three case management pathways on issue, unless the case falls within an excepted class of cases specified in a practice direction. The excepted classes of case which are specified for this purpose are –

(a) uncontested applications;
(b) applications for statutory wills and gifts;
(c) applications made by the Public Guardian;
(d) applications relating to serious medical treatment (for which Practice Direction 9E makes specific provision);
(e) applications in Form COPDOL10; and
(f) applications in Form DLA.

3.2 The scope of the pathways is as follows –

The Personal Welfare Pathway

This will be the normal pathway for a case in which an application (other than an application relating to serious medical treatment) is made to the court to make or authorise one or more decisions and/or actions and/or declarations relating to P's personal welfare only.

The Property and Affairs Pathway

This will be the normal pathway for a case in which an application is made to the Court to make or authorise one or more decisions and/or actions and/or declarations relating to P's property and financial affairs only.

The Mixed Welfare and Property Pathway

This will be the normal pathway for a case in which the court is to be asked to make or authorise one or more decisions and/or actions and/or declarations relating not only to P's property and financial affairs but also P's personal welfare.

Part 4 – The Personal Welfare Pathway

4.1 The Personal Welfare Pathway comprises six stages –

    (a) The pre-issue stage (see **paragraph 4.2**);
    (b) The point of issue of the application (see **paragraph 4.3**);
    (c) Case management on issue (see **paragraph 4.4**);
    (d) The Case Management Conference (see **paragraph 4.5**);
    (e) The Final Management Hearing (see **paragraph 4.6**);
    (f) The Final Hearing (see **paragraph 4.7**).

The pre-issue stage

4.2

(1) *In all cases*

The applicant must take all necessary steps to –

    (a) identify all potential respondents to the proceedings which the applicant proposes to start, and any other interested parties;
    (b) notify P (where possible) and the potential respondents and other interested parties identified in accordance with sub-paragraph (a) of the applicant's intention to start the proceedings unless the matters which the court would be asked to determine can be resolved without the need for proceedings;
    (c) explain to those notified in accordance with sub-paragraph (b) the nature of the proceedings which the applicant proposes to start, and the matters which the court would be asked to determine in those proceedings;
    (d) set out the applicant's proposals for resolving those matters without the need for proceedings;
    (e) engage with those notified in accordance with sub-paragraph (b) to resolve those matters as far as possible;
    (f) ensure, where it is not possible to resolve those matters without starting proceedings, that all the documents and information required by paragraph 4.3 will be ready to be included with the application.

(2) *Additionally, in urgent cases*

Where the applicant intends to make an urgent or interim application, the applicant must consider –

    (a) why the case is urgent and what the consequences will be if the case is not treated as urgent;
    (b) if any of the steps in paragraph 4.2(1) cannot be taken, why this is the case and what the consequences would be if those steps were taken;
    (c) whether there is any specific deadline, and what that deadline is;

(d) whether there are issues which are not urgent and how those could be separated from those which are urgent.

The point of issue of the application

4.3

(1) *In all cases*

The applicant must include in the application, or refer in the application to and file with it, the following documents or information –

(a) a draft order or explanation of the order that is sought;
(b) a clear explanation of why an order, and the specific order sought, is required;
(c) an explanation of the nature of the dispute;
(d) a statement of what is expected of P's family and/or other connected individuals;
(e) the names of the key people involved in the case, and the nature of their involvement;
(f) a list of the options for P;
(g) a needs assessment, including where appropriate a risk assessment;
(h) a support plan for P, with a time line, including where appropriate a transfer plan;
(i) evidence that the key individuals and agencies have been consulted;
(j) confirmation that a best interests meeting has taken place, and a copy of the minutes of that meeting;
(k) any relevant medical evidence;
(l) except in applications under section 21A of the Act, a report from a medical practitioner or other appropriately qualified professional on P's litigation capacity and capacity to make decisions on the issues in the case;
(m) an explanation of how P can be supported to maximise any decision-making capacity which P has (if possible);
(n) an indication of whether there is likely to be a public law challenge in the case, and if so, the nature of the challenge which is anticipated;
(o) a statement of how it is proposed that P will be involved in the case.

(2) *Additionally, in urgent cases*

Where the application is urgent, the applicant must include in the application, or refer in the application to and file with it, the following information or documents in addition to those in paragraph 4.3(1) –

(a) an explanation of why the case is urgent and what the consequences will be if the case is not treated as urgent;
(b) if any of the steps in paragraph 4.2(1) have not been taken, why this is the case and what the consequences would be if those steps were taken;
(c) confirmation of any specific deadline;
(d) information identifying and separating the issues which are urgent from those which are not urgent.

The case management on issue

4.4

(1) *In all cases*

Upon issue of the application, the papers will be placed before a judge for gatekeeping and initial case management directions. These will include –

(a) gatekeeping: allocating the case to the correct level of judge, having regard to any guidance issued in relation to allocation of Court of Protection cases to High Court Judges;
(b) listing for a Case Management Conference within 28 days (unless the matter is urgent, in which case paragraph 4.4(2) applies);
(c) directions to ensure the Case Management Conference is utilised properly;
(d) considering whether it is necessary for P to be joined as a party, and whether any other persons should be invited to attend the Case Management Conference so that they may apply to be joined (but not making any order for any person other than P to be joined at this stage);
(e) directing the parties to consider who can act as litigation friend or rule 1.2 (as numbered in the modified Pilot Parts 1–5) representative for P if necessary;
(f) considering what details of P's estate should be provided for the purposes of securing litigation funding or otherwise;
(g) considering whether an advocates' meeting should take place before the case management conference, and ordering such a meeting if appropriate;
(h) ordering the preparation of a core bundle (which must not exceed 150 pages, unless the court directs otherwise) for the Case Management Conference.

(2) *In urgent cases*

Where the application is urgent –

(a) if the case is within a category which must be heard by a High Court Judge in accordance with any guidance issued in relation to allocation of Court of Protection cases to High Court Judges, it must be transferred to a High Court Judge;
(b) the case will be listed urgently in accordance with the judge's directions.

The case management conference

4.5

At the Case Management Conference, the court will –

(a) record the issues in dispute;
(b) record what has been agreed between the parties;
(c) record which issues are not to be the subject of adjudication in the case;
(d) consider the appropriate judge for the case;
(e) allocate a judge to the case;
(f) actively consider and decide, having regard to rule 1.2 (as numbered in the modified Pilot Parts 1–5), how P is to be involved in the case;
(g) consider whether a litigation friend is required for P, and if so, who is to be the litigation friend, and if the Official Solicitor is to be the litigation friend, declare that the appointment of the Official Solicitor is a last resort;
(h) determine who should be a party;
(i) set a timetable for the proceedings;
(j) fix a date for the Final Management Hearing, and set a target date for the Final Hearing or fix a trial window as appropriate;
(k) consider whether a further best interests meeting is required, and if so, give directions for that meeting;

(l) give directions for evidence, including disclosure and expert reports (if appropriate having regard to sub-paragraph (m));
(m) actively consider whether a section 49 report or the use of a rule 1.2 (as numbered in the modified Pilot Parts 1–5) representative could achieve a better result than the use of an expert;
(n) consider whether there should be a public hearing;
(o) give any other directions as appropriate to further the overriding objective.

The final management hearing

4.6

(1) A Final Management Hearing will be listed to enable the court to determine whether the case can be resolved, and if not, to ensure that the trial is properly prepared, giving directions as necessary for that purpose.

(2) A meeting should take place at least five days before the Final Management Hearing between advocates and, so far as practicable, any unrepresented parties, with the purpose of resolving or narrowing the issues to be determined at the Final Management Hearing, addressing each of the matters required by Practice Direction Pilot 4B and preparing a draft order.

(3) The applicant (or, if the applicant is not represented but the respondent is represented, the respondent) must, not later than 3 days before the Final Management Hearing, file a core bundle, which must comply with the requirements of Practice Direction Pilot 4B and in particular include the documents specified in paragraphs 4.2 and 4.3 of that Practice Direction.

(4) If sub-paragraph (3) has not been complied with, or any other directions have not been complied with, the court will consider whether to adjourn the hearing, and if it does so, will consider making an order as to costs.

The final hearing

4.7

(1) Unless otherwise directed by the court, a meeting should take place at least five days before the Final Hearing between advocates and, so far as practicable, any unrepresented parties, with the purpose of resolving or narrowing the issues to be determined at the Final Hearing.

(2) The applicant (or, if the applicant is not represented but the respondent is represented, the respondent) must, not later than 3 days before the Final Hearing, file a bundle, which must –

(a) comply with the requirements of Practice Direction Pilot 4B, with particular reference to paragraphs 4.6 and 4.7 of that Practice Direction; and
(b) not generally exceed 350 pages and in any event not contain more than one copy of the same document.

(3) If sub-paragraph (2) has not been complied with, or any other directions have not been complied with, the court will consider whether to adjourn the hearing, and if it does so, will consider making an order as to costs.

Part 5 – The Property and Affairs Pathway

5.1

(1) The Property and Affairs Pathway commences at a later stage than the Personal Welfare Pathway. It is recognised that contentious property and affairs applications tend to arise when a routine application is made, for example for the appointment of a deputy, and that application is opposed. The vast majority of applications, however, remain unopposed, and there is not the need for a pre-issue stage which there is in personal welfare cases.

(2) The Property and Affairs Pathway comprises four stages –
   (a) *When the application becomes contested* (see **paragraph 5.2**);
   (b) *Case management on allocation to pathway* (see **paragraph 5.3**);
   (c) *The Dispute Resolution Hearing* (see **paragraph 5.4**);
   (d) *The Final Hearing* (see **paragraph 5.5**).

(3) Urgent applications are less likely in property and affairs cases; but **paragraph 5.6** contains provision for their management.

When the application becomes contested

5.2

(1) When the court is notified in Form COP5 that a property and affairs application is opposed, or that the respondent wishes to seek a different order from that applied for, the case must be allocated to the Property and Affairs Pathway.

(2) A copy of the notification in Form COP5 must be served by the court on the applicant together with the order allocating the case to the Property and Affairs Pathway (see paragraph 5.3; and see also paragraph 2.1(c) which disapplies rule 72(5) and (7)).

Case management on allocation to pathway

5.3

(1) Following notification in Form COP5 that the case is contested, the papers will be placed before a judge who will allocate the case to the Property and Affairs Pathway and either –
   (a) list the case for a Dispute Resolution Hearing; or
   (b) transfer the case to the most appropriate regional court outside the Central Office and Registry for listing of the Dispute Resolution Hearing and future case management.

(2) The judge will also order the respondent to file a summary of the reasons for opposing the application or for seeking a different order, if the reasons are not clear from Form COP5 submitted by the respondent.

The dispute resolution hearing

5.4

(1) All parties must attend the Dispute Resolution Hearing, unless the court directs otherwise; but the Dispute Resolution Hearing is not an attended hearing for the purposes of Practice Direction – Transparency Pilot.

(2) The Dispute Resolution Hearing will normally take place before a District Judge.

(3) The purpose of the Dispute Resolution Hearing is to enable the court to determine whether the case can be resolved and avoid unnecessary litigation, and so –

 (a) in order for the Dispute Resolution Hearing to be effective, parties must approach it openly and without reserve; and
 (b) the content of the hearing is not to be disclosed and evidence of anything said or of any admission made in the course of the hearing will not be admissible in evidence, except at the trial of a person for an offence committed at the hearing.

(4) The court will give its view on the likely outcome of the proceedings.

(5) If the parties reach agreement to settle the case, the court will make a final order if it considers it in P's best interests.

(6) If the parties do not reach agreement, the court will give directions for the management of the case and for a Final Hearing, having regard to the list of matters in paragraph 4.5, and the requirements of Practice Direction Pilot 4B in relation to the preparation of a bundle.

(7) The Final Hearing must be listed before a different judge, and the judge will mark the order accordingly.

The final hearing

5.5

The final hearing will take place in accordance with the directions given at or following the Dispute Resolution Hearing.

Urgent applications

5.6

(1) Where a property and affairs application is urgent, the applicant should bear in mind the obligation on parties to co-operate in rule 1.4(2)(c) (as numbered in the modified Pilot Parts 1–5).

(2) The applicant must include in the application, or refer in the application to and file with it, the following information or documents –

 (a) an explanation of why the case is urgent and what the consequences will be if the case is not treated as urgent;
 (b) if the application is made without notice, an explanation why it was not possible to make the application on notice, and what the consequences would be if the application were to proceed on notice and the order or an interim order were not made immediately;
 (c) confirmation of any specific deadline;
 (d) information identifying and separating the issues which are urgent from those which are not urgent.

(3) On issue, the case will be listed urgently in accordance with the judge's directions after considering the papers, which may, if the matter appears or is confirmed to be contentious, be that –

(a) the case will proceed to a Dispute Resolution Hearing but listed urgently; or
(b) the case may be listed for an interim hearing to decide the urgent matter or matters in the case, and the court can decide at that hearing whether any further hearing is necessary and if so, whether that further hearing should include a Dispute Resolution Hearing or not.

Part 6 – The Mixed Welfare and Property Pathway

6.1

(1) Where a case contains both personal welfare and property and affairs elements, the court has the power to use whichever of the personal welfare or the property and affairs pathway it considers most suitable, or to direct the use of elements of both those pathways if it considers that appropriate.

(2) The Mixed Welfare and Property Pathway, therefore, comprises two stages before the court makes a decision about which pathway, or a mixture of elements of both pathways, is most appropriate –

The *pre-issue stage*, during which the prospective parties are expected to identify which pathway is most appropriate to the case and to comply with the requirements of that pathway and seek to resolve issues as far as possible;

The *point of issue of the application*, for which the parties must file a list of issues to allow the court to identify which pathway, or mixture of elements, is most appropriate.

(3) Case management: On issue of the application, the papers will be placed before a judge who will either –

(a) order the case to be allocated to a pathway and give directions accordingly; or
(b) give directions as to the elements of each pathway which are to apply and the procedure the case will follow.

ANNEX A: PILOT PARTS 1–5

Pilot Part 1 – The Overriding Objective

Contents of this Part

The overriding objective	Rule 1.1
Participation of P	Rule 1.2
Duties to further the overriding objective	
Court's duty to manage cases	Rule 1.3
The duty of the parties	Rule 1.4
The duty of legal representatives	Rule 1.5
The duty of unrepresented litigants	Rule 1.6

Overriding objective

1.1

(1) These Rules have the overriding objective of enabling the court to deal with a case justly and at proportionate cost, having regard to the principles contained in the Act.

(2) The court must seek to give effect to the overriding objective when it –

    (a) exercises any power under the Rules; or
    (b) interprets any rule or practice direction.

(3) Dealing with a case justly and at proportionate cost includes, so far as is practicable –

    (a) ensuring that it is dealt with expeditiously and fairly;
    (b) ensuring that P's interests and position are properly considered;
    (c) dealing with the case in ways which are proportionate to the nature, importance and complexity of the issues;
    (d) ensuring that the parties are on an equal footing;
    (e) saving expense;
    (f) allotting to it an appropriate share of the court's resources, while taking account of the need to allot resources to other cases; and
    (g) enforcing compliance with rules, practice directions and orders.

Participation of P

1.2

(1) The court must in each case, on its own initiative or on the application of any person, consider whether it should make one or more of the directions in paragraph (2), having regard to –

    (a) the nature and extent of the information before the court;
    (b) the issues raised in the case;
    (c) whether a matter is contentious; and
    (d) whether P has been notified in accordance with the provisions of Part 7 and what, if anything, P has said or done in response to such notification.

(2) The directions are that –

    (a) P should be joined as a party;
    (b) P's participation should be secured by the appointment of an accredited legal representative to represent P in the proceedings and to discharge such other functions as the court may direct;
    (c) P's participation should be secured by the appointment of a representative whose function shall be to provide the court with information as to the matters set out in section 4(6) of the Act and to discharge such other functions as the court may direct;
    (d) P should have the opportunity to address (directly or indirectly) the judge determining the application and, if so directed, the circumstances in which that should occur;
    (e) P's interests and position can properly be secured without any direction under sub-paragraphs (a) to (d) being made or by the making of an alternative direction meeting the overriding objective.

(3) Any appointment or directions made pursuant to paragraph (2)(b) to (e) may be made for such period or periods as the court thinks fit.

(4) Unless P has capacity to conduct the proceedings, an order joining P as a party shall only take effect –
   (a) on the appointment of a litigation friend on P's behalf; or
   (b) if the court so directs, on or after the appointment of an accredited legal representative.

(5) If the court has directed that P should be joined as a party but such joinder does not occur because no litigation friend or accredited legal representative is appointed, the court shall record in a judgment or order –
   (a) the fact that no such appointment was made; and
   (b) the reasons given for that appointment not being made.

(6) A practice direction may make additional or supplementary provision in respect of any of the matters set out in this rule.

(The appointment of litigation friends, accredited legal representatives and representatives under paragraph (2)(c) is dealt with under Part 17.)

('Accredited legal representative' is defined in rule 2.1.)

Duties to further the overriding objective

Court's duty to manage cases

1.3

(1) The court must further the overriding objective by actively managing cases.

(2) The court must manage a case at all times and in particular –
   (a) when a case file is referred to a judge;
   (b) at every hearing, whether listed by the court on its own initiative or on application by a party;
   (c) at all stages of a final hearing; and
   (d) when considering enforcement measures including committal.

(3) Active case management includes –
   (a) considering the appropriate case pathway for the case;
   (b) ensuring –
      (i) that the appropriate judge is allocated to the case;
      (ii) judicial continuity, so far as practicable;
   (c) avoiding delay and keeping costs down;
   (d) encouraging the parties to co-operate with each other in the conduct of the proceedings;
   (e) identifying at an early stage –
      (i) the issues; and
      (ii) who should be a party to the proceedings;
   (f) deciding promptly –
      (i) which issues need a full investigation and hearing and which do not; and
      (ii) the procedure to be followed in the case;
   (g) deciding the order in which issues are to be resolved;
   (h) encouraging the parties to use an alternative dispute resolution procedure if the court considers that appropriate;
   (i) fixing timetables or otherwise controlling the progress of the case;
   (j) considering whether the likely benefits of taking a particular step justify the cost of taking it;

(k) dealing with as many aspects of the case as the court can on the same occasion;
(l) dealing with the case without the parties needing to attend at court;
(m) making use of technology;
(n) giving directions to ensure that the case proceeds quickly and efficiently;
(o) considering whether any hearing should be heard in public; and
(p) considering whether any document relating to proceedings should be a public document and, if so, whether and to what extent it should be redacted.

(Rules 4.2 to 4.4 make provision about the court's powers to authorise publication of information about proceedings and to order that a hearing be held in public.)

The duty of the parties

1.4

(1) The parties are required to help the court to further the overriding objective.

(2) Without prejudice to the generality of paragraph (1), each party is required to –
   (a) ask the court to take steps to manage the case if –
      (i) an order or direction of the court appears not to deal with an issue; or
      (ii) if a matter including any new circumstances, issue or dispute arises of which the court is unaware;
   (b) identify before issue if the case is within the scope of one of the case pathways and comply with the requirements of the applicable case pathway;
   (c) co-operate with the other parties and with the court in identifying and narrowing the issues that need to be determined by the court, and the timetable for that determination;
   (d) adhere to the timetable set by these Rules and by the court;
   (e) comply with all directions and orders of the court;
   (f) be full and frank in the disclosure of information and evidence to the court (including any disclosure ordered under Part 16);
   (g) co-operate with the other parties in all aspects of the conduct of the proceedings, including in the preparation of bundles.

(3) If the court determines that any party has failed without reasonable excuse to satisfy the requirements of this rule, it may under rule 159 depart from the general rules about costs in so far as they apply to that party.

(Rule 133(2) deals with the requirements of general disclosure.)

The duty of legal representatives

1.5

(1) Legal representatives of parties are required to help the court to further the overriding objective.

(2) Without prejudice to the generality of paragraph (1), a legal representative of a party must –
   (a) comply with any applicable rules, practice directions or orders of the court;
   (b) follow (where appropriate) the applicable case pathway; and
   (c) address whether the case can be swiftly resolved.

The duty of unrepresented litigants
1.6

(1) Without prejudice to the generality of rule 1.4, unrepresented litigants are required to help the court to further the overriding objective.

(2) This includes –
   (a) engaging with the process applicable in the case and co-operating with the court and the other parties;
   (b) seeking the court's direction if an issue or dispute arises in the case;
   (c) presenting their case fairly; and
   (d) seeking early resolution of any dispute where practicable.

Pilot Part 2 – Interpretation and General Provisions

Contents of this Part

Interpretation	Rule 2.1
Court officers	Rule 2.2
Court officers – authorisation	Rule 2.3
Computation of time	Rule 2.4
Application of the Civil Procedure Rules and Family Procedure Rules	Rule 2.5
Pilot schemes	Rule 2.6

Interpretation
2.1

In these Rules –
   'the Act' means the Mental Capacity Act 2005;
   'accredited legal representative' means a legal representative authorised pursuant to a scheme of accreditation approved by the President to represent persons meeting the definition of 'P' in this rule in proceedings before the court;
   'applicant' means a person who makes, or who seeks permission to make, an application to the court;
   'application form' means the document that is to be used to begin proceedings in accordance with Part 9 of these Rules or any other provision of these Rules or the practice directions which requires the use of an application form;
   'application notice' means the document that is to be used to make an application in accordance with Part 10 of these Rules or any other provision of these Rules or the practice directions which requires the use of an application notice;
   'attorney' means the person appointed as such by an enduring power of attorney created, or purporting to have been created, in accordance with the regulations mentioned in paragraph 2 of Schedule 4 to the Act;
   'business day' means a day other than –
      (a) a Saturday, Sunday, Christmas Day or Good Friday; or
      (b) a bank holiday in England and Wales, under the Banking and Financial Dealings Act 1971;
   'child' means a person under 18;
   'court' means the Court of Protection;
   'deputy' means a deputy appointed under the Act;

'donee' means the donee of a lasting power of attorney;
'donor' means the donor of a lasting power of attorney, except where the expression is used in rule 68 or 201(5) (where it means the donor of an enduring power of attorney);
'enduring power of attorney' means an instrument created in accordance with such of the regulations mentioned in paragraph 2 of Schedule 4 to the Act as applied when it was executed;
'filing' in relation to a document means delivering it, by post or otherwise, to the court office;
'hearing' includes a hearing conducted by telephone, video link, or any other method permitted or directed by the court;
'judge' means a judge nominated to be a judge of the court under the Act;
'lasting power of attorney' has the meaning given in section 9 of the Act;
'legal representative' means a –
   (a) barrister;
   (b) solicitor;
   (c) solicitor's employee;
   (d) manager of a body recognised under section 9 of the Administration of Justice Act 1985; or
   (e) person who, for the purposes of the Legal Services Act 2007, is an authorised person in relation to an activity which constitutes the conduct of litigation (within the meaning of that Act),
who has been instructed to act for a party in relation to any application;
'legally aided person' means a person to whom civil legal services (within the meaning of the Legal Aid, Sentencing and Punishment of Offenders Act 2012) have been made available under arrangements made for the purposes of Part 1 of that Act;
'order' includes a declaration made by the court;
'P' means –
   (a) any person (other than a protected party) who lacks or, so far as consistent with the context, is alleged to lack capacity to make a decision or decisions in relation to any matter that is the subject of an application to the court; and
   (b) a relevant person as defined by paragraph 7 of Schedule A1 to the Act,
and references to a person who lacks capacity are to be construed in accordance with the Act;
'party' is to be construed in accordance with rule 3;
'personal welfare' is to be construed in accordance with section 17 of the Act;
'President' and 'Vice-President' refer to those judges appointed as such under section 46(3)(a) and (b) of the Act;
'property and affairs' is to be construed in accordance with section 18 of the Act;
'protected party' means a party or an intended party (other than P or a child) who lacks capacity to conduct the proceedings;
'representative' means a person appointed under rule 1.2(2)(c), except where the context otherwise requires;
'respondent' means a person who is named as a respondent in the application form or notice, as the case may be;
'Senior Judge' means the judge who has been nominated to be Senior Judge under section 46(4) of the Act, and references in these Rules to a circuit judge include the Senior Judge;
'Tier 1 Judge' means any judge nominated to act as a judge of the Court of Protection under section 46 of the Act who is neither a Tier 2 Judge nor a Tie 3 Judge;
'Tier 2 Judge' means –

(a) the Senior Judge; and
(b) such other judges nominated to act as a judge of the Court of Protection under section 46 Act as may be set out in the relevant practice direction;

'Tier 3 Judge' means –
(a) the President;
(b) the Vice-President; and
(c) such other judges nominated to act as a judge of the Court of Protection under section 46 Act as may be set out in the relevant practice direction;

'Visitor' means a person appointed as such by the Lord Chancellor under section 61 of the Act.

Court officers

2.2

(1) Where these Rules permit or require the court to perform an act of a purely formal or administrative character, that act may be performed by a court officer.

(2) A requirement that a court officer carry out any act at the request of any person is subject to the payment of any fee required by a fees order for the carrying out of that act.

Court officers – authorisation

2.3

(1) The Senior Judge or the President or Vice-President may authorise a court officer to exercise the jurisdiction of the court in such circumstances as may be set out in the relevant practice direction.

(2) A court officer who has been authorised under paragraph (1) –

(a) must refer to a judge any application, proceedings or any question arising in any application or proceedings which ought, in the officer's opinion, to be considered by a judge;
(b) may not deal with any application or proceedings or any question arising in any application or proceedings by way of a hearing; and
(c) may not deal with an application for the reconsideration of an order made by that court officer or another court officer.

Computation of time

2.4

(1) This rule shows how to calculate any period of time which is specified) –

(a) by these Rules;
(b) by a practice direction; or
(c) in an order or direction of the court.

(2) A period of time expressed as a number of days must be computed as clear days.

(3) In this rule, 'clear days' means that in computing the number of days) –

(a) the day on which the period begins; and
(b) if the end of the period is defined by reference to an event, the day on which that event occurs,

are not included.

(4) Where the specified period is 7 days or less, and would include a day which is not a business day, that day does not count.

(5) When the specified period for doing any act at the court office ends on a day on which the office is closed, that act will be done in time if done on the next day on which the court office is open.

Application of the Civil Procedure Rules and Family Procedure Rules

2.5

(1) In any case not expressly provided for by these Rules or the practice directions made under them, the court may apply either the Civil Procedure Rules 1998 or the Family Procedure Rules 2010 (including in either case the practice directions made under them) with any necessary modifications, in so far as is necessary to further the overriding objective.

(2) A reference in these Rules to the Civil Procedure Rules 1998 or to the Family Procedure Rules 2010 is to the version of those rules in force at the date specified for the purpose of that reference in the relevant practice direction.

Pilot schemes

2.6

(1) Practice directions may make provision for the operation of pilot schemes for assessing the use of new practices and procedures in connection with proceedings –

    (a) for specified periods; and
    (b) in relation to proceedings –
        (i)   in specified parts of the country; or
        (ii) relating to specified types of application.

(2) Practice directions may modify or disapply any provision of these Rules during the operation of such pilot schemes.

Pilot Part 3 – Managing the Case

Contents of this Part

The court's general powers of case management	Rule 3.1
Case management – unrepresented parties	Rule 3.2
Court's power to dispense with requirement of any rule	Rule 3.3
Exercise of powers on the court's own initiative	Rule 3.4
General power of the court to rectify matters where there has been an error of procedure	Rule 3.5
Dealing with the application	Rule 3.6
Directions	Rule 3.7
Allocation of proceedings	
Court's jurisdiction in certain kinds of cases to be exercised by certain judges	Rule 3.8
Allocation of cases to case pathways	Rule 3.9

Practice Direction – Case Management Pilot **PD**

The court's general powers of case management

3.1

(1) The list of powers in this rule is in addition to any powers given to the court by any other rule or practice direction or by any other enactment or any powers it may otherwise have.

(2) The court may –

    (a) extend or shorten the time for compliance with any rule, practice direction, or court order or direction (even if an application for extension is made after the time for compliance has expired);

    (b) adjourn or bring forward a hearing;

    (c) require P, a party, a party's legal representative or litigation friend, or P's rule 1.2 representative, to attend court;

    (d) hold a hearing and receive evidence by telephone or any other method of direct oral communication;

    (e) stay the whole or part of any proceedings or judgment either generally or until a specified date or event;

    (f) consolidate proceedings;

    (g) hear two or more applications on the same occasion;

    (h) direct a separate hearing of any issue;

    (i) decide the order in which issues are to be heard;

    (j) exclude an issue from consideration;

    (k) dismiss or give judgment on an application after a decision is made on a preliminary basis;

    (l) direct any party to file and serve an estimate of costs; and

    (m) take any step or give any direction for the purpose of managing the case and furthering the overriding objective.

(3) A judge to whom a matter is allocated may, if the judge considers that the matter is one which ought properly to be dealt with by another judge, transfer the matter to such a judge.

(4) Where the court gives directions it may take into account whether or not a party has complied with any rule or practice direction.

(5) The court may make any order it considers appropriate even if a party has not sought that order.

(6) A power of the court under these Rules to make an order includes a power to vary or revoke the order.

(Rules 1.3 to 1.6 concern the duty of the court to further the overriding objective by actively managing cases, and the duty of parties, legal representatives and unrepresented litigants to assist the court in furthering the overriding objective.)

Case management – unrepresented parties

3.2

(1) This rule applies in any proceedings where at least one party is unrepresented.

(2) When the court is exercising any powers of case management, it must have regard to the fact that at least one party is unrepresented.

(3) The court must adopt such procedure at any hearing as it considers appropriate to further the overriding objective.

(4) At any hearing when the court is taking evidence this may include –

(a) ascertaining from an unrepresented party the matters about which the witness may be able to give evidence or on which the witness ought to be cross-examined; and
(b) putting or causing to be put, to the witness such questions as may appear to the court to be proper.

Court's power to dispense with requirement of any rule

3.3

In addition to its general powers and the powers listed in rule 3.1, the court may dispense with the requirements of any rule.

Exercise of powers on the court's own initiative

3.4

(1) Except where these Rules or another enactment make different provision, the court may exercise its powers on its own initiative.

(2) The court may make an order on its own initiative without hearing the parties or giving them the opportunity to make representations.

(3) Where the court proposes to make an order on its own initiative it may give the parties and any other person it thinks fit an opportunity to make representations and, where it does so, must specify the time by which, and the manner in which, the representations must be made.

(4) Where the court proposes –
(a) to make an order on its own initiative; and
(b) to hold a hearing to decide whether to make the order,
it must give the parties and may give any other person it thinks likely to be affected by the order at least 3 days' notice of the hearing.

General power of the court to rectify matters where there has been an error of procedure

3.5

Where there has been an error of procedure, such as a failure to comply with a rule or practice direction –
(a) the error does not invalidate any step taken in the proceedings unless the court so orders; and
(b) the court may waive the error or require it to be remedied or may make such other order as appears to the court to be just.

Dealing with the application

3.6

(1) This rule and rule 3.7 are subject to any provision made by a practice direction in respect of the case pathway to which the case is allocated.

(2) As soon as practicable after any application has been issued the court shall consider how to deal with it.

(3) Where permission to start proceedings is required, and whether or not it has been applied for, the court's consideration under paragraph (2) shall include whether to grant or refuse permission without a hearing, or to direct a hearing to consider whether permission should be granted.

(4) The court may deal with an application or any part of an application at a hearing or without a hearing.

(5) In considering whether it is necessary to hold a hearing, the court shall, as appropriate, have regard to –

- (a) the nature of the proceedings and the orders sought;
- (b) whether the application is opposed by a person who appears to the court to have an interest in matters relating to P's best interests;
- (c) whether the application involves a substantial dispute of fact;
- (d) the complexity of the facts and the law;
- (e) any wider public interest in the proceedings;
- (f) the circumstances of P and of any party, in particular as to whether their rights would be adequately protected if a hearing were not held;
- (g) whether the parties agree that the court should dispose of the application without a hearing; and
- (h) any other matter specified in the relevant practice direction.

(6) Where the court considers that a hearing is necessary it shall –

- (a) give notice of the hearing date to the parties and to any other person it directs;
- (b) state what is to be dealt with at the hearing, including whether the matter is to be disposed of at that hearing; and
- (c) consider whether it is appropriate –
  - (i) for the hearing or any part of it to be in public; and
  - (ii) to make any order under rule 4.1, 4.2 or 4.3.

(The practice direction Practice Direction – Case Management Pilot makes provision in relation to case management pathways.)

Directions

3.7

(1) The court may –

- (a) give directions in writing; or
- (b) set a date for a directions hearing; and
- (c) do anything else that may be set out in a practice direction.

(2) When giving directions the court may do any of the following –

- (a) require a report under section 49 of the Act and give directions as to any such report;
- (b) give directions as to any requirements contained in these Rules or a practice direction for the giving of notification to any person or for that person to do anything in response to a notification;
- (c) if the court considers that any other person or persons should be a party to the proceedings, give directions joining them as a party;
- (d) if the court considers that any party to the proceedings should not be a party, give directions for that person's removal as a party;
- (e) give directions for the management of the case and set a timetable for the steps to be taken between the giving of directions and the hearing;

(f) subject to rule 3.8, give directions as to the type of judge who is to hear the case;
(g) give directions as to whether the proceedings or any part of them are to be heard in public, or as to whether any particular person should be permitted to attend the hearing, or as to whether any publication of the proceedings is to be permitted;
(h) give directions as to the disclosure of documents, service of witness statements and any expert evidence;
(i) give directions as to the attendance of witnesses and as to whether, and the extent to which, cross-examination will be permitted at any hearing; and
(j) give such other directions as the court may think fit.

(3) The court may give directions at any time –

(a) on its own initiative; or
(b) on the application of a party.

(4) Subject to paragraphs (5) and (6) and unless these Rules or a practice direction provide otherwise or the court directs otherwise, the time specified by a rule or by the court for a person to do any act may be varied by the written agreement of the parties.

(5) A party must apply to the court if that party wishes to vary –

(a) the date the court has fixed for the final hearing; or
(b) the period within which the final hearing is to take place.

(6) The time specified by a rule or practice direction or by the court may not be varied by the parties if the variation would make it necessary to vary the date the court has fixed for any hearing or the period within which the final hearing is to take place.

(Participation of P in proceedings is addressed in rule 1.2 (participation of P) and Part 17 (litigation friends and rule 1.2 representatives).)

Allocation of proceedings

Court's jurisdiction in certain kinds of cases to be exercised by certain judges

3.8

(1) A practice direction made under this rule may specify certain categories of case to be dealt with by a specific judge or a specific class of judges.

(2) Applications in any matter other than those specified in the practice direction referred to in paragraph (1) may be dealt with by any judge.

Allocation of cases to case pathways

3.9

(1) This rule provides for the allocation of cases to case pathways.

(2) There are three case pathways –

(a) the Personal Welfare Pathway;
(b) the Property and Affairs Pathway;
(c) the Mixed Welfare and Property Pathway.

(3) Each case shall on issue be allocated to one of the three case pathways unless (subject to paragraph (5)) it is in an excepted class of cases.

(4) Excepted classes of case may be specified in a practice direction.

(5) The court may direct that a case shall be allocated to a case pathway notwithstanding that it is in an excepted class of cases.

(6) A practice direction may make provision for –

 (a) the scope of each case pathway; and
 (b) how cases in each case pathway are to be managed.

(The practice direction Practice Direction – Case Management Pilot makes provision in relation to the case pathways and excepted classes of case.)

Pilot Part 4 – Hearings

Contents of this Part

Private hearings
General rule – hearing to be in private   Rule 4.1

Court's general power to authorise publication of information about proceedings   Rule 4.2

Power to order a public hearing
Court's power to order that a hearing be held in public   Rule 4.3

Supplementary
Supplementary provisions relating to public or private hearings   Rule 4.4

Private hearings

General rule – hearing to be held in private

4.1

(1) The general rule is that a hearing is to be held in private.

(2) A private hearing is a hearing which only the following persons are entitled to attend –

 (a) the parties;
 (b) P (whether or not a party);
 (c) any person acting in the proceedings as a litigation friend;
 (d) any legal representative of a person specified in any of sub-paragraphs (a) to (c); and
 (e) any court officer.

(3) In relation to a private hearing, the court may make an order –

 (a) authorising any person, or class of persons, to attend the hearing or a part of it; or
 (b) excluding any person, or class of persons, from attending the hearing or a part of it.

Court's general power to authorise publication of information about proceedings

4.2

(1) For the purposes of the law relating to contempt of court, information relating to proceedings held in private (whether or not contained in a document filed with the court) may be communicated in accordance with paragraph (2) or (3).

(2) The court may make an order authorising –

    (a) the publication or communication of such information or material relating to the proceedings as it may specify; or

    (b) the publication of the text or a summary of the whole or part of a judgment or order made by the court.

(3) Subject to any direction of the court, information referred to in paragraph (1) may be communicated in accordance with Practice Direction Pilot 4A.

(4) Where the court makes an order under paragraph (2) it may do so on such terms as it thinks fit, and in particular may –

    (a) impose restrictions on the publication of the identity of –
        (i) any party;
        (ii) P (whether or not a party);
        (iii) any witness; or
        (iv) any other person;

    (b) prohibit the publication of any information that may lead to any such person being identified;

    (c) prohibit the further publication of any information relating to the proceedings from such date as the court may specify; or

    (d) impose such other restrictions on the publication of information relating to the proceedings as the court may specify.

(5) The court may on its own initiative or upon request authorise communication –

    (a) for the purposes set out in Practice Direction Pilot 4A; or
    (b) for such other purposes as it considers appropriate,

of information held by it.

Power to order a public hearing

Court's power to order that a hearing be held in public

4.3

(1) The court may make an order –

    (a) for a hearing to be held in public;
    (b) for a part of a hearing to be held in public; or
    (c) excluding any person, or class of persons, from attending a public hearing or a part of it.

(2) Where the court makes an order under paragraph (1), it may in the same order or by a subsequent order –

    (a) impose restrictions on the publication of the identity of –
        (i) any party;
        (ii) P (whether or not a party);
        (iii) any witness; or

(iv) any other person;
 (b) prohibit the publication of any information that may lead to any such person being identified;
 (c) prohibit the further publication of any information relating to the proceedings from such date as the court may specify; or
 (d) impose such other restrictions on the publication of information relating to the proceedings as the court may specify.

Supplementary

Supplementary provisions relating to public or private hearings

4.4

(1) An order under rule 4.1, 4.2 or 4.3 may be made –
 (a) only where it appears to the court that there is good reason for making the order;
 (b) at any time; and
 (c) either on the court's own initiative or on an application made by any person in accordance with Part 10.

(2) A practice direction may make further provision in connection with –
 (a) private hearings;
 (b) public hearings; or
 (c) the publication of information about any proceedings.

Pilot Part 5 – Court documents

Contents of this Part

Documents used in court proceedings	Rule 5.1
Documents required to be verified by a statement of truth	Rule 5.2
Position statement not required to be verified by statement of truth	Rule 5.3
Failure to verify a document	Rule 5.4
Failure to verify a witness statement	Rule 5.5
False statements	Rule 5.6
Personal details	Rule 5.7
Supply of documents to a party from court records	Rule 5.8
Supply of documents to a non-party from court records	Rule 5.9
Subsequent use of court documents	Rule 5.10
Editing information in court documents	Rule 5.11
Public Guardian to be supplied with court documents relevant to supervision of deputies	Rule 5.12
Provision of court order to Public Guardian	Rule 5.13
Amendment of application	Rule 5.14
Clerical mistakes or slips	Rule 5.15
Endorsement of amendment	Rule 5.16

Documents used in court proceedings

5.1

(1) The court will seal or otherwise authenticate with the stamp of the court the following documents on issue –

    (a) an application form;
    (b) an application notice;
    (c) an order; and
    (d) any other document which a rule or practice direction requires to be sealed or stamped.

(2) Where these Rules or any practice direction require a document to be signed, that requirement is satisfied if the signature is printed by computer or other mechanical means.

(3) A practice direction may make provision for documents to be filed or sent to the court by –

    (a) facsimile; or
    (b) other means.

Documents required to be verified by a statement of truth

5.2

(1) The following documents must be verified by a statement of truth –

    (a) an application form, an application notice, an appellant's notice or a respondent's notice, where the applicant seeks to rely upon matters set out in the document as evidence;
    (b) a witness statement;
    (c) a certificate of –
        (i) service or non-service; or
        (ii) notification or non-notification;
    (d) a deputy's declaration; and
    (e) any other document required by a rule or practice direction to be so verified.

(2) Subject to paragraph (3), a statement of truth is a statement that –

    (a) the party putting forward the document;
    (b) in the case of a witness statement, the maker of the witness statement; or
    (c) in the case of a certificate referred to in paragraph (1)(c), the person who signs the certificate,

believes that the facts stated in the document being verified are true.

(3) If a party is conducting proceedings with a litigation friend, the statement of truth in –

    (a) an application form;
    (b) an application notice; or
    (c) an appellant's notice or a respondent's notice,

is a statement that the litigation friend believes that the facts stated in the document being verified are true.

(4) The statement of truth must be signed –

(a) in the case of an application form, an application notice, an appellant's notice or a respondent's notice –
  (i) by the party or litigation friend; or
  (ii) by the legal representative on behalf of the party or litigation friend; and
(b) in the case of a witness statement, by the maker of the statement.

(5) A statement of truth which is not contained in the document which it verifies must clearly identify that document.

(6) A statement of truth in an application form, an application notice, an appellant's notice or a respondent's notice may be made by –

(a) a person who is not a party; or
(b) two or more parties jointly,

where this is permitted by a relevant practice direction.

Position statement not required to be verified by statement of truth

5.3

Nothing in these Rules requires a position statement to be verified by a statement of truth.

Failure to verify a document

5.4

If an application form, an application notice, an appellant's notice or a respondent's notice is not verified by a statement of truth, the applicant (or appellant or respondent as the case may be) may not rely upon the document as evidence of any of the matters set out in it unless the court permits.

Failure to verify a witness statement

5.5

If a witness statement is not verified by a statement of truth, it shall not be admissible in evidence unless the court permits.

False statements

5.6

(1) Proceedings for contempt of court may be brought against a person if that person makes, or causes to be made, a false statement in a document verified by a statement of truth without an honest belief in its truth.

(2) Proceedings under this rule may be brought only –

(a) by the Attorney General; or
(b) with the permission of the court.

Personal details

5.7

(1) Where a party does not wish to reveal –

(a) his or her home address or telephone number;
(b) P's home address or telephone number;
(c) the name of the person with whom P is living (if that person is not the applicant); or
(d) the address or telephone number of his or her place of business, or the place of business of any of the persons mentioned in sub-paragraphs (b) or (c),

that party must provide those particulars to the court.

(2) Where paragraph (1) applies, the particulars given will not be revealed to any person unless the court so directs.

(3) Where a party changes home address during the course of the proceedings, that party must give notice in writing of the change to the court.

(4) Where a party does not reveal his or her home address, that party must nonetheless provide an address for service which must be within the jurisdiction of the court.

Supply of documents to a party from court records

5.8

Unless the court orders otherwise, a party to proceedings may inspect or obtain from the records of the court a copy of –

(a) any document filed by a party to the proceedings; or
(b) any communication in the proceedings between the court and –
    (i) a party to the proceedings; or
    (ii) another person.

Supply of documents to a non-party from court records

5.9

(1) Subject to rules 5.12 and 4.3(2), a person who is not a party to proceedings may inspect or obtain from the court records a copy of any judgment or order given or made in public.

(2) The court may, on an application made to it, authorise a person who is not a party to proceedings to –

(a) inspect any other documents in the court records; or
(b) obtain a copy of any such documents, or extracts from such documents.

(3) A person making an application for an authorisation under paragraph (2) must do so in accordance with Part 10.

(4) Before giving an authorisation under paragraph (2), the court will consider whether any document is to be provided on an edited basis.

Subsequent use of court documents

5.10

(1) Where a document has been filed or disclosed, a party to whom it was provided may use the document only for the purpose of the proceedings in which it was filed or disclosed, except where –

(a) the document has been read to or by the court or referred to at a public hearing; or
(b) the court otherwise permits.

(2) Paragraph (1)(a) is subject to any order of the court made under rule 4.3(2).

Editing information in court documents
5.11

(1) A party may apply to the court for an order that a specified part of a document is to be edited prior to the document's service or disclosure.

(2) An order under paragraph (1) may be made at any time.

(3) Where the court makes an order under this rule any subsequent use of that document in the proceedings shall be of the document as edited, unless the court directs otherwise.

(4) An application under this rule must be made in accordance with Part 10.

Public Guardian to be supplied with court documents relevant to supervision of deputies
5.12

(1) This rule applies in any case where the court makes an order –
  (a) appointing a person to act as a deputy; or
  (b) varying an order under which a deputy has been appointed.

(2) Subject to paragraphs (3) and (6), the Public Guardian is entitled to be supplied with a copy of qualifying documents if the Public Guardian reasonably considers that it is necessary to have regard to them in connection with the discharge of the Public Guardian's functions under section 58 of the Act in relation to supervision of deputies.

(3) The court may direct that the right to be supplied with documents under paragraph (2) does not apply in relation to such one or more documents, or descriptions of documents, as the court may specify.

(4) A direction under paragraph (3) or (6) may be given –
  (a) either on the court's own initiative or on an application made to it; and
  (b) either –
    (i) at the same time as the court makes the order which appoints the deputy, or which varies it; or
    (ii) subsequently.

(5) 'Qualifying documents' means documents which –
  (a) are filed in court in connection with the proceedings in which the court makes the order referred to in paragraph (1); and
  (b) are relevant to –
    (i) the decision to appoint the deputy;
    (ii) any powers conferred on the deputy;
    (iii) any duties imposed on the deputy; or
    (iv) any other terms applying to those powers and duties which are contained in the order.

(6) The court may direct that any document is to be provided to the Public Guardian on an edited basis.

Provision of court order to Public Guardian

5.13

Any order of the court requiring the Public Guardian to do something, or not to do something, must be served on the Public Guardian as soon as practicable and in any event not later than 7 days after the order was made.

Amendment of application

5.14

(1) The court may allow or direct an applicant, at any stage of the proceedings, to amend the application form or notice.

(2) The amendment may be effected by making in writing the necessary alterations to the application form or notice, but if the amendments are so numerous or of such a nature or length that written alteration would make it difficult or inconvenient to read, a fresh document amended as allowed or directed may be issued.

Clerical mistakes or slips

5.15

The court may at any time correct any clerical mistakes in an order or direction or any error arising in an order or direction from any accidental slip or omission.

Endorsement of amendment

5.16

Where an application form or notice, order or direction has been amended under this Part, a note shall be placed on it showing the date on which it was amended, and the alteration shall be sealed.

ANNEX B1: MODIFICATIONS TO PART 15

Part 15 (experts) is amended as follows.

(a) For rules 121 (duty to restrict expert evidence) and 122 (experts – overriding duty to the court) substitute –

'121 Duty to restrict expert evidence

(1) Expert evidence shall be restricted to that which is necessary to assist the court to resolve the issues in the proceedings.

(2) The court may give permission to file or adduce expert evidence as mentioned in rule 120(1) and 123(1) only if satisfied that the evidence –

(a) is necessary to assist the court to resolve the issues in the proceedings; and

(b) cannot otherwise be provided.

122 Experts – overriding duty to the court

(1) It is the duty of the expert to help the court on the matters within the expert's expertise.

(2) This duty overrides any obligation to the person from whom the expert has received instructions or by whom the expert is paid.'

(b) In rule 123 (court's power to restrict expert evidence), for paragraphs (2) and (3) substitute –

'(2) When a party applies for a direction under this rule, that party must –

  (a) the expert evidence is to relate;
  (b) where practicable, identify the expert in that field upon whose evidence the party wishes to rely;
  (c) provide any other material information about the expert;
  (d) state whether the expert evidence could be obtained from a single joint expert;
  (e) provide any other information or documents required by a practice direction; and
  (f) provide a draft letter of instruction to the expert.

(2A) When deciding whether to give permission as mentioned in paragraph (1), the court is to have regard in particular to –

  (a) the issues to which the expert evidence would relate;
  (b) the questions which the expert would answer;
  (c) the impact which giving permission would be likely to have on the timetable, duration and conduct of the proceedings;
  (d) any failure to comply with any direction of the court about expert evidence; and
  (e) the cost of the expert evidence.

(3) Where a direction is given under this rule, the court shall specify –

  (a) the field or fields in respect of which the expert evidence is to be provided;
  (b) the questions which the expert is required to answer; and
  (c) the date by which the expert is to provide the evidence.'

(c) In rule 125 (written questions to experts), in paragraph (2), omit 'and' at the end of sub-paragraph (b) and at the end of sub-paragraph (c) insert –

'; and

  (d) must be copied and sent to the other parties at the same time as they are sent to the expert.'

(d) In rule 131 (instructions to a single joint expert), for paragraphs (1) and (2) substitute –

'(1) Where the court gives a direction under rule 130 for a single joint expert to be used, the instructions are to be contained in a jointly agreed letter unless the court directs otherwise.

(1A) Where the instructions are to be contained in a jointly agreed letter, in default of agreement the instructions may be determined by the court on the written request of any instructing party copied to the other instructing parties.

(2) Where the court permits the instructing parties to give separate instructions to a single joint expert, unless the court directs otherwise, when an instructing party gives instructions to the expert, that party must at the same time send a copy of the

instructions to the other instructing party or parties.'

ANNEX B2: PART 15 AS MODIFIED

PART 15
EXPERTS

119 References to expert

A reference to an expert in this Part –

(a) is to an expert who has been instructed to give or prepare evidence for the purpose of court proceedings; but
(b) does not include any person instructed to make a report under section 49 of the Act.

120 Restriction on filing an expert's report

(1) No person may file expert evidence unless the court or a practice direction permits, or if it is filed with the application form and is evidence –

(a) that P is a person who lacks capacity to make a decision or decisions in relation to the matter or matters to which the application relates;
(b) as to P's best interests; or
(c) that is required by any rule or practice direction to be filed with the application form.

(2) An applicant may only rely on any expert evidence so filed in support of the application form to the extent and for the purposes that the court allows.

(Rule 64(a) requires the applicant to file any evidence upon which the applicant wishes to rely with the application form.)

121 Duty to restrict expert evidence

(1) Expert evidence shall be restricted to that which is necessary to assist the court to resolve the issues in the proceedings.

(2) The court may give permission to file or adduce expert evidence as mentioned in rule 120(1) and 123(1) only if satisfied that the evidence –

(a) is necessary to assist the court to resolve the issues in the proceedings; and
(b) cannot otherwise be provided.

122 Experts – overriding duty to the court

(1) It is the duty of the expert to help the court on the matters within the expert's expertise.

(2) This duty overrides any obligation to the person from whom the expert has received instructions or by whom the expert is paid.

123 Court's power to restrict expert evidence

(1) Subject to rule 120, no party may file or adduce expert evidence unless the court or a practice direction permits.

(2) When a party applies for a direction under this rule, that party must –

    (a) identify the field in respect of which that party wishes to rely upon expert evidence, and the issues to which the expert evidence is to relate;

    (b) where practicable, identify the expert in that field upon whose evidence the party wishes to rely;

    (c) provide any other material information about the expert;

    (d) state whether the expert evidence could be obtained from a single joint expert;

    (e) provide any other information or documents required by a practice direction; and

    (f) provide a draft letter of instruction to the expert.

(2A) When deciding whether to give permission as mentioned in paragraph (1), the court is to have regard in particular to –

    (a) the issues to which the expert evidence would relate;

    (b) the questions which the expert would answer;

    (c) the impact which giving permission would be likely to have on the timetable, duration and conduct of the proceedings;

    (d) any failure to comply with any direction of the court about expert evidence; and

    (e) the cost of the expert evidence.

(3) Where a direction is given under this rule, the court shall specify –

    (a) the field or fields in respect of which the expert evidence is to be provided;

    (b) the questions which the expert is required to answer; and

    (c) the date by which the expert is to provide the evidence.

(4) The court may specify the person who is to provide the evidence referred to in paragraph (3).

(5) Where a direction is given under this rule for a party to call an expert or put in evidence an expert's report, the court shall give directions for the service of the report on the parties and on such other persons as the court may direct.

(6) The court may limit the amount of the expert's fees and expenses that the party who wishes to rely upon the expert may recover from any other party.

124 General requirement for expert evidence to be given in a written report

Expert evidence is to be given in a written report unless the court directs otherwise.

125 Written questions to experts

(1) A party may put written questions to –

    (a) an expert instructed by another party; or

    (b) a single joint expert appointed under rule 130.

about a report prepared by such a person.

(2 Written questions under paragraph (1) –

    (a) may be put once only;

(b) must be put within 28 days beginning with the date on which the expert's report was served;
(c) must be for the purpose only of clarification of the report; and
(d) must be copied and sent to the other parties at the same time as they are sent to the expert.

(3) Paragraph (2) does not apply in any case where –

(a) the court permits it to be done on a further occasion;
(b) the other party or parties agree; or
(c) any practice direction provides otherwise.

(4) An expert's answers to questions put in accordance with paragraph (1) shall be treated as part of the expert's report.

(5) Paragraph (6) applies where –

(a) a party has put a written question to an expert instructed by another party in accordance with this rule; and
(b) the expert does not answer that question.

(6) The court may make one or both of the following orders in relation to the party who instructed the expert –

(a) that the party may not rely upon the evidence of that expert; or
(b) that the party may not recover the fees and expenses of that expert, or part of them, from any other party.

(7) Unless the court directs otherwise, and subject to any final costs order that may be made, the instructing party is responsible for the payment of the expert's fees and expenses, including the expert's costs of answering questions put by any other party.

126 Contents of expert's report

(1) The court may give directions as to the matters to be covered in an expert's report.

(2) An expert's report must comply with the requirements set out in the relevant practice direction.

(3) At the end of an expert's report there must be a statement that the expert –

(a) understands his or her duty to the court; and
(b) has complied with that duty.

(4) The expert's report must state the substance of all material instructions, whether written or oral, on the basis of which the report was written.

(5) The instructions to the expert shall not be privileged against disclosure.

127 Use by one party of expert's report disclosed by another

Where a party has disclosed an expert's report, any party may use that expert's report as evidence at any hearing in the proceedings.

128 Discussions between experts

(1) The court may, at any stage, direct a discussion between experts for the purpose of requiring the experts to –

(a) identify and discuss the expert issues in the proceedings; and
(b) where possible, reach an agreed opinion on those issues.

(2) The court may specify the issues which the experts must discuss.

(3) The court may direct that following a discussion between the experts they must prepare a statement for the court showing –

(a) those issues on which they agree; and
(b) those issues on which they disagree and a summary of their reasons for disagreeing.

(4) Unless the court directs otherwise, the content of the discussions between experts may be referred to at any hearing or at any stage in the proceedings.

129 Expert's right to ask court for directions

(1) An expert may file a written request for directions to assist in carrying out the expert's functions as an expert.

(2) An expert must, unless the court directs otherwise, provide a copy of any proposed request for directions under paragraph (1) –

(a) to the party instructing the expert, at least 7 days before filing the request; and
(b) to all other parties, at least 4 days before filing it.

(3) The court, when it gives directions, may also direct that a party be served with a copy of the directions.

130 Court's power to direct that evidence is to be given by a single joint expert

(1) Where two or more parties wish to submit expert evidence on a particular issue, the court may direct that the evidence on that issue is to be given by one expert only.

(2) The parties wishing to submit the expert evidence are called 'the instructing parties'.

(3) Where the instructing parties cannot agree who should be the expert, the court may –

(a) select the expert from a list prepared or identified by the instructing parties or
(b) direct the manner by which the expert is to be selected.

131 Instructions to a single joint expert

(1) Where the court gives a direction under rule 130 for a single joint expert to be used, the instructions are to be contained in a jointly agreed letter unless the court directs otherwise.

(1A) Where the instructions are to be contained in a jointly agreed letter, in default of agreement the instructions may be determined by the court on the written request of any instructing party copied to the other instructing parties.

(2) Where the court permits the instructing parties to give separate instructions to a single joint expert, unless the court directs otherwise, when an instructing party

gives instructions to the expert, that party must at the same time send a copy of the instructions to the other instructing party or parties.

(3) The court may give directions about –

(a) the payment of the expert's fees and expenses; and
(b) any inspection, examination or experiments which the expert wishes to carry out.

(4) The court may, before an expert is instructed, limit the amount that can be paid by way of fees and expense to the expert.

(5) Unless the court directs otherwise, and subject to any final costs order that may be made, the instructing parties are jointly and severally liable for the payment of the expert's fees and expenses.'

ANNEX C: MODIFICATION OF REFERENCES ELSEWHERE IN THE COPR TO RULES IN THE NEW PARTS 1–5 AS MODIFIED

Location of reference	Rule referred to	Change reference to
Rule 33 (words in parentheses after rule)	3A	1.2
Rule 41A(a)	3A	1.2
Rule 54 (words in parentheses after rule)	84(1A)	3.6(3)
Rule 88 (words in parentheses after rule)	3A	1.2
Rule 89(6)	7A	2.3
Rule 89 (words in parentheses after rule)	7A(2)(c)	2.3(2)(c)
Rule 99 (words in parentheses after rule)	11	5.2
Part 17 heading	3A	1.2
Rule 143 (words in parentheses after rule)	3A	1.2
Part 17 Section 2 heading	3A	1.2
Rule 146A	3A	1.2
Rule 147 heading	3A	1.2
Rule 148 heading	3A	1.2
Rule 148 (words in parentheses after rule)	3A	1.2

Location of reference	Rule referred to	Change reference to
Rule 148A heading	3A	1.2
Rule 148B heading (twice)	3A	1.2
Rule 148C heading	3A	1.2
Rule 149 heading	3A	1.2
Rule 171(2)	84(3)	3.6(5)
Rule 171A(3)	7A	2.3
Rule 171A (words in parentheses after rule)	7A	2.3
Rule 188(2)	90(1)	4.1(1)

ANNEX D: MODIFICATIONS OF PRACTICE DIRECTIONS

Table A

Practice directions which supplement Parts of the CoPR now in the modified Parts 1-5 are renumbered as follows –

Practice Direction number	Supplementing	Supplementing in modified Parts 1–5	Change Practice Direction number to
2A	Part	Pilot Part 1	Pilot 1A
3A	Part 3	Pilot Part 2	Pilot 2A
3B	Part 3	Pilot Part 2	Pilot 2B
3C	Part 3	Pilot Part 2	Pilot 2C
4A	Part 4	Pilot Part 5	Pilot 5A
4B	Part 4	Pilot Part 5	Pilot 5B
12A	Part 12	Pilot Part 3	Pilot 3A
13A	Part 13	Pilot Part 4	Pilot 4A
13B	Part 13	Pilot Part 4	Pilot 4B

Table B

References in practice directions to rules of Parts which are renumbered as part of the modifications are modified as follows:

Practice Direction	Location of reference	Rule or Part referred to	Change reference to
Pilot 1A	Heading	Part 2	Pilot Part 1
	Paragraph 2	Rule 3A	Rule 1.2
	Paragraph 3	Rule 3A(2)(e)	Rule 1.2(2)(e)
	Paragraph 5	Rule 3A	Rule 1.2
	Paragraph 7	Rule 3A(2)(b) to (e)	Rule 1.2(2)(b) to (e)
	Paragraph 8	Rule 3A	Rule 1.2
	Paragraph 8	Rule 3A(2)(b)	Rule 1.2(2)(b)
	Paragraph 8	Rule 3A(2)(c)	Rule 1.2(2)(c)
	Paragraph 8	Rule 3A	Rule 1.2
	Paragraph 9	Rule 6	Rule 2.1
	Paragraph 12	Rule 3A(2)(c)	Rule 1.2(2)(c)
	Paragraph 12	Rule 3A(2)(d) or (e)	Rule 1.2(2)(d) or (e)
	Paragraph 13 (three times)	Rule 3A	Rule 1.2
Pilot 2A	Heading	Part 3	Pilot Part 2
	Paragraph 1.1	Rule 7A	Rule 2.3
	Paragraph 1.2	Rule 7A(1)	Rule 2.3(1)
	Paragraph 3(a)	Rule 25(2)(a)	Rule 3.1(2)(a)
	Paragraph 3(b)	Rule 25(2)(m)	Rule 3.1(2)(m)
	Paragraph 3(c)	Rule 25(5)	Rule 3.1(5)
	Paragraph 3(d)	Rule 25(6)	Rule 3.1(6)
Pilot 2B	Heading	Part 3	Pilot Part 2
	Paragraph 1.1	Rule 6	Rule 2.1
Pilot 2C	Heading	Part 3	Pilot Part 2
	Paragraph 1	Rule 9(2)	Rule 2.5(2)
Pilot 3A	Heading	Part 12	Pilot Part 3

Court of Protection Rules 2007 **PD**

	Paragraph 1	Rule 86	Rule 3.8
Pilot 4A	Heading	Part 13	Pilot Part 4
	Paragraph 2	Rules 90 to 92	Rules 4.1 to 4.3
	Part 1 heading	Rules 90, 91 or 92	Rules 4.1, 4.2 or 4.3
	Paragraph 4	Rules 90, 91 or 92	Rules 4.1, 4.2 or 4.3
	Paragraph 5	Rules 90 to 92	Rules 4.1 to 4.3
	Paragraph 6	Rules 90, 91 or 92	Rules 4.1, 4.2 or 4.3
	Paragraph 7	Rule 91(1)	Rule 4.2(1)
	Paragraph 7	Rule 91	Rule 4.2
	Paragraph 9	Rule 92	Rule 4.3
	Paragraph 11	Rule 92(2)	Rule 4.3(2)
	Paragraph 12(a)(i),	Rule 91(3)	Rule 4.2(4)
	Paragraph 12(b)(i)	Rule 92(2)	Rule 4.3(2)
	Paragraph 15	Rule 19	Rule 5.11
	Paragraph 30	Rule 91	Rule 4.2
	Paragraph 33(c)	Rule 3A	Rule 1.2
Pilot 4B	Heading	Part 13	Pilot Part 4
Pilot 5A	Heading	Part 4	Pilot Part 5
	Paragraph 1	Rule 10(2)	Rule 5.1(2)
	Paragraph 8	Rule 19	Rule 5.11
Pilot 5B	Heading	Part 4	Pilot Part 5
	Paragraph 1	Rule 11	Rule 5.2
	Paragraph 1	Rule 11(1)	Rule 5.2(1)
	Paragraph 6(a)	Rule 19	Rule 5.11
	Paragraph 16 – words in parentheses after paragraph	Rule 14	Rule 5.6

PART IV

7A	Paragraph 2(d)	Rule 3A	Rule 1.2
8A	Paragraph 4	Rule 84(4)(a)	Rule 3.6(6)(a)
9A	Paragraph 2(c)	Rule 19	Rule 5.11
	Paragraph 3	Rule 19	Rule 5.11
	Paragraph 5	Rule 19	Rule 5.11
	Paragraph 6	Rule 11	Rule 5.2
	Paragraph 8	Rule 14	Rule 5.6
	Paragraph 8 – words in parentheses after paragraph	Practice Direction B accompanying Part 4	Practice Direction Pilot 5B
	Paragraph 13	Rule 10	Rule 5.1
	Paragraph 13	Practice Direction A accompanying Part 4	Practice Direction Pilot 5A
9H	Paragraph 6 – words in parentheses after paragraph	Practice Direction B accompanying Part 4	Practice Direction Pilot 5B
10A	Paragraph 3	Rule 19	Rule 5.11
	Paragraph 6	Rules 90 to 92	Rules 4.1 to 4.3
10B	Paragraph 14	Part 12	Pilot Part 3
10AA	Paragraph 49	Part 13	Pilot Part 4
	Paragraph 49	Practice Direction A to Part 13	Practice Direction Pilot 4A
	Paragraph 49	Rule 92	Rule 4.3
	Paragraph 49	Rule 93	Rule 4.4
11A	Paragraph 8 – words in parentheses after paragraph	Practice Direction 12A	Practice Direction Pilot 3A
14A	Paragraph 2	Rule 19	Rule 5.11
	Paragraph 3(a)	Rule 19	Rule 5.11

	Paragraph 33	Rule 19	Rule 5.11
	Paragraph 34(a)	Rule 19	Rule 5.11
	Paragraph 44 – words in parentheses after paragraph	Practice Direction B accompanying Part 4	Practice Direction Pilot 5B
	Paragraph 45	Rule 14	Rule 5.6
14D	Paragraph 7	Rule 23	Rule 5.15
14E	Paragraph 1(b)	Rule 85(2)(a)	Rule 3.7(2)(a)
	Paragraph 14	Rule 19	Rule 5.11
14E (Pilot)	Paragraph 1(b)	Rule 85(2)(a)	Rule 3.7(2)(a)
	Paragraph 3(b)	Rule 3A	Rule 1.2
	Paragraph 3(b)	Rule 3A(5)	Rule 1.2(5)
	Paragraph 21	Rule 19	Rule 5.11
	Annex (draft order) paragraph 10(c)	Rule 3A	Rule 1.2
	Annex (draft order) paragraph 17	Rule 3A(5)	Rule 1.2(5)
15A	Paragraph 12	Rule 14	Rule 5.6
	Paragraph 12 – words in parentheses after paragraph	Practice Direction B accompanying Part 4	Practice Direction Pilot 5B
17B	Heading	Rule 3A	Rule 1.2
20B	Paragraph 1.2	Rule 6 and Practice Direction 3B	Rule 2.1 and Practice Direction Pilot 2B
Practice Direction – Transparency Pilot	Heading	Part 13	Pilot Part 4
	Paragraph 1.1	Rule 9A	Rule 2.6

PART IV COURT OF PROTECTION PRACTICE 2016

	Paragraph 1.2	Part 13 and Practice Direction 13A	Pilot Part 4 and Practice Direction Pilot 4A
	Heading above paragraph 2.1	Rule 92(1)(a) and (2)	Rule 4.3(1)(a) and (2)
	Paragraph 2.1(a)	Rule 92(1)(a)	Rule 4.3(1)(a)
	Paragraph 2.1(b)	Rule 92(2)	Rule 4.3(2)
	Paragraph 2.4	Rule 92(1)(b) or (c)	Rule 4.3(1)(b) or (c)
Practice Direction – Section 49 Reports Pilot	Paragraph 1.1	Rule 9A	Rule 2.6

1072

Practice Direction – Section 49 Reports Pilot

This Practice Direction supplements Part 14 of the Court of Protection Rules 2007

Note—This pilot Practice Direction is published in draft format for information only; it will not be signed or come into force until June 2016. Further amendments may be made to the pilot Practice Direction during that time. The final pilot Practice Direction will be available on the Courts and Tribunals Judiciary website when the pilot commences.

1.1 This Practice Direction is made under rule 9A of the Court of Protection Rules 2007 ('CoPR'). It provides for a pilot scheme for a revised approach to applications for, and the court's consideration on its own initiative of, orders requiring a report under section 49 of the Act.

1.2 Where the pilot scheme operates, Practice Direction 14E (Pilot) as set out in the Schedule will apply instead of Practice Direction 14E.

1.3 The pilot scheme is to –
   (a) operate from [DATE A] to [DATE B];
   (b) apply in every case in which, on or after [DATE A] –
      (i) an application is made for an order requiring a section 49 report; or
      (ii) the court considers on its own initiative whether to make such an order.

SCHEDULE

Practice Direction 14A (Pilot)

This Practice Direction supplements Part 14 of the Court of Protection Rules 2007

General

1 Attention is drawn to –
   (a) section 49 of the Act – which makes provision for the court to require a report in proceedings brought in respect of P where the court is considering a question relating to P;
   (b) rule 85(2)(a) – which provides that the court, when giving directions, may require a section 49 report and give directions about any such report;
   (c) rule 117 – which sets out the duties of a person required to prepare a section 49 report and specifies to whom the report may be sent; and
   (d) rule 118 – which makes provision for the court to permit written questions to be put to a person who has made a section 49 report.

The court's direction for a report

2 The Annex to this Practice Direction contains the form of an order requiring a report under section 49 of the Act and the forms of directions relating to the report. When requiring a section 49 report, the court will as far as possible base its order and directions on those forms. For practical reasons, the order should be self-contained and not form part of other directions.

3 The following are common factors which the court may consider when deciding whether to order a section 49 report –
   (a) where P objects to the substantive application or wishes to be heard by the court and does not qualify for legal aid;

(b) where it has not been possible to appoint a litigation friend or rule 3A representative, including where the court has made a direction under rule 3A(5);
(c) where a party is a litigant in person and does not qualify for legal aid;
(d) where the public body has recent knowledge of P; or it is reasonably expected that they have recent knowledge of P; or should have knowledge due to their statutory responsibilities under housing, social and/or health care legislation;
(e) the role of the public body is likely to be relevant to the decisions which the court will be asked to make;
(f) the application relates to an attorney or deputy and involves the exercise of the functions of the Public Guardian;
(g) evidence before the court does not adequately confirm the position regarding P's capacity or where it is borderline; or if information is required to inform any best interests decision to be made in relation to P by the court.

Reports by Public Guardian or a Court of Protection Visitor

4 Where a report is to be prepared by either the Public Guardian or a Court of Protection Visitor, a copy of the approved order, the directions and the information described in paragraph 14 below will be sent by the Court to the Public Guardian.

5 In the case of a report which is to be made by a Court of Protection Visitor, the Public Guardian must ensure that a person is nominated from the panel of the General Visitors or the panel of Special Visitors, as appropriate.

6 The nomination of a Court of Protection Visitor should be made before the end of the period of 7 days beginning with the date on which the Public Guardian received a copy of the order.

Reports under arrangements made by a local authority or an NHS body

7 Wherever practicable, before making an application for an order requiring a report under section 49, a party to proceedings should use their best endeavours to:

(a) make contact with an appropriate person within the relevant local authority or NHS body so they are made aware that an application is to be made; its purpose; and the issues or questions which are hoped to be addressed within the report;
(b) identify a named person or by reference to their office ('the senior officer') within the relevant local authority or NHS body who will be able to receive the court order on its behalf; and
(c) enquire as to the reasonableness and time scales for providing the report should the court order it.

8 The party making the application must submit a draft letter of instructions for the purpose of accompanying the order.

9 The court will make enquiry of the party making the application as to what efforts have been made to comply with paragraph 7 above, and the response of the relevant local authority or NHS body, and will take this into consideration before making an order.

10 Where a report is to be prepared under arrangements made by a local authority or an NHS body, a copy of the approved order (which is binding, notwithstanding

that it may not yet be sealed), the information described in paragraph 14 below and the accompanying letter of instruction will be served by either (i) the party who made the application for a section 49 report or (ii) in the event that no party made the application, by the party determined by the court to be the most appropriate party to arrange service on the senior officer as soon as is reasonably practicable but in any event within 48 hours of the making of the order.

11 Upon receipt of the order the senior officer must ensure that –

(a) a person with appropriate expertise/knowledge is nominated to make the report; and
(b) the parties are notified of the name and contact details of the nominated person as soon as practicable.

12 The nomination should be made before the end of the period of 7 days beginning with the date on which the senior officer received a copy of the order.

13 The order must follow the format as set out in the Annex to this Practice Direction and specify the matters required to be addressed in paragraphs 9 and 10 therein.

Access to Information and interview P

14 The court will generally provide, or give permission to the party applying for the section 49 order to provide, to the person who is to produce a report –

(a) a copy of the application form, its annexes and any supporting evidence as may be redacted by direction of the court;
(b) the name and contact details of P;
(c) the name and contact details of the parties;
(d) the name and contact details of any legal representative of a person specified in (b) or (c); and
(e) name and contact details of such other persons who are reasonably likely to be able to provide assistance to the nominated person for the completion of the report.

15 The court order requiring the report, the directions relating to it and the information described in paragraph 14 will generally be sent when the order is served by the party who is required to do so, by first class mail, electronic mail or by facsimile. If the circumstances warrant a different form of communication, the documents and information will also be sent by first class mail, electronic mail or by facsimile at the first available opportunity.

16 Section 49(7) of the Act sets out other documents relating to P which the Public Guardian or a Court of Protection Visitor may examine or take copies of for the purpose of making the report. Where appropriate, the order may also allow the same documents to be examined and copied by the nominated person who is to prepare the section 49 report under arrangements made by the relevant local authority or NHS body.

17 Sections 49(8) and (9) of the Act sets out that the Public Guardian or a Court of Protection Visitor may interview P in private. Where appropriate, the order may also allow P to be interviewed in private by the nominated person who is to prepare the section 49 report under arrangements made by the relevant local authority or NHS body.

The contents of the report

18 The person required to prepare a section 49 report must –

   (a) prepare it having regard to the provisions of rule 117;
   (b) produce it in the manner specified in this Practice Direction (subject to any directions given by the court); and
   (c) produce it in accordance with the timetable set out in the court's directions.

19 The report should contain four main sections. These are –

   (a) the details of the person who prepared the report;
   (b) the details of P;
   (c) the matters and material considered in preparing the report; and
   (d) the conclusions reached.

20 In the first section (details of the person who prepared the report), the report should –

   (a) state the full name of the person who prepared the report;
   (b) state whether that person was appointed under section 49(2) or (3) of the Act;
   (c) state whether that person is –
       (i) the Public Guardian;
       (ii) a General Visitor;
       (iii) a Special Visitor;
       (iv) an officer, employee or other person nominated by a local authority; or
       (v) an officer, employee, or other person nominated by an NHS body;
   (d) state that person's occupation or employment (for example, social worker employed by a local authority or general practitioner in private practice); and
   (e) list that person's qualifications and experience.

21 In the second section (P's details), the report should (unless an order to the contrary pursuant to rule 19 has been made) –

   (a) state P's full name, date of birth and present place of residence;
   (b) state P's nationality, racial origin, cultural background and religious persuasion (if appropriate);
   (c) identify P's immediate family (specifying their relationship to P and contact details;
   (d) identify any other person who has a significant role in P's life (for example, a close friend or a carer) specifying their role and contact details; and
   (e) give a summary of P's medical history.

22 In the third section (matters and material considered), the report should –

   (a) list any interview conducted with P (specifying time and place);
   (b) list any interview conducted with one or more persons other than P (specifying time and place);
   (c) state –
       (i) whether any examination of P was conducted by a Special Visitor under section 49(9) of the Act; and
       (ii) the name and qualifications of any person who assisted with any such examination;
   (d) give a summary of any key events in P's life which appear to have a direct bearing on the matters to be dealt with in the report;

(e) set out the details of any of the following material which was relied on in the preparation of the report –
  (i) any literature or other material;
  (ii) any records obtained under section 49(7) of the Act;
(f) set out the details of facts and opinions relied on in the preparation of the report (ensuring that there is a clear distinction between the two);
(g) where there is a range of opinion on an issue addressed in the report –
  (i) summarise the range of opinion;
  (ii) state the views held by the person who prepared the report and give reasons for them; and
(h) indicate which of the facts are within the knowledge of the person who prepared the report.

23 In the fourth section (conclusions), the report should –

(a) identify any issues or questions which were specified in the directions given by the court as being matters in which the court had a particular interest;
(b) address clearly such issues or questions;
(c) state clearly all conclusions reached by the person who prepared the report;
(d) state clearly the recommendations made by the person who prepared the report; and
(e) contain a statement of truth in the following terms –
'I confirm that insofar as the facts stated in my report are within my own knowledge I have made clear which they are, and I believe them to be true, and that the opinions I have expressed represent my true and complete professional opinion.'

ANNEX

Order for section 49 report

Requirement for section 49 report

1 A report is required pursuant to section 49 of the Mental Capacity Act 2005 in relation to [*insert name of P*], under Court of Protection case number [*insert case number*].

Person required to prepare the report (the author)

2 The report must be prepared by [the Public Guardian] [a Court of Protection Visitor who is a General Visitor] [a Court of Protection Visitor who is a Special Visitor] [a person nominated by the local authority] [XX, a person nominated by the local authority and considered by them to have the appropriate expertise/knowledge to provide the report][a person nominated by the NHS body][YY, a person nominated by the NHS body and considered by them to have the appropriate expertise/knowledge to provide the report].

3 [In the case of a report to be prepared by [a Special Visitor, the Visitor] [a medically qualified practitioner, the practitioner] may carry out in private a [medical] [psychiatric] [psychological] examination of P's capacity or condition].

Producing the report

4 [The report must be made to the court in writing] [The report must be made orally to the court].

5 The report must be produced on or before [*insert date*].

6 [Where the report is made in writing, it must be delivered to the court by [first class post][electronic mail][facsimile].

Context of report

7 The court has received an application for the following [order/direction/declaration]:

[*insert brief details of application*, for example,
- (a) XY be [appointed][removed] as the [deputy][attorney] for property and affairs/personal welfare for [*insert the name of P*];
- (b) [*insert the name of P*] lacks mental capacity to [*insert decision, for example conduct the proceedings/ objects to* .... / *decide where to reside*];
- (a) it is in the best interests of [*insert the name of P*] that [*insert issue*];
- (b) it is lawful in respect of [*insert name of P*] that [*insert issue*].

8 [*insert case summary*].

Content of report

9 Subject to any directions given under paragraph 11, the report must contain all the material required by relevant practice direction and be prepared in the form there specified.

10 The court is particularly interested in the following issues or questions and these must also be addressed in the report:

[*for example*
- (a) whether [*insert the name of P*] has capacity in accordance with sections 2 and 3 of the Mental Capacity Act 2005, to [*insert issue, for example, object to/conduct proceedings/decide where to live*];
- (b) if [he/she] lacks capacity, ascertain to the extent it is practicable and appropriate [his/her] present wishes and feelings and the beliefs and values that would be likely to influence [him/her] with regard to [*insert the matter to which the application relates*];
- (c) if [he/she] lacks capacity, ascertain [his/her] present wishes and feelings as to how [his /her] participation could be secured by the appointment of a representative pursuant to Rule 3A;
- (d) whether [he/she] should have the opportunity to address (directly or indirectly) the judge determining the application and the circumstances in which that should occur;
- (e) describe [*insert the name of P*]'s circumstances;
- (f) what services and support would be provided to [*insert the name of P*]/funded for [*insert the name of P*] by [*insert the name of the public body*];
- (g) whether what is sought by the application could be effectively achieved in a way which is less restrictive of [*insert name of P*]'s rights and freedom;
- (h) the Public Guardian's views as to ....].

11 The report need not address the following:

[(a)   ;
(b)   ].

Persons to whom report is likely to be disclosed

12 The report is to be prepared on the assumption that the court will pursuant to rule 117(4) send a copy of it to the parties and such other persons as the court may direct. The court further directs that the report be sent to [*insert the name of P*][*members of P's family*][*XX County Council/ NHS Hospital Trust/ Clinical Commissioning Group/Local Health Board*][the parties only] [the parties and their legal representatives] [*such other persons as the court may direct*].
]

Persons to contact

13 The author of the report is authorised to contact and seek to interview the following person(s) for the purpose of preparing the report, with their contact details provided with this order:

   (a) [*insert the name of P*] [in private][in the presence of XX];
   (b) [the parties];
   (c) [their legal representatives];
   (d) [*Others which may include* for example, *family, care and health providers*].

14 The author of the report [may interview [*insert the name of P*] in private] [may not interview [*insert the name of P*]].

Access to records

15 For the purpose of enabling the author to prepare the report, [he/she] is authorised to examine and have a copy of the following, which relate to [insert the name of P] and are relevant to the application:

    [for example,
   (a) a copy of the application form, its annexes and any supporting evidence [*such papers may be redacted as required by the court*];
   (b) any health record;
   (c) any record of, or held by, a local authority and compiled in connection with a social services function, and
   (d) any record held by a person registered under Part 2 of the Care Standards Act 2000 or Chapter 2 of Part 1 of the Health and Social Care Act 2008.]

Where a report is made under arrangements by a local authority or NHS Body

16 [The party who made the application for a section 49 report] [the party the court decides is the most appropriate] shall serve a copy of the order on [the senior officer who will accept this order on behalf of the [*insert name of public body*] and who will inform the court of the name of the person who will prepare the report] [XX being the person identified as having the appropriate expertise/knowledge to provide the report] within 7 days of service of this order, notwithstanding that in the event the order has not been sealed by the court, it shall be binding.

Record of lack of representation

17 Pursuant to rule 3A(5), the Court records that [insert name of P] has been directed to be joined as a party but such joinder has not occurred because no litigation friend or accredited legal representative has been appointed because [insert reasons].

Other directions

18

[(a) This order having been made without a hearing or without notice to any person affected by it; P, any party to the proceedings and any person affected by this order may apply to the court within 21 days of the order being served for reconsideration of this order pursuant to rule 89 of the Court of Protection Rules 2007 by filing an application notice (Form COP9) in accordance with Part 10 of those Rules]

[*or*]

[(a) This order having been made [at an attended hearing] (*or if urgent*) [at an urgent hearing] leave to any person adversely affected by this order to apply to the court within 7 days of the order being served, to set aside, vary or stay the relevant disputed provision of this order by filing an application notice (Form COP9) in accordance with Part 10 of the Court of Protection Rules 2007];

[(b)   ]

PART V

Other Statutory Instruments, Practice Directions and guidance

PART V

Other Statutory Instruments, Practice Directions and guidance

PART V: Other Statutory Instruments, Practice Directions and guidance

Contents

Statutory Instruments and Practice Directions	1085
Civil Procedure Rules 1998	1085
Practice Direction 21 – Children and Protected Parties	1107
Practice Direction 44 – General Rules About Costs	1123
Practice Direction 46 – Costs Special Cases	1142
Practice Direction 47 – Procedure for Detailed Assessment of Costs and Default Provisions	1158
Practice Direction 48 – Part 2 of The Legal Aid, Sentencing and Punishment of Offenders Act 2012 Relating to Civil Litigation Funding And Costs: Transitional Provision And Exceptions	1178
Practice Direction 52A – Appeals: General Provisions	1189
Practice Direction 52C – Appeals to the Court of Appeal	1197
Mental Capacity Act 2005 (Independent Mental Capacity Advocates) (General) Regulations 2006	1262
Court of Protection Fees Order 2007	1265
Lasting Powers of Attorney, Enduring Powers of Attorney and Public Guardian Regulations 2007	1276
Mental Capacity Act 2005 (Transfer of Proceedings) Order 2007	1300
Mental Capacity Act 2005 (Transitional and Consequential Provisions) Order 2007	1303
Public Guardian (Fees, etc) Regulations 2007	1321
Mental Capacity (Deprivation of Liberty: Appointment of Relevant Person's Representative) Regulations 2008	1326
Mental Capacity (Deprivation of Liberty: Standard Authorisations, Assessments and Ordinary Residence) Regulations 2008	1332
Family Procedure Rules 2010	1341
Practice Direction 6B – Service out of the Jurisdiction	1345
Practice Direction 6C – Disclosure of Addresses by Government Departments 13 February 1989 as amended by Practice Direction 20 July 1995	1368
Court Funds Rules 2011	1373

Public Guardian Practice Notes — 1390

Public Guardian Practice Note No 1 of 2010: Deputies and Attorneys: Release of Visit Reports — 1390

Public Guardian Practice Note No 2 of 2010: Deputies and Attorneys: The Independent Safeguarding Authority — 1393

Public Guardian Practice Note No 1 of 2011: Court of Protection Costs: The Public Guardian and Costs in Court of Protection Proceedings — 1396

Public Guardian Practice Note No 2 of 2011: Updating Public Guardian Registers: Notification of Death — 1399

Public Guardian Practice Note No 1 of 2012: Deputy Final Reports: Requesting the LPA, EPA Final Report pursuant to Regulation 40 of the LPA, EPA and Public Guardian Regulations 2007 — 1403

Public Guardian Practice Note No 2 of 2012 (updated September 2015): Gifts: Deputies and EPA/LPA Attorneys — 1407

Public Guardian Practice Note No 3 of 2012: Surety Bonds: Statement of Surety Bonds Expectations of the Public Guardian — 1415

Public Guardian Practice Note No 1 of 2016: Public Authority Deputyship Responsibilities — 1418

Public Guardian Practice Note No 2 of 2016: Public Guardian Practice Note No 2 of 2016: OPG's Approach to Solicitor Client Accounts — 1419

Law Society Practice Notes — 1420

Law Society Practice Note of 8 December 2011: Lasting Powers of Attorney — 1420

Law Society Practice Note of 13 June 2013: Financial Abuse — 1440

Law Society Practice Note of 17 March 2014: Mental Capacity: International Aspects — 1456

Law Society Practice Note of 2 July 2015: Meeting the Needs of Vulnerable Clients — 1462

Other Guidance — 1484

Practice Direction of 24 March 2012: Citation of Authorities — 1484

Practice Guidance of 16 January 2014: Transparency in the Court of Protection – Publication of Judgments — 1486

Guidance Note: Acting as a litigation friend in the Court of Protection — 1490

Practice Direction of 26 March 2015: Committal for Contempt of Court – Open Court — 1505

Practice Guidance of 24 June 2015: Committal for Contempt of Court – Open Court — 1508

Statutory Instruments and Practice Directions

Civil Procedure Rules 1998, SI 1998/3132

****

PART 21
CHILDREN AND PROTECTED PARTIES

Overview—Part 21 contains provisions which apply in proceedings involving children and protected parties. The general rule is that a child must have a litigation friend to conduct proceedings on his behalf unless the court orders otherwise. A protected party must always have a litigation friend. The test for whether a person is a protected party for the purposes of CPR 21 is that defined by sections 2 and 3 of the Mental Capacity Act 2005, namely whether, by reason of an impairment or disturbance in the functioning of the mind or brain, he lacks capacity at the material time to make a decision because he is unable to understand, retain, use or weigh relevant information or communicate his decision. Part 21 contains provisions which regulate the appointment and replacement of litigation friends and the termination of their appointment. There are specific provisions which deal with the compromise of claims involving children and protected parties and the control of money recovered by children and protected parties (a protected party who lacks capacity to manage and control money recovered by him or on his behalf is defined as a 'protected beneficiary'). There are also provisions which regulate the payment to litigation friends from money recovered on behalf of children and protected parties of certain costs and expenses which are no longer recoverable from an opponent by virtue of the changes brought about by the Legal Aid, Sentencing and Punishment of Offenders Act 2012.

Those provisions that relate only to children are generally omitted below

Procedural Guide—See Guide PG5, set out in Part II of this work.

21.1 Scope of this Part

(1) This Part –
    (a) contains special provisions which apply in proceedings involving children and protected parties;
    (b) sets out how a person becomes a litigation friend; and
    (c) does not apply to –
        (i) proceedings under Part 75;
        (ii) enforcement of specified debts by taking control of goods; or
        (iii) applications in relation to enforcement or specified debts by taking control of goods,
    where one of the parties to the proceedings is a child.

(2) In this Part –
    (a) 'the 2005 Act' means the Mental Capacity Act 2005;
    (b) 'child' means a person under 18;
    (c) 'lacks capacity' means lacks capacity within the meaning of the 2005 Act;
    (d) 'protected party' means a party, or an intended party, who lacks capacity to conduct the proceedings;
    (e) 'protected beneficiary' means a protected party who lacks capacity to manage and control any money recovered by him or on his behalf or for his benefit in the proceedings.
    (f) 'specified debts' has the same meaning as in rule 75.1(2)(e); and

(g) 'taking control of goods' means using the procedure to take control of goods contained in Schedule 12 to the Tribunals, Courts and Enforcement Act 2007.

(Rules 6.13 and 6.25 contain provisions about the service of documents on children and protected parties.)

(Rule 46.4 deals with costs where money is payable by or to a child or protected party.)

Amendments—SI 2003/3361; SI 2007/2204; SI 2008/2178; SI 2013/1974; SI 2014/407.

Procedural Guide—See Guide 6, set out in Part II of this work.

Practice Direction—See generally Practice Direction 21.

'Part 75' (r 21.1(1)(c))—This deals with traffic enforcement.

Background—The Civil Procedure Rules 1998 (CPR) Part 21 made special provision for two categories of litigant:

(1) 'children' who are, by reason of age, deemed incapable of acting personally unless permitted by the court; and
(2) 'patients' who were treated as being incapable of conducting the proceedings.

For the purpose of the then CPR, 'patient' meant 'a person who, by reason of mental disorder within the meaning of the Mental Health Act 1983 is incapable of managing and administering his property and affairs'. This test was also used to establish the jurisdiction of the former Court of Protection to administer the property and affairs of patients under the Mental Health Act 1983 (MHA 1983), Part VII (ss 93–11). 'Mental disorder' was defined by MHA 1983, s 1(2) as 'mental illness, arrested or incomplete development of mind, psychopathic disorder and any other disorder or disability of mind'. Nothing in the definition was to be construed as implying that a person may be dealt with as suffering from mental disorder by reason only of 'promiscuity or other immoral conduct, sexual deviancy or dependence on alcohol or drugs' (MHA 1983, s 1(3)).

Following the 2007 rule amendments the term 'patient' was replaced by 'protected party' and a new definition applies. This became necessary because of the implementation of the Mental Capacity Act 2005 (MCA 2005).

Mental Capacity Act 2005—This legislation established from 1 October 2007 a comprehensive statutory framework for decisions to be made by and on behalf of those whose capacity to make their own decisions is in doubt. A regional Court of Protection has jurisdiction to make declarations or decisions or to appoint a deputy to make decisions on the person's behalf. A number of district judges and circuit judges are appointed to sit in the new Court and difficult capacity issues may be referred to them.

The general principles that apply within the mental capacity jurisdiction are to be found in the MCA 2005, ss 1–4. They include a new test of 'incapacity' and a 'best interests' approach to any delegated decision-making according to a checklist of factors, thus now incorporated into Part 21. (For an overview of the Act see Section 3 of this book.)

Persons who lack capacity—There are basically three categories of person who may come within the definition of a protected party, namely those with:

(1) a mental illness – the largest group comprises elderly people who become mentally impaired (e g by senile dementia or Alzheimer's disease);
(2) learning disabilities – the previous term was 'mental handicap'; and
(3) brain damage – the courts generally encounter persons with an acquired brain injury. If the damage was caused during the developmental years (e g in childbirth) this will be classed as learning disabilities.

Scope of provision—A representative known as a 'litigation friend' must generally be appointed to conduct the proceedings in the name and on behalf of a child or protected party, and any settlement or compromise must be approved by the Court.

'child' (r 21.1(2)(a))—Defined as 'a person under 18' by r 21.1(2)(a). There is provision for the child to act personally even before attaining that age (r 21.2(3)) but approval of the Court is required and may subsequently be withdrawn (r 21.2(5)).

'**protected party**' (r 21.1(2)(d))—Means 'a party, or an intended party, who lacks capacity [within the meaning of MCA 2005] to conduct the proceedings'. Lack of capacity is also defined (see below).

'**protected beneficiary**' (r 21.1(2)(e))—Means 'a protected party who lacks capacity to manage and control any money recovered by him or on his behalf or for his benefit in the proceedings'. It was necessary to introduce this additional definition because of the decision-specific nature of tests of capacity. A party may lack capacity to conduct the proceedings but nevertheless have the capacity to manage and control his or her money. However, this definition is insufficient for two reasons. First, there is an assumption that only a person who is a protected party may be incapable of financial management. The rule fails to make allowance for the converse, namely that a litigant who has capacity to conduct court proceedings may not have capacity to manage his or her financial affairs. This situation might arise, for example, where a wealthy man with complex financial affairs wished to bring a small claim.

Secondly, if the approach of the civil court is to be compatible with that of the Court of Protection it becomes necessary to aggregate the damages recovered with the existing wealth of the protected party and then to decide whether there is capacity to manage the entirety. The rules committee has only looked at this from the perspective of a brain injured litigant who recovers a substantial sum and did not previously have any personal savings or income of significance.

'**child**' or '**protected party**'—It is possible for a child also to be a protected party and this may be relevant if that condition will continue to subsist on ceasing to be a child (e g with regard to the disposal of money awarded to the child). Thus a child who has severe learning disabilities will continue to be a protected party even after attaining the age of 18.

'**litigation friend**' (r 21.1(1)(b))—This expression is used for the representative, whether the party is a claimant or defendant, and replaces both 'next friend' and 'guardian ad litem' used in previous rules.

'**lacks capacity**'—This term is expressly defined as being 'within the meaning of the Mental Capacity Act 2005' so as to incorporate the principles that apply within that legislation and the jurisprudence that will develop in the new mental capacity jurisdiction. Nevertheless, many of the principles that have evolved under previous case-law are still relevant. MCA 2005, s 2(1) sets out the definition:

'A person lacks capacity in relation to a matter if at the material time he is unable to make a decision for himself in relation to the matter because of an impairment of, or a disturbance in the functioning of, the mind or brain.'

This is a two-stage test, because it must be established, first, that there is an impairment of, or disturbance in the functioning of, the person's mind or brain (the diagnostic threshold); and, secondly, that the impairment or disturbance is sufficient to render the person incapable of making that particular decision. The impairment or disturbance may be permanent or temporary and no reference is made to the degree of impairment or disturbance. This provides a useful screening process – merely being eccentric is not a basis for being deprived of one's right to conduct litigation.

MCA 2005, s 3(1) provides that a person is unable to make a decision if unable to:

- understand the information relevant to the decision;
- retain that information;
- use or weigh that information as part of the process of making the decision; or
- communicate his or her decision (whether by talking, using sign language or any other means).

Explanations must be provided in ways appropriate to the person's circumstances (using simple language, visual aids or any other means). This is not a significant change of approach because it was previously held (in regard to medical treatment though the test was no doubt universal) that the individual must be able to (a) understand and retain information, and (b) weigh that information in the balance to arrive at a choice (per Butler-Sloss LJ in *Re MB* [1997] 2 FLR 426, CA).

'**conduct the proceedings**'—Tests of capacity are now seen as being decision-specific, so it is the capacity of the party to conduct the particular proceedings that is relevant rather than capacity to manage and administer his or her property and affairs in general (as defined under the former test). Thus a person might be a protected party for complex personal injury proceedings yet not for a simultaneous small claim.

Even under the former rule, the Court of Appeal concentrated on the issue-specific nature of tests of capacity and decided that the test related to the individual and his immediate problems. Thus Chadwick LJ in *Masterman-Lister v Brutton & Co and Jewell & anor* [2003] 1 WLR 1511 stated:

'[T]he test to be applied ... is whether the party to legal proceedings is capable of understanding, with the assistance of such proper explanation from legal advisers and experts in other disciplines as the case may require, the issues on which his consent or decision is likely to be necessary in the course of those proceedings. If he has capacity to understand that which he needs to understand in order to pursue or defend a claim, I can see no reason why the law – whether substantive or procedural – should require the interposition of a next friend or guardian ad litem (or, as such a person is now described in the Civil Procedure Rules, a litigation friend).'

Presumptions as to capacity—Adults are presumed competent until the contrary is proved. This is relevant to the burden of proof. In general the person who alleges that an individual lacks capacity must prove this (upon the balance of probabilities rather than beyond reasonable doubt). Capacity, because it can vary, must be assessed at the time that the decision is to be taken. If an individual has previously been found to lack capacity, there is no presumption of continuance, but if there is clear evidence of incapacity for a considerable period, then the burden of proof may be more easily discharged even though it remains on whoever asserts incapacity.

Doubts about capacity may arise for several reasons but these should not be confused with tests of capacity. Thus the status of the individual (being elderly and living in a nursing home), the outcome of a decision (one that no person in his or her right mind would be expected to reach) or appearance, behaviour or conversation may cause capacity to be questioned, but these factors do not determine capacity. It is not unusual for outward appearances to create a false impression of lack of capacity (eg physical disabilities may obstruct the power of speech or movement) even where mental capacity is not affected. Conversely, a person may appear capable through social training and experience when in reality he or she lacks the understanding needed to make decisions. In all these situations a proper assessment of capacity should be made.

Mental disorder—The existence of a mental disorder is no longer a criterion for a person being treated as incapable of conducting proceedings. The new diagnostic threshold of 'an impairment of, or a disturbance in the functioning of, the mind or brain' was introduced because the term 'mental disorder' has acquired distinct interpretations in the context of treatment under the Mental Health legislation. Being mentally disordered does not necessarily result in a person being a protected party, and an assessment of capacity must still be made. Thus:

(a) an individual may be sectioned under the provisions of MHA 1983 yet not be a protected party as regards court proceedings because the criteria are different (consider *Re C (Adult: Refusal of Medical Treatment)* [1994] 1 FLR 31); and

(b) an individual with learning disabilities may still have the capacity to conduct litigation depending on the complexity and the support available.

Communication difficulties—Other methods of communication should always be attempted when necessary and an interpreter may be provided for those with communication difficulties in the same way as for those who do not understand the language used in court.

Physical disabilities—Where the ability of an individual to conduct or participate in proceedings is impaired due to physical disabilities, steps can be taken by the court to overcome these. Thus the loop system may be provided for those who are hard of hearing and enlarged print may be used in all documents for those whose sight is impaired. If necessary, hearings should be conducted in a courtroom or chambers with disabled access but they may now be conducted elsewhere should the need arise (r 2.7).

Tests of capacity—There is no universal test of capacity. Legal capacity depends on understanding rather than wisdom; the quality of the decision is irrelevant as long as the person understands what he or she is deciding. Legal tests vary according to the particular transaction or act involved but are generally issue-specific, ie they relate to the matters which the individual is required to understand. As capacity depends on time and context, a decision as to capacity in one context does not bind a court that has to consider the same issue in a different context.

A person found to be a protected party may nevertheless be capable of getting married, signing an enduring power of attorney (*Re K; Re F* [1988] 2 FLR 15) or consenting to medical treatment (*Re MB* [1997] 2 FLR 426, CA), because the matters to be taken into account are different. For a full explanation of the various tests that apply for different purposes reference should be made to the joint Law Society and BMA publication *Assessment of Mental Capacity: Guidance for doctors and lawyers* (4th edn 2015).

Assessment of capacity—Mental capacity is a question of fact so any issue of capacity can only be determined by a judge in legal proceedings acting not as a medical expert, but as a lay person influenced by personal observation and on the basis of evidence not only from doctors, but also those who know the individual. For comprehensive guidance as to the manner in which capacity should be assessed reference should be made to *Assessment of Mental Capacity: Guidance for doctors and lawyers* (above).

The mental abilities required to conduct litigation have been identified as comprising the ability to recognise a problem, obtain and receive, understand and retain relevant information, including advice; the ability to weigh the information (including that derived from advice) in the balance in reaching a decision; and the ability to communicate that decision (*Masterman-Lister*, see above).

The approach adopted by Boreham J in *White v Fell* (1987) (unreported) was referred to by the Court of Appeal with approval and may still be of assistance:

'The expression "incapable of managing her own affairs and property" must be construed in a common sense way as a whole. It does not call for proof of complete incapacity. On the other hand it is not enough to prove that the Plaintiff is now substantially less capable of managing her own affairs and property than she would have been had the accident not occurred.'

But 'understanding' is not by itself sufficient because the individual needs to be able to use or apply that understanding in making decisions. Thus in *Mitchell v Alasia* [2005] EWHC 11 (QB), Cox J relied on qualities such as impulsiveness and volatility when deciding that the claimant was by reason of his mental disorder incapable of managing and administering his own affairs. And in *Lindsay v Wood* [2006] EWHC 2895 (QB), Stanley Burnton J observed that:

'When considering the question of capacity, psychiatrists and psychologists will normally wish to take into account all aspects of the personality and behaviour of the person in question, including vulnerability to exploitation.'

For an early decision on the test of capacity in regard to a brain-injured claimant see *Saulle v Nouvet* [2007] EWHC 2902 (QB).

Guidance on the approach to capacity issues (in child care proceedings but of more general application) is to be found in *RP v Nottingham City Council & Official Solicitor* [2008] EWCA Civ 462, [2008] 2 FLR 1516.

Time-specific assessment—In *Saulle v Nouvet* [2007] EWHC 2902 (QB), Mr Andrew Edis QC sitting as a Deputy Judge of the High Court dealt with the fact that circumstances might change and made the following observations:

'... the Court must focus on the matters which arise for decision now, and on the Claimant's capacity to deal with them now. I am required not to attempt to foretell the future and provide for situations which may arise when he may have to take some other decision at some other time when his mental state may be different ... I consider that [Dr X] may well be right when he suggests that there may be times in the future when the Claimant will lack capacity to make particular decisions, and note his concern that if that happens when he does not have the support of his family for any reason, he may not come to the attention of the Court of Protection until it is too late. This is a risk against which the old test for capacity used by the Court of Protection under Part VII of the 1983 Act used to guard. The modern law is different.'

Ability to rely upon advice—The extent to which an individual with impaired capacity may rely upon the advice of others was considered by Boreham J in *White v Fell* (1987) (unreported but quoted by Wright J in *Masterman-Lister*, at first instance [2002] EWHC 417 (QB)):

'Few people have the capacity to manage all their affairs unaided. In matters of law, particularly litigation, medicine, and given sufficient resources, finance professional advice is almost universally needed and sought ... [S]he may not understand all the intricacies of litigation, or of a settlement, or of a wise investment policy ... But if that were the appropriate test then quite a substantial proportion of the adult population might be regarded as under disability.'

Medical evidence—Legal practitioners and judges should not jump to conclusions about whether there is an impairment of, or a disturbance in the functioning of, the mind or brain without appropriate evidence, especially in the case of litigants who may merely be stubborn or eccentric. The evidence of a suitably qualified person is required as to the diagnosis, and this evidence will generally extend to the issue of capacity. In *Masterman-Lister* (see above) Kennedy LJ said that 'even where the issue does not seem to be contentious, a district judge who is responsible for case management will almost certainly require the assistance of a medical report before being able to be satisfied that incapacity exists'.

Usually this expert will be a person with medical qualifications and ideally a psychiatrist. However, a psychologist, especially if of an appropriate speciality, may be better qualified in respect of a person with learning disabilities. Such opinion is merely part of the evidence and the factual evidence of a carer or social worker may also be relevant and even more persuasive. The typical general medical practitioner has little knowledge of mental capacity and the various legal tests that apply, so the appropriate test should be spelt out, and it should be explained that different tests apply to different types of decision.

Any doctor or other medical witness asked to assist in relation to capacity needs to know the area of the alleged protected party's activities in relation to which his or her advice is sought (*Masterman-Lister*, see above). All relevant information should be provided, so when the test is whether the individual is incapable of conducting civil proceedings the doctor must be given some idea of the nature and complexity of those proceedings. The doctor will need to know what decisions the individual will be called upon to make for the conduct of that litigation. Only then can the doctor express an opinion whether the individual is capable of giving instructions.

Issues as to capacity—There is unlikely to be any issue as to whether a party is a child. The rules make no express provision as to issues regarding whether a party is a protected party. Such an issue may be raised by the court or one of the parties, or by a litigation friend if there is doubt about whether a party has recovered capacity. It will then be necessary for the proceedings to be stayed until the issue is resolved, and the court may order an inquiry to be made in the proceedings to determine the issue. Notice should be given to the party alleged to be a protected party in case he or she wishes to contest this or arrange representation. This inquiry would normally be heard before a district judge who can compel the attendance of witnesses (including medical attendants and the claimant or defendant him or herself) and the production of documents. Where there are practical difficulties in obtaining medical evidence the Official Solicitor may be consulted. The court can also direct the Official Solicitor to make inquiries and to report about such matters as the court thinks fit (*Harbin v Masterman* [1896] 1 Ch 351, CA).

Courts should always, as a matter of practice, at the first convenient opportunity investigate the question of capacity whenever there is any reason to suspect that it may be absent (eg significant head injury) other than in cases where the Court of Protection has already accepted jurisdiction. Although medical evidence will be required (see above), the judge may consider that he would be assisted by seeing the person alleged to lack capacity (*Masterman-Lister*, see above).

Where, understandably, a claimant's legal team is unable to present a positive case as to whether their client is a protected party, consideration should be given to seeking an order of the court directing the Official Solicitor to review the evidence, to appoint his or her own medical expert, and to appear and make such submissions as he considers appropriate (*Lindsay v Wood* [2006] EWHC 2895 (QB)). The *Masterman-Lister* decision has been explored by the Court of Appeal in a subsequent case where a 50/50 settlement was agreed and proceedings later commenced with a litigation friend to assess quantum (*Bailey v Warren* [2006] EWCA Civ 51).

While evidence is required to support an application for the appointment of a litigation friend, it does not follow that the other party to the litigation is then entitled to put in evidence disputing the basis for the appointment. It cannot properly be contended that a defendant is at risk of suffering prejudice from the appointment of a litigation friend for the claimant (*Folks v Faizey* [2006] EWCA Civ 381) although in a claim for damages following a brain injury where the quantum of damages will also be affected by a finding that the claimant is a protected beneficiary the court may permit the defendant to present evidence and submissions.

Human rights—When a person is treated as a protected party, whether or not as a result of an order of the court, he or she is thereby deprived of important rights, long cherished by English law and now safeguarded by the European Convention on Human Rights (ECHR). Although the CPR do not contain any requirement for a judicial determination of the question, courts should always, as a matter of practice, at the first convenient opportunity investigate the question of capacity whenever there is any reason to suspect that it may be absent, other than in cases where the Court of Protection is already involved (*Masterman-Lister*, see above).

21.2 Requirement for a litigation friend in proceedings by or against children and protected parties

(1) A protected party must have a litigation friend to conduct proceedings on his behalf.

(2) A child must have a litigation friend to conduct proceedings on his behalf unless the court makes an order under paragraph (3).

(3) The court may make an order permitting a child to conduct proceedings without a litigation friend.

(4) An application for an order under paragraph (3) –
   (a) may be made by the child;
   (b) if the child already has a litigation friend, must be made on notice to the litigation friend; and
   (c) if the child has no litigation friend, may be made without notice.

(5) Where –
   (a) the court has made an order under paragraph (3); and
   (b) it subsequently appears to the court that it is desirable for a litigation friend to conduct the proceedings on behalf of the child,

the court may appoint a person to be the child's litigation friend.

Amendments—SI 2007/2204.

Practice Direction—See generally Practice Direction 21.

Scope of provision—The general rule is that a child or protected party may only conduct proceedings, whether as claimant or defendant, by a litigation friend. This applies equally to counterclaims and additional claims under Part 20 (r 20.3(1)). The rule only refers to 'a litigation friend' so a child or protected party may not have more than one in any particular proceedings. There is nothing to prevent that party having a different litigation friend in other proceedings of a different nature, unless a deputy (formerly a receiver) has been appointed in which event he or she should generally be the only litigation friend for the protected party unless the Court of Protection otherwise orders.

Verification that a party is a child or protected party—Practice Direction 21, para 2.3 requires the litigation friend to state in the 'certificate of suitability' that he or she consents to act and knows or believes the party to be a child or protected party. The grounds for this belief must be stated and if based upon medical opinion this document must be attached. It is unlikely to be difficult to ascertain the age of a party, but there may be doubt as to whether a party is a protected party (see the notes to r 21.1 for the procedure then to be adopted).

Even where the issue does not seem to be contentious, a district judge who is responsible for case management will generally require the assistance of a medical report before being able to be satisfied that incapacity exists. An admission by a person alleged to lack capacity will carry little weight. It may assist for the judge to see the person alleged to lack capacity (*Masterman-Lister*, see discussion at notes to r 21.1).

Notification to the child or protected party—Neither the CPR nor the Practice Directions actually provide that a child or protected party must be given notice of the proceedings, unless (in the case of a protected party) the court is involved in the appointment of the litigation friend, so it is possible for proceedings in the name of a child or protected party to be commenced or defended without the personal knowledge of that party. Reliance is placed on the certificate of suitability (see above) and upon service on the parent or guardian of the child, or the person with whom the protected party resides or in whose care he or she is (see also Practice Direction 21, para 2.4). It cannot be assumed that this person will inform the protected party in every situation where this would be prudent.

The protected party as a party—An adult who has the necessary capacity will not be a protected party even if mentally disordered so there is no need for a comparable provision whereby the court may authorise a protected party to conduct proceedings. However, the court may permit proceedings to continue (to a limited extent) even though a litigation friend has not been appointed and may validate proceedings that have continued in breach of the requirements (r 21.3). If the protected party recovers capacity, the appointment of the litigation friend may be terminated by the court order under r 21.9(2), (3).

Duty of litigation friend—The duty of a litigation friend was set out in Practice Direction 21, para 2.1 as being 'fairly and competently to conduct proceedings on behalf of a child or protected party. He must have no interest in the proceedings adverse to that of the child or protected party and all steps and decisions he takes in the proceedings must be taken for the benefit of the child or protected party'. This latter statement was omitted when amendments were made following the implementation of the MCA 2005 which imposes a duty to act in the 'best interests' of the protected party as defined in MCA 2005.

Status of litigation friend—As the appointment is to 'conduct proceedings ... on behalf' of the child or protected party, subject to the provisions of the rules, any act which in the ordinary conduct of any proceedings is required or authorised to be done by a party shall or may be done by the litigation friend. Unless the litigation friend is also a deputy (formerly a receiver) appointed by the Court of Protection or an attorney under a lasting or registered enduring power of attorney, he or she will have no status in regard to the affairs of the protected party outside the proceedings in which he or she is appointed. It follows that if money is awarded to a child or protected party the litigation friend has no authority to receive or expend that money. The money may only be dealt with pursuant to the directions of the court and in this respect reference must be made to r 21.11. Similarly, any settlement or compromise will have to be approved by the court under r 21.10.

Statement of truth—CPR Part 22 makes provision for certain documents to be verified by a 'statement of truth'. If a party is a child or a protected party it will be the litigation friend (or legal representative on his or her behalf) who makes and signs this statement (r 22.1(5), (6)).

Need for a solicitor—There is no requirement in the CPR for a solicitor to act on behalf of a child or protected party whose proceedings are being conducted by a litigation friend. Nevertheless, in a complex or high value case the court may consider that the litigation friend who acts without a solicitor is not 'suitable' within r 21.4(3) and appoint someone else under r 21.7(1)(c).

21.3 Stage of proceedings at which a litigation friend becomes necessary

(1) This rule does not apply where the court has made an order under rule 21.2(3).

(2) A person may not, without the permission of the court –

    (a) make an application against a child or protected party before proceedings have started; or

    (b) take any step in proceedings except –

        (i) issuing and serving a claim form; or

        (ii) applying for the appointment of a litigation friend under rule 21.6,

until the child or protected party has a litigation friend.

(3) If during proceedings a party lacks capacity to continue to conduct proceedings, no party may take any further step in the proceedings without the permission of the court until the protected party has a litigation friend.

(4) Any step taken before a child or protected party has a litigation friend has no effect unless the court orders otherwise.

Amendments—SI 2007/2204.

Scope of provision—The general principle is that a litigation friend must be appointed before any step is taken in proceedings involving a protected party.

Exceptions—The court has a discretion to permit specified steps to be taken before a litigation friend is appointed ('without the permission of the court' (r 21.3(2), (3)) or retrospectively to approve any steps that have been taken without such appointment ('unless the court otherwise orders' (r 21.3(4)). This alleviates the problem under former rules that, where the disability was not identified by the parties or their solicitors or arose during the proceedings without their knowledge, steps taken had no effect and liabilities could arise in respect of abortive costs.

Implications—It is now possible to make urgent orders in proceedings involving a child or protected party before the appointment of a litigation friend, but the court should be made fully aware of all relevant circumstances. Where it is realised during the course of proceedings that a party is (and has been) a child or a protected party, then, provided everyone has acted in good faith and there has been no manifest disadvantage to the party subsequently found to have been a protected party, it is likely that the court will regularise the position retrospectively (*Masterman-Lister*, see discussion at notes to r 21.1). This might be the case where the proceedings have effectively been guided throughout by the person now being appointed as litigation friend. Proceedings inappropriately conducted by the child or protected party or an unsuitable person on his or her behalf will be treated as being of no effect and further proceedings may then be commenced in proper form (the Limitation Acts are unlikely to apply). A compromise of the claim of a person who is declared subsequently not to have had capacity at the time of the agreement will be invalidated even where the person's lack of capacity was unknown to anyone acting for either party at that time (*Dunhill v Burgin (Nos 1 and 2)* [2014] UKSC 18, [2014] COPLR 199). Although the court has the power to validate retrospectively any step under r 21.3(4) the Supreme Court decided that this must depend upon the particular facts and declined to validate the settlement finally disposing of the claim.

Effect on timetable—Until there is a litigation friend no party may take any step in the proceedings so it is assumed that any timetable is suspended. When the court appoints the litigation friend it may be prudent to consider further directions as to the future conduct of the proceedings.

Cessation of appointment of litigation friend upon death of protected party—A litigation friend has no standing to act on behalf of a protected party who has died. Any step taken on behalf of the deceased person is a nullity in the absence of an order pursuant to CPR 19.8(1). Furthermore the grant of letters of administration does not retrospectively validate any step take between death and the grant (*Hussain & Qutb v Bank of Scotland* [2012] EWCA Civ 264 and *Millburn-Snell v Evans* [2011] EWCA Civ 577).

21.4 Who may be a litigation friend without a court order

(1) This rule does not apply if the court has appointed a person to be a litigation friend.

(2) A deputy appointed by the Court of Protection under the 2005 Act with power to conduct proceedings on the protected party's behalf is entitled to be the litigation friend of the protected party in any proceedings to which his power extends.

(3) If nobody has been appointed by the court or, in the case of a protected party, has been appointed as a deputy as set out in paragraph (2), a person may act as a litigation friend if he –

(a) can fairly and competently conduct proceedings on behalf of the child or protected party;
(b) has no interest adverse to that of the child or protected party; and
(c) where the child or protected party is a claimant, undertakes to pay any costs which the child or protected party may be ordered to pay in relation to the proceedings, subject to any right he may have to be repaid from the assets of the child or protected party.

Amendments—SI 2007/2204.

Scope of provision—This rule identifies who may act as a litigation friend without an order appointing him.

Authorised person—Any person authorised under MCA 2005 (ie as a deputy appointed by the Court of Protection) to conduct legal proceedings in the name or on behalf of a protected party is entitled to become the litigation friend in accordance with such authority. An office copy of the order or other authorisation sealed with the official seal of the Court of Protection should be filed. Care should be taken to examine this document because simply being appointed a deputy does not by itself give authority to conduct proceedings. It is not clear if the Court has power to appoint someone else (as under the former rules), but this situation is unlikely to arise and conflict between the court dealing with the litigation and the Court of Protection should be avoided.

Attorneys—An attorney under a registered enduring power of attorney (EPA) or a lasting power of attorney (LPA) is not specifically mentioned but would be an obvious person to act as litigation friend because he or she will control the financial affairs of the protected party (see MCA 2005) and there will, in consequence, be no need for a deputy. An ordinary power of attorney is of no significance because it ceases to have effect upon the incapacity of the donor, but of course the person acting may otherwise be suitable as litigation friend. If an EPA is registered this would normally indicate that the donor is a protected party, but that is not the case for an LPA because registration may take place at an earlier stage.

The court controls its own procedures and principles of agency do not apply. So a power of attorney cannot confer a right to conduct litigation or of audience (*Gregory v Turner, R (on the application of Morris) v North Somerset Council* [2003] EWCA Civ 183). A litigation friend does not have to act by a solicitor and can conduct the litigation on behalf of the protected party: *Gregory v Turner*, para 63. A litigation friend who does not otherwise have a right of audience requires the permission of the court to act as an advocate on behalf of the protected party: *Gregory v Turner*, para 64.

Suitability—There can be no doubt as to the suitability of a person authorised by the Court of Protection (if doubt arises the matter should be referred back to that Court). The rule helpfully sets out the criteria whereby other persons may be regarded as suitable to act as litigation friend (r 21.4(3)), but the court may not waive any of these criteria which the proposed person is unable to satisfy (*R (on the application of Hussain) v Birmingham City Council* [2002] EWHC 949 (Admin)). These criteria feature throughout Part 21, as amplified by Practice Direction 21, para 2.1, and the court must be satisfied that they are complied with before appointing a litigation friend. They may be relied upon where there is a dispute as to who should be appointed. Apart from this there is no restriction on who may be a litigation friend save that the person appointed must not be a child or a protected party and (in practice) should normally be within the jurisdiction. The litigation friend should not have any personal involvement in the proceedings, but see *Spurling v Broadhurst* [2012] EWHC 2883 (Ch). If the court becomes aware of the person's unsuitability it may remove him or her under r 21.7 and substitute another person as litigation friend, but there is no express duty to monitor the situation.

Undertaking as to costs (r 21.4(3)(c))—This undertaking is required from the litigation friend of a claimant (unless appointed by the Court of Protection) but not a defendant, and this is confirmed in Practice Direction 21, para 2.2(e) and 2.3(4). It will also be required when a counterclaim or additional claim is made by a protected party because this is to be treated as if it were a claim for the purpose of the Rules (r 20.3(1) as interpreted by r 20.2(2)(a)). The undertaking is contained in Form N235, Certificate of Suitability of Litigation Friend. A mother's undertaking to meet any liability in costs 'if her circumstances were to change, enabling her to afford them' did not satisfy the requirement of r 21.4(3)(c) and she was, accordingly, ineligible for appointment as a litigation friend (*R (on the application of Hussain) v Birmingham City Council*, above).

The requirement imposes a severe limitation upon the ability of a child or protected party to bring a claim. Query whether it amounts to discrimination against a person with a mental disability contrary to the Disability Discrimination Act 1995 or will otherwise be in breach of the Human Rights Act 1998. The Court of Protection Rules 2007, SI 2007/1744 (the latest court rules to be produced) do not require this undertaking. The litigation friend is, in effect, expected to provide an indemnity so may wish to be protected by a Public Funding certificate or an after-the-event (ATE) insurance indemnity policy, or otherwise be in control of adequate funds held by the child or protected party. One way of circumventing the undertaking in the case of a protected party is to obtain the authority of the Court of Protection to bring the proceedings. The Court has a general discretion as to costs and will take into account the role of the litigation friend but may have power to impose a personal costs liability in case of misconduct quite apart from the undertaking. Further difficulties arise in regard to conditional fee arrangements.

Costs order against litigation friend—An order for costs should not be made against a litigation friend personally without giving him or her a chance to be heard. This probably means adopting the r 46.2 procedure since the litigation friend is not otherwise a party. Such approach will only be appropriate when the litigation friend has misbehaved in the proceedings. The undertaking to pay the child or protected party's costs (if given) is quite different from a personal costs order.

Personal liability of solicitor for costs—A solicitor who acts in any proceedings for or on behalf of a child or protected party without a litigation friend may be held personally liable to pay any wasted costs of the proceedings incurred by the other party, even though the solicitor may not have been aware that the person for whom he or she has been acting is in fact a child or a protected party (*Yonge v Toynbee* [1910] 1 KB 215, CA). However, provided everyone has acted in good faith and there has been no manifest disadvantage to the party subsequently found to have been a child or protected party, it is likely that the court will regularise the position retrospectively (*Masterman-Lister*, see discussion at notes to r 21.1).

21.5 How a person becomes a litigation friend without a court order

(1) If the court has not appointed a litigation friend, a person who wishes to act as a litigation friend must follow the procedure set out in this rule.

(2) A deputy appointed by the Court of Protection under the 2005 Act with power to conduct proceedings on the protected party's behalf must file an official copy(GL) of the order of the Court of Protection which confers his power to act either –

 (a) where the deputy is to act as a litigation friend for a claimant, at the time the claim is made; or
 (b) where the deputy is to act as a litigation friend for a defendant, at the time when he first takes a step in the proceedings on behalf of the defendant.

(3) Any other person must file a certificate of suitability stating that he satisfies the conditions specified in rule 21.4(3) either –

 (a) where the person is to act as a litigation friend for a claimant, at the time when the claim is made; or
 (b) where the person is to act as a litigation friend for a defendant, at the time when he first takes a step in the proceedings on behalf of the defendant.

(4) The litigation friend must –

 (a) serve the certificate of suitability on every person on whom, in accordance with rule 6.13 (service on a parent, guardian etc.), the claim form should be served; and
 (b) file a certificate of service when filing the certificate of suitability.

 (Rules 6.17 and 6.29 set out the details to be contained in a certificate of service.)

Amendments—SI 2007/2204; SI 2008/2178.

Practice Direction—See generally Practice Direction 21.

Scope of provision—This rule sets out the procedural steps for the appointment of a litigation friend otherwise than by a court order. It will be relied upon in most cases.

No need for court appointment of litigation friend—A litigation friend may be appointed simply by filing the relevant documents. The certificate is a prerequisite for appointment without a court order, but will not be conclusive in the event of a dispute as to suitability. It is strange that there is no requirement for the child or protected party to be personally notified that proceedings are being brought or defended in his or her name because he or she may wish to make representations as to who the litigation friend should be or dispute that he or she is a protected party (see generally the provisions as to service in CPR Part 6). It is now good practice for anyone intending to become a litigation friend to serve upon or draw to the attention of the intended protected party the notice of his or her intention to act as litigation friend and certificate of suitability unless there is no prospect of a relevant response and the court may require confirmation of this. The Court of Appeal has recommended a change in the rules so that a person cannot become a protected party without knowing what is going on (see *Masterman-Lister* at notes to r 21.1).

'certificate of suitability' (r 21.5(3))—This document confirms that the person to be appointed meets the criteria whereby a person may be regarded as suitable for appointment as litigation friend (r 21.4(3)). As to suitability, see note to r 21.4. The certificate is not required where the person is a deputy authorised by the Court of Protection to conduct the proceedings (see note to r 21.4).

Deputy appointed by the Court of Protection—An official copy of the order of the Court of Protection, which confers the person's power to act, must be filed. The rules do not contemplate the Court of Protection authorising a person to conduct proceedings without appointing him or her to be a deputy, but this could happen. Presumably the Court would ensure that this person was appointed and exclude any competing application.

'certificate of service' (r 21.5(4)(b))—Rule 6.13 clarifies the persons on whom the certificate of suitability (when required) must be served in accordance with this rule. The alleged protected party is not included (but see note '*No need for court appointment of litigation friend*' above).

Forms—Form N235 (Certificate of suitability of litigation friend).

21.6 How a person becomes a litigation friend by court order

(1) The court may make an order appointing a litigation friend.

(2) An application for an order appointing a litigation friend may be made by –
   (a) a person who wishes to be the litigation friend; or
   (b) a party.

(3) Where –
   (a) a person makes a claim against a child or protected party;
   (b) the child or protected party has no litigation friend;
   (c) the court has not made an order under rule 21.2(3) (order that a child can conduct proceedings without a litigation friend); and
   (d) either –
       (i) someone who is not entitled to be a litigation friend files a defence; or
       (ii) the claimant wishes to take some step in the proceedings,

the claimant must apply to the court for an order appointing a litigation friend for the child or protected party.

(4) An application for an order appointing a litigation friend must be supported by evidence.

(5) The court may not appoint a litigation friend under this rule unless it is satisfied that the person to be appointed satisfies the conditions in rule 21.4(3).

Amendments—SI 2007/2204.

Practice Direction—See generally Practice Direction 21.

Scope of provision—This rule sets out the procedural steps for the appointment of a litigation friend by a court order, that is, where it has not been possible to appoint a litigation friend under r 21.5. The court must be satisfied that the person to be appointed is suitable for appointment in accordance with the criteria set out in r 21.4(3). Although the rules do not so provide, the application should be served upon or at least brought to the notice of the party unless there is no prospect of a relevant response (see note '*No need for court appointment of litigation friend*' under r 21.5).

Official Solicitor—The Official Solicitor should be approached in case of difficulty and may be appointed if he or she consents, but in practice he or she will only consent if there is no one else suitable and willing to act. The Official Solicitor cannot be compelled to act as anybody's litigation friend (*Bradbury & Ors v Paterson & Ors* [2014] EWHC 3992 (QB)). It is not necessary to approach the Official Solicitor in all cases and the court will not be concerned to ascertain whether he or she has declined to consent before appointing someone else. The Official Solicitor should not be appointed without his or her consent, which will not usually be forthcoming until provision is made for payment of his or her costs (Practice Direction 21, para 3.4). Save in the most urgent of cases, it is unlikely that the Official Solicitor will be able to complete his or her inquiries in less than 3 months. Accordingly, a lengthy adjournment of the proceedings might become necessary and a substantive hearing should not be fixed within such period of the Official Solicitor's initial appointment without consulting him or her. Where the circumstances of the case justify the involvement of the Official Solicitor, a completed questionnaire and copy of the order appointing him or her (subject to his or her consent) together with a copy of the court file should be sent to the Official Solicitor's office. The Official Solicitor may be contacted at 81 Chancery Lane, London WC2A 1DD; Tel: 020 7911 7127; Fax: 020 7911 7105.

Service—See r 21.8(1) and (2) for the special rules that apply to an application for appointment by the court of a litigation friend. The (alleged) protected party must be served on a first application to appoint a litigation friend unless the court orders otherwise, but there is still no requirement for a child to be notified of proceedings to be conducted in his or her name and on his or her behalf even though the child may be approaching 18 (see note to r 21.2).

Evidence—Practice Direction 21, para 3.4 clarifies the evidence required. This will presumably include evidence that the party is a child or protected party although this is not expressly stated.

Suitability—See note to r 21.4. The court may appoint the person proposed or any other person who complies with the conditions specified in r 21.4(3) (r 21.8(4)). Thus, the criteria of suitability in r 21.4(3) must be satisfied even though r 21.4(1) expressly states that the rule does not apply if the court has appointed a person to be a litigation friend.

21.7 Court's power to change a litigation friend and to prevent person acting as a litigation friend

(1) The court may –

    (a) direct that a person may not act as a litigation friend;
    (b) terminate a litigation friend's appointment; or
    (c) appoint a new litigation friend in substitution for an existing one.

(2) An application for an order under paragraph (1) must be supported by evidence.

(3) The court may not appoint a litigation friend under this rule unless it is satisfied that the person to be appointed satisfies the conditions in rule 21.4(3).

Amendments—SI 2007/2204.

Scope of provision—The court may prevent a person from being a litigation friend or replace a litigation friend during the course of proceedings whether or not appointed by an order. See '*Suitability*' below. Any dispute as to who should be the litigation friend would be dealt with under this provision.

Service—See r 21.8(1) and (3). See generally note to r 21.6 as to service. Although this does not include the protected party, it is good practice to consult this person as capacity is not an 'all or nothing' concept.

Suitability—See note to r 21.4. The court may appoint the person proposed or any other person who complies with the conditions specified in r 21.4(3) (r 21.8(4)). Thus, the criteria of suitability in r 21.4(3) must be satisfied even though r 21.4(1) expressly states that the rule does not apply if the court has appointed a person to be a litigation friend.

Applications—This rule contemplates an application by a party or presumably a non-party such as an alternative representative for the child or protected party. The court may, as part of its case management powers, initiate the process (r 3.3) and has a duty to do so where it is satisfied that an existing litigation friend has become disabled by conflict of interest (*Zarbafi v Zarbafi* [2014] EWCA Civ 1267. Concern as to an actual or potential litigation friend does not necessarily mean that there is someone with an interest in making the application.

Termination—The rules express no limit on the power to terminate the appointment and if the litigation friend manifestly acts contrary to the child's or the protected party's best interests, the court will remove him or her, even though neither his or her good faith nor diligence is in issue (*Re A (Conjoined Twins: Medical Treatment) (No 2)* [2001] 1 FLR 267, CA). The court's power to terminate the appointment is not restricted by any requirement to identify a substitute litigation friend and a litigation friend who is unwilling to continue to act would be unlikely to satisfy the condition of being a person who can 'fairly and competently conduct the proceedings on behalf of the . . . protected party'.(*Bradbury & Ors v Paterson & Ors* [2014] EWHC 3992 (QB)). In respect of mentally incapable adults, what are this person's best interests has now been clarified by MCA 2005, s 4.

21.8 Appointment of a litigation friend by court order – supplementary

(1) An application for an order under rule 21.6 or 21.7 must be served on every person on whom, in accordance with rule 6.13 (service on parent, guardian etc.), the claim form must be served.

(2) Where an application for an order under rule 21.6 is in respect of a protected party, the application must also be served on the protected party unless the court orders otherwise.

(3) An application for an order under rule 21.7 must also be served on –

    (a) the person who is the litigation friend, or who is purporting to act as the litigation friend, when the application is made; and

    (b) the person who it is proposed should be the litigation friend, if he is not the applicant.

(4) On an application for an order under rule 21.6 or 21.7, the court may appoint the person proposed or any other person who satisfies the conditions specified in rule 21.4(3).

Amendments—SI 2007/2204; SI 2008/2178.

Scope of provision—This rule supplements r 6.13 (which deals with service of the proceedings) and also provides that the court is not obliged to appoint the person proposed but may appoint any other person who complies with the conditions specified in r 21.4(3). Although the rules do not so provide, the application should be served upon or at least brought to the notice of the party unless there is no prospect of a relevant response (see note '*No need for court appointment of litigation friend*' under r 21.5).

Service—Service of the application on the parent or guardian of the child, or the person with whom the protected party resides or in whose care he is, is required in all cases. The application under r 21.6 to appoint a litigation friend must actually be served on the protected party (unless the court orders otherwise) but this is not a universal provision. Where it is proposed to change the litigation friend both the existing and intended litigation friend must be served (but not apparently the protected party). There is no requirement to serve a child in any of these situations, but see the note to r 21.2.

Who is appointed—The court may decide to appoint any other person who meets the criteria set out in r 21.4(3) and is willing to act.

21.9 Procedure where appointment of a litigation friend ceases

(1) When a child who is not a protected party reaches the age of 18, the litigation friend's appointment ceases.

(2) Where a protected party regains or acquires capacity to conduct the proceedings, the litigation friend's appointment continues until it is ended by court order.

(3) An application for an order under paragraph (2) may be made by –

    (a) the former protected party;
    (b) the litigation friend; or
    (c) a party.

(4) The child or protected party in respect of whom the appointment to act has ceased must serve notice on the other parties –

    (a) stating that the appointment of his litigation friend to act has ceased;
    (b) giving his address for service; and
    (c) stating whether or not he intends to carry on the proceedings.

(5) If the child or protected party does not serve the notice required by paragraph (4) within 28 days after the day on which the appointment of the litigation friend ceases the court may, on application, strike out any claim brought by or defence raised by the child or protected party.

(6) The liability of a litigation friend for costs continues until –

    (a) the person in respect of whom his appointment to act has ceased serves the notice referred to in paragraph (4); or
    (b) the litigation friend serves notice on the parties that his appointment to act has ceased.

Amendments—SI 2007/2204.

Practice Direction—See generally Practice Direction 21.

Scope of provision—This rule makes provision for a party ceasing to be a child or protected party.

Child—There will be no need for a litigation friend when the child attains 18 (unless the child is also a protected party) so the appointment then ceases automatically. If this party does not by notice under r 21.9(4) continue the proceedings they may be struck out. There is no express requirement for the child to be notified of the existence of the proceedings up to that point, but notice of an application to strike out under r 21.9(5) must presumably be given to the party formerly a child. The litigation friend will remain liable for costs unless the child gives notice as aforesaid or the litigation friend gives notice under r 21.9(6)(b) which must also be given to the party formerly a child.

Protected party—The position is different in respect of a protected party who recovers capacity. The litigation friend will only be removed by court order following an application under r 21.9(3) and evidence will be required as to capacity. Notice must still be served by the former protected party under r 21.9(4) or the proceedings may be struck out, and the litigation friend will remain liable for costs until that notice is served or he or she serves his or her own notice under r 21.9(6)(b).

Liability of litigation friend for costs—The litigation friend of a claimant may have had to give an undertaking as to costs pursuant to r 21.4(3)(c). This liability continues until notice is served on the other parties either by the claimant or the former litigation friend as mentioned above. Presumably the reference in r 21.9(6) to 'The liability of a litigation friend for costs ...' refers to such undertaking and is not sufficient to create any additional liability. It is not clear whether, when discharged, the litigation friend is released from all liability for costs or only costs incurred from that date, although it is probably the latter.

Relationship between the civil court and the Court of Protection—Doubt may arise in a brain injury claim as to whether the claimant lacks or continues to lack capacity either to litigate or to manage property and affairs. This may be relevant as to the need for a litigation friend and also the quantum of damages to be awarded. In *Saulle v Nouvet* [2007] EWHC 2902 (QB), Mr Andrew Edis QC sitting as a deputy judge of the High Court assumed that the civil court must deal with both assessments of capacity but although that court can make a definitive decision as to capacity to litigate it cannot make a decision as to capacity to manage financial affairs that will be binding on the Court of Protection. Conversely, the Court of Protection has a statutory power to make declarations as to present (but not past) capacity which may relate to both litigation and management of financial affairs and any such declarations are likely to be followed by a civil court. In substantial personal injury claims where the quantum of damages may be affected by the involvement of the Court of Protection there are therefore advantages in the civil court referring both issues of capacity to the Court of Protection for determination. However, where the amount of money involved would not normally trigger the intervention of the Court of Protection it is proportionate and desirable for the civil court to adjudicate on both aspects of capacity (ie to decide whether the litigant is a protected party and if so whether he or she is also a protected beneficiary).

Where there is a reference to the Court of Protection in regard to capacity issues the proceedings should be stayed pending the outcome. It is likely that the defendant will be made a party to the Court of Protection proceedings in view of the financial interest and the advocates in the civil proceedings will thus have a right of audience. The position is different in respect of a dispute as to best welfare interests and in that event the defendants in civil proceedings would not be permitted to become parties to any Court of Protection proceedings. For a full explanation see the judgment of Bodey J in *Re SK* [2012] EWHC 1990 (COP), [2012] COPLR 712.

21.10 Compromise etc. by or on behalf of a child or protected party

(1) Where a claim is made –

    (a) by or on behalf of a child or protected party; or

    (b) against a child or protected party,

no settlement, compromise or payment (including any voluntary interim payment) and no acceptance of money paid into court shall be valid, so far as it relates to the claim by, on behalf of or against the child or protected party, without the approval of the court.

(2) Where –

    (a) before proceedings in which a claim is made by or on behalf of, or against, a child or protected party (whether alone or with any other person) are begun, an agreement is reached for the settlement of the claim; and

    (b) the sole purpose of proceedings is to obtain the approval of the court to a settlement or compromise of the claim,

the claim must –

    (i) be made using the procedure set out in Part 8 (alternative procedure for claims); and

    (ii) include a request to the court for approval of the settlement or compromise.

(3) In proceedings to which Section II or Section III of Part 45 applies, the court will not make an order for detailed assessment of the costs payable to the child or protected party but will assess the costs in the manner set out in that Section.

    (Rule 46.4 contains provisions about costs where money is payable to a child or protected party.)

Amendments—SI 2004/3419; SI 2007/2204; SI 2010/621; SI 2013/262.

Practice Direction—See generally Practice Direction 21.

Scope of provision—This provision ensures that the approval of the court is obtained to any settlement or compromise on behalf of a child or protected party, and extends to accepting any Part 36 offer. It applies to claims other than for money and where the claim is made against the child or protected party. Without this approval the settlement, compromise or payment of any claim is wholly invalid and unenforceable, and is made entirely at the risk of the parties and their solicitors. An unexpected consequence is that the acceptance by a defendant of a Part 36 offer to settle made by a litigation friend (including a partial settlement relating to liability) may be withdrawn before court approval is obtained (*Drinkall v Whitwood* [2003] EWCA Civ 1547).

Setting aside a settlement—Although there is a public interest in the finality of litigation, there is also a public interest in the protection of vulnerable people who lack the mental state to conduct litigation, so a compromise may be set aside many years later where, unknown to the parties, the claimant was a protected party at the time. The test is whether the claimant has capacity to conduct the proceedings, not whether the claimant agrees to the compromise (*Dunhill v Burgin (Nos 1 and 2)* [2014] UKSC 18, [2014] COPLR 199). Following *Dietz v Lennin Chemicals Ltd* [1969] 1 AC 170, the Supreme Court held that r 21.10 was intra vires and, in the case of both children and protected parties, prevailed over the general rule that a contract would be binding if the incapacity of a party was not known to the other party. However, even in a case where a claimant has not been declared to lack capacity the court may consider it appropriate to approve a settlement in the exercise of its inherent jurisdiction thereby ensuring that the settlement is valid in the event that it is later determined that the claimant lacked capacity (*Coles v Perfect* [2013] EWHC 1955 (QB), Teare J).

Test of capacity—Where a compromise is to be negotiated outside court the Supreme Court in *Dunhill v Burgin,* above, confirmed that the proper question, as settled by *Masterman-Lister v Brutton & Co and Jewell & anor* [2003] 1 WLR 1511 and *Bailey v Warren* [2006] EWCA Civ 51 was whether the claimant had the necessary capacity to conduct the proceedings (ie. to litigate). The test of litigation capacity is the capacity to conduct the claim which the claimant in fact has, rather than to conduct the claim as formulated by the claimant's lawyers.

Purpose—There are three distinct reasons for this provision:

(1) to enable defendants to obtain a valid discharge from the claim;
(2) to protect children and protected parties from any lack of skill and experience on the part of their advisers which might lead to a settlement of a money claim for less than it is worth (*Black v Yates* [1992] QB 526 and *Dunhill v Burgin*, above); and
(3) to ensure that solicitors and counsel are paid their proper costs and fees, and no more (this extends to both overcharging and recommending an unfavourable settlement influenced by an attractive costs offer).

Early settlements—Where a compromise or settlement is reached before proceedings are begun the Part 8 procedure is used to seek approval of the court (r 21.10(2)). This does not prevent the settlement of small claims (e.g. under £1,000) by payment to parents or carers prior to any proceedings on the basis of their indemnity and that may be appropriate to avoid disproportionate costs, but there are risks especially if the true value of the claim was not recognised.

Late settlements—Where the compromise or settlement is reached after the proceedings have been commenced, approval is sought by way of an application in the course of those proceedings. It would be an abuse of the process of the court for the parties and their solicitors in any subsisting proceedings to make or act on any such settlement, compromise or payment without the court's approval.

Hearing—The hearing will usually be before the Master or district judge in claims involving a child but before a Master, designated civil judge or his or her nominee in the case of a protected party (Practice Direction 21, paras 5.6 and 6.5). In practice, subject to financial limits, most district judges have been nominated to hear these applications. Very large claims in the High Court may be dealt with by High Court judges.

The hearing (except for very small sums when a hearing may be dispensed with) should generally be attended by the litigation friend and child or protected party unless there is good reason to the contrary. The court will wish to be satisfied that the settlement or compromise is one that should be approved and may wish to ascertain the views of the litigation friend (and the child if of sufficient maturity and understanding) and inspect any scars which feature in a personal injuries claim. A written opinion from counsel or a suitably experienced solicitor as to liability and quantum will be helpful and may be required.

Costs—The requirement for court approval extends to costs (r 46.4). There will be a detailed assessment (r 46.4), but in certain circumstances this may be dispensed with (Practice Direction Costs, para 2.1). The claimant's solicitor does not usually seek any costs over and above those recovered from the defendant, so that the child or protected party receives the full damages without any deduction for costs (this may not be so where conditional fees apply). If such further costs are expressly waived approval of costs may not be required where there has been summary assessment or costs can be agreed or are to be paid by an insurer (Practice Direction Costs, para 2.1). It is not clear how this impinges on obligations under a public funding certificate, but the former practice may continue of the court being invited to record its approval of an agreement as to costs and dispense with assessment.

Need for a public hearing—Although any hearing should normally be held in public to comply with the ECHR, Art 6(1), there are exceptions and hearings involving the interests of a child or protected party may be in private (see r 39.2(3)(d) and Practice Direction 39, paras 1.4A and 1.6). It has been held that the hearing of an application for the approval of a proposed settlement of a personal injury or Fatal Accident Act claim and the basic reasons therefore should be given in open court, although any part of the hearing intended to acquaint the court with the negotiations culminating in the proposed settlement and other details of the claim and the status and medical condition of the claimant should remain private (*Beatham v Carlisle Hospitals NHS Trust* (1999) *The Times*, May 20, QBD, Buckley J).

Setting aside a settlement—Although there is a public interest in the finality of litigation, there is also a public interest in the protection of vulnerable people who lacked the mental state to conduct litigation so a compromise may be set aside many years later where, unknown to the parties, the claimant was a protected party at the time. The test is whether the claimant had capacity to conduct the proceedings not agree to the compromise (*Dunhill v Burgin* [2012] EWCA Civ 397, [2012] COPLR 679).

Varying the settlement—Once the settlement has been approved it is final and cannot be varied or revoked on the ground that an unforeseen event has destroyed the assumption on which it was made pursuant to the case management power of the court under r 3.1(7) (*Roult (by his mother and litigation friend) v North West Strategic Health Authority* [2009] EWCA Civ 444).

Appeals—A decision not to appeal, where permission has been obtained on the express understanding that the possible appellant needs time to consider the matter, and with no consideration moving from the possible respondents, is not a 'compromise' and does not require the approval of the court (*Re A (Conjoined Twins: Medical Treatment) (No 2)* [2001] 1 FLR 267, CA).

Role of the Court of Protection—These provisions apply even where the proceedings are being conducted by the protected party's deputy as litigation friend under the authority of the Court of Protection. In that event the approval of the Master of the former Court of Protection had to be first obtained to proceed with the settlement. This requirement does not apply under the new jurisdiction.

Structured settlement—Where a structured settlement is contemplated reference should be made to Practice Direction 40C.

Provisional damages—See Practice Direction 41, Provisional Damages.

Part 45, Section II—This relates to fixed recoverable costs for road traffic accidents.

Part 45, Section III—This relates to fixed costs for claims pursuant to the Pre-Action Protocol for Low Value Personal Injury Claims in Road Traffic Accidents.

Forms—Form N292 (Order on settlement on behalf of a child or protected party).

21.11 Control of money recovered by or on behalf of a child or protected party

(1) Where in any proceedings –

    (a) money is recovered by or on behalf of or for the benefit of a child or protected party; or

    (b) money paid into court is accepted by or on behalf of a child or protected party, the money will be dealt with in accordance with directions given by the court under this rule and not otherwise.

(2) Directions given under this rule may provide that the money shall be wholly or partly paid into court and invested or otherwise dealt with.

(3) Where money is recovered by or on behalf of a protected party or money paid into court is accepted by or on behalf of a protected party, before giving directions in accordance with this rule, the court will first consider whether the protected party is a protected beneficiary.

Amendments—SI 2007/2204.

Practice Direction—See generally Practice Direction 21, paras 8–10 and 13.

Scope of provision—This rule ensures that there is supervision by the appropriate court of money awarded to or recovered by a child or protected beneficiary. This fund (or the balance after allowing for any money authorised to be released for the immediate benefit of the child or protected beneficiary) will be transferred to the Court Funds Office and applied for the benefit of the claimant in such manner as the court thinks fit (see notes below). Small sums may be released to the parents or carers of a child or protected beneficiary if the court is satisfied that they will invest or use the money for the benefit of the child or protected beneficiary, and this may increasingly become the policy now that lower than market interest rates are obtained on 'special account' making it unattractive to retain the fund in court.

The restriction on the judges who can approve settlements for protected parties (Practice Direction 21, paras 5.6 and 6.5) does not appear to extend to this later stage although in practice the directions will be given in most cases at the same hearing as the approval.

Court Funds Office—The Court Funds Office has now moved from 22 Kingsway, London to Glasgow, G58 1AB, DX: 501757 Cowglen, email: enquiries@cfo.gsi.gov.uk, tel: 0845 223 8500, Fax: 0141 636 4398. Under the Administration of Justice Act 1982, the Court Funds Office acting on behalf of the Accountant General of the Senior Courts, provides investment and banking administration services for clients whose money is held under the control of the civil courts of England and Wales, including the Court of Protection. See the Court Funds Rules 2011 available at: www.justice.gov.uk/about/cfo/ and reproduced in Part V of this work.

'protected beneficiary' (r 21.1(2)(e))—A separate definition is provided because a party may lack capacity to conduct the proceedings and thus be a protected party but, nevertheless, have the capacity to manage money. The protected beneficiary is a protected party who also lacks the capacity to manage and control any money recovered by him or her or on his or her behalf or for his or her benefit in the proceedings. The court must consider the question of mental capacity before it purports to control the money recovered for a protected party.

The definition of a protected beneficiary is insufficient for two reasons. First, there is an assumption (which may not be justified) that only a person who is a protected party may be a protected beneficiary. Secondly, if the approach of the civil court is to be compatible with that of the Court of Protection it becomes necessary to aggregate the damages recovered with the existing wealth of the protected party and then to decide whether there is capacity to manage the entirety.

Procedure—See Practice Direction 21, paras 8–12. The hearing may be in private under r 39.2(3)(d), but initial indications (at least in the High Court) are that approval should be given in public (*Beatham v Carlisle Hospitals NHS Trust* (1999) *The Times*, May 20, QBD).

Order—See Form N292.

Investment and other directions—The court should give directions relating to the fund on the new Form CFO 320 (revised in 2011) as soon as possible after the award is made or settlement approved. This may be at the hearing before a district judge or master approving the settlement, but if the award is made at a trial these directions are likely to be adjourned to a district judge or master in chambers at a later date. Investment directions basically comprise a choice between high interest or equity investment, or a combination of the two. This will be influenced by the use to be made of the fund (e g if periodic payments are to be made) and the period of time that the fund is likely to remain invested (capital growth may be appropriate if the child is young, but accumulation of interest will be the only safe course for a child approaching 18). There is provision to direct that interest or instalments of capital be paid out at regular intervals for the support or maintenance of the child or protected beneficiary. In the case of a child, if a birth certificate is produced 'majority directions' can be given to the effect that the fund be paid out on attaining majority (this will not be appropriate if the child is also or may prove to be a protected beneficiary). The court staff then complete CFO Form 212 which is sent to the Court Funds Office and a local file is created for the fund.

Transfer to another County Court hearing centre—Unless reserved to a particular district judge who has knowledge of the family background, it may be helpful for the file in respect of a continuing fund to be transferred to the hearing centre of the County Court in the area where the child or protected beneficiary lives so that attendance at hearings relating to the application of the fund will be more convenient.

Powers of litigation friend—The role of the litigation friend is restricted to the conduct of the proceedings and his or her powers do not extend to dealing with the financial affairs of the protected beneficiary (*Leather v Kirby* [1965] 1 WLR 1489). He or she should, however, ensure that the fund is properly invested by the court and may have a sufficient continuing interest (eg as a parent or carer) to remain involved in the application of the fund by the court on behalf of the child or protected beneficiary. The person who is the litigation friend may, of course, also be the protected beneficiary's deputy (formerly receiver) or attorney and continue to administer the fund in that capacity.

Control of money: protected beneficiary—If the fund is substantial (over £50,000), or the protected beneficiary already has income or assets which need to be administered, the Court of Protection should administer the entire affairs. Subject to any public funding costs provision, the fund will be transferred to the Court of Protection to the credit of the protected beneficiary to be dealt with as the Court of Protection in its discretion thinks fit. The protected beneficiary's solicitor should approach the Court of Protection at an earlier stage so that there is no delay when the fund becomes available. Where, however, the fund is under £20,000 and there is no other reason to involve the Court of Protection (state benefits can be dealt with by an appointee), it can remain in court and be dealt with as if the protected beneficiary were a child (Practice Direction 21, para 10.2). Between these two figures, the Senior Judge of the Court of Protection should be consulted.

If there is a registered enduring or lasting power of attorney (in which event there will not be a deputy appointed by the Court of Protection), it would normally be appropriate for the attorney or donee who is managing the affairs to receive the fund. There may be concern about this if the fund is very large in relation to the estate that such attorney was appointed to administer, and in that event reference should be made to the Senior Judge of the Court of Protection who may wish to superimpose the appointment of a financial deputy.

Personal injury trust—The civil court should not approve a trust for the damages awarded to a protected beneficiary, although the Court of Protection may do so. For an analysis of the (uncommon) circumstances in which a trust may be authorised see *Re HM (A child)* [2012] WTLR 281 (also reported on Lawtel 27/1/12 and in *Court of Protection Practice 2016*).

Need for Court of Protection involvement—Someone who is treated as a protected party and has a litigation friend does not necessarily need to come under the jurisdiction of the Court of Protection. Conversely, a person within the jurisdiction of the Court of Protection is likely to require a litigation friend for civil proceedings. However, decision-specific tests of capacity must be applied.

21.12 Expenses incurred by a litigation friend

(1) In proceedings to which rule 21.11 applies, a litigation friend who incurs expenses on behalf of a child or protected party in any proceedings is entitled on application to recover the amount paid or payable out of any money recovered or paid into court to the extent that it –

    (a) has been reasonably incurred; and
    (b) is reasonable in amount.

(2) Expenses may include all or part of –

    (a) a premium in respect of a costs insurance policy (as defined by section 58C(5) of the Courts and Legal Services Act 1990)

(b) interest on a loan taken out to pay a premium in respect of a costs insurance policy or other recoverable disbursement.

(3) No application may be made under the rule for expenses that –

(a) are of a type that may be recoverable on an assessment of costs payable by or out of money belonging to a child or protected party; but
(b) are disallowed in whole or in part on such an assessment.

(Costs and expenses which are also 'costs' as defined in rule 44.1(1) are subject to rule 46.4(2) and (3).)

(4) In deciding whether the costs or expenses were reasonably incurred and reasonable in amount, the court will have regard to all the circumstances of the case including the factors set out in rule 44.5(3) and rule 46.9.

(5) When the court is considering the factors to be taken into account in assessing the reasonableness of the costs or expenses, it will have regard to the facts and circumstances as they reasonably appeared to the litigation friend or to the child's or protected party's legal representative when the cost or expense was incurred.

(6) Subject to paragraph (7), where the claim is settled or compromised, or judgment is given, on terms that an amount not exceeding £5,000 is paid to the child or protected party, the total amount the litigation friend may recover under paragraph (1) must not exceed 25% of the sum so agreed or awarded, unless the court directs otherwise. Such total amount must not exceed 50% of the sum so agreed or awarded.

(7) The amount which the litigation friend may recover under paragraph (1) in respect of costs must not (in proceedings at first instance) exceed 25% of the amount of the sum agreed or awarded in respect of –

(a) general damages for pain, suffering and loss of amenity; and
(b) damages for pecuniary loss other than future pecuniary loss, net of any sums recoverable by the Compensation Recovery Unit of the Department for Work and Pensions.

(8) Except in a case in which the costs payable to a child or protected party are fixed by these rules, no application may be made under this rule for a payment out of the money recovered by the child or protected party until the costs payable to the child or protected party have been assessed or agreed.

Amendments—SI 2007/2204; SI 2013/262; SI 2013/1974; SI 2014/3299.

Practice Direction—See generally Practice Direction 21, para 11.

Scope of provision—This rule clarifies the approach to be adopted by the court when a litigation friend seeks approval to deduct from the damages any expenses that are not recoverable from the defendant. For the purposes of this rule the success fee under a conditional fee agreement and the sum payable under a damages-based agreement are treated as 'costs' but only in personal injury claims by children where the damages recovered do not exceed £25,000. The treatment of such 'costs' does not extend to claims by protected parties. Expenses may include an insurance premium (and interest on a loan to fund the premium) in respect of costs insurance policies permitted by s 58C(5) of the Courts and Legal Services Act 1990 (essentially those in claims for clinical negligence). The rule is silent as to the recoverability of insurance premiums in respect of other insurance policies.

There has in the past been a difference of approach by district judges when approving settlements, but there is no reason why a child or protected party should be in a better position than any other claimant in such respect. If the costs and expenses were reasonably incurred at the inception of the claim and are reasonable in amount then the litigation friend should be indemnified. However, if the amounts were unreasonable this may reflect on the advice initially given by the solicitors involved. There is no procedure whereby such costs and expenses may be approved in advance.

The amount that the litigation friend may recover from a child in respect of the success fee under a conditional fee agreement or the sum payable under a damages-based agreement is limited to 25% of the aggregate of any awards of general damages for pain, suffering and loss of amenity and damages for past pecuniary loss (net of any sums recoverable by the CRU). Otherwise there is a limit of 25 per cent on the amount that may be deducted from damages not exceeding £5,000, although the court has a discretion to increase this up to 50 per cent.

Summary assessment—Rule 46.4(5)(b) provides that the costs and expenses which the litigation friend is seeking to recover from a child under this rule may be assessed summarily. The summary assessment may be undertaken at the conclusion of a hearing at which damages to be paid to the child are assessed, at an approval hearing pursuant to r.21.10 or at any time thereafter. Any application for payment out must be supported by a witness statement setting out (1) the nature of the cost or expense and (2) the reasons why the cost or expense was incurred (PD21, para 11.2). Where the litigation friend is seeking payment of a success fee under a conditional fee agreement or a sum payable under a damages-based agreement the witness statement must also include (or be accompanied by) (1) a copy of the CFA or DBA, (2) the risk assessment by reference to which the success fee was determined, (3) the reasons why the particular funding model was adopted, (4) the advice given to the litigation friend in relation to funding arrangements, (5) details of any costs agreed, recovered or fixed costs recoverable by the child and (6) a breakdown of the heads of damage and any CRU payment (PD21, para 11.3).

21.13 Appointment of a guardian of a child's estate

(1) The court may appoint the Official Solicitor to be a guardian of a child's estate where –

 (a) money is paid into court on behalf of the child in accordance with directions given under rule 21.11 (control of money received by a child or protected party);
 (b) the Criminal Injuries Compensation Authority notifies the court that it has made or intends to make an award to the child;
 (c) a court or tribunal outside England and Wales notifies the court that it has ordered or intends to order that money be paid to the child;
 (d) the child is absolutely entitled to the proceeds of a pension fund; or
 (e) in any other case, such an appointment seems desirable to the court.

(2) The court may not appoint the Official Solicitor under this rule unless –

 (a) the persons with parental responsibility (within the meaning of section 3 of the Children Act 1989) agree; or
 (b) the court considers that their agreement can be dispensed with.

(3) The Official Solicitor's appointment may continue only until the child reaches 18.

Amendments—Inserted by SI 2007/2204.

Practice Direction 21 – Children and Protected Parties

This Practice Direction supplements CPR 1998 Part 21 (PD21)

General

1.1 In proceedings where one of the parties is a protected party, the protected party should be referred to in the title to the proceedings as 'A.B. (a protected party by C.D. his litigation friend)'.

1.2 In proceedings where one of the parties is a child, where –

(1) the child has a litigation friend, the child should be referred to in the title to the proceedings as 'A.B. (a child by C.D. his litigation friend)'; or
(2) the child is conducting the proceedings on his own behalf, the child should be referred to in the title as 'A.B. (a child)'.

1.3 A settlement of a claim by a child includes an agreement on a sum to be apportioned to a dependent child under the Fatal Accidents Act 1976.

The Litigation Friend

2.1 A person may become a litigation friend –

(a) without a court order under rule 21.5, or
(b) by a court order under rule 21.6.

2.2 A person who wishes to become a litigation friend without a court order pursuant to rule 21.5(3) must file a certificate of suitability in Practice Form N235 –

(a) stating that he consents to act,
(b) stating that he knows or believes that the [claimant] [defendant] [is a child][lacks capacity to conduct the proceedings],
(c) in the case of a protected party, stating the grounds of his belief and, if his belief is based upon medical opinion or the opinion of another suitably qualified expert, attaching any relevant document to the certificate,
(d) stating that he can fairly and competently conduct proceedings on behalf of the child or protected party and has no interest adverse to that of the child or protected party, and
(e) where the child or protected party is a claimant, undertaking to pay any costs which the child or protected party may be ordered to pay in relation to the proceedings, subject to any right he may have to be repaid from the assets of the child or protected party.

2.3 The certificate of suitability must be verified by a statement of truth.

(Part 22 contains provisions about statements of truth.)

2.4 The litigation friend is not required to serve the document referred to in paragraph 2.2(c) when he serves a certificate of suitability on the person to be served under rule 21.5(4)(a).

Application for a Court Order Appointing a Litigation Friend

3.1 Rule 21.6 sets out who may apply for an order appointing a litigation friend.

3.2 An application must be made in accordance with Part 23 and must be supported by evidence.

3.3 The evidence in support must satisfy the court that the proposed litigation friend –

(1) consents to act,
(2) can fairly and competently conduct proceedings on behalf of the child or protected party,
(3) has no interest adverse to that of the child or protected party, and
(4) where the child or protected party is a claimant, undertakes to pay any costs which the child or protected party may be ordered to pay in relation to the proceedings, subject to any right he may have to be repaid from the assets of the child or protected party.

3.4 Where it is sought to appoint the Official Solicitor as the litigation friend, provision must be made for payment of his charges.

Procedure where the Need for a Litigation Friend Has Come to an End

4.1 Rule 21.9 deals with the situation where the need for a litigation friend comes to an end during the proceedings because either –

(1) a child who is not also a protected party reaches the age of 18 (full age) during the proceedings, or
(2) a protected party regains or acquires capacity to conduct the proceedings.

4.2 A child on reaching full age must serve on the other parties to the proceedings and file with the court a notice –

(1) stating that he has reached full age,
(2) stating that his litigation friend's appointment has ceased,
(3) giving an address for service, and
(4) stating whether or not he intends to carry on with or continue to defend the proceedings.

4.3 If the notice states that the child intends to carry on with or continue to defend the proceedings he must subsequently be described in the proceedings as 'A.B. (formerly a child but now of full age)'.

4.4 Whether or not a child having reached full age serves a notice in accordance with rule 21.9(4) and paragraph 4.2 above, a litigation friend may, at any time after the child has reached full age, serve a notice on the other parties that his appointment has ceased.

4.5 Where a protected party regains or acquires capacity to conduct the proceedings, an application under rule 21.9(3) must be made for an order under rule 21.9(2) that the litigation friend's appointment has ceased.

4.6 The application must be supported by the following evidence –

(1) a medical report or other suitably qualified expert's report indicating that the protected party has regained or acquired capacity to conduct the proceedings,
(2) a copy of any relevant order or declaration of the Court of Protection, and
(3) if the application is made by the protected party, a statement whether or not he intends to carry on with or continue to defend the proceedings.

4.7 An order under rule 21.9(2) must be served on the other parties to the proceedings. The former protected party must file with the court a notice –

(1) stating that his litigation friend's appointment has ceased,
(2) giving an address for service, and
(3) stating whether or not he intends to carry on with or continue to defend the proceedings.

Settlement or Compromise by or on behalf of a Child or Protected Party Before the Issue of Proceedings

5.1 Where a claim by or on behalf of a child or protected party has been dealt with by agreement before the issue of proceedings and only the approval of the court to the agreement is sought, the claim must, in addition to containing the details of the claim and satisfying the requirements of rule 21.10(2), include the following –

(1) subject to paragraph 5.3, the terms of the settlement or compromise or have attached to it a draft consent order in Practice Form N292;
(2) details of whether and to what extent the defendant admits liability;
(3) the age and occupation (if any) of the child or protected party;
(4) the litigation friend's approval of the proposed settlement or compromise,
(5) a copy of any financial advice relating to the proposed settlement; and
(6) in a personal injury case arising from an accident –
  (a) details of the circumstances of the accident,
  (b) medical and quantum reports and joint statements material to the opinion required by paragraph 5.2
  (c) where appropriate, a schedule of any past and future expenses and losses claimed and any other relevant information relating to the personal injury as set out in Practice Direction 16, and
  (d) where considerations of liability are raised –
    (i) any evidence or reports in any criminal proceedings or in an inquest, and
    (ii) details of any prosecution brought.

5.2 (1) An opinion on the merits of the settlement or compromise given by counsel or solicitor acting for the child or protected party must, except in very clear cases, be obtained.
(2) A copy of the opinion and, unless the instructions on which it was given are sufficiently set out in it, a copy of the instructions, must be supplied to the court.

5.3 Where in any personal injury case a claim for damages for future pecuniary loss is settled, the provisions in paragraphs 5.4 and 5.5 must in addition be complied with.

5.4 The court must be satisfied that the parties have considered whether the damages should wholly or partly take the form of periodical payments.

5.5 Where the settlement includes provision for periodical payments, the claim must –

(1) set out the terms of the settlement or compromise; or
(2) have attached to it a draft consent order,

which must satisfy the requirements of rules 41.8 and 41.9 as appropriate.

5.6 Applications for the approval of a settlement or compromise will normally be heard by –

(1) a Master or a District Judge in proceedings involving a child; and
(2) a Master, Designated Civil Judge or his nominee in proceedings involving a protected party.

(For information about provisional damages claims see Part 41 and Practice Direction 41A.)

Settlement or Compromise by or on behalf of a Child or Protected Party After Proceedings Have Been Issued

6.1 Where in any personal injury case a claim for damages for future pecuniary loss, by or on behalf of a child or protected party, is dealt with by agreement after proceedings have been issued, an application must be made for the court's approval of the agreement.

6.2 The court must be satisfied that the parties have considered whether the damages should wholly or partly take the form of periodical payments.

6.3 Where the settlement includes provision for periodical payments, an application under paragraph 6.1 must –

(1) set out the terms of the settlement or compromise; or
(2) have attached to it a draft consent order,

which must satisfy the requirements of rules 41.8 and 41.9 as appropriate.

6.4 The court must be supplied with –

(1) an opinion on the merits of the settlement or compromise given by counsel or solicitor acting for the child or protected party, except in very clear cases; and
(2) a copy of any financial advice; and
(3) documentary evidence material to the opinion referred to at paragraph 6.4(1).

6.5 Applications for the approval of a settlement or compromise, except at the trial, will normally be heard by –

(1) a Master or a District Judge in proceedings involving a child; and
(2) a Master, Designated Civil Judge or his nominee in proceedings involving a protected party.

Apportionment under the Fatal Accidents Act 1976

7.1 A judgment on or settlement in respect of a claim under the Fatal Accidents Act 1976 must be apportioned between the persons by or on whose behalf the claim has been brought.

7.2 Where a claim is brought on behalf of a dependent child or children, any settlement (including an agreement on a sum to be apportioned to a dependent child under the Fatal Accidents Act 1976) must be approved by the court.

7.3 The money apportioned to any dependent child must be invested on the child's behalf in accordance with rules 21.10 and 21.11 and paragraphs 8 and 9 below.

7.4 In order to approve an apportionment of money to a dependent child, the court will require the following information:

(1) the matters set out in paragraphs 5.1(2) and (3), and
(2) in respect of the deceased –
    (a) where death was caused by an accident, the matters set out in paragraphs 5.1(6)(a), (b) and (c), and
    (b) his future loss of earnings, and
(3) the extent and nature of the dependency.

Control of Money Recovered By or On Behalf of a Child or Protected Party

8.1 When giving directions under rule 21.11, the court –
   (1) may direct the money to be paid into court for investment,
   (2) may direct that certain sums be paid direct to the child or protected beneficiary, his litigation friend or his legal representative for the immediate benefit of the child or protected beneficiary or for expenses incurred on his behalf, and
   (3) may direct that the application in respect of the investment of the money be transferred to a local district registry.

8.2 The court will consider the general aims to be achieved for the money in court (the fund) by investment and will give directions as to the type of investment.

8.3 Where a child also lacks capacity to manage and control any money recovered by him or on his behalf in the proceedings, and is likely to remain so on reaching full age, his fund should be administered as a protected beneficiary's fund.

8.4 Where a child or protected beneficiary is in receipt of publicly funded legal services the fund will be subject to a first charge under section 10 of the Access to Justice Act 1999 (statutory charge) and an order for the investment of money on the child's or protected beneficiary's behalf must contain a direction to that effect.

Investment On Behalf of a Child

9.1 At the hearing of an application for the approval of a settlement or compromise the litigation friend or his legal representative must provide, in addition to the information required by paragraphs 5 and 6 –
   (1) a CFO form 320 (initial application for investment of damages) for completion by the judge hearing the application; and
   (2) any evidence or information which the litigation friend wishes the court to consider in relation to the investment of the award for damages.

9.2 Following the hearing in paragraph 9.1, the court will forward to the Court Funds Office a request for investment decision (form 212) and the Court Funds Office will make the appropriate investment.

9.3 Where an award for damages for a child is made at trial, unless paragraph 9.7 applies, the trial judge will –
   (1) direct the money to be paid into court and placed into the special investment account until further investment directions have been given by the court;
   (2) direct the litigation friend to make an application to a Master or District Judge for further investment directions; and
   (3) give such other directions as the trial judge thinks fit, including a direction that the hearing of the application for further investment directions will be fixed for a date within 28 days from the date of the trial.

9.4 The application under paragraph 9.3(2) must be made by filing with the court –
   (1) a completed CFO form 320; and
   (2) any evidence or information which the litigation friend wishes the court to consider in relation to the investment of the award for damages.

9.5 The application must be sent in proceedings in the Royal Courts of Justice to the Masters' Support Unit (Room E16) at the Royal Courts of Justice.

9.6 If the application required by paragraph 9.3(2) is not made to the court, the money paid into court in accordance with paragraph 9.3(1) will remain in the special investment account subject to any further order of the court or paragraph 9.8.

9.7 If the money to be invested is very small the court may order it to be paid direct to the litigation friend to be put into a building society account (or similar) for the child's use.

9.8 If the money is invested in court, it must be paid out to the child on application when he reaches full age.

Investment On Behalf of a Protected Beneficiary

10.1 The Court of Protection has jurisdiction to make decisions in the best interests of a protected beneficiary. Fees may be charged for the administration of funds and these must be provided for in any settlement.

10.2
(1) Where the sum to be invested for the benefit of the protected beneficiary is £50,000 or more (save where under paragraph 10.2A the Court of Protection has authorised a sum of £50,000 or more to be dealt with under subparagraph (2) below) unless a person with authority as –
   (a) the attorney under a registered enduring power of attorney;
   (b) the donee of a lasting power of attorney; or
   (c) the deputy appointed by the Court of Protection,
   to administer or manage the protected beneficiary's financial affairs has been appointed, the order approving the settlement will contain a direction to the litigation friend to apply to the Court of Protection for the appointment of a deputy, after which the fund will be dealt with as directed by the Court of Protection; or
(2) Where the sum to be invested for the benefit of the protected party is under £50,000, or such sum as may be authorised by the Court of Protection under paragraph 10.2A, it may be retained in court and invested in the same way as the fund of a child.

10.2A The Court of Protection may authorise a sum of £50,000 or more to be retained in court and invested it the same way as the fund of a child under subparagraph 10.2(2), either of its own initiative or at the request of the judge giving investment directions in respect of the protected beneficiary.

10.3 A form of order transferring the fund to the Court of Protection is set out in practice form N292.

10.4 In order for the Court Funds Office to release a fund which is subject to the statutory charge, the litigation friend or his legal representative or the person with authority referred to in paragraph 10.2(1) must provide the appropriate regional office of the Legal Services Commission with an undertaking in respect of a sum to cover their costs, following which the regional office will advise the Court Funds Office in writing of that sum, enabling them to transfer the balance to the Court of Protection on receipt of a CFO form 200 payment schedule authorised by the court.

10.5 The CFO form 200 should be completed and presented to the court where the settlement or trial took place for authorisation, subject to paragraphs 10.6 and 10.7.

10.6 Where the settlement took place in the Royal Courts of Justice the CFO form 200 must be completed and presented for authorisation –
(1) on behalf of a child, in the Masters' Support Unit, Room E105, and

(2) on behalf of a protected beneficiary, in the Judgment and Orders Section in the Action Department, Room E17.

10.7 Where the trial took place in the Royal Courts of Justice, the CFO form 200 is completed and authorised by the court officer.

Costs or expenses Incurred by a Litigation Friend

11.1 A litigation friend may make a claim for costs or expenses under rule 21.12(1) –

- (1) where the court has ordered an assessment of costs under rule 46.4(2), at the detailed assessment hearing;
- (1A) where the court has assessed the costs to be paid by the child by way of summary assessment under rule 46.4(5)(b), at the conclusion of the hearing at which damages to be paid to the child are assessed or at the hearing to approve the compromise or settlement under Part 21, or at any time thereafter;
- (2) where the litigation friend's expenses are not of a type which would be recoverable as costs on an assessment of costs between the parties, to the Master or District Judge at the hearing to approve the settlement or compromise under Part 21 (the Master or District Judge may adjourn the matter to the costs judge); or
- (3) where an assessment of costs under rule 46.4(2) is not required, and no approval under Part 21 is necessary, by a Part 23 application supported by a witness statement to a Costs Judge or District Judge as appropriate.

11.2 In all circumstances, the litigation friend must support a claim for payment out in relation to costs or expenses by filing a witness statement setting out –

- (1) the nature and amount of the costs or expense; and
- (2) the reason the costs or expense were incurred.

11.3 Where the application is for payment out of the damages in respect of costs pursuant to rule 21.12(1A) the witness statement must also include (or be accompanied by) –

- (1) a copy of the conditional fee agreement or damages based agreement;
- (2) the risk assessment by reference to which the success fee was determined;
- (3) the reasons why the particular funding model was selected;
- (4) the advice given to the litigation friend in relation to funding arrangements;
- (5) details of any costs agreed, recovered or fixed costs recoverable by the child; and
- (6) confirmation of the amount of the sum agreed or awarded in respect of –
  - (a) general damages for pain, suffering and loss of amenity; and
  - (b) damages for pecuniary loss other than future pecuniary loss,

net of any sums recoverable by the Compensation Recovery Unit of the Department for Work and Pensions.

Guardian's Accounts

12 Paragraph 8 of the practice direction supplementing Part 40 (Judgments and Orders) deals with the approval of the accounts of a guardian of assets of a child.

Payment out of Funds in Court

13.1 Applications to a Master or district judge –

(1) for payment out of money from the fund for the benefit of the child, or
(2) to vary an investment strategy,

may be dealt with without a hearing unless the court directs otherwise.

13.2 When the child reaches full age –

(1) where his fund in court is a sum of money, it will be paid out to him on application; or
(2) where his fund is in the form of investments other than money (for example shares or unit trusts), the investments will on application be –
    (a) sold and the proceeds of sale paid out to him; or
    (b) transferred into his name.

13.3 Where the fund is administered by the Court of Protection, any payment out of money from that fund must be in accordance with any decision or order of the Court of Protection.

13.4 If an application is required for the payment out of money from a fund administered by the Court of Protection, that application must be made to the Court of Protection.

(For further information on payments out of court, see the practice direction supplementing Part 37.)

****

PART 44
GENERAL RULES ABOUT COSTS

Note—Below are the new costs rules that were brought into force in April 2013.

Section 1 – General

44.1 Interpretation and application

(1) In Parts 44 to 47, unless the context otherwise requires –
    'authorised court officer' means any officer or –
        (i) the County Court;
        (ii) a district registry;
        (iii) the Family Court;
        (iiia) the High Court; or
        (iv) the Costs Office,
    whom the Lord Chancellor has authorised to assess costs;
    'costs' includes fees, charges, disbursements, expenses, remuneration, reimbursement allowed to a litigant in person under rule 46.5 and any fee or reward charged by a lay representative for acting on behalf of a party in proceedings allocated to the small claims track;
    'costs judge' means a taxing master of the Senior Courts;
    'Costs Office' means the Senior Courts Costs Office;
    'costs officer' means –
        (i) a costs judge;
        (ii) a District Judge; or
        (iii) an authorised court officer;
    'detailed assessment' means the procedure by which the amount of costs is decided by a costs officer in accordance with Part 47;

'the Director (legal aid)' means the person designated as the Director of Legal Aid Casework pursuant to section 4 of the Legal Aid, Sentencing and Punishment of Offenders Act 2012, or a person entitled to exercise the functions of the Director;

'fixed costs' means costs the amounts of which are fixed by these rules whether or not the court has a discretion to allow some other or no amount, and include –
  (i) the amounts which are to be allowed in respect of legal representatives' charges in the circumstances set out in Section I of Part 45;
  (ii) fixed recoverable costs calculated in accordance with rule 45.11;
  (iii) the additional costs allowed by rule 45.18;
  (iv) fixed costs determined under rule 45.21;
  (v) costs fixed by rules 45.37 and 45.38;

'free of charge' has the same meaning as in section 194(10) of the 2007 Act;

'fund' includes any estate or property held for the benefit of any person or class of person and any fund to which a trustee or personal representative is entitled in that capacity;

'HMRC' means HM Revenue and Customs;

'legal aid' means civil legal services made available under arrangements made for the purposes of Part 1 of the Legal Aid, Sentencing and Punishment of Offenders Act 2012;

'paying party' means a party liable to pay costs;

'the prescribed charity' has the same meaning as in section 194(8) of the 2007 Act;

'pro bono representation' means legal representation provided free of charge;

'receiving party' means a party entitled to be paid costs;

'summary assessment' means the procedure whereby costs are assessed by the judge who has heard the case or application;

'VAT' means Value Added Tax;

'the 2007 Act' means the Legal Services Act 2007.

('Legal representative' has the meaning given in rule 2.3.)

(2) The costs to which Parts 44 to 47 apply include –
  (a) the following costs where those costs may be assessed by the court –
    (i) costs of proceedings before an arbitrator or umpire;
    (ii) costs of proceedings before a tribunal or other statutory body; and
    (iii) costs payable by a client to their legal representative; and
  (b) costs which are payable by one party to another party under the terms of a contract, where the court makes an order for an assessment of those costs.

(3) Where advocacy or litigation services are provided to a client under a conditional fee agreement, costs are recoverable under Parts 44 to 47 notwithstanding that the client is liable to pay the legal representative's fees and expenses only to the extent that sums are recovered in respect of the proceedings, whether by way of costs or otherwise.

Amendments—Inserted by SI 2013/262. Amended by SI 2014/407.

44.2 Court's discretion as to costs

(1) The court has discretion as to –
  (a) whether costs are payable by one party to another;

(b) the amount of those costs; and
(c) when they are to be paid.

(2) If the court decides to make an order about costs –

(a) the general rule is that the unsuccessful party will be ordered to pay the costs of the successful party; but
(b) the court may make a different order.

(3) The general rule does not apply to the following proceedings –

(a) proceedings in the Court of Appeal on an application or appeal made in connection with proceedings in the Family Division; or
(b) proceedings in the Court of Appeal from a judgment, direction, decision or order given or made in probate proceedings or family proceedings.

(4) In deciding what order (if any) to make about costs, the court will have regard to all the circumstances, including –

(a) the conduct of all the parties;
(b) whether a party has succeeded on part of its case, even if that party has not been wholly successful; and
(c) any admissible offer to settle made by a party which is drawn to the court's attention, and which is not an offer to which costs consequences under Part 36 apply.

(5) The conduct of the parties includes –

(a) conduct before, as well as during, the proceedings and in particular the extent to which the parties followed the Practice Direction – Pre-Action Conduct or any relevant pre-action protocol;
(b) whether it was reasonable for a party to raise, pursue or contest a particular allegation or issue;
(c) the manner in which a party has pursued or defended the case or a particular allegation or issue; and
(d) whether a claimant who has succeeded in the claim, in whole or in part, exaggerated its claim.

(6) The orders which the court may make under this rule include an order that a party must pay –

(a) a proportion of another party's costs;
(b) a stated amount in respect of another party's costs;
(c) costs from or until a certain date only;
(d) costs incurred before proceedings have begun;
(e) costs relating to particular steps taken in the proceedings;
(f) costs relating only to a distinct part of the proceedings; and
(g) interest on costs from or until a certain date, including a date before judgment.

(7) Before the court considers making an order under paragraph (6)(f), it will consider whether it is practicable to make an order under paragraph (6)(a) or (c) instead.

(8) Where the court orders a party to pay costs subject to detailed assessment, it will order that party to pay a reasonable sum on account of costs, unless there is good reason not to do so.

Amendments—Inserted by SI 2013/262.

44.3 Basis of assessment

(1) Where the court is to assess the amount of costs (whether by summary or detailed assessment) it will assess those costs –

    (a) on the standard basis; or
    (b) on the indemnity basis,

but the court will not in either case allow costs which have been unreasonably incurred or are unreasonable in amount.

> (Rule 44.5 sets out how the court decides the amount of costs payable under a contract.)

(2) Where the amount of costs is to be assessed on the standard basis, the court will –

    (a) only allow costs which are proportionate to the matters in issue. Costs which are disproportionate in amount may be disallowed or reduced even if they were reasonably or necessarily incurred; and
    (b) resolve any doubt which it may have as to whether costs were reasonably and proportionately incurred or were reasonable and proportionate in amount in favour of the paying party.

> (Factors which the court may take into account are set out in rule 44.4.)

(3) Where the amount of costs is to be assessed on the indemnity basis, the court will resolve any doubt which it may have as to whether costs were reasonably incurred or were reasonable in amount in favour of the receiving party.

(4) Where –

    (a) the court makes an order about costs without indicating the basis on which the costs are to be assessed; or
    (b) the court makes an order for costs to be assessed on a basis other than the standard basis or the indemnity basis,

the costs will be assessed on the standard basis.

(5) Costs incurred are proportionate if they bear a reasonable relationship to –

    (a) the sums in issue in the proceedings;
    (b) the value of any non-monetary relief in issue in the proceedings;
    (c) the complexity of the litigation;
    (d) any additional work generated by the conduct of the paying party; and
    (e) any wider factors involved in the proceedings, such as reputation or public importance.

(6) Where the amount of a solicitor's remuneration in respect of non-contentious business is regulated by any general orders made under the Solicitors Act 1974, the amount of the costs to be allowed in respect of any such business which falls to be assessed by the court will be decided in accordance with those general orders rather than this rule and rule 44.4.

(7) Paragraphs (2)(a) and (5) do not apply in relation to –

    (a) cases commenced before 1 April 2013; or
    (b) costs incurred in respect of work done before 1 April 2013,

and in relation to such cases or costs, rule 44.4.(2)(a) as it was in force immediately before 1 April 2013 will apply instead.

Amendments—Inserted by SI 2013/262. Amended by SI 2013/515.

44.4 Factors to be taken into account in deciding the amount of costs

(1) The court will have regard to all the circumstances in deciding whether costs were –

  (a) if it is assessing costs on the standard basis –
    (i) proportionately and reasonably incurred; or
    (ii) proportionate and reasonable in amount, or
  (b) if it is assessing costs on the indemnity basis –
    (i) unreasonably incurred; or
    (ii) unreasonable in amount.

(2) In particular, the court will give effect to any orders which have already been made.

(3) The court will also have regard to –

  (a) the conduct of all the parties, including in particular –
    (i) conduct before, as well as during, the proceedings; and
    (ii) the efforts made, if any, before and during the proceedings in order to try to resolve the dispute;
  (b) the amount or value of any money or property involved;
  (c) the importance of the matter to all the parties;
  (d) the particular complexity of the matter or the difficulty or novelty of the questions raised;
  (e) the skill, effort, specialised knowledge and responsibility involved;
  (f) the time spent on the case;
  (g) the place where and the circumstances in which work or any part of it was done; and
  (h) the receiving party's last approved or agreed budget.

   (Rule 35.4(4) gives the court power to limit the amount that a party may recover with regard to the fees and expenses of an expert.)

Amendments—Inserted by SI 2013/262.

44.5 Amount of costs where costs are payable under a contract

(1) Subject to paragraphs (2) to (4), where the court assesses (whether by summary or detailed assessment) costs which are payable by the paying party to the receiving party under the terms of a contract, the costs payable under those terms are, unless the contract expressly provides otherwise, to be presumed to be costs which –

  (a) have been reasonably incurred; and
  (b) are reasonable in amount,

and the court will assess them accordingly.

(2) The presumptions in paragraph (1) are rebuttable.

(3) Paragraph (1) does not apply where the contract is between a solicitor and client.

Amendments—Inserted by SI 2013/262.

44.6 Procedure for assessing costs

(1) Where the court orders a party to pay costs to another party (other than fixed costs) it may either –

(a) make a summary assessment of the costs; or
(b) order detailed assessment of the costs by a costs officer,

unless any rule, practice direction or other enactment provides otherwise.

(Practice Direction 44 – General rules about costs sets out the factors which will affect the court's decision under paragraph (1).)

(2) A party may recover the fixed costs specified in Part 45 in accordance with that Part.

Amendments—Inserted by SI 2013/262.

44.7 Time for complying with an order for costs

A party must comply with an order for the payment of costs within 14 days of –

(a) the date of the judgment or order if it states the amount of those costs;
(b) if the amount of those costs (or part of them) is decided later in accordance with Part 47, the date of the certificate which states the amount; or
(c) in either case, such other date as the court may specify.

(Part 47 sets out the procedure for detailed assessment of costs.)

Amendments—Inserted by SI 2013/262.

44.8 Legal representative's duty to notify the party

Where –

(a) the court makes a costs order against a legally represented party; and
(b) the party is not present when the order is made,

the party's legal representative must notify that party in writing of the costs order no later than 7 days after the legal representative receives notice of the order.

(Paragraph 10.1 of Practice Direction 44 defines 'party' for the purposes of this rule.)

Amendments—Inserted by SI 2013/262.

44.9 Cases where costs orders deemed to have been made

(1) Subject to paragraph (2), where a right to costs arises under –

(a1) rule 3.7B (sanctions for dishonouring cheque);
(a) rule 3.7 (defendant's right to costs where claim is struck out for non-payment of fees);
(b) rule 36.13(1) or (2) (claimant's entitlement to costs where a Part 36 offer is accepted); or
(c) rule 38.6 (defendant's right to costs where claimant discontinues),

a costs order will be deemed to have been made on the standard basis.

(2) Paragraph 1(b) does not apply where a Part 36 offer is accepted before the commencement of proceedings.

(3) Where such an order is deemed to be made in favour of a party with pro bono representation, that party may apply for an order under section 194(3) of the 2007 Act.

(4) Interest payable under section 17 of the Judgments Act 1838 or section 74 of the County Courts Act 1984 on the costs deemed to have been ordered under paragraph (1) will begin to run from the date on which the event which gave rise to the entitlement to costs occurred.

Amendments—Inserted by SI 2013/262. Amended by SI 2013/1974; SI 2014/3299.

44.10 Where the court makes no order for costs

(1) Where the court makes an order which does not mention costs –

    (a) subject to paragraphs (2) and (3), the general rule is that no party is entitled –
        (i) to costs; or
        (ii) to seek an order under section 194(3) of the 2007 Act,

in relation to that order; but

    (b) this does not affect any entitlement of a party to recover costs out of a fund held by that party as trustee or personal representative, or under any lease, mortgage or other security.

(2) Where the court makes –

    (a) an order granting permission to appeal;
    (b) an order granting permission to apply for judicial review; or
    (c) any other order or direction sought by a party on an application without notice,

and its order does not mention costs, it will be deemed to include an order for applicant's costs in the case.

(3) Any party affected by a deemed order for costs under paragraph (2) may apply at any time to vary the order.

(4) The court hearing an appeal may, unless it dismisses the appeal, make orders about the costs of the proceedings giving rise to the appeal as well as the costs of the appeal.

(5) Subject to any order made by the transferring court, where proceedings are transferred from one court to another, the court to which they are transferred may deal with all the costs, including the costs before the transfer.

Amendments—Inserted by SI 2013/262.

44.11 Court's powers in relation to misconduct

(1) The court may make an order under this rule where –

    (a) a party or that party's legal representative, in connection with a summary or detailed assessment, fails to comply with a rule, practice direction or court order; or
    (b) it appears to the court that the conduct of a party or that party's legal representative, before or during the proceedings or in the assessment proceedings, was unreasonable or improper.

(2) Where paragraph (1) applies, the court may –

    (a) disallow all or part of the costs which are being assessed; or

(b) order the party at fault or that party's legal representative to pay costs which that party or legal representative has caused any other party to incur.

(3) Where –
   (a) the court makes an order under paragraph (2) against a legally represented party; and
   (b) the party is not present when the order is made,

the party's legal representative must notify that party in writing of the order no later than 7 days after the legal representative receives notice of the order.

Amendments—Inserted by SI 2013/262.

44.12 Set off

Where a party entitled to costs is also liable to pay costs, the court may assess the costs which that party is liable to pay and either –
   (a) set off the amount assessed against the amount the party is entitled to be paid and direct that party to pay any balance; or
   (b) delay the issue of a certificate for the costs to which the party is entitled until the party has paid the amount which that party is liable to pay.

Amendments—Inserted by SI 2013/262.

Section II – Qualified One-Way Costs Shifting

44.13 Qualified one-way costs shifting: scope and interpretation

(1) This Section applies to proceedings which include a claim for damages –
   (a) for personal injuries;
   (b) under the Fatal Accidents Act 1976; or
   (c) which arises out of death or personal injury and survives for the benefit of an estate by virtue of section 1(1) of the Law Reform (Miscellaneous Provisions) Act 1934,

but does not apply to applications pursuant to section 33 of the Senior Courts Act 1981 or section 52 of the County Courts Act 1984 (applications for pre-action disclosure), or where rule 44.17 applies.

(2) In this Section, 'claimant' means a person bringing a claim to which this Section applies or an estate on behalf of which such a claim is brought, and includes a person making a counterclaim or an additional claim.

Amendments—Inserted by SI 2013/262.

44.14 Effect of qualified one-way costs shifting

(1) Subject to rules 44.15 and 44.16, orders for costs made against a claimant may be enforced without the permission of the court but only to the extent that the aggregate amount in money terms of such orders does not exceed the aggregate amount in money terms of any orders for damages and interest made in favour of the claimant.

(2) Orders for costs made against a claimant may only be enforced after the proceedings have been concluded and the costs have been assessed or agreed.

(3) An order for costs which is enforced only to the extent permitted by paragraph (1) shall not be treated as an unsatisfied or outstanding judgment for the purposes of any court record.

Amendments—Inserted by SI 2013/262.

44.15 Exceptions to qualified one-way costs shifting where permission not required

Orders for costs made against the claimant may be enforced to the full extent of such orders without the permission of the court where the proceedings have been struck out on the grounds that –

  (a) the claimant has disclosed no reasonable grounds for bringing the proceedings;
  (b) the proceedings are an abuse of the court's process; or
  (c) the conduct of –
    (i) the claimant; or
    (ii) a person acting on the claimant's behalf and with the claimant's knowledge of such conduct,

is likely to obstruct the just disposal of the proceedings.

Amendments—Inserted by SI 2013/262.

44.16 Exceptions to qualified one-way costs shifting where permission required

(1) Orders for costs made against the claimant may be enforced to the full extent of such orders with the permission of the court where the claim is found on the balance of probabilities to be fundamentally dishonest.

(2) Orders for costs made against the claimant may be enforced up to the full extent of such orders with the permission of the court, and to the extent that it considers just, where –

  (a) the proceedings include a claim which is made for the financial benefit of a person other than the claimant or a dependant within the meaning of section 1(3) of the Fatal Accidents Act 1976 (other than a claim in respect of the gratuitous provision of care, earnings paid by an employer or medical expenses); or
  (b) a claim is made for the benefit of the claimant other than a claim to which this Section applies.

(3) Where paragraph (2)(a) applies, the court may, subject to rule 46.2, make an order for costs against a person, other than the claimant, for whose financial benefit the whole or part of the claim was made.

Amendments—Inserted by SI 2013/262.

44.17 Transitional provision

This Section does not apply to proceedings where the claimant has entered into a pre-commencement funding arrangement (as defined in rule 48.2).

Section III — Damages-based agreements

44.18 Award of costs where there is a damages-based agreement

(1) The fact that a party has entered into a damages-based agreement will not affect the making of any order for costs which otherwise would be made in favour of that party.

(2) Where costs are to be assessed in favour of a party who has entered into a damages-based agreement –

  (a) the party's recoverable costs will be assessed in accordance with rule 44.3; and
  (b) the party may not recover by way of costs more than the total amount payable by that party under the damages-based agreement for legal services provided under that agreement.

Amendments—Inserted by SI 2013/262.

Practice Direction 44 – General Rules About Costs

This Practice Direction supplements CPR 1998 Part 44 (PD44)

SECTION I – GENERAL
SUBSECTION 1 OF THIS PRACTICE DIRECTION

Documents and Forms

1.1 In respect of any document which is required by Practice Directions 44 to 47 to be signed by a party or that party's legal representative, the provisions of Practice Direction 22 relating to who may sign apply as if the document in question was a statement of truth. Statements of truth are not required in assessment proceedings unless a rule of Practice Direction so requires or the court so orders.

> (Practice Direction 22 makes provision for cases in which a party is a child, a protected party or a company or other corporation and cases in which a document is signed on behalf of a partnership.)

1.2 Form N260 is a model form of Statement of Costs to be used for summary assessments.

> (Further details about Statements of Costs are given in paragraph 9.5 below.)

Precedents A, B and C in the Schedule of Costs Precedents annexed to this Practice Direction are model forms of bills of costs to be used for detailed assessments. A party wishing to rely upon a bill which departs from the model forms should include in the background information of the bill an explanation for that departure.

> (Further details about bills of costs are given in Practice Direction 47.)

SUBSECTION 2 OF THIS PRACTICE DIRECTION – SPECIAL PROVISIONS RELATING TO VAT

Scope of this subsection

2.1 This subsection deals with claims for VAT) which are made in respect of costs being dealt with by way of summary assessment or detailed assessment.

VAT Registration Number

2.2 The number allocated by HMRC to every person registered under the Value Added Tax Act 1994 (except a Government Department) must appear in a prominent place at the head of every statement, bill of costs, fee sheet, account or voucher on which VAT is being included as part of a claim for costs.

Entitlement to VAT on Costs

2.3 VAT should not be included in a claim for costs if the receiving party is able to recover the VAT as input tax. Where the receiving party is able to obtain credit from HMRC for a proportion of the VAT as input tax, only that proportion which is not eligible for credit should be included in the claim for costs.

2.4 The receiving party has responsibility for ensuring that VAT is claimed only when the receiving party is unable to recover the VAT or a proportion thereof as input tax.

2.5 Where there is a dispute as to whether VAT is properly claimed the receiving party must provide a certificate signed by the legal representatives or the auditors of the receiving party substantially in the form illustrated in Precedent F in the Schedule of Costs Precedents annexed to Practice Direction 47. Where the receiving party is a litigant in person who is claiming VAT, evidence to support the claim (such as a letter from HMRC) must be produced at the hearing at which the costs are assessed.

2.6 Where there is a dispute as to whether any service in respect of which a charge is proposed to be made in the bill is zero rated or exempt from VAT, reference should be made to HMRC and its view obtained and made known at the hearing at which the costs are assessed. Such enquiry should be made by the receiving party. In the case of a bill from a solicitor to the solicitor's legal representative's own client, such enquiry should be made by the client.

Form of bill of costs where VAT rate changes

2.7 Where there is a change in the rate of VAT, suppliers of goods and services are entitled by sections 88(1) and 88(2) of the Value Added Tax Act 1994 in most circumstances to elect whether the new or the old rate of VAT should apply to a supply where the basic and actual tax points span a period during which the rate changed.

2.8 It will be assumed, unless a contrary indication is given in writing, that an election to take advantage of the provisions mentioned in paragraph 2.7 and to charge VAT at the lower rate has been made. In any case in which an election to charge at the lower rate is not made, such a decision must be justified to the court assessing the costs.

Apportionment

2.9 Subject to 2.7 and 2.8, all bills of costs, fees and disbursements on which VAT is included must be divided into separate parts so as to show work done before, on and after the date or dates from which any change in the rate of VAT takes effect. Where, however, a lump sum charge is made for work which spans a period during which there has been a change in VAT rates, and paragraphs 2.7 and 2.8 above do not apply, reference should be made to paragraphs 30.7 or 30.8 of the VAT Guide (Notice 700) (or any revised edition of that notice) published by HMRC. If necessary, the lump sum should be apportioned. The totals of profit costs and disbursements in each part must be carried separately to the summary.

Change in VAT rate between the conclusion of a detailed settlement and the issue of a final certificate

2.10 Should there be a change in the rate between the conclusion of a detailed assessment and the issue of the final costs certificate, any interested party may apply for the detailed assessment to be varied so as to take account of any increase or reduction in the amount of tax payable. Once the final costs certificate has been issued, no variation under this paragraph will be permitted.

Disbursements not classified as such for VAT purposes

2.11

(1) Legal representatives often make payments to third parties for the supply of goods or services where no VAT was chargeable on the supply by the third party: for example, the cost of meals taken and travel costs. The question whether legal representatives should include VAT in respect of these payments when invoicing their clients or in claims for costs between litigants should be decided in accordance with this Practice Direction and with the criteria set out in the VAT Guide (Notice 700).

(2) Payments to third parties which are normally treated as part of the legal representative's overheads (for example, postage costs and telephone costs) will not be treated as disbursements. The third party supply should be included as part of the costs of the legal representatives' legal services and VAT must be added to the total bill charged to the client.

(3) Disputes may arise in respect of payments made to a third party which the legal representative shows as disbursements in the invoice delivered to the receiving party. Some payments, although correctly described as disbursements for some purposes, are not classified as disbursements for VAT purposes. Items not classified as disbursements for VAT purposes must be shown as part of the services provided by the legal representative and, therefore, VAT must be added in respect of them whether or not VAT was chargeable on the supply by the third party.

(4) Guidance as to the circumstances in which disbursements may or may not be classified as disbursements for VAT purposes is given in the VAT Guide (Notice 700, paragraph 25.1). One of the key issues is whether the third party supply –

(a) was made to the legal representative (and therefore subsumed in the onward supply of legal services); or

(b) was made direct to the receiving party (the third party having no right to demand payment from the legal representative, who makes the payment only as agent for the receiving party).

(5) Examples of payments under subparagraph (4)(a) are: travelling expenses,

such as an airline ticket, and subsistence expenses, such as the cost of meals, where the person travelling and receiving the meals is the legal representative. The supplies by the airline and the restaurant are supplies to the legal representative, not to the client.

(6) Payments under subparagraph (4)(b) are classified as disbursements for VAT purposes and, therefore, the legal representative need not add VAT in respect of them. Simple examples are payments by a legal representative of court fees and payment of fees to an expert witness.

Litigants in person

2.12 Where a litigant acts in person, that litigant is not treated for the purposes of VAT as having supplied services and therefore no VAT is chargeable in respect of work done by that litigant (even where, for example, that litigant is a solicitor or other legal representative). Consequently in such circumstances a bill of costs should not claim any VAT.

Government Departments

2.13 On an assessment between parties, where costs are being paid to a Government Department in respect of services rendered by its legal staff, VAT should not be added.

Payment pursuant to an order under section 194(3) of the 2007 Act

2.14 Where an order is made under section 194(3) of the 2007 Act, any bill presented for agreement or assessment pursuant to that order must not include a claim for VAT.

SUBSECTION 3 OF THIS PRACTICE DIRECTION

Costs Budgets

3.1 In any case where the parties have filed budgets in accordance with Practice Direction 3E but the court has not made a costs management order under rule 3.15, the provisions of this subsection shall apply

3.2 If there is a difference of 20% or more between the costs claimed by a receiving party on detailed assessment and the costs shown in a budget filed by that party, the receiving party must provide a statement of the reasons for the difference with the bill of costs.

3.3 If a paying party –
   (a) claims to have reasonably relied on a budget filed by a receiving party; or
   (b) wishes to rely upon the costs shown in the budget in order to dispute the reasonableness or proportionality of the costs claimed,

the paying party must serve a statement setting out the case in this regard in that party's points of dispute.

3.4 On an assessment of the costs of a party, the court will have regard to the last approved or agreed budget, and may have regard to any other budget previously filed by that party, or by any other party in the same proceedings. Such other budgets may be taken into account when assessing the reasonableness and proportionality of any costs claimed.

3.5 Subject to paragraph 3.4, paragraphs 3.6 and 3.7 apply where there is a difference of 20% or more between the costs claimed by a receiving party and the costs shown in a budget filed by that party.

3.6 Where it appears to the court that the paying party reasonably relied on the budget, the court may restrict the recoverable costs to such sum as is reasonable for the paying party to pay in the light of that reliance, notwithstanding that such sum is less than the amount of costs reasonably and proportionately incurred by the receiving party.

3.7 Where it appears to the court that the receiving party has not provided a satisfactory explanation for that difference, the court may regard the difference between the costs claimed and the costs shown in the budget as evidence that the costs claimed are unreasonable or disproportionate.

SUBSECTION 4 OF THIS PRACTICE DIRECTION – COURT'S DISCRETION AS TO COSTS: RULE 44.2

Court's Discretion as to Costs

4.1 The court may make an order about costs at any stage in a case.

4.2 There are certain costs orders which the court will commonly make in proceedings before trial. The following table sets out the general effect of these orders. The table is not an exhaustive list of the orders which the court may make.

Term	Effect
Costs Costs in any event	The party in whose favour the order is made is entitled to the costs in respect of the part of the proceedings to which the order relates, whatever other costs orders are made in the proceedings.
Costs in the case Costs in the application	The party in whose favour the court makes an order for costs at the end of the proceedings is entitled to his costs of the part of the proceedings to which the order relates.
Costs reserved	The decision about costs is deferred to a later occasion, but if no later order is made the costs will be costs in the case.
Claimant's/defendant's costs in the case/application	If the party in whose favour the costs order is made is awarded costs at the end of the proceedings, that party is entitled to his costs of the part of the proceedings to which the order relates. If any other party is awarded costs at the end of the proceedings, the party in whose favour the final costs order is made is not liable to pay the costs of any other party in respect of the part of the proceedings to which the order relates.

Term	Effect
Costs thrown away	Where, for example, a judgment or order is set aside, the party in whose favour the costs order is made is entitled to the costs which have been incurred as a consequence. This includes the costs of – (a) preparing for and attending any hearing at which the judgment or order which has been set aside was made; (b) preparing for and attending any hearing to set aside the judgment or order in question; (c) preparing for and attending any hearing at which the court orders the proceedings or the part in question to be adjourned; (d) any steps taken to enforce a judgment or order which has subsequently been set aside.
Costs of and caused by	Where, for example, the court makes this order on an application to amend a statement of case, the party in whose favour the costs order is made is entitled to the costs of preparing for and attending the application and the costs of any consequential Amendment to his own statement of case.
Costs here and below	The party in whose favour the costs order is made is entitled not only to his costs in respect of the proceedings in which the court makes the order but also to his costs of the proceedings in any lower court. In the case of an appeal from a Divisional Court the party is not entitled to any costs incurred in any court below the Divisional Court.
No order as to costs Each party to pay his own costs	Each party is to bear his own costs of the part of the proceedings to which the order relates whatever costs order the court makes at the end of the proceedings.

SUBSECTION 5 OF THIS PRACTICE DIRECTION – FEES OF COUNSEL

Fees of Counsel

5.1 (1) When making an order for costs the court may state an opinion as to whether or not the hearing was fit for the attendance of one or more counsel, and, if it does so, the court conducting a detailed assessment of those costs will have regard to the opinion stated.

(2) The court will generally express an opinion only where –
   (a) the paying party asks it to do so;
   (b) more than one counsel appeared for a party; or
   (c) the court wishes to record its opinion that the case was not fit for the attendance of counsel.

5.2 (1) Where the court refers any matter to the conveyancing counsel of the court the fees payable to counsel in respect of the work done or to be done will be assessed by the court in accordance with rule 44.2.
  (2) An appeal from a decision of the court in respect of the fees of such counsel will be dealt with under the general rules as to appeals set out in Part 52. If the appeal is against the decision of an authorised court officer, it will be dealt with in accordance with rules 47.22 to 47.24.

SUBSECTION 6 OF THIS PRACTICE DIRECTION – BASIS OF ASSESSMENT: RULE 44.3

Costs on the indemnity basis

6.1 If costs are awarded on the indemnity basis, the court assessing costs will disallow any costs –

  (a) which it finds to have been unreasonably incurred; or
  (b) which it considers to be unreasonable in amount.

Costs on the standard basis

6.2 If costs are awarded on the standard basis, the court assessing costs will disallow any costs –

  (a) which it finds to have been unreasonably incurred;
  (b) which it considers to be unreasonable in amount;
  (c) which it considers to have been disproportionately incurred or to be disproportionate in amount; or
  (d) about which it has doubts as to whether they were reasonably or proportionately incurred, or whether they are reasonable and proportionate in amount.

SUBSECTION 7 – AMOUNT OF COSTS WHERE COSTS ARE PAYABLE PURSUANT TO A CONTRACT: RULE 44.5

Application of rule 44.5

7.1 Rule 44.5 only applies if the court is assessing costs payable under a contract. It does not –

  (a) require the court to make an assessment of such costs; or
  (b) require a mortgagee to apply for an order for those costs where there is a contractual right to recover out of the mortgage funds.

Costs relating to a mortgage

7.2 (1) The following principles apply to costs relating to a mortgage.
  (2) An order for the payment of costs of proceedings by one party to another is always a discretionary order: section 51 of the Senior Courts Act 1981 ('the section 51 discretion').
  (3) Where there is a contractual right to the costs, the discretion should ordinarily be exercised so as to reflect that contractual right.
  (4) The power of the court to disallow a mortgagee's costs sought to be added to the mortgage security is a power that does not derive from section 51, but from the power of the courts of equity to fix the terms on which redemption will be allowed.

(5) A decision by a court to refuse costs in whole or in part to a mortgagee may be –
   (a) a decision in the exercise of the section 51 discretion;
   (b) a decision in the exercise of the power to fix the terms on which redemption will be allowed;
   (c) a decision as to the extent of a mortgagee's contractual right to add the mortgagee's costs to the security; or
   (d) a combination of two or more of these things.
(6) A mortgagee is not to be deprived of a contractual or equitable right to add costs to the security merely by reason of an order for payment of costs made without reference to the mortgagee's contractual or equitable rights, and without any adjudication as to whether or not the mortgagee should be deprived of those costs.

7.3 (1) Where the contract entitles a mortgagee to –
   (a) add the costs of litigation relating to the mortgage to the sum secured by it; or
   (b) require a mortgagor to pay those costs,
   the mortgagor may make an application for the court to direct that an account of the mortgagee's costs be taken.
   (Rule 25.1(1)(n) provides that the court may direct that a party file an account.)
(2) The mortgagor may then dispute an amount in the mortgagee's account on the basis that it has been unreasonably incurred or is unreasonable in amount.
(3) Where a mortgagor disputes an amount, the court may make an order that the disputed costs are assessed under rule 44.5.

SUBSECTION 8 OF THIS PRACTICE DIRECTION -PROCEDURE FOR ASSESSING COSTS: RULE 44.6

Procedure for Assessing Costs

8.1 Subject to paragraph 8.3, where the court does not order fixed costs (or no fixed costs are provided for) the amount of costs payable will be assessed by the court. Rule 44.6 allows the court making an order about costs either –
   (a) to make a summary assessment of the amount of the costs; or
   (b) to order the amount to be decided in accordance with Part 47 (a detailed assessment).

8.2 An order for costs will be treated as an order for the amount of costs to be decided by a detailed assessment unless the order otherwise provides.

8.3 Where a party is entitled to costs some of which are fixed costs and some of which are not, the court will assess those costs which are not fixed. For example, the court will assess the disbursements payable in accordance with rules 45.12 or 45.19. The decision whether such assessment should be summary or detailed will be made in accordance with paragraphs 9.1 to 9.10 of this Practice Direction.

SUBSECTION 9 OF THIS PRACTICE DIRECTION – SUMMARY ASSESSMENT: GENERAL PROVISIONS

When the court should consider whether to make a summary assessment

9.1 Whenever a court makes an order about costs which does not provide only for fixed costs to be paid the court should consider whether to make a summary assessment of costs.

Timing of summary assessment

9.2 The general rule is that the court should make a summary assessment of the costs –

(a) at the conclusion of the trial of a case which has been dealt with on the fast track, in which case the order will deal with the costs of the whole claim; and

(b) at the conclusion of any other hearing, which has lasted not more than one day, in which case the order will deal with the costs of the application or matter to which the hearing related. If this hearing disposes of the claim, the order may deal with the costs of the whole claim,

unless there is good reason not to do so, for example where the paying party shows substantial grounds for disputing the sum claimed for costs that cannot be dealt with summarily.

Summary assessment of mortgagee's costs

9.3 The general rule in paragraph 9.2 does not apply to a mortgagee's costs incurred in mortgage possession proceedings or other proceedings relating to a mortgage unless the mortgagee asks the court to make an order for the mortgagee's costs to be paid by another party.

(Paragraphs 7.2 and 7.3 deal in more detail with costs relating to mortgages.)

Consent orders

9.4 Where an application has been made and the parties to the application agree an order by consent without any party attending, the parties should seek to agree a figure for costs to be inserted in the consent order or agree that there should be no order for costs.

Duty of parties and legal representatives

9.5 (1) It is the duty of the parties and their legal representatives to assist the judge in making a summary assessment of costs in any case to which paragraph 9.2 above applies, in accordance with the following subparagraphs.

(2) Each party who intends to claim costs must prepare a written statement of those costs showing separately in the form of a schedule –

(a) the number of hours to be claimed;
(b) the hourly rate to be claimed;
(c) the grade of fee earner;
(d) the amount and nature of any disbursement to be claimed, other than counsel's fee for appearing at the hearing;

      (e) the amount of legal representative's costs to be claimed for attending or appearing at the hearing;
      (f) counsel's fees; and
      (g) any VAT to be claimed on these amounts.
(3) The statement of costs should follow as closely as possible Form N260 and must be signed by the party or the party's legal representative. Where a party is –
      (a) an assisted person;
      (b) a LSC funded client;
      (c) a person for who civil legal services (within the meaning of Part 1 of the Legal Aid, Sentencing and Punishment of Offenders Act 2012) are provided under arrangements made for the purposes of that Part of that Act; or
      (d) represented by a person in the party's employment,
the statement of costs need not include the certificate appended at the end of Form N260.
(4) The statement of costs must be filed at court and copies of it must be served on any party against whom an order for payment of those costs is intended to be sought as soon as possible and in any event –
      (a) for a fast track trial, not less than 2 days before the trial; and
      (b) for all other hearings, not less than 24 hours before the time fixed for the hearing.

9.6 The failure by a party, without reasonable excuse, to comply with paragraph 9.5 will be taken into account by the court in deciding what order to make about the costs of the claim, hearing or application, and about the costs of any further hearing or detailed assessment hearing that may be necessary as a result of that failure.

No summary assessment by a costs officer

9.7 The court awarding costs cannot make an order for a summary assessment of costs by a costs officer. If a summary assessment of costs is appropriate but the court awarding costs is unable to do so on the day, the court may give directions as to a further hearing before the same judge.

Assisted persons

9.8 The court will not make a summary assessment of the costs of a receiving party who is an assisted person or LSC funded client or who is a person for whom civil legal services (within the meaning of Part 1 of the Legal Aid, Sentencing and Punishment of Offenders Act 2012) are provided under arrangements made for the purposes of that Part of that Act.

Children or protected parties

9.9 (1) The court will not make a summary assessment of the costs of a receiving party who is a child or protected party within the meaning of Part 21 unless the legal representative acting for the child or protected party has waived the right to further costs (see Practice Direction 46 paragraph 2.1).
    (2) The court may make a summary assessment of costs payable by a child or protected party.

Disproportionate or unreasonable costs

9.10 The court will not give its approval to disproportionate or unreasonable costs. When the amount of the costs to be paid has been agreed between the parties the order for costs must state that the order is by consent.

SUBSECTION 10 OF THIS PRACTICE DIRECTION – LEGAL REPRESENTATIVE'S DUTY TO NOTIFY PARTY: RULE 44.8

Legal Representative's Duty to Notify Party: Rule 44.8

10.1 For For the purposes of rule 44.8 and paragraph 10.2, 'party' includes any person (for example, an insurer, a trade union or the LSC or Lord Chancellor) who has instructed the legal representative to act for the party or who is liable to pay the legal representative's fees.

10.2 A legal representative who notifies a party of an order under rule 44.8 must also explain why the order came to be made.

10.3 Although rule 44.8 does not specify any sanction for breach of the rule the court may, either in the order for costs itself or in a subsequent order, require the legal representative to produce to the court evidence showing that the legal representative took reasonable steps to comply with the rule.

SUBSECTION 11 OF THIS PRACTICE DIRECTION – COURT'S POWERS IN RELATION TO MISCONDUCT: RULE 44.11

Court's Powers In Relation To Misconduct: Rule 44.11

11.1 Before making an order under rule 44.11, the court must give the party or legal representative in question a reasonable opportunity to make written submissions or, if the legal representative so desires, to attend a hearing.

11.2 Conduct which is unreasonable or improper includes steps which are calculated to prevent or inhibit the court from furthering the overriding objective.

11.3 Although rule 44.11(3) does not specify any sanction for breach of the obligation imposed by the rule the court may, either in the order under rule 44.11(2) or in a subsequent order, require the legal representative to produce to the court evidence that the legal representative took reasonable steps to comply with the obligation.

SUBSECTION 12 OF THIS PRACTICE DIRECTION – QUALIFIED ONE-WAY COSTS SHIFTING

Qualified One-Way Costs Shifting

12.1 This subsection applies to proceedings to which Section II of Part 44 applies.

12.2 Examples of claims made for the financial benefit of a person other than the claimant or a dependant within the meaning of section 1(3) of the Fatal Accidents Act 1976 within the meaning of rule 44.16(2) are subrogated claims and claims for credit hire.

12.3 'Gratuitous provision of care' within the meaning of rule 44.16(2)(a) includes the provision of personal services rendered gratuitously by persons such as relatives and friends for things such as personal care, domestic assistance, childminding, home maintenance and decorating, gardening and chauffeuring.

12.4 In a case to which rule 44.16(1) applies (fundamentally dishonest claims) –

(a) the court will normally direct that issues arising out of an allegation that the claim is fundamentally dishonest be determined at the trial;
(b) where the proceedings have been settled, the court will not, save in exceptional circumstances, order that issues arising out of an allegation that the claim was fundamentally dishonest be determined in those proceedings;
(c) where the claimant has served a notice of discontinuance, the court may direct that issues arising out of an allegation that the claim was fundamentally dishonest be determined notwithstanding that the notice has not been set aside pursuant to rule 38.4;
(d) the court may, as it thinks fair and just, determine the costs attributable to the claim having been found to be fundamentally dishonest.

12.5 The court has power to make an order for costs against a person other than the claimant under section 51(3) of the Senior Courts Act 1981 and rule 46.2. In a case to which rule 44.16(2)(a) applies (claims for the benefit of others) –

(a) the court will usually order any person other than the claimant for whose financial benefit such a claim was made to pay all the costs of the proceedings or the costs attributable to the issues to which rule 44.16(2)(a) applies, or may exceptionally make such an order permitting the enforcement of such an order for costs against the claimant.
(b) the court may, as it thinks fair and just, determine the costs attributable to claims for the financial benefit of persons other than the claimant.

12.6 In proceedings to which rule 44.16 applies, the court will normally order the claimant or, as the case may be, the person for whose benefit a claim was made to pay costs notwithstanding that the aggregate amount in money terms of such orders exceeds the aggregate amount in money terms of any orders for damages, interest and costs made in favour of the claimant.

12.7 Assessments of costs may be on a standard or indemnity basis and may be subject to a summary or detailed assessment.

****

PART 46
COSTS – SPECIAL CASES

Section I – Costs Payable by or to Particular Persons

46.1 Pre-commencement disclosure and orders for disclosure against a person who is not a party

(1) This paragraph applies where a person applies –

(a) for an order under –
  (i) section 33 of the Senior Courts Act 1981; or
  (ii) section 52 of the County Courts Act 1984,

(which give the court powers exercisable before commencement of proceedings); or

(b) for an order under –
  (i) section 34 of the Senior Courts Act 1981; or
  (ii) section 53 of the County Courts Act 1984,

(which give the court power to make an order against a non-party for disclosure of documents, inspection of property etc.).

(2) The general rule is that the court will award the person against whom the order is sought that person's costs –

   (a) of the application; and
   (b) of complying with any order made on the application.

(3) The court may however make a different order, having regard to all the circumstances, including–

   (a) the extent to which it was reasonable for the person against whom the order was sought to oppose the application; and
   (b) whether the parties to the application have complied with any relevant pre-action protocol.

Amendments—Inserted by SI 2013/262.

46.2 Costs orders in favour of or against non-parties

(1) Where the court is considering whether to exercise its power under section 51 of the Senior Courts Act 1981 (costs are in the discretion of the court) to make a costs order in favour of or against a person who is not a party to proceedings, that person must –

   (a) be added as a party to the proceedings for the purposes of costs only; and
   (b) be given a reasonable opportunity to attend a hearing at which the court will consider the matter further.

(2) This rule does not apply –

   (a) where the court is considering whether to –
      (i) make an order against the Lord Chancellor in proceedings in which the Lord Chancellor has provided legal aid to a party to the proceedings;
      (ii) make a wasted costs order (as defined in rule 46.8); and
   (b) in proceedings to which rule 46.1 applies (pre-commencement disclosure and orders for disclosure against a person who is not a party).

Amendments—Inserted by SI 2013/262.

46.3 Limitations on court's power to award costs in favour of trustee or personal representative

(1) This rule applies where –

   (a) a person is or has been a party to any proceedings in the capacity of trustee or personal representative; and
   (b) rule 44.5 does not apply.

(2) The general rule is that that person is entitled to be paid the costs of those proceedings, insofar as they are not recovered from or paid by any other person, out of the relevant trust fund or estate.

(3) Where that person is entitled to be paid any of those costs out of the fund or estate, those costs will be assessed on the indemnity basis.

Amendments—Inserted by SI 2013/262.

46.4 Costs where money is payable by or to a child or protected party

(1) This rule applies to any proceedings where a party is a child or protected party and –

    (a) money is ordered or agreed to be paid to, or for the benefit of, that party; or
    (b) money is ordered to be paid by that party or on that party's behalf.

('Child' and 'protected party' have the same meaning as in rule 21.1(2).)

(2) The general rule is that –

    (a) the court must order a detailed assessment of the costs payable by, or out of money belonging to, any party who is a child or protected party; and
    (b) on an assessment under paragraph (a), the court must also assess any costs payable to that party in the proceedings, unless –
        (i) the court has issued a default costs certificate in relation to those costs under rule 47.11; or
        (ii) the costs are payable in proceedings to which Section II or Section III of Part 45 applies.

(3) The court need not order detailed assessment of costs in the circumstances set out in paragraph (5) or in Practice Direction 46.

(4) Where –

    (a) a claimant is a child or protected party; and
    (b) a detailed assessment has taken place under paragraph (2)(a), the only amount payable by the child or protected party is the amount which the court certifies as payable.

(5) Where the costs payable comprise only the success fee claimed by the child's or protected party's legal representative under a conditional fee agreement or the balance of any payment under a damages based agreement, the court may direct that –

    (a) the assessment procedure referred to in rule 46.10 and paragraph 6 of Practice Direction 46 shall not apply; and
    (b) such costs be assessed summarily.

(This rule applies to a counterclaim by or on behalf of a child or protected party by virtue of rule 20.3)

Amendments—Inserted by SI 2013/262. Amended by SI 2015/670.

46.5 Litigants in person

(1) This rule applies where the court orders (whether by summary assessment or detailed assessment) that the costs of a litigant in person are to be paid by any other person.

(2) The costs allowed under this rule will not exceed, except in the case of a disbursement, two-thirds of the amount which would have been allowed if the litigant in person had been represented by a legal representative.

(3) The litigant in person shall be allowed –

    (a) costs for the same categories of –
        (i) work; and
        (ii) disbursements,

which would have been allowed if the work had been done or the disbursements had been made by a legal representative on the litigant in person's behalf;

(b) the payments reasonably made by the litigant in person for legal services relating to the conduct of the proceedings; and

(c) the costs of obtaining expert assistance in assessing the costs claim.

(4) The amount of costs to be allowed to the litigant in person for any item of work claimed will be –

(a) where the litigant can prove financial loss, the amount that the litigant can prove to have been lost for time reasonably spent on doing the work; or

(b) where the litigant cannot prove financial loss, an amount for the time reasonably spent on doing the work at the rate set out in Practice Direction 46.

(5) A litigant who is allowed costs for attending at court to conduct the case is not entitled to a witness allowance in respect of such attendance in addition to those costs.

(6) For the purposes of this rule, a litigant in person includes –

(a) a company or other corporation which is acting without a legal representative; and

(b) any of the following who acts in person (except where any such person is represented by a firm in which that person is a partner) –

 (i) a barrister,
 (ii) a solicitor,
 (iii) a solicitor's employee,
 (iv) a manager of a body recognised under section 9 of the Administration of Justice Act 1985; or
 (v) a person who, for the purposes of the 2007 Act, is an authorised person in relation to an activity which constitutes the conduct of litigation (within the meaning of that Act).

Amendments—Inserted by SI 2013/262.

46.6 Costs where the court has made a group litigation order

(1) This rule applies where the court has made a Group Litigation Order ('GLO').

(2) In this rule –

(a) 'individual costs' means costs incurred in relation to an individual claim on the group register;

(b) 'common costs' means –
 (i) costs incurred in relation to the GLO issues;
 (ii) individual costs incurred in a claim while it is proceeding as a test claim, and
 (iii) costs incurred by the lead legal representative in administering the group litigation; and

(c) 'group litigant' means a claimant or defendant, as the case may be, whose claim is entered on the group register.

(3) Unless the court orders otherwise, any order for common costs against group litigants imposes on each group litigant several liability for an equal proportion of those common costs.

(4) The general rule is that a group litigant who is the paying party will, in addition to any liability to pay the receiving party, be liable for –

(a) the individual costs of that group litigant's claim; and
(b) an equal proportion, together with all the other group litigants, of the common costs.

(5) Where the court makes an order about costs in relation to any application or hearing which involved –

(a) one or more GLO issues; and
(b) issues relevant only to individual claims,

the court will direct the proportion of the costs that is to relate to common costs and the proportion that is to relate to individual costs.

(6) Where common costs have been incurred before a claim is entered on the group register, the court may order the group litigant to be liable for a proportion of those costs.

(7) Where a claim is removed from the group register, the court may make an order for costs in that claim which includes a proportion of the common costs incurred up to the date on which the claim is removed from the group register.

(Part 19 sets out rules about group litigation.)

Amendments—Inserted by SI 2013/262. Amended by SI 2013/1974.

46.7 Orders in respect of pro bono representation

(1) Where the court makes an order under section 194(3) of the 2007 Act –

(a) the court may order the payment to the prescribed charity of a sum no greater than the costs specified in Part 45 to which the party with pro bono representation would have been entitled in accordance with that Part and in respect of that representation had it not been provided free of charge; or
(b) where Part 45 does not apply, the court may determine the amount of the payment (other than a sum equivalent to fixed costs) to be made by the paying party to the prescribed charity by –
  (i) making a summary assessment; or
  (ii) making an order for detailed assessment,

of a sum equivalent to all or part of the costs the paying party would have been ordered to pay to the party with pro bono representation in respect of that representation had it not been provided free of charge.

(2) Where the court makes an order under section 194(3) of the 2007 Act, the order must direct that the payment by the paying party be made to the prescribed charity.

(3) The receiving party must send a copy of the order to the prescribed charity within 7 days of receipt of the order.

(4) Where the court considers making or makes an order under section 194(3) of the 2007 Act, Parts 44 to 47 apply, where appropriate, with the following modifications –

(a) references to 'costs orders', 'orders about costs' or 'orders for the payment of costs' are to be read, unless otherwise stated, as if they refer to an order under section 194(3);
(b) references to 'costs' are to be read, as if they referred to a sum equivalent to the costs that would have been claimed by, incurred by or awarded to the

party with pro bono representation in respect of that representation had it not been provided free of charge; and

(c) references to 'receiving party' are to be read, as meaning a party who has pro bono representation and who would have been entitled to be paid costs in respect of that representation had it not been provided free of charge.

Amendments—Inserted by SI 2013/262. Amended by SI 2013/1974.

Section II – Costs Relating to Legal representatives

46.8 Personal liability of legal representative for costs – wasted costs orders

(1) This rule applies where the court is considering whether to make an order under section 51(6) of the Senior Courts Act 1981 (court's power to disallow or (as the case may be) order a legal representative to meet, 'wasted costs').

(2) The court will give the legal representative a reasonable opportunity to make written submissions or, if the legal representative prefers, to attend a hearing before it makes such an order.

(3) When the court makes a wasted costs order, it will –

  (a) specify the amount to be disallowed or paid; or
  (b) direct a costs judge or a District Judge to decide the amount of costs to be disallowed or paid.

(4) The court may direct that notice must be given to the legal representative's client, in such manner as the court may direct –

  (a) of any proceedings under this rule; or
  (b) of any order made under it against his legal representative.

Amendments—Inserted by SI 2013/262. Amended by SI 2014/407.

46.9 Basis of detailed assessment of solicitor and client costs

(1) This rule applies to every assessment of a solicitor's bill to a client except a bill which is to be paid out of the Community Legal Service Fund under the Legal Aid Act 1988 or the Access to Justice Act 1999.

(2) Section 74(3) of the Solicitors Act 1974 applies unless the solicitor and client have entered into a written agreement which expressly permits payment to the solicitor of an amount of costs greater than that which the client could have recovered from another party to the proceedings.

(3) Subject to paragraph (2), costs are to be assessed on the indemnity basis but are to be presumed–

  (a) to have been reasonably incurred if they were incurred with the express or implied approval of the client;
  (b) to be reasonable in amount if their amount was expressly or impliedly approved by the client;
  (c) to have been unreasonably incurred if –
    (i) they are of an unusual nature or amount; and
    (ii) the solicitor did not tell the client that as a result the costs might not be recovered from the other party.

(4) Where the court is considering a percentage increase on the application of the client, the court will have regard to all the relevant factors as they reasonably appeared to the solicitor or counsel when the conditional fee agreement was entered into or varied.

Amendments—Inserted by SI 2013/262.

46.10 Assessment procedure

(1) This rule sets out the procedure to be followed where the court has made an order under Part III of the Solicitors Act 1974 for the assessment of costs payable to solicitor by the solicitor's client.

(2) The solicitor must serve a breakdown of costs within 28 days of the order for costs to be assessed.

(3) The client must serve points of dispute within 14 days after service on him of the breakdown of costs.

(4) The solicitor must serve any reply within 14 days of service on the solicitor of the points of dispute.

(5) Either party may file a request for a hearing date –

    (a) after points of dispute have been served; but
    (b) no later than 3 months after the date of the order for the costs to be assessed.

(6) This procedure applies subject to any contrary order made by the court.

Amendments—Inserted by SI 2013/262.

Section III – Costs on Allocation and Re-allocation

46.11 Costs on the small claims track and fast track

(1) Part 27 (small claims) and Part 45 Section VI (fast track trial costs) contain special rules about –

    (a) liability for costs;
    (b) the amount of costs which the court may award; and
    (c) the procedure for assessing costs.

(2) Once a claim is allocated to a particular track, those special rules shall apply to the period before, as well as after, allocation except where the court or a practice direction provides otherwise.

Amendments—Inserted by SI 2013/262.

46.12 Limitation on amount court may allow where a claim allocated to the fast track settles before trial

(1) Where the court –

    (a) assesses costs in relation to a claim which –
        (i) has been allocated to the fast track; and
        (ii) settles before the start of the trial; and

(b) is considering the amount of costs to be allowed in respect of a party's advocate for preparing for the trial,

it may not allow, in respect of those advocate's costs, an amount that exceeds the amount of fast track trial costs which would have been payable in relation to the claim had the trial taken place.

(2) When deciding the amount to be allowed in respect of the advocate's costs, the court will have regard to –

    (a) when the claim was settled; and
    (b) when the court was notified that the claim had settled.

(3) In this rule, 'advocate' and 'fast track trial costs' have the meanings given to them by Part 45 Section VI.

Amendments—Inserted by SI 2013/262.

46.13 Costs following allocation, re-allocation and non-allocation

(1) Any costs orders made before a claim is allocated will not be affected by allocation.

(2) Where –

    (a) a claim is allocated to a track; and
    (b) the court subsequently re-allocates that claim to a different track,

then unless the court orders otherwise, any special rules about costs applying –

        (i) to the first track, will apply to the claim up to the date of re-allocation; and
        (ii) to the second track, will apply from the date of re-allocation.

Where the court is assessing costs on the standard basis of a claim which concluded without being allocated to a track, it may restrict those costs to costs that would have been allowed on the track to which the claim would have been allocated if allocation had taken place.

Amendments—Inserted by SI 2013/262.

Section IV – Costs-Only Proceedings

46.14 Costs-only proceedings

(1) This rule applies where –

    (a) the parties to a dispute have reached an agreement on all issues (including which party is to pay the costs) which is made or confirmed in writing; but
    (b) they have failed to agree the amount of those costs; and
    (c) no proceedings have been started.

(2) Where this rule applies, the procedure set out in this rule must be followed.

(3) Proceedings under this rule are commenced by issuing a claim form in accordance with Part 8.

(4) The claim form must contain or be accompanied by the agreement or confirmation.

(5) In proceedings to which this rule applies the court may make an order for the payment of costs the amount of which is to be determined by assessment and/or, where appropriate, for the payment of fixed costs.

(6) Where this rule applies but the procedure set out in this rule has not been followed by a party –

(a) that party will not be allowed costs greater than those that would have been allowed to that party had the procedure been followed; and
(b) the court may award the other party the costs of the proceedings up to the point where an order for the payment of costs is made.

(7) Rule 44.6 (amount of costs where costs are payable pursuant to a contract) does not apply to claims started under the procedure in this rule.

Amendments—Inserted by SI 2013/262.

Section V – Costs in Claims for Judicial Review

46.15 Claims for judicial review: costs against interveners

(1) In this rule the terms 'intervener' and 'relevant party' have the same meaning as in section 87 of the Criminal Justice and Courts Act 2015 ('the 2015 Act').

(2) A relevant party may apply to the court for an order for an intervener to pay costs in accordance with section 87 of the 2015 Act.

(Section 87 of the 2015 Act applies to judicial review proceedings in the High Court and Court of Appeal.)

(Rule 54.17 makes provision for any person to be able to apply for permission to file evidence or make representations at the hearing of a judicial review.)

Amendments—Inserted by SI 2015/670.

Practice Direction 46 – Costs Special Cases

This Practice Direction supplements CPR 1998 Part 46 (PD46)

Awards of Costs In Favour Of a Trustee or Personal Representative: Rule 46.3

1.1 A trustee or personal representative is entitled to an indemnity out of the relevant trust fund or estate for costs properly incurred. Whether costs were properly incurred depends on all the circumstances of the case including whether the trustee or personal representative ('the trustee') –

(a) obtained directions from the court before bringing or defending the proceedings;
(b) acted in the interests of the fund or estate or in substance for a benefit other than that of the estate, including the trustee's own; and
(c) acted in some way unreasonably in bringing or defending, or in the conduct of, the proceedings.

1.2 The trustee is not to be taken to have acted for a benefit other than that of the fund by reason only that the trustee has defended a claim in which relief is sought against the trustee personally.

Costs Where Money Is Payable By Or To A Child Or Protected Party: Rule 46.4

2.1 The circumstances in which the court need not order the detailed assessment of costs under rule 46.4(2) are as follows –

  (a) where there is no need to do so to protect the interests of the child or protected party or their estate;
  (b) where another party has agreed to pay a specified sum in respect of the costs of the child or protected party and the legal representative acting for the child or protected party has waived the right to claim further costs;
  (c) where the court has decided the costs payable to the child or protected party by way of summary assessment and the legal representative acting for the child or protected party has waived the right to claim further costs;
  (d) where an insurer or other person is liable to discharge the costs which the child or protected party would otherwise be liable to pay to the legal representative and the court is satisfied that the insurer or other person is financially able to discharge those costs; and
  (e) where the court has given a direction for summary assessment pursuant to rule 46.34(5).

Litigants In Person: Rule 46.5

3.1 In order to qualify as an expert for the purpose of rule 46.5(3)(c) (expert assistance in connection with assessing the claim for costs), the person in question must be a –

  (a) barrister;
  (b) solicitor;
  (c) Fellow of the Institute of Legal Executives;
  (d) Fellow of the Association of Costs Lawyers;
  (e) law costs draftsman who is a member of the Academy of Experts;
  (f) law costs draftsman who is a member of the Expert Witness Institute.

3.2 Where a self represented litigant wishes to prove that the litigant has suffered financial loss, the litigant should produce to the court any written evidence relied on to support that claim, and serve a copy of that evidence on any party against whom the litigant seeks costs at least 24 hours before the hearing at which the question may be decided.

3.3 A self represented litigant who commences detailed assessment proceedings under rule 47.5 should serve copies of that written evidence with the notice of commencement.

3.4 The amount, which may be allowed to a self represented litigant under rule 45.39(5)(b) and rule 46.5(4)(b), is £19 per hour.

Orders In Respect Of Pro Bono Representation: Rule 46.7

4.1 Where an order is sought under section 194(3) of the Legal Services Act 2007 the party who has pro bono representation must prepare, file and serve a written statement of the sum equivalent to the costs that party would have claimed for that legal representation had it not been provided free of charge.

Personal Liability Of Legal Representative For Costs – Wasted Costs Orders: Rule 46.8

5.1 A wasted costs order is an order –

(a) that the legal representative pay a sum (either specified or to be assessed) in respect of costs to a party; or
(b) for costs relating to a specified sum or items of work to be disallowed.

5.2 Rule 46.8 deals with wasted costs orders against legal representatives. Such orders can be made at any stage in the proceedings up to and including the detailed assessment proceedings. In general, applications for wasted costs are best left until after the end of the trial.

5.3 The court may make a wasted costs order against a legal representative on its own initiative.

5.4 A party may apply for a wasted costs order –

(a) by filing an application notice in accordance with Part 23; or
(b) by making an application orally in the course of any hearing.

5.5 It is appropriate for the court to make a wasted costs order against a legal representative, only if –

(a) the legal representative has acted improperly, unreasonably or negligently;
(b) the legal representative's conduct has caused a party to incur unnecessary costs, or has meant that costs incurred by a party prior to the improper, unreasonable or negligent act or omission have been wasted;
(c) it is just in all the circumstances to order the legal representative to compensate that party for the whole or part of those costs.

5.6 The court will give directions about the procedure to be followed in each case in order to ensure that the issues are dealt with in a way which is fair and as simple and summary as the circumstances permit.

5.7 As a general rule the court will consider whether to make a wasted costs order in two stages –

(a) at the first stage the court must be satisfied –
 (i) that it has before it evidence or other material which, if unanswered, would be likely to lead to a wasted costs order being made; and
 (ii) the wasted costs proceedings are justified notwithstanding the likely costs involved;
(b) at the second stage, the court will consider, after giving the legal representative an opportunity to make representations in writing or at a hearing, whether it is appropriate to make a wasted costs order in accordance with paragraph 5.5 above.

5.8 The court may proceed to the second stage described in paragraph 5.7 without first adjourning the hearing if it is satisfied that the legal representative has already had a reasonable opportunity to make representations.

5.9 On an application for a wasted costs order under Part 23 the application notice and any evidence in support must identify –

(a) what the legal representative is alleged to have done or failed to do; and

(b) the costs that the legal representative may be ordered to pay or which are sought against the legal representative.

Assessment of Solicitor and Client Costs: Rules 46.9 and 46.10

6.1 A client and solicitor may agree whatever terms they consider appropriate about the payment of the solicitor's charges. If however, the costs are of an unusual nature, either in amount or the type of costs incurred, those costs will be presumed to have been unreasonably incurred unless the solicitor satisfies the court that the client was informed that they were unusual and that they might not be allowed on an assessment of costs between the parties. That information must have been given to the client before the costs were incurred.

6.2 Costs as between a solicitor and client are assessed on the indemnity basis. The presumptions in rule 46.9(3) are rebuttable.

6.3 If a party fails to comply with the requirements of rule 46.10 concerning the service of a breakdown of costs or points of dispute, any other party may apply to the court in which the detailed assessment hearing should take place for an order requiring compliance. If the court makes such an order, it may –

(a) make it subject to conditions including a condition to pay a sum of money into court; and
(b) specify the consequence of failure to comply with the order or a condition.

6.4 The procedure for obtaining an order under Part III of the Solicitors Act 1974 is by a Part 8 claim, as modified by rule 67.3 and Practice Direction 67. Precedent J of the Schedule of Costs Precedents is a model form of claim form. The application must be accompanied by the bill or bills in respect of which assessment is sought, and, if the claim concerns a conditional fee agreement, a copy of that agreement. If the original bill is not available a copy will suffice.

6.5 Model forms of order, which the court may make, are set out in Precedents K, L and M of the Schedule of Costs Precedents.

6.6 The breakdown of costs referred to in rule 46.10 is a document which contains the following information –

(a) details of the work done under each of the bills sent for assessment; and
(b) in applications under Section 70 of the Solicitors Act 1974, a cash account showing money received by the solicitor to the credit of the client and sums paid out of that money on behalf of the client but not payments out which were made in satisfaction of the bill or of any items which are claimed in the bill.

6.7 Precedent P of the Schedule of Costs Precedents is a model form of breakdown of costs. A party who is required to serve a breakdown of costs must also serve–

(a) copies of the fee notes of counsel and of any expert in respect of fees claimed in the breakdown, and
(b) written evidence as to any other disbursement which is claimed in the breakdown and which exceeds £250.

6.8 The provisions relating to default costs certificates (rule 47.11) do not apply to cases to which rule 46.10 applies.

6.9 The time for requesting a detailed assessment hearing is within 3 months after the date of the order for the costs to be assessed.

6.10 The form of request for a hearing date must be in Form N258C. The request must be accompanied by copies of –

    (a)   the order sending the bill or bills for assessment;
    (b)   the bill or bills sent for assessment;
    (c)   the solicitor's breakdown of costs and any invoices or accounts served with that breakdown;
    (d)   a copy of the points of dispute;
    (e)   a copy of any replies served;
    (f)   a statement signed by the party filing the request or that party's legal representative giving the names and addresses for service of all parties to the proceedings.

6.11 The request must include the estimated length of hearing.

6.12 On receipt of the request the court will fix a date for the hearing, or will give directions.

6.13 The court will give at least 14 days' notice of the time and place of the detailed assessment hearing.

6.14 Unless the court gives permission, only the solicitor whose bill it is and parties who have served points of dispute may be heard and only items specified in the points of dispute may be raised.

6.15 If a party wishes to vary that party's breakdown of costs, points of dispute or reply, an amended or supplementary document must be filed with the court and copies of it must be served on all other relevant parties. Permission is not required to vary a breakdown of costs, points of dispute or a reply but the court may disallow the variation or permit it only upon conditions, including conditions as to the payment of any costs caused or wasted by the variation.

6.16 Unless the court directs otherwise the solicitor must file with the court the papers in support of the bill not less than 7 days before the date for the detailed assessment hearing and not more than 14 days before that date.

6.17 Once the detailed assessment hearing has ended it is the responsibility of the legal representative appearing for the solicitor or, as the case may be, the solicitor in person to remove the papers filed in support of the bill.

6.18 If, in the course of a detailed assessment hearing of a solicitor's bill to that solicitor's client, it appears to the court that in any event the solicitor will be liable in connection with that bill to pay money to the client, it may issue an interim certificate specifying an amount which in its opinion is payable by the solicitor to the client.

6.19 After the detailed assessment hearing is concluded the court will –

    (a)   complete the court copy of the bill so as to show the amount allowed;
    (b)   determine the result of the cash account;
    (c)   award the costs of the detailed assessment hearing in accordance with Section 70(8) of the Solicitors Act 1974; and
    (d)   issue a final costs certificate.

Costs on the Small Claims and Fast Tracks: Rule 46.11

7.1 (1) Before a claim is allocated to either the small claims track or the fast track the court is not restricted by any of the special rules that apply to that track but see paragraph 8.2 below.

    (2)   Where a claim has been so allocated, the special rules which relate to that

track will apply to work done before as well as after allocation save to the extent (if any) that an order for costs in respect of that work was made before allocation.

(3) Where a claim, issued for a sum in excess of the normal financial scope of the small claims track, is allocated to that track only because an admission of part of the claim by the defendant reduces the amount in dispute to a sum within the normal scope of that track; on entering judgment for the admitted part before allocation of the balance of the claim the court may allow costs in respect of the proceedings down to that date.

Costs Following Allocation, Re-Allocation and Non-Allocation: Rule 46.13

8.1 Before reallocating a claim from the small claims track to another track, the court must decide whether any party is to pay costs to the date of the order to re-allocate in accordance with the rules about costs contained in Part 27 If it decides to make such an order the court will make a summary assessment of those costs in accordance with that Part.

8.2 Where a settlement is reached or a Part 36 offer accepted in a case which has not been allocated but would, if allocated, have been suitable for allocation to the small claims track, rule 46.13 enables the court to allow only small claims track costs in accordance with rule 27.14. This power is not exercisable if the costs are to be paid on the indemnity basis.

Costs-Only Proceedings: Rule 46.14

9.1 A claim form under rule 46.14 should not be issued in the High Court unless the dispute to which the agreement relates was of such a value or type that proceedings would have been commenced in the High Court.

9.2 A claim form which is to be issued in the High Court at the Royal Courts of Justice will be issued in the Costs Office.

9.3 Attention is drawn to rule 8.2 (in particular to paragraph (b)(ii)) and to rule 46.14(3). The claim form must –

(a) identify the claim or dispute to which the agreement relates;
(b) state the date and terms of the agreement on which the claimant relies;
(c) set out or attach a draft of the order which the claimant seeks;
(d) state the amount of the costs claimed.

9.4 Unless the court orders otherwise or Section II of Part 45 applies the costs will be treated as being claimed on the standard basis.

9.5 The evidence required under rule 8.5 includes copies of the documents on which the claimant relies to prove the defendant's agreement to pay costs.

9.6 A costs judge or a District Judge has jurisdiction to hear and decide any issue which may arise in a claim issued under this rule irrespective of the amount of the costs claimed or of the value of the claim to which the agreement to pay costs relates. The court may make an order by consent under paragraph 9.8, or an order dismissing a claim under paragraph 9.10 below.

9.7 When the time for filing the defendant's acknowledgement of service has expired, the claimant may request in writing that the court make an order in the terms of the claim, unless the defendant has filed an acknowledgement of service stating the intention to contest the claim or to seek a different order.

9.8 Rule 40.6 applies where an order is to be made by consent. An order may be made by consent in terms which differ from those set out in the claim form.

9.9 Where costs are ordered to be assessed, the general rule is that this should be by detailed assessment. However when an order is made under this rule following a hearing and the court is in a position to summarily assess costs it should generally do so.

9.10 If the defendant opposes the claim the defendant must file a witness statement in accordance with rule 8.5(3). The court will then give directions including, if appropriate, a direction that the claim shall continue as if it were a Part 7 claim. A claim is not treated as opposed merely because the defendant disputes the amount of the claim for costs.

9.11 A claim issued under this rule may be dealt with without being allocated to a track. Rule 8.9 does not apply to claims issued under this rule.

9.12 Where there are other issues nothing in rule 46.14 prevents a person from issuing a claim form under Part 7 or Part 8 to sue on an agreement made in settlement of a dispute where that agreement makes provision for costs, nor from claiming in that case an order for costs or a specified sum in respect of costs but the 'costs only' procedure in rule 46.14 must be used where the sole issue is the amount of costs.

PART 47
PROCEDURE FOR DETAILED ASSESSMENT OF COSTS AND DEFAULT PROVISIONS

Section I – General Rules about Detailed Assessment

47.1 Time when detailed assessment may be carried out

The general rule is that the costs of any proceedings or any part of the proceedings are not to be assessed by the detailed procedure until the conclusion of the proceedings but the court may order them to be assessed immediately.

> (Practice Direction 47 gives further guidance about when proceedings are concluded for the purpose of this rule.)

Amendments—Inserted by SI 2013/262.

47.2 No stay of detailed assessment where there is an appeal

Detailed assessment is not stayed pending an appeal unless the court so orders.

Amendments—Inserted by SI 2013/262.

47.3 Powers of an authorised court officer

(1) An authorised court officer has all the powers of the court when making a detailed assessment, except –

    (a) power to make a wasted costs order as defined in rule 46.8;
    (b) power to make an order under –
        (i) rule 44.11 (powers in relation to misconduct);
        (ii) rule 47.8 (sanction for delay in commencing detailed assessment proceedings);

(iii) paragraph (2) (objection to detailed assessment by authorised court officer); and
(c) power to make a detailed assessment of costs payable to a solicitor by that solicitor's client, unless the costs are being assessed under rule 46.5 (costs where money is payable to a child or protected party).

(2) Where a party objects to the detailed assessment of costs being made by an authorised court officer, the court may order it to be made by a costs judge or a District Judge.

(Practice Direction 47 sets out the relevant procedure.)

| Senior Executive Officers | £30,000 (excluding VAT) |
| Principal Officers | £75,000 (excluding VAT) |

Amendments—Inserted by SI 2013/262. Amended by SI 2014/407.

47.4 Venue for detailed assessment proceedings

(1) All applications and requests in detailed assessment proceedings must be made to or filed at the appropriate office.

(Practice Direction 47 sets out the meaning of 'appropriate office' in any particular case)

(2) The court may direct that the appropriate office is to be the Costs Office.

(3) In the County Court, a court may direct that another County Court hearing centre is to be the appropriate office.

(4) A direction under paragraph (3) may be made without proceedings being transferred to that court.

(Rule 30.2 makes provision for the transfer within the County Court of proceedings for detailed assessment of costs.)

Amendments—Inserted by SI 2013/262. Amended by SI 2014/407.

Section II – Costs Payable by one Party to Another – Commencement of Detailed Assessment Proceedings

47.5 Application of this Section

This Section of Part 47 applies where a cost officer is to make a detailed assessment of –
(a) costs which are payable by one party to another; or
(b) the sum which is payable by one party to the prescribed charity pursuant to an order under section 194(3) of the 2007 Act.

Amendments—Inserted by SI 2013/262.

47.6 Commencement of detailed assessment proceedings

(1) Detailed assessment proceedings are commenced by the receiving party serving on the paying party –
(a) notice of commencement in the relevant practice form;
(b) a copy of the bill of costs; and

(c) if a costs management order has been made, a breakdown of the costs claimed for each phase of the proceedings.

(Rule 47.7 sets out the period for commencing detailed assessment proceedings)

(2) The receiving party must also serve a copy of the notice of commencement and the bill on any other relevant persons specified in Practice Direction 47.

(3) A person on whom a copy of the notice of commencement is served under paragraph (2) is a party to the detailed assessment proceedings (in addition to the paying party and the receiving party).

(Practice Direction 47 deals with – other documents which the party must file when requesting detailed assessment; the court's powers where it considers that a hearing may be necessary; the form of a bill; and the length of notice which will be given if a hearing date is fixed.)

(Paragraphs 7B.2 to 7B.7 of the Practice Direction – Civil Recovery Proceedings contain provisions about detailed assessment of costs in relation to civil recovery orders.)

Amendments—SI 2015/1569.

Scope of provision—Detailed assessment proceedings are commenced by serving a notice of commencement in Form N252 together with a bill and the other documents referred to in PD47 paras 5.2. See PD47, paras 5.1–5.22 and the commentary thereto for detail of the form and content of the notice of commencement and bill.

47.7 Period for commencing detailed assessment proceedings

The following table shows the period for commencing detailed assessment proceedings.

Source of right to detailed assessment	Time by which detailed assessment proceedings must be commenced
Judgment, direction, order, award or other determination	3 months after the date of the judgment etc. Where detailed assessment is stayed pending an appeal, 3 months after the date of the order lifting the stay
Discontinuance under Part 38	3 months after the date of service of notice of discontinuance under rule 38.3; or 3 months after the date of the dismissal of application to set the notice of discontinuance aside under rule 38.4
Acceptance of an offer to settle under Part 36	3 months after the date when the right to costs arose

Amendments—Inserted by SI 2013/262.

47.8 Sanction for delay in commencing detailed assessment proceedings

(1) Where the receiving party fails to commence detailed assessment proceedings within the period specified –

(a) in rule 47.7; or
(b) by any direction of the court,

the paying party may apply for an order requiring the receiving party to commence detailed assessment proceedings within such time as the court may specify.

(2) On an application under paragraph (1), the court may direct that, unless the receiving party commences detailed assessment proceedings within the time specified by the court, all or part of the costs to which the receiving party would otherwise be entitled will be disallowed.

(3) If –

    (a) the paying party has not made an application in accordance with paragraph (1); and

    (b) the receiving party commences the proceedings later than the period specified in rule 47.7,

the court may disallow all or part of the interest otherwise payable to the receiving party under –

    (i) section 17 of the Judgments Act 1838; or
    (ii) section 74 of the County Courts Act 1984,

but will not impose any other sanction except in accordance with rule 44.11 (powers in relation to misconduct).

(4) Where the costs to be assessed in a detailed assessment are payable out of the Community Legal Service Fund, this rule applies as if the receiving party were the solicitor to whom the costs are payable and the paying party were the Legal Services Commission.

Amendments—Inserted by SI 2013/262.

47.9 Points of dispute and consequence of not serving

(1) The paying party and any other party to the detailed assessment proceedings may dispute any item in the bill of costs by serving points of dispute on –

    (a) the receiving party; and
    (b) every other party to the detailed assessment proceedings.

(2) The period for serving points of dispute is 21 days after the date of service of the notice of commencement.

(3) If a party serves points of dispute after the period set out in paragraph (2), that party may not be heard further in the detailed assessment proceedings unless the court gives permission.

    (Practice Direction 47 sets out requirements about the form of points of dispute)

(4) The receiving party may file a request for a default costs certificate if –

    (a) the period set out in paragraph (2) for serving points of dispute has expired; and
    (b) the receiving party has not been served with any points of dispute.

(5) If any party (including the paying party) serves points of dispute before the issue of a default costs certificate the court may not issue the default costs certificate.

    (Section IV of this Part sets out the procedure to be followed after points of dispute have been served).

Amendments—Inserted by SI 2013/262.

47.10 Procedure where costs are agreed

(1) If the paying party and the receiving party agree the amount of costs, either party may apply for a costs certificate (either interim or final) in the amount agreed.

> (Rule 47.16 and rule 47.17 contain further provisions about interim and final costs certificates respectively)

(2) An application for a certificate under paragraph (1) must be made to the court which would be the venue for detailed assessment proceedings under rule 47.4.

Amendments—Inserted by SI 2013/262.

Section III – Costs Payable by One Party to Another – Default Provisions

47.11 Default costs certificate

(1) Where the receiving party is permitted by rule 47.9 to obtain a default costs certificate, that party does so by filing a request in the relevant practice form.

> (Practice Direction 47 deals with the procedure by which the receiving party may obtain a default costs certificate.)

(2) A default costs certificate will include an order to pay the costs to which it relates.

(3) Where a receiving party obtains a default costs certificate, the costs payable to that party for the commencement of detailed assessment proceedings will be the sum set out in Practice Direction 47.

(4) A receiving party who obtains a default costs certificate in detailed assessment proceedings pursuant to an order under section 194(3) of the 2007 Act must send a copy of the default costs certificate to the prescribed charity.

Amendments—Inserted by SI 2013/262.

47.12 Setting aside a default costs certificate

(1) The court will set aside a default costs certificate if the receiving party was not entitled to it.

(2) In any other case, the court may set aside or vary a default costs certificate if it appears to the court that there is some good reason why the detailed assessment proceedings should continue.

> (Practice Direction 47 contains further details about the procedure for setting aside a default costs certificate and the matters which the court must take into account)

(3) Where the court sets aside or varies a default costs certificate in detailed assessment proceedings pursuant to an order under section 194(3) of the Legal Services Act 2007, the receiving party must send a copy of the order setting aside or varying the default costs certificate to the prescribed charity.

Amendments—Inserted by SI 2013/262.

Section IV – Costs Payable by One Party to Another – Procedure where Points of Dispute are Served

47.13 Optional Reply

(1) Where any party to the detailed assessment proceedings serves points of dispute, the receiving party may serve a reply on the other parties to the assessment proceedings.

(2) The receiving party may do so within 21 days after being served with the points of dispute to which the reply relates.

(Practice Direction 47 sets out the meaning of 'reply'.)

Amendments—Inserted by SI 2013/262.

47.14 Detailed assessment hearing

(1) Where points of dispute are served in accordance with this Part, the receiving party must file a request for a detailed assessment hearing within 3 months of the expiry of the period for commencing detailed assessment proceedings as specified –
  (a) in rule 47.7; or
  (b) by any direction of the court.

(2) Where the receiving party fails to file a request in accordance with paragraph (1), the paying party may apply for an order requiring the receiving party to file the request within such time as the court may specify.

(3) On an application under paragraph (2), the court may direct that, unless the receiving party requests a detailed assessment hearing within the time specified by the court, all or part of the costs to which the receiving party would otherwise be entitled will be disallowed.

(4) If –
  (a) the paying party has not made an application in accordance with paragraph (2); and
  (b) the receiving party files a request for a detailed assessment hearing later than the period specified in paragraph (1),

the court may disallow all or part of the interest otherwise payable to the receiving party under –
  (i) section 17 of the Judgments Act 1838; or
  (ii) section 74 of the County Courts Act 1984,

but will not impose any other sanction except in accordance with rule 44.11 (powers in relation to misconduct).

(5) No party other than –
  (a) the receiving party;
  (b) the paying party; and
  (c) any party who has served points of dispute under rule 47.9,

may be heard at the detailed assessment hearing unless the court gives permission.

(6) Only items specified in the points of dispute may be raised at the hearing, unless the court gives permission.

(7) If an assessment is carried out at more than one hearing, then for the purposes of rule 52.4 time for appealing shall not start to run until the conclusion of the final hearing, unless the court orders otherwise.

>(Practice Direction 47 specifies other documents which must be filed with the request for hearing and the length of notice which the court will give when it fixes a hearing date.)

Amendments—Inserted by SI 2013/262.

47.15 Provisional Assessment

(1) This rule applies to any detailed assessment proceedings commenced in the High Court or a county court on or after 1 April 2013 in which the costs claimed are the amount set out in paragraph 14.1 of the practice direction supplementing this Part, or less.

(2) In proceedings to which this rule applies, the parties must comply with the procedure set out in Part 47 as modified by paragraph 14 Practice Direction 47.

(3) The court will undertake a provisional assessment of the receiving party's costs on receipt of Form N258 and the relevant supporting documents specified in Practice Direction 47.

(4) The provisional assessment will be based on the information contained in the bill and supporting papers and the contentions set out in Precedent G (the points of dispute and any reply).

(5) In proceedings which do not go beyond provisional assessment, the maximum amount the court will award to any party as costs of the assessment (other than the costs of drafting the bill of costs) is £1,500 together with any VAT thereon and any court fees paid by that party.

(6) The court may at any time decide that the matter is unsuitable for a provisional assessment and may give directions for the matter to be listed for hearing. The matter will then proceed under rule 47.14 without modification.

(7) When a provisional assessment has been carried out, the court will send a copy of the bill, as provisionally assessed, to each party with a notice stating that any party who wishes to challenge any aspect of the provisional assessment must, within 21 days of the receipt of the notice, file and serve on all other parties a written request for an oral hearing. If no such request is filed and served within that period, the provisional assessment shall be binding upon the parties, save in exceptional circumstances.

(8) The written request referred to in paragraph (7) must –

 (a) identify the item or items in the court's provisional assessment which are sought to be reviewed at the hearing; and
 (b) provide a time estimate for the hearing.

(9) The court then will fix a date for the hearing and give at least 14 days' notice of the time and place of the hearing to all parties.

(10) Any party which has requested an oral hearing, will pay the costs of and incidental to that hearing unless –

 (a) it achieves an adjustment in its own favour by 20% or more of the sum provisionally assessed; or
 (b) the court otherwise orders.

Amendments—Inserted by SI 2013/262. Amended by SI 2013/1974.

Section V – Interim Costs Certificate and Final Costs Certificate.

47.16 Power to issue an interim certificate

(1) The court may at any time after the receiving party has filed a request for a detailed assessment hearing –

(a) issue an interim costs certificate for such sum as it considers appropriate or
(b) amend or cancel an interim certificate.

(2) An interim certificate will include an order to pay the costs to which it relates, unless the court orders otherwise.

(3) The court may order the costs certified in an interim certificate to be paid into court.

(4) Where the court –

(a) issues an interim costs certificate; or
(b) amends or cancels an interim certificate,

in detailed assessment proceedings pursuant to an order under section 194(3) of the 2007 Act, the receiving party must send a copy of the interim costs certificate or the order amending or cancelling the interim costs certificate to the prescribed charity.

Amendments—Inserted by SI 2013/262.

47.17 Final costs certificate

(1) In this rule a 'completed bill' means a bill calculated to show the amount due following the detailed assessment of the costs.

(2) The period for filing the completed bill is 14 days after the end of the detailed assessment hearing.

(3) When a completed bill is filed the court will issue a final costs certificate and serve it on the parties to the detailed assessment proceedings.

(4) Paragraph (3) is subject to any order made by the court that a certificate is not to be issued until other costs have been paid.

(5) A final costs certificate will include an order to pay the costs to which it relates, unless the court orders otherwise.

(Practice Direction 47 deals with the form of a final costs certificate)

(6) Where the court issues a final costs certificate in detailed assessment proceedings pursuant to an order under section 194(3) of the 2007 Act, the receiving party must send a copy of the final costs certificate to the prescribed charity.

Amendments—Inserted by SI 2013/262.

Section VI – Detailed Assessment Procedure for Costs of a LSC Funded Client or an Assisted Person Where Costs are Payable out of the Community Legal Service Fund

47.18 (1) Where the court is to assess costs of a LSC funded client or an assisted person which are payable out of the Community Legal Services Fund, that person's solicitor may commence detailed assessment proceedings by filing a request in the relevant practice form.

(2) A request under paragraph (1) must be filed within 3 months after the date when the right to detailed assessment arose.

(3) The solicitor must also serve a copy of the request for detailed assessment on the LSC funded client or the assisted person, if notice of that person's interest has been given to the court in accordance with community legal service or legal aid regulations.

(4) Where the solicitor has certified that the LSC funded client or that person wishes to attend an assessment hearing, the court will, on receipt of the request for assessment, fix a date for the assessment hearing.

(5) Where paragraph (3) does not apply, the court will, on receipt of the request for assessment provisionally assess the costs without the attendance of the solicitor, unless it considers that a hearing is necessary.

(6) After the court has provisionally assessed the bill, it will return the bill to the solicitor.

(7) The court will fix a date for an assessment hearing if the solicitor informs the court, within 14 days after receiving the provisionally assessed bill, that the solicitor wants the court to hold such a hearing.

Amendments—Inserted by SI 2013/262.

47.19 Detailed assessment procedure where costs are payable out of a fund other than the community legal service fund

(1) Where the court is to assess costs which are payable out of a fund other than the Community Legal Service Fund, the receiving party may commence detailed assessment proceedings by filing a request in the relevant practice form.

(2) A request under paragraph (1) must be filed within 3 months after the date when the right to detailed assessment arose.

(3) The court may direct that the party seeking assessment serve a copy of the request on any person who has a financial interest in the outcome of the assessment.

(4) The court will, on receipt of the request for assessment, provisionally assess the costs without the attendance of the receiving party, unless the court considers that a hearing is necessary.

(5) After the court has provisionally assessed the bill, it will return the bill to the receiving party.

(6) The court will fix a date for an assessment hearing if the receiving party informs the court, within 14 days after receiving the provisionally assessed bill, that the receiving party wants the court to hold such a hearing.

Amendments—Inserted by SI 2013/262.

Section VII – Costs of Detailed Assessment Proceedings

47.20 Liability for costs of detailed assessment proceedings

(1) The receiving party is entitled to the costs of the detailed assessment proceedings except where –

    (a) the provisions of any Act, any of these Rules or any relevant practice direction provide otherwise; or

    (b) the court makes some other order in relation to all or part of the costs of the detailed assessment proceedings.

(2) Paragraph (1) does not apply where the receiving party has pro bono representation in the detailed assessment proceedings but that party may apply for an order in respect of that representation under section 194(3) of the 2007 Act.

(3) In deciding whether to make some other order, the court must have regard to all the circumstances, including –

    (a) the conduct of all the parties;

    (b) the amount, if any, by which the bill of costs has been reduced; and

    (c) whether it was reasonable for a party to claim the costs of a particular item or to dispute that item.

(4) The provisions of Part 36 apply to the costs of detailed assessment proceedings with the following modifications –

    (a) 'claimant' refers to 'receiving party' and 'defendant' refers to 'paying party';

    (b) 'trial' refers to 'detailed assessment hearing';

    (c) a detailed assessment hearing is 'in progress' from the time when it starts until the bill of costs has been assessed or agreed

    (d) for rule 36.14(7) substitute 'If such sum is not paid within 14 days of acceptance of the offer, or such other period as has been agreed, the receiving party may apply for a final costs certificate for the unpaid sum';

    (e) a reference to 'judgment being entered' is to the completion of the detailed assessment, and references to a 'judgment' being advantageous or otherwise are to the outcome of the detailed assessment.

(5) The court will usually summarily assess the costs of detailed assessment proceedings at the conclusion of those proceedings.

(6) Unless the court otherwise orders, interest on the costs of detailed assessment proceedings will run from the date of default, interim or final costs certificate, as the case may be.

(7) For the purposes of rule 36.17, detailed assessment proceedings are to be regarded as an independent claim.

Amendments—Inserted by SI 2013/262. Amended by SI 2014/3299.

Section VIII – Appeals from Authorised Court Officers in Detailed Assessment Proceedings

47.21 Right to appeal

(1) Any party to detailed assessment proceedings may appeal against a decision of an authorised court officer in those proceedings.

Amendments—Inserted by SI 2013/262.

47.22 Court to hear appeal

An appeal against a decision of an authorised court officer lies to a costs judge or a District Judge of the High Court.

Amendments—Inserted by SI 2013/262. Amended by SI 2014/407.

47.23 Appeal procedure

(1) The appellant must file an appeal notice within 21 days after the date of the decision against which it is sought to appeal.

(2) On receipt of the appeal notice, the court will –

(a) serve a copy of the notice on the parties to the detailed assessment proceedings; and
(b) give notice of the appeal hearing to those parties.

Amendments—Inserted by SI 2013/262.

47.24 Powers of the court on appeal

On an appeal from an authorised court officer the court will –

(a) re-hear the proceedings which gave rise to the decision appealed against; and
(b) make any order and give any directions as it considers appropriate.

Amendments—Inserted by SI 2013/262.

Practice Direction 47 – Procedure for Detailed Assessment of Costs and Default Provisions

This Practice Direction supplements CPR 1998 Part 47 (PD47)

Time When Assessment May Be Carried Out: Rule 47.1

1.1 For the purposes of rule 47.1, proceedings are concluded when the court has finally determined the matters in issue in the claim, whether or not there is an appeal, or made an award of provisional damages under Part 41.

1.2 The court may order or the parties may agree in writing that, although the proceedings are continuing, they will nevertheless be treated as concluded.

1.3 A party who is served with a notice of commencement (see paragraph 5.2 below) may apply to a costs judge or a District Judge to determine whether the party who served it is entitled to commence detailed assessment proceedings. On hearing such an application the orders which the court may make include: an order allowing the detailed assessment proceedings to continue, or an order setting aside the notice of commencement.

1.4 A costs judge or a District Judge may make an order allowing detailed assessment proceedings to be commenced where there is no realistic prospect of the claim continuing.

No Stay of Detailed Assessment Where There is an Appeal: Rule 47.2

2 An application to stay the detailed assessment of costs pending an appeal may be made to the court whose order is being appealed or to the court which will hear the appeal.

Powers of an Authorised Court Officer: Rule 47.3

3.1 The court officers authorised by the Lord Chancellor to assess costs in the Costs Office and the Principal Registry of the Family Division are authorised to deal with claims where the base costs excluding VAT do not exceed £35,000 in the case of senior executive officers, or their equivalent, and £110,000 in the case of principal officers.

3.2 Where the receiving party, paying party and any other party to the detailed assessment proceedings who has served points of dispute are agreed that the assessment should not be made by an authorised court officer, the receiving party should so inform the court when requesting a hearing date. The court will then list the hearing before a costs judge or a District Judge.

3.3 In any other case a party who objects to the assessment being made by an authorised court officer must make an application to the costs judge or District Judge under Part 23 setting out the reasons for the objection.

Venue for Detailed Assessment Proceedings: Rule 47.4

4.1 For the purposes of rule 47.4(1) the 'appropriate office' means –

(a) the district registry or the County Court hearing centre in which the case was being dealt with when the judgment or order was made or the event occurred which gave rise to the right to assessment, or to which it has subsequently been transferred;

(b) where a tribunal, person or other body makes an order for the detailed assessment of costs, the County Court hearing centre (subject to paragraph 4.2); or

(c) in all other cases, including Court of Appeal cases, the Costs Office.

4.2 (1) This paragraph applies where the appropriate office is any of the following County Court hearing centres: Barnet, Bow, Brentford, Bromley, Central London, Clerkenwell and Shoreditch, Croydon, Edmonton, Ilford, Kingston, Lambeth, Mayors and City of London, Romford, Uxbridge, Wandsworth, West London, Willesden and Woolwich.

(2) Where this paragraph applies –

(a) the receiving party must file any request for a detailed assessment hearing in the Costs Office and, for all purposes relating to that detailed assessment (other than the issue of default costs certificates and applications to set aside default costs certificates), the Costs Office will be treated as the appropriate office in that case;
(b) default costs certificates should be issued and applications to set aside default costs certificates should be issued and heard in the relevant County Court hearing centre; and
(c) unless an order is made under rule 47.4(2) directing that the Costs Office as part of the High Court shall be the appropriate office, an appeal from any decision made by a costs judge shall lie to the Designated Civil Judge for the London Group of County Court hearing centres or such judge as the Designated Civil Judge shall nominate. The appeal notice and any other relevant papers should be lodged at the Central London Civil Justice Centre.

4.3 (1) A direction under rule 47.4(2) or (3) specifying a particular court, registry or office as the appropriate office may be given on application or on the court's own initiative.
(2) Unless the Costs Office is the appropriate office for the purposes of rule 47.4(1) an order directing that an assessment is to take place at the Costs Office will be made only if it is appropriate to do so having regard to the size of the bill of costs, the difficulty of the issues involved, the likely length of the hearing, the cost to the parties and any other relevant matter.

Paragraph 4.2(2)(ii)—Default cost certificates are to be dealt with in the relevant county court and not the Costs Office.

Commencement of Detailed Assessment Proceedings: Rule 47.6

5.1 Precedents A, B, C and D in the Schedule of Costs Precedents annexed to this Practice Direction are model forms of bills of costs for detailed assessment.

5.1A Precedent Q in the Schedule of Costs Precedents annexed to this Practice Direction is a model form of breakdown of the costs claimed for each phase of the proceedings.

5.2 The receiving party must serve on the paying party and all the other relevant persons the following documents –

(a) a notice of commencement in Form N252;
(b) a copy of the bill of costs;
(c) copies of the fee notes of counsel and of any expert in respect of fees claimed in the bill;
(d) written evidence as to any other disbursement which is claimed and which exceeds £500;
(e) a statement giving the name and address for service of any person upon whom the receiving party intends to serve the notice of commencement;
(f) if a costs management order has been made, a breakdown of the costs claimed for each phase of the proceedings.

5.3 The notice of commencement must be completed to show as separate items –

(a) the total amount of the costs claimed in the bill;
(b) the extra sum which will be payable by way of fixed costs and court fees if a default costs certificate is obtained.

5.4 Where the notice of commencement is to be served outside England and Wales the date to be inserted in the notice of commencement for the paying party to send points of dispute is a date (not less than 21 days from the date of service of the notice) which must be calculated by reference to Section IV of Part 6 as if the notice were a claim form and as if the date to be inserted was the date for the filing of a defence.

5.5 (1) For the purposes of rule 47.6(2) a 'relevant person' means –
  (a) any person who has taken part in the proceedings which gave rise to the assessment and who is directly liable under an order for costs made against that person;
  (b) any person who has given to the receiving party notice in writing that that person has a financial interest in the outcome of the assessment and wishes to be a party accordingly;
  (c) any other person whom the court orders to be treated as such.
 (2) Where a party is unsure whether a person is or is not a relevant person, that party may apply to the appropriate office for directions.
 (3) The court will generally not make an order that the person in respect of whom the application is made will be treated as a relevant person, unless within a specified time that person applies to the court to be joined as a party to the assessment proceedings in accordance with Part 19 (Parties and Group Litigation).

5.6 Where –
  (a) the bill of costs is capable of being copied electronically; and
  (b) before the detailed assessment hearing,

a paying party requests an electronic copy of the bill, the receiving party must supply the paying party with a copy in its native format (for example, in Excel or an equivalent) free of charge not more than 7 days after receipt of the request.

Form and Contents of Bills of Costs – General

5.7 A bill of costs may consist of such of the following sections as may be appropriate –
  (1) title page;
  (2) background information;
  (3) items of costs claimed under the headings specified in paragraph 5.12;
  (4) summary showing the total costs claimed on each page of the bill;
  (5) schedules of time spent on non-routine attendances; and
  (6) the certificates referred to in paragraph 5.21.

If the only dispute between the parties concerns disbursements, the bill of costs shall be limited to items (1) and (2) above, a list of the disbursements in issue and brief written submissions in respect of those disbursements.

5.8 Where it is necessary or convenient to do so, a bill of costs may be divided into two or more parts, each part containing sections (2), (3) and (4) above. Circumstances in which it will be necessary or convenient to divide a bill into parts include the following –
  (1) Where the receiving party acted in person during the course of the proceedings (whether or not that party also had a legal representative at that time) the bill must be divided into different parts so as to distinguish between;
    (a) the costs claimed for work done by the legal representative; and

(b) the costs claimed for work done by the receiving party in person.
(2) Where the receiving party had pro bono representation for part of the proceedings and an order under section 194(3) of the Legal Services Act 2007 has been made, the bill must be divided into different parts so as to distinguish between –
   (a) the sum equivalent to the costs claimed for work done by the legal representative acting free of charge; and
   (b) the costs claimed for work not done by the legal representative acting free of charge.
(3) Where the receiving party was represented by different legal representatives during the course of the proceedings, the bill must be divided into different parts so as to distinguish between the costs payable in respect of each legal representative.
(4) Where the receiving party obtained legal aid or LSC funding or is a person for whom civil legal services (within the meaning of Part 1 of the Legal Aid, Sentencing and Punishment of Offenders Act 2012) were provided under arrangements made for the purposes of that Part of that Act in respect of all or part of the proceedings the bill must be divided into separate parts so as to distinguish between –
   (a) costs claimed before legal aid or LSC funding was granted or after civil legal services were provided;
   (b) costs claimed after legal aid or LSC funding was granted or after civil legal services were provided; and
   (c) any costs claimed after legal aid or LSC funding ceased or after civil legal services ceased to be provided.
(5) Where the bill covers costs payable under an order or orders under which there are different paying parties the bill must be divided into parts so as to deal separately with the costs payable by each paying party.
(6) Where the bill covers costs payable under an order or orders, in respect of which the receiving party wishes to claim interest from different dates, the bill must be divided to enable such interest to be calculated.

5.9 Where a party claims costs against another party and also claims costs against the LSC or Lord Chancellor only for work done in the same period, the costs claimed against the LSC or Lord Chancellor only can be claimed either in a separate part of the bill or in additional columns in the same part of the bill. Precedents B and C in the Schedule of Costs Precedents annexed to this Practice Direction show how bills should be drafted when costs are claimed against the LSC only.

Form and Content of Bills of Costs: Title page

5.10 The title page of the bill of costs must set out –
(1) the full title of the proceedings;
(2) the name of the party whose bill it is and a description of the document showing the right to assessment (as to which see paragraph 13.3 of this Practice Direction);
(3) if VAT is included as part of the claim for costs, the VAT number of the legal representative or other person in respect of whom VAT is claimed;
(4) details of all legal aid certificates, LSC certificates, certificates recording the determinations of the Directions of Legal Aid Casework and relevant amendment certificates in respect of which claims for costs are included in the bill.

Form and Content of Bills of Costs: Background information

5.11 The background information included in the bill of costs should set out –

(1) a brief description of the proceedings up to the date of the notice of commencement;
(2) a statement of the status of the legal representatives' employee in respect of whom costs are claimed and (if those costs are calculated on the basis of hourly rates) the hourly rates claimed for each such person.
(3) a brief explanation of any agreement or arrangement between the receiving party and his legal representatives, which affects the costs claimed in the bill.

Form and Content of Bills of Costs: Heads of costs

5.12 The bill of costs may consist of items under such of the following heads as may be appropriate –

(1) attendances at court and upon counsel up to the date of the notice of commencement;
(2) attendances on and communications with the receiving party;
(3) attendances on and communications with witnesses including any expert witness;
(4) attendances to inspect any property or place for the purposes of the proceedings;
(5) attendances on and communications with other persons, including offices of public records;
(6) communications with the court and with counsel;
(7) work done on documents:
(8) work done in connection with negotiations with a view to settlement if not already covered in the heads listed above;
(9) attendances on and communications with London and other agents and work done by them;
(10) other work done which was of or incidental to the proceedings and which is not already covered in the heads listed above.

5.13 In respect of each of the heads of costs –

(1) 'communications' means letters out e-mails out and telephone calls;
(2) communications, which are not routine communications, must be set out in chronological order;
(3) routine communications must be set out as a single item at the end of each head;

5.14 Routine communications are letters out, e-mails out and telephone calls which because of their simplicity should not be regarded as letters or e-mails of substance or telephone calls which properly amount to an attendance.

5.15 Each item claimed in the bill of costs must be consecutively numbered.

5.16 In each part of the bill of costs which claims items under head (1) in paragraph 5.12 (attendances at court and upon counsel) a note should be made of –

(1) all relevant events, including events which do not constitute chargeable items;
(2) any orders for costs which the court made (whether or not a claim is made in respect of those costs in this bill of costs).

5.17 The numbered items of costs may be set out on paper divided into columns. Precedents A, B and C in the Schedule of Costs Precedents annexed to this Practice Direction illustrate various model forms of bills of costs.

5.18 In respect of heads (2) to (10) in paragraph 5.12 above, if the number of attendances and communications other than routine communications is twenty or more, the claim for the costs of those items in that section of the bill of costs should be for the total only and should refer to a schedule in which the full record of dates and details is set out. If the bill of costs contains more than one schedule each schedule should be numbered consecutively.

5.19 The bill of costs must not contain any claims in respect of costs or court fees which relate solely to the detailed assessment proceedings other than costs claimed for preparing and checking the bill.

5.20 The summary must show the total profit costs and disbursements claimed separately from the total VAT claimed. Where the bill of costs is divided into parts the summary must also give totals for each part. If each page of the bill gives a page total the summary must also set out the page totals for each page.

5.21 The bill of costs must contain such of the certificates, the texts of which are set out in Precedent F of the Schedule of Costs Precedents annexed to this Practice Direction, as are appropriate.

5.22 The following provisions relate to work done by legal representatives –

(1) Routine letters out, routine e-mails out and routine telephone calls will in general be allowed on a unit basis of 6 minutes each, the charge being calculated by reference to the appropriate hourly rate. The unit charge for letters out and e-mails out will include perusing and considering the routine letters in or e-mails in.

(2) The court may, in its discretion, allow an actual time charge for preparation of electronic communications sent by legal representatives, which properly amount to attendances provided that the time taken has been recorded.

(3) Local travelling expenses incurred by legal representatives will not be allowed. The definition of 'local' is a matter for the discretion of the court. As a matter of guidance, 'local' will, in general, be taken to mean within a radius of 10 miles from the court dealing with the case at the relevant time. Where travelling and waiting time is claimed, this should be allowed at the rate agreed with the client unless this is more than the hourly rate on the assessment.

(4) The cost of postage, couriers, out-going telephone calls, fax and telex messages will in general not be allowed but the court may exceptionally in its discretion allow such expenses in unusual circumstances or where the cost is unusually heavy.

(5) The cost of making copies of documents will not in general be allowed but the court may exceptionally in its discretion make an allowance for copying in unusual circumstances or where the documents copied are unusually numerous in relation to the nature of the case. Where this discretion is invoked the number of copies made, their purpose and the costs claimed for them must be set out in the bill.

(6) Agency charges as between principal legal representatives and their agents will be dealt with on the principle that such charges, where appropriate, form part of the principal legal representative's charges. Where these charges relate to head (1) in paragraph 5.12 (attendances at court and on

counsel) they must be included in their chronological order in that head. In other cases they must be included in head (9) (attendances on London and other agents).

Period for Commencing Detailed Assessment Proceedings: Rule 47.7

6.1 The time for commencing the detailed assessment proceedings may be extended or shortened either by agreement (rule 2.11) or by the court (rule 3.1(2)(a)). Any application is to the appropriate office.

6.2 The detailed assessment proceedings are commenced by service of the documents referred to. Permission to commence assessment proceedings out of time is not required.

Sanction For Delay In Commencing Detailed Assessment Proceedings: Rule 47.8

7 An application for an order under rule 47.8 must be made in writing and be issued in the appropriate office. The application notice must be served at least 7 days before the hearing.

Points of Dispute and Consequences Of Not Serving: Rule 47.9

8.1 Time for service of points of dispute may be extended or shortened either by agreement (rule 2.11) or by the court (rule 3.1(2)(a)). Any application is to the appropriate office.

8.2 Points of dispute must be short and to the point. They must follow Precedent G in the Schedule of Costs Precedents annexed to this Practice Direction, so far as practicable. They must:
   (a) identify any general points or matters of principle which require decision before the individual items in the bill are addressed; and
   (b) identify specific points, stating concisely the nature and grounds of dispute.

Once a point has been made it should not be repeated but the item numbers where the point arises should be inserted in the left hand box as shown in Precedent G.

8.3 The paying party must state in an open letter accompanying the points of dispute what sum, if any, that party offers to pay in settlement of the total costs claimed. The paying party may also make an offer under Part 36.

Procedure Where Costs are Agreed and On Discontinuance: Rule 47.10

9.1 Where the parties have agreed terms as to the issue of a costs certificate (either interim or final) they should apply under rule 40.6 (Consent judgments and orders) for an order that a certificate be issued in the terms set out in the application. Such an application may be dealt with by a court officer, who may issue the certificate.

9.2 Where in the course of proceedings the receiving party claims that the paying party has agreed to pay costs but that the paying party will neither pay those costs nor join in a consent application under paragraph 9.1, the receiving party may apply under Part 23 for a certificate either interim or final to be issued.

9.3 Nothing in rule 47.10 prevents parties who seek a judgment or order by consent from including in the draft a term that a party shall pay to another party a specified sum in respect of costs.

9.4 (1) The receiving party may discontinue the detailed assessment proceedings in accordance with Part 38 (Discontinuance).
(2) Where the receiving party discontinues the detailed assessment proceedings before a detailed assessment hearing has been requested, the paying party may apply to the appropriate office for an order about the costs of the detailed assessment proceedings.
(3) Where a detailed assessment hearing has been requested the receiving party may not discontinue unless the court gives permission.
(4) A bill of costs may be withdrawn by consent whether or not a detailed assessment hearing has been requested.

Default Costs Certificate: Rule 47.11

10.1
(1) A request for the issue of a default costs certificate must be made in Form N254 and must be signed by the receiving party or his legal representative.
(2) The request must be accompanied by a copy of the document giving the right to detailed assessment and must be filed at the appropriate office. (Paragraph 13.3 below identifies the appropriate documents).

10.2 A default costs certificate will be in Form N255.

10.3 Attention is drawn to Rules 40.3 (Drawing up and Filing of Judgments and Orders) and 40.4 (Service of Judgments and Orders) which apply to the preparation and service of a default costs certificate. The receiving party will be treated as having permission to draw up a default costs certificate by virtue of this Practice Direction.

10.4 The issue of a default costs certificate does not prohibit, govern or affect any detailed assessment of the same costs which are payable out of the Community Legal Service Fund of by the Lord Chancellor under Part 1 of the Legal Aid, Sentencing and Punishment of Offenders Act 2012.

10.5 An application for an order staying enforcement of a default costs certificate may be made either –
(a) to a costs judge or District Judge of the court office which issued the certificate; or
(b) to the court (if different) which has general jurisdiction to enforce the certificate.

10.6 Proceedings for enforcement of default costs certificates may not be issued in the Costs Office.

Default Costs Certificate: Fixed Costs on the Issue of a Default Costs Certificate

10.7 Unless paragraph 1.2 of Practice Direction 45 (Fixed Costs in Small Claims) applies or unless the court orders otherwise, the fixed costs to be included in a default costs certificate are £80 plus a sum equal to any appropriate court fee payable on the issue of the certificate.

10.8 The fixed costs included in a certificate must not exceed the maximum sum specified for costs and court fee in the notice of commencement.

Setting Aside Default Costs Certificate: Rule 47.12

11.1 A court officer may set aside a default costs certificate at the request of the receiving party under rule 47.12. A costs judge or a District Judge will make any other order or give any directions under this rule.

11.2

(1) An application for an order under rule 47.12(2) to set aside or vary a default costs certificate must be supported by evidence.
(2) In deciding whether to set aside or vary a certificate under rule 47.12(2) the matters to which the court must have regard include whether the party seeking the order made the application promptly.
(3) As a general rule a default costs certificate will be set aside under rule 47.12 only if the applicant shows a good reason for the court to do so and if the applicant files with the application a copy of the bill, a copy of the default costs certificate and a draft of the points of dispute the applicant proposes to serve if the application is granted.

11.3 Attention is drawn to rule 3.1(3) (which enables the court when making an order to make it subject to conditions) and to rule 44.2(8) (which enables the court to order a party whom it has ordered to pay costs to pay an amount on account before the costs are assessed). A costs judge or a District Judge may exercise the power of the court to make an order under rule 44.2(8) although he did not make the order about costs which led to the issue of the default costs certificate.

Optional Reply: Rule 47.13

12.1 A reply served by the receiving party under Rule 47.13 must be limited to points of principle and concessions only. It must not contain general denials, specific denials or standard form responses.

12.2 Whenever practicable, the reply must be set out in the form of Precedent G.

Detailed Assessment Hearing: Rule 47.14

13.1 The time for requesting a detailed assessment hearing is within 3 months of the expiry of the period for commencing detailed assessment proceedings.

13.2 The request for a detailed assessment hearing must be in Form N258. The request must be accompanied by –

(a) a copy of the notice of commencement of detailed assessment proceedings;
(b) a copy of the bill of costs,
(c) the document giving the right to detailed assessment (see paragraph 13.3 below);
(d) a copy of the points of dispute, annotated as necessary in order to show which items have been agreed and their value and to show which items remain in dispute and their value;
(e) as many copies of the points of dispute so annotated as there are persons who have served points of dispute;
(f) a copy of any replies served;
(g) copies of all orders made by the court relating to the costs which are to be assessed;
(h) copies of the fee notes and other written evidence as served on the paying party in accordance with paragraph 5.2 above;
(i) where there is a dispute as to the receiving party's liability to pay costs to

the legal representatives who acted for the receiving party, any agreement, letter or other written information provided by the legal representative to the client explaining how the legal representative's charges are to be calculated;

(j) a statement signed by the receiving party or the legal representative giving the name, address for service, reference and telephone number and fax number, if any, of –
   (i) the receiving party;
   (ii) the paying party;
   (iii) any other person who has served points of dispute or who has given notice to the receiving party under paragraph 5.5(1)(b) above;
   and giving an estimate of the length of time the detailed assessment hearing will take;

(k) where the application for a detailed assessment hearing is made by a party other than the receiving party, such of the documents set out in this paragraph as are in the possession of that party;

(l) where the court is to assess the costs of an assisted person or LSC funded client or person to whom civil legal aid services (within the meaning of Part 1 of the Legal Aid, Sentencing and Punishment of Offenders Act 2012) are provided under arrangement made for the purposes of that Part of that Act –
   (i) the legal aid certificate, LSC certificate, the certificate recording the determination of the Direction of Legal Aid Casework and relevant amendment certificates, any authorities and any certificates of discharge or revocation or withdrawal;
   (ii) a certificate, in Precedent F(3) of the Schedule of Costs Precedents;
   (iii) if that person has a financial interest in the detailed assessment hearing and wishes to attend, the postal address of that person to which the court will send notice of any hearing;
   (iv) if the rates payable out of the LSC fund or by the Lord Chancellor under Part 1 of the Legal Aid, Sentencing and Punishment of Offenders Act 2012 are prescribed rates, a schedule to the bill of costs setting out all the items in the bill which are claimed against other parties calculated at the legal aid prescribed rates with or without any claim for enhancement: (further information as to this schedule is set out in paragraph 17 of this Practice Direction);
   (v) a copy of any default costs certificate in respect of costs claimed in the bill of costs.

(m) if a costs management order has been made, a breakdown of the costs claimed for each phase of the proceedings.

13.3 'The document giving the right to detailed assessment' means such one or more of the following documents as are appropriate to the detailed assessment proceedings –

(a) a copy of the judgment or order of the court or tribunal giving the right to detailed assessment;
(b) a copy of the notice served under rule 3.7 (sanctions for non-payment of certain fees) where a claim is struck out under that rule;
(c) a copy of the notice of acceptance where an offer to settle is accepted under Part 36 (Offers to settle);
(d) a copy of the notice of discontinuance in a case which is discontinued under Part 38 (Discontinuance);

(e) a copy of the award made on an arbitration under any Act or pursuant to an agreement, where no court has made an order for the enforcement of the award;
(f) a copy of the order, award or determination of a statutorily constituted tribunal or body.

13.4 On receipt of the request for a detailed assessment hearing the court will fix a date for the hearing, or, if the costs officer so decides, will give directions or fix a date for a preliminary appointment.

13.5 Unless the court otherwise orders, if the only dispute between the parties concerns disbursements, the hearing shall take place in the absence of the parties on the basis of the documents and the court will issue its decision in writing.

13.6 The court will give at least 14 days' notice of the time and place of the detailed assessment hearing to every person named in the statement referred to in paragraph 13.2(j) above.

13.7 If either party wishes to make an application in the detailed assessment proceedings the provisions of Part 23 apply.

13.8

(1) This paragraph deals with the procedure to be adopted where a date has been given by the court for a detailed assessment hearing and –
  (a) the detailed assessment proceedings are settled; or
  (b) a party to the detailed assessment proceedings wishes to apply to vary the date which the court has fixed; or
  (c) the parties to the detailed assessment proceedings agree about changes they wish to make to any direction given for the management of the detailed assessment proceedings.
(2) If detailed assessment proceedings are settled, the receiving party must give notice of that fact to the court immediately, preferably by fax.
(3) A party who wishes to apply to vary a direction must do so in accordance with Part 23.
(4) If the parties agree about changes they wish to make to any direction given for the management of the detailed assessment proceedings –
  (a) they must apply to the court for an order by consent; and
  (b) they must file a draft of the directions sought and an agreed statement of the reasons why the variation is sought; and
  (c) the court may make an order in the agreed terms or in other terms without a hearing, but it may direct that a hearing is to be listed.

13.10

(1) If a party wishes to vary that party's bill of costs, points of dispute or a reply, an amended or supplementary document must be filed with the court and copies of it must be served on all other relevant parties.
(2) Permission is not required to vary a bill of costs, points of dispute or a reply but the court may disallow the variation or permit it only upon conditions, including conditions as to the payment of any costs caused or wasted by the variation.

13.11 Unless the court directs otherwise the receiving party must file with the court the papers in support of the bill not less than 7 days before the date for the detailed assessment hearing and not more than 14 days before that date.

13.12 The papers to be filed in support of the bill and the order in which they are to be arranged are as follows –

(i) instructions and briefs to counsel arranged in chronological order together with all advices, opinions and drafts received and response to such instructions;
(ii) reports and opinions of medical and other experts;
(iii) any other relevant papers;
(iv) a full set of any relevant statements of case
(v) correspondence, file notes and attendance notes;

13.13 The court may direct the receiving party to produce any document which in the opinion of the court is necessary to enable it to reach its decision. These documents will in the first instance be produced to the court, but the court may ask the receiving party to elect whether to disclose the particular document to the paying party in order to rely on the contents of the document, or whether to decline disclosure and instead rely on other evidence.

13.14 Once the detailed assessment hearing has ended it is the responsibility of the receiving party to remove the papers filed in support of the bill.

Provisional Assessment: Rule 47.15

14.1 The amount of costs referred to in rule 47.15(1) is £75,000.

14.2 The following provisions of Part 47 and this Practice Direction will apply to cases falling within rule 47.15 –

(1) rules 47.1, 47.2, 47.4 to 47.13, 47.14 (except paragraphs (6) and (7)), 47.16, 47.17, 47.20 and 47.21; and
(2) paragraphs 1, 2, 4 to 12, 13 (with the exception of paragraphs 13.4 to 13.7, 13.9, 13.11 and 13.14), 15, and 16, of this Practice Direction.

14.3 In cases falling within rule 47.15, when the receiving party files a request for a detailed assessment hearing, that party must file –

(a) the request in Form N258;
(b) the documents set out at paragraphs 8.3 and 13.2 of this Practice Direction;
(c) an additional copy of the bill, including a statement of the costs claimed in respect of the detailed assessment drawn on the assumption that there will not be an oral hearing following the provisional assessment;
(d) the offers made (those marked 'without prejudice save as to costs' or made under Part 36 must be contained in a sealed envelope, marked 'Part 36 or similar offers', but not indicating which party or parties have made them);
(e) completed Precedent G (points of dispute and any reply).

14.4

(1) On receipt of the request for detailed assessment and the supporting papers, the court will use its best endeavours to undertake a provisional assessment within 6 weeks. No party will be permitted to attend the provisional assessment.
(2) Once the provisional assessment has been carried out the court will return Precedent G (the points of dispute and any reply) with the court's decisions noted upon it. Within 14 days of receipt of Precedent G the parties must agree the total sum due to the receiving party on the basis of the court's decisions. If the parties are unable to agree the arithmetic, they must refer the dispute back to the court for a decision on the basis of written submissions.

14.5 When considering whether to depart from the order indicated by rule 47.15(10) the court will take into account the conduct of the parties and any offers made.

14.6 If a party wishes to be heard only as to the order made in respect of the costs of the initial provisional assessment, the court will invite each side to make written submissions and the matter will be finally determined without a hearing. The court will decide what if any order for costs to make in respect of this procedure.

Power to Issue An Interim Certificate: Rule 47.16

15 A party wishing to apply for an interim certificate may do so by making an application in accordance with Part 23.

Final Costs Certificate: Rule 47.17

16.1 At the detailed assessment hearing the court will indicate any disallowance or reduction in the sums claimed in the bill of costs by making an appropriate note on the bill.

16.2 The receiving party must, in order to complete the bill after the detailed assessment hearing make clear the correct figures agreed or allowed in respect of each item and must re-calculate the summary of the bill appropriately.

16.3 The completed bill of costs must be filed with the court no later than 14 days after the detailed assessment hearing.

16.4 At the same time as filing the completed bill of costs, the party whose bill it is must also produce receipted fee notes and receipted accounts in respect of all disbursements except those covered by a certificate in Precedent F(5) in the Schedule of Costs Precedents annexed to this Practice Direction.

16.5 No final costs certificate will be issued until all relevant court fees payable on the assessment of costs have been paid.

16.6 If the receiving party fails to file a completed bill in accordance with rule 47.17 the paying party may make an application under Part 23 seeking an appropriate order under rule 3.1.

16.7 A final costs certificate will show –

(a) the amount of any costs which have been agreed between the parties or which have been allowed on detailed assessment;
(b) where applicable the amount agreed or allowed in respect of VAT on such costs.

This provision is subject to any contrary statutory provision relating to costs payable out of the Community Legal Service Fund or by the Lord Chancellor under Part 1 of the Legal Aid, Sentencing and Punishment of Offenders Act 2012.

16.8 A final costs certificate will include disbursements in respect of the fees of counsel only if receipted fee notes or accounts in respect of those disbursements have been produced to the court and only to the extent indicated by those receipts.

16.9 Where the certificate relates to costs payable between parties a separate certificate will be issued for each party entitled to costs.

16.10 Form N257 is a model form of interim costs certificate and Form N256 is a model form of final costs certificate.

16.11 An application for an order staying enforcement of an interim costs certificate or final costs certificate may be made either –

(a) to a costs judge or District Judge of the court office which issued the certificate; or
(b) to the court (if different) which has general jurisdiction to enforce the certificate.

16.12 An interim or final costs certificate may be enforced as if it were a judgment for the payment of an amount of money. However, proceedings for the enforcement of interim costs certificates or final costs certificates may not be issued in the Costs Office.

Detailed Assessment Procedure Where Costs Are Payable Out of The Community Legal Service Fund or by the Lord Chancellor under Part 1 of the Legal Aid, Sentencing and Punishment of Offenders Act 2012: Rule 47.18

17.1 The time for requesting a detailed assessment under rule 47.18 is within 3 months after the date when the right to detailed assessment arose.

17.2

(1) The request for a detailed assessment of costs must be in Form N258A. The request must be accompanied by –
 (a) a copy of the bill of costs;
 (b) the document giving the right to detailed assessment (see paragraph 13.3 above);
 (c) copies of all orders made by the court relating to the costs which are to be assessed;
 (d) copies of any fee notes of counsel and any expert in respect of fees claimed in the bill;
 (e) written evidence as to any other disbursement which is claimed and which exceeds £500;
 (f) the legal aid certificates, LSC certificates, certificates recording the determinations of the Direction of Legal Aid Casework, any relevant amendment certificates, any authorities and any certificates of discharge, revocation or withdrawal and;
 (g) a statement signed by the legal representative giving the representative's name, address for service, reference, telephone number, fax number, e-mail address where available and, if the assisted person has a financial interest in the detailed assessment and wishes to attend, giving the postal address of that person, to which the court will send notice of any hearing.
(2) The relevant papers in support of the bill as described in paragraph 13.12 must only be lodged if requested by the costs officer.

17.3 Where the court has provisionally assessed a bill of costs it will send to the legal representative a notice, in Form N253 annexed to this practice direction, of the amount of costs which the court proposes to allow together with the bill itself. The legal representative should, if the provisional assessment is to be accepted, then complete the bill.

17.4 If the solicitor whose bill it is, or any other party wishes to make an application in the detailed assessment proceedings, the provisions of Part 23 applies.

17.5 It is the responsibility of the legal representative to complete the bill by entering in the bill the correct figures allowed in respect of each item, recalculating the summary of the bill appropriately and completing the Community Legal Service assessment certificate (Form EX80A).

Costs Payable by the Legal Services Commission or Lord Chancellor at Prescribed Rates

17.6 Where the costs of an assisted person or LSC funded client or person to whom civil legal services (within the meaning of Part 1 of the Legal Aid, Sentencing and Punishment of Offenders Act 2012) are provided under arrangements made for the purposes of that Part of that Act are payable by another person but costs can be claimed against the LSC or Lord Chancellor at prescribed rates (with or without enhancement), the solicitor of the assisted person or LSC funded client or person to whom civil legal services are provided must file a legal aid/ LSC schedule in accordance with paragraph 13.2(l) above. The schedule should follow as closely as possible Precedent E of the Schedule of Costs Precedents annexed to this Practice Direction.

17.7 The schedule must set out by reference to the item numbers in the bill of costs, all the costs claimed as payable by another person, but the arithmetic in the schedule should claim those items at prescribed rates only (with or without any claim for enhancement).

17.8 Where there has been a change in the prescribed rates during the period covered by the bill of costs, the schedule (as opposed to the bill) should be divided into separate parts, so as to deal separately with each change of rate. The schedule must also be divided so as to correspond with any divisions in the bill of costs.

17.9 If the bill of costs contains additional columns setting out costs claimed against the LSC or Lord Chancellor only, the schedule may be set out in a separate document or, alternatively, may be included in the additional columns of the bill.

17.10 The detailed assessment of the legal aid/LSC schedule will take place immediately after the detailed assessment of the bill of costs but on occasions, the court may decide to conduct the detailed assessment of the legal aid/LSC schedule separately from any detailed assessment of the bill of costs. This will occur, for example, where a default costs certificate is obtained as between the parties but that certificate is not set aside at the time of the detailed assessment of the legal aid costs.

17.11 Where costs have been assessed at prescribed rates it is the responsibility of the legal representative to enter the correct figures allowed in respect of each item and to recalculate the summary of the legal aid/ LSC schedule.

Detailed Assessment Procedure Where Costs Are Payable Out of A Fund or by the Lord Chancellor under Part 1 of the Legal Aid, Sentencing and Punishment of Offenders Act 2012: Rule 47.19

18.1 Rule 47.19 enables the court to direct under rule 47.19(3) that the receiving party must serve a copy of the request for assessment and copies of the documents which accompany it, on any person who has a financial interest in the outcome of the assessment.

18.2 A person has a financial interest in the outcome of the assessment if the assessment will or may affect the amount of money or property to which that person is or may become entitled out of the fund. Where an interest in the fund is itself held by a trustee for the benefit of some other person, that trustee will be treated as the person having such a financial interest unless it is not appropriate to do so. 'Trustee' includes a personal representative, receiver or any other person acting in a fiduciary capacity.

18.3 The request for a detailed assessment of costs out of the fund should be in Form N258B, be accompanied by the documents set out at paragraph 17.2(1) (a) to (e) and the following –

(a) a statement signed by the receiving party giving his name, address for service, reference, telephone number,
(b) a statement of the postal address of any person who has a financial interest in the outcome of the assessment; and
(c) if a person having a financial interest is a child or protected party, a statement to that effect.

18.4 The court will decide, having regard to the amount of the bill, the size of the fund and the number of persons who have a financial interest, which of those persons should be served and may give directions about service and about the hearing. The court may dispense with service on all or some of those persons.

18.5 Where the court makes an order dispensing with service on all such persons it may proceed at once to make a provisional assessment, or, if it decides that a hearing is necessary, give appropriate directions. Before deciding whether a hearing is necessary, the court may require the receiving party to provide further information relating to the bill.

18.6

(1) The court will send the provisionally assessed bill to the receiving party with a notice in Form N253. If the receiving party is legally represented the legal representative should, if the provisional assessment is to be accepted, then complete the bill.
(2) The court will fix a date for a detailed assessment hearing, if the receiving party informs the court within 14 days after receiving the notice in Form N253, that the receiving party wants the court to hold such a hearing.

18.7 The court will give at least 14 days' notice of the time and place of the hearing to the receiving party and to any person who has a financial interest and who has been served with a copy of the request for assessment.

18.8 If any party or any person who has a financial interest wishes to make an application in the detailed assessment proceedings, the provisions of Part 23 (General Rules about Applications for Court Orders) apply.

18.9 If the receiving party is legally represented the legal representative must complete the bill by inserting the correct figures in respect of each item and must recalculate the summary of the bill.

Costs Of Detailed Assessment Proceedings – Rule 47.20: Offers to Settle Under Part 36 or Otherwise

19 Where an offer to settle is made, whether under Part 36 or otherwise, it should specify whether or not it is intended to be inclusive of the cost of preparation of the bill, interest and VAT. Unless the offer states otherwise it will be treated as being inclusive of these.

Appeals from Authorised Court Officers in Detailed Assessment Proceedings: Rules 47.22 To 47.25

20.1 This Section relates only to appeals from authorised court officers in detailed assessment proceedings. All other appeals arising out of detailed assessment proceedings (and arising out of summary assessments) are dealt with in accordance with Part 52 and Practice Directions 52A to 52E. The destination of appeals is dealt with in accordance with the Access to Justice Act 1999 (Destination of Appeals) Order 2000.

20.2 In respect of appeals from authorised court officers, there is no requirement to obtain permission, or to seek written reasons.

20.3 The appellant must file a notice which should be in Form N161 (an appellant's notice).

20.4 The appeal will be heard by a costs judge or a District Judge of the High Court, and is a re-hearing.

20.5 The appellant's notice should, if possible, be accompanied by a suitable record of the judgment appealed against. Where reasons given for the decision have been officially recorded by the court an approved transcript of that record should accompany the notice. Where there is no official record the following documents will be acceptable –

(a) the officer's comments written on the bill;
(b) advocates' notes of the reasons agreed by the respondent if possible and approved by the authorised court officer.

When the appellant was unrepresented before the authorised court officer, it is the duty of any advocate for the respondent to make a note of the reasons promptly available, free of charge to the appellant where there is no official record or if the court so directs. Where the appellant was represented before the authorised court officer, it is the duty of the appellant's own former advocate to make a note available. The appellant should submit the note of the reasons to the costs judge or District Judge hearing the appeal.

20.6 Where the appellant is not able to obtain a suitable record of the authorised court officer's decision within the time in which the appellant's notice must be filed, the appellant's notice must still be completed to the best of the appellant's ability. It may however be amended subsequently with the permission of the costs judge or District Judge hearing the appeal.

Schedule of Costs Precedents

A: Model form of bill of costs (receiving party's solicitor and counsel on CFA terms)

B: Model form of bill of costs (detailed assessment of additional liability only)

C: Model form of bill of costs (payable by Defendant and the LSC)

D: Model form of bill of costs (alternative form, single column for amounts claimed, separate parts for costs payable by the LSC only)

E: Legal Aid/LSC Schedule of Costs

F: Certificates for including in bill of costs

G: Points of dispute served by the defendant

H: Points of dispute served by the defendant

Guidance notes on Precedent H

J: Solicitors Act 1974: Part 8 claim form under Part III of the Act

K: Solicitors Act 1974: order for delivery of bill

L: Solicitors Act 1974: order for detailed assessment (client)

M: Solicitors Act 1974: order for detailed assessment (solicitors)

P: Solicitors Act 1974: breakdown of costs

Costs Precedents—All of the Costs Precedents can be accessed on the *Court of Protection Practice* CD-ROM or via *Court of Protection Practice* Online.

PART 48
PART 2 OF THE LEGAL AID, SENTENCING AND PUNISHMENT OF OFFENDERS ACT 2012 RELATING TO CIVIL LITIGATION FUNDING AND COSTS: TRANSITIONAL PROVISION IN RELATION TO PRE-COMMENCEMENT FUNDING ARRANGEMENTS

48.1 (1) The provisions of CPR Parts 43 to 48 relating to funding arrangements, and the attendant provisions of the Costs Practice Direction, will apply in relation to a pre-commencement funding arrangement as they were in force immediately before 1 April 2013, with such modifications (if any) as may be made by a practice direction on or after that date.

(2) A reference in rule 48.2 to a rule is to that rule as it was in force immediately before 1 April 2013.

Amendments—Inserted by SI 2013/262.

48.2 (1) A pre-commencement funding arrangement is –
  (a) in relation to proceedings other than insolvency-related proceedings, publication and privacy proceedings or a mesothelioma claim –
    (i) a funding arrangement as defined by rule 43.2(1)(k)(i) where –
      (aa) the agreement was entered into before 1 April 2013 specifically for the purposes of the provision to the person by whom the success fee is payable of advocacy or litigation services in relation to the matter that is the subject of the proceedings in which the costs order is to be made; or
      (bb) the agreement was entered into before 1 April 2013 and advocacy or litigation services were provided to that person under the agreement in connection with that matter before 1 April 2013;
    (ii) a funding arrangement as defined by rule 43.2(1)(k)(ii) where the party seeking to recover the insurance premium took out the insurance policy in relation to the proceedings before 1 April 2013;
    (iii) a funding arrangement as defined by rule 43.2(1)(k)(iii) where the agreement with the membership organisation to meet the costs was made before 1 April 2013 specifically in respect of the costs of other parties to proceedings relating to the matter which is the subject of the proceedings in which the costs order is to be made;
  (b) in relation to insolvency-related proceedings, publication and privacy proceedings or a mesothelioma claim –
    (i) a funding arrangement as defined by rule 43.2(1)(k)(i) where –

(aa) the agreement was entered into before the relevant date specifically for the purposes of the provision to the person by whom the success fee is payable of advocacy or litigation services in relation to the matter that is the subject of the proceedings in which the costs order is to be made; or
(bb) the agreement was entered into before the relevant date and advocacy or litigation services were provided to that person under the agreement in connection with that matter before the relevant date;
(ii) a funding arrangement as defined by rule 43.2(1)(k)(ii) where the party seeking to recover the insurance premium took out the insurance policy in relation to the proceedings before the relevant date.

(2) In paragraph (1) –
  (a) 'insolvency-related proceedings' means any proceedings –
      (i) in England and Wales brought by a person acting in the capacity of –
          (aa) a liquidator of a company which is being wound up in England and Wales or Scotland under Parts V or VI of the Insolvency Act 1986; or
          (bb) a trustee of a bankrupt's estate under Part IX of the Insolvency Act 1986; and
      (ii) brought by a person acting in the capacity of an administrator appointed pursuant to the provisions of Part II of the Insolvency Act 1986;
      (iii) in England and Wales brought by a company which is being wound up in England and Wales or Scotland under Parts IV or V of the Insolvency Act 1986; or
      (iv) brought by a company which has entered administration under Part II of the Insolvency Act 1986;
  (b) 'news publisher' means a person who publishes a newspaper, magazine or website containing news or information about or comment on current affairs;
  (c) 'publication and privacy proceedings' means proceedings for –
      (i) defamation;
      (ii) malicious falsehood;
      (iii) breach of confidence involving publication to the general public;
      (iv) misuse of private information; or
      (v) harassment, where the defendant is a news publisher.
  (d) 'a mesothelioma claim' is a claim for damages in respect of diffuse mesothelioma (within the meaning of the Pneumoconiosis etc. (Workers' Compensation) Act 1979; and
  (e) 'the relevant date' is the date on which sections 44 and 46 of the Legal Aid, Sentencing and Punishment of Offenders Act 2012 came into force in relation to proceedings of the sort in question.

Amendments—Inserted by SI 2013/262.

Practice Direction 48 – Part 2 of The Legal Aid, Sentencing and Punishment of Offenders Act 2012 Relating to Civil Litigation Funding And Costs: Transitional Provision And Exceptions

This Practice Direction supplements CPR 1998 Part 48 (PD48)

Transitional Provisions: General

1.1 Sections 44 and 46 of the Legal Aid, Sentencing and Punishment of Offenders Act 2012 ('the 2012 Act') make changes to the effect that a costs order may not include, respectively, provision requiring the payment by one party of all or part of a success fee payable by another party under a conditional fee agreement or of an amount in respect of all or part of the premium of a costs insurance policy taken out by another party. These changes come into force on 1 April 2013.

1.2 Sections 44(6) and 46(3) of the 2012 Act make saving provisions to the effect, respectively, that these changes do not apply so as to prevent a costs order including such provision where the conditional fee agreement in relation to the proceedings was entered into (or, in relation to a collective conditional fee agreement, services were provided to the party under the agreement), or the costs insurance policy in relation to the proceedings taken out, before the date on which the changes come into force.

1.3 The provisions in the CPR relating to funding arrangements have accordingly been revoked (either in whole or in part as they relate to funding arrangements) with effect from 1 April 2013; but they will remain relevant, and will continue to have effect notwithstanding the revocations, after that date for those cases covered by the saving provisions.

1.4 The provisions in the CPR in force prior to 1 April 2012 relating to funding arrangements include –

(a) CPR 43.2(1)(a), (k), (l), (m), (n), (o), 43.2(3) and 43.2(4);
(b) CPR 44.3A, 44.3B, 44.12B, 44.15 and 44.16;
(c) CPR 45.8, 45.10, 45.12, 45.13, Sections III to V (45.15 to 45.19, 45.20 to 22 and 45.23 to 26), 45.28 and 45.31 to 45.40;
(d) CPR 46.3;
(e) CPR 48.8.

Mesothelioma claims

2.1 By virtue of section 48 of the 2012 Act, the changes relating to recoverable success fees and insurance premiums which are made by sections 44 and 46 of the Act may not be commenced, and accordingly will not apply, in relation to mesothelioma claims (defined by section 48(2) of the Act as having the same meaning as in the Pneumoconiosis etc. (Workers' Compensation) Act 1979) until such time as a review has been carried out and the conclusions of that review published. It will accordingly remain possible for a costs order in favour of a party to such proceedings to include provision requiring the payment of success fees and premiums under after the event costs insurance policies, and so the provisions of the CPR relating to funding arrangements as in force immediately prior to 1 April 2013

Practice Direction – Civil Litigation Funding and Costs: Transitional Provision and Exceptions **PD48**

will continue to apply in relation to such proceedings, whether commenced before or after 1 April 2013. This will include the provision for fixed recoverable success fees in respect of employers' liability disease claims in Section V of Part 45 (CPR 45.23 to 45.26), which will otherwise cease to apply other than to claims in which a CFA was entered into or a costs insurance policy taken out before 1 April 2013).

2.2 On the later date when sections 44 and 46 are brought into force in relation to mesothelioma claims, the saving provisions of sections 44(6) and 44(3) will have effect in relation to funding arrangements in such claims as they do more generally, save that the operative date for the saving provisions will not be 1 April 2013 but the later date.

Insolvency-related proceedings and publication and privacy proceedings

3.1 Sections 44 and 46 of the 2012 Act are not being commenced immediately in relation to certain proceedings related to insolvency. Until such time as those sections are commenced in relation to those proceedings, therefore, they are in a similar position as regards funding arrangements to mesothelioma claims.

3.2 Similarly, sections 44 and 46 of the 2012 Act are not being commenced immediately in respect of publication and privacy proceedings, which will accordingly be in a similar position as regards funding arrangements to mesothelioma claims and insolvency-related proceedings until such time as those sections are commenced in relation to them.

New provision in relation to clinical negligence claims

4.1 Section 46 of the 2012 Act enables the Lord Chancellor by regulations to provide that a costs order may include provision requiring the payment of an amount in respect of all or part of the premium of a costs insurance policy, where –

 (a) the order is made in favour of a party to clinical negligence proceedings of a prescribed description;
 (b) the party has taken out a costs insurance policy insuring against the risk of incurring a liability to pay for one or more expert reports in respect of clinical negligence in connection with the proceedings (or against that risk and other risks);
 (c) the policy is of a prescribed description;
 (d) the policy states how much of the premium relates to the liability to pay for such an expert report or reports, and the amount to be paid is in respect of that part of the premium.

4.2 The regulations made under the power are the Recovery of Costs Insurance Premiums in Clinical Negligence Proceedings Regulations 2012 (S.I. 2012/92). The regulations relate only to clinical negligence cases where a costs insurance policy is taken out on or after 1 April 2013, so the provisions in force in the CPR prior to 1 April 2013 relating to funding arrangements will not apply.

****

PART 52
APPEALS

Section I

General Rules about Appeals

52.1 Scope and interpretation

(1) The rules in this Part apply to appeals to –
  (a) the civil division of the Court of Appeal;
  (b) the High Court; and
  (c) the County Court.

(2) This Part does not apply to an appeal in detailed assessment proceedings against a decision of an authorised court officer.

   (Rules 47.21 to 47.24 deal with appeals against a decision of an authorised court officer in detailed assessment proceedings)

(3) In this Part –
  (a) 'appeal' includes an appeal by way of case stated;
  (b) 'appeal court' means the court to which an appeal is made;
  (c) 'lower court' means the court, tribunal or other person or body from whose decision an appeal is brought;
  (d) 'appellant' means a person who brings or seeks to bring an appeal;
  (e) 'respondent' means –
     (i) a person other than the appellant who was a party to the proceedings in the lower court and who is affected by the appeal; and
     (ii) a person who is permitted by the appeal court to be a party to the appeal; and
  (f) 'appeal notice' means an appellant's or respondent's notice.

(4) This Part is subject to any rule, enactment or practice direction which sets out special provisions with regard to any particular category of appeal.

Amendments—Inserted by SI 2000/221. Amended by SI 2000/2092; SI 2005/3515; SI 2013/1974; SI 2014/407.

52.2 Parties to comply with Practice Directions 52A to 52E

All parties to an appeal must comply with Practice Directions 52A to 52E.

Amendments—Inserted by SI 2000/221. Amended by SI 2009/3390; SI 2012/2208.

52.3 Permission

(1) An appellant or respondent requires permission to appeal –
  (a) where the appeal is from a decision of a judge in the County Court, family court or the High Court, except where the appeal is against –
     (i) a committal order;
     (ii) a refusal to grant habeas corpus; or
     (iii) a secure accommodation order made under section 25 of the Children Act 1989; or

(b) as provided by Practice Direction 52.

(Other enactments may provide that permission is required for particular appeals)

(2) An application for permission to appeal may be made –

(a) to the lower court at the hearing at which the decision to be appealed was made; or
(b) to the appeal court in an appeal notice.

(Rule 52.4 sets out the time limits for filing an appellant's notice at the appeal court. Rule 52.5 sets out the time limits for filing a respondent's notice at the appeal court. Any application for permission to appeal to the appeal court must be made in the appeal notice (see rules 52.4(1) and 52.5(3))

(Rule 52.13(1) provides that permission is required from the Court of Appeal for all appeals to that court from a decision of the County Court, family court or the High Court which was itself made on appeal)

(3) Where the lower court refuses an application for permission to appeal –,

(a) a further application for permission may be made to the appeal court; and
(b) the order refusing permission will specify –
    (i) the court to which any further application for permission should be made; and
    (ii) the level of the judge who should hear the application.

(4) Subject to paragraph (4A) and except where a rule or practice direction provides otherwise, where the appeal court, without a hearing, refuses permission to appeal, the person seeking permission may request the decision to be reconsidered at a hearing.

(4A)

(a) Where a judge of the Court of Appeal or of the High Court, a Designated Civil Judge or a Specialist Circuit Judge refuses permission to appeal without a hearing and considers that the application is totally without merit, the judge may make an order that the person seeking permission may not request the decision to be reconsidered at a hearing.
(b) For the purposes of subparagraph (a) 'Specialist Circuit Judge' means any Circuit Judge in the County Court nominated to hear cases in the Mercantile, Chancery or Technology and Construction Court lists.

(4B) Rule 3.3(5) will not apply to an order that the person seeking permission may not request the decision to be reconsidered at a hearing made under paragraph (4A).

(5) A request under paragraph (4) must be filed within seven days after service of the notice that permission has been refused.

(6) Permission to appeal may be given only where –

(a) the court considers that the appeal would have a real prospect of success; or
(b) there is some other compelling reason why the appeal should be heard.

(7) An order giving permission may –

(a) limit the issues to be heard; and
(b) be made subject to conditions.

(Rule 3.1(3) also provides that the court may make an order subject to conditions)

(Rule 25.15 provides for the court to order security for costs of an appeal)

Amendments—Inserted by SI 2000/221. Amended by SI 2005/3515; SI 2006/1689; SI 2008/2178; SI 2009/3390; SI 2012/2208; SI 2014/407; SI 2014/879; SI 2014/2044.

52.4 Appellant's notice

(1) Where the appellant seeks permission from the appeal court it must be requested in the appellant's notice.

(2) The appellant must file the appellant's notice at the appeal court within –
   (a) such period as may be directed by the lower court (which may be longer or shorter than the period referred to in sub-paragraph (b); or
   (b) where the court makes no such direction, 21 days after the date of the decision of the lower court that the appellant wishes to appeal.

(3) Subject to paragraph (4) and unless the appeal court orders otherwise, an appellant's notice must be served on each respondent –
   (a) as soon as practicable; and
   (b) in any event not later than 7 days,

after it is filed.

(4) Where an appellant seeks permission to appeal against a decision to refuse to grant an interim injunction under section 41 of the Policing and Crime Act 2009 the appellant is not required to serve the appellant's notice on the respondent.

Amendments—Inserted by SI 2000/221. Amended by SI 2005/3515; SI 2010/1953.

52.5 Respondent's notice

(1) A respondent may file and serve a respondent's notice.

(2) A respondent who –
   (a) is seeking permission to appeal from the appeal court; or
   (b) wishes to ask the appeal court to uphold the order of the lower court for reasons different from or additional to those given by the lower court,

must file a respondent's notice.

(3) Where the respondent seeks permission from the appeal court it must be requested in the respondent's notice.

(4) A respondent's notice must be filed within –
   (a) such period as may be directed by the lower court; or
   (b) where the court makes no such direction, 14 days, after the date in paragraph (5).

(5) The date referred to in paragraph (4) is –
   (a) the date the respondent is served with the appellant's notice where –
      (i) permission to appeal was given by the lower court; or
      (ii) permission to appeal is not required;
   (b) the date the respondent is served with notification that the appeal court has given the appellant permission to appeal; or
   (c) the date the respondent is served with notification that the application for permission to appeal and the appeal itself are to be heard together.

(6) Unless the appeal court orders otherwise a respondent's notice must be served on the appellant and any other respondent –

  (a) as soon as practicable; and
  (b) in any event not later than 7 days,

after it is filed.

(7) This rule does not apply where rule 52.4(4) applies.

Amendments—Inserted by SI 2000/221. Amended by SI 2010/1953.

52.5A Transcripts at public expense

(1) Subject to paragraph (2), the lower court or the appeal court may direct, on the application of a party to the proceedings, that an official transcript of the judgment of the lower court, or of any part of the evidence or the proceedings in the lower court, be obtained at public expense for the purposes of an appeal.

(2) Before making a direction under paragraph (1), the court must be satisfied that –

  (a) the applicant qualifies for fee remission or is otherwise in such poor financial circumstances that the cost of obtaining a transcript would be an excessive burden; and
  (b) it is necessary in the interests of justice for such a transcript to be obtained.

Amendments—Inserted by SI 2014/2044.

52.6 Variation of time

(1) An application to vary the time limit for filing an appeal notice must be made to the appeal court.

(2) The parties may not agree to extend any date or time limit set by –

  (a) these Rules;
  (b) Practice Direction 52; or
  (c) an order of the appeal court or the lower court.

  (Rule 3.1(2)(a) provides that the court may extend or shorten the time for compliance with any rule, practice direction or court order (even if an application for extension is made after the time for compliance has expired))

  (Rule 3.1(2)(b) provides that the court may adjourn or bring forward a hearing)

Amendments—Inserted by SI 2000/221. Amended by SI 2009/3390.

52.7 Stay(GL)

Unless –

  (a) the appeal court or the lower court orders otherwise; or
  (b) the appeal is from the Immigration and Asylum Chamber of the Upper Tribunal,

an appeal shall not operate as a stay of any order or decision of the lower court.

Amendments—Inserted by SI 2000/221. Amended by SI 2006/1689; SI 2009/3390.

52.8 Amendment of appeal notice

An appeal notice may not be amended without the permission of the appeal court.

Amendments—Inserted by SI 2000/221.

52.9 Striking out^(GL) appeal notices and setting aside or imposing conditions on permission to appeal

(1) The appeal court may –

    (a) strike out the whole or part of an appeal notice;
    (b) set aside^(GL) permission to appeal in whole or in part;
    (c) impose or vary conditions upon which an appeal may be brought.

(2) The court will only exercise its powers under paragraph (1) where there is a compelling reason for doing so.

(3) Where a party was present at the hearing at which permission was given they may not subsequently apply for an order that the court exercise its powers under sub-paragraphs (1)(b) or (1)(c).

Amendments—Inserted by SI 2000/221. Amended by SI 2014/2044.

52.9A Orders to limit the recoverable costs of an appeal

(1) In any proceedings in which costs recovery is normally limited or excluded at first instance, an appeal court may make an order that the recoverable costs of an appeal will be limited to the extent which the court specifies.

(2) In making such an order the court will have regard to –

    (a) the means of both parties;
    (b) all the circumstances of the case; and
    (c) the need to facilitate access to justice.

(3) If the appeal raises an issue of principle or practice upon which substantial sums may turn, it may not be appropriate to make an order under paragraph (1).

(4) An application for such an order must be made as soon as practicable and will be determined without a hearing unless the court orders otherwise.

Amendments—Inserted by SI 2013/262.

52.10 Appeal court's powers

(1) In relation to an appeal the appeal court has all the powers of the lower court.

    (Rule 52.1(4) provides that this Part is subject to any enactment that sets out special provisions with regard to any particular category of appeal – where such an enactment gives a statutory power to a tribunal, person or other body it may be the case that the appeal court may not exercise that power on an appeal)

(2) The appeal court has power to –

    (a) affirm, set aside or vary any order or judgment made or given by the lower court;
    (b) refer any claim or issue for determination by the lower court;
    (c) order a new trial or hearing;

(d) make orders for the payment of interest;
(e) make a costs order.

(3) In an appeal from a claim tried with a jury the Court of Appeal may, instead of ordering a new trial –

(a) make an order for damages; or
(b) vary an award of damages made by the jury.

(4) The appeal court may exercise its powers in relation to the whole or part of an order of the lower court.

(5) If the appeal court –

(a) refuses an application for permission to appeal;
(b) strikes out an appellant's notice; or
(c) dismisses an appeal,

and it considers that the application, the appellant's notice or the appeal is totally without merit, the provisions of paragraph (6) must be complied with.

(6) Where paragraph (5) applies –

(a) the court's order must record the fact that it considers the application, the appellant's notice or the appeal to be totally without merit; and
(b) the court must at the same time consider whether it is appropriate to make a civil restraint order.

(Part 3 contains general rules about the court's case management powers)

Amendments—Inserted by SI 2000/221. Amended by SI 2004/2072.

52.11 Hearing of appeals

(1) Every appeal will be limited to a review of the decision of the lower court unless –

(a) a practice direction makes different provision for a particular category of appeal; or
(b) the court considers that in the circumstances of an individual appeal it would be in the interests of justice to hold a re-hearing.

(2) Unless it orders otherwise, the appeal court will not receive –

(a) oral evidence; or
(b) evidence which was not before the lower court.

(3) The appeal court will allow an appeal where the decision of the lower court was –

(a) wrong; or
(b) unjust because of a serious procedural or other irregularity in the proceedings in the lower court.

(4) The appeal court may draw any inference of fact which it considers justified on the evidence.

(5) At the hearing of the appeal a party may not rely on a matter not contained in his appeal notice unless the appeal court gives permission.

Amendments—Inserted by SI 2000/221.

52.12 Non-disclosure of Part 36 offers and payments

(1) The fact that a Part 36 offer or payment into court has been made must not be disclosed to any judge of the appeal court who is to hear or determine –

(a) an application for permission to appeal; or
(b) an appeal,

until all questions (other than costs) have been determined.

(2) Paragraph (1) does not apply if the Part 36 offer or payment into court is relevant to the substance of the appeal.

(3) Paragraph (1) does not prevent disclosure in any application in the appeal proceedings if disclosure of the fact that a Part 36 offer or payment into court has been made is properly relevant to the matter to be decided.

> (Rule 36.4 has the effect that a Part 36 offer made in proceedings at first instance will not have consequences in any appeal proceedings. Therefore, a fresh Part 36 offer needs to be made in appeal proceedings. However, rule 52.12 applies to a Part 36 offer whether made in the original proceedings or in the appeal.)

Amendments—Inserted by SI 2000/221. Amended by SI 2003/3361; SI 2006/3435; SI 2014/3299.

52.12A Statutory appeals – court's power to hear any person

(1) In a statutory appeal, any person may apply for permission –

(a) to file evidence; or
(b) to make representations at the appeal hearing.

(2) An application under paragraph (1) must be made promptly.

Amendments—Inserted by SI 2007/2204.

Section II
Special Provisions Applying to the Court of Appeal

52.13 Second appeals to the court

(1) Permission is required from the Court of Appeal for any appeal to that court from a decision of the County Court, family court or the High Court which was itself made on appeal.

(2) The Court of Appeal will not give permission unless it considers that –

(a) the appeal would raise an important point of principle or practice; or
(b) there is some other compelling reason for the Court of Appeal to hear it.

Amendments—Inserted by SI 2000/221. Amended by SI 2014/407; SI 2014/879.

52.14 Assignment of appeals to the Court of Appeal

(1) Where the court from or to which an appeal is made or from which permission to appeal is sought ('the relevant court') considers that –

(a) an appeal which is to be heard by the County Court or the High Court would raise an important point of principle or practice; or
(b) there is some other compelling reason for the Court of Appeal to hear it,

the relevant court may order the appeal to be transferred to the Court of Appeal.

> (The Master of the Rolls has the power to direct that an appeal which would be heard by the County Court or the High Court should be heard instead by the Court of Appeal – see section 57 of the Access to Justice Act 1999)

(2) The Master of the Rolls or the Court of Appeal may remit an appeal to the court in which the original appeal was or would have been brought.

Amendments—Inserted by SI 2000/221. Amended by SI 2014/407.

52.15 Judicial review appeals from the High Court

(1) Where permission to apply for judicial review has been refused at a hearing in the High Court, the person seeking that permission may apply to the Court of Appeal for permission to appeal.

(1A) Where permission to apply for judicial review of a decision of the Upper Tribunal has been refused by the High Court or where permission to apply for judicial review has been refused and recorded as totally without merit in accordance with rule 23.12 –

  (a) the applicant may apply to the Court of Appeal for permission to appeal;
  (b) the application will be determined on paper without an oral hearing.

(2) An application in accordance with paragraphs (1) or (1A) must be made within 7 days of the decision of the High Court to refuse to give permission to apply for judicial review or, in the case of an application under paragraph (1A), within 7 days of service of the order of the High Court refusing permission to apply for judicial review.

(3) On an application under paragraph (1) or (1A), the Court of Appeal may, instead of giving permission to appeal, give permission to apply for judicial review.

(4) Where the Court of Appeal gives permission to apply for judicial review in accordance with paragraph (3), the case will proceed in the High Court unless the Court of Appeal orders otherwise.

Amendments—Inserted by SI 2000/221. Amended by SI 2012/2208; SI 2013/1412; SI 2014/2044.

52.15A Judicial review appeals from the Upper Tribunal

(1) Where permission to bring judicial review proceedings has been refused by the Upper Tribunal and permission to appeal has been refused by the Upper Tribunal, an application for permission to appeal may be made to the Court of Appeal.

(2) Where an application for permission to bring judicial review proceedings has been recorded by the Upper Tribunal as being completely without merit and an application for permission to appeal is made to the Court of Appeal in accordance with paragraph (1) above, the application will be determined on paper without an oral hearing.

> (The time limits for filing an appellant's notice under rule 52.15A(1) are set out in Practice Direction 52D.)

Amendments—Inserted by SI 2014/2044.

52.16 Who may exercise the powers of the Court of Appeal

(1) A court officer assigned to the Civil Appeals Office who is –

    (a)   a barrister; or

    (b)   a solicitor

may exercise the jurisdiction of the Court of Appeal with regard to the matters set out in paragraph (2) with the consent of the Master of the Rolls.

(2) The matters referred to in paragraph (1) are –

    (a)   any matter incidental to any proceedings in the Court of Appeal;

    (b)   any other matter where there is no substantial dispute between the parties; and

    (c)   the dismissal of an appeal or application where a party has failed to comply with any order, rule or practice direction.

(3) A court officer may not decide an application for –

    (a)   permission to appeal;

    (b)   bail pending an appeal;

    (c)   an injunction[GL];

    (d)   a stay[GL] of any proceedings, other than a temporary stay of any order or decision of the lower court over a period when the Court of Appeal is not sitting or cannot conveniently be convened.

(4) Decisions of a court officer may be made without a hearing.

(5) A party may request any decision of a court officer to be reviewed by the Court of Appeal.

(6) At the request of a party, a hearing will be held to reconsider a decision of –

    (a)   a single judge; or

    (b)   a court officer,

made without a hearing.

(6A) A request under paragraph (5) or (6) must be filed within 7 days after the party is served with notice of the decision.

(7) A single judge may refer any matter for a decision by a court consisting of two or more judges.

> (Section 54(6) of the Senior Courts Act 1981 provides that there is no appeal from the decision of a single judge on an application for permission to appeal)
>
> (Section 58(2) of the Senior Courts Act 1981 provides that there is no appeal to the Supreme Court from decisions of the Court of Appeal that –
>
>   (a)   are taken by a single judge or any officer or member of staff of that court in proceedings incidental to any cause or matter pending before the civil division of that court; and
>
>   (b)   do not involve the determination of an appeal or of an application for permission to appeal,
>
> and which may be called into question by rules of court. Rules 52.16(5) and (6) provide the procedure for the calling into question of such decisions)

Amendments—Inserted by SI 2000/221. Amended by SI 2003/3361; CRA 2005, Sch 11, para 1(2); SI 2009/2092.

Section III
Provisions about Reopening Appeals

52.17 Reopening of final appeals

(1) The Court of Appeal or the High Court will not reopen a final determination of any appeal unless –

 (a) it is necessary to do so in order to avoid real injustice;
 (b) the circumstances are exceptional and make it appropriate to reopen the appeal; and
 (c) there is no alternative effective remedy.

(2) In paragraphs (1), (3), (4) and (6), 'appeal' includes an application for permission to appeal.

(3) This rule does not apply to appeals to the County Court.

(4) Permission is needed to make an application under this rule to reopen a final determination of an appeal even in cases where under rule 52.3(1) permission was not needed for the original appeal.

(5) There is no right to an oral hearing of an application for permission unless, exceptionally, the judge so directs.

(6) The judge will not grant permission without directing the application to be served on the other party to the original appeal and giving him an opportunity to make representations.

(7) There is no right of appeal or review from the decision of the judge on the application for permission, which is final.

(8) The procedure for making an application for permission is set out in Practice Direction 52.

Amendments—Inserted by SI 2003/2113. Amended by SI 2009/3390; SI 2014/407.

****

Practice Direction 52A – Appeals: General Provisions

This Practice Direction supplements CPR Part 52

Amendments—CPR Update 59.

SECTION 1: PRACTICE DIRECTIONS SUPPLEMENTING PART 52

1.1 There are five Practice Directions supplementing Part 52 –

- PD52A – Appeals: general provisions
- PD52B – Appeals in the County Court and the High Court
- PD52C – Appeals to the Court of Appeal
- PD52D – Statutory appeals and appeals subject to special provision
- PD52E – Appeals by way of case stated

Amendments—CPR Update 69.

SECTION 2: INTRODUCTION

2.1 These Practice Directions apply to all appeals to which Part 52 applies.

2.2 Part 52 complements the provisions of sections 54 to 57 of the Access to Justice Act 1999 and provides a uniform procedure for appeals in the County Court and the High Court and a modified procedure for the Civil Division of the Court of Appeal. Part 52 does not apply to –

(a) family proceedings in the High Court or County Court but does apply to appeals to the Court of Appeal from decisions made in family proceedings with such modifications as may be required;

(b) appeals in detailed assessment proceedings against the decision of an authorised court officer.

Amendments—CPR Update 69.

SECTION 3: DESTINATIONS OF APPEAL

3.1 Section 56 of the Access to Justice Act 1999 enables the Lord Chancellor by Order to specify the destinations of appeal in different cases. The Access to Justice Act 1999 (Destination of Appeals) Order 2000, SI 2000/1071 made under section 56, specifies the general destinations of appeal which apply subject to any statutory provision to the contrary. The destinations of appeal provided by that Order are explained in the following paragraphs of this section of this Practice Direction.

3.2 'Statutory appeals' and 'Appeals by way of case stated' are dealt with in PD52D – refer to those provisions for the appropriate court to which such an appeal may lie.

3.3 The court or judge to which an appeal is to be made (subject to obtaining any necessary permission) is set out in the tables below –

- Table 1 deals with appeals in proceedings other than family and insolvency proceedings;
- Table 2 deals with appeals in insolvency proceedings; and
- Table 3 deals with appeals in family proceedings which may be heard in the Family Division and to which the CPR may apply.

3.4 Definitions of terms and abbreviations used in Tables 1, 2 and 3:

'Destination': the court to which the appeal lies.
'Pt 7 Claim (not MT)': Part 7 Claim, other than a claim allocated to the multitrack.
'Pt 7 Claim (MT)': Part 7 Claim, allocated to the multi-track.
'Pt 8 Claim (not MT)': Part 8 Claim, other than a claim allocated to the multitrack.
'Pt 8 Claim (MT)': Part 8 Claim, allocated to the multi-track.
'DJ': District Judge.
'CJ': Circuit Judge including a recorder or a District Judge who is exercising the jurisdiction of a Circuit Judge with the permission of the Designated Civil Judge in respect of the case.
'CJ (CC)': Circuit Judge in the County Court.
'Master': Master, District Judge sitting in a district registry or any other judge referred to in article 2 of the Destination of Appeals Order.
'Final': A final decision within the meaning of paragraphs 3.6 to 3.8 of this Practice Direction.
'Interim': A decision that is not a final decision within the meaning of paragraphs 3.6 to 3.8 of this Practice Direction.
'HCJ': single judge of the High Court.

Appeals: General Provisions (CPR Part 52) **PD52A**

'HCJ(FD)': single judge of the family Division of the High Court.
'CA': Court of Appeal.
'Other': Claims or originating or pre-action applications started otherwise than by a Part 7 or Part 8 claim (for example an application under Part 23).
'Specialist': Specialist proceedings (under the Companies Act 1985 or the Companies Act 1989 or to which Sections I, II or III of Part 57 or any of Parts 58,59,60, 62 or 63 apply).

(Note: Tables 1, 2 and 3 do not include so-called 'leap frog' appeals either to the Court of Appeal pursuant to section 57 of the Access to Justice Act 1999 or to the Supreme Court pursuant to section 13 of the Administration of Justice Act 1969.)

3.5 The destinations in the tables set out below apply whether the decision is interim or final. For the meaning of 'final decision' for the purposes of this table see paragraphs 3.6 to 3.8 below.

Table 1: Proceedings other than family or insolvency proceedings

Court	Deciding judge	Nature of claim	Interim/final	Destination
County	DJ	Pt 7 Claim	Interim	CJ (CC)
		Pt 7 Claim (not MT)	Final	
		Pt 7 Claim (MT)	Final	CA
		Pt 8 Claim	Interim/final	CJ (CC)
		Other	Interim/final	
		Specialist	Interim	
			Final	CA
	CJ	Pt 7 Claim	Interim	HCJ
		Pt 7 Claim (not MT)	Final	
		Pt 7 Claim (MT)	Final	CA
		Pt 8 Claim	Interim/final	HCJ
		Other	Interim/final	
		Specialist	Interim	
			Final	CA

Court	Deciding judge	Nature of claim	Interim/final	Destination
High	Master	Pt 7 Claim	Interim	HCJ
	Pt 7 Claim (not MT)		Final	
		Pt 7 Claim (MT)	Final	CA
		Pt 8 Claim	Interim/final	HCJ
	Other		Interim/final	
	Specialist		Interim	
			Final	CA
	HCJ	Any	Interim/final	CA

Table 2: Insolvency proceedings

Court	Deciding judge	Destination
County	DJ or CJ	HCJ
High	Registrar	
	HCJ	CA

Table 3: Family proceedings in the Principal Registry of the Family Division and to which the CPR will apply

The proceedings to which this table applies include proceedings under the Inheritance (Provision for Family and Dependants) Act 1975 and proceedings under the Trusts of Land and Appointment of Trustees Act 1996.

Deciding judge	Nature of claim	Decision under appeal	Destination
DJ	Part 7 Claim (not MT)	Any decision other than a final decision	HCJ (FD)
	Part 7 Claim (MT)	Final decision	CA
	Part 8 Claim (not MT)	Any decision	HCJ (FD)
	Part 8 Claim (MT)		
HCJ (FD)	Any	Any decision	CA

3.6 A 'final decision' is a decision of a court that would finally determine (subject to any possible appeal or detailed assessment of costs) the entire proceedings whichever way the court decided the issues before it.

3.7 A decision is to be treated as a final decision for destination of appeal purposes where it –

(a) is made at the conclusion of part of a hearing or trial which has been split into parts; and
(b) would, if it had been made at the conclusion of that hearing or trial, have been a final decision.

3.8 (1) The following are examples of final decisions –

- a judgment on liability at the end of a split trial;
- a judgment at the conclusion of an assessment of damages following a judgment on liability.

(2) The following are examples of decisions that are not final –

- a case management decision (within the meaning of paragraph 4.6);
- a grant or refusal of interim relief;
- summary judgment;
- striking out a claim or statement of case;
- a summary or detailed assessment of costs;
- an order for the enforcement of a final decision.

Filing appellant's notice in wrong court

3.9 (1) Where a party attempts to file an appellant's notice in a court which does not have jurisdiction to issue the notice, a court officer may notify that party in writing that the appeal court does not have jurisdiction in respect of the notice.

(2) Before notifying a person under paragraph (1) the court officer must confer –

(a) with a judge of the appeal court; or
(b) where the Court of Appeal is the appeal court, with a court officer who exercises the jurisdiction of that Court under rule 52.16.

(3) Where a court officer, in the Court of Appeal, notifies a person under paragraph (1), rule 52.16(5) and (6) shall not apply.

Amendments—CPR Update 69.

SECTION 4: OBTAINING PERMISSION TO APPEAL

Where to apply for permission

4.1 An application for permission to appeal may be made –

(a) to the lower court at the hearing at which the decision to be appealed against is given (in which case the lower court may adjourn the hearing to give a party an opportunity to apply for permission to appeal); or
(b) where the lower court refuses permission to appeal or where no application is made to the lower court, to the appeal court in accordance with rule 52.4.

Form

4.2 An application for permission to appeal to the appeal court must be made using an appellant's notice (form N161 or N164 (small claims track)).

Appeals from Masters and District Judges of High Court

4.3 In relation to appeals from Masters or District Judges of the High Court: appeals, applications for permission and any other applications in the appeal may be heard and directions in the appeal may be given by a High Court Judge or by any person authorised under section 9 of the Senior Courts Act 1981 to act as a judge of the High Court.

Where the lower court is the County Court

4.4 Where the lower court is the County Court –

(a) subject to sub-paragraph (b), appeals and applications for permission to appeal will be heard by a High Court Judge or by a person authorised under paragraphs (1), (2) or (4) of the Table in section 9(1) of the Senior Courts Act 1981 to act as a judge of the High Court;

(b) an appeal or application for permission to appeal from the decision of a recorder may be heard by a Designated Civil Judge who is authorised under paragraph (5) of the Table in section 9(1) of the Senior Courts Act 1981 to act as a judge of the High Court; and

(c) other applications in the appeal may be heard and directions in the appeal may be given either by a High Court Judge or by any person authorised under section 9 of the Senior Courts Act 1981 to act as a judge of the High Court.

4.5 The Designated Civil Judge in consultation with the Presiding Judge has responsibility for allocating appeals from decisions of District Judges to Circuit Judges.

Appeal in relation to case management decision

4.6 Where the application is for permission to appeal from a case management decision, the court dealing with the application may take into account whether –

(a) the issue is of sufficient significance to justify the costs of an appeal;
(b) the procedural consequences of an appeal (e.g. loss of trial date) outweigh the significance of the case management decision;
(c) it would be more convenient to determine the issue at or after trial.

Case management decisions include decisions made under rule 3.1(2) and decisions about disclosure, filing of witness statements or experts' reports, directions about the timetable of the claim, adding a party to a claim and security for costs.

Second appeal

4.7 An application for permission to appeal from a decision of the High Court or the County Court which was itself made on appeal is a second appeal and must be made to the Court of Appeal. If permission to appeal is granted the appeal will be heard by the Court of Appeal.

Amendments—CPR Updates 60, 69.

SECTION 5: SKELETON ARGUMENTS

5.1 (1) The purpose of a skeleton argument is to assist the court by setting out as concisely as practicable the arguments upon which a party intends to rely.

(2) A skeleton argument must –

- be concise;
- both define and confine the areas of controversy;
- be set out in numbered paragraphs;
- be cross-referenced to any relevant document in the bundle;
- be self-contained and not incorporate by reference material from previous skeleton arguments;
- not include extensive quotations from documents or authorities.

(3) Documents to be relied on must be identified.

(4) Where it is necessary to refer to an authority, a skeleton argument must –

(a) state the proposition of law the authority demonstrates; and
(b) identify the parts of the authority that support the proposition.

If more than one authority is cited in support of a given proposition, the skeleton argument must briefly state why.

(5) The cost of preparing a skeleton argument which –

(a) does not comply with the requirements set out in this paragraph; or
(b) was not filed within the time limits provided by this Practice Direction (or any further time granted by the court),

will not be allowed on assessment except as directed by the court.

5.2 The parties should consider what other information the appeal court will need. This may include a list of persons who feature in the case or glossaries of technical terms. A chronology of relevant events will be necessary in most appeals.

5.3 Any statement of costs must show the amount claimed for the skeleton argument separately.

Amendments—CPR Update 66.

SECTION 6: DISPOSING OF APPLICATIONS AND APPEALS BY CONSENT

Dismissal of applications or appeals by consent

6.1 An appellant who does not wish to pursue an application or appeal may request the appeal court to dismiss the application or the appeal. If such a request is granted it will usually be subject to an order that the appellant pays the costs of the application or appeal.

6.2 If the appellant wishes to have the application or appeal dismissed without costs, his request must be accompanied by a letter signed by the respondent stating that the respondent so consents.

6.3 Where a settlement has been reached disposing of the application or appeal, the parties may make a joint request to the court for the application or appeal to be dismissed by consent. If the request is granted the application or appeal will be dismissed.

Allowing unopposed appeals or applications on paper

6.4 The appeal court will not normally make an order allowing an appeal unless satisfied that the decision of the lower court was wrong or unjust because of a serious procedural or other irregularity. The appeal court may, however, set aside or vary the order of the lower court by consent and without determining the merits of the appeal if it is satisfied that there are good and sufficient reasons for so doing. Where the appeal court is requested by all parties to allow an application or an appeal the court may consider the request on the papers. The request should set out the relevant history of the proceedings and the matters relied on as justifying the order and be accompanied by a draft order.

Disposal of applications and appeals involving children or protected parties

6.5 Where one of the parties is a child or protected party, any disposal of an application or the appeal requires the court's approval. A draft order signed by the parties' solicitors should be sent to the appeal court, together with an opinion from the advocate acting on behalf of the child or protected party and, in the case of a protected party, any relevant documents prepared for the Court of Protection.

SECTION 7: REOPENING APPEALS (RULE 52.17)

7.1 A party applying for permission to reopen an appeal or an application for permission to appeal must apply for such permission from the court whose decision the party wishes to reopen.

7.2 The application for permission must be made by application notice and be supported by written evidence, verified by a statement of truth. A copy of the application for permission must not be served on any other party to the original appeal unless the court so directs.

7.3 Where the court directs that the application for permission is to be served on another party, that party may, within 14 days of the service on him of the copy of the application, file and serve a written statement either supporting or opposing the application.

7.4 The application for permission will be considered on paper by a single judge.

SECTION 8: TRANSITIONAL PROVISIONS

8.1 This Practice Direction and Practice Directions 52B, 52C, 52D and 52E shall come into force on 1 October 2012 and shall apply to all appeals where –

(a) the appeal notice was filed; or
(b) permission to appeal was given

on or after that date.

8.2 The appeal court may at any time direct that, in relation to any appeal, one or more of Practice Directions 52A, 52B, 52C, 52D or 52E shall apply irrespective of the date on which the appeal notice was filed or permission to appeal was given.

****

Practice Direction 52C – Appeals to the Court of Appeal

This Practice Direction supplements CPR Part 52

Amendments—CPR Update 59.

Contents of this Practice Direction

This Practice Direction is divided into the following sections:
1. Introduction and interpretation
2. Starting an appeal to the Court of Appeal, Grounds of Appeal and Skeleton Arguments
3. Respondent's notice and respondent's skeleton argument
4. Procedure where permission to appeal is sought from the Court of Appeal
5. Timetable
6. Management of the appeal
7. Bundles, amendment and supplementary skeleton arguments

SECTION 1: INTRODUCTION AND INTERPRETATION

1 In this Practice Direction –
'appeal notice' means either an appellant's notice in form N161 or a respondent's notice in form N162;
'appellant's notice' means an appeal notice filed by an appellant and a 'respondent's notice' means an appeal notice filed by a respondent;
'hearing date' means the date on which the appeal is listed to be heard, including a 'floating' date over two or more days;
'listing window notification' means the letter sent by the Civil Appeals Office in accordance with Section 5: Timetable Part 1 notifying the parties of the window within which the appeal is likely to be heard; and 'date of the listing window notification' means the date of such letter;
'replacement skeleton argument' means a skeleton argument which has been amended in order to include cross references to the appeal bundle and is lodged and served in accordance with the timetable at Section 5 Part 2.

2 The court may make such directions as the case may require and such directions will prevail over any provision of this practice direction.

SECTION 2: STARTING AN APPEAL TO THE COURT OF APPEAL

Filing the Appellant's Notice and accompanying documents

3 (1) An appellant's notice (Form N161) must be filed and served in all cases. The appellant's notice must be accompanied by the appropriate fee or, if appropriate, a fee remission certificate.

(2) The appellant's notice and accompanying documents must be filed in the Civil Appeals Office Registry, Room E307, Royal Courts of Justice, Strand, London, WC2A 2LL.

(3) At the same time as filing an appellant's notice, the appellant must provide for the use of the court three copies of the appellant's notice and one copy of each of the following –

   (a)   the sealed order or tribunal determination being appealed;
   (b)   any order granting or refusing permission to appeal, together with a copy of the judge's or tribunal's reasons for granting or refusing permission to appeal;
   (c)   any witness statements or affidavits relied on in support of any application included in the appellant's notice;
   (d)   in cases where the decision of the lower court was itself made on appeal, the first order, the reasons given by the judge who made it, and the appellant's notice of appeal against that order;
   (e)   in a claim for judicial review or a statutory appeal, the original decision which was the subject of the application to the lower court;
   (f)   the order allocating the case to a track (if any);
   (g)   the appellant's skeleton argument in support of the appeal;
   (h)   the approved transcript of the judgment.

(4) The appellant must also provide to the court one copy of the appellant's notice for each respondent for sealing by the court and return to the appellant for service.

(5) Where the appellant applies for permission to appeal, additional documents are required: see Section 4 of this Practice Direction.

(6) Provisions in relation to the skeleton argument are set out in paragraph 31.

Extension of time for filing appellant's notice

4 (1) Where the time for filing an appellant's notice has expired, the appellant must –

   (a)   file the appellant's notice; and
   (b)   include in that appellant's notice an application for an extension of time.

(2) The appellant's notice must state the reason for the delay and the steps taken prior to the application being made.

(3) Where the appellant's notice includes an application for an extension of time and permission to appeal has been given or is not required, the respondent has the right to oppose that application and to be heard at any hearing of that application. In respect of any application to extend time –

   (a)   The respondent must –
         (i)   be served with a copy of any evidence filed in support of the application; and
         (ii)   inform the court in writing of any objections to the grant of the extension of time within 7 days of being served with the appellant's notice.
   (b)   A respondent who unreasonably opposes an application for an extension of time may be ordered to pay the costs of the application.
   (c)   An application for an extension of time will normally be determined without a hearing unless the court directs otherwise.

Grounds of Appeal

5 (1) The grounds of appeal must identify as concisely as possible the respects in which the judgment of the court below is –

(a) wrong; or
(b) unjust because of a serious procedural or other irregularity, as required by rule 52.11(3).

(2) The reasons why the decision under appeal is wrong or unjust must not be included in the grounds of appeal and must be confined to the skeleton argument.

Second appeals

5A An application to make a second appeal must identify in the grounds of appeal –
(a) the important point of principle or practice, or
(b) the compelling reason

which is said to justify the grant of permission to appeal.

Amendments—CPR Update 60.

Non-availability of documents

6 (1) If the appellant is unable to provide any of the necessary documents in time, the appellant must complete the appeal notice on the basis of the available documents. The notice may be amended subsequently with the permission of the court (see paragraph 30).

(2) Any application for a transcript at public expense should be made within the appellant's notice.

Amendments—CPR Update 75.

Service on the respondent

7.1 The Civil Appeals Office will not serve documents. Where service is required by the Rules or this Practice Direction, it must be effected by the parties.

7.1A The appellant's skeleton argument in respect of an application for permission to appeal must be served on each respondent at the same time as service of the appellant's notice.

7.2 The evidence in support of any application made in an appellant's notice must be filed and served with the appellant's notice.

7.3 An application for an order to dispense with service of the appellant's notice under rule 6.28 must be made in the appeal notice or, thereafter, by application notice under Part 23.

Amendments—CPR Updates 66, 75.

SECTION 3: RESPONDENT'S NOTICE (RULE 52.5) AND RESPONDENT'S SKELETON ARGUMENT

Respondent's notice

8 (1) A respondent who seeks to appeal against any part of the order made by the court below must file an appeal notice.

(2) A respondent who seeks a variation of the order of the lower court must file an appeal notice and must obtain permission to appeal.

(3) A respondent who seeks to contend that the order of the court below should be upheld for reasons other than those given by that court must file a respondent's notice.

(4) The notice may be amended subsequently with the permission of the court (see paragraph 30).

Skeleton argument to be lodged with the respondent's notice

9 A respondent who files a respondent's notice must, within 14 days of filing the notice, lodge a skeleton argument with the court and serve a copy of the skeleton argument on every other party to the appeal.

(Provisions in relation to the skeleton argument are set out in paragraph 31.)

Documents to be filed with respondent's notice

10 The respondent must file the following documents with the respondent's notice –

 (a) two additional copies of the respondent's notice for the court; and
 (b) one copy each for the appellant and any other respondents.

Applications within respondent's notice

11 (1) A respondent may include an application within a respondent's notice.

(2) The parties must consider whether it would be more convenient for any application to be listed with the appeal or whether the application needs to be considered in advance.

(3) Where parties consider that the time estimate for the appeal will be affected by listing the application with the appeal, they must inform the court without delay.

Time limits: rule 52.5(4) and (5)

12 Where an extension of time is required, the respondent must apply in the respondent's notice and explain the delay.

Respondent's skeleton argument (where no respondent's notice filed)

13 (1) In all cases where the respondent is legally represented and proposes to address the court, the respondent must lodge and serve a skeleton argument.

(2) A respondent's skeleton argument must be lodged and served in accordance with Part 1 of the Timetable in Section 5.

(Provisions in relation to the skeleton argument are set out in paragraph 31.)

SECTION 4: PROCEDURE WHERE PERMISSION TO APPEAL IS SOUGHT FROM THE COURT OF APPEAL

Documents for use on an application for permission

14 (1) Within 14 days of filing the appeal notice the appellant must lodge a bundle containing only those documents which are necessary for the court to determine that application.

(2) The bundle of documents must –

Appeals to the Court of Appeal (CPR Part 52) **PD52C**

    (a)   be paginated and in chronological order;
    (b)   contain an index at the front.

Determination of applications for permission to appeal

15 (1) Applications for permission to appeal will generally be considered by the court without a hearing in the first instance. The court will notify the parties of the decision and the reasons for it.

(2) If permission is refused the appellant is entitled to have the decision reconsidered at an oral hearing, except where the rules otherwise provide. The hearing may be before the same judge.

(3) A request for the decision to be reconsidered at an oral hearing must be filed within 7 days after service of the letter giving notice that permission has been refused.

A copy of the request must be served by the appellant on the respondent at the same time.

Amendments—CPR Update 75.

Permission hearing

16 (1) Where an appellant who is represented makes a request for a decision to be reconsidered at an oral hearing, the appellant's advocate must at least 4 days before the hearing file a brief written statement –

    (a)   informing the court and the respondent of the points which are to be raised at the hearing; and
    (b)   setting out the reasons why permission should be granted notwithstanding the reasons given for the refusal of permission.

(2) The court will notify the respondent of the hearing but the respondent is not expected to attend unless the court so directs.

(3) If the court directs the respondent to attend the permission hearing, the appellant must supply the respondent with a copy of the skeleton argument and any documents to which the appellant intends to refer.

Appellant in receipt of services funded by the Legal Services Commission applying for permission to appeal

17 Where the appellant is in receipt of services funded by the Legal Services Commission and permission to appeal has been refused by the court without a hearing, the appellant must send a copy of the court's reasons for refusing permission to the Legal Services Commission as soon as it has been received. The court will require confirmation that this has been done if a hearing is requested to re-consider the application.

Note—The Legal Aid Agency replaced the Legal Services Commission on 1 April 2013.

Limited permission: rule 52.3

18 (1) If, under rule 52.3(7), the court grants permission to appeal on some issues only, it will –

    (a)   refuse permission on any remaining issues; or

(b) adjourn the application in respect of those issues to the hearing of the appeal.

(2) If the court adjourns the application under sub-paragraph (1)(b), the appellant must inform the court and the respondent in writing, within 14 days after the date of the court's order, whether the appellant intends to pursue the application. If the appellant intends to pursue the application, the parties must include in any time estimate for the appeal hearing an allowance for the adjourned application.

(3) If the court refuses permission to appeal on the remaining issues without a hearing and the applicant wishes to have that decision reconsidered at an oral hearing, the time limit in rule 52.3(5) applies. Any application for an extension of this time should be made promptly. When hearing the appeal on the issues for which permission has been given the court will not normally grant an application to extend time in relation to the remaining issues.

Respondent need not take any action when served with an appellant's notice

19 Unless the court directs otherwise, a respondent need not take any action when served with an appellant's notice until notified that permission to appeal has been granted.

Respondent's costs of permission applications

20 (1) In most cases an application for permission to appeal will be determined without the need for the respondent to file submissions or attend a hearing. In such circumstances an order for costs will not normally be made in favour of a respondent who voluntarily makes submissions or attends a hearing.

(2) If the court directs the respondent to file submissions or attend a hearing, it will normally award costs to the respondent if permission is refused.

SECTION 5: TIMETABLE

21 Subject to any specific directions that may be given by the court, the timetable for the conduct of an appeal after the date of the listing window notification is set out below:

Timetable Part 1: Listing window notification to lodging bundle

Period within which step is to be taken	Action	Cross reference to relevant provisions in this Practice Direction
Within 14 days of service of: (i) the appellant's notice if permission has been given by the lower court or is not needed;	**Respondent's notice** (if any) must be filed and served	Paragraph 8 (respondent's notice)

Period within which step is to be taken	Action	Cross reference to relevant provisions in this Practice Direction
(ii) notification that permission has been granted by the Court of Appeal; or (iii) notification that the permission application will be listed with the appeal to follow		
Within 14 days of filing a respondent's notice	**If respondent has filed a respondent's notice**, respondent must lodge and serve a skeleton argument on every other party	Paragraph 9 (skeleton argument to be lodged with the respondent's notice or within 14 days of filing respondent's notice)
7 days after date of listing window notification	Appellant must serve **proposed bundle index** on every respondent	Paragraph 27 (bundle of documents)
14 days after date of listing window notification	**Appeal questionnaire** must be filed and served on every respondent	Paragraph 1 (listing window notification defined) Paragraph 23 (Appeal questionnaire)
7 days after service of Appellant's Appeal Questionnaire	**If a respondent disagrees with appellant's time estimate**, that respondent must file and serve on every other party its own time estimate	Paragraph 24 (time estimate)
21 days after listing window notification	**Appeal skeleton**: appellant must serve on every respondent an appeal skeleton (without bundle cross references)	Paragraph 31 (skeleton argument)

Period within which step is to be taken	Action	Cross reference to relevant provisions in this Practice Direction
21 days after date of the listing window notification	**Agree bundle**: the respondent must either agree the contents of the appeal bundle or notify the appellant of the documents that the respondent considers should be included in, or removed from, the appeal bundle by sending a revised index. If there is no agreement in relation to inclusion of a particular document, it must be placed in a supplemental bundle prepared by the party who has proposed its inclusion.	Paragraph 27 (bundle of documents) Paragraph 28 (bundle: Appeals from Upper Tribunal Immigration and Asylum Chamber)
42 days after date of listing window notification	**Where Respondent has not filed a respondent's notice**, respondent must lodge skeleton argument and serve on every other party	Paragraph 13 (respondent's skeleton argument (where no Respondent's Notice filed)) Paragraph 31 (skeleton argument)

Timetable Part 2: Steps to be taken once hearing date fixed: lodging bundles, supplemental skeletons and bundles of authorities

Time before hearing date when step is to be taken	Action	Cross reference to relevant provisions in this Practice Direction
No later than 42 days before the appeal hearing	Lodge, as directed by the court, the appropriate number of appeal bundles and serve a copy on all other parties to the appeal	Paragraph 27 (bundle of documents) Paragraph 28 (bundle: Appeals from Upper Tribunal Immigration and Asylum Chamber)

Appeals to the Court of Appeal (CPR Part 52) **PD52C**

Time before hearing date when step is to be taken	Action	Cross reference to relevant provisions in this Practice Direction
No later than 14 days before date of appeal hearing	Appellant must lodge and serve replacement skeleton argument	Paragraph 1 (replacement skeleton argument defined)
		Paragraph 31 (skeleton argument content, length and format)
		Paragraph 32 (supplementary skeleton argument)
No later than 7 days before the date of the hearing	Respondent must lodge and serve replacement skeleton argument	Paragraph 1 (replacement skeleton argument defined)
		Paragraph 32 (supplementary skeleton argument)
No later than 7 days before date of appeal hearing	Bundles of authorities must be lodged	Paragraph 29 (bundle of authorities)
No later than 7 days before the date of the hearing	Every document needed for the appeal hearing (if not already lodged or filed) must be lodged or filed and served on all other parties to the appeal	

Amendments—CPR Update 66.

SECTION 6: MANAGEMENT OF THE APPEAL

Listing and hear-by dates

22 The hear-by date is the last day of the listing window.

Appeal Questionnaire

23 The appellant must complete and file the Appeal Questionnaire and serve it on the respondent within 14 days after the date of the listing window notification.

Time estimates

24 If the respondent disagrees with the appellant's time estimate, the respondent must inform the court within 7 days of service of the Appeal Questionnaire. In the absence of such notification the respondent will be deemed to have accepted the appellant's time estimate.

Multiple Appeals

25 (1) If two or more appeals are pending in the same or related proceedings, the parties must seek directions as to whether they should be heard together or consecutively by the same judges.

(2) Whether appeals are heard together or consecutively, the parties must attempt to agree a single appeal bundle or set of bundles for all the appeals and seek directions if they are unable to do so.

Expedition

26 (1) The court may direct that the hearing of an appeal be expedited.

(2) The court will deal with requests for expedition without a hearing. Requests for expedition must be made by letter setting out succinctly the grounds on which expedition is sought. The letter (or, if time is particularly short, email) must be marked for the immediate attention of the court and copied to the other parties to the appeal.

(3) If an expedited appeal hearing is required as a matter of extreme urgency, the Civil Appeals Office must be informed as soon as possible. If necessary, parties or their legal representatives should call the Royal Courts of Justice switchboard on 020 7947 6000 and ask a member of the security staff to contact the Duty Judge.

(4) An expedited hearing will be listed at the convenience of the court and not according to the availability of counsel.

SECTION 7: BUNDLES, AMENDMENT AND SKELETON ARGUMENTS

Bundle of documents

27 (1) The appellant must lodge an appeal bundle which must contain only those documents relevant to the appeal. The bundle must –

(a) be paginated and in chronological order;
(b) contain an index at the front.

(2) Documents relevant to the appeal: Subject to any order made by the court, the following documents must be included in the appeal bundle –

(a) a copy of the appellant's notice;
(b) a copy of any respondent's notice;
(c) a copy of any appellant's or respondent's skeleton argument;
(d) a copy of the order under appeal;
(e) a copy of the order of the lower court granting or refusing permission to appeal together with a copy of the judge's reasons, if any, for granting or refusing permission;
(f) a copy of any order allocating the case to a track;
(g) the approved transcript of the judgment of the lower court (except in appeals in cases which were allocated to the small claims track but subject to any order of the court).

(3) Documents which may be included: The following documents should also be considered for inclusion in the appeal bundle but should be included only where relevant to the appeal –

(a) statements of case;
(b) application notices;
(c) other orders made in the case;
(d) a chronology of relevant events;
(e) witness statements made in support of any application made in the appellant's notice;
(f) other witness statements;
(g) other documents which the appellant or respondent consider relevant to the appeal.

(4) Bundles not to include originals: Unless otherwise directed, the appeal bundle should not include original material such as original documents, photographs and recorded media. Such material should be provided to the court, if necessary, at the hearing.

(5) Destruction of bundles: Bundles lodged with the court will not be returned to the parties but will be destroyed in the confidential waste system at the conclusion of the proceedings and without further notification.

Appeals from the Upper Tribunal Immigration and Asylum Chamber

28 (1) In an appeal from the Immigration and Asylum Chamber of the Upper Tribunal (other than an appeal relating to a claim for judicial review):

(a) the Immigration and Asylum Chamber of the Upper Tribunal, upon request, shall send to the Civil Appeals Office copies of the documents which were before the relevant Tribunal when it considered the appeal;
(b) the appellant is not required to file an appeal bundle;
(c) the appellant must file with the appellant's notice the documents specified in paragraph 3(3)(a) to (e) and (g) of this Practice Direction.

Amendments—CPR Update 81.

Bundle of authorities

29 (1) After consultation with any opposing advocate, the appellant's advocate must file a bundle containing photocopies of the authorities upon which each party will rely at the hearing.

(2) The most authoritative report of each authority must be used in accordance with the Practice Direction on Citation of Authorities (2012) and must have the relevant passages marked by a vertical line in the margin.

(3) Photocopies of authorities should not be in landscape format and the type should not be reduced in size.

(4) The bundle should not –

(a) include authorities for propositions not in dispute; or
(b) contain more than 10 authorities unless the issues in the appeal justify more extensive citation.

(5) A bundle of authorities must bear a certificate by the advocates responsible for arguing the case that the requirements of sub-paragraphs (2) to (4) of this paragraph have been complied with in respect of each authority included.

Amendment of appeal notice: rule 52.8

30 (1) An appeal notice may not be amended without the permission of the court.

(2) An application for permission to amend made before permission to appeal has been considered will normally be determined without a hearing.

(3) An application for permission to amend (after permission to appeal has been granted) and any submissions in opposition will normally be dealt with at the hearing unless that would cause unnecessary expense or delay, in which case a request should be made for the application to amend to be heard in advance.

(4) Legal representatives must –
   (a) inform the court at the time they make the application if the existing time estimate is affected by the proposed amendment; and
   (b) attempt to agree any revised time estimate no later than 7 days after service of the application.

Skeleton argument

31 (1) Any skeleton argument must comply with the provisions of Section 5 of Practice Direction 52A and must:
   (a) not normally exceed 25 pages (excluding front sheets and back sheets);
   (b) be printed on A4 paper in not less than 12 point font and 1.5 line spacing.

(2) Where an appellant has filed a skeleton argument in support of an application for permission to appeal, the same skeleton argument may be relied upon in the appeal or the appellant may file an appeal skeleton argument (Timetable Section 5, Part 1).

(3) At the hearing the court may refuse to hear argument on a point not included in a skeleton argument filed within the prescribed time.

(4) The court may disallow the cost of preparing an appeal skeleton argument which does not comply with these requirements or was not filed within the prescribed time.

Supplementary skeleton arguments

32 (1) A party may file a supplementary skeleton argument only where strictly necessary and only with the permission of the court

(2) If a party wishes to rely on a supplementary skeleton argument, it must be lodged and served as soon as practicable. It must be accompanied by a request for permission setting out the reasons why a supplementary skeleton argument is necessary and why it could not reasonably have been lodged earlier.

(3) Only exceptionally will the court allow the use of a supplementary skeleton argument if lodged later than 7 days before the hearing.

****

PART 70
GENERAL RULES ABOUT ENFORCEMENT OF JUDGMENTS AND ORDERS

70.1 Scope of this Part and interpretation

(1) This Part contains general rules about enforcement of judgments and orders.

(Rules about specific methods of enforcement are contained in Parts 71 to 73, 81, 83 and 84 and Schedule 2 CCR Orders 27 and 28)

(2) In this Part and in Parts 71 to 73 –

(a) 'judgment creditor' means a person who has obtained or is entitled to enforce a judgment or order;
(b) 'judgment debtor' means a person against whom a judgment or order was given or made;
(c) 'judgment or order' includes an award which the court has –
  (i) registered for enforcement;
  (ii) ordered to be enforced; or
  (iii) given permission to enforce
  as if it were a judgment or order of the court, and in relation to such an award, 'the court which made the judgment or order' means the court which registered the award or made such an order; and
(d) 'judgment or order for the payment of money' includes a judgment or order for the payment of costs, but does not include a judgment or order for the payment of money into court.

Amendments—Inserted by SI 2001/2792. Amended by SI 2002/2058; SI 2014/407.

70.2 Methods of enforcing judgments or orders

(1) Practice Direction 70 sets out methods of enforcing judgments or orders for the payment of money.

(2) A judgment creditor may, except where an enactment, rule or practice direction provides otherwise –

(a) use any method of enforcement which is available; and
(b) use more than one method of enforcement, either at the same time or one after another.

Amendments—Inserted by SI 2001/2792. Amended by SI 2009/3390.

70.2A Court may order act to be done at expense of disobedient party

(1) In this rule 'disobedient party' means a party who has not complied with a mandatory order, an injunction or a judgment or order for the specific performance of a contract.

(2) Subject to paragraph (4), if a mandatory order, an injunction or a judgment or order for the specific performance of a contract is not complied with, the court may direct that the act required to be done may, so far as practicable, be done by another person, being –

(a) the party by whom the order or judgment was obtained; or
(b) some other person appointed by the court.

(3) Where paragraph (2) applies –

(a) the costs to another person of doing the act will be borne by the disobedient party;
(b) upon the act being done the expenses incurred may be ascertained in such manner as the court directs; and
(c) execution may issue against the disobedient party for the amount so ascertained and for costs.

(4) Paragraph (2) is without prejudice to –

(a) the court's powers under section 39 of the Senior Courts Act 1981; and
(b) the court's powers to punish the disobedient party for contempt.

Amendments—Inserted by SI 2014/407.

70.3 Transfer of proceedings for enforcement

(1) Subject to rule 83.17, a judgment creditor wishing to enforce a High Court judgment or order in the County Court must apply to the High Court for an order transferring the proceedings.

(2) A practice direction may make provisions about the transfer of proceedings for enforcement.

(Rule 83.19 contains provisions about the transfer of County Court proceedings to the High Court for enforcement)

Amendments—Inserted by SI 2001/2792. Amended by SI 2014/407.

70.4 Enforcement of judgment or order by or against non-party

If a judgment or order is given or made in favour of or against a person who is not a party to proceedings, it may be enforced by or against that person by the same methods as if he were a party.

Amendments—Inserted by SI 2001/2792.

70.5 Enforcement of decisions of bodies other than the High Court and the County Court and compromises enforceable by enactment

(1) This rule applies, subject to paragraph (2), where an enactment provides that –

(a) a decision of a court, tribunal, body or person other than the High Court or a County Court; or
(b) a compromise,

may be enforced as if it were a court order or that any sum of money payable under that decision or compromise may be recoverable as if payable under a court order.

(2) This rule does not apply to –

(a) any judgment to which Part 74 applies;
(b) arbitration awards;
(c) any order to which RSC Order 115 applies; or
(d) proceedings to which Part 75 (traffic enforcement) applies.

(2A) Unless paragraph (3) applies, a party may enforce the decision or compromise by applying for a specific method of enforcement under Parts 71 to 73, 81, 83 and 84 and Schedule 2 CCR Orders 27 and 28 and must –

(a) file with the court a copy of the decision or compromise being enforced; and
(b) provide the court with the information required by Practice Direction 70.

(3) If an enactment provides that a decision or compromise is enforceable or a sum of money is recoverable if a court so orders, an application for such an order must be made in accordance with paragraphs (4) to (7A) of this rule.

(4) The application –
  (a) may, unless paragraph (4A) applies, be made without notice; and
  (b) must be made to the court for the district where the person against whom the order is sought, resides or carries on business, unless the court otherwise orders.

(4A) Where a compromise requires a person to whom a sum of money is payable under the compromise to do anything in addition to discontinuing or not starting proceedings ('a conditional compromise'), an application under paragraph (4) must be made on notice.

(5) The application notice must –
  (a) be in the form; and
  (b) contain the information
required by Practice Direction 70.

(6) A copy of the decision or compromise must be filed with the application notice.

(7) An application other than in relation to a conditional compromise may be dealt with by a court officer without a hearing.

(7A) Where an application relates to a conditional compromise, the respondent may oppose it by filing a response within 14 days of service of the application notice and if the respondent –
  (a) does not file a response within the time allowed, the court will make the order; or
  (b) files a response within the time allowed, the court will make such order as appears appropriate.

(8) If an enactment provides that a decision or compromise may be enforced in the same manner as an order of the High Court if it is registered, any application to the High Court for registration must be made in accordance with Practice Direction 70.

Amendments—Inserted by SI 2001/2792. Substituted by SI 2008/3327. Amended by SI 2009/3390; SI 2014/407.

70.6 Effect of setting aside judgment or order

If a judgment or order is set aside, any enforcement of the judgment or order shall cease to have effect unless the court otherwise orders.

Amendments—Inserted by SI 2001/2792.

****

PART 71
ORDERS TO OBTAIN INFORMATION FROM JUDGMENT DEBTORS

71.1 Scope of this Part

This Part contains rules which provide for a judgment debtor to be required to attend court to provide information, for the purpose of enabling a judgment creditor to enforce a judgment or order against him.

Amendments—Inserted by SI 2001/2792.

71.2 Order to attend court

(1) A judgment creditor may apply for an order requiring –

    (a) a judgment debtor; or
    (b) if a judgment debtor is a company or other corporation, an officer of that body;
    to attend court to provide information about –
        (i) the judgment debtor's means; or
        (ii) any other matter about which information is needed to enforce a judgment or order.

(2) An application under paragraph (1) –

    (a) may be made without notice; and
    (b) must be issued in the court or County Court hearing centre which made the judgment or order which it is sought to enforce, except that –
        (i) if the proceedings have since been transferred to a different court or hearing centre, it must be issued in that court; or
        (ii) subject to subparagraph (b)(i), if it is to enforce a judgment made in the County Court Money Claims Centre, it must be issued in accordance with section 2 of Practice Direction 70.

(3) The application notice must –

    (a) be in the form; and
    (b) contain the information

required by Practice Direction 71.

(4) An application under paragraph (1) may be dealt with by a court officer without a hearing.

(5) If the application notice complies with paragraph (3), an order to attend court will be issued in the terms of paragraph (6).

(6) A person served with an order issued under this rule must –

    (a) attend court at the time and place specified in the order;
    (b) when he does so, produce at court documents in his control which are described in the order; and
    (c) answer on oath such questions as the court may require.

(7) An order under this rule will contain a notice in the following terms , or in terms to substantially the same effect –

    If you the within-named [ ] do not comply with this order you may be held to be in contempt of court and imprisoned or fined, or your assets may be seized.

Amendments—Inserted by SI 2001/2792. Amended by SI 2009/3390; SI 2012/505; SI 2012/2208; SI 2014/407.

71.3 Service of order

(1) An order to attend court must, unless the court otherwise orders, be served personally on the person ordered to attend court not less than 14 days before the hearing.

(2) If the order is to be served by the judgment creditor, he must inform the court not less than 7 days before the date of the hearing if he has been unable to serve it.

Amendments—Inserted by SI 2001/2792.

71.4 Travelling expenses

(1) A person ordered to attend court may, within 7 days of being served with the order, ask the judgment creditor to pay him a sum reasonably sufficient to cover his travelling expenses to and from court.

(2) The judgment creditor must pay such a sum if requested.

Amendments—Inserted by SI 2001/2792.

71.5 Judgment creditor's affidavit

(1) The judgment creditor must file an affidavit$^{(GL)}$ or affidavits –

   (a) by the person who served the order (unless it was served by the court) giving details of how and when it was served;
   (b) stating either that –
      (i) the person ordered to attend court has not requested payment of his travelling expenses; or
      (ii) the judgment creditor has paid a sum in accordance with such a request; and
   (c) stating how much of the judgment debt remains unpaid.

(2) The judgment creditor must either –

   (a) file the affidavit$^{(GL)}$ or affidavits not less than 2 days before the hearing; or
   (b) produce it or them at the hearing.

Amendments—Inserted by SI 2001/2792.

71.6 Conduct of the hearing

(1) The person ordered to attend court will be questioned on oath.

(2) The questioning will be carried out by a court officer unless the court has ordered that the hearing shall be before a judge.

(3) The judgment creditor or his representative –

   (a) may attend and ask questions where the questioning takes place before a court officer; and
   (b) must attend and conduct the questioning if the hearing is before a judge.

Amendments—Inserted by SI 2001/2792.

71.7 Adjournment of the hearing

If the hearing is adjourned, the court will give directions as to the manner in which notice of the new hearing is to be served on the judgment debtor.

Amendments—Inserted by SI 2001/2792.

71.8 Failure to comply with order

(1) If a person against whom an order has been made under rule 71.2 –

    (a) fails to attend court;
    (b) refuses at the hearing to take the oath or to answer any question; or
    (c) otherwise fails to comply with the order;

the court will refer the matter to a High Court judge or Circuit Judge.

(2) That judge may, subject to paragraphs (3) and (4), make a committal order against the person.

(3) A committal order for failing to attend court may not be made unless the judgment creditor has complied with rules 71.4 and 71.5.

(4) If a committal order is made, the judge will direct that –

    (a) the order shall be suspended provided that the person –
        (i) attends court at a time and place specified in the order; and
        (ii) complies with all the terms of that order and the original order; and
    (b) if the person fails to comply with any term on which the committal order is suspended, he shall be brought before a judge to consider whether the committal order should be discharged.

    (Part 81 contains provisions in relation to committal.)

Amendments—Inserted by SI 2001/2792. Amended by SI 2001/4015; SI 2012/2208; SI 2014/407.

****

PART 72
THIRD PARTY DEBT ORDERS

72.1 Scope of this Part and interpretation

(1) This Part contains rules which provide for a judgment creditor to obtain an order for the payment to him of money which a third party who is within the jurisdiction owes to the judgment debtor.

(2) In this Part, 'bank or building society' includes any person carrying on a business in the course of which he lawfully accepts deposits in the United Kingdom.

Amendments—Inserted by SI 2001/2792. Amended by SI 2001/4015.

72.2 Third party debt order

(1) Upon the application of a judgment creditor, the court may make an order (a 'final third party debt order') requiring a third party to pay to the judgment creditor –

   (a) the amount of any debt due or accruing due to the judgment debtor from the third party; or
   (b) so much of that debt as is sufficient to satisfy the judgment debt and the judgment creditor's costs of the application.

(2) The court will not make an order under paragraph 1 without first making an order (an 'interim third party debt order') as provided by rule 72.4(2).

(3) In deciding whether money standing to the credit of the judgment debtor in an account to which section 40 of the Senior Courts Act 1981 or section 108 of the County Courts Act 1984 relates may be made the subject of a third party debt order, any condition applying to the account that a receipt for money deposited in the account must be produced before any money is withdrawn will be disregarded.

> (Section 40(3) of the Senior Courts Act 1981 and section 108(3) of the County Courts Act 1984 contain a list of other conditions applying to accounts that will also be disregarded)

Amendments—Inserted by SI 2001/2792. Amended by Constitutional Reform Act 2005, s 59(5), Sch 11, para 1(2).

72.3 Application for third party debt order

(1) An application for a third party debt order –

   (a) may be made without notice; and
   (b) must be issued in the court which made the judgment or order which it is sought to enforce, except that –
       (i) if the proceedings have since been transferred to a different court, it must be issued in that court; or
       (ii) subject to subparagraph (b)(i), if it is to enforce a judgment made in the County Court Money Claims Centre, it must be issued in accordance with section 2 of Practice Direction 70.

(2) The application notice must –

   (a) (i) be in the form; and
       (ii) contain the information
       required by Practice Direction 72; and
   (b) be verified by a statement of truth.

Amendments—Inserted by SI 2001/2792. Amended by SI 2009/3390; SI 2012/505; SI 2014/407.

72.4 Interim third party debt order

(1) An application for a third party debt order will initially be dealt with by a judge without a hearing.

(2) The judge may make an interim third party debt order –

   (a) fixing a hearing to consider whether to make a final third party debt order; and

(b) directing that until that hearing the third party must not make any payment which reduces the amount he owes the judgment debtor to less than the amount specified in the order.

(3) An interim third party debt order will specify the amount of money which the third party must retain, which will be the total of –

(a) the amount of money remaining due to the judgment creditor under the judgment or order; and
(b) an amount for the judgment creditor's fixed costs of the application, as specified in Practice Direction 72.

(4) An interim third party debt order becomes binding on a third party when it is served on him.

(5) The date of the hearing to consider the application shall be not less than 28 days after the interim third party debt order is made.

Amendments—Inserted by SI 2001/2792. Amended by SI 2009/3390.

72.5 Service of interim order

(1) Copies of an interim third party debt order, the application notice and any documents filed in support of it must be served –

(a) on the third party, not less than 21 days before the date fixed for the hearing; and
(b) on the judgment debtor not less than –
    (i) 7 days after a copy has been served on the third party; and
    (ii) 7 days before the date fixed for the hearing.

(2) If the judgment creditor serves the order, he must either –

(a) file a certificate of service not less than 2 days before the hearing; or
(b) produce a certificate of service at the hearing.

Amendments—Inserted by SI 2001/2792.

72.6 Obligations of third parties served with interim order

(1) A bank or building society served with an interim third party debt order must carry out a search to identify all accounts held with it by the judgment debtor.

(2) The bank or building society must disclose to the court and the creditor within 7 days of being served with the order, in respect of each account held by the judgment debtor –

(a) the number of the account;
(b) whether the account is in credit; and
(c) if the account is in credit –
    (i) whether the balance of the account is sufficient to cover the amount specified in the order;
    (ii) the amount of the balance at the date it was served with the order, if it is less than the amount specified in the order; and
    (iii) whether the bank or building society asserts any right to the money in the account, whether pursuant to a right of set-off or otherwise, and if so giving details of the grounds for that assertion.

(3) If –

(a) the judgment debtor does not hold an account with the bank or building society; or
(b) the bank or building society is unable to comply with the order for any other reason (for example, because it has more than one account holder whose details match the information contained in the order, and cannot identify which account the order applies to),

the bank or building society must inform the court and the judgment creditor of that fact within 7 days of being served with the order.

(4) Any third party other than a bank or building society served with an interim third party debt order must notify the court and the judgment creditor in writing within 7 days of being served with the order, if he claims –

(a) not to owe any money to the judgment debtor; or
(b) to owe less than the amount specified in the order.

Amendments—Inserted by SI 2001/2792. Amended by SI 2001/4015.

72.7 Arrangements for debtors in hardship

(1) If –

(a) a judgment debtor is an individual;
(b) he is prevented from withdrawing money from his account with a bank or building society as a result of an interim third party debt order; and
(c) he or his family is suffering hardship in meeting ordinary living expenses as a result,

the court may, on an application by the judgment debtor, make an order permitting the bank or building society to make a payment or payments out of the account ('a hardship payment order').

(2) An application for a hardship payment order may be made –

(a) in High Court proceedings, at the Royal Courts of Justice or to any district registry; and
(b) in County Court proceedings, to any County Court.

(3) A judgment debtor may only apply to one court for a hardship payment order.

(4) An application notice seeking a hardship payment order must –

(a) include detailed evidence explaining why the judgment debtor needs a payment of the amount requested; and
(b) be verified by a statement of truth.

(5) Unless the court orders otherwise, the application notice –

(a) must be served on the judgment creditor at least 2 days before the hearing; but
(b) does not need to be served on the third party.

(6) A hardship payment order may –

(a) permit the third party to make one or more payments out of the account; and
(b) specify to whom the payments may be made.

Amendments—Inserted by SI 2001/2792. Amended by SI 2014/407.

72.8 Further consideration of the application

(1) If the judgment debtor or the third party objects to the court making a final third party debt order, he must file and serve written evidence stating the grounds for his objections.

(2) If the judgment debtor or the third party knows or believes that a person other than the judgment debtor has any claim to the money specified in the interim order, he must file and serve written evidence stating his knowledge of that matter.

(3) If –

  (a) the third party has given notice under rule 72.6 that he does not owe any money to the judgment debtor, or that the amount which he owes is less than the amount specified in the interim order; and
  (b) the judgment creditor wishes to dispute this,

the judgment creditor must file and serve written evidence setting out the grounds on which he disputes the third party's case.

(4) Written evidence under paragraphs (1), (2) or (3) must be filed and served on each other party as soon as possible, and in any event not less than 3 days before the hearing.

(5) If the court is notified that some person other than the judgment debtor may have a claim to the money specified in the interim order, it will serve on that person notice of the application and the hearing.

(6) At the hearing the court may –

  (a) make a final third party debt order;
  (b) discharge the interim third party debt order and dismiss the application;
  (c) decide any issues in dispute between the parties, or between any of the parties and any other person who has a claim to the money specified in the interim order; or
  (d) direct a trial of any such issues, and if necessary give directions.

Amendments—Inserted by SI 2001/2792.

72.9 Effect of final third party order

(1) A final third party debt order shall be enforceable as an order to pay money.

(2) If –

  (a) the third party pays money to the judgment creditor in compliance with a third party debt order; or
  (b) the order is enforced against him,

the third party shall, to the extent of the amount paid by him or realised by enforcement against him, be discharged from his debt to the judgment debtor.

(3) Paragraph (2) applies even if the third party debt order, or the original judgment or order against the judgment debtor, is later set aside.

Amendments—Inserted by SI 2001/2792.

72.10 Money in court

(1) If money is standing to the credit of the judgment debtor in court –

(a) the judgment creditor may not apply for a third party debt order in respect of that money; but
(b) he may apply for an order that the money in court, or so much of it as is sufficient to satisfy the judgment or order and the costs of the application, be paid to him.

(2) An application notice seeking an order under this rule must be served on –

(a) the judgment debtor; and
(b) the Accountant General at the Court Funds Office.

(3) If an application notice has been issued under this rule, the money in court must not be paid out until the application has been disposed of.

Amendments—Inserted by SI 2001/2792.

72.11 Costs

If the judgment creditor is awarded costs on an application for an order under rule 72.2 or 72.10 –

(a) he shall, unless the court otherwise directs, retain those costs out of the money recovered by him under the order; and
(b) the costs shall be deemed to be paid first out of the money he recovers, in priority to the judgment debt.

Amendments—Inserted by SI 2001/2792.

****

PART 73
CHARGING ORDERS, STOP ORDERS AND STOP NOTICES

73.1 Scope of this Part and interpretation

(1) This Part contains rules which provide for a judgment creditor to enforce a judgment by obtaining –

(a) a charging order (Section I);
(b) a stop order (Section II); or
(c) a stop notice (Section III),

over or against the judgment debtor's interest in an asset.

(2) In this Part –

(a) 'the 1979 Act' means the Charging Orders Act 1979;
(b) 'the 1992 Regulations' means the Council Tax (Administration and Enforcement) Regulations 1992;
(c) 'funds in court' includes securities held in court;
(d) 'securities' means securities of any of the kinds specified in section 2(2)(b) of the 1979 Act.

Amendments—Inserted by SI 2001/2792.

Section I – Charging Orders

73.2 Scope of this Section

This Section applies to an application by a judgment creditor for a charging order under –

(a) section 1 of the 1979 Act; or
(b) regulation 50 of the 1992 Regulations.

Amendments—Inserted by SI 2001/2792.

73.3 Application for charging order

(1) An application for a charging order may be made without notice.

(2) An application for a charging order must be issued in the court of County Court hearing centre which made the judgment or order which it is sought to enforce, unless –

(a) the proceedings have since been transferred to a different court, in which case the application must be issued in that court;
(b) the application is made under the 1992 Regulations, in which event it must be issued in the County Court for the district in which the relevant dwelling (as defined in regulation 50(3)(b) of those Regulations) is situated;
(c) the application is for a charging order over an interest in a fund in court, in which [event][1] it must be issued in the court in which the claim relating to that fund is or was proceeding;
(d) the application is to enforce a judgment or order of the High Court and it is required by section 1(2) of the 1979 Act to be made to a County Court; or
(e) the application is to enforce a judgment made in the County Court Money Claims Centre, in which event the application must be issued in accordance with section 2 of Practice Direction 70.

(3) Subject to paragraph (2), a judgment creditor may apply for a single charging order in respect of more than one judgment or order against the same debtor.

(4) The application notice must –

(a) (i) be in the form; and
(ii) contain the information,
required by Practice Direction 73; and
(b) be verified by a statement of truth.

Amendments—Inserted by SI 2001/2792; SI 2009/3390; SI 2012/505; SI 2014/407.

73.4 Interim charging order

(1) An application for a charging order will initially be dealt with by a judge without a hearing.

(2) The judge may make an order (an 'interim charging order') –

(a) imposing a charge over the judgment debtor's interest in the asset to which the application relates; and

---

[1] Amendment: Civil Procedure (Amendment) Rules 2012, SI 2012/505, with effect from 19 March 2012.

(b) fixing a hearing to consider whether to make a final charging order as provided by rule 73.8(2)(a).

Amendments—Inserted by SI 2001/2792.

73.5 Service of interim order

(1) Copies of the interim charging order, the application notice and any documents filed in support of it must, not less than 21 days before the hearing, be served on the following persons –

- (a) the judgment debtor;
- (b) such other creditors as the court directs;
- (c) if the order relates to an interest under a trust, on such of the trustees as the court directs;
- (d) if the interest charged is in securities other than securities held in court, then –
  - (i) in the case of stock for which the Bank of England keeps the register, the Bank of England;
  - (ii) in the case of government stock to which (i) does not apply, the keeper of the register;
  - (iii) in the case of stock of any body incorporated within England and Wales, that body;
  - (iv) in the case of stock of any body incorporated outside England and Wales or of any state or territory outside the United Kingdom, which is registered in a register kept in England and Wales, the keeper of that register;
  - (v) in the case of units of any unit trust in respect of which a register of the unit holders is kept in England and Wales, the keeper of that register; and
- (e) if the interest charged is in funds in court, the Accountant General at the Court Funds Office.

(2) If the judgment creditor serves the order, he must either –

- (a) file a certificate of service not less than 2 days before the hearing; or
- (b) produce a certificate of service at the hearing.

Amendments—Inserted by SI 2001/2792.

73.6 Effect of interim order in relation to securities

(1) If a judgment debtor disposes of his interest in any securities, while they are subject to an interim charging order which has been served on him, that disposition shall not, so long as that order remains in force, be valid as against the judgment creditor.

(2) A person served under rule 73.5(1)(d) with an interim charging order relating to securities must not, unless the court gives permission –

- (a) permit any transfer of any of the securities; or
- (b) pay any dividend, interest or redemption payment relating to them.

(3) If a person acts in breach of paragraph (2), he will be liable to pay to the judgment creditor

(a) the value of the securities transferred or the amount of the payment made (as the case may be); or
(b) if less, the amount necessary to satisfy the debt in relation to which the interim charging order was made.

Amendments—Inserted by SI 2001/2792.

73.7 Effect of interim order in relation to funds in court

If a judgment debtor disposes of his interest in funds in court while they are subject to an interim charging order which has been served on him and on the Accountant General in accordance with rule 73.5(1), that disposition shall not, so long as that order remains in force, be valid as against the judgment creditor.

Amendments—Inserted by SI 2001/2792.

73.8 Further consideration of the application

(1) If any person objects to the court making a final charging order, he must –

(a) file; and
(b) serve on the applicant,

written evidence stating the grounds of his objections, not less than 7 days before the hearing.

(2) At the hearing the court may –

(a) make a final charging order confirming that the charge imposed by the interim charging order shall continue, with or without modification;
(b) discharge the interim charging order and dismiss the application;
(c) decide any issues in dispute between the parties, or between any of the parties and any other person who objects to the court making a final charging order; or
(d) direct a trial of any such issues, and if necessary give directions.

(3) If the court makes a final charging order which charges securities other than securities held in court, the order will include a stop notice unless the court otherwise orders.

(Section III of this Part contains provisions about stop notices)

(4) Any order made at the hearing must be served on all the persons on whom the interim charging order was required to be served.

Amendments—Inserted by SI 2001/2792.

73.9 Discharge or variation of order

(1) Any application to discharge or vary a charging order must be made to the court which made the charging order.

> (Section 3(5) of the 1979 Act and regulation 51(4) of the 1992 Regulations provide that the court may at any time, on the application of the debtor, or of any person interested in any property to which the order relates, or (where the 1992 Regulations apply) of the authority, make an order discharging or varying the charging order)

(2) The court may direct that –

    (a) any interested person should be joined as a party to such an application; or
    (b) the application should be served on any such person.

(3) An order discharging or varying a charging order must be served on all the persons on whom the charging order was required to be served.

Amendments—Inserted by SI 2001/2792.

73.10 Enforcement of charging order by sale

(1) Subject to the provisions of any enactment, the court may, upon a claim by a person who has obtained a charging order over an interest in property, order the sale of the property to enforce the charging order.

(2) A claim for an order for sale under this rule should be made to the court which made the charging order, unless that court does not have jurisdiction to make an order for sale.

    (A claim under this rule is a proceeding for the enforcement of a charge, and section 23(c) of the County Courts Act 1984 provides the extent of the County Court's jurisdiction to hear and determine such proceedings)

(3) The claimant must use the Part 8 procedure.

(4) A copy of the charging order must be filed with the claim form.

(5) The claimant's written evidence must include the information required by Practice Direction 73.

Amendments—Inserted by SI 2001/2792. Amended by SI 2009/3390; SI 2014/407.

Section II – Stop Orders

73.11 Interpretation

In this Section, 'stop order' means an order of the High Court not to take, in relation to funds in court or securities specified in the order, any of the steps listed in section 5(5) of the 1979 Act.

Amendments—Inserted by SI 2001/2792.

73.12 Application for stop order

(1) The High Court may make –

    (a) a stop order relating to funds in court, on the application of any person –
        (i) who has a mortgage or charge on the interest of any person in the funds; or
        (ii) to whom that interest has been assigned; or
        (iii) who is a judgment creditor of the person entitled to that interest; or
    (b) a stop order relating to securities other than securities held in court, on the application of any person claiming to be beneficially entitled to an interest in the securities.

(2) An application for a stop order must be made –

    (a) by application notice in existing proceedings; or

(b) by Part 8 claim form if there are no existing proceedings in the High Court.

(3) The application notice or claim form must be served on –
    (a) every person whose interest may be affected by the order applied for; and
    (b) either –
        (i) the Accountant General at the Court Funds Office, if the application relates to funds in court; or
        (ii) the person specified in rule 73.5(1)(d), if the application relates to securities other than securities held in court.

Amendments—Inserted by SI 2001/2792.

73.13 Stop order relating to funds in court

A stop order relating to funds in court shall prohibit the transfer, sale, delivery out, payment or other dealing with –
    (a) the funds or any part of them; or
    (b) any income on the funds.

Amendments—Inserted by SI 2001/2792.

73.14 Stop order relating to securities

(1) A stop order relating to securities other than securities held in court may prohibit all or any of the following steps –
    (a) the registration of any transfer of the securities;
    (b) the making of any payment by way of dividend, interest or otherwise in respect of the securities; and
    (c) in the case of units of a unit trust, any acquisition of or other dealing with the units by any person or body exercising functions under the trust.

(2) The order shall specify –
    (a) the securities to which it relates;
    (b) the name in which the securities stand;
    (c) the steps which may not be taken; and
    (d) whether the prohibition applies to the securities only or to the dividends or interest as well.

Amendments—Inserted by SI 2001/2792.

73.15 Variation or discharge of order

(1) The court may, on the application of any person claiming to have a beneficial interest in the funds or securities to which a stop order relates, make an order discharging or varying the order.

(2) An application notice seeking the variation or discharge of a stop order must be served on the person who obtained the order.

Amendments—Inserted by SI 2001/2792.

Section III – Stop Notices

73.16 General

In this Section –

(a) 'stop notice' means a notice issued by the court which requires a person or body not to take, in relation to securities specified in the notice, any of the steps listed in section 5(5) of the 1979 Act, without first giving notice to the person who obtained the notice; and

(b) 'securities' does not include securities held in court.

Amendments—Inserted by SI 2001/2792.

73.17 Request for stop notice

(1) The High Court may, on the request of any person claiming to be beneficially entitled to an interest in securities, issue a stop notice.

(A stop notice may also be included in a final charging order, by either the High Court or a County Court, under rule 73.8(3))

(2) A request for a stop notice must be made by filing –

(a) a draft stop notice; and
(b) written evidence which –
 (i) identifies the securities in question;
 (ii) describes the applicant's interest in the securities; and
 (iii) gives an address for service for the applicant.

(A sample form of stop notice is annexed to [Practice Direction 73])

(3) If a court officer considers that the request complies with paragraph (2), he will issue a stop notice.

(4) The applicant must serve copies of the stop notice and his written evidence on the person to whom the stop notice is addressed.

Amendments—Inserted by SI 2001/2792. Amended by SI 2009/3390; SI 2009/3390.

73.18 Effect of stop notice

(1) A stop notice –

(a) takes effect when it is served in accordance with rule 73.17(4); and
(b) remains in force unless it is withdrawn or discharged in accordance with rule 73.20 or 73.21.

(2) While a stop notice is in force, the person on whom it is served –

(a) must not –
 (i) register a transfer of the securities described in the notice; or
 (ii) take any other step restrained by the notice,

without first giving 14 days' notice to the person who obtained the stop notice; but

(b) must not, by reason only of the notice, refuse to register a transfer or to take any other step, after he has given 14 days' notice under paragraph (2)(a) and that period has expired.

Amendments—Inserted by SI 2001/2792.

73.19 Amendment of stop notice

(1) If any securities are incorrectly described in a stop notice which has been obtained and served in accordance with rule 73.17, the applicant may request an amended stop notice in accordance with that rule.

(2) The amended stop notice takes effect when it is served.

Amendments—Inserted by SI 2001/2792.

73.20 Withdrawal of stop notice

(1) A person who has obtained a stop notice may withdraw it by serving a request for its withdrawal on –

(a) the person or body on whom the stop notice was served; and
(b) the court which issued the stop notice.

(2) The request must be signed by the person who obtained the stop notice, and his signature must be witnessed by a practising solicitor.

Amendments—Inserted by SI 2001/2792.

73.21 Discharge or variation of stop notice

(1) The court may, on the application of any person claiming to be beneficially entitled to an interest in the securities to which a stop notice relates, make an order discharging or varying the notice.

(2) An application to discharge or vary a stop notice must be made to the court which issued the notice.

(3) The application notice must be served on the person who obtained the stop notice.

Amendments—Inserted by SI 2001/2792.

73.22 Practice Direction 73 makes provision for the procedure to be followed when applying for an order under section 23 of the Partnership Act 1890.

Amendments—Inserted by SI 2006/1689. Amended by SI 2009/3390.

****

PART 83
WRITS AND WARRANTS – GENERAL PROVISIONS

Section I – Scope and Interpretation

83.1 Scope and interpretation

(1) This Part contains general rules about writs and warrants as follows –

(a) Section II relates to writs and warrants;
(b) Section III relates to writs only; and
(c) Section IV relates to warrants only.

(2) In this Part –

(a) 'the Act' means the Tribunals, Courts and Enforcement Act 2007;
(b) 'the creditor' means a person who has obtained or who is entitled to enforce a judgment or order;
(c) 'the debtor' means a person against whom a judgment or order was given or made;
(d) 'enforcement agent' has the meaning given in paragraph 2(1) of Schedule 12;
(e) 'enforcement officer' means an individual who is authorised to act as an enforcement officer under Schedule 7 to the Courts Act 2003;
(f) 'relevant enforcement officer' means –
  (i) in relation to a writ of execution or a writ of control which is directed to a single enforcement officer, that officer; and
  (ii) in relation to a writ of execution or writ of control which is directed to two or more enforcement officers, the officer to whom the writ is allocated;
(g) 'Schedule 12' means Schedule 12 to the Act;
(h) 'TCG procedure' means the procedure in Schedule 12 to take control of goods and sell them to recover a sum in accordance with that Schedule and regulations made under it;
(i) 'TCG Regulations' means the Taking Control of Goods Regulations 2013;
(j) 'warrant of control' is to be construed in accordance with section 62(4) of the Act;
(k) 'writ of control' is to be construed in accordance with section 62(4) of the Act;
(l) 'writ of execution' includes –
  (i) a writ of possession;
  (ii) a writ of delivery;
  (iii) a writ of sequestration;
  (iv) a writ of fieri facias de bonis ecclesiasticis,
and any further writ in aid of any such writs, but does not include a writ of control.

Amendments—Inserted by SI 2014/407.

Note—See note to r 184 of the Court of Protection Rules reproduced in Part IV of this work.

Section II – Writs and Warrants

83.2 Writs and warrants of control, writs of execution, warrants of delivery and warrants of possession – permission to issue certain writs or warrants

(1) This rule applies to –

  (a) writs and warrants of control;
  (b) writs of execution;
  (c) warrants of delivery;
  (d) warrants of possession.

(2) A writ or warrant to which this rule applies is referred to in this rule as a 'relevant writ or warrant'.

(3) A relevant writ or warrant must not be issued without the permission of the court where –

  (a) six years or more have elapsed since the date of the judgment or order;

(b) any change has taken place, whether by death or otherwise, in the parties –
  (i) entitled to enforce the judgment or order; or
  (ii) liable to have it enforced against them;
(c) the judgment or order is against the assets of a deceased person coming into the hands of that person's executors or administrators after the date of the judgment or order, and it is sought to issue execution against such assets;
(d) any goods to be seized under a relevant writ or warrant are in the hands of a receiver appointed by a court or sequestrator;
(e) under the judgment or order, any person is entitled to a remedy subject to the fulfilment of any condition, and it is alleged that the condition has been fulfilled; or
(f) the permission sought is for a writ of control or writ of execution, and that writ is to be in aid of another writ of control or execution.

(4) An application for permission may be made in accordance with Part 23 and must –
  (a) identify the judgment or order to which the application relates;
  (b) if the judgment or order is for the payment of money, state the amount originally due and, if different, the amount due at the date the application notice is filed;
  (c) where the case falls within paragraph (3)(a), state the reasons for the delay in enforcing the judgment or order;
  (d) where the case falls within paragraph (3)(b), state the change which has taken place in the parties entitled or liable to execution since the date of the judgment or order;
  (e) where the case falls within paragraph (3)(c) or (d), state that a demand to satisfy the judgment or order was made on the person liable to satisfy it and that that person has refused or failed to do so;
  (f) give such other information as is necessary to satisfy the court that the applicant is entitled to proceed to execution on the judgment or order, and that the person against whom it is sought to issue execution is liable to execution on it.

(5) An application for permission may be made without notice being served on any other party unless the court directs otherwise.

(6) If because of one event, an applicant seeks permission under paragraph (3)(b) to enforce more than one judgment or order, the applicant need only make one application for permission.

(7) Where paragraph (6) applies –
  (a) a schedule must be attached to the application for permission, specifying all the judgments or orders in respect of which the application for permission is made; and
  (b) if the application notice is directed to be served on any person, it need set out only such part of the application as affects that person.

(8) Paragraph (3) is without prejudice to section 2 of the Reserve and Auxiliary Forces (Protection of Civil Interests) Act 1951 and any enactment, rule or direction by virtue of which a person is required to obtain the permission of the court for the issue of a warrant or to proceed to execution or otherwise to the enforcement of a judgment or order.

(7A) Where –

(a) the court grants permission, under this rule or otherwise, for the issue of a writ of execution or writ of control ('the permission order'); and
(b) the writ is not issued within one year after the date of the permission order, the permission order will cease to have effect.

(7B) Where a permission order has ceased to have effect, the court may grant a fresh permission order.

Amendments—Inserted by SI 2014/407. Amended by SI 2014/867.

83.2A Application for permission to issue a writ of sequestration

Notwithstanding anything in rule 83.2, an application for permission to issue a writ of sequestration must be made in accordance with Part 81 and in particular Section 7 of that Part.

Amendments—Inserted by SI 2014/867.

83.3 Writs and warrants other than those conferring a power to use the TCG procedure – duration and priority

(1) This rule applies to –

   (a) writs of execution;
   (b) warrants of possession; and
   (c) warrants of delivery,

other than writs of execution or warrants that confer a power to use the TCG procedure.

(2) A writ or warrant to which this rule applies is referred to in this rule as a 'relevant writ or warrant', 'relevant writ' or 'relevant warrant' as appropriate.

(3) Subject to paragraph (4), for the purposes of execution, a writ or warrant will be valid for the period of 12 months beginning with the date of its issue.

(4) The court may extend the relevant writ or warrant from time to time for a period of 12 months at any one time.

(5) If the application is made before the expiry of the period of 12 months, the period of extension will begin on the day after the expiry.

(6) If the application is made after the expiry of the period of 12 months, any period of extension will begin on any day after the expiry that the court may allow.

(7) Before a relevant writ that has been extended is executed –

   (a) the court will seal the writ; or
   (b) the applicant for the extension order must serve a notice sealed as described in subparagraph (a) on the relevant enforcement officer informing that officer of the making of the extension order and the date of that order.

(8) In relation to a relevant warrant, the court will endorse the warrant with a note of the renewal or extension.

(9) Irrespective of whether it has been extended under paragraph (4) –

   (a) the priority of a relevant writ will be determined by reference to the time it is originally received by the person who is under a duty to endorse it; and

(b) the priority of a relevant warrant will be determined by reference to the date on which it was originally issued.

(10) The production of the following will be evidence that the relevant writ or warrant has been extended –

(a) the writ sealed in accordance with paragraph (7)(a);
(b) the notice sealed in accordance with paragraph (7)(b);
(c) the warrant endorsed in accordance with paragraph (8).

(11) If, during the validity of a relevant writ, a person makes an application under Part 85 in relation to an execution under that writ, the validity of the writ will be extended until the expiry of 12 months from the conclusion of the proceedings under Part 85.

Amendments—Inserted by SI 2014/407.

83.4 Writs and warrants conferring a power to use the TCG procedure – duration and priority

(1) This rule applies to –

(a) a writ of control;
(b) a warrant of control; and
(c) any other writ or warrant that confers power to use the TCG procedure.

(2) A writ or warrant to which this rule applies is referred to in this rule as a 'relevant writ or warrant', 'relevant writ' or 'relevant warrant' as appropriate.

(3) A relevant writ or warrant will be valid for the period in which an enforcement agent may take control of the goods in question, as specified in regulation 9(1) of the TCG Regulations.

(4) If a period in which to take control of goods is extended by the court under regulation 9(3) of the TCG Regulations, the validity of the relevant writ or warrant will be extended for the same period.

(Rule 84.5 contains provisions about applications to the court requesting a time extension.)

(5) Irrespective of whether it has been extended under regulation 9(3) of the TCG Regulations –

(a) the priority of a relevant writ will be determined by reference to the time it is originally received by the person who is under a duty to endorse it; and
(b) the priority of a relevant warrant will be determined by reference to the date on which it was originally issued.

(6) The production of –

(a) the extension order granted under regulation 9(3) of the TCG Regulations, or a copy of it; or
(b) the relevant writ or warrant endorsed in accordance with rule 84.5(3)(b), or a copy of it,

will be evidence that the writ or warrant has been extended.

(7) If, during the validity of a relevant writ or warrant, a person makes an application under Part 85 in relation to goods taken into control under that writ or warrant, the validity of the writ or warrant will be extended until the expiry of 12 months from the conclusion of the proceedings under Part 85.

Amendments—Inserted by SI 2014/407.

83.5 Writs and warrants – separate enforcement of costs

(1) Where –

  (a) judgment is given or an order made for –
    (i) payment of a sum otherwise than by instalments ('the sum'); and
    (ii) costs to be assessed; and
  (b) default is made in payment of the sum before the costs have been assessed,

a writ of control or warrant of control (as appropriate) may be issued for the recovery of the sum.

(2) If –

  (a) paragraph (1) applies;
  (b) a writ or warrant is issued for the recovery of the sum;
  (c) the costs are assessed; and
  (d) default is made in payment of the costs,

a separate writ of control or warrant of control may be issued for the recovery of the costs.

(3) A party entitled to enforce a judgment or order of the High Court for –

  (a) the delivery of any property, other than money; or
  (b) possession of any property,

may issue a separate writ of control to enforce payment of any damages or costs awarded to that party by that judgment or order.

(4) A party entitled to enforce a judgment or order of the County Court by warrant of delivery may issue a separate warrant of control to enforce payment of any damages or costs awarded to that party by that judgment or order.

Amendments—Inserted by SI 2014/407.

83.6 Writs and warrants – levying execution on certain days

(1) This rule applies to writs and warrants other than –

  (a) writs of control;
  (b) warrants of control; and
  (c) writs or warrants in relation to an Admiralty claim in rem.

(2) Where a writ or warrant is not a writ of control or warrant of control but nevertheless confers the power to use the TCG procedure, this rule applies to the parts of the writ or warrant that do not confer the power to use the TCG Procedure.

(3) Unless the court orders otherwise, a writ or warrant to enforce a judgment or order must not be executed on a Sunday, Good Friday or Christmas Day.

Amendments—Substituted by SI 2014/2044.

83.7 Writs of control and warrants – power to stay execution or grant other relief

(1) At the time that a judgment or order for payment of money is made or granted, or at any time thereafter, the debtor or other party liable to execution of a writ of control or a warrant may apply to the court for a stay of execution.

(2) The power of the court to stay execution of a warrant of control may be exercised by a District Judge, or a court officer where paragraph (10) applies, and the power of the court to stay execution of any other warrant or of a writ of control may be exercised by a Master or District Judge.

(3) Where the application for a stay of execution is made on the grounds of the applicant's inability to pay, the witness statement required by paragraph (6)(b) must disclose the debtor's means.

(4) If the court is satisfied that –

(a) there are special circumstances which render it inexpedient to enforce the judgment or order; or
(b) the applicant is unable from any reason to pay the money,

then, notwithstanding anything in paragraph (5) or (6), the court may by order stay the execution of the judgment or order, either absolutely or for such period and subject to such conditions as the court thinks fit.

(5) An application under this rule, if not made at the time the judgment is given or order made –

(a) must be made in accordance with Part 23, as modified by paragraphs (6) to (14); and
(b) may be made even if the party liable to execution did not acknowledge service of the claim form or serve a defence or take any previous part in the proceedings.

(6) The grounds on which an application under this rule is made must –

(a) be set out in the application notice; and
(b) be supported by a witness statement made by or on behalf of the applicant substantiating the grounds.

(7) Paragraphs (8) to (15) apply to applications in the County Court.

(8) Where the debtor makes an application in the County Court, the court will –

(a) send the creditor a copy of the debtor's application (and statement of means); and
(b) require the creditor to notify the court in writing whether or not the creditor objects to the application, within 14 days of service of the notification, giving reasons for any objection the creditor may have to the granting of the application.

(9) If the creditor does not notify the court of any objection within the time stated, the court officer may make an order suspending the warrant on terms of payment.

(10) Upon receipt of a notice by the creditor under paragraph (8)(b), the court officer may, if the creditor agrees, or objects only to the terms offered, determine the date and rate of payment and make an order suspending the warrant on terms of payment.

(11) Any party affected by an order made under paragraph (10) may, within 14 days of service of the order on that party and giving reasons, apply on notice for the order to be reconsidered.

(12) If a party applies for the order to be reconsidered, the court will –
  (a) fix a day for the hearing of the application before the District Judge; and
  (b) give to the creditor and the debtor not less than 8 days' notice of the day so fixed.

(13) On hearing an application under paragraph (11), the District Judge may confirm the order or set it aside and make such new order as the court thinks fit.

(14) Where the creditor states in the notice under paragraph (8)(b) that the creditor wishes the enforcement agent to proceed to execute the warrant, the court will –
  (a) fix a day for a hearing before the District Judge of the debtor's application; and
  (b) give to the creditor and to the debtor not less than 2 days' notice of the day so fixed.

(15) Where an order is made by the District Judge suspending a warrant of execution, the debtor may be ordered to pay the costs of the warrant and any fees or expenses incurred before its suspension and the order may authorise the sale of a sufficient portion of any goods seized to cover such costs, fees and expenses and the expenses of sale.

Amendments—Inserted by SI 2014/407.

83.8 Writs and warrants – information about execution of the writ or warrant

(1) If the creditor or debtor serves notice on the enforcement agent or enforcement officer requiring reasonable information about the execution of a writ or warrant, the enforcement agent or enforcement officer must send such information to the creditor or debtor within 7 days of service of the notice.

(2) If the enforcement agent or enforcement officer fails to comply with the notice, the party who served the notice may apply to the court for an order directing the enforcement agent or enforcement officer to comply with the notice.

Amendments—Inserted by SI 2014/407.

Section III – Writs

83.9 Issue of writs of execution and writs of control

(1) In this rule 'the appropriate office' means –
  (a) where the proceedings in which execution is to issue are in a District Registry, that Registry;
  (b) where the proceedings are in the Principal Registry of the Family Division, that Registry;
  (c) where the proceedings are Admiralty proceedings or commercial proceedings which are not in a District Registry, the Admiralty and Commercial Registry;
  (ca) where the proceedings are in the Chancery Division, Chancery Chambers;
  (d) in any other case, the Central Office of the Senior Courts.

(2) Issue of a writ of execution or control takes place on its being sealed by a court officer of the appropriate office.

(3) Before a writ is issued a request for its issue must be filed.

(4) The request must be signed –
   (a) by the person entitled to execution, if acting in person; or
   (b) by or on behalf of the solicitor of the person entitled to execution.

(5) The writ will not be sealed unless at the time it is presented for sealing –
   (a) the person presenting the writ produces –
      (i) the judgment or order on which the writ is to issue, or an office copy of it;
      (ii) where permission was required for the writ to be issued, the order granting such permission or evidence of the granting of it;
      (iii) where judgment on failure to acknowledge service has been entered against a State, as defined in section 14 of the State Immunity Act 1978, evidence that the State has been served in accordance with rule 40.10 and that the judgment has taken effect; and
   (b) the court officer authorised to seal it is satisfied that the period, if any, specified in the judgment or order for the payment of any money or the doing of any other act under the judgment or order has expired.

(6) Every writ of execution or control will bear the date of the day on which it is issued.

Amendments—Inserted by SI 2014/407. Amended by SI 2014/2044.

83.10 Writs of control and writs of delivery – description of parties

(1) This rule applies where the name or address of the creditor or debtor as given in the request for the issue of the following differs from that person's name or address in the judgment or order sought to be enforced –

   (a) a writ of control;
   (b) writ of delivery.

(2) If the creditor files a witness statement that satisfies the court officer that the name or address as given in the request is applicable to the person concerned, the creditor or the debtor will be described in the writ as 'CD of name and address as given in the request suing or sued as AD of name and address in the judgment or order'.

Amendments—Inserted by SI 2014/407.

83.11 Writs relating to ecclesiastical property

(1) In this rule, 'a writ relating to ecclesiastical property' means –

   (a) a writ of fieri facias de bonis ecclesiasticis; or
   (b) a writ of sequestrari de bonis ecclesiasticis.

(2) This rule applies where it appears upon the return of any writ of control that the person against whom the writ was issued –

   (a) has no goods or chattels in the district of the relevant enforcement officer; but

(b) is the incumbent of a benefice named in the return.

(3) After the writ and return have been filed, the party by whom the writ of control was issued may issue a writ relating to ecclesiastical property.

(4) Any such writ must be directed and delivered to the bishop of the diocese within which that benefice is, to be executed by that bishop.

(5) The only fees allowed to the bishop or diocesan officer for the execution of the writ are those authorised by or under any enactment, including any measure of the General Synod.

Amendments—Inserted by SI 2014/407.

83.12 Writs other than those conferring a power to use the TCG procedure – order for sale otherwise than by auction

(1) This rule applies in relation to writs that do not confer a power to use the TCG procedure.

(2) A court order under paragraph 10 of Schedule 7 to the Courts Act 2003 that a sale of goods seized under an execution may be made otherwise than by public auction may be made on the application of –

(a) the person at whose instance the writ of execution under which the sale is to be made was issued;
(b) the person against whom that writ was issued (in this rule referred to as 'the judgment debtor'); or
(c) if the writ was directed to one or more enforcement officers, the relevant enforcement officer.

(3) Such an application must be made in accordance with Part 23.

(4) Where the applicant for an order under this rule is not the enforcement officer, the enforcement officer must, on the demand of the applicant, send to the applicant a list, stating –

(a) whether the enforcement officer has notice of the issue of another writ or writs of execution against the goods of the judgment debtor; and
(b) so far as is known to the enforcement officer, the name and address of every creditor who has obtained the issue of another such writ of execution.

(5) Where the enforcement officer is the applicant, the enforcement officer must prepare such a list.

(6) Not less than 3 days before the hearing, the applicant must serve the application notice on each of the other persons by whom the application might have been made and on every person named in the list prepared under paragraph (4) or (5).

(7) Service of the application notice on a person named in the list prepared under paragraph (4) or (5) is notice to that person for the purpose of paragraph 10(3) of Schedule 7 to the Courts Act 2003.

(8) The applicant must produce the list prepared under paragraph (4) or (5) to the court on the hearing of the application.

(9) Every person on whom the application notice was served may attend and be heard on the hearing of the application.

Amendments—Inserted by SI 2014/407.

83.13 Enforcement in the High Court of a judgment or order for possession of land

(1) A judgment or order for the giving of possession of land may be enforced in the High Court by one or more of the following means –

   (a) writ of possession;
   (b) in a case in which rule 81.4 applies, an order of committal;
   (c) in a case in which rule 81.20 applies, writ of sequestration.

(2) Subject to paragraphs (3), (5) and (6), a writ of possession to enforce a judgment or order for the giving of possession of any land will not be issued without the permission of the court.

(3) The court's permission is not required for the issue of a writ of possession in a possession claim against trespassers under Part 55 unless the writ is to be issued after the expiry of three months from the date of the order.

(4) An application for permission under paragraph (3) may be made without notice being served on any other party unless the court orders otherwise.

(5) The courts' permission to issue a writ of restitution in aid of a writ of possession is required whether or not permission was required for the writ of possession.

(6) The court's permission is not required for the issue of a writ of possession to enforce a judgment or order for the giving of possession of any land where the judgment or order was given or made in proceedings in which there is a claim for –

   (a) payment of moneys secured by the mortgage;
   (b) sale of the mortgaged property;
   (c) foreclosure;
   (d) delivery of possession (whether before or after foreclosure or without foreclosure) to the mortgagee by the mortgagor or by any other person who is alleged to be in possession of the property;
   (e) redemption;
   (f) reconveyance of the land or its release from the security; or
   (g) delivery of possession by the mortgagee.

(7) In paragraph (6) 'mortgage' includes a legal or equitable mortgage and a legal or equitable charge, and reference to a mortgagor, a mortgagee and mortgaged land is to be interpreted accordingly.

(8) Permission referred to in paragraph (2) will not be granted unless it is shown –

   (a) that every person in actual possession of the whole or any part of the land ('the occupant') has received such notice of the proceedings as appears to the court sufficient to enable the occupant to apply to the court for any relief to which the occupant may be entitled; and
   (b) if the operation of the judgment or order is suspended by section 16(2) of the Landlord and Tenant Act 1954, that the applicant has not received notice in writing from the tenant that the tenant desires that the provisions of section 16(2)(a) and (b) of that subsection shall have effect.

(9) A writ of possession may include provision for enforcing the payment of any money adjudged or ordered to be paid by the judgment or order which is to be enforced by the writ.

Amendments—Inserted by SI 2014/407.

83.14 Enforcement in the High Court of a judgment or order for delivery of goods

(1) A judgment or order for the delivery of any goods which does not give a person against whom the judgment is given or order made the alternative of paying the assessed value of the goods may be enforced in the High Court by one or more of the following means –

- (a) writ of delivery to recover the goods without alternative provision for recovery of the assessed value of those goods ('writ of specific delivery');
- (b) in a case in which rule 81.4 applies, an order of committal;
- (c) in a case in which rule 81.20 applies, writ of sequestration.

(2) A judgment or order for the delivery of any goods or payment of their assessed value may be enforced by one or more of the following means –

- (a) writ of delivery to recover the goods or their assessed value;
- (b) by order of the court, writ of specific delivery;
- (c) in a case in which rule 81.20 applies, writ of sequestration.

(3) An application for an order under paragraph (2)(b) must be made in accordance with Part 23, and must be served on the defendant against whom the judgment or order sought to be enforced was given or made.

(4) A writ of specific delivery, and a writ of delivery to recover any goods or their assessed value, may include provision for enforcing the payment of any money adjudged or ordered to be paid by the judgment or order which is to be enforced by the writ.

(5) A judgment or order for the payment of the assessed value of any goods may be enforced by the same means as any other judgment or order for the payment of money.

(6) This rule applies to writs in aid of writs of delivery.

Amendments—Inserted by SI 2014/407.

Section IV – Warrants

83.15 Application for warrant of control or warrant of delivery

(1) In this rule, 'instalment order' means an order for payment of a sum of money by instalments.

(2) This rule applies in relation to –

- (a) warrants of control; and
- (b) warrants of delivery.

(3) A creditor may apply for a warrant to be issued by filing a request.

(4) A request for a warrant of control or delivery –

- (a) may be made without notice; and
- (b) must be made to –
  - (i) the County Court hearing centre where the judgment or order which it is sought to enforce was made; or
  - (ii) the County Court hearing centre to which the proceedings have since been transferred.

(5) Subject to paragraph (4)(b)(ii), a request for a warrant of control to enforce a judgment or order made at the County Court Money Claims Centre must be made to that office.

(6) In the request, the creditor must certify –

    (a)   the amount remaining due under the judgment or order; and
    (b)   where the order made is an instalment order –
        (i)   that the whole or part of any instalment due remains unpaid; and
        (ii)   the amount for which the warrant is to be issued.

(7) The court officer may discharge the functions of the District Judge under section 85(2) of the County Courts Act 1984 of issuing a warrant.

(8) Unless an instalment order has been made and paragraphs (9) and (10) apply, any warrant issued must be issued for the whole of the sum of money and costs remaining unpaid, and may not be issued for part of the sum.

(9) Where the court has made an instalment order and default has been made in payment of an instalment, then subject to paragraph (10), a warrant of control may be issued for –

    (a)   the whole of the sum of money and costs then remaining unpaid; or
    (b)   for such part of the sum as the creditor may request, which must not be less than the greater of –
        (i)   £50; or
        (ii)   the amount of one monthly instalment or, as the case may be, four weekly instalments.

(10) Where an instalment order has been made, no warrant will be issued unless at the time when it is issued –

    (a)   the whole or part of an instalment which has already become due remains unpaid; and
    (b)   any warrant previously issued for part of the sum of money and costs has expired, been satisfied or abandoned.

Amendments—Inserted by SI 2014/407.

83.16 Warrant of control or warrant of delivery – opposition by debtor and debtor's request for transfer

The court may, on an application by a debtor who wishes to oppose a request for a warrant of control or warrant of delivery, transfer it to the County Court hearing centre serving the address where the debtor resides or carries on business, or to another court.

Amendments—Inserted by SI 2014/407.

83.17 Warrant of control or warrant of delivery – execution of High Court judgment

(1) Where it is desired to enforce by warrant of control or warrant of delivery –

    (a)   a judgment or order of the High Court; or
    (b)   a judgment, order, decree or award which is or has become enforceable as if it were a judgment of the High Court,

the request referred to in rule 83.15(3) may be filed in the County Court hearing centre which serves the address where execution is to be levied.

(2) Subject to paragraph (3), any restriction imposed by these rules on the issue of execution will apply as if the judgment, order, decree or award were a judgment or order of the County Court.

(3) Permission to issue execution will not be required if permission has already been given by the High Court.

(4) Notice of the issue of the warrant will be sent by the County Court to the High Court.

Amendments—Inserted by SI 2014/407.

83.18 Warrants of control and warrants of delivery – description of parties

(1) This rule applies where the name or address of the creditor or debtor as given in the request for the issue of the following differs from that person's name or address in the judgment or order sought to be enforced –

(a) a warrant of control;
(b) a warrant of delivery.

(2) If the creditor files a witness statement that satisfies the court officer that the name or address as given in the request is applicable to the person concerned, the creditor or the debtor will be described in the warrant as 'CD of name and address as given in the request suing or sued as AD of name and address in the judgment or order'.

Amendments—Inserted by SI 2014/407.

83.19 Creditor's request for transfer to the High Court for enforcement

(1) This rule applies where the creditor makes a request for a certificate of judgment under rule 40.14A(1) for the purpose of enforcing the judgment or order in the High Court –

(a) by execution against goods; or
(b) where the judgment or order to be enforced is an order for possession of land made in a possession claim against trespassers.

(2) The grant of a certificate by the court will take effect as an order to transfer the proceedings to the High Court and the transfer will have effect on the grant of that certificate.

(3) On the transfer of proceedings in accordance with paragraph (2), the County Court will –

(a) give notice to the debtor or the person against whom the possession order was made that the proceedings have been transferred; and
(b) make an entry of the fact of transfer in the court records.

(4) In a case where a request for a certificate of judgment is made under rule 40.14A(1) for the purpose of enforcing a judgment or order in the High Court

and any of the following proceedings are pending, the request for the certificate will not be dealt with until those proceedings are determined –

    (a)   an application for a variation in the date or rate of payment of money due under a judgment or order;
    (b)   an application under either rule 39.3(3) or rule 13.4;
    (c)   a request for an administration order; or
    (d)   an application for a stay of execution under section 88 of the County Courts Act 1984.

Amendments—Inserted by SI 2014/407.

83.20 Warrants of control – bankruptcy or winding up of debtor

(1) This rule applies where the enforcement agent responsible for the execution of a warrant of control is required by any provision of the Insolvency Act 1986 or any other enactment relating to insolvency to retain the proceeds of sale of goods sold under the warrant or money paid in order to avoid a sale.

(2) The enforcement agent will, as soon as practicable after the sale or the receipt of the money, send notice to the creditor and the court.

(3) Where the enforcement agent responsible for the execution of a warrant –

    (a)   receives notice that –
        (i)   a bankruptcy order has been made against the debtor; or
        (ii)   if the debtor is a company –
            (aa)   a provisional liquidator has been appointed; or
            (bb)   an order has been made or a resolution passed for the winding up of the company;
    (b)   withdraws from possession of goods seized; or
    (c)   pays over to –
        (i)   the official receiver or trustee in bankruptcy; or
        (ii)   if the debtor is a company, the liquidator,
        the proceeds of sale of goods sold under the warrant or money paid in order to avoid a sale or seized or received in part satisfaction of the warrant,

the enforcement agent must send notice to the creditor and the court.

Amendments—Inserted by SI 2014/407.

83.21 Warrants where the debtor is a farmer

(1) This rule applies if –

    (a)   any of the following warrants has been issued –
        (i)   a warrant of control;
        (ii)   any other warrant conferring the power to use the TCG procedure; or
        (iii)   a warrant of delivery; and
    (b)   the enforcement agent has reason to believe that the debtor is a farmer.

(2) If requested to do so by the court or enforcement agent, the creditor must provide the court or enforcement agent with an official certificate, dated not more than three days beforehand, of the result of a search at the Land Registry as to the existence of any charge registered against the debtor under the Agricultural Credits Act 1928.

(3) If the creditor fails to provide the official certificate referred to in paragraph (2) within 7 days of receipt of the request, the court, of its own motion or on the application of the enforcement agent, may order the creditor to provide the certificate.

Amendments—Inserted by SI 2014/407.

83.22 Warrants – withdrawal and suspension of warrant at creditor's request

(1) This rule applies if any of the following warrants has been issued –
   (a) a warrant of control;
   (b) any other warrant conferring the power to use the TCG procedure; or
   (c) a warrant of delivery.

(2) Where a creditor requests the court to withdraw the warrant, subject to the following paragraphs of this rule –
   (a) the creditor will be treated as having abandoned the goods; and
   (b) the court will mark the warrant as withdrawn by request of the creditor.

(3) Where the request is made in consequence of an application having been made under Part 85, the enforcement power ceases to be exercisable in respect of the goods claimed.

(4) If the court is requested by the creditor to suspend the warrant because of an arrangement with the debtor, the court will mark the warrant as suspended by request of the creditor and the creditor may subsequently apply to the court for it to be re-issued.

(5) Nothing in this rule will prejudice any right of the creditor to apply for the issue of a fresh warrant or will authorise the re-issue of a warrant which has been withdrawn or has expired or has been superseded by the issue of a fresh warrant.

Amendments—Inserted by SI 2014/407.

83.23 Warrants of delivery

(1) In this rule 'warrant of specific delivery' means a warrant to recover goods without alternative provision for recovery of their value.

(2) Except where an act or rule provides otherwise, a judgment or order for the delivery of any goods will be enforceable by warrant of delivery in accordance with this rule.

(3) If the judgment or order does not give the person against whom it was given or made the alternative of paying the value of the goods, it may be enforced by a warrant of specific delivery.

(4) If the judgment or order is for the delivery of the goods or payment of their value, it may be enforced by a warrant of delivery to recover the goods or their value.

(5) Where a warrant of delivery is issued, the creditor will be entitled, by the same or a separate warrant, to execution against the debtor's goods for any money payable under the judgment or order which is to be enforced by the warrant of delivery.

(6) Where –

(a) a judgment or order is given or made for the delivery of goods or payment of their value; and
(b) a warrant is issued to recover the goods or their value,

money paid into court under the warrant will be appropriated first to any sum of money and costs awarded.

Amendments—Inserted by SI 2014/407.

83.24 Warrants of delivery other than those conferring a power to use the TCG procedure – notice and inventory requirements

(1) This rule applies where –
  (a) a warrant of delivery has been issued for the whole or part of a sum of money and costs; and
  (b) the warrant does not confer power to use the TCG procedure.

(2) Unless the court orders otherwise, the enforcement agent –
  (a) must serve the debtor with a notice warning of the warrant; and
  (b) must not levy the warrant until at least 7 days after service of the notice.

(3) Upon levying execution of the warrant, the enforcement agent must leave notice of the warrant at the place where it has been executed.

(4) If the enforcement agent removes the goods, the enforcement agent must deliver or send to the debtor an inventory of the goods removed sufficient for the debtor to identify the goods.

(5) The inventory must be delivered or sent to the debtor within 7 days of the goods being seized by –
  (a) delivery to the debtor personally;
  (b) sending the inventory by post to the debtor's place of residence; or
  (c) where the debtor's place of residence is not known, by leaving the inventory for, or sending it to, the debtor at the place from which the goods were removed.

(6) If the enforcement agent fails to supply an inventory in accordance with this rule, the debtor may make an application to the court using the procedure in Part 23, for an order requiring the enforcement agent to do so.

Amendments—Inserted by SI 2014/407.

83.25 Warrants of delivery conferring a power to use the TCG procedure – notice of enforcement and inventory requirements

(1) Where a warrant of delivery confers the power to use the TCG procedure, this rule applies in relation to the parts of the warrant that do not confer that power.

(2) Subject to paragraph (4), the enforcement agent must send a warning notice to the person against whom the warrant is issued not less than 7 clear days before the enforcement agent executes the warrant.

(3) Where the period referred to in paragraph (2) includes a Sunday, bank holiday, Good Friday or Christmas Day, that day does not count in calculating that period.

(4) The court may order that a specified shorter period of notice be given to the debtor.

(5) The enforcement agent may apply for the order by way of application under Part 23 and may make the application as part of an application under rule 84.4.

(6) Upon executing the warrant, the enforcement agent must give to the debtor or leave for the debtor at the place where the warrant is being executed, notice about the execution.

(7) As soon as reasonably practicable, and in any event within 7 days of execution of the warrant, the enforcement agent must provide the debtor with a written inventory of goods taken with a description of the goods to enable the debtor to identify the goods correctly.

(8) If the enforcement agent fails to provide –

    (a) notice of execution under paragraph (6); or
    (b) an inventory under paragraph (7) within 7 days of execution,

the debtor may make an application to the court under Part 23 for an order requiring the enforcement agent to supply the notice or inventory as appropriate.

    (Regulations 6 and 30 to 33 of the TCG Regulations contain notice and inventory requirements that apply in relation to the use of the TCG procedure.)

Amendments—Inserted by SI 2014/407.

83.26 Warrants of possession

(1) A judgment or order for the recovery of land will be enforceable by warrant of possession.

(2) An application for a warrant of possession –

    (a) may be made without notice; and
    (b) must be made to –
        (i) the County Court hearing centre where the judgment or order which it is sought to enforce was made; or
        (ii) the County Court hearing centre to which the proceedings have since been transferred.

(3) The court may, on an application by a debtor who wishes to oppose an application for a warrant of possession, transfer it to the County Court hearing centre serving the address where the debtor resides or carries on business, or to another court.

(4) Without prejudice to paragraph (7), the person applying for a warrant of possession must file a certificate that the land which is subject of the judgment or order has not been vacated.

(5) When applying for a warrant of possession of a dwelling-house subject to a mortgage, the claimant must certify that notice has been given in accordance with the Dwelling Houses (Execution of Possession Orders by Mortgagees) Regulations 2010.

(6) Where a warrant of possession is issued, the creditor will be entitled, by the same or a separate warrant, to execution against the debtor's goods for any money payable under the judgment or order which is to be enforced by the warrant of possession.

(7) In a case to which paragraph (6) applies or where an order for possession has been suspended on terms as to payment of a sum of money by instalments, the creditor must in the request certify –

    (a) the amount of money remaining due under the judgment or order; and
    (b) that the whole or part of any instalment due remains unpaid.

(8) A warrant of restitution may be issued, with the permission of the court, in aid of any warrant of possession.

(9) An application for permission under paragraph (8) may be made without notice being served on any other party and must be supported by evidence of –

    (a) wrongful re-entry into possession following the execution of the warrant of possession; and
    (b) such further facts as would, in the High Court, enable the creditor to have a writ of restitution issued.

(10) A warrant of possession to enforce an order for possession in a possession claim against a trespasser under Part 55 ('a warrant of possession against a trespasser') may be issued at any time after the date on which possession is ordered to be given.

(11) No warrant of possession against a trespasser may be issued after the expiry of 3 months from the date of the order without the permission of the court.

(12) Unless the court otherwise directs, an application for permission under paragraph (11) may be made without notice to any other party.

Amendments—Inserted by SI 2014/407.

83.27 Saving for enforcement by committal

Nothing in rules 83.23 and 83.26 prejudices any power to enforce a judgment or order for the delivery of goods or the recovery of land by any order of committal.

Amendments—Inserted by SI 2014/407.

83.28 Suspension of part warrant

(1) This rule applies where a warrant issued for part of a sum of money and costs payable under a judgment or order is suspended on payment of instalments.

    (2) Unless the court otherwise directs, the judgment or order will be treated as suspended on those terms as respects the whole of the sum of money and costs then remaining unpaid.

Amendments—Inserted by SI 2014/407.

83.29 Concurrent warrants

Two or more warrants of control may be issued concurrently for execution by two or more different enforcement agents, but –

    (a) no more may be levied under all the warrants together than is authorised to be levied under one of them; and
    (b) unless the court orders otherwise, the costs of more than one warrant will not be allowed against the debtor.

Amendments—Inserted by SI 2014/407.

****

PART 84
ENFORCEMENT BY TAKING CONTROL OF GOODS

Section I – Scope and Interpretation

84.1 Scope

This Part contains rules in relation to enforcement by taking control of goods using the procedure in Schedule 12 to the Tribunals, Courts and Enforcement Act 2007.

Amendments—Inserted by SI 2014/407.

Note—See note to r 184 of the Court of Protection Rules reproduced in Part IV of this work.

84.2 Interpretation

In this Part –

(a) 'the Act' means the Tribunals Courts and Enforcement Act 2007;
(b) 'Schedule 12' means Schedule 12 to the Act;
(c) 'creditor' has the meaning given in paragraph 1(6) of Schedule 12;
(d) 'co-owner' has the meaning given in paragraph 3(1) of Schedule 12;
(e) 'debtor' has the meaning given in paragraph 1(5) of Schedule 12;
(f) 'enforcement agent' has the meaning given in paragraph 2(1) of Schedule 12;
(g) 'Fees Regulations' means the Taking Control of Goods (Fees) Regulations 2014;
(h) 'TCG Regulations' means the Taking Control of Goods Regulations 2013;
(i) 'writ of control' and 'warrant of control' are to be construed in accordance with section 62(4) of the Act.

Amendments—Inserted by SI 2014/407.

Section II – Where and How to make Applications

84.3 Where and how to make applications

(1) This rule sets out where and how applications referred to in this Part must be made.

(2) Applications referred to in this Part must be made in accordance with the procedure in Part 23 as modified by this Part.

(3) Where there are no pre-existing proceedings, an application referred to in this Part must be made to the County Court.

(4) Where there are pre-existing proceedings, the application must be made to the High Court or the County Court in accordance with rule 23.2.

Amendments—Inserted by SI 2014/407.

Section III – Taking Control of Goods

84.4 Notice of enforcement prior to taking control of goods – application for notice period of less than the minimum period

(1) This rule applies where a person seeks an order under regulation 6(3) of the TCG Regulations that a shorter notice period than the minimum period for taking control of goods set out in regulation 6(1) of those Regulations be given to the debtor.

(2) The person may make an application for the order.

(3) The application –
   (a) may be made without notice; and
   (b) must be accompanied by evidence demonstrating that if the order is not made, it is likely that goods of the debtor will be moved or otherwise disposed of, in order to avoid the enforcement agent taking control of the goods.

Amendments—Inserted by SI 2014/407.

84.5 Application to extend the period in which to take control of goods

(1) An application under regulation 9(4) of the TCG Regulations (application to extend the period in which to take control of goods) must be accompanied by –
   (a) a witness statement made by the person making the application that no previous application under regulation 9(4) has been made to extend that period; and
   (b) the applicant's grounds for not taking control of goods of the debtor during the period specified in regulation 9(1).

(2) If –
   (a) the application is made before the expiry of the period specified in regulation 9(1); and
   (b) the court orders the period of extension,

the period of extension will start on the day after the expiry of the period specified in regulation 9(1), or on such later day as the court may order.

(3) If the court orders the period of extension –
   (a) the applicant must serve a copy of the extension order on the debtor, and on the creditor, enforcement agent or enforcement officer as appropriate; and
   (b) if the goods are to be taken into control by virtue of a warrant or writ of control, or of any other writ or warrant conferring the power to use the procedure in Schedule 12, the court will endorse on the warrant or writ a note of the extension.

Amendments—Inserted by SI 2014/407.

84.6 Application to take control of goods during prohibited hours

An application by the enforcement agent under regulation 13(2)(a) of the TCG Regulations for an order allowing goods to be taken into control during hours prohibited by regulation 13(1) of those Regulations –

(a) may be made without notice; and
(b) must be accompanied by evidence demonstrating that if the order is not made, it is likely that goods of the debtor will be moved or otherwise disposed of, in order to avoid the enforcement agent taking control of the goods.

Amendments—Inserted by SI 2014/407.

84.7 Application to enter, re-enter or remain on premises otherwise than during permitted hours

An application by the enforcement agent under regulation 22(5) of the TCG Regulations for an order allowing the enforcement agent to enter, re-enter or remain on premises at times other than those permitted by regulation 22(2), (3) or (4) of those Regulations– –

(a) may be made without notice; and
(b) must be accompanied by evidence demonstrating that if the order is not made, it is likely that goods of the debtor will be moved or otherwise disposed of, in order to avoid the enforcement agent taking control of the goods.

Amendments—Inserted by SI 2014/407.

84.8 Notice of intention to re-enter premises – application for notice period of less than the minimum period

(1) This rule applies where a person seeks an order under regulation 25(3) of the TCG Regulations that a shorter notice period than the minimum period for re-entering premises set out in regulation 25(1) of those Regulations be given to the debtor.

(2) The person may make an application for the order.

(3) The application –

(a) may be made without notice; and
(b) must be accompanied by evidence demonstrating that if the order is not made, it is likely that goods of the debtor will be moved to be disposed of, in order to avoid the enforcement agent inspecting or removing the goods.

Amendments—Inserted by SI 2014/407.

84.9 Application for a warrant to enter premises – conditions to be satisfied before a warrant may be issued

(1) This rule applies to an application by an enforcement agent for –

(a) the issue of a warrant under paragraph 15(1) of Schedule 12;
(b) the issue of a warrant under paragraph 20(2) of Schedule 12 allowing the use of reasonable force to enter premises; or
(c) the inclusion in a warrant power under paragraph 21(2) of Schedule 12 to use reasonable force to enter premises.

(2) Where the application is for the issue of a warrant under paragraph 15(1) of Schedule 12, the enforcement agent must provide the court with sufficient evidence and information to satisfy the court that the conditions in paragraph 15(2) of Schedule 12 are met.

(3) Where the application is for the issue of a warrant under paragraph 20(2) or 21(2) of Schedule 12, the enforcement agent must provide the court with sufficient evidence and information to satisfy the court that the conditions set out in regulation 28(2) of the TCG Regulations have been met.

Amendments—Inserted by SI 2014/407.

84.10 Application for a warrant allowing reasonable force in relation to goods on the highway – conditions to be satisfied before a warrant may be issued

(1) This rule applies to an application by an enforcement agent for the issue of a warrant under paragraph 31(1) of Schedule 12 allowing the use of reasonable force in relation to goods on the highway.

(2) The enforcement agent must provide the court with sufficient evidence and information to satisfy the court that the conditions set out in regulation 29(2) of the TCG Regulations have been met.

Amendments—Inserted by SI 2014/407.

84.11 Application for sale otherwise than by public auction

(1) This rule applies to an application by an enforcement agent for an order for sale otherwise than by public auction under paragraph 41(2) of Schedule 12 ('alternative sale application').

(2) Where the enforcement agent has made a statement to the court under paragraph 41(4) of Schedule 12 (reason to believe that an enforcement power has become exercisable by another creditor against the debtor or co-owner), the alternative sale application must be accompanied by –

   (a) a list of the name and address of every other creditor that the enforcement agent has reason to believe has an exercisable enforcement power against the debtor or co-owner and a explanation of why the enforcement agent has such a belief; and
   (b) a copy of the notice of application required by paragraph 41(5) of Schedule 12 and proof that the notice has been served on such other creditors not less than 4 days before the day fixed for the hearing of the application.

(3) Every person to whom notice of the application was given may attend and be heard on the hearing of the application.

Amendments—Inserted by SI 2014/407.

84.12 Application in relation to disposal of abandoned goods

(1) This rule applies to an application by the enforcement agent under regulation 47(5) of the TCG Regulations for an order for the disposal of goods abandoned by the debtor.

(2) If the enforcement agent applies for an order for disposal by way of donation to a charitable organisation or destruction of goods, the enforcement agent must explain in the application why the enforcement agent does not wish the goods to be made available for a further period of collection.

Amendments—Inserted by SI 2014/407.

84.13 Application by the debtor for a remedy in relation to goods taken into control

(1) This rule applies where the debtor wishes to bring proceedings under paragraph 66 of Schedule 12 for –

   (a) breach of a provision of Schedule 12; or
   (b) enforcement action taken under a defective instrument.

(2) The debtor may bring proceedings by way of an application.

(3) The application must be accompanied by evidence of how –

   (a) the provisions of Schedule 12 are alleged to have been breached; or
   (b) the instrument is alleged to be defective.

Amendments—Inserted by SI 2014/407.

84.14 Application by the enforcement agent for exceptional disbursements

(1) This rule applies to an application by an enforcement agent for exceptional disbursements under regulation 10 of the Fees Regulations.

(2) The application must be accompanied by –

   (a) evidence of the creditor's consent to the application; and
   (b) evidence that the disbursements to which the application relate are necessary for effective enforcement of the sum to be recovered, having regard to all the circumstances including –
      (i) the amount of the sum to be recovered; and
      (ii) the nature and value of the goods which have been taken into control, or which it is sought to take into control.

(3) Where the application is made before the goods are taken into control, it may be made without notice.

Amendments—Inserted by SI 2014/407.

84.15 Application where there is a dispute regarding a co-owner's share of proceeds

(1) This rule applies to an application under regulation 15 of the Fees Regulations to determine the amount of the proceeds payable to a co-owner.

(2) The applicant must file with the application –

    (a) evidence of the enforcement power;
    (b) a copy of the itemised list of goods sold or otherwise disposed of required by regulation 14(1)(a) of the Fees Regulations;
    (c) a copy of the statement of the sum received in relation to each item required by regulation 14(1)(b)(i) of the Fees Regulations;
    (d) a copy of the statement of the proceeds required by regulation 14(1)(b)(ii) of the Fees Regulations;
    (e) a copy of the statement of the application of the proceeds required by regulation 14(1)(b)(iii) of the Fees Regulations;
    (f) evidence that the share of proceeds paid to the co-owner was not proportionate to the co-owner's interest in the goods sold.

(3) The applicant must serve a copy of the application notice in accordance with table 1.

Table 1

Applicant	Those to be served with a copy of the application notice
Co-owner	Any other co-owners; creditor; debtor; enforcement agent
Creditor	Co-owners; debtor; enforcement agent
Debtor	Co-owners; creditor; enforcement agent
Enforcement agent	Co-owners; creditor; debtor

Amendments—Inserted by SI 2014/407.

84.16 Disputes about the amount of fees or disbursements recoverable under the Fees Regulations

(1) This rule applies where –

    (a) there is a dispute about the amount of fees or disbursements, other than exceptional disbursements, recoverable under the Fees Regulations; and
    (b) a party wishes the court to assess the amounts recoverable under regulation 16 of the Fees Regulations.

(2) A party may make an application to the court to assess the amounts.

(3) The application must be accompanied by –

    (a) evidence of the amount of fees or disbursements in dispute;
    (b) evidence that the fees or disbursements in dispute were not applicable, as the debt had been settled before the stage where it would have been necessary to incur those fees or expenses;
    (c) evidence that, because the enforcement agent was instructed to use the TCG procedure in relation to the same debtor but in respect of more than one enforcement power where the enforcement powers could reasonably be exercised at the same time, regulation 11 of the Fees Regulations should have been applied;

(d) evidence that the fee due and any disbursements for the enforcement stage, first enforcement stage, or first and second enforcement stage, as appropriate, are not recoverable under regulation 12 of the Fees Regulations; or
(e) where the dispute concerns the amount of the percentage fee, calculated in accordance with regulation 7 of the Fees Regulations, evidence of the amount of the sum to be recovered.

Amendments—Inserted by SI 2014/407.

Section IV – Proceedings in relation to certificates under section 64 of the 2007 Act Interpretation

84.17 In this Section –
(a) 'Certification Regulations' means the Certification of Enforcement Agents Regulations 2014;
(b) 'applicant', 'certificate', 'certificated person' and 'complainant' have the meanings given in regulation 2 of the Certification Regulations.

Amendments—Inserted by SI 2014/482, subject to transitional provisions.

84.18 Application for issue of a certificate under section 64 of the 2007 Act

(1) This rule applies to an application for the issue of a certificate under section 64 of the 2007 Act.

(2) The application must be made to the County Court Business Centre, using the relevant form prescribed in Practice Direction 4.

(3) The application must specify one of the County Court hearing centres listed in Practice Direction 84 as the centre at which the application is to be heard.

(4) The application must, in addition to the matters specified in rule 23.6, provide evidence that the applicant fulfils the requirements of regulation 3(b) of the Certification Regulations, and in particular –

(a) the application must be accompanied by the documents specified in Practice Direction 84; and
(b) the additional documents specified in Practice Direction 84 must be produced to the court on the day of the hearing.

(5) If any reasons have been submitted to the court in response to the notice of the application required by regulation 4(5) of the Certification Regulations, a copy of those reasons must be sent to the applicant at least 7 days before the hearing, and the applicant may respond both in writing and at the hearing.

(6) The applicant must also file such further evidence as the court may direct.

(7) The applicant must attend for examination on the day of the hearing.

(8) Rules 23.2, 23.4, 23.7, 23.8, 23.9 and 23.10 do not apply to an application to which this rule applies.

Amendments—Inserted by SI 2014/482, subject to transitional provisions.

84.19 Issue of replacement certificates and surrender of certificates

(1) Where changes are required to be notified and the certificate produced under regulation 8 of the Certification Regulations, the changes must be notified to, and the certificate produced at, the County Court hearing centre at which the certificate was issued.

(2) Where a certificate is required to be surrendered under regulation 12 of the Certification Regulations, the certificate must be surrendered to the County Court hearing centre at which the certificate was issued.

Amendments—Inserted by SI 2014/, subject to transitional provisions.

84.20 Complaints as to fitness to hold a certificate

(1) This rule applies to a complaint under regulation 9(1) of the Certification Regulations.

(2) The complaint must be submitted to the County Court hearing centre at which the certificate was issued, using the relevant form prescribed in Practice Direction 4.

(3) A copy of the complaint must be sent to the applicant at least 14 days before the hearing, and the applicant may respond both in writing and at the hearing.

(4) The complainant is not liable for any costs incurred by the certificated person in responding to the complaint, unless paragraph (5) applies.

(5) The court may order the complainant to pay such costs as it considers reasonable if it is satisfied that the complaint –

(a) discloses no reasonable grounds for considering that the certificated person is not a fit person to hold a certificate; and
(b) amounts to an abuse of the court's process.

Amendments—Inserted by SI 2014/482, subject to transitional provisions.
****

PART 85
CLAIMS ON CONTROLLED GOODS AND EXECUTED GOODS

Section I – Scope and Interpretation

85.1 Scope

(1) This Part contains rules about claims on controlled goods and executed goods as follows –

(a) Section II sets out the mode of application for claims under this Part;
(b) Section III relates to the procedure for making claims to controlled goods;
(c) Section IV relates to the procedure for making claims against executed goods;
(d) Section V relates to the procedure for a debtor making a claim to exempt goods;
(e) Section VI relates to the powers of the court hearing any application under this Part.

(2) The rules in this Part apply where –

(a) a person makes an application to the court claiming that goods of which control has been taken belong to that person and not to the debtor;
(b) a person makes an application to the court claiming that goods, money or chattels taken or intended to be taken under a writ of execution or the proceeds or value of such goods or chattels belong to that person and not to the debtor; and
(c) a debtor, whose goods have been made subject to an enforcement power under an enactment, writ or warrant of control or have been taken or are intended to be taken under a writ of execution, claims that such goods or any of them are exempt goods.

Amendments—Inserted by SI 2014/407.

Note—See note to r 184 of the Court of Protection Rules reproduced in Part IV of this work.

85.2 Interpretation

(1) In this Part –
  (a) 'the Act' means the Tribunals, Courts and Enforcement Act 2007;
  (b) 'claim to controlled goods' is a claim made under paragraph 60(1) of Schedule 12;
  (c) 'a claim to exempt goods' means a claim by a debtor whose goods have been subject to an enforcement power under an enactment, writ or warrant of control or the right to execute conferred by a writ of execution, that such goods are exempt goods;
  (d) 'claimant to controlled goods' means any person making a claim to controlled goods;
  (e) 'claimant to executed goods' means any person making a claim to executed goods;
  (f) 'the court' has the meaning given in paragraph 60(8) of Schedule 12, in respect of a claim to controlled goods;
  (g) 'debtor's home court' means the Central Office or District Registry of the High Court or the County Court hearing centre serving the address where the debtor resides or carries on business;
  (h) 'enforcement agent' has the meaning given in paragraph 2(1) of Schedule 12;
  (i) 'enforcement officer' means an individual who is authorised to act as an enforcement officer under the Courts Act 2003;
  (j) 'executed goods' means goods subject to a writ of execution;
  (k) 'exempt goods' –
    (i) in respect of controlled goods has the meaning given in paragraph 3(1) of Schedule 12 and defined in regulations 4 and 5 of the TCG Regulations; and
    (ii) in respect of executed goods has the meaning given in paragraph 9(3) of Schedule 7 to the Courts Act 2003;
  (l) 'goods subject to enforcement' refers to either controlled goods or executed goods;
  (m) 'relevant enforcement officer' means –
    (i) in relation to a writ of execution which is directed to a single enforcement officer, that officer; and
    (ii) in relation to a writ of execution which is directed to two or more enforcement officers, the officer to whom the writ is allocated;
  (n) 'required payments' has the meaning given in paragraph 60(4) of Schedule 12;

(o) 'Schedule 12' means Schedule 12 to the Act;
(p) 'TCG Regulations' means the Taking Control of Goods Regulations 2013;
(q) 'warrant of control' is to be construed in accordance with section 62(4) of the Act;
(r) 'writ of control' is to be construed in accordance with section 62(4) of the Act;
(s) 'writ of execution' includes –
  (i) a writ of possession;
  (ii) a writ of delivery;
  (iii) a writ of sequestration;
  (iv) writs relating to ecclesiastical property, namely –
    (aa) a writ of fieri facias de bonis ecclesiasticis;
    (bb) a writ of sequestrari de bonis ecclesiasticis,
  and any further writ in aid of any such writs, but does not include a writ of control;
(t) the following words or phrases have the meaning given in paragraph 1 of Schedule 12, in respect of a claim to controlled goods –
  (i) 'creditor';
  (ii) 'debt';
  (iii) 'debtor';
  (iv) 'enforcement power';
(u) the following words or phrases have the meaning given in paragraph 3(1) of Schedule 12 –
  (i) 'control';
  (ii) 'controlled goods';
  (iii) 'co-owner';
  (iv) 'disposal';
  (v) 'interest';
  (vi) 'money';
  (vi) 'premises';
  (vii) 'securities'.

Amendments—Inserted by SI 2014/407.

Section II – Mode of Application for Claims under this Part

85.3 Mode of application for claims under this Part

Any claim under this Part must be made by an application in accordance with Part 23.

Amendments—Inserted by SI 2014/407.

Section III – Procedure for making a claim to controlled goods

85.4 Procedure for making a claim to controlled goods

(1) Any person making a claim under paragraph 60(1) of Schedule 12 must, as soon as practicable but in any event within 7 days of the goods being removed under the exercise of an enforcement power, give notice in writing of their claim to the enforcement agent who has taken control of the goods ('the notice of claim to controlled goods') and must include in such notice –

(a) their full name and address, and confirmation that such address is their address for service;
(b) a list of all those goods in respect of which they make such a claim; and
(c) the grounds of their claim in respect of each item.

(2) On receipt of a notice of claim to controlled goods which complies with paragraph (1) the enforcement agent must within 3 days give notice of such claim to –

(a) the creditor; and
(b) any other person making a claim to the controlled goods under paragraph (1) ('any other claimant to the controlled goods');

(3) The creditor, and any other claimant to the controlled goods, must, within 7 days after receiving the notice of claim to controlled goods, give notice in writing to the enforcement agent informing them whether the claim to controlled goods is admitted or disputed in whole or in part.

(4) The enforcement agent must notify the claimant to the controlled goods in writing within 3 days of receiving the notice in paragraph (3) whether the claim to controlled goods is admitted or disputed in whole or in part.

(5) A creditor who gives notice in accordance with paragraph (3) admitting a claim to controlled goods is not liable to the enforcement agent for any fees and expenses incurred by the enforcement agent after receipt of that notice by the enforcement agent.

(6) If an enforcement agent receives a notice from a creditor under paragraph (3) admitting a claim to controlled goods the following applies –

(a) the enforcement power ceases to be exercisable in respect of such controlled goods; and
(b) as soon as reasonably practicable the enforcement agent must make the goods available for collection by the claimant to controlled goods if they have been removed from where they were found.

(7) Where the creditor, or any other claimant to controlled goods to whom a notice of claim to controlled goods was given, fails, within the period mentioned in paragraph (3), to give the required notice, the enforcement agent may seek –

(a) the directions of the court by way of an application; and
(b) an order preventing the bringing of any claim against them for, or in respect of, their having taken control of any of the goods or having failed so to do.

Amendments—Inserted by SI 2014/407.

85.5 Procedure for making a claim to controlled goods where the claim is disputed

(1) Where a creditor, or any other claimant to controlled goods to whom a notice of claim to controlled goods was given, gives notice under rule 85.4(3) that the claim to controlled goods, or any part of it, is disputed, and wishes to maintain their claim to the controlled goods, the following procedure will apply.

(2) The claimant to controlled goods must make an application which must be supported by –

(a) a witness statement –

(i) specifying any money;
(ii) describing any goods claimed; and
(iii) setting out the grounds upon which their claim to the controlled goods is based; and
(b) copies of any supporting documents that will assist the court to determine the claim.

(3) In the High Court the claimant to controlled goods must serve the application notice and supporting witness statements and exhibits on –

(a) the creditor;
(b) any other claimant to controlled goods of whom the claimant to controlled goods is aware; and
(c) the enforcement agent.

(4) In the County Court when the application is made the claimant to controlled goods must provide to the court the addresses for service of –

(a) the creditor;
(b) any other claimant to controlled goods of whom the claimant to controlled goods is aware; and
(c) the enforcement agent,

('the respondents'), and the court will serve the application notice and any supporting witness statement and exhibits on the respondents.

(5) An application under paragraph (2) must be made to the court which issued the writ or warrant conferring power to take control of the controlled goods, or, if the power was conferred under an enactment, to the debtor's home court.

(6) The claimant to controlled goods must make the required payments on issue of the application in accordance with paragraph 60(4)(a) of Schedule 12, unless such claimant seeks a direction from the court that the required payment be a proportion of the value of the goods, in which case they must seek such a direction immediately after issue of the application, on notice to the creditor and to the enforcement agent.

(7) The application notice will be referred to a Master or District Judge.

(8) On receipt of an application for a claim to controlled goods, the Master or District Judge may –

(a) give directions for further evidence from any party;
(b) list a hearing to give directions;
(c) list a hearing of the application;
(d) determine the amount of the required payments, make directions or list a hearing to determine any issue relating to the amount of the required payments or the value of the controlled goods;
(e) stay, or dismiss, the application if the required payments have not been made;
(f) make directions for the retention, sale or disposal of the controlled goods;
(g) give directions for determination of any issue raised by a claim to controlled goods.

Amendments—Inserted by SI 2014/407.

Section IV – Procedure for making a Claim against Executed Goods

85.6 Procedure for making a claim against executed goods

(1) A claimant to executed goods must, as soon as practicable but in any event within 7 days of the goods being removed by the enforcement officer, give notice in writing of their claim to the relevant enforcement officer ('the notice of claim to executed goods') and must include in such notice –

(a) their full name and address, and confirmation that such address is their address for service;
(b) a list of all those goods in respect of which they make such a claim; and
(c) the grounds of their claim in respect of each item.

(2) On receipt of a notice of claim to executed goods which complies with paragraph (1) the enforcement officer must within 3 days give notice of such claim to –

(a) the creditor; and
(b) any other person making a claim to the executed goods under paragraph (1) ('any other claimant to the executed goods').

(3) The creditor, and any other claimant to executed goods, must, within 7 days after receiving the notice of claim to the executed goods, give notice in writing to the enforcement officer informing them whether the claim to the executed goods is admitted or disputed in whole or in part.

(4) The enforcement officer must notify the claimant to executed goods in writing within 3 days of receiving the notice in paragraph (3) whether the claim to executed goods is admitted or disputed in whole or in part.

(5) A creditor who gives notice in accordance with paragraph (3) admitting a claim to executed goods is not liable to the enforcement officer for any fees and expenses incurred by the enforcement officer after receipt of that notice by the enforcement officer.

(6) If an enforcement officer receives a notice from a creditor under paragraph (3) admitting a claim to executed goods the following applies –

(a) the writ of execution ceases to be exercisable in respect of such executed goods; and
(b) as soon as reasonably practicable the enforcement officer must make the goods available for collection by the claimant to executed goods if the enforcement officer has removed the goods from where they were found.

(7) Where the creditor, or any other claimant to executed goods to whom a notice of claim to executed goods was given, fails, within the period mentioned in paragraph (3), to give the required notice, the enforcement officer may seek –

(a) the directions of the court by way of an application; and
(b) an order preventing the bringing of any claim against them for, or in respect of, the seizure of the executed goods or their having failed so to do.

(8) An application under paragraph (7) must be made to the court which issued the writ of execution.

Amendments—Inserted by SI 2014/407.

85.7 Procedure for making a claim to executed goods where the claim is disputed

(1) Where a creditor, or any other claimant to executed goods to whom a notice of claim to executed goods was given, gives notice under rule 85.6(3) that the claim to executed goods, or any part of it, is disputed, and wishes to maintain their claim, the following procedure will apply.

(2) The claimant to executed goods must make an application by application notice which must be supported by –

(a) a witness statement –
  (i) specifying any money;
  (ii) describing any goods claimed; and
  (iii) setting out the grounds upon which the claim to the executed goods is based; and
(b) copies of any supporting documents that will assist the court to determine the claim.

(3) The claimant to executed goods must serve the application notice and supporting witness statements and exhibits on –

(a) the creditor;
(b) any other claimant to the executed goods of whom they are aware; and
(c) the relevant enforcement officer.

(4) An application under paragraph (2) must be made to the court which issued the writ of execution.

(5) The application notice will be referred to a Master or District Judge of a District Registry.

(6) On receipt of an application for a claim to executed goods, the Master or District Judge may –

(a) give directions for further evidence from any party;
(b) list a hearing to give directions;
(c) list a hearing of the application;
(d) make directions for the retention, sale or disposal of the executed goods; and
(e) give directions for determination of any issue raised by a claim to executed goods.

  (Rule 83.3(11) provides that the validity of a writ of execution is automatically extended following an application under paragraph (2) until 12 months from the conclusion of the application proceedings.)

Amendments—Inserted by SI 2014/407.

Section V – Procedure for a Debtor making a Claim to Exempt Goods

85.8 Procedure for a debtor making a claim to exempt goods

(1) A debtor making a claim to exempt goods must, as soon as practicable and in any event within 7 days of the removal of the goods, give notice in writing of the claim to exempt goods ('notice of claim to exempt goods') to the enforcement agent who has taken control of the goods or relevant enforcement officer and must include in such notice –

(a) their full name and address and that address is their address for service;

(b) a list of all those goods in respect of which they make such a claim; and
(c) the grounds of the claim in respect of each item.

(2) On receipt of a notice of claim to exempt goods, the enforcement agent or relevant enforcement officer must within 3 days give notice of such claim to –

(a) the creditor; and
(b) any other person making a claim under rule 85.4 or 85.6 to the goods subject to enforcement ('any other claimant to the goods subject to enforcement').

(3) The creditor, and any other claimant to the goods subject to enforcement, must, within 7 days after receiving the notice of claim to exempt goods, give notice in writing to the enforcement agent or relevant enforcement officer informing them whether the claim to exempt goods is admitted or disputed in whole or in part.

(4) The enforcement agent or relevant enforcement officer must notify the debtor in writing within 3 days of receiving the notice in paragraph (3) whether the claim to exempt goods is admitted or disputed in whole or in part.

(5) A creditor who gives notice in accordance with paragraph (3) admitting a claim to controlled goods or to executed goods is not liable to the enforcement agent or officer for any fees and expenses incurred by the enforcement agent or officer after receipt of that notice by the enforcement agent or officer.

(6) If an enforcement agent or relevant enforcement officer receives a notice from a creditor and from any other claimant to the goods subject to enforcement under paragraph (3) admitting a claim to exempt goods the following applies –

(a) the enforcement power ceases to be exercisable, and the right to execute conferred by any writ of execution ceases to have effect, in respect of such exempt goods;
(b) as soon as reasonably practicable the enforcement agent or relevant enforcement officer must make the goods available for collection by the debtor if the enforcement agent or officer has removed them from where they were found.

(7) Where the creditor, or any other claimant to the goods subject to enforcement to whom notice of claim to exempt goods was given, fails, within the period mentioned in paragraph (3), to give the required notice, the enforcement agent or relevant enforcement officer may seek –

(a) the directions of the court by way of an application; and
(b) an order preventing the bringing of any claim against them for, or in respect of, their having taken control of or seized by execution any of the goods or their having failed to do so.

(8) An application under paragraph (7) must be made to the court which issued the writ or warrant conferring power to take control of controlled goods, or the writ of execution or, if the power to take control of controlled goods was conferred under an enactment, to the County Court hearing centre which is the debtor's home court.

Amendments—Inserted by SI 2014/407.

85.9 Procedure for making a claim to exempt goods where the claim is disputed

(1) Where a creditor, or any other claimant to goods subject to enforcement to whom notice of a claim to exempt goods was given, gives notice under rule 85.8 that

the claim to exempt goods, or any part of it, is disputed, and wishes to maintain their claim on the goods subject to enforcement, the following procedure will apply.

(2) The debtor must make an application within 7 days of receiving the notice under rule 85.8(3) which must be supported by –

   (a)   a witness statement –
        (i)   describing any goods to which a claim to exempt goods is made; and
        (ii)   setting out the grounds upon which such claim is based; and
   (b)   copies of any supporting documents that will assist the court to determine such claim.

(3) In the High Court the debtor must serve the application notice and supporting witness statements and exhibits on –

   (a)   the creditor;
   (b)   any other claimant to the goods subject to enforcement of whom they are aware; and
   (c)   the enforcement agent or relevant enforcement officer.

(4) In the County Court the debtor must provide to the court when the application is made the addresses for service of –

   (a)   the creditor;
   (b)   any other claimant to controlled goods of whom the debtor is aware; and
   (c)   the enforcement agent,

       ('the respondents'), and the court will serve the application notice and supporting witness statements and exhibits on the respondents.

(5) An application under paragraph (2) must be made to the court which issued the writ or warrant conferring power to take control of controlled goods or the writ of execution or if the power to take control of controlled goods was conferred under an enactment, to the debtor's home court.

(6) The application notice will be referred to a Master or District Judge.

(7) On receipt of an application for a claim to exempt goods, the Master or District Judge may –

   (a)   give directions for further evidence;
   (b)   list a hearing to give directions;
   (c)   list a hearing of the application;
   (d)   make directions for the retention, sale or disposal of the goods subject to the claim to exempt goods;
   (e)   give directions for determination of any issue raised by the exempt goods claim.

Amendments—Inserted by SI 2014/407.

Section VI – Powers of the Court hearing any application under this Part

85.10 Directions and determination of claims

(1) At any hearing of any application under this Part the court may –

   (a)   determine an application summarily; or
   (b)   give directions for the determination of any issue raised by such application;

(c) order that any issue between any parties to a claim to goods subject to enforcement be stated and tried, and give all necessary directions for trial;
(d) give directions for the purpose of determining the amount of the required payments or any underpayment of the required payments pursuant to paragraph 60(5) of Schedule 12 and regulation 49 of the TCG Regulations;
(e) summarily determine the amount of the required payments or any underpayment of the required payments pursuant to paragraph 60(5) of Schedule 12 and regulation 49 of the TCG Regulations;
(f) make directions for the retention, sale or disposal of goods subject to enforcement and for the payment of any proceeds of sale; or
(g) make any order that the court considers appropriate.

(2) Where a claimant to goods subject to enforcement or a debtor making a claim to exempt goods does not appear at any hearing listed on the application or, having appeared, fails or refuses to comply with an order made in the proceedings, the court may make an order declaring such claimant, or the debtor, and all persons claiming under them, for ever barred from prosecuting their claim against the creditor or any other claimant to the goods subject to enforcement, but such an order will not affect the rights of any other claimants to the goods subject to enforcement as between themselves.

(3) Where a claimant to goods subject to enforcement alleges that they are entitled, under a bill of sale or otherwise, to the controlled goods or to the executed goods by way of security for debt, the court may order those goods or any part thereof to be sold and may direct that the proceeds of sale be applied in such manner and on such terms as may be just and as may be specified in the order.

(4) Nothing in this rule limits the court's case management powers to make any other directions permissible under these Rules.

Amendments—Inserted by SI 2014/407.

85.11 Trial of issue

(1) Part 39 will, with the necessary modifications, apply to the trial of an issue in an application under this Part as it applies to the trial of a claim.

(2) The court by which an issue is tried may give such judgment or make such order as finally to dispose of all questions arising in the application.

(3) Practice Direction 2B applies to the trial of an issue in an application under this Part.

Amendments—Inserted by SI 2014/407.

85.12 Costs

(1) The court may in or for the purposes of any application under this Part make such order as to costs as it thinks just.

(2) Where a claimant to goods subject to enforcement or a debtor in a claim to exempt goods fails to appear at a hearing, the court may direct that the enforcement agent's or officer's costs and creditor's costs will be assessed by a Master, District Judge, Costs judge or Costs officer.

(3) In a claim to controlled goods a debtor may request the court to assess the costs incurred by an enforcement agent, in which case the court will apply the Taking Control of Goods (Fees) Regulations 2014 to such assessment.

(4) In a claim to executed goods a debtor may request the court to assess the costs incurred by an enforcement officer, in which case the court will apply Schedule 3 of the High Court Enforcement Officers Regulations 2004 to such assessment, save in relation to the costs of execution of writs of sequestration and writs relating to ecclesiastical property.

Amendments—Inserted by SI 2014/407.

****

Mental Capacity Act 2005 (Independent Mental Capacity Advocates) (General) Regulations 2006, SI 2006/1832

1 Citation, commencement and extent

(1) These Regulations may be cited as the Mental Capacity Act 2005 (Independent Mental Capacity Advocates) (General) Regulations 2006.

(2) These Regulations shall come into force –

    (a) for the purpose of enabling the Secretary of State to make arrangements under section 35 of the Act, and for the purpose of enabling local authorities to approve IMCAs, on 1 November 2006, and

    (b) for all other purposes, on 1 April 2007.

(3) These Regulations apply in relation to England only.

2 Interpretation

(1) In these Regulations –

    'the Act' means the Mental Capacity Act 2005; and
    'IMCA' means an independent mental capacity advocate.

(2) In these Regulations, references to instructions given to a person to act as an IMCA are to instructions given under sections 37 to 39 of the Act or under regulations made by virtue of section 41 of the Act.

3 Meaning of NHS Body

(1) For the purposes of sections 37 and 38 of the Act, 'NHS body' means a body in England which is –

    (a) … ;
    (b) an NHS foundation trust;
    (ba) a clinical commissioning group
    (bb) the National Health Service Commissioning Board

(bc) a local authority (within the meaning of section 2B of the National Health Service Act 2006) acting in the exercise of public health functions (within the meaning of that Act)
(c) … ;
(d) an NHS Trust; or
(e) a Care Trust.

(2) In this regulation –

'Care Trust' means a body designated as a Care Trust under section 45 of the Health and Social Care Act 2001;
'clinical commissioning group' means a body established under section 14D of the National Health Service Act 2006;
'NHS foundation trust' has the meaning given in section 1 of the Health and Social Care (Community Health and Standards) Act 2003;
'NHS trust' means a body established under section 5 of the National Health Service and Community Care Act 1990;

Amendments—SI 2013/235.

4 Meaning of serious medical treatment

(1) This regulation defines serious medical treatment for the purposes of section 37 of the Act.

(2) Serious medical treatment is treatment which involves providing, withdrawing or withholding treatment in circumstances where –

(a) in a case where a single treatment is being proposed, there is a fine balance between its benefits to the patient and the burdens and risks it is likely to entail for him,
(b) in a case where there is a choice of treatments, a decision as to which one to use is finely balanced, or
(c) what is proposed would be likely to involve serious consequences for the patient.

5 Appointment of independent mental capacity advocates

(1) No person may be appointed to act as an IMCA for the purposes of sections 37 to 39 of the Act, or regulations made by virtue of section 41 of the Act, unless –

(a) he is for the time being approved by a local authority on the grounds that he satisfies the appointment requirements, or
(b) he belongs to a class of persons which is for the time being approved by a local authority on the grounds that all persons in that class satisfy the appointment requirements.

(2) The appointment requirements, in relation to a person appointed to act as an IMCA, are that –

(a) he has appropriate experience or training or an appropriate combination of experience and training;
(b) he is a person of integrity and good character; and
(c) he is able to act independently of any person who instructs him.

(3) Before a determination is made in relation to any person for the purposes of paragraph (2)(b), there must be obtained, in respect of that person, an enhanced criminal record certificate issued pursuant to section 113B of the Police Act 1997 which includes –

(a) where the determination is in respect of a person's appointment as an IMCA for a person who has not attained the age of 18, suitability information relating to children (within the meaning of section 113BA of the Police Act 1997);
(b) where the determination is in respect of a person's appointment as an IMCA for a person who has attained the age of 18, suitability information relating to vulnerable adults (within the meaning of section 113BB of that Act).]

Amendments—SI 2009/2376.

6 Functions of an independent mental capacity advocate

(1) This regulation applies where an IMCA has been instructed by an authorised person to represent a person ('P').

(2) 'Authorised person' means a person who is required or enabled to instruct an IMCA under sections 37 to 39 of the Act or under regulations made by virtue of section 41of the Act.

(3) The IMCA must determine in all the circumstances how best to represent and support P.

(4) In particular, the IMCA must –
 (a) verify that the instructions were issued by an authorised person;
 (b) to the extent that it is practicable and appropriate to do so –
  (i) interview P, and
  (ii) examine the records relevant to P to which the IMCA has access under section 35(6) of the Act;
 (c) to the extent that it is practicable and appropriate to do so, consult –
  (i) persons engaged in providing care or treatment for P in a professional capacity or for remuneration, and
  (ii) other persons who may be in a position to comment on P's wishes, feelings, beliefs or values; and
 (d) take all practicable steps to obtain such other information about P, or the act or decision that is proposed in relation to P, as the IMCA considers necessary.

(5) The IMCA must evaluate all the information he has obtained for the purpose of –
 (a) ascertaining the extent of the support provided to P to enable him to participate in making any decision about the matter in relation to which the IMCA has been instructed;
 (b) ascertaining what P's wishes and feelings would be likely to be, and the beliefs and values that would be likely to influence P, if he had capacity in relation to the proposed act or decision;
 (c) ascertaining what alternative courses of action are available in relation to P;
 (d) where medical treatment is proposed for P, ascertaining whether he would be likely to benefit from a further medical opinion.

(6) The IMCA must prepare a report for the authorised person who instructed him.

(7) The IMCA may include in the report such submissions as he considers appropriate in relation to P and the act or decision which is proposed in relation to him.

7 Challenges to decisions affecting persons who lack capacity

(1) This regulation applies where –
> (a) an IMCA has been instructed to represent a person ('P') in relation to any matter, and
> (b) a decision affecting P (including a decision as to his capacity) is made in that matter.

(2) The IMCA has the same rights to challenge the decision as he would have if he were a person (other than an IMCA) engaged in caring for P or interested in his welfare.

Court of Protection Fees Order 2007, SI 2007/1745

1 Citation and commencement

This Order may be cited as the Court of Protection Fees Order 2007 and comes into force on 1 October 2007.

2 Interpretation

In this Order –
> 'the Act' means the Mental Capacity Act 2005;
> 'appellant' means the person who brings or seeks to bring an appeal;
> 'court' means the Court of Protection;
> 'P' means any person (other than a protected party) who lacks or, so far as consistent with the context, is alleged to lack capacity to make a decision or decisions in relation to any matter that is the subject of an application to the court and references to a person who lacks capacity are to be construed in accordance with the Act;
> 'protected party' means a party or an intended party (other than P or a child) who lacks capacity to conduct the proceedings;
> 'the Regulations' means the Lasting Powers of Attorney, Enduring Powers of Attorney and Public Guardian Regulations 2007; and
> 'the Rules' means the Court of Protection Rules 2007.

3 Schedule of fees

The fees set out in the Schedule 1 to this Order shall apply in accordance with the following provisions of this Order.

Amendments—SI 2013/2302.

4 Application fee

(1) An application fee shall be payable by the applicant on making an application under Part 9 of the Rules (how to start proceedings) in accordance with the following provisions of this article.

(2) Where permission to start proceedings is required under Part 8 of the Rules (permission), the fee prescribed by paragraph (1) shall be payable on making an application for permission.

(3) The fee prescribed by paragraph (1) shall not be payable where the application is made under –

- (a) rule 67 of the Rules (applications relating to lasting powers of attorney) by –
  - (i) the donee of a lasting power of attorney, or
  - (ii) a person named in a statement made by the donor of a lasting power of attorney in accordance with paragraph 2(1)(c)(i) of Part 1 of Schedule 1 to the Act,

and is solely in respect of an objection to the registration of a lasting power of attorney; or

- (b) rule 68 of the Rules (applications relating to enduring powers of attorney) by –
  - (i) a donor of an enduring power of attorney,
  - (ii) an attorney under an enduring power of attorney, or
  - (iii) a person listed in paragraph 6(1) of Part 3 of Schedule 4 to the Act, and is solely in respect of an objection to the registration of an enduring power of attorney.

(4) The fee prescribed by paragraph (1) shall not be payable where the application is made by the Public Guardian.

(5) Where a fee has been paid under paragraph (1) it shall be refunded where P dies within five days of the application being filed.

5 Appeal fee

(1) An appeal fee shall be payable by the appellant on the filing of an appellant's notice under Part 20 of the Rules (appeals) in accordance with the following provisions of this article.

(2) The fee prescribed by paragraph (1) shall not be payable where the appeal is –

- (a) brought by the Public Guardian; or
- (b) an appeal against a decision of a nominated officer made under rule 197 of the Rules (appeal against a decision of a nominated officer).

(3) The fee prescribed by paragraph (1) shall be refunded where P dies within five days of the appellant's notice being filed.

6 Hearing fees

(1) A hearing fee shall be payable by the applicant where the court has –

- (a) held a hearing in order to determine the case; and
- (b) made a final order, declaration or decision.

(2) A hearing fee shall be payable by the appellant in relation to an appeal where the court has –

(a) held a hearing in order to determine the appeal; and
(b) made a final order, declaration or decision in relation to the appeal.

(3) The fees prescribed by paragraphs (1) and (2) shall not be payable where the hearing is in respect of an application or appeal brought by the Public Guardian.

(4) The fee prescribed by paragraph (2) shall not be payable where the hearing is in respect of an appeal against a decision of a nominated officer made under rule 197 of the Rules (appeal against a decision of a nominated officer).

(5) The fee prescribed by paragraph (1) shall not be payable where the applicant was not required to pay an application fee under Article 4(1) by virtue of Article 4(3).

(6) The fees prescribed by paragraphs (1) and (2) shall be payable by the applicant or appellant as the case may be within 30 days of the date of the invoice for the fee.

7 Fee for request for copy of court document

(1) A fee for a copy of a court document shall be payable by the person requesting the copy of the document.

(2) *(revoked)*

(3) The fees prescribed by paragraph (1) shall be payable at the time the request for the copy is made to the court.

Amendments—SI 2009/513.

8 Remissions and part remissions

Schedule 2 applies for the purpose of ascertaining whether a party is entitled to a remission or part remission of a fee prescribed by this Order.

Amendments—Substituted by SI 2013/2302.

9 *(revoked)*

10 Transitional provision

(1) In this article 'Court of Protection' means the office of the Supreme Court called the Court of Protection which ceases to exist under section 45(6) of the Act.

(2) Where a hearing that takes place on or after 1 October 2007 was listed by the Court of Protection before 1 October 2007, no hearing fee shall be payable under Article 6.

SCHEDULE 1
FEES TO BE TAKEN

Column 1	Column 2
Application fee (Article 4)	£400.00
Appeal fee (Article 5)	£400.00
Hearing fees (Article 6)	£500.00
Copy of a document fee (Article 7(1))	£5.00

Amendments—SI 2009/513; SI 2013/2302.

SCHEDULE 2
REMISSIONS AND PART REMISSIONS

1 Interpretation

(1) In this Schedule –

'child' means a person –
   (a) whose main residence is with a party and who is aged –
      (i) under 16 years; or
      (ii) 16 to 19 years; and is –
         (aa) not married or in a civil partnership; and
         (bb) enrolled or accepted in full-time education that is not advanced education, or approved training; or
   (b) in respect of whom a party or their partner pays child support maintenance or periodic payments in accordance with a maintenance agreement,
and 'full-time education', 'advanced education' and 'approved training' have the meaning given by the Child Benefit (General) Regulations 2006;
'child support maintenance' has the meaning given in section 3(6) of the Child Support Act 1991;
'couple' has the meaning given in section 3(5A) of the Tax Credits Act 2002;
'disposable capital' has the meaning given in paragraph 5;
'excluded benefits' means any of the following –
   (a) any of the following benefits payable under the Social Security Contributions and Benefits Act 1992 or the corresponding provisions of the Social Security Contributions and Benefits (Northern Ireland) Act 1992 –
      (i) attendance allowance under section 64;
      (ii) severe disablement allowance;
      (iii) carer's allowance;
      (iv) disability living allowance;
      (v) constant attendance allowance under section 104 as an increase to a disablement pension;
      (vi) any payment made out of the social fund;
      (vii) housing benefit;
      (viii) widowed parents allowance;

(b) any of the following benefit payable under the Tax Credits Act 2002 –
  (i) any disabled child element or severely disabled child element of the child tax credit;
  (ii) any childcare element of the working tax credit;
(c) any direct payment made under the Community Care, Services for Carers and Children's Services (Direct Payments) (England) Regulations 2009, the Community Care, Services for Carers and Children's Services (Direct Payments) (Wales) Regulations 2011, the Carers and Direct Payments Act (Northern Ireland) 2002, or section 12B(1) of the Social Work (Scotland) Act 1968;
(d) a back to work bonus payable under section 26 of the Jobseekers Act 1995, or article 28 of the Jobseekers (Northern Ireland) Order 1995;
(e) any exceptionally severe disablement allowance paid under the Personal Injuries (Civilians) Scheme 1983;
(f) any payments from the Industrial Injuries Disablement Benefit;
(g) any pension paid under the Naval, Military and Air Forces etc. (Disablement and Death) Service Pension Order 2006;
(h) any payment made from the Independent Living Funds;
(i) any payment made from the Bereavement Allowance;
(j) any financial support paid under an agreement for the care of a foster child;
(k) any housing credit element of pension credit;
(l) any armed forces independence payment;
(m) any personal independence payment payable under the Welfare Reform Act 2012;
(n) any payment on account of benefit as defined in the Social Security (Payments on Account of Benefit) Regulations 2013;
(o) any of the following amounts, as defined by the Universal Credit Regulations 2013, that make up an award of universal credit –
  (i) an additional amount to the child element in respect of a disabled child;
  (ii) a housing costs element;
  (iii) a childcare costs element;
  (iv) a carer element;
  (v) a limited capability for work or limited capacity for work and work-related activity element.

'family help (higher)' has the meaning given in paragraph 15(3) of the Civil Legal Aid (Merits Criteria) Regulations 2013;

'family help (lower)' has the meaning given in paragraph 15(2) of the Civil Legal Aid (Merits Criteria) Regulations 2013;

'gross monthly income' has the meaning given in paragraph 13;

'Independent Living Funds' means the funds listed at regulation 20(2)(b) of the Criminal Legal Aid (Financial Resources) Regulations 2013;

'legal representation' has the meaning given in paragraph 18(2) of the Civil Legal Aid (Merits Criteria) Regulations 2013;

'maintenance agreement' has the meaning given in subsection 9(1) of the Child Support Act 1991;

'partner' means a person with whom the party lives as a couple and includes a person with whom the party is not currently living but from whom the party is not living separate and apart;

'party' means the individual who would, but for this Schedule, be liable to pay a fee under this Order;

'restraint order' means –

(a) an order under section 42(1A) of the Senior Courts Act 1981;
(b) an order under section 33 of the Employment Tribunals Act 1996;
(c) a civil restraint order made under rule 3.11 of the Civil Procedure Rules 1998, or a practice direction made under that rule; or
(d) a civil restraint order under rule 4.8 of the Family Procedure Rules 2010, or the practice direction referred to in that rule.

(2) References to remission of a fee are to be read as including references to a part remission of a fee as appropriate and remit and remitted shall be construed accordingly.

2 Fee remission

If a party satisfies the disposable capital test, the amount of any fee remission is calculated by applying the gross monthly income test.

Disposable capital test

3 Disposable capital test

(1) Subject to paragraph 4, a party satisfies the disposable capital test if –
(a) the fee payable by the party and for which an application for remission is made, falls within a fee band set out in column 1 of Table 1; and
(b) the party's disposable capital is less than the amount in the corresponding row of column 2.

Table 1

Column 1 (fee band)	Column 2 (disposable capital)
Up to and including £1,000	£3,000
£1,001 to £1,335	£4,000
£1,336 to £1,665	£5,000
£1,666 to £2,000	£6,000
£2,001 to £2,330	£7,000
£2,331 to £4,000	£8,000
£4,001 to £5,000	£10,000
£5,001 to £6,000	£12,000
£6,001 to £7,000	£14,000
£7,001 or more	£16,000

4 Subject to paragraph 14, if a party or their partner is aged 61 or over, that party satisfies the disposable capital test if that party's disposable capital is less than £16,000.

5 Disposable capital

Subject to paragraph 14, disposable capital is the value of every resource of a capital nature belonging to the party on the date on which the application for remission is made, unless it is treated as income by this Order, or it is disregarded as excluded disposable capital.

6 Disposable capital – non-money resources

The value of a resource of a capital nature that does not consist of money is calculated as the amount which that resource would realise if sold, less –

(a) 10% of the sale value; and
(b) the amount of any borrowing secured against that resource that would be repayable on sale.

7 Disposable capital – resources held outside the United Kingdom

(1) Capital resources in a country outside the United Kingdom count towards disposable capital.

(2) If there is no prohibition in that country against the transfer of a resource into the United Kingdom, the value of that resource is the amount which that resource would realise if sold in that country, in accordance with paragraph 6.

(3) If there is a prohibition in that country against the transfer of a resource into the United Kingdom, the value of that resource is the amount that resource would realise if sold to a buyer in the United Kingdom.

8 Disposable capital – foreign currency resources

Where disposable capital is held in currency other than sterling, the cost of any banking charge or commission that would be payable if that amount were converted into sterling, is deducted from its value.

9 Disposable capital – jointly owned resources

Where any resource of a capital nature is owned jointly or in common, there is a presumption that the resource is owned in equal shares, unless evidence to the contrary is produced.

10 Excluded disposable capital

The following things are excluded disposable capital –

(a) a property which is the main or only dwelling occupied by the party;
(b) the household furniture and effects of the main or only dwelling occupied by the party;

(c) articles of personal clothing;
(d) any vehicle, the sale of which would leave the party, or their partner, without motor transport;
(e) tools and implements of trade, including vehicles used for business purposes;
(f) the capital value of the party's or their partner's business, where the party or their partner is self-employed;
(g) the capital value of any funds or other assets held in trust, where the party or their partner is a beneficiary without entitlement to advances of any trust capital;
(h) a jobseeker's back to work bonus;
(i) a payment made as a result of a determination of unfair dismissal by a court or tribunal, or by way of settlement of a claim for unfair dismissal;
(j) any compensation paid as a result of a determination of medical negligence or in respect of any personal injury by a court, or by way of settlement of a claim for medical negligence or personal injury;
(k) the capital held in any personal or occupational pension scheme;
(l) any cash value payable on surrender of a contract of insurance;
(m) any capital payment made out of the Independent Living Funds;
(n) any bereavement payment;
(o) any capital insurance or endowment lump sum payments that have been paid as a result of illness, disability or death;
(p) any student loan or student grant;
(q) any payments under the criminal injuries compensation scheme.

Gross monthly income test

11 Remission of fees – gross monthly income

(1) If a party satisfies the disposable capital test, no fee is payable under this Order if, at the time when the fee would otherwise be payable, the party or their partner has the number of children specified in column 1 of Table 2 and –

(a) if the party is single, their gross monthly income does not exceed the amount set out in the appropriate row of column 2; or
(b) if the party is one of a couple, the gross monthly income of that couple does not exceed the amount set out in the appropriate row of column 3.

Table 2

Column 1 Number of children of party	Column 2 Single	Column 3 Couple
no children	£1,085	£1,245
1 child	£1,330	£1,490
2 children	£1,575	£1,735

(2) If a party or their partner has more than 2 children, the relevant amount of gross monthly income is the appropriate amount specified in Table 2 for 2 children, plus the sum of £245 for each additional child.

(3) For every £10 of gross monthly income received above the appropriate amount in Table 2, including any additional amount added under sub-paragraph (2), the party must pay £5 towards the fee payable, up to the maximum amount of the fee payable.

(4) This paragraph is subject to paragraph 12.

12 Gross monthly income cap

(1) No remission is available if a party or their partner has the number of children specified in column 1 of Table 3 and –

 (a) if the party is single, their gross monthly income exceeds the amount set out in the appropriate row of column 2 of Table 3; or
 (b) if the party is one of a couple, the gross monthly income of that couple exceeds the amount set out in the appropriate row of column 3 of Table 3.

Table 3

Column 1 Number of children of party	Column 2 Single	Column 3 Couple
no children	£5,085	£5,245
1 child	£5,330	£5,490
2 children	£5,575	£5,735

(2) If a party or their partner has more than 2 children, the relevant amount of gross monthly income is the appropriate amount specified in Table 3 for 2 children, plus the sum of £245 for each additional child.

13 Gross monthly income

(1) Subject to paragraph 14, gross monthly income means the total monthly income, for the month preceding that in which the application for remission is made, from all sources, other than receipt of any of the excluded benefits.

(2) Income from a trade, business or gainful occupation other than an occupation at a wage or salary is calculated as –

 (a) the profits which have accrued or will accrue to the party; and
 (b) the drawings of the party;

in the month preceding that in which the application for remission is made.

(3) In calculating profits under sub-paragraph (2)(a), all sums necessarily expended to earn those profits are deducted.

General

14 Resources and income treated as the party's resources and income

(1) Subject to sub-paragraphs (2) to (5), the disposable capital and gross monthly income of a partner is to be treated as disposable capital and gross monthly income of the party.

(2) Where the partner of the party has a contrary interest to the party in the matter to which the fee relates, the disposable capital and gross monthly income of that partner is not treated as the disposable capital and gross monthly income of the party.

(3) Where proceedings are brought concerning the property and affairs of 'P', for the purpose of determining whether a party is entitled to a remission or part remission of a fee in accordance with this Schedule –

(a) the disposable capital and gross monthly income of the person bringing those proceedings is not treated as the disposable capital and gross monthly income of the party;
(b) the disposable capital and gross monthly income of 'P' is to be treated as the disposable capital of the party; and
(c) the disposable capital and gross monthly income of the partner of 'P', if any, is not treated as the disposable capital and gross monthly income of the party.

(4) Where proceedings are brought concerning the personal welfare of 'P', for the purpose of determining whether a party is entitled to a remission or part remission of a fee in accordance with this Schedule, the disposable capital and gross monthly income of a partner, if any, is not treated as the disposable capital and gross monthly income of the party, where that partner is 'P' who is the subject of those proceedings in which the fee is payable.

(5) Where proceedings concern both the property and affairs of 'P' and their personal welfare, their disposable capital and gross monthly income shall be treated in accordance with sub-paragraph (3).

15 Application for remission of a fee

(1) An application for remission of a fee must be made at the time when the fee would otherwise be payable.

(2) Where an application for remission of a fee is made, the party must –

(a) indicate the fee to which the application relates;
(b) declare the amount of their disposable capital; and
(c) provide documentary evidence of their gross monthly income and the number of children relevant for the purposes of paragraphs 11 and 12.

(3) Where an application for remission of a fee is made on or before the date on which a fee is payable, the date for payment of the fee is disapplied.

(4) Where an application for remission is refused, or if part remission of a fee is granted, the amount of the fee which remains unremitted must be paid within the period notified in writing to the party.

16 Remission in exceptional circumstances

A fee specified in this Order may be remitted where the Lord Chancellor is satisfied that there are exceptional circumstances which justify doing so.

17 Refunds

(1) Subject to sub-paragraph (3), where a party pays a fee at a time when that party would have been entitled to a remission if they had provided the documentary evidence required by paragraph 15, the fee, or the amount by which the fee would have been reduced as the case may be, must be refunded if documentary evidence relating to the time when the fee became payable is provided at a later date.

(2) Subject to sub-paragraph (3), where a fee has been paid at a time when the Lord Chancellor, if all the circumstances had been known, would have remitted the fee under paragraph 15, the fee or the amount by which the fee would have been reduced, as the case may be, must be refunded to the party.

(3) No refund shall be made under this paragraph unless the party who paid the fee applies within 3 months of the date of the order of the court which finally disposed of the proceedings.

(4) The Lord Chancellor may extend the period of 3 months mentioned in sub-paragraph (3) if the Lord Chancellor considers that there is a good reason for a refund being made after the end of the period of 3 months.

18 Legal Aid

A party is not entitled to a fee remission if, under Part 1 of the Legal Aid, Sentencing and Punishment of Offenders Act 2012, they are in receipt of the following civil legal services –

   (a) Legal representation; or
   (b) Family help (higher); or
   (c) Family help (lower) in respect of applying for a consent order.

19 Vexatious litigants

(1) This paragraph applies where –

   (a) a restraint order is in force against a party; and
   (b) that party makes an application for permission to –
      (i) issue proceedings or take a step in proceedings as required by the restraint order;
      (ii) apply for amendment or discharge of the order; or
      (iii) appeal the order.

(2) The fee prescribed by this Order for the application is payable in full.

(3) If the party is granted permission, they are to be refunded the difference between –

   (a) the fee paid; and
   (b) the fee that would have been payable if this Schedule had been applied without reference to this paragraph.

20 Exceptions

No remissions or refunds are available in respect of the fee payable for –

(a) copy or duplicate documents;
(b) searches.

Amendments—Schedule inserted by SI 2013/2302. Amended by SI 2013/2302; SI 2014/590.

Lasting Powers of Attorney, Enduring Powers of Attorney and Public Guardian Regulations 2007, SI 2007/1253

ARRANGEMENT OF REGULATIONS

PART 1
PRELIMINARY

Regulation	Page
1 Citation and commencement	1278
2 Interpretation	1278
3 Minimal differences from forms prescribed in these Regulations	1278
4 Computation of time	1279

PART 2
LASTING POWERS OF ATTORNEY

Instruments intended to create a lasting power of attorney

5 Forms for lasting powers of attorney	1279
6 Maximum number of people to notify	1279
8 Persons who may provide an LPA certificate	1279
9 Execution of instrument	1280

Registering the instrument

10 Notice to be given by a person about to apply for registration of lasting power of attorney	1281
11 Application for registration	1282
12	1283
13 Notice of receipt of application for registration	1283
14 Objection to registration: notice to Public Guardian to be given by the donee of the power or a person to notify	1283
14A Objection to registration: notice to Public Guardian to be given by the donor	1284
15 Objection to registration: application to the court	1284
16 Notifying applicants of non-registration of lasting power of attorney	1285
17 Notice to be given on registration of lasting power of attorney	1285

Post-registration

18 Changes to instrument registered as lasting power of attorney	1286
19 Loss or destruction of instrument registered as lasting power of attorney	1286
20 Disclaimer of appointment by a donee of lasting power of attorney	1286
21 Revocation by donor of lasting power of attorney	1287

22	Revocation of a lasting power of attorney on death of donor	1287

PART 3
ENDURING POWERS OF ATTORNEY

23	Notice of intention to apply for registration of enduring power of attorney	1287
24	Application for registration	1288
25	Notice of objection to registration	1288
26	Notifying applicants of non-registration of enduring power of attorney	1288
27	Registration of instrument creating an enduring power of attorney	1289
28	Objection or revocation not applying to all joint and several attorneys	1289
29	Loss or destruction of instrument registered as enduring power of attorney	1289

PART 4
FUNCTIONS OF THE PUBLIC GUARDIAN

The registers

30	Establishing and maintaining the registers	1289
31	Disclosure of information on a register: search by the Public Guardian	1290
32	Disclosure of additional information held by the Public Guardian	1290

Security for discharge of functions

33	Persons required to give security for the discharge of their functions	1291
34	Security given under regulation 33(2)(a): requirement for endorsement	1291
35	Security given under regulation 33(2)(a): maintenance or replacement	1292
36	Enforcement following court order of any endorsed security	1293
37	Discharge of any endorsed security	1293

Deputies

38	Application for additional time to submit a report	1293
39	Content of reports	1294
40	Power to require final report on termination of appointment	1294
41	Power to require information from deputies	1295
42	Right of deputy to require review of decisions made by the Public Guardian	1295

Miscellaneous functions

43	Applications to the Court of Protection	1296
44	Visits by the Public Guardian or by Court of Protection Visitors at his direction	1296
45	Functions in relation to persons carrying out specific transactions	1297
46	Power to require information from donees of lasting power of attorney	1297
47	Power to require information from attorneys under enduring power of attorney	1297
48	Other functions in relation to enduring powers of attorney	1298
	Schedule 1 – Form of Lasting Power of Attorney	1298
	Schedule 2	1299
	Form of Notice of Intention to Register Lasting Power of Attorney (Form LPA3)	1299
	Schedule 3 – Form to Register Certain Lasting Powers of Attorney (Form LP2)	1299
	Schedule 4	1299
	Form of Notices of Application to Register a Lasting Power of Attorney	1299
	Schedule 5 – Notice of Registration of a Lasting Power of Attorney (LPA 004)	1299
	Schedule 6	1300

Form of Disclaimer by a Proposed or Acting Attorney under a Lasting Power of Attorney (Form LPA005) 1300
Schedule 7 – Notice of Intention to Apply for Registration of an Enduring Power of Attorney (EP1 PG) 1300
Schedule 8 – Application to Register an Enduring Power of Attorney (EP2 PG) 1300

PART 1
PRELIMINARY

1 Citation and commencement

(1) These Regulations may be cited as the Lasting Powers of Attorney, Enduring Powers of Attorney and Public Guardian Regulations 2007.

(2) These Regulations shall come into force on 1 October 2007.

2 Interpretation

(1) In these Regulations –

'the Act' means the Mental Capacity Act 2005;
'court' means the Court of Protection;
'LPA certificate', in relation to an instrument made with a view to creating a lasting power of attorney, means the certificate which is required to be included in the instrument by virtue of paragraph 2(1)(e) of Schedule 1 to the Act;
'person to notify', in relation to an instrument made with a view to creating a lasting power of attorney, means a person who, under Schedule 1, paragraph 2(1)(c)(i) of the Act, is named in the instrument as being a person to be notified of any application for the registration of the instrument;
'prescribed information', in relation to any instrument intended to create a lasting power of attorney, means the information contained in the form used for the instrument which appears under the heading 'Section 8 – Your legal rights and responsibilities'.

Amendments—SI 2015/899.

3 Minimal differences from forms prescribed in these Regulations

(1) In these Regulations, any reference to a form –

(a) in the case of a form set out in Schedules 1 to 7 to these Regulations, is to be regarded as including a Welsh version of that form; and
(b) in the case of a form set out in Schedules 2 to 7 to these Regulations, is to be regarded as also including –
 (i) a form to the same effect but which differs in an immaterial respect in form or mode of expression;
 (ii) a form to the same effect but with such variations as the circumstances may require or the court or the Public Guardian may approve; or
 (iii) a Welsh version of a form within (i) or (ii).

4 Computation of time

(1) This regulation shows how to calculate any period of time which is specified in these Regulations.

(2) A period of time expressed as a number of days must be computed as clear days.

(3) Where the specified period is 7 days or less, and would include a day which is not a business day, that day does not count.

(4) When the specified period for doing any act at the office of the Public Guardian ends on a day on which the office is closed, that act will be done in time if done on the next day on which the office is open.

(5) In this regulation –

'business day' means a day other than –
  (a) a Saturday, Sunday, Christmas Day or Good Friday; or
  (b) a bank holiday under the Banking and Financial Dealings Act 1971, in England and Wales; and

'clear days' means that in computing the number of days –
  (a) the day on which the period begins, and
  (b) if the end of the period is defined by reference to an event, the day on which that event occurs,
are not included.

PART 2
LASTING POWERS OF ATTORNEY

Instruments intended to create a lasting power of attorney

5 Forms for lasting powers of attorney

The forms set out in Parts 1 and 2 of Schedule 1 to these Regulations are the forms which, in the circumstances to which they apply, are to be used for instruments intended to create a lasting power of attorney.

6 Maximum number of people to notify

The maximum number of named persons that the donor of a lasting power of attorney may specify in the instrument intended to create the power is 5.

Amendments—SI 2015/899.

7 (*revoked*)

8 Persons who may provide an LPA certificate

(1) Subject to paragraph (3), the following persons may give an LPA certificate –

  (a) a person chosen by the donor as being someone who has known him personally for the period of at least two years which ends immediately before the date on which that person signs the LPA certificate;
  (b) a person chosen by the donor who, on account of his professional skills and

expertise, reasonably considers that he is competent to make the judgments necessary to certify the matters set out in paragraph (2)(1)(e) of Schedule 1 to the Act.

(2) The following are examples of persons within paragraph (1)(b) –

    (a) a registered health care professional;
    (b) a barrister, solicitor or advocate called or admitted in any part of the United Kingdom;
    (c) a registered social worker; or
    (d) an independent mental capacity advocate.

(3) A person is disqualified from giving an LPA certificate in respect of any instrument intended to create a lasting power of attorney if that person is –

    (a) a family member of the donor;
    (b) a donee of that power;
    (c) a donee of –
        (i) any other lasting power of attorney, or
        (ii) an enduring power of attorney,
    which has been executed by the donor (whether or not it has been revoked);
    (d) a family member of a donee within sub-paragraph (b);
    (e) a director or employee of a trust corporation acting as a donee within sub-paragraph (b);
    (f) a business partner or employee of –
        (i) the donor, or
        (ii) a donee within sub-paragraph (b);
    (g) an owner, director, manager or employee of any care home in which the donor is living when the instrument is executed; or
    (h) a family member of a person within sub-paragraph (g).

(4) In this regulation –

    'care home' has the meaning given in section 3 of the Care Standards Act 2000;
    'registered health care professional' means a person who is a member of a profession regulated by a body mentioned in section 25(3) of the National Health Service Reform and Health Care Professions Act 2002; and
    'registered social worker' means a person registered as a social worker in a register maintained by –
        (a) the Health and Care Professions Council;
        (b) the Care Council for Wales;
        (c) the Scottish Social Services Council; or
        (d) the Northern Ireland Social Care Council.

Amendments—SI 2012/1479.

9 Execution of instrument

(1) An instrument intended to create a lasting power of attorney must be executed in accordance with this regulation.

(2) The donor must read (or have read to him) all the prescribed information.

(3) As soon as reasonably practicable after the steps required by paragraph (2) have been taken, the donor must –

    (a) complete the provisions of Sections 1 to 7 of the instrument that apply to him (or direct another person to do so); and
    (b) subject to paragraph (7), in the presence of a witness –

(i) sign Section 9 of the instrument if the instrument is intended to create a lasting power of attorney for property and financial affairs (Form LP1F); or
(ii) sign Sections 5 and 9 of the instrument if the instrument is intended to create a lasting power of attorney for health and welfare (Form LP1H);

(4) As soon as reasonably practicable after the steps required by paragraph (3) have been taken –

(a) the person giving an LPA certificate,
(b) ....

must complete the LPA certificate at Section 10 of the instrument and sign it.

(5) As soon as reasonably practicable after the steps required by paragraph (4) have been taken –

(a) the donee, or
(b) if more than one, each of the donees,

must read (or have read to him) all the prescribed information.

(6) As soon as reasonably practicable after the steps required by paragraph (5) have been taken, the donee or, if more than one, each of them –

(a) must complete the provisions of Section 11 of the instrument that apply to him (or direct another person to do so); and
(b) subject to paragraph (7), must sign Section 11 of the instrument in the presence of a witness.

(7) If the instrument is to be signed by any person at the direction of the donor, or at the direction of any donee, the signature must be done in the presence of two witnesses.

(8) For the purposes of this regulation –

(a) the donor may not witness any signature required for the power;
(b) a donee may not witness any signature required for the power apart from that of another donee.

(9) A person witnessing a signature must –

(a) sign the instrument; and
(b) give his full name and address.

(10) Any reference in this regulation to a person signing an instrument (however expressed) includes his signing it by means of a mark made on the instrument at the appropriate place.

Amendments—SI 2015/899.

Registering the instrument

10 Notice to be given by a person about to apply for registration of lasting power of attorney

Schedule 2 to these Regulations sets out the form of notice (Form LPA3) which must be given by a donor or donee who is about to make an application for the registration of an instrument intended to create a lasting power of attorney.

Amendments—SI 2015/899.

11 Application for registration

(1) An application to the Public Guardian for the registration of an instrument intended to create a lasting power of attorney that is in Form LP1F or LP1H must be made by completion of Sections 12 and 13, the relevant parts of Section 14 and Section 15 of that Form.

(2) An application to the Public Guardian for the registration of an instrument intended to create a lasting power of attorney that is in a pre-July 2015 form must be made by using Form LP2 set out in Schedule 3 to these Regulations.

(3) An application to the Public Guardian for the registration of an instrument intended to create a lasting power of attorney where the application is a repeat application ('a reduced fee repeat application') may only be made if –

(a) the initial application for the registration of a lasting power of attorney is made on or after 1 October 2011;
(b) the initial application was returned to the applicant as invalid;
(c) the reduced fee repeat application is submitted for registration within three months of the date on which the initial application was returned to the applicant as invalid; and
(d) the reduced fee for such applications applies.

(4) Where the initial application for the registration of the lasting power of attorney was made in accordance with paragraph (1) using Form LP1F or LP1H, a reduced fee repeat application must also be made by the completion of Form LP1F or LP1H as appropriate, including completion of the repeat application option in Section 14 of that Form.

(5) Where the initial application for the registration of the lasting power of attorney was made in accordance with paragraph (2) using a pre-July 2015 form, a reduced fee repeat application must be made by the completion of Form LP1F or LP1H as appropriate, including completion of the repeat application option in Section 14 of that Form.

(6) Where the instrument to be registered which is sent with the application is neither –

(a) the original instrument intended to create the power; nor
(b) a certified copy of it,

the Public Guardian must not register the instrument unless the court directs the Public Guardian to do so.

(7) In this regulation –

(a) 'pre-July 2015 form' means a valid instrument intended to create a lasting power of attorney that is not in Form LP1F or LP1H but that complies with these Regulations as they were in force immediately before 1 July 2015; and
(b) 'certified copy' means a photographic or other facsimile copy which is certified as an accurate copy by –
   (i) the donor; or
   (ii) a solicitor or notary.

Amendments—Last substituted by SI 2015/899.

12 The period at the end of which the Public Guardian must register an instrument in accordance with paragraph 5 of Schedule 1 to the Act is the period of 4 weeks beginning with –

  (a) the date on which the Public Guardian gave the notice or notices under paragraph 7 or 8 of Schedule 1 to the Act of receipt of an application for registration; or
  (b) if notices were given on more than one date, the latest of those dates.

Amendments—SI 2013/506.

13 Notice of receipt of application for registration

(1) Part 1 of Schedule 4 to these Regulations sets out the form of notice ('LPA 003A') which the Public Guardian must give to the donee (or donees) when the Public Guardian receives an application for the registration of a lasting power of attorney.

(2) Part 2 of Schedule 4 sets out the form of notice ('LPA 003B') which the Public Guardian must give to the donor when the Public Guardian receives such an application.

(3) Where it appears to the Public Guardian that there is good reason to do so, the Public Guardian must also provide (or arrange for the provision of) an explanation to the donor of –

  (a) the notice referred to in paragraph (2) and what the effect of it is; and
  (b) why it is being brought to his attention.

(4) Any information provided under paragraph (3) must be provided –

  (a) to the donor personally; and
  (b) in a way that is appropriate to the donor's circumstances (for example using simple language, visual aids or other appropriate means).

14 Objection to registration: notice to Public Guardian to be given by the donee of the power or a person to notify

(1) This regulation deals with any objection to the registration of an instrument as a lasting power of attorney which is to be made to the Public Guardian by the donee of the power or a person to notify.

(2) Where the donee of the power or a person to notify –

  (a) is entitled to receive notice under paragraph 6, 7 or 8 of Schedule 1 to the Act of an application for the registration of the instrument, and
  (b) wishes to object to registration on a ground set out in paragraph 13(1) of Schedule 1 to the Act,

he must do so before the end of the period of 3 weeks beginning with the date on which the notice is given.

(3) A notice of objection must be given in writing, setting out –

  (a) the name and address of the objector;
  (b) … the name and address of the donor of the power;
  (c) if known, the name and address of the donee (or donees); and
  (d) the ground for making the objection.

(4) The Public Guardian must notify the objector as to whether he is satisfied that the ground of the objection is established.

(5) At any time after receiving the notice of objection and before giving the notice required by paragraph (4), the Public Guardian may require the objector to provide such further information, or produce such documents, as the Public Guardian reasonably considers necessary to enable him to determine whether the ground for making the objection is established.

(6) Where –
   (a) the Public Guardian is satisfied that the ground of the objection is established, but
   (b) by virtue of section 13(7) of the Act, the instrument is not revoked,

the notice under paragraph (4) must contain a statement to that effect.

(7) Nothing in this regulation prevents an objector from making a further objection under paragraph 13 of Schedule 1 to the Act where –
   (a) the notice under paragraph (4) indicates that the Public Guardian is not satisfied that the particular ground of objection to which that notice relates is established; and
   (b) the period specified in paragraph (2) has not expired.

Amendments—SI 2007/2161; SI 2015/899; SI 2013/506.

14A Objection to registration: notice to Public Guardian to be given by the donor

(1) This regulation deals with any objection to the registration of an instrument as a lasting power of attorney which is to be made to the Public Guardian by the donor of the power.

(2) Where the donor of the power –
   (a) is entitled to receive notice under paragraph 8 of Schedule 1 to the Act of an application for the registration of the instrument, and
   (b) wishes to object to the registration

he must do so before the end of the period of 3 weeks beginning with the date on which the notice is given.

(3) The donor of the power must give notice of his objection in writing to the Public Guardian, setting out –
   (a) the name and address of the donor of the power
   (b) if known, the name and address of the donee (or donees); and
   (c) the ground for making the objection.

Amendments—Inserted by SI 2007/2161. Amended by SI 2013/506.

15 Objection to registration: application to the court

(1) This regulation deals with any objection to the registration of an instrument as a lasting power of attorney which is to be made to the court.

(2) The grounds for making an application to the court are –

(a) that one or more of the requirements for the creation of a lasting power of attorney have not been met;
(b) that the power has been revoked, or has otherwise come to an end, on a ground other than the grounds set out in paragraph 13(1) of Schedule 1 to the Act;
(c) any of the grounds set out in paragraph (a) or (b) of section 22(3) of the Act.

(3) Where any person –

(a) is entitled to receive notice under paragraph 6, 7 or 8 of Schedule 1 to the Act of an application for the registration of the instrument, and
(b) wishes to object to registration on one or more of the grounds set out in paragraph (2),

he must make an application to the court before the end of the period of 3 weeks beginning with the date on which the notice is given.

(4) The notice of an application to the court, which a person making an objection to the court is required to give to the Public Guardian under paragraph 13(3)(b)(ii) of Schedule 1 to the Act, must be in writing.

Amendments—SI 2013/506.

16 Notifying applicants of non-registration of lasting power of attorney

Where the Public Guardian is prevented from registering an instrument as a lasting power of attorney by virtue of –

(a) paragraph 11(1) of Schedule 1 to the Act (instrument not made in accordance with Schedule),
(b) paragraph 12(2) of that Schedule (deputy already appointed),
(c) paragraph 13(2) of that Schedule (objection by donee or named person on grounds of bankruptcy, disclaimer, death etc),
(d) paragraph 14(2) of that Schedule (objection by donor), or
(e) regulation 11(2) of these Regulations (application for registration not accompanied by original instrument or certified copy),

he must notify the person (or persons) who applied for registration of that fact.

17 Notice to be given on registration of lasting power of attorney

(1) Where the Public Guardian registers an instrument as a lasting power of attorney, he must –

(a) retain a copy of the instrument; and
(b) return to the person (or persons) who applied for registration the original instrument, or the certified copy of it, which accompanied the application for registration.

(2) Schedule 5 to these Regulations sets out the form of notice ('LPA 004') which the Public Guardian must give to the donor and donee (or donees) when the Public Guardian registers an instrument.

(3) Where it appears to the Public Guardian that there is good reason to do so, the Public Guardian must also provide (or arrange for the provision of) an explanation to the donor of –

(a) the notice referred to in paragraph (2) and what the effect of it is; and
(b) why it is being brought to his attention.

(4) Any information provided under paragraph (3) must be provided –
(a) to the donor personally; and
(b) in a way that is appropriate to the donor's circumstances (for example using simple language, visual aids or other appropriate means).

(5) 'Certified copy' is to be construed in accordance with regulation 11(3).

Post-registration

18 Changes to instrument registered as lasting power of attorney

(1) This regulation applies in any case where any of paragraphs 21 to 24 of Schedule 1 to the Act requires the Public Guardian to attach a note to an instrument registered as a lasting power of attorney.

(2) The Public Guardian must give a notice to the donor and the donee (or, if more than one, each of them) requiring him to deliver to the Public Guardian –
(a) the original instrument which was sent to the Public Guardian for registration;
(b) any office copy of that registered instrument; and
(c) any certified copy of that registered instrument.

(3) On receipt of the document, the Public Guardian must –
(a) attach the required note; and
(b) return the document to the person from whom it was obtained.

Amendments—SI 2009/1884.

19 Loss or destruction of instrument registered as lasting power of attorney

(1) This regulation applies where –
(a) a person is required by or under the Act to deliver up to the Public Guardian any of the following documents –
   (i) an instrument registered as a lasting power of attorney;
   (ii) an office copy of that registered instrument;
   (iii) a certified copy of that registered instrument; and
(b) the document has been lost or destroyed.

(2) The person required to deliver up the document must provide to the Public Guardian in writing –
(a) if known, the date of the loss or destruction and the circumstances in which it occurred;
(b) otherwise, a statement of when he last had the document in his possession.

20 Disclaimer of appointment by a donee of lasting power of attorney

(1) Schedule 6 to these Regulations sets out the form ('LPA 005') which a donee of an instrument registered as a lasting power of attorney must use to disclaim his appointment as donee.

(2) The donee must send –

  (a) the completed form to the donor; and
  (b) a copy of it to –
   (i) the Public Guardian; and
   (ii) any other donee who, for the time being, is appointed under the power.

21 Revocation by donor of lasting power of attorney

(1) A donor who revokes a lasting power to attorney must –

  (a) notify the Public Guardian that he has done so; and
  (b) notify the donee (or, if more than one, each of them) of the revocation.

(2) Where the Public Guardian receives a notice under paragraph (1)(a), he must cancel the registration of the instrument creating the power if he is satisfied that the donor has taken such steps as are necessary in law to revoke it.

(3) The Public Guardian may require the donor to provide such further information, or produce such documents, as the Public Guardian reasonably considers necessary to enable him to determine whether the steps necessary for revocation have been taken.

(4) Where the Public Guardian cancels the registration of the instrument he must notify –

  (a) the donor; and
  (b) the donee or, if more than one, each of them.

22 Revocation of a lasting power of attorney on death of donor

(1) The Public Guardian must cancel the registration of an instrument as a lasting power of attorney if he is satisfied that the power has been revoked as a result of the donor's death.

(2) Where the Public Guardian cancels the registration of an instrument he must notify the donee or, if more than one, each of them.

PART 3
ENDURING POWERS OF ATTORNEY

23 Notice of intention to apply for registration of enduring power of attorney

(1) Schedule 7 to these Regulations sets out the form of notice ('EP1PG') which an attorney (or attorneys) under an enduring power of attorney must give of his intention to make an application for the registration of the instrument creating the power.

(2) In the case of the notice to be given to the donor, the attorney must also provide (or arrange for the provision of) an explanation to the donor of –

  (a) the notice and what the effect of it is; and
  (b) why it is being brought to his attention.

(3) The information provided under paragraph (2) must be provided –

(a) to the donor personally; and
(b) in a way that is appropriate to the donor's circumstances (for example using simple language, visual aids or other appropriate means).

24 Application for registration

(1) Schedule 8 to these Regulations sets out the form ('EP2PG') which must be used for making an application to the Public Guardian for the registration of an instrument creating an enduring power of attorney.

(1A) The Public Guardian must not register an instrument where only a certified copy of the instrument is sent with the application, unless the applicant verifies that he cannot produce the original instrument because it has been lost or, as the case may be, destroyed.

(2) Where the instrument to be registered which is sent with the application is neither –

(a) the original instrument creating the power, nor
(b) a certified copy of it in relation to which paragraph (1A) has been complied with,

the Public Guardian must not register the instrument unless the court directs him to do so.

(3) 'Certified copy', in relation to an enduring power of attorney, means a copy certified in accordance with section 3 of the Powers of Attorney Act 1971.

Amendments—SI 2010/1063.

25 Notice of objection to registration

(1) This regulation deals with any objection to the registration of an instrument creating an enduring power of attorney which is to be made to the Public Guardian under paragraph 13(4) of Schedule 4 to the Act.

(2) A notice of objection must be given in writing, setting out –

(a) the name and address of the objector;
(b) if different, the name and address of the donor of the power;
(c) if known, the name and address of the attorney (or attorneys); and
(d) the ground for making the objection.

26 Notifying applicants of non-registration of enduring power of attorney

Where the Public Guardian is prevented from registering an instrument creating an enduring power of attorney by virtue of –

(a) paragraph 13(2) of Schedule 4 to the Act (deputy already appointed),
(b) paragraph 13(5) of that Schedule (receipt by Public Guardian of valid notice of objection from person entitled to notice of application to register),
(c) paragraph 13(7) of that Schedule (Public Guardian required to undertake appropriate enquiries in certain circumstances), or
(d) regulation 24(2) of these Regulations (application for registration not accompanied by original instrument or certified copy),

he must notify the person (or persons) who applied for registration of that fact.

27 Registration of instrument creating an enduring power of attorney

(1) Where the Public Guardian registers an instrument creating an enduring power of attorney, he must –

(a) retain a copy of the instrument; and
(b) return to the person (or persons) who applied for registration the original instrument, or the certified copy of it, which accompanied the application.

(2) 'Certified copy' has the same meaning as in regulation 24(3).

28 Objection or revocation not applying to all joint and several attorneys

In a case within paragraph 20(6) or (7) of Schedule 4 to the Act, the form of the entry to be made in the register in respect of an instrument creating the enduring power of attorney is a stamp bearing the following words (inserting the information indicated, as appropriate) –

'THE REGISTRATION OF THIS ENDURING POWER OF ATTORNEY IS QUALIFIED AND EXTENDS TO THE APPOINTMENT OF ……….(insert name of attorney(s) not affected by ground(s) of objection or revocation) ONLY AS THE ATTORNEY(S) OF ………… (insert name of donor)'.

29 Loss or destruction of instrument registered as enduring power of attorney

(1) This regulation applies where –

(a) a person is required by or under the Act to deliver up to the Public Guardian any of the following documents –
    (i) an instrument registered as an enduring power of attorney;
    (ii) an office copy of that registered instrument; or
    (iii) a certified copy of that registered instrument; and
(b) the document has been lost or destroyed.

(2) The person who is required to deliver up the document must provide to the Public Guardian in writing –

(a) if known, the date of the loss or destruction and the circumstances in which it occurred;
(b) otherwise, a statement of when he last had the document in his possession.

PART 4
FUNCTIONS OF THE PUBLIC GUARDIAN

The registers

30 Establishing and maintaining the registers

(1) In this Part 'the registers' means –

(a) the register of lasting powers of attorney,

(b) the register of enduring powers of attorney, and
(c) the register of court orders appointing deputies,

which the Public Guardian must establish and maintain.

(2) On each register the Public Guardian may include –

(a) such descriptions of information about a registered instrument or a registered order as the Public Guardian considers appropriate; and
(b) entries which relate to an instrument or order for which registration has been cancelled.

31 Disclosure of information on a register: search by the Public Guardian

(1) Any person may, by an application made under paragraph (2), request the Public Guardian to carry out a search of one or more of the registers.

(2) An application must –

(a) state –
   (i) the register or registers to be searched;
   (ii) the name of the person to whom the application relates; and
   (iii) such other details about that person as the Public Guardian may require for the purpose of carrying out the search; and
(b) be accompanied by any fee provided for under section 58(4)(b) of the Act.

(3) The Public Guardian may require the applicant to provide such further information, or produce such documents, as the Public Guardian reasonably considers necessary to enable him to carry out the search.

(4) As soon as reasonably practicable after receiving the application –

(a) the Public Guardian must notify the applicant of the result of the search; and
(b) in the event that it reveals one or more entries on the register, the Public Guardian must disclose to the applicant all the information appearing on the register in respect of each entry.

32 Disclosure of additional information held by the Public Guardian

(1) This regulation applies in any case where, as a result of a search made under regulation 31, a person has obtained information relating to a registered instrument or a registered order which confers authority to make decisions about matters concerning a person ('P').

(2) On receipt of an application made in accordance with paragraph (4), the Public Guardian may, if he considers that there is good reason to do so, disclose to the applicant such additional information as he considers appropriate.

(3) 'Additional information' means any information relating to P –

(a) which the Public Guardian has obtained in exercising the functions conferred on him under the Act; but
(b) which does not appear on the register.

(4) An application must state –

(a) the name of P;

(b) the reasons for making the application; and
(c) what steps, if any, the applicant has taken to obtain the information from P.

(5) The Public Guardian may require the applicant to provide such further information, or produce such documents, as the Public Guardian reasonably considers necessary to enable him to determine the application.

(6) In determining whether to disclose any additional information relating to P, the Public Guardian must, in particular, have regard to –

(a) the connection between P and the applicant;
(b) the reasons for requesting the information (in particular, why the information cannot or should not be obtained directly from P);
(c) the benefit to P, or any detriment he may suffer, if a disclosure is made; and
(d) any detriment that another person may suffer if a disclosure is made.

Amendments—SI 2009/1884.

Security for discharge of functions

33 Persons required to give security for the discharge of their functions

(1) This regulation applies in any case where the court orders a person ('S') to give to the Public Guardian security for the discharge of his functions.

(2) The security must be given by S –

(a) by means of a bond which is entered into in accordance with regulation 34; or
(b) in such other manner as the court may direct.

(3) For the purposes of paragraph (2)(a), S complies with the requirement to give the security only if –

(a) the endorsement required by regulation 34(2) has been provided; and
(b) the person who provided it has notified the Public Guardian of that fact.

(4) For the purposes of paragraph (2)(b), S complies with the requirement to give the security –

(a) in any case where the court directs that any other endorsement must be provided, only if –
   (i) that endorsement has been provided; and
   (ii) the person who provided it has notified the Public Guardian of that fact;
(b) in any case where the court directs that any other requirements must be met in relation to the giving of the security, only if the Public Guardian is satisfied that those other requirements have been met.

34 Security given under regulation 33(2)(a): requirement for endorsement

(1) This regulation has effect for the purposes of regulation 33(2)(a).

(2) A bond is entered into in accordance with this regulation only if it is endorsed by –

(a) an authorised insurance company; or
(b) an authorised deposit-taker.

(3) A person may enter into the bond under –
   (a) arrangements made by the Public Guardian; or
   (b) other arrangements which are made by the person entering into the bond or on his behalf.

(4) The Public Guardian may make arrangements with any person specified in paragraph (2) with a view to facilitating the provision by them of bonds which persons required to give security to the Public Guardian may enter into.

(5) In this regulation –

'authorised insurance company' means –
   (a) a person who has permission under Part 4 of the Financial Services and Markets Act 2000 to effect or carry out contracts of insurance;
   (b) an EEA firm of the kind mentioned in paragraph 5(d) of Schedule 3 to that Act, which has permission under paragraph 15 of that Schedule to effect or carry out contracts of insurance;
   (c) a person who carries on insurance market activity (within the meaning given in section 316(3) of that Act); and

'authorised deposit-taker' means –
   (a) a person who has permission under Part 4 of the Financial Services and Markets Act 2000 to accept deposits;
   (b) an EEA firm of the kind mentioned in paragraph 5(d) of Schedule 3 to that Act, which has permission under paragraph 15 of that Schedule to accept deposits.

(6) The definitions of 'authorised insurance company' and 'authorised deposit-taker' must be read with –
   (a) section 22 of the Financial Services and Markets Act 2000;
   (b) any relevant order under that section; and
   (c) Schedule 2 to that Act.

35 Security given under regulation 33(2)(a): maintenance or replacement

(1) This regulation applies to any security given under regulation 33(2)(a).

(2) At such times or at such intervals as the Public Guardian may direct by notice in writing, any person ('S') who has given the security must satisfy the Public Guardian that any premiums payable in respect of it have been paid.

(3) Where S proposes to replace a security already given by him, the new security is not to be regarded as having been given until the Public Guardian is satisfied that –
   (a) the requirements set out in sub-paragraphs (a) and (b) of regulation 33(3) have been met in relation to it; and
   (b) no payment is due from S in connection with the discharge of his functions.

(4) The Public Guardian must, if satisfied as to the matters in paragraph (3), provide written notice of that fact to S within 2 weeks of being given notification in accordance with regulation 33(3)(b) in relation to the new security.

Amendments—SI 2013/506.

36 Enforcement following court order of any endorsed security

(1) This regulation applies to any security given to the Public Guardian in respect of which an endorsement has been provided.

(2) Where the court orders the enforcement of the security, the Public Guardian must –

(a) notify any person who endorsed the security of the contents of the order; and
(b) notify the court when payment has been made of the amount secured.

37 Discharge of any endorsed security

(1) This regulation applies to any security given by a person ('S') to the Public Guardian in respect of which an endorsement has been provided.

(2) The security may be discharged if the court makes an order discharging it.

(3) Otherwise the security may not be discharged –

(a) if the person on whose behalf S was appointed to act dies, until the end of the period of 2 years beginning on the date of his death; or
(b) in any other case, until the end of the period of 7 years beginning on whichever of the following dates first occurs –
   (i) if S dies, the date of his death;
   (ii) if the court makes an order which discharges S but which does not also discharge the security under paragraph (2), the date of the order;
   (iii) the date when S otherwise ceases to be under a duty to discharge the functions in respect of which he was ordered to give security.

(3A) Where S has replaced a security ('the original security') previously given by S and the Public Guardian has provided notice in accordance with regulation 35(4), the original security shall stand discharged 2 years from the date on which that notice was issued unless discharged by earlier order of the court upon application under paragraph (2).

(4) For the purposes of paragraph (3), if a person takes any step with a view to discharging the security before the end of the period specified in that paragraph, the security is to be treated for all purposes as if it were still in place.

(5) For the purposes of paragraph (3A), if a person takes any step otherwise than under paragraph (2) with a view to discharging the original security before the end of the period specified paragraph (3A), the security is to be treated for all purposes as if it were still in place.

Amendments—SI 2010/1063; SI 2013/506.

Deputies

38 Application for additional time to submit a report

(1) This regulation applies where the court requires a deputy to submit a report to the Public Guardian and specifies a time or interval for it to be submitted.

(2) A deputy may apply to the Public Guardian requesting more time for submitting a particular report.

(3) An application must –

(a) state the reason for requesting more time; and
(b) contain or be accompanied by such information as the Public Guardian may reasonably require to determine the application.

(4) In response to an application, the Public Guardian may, if he considers it appropriate to do so, undertake that he will not take steps to secure performance of the deputy's duty to submit the report at the relevant time on the condition that the report is submitted on or before such later date as he may specify.

39 Content of reports

(1) Any report which the court requires a deputy to submit to the Public Guardian must include such material as the court may direct.

(2) The report must also contain or be accompanied by –

(a) specified information or information of a specified description; or
(b) specified documents or documents of a specified description.

(3) But paragraph (2) –

(a) extends only to information or documents which are reasonably required in connection with the exercise by the Public Guardian of functions conferred on him under the Act; and
(b) is subject to paragraph (1) and to any other directions given by the court.

(4) Where powers as respects a person's property and affairs are conferred on a deputy under section 16 of the Act, the information specified by the Public Guardian under paragraph (2) may include accounts which –

(a) deal with specified matters; and
(b) are provided in a specified form.

(5) The Public Guardian may require –

(a) any information provided to be verified in such manner, or
(b) any document produced to be authenticated in such manner,

as he may reasonably require.

(6) 'Specified' means specified in a notice in writing given to the deputy by the Public Guardian.

40 Power to require final report on termination of appointment

(1) This regulation applies where –

(a) the person on whose behalf a deputy was appointed to act has died;
(b) the deputy has died;
(c) the court has made an order discharging the deputy; or
(d) the deputy otherwise ceases to be under a duty to discharge the functions to which his appointment relates.

(2) The Public Guardian may require the deputy (or, in the case of the deputy's death, his personal representatives) to submit a final report on the discharge of his functions.

(3) A final report must be submitted –

(a) before the end of such reasonable period as may be specified; and

(b) at such place as may be specified.

(4) The Public Guardian must consider the final report, together with any other information that he may have relating to the discharge by the deputy of his functions.

(5) Where the Public Guardian is dissatisfied with any aspect of the final report he may apply to the court for an appropriate remedy (including enforcement of security given by the deputy).

(6) 'Specified' means specified in a notice in writing given to the deputy or his personal representatives by the Public Guardian.

41 Power to require information from deputies

(1) This regulation applies in any case where –
   (a) the Public Guardian has received representations (including complaints) about –
      (i) the way in which a deputy is exercising his powers; or
      (ii) any failure to exercise them; or
   (b) it appears to the Public Guardian that there are other circumstances which –
      (i) give rise to concerns about, or dissatisfaction with, the conduct of the deputy (including any failure to act); or
      (ii) otherwise constitute good reason to seek information about the deputy's discharge of his functions.

(2) The Public Guardian may require the deputy –
   (a) to provide specified information or information of a specified description; or
   (b) to produce specified documents or documents of a specified description.

(3) The information or documents must be provided or produced –
   (a) before the end of such reasonable period as may be specified; and
   (b) at such place as may be specified.

(4) The Public Guardian may require –
   (a) any information provided to be verified in such manner, or
   (b) any document produced to be authenticated in such manner,

as he may reasonably require.

(5) 'Specified' means specified in a notice in writing given to the deputy by the Public Guardian.

42 Right of deputy to require review of decisions made by the Public Guardian

(1) A deputy may require the Public Guardian to reconsider any decision he has made in relation to the deputy.

(2) The right under paragraph (1) is exercisable by giving notice of exercise of the right to the Public Guardian before the end of the period of 14 days beginning with the date on which notice of the decision is given to the deputy.

(3) The notice of exercise of the right must –

(a) state the grounds on which reconsideration is required; and
   (b) contain or be accompanied by any relevant information or documents.

(4) At any time after receiving the notice and before reconsidering the decision to which it relates, the Public Guardian may require the deputy to provide him with such further information, or to produce such documents, as he reasonably considers necessary to enable him to reconsider the matter.

(5) The Public Guardian must give to the deputy –

   (a) written notice of his decision on reconsideration, and
   (b) if he upholds the previous decision, a statement of his reasons.

Miscellaneous functions

43 Applications to the Court of Protection

The Public Guardian has the function of making applications to the court in connection with his functions under the Act in such circumstances as he considers it necessary or appropriate to do so.

44 Visits by the Public Guardian or by Court of Protection Visitors at his direction

(1) This regulation applies where the Public Guardian visits, or directs a Court of Protection Visitor to visit, any person under any provision of the Act or these Regulations.

(2) The Public Guardian must notify (or make arrangements to notify) the person to be visited of –

   (a) the date or dates on which it is proposed that the visit will take place;
   (b) to the extent that it is practicable to do so, any specific matters likely to be covered in the course of the visit; and
   (c) any proposal to inform any other person that the visit is to take place.

(3) Where the visit is to be carried out by a Court of Protection Visitor –

   (a) the Public Guardian may –
      (i) give such directions to the Visitor, and
      (ii) provide him with such information concerning the person to be visited,

as the Public Guardian considers necessary for the purposes of enabling the visit to take place and the Visitor to prepare any report the Public Guardian may require; and

   (b) the Visitor must seek to carry out the visit and take all reasonable steps to obtain such other information as he considers necessary for the purpose of preparing a report.

(4) A Court of Protection Visitor must submit any report requested by the Public Guardian in accordance with any timetable specified by the Public Guardian.

(5) If he considers it appropriate to do so, the Public Guardian may, in relation to any person interviewed in the course of preparing a report –

   (a) disclose the report to him; and
   (b) invite him to comment on it.

45 Functions in relation to persons carrying out specific transactions

(1) This regulation applies where, in accordance with an order made under section 16(2)(a) of the Act, a person ('T') has been authorised to carry out any transaction for a person who lacks capacity.

(2) The Public Guardian has the functions of –

  (a) receiving any reports from T which the court may require;
  (b) dealing with representations (including complaints) about –
    (i) the way in which the transaction has been or is being carried out; or
    (ii) any failure to carry it out.

(3) Regulations 38 to 41 have effect in relation to T as they have effect in relation a deputy.

46 Power to require information from donees of lasting power of attorney

(1) This regulation applies where it appears to the Public Guardian that there are circumstances suggesting that the donee of a lasting power of attorney may –

  (a) have behaved, or may be behaving, in a way that contravenes his authority or is not in the best interests of the donor of the power,
  (b) be proposing to behave in a way that would contravene that authority or would not be in the donor's best interests, or
  (c) have failed to comply with the requirements of an order made, or directions given, by the court.

(2) The Public Guardian may require the donee –

  (a) to provide specified information or information of a specified description; or
  (b) to produce specified documents or documents of a specified description.

(3) The information or documents must be provided or produced –

  (a) before the end of such reasonable period as may be specified; and
  (b) at such place as may be specified.

(4) The Public Guardian may require –

  (a) any information provided to be verified in such manner, or
  (b) any document produced to be authenticated in such manner,

as he may reasonably require.

(5) 'Specified' means specified in a notice in writing given to the donee by the Public Guardian.

47 Power to require information from attorneys under enduring power of attorney

(1) This regulation applies where it appears to the Public Guardian that there are circumstances suggesting that, having regard to all the circumstances (and in particular the attorney's relationship to or connection with the donor) the attorney under a registered enduring power of attorney may be unsuitable to be the donor's attorney.

(2) The Public Guardian may require the attorney –

(a) to provide specified information or information of a specified description; or
(b) to produce specified documents or documents of a specified description.

(3) The information or documents must be provided or produced –
(a) before the end of such reasonable period as may be specified; and
(b) at such place as may be specified.

(4) The Public Guardian may require –
(a) any information provided to be verified in such manner, or
(b) any document produced to be authenticated in such manner,

as he may reasonably require.

(5) 'Specified' means specified in a notice in writing given to the attorney by the Public Guardian.

48 Other functions in relation to enduring powers of attorney

(1) The Public Guardian has the following functions –

(a) directing a Court of Protection Visitor –
   (i) to visit an attorney under a registered enduring power of attorney, or
   (ii) to visit the donor of a registered enduring power of attorney,

and to make a report to the Public Guardian on such matters as he may direct;

(b) dealing with representations (including complaints) about the way in which an attorney under a registered enduring power of attorney is exercising his powers.

(2) The functions conferred by paragraph (1) may be discharged in co-operation with any other person who has functions in relation to the care or treatment of P.

Amendments—SI 2010/1063.

SCHEDULE 1
FORM OF LASTING POWER OF ATTORNEY

PART 1: FORM OF LASTING POWER OF ATTORNEY FOR PROPERTY AND FINANCIAL AFFAIRS (FORM LP1F)

This form can be found in Part VII of this work.

PART 2: FORM OF LASTING POWER OF ATTORNEY FOR HEALTH AND WELFARE (FORM LP1H)

This form can be found in Part VII of this work.

Amendments—Last substituted by SI 2015/899.

SCHEDULE 2

FORM OF NOTICE OF INTENTION TO REGISTER LASTING POWER OF ATTORNEY (FORM LPA3)

This form can be found in Part VII of this work.

Amendments—Substituted by SI 2015/899.

SCHEDULE 3
FORM TO REGISTER CERTAIN LASTING POWERS OF ATTORNEY (FORM LP2)

This form can be found in Part VII of this work.

Amendments—Substituted by SI 2015/899.

SCHEDULE 4

FORM OF NOTICES OF APPLICATION TO REGISTER A LASTING POWER OF ATTORNEY

PART 1: FORM OF NOTICE TO ATTORNEY: APPLICATION TO REGISTER A LASTING POWER OF ATTORNEY (FORM LPA003A)

This form can be found in Part VII of this work.

PART 2: FORM OF NOTICE TO DONOR: APPLICATION TO REGISTER A LASTING POWER OF ATTORNEY (FORM LPA003B)

This form can be found in Part VII of this work.

Amendments—Substituted by SI 2015/899.

SCHEDULE 5
NOTICE OF REGISTRATION OF A LASTING POWER OF ATTORNEY (LPA 004)

This form can be found in Part VII of this work.

SCHEDULE 6

FORM OF DISCLAIMER BY A PROPOSED OR ACTING ATTORNEY UNDER A LASTING POWER OF ATTORNEY (FORM LPA005)

This form can be found in Part VII of this work.

Amendments—Substituted by SI 2015/899.

SCHEDULE 7
NOTICE OF INTENTION TO APPLY FOR REGISTRATION OF AN ENDURING POWER OF ATTORNEY (EP1 PG)

This form can be found in Part VII of this work.

Amendments—SI 2007/2051; SI 2010/1063.

SCHEDULE 8
APPLICATION TO REGISTER AN ENDURING POWER OF ATTORNEY (EP2 PG)

This form can be found in Part VII of this work.

Amendments—SI 2010/1063.

Mental Capacity Act 2005 (Transfer of Proceedings) Order 2007, SI 2007/1899

ARRANGEMENT OF ARTICLES

Article		Page
1	Citation and commencement	1300
2	Transfers from the Court of Protection to a court having jurisdiction under the Children Act	1301
3	Transfers from a court having jurisdiction under the Children Act to the Court of Protection	1302
4	Avoidance of double liability for fees	1303

1 Citation and commencement

(1) This Order may be cited as the Mental Capacity Act 2005 (Transfer of Proceedings) Order 2007.

(2) This Order shall come into force on 1 October 2007.

(3) In this Order 'the Children Act' means the Children Act 1989.

Scope of provision—The Children Act 1989 allows the court to make decisions in relation to people under 18 years. The typical application under the Act will concern where the child should reside and the terms of contact between a parent and the child. However, the Act does allow the court to make other decisions relating to a child.

The Court of Protection will normally be called upon to exercise its powers in relation to a person over 16 years. However, the Mental Capacity Act 2005 (MCA 2005), s 18(3) allows the Court to exercise its powers in relation to property and finance matters over a person under 16.

The purpose of this Order is to allow a case to be dealt by the court best placed to deal with the issues relating to a young person. There may also be instances where a child is of an age where the Children Act 1989 will no longer apply in the near future but the court still needs to be involved with that person's life in one way or another.

Many of the judges nominated to sit in the Court of Protection also exercise jurisdiction in children's cases. This will either allow a case to be followed through by the same judge or by another judge who will readily appreciate the issues.

2 Transfers from the Court of Protection to a court having jurisdiction under the Children Act

(1) This article applies to any proceedings in the Court of Protection which relate to a person under 18.

(2) The Court of Protection may direct the transfer of the whole or part of the proceedings to a court having jurisdiction under the Children Act where it considers that in all the circumstances, it is just and convenient to transfer the proceedings.

(3) In making a determination, the Court of Protection must have regard to –

    (a)   whether the proceedings should be heard together with other proceedings that are pending in a court having jurisdiction under the Children Act;

    (b)   whether any order that may be made by a court having jurisdiction under that Act is likely to be a more appropriate way of dealing with the proceedings;

    (c)   the need to meet any requirements that would apply if the proceedings had been started in a court having jurisdiction under the Children Act; and

    (d)   any other matter that the court considers relevant.

(4) The Court of Protection –

    (a)   may exercise the power to make an order under paragraph (2) on an application or on its own initiative; and

    (b)   where it orders a transfer, must give reasons for its decision.

(5) Any proceedings transferred under this article –

    (a)   are to be treated for all purposes as if they were proceedings under the Children Act which had been started in a court having jurisdiction under that Act; and

    (b)   are to be dealt with after the transfer in accordance with directions given by a court having jurisdiction under that Act.

Scope of provision—This article deals with a case in the Court of Protection. It sets out the matters to which the Court must have regard when considering the transfer of a case to a children's court.

The children's court could be the High Court, the county court or the Family Proceedings Court. Article 2(3) sets out the matters to which the Court of Protection must have regard.

'whether the proceedings should be heard together with [other proceedings in the children's court]' (art 2(3)(a) —If there are other linked or connected proceedings, it may be more sensible for them to be dealt with in one court.

For example:

There are two children, X and Y. X suffered brain damage at birth, the father is his deputy and X's affairs are the subject of the Court of Protection. Y is healthy and not subject to the Court.

The parents are to divorce. There are ancillary relief proceedings and a dispute about residence and contact concerning both children.

One of the assets is the matrimonial home which was partially purchased with funds from X's fund in court after permission was given by the Court of Protection. X has an interest in the property. Issues have arisen concerning this property.

Both parents want residence of X and Y and there are also problems with contact.

It is clearly desirable in this case for all the family litigation to be heard in one court. The Court of Protection has no jurisdiction to deal with ancillary relief or matters concerning Y so matters concerning X could be transferred to be heard in the children's court by a family judge who is also nominated to hear Court of Protection matters.

'**whether any order [made by the children's court] is likely to be a more appropriate way of dealing with the proceedings**' (art 2(3)(b))—It is important to examine the powers and remedies available in both jurisdictions to see whether the children's court would be a better forum for a matter to be adjudicated. For example, the Court of Protection cannot order a CAFCASS report or order the parents to attend a conciliation hearing which many courts offer.

Overall, it may be felt that a children's dispute should be dealt with in a court which regularly deals with such disputes rather than the Court of Protection.

Under the Children Act 1989, the welfare principle will apply and the child's interests are paramount. The court would have to consider if this principle is more appropriate than simply applying the best interests test under MCA 2005.

'**the need to meet any requirements that would apply if the proceedings had been started in [the children's court]**' (art 2(3)(c))—For example, a child has a deputy who is a solicitor; an issue has arisen as to where the child should live. The deputy could not make an application in the family court without the permission of the Court of Protection and of the family court.

'**any other matter that the court considers relevant**' (art 2(3)(d))—This will depend on the circumstances and the facts of each case. When considering the issue of transfer, the court must have regard to P's best interests.

3 Transfers from a court having jurisdiction under the Children Act to the Court of Protection

(1) This article applies to any proceedings in a court having jurisdiction under the Children Act which relate to a person under 18.

(2) A court having jurisdiction under the Children Act may direct the transfer of the whole or part of the proceedings to the Court of Protection where it considers that in all circumstances, it is just and convenient to transfer the proceedings.

(3) In making a determination, the court having jurisdiction under the Children Act must have regard to –

    (a)   whether the proceedings should be heard together with other proceedings that are pending in the Court of Protection;

    (b)   whether any order that may be made by the Court of Protection is likely to be a more appropriate way of dealing with the proceedings;

    (c)   the extent to which any order made as respects a person who lacks capacity is likely to continue to have effect when that person reaches 18; and

    (d)   any other matter that the court considers relevant.

(4) A court having jurisdiction under the Children Act –

    (a)   may exercise the power to make an order under paragraph (2) on an application or on its own initiative; and

    (b)   where it orders a transfer, must give reasons for its decision.

(5) Any proceedings transferred under this article –

(a) are to be treated for all purposes as if they were proceedings under the Mental Capacity Act 2005 which had been started in the Court of Protection; and
(b) are to be dealt with after the transfer in accordance with directions given by the Court of Protection.

Scope of provision—This article deals with transfer from the children's court to the Court of Protection. The same criteria are applied as in art 2.

4 Avoidance of double liability for fees

Any fee paid for the purpose of starting any proceedings that are transferred under article 2 or 3 is to be treated as if it were the fee that would have been payable if the proceedings had started in the court to which the transfer is made.

Mental Capacity Act 2005 (Transitional and Consequential Provisions) Order 2007, SI 2007/1898

1 Citation and commencement

This Order may be cited as the Mental Capacity Act 2005 (Transitional and Consequential Provisions) Order 2007, and comes into force on 1 October 2007.

2 Interpretation

In this Order –

(a) 'the Act' means the Mental Capacity Act 2005; and
(b) 'Court of Protection' refers
 (i) the first time the expression appears in article 4, to the office of the Supreme Court called the Court of Protection mentioned in section 45(6) of the Act, and
 (ii) where the expression appears in articles 3, 4(a) and (b), to the superior court of record established by section 45(1) of the Act.

3 Proceedings begun in the High Court before 1 October 2007

(1) This article applies to any proceedings about P's personal welfare begun in the High Court before 1 October 2007 in respect of which the Court of Protection would, but for this article, have jurisdiction on and after that date under section 16 of the Act.

(2) The proceedings may continue to be dealt with, until they are finally decided, in accordance with the arrangements existing immediately before 1 October 2007.

(3) For the purposes of paragraph (2), an application is finally decided when it is determined and there is no possibility of the determination being reversed or varied on an appeal.

(4) In dealing with proceedings under this article, the High Court retains all the powers and jurisdiction in relation to any matter that is the subject of the proceedings that it had immediately before the commencement of the Act.

(5) In this article –

 (a) 'P' means any person (other than a protected party) who lacks, or so far as consistent with the context is alleged to lack, capacity to make a decision or decisions in relation to any matter that is the subject of an application to the court and references to a person who lacks capacity are to be construed in accordance with the Act;
 (b) 'personal welfare' is to be construed in accordance with section 17 of the Act; and
 (c) 'protected party' means a party, or an intended party (other than P or a child), who lacks capacity to conduct the proceedings.

4 Senior Judge of the Court of Protection

The person who, immediately before the commencement of Part 2 of the Act, holds the office of Master of the Court of Protection, shall be treated as –

 (a) being a circuit judge nominated under section 46(1) of the Act to exercise the jurisdiction of the Court of Protection; and
 (b) having been appointed the Senior Judge of the Court of Protection under section 46(4) of the Act.

5 Advance decisions to refuse life-sustaining treatment

(1) An advance decision refusing life-sustaining treatment shall be treated as valid and applicable to a treatment and does not have to satisfy the requirements mentioned in paragraph (3) if the conditions in paragraph (2) are met.

(2) The conditions that must be met are that –

 (a) a person providing health care for a person ('P') reasonably believes that –
  (i) P has made the advance decision refusing life-sustaining treatment before 1 October 2007, and
  (ii) P has lacked the capacity to comply with the provisions mentioned in paragraph (3) since 1 October 2007;
 (b) the advance decision is in writing;
 (c) P has not –
  (i) withdrawn the decision at a time when he had capacity to do so, or
  (ii) done anything else clearly inconsistent with the advance decision remaining his fixed decision;
 (d) P does not have the capacity to give or refuse consent to the treatment in question at the material time;
 (e) the treatment in question is the treatment specified in the advance decision;
 (f) any circumstances specified in the advance decision are present; and
 (g) there are no reasonable grounds for believing that circumstances exist which P did not anticipate at the time of the advance decision and which would have affected his decision had he anticipated them.

(3) The requirements that do not have to be satisfied are as follows –

 (a) the requirement for the decision to be verified by a statement by P to the

effect that the advance decision is to apply to that treatment even if life is at risk (section 25(5)(a) of the Act); and
(b) the requirement for a signed and witnessed advance decision (section 25(6)(b) to (d) of the Act).

(4) In this article, 'advance decision' has the meaning given in section 24(1) of the Act.

6 Minor and consequential amendments

Schedule 1 contains minor and consequential amendments.

SCHEDULE 1
MINOR AND CONSEQUENTIAL AMENDMENTS

Article 6

1 Trustee Savings Bank Life Annuity Regulations 1930

In regulation 16(2) of the Trustee Savings Bank Life Annuity Regulations 1930 –
(a) for the words 'a person who is incapable, by reason of mental disorder within the meaning of the Mental Health Act 1959, of managing and administering his property and affairs' substitute 'a person who lacks mental capacity within the meaning of the Mental Capacity Act 2005 to administer and manage his property and affairs'; and
(b) for the word 'receiver' substitute 'deputy'.

2 Savings Contract Regulations 1969

(1) The Savings Contract Regulations 1969 are amended in accordance with this paragraph.

(2) In regulation 2(1) (interpretation), omit the entries for 'mentally disordered person' and 'receiver' and, in the appropriate alphabetical position, insert –
(a) ' "deputy" in the application of these Regulations to England and Wales, means, in relation to any decision made for a person who lacks capacity, a deputy appointed by the Court of Protection for that person with power to make decisions in relation to the matters in question;'; and
(b) ' "person who lacks capacity" means a person who lacks capacity within the meaning of the Mental Capacity Act 2005;'.

(3) In regulation 7 (payment in case of mentally disordered persons) –
(a) in the title, for 'mentally disordered persons' substitute 'persons who lack capacity'; and
(b) in paragraphs (1) and (2) in each place –
(i) for 'mentally disordered person' substitute 'person who lacks capacity', and
(ii) for 'receiver' substitute 'deputy'.

(4) In regulation 12 (persons under disability) –

(a) for 'mentally disordered person' substitute 'person who lacks capacity'; and
(b) for 'receiver' substitute 'deputy'.

(5) In regulation 27 (application to Scotland) –

(a) in paragraph (a), for 'mentally disordered person' substitute 'person who lacks capacity'; and
(b) in paragraph (b), for 'receiver in relation to a mentally disordered person' substitute 'deputy in relation to a person who lacks capacity'.

(6) In regulation 28(2) (application to Northern Ireland) –

(a) in sub-paragraph (a), for 'mentally disordered person' substitute 'person who lacks capacity'; and
(b) in sub-paragraph (b), for 'receiver in relation to a mentally disordered person' substitute 'deputy in relation to a person who lacks capacity'.

(7) In regulation 29(2)(a) (application to the Isle of Man), for 'receiver in relation to a mentally disordered person' substitute 'deputy in relation to a person who lacks capacity'.

(8) In regulation 30 (application to the Channel Islands) –

(a) in paragraphs (2)(a) and (3)(a), for 'mentally disordered person' substitute 'person who lacks capacity'; and
(b) in paragraphs (2)(b) and (3)(b), for 'receiver in relation to a mentally disordered person' substitute 'deputy in relation to a person who lacks capacity'.

3 Pensions Increase (Judicial Pensions) Regulations 1972

In paragraph 9 of the Schedule to the Pensions Increase (Judicial Pensions) Regulations 1972, omit the reference to a Master of the Court of Protection except in the case of a person holding that office immediately before the commencement of this paragraph or who had previously retired from that office or died.

4 National Savings Bank Regulations 1972

(1) The National Savings Bank Regulations 1972 are amended in accordance with this paragraph.

(2) In regulation 2(1) (interpretation), omit the entries for 'mentally disordered person' and 'receiver' and, in the appropriate alphabetical position, insert –

(a) ' "deputy" in the application of these Regulations to England and Wales, means, in relation to any decision made for a person who lacks capacity, a deputy appointed by the Court of Protection for that person with power to make decisions in relation to the matters in question;'; and
(b) ' "person who lacks capacity" means a person who lacks capacity within the meaning of the Mental Capacity Act 2005;'.

(3) In regulation 7 (mentally disordered persons) –

(a) in the title, for 'Mentally disordered persons' substitute 'Persons who lack capacity';
(b) in paragraph (1), for 'mentally disordered person, by his receiver' substitute 'person who lacks capacity, by his deputy';

(c) in paragraphs (2), (3) and (4) in each place –
  (i) for 'mentally disordered person' substitute 'person who lacks capacity', and
  (ii) for 'receiver' substitute 'deputy';

(4) In regulation 8(4)(c) (joint accounts) –
  (a) for 'mentally disordered person' substitute 'person who lacks capacity'; and
  (b) for 'receiver' substitute 'deputy'.

(5) In regulation 9(4) (trust accounts) –
  (a) for both references to 'mentally disordered person' substitute 'person who lacks capacity'; and
  (b) for 'receiver' substitute 'deputy'.

(6) In regulation 37(1)(b) (payment under nomination) –
  (a) for 'mentally disordered person' substitute 'person who lacks capacity'; and
  (b) for 'receiver' substitute 'deputy'.

(7) In regulation 45 (persons under disability) –
  (a) for 'mentally disordered person' substitute 'person who lacks capacity'; and
  (b) for 'receiver' substitute 'deputy'.

(8) In regulation 57(2)(a) (application to the Isle of Man), for 'receiver in relation to a mentally disordered person' substitute 'deputy in relation to a person who lacks capacity'.

(9) In regulation 58 (application to the Channel Islands) –
  (a) in paragraphs (2)(a) and (3)(a), for 'mentally disordered person' substitute 'person who lacks capacity'; and
  (b) in paragraphs (2)(b) and (3)(b), for 'receiver in relation to a mentally disordered person' substitute 'deputy in relation to a person who lacks capacity'.

5 Premium Savings Bond Regulations 1972

(1) The Premium Savings Bond Regulations 1972 are amended in accordance with this paragraph.

(2) In regulation 2(1) (interpretation), omit the entries for 'mentally disordered person' and 'receiver' and, in the appropriate alphabetical position, insert –
  (a) ' "deputy" in the application of these Regulations to England and Wales, means, in relation to any decision made for a person who lacks capacity, a deputy appointed by the Court of Protection for that person with power to make decisions in relation to the matters in question;'; and
  (b) ' "person who lacks capacity" means a person who lacks capacity within the meaning of the Mental Capacity Act 2005;'.

(3) In regulation 4 (persons entitled to purchase and hold bonds) –
  (a) in paragraph (3)(b), for 'mentally disordered person, by his receiver' substitute 'a person who lacks capacity, by his deputy', and

(b) in paragraph (5)(b), for 'mentally disordered person' substitute 'person who lacks capacity'.

(4) In regulation 10 (payment in case of mentally disordered persons) –

   (a) in the title, for 'Mentally disordered persons' substitute 'Persons who lack capacity';

   (b) in paragraph (1) –

      (i) for 'mentally disordered person' substitute 'person who lacks capacity', and

      (ii) for 'receiver' substitute 'deputy'; and

   (c) in paragraph (2), for 'mentally disordered person for whose estate no receiver' substitute 'person who lacks capacity for whom no deputy has been appointed in relation to his property and affairs'.

(5) In regulation 16 (persons under disability) –

   (a) for 'mentally disordered person' substitute 'person who lacks capacity'; and

   (b) for 'receiver' substitute 'deputy'.

(6) In regulation 31 (application to Scotland) –

   (a) in paragraph (a), for 'mentally disordered person' substitute 'person who lacks capacity'; and

   (b) in paragraph (b), for 'receiver in relation to a mentally disordered person' substitute 'deputy in relation to a person who lacks capacity'.

(7) In regulation 32(2) (application to Northern Ireland) –

   (a) in paragraph (a), for 'mentally disordered person' substitute 'person who lacks capacity'; and

   (b) in paragraph (b), for 'receiver in relation to a mentally disordered person' substitute 'deputy in relation to a person who lacks capacity'.

(8) In regulation 33(2)(a) (application to the Isle of Man), for 'receiver in relation to a mentally disordered person' substitute 'deputy in relation to a person who lacks capacity'.

(9) In regulation 34 (application to the Channel Islands) –

   (a) in paragraphs (2)(a) and (3)(a), for 'mentally disordered person' substitute 'person who lacks capacity'; and

   (b) in paragraphs (2)(b) and (3)(b), for 'receiver in relation to a mentally disordered person' substitute 'deputy in relation to a person who lacks capacity'.

6 National Savings Stock Register Regulations 1976

(1) The National Savings Stock Register Regulations 1976 are amended in accordance with this paragraph.

(2) In regulation 2(1) (interpretation), omit the entries for 'mentally disordered person' and 'receiver' and, in the appropriate alphabetical position, insert –

   (a) ' "deputy" in the application of these Regulations to England and Wales, means, in relation to any decision made for a person who lacks capacity, a deputy appointed by the Court of Protection for that person with power to make decisions in relation to the matters in question;'; and

   (b) ' "person who lacks capacity" means a person who lacks capacity within

the meaning of the Mental Capacity Act 2005;'.
(3) In regulation 31 (persons under disability) –
   (a) in paragraphs (1) and (2) in each place –
      (i) for 'mentally disordered person' substitute 'person who lacks capacity'; and
      (ii) for 'receiver' substitute 'deputy'; and
   (b) in paragraphs (3) and (4), for 'mentally disordered person' substitute 'person who lacks capacity'.

(4) In regulation 59 (application to Scotland) –
   (a) in paragraph (a), for 'mentally disordered person' substitute 'person who lacks capacity'; and
   (b) in paragraph (b), for 'receiver in relation to a mentally disordered person' substitute 'deputy in relation to a person who lacks capacity'.

(5) In regulation 60(2) (application to Northern Ireland) –
   (a) in paragraph (a), for 'mentally disordered person' substitute 'person who lacks capacity'; and
   (b) in paragraph (b), for 'receiver in relation to a mentally disordered person' substitute 'deputy in relation to a person who lacks capacity'.

(6) In regulation 61(2)(a) (application to the Isle of Man), for 'receiver in relation to a mentally disordered person' substitute 'deputy in relation to a person who lacks capacity'.

(7) In regulation 62 (application to the Channel Islands) –
   (a) in paragraphs (2)(a) and (3)(a), for 'mentally disordered person' substitute 'person who lacks capacity'; and
   (b) in paragraphs (2)(b) and (3)(b), for 'receiver in relation to a mentally disordered person' substitute 'deputy in relation to a person who lacks capacity'.

7 Motor Vehicles (Tests) Regulations 1981

In regulation 9(1)(c) (cessations: general) of the Motor Vehicles (Tests) Regulations 1981, for the words from 'patient' to 'Mental Health Act 1983' substitute 'person who lacks capacity (within the meaning of the Mental Capacity Act 2005) to carry on the activities covered by the authorisation'.

8 The Mental Health Review Tribunal Rules 1983

For rule 7(c) (notice to other persons interested) of the Mental Health Review Tribunal Rules 1983, substitute –

'(c) where there is an extant order of either –
   (i) the office of the Supreme Court called the Court of Protection mentioned in section 45(6) of the Mental Capacity Act 2005, or
   (ii) the superior court of record established by section 45(1) of the Mental Capacity Act 2005, to the court referred to in sub-paragraph (ii) of this rule;'

9 Savings Certificates (Yearly Plan) Regulations 1984

(1) The Savings Certificates (Yearly Plan) Regulations 1984 are amended in accordance with this paragraph.

(2) In regulation 2 (interpretation), omit the entries for 'mentally disordered person' and 'receiver' and, in the appropriate alphabetical position, insert –

- (a) ' "deputy" in the application of these Regulations to England and Wales, means, in relation to any decision made for a person who lacks capacity, a deputy appointed by the Court of Protection for that person with power to make decisions in relation to the matters in question;'; and
- (b) ' "person who lacks capacity" means a person who lacks capacity within the meaning of the Mental Capacity Act 2005;'.

(3) In regulation 4(2)(b) (persons entitled to enter into agreements and to hold certificates), for 'mentally disordered person, by his receiver' substitute 'person who lacks capacity, by his deputy'.

(4) In regulation 5(2) (maximum payments), for 'mentally disordered person' substitute 'person who lacks capacity'.

(5) In regulation 8 (repayment in case of persons under 7 years of age and mentally disordered persons) –

- (a) in the title, for 'mentally disordered persons' substitute 'persons who lack capacity';
- (b) in paragraph (2), for 'mentally disordered person, by his receiver' substitute 'person who lacks capacity, by his deputy'; and
- (c) in paragraph (3), for 'mentally disordered person for whose estate no receiver' substitute 'person who lacks capacity for whom no deputy'.

(6) In regulation 9(1)(a) (repayment in case of joint trustees) –

- (a) for 'mentally disordered person' substitute 'person who lacks capacity'; and
- (b) for 'receiver' substitute 'deputy'.

(7) In regulation 10(1)(a) (repayment in case of certificate held by person jointly) –

- (a) for 'mentally disordered person' substitute 'person who lacks capacity'; and
- (b) for 'receiver' substitute 'deputy'.

(8) In regulation 18 (persons under disability) –

- (a) for 'mentally disordered person' substitute 'person who lacks capacity'; and
- (b) for 'receiver' substitute 'deputy'.

(9) In regulation 33 (application to Scotland) –

- (a) in paragraph (a), for 'mentally disordered person' substitute 'person who lacks capacity'; and
- (b) in paragraph (b), for 'receiver in relation to a mentally disordered person' substitute 'deputy in relation to a person who lacks capacity'.

(10) In regulation 34(2) (application to Northern Ireland) –

- (a) in paragraph (a), for 'mentally disordered person' substitute 'person who lacks capacity'; and
- (b) in paragraph (b), for 'receiver in relation to a mentally disordered person' substitute 'deputy in relation to a person who lacks capacity'.

(11) In regulation 35(2)(a) (application to the Isle of Man), for 'receiver in relation to a mentally disordered person' substitute 'deputy in relation to a person who lacks capacity'.

(12) In regulation 36 (application to the Channel Islands) –

(a) in paragraphs (2)(a) and (3)(a), for 'mentally disordered person' substitute 'person who lacks capacity'; and
(b) in paragraphs (2)(b) and (3)(b), for 'receiver in relation to a mentally disordered person' substitute 'deputy in relation to a person who lacks capacity'.

10 Road Vehicles (Construction and Use) Regulations 1986

In paragraph 5(1)(c) of Part 1 of Schedule 3B (authorised sealers) to the Road Vehicles (Construction and Use) Regulations 1986, for the words from 'patient' to 'Mental Health Act 1983, substitute 'person who lacks capacity (within the meaning of the Mental Capacity Act 2005) to carry on the activities covered by the authorisation'.

11 Operation of Public Service Vehicles (Partnership) Regulations 1986

On the entry as to section 57(2) of the Public Passenger Vehicles Act 1981, in column 2 of Part 1 of the Schedule to the Operation of Public Service Vehicles (Partnership) Regulations 1986, for the words from 'patient' to 'Mental Health Act 1983', substitute 'person who lacks capacity (within the meaning of the Mental Capacity Act 2005) to carry on the activities covered by the licence'.

12 Insolvency Rules 1986

(1) The Insolvency Rules 1986 are amended in accordance with this paragraph.

(2) In rule 4.214 (witness unfit for examination) –

(a) in paragraph (1) –
 (i) omit the words 'mental disorder or', and
 (ii) before 'is suffering' insert 'is a person who lacks capacity within the meaning of the Mental Capacity Act 2005 or', and
(b) in paragraph (3)(a), for the words 'patient within the meaning of the Mental Health Act 1983' substitute 'person who lacks capacity within the meaning of the Mental Capacity Act 2005'.

(3) In rule 6.174 (bankrupt unfit for examination) –

(a) in paragraph (1) –
 (i) omit the words 'mental disorder or', and
 (ii) before 'is suffering' insert 'is a person who lacks capacity within the meaning of the Mental Capacity Act 2005 or', and
(b) in paragraph (3)(a), for the words 'patient within the meaning of the Mental Health Act 1983', substitute 'person who lacks capacity within the meaning of the Mental Capacity Act 2005'.

(4) In the heading to Part 7 of Chapter 7, for 'Persons Incapable of Managing their Affairs', substitute 'Persons who Lack Capacity to Manage their Affairs'.

(5) In rule 7.43 (introductory) –

   (a) in paragraph (1), for 'is incapable of managing and administering his property and affairs', substitute 'lacks capacity within the meaning of the Mental Capacity Act 2005 to manage and administer his property and affairs'; and

   (b) in paragraph (1)(a), for 'mental disorder within the meaning of the Mental Health Act 1983', substitute 'lacking capacity within the meaning of the Mental Capacity Act 2005'.

(6) In paragraph 4.64 of Part 4 of Schedule 4, Forms Index (companies winding up) –

   (a) after the words 'person who', insert 'lacks capacity to manage and administer his property and affairs or'; and

   (b) for the words 'mental disorder or', substitute 'a'.

(7) In paragraph 6.57 of Part 6 of Schedule 4, Forms Index (bankruptcy) –

   (a) after the words 'bankrupt who', insert 'lacks capacity to manage and administer his property and affairs or'; and

   (b) for the words 'mental disorder or', substitute 'a'.

(8) For form 4.64 in Schedule 4 (forms), substitute the form in Schedule 2 (Part 1).

(9) For form 6.57 in Schedule 4 (forms), substitute the form in Schedule 2 (Part 2).

13 Non-contentious Probate Rules 1987

(1) Rule 31 (grant to attorneys) and 35 (grants in case of mental incapacity) of the Non-contentious Probate Rules 1987 are amended in accordance with this paragraph.

(2) For rule 31(3) substitute –

'(3) Where the donor referred to in paragraph (1) above lacks capacity within the meaning of the Mental Capacity Act 2005 and the attorney is acting under an enduring power of attorney or lasting power of attorney, the application shall be made in accordance with rule 35.'

(3) For rule 35, in the title, for the words 'mental incapacity' substitute 'lack of mental capacity'.

(4) In rule 35(1), for the words 'incapable person' substitute 'person who lacks capacity within the meaning of the Mental Capacity Act 2005'.

(5) In rule 35(2) –

   (a) for the words 'is by reason of mental incapacity incapable of managing', substitute 'lacks capacity within the meaning of the Mental Capacity Act 2005 to manage';

   (b) for each reference to an incapable person substitute a reference to a person who lacks capacity within the meaning of the Mental Capacity Act 2005; and

   (c) at the end of sub-paragraph (b), insert 'or lasting power of attorney'.

(6) In rule 35(4), for the words 'incapable person', substitute 'person who lacks capacity within the meaning of the Mental Capacity Act 2005'.

14 Judicial Pension (Preservation of Benefits) Order 1988

In Schedule 2 to the Judicial Pension (Preservation of Benefits) Order 1988, omit the reference to a Master of the Court of Protection except in the case of a person holding that office immediately before the commencement of this paragraph or who had previously retired from that office or died.

15 Judicial Pensions (Requisite Benefits) Order 1988

In Schedule 2 (office) to the Judicial Pensions (Requisite Benefits) Order 1988, omit the reference to a Master of the Court of Protection except in the case of a person holding that office immediately before the commencement of this paragraph or who had previously retired from that office or died.

16 Church of England Pensions Regulations 1988

(1) Regulation 30 (payment of pensions in respect of persons suffering from mental disorder) of the Church of England Pensions Regulations 1988 is amended in accordance with this paragraph.

(2) In paragraph (1) –

 (a) for the words 'is incapable by reason of mental disorder within the meaning of the Mental Health Act, 1983, of managing and administering', substitute 'lacks capacity (within the meaning of the Mental Capacity Act 2005) to manage and administer'; and

 (b) in sub-paragraph (a), for the words 'suffering from mental disorder', substitute 'a person lacking capacity (within the meaning of the Mental Capacity Act 2005) to manage and administer his property and affairs'.

(3) In paragraph (2) –

 (a) for the words 'authority having jurisdiction under Part VII of the Mental Health Act, 1983', substitute 'Court of Protection'; and

 (b) for each reference to 'that authority' substitute a reference to 'the Court of Protection'.

(4) In paragraph (3) –

 (a) for the words 'the authority having jurisdiction under Part VII of the Mental Health Act, 1983 give', substitute 'the Court of Protection gives'; and

 (b) for the words 'that authority', substitute 'the Court of Protection'.

17 Savings Certificates Regulations 1991

(1) The Savings Certificates Regulations 1991 are amended in accordance with this paragraph.

(2) In regulation 2(1) (interpretation), omit the entries for 'mentally disordered person' and 'receiver' and, in the appropriate alphabetical position, insert –

 (a) ' "deputy" in the application of these Regulations to England and Wales, means, in relation to any decision made for a person who lacks capacity, a deputy appointed by the Court of Protection for that person with power to make decisions in relation to the matters in question;'; and

(b) ' "person who lacks capacity" means a person who lacks capacity within the meaning of the Mental Capacity Act 2005;'.

(3) In regulation 4(2)(c) (persons entitled to purchase and hold certificates), for 'mentally disordered person, by his receiver' substitute 'person who lacks capacity, by his deputy'.

(4) In regulation 9 (repayment in case of persons under 7 years of age and mentally disordered persons) –

(a) in the title, for 'mentally disordered persons' substitute 'persons who lack capacity';
(b) in paragraph (2), for 'mentally disordered person shall be made by his receiver' substitute 'person who lacks capacity shall be made by his deputy'; and
(c) in paragraph (4), for the words from 'mentally disordered person for' to 'of the mentally disordered person' substitute 'person who lacks capacity in respect of whom no deputy has been appointed, the Director of Savings may, if he thinks fit, pay the whole or any part of the amount repayable in respect of the certificate to any person who satisfies him that he will apply the payment for the maintenance or otherwise for the benefit of the person who lacks capacity'.

(5) In regulation 10(1)(a) (repayment in case of certificate held by persons jointly) –

(a) for 'mentally disordered person' substitute 'person who lacks capacity'; and
(b) for 'receiver' substitute 'person who lacks capacity'.

(6) In regulation 18 (persons under disability) –

(a) for 'mentally disordered person' substitute 'person who lacks capacity'; and
(b) for 'receiver' substitute 'deputy'.

(7) In regulation 33 (application to Scotland) –

(a) in paragraph (a), for 'mentally disordered person' substitute 'person who lacks capacity'; and
(b) in paragraph (b), for 'receiver in relation to a mentally disordered person' substitute 'deputy in relation to a person who lacks capacity'.

(8) In regulation 34 (application to Northern Ireland) –

(a) in paragraph (b), for 'mentally disordered person' substitute 'person who lacks capacity'; and
(b) in paragraph (c), for 'receiver in relation to a mentally disordered person' substitute 'deputy in relation to a person who lacks capacity'.

(9) In regulation 35(2) (application to the Isle of Man) –

(a) in paragraph (a), for 'mentally disordered person' substitute 'person who lacks capacity'; and
(b) in paragraph (b), for 'receiver in relation to any act or thing done in respect of a mentally disordered person shall be construed as a reference to a receiver' substitute 'deputy in relation to any decision made for a person who lacks capacity shall be construed as a reference to a deputy'.

(10) In regulation 36 (application to the Channel Islands) –

(a) in paragraphs (2)(a) and (3)(a), for 'mentally disordered person' substitute 'person who lacks capacity'; and

(b) in paragraphs (2)(b) and (3)(b), for 'receiver in relation to a mentally disordered person' substitute 'deputy in relation to a person who lacks capacity'.

(11) In paragraph 2 of Part 1 of Schedule 1 (persons entitled to hold index-linked certificates to be purchased before 7 September 1981), for 'receiver on behalf of and in the name of a mentally disordered person' substitute 'deputy on behalf of and in the name of a person who lacks capacity'.

18 Savings Certificates (Children's Bonus Bonds) Regulations 1991

(1) The Savings Certificates (Children's Bonus Bonds) Regulations 1991 are amended in accordance with this paragraph.

(2) In regulation 2(1) (interpretation), omit the entries for 'mentally disordered person' and 'receiver' and, in the appropriate alphabetical position, insert –

(a) ' "deputy" in the application of these Regulations to England and Wales, means, in relation to any decision made for a person who lacks capacity, a deputy appointed by the Court of Protection for that person with power to make decisions in relation to the matters in question;'; and
(b) ' "person who lacks capacity" means a person who lacks capacity within the meaning of the Mental Capacity Act 2005;'.

(3) In regulation 8(2) (repayment in case of persons under 16 years of age), for 'mentally disordered person' substitute 'person who lacks capacity'.

(4) In regulation 9 (repayment in case of mentally disordered persons) –

(a) in the title, for 'mentally disordered persons' substitute 'persons who lack capacity';
(b) in paragraph (1), for 'mentally disordered person shall be made by his receiver' substitute 'person who lacks capacity shall be made by his deputy'; and
(c) in paragraph (2), for 'mentally disordered person for whose estate no receiver' substitute 'person who lacks capacity for whom no deputy'.

(5) In regulation 15 (persons under disability) –

(a) for 'mentally disordered person' substitute 'person who lacks capacity'; and
(b) for 'receiver' substitute 'deputy'.

(6) In regulation 29 (application to Scotland) –

(a) in paragraph (a), for 'mentally disordered person' substitute 'person who lacks capacity'; and
(b) in paragraph (b), for 'receiver in relation to a mentally disordered person' substitute 'deputy in relation to a person who lacks capacity'.

(7) In regulation 30 (application to Northern Ireland) –

(a) n paragraph (a), for 'mentally disordered person' substitute 'person who lacks capacity'; and
(b) in paragraph (b), for 'receiver in relation to a mentally disordered person' substitute 'deputy in relation to a person who lacks capacity'.

(8) In regulation 31(2) (application to the Isle of Man) –

(a) in paragraph (a), for 'mentally disordered person' substitute 'person who lacks capacity'; and
(b) in paragraph (b), for 'receiver in relation to any act or thing done in respect of a mentally disordered person shall be construed as a reference to a receiver' substitute 'deputy in relation to any decision made for a person who lacks capacity shall be construed as a reference to a deputy'.

(9) In regulation 32 (application to the Channel Islands) –
(a) in paragraphs (2)(a) and (3)(a), for 'mentally disordered person' substitute 'person who lacks capacity'; and
(b) in paragraphs (2)(b) and (3)(b), for 'receiver in relation to a mentally disordered person' substitute 'deputy in relation to a person who lacks capacity'.

19 Judicial Pensions (Transfer Between Judicial Pension Schemes) Regulations 1995

In Schedule 2 (existing judicial scheme judicial offices included in each arrangement) to the Judicial Pensions (Transfer Between Judicial Pension Schemes) Regulations 1995, under the cross-heading 'District Judiciary Scheme', omit the reference to a Master of the Court of Protection except in the case of a person holding that office immediately before the commencement of this paragraph or who had previously retired from that office or died.

20 Judicial Pensions (Additional Voluntary Contributions) Regulations 1995

In Schedule 4 (existing judicial scheme judicial offices included in each arrangement) to the Judicial Pensions (Additional Voluntary Contributions) Regulations 1995, under the cross-heading 'District Judiciary Scheme', omit the reference to a Master of the Court of Protection except in the case of a person holding that office immediately before the commencement of this paragraph or who had previously retired from that office or died.

21 Goods Vehicles (Licensing of Operators) Regulations 1995

(1) Regulations 29 (partnerships) and 31 (continuance of licence on death, bankruptcy etc) of the Goods Vehicles (Licensing of Operators) Regulations 1995 are amended in accordance with this paragraph.

(2) In regulation 29(11)(b), for the words from 'patient' to 'Mental Health Act 1983', substitute 'person who lacks capacity (within the meaning of the Mental Capacity Act 2005) to carry on the activities covered by the licence'.

(3) In regulation 31 –
(a) in paragraph (2), for the words from 'patient' to 'Mental Health Act 1983', substitute 'person who lacks capacity (within the meaning of the Mental Capacity Act 2005) to carry on the activities covered by the licence'; and
(b) in paragraph (3), for the words from 'patient' to 'Mental Health Act 1983', substitute 'person who lacks capacity (within the meaning of the Mental Capacity Act 2005) to carry on the activities covered by the licence'.

22 Landfill Tax Regulations 1996

For regulation 33(1C)(a) (bodies eligible for approval) of the Landfill Tax Regulations 1996, substitute –

> '(a) in England and Wales, the person lacks capacity within the meaning of the Mental Capacity Act 2005 to administer and manage his property and affairs;'.

23 (revoked)

24 General Chiropractic Council (Constitution and Procedure) Rules Order 1999

In rule 2 (grounds of removal) of the General Chiropractic Council (Constitution and Procedure) Rules Order of Council 1999, in paragraph (1)(d) for 'or is otherwise incapable, by reason of mental disorder, of properly managing his property or affairs', substitute 'or lacks capacity within the meaning of the Mental Capacity Act 2005, to properly manage his property or affairs'.

25 Health Service Medicines (Price Control Appeals) Regulations 2000

In regulation 7 (appointment of tribunal) of the Health Service Medicines (Price Control Appeals) Regulations 2000, in paragraph (3)(b), for 'incapacity' substitute 'lack of capacity (within the meaning of the Mental Capacity Act 2005)'.

26 Ionising Radiation (Medical Exposure) Regulations 2000

In regulation 7 (optimisation) of the Ionising Radiation (Medical Exposure) Regulations 2000 –

(a) in paragraph (5)(b), after 'capacity' insert '(within the meaning of the Mental Capacity Act 2005 in the case of a child aged sixteen or seventeen)'; and
(b) in paragraph (5)(c), after 'capacity' insert '(within the meaning of the Mental Capacity Act 2005)'.

27 Carers (Services) and Direct Payments (Amendment) (England) Regulations 2001

For regulation 2(2) (services of an intimate nature and prescribed circumstances) of the Carers (Services) and Direct Payments (Amendment) (England) Regulations 2001, substitute –

> '(2) Where a service (A) is being delivered to the person cared for, a service of an intimate nature may be provided if –
>
> (a) during the delivery of service A, the person cared for asks the person delivering that service to provide a service of an intimate nature;
> (b) the person lacks capacity (within the meaning of the Mental Capacity Act 2005) to consent to the provision of a service of an intimate nature and it is provided in accordance with the principles of that Act; or
> (c) except where sub-paragraph (b) applies, the person cared for is in a

situation in which he is likely to suffer serious personal harm unless a service of an intimate nature is provided to him and the person providing service A reasonably believes that it is necessary to provide a service of an intimate nature because the likelihood of serious personal harm to the person cared for is imminent.'.

28–30 (*revoked*)

31 Land Registration Rules 2003

(1) Rule 61 (documents executed by attorney) of, and Schedule 3 (forms referred to in rule 206) to, the Land Registration Rules 2003 are amended in accordance with this paragraph.

(2) In rule 61 –

(a) for paragraph (1)(c) substitute –

'(c) a document which under section 4 of the Evidence and Powers of Attorney Act 1940, paragraph 16 of Part 2 of Schedule 1, or paragraph 15(3) of Part 5 of Schedule 4 to the Mental Capacity Act 2005 is sufficient evidence of the contents of the power, or'; and

(b) for paragraph (2) substitute –

'(2) If an order or direction under section 22 or 23 of, or paragraph 16 of Part 5 of Schedule 4 to, the Mental Capacity Act 2005 has been made with respect to a power or the donor of the power or the attorney appointed under it, the order or direction must be produced to the registrar.'.

(3) In Schedule 3 –

(a) in Form 1 (certificate as to execution of power of attorney (rule 61)) –

(i) for the first bullet point substitute –

'the power of attorney ('the power') is in existence and is made and, where required, has been registered under (*state statutory provisions under which the power is made and, where required, has been registered, if applicable*),', and

(ii) in the fourth bullet point, for the words 'or section 7(3) of the Enduring Powers of Attorney Act 1985', substitute –

', paragraph 16 of Part 2 of Schedule 1, or paragraph 15(3) of Part 5 of Schedule 4 to the Mental Capacity Act 2005'; and

(b) in Form 2 (statutory declaration/certificate as to non-revocation for powers more than 12 months old at the date of the disposition for which they are used (rule 62) –

(i) in the third bullet point, for the words 'valid enduring power', substitute 'valid lasting or enduring power of attorney',

(ii) after the third bullet point, insert –

'Where the power is in the form prescribed for a lasting power of attorney –

that a lasting power of attorney was not created, or

of circumstances which, if the lasting power of attorney had been created, would have terminated the attorney's authority to act as an attorney, or', and

(iii) in the heading immediately before the fourth bullet point, after the words 'enduring power', insert 'of attorney'.

32 National Health Service (Travel Expenses and Remission of Charges) Regulations 2003

In regulation 7 (claims to entitlement) of the National Health Service (Travel Expenses and Remission of Charges) Regulations 2003, for paragraph (3), substitute –

'(3) A claim may be made on behalf of another person where that person –
  (a) is unable by reason of physical incapacity; or
  (b) lacks capacity within the meaning of the Mental Capacity Act 2005,
to make the claim himself.'.

33 Child Trust Funds Regulations 2004

In regulation 33A(2) (the official solicitor or accountant of court to be the person who has the authority to manage an account) of the Child Trust Funds Regulations 2004, in Condition 4 –
  (a) in sub-paragraph (a), for the word 'receiver' substitute 'deputy';
  (b) for sub-paragraph (b), substitute '(b) determined that such a person lacks capacity within the meaning of the Mental Capacity Act 2005 to manage the child's property and affairs'; and
  (c) in the modifications of condition 4 for Scotland –
    (i) in sub-paragraph (b), for the word 'receiver' substitute 'deputy'; and
    (ii) in sub-paragraph (c), for the word 'patient' substitute 'person lacking capacity'.

34 National Health Service (Complaints) Regulations 2004

In regulation 8 (person who may make complaints) of the National Health Service (Complaints) Regulations 2004 –
  (a) in paragraph (2)(c), omit 'or mental' and 'or';
  (b) after paragraph (2)(c), insert –
    '(cc) is unable because he lacks capacity within the meaning of the Mental Capacity Act 2005 to make the complaint himself; or';
  (c) in paragraph (3), after 'who is' insert 'physically'; and
  (d) after paragraph (3) insert –

'(3A) In the case of a patient or person affected who lacks capacity within the meaning of the Mental Capacity Act 2005 the representative must be either a person appointed or authorised to act on his behalf under the 2005 Act or another person who, in the opinion of the complaints manager, had or has a sufficient interest in his welfare and is a suitable person to act as representative'.

35 Commonhold Regulations 2004

(1) In the table of contents in Schedule 2 (articles of association) to the Commonhold Regulations 2004, under the heading 'Votes of Members', for the words 'Entitlement to vote –Mental Capacity' substitute 'Entitlement to vote –lack of mental capacity'.

(2) In the title to article 29 of Schedule 2 (articles of association) to the Commonhold Regulations 2004, for the words 'mental incapacity' substitute 'lack of mental capacity'.

(3) In article 29 of Schedule 2 (articles of association) to the Commonhold Regulations 2004, for each reference to 'receiver' substitute a reference to 'deputy'.

36 (*revoked*)

37 Damages (Variation of Periodical Payments) Order 2005

For article 3(d) (defendant's financial resources) of the Damages (Variation of Periodical Payments) Order 2005, substitute –

'(d) the order is made by consent and the claimant is neither a child, nor a person who lacks capacity within the meaning of the Mental Capacity Act 2005 to administer and manage his property and affairs nor a patient within the meaning of Part VII of the Mental Health (Northern Ireland) Order 1986,'.

38 Disability Discrimination (Service Providers and Public Authorities Carrying Out Functions) Regulations 2005

In regulation 3(b) (circumstances in which mental incapacity justification does not apply) of the Disability Discrimination (Service Providers and Public Authorities Carrying Out Functions) Regulations 2005, for the words 'functions conferred by or under Part 7 of the Mental Health Act 1983', substitute 'being a deputy appointed by the Court of Protection'.

39 Disability Discrimination (Private Clubs etc) Regulations 2005

(1) In regulation 3(b) (circumstances in which mental incapacity justification does not apply) of the Disability Discrimination (Private Clubs etc) Regulations 2005, for the words 'functions conferred by or under Part 7 of the Mental Health Act 1983', substitute 'being a deputy appointed by the Court of Protection'.

(2) In regulation 13(3)(b) (duty of associations to make adjustments: justification) of these regulations, for the words 'functions conferred by or under Part 7 of the Mental Health Act 1983', substitute 'being a deputy appointed by the Court of Protection'.

40 Disability Discrimination (Premises) Regulations 2006

In regulation 2(b) (circumstances in which mental incapacity justification does not apply) of the Disability Discrimination (Premises) Regulations 2006, for the words 'functions conferred by or under Part 7 of the Mental Health Act 1983', substitute 'being a deputy appointed by the Court of Protection'.

Amendments—SI 2008/2836; SI 2010/807.

****

Public Guardian (Fees, etc) Regulations 2007,
SI 2007/2051

ARRANGEMENT OF REGULATIONS

Regulation	Page
1 Citation and commencement	1321
2 Interpretation	1321
3 Schedule of fees	1322
4 Fee for application to register an enduring power of attorney	1322
4A Enduring power of attorney office copy fee	1322
5 Fees for application to register a lasting power of attorney and repeat application to register	1322
5A Lasting power of attorney office copy fee	1323
8 Appointment of deputy: assessment and supervision fees	1323
9 Exemptions	1324
10 Reductions and remissions	1324
11 Transitional provision	1325
12 Amendment to Schedule 7 of the Lasting Powers of Attorney, Enduring Powers of Attorney and Public Guardian Regulations 2007	1325
Schedule – Fees to be taken	1325

1 Citation and commencement

These Regulations may be cited as the Public Guardian (Fees, etc) Regulations 2007 and shall come into force on 1 October 2007.

2 Interpretation

In these Regulations –

'the Act' means the Mental Capacity Act 2005;
'court' means the Court of Protection;
'office copy' means a true copy of the original marked by the Public Guardian as being an office copy;
'P' means the person in respect of whom a deputy has been appointed under section 16 of the Act; and
'Public Guardian' means the officer appointed in accordance with section 57 of the Act;
'the registers' means –
  (a) the register of lasting powers of attorney,
  (b) the register of enduring powers of attorney, and
  (c) the register of court orders appointing deputies,

established and maintained by the Public Guardian under section 58(1)(a) and (b) of and paragraph 14 of Schedule 4 to the Act.

Amendments—SI 2009/514.

3 Schedule of fees

The fees set out in the Schedule to these Regulations shall apply in accordance with the following provisions of these Regulations.

4 Fee for application to register an enduring power of attorney

(1) A fee for the registration of an enduring power of attorney shall be payable by the person seeking to register the enduring power of attorney under regulation 24 of the Lasting Powers of Attorney, Enduring Powers of Attorney and Public Guardian Regulations 2007 (application for registration).

(2) The fee prescribed by paragraph (1) shall be payable upon the application to register the enduring power of attorney.

Amendments—SI 2011/2189.

4A Enduring power of attorney office copy fee

(1) A fee for an office copy of an enduring power of attorney registered under paragraph 13 in Part 4 of Schedule 4 to the Mental Capacity Act 2005 shall be payable by the person requesting the office copy.

(2) The fee prescribed by paragraph (1) shall be payable at the time the request for an office copy is made.

Amendments—Inserted by SI 2009/514.

5 Fees for application to register a lasting power of attorney and repeat application to register

(1) A fee for the registration of a lasting power of attorney shall be payable by the person seeking to register the lasting power of attorney under regulation 11 of the Lasting Powers of Attorney, Enduring Powers of Attorney and Public Guardian Regulations 2007 (application for registration).

(1A) A reduced fee for an application to register a lasting power of attorney shall be payable where the application is a repeat application in the following circumstances –

(a) the initial application to register a lasting power of attorney is made on or after 1 October 2011;
(b) the initial application is returned to the applicant as invalid; and
(c) the repeat application to register is submitted within 3 months of the date on which the invalid application was returned to the applicant.

(2) The fee prescribed by –

(a) paragraph (1) shall be payable upon the application to register the lasting power of attorney; and
(b) paragraph (1A) shall be payable upon the submission of the repeat application to register.

Amendments—SI 2011/2189.

5A Lasting power of attorney office copy fee

(1) A fee for an office copy of a lasting power of attorney registered under Part 2 of Schedule 1 to the Mental Capacity Act 2005 shall be payable by the person requesting the office copy.

(2) The fee prescribed by paragraph (1) shall be payable at the time the request for an office copy is made.

Amendment—Inserted by SI 2009/514.

6–7 (revoked)

8 Appointment of deputy: assessment and supervision fees

(1) This regulation applies where –

   (a) the court has appointed a deputy under section 16 of the Act (powers to make decisions and appoint deputies: general); …

   (b) …

(2) Where paragraph (1) applies the Public Guardian shall assess the level of supervision required under section 58(1)(c) of the Act.

(3) The levels of supervision are –

   (a) general; and;

   (b) minimal

(3A) Where the Public Guardian makes an assessment in accordance with paragraph (2) a fee shall be payable by P within 30 days of the date of the invoice for the fee.

(4) Where the level of supervision assessed by the Public Guardian in accordance with paragraph (2) is –

   (a) 'general', an annual supervision fee shall be payable by P until the appointment of the deputy is terminated; and

   (b) 'minimal', an annual administration fee shall be payable by P until the appointment of the deputy is terminated.

(5) Subject to paragraphs (6) and (7), the appropriate supervision fee prescribed by paragraph (4) shall be due on 31 March each year and shall be payable by P within 30 days of the date of the invoice for the fee.

(6) Where the period for which the fee prescribed by paragraph (4) is payable is less than one year, the amount of the fee payable shall be such proportion of the full fee as that period bears to one year.

(7) Where the deputy's appointment terminates, the appropriate fee prescribed by paragraph (4) shall be due on the date of termination and shall be payable within 30 days of the date of the invoice for the fee.

(8) In the event of termination of the appointment due to P's death, the appropriate fee prescribed by paragraphs (3A) and (4) shall be payable by P's estate.

Amendments—SI 2009/514; SI 2011/2189.

9 Exemptions

(1) Subject to paragraphs (2) and (2A) no fee shall be payable under these regulations when, at the time when the fee would otherwise become payable, the relevant person is in receipt of any qualifying benefit.

(2) Paragraph (1) does not apply to a person who has an award of damages in excess of £16,000 which has been disregarded for the purposes of determining eligibility for that benefit.

(2A) Paragraph (1) does not apply to the office copy fees prescribed by regulations 4A and 5A.

(3) For the purposes of regulation 4 the relevant person is the donor of the enduring power of attorney.

(4) For the purposes of regulation 5 the relevant person is the donor of the lasting power of attorney.

(5) For the purposes of regulation 6 the relevant person is the person making the application.

(6) the purposes of regulations 7 and 8 the relevant person is P.

(7) The following are qualifying benefits for the purposes of paragraph (1) –

(a) income support under the Social Security Contributions and Benefits Act 1992;
(b) working tax credit, provided that –
   (i) child tax credit is being paid to the relevant person, or to a couple (as defined in section 3(5)(A) of the Tax Credits Act 2002) which includes the relevant person; or
   (ii) there is a disability element or severe disability element (or both) to the tax credit received by the relevant person;
(c) income-based job-seeker's allowance under the Jobseekers Act 1995;
(d) guarantee credit under the State Pensions Credit Act 2002;
(e) council tax benefit under the Social Security Contributions and Benefits Act 1992; …
(f) housing benefit under the Social Security Contributions and Benefits Act 1992; and
(g) income-related employment and support allowance under Part 1 of the Welfare Reform Act 2007.

Amendments—SI 2007/2616; SI 2009/514; SI 2011/2189.

10 Reductions and remissions

(1) Where it appears to the Public Guardian that the payment of any fee prescribed by these Regulations would, owing to the exceptional circumstances of the particular case, involve undue hardship, he may reduce or remit the fee in that case.

(1A) Where, at the time that a fee under these Regulations is payable, the relevant person (or a couple which includes the relevant person) is in receipt of universal credit under the Welfare Reform Act 2012, the Public Guardian may reduce or remit that fee.

(1B) Paragraph (1A) does not apply to the office copy fees prescribed by regulations 4A and 5A.

(1C) In paragraph (1A) –

(a) paragraphs (3) to (6) of regulation 9 apply for the purpose of determining who is the relevant person;
(b) 'couple' has the meaning given in section 39 of the Welfare Reform Act 2012.

(2) An application for the reduction or remission of any fee paid under regulation 8 (appointment of deputy assessment and supervision fees) must be made to the Public Guardian within 6 months after the date of the invoice in respect of that fee.

Amendment—SI 2010/1062; SI 2011/2189; SI 2013/1748.

11 Transitional provision

(1) In respect of the administration fee that would have been payable under rule 78 of the Court of Protection Rules 2001 on 31 March 2008, the appropriate proportion of that fee shall be due on 30 September 2007 and shall be payable within 30 days of the date of the invoice for the fee.

(2) Where the period for which the fee prescribed by paragraph (1) is payable is less than six months, the amount of the fee payable shall be such proportion of that fee as that period bears to six months.

12 Amendment to Schedule 7 of the Lasting Powers of Attorney, Enduring Powers of Attorney and Public Guardian Regulations 2007

(1) Schedule 7 of the Lasting Powers of Attorney, Enduring Powers of Attorney and Public Guardian Regulations 2007 is amended as follows.

(2) For paragraph 1 of Form EP1PG substitute 'You have the right to object to the proposed registration on one or more of the grounds set out below. You must notify the Office of the Public Guardian of your objection within five weeks from the day this notice was given to you. You may make an application to the Court of Protection under rule 68 of the Court of Protection Rules 2007 for a decision on the matter. No fee is payable for such an application. If you do not make such an application, the Public Guardian will ask for the court's directions about registration.'

Regulation 3

SCHEDULE
FEES TO BE TAKEN

Column 1	Column 2
Fee for application to register an enduring power of attorney (regulation 4)	£110.00
Enduring power of attorney office copy fee (regulation 4A)	£25.00
Fee for application to register a lasting power of attorney (regulation 5)	£110.00

Reduced fee for repeat application to register a lasting power of attorney(regulation 5)	£55.00
Lasting power of attorney office copy fee (regulation 5A)	£35.00
Deputy assessment fee (regulation 8)	£100.00
general supervision (regulation 8)	£320.00
minimal supervision (regulation 8)	£35.00

Amendments—SI 2009/514; SI 2010/1062; SI 2013/1748.

Mental Capacity (Deprivation of Liberty: Appointment of Relevant Person's Representative) Regulations 2008, SI 2008/1315

ARRANGEMENT OF REGULATIONS

Regulation	Page
1 Citation, commencement and application	1327
2 Interpretation	1327

PART 1
SELECTION OF REPRESENTATIVES

3 Selection of a person to be a representative – general	1327
4 Determination of capacity	1328
5 Selection by the relevant person	1328
6 Selection by a donee or deputy	1328
7 Confirmation of eligibility of family member, friend or carer and recommendation to the supervisory body	1329
8 Selection by the best interests assessor	1329
9 Selection by the supervisory body	1329

PART 2
APPOINTMENT OF REPRESENTATIVES

10 Commencement of appointment procedure	1330
11 Appointment of representative	1330
12 Formalities of appointing a representative	1330
13 Termination of representative's appointment	1331
14 Formalities of termination of representative's appointment	1331
15 Payment to a representative	1331

1 Citation, commencement and application

(1) These Regulations may be cited as the Mental Capacity (Deprivation of Liberty: Appointment of Relevant Person's Representative) Regulations 2008 and shall come into force on 3 November 2008.

(2) These Regulations apply in relation to England only.

2 Interpretation

In these Regulations –

'best interests assessor' means a person selected to carry out a best interests assessment under paragraph 38 of Schedule A1 to the Act;
'donee' is a person who has a lasting power of attorney conferred on them by the relevant person, giving that donee the authority to make decisions about the relevant person's personal welfare;
'the Act' means the Mental Capacity Act 2005; and
'the relevant person's managing authority' means the managing authority that has made the application for a standard authorisation in respect of the relevant person.

PART 1
SELECTION OF REPRESENTATIVES

3 Selection of a person to be a representative – general

(1) In addition to any requirements in regulations 6 to 9 and 11, a person can only be selected to be a representative if they are –

(a) 18 years of age or over;
(b) able to keep in contact with the relevant person;
(c) willing to be the relevant person's representative;
(d) not financially interested in the relevant person's managing authority;
(e) not a relative of a person who is financially interested in the managing authority;
(f) not employed by, or providing services to, the relevant person's managing authority, where the relevant person's managing authority is a care home;
(g) not employed to work in the relevant person's managing authority in a role that is, or could be, related to the relevant person's case, where the relevant person's managing authority is a hospital; and
(h) not employed to work in the supervisory body that is appointing the representative in a role that is, or could be, related to the relevant person's case.

(2) For the purposes of this regulation a 'relative' means –

(a) a spouse, ex-spouse, civil partner or ex-civil partner;
(b) a person living with the relevant person as if they were a spouse or a civil partner;
(c) a parent or child;
(d) a brother or sister;
(e) a child of a person falling within sub-paragraphs (a), (b) or (d);
(f) a grandparent or grandchild;
(g) a grandparent-in-law or grandchild-in-law;
(h) an uncle or aunt;

(i) a brother-in-law or sister-in-law;
(j) a son-in-law or daughter-in-law;
(k) a first cousin; or
(l) a half-brother or half-sister.

(3) For the purposes of this regulation –
(a) the relationships in paragraph (2)(c) to (k) include step relationships;
(b) references to step relationships and in-laws in paragraph (2) are to be read in accordance with section 246 of the Civil Partnership Act 2004;
(c) a person has a financial interest in a managing authority where –
   (i) that person is a partner, director, other office-holder or major shareholder of the managing authority that has made the application for a standard authorisation, and
   (ii) the managing authority is a care home or independent hospital; and
(d) a major shareholder means –
   (i) any person holding one tenth or more of the issued shares in the managing authority, where the managing authority is a company limited by shares, and
   (ii) in all other cases, any of the owners of the managing authority.

4 Determination of capacity

The best interests assessor must determine whether the relevant person has capacity to select a representative.

5 Selection by the relevant person

(1) Where the best interests assessor determines that the relevant person has capacity, the relevant person may select a family member, friend or carer.

(2) Where the relevant person does not wish to make a selection under paragraph (1), regulation 8 applies.

6 Selection by a donee or deputy

(1) Where –
(a) the best interests assessor determines that the relevant person lacks capacity to select a representative; and
(b) the relevant person has a donee or deputy and the donee's or deputy's scope of authority permits the selection of a family member, friend or carer of the relevant person,

the donee or deputy may select such a person.

(2) A donee or deputy may select himself or herself to be the relevant person's representative.

(3) Where a donee or deputy does not wish to make a selection under paragraph (1) or (2), regulation 8 applies.

7 Confirmation of eligibility of family member, friend or carer and recommendation to the supervisory body

(1) The best interests assessor must confirm that a person selected under regulation 5(1) or 6(1) or (2) is eligible to be a representative.

(2) Where the best interests assessor confirms the selected person's eligibility under paragraph (1), the assessor must recommend the appointment of that person as a representative to the supervisory body.

(3) Where the best interests assessor is unable to confirm the selected person's eligibility under paragraph (1), the assessor must –

  (a) advise the person who made the selection of that decision and give the reasons for it; and
  (b) invite them to make a further selection.

8 Selection by the best interests assessor

(1) The best interests assessor may select a family member, friend or carer as a representative where paragraph (2) applies.

(2) The best interests assessor may make a selection where –

  (a) the relevant person has the capacity to make a selection under regulation 5(1) but does not wish to do so;
  (b) the relevant person's donee or deputy does not wish to make a selection under regulation 6(1) or (2); or
  (c) the relevant person lacks the capacity to make a selection and –
    (i) does not have a donee or deputy, or
    (ii) has a donee or deputy but the donee's or deputy's scope of authority does not permit the selection of a representative.

(3) Where the best interests assessor selects a person in accordance with paragraph (2), the assessor must recommend that person for appointment as a representative to the supervisory body.

(4) But the best interests assessor must not select a person under paragraph (2) where the relevant person, donee or deputy objects to that selection.

(5) The best interests assessor must notify the supervisory body if they do not select a person who is eligible to be a representative.

9 Selection by the supervisory body

(1) Where a supervisory body is given notice under regulation 8(5), it may select a person to be the representative, who –

  (a) would be performing the role in a professional capacity;
  (b) has satisfactory skills and experience to perform the role;
  (c) is not a family member, friend or carer of the relevant person;
  (d) is not employed by, or providing services to, the relevant person's managing authority, where the relevant person's managing authority is a care home;
  (e) is not employed to work in the relevant person's managing authority in a role that is, or could be, related to the relevant person's case, where the relevant person's managing authority is a hospital; and
  (f) is not employed by the supervisory body.

(2) The supervisory body must be satisfied that there is in respect of the person –

    (a) an enhanced criminal record certificate issued pursuant to section 113B of the Police Act 1997 (enhanced criminal record certificates);or

    (b) if the purpose for which the certificate is required is not one prescribed under subsection (2) of that section, a criminal record certificate issued pursuant to section 113A of that Act (criminal record certificates).

Amendments—SI 2008/2368.

PART 2
APPOINTMENT OF REPRESENTATIVES

10 Commencement of appointment procedure

The procedure for appointing a representative must begin as soon as –

    (a) a best interests assessor is selected by the supervisory body for the purposes of a request for a standard authorisation; or

    (b) a relevant person's representative's appointment terminates, or is to be terminated, under regulation 14 and the relevant person remains subject to a standard authorisation.

11 Appointment of representative

Except where regulation 9 applies, a supervisory body may not appoint a representative unless the person is recommended to it under regulations 7 or 8.

12 Formalities of appointing a representative

(1) The offer of an appointment to a representative must be made in writing and state –

    (a) the duties of a representative to –
        (i) maintain contact with the relevant person,
        (ii) represent the relevant person in matters relating to, or connected with, the deprivation of liberty, and
        (iii) support the relevant person in matters relating to, or connected with, the deprivation of liberty; and
    (b) the length of the period of the appointment.

(2) The representative must inform the supervisory body in writing that they are willing to accept the appointment and that they have understood the duties set out in sub-paragraph (1)(a).

(3) The appointment must be made for the period of the standard authorisation.

(4) The supervisory body must send copies of the written appointment to –

    (a) the appointed person;
    (b) the relevant person;
    (c) the relevant person's managing authority;
    (d) any donee or deputy of the relevant person;
    (e) any independent mental capacity advocate appointed in accordance with sections 37 to 39D of the Act, involved in the relevant person's case; and

(f) every interested person named by the best interests assessor in their report as somebody the assessor has consulted in carrying out the assessment.

13 Termination of representative's appointment

A person ceases to be a representative if –

(a) the person dies;
(b) the person informs the supervisory body that they are no longer willing to continue as representative;
(c) the period of the appointment ends;
(d) a relevant person who has selected a family member, friend or carer under regulation 5(1) who has been appointed as their representative informs the supervisory body that they object to the person continuing to be a representative;
(e) a donee or deputy who has selected a family member, friend or carer of the relevant person under regulation 6(1) who has been appointed as a representative informs the supervisory body that they object to the person continuing to be a representative;
(f) the supervisory body terminates the appointment because it is satisfied that the representative is not maintaining sufficient contact with the relevant person in order to support and represent them;
(g) the supervisory body terminates the appointment because it is satisfied that the representative is not acting in the best interests of the relevant person; or
(h) the supervisory body terminates the appointment because it is satisfied that the person is no longer eligible or was not eligible at the time of appointment, to be a representative.

14 Formalities of termination of representative's appointment

(1) Where a representative's appointment is to be terminated for a reason specified in paragraphs (c) to (h) of regulation 13, the supervisory body must inform the representative of –

(a) the pending termination of the appointment;
(b) the reasons for the termination of the appointment; and
(c) the date on which the appointment terminates.

(2) The supervisory body must send copies of the termination of the appointment to –

(a) the relevant person;
(b) the relevant person's managing authority;
(c) any donee or deputy of the relevant person;
(d) any independent mental capacity advocate appointed in accordance with sections 37 to 39D of the Act, involved in the relevant person's case; and
(e) every interested person named by the best interests assessor in their report as somebody the assessor has consulted in carrying out the assessment.

15 Payment to a representative

A supervisory body may make payments to a representative appointed following a selection under regulation 9.

Mental Capacity (Deprivation of Liberty: Standard Authorisations, Assessments and Ordinary Residence) Regulations 2008, SI 2008/1858

ARRANGEMENT OF REGULATIONS

PART 1
PRELIMINARY

Regulation	Page
1 Citation, commencement and application	1333
2 Interpretation	1333

PART 2
ELIGIBILITY TO CARRY OUT ASSESSMENTS

3 Eligibility – general	1333
4 Eligibility to carry out a mental health assessment	1334
5 Eligibility to carry out a best interests assessment	1334
6 Eligibility to carry out a mental capacity assessment	1335
7 Eligibility to carry out an eligibility assessment	1335
8 Eligibility to carry out an age assessment	1335
9 Eligibility to carry out a no refusals assessment	1335

PART 3
SELECTION OF ASSESSORS

10 Selection of assessors – relatives	1335
11 Selection of assessors – financial interest	1336
12 Selection of best interests assessors	1336

PART 4
ASSESSMENTS

13 Time frame for assessments	1336
14 Time limit for carrying out an assessment to decide whether or not there is an unauthorised deprivation of liberty	1337
15 Relevant eligibility information	1337

PART 5
REQUESTS FOR A STANDARD AUTHORISATION

16 Information to be provided in a request for a standard authorisation	1337

PART 6
SUPERVISORY BODIES: CARE HOMES AND HOSPITALS

17 Application and Interpretation of Part 6	1338
18 Arrangements where there is a question as to the ordinary residence	1339
19 Effect of change in supervisory body following determination of any question about ordinary residence	1339

PART 1
PRELIMINARY

1 Citation, commencement and application

(1) These Regulations may be cited as the Mental Capacity (Deprivation of Liberty: Standard Authorisations, Assessments and Ordinary Residence) Regulations 2008 and shall come into force on 3 November 2008.

(2) These Regulations apply in relation to England only.

2 Interpretation

In these Regulations –
> 'approved mental health professional' means a person approved under section 114(1) of the Mental Health Act 1983 to act as an approved mental health professional for the purposes of that Act;
> 'best interests assessor' means a person selected to carry out a best interests assessment under paragraph 38 of Schedule A1 to the Act;
> 'the Act' means the Mental Capacity Act 2005.

Amendments—SI 2012/1479.

PART 2
ELIGIBILITY TO CARRY OUT ASSESSMENTS

3 Eligibility – general

(1) In addition to any requirement in regulations 4 to 9, a person is eligible to carry out an assessment where paragraphs (2) to (4) are met.

(2) The person must satisfy the supervisory body that there is in force in relation to that person an adequate and appropriate indemnity arrangement which provides cover in respect of any liabilities that might arise in connection with carrying out the assessment.

(2A) For the purposes of this regulation, an 'indemnity arrangement' may comprise –
  (a) a policy of insurance;
  (b) an arrangement made for the purposes of indemnifying a person; or
  (c) a combination of a policy of insurance and an arrangement made for the purposes of indemnifying a person.

(3) The supervisory body must be satisfied that the person has the skills and experience appropriate to the assessment to be carried out which must include, but are not limited to, the following –
  (a) an applied knowledge of the Mental Capacity Act 2005 and related Code of Practice; and
  (b) the ability to keep appropriate records and to provide clear and reasoned reports in accordance with legal requirements and good practice.

(4) The supervisory body must be satisfied that there is in respect of the person –
  (a) an enhanced criminal record certificate issued under section 113B of the Police Act 1997 (enhanced criminal record certificates); or
  (b) if the purpose for which the certificate is required is not one prescribed

under subsection (2) of that section, a criminal record certificate issued pursuant to section 113A of that Act (criminal record certificates).

Amendments—SI 2009/827.

4 Eligibility to carry out a mental health assessment

(1) A person is eligible to carry out a mental health assessment if paragraphs (2) and (3) are met.

(2) The person must be –

    (a) approved under section 12 of the Mental Health Act 1983; or
    (b) a registered medical practitioner who the supervisory body is satisfied has at least three years post registration experience in the diagnosis or treatment of mental disorder.

(3) The supervisory body must be satisfied that the person has successfully completed the Deprivation of Liberty Safeguards Mental Health Assessors training programme made available by the Royal College of Psychiatrists.

(4) Except in the 12 month period beginning with the date the person has successfully completed the programme referred to in paragraph (3), the supervisory body must be satisfied that the person has, in the 12 months prior to selection, completed further training relevant to their role as a mental health assessor.

5 Eligibility to carry out a best interests assessment

(1) A person is eligible to carry out a best interests assessment if paragraphs (2) and (3) are met.

(2) The person must be one of the following –

    (a) an approved mental health professional;
    (b) *(revoked)*
    (c) a first level nurse, registered in Sub-Part 1 of the Nurses' Part of the Register maintained under article 5 of the Nursing and Midwifery Order 2001;
    (d) an occupational therapist registered in Part 6, or a social worker registered in Part 16, of the register maintained under article 5 of the Health and Social Work Professions Order 2001; or
    (e) a chartered psychologist who is listed in the British Psychological Society's Register of Chartered Psychologists and who holds a relevant practising certificate issued by that Society.

(3) The supervisory body must be satisfied that the person –

    (a) is not suspended from the register or list relevant to the person's profession mentioned in paragraph (2);
    (b) has at least two years post registration experience in one of the professions mentioned in paragraph (2);
    (c) has successfully completed training that has been approved by the Secretary of State to be a best interests assessor;
    (d) except in the 12 month period beginning with the date the person has successfully completed the training referred to in sub-paragraph (c), the

supervisory body must be satisfied that the person has, in the 12 months prior to selection, completed further training relevant to their role as a best interests assessor; and

(e) has the skills necessary to obtain, evaluate and analyse complex evidence and differing views and to weigh them appropriately in decision making.

Amendments—SI 2012/1479.

6 Eligibility to carry out a mental capacity assessment

A person is eligible to carry out a mental capacity assessment if that person is eligible to carry out –

(a) a mental health assessment; or
(b) a best interests assessment.

7 Eligibility to carry out an eligibility assessment

A person is eligible to carry out an eligibility assessment if that person is –

(a) approved under section 12 of the Mental Health Act 1983 and is eligible to carry out a mental health assessment; or
(b) an approved mental health professional and is eligible to carry out a best interests assessment.

8 Eligibility to carry out an age assessment

A person is eligible to carry out an age assessment if that person is eligible to carry out a best interests assessment.

9 Eligibility to carry out a no refusals assessment

A person is eligible to carry out a no refusals assessment if that person is eligible to carry out a best interests assessment.

PART 3
SELECTION OF ASSESSORS

10 Selection of assessors – relatives

(1) A supervisory body must not select a person to carry out an assessment if the person is –

(a) a relative of the relevant person; or
(b) a relative of a person who is financially interested in the care of the relevant person.

(2) For the purposes of this regulation a 'relative' means –

(a) a spouse, ex-spouse, civil partner or ex-civil partner;
(b) a person living with the relevant person as if they were a spouse or a civil partner;
(c) a parent or child;
(d) a brother or sister;

(e) a child of a person falling within sub-paragraphs (a), (b) or (d);
(f) a grandparent or grandchild;
(g) a grandparent-in-law or grandchild-in-law;
(h) an uncle or aunt;
(i) a brother-in-law or sister-in-law;
(j) a son-in-law or daughter-in-law;
(k) a first cousin; or
(l) a half-brother or half-sister.

(3) For the purposes of this regulation –
   (a) the relationships in paragraph (2)(c) to (k) include step relationships;
   (b) references to step relationships and in-laws in paragraph (2) are to be read in accordance with section 246 of the Civil Partnership Act 2004; and
   (c) financial interest has the meaning given in regulation 11.

11 Selection of assessors – financial interest

(1) A supervisory body must not select a person to carry out an assessment where the person has a financial interest in the case.

(2) A person has a financial interest in a case where –
   (a) that person is a partner, director, other office-holder or major shareholder of the managing authority that has made the application for a standard authorisation; and
   (b) the managing authority is a care home or independent hospital.

(3) A major shareholder means –
   (a) any person holding one tenth or more of the issued shares in the managing authority, where the managing authority is a company limited by shares; and
   (b) in all other cases, any of the owners of the managing authority.

12 Selection of best interests assessors

(1) A supervisory body must not select a person to carry out a best interests assessment if that person is involved in the care, or making decisions about the care, of the relevant person.

(2) Where the managing authority and supervisory body are both the same body, the supervisory body must not select a person to carry out a best interests assessment who is employed by it or who is providing services to it.

PART 4
ASSESSMENTS

13 Time frame for assessments

(1) Except as provided in paragraph (2), all assessments required for a standard authorisation must be completed within the period of 21 days beginning with the date that the supervisory body receives a request for such an authorisation.

(2) Where a supervisory body receives a request for a standard authorisation and the managing authority has given an urgent authorisation under paragraph 76 of

Schedule A1 to the Act, the assessments required for that standard authorisation must be completed within the period during which the urgent authorisation is in force.

14 Time limit for carrying out an assessment to decide whether or not there is an unauthorised deprivation of liberty

Subject to paragraph 69(3) to (5) of Schedule A1 to the Act, an assessment required under that paragraph must be completed within the period of 7 days beginning with the date that the supervisory body receives the request from an eligible person.

15 Relevant eligibility information

(1) This regulation applies where an individual is being assessed and the eligibility assessor and the best interests assessor are not the same person.

(2) The eligibility assessor must request that the best interests assessor provides any relevant eligibility information that the best interests assessor may have.

(3) The best interests assessor must comply with any request made under this regulation.

(4) In this regulation 'eligibility assessor' means a person selected to carry out the eligibility assessment under paragraph 46 of Schedule A1 to the Act.

PART 5
REQUESTS FOR A STANDARD AUTHORISATION

16 Information to be provided in a request for a standard authorisation

(1) A request for a standard authorisation must include the following information –

    (a) the name and gender of the relevant person;
    (b) the age of the relevant person or, where this is not known, whether the managing authority believes that the relevant person is aged 18 years or older;
    (c) the address and telephone number where the relevant person is currently located;
    (d) the name, address and telephone number of the managing authority and the name of the person within the managing authority who is dealing with the request;
    (e) the purpose for which the authorisation is requested;
    (f) the date from which the standard authorisation is sought; and
    (g) whether the managing authority has given an urgent authorisation under paragraph 76 of Schedule A1 to the Act and, if so, the date on which it expires.

(2) Except as provided for in paragraph (3), a request for a standard authorisation must include the following information if it is available or could reasonably be obtained by the managing authority –

    (a) any medical information relating to the relevant person's health that the managing authority considers to be relevant to the proposed restrictions to the relevant person's liberty;

(b) the diagnosis of the mental disorder (within the meaning of the Mental Health Act 1983 but disregarding any exclusion for persons with learning disability) that the relevant person is suffering from;
(c) any relevant care plans and relevant needs assessments;
(d) the racial, ethnic or national origins of the relevant person;
(e) whether the relevant person has any special communication needs;
(f) details of the proposed restrictions on the relevant person's liberty;
(g) whether section 39A of the Act (person becomes subject to Schedule A1) applies;
(h) where the purpose of the proposed restrictions to the relevant person's liberty is to give treatment, whether the relevant person has made an advance decision that may be valid and applicable to some or all of that treatment;
(i) whether the relevant person is subject to –
   (i) the hospital treatment regime,
   (ii) the community treatment regime, or
   (iii) the guardianship regime;
(j) the name, address and telephone number of –
   (i) anyone named by the relevant person as someone to be consulted about his welfare,
   (ii) anyone engaged in caring for the person or interested in his welfare,
   (iii) any donee of a lasting power of attorney granted by the person,
   (iv) any deputy appointed for the person by the court, and
   (v) any independent mental capacity advocate appointed in accordance with sections 37 to 39D of the Act; and
(k) whether there is an existing authorisation in relation to the detention of the relevant person and, if so, the date of the expiry of that authorisation.

(3) Where –

(a) there is an existing authorisation in force in relation to the detention of the relevant person; and
(b) the managing authority makes a request in accordance with paragraph 30 of Schedule A1 to the Act for a further standard authorisation in relation to the same relevant person,

the request need not include any of the information mentioned in paragraph (2)(a) to (j) if that information remains the same as that supplied in relation to the request for the existing authorisation.

(4) In this regulation 'existing authorisation' has the same meaning as in paragraph 29 of Schedule A1 to the Act.

PART 6
SUPERVISORY BODIES: CARE HOMES AND HOSPITALS

Disputes about the Place of Ordinary Residence

17 Application and Interpretation of Part 6

(1) This Part applies where –
   (a) a local authority ('local authority A') receives a request from –

(i) a care home or hospital for a standard authorisation under paragraph 24, 25 or 30 of Schedule A1 to the Act, or
(ii) an eligible person to decide whether or not there is an unauthorised deprivation of liberty in a care home or hospital under paragraph 68 of Schedule A1 to the Act;
(b) local authority A wishes to dispute that it is the supervisory body; and
(c) a question as to the ordinary residence of the relevant person is to be determined by the Secretary of State under paragraph 183 of Schedule A1 to the Act.

(2) In this Part –
(a) 'local authority A' has the meaning given in paragraph (1); and
(b) 'local authority C' has the meaning given in regulation 18(2).

Amendments—SI 2013/235.

Note—These Regulations were amended with effect from 1 April 2013 to provide for amendments consequential to the coming into force of the provisions of the Health and Social Act 2012, which abolished Primary Care Trusts in England and necessitated the transfer of supervisory body responsibilities in England to local authorities for deprivations of liberty occurring in hospitals.

18 Arrangements where there is a question as to the ordinary residence

(1) Local authority A must act as supervisory body in relation to a request mentioned in regulation 17(1)(a) until the determination of the question as to the ordinary residence of the relevant person.

(2) But where another local authority ('local authority C') agrees to act as the supervisory body in place of local authority A, that local authority shall become the supervisory body until the determination of the question as to the ordinary residence of the relevant person.

(3) When the question about the ordinary residence of the relevant person has been determined, the local authority which has been identified as the supervisory body shall become the supervisory body.

19 Effect of change in supervisory body following determination of any question about ordinary residence

(1) Where the question of ordinary residence of the relevant person is determined in accordance with paragraph 183(3) of Schedule A1 to the Act, and another local authority ('local authority B') becomes the supervisory body in place of local authority A or local authority C, as the case may be, paragraphs (3) to (6A) shall apply.

(2) Where the question of ordinary residence of the relevant person is determined in accordance with paragraph 183(3) of Schedule A1 to the Act and local authority C remains the supervisory body, paragraphs (7) to (10) shall apply.

(3) Local authority B shall be treated as the supervisory body that received the request mentioned in regulation 17(1)(a) and must comply with the time limits specified in –

(a) regulation 13 for carrying out the assessments required for a standard authorisation; or

(b) regulation 14 for carrying out an assessment required under paragraph 69 of Schedule A1 to the Act,

as the case may be, where the assessments have still to be completed.

(4) Anything done by or in relation to local authority A or local authority C in connection with the authorisation or request, as the case may be, has effect, so far as is necessary for continuing its effect after the change, as if done by or in relation to local authority B.

(5) Anything which relates to the authorisation or request and which is in the process of being done by or in relation to local authority A or local authority C at the time of the change may be continued by or in relation to local authority B.

(6) But –

(a) local authority A or local authority C does not, by virtue of this regulation, cease to be liable for anything done by it in connection with the authorisation or request before the change; and

(b) local authority B does not, by virtue of this regulation, become liable for any such thing.

(6A) Local authority A or local authority C shall be entitled to recover from local authority B expenditure incurred in exercising functions as the supervisory body.

(7) Local authority C shall be treated as the supervisory body that received the request mentioned in regulation 17(1)(a) and must comply with the time limits specified in –

(a) regulation 13 for carrying out the assessments required for a standard authorisation; or

(b) regulation 14 for carrying out an assessment required under paragraph 69 of Schedule A1 to the Act,

as the case may be, where the assessments have still to be completed.

(8) Anything done by or in relation to local authority A in connection with the authorisation or request, as the case may be, has effect, so far as is necessary for continuing its effect after the change, as if done by or in relation to local authority C.(9) Anything which relates to the authorisation or request and which is in the process of being done by or in relation to local authority A at the time of the change may be continued by or in relation to local authority C.

(9) Anything which relates to the authorisation or request and which is in the process of being done by or in relation to local authority A at the time of the change may be continued by or in relation to local authority C.

(10) But –

(a) local authority A does not, by virtue of this regulation, cease to be liable for anything done by it in connection with the authorisation or request before the change; and

(b) local authority C does not, by virtue of this regulation, become liable for any such thing.

Amendments—SI 2009/827.

Family Procedure Rules 2010, SI 2010/2955

ARRANGEMENT OF RULES

Chapter 4

Rule		Page
	Service Out of the Jurisdiction	
6.40	Scope and interpretation	1341
6.41	Permission to serve not required	1341
6.42	Period for acknowledging service or responding to application where application is served out of the jurisdiction	1342
6.43	Method of service – general provisions	1342
6.44	Service in accordance with the Service Regulation	1342
6.45	Service through foreign governments, judicial authorities and British Consular authorities	1343
6.46	Procedure where service is to be through foreign governments, judicial authorities and British Consular authorities	1344
6.47	Translation of application form or other document	1344
6.48	Undertaking to be responsible for expenses of the Foreign and Commonwealth Office	1345

Practice Direction 6B – Service out of the Jurisdiction — 1345

Practice Direction 6C – Disclosure of Addresses by Government Departments 13 February 1989 as amended by Practice Direction 20 July 1995 — 1368

****

Chapter 4

Service Out of the Jurisdiction

6.40 Scope and interpretation

(1) This Chapter contains rules about –
   (a) service of application forms and other documents out of the jurisdiction; and
   (b) the procedure for service.

   ('Jurisdiction' is defined in rule 2.3.)

(2) In this Chapter –

'application form' includes an application notice;
'Commonwealth State' means a State listed in Schedule 3 to the British Nationality Act 1981; and
'the Hague Convention' means the Convention on the service abroad of judicial and extra-judicial documents in civil or commercial matters signed at the Hague on November 15, 1965.

6.41 Permission to serve not required

Any document to be served for the purposes of these rules may be served out of the jurisdiction without the permission of the court.

6.42 Period for acknowledging service or responding to application where application is served out of the jurisdiction

(1) This rule applies where, under these rules, a party is required to file –

(a) an acknowledgment of service; or
(b) an answer to an application,

and sets out the time period for doing so where the application is served out of the jurisdiction.

(2) Where the applicant serves an application on a respondent in –

(a) Scotland or Northern Ireland; or
(b) a Member State or Hague Convention country within Europe,

the period for filing an acknowledgment of service or an answer to an application is 21 days after service of the application.

(3) Where the applicant serves an application on a respondent in a Hague Convention country outside Europe, the period for filing an acknowledgment of service or an answer to an application is 31 days after service of the application.

(4) Where the applicant serves an application on a respondent in a country not referred to in paragraphs (2) and (3), the period for filing an acknowledgment of service or an answer to an application is set out in Practice Direction 6B.

6.43 Method of service – general provisions

(1) This rule contains general provisions about the method of service of an application for a matrimonial or civil partnership order, or other document, on a party out of the jurisdiction.

Where service is to be effected on a party in Scotland or Northern Ireland

(2) Where a party serves an application form or other document on a party in Scotland or Northern Ireland, it must be served by a method permitted by Chapter 2 (and references to 'jurisdiction' in that Chapter are modified accordingly) or Chapter 3 of this Part and rule 6.26(5) applies.

Where service is to be effected on a respondent out of the United Kingdom

(3) Where the applicant wishes to serve an application form, or other document, on a respondent out of the United Kingdom, it may be served by any method –

provided for by –
rule 6.44 (service in accordance with the Service Regulation);
rule 6.45 (service through foreign governments, judicial authorities and British Consular authorities); or
permitted by the law of the country in which it is to be served.

(4) Nothing in paragraph (3) or in any court order authorises or requires any person to do anything which is contrary to the law of the country where the application form, or other document, is to be served.

6.44 Service in accordance with the Service Regulation

(1) This rule applies where the applicant wishes to serve the application form, or other document, in accordance with the Service Regulation.

(2) The applicant must file –
   (a) the application form or other document;
   (b) any translation; and
   (c) any other documents required by the Service Regulation.

(3) When the applicant files the documents referred to in paragraph (2), the court officer will –
   (a) seal$^{(GL)}$, or otherwise authenticate with the stamp of the court, the copy of the application form; and
   (b) forward the documents to the Senior Master of the Queen's Bench Division.

(4) In addition to the documents referred to in paragraph (2), the applicant may file a photograph of the person to be served if the applicant considers that it would assist in ensuring effective service.

(The Service Regulation is annexed to Practice Direction 6B.)

(Article 20(1) of the Service Regulation provides that the Regulation prevails over other provisions contained in any other agreement or arrangement concluded by Member States.)

Amendments—SI 2011/1328.

6.45 Service through foreign governments, judicial authorities and British Consular authorities

(1) Where the applicant wishes to serve an application form, or other document, on a respondent in any country which is a party to the Hague Convention, it may be served –
   (a) through the authority designated under the Hague Convention in respect of that country; or
   (b) if the law of that country permits –
      (i) through the judicial authorities of that country; or
      (ii) through a British Consular authority in that country.

(2) Where the applicant wishes to serve an application form, or other document, on a respondent in any country which is not a party to the Hague Convention, it may be served, if the law of that country so permits –
   (a) through the government of that country, where that government is willing to serve it; or
   (b) through a British Consular authority in that country.

(3) Where the applicant wishes to serve an application form, or other document, in –
   (a) any Commonwealth State which is not a party to the Hague Convention;
   (b) the Isle of Man or the Channel Islands; or
   (c) any British Overseas Territory,

the methods of service permitted by paragraphs (1)(b) and (2) are not available and the applicant or the applicant's agent must effect service on a respondent in accordance with rule 6.43 unless Practice Direction 6B provides otherwise.

(4) This rule does not apply where service is to be effected in accordance with the Service Regulation.

(A list of British overseas territories is reproduced in Practice Direction 6B.)

6.46 Procedure where service is to be through foreign governments, judicial authorities and British Consular authorities

(1) This rule applies where the applicant wishes to serve an application form, or other document, under rule 6.45(1) or (2).

(2) Where this rule applies, the applicant must file –

    (a) a request for service of the application form, or other document, by specifying one or more of the methods in rule 6.45(1) or (2);

    (b) a copy of the application form or other document;

    (c) any other documents or copies of documents required by Practice Direction 6B; and

    (d) any translation required under rule 6.47.

(3) When the applicant files the documents specified in paragraph (2), the court officer will –

    (a) seal$^{(GL)}$, or otherwise authenticate with the stamp of the court, the copy of the application form or other document; and

    (b) forward the documents to the Senior Master of the Queen's Bench Division.

(4) The Senior Master will send documents forwarded under this rule –

    (a) where the application form, or other document, is being served through the authority designated under the Hague Convention, to that authority; or

    (b) in any other case, to the Foreign and Commonwealth Office with a request that it arranges for the application form or other document to be served.

(5) An official certificate which –

    (a) states that the method requested under paragraph (2)(a) has been performed and the date of such performance;

    (b) states, where more than one method is requested under paragraph (2)(a), which method was used; and

    (c) is made by –

        (i) a British Consular authority in the country where the method requested under paragraph (2)(a) was performed;

        (ii) the government or judicial authorities in that country; or

        (iii) the authority designated in respect of that country under the Hague Convention,

is evidence of the facts stated in the certificate.

(6) A document purporting to be an official certificate under paragraph (5) is to be treated as such a certificate, unless it is proved not to be.

6.47 Translation of application form or other document

(1) Except where paragraphs (4) and (5) apply, every copy of the application form, or other document, filed under rule 6.45 (service through foreign governments, judicial authorities and British Consular authorities) must be accompanied by a translation of the application form or other document.

(2) The translation must be –

    (a) in the official language of the country in which it is to be served; or

    (b) if there is more than one official language of that country, in any official language which is appropriate to the place in the country where the application form or other document is to be served.

(3) Every translation filed under this rule must be accompanied by a statement by the person making it that it is a correct translation, and the statement must include that person's name, address and qualifications for making the translation.

(4) The applicant is not required to file a translation of the application form, or other document, filed under rule 6.45 where it is to be served in a country of which English is an official language.

(5) The applicant is not required to file a translation of the application form or other document filed under rule 6.45 where –

(a) the person on whom the document is to be served is able to read and understand English; and
(b) service of the document is to be effected directly on that person.

(This rule does not apply to service in accordance with the Service Regulation which contains its own provisions about the translation of documents.)

6.48 Undertaking to be responsible for expenses of the Foreign and Commonwealth Office

Every request for service filed under rule 6.46 (procedure where service is to be through foreign governments, judicial authorities etc.) must contain an undertaking by the person making the request –

(a) to be responsible for all expenses incurred by the Foreign and Commonwealth Office or foreign judicial authority; and
(b) to pay those expenses to the Foreign and Commonwealth Office or foreign judicial authority on being informed of the amount.

****

Practice Direction 6B – Service out of the Jurisdiction

This Practice Direction supplements FPR 2010 Part 6, Chapter 4 (PD6B)

Scope of this Practice Direction

1.1 This Practice Direction supplements Chapter 4 (service out of the jurisdiction) of Part 6.

(Practice Direction 6A contains relevant provisions supplementing rule 6.43(2) in relation to the method of service on a party in Scotland or Northern Ireland.)

Service in other Member States of the European Union

2.1 Where service is to be effected in another Member of State of the European Union, the Service Regulation applies.

2.2 The Service Regulation is Regulation (EC) No. 1393/2007 of the European Parliament and of the Council of 13 November 2007 on the service in the Member

States of judicial and extrajudicial documents in civil or commercial matters (service of documents), and repealing Council Regulation (EC) no. 1348/2000, as amended from time to time and as applied by the Agreement made on 19 October 2005 between the European Community and the Kingdom of Denmark on the service of judicial and extrajudicial documents in civil and commercial matters.

2.3 The Service Regulation is annexed to this Practice Direction.

> (Article 20(1) of the Service Regulation provides that the Regulation prevails over other provisions contained in bilateral or multilateral agreements or arrangements concluded by the Member of States and in particular Article IV of the protocol to the Brussels Convention of 1968 and the Hague Convention of 15 November 1965)

Documents to be filed under rule 6.46(2)

3.1 A duplicate of –

(a) the application form or other document to be served under rule 6.45(1) or (2);
(b) any documents accompanying the application or other document referred to in paragraph (a); and
(c) any translation required by rule 6.47;

must be provided for each party to be served out of the jurisdiction, together with forms for responding to the application.

3.2 Some countries require legalisation of the document to be served and some require a formal letter of request which must be signed by the Senior Master. Any queries on this should be addressed to the Foreign Process Section (Room E02) at the Royal Courts of Justice.

Service in a Commonwealth State or British Overseas Territory

4.1 The judicial authorities of certain Commonwealth States which are not a party to the Hague Convention require service to be in accordance with rule 6.45(1)(b)(i) and not 6.45(3). A list of such countries can be obtained from the Foreign Process Section (Room E02) at the Royal Courts of Justice.

4.2 The list of British overseas territories is contained in Schedule 6 to the British Nationality Act 1981. For ease of reference these are –

(a) Anguilla;
(b) Bermuda;
(c) British Antarctic Territory;
(d) British Indian Ocean Territory;
(e) Cayman Islands;
(f) Falkland Islands;
(g) Gibraltar;
(h) Montserrat;
(i) Pitcairn, Henderson, Ducie and Oeno Islands;
(j) St. Helena, Ascension and Tristan da Cunha;
(k) South Georgia and the South Sandwich Islands;
(l) Sovereign Base Areas of Akrotiri and Dhekelia;
(m) Turks and Caicos Islands;
(n) Virgin Islands.

Period for responding to an application form

5.1 Where rule 6.42 applies, the period within which the respondent must file an acknowledgment of service or an answer to the application is the number of days listed in the Table after service of the application.

5.2 Where an application is served out of the jurisdiction any statement as to the period for responding to the claim contained in any of the forms required by the Family Procedure Rules to accompany the application must specify the period prescribed under rule 6.42.

Service of application notices and orders

6.1 The provisions of Chapter 4 of Part 6 (special provisions about service out of the jurisdiction) also apply to service out of the jurisdiction of an application notice or order.

6.2 Where an application notice is to be served out of the jurisdiction in accordance with Chapter 4 of Part 6 the court must have regard to the country in which the application notice is to be served in setting the date for the hearing of the application and giving any direction about service of the respondent's evidence.

Period for responding to an application notice

7.1 Where an application notice or order is served out of the jurisdiction, the period for responding is 7 days less than the number of days listed in the Table.

Further information

8.1 Further information concerning service out of the jurisdiction can be obtained from the Foreign Process Section, Room E02, Royal Courts of Justice, Strand, London WC2A 2LL (telephone 020 7947 6691).

Table

Place or country	Number of days
Afghanistan	23
Albania	25
Algeria	22
Andorra	21
Angola	22
Anguilla	31
Antigua and Barbuda	23
Antilles (Netherlands)	31
Argentina	22

PART V   COURT OF PROTECTION PRACTICE 2016

Place or country	Number of days
Armenia	21
Ascension Island	31
Australia	25
Austria	21
Azerbaijan	22
Azores	23
Bahamas	22
Bahrain	22
Balearic Islands	21
Bangladesh	23
Barbados	23
Belarus	21
Belgium	21
Belize	23
Benin	25
Bermuda	31
Bhutan	28
Bolivia	23
Bosnia and Herzegovina	21
Botswana	23
Brazil	22
British Virgin Islands	31
Brunei	25
Bulgaria	23
Burkina Faso	23
Burma	23
Burundi	22

Practice Direction 6B – Service out of the Jurisdiction **PD6B**

Place or country	Number of days
Cambodia	28
Cameroon	22
Canada	22
Canary Islands	22
Cape Verde	25
Caroline Islands	31
Cayman Islands	31
Central African Republic	25
Chad	25
Chile	22
China	24
China (Hong Kong)	31
China (Macau)	31
China (Taiwan)	23
China (Tibet)	34
Christmas Island	27
Cocos (Keeling) Islands	41
Colombia	22
Comoros	23
Congo (formerly Congo Brazzaville or French Congo)	25
Congo (Democratic Republic)	25
Corsica	21
Costa Rica	23
Croatia	21
Cuba	24
Cyprus	31

PART V

Place or country	Number of days
Czech Republic	21
Denmark	21
Djibouti	22
Dominica	23
Dominican Republic	23
East Timor	25
Ecuador	22
Egypt	22
El Salvador	25
Equatorial Guinea	23
Eritrea	22
Estonia	21
Ethiopia	22
Falkland Islands and Dependencies	31
Faroe Islands	31
Fiji	23
Finland	24
France	21
French Guyana	31
French Polynesia	31
French West Indies	31
Gabon	25
Gambia	22
Georgia	21
Germany	21
Ghana	22
Gibraltar	31

Place or country	Number of days
Greece	21
Greenland	31
Grenada	24
Guatemala	24
Guernsey	21
Guinea	22
Guinea-Bissau	22
Guyana	22
Haiti	23
Holland (Netherlands)	21
Honduras	24
Hungary	22
Iceland	22
India	23
Indonesia	22
Iran	22
Iraq	22
Ireland (Republic of)	21
Ireland (Northern)	21
Isle of Man	21
Israel	22
Italy	21
Ivory Coast	22
Jamaica	22
Japan	23
Jersey	21
Jordan	23

Place or country	Number of days
Kazakhstan	21
Kenya	22
Kiribati	23
Korea (North)	28
Korea (South)	24
Kosovo	21
Kuwait	22
Kyrgyzstan	21
Laos	30
Latvia	21
Lebanon	22
Lesotho	23
Liberia	22
Libya	21
Liechtenstein	21
Lithuania	21
Luxembourg	21
Macedonia	21
Madagascar	23
Madeira	31
Malawi	23
Malaysia	24
Maldives	26
Mali	25
Malta	21
Mariana Islands	26
Marshall Islands	32

Place or country	Number of days
Mauritania	23
Mauritius	22
Mexico	23
Micronesia	23
Moldova	21
Monaco	21
Mongolia	24
Montenegro	21
Montserrat	31
Morocco	22
Mozambique	23
Namibia	23
Nauru	36
Nepal	23
Netherlands	21
Nevis	24
New Caledonia	31
New Zealand	26
New Zealand Island Territories	50
Nicaragua	24
Niger (Republic of)	25
Nigeria	22
Norfolk Island	31
Norway	21
Oman (Sultanate of)	22
Pakistan	23
Palau	23

Place or country	Number of days
Panama	26
Papua New Guinea	26
Paraguay	22
Peru	22
Philippines	23
Pitcairn, Henderson, Ducie and Oeno Islands	31
Poland	21
Portugal	21
Portuguese Timor	31
Puerto Rico	23
Qatar	23
Reunion	31
Romania	22
Russia	21
Rwanda	23
Sabah	23
St. Helena	31
St Kitts and Nevis	24
St Lucia	24
St Pierre and Miquelon	31
St Vincent and the Grenadines	24
Samoa (USA Territory) (See also Western Samoa)	30
San Marino	21
Sao Tome and Principe	25
Sarawak	28
Saudi Arabia	24
Scotland	21

Place or country	Number of days
Senegal	22
Serbia	21
Seychelles	22
Sierra Leone	22
Singapore	22
Slovakia	21
Slovenia	21
Society Islands (French Polynesia)	31
Solomon Islands	29
Somalia	22
South Africa	22
South Georgia (Falkland Island Dependencies)	31
South Orkneys	21
South Shetlands	21
Spain	21
Spanish Territories of North Africa	31
Sri Lanka	23
Sudan	22
Surinam	22
Swaziland	22
Sweden	21
Switzerland	21
Syria	23
Tajikistan	21
Tanzania	22
Thailand	23
Togo	22

Place or country	Number of days
Tonga	30
Trinidad and Tobago	23
Tristan Da Cunha	31
Tunisia	22
Turkey	21
Turkmenistan	21
Turks & Caicos Islands	31
Tuvalu	23
Uganda	22
Ukraine	21
United Arab Emirates	22
United States of America	22
Uruguay	22
Uzbekistan	21
Vanuatu	29
Vatican City State	21
Venezuela	22
Vietnam	28
Virgin Islands – USA	24
Wake Island	25
Western Samoa	34
Yemen (Republic of)	30
Zaire	25
Zambia	23
Zimbabwe	22

ANNEX – SERVICE REGULATION (RULE 6.44)

Council Regulation (EC) No 1393/2007 of 13 November 2007 on the service in the Member States of judicial and extrajudicial documents in civil or commercial matters (service of documents), and repealing Council Regulation (EC) No 1348/2000

THE EUROPEAN PARLIAMENT AND THE COUNCIL OF THE EUROPEAN UNION,

Having regard to the Treaty establishing the European Community, and in particular Article 61(c) and Article 67(5), second indent, thereof,

Having regard to the proposal from the Commission,

Having regard to the opinion of the European Economic and Social Committee,

Acting in accordance with the procedure laid down in Article 251 of the Treaty,

Whereas:

(1) The Union has set itself the objective of maintaining and developing the Union as an area of freedom, security and justice, in which the free movement of persons is assured. To establish such an area, the Community is to adopt, among others, the measures relating to judicial cooperation in civil matters needed for the proper functioning of the internal market.

(2) The proper functioning of the internal market entails the need to improve and expedite the transmission of judicial and extrajudicial documents in civil or commercial matters for service between the Member States.

(3) The Council, by an Act dated 26 May 1997, drew up a Convention on the service in the Member States of the European Union of judicial and extrajudicial documents in civil or commercial matters and recommended it for adoption by the Member States in accordance with their respective constitutional rules. That Convention has not entered into force. Continuity in the results of the negotiations for conclusion of the Convention should be ensured.

(4) On 29 May 2000 the Council adopted Regulation (EC) No 1348/2000 on the service in the Member States of judicial and extrajudicial documents in civil or commercial matters. The main content of that Regulation is based on the Convention.

(5) On 1 October 2004 the Commission adopted a report on the application of Regulation (EC) No 1348/2000. The report concludes that the application of Regulation (EC) No 1348/2000 has generally improved and expedited the transmission and the service of documents between Member States since its entry into force in 2001, but that nevertheless the application of certain provisions is not fully satisfactory.

(6) Efficiency and speed in judicial procedures in civil matters require that judicial and extrajudicial documents be transmitted directly and by rapid means between local bodies designated by the Member States. Member States may indicate their intention to designate only one transmitting or receiving agency or one agency to perform both functions, for a period of five years. This designation may, however, be renewed every five years.

(7) Speed in transmission warrants the use of all appropriate means, provided that certain conditions as to the legibility and reliability of the document received are observed. Security in transmission requires that the document to be transmitted be accompanied by a standard form, to be completed in the official language or one of

the official languages of the place where service is to be effected, or in another language accepted by the Member State in question.

(8) This Regulation should not apply to service of a document on the party's authorised representative in the Member State where the proceedings are taking place regardless of the place of residence of that party.

(9) The service of a document should be effected as soon as possible, and in any event within one month of receipt by the receiving agency.

(10) To secure the effectiveness of this Regulation, the possibility of refusing service of documents should be confined to exceptional situations.

(11) In order to facilitate the transmission and service of documents between Member States, the standard forms set out in the Annexes to this Regulation should be used.

(12) The receiving agency should inform the addressee in writing using the standard form that he may refuse to accept the document to be served at the time of service or by returning the document to the receiving agency within one week if it is not either in a language which he understands or in the official language or one of the official languages of the place of service. This rule should also apply to the subsequent service once the addressee has exercised his right of refusal. These rules on refusal should also apply to service by diplomatic or consular agents, service by postal services and direct service. It should be established that the service of the refused document can be remedied through the service on the addressee of a translation of the document.

(13) Speed in transmission warrants documents being served within days of receipt of the document. However, if service has not been effected after one month has elapsed, the receiving agency should inform the transmitting agency. The expiry of this period should not imply that the request be returned to the transmitting agency where it is clear that service is feasible within a reasonable period.

(14) The receiving agency should continue to take all necessary steps to effect the service of the documents also in cases where it has not been possible to effect service within the month, for example, because the defendant has been away from his home on holiday or away from his office on business. However, in order to avoid an open-ended obligation for the receiving agency to take steps to effect the service of a document, the transmitting agency should be able to specify a time limit in the standard form after which service is no longer required.

(15) Given the differences between the Member States as regards their rules of procedure, the material date for the purposes of service varies from one Member State to another. Having regard to such situations and the possible difficulties that may arise, this Regulation should provide for a system where it is the law of the Member State addressed which determines the date of service. However, where according to the law of a Member State a document has to be served within a particular period, the date to be taken into account with respect to the applicant should be that determined by the law of that Member State. This double date system exists only in a limited number of Member States. Those Member States which apply this system should communicate this to the Commission, which should publish the information in the *Official Journal of the European Union* and make it available through the European Judicial Network in Civil and Commercial Matters established by Council Decision 2001/470/EC.

(16) In order to facilitate access to justice, costs occasioned by recourse to a judicial officer or a person competent under the law of the Member State addressed should correspond to a single fixed fee laid down by that Member State in advance which

respects the principles of proportionality and non-discrimination. The requirement of a single fixed fee should not preclude the possibility for Member States to set different fees for different types of service as long as they respect these principles.

(17) Each Member State should be free to effect service of documents directly by postal services on persons residing in another Member State by registered letter with acknowledgement of receipt or equivalent.

(18) It should be possible for any person interested in a judicial proceeding to effect service of documents directly through the judicial officers, officials or other competent persons of the Member State addressed, where such direct service is permitted under the law of that Member State.

(19) The Commission should draw up a manual containing information relevant for the proper application of this Regulation, which should be made available through the European Judicial Network in Civil and Commercial Matters. The Commission and the Member States should do their utmost to ensure that this information is up to date and complete especially as regards contact details of receiving and transmitting agencies.

(20) In calculating the periods and time limits provided for in this Regulation, Regulation (EEC, Euratom) No 1182/71 of the Council of 3 June 1971 determining the rules applicable to periods, dates and time limits should apply.

(21) The measures necessary for the implementation of this Regulation should be adopted in accordance with Council Decision 1999/468/EC of 28 June 1999 laying down the procedures for the exercise of implementing powers conferred on the Commission.

(22) In particular, power should be conferred on the Commission to update or make technical amendments to the standard forms set out in the Annexes. Since those measures are of general scope and are designed to amend/delete non-essential elements of this Regulation, they must be adopted in accordance with the regulatory procedure with scrutiny provided for in Article 5a of Decision 1999/468/EC.

(23) This Regulation prevails over the provisions contained in bilateral or multilateral agreements or arrangements having the same scope, concluded by the Member States, and in particular the Protocol annexed to the Brussels Convention of 27 September 1968 and the Hague Convention of 15 November 1965 in relations between the Member States party thereto. This Regulation does not preclude Member States from maintaining or concluding agreements or arrangements to expedite or simplify the transmission of documents, provided that they are compatible with this Regulation.

(24) The information transmitted pursuant to this Regulation should enjoy suitable protection. This matter falls within the scope of Directive 95/46/EC of the European Parliament and of the Council of 24 October 1995 on the protection of individuals with regard to the processing of personal data and on the free movement of such data, and of Directive 2002/58/EC of the European Parliament and of the Council of 12 July 2002 concerning the processing of personal data and the protection of privacy in the electronic communications sector (Directive on privacy and electronic communications).

(25) No later than 1 June 2011 and every five years thereafter, the Commission should review the application of this Regulation and propose such amendments as may appear necessary.

(26) Since the objectives of this Regulation cannot be sufficiently achieved by the Member States and can therefore, by reason of the scale or effects of the action, be

better achieved at Community level, the Community may adopt measures, in accordance with the principle of subsidiarity as set out in Article 5 of the Treaty. In accordance with the principle of proportionality, as set out in that Article, this Regulation does not go beyond what is necessary in order to achieve those objectives.

(27) In order to make the provisions more easily accessible and readable, Regulation (EC) No 1348/2000 should be repealed and replaced by this Regulation.

(28) In accordance with Article 3 of the Protocol on the position of the United Kingdom and Ireland, annexed to the Treaty on European Union and to the Treaty establishing the European Community, the United Kingdom and Ireland are taking part in the adoption and application of this Regulation.

(29) In accordance with Articles 1 and 2 of the Protocol on the position of Denmark, annexed to the Treaty on European Union and to the Treaty establishing the European Community, Denmark does not take part in the adoption of this Regulation and is not bound by it or subject to its application,

HAVE ADOPTED THIS REGULATION:

Note—The EC Treaty has become the Treaty on the Functioning of the European Union (TFEU) and the Articles have been re-numbered: Art 5 is replaced, in substance, by Art 5 of the Treaty on the European Union; Art 61 is now Art 67 TFEU; Art 67 is repealed; and Art 251 is now Art 294 TFEU.

CHAPTER I
GENERAL PROVISIONS

ARTICLE 1
SCOPE

1 This Regulation shall apply in civil and commercial matters where a judicial or extrajudicial document has to be transmitted from one Member State to another for service there. It shall not extend in particular to revenue, customs or administrative matters or to liability of the State for actions or omissions in the exercise of state authority (*acta iure imperii*).

2 This Regulation shall not apply where the address of the person to be served with the document is not known.

3 In this Regulation, the term 'Member State' shall mean the Member States with the exception of Denmark.

ARTICLE 2
TRANSMITTING AND RECEIVING AGENCIES

1 Each Member State shall designate the public officers, authorities or other persons, hereinafter referred to as 'transmitting agencies', competent for the transmission of judicial or extra-judicial documents to be served in another Member State.

2 Each Member State shall designate the public officers, authorities or other persons, hereinafter referred to as 'receiving agencies', competent for the receipt of judicial or extrajudicial documents from another Member State.

3 A Member State may designate one transmitting agency and one receiving agency, or one agency to perform both functions. A federal State, a State in which several legal systems apply or a State with autonomous territorial units shall be free

to designate more than one such agency. The designation shall have effect for a period of five years and may be renewed at five-year intervals.

4 Each Member State shall provide the Commission with the following information:

(a) the names and addresses of the receiving agencies referred to in paragraphs 2 and 3;
(b) the geographical areas in which they have jurisdiction;
(c) the means of receipt of documents available to them; and
(d) the languages that may be used for the completion of the standard form set out in Annex I.

Member States shall notify the Commission of any subsequent modification of such information.

ARTICLE 3
CENTRAL BODY

Each Member State shall designate a central body responsible for:

(a) supplying information to the transmitting agencies;
(b) seeking solutions to any difficulties which may arise during transmission of documents for service;
(c) forwarding, in exceptional cases, at the request of a transmitting agency, a request for service to the competent receiving agency.

A federal State, a State in which several legal systems apply or a State with autonomous territorial units shall be free to designate more than one central body.

CHAPTER II
JUDICIAL DOCUMENTS

SECTION 1
TRANSMISSION AND SERVICE OF JUDICIAL DOCUMENTS

ARTICLE 4
TRANSMISSION OF DOCUMENTS

1 Judicial documents shall be transmitted directly and as soon as possible between the agencies designated pursuant to Article 2.

2 The transmission of documents, requests, confirmations, receipts, certificates and any other papers between transmitting agencies and receiving agencies may be carried out by any appropriate means, provided that the content of the document received is true and faithful to that of the document forwarded and that all information in it is easily legible.

3 The document to be transmitted shall be accompanied by a request drawn up using the standard form set out in Annex I. The form shall be completed in the official language of the Member State addressed or, if there are several official languages in that Member State, the official language or one of the official languages of the place where service is to be effected, or in another language which that Member State has indicated it can accept. Each Member State shall indicate the official language or languages of the institutions of the European Union other than its own which is or are acceptable to it for completion of the form.

4 The documents and all papers that are transmitted shall be exempted from legalisation or any equivalent formality.

5 When the transmitting agency wishes a copy of the document to be returned together with the certificate referred to in Article 10, it shall send the document in duplicate.

ARTICLE 5
TRANSLATION OF DOCUMENTS

1 The applicant shall be advised by the transmitting agency to which he forwards the document for transmission that the addressee may refuse to accept it if it is not in one of the languages provided for in Article 8.

2 The applicant shall bear any costs of translation prior to the transmission of the document, without prejudice to any possible subsequent decision by the court or competent authority on liability for such costs.

ARTICLE 6
RECEIPT OF DOCUMENTS BY RECEIVING AGENCY

1 On receipt of a document, a receiving agency shall, as soon as possible and in any event within seven days of receipt, send a receipt to the transmitting agency by the swiftest possible means of transmission using the standard form set out in Annex I.

2 Where the request for service cannot be fulfilled on the basis of the information or documents transmitted, the receiving agency shall contact the transmitting agency by the swiftest possible means in order to secure the missing information or documents.

3 If the request for service is manifestly outside the scope of this Regulation or if non-compliance with the formal conditions required makes service impossible, the request and the documents transmitted shall be returned, on receipt, to the transmitting agency, together with the notice of return using the standard form set out in Annex I.

4 A receiving agency receiving a document for service but not having territorial jurisdiction to serve it shall forward it, as well as the request, to the receiving agency having territorial jurisdiction in the same Member State if the request complies with the conditions laid down in Article 4(3) and shall inform the transmitting agency accordingly using the standard form set out in Annex I. That receiving agency shall inform the transmitting agency when it receives the document, in the manner provided for in paragraph 1.

ARTICLE 7
SERVICE OF DOCUMENTS

1 The receiving agency shall itself serve the document or have it served, either in accordance with the law of the Member State addressed or by a particular method requested by the transmitting agency, unless that method is incompatible with the law of that Member State.

2 The receiving agency shall take all necessary steps to effect the service of the document as soon as possible, and in any event within one month of receipt. If it has not been possible to effect service within one month of receipt, the receiving agency shall:

    (a)   immediately inform the transmitting agency by means of the certificate in the standard form set out in Annex I, which shall be drawn up under the conditions referred to in Article 10(2); and

(b) continue to take all necessary steps to effect the service of the document, unless indicated otherwise by the transmitting agency, where service seems to be possible within a reasonable period of time.

ARTICLE 8
REFUSAL TO ACCEPT A DOCUMENT

1 The receiving agency shall inform the addressee, using the standard form set out in Annex II, that he may refuse to accept the document to be served at the time of service or by returning the document to the receiving agency within one week if it is not written in, or accompanied by a translation into, either of the following languages:

(a) a language which the addressee understands; or
(b) the official language of the Member State addressed or, if there are several official languages in that Member State, the official language or one of the official languages of the place where service is to be effected.

2 Where the receiving agency is informed that the addressee refuses to accept the document in accordance with paragraph 1, it shall immediately inform the transmitting agency by means of the certificate provided for in Article 10 and return the request and the documents of which a translation is requested.

3 If the addressee has refused to accept the document pursuant to paragraph 1, the service of the document can be remedied through the service on the addressee in accordance with the provisions of this Regulation of the document accompanied by a translation into a language provided for in paragraph 1. In that case, the date of service of the document shall be the date on which the document accompanied by the translation is served in accordance with the law of the Member State addressed. However, where according to the law of a Member State, a document has to be served within a particular period, the date to be taken into account with respect to the applicant shall be the date of the service of the initial document determined pursuant to Article 9(2).

4 Paragraphs 1, 2 and 3 shall also apply to the means of transmission and service of judicial documents provided for in Section 2.

5 For the purposes of paragraph 1, the diplomatic or consular agents, where service is effected in accordance with Article 13, or the authority or person, where service is effected in accordance with Article 14, shall inform the addressee that he may refuse to accept the document and that any document refused must be sent to those agents or to that authority or person respectively.

ARTICLE 9
DATE OF SERVICE

1 Without prejudice to Article 8, the date of service of a document pursuant to Article 7 shall be the date on which it is served in accordance with the law of the Member State addressed.

2 However, where according to the law of a Member State a document has to be served within a particular period, the date to be taken into account with respect to the applicant shall be that determined by the law of that Member State.

3 Paragraphs 1 and 2 shall also apply to the means of transmission and service of judicial documents provided for in Section 2.

ARTICLE 10
CERTIFICATE OF SERVICE AND COPY OF THE DOCUMENT SERVED

1 When the formalities concerning the service of the document have been completed, a certificate of completion of those formalities shall be drawn up in the standard form set out in Annex I and addressed to the transmitting agency, together with, where Article 4(5) applies, a copy of the document served.

2 The certificate shall be completed in the official language or one of the official languages of the Member State of origin or in another language which the Member State of origin has indicated that it can accept. Each Member State shall indicate the official language or languages of the institutions of the European Union other than its own which is or are acceptable to it for completion of the form.

ARTICLE 11
COSTS OF SERVICE

1 The service of judicial documents coming from a Member State shall not give rise to any payment or reimbursement of taxes or costs for services rendered by the Member State addressed.

2 However, the applicant shall pay or reimburse the costs occasioned by:

(a) recourse to a judicial officer or to a person competent under the law of the Member State addressed;
(b) the use of a particular method of service.

Costs occasioned by recourse to a judicial officer or to a person competent under the law of the Member State addressed shall correspond to a single fixed fee laid down by that Member State in advance which respects the principles of proportionality and non-discrimination. Member States shall communicate such fixed fees to the Commission.

SECTION 2
OTHER MEANS OF TRANSMISSION AND SERVICE OF JUDICIAL DOCUMENTS

ARTICLE 12
TRANSMISSION BY CONSULAR OR DIPLOMATIC CHANNELS

Each Member State shall be free, in exceptional circumstances, to use consular or diplomatic channels to forward judicial documents, for the purpose of service, to those agencies of another Member State which are designated pursuant to Articles 2 or 3.

ARTICLE 13
SERVICE BY DIPLOMATIC OR CONSULAR AGENTS

1 Each Member State shall be free to effect service of judicial documents on persons residing in another Member State, without application of any compulsion, directly through its diplomatic or consular agents.

2 Any Member State may make it known, in accordance with Article 23(1), that it is opposed to such service within its territory, unless the documents are to be served on nationals of the Member State in which the documents originate.

ARTICLE 14
SERVICE BY POSTAL SERVICES

Each Member State shall be free to effect service of judicial documents directly by postal services on persons residing in another Member State by registered letter with acknowledgement of receipt or equivalent.

ARTICLE 15
DIRECT SERVICE

Any person interested in a judicial proceeding may effect service of judicial documents directly through the judicial officers, officials or other competent persons of the Member State addressed, where such direct service is permitted under the law of that Member State.

CHAPTER III

EXTRAJUDICIAL DOCUMENTS

ARTICLE 16
TRANSMISSION

Extrajudicial documents may be transmitted for service in another Member State in accordance with the provisions of this Regulation.

CHAPTER IV
FINAL PROVISIONS

ARTICLE 17
IMPLEMENTING RULES

Measures designed to amend non-essential elements of this Regulation relating to the updating or to the making of technical amendments to the standard forms set out in Annexes I and II shall be adopted in accordance with the regulatory procedure with scrutiny referred to in Article 18(2).

ARTICLE 18
COMMITTEE

1 The Commission shall be assisted by a committee.

2 Where reference is made to this paragraph, Article 5a(1) to (4), and Article 7 of Decision 1999/468/EC shall apply, having regard to the provisions of Article 8 thereof.

ARTICLE 19
DEFENDANT NOT ENTERING AN APPEARANCE

1 Where a writ of summons or an equivalent document has had to be transmitted to another Member State for the purpose of service under the provisions of this Regulation and the defendant has not appeared, judgment shall not be given until it is established that:

(a) the document was served by a method prescribed by the internal law of the

Member State addressed for the service of documents in domestic actions upon persons who are within its territory; or

(b) the document was actually delivered to the defendant or to his residence by another method provided for by this Regulation; and that in either of these cases the service or the delivery was effected in sufficient time to enable the defendant to defend.

2 Each Member State may make it known, in accordance with Article 23(1), that the judge, notwithstanding the provisions of paragraph 1, may give judgment even if no certificate of service or delivery has been received, if all the following conditions are fulfilled:

(a) the document was transmitted by one of the methods provided for in this Regulation;
(b) a period of time of not less than six months, considered adequate by the judge in the particular case, has elapsed since the date of the transmission of the document;
(c) no certificate of any kind has been received, even though every reasonable effort has been made to obtain it through the competent authorities or bodies of the Member State addressed.

3 Notwithstanding paragraphs 1 and 2, the judge may order, in case of urgency, any provisional or protective measures.

4 When a writ of summons or an equivalent document has had to be transmitted to another Member State for the purpose of service under the provisions of this Regulation and a judgment has been entered against a defendant who has not appeared, the judge shall have the power to relieve the defendant from the effects of the expiry of the time for appeal from the judgment if the following conditions are fulfilled:

(a) the defendant, without any fault on his part, did not have knowledge of the document in sufficient time to defend, or knowledge of the judgment in sufficient time to appeal; and
(b) the defendant has disclosed a *prima facie* defence to the action on the merits.

An application for relief may be filed only within a reasonable time after the defendant has knowledge of the judgment.

Each Member State may make it known, in accordance with Article 23(1), that such application will not be entertained if it is filed after the expiry of a time to be stated by it in that communication, but which shall in no case be less than one year following the date of the judgment.

5 Paragraph 4 shall not apply to judgments concerning the status or capacity of persons.

ARTICLE 20
RELATIONSHIP WITH AGREEMENTS OR ARRANGEMENTS TO WHICH MEMBER STATES ARE PARTY

1 This Regulation shall, in relation to matters to which it applies, prevail over other provisions contained in bilateral or multilateral agreements or arrangements concluded by the Member States, and in particular Article IV of the Protocol to the Brussels Convention of 1968 and the Hague Convention of 15 November 1965.

2 This Regulation shall not preclude individual Member States from maintaining or concluding agreements or arrangements to expedite further or simplify the transmission of documents, provided that they are compatible with this Regulation.

3 Member States shall send to the Commission:

(a) a copy of the agreements or arrangements referred to in paragraph 2 concluded between the Member States as well as drafts of such agreements or arrangements which they intend to adopt; and

(b) any denunciation of, or amendments to, these agreements or arrangements.

ARTICLE 21
LEGAL AID

This Regulation shall not affect the application of Article 23 of the Convention on civil procedure of 17 July 1905, Article 24 of the Convention on civil procedure of 1 March 1954 or Article 13 of the Convention on international access to justice of 25 October 1980 between the Member States party to those Conventions.

ARTICLE 22
PROTECTION OF INFORMATION TRANSMITTED

1 Information, including in particular personal data, transmitted under this Regulation shall be used by the receiving agency only for the purpose for which it was transmitted.

2 Receiving agencies shall ensure the confidentiality of such information, in accordance with their national law.

3 Paragraphs 1 and 2 shall not affect national laws enabling data subjects to be informed of the use made of information transmitted under this Regulation.

4 This Regulation shall be without prejudice to Directives 95/46/EC and 2002/58/EC.

ARTICLE 23
COMMUNICATION AND PUBLICATION

1 Member States shall communicate to the Commission the information referred to in Articles 2, 3, 4, 10, 11, 13, 15 and 19. Member States shall communicate to the Commission if, according to their law, a document has to be served within a particular period as referred to in Articles 8(3) and 9(2).

2 The Commission shall publish the information communicated in accordance with paragraph 1 in the *Official Journal of the European Union* with the exception of the addresses and other contact details of the agencies and of the central bodies and the geographical areas in which they have jurisdiction.

3 The Commission shall draw up and update regularly a manual containing the information referred to in paragraph 1, which shall be available electronically, in particular through the European Judicial Network in Civil and Commercial Matters.

ARTICLE 24
REVIEW

No later than 1 June 2011, and every five years thereafter, the Commission shall present to the European Parliament, the Council and the European Economic and Social Committee a report on the application of this Regulation, paying special attention to the effectiveness of the agencies designated pursuant to Article 2 and to the practical application of Article 3(c) and Article 9. The report shall be accompanied if need be by proposals for adaptations of this Regulation in line with the evolution of notification systems.

ARTICLE 25
REPEAL

1 Regulation (EC) No 1348/2000 shall be repealed as from the date of application of this Regulation.

2 References made to the repealed Regulation shall be construed as being made to this Regulation and should be read in accordance with the correlation table in Annex III.

ARTICLE 26
ENTRY INTO FORCE

This Regulation shall enter into force on the 20th day following its publication in the *Official Journal of the European Union*.

It shall apply from 13 November 2008 with the exception of Article 23 which shall apply from 13 August 2008.

This Regulation shall be binding in its entirety and directly applicable in the Member States in accordance with the Treaty establishing the European Community.

Done at Strasbourg, 13 November 2007.

For the European Parliament

The President

H.-G. PÖTTERING

For the Council

The President

M. LOBO ANTUNES

Practice Direction 6C – Disclosure of Addresses by Government Departments 13 February 1989 as amended by Practice Direction 20 July 1995

This Practice Direction supplements FPR 2010 Part 6 (PD6C)

The arrangements set out in the Registrar's Direction of 26 April 1988 whereby the court may request the disclosure of addresses by government departments have been further extended.

These arrangements will now cover:

    (a) tracing the address of a person in proceedings against whom another person is seeking to obtain or enforce an order for financial provision either for himself or herself or for the children of the former marriage; and,

    (b) tracing the whereabouts of a child, or the person with whom the child is said to be, in proceedings under the Child Abduction and Custody Act 1985 or in which a [Part I order] is being sought or enforced.

Requests for such information will be made officially by the district judge. The request, in addition to giving the information mentioned below, should certify:

1 *In financial provision applications* either

    (a) that a financial provision order is in existence, but cannot be enforced because the person against whom the order has been made cannot be traced; or

    (b) that the applicant has filed or issued a notice, petition or originating summons containing an application for financial provision which cannot be served because the respondent cannot be traced.

A 'financial provision order' means any of the orders mentioned in s 21 of the Matrimonial Causes Act 1973, except an order under s 27(6) of that Act.

2 *In wardship proceedings* that the child is the subject of wardship proceedings and cannot be traced, and is believed to be with the person whose address is sought.

3 *(deleted)*

The following notes set out the information required by those departments which are likely to be of the greatest assistance to an applicant.

(1) Department of Social Security

The department most likely to be able to assist is the Department of Social Security, whose records are the most comprehensive and complete. The possibility of identifying one person amongst so many will depend on the particulars given. An address will not be supplied by the department unless it is satisfied from the particulars given that the record of the person has been reliably identified.

The applicant or his solicitor should therefore be asked to supply as much as possible of the following information about the person sought:

    (i) National Insurance number;
    (ii) surname;
    (iii) forenames in full;
    (iv) date of birth (or, if not known, approximate age);
    (v) last known address, with date when living there;
    (vi) any other known address(es) with dates;
    (vii) if the person sought is a war pensioner, his war pension and service particulars (if known);

and in applications for financial provision:

    (viii) the exact date of the marriage and the wife's forenames.

Enquiries should be sent by the [district judge] to:

Contribution Agency

Special Section A, Room 101B

Longbenton

Newcastle upon Tyne

NE98 1YX

The department will be prepared to search if given full particulars of the person's name and date of birth, but the chances of accurate identification are increased by the provision of more identifying information.

Second requests for records to be searched, provided that a reasonable interval has elapsed, will be met by the Department of Social Security.

Income Support/Supplementary Benefit

Where, in the case of applications for financial provision, the wife is or has been in receipt of income support/supplementary benefit, it would be advisable in the first instance to make enquiries of the manager of the local Social Security office for the area in which she resides in order to avoid possible duplication of enquiries.

(2) Office for National Statistics

National Health Service Central Register

The Office for National Statistics administers the National Health Service Central Register for the Department of Health. The records held in the Central Register include individuals' names, with dates of birth and National Health Service number, against a record of the Family Practitioner Committee area where the patient is currently registered with a National Health Service doctor. The Central Register does not hold individual patients' addresses, but can advise courts of the last Family Practitioner Committee area registration. Courts can then apply for information about addresses to the appropriate Family Practitioner Committee for independent action.

When application is made for the disclosure of Family Practitioner Committee area registrations from these records the applicant or his solicitor should supply as much as possible of the following information about the person sought:

(i) National Health Service number;
(ii) surname;
(iii) forenames in full;
(iv) date of birth (or, if not known, approximate age);
(v) last known address;
(vi) mother's maiden name.

Enquiries should be sent by the district judge to:

The Office for National Statistics
National Health Service Central Register
Smedley Hydro, Trafalgar Road
Southport
Merseyside
PR8 2HH

(3) Passport Office

If all reasonable enquiries, including the aforesaid methods, have failed to reveal an address, or if there are strong grounds for believing that the person sought may have made a recent application for a passport, enquiries may be made to the Passport Office. The applicant or his solicitor should provide as much of the following information about the person as possible:

(i) surname;
(ii) forenames in full;
(iii) date of birth (or, if not known, approximate age);
(iv) place of birth;
(v) occupation;
(vi) whether known to have travelled abroad, and, if so, the destination and dates;
(vii) last known address, with date living there;
(viii) any other known address(es), with dates.

The applicant or his solicitor must also undertake in writing that information given in response to the enquiry will be used solely for the purpose for which it was requested, ie to assist in tracing the husband in connection with the making or enforcement of a financial provision order or in tracing a child in connection with a [Part 1 order] or wardship proceedings, as the case may be.

Enquiries should be sent to:

The Chief Passport Officer
UK Passport Agency
Home Office
Clive House, Petty France
London
SW1H 9HD

(4) Ministry of Defence

In cases where the person sought is known to be serving or to have recently served in any branch of HM Forces, the solicitor representing the applicant may obtain the address for service of financial provision or Part I and wardship proceedings direct from the appropriate service department. In the case of army servicemen, the solicitor can obtain a list of regiments and of the various manning and record offices from the Officer in Charge, Central Manning Support Office, Higher Barracks, Exeter EC4 4ND.

The solicitor's request should be accompanied by a written undertaking that the address will be used for the purpose of service of process in those proceedings and that so far as is possible the solicitor will disclose the address only to the court and not to the applicant or any other person, except in the normal course of the proceedings.

Alternatively, if the solicitor wishes to serve process on the person's commanding officer under the provisions contained in s 101 of the Naval Act 1957, s 153 of the Army Act 1955 and s 153 of the Air Force Act 1955 (all of which as amended by s 62 of the Armed Forces Act 1971) he may obtain that officer's address in the same way.

Where the applicant is acting in person the appropriate service department is prepared to disclose the address of the person sought, or that of his commanding officer, to a [district judge] on receipt of an assurance that the applicant has given an undertaking that the information will be used solely for the purpose of serving process in the proceedings.

In all cases, the request should include details of the person's full name, service number, rank or rating, and his ship, arm or trade, corps, regiment or unit or as much of this information as is available. The request should also include details of his date of birth, or, if not known, his age, his date of entry into the service and, if no longer serving, the date of discharge, and any other information, such as his last known address. Failure to quote the service number and the rank or rating may result in failure to identify the serviceman or at least in considerable delay.

Enquiries should be addressed as follows:

(a)	Officers of Royal Navy and Women's Royal Naval Service	The Naval Secretary, Room 161, Victory Building, HM Naval Base, Portsmouth, Hants PO1 3LS
	Ratings in the Royal Navy, WRNS Ratings, QARNNS Ratings	Captain, Naval Drafting, Centurion Building, Grange Road, Gosport, Hants PO13 9XA
	RN Medical and Dental Officers	The Medical Director General (Naval), Room 114, Victory Building, HM Naval Base, Portsmouth, Hants PO1 3LS
	Naval Chaplains	Director General, Naval Chaplaincy Service, Room 201, Victory Building, HM Naval Base, Portsmouth, Hants PO1 3LS
(b)	Royal Marine Officers	The Naval Secretary, Room 161, Victory Building, HM Naval Base, Portsmouth, Hants PO1 3LS
	Royal Marine Ranks	HQRM (DRORM), West Battery, Whale Island, Portsmouth, Hants PO2 8DX
(c)	Army Officers (including WRAC and QARANC)	Army Officer Documentation Office, Index Department, Room F7, Government Buildings, Stanmore, Middlesex
	Other Ranks, Army	The Manning and Record Office which is appropriate to the Regiment or Corps

| (d) | Royal Air Force Officers and Other Ranks, Women's Royal Air Force Officers and Other Ranks (including PMRA FNS) | Ministry of Defence, RAF Personnel Management, 2b1(a) (RAF), Building 248, RAF Innsworth, Gloucester, GL3 1EZ |

General notes

Records held by other departments are less likely to be of use, either because of their limited scope or because individual records cannot readily be identified. If, however, the circumstances suggest that the address may be known to another department, application may be made to it by the [district judge], all relevant particulars available being given.

When the department is able to supply the address of the person sought to the [district judge], it will be passed on by him to the applicant's solicitor (or, in proper cases, direct to the applicant if acting in person) on an understanding to use it only for the purpose of the proceedings.

Nothing in this practice direction affects the service in matrimonial causes of petitions which do not contain any application for financial provision, etc. The existing arrangements whereby the Department of Social Security will at the request of the solicitor forward a letter by ordinary post to a party's last known address remain in force in such cases.

The Registrar's Direction of 26 April 1988 is hereby revoked.

Issued in its original form with the concurrence of the Lord Chancellor.

Court Funds Rules 2011, SI 2011/1734

ARRANGEMENT OF RULES

PART 1
PRELIMINARY, INTERPRETATION AND GENERAL PROVISIONS

Rule		Page
1	Citation, commencement, revocation and transition	1375
2	Application of the Rules	1375
3	Interpretation	1375
4	Court Funds Office	1376
5	Discharge of Accountant General's functions	1376

PART 2
DEPOSIT OF FUNDS IN COURT

6	Documents accompanying deposit of funds in court	1376
7	Deposit of funds	1378
8	Deposit of funds at a District Registry or county court or the Mayor's and City of London Court	1378
9	Promissory notes	1378
10	Refusal to accept a deposit	1379

PART 3
ACCOUNTS AND INVESTMENTS

11	Interest bearing accounts	1379
12	Transfer between accounts	1379
13	Accrual of interest	1380
14	Investment	1380
15	Investment in securities	1381
16	Foreign currency	1381
17	Authority to direct investment	1381
18	Timing of investment	1382
19	Payment of charges when dealing with securities	1382
20	Conversion and allotment of securities	1382
21	Securities of a dissolved company	1383

PART 4
PAYMENT OUT FROM A FUND IN COURT

22	Documents required for payment	1383
23	Interest on payments	1384
24	Payment to a representative of a deceased person	1384
25	Payment of funeral expenses	1385
26	Payment of inheritance tax	1385
27	Payment in respect of CPR Part 36 (offers to settle)	1385
28	Payment where the claimant's legal representation has been funded by the Legal Services Commission or provided under arrangements made for the purposes of Part 1 of the Legal Aid, Sentencing and Punishment of Offenders Act 2012	1386
29	Remaining balance	1386
30	Time for making payments	1386
31	Regular payments	1386
32	Method of payment	1387
33	Dealing with a fund in court before the receipt of a payment schedule	1387
34	Refusal to make a payment	1387
35	Identification of payees	1387

PART 5
UNCLAIMED FUNDS IN COURT

36	Transfer to the unclaimed funds account	1388
37	Disposal of unclaimed securities and effects	1388
38	Converting unclaimed foreign currency	1388
39	Unclaimed county court money	1388
40	List of unclaimed funds in court and money	1388
41	Payment out of an unclaimed funds account	1389

PART 6
MISCELLANEOUS PROVISIONS

42	Information about a fund in court	1389
43	Statement of account	1389
44	Court's obligations in respect of deposit and payment schedules	1389
45	Transfer between courts	1389
46	National Debt Commissioners	1390

PART 1
PRELIMINARY, INTERPRETATION AND GENERAL PROVISIONS

1 Citation, commencement, revocation and transition

(1) These Rules may be cited as the Court Funds Rules 2011 and shall come into force on 3 October 2011.

(2) The Rules specified in the schedule to these Rules are revoked, except that they continue to apply to such extent as may be necessary for giving effect to any order, direction or request made before 3 October 2011.

2 Application of the Rules

These Rules apply to funds deposited or to be deposited in court:

(a) under an enactment; or
(b) in respect of proceedings in:
 (i) a county court;
 (ii) the High Court;
 (iii) the Civil Division of the Court of Appeal;
 (iv) the Court of Protection; or
 (iv) the family court.

Amendments—SI 2014/879.

3 Interpretation

(1) Expressions used in these Rules that are also used in the Civil Procedure Rules 1998 shall have the same meaning as they have in those Rules.

(2) In these Rules:

'Accountant General' means the Accountant General of the Senior Courts or a person appointed under rule 5;
'Authenticated' means authenticated with a stamp issued by the Accountant General;
'Child' means a person under 18;
'Common investment fund' means a fund established by a scheme made under section 42 of the Administration of Justice Act 1982;
'Court' means any court listed in rule 2(b);
'CPR' means the Civil Procedure Rules 1998;
'Deposit schedule' means a schedule to an order directing that a fund be deposited in court;
'Deputy' means a person who makes decisions on behalf of a person who lacks capacity and who has been:
 (a) appointed by a court under section 16(2)(b) of the Mental Capacity Act 2005; or
 (b) deemed to be so appointed by virtue of paragraph 1 of schedule 5 to that Act;
'Foreign currency' means currency other than sterling;
'Fund' means money (including foreign currency), securities or effects;
'Fund in court' means a fund deposited in court in accordance with Part 2 of these Rules;

'Investment manager' means a person appointed by a deputy to make decisions as to the investment of a fund in court on behalf of a person who lacks capacity;

'Order' means an order or direction made under the seal of a court;

'Payment schedule' means a schedule to an order directing a payment from, or a dealing with, a fund in court;

'Person who lacks capacity' means a person who:

    (a)   immediately before 1st October 2007 was a patient within the meaning of Part VII of the Mental Health Act 1983; or

    (b)   a court has found lacks capacity within the meaning of the Mental Capacity Act 2005 in relation to a fund in court held or to be held on that person's behalf; and

'Written request' means a request made on a form approved by the Accountant General to:

    (a)   deposit funds in court;

    (b)   deal with a fund in court; or

    (c)   receive payment from a fund in court.

(3) In these Rules, where two or more deputies are appointed in relation to a person who lacks capacity:

    (a)   the word 'deputy' refers to those deputies acting jointly if and to the extent that joint action is required by the terms of their appointment; and

    (b)   any rule permitting the Accountant General to refuse to:

        (i)   follow a direction given by a deputy; or

        (ii) undertake any other act at the request of a deputy,

includes a power to refuse to do so on the ground that, while the terms of appointment require the deputies to act jointly, the direction or request was not jointly made.

4 Court Funds Office

The office of the Accountant General shall continue to be known as the Court Funds Office.

5 Discharge of Accountant General's functions

The Accountant General may appoint one or more persons to do anything that may be done by the Accountant General under these Rules.

PART 2
DEPOSIT OF FUNDS IN COURT

6 Documents accompanying deposit of funds in court

(1) The general rule is that the Accountant General shall only accept a deposit of a fund if provided with:

    (a)   a deposit schedule signed and authenticated by a court; or

    (b)   (i)   a written request; and

        (ii) a sealed copy of the court order authorising the deposit.

(2) The general rule does not apply if a fund is deposited in court under one of the following paragraphs in this rule.

(3) Where the deposit is made under CPR rule 37.2 (which provides that there must be a payment into court where a defendant wishes to rely on a defence of tender before claim) the Accountant General shall only accept the deposit if provided with:

(a) a written request;
(b) a sealed copy of the claim form; and
(c) a copy of the defence.

(4) Where the deposit is made under CPR rule 61.11(18) (which provides that the claimant may constitute a limitation fund by making a payment into court) the Accountant General shall only accept the deposit if provided with a written request sealed by a court.

(5) Where the deposit is made under the Life Assurance Companies (Payment into Court) Act 1896, the Accountant General shall only accept the deposit if provided with:

(a) a deposit schedule signed and authenticated by a court; and
(b) a copy of the witness statement or affidavit filed in accordance with CPR rule 37.4 (which relates to payment into court under enactments).

(6) Where the deposit is made under the Trustee Act 1925(b), the Accountant General shall only accept the deposit if provided with:

(a) (i) a deposit schedule signed and authenticated by a court; and
    (ii) a copy of the witness statement or affidavit filed in accordance with CPR rule 37.4;

or

(b) (i) a written request; and
    (ii) a sealed copy of the court order authorising the deposit.

(7) Where the deposit is made under any other enactment that requires specific authority for a fund to be deposited in court, the Accountant General shall only accept the deposit if provided with:

(a) a written request; and
(b) the document authorising the deposit.

(8) Where the deposit is made by a deputy, the Accountant General shall only accept the deposit if provided with:

(a) a written request; and
(b) a sealed copy of the order appointing the deputy.

(9) The Accountant General shall only accept the deposit of foreign currency in court if provided with:

(a) a deposit schedule signed and authenticated by a court authorising the deposit of that currency; or
(b) (i) a written request; and
    (ii) a sealed copy of the court order authorising the deposit of that currency.

(10) A sealed copy of a court order is not required where the written request is made by the Admiralty Marshal.

(11) A sealed copy of a court order is not required where the written request has been sealed by the court that made the order.

7 Deposit of funds

(1) Where a fund is to be deposited in court, it shall be sent to the Court Funds Office unless:

 (a) it is deposited in accordance with rule 8; or
 (b) the Accountant General directs otherwise.

(2) Where the fund to be deposited at the Court Funds Office is money, it shall be deposited by means of a cheque or bankers' draft unless the Accountant General directs otherwise.

(3) Any cheque or banker's draft shall be made payable to the Accountant General of the Senior Courts.

8 Deposit of funds at a District Registry or county court or the Mayor's and City of London Court

(1) A fund may be deposited at a District Registry or county court or the Mayor's and City of London Court in accordance with this rule.

(2) A fund may be deposited at a District Registry or county court:

 (a) in respect of proceedings at that District Registry or county court by a litigant in person without a current account; or
 (b) where an enactment authorises a deposit at a District Registry or county court.

(3) A fund may only be deposited under paragraph (2)(a) as cash.

(4) A fund may only be deposited under paragraph (2)(b):

 (a) by means of a cheque or banker's draft made payable to the Accountant General of the Senior Courts;
 (b) as securities; or
 (c) as cash, if deposited by a person without a current account.

(5) In addition, a fund may be deposited as cash at the Mayor's and City of London Court:

 (a) in respect of proceedings at the Royal Courts of Justice, by a litigant in person without a current account; or
 (b) by a person who is required by or under an enactment to give security for costs in respect of proceedings for an election petition.

(6) The Accountant General shall only accept a deposit made under this rule if the documents required under rule 6 are provided with the deposit.

(7) The District Registry, county court or the Mayor's and City of London Court, as the case may be, shall forward the deposit to the Accountant General within one working day of receipt, together with:

 (a) any document provided to comply with rule 6; and
 (b) confirmation of the date of receipt.

9 Promissory notes

A fund may not be deposited by way of a promissory note.

10 Refusal to accept a deposit

The Accountant General shall refuse to accept a deposit if:

   (a) the person requesting the deposit has not complied with these Rules; or
   (b) there is any other good reason to do so.

PART 3
ACCOUNTS AND INVESTMENTS

11 Interest bearing accounts

(1) The Accountant General shall maintain two interest bearing accounts; a basic account and a special account.

(2) The Accountant General shall invest money in a basic account unless:

   (a) a court directs otherwise;
   (b) it is invested in a special account;
   (c) it is transferred to an account of unclaimed funds; or
   (d) it amounts to less than £10.

(3) Subject to rule 12(2), the Accountant General shall invest money to which a child or person who lacks capacity is entitled in a special account unless:

   (a) a court directs otherwise;
   (b) a deputy or investment manager directs otherwise;
   (c) it is transferred to an account of unclaimed funds; or
   (d) it amounts to less than £10.

(4) If the Accountant General appoints the Director of Savings under rule 5, from the date of the appointment paragraphs (2)(d) and (3)(d) shall cease to have effect.

12 Transfer between accounts

(1) Paragraph (2) applies where a child or person who lacks capacity has become entitled to money held in a basic account.

(2) The Accountant General shall only transfer the money to a special account if provided with a payment schedule signed and authenticated by the court directing such transfer.

(3) The transfer under paragraph (2) shall only take effect from the date on which the payment schedule is received by the Court Funds Office.

(4) Paragraph (5) applies where a person who is entitled to money in a special account:

   (a) dies;
   (b) ceases to be a child; or
   (c) ceases to be a person who lacks capacity.

(5) The Accountant General shall transfer the money to a basic account.

(6) The transfer under paragraph (5) shall take effect from the date on which the person died or ceased to be a child or a person who lacks capacity.

13 Accrual of interest

(1) In this rule, the effective date means:

(a) in the case of a deposit made by cheque or banker's draft, the date on which the cheque or bankers' draft is received by the Court Funds Office;
(b) where the Accountant General has directed under rule 7(1)(b) that the deposit is to be made at a bank, the date on which the deposit is credited to the Accountant General's account;
(c) in the case of a deposit made under rule 8, the date of its receipt in the court office; or
(d) such other date as the Accountant General may determine.

(2) Subject to paragraph (3) and rule 16(2), interest shall accrue on a daily basis from the effective date until the day before money is withdrawn from the account.

(3) Interest shall cease to accrue from the date on which a claimant accepts an offer under CPR Part 36.

(4) Unless the Accountant General directs otherwise, accrued interest shall be credited:

(a) to a basic account, on the last Friday in March and September;
(b) to a special account, on the last Friday in May and November;
(c) when money is withdrawn from an account;
(d) when money is transferred from a basic account to a special account;
(e) when money is transferred from a special account to a basic account; and
(f) when an account is closed.

(5) The Accountant General shall credit accrued interest without deducting income tax.

(6) If the Accountant General appoints the Director of Savings under rule 5, from the date of the appointment:

(a) paragraph (4)(a), (b) and (c) shall cease to have effect;
(b) accrued interest shall be credited to a basic account on 31 March and 30 September; and
(c) accrued interest shall be credited to a special account on 31 May and 30 November.

14 Investment

(1) Except where rule 15 applies, the Accountant General may only invest or reinvest a fund in court in:

(a) a basic account;
(b) a special account; or
(c) a common investment fund.

(2) Except where rule 15 applies, the Accountant General may only invest money in a common investment fund if it:

(a) amounts to £10,000 or more; and
(b) is held on behalf of:
    (i) a child who, on the date on which the investment policy is approved by a court, has 5 years or more until their 18th birthday; or

(ii) a person who lacks capacity who a court, deputy or investment manager has reason to believe will require the investment to be held for 5 years or more.

15 Investment in securities

(1) This rule applies where a fund in court was invested by the Accountant General in any of the following ways before 3 October 2011 and remained so invested immediately before that date:

(a) in any manner specified in Part I, paragraphs 1 to 10 and 12 of Part II and paragraphs 2, 2A and 3 of Part III of schedule 1 to the Trustee Act 1961, as supplemented by the provisions of Part IV of that schedule;
(b) in investment trust ordinary shares;
(c) in securities (other than common investment fund units) where the person entitled to the securities is subject to an order of the Court of Protection; or
(d) in a common investment fund.

(2) The Accountant General may continue to invest or reinvest the fund in court in the ways mentioned in paragraph (1).

(3) The Accountant General may not invest or reinvest the fund in court in accordance with paragraph (2) if the cost would be disproportionate to the amount to be invested or reinvested.

16 Foreign currency

(1) The Accountant General shall invest or reinvest foreign currency in an interest bearing account in such currency if provided with:

(a) a payment schedule signed and authenticated by a court directing the investment or reinvestment of the foreign currency; or
(b) written directions in accordance with rule 17(2) directing the investment or reinvestment of the foreign currency.

(2) Interest shall accrue on money invested or reinvested under paragraph (1) from the date on which the Accountant General is provided with either the payment schedule or written directions directing the investment or reinvestment of the foreign currency.

(3) The Accountant General shall pay any charge incurred in placing foreign currency into a foreign currency account from the account in which the foreign currency is held.

(4) Unless a court, deputy or investment manager directs otherwise, the Accountant General shall convert dividend payments received in a foreign currency into sterling and invest the proceeds in accordance with this Part.

17 Authority to direct investment

(1) Subject to paragraph (2), the Accountant General shall invest or reinvest a fund in court in accordance with a written request from a court.

(2) The Accountant General shall invest or reinvest a fund in court that is subject to an order of the Court of Protection in accordance with written directions from:

(a) the Court of Protection;

(b) a deputy; or
(c) an investment manager.

(3) If a deputy appoints an investment manager, the deputy must send in writing to the Accountant General:

(a) authority for the investment manager to give directions for the investment of a fund in court; and
(b) contact details of the investment manager.

(4) The Accountant General may not comply with a direction given under paragraph (2)(b) if:

(a) the deputy gave the direction without authority to do so;
(b) the Court of Protection has made a contrary direction; or
(c) there is any other good reason for not complying.

(5) The Accountant General may not comply with a direction given under paragraph (2)(c) if:

(a) a deputy appointed the investment manager without authority to do so;
(b) the deputy has not complied with paragraph (3);
(c) the investment manager gave the direction without authority to do so;
(d) the Court of Protection has made a contrary direction; or
(e) there is any other good reason for not complying.

18 Timing of investment

The Accountant General shall comply with any order, direction or request for investment as soon as is practicable.

19 Payment of charges when dealing with securities

Unless a court directs otherwise, the Accountant General shall pay any charge incurred when dealing with securities from the fund in court of the person on whose behalf the Accountant General is dealing.

20 Conversion and allotment of securities

(1) Where nobody else is able to give directions, the Accountant General may apply to the appropriate court for directions on how to deal with a conversion or allotment of securities.

(2) Where a security in court has been converted into another security, the Accountant General shall write off the original security and replace it with the whole, or where appropriate a proportionate part, of the substituted security.

(3) Unless the court directs otherwise, the Accountant General shall deal with any substituted security and dividends, so far as is practicable, in the same manner as the original security and dividends.

(4) Where an allotment is made in respect of a security in court the Accountant General shall:

(a) credit the whole, or a proportionate part, of the allotment to the account of the original security if the allotment is fully paid;
(b) sell the allotment and credit the whole, or a proportionate part, of the

proceeds of sale to the appropriate account or otherwise as the court may direct if the allotment is not fully paid; or

(c) sell any non-apportionable security and credit the proceeds to the appropriate account.

21 Securities of a dissolved company

The Accountant General shall write off the securities of any company that has been struck off the company register in the country in which the company is incorporated.

PART 4
PAYMENT OUT FROM A FUND IN COURT

22 Documents required for payment

(1) The general rule is that the Accountant General shall make a payment from a fund in court if provided with a payment schedule signed and authenticated by a court.

(2) The general rule does not apply if a payment is made under one of the following paragraphs in this rule.

(3) Subject to paragraphs (6) and (7), where a deputy has been appointed, the Accountant General shall only make a payment from a fund in court if provided with:

    (a) a written request from the deputy; and
    (b) a sealed copy of the court order authorising the payment.

(4) Where an enactment requires specific authority for payment, the Accountant General shall only make a payment from a fund in court if provided with:

    (a) a written request; and
    (b) any authority required to permit payment under the enactment.

(5) Where a court has ordered that a person may apply directly to the Court Funds Office for payment of a fund in court on or after reaching their majority, the Accountant General shall only make a payment from the fund in court if provided with a written request from that person.

(6) Where the Court of Protection is satisfied that a person no longer lacks capacity in relation to a fund in court to which that person is entitled, the Accountant General shall only make a payment from the fund in court if provided with:

    (a) a written request; and
    (b) a sealed copy of the court order.

(7) Where the Court of Protection has ordered a payment from a fund in court be made to a person other than the person entitled to the fund in court or a deputy, the Accountant General shall only make a payment from the fund in court if provided with:

    (a) a payment schedule signed and authenticated by the court; or
    (b) (i) a written request; and
        (ii) a sealed copy of the court order authorising the payment.

23 Interest on payments

Where rule 22 applies, the Accountant General shall deal with any interest in accordance with:

(a) the payment schedule; or
(b) the other authority for payment.

24 Payment to a representative of a deceased person

(1) This rule applies where a person entitled to a fund in court dies.

(2) Where a grant of representation has been obtained, the Accountant General shall pay out the fund in court to the personal representative of the deceased if provided with:

(a) a written request; and
(b) a sealed copy of the grant of representation.

(3) Where a grant of representation has been obtained by two or more persons, the Accountant General shall only pay out the fund in court if provided with:

(a) the documents required under paragraph (2);
(b) the written consent of each living person named as a personal representative in the grant of representation; and
(c) a copy of the death certificate of any deceased person who was named as a personal representative in the grant of representation.

(4) Where the value of the estate is less than £5,000 and the person dies testate, the Accountant General shall pay out the fund in court to the person who claims to have the right to a grant of probate if provided with:

(a) a written request;
(b) a copy of the will of the deceased; and
(c) a copy of the death certificate of the deceased.

(5) Where the value of the estate is less than £5,000 and two or more persons have a right to a grant of probate, the Accountant General shall only pay out the fund in court if provided with:

(a) the documents required under paragraph (4);
(b) the written consent of each living person who has been named as an executor in the deceased's will; and
(c) a copy of the death certificate of any deceased person who was named as an executor in the deceased's will.

(6) Where the value of the estate is less than £5,000 and the person dies intestate, the Accountant General shall pay out the fund in court to the person who claims to have a prior right to a grant of letters of administration if provided with:

(a) a written request;
(b) a written declaration of kinship; and
(c) a copy of the death certificate of the deceased.

(7) Where the value of the estate is less than £5,000 and two or more persons claim to have a prior right to a grant of letters of administration, the Accountant General shall only pay out the fund in court if provided with:

(a) the documents required under paragraph (6);

(b) the written consent of each person who appears to have a prior right to a grant of letters of administration; and
(c) a written declaration of kinship of each such person.

25 Payment of funeral expenses

(1) This rule applies where a person who is entitled to a fund in court and subject to an order of the Court of Protection dies.

(2) The Accountant General shall make a payment from the fund in court of the deceased to a funeral director in respect of reasonable funeral expenses if provided with:

(a) a funeral invoice; and
(b) a written request from:
　(i) an executor of the deceased's estate; or
　(ii) the person who arranged the funeral if the deceased died intestate.

26 Payment of inheritance tax

(1) This rule applies where a person who is entitled to a fund in court and subject to an order of the Court of Protection dies.

(2) The Accountant General shall make a payment from the fund in court of the deceased to Her Majesty's Revenue and Customs in respect of all or part of the inheritance tax due on the deceased's estate if provided with:

(a) the completed relevant form from Her Majesty's Revenue and Customs; and
(b) a written request from:
　(i) an executor of the deceased's estate; or
　(ii) a person who appears to have a prior right to a grant of letters of administration of the estate if the deceased died intestate.

27 Payment in respect of CPR Part 36 (offers to settle)

(1) This rule applies where:

(a) a payment is to be made to a claimant out of a fund in court under CPR Part 36; and
(b) the permission of a court is not required for the payment.

(2) Subject to rule 28(3), where a defendant has deposited money under a court order or in support of a defence of tender before claim and a CPR Part 36 offer is subsequently accepted, the Accountant General shall make a payment from a fund in court if provided with:

(a) a written request from the claimant; and
(b) written confirmation from the defendant that all, or part, of the fund in court may be used to satisfy the offer (in whole or in part).

(3) Subject to rule 28(3), where a CPR Part 36 deposit has been made and the CPR Part 36 offer has been accepted, the Accountant General shall make a payment from a fund in court if provided with a written request from the claimant.

(4) The Accountant General shall pay any accrued interest remaining in court following a payment under paragraph (2) or (3) or rule 28(2) to the defendant.

(5) The Accountant General may not make any payment under this rule where more than one defendant is sued jointly and not all of the defendants have deposited money in court unless:

(a) the claimant has also discontinued the claim against the defendants who have not deposited money in court; and
(b) the Accountant General is provided with a copy of:
   (i) the notice of discontinuance; and
   (ii) the written consent to the discontinuance of each of those defendants.

28 Payment where the claimant's legal representation has been funded by the Legal Services Commission or provided under arrangements made for the purposes of Part 1 of the Legal Aid, Sentencing and Punishment of Offenders Act 2012

(1) This rule applies where:

(a) a payment is to be made to a claimant out of a fund in court under CPR Part 36;
(b) the claimant's legal representation has been funded by the Legal Services Commission or provided under arrangements made for the purposes of Part 1 of the Legal Aid, Sentencing and Punishment of Offenders Act 2012; and
(c) regulation 18(1) of the Community Legal Services (Costs) Regulations 2000 or regulation 13(1) of the Civil Legal Aid (Statutory Charge) Regulations 2013 applies to the fund in court.

(2) Where the claimant is legally represented, the Accountant General shall pay the amount to be paid out under rule 27(2) or (3) to the claimant's legal representative.

(3) Where the claimant is no longer legally represented, the Accountant General shall only make a payment from a fund in court if provided with a payment schedule signed and authenticated by a court.

Amendments—SI 2013/534, reg 14(1), Sch, Pt 1, para 9(a)–(c).

29 Remaining balance

The remaining balance of a fund in court (if any) after a payment under rule 27 or 28(2) shall be paid out in accordance with rule 22.

30 Time for making payments

The Accountant General shall make any payment as soon as practicable after receipt of:

(a) the payment schedule; or
(b) the other authority for payment.

31 Regular payments

Where a payment schedule directs that regular payments are to be made, the payment schedule shall state the dates on which the payments shall be made.

32 Method of payment

(1) In this rule:

'BACS' means the method of payment known as 'Banks Automated Clearing System' by which money is transferred from one bank in the United Kingdom to another; and

'International money transfer' means a method of payment in which money is transferred from a bank in the United Kingdom to a bank outside the United Kingdom by means of an automated system.

(2) Unless the Accountant General directs otherwise, payment out from a fund in court shall be made by:

(a) BACS;
(b) international money transfer;
(c) cheque; or
(d) warrant.

(3) The Accountant General may deduct any charges incurred in paying money out of court from the fund in court from which the payment was made.

33 Dealing with a fund in court before the receipt of a payment schedule

(1) Paragraph 2 applies where the Accountant General has dealt with a fund in court after the date of a court order but before the receipt of the related payment schedule.

(2) The Accountant General shall, if reasonably practicable, deal with an asset that is not mentioned in the payment schedule in accordance with the payment schedule.

34 Refusal to make a payment

The Accountant General may not make a payment if:

(a) the identity or entitlement of a person claiming to be entitled to a payment is in doubt;
(b) the request for payment is outside the scope of a deputy's power;
(c) the person requesting payment has not complied with these Rules; or
(d) there is any other good reason to do so.

35 Identification of payees

(1) If the Accountant General, in accordance with rule 34(a), does not make a payment, the Accountant General may require the personal attendance of the person claiming to be entitled to the payment at a court in order to provide evidence of their identity or entitlement.

(2) The Accountant General may not pay a person who changes their name before a fund in court has been paid, unless that person provides the Accountant General with evidence of their change of name.

PART 5
UNCLAIMED FUNDS IN COURT

36 Transfer to the unclaimed funds account

(1) The Accountant General may transfer an unclaimed fund in court to an account of unclaimed funds.

(2) Subject to paragraph (3), a fund in court shall be treated as unclaimed if:

  (a) it has not been dealt with for ten years other than:
  (i)   being credited with accrued interest or dividends; or
  (ii) by a compulsory dealing in securities; or
  (b) the Accountant General is, at any time, satisfied that all reasonable steps have been taken to trace the person entitled to the fund in court and that person cannot be traced.

(3) Where a fund in court is held on behalf of a child and the child's date of birth is known, paragraph (2)(a) shall not apply until the child's 18th birthday.

37 Disposal of unclaimed securities and effects

(1) The Accountant General may sell any unclaimed securities (including common investment fund units) or effects to be transferred under rule 36 and pay the proceeds into an account of unclaimed funds.

(2) The Accountant General shall write off any securities or effects transferred under rule 36 which have no value.

38 Converting unclaimed foreign currency

The Accountant General shall convert any foreign currency to be transferred under rule 36 into sterling and pay the proceeds into an account of unclaimed funds.

39 Unclaimed county court money

(1) Money paid into a county court other than under rule 8 may be treated as unclaimed if it has not been dealt with for a period of one year immediately before 1st March in any year.

(2) The Accountant General shall accept a deposit of money treated by a county court as unclaimed under paragraph (1) if provided with a written request from an officer of that court.

(3) The Accountant General shall place money that has been deposited under paragraph (2) to an account of unclaimed funds.

(4) Each county court shall maintain a list of monies deposited under paragraph (2), which may be inspected at that court's office.

40 List of unclaimed funds in court and money

The Accountant General shall maintain a list of funds in court transferred under rule 36(1) and of money deposited under rule 39(2).

41 Payment out of an unclaimed funds account

(1) The Accountant General shall make a payment out of an account of unclaimed funds if provided with a payment schedule signed and authenticated by a court.

(2) Subject to paragraph (3), money paid out of an account of unclaimed funds shall be credited with simple interest at the rate of interest payable on a basic account at the date of payment, from the date on which the money was transferred to an account of unclaimed funds.

(3) The Accountant General may not credit any interest to unclaimed money deposited under rule 39(2).

PART 6
MISCELLANEOUS PROVISIONS

42 Information about a fund in court

The Accountant General shall, on receipt of a request in writing, provide information about a fund in court to:

(a) a person who is entitled to the fund in court; or
(b) a person who the Accountant General considers to have a valid reason for requesting the information.

43 Statement of account

(1) Paragraph (2) applies where a child or a person who lacks capacity is entitled to a fund in court.

(2) The Accountant General shall send a statement of account to the child or person who lacks capacity:

(a) on an annual basis; and
(b) at such other times as the Accountant General considers appropriate.

44 Court's obligations in respect of deposit and payment schedules

(1) Where an order has been made in respect of a fund in court, an officer of the court which made the order shall:

(a) sign and authenticate the deposit schedule or payment schedule, as the case may be; and
(b) send it to the Accountant General.

(2) Where the court amends a deposit schedule or payment schedule, an officer of the court which made the order shall:

(a) sign and seal the amendment; and
(b) send it to the Accountant General.

45 Transfer between courts

Where proceedings in which a fund has been deposited in court are transferred to another court, the court to which the proceedings are transferred must notify the Accountant General of the transfer.

46 National Debt Commissioners

(1) The Accountant General shall transfer to the National Debt Commissioners:

(a) money held in the account of the Accountant General (the 'operational account') that exceeds the amount reasonably required to satisfy current demands; and
(b) non-apportionable sums received in respect of securities.

(2) The National Debt Commissioners shall transfer to the Accountant General such amount as the Accountant General may request in writing if the balance of the operational account is less than the amount reasonably required to satisfy current demands.

(3) As soon as is practicable after half-yearly interest accruing on money invested in a basic or special account has been credited to the appropriate accounts the Accountant General shall certify to the National Debt Commissioners the amount required to credit interest on those accounts.

(4) When the Accountant General has informed the National Debt Commissioners of the amount required in paragraph (3), the National Debt Commissioners shall credit that amount to the account into which the money transferred under paragraph (1) was invested.

Public Guardian Practice Notes

Public Guardian Practice Note No 1 of 2010: Deputies and Attorneys: Release of Visit Reports

1 Summary

1.1 This practice note details when a copy of a Court of Protection Visitor's report may be released, and to whom it may be released. Regulations allow the Public Guardian discretion to release a copy of a visit report to parties interviewed by the Visitor in the course of preparing the report. A visit report may be made available to parties included in a Public Guardian application to Court, or supplied to the Police or a Local Authority in an investigation. Personal information contained within a visit report may be released following a Data Protection Act subject access request.

1.2 The Court of Protection can order reports by a Visitor to assist its decision making. Reports produced for the Court can only be released with the permission of the Court.

1.3 Reports produced by the former Lord Chancellor's Visitors prior to the Introduction of the Mental Capacity Act 2005 on 1 October 2007 are records of the Court of Protection, and can only be released with the permission of the Court.

2 Court of Protection Visitors

2.1 Court of Protection Visitors are statutory roles, created by Section 61 of the Mental Capacity Act 2005. There are two types of Visitors: Special Visitors and

General Visitors. Special Visitors are medically qualified, with experience of mental incapacity, whilst General Visitors are not required to be medically qualified, but usually have experience of mental incapacity.

2.2 The panel of Visitors is administered by the Office of the Public Guardian (OPG). Visitors are mainly engaged on contracts for service, although a small number of general visitors are employed directly by the OPG. They carry out visits throughout England and Wales.

2.3 Court of Protection Visitors can visit people who have a Deputy appointed by the Court of Protection; Deputies; Donors and Attorneys under registered Lasting or Enduring Powers of Attorney. They supply independent reports to the Public Guardian to assist him in his role of supervising Deputies and investigating concerns about the actions of a Deputy or Attorney, and to the Court of Protection to assist it in its decision making.

3 Release of a report by the Public Guardian

3.1 The Public Guardian may commission a report by a Court of Protection Visitor as part of his supervision of Deputies, or investigations into concerns about the actions of a Deputy or Attorney. Regulation 44 of the Lasting Powers of Attorney, Enduring Powers of Attorney and Public Guardian Regulations allows the Public Guardian, if he considers it appropriate to do so, to release a Visitor's report to any person interviewed in the course of preparing a report, and invite him/her to comment on it. This could include the Deputy, client, donor, attorney or any third party interviewed by the visitor such as a relative or carer.

3.2 Requests for a copy of a visit report should be made in writing to the OPG. The request will be dealt with by a senior manager within the OPG who has delegated authority to release reports by the Public Guardian. Release of the report is discretionary, and may be refused. For example, if the report contains: information about a third party that may breach their data protection rights; or information that was disclosed in confidence to the Visitor by a third party; or information that may be harmful to anyone named in the report. The OPG operates a whistle blowing policy that protects the identity of people making allegations of abuse, which in part enables the Public Guardian to perform his statutory duty to investigate such allegations fully.

A visit report may therefore sometimes be released with parts 'redacted', i.e. with parts removed.

3.3 Release of reports to other Court of Protection Visitors

Reports prepared for the Public Guardian since October 2007 may be released to a Visitor subsequently asked to visit in the same case as part of the Public Guardian's supervisory or investigatory duties.

3.4 Release of reports to the Police

Reports prepared for the Public Guardian since October 2007 may be released to the Police if they are investigating whether a crime has taken place.

3.5 Release of reports to Local Authorities

The OPG has a protocol governing working arrangements with Local Authorities in their role as lead agencies for safeguarding vulnerable adults.

Information from a visit report may be shared with a Local Authority where the OPG deems it necessary to safeguard a vulnerable adult, to prevent or respond to abuse, to safeguard other vulnerable adults or deal with a perpetrator of abuse.

4 Reports in Public Guardian Court applications

4.1 Visit reports prepared for the Public Guardian may be used as evidence in applications to the Court of Protection. In that case, a copy of the report is served by the applicant on the parties to the application, unless a judge orders otherwise.

5 Release of a report under the Data Protection Act

5.1 The Data Protection Act (Section 7) gives individuals the right to request personal information that is held by either public or private organisations. This may be:

- Information about themselves (known as a subject access request)
- Information about the person the individual is acting for under a registered Enduring Power of Attorney or Lasting Power of Attorney, or Court of Protection Deputyship.

5.2 There is information on how to make a Data Protection Act subject access request on the OPG website at www.publicguardian.gov.uk. A fee is payable. If a visit report is released following a Data Protection Act request, then information that does not relate to the data subject and the names of some third parties will be redacted in accordance with the principles of the Data Protection Act.

6 Court of Protection reports

6.1 Visitors' reports prepared for the Court are provided to parties to the proceedings under rule 117 of the Court rules, unless the Court orders otherwise. Parties to the proceedings are defined as the applicant, the respondent and anyone joined as a party, and to others that the Court may direct.

6.2 Under Rule 17 of the Court Rules, an application may be made to the Court for a copy of a report (or other records of the Court) by someone who is not a party to proceedings. The Court may provide documents on an edited basis.

6.3 An application should be made on form COP9 and no fee is payable. Further details of how to make an application to the Court of Protection can be found on Her Majesty's Court Service website at www.hmcourts-service.gov.uk. The Court Enquiry Service can be contacted on 0300 456 4600.

7 Reports made before 1 October 2007

7.1 All reports made by the former Lord Chancellor's Visitors before implementation of the Mental Capacity Act on 1 October 2007 are records of the Court of Protection, and can only be released with the permission of the Court. An application to the Court can be made as detailed above.

Public Guardian Practice Note No 2 of 2010: Deputies and Attorneys: The Independent Safeguarding Authority

1 Summary

1.1 This practice note details the Public Guardian's policy on exchange of information with the Independent Safeguarding Authority.

1.2 The Safeguarding Vulnerable Groups Act 2006 established a system for regulating people who engage in some activities in relation to children and vulnerable adults. People acting as Deputies and Attorneys are covered by the Act. The Public Guardian is a supervisory authority under the Act and has duties and powers relating to obtaining information from and providing information to the Independent Safeguarding Authority (ISA).

1.3 The Public Guardian will refer a Deputy or Attorney to the ISA where they have committed a relevant offence. They will also refer a Deputy or Attorney to the ISA where they have evidence that the Deputy or Attorney has engaged or is likely to engage in behaviour which will cause harm or risk of harm to a child or vulnerable adult.

1.4 The Public Guardian will make enquiries with the ISA where he is investigating the actions of a Deputy or Attorney and he has concerns that the individual may cause harm to a child or vulnerable adult; and where the Court of Protection requests the Public Guardian makes enquiries and those enquiries are in connection with the Public Guardian's functions. Enquiries will be made as appropriate and may include whether a deputy or attorney is on a barred list, or is being considered for inclusion on the barred list, or whether a deputy or attorney is registered with the ISA in connection with another regulated activity.

2 The Independent Safeguarding Authority (ISA)

2.2 The Independent Safeguarding Authority's (ISA) role is to help prevent unsuitable people from working with children and vulnerable adults. They assess individuals working or wishing to work in activities covered by the Safeguarding Vulnerable Groups Act and make decisions and maintain the list of people barred from working with children and vulnerable adults. 2

2.3 On the 15 June 2010 the Government announced its intention to review the scheme and implementation has been halted whilst the review is carried out. However, regulations introduced in October 2009 continue to apply, and the ISA is continuing to operate and maintain the barred lists whilst the review is being carried out.

More information about the ISA can be found at www.isa-gov.org.uk

Note—OPG Practice Note No 2 of 2010 was issued without para 2.1.

3 Deputies and Attorneys and the Safeguarding Vulnerable Groups Act

3.1 People who are classed as vulnerable adults under the Safeguarding Vulnerable Groups Act include donors of lasting and enduring powers of attorney which are registered or an application has been made to register, and people for whom the Court of Protection has appointed a Deputy (including children with a Court appointed Deputy). Deputies and Attorneys carry out what is called 'regulated activity' when making decisions on behalf of the person they are appointed to act for.

3.2 Deputies and Attorneys are not obliged to register with the ISA, but it is a criminal offence if someone acts as a Deputy or Attorney if they are have been barred by the ISA.

4 The Public Guardian's duties and powers under the Safeguarding Vulnerable Groups Act

4.1 The Public Guardian is a 'supervisory authority' under the Safeguarding Vulnerable Groups Act, and has certain powers and duties in relation to the Act, introduced on 12 October 2009. His duties are to:

- Provide the ISA with certain information if he believes that someone is engaged in regulated activity and may harm a child or vulnerable adult;
- Provide information to the ISA if the ISA are considering whether to include someone on the barred list or remove them from the list.

4.2 His powers are to:

- Apply to the ISA for information as to whether someone is on a barred list, or is being considered for inclusion on the barred list, or is registered with the ISA;
- Ask the ISA to provide him with information which is relevant to the exercise of his functions as Public Guardian.

4.3 The Public Guardian does not decide whether someone should be placed onto the barred list – this is decided by the ISA.

5 When the Public Guardian will make a referral to the ISA

5.1 The Public Guardian **must** make a referral to the ISA when an individual has received a caution or conviction for a relevant offence. The list of relevant offences is set out in regulations and can be accessed on the ISA website. The most likely situation which will prompt an automatic Public Guardian referral to the ISA is where he is aware that someone has been cautioned or convicted for the ill treatment or neglect of someone who lacks mental capacity.

5.2 The Public Guardian can also make a referral to the ISA where there is sufficient evidence that someone has engaged in *relevant conduct* and satisfies a *harm test*. ISA guidance says that harm includes financial harm, neglect, and physical harm. Examples of relevant conduct include unauthorised withdrawals from a vulnerable adult's account, theft, fraud, exploitation, failure to administer reasonable care, unmet social or care needs, use of inappropriate restraint, and under or overuse of medication.

5.3 An ISA referral will be considered when the Public Guardian is investigating the conduct of a Deputy or Attorney and will depend on the circumstances of the case. A referral will be made when a Deputy or Attorney has been cautioned or convicted of a crime against the person whose affairs they manage. This includes theft, fraud and abuse of position. In other cases, the following factors will be taken into account when considering a referral:

- Whether there is compelling evidence that the Deputy or Attorney poses a risk of harm to children or vulnerable adults;

- Whether someone has communicated something in his/her thoughts, beliefs or attitudes that indicates a risk of harm directly in relation to children or vulnerable adults;
- The specific behaviour that may give rise to risk or harm to a child or vulnerable adult;
- Whether the action taken by the OPG has removed the risk or harm, or whether there is an ongoing risk;
- The likelihood and risk of the behaviour being repeated against a child or vulnerable adult;
- The level of harm the behaviour is likely to cause if it is repeated.

5.4 The information that the ISA require on a referral is specified in legislation. The OPG will use the ISA's standard referral form when providing information to the ISA, and will not notify the individual that a referral has been made.

6 When the Public Guardian will ask the ISA for information about an individual

6.1 The Public Guardian can ask the ISA whether someone is on a barred list, or is being considered for inclusion on the barred list or whether a deputy or attorney is registered with the ISA in connection with another regulated activity. Enquiries will be made as appropriate where the OPG are investigating the actions of someone who is on the registers of Deputies, Lasting Powers of Attorney or Enduring Powers of Attorney and they have concerns that the individual may cause harm to a child or vulnerable adult. The Public Guardian will also make enquiries where he has reason to believe that an attorney under an Enduring Power of Attorney or Lasting Power of Attorney which is the subject of an application to register is on a barred list, or if the court requests him to make enquiries concerning an individual who has applied to be a Deputy.

6.2 The OPG will consider the information supplied by the ISA when determining the appropriate action during or on conclusion of an investigation into the actions of a Deputy or Attorney. Where the ISA confirm that a Deputy or Attorney is on the barred list, the Public Guardian will make an application to the Court of Protection for their removal as Deputy or Attorney.

7 The Court of Protection

7.1 The Court of Protection is not a supervisory authority or regulated activity provider under the Safeguarding Vulnerable Groups Act, and is not included in the arrangements the OPG has with the ISA. However, the Court may request the Public Guardian to make enquiries with the ISA if those enquiries are in connection with the Public Guardian's functions.

# Public Guardian Practice Note No 1 of 2011: Court of Protection Costs: The Public Guardian and Costs in Court of Protection Proceedings

1 Summary

Since the implementation of the Mental Capacity Act (MCA) in October 2007, the Public Guardian (PG) has made an increasing number of applications to the Court of Protection in pursuance of his statutory functions under the Act.

The Public Guardian has historically only sought payment of his costs in a handful of cases where he had instructed Counsel due to the complexity of the cases. In other cases, although the costs of the Public Guardian have often been low, these costs have effectively been borne by all other users of OPG services as a cross-subsidy from OPG fees.

In order to address this situation, this Practice Note sets out the future policy of the Public Guardian with regard to the costs of the OPG of making applications to the Court of Protection. This policy will also apply to applications made by other parties to which the Public Guardian has been joined.

It is important to note that the awarding of costs is at the discretion of the Court and is not within the jurisdiction or discretion of the Public Guardian. In this regard the Public Guardian is in the same position as all other Court users.

2 The Court of Protection Rules relating to Costs

Costs in the Court of Protection are governed by Part 19 of the Court of Protection Rules 2007.

Rule 156, applying to property and affairs, states:

> 'Where the proceedings concern P's property and affairs the general rule is that the costs of the proceedings or of that part of the proceedings that concerns P's property and affairs, shall be paid by P or charged to his estate'

Rule 157 sets the starting point for costs orders relating to personal welfare:

> 'Where the proceedings concern P's personal welfare the general rule is that there will be no order as to the costs of the proceedings or of that part of the proceedings that concerns P's personal welfare.'

Rule 159 sets out the circumstances in which the Court may depart from the general rules:

> '(1) The court may depart from rules 156 to 158 if the circumstances so justify, and in deciding whether departure is justified the court will have regard to all the circumstances, including –
>
> (a) the conduct of the parties;
> (b) whether a party has succeeded on part of his case, even if he has not been wholly successful; and
> (c) the role of any public body involved in the proceedings.
>
> (2) The conduct of the parties includes –
>
> (a) conduct before, as well as during, the proceedings;
> (b) whether it was reasonable for a party to raise, pursue or contest a particular issue;

(c) the manner in which a party has made or responded to an application or a particular issue; and
(d) whether a party who has succeeded in his application or response to an application, in whole or in part, exaggerated any matter contained in his application or response.

(3) Without prejudice to rules 156 to 158 and the foregoing provisions of this rule, the court may permit a party to recover their fixed costs in accordance with the relevant practice direction.'

3 The Public Guardian as a Litigant in the Court of Protection

A person is a 'litigant in person' during any stage of proceedings in court in which he or she is not represented by a solicitor or firm of solicitors. For this purpose the term 'litigant in person' may include a company or other corporation, a barrister, a solicitor, a solicitor's employee or other authorised litigator who is acting for himself[1].

[1] Senior Court Costs Office guidance

The Public Guardian is an 'authorised litigator' as defined by the Senior Court Costs Office guidance because it is his statutory function to make applications to the Court of Protection. This function is set out at Regulation 43 of the Lasting Powers of Attorney, Enduring Powers of Attorney and Public Guardian Regulations 2007:

'43 The Public Guardian has the function of making applications to the court in connection with his functions under the Act in such circumstances as he considers it necessary or appropriate to do so.'

The costs recoverable by parties in respect of periods when they are or were litigants in person are governed by the Litigants in Person (Costs and Expenses) Act 1975 and by Civil Procedure Rule 48.6 (applicable where the Court of Protection orders the costs of a litigant in person to be paid by another). The costs of litigants in person include –

(i) Out of pocket expenses such as court fees (although the OPG is currently exempt from payment of these), cost of travel to and from Court, witness fees/expenses and the cost of expert reports (which could include Court of Protection and Special Medical Visitor reports).
(ii) Payments made to obtain expert assistance in connection with assessing the claim for costs.
(iii) Costs for work done by the litigant in person which caused him or her pecuniary loss. For example, a litigant in person who is in employment might lose a day's pay through attending a court hearing or through going on a long journey to interview an essential witness. For the Public Guardian this could include, for example, paying the costs of a Special Medical Visitor for preparing a report and for attending Court if required.
(iv) Costs for work done by a litigant in person which did not cause him or her any pecuniary loss (for example, if the work was done during leisure time).

The Public Guardian does not seek to recover salary costs of staff involved in making the application to court.

4 Instructing Counsel

The Public Guardian is very mindful of Rules 3 and 4 of the Court of Protection Rules 2007 and of the need to keep costs of Court of Protection hearings to a minimum.

The general policy of the Public Guardian is that he will be represented at Court of Protection hearings by a member of OPG staff.

However, it will be the general policy of the Public Guardian to instruct Counsel in the following circumstances –

- Where the issues involved are legally complex.
- Where the case is particularly hostile or contentious and cross-examination of witnesses is likely to be required

In such cases, the Public Guardian is entitled to seek the recovery of costs of fees paid to a barrister for advocacy, drafting and advisory work. This is referred to in Bar Council guidance on the recovery of costs in non-solicitor cases and falls generally within the out-of-pocket expenses category referred to at 3 above.

5 When will the Public Guardian Claim Costs?

The Public Guardian will consider each case on its merits and will always consider the best interests of the incapacitated person ('P') when deciding whether to claim the OPG's costs of a Court application.

Court applications are resource intensive and may cause the OPG to incur administrative and legal costs, and out of pocket expenses, particularly when an attended hearing takes place. However, the Public Guardian will only seek to claim costs where it is objectively fair and reasonable to do so.

Whilst it is not possible for this Practice Note to be completely prescriptive, the Public Guardian will generally seek an Order for payment of his costs, where the outcome of the application vindicates it having been made, in the following circumstances –

- Where an application to Court is necessitated by the actions of another party – for example, a failure by a Deputy or Attorney to exercise their powers appropriately or to provide information legitimately demanded by the Public Guardian in pursuance of his statutory functions.

This is a very broad statement of policy and the Public Guardian reserves the right to adapt his course of action as circumstances and proceedings dictate.

6 Who will pay the Public Guardian's Costs?

It is firstly important to reiterate that the awarding of costs is at the discretion of the Court of Protection and is not within the jurisdiction or discretion of the Public Guardian.

When determining who to claim costs against, the Public Guardian will take into account whether the actions of a particular party have necessitated the application and/or their conduct falls within the scope of Rule 159 – in which case he may claim costs against that particular party.

Again, this is a very broad statement of policy and the Public Guardian reserves the right to adapt his course of action as circumstances and proceedings dictate.

7 Giving Notice of Costs Applications

The Public Guardian will generally state in his originating application to the Court if he intends to seek a costs Order that varies from the usual costs provisions set out in Rule 156. However, as a case progresses the Public Guardian reserves the right to alter his original stance to take into account the provisions of Rule 159 of the Court of Protection Rules 2007, namely (i) the success, or otherwise, of his application, and (ii) the conduct of the relevant parties during the application process.

Notice of any change of position on costs will be given at the earliest possible opportunity to all parties to the application.

8 Challenging the Costs of the Public Guardian

In cases where the Public Guardian is awarded all or part of his costs of an application by the Court of Protection, the OPG will seek payment as follows –

(i) Where costs are awarded from P's estate, the OPG will demand payment within 28 days from the Deputy or Attorney if one is in place, and otherwise from the new Deputy when appointed.
(ii) Where costs are awarded against another party personally the OPG will invoice that party and will demand payment within 28 days.

If any party wishes to challenge the level of costs invoiced by the OPG then that party must apply to the Court of Protection (this can be done orally at a hearing if the costs order is made in this way) for an Order that the costs of the Public Guardian should be formally assessed by the Senior Court Costs Office. Parties should be aware that this will incur the relevant assessment fee (Rule 161 CoP Rules 2007) – currently £110 if the bill does not exceed £3,000 (excluding VAT and disbursements) or £220 if it does – and that this fee may be payable by the person requesting the assessment. It is possible, although the OPG will seek to avoid this, that the OPG may also have to incur the costs of instructing a costs draftsman to prepare its file for assessment. These additional costs could also ultimately be payable by the person requesting the assessment.

If the Public Guardian incurs Counsel's costs then this aspect of the Public Guardian's bill can also be challenged by way of the assessment process set out in the paragraph above.

9 Enforcement of Costs Orders

It will be the general policy of the Public Guardian to seek to enforce all costs Orders made by the Court of Protection in his favour. Where necessary, this will include the issuing of proceedings in another Court for recovery of monies owed.

Public Guardian Practice Note No 2 of 2011: Updating Public Guardian Registers: Notification of Death

1 Summary

1.1 The Public Guardian is responsible for maintaining a register of attorneys acting under a registered power of attorney and deputies appointed by the Court of Protection. This practice note outlines the requirements for notifying the Office of the Public Guardian (OPG) of deaths affecting the registers.

2 When to notify the Public Guardian of a death

2.1 The following deaths should be notified to the Office of the Public Guardian:

- Death of the donor of a registered Enduring or Lasting Power or Attorney
- Death of an attorney acting under a registered Enduring or Lasting Power of Attorney
- Death of a replacement attorney (but see paragraph 5)
- Death of a deputy appointed by the Court of Protection
- Death of someone for whom the Court of Protection has appointed a deputy (P)

3 Death of a donor of a registered Enduring or Lasting Power of Attorney

3.1 The Public Guardian is obliged to cancel the registration of an Enduring or a Lasting Power of Attorney if he is satisfied that the power has been revoked as a result of the donor's death.

3.2 The OPG require proof of the donor's death (see paragraph 8) and the EPA or LPA (the instrument) should be returned to the office for cancellation.

3.3 The OPG will notify the attorney/s accordingly.

4 Death of an attorney acting under a registered Enduring or Lasting Power of Attorney

4.1 If the attorney was a sole attorney, his/her death revokes the power. The OPG require proof of the attorney's death (see paragraph 8) and the EPA or LPA should be returned to the office for cancellation.

4.2 If the attorney was appointed to act jointly (i.e. s/he could only act together with someone else), then his/her death revokes the power. The OPG will require proof of the attorney's death (see paragraph 8) and the instrument should be returned to the office for cancellation.

4.3 If the attorney acting under an LPA was appointed jointly and severally with another attorney or attorneys (i.e. s/he could act independently or in conjunction with the other attorneys), then the LPA is still valid.

4.4 If a replacement attorney has been appointed, then the LPA is still valid provided there is a surviving attorney. The OPG will require proof of the attorney's death (see paragraph 8) and return of the instrument to activate the replacement attorney. They will stamp and return the instrument accordingly.

4.5 In the case of EPAs, the successor attorney only needs to show the death certificate to financial institutions to demonstrate entitlement to act.

5 Death of a replacement attorney

5.1 Proof of a death of a replacement attorney will not be required if the main attorney or attorneys continue to act. Proof of death of a replacement attorney will only be required if the original attorney subsequently dies or ceases to act for any reason, which would render the LPA invalid. If that happens, the LPA will need to be returned to the OPG for cancellation, together with the required proof of death.

6 Death of a deputy appointed by the Court of Protection

6.1 The Public Guardian must be notified of the death of a deputy appointed by the Court of Protection so that the register of Deputies can be updated.

6.2 The OPG will require proof of death (see paragraph 8)

6.3 The Public Guardian's jurisdiction ends on the death of a deputy unless s/he was jointly and severally appointed or/and until the Court appoints a replacement deputy. However, the Public Guardian can request a final report from the deputy's personal representatives and can apply to Court for an appropriate remedy if he is dissatisfied with any aspect of the final report. This is irrespective of any other party applying to Court to be appointed as deputy.

7 Death of someone for whom the Court has appointed a deputy

7.1 The Public Guardian must be notified of the death of someone for who the Court has appointed a Deputy so that the register of Deputies can be updated. The death will bring the deputyship to an end although the Public Guardian can request a final report from the deputy. The OPG will require proof of death (see paragraph 8)

8 Proof of death

8.1 In all cases, the correspondent must provide the OPG's case reference number, full name, date of birth and last address of the deceased person, together with any of the following proof of death:

- A completed solicitors' death verification form
- A copy of a letter from someone who is able to confirm the date of death, for example :
  - A solicitor, barrister or advocate authorised to practice in the country where the declaration is made
  - A legal Executive who is a member of the Institute of Legal Executives
  - A Willwriter who is a member of either: the Society of Willwriters, the Institute of Professional Willwriters or the European Association of Willwriters
  - A doctor or surgeon registered in the country where the declaration is made
  - A notary public or any person allowed to administer oaths in the country where the declaration is made
  - A Magistrate
  - A Chartered accountant
  - A funeral director
  - An officer of a bank (a letter on headed paper is acceptable)
  - An officer of the Department of Work and Pensions responsible for administering benefits
  - A social worker registered to practice in the country where the declaration is made
  - A local government officer responsible for administering benefits or council tax
  - A care home manager or owner
  - A letter from a consular or embassy official, if the person died abroad

(N.B. the above list is not exhaustive, and other forms of confirmation may be accepted at the OPG's discretion)

- A certificate issued by the Registrar General, a Superintendent Registrar or a Registrar of Births and Deaths
- The equivalent of a certificate issued abroad by the appropriate registration authority if the person died abroad

8.2 The OPG preference is not to receive original certificates, but should these be sent, they will be returned to the sender on receipt.

9 Process followed by the OPG when a death is reported

9.1 When a death is reported to the OPG by telephone, the caller will be advised to send in written verification of the date of death. The OPG's electronic record will be updated straight away to note the date of death, if known, and, if the caller does not know the date of death, then date of death is recorded as the date of the call. However, a phone call is not regarded as strong enough proof of death and the OPG will require proof as set out in paragraph 8.1 above in order to stop any further registration process or routine correspondence.

9.2 Once notified of a death, the OPG will send a letter to the appropriate person. If the death cancels a power of attorney, the OPG will ask for the return of the instrument for cancellation, and will notify the attorneys if applicable. If the person who died is someone with a Deputy, then the letter will advise the Deputy of any further action he or she should take. In both cases, the OPG will request verification of the date of death if this hasn't already been provided.

9.3 The Public Guardian's jurisdiction ends once a deputy has died. If it is necessary to appoint a new deputy, then the OPG will advise the next of kin that an application to the Court of Protection is needed. If it is unclear whether anyone will make the necessary application, then the OPG will advise the person's local authority adult care services so that they can take any necessary action under their protection of vulnerable adults procedures.

10 OPG Fees

10.1 EPA and LPA registration fees are payable on application and no refund is available should either donor or attorney die after the application has been scanned onto the system. This applies to all registration fees regardless of whether the application was invalid, imperfect or withdrawn before registration. The registration fee is recoverable from the estate if the donor dies before the fee is paid.

10.2 In cases where notification of death is received before the date an application is scanned onto the OPG's systems, a full refund will be agreed.

Notification can be by telephone initially, provided it is followed up by one of the accepted forms of proof of death (see paragraph 8 for a list) which must be sent within 10 days of the death. A refund will not be paid until proof of death is received.

10.3 An application for fee remission can still be submitted after the death of the donor and must be accompanied by supporting evidence.

10.4 The deputy fee is one-off payment for placing the Deputy's details on a register and carrying out a risk assessment to determine the appropriate supervision regime. The invoice will be sent out when the assessment is carried out and the fee is not refundable if the deputy or person for whom the Court has appointed dies after the assessment has been made.

10.5 If the person who lacks capacity dies, supervision fees will be calculated on a pro-rata basis up to the date of death and an invoice will be sent to the deputy to arrange payment.

10.6 If the deputy dies supervision fees will be calculated up to the date of death and the new deputy will be invoiced for the outstanding fees when appointed.

Public Guardian Practice Note No 1 of 2012: Deputy Final Reports: Requesting the LPA, EPA Final Report pursuant to Regulation 40 of the LPA, EPA and Public Guardian Regulations 2007

1 Summary

The Mental Capacity Act 2005 ('the Act') and the associated Lasting Power of Attorney, Enduring Power of Attorney and Public Guardian Regulations 2007 ('the Regulations') formally set out the functions of the Public Guardian as a statutory office-holder. Although the requirement for Court-appointed Deputies to report annually to the Public Guardian is now a well-established one, the circumstances in which a final report may be sought by the Public Guardian are considered to be less well-known.

In order to provide clarity around this issue, this Practice Note sets out the general policy of the Public Guardian with regard to the requesting of a final report from an outgoing Deputy or, where the Deputy is deceased, from the administrator(s) of the deceased Deputy's estate.

This Practice Note does **not** address any matters relating to the provision by Deputies of an annual report to the Public Guardian as part of the Public Guardian's general supervisory function.

2 The Public Guardian's Powers

The powers of the Public Guardian in respect of reports from Deputies derive from both the Act and from the Regulations.

Where the Court of Protection has ordered a Deputy to report to the Public Guardian, section 58(1)(f) of the Act gives the Public Guardian power to receive those reports as part of his general supervisory function pursuant to Section 58(1)(c) of the Act.

Section 58(1)(f) usually covers reports provided by Deputies to the Public Guardian on an annual basis but it does also cover cases where the Court directs the provision of a final report to the Public Guardian. Those cases are covered at section 9 below.

Regulation 40 provides the Public Guardian with specific additional powers in respect of requesting a final report –

> **'40 Power to require final report on termination of appointment**
>
> (1) This regulation applies where –
>
>   (a)   the person on whose behalf a deputy was appointed to act has died;
>   (b)   the deputy has died;
>   (c)   the court has made an order discharging the deputy; or
>   (d)   the deputy otherwise ceases to be under a duty to discharge the functions to which his appointment relates.
>
> (2) The Public Guardian may require the deputy (or, in the case of the deputy's death, his personal representatives) to submit a final report on the discharge of his function.
>
> …

'(4) The Public Guardian must consider the final report, together with any other information that he may have relating to the discharge by the deputy of his functions.'

What this Regulation means is that, in circumstances where the Court has not made an Order directing a final report, the Public Guardian has legal power to require an outgoing Deputy (or his personal representative(s) in the event of the Deputy's death) to provide a final report of his activities as Deputy. It gives the Public Guardian power to examine the final report in conjunction with any existing information held by the Office of the Public Guardian ('OPG') regarding the way in which the Deputy had exercised his powers.

3

When will the Public Guardian seek a Final Report? It is firstly important to emphasise that Regulation 40 does not place any mandatory obligation upon the Public Guardian to seek a final report. The matter will therefore be at the discretion of the Public Guardian on a case-by-case basis. The Public Guardian will consider each case on its merits and, where the incapacitated person ('P') is still alive, will always consider the best interests of that person when deciding whether to request a final report.

There will be some cases where the Public Guardian will exercise his discretion not to seek a final report. This could be, for example, in cases where the time period between the filing of the last annual report and the discharge/death of the Deputy is a short one and, additionally, there are no existing concerns about the handling of the Deputyship.

In cases where P has died and where there is no security bond in place, it is unlikely that the Public Guardian will call for a final report because, if the report were to be unsatisfactory there would be no application that the Public Guardian could make to the Court as the Court would no longer have jurisdiction. In these cases it will be the policy of the Public Guardian to liaise with P's personal representatives to advise them of their right to call for an account from the former deputy if they wish.

In cases where P has died and a security bond is in place, the Public Guardian will assess the situation on a case-by-case basis. In some of these cases the OPG will consult with P's personal representatives as to whether it is more appropriate for the personal representatives to exercise their right to call for an account from the former deputy (and to apply to the Court if the report is unsatisfactory).

This is a very broad statement of policy and the Public Guardian reserves the right to adapt his course of action as circumstances dictate.

4 How long will I be given to provide the Final Report?

'A final report must be submitted –

(a) before the end of such reasonable period as may be specified; and
(b) at such place as may be specified.'

The Public Guardian will comply with Regulation 40(6) which states that he will give notice in writing of the period of time allowed for the preparation of the report and the details of the address for the report to be submitted to.

It is not possible for this Practice Note to be completely prescriptive as cases will vary in terms of complexity and urgency. The Public Guardian's default position is that he will usually permit a period of at least 21 calendar days for the lodging of a final report.

However, in cases where urgency is identified, the Public Guardian reserves the right to reduce this time period accordingly.

The Public Guardian will consider written requests for an extension of time on a case-by-case basis.

5

What time period will the Final Report cover? Where the Public Guardian exercises his discretion to request a final report, it will be his policy to request a report that covers the entirety of the period of time elapsed since the end date of the last report lodged with the OPG.

It will be the policy of the Public Guardian to request that the final report includes all of the former Deputy's activities up to and including the date on which the report is signed by the person preparing it.

In cases where the last annual report was filed within the preceding 12 months it follows that the final report will be for a shorter period than usual. In other cases, where annual reports are pending, the final report period could be for a period considerably longer than 12 months.

In cases where no reports have ever been lodged, a final report will be requested that covers the entirety of the period of the deputyship, up to and including the date upon which the report is signed by the person preparing it.

6 What format will the Final Report take?

It will be the general policy of the Public Guardian to request a final report in the format of an OPG annual deputy report.

The Public Guardian may also require that:

- The report must contain or be accompanied by:
  (a) specified information or information of a specified description; or
  (b) specified documents or documents of a specified description.
- The report includes accounts which deal with specified matters and which are provided in a specified form.
- Information or documents provided be verified or authenticated in such manner as he may reasonably require.

7 What will happen if the Final Report is not provided?

It is possible for this Practice Note to be completely prescriptive as circumstances will vary from case to case.

However, outgoing Deputies and administrators of deceased Deputy's estates should be aware of the wording of Regulation 40(5):

> '(5) Where the Public Guardian is dissatisfied with any aspect of the final report he may apply to the court for an appropriate remedy (including enforcement of security given by the deputy).'

It therefore follows that if a final report is requested, but not provided, it is within the Public Guardian's powers to apply to the Court for further directions. It is not possible for this Practice Note to be completely prescriptive as these applications will vary from case to case, but applications by the Public Guardian will include:

- Applications for the forfeiture of the Deputy security bond in its full amount – it is the view of the Public Guardian that a former Deputy cannot escape liability under the Deputy security bond by refusing or failing to provide a report and that it is for the former Deputy, or his personal representative(s), to prove to the Court that there has been no loss to the estate.
- Applications for an order directing the former deputy to account to any new Deputy within a specific timescale and with specific requirements.

These applications could also seek an Order granting any new Deputy specific powers to investigate the former Deputy and to take remedial action (if required) against the former Deputy or his estate, particularly where there is evidence or indication of loss over and above the amount of the security bond.

In these cases the Public Guardian may consult with any new Deputy as to whether the new Deputy is better-placed to take remedial action, which may include an application to the Court.

8 What will happen if the Public Guardian is not satisfied with the Final Report.

In cases where a final report is provided but the Public Guardian is not satisfied with the report, it will be his general policy to apply to the Court for '*an appropriate remedy*' as per Regulation 40(5). This will include applications to the Court of Protection as set out at section 7 above.

9 What is the Public Guardian's role where the Court has ordered a final report.

Where the Court directs a discharged Deputy to lodge a final report with the OPG it is the role of Public Guardian to receive the report pursuant to S58(1)(f) of the Act and to determine whether or not he is satisfied with it.

The Court may set a timescale for the lodging of the report with the OPG. Discharged deputies should be aware that Regulation 38 provides for an application to the Public Guardian for an extension of time for the lodging of the final report –

38 Application for additional time to submit a report

(1) This regulation applies where the court requires a deputy to submit a report to the Public Guardian and specifies a time or interval for it to be submitted.

(2) A deputy may apply to the Public Guardian requesting more time for submitting a particular report.

(3) An application must –

   (a) state the reason for requesting more time; and
   (b) contain or be accompanied by such information as the Public Guardian may reasonably require to determine the application.

(4) In response to an application, the Public Guardian may, if he considers it appropriate to do so, undertake that he will not take steps to secure performance of the deputy's duty to submit the report at the relevant time on the condition that the report is submitted on or before such date as he may specify.

If the Public Guardian has set the timescale for the provision of the final report, it will be his policy to consider requests in writing for an extension of time on a case-by-case basis.

If the Court has not set a timescale for the lodging of the final report the Public Guardian will write to the discharged deputy seeking the lodging of the final report in accordance with the terms of sections 4, 5 and 6 of this Practice Notes.

If the report is not lodge with the OPG within the timeframe set by the Court of Protection or by the OPG, the Public Guardian will consider whether to apply to the Court for further directions. This could include applications to the Court of Protection as set out at section 7 above.

In some cases the Public Guardian may decide, based upon existing information held by the OPG, for example recent satisfactory accounts, not to pursue the discharged Deputy (or his estate) for the outstanding final report and it will be the policy of the Public Guardian in those cases not to take any further action. It would remain open to the discharged Deputy, or the administrators of his estate, to apply to the Court for an Order formally waiving the requirement of the Deputy to lodge a final report.

In other cases where the final report is not received, and where the OPG is unable to form an opinion as to how the discharged deputy had managed his/her responsibilities, it will be the policy of the Public Guardian to apply to the Court for further directions. This could include applications to the Court of Protections as set out at section 7 above.

In cases where a final report is provided but the Public Guardian is not satisfied with the report, the Public Guardian will consider whether he should apply to the Court as set out at section 7 above. In these cases the Public Guardian may consult with any new Deputy as to whether the new Deputy is better-placed to take remedial action, which may include an application to the Court.

Public Guardian Practice Note No 2 of 2012 (updated September 2015): Gifts: Deputies and EPA/LPA Attorneys

1 Summary

The primary duty of a deputy or an attorney is to make decisions in the best interests of the person for whom they have been appointed (referred to as 'P'). The deputy/attorney has a duty to protect P's interests, to administer their financial affairs and property for P's benefit, to keep their own money separate from P's, and a duty not to take advantage of their position as deputy or attorney.

This Practice Note summarises the position of deputies and attorneys and gifts. It gives guidance on how they should approach this issue, but it must not be treated as legal advice.

There can be no generalised approach to gifts. Each decision must be made considering its own context and timing. As with all decisions a deputy or attorney makes, the overriding test is whether this is in P's best interests. Best interests must be determined on each occasion taking into account all the relevant circumstances and in particular taking into account the steps outlined in s 4 of the Mental Capacity Act: www.legislation.gov.uk/ukpga/2005/9/pdfs/ukpga_20050009_en.pdf

This Practice Note includes the practice and policies that the Office of the Public Guardian ('the OPG') follows when deputies or attorneys have exceeded their authority by making excessive gifts and explains the consequences of this.

2 What is meant by a Gift?

A deputy or an attorney makes a gift when they transfer money, property or possessions from P to themselves or to other people. It can include making an interest free loan, as the waived interest is in effect a gift.

A gift includes creating a trust of P's property and varying the will of a deceased person so as to divert P's interest in the estate to someone else by a deed of variation. Both of these require an application to the Court of Protection.

3 Deputies and Gifts

A deputy's main duty is to provide for P's needs. Their main focus should be on maintaining and providing for P.

A deputy's powers are set out in the Order appointing them as a deputy.

Deputies should carefully check the terms of their Order and seek advice from the OPG or from solicitors if they need clarification of their powers.

A deputy has no power to make gifts other than that contained in their Order of appointment. Most Deputy Orders give quite limited powers to make gifts. A deputy order usually allows the deputy to:

- Make gifts on customary occasions to relatives or persons connected to P provided that the value of the gift is not unreasonable having regard to all the circumstances and, in particular, the size of the estate
- Make gifts to charities which P might have made, provided that the gift is not unreasonable having regard to all the circumstances and, in particular, the size of the estate

A deputy is not obliged to make gifts.

A deputy who wants to make gifts of money or property which exceed the terms of their order – whether or not they will benefit directly or indirectly – must apply to the Court of Protection for authority to make the gift.

4 Attorneys and Gifts

Registered Enduring Powers of Attorney (EPAs)

An EPA attorney's main duty is to provide for P's needs. Their main focus should be on maintaining and providing for P.

The Mental Capacity Act says that an EPA attorney may:

- Make gifts of a seasonal nature, or on an anniversary of a birth, marriage or civil partnership;

- These seasonal or anniversary gifts may be made to persons (including the Attorney) who are related to or connected to P;
- Make gifts to any charity to whom P made or might have been expected to make gifts.

The value of each gift should not be unreasonable having regard to all the circumstances and in particular the size of P's estate.

An attorney is not obliged to make any gifts.

The attorney is obliged to follow any restrictions or conditions in the EPA about gifts.

The restrictions on gifts also apply to unregistered EPAs, provided P still has capacity to make decisions, and has agreed to the EPA being used by the attorney.

Registered Property & Financial Affairs Lasting Powers of Attorney (LPA)

A Property & Financial Affairs LPA attorney's main duty is to provide for P's needs.

Their main focus should be on maintaining and providing for P.

The Mental Capacity Act prescribes that an attorney has no authority to make gifts except in the following limited circumstances:

- A Property & Financial Affairs LPA attorney may only make gifts on customary occasions.
- Customary occasions are the occasion or anniversary of a birth, a marriage or the formation of a civil partnership, or any other occasion on which presents are customarily given within families or among friends or associates.
- These gifts may be made to persons (including the attorney) who are related to or connected with P.
- Gifts may also be made to any charity to whom P made or might have been expected to make gifts.
- The value of each gift should not be unreasonable having regard to all the circumstances and, in particular, the size of P's estate.

An Attorney is not obliged to make any gifts.

The Attorney is obliged to follow any restrictions or conditions in the LPA about gifts.

5 Applying to the Court of Protection

Deputies and attorneys should apply to the Court of Protection where they want to make gifts which they do not have the authority to make under their deputy order or their EPA/LPA. The Public Guardian cannot approve a gift or a loan. Only the Court of Protection can do this.

The Court of Protection cannot give informal advice on whether a deputy or attorney can make a gift. A formal application must always be made. Application forms can be obtained from the Court or from the HM Courts & Tribunals Service website: http://hmctsformfinder.justice.gov.uk/HMCTS/FormFinder.do

Practice Direction F to Part 9 of the Court of Protection Rules 2007 explains the procedure relating to gift applications: http://www.justice.gov.uk/downloads/courts/court-of-protection/Court_Rules_2007.pdf

6 Guidance on Gifts: Deputies and Attorneys

The Mental Capacity Act does not define what is a 'reasonable' or 'unreasonable' gift. Deputies and attorneys are expected to decide how much is reasonable. It is not possible for the Public Guardian to give precise figures or guidance.

The reasonableness of a gift depends very much on P's particular circumstances which includes consideration of their liquid capital; whether they own a property and what will happen to it; their income and expenditure and whether there is a sizable gap between the two; their care and accommodation costs and whether these are likely to change; their age and life expectancy; their future needs; the terms of their Will and so on.

Any gift or transfer of real property, (e g land or a house) either the whole property or a part share, is almost certainly outside the powers of the deputy or attorney (notwithstanding P's previously expressed wishes) and the deputy or attorney will need to apply to the Court of Protection for authority to make the gift or transfer.

Deputies and attorneys may choose to gift personal possessions or furniture of modest or sentimental value to family members, for example when disposing of the contents of P's house, provided that the items are of modest value. Items of significant monetary value should not be gifted unless authorised by the Court.

It is suggested that deputies and attorneys consider the following factors when deciding whether to make a gift: (This is not an exhaustive list.)

The occasion of the gift

Does the gift relate to a customary occasion such as a birthday, anniversary or some recognised family occasion?

Does the gift relate to charitable giving?

If neither of the above, it is likely that the deputy or attorney will need to apply to Court. For example, most gifts made for tax planning purposes require a court application.

The amount of the gift

Is the proposed gift for a reasonable amount? This should be a reasonable amount that would normally be incurred on a customary occasion or in relation to charitable giving. Is it affordable? Is it line with the sort of gift which P used to make before they

began to lose capacity to make their own decisions? Will it impact on P's future needs? Is the amount reasonable taking into account all of P's current circumstances?

P's Financial Circumstances

The deputy or attorney should consider P's financial circumstances, not simply in terms of their capital/savings but also their present and future needs. The issues to be considered include (and this is not an exhaustive list):

- Whether P's income covers their usual expenditure? If not, how much is the shortfall?
- How much are the total assets?
- The cost of P's care and accommodation
- Whether P owns a property and what will happen to it

- P's likely future financial needs and how these may change (for example, whether entitlement to Continuing Health Care funding will be reviewed in future)

The Recipient(s) of the Gift

Is the deputy/attorney treating members of the family equally in making gifts? If not, is there a good reason for this?

Is the deputy/attorney taking advantage of their position by making gifts only to themselves and not considering making gifts to others?

Is the deputy/attorney proposing to make gifts to persons who are not relatives and who are not closely connected to P? Did P make gifts to them before they began to lose capacity to make their own decisions?

P's Will

If the deputy or attorney is aware of the contents of P's Will, they should try to take this into account when considering gifts, as this may be an indication of P's wishes.

However, taking the Will into account does not mean a deputy or attorney can gift P's assets according to the Will in P's lifetime.

7 Deputies and Provision for the Needs of Others

Most Deputy Orders enable the deputy to make provision for the 'needs' of anyone who is related or connected to P. The deputy may only do this if P had provided for those needs in the past or if P might have been expected to provide for those needs.

Most Deputy Orders do not define what is meant by 'needs' but it is generally intended to cover situations such as maintaining spouses or dependent relatives and other circumstances where there is evidence that P has made financial provision for others for particular reasons in the past and that they would be likely to do so again in the future.

The deputy should apply to the Court if there is any doubt as to whether they can rely on this provision in the Order.

The deputy must comply with any restrictions in the Order.

8 Attorneys and Provision for the Needs of Others

Enduring Powers of Attorney

The Mental Capacity Act allows an EPA attorney to benefit themselves or other persons if P might be expected to provide for his or that person's needs. The Attorney may do whatever P might be expected to do to meet those needs.

The Mental Capacity Act does not define what is meant by 'needs' but it is generally intended to cover situations such as maintaining spouses or dependent relatives and other circumstances where there is evidence that P has made financial provision for others for particular reasons in the past and that they would be likely to do so again in the future.

The attorney should apply to the Court if there is any doubt as to whether they can rely on this provision in the EPA.

The attorney must comply with any restrictions in the EPA.

Lasting Powers of Attorney

The Mental Capacity Act does not expressly permit an LPA attorney to benefit themselves or other persons by providing for their needs. However, the Court of Protection has confirmed that an LPA attorney may provide for the needs of family members if P is legally obliged to maintain them, as in the case of P's spouse, civil partner or minor child. An application to Court will be necessary if an attorney wishes to maintain anyone else.

9 P's Capacity to Make or Authorise Gifts

A deputy order or registered EPA/LPA does not necessarily prevent P from making or authorising gifts themselves. Deputies and attorneys are expected to use care and caution where P expresses a wish to make gifts. There are specific legal tests of capacity to make a gift and it is advisable to seek legal advice and/or to arrange for a mental capacity assessment to be carried out to ensure that P has the capacity to make this decision, especially where a substantial gift is proposed.

Section 3 of the Mental Capacity Act requires P to be able to understand the information relevant to the decision, retain that information, use or weigh that information, and communicate his decision in order to have the capacity to make a decision. The information relevant to a decision includes information about the reasonably foreseeable consequences of deciding one way or another and of failing to make the decision. Further guidance can be found in the Mental Capacity Code of Practice.

The Public Guardian may ask the deputy or attorney to explain the steps they took to ascertain that P had the capacity to make or authorise the gift.

Wherever possible deputies and attorneys should try to involve P in the decision making process when gifts are contemplated. Even if P lacks capacity to make the decision, they may have views on matters affecting the decision, and on what outcome would be preferred. Their involvement can help work out what would be in their best interests. The Mental Capacity Act Code of Practice includes guidance on how to approach this (5.21–5.24): www.justice.gov.uk/downloads/protecting-thevulnerable/mca/mca-code-practice-0509.pdf

10 The Consequences of Making Unauthorised Gifts

The Public Guardian can investigate and ask for an account of any gifts made. Both deputies and attorneys should keep a record of any gifts made and the circumstances of such, so that they are in a position to give an account if asked. A deputy should include the detail of gifts in any annual account they submit to the Public Guardian.

If the deputy/attorney makes excessive gifts, the Public Guardian may:

- Apply to the Court of Protection for removal of the deputy or attorney (and, if appropriate, ask the court to arrange for a deputy or new deputy to be appointed)
- Apply to the Court of Protection for the security bond of a deputy to be called in
- Instruct the deputy/attorney to apply for retrospective approval from the Court of Protection in circumstances where such an application would have a reasonable prospect of success
- Request the deputy/attorney to seek the return of the gifts and restitution of P's assets

- Refer the matter to the police or other relevant regulatory or safeguarding bodies.

A new deputy may be authorised to take legal action to recover the money gifted. In some cases the Police may be asked to investigate.

Deprivation of Assets

If the local authority arranges for P to enter a care home on a permanent basis, P will be means tested to see whether they should make a contribution towards the cost of their care. The local authority calculates this using their income, savings and other capital.

Transferring an asset out of P's name does not necessarily mean that it will not be taken into account in this means test. The local authority can, when assessing a resident's eligibility for assistance, look for evidence of deliberate, or intentional, deprivation of capital and assets.

The same principles apply where there is a deprivation of assets with a view to claiming means-tested benefits.

Security bond – Deputies

Most deputy orders require the deputy to take out a security bond. The bond is a form of insurance which protects P's estate against financial mismanagement by the deputy.

If a deputy makes excessive and unauthorised gifts of money and property, the Public Guardian – or any other person with a sufficient interest – may apply to the Court of Protection for an order enforcing the bond to recover the loss.

If the Court makes such an order, the insurance company will reimburse P but they will seek to recover the money personally from the deputy. The insurance company may take further Civil Court proceedings against the deputy to achieve this.

The Criminal Law

Where excessive and unauthorised gifts have been made by a deputy or an Attorney, the Public Guardian will consider asking the Police to investigate.

Fraud by Abuse of Position is a criminal offence under Section 4 of the Fraud Act 2006. This applies to anyone who holds a position in which they are expected to safeguard, and not act against, the financial interests of another person. Deputies and attorneys are in this position.

The Fraud Act makes it a criminal offence to dishonestly abuse that position, where the person intends to make a gain for themselves or others, or to cause a loss to P, or to expose P to a risk of loss.

11 Deputies: Supervision and Investigation

Supervision

The Public Guardian supervises deputies. The degree of supervision varies according to the circumstances of the case.

Where the Public Guardian considers that a deputy has exceeded their authority by making unauthorised gifts or charging unreasonable expenses, the Public Guardian may increase the deputy's supervision level. The Public Guardian may also take action to ensure that the deputy complies with their duties, for example by warning the deputy and advising them how to approach this in future. In serious cases the OPG Compliance Unit may be asked to investigate.

Investigation

Section 58 of the Mental Capacity Act 2005 and Regulation 41 of the LPA, EPA and Public Guardian Regulations 2007 give the Public Guardian power to investigate complaints and concerns about a deputy's failure to comply with their duties and to require the deputy to supply information and documents.

Outcomes

Occasionally the matter can be resolved by the deputy or whoever has received unauthorised gifts paying back the money. The deputy may be given a warning and their supervision level increased. Sometimes the Public Guardian will ask the deputy to apply to the Court for retrospective approval to gifts. In the most serious cases, the Police may be alerted and the Public Guardian may apply to the Court of Protection for an order:

- Discharging the deputy or
- Suspending the deputy and freezing accounts and/or
- Directing the deputy to account and supply information to the Public Guardian and/or
- Enforcing the security bond

The Court may arrange a hearing before a judge which the deputy will be expected to attend to explain their actions.

12 Attorneys: Compliance and Investigation

Investigation

The OPG Compliance Unit investigates concerns the way in which an attorney is exercising their powers. Section 58 of the Mental Capacity Act and Regulation 46–48 of the LPA, EPA and Public Guardian Regulations give the Public Guardian powers to investigate attorneys and to require attorneys so supply information, accounts, and documents.

Where the Public Guardian concludes that an attorney has exceeded their authority by making excessive gifts or charging unreasonable expenses, the Public Guardian may take action to remedy the situation.

Outcomes

Occasionally the matter can be resolved by the attorney or whoever has received unauthorised gifts paying back the money. The attorney may be given a warning.

Sometimes the Public Guardian will ask the attorney to apply to the Court for retrospective approval to gifts. In the most serious cases, the police may be alerted and the Public Guardian may apply to the Court of Protection for an order:

- Revoking the EPA/LPA and, if appropriate, arranging for the appointment of a deputy to investigate further and consider whether funds can be recovered, or
- Suspending the attorney's authority and freezing accounts and/or

- Directing the attorney to account and supply information to the Public Guardian or to the Court

The Court may arrange a hearing before a judge which the attorney will be expected to attend to explain their actions.

Alan Eccles
Public Guardian and Chief Executive

Public Guardian Practice Note No 3 of 2012: Surety Bonds: Statement of Surety Bonds Expectations of the Public Guardian

1 Introduction

The Mental Capacity Act 2005 (MCA) makes provision for ways in which decisions can be made on behalf of people in circumstances where they may be incapable of making such decisions personally. In such cases, where the person, (referred to as 'P'), has property or finances and no attorney in place it will be necessary to apply to the Court of Protection (the Court) for an appropriate order.

Where the Court makes a one off order or appoints a deputy to manage P's property and affairs, it may require security be given by way of a surety bond for the protection of P's assets. The Court will decide the value of the surety bond.

The Public Guardian was created under the MCA on 1 October 2007. The Office of the Public Guardian (OPG) is an Executive Agency of the Ministry of Justice that supports the Public Guardian in the discharge of his duties. The Public Guardian has a number of statutory functions, which includes receiving security which the Court requires a deputy or any other person to give. The Public Guardian can also apply to the Court to enforce the bond where the Deputy is in breach of duty.

The regulations that deal with security are set out at Annex A and can be found in full at:

The Lasting Powers of Attorney, Enduring Powers of Attorney and Public Guardian Regulations 2007 (2007 No. 1253)

The Lasting Powers of Attorney, Enduring Powers of Attorney and Public Guardian (Amendment) Regulations 2010 (2010 No. 1063)

2 The Scheme

Regulation 34(4) allows the Public Guardian to make arrangements to facilitate the provision of bonds. The arrangement is commonly called 'the Scheme'. The Scheme provides suitable surety bonds for the purposes of security to all deputies appointed by the Court. From October 2012, the Scheme is administered by Deputy Bond Services. Deputies are not bound to enter into an arrangement within the Scheme and can seek their own arrangements.

3 The purpose of this document

This document sets out the Public Guardian's expectations for any company seeking to provide bonds outside of the Scheme. Providers need to demonstrate to deputies wishing to move outside the Scheme that they understand the unique nature of deputy bonds, they meet the requirements of the Regulations, and provide the requisite protection for 'P'. The OPG has no contract with any provider outside the Scheme and does not provide any endorsement or promotion of products offered.

The order giving the authority to act as a deputy will not be released until the Court and OPG are satisfied that appropriate security is in place. To ease this process the OPG would expect to agree that the provider and product meet the requirements in the regulations and the Public Guardian's expectations before it is in use. Otherwise the matter will have to be dealt with on a case by case basis, which may delay the appointment of a deputy. Providers who satisfy the requirements in the Regulations and have agreed to meet the Public Guardian's expectations will be placed on a list maintained by the OPG and made available to the Court of Protection.

The OPG would expect to review regularly that a provider is meeting the requirements and the Public Guardian's expectations, usually annually.

4 Expectations for providers

1 Providers will need to be able to endorse a bond as set out in regulation 34.

2 The Public Guardian expects bond providers to maintain full membership of British Insurers Brokers Association (BIBA) or successor or equivalent association.

5 Expectations for the Bond

The security given by the bond is solely for the protection of P, and there is no protection for the deputy. These expectations provide assurance that the protection is robust and continuous throughout the deputyship. Bond providers should understand the following:

- The amount of security required is set by the Court and cannot be varied by the bond provider or the OPG;
- Neither the OPG or the Court are party to the bond, which is between the deputy and the bond provider;
- Once entered into, the bond cannot be cancelled by either party for any reason;
- The bond can only be discharged by the Court;
- Upon cessation of the deputyship the bond will lapse in line with the timescales in regulation 37(3) as amended;
- To discharge a bond outside these timescales will require one of the parties to make an application to the Court.

6 Enforcement

Where a deputy fails in his or her duties, the bond can be enforced if required. Bond providers should understand the following:

- The Court can call in all or part of the bond up to the limit secured. There is no requirement to prove fraud and the loss may not be quantifiable;
- The Court may order an interim payment, i.e. that part of the bond is called in pending quantification of the loss;
- The Insurer must pay on demand without further investigation;
- Notification will be via a Court Order;
- It is expected that Insurers will have the right to recover the amount they have paid out, plus their expenses, from the deputy. This is a matter for the insurer and in which the Public Guardian or Court play no part.

7 Deputies wishing to change provider

Where a deputy wishes to change bond provider, Regulation 5(3) provides that the Public Guardian must be satisfied that certain requirements have been met. Providers are expected to inform the OPG of any deputies wishing to change providers.

- The Public Guardian expects providers to ensure that deputies wishing to change provider understand whether the insurer will accept retrospective liability for any loss during the deputyship, no matter when it occurred. If retrospective liability is not accepted, the Public Guardian expects providers to make it clear that unless the previous bond is discharged, the deputy may be liable to pay premiums for both bonds.

8 Changes to the Amount of Security

Bond providers should understand the following:

- The Court can change the amount of security required at any time. This is most common where an application is made to increase the deputy's access to funds. The Public Guardian considers it preferable, to ensure protection of P, that the wording of the bond ensures that the deputy accepts any increased security and premium without the need for further documents to be signed.

Should this not be the case, bond providers should ensure that a process is in place for notifying the Public Guardian where changes in security ordered by the Court have not been effected.

9 Exchange of Information

There are requirements for exchange of information within the regulations. The OPG would look to agree an appropriate method of electronic transfer of information with providers who can meet the above expectations.

The OPG would seek an information sharing agreement between the provider, the Court and itself. The agreement would be expected to cover notification of a bond being put in place, the cessation of a deputyship, enforcement of bonds, and the format and layout of the information. It would also seek to agree timescales for transfer of information and to replying to information requests from the OPG and the Court

10 Complaints

The Public Guardian expects bond providers to set out a clear complaints procedure, available on its website, which meets the requirements of both the Financial Services Authority and Financial Ombudsman Service.

Annex A
Public Guardian Regulations 33–37

The Lasting Powers of Attorney, Enduring Powers of Attorney and Public Guardian Regulations 2007 are set out earlier in this Part.

Public Guardian Practice Note No 1 of 2016: Public Authority Deputyship Responsibilities

Summary

Public authorities are reminded of their legal obligations and duty of care when appointed as a deputy by the Court of Protection to manage the financial affairs of people who lack mental capacity. Delegation of duties outside the public authority is not permitted, and caution should be taken when contracting with or referring vulnerable clients to external deputyship providers.

Delegation of duties: the Mental Capacity Act and Code of Practice

Public authorities appointed by the Court of Protection to manage the finances and property of people who lack mental capacity are responsible for the income and assets of vulnerable people to the value of many millions of pounds.

They are obliged to act in accordance with the Mental Capacity Act 2005, its associated regulations, and the Mental Capacity Act Code of Practice.

Where the named deputy is the director of adult services or another public authority officer, they may delegate duties to other public authority staff, but remain accountable for actions and decisions in relation to those clients.

Duties cannot be delegated to organisations outside the public authority.

Important factors to note

Public authorities considering changing from direct provision of a deputyship service are advised to carefully consider the options available locally to ensure that vulnerable clients are not exposed to risk of financial abuse.

If entering into contractual arrangements with an external provider, the public authority will wish to satisfy itself that the provider is fit to handle the finances of vulnerable people.

Checks may involve ensuring that appropriate criminal checks of individuals employed by providers have been carried out using the Disclosure and Barring Service.

The enhanced check will disclose the same information as a standard check but will also include local police information that is relevant and ought to be disclosed.

Public authorities may also have strong links with their local police through their safeguarding boards, which could provide an opportunity to discuss such cases prior to appointment.

Any public authority wishing to retire as deputy from their existing cases must apply to the Court of Protection, in which case the court will expect the public authority to demonstrate that an appropriate alternative deputy has been identified, if one is still required.

Failure to address these issues may result in safeguarding concerns and expose the public authority to reputational, and in some cases, financial risk.

Public Guardian Practice Note No 2 of 2016: Public Guardian Practice Note No 2 of 2016: OPG's Approach to Solicitor Client Accounts

Summary

Some solicitor deputies may have received correspondence from OPG concerning the use of their client accounts to manage deputyship funds, and the interaction between a deputy's duties under the Mental Capacity Act 2005 (MCA), SRA Accounts Rules 2011 (SARs) and the MCA Code of Practice.

This note clarifies OPG's position.

Context

Rule 14.5 SARs provides as follows:

> 'You must not provide banking facilities through a client account. Payments into, and transfers or withdrawals from a client account must be in respect of instructions relating to an underlying transaction (and the funds arising from) or to a service forming part of your normal regulated activities.'

We have clarified the purpose of this provision with the SRA and understand that it is intended to prevent client accounts being used for improper or criminal purposes including fraud and money laundering. It does not restrict the use of client accounts where there is a reasonable connection to an underlying legal transaction or recognised professional duties of a solicitor which you are providing. (Further guidance on this may be obtained from the SRA.)

The MCA Code of Practice suggests that funds should not be 'mixed' with those of other people. This would include not mixing them with the funds of other clients unless good reasons were provided.

OPG is of the view that holding monies on general client account does not constitute good reason, even when the protection that holding money in a solicitor's client account is taken into consideration, for example the requirement for most firms to obtain an independent accountant's report. The same protection would be afforded to a separate or designated client account that is segregated from the general account.

Clarification

OPG's first clarification is that we have no objection in principle to use of general client accounts as a temporary or holding position prior to deputies setting up segregated client accounts or separate bank accounts as expected, to manage ongoing transactions.

Solicitor deputies are reminded that there are factors other than the SARs that they may wish to consider.

The first is that in addition to SRA requirements, OPG will need to be satisfied that deputies have proper safeguards in place to protect deputyship funds. Deputies act under the authority of the court on behalf of vulnerable people, and extra care may need to be taken around who can authorise payments from deputyship funds.

Setting up a separate bank account for a deputyship with named signatories may be simpler in practice.

Secondly, a deputy has a general duty to act in the incapacitated person's best interests, which can include managing their funds to gain the best return. There will be cases where large balances in a client account will not represent the best investment strategy for a client. In these cases OPG will question the appropriateness of keeping significant excess funds in this way.

Professional deputies are reminded of OPG's standards for professional deputies, which can be accessed at:

https://www.gov.uk/government/publications/ office-of-the-public-guardian-deputy-standards

Standard 1a (9) states:

> 'Open a deputyship account in the client's name with the deputy named as such on the account. Ensure that all funds held for the client are held in accounts and/or investments in their name and kept separate from the funds of the deputy or other parties.'

OPG's second clarification is that solicitor deputies are reminded that their management of funds should be organised with the best interests of their client in mind.

OPG continues to work with professional deputies to ensure that our supervision is proportionate and appropriate, and if you have any comments on this note or any other matter then please contact us.

Law Society Practice Notes

Law Society Practice Note of 8 December 2011: Lasting Powers of Attorney

(© The Law Society 2011)

1 Introduction

1.1 Who should read this practice note?

Solicitors who advise clients on drawing up a Lasting Power of Attorney (LPA), and solicitors who are acting as an attorney under an LPA.

1.2 What are the issues?

Any solicitor intending to give advice about an LPA or act as an attorney under an LPA must be aware of the provisions in the Mental Capacity Act 2005 (MCA 2005) and the Mental Capacity Act 2005 Code of Practice (the Code of Practice). Solicitors should also be familiar with the relevant guidance produced by the Office of the Public Guardian (OPG).

The practice note provides an overview of LPAs, and also covers the ongoing arrangements for Enduring Powers of Attorney (EPA). It does not deal with situations with an international element, for example using an LPA to sell a foreign property, or a non-UK individual who wishes to make an LPA.

1.3 Professional Conduct

The following sections of the SRA Code are relevant to this issue:
- Chapter 1 on Client Care
- Chapter 4 on Confidentiality and disclosure

1.4 Status of this practice note

Practice notes are issued by the Law Society for the use and benefit of its members. They represent the Law Society's view of good practice in a particular area. They are not intended to be the only standard of good practice that solicitors can follow. You are not required to follow them, but doing so will make it easier to account to oversight bodies for your actions.

Practice notes are not legal advice, nor do they necessarily provide a defence to complaints of misconduct or of inadequate professional service. While care has been taken to ensure that they are accurate, up to date and useful, the Law Society will not accept any legal liability in relation to them.

For queries or comments on this practice note contact the Law Society's Practice Advice Service.

1.5 Terminology in this practice note

Must – A specific requirement in legislation or of a principle, rule, outcome or other mandatory provision in the SRA Handbook. You must comply, unless there are specific exemptions or defences provided for in relevant legislation or the SRA Handbook.

Should –
- Outside of a regulatory context, good practice for most situations in the Law Society's view.
- In the case of the SRA Handbook, an indicative behaviour or other non-mandatory provision (such as may be set out in notes or guidance).

These may not be the only means of complying with legislative or regulatory requirements and there may be situations where the suggested route is not the best possible route to meet the needs of your client. However, if you do not follow the suggested route, you should be able to justify to oversight bodies why the alternative approach you have taken is appropriate, either for your practice, or in the particular retainer.

May – A non-exhaustive list of options for meeting your obligations or running your practice. Which option you choose is determined by the profile of the individual practice, client or retainer. You may be required to justify why this was an appropriate option to oversight bodies.

SRA Code SRA Code of Conduct 2011

SRA -Solicitors Regulation Authority

IB indicative behaviour

LPA Lasting Powers of Attorney

EPA Enduring Powers of Attorney
MCA2005 Mental Capacity Act 2005

2 SRA Principles

There are ten mandatory principles which apply to all those the SRA regulates and to all aspects of practice. The principles can be found in the SRA Handbook.

The principles apply to solicitors or managers of authorised bodies who are practising from an office outside the UK. They also apply if you are a lawyer-controlled body practising from an office outside the UK.

3 Powers of Attorney

3.1 Lasting Powers of Attorney

There are two separate prescribed forms for Lasting Powers of Attorneys (LPAs) available from the Ministry of Justice website:

- property and financial affairs LPA, and
- health and welfare LPA.

3.1.1 Property and financial affairs LPAs

A property and financial affairs LPA can be used to appoint attorneys to make a range of decisions, including:

- the buying and selling of property
- operating a bank account
- dealing with tax affairs, and
- claiming benefits.

See paragraphs 7.32–7.39 of the Code of Practice for more information.

3.1.2 Health and welfare LPAs

A health and welfare LPA can be used to appoint attorneys to make decisions on, for example:

- where the donor should live
- day-to-day care (including for example, diet and dress), and
- whether to give or refuse consent to medical treatment.

See paragraphs 7.21–7.31 of the Code of Practice for more information.

All LPAs must be registered with the Office of the Public Guardian before they can be used.

3.2 Enduring Powers of Attorney

The MCA 2005 repealed the Enduring Powers of Attorney Act 1985 and it is no longer possible to create a new EPA.

However, valid EPAs that were executed before the MCA 2005 came into force on 1 October 2007 will continue to be valid even if they have not been registered.

See section 17 Enduring Powers of Attorney for further information.

3.3 Ordinary Powers of Attorney

Section 10 of the Power of Attorney Act 1971 provides for the making of an Ordinary Power of Attorney (OPA) to manage the donor's affairs. An OPA is usually made when it is difficult for the donor to manage their affairs, for example because of a physical disability or when the donor is travelling abroad.

4 The donor's capacity

4.1 Assessing capacity

You should be satisfied that the donor has the mental capacity to make a power of attorney. It is important that the donor is aware of the implications of their actions and should be alerted to possibilities of exploitation.

When assessing a client's capacity to create an LPA you should refer to sections 2 and 3 of the MCA 2005 and chapters 2–4 of the Code of Practice. See also the 2010 judgment of the Senior Judge of the Court of Protection in Re Collis (unreported), 27 October 2010, Court of Protection.

For further guidance, see Assessment of Mental Capacity: a practical guide for doctors and lawyers (Law Society 2010).

4.2 Where there is doubt about a donor's capacity

If there is doubt about the donor's capacity, a medical opinion should be considered. In cases where the LPA is being contested, for example by a family member, it may be necessary for the matter to be decided by the Court of Protection if the dispute cannot be resolved by other means.

You may want to ask the donor to give advance consent in writing authorising you to contact the donor's GP or any other medical practitioner if the need for medical evidence should arise at a later date to assess whether the donor has capacity to make a particular decision.

4.3 Incapacity: the functional and time-specific test

Unlike the EPA regime where registration demonstrates to a third party that the attorney has responsibility and the authority to make decisions relating to the donor's property and affairs, the MCA 2005 provisions for LPAs do not have such a readily identifiable point where the attorney(s) takes over.

This is because sections 2 and 3 of the MCA 2005 sets out a 'functional and time-specific' test of incapacity, which means capacity will vary according to the particular decision to be taken at the particular time.

For example, a donor may be able to make decisions about household spending but not about selling their home. One month later their capacity to make these decisions may have changed – either improved or become worse. There will not often be any one point where a person loses capacity to make all decisions.

Instead, the MCA 2005 sets out a joint approach where the attorney and the donor work together. The starting assumption must always be that a donor has the capacity to make a decision, unless it can be established that they lack capacity (section 1(2) MCA 2005).

A donor should not be treated as unable to make a decision unless all practical steps to help him or her to do so have been taken without success (section 1(3)

MCA 2005). Involving the donor as fully as practicable could involve deferring making a decision or setting up further assistance in order to enable the donor to make a decision.

This may be particularly relevant for health and welfare LPAs as these only operate where the person lacks capacity to make the decision.

Further guidance is provided in chapters 2 and 3 of the Code of Practice.

4.4 Acting in the donor's best interests

Where it is established that the donor lacks the capacity to make a particular decision, section 4 of the MCA 2005 requires the attorney to act in the donor's 'best interests', taking into account the relevant circumstances.

The MCA 2005 sets out a checklist of factors that should be considered by a person deciding what is in the best interests of a person who lacks capacity.

This includes, where practicable and appropriate to do so, consulting with the relatives, carers and others who have an interest in the donor's welfare.

It also includes, where reasonably practicable, permitting and encouraging the donor to participate as fully as possible or improving their ability to participate in making the decision.

Further guidance on best interests is provided in chapter 5 of the Code of Practice.

5 Risk of abuse

You should, when advising clients of the benefits of LPAs, also inform them of the risks of abuse, particularly the risk that the attorney(s) could misuse the power.

You should discuss with the donor appropriate measures to safeguard against the LPA being misused or exploited.

You may also notify other family members or friends (who are not named persons to be notified of an application to register the LPA) of:

- the existence of the power
- why they have chosen the attorney(s), and
- how the donor intends it to be used.

This may help to guard against the possibility of abuse by an attorney and may also reduce the risk of conflict between family members at a later stage.

5.1 Deputyships

There may be situations where a deputyship (once the person has lost capacity) could be viewed as being more appropriate and protective than the creation of an LPA. This may be advisable, for example:

- where the assets are more substantial or complex than family members are accustomed to handle and there is no suitable professional to appoint as attorney, or
- in cases where litigation may lead to a substantial award of damages for personal injury.

It is important to be aware, however, that the court will not approve a deputyship application as a matter of course and that, particularly for health and welfare matters, is likely to be reluctant to do so. See *G v E* [2010] EWHC 2512 (COP).

6 Taking instructions for an LPA

Where you are instructed to prepare an LPA, the donor is the client. You should ensure that you have taken and recorded the instructions from the client.

You must not accept instructions where you have reasonable grounds to suspect that those instructions have been given by the client under duress or undue influence.

You must also not act on instructions until you are satisfied that the instructions represent the client's wishes (IB 1.28, see Outcomes in Chapter 1 – Client Care SRA Code of Conduct 2011).

6.1 Verifying instructions

You should be instructed by the client. When asked to prepare an LPA on written instructions al one, you should always consider carefully whether these instructions are sufficient, or whether you should see the client to discuss the instructions with them.

Where instructions for the preparation of an LPA are given by someone other than the client, you should not proceed without checking that the client agrees with the instructions given (IB 1.25, see Outcomes in Chapter 1 – Client Care SRA Code of Conduct 2011).

If you have doubts you should attempt to see the client alone or take other appropriate steps to confirm:

- the instructions with the client personally after offering appropriate advice, and
- that the donor has the necessary capacity to make the power (see section 3 above).

6.2 Your duty to the donor after the LPA is registered

Once the LPA has been registered and the donor lacks the capacity to make the relevant decision, instructions may be accepted from the attorney(s) however your duties to the donor still remain in place.

It is important to obtain clear instructions from the donor at the time of drafting the LPA as to whom and on what basis any copy of the registered LPA can be released.

7 Drafting the LPA

7.1 Choice of attorney(s)

The choice of attorney(s) is clearly a personal decision for the donor, but it is important for you to advise the donor of the various options available, and to stress the need for the attorney(s) to be trustworthy.

The donor should be advised that the appointment of a sole attorney may provide greater opportunity for abuse and exploitation than appointing more than one attorney.

You should ask questions about the donor's relationship with the proposed attorney(s) including any replacement attorney and, depending on which type of LPA is being created, whether the attorney(s) has the skills required to manage the donor's property and financial affairs or to make decisions about the donor's health and welfare.

The donor should be advised to consider the suitability of appointing a family member or someone independent of the family, or a combination of both.

If the donor wishes to create both a property and financial affairs LPA and a health and welfare LPA you may wish to advise them to consider appointing different attorneys for each LPA.

7.2 More than one attorney

Where more than one attorney is to be appointed, they may be authorised to act 'jointly', or 'jointly and severally', or 'jointly in respect of some matters and jointly and severally in respect of others' (section 10(4) MCA 2005).

If more than one attorney has been appointed and it is not stated whether they are appointed jointly or jointly and severally, they will be treated on the basis that they are appointed jointly when the LPA is registered.

This default position does not extend to EPAs and failure to specify on the prescribed form whether the attorneys should act jointly or jointly and severally would normally invalidate the instrument as an enduring power.

The differences between a 'joint' and 'joint and several' appointment should be explained to the donor. You should explain to your client that when making a joint appointment:

- joint attorneys must all act together and not separately
- the LPA will terminate if any one of the attorneys disclaims, dies, becomes bankrupt (bankruptcy only applies to property and financial affairs LPAs), or lacks capacity
- unless the LPA specifically states otherwise it will also terminate with the dissolution or annulment of the marriage or civil partnership between the donor and the attorney, and
- joint appointments may provide a safeguard against possible abuse, since each attorney will be able to oversee the actions of the other(s).

You should explain to your client that, when making a joint and several appointment:

- that joint and several attorneys can all act together but can also act independently if they wish, and
- the LPA will not be automatically terminated by the disclaimer, death, bankruptcy, dissolution/annulment of marriage/civil partnership, or incapacity of one attorney. In these circumstances the LPA would continue and the remaining attorney(s) can continue to act.

Your client may wish for their attorneys appointed under an LPA to act jointly in respect of some matters and jointly and severally in respect of others.

You should advise your client that the court may not accept this arrangement if it believes that such an arrangement fetters the LPA by providing the attorneys with unreasonable discretion.

The donor may have to make difficult choices as to which member(s) of the family or others to appoint as their attorney. You may wish to inform the donor that it is possible to allow some flexibility, for example the donor may wish to appoint:

A family member and a professional to act jointly and severally, for example with the family member dealing with day-to-day matters, and the professional dealing with more complex decisions.

However you may wish to highlight that the donor and the attorneys should consider the potential for conflict that could arise from this arrangement.

A professional attorney will have a higher duty of care and will usually be remunerated and this could create tension between the attorneys.

Further problems could arise if for example, the professional wishes to take a cautious approach and perhaps seek a court declaration or medical opinion, which would result in costs being incurred.

Their spouse or civil partner as attorney, with their adult child(ren) appointed as replacement attorneys should the spouse or civil partner die or become incapacitated.

Alternatively, the donor could appoint everyone to act jointly and severally, with an informal understanding that the children will not act while the spouse or civil partner is able to do so.

Extended time may be needed to explain the benefits and drawbacks of requiring specific decisions to be made jointly, and jointly and severally, as these areas can be confusing for the donor and attorneys.

7.3 Guidance, restrictions and conditions

As well as allowing for the specification of restrictions and conditions on the authority of attorney(s), the prescribed forms for LPAs also allow guidance to be provided to the attorney(s) when making decisions in the donor's best interests.

Any restrictions or conditions, if deemed valid, will be binding on the attorney(s) and can only be overturned by the court, whereas the guidance, although clearly pertinent, is not binding on the attorney(s).

You should ensure that you make the distinction between restrictions/conditions and guidance clear to the client. It is important that the drafting of this section reflects this distinction and that the language used does not suggest that any guidance is binding.

It is also important to inform the client that guidance within an LPA will be public and therefore visible to third parties. It also means that if the donor wishes to change the guidance, and does so in a side letter, for example, the previous guidance will remain in the LPA, apparently still valid, unless a new LPA is made.

You should explain to the client, and if practicable the attorney(s) that because guidance is not binding, the attorney(s) are entitled to act differently from suggestions within the guidance section of the LPA.

In this situation, the attorney(s) may conclude that, having used the 'best interests checklist' set out in section 4 of the MCA 2005, it would be in the overall best interests of the donor to act differently from the guidance.

However it should also be stressed that the guidance must be considered in assessing the best interests of the donor.

As a registered property and financial affairs LPA can be used whilst the donor retains capacity, restrictions that attempt to limit the attorney's power to use the LPA whilst the donor still has capacity are difficult to draft.

You should explain that this type of restriction may not be accepted by the court and might be rejected as unworkable by financial institutions.

If the donor does not trust the attorney to only act when appropriate this may raise questions as to the appropriateness of their appointment.

8 Certificate providers

A valid LPA must include a certificate completed by an independent third party known as the 'certificate provider' confirming that, in their opinion:

- the donor understands the purpose of the LPA and the scope of the authority conferred under it
- no fraud or undue pressure is being used to induce the donor to create the LPA, and
- there is nothing else that would prevent the LPA being created.

You should inform the donor that choosing a suitable certificate provider is an important safeguard and without the certificate the LPA cannot be registered and used. The choice of certificate provider is clearly a personal decision for the donor, but it is important for you to advise the donor of the various options available.

A certificate provider cannot be:

- under 18
- a member of the donor's or attorney's family
- a business partner or paid employee of the donor or attorney(s)
- an attorney appointed in this or another LPA or any EPA made by the donor
- the owner, director, manager or an employee of a care home in which the donor lives or their family member
- a director or employee of a trust corporation appointed as attorney in this LPA (this only applies to someone certifying a property and financial affairs LPA).

A person who signs an LPA as a certificate provider will also need to be able to demonstrate that they:

- understand what is involved in making an LPA
- understand the effect of making an LPA
- have the skills to assess that the donor understands what an LPA is and what is involved in making an LPA
- can assess that the donor also understands the contents of their LPA and what powers they are giving to the attorney(s)
- can verify that the donor is under no undue pressure by anyone to make the LPA, and
- have sufficient knowledge and understanding of the donor's affairs to able to be satisfied that no fraud was involved in the creation of the LPA.

It is important that the certificate provider is aware of the significance of making clear notes relating to the certification of the LPA. These notes should be kept for as long as is necessary and at least until the LPA is registered, in case there is a challenge against the validity of the LPA.

8.1 If you provide a certificate as a professional

Solicitors are one of the professional groups permitted to act as a certificate provider. However, you must ensure, on the facts of the particular case, that you do not fall into one of the excluded categories.

In particular, you cannot provide a certificate if you are:

- a business partner or paid employee of the attorney(s), this includes firms operating as Limited Liability Partnerships or limited companies (despite being a separate legal entity), or
- an attorney appointed under any LPA or EPA made by the donor. This would mean, for example, that you could not provide a certificate if in the past the client executed an EPA in favour of you, even though the EPA was never used or registered or was revoked.

Before signing the certificate you should take a suitably detailed personal and financial history from the donor, and if necessary insist on seeing them on their own, to satisfy the requirements concerning undue pressure and fraud. This may have both time and cost implications.

You should also be aware that if, for example, a family member objects to the LPA during the registration process then the certificate provider may be called to the Court of Protection to account for their opinion.

You should retain any notes you have made in your role as a certificate provider for as long as is necessary and at least until the LPA is registered, and provide these to the Court of Protection if they are relevant to any challenge regarding the LPA.

8.2 If you provide a certificate as a 'non-professional'

As a solicitor or retired solicitor, you may be approached by clients, former clients, friends or acquaintances asking you to provide a certificate on the basis that you have known them personally over the last two years. You should exercise considerable caution before providing a certificate on this basis.

The guidance given on the LPA instrument suggests that the requirement to know the donor 'personally' means the certificate provider should have known the donor 'for at least two years and as more than an acquaintance'.

A non-professional certificate provider may be called to the Court of Protection to account for their opinion if, for example, a family member objects to the LPA. The court may expect a higher standard of care and skill if the certificate has been provided by a solicitor and the donor is their client or former client.

If you have retired from practice you should consider why the donor has asked you to be their certificate provider. You should ensure that the donor has not specifically chosen you based on the skills and knowledge you have developed when practising as a solicitor as opposed to you having known them personally for the last two years.

9 Registering the LPA

An LPA is not created unless the instrument purporting to confer authority has been registered by the Office of the Public Guardian (OPG).

You should explain to the donor and, where practicable, the attorney(s) that the LPA cannot be used until it has been registered. The LPA can be registered anytime after it has been completed and signed by all those who are required to sign.

It is important that you clearly explain to the donor the implications of not registering the LPA shortly after it has been made. For example, if the donor of an unregistered health and welfare LPA faced a medical emergency their attorney(s) would not be authorised to act on their behalf until the power is registered, which at the very least would take approximately 13 weeks.

Refer to the health and in capacity law section of the Directgov website for current registration times.

You should inform the donor that a fee will be payable for the registration of the LPA and that a separate fee will be charged for a property and affairs LPA and for a personal welfare LPA even if they have been made by the same donor.

Once registered, a property and financial affairs LPA can be used while the donor still has capacity, unless it specifies otherwise, while a health and welfare LPA can only be used when the donor no longer has capacity to make the particular decision affecting their healthcare or personal welfare.

9.1 Time limits for registration

There is no time limit for making the application to register the LPA. The application can be made by the donor, or all the attorneys if the LPA is a joint power, or if a joint and several power by any of the attorneys.

9.2 Notifying named persons of an application to register an LPA

You should explain to the donor that they can name up to five people to be notified when an application to register the LPA is made. An attorney or replacement attorney appointed in the LPA cannot be specified as a named person.

If the donor decides not to include anyone to be notified then a second person will be needed to provide an additional certificate. You should advise the donor that including a named person may be a safeguard, particularly if the power is not registered shortly following execution, because if the donor lacks capacity at the time of registration they will be relying on these people to raise concerns.

You should advise the donor to make their named person(s) aware of the LPA, and what is required of them when an application to register is made, before the LPA is completed.

This will ensure that where a person does not wish to take on this role, someone else can be appointed. The donor may also tell their named person(s) who they have appointed as attorney(s). This allows the person(s) to raise any queries or concerns with the donor and may reduce objections when the application to register the LPA is made, avoiding extra costs and delays.

The donor or the attorney(s) making the application to register must give notice on the prescribed form (LPA001) to everyone named by the donor in the LPA as a person who should be notified of an application to register.

9.3 Verifying the registration

The registered LPA document will be stamped on every page by the OPG. You should check that each page has been stamped and that there are no missing pages, or unintentional additional pages attached.

9.4 The LPA register and disclosure of information

The OPG is responsible for maintaining a register of all LPAs, EPAs and court appointed deputies.

You should inform the donor that a registered LPA is a public document and certain information about their LPA will be available to anyone who applies to search the register.

10 Attorneys

10.1 Duties and responsibilities of attorneys

An attorney has a duty to act within the scope of their powers set out in the LPA. The authority conferred by the LPA is also subject to the provisions of the MCA 2005, in particular section 1 (the principles) and section 4 (best interests). Attorneys and anyone acting in a professional capacity in relation to the person who lacks capacity also have a specific obligation to have regard to the Code of Practice (section 42(4) MCA 2005).

In addition, attorneys have a duty:

- of care
- to carry out the donor's instructions
- not to take advantage of the position of the attorney
- not to delegate unless authorised to do so
- of good faith
- of confidentiality
- to comply with directions of the Court of Protection
- not to disclaim without notifying the donor, the other attorneys, and the Public Guardian, and
- complying with the relevant guidance.

In relation to a property and financial affairs LPA there is also a duty to:

- keep accounts, and
- keep the donor's money and property separate from their own.

According to paragraph 7.59 of the Code of Practice:

- If attorneys are being paid for their services, they should demonstrate a higher degree of care and skill.
- Attorneys who undertake their duties in the course of their professional work (such as solicitors or corporate trustees) must display professional competence and follow their profession's rules and standards.

Further guidance on the duties and responsibilities of attorneys is provided in Chapter 7 of the Code of Practice.

10.2 Delegation by the attorney

It is a basic principle of the law of agency that an attorney cannot delegate their authority. Alternatively, this could be expressed as a duty on the part of an agent to perform their functions personally.

Such a duty is imposed because of the discretion and trust reposed in the attorney(s) by the donor.

There are exceptions to this general rule and, like any other agent, an attorney acting under an LPA has an implied power in certain circumstances to delegate:

- any functions which are of a purely administrative nature and do not involve or require the exercise of discretion
- any functions which the donor would not expect the attorney to attend to personally, or
- through necessity or unforeseen circumstances, although caution should be exercised before relying on this exception.

In *Re Putt*, (unreported), 22 March 2011, Court of Protection, the court rejected a delegation clause which authorised the attorney to delegate his functions where it was not strictly necessary or expedient to do so. Delegation and substitution are not interchangeable.

See 7.61 of the Code of Practice.

10.3 Replacement attorney

Whilst an LPA cannot provide for an attorney to make a substitute or successor appointment, it can appoint a replacement attorney to act if any of the attorneys under a joint and several LPA cannot continue to act.

If the donor of an LPA wishes to appoint a replacement attorney(s), they should clearly state how replacements are to be appointed and how they are to act, for example solely or jointly. If the donor has more than one attorney, he or she can specify who the replacement attorney can and cannot replace. The donor can only appoint a replacement attorney for the original attorneys.

In *Re Druce*, (unreported), 31 May 2011, Court of Protection, the court stated that 'there is nothing in section 10(8)(b) of the MCA 2005, which deals with the appointment of replacement attorneys, to displace the fundamental principle that the survivor of joint attorneys cannot act. Where one of the original joint attorneys can no longer act, the replacement(s) will step in and act alone, to the exclusion of the surviving original attorney'.

You should advise the donor that when considering whether a replacement attorney should be appointed, it is important that the donor chooses someone they know well and trust to make decisions in their best interests in the same way as would be the case for their first choice attorney(s).

10.4 Solicitor-attorneys and costs

Where you are appointed as the attorney of an LPA you should discuss with the donor your current terms and conditions of business (including charging rates and the frequency of billing) and have these approved by the donor at the time of granting the power.

You should ensure that the donor is aware that there is a likelihood that the costs provided may change with time. The donor should also be provided with sufficient information regarding the options for appointing a lay attorney, such as a family member.

The prescribed forms for LPAs include a section where the donor can confirm that they have agreed for their attorney to be paid a fee and set out the arrangements which have been agreed.

Decisions about payments should be recorded here with the appropriate level of detail, as necessary.

10.5 Disclaiming an appointment

An attorney or proposed attorney can disclaim their appointment by completing the prescribed form (LPA005) which must be sent to the donor and copied to the OPG and any other attorney(s) appointed under the power.

10.6 Retirement as attorney

Before agreeing to act as an attorney in your capacity as a professional solicitor, you should consider how matters will be dealt with if you retire from practice.

11 Property and financial affairs LPAs

11.1 Limiting the LPA

The donor can limit the power of the LPA by specifying that the LPA only grants authority to the attorney(s) to deal with certain specific assets.

11.2 Gifts

Section 12 of the MCA 2005 gives the attorney(s) limited authority to make gifts of the donor's money or property:

- The recipient of the gift must be either an individual who is related to or connected with the donor (including the attorney(s)), or a charity to which the donor actually made gifts or might be expected to make gifts if they had capacity.
- The timing of the gift must occur within the prescribed parameters. A gift to charity can be made at any time of the year, but a gift to an individual must be of a seasonal nature, or made on the occasion of a birth or marriage/civil partnership, or on the anniversary of a birth or marriage/civil partnership.
- The value of the gift must not be unreasonable having regard to all the circumstances and in particular the size of the donor's estate.

The donor cannot confer wider authority on the attorney than that specified in section 12, but it is open to the donor to restrict or exclude the authority which would otherwise be available to the attorney(s) under that section.

The donor may include guidance in the power on the circumstances in which the attorney(s) may make gifts of money or property but these should not exceed the limits specified in section 12.

Any attempt to expand or circumvent the scope of the provisions of section 12 is likely to be challenged by the Public Guardian. Circumventing section 12 by inserting what is in effect a restriction in the guidance section is also likely to be rejected by the court.

The Court of Protection can authorise the attorney(s) to act so as to benefit themselves or others, otherwise than in accordance with section 12, provided that there are no restrictions in the LPA itself and the court is satisfied that this would be in the donor's best interests (section 23(4) MCA 2005).

Solicitors must also take account of the professional rules concerning gifts from clients (IB 1.9, see Outcomes in Chapter 1 – Client Care SRA Code of Conduct 2011).

11.3 Investment business

Unless the power is restricted to exclude investments as defined by the Financial Services and Markets Act 2000, the attorney(s) may need to consider the investment business implications of their appointment. If you are an attorney and conducting investment business you will need to be authorised under the Financial Services and Markets Act 2000.

In addition, you will need to consider whether the SRA Financial Services (Scope) Rules 2001 apply.

11.4 Trusteeships held by the donor

The solicitor should ask whether the donor holds:

- any trusteeships, and
- any property jointly with others.

In cases of jointly owned property you should exercise caution and consider any concerns or problems that may arise from your actions which affect the other joint owner.

Under the Trustee Delegation Act 1999 (the 1999 Act) the general rule is that any trustee functions delegated to an attorney must comply with the provisions of section 25 of the Trustee Act 1925, as amended by the 1999 Act.

However, section 1(1) of the 1999 Act provides an exception to this general rule. An attorney can exercise a trustee function of the donor if it relates to land, or the capital proceeds or income from land, in which the donor has a beneficial interest.

The transfer or deed must be made to two distinct trustees, not one person acting in two different capacities, subject to any provision to the contrary contained in the trust instrument or the power of attorney itself.

11.5 Disclosure of the donor's will

You are under a duty to keep your clients' affairs confidential (Chapter 4 – Confidentiality and disclosure SRA Code of Conduct 2011). However, the attorney(s) may need to know about the contents of the donor's will in order to avoid acting in a manner contrary to the testamentary intentions of the donor for example, by the sale of an asset specifically bequeathed, when other assets that fell into residue could be disposed of instead.

The question of disclosure of the donor's will should be discussed at the time of making the LPA, and instructions should be obtained as to whether disclosure is denied, or the circumstances in which it is permitted. If no sufficient authority is available the attorney(s) should apply to the Court of Protection for a specific order for the contents of the will to be disclosed.

The attorney(s) also has a common law duty to keep the donor's affairs (including the contents of a will) confidential.

11.6 Money laundering

The preparation of an LPA for clients does not itself constitute a 'financial transaction' for the purposes of the Money Laundering Regulations 2007. However, a solicitor acting for property and financial affairs LPA attorney, or acting as an attorney themselves, is likely to be undertaking 'relevant business'.

For further advice see the Law Society's practice note on Anti-money laundering.

11.7 Statutory wills

An attorney cannot execute a will on the donor's behalf because the Wills Act 1837 requires a will to be signed by the testator personally or by someone in their presence and at their direction.

Where a person lacks testamentary capacity, the Court of Protection can order the execution of a statutory will on their behalf. The court's will-making jurisdiction is conferred by section 18 of the MCA 2005.

12 Health and welfare LPAs

12.1 Scope

An attorney appointed in a registered health and welfare LPA has no authority to make a decision which the donor has capacity to make for himself or herself. This is not the case for a registered property and financial affairs power and you should ensure that your client understands the difference.

Clients also need to know that, unless the donor adds restrictions or conditions, the attorney(s) of a health and welfare LPA will have authority to make almost all personal welfare and healthcare decisions. Important exceptions include:

- decisions relating to life-sustaining treatment, unless the LPA expressly authorises this, and
- cases where a valid and applicable advance decision made by the donor to refuse the proposed treatment takes precedence.

A health and welfare LPA is a powerful document because of the wide ranging decisions that can be made on behalf of the donor and therefore clients need to be in a position to make an informed decision about the scope of the power.

In addition to considering the scope of authority with you, clients may also want to discuss it with, for example, their prospective attorney(s) and, where appropriate, their GP or any relevant health or social care professionals.

A health and welfare LPA can be limited to specific decisions and it may be helpful to create a checklist of questions and a range of suggested clauses which the client might wish to consider when creating a health and welfare LPA.

The guidance box in section 7 of the prescribed form enables clients to set out their wishes and preferences for personal care, including healthcare, in a way that is not legally binding but which their attorney(s) will take into account in deciding best interests.

For example, the donor may wish to include guidance stating that the attorney should not accommodate the donor at another location without consulting specific members of the family.

When drafting the LPA you should ensure that the client's instructions are clear and comprehensible to any health or social care professional who enquires about the scope of an attorney's authority under the LPA.

12.2 Life-sustaining treatment

Decisions to give or refuse consent to life-sustaining treatment can only be made by the attorney(s) if the donor has specifically conferred this authority in section 5 of the prescribed form in the presence of a witness. The witness must be over 18 and cannot be an attorney appointed in the instrument.

Life-sustaining treatment is defined in section 4(10) of the MCA 2005 as '*treatment which in the view of a person providing health care for the person concerned is necessary to sustain life*'.

Further guidance is provided in paragraphs 5.29–5.36 of the Code of Practice.

12.3 Relationship with advance decisions and advance statements

12.3.1 Advance decisions ('living wills')

Some clients may ask about making a 'living will' – which is described in the MCA 2005 as an 'advance decision' – and whether they should make an advance decision rather than a health and welfare LPA or vice versa.

An advance decision allows a person, provided they have capacity, to refuse medical treatment that might be given at a time in the future when they lack capacity to refuse that treatment. If an advance decision is both valid and applicable in the particular circumstances, it has the same effect as a contemporaneous refusal of treatment by a person with capacity. This means that the treatment specified in the decision cannot lawfully be given.

Further information and guidance is provided in chapter 9 of the Code of Practice.

Possible points for the client to consider include:

- A health and welfare LPA allows a donor to give general authority for the attorney(s) to give or refuse consent to life-sustaining treatment where Option A, section 5, of the prescribed form is completed. Unlike an advance decision it is not necessary to specify a particular treatment or particular circumstances where treatment is refused. This of course requires a high degree of trust by the donor towards the attorney(s).
- Under a health and welfare LPA the attorney(s) must make decisions in the donor's best interests? and follow the checklist in section 4 of the MCA 2005 which includes consultation with those close to the person who lacks capacity. Where an advance decision is being followed the best interests principle does not apply – if it is valid and applicable it must be respected even if the healthcare professionals think it goes against the person's best interests.
- There are stringent requirements for completing and registering an LPA whereas the MCA 2005 does not impose any particular formalities concerning advance decisions except for decisions relating to life-sustaining treatment. This relative informality may be attractive for some clients but it can also lead to uncertainty over whether an advance decision exists or is valid.

In some cases when dealing with a seriously or terminally ill person it may be prudent to consider with them whether to combine a health and welfare LPA with an advance decision. The LPA may take time to register, but the advance decision takes effect immediately and can be used before the LPA has been registered.

Clients should be made aware that where a person makes a health and welfare LPA (regardless of whether it provides authority to give or refuse consent to life-sustaining treatment) and subsequently makes an advance decision, which is valid and applicable in the circumstances, the advance decision takes priority.

A health and welfare LPA made after an advance decision will make the advance decision invalid if the LPA gives the attorney authority to make decisions about the same treatment.

If necessary, you may need to advise that the law relating to euthanasia and assisted suicide has not been changed, and the introduction of health and welfare LPAs and advance decisions does not legitimise euthanasia.

Clients may also want information about registering their decision in relation to organ donation. The NHS Organ Donor Register website has further information about signing-up online and carrying a donor card.

12.3.2 Advance statements

You should advise the donor that the MCA 2005 provides for creation of an 'advance statement' (as distinct from an 'advance decision'), which enables a person with capacity to set out their wishes and feelings in writing about, for example, the care and treatment they would like to receive should they lose capacity in the future.

Advance statements are not legally binding but should be taken into account by decision makers – including attorney(s) – when making best interest decisions under section 4(6) of the MCA 2005. A client could decide to make an advance statement as a separate exercise to providing guidance for their attorney in section 7 of the prescribed form.

Further information on advance statements is provided in paragraphs 5.37–5.45 of the Code of Practice.

13 Using the prescribed LPA forms

The current prescribed LPA forms can be found on the Ministry of Justice website.

An LPA may be refused registration because of a defect in the form or the wording of the instrument. In some cases, registration may be possible after the filing of further evidence to overcome the defect.

Where you have assisted a donor in drawing up an LPA which is subsequently refused registration because of a material defect you may find it alleged that you should be liable for the additional costs of deputyship, since at that point the donor may not have the capacity to execute a new LPA.

Once the LPA has been signed any mistakes or errors cannot simply be corrected, even if the donor still has capacity, although on occasion and for minor points the OPG may suggest this as a solution and accept the amended document.

14 Executing the LPA

An LPA must be executed by the donor, the certificate provider and the attorney(s) in the correct order. In *Re Sporne*, (unreported), 13 October 2009, Court of Protection, where Part C of the LPA was signed before Part B and the donor subsequently lost capacity, the Court of Protection refused to exercise its discretion to validate the LPA (under paragraph 3(2) of schedule 1 of the MCA 2005) as it was a significant procedural error.

Execution by the donor, certificate provider and attorney(s) need not take place simultaneously but the regulations require that each stage must take place as soon as reasonably practicable after the previous stage.

(Note, that for section 5 'life-sustaining treatment' of a health and welfare LPA must be signed and witnessed at the same time.)

14.1 Witnesses

Execution by the donor and the attorney(s) must take place in the presence of a witness (but not necessarily the same witness) who must sign Part A and/or Part C of the prescribed form as appropriate, and give their full name and address. There are various restrictions as to who can act as a witness, in particular:

- the donor and attorney/replacement attorney must not witness each other's signature
- it is not advisable for the donor's spouse or civil partner to witness the donor's signature because of the rules of evidence relating to compellability.

There are specific provisions in relation to a donor who is unable to sign. See the LPA form and supporting guidance for more information.

15 Relationship between property and financial affairs and health and welfare LPAs

Depending on the decision to be made, an attorney may reasonably be expected to consult with the attorney(s) of any other LPA made by the donor, whenever the donor's best interests are being considered (section 4(7)(c), MCA 2005 and paragraph 5.55 of the Code of Practice). It is also likely that EPA attorney(s) would also be consulted.

Attorneys should also be aware that the demarcation between decisions made under a property and financial affairs LPA and a health and welfare LPA may not always be clear, for example, where the donor lives is a welfare decision which also has financial implications. If there are conflicts then an application can be made to the Court of Protection to resolve the issue but this should only be considered as a last resort.

16 Reporting suspected abuse of an LPA

If you suspect that an attorney may be misusing an LPA or acting dishonestly you should contact the Compliance and Regulations Unit of the OPG immediately.

You should also contact the police if you suspect psychological, physical or sexual abuse, theft or fraud.

It may also be necessary, particularly in cases involving health and welfare LPAs, to refer the matter to the local authority Adult Protection Unit.

Further guidance is provided in paragraphs 7.69–7.74 and Chapter 14 of the Code of Practice.

17 Enduring Powers of Attorney

The Enduring Powers of Attorney Act 1985 was repealed by the MCA 2005, but it was reintroduced almost in its entirety in Schedule 4 of the MCA 2005. The amendments take account of the changes to the Court of Protection and the new role of the Office of the Public Guardian in the registration process.

It is not possible to make new EPAs, although the operation of existing EPAs made before 1 October 2007 will fall under Schedule 4 of the MCA 2005.

An EPA can only authorise attorneys to make decisions about the donor's property and financial affairs. EPA attorneys have no authority to make health and welfare decisions for the donor.

If the donor has full mental capacity an EPA does not have to be registered before you can use it, unless there is an express condition requiring registration.

The EPA must be registered with the OPG as soon as the donor starts to lose capacity.

Registration of an EPA may be cancelled on the donor's recovery.

17.1 Duties under an EPA

The principles of the MCA 2005 are specifically excluded from applying to an EPA attorney (Schedule 4, paragraph 1(1) MCA 2005). However under the law of agency, the EPA attorney has certain duties to the donor (some of these are indicated in section 10.1 above). Further guidance is available in paragraphs 7.58–7.68 of the Code of Practice.

According to paragraph 7.5 of the Code of Practice, EPA attorneys do not have a legal duty to have regard to the Code, but the Code's guidance will still be helpful to them.

17.2 Solicitors acting as an EPA attorney

If you are acting as an EPA attorney you may be considered to have a duty to have regard to the Code of Practice since you will be acting in a 'professional capacity' for the purposes of section 42(4)(e) of the MCA 2005.

This is not straightforward because under Schedule 4 of the MCA 2005 the EPA must be registered when a person is becoming or has become incapable of managing their own affairs and from this point on it is the attorney who manages the donor's affairs. This is different to the concept of incapacity used in the rest of the MCA 2005 which is both function and time-specific. It appears that the Code will therefore selectively apply to the professional EPA attorney as there will not be a requirement to assess capacity on each decision being made.

17.3 Acting in the donor's best interests

Under an EPA, an attorney has a common law duty to act in the donor's best interests. This duty is reinforced by paragraph 5.2 of the Code of Practice which states that the best interests principle 'covers all aspects of financial, personal welfare and healthcare decision-making and actions. It applies to anyone making decisions or acting under the provisions of the Act, including attorneys appointed under a Lasting Power of Attorney or registered Enduring Power of Attorney'.

However, Paragraph 1(1) of Schedule 4 of the MCA 2005 is somewhat ambiguous, stating that: 'Where an individual has created a power of attorney which is an enduring power within the meaning of this schedule? And, accordingly, section 1 of this Act does not apply'.

You should therefore err on the side of caution and take into the account the best interests principle.

The attorney of an EPA is not specifically named as a person to be consulted when a decision-maker is making a best interests determination under section 4 of the MCA 2005. However it is likely that in the majority of cases any EPA attorney appointed by the attorney will be considered to be a person who is 'interested in his welfare' for the purposes of section 4(7)(b) of the MCA 2005, and therefore would be consulted.

This appears to be confirmed in paragraph 5.55 of the Code of Practice.

17.4 EPA Register

The OPG is responsible for maintaining a register of EPAs which can be searched by any person on payment of a fee.

Law Society Practice Note of 13 June 2013: Financial Abuse

(© The Law Society 2013)

1 Introduction

1.1 Who should read this practice note?

All solicitors who advise clients that are or may be at risk of financial abuse, in particular those conducting private client work involving financial planning, execution of wills or LPAs.

1.2 What is the issue?

As a result of economic recession, social change and advances in technology the risk of financial abuse is increasing. Solicitors are well placed to identify possible or actual financial abuse in the context of particular retainers.

You have a responsibility to be aware of financial abuse and to understand your role in both preventing it and taking action to protect clients who have been financially abused.

Financial abuse covers a wide variety of activities from mishandling finances to fraud, but may broadly be described as a violation of an individual's rights relating to their financial affairs or assets.

Anyone can be a victim of financial abuse, but particular groups may be especially at risk. Age and specific disabilities may have an impact on the individual's capacity to make decisions which places them at increased risk of abuse.

People with learning disabilities or other conditions that have led to cognitive impairment, and in some instances, people who have poor mental health may also be particularly at risk.

This practice note is aimed to assist you in identifying and acting upon suspected or actual financial abuse in the course of your practice.

The SRA has published a Handbook, which sets out all the SRA's regulatory requirements. It outlines the ethical standards that the SRA expects of law firms and practitioners and the outcomes that the SRA expects them to achieve for their clients.

An overview of outcomes-focused regulation (OFR) can be found on the Law Society's website. This provides information on what the SRA Handbook contains, including a summary of the chapters in the Code of Conduct and a summary of the reporting requirements included throughout the Handbook.

2 Financial Abuse

2.1 What is financial abuse?

There is no statutory definition of financial abuse. However, statutory guidance published by the Department of Health entitled 'No Secrets' defines financial abuse as follows:

> 'Financial or material abuse, including theft, fraud, exploitation, pressure in connection with wills, property or inheritance or financial transactions, or the misuse or misappropriation of property, possessions or benefits. (DH/Home Office, 2000)'

More information about 'No Secrets' can be found in 6.3.1 Codes of practice.

2.2 Forms of financial abuse

'No Secrets' is the English guidance to local authorities on safeguarding, and it identifies financial or material abuse as including a range of activities, which are listed below with examples of how they might manifest in practice.

In Wales, the applicable guidance is 'In Safe Hands', and for cross-border cases, it should be noted that the Scottish legislative regime is different.

- **Theft** – either physically, or through transfer of funds from the vulnerable person
- **misappropriation or misuse of money or property** – for example, improper use of money or assets when handling it for a vulnerable person under informal arrangements
- **exerting undue influence to give away assets or gifts** – this can include placing inappropriate pressure on a vulnerable person to change their will, or make gifts they otherwise would not or signing over the family home to one relative when the older person is about to go into residential care
- **putting undue pressure on the older person to accept lower-cost/lower-quality services** in order to preserve more financial resources to be passed to beneficiaries on death
- **carrying out unnecessary work and/or overcharging** – for example, tradesmen advising repairs for non-existent problems to property, or offering a service such as will writing accompanied by pressure selling, work for which is overcharged, and/or charged in advance
- **misuse of older persons' assets by professionals** – for example, by accountants or legal professionals with access to client funds
- **misuse of enduring/lasting powers of attorney** – use other than as intended or further than as limited by the document
- **misuse of welfare benefits** by appointees appointed to manage such benefits on behalf of a person lacking capacity to manage them
- **misuse of Direct Payments** by paid carers or family members instead of using the money for the benefit of the recipient
- **salesmen encouraging certain people with learning disabilities who may lack capacity for their finances to enter into contracts or changing suppliers** (for example for mobile phone services) when they do not understand their contractual responsibilities. This can also arise with older people, who may have limited capability to understand such contracts
- **apparent theft or loss of possessions**, for example in contexts such as hospitals or care homes, or where people have carers at home.

Assumptions that a person is fully protected once in these contexts should be avoided, as they can remain vulnerable to any of the above forms of abuse.

3 Identification of adults vulnerable to abuse and precautions to be taken

3.1 Groups at particular risk

Although anyone can be the victim of financial abuse, certain groups are particularly at risk.

3.1.1 Older people

In particular, older people are extremely vulnerable to financial abuse whether perpetrated by relatives, carers or strangers.

You should not assume that any person accompanying your client has their best interests at heart You should be alert to the nature of the instructions you receive and the manner or behaviour of someone who accompanies the client.

A study found the following factors predispose an older person to financial abuse. This is not an exhaustive list and some factors may apply to persons other than older people:

- advanced age
- stroke
- dementia or other cognitive impairment
- physical, mental or emotional distress
- depression
- recent loss of spouse or divorce
- social isolation
- middle or upper income bracket
- taking multiple medications
- frailty.

More information on the study, 'Strategy for Recognising, Preventing and Dealing with the Abuse of Older and Vulnerable People', *Solicitors for the Elderly*, January 2010 can be found at section 6.3.3.

You may also need to consider a client's background in order to assess their capability. For example, some older women may not have had an involvement in the family finances, so a partner's death can have a greater impact on their capability than is immediately evident.

3.1.2 Other vulnerable adults

While older people may be particularly vulnerable other groups may also be vulnerable to financial abuse, including individuals with learning disabilities, poor mental health and acquired brain injury (eg stroke).

People with sensory impairments may also be at particular risk of abuse, especially where they are relying on others for information and assistance managing their affairs.

Government guidance and case law commonly cite the Law Commission Report *Who decides?: making decisions on behalf of mentally incapacitated adults* (1997) when defining 'vulnerable adults'.

Under this definition, a vulnerable adult is a person over 18 years of age who:

> 'is or may be in need of community care services by reason of mental or other disability, age or illness and who is or may be unable to take care himself or herself, or unable to protect himself or herself against significant harm or serious exploitation.'

More information can be found at 6.5.1 Law Commission Report.

The Law Society acknowledges the view of many stakeholders that use of the word 'vulnerable' can be perceived as negative and can undermine the fact that the fault of any abuse lies solely with the perpetrator.

'Vulnerable adults' has been used in this document only for clarity as the existing legal term used in applicable guidance, and is only intended to refer to people at greater risk of financial abuse.

Capacity can fluctuate over time alongside other circumstances such mental health problems, and you should therefore assess capacity at the point a decision is being made by the client.

People with fluctuating mental health conditions may be aware that their capacity to instruct and to manage their financial affairs can vary, and may want advice to help them plan for times when they lack capacity. See section 3.3.2 on 'Capacity to instruct a solicitor' for further details.

3.2 What to be alert for – known indicators for abusive activity

Financial abuse indicators can include the following scenarios and even though these indicators have been set out for elderly persons, they can also be found in financial abuse of other client groups such as people with learning disability etc:

- signatures on cheques, or other documents that do not resemble the vulnerable person's signature or are signed when the person is unable to write
- any sudden changes in bank accounts, including unexplained withdrawals of large sums of money by a person accompanying the vulnerable person
- the sudden inclusion of additional names on an vulnerable person's bank accounts or benefits payments – often these individuals are unrelated to the older person
- abrupt changes to or creation of wills that leave most or all of the assets to a new friend or only one relative
- the sudden appearance of previously uninvolved relatives claiming their rights to a vulnerable person's affairs and possessions
- unexplained sudden transfers of assets to a family member or someone outside the family
- numerous small sums of cash being 'given' to, or money regularly disappearing after visits from a relative or neighbour
- numerous unpaid bills when someone else is supposed to be paying bills for the vulnerable person
- unusual concern by someone that an excessive amount of money is being expended on the care of the vulnerable person
- lack of amenities such as TV, personal grooming items, appropriate clothing items, that the vulnerable person should be able to afford
- the unexplained disappearance of funds or valuables such as jewellery
- deliberate isolation of a vulnerable person from their friends and family, resulting in the carer alone having total control.

From 'A Strategy for Recognising, Preventing and Dealing with the Abuse of Older and Vulnerable People', *Solicitors for the Elderly*, January 2010. See further information at 6.3.3 Third party guidance.

While solicitors may be more likely to notice some indicators than others, depending on the nature of their practice (for example, with regard to will making, gifts or transfer of assets), they may also become aware of others during the course of their work for a client.

Mental health awareness training and disability equality training can assist in identifying potential abuse. You may wish to dedicate some of your CPD hours to such courses to develop this awareness.

3.3 Identification and the assessment of capacity

Clients who may exhibit particular vulnerability to financial abuse may also lack capacity to provide instructions for a transaction.

Clients who lack capacity may be at greater risk of abuse; for example, they may not understand the risks and consequences of making a substantial gift of their assets or of transferring their family home into the names of relatives.

Solicitors are service providers under equality legislation and you should use plain English when speaking or writing to the client about measures that would protect them from abuse.

If your client does lack capacity, then your role and obligations are different to when the client has capacity. The assessment of mental capacity is governed by the Mental Capacity Act 2005 (MCA 2005).

3.3.1 Principles

The MCA 2005 sets out a number of principles for its application, the first three of which act as a starting point for assessing capacity:

- A person must be assumed to have capacity unless it is established that he lacks capacity – Section 1(2)
- A person is not to be treated as unable to make a decision unless all practicable steps to help him to do so have been taken without success – Section 1(3)
- A person is not to be treated as unable to make a decision merely because he makes an unwise decision ° Section 1(4)

The MCA 2005 Code of Practice provides a comprehensive explanation of how these principles are applied.

3.3.2 Capacity to instruct the solicitor

If you are in any doubt as to whether a client has capacity to provide instructions, you must perform a capacity assessment before any instructions are acted upon.

The assessment should be conducted with the client alone without other family members being present. It should not be assumed that anyone accompanying the client has their best interests at heart.

However, it may be useful to observe how any relative or friend who has accompanied the client behaves towards the client and vice versa to identify whether there is the possibility of undue influence or pressure.

Section 2(1) of the MCA sets out a two stage test for establishing a lack of capacity, explained in the Code of Practice as determining whether:

- they have an impairment or disturbance (for example, a disability, condition or trauma) that affects the way their mind or brain works, and
- the impairment or disturbance means that they are unable to make a specific decision at the time it needs to be made.

Further information can be found in section 6.3.1 Codes of practice.

An impairment or disturbance can be temporary, and the relevant time for establishing whether one exists is the time the decision needs to be made.

For a person to lack capacity to make a specific decision, it must be established on the balance of probabilities that they are unable:

- to understand the information relevant to the decision, or,;
- to retain the information, or,;
- to use or weigh up the information as part of the process of making the decision, or
- to communicate the decision (whether by talking, sign language, or any other means).

Most importantly, section 3(4) states that the information relevant to a decision includes information about the reasonably foreseeable consequences of deciding one way or the other or failing to make a decision.

This provision is useful for assessing people with borderline or fluctuating capacity. If the person fails any one of the elements listed above, then they are treated as lacking capacity for that decision.

3.3.3 MCA 2005 and undue influence or misuse of power

Under MCA 2005, there remain a number of decisions where case law determines whether or not the person has the capacity to decide a matter.

This includes capacity to make a will (*Banks v Goodfellow* (1870) LR 5 QB 549) and capacity to instruct a solicitor to take legal proceedings (*Masterman-Lister v Brutton & Co* [2002] EWCA Civ 1889).

There are a minority of cases where a person may appear to have capacity under the MCA 2005 test but actually lacks capacity when they come under pressure from powerful relatives or friends. This can happen for example, to someone in the early stages of dementia or with a mild learning disability.

In *DL v A Local Authority & Ors* [2012] EWCA Civ 253 the Court of Appeal used its inherent jurisdiction to protect such vulnerable adults.

Since then, the inherent jurisdiction has been used infrequently to protect this group of people.

FURTHER STEPS IN ASSESSING CAPACITY

In addition to the principles set out at the start of this section, the following list provides a summary of the relevant issues and actions you should bear in mind when assessing capacity.

The threshold test for establishing lack of capacity will vary depending on the seriousness of the decision being made, which for example may be of a different level when making a will, gift or lasting power of attorney.

Similarly, the formality of the assessment should relate to the seriousness of the decision. The assessment of capacity form (COP3) requires the form to be completed by a 'practitioner', which could be a psychologist, psychiatrist, or other registered medical practitioner. In some circumstances it can be signed by a registered therapist such as a speech therapist or occupational therapist.

When choosing a health professional to conduct a capacity assessment of your client, you should make sure he or she has a good understanding of the Mental Capacity Act.

While there is an assumption of capacity under the MCA principles, you must be satisfied that the client has the requisite capacity to provide a given instruction.

You should not express a view on a client's capacity before conducting a formal assessment with them.

You should be careful to distinguish between the ability to express a choice (eg one beneficiary over another) and the capacity to understand the consequences and effects of a transaction involving the client's own interests. Under the MCA principles above, their choice does not have to be a wise one or one that you agree with.

If the client's capacity is in doubt, you should obtain a medical or other expert opinion (relevant to the matter affecting the client's capacity) when making the assessment of capacity in relation to specific decisions. This could be a specialist medical opinion, eg from a psychiatrist or geriatrician , a psychologist specialising in learning disability, or a neuro-psychiatrist or neuro-psychologist for a person with an acquired brain injury.

Your client might have had contact with local authority social services who may have already completed a pro forma assessment of capacity for the relevant issue. This should be shared free of charge with you upon request (subject to your client's consent) and provides a good reference point in deciding whether or not it will be necessary to proceed to arrange a further professional opinion on your client's capacity.

Where social care or minor financial decisions are involved, such as a decision to move into residential care, or relating to contact with certain family members, a capacity assessment form can be completed by the local authority social worker.

For treatment decisions or major financial decisions, you may prefer to consult the treating psychiatrist, rehabilitation consultant or general practitioner. You should approach medical or social professionals who know the client well, especially if the client presents as if they have capacity, but appears unduly influenced or intimidated when in the presence of a particular relative.

The Law Society and British Medical Association book *Assessment of Mental Capacity* (3rd Edition) provides guidance on how lawyers and health and social care professionals can ensure this process is thorough and best ensures the protection of your client.

You should be aware of Data Protection Act obligations and the Solicitors' Code of Conduct when seeking medical or other opinions. More information about the data protection act can be found at 6.3.2.

WHAT HAPPENS WHEN SOMEONE LACKS CAPACITY

If a person lacks capacity to make a decision, then the best interests principle applies.

Those close to the family should be consulted, and the views and wishes of the person lacking capacity should be taken into account before family or professionals can proceed to make a best interests decision on behalf of the person (see s 5 of the MCA 2005).

You should continue to consult and involve a person who lacks capacity to instruct in decisions and further steps to be taken. Ensuring that a person has an independent advocate can assist in this regard.

Any substantial financial transaction will require Court of Protection involvement if the client lacks capacity (see sections below on Powers of Attorneys and deputyship).

However, if you determine on your own assessment that it appears the client lacks capacity to instruct you, then you should discuss the need to obtain a formal assessment of capacity from a relevant professional with your client.

4 Taking action to prevent abuse

If you suspect financial abuse, deciding on the appropriate action will not always be a straightforward decision. This is especially so when taking into account the rules of client confidentiality.

Iif your client does not have capacity to make the relevant decision or take the action that they want to take, then arguably your duty of care to protect that person in the public interest has to be weighed against the duty of confidentiality.

It is important to work and plan together with a client to prevent financial abuse, for example by taking precautionary measures to protect against financial abuse during periods when the client anticipates they may be unwell.

This could include:

- making an LPA
- making arrangements for two signatures to be required for withdrawal of sums above a certain amount.

These planning decisions need to be taken carefully, and balanced against the risk of the client being exposed to a greater risk of financial abuse (for example, by their attorney).

If you have a reasonable belief that an offence has been committed against your client and you have their consent to notify the police and other appropriate authorities you should do so.

Other methods of protecting your client from financial abuse are detailed in the sections below.

4.1 Powers of attorney

Lasting powers of attorney (which continue to be valid after the person loses capacity, unlike a power of attorney) enable an adult to appoint a third party to exercise decision-making powers on behalf of the donor.

It is important that clients understand the risks as well as the benefits of granting these powers, and you should be aware of the potential for their abuse and build in appropriate safeguards.

You should take special care if a client arrives with a new friend or long lost relative who they wish to nominate as their financial attorney, particularly when there is a complex portfolio of assets or large assets.

This person may be taking advantage of the client. In this situation you may decide to enquire into the nature of the relationship with the client. Such a decision will be within your professional judgement and may assist in ascertaining whether the relationship is genuine or not, and that the instructions are in the interests of the client.

You should note that a specific capacity test applies to making a lasting power of attorney.

The same principles apply to enduring powers of attorney executed before the implementation of the MCA, as these are still lawful.

For further information on lasting powers of attorney, including client's capacity to make them, and building in safeguards against abuse, solicitors should refer to the Law Society Lasting powers of attorney practice note.

4.2 Gifts

Clients should be made aware of the nature of any gift as an outright transfer, and should be made aware of the risks any substantial transfers may increase regarding their ability to support themselves independently.

Potential beneficiaries of the client's will, such as family members, may have encouraged the client to make a gift in order to avoid taxes or nursing home fees.

As well as advising the client of the risks to their future independence that such gifts might entail, it may not be an effective way to avoid tax.

Further, the local authority may treat this gift as a deliberate deprivation of assets for the purpose of avoiding paying residential or nursing home fees, which results in the local authority charging full fees to the client.

For further information on gifts of assets, solicitors should refer to the Law Society Making gifts of assets practice note.

4.3 Wills

When drafting wills, you should be particularly alert for potential abuse in the following instances:

- where the person making the will is not being allowed individual access to the you
- where instructions come from a third party
- where instructions are coming from a third party who is to benefit from the will
- where a third party is always present at an interview with the solicitor
- where a third party is using their own solicitor to prepare a will for a vulnerable person who has previously had their own solicitor.

4.4 Estate administration

You should always be aware of the potential for abuse where an elderly person wishes to appoint an attorney for the purposes of taking out a grant of probate or letters of administration.

Notice should also be taken of substantial 'interference' or influence where a third party is becoming involved in the administration of an unconnected person's estate where they do not benefit or have no indirect benefit.

4.5 Mis-selling

Some groups at particular risk may lack capacity for their finances to enter into contracts, to change suppliers or to understand their contractual responsibilities.

If you suspect your client has been mis-sold a product or service, you may wish to consider approaching the relevant ombudsman. For example, for mis-selling of financial products, you or the client can contact the Financial Ombudsman. More information about the Financial Ombudsman can be found at 6.4.2 Financial ombudsman.

4.6 Language and cultural barriers

You should take great care to correctly identify the relationship between clients and any person accompanying them.

The exact nature of relationships can become confused when interpretation is necessary for communication with the client, or where the client is from a cultural background that identifies such relationships differently (for example, using familial language to describe someone not formally related to the client).

If you are concerned that the client's wishes are not being communicated accurately by someone that they have elected to translate for them, you should consider whether to engage an independent translator.

It is also important to ensure that contractual terms and consequences are clearly understood by clients from cultural backgrounds that may hold different understandings of contractual and propriety concepts.

5 Addressing suspected abuse – what steps to take

5.1 Confidentiality

General guidance on the common law of confidentiality, data protection and freedom of information principles is available in *SCIE Report 50: Safeguarding adults at risk of harm* and *No Secrets*.

It is important to note that guidance available on confidentiality has been substantially reduced under the new SRA Code. Chapter 4, Outcome 1 requires that:

> 'the affairs of the clients are kept confidential by you and your firm unless disclosure is required by or permitted by law or the client consents;'

There are no specific exceptions to this outcome in the Code that relate to permitting disclosure so as to protect a client without capacity from abuse committed by a third party, nor does the code detail any relevant indicative behaviours. The Law Society is currently seeking to address this shortfall in protection for clients.

For advice on the Code of Conduct, solicitors should call the SRA professional ethics helpline on 0370 606 2577.

Solicitors may also find it useful to review the ICO guidance on disclosure under the Data Protection Act and the OPG Safeguarding Policy on sharing of information (section 7.3.2 below).

5.2 Office of the Public Guardian

The Office of the Public Guardian (OPG) has responsibility for investigating concerns about the actions of registered attorneys and deputies (or where the Court has authorised an action under a single order).

It has an investigations unit with a dedicated phone number which can be found at section 7.4.1 below. Its Safeguarding Vulnerable Adults policy outlines what they can do if investigating any of the above.

It could take any of the following actions:

- apply to the Court for the **suspension, discharge or replacement of a deputy**
- apply to the Court for an **Order to be varied or for a deputy's security bond to be called in or varied**
- apply to the Court for a **revocation of a power of attorney**
- inform the **police**, where a crime may have been committed
- require a deputy to **provide a final report** where the person he or she was acting for has died or the deputy has been discharged.
- monitor the situation through ongoing close **supervision** of the deputy in the case
- inform **external agencies**. This will include notifying any professional body, where the perpetrator is a member, and the Independent Safeguarding Authority (from October 2009).

The OPG policy sets the following time limits for local authorities:

- same-day referral to adult social care teams or relevant outside organisations
- the next day for any decision to investigate, and
- five working days to formulate a multi-agency plan for assessing the risk and addressing any immediate protection needs.

In practice, if the local authority have already placed the vulnerable adult into safeguarding, and are planning legal action against the suspected abuser, the OPG and the local authority will work together to decide which agency will take the lead for action.

If there are concerns about a person who is outside of the scope of an OPG investigation, the policy states that the informant should always be told:

- when the OPG's action has completed, or
- when the matter has been referred to another agency for investigation, and
- if it has been referred, who it has been referred to.

More information about persons outside the scope can be found in 5.2.1.

There may be situations where the person subject to abuse lacks capacity but the Public Guardian lacks jurisdiction to intervene as they do not have an appointed deputy or attorney.

In these circumstances you may want to consider or advise on an application to the court. The court has wide powers which may be exercised to protect someone who lacks capacity. This includes powers to appoint a deputy, make declarations of capacity, or prohibit named persons from contacting someone who lacks capacity.

The Government is consulting on legislation in response to the Law Commission's report on the review of Adult Social Care law, which contained a number of proposals on safeguarding.

You should remain alert to any changes in this area of law.

5.2.1 Examples of persons outside the scope of the OPG

AN UNREGISTERED EPA

The OPG will normally make a referral to the Adult Social Care Department of the local authority of the area where the vulnerable person lives. If the donor of the EPA lacks capacity to make decisions, the OPG may advise that an application is made to the Court of Protection for revocation of the EPA and the appointment of a deputy. The court will sometimes order the Public Guardian to provide a report under Section 49 of the Mental Capacity Act in such cases.

A FORMER RECEIVER OR DEPUTY

The OPG will normally advise the current deputy to deal with the matter. Where a deputy has been discharged, or has died, or the vulnerable adult has died, the OPG can call for a final report from the former deputy (or the personal representatives if the deputy has died). If the Public Guardian is not satisfied, he may apply to the Court of Protection for enforcement of the security bond. This only applies to deaths/discharges after 1 October 2007.

ANY OTHER PERSON

The OPG will make a referral to Adult Social Care and if the vulnerable adult has an appointed deputy then the OPG will want to be kept informed of the situation and could contribute to the action by monitoring the situation through supervision of the deputy and visits to the vulnerable adult from a Court of Protection Visitor.

APPOINTEES

The OPG will make a referral to the Department for Work and Pensions and to Adult Social Care.

5.3 Litigation

If litigation is contemplated, you should consult with family members to see if an appropriate individual is able to act as a litigation friend.

If there is no family or no one who does not present a potential conflict of interest with the client eg the relative is the suspected abuser, then you should contact the Official Solicitor. The Official Solicitor can be appointed as litigation friend, if proceedings need to be taken.

5.4 Deputyship

If the client has assets that need protecting and lacks capacity to manage their assets, an application should be made to the Court of Protection for a deputy to be appointed.

The Court will give wide ranging powers to the deputy to manage the client's bank accounts, sell property, and manage other assets.

If there is a need for a court order appointing a deputy, then if no suitable individual can be found or no relative is willing to act as deputy, or you do not provide such a service, then one option would be to contact the local authority's adult care solicitor to ask whether the local authority Deputyship team is willing to act as deputy.

Failing this, an application can be made for a 'panel deputy' to be appointed.

A panel deputy is a member of an approved list of deputies (mostly solicitors) with specialist knowledge of the MCA 2005.

A list of panel deputies can be found on the justice.gov website, and the Court of Protection has access to a Panel of Deputies who may be called on where there is no-one else willing or able to take on the role of deputy.

You should consider whether it is appropriate for an application to be made for a statutory will.

5.5 Appointeeship

If a client is in receipt of a state pension and/or benefits, an application can be made to the Department of Works and Pensions for a suitable relative to be appointed as the appointee of the client's benefits if:

- the client does not have capacity to manage them any longer, or
- there are concerns that these are being mismanaged..

If there is no relative or no suitable relative, then the local authority may agree to be appointed as appointee of the benefits and pension.

If you have concerns that the benefits are being mismanaged, then you should consider reporting these concerns to the Department of Works and Pensions who will investigate whether or not the current appointee is a suitable person to continue to act as appointee.

You can contact the Pensions Service on 0845 6060265 for those over 60 if they suspect abuse and want to apply for appointeeship.

For those under 60 there are a number of potential remedies and the contact number is 0845 6088506.

The DWP benefit fraud hotline can be contacted on 0800 854 440. There is also a DLA and Attendance Allowance hotline which can be contacted on 08457 123456.

On contacting these hotlines, you will be informed of the appropriate office to send a fax with a letter and/or application to take over appointeeship or report concerns.

5.6 The role of the local authority

Under No Secrets, the lead agency responsible for arranging safeguarding procedures to take protective action for a vulnerable adult is the local authority adult care department.

The local authority can arrange an initial strategy meeting which is attended by relevant professionals, both statutory and voluntary, dealing with the vulnerable adult with a view to deciding immediate measures to prevent or stop the financial abuse.

Later, a case conference will be held to examine the effectiveness of the measures and decide further strategies.

It is important that the vulnerable adult's capacity to make relevant decisions, such as decisions to protect themselves against abuse, capacity to manage their finances and assets is assessed as soon as possible so that the outcome will determine the available legal options such as using the Court of Protection or not.

5.7 Abuse and neglect by legal professionals

If you suspect abuse or neglect by another legal professional, you should contact the SRA for guidance. For more information see 6.2.2.

5.8 Criminal offences

Where you suspect an appointee is not using their powers for the benefit of the vulnerable adult then you should notify the DWP.

If you suspect a criminal offence may be taking place, contact your local safeguarding team or the police. However, the police may ask that no action be taken while they investigate and gather evidence against the perpetrator before the perpetrator realises that the police are investigating.

The difficulty with this approach is that you may have a duty of care to apply for deputyship in the interim to protect the assets from being further dissipated by the perpetrator. If the perpetrator is a deputy or attorney, the OPG will want to launch an investigation.

Generally local uathority solicitors will cooperate with the police. You should make clear that they must take interim steps to apply to the Court of Protection if there are sufficient assets to make it worthwhile appointing a deputyship. If not, they must notify DWP to stop paying the adult's benefits to the perpetrator as the appointee.

Local authorities may also be able to assist, by considering what protective action might be needed in cases of financial abuse; this action can include applying for interim deputyship orders or a single order.

6 Further information

6.1 Law Society

6.1.1 Law Society Practice Advice Service

The Law Society Practice Advice Service provides a dedicated support line for Law Society members and employees of law firms.

6.1.2 Law Society practice notes
- Making gifts of assets practice note
- Lasting powers of attorney practice note

6.1.3 Law Society publications

Assessment of Mental Capacity, 3rd Edition (2009)

Anti-Money Laundering Toolkit

Lexcel Financial Management and Business Planning Toolkit

6.2 Solicitors Regulation Authority

6.2.1 Professional Ethics Helpline

Contact the Solicitors Regulation Authority's Professional ethics helpline for advice on conduct issues.

6.2.2 Reporting another professional

The SRA provides guidance reporting misconduct.

6.3 Guidance

6.3.1 Codes of practice

Mental Capacity Act 2005 Code of Practice

No Secrets – Department of Health and Home Office guidance on developing and implementing multi-agency policies and procedures to protect vulnerable adults from abuse (2010) (now on national archives website)

In Safe Hands – Welsh Government guidance on adult protection procedures

SCIE Report 50: Safeguarding adults at risk of harm – Social Care Institute for Excellence guidance on safeguarding which includes information on financial abuse against vulnerable adults (2011).

6.3.2 Data protection

- Information Commissioner guidance on disclosure
- ICO guidance on releasing information to prevent or detect crime (section 29), Data Protection Act
- OPG safeguarding policy on sharing of information, section 8.8

6.3.3 Third party guidance

'A Strategy for Recognising, Preventing and Dealing with the Abuse of Older and Vulnerable People' (PDF), *Solicitors for the Elderly* (January 2010)

6.4 Useful contacts

6.4.1 Office of the Public Guardian

Office of the Public Guardian Investigations Unit contact details, Policy Guidance, the Procedures and Practice Guidance and the Protocol for working with Local Authorities.

6.4.2 Other groups

- Action on Elder Abuse
- Age UK
- Financial Ombudsman
- Mencap
- Mind
- Office of the Public Guardian: OPG on Justice.gov and OPG on GOV.uk
- Solicitors for the Elderly

6.5 Other resources

6.5.1 Law Commission report

Law Commission report: 'Who decides?: making decisions on behalf of mentally incapacitated adults' (1997)

6.6 Acknowledgements

The Law Society acknowledges the Mental Health and Disability Committee for its help in developing this practice note.

The Law Society would like to express its gratitude to the following organisations for their assistance in reviewing the practice note:

- Action Against Elder Abuse
- Age UK
- ADASS
- The Local Government Association
- MIND
- The Office of the Public Guardian
- The Official Solicitor

7 Terminology

Must

A specific requirement in legislation or of a principle, rule, outcome or other mandatory provision in the SRA Handbook. You must comply, unless there are specific exemptions or defences provided for in relevant legislation or the SRA Handbook.

Should

- Outside of a regulatory context, good practice for most situations in the Law Society's view.
- In the case of the SRA Handbook, an indicative behaviour or other non-mandatory provision (such as may be set out in notes or guidance).

These may not be the only means of complying with legislative or regulatory requirements and there may be situations where the suggested route is not the best possible route to meet the needs of your client. However, if you do not follow the suggested route, you should be able to justify to oversight bodies why the alternative approach you have taken is appropriate, either for your practice, or in the particular retainer.

May

A non-exhaustive list of options for meeting your obligations or running your practice. Which option you choose is determined by the profile of the individual practice, client or retainer. You may be required to justify why this was an appropriate option to oversight bodies.

Law Society Practice Note of 17 March 2014: Mental Capacity: International Aspects

(© The Law Society 2014)

1 Introduction

1.1 Who should read this practice note?

This practice note is for solicitors who don't regularly give advice to clients who:

- are moving abroad
- are retiring abroad
- own property or other assets overseas

They may nonetheless be presented with a mental capacity issue which involves an overseas element.

1.2 What is the issue?

The problems that arise where a client has moved overseas, or owns assets abroad and loses mental capacity are not new. However the increasing number of elderly people in England and Wales, combined with the fact that many more people own property abroad, means that solicitors whose practice does not routinely deal with international issues are increasingly finding themselves faced with cases of this sort.

The purpose of this practice note is to give you a basic practical starting point in such cases. It is important to appreciate however, that this is a complex, specialist topic and that you cannot advise without knowing or consulting the appropriate legal resources.

If neither you nor your firm are familiar with this area of practice you should consider carefully whether it is appropriate for you to give advice. In that context, this practice note aims to give some initial practical assistance.

This practice note relates only to Lasting Powers of Attorney for Property and Financial Affairs (LPAs) and Enduring Powers of Attorney (EPAs), as well as some aspects of deputyship. It does not deal with Health and Welfare Lasting Powers of Attorney, where different or additional issues can arise.

2 Private international law and the Hague Convention XXXV of 13 January 2000

The approach to mental capacity in other jurisdictions may not be the same as it is in England and Wales, and may differ considerably from the provisions of the Mental Capacity Act 2005 (the Act).

Private international law issues that arise when an individual living, or owning property, abroad loses capacity include:

(a) which country's courts have jurisdiction to make orders in relation to that person's property and affairs
(b) whether a foreign jurisdiction will recognise and enforce either
   (i) the orders of the courts of England and Wales or
   (ii) an LPA or EPA which is valid in England and Wales

The Hague Convention XXXV of 13 January 2000 on the International Protection of Adults (the convention) seeks to provide solutions in cross-border mental capacity cases. The convention has been ratified by a number of European states (for example France and Germany), but only Scotland has ratified it within the UK.

Scotland and Northern Ireland are each jurisdictions separate from England and Wales for this purpose.

3 Loss of mental capacity in cases involving foreign jurisdictions

In a case where an individual has purchased property overseas and has since lost mental capacity, it may become necessary to sell the foreign property – for example, to pay for care costs.

3.1 Enduring Power of Attorney or Lasting Power of Attorney

The first step will generally be to ascertain whether the individual made the local equivalent of an EPA or LPA in the foreign jurisdiction. If they did, then taking local advice on the possibility of using this local power is likely to be the simplest way forward.

If the individual did not make the local equivalent of an EPA or an LPA but does have an EPA or LPA which has been registered with the Office of the Public Guardian (or by the Court of Protection in the case of an EPA registered before 1 October 2007), that EPA or LPA may be acceptable in the foreign jurisdiction.

You will need to obtain advice in the local jurisdiction to ascertain whether the EPA or LPA is acceptable or not. See section 6: obtaining foreign advice.

3.2 Local requirements

If an EPA or LPA is acceptable in the foreign jurisdiction, local requirements may still have to be met before it can be used.

Precisely what these requirements will be will depend on the advice received on the relevant foreign law. Lawyers or notaries in different jurisdictions may express those requirements differently; for example, they may be more or less cautious.

3.2.1 Certification

In some countries, third parties placing reliance on a registered EPA or LPA may be required to have a copy of the EPA/LPA certified as a true copy and then have an apostille affixed to it by the Foreign Commonwealth Office (FCO). See section 4 for more information about this process.

3.2.2 Translation

An English or Welsh EPA or LPA may have to be translated into the language of the foreign jurisdiction, and a notarial certificate obtained verifying the accuracy of the translation.

Most legal translation companies can arrange this. Alternatively, you could use a general notary public with the requisite language skills, or a firm of scrivener notaries (public notaries who are proficient in one or more foreign languages and have some familiarity with the legal requirements of those countries).

Such notaries will often be able to provide both the translation and the notarial services under one roof, at least in the case of the most common European languages, such as French and Spanish.

3.3 Deputyship order

If the individual who has lost mental capacity does not have an EPA or LPA in the form prescribed in England and Wales, it may be possible to apply to the Court of Protection for a deputyship order, which may be recognised in the foreign jurisdiction.

This approach is only likely to be appropriate, however, if the individual concerned is habitually resident in England and Wales and merely owns assets in the other jurisdiction.

Recognition of the order and the deputy's powers may not be automatic and a formal application to the local court of equivalent jurisdiction to the Court of Protection will probably be required.

If the foreign court is satisfied as to the deputy's standing, courses open to it include:

- confirming the deputy's authority, providing him with the appropriate authority to act within the overseas jurisdiction
- appointing a local guardian to act and account ultimately to the deputy for any assets realised.

If the individual is habitually resident in the foreign jurisdiction but has some assets in England and Wales, then it may be possible in certain circumstances to bring an application for a deputyship order in the English court to cover the overseas property. However, this is not a straightforward procedure.

Even if available, the order may not be recognised in the foreign jurisdiction and so specific local advice will be needed in each case. See section 6: Obtaining foreign advice.

In the majority of cases, the better course will be to bring the equivalent of deputyship proceedings in either the jurisdiction where the individual is habitually resident or in the jurisdiction where the asset is situated.

You may need to take a similar approach in cases where, although an individual has an EPA or LPA, that power of attorney is not recognised in the foreign jurisdiction.

4 Advising clients before they move abroad or buy property overseas

If you are advising a client who is intending to live overseas, or wants to own a property or other assets abroad, there will be some cases where it is appropriate to raise the possibility of subsequent loss of mental capacity with them. In such cases, you should ideally raise this matter before their departure or purchase: planning ahead can avoid difficulties later on.

You should bear in mind that the advice that may be needed in an international or cross-border situation will be more wide-ranging and specialist than issues simply relating to mental capacity. This is beyond the scope of this practice note.

4.1 Instructing a foreign lawyer

If, in a case that involves a foreign jurisdiction, your client wishes to address the issue of possible future mental incapacity, they will generally need to instruct (probably with your assistance) an appropriate professional in the jurisdiction where they intend to live or own property, so that the professional can advise them of local requirements.

Many jurisdictions have well-developed laws governing the loss of mental capacity and allow an individual to make arrangements in advance to deal with such an event.

For example, many states in the USA permit a person to execute a Durable Power of Attorney, which is akin to an LPA, by which they can appoint an attorney to act in relation to their property and affairs if they lose mental capacity.

Not all jurisdictions have the equivalents of EPAs or LPAs. Despite this, as explained above, in some cases the foreign jurisdiction may recognise an EPA or LPA made under the law of England and Wales, provided certain local formalities or other requirements are met.

See section 6 on obtaining foreign advice.

4.2 Advising on the law of a foreign jurisdiction

Your client may ask you to advise on whether the EPA or LPA that they have already made (or which they now plan to make) will be recognised in the foreign jurisdiction. This is not advice that a solicitor practising only in England and Wales is qualified to give, as the answer will depend on the law of the foreign jurisdiction in question.

The client may or may not be prepared to incur the cost and effort of taking local advice at that stage, given that loss of mental capacity is only a possibility. If they decide against taking advice at that time, but wish to press ahead with making the power, the following two pointers may help:

- As a general rule, if a client who is moving abroad wishes to make a LPA then a better outcome is likely if they make that LPA while they are still habitually resident in the UK, rather than after they have left.
- It is likely to be useful to include a choice of law clause in the LPA, designating the law of England and Wales as the applicable law. This is because a key question in the foreign jurisdiction will be to know what law the document states it is governed by – something which is not explicitly stated on the current LPA form.

You may wish to consider using the following clause which has been agreed by the Office of the Public Guardian:

'This LPA is made in accordance with and governed by the law of England and Wales, which I specify shall be the law applicable to the existence, extent, modification and extinction of this power'.

For want of a better place, the clause probably has to go in the space on the form for restrictions and conditions.

5 Notarisation, certification, the apostille and legalisation

Currently, the primary mechanism for recognition of documents such as EPAs and LPAs internationally is first to obtain a certificate attached to the document and given by a public notary, or sometimes by a solicitor, usually as to the nature or status of the document.

The apostille is a certificate issued by the FCO and attached to the certificate issued by the public notary (or by the solicitor in appropriate cases) as confirmation that the signature, seal or stamp on the document is genuine.

The apostille does not certify the authenticity of the document or give approval of its content. It only confirms the status of the person who gave the certificate.

In the case of an EPA or LPA, the apostille will confirm that the public notary or solicitor who has given the certificate is known to the FCO.

Where a notarial certificate is given by a public notary qualified in England and Wales the public notary may be able to assist in formulating the appropriate form of notarial certificate (though the precise certificate that is required will depend on the advice of the local notary or lawyer), and he or she will also be able to obtain the apostille.

In some cases the foreign lawyer or notary may require the certificate to be one of due execution, again with an apostille affixed. However a certificate of due execution can generally only be given if the power was originally signed before the notary (ie the public notary must have given the certificate at the time of signing).

5.1 Registering with the Foreign Commonwealth Office

The signatures of all public notaries are already registered with the FCO. If a solicitor wishes to register their signature with the FCO they need to provide the FCO with the required evidence.

Provided evidence of a solicitor's identity and signature has been accepted by the FCO, then the FCO will affix an apostille to a solicitor's certificate, verifying the solicitor's identity.

In some cases using a solicitor's certificate may be attractive because it may be simpler and cheaper than the involvement of a public notary.

You should be aware, however, that some jurisdictions, particularly those based on civil law, may refuse to recognise a certificate that has been given by a solicitor rather than a public notary. Before adopting this approach you need to consider whether a solicitor's certificate will be acceptable in the jurisdiction in which you propose to use the document.

5.2 Obtaining an apostille

If you are not using a public notary, and are not a solicitor who subscribes to the FCO's premium service to obtain apostilles, then an apostille can be obtained by making a postal application to the FCO at Milton Keynes. Details can be obtained from the FCO's website.

6 Obtaining foreign advice

In all circumstances where advice on the law of a foreign jurisdiction is needed it should be obtained from a practitioner suitably qualified in the law of that jurisdiction.

Unless you are dual qualified it is not appropriate for you to try to provide advice on the local law yourself, even if you have previous practical experience of that jurisdiction. The law or formalities may have changed, or the particular notary or lawyer with whom the attorney or deputy will have to work (for example to sell the property) may insist on requirements different from those imposed in the last case.

Details of advisers in foreign jurisdictions can be found from a number of sources, including:

- the Society of Trust & Estate Practitioners
- some of the legal directories
- chambers of notaries or local law societies in the jurisdiction in question
- the International Union of Notaries which lists notaries working in jurisdictions throughout the world.

You can get details of public notaries practising within England and Wales from the Notaries Society and a list of scrivener notaries is maintained by the Society of Scrivener Notaries.

7 Time and expense

Cross-border issues will inevitably add to costs. Your client may require advice not only from you but also in the local jurisdiction, and may also have to provide notarised and translated documents.

In addition, matters are likely to take longer than they would if there were no foreign element.

The client should appreciate that different time zones, language differences and local procedures may all affect the speed and cost with which matters can be concluded.

8 More Information

8.1 References

8.1.1 Legislation

Mental Capacity Act 2005

8.1.2 Conventions

The Hague Convention XXXV of 13 January 2000 on the International Protection of Adults

8.1.3 Websites
- Public notaries in England and Wales
- Scrivener notaries in England and Wales
- Foreign Notaries registered with the International Union of Notaries
- Trust and estate practitioners overseas
- Foreign and Commonwealth Office

8.1.4 Books
- *Court of Protection Practice*, appendix 1
- *Assessment of Mental Capacity*, 3rd edition

8.2 Further products and support

8.2.1 Practice Advice

The Law Society provides support to solicitors on a wide range of areas of legal practice. The service is staffed by solicitors and can be contacted on 020 7320 5675 from 09.00 to 17.00 on weekdays.

Visit the Practice Advice Service.

8.2.2 Professional Ethics Helpline

Solicitors Regulation Authority's Professional Ethics Helpline gives advice on conduct issues.

9 Terminology in this practice note

Must – A specific requirement in legislation or of a principle, rule, outcome or other mandatory provision in the SRA Handbook. You must comply, unless there are specific exemptions or defences provided for in relevant legislation or the SRA Handbook.

Should –

- Outside of a regulatory context, good practice for most situations in the Law Society's view.
- In the case of the SRA Handbook, an indicative behaviour or other non-mandatory provision (such as may be set out in notes or guidance).

These may not be the only means of complying with legislative or regulatory requirements and there may be situations where the suggested route is not the best possible route to meet the needs of your client. However, if you do not follow the suggested route, you should be able to justify to oversight bodies why the alternative approach you have taken is appropriate, either for your practice, or in the particular retainer.

May – A non-exhaustive list of options for meeting your obligations or running your practice. Which option you choose is determined by the profile of the individual practice, client or retainer. You may be required to justify why this was an appropriate option to oversight bodies.

SRA Code – SRA Code of Conduct 2011

SRA – Solicitors Regulation Authority

****

Law Society Practice Note of 2 July 2015: Meeting the Needs of Vulnerable Clients

(© The Law Society 2015)

1 Introduction

1.1 Who should read this practice note?

This practice note is essential reading for all solicitors, practice managers and legal support staff, particularly if you do not act for vulnerable clients on a regular basis.

1.2 What is the issue?

Some clients have difficulty accessing and using legal services. Research has concluded that solicitors need to adapt their practices to identify and meet the needs of vulnerable clients.

1.3 Who are vulnerable clients?

The terms vulnerable and vulnerability are used here as a shorthand to address a range of situations which could affect any client who is at a disadvantage because of factors that affect their access to, and use of, legal services.

Please note that this practice note does not provide specific advice in relation to children or the needs of vulnerable defendants in criminal proceedings.

The possibility of vulnerability should be considered whenever you are consulted or instructed by a client in any matter.

This practice note focuses on three broad categories of vulnerable clients.

They are:

- clients who have capacity to make decisions and provide you with instructions, but by reason of a range of mental and/or physical disabilities require enhanced support to engage your services and give you instructions – sections 2 and 3
- clients who lack mental capacity to make decisions and provide you with instructions, for whom a range of statutory and other safeguards must be followed – section 4
- clients who are vulnerable to undue influence or duress and who may or may not have mental capacity to make decisions and provide you with instructions – section 6

1.4 Compliance with regulatory and legislative obligations

Section 5 of this note discusses independent third party support for vulnerable clients which can often be crucial in assisting you in obtaining the best possible legal outcome for them.

1.4.1 There are ten mandatory principles which apply to all those the Solicitors Regulation Authority (SRA) regulates and to all aspects of practice. The principles can be found in the SRA Handbook. You should always bear these principles in mind and use them as your starting point. Failure to meet your professional duties within the SRA Handbook may result in SRA sanctions or a referral to the Solicitors' Disciplinary Tribunal.

1.4.2 In addition, if you fail to meet the needs of a vulnerable client you could be at risk of:
- A discrimination claim or a claim for a failure to make reasonable adjustments under the Equality Act 2010, which could result in sanctions including damages.
- A claim for damages or compensation against you or your firm if you act on the instructions of a client lacking capacity to make relevant decisions, having failed to satisfy yourself as to the client's capacity to instruct you or failing to document your assessment of the client's capacity, leaving the validity of the transaction open to challenge.
- A complaint against you to the Legal Ombudsman, which could result in your name being published and/or you having to pay financial compensation. The ombudsman will refer complaints about discrimination to the SRA.
- Reputational risk – your practice's reputation is inextricably linked to the way in which you treat your clients. Conversely, a practice with an inclusive ethos will not only attract a wider group of clients but also a more diverse workforce bringing benefits to the business.
- Liability to other parties for breach of warrant of authority.[1]

1 *Blankley v Central Manchester & Manchester Children's University Hospitals NHS Trust* [2015] EWCA Civ 18

    1.4.3 This practice note will help you to recognise and meet your duties under the Mental Capacity Act 2005 and the Equality Act 2010.

2 Identifying the vulnerable client

2.1 Vulnerability indicators

Risk factors may be short or long-term, and can fluctuate over time depending on the circumstances. The following are offered as examples of risk factors and are not an exhaustive list:

- advanced age, children and young people
- physical disabilities or ill-health
- cognitive impairment
- loss of mental capacity to make relevant decisions
- mental health problems
- learning disabilities
- sensory impairment
- dementia
- acquired brain injury caused for example by a stroke or head injury
- severe facial or other disfigurement
- difficulty in accessing and/or understanding complex information, for example, because of psychological or emotional factors such as stress or bereavement
- communication difficulties, including no or limited speech, English as a foreign language, limited ability to read or write and illiteracy
- experience of domestic violence or sexual abuse
- heavy reliance on others (family or friends) for necessary care, support or accommodation
- long-term alcohol or drug abuse
- exposure to financial abuse

Some people may be affected by more than one risk factor – for example, many people with a learning disability have hearing and/or visual problems that can affect their communication and understanding.

Any one or more of these risk factors may mean that your client is vulnerable and may require your assistance to express their wishes, understand relevant advice and provide you with instructions, or that they may lack capacity to make relevant decisions and to give your instructions.

2.2 Signs of vulnerability: what to look out for

It may not always be easy to identify vulnerability. Some signs may be obvious while others are only just perceptible or hidden. You should not assume that your client will tell you of any difficulties. Simple observation will identify many mobility problems, physical or sensory disabilities or more severe impairment of mental capacity. It is important not to feel inhibited about asking for more information for fear of being intrusive – many clients will be open about any disability they have or specific assistance they require, or will be if asked, and will be glad to discuss how you can best meet their needs.

The Law Society practice note on financial abuse provides further guidance on the identification of adults at risk of financial abuse.

2.3 Identifying the needs of your client

Once you are aware that there are risk factors present, you can help your client to access your services and overcome any disadvantage caused by these risk factors. You should tactfully try to identify the needs of your client to find out whether they:

- have any requirements or preferences for communicating with you
- have any requirements to access your services, for example, to overcome mobility problems or hearing or sight difficulties
- have any requirements in terms of how services are provided, such as documents written in clear and simple language or information given orally
- understand and can act on the information and advice provided, or whether they may need support to do this, for example, from an advocacy service or interpreter.

Carers or family members may also be able to provide helpful information but in the first instance you should always seek to discuss these matters with the client alone, unless the client lacks capacity give you instructions (see Section 5).

3 Enabling vulnerable clients to access your services

3.1 Areas to think about

Ensuring that your practice provides an accessible service to vulnerable clients will mean considering many different aspects of your practice including:

- Marketing/making use of local links: advertising the services that you offer and the ways in which you can assist vulnerable clients and their families and carers. Many vulnerable potential clients will not have access to the internet.
- Website accessibility: conversely, for many clients, your website will be an important source of information about your practice and the services that it offers. If your website is not easy to read or navigate or if its content is difficult to understand, you may put off potential clients[2].

2   The World Wide Web Consortium produces recommendations for website accessibility

- Accessibility to and around your premises: are your premises easy to find and to access? Would older clients and clients with sensory and mobility difficulties be able to access your building? Are the floors and corridors clear? Are your rooms well lit? This is particularly important for clients who may be lip reading. Do you have meeting rooms large enough to accommodate clients who may bring other family members, carers or advocates with them? The Centre for Accessible Environments can provide you with information about registered access audits.
- Ensuring compliance with your statutory obligations to make reasonable adjustments and avoidance of disability discrimination in charging for reasonable adjustments.
- Training for staff who may have contact with clients on accessibility, disability and deaf awareness, reasonable adjustments, mental capacity, recognising vulnerability, conflicts between clients and carers, safeguarding and financial abuse.
- Flexibility around appointment times, duration and location.
- Willingness to visit clients at home may put them at ease and aid communication, for example, where your clients have dementia or mental health problems.
- Accessibility of written communications, for example, client care letters, letters of advice, costs information, written clearly and free from 'legal jargon'.
- Anticipating accessibility issues that may arise at tribunal, hospital or court hearings.

- The use of support professionals or independent advocates who can assist, for example, clients with a learning disability, throughout the legal process, including at the initial advice stage.
- Appropriate safeguards when using semi-automated systems.
- Obtaining feedback from clients on how to improve the service you offer.

3.2 Tailored and appropriate communication

> 'He more or less explained a lot of it to me without some of the jargon that you would get with most. Some solicitors they go through all this jargon and you think 'what are they on about', you know, and he did explain a lot of it to me as well'.[3]

[3] Norah Fry Centre Research, What happens when people with learning disabilities access legal services?

The 'reasonable adjustments' duty under the Equality Act 2010 is anticipatory: you must anticipate the needs of people with particular types of disability as well as making tailored reasonable adjustments for individuals. This means you need to be prepared: you should know, for example, how to find and engage a sign language interpreter.[4]

[4] The Law Society practice note on providing services to deaf/hard of hearing people provides more guidance

Types of adjustments that could aid communication with your clients include:

- allowing extra time for meetings with clients who may need longer to understand what you are explaining, or who have a speech impairment, or who are communicating through a third party
- explaining issues without using legal jargon
- enlisting the help of an appropriate third party
- providing information in large print, Braille, audio, DVD or easy-read format
- providing written text on a coloured rather than a white background; this can be particularly helpful for dyslexic clients or those with a visual impairment and they can advise you as to which colours to use
- providing a sign language interpreter, lip-speaker or deaf-blind communicator
- providing a reader for clients with visual impairments
- installing an induction loop or having a portable one available
- conducting conversations with clients using the text relay system
- providing a digital recorder, dictaphone or electronic notetaker, or
- not requiring the client to make complaints or other requests in writing.

3.3 Assisting vulnerable clients in the course of court proceedings

3.3.1 Criminal cases

Special considerations and measures apply to vulnerable defendants and witnesses in criminal and family cases. These are especially relevant if you are carrying out any advocacy on behalf of a vulnerable client or instructing counsel to do so. The Advocacy Training Council has developed specialist toolkits under the Advocates Gateway programme which provide valuable advice on supporting vulnerable clients throughout the trial or hearing process. The toolkits can be accessed at *www.theadvocatesgateway.org/toolkits*.

A range of 'special measures' apply to vulnerable and intimidated witnesses (but not defendants) in criminal cases pursuant to sections 16 to 33 of the Youth Justice and

Criminal Evidence Act 1999, including screens to shield the witness from the defendant, use of a live link, exclusion of the public from the courtroom, and the removal of wigs and gowns in the Crown Court. The court may appoint an intermediary to assist a vulnerable witness to give their evidence at court and facilitate communication; the intermediary may explain questions or answers so far as is necessary to enable them to be understood by the witness or the questioner, without changing the substance of the evidence.

The Coroners and Justice Act 2009 extended intermediaries to the evidence of defendants, but this provision is not yet in force. However, the courts have a common law duty to appoint an intermediary to ensure that a vulnerable child defendant can have a fair trial (see *R (C) v Sevenoaks Youth Court* [2009] EWHC 3088 (Admin); and *R (OP) v SS Justice, Cheltenham MC, and CPS (Just for Kids Law intervening)* [2014] EWHC 1944 (Admin)).

3.3.2 Family cases

Intermediaries have also been used in civil cases, in particular in the Family Court, for both children and vulnerable adults.

4 Clients who may lack mental capacity

4.1 What is capacity?

Mental capacity is the ability to make a decision – both day-to-day decisions and more significant decisions that may have legal consequences, such as buying property, entering into a contract, making a will, bringing or defending legal proceedings or seeking a divorce. Capacity is decision-specific, so a client may have capacity to make a simple decision but does not have capacity to make a complex decision or a decision that has significant consequences or carries significant risk.

If you reasonably entertain a doubt about your client's capacity to give proper instructions, it is your professional duty to satisfy yourself that the client either has or does not have the capacity to give instructions.[5] The statutory test of capacity to make a decision is contained in section 2(1) MCA 2005 which is set out at paragraph 4.3 below. There continues to be judicial debate as to the relationship between the statutory capacity test and common law tests of capacity although the High Court has clarified the position on the test for capacity to make a will and to make a lifetime gift (both of which are addressed at paragraphs 4.5.1 and 4.5.2 respectively).

5 *RP v Nottingham City Council and Official Solicitor* [2008] EWCA Civ 462

The test of capacity to conduct proceedings is set out in paragraph 4.5.3 below.

4.2 Mental Capacity Act 2005 – the statutory principles

Section 1 MCA 2005 contains the first three principles that are the starting point for assessing capacity:

1. A person must be assumed to have capacity unless it is established that he lacks capacity.
2. A person is not to be treated as unable to make a decision unless all practicable steps to help him to do so have been taken without success.
3. A person is not to be treated as unable to make a decision merely because he makes an unwise decision.

The starting point is the presumption that an adult client has full legal capacity to make their own decisions. Where there is doubt as to a person's capacity, the burden of proof is on the person seeking to establish a lack of capacity, on the balance of probabilities.

A person must be given all appropriate help and support to enable them to make their own decisions or, in the event that they are assessed as lacking capacity to make the decision in question, to maximise their participation in any decision making process. An unwise decision should not, by itself be sufficient to indicate lack of capacity. However, doubt may be raised as to the person's capacity if, for example, their decision is out of character.

4.3 Mental Capacity Act – the legal test for capacity to make decisions

You should be aware that a lack of capacity cannot be established merely because of a person's age or appearance or their condition or an aspect of their behaviour. Section 2(1) of the MCA 2005 states that:

> '... a person lacks capacity in relation to a matter if at the material time he is unable to make a decision for himself in relation to the matter because of an impairment of, or a disturbance in the functioning of, the mind or brain.'[6]

6   PC & Anor v City of York Council [2013] EWCA Civ 478

Capacity is therefore both decision specific and time specific and the inability to make the decision in question must be because of 'an impairment of, or a disturbance in the functioning of the mind or brain'.

Although there is one test of capacity, the statutory Code of Practice which supports the MCA 2005 identifies two elements: the 'diagnostic' and the 'functional' elements.

- Does the person have an impairment or disturbance that affects the way their mind or brain works?
- Does the impairment or disturbance mean that they are unable to make a specific decision at the time it needs to be made for one or more of the reasons set out in section 3 MCA 2005?

It is important to understand that a person is only considered to lack capacity for the purposes of the MCA 2005 if their inability to make a decision is because of an impairment or a disturbance in, the functioning of, the mind or brain.

Section 3 MCA 2005 defines what it means to be unable to make a decision.

In deciding whether the person is unable to make a decision the following four factors must be considered:

- Does the person understand the information relevant to the decision?
- Can the person retain the information?
- Can the person use or weigh up the information as part of the process of making the decision?
- Can the person communicate their decision (whether by talking, sign language, or any other means)?

Information relevant to a decision will include the particular nature of the decision in question, the purpose for which it is needed, the effect(s) of the decision and the likely consequences of deciding one way or another or of making no decision at all (MCA 2005 s 3(4)). You must provide an explanation of the relevant information in ways that are appropriate to the person's circumstances, using the most appropriate form of communication to help the person understand.

Retaining information for even a short time may be sufficient in the context of some decisions. It depends on what is necessary for the decision in question.

You can find further guidance about the MCA 2005 test of capacity in chapter 4 of the MCA 2005 Code of Practice.

Section 6 of this practice note addresses the position where a client has capacity to make the material decisions but is vulnerable to the influence of those around them.

4.4 Capacity to instruct a solicitor to carry out specific instructions

You must be satisfied that your client has capacity to give you instructions on the matter in question. If you have any doubt as to whether a client has capacity to provide an instruction or instructions, you must undertake a capacity assessment before any instructions are acted upon. To do otherwise may place you at risk of the sanctions set out at paragraph 1.4.2 above.

Different levels of capacity are required for different transactions. For example, different considerations apply to making a gift than in conducting litigation. You must assess the client''s understanding in the context of the transaction upon which you are instructed, applying the relevant legal test of capacity (see paragraph 4.5 below) and then consider whether the client is able to provide you with instructions on what they wish to do.

Even if you are satisfied that your client has the necessary mental capacity to make a specific decision, you may still need to be alert to the possibility of the client being subject to undue influence (see section 6).

If your client lacks capacity instruct you your role, your obligations and responsibilities are different from when you are acting for a client with capacity (see paragraph 4.7 below).

4.5 Other legal tests of capacity

4.5.1 Capacity to make a will

The High Court in *Walker v Badmin* [2014] All ER (D) 258 reviewed various conflicting decisions on whether the correct test of capacity is the MCA 2005 test or that established in the case of *Banks v Goodfellow* QBD 1870. It was concluded that the *Banks v Goodfellow* test is the correct test, although it is possible that an appellate court might reach a different conclusion. This test is set out below:

The testator must:

a. understand the nature of his act (of making a will) and its effects;
b. understand the extent of the property in his estate. be able to comprehend and appreciate the claims to which he ought to give effect; and
c. that no disorder of his mind 'shall poison his affections, perverse his sense of right, or his will in disposing of his property'.

4.5.2 Capacity to make a lifetime gift

As in the case of wills there has been uncertainty as to whether the common law test has been superseded by the MCA 2005 test. The High Court in *Kicks v Leigh* [2014] EWHC 3926 (Ch) reviewed the conflicting case law and concluded that the common law test is the correct test. Again, it is possible that an appellate court might reach a different conclusion.

The common law test is set out in *Re Beaney* [1978] 2 All ER 595 which says that the degree of understanding required for the making of a valid lifetime gift is relative to the transaction which is to be carried out. If the subject matter and value of the gift is trivial in relation to the donor's other assets a low degree of understanding is sufficient. However, if the effect of the gift is to dispose of the donor's only asset of value and so pre-empt the devolution of his estate under his will or on his intestacy, the degree of understanding required is as high as that required for a will and the donor has to understand the claims of all potential donees and the extent of the property to be disposed of.

4.5.3 Capacity to conduct proceedings

(NB this section does not cover criminal proceedings)

Formally, the test of capacity to conduct proceedings will vary according to the type of court. However, as the Supreme Court has made clear in *Dunhill v Burgin* [2014] UKSC 18, there is unlikely to be any real difference whether the test is the statutory test applied under the MCA 2005 (as is applied in civil proceedings) or the common law.

The key question therefore remains as set out in the judgment of Chadwick LJ in *Masterman-Lister v Brutton & Co* [2003] 3 All ER 162, namely whether:

> 'a party to legal proceedings is capable of understanding, with the assistance of such proper explanation (in broad terms and simple language) from legal advisers and other experts as the case may require, the matters on which their consent or decision was likely to be necessary in the course of those proceedings.'

This test applies to the proceedings as a whole and not at each step in the conduct of the proceedings.[7]

7   *Masterman-Lister v Brutton & Co* [2003] 3 All ER 162 confirmed in *Dunhill v Burgin* [2014] UKSC 18

The test of lack of capacity to conduct proceedings is the statutory test under the MCA 2005. However, the principles that evolved under the common law continue to be of assistance in applying the statutory test.

Capacity depends on time and context and should not be determined in the abstract. The question is always whether the litigant has capacity to conduct proceedings in relation to the particular proceedings in which he is involved and not other proceedings or their ability to make decisions in general.[8]

8   *Sheffield City Council v E and another* [2005] Fam 326 per Munby J at para 38

The following are some of the factors that may be relevant, for example, in assessing a client's capacity to conduct civil proceedings:

- The client would need to understand how the proceedings were to be funded.
- The party would need to know about the chances of not succeeding and the risk of an adverse order as to costs.
- The client would need to have capacity to make the sort of decisions that arise in litigation.
- The client would need to have the capacity to give proper instructions for, and to approve the particulars of claim, and to approve a compromise.
- For a client to have capacity to approve a compromise, they would need insight into the compromise, an ability to instruct solicitors to advise them on it, and an understanding of the solicitor's advice and an ability to weigh that advice before making a decision.

The Supreme Court also made clear in *Dunhill v Burgin* that the test must be applied to the claim that the party in fact has, not to the claim as formulated by their lawyers.

If your client is a party to but lacks capacity to conduct proceedings in the County Court, High Court, Family Court or Court of Protection a litigation friend must be appointed to give instructions and otherwise conduct the proceedings on their behalf.[9] The rules that govern the procedures vary according to the court or tribunal that the party is before.

9   Part 21 Civil Procedure Rules 1998, Part 15 Family Procedure Rules 2010, Part 17 Court of Protection Rules 2007

4.6 Assessing capacity

It is for you to decide whether a client has capacity to instruct you and whether you can accept and act on the client's instructions. Although the MCA 2005 guiding principle is the presumption of capacity you would not be acting in your client's best interests when you knew or should have known that there were grounds to doubt their capacity without first satisfying yourself that the client does indeed have the requisite capacity – see paragraph 1.4.2 above.

You must apply the relevant legal test in respect of each particular transaction at the time the decision needs to be made.

The assessment should be conducted whenever possible with the client alone. You should not assume that anyone accompanying the client (including a family member) has their genuine interests at heart.

It may be useful if you also observe how any relative or friend who has accompanied the client behaves towards the client and vice versa as that may identify whether there is the risk of undue influence or pressure.

If you are concerned about a client's capacity, especially in relation to a decision with serious consequences either for them or other people, it is advisable to seek the opinion of an appropriately qualified professional. Where possible, you should choose a professional who knows your client and has expertise relevant to your client's condition. You should explain to the professional the legal test of capacity and ask for an opinion as to how the client's medical condition may affect their ability to make the decision in question.

Testamentary capacity

Where a will is prepared for an elderly or seriously ill client, the courts have developed the '*golden rule*', which should be considered as guidance only. This provides that the will should be approved or witnessed by a medical practitioner, regardless of how tactless or difficult it may be to explain this precautionary measure to your client.[10] The aim of the rule is to minimise or avoid post-death disputes about the capacity of the testator.

10   Templeman in *Kenward v Adams* [1975] CLY 3591; *The Times*, 29 November, 1975

Ultimately, you must satisfy yourself that your client has the requisite testamentary capacity. You should therefore make and retain detailed and contemporaneous attendance notes, which confirm the steps you have taken to explore their capacity, the evidence you have collated, the circumstances and the rationale for your decision.

If there is a doubt about whether a client has capacity to make a particular decision, it is advisable to see the client personally in order to satisfy yourself that your client has capacity to make the decision you are concerned with.

4.6.1 Techniques for assessing capacity

How and when you see the client may be important, for example, choosing the time of day when the client is most alert and seeing them in the place where they feel most comfortable. There may be times or intervals in the day when your client may be more lucid than others; it is important to recognise that capacity can fluctuate significantly during the course of one day.

To put your client at ease, you might first chat about matters other than the business that you intend to carry out. It is helpful to know from other sources (such as family or carers) something of the client's family background and career so that you can verify the client's recollection. You should also ask a few questions about current affairs and past events. You should prepare and retain detailed and contemporaneous notes of any attendances. It is also helpful to record the questions you ask the client and the client's response, using the client's own words if possible.

At any subsequent interview you should seek to discuss some of the same matters and see if there is consistency in what the client says. You should also seek detailed instructions again – if they are materially different there is a good chance that the client may lack capacity in respect of that particular transaction.

Remember that you are testing the client's understanding of the decision to be made at the time it is made, not whether you agree with the client.

See also the guidance on assessing capacity in the Law Society practice note, Financial abuse.

4.6.2 Obtaining a medical or other expert opinion

You should inform your client of any concerns that you have about their capacity, the purpose of any capacity assessment, and the implications if they are found to lack such capacity.

If your client is a party to proceedings you may require the permission of the court to obtain an expert opinion.

When obtaining a medical or other expert opinion you must provide the client's written consent or confirm that the client has agreed to be assessed: You will also need to:

- explain clearly the purpose of the assessment and appropriate test of capacity
- with the consent of the client, supply sufficient background information to enable the expert to make an informed assessment – the information the expert receives may well affect their opinion, which places the onus on you to provide the right information
- set out any concerns about the client, especially about the appropriateness of the proposed decision and whether the expert is in fact being asked to confirm your opinion
- ask the expert to set out how the client's condition may affect their ability to make the decision in question, giving reasons for their conclusions
- provide a timescale for any response, especially if the matter is urgent
- actively chase the expert for the report, if there is any delay, and
- let the expert know if and how they are to be paid for the opinion.

In some circumstances, it may be more relevant to obtain an opinion from a professional other than a medical practitioner, such as a social worker, clinical psychologist or speech and language therapist, depending on the client's particular condition and the decision in question. However, the same considerations apply in relation to all appropriately qualified professionals.

There may be occasions when the client objects to you obtaining a report. If you still have serious concerns that the client lacks capacity to provide you with instructions and you have taken all reasonable steps to encourage your client to obtain a report, you must explain to your client in writing that you are unable to act for him, or to continue to act for him without a report being obtained and explain the legal consequences.

If proceedings are being contemplated, or if you are concerned your client has lost capacity during the course of proceedings, an application can be made to the court for a determination of whether the client lacks capacity to conduct the proceedings. The court may then order an assessment. However, if the client refuses to undergo medical assessment then there is no power to order an individual to comply with an assessment of capacity. In some cases the judge will have to form a view as to capacity without the benefit of any external expertise, although the courts have emphasised that judges should be slow to do so because of the seriousness of the consequences for the person.[11]

11   *Baker Tilly v Makar* [2013] EWHC 759 (QB)

The Official Solicitor has a standard form of report (Certificate of Capacity to Conduct the Proceedings) for recording the assessment of the mental capacity of an adult to conduct their own proceedings where that adult is a party or intended party to proceedings in the Family Court, the High Court, a county court or the Court of Appeal. The certificate has guidance notes for the assessor and can be sent with the letter of instruction.

4.7 What happens when a client lacks capacity to give you instructions?

If you consider that a potential client lacks capacity to give you instructions, you may be entitled to decline to act on their behalf. If you do wish to act on their behalf, you must first make sure that you are able to identify a person who has the requisite authority to give you instructions (see paragraph 4.7.1 below).

If you consider that an existing client has lost the capacity to continue to give you instructions, then the following considerations apply:

- generally a retainer terminates by operation of law when a client loses the capacity to give or confirm instructions
- however, there may be exceptions to this rule (in particular where the retainer has provided for the potential loss of such capacity).[12]

12   See *Blankley v Central Manchester and Manchester Children"s University Hospitals NHS Trust* [2015] EWCA Civ 18

Where an existing client loses capacity to instruct you, you should as far as practicable take action to protect your client's interests. As set out below, if you are to continue to act, you need to make sure that you have identified a person who is able to give you instructions.

If you remain doubtful as to the correct course of action you should contact the SRA Ethics Helpline.

4.7.1 Taking instructions on behalf of a client who lacks capacity

Depending on the circumstances of the case, you may be able to act, or continue to act on behalf of a client lacking capacity to instruct you by obtaining your instructions from a litigation friend, attorney or court appointed deputy. For example:

- You may act under the instructions of an attorney (such as a family member) appointed under a registered enduring power of attorney (EPA) or lasting power of attorney (LPA), provided the decision in question is within the scope of their authority. You may act under the instructions of a court appointed deputy (depending upon the scope of the deputy's authority).
- You may continue to conduct legal proceedings on the client's behalf acting on the instructions of a litigation friend appointed by the court.
- Where there are no current proceedings, but where proceedings are contemplated, you may be able to identify a third party who can give instructions on the client's behalf, as a proposed litigation friend. The proposed litigation friend is able to sign an application for legal aid on behalf of the client: see Regulation 22 of the Civil Legal Aid (Procedure) Regulations 2012 and paragraph 3.12 of the Standard Civil Contract 2014.

You should also be aware that the new Rule 3A within the Court of Protection Rules allows the Court of Protection in some cases to appoint an accredited legal representative to act for a client without a litigation friend (assuming that a panel of representatives will have been created).

See paragraph 5.3 below for more detail about taking instructions from an agent.

5 The role of carers and other third parties

5.1 Carers of vulnerable people

Carers can play a valuable role in supporting vulnerable people to access legal services and to make relevant decisions for themselves. Carers may also be able to assist with communication and help you to identify what reasonable adjustments could be made to assist the client. In practice, the definition of a carer has a wide meaning and includes informal carers such as relatives or friends providing personal care or supervision either full time or merely on a casual basis, as well as professional carers such as care workers, social workers and community nurses.

In the first instance, you should seek to obtain information and discuss matters with the client alone, being especially mindful of the principle of client confidentiality and the need for consent if confidentiality is to be waived.

5.2 Taking instructions: the involvement of carers

It is important to be clear about who your client is, whenever relatives or other carers seek to give instructions on their behalf. As a general rule, you can act only on a client's instructions. No one, whether a family member or professional, has the right to give instructions or make decisions about another person's property, financial or legal affairs unless they have been given formal authority to do so either by the client or by a court (for example an attorney acting under and EPA or LPA, a litigation friend or deputy).

For further information please see the Law Society practice note, lasting powers of attorney.

5.3 Taking instructions from an agent

In some cases where the client lacks capacity to give instructions, you may be taking instructions from an agent such as an attorney (if it is within the scope of their authority) or a deputy (if it is within the scope of their authority). The person for whom the attorney or deputy is acting (the principal) is still your client and you must act in the client's best interests.

If you are concerned that the instructions you are given by the agent are not in your client's best interests or that there is a conflict of interest, you should inform the agent of your concerns. If necessary, you should decline to act on the instructions of the agent if you continue to believe that these are not in the client's best interests. You will have to decide whether you can continue to act for the client, or alternatively for the agent on the basis that another independent solicitor will be appointed to represent the principal.

In certain situations, you will be deemed to be acting for the agent rather than the principal. These include:

- where you have been instructed by an attorney to apply to the Office of the Public Guardian for registration of the EPA or LPA where a prospective deputy instructs you to apply to the Court of Protection for the appointment of a deputy
- where you represent the deputy, attorney or other party to Court of Protection proceedings when there is a conflict of interest – in such a situation, you may act for the party to the proceedings and the Court of Protection may, if no other party is available and in the last resort, appoint the Official Solicitor or another independent person to act as litigation friend to represent the interests of the principal
- where you believe there is a conflict of interest and that you must act for the agent rather than the principal (who should then be separately represented).

5.3.1 Attorneys

While they still have capacity to do so, adults aged 18 and over may make an LPA appointing their chosen attorney(s) to make specific decisions on their behalf. The attorney's role and powers will depend on the type of power of attorney made and whether the donor has specified any restrictions in the attorney's authority to act. In the case of a health and welfare LPA attorneys must always consider whether the donor can in fact make the decision themselves and should only act in their best interests if the donor is unable to. It is also important to note that attorneys are not entitled as of right to act as litigation friends and must be appointed in the normal way (see para 5.4.3 below).

Further information on the various forms of LPA and their effect please see the Law Society practice note on lasting powers of attorney.

5.3.2 Deputies

Where there is an ongoing need for decisions to be made on behalf of a person lacking capacity to make such decisions, and the person has not previously made an LPA or EPA appointing an attorney to make the relevant decisions, the Court of Protection may appoint a deputy with authority to make those decisions.

Court appointed deputies can be given wide powers, including the power to conduct legal proceedings on behalf of a person lacking capacity if authorised by the court to do so. The scope of the deputy's authority will be specified in their order of appointment. Deputies can be appointed to make decisions either in respect of property and financial affairs or in respect of the health and welfare of the patient, or occasionally both. However, the court is required under the MCA wherever possible to make a single decision in preference to the appointment of a deputy, so the appointment of health and welfare deputies is rare.

Deputies must always act in the best interests of the person lacking capacity and in accordance with the MCA 2005 principles (see above) and must have regard to the guidance given in the MCA Code of Practice, in particular Chapter 8.

5.3.3 Litigation friends

People who lack capacity to conduct proceedings may become parties to proceedings in the High Court, the county courts and the Family Court, as well as in the Court of Protection. Litigation friends are appointed to give instructions and otherwise conduct the proceedings on their behalf. They will stand in the shoes of the individual lacking capacity and give instructions on their behalf. A litigation friend can be a family member or professional, but will not (save in exceptional circumstances) be the solicitor themselves.[13] The Official Solicitor is the litigation friend of last resort, and more detail about his role is available at *https://www.gov.uk/government/organisations/official-solicitor-and-public-trustee/about*. Guidance about the role of litigation friends in the Court of Protection is available at *http://www.law.manchester.ac.uk/about/news/litigation-friend-guidance/*.

---

13 If a suitable panel is established, it may in due course be possible for solicitors to be appointed directly to represent the subject of proceedings before the Court of Protection as 'accredited legal representatives'.

5.4 Advocates

There are a range of independent advocates appointed under the MCA 2005, the Mental Health Act 1983 and also the Care Act 2014 who may be involved with vulnerable clients. Aside from statutory advocates many advocates are also appointed from the voluntary sector on a privately paid basis and often from personal care budgets. It is always important to check the basis upon which the advocate has been commissioned to provide the services to your client, because each will be providing a somewhat different function.

Advocates will often play a vital role in supporting vulnerable clients, and may well play a particularly important role in assisting the client to communicate with you for purposes of providing instructions. However, an advocate will never, by virtue of their role alone, be in a position to provide you with those instructions.

5.5 Appropriate Adults in criminal matters

Under the Police and Criminal Evidence Act 1984 (PACE) Codes of Practice, police custody sergeants must secure an Appropriate Adult (AA) to safeguard the rights and welfare of vulnerable people (children aged 10–17 and mentally vulnerable adults) who are detained and questioned by the police. The role includes:

- to support, advise and assist the detained person, particularly while they are being questioned
- to observe whether the police are acting properly, fairly and with respect for the rights of the detained person – and to tell them if they are not

- to assist with communication between the detained person and the police
- to ensure that the detained person understands their rights and that the AA has a role in protecting those rights.

An AA should be someone who is completely independent of the police and, where possible the vulnerable person (although parents often do act as AA for a child or young person). It is desirable that they should have a sound understanding of, and experience or training in, dealing with the needs of juveniles, vulnerable adults or mentally disordered people. An AA cannot, merely because of their position, give instructions to a solicitor on behalf of the individuals they are to assist.

6 Influence and undue influence

There are a significant class of people who are unable to take their own decisions but whose inability to do so stems from the influence exercised over them by others (for example family members), rather than from an impairment of, or disturbance in, their mind or brain.

The law treats such vulnerable individuals differently to those lacking capacity for the purposes of the MCA 2005: because the person has capacity to make their own decision, no other person may take decisions on their behalf.

In these circumstances it is possible for any person or body concerned as to whether the individual is under duress to seek the assistance of the High Court to provide its protection under its inherent jurisdiction.[14] The High Court has the power to grant injunctive or other relief with the aim of putting in place a framework to enable the individual to make their own decisions.

14 See *Re L (Vulnerable Adults with Capacity: Court's Jurisdiction)* [2012] EWCA Civ 253

In your first meeting with a vulnerable client, information may come from an intermediary, such as a family member, carer or concerned neighbour. In the majority of cases their assistance is well intentioned and they will be communicating on behalf of, and with the consent of, the client.

However, you should be aware of the possibility of conflicts of interest or, in some cases, undue influence. Your overriding duty is to your client and you must ensure that your instructions are from your client, free of undue influence of others. So, if your client has capacity to do so, you should confirm your instructions directly with the client by seeing them on their own, especially if detailed information has been provided by someone else.

Clients may seek legal advice (for example to make a will, an LPA or a significant gift) because they have been influenced or told by someone, such as a family member, that they ought to do so. Such 'influence' may be well-intentioned and sensible. However, if you suspect that a client's instructions are the result of coercion or pressure ('undue influence'), you need to exercise your professional judgment as to whether you can proceed or continue to act on the client's behalf.

Your duties in relation to assessing the possibility of undue influence bearing upon your client are underpinned by the indicative behaviours in chapter 1 of the SRA Code. In particular IB 1.6 and IB 1.28 directly address the issue of undue influence:

- IB (1.6) 'in taking instructions and during the course of the retainer, [have] proper regard to your client's mental capacity or other vulnerability, such as incapacity or duress.'
- IB (1.28) '"acting for a client when there are reasonable grounds for believing that the instructions are affected by duress or undue influence

without satisfying yourself that they represent the client's wishes"... would demonstrate that you have failed to comply with the Code.'

6.1 Presumption of undue influence

6.1.1 Gifts

Undue influence may be a factor even when there is no evidence of any coercion or pressure. If an individual is contemplating making a significant lifetime gift, undue influence is presumed where there is a relationship of trust and confidence between the client and the recipient of the gift, (for example, care giver and care receiver, patient and doctor, solicitor and client), and the proposed gift requires an explanation (for example, it is an absurdly generous gift, or a gift of their main asset, such as their home, perhaps to just one of their children).

Once the presumption of undue influence has arisen, it is not sufficient for the recipient to demonstrate that the individual had capacity to make the gift, and that there was no actual coercion or influence. It is important that the individual has their own independent legal advice, considering all the relevant information and risks, before making a free and fully informed decision to go ahead with the gift.

6.1.2 Testamentary dispositions

This 'presumption' of undue influence does not arise for testamentary dispositions. Persuading an individual to include a specific individual as a beneficiary in their will would not necessarily amount to undue influence. Coercive behaviour is usually required.

However, if the client is particularly elderly or frail, then less obviously aggressive methods might amount to undue influence.

6.2 No actual evidence of undue influence but concerns remain

Where there is no evidence of undue influence or pressure[15] but the client appears to want to continue with a transaction that you consider to be against their best interests, you should see the client alone (or with a neutral third party if the client wishes someone else to be present to support them or assist communication). In doing so you should explain the consequences of the instructions the client has given and get confirmation (preferably in writing) that the client wishes to proceed.

15 See *A Local Authority v DL & Ors* [2011] EWHC 1022 (Fam)

You should be mindful in circumstances such as these that a core principle of the MCA 2005 (and the common law) is that a decision you may consider to be unwise may nonetheless be a capacitous decision. It is therefore important that you probe carefully as to the driver for the decision where your suspicions are raised and keep a detailed note of your discussion.

It may be preferable to use an independent advocate or interpreter or other assistance from an independent source, rather than relying on a family member or carer to communicate the client's wishes.

7 Case studies for practitioners

A Working with disabled clients

Mrs Jones' marriage has broken down after forty years and she decides to seek legal advice about a divorce. She has a severe visual impairment but does not want anyone to know that she is thinking about a divorce, so she wants to meet with a solicitor on her own. She telephones a local solicitor's firm to book an appointment and is put through to the team secretary of the firm's family law department, Ms Clare Robinson.

Clare takes some details from her and explains that the first available appointment is the following Tuesday at 09:00. Mrs Jones asks if she could have a later appointment because, as a result of her visual impairment, she finds it easier to travel around when the streets are less busy. Clare asks if she would prefer a home visit. Mrs Jones is grateful for the offer but explains that she does not want her husband to know anything about the visit. She says that she is able to find her way to the office but asks if a member of staff can guide her into the building from the street as she is not familiar with the office. She also asks if any written documentation can be sent by e-mail or provided in large print format. Clare assures her that this will not be a problem. She also asks if the firm could provide a digital recorder for her to record any meetings so that she can remind herself of discussions and key points that are made. Clare says the firm would be happy to lend her a digital recorder for these purposes and can also let her use it to record instructions rather than e-mailing them if that would be easier for her, but will ask for it back when the matter is completed.

Clare makes the appointment for later on Tuesday and then explains Mrs Jones' needs to Mrs Temple, the solicitor who will be acting for Mrs Jones. She also speaks to the reception staff to make them aware of Mrs Jones' additional needs and Mary Baker, the lead receptionist, says she will wait outside the office to greet Mrs Jones.

On the morning of her appointment, Clare reminds the reception staff that Mrs Jones is coming in and discovers that Mary is off sick and that reception is short staffed as a result. She therefore waits outside for Mrs Jones herself, having checked that the reception area, toilets and meeting room are free from clutter and other trip hazards. At the meeting Mrs Temple provides Mrs Jones with the digital recorder. She advises her about divorce proceedings and how to approach the division of money and assets. She discusses with her whether she will need additional support given that she will now be living on her own.

Mrs Jones is so impressed by the firm's service that she recommends the firm to her local support group for people who are visually impaired.

B Working with clients who may lack capacity

Tom O'Sullivan was 38 years old when he was involved in a road traffic accident. On his way home from work as a graphic designer, he was knocked off his bicycle by a lorry turning left across the cycle lane he was travelling in. He suffered a severe closed head injury, a fractured shoulder and massive bruising to both legs. He was in hospital for nearly 6 months and then had several months attending out-patient appointments for physiotherapy and other forms of rehabilitation. When he returned to work over a year after the accident he was only able to perform routine clerical work. In order to keep up mortgage payments and provide for their two young children, Tom's wife returned to full-time work. After a few months of becoming increasingly frustrated with his mundane job, Tom resigned and has barely worked since then.

Shortly after the accident, with the help of his father and supported by his wife, Tom seeks advice from you about claiming damages against the lorry driver and the company that employed him. It took some time to gather together the medical reports and the information in relation to financial loss, but eventually the claim is issued almost three years after the accident. Although by that time Tom had largely recovered from his physical injuries, he complained that he continued to suffer from a complete loss of the senses of smell and taste, some hearing loss, forgetfulness, headaches, anxiety and mood swings. However, he seemed able to provide accurate information relating to the claim and to understand the advice given to him by you and counsel.

The defence denied liability and alleged contributory negligence as Tom had had an after-work drink before cycling home. Tom's counsel had advised that this could be assessed as high as 50 per cent. Following negotiations, the defence made a payment into court and Tom, accompanied by his wife, father and solicitor attended a conference at counsel's office to discuss the offer. During the course of the meeting Tom became increasingly angry, distressed and tearful, but continued to ask relevant questions and put forward cogent arguments for seeking a higher offer. Counsel expresses some concern about Tom's behaviour.

After the conference, you receive a phone call from Tom's wife, saying that she was concerned about personality changes since the accident and particularly his mood swings and depression which had got worse since the conference. She also let slip that he had talked about committing suicide, although he had asked her not to tell anyone for fear of upsetting the family. She asks you to speed up the negotiations and reach a settlement – any settlement – as soon as possible, even if they could not get the amount of damages they wanted, as she was worried about the effect of prolonged court proceedings on Tom's condition.

Points for consideration about litigation and settlement

- You should ask to see Tom alone to make a careful assessment of Tom's capacity to give you instructions, and to consider whether the presumption of capacity continues to apply or was rebutted by the new information about Tom's condition and behaviour.
- You should notify counsel of your concerns and keep counsel apprised of the steps that are being taken to ascertain whether Tom has litigation capacity to conduct the proceedings.
- You will probably decide to seek an expert opinion, for example from a consultant in neuropsychiatric rehabilitation, to assess how Tom's brain injury may be affecting his ability to provide you with instructions. The letter of instruction to the expert should set out clearly the issues relating to his claim and the decisions required of him. The solicitor should also refer to the judgments in *Dunhill v Burgin* [2014] UKSC 18 and *Masterman-Lister v Brutton & Co (Nos. 1 and 2)* [2002] EWCA Civ 1889. You will need to seek Tom's consent to the examination by carefully explaining to him that any settlement could be invalid if he were later found to lack capacity to conduct the legal proceedings.
- If Tom refuses to consent to the medical examination, you will need to make your own assessment of Tom's capacity based on the available evidence. With or without a medical opinion you should keep a careful record of the assessment of capacity and the reasons for the conclusions reached.

- If you conclude that Tom continues to have capacity to conduct the proceedings, then you can continue to act on Tom's instructions. You should discuss with Tom his wife's concerns and the possible effect of the court proceedings and how Tom can best be supported during the process by you or a third party.
- If you conclude that Tom now lacks capacity to conduct the proceedings, a litigation friend must be appointed to conduct the proceedings on his behalf. The solicitor should discuss with Tom, his wife and his father who might be the most appropriate person to ask the court to be appointed as Tom's litigation friend.
- If you consider that there is no one among Tom's family or friends who is able to conduct the case and has no conflict of interest, you may wish to contact the Official Solicitor who is the last resort litigation friend. The Official Solicitor will require confirmation that Tom lacks litigation capacity to conduct the proceedings and information on how Tom's legal costs are to be paid.
- If you conclude that Tom now lacks capacity to conduct the proceedings and Tom continues to assert his own capacity to instruct you, you should inform the court hearing the claim and an application should be made to determine if Tom has lost capacity and, if so, for the appointment of a litigation friend.

C Working with clients who may be vulnerable to undue influence

Mrs Bryan is 79 and has early onset dementia. Her previous solicitor acted for her and her late husband in the preparation of their wills.

Mrs Bryan's son Don has arranged an appointment for his mother at your offices to review her will, following the death of her husband. She is brought to the meeting by Don, who remains in the waiting room, while you see Mrs Bryan alone. She tells you during your meeting that she has recently rented out her own home and has moved in to live with Don, and his family. Neither Mrs Bryan nor her son Don are existing clients of your firm.

You receive a letter from Mrs Bryan shortly after the meeting, telling you that as she has decided to live with Don permanently, that she is selling her own house and would like you to handle the conveyancing. She further advises you that she is using the proceeds of sale to pay towards an extension, a conservatory and replacement windows and a new kitchen in Don's property.

Points for consideration:

As Mrs Bryan's arrangements and plans may result in some vulnerability, you should consider the following action:

- You should (with Mrs Bryan's authority) obtain a copy of her previous will, and discuss her reasons both for the change in solicitor and any substantive changes to the terms of her will.
- You should have a further face-to-face meeting with Mrs Bryan, to discuss her plans for her property and assess her mental capacity to provide instructions to you in relation to each of the proposed transactions. If you are in doubt, you should seek a medical opinion about her capacity to make the relevant decisions and to instruct you. Your instructions to the medical professional must set out the specific criteria to be considered for each transaction.
- Mrs Bryan will need advice (inter alia) on whether she should have a legal

- or beneficial interest in her son's house in exchange for her planned contribution, as she will need an 'exit plan' should the living arrangement break down for any reason.
- You should also consider whether Mrs Bryan may be at risk of undue influence, most obviously in relation to the money she is planning to 'gift' to Don to spend on his property, where the presumption of undue influence may arise. She may be dependent on Don and his family for her care and accommodation. She may not be entirely happy with the planned course of action but feel unable to express that to her family.
- You should endeavour to see Mrs Bryan alone, to enable her to explore fully the risks and benefits of the proposed transactions

D Working with clients with learning disability

John and Mary Smith need advice about possible care proceedings being taken in respect of their two year-old child. They have received a pre-proceedings letter from the local authority which urges them to take legal advice and which gives your firm's name (among others) as appropriate specialists. An appointment has been made, by telephone, by an independent advocate Mrs Jones, who said she was calling on behalf of the Smiths as they both have learning disabilities and find formal telephone conversations and correspondence problematic. She has left her contact number.

Although you are a very experienced care proceedings lawyer, you have not worked with clients with learning disabilities before, or with an independent advocate. Colleagues tell you that, in general terms, independent advocates help the people they work with to participate in decisions that affect their lives, to understand what they are being told and enable them to make their views, opinions and decisions known.

Your colleagues say that, similarly to working with intermediaries in court, having the assistance of an independent advocate is essential for ensuring that you can communicate effectively with your clients and that they can communicate effectively with you.

Points for consideration:

- Recent case law involving parents with learning difficulties (for example *A Father v SBC & Others* [2014] EWFC 6) emphasises the need to ensure that the processes by which decisions about the children are made are fair and that the parents are sufficiently involved in that process. The Human Rights Act 1998 and the Equality Act 2010 are therefore likely to be particularly relevant for your clients.
- All aspects of this case, including the Smiths' contact with you and the local authority, how meetings and correspondence are managed, what services are offered, how decisions are reached, what adjustments have been made, will be pertinent when considering whether there has been compliance with the legislation.

Before the meeting

- Check if the advocate will be attending with the Smiths. Ask what you can do, at this stage, to ensure the Smiths will be able to participate fully. For example, normally, your new clients are asked to complete some paperwork while waiting for their appointment and they are given some generic information about the firm's client services and legal aid. Consider sending this paperwork to Mrs Jones, in advance of the meeting, together

with a list of questions you will be asking the Smiths, expressed in plain English. You could also provide and Easyread version for the Smiths. This will give your clients an opportunity to think about their answers, before the meeting.
- Check the Working Together with Parents Network website for a wide range of information and resources relating to parents with learning disabilities.
- Start to consider likely case management issues that will arise in the office and at court including the Advocates Gateway resources and toolkits referenced at paragraph 3.3 above.

At the meeting
- Ensure the Smiths are happy for Mrs Jones to be present at the meeting.
- Check with the Smiths how you can make communication effective, for you both, during the meeting and with any follow up correspondence or actions.
- Consider whether there is any conflict of interest as between the Smiths or the potential for a conflict to arise.
- If you believe that the mental capacity of one or both of the Smiths to be at issue follow the relevant guidance contained within section 4 of this practice note.
- Without making assumptions about the degree of learning disability a client has, or how this impacts on their ability to engage with you, you know that the following steps are likely to be useful, and may be essential: you may need to repeat things several times, sometimes re-phrasing, but always using short sentences, one concrete idea at a time, in a logical and clear order; you may have to take into account a reduced ability to read, write, concentrate, process and recall information and a difficulty with organisational skills such as time-keeping.
- You will need to check understanding frequently – not by asking questions that only require a yes/no answer, but by asking short, simple, open questions designed to elicit from your client, for example: what they have understood to be happening, or what they will need to do, or what next steps you will be taking on their behalf.
- Explain to the Smiths the role of the different professionals such as the children's guardian.
- Check that the Smiths know where the court building is and how to get there for hearings.

****

Other Guidance

Practice Direction of 24 March 2012: Citation of Authorities

Preamble

1 This Practice Direction is issued in order to clarify the practice and procedure governing the citation of authorities and applies throughout the Senior Courts of England and Wales, including the Crown Court, in county courts and in magistrates' courts.

Repeal

2 Practice Direction (Court of Appeal: Citation of Authority) [1995] 1 WLR 1096 of 22 June 1995, Practice Statement (Court of Appeal: Authorities) [1996] 1 WLR 854 of 15 May 1996, paragraph 8 of Practice Statement (Supreme Court: Judgments) [1998] 1 WLR 825 of 22 April 1998, paragraph 3 of Practice Direction (Judgments: Form and Citation) [2001] 1 WLR 194 of 11 January 2001, and, in so far as they remain in force, paragraphs 10.1 and 10.2 of Practice Direction ((Court of Appeal (Civil Division)) [1999] 1 WLR 1027 of 19 April 1999 are hereby revoked.

Variation

3 Practice Direction (Criminal Proceedings: Consolidation) [2002] 1 WLR 2870 of 8 July 2002 (as amended) is varied so that all references to paragraph 10.1 of Practice Direction (Court of Appeal (Civil Division)) [1999] 1 WLR 1027; [1999] 2 All ER 490 are to read as references to paragraphs 5–13 of this Practice Direction.

4 Practice Direction 52 supplementing CPR Pt 52 is varied so that paragraph 15.11(2) reads as follows:

> '(2) The bundle of authorities should comply with the requirements of Practice Direction: Citation of Authorities (2012) and in general –
>
> (a) have the relevant passages of the authorities marked;
> (b) not include authorities for propositions not in dispute; and
> (c) not contain more than 10 authorities unless the scale of the appeal warrants more extensive citation.'

Citation of Authority

5 When authority is cited, whether in written or oral submissions, the following practice should be followed.

6 Where a judgment is reported in the Official Law Reports (AC, QB, Ch, Fam) published by the Incorporated Council of Law Reporting for England and Wales, that report must be cited. These are the most authoritative reports; they contain a summary of the argument. Other series of reports and official transcripts of judgment may only be used when a case is not reported in the Official Law Reports.

7 If a judgment is not (or not yet) reported in the Official Law Reports but it is reported in the Weekly Law Reports (WLR) or the All England Law Reports (All ER) that report should be cited. If the case is reported in both the WLR and the All ER either report may properly be cited.

8 If a judgment is not reported in the Official Law Reports, the WLR, or the All ER, but it is reported in any of the authoritative specialist series of reports which contain a headnote and are made by individuals holding a Senior Courts qualification (for the purposes of section 115 of the Courts and Legal Services Act 1990), the specialist report should be cited.

9 Where a judgment is not reported in any of the reports referred to in paragraphs [6] to [8] above, but is reported in other reports, they may be cited.

10 Where a judgment has not been reported, reference may be made to the official transcript if that is available, not the handed-down text of the judgment, as this may have been subject to late revision after the text was handed down. Official transcripts may be obtained from, for instance, BAILII (http://www.bailii.org/). An unreported case should not usually be cited unless it contains a relevant statement of legal principle not found in reported authority.

11 Occasions arise when one report is fuller than another, or when there are discrepancies between reports. On such occasions, the practice outlined above need not be followed, but the court should be given a brief explanation why this course is being taken, and the alternative references should be given.

12 If a judgment under appeal has been reported before the hearing but after skeleton arguments have been filed with the court, and counsel wish to argue from the published report rather than from the official transcript, the court should be provided with photocopies of the report for the use of the court.

13 Judgments reported in any series of reports, including those of the Incorporated Council of Law Reporting, should be provided either by way of a photocopy of the published report or by way of a copy of a reproduction of the judgment in electronic form that has been authorised by the publisher of the relevant series, but in any event (1) the report must be presented to the court in an easily legible form (a 12-point font is preferred but a 10- or 11-point font is acceptable) and (2) the advocate presenting the report is satisfied that it has not been reproduced in a garbled form from the data source. In any case of doubt the court will rely on the printed text of the report (unless the editor of the report has certified that an electronic version is more accurate because it corrects an error contained in an earlier printed text of the report).

14 This Direction is made by the Lord Chief Justice with the agreement of the Master of the Rolls and the President of the Family Division. It is issued in accordance with the procedure laid down in Part 1 of Schedule 2 to the Constitutional Reform Act 2005.

The Right Honourable
The Lord Judge
The Lord Chief Justice of England and Wales

Practice Guidance of 16 January 2014: Transparency in the Court of Protection – Publication of Judgments

The purpose of this Guidance

1 This Guidance (together with similar Guidance issued at the same time for the family courts) is intended to bring about an immediate and significant change in practice in relation to the publication of judgments in family courts and the Court of Protection.

2 In both courts there is a need for greater transparency in order to improve public understanding of the court process and confidence in the court system. At present too few judgments are made available to the public, which has a legitimate interest in being able to read what is being done by the judges in its name. The Guidance will have the effect of increasing the number of judgments available for publication (even if they will often need to be published in appropriately anonymised form).

3 In July 2011 Sir Nicholas Wall P issued, jointly with Bob Satchwell, Executive Director of the Society of Editors, a paper, *The Family Courts: Media Access & Reporting* (Media Access & Reporting), setting out a statement of the current state of the law. In their preface they recognised that the debate on increased transparency and public confidence in the family courts would move forward and that future consideration of this difficult and sensitive area would need to include the questions of access to and reporting of proceedings by the media, whilst maintaining the privacy of the families involved. The paper is to be found at: http://www.judiciary.gov.uk/Resources/JCO/Documents/Guidance/family-courts¬media-july2011.pdf

4 In April 2013 I issued a statement, *View from the President's Chambers: the Process of Reform*, [2013] Fam Law 548, in which I identified transparency as one of the three strands in the reforms which the family justice system is currently undergoing. I said:

'I am determined to take steps to improve access to and reporting of family proceedings. I am determined that the new Family Court should not be saddled, as the family courts are at present, with the charge that we are a system of secret and unaccountable justice. Work, commenced by my predecessor, is well underway. I hope to be in a position to make important announcements in the near future.'

5 That applies just as much to the issue of transparency in the Court of Protection.

6 Very similar issues arise in both the Family Court (as it will be from April 2014) and the Court of Protection in relation to the need to protect the personal privacy of children and vulnerable adults. The applicable rules differ, however, and this is something that needs attention. My starting point is that so far as possible the same rules and principles should apply in both the family courts (in due course the Family Court) and the Court of Protection.

7 I propose to adopt an incremental approach. Initially I am issuing this Guidance. This will be followed by further Guidance and in due course more formal Practice Directions and changes to the Rules (the Court of Protection Rules 2007 and the Family Procedure Rules 2010). Changes to primary legislation are unlikely in the near future.

8 As provided in paragraph 14 below, this Guidance applies only to judgments delivered by certain judges. In due course consideration will be given to extending it to judgments delivered by other judges.

The legal framework

9 The effect of section 12 of the Administration of Justice Act 1960 is that it is a contempt of court to publish a judgment in a Court of Protection case unless either the judgment has been delivered in public or, where delivered in private, the judge has authorised publication. In the latter case, the judge normally gives permission for the judgment to be published on condition that the published version protects the anonymity of the person who is subject of the proceedings and members of their family.

10 In every case the terms on which publication is permitted are a matter for the judge and will be set out by the judge in a rubric at the start of the judgment.

11 The normal terms as described in paragraph 9 may be appropriate in a case where no-one wishes to discuss the proceedings otherwise than anonymously. But they may be inappropriate, for example, where family members wish to discuss their experiences in public, identifying themselves and making use of the judgment. Equally, they may be inappropriate in cases where findings have been made against a person and someone else contends and/or the court concludes that it is in the public interest for that person to be identified in any published version of the judgment.

12 If any party wishes to identify himself or herself, or any other party or person, as being a person referred to in any published version of the judgment, their remedy is to seek an order of the court and a suitable modification of the rubric: Media Access & Reporting, para 82; *Re RB (Adult) (No 4)* [2011] EWHC 3017 (Fam), [2012] 1 FLR 466, paras [17], [19].

13 Nothing in this Guidance affects the exercise by the judge in any particular case of whatever powers would otherwise be available to regulate the publication of material relating to the proceedings. For example, where a judgment is likely to be used in a way that would defeat the purpose of any anonymisation, it is open to the judge to refuse to publish the judgment or to make an order restricting its use.

Guidance

14 This Guidance takes effect from 3 February 2014. It applies to all judgments in the Court of Protection delivered by the Senior Judge, nominated Circuit Judges and High Court Judges.

15 The following paragraphs of this Guidance distinguish between two classes of judgment:

(i) those that the judge *must* ordinarily allow to be published (paragraphs 16 and 17); and
(ii) those that *may* be published (paragraph 18).

16 Permission to publish a judgment should always be given whenever the judge concludes that publication would be in the public interest and whether or not a request has been made by a party or the media.

17 Where a judgment relates to matters set out in the Schedule below and a written judgment already exists in a publishable form or the judge has already ordered that

the judgment be transcribed, the starting point is that permission should be given for the judgment to be published unless there are compelling reasons why the judgment should not be published.

Schedule

Judgments arising from:

(i) any application for an order involving the giving or withholding of serious medical treatment and any other hearing held in public;

(ii) any application for a declaration or order involving a deprivation or possible deprivation of liberty;

(iii) any case where there is a dispute as to who should act as an attorney or a deputy;

(iv) any case where the issues include whether a person should be restrained from acting as an attorney or a deputy or that an appointment should be revoked or his or her powers should be reduced;

(v) any application for an order that an incapacitated adult (P) be moved into or out of a residential establishment or other institution;

(vi) any case where the sale of P's home is in issue

(vii) any case where a property and affairs application relates to assets (including P's home) of £1 million or more or to damages awarded by a court sitting in public;

(viii) any application for a declaration as to capacity to marry or to consent to sexual relations;

(ix) any application for an order involving a restraint on publication of information relating to the proceedings.

18 In all other cases, the starting point is that permission may be given for the judgment to be published whenever a party or an accredited member of the media applies for an order permitting publication, and the judge concludes that permission for the judgment to be published should be given.

19 In deciding whether and if so when to publish a judgment, the judge shall have regard to all the circumstances, the rights arising under any relevant provision of the European Convention on Human Rights, including Articles 6 (right to a fair hearing), 8 (respect for private and family life) and 10 (freedom of expression), and the effect of publication upon any current or potential criminal proceedings.

20 In all cases where a judge gives permission for a judgment to be published:

(i) public authorities and expert witnesses should be named in the judgment approved for publication, unless there are compelling reasons why they should not be so named;

(ii) the person who is the subject of proceedings in the Court of Protection and other members of their family should not normally be named in the judgment approved for publication unless the judge otherwise orders;

(iii) anonymity in the judgment as published should not normally extend beyond protecting the privacy of the adults who are the subject of the proceedings and other members of their families, unless there are compelling reasons to do so.

21 Unless the judgment is already in anonymised form, any necessary anonymisation of the judgment shall be carried out as the judge orders. The version approved for publication will contain such rubric as the judge specifies. Unless the rubric specified by the judge provides expressly to the contrary every published judgment shall be deemed to contain the following rubric:

'This judgment was delivered in private. The judge has given leave for this version of the judgment to be published on condition that (irrespective of what is contained in the judgment) in any published version of the judgment the anonymity of the incapacitated person and members of their family must be strictly preserved. All persons, including representatives of the media, must ensure that this condition is strictly complied with. Failure to do so will be a contempt of court.'

22 The judge will need to consider who should be ordered to bear the cost of transcribing the judgment. Unless the judge otherwise orders:

(i) in cases falling under paragraph 18, the cost of transcribing the judgment shall be borne by the party or person applying for publication of the judgment;

(ii) in other cases, the cost of transcribing the judgment shall be at public expense.

23 In all cases where permission is given for a judgment to be published, the version of the judgment approved for publication shall be made available, upon payment of any appropriate charge that may be required, to any person who requests a copy. Where a judgment to which paragraph 16 or 17 applies is approved for publication, it shall as soon as reasonably practicable be placed by the court on the BAILII website. Where a judgment to which paragraph 18 applies is approved for publication, the judge shall consider whether it should be placed on the BAILII website and, if so, it shall as soon as reasonably practicable be placed by the court on the BAILII website.

Sir James Munby, President of the Court of Protection

Guidance Note: Acting as a litigation friend in the Court of Protection

This Guidance, commissioned by the Department of Health, aims (inter alia) to enable more people to consider taking up the role of litigation friend for 'P' in the Court of Protection. It was written for non-legal advocates such as Independent Mental Capacity Advocates ('IMCAs') and Relevant Person's Representatives ('RPRs') as well as family members or friends of P and is of most relevance to applications relating to P's health and welfare (including those relating to deprivation of liberty). Extracts from the Guidance are reproduced here by permission of the author Alex Ruck Keene, Barrister of Thirty Nine Essex Street (a contributor to this book). The full Guidance is available at: www.law.manchester.ac.uk/medialibrary/Main%20site/LAC/Acting-as-a-Litigation-Friend-in-the-Court-of-Protection-October-2014.pdf

C Who can be a litigation friend for P in proceedings before the Court of Protection?

The criteria – introduction

25 In principle, anyone can act as a litigation friend for P (or indeed any other party to proceedings before the Court of Protection) if they:

1 Are able to conduct proceedings on behalf of P competently and fairly;
2 Have no interests adverse to that of P; and
3 Agree to act as litigation friend.

The Official Solicitor

****

28 … The Official Solicitor … applies strict acceptance criteria deciding whether to accept an invitation to act as litigation friend … in relation to P:

1 There must be evidence or a finding with regard to P's lack of relevant decision making capacity;
2 There must be no one else suitable and willing to act as litigation friend;
3 The Official Solicitor must be satisfied that there is security for the costs of legal representation of P or the case falls in one of the classes in which, exceptionally, he funds the litigation services out of, or partially out of, his budget …

29 All three of these criteria are applied strictly, which means that there are a significant number of cases in which the Official Solicitor will not act as litigation friend because:

- There is someone else who is suitable and willing to act as litigation friend; or
- … P is not eligible for legal aid and the Official Solicitor considers that they do not have sufficient money or disposable assets to be able to meet the costs of legal representation.

****

The criteria in more detail (1) suitability

31 The courts have considered the criteria for being a litigation friend in a number of cases, and have given the following guidance:

- The mere fact that a person (for instance a family member) has strong views as to where P's best interests lie does not automatically disqualify them from acting as P's litigation friend, especially where competent legal representatives are instructed by that (proposed) litigation friend:[1]
- However, where there is a family dispute concerning P's best interests, it would be rare for it to be appropriate for a family member to be appointed as P's litigation friend in proceedings relating to that dispute. If they were to be so appointed, they would have 'to demonstrate that he or she can, as P's litigation friend, take a balanced and even-handed approach to the relevant issues.'[2]

1 *AVS v NHS Foundation Trust and P PCT* [2011] EWCA Civ 7; [2011] COPLR Con Vol 219, at paragraph 28 per Ward LJ See also *WCC v AB and SB* [2013] COPLR 157 and *Westminster City Council v Manuela Sykes* [2014] EWHC B9 (COP).
2 *Re UF* [2013] EWHC 4289 (COP); [2014] COPLR forthcoming at paragraph 23 per Charles J.

32 There are reported cases in which IMCAs[3] and RPRs[4] have acted as litigation friends, and these cases represent the tip of the iceberg. The Court of Protection has recognised that there can be positive benefits to the appointment of such advocates to act as litigation friend for P. In AB v LCC (a case under s.21A MCA 2005), Mostyn J identified the following advantages to a paid RPR acting as litigation friend for P in such an application:

'i) they will probably have met the detained person;
ii) they provide continuity;
iii) it may be cost effective if having been involved it avoids the duplication of work by a publicly funded litigation friend;
iv) they may often be situated local to the geographical area where the detained person resides;
v) It does not require the detained person to meet yet more people which may be unsettling or confusing.'[5]

3 *Re M (Best Interests: Deprivation of Liberty)* [2013] EHWC 3456 (COP).
4 *AB v LCC (A Local Authority) and the Care Manager of BCH* [2011] EWHC 3151 (COP); [2012] COPLR 314.
5 At paragraph 43. Mostyn J also identified a number of disadvantages, but concluded that 'in many cases…the RPR can well fulfil [the litigation friend] role' (paragraph 45).

33 Advocates have also themselves identified positive benefits to acting as a litigation friend. In informal research conducted for purposes of writing this Guidance, those who have acted as litigation friends have emphasised, in particular, the added value that they feel that they can bring:

- from prior knowledge of and familiarity with P (where they had previously been involved with P through, for instance, an IMCA instruction);
- from their expertise in and understanding of the application of the MCA 2005 to health and social care;
- from the fact that they are in general, especially where P lives far from London, likely to be able to visit P more often than would a case-worker allocated the case in the Official Solicitor's office. The Official Solicitor will almost invariably appoint solicitors who are based locally and

therefore able to visit P, but advocates have identified a difference between solicitors reporting upon a visit and the litigation friend themselves being able to visit.

34 These advantages apply whether or not the advocate brings the application in P's name or agrees to act as litigation friend in proceedings brought by another person or body.

35 It is also important in this regard that the ability of an IMCA to act as litigation friend for P to bring an application to the Court of Protection... acts as a vital extension to their role in advocating for P's interests in decision-making involving public bodies:

- IMCAs are more often than not the only independent person involved whose sole function is to represent the person and to advocate for them in decision-making. Their right to challenge decisions extends as far as taking an issue to the Court of Protection. Further, because they can – in appropriate circumstances – take a challenge in P's name as P's litigation friend means that they can bring a challenge without the pressure of facing the additional costs that would be likely to be incurred if they applied in their own name;[6]
- If an IMCA considers that all avenues have not been exhausted in reaching the decision that is in P's best interests on an informal basis,[7] then – again – the potential for making an application to the Court of Protection in P's name can serve as a vital tool to ensure that they are fulfilling their responsibilities to P. Even if the IMCA goes no further than seeking legal advice as to whether an application is, in fact, appropriate, seeking such legal advice can – itself – be extremely useful in ensuring that the issues being considered in the informal decision-making process have properly been identified;
- By acting as litigation friend, the IMCA can also further P's interests by making an application to the Court of Protection where they consider that a delay in informal decision-making is having a negative impact on P. Conversely, where the application has been brought by someone else, an IMCA can assist to 'unlock' the situation by agreeing to act as a litigation friend and moving to minimise the delays to the resolution of the proceedings.

6 And also the need to pay court fees: discussed further at paragraph 153 below.
7 I.e. outside the Court of Protection as part of the process that must be followed for those doing acts in connection with the care and treatment or that individual can rely upon the defence contained in s 5 of the MCA 2005.

36 In short, therefore, paid RPRs and IMCAs in particular, should see the opportunity to act as a litigation friend for P (whether to bring a challenge on P's behalf or to accept an invitation to act) as a way to deploy their knowledge and expertise so as to bring real benefits to P. Above all, an advocate who knows P – or a family member – will be able to use that knowledge so as to be able to ensure that the 'real' P is at the heart of the proceedings.

37 It is very important to note, though, that the role of a statutory advocate and that of a litigation friend, whilst similar, are not the same. This gives rise to two issues:

- If they are to continue in the role for which they were previously appointed,[8] the advocate must be satisfied that they have the time to dedicate both to that role and to the separate task of acting as litigation friend;
- Equally importantly, and as discussed further in chapter E below, a

litigation friend is not, solely, P's advocate before the court in the sense of advancing arguments based upon their understanding of P's wishes and feelings. In some cases, an advocate may wish to retain the freedom to advocate P's wishes and feelings strongly to the court in their capacity as advocate without having to proceed by the more limited and specific task appointed to a litigation friend. In such a case, the advocate should consider carefully whether they should continue their original role and allow someone else to act as litigation friend. In some cases, an advocate may also feel that there are other reasons why they would find it hard to take on the role of litigation friend whilst still continuing to act as advocate.

8   Which will depend very much upon the nature of the appointment.

38 It is also important to remember that it is also always possible for the advocate themselves to bring proceedings:[9]

- In the case of an advocate other than an RPR, they would need the permission of the court; an RPR does not need permission to bring an application.[10] If an advocate brings proceedings themselves, they would be treated as any other party to the proceedings, and could (within reason) argue the case that they wanted to advocate as to where P's best interests lay as strongly as they wished. As we will see, a litigation friend appointed to act for P has a somewhat more limited function.
- An advocate bringing the application themselves would have to fund the application and the proceedings themselves or to secure funding for this purpose, as well as to pay any court fees (for more on funding, see chapter I). In such a case, it is suggested that if the advocate is employed by an organisation, the organisation should meet the costs of the application, but that would be a matter for resolution between the advocate and their employer (and the organisation would, itself, have to consider where it is to obtain funding for this purpose);
- Whilst the matters above means, realistically, that in most cases the advocate would not be able to bring an application themselves, it is always important to remember that this is – technically – an option;
- The advocate should always therefore ask themselves as part of their consideration of whether to take on the role of litigation friend so as to bring an application in P's name why they cannot bring the application themselves in their own right.

9   Specific provisions have been made in relation to IMCAs. Regulation 7 of The Mental Capacity Act 2005 (Independent Mental Capacity Advocates) (General) Regulations 2006 (SI 2006/1832) provides that if an IMCA has been instructed to represent a person ('P') in relation to any matter, and (b) a decision affecting P (including a decision as to his capacity) is made in that matter, an IMCA has the same rights to bring a challenge as a person caring for P or interested in his welfare:
10 Rule 51(2A) of the Court of Protection Rules 2007.

39 Even when an advocate – and, indeed, any litigation friend – has been appointed to act as litigation friend, they must always keep in mind the possibility that they may, at some stage, cease to meet the suitability criteria …

The criteria in more detail (2) agreement

40 No one can be forced to act as litigation friend, and a litigation friend must either (a) actively put themselves forward to act as one (for instance by bringing an application in P's name as P's litigation friend; or (b) agree to an invitation. These two situations merit separate consideration.

1   An advocate proposing themselves as litigation friend for P in bringing an application is – self-evidently – agreeing to act as P's litigation friend. Because the advocate is 'making the running,' they will need to be satisfied that they have in place the necessary arrangements to meet the costs both of acting as litigation friend and of instructing solicitors …;

2   An IMCA who is being asked to act as a litigation friend for P is in a slightly different position. They are, in effect, in a position of some power, because they are presumably being asked to act as litigation friend so as to allow the proceedings to go forward. In such a case, the proposed litigation friend is quite entitled to say that they will only act if they are given sufficient funding to allow them to instruct legal representatives.[11] This is, in essence, exactly what the Official Solicitor does. In such a situation, what will then happen will depend upon whether P is eligible for legal aid:

- If P is eligible for legal aid, then an order will be made entitling the litigation friend to sign the relevant paperwork on P's behalf so as to receive legal aid which covers the cost of the fees incurred by the legal representatives;
- If P is not entitled to legal aid, then an order will be made making it clear that the litigation friend is entitled to spend a certain amount of P's money on legal fees. In either case, the fees that are actually incurred by the lawyers will be scrutinised carefully by the court at the end of the case. This will primarily be a matter for the legal representatives to address, but one of the litigation friend's roles is always to have in mind whether the steps that are being taken by the lawyers are necessary and proportionate.

3   It is therefore suggested that, in a case where an advocate is invited by the court to act as a litigation friend in a case brought by a public authority, the advocate can quite properly make that appointment conditional on receiving funding from the relevant public authority to allow them to spend adequate time upon their role as litigation friend. In other words, the advocate can say 'I am not happy to accept the invitation to act as litigation friend for P without payment for my time, so as to ensure that my other clients can continue to receive IMCA services.'

4   In informal research conducted for purposes of writing this Guidance, a frequent concern expressed by IMCAs was that, by accepting an invitation to act as litigation friend, they might somehow end up being required to pay the costs of one or more of the other parties to the proceedings. Whilst it exists, this risk is, in reality, very small (as explained further at paragraphs 138–139). To make the risk even smaller, IMCAs in cases brought by public authorities routinely ask for and are given undertakings – i.e. are promised – by the public authorities that the public authority in question will not seek to make them pay any of their costs. It is quite proper to make the giving of such an undertaking a pre-condition of agreeing to act as a litigation friend.

[11] Whether a litigation friend has to instruct lawyers is discussed at paragraphs 47–50 below.

41 It is important to emphasise that in agreeing either to put themselves forward to act as litigation friend or agreeing to accept an invitation to act as litigation friend, an advocate must take into account that:

1   They must be satisfied that they can conduct the litigation 'competently.' There is no definition in the MCA 2005 or the Court of Protection Rules as to what constitutes 'competence' for these purposes. It is suggested that it does not equate to perfection, but rather to approaching the task with suitable degree of detachment to be able to make objective decisions, as

well as suitable knowledge of the principles of the MCA 2005. It is also suggested that conducting litigation competently also involves the litigation friend being able to dedicate adequate time to devote to the task and to being aware when it is necessary to obtain legal advice and/or representation (and having access to such advice/representation); and

2   Whilst it might superficially seem better to take on a case to meet an immediate need even if the advocate has doubts as to whether they will be able to take the matter to a conclusion, care needs to be taken here. In general, it may very well cause disruption to the proceedings further down the line if the advocate then withdraws as litigation friend, and a judge is likely to look rather dimly upon someone withdrawing (for instance) on the basis that the workload was more than was anticipated. However, there may be circumstances in which unless the advocate acts as litigation friend for purposes of getting a matter to court, it simply will not get there and the advocate may at that point feel that the priority is to bring P's situation to the attention of the court even if they cannot then take it further forward. The IMCA or other advocate in such a case may well be justified then in bringing the application and making very clear from the outset that they are not in a position to do more than put the matter before the court. This is discussed further at paragraph 50 below.

****

D Becoming a litigation friend and instructing lawyers

How is a litigation friend appointed?

43   There are two ways in which a litigation friend can be appointed: without a court order and with one:

1   If there is no deputy, a person can become a litigation friend for a protected party or for a child without a court order if they file and serve a certificate of suitability (with a statement of truth) on a form COP 22, which must also include the information set out in Practice Direction 17A.[12]

2   A person can only be appointed to act as litigation friend for P with a court order.

12   In particular that the litigation friend knows or believes that the child or protected party lacks capacity to conduct the proceedings themselves, and the grounds of that belief set out above. If the belief is based upon medical opinion, or the opinion of another suitably qualified expert, the document should be attached to the certificate.

44   An order appointing a person as a litigation friend for P (if P is joined to the proceedings) can be made either at the court's own initiative or upon application by any person (i.e. not just by the proposed litigation friend). Any application must be supported by evidence that will allow the court to be satisfied (as it must also be satisfied if it is contemplating making the order of its own initiative) that:

- The proposed litigation friend can fairly and competently conduct proceedings on behalf of the individual in question;
- The proposed litigation friend has no interests adverse to the individual in question; and
- The proposed litigation friend consents to the appointment.

45   Perhaps curiously, a person other than the Official Solicitor who either actively advances themselves to act as litigation friend for P or whom the court is contemplating of its own motion appointing to act for P does not, formally, need to

file and serve a certificate of suitability, although (as set out above) the court will still need to be satisfied that they meet the criteria for appointment before making the order.

46 Although this power is rarely exercised, it should be noted that, if the court considers that it requires further evidence before it can grant someone's application to be appointed as litigation friend, it will make directions to enable to such evidence to be obtained.

Does a litigation friend need to instruct lawyers?

47 In a judgment given in August 2014,[13] the President of the Court of Protection held that a 'lay' litigation friend[14] does not need to instruct solicitors in order to act as litigation friend and to conduct proceedings on behalf of P. In other words, a 'lay' litigation friend does not need to instruct solicitors in order – for instance – to issue an application in the Court of Protection. However, the President also held that a 'lay' litigation friend[15] will need the permission of the court to act as an advocate on behalf of P – in other words – to address the court. If they do not, they will be committing a criminal offence.

13 *Re X and Ors (Deprivation of Liberty)* [2014] EWCOP 25 and [2014] EWCOP 37.
14 I.e. a litigation friend who is not, themselves, a practising lawyer or appropriately qualified legal executive.
15 Or a legally qualified litigation friend who does not have rights of audience.

48 Lay litigation friends will also need to be aware that, as matters stand, they may encounter difficulties in seeking to instruct a barrister to appear on their behalf as an advocate without instructing a solicitor. The rules in this regard regarding what is called 'direct access' or 'Public Access'[16] – i.e. instructing a barrister without using a solicitor – were not designed with this situation in mind, and the legal position in this regard is not clear.

16 For more details about the Public Access scheme and a list of barristers who offer their services on this basis, see www.barcouncil.org.uk/instructing-a-barrister/public-access/. There is no specific category identified as 'Court of Protection' or 'Mental Capacity' work in the directory, but at least some of those who offer services under the 'Mental Health' heading will be able to act in cases before the Court of Protection.

49 Informal research conducted for purposes of writing this advice found that some experienced IMCAs would consider acting without a solicitor in a straightforward case (and, indeed, that some had already done so). Courts are – in general – careful not to allow those who are not legally qualified but who are receiving money for their services to appear as advocates before them. However, and although no guidance has been issued as to when permission should be granted to a litigation friend to act as an advocate and formally to address the court, there is no reason why an experienced IMCA should not seek such permission in an appropriate case.

50 There is, therefore, a very important place for litigation friends to conduct proceedings without the need to act through lawyers (seeking appropriate permission to address the court), and it may well be that the practice spreads as IMCAs and other advocates become more familiar with acting as litigation friends. Examples of situations where an IMCA (or other advocate) may well consider acting as a litigation friend without a solicitor would be:

- Where a public authority has made an application for an order authorising the deprivation of a person's liberty in a supported living placement (i.e. outside the scope of the 'DoLS regime'), P has been joined to the proceedings, and there is no serious dispute as to whether the deprivation of liberty is in P's best interests;[17]

- Where there is a dispute about a limited single issue (for example contact between P and a family member) which has been brought before the court by a local authority, where the IMCA has sufficient familiarity with P's circumstances and wishes and feelings, and where the IMCA does not consider that there is any mismatch between P's wishes and feelings and where their best interests may ultimately lie;
- For the more limited purpose of bringing a sufficiently urgent and serious dispute to the attention of the court where, as in the circumstances set out at paragraph 92 below, no other person/body (and, in particular the public body with statutory responsibility for P) is prepared to make the application. In such case, the advocate should make clear in their application the efforts that they have gone to persuade the public authority to bring proceedings, and indicate whether
  (1) they would be prepared to continue acting as litigation friend for P in the event that the public authority, in fact, takes over as applicant (and, if so, whether they would be prepared to continue acting without the benefit of legal representation – it may well be that an advocate would feel more comfortable acting without the benefit of such representation if they are not 'making the running' in the proceedings);
  (2) they would wish to cease acting as litigation friend upon the matter being before the court and a suitable alternative litigation friend being identified – most obviously –instance – the Official Solicitor.[18]

17 For more on the role of a litigation friend in cases involving a deprivation of liberty, see further paragraphs 74–76 below.
18 If the proposal is the advocate ceases to act as litigation friend in favour of the Official Solicitor, it would be very sensible for the advocate to identify whether P is eligible for legal aid and/or otherwise in a position to meet the Official Solicitor's legal costs, because, as noted at paragraph 28 above, the Official Solicitor will not accept an invitation to act as litigation friend without a guarantee that his legal costs will be met.

51 Subject to the caveat that spending P's money always requires the authority of the court (or an attorney/deputy with appropriate authority), it would always be open to an advocate to instruct solicitors for limited purposes – for instance, to provide initial advice or to draft an application. Equally, most reputable community care solicitors will usually provide an initial consultation for free, and an advocate may well be able to gauge during the course of that consultation whether they feel confident to be able to proceed without the benefit of further legal representation.

52 It should be noted that a professional litigation friend (i.e. a litigation friend other than a carer or family member acting voluntarily) acting as both litigation friend and, in effect, P's solicitor for purposes of conducting the litigation may well feel that they should be entitled to greater reimbursement, not least because of the greater time that they will no doubt spend on the case. For instance, drafts of witness statements are often prepared by solicitors instructed by the litigation friend; if solicitors are not instructed, then the advocate will not just be considering what stance to take on P's behalf and what evidence to give in the witness statement, but will also have to spend time drafting the statement. However, a litigation friend in such a situation will need to be aware that they may well be limited in what they can recover by way of reimbursement for their time spent on these legal tasks. This is discussed further at paragraph 163 below.

53 A final complication is that the judgment in Re X noted above is currently under appeal, and it may be that the Court of Appeal takes a different approach to the question of whether litigation friends can act without the benefit of lawyers. Any

litigation friend who is considering conducting proceedings without a lawyer should therefore double-check the position by making use of the resources outlined in the last section of this Guidance.

54 Whilst it may well be that the picture will change in future, the informal research conducted for purposes of producing this Guidance suggests it is perhaps more likely for the time being that most litigation friends will want to obtain the benefit of legal representation, and the rest of this Guidance is for the most part predicated upon the basis that the litigation friend will instruct solicitors to advise and represent them.

****

E What does a litigation friend do?

What are the duties imposed by the law?

66 Unhelpfully, there is no guidance contained in the MCA 2005 or in any of the supporting materials as to how a litigation friend should discharge their duties, and it is therefore necessary to look more widely for guidance upon this question. This area of the law is not straightforward, and the litigation friend should seek specific legal advice both at the outset and in relation to any specific points that may arise. What follows, however, is a summary of what appears – as matters presently stand – to be the proper approach to take when a litigation friend acts for P. It focuses primarily upon the practical steps, rather than examining the legal questions in any detail.

67 It is perhaps easiest to start by identifying what a litigation friend is not. They are not:

- a party themselves. They must always remember that they act on behalf of P, and subject to the duty to conduct the litigation fairly and competently on P's behalf;
- the advocate of the party on whose behalf they act, whether (a) a lay advocate; (b) a statutory advocate;[19] or (c) a legally qualified advocate authorised to carry out the conduct of litigation – they are 'a great deal more;'[20] or
- the equivalent of a children's guardian appointed in certain categories of family proceedings to represent the interests of a child.[21] The duties of such a guardian are wide-ranging[22] but, crucially, involve an investigatory and reporting role that is very different to that of a litigation friend; or
- a person discharging the function of a 'McKenzie friend'.[23] Such a friend can only assist a person who has litigation capacity.

19 Such as an IMCA or an Independent Mental Health Advocate discharging functions under the MHA 1983.
20 *RP v Nottingham City Council and the Official Solicitor (Mental Capacity of Parent)* [2008] EWCA Civ 462; [2008] 2 FLR 1516 at paragraph 129 per Wall LJ.
21 Under Children Act (CA) 1989, s 5; see also FPR 2010, Pt 14 and FPR, rr 16.3 and 16.4.
22 They are set out in Practice Direction 16A to the FPR 2010.
23 A 'McKenzie Friend' is someone who provides reasonable assistance to a litigant in person. A McKenzie friend does not represent the litigant but can sit beside them in court and 'quietly assist'. See the Practice Guidance: McKenzie Friends (Civil and Family Courts), issued by the Master of the Rolls and the President of the Family Division on 12th July 2010.

68 In order to discharge their functions and to give instructions to legal representatives, a litigation friend acting on behalf of P will have to form a view as to:

- whether P has capacity to take the decisions in issue (if they form the view that P has, in fact, got capacity to litigate, then, ... they must bring that matter to the attention of the court as soon as possible); and
- if P lacks capacity to take the decisions in issue, where P's best interests lie. In this regard, the litigation friend may well find it useful to draw up a balance sheet to identify the risks and benefits of the various options before the court. Such balance sheets are regularly used by the judges seeking to identify where P's best interests lie, and it can be extremely useful for the litigation friend to have drawn up a balance sheet themselves at an earlier stage, both to ensure that they have considered all the material matters and to assist in putting a case on P's behalf to the court ...

69 Whilst the litigation friend can – and should – proceed upon the basis of the views concluded upon the two issues set out above, and (where appropriate) to put a case as to both to the court, it is vital that:

- the litigation friend does not thereby seek to take on an investigatory role, a role that was specifically not provided for in the MCA 2005 or the Court of Protection Rules 2007. This does not mean that a litigation friend could not properly visit P and provide what is known as an attendance note of their visit – i.e. a note of their conversation with P – to put before the court. Indeed, this would usually be a very important part of the functions of a litigation friend. Rather, this means that the litigation friend should not seek to carry out extensive 'detective' work so as to be able (in essence) to put an expert report to the court for it to accept or reject;
- whether by taking on an investigatory role or otherwise, the litigation friend does not seek to pre-empt the court's determination upon the issues in the case by seeking to impose themselves as decision-maker.

70 The need for a litigation friend to be careful to remember the limits of their role is particularly important where:

- the assessment either of capacity or of best interests is finely balanced; or
- P has very strong views which conflict with the litigation friend's assessment of the relevant issue.

71 In respect of this latter category of case (which is not unusual), as the law stands at present, it appears clear that a litigation friend is not bound to advance a case to the court that they properly consider – after suitably anxious consideration – to be unarguable.[24] In other words, the litigation friend could properly conclude that (for instance) even if P very strongly wishes to have contact with an abusive family member, the risk posed by that abusive family member was such that the litigation friend could not properly argue that such contact was in P's best interests.

24 See in this regard *RP v United Kingdom (Application no. 38245/08, decision of 9 October 2012)*; [2013] 1 FLR 744, at paragraph 76.

72 However, it is important to recognise that, if P has a strong view as to what they wish the court to do but the litigation friend properly considers that (a) P does not have capacity to make the decision in question; and (b) that such a view is unarguable, then there is a tension between the position of the litigation friend and P's rights under Articles 6 and 8 of the European Convention on Human Rights ('ECHR'):

- A person who has capacity to conduct their own litigation has the right under Articles 6 and 8 ECHR to advance to the court any argument that they wish as to the decision the judge should reach (subject to the court's

powers to manage cases so that entirely meritless arguments are given short shrift as to not to occupy disproportionate amounts of time and expense);
- The fact that a litigation friend is appointed to act on P's behalf and thereby to act – in part (and for proper reasons) – as a filter or check upon the ability of P to advance their wishes and feelings to the court as arguments as to what outcome should be reached is, inevitably, an interference with their rights under Articles 6 and 8 ECHR;[25]
- As the law currently stands, a litigation friend is entitled – properly – to advance arguments that conflict with P's wishes and feelings without breaching their rights under Articles 6 and 8 ECHR. However, it is equally important to recognise that the stronger the conflict between the arguments advanced in P's name to the court and P's own wishes and feelings, the greater the interference with P's rights and the more important the need for the litigation friend to proceed with caution and to make P's own wishes clear to the court.

25 In some other ways, it is an important safeguard of their rights, ensuring that the court procedures are conducted in such a way that their participation is secured insofar as possible.

73 In a case where there is clear conflict between what P would like to happen and what the litigation friends considers that they have to submit to the court:
- The litigation friend should consider very carefully whether to concede the issue (i.e. whether actively to agree to the course of action with which P does not agree), or whether, rather, simply to say to the court that they will leave it to the court to decide. Whilst little might appear to turn on this distinction, it can be very important for P not to hear their litigation friend appearing actively to argue for the opposite course of action to that they wish; and
- The litigation friend is under a particularly important duty to make sure that P's views are relayed as clearly as possible to the court.[26] It would, in many cases, be appropriate in such a case for the litigation friend to make clear that it the court needs to hear directly from P themselves.

26 This was emphasised in *RP v United Kingdom* at paragraph 76.

Deprivation of liberty cases – the principles

74 It is suggested that litigation friends should be particularly careful to ensure that they seek to uphold P's right to liberty under Article 5 ECHR, especially in cases brought under s.21A MCA 2005 in relation to authorisations granted under the DOLS regime (i.e. appeals against authorisations under Schedule A1 to the MCA 2005).

75 Article 5 ECHR provides legal safeguards to those deprived of their liberty by the state. This applies to those subject to DOLS authorisations in the same way as it does to those detained under the MHA 1983. One such safeguard is set out in Article 5(4) and is the ability to challenge the detention before a court able to order the person's release if the detention is not lawful.

Deprivation of liberty cases – what a litigation friend should do

76 In the circumstances, and taking into account, in particular, the case-law from the European Court of Human Rights as to the nature of the obligations imposed by both Articles 5(1) and 5(4) ECHR,[27] it is suggested that in a case involving a deprivation of liberty:

- a litigation friend for P must always consider testing whether it is correct that the assertion implicit in a request that the court uphold an authorisation or otherwise approve a deprivation of liberty that the regime in question is the least restrictive option. In other words, and to use the language of the European Court of Human Rights, the litigation friend must consider testing whether other, less severe measures have been considered and found to be insufficient to safeguard the individual interest which might require that the person concerned be detained;[28]
- Where P wishes to challenge that deprivation, then it is suggested that the litigation friend is, in fact, obliged to do so unless satisfied, after the most careful deliberation, that there truly is no properly arguable case that the deprivation of liberty does not represent the least restrictive requirement.[29] If this is the case, then it is further suggested that it would never be appropriate for the litigation friend actively to concede that the deprivation of liberty was in P's best interests. At most, it suggested that the litigation friend could leave it to the judge to decide (having ensured that P's views were relayed to the court). This would most likely require an oral hearing.

27 See, in particular, *Stanev v Bulgaria* [2012] ECHR 46 at paragraph 143.
28 As did the Official Solicitor in *Y County Council v ZZ* [2013] COPLR 463, in which ZZ vigorously disputed the necessity for the restrictions imposed upon him – primarily so as to secure against the risk that he would commit sexual offences against children.
29 Note in this regard the observation of Moses LJ in *TA v AA and Knowsley Metropolitan Borough Council* [2014] EWCA 1661 in relation to an application under s 21A of the MCA 2005: '75. But it may be useful, to prevent any repetition of this unfortunate history, to record that the Official Solicitor did not in these proceedings dispute the proposition that HHJ Gore QC was required to determine the appeal and could not lawfully refuse to consider it, however obvious the outcome and however short the hearing and disposal of the appeal. [...] I need only emphasise that due and proper consideration of an appeal under section 21A of the MCA 2005 may not require any lengthy consideration. A full hearing is not necessarily a lengthy, time consuming or expensive hearing.' In other words, it is quite proper for a litigation friend to take the steps they consider necessary to ensure to advance P's objections to a deprivation of liberty even if they have only very limited prospects of success, in the knowledge that the court will be able to calibrate its consideration of the application appropriately.

****

How to decide what instructions to give

79 If P is capable of expressing wishes and feelings, it is vitally important that the litigation friend takes all reasonable steps to ascertain them. This is for two reasons: (1) to inform the litigation friend in their consideration of where P's best interests lie; and (2) to ensure that the litigation friend can then place those views before the court.

80 IMCAs are particularly well-placed in this regard because the process of deciding what instructions to give is closely allied to the process of preparing a report pursuant to an instruction under one of the relevant provisions of the MCA 2005 for purposes of decision-making outside the scope of the court.

81 If the litigation friend is not already acquainted and familiar with P, this may well involve enlisting the assistance of P's support workers or family members who are familiar with P, although the litigation friend must always be careful to ensure that – so far as possible – they are receiving P's wishes and feelings unmediated by anyone else.

82 As noted, P's wishes and feelings – whilst vitally important   will not necessarily be determinative of the approach that the litigation friend will take on

their behalf. The litigation friend should also ensure that they have considered the other evidence that is available (and the evidence that might become available).

83 In many cases, the litigation friend – and, in turn, the court – will want to have independent evidence to assist in the assessment of where P's best interests lie, either by way of a report prepared under s.49 MCA 2005 or a report from a suitably qualified expert. This is addressed further in Chapter G below. One of the litigation friend's most important tasks is gauging – and then informing the court – whether such evidence is required (and, if so, what evidence).

84 Assuming that the litigation friend has instructed lawyers, they should seek advice as to any points upon which they are unclear, and should enlist the assistance of the lawyers in (for instance) reviewing relevant documentation. It is ultimately, however, for the litigation friend to decide what instructions to give.

85 Finally, the litigation friend should always keep matters under review and allow for the possibility either that matters evolve or that (as often happens) new evidence sheds very different light upon the picture that was initially presented. This is particularly important as regards the position that the litigation friend is intending to adopt towards the 'ultimate' questions in the application – i.e. whether P has capacity to take the relevant decision(s), and the decision(s) that the Court is being asked to take on P's behalf. The Official Solicitor almost invariably expresses all his views as (in essence) subject to confirmation having heard all the evidence at the end of the final hearing; there is a great deal to be said to following this practice.

F When is it appropriate to bring a case to the Court of Protection as litigation friend for P?

86 In this section, we cover the position where an advocate or a family member/carer is considering bringing a case on behalf of P as litigation friend (rather than the position where proceedings are already on foot and the advocate or family member/care is being invited to act as litigation friend).

When should matters go to the Court of Protection?

87 There are, in very broad terms, two reasons why applications should be brought to the Court of Protection:

1 There is a dispute that cannot be resolved by the informal and collaborative decision-making structures established by the MCA 2005;[30]
2 The decision in question is one that is particularly difficult or serious;

[30] See *G v E (Deputyship and Litigation Friend)* [2010] EWHC 2512 (COP) at paragraph 57.

88 A specific sub-set of cases in the first category is cases concerning people deprived of their liberty in care homes and hospitals under authorisations granted under Schedule A1. The importance of securing the right under Article 5(4) ECHR of those deprived of their liberty in such settings to an independent judicial review of the lawfulness of their detention cannot be over-emphasised, and the role played by RPRs and IMCAs here is particularly important, especially the role of IMCAs appointed under s.39D MCA 2005 to assist unpaid RPRs. So as to render the Article 5(4) ECHR rights of detained residents effective, it is particularly important in such cases that:

- where appropriate, the detained person is enabled to bring a challenge to the Court of Protection under s.21A MCA 2005; and
- any litigation friend appointed to act on that person's behalf in the proceedings follows the guidance set out at paragraphs 74–77 above and is

tenacious in ensuring that the evidence advanced in support of the deprivation of liberty is properly tested.

89 It is sometimes easy to overlook the second category of case outlined above and to think that the Court of Protection exists solely to resolve disputes. That is an extremely important function, but focussing too much upon the court as a forum to turn to only as a last resort to resolve disputes can blur the fact that, as judges have said on numerous occasions, their function can also be to take decisions on behalf of P that public authorities feel are too risky for them properly to be able to take themselves. As Peter Jackson J said in Re M (Deprivation of Liberty),[31] in the context of a case where the choice facing the commissioning bodies was depriving a diabetic woman in a care home where she was desperately unhappy or allowing her to return home where she would undoubtedly be non-compliant with her medication and be at very high risk of death:

> '... my decision [to decide on the woman's behalf that she should go home] implies no criticism whatever of any of the witnesses from the local authority or by the CCG. I understand the position taken and the reasons for it; indeed it would be difficult for them to have taken a different view on the facts of the case. There are risks either way and it is perfectly appropriate that responsibility for the outcome should fall on the shoulders of the court and not on the shoulders of the parties.'

31 [2013] EWHC 3456 (COP).

90 That a matter comes to the Court of Protection is therefore not necessarily a sign of 'failure.' Indeed, in the case of certain medical decisions,[32] the matter has to come to court.

32 Namely (a) decisions about the proposed withholding or withdrawal of artificial nutrition and hydration from a person in a permanent vegetative state or a minimally conscious state; (b) cases involving organ or bone marrow donation by a person who lacks capacity to consent; and (c) cases involving non-therapeutic sterilisation of a person who lacks capacity to consent. Practice Direction 9E to the Court of Protection Rules 2007. See also the guidance endorsed in *NHS Trust v FG* [2014] EWCOP 30.

Alternatives to the Court of Protection

91 If the case falls into the first category set about above, i.e. a dispute about where P's best interests may lie, then it is necessary to ensure that all alternative options have been explored to resolve that dispute before going to the Court of Protection. The Code of Practice to the MCA 2005 explores some of these options at Chapter 15. An option that is not set out in the Code of Practice that can be particularly useful in disputes about welfare is the commissioning (by the relevant local authority) of a report from an independent social worker. Obtaining such a report can provide the reassurance to the family of the individual in question that the option being advanced by the local authority is, indeed, in their best interests; it can, on occasion, also lead to suggestions as to alternative options that the local authority might not have considered.

****

APPENDIX A: CHECKLISTS

Advocate considering bringing application on behalf of P

1   Consider whether P has the capacity to conduct the proceedings.

2   (If a professional advocate, e.g. IMCA), identify basis upon which the work to be done as litigation friend is to be funded.
3   Identify the issues that may require resolution by the Court of Protection – is the issue actually one for that court?
4   Identify whether other steps may be possible to resolve issues without application to the Court of Protection – e.g. Alternative Dispute Resolution.
5   (Where relevant) take – and document – appropriate steps to require public authority to bring the application.
6   If those steps have not succeeded, contact Official Solicitor's office to see whether Official Solicitor would apply on P's behalf as litigation friend.
7   Consider whether necessary to instruct solicitors:
    a   make use (where possible) of any initial free consultation offered by appropriately qualified solicitors' firm;
    b   confirm whether P is eligible for public funding (legal aid);
    c   if P is not eligible for public funding, need to consider (with legal advice) steps necessary to secure mechanism for legal costs to be met out of P's assets
8   Consider, with care, whether advocate can fulfil the requirements set out in the COP22 certificate of suitability.
9   If P eligible for public funding, ensure that solicitors instructed have taken appropriate steps to apply for public funding.
10 Investigate whether P eligible for any fee remission and take appropriate steps when applying in P's name for such exemption.
11 If acting without solicitors, complete necessary COP forms (in a welfare case, COP1 and COP1B and, if necessary, a COP9 witness statement), and take steps to have COP3 form completed (addressing P's lack of capacity). Complete also the COP22 certificate of suitability. If instructing solicitors, ensure that solicitors have properly explained the contents of the forms and (in particular) the relief sought from the court – i.e. the orders and/or declarations.
12 Make clear why the application is brought in P's name (as opposed, for instance, by the IMCA personally) and what contact has been had with the Official Solicitor's office to investigate whether the Official Solicitor will act on P's behalf as applicant.
13 If advocate is bringing application solely for purposes of ensuring that a matter comes to the attention of the court, make this very clear in the application.
14 Once matter is before the court, ensure that all stages the focus is upon (1) the actual issues that need to be resolved; and (2) that those procedural steps – and only those steps – required to resolve those issues are taken.

Advocate invited to consider acting as litigation friend for P in proceedings brought by another person/body

1   Consider whether P has the capacity to conduct the proceedings.
2   Consider whether P (If a professional advocate, e.g. IMCA), identify basis upon which the work to be done as litigation friend is to be funded:
    a   If this is to be by way of funding from another party (e.g. local authority applicant), take appropriate steps to secure confirmation of this in writing;
    b   If this is to be by way of funding from P's own assets, take steps to confirm with the court whether this would meet with approval, noting that it would be unusual for the court to approve payment for the costs of acting as litigation friend for P's own assets.

3 Consider whether necessary to instruct solicitors:
   a   make use (where possible) of any initial free consultation offered by appropriately qualified solicitors' firm;
   b   confirm whether P is eligible for public funding (legal aid);
   c   if P is not eligible for public funding, need to consider (with legal advice) steps necessary to secure mechanism for legal costs to be met either by another party to the proceedings or out of P's assets.
4 Consider, with care, whether advocate can fulfil the requirements set out in the COP22 certificate of suitability.
5 (If appropriate) seek undertaking from applicant that they will not seek any legal costs against the litigation friend personally if they were to accept the appointment.
6 Having consented to invitation and having been appointed, ensure that all stages the focus is upon (1) the actual issues that need to be resolved; and (2) that those procedural steps – and only those steps – required to resolve those issues are taken.

Practice Direction of 26 March 2015: Committal for Contempt of Court – Open Court

Note—For answers to various questions that have arisen on the application and interpretation of this Practice Direction, see the Practice Guidance of 24 June 2015, which is set out below.

Preamble

1 This Practice Direction applies to all proceedings for committal for contempt of court, including contempt in the face of the court, whether arising under any statutory or inherent jurisdiction and, particularly, supplements the provisions relating to contempt of court in the Civil Procedure Rules 1998, the Family Procedure Rules 2010, the Court of Protection Rules 2007, and the Criminal Procedure Rules 2014 and any related Practice Directions supplementing those various provisions. It applies in all courts in England and Wales, including the Court of Protection, and supersedes the *Practice Guidance: Committal for Contempt* [2013] 1 WLR 1326, dated 3 May 2013; *Practice Guidance (Committal Proceedings: Open Court) (No 2)* [2013] 1 WLR 1753, dated 4 June 2013; and *President's Circular: Committals* (*The Family Court Practice 2014* at p 2976), dated 2 August 2013.

2 Any reference in this Practice Direction to a judgment includes reference to written reasons provided in accordance with rule 27.2 of the Family Procedure Rules 2010.

Open Justice

3 Open justice is a fundamental principle. The general rule is that hearings are carried out in, and judgments and orders are made in, public. This rule applies to all hearings, whether on application or otherwise, for committal for contempt irrespective of the court in which they are heard or of the proceedings in which they arise.

4 Derogations from the general principle can only be justified in exceptional circumstances, when they are strictly necessary as measures to secure the proper administration of justice. Derogations shall, where justified, be no more than strictly necessary to achieve their purpose.

Committal Hearings – in Public

5 (1) All committal hearings, whether on application or otherwise and whether for contempt in the face of the court or any other form of contempt, shall be listed and heard in public.
 (2) They shall, except where paragraph 5(3) applies, be listed in the public court list as follows:
 FOR HEARING IN OPEN COURT
 Application by (*full name of applicant*) for
 the Committal to prison of
 (*full name of the person alleged to be in contempt*)
 (3) In those cases where the person alleged to be in contempt is subject to arrest for an alleged breach of an order, including a location or collection order or an order made under the Family Law Act 1996, the hearing shall be listed in the public court list as follows:
 FOR HEARING IN OPEN COURT [*add, where there has been a remand in custody:* in accordance with the order of (name of judge) dated *(date)*]
 Proceedings for the Committal to prison of
 (*full name of the person alleged to be in contempt*)
 who was arrested on (*date*) in accordance with and for alleged breach of a [location/collection/Family Law Act 1996/other] order made by (*name of judge*) on (*date*).

6 Where it is not possible to publish the details required by paragraph 5(3) in the public court list in the usual way the day before the hearing ie, in such circumstances where the alleged contemnor is produced at court by the Tipstaff or a constable on the morning of the hearing, having been arrested over night, the following steps should be taken:

 (1) Where, as in the Royal Courts of Justice, the public court list is prepared and accessible in electronic form, it should be updated with the appropriate entry as soon as the court becomes aware that the matter is coming before it;
 (2) Notice of the hearing should at the same time be placed outside the door of the court in which the matter is being, or is to be heard, and at whatever central location in the building the various court lists are displayed;
 (3) Notice should be given to the national print and broadcast media, via the Press Association's CopyDirect service, of the fact that the hearing is taking or is shortly due to take place.

If an alleged contemnor is produced at court, having been arrested overnight, the person shall immediately be produced before a judge who shall sit in public.

7 Where the committal hearing is brought by way of application notice, the court may authorise any person who is not a party to proceedings to obtain a copy of the application notice, upon request and subject to payment of any appropriate fee. Authorisation shall be granted in all but exceptional circumstances. Where authorisation is refused, the reasons for that refusal shall be set out in writing by the judge and supplied to the person who made the request.

Committal Hearings – in Private

8 Where the court, either on application or otherwise, is considering derogating from the general rule and holding a committal hearing in private, or imposing any other such derogation from the principle of open justice:

(1) it shall in all cases before the hearing takes place, notify the national print and broadcast media, via the Press Association's CopyDirect service, of the fact of the committal hearing (whether it is brought on application or otherwise) when and where it is listed for hearing, and the nature of the proposed derogation; and

(2) at the outset of the committal hearing the court shall hear submissions from the parties and/or the media on the question whether to impose the proposed derogation.

9 In considering the question whether there are exceptional circumstances justifying a derogation from the general rule, and whether that derogation is no more than strictly necessary the fact that the committal hearing is made in the Court of Protection or in any proceedings relating to a child does not of itself justify the matter being heard in private. Moreover the fact that the hearing may involve the disclosure of material which ought not to be published does not of itself justify hearing the application in private if such publication can be restrained by an appropriate order.

10 Where the court decides to exercise its discretion to derogate from the general rule, and particularly where it decides to hold a committal hearing in private, it shall, before it continues to do so, sit in public in order to give a reasoned public judgment setting out why it is doing so.

11 Where, having decided to exercise its discretion to hold a committal hearing in private, the court further decides that the substantive committal application is to be adjourned to a future date, the adjourned hearing shall be listed in the public court list as follows:

> FOR HEARING IN PRIVATE
> In accordance with the order of (*name of judge*) dated (*date*)
> [On the application of (*full name of applicant*)]
> Proceedings for the Committal to prison of
> (*full name of the person alleged to be in contempt*)

12 Orders directing a committal hearing be heard in private or of other such derogations from the principle of open justice shall not be granted by consent of the parties: see *JIH v News Group Newspapers* [2011] EWCA Civ 42, [2011] 1 WLR 1645 at [21].

Judgments

13 (1) In all cases, irrespective of whether the court has conducted the hearing in public or in private, and the court finds that a person has committed a contempt of court, the court shall at the conclusion of that hearing sit in public and state:

    (i) the name of that person;
    (ii) in general terms the nature of the contempt of court in respect of which the committal order, which for this purpose includes a suspended committal order, is being made;
    (iii) the punishment being imposed; and
    (iv) provide the details required by (i) to (iii) to the national media, via the

CopyDirect service, and to the Judicial Office, at *judicialwebupdates@judiciary.gsi.gov.uk*, for publication on the website of the Judiciary of England and Wales.

(2) There are no exceptions to these requirements. There are never any circumstances in which any one may be committed to custody or made subject to a suspended committal order without these matters being stated by the court sitting in public.

14 In addition to the requirements at paragraph 13, the court shall, in respect of all committal decisions, also either produce a written judgment setting out its reasons or ensure that any oral judgment is transcribed, such transcription to be ordered the same day as the judgment is given and prepared on an expedited basis. It shall do so irrespective of its practice prior to this Practice Direction coming into force and irrespective of whether or not anyone has requested this.

15 Copies of the written judgment or transcript of judgment shall then be provided to the parties and the national media via the CopyDirect service. Copies shall also be supplied to BAILII and to the Judicial Office at *judicialwebupdates@judiciary.gsi.gov.uk* for publication on their websites as soon as reasonably practicable.

16 Advocates and the judge (except judges and justices of the peace in the Magistrates' courts) shall be robed for all committal hearings.

This Direction is made by the Lord Chief Justice, following consultation with the Master of the Rolls, President of the Queen's Bench Division, President of the Family Division and of the Court of Protection, and Chancellor of the High Court. It is issued in accordance with the procedure laid down in Part 1 of Schedule 2 to the Constitutional Reform Act 2005.

Lord Thomas LCJ

Practice Guidance of 24 June 2015: Committal for Contempt of Court – Open Court

Preamble

1 This Practice Guidance answers various questions which have arisen on the application and interpretation of the Practice Direction: *Committal for Contempt – Open Court*, dated 26 March 2015 (the Committal PD).

Press Notification – Hearings

2 The Committal PD only requires the press to be notified before a committal hearing in two circumstances:

(1) where it is not possible to list the committal hearing in the public court list in the usual way the day before the hearing is to take place, see paragraph 6 of the Committal PD; and
(2) where, in advance of a hearing, the court, either on application or of its own initiative, is considering holding the committal hearing in private, see paragraph 8 of the Committal PD.

3 Press notification of a committal hearing is not therefore required in respect of all committal hearings.

Judgments

4 Paragraph 13 of the Committal PD only applies where the court finds that a person has committed a contempt of court and makes either an order for committal or a suspended committal order, see specifically paragraph 13(1)(ii). It does not apply where the court makes any other order having found a person has committed a contempt of court.

5 Where paragraph 13 applies, the following format for providing the required information should be used:

'Pursuant to paragraph 13 of Practice Direction: Committal for Contempt of Court – Open Court

In relation to [insert case number] on [insert date], at [insert court] I, [insert title and name of judge] sentence [insert name of individual subject to the committal or suspended committal order], to [an immediate/suspended custodial sentence] of [insert term of sentence] for contempt of court. The basis of that sentence was that [short, general reasons].'

6 For the purposes of paragraph 14 of the Committal PD, where it is not the usual practice of a court to give reasoned judgments because, for instance, it is not a court of record, the judgment, should set out the information required by paragraph 13(1)(i)–(iii) of the PD with short, written, reasons why the court arrived at its decision. Annex 1 to this Guidance contains a judgment pro forma for this purpose. This may be of particular assistance in the County Court and Magistrates' courts.

Application to proceedings under CPR r 71 and CCR O 27 and FPR rr 33.19, 33.19A and 33.23

7 The Committal PD applies to committal hearings, see paragraph 5(1) of the Committal PD.

8 The Committal PD does not apply to orders made on a written reference to a High Court judge or Circuit judge under the procedure set out in CPR r 71.8(1) and r 71.8(2) and CPR PD71, paragraph 6 and 7. It does not as CPR r 71 provides a process whereby any committal order made on such a written reference must be suspended on terms, amongst other things, that the person subject to the order attend court and is therefore capable of challenge before enforcement: see CPR r 71.8(3) and r 71.8(4) and *Broomleigh Housing Association Ltd v Okonkwo* [2010] EWCA Civ 1113 at [22]. The Committal PD does, as a consequence, apply to any hearing under CPR r 71.8(4)(b)).

9 The Committal PD applies to the attachment of earnings procedure under CCR O 27 r 7 and O 27 r 7A as it does to CPR r 71. It therefore only applies to the adjourned hearing referred to in CCR O 27 r 7B and to any further hearing to deal with a suspended committal order made under that provision.

10 Paragraphs 7–9 apply to FPR rr 33.19, 33.19A and 33.23 in so far as they apply the procedure in CCR O 27 and CPR r 71 to proceedings to which the Family Procedure Rules 2010 apply.

Applications to proceedings under the Policing and Crime Act 2009 and the Anti-Social Behaviour, Crime and Policing Act 2014

11 The Policing and Crime Act 2009 makes provision for civil injunctions to be made in respect of gang-related violence. The Anti-Social Behaviour, Crime and Policing Act 2014 makes provision for civil injunctions to be made in respect of certain types of anti-social behaviour.

12 The Committal PD applies to committal hearings in respect of adults who are alleged to have breached injunctions made under the 2009 Act and the 2014 Act. It does not however apply to hearings arising from alleged breaches of injunctions made under either the 2009 Act or the 2014 Act by individuals under the age of 18 as they are not applications for committal to prison for contempt, but are rather applications for a supervision or detention order under the statutory procedure set out in schedule 5A of the 2009 Act and schedule 2 of the 2014 Act.

13 In certain circumstances section 43 of the 2009 Act and section 9 of 2014 Act may require breach of an injunction to be dealt with by a judge outside the court's normal opening hours, ie, in the evening, at a weekend or on a bank holiday.

14 Where an 'out of hours' court is open and available, such matters should be listed and heard at that court 'out of hours'. Paragraph 6(3) of the Committal PD applies to such listings.

15 Where no 'out of hours' court is open and available, the judge should consider whether the matter can properly be dealt with, at a location other than an open court, through exercise of the power to remand on bail or in custody, provided under section 43(5) and schedule 5 of the 2009 or section 9(5) and schedule 1 of the 2014 Act. Use of the remand power does not engage the notification requirements of paragraphs 5, 6, 13 or 15 of the Committal PD. Those requirements will be met when the matter comes back before the court as specified below.

16 Where breach of an injunction is dealt with by way of remand on bail, the committal hearing should be listed, in accordance with the provisions of the Committal PD, at the first convenient date when the court is sitting.

17 Where breach of an injunction is dealt with by way of remand in custody, the committal hearing should be listed for hearing, within any applicable statutory time limit and in accordance with the provisions of the Committal PD, in the nearest appropriate court to the place of custody on the first convenient date when the court is sitting.

Review

18 The operation of the Committal PD will be subject to review in October 2015.

Lord Thomas LCJ

****

PART VI

Codes of Practice

PART VI

Codes of Practice

PART VI: Codes of Practice

Contents

Mental Capacity Act 2005: Code of Practice   1515

Mental Capacity Act 2005: Deprivation of Liberty Safeguards Code of Practice   1753

Mental Capacity Act 2005: Code of Practice

Issued by the Lord Chancellor on 23 April 2007 in accordance with sections 42 and 43 of the Act

FOREWORD BY LORD FALCONER

The Mental Capacity Act 2005 is a vitally important piece of legislation, and one that will make a real difference to the lives of people who may lack mental capacity. It will empower people to make decisions for themselves wherever possible, and protect people who lack capacity by providing a flexible framework that places individuals at the very heart of the decision-making process. It will ensure that they participate as much as possible in any decisions made on their behalf, and that these are made in their best interests. It also allows people to plan ahead for a time in the future when they might lack the capacity, for any number of reasons, to make decisions for themselves.

The Act covers a wide range of decisions and circumstances, but legislation alone is not the whole story. We have always recognised that the Act needs to be supported by practical guidance, and the Code of Practice is a key part of this. It explains how the Act will operate on a day-to-day basis and offers examples of best practice to carers and practitioners.

Many individuals and organisations have read and commented upon earlier drafts of the Code of Practice and I am very grateful to all those who contributed to this process. This Code of Practice is a better document as a result of this input.

A number of people will be under a formal duty to have regard to the Code: professionals and paid carers for example, or people acting as attorneys or as deputies appointed by the Court of Protection. But for many people, the most important relationships will be with the wide range of less formal carers, the close family and friends who know the person best, some of whom will have been caring for them for many years. The Code is also here to provide help and guidance for them. It will be crucial to the Code's success that all those relying upon it have a document that is clear and that they can understand. I have been particularly keen that we do all we can to achieve this.

The Code of Practice will be important in shaping the way the Mental Capacity Act 2005 is put into practice and I strongly encourage you to take the time to read and digest it.

INTRODUCTION

The Mental Capacity Act 2005, covering England and Wales, provides a statutory framework for people who lack capacity to make decisions for themselves, or who have capacity and want to make preparations for a time when they may lack capacity in the future. It sets out who can take decisions, in which situations, and how they should go about this. The Act received Royal Assent on 7 April 2005 and will come into force during 2007.

The legal framework provided by the Mental Capacity Act 2005 is supported by this Code of Practice (the Code), which provides guidance and information about how the Act works in practice. Section 42 of the Act requires the Lord Chancellor to produce a Code of Practice for the guidance of a range of people with different duties and functions under the Act. Before the Code is prepared, section 43 requires that the Lord Chancellor must have consulted the National Assembly for Wales and such other persons as he considers appropriate. The Code is also subject to the approval of Parliament and must have been placed before both Houses of Parliament for a 40-day period without either House voting against it. This Code of Practice has been produced in accordance with these requirements.

The Code has statutory force, which means that certain categories of people have a legal duty to have regard to it when working with or caring for adults who may lack capacity to make decisions for themselves. These categories of people are listed below.

How should the Code of Practice be used?

The Code of Practice provides guidance to anyone who is working with and/or caring for adults who may lack capacity to make particular decisions. It describes their responsibilities when acting or making decisions on behalf of individuals who lack the capacity to act or make these decisions for themselves. In particular, the Code of Practice focuses on those who have a duty of care to someone who lacks the capacity to agree to the care that is being provided.

Who is the Code of Practice for?

The Act does not impose a legal duty on anyone to 'comply' with the Code – it should be viewed as guidance rather than instruction. But if they have not followed relevant guidance contained in the Code then they will be expected to give good reasons why they have departed from it.

Certain categories of people are legally required to 'have regard to' relevant guidance in the Code of Practice. That means they must be aware of the Code of Practice when acting or making decisions on behalf of someone who lacks capacity to make a decision for themselves, and they should be able to explain how they have had regard to the Code when acting or making decisions.

The categories of people that are required to have regard to the Code of Practice include anyone who is:

- an attorney under a Lasting Power of Attorney (LPA) (see chapter 7)
- a deputy appointed by the new Court of Protection (see chapter 8)
- acting as an Independent Mental Capacity Advocate (see chapter 10)
- carrying out research approved in accordance with the Act (see chapter 11)
- acting in a professional capacity for, or in relation to, a person who lacks capacity working
- being paid for acts for or in relation to a person who lacks capacity.
- The last two categories cover a wide range of people. People acting in a professional capacity may include:
- a variety of healthcare staff (doctors, dentists, nurses, therapists, radiologists, paramedics etc)
- social care staff (social workers, care managers, etc)
- others who may occasionally be involved in the care of people who lack capacity to make the decision in question, such as ambulance crew, housing workers, or police officers.

People who are being paid for acts for or in relation to a person who lacks capacity may include:

- care assistants in a care home
- care workers providing domiciliary care services, and
- others who have been contracted to provide a service to people who lack capacity to consent to that service.

However, the Act applies more generally to everyone who looks after, or cares for, someone who lacks capacity to make particular decisions for themselves. This includes family carers or other carers. Although these carers are not legally required to have regard to the Code of Practice, the guidance given in the Code will help them to understand the Act and apply it. They should follow the guidance in the Code as far as they are aware of it.

What does 'lacks capacity' mean?

One of the most important terms in the Code is 'a person who lacks capacity'.

Whenever the term 'a person who lacks capacity' is used, it means **a person who lacks capacity to make a particular decision or take a particular action for themselves at the time the decision or action needs to be taken.**

This reflects the fact that people may lack capacity to make some decisions for themselves, but will have capacity to make other decisions. For example, they may have capacity to make small decisions about everyday issues such as what to wear or what to eat, but lack capacity to make more complex decisions about financial matters.

It also reflects the fact that a person who lacks capacity to make a decision for themselves at a certain time may be able to make that decision at a later date. This may be because they have an illness or condition that means their capacity changes. Alternatively, it may be because at the time the decision needs to be made, they are unconscious or barely conscious whether due to an accident or being under anaesthetic or their ability to make a decision may be affected by the influence of alcohol or drugs.

Finally, it reflects the fact that while some people may always lack capacity to make some types of decisions – for example, due to a condition or severe learning disability that has affected them from birth – others may learn new skills that enable them to gain capacity and make decisions for themselves.

Chapter 4 provides a full definition of what is meant by 'lacks capacity'.

What does the Code of Practice actually cover?

The Code explains the Act and its key provisions.

- Chapter 1 introduces the Mental Capacity Act 2005.
- Chapter 2 sets out the five statutory principles behind the Act and the way they affect how it is put in practice.
- Chapter 3 explains how the Act makes sure that people are given the right help and support to make their own decisions.
- Chapter 4 explains how the Act defines 'a person who lacks capacity to make a decision' and sets out a single clear test for assessing whether a person lacks capacity to make a particular decision at a particular time.
- Chapter 5 explains what the Act means by acting in the best interests of someone lacking capacity to make a decision for themselves, and describes the checklist set out in the Act for working out what is in someone's best interests.
- Chapter 6 explains how the Act protects people providing care or treatment for someone who lacks the capacity to consent to the action being taken.
- Chapter 7 shows how people who wish to plan ahead for the possibility that they might lack the capacity to make particular decisions for themselves in the future are able to grant Lasting Powers of Attorney (LPAs) to named individuals to make certain decisions on their behalf, and how attorneys appointed under an LPA should act.
- Chapter 8 describes the role of the new Court of Protection, established under the Act, to make a decision or to appoint a

decision-maker on someone's behalf in cases where there is no other way of resolving a matter affecting a person who lacks capacity to make the decision in question.
- Chapter 9 explains the procedures that must be followed if someone wishes to make an advance decision to refuse medical treatment to come into effect when they lack capacity to refuse the specified treatment.
- Chapter 10 describes the role of Independent Mental Capacity Advocates appointed under the Act to help and represent particularly vulnerable people who lack capacity to make certain significant decisions. It also sets out when they should be instructed.
- Chapter 11 provides guidance on how the Act sets out specific safeguards and controls for research involving, or in relation to, people lacking capacity to consent to their participation.
- Chapter 12 explains those parts of the Act which can apply to children and young people and how these relate to other laws affecting them.
- Chapter 13 explains how the Act relates to the Mental Health Act 1983.
- Chapter 14 sets out the role of the Public Guardian, a new public office established by the Act to oversee attorneys and deputies and to act as a single point of contact for referring allegations of abuse in relation to attorneys and deputies to other relevant agencies.
- Chapter 15 examines the various ways that disputes over decisions made under the Act or otherwise affecting people lacking capacity to make relevant decisions can be resolved.
- Chapter 16 summarises how the laws about data protection and freedom of information relate to the provisions of the Act.

What is the legal status of the Code?

Where does it apply?

The Act and therefore this Code applies to everyone it concerns who is habitually resident or present in England and Wales. However, it will also be possible for the Court of Protection to consider cases which involve persons who have assets or property outside this jurisdiction, or who live abroad but have assets or property in England or Wales.

What happens if people don't comply with it?

There are no specific sanctions for failure to comply with the Code. But a failure to comply with the Code can be used in evidence before a court or tribunal in any civil or criminal proceedings, if the court or tribunal considers it to be relevant to those proceedings. For example, if a court or tribunal believes that anyone making decisions for someone who lacks capacity has not acted in the best interests of the person they care for, the court can use the person's failure to comply with the Code as evidence.

That's why it's important that anyone working with or caring for a person who lacks capacity to make specific decisions should become familiar with the Code.

Where can I find out more?

The Code of Practice is not an exhaustive guide or complete statement of the law. Other materials have been produced by the Department for Constitutional Affairs, the Department of Health and the Office of the Public Guardian to help explain aspects of the Act from different perspectives and for people in different situations. These include guides for family carers and other carers and basic information of interest to the general public. Professional organisations may also produce specialist information and guidance for their members.

The Code also provides information on where to get more detailed guidance from other sources. A list of contact details is provided in Annex A and further information appears in the footnotes to each chapter. References made and any links provided to material or organisations do not form part of the Code and do not attract the same legal status. Signposts to further information are provided for assistance only and references made should not suggest that the Department for Constitutional Affairs endorses such material.

Using the code

References in the Code of Practice

Throughout the Code of Practice, the Mental Capacity Act 2005 is referred to as 'the Act' and any sections quoted refer to this Act unless otherwise stated. References are shown as follows: section 4(1). This refers to the section of the Act. The subsection number is in brackets.

Where reference is made to provisions from other legislation, the full title of the relevant Act will be set out, for example 'the Mental Health Act 1983', unless otherwise stated. (For example, in chapter 13, the Mental Health Act 1983 is referred to as MHA and the Mental Capacity Act as MCA.) The Code of Practice is sometimes referred to as the Code.

Scenarios used in the Code of Practice

The Code includes many boxes within the text in which there are scenarios, using imaginary characters and situations. These are intended to help illustrate what is meant in the main text. The scenarios should not in any way be taken as templates for decisions that need to be made in similar situations.

Alternative formats and further information

The Code is also available in Welsh and can be made available in other formats on request.

****

1 WHAT IS THE MENTAL CAPACITY ACT 2005?

1.1 The Mental Capacity Act 2005 (the Act) provides the legal framework for acting and making decisions on behalf of individuals who lack the mental capacity to make particular decisions for themselves. Everyone working with and/or caring for an adult who may lack capacity to make specific decisions must comply with this Act when making decisions or acting for that person, when the person lacks the capacity to make a particular decision for themselves. The same rules apply whether the decisions are life-changing events or everyday matters.

1.2 The Act's starting point is to confirm in legislation that it should be assumed that an adult (aged 16 or over) has full legal capacity to make decisions for themselves (the right to autonomy) unless it can be shown that they lack capacity to make a decision for themselves at the time the decision needs to be made. This is known as the presumption of capacity. The Act also states that people must be given all appropriate help and support to enable them to make their own decisions or to maximise their participation in any decision-making process.

1.3 The underlying philosophy of the Act is to ensure that any decision made, or action taken, on behalf of someone who lacks the capacity to make the decision or act for themselves is made in their best interests.

1.4 The Act is intended to assist and support people who may lack capacity and to discourage anyone who is involved in caring for someone who lacks capacity from being overly restrictive or controlling. But the Act also aims to balance an individual's right to make decisions for themselves with their right to be protected from harm if they lack capacity to make decisions to protect themselves.

1.5 The Act sets out a legal framework of how to act and make decisions on behalf of people who lack capacity to make specific decisions for themselves. It sets out some core principles and methods for making decisions and carrying out actions in relation to personal welfare, healthcare and financial matters affecting people who may lack capacity to make specific decisions about these issues for themselves.

1.6 Many of the provisions in the Act are based upon existing common law principles (i.e. principles that have been established through decisions made by courts in individual cases). The Act clarifies and improves upon these principles and builds on current good practice which is based on the principles.

1.7 The Act introduces several new roles, bodies and powers, all of which will support the Act's provisions. These include:
- Attorneys appointed under Lasting Powers of Attorney (see chapter 7)
- The new Court of Protection, and court-appointed deputies (see chapter 8)
- Independent Mental Capacity Advocates (see chapter 10).

The roles, bodies and powers are all explained in more depth in the specific chapters of the Code highlighted above.

What decisions are covered by the Act, and what decisions are excluded?

1.8 The Act covers a wide range of decisions made, or actions taken, on behalf of people who may lack capacity to make specific decisions for themselves. These can be decisions about day-to-day matters – like what to wear, or what to buy when doing the weekly shopping – or decisions about major life-changing events, such as whether the person should move into a care home or undergo a major surgical operation.

1.9 There are certain decisions which can never be made on behalf of a person who lacks capacity to make those specific decisions. This is because they are either so personal to the individual concerned, or governed by other legislation.

1.10 Sections 27–29 and 62 of the Act set out the specific decisions which can never be made or actions which can never be carried out under the Act, whether by family members, carers, professionals, attorneys or the Court of Protection. These are summarised below.

Decisions concerning family relationships (section 27)

Nothing in the Act permits a decision to be made on someone else's behalf on any of the following matters:
- consenting to marriage or a civil partnership
- consenting to have sexual relations
- consenting to a decree of divorce on the basis of two years' separation
- consenting to the dissolution of a civil partnership
- consenting to a child being placed for adoption or the making of an adoption order
- discharging parental responsibility for a child in matters not relating to the child's property, or
- giving consent under the Human Fertilisation and Embryology Act 1990.

Mental Health Act matters (section 28)

Where a person who lacks capacity to consent is currently detained and being treated under Part 4 of the Mental Health Act 1983, nothing in the Act authorises anyone to:
- give the person treatment for mental disorder, or
- consent to the person being given treatment for mental disorder.

Further guidance is given in chapter 13 of the Code.

Voting rights (section 29)

Nothing in the Act permits a decision on voting, at an election for any public office or at a referendum, to be made on behalf of a person who lacks capacity to vote.

Unlawful killing or assisting suicide (section 62)

For the avoidance of doubt, nothing in the Act is to be taken to affect the law relating to murder, manslaughter or assisting suicide.

1.11 Although the Act does not allow anyone to make a decision about these matters on behalf of someone who lacks capacity to make such a decision for themselves (for example, consenting to have sexual relations), this does not prevent action being taken to protect a vulnerable person from abuse or exploitation.

How does the Act relate to other legislation?

1.12 The Mental Capacity Act 2005 will apply in conjunction with other legislation affecting people who may lack capacity in relation to specific matters. This means that healthcare and social care staff acting under the Act should also be aware of their obligations under other legislation, including (but not limited to) the:
- Care Standards Act 2000
- Data Protection Act 1998
- Disability Discrimination Act 1995
- Human Rights Act 1998
- Mental Health Act 1983
- National Health Service and Community Care Act 1990
- Human Tissue Act 2004.

What does the Act say about the Code of Practice?

1.13 Section 42 of the Act sets out the purpose of the Code of Practice, which is to provide guidance for specific people in specific circumstances. Section 43 explains the procedures that had to be followed in preparing the Code and consulting on its contents, and for its consideration by Parliament.

Section 42, subsections (4) and (5), set out the categories of people who are placed under a legal duty to 'have regard to' the Code and gives further information about the status of the Code. More details can be found in the Introduction, which explains the legal status of the Code.

2 WHAT ARE THE STATUTORY PRINCIPLES AND HOW SHOULD THEY BE APPLIED?

Section 1 of the Act sets out the five 'statutory principles' – the values that underpin the legal requirements in the Act. The Act is intended to be enabling and supportive of people who lack capacity, not restricting or controlling of their lives. It aims to protect people who lack capacity to make particular decisions, but also to maximise their ability to make decisions, or to participate in decision-making, as far as they are able to do so.

The five statutory principles are:
1. A person must be assumed to have capacity unless it is established that they lack capacity.
2. A person is not to be treated as unable to make a decision unless all practicable steps to help him to do so have been taken without success.
3. A person is not to be treated as unable to make a decision merely because he makes an unwise decision.
4. An act done, or decision made, under this Act for or on behalf of a person who lacks capacity must be done, or made, in his best interests.
5. Before the act is done, or the decision is made, regard must be had to whether the purpose for which it is needed can be as effectively achieved in a way that is less restrictive of the person's rights and freedom of action.

This chapter provides guidance on how people should interpret and apply the statutory principles when using the Act. Following the principles and applying them to the Act's framework for decision-making will help to ensure not only that appropriate action is taken in individual cases, but also to point the way to solutions in difficult or uncertain situations.

> In this chapter, as throughout the Code, a person's capacity (or lack of capacity) refers specifically to their capacity to make a particular decision at the time it needs to be made.

Quick summary

- Every adult has the right to make their own decisions if they have the capacity to do so. Family carers and healthcare or social care staff must assume that a person has the capacity to make decisions, unless it can be established that the person does not have capacity.
- People should receive support to help them make their own decisions. Before concluding that individuals lack capacity to make a particular decision, it is important to take all possible steps to try to help them reach a decision themselves.
- People have the right to make decisions that others might think are unwise. A person who makes a decision that others think is unwise should not automatically be labelled as lacking the capacity to make a decision.
- Any act done for, or any decision made on behalf of, someone who lacks capacity must be in their best interests.
- Any act done for, or any decision made on behalf of, someone who lacks capacity should be an option that is less restrictive of their basic rights and freedoms – as long as it is still in their best interests.

What is the role of the statutory principles?

2.1 The statutory principles aim to:
- protect people who lack capacity and
- help them take part, as much as possible, in decisions that affect them.

They aim to assist and support people who may lack capacity to make particular decisions, not to restrict or control their lives.

2.2 The statutory principles apply to any act done or decision made under the Act. When followed and applied to the Act's decision-making framework, they will help people take appropriate action in individual cases. They will also help people find solutions in difficult or uncertain situations.

How should the statutory principles be applied?

Principle 1: *'A person must be assumed to have capacity unless it is established that he lacks capacity.' (section 1(2))*

2.3 This principle states that every adult has the right to make their own decisions – unless there is proof that they lack the capacity to make a particular decision when it needs to be made. This has been a fundamental principle of the common law for many years and it is now set out in the Act.

2.4 It is important to balance people's right to make a decision with their right to safety and protection when they can't make decisions to protect themselves. But the starting assumption must always be that an individual has the capacity, until there is proof that they do not. Chapter 4 explains the Act's definition of 'lack of capacity' and the processes involved in assessing capacity.

> **Scenario: Assessing a person's capacity to make decisions**
>
> When planning her retirement, Mrs Arnold made and registered a Lasting Power of Attorney (LPA) – a legal process that would allow her son to manage her property and financial affairs if she ever lacked capacity to manage them herself. She has now been diagnosed with dementia, and her son is worried that she is becoming confused about money.
>
> Her son must assume that his mother has capacity to manage her affairs. Then he must consider each of Mrs Arnold's financial decisions as she makes them, giving her any help and support she needs to make these decisions herself.
>
> Mrs Arnold's son goes shopping with her, and he sees she is quite capable of finding goods and making sure she gets the correct change. But when she needs to make decisions about her investments, Mrs Arnold gets confused – even though she has made such decisions in the past. She still doesn't understand after her son explains the different options.
>
> Her son concludes that she has capacity to deal with everyday financial matters but not more difficult affairs at this time. Therefore, he is able to use the LPA for the difficult financial decisions his mother can't make. But Mrs Arnold can continue to deal with her other affairs for as long as she has capacity to do so.

2.5 Some people may need help to be able to make a decision or to communicate their decision. However, this does not necessarily mean that they cannot make that decision – unless there is proof that they do lack capacity to do so. Anyone who believes that a person lacks capacity should be able to prove their case. Chapter 4 explains the standard of proof required.

Principle 2: *'A person is not to be treated as unable to make a decision unless all practicable steps to help him to do so have been taken without success.' (section 1(3))*

2.6 It is important to do everything practical (the Act uses the term 'practicable') to help a person make a decision for themselves before concluding that they lack capacity to do so. People with an illness or disability affecting their ability to make a decision should receive support to help them make as many decisions as they can. This principle aims to stop people being automatically labelled as lacking capacity to make particular decisions. Because it encourages individuals to play as big a role as possible in decision-making, it also helps prevent unnecessary interventions in their lives.

2.7 The kind of support people might need to help them make a decision varies. It depends on personal circumstances, the kind of decision that has to be made and the time available to make the decision. It might include:
- using a different form of communication (for example, non-verbal communication)
- providing information in a more accessible form (for example, photographs, drawings, or tapes)
- treating a medical condition which may be affecting the person's capacity or
- having a structured programme to improve a person's capacity to make particular decisions (for example, helping a person with learning disabilities to learn new skills).

Chapter 3 gives more information on ways to help people make decisions for themselves.

Scenario: Taking steps to help people make decisions for themselves

Mr Jackson is brought into hospital following a traffic accident. He is conscious but in shock. He cannot speak and is clearly in distress, making noises and gestures.

From his behaviour, hospital staff conclude that Mr Jackson currently lacks capacity to make decisions about treatment for his injuries, and they give him urgent treatment. They hope that after he has recovered from the shock they can use an advocate to help explain things to him.

However, one of the nurses thinks she recognises some of his gestures as sign language, and tries signing to him. Mr Jackson immediately becomes calmer, and the doctors realise that he can communicate in sign language. He can also answer some written questions about his injuries.

The hospital brings in a qualified sign-language interpreter and concludes that Mr Jackson has the capacity to make decisions about any further treatment.

2.8 Anyone supporting a person who may lack capacity should not use excessive persuasion or 'undue pressure'.[1] This might include behaving in a manner which is overbearing or dominating, or seeking to influence the person's decision, and could push a person into making a decision they might not otherwise have made. However, it is important to provide appropriate advice and information.

1   Undue influence in relation to consent to medical treatment was considered in *Re T (Adult: Refusal of Treatment)* [1992] 2 FLR 458 and in financial matters in *Royal Bank of Scotland v Etridge* [2001] UKHL 44, [2001] 2 FLR 1364.

Scenario: Giving appropriate advice and support

Sara, a young woman with severe depression, is getting treatment from mental health services. Her psychiatrist determines that she has capacity to make decisions about treatment, if she gets advice and support.

Her mother is trying to persuade Sara to agree to electro-convulsive therapy (ECT), which helped her mother when she had clinical depression in the past. However, a friend has told Sara that ECT is 'barbaric'.

The psychiatrist provides factual information about the different types of treatment available and explains their advantages and disadvantages. She also describes how different people experience different reactions or side effects. Sara is then able to consider what treatment is right for her, based on factual information rather than the personal opinions of her mother and friend.

2.9 In some situations treatment cannot be delayed while a person gets support to make a decision. This can happen in emergency situations or when an urgent decision is required (for example, immediate medical treatment). In these situations, the only practical and appropriate steps might be to keep a person informed of what is happening and why.

Principle 3: *'A person is not to be treated as unable to make a decision merely because he makes an unwise decision.' (section 1(4))*

2.10 Everybody has their own values, beliefs, preferences and attitudes. A person should not be assumed to lack the capacity to make a decision just because other people think their decision is unwise. This applies even if family members, friends or healthcare or social care staff are unhappy with a decision.

Scenario: Allowing people to make decisions that others think are unwise

Mr Garvey is a 40-year-old man with a history of mental health problems. He sees a Community Psychiatric Nurse (CPN) regularly. Mr Garvey decides to spend £2,000 of his savings on a camper van to travel around Scotland for six months. His CPN is concerned that it will be difficult to give Mr Garvey continuous support and treatment while travelling, and that his mental health might deteriorate as a result.

> However, having talked it through with his CPN, it is clear that Mr Garvey is fully aware of these concerns and has the capacity to make this particular decision. He has decided he would like to have a break and thinks this will be good for him.
>
> Just because, in the CPN's opinion, continuity of care might be a wiser option, it should not be assumed that Mr Garvey lacks the capacity to make this decision for himself.

2.11 There may be cause for concern if somebody:
- repeatedly makes unwise decisions that put them at significant risk of harm or exploitation or
- makes a particular unwise decision that is obviously irrational or out of character.

These things do not necessarily mean that somebody lacks capacity. But there might be need for further investigation, taking into account the person's past decisions and choices. For example, have they developed a medical condition or disorder that is affecting their capacity to make particular decisions? Are they easily influenced by undue pressure? Or do they need more information to help them understand the consequences of the decision they are making?

> **Scenario: Decisions that cause concern**
>
> Cyril, an elderly man with early signs of dementia, spends nearly £300 on fresh fish from a door-to-door salesman. He has always been fond of fish and has previously bought small amounts in this way. Before his dementia, Cyril was always very careful with his money and would never have spent so much on fish in one go.
>
> This decision alone may not automatically mean Cyril lacks capacity to manage all aspects of his property and affairs. But his daughter makes further enquiries and discovers Cyril has overpaid his cleaner on several occasions – something he has never done in the past. He has also made payments from his savings that he cannot account for.
>
> His daughter decides it is time to use the registered Lasting Power of Attorney her father made in the past. This gives her the authority to manage Cyril's property and affairs whenever he lacks the capacity to manage them himself. She takes control of Cyril's chequebook to protect him from possible exploitation, but she can still ensure he has enough money to spend on his everyday needs.

Principle 4: *'An act done, or decision made, under this Act for or on behalf of a person who lacks capacity must be done, or made, in his best interests.'* *(section 1(5))*

2.12 The principle of acting or making a decision in the best interests of a person who lacks capacity to make the decision in question is a well-established principle in the common law.[2] This principle is now set out in the Act, so that a person's best interests must be the basis for all decisions made and actions carried out on their behalf in situations where they lack capacity to make those particular decisions for themselves. The only exceptions to this are around research (see chapter 11) and advance decisions to refuse treatment (see chapter 9) where other safeguards apply.

[2] See for example *Re MB (Medical Treatment)* [1997] 2 FLR 426, CA; *Re A (Male Sterilisation)* [2000] 1 FLR 549, CA; *Re S (Sterilisation: Patient's Best Interests)* [2000] 2 FLR 389.

2.13 It is impossible to give a single description of what 'best interests' are, because they depend on individual circumstances. However, section 4 of the Act sets out a checklist of steps to follow in order to determine what is in the best interests of a person who lacks capacity to make the decision in question each time someone acts or makes a decision on that person's behalf. See chapter 5 for detailed guidance and examples.

Principle 5: *'Before the act is done, or the decision is made, regard must be had to whether the purpose for which it is needed can be as effectively achieved in a way that is less restrictive of the person's rights and freedom of action.' (section 1(6))*

2.14 Before somebody makes a decision or acts on behalf of a person who lacks capacity to make that decision or consent to the act, they must always question if they can do something else that would interfere less with the person's basic rights and freedoms. This is called finding the 'less restrictive alternative'. It includes considering whether there is a need to act or make a decision at all.

2.15 Where there is more than one option, it is important to explore ways that would be less restrictive or allow the most freedom for a person who lacks capacity to make the decision in question. However, the final decision must always allow the original purpose of the decision or act to be achieved.

2.16 Any decision or action must still be in the best interests of the person who lacks capacity. So sometimes it may be necessary to choose an option that is not the least restrictive alternative if that option is in the person's best interests. In practice, the process of choosing a less restrictive option and deciding what is in the person's best interests will be combined. But both principles must be applied each time a decision or action may be taken on behalf of a person who lacks capacity to make the relevant decision.

Scenario: Finding a less restrictive option

Sunil, a young man with severe learning disabilities, also has a very severe and unpredictable form of epilepsy that is associated with drop attacks. This can result in serious injury. A neurologist has advised

> that, to limit the harm that might come from these attacks, Sunil should either be under constant close observation, or wear a protective helmet.
>
> After assessment, it is decided that Sunil lacks capacity to decide on the most appropriate course of action for himself. But through his actions and behaviour, Sunil makes it clear he doesn't like to be too closely observed – even though he likes having company.
>
> The staff of the home where he lives consider various options, such as providing a special room for him with soft furnishings, finding ways to keep him under close observation or getting him to wear a helmet. In discussion with Sunil's parents, they agree that the option that is in his best interests, and is less restrictive, will be the helmet – as it will enable him to go out, and prevent further harm.

3 HOW SHOULD PEOPLE BE HELPED TO MAKE THEIR OWN DECISIONS?

Before deciding that someone lacks capacity to make a particular decision, it is important to take all practical and appropriate steps to enable them to make that decision themselves (statutory principle 2, see chapter 2). In addition, as section 3(2) of the Act underlines, these steps (such as helping individuals to communicate) must be taken in a way which reflects the person's individual circumstances and meets their particular needs. This chapter provides practical guidance on how to support people to make decisions for themselves, or play as big a role as possible in decision-making.

> In this chapter, as throughout the Code, a person's capacity (or lack of capacity) refers specifically to their capacity to make a particular decision at the time it needs to be made.

Quick summary

To help someone make a decision for themselves, check the following points:

Providing relevant information
- Does the person have all the relevant information they need to make a particular decision?
- If they have a choice, have they been given information on all the alternatives?

Communicating in an appropriate way
- Could information be explained or presented in a way that is easier for the person to understand (for example, by using simple language or visual aids)?
- Have different methods of communication been explored if required, including non-verbal communication?
- Could anyone else help with communication (for example, a family member, support worker, interpreter, speech and language therapist or advocate)?

Making the person feel at ease
- Are there particular times of day when the person's understanding is better?
- Are there particular locations where they may feel more at ease?
- Could the decision be put off to see whether the person can make the decision at a later time when circumstances are right for them?

Supporting the person
- Can anyone else help or support the person to make choices or express a view?

How can someone be helped to make a decision?

3.1 There are several ways in which people can be helped and supported to enable them to make a decision for themselves. These will vary depending on the decision to be made, the time-scale for making the decision and the individual circumstances of the person making it.

3.2 The Act applies to a wide range of people with different conditions that may affect their capacity to make particular decisions. So, the appropriate steps to take will depend on:
- a person's individual circumstances (for example, somebody with learning difficulties may need a different approach to somebody with dementia)
- the decision the person has to make and
- the length of time they have to make it.

3.3 Significant, one-off decisions (such as moving house) will require different considerations from day-to-day decisions about a person's care and welfare. However, the same general processes should apply to each decision.

3.4 In most cases, only some of the steps described in This chapter will be relevant or appropriate, and the list included here is not exhaustive. It is up to the people (whether family carers, paid carers, healthcare staff or anyone else) caring for or supporting an individual to consider what is possible and appropriate in individual cases. In all cases it is extremely important to find the most effective way of communicating with the person concerned. Good communication is essential for explaining relevant information in an appropriate way and for ensuring that the steps being taken meet an individual's needs.

3.5 Providing appropriate help with decision-making should form part of care planning processes for people receiving health or social care services. Examples include:
- Person Centred Planning for people with learning disabilities
- the Care Programme Approach for people with mental disorders
- the Single Assessment Process for older people in England, and
- the Unified Assessment Process in Wales.

What happens in emergency situations?

3.6 Clearly, in emergency medical situations (for example, where a person collapses with a heart attack or for some unknown reason and is brought unconscious into a hospital), urgent decisions will have to be made and immediate action taken in the person's best interests. In these situations, it may not be practical or appropriate to delay the treatment while trying to help the person make their own decisions, or to consult with any known attorneys or deputies. However, even in emergency situations, healthcare staff should try to communicate with the person and keep them informed of what is happening.

What information should be provided to people and how should it be provided?

3.7 Providing relevant information is essential in all decision-making. For example, to make a choice about what they want for breakfast, people need to know what food is available. If the decision concerns medical treatment, the doctor must explain the purpose and effect of the course of treatment and the likely consequences of accepting or refusing treatment.

3.8 All practical and appropriate steps must be taken to help people to make a decision for themselves. Information must be tailored to an individual's needs and abilities. It must also be in the easiest and most appropriate form of communication for the person concerned.

What information is relevant?

3.9 The Act cannot state exactly what information will be relevant in each case. Anyone helping someone to make a decision for themselves should therefore follow these steps.
- Take time to explain anything that might help the person make a decision. It is important that they have access to all the information they need to make an informed decision.

- Try not to give more detail than the person needs – this might confuse them. In some cases, a simple, broad explanation will be enough. But it must not miss out important information.
- What are the risks and benefits? Describe any foreseeable consequences of making the decision, and of not making any decision at all.
- Explain the effects the decision might have on the person and those close to them – including the people involved in their care.
- If they have a choice, give them the same information in a balanced way for all the options.
- For some types of decisions, it may be important to give access to advice from elsewhere. This may be independent or specialist advice (for example, from a medical practitioner or a financial or legal adviser). But it might simply be advice from trusted friends or relatives.

Communication – general guidance

3.10 To help someone make a decision for themselves, all possible and appropriate means of communication should be tried.
- Ask people who know the person well about the best form of communication (try speaking to family members, carers, day centre staff or support workers). They may also know somebody the person can communicate with easily, or the time when it is best to communicate with them.
- Use simple language. Where appropriate, use pictures, objects or illustrations to demonstrate ideas.
- Speak at the right volume and speed, with appropriate words and sentence structure. It may be helpful to pause to check understanding or show that a choice is available.
- Break down difficult information into smaller points that are easy to understand. Allow the person time to consider and understand each point before continuing.
- It may be necessary to repeat information or go back over a point several times.
- Is help available from people the person trusts (relatives, friends, GP, social worker, religious or community leaders)? If so, make sure the person's right to confidentiality is respected.
- Be aware of cultural, ethnic or religious factors that shape a person's way of thinking, behaviour or communication. For example, in some cultures it is important to involve the community in decision-making. Some religious beliefs (for example, those of Jehovah's Witnesses or Christian Scientists) may influence the person's approach to medical treatment and information about treatment decisions.
- If necessary, consider using a professional language interpreter. Even if a person communicated in English or Welsh in the past, they may have lost some verbal skills (for example, because of

dementia). They may now prefer to communicate in their first language. It is often more appropriate to use a professional interpreter rather than to use family members.
- If using pictures to help communication, make sure they are relevant and the person can understand them easily. For example, a red bus may represent a form of transport to one person but a day trip to another.
- Would an advocate (someone who can support and represent the person) improve communication in the current situation? (See chapters 10 and 15 for more information about advocates.)

Scenario: Providing relevant information

Mrs Thomas has Alzheimer's disease and lives in a care home. She enjoys taking part in the activities provided at the home. Today there is a choice between going to a flower show, attending her usual pottery class or watching a DVD. Although she has the capacity to choose, having to decide is making her anxious.

The care assistant carefully explains the different options. She tells Mrs Thomas about the DVD she could watch, but Mrs Thomas doesn't like the sound of it. The care assistant shows her a leaflet about the flower show. She explains the plans for the day, where the show is being held and how long it will take to get there in the mini-van. She has to repeat this information several times, as Mrs Thomas keeps asking whether they will be back in time for supper. She also tells Mrs Thomas that one of her friends is going on the trip.

At first, Mrs Thomas is reluctant to disturb her usual routine. But the care assistant reassures her she will not lose her place at pottery if she misses a class. With this information, Mrs Thomas can therefore choose whether or not to go on the day trip.

Helping people with specific communication or cognitive problems

3.11 Where people have specific communication or cognitive problems, the following steps can help:
- Find out how the person is used to communicating. Do they use picture boards or Makaton (signs and symbols for people with communication or learning difficulties)? Or do they have a way of communicating that is only known to those close to them?
- If the person has hearing difficulties, use their preferred method of communication (for example, visual aids, written messages or sign language). Where possible, use a qualified interpreter.
- Are mechanical devices such as voice synthesisers, keyboards or other computer equipment available to help?

- If the person does not use verbal communication skills, allow more time to learn how to communicate effectively.
- For people who use non-verbal methods of communication, their behaviour (in particular, changes in behaviour) can provide indications of their feelings.
- Some people may prefer to use non-verbal means of communication and can communicate most effectively in written form using computers or other communication technologies. This is particularly true for those with autistic spectrum disorders.
- For people with specific communication difficulties, consider other types of professional help (for example, a speech and language therapist or an expert in clinical neuropsychology).

> **Scenario: Helping people with specific communication difficulties**
>
> David is a deafblind man with learning disabilities who has no formal communication. He lives in a specialist home. He begins to bang his head against the wall and repeats this behaviour throughout the day. He has not done this before.
>
> The staff in the home are worried and discuss ways to reduce the risk of injury. They come up with a range of possible interventions, aimed at engaging him with activities and keeping him away from objects that could injure him. They assess these as less restrictive ways to ensure he is safe. But David lacks the capacity to make a decision about which would be the best option.
>
> The staff call in a specialist in challenging behaviour, who says that David's behaviour is communicative. After investigating this further, staff discover he is in pain because of tooth decay. They consult a dentist about how to resolve this, and the dentist decides it is in David's best interests to get treatment for the tooth decay. After treatment, David's head-banging stops.

What steps should be taken to put a person at ease?

3.12 To help put someone at ease and so improve their ability to make a decision, careful consideration should be given to both location and timing.

Location

3.13 In terms of location, consider the following:
- Where possible, choose a location where the person feels most at ease. For example, people are usually more comfortable in their own home than at a doctor's surgery.

- Would the person find it easier to make their decision in a relevant location? For example, could you help them decide about medical treatment by taking them to hospital to see what is involved?
- Choose a quiet location where the discussion can't be easily interrupted.
- Try to eliminate any background noise or distractions (for example, the television or radio, or people talking).
- Choose a location where the person's privacy and dignity can be properly respected.

Timing

3.14 In terms of timing, consider the following:
- Try to choose the time of day when the person is most alert – some people are better in the mornings, others are more lively in the afternoon or early evening. It may be necessary to try several times before a decision can be made.
- If the person's capacity is likely to improve in the foreseeable future, wait until it has done so – if practical and appropriate. For example, this might be the case after treatment for depression or a psychotic episode. Obviously, this may not be practical and appropriate if the decision is urgent.
- Some medication could affect a person's capacity (for example, medication which causes drowsiness or affects memory). Can the decision be delayed until side effects have subsided?
- Take one decision at a time – be careful to avoid making the person tired or confused.
- Don't rush – allow the person time to think things over or ask for clarification, where that is possible and appropriate.
- Avoid or challenge time limits that are unnecessary if the decision is not urgent. Delaying the decision may enable further steps to be taken to assist people to make the decision for themselves.

Scenario: Getting the location and timing right

Luke, a young man, was seriously injured in a road traffic accident and suffered permanent brain damage. He has been in hospital several months, and has made good progress, but he gets very frustrated at his inability to concentrate or do things for himself.

Luke now needs surgical treatment on his leg. During the early morning ward round, the surgeon tries to explain what is involved in the operation. She asks Luke to sign a consent form, but he gets angry and says he doesn't want to talk about it.

> His key nurse knows that Luke becomes more alert and capable later in the day. After lunch, she asks him if he would like to discuss the operation again. She also knows that he responds better one-to-one than in a group. So she takes Luke into a private room and repeats the information that the surgeon gave him earlier. He understands why the treatment is needed, what is involved and the likely consequences. Therefore, Luke has the capacity to make a decision about the operation.

Support from other people

3.15 In some circumstances, individuals will be more comfortable making decisions when someone else is there to support them.
- Might the person benefit from having another person present? Sometimes having a relative or friend nearby can provide helpful support and reduce anxiety. However, some people might find this intrusive, and it could increase their anxiety or affect their ability to make a free choice. Find ways of getting the person's views on this, for example, by watching their behaviour towards other people.
- Always respect a person's right to confidentiality.

> *Scenario: Getting help from other people*
>
> Jane has a learning disability. She expresses herself using some words, facial expressions and body language. She has lived in her current community home all her life, but now needs to move to a new group home. She finds it difficult to discuss abstract ideas or things she hasn't experienced. Staff conclude that she lacks the capacity to decide for herself which new group home she should move to.
>
> The staff involve an advocate to help Jane express her views. Jane's advocate spends time with her in different environments. The advocate uses pictures, symbols and Makaton to find out the things that are important to Jane, and speaks to people who know Jane to find out what they think she likes. She then supports Jane to show their work to her care manager, and checks that the new homes suggested for her are able to meet Jane's needs and preferences.
>
> When the care manager has found some suitable places, Jane's advocate visits the homes with Jane. They take photos of the houses to help her distinguish between them. The advocate then uses the photos to help Jane work out which home she prefers. Jane's own feelings can now play an important part in deciding what is in her best interests – and so in the final decision about where she will live.

What other ways are there to enable decision-making?

3.16 There are other ways to help someone make a decision for themselves.

- Many people find it helpful to talk things over with people they trust – or people who have been in a similar situation or faced similar dilemmas. For example, people with learning difficulties may benefit from the help of a designated support worker or being part of a support network.
- If someone is very distressed (for example, following a death of someone close) or where there are long-standing problems that affect someone's ability to understand an issue, it may be possible to delay a decision so that the person can have psychological therapy, if needed.
- Some organisations have produced materials to help people who need support to make decisions and for those who support them. Some of this material is designed to help people with specific conditions, such as Alzheimer's disease or profound learning disability.
- It may be important to provide access to technology. For example, some people who appear not to communicate well verbally can do so very well using computers.

Scenario: Making the most of technology

Ms Patel has an autistic spectrum disorder. Her family and care staff find it difficult to communicate with her. She refuses to make eye contact, and gets very upset and angry when her carers try to encourage her to speak.

One member of staff notices that Ms Patel is interested in the computer equipment. He shows her how to use the keyboard, and they are able to have a conversation using the computer. An IT specialist works with her to make sure she can make the most of her computing skills to communicate her feelings and decisions.

---

4 HOW DOES THE ACT DEFINE A PERSON'S CAPACITY TO MAKE A DECISION AND HOW SHOULD CAPACITY BE ASSESSED?

This chapter explains what the Act means by 'capacity' and 'lack of capacity'. It provides guidance on how to assess whether someone has the capacity to make a decision, and suggests when professionals should be involved in the assessment.

> In this chapter, as throughout the Code, a person's capacity (or lack of capacity) refers specifically to their capacity to make a particular decision at the time it needs to be made

Quick summary

This checklist is a summary of points to consider when assessing a person's capacity to make a specific decision. Readers should also refer to the more detailed guidance in this chapter and chapters 2 and 3.

Presuming someone has capacity
- The starting assumption must always be that a person has the capacity to make a decision, unless it can be established that they lack capacity.

Understanding what is meant by capacity and lack of capacity
- A person's capacity must be assessed specifically in terms of their capacity to make a particular decision at the time it needs to be made.

Treating everyone equally
- A person's capacity must not be judged simply on the basis of their age, appearance, condition or an aspect of their behaviour.

Supporting the person to make the decision for themselves
- It is important to take all possible steps to try to help people make a decision for themselves (see chapter 2, principle 2, and chapter 3).

Assessing capacity

Anyone assessing someone's capacity to make a decision for themselves should use the two-stage test of capacity.
- Does the person have an impairment of the mind or brain, or is there some sort of disturbance affecting the way their mind or brain works? (It doesn't matter whether the impairment or disturbance is temporary or permanent.)
- If so, does that impairment or disturbance mean that the person is unable to make the decision in question at the time it needs to be made?

Assessing ability to make a decision
- Does the person have a general understanding of what decision they need to make and why they need to make it?
- Does the person have a general understanding of the likely consequences of making, or not making, this decision?

- Is the person able to understand, retain, use and weigh up the information relevant to this decision?
- Can the person communicate their decision (by talking, using sign language or any other means)? Would the services of a professional (such as a speech and language therapist) be helpful?

Assessing capacity to make more complex or serious decisions
- Is there a need for a more thorough assessment (perhaps by involving a doctor or other professional expert)?

What is mental capacity?

4.1 Mental capacity is the ability to make a decision.
- This includes the ability to make a decision that affects daily life – such as when to get up, what to wear or whether to go to the doctor when feeling ill – as well as more serious or significant decisions.
- It also refers to a person's ability to make a decision that may have legal consequences – for them or others. Examples include agreeing to have medical treatment, buying goods or making a will.

4.2 The starting point must always be to assume that a person has the capacity to make a specific decision (see chapter 2, principle 1). Some people may need help to be able to make or communicate a decision (see chapter 3). But this does not necessarily mean that they lack capacity to do so. What matters is their ability to carry out the processes involved in making the decision – and not the outcome.

What does the Act mean by 'lack of capacity'?

4.3 Section 2(1) of the Act states:
> 'For the purposes of this Act, a person lacks capacity in relation to a matter if at the material time he is unable to make a decision for himself in relation to the matter because of an impairment of, or a disturbance in the functioning of, the mind or brain.'

This means that a person lacks capacity if:
- they have an impairment or disturbance (for example, a disability, condition or trauma) that affects the way their mind or brain works, and
- the impairment or disturbance means that they are unable to make a specific decision at the time it needs to be made.

4.4 An assessment of a person's capacity must be based on their ability to make a specific decision at the time it needs to be made, and not their ability to make decisions in general. Section 3 of the Act defines what it means to be unable to make a decision (this is explained in paragraph 4.14 below).

4.5 Section 2(2) states that the impairment or disturbance does not have to be permanent. A person can lack capacity to make a decision at the time it needs to be made even if:
- the loss of capacity is partial
- the loss of capacity is temporary
- their capacity changes over time.

A person may also lack capacity to make a decision about one issue but not about others.

4.6 The Act generally applies to people who are aged 16 or older. Chapter 12 explains how the Act affects children and young people – in particular those aged 16 and 17 years.

What safeguards does the Act provide around assessing someone's capacity?

4.7 An assessment that a person lacks capacity to make a decision must never be based simply on:
- their age
- their appearance
- assumptions about their condition, or
- any aspect of their behaviour. (section 2(3))

4.8 The Act deliberately uses the word 'appearance', because it covers all aspects of the way people look. So for example, it includes the physical characteristics of certain conditions (for example, scars, features linked to Down's syndrome or muscle spasms caused by cerebral palsy) as well as aspects of appearance like skin colour, tattoos and body piercings, or the way people dress (including religious dress).

4.9 The word 'condition' is also wide-ranging. It includes physical disabilities, learning difficulties and disabilities, illness related to age, and temporary conditions (for example, drunkenness or unconsciousness). Aspects of behaviour might include extrovert (for example, shouting or gesticulating) and withdrawn behaviour (for example, talking to yourself or avoiding eye contact).

Scenario: Treating everybody equally

Tom, a man with cerebral palsy, has slurred speech. Sometimes he also falls over for no obvious reason

One day Tom falls in the supermarket. Staff call an ambulance, even though he says he is fine. They think he may need treatment after his fall.

When the ambulance comes, the ambulance crew know they must not make assumptions about Tom's capacity to decide about treatment,

> based simply on his condition and the effects of his disability. They talk to him and find that he is capable of making healthcare decisions for himself.

What proof of lack of capacity does the Act require?

4.10 Anybody who claims that an individual lacks capacity should be able to provide proof. They need to be able to show, *on the balance of probabilities*, that the individual lacks capacity to make a particular decision, at the time it needs to be made (section 2(4)). This means being able to show that it is more likely than not that the person lacks capacity to make the decision in question.

What is the test of capacity?

To help determine if a person lacks capacity to make particular decisions, the Act sets out a two-stage test of capacity.

Stage 1: Does the person have an impairment of, or a disturbance in the functioning of, their mind or brain?

4.11 Stage 1 requires proof that the person has an impairment of the mind or brain, or some sort of or disturbance that affects the way their mind or brain works. If a person does not have such an impairment or disturbance of the mind or brain, they will not lack capacity under the Act.

4.12 Examples of an impairment or disturbance in the functioning of the mind or brain may include the following:
- conditions associated with some forms of mental illness
- dementia
- significant learning disabilities
- the long-term effects of brain damage
- physical or medical conditions that cause confusion, drowsiness or loss of consciousness
- delirium
- concussion following a head injury, and
- the symptoms of alcohol or drug use.

> *Scenario: Assessing whether an impairment or disturbance is affecting someone's ability to make a decision*
>
> Mrs Collins is 82 and has had a stroke. This has weakened the left-hand side of her body. She is living in a house that has been the family home for years. Her son wants her to sell the house and live with him.

> Mrs Collins likes the idea, but her daughter does not. She thinks her mother will lose independence and her condition will get worse. She talks to her mother's consultant to get information that will help stop the sale. But he says that although Mrs Collins is anxious about the physical effects the stroke has had on her body, it has not caused any mental impairment or affected her brain, so she still has capacity to make her own decision about selling her house.

Stage 2: Does the impairment or disturbance mean that the person is unable to make a specific decision when they need to?

4.13 For a person to lack capacity to make a decision, the Act says their impairment or disturbance must affect their ability to make the specific decision when they need to. But first people must be given all practical and appropriate support to help them make the decision for themselves (see chapter 2, principle 2). Stage 2 can only apply if all practical and appropriate support to help the person make the decision has failed. See chapter 3 for guidance on ways of helping people to make their own decisions.

What does the Act mean by 'inability to make a decision'?

4.14 A person is unable to make a decision if they cannot:
1. understand information about the decision to be made (the Act calls this 'relevant information')
2. retain that information in their mind
3. use or weigh that information as part of the decision-making process, or
4. communicate their decision (by talking, using sign language or any other means). See section 3(1).

4.15 These four points are explained in more detail below. The first three should be applied together. If a person cannot do any of these three things, they will be treated as unable to make the decision. The fourth only applies in situations where people cannot communicate their decision in any way.

Understanding information about the decision to be made

4.16 It is important not to assess someone's understanding before they have been given relevant information about a decision. Every effort must be made to provide information in a way that is most appropriate to help the person to understand. Quick or inadequate explanations are not acceptable unless the situation is urgent (see chapter 3 for some practical steps). Relevant information includes:
- the nature of the decision
- the reason why the decision is needed, and
- the likely effects of deciding one way or another, or making no decision at all.

4.17 Section 3(2) outlines the need to present information in a way that is appropriate to meet the individual's needs and circumstances. It also stresses the importance of explaining information using the most effective form of communication for that person (such as simple language, sign language, visual representations, computer support or any other means).

4.18 For example:
- a person with a learning disability may need somebody to read information to them. They might also need illustrations to help them to understand what is happening. Or they might stop the reader to ask what things mean. It might also be helpful for them to discuss information with an advocate.
- a person with anxiety or depression may find it difficult to reach a decision about treatment in a group meeting with professionals. They may prefer to read the relevant documents in private. This way they can come to a conclusion alone, and ask for help if necessary.
- someone who has a brain injury might need to be given information several times. It will be necessary to check that the person understands the information. If they have difficulty understanding, it might be useful to present information in a different way (for example, different forms of words, pictures or diagrams). Written information, audiotapes, videos and posters can help people remember important facts.

4.19 Relevant information must include what the likely consequences of a decision would be (the possible effects of deciding one way or another) – and also the likely consequences of making no decision at all (section 3(4)). In some cases, it may be enough to give a broad explanation using simple language. But a person might need more detailed information or access to advice, depending on the decision that needs to be made. If a decision could have serious or grave consequences, it is even more important that a person understands the information relevant to that decision.

Scenario: Providing relevant information in an appropriate format

Mr Leslie has learning disabilities and has developed an irregular heartbeat. He has been prescribed medication for this, but is anxious about having regular blood tests to check his medication levels. His doctor gives him a leaflet to explain:
- the reason for the tests
- what a blood test involves
- the risks in having or not having the tests, and
- that he has the right to decide whether or not to have the test.

The leaflet uses simple language and photographs to explain these things. Mr Leslie's carer helps him read the leaflet over the next few days, and checks that he understands it.

> Mr Leslie goes back to tell the doctor that, even though he is scared of needles, he will agree to the blood tests so that he can get the right medication. He is able to pick out the equipment needed to do the blood test. So the doctor concludes that Mr Leslie can understand, retain and use the relevant information and therefore has the capacity to make the decision to have the test.

Retaining information

4.20 The person must be able to hold the information in their mind long enough to use it to make an effective decision. But section 3(3) states that people who can only retain information for a short while must not automatically be assumed to lack the capacity to decide – it depends on what is necessary for the decision in question. Items such as notebooks, photographs, posters, videos and voice recorders can help people record and retain information.

> *Scenario: Assessing a person's ability to retain information*
>
> Walter, an elderly man, is diagnosed with dementia and has problems remembering things in the short term. He can't always remember his great-grandchildren's names, but he recognises them when they come to visit. He can also pick them out on photographs.
>
> Walter would like to buy premium bonds (a type of financial investment) for each of his great-grandchildren. He asks his solicitor to make the arrangements. After assessing his capacity to make financial decisions, the solicitor is satisfied that Walter has capacity to make this decision, despite his short-term memory problems.

Using or weighing information as part of the decision-making process

4.21 For someone to have capacity, they must have the ability to weigh up information and use it to arrive at a decision. Sometimes people can understand information but an impairment or disturbance stops them using it. In other cases, the impairment or disturbance leads to a person making a specific decision without understanding or using the information they have been given.[3]

3 This issue has been considered in a number of court cases, including *Re MB* [1997] 2 FLR 426, CA; *R v Collins and Ashworth Hospital Authority ex parte Brady* [2001] 58 BMLR 173.

4.22 For example, a person with the eating disorder anorexia nervosa may understand information about the consequences of not eating. But their compulsion not to eat might be too strong for them to ignore. Some people who have serious brain damage might make impulsive decisions regardless of information they have been given or their understanding of it.

Inability to communicate a decision in any way

4.23 Sometimes there is no way for a person to communicate. This will apply to very few people, but it does include:
- people who are unconscious or in a coma, or
- those with the very rare condition sometimes known as 'locked-in syndrome', who are conscious but cannot speak or move at all.

If a person cannot communicate their decision in any way at all, the Act says they should be treated as if they are unable to make that decision.

4.24 Before deciding that someone falls into this category, it is important to make all practical and appropriate efforts to help them communicate. This might call for the involvement of speech and language therapists, specialists in non-verbal communication or other professionals. Chapter 3 gives advice for communicating with people who have specific disabilities or cognitive problems.

4.25 Communication by simple muscle movements can show that somebody can communicate and may have capacity to make a decision.[4] For example, a person might blink an eye or squeeze a hand to say 'yes' or 'no'. In these cases, assessment must use the first three points listed in paragraph 4.14, which are explained in more depth in paragraphs 4.16–4.22.

[4] This was demonstrated in the case *Re AK (Adult Patient) (Medical Treatment: Consent)* [2001] 1 FLR 129.

What other issues might affect capacity?

People with fluctuating or temporary capacity

4.26 Some people have fluctuating capacity – they have a problem or condition that gets worse occasionally and affects their ability to make decisions. For example, someone who has manic depression may have a temporary manic phase which causes them to lack capacity to make financial decisions, leading them to get into debt even though at other times they are perfectly able to manage their money. A person with a psychotic illness may have delusions that affect their capacity to make decisions at certain times but disappear at others. Temporary factors may also affect someone's ability to make decisions. Examples include acute illness, severe pain, the effect of medication, or distress after a death or shock. More guidance on how to support someone with fluctuating or temporary capacity to make a decision can be found in chapter 3, particularly paragraphs 3.12–3.16. More information about factors that may indicate that a person may regain or develop capacity in the future can be found at paragraph 5.28.

4.27 As in any other situation, an assessment must only examine a person's capacity to make a particular decision when it needs to be made. It may be possible to put off the decision until the person has the capacity to make it (see also guidance on best interests in chapter 5).

Ongoing conditions that may affect capacity

4.28 Generally, capacity assessments should be related to a specific decision. But there may be people with an ongoing condition that affects their ability to make certain decisions or that may affect other decisions in their life. One decision on its own may make sense, but may give cause for concern when considered alongside others.

4.29 Again, it is important to review capacity from time to time, as people can improve their decision-making capabilities. In particular, someone with an ongoing condition may become able to make some, if not all, decisions. Some people (for example, people with learning disabilities) will learn new skills throughout their life, improving their capacity to make certain decisions. So assessments should be reviewed from time to time. Capacity should always be reviewed:
- whenever a care plan is being developed or reviewed
- at other relevant stages of the care planning process, and
- as particular decisions need to be made.

4.30 It is important to acknowledge the difference between:
- unwise decisions, which a person has the right to make (chapter 2, principle 3), and
- decisions based on a lack of understanding of risks or inability to weigh up the information about a decision.

Information about decisions the person has made based on a lack of understanding of risks or inability to weigh up the information can form part of a capacity assessment – particularly if someone repeatedly makes decisions that put them at risk or result in harm to them or someone else.

Scenario: Ongoing conditions

Paul had an accident at work and suffered severe head injuries. He was awarded compensation to pay for care he will need throughout his life as a result of his head injury. An application was made to the Court of Protection to consider how the award of compensation should be managed, including whether to appoint a deputy to manage Paul's financial affairs. Paul objected as he believed he could manage his life and should be able to spend his money however he liked.

He wrote a list of what he intended to spend his money on. This included fully-staffed luxury properties and holiday villas, cars with chauffeurs, jewellery and various other items for himself and his

> family. But spending money on all these luxury items would not leave enough money to cover the costs of his care in future years.
>
> The court judged that Paul had capacity to make day-to-day financial decisions, but he did not understand why he had received compensation and what the money was supposed to be used for. Nor did he understand how buying luxuries now could affect his future care. The court therefore decided Paul lacked capacity to manage large amounts of money and appointed a deputy to make ongoing financial decisions relating to his care. But it gave him access to enough funds to cover everyday needs and occasional treats.

What other legal tests of capacity are there?

4.31 The Act makes clear that the definition of 'lack of capacity' and the two-stage test for capacity set out in the Act are 'for the purposes of this Act'. This means that the definition and test are to be used in situations covered by this Act. Schedule 6 of the Act also amends existing laws to ensure that the definition and test are used in other areas of law not covered directly by this Act.

For example, Schedule 6, paragraph 20 allows a person to be disqualified from jury service if they lack the capacity (using this Act's definition) to carry out a juror's tasks.

4.32 There are several tests of capacity that have been produced following judgments in court cases (known as common law tests).[5] These cover:

- capacity to make a will[6]
- capacity to make a gift[7]
- capacity to enter into a contract[8]
- capacity to litigate (take part in legal cases),[9] and
- capacity to enter into marriage.[10]

5   For details, see British Medical Association & Law Society, *Assessment of Mental Capacity: Guidance for Doctors and Lawyers* (BMA, 1995; BMJ Books, 2nd edn, 2004; Law Society Publishing, 3rd edn, 2009).
6   *Banks v Goodfellow* (1870) LR 5 QB 549.
7   *Re Beaney (deceased)* [1978] 1 WLR 770.
8   *Boughton v Knight* (1873) LR 3 PD 64.
9   *Masterman-Lister v Brutton & Co and Jewell & anor* [2003] 1 WLR 1511.
10 *Sheffield City Council v E* [2004] EWHC 2808 (Fam), [2005] 1 FLR 965.

4.33 The Act's new definition of capacity is in line with the existing common law tests, and the Act does not replace them. When cases come before the court on the above issues, judges can adopt the new definition if they think it is appropriate. The Act will apply to all other cases relating to financial, healthcare or welfare decisions.

When should capacity be assessed?

4.34 Assessing capacity correctly is vitally important to everyone affected by the Act. Someone who is assessed as lacking capacity may be denied their right to make a specific decision – particularly if others think that the decision would not be in their best interests or could cause harm. Also, if a person lacks capacity to make specific decisions, that person might make decisions they do not really understand. Again, this could cause harm or put the person at risk. So it is important to carry out an assessment when a person's capacity is in doubt. It is also important that the person who does an assessment can justify their conclusions. Many organisations will provide specific professional guidance for members of their profession.[11]

11 See for example, British Medical Association & Law Society, *Assessment of Mental Capacity: Guidance for Doctors and Lawyers* (BMA, 1995; BMJ Books, 2nd edn, 2004; Law Society Publishing, 3rd edn, 2009); the Joint Royal Colleges Ambulance Service Liaison Committee Clinical Practice Guidelines (JRCALC, available online at www2.warwick.ac.uk/fac/med/research/hsri/ emergencycare/jrcalc_2006/clinical_guidelines_2006.pdf) and British Psychological Society, *Guidelines on assessing capacity* (BPS, 2006 available online at www.bps.org.uk).

4.35 There are a number of reasons why people may question a person's capacity to make a specific decision:
- the person's behaviour or circumstances cause doubt as to whether they have the capacity to make a decision
- somebody else says they are concerned about the person's capacity, or
- the person has previously been diagnosed with an impairment or disturbance that affects the way their mind or brain works (see paragraphs 4.11–4.12 above), and it has already been shown they lack capacity to make other decisions in their life.

4.36 The starting assumption must be that the person has the capacity to make the specific decision. If, however, anyone thinks a person lacks capacity, it is important to then ask the following questions:
- Does the person have all the relevant information they need to make the decision?
- If they are making a decision that involves choosing between alternatives, do they have information on all the different options?
- Would the person have a better understanding if information was explained or presented in another way?
- Are there times of day when the person's understanding is better?
- Are there locations where they may feel more at ease?
- Can the decision be put off until the circumstances are different and the person concerned may be able to make the decision?
- Can anyone else help the person to make choices or express a view (for example, a family member or carer, an advocate or someone to help with communication)?

4.37 Chapter 3 describes ways to deal with these questions and suggest steps which may help people make their own decisions. If all practical and appropriate steps fail, an assessment will then be needed of the person's capacity to make the decision that now needs to be made.

Who should assess capacity?

4.38 The person who assesses an individual's capacity to make a decision will usually be the person who is directly concerned with the individual at the time the decision needs to be made. This means that different people will be involved in assessing someone's capacity to make different decisions at different times.

For most day-to-day decisions, this will be the person caring for them at the time a decision must be made. For example, a care worker might need to assess if the person can agree to being bathed. Then a district nurse might assess if the person can consent to have a dressing changed.

4.39 For acts of care or treatment (see chapter 6), the assessor must have a 'reasonable belief' that the person lacks capacity to agree to the action or decision to be taken (see paragraphs 4.44–4.45 for a description of reasonable belief).

4.40 If a doctor or healthcare professional proposes treatment or an examination, they must assess the person's capacity to consent. In settings such as a hospital, this can involve the multi-disciplinary team (a team of people from different professional backgrounds who share responsibility for a patient). But ultimately, it is up to the professional responsible for the person's treatment to make sure that capacity has been assessed.

4.41 For a legal transaction (for example, making a will), a solicitor or legal practitioner must assess the client's capacity to instruct them. They must assess whether the client has the capacity to satisfy any relevant legal test. In cases of doubt, they should get an opinion from a doctor or other professional expert.

4.42 More complex decisions are likely to need more formal assessments (see paragraph 4.54 below). A professional opinion on the person's capacity might be necessary. This could be, for example, from a psychiatrist, psychologist, a speech and language therapist, occupational therapist or social worker. But the final decision about a person's capacity must be made by the person intending to make the decision or carry out the action on behalf of the person who lacks capacity – not the professional, who is there to advise.

4.43 Any assessor should have the skills and ability to communicate effectively with the person (see chapter 3). If necessary, they should get professional help to communicate with the person.

Scenario: Getting help with assessing capacity

Ms Dodd suffered brain damage in a road accident and is unable to speak. At first, her family thought she was not able to make decisions. But they soon discovered that she could choose by pointing at things, such as the clothes she wants to wear or the food she prefers. Her

> behaviour also indicates that she enjoys attending a day centre, but she refuses to go swimming. Her carers have assessed her as having capacity to make these decisions.
>
> Ms Dodd needs hospital treatment but she gets distressed when away from home. Her mother feels that Ms Dodd is refusing treatment by her behaviour, but her father thinks she lacks capacity to say no to treatment that could improve her condition.
>
> The clinician who is proposing the treatment will have to assess Ms Dodd's capacity to consent. He gets help from a member of staff at the day centre who knows Ms Dodd's communication well and also discusses things with her parents. Over several meetings the clinician explains the treatment options to Ms Dodd with the help of the staff member. The final decision about Ms Dodd's capacity rests with the clinician, but he will need to use information from the staff member and others who know Ms Dodd well to make this assessment.

What is 'reasonable belief' of lack of capacity?

4.44 Carers (whether family carers or other carers) and care workers do not have to be experts in assessing capacity. But to have protection from liability when providing care or treatment (see chapter 6), they must have a 'reasonable belief' that the person they care for lacks capacity to make relevant decisions about their care or treatment (section 5(1)). To have this reasonable belief, they must have taken 'reasonable' steps to establish that that the person lacks capacity to make a decision or consent to an act at the time the decision or consent is needed. They must also establish that the act or decision is in the person's best interests (see chapter 5).
They do not usually need to follow formal processes, such as involving a professional to make an assessment. However, if somebody challenges their assessment (see paragraph 4.63 below), they must be able to describe the steps they have taken. They must also have objective reasons for believing the person lacks capacity to make the decision in question.

4.45 The steps that are accepted as 'reasonable' will depend on individual circumstances and the urgency of the decision. Professionals, who are qualified in their particular field, are normally expected to undertake a fuller assessment, reflecting their higher degree of knowledge and experience, than family members or other carers who have no formal qualifications. See paragraph 4.36 for a list of points to consider when assessing someone's capacity. The following may also be helpful:
- Start by assuming the person has capacity to make the specific decision. Is there anything to prove otherwise?
- Does the person have a previous diagnosis of disability or mental disorder? Does that condition now affect their capacity

to make this decision? If there has been no previous diagnosis, it may be best to get a medical opinion.
- Make every effort to communicate with the person to explain what is happening.
- Make every effort to try to help the person make the decision in question.
- See if there is a way to explain or present information about the decision in a way that makes it easier to understand. If the person has a choice, do they have information about all the options?
- Can the decision be delayed to take time to help the person make the decision, or to give the person time to regain the capacity to make the decision for themselves?
- Does the person understand what decision they need to make and why they need to make it?
- Can they understand information about the decision? Can they retain it, use it and weigh it to make the decision?
- Be aware that the fact that a person agrees with you or assents to what is proposed does not necessarily mean that they have capacity to make the decision.

What other factors might affect an assessment of capacity?

4.46 It is important to assess people when they are in the best state to make the decision, if possible. Whether this is possible will depend on the nature and urgency of the decision to be made. Many of the practical steps suggested in chapter 3 will help to create the best environment for assessing capacity. The assessor must then carry out the two stages of the test of capacity (see paragraphs 4.11–4.25 above).

4.47 In many cases, it may be clear that the person has an impairment or disturbance in the functioning of their mind or brain which could affect their ability to make a decision. For example, there might be a past diagnosis of a disability or mental disorder, or there may be signs that an illness is returning. Old assumptions about an illness or condition should be reviewed. Sometimes an illness develops gradually (for example, dementia), and it is hard to know when it starts to affect capacity. Anyone assessing someone's capacity may need to ask for a medical opinion as to whether a person has an illness or condition that could affect their capacity to make a decision in this specific case.

Scenario: *Getting a professional opinion*

Mr Elliott is 87 years old and lives alone. He has poor short-term memory, and he often forgets to eat. He also sometimes neglects his personal hygiene. His daughter talks to him about the possibility of moving into residential care. She decides that he understands the

> reasons for her concerns as well as the risks of continuing to live alone and, having weighed these up, he has the capacity to decide to stay at home and accept the consequences.
>
> Two months later, Mr Elliott has a fall and breaks his leg. While being treated in hospital, he becomes confused and depressed. He says he wants to go home, but the staff think that the deterioration in his mental health has affected his capacity to make this decision at this time. They think he cannot understand the consequences or weigh up the risks he faces if he goes home. They refer him to a specialist in old age psychiatry, who assesses whether his mental health is affecting his capacity to make this decision. The staff will then use the specialist's opinion to help their assessment of Mr Elliott's capacity.

4.48 Anyone assessing someone's capacity must not assume that a person lacks capacity simply because they have a particular diagnosis or condition. There must be proof that the diagnosed illness or condition affects the ability to make a decision when it needs to be made. The person assessing capacity should ask the following questions:
- Does the person have a general understanding of what decision they need to make and why they need to make it?
- Do they understand the likely consequences of making, or not making, this decision?
- Can they understand and process information about the decision? And can they use it to help them make a decision?

In borderline cases, or where there is doubt, the assessor must be able to show that it is more likely than not that the answer to these questions is 'no'.

What practical steps should be taken when assessing capacity?

4.49 Anyone assessing someone's capacity will need to decide which of these steps are relevant to their situation.
- They should make sure that they understand the nature and effect of the decision to be made themselves. They may need access to relevant documents and background information (for example, details of the person's finances if assessing capacity to manage affairs). See chapter 16 for details on access to information.
- They may need other relevant information to support the assessment (for example, healthcare records or the views of staff involved in the person's care).
- Family members and close friends may be able to provide valuable background information (for example, the person's past behaviour and abilities and the types of decisions they can

currently make). But their personal views and wishes about what they would want for the person must not influence the assessment.
- They should again explain to the person all the information relevant to the decision. The explanation must be in the most appropriate and effective form of communication for that person.
- Check the person's understanding after a few minutes. The person should be able to give a rough explanation of the information that was explained. There are different methods for people who use nonverbal means of communication (for example, observing behaviour or their ability to recognise objects or pictures).
- Avoid questions that need only a 'yes' or 'no' answer (for example, did you understand what I just said?). They are not enough to assess the person's capacity to make a decision. But there may be no alternative in cases where there are major communication difficulties. In these cases, check the response by asking questions again in a different way.
- Skills and behaviour do not necessarily reflect the person's capacity to make specific decisions. The fact that someone has good social or language skills, polite behaviour or good manners doesn't necessarily mean they understand the information or are able to weigh it up.
- Repeating these steps can help confirm the result.

4.50 For certain kinds of complex decisions (for example, making a will), there are specific legal tests (see paragraph 4.32 above) in addition to the two-stage test for capacity. In some cases, medical or psychometric tests may also be helpful tools (for example, for assessing cognitive skills) in assessing a person's capacity to make particular decisions, but the relevant legal test of capacity must still be fulfilled.

When should professionals be involved?

4.51 Anyone assessing someone's capacity may need to get a professional opinion when assessing a person's capacity to make complex or major decisions. In some cases this will simply involve contacting the person's general practitioner (GP) or family doctor. If the person has a particular condition or disorder, it may be appropriate to contact a specialist (for example, consultant psychiatrist, psychologist or other professional with experience of caring for patients with that condition). A speech and language therapist might be able to help if there are communication difficulties. In some cases, a multi-disciplinary approach is best. This means combining the skills and expertise of different professionals.

4.52 Professionals should never express an opinion without carrying out a proper examination and assessment of the person's capacity to make the decision. They must apply the appropriate test of capacity. In some cases, they will need to meet the person more than once – particularly if the person has communication difficulties. Professionals can get background information from a person's family and carers. But the personal views of these people about what they want for the person who lacks capacity must not influence the outcome of that assessment.

4.53 Professional involvement might be needed if:
- the decision that needs to be made is complicated or has serious consequences
- an assessor concludes a person lacks capacity, and the person challenges the finding
- family members, carers and/or professionals disagree about a person's capacity
- there is a conflict of interest between the assessor and the person being assessed
- the person being assessed is expressing different views to different people – they may be trying to please everyone or telling people what they think they want to hear
- somebody might challenge the person's capacity to make the decision – either at the time of the decision or later (for example, a family member might challenge a will after a person has died on the basis that the person lacked capacity when they made the will)
- somebody has been accused of abusing a vulnerable adult who may lack capacity to make decisions that protect them
- a person repeatedly makes decisions that put them at risk or could result in suffering or damage.

Scenario: Involving professional opinion

Ms Ledger is a young woman with learning disabilities and some autistic spectrum disorders. Recently she began a sexual relationship with a much older man, who is trying to persuade her to move in with him and come off the pill. There are rumours that he has been violent towards her and has taken her bankbook.

Ms Ledger boasts about the relationship to her friends. But she has admitted to her key worker that she is sometimes afraid of the man. Staff at her sheltered accommodation decide to make a referral under the local adult protection procedures. They arrange for a clinical psychologist to assess Ms Ledger's understanding of the relationship and her capacity to consent to it.

4.54 In some cases, it may be a legal requirement, or good professional practice, to undertake a formal assessment of capacity. These cases include:

- where a person's capacity to sign a legal document (for example, a will), could later be challenged, in which case an expert should be asked for an opinion[12]

12 Kenward v Adams (1975) The Times, 29 November.

- to establish whether a person who might be involved in a legal case needs the assistance of the Official Solicitor or other litigation friend (somebody to represent their views to a court and give instructions to their legal representative) and there is doubt about the person's capacity to instruct a solicitor or take part in the case[13]

13 Civil Procedure Rules 1998, r 21.1.

- whenever the Court of Protection has to decide if a person lacks capacity in a certain matter
- if the courts are required to make a decision about a person's capacity in other legal proceedings[14]
- if there may be legal consequences of a finding of capacity (for example, deciding on financial compensation following a claim for personal injury).

14 Masterman-Lister v Brutton & Co and Jewell & anor [2003] 1 WLR 1511, at [54].

Are assessment processes confidential?

4.55 People involved in assessing capacity will need to share information about a person's circumstances. But there are ethical codes and laws that require professionals to keep personal information confidential. As a general rule, professionals must ask their patients or clients if they can reveal information to somebody else – even close relatives. But sometimes information may be disclosed without the consent of the person who the information concerns (for example, to protect the person or prevent harm to other people).[15]

15 For example, in the circumstances discussed in W v Egdell [1990] Ch 359, at [848]; R (S) v Plymouth City Council and C [2002] EWCA Civ 388, [2002] 1 FLR 1177, at [49].

4.56 Anyone assessing someone's capacity needs accurate information concerning the person being assessed that is relevant to the decision the person has to make. So professionals should, where possible, make relevant information available. They should make every effort to get the person's permission to reveal relevant information. They should give a full explanation of why this is necessary, and they should tell the person about the risks and consequences of revealing, and not revealing information. If the person is unable to give permission, the professional might still be allowed to provide information that will help make an accurate assessment of the person's capacity to make the specific decision. Chapter 16 has more detail on how to access information.

What if someone refuses to be assessed?

4.57 There may be circumstances in which a person whose capacity is in doubt refuses to undergo an assessment of capacity or refuses to be examined by a doctor or other professional. In these circumstances, it might help to explain to someone refusing an assessment why it is needed and what the consequences of refusal are. But threats or attempts to force the person to agree to an assessment are not acceptable.

4.58 If the person lacks capacity to agree or refuse, the assessment can normally go ahead, as long as the person does not object to the assessment, and it is in their best interests (see chapter 5).

4.59 Nobody can be forced to undergo an assessment of capacity. If someone refuses to open the door to their home, it cannot be forced. If there are serious worries about the person's mental health, it may be possible to get a warrant to force entry and assess the person for treatment in hospital – but the situation must meet the requirements of the Mental Health Act 1983 (section 135). But simply refusing an assessment of capacity is in no way sufficient grounds for an assessment under the Mental Health Act 1983 (see chapter 13).

Who should keep a record of assessments?

4.60 Assessments of capacity to take day-to-day decisions or consent to care require no formal assessment procedures or recorded documentation. Paragraphs 4.44–4.45 above explain the steps to take to reach a 'reasonable belief' that someone lacks capacity to make a particular decision. It is good practice for paid care workers to keep a record of the steps they take when caring for the person concerned.

Professional records

4.61 It is good practice for professionals to carry out a proper assessment of a person's capacity to make particular decisions and to record the findings in the relevant professional records.
- A doctor or healthcare professional proposing treatment should carry out an assessment of the person's capacity to consent (with a multi-disciplinary team, if appropriate) and record it in the patient's clinical notes.
- Solicitors should assess a client's capacity to give instructions or carry out a legal transaction (obtaining a medical or other professional opinion, if necessary) and record it on the client's file.
- An assessment of a person's capacity to consent or agree to the provision of services will be part of the care planning processes for health and social care needs, and should be recorded in the relevant documentation. This includes:
    - Person Centred Planning for people with learning disabilities

- the Care Programme Approach for people with mental illness
- the Single Assessment Process for older people in England, and
- the Unified Assessment Process in Wales.

Formal reports or certificates of capacity

4.62 In some cases, a more detailed report or certificate of capacity may be required, for example,
- for use in court or other legal processes
- as required by Regulations, Rules or Orders made under the Act.

How can someone challenge a finding of lack of capacity?

4.63 There are likely to be occasions when someone may wish to challenge the results of an assessment of capacity. The first step is to raise the matter with the person who carried out the assessment. If the challenge comes from the individual who is said to lack capacity, they might need support from family, friends or an advocate. Ask the assessor to:
- give reasons why they believe the person lacks capacity to make the decision, and
- provide objective evidence to support that belief.

4.64 The assessor must show they have applied the principles of the Mental Capacity Act (see chapter 2). Attorneys, deputies and professionals will need to show that they have also followed guidance in this chapter.

4.65 It might be possible to get a second opinion from an independent professional or another expert in assessing capacity. Chapter 15 has other suggestions for dealing with disagreements. But if a disagreement cannot be resolved, the person who is challenging the assessment may be able to apply to the Court of Protection. The Court of Protection can rule on whether a person has capacity to make the decision covered by the assessment (see chapter 8).

5 WHAT DOES THE ACT MEAN WHEN IT TALKS ABOUT 'BEST INTERESTS'?

One of the key principles of the Act is that any act done for, or any decision made on behalf of a person who lacks capacity must be done, or made, in that person's *best interests*. That is the same whether the person making the decision or acting is a family carer, a paid care worker, an attorney, a court-appointed deputy, or a healthcare professional, and whether the decision is a minor issue – like what to wear – or a major issue, like whether to provide particular healthcare.

As long as these acts or decisions are in the best interests of the person who lacks capacity to make the decision for themselves, or to consent to acts concerned with their care or treatment, then the decision-maker or carer will be protected from liability.

There are exceptions to this, including circumstances where a person has made an advance decision to refuse treatment (see chapter 9) and, in specific circumstances, the involvement of a person who lacks capacity in research (see chapter 11). But otherwise the underpinning principle of the Act is that all acts and decisions should be made in the best interests of the person without capacity.

Working out what is in someone else's best interests may be difficult, and the Act requires people to follow certain steps to help them work out whether a particular act or decision is in a person's best interests. In some cases, there may be disagreement about what someone's best interests really are. As long as the person who acts or makes the decision has followed the steps to establish whether a person has capacity, and done everything they reasonably can to work out what someone's best interests are, the law should protect them.

This chapter explains what the Act means by 'best interests' and what things should be considered when trying to work out what is in someone's best interests. It also highlights some of the difficulties that might come up in working out what the best interests of a person who lacks capacity to make the decision actually are.

> In this chapter, as throughout the Code, a person's capacity (or lack of capacity) refers specifically to their capacity to make a particular decision at the time it needs to be made.

Quick summary

A person trying to work out the best interests of a person who lacks capacity to make a particular decision ('lacks capacity') should:

Encourage participation
- do whatever is possible to permit and encourage the person to take part, or to improve their ability to take part, in making the decision

Identify all relevant circumstances
- try to identify all the things that the person who lacks capacity would take into account if they were making the decision or acting for themselves

Find out the person's views
- try to find out the views of the person who lacks capacity, including:

- the person's past and present wishes and feelings – these may have been expressed verbally, in writing or through behaviour or habits.
- any beliefs and values (e.g. religious, cultural, moral or political) that would be likely to influence the decision in question.
- any other factors the person themselves would be likely to consider if they were making the decision or acting for themselves.

Avoid discrimination
- not make assumptions about someone's best interests simply on the basis of the person's age, appearance, condition or behaviour.

Assess whether the person might regain capacity
- consider whether the person is likely to regain capacity (e.g. after receiving medical treatment). If so, can the decision wait until then?

If the decision concerns life-sustaining treatment
- not be motivated in any way by a desire to bring about the person's death. They should not make assumptions about the person's quality of life.

Consult others
- if it is practical and appropriate to do so, consult other people for their views about the person's best interests and to see if they have any information about the person's wishes and feelings, beliefs and values. In particular, try to consult:
  - anyone previously named by the person as someone to be consulted on either the decision in question or on similar issues
  - anyone engaged in caring for the person
  - close relatives, friends or others who take an interest in the person's welfare
  - any attorney appointed under a Lasting Power of Attorney or Enduring Power of Attorney made by the person
  - any deputy appointed by the Court of Protection to make decisions for the person.
- For decisions about major medical treatment or where the person should live and where there is no-one who fits into any of the above categories, an Independent Mental Capacity Advocate (IMCA) must be consulted. (See chapter 10 for more information about IMCAs.)
- When consulting, remember that the person who lacks the capacity to make the decision or act for themselves still has a right to keep their affairs private – so it would not be right to share every piece of information with everyone.

Avoid restricting the person's rights
- see if there are other options that may be less restrictive of the person's rights.

Take all of this into account
- weigh up all of these factors in order to work out what is in the person's best interests.

What is the best interests principle and who does it apply to?

5.1 The best interests principle underpins the Mental Capacity Act. It is set out in section 1(5) of the Act.

> 'An act done, or decision made, under this Act for or on behalf of a person who lacks capacity must be done, or made, in his best interests.'

The concept has been developed by the courts in cases relating to people who lack capacity to make specific decisions for themselves, mainly decisions concerned with the provision of medical treatment or social care.

5.2 This principle covers all aspects of financial, personal welfare and healthcare decision-making and actions. It applies to anyone making decisions or acting under the provisions of the Act, including:
- family carers, other carers and care workers
- healthcare and social care staff
- attorneys appointed under a Lasting Power of Attorney or registered Enduring Power of Attorney
- deputies appointed by the court to make decisions on behalf of someone who lacks capacity, and
- the Court of Protection.

5.3 However, as chapter 2 explained, the Act's first key principle is that people must be assumed to have capacity to make a decision or act for themselves unless it is established that they lack it. That means that working out a person's best interests is only relevant when that person has been assessed as lacking, or is reasonably believed to lack, capacity to make the decision in question or give consent to an act being done.

People with capacity are able to decide for themselves what they want to do. When they do this, they might choose an option that other people don't think is in their best interests. That is their choice and does not, in itself, mean that they lack capacity to make those decisions.

Exceptions to the best interests principle

5.4 There are two circumstances when the best interests principle will not apply. The first is where someone has previously made an advance decision to refuse medical treatment while they had the capacity to do so. Their advance decision should be respected when they lack capacity, even if others think that the decision to refuse treatment is not in their best interests (guidance on advance decisions is given in chapter 9).

The second concerns the involvement in research, in certain circumstances, of someone lacking capacity to consent (see chapter 11).

What does the Act mean by best interests?

5.5 The term 'best interests' is not actually defined in the Act. This is because so many different types of decisions and actions are covered by the Act, and so many different people and circumstances are affected by it.

5.6 Section 4 of the Act explains how to work out the best interests of a person who lacks capacity to make a decision at the time it needs to be made. This section sets out a checklist of common factors that must always be considered by anyone who needs to decide what is in the best interests of a person who lacks capacity in any particular situation. This checklist is only the starting point: in many cases, extra factors will need to be considered.

5.7 When working out what is in the best interests of the person who lacks capacity to make a decision or act for themselves, decision-makers must take into account all relevant factors that it would be reasonable to consider, not just those that they think are important. They must not act or make a decision based on what they would want to do if they were the person who lacked capacity.

Scenario: Whose best interests?

Pedro, a young man with a severe learning disability, lives in a care home. He has dental problems which cause him a lot of pain, but refuses to open his mouth for his teeth to be cleaned.

The staff suggest that it would be a good idea to give Pedro an occasional general anaesthetic so that a dentist can clean his teeth and fill any cavities. His mother is worried about the effects of an anaesthetic, but she hates to see him distressed and suggests instead that he should be given strong painkillers when needed.

While the views of Pedro's mother and carers are important in working out what course of action would be in his best interests, the decision must *not* be based on what would be less stressful for them. Instead, it must focus on Pedro's best interests.

Having talked to others, the dentist tries to find ways of involving Pedro in the decision, with the help of his key worker and an advocate, to try to find out the cause and location of the problem and to explain

> to him that they are trying to stop the pain. The dentist tries to find out if any other forms of dental care would be better, such as a mouthwash or dental gum.
>
> The dentist concludes that it would be in Pedro's best interests for:
> - proper investigation to be carried out under anaesthetic so that immediate treatment can be provided
> - options for his future dental care to be reviewed by the care team, involving Pedro as far as possible.

Who can be a decision-maker?

5.8 Under the Act, many different people may be required to make decisions or act on behalf of someone who lacks capacity to make decisions for themselves. The person making the decision is referred to throughout this chapter, and in other parts of the Code, as the 'decision-maker', and it is the decision-maker's responsibility to work out what would be in the best interests of the person who lacks capacity.
- For most day-to-day actions or decisions, the decision-maker will be the carer most directly involved with the person at the time.
- Where the decision involves the provision of medical treatment, the doctor or other member of healthcare staff responsible for carrying out the particular treatment or procedure is the decision-maker.
- Where nursing or paid care is provided, the nurse or paid carer will be the decision-maker.
- If a Lasting Power of Attorney (or Enduring Power of Attorney) has been made and registered, or a deputy has been appointed under a court order, the attorney or deputy will be the decision-maker, for decisions within the scope of their authority.

5.9 What this means is that a range of different decision-makers may be involved with a person who lacks capacity to make different decisions.

5.10 In some cases, the same person may make different types of decision for someone who lacks capacity to make decisions for themselves. For instance, a family carer may carry out certain acts in caring for the person on a day-to-day basis, but if they are also an attorney, appointed under a Lasting Power of Attorney (LPA), they may also make specific decisions concerning the person's property and affairs or their personal welfare (depending on what decisions the LPA has been set up to cover).

5.11 There are also times when a joint decision might be made by a number of people. For example, when a care plan for a person who lacks capacity to make relevant decisions is being put together, different healthcare or social care staff might be involved in making decisions or recommendations about the person's care package. Sometimes these decisions will be made by a team of healthcare or social care staff as a whole. At other times, the decision will be made by a specific individual within the team. A different member of the team may then implement that decision, based on what the team has worked out to be the person's best interests.

5.12 No matter who is making the decision, the most important thing is that the decision-maker tries to work out what would be in the best interests of the person who lacks capacity.

Scenario: Coming to a joint decision

Jack, a young man with a brain injury, lacks capacity to agree to a rehabilitation programme designed to improve his condition. But the healthcare and social care staff who are looking after him believe that he clearly needs the programme, and have obtained the necessary funding from the Primary Care Trust.

However, Jack's family want to take him home from hospital as they believe they can provide better care for him at home.

A 'best interests' case conference is held, involving Jack, his parents and other family members and the relevant professionals, in order to decide what course of action would be in the Jack's best interests.

A plan is developed to enable Jack to live at home, but attend the day hospital every weekday. Jack seems happy with the proposals and both the family carers and the healthcare and social care staff are satisfied that the plan is in his best interests.

What must be taken into account when trying to work out someone's best interests?

5.13 Because every case – and every decision – is different, the law can't set out all the factors that will need to be taken into account in working out someone's best interests. But section 4 of the Act sets out some common factors that must always be considered when trying to work out someone's best interests. These factors are summarised in the checklist here:
- Working out what is in someone's best interests cannot be based simply on someone's age, appearance, condition or behaviour. (see paragraphs 5.16–5.17).
- All relevant circumstances should be considered when working out someone's best interests (paragraphs 5.18–5.20).
- Every effort should be made to encourage and enable the person who lacks capacity to take part in making the decision (paragraphs 5.21–5.24).

- If there is a chance that the person will regain the capacity to make a particular decision, then it may be possible to put off the decision until later if it is not urgent (paragraphs 5.25–5.28).
- Special considerations apply to decisions about life-sustaining treatment (paragraphs 5.29–5.36).
- The person's past and present wishes and feelings, beliefs and values should be taken into account (paragraphs 5.37–5.48).
- The views of other people who are close to the person who lacks capacity should be considered, as well as the views of an attorney or deputy (paragraphs 5.49–5.55).

It's important not to take shortcuts in working out best interests, and a proper and objective assessment must be carried out on every occasion. If the decision is urgent, there may not be time to examine all possible factors, but the decision must still be made in the best interests of the person who lacks capacity. Not all the factors in the checklist will be relevant to all types of decisions or actions, and in many cases other factors will have to be considered as well, even though some of them may then not be found to be relevant.

5.14 What is in a person's best interests may well change over time. This means that even where similar actions need to be taken repeatedly in connection with the person's care or treatment, the person's best interests should be regularly reviewed.

5.15 Any staff involved in the care of a person who lacks capacity should make sure a record is kept of the process of working out the best interests of that person for each relevant decision, setting out:
- how the decision about the person's best interests was reached
- what the reasons for reaching the decision were
- who was consulted to help work out best interests, and
- what particular factors were taken into account.

This record should remain on the person's file.

For major decisions based on the best interests of a person who lacks capacity, it may also be useful for family and other carers to keep a similar kind of record.

What safeguards does the Act provide around working out someone's best interests?

5.16 Section 4(1) states that anyone working out someone's best interests must not make unjustified assumptions about what their best interests might be simply on the basis of the person's age, appearance, condition or any aspect of their behaviour. In this way, the Act ensures that people who lack capacity to make decisions for themselves are not subject to discrimination or treated any less favourably than anyone else.

5.17 'Appearance' is a broad term and refers to all aspects of physical appearance, including skin colour, mode of dress and any visible medical problems, disfiguring scars or other disabilities. A person's 'condition' also covers a range of factors including physical disabilities, learning difficulties or disabilities, age-related illness or temporary conditions (such as drunkenness or unconsciousness). 'Behaviour' refers to behaviour that might seem unusual to others, such as talking too loudly or laughing inappropriately.

Scenario: Following the checklist

Martina, an elderly woman with dementia, is beginning to neglect her appearance and personal hygiene and has several times been found wandering in the street unable to find her way home. Her care workers are concerned that Martina no longer has capacity to make appropriate decisions relating to her daily care. Her daughter is her personal welfare attorney and believes the time has come to act under the Lasting Power of Attorney (LPA).

She assumes it would be best for Martina to move into a care home, since the staff would be able to help her wash and dress smartly and prevent her from wandering.

However, it cannot be assumed *simply on the basis of her age, condition, appearance or behaviour* either that Martina lacks capacity to make such a decision or that such a move would be in her best interests.

Instead, steps must be taken to assess her capacity. If it is then agreed that Martina lacks the capacity to make this decision, all the relevant factors in the best interests' checklist must be considered to try to work out what her best interests would be.

Her daughter must therefore consider:

- Martina's past and present wishes and feelings
- the views of the people involved in her care
- any alternative ways of meeting her care needs effectively which might be less restrictive of Martina's rights and freedoms, such as increased provision of home care or attendance at a day centre.

By following this process, Martina's daughter can then take decisions on behalf of her mother and in her best interests, when her mother lacks the capacity to make them herself, on any matters that fall under the authority of the LPA.

How does a decision-maker work out what 'all relevant circumstances' are?

5.18 When trying to work out someone's best interests, the decision-maker should try to identify all the issues that would be most relevant to the individual who lacks capacity and to the particular decision, as well as those in the 'checklist'. Clearly, it is not always possible or practical to investigate in depth every issue which may have some relevance to the person who lacks capacity or the decision in question. So relevant circumstances are defined in section 4(11) of the Act as those:

> '(a) of which the person making the determination is aware, and (b) which it would be reasonable to regard as relevant.'

5.19 The relevant circumstances will of course vary from case to case. For example, when making a decision about major medical treatment, a doctor would need to consider the clinical needs of the patient, the potential benefits and burdens of the treatment on the person's health and life expectancy and any other factors relevant to making a professional judgement.[16] But it would not be reasonable to consider issues such as life expectancy when working out whether it would be in someone's best interests to be given medication for a minor problem.

16 *An NHS Trust v S* [2003] EWHC 365 (Fam), at [47].

5.20 Financial decisions are another area where the relevant circumstances will vary. For example, if a person had received a substantial sum of money as compensation for an accident resulting in brain injury, the decision-maker would have to consider a wide range of circumstances when making decisions about how the money is spent or invested, such as:

- whether the person's condition is likely to change
- whether the person needs professional care, and
- whether the person needs to live somewhere else to make it easier
for them.

These kinds of issues can only be decided on a case-by-case basis.

How should the person who lacks capacity be involved in working out their best interests?

5.21 Wherever possible, the person who lacks capacity to make a decision should still be involved in the decision-making process (section 4(4)).

5.22 Even if the person lacks capacity to make the decision, they may have views on matters affecting the decision, and on what outcome would be preferred. Their involvement can help work out what would be in their best interests.

5.23 The decision-maker should make sure that all practical means are used to enable and encourage the person to participate as fully as possible in the decision-making process and any action taken as a result, or to help the person improve their ability to participate.

5.24 Consulting the person who lacks capacity will involve taking time to explain what is happening and why a decision needs to be made. Chapter 3 includes a number of practical steps to assist and enable

decision-making which may be also be helpful in encouraging greater participation. These include:
- using simple language and/or illustrations or photographs to help the person understand the options
- asking them about the decision at a time and location where the person feels most relaxed and at ease
- breaking the information down into easy-to-understand points
- using specialist interpreters or signers to communicate with the person.

This may mean that other people are required to communicate with the person to establish their views. For example, a trusted relative or friend, a full-time carer or an advocate may be able to help the person to express wishes or aspirations or to indicate a preference between different options.

More information on all of these steps can be found in chapter 3.

> **Scenario: Involving someone in working out their best interests**
>
> The parents of Amy, a young woman with learning difficulties, are going through a divorce and are arguing about who should continue to care for their daughter. Though she cannot understand what is happening, attempts are made to see if Amy can give some indication of where she would prefer to live.
>
> An advocate is appointed to work with Amy to help her understand the situation and to find out her likes and dislikes and matters which are important to her. With the advocate's help, Amy is able to participate in decisions about her future care.

How do the chances of someone regaining and developing capacity affect working out what is in their best interests?

5.25 There are some situations where decisions may be deferred, if someone who currently lacks capacity may regain the capacity to make the decision for themselves. Section 4(3) of the Act requires the decision-maker to consider:
- whether the individual concerned is likely to regain the capacity to make that particular decision in the future, and
- if so, when that is likely to be.

It may then be possible to put off the decision until the person can make it for themselves.

5.26 In emergency situations – such as when urgent medical treatment is needed – it may not be possible to wait to see if the person may regain capacity so they can decide for themselves whether or not to have the urgent treatment.

5.27 Where a person currently lacks capacity to make a decision relating to their day-to-day care, the person may – over time and with the right support – be able to develop the skills to do so.

Though others may need to make the decision on the person's behalf at the moment, all possible support should be given to that person to enable them to develop the skills so that they can make the decision for themselves in the future.

> **Scenario: Taking a short-term decision for someone who may regain capacity**
>
> Mr Fowler has suffered a stroke leaving him severely disabled and unable to speak. Within days, he has shown signs of improvement, so with intensive treatment there is hope he will recover over time. But at present both his wife and the hospital staff find it difficult to communicate with him and have been unable to find out his wishes.
>
> He has always looked after the family finances, so Mrs Fowler suddenly discovers she has no access to his personal bank account to provide the family with money to live on or pay the bills. Because the decision can't be put off while efforts are made to find effective means of communicating with Mr Fowler, an application is made to the Court of Protection for an order that allows Mrs Fowler to access Mr Fowler's money.
>
> The decision about longer-term arrangements, on the other hand, can be delayed until alternative methods of communication have been tried and the extent of Mr Fowler's recovery is known.

5.28 Some factors which may indicate that a person may regain or develop capacity in the future are:
- the cause of the lack of capacity can be treated, either by medication or some other form of treatment or therapy
- the lack of capacity is likely to decrease in time (for example, where it is caused by the effects of medication or alcohol, or following a sudden shock)
- a person with learning disabilities may learn new skills or be subject to new experiences which increase their understanding and ability to make certain decisions
- the person may have a condition which causes capacity to come and go at various times (such as some forms of mental illness) so it may be possible to arrange for the decision to be made during a time when they do have capacity
- a person previously unable to communicate may learn a new form of communication (see chapter 3).

How should someone's best interests be worked out when making decisions about life-sustaining treatment?

5.29 A special factor in the checklist applies to decisions about treatment which is necessary to keep the person alive ('life-sustaining treatment') and this is set out in section 4(5) of the Act. The fundamental rule is that anyone who is deciding whether or not life-sustaining treatment is in the best interests of someone who lacks capacity to consent to or refuse such treatment must not be motivated by a desire to bring about the person's death.

5.30 Whether a treatment is 'life-sustaining' depends not only on the type of treatment, but also on the particular circumstances in which it may be prescribed. For example, in some situations giving antibiotics may be life-sustaining, whereas in other circumstances antibiotics are used to treat a non-life-threatening condition. It is up to the doctor or healthcare professional providing treatment to assess whether the treatment is life-sustaining in each particular situation.

5.31 All reasonable steps which are in the person's best interests should be taken to prolong their life. There will be a limited number of cases where treatment is futile, overly burdensome to the patient or where there is no prospect of recovery. In circumstances such as these, it may be that an assessment of best interests leads to the conclusion that it would be in the best interests of the patient to withdraw or withhold life-sustaining treatment, even if this may result in the person's death. The decision-maker must make a decision based on the best interests of the person who lacks capacity. They must not be motivated by a desire to bring about the person's death for whatever reason, even if this is from a sense of compassion. Healthcare and social care staff should also refer to relevant professional guidance when making decisions regarding life-sustaining treatment.

5.32 As with all decisions, before deciding to withdraw or withhold life-sustaining treatment, the decision-maker must consider the range of treatment options available to work out what would be in the person's best interests. All the factors in the best interests checklist should be considered, and in particular, the decision-maker should consider any statements that the person has previously made about their wishes and feelings about life-sustaining treatment.

5.33 Importantly, section 4(5) cannot be interpreted to mean that doctors are under an obligation to provide, or to continue to provide, life-sustaining treatment where that treatment is not in the best interests of the person, even where the person's death is foreseen. Doctors must apply the best interests' checklist and use their professional skills to decide whether life-sustaining treatment is in the person's best interests. If the doctor's assessment is disputed, and there is no other way of resolving the dispute, ultimately the Court of Protection may be asked to decide what is in the person's best interests.

5.34 Where a person has made a written statement in advance that requests particular medical treatments, such as artificial nutrition and hydration (ANH), these requests should be taken into account by the treating doctor in the same way as requests made by a patient who has the capacity to make such decisions. Like anyone else involved in making this decision, the doctor must weigh written statements alongside all other relevant factors to decide whether it is in the best interests of the patient to provide or continue life-sustaining treatment.

5.35 If someone has made an advance decision to refuse life-sustaining treatment, specific rules apply. More information about these can be found in chapter 9 and in paragraph 5.45 below.

5.36 As mentioned in paragraph 5.33 above, where there is any doubt about the patient's best interests, an application should be made to the Court of Protection for a decision as to whether withholding or withdrawing life-sustaining treatment is in the patient's best interests.

How do a person's wishes and feelings, beliefs and values affect working out what is in their best interests?

5.37 Section 4(6) of the Act requires the decision-maker to consider, as far as they are 'reasonably ascertainable':

'(a) the person's past and present wishes and feelings (and in particular, any relevant written statements made by him when he had capacity),

(b) the beliefs and values that would be likely to influence his decision if he had capacity, and

(c) the other factors that he would be likely to consider if he were able to do so.'

Paragraphs 5.38–5.48 below give further guidance on each of these factors.

5.38 In setting out the requirements for working out a person's 'best interests', section 4 of the Act puts the person who lacks capacity at the centre of the decision to be made. Even if they cannot make the decision, their wishes and feelings, beliefs and values should be taken fully into account – whether expressed in the past or now. But their wishes and feelings, beliefs and values will not necessarily be the deciding factor in working out their best interests. Any such assessment must consider past and current wishes and feelings, beliefs and values alongside all other factors, but the final decision must be based entirely on what is in the person's best interests.

Scenario: Considering wishes and feelings as part of best interests

Andre, a young man with severe learning disabilities who does not use any formal system of communication, cuts his leg while outdoors. There is some earth in the wound. A doctor wants to give him a tetanus jab, but Andre appears scared of the needle and pushes it away.

> Assessments have shown that he is unable to understand the risk of infection following his injury, or the consequences of rejecting the injection.
>
> The doctor decides that it is in the Andre's best interests to give the vaccination. She asks a nurse to comfort Andre, and if necessary, restrain him while she gives the injection. She has objective reasons for believing she is acting in Andre's best interests, and for believing that Andre lacks capacity to make the decision for himself. So she should be protected from liability under section 5 of the Act (see chapter 6).

What is 'reasonably ascertainable'?

5.39 How much someone can learn about a person's past and present views will depend on circumstances and the time available. 'Reasonably ascertainable' means considering all possible information in the time available. What is available in an emergency will be different to what is available in a non-emergency. But even in an emergency, there may still be an opportunity to try to communicate with the person or his friends, family or carers (see chapter 3 for guidance on helping communication).

What role do a person's past and present wishes and feelings play?

5.40 People who cannot express their current wishes and feelings in words may express themselves through their behaviour. Expressions of pleasure or distress and emotional responses will also be relevant in working out what is in their best interests. It is also important to be sure that other people have not influenced a person's views. An advocate could help the person make choices and express their views.

5.41 The person may have held strong views in the past which could have a bearing on the decision now to be made. All reasonable efforts must be made to find out whether the person has expressed views in the past that will shape the decision to be made. This could have been through verbal communication, writing, behaviour or habits, or recorded in any other way (for example, home videos or audiotapes).

5.42 Section 4(6)(a) places special emphasis on written statements the person might have made before losing capacity. These could provide a lot of information about a person's wishes. For example, these statements could include information about the type of medical treatment they would want in the case of future illness, where they would prefer to live, or how they wish to be cared for.

5.43 The decision-maker should consider written statements carefully. If their decision does not follow something a person has put in writing, they must record the reasons why. They should be able to justify their reasons if someone challenges their decision.

5.44 A doctor should take written statements made by a person before losing capacity which request specific treatments as seriously as those made by people who currently have capacity to make treatment decisions. But they would not have to follow a written request if they think the specific treatment would be clinically unnecessary or not appropriate for the person's condition, so not in the person's best interests.

5.45 It is important to note the distinction between a written statement expressing treatment preferences and a statement which constitutes an advance decision to refuse treatment. This is covered by section 24 of the Act, and it has a different status in law. Doctors cannot ignore a written statement that is a valid advance decision to refuse treatment. An advance decision to refuse treatment must be followed if it meets the Act's requirements and applies to the person's circumstances. In these cases, the treatment must not be given (see chapter 9 for more information). If there is not a valid and applicable advance decision, treatment should be provided based on the person's best interests.

What role do beliefs and values play?

5.46 Everybody's values and beliefs influence the decisions they make. They may become especially important for someone who lacks capacity to make a decision because of a progressive illness such as dementia, for example. Evidence of a person's beliefs and values can be found in things like their:
- cultural background
- religious beliefs
- political convictions, or
- past behaviour or habits.

Some people set out their values and beliefs in a written statement while they still have capacity.

Scenario: Considering beliefs and values

Anita, a young woman, suffers serious brain damage during a car accident. The court appoints her father as deputy to invest the compensation she received. As the decision-maker he must think about her wishes, beliefs and values before deciding how to invest the money.

Anita had worked for an overseas charity. Her father talks to her former colleagues. They tell him how Anita's political beliefs shaped her work and personal beliefs, so he decides not to invest in the bonds that a financial adviser had recommended, because they are from

> companies Anita would not have approved of. Instead, he employs an ethical investment adviser to choose appropriate companies in line with her beliefs.

What other factors should a decision-maker consider?

5.47 Section 4(6)(c) of the Act requires decision-makers to consider any other factors the person who lacks capacity would consider if they were able to do so. This might include the effect of the decision on other people, obligations to dependants or the duties of a responsible citizen.

5.48 The Act allows actions that benefit other people, as long as they are in the best interests of the person who lacks capacity to make the decision. For example, having considered all the circumstances of the particular case, a decision might be made to take a blood sample from a person who lacks capacity to consent, to check for a genetic link to cancer within the family, because this might benefit someone else in the family. But it might still be in the best interests of the person who lacks capacity. 'Best interests' goes beyond the person's medical interests.

For example, courts have previously ruled that possible wider benefits to a person who lacks capacity to consent, such as providing or gaining emotional support from close relationships, are important factors in working out the person's own best interests.[17] If it is likely that the person who lacks capacity would have considered these factors themselves, they can be seen as part of the person's best interests.

17 See for example *Re Y (Mental Patient: Bone Marrow Donation)* [1996] 2 FLR 787; sub nom Re Y (Mental Incapacity: Bone Marrow Transplant) and *Re A (Male Sterilisation)* [2000] 1 FLR 549, CA.

Who should be consulted when working out someone's best interests?

5.49 The Act places a duty on the decision-maker to consult other people close to a person who lacks capacity, where practical and appropriate, on decisions affecting the person and what might be in the person's best interests. This also applies to those involved in caring for the person and interested in the person's welfare. Under section 4(7), the decision-maker has a duty to take into account the views of the following people, where it is practical and appropriate to do so:
- anyone the person has previously named as someone they want to be consulted
- anyone involved in caring for the person
- anyone interested in their welfare (for example, family carers, other close relatives, or an advocate already working with the person)

- an attorney appointed by the person under a Lasting Power of Attorney, and
- a deputy appointed for that person by the Court of Protection.

5.50 If there is no-one to speak to about the person's best interests, in some circumstances the person may qualify for an Independent Mental Capacity Advocate (IMCA). For more information on IMCAs, see chapter 10.

5.51 Decision-makers must show they have thought carefully about who to speak to. If it is practical and appropriate to speak to the above people, they must do so and must take their views into account. They must be able to explain why they did not speak to a particular person – it is good practice to have a clear record of their reasons. It is also good practice to give careful consideration to the views of family carers, if it is possible to do so.

5.52 It is also good practice for healthcare and social care staff to record at the end of the process why they think a specific decision is in the person's best interests. This is particularly important if healthcare and social care staff go against the views of somebody who has been consulted while working out the person's best interests.

5.53 The decision-maker should try to find out:
- what the people consulted think is in the person's best interests in this matter, and
- if they can give information on the person's wishes and feelings, beliefs and values.

5.54 This information may be available from somebody the person named before they lost capacity as someone they wish to be consulted. People who are close to the person who lacks capacity, such as close family members, are likely to know them best. They may also be able to help with communication or interpret signs that show the person's present wishes and feelings. Everybody's views are equally important – even if they do not agree with each other. They must be considered alongside the views of the person who lacks capacity and other factors. See paragraphs 5.62–5.69 below for guidance on dealing with conflicting views.

Scenario: Considering other people's views

Lucia, a young woman with severe brain damage, is cared for at home by her parents and attends a day centre a couple of days each week. The day centre staff would like to take some of the service users on holiday. They speak to Lucia's parents as part of the process of assessing whether the holiday would be in her best interests.

The parents think that the holiday would be good for her, but they are worried that Lucia gets very anxious if she is surrounded by strangers who don't know how to communicate with her. Having tried to seek

> Lucia's views and involve her in the decision, the staff and parents agree that a holiday would be in her best interests, as long as her care assistant can go with her to help with communication.

5.55 Where an attorney has been appointed under a Lasting Power of Attorney or Enduring Power of Attorney, or a deputy has been appointed by a court, they must make the decisions on any matters they have been appointed to deal with. Attorneys and deputies should also be consulted, if practical and appropriate, on other issues affecting the person who lacks capacity.

For instance, an attorney who is appointed only to look after the person's property and affairs may have information about the person's beliefs and values, wishes and feelings, that could help work out what would be in the person's best interests regarding healthcare or treatment decisions. (See chapters 7 and 8 for more information about the roles of attorneys and deputies.)

How can decision-makers respect confidentiality?

5.56 Decision-makers must balance the duty to consult other people with the right to confidentiality of the person who lacks capacity. So if confidential information is to be discussed, they should only seek the views of people who it is appropriate to consult, where their views are relevant to the decision to be made and the particular circumstances.

5.57 There may be occasions where it is in the person's best interests for personal information (for example, about their medical condition, if the decision concerns the provision of medical treatment) to be revealed to the people consulted as part of the process of working out their best interests (further guidance on this is given in chapter 16). Healthcare and social care staff who are trying to determine a person's best interests must follow their professional guidance, as well as other relevant guidance, about confidentiality.

When does the best interests principle apply?

5.58 Section 1(5) of the Act confirms that the principle applies to any act done, or any decision made, on behalf of someone where there is reasonable belief that the person lacks capacity under the Act. This covers informal day-to-day decisions and actions as well as decisions made by the courts.

Reasonable belief about a person's best interests

5.59 Section 4(9) confirms that if someone acts or makes a decision in the reasonable belief that what they are doing is in the best interests of the person who lacks capacity, then – provided they have followed the checklist in section 4 – they will have complied with the best interests principle set out in the Act. Coming to an incorrect conclusion about a person's capacity or best interests does not necessarily mean that the decision-maker would not get protection from liability (this is explained in chapter 6). But they must be able to show that it was reasonable for them to think that the person lacked capacity and that they were acting in the person's best interests at the time they made their decision or took action.

5.60 Where there is a need for a court decision, the court is likely to require formal evidence of what might be in the person's best interests. This will include evidence from relevant professionals (for example, psychiatrists or social workers). But in most day-to-day situations, there is no need for such formality. In emergency situations, it may not be practical or possible to gather formal evidence.

5.61 Where the court is not involved, people are still expected to have reasonable grounds for believing that they are acting in somebody's best interests. This does not mean that decision-makers can simply impose their own views. They must have objective reasons for their decisions – and they must be able to demonstrate them. They must be able to show they have considered all relevant circumstances and applied all elements of the best interests checklist.

Scenario: Demonstrating reasonable belief

Mrs Prior is mugged and knocked unconscious. She is brought to hospital without any means of identification. She has head injuries and a stab wound, and has lost a lot of blood. In casualty, a doctor arranges an urgent blood transfusion. Because this is necessary to save her life, the doctor believes this is in her best interests.

When her relatives are contacted, they say that Mrs Prior's beliefs meant that she would have refused all blood products. But since Mrs Prior's handbag had been stolen, the doctor had no idea who the woman was nor what her beliefs her. He needed to make an immediate decision and Mrs Prior lacked capacity to make the decision for herself. Therefore he had reasonable grounds for believing that his action was in his patient's best interests – and so was protected from liability.

Now that the doctor knows Mrs Prior's beliefs, he can take them into account in future decisions about her medical treatment if she lacks capacity to make them for herself. He can also consult her family, now that he knows where they are.

What problems could arise when working out someone's best interests?

5.62 It is important that the best interests principle and the statutory checklist are flexible. Without flexibility, it would be impossible to prioritise factors in different cases – and it would be difficult to ensure that the outcome is the best possible for the person who lacks capacity to make the particular decision. Some cases will be straightforward. Others will require decision-makers to balance the pros and cons of all relevant factors.[18] But this flexibility could lead to problems in reaching a conclusion about a person's best interests.

18 Re A (Male Sterilisation) [2000] 1 FLR 549.

What happens when there are conflicting concerns?

5.63 A decision-maker may be faced with people who disagree about a person's best interests. Family members, partners and carers may disagree between themselves. Or they might have different memories about what views the person expressed in the past. Carers and family might disagree with a professional's view about the person's care or treatment needs.

5.64 The decision-maker will need to find a way of balancing these concerns or deciding between them. The first approach should be to review all elements of the best interests checklist with everyone involved. They should include the person who lacks capacity (as much as they are able to take part) and anyone who has been involved in earlier discussions. It may be possible to reach an agreement at a meeting to air everyone's concerns. But an agreement in itself might not be in the person's best interests. Ultimate responsibility for working out best interests lies with the decision-maker.

Scenario: Dealing with disagreement

Some time ago, Mr Graham made a Lasting Power of Attorney (LPA) appointing his son and daughter as joint attorneys to manage his finances and property. He now has Alzheimer's disease and has moved into private residential care. The son and daughter have to decide what to do with Mr Graham's house.

His son thinks it is in their father's best interests to sell it and invest the money for Mr Graham's future care. But his daughter thinks it is in Mr Graham's best interests to keep the property, because he enjoys visiting and spending time in his old home.

After making every effort to get Mr Graham's views, the family meets to discuss all the issues involved. After hearing other family views, the attorneys agree that it would be in their father's best interests to keep the property for so long as he is able to enjoy visiting it.

Family, partners and carers who are consulted

5.65 If disagreement continues, the decision-maker will need to weigh up the views of different parties. This will depend entirely upon the circumstances of each case, the people involved and their relationship with the person who lacks capacity. Sometimes the decision-maker will find that carers have an insight into how to interpret a person's wishes and feelings that can help them reach a decision.

5.66 At the same time, paid care workers and voluntary sector support workers may have specialist knowledge about up-to-date care options or treatments. Some may also have known the person for many years.

5.67 People with conflicting interests should not be cut out of the process (for example, those who stand to inherit from the person's will may still have a right to be consulted about the person's care or medical treatment). But decision-makers must always ensure that the interests of those consulted do not overly influence the process of working out a person's best interests. In weighing up different contributions, the decision-maker should consider:

- how long an individual has known the person who lacks capacity, and
- what their relationship is.

Scenario: Settling disagreements

Robert is 19 and has learning disabilities and autism. He is about to leave his residential special school. His parents want Robert to go to a specialist unit run by a charitable organisation, but he has been offered a place in a local supported living scheme. The parents don't think Robert will get appropriate care there.

The school sets up a 'best interests' meeting. People who attend include Robert, his parents, teachers from his school and professionals involved in preparing Robert's care plan. Robert's parents and teachers know him best. They set out their views and help Robert to communicate where he would like to live.

Social care staff identify some different placements within the county. Robert visits these with his parents. After further discussion, everyone agrees that a community placement near his family home would be in Robert's best interests.

Settling disputes about best interests

5.68 If someone wants to challenge a decision-maker's conclusions, there are several options:

- Involve an advocate to act on behalf of the person who lacks capacity to make the decision (see paragraph 5.69 below).
- Get a second opinion.
- Hold a formal or informal 'best interests' case conference.
- Attempt some form of mediation (see chapter 15).
- Pursue a complaint through the organisation's formal procedures.

Ultimately, if all other attempts to resolve the dispute have failed, the court might need to decide what is in the person's best interests. Chapter 8 provides more information about the Court of Protection.

Advocacy

5.69 An advocate might be useful in providing support for the person who lacks capacity to make a decision in the process of working out their best interests, if:
- the person who lacks capacity has no close family or friends to take an interest in their welfare, and they do not qualify for an Independent Mental Capacity Advocate (see chapter 10)
- family members disagree about the person's best interests
- family members and professionals disagree about the person's best interests
- there is a conflict of interest for people who have been consulted in the best interests assessment (for example, the sale of a family property where the person lives)
- the person who lacks capacity is already in contact with an advocate
- the proposed course of action may lead to the use of restraint or other restrictions on the person who lacks capacity
- there is a concern about the protection of a vulnerable adult.

6 WHAT PROTECTION DOES THE ACT OFFER FOR PEOPLE PROVIDING CARE OR TREATMENT?

Section 5 of the Act allows carers, healthcare and social care staff to carry out certain tasks without fear of liability. These tasks involve the personal care, healthcare or treatment of people who lack capacity to consent to them. The aim is to give legal backing for acts that need to be carried out in the best interests of the person who lacks capacity to consent.[19]

19 The provisions of section 5 are based on the common law 'doctrine of necessity' as set out in *Re F (Mental Patient: Sterilisation)* [1989] 2 FLR 376.

This chapter explains:
- how the Act provides protection from liability
- how that protection works in practice
- where protection is restricted or limited, and
- when a carer can use a person's money to buy goods or services without formal permission.

> In this chapter, as throughout the Code, a person's capacity (or lack of capacity) refers specifically to their capacity to make a particular decision at the time it needs to be made.

Quick summary

The following steps list all the things that people providing care or treatment should bear in mind to ensure they are protected by the Act.

Acting in connection with the care or treatment of someone who lacks capacity to consent
- Is the action to be carried out in connection with the care or treatment of a person who lacks capacity to give consent to that act?
- Does it involve major life changes for the person concerned? If so, it will need special consideration.
- Who is carrying out the action? Is it appropriate for that person to do so at the relevant time?

Checking whether the person has capacity to consent
- Have all possible steps been taken to try to help the person make a decision for themselves about the action?
- Has the two-stage test of capacity been applied?
- Are there reasonable grounds for believing the person lacks capacity to give permission?

Acting in the person's best interests
- Has the best interests checklist been applied and all relevant circumstances considered?
- Is a less restrictive option available?
- Is it reasonable to believe that the proposed act is in the person's best interests?

Understanding possible limitations on protection from liability
- If restraint is being considered, is it necessary to prevent harm to the person who lacks capacity, and is it a proportionate response to the likelihood of the person suffering harm – and to the seriousness of that harm?
- Could the restraint be classed as a 'deprivation of the person's liberty'?
- Does the action conflict with a decision that has been made by an attorney or deputy under their powers?

Paying for necessary goods and services
- If someone wishes to use the person's money to buy goods or pay for services for someone who lacks capacity to do so themselves, are those goods or services necessary and in the person's best interests?
- Is it necessary to take money from the person's bank or building society account or to sell the person's property to pay for goods or services? If so, formal authority will be required.

What protection do people have when caring for those who lack capacity to consent?

6.1 Every day, millions of acts are done to and for people who lack capacity either to:
- take decisions about their own care or treatment, or
- consent to someone else caring for them.

Such acts range from everyday tasks of caring (for example, helping someone to wash) to life-changing events (for example, serious medical treatment or arranging for someone to go into a care home). In theory, many of these actions could be against the law. Legally, people have the right to stop others from interfering with their body or property unless they give permission. But what happens if someone lacks capacity to give permission? Carers who dress people who cannot dress themselves are potentially interfering with someone's body without their consent, so could theoretically be prosecuted for assault. A neighbour who enters and cleans the house of a person who lacks capacity could be trespassing on the person's property.

6.2 Section 5 of the Act provides 'protection from liability'. In other words, it protects people who carry out these actions. It stops them being prosecuted for acts that could otherwise be classed as civil wrongs or crimes. By protecting family and other carers from liability, the Act allows necessary caring acts or treatment to take place as if a person who lacks capacity to consent had consented to them. People providing care of this sort do not therefore need to get formal authority to act.

6.3 Importantly, section 5 does not give people caring for or treating someone the power to make any other decisions on behalf of those who lack capacity to make their own decisions. Instead, it offers protection from liability so that they can act in connection with the person's care or treatment. The power to make decisions on behalf of someone who lacks capacity can be granted through other parts of the Act (such as the powers granted to attorneys and deputies, which are explained in chapters 7 and 8).

What type of actions might have protection from liability?

6.4 Section 5(1) provides possible protection for actions carried out *in connection with care or treatment*. The action may be carried out on behalf of someone who is believed to lack capacity to give permission for the action, so long as it is in that person's best interests (see chapter 5). The Act does not define 'care' or 'treatment'. They should be given their normal meaning. However, section 64(1) makes clear that treatment includes diagnostic or other procedures.

6.5 Actions that might be covered by section 5 include:

Personal care

- helping with washing, dressing or personal hygiene
- helping with eating and drinking
- helping with communication
- helping with mobility (moving around)
- helping someone take part in education, social or leisure activities
- going into a person's home to drop off shopping or to see if they are alright
- doing the shopping or buying necessary goods with the person's money
- arranging household services (for example, arranging repairs or maintenance for gas and electricity supplies)
- providing services that help around the home (such as homecare or meals on wheels)
- undertaking actions related to community care services (for example, day care, residential accommodation or nursing care) – but see also paragraphs 6.7–6.14 below
- helping someone to move home (including moving property and clearing the former home).

Healthcare and treatment

- carrying out diagnostic examinations and tests (to identify an illness, condition or other problem)
- providing professional medical, dental and similar treatment
- giving medication
- taking someone to hospital for assessment or treatment
- providing nursing care (whether in hospital or in the community)
- carrying out any other necessary medical procedures (for example, taking a blood sample) or therapies (for example, physiotherapy or chiropody)
- providing care in an emergency.

6.6 These actions only receive protection from liability if the person is reasonably believed to lack capacity to give permission for the action. The action must also be in the person's best interests and follow the Act's principles (see paragraph 6.26 onwards).

6.7 Some acts in connection with care or treatment may cause major life changes with significant consequences for the person concerned. Those requiring particularly careful consideration include a change of residence, perhaps into a care home or nursing home, or major decisions about healthcare and medical treatment. These are described in the following paragraphs.

A change of residence

6.8 Sometimes a person cannot get sufficient or appropriate care in their own home, and they may have to move – perhaps to live with relatives or to go into a care home or nursing home. If the person lacks capacity to consent to a move, the decision-maker(s) must consider whether the move is in the person's best interests (by referring to the best interests checklist in chapter 5 and in particular the person's past and present wishes and feelings, as well as the views of other relevant people). The decision-maker(s) must also consider whether there is a less restrictive option (see chapter 2, principle 5).
This may involve speaking to:
- anyone currently involved in the person's care
- family carers and other family members close to the person and interested in their welfare
- others who have an interest in the person's welfare
- anyone the person has previously named as someone to be consulted, and
- an attorney or deputy who has been legally appointed to make particular decisions on their behalf.

6.9 Some cases will require an Independent Mental Capacity Advocate (IMCA). The IMCA represents and supports the person who lacks capacity and they will provide information to make sure the final decision is in the person's best interests (see chapter 10). An IMCA is needed when there is no-one close to the person who lacks capacity to give an opinion about what is best for them, and:
- an NHS body is proposing to provide serious medical treatment or
- an NHS body or local authority is proposing to arrange accommodation in hospital or a care home or other longer-term accommodation and
  – the person will stay in hospital longer than 28 days, or
  – they will stay in a care home for more than eight weeks.

There are also some circumstances where an IMCA may be appointed on a discretionary basis. More guidance is available in chapter 10.

6.10 Sometimes the final outcome may not be what the person who lacks capacity wanted. For example, they might want to stay at home, but those caring for them might decide a move is in their best interests. In all cases, those making the decision must first consider other options that might restrict the person's rights and freedom of action less (see chapter 2, principle 5).

6.11 In some cases, there may be no alternative but to move the person. Such a move would normally require the person's formal consent if they had capacity to give, or refuse, it. In cases where a person lacks capacity to consent, section 5 of the Act allows carers to carry out actions relating to the move – as long as the Act's principles and the requirements for working out best interests have been followed. This applies even if the person continues to object to the move.

However, section 6 places clear limits on the use of force or restraint by only permitting restraint to be used (for example, to transport the person to their new home) where this is necessary to protect the person from harm and is a proportionate response to the risk of harm (see paragraphs 6.40–6.53). Any action taken to move the person concerned or their property could incur liability unless protected under section 5.

6.12 If there is a serious disagreement about the need to move the person that cannot be settled in any other way, the Court of Protection can be asked to decide what the person's best interests are and where they should live. For example, this could happen if members of a family disagree over what is best for a relative who lacks capacity to give or deny permission for a move.

6.13 In some circumstances, being placed in a hospital or care home may deprive the person of their liberty (see paragraphs 6.49–6.53). If this is the case, there is no protection from liability – even if the placement was considered to be in the best interests of the person (section 6(5)). It is up to the decision-maker to first look at a range of alternative and less restrictive options to see if there is any way of avoiding taking away the person's liberty.

6.14 If there is no alternative way of caring for the person, specific authority will be required to keep the person in a situation which deprives them of their liberty. For instance, sometimes the Court of Protection might be prepared to grant an order of which a consequence is the deprivation of a person's liberty – if it is satisfied that this is in the person's best interests. In other cases, if the person needs treatment for a mental disorder and meets the criteria for detention under the Mental Health Act 1983, this may be used to admit or keep the person in hospital (see chapter 13).

Healthcare and treatment decisions

6.15 Section 5 also allows actions to be taken to ensure a person who lacks capacity to consent receives necessary medical treatment. This could involve taking the person to hospital for out-patient treatment or arranging for admission to hospital. Even if a person who lacks capacity to consent objects to the proposed treatment or admission to hospital, the action might still be allowed under section 5 (but see paragraphs 6.20 and 6.22 below). But there are limits about whether force or restraint can be used to impose treatment (see paragraphs 6.40–6.53).

6.16 Major healthcare and treatment decisions – for example, major surgery or a decision that no attempt is to be made to resuscitate the patient (known as 'DNR' decisions) – will also need special consideration. Unless there is a valid and applicable advance decision to refuse the specific treatment, healthcare staff must carefully work out what would be in the person's best interests (see chapter 5). As part of the process of working this out, they will need to consider (where practical and appropriate):

- the past and present wishes and feelings, beliefs and values of the person who lacks capacity to make the treatment decision, including any advance statement the person wrote setting out their wishes when they had capacity
- the views of anyone previously named by the person as someone to be consulted
- the views of anyone engaged in caring for the person
- the views of anyone interested in their welfare, and
- the views of any attorney or deputy appointed for the person.

In specific cases where there is no-one else available to consult about the person's best interests, an IMCA must be appointed to support and represent the person (see paragraph 6.9 above and chapter 10).

Healthcare staff must also consider whether there are alternative treatment options that might be less intrusive or restrictive (see chapter 2, principle 5). When deciding about the provision or withdrawal of life-sustaining treatment, anyone working out what is in the best interests of a person who lacks capacity must not be motivated by a desire to bring about the person's death (see chapter 5).

6.17 Multi-disciplinary meetings are often the best way to decide on a person's best interests. They bring together healthcare and social care staff with different skills to discuss the person's options and may involve those who are closest to the person concerned. But final responsibility for deciding what is in a person's best interest lies with the member of healthcare staff responsible for the person's treatment. They should record their decision, how they reached it and the reasons for it in the person's clinical notes. As long as they have recorded objective reasons to show that the decision is in the person's best interests, and the other requirements of section 5 of the Act are met, all healthcare staff taking actions in connection with the particular treatment will be protected from liability.

6.18 Some treatment decisions are so serious that the court has to make them – unless the person has previously made a Lasting Power of Attorney appointing an attorney to make such healthcare decisions for them (see chapter 7) or they have made a valid advance decision to refuse the proposed treatment (see chapter 9). The Court of Protection must be asked to make decisions relating to:[20]

- the proposed withholding or withdrawal of artificial nutrition and
  hydration (ANH) from a patient in a permanent vegetative state (PVS)
- cases where it is proposed that a person who lacks capacity to consent should donate an organ or bone marrow to another person
- the proposed non-therapeutic sterilisation of a person who lacks
  capacity to consent (for example, for contraceptive purposes)
- cases where there is a dispute about whether a particular treatment
  will be in a person's best interests.

See paragraphs 8.18–8.24 for more details on these types of cases.

20 The procedures resulting from those court judgements are set out in a Practice Note from the Official Solicitor (available at www.officialsolicitor.gov.uk) and will be set out in a Practice Direction from the new Court of Protection.

6.19 This last category may include cases that introduce ethical dilemmas concerning untested or innovative treatments (for example, new treatments for variant Creutzfeldt-Jakob Disease (CDJ)) where it is not known if the treatment will be effective, or certain cases involving a termination of pregnancy. It may also include cases where there is conflict between professionals or between professionals and family members which cannot be resolved in any other way.

Where there is conflict, it is advisable for parties to get legal advice, though they may not necessarily be able to get legal aid to pay for this advice. Chapter 8 gives more information about the need to refer cases to court for a decision.

Who is protected from liability by section 5?

6.20 Section 5 of the Act is most likely to affect:
- family carers and other kinds of carers
- care workers
- healthcare and social care staff, and
- others who may occasionally be involved in the care or treatment of a person who lacks capacity to consent (for example, ambulance staff, housing workers, police officers and volunteer support workers).

6.21 At any time, it is likely that several people will be carrying out tasks that are covered by section 5 of the Act. Section 5 does not:
- give one person more rights than another to carry out tasks
- specify who has the authority to act in a specific instance
- allow somebody to make decisions relating to subjects other than the care or treatment of the person who lacks capacity, or
- allow somebody to give consent on behalf of a person who lacks capacity to do so.

6.22 To receive protection from liability under section 5, all actions must be related to the care or treatment of the person who lacks capacity to consent. Before taking action, carers must first reasonably believe that:
- the person lacks the capacity to make that particular decision at the time it needs to be made, and
- the action is in the person's best interests.

This is explained further in paragraphs 6.26–6.34 below.

> **Scenario: Protecting multiple carers**
>
> Mr Rose, an older man with dementia, gets help from several people. His sister sometimes cooks meals for him. A district nurse visits him to change the dressing on a pressure sore, and a friend often takes Mr Rose to the park, guiding him when they cross the road. Each of these individuals would be protected from liability under section 5 of the Act – but only if they take reasonable steps to check that he lacks capacity to consent to the actions they take and hold a reasonable belief that the actions are in Mr Rose's best interests.

6.23 Section 5 may also protect carers who need to use the person's money to pay for goods or services that the person needs but lacks the capacity to purchase for themselves. However, there are strict controls over who may have access to another person's money. See paragraphs 6.56–6.66 for more information.

6.24 Carers who provide personal care services must not carry out specialist procedures that are normally done by trained healthcare staff. If the action involves medical treatment, the doctor or other member of healthcare staff with responsibility for the patient will be the decision-maker who has to decide whether the proposed treatment is in the person's best interests (see chapter 5). A doctor can delegate responsibility for giving the treatment to other people in the clinical team who have the appropriate skills or expertise. People who do more than their experience or qualifications allow may not be protected from liability.

Care planning

6.25 Decisions about a person's care or treatment are often made by a multi-disciplinary team (a team of professionals with different skills that contribute to a person's care), by drawing up a care plan for the person. The preparation of a care plan should always include an assessment of the person's capacity to consent to the actions covered by the care plan, and confirm that those actions are agreed to be in the person's best interests. Healthcare and social care staff may then be able to assume that any actions they take under the care plan are in the person's best interests, and therefore receive protection from liability under section 5. But a person's capacity and best interests must still be reviewed regularly.

What steps should people take to be protected from liability?

6.26 As well as taking the following steps, somebody who wants to be protected from liability should bear in mind the statutory principles set out in section 1 of the Act (see chapter 2).

6.27 First, reasonable steps must be taken to find out whether a person has the capacity to make a decision about the proposed action (section 5(1)(a)). If the person has capacity, they must give their consent for anyone to take an action on their behalf, so that the person taking the action is protected from liability. For guidance on what is classed as 'reasonable steps', see paragraphs 6.29–6.34. But reasonable steps must always include:
- taking all practical and appropriate steps to help people to make a decision about an action themselves, and
- applying the two-stage test of capacity (see chapter 4).

The person who is going to take the action must have a 'reasonable belief' that the individual lacks capacity to give consent for the action at the time it needs to be taken.

6.28 Secondly, the person proposing to take action must have reasonable grounds for believing that the action is in the best interests of the person who lacks capacity. They should apply all elements of the best interests checklist (see chapter 5), and in particular
- consider whether the person is likely to regain capacity to make this decision in the future. Can the action wait until then?
- consider whether a less restrictive option is available (chapter 2, principle 5), and
- have objective reasons for thinking an action is in the best interests of the person who lacks capacity to consent to it.

What is 'reasonable'?

6.29 As explained in chapter 4, anyone assessing a person's capacity to make decisions for themselves or give consent must focus wholly on whether the person has capacity to make a specific decision at the time it needs to be made and not the person's capacity to make decisions generally. For example, a carer helping a person to dress can assess a person's capacity to agree to their help by explaining the different options (getting dressed or staying in nightclothes), and the consequences (being able to go out, or staying in all day).

6.30 Carers do not have to be experts in assessing capacity. But they must be able to show that they have taken *reasonable steps* to find out if the person has the capacity to make the specific decision. Only then will they have *reasonable grounds for believing* the person lacks capacity in relation to that particular matter. See paragraphs 4.44–4.45 for guidance on what is classed as 'reasonable' – although this will vary, depending on circumstances.

6.31 For the majority of decisions, formal assessment processes are unlikely to be required. But in some circumstances, professional practice requires some formal procedures to be carried out (for example, where consent to medical treatment is required, the doctor will need to assess – and record the person's capacity to consent). Under section 5, carers and professionals will be protected from liability as long as they are able to provide some objective reasons that explain why they believe that the person lacks capacity to consent to the action. If somebody challenges their belief, both carers and professionals will be protected from liability as long as they can show that they took steps to find out whether the person has capacity and that they have a reasonable belief that the person lacks capacity.

6.32 Similarly, carers, relatives and others involved in caring for someone who lacks capacity must have *reasonable grounds for believing* that their action is in the person's best interests. They must not simply impose their own views. They must be able to show that they considered all relevant circumstances and applied the best interests checklist. This includes showing that they have tried to involve the person who lacks capacity, and find out their wishes and feelings, beliefs and values. They must also have asked other people's opinions, where practical and appropriate. If somebody challenges their decision, they will be protected from liability if they can show that it was reasonable for them to believe that their action was in the person's best interests – in all the circumstances of that particular case.

6.33 If healthcare and social care staff are involved, their skills and knowledge will affect what is classed as 'reasonable'. For example, a doctor assessing somebody's capacity to consent to treatment must demonstrate more skill than someone without medical training. They should also record in the person's healthcare record the steps they took and the reasons for the finding. Healthcare and social care staff should apply normal clinical and professional standards when deciding what treatments to offer. They must then decide whether the proposed treatment is in the best interests of the person who lacks capacity to consent. This includes considering all relevant circumstances and applying the best interests checklist (see chapter 5).

6.34 Healthcare and social care staff can be said to have 'reasonable grounds for believing' that a person lacks capacity if:
- they are working to a person's care plan, and
- the care planning process involved an assessment of the person's capacity to make a decision about actions in the care plan.

It is also reasonable for them to assume that the care planning process assessed a person's best interests. But they should still make every effort to communicate with the person to find out if they still lack capacity and the action is still in their best interests.

> **Scenario: Working with a care plan**
>
> Margaret, an elderly woman, has serious mental health and physical problems. She lives in a nursing home and a care plan has been prepared by the multi-disciplinary team, in consultation with her relatives in deciding what course of action would be in Margaret's best interests. The care plan covers the medication she has been prescribed, the physiotherapy she needs, help with her personal care and other therapeutic activities such as art therapy.
>
> Although attempts were made to involve Margaret in the care planning process, she has been assessed by the doctor responsible for her care as lacking capacity to consent to most aspects of her care plan. The care plan can be relied on by the nurse or care assistant who administers the medication, by the physiotherapist and art therapist, and also by the care assistant who helps with Margaret's personal care, providing them with reasonable grounds for believing that they are acting in her best interests.
>
> However, as each act is performed, they must all take reasonable steps to communicate with Margaret to explain what they are doing and to ascertain whether she has the capacity to consent to the act in question. If they think she does, they must stop the treatment unless or until Margaret agrees that it should continue.

What happens in emergency situations?

6.35 Sometimes people who lack capacity to consent will require emergency medical treatment to save their life or prevent them from serious harm. In these situations, what steps are 'reasonable' will differ to those in non-urgent cases. In emergencies, it will almost always be in the person's best interests to give urgent treatment without delay. One exception to this is when the healthcare staff giving treatment are satisfied that an advance decision to refuse treatment exists (see paragraph 6.37).

What happens in cases of negligence?

6.36 Section 5 does not provide a defence in cases of negligence – either in carrying out a particular act or by failing to act where necessary. For example, a doctor may be protected against a claim of battery for carrying out an operation that is in a person's best interests. But if they perform the operation negligently, they are not protected from a charge of negligence. So the person who lacks capacity has the same rights in cases of negligence as someone who has consented to the operation.

What is the effect of an advance decision to refuse treatment?

6.37 Sometimes people will make an advance decision to refuse treatment while they still have capacity to do so and before they need that particular treatment. Healthcare staff must respect this decision if it is valid and applies to the proposed treatment.

6.38 If healthcare staff are satisfied that an advance decision is valid and applies to the proposed treatment, they are not protected from liability if they give any treatment that goes against it. But they are protected from liability if they did not know about an advance decision or they are not satisfied that the advance decision is valid and applies in the current circumstances (section 26(2)). See chapter 9 for further guidance.

What limits are there on protection from liability?

6.39 Section 6 imposes some important limitations on acts which can be carried out with protection from liability under section 5 (as described in the first part of this chapter). The key areas where acts might not be protected from liability are where there is inappropriate use of restraint or where a person who lacks capacity is deprived of their liberty.

Using restraint

6.40 Section 6(4) of the Act states that someone is using restraint if they:
- use force – or threaten to use force – to make someone do something that they are resisting, or
- restrict a person's freedom of movement, whether they are resisting or not.

6.41 Any action intended to restrain a person who lacks capacity will not attract protection from liability unless the following two conditions are met:
- the person taking action must reasonably believe that restraint is *necessary* to prevent *harm* to the person who lacks capacity, and
- the amount or type of restraint used and the amount of time it lasts must be a *proportionate response* to the likelihood and seriousness of harm.

See paragraphs 6.44–6.48 for more explanation of the terms *necessary, harm* and a *proportionate response*.

6.42 Healthcare and social care staff should also refer to:

- professional and other guidance on restraint or physical intervention, such as that issued by the Department of Health[21] or Welsh Assembly Government,[22] and
- limitations imposed by regulations and standards, such as the national minimum standards for care services (see chapter 14).

21 For guidance on using restraint with people with learning disabilities and autistic spectrum disorder, see *Guidance for restrictive physical interventions* (published by the Department of Health and Department for Education and Skills and available at www.dh.gov.uk/assetRoot/ 04/06/84/61/04068461.pdf).
22 In Wales, the relevant guidance is the Welsh Assembly Government's *Framework for restrictive physical intervention policy and practice* (available at www.childrenfirst.wales. gov.uk/content/framework/phys-int-e.pdf).

6.43 In addition to the requirements of the Act, the common law imposes a duty of care on healthcare and social care staff in respect of all people to whom they provide services. Therefore if a person who lacks capacity to consent has challenging behaviour, or is in the acute stages of illness causing them to act in way which may cause harm to others, staff may, under the common law, take appropriate and necessary action to restrain or remove the person, in order to prevent harm, both to the person concerned and to anyone else. However, within this context, the common law would not provide sufficient grounds for an action that would have the effect of depriving someone of their liberty (see paragraphs 6.49–6.53).

When might restraint be 'necessary'?

6.44 Anybody considering using restraint must have objective reasons to justify that restraint is necessary. They must be able to show that the person being cared for is likely to suffer harm unless proportionate restraint is used. A carer or professional must not use restraint just so that they can do something more easily. If restraint is necessary to prevent harm to the person who lacks capacity, it must be the minimum amount of force for the shortest time possible.

Scenario: Appropriate use of restraint

Derek, a man with learning disabilities, has begun to behave in a challenging way. Staff at his care home think he might have a medical condition that is causing him distress. They take him to the doctor, who thinks that Derek might have a hormone imbalance. But the doctor needs to take a blood test to confirm this, and when he tries to take the test Derek attempts to fight him off.

The results might be negative – so the test might not be necessary. But the doctor decides that a test is in Derek's best interests, because failing to treat a problem like a hormone imbalance might make it

> worse. It is therefore in Derek's best interests to restrain him to take the blood test. The temporary restraint is in proportion to the likely harm caused by failing to treat a possible medical condition.

What is 'harm'?

6.45 The Act does not define 'harm', because it will vary depending on the situation. For example,
- a person with learning disabilities might run into a busy road without warning, if they do not understand the dangers of cars
- a person with dementia may wander away from home and get lost, if they cannot remember where they live
- a person with manic depression might engage in excessive spending during a manic phase, causing them to get into debt
- a person may also be at risk of harm if they behave in a way that encourages others to assault or exploit them (for example, by behaving in a dangerously provocative way).

6.46 Common sense measures can often help remove the risk of harm (for example, by locking away poisonous chemicals or removing obstacles). Also, care planning should include risk assessments and set out appropriate actions to try to prevent possible risks. But it is impossible to remove all risk, and a proportionate response is needed when the risk of harm does arise.

What is a 'proportionate response'?

6.47 A 'proportionate response' means using the least intrusive type and minimum amount of restraint to achieve a specific outcome in the best interests of the person who lacks capacity. On occasions when the use of force may be necessary, carers and healthcare and social care staff should use the minimum amount of force for the shortest possible time.

For example, a carer may need to hold a person's arm while they cross the road, if the person does not understand the dangers of roads. But it would not be a proportionate response to stop the person going outdoors at all. It may be appropriate to have a secure lock on a door that faces a busy road, but it would not be a proportionate response to lock someone in a bedroom all the time to prevent them from attempting to cross the road.

6.48 Carers and healthcare and social care staff should consider less restrictive options before using restraint. Where possible, they should ask other people involved in the person's care what action they think is necessary to protect the person from harm. For example, it may be appropriate to get an advocate to work with the person to see if they can avoid or minimise the need for restraint to be used.

> **Scenario: Avoiding restraint**
>
> Oscar has learning disabilities. People at the college he attends sometimes cannot understand him, and he gets frustrated. Sometimes he hits the wall and hurts himself.
>
> Staff don't want to take Oscar out of class, because he says he enjoys college and is learning new skills. They have allowed his support worker to sit with him, but he still gets upset. The support worker could try to hold Oscar back. But she thinks this is too forceful, even though it would stop him hurting himself.
>
> Instead, she gets expert advice from members of the local community team. Observation helps them understand Oscar's behaviour better. They come up with a support strategy that reduces the risk of harmful behaviour and is less restrictive of his freedom.

When are acts seen as depriving a person of their liberty?

6.49 Although section 5 of the Act permits the use of restraint where it is necessary under the above conditions, section 6(5) confirms that there is no protection under the Act for actions that result in someone being deprived of their liberty (as defined by Article 5(1) of the European Convention on Human Rights). This applies not only to public authorities covered by the Human Rights Act 1998 but to everyone who might otherwise get protection under section 5 of the Act. It also applies to attorneys or deputies – they cannot give permission for an action that takes away a person's liberty.

6.50 Sometimes there is no alternative way to provide care or treatment other than depriving the person of their liberty. In this situation, some people may be detained in hospital under the Mental Health Act 1983– but this only applies to people who require hospital treatment for a mental disorder (see chapter 13). Otherwise, actions that amount to a deprivation of liberty will not be lawful unless formal authorisation is obtained.

6.51 In some cases, the Court of Protection might grant an order that permits the deprivation of a person's liberty, if it is satisfied that this is in a person's best interests.

6.52 It is difficult to define the difference between actions that amount to a restriction of someone's liberty and those that result in a deprivation of liberty. In recent legal cases, the European Court of Human Rights said that the difference was 'one of degree or intensity, not one of nature or substance'.[23] There must therefore be particular factors in the specific situation of the person concerned which provide the 'degree' or 'intensity' to result in a deprivation of liberty. In practice, this can relate to:

- the type of care being provided
- how long the situation lasts

- its effects, or
- the way in a particular situation came about.[24]

The European Court of Human Rights has identified the following as factors contributing to deprivation of liberty in its judgments on cases to date:

- restraint was used, including sedation, to admit a person who is resisting
- professionals exercised complete and effective control over care and movement for a significant period
- professionals exercised control over assessments, treatment, contacts and residence
- the person would be prevented from leaving if they made a meaningful attempt to do so
- a request by carers for the person to be discharged to their care was refused
- the person was unable to maintain social contacts because of restrictions placed on access to other people
- the person lost autonomy because they were under continuous supervision and control.[25]

23 HL v The United Kingdom (Application no 45508/99) (2004) 40 EHRR 761, ECHR, at [89].
24 In HL v The United Kingdom (also known as the 'Bournewood' case), the European Court said that 'the key factor in the present case [is] that the health care professionals treating and managing the applicant exercised complete and effective control over his care and movements'. They found 'the concrete situation was that the applicant was under continuous supervision and control and was not free to leave.'
25 These are listed in the Department of Health's draft illustrative Code of Practice guidance about the proposed safeguards. www.dh.gov.uk/assetRoot/04/14/17/64/04141764.pdf

6.53 The Government has announced that it intends to amend the Act to introduce new procedures and provisions for people who lack capacity to make relevant decisions but who need to be deprived of their liberty, in their best interests, otherwise than under the Mental Health Act 1983 (the so-called 'Bournewood provisions'). This chapter will be fully revised in due course to reflect those changes. Information about the Government's current proposals in respect of the Bournewood safeguards is available on the Department of Health website. This information includes draft illustrative Code of Practice guidance about the proposed safeguards. See paragraphs 13.52–13.55 for more details.

How does section 5 apply to attorneys and deputies?

6.54 Section 5 does not provide protection for actions that go against the decision of someone who has been authorised to make decisions for a person who lacks capacity to make such decision for themselves. For instance, if someone goes against the decision of an attorney acting under a Lasting Power of Attorney (LPA) (see chapter 7) or a deputy appointed by the Court of Protection (see chapter 8), they will not be protected under section 5.

6.55 Attorneys and deputies must only make decisions within the scope of the authority of the LPA or court order. Sometimes carers or healthcare and social care staff might feel that an attorney or deputy is making decisions they should not be making, or that are not in a person's best interests. If this is the case, and the disagreement cannot be settled any other way, either the carers, the staff or the attorney or deputy can apply to the Court of Protection. If the dispute concerns the provision of medical treatment, medical staff can still give life-sustaining treatment, or treatment which stops a person's condition getting seriously worse, while the court is coming to a decision (section 6(6)).

Who can pay for goods or services?

6.56 Carers may have to spend money on behalf of someone who lacks capacity to purchase necessary goods or services. For example, they may need to pay for a milk delivery or for a chiropodist to provide a service at the person's home. In some cases, they might have to pay for more costly arrangements such as house repairs or organising a holiday. Carers are likely to be protected from liability if their actions are properly taken under section 5, and in the best interests of the person who lacks capacity.

6.57 In general, a contract entered into by a person who lacks capacity to make the contract cannot be enforced if the other person knows, or must be taken to have known, of the lack of capacity. Section 7 of the Act modifies this rule and states that where the contract is for 'necessary' goods or services for a person who lacks capacity to make the arrangements for themselves, that person must pay a reasonable price for them.

What are necessary goods and services?

6.58 'Necessary' means something that is suitable to the person's condition in life (their place in society, rather than any mental or physical condition) and their actual requirements when the goods or services are provided (section 7(2)). The aim is to make sure that people can enjoy a similar standard of living and way of life to those they had before lacking capacity. For example, if a person who now lacks capacity previously chose to buy expensive designer clothes, these are still necessary goods – as long as they can still afford them. But they would not be necessary for a person who always wore cheap clothes, no matter how wealthy they were.

6.59 Goods are not necessary if the person already has a sufficient supply of them. For example, buying one or two new pairs of shoes for a person who lacks capacity could be necessary. But a dozen pairs would probably not be necessary.

How should payments be arranged?

6.60 If a person lacks capacity to arrange for payment for necessary goods and services, sections 5 and 8 allow a carer to arrange payment on their behalf.

6.61 The carer must first take reasonable steps to check whether a person can arrange for payment themselves, or has the capacity to consent to the carer doing it for them. If the person lacks the capacity to consent or pay themselves, the carer must decide what goods or services would be necessary for the person and in their best interests. The carer can then lawfully deal with payment for those goods and services in one of three ways:

- If neither the carer nor the person who lacks capacity can produce the necessary funds, the carer may promise that the person who lacks capacity will pay. A supplier may not be happy with this, or the carer may be worried that they will be held responsible for any debt. In such cases, the carer must follow the formal steps in paragraphs 6.62–6.66 below.
- If the person who lacks capacity has cash, the carer may use that money to pay for goods or services (for example, to pay the milkman or the hairdresser).
- The carer may choose to pay for the goods or services with their own money. The person who lacks capacity must pay them back. This may involve using cash in the person's possession or running up an IOU. (This is not appropriate for paid care workers, whose contracts might stop them handling their clients' money.) The carer must follow formal steps to get money held in a bank or building society account (see paragraphs 6.63–6.66 below).

6.62 Carers should keep bills, receipts and other proof of payment when paying for goods and services. They will need these documents when asking to get money back. Keeping appropriate financial records and documentation is a requirement of the national minimum standards for care homes or domiciliary care agencies.

Access to a person's assets

6.63 The Act does not give a carer or care worker access to a person's income or assets. Nor does it allow them to sell the person's property.

6.64 Anyone wanting access to money in a person's bank or building society will need formal legal authority. They will also need legal authority to sell a person's property. Such authority could be given in a Lasting Power of Attorney (LPA) appointing an attorney to deal with property and affairs, or in an order of the Court of Protection (either a single decision of the court or an order appointing a deputy to make financial decisions for the person who lacks capacity to make such decisions).

> **Scenario: Being granted access to a person's assets**
>
> A storm blew some tiles off the roof of a house owned by Gordon, a man with Alzheimer's disease. He lacks capacity to arrange for repairs and claim on his insurance. The repairs are likely to be costly.
>
> Gordon's son decides to organise the repairs, and he agrees to pay because his father doesn't have enough cash available. The son could then apply to the Court of Protection for authority to claim insurance on his father's behalf and for him to be reimbursed from his father's bank account to cover the cost of the repairs once the insurance payment had been received.

6.65 Sometimes another person will already have legal control of the finances and property of a person who lacks capacity to manage their own affairs. This could be an attorney acting under a registered EPA or an appropriate LPA (see chapter 7) or a deputy appointed by the Court of Protection (see chapter 8). Or it could be someone (usually a carer) that has the right to act as an 'appointee' (under Social Security Regulations) and claim benefits for a person who lacks capacity to make their own claim and use the money on the person's behalf. But an appointee cannot deal with other assets or savings from sources other than benefits.

6.66 Section 6(6) makes clear that a family carer or other carer cannot make arrangements for goods or services to be supplied to a person who lacks capacity if this conflicts with a decision made by someone who has formal powers over the person's money and property, such as an attorney or deputy acting within the scope of their authority. Where there is no conflict and the carer has paid for necessary goods and services the carer may ask for money back from an attorney, a deputy or where relevant, an appointee.

7 WHAT DOES THE ACT SAY ABOUT LASTING POWERS OF ATTORNEY?

This chapter explains what Lasting Powers of Attorney (LPAs) are and how they should be used. It also sets out:

- how LPAs differ from Enduring Powers of Attorney (EPAs)
- the types of decisions that people can appoint attorneys to make (attorneys are also called 'donees' in the Act)
- situations in which an LPA can and cannot be used
- the duties and responsibilities of attorneys
- the standards required of attorneys, and
- measures for dealing with attorneys who don't meet appropriate standards.

This chapter also explains what should happen to EPAs that were made before the Act comes into force.

> In this chapter, as throughout the Code, a person's capacity (or lack of capacity) refers specifically to their capacity to make a particular decision at the time it needs to be made.

Quick summary

Anyone asked to be an attorney should:
- consider whether they have the skills and ability to act as an attorney (especially if it is for a property and affairs LPA)
- ask themselves whether they actually want to be an attorney and take on the duties and responsibilities of the role.

Before acting under an LPA, attorneys must:
- make sure the LPA has been registered with the Public Guardian
- take all practical and appropriate steps to help the donor make the particular decision for themselves.

When acting under an LPA:
- make sure that the Act's statutory principles are followed
- check whether the person has the capacity to make that particular decision for themselves. If they do:
  – a personal welfare LPA cannot be used – the person must make the decision
  – a property and affairs LPA can be used even if the person has capacity to make the decision, unless they have stated in the LPA that they should make decisions for themselves when they have capacity to do so.

At all times, remember:
- anything done under the authority of the LPA must be in the person's best interests
- anyone acting as an attorney must have regard to guidance in this Code of Practice that is relevant to the decision that is to be made
- attorneys must fulfil their responsibilities and duties to the person who lacks capacity.

What is a Lasting Power of Attorney (LPA)?

7.1 Sometimes one person will want to give another person authority to make a decision on their behalf. A power of attorney is a legal document that allows them to do so. Under a power of attorney, the chosen person (the attorney or donee) can make decisions that are as valid as one made by the person (the donor).

7.2 Before the Enduring Powers of Attorney Act 1985, every power of attorney automatically became invalid as soon as the donor lacked the capacity to make their own decision. But that Act introduced the Enduring Power of Attorney (EPA). An EPA allows an attorney to make decisions about property and financial affairs even if the donor lacks capacity to manage their own affairs.

7.3 The Mental Capacity Act replaces the EPA with the Lasting Power of Attorney (LPA). It also increases the range of different types of decisions that people can authorise others to make on their behalf. As well as property and affairs (including financial matters), LPAs can also cover personal welfare (including healthcare and consent to medical treatment) for people who lack capacity to make such decisions for themselves.

7.4 The donor can choose one person or several to make different kinds of decisions. See paragraphs 7.21–7.31 for more information about personal welfare LPAs. See paragraphs 7.32–7.42 for more information about LPAs on property and affairs.

How do LPAs compare to EPAs?

7.5 There are a number of differences between LPAs and EPAs. These are summarised as follows:
- EPAs only cover property and affairs. LPAs can also cover personal welfare.
- Donors must use the relevant specific form (prescribed in regulations) to make EPAs and LPAs. There are different forms for EPAs, personal welfare LPAs and property and affairs LPAs.
- EPAs must be registered with the Public Guardian when the donor can no longer manage their own affairs (or when they start to lose capacity). But LPAs can be registered at any time before they are used – before or after the donor lacks capacity to make particular decisions that the LPA covers. If the LPA is not registered, it can't be used.
- EPAs can be used while the donor still has capacity to manage their own property and affairs, as can property and affairs LPAs, so long as the donor does not say otherwise in the LPA. But personal welfare LPAs can only be used once the donor lacks capacity to make the welfare decision in question.
- Once the Act comes into force, only LPAs can be made but existing EPAs will continue to be valid. There will be different laws and procedures for EPAs and LPAs.
- Attorneys making decisions under a registered EPA or LPA must follow the Act's principles and act in the best interests of the donor.
- The duties under the law of agency apply to attorneys of both EPAs and LPAs (see paragraphs 7.58–7.68 below).
- Decisions that the courts have made about EPAs may also affect how people use LPAs.

- Attorneys acting under an LPA have a legal duty to have regard to the guidance in this Code of Practice. EPA attorneys do not. But the Code's guidance will still be helpful to them.

How does a donor create an LPA?

7.6 The donor must also follow the right procedures for creating and registering an LPA, as set out below. Otherwise the LPA might not be valid. It is not always necessary to get legal advice. But it is a good idea for certain cases (for example, if the donor's circumstances are complicated).

7.7 Only adults aged 18 or over can make an LPA, and they can only make an LPA if they have the capacity to do so. For an LPA to be valid:
- the LPA must be a written document set out in the statutory form prescribed by regulations[26]
- the document must include prescribed information about the nature and effect of the LPA (as set out in the regulations)
- the donor must sign a statement saying that they have read the prescribed information (or somebody has read it to them) and that they want the LPA to apply when they no longer have capacity
- the document must name people (not any of the attorneys) who should be told about an application to register the LPA, or it should say that there is no-one they wish to be told
- the attorneys must sign a statement saying that they have read the prescribed information and that they understand their duties – in particular the duty to act in the donor's best interests
- the document must include a certificate completed by an independent third party,[27] confirming that:
  - in their opinion, the donor understands the LPA's purpose
  - nobody used fraud or undue pressure to trick or force the donor into making the LPA and
  - there is nothing to stop the LPA being created.

26 The prescribed forms will be available from the Office of the Public Guardian (OPG) or from legal stationers.
27 Details of who may and who may not be a certificate provider will be available in regulations. The OPG will produce guidance for certificate providers on their role.

Who can be an attorney?

7.8 A donor should think carefully before choosing someone to be their attorney. An attorney should be someone who is trustworthy, competent and reliable. They should have the skills and ability to carry out the necessary tasks.

7.9 Attorneys must be at least 18 years of age. For property and affairs LPAs, the attorney could be either:
- an individual (as long as they are not bankrupt at the time the LPA is made), or

- a trust corporation (often parts of banks or other financial institutions).

If an attorney nominated under a property and affairs LPA becomes bankrupt at any point, they will no longer be allowed to act as an attorney for property and affairs. People who are bankrupt can still act as an attorney for personal welfare LPAs.

7.10 The donor must name an individual rather than a job title in a company or organisation, (for example, 'The Director of Adult Services' or 'my solicitor' would not be sufficient). A paid care worker (such as a care home manager) should not agree to act as an attorney, apart from in unusual circumstances (for example, if they are the only close relative of the donor).

7.11 Section 10(4) of the Act allows the donor to appoint two or more attorneys and to specify whether they should act 'jointly', 'jointly and severally', or 'jointly in respect of some matters and jointly and severally in respect of others'.

- Joint attorneys must always act together. All attorneys must agree decisions and sign any relevant documents.
- Joint and several attorneys can act together but may also act independently if they wish. Any action taken by any attorney alone is as valid as if they were the only attorney.

7.12 The donor may want to appoint attorneys to act jointly in some matters but jointly and severally in others. For example, a donor could choose to appoint two or more financial attorneys jointly and severally. But they might say then when selling the donor's house, the attorneys must act jointly. The donor may appoint welfare attorneys to act jointly and severally but specify that they must act jointly in relation to giving consent to surgery. If a donor who has appointed two or more attorneys does not specify how they should act, they must always act jointly (section 10(5)).

7.13 Section 10(8) says that donors may choose to name replacement attorneys to take over the duties in certain circumstances (for example, in the event of an attorney's death). The donor may name a specific attorney to be replaced, or the replacements can take over from any attorney, if necessary. Donors cannot give their attorneys the right to appoint a substitute or successor.

How should somebody register and use an LPA?

7.14 An LPA must be registered with the Office of the Public Guardian (OPG) before it can be used. An unregistered LPA will not give the attorney any legal powers to make a decision for the donor. The donor can register the LPA while they are still capable, or the attorney can apply to register the LPA at any time.

7.15 There are advantages in registering the LPA soon after the donor makes it (for example, to ensure that there is no delay when the LPA needs to be used). But if this has not been done, an LPA can be registered after the donor lacks the capacity to make a decision covered by the LPA.

7.16 If an LPA is unregistered, attorneys must register it before making any decisions under the LPA. If the LPA has been registered but not used for some time, the attorney should tell the OPG when they begin to act under it – so that the attorney can be sent relevant, up-to-date information about the rules governing LPAs.

7.17 While they still have capacity, donors should let the OPG know of permanent changes of address for the donor or the attorney or any other changes in circumstances. If the donor no longer has capacity to do this, attorneys should report any such changes to the OPG. Examples include an attorney of a property and affairs LPA becoming bankrupt or the ending of a marriage between the donor and their attorney. This will help keep OPG records up to date, and will make sure that attorneys do not make decisions that they no longer have the authority to make.

What guidance should an attorney follow?

7.18 Section 9(4) states that attorneys must meet the requirements set out in the Act. Most importantly, they have to follow the statutory principles (section 1) and make decisions in the best interests of the person who lacks capacity (section 4). They must also respect any conditions or restrictions that the LPA document contains. See chapter 2 for guidance on how to apply the Act's principles.

7.19 Chapter 3 gives suggestions of ways to help people make their own decisions in accordance with the Act's second principle. Attorneys should also refer to the guidance in chapter 4 when assessing the donor's capacity to make particular decisions, and in particular, should follow the steps suggested for establishing a 'reasonable belief' that the donor lacks capacity (see paragraphs 4.44–4.45). Assessments of capacity or best interests must not be based merely on:
- a donor's age or appearance, or
- unjustified assumptions about any condition they might have or their behaviour.

7.20 When deciding what is in the donor's best interests, attorneys should refer to the guidance in chapter 5. In particular, they must consider the donor's past and present wishes and feelings, beliefs and values. Where practical and appropriate, they should consult with:
- anyone involved in caring for the donor
- close relatives and anyone else with an interest in their welfare
- other attorneys appointed by the donor.

See paragraphs 7.52–7.68 for a description of an attorney's duties.

Scenario: Making decisions in a donor's best interests

Mr Young has been a member of the Green Party for a long time. He has appointed his solicitor as his attorney under a property and affairs

LPA. But Mr Young did not state in the LPA that investments made on his behalf must be ethical investments. When the attorney assesses his client's best interests, however, the attorney considers the donor's past wishes, values and beliefs. He makes sure that he only invests in companies that are socially and environmentally responsible.

What decisions can an LPA attorney make?
Personal welfare LPAs

7.21 LPAs can be used to appoint attorneys to make decisions about personal welfare, which can include healthcare and medical treatment decisions. Personal welfare LPAs might include decisions about:
- where the donor should live and who they should live with
- the donor's day-to-day care, including diet and dress
- who the donor may have contact with
- consenting to or refusing medical examination and treatment on the donor's behalf
- arrangements needed for the donor to be given medical, dental or optical treatment
- assessments for and provision of community care services
- whether the donor should take part in social activities, leisure activities, education or training
- the donor's personal correspondence and papers
- rights of access to personal information about the donor, or
- complaints about the donor's care or treatment.

7.22 The standard form for personal welfare LPAs allows attorneys to make decisions about anything that relates to the donor's personal welfare. But donors can add restrictions or conditions to areas where they would not wish the attorney to have the power to act. For example, a donor might only want an attorney to make decisions about their social care and not their healthcare. There are particular rules for LPAs authorising an attorney to make decisions about life-sustaining treatment (see paragraphs 7.30–7.31 below).

7.23 A general personal welfare LPA gives the attorney the right to make all of the decisions set out above although this is not a full list of the actions they can take or decisions they can make. However, a personal welfare LPA can only be used at a time when the donor lacks capacity to make a specific welfare decision.

Scenario: Denying attorneys the right to make certain decisions

Mrs Hutchison is in the early stages of Alzheimer's disease. She is anxious to get all her affairs in order while she still has capacity to do so. She makes a personal welfare LPA, appointing her daughter as attorney. But Mrs Hutchison knows that her daughter doesn't always

> get on with some members of the family – and she wouldn't want her daughter to stop those relatives from seeing her.
>
> She states in the LPA that her attorney does not have the authority to decide who can contact her or visit her. If her daughter wants to prevent anyone having contact with Mrs Hutchison, she must ask the Court of Protection to decide.

7.24 Before making a decision under a personal welfare LPA, the attorney must be sure that:
- the LPA has been registered with the OPG
- the donor lacks the capacity to make the particular decision or the attorney reasonably believes that the donor lacks capacity to take the decisions covered by the LPA (having applied the Act's principles), and
- they are making the decision in the donor's best interests.

7.25 When healthcare or social care staff are involved in preparing a care plan for someone who has appointed a personal welfare attorney, they must first assess whether the donor has capacity to agree to the care plan or to parts of it. If the donor lacks capacity, professionals must then consult the attorney and get their agreement to the care plan. They will also need to consult the attorney when considering what action is in the person's best interests.

Personal welfare LPAs that authorise an attorney to make healthcare decisions

7.26 A personal welfare LPA allows attorneys to make decisions to accept or refuse healthcare or treatment unless the donor has stated clearly in the LPA that they do not want the attorney to make these decisions.

7.27 Even where the LPA includes healthcare decisions, attorneys do not have the right to consent to or refuse treatment in situations where:
- **the donor has capacity to make the particular healthcare decision (section 11(7)(a))**
  An attorney has no decision-making power if the donor can make their own treatment decisions.
- **the donor has made an advance decision to refuse the proposed treatment (section 11(7)(b))**
  An attorney cannot consent to treatment if the donor has made a valid and applicable advance decision to refuse a specific treatment (see chapter 9). But if the donor made an LPA after the advance decision, and gave the attorney the right to consent to or refuse the treatment, the attorney can choose not to follow the advance decision.

- **a decision relates to life-sustaining treatment (section 11(7)(c))**
  An attorney has no power to consent to or refuse life-sustaining treatment, unless the LPA document expressly authorises this (See paragraphs 7.30–7.31 below.)
- **the donor is detained under the Mental Health Act (section 28)**
  An attorney cannot consent to or refuse treatment for a mental disorder for a patient detained under the Mental Health Act 1983 (see also chapter 13).

7.28 LPAs cannot give attorneys the power to demand specific forms of medical treatment that healthcare staff do not believe are necessary or appropriate for the donor's particular condition.

7.29 Attorneys must always follow the Act's principles and make decisions in the donor's best interests. If healthcare staff disagree with the attorney's assessment of best interests, they should discuss the case with other medical experts and/or get a formal second opinion. Then they should discuss the matter further with the attorney. If they cannot settle the disagreement, they can apply to the Court of Protection (see paragraphs 7.45–7.49 below). While the court is coming to a decision, healthcare staff can give life-sustaining treatment to prolong the donor's life or stop their condition getting worse.

Personal welfare LPAs that authorise an attorney to make decisions about life-sustaining treatment

7.30 An attorney can only consent to or refuse life-sustaining treatment on behalf of the donor if, when making the LPA, the donor has specifically stated in the LPA document that they want the attorney to have this authority.

7.31 As with all decisions, an attorney must act in the donor's best interests when making decisions about such treatment. This will involve applying the best interests checklist (see chapter 5) and consulting with carers, family members and others interested in the donor's welfare. In particular, the attorney must not be motivated in any way by the desire to bring about the donor's death (see paragraphs 5.29–5.36). Anyone who doubts that the attorney is acting in the donor's best interests can apply to the Court of Protection for a decision.

Scenario: Making decisions about life-sustaining treatment

Mrs Joshi has never trusted doctors. She prefers to rely on alternative therapies. Because she saw her father suffer after invasive treatment for cancer, she is clear that she would refuse such treatment herself.

> She is diagnosed with cancer and discusses her wishes with her husband. Mrs Joshi knows that he would respect her wishes if he ever had to make a decision about her treatment. She makes a personal welfare LPA appointing him as her attorney with authority to make all her welfare and healthcare decisions. She includes a specific statement authorising him to consent to or refuse life-sustaining treatment.
>
> He will then be able to consider her views and make decisions about treatment in her best interests if she later lacks capacity to make those decisions herself.

Property and affairs LPAs

7.32 A donor can make an LPA giving an attorney the right to make decisions about property and affairs (including financial matters). Unless the donor states otherwise, once the LPA is registered, the attorney is allowed to make all decisions about the donor's property and affairs even if the donor still has capacity to make the decisions for themselves. In this situation, the LPA will continue to apply when the donor no longer has capacity.

7.33 Alternatively a donor can state in the LPA document that the LPA should only apply when they lack capacity to make a relevant decision. It is the donor's responsibility to decide how their capacity should then be assessed. For example, the donor may trust the attorney to carry out an assessment, or they may say that the LPA only applies if their GP or another doctor confirms in writing that they lack capacity to make specific decisions about property or finances. Financial institutions may wish to see the written confirmation before recognising the attorney's authority to act under the LPA.

7.34 The fact that someone has made a property and affairs LPA does not mean that they cannot continue to carry out financial transactions for themselves. The donor may have full capacity, but perhaps anticipates that they may lack capacity at some future time. Or they may have fluctuating or partial capacity and therefore be able to make some decisions (or at some times), but need an attorney to make others (or at other times). The attorney should allow and encourage the donor to do as much as possible, and should only act when the donor asks them to or to make those decisions the donor lacks capacity to make. However, in other cases, the donor may wish to hand over responsibility for all decisions to the attorney, even those they still have capacity to make.

7.35 If the donor restricts the decisions an attorney can make, banks may ask the attorney to sign a declaration that protects the bank from liability if the attorney misuses the account.[28]

---

[28] See British Banking Association's guidance for bank staff on *'Banking for mentally Incapacitated and learning disabled customers'*.

7.36 If a donor does not restrict decisions the attorney can make, the attorney will be able to decide on any or all of the person's property and financial affairs. This might include:
- buying or selling property
- opening, closing or operating any bank, building society or other account
- giving access to the donor's financial information
- claiming, receiving and using (on the donor's behalf) all benefits, pensions, allowances and rebates (unless the Department for Work and Pensions has already appointed someone and everyone is happy for this to continue)
- receiving any income, inheritance or other entitlement on behalf of the donor
- dealing with the donor's tax affairs
- paying the donor's mortgage, rent and household expenses
- insuring, maintaining and repairing the donor's property
- investing the donor's savings
- making limited gifts on the donor's behalf (but see paragraphs 7.40–7.42 below)
- paying for private medical care and residential care or nursing home fees
- applying for any entitlement to funding for NHS care, social care or adaptations
- using the donor's money to buy a vehicle or any equipment or other help they need
- repaying interest and capital on any loan taken out by the donor.

7.37 A general property and affairs LPA will allow the attorney to carry out any or all of the actions above (although this is not a full list of the actions they can take). However, the donor may want to specify the types of powers they wish the attorney to have, or to exclude particular types of decisions. If the donor holds any assets as trustee, they should get legal advice about how the LPA may affect this.

7.38 The attorney must make these decisions personally and cannot generally give someone else authority to carry out their duties (see paragraphs 7.61–7.62 below). But if the donor wants the attorney to be able to give authority to a specialist to make specific decisions, they need to state this clearly in the LPA document (for example, appointing an investment manager to make particular investment decisions).

7.39 Donors may like to appoint someone (perhaps a family member or a professional) to go through their accounts with the attorney from time to time. This might help to reassure donors that somebody will check their financial affairs when they lack capacity to do so. It may also be helpful for attorneys to arrange a regular check that everything is being done properly. The donor should ensure that the person is willing to carry out this role and is prepared to ask for the accounts if the attorney does not provide them. They should include this arrangement in the signed LPA document. The LPA should also say whether the person can charge a fee for this service.

What gifts can an attorney make under a property and affairs LPA?

7.40 An attorney can only make gifts of the donor's money or belongings to people who are related to or connected with the donor (including the attorney) on specific occasions, including:
- births or birthdays
- weddings or wedding anniversaries
- civil partnership ceremonies or anniversaries, or
- any other occasion when families, friends or associates usually give presents (section 12(3)(b)).

7.41 If the donor previously made donations to any charity regularly or from time to time, the attorney can make donations from the person's funds. This also applies if the donor could have been expected to make such payments (section 12(2)(b)). But the value of any gift or donation must be reasonable and take into account the size of the donor's estate. For example, it would not be reasonable to buy expensive gifts at Christmas if the donor was living on modest means and had to do without essential items in order to pay for them.

7.42 The donor cannot use the LPA to make more extensive gifts than those allowed under section 12 of the Act. But they can impose stricter conditions or restrictions on the attorney's powers to make gifts. They should state these restrictions clearly in the LPA document when they are creating it. When deciding on appropriate gifts, the attorney should consider the donor's wishes and feelings to work out what would be in the donor's best interests. The attorney can apply to the Court of Protection for permission to make gifts that are not included in the LPA (for example, for tax planning purposes).

Are there any other restrictions on attorneys' powers?

7.43 Attorneys are not protected from liability if they do something that is intended to restrain the donor, unless:
- the attorney reasonably believes that the donor lacks capacity to make the decision in question, and
- the attorney reasonably believes that restraint is necessary to prevent harm to the donor, and
- the type of restraint used is in proportion to the likelihood and the seriousness of the harm.

If an attorney needs to make a decision or take action which may involve the use of restraint, they should take account of the guidance set out in chapter 6.

7.44 Attorneys have no authority to take actions that result in the donor being deprived of their liberty. Any deprivation of liberty will only be lawful if this has been properly authorised and there is other protection available for the person who lacks capacity. An example would be the protection around detention under the Mental Health Act 1983 (see chapter 13) or a court ruling. Chapter 6 gives more guidance on working out whether an action is restraint or a deprivation of liberty.

What powers does the Court of Protection have over LPAs?

7.45 The Court of Protection has a range of powers to:
- determine whether an LPA is valid
- give directions about using the LPA, and
- to remove an attorney (for example, if the attorney does not act in the best interests of the donor).

Chapter 8 gives more information about the Court of Protection's powers.

7.46 If somebody has doubts over whether an LPA is valid, they can ask the court to decide whether the LPA:
- meets the Act's requirements
- has been revoked (cancelled) by the donor, or
- has come to an end for any other reason.

7.47 The court can also stop somebody registering an LPA or rule that an LPA is invalid if:
- the donor made the LPA as a result of undue pressure or fraud, or
- the attorney behaves, has behaved or is planning to behave in a way that goes against their duties or is not in the donor's best interests.

7.48 The court can also clarify an LPA's meaning, if it is not clear, and it can tell attorneys how they should use an LPA. If an attorney thinks that an LPA does not give them enough powers, they can ask the court to extend their powers – if the donor no longer has capacity to authorise this. The court can also authorise an attorney to give a gift that the Act does not normally allow (section 12(2)), if it is in the donor's best interests.

7.49 All attorneys should keep records of their dealings with the donor's affairs (see also paragraph 7.67 below). The court can order attorneys to produce records (for example, financial accounts) and to provide specific reports, information or documentation. If somebody has concerns about an attorney's payment or expenses, the court could resolve the matter.

What responsibilities do attorneys have?

7.50 A donor cannot insist on somebody agreeing to become an attorney. It is down to the proposed attorney to decide whether to take on this responsibility. When an attorney accepts the role by signing the LPA document, this is confirmation that they are willing to act under the LPA once it is registered. An attorney can withdraw from the appointment if they ever become unable or unwilling to act, but if the LPA has been registered they must follow the correct procedures for withdrawing. (see paragraph 7.66 below).

7.51 Once the attorney starts to act under an LPA, they must meet certain standards. If they don't carry out the duties below, they could be removed from the role. In some circumstances they could face charges of fraud or negligence.

What duties does the Act impose?

7.52 Attorneys acting under an LPA have a duty to:
- follow the Act's statutory principles (see chapter 2)
- make decisions in the donor's best interests
- have regard to the guidance in the Code of Practice
- only make those decisions the LPA gives them authority to make.

Principles and best interests

7.53 Attorneys must act in accordance with the Act's statutory principles (section 1) and in the best interests of the donor (the steps for working out best interests are set out in section 4). In particular, attorneys must consider whether the donor has capacity to make the decision for themselves. If not, they should consider whether the donor is likely to regain capacity to make the decision in the future. If so, it may be possible to delay the decision until the donor can make it.

The Code of Practice

7.54 As well as this chapter, attorneys should pay special attention to the following guidance set out in the Code:
- chapter 2, which sets out how the Act's principles should be applied
- chapter 3, which describes the steps which can be taken to try to
  help the person make decisions for themselves
- chapter 4, which describes the Act's definition of lack of capacity
  and gives guidance on assessing capacity, and
- chapter 5, which gives guidance on working out the donor's best interests.

7.55 In some circumstances, attorneys might also find it useful to refer to guidance in:
- chapter 6, which explains when attorneys who have caring responsibilities may have protection from liability and gives

guidance on the few circumstances when the Act allows restraint in connection with care and treatment
- chapter 8, which gives a summary of the Court of Protection's powers relating to LPAs
- chapter 9, which explains how LPAs may be affected if the donor has made an advance decision to refuse treatment, and
- chapter 15, which describes ways to settle disagreements.

Only making decisions covered by an LPA

7.56 A personal welfare attorney has no authority to make decisions about a donor's property and affairs (such as their finances). A property and affairs attorney has no authority in decisions about a donor's personal care. (But the same person could be appointed in separate LPAs to carry out both these roles.) Under any LPA, the attorney will have authority in a wide range of decisions. But if a donor includes restrictions in the LPA document, this will limit the attorney's authority (section 9(4)(b)). If the attorney thinks that they need greater powers, they can apply to the Court of Protection which may decide to give the attorney the authority required or alternatively to appoint the attorney as a deputy with the necessary powers (see chapter 8).

7.57 It is good practice for decision-makers to consult attorneys about any decision or action, whether or not it is covered by the LPA. This is because an attorney is likely to have known the donor for some time and may have important information about their wishes and feelings. Researchers can also consult attorneys if they are thinking about involving the donor in research (see chapter 11).

Scenario: Consulting attorneys

Mr Varadi makes a personal welfare LPA appointing his son and daughter as his joint attorneys. He also makes a property and affairs LPA, appointing his son and his solicitor to act jointly and severally. He registers the property and affairs LPA straight away, so his attorneys can help with financial decisions.

Two years later, Mr Varadi has a stroke, is unable to speak and has difficulty communicating his wishes. He also lacks the capacity to make decisions about treatment. The attorneys apply to register the personal welfare LPA. Both feel that they should delay decisions about Mr Varadi's future care, because he might regain capacity to make the decisions himself. But they agree that some decisions cannot wait.

Although the solicitor has no authority to make welfare decisions, the welfare attorneys consult him about their father's best interests. They speak to him about immediate treatment decisions and their suggestion

> to delay making decisions about his future care. Similarly, the property and affairs attorneys consult the daughter about the financial decisions that Mr Varadi does not have the capacity to make himself.

What are an attorney's other duties?

7.58 An attorney appointed under an LPA is acting as the chosen agent of the donor and therefore, under the law of agency, the attorney has certain duties towards the donor. An attorney takes on a role which carries a great deal of power, which they must use carefully and responsibly. They have a duty to:
- apply certain standards of care and skill (duty of care) when making decisions
- carry out the donor's instructions
- not take advantage of their position and not benefit themselves, but benefit the donor (fiduciary duty)
- not delegate decisions, unless authorised to do so
- act in good faith
- respect confidentiality
- comply with the directions of the Court of Protection
- not give up the role without telling the donor and the court.

In relation to property and affairs LPAs, they have a duty to:
- keep accounts
- keep the donor's money and property separate from their own.

Duty of care

7.59 'Duty of care' means applying a certain standard of care and skill – depending on whether the attorney is paid for their services or holds relevant professional qualifications.
- Attorneys who are not being paid must apply the same care, skill and diligence they would use to make decisions about their own life. An attorney who claims to have particular skills or qualifications must show greater skill in those particular areas than someone who does not make such claims.
- If attorneys are being paid for their services, they should demonstrate a higher degree of care and skill.
- Attorneys who undertake their duties in the course of their professional work (such as solicitors or corporate trustees) must display professional competence and follow their profession's rules and standards.

Fiduciary duty

7.60 A fiduciary duty means attorneys must not take advantage of their position. Nor should they put themselves in a position where their personal interests conflict with their duties. They also must not allow any other influences to affect the way in which they act as an attorney. Decisions should always benefit the donor, and not the attorney. Attorneys must not profit or get any personal benefit from their position, apart from receiving gifts where the Act allows it, whether or not it is at the donor's expense.

Duty not to delegate

7.61 Attorneys cannot usually delegate their authority to someone else. They must carry out their duties personally. The attorney may seek professional or expert advice (for example, investment advice from a financial adviser or advice on medical treatment from a doctor). But they cannot, as a general rule, allow someone else to make a decision that they have been appointed to make, unless this has been specifically authorised by the donor in the LPA.

7.62 In certain circumstances, attorneys may have limited powers to delegate (for example, through necessity or unforeseen circumstances, or for specific tasks which the donor would not have expected the attorney to attend to personally). But attorneys cannot usually delegate any decisions that rely on their discretion.

Duty of good faith

7.63 Acting in good faith means acting with honesty and integrity. For example, an attorney must try to make sure that their decisions do not go against a decision the donor made while they still had capacity (unless it would be in the donor's best interests to do so).

Duty of confidentiality

7.64 Attorneys have a duty to keep the donor's affairs confidential, unless:
- before they lost capacity to do so, the donor agreed that some personal or financial information may be revealed for a particular purpose (for example, they have named someone they want to check their financial accounts), or
- there is some other good reason to release it (for example, it is in the public interest or the best interests of the person who lacks capacity, or there is a risk of harm to the donor or others).

In the latter circumstances, it may be advisable for the attorney to get legal advice. Chapter 16 gives more information about confidentiality.

Duty to comply with the directions of the Court of Protection

7.65 Under sections 22 and 23 of the Act, the Court of Protection has wide-ranging powers to decide on issues relating to the operation or validity of an LPA. It can also:
- give extra authority to attorneys

- order them to produce records (for example, financial accounts), or
- order them to provide specific information or documentation to the court.

Attorneys must comply with any decision or order that the court makes.

Duty not to disclaim without notifying the donor and the OPG

7.66 Once someone becomes an attorney, they cannot give up that role without notifying the donor and the OPG. If they decide to give up their role, they must follow the relevant guidance available from the OPG.

Duty to keep accounts

7.67 Property and affairs attorneys must keep accounts of transactions carried out on the donor's behalf. Sometimes the Court of Protection will ask to see accounts. If the attorney is not a financial expert and the donor's affairs are relatively straightforward, a record of the donor's income and expenditure (for example, through bank statements) may be enough. The more complicated the donor's affairs, the more detailed the accounts may need to be.

Duty to keep the donor's money and property separate

7.68 Property and affairs attorneys should usually keep the donor's money and property separate from their own or anyone else's. There may be occasions where donors and attorneys have agreed in the past to keep their money in a joint bank account (for example, if a husband is acting as his wife's attorney). It might be possible to continue this under the LPA. But in most circumstances, attorneys must keep finances separate to avoid any possibility of mistakes or confusion.

How does the Act protect donors from abuse?

What should someone do if they think an attorney is abusing their position?

7.69 Attorneys are in a position of trust, so there is always a risk of them abusing their position. Donors can help prevent abuse by carefully choosing a suitable and trustworthy attorney. But others have a role to play in looking out for possible signs of abuse or exploitation, and reporting any concerns to the OPG. The OPG will then follow this up in co-operation with relevant agencies.

7.70 Signs that an attorney may be exploiting the donor (or failing to act in the donor's best interests) include:

- stopping relatives or friends contacting the donor – for example, the attorney may prevent contact or the donor may suddenly refuse visits or telephone calls from family and friends for no reason
- sudden unexplained changes in living arrangements (for example, someone moves in to care for a donor they've had little contact with)
- not allowing healthcare or social care staff to see the donor
- taking the donor out of hospital against medical advice, while the donor is having necessary medical treatment
- unpaid bills (for example, residential care or nursing home fees)
- an attorney opening a credit card account for the donor
- spending money on things that are not obviously related to the donor's needs
- the attorney spending money in an unusual or extravagant way
- transferring financial assets to another country.

7.71 Somebody who suspects abuse should contact the OPG immediately. The OPG may direct a Court of Protection Visitor to visit an attorney to investigate. In cases of suspected physical or sexual abuse, theft or serious fraud, the person should contact the police. They might also be able to refer the matter to the relevant local adult protection authorities.

7.72 In serious cases, the OPG will refer the matter to the Court of Protection. The court may revoke (cancel) the LPA or (through the OPG) prevent it being registered, if it decides that:
- the LPA does not meet the legal requirements for creating an LPA
- the LPA has been revoked or come to an end for any other reason
- somebody used fraud or undue pressure to get the donor to make the LPA
- the attorney has done something that they do not have authority to do, or
- the attorney has behaved or is planning to behave in a way that is not in the donor's best interests.

The court might then consider whether the authority previously given to an attorney can be managed by:
- the court making a single decision, or
- appointing a deputy.

What should an attorney do if they think someone else is abusing the donor?

7.73 An attorney who thinks someone else is abusing or exploiting the donor should report it to the OPG and ask for advice on what action they should take. They should contact the police if they suspect physical or sexual abuse, theft or serious fraud. They might also be able to refer the matter to local adult protection authorities.

7.74 Chapter 13 gives more information about protecting vulnerable people from abuse, ill treatment or neglect. It also discusses the duties and responsibilities of the various agencies involved, including the OPG and local authorities. In particular, it is a criminal offence (with a maximum penalty of five years' imprisonment, a fine, or both) for anyone (including attorneys) to wilfully neglect or ill-treat a person in their care who lacks capacity to make decisions for themselves (section 44).

What happens to existing EPAs once the Act comes into force?

7.75 Once the Act comes into force, it will not be possible to make new EPAs. Only LPAs can then be made.

7.76 Some donors will have created EPAs before the Act came into force with the expectation that their chosen attorneys will manage their property and affairs in the future, whether or not they have capacity to do so themselves.

7.77 If donors still have capacity after the Act comes into force, they can cancel the EPA and make an LPA covering their property and affairs. They should also notify attorneys and anyone else aware of the EPA (for example, a bank) that they have cancelled it.

7.78 Some donors will choose not to cancel their EPA or they may already lack the capacity to do so. In such cases, the Act allows existing EPAs, whether registered or not, to continue to be valid so that attorneys can meet the donor's expectations (Schedule 4). An EPA must be registered with the OPG when the attorney thinks the donor lacks capacity to manage their own affairs, or is beginning to lack capacity to do so.

7.79 EPA attorneys may find guidance in this chapter helpful. In particular, all attorneys must comply with the duties described in paragraphs 7.58–7.68 above. EPA attorneys can also be found liable under section 44 of the new Act, which sets out the new criminal offences of ill treatment and wilful neglect. The OPG has produced guidance on EPAs (see Annex A for details of publications and contact information).

8 WHAT IS THE ROLE OF THE COURT OF PROTECTION AND COURT-APPOINTED DEPUTIES?

This chapter describes the role of the Court of Protection and the role of court-appointed deputies. It explains the powers that the court has and how to make an application to the court. It also looks at how the court appoints a deputy to act and make decisions on behalf of someone who lacks capacity to make those decisions. In particular, it gives guidance on a deputy's duties and the consequences of not carrying them out responsibly.

The Office of the Public Guardian (OPG) produces detailed guidance for deputies. See the Annex for more details of the publications and how to get them. Further details on the court's procedures are given in the Court of Protection Rules and Practice Directions issued by the court.

> In this chapter, as throughout the Code, a person's capacity (or lack of capacity) refers specifically to their capacity to make a particular decision at the time it needs to be made.

Quick summary

The Court of Protection has powers to:
- decide whether a person has capacity to make a particular decision for themselves
- make declarations, decisions or orders on financial or welfare matters affecting people who lack capacity to make such decisions
- appoint deputies to make decisions for people lacking capacity to make those decisions
- decide whether an LPA or EPA is valid, and
- remove deputies or attorneys who fail to carry out their duties.

Before accepting an appointment as a deputy, a person the court nominates should consider whether:
- they have the skills and ability to carry out a deputy's duties (especially in relation to property and affairs)
- they actually want to take on the duties and responsibilities.

Anyone acting as a deputy must:
- make sure that they only make those decisions that they are authorised to make by the order of the court
- make sure that they follow the Act's statutory principles, including:
  - considering whether the person has capacity to make a particular decision for themselves. If they do, the deputy should allow them to do so unless the person agrees that the deputy should make the decision
  - taking all possible steps to try to help a person make the particular decision
- always make decisions in the person's best interests
- have regard to guidance in the Code of Practice that is relevant to the situation
- fulfil their duties towards the person concerned (in particular the duty of care and fiduciary duties to respect the degree of trust placed in them by the court).

What is the Court of Protection?

8.1 Section 45 of the Act sets up a specialist court, the Court of Protection, to deal with decision-making for adults (and children in a few cases) who may lack capacity to make specific decisions for themselves. The new Court of Protection replaces the old court of the same name, which only dealt with decisions about the property and financial affairs of people lacking capacity to manage their own affairs. As well as property and affairs, the new court also deals with serious decisions affecting healthcare and personal welfare matters. These were previously dealt with by the High Court under its inherent jurisdiction.

8.2 The new Court of Protection is a superior court of record and is able to establish precedent (it can set examples for future cases) and build up expertise in all issues related to lack of capacity. It has the same powers, rights, privileges and authority as the High Court. When reaching any decision, the court must apply all the statutory principles set out in section 1 of the Act. In particular, it must make a decision in the best interests of the person who lacks capacity to make the specific decision. There will usually be a fee for applications to the court.[29]

29 Details of the fees charged by the court, and the circumstances in which the fees may be waived or remitted, are available from the Office of the Public Guardian (OPG).

How can somebody make an application to the Court of Protection?

8.3 In most cases concerning personal welfare matters, the core principles of the Act and the processes set out in chapters 5 and 6 will be enough to:
- help people take action or make decisions in the best interests of someone who lacks capacity to make decisions about their own care or treatment, or
- find ways of settling disagreements about such actions or decisions.

But an application to the Court of Protection may be necessary for:
- particularly difficult decisions
- disagreements that cannot be resolved in any other way (see chapter 15), or
- situations where ongoing decisions may need to be made about the personal welfare of a person who lacks capacity to make decisions for themselves.

8.4 An order of the court will usually be necessary for matters relating to the property and affairs (including financial matters) of people who lack capacity to make specific financial decisions for themselves, unless:
- their only income is state benefits (see paragraph 8.36 below), or

- they have previously made an Enduring Power of Attorney (EPA) or a Lasting Power of Attorney (LPA) to give somebody authority to manage their property and affairs (see chapter 7).

8.5 Receivers appointed by the court before the Act commences will be treated as deputies. But they will keep their existing powers and duties. They must meet the requirements set out in the Act and, in particular, follow the statutory principles and act in the best interests of the person for whom they have been appointed. They must also have regard to guidance in this chapter and other parts of the Code of Practice. Further guidance for receivers is available from the OPG.

Cases involving young people aged 16 or 17

8.6 Either a court dealing with family proceedings or the Court of Protection can hear cases involving people aged 16 or 17 who lack capacity. In some cases, the Court of Protection can hear cases involving people younger than 16 (for example, when somebody needs to be appointed to make longer-term decisions about their financial affairs). Under section 21 of the Mental Capacity Act, the Court of Protection can transfer cases concerning children to a court that has powers under the Children Act 1989. Such a court can also transfer cases to the Court of Protection, if necessary. Chapter 12 gives more detail on cases where this might apply.

Who should make the application?

8.7 The person making the application will vary, depending on the circumstances. For example, a person wishing to challenge a finding that they lack capacity may apply to the court, supported by others where necessary. Where there is a disagreement among family members, for example, a family member may wish to apply to the court to settle the disagreement – bearing in mind the need, in most cases, to get permission beforehand (see paragraphs 8.11–8.12 below).

8.8 For cases about serious or major decisions concerning medical treatment (see paragraphs 8.18–8.24 below), the NHS Trust or other organisation responsible for the patient's care will usually make the application. If social care staff are concerned about a decision that affects the welfare of a person who lacks capacity, the relevant local authority should make the application.

8.9 For decisions about the property and affairs of someone who lacks capacity to manage their own affairs, the applicant will usually be the person (for example, family carer) who needs specific authority from the court to deal with the individual's money or property.

8.10 If the applicant is the person who is alleged to lack capacity, they will always be a party to the court proceedings. In all other cases, the court will decide whether the person who lacks, or is alleged to lack, capacity should be involved as a party to the case. Where the person is a party to the case, the court may appoint the Official Solicitor to act for them.

Who must ask the court for permission to make an application?

8.11 As a general rule, potential applicants must get the permission of the Court of Protection before making an application (section 50). People who the Act says do not need to ask for permission include:
- a person who lacks, or is alleged to lack, capacity in relation to a specific decision or action (or anyone with parental responsibility, if the person is under 18 years)
- the donor of the LPA an application relates to – or their attorney
- a deputy who has been appointed by the court to act for the person concerned, and
- a person named in an existing court order relating to the application.

The Court of Protection Rules also set out specific types of cases where permission is not required.

8.12 When deciding whether to give permission for an application, the court must consider:
- the applicant's connection to the person the application is about
- the reasons for the application
- whether a proposed order or direction of the court will benefit the person the application is about, and
- whether it is possible to get that benefit another way.

Scenario: Considering whether to give permission for an application

Sunita, a young Asian woman, has always been close to her older brother, who has severe learning disabilities and lives in a care home. Two years ago, Sunita married a non-Asian man, and her family cut off contact with her. She still wants to visit her brother and to be consulted about his care and what is in his best interests. But the family is not letting her. The Court of Protection gives Sunita permission to apply to the court for an order allowing her contact with her brother.

What powers does the Court of Protection have?

8.13 The Court of Protection may:
- make declarations, decisions and orders on financial and welfare matters affecting people who lack, or are alleged to lack, capacity (the lack of capacity must relate to the particular issue being presented to the court)

- appoint deputies to make decisions for people who lack capacity to make those decisions
- remove deputies or attorneys who act inappropriately.

The Court can also hear cases about LPAs and EPAs. The court's powers concerning EPAs are set out in Schedule 4 of the Act.

8.14 The court must always follow the statutory principles set out in section 1 of the Act (see chapter 2) and make the decision in the best interests of the person concerned (see chapter 5).

What declarations can the court make?

8.15 Section 15 of the Act provides the court with powers to make a declaration (a ruling) on specific issues. For example, it can make a declaration as to whether a person has capacity to make a particular decision or give consent for or take a particular action. The court will require evidence of any assessment of the person's capacity and may wish to see relevant written evidence (for example, a diary, letters or other papers). If the court decides the person has capacity to make that decision, they will not take the case further. The person can now make the decision for themselves.

8.16 Applications concerning a person's capacity are likely to be rare – people can usually settle doubts and disagreements informally (see chapters 4 and 15). But an application may be relevant if:
- a person wants to challenge a decision that they lack capacity
- professionals disagree about a person's capacity to make a specific (usually serious) decision
- there is a dispute over whether the person has capacity (for example, between family members).

8.17 The court can also make a declaration as to whether a specific act relating to a person's care or treatment is lawful (either where somebody has carried out the action or is proposing to). Under section 15, this can include an omission or failure to provide care or treatment that the person needs.

This power to decide on the lawfulness of an act is particularly relevant for major medical treatment cases where there is doubt or disagreement over whether the treatment would be in the person's best interests. Healthcare staff can still give life-sustaining treatment, or treatment which stops a person's condition getting seriously worse, while the court is coming to a decision.

Serious healthcare and treatment decisions

8.18 Prior to the Act coming into force, the courts decided that some decisions relating to the provision of medical treatment were so serious that in each case, an application should be made to the court for a declaration that the proposed action was lawful before that action was taken. Cases involving any of the following decisions should therefore be brought before a court:

- decisions about the proposed withholding or withdrawal of artificial nutrition and hydration (ANH) from patients in a permanent vegetative state (PVS)
- cases involving organ or bone marrow donation by a person who lacks capacity to consent
- cases involving the proposed non-therapeutic sterilisation of a person who lacks capacity to consent to this (e.g. for contraceptive purposes) and
- all other cases where there is a doubt or dispute about whether a particular treatment will be in a person's best interests.

8.19 The case law requirement to seek a declaration in cases involving the withholding or withdrawing of artificial nutrition and hydration to people in a permanent vegetative state is unaffected by the Act[30] and as a matter of practice, these cases should be put to the Court of Protection for approval.

30 *Airedale NHS Trust v Bland* [1993] 1 FLR 1026.

8.20 Cases involving organ or bone marrow donation by a person who lacks capacity to consent should also be referred to the Court of Protection. Such cases involve medical procedures being performed on a person who lacks capacity to consent but which would benefit a third party (though would not necessarily directly or physically benefit the person who lacks capacity). However, sometimes such procedures may be in the person's overall best interests (see chapter 5). For example, the person might receive emotional, social and psychological benefits as a result of the help they have given, and in some cases the person may experience only minimal physical discomfort.

8.21 A prime example of this is the case of *Re Y*[31] where it was found to be in Y's best interests for her to donate bone marrow to her sister. The court decided that it was in Y's best interests to continue to receive strong emotional support from her mother, which might be diminished if her sister's health were to deteriorate further, or she were to die.

Further details on this area are available in Department of Health or Welsh Assembly guidance.[32]

31 *Re Y (Mental Patient: Bone Marrow Donation)* [1996] 2 FLR 787; sub nom Re Y (Mental Incapacity: Bone Marrow Transplant).
32 Reference Guide to Consent for Examination or Treatment, Department of Health, March 2001: www.dh.gov.uk/PublicationsAndStatistics/Publications/PublicationsPolicyAnd Guidance/PublicationsPolicyAndGuidanceArticle/fs/en?CONTENT_ID=4006757&chk= snmdw8

8.22 Non-therapeutic sterilisation is the sterilisation for contraceptive purposes of a person who cannot consent. Such cases will require a careful assessment of whether such sterilisation would be in the best interests of the person who lacks capacity and such cases should continue to be referred to the court.[33] The court has also given guidance on when certain termination of pregnancy cases should be brought before the court.[34]

33 See e.g. *Re A (Medical Treatment: Male Sterilisation)* [2000] 1 FLR 549, where a mother applied for a declaration that a vasectomy was in the best interests of A, her son, (who had

Down's syndrome and was borderline between significant and severe impairment of intelligence), in the absence of his consent. After balancing the burdens and benefits of the proposed vasectomy to A, the Court of Appeal held that the vasectomy would not be in A's best interests.

34 *D v An NHS Trust (Medical Treatment: Consent: Termination)* [2003] EWHC 2793 (Fam), [2004] 1 FLR 1110.

8.23 Other cases likely to be referred to the court include those involving ethical dilemmas in untested areas (such as innovative treatments for variant CJD), or where there are otherwise irresolvable conflicts between healthcare staff, or between staff and family members.

8.24 There are also a few types of cases that should generally be dealt with by the court, since other dispute resolution methods are unlikely to be appropriate (see chapter 15). This includes, for example, cases where it is unclear whether proposed serious and/or invasive medical treatment is likely to be in the best interests of the person who lacks capacity to consent.

What powers does the court have to make decisions and appoint deputies?

8.25 In cases of serious dispute, where there is no other way of finding a solution or when the authority of the court is needed in order to make a particular decision or take a particular action, the court can be asked to make a decision to settle the matter using its powers under section 16.

However, if there is a need for ongoing decision-making powers and there is no relevant EPA or LPA, the court may appoint a deputy to make future decisions. It will also state what decisions the deputy has the authority to make on the person's behalf.

8.26 In deciding what type of order to make, the court must apply the Act's principles and the best interests checklist. In addition, it must follow two further principles, intended to make any intervention as limited as possible:

- Where possible, the court should make the decision itself in preference to appointing a deputy.
- If a deputy needs to be appointed, their appointment should be as limited in scope and for as short a time as possible.

What decisions can the court make?

8.27 In some cases, the court must make a decision, because someone needs specific authority to act and there is no other route for getting it. These include cases where:

- there is no EPA or property and affairs LPA in place and someone needs to make a financial decision for a person who lacks capacity to make that decision (for example, the decision to terminate a tenancy agreement), or
- it is necessary to make a will, or to amend an existing will, on behalf of a person who lacks capacity to do so.

8.28 Examples of other types of cases where a court decision might be appropriate include cases where:
- there is genuine doubt or disagreement about the existence, validity or applicability of an advance decision to refuse treatment (see chapter 9)
- there is a major disagreement regarding a serious decision (for example, about where a person who lacks capacity to decide for themselves should live)
- a family carer or a solicitor asks for personal information about someone who lacks capacity to consent to that information being revealed (for example, where there have been allegations of abuse of a person living in a care home)
- someone suspects that a person who lacks capacity to make decisions to protect themselves is at risk of harm or abuse from a named individual (the court could stop that individual contacting the person who lacks capacity).

8.29 Anyone carrying out actions under a decision or order of the court must still also follow the Act's principles.

> **Scenario: Making a decision to settle disagreements**
>
> Mrs Worrell has Alzheimer's disease. Her son and daughter argue over which care home their mother should move to. Although Mrs Worrell lacks the capacity to make this decision herself, she has enough money to pay the fees of a care home.
>
> Her solicitor acts as attorney in relation to her financial affairs under a registered EPA. But he has no power to get involved in this family dispute – nor does he want to get involved.
>
> The Court of Protection makes a decision in Mrs Worrell's best interests, and decides which care home can best meet her needs. Once this matter is resolved, there is no need to appoint a deputy.

What powers does the court have in relation to LPAs?

8.30 The Court of Protection can determine the validity of an LPA or EPA and can give directions as to how an attorney should use their powers under an LPA (see chapter 7). In particular, the court can cancel an LPA and end the attorney's appointment. The court might do this if the attorney was not carrying out their duties properly or acting in the best interests of the donor. The court must then decide whether it is necessary to appoint a deputy to take over the attorney's role.

What are the rules for appointing deputies?

8.31 Sometimes it is not practical or appropriate for the court to make a single declaration or decision. In such cases, if the court thinks that somebody needs to make future or ongoing decisions for someone whose condition makes it likely they will lack capacity to make some further decisions in the future, it can appoint a deputy to act for and make decisions for that person. A deputy's authority should be as limited in scope and duration as possible (see paragraphs 8.35–8.39 below).

How does the court appoint deputies?

8.32 It is for the court to decide who to appoint as a deputy. Different skills may be required depending on whether the deputy's decisions will be about a person's welfare (including healthcare), their finances or both. The court will decide whether the proposed deputy is reliable and trustworthy and has an appropriate level of skill and competence to carry out the necessary tasks.

8.33 In the majority of cases, the deputy is likely to be a family member or someone who knows the person well. But in some cases the court may decide to appoint a deputy who is independent of the family (for example, where the person's affairs or care needs are particularly complicated). This could be, for example, the Director of Adult Services in the relevant local authority (but see paragraph 8.60 below) or a professional deputy. The OPG has a panel of professional deputies (mainly solicitors who specialise in this area of law) who may be appointed to deal with property and affairs if the court decides that would be in the person's best interests.

When might a deputy need to be appointed?

8.34 Whether a person who lacks capacity to make specific decisions needs a deputy will depend on:
- the individual circumstances of the person concerned
- whether future or ongoing decisions are likely to be necessary, and
- whether the appointment is for decisions about property and affairs or personal welfare.

Property and affairs

8.35 The court will appoint a deputy to manage a person's property and affairs (including financial matters) in similar circumstances to those in which they would have appointed a receiver in the past. If a person who lacks capacity to make decisions about property and affairs has not made an EPA or LPA, applications to the court are necessary:

- for dealing with cash assets over a specified amount that remain after any debts have been paid
- for selling a person's property, or
- where the person has a level of income or capital that the court thinks a deputy needs to manage.

8.36 If the only income of a person who lacks capacity is social security benefits and they have no property or savings, there will usually be no need for a deputy to be appointed. This is because the person's benefits can be managed by an appointee, appointed by the Department for Work and Pensions to receive and deal with the benefits of a person who lacks capacity to do this for themselves. Although appointees are not covered by the Act, they will be expected to act in the person's best interests and must do so if they are involved in caring for the person. If the court does appoint a property and affairs deputy for someone who has an appointee, it is likely that the deputy would take over the appointee's role.

8.37 Anybody considered for appointment as a property and affairs deputy will need to sign a declaration giving details of their circumstances and ability to manage financial affairs. The declaration will include details of the tasks and duties the deputy must carry out. The deputy must assure the court that they have the skills, knowledge and commitment to carry them out.

Personal welfare (including healthcare)

8.38 Deputies for personal welfare decisions will only be required in the most difficult cases where:
- important and necessary actions cannot be carried out without the court's authority, or
- there is no other way of settling the matter in the best interests of the person who lacks capacity to make particular welfare decisions.

8.39 Examples include when:
- someone needs to make a series of linked welfare decisions over time and it would not be beneficial or appropriate to require all of those decisions to be made by the court. For example, someone (such as a family carer) who is close to a person with profound and multiple learning disabilities might apply to be appointed as a deputy with authority to make such decisions
- the most appropriate way to act in the person's best interests is to have a deputy, who will consult relevant people but have the final authority to make decisions
- there is a history of serious family disputes that could have a detrimental effect on the person's future care unless a deputy is appointed to make necessary decisions
- the person who lacks capacity is felt to be at risk of serious harm if left in the care of family members. In these rare cases, welfare decisions may need to be made by someone

independent of the family, such as a local authority officer. There may even be a need for an additional court order prohibiting those family members from having contact with the person.

Who can be a deputy?

8.40 Section 19(1) states that deputies must be at least 18 years of age. Deputies with responsibility for property and affairs can be either an individual or a trust corporation (often parts of banks or other financial institutions). No-one can be appointed as a deputy without their consent.

8.41 Paid care workers (for example, care home managers) should not agree to act as a deputy because of the possible conflict of interest – unless there are exceptional circumstances (for example, if the care worker is the only close relative of the person who lacks capacity). But the court can appoint someone who is an office-holder or in a specified position (for example, the Director of Adult Services of the relevant local authority). In this situation, the court will need to be satisfied that there is no conflict of interest before making such an appointment (see paragraphs 8.58–8.60).

8.42 The court can appoint two or more deputies and state whether they should act 'jointly', 'jointly and severally' or 'jointly in respect of some matters and jointly and severally in respect of others' (section 19 (4)(c)).

- Joint deputies must always act together. They must all agree decisions or actions, and all sign any relevant documents.
- Joint and several deputies can act together, but they may also act independently if they wish. Any action taken by any deputy alone is as valid as if that person were the only deputy.

8.43 Deputies may be appointed jointly for some issues and jointly and severally for others. For example, two deputies could be appointed jointly and severally for most decisions, but the court might rule that they act jointly when selling property.

Scenario: Acting jointly and severally

Toby had a road accident and suffered brain damage and other disabilities. He gets financial compensation but lacks capacity to manage this amount of money or make decisions about his future care. His divorced parents are arguing about where their son should live and how his compensation money should be used. Toby has always been close to his sister, who is keen to be involved but is anxious about dealing with such a large amount of money.

The court decides where Toby will live. It also appoints his sister and a solicitor as joint and several deputies to manage his property and

> affairs. His sister can deal with any day-to-day decisions that Toby lacks capacity to make, and the solicitor can deal with more complicated matters.

What happens if a deputy can no longer carry out their duties?

8.44 When appointing a deputy, the court can also appoint someone to be a successor deputy (someone who can take over the deputy's duties in certain situations). The court will state the circumstances under which this could occur. In some cases it will also state a period of time in which the successor deputy can act. Appointment of a successor deputy might be useful if the person appointed as deputy is already elderly and wants to be sure that somebody will take over their duties in the future, if necessary.

> **Scenario: Appointing a successor deputy**
>
> Neil, a man with Down's syndrome, inherits a lot of money and property. His parents were already retired when the court appointed them as joint deputies to manage Neil's property and affairs. They are worried about what will happen to Neil when they cannot carry out their duties as deputies any more. The court agrees to appoint other relatives as successor deputies. They will then be able to take over as deputies after the parents' death or if his parents are no longer able to carry out the deputy's role.

Can the court protect people lacking capacity from financial loss?

8.45 Under section 19(9)(a) of the Act the court can ask a property and affairs deputy to provide some form of security (for example, a guarantee bond) to the Public Guardian to cover any loss as a result of the deputy's behaviour in carrying out their role. The court can also ask a deputy to provide reports and accounts to the Public Guardian, as it sees fit.

Are there any restrictions on a deputy's powers?

8.46 Section 20 sets out some specific restrictions on a deputy's powers. In particular, a deputy has no authority to make decisions or take action:
- if they do something that is intended to restrain the person who lacks capacity – apart from under certain circumstances (guidance on the circumstances when restraint might be permitted is given in chapter 6)[35]
- if they think that the person concerned has capacity to make the particular decision for themselves

- if their decision goes against a decision made by an attorney acting under a Lasting Power of Attorney granted by the person before they lost capacity, or
- to refuse the provision or continuation of life-sustaining treatment for a person who lacks capacity to consent – such decisions must be taken by the court.

If a deputy thinks their powers are not enough for them to carry out their duties effectively, they can apply to the court to change their powers. See paragraph 8.54 below.

35 It is worth noting that there is a drafting error in section 20 of the Act. The word 'or' in section 20(11)(a) should have been 'and' in order to be consistent with sections 6(3)(a) and 11(4)(a). The Government will make the necessary amendment to correct this error at the earliest available legislative opportunity.

What responsibilities do deputies have?

8.47 Once a deputy has been appointed by the court, the order of appointment will set out their specific powers and the scope of their authority. On taking up the appointment, the deputy will assume a number of duties and responsibilities and will be required to act in accordance with certain standards. Failure to comply with the duties set out below could result in the Court of Protection revoking the order appointing the deputy and, in some circumstances, the deputy could be personally liable to claims for negligence or criminal charges of fraud.

8.48 Deputies should always inform any third party they are dealing with that the court has appointed them as deputy. The court will give the deputy official documents to prove their appointment and the extent of their authority.

8.49 A deputy must act whenever a decision or action is needed and it falls within their duties as set out in the court order appointing them. A deputy who fails to act at all in such situations could be in breach of duty.

What duties does the Act impose?

8.50 Deputies must:
- follow the Act's statutory principles (see chapter 2)
- make decisions or act in the best interests of the person who lacks capacity
- have regard to the guidance in this Code of Practice
- only make decisions the Court has given them authority to make.

Principles and best interests

8.51 Deputies must act in accordance with the Act's statutory principles (section 1) and in particular the best interests of the person who lacks capacity (the steps for working out best interests are set out in section 4). In particular, deputies must consider whether the person has capacity to make the decision for themselves. If not, they should consider whether the person is likely to regain capacity to make the decision in the future. If so, it may be possible to delay the decision until the person can make it.

The Code of Practice

8.52 As well as this chapter, deputies should pay special attention to the following guidance set out in the Code:
- chapter 2, which sets out how the Act's principles should be applied
- chapter 3, which describes the steps which can be taken to try to help the person make decisions for themselves
- chapter 4, which describes the Act's definition of lack of capacity
  and gives guidance on assessing capacity, and
- chapter 5, which gives guidance on working out someone's best interests.

8.53 In some situations, deputies might also find it useful to refer to guidance in:
- chapter 6, which explains when deputies who have caring responsibilities may have protection from liability and gives guidance on the few circumstances when the Act allows restraint in connection with care and treatment, and
- chapter 15, which describes ways to settle disagreements.

Only making decisions the court authorises a deputy to make

8.54 A deputy has a duty to act only within the scope of the actual powers given by the court, which are set out in the order of appointment. It is possible that a deputy will think their powers are not enough for them to carry out their duties effectively. In this situation, they must apply to the court either to:
- ask the court to make the decision in question, or
- ask the court to change the deputy's powers.

What are a deputy's other duties?

8.55 Section 19(6) states that a deputy is to be treated as 'the agent' of the person who lacks capacity when they act on their behalf. Being an agent means that the deputy has legal duties (under the law of agency) to the person they are representing. It also means that when they carry out tasks within their powers, they are not personally liable to third parties.

8.56 Deputies must carry out their duties carefully and responsibly. They have a duty to:
- act with due care and skill (duty of care)

- not take advantage of their situation (fiduciary duty)
- indemnify the person against liability to third parties caused by the deputy's negligence
- not delegate duties unless authorised to do so
- act in good faith
- respect the person's confidentiality, and
- comply with the directions of the Court of Protection.

Property and affairs deputies also have a duty to:
- keep accounts, and
- keep the person's money and property separate from own finances.

Duty of care

8.57 'Duty of care' means applying a certain standard of care and skill – depending on whether the deputy is paid for their services or holds relevant professional qualifications.
- Deputies who are not being paid must use the same care, skill and diligence they would use when making decisions for themselves or managing their own affairs. If they do not, they could be held liable for acting negligently. A deputy who claims to have particular skills or qualifications must show greater skill in those particular areas than a person who does not make such claims.
- If deputies are being paid for their services, they are expected to demonstrate a higher degree of care or skill when carrying out their duties.
- Deputies whose duties form part of their professional work (for example, solicitors or accountants) must display normal professional competence and follow their profession's rules and standards.

Fiduciary duty

8.58 A fiduciary duty means deputies must not take advantage of their position. Nor should they put themselves in a position where their personal interests conflict with their duties. For example, deputies should not buy property that they are selling for the person they have been appointed to represent. They should also not accept a third party commission in any transactions. Deputies must not allow anything else to influence their duties. They cannot use their position for any personal benefit, whether or not it is at the person's expense.

8.59 In many cases, the deputy will be a family member. In rare situations, this could lead to potential conflicts of interests. When making decisions, deputies should follow the Act's statutory principles and apply the best interests checklist and not allow their own personal interests to influence the decision.

8.60 Sometimes the court will consider appointing the Director of Adult Services in England or Director of Social Services in Wales of the relevant local authority as a deputy. The court will need to be satisfied that the authority has arrangements to avoid possible conflicts of interest. For example where the person for whom a financial deputy is required receives community care services from the local authority, the court will wish to be satisfied that decisions about the person's finances will be made in the best interests of that person, regardless of any implications for the services provided.

Duty not to delegate

8.61 A deputy may seek professional or expert advice (for example, investment advice from a financial adviser or a second medical opinion from a doctor). But they cannot give their decision-making responsibilities to someone else. In certain circumstances, the court will authorise the delegation of specific tasks (for example, appointing a discretionary investment manager for the conduct of investment business).

8.62 In certain circumstances, deputies may have limited powers to delegate (for example, through necessity or unforeseen circumstances, or for specific tasks which the court would not have expected the deputy to attend to personally). But deputies cannot usually delegate any decisions that rely on their discretion. If the deputy is the Director of Adult Services in England or Director of Social Services in Wales, or a solicitor, they can delegate specific tasks to other staff. But the deputy is still responsible for any actions or decisions taken, and can therefore be held accountable for any errors that are made.

Duty of good faith

8.63 Acting in good faith means acting with honesty and integrity. For example, a deputy must try to make sure that their decisions do not go against a decision the person made while they still had capacity (unless it would be in the person's best interests to do so).

Duty of confidentiality

8.64 Deputies have a duty to keep the person's affairs confidential, unless:
- before they lost capacity to do so, the person agreed that information could be revealed where necessary
- there is some other good reason to release information (for example, it is in the public interest or in the best interests of the person who lacks capacity, or where there is a risk of harm to the person concerned or to other people)

In the latter circumstances, it is advisable for the deputy to contact the OPG for guidance or get legal advice. See chapter 16 for more information about revealing personal information.

Duty to comply with the directions of the Court of Protection

8.65 The Court of Protection may give specific directions to deputies about how they should use their powers. It can also order deputies to provide reports (for example, financial accounts or reports on the welfare of the person who lacks capacity) to the Public Guardian at any time or at such intervals as the court directs. Deputies must comply with any direction of the court or request from the Public Guardian.

Duty to keep accounts

8.66 A deputy appointed to manage property and affairs is expected to keep, and periodically submit to the Public Guardian, correct accounts of all their dealings and transactions on the person's behalf.

Duty to keep the person's money and property separate

8.67 Property and affairs deputies should usually keep the person's money and property separate from their own or anyone else's. This is to avoid any possibility of mistakes or confusion in handling the person's affairs. Sometimes there may be good reason not to do so (for example, a husband might be his wife's deputy and they might have had a joint account for many years).

Changes of contact details

8.68 A deputy should inform the OPG of any changes of contact details or circumstances (for the deputy or the person they are acting for). This will help make sure that the OPG has up-to-date records. It will also allow the court to discharge people who are no longer eligible to act as deputies.

Who is responsible for supervising deputies?

8.69 Deputies are accountable to the Court of Protection. The court can cancel a deputy's appointment at any time if it decides the appointment is no longer in the best interests of the person who lacks capacity.

8.70 The OPG is responsible for supervising and supporting deputies. But it must also protect people lacking capacity from possible abuse or exploitation. Anybody who suspects that a deputy is abusing their position should contact the OPG immediately. The OPG may instruct a Court of Protection Visitor to visit a deputy to investigate any matter of concern. It can also apply to the court to cancel a deputy's appointment.

8.71 The OPG will consider carefully any concerns or complaints against deputies. But if somebody suspects physical or sexual abuse or serious fraud, they should contact the police and/or social services immediately, as well as informing the OPG. Chapter 14 gives more information about the role of the OPG. It also discusses the protection of vulnerable people from abuse, ill treatment or wilful neglect and the responsibilities of various relevant agencies.

9 WHAT DOES THE ACT SAY ABOUT ADVANCE DECISIONS TO REFUSE TREATMENT?

This chapter explains what to do when somebody has made an advance decision to refuse treatment. It sets out:

- what the Act means by an 'advance decision'
- guidance on making, updating and cancelling advance decisions
- how to check whether an advance decision exists
- how to check that an advance decision is valid and that it applies to current circumstances
- the responsibilities of healthcare professionals when an advance decision exists
- how to handle disagreements about advance decisions.

In this chapter, as throughout the Code, a person's capacity (or lack of capacity) refers specifically to their capacity to make a particular decision at the time it needs to be made.

Quick summary

- An advance decision enables someone aged 18 and over, while still capable, to refuse specified medical treatment for a time in the future when they may lack the capacity to consent to or refuse that treatment.
- An advance decision to refuse treatment must be valid and applicable to current circumstances. If it is, it has the same effect as a decision that is made by a person with capacity: healthcare professionals must follow the decision.
- Healthcare professionals will be protected from liability if they:
  - stop or withhold treatment because they reasonably believe that an advance decision exists, and that it is valid and applicable
  - treat a person because, having taken all practical and appropriate steps to find out if the person has made an advance decision to refuse treatment, they do not know or are not satisfied that a valid and applicable advance decision exists.

- People can only make an advance decision under the Act if they are 18 or over and have the capacity to make the decision. They must say what treatment they want to refuse, and they can cancel their decision – or part of it – at any time.
- If the advance decision refuses life-sustaining treatment, it must:
  - be in writing (it can be written by a someone else or recorded in healthcare notes)
  - be signed and witnessed, and
  - state clearly that the decision applies even if life is at risk.
- To establish whether an advance decision is valid and applicable, healthcare professionals must try to find out if the person:
  - has done anything that clearly goes against their advance decision
  - has withdrawn their decision
  - has subsequently conferred the power to make that decision on an attorney, or
  - would have changed their decision if they had known more about the current circumstances.
- Sometimes healthcare professionals will conclude that an advance decision does not exist, is not valid and/or applicable – but that it is an expression of the person's wishes. The healthcare professional must then consider what is set out in the advance decision as an expression of previous wishes when working out the person's best interests (see chapter 5).
- Some healthcare professionals may disagree in principle with patients' decisions to refuse life-sustaining treatment. They do not have to act against their beliefs. But they must not simply abandon patients or act in a way that that affects their care.
- Advance decisions to refuse treatment for mental disorder may not apply if the person who made the advance decision is or is liable to be detained under the Mental Health Act 1983.

How can someone make an advance decision to refuse treatment?

What is an advance decision to refuse treatment?

9.1 It is a general principle of law and medical practice that people have a right to consent to or refuse treatment. The courts have recognised that adults have the right to say in advance that they want to refuse treatment if they lose capacity in the future – even if this results in their death. A valid and applicable advance decision to refuse treatment has the same force as a contemporaneous decision. This has been a fundamental principle of the common law for many years and it is now set out in the Act. Sections 24–26 of the Act set out the when a person can make an advance decision to refuse treatment. This applies if:
- the person is 18 or older, and
- they have the capacity to make an advance decision about treatment.

Information on advance decisions to refuse treatment made by young people (under the age of 18) will be available at www.dh.gov.uk/consent

9.2 Healthcare professionals must follow an advance decision if it is valid and applies to the particular circumstances. If they do not, they could face criminal prosecution (they could be charged for committing a crime) or civil liability (somebody could sue them).

9.3 Advance decisions can have serious consequences for the people who make them. They can also have an important impact on family and friends, and professionals involved in their care. Before healthcare professionals can apply an advance decision, there must be proof that the decision:

- exists
- is valid, and
- is applicable in the current circumstances.

These tests are legal requirements under section 25(1). Paragraphs 9.38–9.44 explain the standard of proof the Act requires.

Who can make an advance decision to refuse treatment?

9.4 It is up to individuals to decide whether they want to refuse treatment in advance. They are entitled to do so if they want, but there is no obligation to do so. Some people choose to make advance decisions while they are still healthy, even if there is no prospect of illness. This might be because they want to keep some control over what might happen to them in the future. Others may think of an advance decision as part of their preparations for growing older (similar to making a will). Or they might make an advance decision after they have been told they have a specific disease or condition.

Many people prefer not to make an advance decision, and instead leave healthcare professionals to make decisions in their best interests at the time a decision needs to be made. Another option is to make a Lasting Power of Attorney. This allows a trusted family member or friend to make personal welfare decisions, such as those around treatment, on someone's behalf, and in their best interests if they ever lose capacity to make those decisions themselves (see paragraph 9.33 below and chapter 7).

9.5 People can only make advance decisions to refuse treatment. Nobody has the legal right to demand specific treatment, either at the time or in advance. So no-one can insist (either at the time or in advance) on being given treatments that healthcare professionals consider to be clinically unnecessary, futile or inappropriate. But people can make a request or state their wishes and preferences in advance. Healthcare professionals should then consider the request when deciding what is in a patient's best interests (see chapter 5) if the patient lacks capacity.

9.6 Nobody can ask for and receive procedures that are against the law (for example, help with committing suicide). As section 62 sets out, the Act does not change any of the laws relating to murder, manslaughter or helping someone to commit suicide.

Capacity to make an advance decision

9.7 For most people, there will be no doubt about their capacity to make an advance decision. Even those who lack capacity to make some decisions may have the capacity to make an advance decision. In some cases it may be helpful to get evidence of a person's capacity to make the advance decision (for example, if there is a possibility that the advance decision may be challenged in the future). It is also important to remember that capacity can change over time, and a person who lacks capacity to make a decision now might be able to make it in the future.

Chapter 3 explains how to assess a person's capacity to make a decision.

Scenario: Respecting capacity to make an advance decision

Mrs Long's family has a history of polycystic ovary syndrome. She has made a written advance decision refusing any treatment or procedures that might affect her fertility. The document states that her ovaries and uterus must not be removed. She is having surgery to treat a blocked fallopian tube and, during the consent process, she told her doctor about her advance decision.

During surgery the doctor discovers a solid mass that he thinks might be cancerous. In his clinical judgement, he thinks it would be in Mrs Long's best interests for him to remove the ovary. But he knows that Mrs Long had capacity when she made her valid and applicable advance decision, so he must respect her rights and follow her decision. After surgery, he can discuss the matter with Mrs Long and advise her about treatment options.

9.8 In line with principle 1 of the Act, that 'a person must be assumed to have capacity unless it is established that he lacks capacity', healthcare professionals should always start from the assumption that a person who has made an advance decision had capacity to make it, unless they are aware of reasonable grounds to doubt the person had the capacity to make the advance decision at the time they made it. If a healthcare professional is not satisfied that the person had capacity at the time they made the advance decision, or if there are doubts about its existence, validity or applicability, they can treat the person without fear of liability. It is good practice to record their decisions and the reasons for them. The Act does not require them to record their assessment of the person's capacity at the time the decision was made, but it would be good practice to do so.

9.9 Healthcare professionals may have particular concerns about the capacity of someone with a history of suicide attempts or suicidal thoughts who has made an advance decision. It is important to remember that making an advance decision which, if followed, may result in death does not necessarily mean a person is or feels suicidal. Nor does it necessarily mean the person lacks capacity to make the advance decision. If the person is clearly suicidal, this may raise questions about their capacity to make an advance decision at the time they made it.

What should people include in an advance decision?

9.10 There are no particular formalities about the format of an advance decision. It can be written or verbal, unless it deals with life-sustaining treatment, in which case it must be written and specific rules apply (see paragraphs 9.24–9.28 below).

9.11 An advance decision to refuse treatment:
- must state precisely what treatment is to be refused – a statement giving a general desire not to be treated is not enough
- may set out the circumstances when the refusal should apply – it is helpful to include as much detail as possible
- will only apply at a time when the person lacks capacity to consent to or refuse the specific treatment.

Specific rules apply to life-sustaining treatment.

9.12 People can use medical language or everyday language in their advance decision. But they must make clear what their wishes are and what treatment they would like to refuse.

9.13 An advance decision refusing all treatment in any situation (for example, where a person explains that their decision is based on their religion or personal beliefs) may be valid and applicable.

9.14 It is recommended that people who are thinking about making an advance decision get advice from:
- healthcare professionals (for example, their GP or the person most closely involved with current healthcare or treatment), or
- an organisation that can provide advice on specific conditions or situations (they might have their own format for recording an advance decision).

But it is up to the person whether they want to do this or not. Healthcare professionals should record details of any discussion on healthcare records.

9.15 Some people may also want to get legal advice. This will help them make sure that they express their decision clearly and accurately. It will also help to make sure that people understand their advance decision in the future.

9.16 It is a good idea to try to include possible future circumstances in the advance decision. For example, a woman may want to state in the advance decision whether or not it should still apply if she later becomes pregnant. If the document does not anticipate a change in circumstance, healthcare professionals may decide that it is not applicable if those particular circumstances arise.

9.17 If an advance decision is recorded on a patient's healthcare records, it is confidential. Some patients will tell others about their advance decision (for example, they might tell healthcare professionals, friends or family). Others will not. People who do not ask for their advance decision to be recorded on their healthcare record will need to think about where it should be kept and how they are going to let people know about their decision.

Written advance decisions

9.18 A written document can be evidence of an advance decision. It is helpful to tell others that the document exists and where it is. A person may want to carry it with them in case of emergency, or carry a card, bracelet or other indication that they have made an advance decision and explaining where it is kept.

9.19 There is no set form for written advance decisions, because contents will vary depending on a person's wishes and situation. But it is helpful to include the following information:
- full details of the person making the advance decision, including date of birth, home address and any distinguishing features (in case healthcare professionals need to identify an unconscious person, for example)
- the name and address of the person's GP and whether they have a copy of the document
- a statement that the document should be used if the person ever lacks capacity to make treatment decisions
- a clear statement of the decision, the treatment to be refused and the circumstances in which the decision will apply
- the date the document was written (or reviewed)
- the person's signature (or the signature of someone the person has asked to sign on their behalf and in their presence)
- the signature of the person witnessing the signature, if there is one (or a statement directing somebody to sign on the person's behalf).

See paragraphs 9.24–9.28 below if the advance decision deals with life-sustaining treatment.

9.20 Witnessing the person's signature is not essential, except in cases where the person is making an advance decision to refuse life-sustaining treatment. But if there is a witness, they are witnessing the signature and the fact that it confirms the wishes set out in the advance decision. It may be helpful to give a description of the relationship between the witness and person making the advance decision. The role of the witness is to witness the person's signature, it is not to certify that the person has the capacity to make the advance decision – even if the witness is a healthcare professional or knows the person.

9.21 It is possible that a professional acting as a witness will also be the person who assesses the person's capacity. If so, the professional should also make a record of the assessment, because acting as a witness does not prove that there has been an assessment.

Verbal advance decisions

9.22 There is no set format for verbal advance decisions. This is because they will vary depending on a person's wishes and situation. Healthcare professionals will need to consider whether a verbal advance decision exists and whether it is valid and applicable (see paragraphs 9.38– 9.44).

9.23 Where possible, healthcare professionals should record a verbal advance decision to refuse treatment in a person's healthcare record. This will produce a written record that could prevent confusion about the decision in the future. The record should include:
- a note that the decision should apply if the person lacks capacity to make treatment decisions in the future
- a clear note of the decision, the treatment to be refused and the circumstances in which the decision will apply
- details of someone who was present when the oral advance decision was recorded and the role in which they were present (for example, healthcare professional or family member), and
- whether they heard the decision, took part in it or are just aware that it exists.

What rules apply to advance decisions to refuse life-sustaining treatment?

9.24 The Act imposes particular legal requirements and safeguards on the making of advance decisions to refuse life-sustaining treatment. Advance decisions to refuse life-sustaining treatment must meet specific requirements:
- They must be put in writing. If the person is unable to write, someone else should write it down for them. For example, a family member can write down the decision on their behalf, or a healthcare professional can record it in the person's healthcare notes.
- The person must sign the advance decision. If they are unable to sign, they can direct someone to sign on their behalf in their presence.
- The person making the decision must sign in the presence of a witness to the signature. The witness must then sign the document in the presence of the person making the advance decision. If the person making the advance decision is unable

to sign, the witness can witness them directing someone else to sign on their behalf. The witness must then sign to indicate that they have witnessed the nominated person signing the document in front of the person making the advance decision.
- The advance decision must include a clear, specific written statement from the person making the advance decision that the advance decision is to apply to the specific treatment even if life is at risk.
- If this statement is made at a different time or in a separate document to the advance decision, the person making the advance decision (or someone they have directed to sign) must sign it in the presence of a witness, who must also sign it.

9.25 Section 4(10) states that life-sustaining treatment is treatment which a healthcare professional who is providing care to the person regards as necessary to sustain life. This decision will not just depend on the type of treatment. It will also depend on the circumstances in which the healthcare professional is giving it. For example, in some situations antibiotics may be life-sustaining, but in others they can be used to treat conditions that do not threaten life.

9.26 Artificial nutrition and hydration (ANH) has been recognised as a form of medical treatment. ANH involves using tubes to provide nutrition and fluids to someone who cannot take them by mouth. It bypasses the natural mechanisms that control hunger and thirst and requires clinical monitoring. An advance decision can refuse ANH. Refusing ANH in an advance decision is likely to result in the person's death, if the advance decision is followed.

9.27 It is very important to discuss advance decisions to refuse life-sustaining treatment with a healthcare professional. But it is not compulsory. A healthcare professional will be able to explain:
- what types of treatment may be life-sustaining treatment, and in what circumstances
- the implications and consequences of refusing such treatment (see also paragraph 9.14).

9.28 An advance decision cannot refuse actions that are needed to keep a person comfortable (sometimes called basic or essential care). Examples include warmth, shelter, actions to keep a person clean and the offer of food and water by mouth. Section 5 of the Act allows healthcare professionals to carry out these actions in the best interests of a person who lacks capacity to consent (see chapter 6). An advance decision can refuse artificial nutrition and hydration.

When should someone review or update an advance decision?

9.29 Anyone who has made an advance decision is advised to regularly review and update it as necessary. Decisions made a long time in advance are not automatically invalid or inapplicable, but they may raise doubts when deciding whether they are valid and applicable. A written decision that is regularly reviewed is more likely to be valid and applicable to current circumstances – particularly for progressive illnesses. This is because it is more likely to have taken on board changes that have occurred in a person's life since they made their decision.

9.30 Views and circumstances may change over time. A new stage in a person's illness, the development of new treatments or a major change in personal circumstances may be appropriate times to review and update an advance decision.

How can someone withdraw an advance decision?

9.31 Section 24(3) allows people to cancel or alter an advance decision at any time while they still have capacity to do so. There are no formal processes to follow. People can cancel their decision verbally or in writing, and they can destroy any original written document. Where possible, the person who made the advance decision should tell anybody who knew about their advance decision that it has been cancelled. They can do this at any time. For example, they can do this on their way to the operating theatre or immediately before being given an anaesthetic. Healthcare professionals should record a verbal cancellation in healthcare records. This then forms a written record for future reference.

How can someone make changes to an advance decision?

9.32 People can makes changes to an advance decision verbally or in writing (section 24(3)) whether or not the advance decision was made in writing. It is good practice for healthcare professionals to record a change of decision in the person's healthcare notes. But if the person wants to change an advance decision to include a refusal of life-sustaining treatment, they must follow the procedures described in paragraphs 9.24–9.28.

How do advance decisions relate to other rules about decision-making?

9.33 A valid and applicable advance decision to refuse treatment is as effective as a refusal made when a person has capacity. Therefore, an advance decision overrules:
- the decision of any personal welfare Lasting Power of Attorney (LPA) made before the advance decision was made. So an attorney cannot give consent to treatment that has been refused in an advance decision made after the LPA was signed
- the decision of any court-appointed deputy (so a deputy cannot give consent to treatment that has been refused in an advance decision which is valid and applicable)
- the provisions of section 5 of the Act, which would otherwise allow healthcare professionals to give treatment that they believe is in a person's best interests.

9.34 An LPA made after an advance decision will make the advance decision invalid, if the LPA gives the attorney the authority to make decisions about the same treatment (see paragraph 9.40).

9.35 The Court of Protection may make declarations as to the existence, validity and applicability of an advance decision, but it has no power to overrule a valid and applicable advance decision to refuse treatment.

9.36 Where an advance decision is being followed, the best interests principle (see chapter 5) does not apply. This is because an advance decision reflects the decision of an adult with capacity who has made the decision for themselves. Healthcare professionals must follow a valid and applicable advance decision, even if they think it goes against a person's best interests.

Advance decisions regarding treatment for mental disorder

9.37 Advance decisions can refuse any kind of treatment, whether for a physical or mental disorder. But generally an advance decision to refuse treatment for mental disorder can be overruled if the person is detained in hospital under the Mental Health Act 1983, when treatment could be given compulsorily under Part 4 of that Act. Advance decisions to refuse treatment for other illnesses or conditions are not affected by the fact that the person is detained in hospital under the Mental Health Act. For further information see chapter 13.

How can somebody decide on the existence, validity and applicability of advance decisions?

Deciding whether an advance decision exists

9.38 It is the responsibility of the person making the advance decision to make sure their decision will be drawn to the attention of healthcare professionals when it is needed. Some people will want their decision to be recorded on their healthcare records. Those who do not will need to find other ways of alerting people that they have made an advance decision and where somebody will find any written document and supporting evidence. Some people carry a card or wear a bracelet. It is also useful to share this information with family and friends, who may alert healthcare professionals to the existence of an advance decision. But it is not compulsory. Providing their GP with a copy of the written document will allow them to record the decision in the person's healthcare records.

9.39 It is important to be able to establish that the person making the advance decision was 18 or over when they made their decision, and that they had the capacity to make that decision when they made it, in line with the two-stage test for capacity set out in chapter 3. But as explained in paragraphs 9.7–9.9 above, healthcare professionals should always start from the assumption that the person had the capacity to make the advance decision.

Deciding whether an advance decision is valid

9.40 An existing advance decision must still be valid at the time it needs to be put into effect. Healthcare professionals must consider the factors in section 25 of the Act before concluding that an advance decision is valid. Events that would make an advance decision invalid include those where:
- the person withdrew the decision while they still had capacity to do so
- after making the advance decision, the person made a Lasting Power of Attorney (LPA) giving an attorney authority to make treatment decisions that are the same as those covered by the advance decision (see also paragraph 9.33)
- the person has done something that clearly goes against the advance decision which suggests that they have changed their mind.

Scenario: Assessing whether an advance decision is valid

A young man, Angus, sees a friend die after prolonged hospital treatment. Angus makes a signed and witnessed advance decision to refuse treatment to keep him alive if he is ever injured in this way. The advance decision includes a statement that this will apply even if his life is at risk.

A few years later, Angus is seriously injured in a road traffic accident. He is paralysed from the neck down and cannot breathe without the help of a machine. At first he stays conscious and gives permission to be treated. He takes part in a rehabilitation programme. Some months later he loses consciousness.

At this point somebody finds his written advance decision, even though Angus has not mentioned it during his treatment. His actions before his lack of capacity obviously go against the advance decision. Anyone assessing the advance decision needs to consider very carefully the doubt this has created about the validity of the advance decision, and whether the advance decision is valid and applicable as a result.

Deciding whether an advance decision is applicable

9.41 To be applicable, an advance decision must apply to the situation in question and in the current circumstances. Healthcare professionals must first determine if the person still has capacity to accept or refuse treatment at the relevant time (section 25(3)). If the person has capacity, they can refuse treatment there and then. Or they can change their decision and accept treatment. The advance decision is not applicable in such situations.

9.42 The advance decision must also apply to the proposed treatment. It is not applicable to the treatment in question if (section 25(4)):
- the proposed treatment is not the treatment specified in the advance decision
- the circumstances are different from those that may have been set out in the advance decision, or
- there are reasonable grounds for believing that there have been changes in circumstance, which would have affected the decision if the person had known about them at the time they made the advance decision.

9.43 So when deciding whether an advance decision applies to the proposed treatment, healthcare professionals must consider:
- how long ago the advance decision was made, and
- whether there have been changes in the patient's personal life (for example, the person is pregnant, and this was not anticipated when they made the advance decision) that might affect the validity of the advance decision, and
- whether there have been developments in medical treatment that the person did not foresee (for example, new medications, treatment or therapies).

9.44 For an advance decision to apply to life-sustaining treatment, it must meet the requirements set out in paragraphs 9.24–9.28.

Scenario: Assessing if an advance decision is applicable

Mr Moss is HIV positive. Several years ago he began to have AIDS-related symptoms. He has accepted general treatment, but made an advance decision to refuse specific retro-viral treatments, saying he didn't want to be a 'guinea pig' for the medical profession. Five years later, he is admitted to hospital seriously ill and keeps falling unconscious.

The doctors treating Mr Moss examine his advance decision. They are aware that there have been major developments in retro-viral treatment recently. They discuss this with Mr Moss's partner and both agree that there are reasonable grounds to believe that Mr Moss may have changed his advance decision if he had known about newer treatment options. So the doctors decide the advance decision does not apply to the new retro-virals and give him treatment.

If Mr Moss regains his capacity, he can change his advance decision and accept or refuse future treatment.

What should healthcare professionals do if an advance decision is not valid or applicable?

9.45 If an advance decision is not valid or applicable to current circumstances:
- healthcare professionals must consider the advance decision as part of their assessment of the person's best interests (see chapter 5) if they have reasonable grounds to think it is a true expression of the person's wishes, and
- they must not assume that because an advance decision is either invalid or not applicable, they should always provide the specified treatment (including life-sustaining treatment) – they must base this decision on what is in the person's best interests.

What happens to decisions made before the Act comes into force?

9.46 Advance decisions made before the Act comes into force may still be valid and applicable. Healthcare professionals should apply the rules in the Act to advance decisions made before the Act comes into force, subject to the transitional protections that will apply to advance decisions that refuse life-sustaining treatment. Further guidance will be available at www.dh.gov.uk/consent.

What implications do advance decisions have for healthcare professionals?

What are healthcare professionals' responsibilities?

9.47 Healthcare professionals should be aware that:
- a patient they propose to treat may have refused treatment in advance, and
- valid and applicable advance decisions to refuse treatment have the same legal status as decisions made by people with capacity at the time of treatment.

9.48 Where appropriate, when discussing treatment options with people who have capacity, healthcare professionals should ask if there are any specific types of treatment they do not wish to receive if they ever lack capacity to consent in the future.

9.49 If somebody tells a healthcare professional that an advance decision exists for a patient who now lacks capacity to consent, they should make reasonable efforts to find out what the decision is. Reasonable efforts might include having discussions with relatives of the patient, looking in the patient's clinical notes held in the hospital or contacting the patient's GP.

9.50 Once they know a verbal or written advance decision exists, healthcare professionals must determine whether:
- it is valid (see paragraph 9.40), and
- it is applicable to the proposed treatment (see paragraphs 9.41–9.44).

9.51 When establishing whether an advance decision applies to current circumstances, healthcare professionals should take special care if the decision does not seem to have been reviewed or updated for some time. If the person's current circumstances are significantly different from those when the decision was made, the advance decision may not be applicable. People close to the person concerned, or anyone named in the advance decision, may be able to help explain the person's prior wishes.

9.52 If healthcare professionals are satisfied that an advance decision to refuse treatment exists, is valid and is applicable, they must follow it and not provide the treatment refused in the advance decision.

9.53 If healthcare professionals are not satisfied that an advance decision exists that is both valid and applicable, they can treat the person without fear of liability. But treatment must be in the person's best interests (see chapter 5). They should make clear notes explaining why they have not followed an advance decision which they consider to be invalid or not applicable.

9.54 Sometimes professionals can give or continue treatment while they resolve doubts over an advance decision. It may be useful to get information from someone who can provide information about the person's capacity when they made the advance decision. The Court of Protection can settle disagreements about the existence, validity or applicability of an advance decision. Section 26 of the Act allows healthcare professionals to give necessary treatment, including life-sustaining treatment, to stop a person's condition getting seriously worse while the court decides.

Do advance decisions apply in emergencies?

9.55 A healthcare professional must provide treatment in the patient's best interests, unless they are satisfied that there is an advance decision that is:
- valid, and
- applicable in the circumstances.

9.56 Healthcare professionals should not delay emergency treatment to look for an advance decision if there is no clear indication that one exists. But if it is clear that a person has made an advance decision that is likely to be relevant, healthcare professionals should assess its validity and applicability as soon as possible. Sometimes the urgency of treatment decisions will make this difficult.

When can healthcare professionals be found liable?

9.57 Healthcare professionals must follow an advance decision if they are satisfied that it exists, is valid and is applicable to their circumstances. Failure to follow an advance decision in this situation could lead to a claim for damages for battery or a criminal charge of assault.

9.58 But they are protected from liability if they are not:
- aware of an advance decision, or
- satisfied that an advance decision exists, is valid and is applicable to the particular treatment and the current circumstances (section 26(2)).

If healthcare professionals have genuine doubts, and are therefore not 'satisfied', about the existence, validity or applicability of the advance decision, treatment can be provided without incurring liability.

9.59 Healthcare professionals will be protected from liability for failing to provide treatment if they 'reasonably believe' that a valid and applicable advance decision to refuse that treatment exists. But they must be able to demonstrate that their belief was reasonable (section 26(3)) and point to reasonable grounds showing why they believe this. Healthcare professionals can only base their decision on the evidence that is available at the time they need consider an advance decision.

9.60 Some situations might be enough in themselves to raise concern about the existence, validity or applicability of an advance decision to refuse treatment. These could include situations when:
- a disagreement between relatives and healthcare professionals about whether verbal comments were really an advance decision
- evidence about the person's state of mind raises questions about their capacity at the time they made the decision (see paragraphs 9.7–9.9)
- evidence of important changes in the person's behaviour before they lost capacity that might suggest a change of mind.

In cases where serious doubt remains and cannot be resolved in any other way, it will be possible to seek a declaration from the court.

What if a healthcare professional has a conscientious objection to stopping or providing life-sustaining treatment?

9.61 Some healthcare professionals may disagree in principle with patients' rights to refuse life-sustaining treatment. The Act does not change the current legal situation. They do not have to do something that goes against their beliefs. But they must not simply abandon patients or cause their care to suffer.

9.62 Healthcare professionals should make their views clear to the patient and the healthcare team as soon as someone raises the subject of withholding, stopping or providing life-sustaining treatment. Patients who still have capacity should then have the option of transferring their care to another healthcare professional, if it is possible to do this without affecting their care.

9.63 In cases where the patient now lacks capacity but has made a valid and applicable advance decision to refuse treatment which a doctor or health professional cannot, for reasons of conscience, comply with, arrangements should be made for the management of the patient's care to be transferred to another healthcare professional.[36] Where a transfer cannot be agreed, the Court of Protection can direct those responsible for the person's healthcare (for example, a Trust, doctor or other health professional) to make arrangements to take over responsibility for the person's healthcare (section 17(1)(e)).

[36] Re B (Adult: Refusal of Medical Treatment) [2002] EWHC 429 (Fam), [2002] 1 FLR 1090, at [100(viii)].

What happens if there is a disagreement about an advance decision?

9.64 It is ultimately the responsibility of the healthcare professional who is in charge of the person's care when the treatment is required to decide whether there is an advance decision which is valid and applicable in the circumstances. In the event of disagreement about an advance decision between healthcare professionals, or between healthcare professionals and family members or others close to the person, the senior clinician must consider all the available evidence. This is likely to be a hospital consultant or the GP where the person is being treated in the community.

9.65 The senior clinician may need to consult with relevant colleagues and others who are close to or familiar with the patient. All staff involved in the person's care should be given the opportunity to express their views. If the person is in hospital, their GP may also have relevant information.

9.66 The point of such discussions should not be to try to overrule the person's advance decision but rather to seek evidence concerning its validity and to confirm its scope and its applicability to the current circumstances. Details of these discussions should be recorded in the person's healthcare records. Where the senior clinician has a reasonable belief that an advance decision to refuse medical treatment is both valid and applicable, the person's advance decision should be complied with.

When can somebody apply to the Court of Protection?

9.67 The Court of Protection can make a decision where there is genuine doubt or disagreement about an advance decision's existence, validity or applicability. But the court does not have the power to overturn a valid and applicable advance decision.

9.68 The court has a range of powers (sections 16–17) to resolve disputes concerning the personal care and medical treatment of a person who lacks capacity (see chapter 8). It can decide whether:
- a person has capacity to accept or refuse treatment at the time it is proposed
- an advance decision to refuse treatment is valid
- an advance decision is applicable to the proposed treatment in the current circumstances.

9.69 While the court decides, healthcare professionals can provide life-sustaining treatment or treatment to stop a serious deterioration in their condition. The court has emergency procedures which operate 24 hours a day to deal with urgent cases quickly. See chapter 8 for guidance on applying to the court.

10 WHAT IS THE NEW INDEPENDENT MENTAL CAPACITY ADVOCATE SERVICE AND HOW DOES IT WORK?

This chapter describes the new Independent Mental Capacity Advocate (IMCA) service created under the Act. The purpose of the IMCA service is to help particularly vulnerable people who lack the capacity to make important decisions about serious medical treatment and changes of accommodation, and who have no family or friends that it would be appropriate to consult about those decisions. IMCAs will work with and support people who lack capacity, and represent their views to those who are working out their best interests.

The chapter provides guidance both for IMCAs and for everyone who may need to instruct an IMCA. It explains how IMCAs should be appointed. It also explains the IMCA's duties and the situations when an IMCA should be instructed. Both IMCAs and decision-makers are required to have regard to the Code of Practice.

> In this chapter, as throughout the Code, a person's capacity (or lack of capacity) refers specifically to their capacity to make a particular decision at the time it needs to be made.

Quick summary

Understanding the role of the IMCA service
- The aim of the IMCA service is to provide independent safeguards for people who lack capacity to make certain important decisions and, at the time such decisions need to be made, have no-one else (other than paid staff) to support or represent them or be consulted.
- IMCAs must be independent.

Instructing and consulting an IMCA
- An IMCA must be instructed, and then consulted, for people lacking capacity who have no-one else to support them (other than paid staff), whenever:
  - an NHS body is proposing to provide serious medical treatment, or
  - an NHS body or local authority is proposing to arrange accommodation (or a change of accommodation) in hospital or a care home, and

- the person will stay in hospital longer than 28 days, or
- they will stay in the care home for more than eight weeks.
- An IMCA may be instructed to support someone who lacks capacity to make decisions concerning:
  - care reviews, where no-one else is available to be consulted
  - adult protection cases, whether or not family, friends or others are involved

Ensuring an IMCA's views are taken into consideration

- The IMCA's role is to support and represent the person who lacks capacity. Because of this, IMCAs have the right to see relevant healthcare and social care records.
- Any information or reports provided by an IMCA must be taken into account as part of the process of working out whether a proposed decision is in the person's best interests.

What is the IMCA service?

10.1 Sections 35–41 of the Act set up a new IMCA service that provides safeguards for people who:
- lack capacity to make a specified decision at the time it needs to be made
- are facing a decision on a long-term move or about serious medical treatment and
- have nobody else who is willing and able to represent them or be consulted in the process of working out their best interests.

10.2 Regulations made under the Act also state that IMCAs may be involved in other decisions, concerning:
- a care review, or
- an adult protection case.

In adult protection cases, an IMCA may be appointed even where family members or others are available to be consulted.

10.3 Most people who lack capacity to make a specific decision will have people to support them (for example, family members or friends who take an interest in their welfare). Anybody working out a person's best interests must consult these people, where possible, and take their views into account (see chapter 5). But if a person who lacks capacity has nobody to represent them or no-one who it is appropriate to consult, an IMCA must be instructed in prescribed circumstances. The prescribed circumstances are:
- providing, withholding or stopping serious medical treatment
- moving a person into long-term care in hospital or a care home (see 10.11 for definition), or
- moving the person to a different hospital or care home.

The only exception to this can be in situations where an urgent decision is needed. Further details on the situations where there is a duty to instruct an IMCA are given in paragraphs 10.40–10.58.

In other circumstances, an IMCA *may* be appointed for the person (see paragraphs 10.59–10.68). These include:

- care reviews or
- adult protection cases.

10.4 The IMCA will:
- be independent of the person making the decision
- provide support for the person who lacks capacity
- represent the person without capacity in discussions to work out whether the proposed decision is in the person's best interests
- provide information to help work out what is in the person's best interests (see chapter 5), and
- raise questions or challenge decisions which appear not to be in the best interests of the person.

The information the IMCA provides must be taken into account by decision-makers whenever they are working out what is in a person's best interests. See paragraphs 10.20–10.39 for more information on an IMCA's role. For more information on who is a decision-maker, see chapter 5.

10.5 The IMCA service will build on good practice in the independent advocacy sector. But IMCAs have a different role from many other advocates. They:
- provide statutory advocacy
- are instructed to support and represent people who lack capacity to make decisions on specific issues
- have a right to meet in private the person they are supporting
- are allowed access to relevant healthcare records and social care records
- provide support and representation specifically while the decision is being made, and
- act quickly so their report can form part of decision-making.

Who is responsible for delivering the service?

10.6 The IMCA service is available in England and Wales. Both countries have regulations for setting up and managing the service.
- England's regulations[37] are available at www.opsi.gov.uk/si/si200618.htm and www.opsi.gov.uk/si/dsis2006.htm.
- The regulations for Wales[38] are available at www.new.wales.gov.uk/consultations/closed/healandsoccarecloscons/.

Guidance has been issued to local health boards and local authorities involved in commissioning IMCA services for their area.

---

37 *The Mental Capacity Act 2005 (Independent Mental Capacity Advocate) (General) Regulations 2006* (SI 2006/1832). The 'General Regulations'. These regulations set out the details on how the IMCA will be appointed, the functions of the IMCA, including their role in challenging the decision-maker and include definitions of 'serious medical treatment' and 'NHS body'.

The Mental Capacity Act 2005 (Independent Mental Capacity Advocate) (Expansion of Role) Regulations 2006 (SI 2006/2883). The 'Expansion Regulations'. These regulations specify the circumstances in which local authorities and NHS bodies may provide the IMCA service on a discretionary basis. These include involving the IMCA in a care review and in adult protection cases.

38 The Mental Capacity Act 2005 (Independent Mental Capacity Advocate) (Wales)

Regulations 2007 (SI 2007/852 (W.77)). These regulations will remain in draft form until they are made by the National Assembly for Wales. The target coming into force date is 1 October 2007. Unlike the two sets of English regulations there will be one set only for Wales. Although the Welsh regulations will remain in draft form until the coming into force date, these have been drafted to give effect to similar and corresponding provisions to the regulations in England.

10.7 In England the Secretary of State for Health delivers the service through local authorities, who work in partnership with NHS organisations. Local authorities have financial responsibility for the service. In Wales the National Assembly for Wales delivers the service through local health boards, who have financial responsibility for the service and work in partnership with local authority social services departments and other NHS organisations. The service is commissioned from independent organisations, usually advocacy organisations.

10.8 Local authorities or NHS organisations are responsible for instructing an IMCA to represent a person who lacks capacity. In these circumstances they are called the 'responsible body'.

10.9 For decisions about serious medical treatment, the responsible body will be the NHS organisation providing the person's healthcare or treatment. But if the person is in an independent or voluntary sector hospital, the responsible body will be the NHS organisation arranging and funding the person's care, which should have arrangements in place with the independent or voluntary sector hospital to ensure an IMCA is appointed promptly.

10.10 For decisions about admission to accommodation in hospital for 28 days or more, the responsible body will be the NHS body that manages the hospital. For admission to an independent or voluntary sector hospital for 28 days or more, the responsible body will be the NHS organisation arranging and funding the person's care. The independent or voluntary hospital must have arrangements in place with the NHS organisation to ensure that an IMCA can be appointed without delay.

10.11 For decisions about moves into long-term accommodation[39] (for eight weeks or longer), or about a change of accommodation, the responsible body will be either:
- the NHS body that proposes the move or change of accommodation (e.g. a nursing home), or
- the local authority that has carried out an assessment of the person under the NHS and Community Care Act 1990 and decided the move may be necessary.

39 This may be accommodation in a care home, nursing home, ordinary and sheltered housing, housing association or other registered social housing or in private sector housing provided by a local authority or in hostel accommodation.

10.12 Sometimes NHS organisations and local authorities will make decisions together about moving a person into long-term care. In these cases, the organisation that must instruct the IMCA is the one that is ultimately responsible for the decision to move the person. The IMCA to be instructed is the one who works wherever the person is at the time that the person needs support and representation.

What are the responsible body's duties?

10.13 The responsible body:
- *must* instruct an IMCA to support and represent a person in the situations set out in paragraphs 10.40–10.58
- *may* decide to instruct an IMCA in situations described in paragraphs 10.59–10.68
- *must*, in all circumstances when an IMCA is instructed, take properly into account the information that the IMCA provides when working out whether the particular decision (such as giving, withholding or stopping treatment, changing a person's accommodation, or carrying out a recommendation following a care review or an allegation requiring adult protection) is in the best interests of the person who lacks capacity.

10.14 The responsible body should also have procedures, training and awareness programmes to make sure that:
- all relevant staff know when they need to instruct an IMCA and are able to do so promptly
- all relevant staff know how to get in touch with the IMCA service and know the procedure for instructing an IMCA
- they record an IMCA's involvement in a case and any information the IMCA provides to help decision-making
- they also record how a decision-maker has taken into account the IMCA's report and information as part of the process of working out the person's best interests (this should include reasons for disagreeing with that advice, if relevant)
- they give access to relevant records when requested by an IMCA under section 35(6)(b) of the Act
- the IMCA gets information about changes that may affect the support and representation the IMCA provides
- decision-makers let all relevant people know when an IMCA is working on a person's case, and
- decision-makers inform the IMCA of the final decision taken and the reason for it.

10.15 Sometimes an IMCA and staff working for the responsible body might disagree. If this happens, they should try to settle the disagreement through discussion and negotiation as soon as possible. If they cannot do this, they should then follow the responsible body's formal procedures for settling disputes or complaints (see paragraphs 10.34 to 10.39 below).

10.16 In some situations the IMCA may challenge a responsible body's decision, or they may help somebody who is challenging a decision. The General Regulations in England and the Regulations in Wales set out when this may happen (see also chapter 15). If there is no other way of resolving the disagreement, the decision may be challenged in the Court of Protection.

Who can be an IMCA?

10.17 In England, a person can only be an IMCA if the local authority approves their appointment. In Wales, the local health board will provide approval. Qualified employees of an approved organisation can act as IMCAs. Local authorities and health boards will usually commission independent advocacy organisations to provide the IMCA service. These organisations will work to appropriate organisational standards set through the contracting/commissioning process.

10.18 Individual IMCAs must:
- have specific experience
- have IMCA training
- have integrity and a good character, and
- be able to act independently.

All IMCAs must complete the IMCA training in order that they can work as an independent mental capacity advocate. A national advocacy qualification is also being developed, which will include the IMCA training.

Before a local authority or health board appoints an IMCA, they must carry out checks with the Criminal Records Bureau (CRB) to get a criminal record certificate or enhanced criminal record certificate for that individual.[40]

[40] IMCAs were named as a group that is subject to mandatory checking under the new vetting and barring system in the Safeguarding Vulnerable Groups Act 2006. Roll-out of the bulk of the scheme will take place in 2008.

10.19 IMCAs must be independent. People cannot act as IMCAs if they:
- care for or treat (in a paid or professional capacity) the person they will be representing (this does not apply if they are an existing advocate acting for that person), or
- have links to the person instructing them, to the decision-maker or to other individuals involved in the person's care or treatment that may affect their independence.

What is an IMCA's role?

10.20 An IMCA must decide how best to represent and support the person who lacks capacity that they are helping. They:
- must confirm that the person instructing them has the authority to do so
- should interview or meet in private the person who lacks capacity, if possible
- must act in accordance with the principles of the Act (as set out in section 1 of the Act and chapter 2 of the Code) and take account of relevant guidance in the Code
- may examine any relevant records that section 35(6) of the Act gives them access to
- should get the views of professionals and paid workers providing care or treatment for the person who lacks capacity

- should get the views of anybody else who can give information about the wishes and feelings, beliefs or values of the person who lacks capacity
- should get hold of any other information they think will be necessary
- must find out what support a person who lacks capacity has had to help them make the specific decision
- must try to find out what the person's wishes and feelings, beliefs and values would be likely to be if the person had capacity
- should find out what alternative options there are
- should consider whether getting another medical opinion would help the person who lacks capacity, and
- must write a report on their findings for the local authority or NHS body.

10.21 Where possible, decision-makers should make decisions based on a full understanding of a person's past and present wishes. The IMCA should provide the decision-maker with as much of this information as possible – and anything else they think is relevant. The report they give the decision-maker may include questions about the proposed action or may include suggested alternatives, if they think that these would be better suited to the person's wishes and feelings.

10.22 Another important part of the IMCA's role is communicating their findings. Decision-makers should find the most effective way to enable them to do this. In some of the IMCA pilot areas,[41] hospital discharge teams added a 'Need to instruct an IMCA?' question on their patient or service user forms. This allowed staff to identify the need for an IMCA as early as possible, and to discuss the timetable for the decision to be made. Some decisions need a very quick IMCA response, others will allow more time. In the pilot areas, IMCA involvement led to better informed discharge planning, with a clearer focus on the best interests of a person who lacked capacity. It did not cause additional delays in the hospital discharge.

41 For further information see www.dh.gov.uk/imca

Representing and supporting the person who lacks capacity

10.23 IMCAs should take account of the guidance in chapter 5.
- IMCAs should find out whether the decision-maker has given all practical and appropriate support to help the person who lacks capacity to be involved as much as possible in decision-making. If the person has communication difficulties, the IMCA should also find out if the decision-maker has obtained any specialist help (for example, from a speech and language therapist).
- Sometimes an IMCA may find information to suggest a person might regain capacity in the future, either so they can make the

decision themselves or be more involved in decision-making. In such a situation, the IMCA can ask the decision-maker to delay the decision, if it is not urgent.
- The IMCA will need to get as much information as possible about the person's wishes, feelings, beliefs and values – both past and present. They should also consider the person's religion and any cultural factors that may influence the decision.

10.24 Sometimes a responsible body will not have time to instruct an IMCA (for example in an emergency or if a decision is urgent). If this is the case, this should be recorded, with the reason an IMCA has not been instructed. Where the decision concerns a move of accommodation, the local authority must appoint an IMCA as soon as possible afterwards. Sometimes the IMCA will not have time to carry out full investigations. In these situations, the IMCA must make a judgement about what they can achieve in the time available to support and represent the person who lacks capacity.

10.25 Sometimes an IMCA might not be able to get a good picture of what the person might want. They should still try to make sure the decision-maker considers all relevant information by:
- raising relevant issues and questions, and
- providing additional, relevant information to help the final decision.

Finding and evaluating information

10.26 Section 35(6) provides IMCAs with certain powers to enable them to carry out their duties. These include:
- the right to have an interview in private with the person who lacks capacity, and
- the right to examine, and take copies of, any records that the person holding the record thinks are relevant to the investigation (for example, clinical records, care plans, social care assessment documents or care home records).

10.27 The IMCA may also need to meet professionals or paid carers providing care or treatment for the person who lacks capacity. These people can help assess the information in case records or other sources. They can also comment on possible alternative courses of action. Ultimately, it is the decision-maker's responsibility to decide whether a proposed course of action is in the person's best interests. However, the Act requires the decision-maker to take account of the reports made and information given by the IMCA. In most cases a decision on the person's best interests will be made through discussion involving all the relevant people who are providing care or treatment, as well as the IMCA.

Finding out the person's wishes and feelings, beliefs and values

10.28 The IMCA needs to try and find out what the person's wishes and feelings might be, and what their underlying beliefs and values might also be. The IMCA should try to communicate both verbally and non-verbally with the person who may lack capacity, as appropriate. For example, this might mean using pictures or photographs. But there will be cases where the person cannot communicate at all (for example, if they are unconscious). The IMCA may also talk to other professionals or paid carers directly involved in providing present or past care or treatment. The IMCA might also need to examine health and social care records and any written statements of preferences the person may have made while they still had capacity to do so.

Chapter 5 contains further guidance on finding out the views of people who lack capacity. Chapter 3 contains further guidance on helping someone to make their own decision.

Considering alternative courses of action

10.29 The IMCA will need to check whether the decision-maker has considered all possible options. They should also ask whether the proposed option is less restrictive of the person's rights or future choices or would allow them more freedom (chapter 2, principle 5).

10.30 The IMCA may wish to discuss possible options with other professionals or paid carers directly involved in providing care or treatment for the person. But they must respect the confidentiality of the person they are representing.

Scenario: Using an IMCA

Mrs Nolan has dementia. She is being discharged from hospital. She has no close family or friends. She also lacks the capacity to decide whether she should return home or move to a care home. The local authority instructs an IMCA.

Mrs Nolan tells the IMCA that she wants to go back to her own home, which she can remember and describe. But the hospital care team thinks she needs additional support, which can only be provided in a care home.

The IMCA reviewed all the assessments of Mrs Nolan's needs, spoke to people involved in her care and wrote a report stating that Mrs Nolan had strong and clear wishes. The IMCA also suggested that a care package could be provided to support Mrs Nolan if she were allowed to return home. The care manager now has to decide what is in Mrs Nolan's best interests. He must consider the views of the hospital care team and the IMCA's report.

Getting a second medical opinion

10.31 For decisions about serious medical treatment, the IMCA may consider seeking a second medical opinion from a doctor with appropriate expertise. This puts a person who lacks the capacity to make a specific decision in the same position as a person who has capacity, who has the right to request a second opinion.

What happens if the IMCA disagrees with the decision-maker?

10.32 The IMCA's role is to support and represent their client. They may do this through asking questions, raising issues, offering information and writing a report. They will often take part in a meeting involving different healthcare and social care staff to work out what is in the person's best interests. There may sometimes be cases when an IMCA thinks that a decision-maker has not paid enough attention to their report and other relevant information and is particularly concerned about the decision made. They may then need to challenge the decision.

10.33 An IMCA has the same rights to challenge a decision as any other person caring for the person or interested in his welfare. The right of challenge applies both to decisions about lack of capacity and a person's best interests.

10.34 Chapter 15 sets out how disagreements can be settled. The approach will vary, depending on the type and urgency of the disagreement. It could be a formal or informal approach.

Disagreements about health care or treatment
- Consult the Patient Advice and Liaison Service (England)
- Consult the Community Health Council (Wales)
- Use the NHS Complaints Procedure
- Refer the matter to the local continuing care review panel
- Engage the services of the Independent Complaints Advocacy Service (England) or another advocate.

Disagreements about social care
- Use the care home's complaints procedure (if the person is in a care home)
- Use the local authority complaints procedure.

10.35 Before using these formal methods, the IMCA and the decision-maker should discuss the areas they disagree about – particularly those that might have a serious impact on the person the IMCA is representing. The IMCA and decision-maker should make time to listen to each other's views and to understand the reason for the differences. Sometimes these discussions can help settle a disagreement.

10.36 Sometimes an IMCA service will have a steering group, with representatives from the local NHS organisations and the local authority. These representatives can sometimes negotiate between two differing views. Or they can clarify policy on a certain issue.

They should also be involved if an IMCA believes they have discovered poor practice on an important issue.

10.37 IMCAs may use complaints procedures as necessary to try to settle a disagreement – and they can pursue a complaint as far as the relevant ombudsman if needed. In particularly serious or urgent cases, an IMCA may seek permission to refer a case to the Court of Protection for a decision. The Court will make a decision in the best interests of the person who lacks capacity.

10.38 The first step in making a formal challenge is to approach the Official Solicitor (OS) with the facts of the case. The OS can decide to apply to the court as a litigation friend (acting on behalf of the person the IMCA is representing). If the OS decides not to apply himself, the IMCA can ask for permission to apply to the Court of Protection. The OS can still be asked to act as a litigation friend for the person who lacks capacity.

10.39 In extremely serious cases, the IMCA might want to consider an application for judicial review in the High Court. This might happen if the IMCA thinks there are very serious consequences to a decision that has been made by a public authority. There are time limits for making an application, and the IMCA would have to instruct solicitors – and may be liable for the costs of the case going to court. So IMCAs should get legal advice before choosing this approach. The IMCA can also ask the OS to consider making the claim.

What decisions require an IMCA?

10.40 There are three types of decisions which require an IMCA to be instructed for people who lack capacity. These are:
- decisions about providing, withholding or stopping serious medical treatment
- decisions about whether to place people into accommodation (for example a care home or a long stay hospital), and
- decisions about whether to move people to different long stay accommodation.

For these decisions all local authorities and all health bodies must refer the same kinds of decisions to an IMCA for anyone who lacks capacity and qualifies for the IMCA service.

10.41 There are two further types of decisions where the responsible body has the power to instruct an IMCA for a person who lacks capacity. These are decisions relating to:
- care reviews and
- adult protection cases.

In such cases, the relevant local authority or NHS body must decide in each individual case whether it would be of particular benefit to the person who lacks capacity to have an IMCA to support them. The factors which should be considered are explained in paragraphs 10.59–10.68.[42]

[42] See chapter 11 for information about the role of 'consultees' when research is proposed

involving a person who lacks capacity to make a decision about whether to agree to take part in research. In certain situations IMCAs may be involved as consultees for research purposes.

Decisions about serious medical treatment

10.42 Where a serious medical treatment decision is being considered for a person who lacks the capacity to consent, and who qualifies for additional safeguards, section 37 of the Act imposes a duty on the NHS body to instruct an IMCA. NHS bodies must instruct an IMCA whenever they are proposing to take a decision about 'serious medical treatment', or proposing that another organisation (such as a private hospital) carry out the treatment on their behalf, if:
- the person concerned does not have the capacity to make a decision about the treatment, and
- there is no-one appropriate to consult about whether the decision is in the person's best interests, other than paid care staff.

10.43 Regulations for England and Wales set out the definition of 'serious medical treatment' for decisions that require an IMCA. It includes treatments for both mental and physical conditions.

Serious medical treatment is defined as treatment which involves giving new treatment, stopping treatment that has already started or withholding treatment that could be offered in circumstances where:
- if a single treatment is proposed there is a fine balance between the likely benefits and the burdens to the patient and the risks involved
- a decision between a choice of treatments is finely balanced, or
- what is proposed is likely to have serious consequences for the patient.

10.44 'Serious consequences' are those which could have a serious impact on the patient, either from the effects of the treatment itself or its wider implications. This may include treatments which:
- cause serious and prolonged pain, distress or side effects
- have potentially major consequences for the patient (for example, stopping life-sustaining treatment or having major surgery such as heart surgery), or
- have a serious impact on the patient's future life choices (for example, interventions for ovarian cancer).

10.45 It is impossible to set out all types of procedures that may amount to 'serious medical treatment', although some examples of medical treatments that might be considered serious include:
- chemotherapy and surgery for cancer
- electro-convulsive therapy
- therapeutic sterilisation
- major surgery (such as open-heart surgery or brain/neuro-surgery)
- major amputations (for example, loss of an arm or leg)

- treatments which will result in permanent loss of hearing or sight
- withholding or stopping artificial nutrition and hydration, and
- termination of pregnancy.

These are illustrative examples only, and whether these or other procedures are considered serious medical treatment in any given case, will depend on the circumstances and the consequences for the patient. There are also many more treatments which will be defined as serious medical treatments under the Act's regulations. Decision-makers who are not sure whether they need to instruct an IMCA should consult their colleagues.

10.46 The only situation in which the duty to instruct an IMCA need not be followed, is when an urgent decision is needed (for example, to save the person's life). This decision must be recorded with the reason for the non-referral. Responsible bodies will however still need to instruct an IMCA for any serious treatment that follows the emergency treatment.

10.47 While a decision-maker is waiting for the IMCA's report, they must still act in the person's best interests (for example, to give treatment that stops the person's condition getting worse).

Scenario: Using an IMCA for serious medical treatment

Mr Jones had a fall and suffered serious head injuries. Hospital staff could not find any family or friends. He needed urgent surgery, but afterwards still lacked capacity to accept or refuse medical treatment.

The hospital did not involve an IMCA in the decision to operate, because it needed to make an emergency decision. But it did instruct an IMCA when it needed to carry out further serious medical treatment.

The IMCA met with Mr Jones looked at his case notes and reviewed the options with the consultant. The decision-maker then made the clinical decision about Mr Jones' best interests taking into account the IMCA's report.

10.48 Some decisions about medical treatment are so serious that the courts need to make them (see chapter 8). But responsible bodies should still instruct an IMCA in these cases. The OS may be involved as a litigation friend of the person who lacks capacity.

10.49 Responsible bodies do not have to instruct an IMCA for patients detained under the Mental Health Act 1983, if:
- the treatment is for mental disorder, and
- they can give it without the patient's consent under that Act.

10.50 If serious medical treatment proposed for the detained patient is not for their mental disorder, the patient then has a right to an IMCA – as long as they meet the Mental Capacity Act's requirements. So a detained patient without capacity to consent to cancer treatment, for example, should qualify for an IMCA if there are no family or friends whom it would be appropriate to consult.

Decisions about accommodation or changes of residence

10.51 The Act imposes similar duties on NHS bodies and local authorities who are responsible for long-term accommodation decisions for a person who lacks the capacity to agree to the placement and who qualifies for the additional safeguard of an IMCA. The right to an IMCA applies to decisions about long-term accommodation in a hospital or care home if it is:
- provided or arranged by the NHS, or
- residential care that is provided or arranged by the local authority or provided under section 117 of the Mental Health Act 1983, or
- a move between such accommodation.

10.52 Responsible bodies have a duty to instruct an IMCA if:
- an NHS organisation proposes to place a person who lacks capacity in a hospital – or to move them to another hospital – for longer than 28 days, or
- an NHS organisation proposes to place a person who lacks capacity in a care home – or to move them to a different care home – for what is likely to be longer than eight weeks.

In either situation the other qualifying conditions apply. So, if the accommodation is for less than 28 days in a hospital or less than 8 weeks in a care home, then an IMCA need not be appointed.

10.53 The duty also applies if a local authority carries out an assessment under section 47 of the NHS and Community Care Act 1990, and it decides to:
- provide care services for a person who lacks capacity in the form of residential accommodation in a care home or its equivalent (see paragraph 10.11) which is likely to be longer than eight weeks, or
- move a person who lacks capacity to another care home or its equivalent for a period likely to exceed eight weeks.

10.54 In some cases, a care home may decide to de-register so that they can provide accommodation and care in a different way. If a local authority makes the new arrangements, then an IMCA should still be instructed if a patient lacks capacity and meets the other qualifying conditions.

10.55 Sometimes a person's placement will be longer than expected. The responsible body should involve an IMCA as soon as they realise the stay will be longer than 28 days or eight weeks, as appropriate.

10.56 People who fund themselves in long-term accommodation have the same rights to an IMCA as others, if the local authority:
- carries out an assessment under section 47 of the NHS and Community Care Act 1990, and

- decides it has a duty to the person (under either section 21 or 29 of the National Assistance Act 1947 or section 117 of the Mental Health Act 1983).

10.57 Responsible bodies can only put aside the duty to involve an IMCA if the placement or move is urgent (for example, an emergency admission to hospital or possible homelessness). The decision-maker must involve an IMCA as soon as possible after making an emergency decision, if:
- the person is likely to stay in hospital for longer than 28 days, or
- they will stay in other accommodation for longer than eight weeks.

10.58 Responsible bodies do not have to involve IMCAs if the person in question is going to be required to stay in the accommodation under the Mental Health Act 1983. But if a person is discharged from detention, they have a right to an IMCA in future accommodation decisions (if they meet the usual conditions set out in the Act).

When can a local authority or NHS body decide to instruct an IMCA?

10.59 The Expansion Regulations have given local authorities and NHS bodies the power to apply the IMCA role to two further types of decisions:
- a care review, and
- adult protection cases that involve vulnerable people.

10.60 In these situations, the responsible body must consider in each individual case whether to instruct an IMCA. Where an IMCA is instructed:
- the decision-maker must be satisfied that having an IMCA will be of particular benefit to the person who lacks capacity
- the decision-maker must also follow the best interests checklist, including getting the views of anyone engaged in caring for a person when assessing their best interests, and
- the decision-maker must consider the IMCA's report and related information when making a decision.

10.61 Responsible bodies are expected to take a strategic approach in deciding when they will use IMCAs in these two additional situations. They should establish a policy locally for determining these decisions, setting out the criteria for appointing an IMCA including the issues to be taken into account when deciding if an IMCA will be of particular benefit to the person concerned. However, decision-makers will need to consider each case separately to see if the criteria are met. Local authorities or NHS bodies may want to publish their approach for ease of access, setting out the ways they intend to use these additional powers and review it periodically.

Involving an IMCA in care reviews

10.62 A responsible body can instruct an IMCA to support and represent a person who lacks capacity when:
- they have arranged accommodation for that person
- they aim to review the arrangements (as part of a care plan or otherwise), and
- there are no family or friends who it would be appropriate to consult.

10.63 Section 7 of the Local Authority Social Services Act 1970 sets out current requirements for care reviews. It states that there should be a review 'within three months of help being provided or major changes made to services'. There should then be a review every year – or more often, if needed.

10.64 Reviews should relate to decisions about accommodation:
- for someone who lacks capacity to make a decision about accommodation
- that will be provided for a continuous period of more than 12 weeks
- that are not the result of an obligation under the Mental Health Act 1983, and
- that do not relate to circumstances where sections 37 to 39 of the Act would apply.

10.65 Where the person is to be detained or required to live in accommodation under the Mental Health Act 1983, an IMCA will not be needed since the safeguards available under that Act will apply.

Involving IMCAs in adult protection cases

10.66 Responsible bodies have powers to instruct an IMCA to support and represent a person who lacks capacity where it is alleged that:
- the person is or has been abused or neglected by another person, or
- the person is abusing or has abused another person.

The responsible bodies can only instruct an IMCA if they propose to take, or have already taken, protective measures. This is in accordance with adult protection procedures set up under statutory guidance.[43]

---

43 Published guidance: No secrets: Guidance on developing and implementing multi-agency policies and procedures to protect vulnerable adults from abuse for England (on the Department of Health website) and In safe hands in Wales.

No secrets applies to adults aged 18 or over. The Children Act 1989 applies to 16 and 17 year olds who may be facing abuse. Part V of the Act covers the Protection of Children, which includes at section 47 the duty to investigate by a local authority in order to decide whether they should take any action to safeguard or promote a child's welfare where he or she requires protection or may suffer harm. See also chapter 12 of this Code.10.67 In adult protection cases (and no other cases), access to IMCAs is not restricted to people who have no-one else to support or represent them. People who lack capacity who have family and friends can still have an IMCA to support them in the adult protection procedures.

10.68 In some situations, a case may start out as an adult protection case where a local authority may consider whether or not to involve an IMCA under the criteria they have set – but may then become a case where the allegations or evidence give rise to the question of whether the person should be moved in their best interests. In these situations the case has become one where an IMCA must be involved if there is no-one else appropriate to support and represent the person in this decision.

Who qualifies for an IMCA?

10.69 Apart from the adult protection cases discussed above, IMCAs are only available to people who:
- lack capacity to make a specific decision about serious medical treatment or long-term accommodation, *and*
- have no family or friends who are available and appropriate to support or represent them apart from professionals or paid workers providing care or treatment, *and*
- have not previously named someone who could help with a decision, *and*
- have not made a Lasting Power of Attorney or Enduring Power of Attorney (see paragraph 10.70 below).

10.70 The Act says that IMCAs cannot be instructed if:
- a person who now lacks capacity previously named a person that should be consulted about decisions that affect them, and that person is available and willing to help
- the person who lacks capacity has appointed an attorney, either under a Lasting Power of Attorney or an Enduring Power of Attorney, and the attorney continues to manage the person's affairs
- the Court of Protection has appointed a deputy, who continues to act on the person's behalf.

10.71 However, where a person has no family or friends to represent them, but does have an attorney or deputy who has been appointed solely to deal with their property and affairs, they should not be denied access to an IMCA. The Government is seeking to amend the Act at the earliest opportunity to ensure that, in such circumstances, an IMCA should always be appointed to represent the person's views when they lack the capacity to make decisions relating to serious medical treatment or long-term accommodation moves.

10.72 A responsible body can still instruct an IMCA if the Court of Protection is deciding on a deputy, but none is in place when a decision needs to be made.

> **Scenario: Qualifying for an IMCA**
>
> Ms Lewis, a woman with a history of mental health problems has lived in a care home for several years. Her home will soon close, and she has no-one who could help her. She has become very anxious and now lacks capacity to make a decision about future accommodation. The local authority instructs an IMCA to support her. The IMCA visits Ms Lewis, talks to staff who have been involved in her care and reviews her case notes.
>
> In his report, the IMCA includes the information that Ms Lewis is very close to another client in the care home. The IMCA notes that they could move together – if it is also in the interests of the other client. The local authority now has to decide on the best interests of the client, considering the information that the IMCA has provided.

Will IMCAs be available to people in prisons?

10.73 IMCAs should be available to people who are in prison and lack capacity to make decisions about serious medical treatment or long-term accommodation.

Who is it 'appropriate to consult'?

10.74 The IMCA is a safeguard for those people who lack capacity, who have no-one close to them who 'it would be appropriate to consult'. (This is apart from adult protection cases where this criterion does not apply.) The safeguard is intended to apply to those people who have little or no network of support, such as close family or friends, who take an interest in their welfare or no-one willing or able to be formally consulted in decision-making processes.

10.75 The Act does not define those 'whom it would be appropriate to consult' and the evaluation of the IMCA pilots reported that decision-makers in the local authority and in the NHS, whose decision it is to determine this, sometimes found it difficult to establish when an IMCA was required.[44] Section 4(7) provides that consultation about a person's best interests shall include among others, anyone:
- named by the person as someone to be consulted on a relevant decision
- engaged in caring for them, or
- interested in their welfare (see chapter 4).

44 see www.dh.gov.uk/PolicyAndGuidance/HealthAndSocialCareTopics/SocialCare/IMCA/fs/en

10.76 The decision-maker must determine if it is possible and practical to speak to these people, and those described in paragraph 10.70 when working out whether the proposed decision is in the person's best interests. If it is not possible, practical and appropriate to consult anyone, an IMCA should be instructed.

10.77 There may be situations where a person who lacks capacity has family or friends, but it is not practical or appropriate to consult them. For example, an elderly person with dementia may have an adult child who now lives in Australia, or an older person may have relatives who very rarely visit. Or, a family member may simply refuse to be consulted. In such cases, decision-makers must instruct an IMCA – for serious medical treatment and care moves and record the reason for the decision.

10.78 The person who lacks capacity may have friends or neighbours who know their wishes and feelings but are not willing or able to help with the specific decision to be made. They may think it is too much of a responsibility. If they are elderly and frail themselves, it may be too difficult for them to attend case conferences and participate formally. In this situation, the responsible body should instruct an IMCA, and the IMCA may visit them and enable them to be involved more informally.

10.79 If a family disagrees with a decision-maker's proposed action, this is not grounds for concluding that there is nobody whose views are relevant to the decision.

10.80 A person who lacks capacity and already has an advocate may still be entitled to an IMCA. The IMCA would consult with the advocate. Where that advocate meets the appointment criteria for the IMCA service, they may be appointed to fulfil the IMCA role for this person in addition to their other duties.

11 HOW DOES THE ACT AFFECT RESEARCH PROJECTS INVOLVING A PERSON WHO LACKS CAPACITY?

It is important that research involving people who lack capacity can be carried out, and that is carried out properly. Without it, we would not improve our knowledge of what causes a person to lack or lose capacity, and the diagnosis, treatment, care and needs of people who lack capacity.

This chapter gives guidance on involving people who lack capacity to consent to take part in research. It sets out:

- what the Act means by 'research'
- the requirements that people must meet if their research project involves somebody who lacks capacity
- the specific responsibilities of researchers, and
- how the Act applies to research that started before the Act came into force.

This chapter only deals with research in relation to adults. Further guidance will be provided on how the Act applies in relation to research involving those under the age of 18.

> In this chapter, as throughout the Code, a person's capacity (or lack of capacity) refers specifically to their capacity to make a particular decision at the time it needs to be made.

Quick summary

The Act's rules for research that includes people who lack capacity to consent to their involvement cover:
- when research can be carried out
- the ethical approval process
- respecting the wishes and feelings of people who lack capacity
- other safeguards to protect people who lack capacity
- how to engage with a person who lacks capacity
- how to engage with carers and other relevant people.

This chapter also explains:
- the specific rules that apply to research involving human tissue and
- what to do if research projects have already been given the go-ahead.

The Act applies to all research that is intrusive. 'Intrusive' means research that would be unlawful if it involved a person who had capacity but had not consented to take part. The Act does not apply to research involving clinical trials (testing new drugs).

Why does the Act cover research?

11.1 Because the Act is intended to assist and support people who may lack capacity, the Act protects people who take part in research projects but lack capacity to make decisions about their involvement. It makes sure that researchers respect their wishes and feelings. The Act does not apply to research that involves clinical trials of medicines –because these are covered by other rules.[45]

45 The Medicines for Human Use (Clinical Trials) Regulations 2004.

> *How can research involving people who lack capacity help?*
>
> A high percentage of patients with Down's syndrome lack capacity to agree or refuse to take part in research. Research involving patients with Down's syndrome has shown that they are more likely than other people to get pre-senile dementia. Research has also shown that when this happens the pathological changes that occur in a person with Down's syndrome (changes affecting their body and brain) are similar to those that occur in someone with Alzheimer's disease. This means

> that we now know that treatment similar to that used for memory disorders in patients with Alzheimer's is appropriate to treat dementia in those with Down's syndrome.

What is 'research'?

11.2 The Act does not have a specific definition for 'research'. The Department of Health and National Assembly for Wales publications *Research governance framework for health and social care* both state:

> 'research can be defined as the attempt to derive generalisable new knowledge by addressing clearly defined questions with systematic and rigorous methods.'[46]

Research may:

- provide information that can be applied generally to an illness, disorder or condition
- demonstrate how effective and safe a new treatment is
- add to evidence that one form of treatment works better than another
- add to evidence that one form of treatment is safer than another, or
- examine wider issues (for example, the factors that affect someone's capacity to make a decision).

[46] www.dh.gov.uk/PublicationsAndStatistics/Publications/PublicationsPolicyAndGuidance/PublicationsPolicyAndGuidanceArticle/fx/en?CONTENT_ID=4008777&chk=dMRd/5 and www.word.wales.gov.uk/content/governance/governance-e.htm

11.3 Researchers must state clearly if an activity is part of someone's care and not part of the research. Sometimes experimental medicine or treatment may be performed for the person's benefit and be the best option for their care. But in these cases, it may be difficult to decide whether treatment is research or care. Where there is doubt, the researcher should seek legal advice.

What assumptions can a researcher make about capacity?

11.4 Researchers should assume that a person has capacity, unless there is proof that they lack capacity to make a specific decision (see chapter 3). The person must also receive support to try to help them make their own decision (see chapter 2). The person whose capacity is in question has the right to make decisions that others might not agree with, and they have the right not to take part in research.

What research does the Act cover?

11.5 It is expected that most of the researchers who ask for their research to be approved under the Act will be medical or social care researchers. However, the Act can cover more than just medical and social care research. Intrusive research which does not meet the requirements of the Act cannot be carried out lawfully in relation to people who lack capacity.

11.6 The Act applies to research that:
- is 'intrusive' (if a person taking part had capacity, the researcher would need to get their consent to involve them)
- involves people who have an impairment of, or a disturbance in the functioning of, their mind or brain which makes them unable to decide whether or not to agree to take part in the research (ie they lack capacity to consent), and
- is not a clinical trial covered under the Medicines for Human Use (Clinical Trials) Regulations 2004.

11.7 There are circumstances where no consent is needed to lawfully involve a person in research. These apply to all persons, whether they have capacity or not:
- Sometimes research only involves data that has been anonymised (it cannot be traced back to individuals). Confidentiality and data protection laws do not apply in this case.
- Under the Human Tissue Act 2004, research that deals only with human tissue that has been anonymised does not require consent (see paragraphs 11.37–11.40). This applies to both those who have capacity and those who do not. But the research must have ethical approval, and the tissue must come from a living person.[47]
- If researchers collected human tissue samples before 31 August 2006, they do not need a person's consent to work on them. But they will normally have to get ethical approval.
- Regulations[48] made under section 251 of the NHS Act 2006 (formerly known as section 60 of the Health and Social Care Act 2001[49]) allow people to use confidential patient information without breaking the law on confidentiality by applying to the Patient Information Advisory Group for approval on behalf of the Secretary of State.[50]

48 Health Service (Control of Patient Information) Regulations 2002 Section I. 2002/1438.
49 Section 60 of the Health and Social Care Act 2001 was included in the NHS Act 2006 which consolidated all the previous health legislation still in force.
50 The Patient Information Advisory Group considers applications on behalf of the Secretary of State to allow the common law duty of confidentiality to be aside. It was established under section 61of the Health and Social Care Act 2006 (now known as section 252 of the NHS Act 2006). Further information can be found at www.advisorybodies.doh.gov.uk/PIAG.

Who is responsible for making sure research meets the Act's requirements?

11.8 Responsibility for meeting the Act's requirements lies with:
- the 'appropriate body', as defined in regulations made by the Secretary of State (for regulations applying in England) or the National Assembly for Wales (for regulations applying in Wales) (see paragraph 11.10), and

- the researchers carrying out the research (see paragraphs 11.20–11.40).

How can research get approval?

11.9 Research covered by the Act cannot include people who lack capacity to consent to the research unless:
- it has the approval of 'the appropriate body', and
- it follows other requirements in the Act to:
  – consider the views of carers and other relevant people
  – treat the person's interests as more important than those of science and society, and
  – respect any objections a person who lacks capacity makes during research.

11.10 An 'appropriate body' is an organisation that can approve research projects. In England, the 'appropriate body' must be a research ethics committee recognised by the Secretary of State.[51] In Wales, the 'appropriate body' must be a research ethics committee recognised by the Welsh Assembly Government.

[51] Mental Capacity Act 2005 (Appropriate Body) (England) Regulations 2006.

11.11 The appropriate body can only approve a research project if the research is linked to:
- an impairing condition that affects the person who lacks capacity, or
- the treatment of that condition (see paragraph 11.17)

and:
- there are reasonable grounds for believing that the research would be less effective if only people with capacity are involved, and
- the research project has made arrangements to consult carers and to follow the other requirements of the Act.

11.12 Research must also meet one of two requirements:
1. The research must have some chance of benefiting the person who lacks capacity, as set out in paragraph 11.14 below. The benefit must be in proportion to any burden caused by taking part, or
2. The aim of the research must be to provide knowledge about the cause of, or treatment or care of people with, the same impairing condition – or a similar condition.

If researchers are relying on the second requirement, the Act sets out further requirements that must be met:
- the risk to the person who lacks capacity must be negligible
- there must be no significant interference with the freedom of action or privacy of the person who lacks capacity, and
- nothing must be done to or in relation to the person who lacks capacity which is unduly invasive or restrictive (see paragraphs 11.16–11.19 below).

11.13 An impairing condition:

- is caused by (or may be caused by) an impairment of, or disturbance in the functioning of, the person's mind or brain
- causes (or may cause) an impairment or disturbance of the mind or brain, or
- contributes to (or may contribute to) an impairment or disturbance of the mind or brain.

Balancing the benefit and burden of research

11.14 Potential benefits of research for a person who lacks capacity could include:
- developing more effective ways of treating a person or managing their condition
- improving the quality of healthcare, social care or other services that they have access to
- discovering the cause of their condition, if they would benefit from that knowledge, or
- reducing the risk of the person being harmed, excluded or disadvantaged.

11.15 Benefits may be direct or indirect (for example, the person might benefit at a later date if policies or care packages affecting them are changed because of the research). It might be that participation in the research itself will be of benefit to the person in particular circumstances. For example, if the research involves interviews and the person has the opportunity to express their views, this could be considered of real benefit to a particular individual.

Providing knowledge about causes, treatment or care of people with the same impairing condition or a similar condition

11.16 It is possible for research to be carried out which doesn't actually benefit the person taking part, as long as it aims to provide knowledge about the causes, treatment or care of people with the same impairing condition, or a similar condition. *'Care'* and *'treatment'* are not limited to medical care and treatment. For example, research could examine how day-to-day life in prison affects prisoners with mental health conditions.

11.17 It is the person's actual condition that must be the same or similar in research, not the underlying cause. A *'similar condition'* may therefore have a different cause to that suffered by the participant. For example, research into ways of supporting people with learning disabilities to live more independently might involve a person with a learning disability caused by a head trauma. But its findings might help people with similar learning disabilities that have different causes.

> **Scenario: Research that helps find a cause or treatment**
>
> Mr Neal has Down's syndrome. For many years he has lived in supported housing and worked in a local supermarket. But several months ago, he became aggressive, forgetful and he started to make mistakes at work. His consultant believes that this may indicate the start of Alzheimer's disease.
>
> Mr Neal's condition is now so bad that he does not have capacity to consent to treatment or make other decisions about his care. A research team is researching the cause of dementia in people with Down's syndrome. They would like to involve Mr Neal. The research satisfies the Act's requirement that it is intended to provide knowledge of the causes or treatment of that condition, even though it may not directly benefit Mr Neal. So the approving body might give permission – if the research meets other requirements.

11.18 Any risk to people involved in this category of research must be 'negligible' (minimal). This means that a person should suffer no harm or distress by taking part. Researchers must consider risks to psychological wellbeing as well as physical wellbeing. This is particularly relevant for research related to observations or interviews.

11.19 Research in this category also must not affect a person's freedom of action or privacy in a significant way, and it should not be unduly invasive or restrictive. What will be considered as unduly invasive will be different for different people and different types of research. For example, in psychological research some people may think a specific question is intrusive, but others would not. Actions will not usually be classed as unduly invasive if they do not go beyond the experience of daily life, a routine medical examination or a psychological examination.

> **Scenario: Assessing the risk to research participants**
>
> A research project is studying:
> - how well people with a learning disability make financial decisions, and
> - communication techniques that may improve their decision-making capacity.
>
> Some of the participants lack capacity to agree to take part. The Research Ethics Committee is satisfied that some of these participants may benefit from the study because their capacity to make financial decisions may be improved. For those who will not gain any personal benefit, the Committee is satisfied that:
> - the research meets the other conditions of the Act

> - the research methods (psychological testing and different communication techniques) involve no risk to participants, and
> - the research could not have been carried out as effectively with people who have capacity.

What responsibilities do researchers have?

11.20 Before starting the research, the research team must make arrangements to:
- obtain approval for the research from the 'appropriate body'
- get the views of any carers and other relevant people before involving a person who lacks capacity in research (see paragraphs 11.22–11.28). There is an exception to this consultation requirement in situations where urgent treatment needs to be given or is about to be given
- respect the objections, wishes and feelings of the person, and
- place more importance on the person's interests than on those of science and society.

11.21 The research proposal must give enough information about what the team will do if a person who lacks capacity needs urgent treatment during research and it is not possible to speak to the person's carer or someone else who acts or makes decisions on behalf of the person (see paragraphs 11.32–11.36).

Consulting carers

11.22 Once it has been established that a person lacks capacity to agree to participate, then before they are included in research the researcher must consult with specified people in accordance with section 32 of the Act to determine whether the person should be included in the research.

Who can researchers consult?

11.23 The researcher should as a matter of good practice take reasonable steps to identify someone to consult. That person (the consultee) must be involved in the person's care, interested in their welfare and must be willing to help. They must not be a professional or paid care worker. They will probably be a family member, but could be another person.

11.24 The researcher must take into account previous wishes and feelings that the person might have expressed about who they would, or would not, like involved in future decisions.

11.25 A person is not prevented from being consulted if they are an attorney authorised under a registered Lasting Power of Attorney or are a deputy appointed by the Court of Protection. But that person must not be acting in a professional or paid capacity (for example, person's solicitor).

11.26 Where there is no-one who meets the conditions mentioned at paragraphs 11.23 and 11.25, the researcher must nominate a person to be the consulted. In this situation, they must follow guidance from the Secretary of State for Health in England or the National Assembly for Wales (the guidance will be available from mid-2007). The person who is nominated must have no connection with the research project.

11.27 The researcher must provide the consultee with information about the research project and ask them:
- for advice about whether the person who lacks capacity should take part in the project, and
- what they think the person's feelings and wishes would be, if they had capacity to decide whether to take part.

11.28 Sometimes the consultee will say that the person would probably not take part in the project or that they would ask to be withdrawn. In this situation, the researcher must not include the person in the project, or they should withdraw them from it. But if the project has started, and the person is getting treatment as part of the research, the researcher may decide that the person should not be withdrawn if the researcher reasonably believes that this would cause a significant risk to the person's health. The researcher may decide that the person should continue with the research while the risk exists. But they should stop any parts of the study that are not related to the risk to the person's health.

What other safeguards does the Act require?

11.29 Even when a consultee agrees that a person can take part in research, the researcher must still consider the person's wishes and feelings.

11.30 Researchers must not do anything the person who lacks capacity objects to. They must not do anything to go against any advance decision to refuse treatment or other statement the person has previously made expressing preferences about their care or treatment. They must assume that the person's interests in this matter are more important than those of science and society.

11.31 A researcher must withdraw someone from a project if:
- they indicate in any way that they want to be withdrawn from the project (for example, if they become upset or distressed), or
- any of the Act's requirements are no longer met.

What happens if urgent decisions are required during the research project?

11.32 Anyone responsible for caring for a person must give them urgent treatment if they need it. In some circumstances, it may not be possible to separate the research from the urgent treatment.

11.33 A research proposal should explain to the appropriate body how researchers will deal with urgent decisions which may occur during the project, when there may not be time to carry out the consultations required under the Act. For example, after a patient has arrived in intensive care, the doctor may want to chart the course of an injury by taking samples or measurements immediately and then taking further samples after some type of treatment to compare with the first set.

11.34 Special rules apply where a person who lacks capacity is getting, or about to get, urgent treatment and researchers want to include them in a research project. If in these circumstances a researcher thinks that it is necessary to take urgent action for the purposes of the research, and they think it is not practical to consult someone about it, the researcher can take that action if:
- they get agreement from a registered medical practitioner not involved with the research, or
- they follow a procedure that the appropriate body agreed to at approval stage.

11.35 The medical practitioner may have a connection to the person who lacks capacity (for example, they might be their doctor). But they must not be involved in the research project in any way. This is to avoid conflicts of interest.

11.36 This exception to the duty to consult only applies:
- for as long as the person needs urgent treatment, and
- when the researcher needs to take action urgently for research to be valid.

It is likely to be limited to research into procedures or treatments used in emergencies. It does not apply where the researcher simply wants to act quickly.

What happens for research involving human tissue?

11.37 A person with capacity has to give their permission for someone to remove tissue from their body (for example, taking a biopsy (a sample) for diagnosis or removal of tissue in surgery). The Act allows the removal of tissue from the body of a person who lacks capacity, if it is in their best interests (see chapter 5).

11.38 People with capacity must also give permission for the storage or use of tissue for certain purposes, set out in the Human Tissue Act 2004, (for example, transplants and research). But there are situations in which permission is not required by law:
- research where the samples are anonymised and the research has ethical approval[52]

- clinical audit
- education or training relating to human health
- performance assessment
- public health monitoring, and
- quality assurance.

52 Section 1(9) of the Human Tissue Act 2004.

11.39 If an adult lacks capacity to consent, the Human Tissue Act 2004 says that tissue can be stored or used without seeking permission if the storage or use is:
- to get information relevant to the health of another individual (for example, before conducting a transplant), as long as the researcher or healthcare professional storing or using the human tissue believes they are doing it in the best interests of the person who lacks capacity to consent
- for a clinical trial approved and carried out under the Medicines for Human Use (Clinical Trials) Regulations 2004, or
- for intrusive research:
   - after the Mental Capacity Act comes into force
   - that meets the Act's requirements, and
   - that has ethical approval.

11.40 Tissue samples that were obtained before 31 August 2006 are existing holdings under the Human Tissue Act. Researchers can work with these tissues without seeking permission. But they will still need to get ethical approval. Guidance is available in the Human Tissue Authority Code of Practice on consent.[53]

53 www.hta.gov.uk

What should happen to research that started before the Act came into force?

What if a person has capacity when research starts but loses capacity?

11.41 Some people with capacity will agree to take part in research but may then lose capacity before the end of the project. In this situation, researchers will be able to continue research as long as they comply with the conditions set out in the Mental Capacity Act 2005 (Loss of Capacity During Research Project) (England) Regulations 2007 or equivalent Welsh regulations.
The regulations only apply to tissue and data collected before the loss of capacity from a person who gave consent before 31 March 2008 to join a project that starts before 1 October 2007.

11.42 The regulations do not cover research involving direct intervention (for example, taking of further blood pressure readings) or the taking of further tissue after loss of capacity. Such research must comply with sections 30 to 33 of the Act to be lawful.

11.43 Where the regulations do apply, research can only continue if the project already has procedures to deal with people who lose capacity during the project. An appropriate body must have approved the procedures. The researcher must follow the procedures that have been approved.

11.44 The researcher must also:
- seek out the views of someone involved in the person's care or interested in their welfare and if a carer can't be found they must nominate a consultee (see paragraphs 11.22–11.28)
- respect advance decisions and expressed preferences, wishes or objections that the person has made in the past, and
- treat the person's interests as more important than those of science and society.

The appropriate body must be satisfied that the research project has reasonable arrangements to meet these requirements.

11.45 If at any time the researcher believes that procedures are no longer in place or the appropriate body no longer approves the research, they must stop research on the person immediately.

11.46 Where regulations do apply, research does not have to:
- be linked to an impairing condition of the person
- have the potential to benefit that person, or
- aim to provide knowledge relevant to others with the same or a similar condition.

What happens to existing projects that a person never had capacity to agree to?

11.47 There are no regulations for projects that:
- started before the Act comes into force, and
- a person never had the capacity to agree to.

Projects that already have ethical approval will need to obtain approval from an appropriate body under sections 30 and 31 of the Mental Capacity Act and to comply with the requirements of sections 32 and 33 of that Act by 1 October 2008. Research that does not have ethical approval must get approval from an appropriate body by 1 October 2007 to continue lawfully. This is the case in England and it is expected that similar arrangements will apply in Wales.

12 HOW DOES THE ACT APPLY TO CHILDREN AND YOUNG PEOPLE?

This chapter looks at the few parts of the Act that may affect children under 16 years of age. It also explains the position of young people aged 16 and 17 years and the overlapping laws that affect them.

This chapter does not deal with research. Further guidance will be provided on how the Act applies in relation to research involving those under the age of 18.

Within this Code of Practice, 'children' refers to people aged below 16. 'Young people' refers to people aged 16–17. This differs from the Children Act 1989 and the law more generally, where the term 'child' is used to refer to people aged under 18.

> In this chapter, as throughout the Code, a person's capacity (or lack of capacity) refers specifically to their capacity to make a particular decision at the time it needs to be made.

Quick summary

Children under 16

- The Act does not generally apply to people under the age of 16.
- There are two exceptions:
  - The Court of Protection can make decisions about a child's property or finances (or appoint a deputy to make these decisions) if the child lacks capacity to make such decisions within section 2(1) of the Act and is likely to still lack capacity to make financial decisions when they reach the age of 18 (section 18(3)).
  - Offences of ill treatment or wilful neglect of a person who lacks capacity within section 2(1) can also apply to victims younger than 16 (section 44).

Young people aged 16–17 years

- Most of the Act applies to young people aged 16–17 years, who may lack capacity within section 2(1) to make specific decisions.
- There are three exceptions:
  - Only people aged 18 and over can make a Lasting Power of Attorney (LPA).
  - Only people aged 18 and over can make an advance decision to refuse medical treatment.
  - The Court of Protection may only make a statutory will for a person aged 18 and over.

Care or treatment for young people aged 16–17

- People carrying out acts in connection with the care or treatment of a young person aged 16–17 who lacks capacity to consent within section 2(1) will generally have protection from liability (section 5), as long as the person carrying out the act:
  - has taken reasonable steps to establish that the young person lacks capacity
  - reasonably believes that the young person lacks capacity and that the act is in the young person's best interests, and
  - follows the Act's principles.

- When assessing the young person's best interests (see chapter 5), the person providing care or treatment must consult those involved in the young person's care and anyone interested in their welfare – if it is practical and appropriate to do so. This may include the young person's parents. Care should be taken not to unlawfully breach the young person's right to confidentiality (see chapter 16).
- Nothing in section 5 excludes a person's civil liability for loss or damage, or his criminal liability, resulting from his negligence in carrying out the act.

Legal proceedings involving young people aged 16-17
- Sometimes there will be disagreements about the care, treatment or welfare of a young person aged 16 or 17 who lacks capacity to make relevant decisions. Depending on the circumstances, the case may be heard in the family courts or the Court of Protection.
- The Court of Protection may transfer a case to the family courts, and vice versa.

Does the Act apply to children?

12.1 Section 2(5) of the Act states that, with the exception of section 2(6), as explained below, no powers under the Act may be exercised in relation to a child under 16.

12.2 Care and treatment of children under the age of 16 is generally governed by common law principles. Further information is provide at www.dh.gov.uk/consent.

Can the Act help with decisions about a child's property or finances?

12.3 Section 2(6) makes an exception for some decisions about a child's property and financial affairs. The Court of Protection can make decisions about property and affairs of those under 16 in cases where the person is likely to still lack capacity to make financial decisions after reaching the age of 18. The court's ruling will still apply when the person reaches the age of 18, which means there will not be a need for further court proceedings once the person reaches the age of 18.

12.4 The Court of Protection can:
- make an order (for example, concerning the investment of an award of compensation for the child), and/or
- appoint a deputy to manage the child's property and affairs and to make ongoing financial decisions on the child's behalf.

In making a decision, the court must follow the Act's principles and decide in the child's best interests as set out in chapter 5 of the Code.

> **Scenario: Applying the Act to children**
>
> Tom was nine when a drunk driver knocked him off his bicycle. He suffered severe head injuries and permanent brain damage. He received a large amount of money in compensation. He is unlikely to recover enough to be able to make financial decisions when he is 18. So the Court of Protection appoints Tom's father as deputy to manage his financial affairs in order to pay for the care Tom will need in the future.

What if somebody mistreats or neglects a child who lacks capacity?

12.5 Section 44 covers the offences of ill treatment or wilful neglect of a person who lacks capacity to make relevant decisions (see chapter 14). This section also applies to children under 16 and young people aged 16 or 17. But it only applies if the child's lack of capacity to make a decision for themselves is caused by an impairment or disturbance that affects how their mind or brain works (see chapter 4). If the lack of capacity is solely the result of the child's youth or immaturity, then the ill treatment or wilful neglect would be dealt with under the separate offences of child cruelty or neglect.

Does the Act apply to young people aged 16–17?

12.6 Most of the Act applies to people aged 16 years and over. There is an overlap with the Children Act 1989. For the Act to apply to a young person, they must lack capacity to make a particular decision (in line with the Act's definition of lack of capacity described in chapter 4). In such situations either this Act or the Children Act 1989 may apply, depending upon the particular circumstances. However, there may also be situations where neither of these Acts provides an appropriate solution. In such cases, it may be necessary to look to the powers available under the Mental Health Act 1983 or the High Court's inherent powers to deal with cases involving young people.

12.7 There are currently no specific rules for deciding when to use either the Children Act 1989 or the Mental Capacity Act 2005 or when to apply to the High Court. But, the examples below show circumstances where this Act may be the most appropriate (see also paragraphs 12.21–12.23 below).

- In unusual circumstances it might be in a young person's best interests for the Court of Protection to make an order and/or appoint a property and affairs deputy. For example, this might occur when a young person receives financial compensation and the court appoints a parent or a solicitor as a property and affairs deputy.

- It may be appropriate for the Court of Protection to make a welfare decision concerning a young person who lacks capacity to decide for themselves (for example, about where the young person should live) if the court decides that the parents are not acting in the young person's best interests.
- It might be appropriate to refer a case to the Court of Protection where there is disagreement between a person interested in the care and welfare of a young person and the young person's medical team about the young person's best interests or capacity.

Do any parts of the Act not apply to young people aged 16 or 17?

LPAs

12.8 Only people aged 18 or over can make a Lasting Power of Attorney (LPA) (section 9(2)(c)).

Advance decisions to refuse treatment

12.9 Information on decisions to refuse treatment made in advance by young people under the age of 18 will be available at www.dh.gov.uk/consent.

Making a will

12.10 The law generally does not allow anyone below the age of 18 to make a will. So section 18(2) confirms that the Court of Protection can only make a statutory will on behalf of those aged 18 and over.

What does the Act say about care or treatment of young people aged 16 or 17?

Background information concerning competent young people

12.11 The Family Law Reform Act 1969 presumes that young people have the legal capacity to agree to surgical, medical or dental treatment.[54] This also applies to any associated procedures (for example, investigations, anaesthesia or nursing care).

[54] Family Law Reform Act 1969, s 8(1).

12.12 It does not apply to some rarer types of procedure (for example, organ donation or other procedures which are not therapeutic for the young person) or research. In those cases, anyone under 18 is presumed to lack legal capacity, subject to the test of 'Gillick competence' (testing whether they are mature and intelligent enough to understand a proposed treatment or procedure).[55]

[55] In the case of *Gillick v West Norfolk and Wisbech Area Health Authority and Another* [1986] 1 FLR 224, the court found that a child below 16 years of age will be competent to consent to medical treatment if they have sufficient intelligence and understanding to understand

what is proposed. This test applies in relation to all people under 18 where there is no presumption of competence in relation to the procedure – for example where the procedure is not one referred to in section 8 of the Family Law Reform Act 1969, e.g organ donation.

12.13 Even where a young person is presumed to have legal capacity to consent to treatment, they may not necessarily be able to make the relevant decision. As with adults, decision-makers should assess the young person's capacity to consent to the proposed care or treatment (see chapter 4). If a young person lacks capacity to consent within section 2(1) of the Act because of an impairment of, or a disturbance in the functioning of, the mind or brain then the Mental Capacity Act will apply in the same way as it does to those who are 18 and over. If however they are unable to make the decision for some other reason, for example because they are overwhelmed by the implications of the decision, the Act will not apply to them and the legality of any treatment should be assessed under common law principles.

12.14 If a young person has capacity to agree to treatment, their decision to consent must be respected. Difficult issues can arise if a young person has legal and mental capacity and refuses consent – especially if a person with parental responsibility wishes to give consent on the young person's behalf. The Family Division of the High Court can hear cases where there is disagreement. The Court of Protection has no power to settle a dispute about a young person who is said to have the mental capacity to make the specific decision.

12.15 It may be unclear whether a young person lacks capacity within section 2(1) of the Act. In those circumstances, it would be prudent for the person providing care or treatment for the young person to seek a declaration from the court.

If the young person lacks capacity to make care or treatment decisions

12.16 Under the common law, a person with parental responsibility for a young person is generally able to consent to the young person receiving care or medical treatment where they lack capacity under section 2(1) of the Act. They should act in the young person's best interests.

12.17 However if a young person lacks the mental capacity to make a specific care or treatment decision within section 2(1) of the Act, healthcare staff providing treatment, or a person providing care to the young person, can carry out treatment or care with protection from liability (section 5) whether or not a person with parental responsibility consents.[56] They must follow the Act's principles and make sure that the actions they carry out are in the young person's best interests. They must make every effort to work out and consider the young person's wishes, feelings, beliefs and values – both past and present – and consider all other factors in the best interests checklist (see chapter 5).

56 Nothing in section 5 excludes a person's civil liability for loss or damage, or his criminal liability, resulting from his negligence in doing the Act.

12.18 When assessing a young person's best interests, healthcare staff must take into account the views of anyone involved in caring for the young person and anyone interested in their welfare, where it is practical and appropriate to do so. This may include the young person's parents and others with parental responsibility for the young person. Care should be taken not to unlawfully breach the young person's right to confidentiality (see chapter 16).

12.19 If a young person has said they do not want their parents to be consulted, it may not be appropriate to involve them (for example, where there have been allegations of abuse).

12.20 If there is a disagreement about whether the proposed care or treatment is in the best interests of a young person, or there is disagreement about whether the young person lacks capacity and there is no other way of resolving the matter, it would be prudent for those in disagreement to seek a declaration or other order from the appropriate court (see paragraphs 12.23–12.25 below).

Scenario: Working out a young person's best interests

Mary is 16 and has Down's syndrome. Her mother wants Mary to have dental treatment that will improve her appearance but is not otherwise necessary.

To be protected under section 5 of the Act, the dentist must consider whether Mary has capacity to agree to the treatment and what would be in her best interests. He decides that she is unable to understand what is involved or the possible consequences of the proposed treatment and so lacks capacity to make the decision.

But Mary seems to want the treatment, so he takes her views into account in deciding whether the treatment is in her best interests. He also consults with both her parents and with her teacher and GP to see if there are other relevant factors to take into account.

He decides that the treatment is likely to improve Mary's confidence and self-esteem and is in her best interests.

12.21 There may be particular difficulties where young people with mental health problems require in-patient psychiatric treatment, and are treated informally rather than detained under the Mental Health Act 1983. The Mental Capacity Act and its principles apply to decisions related to the care and treatment of young people who lack mental capacity to consent, including treatment for mental disorder. As with any other form of treatment, somebody assessing a young person's best interests should consult anyone involved in caring for the young person or anyone interested in their welfare, as far as is practical and appropriate. This may include the young person's parents or those with parental responsibility for the young person.

But the Act does not allow any actions that result in a young person being deprived of their liberty (see chapter 6). In such circumstances, detention under the Mental Health Act 1983 and the safeguards provided under that Act might be appropriate (see also chapter 13).

12.22 People may disagree about a young person's capacity to make the specific decision or about their best interests, or it may not be clear whether they lack capacity within section 2(1) or for some other reason. In this situation, legal proceedings may be necessary if there is no other way of settling the disagreement (see chapters 8 and 15). If those involved in caring for the young person or who are interested in the young person's welfare do not agree with the proposed treatment, it may be necessary for an interested party to make an application to the appropriate court.

What powers do the courts have in cases involving young people?

12.23 A case involving a young person who lacks mental capacity to make a specific decision could be heard in the family courts (probably in the Family Division of the High Court) or in the Court of Protection.

12.24 If a case might require an ongoing order (because the young person is likely to still lack capacity when they are 18), it may be more appropriate for the Court of Protection to hear the case. For one-off cases not involving property or finances, the Family Division may be more appropriate.

12.25 So that the appropriate court hears a case, the Court of Protection can transfer cases to the family courts, and vice versa (section 21).

Scenario: Hearing cases in the appropriate court

Shola is 17. She has serious learning disabilities and lacks the capacity to decide where she should live. Her parents are involved in a bitter divorce. They cannot agree on several issues concerning Shola's care – including where she should live. Her mother wants to continue to look after Shola at home. But her father wants Shola to move into a care home.

In this case, it may be more appropriate for the Court of Protection to deal with the case. This is because an order made in the Court of Protection could continue into Shola's adulthood. However an order made by the family court under the Children Act 1989 would end on Shola's eighteenth birthday.

13 WHAT IS THE RELATIONSHIP BETWEEN THE MENTAL CAPACITY ACT AND THE MENTAL HEALTH ACT 1983?

This chapter explains the relationship between the Mental Capacity Act 2005 (MCA) and the Mental Health Act 1983 (MHA). It:
- sets out when it may be appropriate to detain someone under the MHA rather than to rely on the MCA
- describes how the MCA affects people lacking capacity who are also subject to the MHA
- explains when doctors cannot give certain treatments for a mental disorder (in particular, psychosurgery) to someone who lacks capacity to consent to it, and
- sets out changes that the Government is planning to make to both Acts.

It does not provide a full description of the MHA. The MHA has its own Memorandum to explain the Act and its own Code of Practice to guide people about how to use it.[57]

[57] Department of Health & Welsh Office, *Mental Health Act 1983 Code of Practice* (TSO, 1999), www.dh.gov.uk/assetRoot/04/07/49/61/04074961.pdf

> In this chapter, as throughout the Code, a person's capacity (or lack of capacity) refers specifically to their capacity to make a particular decision at the time it needs to be made.

Quick summary

- Professionals may need to think about using the MHA to detain and treat somebody who lacks capacity to consent to treatment (rather than use the MCA), if:
  - it is not possible to give the person the care or treatment they need without doing something that might deprive them of their liberty
  - the person needs treatment that cannot be given under the MCA (for example, because the person has made a valid and applicable advance decision to refuse an essential part of treatment)
  - the person may need to be restrained in a way that is not allowed under the MCA
  - it is not possible to assess or treat the person safely or effectively without treatment being compulsory (perhaps because the person is expected to regain capacity to consent, but might then refuse to give consent)
  - the person lacks capacity to decide on some elements of the treatment but has capacity to refuse a vital part of it – and they have done so, or

- there is some other reason why the person might not get treatment, and they or somebody else might suffer harm as a result.
- Before making an application under the MHA, decision-makers should consider whether they could achieve their aims safely and effectively by using the MCA instead.
- Compulsory treatment under the MHA is not an option if:
  - the patient's mental disorder does not justify detention in hospital, or
  - the patient needs treatment only for a physical illness or disability.
- The MCA applies to people subject to the MHA in the same way as it applies to anyone else, with four exceptions:
  - if someone is detained under the MHA, decision-makers cannot normally rely on the MCA to give treatment for mental disorder or make decisions about that treatment on that person's behalf
  - if somebody can be treated for their mental disorder without their consent because they are detained under the MHA, healthcare staff can treat them even if it goes against an advance decision to refuse that treatment
  - if a person is subject to guardianship, the guardian has the exclusive right to take certain decisions, including where the person is to live, and
  - Independent Mental Capacity Advocates do not have to be involved in decisions about serious medical treatment or accommodation, if those decisions are made under the MHA.
- Healthcare staff cannot give psychosurgery (i.e. neurosurgery for mental disorder) to a person who lacks capacity to agree to it. This applies whether or not the person is otherwise subject to the MHA.

Who does the MHA apply to?

13.1 The MHA provides ways of assessing, treating and caring for people who have a serious mental disorder that puts them or other people at risk. It sets out when:
- people with mental disorders can be detained in hospital for assessment or treatment
- people who are detained can be given treatment for their mental disorder without their consent (it also sets out the safeguards people must get in this situation), and
- people with mental disorders can be made subject to guardianship or after-care under supervision to protect them or other people.

13.2 Most of the MHA does not distinguish between people who have the capacity to make decisions and those who do not. Many people covered by the MHA have the capacity to make decisions for themselves. Most people who lack capacity to make decisions about their treatment will never be affected by the MHA, even if they need treatment for a mental disorder.

13.3 But there are cases where decision-makers will need to decide whether to use the MHA or MCA, or both, to meet the needs of people with mental health problems who lack capacity to make decisions about their own treatment.

What are the MCA's limits?

13.4 Section 5 of the MCA provides legal protection for people who care for or treat someone who lacks capacity (see chapter 6). But they must follow the Act's principles and may only take action that is in a person's best interests (see chapter 5). This applies to care or treatment for physical and mental conditions. So it can apply to treatment for people with mental disorders, however serious those disorders are.

13.5 But section 5 does have its limits. For example, somebody using restraint only has protection if the restraint is:
- necessary to protect the person who lacks capacity from harm, and
- in proportion to the likelihood and seriousness of that harm.

13.6 There is no protection under section 5 for actions that deprive a person of their liberty (see chapter 6 for guidance). Similarly, the MCA does not allow giving treatment that goes against a valid and applicable advance decision to refuse treatment (see chapter 9).

13.7 None of these restrictions apply to treatment for mental disorder given under the MHA – but other restrictions do.

When can a person be detained under the MHA?

13.8 A person may be taken into hospital and detained for assessment under section 2 of the MHA for up to 28 days if:
- they have a mental disorder that is serious enough for them to be detained in a hospital for assessment (or for assessment followed by treatment) for at least a limited period, and
- they need to be detained to protect their health or safety, or to protect others.

13.9 A patient may be admitted to hospital and detained for treatment under section 3 of the MHA if:
- they have a mental illness, severe mental impairment, psychopathic disorder or mental impairment (the MHA sets out definitions for these last three terms)
- their mental disorder is serious enough to need treatment in hospital
- treatment is needed for the person's health or safety, or for the protection of other people – and it cannot be provided without detention under this section, and

- (if the person has a mental impairment or psychopathic disorder) treatment is likely to improve their condition or stop it getting worse.

13.10 Decision-makers should consider using the MHA if, in their professional judgment, they are not sure it will be possible, or sufficient, to rely on the MCA. They do not have to ask the Court of Protection to rule that the MCA does not apply before using the MHA.

13.11 If a clinician believes that they can safely assess or treat a person under the MCA, they do not need to consider using the MHA. In this situation, it would be difficult to meet the requirements of the MHA anyway.

13.12 It might be necessary to consider using the MHA rather than the MCA if:
- it is not possible to give the person the care or treatment they need without carrying out an action that might deprive them of their liberty
- the person needs treatment that cannot be given under the MCA (for example, because the person has made a valid and applicable advance decision to refuse all or part of that treatment)
- the person may need to be restrained in a way that is not allowed under the MCA
- it is not possible to assess or treat the person safely or effectively without treatment being compulsory (perhaps because the person is expected to regain capacity to consent, but might then refuse to give consent)
- the person lacks capacity to decide on some elements of the treatment but has capacity to refuse a vital part of it – and they have done so, or
- there is some other reason why the person might not get the treatment they need, and they or somebody else might suffer harm as a result.

13.13 But it is important to remember that a person cannot be treated under the MHA unless they meet the relevant criteria for being detained. Unless they are sent to hospital under Part 3 of the MHA in connection with a criminal offence, people can only be detained where:
- the conditions summarised in paragraph 13.8 or 13.9 are met
- the relevant people agree that an application is necessary (normally two doctors and an approved social worker), and
- (in the case of section 3) the patient's nearest relative has not objected to the application.

'Nearest relative' is defined in section 26 of the MHA. It is usually, but not always, a family member.

> **Scenario: Using the MHA**
>
> Mr Oliver has a learning disability. For the last four years, he has had depression from time to time, and has twice had treatment for it at a psychiatric hospital. He is now seriously depressed and his care workers are worried about him.
>
> Mr Oliver's consultant has given him medication and is considering electro-convulsive therapy. The consultant thinks this care plan will only work if Mr Oliver is detained in hospital. This will allow close observation and Mr Oliver will be stopped if he tries to leave. The consultant thinks an application should be made under section 3 of the MHA.
>
> The consultant also speaks to Mr Oliver's nearest relative, his mother. She asks why Mr Oliver needs to be detained when he has not needed to be in the past. But after she hears the consultant's reasons, she does not object to the application. An approved social worker makes the application and obtains a second medical recommendation. Mr Oliver is then detained and taken to hospital for his treatment for depression to begin.

13.14 Compulsory treatment under the MHA is not an option if:
- the patient's mental disorder does not justify detention in hospital, or
- the patient needs treatment only for a physical illness or disability.

13.15 There will be some cases where a person who lacks capacity cannot be treated either under the MHA or the MCA – even if the treatment is for mental disorder.

> **Scenario: Deciding whether to use the MHA or MCA**
>
> Mrs Carter is in her 80s and has dementia. Somebody finds her wandering in the street, very confused and angry. A neighbour takes her home and calls her doctor. At home, it looks like she has been deliberately smashing things. There are cuts on her hands and arms, but she won't let the doctor touch them, and she hasn't been taking her medication.
>
> Her doctor wants to admit her to hospital for assessment. Mrs Carter gets angry and says that they'll never keep her in hospital. So the doctor thinks that it might be necessary to use the MHA. He arranges for an approved social worker to visit. The social worker discovers that Mrs Carter was expecting her son this morning, but he has not turned up. They find out that he has been delayed, but could not call because Mrs Carter's telephone has become unplugged.

When she is told that her son is on his way, Mrs Carter brightens up. She lets the doctor treat her cuts – which the doctor thinks it is in her best interests to do as soon as possible. When Mrs Carter's son arrives, the social worker explains the doctor is very worried, especially that Mrs Carter is not taking her medication. The son explains that he will help his mother take it in future. It is agreed that the MCA will allow him to do that. The social worker arranges to return a week later and calls the doctor to say that she thinks Mrs Carter can get the care she needs without being detained under the MHA. The doctor agrees.

How does the MCA apply to a patient subject to guardianship under the MHA?

13.16 Guardianship gives someone (usually a local authority social services department) the exclusive right to decide where a person should live – but in doing this they cannot deprive the person of their liberty. The guardian can also require the person to attend for treatment, work, training or education at specific times and places, and they can demand that a doctor, approved social worker or another relevant person have access to the person wherever they live. Guardianship can apply whether or not the person has the capacity to make decisions about care and treatment. It does not give anyone the right to treat the person without their permission or to consent to treatment on their behalf.

13.17 An application can be made for a person who has a mental disorder to be received into guardianship under section 7 of the MHA when:
- the situation meets the conditions summarised in paragraph 13.18
- the relevant people agree an application for guardianship should be made (normally two doctors and an approved social worker), and
- the person's nearest relative does not object.

13.18 An application can be made in relation to any person who is 16 years or over if:
- they have a mental illness, severe mental impairment, psychopathic disorder or mental impairment that is serious enough to justify guardianship (see paragraph 13.20 below), and
- guardianship is necessary in the interests of the welfare of the patient or to protect other people.

13.19 Applicants (usually approved social workers) and doctors supporting the application will need to determine whether they could achieve their aims without guardianship. For patients who lack capacity, the obvious alternative will be action under the MCA.

13.20 But the fact that the person lacks capacity to make relevant decision is not the only factor that applicants need to consider. They need to consider all the circumstances of the case. They may

conclude that guardianship is the best option for a person with a mental disorder who lacks capacity to make those decisions if, for example:
- they think it is important that one person or authority should be in charge of making decisions about where the person should live (for example, where there have been long-running or difficult disagreements about where the person should live)
- they think the person will probably respond well to the authority and attention of a guardian, and so be more prepared to accept treatment for the mental disorder (whether they are able to consent to it or it is being provided for them under the MCA), or
- they need authority to return the person to the place they are to live (for example, a care home) if they were to go absent.

Decision-makers must never consider guardianship as a way to avoid applying the MCA.

13.21 A guardian has the exclusive right to decide where a person lives, so nobody else can use the MCA to arrange for the person to live elsewhere. Somebody who knowingly helps a person leave the place a guardian requires them to stay may be committing a criminal offence under the MHA. A guardian also has the exclusive power to require the person to attend set times and places for treatment, occupation, education or training. This does not stop other people using the MCA to make similar arrangements or to treat the person in their best interests. But people cannot use the MCA in any way that conflicts with decisions which a guardian has a legal right to make under the MHA. See paragraph 13.16 above for general information about a guardian's powers.

How does the MCA apply to a patient subject to after-care under supervision under the MHA?

13.22 When people are discharged from detention for medical treatment under the MHA, their responsible medical officer may decide to place them on after-care under supervision. The responsible medical officer is usually the person's consultant psychiatrist. Another doctor and an approved social worker must support their application.

13.23 After-care under supervision means:
- the person can be required to live at a specified place (where they can be taken to and returned, if necessary)
- the person can be required to attend for treatment, occupation, education or training at a specific time and place (where they can be taken, if necessary), and
- their supervisor, any doctor or approved social worker or any other relevant person must be given access to them wherever they live.

13.24 Responsible medical officers can apply for after-care under supervision under section 25A of the MHA if:

- the person is 16 or older and is liable to be detained in a hospital for treatment under section 3 (and certain other sections) of the MHA
- the person has a mental illness, severe mental impairment, psychopathic disorder or mental impairment
- without after-care under supervision the person's health or safety would be at risk of serious harm, they would be at risk of serious exploitation, or other people's safety would be at risk of serious harm, and
- after-care under supervision is likely to help make sure the person gets the after-care services they need.

'Liable to be detained' means that a hospital is allowed to detain them. Patients who are liable to be detained are not always actually in hospital, because they may have been given permission to leave hospital for a time.

13.25 After-care under supervision can be used whether or not the person lacks capacity to make relevant decisions. But if a person lacks capacity, decision-makers will need to decide whether action under the MCA could achieve their aims before making an application. The kinds of cases in which after-care under supervision might be considered for patients who lack capacity to take decisions about their own care and treatment are similar to those for guardianship.

How does the Mental Capacity Act affect people covered by the Mental Health Act?

13.26 There is no reason to assume a person lacks capacity to make their own decisions just because they are subject (under the MHA) to:
- detention
- guardianship, or
- after-care under supervision.

13.27 People who lack capacity to make specific decisions are still protected by the MCA even if they are subject to the MHA (this includes people who are subject to the MHA as a result of court proceedings). But there are four important exceptions:
- if someone is liable to be detained under the MHA, decision-makers cannot normally rely on the MCA to give mental health treatment or make decisions about that treatment on someone's behalf
- if somebody can be given mental health treatment without their consent because they are liable to be detained under the MHA, they can also be given mental health treatment that goes against an advance decision to refuse treatment
- if a person is subject to guardianship, the guardian has the exclusive right to take certain decisions, including where the person is to live, and

- Independent Mental Capacity Advocates do not have to be involved in decisions about serious medical treatment or accommodation, if those decisions are made under the MHA.

What are the implications for people who need treatment for a mental disorder?

13.28 Subject to certain conditions, Part 4 of the MHA allows doctors to give patients who are liable to be detained treatment for mental disorders without their consent – whether or not they have the capacity to give that consent. Paragraph 13.31 below lists a few important exceptions.

13.29 Where Part 4 of the MHA applies, the MCA cannot be used to give medical treatment for a mental disorder to patients who lack capacity to consent. Nor can anyone else, like an attorney or a deputy, use the MCA to give consent for that treatment. This is because Part 4 of the MHA already allows clinicians, if they comply with the relevant rules, to give patients medical treatment for mental disorder even though they lack the capacity to consent. In this context, medical treatment includes nursing and care, habilitation and rehabilitation under medical supervision.

13.30 But clinicians treating people for mental disorder under the MHA cannot simply ignore a person's capacity to consent to treatment. As a matter of good practice (and in some cases in order to comply with the MHA) they will always need to assess and record:
- whether patients have capacity to consent to treatment, and
- if so, whether they have consented to or refused that treatment.

For more information, see the MHA Code of Practice.

13.31 Part 4 of the MHA does not apply to patients:
- admitted in an emergency under section 4(4)(a) of the MHA, following a single medical recommendation and awaiting a second recommendation
- temporarily detained (held in hospital) under section 5 of the MHA while awaiting an application for detention under section 2 or section 3
- remanded by a court to hospital for a report on their medical condition under section 35 of the MHA
- detained under section 37(4), 135 or 136 of the MHA in a place of safety, or
- who have been conditionally discharged by the Mental Health Review Tribunal (and not recalled to hospital).

13.32 Since the MHA does not allow treatment for these patients without their consent, the MCA applies in the normal way, even if the treatment is for mental disorder.

13.33 Even when the MHA allows patients to be treated for mental disorders, the MCA applies in the normal way to treatment for physical disorders. But sometimes healthcare staff may decide to focus first on treating a detained patient's mental disorder in the hope that they will get back the capacity to make a decision about treatment for the physical disorder.

13.34 Where people are subject to guardianship or after-care under supervision under the MHA, the MCA applies as normal to all treatment. Guardianship and after-care under supervision do not give people the right to treat patients without consent.

> **Scenario: Using the MCA to treat a patient who is detained under the MHA**
>
> Mr Peters is detained in hospital under section 3 of the MHA and is receiving treatment under Part 4 of the MHA. Mr Peters has paranoid schizophrenia, delusions, hallucinations and thought disorder. He refuses all medical treatment. Mr Peters has recently developed blood in his urine and staff persuaded him to have an ultrasound scan. The scan revealed suspected renal carcinoma.
>
> His consultant believes that he needs a CT scan and treatment for the carcinoma. But Mr Peters refuses a general anaesthetic and other medical procedures. The consultant assesses Mr Peters as lacking capacity to consent to treatment under the MCA's test of capacity. The MHA is not relevant here, because the CT scan is not part of Mr Peters' treatment for mental disorder.
>
> Under section 5 of the MCA, doctors can provide treatment without consent. But they must follow the principles of the Act and believe that treatment is in Mr Peters' best interests.

How does the Mental Health Act affect advance decisions to refuse treatment?

13.35 The MHA does not affect a person's advance decision to refuse treatment, unless Part 4 of the MHA means the person can be treated for mental disorder without their consent. In this situation healthcare staff can treat patients for their mental disorder, even if they have made an advance decision to refuse such treatment.

13.36 But even then healthcare staff must treat a valid and applicable advance decision as they would a decision made by a person with capacity at the time they are asked to consent to treatment. For example, they should consider whether they could use a different type of treatment which the patient has not refused in advance. If healthcare staff do not follow an advance decision, they should record in the patient's notes why they have chosen not to follow it.

13.37 Even if a patient is being treated without their consent under Part 4 of the MHA, an advance decision to refuse other forms of treatment is still valid. Being subject to guardianship or after-care under supervision does not affect an advance decision in any way. See chapter 9 for further guidance on advance decisions to refuse treatment.

> **Scenario: Deciding on whether to follow an advance decision to refuse treatment**
>
> Miss Khan gets depression from time to time and has old physical injuries that cause her pain. She does not like the side effects of medication, and manages her health through diet and exercise. She knows that healthcare staff might doubt her decision-making capacity when she is depressed. So she makes an advance decision to refuse all medication for her physical pain and depression.
>
> A year later, she gets major depression and is detained under the MHA. Her GP (family doctor) tells her responsible medical officer (RMO) at the hospital about her advance decision. But Miss Khan's condition gets so bad that she will not discuss treatment. So the RMO decides to prescribe medication for her depression, despite her advance decision. This is possible because Miss Khan is detained under the MHA.
>
> The RMO also believes that Miss Khan now lacks capacity to consent to medication for her physical pain. He assesses the validity of the advance decision to refuse medication for the physical pain. Her GP says that Miss Khan seemed perfectly well when she made the decision and seemed to understand what it meant. In the GP's view, Miss Khan had the capacity to make the advance decision. The RMO decides that the advance decision is valid and applicable, and does not prescribe medication for Miss Khan's pain – even though he thinks it would be in her best interests. When Miss Khan's condition improves, the consultant will be able to discuss whether she would like to change her mind about treatment for her physical pain.

Does the MHA affect the duties of attorneys and deputies?

13.38 In general, the MHA does not affect the powers of attorneys and deputies. But there are two exceptions:
- they will not be able to give consent on a patient's behalf for treatment under Part 4 of the MHA, where the patient is liable to be detained under the MHA (see 13.28–13.34 above), and
- they will not be able to take decisions:
    - about where a person subject to guardianship should live, or
    - that conflict with decisions that a guardian has a legal right to make.

13.39 Being subject to the MHA does not stop patients creating new Lasting Powers of Attorney (if they have the capacity to do so). Nor does it stop the Court of Protection from appointing a deputy for them.

13.40 In certain cases, people subject to the MHA may be required to meet specific conditions relating to:
- leave of absence from hospital
- after-care under supervision, or
- conditional discharge.

Conditions vary from case to case, but could include a requirement to:
- live in a particular place
- maintain contact with health services, or
- avoid a particular area.

13.41 If an attorney or deputy takes a decision that goes against one of these conditions, the patient will be taken to have gone against the condition. The MHA sets out the actions that could be taken in such circumstances. In the case of leave of absence or conditional discharge, this might involve the patient being recalled to hospital.

13.42 Attorneys and deputies are able to exercise patients' rights under the MHA on their behalf, if they have the relevant authority. In particular, some personal welfare attorneys and deputies may be able to apply to the Mental Health Review Tribunal (MHRT) for the patient's discharge from detention, guardianship or after-care under supervision.

13.43 The MHA also gives various rights to a patient's nearest relative. These include the right to:
- insist that a local authority social services department instructs an approved social worker to consider whether the patient should be made subject to the MHA
- apply for the patient to be admitted to hospital or guardianship
- object to an application for admission for treatment
- order the patient's discharge from hospital (subject to certain conditions) and
- order the patient's discharge from guardianship.

13.44 Attorneys and deputies may not exercise these rights, unless they are themselves the nearest relative. If the nearest relative and an attorney or deputy disagree, it may be helpful for them to discuss the issue, perhaps with the assistance of the patient's clinicians or social worker. But ultimately they have different roles and both must act as they think best. An attorney or deputy must act in the patient's best interests.

13.45 It is good practice for clinicians and others involved in the assessment or treatment of patients under the MHA to try to find out if the person has an attorney or deputy. But this may not always be possible. So attorneys and deputies should contact either:
- the healthcare professional responsible for the patient's treatment (generally known as the patient's RMO)
- the managers of the hospital where the patient is detained

- the person's guardian (normally the local authority social services department), or
- the person's supervisor (if the patient is subject to after-care under supervision).

Hospitals that treat detained patients normally have a Mental Health Act Administrator's office, which may be a useful first point of contact.

Does the MHA affect when Independent Mental Capacity Advocates must be instructed?

13.46 As explained in chapter 10, there is no duty to instruct an Independent Mental Capacity Advocate (IMCA) for decisions about serious medical treatment which is to be given under Part 4 of the MHA. Nor is there a duty to do so in respect of a move into accommodation, or a change of accommodation, if the person in question is to be required to live in it because of an obligation under the MHA. That obligation might be a condition of leave of absence or conditional discharge from hospital or a requirement imposed by a guardian or a supervisor.

13.47 However, the rules for instructing an IMCA for patients subject to the MHA who might undergo serious medical treatment not related to their mental disorder are the same as for any other patient.

13.48 The duty to instruct an IMCA would also apply as normal if accommodation is being planned as part of the after-care under section 117 of the MHA following the person's discharge from detention (and the person is not going to be required to live in it as a condition of after-care under supervision). This is because the person does not have to accept that accommodation.

What is the effect of section 57 of the Mental Health Act on the MCA?

13.49 Section 57 of the MHA states that psychosurgery (neurosurgery for mental disorder) requires:
- the consent of the patient, and
- the approval of an independent doctor and two other people appointed by the Mental Health Act Commission.

Psychosurgery is any surgical operation that destroys brain tissue or the function of brain tissue.

13.50 The same rules apply to other treatments specified in regulations under section 57. Currently, the only treatment included in regulations is the surgical implantation of hormones to reduce a man's sex drive.

13.51 The combined effect of section 57 of the MHA and section 28 of the MCA is, effectively, that a person who lacks the capacity to consent to one of these treatments for mental disorder may never be given it. Healthcare staff cannot use the MCA as an alternative way of giving these kinds of treatment. Nor can an attorney or deputy give permission for them on a person's behalf.

What changes does the Government plan to make to the MHA and the MCA?

13.52 The Government has introduced a Mental Health Bill into Parliament in order to modernise the MHA. Among the changes it proposes to make are:
- some amendments to the criteria for detention, including a new requirement that appropriate medical treatment be available for patients before they can be detained for treatment
- the introduction of supervised treatment in the community for suitable patients following a period of detention and treatment in hospital. This will help make sure that patients get the treatment they need and help stop them relapsing and returning to hospital
- the replacement of the approved social worker with the approved mental health professional. This will open up the possibility of approved mental healthcare professionals being drawn from other disciplines as well as social work. Other changes will open up the possibility of clinicians who are not doctors being approved to take on the role of the responsible medical officer. This role will be renamed the responsible clinician.
- provisions to make it possible for patients to apply to the county court for an unsuitable nearest relative to be replaced, and
- the abolition of after-care under supervision.

13.53 The Bill will also amend the MCA to introduce new procedures and provisions to make relevant decisions but who need to be deprived of their liberty, in their best interests, otherwise than under the Mental Health Act 1983 (the so-called 'Bournewood provisions').[58]

[58] This refers to the European Court of Human Rights judgment (5 October 2004) in the case of *HL v The United Kingdom (Application No 45508/99)* (2004) 40 EHRR 761, ECHR.

13.54 This chapter, as well as chapter 6, will be fully revised in due course to reflect those changes. Information about the Government's current proposals in respect of the Bournewood safeguards is available on the Department of Health website. This information includes draft illustrative Code of Practice guidance about the proposed safeguards.[59]

[59] See www.dh.gov.uk/PublicationsAndStatistics/Publications/PublicationsPolicy AndGuidance/PublicationsPolicyAndGuidanceArticle/fs/en?CONTENT_ID= 4141656&chk=jlw07L

13.55 In the meantime, people taking decisions under both the MCA and the MHA must base those decisions on the Acts as they stand now.

14 WHAT MEANS OF PROTECTION EXIST FOR PEOPLE WHO LACK CAPACITY TO MAKE DECISIONS FOR THEMSELVES?

This chapter describes the different agencies that exist to help make sure that adults who lack capacity to make decisions for themselves are protected from abuse. It also explains the services those agencies provide and how they supervise people who provide care for or make decisions on behalf of people who lack capacity. Finally, it explains what somebody should do if they suspect that somebody is abusing a vulnerable adult who lacks capacity.

> In this chapter, as throughout the Code, a person's capacity (or lack of capacity) refers specifically to their capacity to make a particular decision at the time it needs to be made.

Quick summary

- Always report suspicions of abuse of a person who lacks capacity to the relevant agency.

Concerns about an appointee

- When someone is concerned about the collection or use of social security benefits by an appointee on behalf a person who lacks capacity, they should contact the local Jobcentre Plus. If the appointee is for someone who is over the age of 60, contact The Pension Service.

Concerns about an attorney or deputy

- If someone is concerned about the actions of an attorney or deputy, they should contact the Office of the Public Guardian.

Concerns about a possible criminal offence

- If there is a good reason to suspect that someone has committed a crime against a vulnerable person, such as theft or physical or sexual assault, contact the police.
- In addition, social services should also be contacted, so that they can support the vulnerable person during the investigation.

Concerns about possible ill-treatment or wilful neglect

- The Act introduces new criminal offences of ill treatment or wilful neglect of a person who lacks capacity to make relevant decisions (section 44).
- If someone is not being looked after properly, contact social services.
- In serious cases, contact the police.

Concerns about care standards
- In cases of concern about the standard of care in a care home or an adult placement scheme, or about the care provided by a home care worker, contact social services.
- It may also be appropriate to contact the Commission for Social Care Inspection (in England) or the Care and Social Services Inspectorate for Wales.

Concerns about healthcare or treatment
- If someone is concerned about the care or treatment given to the person in any NHS setting (such as an NHS hospital or clinic) contact the managers of the service.
- It may also be appropriate to make a formal complaint through the NHS complaints procedure (see chapter 15).

What is abuse?

14.1 The word 'abuse' covers a wide range of actions. In some cases, abuse is clearly deliberate and intentionally unkind. But sometimes abuse happens because somebody does not know how to act correctly – or they haven't got appropriate help and support. It is important to prevent abuse, wherever possible. If somebody is abused, it is important to investigate the abuse and take steps to stop it happening.

14.2 Abuse is anything that goes against a person's human and civil rights. This includes sexual, physical, verbal, financial and emotional abuse. Abuse can be:
- a single act
- a series of repeated acts
- a failure to provide necessary care, or
- neglect.

Abuse can take place anywhere (for example, in a person's own home, a care home or a hospital).

14.3 The main types of abuse are:

Type of abuse	Examples
Financial	- theft
- fraud
- undue pressure
- misuse of property, possessions or benefits
- dishonest gain of property, possessions or benefits.

Physical	• slapping, pushing, kicking or other forms of violence
	• misuse of medication (for example, increasing dosage to make someone drowsy)
	• inappropriate punishments (for example, not giving someone a meal because they have been 'bad').
Sexual	• rape
	• sexual assault
	• sexual acts without consent (this includes if a person is not able to give consent or the abuser used pressure).
Psychological	• emotional abuse
	• threats of harm, restraint or abandonment
	• refusing contact with other people
	• intimidation
	• threats to restrict someone's liberty.
Neglect and acts of omission	• ignoring the person's medical or physical care needs
	• failing to get healthcare or social care
	• withholding medication, food or heating.

14.4 The Department of Health and the National Assembly for Wales have produced separate guidance on protecting vulnerable adults from abuse. *No secrets*[60] (England) and *In safe hands*[61] (Wales) both define vulnerable adults as people aged 18 and over who:
- need community care services due to a mental disability, other disability, age or illness, and
- may be unable to take care of themselves or protect themselves against serious harm or exploitation.

This description applies to many people who lack capacity to make decisions for themselves.

[60] Department of Health and Home Office, *No secrets: Guidance on developing and implementing multi-agency policies and procedures to protect vulnerable adults from abuse*, (2000) www.dh.gov.uk/assetRoot/04/07/45/40/04074540.pdf
[61] National Assembly for Wales, *In safe hands: Implementing adult protection procedures in Wales* (update 2003) available to order from http://welshgovernmentpublications.soutron.net/publications/ (Note: new website address inserted by authors).

14.5 Anyone who thinks that someone might be abusing a vulnerable adult who lacks capacity should:
- contact the local social services (see paragraphs 14.27–14.28 below)
- contact the Office of the Public Guardian (see paragraph 14.8 below), or
- seek advice from a relevant telephone helpline[62] or through the Community Legal Service.[63]

Full contact details are provided in Annex A.

62 For example, the Action on Elder Abuse (0808 808 8141), Age Concern (0800 009966) or CarersLine (0808 808 7777).
63 Community Legal Service Direct www.clsdirect.org.uk

14.6 In most cases, local adult protection procedures will say who should take action (see paragraphs 14.28–14.29 below). But some abuse will be a criminal offence, such as physical assault, sexual assault or rape, theft, fraud and some other forms of financial exploitation. In these cases, the person who suspects abuse should contact the police urgently. The criminal investigation may take priority over all other forms of investigation. So all agencies will have to work together to plan the best way to investigate possible abuse.

14.7 The Fraud Act 2006 (due to come into force in 2007) creates a new offence of 'fraud by abuse of position'. This new offence may apply to a range of people, including:
- attorneys under a Lasting Power of Attorney (LPA) or an Enduring Power of Attorney (EPA), or
- deputies appointed by the Court of Protection to make financial decisions on behalf of a person who lacks capacity.

Attorneys and deputies may be guilty of fraud if they dishonestly abuse their position, intend to benefit themselves or others, and cause loss or expose a person to the risk of loss. People who suspect fraud should report the case to the police.

How does the Act protect people from abuse?
The Office of the Public Guardian

14.8 Section 57 of the Act creates a new Public Guardian, supported by staff of the Office of the Public Guardian (OPG). The Public Guardian helps protect people who lack capacity by:
- setting up and managing a register of LPAs
- setting up and managing a register of EPAs
- setting up and managing a register of court orders that appoint deputies
- supervising deputies, working with other relevant organisations (for example, social services, if the person who lacks capacity is receiving social care)
- sending Court of Protection Visitors to visit people who may lack capacity to make particular decisions and those who have formal powers to act on their behalf (see paragraphs 14.10–14.11 below)
- receiving reports from attorneys acting under LPAs and from deputies
- providing reports to the Court of Protection, as requested, and
- dealing with representations (including complaints) about the way in which attorneys or deputies carry out their duties.

14.9 Section 59 of the Act creates a Public Guardian Board to oversee and review how the Public Guardian carries out these duties.

Court of Protection Visitors

14.10 The role of a Court of Protection Visitor is to provide independent advice to the court and the Public Guardian. They advise on how anyone given power under the Act should be, and is, carrying out their duties and responsibilities. There are two types of visitor: General Visitors and Special Visitors. Special visitors are registered medical practitioners with relevant expertise. The court or Public Guardian can send whichever type of visitor is most appropriate to visit and interview a person who may lack capacity. Visitors can also interview attorneys or deputies and inspect any relevant healthcare or social care records. Attorneys and deputies must co-operate with the visitors and provide them with all relevant information. If attorneys or deputies do not co-operate, the court can cancel their appointment, where it thinks that they have not acted in the person's best interests.

> **Scenario: Using a General Visitor**
>
> Mrs Quinn made an LPA appointing her nephew, Ian, as her financial attorney. She recently lost capacity to make her own financial decisions, and Ian has registered the LPA. He has taken control of Mrs Quinn's financial affairs.
>
> But Mrs Quinn's niece suspects that Ian is using Mrs Quinn's money to pay off his own debts. She contacts the OPG, which sends a General Visitor to visit Mrs Quinn and Ian. The visitor's report will assess the facts. It might suggest the case go to court to consider whether Ian has behaved in a way which:
>
> - goes against his authority under the LPA, or
> - is not in Mrs Quinn's best interests.
>
> The Public Guardian will decide whether the court should be involved in the matter. The court will then decide if it requires further evidence. If it thinks that Ian is abusing his position, the court may cancel the LPA.

14.11 Court of Protection Visitors have an important part to play in investigating possible abuse. But their role is much wider than this. They can also check on the general wellbeing of the person who lacks capacity, and they can give support to attorneys and deputies who need help to carry out their duties.

How does the Public Guardian oversee LPAs?

14.12 An LPA is a private arrangement between the donor and the attorney (see chapter 7). Donors should only choose attorneys that they can trust. The OPG provides information to help potential donors understand:
- the impact of making an LPA
- what they can give an attorney authority to do
- what to consider when choosing an attorney.

14.13 The Public Guardian must make sure that an LPA meets the Act's requirements. Before registering an LPA, the OPG will check documentation. For property and affairs LPAs, it will check whether an attorney appointed under the LPA is bankrupt since this would revoke the authority.

14.14 The Public Guardian will not usually get involved once somebody has registered an LPA – unless someone is worried about how an attorney is carrying out their duties. If concerns are raised about an attorney, the OPG works closely with organisations such as local authorities and NHS Trusts to carry out investigations.

How does the Public Guardian supervise deputies?

14.15 Individuals do not choose who will act as a deputy for them. The court will make the decision. There are measures to make sure that the court appoints an appropriate deputy. The OPG will then supervise deputies and support them in carrying out their duties, while also making sure they do not abuse their position.

14.16 When a case comes before the Court of Protection, the Act states that the court should make a decision to settle the matter rather than appoint a deputy, if possible. Deputies are most likely to be needed for financial matters where someone needs continued authority to make decisions about the person's money or other assets. It will be easier for the courts to make decisions in cases where a one-off decision is needed about a person's welfare, so there are likely to be fewer personal welfare deputies. But there will be occasions where ongoing decisions about a person's welfare will be required, and so the court will appoint a personal welfare deputy (see chapter 8).

Scenario: Appointing deputies

Peter was in a motorbike accident that left him permanently and seriously brain-damaged. He has minimal awareness of his surroundings and an assessment has shown that he lacks capacity to make most decisions for himself.

Somebody needs to make several decisions about what treatment Peter needs and where he should be treated. His parents feel that healthcare staff do not always consider their views in decisions about what

> treatment is in Peter's best interests. So they make an application to the court to be appointed as joint personal welfare deputies.
>
> There will be many care or treatment decisions for Peter in the future. The court decides it would not be practical to make a separate decision on each of them. It also thinks Peter needs some continuity in decision-making. So it appoints Peter's parents as joint personal welfare deputies.

14.17 The OPG may run checks on potential deputies if requested to by the court. It will carry out a risk assessment to determine what kind of supervision a deputy will need once they are appointed.

14.18 Deputies are accountable to the court. The OPG supervises the deputy's actions on the court's behalf, and the court may want the deputy to provide financial accounts or other reports to the OPG. The Public Guardian deals with complaints about the way deputies carry out their duties. It works with other relevant agencies to investigate them. Chapter 8 gives detailed information about the responsibilities of deputies.

What happens if someone says they are worried about an attorney or deputy?

14.19 Many people who lack capacity are likely to get care or support from a range of agencies. Even when an attorney or deputy is acting on behalf of a person who lacks capacity, the other carers still have a responsibility to the person to provide care and act in the person's best interests. Anybody who is caring for a person who lacks capacity, whether in a paid or unpaid role, who is worried about how attorneys or deputies carry out their duties should contact the Public Guardian.

14.20 The OPG will not always be the most appropriate organisation to investigate all complaints. It may investigate a case jointly with:
- healthcare or social care professionals
- social services
- NHS bodies
- the Commission for Social Care Inspection in England or the Care and Social Services Inspectorate for Wales (CSSIW)[64]
- the Healthcare Commission in England or the Healthcare Inspectorate for Wales, and
- in some cases, the police.

64 In April 2007, the Care Standards Inspectorate for Wales (CSIW) and the Social Services Inspectorate for Wales (SSIW) came together to form the Care and Social Services Inspectorate for Wales.

14.21 The OPG will usually refer concerns about personal welfare LPAs or personal welfare deputies to the relevant agency. In certain circumstances it will alert the police about a case. When it makes a referral, the OPG will make sure that the relevant agency keeps it informed of the action it takes. It will also make sure that the court has all the information it needs to take possible action against the attorney or deputy.

14.22 Examples of situations in which a referral might be necessary include where:
- someone has complained that a welfare attorney is physically abusing a donor – the OPG would refer this case to the relevant local authority adult protection procedures and possibly the police
- the OPG has found that a solicitor appointed as a financial deputy for an elderly woman has defrauded her estate – the OPG would refer this case to the police and the Law Society Consumer Complaints Service.

How does the Act deal with ill treatment and wilful neglect?

14.23 The Act introduces two new criminal offences: ill treatment and wilful neglect of a person who lacks capacity to make relevant decisions (section 44). The offences may apply to:
- anyone caring for a person who lacks capacity – this includes family carers, healthcare and social care staff in hospital or care homes and those providing care in a person's home
- an attorney appointed under an LPA or an EPA, or
- a deputy appointed for the person by the court.

14.24 These people may be guilty of an offence if they ill-treat or wilfully neglect the person they care for or represent. Penalties will range from a fine to a sentence of imprisonment of up to five years – or both.

14.25 Ill treatment and neglect are separate offences.[65] For a person to be found guilty of ill treatment, they must either:
- have deliberately ill-treated the person, or
- be reckless in the way they were ill-treating the person or not.

It does not matter whether the behaviour was likely to cause, or actually caused, harm or damage to the victim's health.

65 *R v Newington* (1990) 91 Cr App R 247, CA.

14.26 The meaning of 'wilful neglect' varies depending on the circumstances. But it usually means that a person has deliberately failed to carry out an act they knew they had a duty to do.

Scenario: Reporting abuse

Norma is 95 and has Alzheimer's disease. Her son, Brendan, is her personal welfare attorney under an LPA. A district nurse has noticed that Norma has bruises and other injuries. She suspects Brendan may be assaulting his mother when he is drunk. She alerts the police and the local Adult Protection Committee.

> Following a criminal investigation, Brendan is charged with ill-treating his mother. The Public Guardian applies to the court to cancel the LPA. Social services start to make alternative arrangements for Norma's care.

What other measures protect people from abuse?

14.27 Local agencies have procedures that allow them to work together (called multi-agency working) to protect vulnerable adults – in care settings and elsewhere. Most areas have Adult Protection Committees. These committees:
- create policy (including reporting procedures)
- oversee investigations and other activity between agencies
- carry out joint training, and
- monitor and review progress.

Other local authorities have developed multi-agency Adult Protection Procedures, which are managed by a dedicated Adult Protection Co-ordinator.

14.28 Adult Protection Committees and Procedures (APCP) involve representatives from the NHS, social services, housing, the police and other relevant agencies. In England, they are essential points of contact for anyone who suspects abuse or ill treatment of a vulnerable adult. They can also give advice to the OPG if it is uncertain whether an intervention is necessary in a case of suspected abuse. In Wales, APCPs are not necessarily points of contact themselves, but they publish details of points of contact.

Who should check that staff are safe to work with vulnerable adults?

14.29 Under the Safeguarding Vulnerable Groups Act 2006, criminal record checks are now compulsory for staff who:
- have contact with service users in registered care homes
- provide personal care services in someone's home, and
- are involved in providing adult placement schemes.

14.30 Potential employers must carry out a pre-employment criminal record check with the Criminal Records Bureau (CRB) for all potential new healthcare and social care staff. This includes nursing agency staff and home care agency staff.

See Annex A for sources of more detailed information.

14.31 The Protection of Vulnerable Adults (POVA) list has the names of people who have been barred from working with vulnerable adults (in England and Wales). Employers providing care in a residential setting or a person's own home must check whether potential employees are on the list.[66] If they are on the list, they must:
- refuse to employ them, or
- employ them in a position that does not give them regular contact with vulnerable adults.

It is an offence for anyone on the list to apply for a care position. In such cases, the employer should report the person making the application.

66 www.dh.gov.uk/PublicationsAndStatistics/Publications/PublicationsPolicyAndGuidance/
PublicationsPolicyAndGuidanceArticle/fs/en?CONTENT_ID=4085855&chk=p0kQeS

Who is responsible for monitoring the standard of care providers?

14.32 All care providers covered by the Care Standards Act 2000 must register with the Commission for Social Care Inspection in England (CSCI) or the Care and Social Services Inspectorate for Wales (CSSIW).[67] These agencies make sure that care providers meet certain standards. They require care providers to have procedures to protect people from harm or abuse. These agencies can take action if they discover dangerous or unsafe practices that could place people at risk.

67 See footnote 64 above regarding the merger of the Care Standards Inspectorate for Wales and the Social Services Inspectorate for Wales.

14.33 Care providers must also have effective complaints procedures. If providers cannot settle complaints, CSCI or CSSIW can look into them.

14.34 CSCI or CSSIW assesses the effectiveness of local adult protection procedures. They will also monitor the arrangements local councils make in response to the Care Standards Act.

What is an appointee, and who monitors them?

14.35 The Department for Work and Pensions (DWP) can appoint someone (an appointee) to claim and spend benefits on a person's behalf[68] if that person:
- gets social security benefits or pensions
- lacks the capacity to act for themselves
- has not made a property and affairs LPA or an EPA, and
- the court has not appointed a property and affairs deputy.

68 www.dwp.gov.uk/publications/dwp/2005/gl21_apr.pdf

14.36 The DWP checks that an appointee is trustworthy. It also investigates any allegations that an appointee is not acting appropriately or in the person's interests. It can remove an appointee who abuses their position. Concerns about appointees should be raised with the relevant DWP agency (the local Jobcentre Plus, or if the person is aged 60 or over, The Pension Service).

Are there any other means of protection that people should be aware of?

14.37 There are a number of additional means that exist to protect people who lack capacity to make decisions for themselves. Healthcare and social care staff, attorneys and deputies should be aware of:
- National Minimum Standards (for example, for healthcare, care homes, and home care agencies) which apply to both England and Wales (see paragraph 14.38)
- National Service Frameworks, which set out national standards for specific health and care services for particular groups (for example, for mental health services[69] or services for older people[70])
- complaints procedures for all NHS bodies and local councils (see chapter 15)
- Stop Now Orders (also known as Enforcement Orders) that allow consumer protection bodies to apply for court orders to stop poor trading practices (for example, unfair door-step selling or rogue traders).[71]
- The Public Interest Disclosure Act 1998, which encourages people to report malpractice in the workplace and protects people who report malpractice from being sacked or victimised.

69 www.dh.gov.uk/assetRoot/04/07/72/09/04077209.pdf   and   www.wales.nhs.uk/sites3/page.cfm?orgid=438&pid=11071
70 www.dh.gov.uk/assetRoot/04/07/12/83/04071283.pdf   and   www.wales.nhs.uk/sites3/home.cfm?orgid=439&redirect=yes&CFID=298511&CFTOKEN=6985382
71 www.oft.gov.uk/Business/Legal/Stop+Now+Regulations.htm

14.38 Information about all national minimum standards are available on the CSCI[72] and Healthcare Commission websites[73] and the Welsh Assembly Government website. Chapter 15 gives guidance on complaints procedures. Individual local authorities will have their own complaints system in place.

72 www.csci.org.uk/information_for_service_providers/national_minimum_standards/default.htm
73 www.healthcarecommission.org.uk/_db/_documents/The_annual_health_check_in_2006_2007_assessing_and_rating_the_NHS_200609225143.pdf

15 WHAT ARE THE BEST WAYS TO SETTLE DISAGREEMENTS AND DISPUTES ABOUT ISSUES COVERED IN THE ACT?

Sometimes people will disagree about:
- a person's capacity to make a decision
- their best interests
- a decision someone is making on their behalf, or
- an action someone is taking on their behalf.

It is in everybody's interests to settle disagreements and disputes quickly and effectively, with minimal stress and cost. This chapter sets out the different options available for settling disagreements. It also suggests ways to avoid letting a disagreement become a serious dispute. Finally, it sets out when it might be necessary to apply to the Court of Protection and when somebody can get legal funding.

> In this chapter, as throughout the Code, a person's capacity (or lack of capacity) refers specifically to their capacity to make a particular decision at the time it needs to be made.

Quick summary

- When disagreements occur about issues that are covered in the Act, it is usually best to try and settle them before they become serious.
- Advocates can help someone who finds it difficult to communicate their point of view. (This may be someone who has been assessed as lacking capacity.)
- Some disagreements can be effectively resolved by mediation.
- Where there is a concern about healthcare or social care provided to a person who lacks capacity, there are formal and informal ways of complaining about the care or treatment.
- The Health Service Ombudsman or the Local Government Ombudsman (in England) or the Public Services Ombudsman (in Wales) can be asked to investigate some problems that have not been resolved through formal complaints procedures.
- Disputes about the finances of a person who lacks capacity should usually be referred to the Office of the Public Guardian (OPG).
- When other methods of resolving disagreements are not appropriate, the matter can be referred to the Court of Protection.
- There are some decisions that are so serious that the Court of Protection should always make them.

What options are there for settling disagreements?

15.1 Disagreements about healthcare, social or other welfare services may be between:
- people who have assessed a person as lacking capacity to make a decision and the person they have assessed (see chapter 4 for how to challenge an assessment of lack of capacity)
- family members or other people concerned with the care and welfare of a person who lacks capacity
- family members and healthcare or social care staff involved in providing care or treatment
- healthcare and social care staff who have different views about what is in the best interests of a person who lacks capacity.

15.2 In general, disagreements can be resolved by either formal or informal procedures, and there is more information on both in this chapter. However, there are some disagreements and some subjects that are so serious they can only be resolved by the Court of Protection.

15.3 It is usually best to try and settle disagreements before they become serious disputes. Many people settle them by communicating effectively and taking the time to listen and to address worries. Disagreements between family members are often best settled informally, or sometimes through mediation. When professionals are in disagreement with a person's family, it is a good idea to start by:
- setting out the different options in a way that is easy to understand
- inviting a colleague to talk to the family and offer a second opinion
- offering to get independent expert advice
- using an advocate to support and represent the person who lacks capacity
- arranging a case conference or meeting to discuss matters in detail
- listening to, acknowledging and addressing worries, and
- where the situation is not urgent, allowing the family time to think it over.

Further guidance on how to deal with problems without going to court may also be found in the Community Legal Services Information Leaflet 'Alternatives to Court'.[74]

[74] CLS (Community Legal Services) Direct Information Leaflet Number 23, www.clsdirect.org.uk/legalhelp/leaflet23.jsp?lang=en

When is an advocate useful?

15.4 An advocate helps communicate the feelings and views of someone who has communication difficulties. The definition of advocacy set out in the Advocacy Charter adopted by most advocacy schemes is as follows: 'Advocacy is taking action to help people say what they want, secure their rights, represent their interests and obtain services they need. Advocates and advocacy schemes work in partnership with the people they support and take their side. Advocacy promotes social inclusion, equality and social justice.'[75]

An advocate may be able to help settle a disagreement simply by presenting a person's feelings to their family, carers or professionals. Most advocacy services are provided by the voluntary sector and are arranged at a local level. They have no link to any agency involved with the person.

[75] Advocacy across London, *Advocacy Charter* (2002)

15.5 Using advocates can help people who find it difficult to communicate (including those who have been assessed as lacking capacity) to:
- say what they want

- claim their rights
- represent their interests, and
- get the services they need.

15.6 Advocates may also be involved in supporting the person during mediation (see paragraphs 15.7–15.13 below) or helping with complaints procedures. Sometimes people who lack capacity or have been assessed as lacking capacity have a legal right to an advocate, for example:

- when making a formal complaint against the NHS (see paragraph 15.18), and
- where the Act requires the involvement of an Independent Mental Capacity Advocate (IMCA) (see chapter 10).

When is mediation useful?

15.7 A mediator helps people to come to an agreement that is acceptable to all parties. Mediation can help solve a problem at an early stage. It offers a wider range of solutions than the court can – and it may be less stressful for all parties, more cost-effective and quicker. People who come to an agreement through mediation are more likely to keep to it, because they have taken part in decision-making.

15.8 Mediators are independent. They have no personal interest in the outcome of a case. They do not make decisions or impose solutions. The mediator will decide whether the case is suitable for mediation. They will consider the likely chances of success and the need to protect the interests of the person who lacks capacity.

15.9 Any case that can be settled through negotiation is likely to benefit from mediation. It is most suitable when people are not communicating well or not understanding each other's point of view. It can improve relationships and stop future disputes, so it is a good option when it is in the person's interests for people to have a good relationship in the future.

Scenario: Using mediation

Mrs Roberts has dementia and lacks capacity to decide where she should live. She currently lives with her son. But her daughter has found a care home where she thinks her mother will get better care. Her brother disagrees.

Mrs Roberts is upset by this family dispute, and so her son and daughter decide to try mediation. The mediator believes that Mrs Roberts is able to communicate her feelings and agrees to take on the case. During the sessions, the mediator helps them to focus on their mother's best interests rather than imposing their own views. In the

> end, everybody agrees that Mrs Roberts should continue to live with her son. But they agree to review the situation again in six months to see if the care home might then be better for her.

15.10 In mediation, everybody needs to take part as equally as possible so that a mediator can help everyone involved to focus on the person's best interests. It might also be appropriate to involve an advocate to help communicate the wishes of the person who lacks capacity.

15.11 The National Mediation Helpline[76] helps callers to identify an effective means of resolving their difficulty without going to court. It will arrange an appointment with a trained and accredited mediator. The Family Mediation Helpline[77] can provide information on family mediation and referrals to local family mediation services. Family mediators are trained to deal with the emotional, practical and financial needs of those going through relationship breakdown.

76 National Mediation Helpline, Tel: 0845 60 30 809, www.nationalmediationhelpline.com
77 Family Mediation Helpline, Tel: 0845 60 26 627, www.familymediationhelpline.co.uk

15.12 Healthcare and social care staff may also take part in mediation processes. But it may be more appropriate to follow the relevant healthcare or social care complaints procedures (see paragraphs 15.14–15.32).

15.13 In certain situations (mainly family mediation), legal aid may be available to fund mediation for people who meet the qualifying criteria (see paragraphs 15.38–15.44).

How can someone complain about healthcare?

15.14 There are formal and informal ways of complaining about a patient's healthcare or treatment. Healthcare staff and others need to know which methods are suitable in which situations.

15.15 In England, the Patient Advice and Liaison Service (PALS) provides an informal way of dealing with problems before they reach the complaints stage. PALS operate in every NHS and Primary Care Trust in England. They provide advice and information to patients (or their relatives or carers) to try to solve problems quickly. They can direct people to specialist support services (for example, advocates, mental health support teams, social services or interpreting services). PALS do not investigate complaints. Their role is to explain complaints procedures and direct people to the formal NHS complaints process, if necessary. NHS complaints procedures deal with complaints about something that happened in the past that requires an apology or explanation. A court cannot help in this situation, but court proceedings may be necessary in some clinical negligence cases (see paragraph 15.22).

15.16 In Wales, complaints advocates based at Community Health Councils provide advice and support to anyone with concerns about treatment they have had.

Disagreements about proposed treatments

15.17 If a case is not urgent, the supportive atmosphere of the PALS may help settle it. In Wales, the local Community Health Council may be able to help. But urgent cases about proposed serious treatment may need to go to the Court of Protection (see paragraphs 15.35–15.36).

> **Scenario: Disagreeing about treatment or an assessment**
>
> Mrs Thompson has Alzheimer's and does not want a flu jab. Her daughter thinks she should have the injection. The doctor does not want to go against the wishes of his patient, because he believes she has capacity to refuse treatment.
>
> Mrs Thompson's daughter goes to PALS. A member of staff gives her information and advice about what is meant by capacity to consent to or refuse treatment, and tells her how to find out about the flu jab. The PALS staff speak to the doctor, and then they explain his clinical assessment to Mrs Thompson's daughter.
>
> The daughter is still unhappy. PALS staff advise her that the Independent Complaints Advocacy Service can help if she wishes to make a formal complaint.

The formal NHS complaints procedure

15.18 The formal NHS complaints procedure deals with complaints about NHS services provided by NHS organisations or primary care practitioners. As a first step, people should try to settle a disagreement through an informal discussion between:
- the healthcare staff involved
- the person who may lack capacity to make the decision in question (with support if necessary)
- their carers, and
- any appropriate relatives.

If the person who is complaining is not satisfied, the Independent Complaints Advocacy Service (ICAS) may help. In Wales, the complaints advocates based at Community Health Councils will support and advise anyone who wants to make a complaint.

15.19 In England, if the person is still unhappy after a local investigation, they can ask for an independent review by the Healthcare Commission. If the patient involved in the complaint was or is detained under the Mental Health Act 1983, the Mental

Health Act Commission can be asked to look into the complaint. If people are still unhappy after this stage, they can go to the Health Service Ombudsman. More information on how to make a complaint in England is available from the Department of Health.

15.20 In Wales, if patients are still unhappy after a local investigation, they can ask for an independent review of their complaint by independent lay reviewers. After this, they can take their case to the Public Services Ombudsman for Wales. People can take their complaint direct to the Ombudsman if:
- the complaint is about care or treatment that took place after 1 April 2006, and
- they have tried to settle the problem locally first.

The Mental Health Act Commission may also investigate complaints about the care or treatment of detained patients in Wales, if attempts have been made to settle the complaint locally without success.

15.21 Regulations about first trying to settle complaints locally do not apply to NHS Foundation Trusts. But these Trusts are covered by the independent review stage operated by the Healthcare Commission and by the Health Service Ombudsman. People who have a complaint about an NHS Foundation Trust should contact the Trust for advice on how to make a complaint.

Cases of clinical negligence

15.22 The NHS Litigation Authority oversees all clinical negligence cases brought against the NHS in England. It actively encourages people to try other forms of settling complaints before going to court. The National Assembly for Wales also encourages people to try other forms of settling complaints before going to court.

How can somebody complain about social care?

15.23 The social services complaints procedure has been reformed. The reformed procedure came into effect on 1 September 2006 in England and on 1 April 2006 in Wales.

15.24 A service provider's own complaints procedure should deal with complaints about:
- the way in which care services are delivered
- the type of services provided, or
- a failure to provide services.

15.25 Care agencies contracted by local authorities or registered with the Commission for Social Care Inspection (CSCI) in England or Care and Social Services Inspectorate for Wales (CSSIW) are legally obliged to have their own written complaints procedures. This includes residential homes, agencies providing care in people's homes, nursing agencies and adult placement schemes. The procedures should set out how to make a complaint and what to do with a complaint that cannot be settled locally.

Local authority complaints procedures

15.26 For services contracted by a local authority, it may be more appropriate to use the local authority's complaints procedure. A simple example would be a situation where a local authority places a person in a care home and the person's family are not happy with the placement. If their complaint is not about the services the home provides (for example, it might be about the local authority's assessment of the person's needs), it might be more appropriate to use the local authority's complaints procedure.

15.27 As a first step, people should try to settle a disagreement through an informal discussion, involving:
- the professionals involved
- the person who may lack capacity to make the decision in question (with support if necessary)
- their carers, and
- any appropriate relatives.

15.28 If the person making the complaint is not satisfied, the local authority will carry out a formal investigation using its complaints procedure. In England, after this stage, a social service Complaints Review Panel can hear the case. In Wales complaints can be referred to the National Assembly for Wales for hearing by an independent panel.

Other complaints about social care

15.29 People can take their complaint to the CSCI in England or the CSSIW in Wales, if:
- the complaint is about regulations or national minimum standards not being met, and
- the complainants are not happy with the provider's own complaints procedure or the response to their complaint.

15.30 If a complaint is about a local authority's administration, it may be referred to the Commission for Local Administration in England (the Local Government Ombudsman) or the Public Services Ombudsman for Wales.

What if a complaint covers healthcare and social care?

15.31 Taking a complaint through NHS or local authority complaints procedures can be a complicated process – especially if the complaint covers a number of service providers or both healthcare and social care. In such situations, local authorities and the NHS must work together and agree which organisation will lead in handling the complaint. If a person is not happy with the outcome, they can take their case to the Health Service Ombudsman or to the Local Government Ombudsman (in England). There is guidance which sets out how organisations should work together to handle complaints that cover healthcare and social care (in England *Learning from Complaints* and in Wales *Listening and learning*). The Public Services Ombudsman for Wales handles complaints that cover both healthcare and social care.

Who can handle complaints about other welfare issues?

15.32 The Independent Housing Ombudsman deals with complaints about registered social landlords in England. This applies mostly to housing associations. But it also applies to many landlords who manage homes that were formerly run by local authorities and some private landlords. In Wales, the Public Services Ombudsman for Wales deals with complaints about registered social landlords. Complaints about local authorities may be referred to the Local Government Ombudsman in England or the Public Services Ombudsman for Wales. They look at complaints about decisions on council housing, social services, Housing Benefit and planning applications. More information about complaints to an Ombudsman is available on the relevant websites (see Annex A).

What is the best way to handle disagreement about a person's finances?

15.33 Some examples of disagreements about a person's finances are:
- disputes over the amount of money a person who lacks capacity should pay their carer
- disputes over whether a person who lacks capacity should sell their house
- somebody questioning the actions of a carer, who may be using the money of a person who lacks capacity inappropriately or without proper authority
- somebody questioning the actions of an attorney appointed under a Lasting Power of Attorney or an Enduring Power of Attorney or a deputy appointed by the court.

15.34 In all of the above circumstances, the most appropriate action would usually be to contact the Office of the Public Guardian (OPG) for guidance and advice. See chapter 14 for further details on the role of the OPG.

How can the Court of Protection help?

15.35 The Court of Protection deals with all areas of decision-making for adults who lack capacity to make particular decisions for themselves (see chapter 8 for more information about its roles and responsibilities). But the court is not always the right place to settle problems involving people who lack capacity. Other forms of settling disagreements may be more appropriate and less distressing.

15.36 There are some decisions that are so serious that the court should always make them. There are also other types of cases that the court should deal with when another method would generally not be suitable. See chapter 8 for more information about both kinds of cases.

Right of Appeal

15.37 Section 53 of the Act describes the rights of appeal against any decision taken by the Court of Protection. There are further details in the Court of Protection Rules. It may be advisable for anyone who wishes to appeal a decision made by the court to seek legal advice.

Will public legal funding be available?

15.38 Depending on their financial situation, once the Act comes into force people may be entitled to:
- publicly funded legal advice from accredited solicitors or advice agencies
- legal representation before the new Court of Protection (in the most serious cases).

Information about solicitors and organisations who give advice on different areas of law is available from Community Legal Services Direct (CLS Direct).[78] Further information about legal aid and public funding can be obtained from the Legal Services Commission.[79] See Annex A for full contact details.

78 CLS Direct, Tel: 0845 345 4 345, www.clsdirect.org.uk
79 www.legalservices.gov.uk

15.39 People who lack capacity to instruct a solicitor or conduct their own case will need a litigation friend. This person could be a relative, friend, attorney or the Official Solicitor (when no-one else is available). The litigation friend is able to instruct the solicitor and conduct the case on behalf of a person who lacks capacity to give instructions. If the person qualifies for public legal funding, the litigation friend can claim funding on their behalf.

When can someone get legal help?

15.40 Legal help is a type of legal aid (public funding) that pays for advice and assistance on legal issues, including those affecting a person who lacks capacity. But it does not provide representation for a full court hearing, although there is a related form of funding

called 'help at court' under which a legal representative can speak in court on a client's behalf on an informal basis. To qualify for legal help, applicants must show that:
- they get specific social security benefits, or they earn less than a specific amount and do not have savings or other financial assets in excess of a specific amount
- they would benefit sufficiently from legal advice to justify the amount it costs, and
- they cannot get another form of funding.

15.41 Legal help can include:
- help from a solicitor or other representative in writing letters
- in exceptional circumstances, getting a barrister's opinion, and
- assistance in preparing for Court of Protection hearings.

15.42 People cannot get legal help for making a Lasting Power of Attorney or an advance decision to refuse treatment. But they can get general help and information from the OPG. The OPG cannot give legal or specialist advice. For example, they will not be able to advise someone on what powers they should delegate to their attorney under an LPA.

When can someone get legal representation?

15.43 Public funding for legal representation in the Court of Protection will be available from solicitors with a relevant contract – but only for the most serious cases. To qualify, applicants will normally face the same test as for legal help to qualify financially (paragraph 15.40). They will generally have to satisfy more detailed criteria than applicants for legal help, relating, for instance, to their prospects of being successful, to whether legal representation is necessary and to the cost benefit of being represented. They will also have to establish that the case could not be brought or funded in another way and that there are not alternatives to court proceedings that should be explored first.

15.44 Serious personal welfare cases that were previously heard by the High Court will continue to have public funding for legal representation when they are transferred to the Court of Protection. These cases will normally be related to personal liberty, serious welfare decisions or medical treatment for a person who lacks capacity. But legal representation may also be available in other types of cases, depending on the particular circumstances.

16 WHAT RULES GOVERN ACCESS TO INFORMATION ABOUT A PERSON WHO LACKS CAPACITY?

This chapter gives guidance on:
- what personal information about someone who lacks capacity people involved in their care have the right to see, and
- how they can get hold of that information.

This chapter is only a general guide. It does not give detailed information about the law. Nor does it replace professional guidance or the guidance of the Information Commissioner's Office on the Data Protection Act 1998 (this guidance is available on its website, see Annex A). Where necessary, people should take legal advice.

This chapter is mainly for people such as family carers and other carers, deputies and attorneys, who care for or represent someone who lacks capacity to make specific decisions and in particular, lacks capacity to allow information about them to be disclosed. Professionals have their own codes of conduct, and they may have the support of experts in their organisations.

> In this chapter, as throughout the Code, a person's capacity (or lack of capacity) refers specifically to their capacity to make a particular decision at the time it needs to be made.

Quick summary

Questions to ask when requesting personal information about someone who may lack capacity

- Am I acting under a Lasting Power of Attorney or as a deputy with specific authority?
- Does the person have capacity to agree that information can be disclosed? Have they previously agreed to disclose the information?
- What information do I need?
- Why do I need it?
- Who has the information?
- Can I show that:
  - I need the information to make a decision that is in the best interests of the person I am acting for, and
  - the person does not have the capacity to act for themselves?
- Do I need to share the information with anyone else to make a decision that is in the best interests of the person who lacks capacity?
- Should I keep a record of my decision or action?
- How long should I keep the information for?
- Do I have the right to request the information under section 7 of the Data Protection Act 1998?

Questions to ask when considering whether to disclose information

- Is the request covered by section 7 of the Data Protection Act 1998? Is the request being made by a formally authorised representative?

If not:

- Is the disclosure legal?

- Is the disclosure justified, having balanced the person's best interests and the public interest against the person's right to privacy?

Questions to ask to decide whether the disclosure is legal or justified
- Do I (or does my organisation) have the information?
- Am I satisfied that the person concerned lacks capacity to agree to disclosure?
- Does the person requesting the information have any formal authority to act on behalf of the person who lacks capacity?
- Am I satisfied that the person making the request:
  - is acting in the best interests of the person concerned?
  - needs the information to act properly?
  - will respect confidentiality?
  - will keep the information for no longer than necessary?
- Should I get written confirmation of these things?

What laws and regulations affect access to information?

16.1 People caring for, or managing the finances of, someone who lacks capacity may need information to:
- assess the person's capacity to make a specific decision
- determine the person's best interests, and
- make appropriate decisions on the person's behalf.

16.2 The information they need varies depending on the circumstances. For example:
- a daughter providing full-time care for an elderly parent will make decisions based on her own experience and knowledge of her parent
- a deputy may need information from other people. For instance, if they were deciding whether a person needs to move into a care home or whether they should sell the person's home, they might need information from family members, the family doctor, the person's bank and their solicitor to make sure they are making the decision in the person's best interests.

16.3 Much of the information needed to make decisions under the Act is sensitive or confidential. It is regulated by:
- the Data Protection Act 1998
- the common law duty of confidentiality
- professional codes of conduct on confidentiality, and
- the Human Rights Act 1998 and European Convention on Human Rights, in particular Article 8 (the right to respect for private and family life), which means that it is only lawful to reveal someone's personal information if:
  - there is a legitimate aim in doing so
  - a democratic society would think it necessary to do so, and
  - the kind and amount of information disclosed is in relation to the need.

What information do people generally have a right to see?

16.4 Section 7 of the Data Protection Act 1998 gives everyone the right to see personal information that an organisation holds about them. They may also authorise someone else to access their information on their behalf. The person holding the information has a legal duty to release it. So, where possible, it is important to try to get a person's consent before requesting to see information about them.

16.5 A person may have the capacity to agree to someone seeing their personal information, even if they do not have the capacity to make other decisions. In some situations, a person may have previously given consent (while they still had capacity) for someone to see their personal information in the future.

16.6 Doctors and lawyers cannot share information about their clients, or that clients have given them, without the client's consent. Sometimes it is fair to assume that a doctor or lawyer already has someone's consent (for example, patients do not usually expect healthcare staff or legal professionals to get consent every time they share information with a colleague – but staff may choose to get clients' consent in writing when they begin treating or acting for that person). But in other circumstances, doctors and lawyers must get specific consent to 'disclose' information (share it with someone else).

16.7 If someone's capacity changes from time to time, the person needing the information may want to wait until that person can give their consent. Or they may decide that it is not necessary to get access to information at all, if the person will be able to make a decision on their own in the future.

16.8 If someone lacks the capacity to give consent, someone else might still be able to see their personal information. This will depend on:
- whether the person requesting the information is acting as an agent (a representative recognised by the law, such as a deputy or attorney) for the person who lacks capacity
- whether disclosure is in the best interests of the person who lacks capacity, and
- what type of information has been requested.

When can attorneys and deputies ask to see personal information?

16.9 An attorney acting under a valid LPA or EPA (and sometimes a deputy) can ask to see information concerning the person they are representing, as long as the information applies to decisions the attorney has the legal right to make.

16.10 In practice, an attorney or deputy may only require limited information and may not need to make a formal request. In such circumstances, they can approach the information holder informally. Once satisfied that the request comes from an attorney or deputy (having seen appropriate authority), the person holding information should be able to release it. The attorney or deputy can still make a formal request for information in the future.

16.11 The attorney or deputy must treat the information confidentially. They should be extremely careful to protect it. If they fail to do so, the court can cancel the LPA or deputyship.

16.12 Before the Act came into effect, only a few receivers were appointed with the general authority to manage a person's property and affairs. So they needed specific authority from the Court of Protection to ask for access to the person's personal information. Similarly, a deputy who only has authority to act in specific areas only has the right to ask for information relating to decisions in those specific areas. For information relating to other areas, the deputy will need to apply to the Court of Protection.

16.13 Requests for personal information must be in writing, and there might be a fee. Information holders should release it promptly (always within 40 calendar days). Fees may be particularly high for getting copies of healthcare records – particularly where information may be in unusual formats (for example, x-rays). The maximum fee is currently £50. Complaints about a failure to comply with the Data Protection Act 1998 should be directed to the Information Commissioner's Office (see Annex A for contact details).

What limitations are there?

16.14 Attorneys and deputies should only ask for information that will help them make a decision they need to make on behalf of the person who lacks capacity. For example, if the attorney needs to know when the person should take medication, they should not ask to see the entire healthcare record. The person who releases information must make sure that an attorney or deputy has official authority (they may ask for proof of identity and appointment). When asking to see personal information, attorneys and deputies should bear in mind that their decision must always be in the best interests of the person who lacks capacity to make that decision.

16.15 The attorney or deputy may not know the kind of information that someone holds about the person they are representing. So sometimes it might be difficult for them to make a specific request. They might even need to see all the information to make a decision. But again, the 'best interests' principle applies.

Scenario: Giving attorneys access to personal information

Mr Yapp is in the later stages of Alzheimer's disease. His son is responsible for Mr Yapp's personal welfare under a Lasting Power of Attorney. Mr Yapp has been in residential care for a number of years. But his son does not think that the home is able to meet his father's current needs as his condition has recently deteriorated.

> The son asks to see his father's records. He wants specific information about his father's care, so that he can make a decision about his father's best interests. But the manager of the care home refuses, saying that the Data Protection Act stops him releasing personal information.
>
> Mr Yapp's son points out that he can see his father's records, because he is his personal welfare attorney and needs the information to make a decision. The Data Protection Act 1998 requires the care home manager to provide access to personal data held on Mr Yapp.

16.16 The deputy or attorney may find that some information is held back (for example, when this contains references to people other than the person who lacks capacity). This might be to protect another person's privacy, if that person is mentioned in the records. It is unlikely that information relating to another person would help an attorney make a decision on behalf of the person who lacks capacity. The information holder might also be obliged to keep information about the other person confidential. There might be another reason why the person does not want information about them to be released. Under these circumstances, the attorney does not have the right to see that information.

16.17 An information holder should not release information if doing so would cause serious physical or mental harm to anyone – including the person the information is about. This applies to information on health, social care and education records.

16.18 The Information Commissioner's Office can give further details on:
- how to request personal information
- restrictions on accessing information, and
- how to appeal against a decision not to release information.

When can someone see information about healthcare or social care?

16.19 Healthcare and social care staff may disclose information about somebody who lacks capacity only when it is in the best interests of the person concerned to do so, or when there is some other, lawful reason for them to do so.

16.20 The Act's requirement to consult relevant people when working out the best interests of a person who lacks capacity will encourage people to share the information that makes a consultation meaningful. But people who release information should be sure that they are acting lawfully and that they can justify releasing the information. They need to balance the person's right to privacy with what is in their best interests or the wider public interest (see paragraphs 16.24–16.25 below).

16.21 Sometimes it will be fairly obvious that staff should disclose information. For example, a doctor would need to tell a new care worker about what drugs a person needs or what allergies the person has. This is clearly in the person's best interests.

16.22 Other information may need to be disclosed as part of the process of working out someone's best interests. A social worker might decide to reveal information about someone's past when discussing their best interests with a close family member. But staff should always bear in mind that the Act requires them to consider the wishes and feelings of the person who lacks capacity.

16.23 In both these cases, staff should only disclose as much information as is relevant to the decision to be made.

Scenario: Sharing appropriate information

Mr Jeremy has learning disabilities. His care home is about to close down. His care team carries out a careful assessment of his needs. They involve him as much as possible, and use the support of an Independent Mental Capacity Advocate. Following the assessment, he is placed with carers under an adult placement scheme.

The carers ask to see Mr Jeremy's case file, so that they can provide him with appropriate care in his best interests. The care manager seeks Mr Jeremy's consent to disclosure of his notes, but believes that Mr Jeremy lacks capacity to make this decision. She recognises that it is appropriate to provide the carers with sufficient information to enable them to act in Mr Jeremy's best interests. But it is not appropriate for them to see all the information on the case file. Much of it is not relevant to his current care needs. The care manager therefore only passes on relevant information from the file.

16.24 Sometimes a person's right to confidentiality will conflict with broader public concerns. Information can be released if it is in the public interest, even if it is not in the best interests of the person who lacks capacity. It can be difficult to decide in these cases, and information holders should consider each case on its merits. The NHS Code on Confidentiality gives examples of when disclosure is in the public interest. These include situations where disclosing information could prevent, or aid investigation of, serious crimes, or to prevent serious harm, such as spread of an infectious disease. It is then necessary to judge whether the public good that would be achieved by the disclosure outweighs both the obligation of confidentiality to the individual concerned and the broader public interest in the provision of a confidential service.

16.25 For disclosure to be in the public interest, it must be proportionate and limited to the relevant details. Healthcare or social care staff faced with this decision should seek advice from their legal advisers. It is not just things for 'the public's benefit' that are in the public interest – disclosure for the benefit of the person who lacks capacity can also be in the public interest (for example, to stop a person who lacks capacity suffering physical or mental harm).

What financial information can carers ask to see?

16.26 It is often more difficult to get financial information than it is to get information on a person's welfare. A bank manager, for example, is less likely to:
- know the individual concerned
- be able to make an assessment of the person's capacity to consent to disclosure, and
- be aware of the carer's relationship to the person.

So they are less likely than a doctor or social worker to be able to judge what is in a person's best interests and are bound by duties to keep clients' affairs confidential. It is likely that someone wanting financial information will need to apply to the Court of Protection for access to that information. This clearly does not apply to an attorney or a deputy appointed to manage the person's property and affairs, who will generally have the authority (because of their appointment) to obtain all relevant information about the person's property and affairs.

Is information still confidential after someone shares it?

16.27 Whenever a carer gets information, they should treat the information in confidence, and they should not share it with anyone else (unless there is a lawful basis for doing so). In some circumstances, the information holder might ask the carer to give a formal confirmation that they will keep information confidential.

16.28 Where the information is in written form, carers should store it carefully and not keep it for longer than necessary. In many cases, the need to keep the information will be temporary. So the carer should be able to reassure the information holder that they will not keep a permanent record of the information.

What is the best way to settle a disagreement about personal information?

16.29 A carer should always start by trying to get consent from the person whose information they are trying to access. If the person lacks capacity to consent, the carer should ask the information holder for the relevant information and explain why they need it. They may need to remind the information holder that they have to make a decision in the person's best interests and cannot do so without the relevant information.

16.30 This can be a sensitive area and disputes will inevitably arise. Healthcare and social care staff have a difficult judgement to make. They might feel strongly that disclosing the information would not be in the best interests of the person who lacks capacity and would amount to an invasion of their privacy. This may be upsetting for the carer who will probably have good motives for wanting the information. In all cases, an assessment of the interests and needs of the person who lacks capacity should determine whether staff should disclose information.

16.31 If a discussion fails to settle the matter, and the carer still is not happy, there are other ways to settle the disagreement (see chapter 15). The carer may need to use the appropriate complaints procedure. Since the complaint involves elements of data protection and confidentiality, as well as best interests, relevant experts should help deal with the complaint.

16.32 In cases where carers and staff cannot settle their disagreement, the carer can apply to the Court of Protection for the right to access to the specific information. The court would then need to decide if this was in the best interests of the person who lacks capacity to consent. In urgent cases, it might be necessary for the carer to apply directly to the court without going through the earlier stages.

KEY WORDS AND PHRASES USED IN THE CODE

The table below is not a full index or glossary. Instead, it is a list of key terms used in the Code or the Act, and the main references to them. References in bold indicate particularly valuable content for that term.

Acts in connection with care or treatment	Tasks carried out by carers, healthcare or social care staff which involve the personal care, healthcare or medical treatment of people who lack capacity to consent to them – referred to in the Act as 'section 5 acts'.	Chapter 6 2.13–2.14, 4.39 Best interests and _ 5.10, 5,39 Deprivation of liberty and_ 6.39. 6.49–6.52

Advance decision to refuse treatment	A decision to refuse specified treatment made in advance by a person who has capacity to do so. This decision will then apply at a future time when that person lacks capacity to consent to, or refuse, the specified treatment. This is set out in Section 24(1) of the Act. Specific rules apply to advance decisions to refuse life-sustaining treatment.	Chapter 9 (all) Best interests and _ 5.5, 5.35, 5.45 Protection from liability and _ 6.37–6.38 LPAs and _ 7.55 Deputies and _ 8.28 Research and _ 11.30 Young people and _ 12.9 Mental Health Act 13.35–13.37
Adult protection procedures	Procedures devised by local authorities, in conjunction with other relevant agencies, to investigate and deal with allegations of abuse or ill treatment of vulnerable adults, and to put in place safeguards to provide protection from abuse.	Chapter 14 14.6, 14.22, 14.27–28, 14.34 IMCAs and _ 10.66–10.67
After-care under supervision	Arrangements for supervision in the community following discharge from hospital of certain patients previously detained under the Mental Health Act 1983.	Chapter 13 13.22–13.25, 13.34, 13.37, 13.40, 13.42, 13.45, 13.48, 13.52
Agent	A person authorised to act on behalf of another person under the law of agency. Attorneys appointed under an LPA or EPA are agents and court-appointed deputies are deemed to be agents and must undertake certain duties as agents.	LPAs and _ 7.58–7.68 Deputies and _ 8.55–8.68
Appointee	Someone appointed under Social Security Regulations to claim and collect social security benefits or pensions on behalf of a person who lacks capacity to manage their own benefits. An appointee is permitted to use the money claimed to meet the person's needs.	Role of _ 6:65–6.66 Deputies and _ 8.56 Concerns about _ 14:35–14.36

Appropriate body	A committee which is established to advise on, or on matters which include, the ethics of intrusive research in relation to people who lack capacity to consent to it, and is recognised for those purposes by the Secretary of State (in England) or the National Assembly for Wales (in Wales).	Chapter 11 11.8–11.11, 11.20, 11.33–11.34, 11.43–11.47.
Approved Social Worker (ASW)	A specially trained social worker with responsibility for assessing a person's needs for care and treatment under the Mental Health Act 1983. In particular, an ASW assesses whether the person should be admitted to hospital for assessment and/or treatment.	Chapter 13 13.16, 13.22–13.23, 13.43, 13.52
Artificial Nutrition and Hydration (ANH)	Artificial nutrition and hydration (ANH) has been recognised as a form of medical treatment. ANH involves using tubes to provide nutrition and fluids to someone who cannot take them by mouth. It bypasses the natural mechanisms that control hunger and thirst and requires clinical monitoring.	9.26 5.34 6.18 8.18
Attorney	Someone appointed under either a Lasting Power of Attorney (LPA) or an Enduring Power of Attorney (EPA), who has the legal right to make decisions within the scope of their authority on behalf of the person (the donor) who made the Power of Attorney.	Chapter 7 Best interests principle and _ 5.2, 5.13, 5.49, 5.55 Protection from liability as _ 6.54–6.55 Court of Protection and _ 8.30 Advance decisions and _ 9.33 Mental Health Act and _ 13.38–13.45 Public Guardian and _ 14.7–14.14 Legal help and _ 15.39–15.42 Accessing personal information as _ 16.9–16.16

Best interests	Any decisions made, or anything done for a person who lacks capacity to make specific decisions, must be in the person's best interests. There are standard minimum steps to follow when working out someone's best interests. These are set out in section 4 of the Act, and in the non-exhaustive checklist in 5.13.	**Chapter 2 (Principle 4) Chapter 5** Protection from liability and _ 6.4–6.18

Reasonable belief and _ 6.32–6.36

Deprivation of liberty and _ 6.51–6.53

Acting as an attorney and _ 7.19–7.20, 7.29, 7.53

Court of Protection and _ 8.14–8.26

Acting as a deputy and _ 8.50–8.52

Advance decisions and _ 9.4–9.5 |
| **Bournewood provisions** | A name given to some proposed new procedures and safeguards for people who lack capacity to make relevant decisions but who need to be deprived of their liberty, in their best interests, otherwise than under the Mental Health Act 1983. The name refers to a case which was eventually decided by the European Court of Human Rights. | 6.53–6.54

13.53–13.54 |
| **Capacity** | The ability to make a decision about a particular matter at the time the decision needs to be made. The legal definition of a person who lacks capacity is set out in section 2 of the Act. | **Chapter 4** |

Carer	Someone who provides *unpaid* care by looking after a friend or neighbour who needs support because of sickness, age or disability. In this document, the role of the carer is different from the role of a professional care worker.	**Acting as decision-maker 5.8–5.10** **Protection from liability 6.20–6.24** Assessing capacity as 4.44–4.45 Acting with reasonable belief 6.29–6.34 Paying for goods and services 6.56–6.66 Accessing information 16.26–16.32
Care worker	Someone employed to provide personal care for people who need help because of sickness, age or disability. They could be employed by the person themselves, by someone acting on the person's behalf or by a care agency.	Assessing capacity as 4.38, 4.44–4.45 Protection from liability 6.20 Paying for goods and services 6.56–6.66 Acting as an attorney 7.10 Acting as a deputy 8.41
Children Act 1989	A law relating to children and those with parental responsibility for children.	Chapter 12
Complaints Review Panel	A panel of people set up to review and reconsider complaints about health or social care services which have not been resolved under the first stage of the relevant complaints procedure.	15.28
Consultee	A person who is consulted, for example about the involvement in a research project of a person who lacks capacity to consent to their participation in the research.	11.23, 11.28–29, 11.44

Court of Protection	The specialist Court for all issues relating to people who lack capacity to make specific decisions. The Court of Protection is established under section 45 of the Act.	Chapter 8 _ must always make decisions about these issues 6.18 Decisions about life- sustaining treatment 5.33–5.36 LPAs and _ 7.45–7.49 Advance decisions and _ 9.35, 9.54, 9.67–9.69 Decisions regarding children and young people 12.3–12.4, 12.7, 12.10, 12.23–12.25 Access to legal help 15.40–15.44
Court of Protection Visitor	Someone who is appointed to report to the Court of Protection on how attorneys or deputies are carrying out their duties. Court of Protection Visitors are established under section 61 of the Act. They can also be directed by the Public Guardian to visit donors, attorney and deputies under section 58(1)(d).	14.10–14.11 Attorneys and _ 7.71 Deputies and _ 8.71
Criminal Records Bureau (CRB)	An Executive Agency of the Home Office which provides access to criminal record information. Organisations in the public, private and voluntary sectors can ask for the CRB to check candidates for jobs to see if they have any criminal records which would make them unsuitable for certain work, especially that involves children or vulnerable adults. For some jobs, a CRB check is mandatory.	Checking healthcare and social care staff 14.29–14.30 Checking IMCAs 10.18
Data Protection Act 1998	A law controlling the handling of, and access to, personal information, such as medical records, files held by public bodies and financial information held by credit reference agencies.	Chapter 16

Decision-maker	Under the Act, many different people may be required to make decisions or act on behalf of someone who lacks capacity to make decisions for themselves. The person making the decision is referred to throughout the Code, as the 'decision-maker', and it is the decision-maker's responsibility to work out what would be in the best interests of the person who lacks capacity.	Chapter 5 Working with IMCAs 10.4, 10.21–10.29 Applying the MHA 13.3, 13.10, 13.27
Declaration	A kind of order made by the Court of Protection. For example, a declaration could say whether a person has or lacks capacity to make a particular decision, or declaring that a particular act would or would not be lawful. The Court's power to make declarations is set out in section 15 of the Act	8.13–8.19 Advance decisions and _ 9.35
Deprivation of liberty	Deprivation of liberty is a term used in the European Convention on Human Rights about circumstances when a person's freedom is taken away. Its meaning in practice is being defined through case law.	6.49–6.54 Protection from liability 6.13–6.14 Attorneys and _ 7.44 Mental Health Act and _ 13.12, 13.16

Deputy	Someone appointed by the Court of Protection with ongoing legal authority as prescribed by the Court to make decisions on behalf of a person who lacks capacity to make particular decisions as set out in Section 16(2) of the Act.	Chapter 8 Best interests principle and _ 5.2, 5.13, 5.49, 5.55 Protection from liability as _ 6.54–6.55 Attorneys becoming _ 7.56 Advance decisions and _ 9.33 IMCAs and _ 10.70–72 Acting for children and young people 12.4, 12.7 Public Guardian and _ 14.15–14.18 Complaints about 14.19–14.25 Accessing personal information as _ 16.9–16.16
Donor	A person who makes a Lasting Power of Attorney or Enduring Power of Attorney	Chapter 7
Enduring Power of Attorney (EPA)	A Power of Attorney created under the Enduring Powers of Attorney Act 1985 appointing an attorney to deal with the donor's property and financial affairs. Existing EPAs will continue to operate under Schedule 4 of the Act, which replaces the EPA Act 1985.	Chapter 7 See also LPA
Family carer	A family member who looks after a relative who needs support because of sickness, age or disability. It does not mean a professional care-worker employed by a disabled person or a care assistant in a nursing home, for example.	See carer

Family Division of the High Court	The Division of the High Court that has the jurisdiction to deal with all matrimonial and civil partnership matters, family disputes, matters relating to children and some disputes about medical treatment.	12.14, 12.23
Fiduciary duty	Anyone acting under the law of agency will have this duty. In essence, it means that any decision taken or act done as an agent (such as an attorney or deputy) must not benefit themselves, but must benefit the person for whom they are acting.	_ for attorneys 7.58 _ for deputies 8.58
Guardianship	Arrangements, made under the Mental Health Act 1983, for a guardian to be appointed for a person with mental disorder to help ensure that the person gets the care they need in the community.	**13.16–13.21** 13.1, 13.25–13.27, 13.54
Health Service Ombudsman	An independent person whose organisation investigates complaints about National Health Service (NHS) care or treatment in England which have not been resolved through the NHS complaints procedure.	15.19, 15.21, 15.31
Human Rights Act 1998	A law largely incorporating into UK law the substantive rights set out in the European Convention on Human Rights.	6.49 16.3
Human Tissue Act 2004	A law to regulate issues relating to whole body donation and the taking, storage and use of human organs and tissue.	11.7 11.38–11.39
Ill treatment	Section 44 of the Act introduces a new offence of ill treatment of a person who lacks capacity by someone who is caring for them, or acting as a deputy or attorney for them. That person can be guilty of ill treatment if they have deliberately ill-treated a person who lacks capacity, or been reckless as to whether they were ill-treating the person or not. It does not matter whether the behaviour was likely to cause, or actually caused, harm or damage to the victim's health.	14.23–14.26
Independent Complaints Advocacy Service (ICAS)	In England, a service to support patients and their carers who wish to pursue a complaint about their NHS treatment or care.	15.18

Independent Mental Capacity Advocate (IMCA)	Someone who provides support and representation for a person who lacks capacity to make specific decisions, where the person has no-one else to support them. The IMCA service is established under section 35 of the Act and the functions of IMCAs are set out in section 36. It is not the same as an ordinary advocacy service.	Chapter 10 Consulting to work out best interests 5.51 Involvement in changes of residence 6.9 Involvement in serious medical decisions 6.16 MHA and _ 13.46–13.48
Information Commissioner's Office	An independent authority set up to promote access to official information and to protect personal information. It has powers to ensure that the laws about information, such as the Data Protection Act 1998, are followed.	16.13 16.18
Lasting Power of Attorney (LPA)	A Power of Attorney created under the Act (see Section 9(1)) appointing an attorney (or attorneys) to make decisions about the donor's personal welfare (including healthcare) and/or deal with the donor's property and affairs.	Chapter 7 Best interests principle and _ 5.2, 5.13, 5.49, 5.55 Protection from liability as _ 6.54–6.55 Court of Protection and _ 8.30 Advance decisions and _ 9.33 Mental Health Act and _ 13.38–13.45 Public Guardian and _ 14.7–14.14 Legal help and _ 15.39–15.42 Accessing personal information as _ 16.9–16.16

Life-sustaining treatment	Treatment that, in the view of the person providing healthcare, is necessary to keep a person alive See Section 4(10) of the Act.	**Providing or stopping _ in best interests 5.29–5.36** **Advance decisions to refuse _ 9.10–9.11, 9.19–9.20, 9.24–9.28** Protection from liability when providing _ 6.16, 6.55 Attorneys and _ 7.22, 7.27, 7.29-7.30 Deputies and _ 8.17, 8.46 Conscientious objection to stopping _ 9.61–9.63 IMCAs and _ 10.44
Litigation friend	A person appointed by the court to conduct legal proceedings on behalf of, and in the name of, someone who lacks capacity to conduct the litigation or to instruct a lawyer themselves.	4.54 10.38 15.39
Local Government Ombudsman	In England, an independent organisation that investigates complaints about councils and local authorities on most council matters including housing, planning, education and social services.	15.30–15.32
Makaton	A language programme using signs and symbols, for the teaching of communication, language and literacy skills for people with communication and learning difficulties.	3.11
Mediation	A process for resolving disagreements in which an impartial third party (the mediator) helps people in dispute to find a mutually acceptable resolution.	15.7–15.13
Mental capacity	See capacity	

Mental Health Act 1983	A law mainly about the compulsory care and treatment of patients with mental health problems. In particular, it covers detention in hospital for mental health treatment.	**Chapter 13** Deprivation of liberty other than in line with _ 6.50–6.53, 7.44 Attorneys and _ 7.27 Advance decisions and _ 9.37 IMCAs and 10.44, 10.51, 10.56–10.58 Children and young people and _ 12.6, 12.21 Complaints regarding _ 15.19
Mental Health Review Tribunal	An independent judicial body with powers to direct the discharge of patients who are detained under the Mental Health Act 1983.	13.31 13.42
NHS Litigation Authority	A Special Health Authority (part of the NHS), responsible for handling negligence claims made against NHS bodies in England.	15.22

Office of the Public Guardian (OPG)	The Public Guardian is an officer established under Section 57 of the Act. The Public Guardian will be supported by the Office of the Public Guardian, which will supervise deputies, keep a register of deputies, Lasting Powers of Attorney and Enduring Powers of Attorney, check on what attorneys are doing, and investigate any complaints about attorneys or deputies. The OPG replaces the Public Guardianship Office (PGO) that has been in existence for many years.	**14.8–14.22** Registering LPAs with _ 7.14–7.17 Supervision of attorneys by _ 7.69–7.74 Registering EPAs with _ 7.78 Guidance for EPAs _ 7.79 Guidance for receivers_ 8.5 Panel of deputies of _ 8.35 Supervision of deputies by _ 8.69–8.77
Official Solicitor	Provides legal services for vulnerable persons, or in the interests of achieving justice. The Official Solicitor represents adults who lack capacity to conduct litigation in county court or High Court proceedings in England and Wales, and in the Court of Protection.	Helping with formal assessment of capacity 4.54 Acting in applications to the Court of Protection 8.10 Acting as litigation friend 10.38, 15.39
Patient Advice and Liaison Service (PALS)	In England, a service providing information, advice and support to help NHS patients, their families and carers. PALS act on behalf of service users when handling patient and family concerns and can liaise with staff, managers and, where appropriate, other relevant organisations, to find solutions.	15.15–15.17
Permanent vegetative state (PVS)	A condition caused by catastrophic brain damage whereby patients in PVS have a permanent and irreversible lack of awareness of their surroundings and no ability to interact at any level with those around them.	6.18 8.18

Personal welfare	Personal welfare decisions are any decisions about person's healthcare, where they live, what clothes they wear, what they eat and anything needed for their general care and well-being. Attorneys and deputies can be appointed to make decisions about personal welfare on behalf of a person who lacks capacity. Many acts of care are to do with personal welfare.	_ LPAs 7.21–7.31 _ deputies 8.38–8.39 Advance decisions about _ 9.4, 9.35 Role of High Court in decisions about _ 15.44
Property and affairs	Any possessions owned by a person (such as a house or flat, jewellery or other possessions), the money they have in income, savings or investments and any expenditure. Attorneys and deputies can be appointed to make decisions about property and affairs on behalf of a person who lacks capacity.	_ LPAs 7.32–7.42 _ deputies 8.34–8.37 Restrictions on _ LPA 7.56 Duties of _ attorney 7.58, 7.67–7.68 _ EPAs 7.76–7.77 OPG panel of _ deputies 8.35 Duties of _ deputy 8.56, 8.67–8.68 _ of children and young people 12.3–12.4, 12.7
Protection from liability	Legal protection, granted to anyone who has acted or made decisions in line with the Act's principles.	Chapter 6
Protection of Vulnerable Adults (POVA) list	A register of individuals who have abused, neglected or otherwise harmed vulnerable adults in their care or placed vulnerable adults at risk of harm. Providers of care must not offer such individuals employment in care positions.	14.31
Public Services Ombudsman for Wales	An independent body that investigates complaints about local government and NHS organisations in Wales, and the National Assembly for Wales, concerning matters such as housing, planning, education, social services and health services.	15.20 15.30–15.32

Receiver	Someone appointed by the former Court of Protection to manage the property and affairs of a person lacking capacity to manage their own affairs. Existing receivers continue as deputies with legal authority to deal with the person's property and affairs.	8.5 8.35
Restraint	See Section 6(4) of the Act. The use or threat of force to help do an act which the person resists, or the restriction of the person's liberty of movement, whether or not they resist. Restraint may only be used where it is necessary to protect the person from harm and is proportionate to the risk of harm.	6.39–6.44, 6.47–53 Use of _ in moves between accommodation 6.11 Use of _ in healthcare and treatment decisions 6.15 Attorneys and _ 7.43-7.44 Deputies and _ 8.46 MHA and _ 13.5
Statutory principles	The five key principles are set out in Section 1 of the Act. They are designed to emphasise the fundamental concepts and core values of the Act and to provide a benchmark to guide decision-makers, professionals and carers acting under the Act's provisions. The principles generally apply to all actions and decisions taken under the Act.	Chapter 2
Two-stage test of capacity	Using sections 2 and 3 of the Act to assess whether or not a person has capacity to make a decision for themselves at that time.	4.10–4.13 Protection from liability 6.27 Applying _ to advance decisions 9.39
Wilful neglect	An intentional or deliberate omission or failure to carry out an act of care by someone who has care of a person who lacks (or whom the person reasonably believes lacks) capacity to care for themselves. Section 44 introduces a new offence of wilful neglect of a person who lacks capacity.	14.23–14.26

Written statements of wishes and feelings	Written statements the person might have made before losing capacity about their wishes and feelings regarding issues such as the type of medical treatment they would want in the case of future illness, where they would prefer to live, or how they wish to be cared for. They should be used to help find out what someone's wishes and feelings might be, as part of working out their best interests. They are not the same as advance decisions to refuse treatment and are not binding.	5.34 5.37 5.42–5.44

ANNEX A

The following list provides contact details for some organisations that provide information, guidance or materials related to the Code of Practice and the Mental Capacity Act. The list is not exhaustive: many other organisations may also produce their own materials.

British Banking Association

[Provides a leaflet for customers on *'Banking for people who lack capacity to make decisions (England and Wales)'*. Available from www.bba.org.uk/publications/entry/banking-for-people-who-lack-capacity-to-make-decisions-england-and-wales/leaflets/]

Note—Words in square brackets have been amended by the authors to reflect changes to website addresses.

web: www.bba.org.uk
telephone: 020 7216 8800

British Medical Association

[Co-authors (with the Law Society) of *Assessment of Mental Capacity: A Practical Guide for Doctors and Lawyers* (Third edition) (London: The Law Society, 2010). See www.bma.org.uk/ap.nsf/Content/Assessmentmental?OpenDocument& Highlight=2,mental, capacity

Available from The Law Society (www.lawsocietyshop.org.uk/ecom_lawsoc/public/saleproduct.jsf?catalogueCode=9781853287787), price £41.95]

Note—Words in square brackets have been amended by the authors to reflect changes to website addresses.

web: www.bma.org.uk
telephone: 020 7387 4499

British Psychological Society

Publishers of *Guidelines on assessing capacity* – professional guidance available online to members.
web:		www.bps.org.uk
telephone:	(0)116 254 9568

Commission for Social Care Inspection

The Commission for Social Care Inspection (CSCI) registers, inspects and reports on social care services in England.
web:		www.csci.org.uk
telephone:	0845 015 0120 / 0191 233 3323
textphone:	0845 015 2255 / 0191 233 3588

Criminal Records Bureau (CRB)

The CRB runs criminal records checks on people who apply for jobs working with children and vulnerable adults.
web:		www.crb.org.uk
telephone:	0870 90 90 811

Department for Constitutional Affairs

The government department with responsibility for the Mental Capacity Act and the Code of Practice. Also publishes guidance for specific audiences www.dca.gov.uk/legal-policy/mental-capacity/guidance.htm

Department of Health

Publishes guidance for healthcare and social care staff in England. Key publications referenced in the Code include:
- on using restraint with people with learning disabilities and autistic spectrum disorder, see *Guidance for restrictive physical interventions* www.dh.gov.uk/assetRoot/04/06/84/61/04068461.pdf
- on adult protection procedures, see *No secrets: Guidance on developing and implementing multi-agency policies and procedures to protect vulnerable adults from abuse* www.dh.gov.uk/assetRoot/04/07/45/44/04074544.pdf
- on consent to examination and treatment, including advance decisions to refuse treatment www.dh/gov.uk/consent
- [on the Deprivation of Liberty safeguards, a supplement to this Code of Practice www.dh.gov.uk/en/Publicationsandstatistics/Publications/PublicationsPolicyAndGuidance/DH_085476]

- on IMCAs and the IMCA pilots www.dh.gov.uk/imca
- [DH also is responsible for the *Mental Health Act 1983 Code of Practice* (TSO 2008) www.dh.gov.uk/prod_consum_dh/groups/dh_digitalassets/@dh/@en/documents/digitalasset/dh_087073.pdf]

Note—Words in square brackets have been amended by the authors to reflect changes to website addresses.

Direct.gov

Provides free legal information to people living in England and Wales to help them deal with legal problems.

web: www.direct.gov.uk/en/Governmentcitizensandrights/Mentalcapacityandthelaw/index.htm

Note—Community Legal Services Direct no longer exists. The authors have added in this new entry in light of this.

Family Mediation Helpline

Provides general information on family mediation and contact details for mediation services in your local area.

Web: www.familymediationhelpline.co.uk
telephone: 0845 60 26 627

Healthcare Commission

The health watchdog in England, undertaking reviews and investigations into the provision of NHS and private healthcare services.

Web: www.healthcarecommission.org.uk
telephone: 0845 601 3012
switchboard: 020 7448 9200

Healthcare Inspectorate for Wales

Undertakes reviews and investigations into the provision of NHS funded care, either by or for Welsh NHS organisations.

Web: www.hiw.org.uk
email: hiw@wales.gsi.gov.uk
telephone: 029 2092 8850

Housing Ombudsman Service

The Housing Ombudsman Service considers complaints against member organisations, and deals with other housing disputes.

Web: www.ihos.org.uk
email: info@housing-ombudsman.org.uk
telephone: 020 7421 3800

Information Commissioner's Office

The Information Commissioner's Office is the UK's independent authority set up to promote access to official information and to protect personal information.

Web: www.ico.gov.uk
telephone helpline: 08456 30 60 60

Legal Services Commission

Looks after legal aid in England and Wales, and provides information, advice and legal representation.

Web: www.legalservices.gov.uk
See also Community Legal Services Direct.

Local Government Ombudsman

The Local Government Ombudsmen investigate complaints about councils and certain other bodies.

Web: www.lgo.org.uk
telephone: 0845 602 1983

National Mediation Helpline

Provides access to a simple, low cost method of resolving a wide range of disputes.

The National Mediation Helpline is operated on behalf of the Department for Constitutional Affairs (DCA) in conjunction with the Civil Mediation Council (CMC).

Web: www.nationalmediationhelpline.com
telephone: 0845 60 30 809

Office of the Public Guardian

The new Public Guardian is established under the Act and will be supported by the Office of the Public Guardian, which will replace the current Public

Guardianship Office (PGO). The OPG will be an executive agency of the Department for Constitutional Affairs. Amongst its other roles, it provides forms for LPAs and EPAs.

Web: From October 2007, a new website will be created at www.publicguardian.gov.uk

Official Solicitor

Provides legal services for vulnerable people and is able to represent people who lack capacity and act as a litigation friend.

Web: www.officialsolicitor.gov.uk
telephone: 020 7911 7127

Patient Advice and Liaison Service (PALS)

Provides information about the NHS and help resolve concerns or problems with the NHS, including support when making complaints.

Web: www.pals.nhs.uk
The site includes contact details for local PALS offices around the country.

Patient Information Advisory Group

Considers applications on behalf of the Secretary of State to allow the common law duty of confidentiality to be aside.

Web: www.advisorybodies.doh.gov.uk/PIAG

Public Service Ombudsman for Wales

Investigates complaints about local authorities and NHS organisations in Wales, and about the National Assembly Government for Wales.

Web: www.ombudsman-wales.org.uk
telephone: 01656 641 150

Welsh Assembly Government

Produces key pieces of guidance for healthcare and social care staff, including:
- *In safe hands – Implementing Adult Protection Procedures in Wales* (update 2003) [http://welshgovernmentpublications.soutron.net/publications/]
- *Framework for restrictive physical intervention policy and practice* (available for order from [http://welshgovernmentpublications.soutron.net/publications/])

Hard copies of this publication are available from TSO

For more information on the Mental Capacity Act contact [the Office of the Public Guardian]:

9am – 5pm, Mon – Fri

Note—Words in square brackets have been amended by the authors to reflect changes to website addresses.

Telephone:	[0300 456 0300]
or	+44 207 664 7000 (for callers outside UK)
Text Phone:	[0115 934 2778]
Fax:	0870 739 5780 (UK callers)
Email:	[customerservices@publicguardian.gsi.gov.uk]
Website:	[www.justice.gov.uk/about/opg.htm]
Post:	[Office of the Public Guardian PO Box 15118 Birmingham B16 6GX]

Note—Words in square brackets have been amended by the authors to reflect changes to contact information.

Mental Capacity Act 2005: Deprivation of Liberty Safeguards Code of Practice

SUPPLEMENTING THE MAIN MENTAL CAPACITY ACT 2005 CODE OF PRACTICE

Issued by the Lord Chancellor on 26 August 2008 in accordance with sections 42 and 43 of the Act[80]

[80] As was anticipated in the Code of Practice (at para 2), and discussed in detail in Chapter 6 above, the case law upon deprivation of liberty has moved on substantially since it was issued in August 2008. It is likely that the Code of Practice will require updating in light of the decision of the Supreme Court in the conjoined appeals against the decisions of the Court of Appeal in *Cheshire West and Chester Council v P* [2011] EWCA Civ 1257, [2012] COPLR 37 and *P and Q v Surrey County Council* [2011] EWCA Civ 190, [2011] COPLR Con Vol 931. Further, it will also require updating to take into account the abolition of Primary Care Trusts with effect from 1 April 2013 (which means that local authorities will assume the responsibilities of supervisory bodies for those detained in hospital as well as in care homes). A decision has been taken not to annotate this document on a 'running' basis, but it now must be approached with some caution as a guide to the current state of the law.

FOREWORD BY IVAN LEWIS AND EDWINA HART MBE

The Mental Capacity Act 2005 ('the Act') provides a statutory framework for acting and making decisions on behalf of individuals who lack the mental capacity to do so for themselves. It introduced a number of laws to protect these individuals and ensure that they are given every chance to make decisions for themselves. The Act came into force in October 2007.

The Government has added new provisions to the Act: the deprivation of liberty safeguards. The safeguards focus on some of the most vulnerable people in our society: those who for their own safety and in their own best interests need to be accommodated under care and treatment regimes that may have the effect of depriving them of their liberty, but who lack the capacity to consent.

The deprivation of a person's liberty is a very serious matter and should not happen unless it is absolutely necessary, and in the best interests of the person concerned. That is why the safeguards have been created: to ensure that any decision to deprive someone of their liberty is made following defined processes and in consultation with specific authorities.

The new provisions in the Act set out the legal framework of the deprivation of liberty safeguards. This Code of Practice is formally issued by the Lord Chancellor as a Code of Practice under the Mental Capacity Act 2005. It provides guidance and information for those implementing the deprivation of liberty safeguards legislation on a daily basis. In some cases, this will be paid staff, in others those who have been appointed in law to represent individuals who lack capacity to make decisions for themselves (such as deputies or donees of a Lasting Power of Attorney).

Because of this broad audience, the Code of Practice has been written so as to make it as user-friendly as possible – like the main Mental Capacity Act 2005 Code of Practice, issued in April 2007. We are grateful to all those who commented on earlier drafts of the Code to help it achieve that goal.

Ivan Lewis

Edwina Hart

INTRODUCTION

The Mental Capacity Act 2005 ('the Act'), covering England and Wales, provides a statutory framework for acting and making decisions on behalf of people who lack the capacity to make those decisions for themselves. These can be small decisions – such as what clothes to wear – or major decisions, such as where to live.

In some cases, people lack the capacity to consent to particular treatment or care that is recognised by others as being in their best interests, or which will protect them from harm. Where this care might involve depriving vulnerable people of their liberty in either a hospital or a care home, extra safeguards have been introduced, in law, to protect their rights and ensure that the care or treatment they receive is in their best interests.

This Code of Practice helps explain how to identify when a person is, or is at risk of, being deprived of their liberty and how deprivation of liberty may be avoided. It also explains the safeguards that have been put in place to ensure that deprivation of liberty, where it does need to occur, has a lawful basis. In addition, it provides guidance on what someone should do if they suspect that a person who lacks capacity is being deprived of their liberty unlawfully.

These safeguards are an important way of protecting the rights of many vulnerable people and should not be viewed negatively. Depriving someone of their liberty can be a necessary requirement in order to provide effective care or treatment. By following the criteria set out in the safeguards, and explained in this Code of Practice, the decision to deprive someone of their liberty can be made lawfully and properly.

How does this Code of Practice relate to the main Mental Capacity Act 2005 Code of Practice?

This document adds to the guidance in the main Mental Capacity Act 2005 Code of Practice ('the main Code'), which was issued in April 2007, and should be used in conjunction with the main Code. It focuses specifically on the deprivation of liberty safeguards added to the Act. These can be found in sections 4A and 4B of, and Schedules A1 and 1A to, the Act.

Though these safeguards were mentioned in the main Code (particularly in chapters 6 and 13), they were not covered in any detail. That was because, at the time the main Code was published, the deprivation of liberty safeguards were still going through the Parliamentary process as part of the Mental Health Bill.[81]

Although the main Code does not cover the deprivation of liberty safeguards, the principles of that Code, and much of its content, are directly relevant to the deprivation of liberty safeguards. It is important that both the

Act and the main Code are adhered to whenever capacity and best interests issues, and the deprivation of liberty safeguards, are being considered. The deprivation of liberty safeguards are in addition to, and do not replace, other safeguards in the Act.

81 The Mental Health Bill was used as a vehicle to amend the Mental Capacity Act 2005 in order to introduce the deprivation of liberty safeguards. The Bill became the Mental Health Act 2007 following completion of its Parliamentary passage.

How should this Code of Practice be used?

This Code of Practice provides guidance to anyone working with and/or caring for adults who lack capacity, but it particularly focuses on those who have a 'duty of care' to a person who lacks the capacity to consent to the care or treatment that is being provided, where that care or treatment may include the need to deprive the person of their liberty. This Code of Practice is also intended to provide information for people who are, or could become, subject to the deprivation of liberty safeguards, and for their families, friends and carers, as well as for anyone who believes that someone is being deprived of their liberty unlawfully.

In this Code of Practice, as throughout the main Code, references to 'lack of capacity' refer to the capacity to make a particular decision at the time it needs to be made. In the context of the deprivation of liberty safeguards, the capacity is specifically the capacity to decide whether or not to consent to care or treatment which involves being kept in a hospital or care home in circumstances that amount to a deprivation of liberty, at the time that decision needs to be made.

What is the legal status of this Code of Practice?

As with the main Code, this Code of Practice is published by the Lord Chancellor, under sections 42 and 43 of the Mental Capacity Act 2005. The purpose of the main Code is to provide guidance and information about how the Act works in practice.

Both this Code and the main Code have statutory force, which means that certain people are under a legal duty to have regard to them. More details can be found in the Introduction to the main Code, which explains the legal status of the Code and who should have regard to it.

In addition to those for whom the main Code is intended, this Code of Practice specifically focuses on providing guidance for:

- people exercising functions relating to the deprivation of liberty safeguards, and
- people acting as a relevant person's representative[82] under the deprivation of liberty safeguards (see chapter 7).

82 A 'relevant person' is a person who is, or may become, deprived of their liberty in accordance with the deprivation of liberty safeguards.

Scenarios used in this Code of Practice

This Code of Practice includes boxes within the main text containing scenarios, using imaginary characters and situations. These are intended to help illustrate what is meant in the main text. They should not in any way be taken as templates for decisions that need to be made in similar situations. Decisions must always be made on the facts of each individual case.

Alternative formats and further information

This Code of Practice is also available in Welsh and can be made available in other formats on request.

1 WHAT ARE THE DEPRIVATION OF LIBERTY SAFEGUARDS AND WHY WERE THEY INTRODUCED?

The deprivation of liberty safeguards were introduced to provide a legal framework around the deprivation of liberty. Specifically, they were introduced to prevent breaches of the European Convention on Human Rights (ECHR) such as the one identified by the judgment of the European Court of Human Rights (ECtHR) in the case of *HL v the United Kingdom*[83] (commonly referred to as the 'Bournewood' judgment). The case concerned an autistic man (HL) with a learning disability, who lacked the capacity to decide whether he should be admitted to hospital for specific treatment. He was admitted on an informal basis under common law in his best interests, but this decision was challenged by HL's carers. In its judgment, the ECtHR held that this admission constituted a deprivation of HL's liberty and, further, that:

- the deprivation of liberty had not been in accordance with 'a procedure prescribed by law' and was, therefore, in breach of Article 5(1) of the ECHR, and
- there had been a contravention of Article 5(4) of the ECHR because HL had no means of applying quickly to a court to see if the deprivation of liberty was lawful.

To prevent further similar breaches of the ECHR, the Mental Capacity Act 2005 has been amended to provide safeguards for people who lack capacity specifically to consent to treatment or care in either a hospital or a care home[84] that, in their own best interests, can only be provided in circumstances that amount to a deprivation of liberty, and where detention under the Mental Health Act 1983 is not appropriate for the person at that time. These safeguards are referred to in this Code of Practice as 'deprivation of liberty safeguards'.

83 (2004) Application No: 00045508/99.

84 Throughout this document, the term 'care home' means a care home registered under the Care Standards Act 2000.

What are the deprivation of liberty safeguards?

1.1 The deprivation of liberty safeguards provide legal protection for those vulnerable people who are, or may become, deprived of their liberty within the meaning of Article 5 of the ECHR in a hospital or care home, whether placed under public or private arrangements. They do not apply to people detained under the Mental Health Act 1983. The safeguards exist to provide a proper legal process and suitable protection in those circumstances where deprivation of liberty appears to be unavoidable, in a person's own best interests.

1.2 Every effort should be made, in both commissioning and providing care or treatment, to prevent deprivation of liberty. If deprivation of liberty cannot be avoided, it should be for no longer than is necessary.

1.3 The safeguards provide for deprivation of liberty to be made lawful through 'standard' or 'urgent' authorisation processes. These processes are designed to prevent arbitrary decisions to deprive a person of liberty and give a right to challenge deprivation of liberty authorisations.

1.4 The deprivation of liberty safeguards mean that a 'managing authority' (i.e. the relevant hospital or care home – see paragraph 3.1) must seek authorisation from a 'supervisory body' in order to be able lawfully to deprive someone of their liberty. Before giving such an authorisation, the supervisory body must be satisfied that the person has a mental disorder[85] and lacks capacity to decide about their residence or treatment. The supervisory body could be a primary care trust, a local authority, Welsh Ministers or a local health board (LHB) (see paragraph 3.3).

85 As defined in section 1 of the Mental Health Act 1983, a mental disorder is any disorder or disability of the mind, apart from dependence on alcohol and drugs. This includes all learning disabilities. The distinction in the Mental Health Act 1983 between learning disabilities depending on whether or not they are associated with abnormally aggressive or seriously irresponsible behaviour is not relevant.

1.5 A decision as to whether or not deprivation of liberty arises will depend on all the circumstances of the case (as explained more fully in chapter 2). It is neither necessary nor appropriate to apply for a deprivation of liberty authorisation for everyone who is in hospital or a care home simply because the person concerned lacks capacity to decide whether or not they should be there. In deciding whether or not an application is necessary, a managing authority should carefully consider whether any restrictions that are, or will be, needed to provide ongoing care or treatment amount to a deprivation of liberty when looked at together.

1.6 The deprivation of liberty safeguards cover:
- how an application for authorisation should be applied for
- how an application for authorisation should be assessed

- the requirements that must be fulfilled for an authorisation to be given
- how an authorisation should be reviewed
- what support and representation must be provided for people who are subject to an authorisation, and
- how people can challenge authorisations.

Who is covered by these safeguards?

1.7 The safeguards apply to people in England and Wales who have a mental disorder and lack capacity to consent to the arrangements made for their care or treatment, but for whom receiving care or treatment in circumstances that amount to a deprivation of liberty may be necessary to protect them from harm and appears to be in their best interests. A large number of these people will be those with significant learning disabilities, or older people who have dementia or some similar disability, but they can also include those who have certain other neurological conditions (for example as a result of a brain injury).

1.8 In order to come within the scope of a deprivation of liberty authorisation, a person must be detained in a hospital or care home, for the purpose of being given care or treatment in circumstances that amount to a deprivation of liberty. The authorisation must relate to the individual concerned and to the hospital or care home in which they are detained.

1.9 For the purposes of Article 5 of the ECHR, there is no distinction in principle between depriving a person who lacks capacity of their liberty for the purpose of treating them for a physical condition, and depriving them of their liberty for treatment of a mental disorder. There will therefore be occasions when people who lack capacity to consent to admission are taken to hospital for treatment of physical illnesses or injuries, and then need to be cared for in circumstances that amount to a deprivation of liberty. In these circumstances, a deprivation of liberty authorisation must be applied for. Consequently, this Code of Practice must be followed and applied in acute hospital settings as well as care homes and mental health units.

1.10 It is important to bear in mind that, while the deprivation of liberty might be for the purpose of giving a person treatment, a deprivation of liberty authorisation does not itself authorise treatment. Treatment that is proposed following authorisation of deprivation of liberty may only be given with the person's consent (if they have capacity to make the decision) or in accordance with the wider provisions of the Mental Capacity Act 2005. More details of this are contained in paragraphs 5.10 to 5.13 of this Code.

1.11 The safeguards cannot apply to people while they are detained in hospital under the Mental Health Act 1983. The safeguards can, however, apply to a person who has previously been detained in hospital under the Mental Health Act 1983. There are other cases in which people who are – or could be – subject to the Mental Health Act 1983 will not meet the eligibility requirement for the safeguards. Chapter 13 of the main Code contains guidance on the relationship between the Mental Capacity Act 2005 and the Mental Health Act 1983 generally, as does the Code of Practice to the Mental Health Act 1983 itself. Paragraphs 4.40 to 4.57 of the present Code explain the relationship of the deprivation of liberty safeguards to the Mental Health Act 1983, and in particular how to assess if a person is eligible to be deprived of their liberty under the safeguards.

1.12 The safeguards relate only to people aged 18 and over. If the issue of depriving a person under the age of 18 of their liberty arises, other safeguards must be considered – such as the existing powers of the court, particularly those under section 25 of the Children Act 1989, or use of the Mental Health Act 1983.

When can someone be deprived of their liberty?

1.13 Depriving someone who lacks the capacity to consent to the arrangements made for their care or treatment of their liberty is a serious matter, and the decision to do so should not be taken lightly. The deprivation of liberty safeguards make it clear that a person may only be deprived of their liberty:
- in their own best interests to protect them from harm
- if it is a proportionate response to the likelihood and seriousness of the harm, and
- if there is no less restrictive alternative.

1.14 Under no circumstances must deprivation of liberty be used as a form of punishment, or for the convenience of professionals, carers or anyone else. Deprivation of liberty should not be extended due to delays in moving people between care or treatment settings, for example when somebody awaits discharge after completing a period of hospital treatment.

Are there any cultural considerations in implementing the safeguards?

1.15 The deprivation of liberty safeguards should not impact in any different way on different racial or ethnic groups, and care should be taken to ensure that the provisions are not operated in a manner that discriminates against particular racial or ethnic groups. It is up to managing authorities and supervisory bodies to ensure that their staff are aware of their responsibilities in this regard and of the need to ensure that the safeguards are operated fairly and equitably.

1.16 Assessors who carry out deprivation of liberty assessments to help decide whether a person should be deprived of their liberty (see chapter 4) should have the necessary skills and experience to take account of people's diverse backgrounds. Accordingly, they will need to have an understanding of, and respect for, the background of the relevant person. Supervisory bodies must take these factors into account when appointing assessors and must seek to appoint the most suitable available person for each case.

1.17 Interpreters should be available, where necessary, to help assessors to communicate not only with the relevant person but also with people with an interest in their care and treatment. An interpreter should be suitably qualified and experienced to enable them to provide effective language and communication support in the particular case concerned, and to offer appropriate assistance to the assessors involved. Information should be made available in other languages where relevant.

1.18 Any decision about the instruction of Independent Mental Capacity Advocates (see paragraphs 3.22 to 3.28) or relevant person's representatives (see chapter 7) should take account of the cultural, national, racial or ethnic background of the relevant person.

Where do the safeguards apply?

1.19 Although the Bournewood judgment was specifically about a patient who lacked capacity to consent to admission to hospital for mental health treatment, the judgment has wider implications that extend to people who lack capacity and who might be deprived of their liberty either in a hospital or in a care home.

1.20 It will only be lawful to deprive somebody of their liberty elsewhere (for example, in their own home, in supported living arrangements other than in a care home, or in a day centre) when following an order of the Court of Protection on a personal welfare matter. In such a case, the Court of Protection order itself provides a legal basis for the deprivation of liberty. This means that a separate deprivation of liberty authorisation under the processes set out in this Code of Practice is not required. More information about applying to the Court of Protection regarding personal welfare matters is given in chapter 10.

How do the safeguards apply to privately arranged care or treatment?

1.21 Under the Human Rights Act 1998, the duty to act in accordance with the ECHR applies only to public authorities. However, all states that have signed up to the ECHR are obliged to make sure that the rights set out in the ECHR apply to all of their citizens. The Mental Capacity Act 2005 therefore makes it clear that the deprivation of liberty safeguards apply to both publicly and privately arranged care or treatment.

How do the safeguards relate to the rest of the Mental Capacity Act 2005?

1.22 The deprivation of liberty safeguards are in addition to, and do not replace, other safeguards in the Mental Capacity Act 2005. This means that decisions made, and actions taken, for a person who is subject to a deprivation of liberty authorisation must fulfil the requirements of the Act in the same way as for any other person. In particular, any action taken under the deprivation of liberty safeguards must be in line with the principles of the Act:

- A person must be assumed to have capacity to make a decision unless it is established that they lack the capacity to make that decision.
- A person is not to be treated as unable to make a decision unless all practicable steps to help them to do so have been taken without success.
- A person is not to be treated as unable to make a decision merely because they make an unwise decision.
- An act done, or decision made, under the Act for or on behalf of a person who lacks capacity must be done, or made, in their best interests.
- Before the act is done, or the decision is made, regard must be had to whether the purpose for which it is needed can be as effectively achieved in a way that is less restrictive of the person's rights and freedom of action.

These principles are set out in chapter 2 of the main Code and explained in more detail in chapters 3 to 6 of the same document. Paragraph 5.13 of the main Code contains a checklist of factors that need to be taken into account in determining a person's best interests.

2 WHAT IS DEPRIVATION OF LIBERTY?

There is no simple definition of deprivation of liberty. The question of whether the steps taken by staff or institutions in relation to a person amount to a deprivation of that person's liberty is ultimately a legal question, and only the courts can determine the law. This guidance seeks to assist staff and institutions in considering whether or not the steps they are taking, or proposing to take, amount to a deprivation of a person's liberty. The deprivation of liberty safeguards give best interests assessors the authority to make recommendations about proposed deprivations of liberty, and supervisory bodies the power to give authorisations that deprive people of their liberty.

This chapter provides guidance for staff and institutions on how to assess whether particular steps they are taking, or proposing to take, might amount to a deprivation of liberty, based on existing case law. It also considers what other factors may be taken into account when considering the issue of deprivation of liberty, including, importantly, what is permissible under the

Mental Capacity Act 2005 in relation to restraint or restriction. Finally, it provides a summary of some of the most important cases to date.

Further legal developments may occur after this guidance has been issued, and healthcare and social care staff need to keep themselves informed of legal developments that may have a bearing on their practice.

What does case law say to date?

2.1 The European Court of Human Rights (ECtHR) has drawn a distinction between the deprivation of liberty of an individual (which is unlawful, unless authorised) and restrictions on the liberty of movement of an individual.

2.2 The ECtHR made it clear that the question of whether someone has been deprived of liberty depends on the particular circumstances of the case. Specifically, the ECtHR said in its October 2004 judgment in *HL v the United Kingdom*:

> 'to determine whether there has been a deprivation of liberty, the starting-point must be the specific situation of the individual concerned and account must be taken of a whole range of factors arising in a particular case such as the type, duration, effects and manner of implementation of the measure in question. The distinction between a deprivation of, and restriction upon, liberty is merely one of degree or intensity and not one of nature or substance.'

2.3 The difference between deprivation of liberty and restriction upon liberty is one of degree or intensity. It may therefore be helpful to envisage a scale, which moves from 'restraint' or 'restriction' to 'deprivation of liberty'. Where an individual is on the scale will depend on the concrete circumstances of the individual and may change over time. For more information on how the Act defines restraint, see paragraphs 2.8–2.12.

2.4 Although the guidance in this chapter includes descriptions of past decisions of the courts, which should be used to help evaluate whether deprivation of liberty may be occurring, each individual case must be assessed on its own circumstances. No two cases are likely to be identical, so it is important to be aware of previous court judgments and the factors that the courts have identified as important.

2.5 The ECtHR and UK courts have determined a number of cases about deprivation of liberty. Their judgments indicate that the following factors can be relevant to identifying whether steps taken involve more than restraint and amount to a deprivation of liberty. It is important to remember that this list is not exclusive; other factors may arise in future in particular cases.

- Restraint is used, including sedation, to admit a person to an institution where that person is resisting admission.
- Staff exercise complete and effective control over the care and movement of a person for a significant period.

- Staff exercise control over assessments, treatment, contacts and residence.
- A decision has been taken by the institution that the person will not be released into the care of others, or permitted to live elsewhere, unless the staff in the institution consider it appropriate.
- A request by carers for a person to be discharged to their care is refused.
- The person is unable to maintain social contacts because of restrictions placed on their access to other people.
- The person loses autonomy because they are under continuous supervision and control.

There is more information on some relevant cases at the end of this chapter (paragraphs 2.17–2.23).

How can deprivation of liberty be identified?

2.6 In determining whether deprivation of liberty has occurred, or is likely to occur, decision-makers need to consider all the facts in a particular case. There is unlikely to be any simple definition that can be applied in every case, and it is probable that no single factor will, in itself, determine whether the overall set of steps being taken in relation to the relevant person amount to a deprivation of liberty. In general, the decision-maker should always consider the following:
- All the circumstances of each and every case
- What measures are being taken in relation to the individual? When are they required? For what period do they endure? What are the effects of any restraints or restrictions on the individual? Why are they necessary? What aim do they seek to meet?
- What are the views of the relevant person, their family or carers? Do any of them object to the measures?
- How are any restraints or restrictions implemented? Do any of the constraints on the individual's personal freedom go beyond 'restraint' or 'restriction' to the extent that they constitute a deprivation of liberty?
- Are there any less restrictive options for delivering care or treatment that avoid deprivation of liberty altogether?
- Does the cumulative effect of all the restrictions imposed on the person amount to a deprivation of liberty, even if individually they would not?

What practical steps can be taken to reduce the risk of deprivation of liberty occurring?

2.7 There are many ways in which providers and commissioners of care can reduce the risk of taking steps that amount to a deprivation of liberty, by minimising the restrictions imposed and ensuring that

decisions are taken with the involvement of the relevant person and their family, friends and carers. The processes for staff to follow are:
- Make sure that all decisions are taken (and reviewed) in a structured way, and reasons for decisions recorded.
- Follow established good practice for care planning.
- Make a proper assessment of whether the person lacks capacity to decide whether or not to accept the care or treatment proposed, in line with the principles of the Act (see chapter 3 of the main Code for further guidance).
- Before admitting a person to hospital or residential care in circumstances that may amount to a deprivation of liberty, consider whether the person's needs could be met in a less restrictive way. Any restrictions placed on the person while in hospital or in a care home must be kept to the minimum necessary, and should be in place for the shortest possible period.
- Take proper steps to help the relevant person retain contact with family, friends and carers. Where local advocacy services are available, their involvement should be encouraged to support the person and their family, friends and carers.
- Review the care plan on an ongoing basis. It may well be helpful to include an independent element, possibly via an advocacy service, in the review.

What does the Act mean by 'restraint'?

2.8 Section 6(4) of the Act states that someone is using restraint if they:
- use force – or threaten to use force – to make someone do something that they are resisting, or
- restrict a person's freedom of movement, whether they are resisting or not.

2.9 Paragraphs 6.40 to 6.48 of the main Code contain guidance about the appropriate use of restraint. Restraint is appropriate when it is used to prevent harm to the person who lacks capacity and it is a proportionate response to the likelihood and seriousness of harm. Appropriate use of restraint falls short of deprivation of liberty.

2.10 Preventing a person from leaving a care home or hospital unaccompanied because there is a risk that they would try to cross a road in a dangerous way, for example, is likely to be seen as a proportionate restriction or restraint to prevent the person from coming to harm. That would be unlikely, in itself, to constitute a deprivation of liberty. Similarly, locking a door to guard against immediate harm is unlikely, in itself, to amount to a deprivation of liberty.

2.11 The ECtHR has also indicated that the duration of any restrictions is a relevant factor when considering whether or not a person is deprived of their liberty. This suggests that actions that are immediately necessary to prevent harm may not, in themselves, constitute a deprivation of liberty.

2.12 However, where the restriction or restraint is frequent, cumulative and ongoing, or if there are other factors present, then care providers should consider whether this has gone beyond permissible restraint, as defined in the Act. If so, then they must either apply for authorisation under the deprivation of liberty safeguards (as explained in chapter 3) or change their care provision to reduce the level of restraint.

How does the use of restraint apply within a hospital or when taking someone to a hospital or a care home?

Within a hospital

2.13 If a person in hospital for mental health treatment, or being considered for admission to a hospital for mental health treatment, needs to be restrained, this is likely to indicate that they are objecting to treatment or to being in hospital. The care providers should consider whether the need for restraint means the person is objecting (see paragraph 4.46 of this Code for guidance on how to decide whether a person is objecting for this purpose). A person who objects to mental health treatment, and who meets the criteria for detention under the Mental Health Act 1983, is normally ineligible for an authorisation under the deprivation of liberty safeguards. If the care providers believe it is necessary to detain the person, they may wish to consider use of the Mental Health Act 1983.

Taking someone to a hospital or a care home

2.14 Transporting a person who lacks capacity from their home, or another location, to a hospital or care home will not usually amount to a deprivation of liberty (for example, to take them to hospital by ambulance in an emergency.) Even where there is an expectation that the person will be deprived of liberty within the care home or hospital, it is unlikely that the journey itself will constitute a deprivation of liberty so that an authorisation is needed before the journey commences. In almost all cases, it is likely that a person can be lawfully taken to a hospital or a care home under the wider provisions of the Act, as long as it is considered that being in the hospital or care home will be in their best interests.

2.15 In a very few cases, there may be exceptional circumstances where taking a person to a hospital or a care home amounts to a deprivation of liberty, for example where it is necessary to do more than persuade or restrain the person for the purpose of transportation, or where the journey is exceptionally long. In such cases, it may be necessary to seek an order from the Court of Protection to ensure that the journey is taken on a lawful basis.

How should managing authorities avoid unnecessary applications for standard authorisations?

2.16 While it is unlawful to deprive a person of their liberty without authorisation, managing authorities should take into consideration that unnecessary applications for standard authorisations in cases that do not in fact involve depriving a person of liberty may place undue stress upon the person being assessed and on their families or carers. Moreover, consideration must always be given to the possibility of less restrictive options for delivering care or treatment that avoid deprivation of liberty altogether.

Examples of case law

2.17 To provide further guidance, the following paragraphs contain short descriptions of what appear to be the significant features of recent or important cases in England and Wales and the ECtHR dealing with deprivation of liberty. Remember that:
- these descriptions are for guidance only
- only the courts can authoritatively determine the law; and
- the courts are likely to give judgments in cases after this guidance is issued. Staff will need to keep up to date and take account of further relevant legal developments.

Cases where the courts found that the steps taken did not involve a deprivation of liberty

2.18 *LLBC v TG* (judgment of High Court of 14 November 2007)

TG was a 78-year-old man with dementia and cognitive impairment. TG was resident in a care home, but was admitted to hospital with pneumonia and septicaemia. While he was in hospital, there was a dispute between the local authority and TG's daughter and granddaughter about TG's future. The daughter and granddaughter wanted TG to live with them, but the local authority believed that TG needed 24-hour care in a residential care home.

The council obtained an order from the court, directing that TG be delivered to the care home identified as appropriate by the council. Neither the daughter nor granddaughter was informed that a court hearing was taking place. That order was subsequently changed and TG was able to live with his daughter and granddaughter.

TG's daughter and granddaughter claimed that the period of time he had spent at the care home amounted to a deprivation of his liberty. The judge considered that there was no deprivation of liberty, but the case was borderline. The key factors in his decision included:
- The care home was an ordinary care home where only ordinary restrictions of liberty applied.
- The family were able to visit TG on a largely unrestricted basis and were entitled to take him out from the home for outings

- TG was personally compliant and expressed himself as happy in the care home. He had lived in a local authority care home for over three years and was objectively content with his situation there.
- There was no occasion where TG was objectively deprived of his liberty.

The judge said:

> 'Whilst I agree that the circumstances of the present case may be near the borderline between mere restrictions of liberty and Article 5 detention, I have come to the conclusion that, looked at as a whole and having regard to all the relevant circumstances, the placement of TG in Towerbridge falls short of engaging Article 5.'

2.19 *Nielsen v Denmark (ECtHR;* (1988) 11 EHRR 175)

The mother of a 12-year-old boy arranged for his admission to the state hospital's psychiatric ward. The boy had a nervous disorder and required treatment in the form of regular talks and environmental therapy. The treatment given, and the conditions under which it was administered, was appropriate. The duration of treatment was 5½ months. The boy, however, applied to the ECtHR, feeling that he had been deprived of his liberty.

The restrictions placed on the applicant's freedom of movement and contacts with the outside world were not much different from restrictions that might be imposed on a child in an ordinary hospital. The door of the ward was locked to prevent children exposing themselves to danger or running around disturbing other patients. The applicant was free to leave the ward with permission and to go out if accompanied by a member of staff. He was able to visit his family and friends, and towards the end of his stay to go to school.

The Court held:

> 'The restrictions imposed on the applicant were not of a nature or degree similar to the cases of deprivation of liberty specified in paragraph (1) of Article 5. In particular, he was not detained as a person of unsound mind. .... Indeed, the restrictions to which the applicant was subject were no more than the normal requirements for the care of a child of 12 years of age receiving treatment in hospital. The conditions in which the applicant stayed thus did not, in principle, differ from those obtaining in many hospital wards where children with physical disorders are treated.'

It concluded:

> 'the hospitalisation of the applicant did not amount to a deprivation of liberty within the meaning of Article 5, but was a responsible exercise by his mother of her custodial rights in the interests of the child.'

2.20 *HM v Switzerland (ECtHR;* (2002) 38 EHRR 314)

An 84-year-old woman was placed indefinitely in a nursing home by state authorities. She had had the possibility of staying at home and being cared for there, but she and her son had refused to co-operate with the relevant care association, and her living conditions had subsequently deteriorated. The state authorities placed her in the home in order to provide her with necessary medical care and satisfactory living conditions and hygiene.

The woman was not placed in the secure ward of the home but was free to move within the home and to have social contacts with the outside world. She was initially undecided as to what solution she preferred and, after moving into the home, the applicant had agreed to stay there. However, she subsequently applied to the courts saying that she had been deprived of her liberty.

The Court held that she had not been deprived of her liberty:

> 'Bearing these elements in mind, in particular the fact that [the authorities] had ordered the applicant's placement in the nursing home in her own interests in order to provide her with the necessary medical care and satisfactory living conditions and standards of hygiene, and also taking into consideration the comparable circumstances of *Nielsen v Denmark* [see case summary above], the Court concludes that in the circumstances of the present case the applicant's placement in the nursing home did not amount to a deprivation of liberty within the meaning of Article 5(1), but was a responsible measure taken by the competent authorities in the applicant's best interests.'

Cases where the courts have found that the steps taken involve a deprivation of liberty

2.21 *DE and JE v Surrey County Council (SCC)* (High Court judgment of 29 December 2006)

DE was a 76-year-old man who, following a major stroke, had become blind and had significant short-term memory impairment. He also had dementia and lacked capacity to decide where he should live, but was still often able to express his wishes with some clarity and force.

DE was married to JE. In August 2003, DE was living at home with JE. There was an occasion when JE felt that she could not care for DE, and placed him on a chair on the pavement in front of the house and called the police. The local authority then placed him in two care homes, referred to in the judgment of the court as the X home and the Y home.

Within the care homes, DE had a very substantial degree of freedom and lots of contact with the outside world. He was never subject to physical or chemical restraint.

DE repeatedly expressed the wish to live with JE, and JE also wanted DE to live with her. SCC would not agree to DE returning to live with, or visit, JE and made it clear that if JE were to persist in an attempt to remove DE, SCC would contact the police. DE and JE applied to the courts that this was a deprivation of his liberty.

In his judgment, Justice Munby said:

> 'The fundamental issue in this case ... is whether DE has been and is deprived of his liberty to leave the X home and whether DE has been and is deprived of his liberty to leave the Y home. And when I refer to leaving the X home and the Y home, I do not mean leaving for the purpose of some trip or outing approved by SCC or by those managing the institution; I mean leaving in the sense of removing himself permanently in order to live where and with whom he chooses, specifically removing himself to live at home with JE.'

He then said:

> 'DE was not and is not "free to leave", and was and is, in that sense, completely under the control of [the local authority], because, as [counsel for DE] put it, it was and is [the local authority] who decides the essential matters of where DE can live, whether he can leave and whether he can be with JE.'

He concluded:

> 'The simple reality is that DE will be permitted to leave the institution in which [the local authority] has placed him and be released to the care of JE only as and when, – if ever; probably never, – [the local authority] considers it appropriate. [The local authority's] motives may be the purest, but in my judgment, [it] has been and is continuing to deprive DE of his liberty.'

2.22 HL v United Kingdom (ECtHR; (2004) 40 EHRR 761)

A 48-year-old man who had had autism since birth was unable to speak and his level of understanding was limited. He was frequently agitated and had a history of self-harming behaviour. He lacked the capacity to consent to treatment.

For over 30 years, he was cared for in Bournewood Hospital. In 1994, he was entrusted to carers and for three years he lived successfully with his carers. Following an incident of self-harm at a day centre on 22 July 1997, the applicant was taken to Bournewood Hospital where he was re-admitted informally (not under the Mental Health Act 1983).

The carers wished to have the applicant released to their care, which the hospital refused. The carers were unable to visit him.

In its judgment in *HL v the United Kingdom*, the ECtHR said that:

> 'the key factor in the present case [is] that the health care professionals treating and managing the applicant exercised complete and effective control over his care and movements from the moment he presented acute behavioural problems on July 22, 1997 to the date when he was compulsorily detained on October 29, 1997.

> 'His responsible medical officer (Dr M) was clear that, had the applicant resisted admission or tried to leave thereafter, she would have prevented him from doing so and would have considered his involuntary committal under s. 3 of the 1983 Act; indeed, as soon as the Court of Appeal indicated that his appeal would be allowed, he was compulsorily detained under the 1983 Act. The correspondence between the applicant's carers and Dr M reflects both the carer's wish to have the applicant immediately released to their care and, equally, the clear intention of Dr M and the other relevant health care professionals to exercise strict control over his assessment, treatment, contacts and, notably, movement and residence; the applicant would only be released from hospital to the care of Mr and Mrs E as and when those professionals considered it appropriate. ... it was clear from the above noted correspondence that the applicant's contact with his carers was directed and controlled by the hospital, his carers visiting him for the first time after his admission on 2 November 1997.

> 'Accordingly, the concrete situation was that the applicant was under continuous supervision and control and was not free to leave.'

2.23 Storck v Germany (ECtHR; (2005) 43 EHRR 96)

A young woman was placed by her father in a psychiatric institution on occasions in 1974 and 1975. In July 1977, at the age of 18, she was placed again in a psychiatric institution. She was kept in a locked ward and was under the continuous supervision and control of the clinic personnel and was not free to leave the clinic during her entire stay of 20 months. When she attempted to flee, she was shackled. When she succeeded one time, she was brought back by the police. She was unable to maintain regular contact with the outside world.

She applied to the courts on the basis that she had been deprived of her liberty. There was a dispute about whether she consented to her confinement.

The Court noted:

> 'the applicant, on several occasions, had tried to flee from the clinic. She had to be shackled in order to prevent her from absconding and had to be brought back to the clinic by the police when she managed to escape on one occasion. Under these circumstances, the Court is unable to discern any factual basis for the assumption that the applicant – presuming that she had the capacity to consent – agreed to her continued stay in the clinic. In the alternative, assuming that the applicant was no longer capable of consenting following her treatment with strong medication, she cannot, in any event, be considered to have validly agreed to her stay in the clinic.'

2.24 These cases reinforce the need to carefully consider all the specific circumstances of the relevant individual before deciding whether or not a person is being deprived of their liberty. They also underline the vital importance of involving family, friends and carers in this decision-making process: a significant feature of a number of the cases that have come before the courts is a difference of opinion or communication issue between the commissioners or providers of care and family members and carers.

3 HOW AND WHEN CAN DEPRIVATION OF LIBERTY BE APPLIED FOR AND AUTHORISED?

There are some circumstances in which depriving a person, who lacks capacity to consent to the arrangements made for their care or treatment, of their liberty is necessary to protect them from harm, and is in their best interests.

Deprivation of liberty can be authorised by supervisory bodies (primary care trusts (PCTs), local authorities, Welsh Ministers or local health boards (LHBs). To obtain authorisation to deprive someone of their liberty, managing authorities have to apply for an authorisation following the processes set out in this chapter.[86] Once an application has been received, the supervisory body must then follow the assessment processes set out in chapter 4 before it can authorise deprivation of liberty. It should be borne in mind that a deprivation of liberty authorisation does not, in itself, give authority to treat someone. This issue is covered in paragraphs 5.10 to 5.13.

In the vast majority of cases, it should be possible to plan in advance so that a standard authorisation can be obtained before the deprivation of liberty begins. There may, however, be some exceptional cases where the need for the deprivation of liberty is so urgent that it is in the best interests of the person for it to begin while the application is being considered. In that case, the care home or hospital may give an urgent authorisation for up to seven days (see chapter 6).

86 If a person is lawfully deprived of liberty in a care home or hospital as **a consequence of an order of the Court of Protection**, there is no need to apply for an authorisation. However, once the order of the Court of Protection has expired, for lawful deprivation of liberty to continue authorisation must be obtained by following the processes set out in this chapter.

How, in summary, can deprivation of liberty be authorised?

3.1 A **managing authority** has responsibility for applying for authorisation of deprivation of liberty for any person who may come within the scope of the deprivation of liberty safeguards:
- In the case of an NHS hospital, the managing authority is the NHS body responsible for the running of the hospital in which the relevant person is, or is to be, a resident.
- In the case of a care home or a private hospital, the managing authority will be the person registered, or required to be registered, under part 2 of the Care Standards Act 2000 in respect of the hospital or care home.

3.2 If a healthcare or social care professional thinks that an authorisation is needed, they should inform the managing authority. This might be as a result of a care review or needs assessment but could happen at any other time too. (See chapter 9 for guidance on action to take if there is a concern that a person is already being deprived of their liberty, without authorisation.)

3.3 A **supervisory body** is responsible for considering requests for authorisations, commissioning the required assessments (see chapter 4) and, where all the assessments agree, authorising the deprivation of liberty:
- Where the deprivation of liberty safeguards are applied to a person in a hospital situated in England, the supervisory body will be:
  - if a PCT commissions[87] the relevant care or treatment (or it is commissioned on the PCT's behalf), that PCT
  - if the Welsh Ministers or an LHB commissions the relevant care and treatment in England, the Welsh Ministers, or
  - in any other case, the PCT for the area in which the hospital is situated.
- Where the deprivation of liberty safeguards are applied to a person in a hospital situated in Wales, the supervisory body will be the Welsh Ministers or an LHB **unless** a PCT commissions the relevant care and treatment in Wales, in which case the PCT will be the supervisory body.
- Where the deprivation of liberty safeguards are applied to a person in a care home, whether situated in England or Wales,

the supervisory body will be the local authority for the area in which the person is ordinarily resident. However, if the person is not ordinarily resident in the area of any local authority (for example a person of no fixed abode), the supervisory body will be the local authority for the area in which the care home is situated.[88]

87 Guidance on establishing the responsible commissioner can be found at http://www.dh.gov.uk/en/Publicationsandstatistics/Publications/PublicationsPolicyAndGuidance/DH_078466
88 To work out the place of ordinary residence, the usual mechanisms under the National Assistance Act 1948 apply (see www.dh.gov.uk/en/Publicationsandstatistics/Publications/PublicationsPolicyAndGuidance/DH_113627 – new website address inserted by the authors). Any unresolved questions about the ordinary residence of a person will be handled by the Secretary of State or by the Welsh Ministers. Until a decision is made, the local authority that received the application must act as the supervisory body. After the decision is made, the local authority of ordinary residence must become the supervisory body. Regulations 17 to 19 of the Mental Capacity (Deprivation of Liberty: Standard Authorisations, Assessments and Ordinary Residence) Regulations 2008 set out, for England, arrangements that are to have effect while any question as to the ordinary residence of a person is determined in a case in which a local authority has received a request for a standard authorisation or a request to decide whether there is an unauthorised deprivation of liberty.

3.4 There are two types of authorisation: standard and urgent. A managing authority must request a standard authorisation when it appears likely that, at some time during the next 28 days, someone will be accommodated in its hospital or care home in circumstances that amount to a deprivation of liberty within the meaning of Article 5 of the European Convention on Human Rights. The request must be made to the supervisory body. Whenever possible, authorisation should be obtained in advance. Where this is not possible, and the managing authority believes it is necessary to deprive someone of their liberty in their best interests **before** the standard authorisation process can be completed, the managing authority must itself give an urgent authorisation and then obtain standard authorisation within seven calendar days (see chapter 6).

3.5 The flowchart at Annex 1 gives an overview of how the deprivation of liberty safeguards process should operate.

How should managing authorities decide whether to apply for an authorisation?

3.6 Managing authorities should have a procedure in place that identifies:
- whether deprivation of liberty is or may be necessary in a particular case
- what steps they should take to assess whether to seek authorisation
- whether they have taken all practical and reasonable steps to avoid a deprivation of liberty
- what action they should take if they do need to request an authorisation
- how they should review cases where authorisation is or may be necessary, and

- who should take the necessary action.

A flowchart that can be used to help develop such a procedure is at Annex 2.

What is the application process?

3.7 A managing authority must apply for a standard authorisation. The application should be made in writing to the supervisory body. A standard form is available for this purpose.

3.8 In England, the request from a managing authority for a standard authorisation must include:
- the name and gender of the relevant person
- the age of the relevant person or, where this is not known, whether the managing authority reasonably believes that the relevant person is aged 18 years or older
- the address at which the relevant person is currently located, and the telephone number at the address
- the name, address and telephone number of the managing authority and the name of the person within the managing authority who is dealing with the request
- the purpose for which the authorisation is requested
- the date from which the authorisation is sought, and
- whether the managing authority has given an urgent authorisation and, if so, the date on which it expires.

3.9 A request for a standard authorisation must also include, if it is available or could reasonably be obtained by the managing authority:
- any medical information relating to the relevant person's health that the managing authority reasonably considers to be relevant to the proposed restrictions to their liberty
- the diagnosis of the mental disorder (within the meaning of the Mental Health Act 1983 but disregarding any exclusion for persons with learning disability) from which the relevant person is suffering
- any relevant care plans and needs assessments
- the racial, ethnic or national origins of the relevant person
- whether the relevant person has any special communication needs
- details of the proposed restrictions on the relevant person's liberty
- whether it is necessary for an Independent Mental Capacity Advocate (IMCA) to be instructed
- where the purpose of the proposed restrictions to the relevant person's liberty is to give treatment, whether the relevant person has made an advance decision that may be valid and applicable to some or all of that treatment
- whether there is an existing standard authorisation in relation to the detention of the relevant person and, if so, the date of the expiry of that authorisation

- whether the relevant person is subject to any requirements of the Mental Health Act 1983, and
- the name, address and telephone number of:
  - anyone named by the relevant person as someone to be consulted about their welfare
  - anyone engaged in caring for the person or interested in their welfare
  - any donee of a Lasting Power of Attorney ('donee') granted by the person
  - any deputy appointed for the person by the court, and
  - any IMCA who has already been instructed.

If there is an existing authorisation, information that has not changed does not have to be resupplied.

3.10 In Wales, the request from a managing authority for a standard authorisation must include:
- the name of the relevant person
- the name, address and telephone number of the managing authority
- the reasons why the managing authority considers that the relevant person is being or will be detained in circumstances which amount to a deprivation of liberty
- the reasons why the managing authority considers that the relevant person satisfies the qualifying requirements
- details of any urgent authorisation
- information or documents in support of why the relevant person satisfies the qualifying requirements
- the name, address and telephone number of any person who has an interest in the welfare of the relevant person, and
- details of any relevant valid and applicable advance decision.

Where should applications be sent?

3.11 If the application is being made by a care home, the application must be sent to the local authority for the area in which the relevant person is ordinarily resident. If the relevant person is not ordinarily resident in the area of any local authority (for example, is of no fixed abode), if the care home does not know where the person currently lives, or if the person does not live in England or Wales, the application should be sent to the local authority in whose area the care home is located.

3.12 When the application is being made by a hospital:
- if the care is commissioned by a PCT, the application should be sent to that PCT
- if the care is commissioned by the Welsh Ministers, the application should be sent to the LHB for the area in which the relevant person is ordinarily resident
- if the care is commissioned by an LHB, the application should be sent to that LHB, and

- in any other case (for example, care that is commissioned privately), the application should be sent to the PCT for the area in which the relevant hospital is situated.

3.13 An application sent to the wrong supervisory body can be passed on to the correct supervisory body without the managing authority needing to reapply. But the managing authority should make every effort to establish which is the correct supervisory body to minimise delays in handling the application. (Footnote 8 explains how place of ordinary residence is determined and how disputes about the place of ordinary residence will be resolved.)

3.14 The managing authority must keep a written record of each request made for a standard authorisation and the reasons for making the request.

Who should be informed that an application has been made?

3.15 The managing authority should tell the relevant person's family, friends and carers, and any IMCA already involved in the relevant person's case, that it has applied for an authorisation of deprivation of liberty, unless it is impractical or impossible to do so, or undesirable in terms of the interests of the relevant person's health or safety. Anyone who is engaged in caring for the relevant person or interested in their welfare, or who has been named by them as a person to consult, must be given the opportunity to input their views on whether deprivation of liberty is in the best interests of the relevant person, as part of the best interests assessment (see paragraphs 4.58 to 4.76), as far as is practical and appropriate. The views of the relevant person about who to inform and consult should be taken into account.

3.16 The managing authority must notify the supervisory body if it is satisfied that there is no one who should be consulted in determining the relevant person's best interests, except those providing care and treatment for the relevant person in a professional capacity or for remuneration. In such a case, the supervisory body must instruct an IMCA to represent and support the relevant person before any assessments take place (see paragraphs 3.22 to 3.27 regarding the rights and role of an IMCA instructed in these circumstances).

What action does the supervisory body need to take when it receives an application for authorisation?

3.17 When it receives an application for authorisation of deprivation of liberty, the supervisory body must, as soon as is practical and possible:
- consider whether the request is appropriate and should be pursued, and

- seek any further information that it requires from the managing authority to help it with the decision.

If the supervisory body has any doubts about proceeding with the request, it should seek to resolve them with the managing authority.

3.18 Supervisory bodies should have a procedure in place that identifies the action they should take, who should take it and within what timescale. As far as practical and possible, they should communicate the procedure to managing authorities and give them the relevant contact details for making an application. The flowchart at Annex 3 summarises the process that a supervisory body should follow on receipt of a request from a managing authority for a standard deprivation of liberty authorisation.

Can an application for authorisation be made in advance?

3.19 A standard authorisation comes into force when it is given, or at any later time specified in the authorisation. Paragraph 3.4 refers to the timescales for initially applying for authorisations: 28 days are allowed so that authorisations can usually be sought as part of care planning (such as planning of discharge from hospital). There is no statutory limit on how far in advance of the expiry of one authorisation a fresh authorisation can be sought. Clearly, however, an authorisation should not be applied for too far in advance as this may prevent an assessor from making an accurate assessment of what the person's circumstances will be at the time the authorisation will come into force.

3.20 If a supervisory body considers that an application for an authorisation has been made too far in advance, it should raise the matter with the managing authority. The outcome may be an agreement with the managing authority that the application should be withdrawn, to be resubmitted at a more appropriate time.

What happens when the managing authority and the supervisory body are the same organisation?

3.21 In some cases, a single organisation will be both supervisory body and managing authority – for example, where a local authority itself provides a residential care home, rather than purchasing the service from another organisation. This does not prevent it from acting in both capacities. However, in England the regulations specify that in such a situation the best interests assessor cannot be an employee of the supervisory body/managing authority, or providing services to it. For example, in a case involving a local authority care home, the best interests assessor could be an NHS employee or an independent practitioner. (See paragraphs 4.13 and 4.60 for full details of who can be a best interests assessor.) There are similar provisions for Wales.

When should an IMCA be instructed?

3.22 If there is nobody appropriate to consult, other than people engaged in providing care or treatment for the relevant person in a professional capacity[89] or for remuneration, the managing authority must notify the supervisory body when it submits the application for the deprivation of liberty authorisation. The supervisory body must then instruct an IMCA straight away to represent the person. It is particularly important that the IMCA is instructed quickly if an urgent authorisation has been given, so that they can make a meaningful input at a very early stage in the process. (See paragraph 3.28 for other stages in the deprivation of liberty safeguards process when an IMCA must or may be instructed.)

[89] A friend or family member is not considered to be acting in a professional capacity simply because they have been appointed as the person's representative for a previous authorisation.

3.23 Chapter 10 of the main Code ('What is the new Independent Mental Capacity Advocate service and how does it work?') describes the wider rights and role of an IMCA. Supervisory bodies should follow the guidance in that chapter in identifying an IMCA who is suitably qualified to represent the relevant person. However, it is also important to note that an IMCA instructed at this initial stage of the deprivation of liberty safeguards process has additional rights and responsibilities compared to an IMCA more generally instructed under the Mental Capacity Act 2005. IMCAs in this context have the right to:

- as they consider appropriate, give information or make submissions to assessors, which assessors must take into account in carrying out their assessments
- receive copies of any assessments from the supervisory body
- receive a copy of any standard authorisation given by the supervisory body
- be notified by the supervisory body if they are unable to give a standard authorisation because one or more of the deprivation of liberty assessments did not meet the qualifying requirements
- receive a copy of any urgent authorisation from the managing authority
- receive from the managing authority a copy of any notice declining to extend the duration of an urgent authorisation
- receive from the supervisory body a copy of any notice that an urgent authorisation has ceased to be in force, and
- apply to the Court of Protection for permission to take the relevant person's case to the Court in connection with a matter relating to the giving or refusal of a standard or urgent authorisation (in the same way as any other third party can).

The assessment and authorisation processes are described in chapters 4 and 5.

3.24 IMCAs will need to familiarise themselves with the relevant person's circumstances and to consider what they may need to tell any of the assessors during the course of the assessment process.

They will also need to consider whether they have any concerns about the outcome of the assessment process.

3.25 Differences of opinion between an IMCA and an assessor should ideally be resolved while the assessment is still in progress. Where there are significant disagreements between an IMCA and one or more of the assessors that cannot be resolved between them, the supervisory body should be informed before the assessment is finalised. The supervisory body should then consider what action might be appropriate, including perhaps convening a meeting to discuss the matter. Wherever possible, differences of opinion should be resolved informally in order to minimise the need for an IMCA to make an application to the Court of Protection. However, an IMCA should not be discouraged from making an application to the Court of Protection should they consider it necessary. (Chapter 15 of the main Code ('What are the best ways to settle disagreements and disputes about issues covered in the Act?') contains general guidance about the resolution of disputes arising under the Act.)

3.26 An IMCA will also need to consider whether they have any concerns about the giving of an urgent authorisation (see chapter 6), and whether it would be appropriate to challenge the giving of such an authorisation via the Court of Protection.

3.27 Once a relevant person's representative is appointed (see chapter 7), the duties imposed on the IMCA cease to apply. The IMCA may, however, still apply to the Court of Protection for permission to take the relevant person's case to the Court in connection with the giving of a standard authorisation; but, in doing so, the IMCA must take account of the views of the relevant person's representative.

Other circumstances in which an IMCA must or may be instructed

3.28 An IMCA must also be instructed during gaps in the appointment of a relevant person's representative (for instance, if a new representative is being sought – see paragraphs 7.34 to 7.36). In addition, an IMCA may be instructed at any time where:
- the relevant person does not have a paid 'professional' representative
- the relevant person or their representative requests that an IMCA is instructed to help them, or
- a supervisory body believes that instructing an IMCA will help to ensure that the person's rights are protected (see paragraphs 7.37 to 7.41).

4 WHAT IS THE ASSESSMENT PROCESS FOR A STANDARD AUTHORISATION OF DEPRIVATION OF LIBERTY?

When a supervisory body gives a standard authorisation of deprivation of liberty, the managing authority may lawfully deprive the relevant person of their liberty in the hospital or care home named in the authorisation.

This chapter describes the assessments that have to be undertaken in order for a standard authorisation to be given. It also sets out who is eligible to undertake the assessments.

What assessments are required before giving a standard authorisation?

4.1 As soon as the supervisory body has confirmed that the request for a standard authorisation should be pursued, it must obtain the relevant assessments to ascertain whether the qualifying requirements of the deprivation of liberty safeguards are met. The supervisory body has a legal responsibility to select assessors who are both suitable and eligible. Assessments must be completed within 21 days for a standard deprivation of liberty authorisation, or, where an urgent authorisation has been given, before the urgent authorisation expires.

4.2 The assessments (described in paragraphs 4.23 to 4.76) are:
- age assessment (paragraphs 4.23 and 4.24)
- no refusals assessment (paragraphs 4.25 to 4.28)
- mental capacity assessment (paragraphs 4.29 to 4.32)
- mental health assessment (paragraphs 4.33 to 4.39)
- eligibility assessment (paragraphs 4.40 to 4.57), and
- best interests assessment (paragraphs 4.58 to 4.76).

Standard forms are available for completion by each of the assessors.

4.3 If the person being assessed is not currently in the supervisory body's area, the supervisory body should seek, as far as is practical and possible, to arrange to use assessors based near where the person currently is.

Using equivalent assessments

4.4 The Act states that where an 'equivalent assessment' to any of these assessments has already been obtained, it may be relied upon instead of obtaining a fresh assessment.

4.5 An equivalent assessment is an assessment:
- that has been carried out in the last 12 months, not necessarily for the purpose of a deprivation of liberty authorisation (where the required assessment is an age assessment, there is no time limit on the use of an equivalent assessment)
- that meets all the requirements of the deprivation of liberty assessment,

- of which the supervisory body is satisfied that there is no reason to believe that it is no longer accurate, and
- of which the supervisory body has a written copy.

An example would be a recent assessment carried out for the purposes of the Mental Health Act 1983, which could serve as an equivalent to a mental health assessment.

4.6 Great care should be taken in deciding to use an equivalent assessment and this should not be done routinely. The older the assessment is, even if it took place within the last 12 months, the less likely it is to represent a valid equivalent assessment (unless it is an age assessment). For example, only a very recent mental capacity assessment would be appropriate where capacity is known to fluctuate, since one of the principles of the Act is that a person must be assumed to have capacity unless it is established that they lack capacity.

4.7 If an equivalent best interests assessment is used, the supervisory body must also take into account any information given, or submissions made, by the relevant person's representative or an Independent Mental Capacity Advocate (IMCA) instructed under the deprivation of liberty safeguards.

4.8 Supervisory bodies should record the reasons why they have used any equivalent assessment. A standard form is available for this purpose.

When must assessments take place?

4.9 The regulations for England[90] specify that all assessments required for a standard authorisation must be completed within 21 calendar days from the date on which the supervisory body receives a request from a managing authority. The regulations for Wales specify that all assessments required for a standard authorisation must be completed within 21 days from the date the assessors were instructed by the supervisory body.

90 The Mental Capacity (Deprivation of Liberty: Standard Authorisations, Assessments and Ordinary Residence) Regulations 2008.

4.10 However, if an urgent authorisation is already in force, the assessments must be completed before the urgent authorisation expires. The regulations for Wales specify that, where the managing authority has given itself an urgent authorisation and applies for a standard authorisation, the assessors must complete the assessments within five days of the date of instruction.

4.11 Urgent authorisations may be given by managing authorities for an initial period not exceeding seven days. If there are exceptional reasons why it has not been possible to deal with the request for a standard authorisation within the period of the urgent authorisation, they may be extended **by the supervisory body** for up to a further seven days. It is for the supervisory body to decide what constitutes an 'exceptional reason', taking into account all the circumstances of an individual case.

4.12 Supervisory bodies must keep a record of all requests for standard authorisations that they receive and should acknowledge the receipt of requests from managing authorities for standard authorisations.

How should assessors be selected?

4.13 The six assessments do not have to be completed by different assessors. In fact, it is highly unlikely that there will be six separate assessors – not least because it is desirable to minimise the burden on the person being assessed. However, each assessor must make their own decisions, and to ensure that an appropriate degree of objectivity is brought to the assessment process:
- there **must** be a minimum of two assessors
- the mental health and best interests assessors **must** be different people
- the best interests assessor can be an employee of the supervisory body or managing authority, but **must not** be involved in the care or treatment of the person they are assessing nor in decisions about their care
- a potential best interests assessor should not be used if they are in a line management relationship with the professional proposing the deprivation of liberty or the mental health assessor
- none of the assessors may have a financial interest in the case of the person they are assessing (a person is considered to have a financial interest in a case where that person is a partner, director, other office-holder or major shareholder of the managing authority that has made the application for a standard authorisation)
- an assessor **must not** be a relative of the person being assessed, nor of a person with a financial interest in the person's care. For this purpose, a 'relative' is:
    a. a spouse, ex-spouse, civil partner or ex-civil partner
    b. a person living with the relevant person as if they were a spouse or a civil partner
    c. a parent or child
    d. a brother or sister
    e. a child of a person falling within definitions a, b or d
    f. a grandparent or grandchild
    g. a grandparent-in-law or grandchild-in-law
    h. an aunt or uncle
    i. a sister-in-law or brother-in-law
    j. a son-in-law or daughter-in-law
    k. a first cousin, or
    l. a half-brother or half-sister.
    These relationships include step-relationships
- where the managing authority and supervisory body are both the same body (see paragraph 3.21), the supervisory body may

not select to carry out a best interests assessment a person who is employed by the body, or providing services to it, and
- the supervisory body should seek to avoid appointing assessors in any other possible conflict of interests situations that might bring into question the objectivity of an assessment.

4.14 Other relevant factors for supervisory bodies to consider when appointing assessors include:
- the reason for the proposed deprivation of liberty
- whether the potential assessor has experience of working with the service user group from which the person being assessed comes (for example, older people, people with learning disabilities, people with autism, or people with brain injury)
- whether the potential assessor has experience of working with people from the cultural background of the person being assessed, and
- any other specific needs of the person being assessed, for example communication needs.

4.15 Supervisory bodies should ensure that sufficient assessors are available to meet their needs, and must be satisfied in each case that the assessors have the skills, experience, qualifications and training required by regulations to perform the function effectively. The regulations also require supervisory bodies to be satisfied that there is an appropriate criminal record certificate issued in respect of an assessor. It will be useful to keep a record of qualified assessors and their experience and availability. Supervisory bodies should consider making arrangements to ensure that assessors have the necessary opportunities to maintain their skills and knowledge (of legal developments, for example) and share, audit and review their practice.

4.16 Assessors act as individual professionals and are personally accountable for their decisions. Managing authorities and supervisory bodies must not dictate or seek to influence their decisions.

4.17 There is no reason in principle why interviews, examinations and fact-finding required as part of any deprivation of liberty safeguards assessment cannot serve more than one purpose, in order to avoid unnecessary burdens both on the person being assessed and on staff. However, if this does happen, all purposes of the interview or examination should be made clear to the relevant person, and to any family members, friends, carers or advocates supporting them.

Protection against liability

4.18 Nobody can or should carry out an assessment unless they are protected against any liabilities that might arise in connection with carrying out the assessment. Individual assessors will need to satisfy themselves, and any supervisory body that selects them as an assessor, that they are appropriately covered by either employers' or personal insurance.

What is the assessment process?

4.19 As indicated in paragraph 4.2, there are six assessments that must be conducted before a supervisory body can give an authorisation.

4.20 The assessments are set out in the order in which it will normally be most appropriate to complete them. In particular, it is recommended that the best interests assessment, which is likely to be the most time-consuming, is not started until there is a reasonable expectation that the other five qualifying requirements will be met.

4.21 But, ultimately, it is for the supervisory body to decide on the order in which the assessments should be undertaken and, in the light of the time available to complete the overall assessment process, the extent to which they should be undertaken to separate or simultaneous timescales. The supervisory body's decision about how many assessors will undertake the assessments (see paragraph 4.13) will also be a relevant factor.

4.22 The following paragraphs explain the assessment process.

Age assessment

4.23 The purpose of the age assessment is simply to confirm whether the relevant person is aged 18 or over. This is because, as paragraph 1.12 explains, the deprivation of liberty safeguards apply only to people aged 18 or over. For people under the age of 18, a different safeguards process applies. In most cases, this is likely to be a fairly straightforward assessment. If there is any doubt, age should be established by a birth certificate or other evidence that the assessor considers reliable. Where it is not possible to verify with any certainty whether a person is aged 18 or over, the assessor should base the assessment on the best of their knowledge and belief.

4.24 This assessment can be undertaken by anybody whom the supervisory body is satisfied is eligible to be a best interests assessor.

No refusals assessment

4.25 The purpose of the no refusals assessment is to establish whether an authorisation to deprive the relevant person of their liberty would conflict with other existing authority for decision-making for that person.

4.26 The following are instances of a conflict that would mean that a standard authorisation could not be given:
- If the relevant person has made **an advance decision to refuse treatment** that remains valid and is applicable to some or all of the treatment that is the purpose for which the authorisation is requested, then a standard authorisation cannot be given. See sections 24 to 26 of the Mental Capacity Act 2005 and

chapter 9 of the main Code ('What does the Act say about advance decisions to refuse treatment?') for more information about advance decisions and when they are valid and applicable. Remember too that the deprivation of liberty authorisation does not, in itself, provide authority to treat the person (see paragraphs 5.10 to 5.13 of this Code).

- If any part of the proposal to deprive the person of their liberty (including any element of the care plan) would be in conflict with a **valid decision of a donee or a deputy** made within the scope of their authority, then a standard authorisation cannot be given. For example, if a donee or deputy decides that it would not be in the best interests of the relevant person to be in a particular care home, and that decision is within the scope of their authority, then the care plan will need to be reviewed with the donee or deputy.

4.27 If there is any such conflict, the no refusals assessment qualifying requirement will not be met and a standard authorisation for deprivation of liberty cannot be given.

4.28 The no refusals assessment can be undertaken by anybody that the supervisory body is satisfied is eligible to be a best interests assessor.

Mental capacity assessment

4.29 The purpose of the mental capacity assessment is to establish whether the relevant person lacks capacity to decide whether or not they should be accommodated in the relevant hospital or care home to be given care or treatment. The assessment refers specifically to the relevant person's capacity to make this decision at the time it needs to be made. The starting assumption should always be that a person has the capacity to make the decision.

4.30 Sections 1 to 3 of the Act set out how a person's capacity to make decisions should be determined. Chapter 4 of the main Code ('How does the Act define a person's capacity to make a decision and how should capacity be assessed?') gives further guidance on ways to assess capacity. When assessing the capacity of a person being considered for the deprivation of liberty safeguards, these guidelines should be followed.

4.31 The regulations for England specify that the mental capacity assessment can be undertaken by anyone who is eligible to act as a mental health or best interests assessor. In deciding who to appoint for this assessment, the supervisory body should take account of the need for understanding and practical experience of the nature of the person's condition and its impact on decision-making.

4.32 Supervisory bodies may wish to consider using an eligible assessor who already knows the relevant person to undertake this assessment, if they think it would be of benefit. This will primarily arise if somebody involved in the person's care is considered best placed to carry out a reliable assessment, using their knowledge of the person over a period of time. It may also help in reducing any distress that might be caused to the person if they were assessed by somebody they did not know.

Mental health assessment

4.33 The purpose of the mental health assessment is to establish whether the relevant person has a mental disorder within the meaning of the Mental Health Act 1983. That means any disorder or disability of mind, apart from dependence on alcohol or drugs. It includes all learning disabilities. This is not an assessment to determine whether the person requires mental health treatment.

4.34 A distinction can be drawn between the mental health assessment and the mental capacity assessment:
- Although a person must have an impairment or disturbance of the functioning of the mind or brain in order to lack capacity, it does not follow that they automatically have a mental disorder within the meaning of the Mental Health Act 1983.
- The objective of the mental health assessment is to ensure that the person is medically diagnosed as being of 'unsound mind' and so comes within the scope of Article 5 of the European Convention on Human Rights.

4.35 In both England and Wales, the regulations specify that:
- the mental health assessment must be carried out by a doctor, and
- the assessing doctor has to either be approved under section 12 of the Mental Health Act 1983, or be a registered medical practitioner with at least three years' post-registration experience in the diagnosis or treatment of mental disorder, such as a GP with a special interest. This includes doctors who are automatically treated as being section 12 approved because they are approved clinicians under the Mental Health Act 1983.

4.36 To be eligible to undertake assessments, in England a doctor will need to have completed the standard training for deprivation of liberty mental health assessors. Except in the 12 month period beginning with the date the doctor has successfully completed the standard training, the regulations for England also require the supervisory body to be satisfied that the doctor has, in the 12 months prior to selection, completed further training relevant to their role as a mental health assessor. In Wales, a doctor will need to have completed appropriate training and have appropriate skills and experience.

4.37 Supervisory bodies must consider the suitability of the assessor for the particular case (for example, whether they have experience relevant to the person's condition).

4.38 As with the mental capacity assessment, supervisory bodies may wish to consider using an eligible assessor who already knows the relevant person to undertake this assessment, if they think it would be of benefit.

4.39 The mental health assessor is required to consider how the mental health of the person being assessed is likely to be affected by being deprived of their liberty, and to report their conclusions to the best interests assessor. The mental health and best interests assessments cannot be carried out by the same person.

Eligibility assessment

4.40 This assessment relates specifically to the relevant person's status, or potential status, under the Mental Health Act 1983.

4.41 A person is not eligible for a deprivation of liberty authorisation if:
- they are detained as a hospital in-patient under the Mental Health Act 1983, or
- the authorisation, if given, would be inconsistent with an obligation placed on them under the Mental Health Act 1983, such as a requirement to live somewhere else. This will only affect people who are on leave of absence from detention under the Mental Health Act 1983 or who are subject to guardianship, supervised community treatment or conditional discharge.

4.42 Where the proposed authorisation relates to a care home, or to deprivation of liberty in a hospital for non-mental health treatment, the eligibility assessment will simply be a matter of checking that authorisation would not be inconsistent with an obligation placed on the person under the Mental Health Act 1983.

4.43 When a person is subject to guardianship under the Mental Health Act 1983, their guardian can decide where they are to live, but cannot authorise deprivation of liberty and cannot require them to live somewhere where they are deprived of liberty unless that deprivation of liberty is authorised.

4.44 Occasionally, a person who is subject to guardianship and who lacks capacity to make the relevant decisions may need specific care or treatment in a care home or hospital that cannot be delivered without deprivation of liberty. This may be in a care home in which they are already living or in which the guardian thinks they ought to live, or it may be in a hospital where they need to be for physical health care. It may also apply if they need to be in hospital for mental health care. The process for obtaining a deprivation of liberty authorisation and the criteria to be applied are the same as for any other person.

4.45 If the proposed authorisation relates to deprivation of liberty in a hospital **wholly or partly for the purpose of treatment of mental disorder**, then the relevant person will not be eligible if:
- they object to being admitted to hospital, or to some or all the treatment they will receive there for mental disorder, **and**
- they meet the criteria for an application for admission under section 2 or section 3 of the Mental Health Act 1983 (unless an attorney or deputy, acting within their powers, had consented to the things to which the person is objecting).

4.46 In many cases, the relevant person will be able to state an objection. However, where the person is unable to communicate, or can only communicate to a limited extent, assessors will need to consider the person's behaviour, wishes, feelings, views, beliefs and values, both present and past, so far as they can be ascertained (see paragraphs 5.37 to 5.48 of the main Code for guidance on how to do this). If there is reason to think that a person would object if able to do so, then the person should be assumed to be objecting. Occasionally, it may be that the person's behaviour initially suggests an objection, but that this objection is in fact not directed at the treatment at all. In that case, the person should **not** be taken to be objecting.

4.47 Assessors should always bear in mind that their job is simply to establish whether the person objects to treatment or to being in hospital: whether that objection is reasonable or not is not the issue.

4.48 Even where a person does not object and a deprivation of liberty authorisation is possible, it should not be assumed that such an authorisation is invariably the correct course. There may be other factors that suggest that the Mental Health Act 1983 should be used (for example, where it is thought likely that the person will recover relevant capacity and will then refuse to consent to treatment, or where it is important for the hospital managers to have a formal power to retake a person who goes absent without leave). Further guidance on this is given in the Mental Health Act 1983 Code of Practice.

4.49 The eligibility assessor is not required to decide (or even consider) whether an application under the Mental Health Act 1983 would be in the person's best interests.

4.50 If the proposed authorisation relates to deprivation of liberty in a hospital **wholly or partly for the purpose of treatment of mental disorder**, then the person will also not be eligible if they are:
- currently on leave of absence from detention under the Mental Health Act 1983
- subject to supervised community treatment, or
- subject to conditional discharge,

in which case powers of recall under the Mental Health Act 1983 should be used.

4.51 People on leave of absence from detention under the Mental Health Act 1983 or subject to supervised community treatment or conditional discharge are, however, eligible for the deprivation of liberty safeguards if they require treatment in hospital for a physical disorder.

Who can conduct an eligibility assessment?

4.52 The regulations for England specify that the eligibility assessment must be completed by:
- a mental health assessor who is also a section 12 doctor, or

- a best interests assessor who is also an approved mental health professional (AMHP).

4.53 The assessment cannot be carried out by a non-section 12 doctor, even if they are qualified to be a mental health assessor, nor by a non-AMHP, even if they are qualified to be a best interests assessor. This will ensure that the eligibility assessor is sufficiently familiar with the Mental Health Act 1983, which will be particularly important in cases in which it appears that the powers available under the Mental Health Act 1983 may be more appropriate than the deprivation of liberty safeguards.

4.54 The eligibility assessment will often be carried out by the best interests assessor but, where this is not the case, the eligibility assessor must request the best interests assessor to provide any relevant eligibility information that the best interests assessor may have, and the best interests assessor must comply with this request.

What happens when people are assessed as ineligible?

4.55 If the eligibility assessor believes that the relevant person is not eligible, but (on the basis of the report of the best interests assessor) that they should nevertheless be deprived of liberty in their best interests, the eligibility assessor should immediately inform the supervisory body.

4.56 In the case of someone already subject to the Mental Health Act 1983, the eligibility assessor should inform the supervisory body with a view to contact being made with the relevant responsible clinician (i.e. the clinician in overall charge of the person's treatment) or, if the person is subject to guardianship, the relevant local social services authority. Otherwise, the assessor or supervisory body should take steps to arrange for the person to be assessed further with a view to an application being made for admission to hospital under the Mental Health Act 1983. Assessors will need to be familiar with local arrangements for doing this.

4.57 In some cases, even before the eligibility assessment is undertaken, it may be known that there is a chance that the person will have to be assessed with a view to an application under the Mental Health Act 1983 because the eligibility assessment might conclude that they are ineligible for a deprivation of liberty authorisation. In such cases, steps should be taken, where practical and possible, to arrange assessments in a way that minimises the number of separate interviews or examinations the person has to undergo.

Best interests assessment

4.58 The purpose of the best interests assessment is to establish, firstly, whether deprivation of liberty is occurring or is going to occur and, if so, whether:

- it is in the best interests of the relevant person to be deprived of liberty
- it is necessary for them to be deprived of liberty in order to prevent harm to themselves, and
- deprivation of liberty is a proportionate response to the likelihood of the relevant person suffering harm and the seriousness of that harm.

4.59 The best interests assessor is the person who is responsible for assessing what is in the best interests of a relevant person.

4.60 In both England and Wales, the best interests assessment must be undertaken by an AMHP, social worker, nurse, occupational therapist or chartered psychologist with the skills and experience specified in the regulations. In England, this includes at least two years' post-registration experience. In England, the supervisory body must also be satisfied that the assessor:

- is not suspended from the register or list relevant to the person's profession
- has successfully completed training that has been approved[91] by the Secretary of State to be a best interests assessor
- except in the 12 month period beginning with the date the person has successfully completed the approved training, has, in the 12 months prior to selection, completed further training relevant to their role as a best interests assessor, and
- has the skills necessary to obtain, evaluate and analyse complex evidence and differing views and to weigh them appropriately in decision-making.

91 Approved courses can be found at: http://www.dh.gov.uk/en/SocialCare/Deliveringadultsocialcare/MentalCapacity/MentalCapacityActDeprivationofLibertySafeguards/index.htm

4.61 Section 4 of the Mental Capacity Act 2005 sets out the best interests principles that apply for the purpose of the Act. Chapter 5 of the main Code ('What does the Act mean when it talks about "best interests"?') explains this in more detail, and, in particular, paragraph 5.13 of the main Code includes a checklist of factors that need to be taken into account in working out what is in a person's best interests. These principles and guidance apply equally to working out a person's best interests for the purpose of the deprivation of liberty safeguards. However, when it comes to best interests around deprivation of liberty, additional factors apply, including:

- whether any harm to the person could arise if the deprivation of liberty does not take place
- what that harm would be
- how likely that harm is to arise (i.e. is the level of risk sufficient to justify a step as serious as depriving a person of liberty?)
- what other care options there are which could avoid deprivation of liberty, and

- if deprivation of liberty is currently unavoidable, what action could be taken to avoid it in future.

Establishing whether deprivation of liberty is occurring

4.62 The first task of a best interests assessor is to establish whether deprivation of liberty is occurring, or is likely to occur, since there is no point in the assessment process proceeding further if deprivation of liberty is not at issue. If the best interests assessor concludes that deprivation of liberty is **not** occurring and is not likely to occur, they should state in their assessment report to the supervisory body that deprivation of liberty is not in the person's best interests because there is obviously a less restrictive option available. The best interests requirement will therefore not be met in such a case.

4.63 To establish whether deprivation of liberty is occurring, or is likely to occur, the best interests assessor must consult the managing authority of the hospital or care home where the person is, or will be, accommodated and examine any relevant needs assessments and care plans prepared for the person. The best interests assessor must consider whether the care plan and the manner in which it is being, or will be, implemented constitutes a deprivation of liberty. If not, then no deprivation of liberty authorisation is required for that care plan.

4.64 The managing authority and supervisory body must provide the best interests assessor with any needs assessments or care plans that they have undertaken or which have been undertaken on their behalf.

The best interests assessment process

4.65 If the best interests assessor considers that deprivation of liberty is occurring, or is likely to occur, they should start a full best interests assessment. In line with section 4(7) of the Act this involves seeking the views of a range of people connected to the relevant person to find out whether they believe that depriving the relevant person of their liberty is, or would be, in the person's best interests to protect them from harm or to enable them to follow the care plan proposed. The best interests assessor should, as far as is practical and possible, seek the views of:
- anyone the person has previously named as someone they want to be consulted
- anyone involved in caring for the person
- anyone interested in the person's welfare (for example, family carers, other close relatives, or an advocate already working with the person), and
- any donee or deputy who represents the person.

4.66 This may mean that the best interests assessor needs to explain key aspects of the care plan and what it aims to do to the people being consulted. The best interests assessor should then take the views received into account as far as is practical and appropriate. It is essential that the best interests assessor provides an independent and objective view of whether or not there is a genuine justification for deprivation of liberty, taking account of all the relevant views and factors.

4.67 The best interests assessor must state in their assessment the name and address of every interested person whom they have consulted in carrying out the assessment.

4.68 Family and friends may not be confident about expressing their views: it is the responsibility of the best interests assessor to enable them to do so – using support to meet communication or language needs as necessary.

Scenario: Consulting around best interests

Mr Simpson is 60 and has dementia with particularly poor short-term memory, which clinicians agree is most likely to be related to chronic excessive alcohol intake. After initial treatment in hospital, he has been admitted to a care home – a decision which he consented to.

However, though he had the mental capacity to consent to hospital admission, he has no insight into his dementia. He is unable to understand the health and safety implications of continuing to drink, and will do so heavily whenever he has access to alcohol and the money to buy it.

Although Mr Simpson had no access to alcohol in hospital, there is a pub within walking distance of the care home, which he visits and drinks in. When he returns to the home intoxicated, his behaviour can be very distressing and potentially dangerous to other residents. The care home staff believe that if this continues, there may be no other option than to return him to hospital under the Mental Health Act 1983.

The care home staff have asked Mr Simpson to drink only in moderation, but this has not proved successful; and the landlord has been asked not to serve him more than one drink but has refused to do so. The manager of the home is now considering a care plan to prevent Mr Simpson from leaving the home without an escort, and to prevent visits from friends who bring alcohol. He believes this would be in Mr Simpson's best interests.

As the pub is open all day, if this new care plan was adopted, Mr Simpson would be stopped from going out at all without an escort, even though he often goes to the shops and the park as well as the pub. Staffing levels are such that an escort would only be available on some days and for limited periods.

> Mr Simpson's daughter, his closest relative, is concerned that these restrictions are excessive and would amount to a deprivation of liberty. She believes that having a drink and socialising in the pub is her father's 'only remaining pleasure', and is sure that, if he still had capacity, he would choose to carry on drinking, regardless of the health risks.
>
> She requests a best interests meeting to consider whether a less restrictive care plan could still meet his needs.
>
> At this meeting, Mr Simpson's community mental health nurse confirms that Mr Simpson is likely to lack capacity in relation to this particular issue, and advises that if he continues to drink to excess his dementia is likely to advance rapidly and his life expectancy will be reduced. However, small amounts of alcohol will not be significantly harmful.
>
> The consensus is that the proposed restrictions would severely limit Mr Simpson's ability to maintain social contact and to carry on the life he has been used to, and that this would amount to deprivation of liberty. Bearing in mind his daughter's view, it is felt that it would not be in Mr Simpson's best interests to prevent him from having any alcohol at all. However, in view of the health risks and the likelihood that he would otherwise have to be detained in hospital, it would be in Mr Simpson's best interests to ensure that he does not get intoxicated. (The possibility of limiting his access to his money would be unacceptable since he retains the capacity to decide how to spend it in other ways.)
>
> Discussion then focuses on ways of minimising restrictions so that he is still able to visit the pub, but drinks in moderation. The care home key worker says that when she has gone to the pub with Mr Simpson he has been fully co-operative and has had just one drink before coming back with her. It is therefore agreed that the home will provide an escort for him to visit the pub at least three times a week, and the shops and the park at other times, and that his daughter will be able to take him out at any time.
>
> It is agreed that care home staff (in consultation with his daughter) will review Mr Simpson's care plan in two months' time and, if it is felt that increased restrictions are required, consider whether it is then necessary to request an authorisation for deprivation of liberty.

4.69 The best interests assessor must involve the relevant person in the assessment process as much as is possible and practical, and help them to participate in decision-making. The relevant person should be given the support needed to participate, using non-verbal means of communication where needed (see paragraphs 3.10 and 3.11 of the main Code) or the support of speech and language therapists. It may also help to involve others whom the relevant person already trusts and who are used to communicating with the relevant person.

4.70 The best interests assessor will need to consider the conclusions of the mental health assessor about how the person being assessed is likely to be affected by being deprived of their liberty. If the proposed care would involve the person being moved, then the assessor should consider the impact of the upheaval and of the journey itself on the person.

4.71 If the best interests assessment supports deprivation of liberty in the care home or hospital in question, the assessor must state what the maximum authorisation period should be in the case concerned. This must not exceed 12 months. The assessor should set out the reasons for selecting the period stated. This decision will be based on the information obtained during the consultation process – but should also reflect information from the person's care plan about how long any treatment or care will be required in circumstances that amount to a deprivation of liberty. It should also take into account any available indication of how likely it is that the relevant person's circumstances will change, including the expected progression of the illness or disability. The underlying principle is that deprivation of liberty should be for the minimum period necessary so, for the maximum 12-month period to apply, the assessor will need to be confident that there is unlikely to be a change in the person's circumstances that would affect the authorisation within that timescale.

The report of the best interests assessor

4.72 The best interests assessor must provide a report that explains their conclusion and their reasons for it. If they do not support deprivation of liberty, then their report should aim to be as useful as possible to the commissioners and providers of care in deciding on future action (for example, recommending an alternative approach to treatment or care in which deprivation of liberty could be avoided). It may be helpful for the best interests assessor to discuss the possibility of any such alternatives with the providers of care **during the assessment process**.

4.73 If the best interests assessor does not support deprivation of liberty, it would be good practice for their report to be included in the relevant person's care plan or case notes, to ensure that any views about how deprivation of liberty can be avoided are made clear to the providers of care and all relevant staff on an ongoing basis.

4.74 The best interests assessor may recommend that conditions should be attached to the authorisation. For example, they may make recommendations around contact issues, issues relevant to the person's culture or other major issues related to the deprivation of liberty, which – if not dealt with – would mean that the deprivation of liberty would cease to be in the person's best interests. The best interests assessor may also recommend conditions in order to work towards avoiding deprivation of liberty in future. But it is not the best interests assessor's role to specify conditions that do not directly relate to the issue of deprivation of liberty.

4.75 Conditions should not be a substitute for a properly constructed care plan (see paragraph 2.7 on good practice for care planning). In recommending conditions, best interests assessors should aim to impose the minimum necessary constraints, so that they do not unnecessarily prevent or inhibit the staff of the hospital or care home from responding appropriately to the person's needs, whether they remain the same or vary over time. It would be good practice for the best interests assessor to discuss any proposed conditions with the relevant personnel at the home or hospital before finalising the assessment, and to make clear in their report whether the rejection or variation of recommended conditions by the supervisory body would significantly affect the other conclusions they have reached.

4.76 Where possible, the best interests assessor should recommend someone to be appointed as the relevant person's representative (see chapter 7). The assessor should be well placed, as a result of the consultation process, to identify whether there is anybody suitable to take on this role. The appointment of the relevant person's representative cannot take place unless and until an authorisation is given. However, by identifying someone to take on this role at an early stage, the best interests assessor can help to ensure that a representative is appointed as soon as possible.

Scenario: Application for standard authorisation

Mrs Jackson is 87 years old and lives by herself in an isolated bungalow in a rural area. Over the past few years, staff at her local health centre have become increasingly concerned about her wellbeing and ability to look after herself. Her appearance has become unkempt, she does not appear to be eating properly and her house is dirty.

The community mental health team have attempted to gain her trust, but she is unwilling to engage with them. She has refused care workers entry to her home and declined their help with personal hygiene and household chores.

Because it is believed that she is a potential risk to herself, she is admitted to psychiatric hospital under section 2 of the Mental Health Act 1983 for assessment of her mental disorder.

Following the assessment, it is felt that Mrs Jackson requires further treatment for mental disorder. An application is made for her detention to be continued under section 3 of the Mental Health Act 1983. She is prescribed antipsychotic medication, but this seems to have little effect on her behaviour. She remains extremely suspicious of people to the point of being delusional. She is assessed as potentially having mild dementia, most probably of the Alzheimer type, but because there is no obvious benefit from anti-dementia medication, further treatment for mental disorder is felt unnecessary.

Mrs Jackson insists that she wishes to return to her own home, but given past failed attempts to gain her acceptance of support at home and her likely future mental deterioration, transfer to a care home is believed to be most appropriate.

A best interests meeting is held by the mental health team to consider her future care and placement, and the team's approved social worker and the instructed IMCA are invited. The meeting concludes that Mrs Jackson does not have sufficient mental capacity to make an informed decision on her stated wish to return home. There is no advance decision in existence, no Lasting Power of Attorney or court deputy appointed and no practical way of contacting her immediate family.

An appropriate care home is identified. A care plan is developed to give Mrs Jackson as much choice and control over her daily living as possible. However, it is felt that the restrictions still necessary to ensure Mrs Jackson's wellbeing will be so intense and of such duration that a request for a standard deprivation of liberty authorisation should be made by the care home manager (the relevant managing authority).

The best interests assessor agrees that the proposed course of action is in Mrs Jackson's best interests and recommends a standard authorisation for six months in the first instance.

What guidelines are there relating to the work of assessors?

Access to records

4.77 All assessors may, at any reasonable time, examine and take copies of:
- any health record
- any record of, or held by, a local authority that was compiled in accordance with a social services function, and
- any record held by a care home

which they consider may be relevant to their assessment. Assessors should list in their assessment report what records they examined.

Recording and reporting assessments

4.78 As soon as possible after carrying out their assessments, assessors must keep a written record of the assessment and must give copies

of their assessment report(s) to the supervisory body. The supervisory body must in turn give copies of the assessment report(s) to:
- the managing authority
- the relevant person and their representative, and
- any IMCA instructed

at the same time that it gives them copies of the deprivation of liberty authorisation or notification that an authorisation is not to be given (see paragraphs 5.7 and 5.18 respectively).

5 WHAT SHOULD HAPPEN ONCE THE ASSESSMENTS ARE COMPLETE?

If all the assessments in the standard authorisation assessment process indicate that the relevant person meets all the qualifying requirements, then the supervisory body will give a deprivation of liberty authorisation. If any of the qualifying requirements are not met, however, different actions will need to be taken, depending on the circumstances of the individual case.

This chapter identifies potential outcomes of the assessment process and offers guidance on what should happen next.

What action should the supervisory body take if the assessments conclude that the person meets the requirements for authorisation?

5.1 If all the assessments conclude that the relevant person meets the requirements for authorisation, and the supervisory body has written copies of all the assessments, it must give a standard authorisation. A standard form is available for this purpose.

5.2 The supervisory body cannot give a standard authorisation if any of the requirements are not fulfilled.

5.3 The supervisory body must set the period of the authorisation, which may not be longer than that recommended by the best interests assessor (see paragraph 4.71).

5.4 When the supervisory body gives a standard authorisation, it must do so in writing and must state the following:
- the name of the relevant person
- the name of the relevant hospital or care home
- the period during which the authorisation is to be in force (which may not exceed the period recommended by the best interests assessor)
- the purpose for which the authorisation is given (i.e. why the person needs to be deprived of their liberty)
- any conditions subject to which the authorisation is given (see paragraph 5.5), and
- the reason why each qualifying requirement is met.

5.5 The supervisory body may attach conditions to the authorisation. Before deciding whether to give the authorisation subject to conditions, the supervisory body must consider any recommendations made by the best interests assessor (see paragraph 4.74). Where the supervisory body does not attach conditions as recommended by the best interests assessor, it should discuss the matter with the best interests assessor in case the rejection or variation of the conditions would significantly affect the other conclusions the best interests assessor reached in their report.

5.6 It is the responsibility of the supervisory body to appoint a representative for the relevant person (see chapter 7).

5.7 As soon as possible after giving the authorisation, the supervisory body must give a copy of the authorisation to:
- the managing authority
- the relevant person
- the relevant person's representative
- any Independent Mental Capacity Advocate (IMCA) involved, and
- every interested person named by the best interests assessor in their report as somebody they have consulted in carrying out their assessment.

The supervisory body must also keep a written record of any standard authorisation that it gives and of the matters referred to in paragraph 5.4.

5.8 The managing authority must take all practical and possible steps to ensure that the relevant person understands the effect of the authorisation and their rights around it. These include their right to challenge the authorisation via the Court of Protection, their right to request a review, and their right to have an IMCA instructed, along with the process for doing so (see paragraphs 7.37 to 7.41). Appropriate information must be given to the relevant person both orally and in writing. Any written information must also be given to the relevant person's representative. This must happen as soon as possible and practical after the authorisation is given.

How long can an authorisation last?

5.9 A deprivation of liberty should last for the shortest period possible. The best interests assessor should only recommend authorisation for as long as the relevant person is likely to meet all the qualifying requirements. The authorisation may be for quite a short period. A short period may, for example, be appropriate if:
- the reason that the deprivation of liberty is in the person's best interests is because their usual care arrangements have temporarily broken down, or
- there are likely to be changes in the person's mental disorder in the relatively near future (for example, if the person is in rehabilitation following brain injury).

What restrictions exist on authorisations?

5.10 A deprivation of liberty authorisation – whether urgent or standard – relates solely to the issue of deprivation of liberty. It does not give authority to treat people, nor to do anything else that would normally require their consent. The arrangements for providing care and treatment to people in respect of whom a deprivation of liberty authorisation is in force are subject to the wider provisions of the Mental Capacity Act 2005.

5.11 This means that any treatment can only be given to a person who has not given their consent if:
- it is established that the person lacks capacity to make the decision concerned
- it is agreed that the treatment will be in their best interests, having taken account of the views of the person and of people close to them, and, where relevant in the case of serious medical treatment, of any IMCA involved
- the treatment does not conflict with a valid and applicable advance decision to refuse treatment, and
- the treatment does not conflict with a decision made by a donee of Lasting Power of Attorney or a deputy acting within the scope of their powers.

5.12 In deciding what is in a person's best interests, section 4 of the Act applies in the same way as it would if the person was not deprived of liberty. The guidance in chapter 5 of the main Code on assessing best interests is also relevant.

5.13 Life-sustaining treatment, or treatment to prevent a serious deterioration in the person's condition, may be provided while a decision in respect of any relevant issue is sought from the Court of Protection. The need to act in the best interests of the person concerned will continue to apply in the meantime.

Can a person be moved to a different location under a standard authorisation?

5.14 If a person who is subject to a standard authorisation moves to a different hospital or care home, the managing authority of the new hospital or care home must request a new standard authorisation. The application should be made **before** the move takes place.

5.15 If the move has to take place so urgently that this is impossible, the managing authority of the new hospital or care home will need to give an urgent authorisation (see chapter 6).

5.16 The only exception is if the care regime in the new facility will not involve deprivation of liberty.

5.17 These arrangements are not an alternative to applying the provisions of sections 38 and 39 of the Act regarding change of residence.

What happens if an assessment concludes that one of the requirements is not met?

5.18 If any of the assessments conclude that one of the requirements is not met, then the assessment process should stop immediately and authorisation may not be given. The supervisory body should:
- inform anyone still engaged in carrying out an assessment that they are not required to complete it
- notify the managing authority, the relevant person, any IMCA involved and every interested person consulted by the best interests assessor that authorisation has not been given (a standard form is available for this purpose), and
- provide the managing authority, the relevant person and any IMCA involved with copies of those assessments that have been carried out. This must be done as soon as possible, because in some cases different arrangements will need to be made for the person's care.

5.19 If the reason the standard authorisation cannot be given is because the eligibility requirement is not met, it may be necessary to consider making the person subject to the Mental Health Act 1983. If this is the case, it may be possible to use the same assessors to make that decision, thereby minimising the assessment processes.

What are the responsibilities of the managing authority and the commissioners of care if a request for an authorisation is turned down?

5.20 The managing authority is responsible for ensuring that it does not deprive a person of their liberty without an authorisation. The managing authority must comply with the law in this respect: where a request for an authorisation is turned down, it will need to review the relevant person's actual or proposed care arrangements to ensure that a deprivation of liberty is not allowed to either continue or commence.

5.21 Supervisory bodies and other commissioners of care will need to purchase care packages in a way that makes it possible for managing authorities to comply with the outcome of the deprivation of liberty safeguards assessment process when a request for a standard authorisation is turned down.

5.22 The actions that both managing authorities and commissioners of care should consider if a request for an authorisation is turned down will depend on the reason why the authorisation has not been given:
- If the best interests assessor concluded that the relevant person was not in fact being, or likely to be, deprived of liberty, no action is likely to be necessary.
- If the best interests assessor concluded that the proposed or actual deprivation of liberty was not in the relevant person's best interests, the managing authority, in conjunction with the commissioner of the care, will need to consider how the care plan could be changed to avoid deprivation of liberty. (See, for

example, the guidance on practical ways to reduce the risk of deprivation of liberty in paragraph 2.7.) They should examine carefully the reasons given in the best interests assessor's report, and may find it helpful to discuss the matter with the best interests assessor. Where appropriate, they should also discuss the matter with family and carers. If the person is not yet a resident in the care home or hospital, the revised care plan may not involve admission to that facility unless the conditions of care are adapted to be less restrictive and deprivation of liberty will not occur.

- If the mental capacity assessor concluded that the relevant person **has** capacity to make decisions about their care, the care home or hospital will need to consider, in conjunction with the commissioner of the care, how to support the person to make such decisions.
- If the relevant person was identified as not eligible to be subject to a deprivation of liberty authorisation, it may be appropriate to assess whether an application should be made to detain the person under the Mental Health Act 1983.
- If the relevant person does not have a mental disorder as defined in the Mental Health Act 1983, the care plan will need to be modified to avoid a deprivation of liberty, since there would be no lawful basis for depriving a person of liberty in those circumstances.
- Where there is a valid refusal by a donee or deputy, or an applicable and valid advance decision (see paragraphs 4.25 to 4.28), alternative care arrangements will need to be made. If there is a question about the refusal, a decision may be sought from the Court of Protection.
- If the person is under 18, use of the Children Act 1989 may be considered.

5.23 Working out what action should be taken where a request for a standard deprivation of liberty authorisation is turned down in respect of a 'self-funder' may present particular problems, because the managing authority may not be able to make alternative care arrangements without discussing them with those controlling the funding, whether relatives of the person concerned or others. The desired outcome should be the provision of a care regime that does not constitute deprivation of liberty.

5.24 Where the best interests assessor comes to the conclusion that the best interests requirement is not met, but it appears to the assessor that the person being assessed is already being deprived of their liberty, the assessor must inform the supervisory body and explain in their report why they have reached that conclusion. The supervisory body must then inform the managing authority to review the relevant person's care plan immediately so that unauthorised deprivation of liberty does not continue. Any necessary changes must be made urgently to stop what would be an unlawful deprivation of liberty. The steps taken to stop the deprivation of liberty should be recorded in the care plan. Where possible, family, friends and carers should be involved in deciding how to prevent the unauthorised deprivation of liberty from continuing. If the supervisory body has any doubts about whether the matter is being satisfactorily resolved within an appropriately urgent timescale, it should alert the inspection body (see chapter 11).

6 WHEN CAN URGENT AUTHORISATIONS OF DEPRIVATION OF LIBERTY BE GIVEN?

Wherever possible, applications for deprivation of liberty authorisations should be made before the deprivation of liberty commences. However, where deprivation of liberty unavoidably needs to commence before a standard authorisation can be obtained, an urgent authorisation can be given which will make the deprivation of liberty lawful for a short period of time.

This chapter contains guidance on the rules around urgent authorisations.

When can an urgent authorisation be given?

6.1 A managing authority can itself give an urgent authorisation for deprivation of liberty where:
- it is required to make a request to the supervisory body for a standard authorisation, but believes that the need for the person to be deprived of their liberty is so urgent that deprivation needs to begin before the request is made, or
- it has made a request for a standard authorisation, but believes that the need for a person to be deprived of liberty has now become so urgent that deprivation of liberty needs to begin before the request is dealt with by the supervisory body.

This means that an urgent authorisation can never be given without a request for a standard authorisation being made simultaneously. Therefore, before giving an urgent authorisation, a managing authority will need to have a reasonable expectation that the six qualifying requirements for a standard authorisation are likely to be met.

6.2 Urgent authorisations should normally only be used in response to sudden unforeseen needs. However, they can also be used in care planning (for example, to avoid delays in transfer for rehabilitation, where delay would reduce the likely benefit of the rehabilitation).

6.3 However, an urgent authorisation should not be used where there is no expectation that a standard deprivation of liberty authorisation will be needed. Where, for example:
- a person who lacks capacity to make decisions about their care and treatment has developed a mental disorder as a result of a physical illness, and

- the physical illness requires treatment in hospital in circumstances that amount to a deprivation of liberty, and
- the treatment of that physical illness is expected to lead to rapid resolution of the mental disorder such that a standard deprivation of liberty authorisation would not be required,

it would not be appropriate to give an urgent authorisation simply to legitimise the short-term deprivation of liberty.

6.4 Similarly, an urgent deprivation of liberty authorisation should not be given when a person is, for example, in an accident and emergency unit or a care home, and it is anticipated that within a matter of a few hours or a few days the person will no longer be in that environment.

6.5 Any decision to give an urgent authorisation and take action that deprives a person of liberty must be in the person's best interests, as set out in section 4 of the Mental Capacity Act 2005. Where restraint is involved, all actions must comply with the additional conditions in section 6 of the Act (see chapter 6 of the main Code).

6.6 The managing authority must decide the period for which the urgent authorisation is given, but this must not exceed seven days (see paragraphs 6.20 to 6.28 regarding the possible extension of the seven-day period). The authorisation must be in writing and must state:
- the name of the relevant person
- the name of the relevant hospital or care home
- the period for which the authorisation is to be in force, and
- the purpose for which the authorisation is given.

A standard form is available for a managing authority to use to notify a supervisory body that it has given an urgent authorisation.

6.7 Supervisory bodies and managing authorities should have a procedure in place that identifies:
- what actions should be taken when an urgent authorisation needs to be made
- who should take each action, and
- within what timescale.

What records should be kept about urgent authorisations?

6.8 The managing authority must keep a written record of any urgent authorisations given, including details of why it decided to give an urgent authorisation. They must give a copy of the authorisation to the relevant person and any IMCA instructed, and place a copy in the relevant person's records. The managing authority must also seek to ensure that, as far as possible, the relevant person understands the effect of the authorisation and the right to challenge the authorisation via the Court of Protection. Appropriate information must be given both orally and in writing.

6.9 The managing authority should, as far as possible and appropriate, notify the relevant person's family, friends and carers when an urgent authorisation is given in order to enable them to offer informed support to the person.

6.10 The processes surrounding the giving and receiving of urgent authorisations should be clearly recorded, and regularly monitored and audited, as part of a managing authority's or supervisory body's governance structure.

Who should be consulted before giving an urgent authorisation?

6.11 If the managing authority is considering depriving a person of liberty in an emergency and giving an urgent authorisation, they must, as far as is practical and possible, take account of the views of anyone engaged in caring for the relevant person or interested in their welfare. The aim should be to consult carers and family members at as early a stage as possible so that their views can be properly taken into account before a decision to give an urgent authorisation is taken.

6.12 The steps taken to involve family, friends or carers should be recorded in the relevant person's records, along with their views. The views of the carers will be important because their knowledge of the person will put them in a good position to gauge how the person will react to the deprivation of their liberty, and the effect it will have on their mental state. It may also be appropriate to consult any staff who may have some involvement in the person's case.

6.13 The ultimate decision, though, will need to be based on a judgement of what is in the relevant person's best interests. The decision-maker from the managing authority will need to be able to show that they have made a reasonable decision based on their professional judgement and taking account of all the relevant factors. This is an important decision, because it could mean the deprivation of a person's liberty without, at this stage, the full deprivation of liberty safeguards assessment process having taken place. The decision should therefore be taken at a senior level within the managing authority.

Scenario: Urgent authorisation followed by short-term standard authorisation

Mr Baker is 75, widowed and lives near his only family – his daughter. He is admitted to hospital having been found by his daughter on his kitchen floor. He is uncharacteristically confused and is not able to give a reliable history of what has happened. He has a routine physical examination, as well as blood and urine investigations, and is diagnosed as having a urinary tract infection. He is given antibiotics, but his nursing care is complicated by his fluctuating confusion. Once or twice he removes his clothes and walks through the ward naked, and at times he tries to leave the ward, unaware that he is in hospital, and believing that he is late for an important work meeting. During more lucid moments, however, he knows where he is and accepts the need for investigation and treatment in hospital.

The responsible consultant, in consultation with ward nursing staff and Mr Baker's daughter, feels that it would be in his best interests to place him in a side room to protect his dignity, and restrict his movements to ensure he remains on the ward.

However, after two days, his confusion appears to worsen: he starts having hallucinations and has to be restrained more often by staff to prevent him leaving the ward. After assessment by a doctor from the liaison psychiatry team, Mr Baker is prescribed antipsychotic medication for his own and other patients' safety. He does not resist taking this medication. The likely benefits and possible side effects are discussed with his daughter and, on balance, the medication is felt to be in his best interests in order to continue his medical investigations.

Staff become concerned about the level of restriction of liberty Mr Baker is now subject to. In particular, they are concerned about the duration of the restrictions; the fact that Mr Baker no longer has lucid intervals when he can give his consent to ongoing care and treatment in hospital; and the physical restraint that is still being required on occasion.

After discussion between the ward manager and Mr Baker's daughter, the managing authority gives an urgent authorisation and submits a request for a standard authorisation to the supervisory body (PCT). A best interests assessor is appointed, and the liaison psychiatrist provides the mental health and mental capacity assessments. In making all the deprivation of liberty safeguards assessments to see whether the qualifying requirements are met, it is considered that although restraint is being used, this does not mean he is objecting having regard to all the circumstances, so he is not ineligible and a standard authorisation is given.

Can a person be moved into care under an urgent authorisation?

6.14 There may be cases in which managing authorities are considering giving an urgent authorisation to enable them to move the relevant person to a new type of care. This may occur, for example, when considering whether to admit a person living at home or with relatives into a hospital care regime that would deprive them of their liberty, and when the need for admission appears to be so urgent that there would not be enough time to follow the standard authorisation process.

6.15 For some people, such a change of location may have a detrimental effect on their mental health, which might significantly distort the way they come across during any assessment process. In such a case, managing authorities should consider whether giving the urgent authorisation and admitting the person to hospital would outweigh the benefits of leaving the person in their existing location, where any assessment of their needs might be more accurate. This will involve looking carefully at the existing care arrangements and consulting with any carers involved, to establish whether or not the person could safely and beneficially be cared for in their home environment while the assessment process takes place. Where the relevant person is already known to statutory care providers, for example the community mental health team or social services, it will be important to involve them in this decision-making process. The relevant person's GP may also be an important source of knowledge about the person's situation, and may be able to offer a valuable opinion when the appropriateness of moving the person into a different care setting is under consideration.

What happens at the end of an urgent authorisation period?

6.16 An urgent authorisation will terminate at the end of the period for which it is given. As noted above, this is normally a maximum of seven days, but in exceptional circumstances an urgent authorisation can be extended to a maximum of 14 days **by the supervisory body**, as explained in paragraphs 6.20 to 6.28.

6.17 An urgent authorisation will terminate before this time if the standard authorisation applied for is given.

6.18 An urgent authorisation will also terminate if a managing authority receives notice from the supervisory body that the standard authorisation will not be given. It will not then be lawful to continue to deprive the relevant person of their liberty.

6.19 The supervisory body must inform the relevant person and any IMCA instructed that the urgent authorisation has ended. This notification can be combined with the notification to them of the outcome of the application for standard authorisation.

Scenario: Considering an urgent authorisation

Mr Watson is 35. He has autism and learning disabilities. He lives in the family home with his parents. Although he is well settled and generally calm at home, Mr Watson sometimes becomes disturbed when in an unfamiliar and crowded environment.

While his parents are away for a couple of days, and Mr Watson is in the care of a paid carer, he has an accident at home. His carer is concerned that he may have broken his arm and takes him to the A&E

> department at the local hospital, where it is decided that his arm needs to be X-rayed to check for a break. The outcome is that there is no break, just bad bruising, so there is no medical need to admit him.
>
> However, because of the pain he is in and the crowded environment, Mr Watson has become very agitated to the extent that hospital security personnel feel a need to control him physically. The carer tries to restrain him and lead him outside where she says he is likely to be more settled and calm down.
>
> Because restraint is being used, the A&E doctor wonders whether it his duty to use an urgent authorisation or other measure to detain Mr Watson in hospital if he believes it is in his best interests.
>
> He consults a liaison psychiatry nurse, who reassures him that such restraint is permitted under the Mental Capacity Act 2005 where it is necessary to prevent harm to the person himself and so long as it is a proportionate response. The nurse assists the carer with gentle restraint to take Mr Watson to a quieter area. She suggests the doctor phone Mr Watson's parents for further information, and obtains painkillers for Mr Watson.
>
> The doctor speaks to Mr Watson's parents, who believe that Mr Watson does not have the mental capacity to decide on his care and treatment in the current circumstances. They have experienced similar situations many times, and are confident that Mr Watson will calm down once he is back in his home environment. They state that if any more detailed assessment of his mental state is required it should take place there, in the company of the carer whom they know and trust. They reassure the doctor that Mr Watson is highly unlikely to present a danger to himself, his carer or the general public.
>
> The doctor decides that it will be in Mr Watson's best interests to return home with his carer.

How and when can an urgent authorisation be extended?

6.20 If there are exceptional reasons why the request for a standard authorisation cannot be dealt with within the period of the original urgent authorisation, the managing authority may ask the supervisory body to extend the duration of the urgent authorisation for a maximum of a further seven days. The managing authority must keep a written record of the reason for making the request and must notify the relevant person, in writing, that they have made the request. Standard forms are available for managing authorities to request the extension of an urgent authorisation from a supervisory body and for supervisory bodies to record their decision in response to such a request.

6.21 Unless the duration of the urgent authorisation is extended by the supervisory body, or a standard authorisation is given before the urgent authorisation expires, the authority to deprive the person of liberty will cease once the urgent authorisation period has expired. It is therefore essential that any request for an extension of an urgent authorisation is made promptly. This will necessitate good communication between the managing authority and the supervisory body regarding the progress of the standard authorisation assessment process. Particular care may need to be taken where an urgent authorisation is due to expire over the weekend or on a bank holiday, when appropriate people at the managing authority and supervisory body may not be immediately available.

6.22 The supervisory body may only extend the duration of the urgent authorisation if:
- the managing authority has made a request for a standard authorisation
- there are exceptional reasons why it has not yet been possible to make a standard authorisation, and
- it is essential for the deprivation of liberty to continue while the supervisory body makes its decision.

6.23 Extensions can only be granted for exceptional reasons. An example of when an extension would be justified might be where:
- it was not possible to contact a person whom the best interests assessor needed to contact
- the assessment could not be relied upon without their input, and
- extension for the specified period would enable them to be contacted.

6.24 It is for the supervisory body to decide what constitutes an 'exceptional reason', but because of the seriousness of the issues involved, the supervisory body's decision must be soundly based and defensible. It would not, for example, be appropriate to use staffing shortages as a reason to extend an urgent authorisation.

6.25 An urgent authorisation can only be extended once.

6.26 The supervisory body must notify the managing authority of the length of any extension granted and must vary the original urgent authorisation so that it states the extended duration. The supervisory body must also keep a written record of the outcome of the request and the period of the extension.

6.27 The managing authority must give a copy of the varied urgent authorisation to the relevant person and any IMCA instructed, and must seek to ensure that, as far as possible, the relevant person understands the effect of the varied authorisation and the right to challenge the authorisation via the Court of Protection. The appropriate information must be given both orally and in writing.

6.28 If the supervisory body decides not to extend the urgent authorisation, it must inform the managing authority of its decision and the reasons for it. The managing authority must give a copy of the notice to the relevant person and any IMCA involved.

7 WHAT IS THE ROLE OF THE RELEVANT PERSON'S REPRESENTATIVE?

Once a standard deprivation of liberty authorisation has been given, supervisory bodies must appoint the relevant person's representative as soon as possible and practical to represent the person who has been deprived of their liberty.

This chapter explains the role of the relevant person's representative and gives guidance on their selection and appointment.

What is the role of the relevant person's representative?

7.1 The supervisory body must appoint a relevant person's representative for every person to whom they give a standard authorisation for deprivation of liberty. It is important that the representative is appointed at the time the authorisation is given or as soon as possible and practical thereafter.

7.2 The role of the relevant person's representative, once appointed, is:
- to maintain contact with the relevant person, and
- to represent and support the relevant person in all matters relating to the deprivation of liberty safeguards, including, if appropriate, triggering a review, using an organisation's complaints procedure on the person's behalf or making an application to the Court of Protection.

This is a crucial role in the deprivation of liberty process, providing the relevant person with representation and support that is independent of the commissioners and providers of the services they are receiving.

7.3 The best interests principle of the Act applies to the relevant person's representative in the same way that it applies to other people acting or making decisions for people who lack capacity.

How should managing authorities work with the relevant person's representative?

7.4 As soon as possible and practical after a standard deprivation of liberty authorisation is given, the managing authority must seek to ensure that the relevant person and their representative understand:
- the effect of the authorisation
- their right to request a review (see chapter 8)
- the formal and informal complaints procedures that are available to them

- their right to make an application to the Court of Protection to seek variation or termination of the authorisation (see chapter 10), and
- their right, where the relevant person does not have a paid 'professional' representative, to request the support of an Independent Mental Capacity Advocate (IMCA) (see paragraphs 7.37 to 7.41).

7.5 When providing information to the person and their representative, the managing authority should take account of the communication and language needs of both the person and their representative. Provision of information should be seen as an ongoing responsibility, rather than a one-off activity.

Who can be the relevant person's representative?[92]

[92] Requirements relating to the eligibility, selection and appointment of relevant person's representatives are covered in regulations. The regulations for England are The Mental Capacity (Deprivation of Liberty: Appointment of Relevant Person's Representative) Regulations 2008. The regulations for Wales are The Mental Capacity (Deprivation of Liberty: Appointment of Relevant Person's Representative) (Wales) Regulations 2008.

7.6 To be eligible to be the relevant person's representative, a person must be:
- 18 years of age or over
- able to keep in contact with the relevant person, and
- willing to be appointed.

The person must not be:
- financially interested in the relevant person's managing authority (a person is considered to be financially interested where that person is a partner, director, other office-holder or major shareholder of the managing authority)
- a relative of a person who has a financial interest in the relevant person's managing authority (paragraph 4.13 explains what is meant by 'relative')
- employed by, or providing services to, the care home in which the person relevant person is residing
- employed by the hospital in a role that is, or could be, related to the treatment or care of the relevant person, or
- employed to work in the relevant person's supervisory body in a role that is, or could be, related to the relevant person's case.

7.7 The appointment of the relevant person's representative is in addition to, and does not affect, any appointment of a donee or deputy. Similarly, the functions of the representative are in addition to, and do not affect, the authority of any donee, the powers of any deputy or any powers of the court. A donee or deputy may themselves be appointed as the relevant person's representative if they meet the eligibility criteria set out in paragraph 7.6.

7.8 There is no presumption that the relevant person's representative should be the same as the person who is their nearest relative for the purposes of the Mental Health Act 1983, even where the relevant person is likely to be subject simultaneously to an authorisation under these safeguards and a provision of the Mental Health Act 1983. This is because the relevant person's representative is not selected in the same way as the nearest relative under the Mental Health Act 1983, nor do they perform the same role. However, there is nothing to stop the relevant person's representative being the same as their nearest relative under the Mental Health Act 1983.

When should the relevant person's representative be identified?

7.9 The process of identifying a representative must begin as soon as possible.

7.10 Normally, this should be when the best interests assessor is appointed – even if one or more of the other assessments has not yet been completed. This is because the best interests assessor must, as part of the assessment process, identify if there is anyone they would recommend to become the relevant person's representative. The best interests assessor should discuss the representative role with the people interviewed as part of the assessment.

7.11 This does leave a risk that the process to identify a representative might begin in cases where authorisation is not given. Nevertheless, it is important that the process begins, so that the representative can be appointed immediately the authorisation is given or as soon as possible and practical thereafter.

How should the relevant person's representative be selected?

7.12 The best interests assessor should first establish whether the relevant person has the capacity to select their own representative and, if so, invite them to do so. If the relevant person has capacity and selects an eligible person (according to the criteria set out in paragraph 7.6), the best interests assessor must recommend that person to the supervisory body for appointment.

7.13 Alternatively, if the relevant person lacks capacity and there is a donee or deputy with the appropriate authority, the donee or deputy may select the person to be recommended as the relevant person's representative, again subject to the criteria set out in paragraph 7.6. If a donee or deputy selects an eligible person, then the best interests assessor must recommend that person to the supervisory body for appointment.

7.14 It is up to the best interests assessor to confirm whether any representative proposed by the relevant person, a donee or a deputy is eligible. If the best interests assessor decides that a proposed representative is not eligible, they must advise the person who made the selection and invite them to make a further selection.

7.15 If neither the relevant person, nor a donee or deputy, selects an eligible person, then the best interests assessor must consider whether they are able to identify someone eligible who could act as the relevant person's representative.

7.16 In making a recommendation, the assessor should consider, and balance, factors such as:
- Does the relevant person have a preference?
- If they do not have the capacity to express a preference now, is there any written statement made by the relevant person when they had capacity that indicates who they may now want to be their representative?
- Will the proposed representative be able to keep in contact with the relevant person?
- Does the relevant person appear to trust and feel comfortable with the proposed representative?
- Would the proposed representative be able to represent the relevant person effectively?
- Is the proposed representative likely to represent the relevant person's best interests?

In most cases, the best interests assessor will be able to check at the same time that the proposed representative is willing to take on the role.

7.17 It should not be assumed that the representative needs to be someone who supports the deprivation of liberty.

7.18 The best interests assessor must not select a representative where the relevant person, if they have the capacity to do so, or a donee or a deputy acting within the scope of their authority, states they are not content with that selection.

7.19 If the best interests assessor is unable to recommend anybody to be the relevant person's representative, they must notify the supervisory body accordingly. The supervisory body must then itself identify an eligible person to be appointed as the representative. In doing so, the supervisory body may select a person who:
- would be performing the role in a professional capacity
- has satisfactory skills and experience to perform the role
- is not a family member, friend or carer of the relevant person
- is not employed by, or providing services to, the relevant person's managing authority, where the relevant person's managing authority is a care home
- is not employed to work in the relevant person's managing authority in a role that is, or could be, related to the relevant person's case, where the relevant person's managing authority is a hospital
- is not employed to work in the supervisory body that is appointing the representative in a role that is, or could be, related to the relevant person's case, and
- the supervisory body is satisfied that an appropriate criminal record certificate has been issued in respect of.

7.20 The supervisory body may pay a person they select to be the relevant person's representative in the circumstances set out in paragraph 7.19. This service could be commissioned, for example, through an advocacy services provider, ensuring that the service provides effective independent representation for the relevant person.

7.21 When selecting a suitable representative for the relevant person, the best interests assessor or supervisory body should pay particular attention to the communication and cultural needs of the relevant person.

How should the relevant person's representative be appointed?

7.22 The supervisory body must invite, in writing, the person recommended by the best interests assessor to become the relevant person's representative. If the best interests assessor does not recommend anyone, then the supervisory body should identify and appoint someone to undertake the role. If the person is willing to become the representative, the supervisory body must formally appoint them. If the person refuses, a further eligible person must be identified and invited to become the representative. This process must continue until an eligible person is appointed.

7.23 The appointment of the relevant person's representative by the supervisory body must be in writing and set out the role and responsibilities of the relevant person's representative. The letter of appointment should also state the name of the appointed person and the date of expiry of the appointment, which must be for the period of the standard authorisation that has been given. The supervisory body must send copies of the written appointment to:
- the appointed person
- the relevant person
- any donee or deputy of the relevant person
- any IMCA involved
- every interested person named by the best interests assessor in their report as somebody they have consulted in carrying out their assessment, and
- the managing authority of the relevant hospital or care home.

7.24 The relevant person's representative must confirm to the supervisory body in writing that they are willing to accept the appointment and have understood their roles and responsibilities in respect of the relevant person.

How should the work of the relevant person's representative be supported and monitored?

7.25 It is important that the representative has sufficient contact with the relevant person to ensure that the relevant person's best interests are being safeguarded. In order to fulfil their role, therefore, the representative will need to be able to have face-to-face contact with the relevant person. That means that the care home or hospital should accommodate visits by the representative at reasonable times. The name of the person's representative should be recorded in the person's health and social care records.

7.26 Managing authorities and supervisory bodies should inform the relevant person's representative about sources of support and information available to help them in the role, including how to access the support of an IMCA (see paragraphs 7.37 to 7.41).

7.27 If the representative has insufficient contact with the relevant person, for whatever reason, the person may effectively be unable to access important review and appeal rights. For this reason, if the representative does not maintain an appropriate level of contact with the person, the managing authority will need to consider informing the supervisory body. When the managing authority is reviewing the person's care plan, it should consider whether the representative is in sufficient contact with the relevant person to offer effective support. Records kept by managing authorities about frequency of contact will support this consideration.

7.28 Because the appropriate levels and methods of contact between a relevant person and their representative will vary from case to case, this is a matter about which the managing authority will need to exercise discretion. If the managing authority has any concerns, it may be best to raise the matter with the representative initially to see whether any perceived problems can be resolved informally. If after this the representative still does not maintain what the managing authority considers to be an appropriate level of contact with the relevant person, then the managing authority should notify the supervisory body.

When can the appointment of the relevant person's representative be terminated?

7.29 The appointment of the relevant person's representative will be terminated in any of the following circumstances:
- The standard authorisation comes to an end and a new authorisation is not applied for or, if applied for, is not given.
- The relevant person, if they have capacity to do so, objects to the representative continuing in their role and a different person is selected to be their representative instead.
- A donee or deputy, if it is within their authority to do so and the relevant person lacks the capacity to decide, objects to the representative continuing in their role and a different person is selected to be the representative instead.
- The supervisory body becomes aware that the representative is no longer willing or eligible to continue in the role.
- The supervisory body becomes aware that the relevant person's representative is not keeping in touch with the person, is not representing and supporting them effectively or is not acting in the person's best interests.
- The relevant person's representative dies.

7.30 If the supervisory body becomes aware that the representative may not be keeping in touch with the person, is not acting in the relevant person's best interests, or is no longer eligible, it should contact the representative to clarify the position before deciding whether to terminate the appointment.

7.31 When the appointment of the relevant person's representative ends, the supervisory body must give notice to all those listed in paragraph 7.23. This notice should be given as soon as possible, stating when the appointment ended and the reason why.

7.32 When the appointment of a relevant person's representative ends but the lawful deprivation of liberty continues, the supervisory body must appoint a suitable replacement to be the relevant person's representative as soon as possible and practical after they become aware of the vacancy. As before, a person qualified to be a best interests assessor should make a recommendation to the supervisory body and the supervisory body should take account of any such recommendations.

7.33 If the reason for the termination of the former representative's appointment is that they are no longer eligible, the views of the former representative on who might replace them should be sought. The person identified as most suitable should then be invited to accept the appointment. This process should continue until an eligible person is willing to accept appointment.

What happens when there is no relevant person's representative available?

7.34 A person who is being deprived of their liberty will be in a particularly vulnerable position during any gaps in the appointment of the relevant person's representative, since there may be nobody to represent their interests or to apply for a review on their behalf. In these circumstances, if there is nobody who can support and represent the person (other than a person engaged in providing care and treatment for the relevant person in a professional capacity or for remuneration), the managing authority must notify the supervisory body, who must instruct an IMCA to represent the relevant person until a new representative is appointed.

7.35 The role of an IMCA instructed in these circumstances is essentially the same as that of the relevant person's representative. The role of the IMCA in this situation ends when the new relevant person's representative is appointed.

7.36 At any time when the relevant person does not have a representative, it will be particularly important for supervisory bodies to consider exercising their discretion to carry out a review if there is any significant change in the person's circumstances.

When should an IMCA be instructed?

7.37 Both the person who is deprived of liberty under a standard authorisation and their representative have a statutory right of access to an IMCA. It is the responsibility of the supervisory body to instruct an IMCA if the relevant person or their representative requests one. The intention is to provide extra support to the relevant person or a family member or friend acting as their representative if they need it, and to help them make use of the review process or access the Court of Protection safeguards. Where the relevant person has a paid 'professional' representative (see paragraphs 7.19 and 7.20), the need for additional advocacy support should not arise and so there is no requirement for an IMCA to be provided in those circumstances.

7.38 The role of the IMCA is to help represent the relevant person and, in particular, to assist the relevant person and their representative to understand the effect of the authorisation, what it means, why it has been given, why the relevant person meets the criteria for authorisation, how long it will last, any conditions to which the authorisation is subject and how to trigger a review or challenge in the Court of Protection. The IMCA can also provide support with a review (see chapter 8) or with an application to the Court of Protection (see chapter 10), for example to help the person to communicate their views.

7.39 The IMCA will have the right to make submissions to the supervisory body on the question of whether a qualifying requirement should be reviewed, or to give information, or make submissions, to any assessor carrying out a review assessment. Both the person and their representative must be told about the IMCA service and how to request an IMCA.

7.40 An IMCA must be instructed whenever requested by the relevant person or their representative. A request may be made more than once during the period of the authorisation. For example, help may be sought at the start of the authorisation and then again later in order to request a review.

7.41 In addition, if the supervisory body has reason to believe that the review and Court of Protection safeguards might not be used without the support of an IMCA, then they must instruct an IMCA. For example, if the supervisory body is aware that the person has selected a representative who needs support with communication, it should consider whether an IMCA is needed.

8 WHEN SHOULD AN AUTHORISATION BE REVIEWED AND WHAT HAPPENS WHEN IT ENDS?

When a person is deprived of their liberty, the managing authority has a duty to monitor the case on an ongoing basis to see if the person's circumstances change – which may mean they no longer need to be deprived of their liberty.

The managing authority must set out in the care plan clear roles and responsibilities for monitoring and confirm under what circumstances a review is necessary. For example, if a person's condition is changing frequently, then their situation should be reviewed more frequently.

This chapter explains the duties of managing authorities and supervisory bodies in relation to reviewing cases, and what happens when an authorisation ends. The review process is set out in flowchart form at Annex 4.

When should a standard authorisation be reviewed?

8.1 A standard authorisation can be reviewed at any time. The review is carried out by the supervisory body.

8.2 There are certain statutory grounds for carrying out a review. If the statutory grounds for a review are met, the supervisory body must carry out a review. If a review is requested by the relevant person, their representative or the managing authority, the supervisory body must carry out a review. Standard letters are available for the relevant person or their representative to request a review. There is also a standard form available for the managing authority to request a review. A supervisory body can also decide to carry out a review at its own discretion.

8.3 The statutory grounds for a review are:
- The relevant person no longer meets the age, no refusals, mental capacity, mental health or best interests requirements.
- The relevant person no longer meets the eligibility requirement because they now object to receiving mental health treatment in hospital and they meet the criteria for an application for admission under section 2 or section 3 of the Mental Health Act 1983 (see paragraphs 4.45 to 4.48).
- There has been a change in the relevant person's situation and, because of the change, it would be appropriate to amend an existing condition to which the authorisation is subject, delete an existing condition or add a new condition.
- The reason(s) the person now meets the qualifying requirement(s) is(are) different from the reason(s) given at the time the standard authorisation was given.

8.4 Different arrangements apply if the person no longer meets the eligibility requirement because they have been detained under the Mental Health Act, or become subject to a requirement under that Act that conflicts with the authorisation. (See paragraphs 8.19 to 8.21 regarding the short-term suspension of a standard authorisation.)

8.5 A managing authority must request a review if it appears to it that one or more of the qualifying requirements is no longer met, or may no longer be met.

What happens when a review is going to take place?

8.6 The supervisory body must tell the relevant person, their representative and the managing authority if they are going to carry out a review. This must be done either before the review begins or as soon as possible and practical after it has begun. A standard form is available for this purpose.

8.7 The relevant person's records must include information about any formal reviews that have been requested, when they were considered, and the outcome. These records must be retained by the supervisory body.

8.8 Deprivation of liberty can be ended before a formal review. An authorisation only **permits** deprivation of liberty: it does not mean that a person **must be** deprived of liberty where circumstances no longer necessitate it. If a care home or hospital decides that deprivation of liberty is no longer necessary then they must end it immediately, by adjusting the care regime or implementing whatever other change is appropriate. The managing authority should then apply to the supervisory body to review and, if appropriate, formally terminate the authorisation.

How should standard authorisations be reviewed?

8.9 When a supervisory body receives a request for a review, it must first decide which, if any, of the qualifying requirements need to be reviewed. A standard form is available for recording this decision.

8.10 If the supervisory body concludes that none of the qualifying requirements need to be reviewed, no further action is necessary. For example, if there has been a very recent assessment or review and no new evidence has been submitted to show that the relevant person does not meet the criteria, or that circumstances have changed, no review is required.

8.11 If it appears that one or more of the qualifying requirements should be reviewed, the supervisory body must arrange for a separate review assessment to be carried out for each of these requirements.

8.12 The supervisory body must record when a review is requested, what it decides to do (whether it decides to carry out a review or not) and the reasons for its decision.

8.13 In general, review processes should follow the standard authorisation processes – so supervisory bodies should conduct the assessments outlined in chapter 4 of this Code of Practice for each of the qualifying requirements that need to be reviewed.

8.14 Where the supervisory body decides that the best interests requirement should be reviewed solely because details of the **conditions** attached to the authorisation need to be changed, and the review request does not include evidence that there is a significant change in the relevant person's overall circumstances, there is no need for a full reassessment of best interests. The supervisory body can simply vary the conditions attached to the authorisation as appropriate. In deciding whether a full reassessment is necessary, the supervisory body should consider whether the grounds for the authorisation, or the nature of the conditions, are being contested by anyone as part of the review request.

8.15 If the review relates to any of the other requirements, or to a significant change in the person's situation under the best interests requirement, the supervisory body must obtain a new assessment.

8.16 If the assessment shows that the requirement is still met, the supervisory body must check whether the reason that it is met has changed from the reason originally stated on the authorisation. If it has, the supervisory body should make any appropriate amendments to the authorisation. In addition, if the review relates to the best interests requirement, the supervisory body must consider whether any conditions should be changed following the new assessment.

Scenario: The review process

Jo is 29 and sustained severe brain damage in a road traffic collision that killed her parents. She has great difficulty in verbal and written communication. Jo can get very frustrated and has been known to lash out at other people in the nursing care home where she now lives. At first, she regularly attempted to leave the home, but the view of the organisation providing Jo's care was that such a move would place her at serious risk, so she should be prevented from leaving.

Jo was assessed under the deprivation of liberty safeguards and an authorisation was made for six months. That authorisation is not due to end for another three months. However, Jo has made huge progress at the home and her representative is no longer sure that the restrictions are necessary. Care home staff, however, do not think that her improvement reduces the best interests requirement of the deprivation of liberty authorisation.

Jo is assisted by her representative to request a review, in the form of a letter with pictures. The pictures appear to describe Jo's frustration with the legal processes that she perceives are preventing her from moving into her own accommodation.

The supervisory body appoints a best interests assessor to coordinate the review. The best interests assessor considers which of the qualifying requirements needs to be reviewed and by whom. It appears that the best interests assessment, as well as possibly the mental health and mental capacity assessments, should be reviewed.

To assess Jo's mental capacity and her own wishes for the best interests assessment, the best interests assessor feels that specialist help would be beneficial. A speech and language therapist meets with Jo and uses a visual communication system with her. Using this system, the therapist is able to say that in her view Jo is unlikely to

> have capacity to make the decision to leave the care home. The mental health assessment also confirmed that Jo was still considered to have a mental disorder.
>
> The best interests assessor was uncertain, however, whether it was still in Jo's best interests to remain under the deprivation of liberty authorisation. It was not possible to coordinate full updated assessments from the rehabilitation team, who knew her well, in the time limits required. So, because the care home believed that the standard authorisation was still required, and it was a complex case, the best interests assessor recommended to the supervisory body that two conditions should be applied to the standard authorisation:
> - assessments must be carried out by rehabilitation specialists on Jo's clinical progress, and
> - a full case review should be held within one month.
>
> At this review meeting, to which Jo's representative and the best interests assessor were invited, it was agreed that Jo had made such good progress that deprivation of liberty was no longer necessary, because the risks of her having increased freedom had reduced. The standard authorisation was therefore terminated, and a new care plan was prepared which focused on working towards more independent living.

What happens if any of the requirements are not met?

8.17 If any of the requirements are not met, then the authorisation must be terminated immediately.

8.18 The supervisory body must give written notice of the outcome of a review and any changes that have been made to the deprivation of liberty authorisation to:
- the managing authority and the care home or hospital itself
- the relevant person
- the relevant person's representative, and
- any Independent Mental Capacity Advocate (IMCA) involved.

Short-term suspension of authorisation

8.19 There are separate review arrangements for cases in which the eligibility requirement ceases to be met for a short period of time for reasons other than that the person is objecting to receiving mental health treatment in hospital. For example, if the relevant person is detained as a hospital in-patient under the Mental Health Act 1983, the managing authority must notify the supervisory body, who will suspend the authorisation.

8.20 If the relevant person then becomes eligible again within 28 days, the managing authority must notify the supervisory body who will remove the suspension. If no such notice is given within 28 days, then the authorisation will be terminated. Standard forms are available for managing authorities to notify supervisory bodies about the need for suspension of an authorisation, or that a suspension should be lifted.

8.21 If the person ceases to meet the eligibility requirement because they begin to object to receiving mental health treatment in hospital and they meet the criteria for an application for admission under section 2 or section 3 of the Mental Health Act 1983, a review should be started immediately (see paragraph 8.3).

Is a review necessary when the relevant person's capacity fluctuates?

8.22 Guidance about people with fluctuating or temporary capacity is contained in paragraphs 4.26 and 4.27 of the main Code. In the context of deprivation of liberty safeguards, where a relevant person's capacity to make decisions about the arrangements made for their care and treatment fluctuates on a short-term basis, a balance needs to be struck between:
- the need to review and terminate an authorisation if a person regains capacity, and
- spending time and resources constantly reviewing, terminating and then seeking fresh deprivation of liberty authorisations as the relevant person's capacity changes.

8.23 Each case must be treated on its merits. Managing authorities should keep all cases under review: where a person subject to an authorisation is deemed to have regained the capacity to decide about the arrangements made for their care and treatment, the managing authority must assess whether there is consistent evidence of the regaining of capacity on a longer-term basis. This is a clinical judgement that will need to be made by a suitably qualified person.

8.24 Where there is consistent evidence of regaining capacity on this longer-term basis, deprivation of liberty should be lifted immediately, and a formal review and termination of the authorisation sought. However, it should be borne in mind that a deprivation of liberty authorisation carries with it certain safeguards that the relevant person will lose if the authorisation is terminated. Where the regaining of capacity is likely to be temporary, and the authorisation will be required again within a short period of time, the authorisation should be left in place, but with the situation kept under ongoing review.

Scenario: Fluctuating capacity

Walter, an older man with severe depression, is admitted to hospital from a care home. He seems confused and bewildered, but does not object. His family are unable to look after him at home, but they would prefer him to go into a different care home rather than stay in hospital.

> However, there is no alternative placement available, so when the assessment concludes that Walter lacks capacity to make decisions about his care and treatment, the only option seems to be that he should stay on the ward,
>
> Because the care regime in the ward is extremely restrictive – Walter is not allowed to leave the hospital and his movement within the hospital is restricted for his own safety – ward staff think that they need to apply for a deprivation of liberty authorisation which is subsequently given.
>
> However, over time Walter starts to experience lucid passages, during which he expresses relief at being on the ward rather than in the care home. A review meeting is convened and the participants agree that Walter now sometimes has capacity to make decisions about the arrangements made for his care and treatment. As this capacity fluctuates, it is decided, in consultation with his family, that the deprivation of liberty authorisation should remain in place for the time being.
>
> Walter remains on the ward and his progress is such that his family feel they could look after him at home. Walter seems happy with this proposal and the consultant psychiatrist with responsibility for his care agrees to this. The deprivation of liberty authorisation is reviewed and terminated.

What happens when an authorisation ends?

8.25 When an authorisation ends, the managing authority cannot lawfully continue to deprive a person of their liberty.

8.26 If the managing authority considers that a person will still need to be deprived of liberty after the authorisation ends, they need to request a further standard authorisation to begin immediately after the expiry of the existing authorisation.

8.27 There is no statutory time limit on how far in advance of the expiry of one authorisation the managing authority can apply for a renewal authorisation. It will need to be far enough in advance for the renewal authorisation to be given before the existing authorisation ends (but see paragraphs 3.19 and 3.20 about not applying for authorisations too far in advance).

8.28 Once underway, the process for renewing a standard authorisation is the same as that for obtaining an original authorisation, and the same assessment processes must take place. However, the need to instruct an IMCA will not usually arise because the relevant person should at this stage have a representative appointed.

8.29 When the standard authorisation ends, the supervisory body must inform in writing:
- the relevant person

- the relevant person's representative
- the managing authority, and
- every interested person named by the best interests assessor in their report as somebody they have consulted in carrying out their assessment.

9 WHAT HAPPENS IF SOMEONE THINKS A PERSON IS BEING DEPRIVED OF THEIR LIBERTY WITHOUT AUTHORISATION?

It is a serious issue to deprive someone of their liberty without authorisation if they lack the capacity to consent. If anyone believes that a person is being deprived of their liberty without authorisation, they should raise this with the relevant authorities.

If the conclusion is that the person is being deprived of their liberty unlawfully, this will normally result in a change in their care arrangements, or in an application for a deprivation of liberty authorisation being made.

This chapter explains the process for reporting concerns and for assessing whether unauthorised deprivation of liberty is occurring. The flowchart at Annex 3 summarises the process that a supervisory body should follow when it receives a request from somebody other than the managing authority to examine whether or not there is a current unauthorised deprivation of liberty.

What action should someone take if they think a person is being deprived of their liberty without authorisation?

9.1 If the relevant person themselves, any relative, friend or carer or any other third party (such as a person carrying out an inspection visit or a member of an advocacy organisation) believes that a person is being deprived of liberty without the managing authority having applied for an authorisation, they should draw this to the attention of the managing authority. A standard letter is available for this purpose. In the first instance, they should ask the managing authority to apply for an authorisation if it wants to continue with the care regime, or to change the care regime immediately. Given the seriousness of deprivation of liberty, a managing authority must respond within a reasonable time to the request. This would normally mean within 24 hours.

9.2 It may be possible for the managing authority to resolve the matter informally with the concerned person. For example, the managing authority could discuss the case with the concerned person, and perhaps make some adjustment to the care arrangements so that concerns that a deprivation of liberty may be occurring are removed. However, if the managing authority is unable to resolve the issue with the concerned person quickly, they should submit a request for a standard authorisation to the supervisory body.

9.3 If the concerned person has raised the matter with the managing authority, and the managing authority does not apply for an authorisation within a reasonable period, the concerned person can ask the supervisory body to decide whether there is an unauthorised deprivation of liberty. They should:
- tell the supervisory body the name of the person they are concerned about and the name of the hospital or care home, and
- as far as they are able, explain why they think that the person is deprived of their liberty.

A standard letter is available for this purpose.

9.4 In such circumstances, the supervisory body must select and appoint a person who is suitable and eligible to carry out a best interests assessment to consider whether the person is deprived of liberty.

9.5 The supervisory body does not, however, need to arrange such an assessment where it appears to the supervisory body that:
- the request they have received is frivolous or vexatious (for example, where the person is very obviously not deprived of their liberty) or where a very recent assessment has been carried out and repeated requests are received, or
- the question of whether or not there is an unauthorised deprivation of liberty has already been decided, and since that decision, there has been no change of circumstances that would merit the question being considered again.

The supervisory body should record the reasons for their decisions. A standard form is available for this purpose.

9.6 The supervisory body must notify the person who raised the concern, the relevant person, the managing authority of the relevant hospital or care home and any IMCA involved:
- that it has been asked to assess whether or not there is an unauthorised deprivation of liberty
- whether or not it has decided to commission an assessment, and
- where relevant, who has been appointed as assessor.

What happens if somebody informs the supervisory body directly that they think a person is being deprived of their liberty without authorisation?

9.7 If a person raises concerns about a potential unauthorised deprivation of liberty directly with the supervisory body, the supervisory body should immediately arrange a preliminary assessment to determine whether a deprivation of liberty is occurring. The supervisory body should then immediately notify the managing authority, rather than asking the concerned person to contact the managing authority themselves, to ask them to request a standard authorisation in respect of the person who is possibly deprived of liberty. The supervisory body should agree with the managing authority what is a reasonable period within which a standard authorisation should be requested (unless the managing authority is able to resolve the matter informally with the concerned person as described in paragraph 9.2). If the managing authority does not submit an application within the agreed period, and the matter has not been resolved informally, the supervisory body should follow the process set out in paragraphs 9.3 to 9.6 to assess whether unlawful deprivation of liberty is occurring. Even if the concerned person prefers to deal directly with the managing authority, the supervisory body should monitor what happens very closely to ensure that no unlawful deprivation of liberty may be occurring without proper action being taken.

How will the assessment of unlawful deprivation of liberty be conducted?

9.8 An assessment of whether an unlawful deprivation of liberty is occurring must be carried out within seven calendar days. Although the assessment must be completed by somebody who is suitable and eligible to carry out a best interests assessment, it is not a best interests assessment as such. The purpose of the assessment is simply to establish whether unlawful deprivation of liberty is occurring.

9.9 The person nominated to undertake the assessment must consult the managing authority of the relevant hospital or care home, and examine any relevant needs assessments and care plans to consider whether they constitute a deprivation of liberty. They should also speak to the person who raised the concern about why they believe that the relevant person is being deprived of their liberty and consult, as far as is possible, with the relevant person's family and friends. If there is nobody appropriate to consult among family and friends, they should inform the supervisory body who must arrange for an IMCA to be instructed to support and represent the person. A standard form is available for the assessor to record the outcome of their assessment.

What happens once the assessment has been conducted?

9.10 There are three possible outcomes of this assessment. The assessor may conclude that:
- the person is not being deprived of their liberty
- the person is being lawfully deprived of their liberty because authorisation exists (this, though, is an unlikely outcome since the supervisory body should already be aware if any authorisation exists, thus rendering any assessment in response to a third party request unnecessary), or
- the person is being deprived of their liberty unlawfully.

9.11 The supervisory body must notify the following people of the outcome of the assessment:
- the concerned third party who made the request
- the relevant person
- the managing authority of the relevant hospital or care home, and
- any IMCA involved.

A standard form is available for this purpose.

9.12 If the outcome of the assessment is that there is an unauthorised deprivation of liberty, then the full assessment process should be completed as if a standard authorisation for deprivation of liberty had been applied for – unless the managing authority changes the care arrangements so that it is clear that there is no longer any deprivation of liberty.

9.13 If, having considered what could be done to avoid deprivation of liberty, the managing authority decides that the need to continue the deprivation of liberty is so urgent that the care regime should continue while the assessments are carried out, it must give an urgent authorisation and seek a standard authorisation within seven days. The managing authority must supply the supervisory body with the same information it would have had to include in a request for a standard authorisation.

9.14 If the concerned person does not accept the outcome of their request for assessment, they can apply to the Court of Protection to hear their case. See chapter 10 for more details of the role of the Court of Protection.

10 WHAT IS THE COURT OF PROTECTION AND WHEN CAN PEOPLE APPLY TO IT?

To comply with Article 5(4) of the European Convention on Human Rights, anybody deprived of their liberty in accordance with the safeguards described in this Code of Practice is entitled to the right of speedy access to a court that can review the lawfulness of their deprivation of liberty. The Court of Protection, established by the Mental Capacity Act 2005, is the court for this purpose. Chapter 8 of the main Code provides more details on its role, powers and responsibilities.

When can people apply to the Court of Protection about the deprivation of liberty safeguards and who can apply?

Applying before an authorisation is given

10.1 The relevant person, or someone acting on their behalf, may make an application to the Court of Protection **before** a decision has been reached on an application for authorisation to deprive a person of their liberty. This might be to ask the court to declare whether the relevant person has capacity, or whether an act done or proposed to be done in relation to that person is lawful (this may include whether or not the act is or would be in the best interests of the relevant person). It is up to the Court of Protection to decide whether or not to consider such an application in advance of the decision on authorisation.

Applying after an authorisation has been given

10.2 Once a standard authorisation has been given, the relevant person or their representative has the right to apply to the Court of Protection to determine any question relating to the following matters:
- whether the relevant person meets one or more of the qualifying requirements for deprivation of liberty
- the period for which the standard authorisation is to be in force
- the purpose for which the standard authorisation is given, or
- the conditions subject to which the standard authorisation is given.

10.3 Where an urgent authorisation has been given, the relevant person or certain persons acting on their behalf, such as a donee or deputy, has the right to apply to the Court of Protection to determine any question relating to the following matters:
- whether the urgent authorisation should have been given
- the period for which the urgent authorisation is to be in force, or
- the purpose for which the urgent authorisation has been given.

10.4 Where a standard or urgent authorisation has been given, any other person may also apply to the Court of Protection for permission to take the relevant person's case to court to determine whether an authorisation should have been given. However, the Court of Protection has discretion to decide whether or not to consider an application from these people.

10.5 Wherever possible, concerns about the deprivation of liberty should be resolved informally or through the relevant supervisory body's or managing authority's complaints procedure, rather than through the Court of Protection. Chapter 15 of the main Code ('What are the best ways to settle disagreements and disputes about issues covered in the Act?') contains general guidance on how to settle disputes about issues covered in the Mental Capacity Act 2005. The review processes covered in chapter 8 of this Code also provide a way of resolving disputes or concerns, as explained in that chapter.

10.6 The aim should be to limit applications to the Court of Protection to cases that genuinely need to be referred to the court. However, with deprivation of liberty at stake, people should not be discouraged from making an application to the Court of Protection if it proves impossible to resolve concerns satisfactorily through other routes in a timely manner.

How should people apply to the Court of Protection?

10.7 Guidance on the court's procedures, including how to make an application, is given in the Court of Protection Rules and Practice Directions issued by the court.[93]

[93] There will usually be a fee for applications to the court. Details of the fees charged by the court and the circumstances in which fees may be waived or remitted are available from the Office of the Public Guardian (http://www.publicguardian.gov.uk/).

10.8 The following people have an automatic right of access to the Court of Protection and do not have to obtain permission from the court to make an application:
- a person who lacks, or is alleged to lack, capacity in relation to a specific decision or action
- the donor of a Lasting Power of Attorney to whom an application relates, or their donee
- a deputy who has been appointed by the court to act for the person concerned
- a person named in an existing court order[94] to which the application relates, and
- the person appointed by the supervisory body as the relevant person's representative.

[94] Examples of existing court orders include orders appointing a deputy or declarations made by the court in relation to treatment issues.

10.9 All other applicants must obtain the permission of the court before making an application. (See section 50 of the Mental Capacity Act 2005, as amended.) This can be done by completing the appropriate application form.

What orders can the Court of Protection make?

10.10 The court may make an order:
- varying or terminating a standard or urgent authorisation, or
- directing the supervisory body (in the case of a standard authorisation) or the managing authority (in the case of an urgent authorisation) to vary or terminate the authorisation.

What is the role of the Court of Protection in respect of people lacking capacity who are deprived of their liberty in settings other than hospitals or care homes?

10.11 The deprivation of liberty safeguards relate only to circumstances where a person is deprived of their liberty in a hospital or care home. Depriving a person who lacks capacity to consent to the arrangements made for their care or treatment of their liberty in other settings (for example in a person's own home, in supported living arrangements other than in care homes or in a day centre) will only be lawful following an order of the Court of Protection on a best interests personal welfare matter (see paragraph 6.51 of the main Code).

10.12 In such a case, application to the Court of Protection should be made before deprivation of liberty begins. A Court of Protection order will then itself provide a legal basis for the deprivation of liberty. A separate deprivation of liberty authorisation under the processes set out in this Code will not be required.

Is legal aid available to support applications to the Court of Protection in deprivation of liberty safeguards cases?

10.13 Legal aid will be available both for advice and representation before the Court of Protection.

11 HOW WILL THE SAFEGUARDS BE MONITORED?

The deprivation of a person's liberty is a significant issue. The deprivation of liberty safeguards are designed to ensure that a person who lacks capacity to consent to the arrangements made for their care or treatment is suitably protected against arbitrary detention. In order to provide reassurance that the safeguards processes are being correctly operated, it is important for there to be an effective mechanism for monitoring the implementation of the safeguards.

Who will monitor the safeguards?

11.1 Regulations[95] will confer the responsibility for the inspection process of the operation of the deprivation of liberty safeguards in England on a new regulator, the Care Quality Commission, bringing together functions from the existing Commission for Social Care Inspection, the Healthcare Commission and the Mental Health Act Commission. The new body will be established during 2008, subject to the passage of the relevant legislation through Parliament, and is expected to be fully operational by 2009/10 in line with the deprivation of liberty safeguards coming into force.

[95] Draft regulations for England will be consulted upon later. Welsh Ministers are currently considering how they will use their regulation-making powers for Wales.

11.2 In Wales, the functions of monitoring the operation of the deprivation of liberty safeguards will fall to Welsh Ministers. These functions will be performed on their behalf by Healthcare Inspectorate Wales and the Care and Social Services Inspectorate Wales.

What will the inspection bodies do and what powers will they have?

11.3 The inspection bodies for care homes and hospitals will be expected to:
- monitor the manner in which the deprivation of liberty safeguards are being operated by:

- visiting hospitals and care homes in accordance with their existing visiting programme
- interviewing people accommodated in hospitals and care homes to the extent that they consider it necessary to do so, and
- requiring the production of, and inspecting, relevant records relating to the care or treatment of people accommodated in hospitals and care homes
- report annually, summarising their activity and their findings about the operation of the deprivation of liberty safeguards. In England this report will be made to the Secretary of State for Health, and in Wales the report will be made to the Welsh Ministers. It will be for each monitoring body to decide whether there should be a deprivation of liberty safeguards specific report or whether the report should form part of a wider report on the monitoring body's activities.

11.4 The inspection bodies will have the power to require supervisory bodies and managing authorities of hospitals or care homes to disclose information to them.

11.5 The inspection process will not cover the revisiting of individual assessments (other than by way of a limited amount of sampling).

11.6 The inspection process will not constitute an alternative review or appeal process. However, if the inspection body comes across a case where they believe deprivation of liberty may be occurring without an authorisation, they should inform the supervisory body in the same way as any other third party may do.

11.7 The inspection bodies will look at the deprivation of liberty protocols and procedures in place within managing authorities and supervisory bodies. The aim is to use a small amount of sampling to evaluate the effect of these protocols and procedures on individual cases. Monitoring should take place at a time when the monitoring body is visiting the care home or in-patient setting as part of routine operations, not as an exception.

11.8 Supervisory bodies and managing authorities should keep their protocols and procedures under review and supervisory bodies should assess the nature of the authorisations they are giving in light of their local population. This information may be relevant to policy decisions about commissioning care and support services.

CHECKLISTS

Key points for care homes and hospitals (managing authorities)

- Managing authorities need to adapt their care planning processes to incorporate consideration of whether a person has capacity to consent to the services which are to be provided and whether their actions are likely to result in a deprivation of liberty.

- A managing authority must not, except in an urgent situation, deprive a person of liberty unless a standard authorisation has been given by the supervisory body for that specific situation, and remains in force.
- It is up to the managing authority to request such authorisation and implement the outcomes.
- Authorisation should be obtained from the supervisory body in advance of the deprivation of liberty, except in circumstances considered to be so urgent that the deprivation of liberty needs to begin immediately. In such cases, authorisation must be obtained within seven calendar days of the start of the deprivation of liberty.
- A managing authority must ensure that they comply with any conditions attached to the authorisation.
- A managing authority should monitor whether the relevant person's representative maintains regular contact with the person.
- Authorisation of deprivation of liberty should only be sought if it is genuinely necessary for a person to be deprived of liberty in their best interests in order to keep them safe. It is not necessary to apply for authorisations for all admissions to hospitals and care homes simply because the person concerned lacks capacity to decide whether to be admitted.

Key points for local authorities and NHS bodies (supervisory bodies)

- Supervisory bodies will receive applications from managing authorities for standard authorisations of deprivation of liberty. Deprivation of liberty cannot lawfully begin until the supervisory body has given authorisation, or the managing authority has itself given an urgent authorisation.
- Before an authorisation for deprivation of liberty may be given, the supervisory body must have obtained written assessments of the relevant person in order to ensure that they meet the qualifying requirements (including that the deprivation of liberty is necessary to protect them from harm and will be in their best interests).
- Supervisory bodies will need to ensure that sufficient assessors are available to meet the needs of their area and that these assessors have the skills, qualifications, experience and training to perform the function.
- Authorisation may not be given unless all the qualifying requirements are met.
- In giving authorisation, the supervisory body must specify its duration, which may not exceed 12 months and may not be for longer than recommended by the best interests assessor. Deprivation of liberty should not continue for longer than is necessary.
- The supervisory body may attach conditions to the authorisation if it considers it appropriate to do so.
- The supervisory body must give notice of its decision in writing to specified people, and notify others.

- The supervisory body must appoint a relevant person's representative to represent the interests of every person for whom they give a standard authorisation for deprivation of liberty.
- When an authorisation is in force, the relevant person, the relevant person's representative and any IMCA representing the individual have a right at any time to request that the supervisory body reviews the authorisation.

Key points for managing authorities and supervisory bodies

In addition to the above, both managing authorities and supervisory bodies should be aware of the following key points:

- An authorisation may last for a maximum period of 12 months.
- Anyone engaged in caring for the person, anyone named by them as a person to consult, and anyone with an interest in the person's welfare must be consulted in decision-making.
- Before the current authorisation expires, the managing authority may seek a fresh authorisation for up to another 12 months, provided it is established, on the basis of further assessment, that the requirements continue to be met.
- The authorisation should be reviewed, and if appropriate revoked, before it expires if there has been a significant change in the person's circumstances. To this end, the managing authority will be required to ensure that the continued deprivation of liberty of a person remains necessary in the best interests of the person.
- A decision to deprive a person of liberty may be challenged by the relevant person, or by the relevant person's representative, by an application to the Court of Protection. However, managing authorities and supervisory bodies should always be prepared to try to resolve disputes locally and informally. No one should be forced to apply to the court because of failure or unwillingness on the part of a managing authority or supervisory body to engage in constructive discussion.
- If the court is asked to decide on a case where there is a question about whether deprivation of liberty is lawful or should continue to be authorised, the managing authority can continue with its current care regime where it is necessary:
  - for the purpose of giving the person life-sustaining treatment, or
  - to prevent a serious deterioration in their condition while the court makes its decision.
- The complete process of assessing and authorising deprivation of liberty should be clearly recorded, and regularly monitored and audited, as part of an organisation's governance structure.
- Management information should be recorded and retained, and used to measure the effectiveness of the deprivation of liberty processes. This information will also need to be shared with the inspection bodies.

ANNEXES
Annex 1

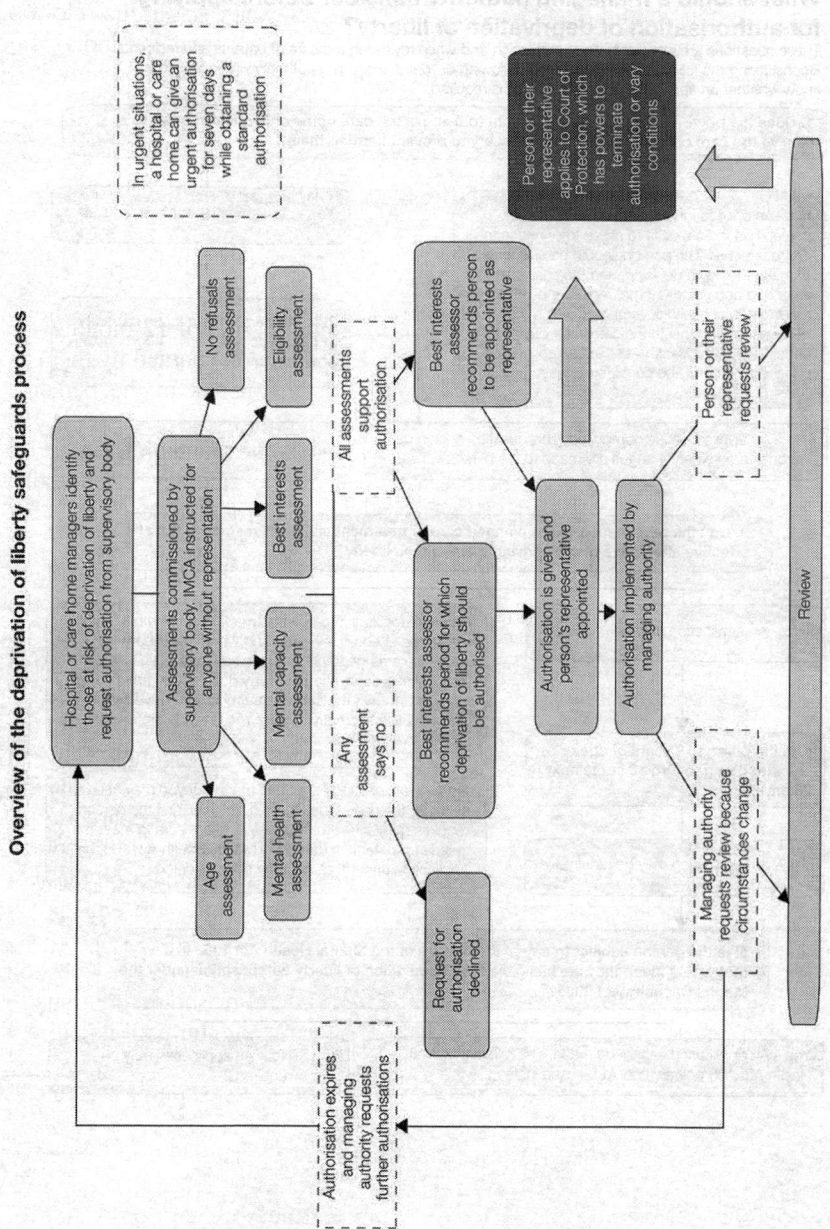

Annex 2

What should a managing authority consider before applying for authorisation of deprivation of liberty?

These questions are relevant **both** at admission **and** when reviewing the care of patients and residents. By considering the following questions in the following or der, a managing authority will be helped to know whether an application for authorisation is required.

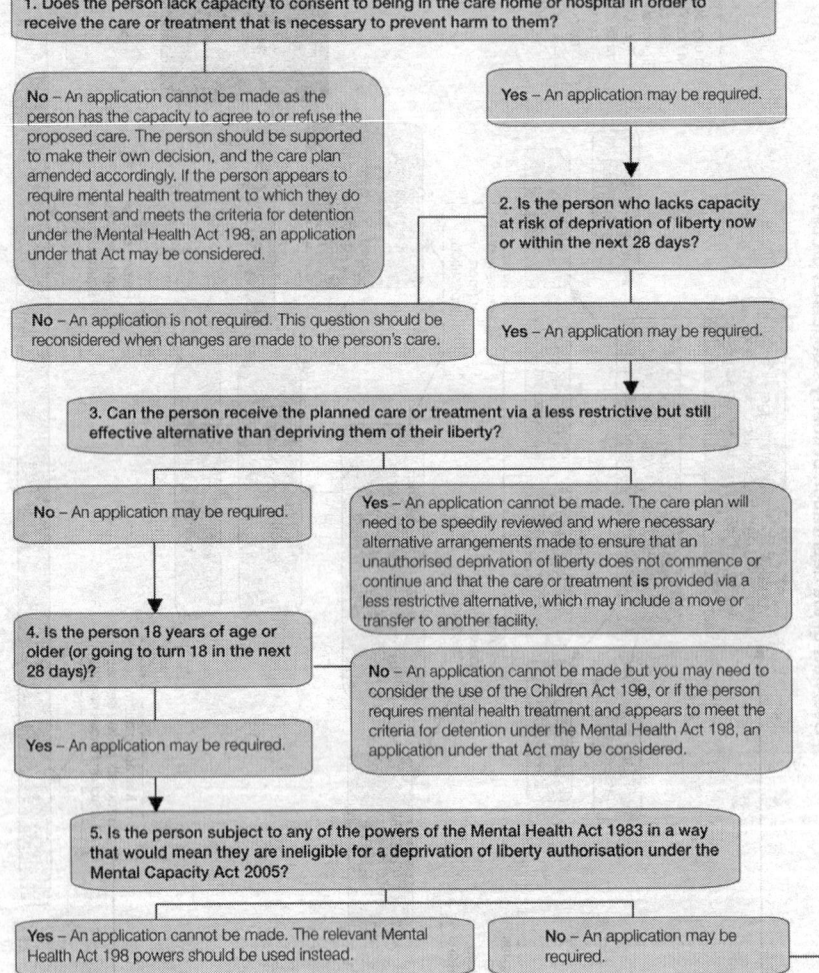

Mental Capacity Act 2005: Deprivation of Liberty Safeguards Code of Practice

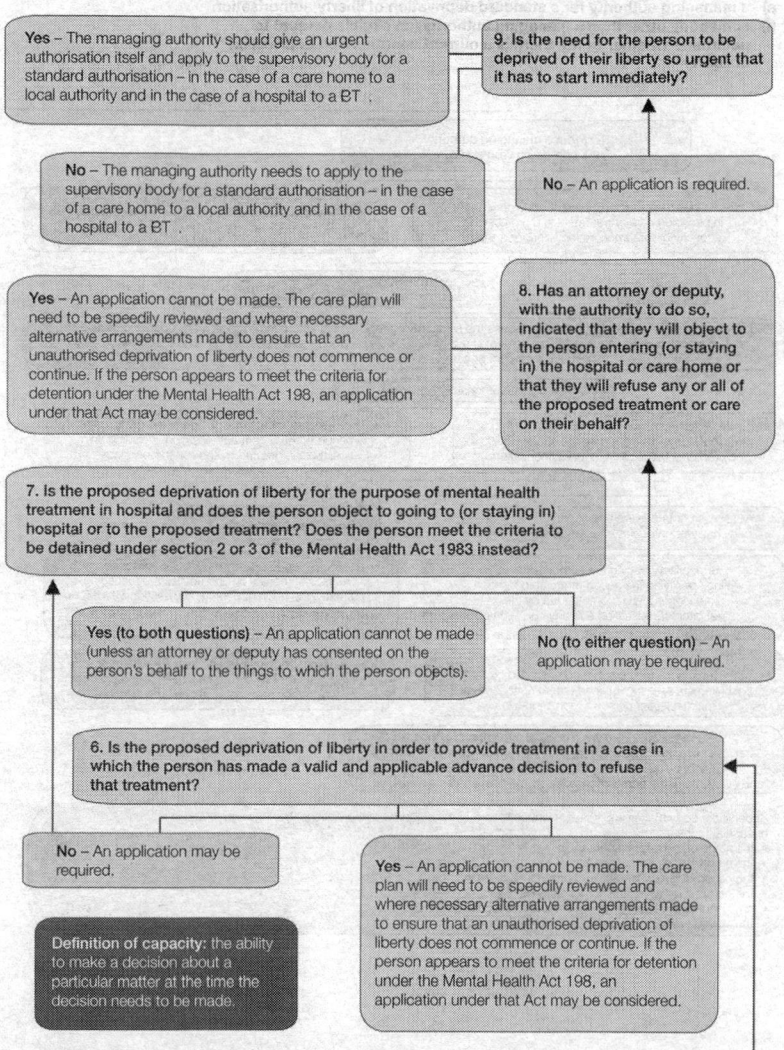

NB: An authorisation only relates to deprivation of liberty and does not give authority for any course of treatment.

Annex 3

Supervisory body action on receipt of a request from:
a) a managing authority for a standard deprivation of liberty authorisation
b) somebody other than a managing authority (an eligible person) to determine whether or not there is a current unauthorised deprivation of liberty

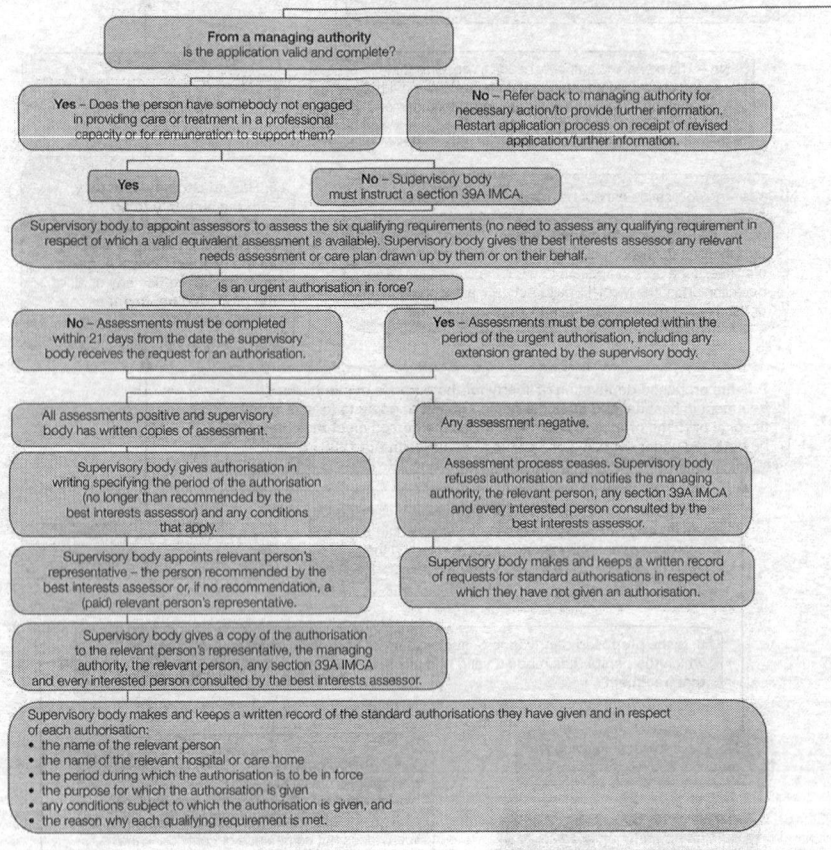

```
                    ┌─────────────────────────────────────┐
                    │ Request received. Supervisory body  │
                    │ makes and keeps written record of   │
                    │ request.                            │
                    └─────────────────────────────────────┘
                                      │
                    ┌─────────────────────────────────────┐
                    │         From an eligible person     │
                    │ Has the eligible person asked the   │
                    │ managing authority to apply for an  │
                    │ authorisation and the managing      │
                    │ authority not done so within a      │
                    │ reasonable period?                  │
                    └─────────────────────────────────────┘
```

Yes – Is the request frivolous or vexatious, or has the question whether or not there has been an unauthorised deprivation of liberty already been decided with no subsequent change of circumstances?

No – Refer the matter back to the eligible person to approach the managing authority.

No – Supervisory body to select a person suitable and eligible to carry out a best interests assessment to assess whether or not there is an unauthorised deprivation of liberty. The assessment must be completed within 7 days.

Yes – Notify the eligible person, the person to whom the request relates and the managing authority that the supervisory body has been asked to decide whether or not there is an unauthorised deprivation of liberty but that it is not to be pursued.

Does the person have somebody not engaged in providing care or treatment in a professional capacity or for remuneration to support them?

Yes

No – Supervisory body must instruct a section 39A IMCA.

Supervisory body to notify the eligible person, the person to whom the request relates, the managing authority and any section 39A IMCA of the decision and who has been appointed to undertake the assessment.

Does assessment confirm that there is a deprivation of liberty?

Yes – Is the deprivation of liberty already authorised?

No – Supervisory body to notify the outcome of the assessment, and give copies of the assessment, to the eligible person, the person to whom the request relates, the managing authority and any section 39A IMCA.

No

Yes – Supervisory body to notify the outcome of the assessment, and give copies of the assessment, to the eligible person, the person to whom the request relates, the managing authority and any section 39A IMCA.

Supervisory body to notify the outcome of the assessment to the eligible person, the person to whom the request relates, the managing authority and any section 39A IMCA.

The managing authority must supply the supervisory body with the information that the managing authority would have had to include in a request for a standard authorisation.

Action must continue as if a request for a standard authorisation had been received from a managing authority.

PART VI

Annex 4

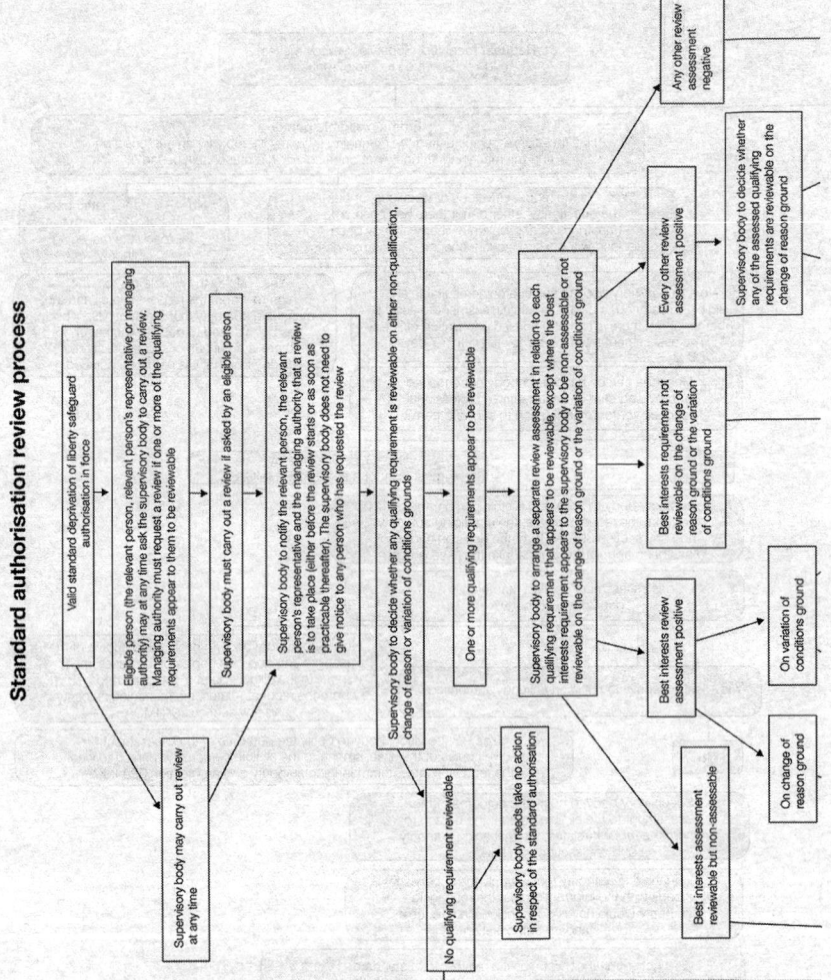

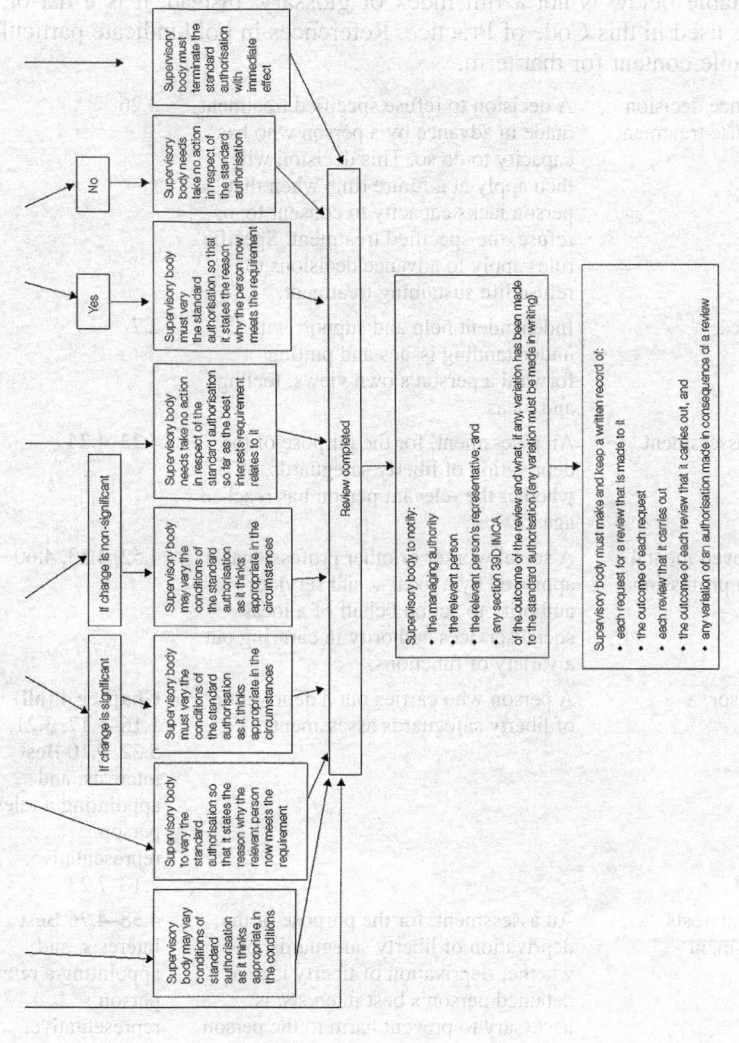

KEY WORDS AND PHRASES USED IN THE CODE OF PRACTICE

The table below is not a full index or glossary. Instead, it is a list of key terms used in this Code of Practice. References in bold indicate particularly valuable content for that term.

Advance decision to refuse treatment	A decision to refuse specified treatment made in advance by a person who has capacity to do so. This decision will then apply at a future time when that person lacks capacity to consent to, or refuse, the specified treatment. Specific rules apply to advance decisions to refuse life sustaining treatment.	4.26
Advocacy	Independent help and support with understanding issues and putting forward a person's own views, feelings and ideas.	2.7
Age assessment	An assessment, for the purpose of the deprivation of liberty safeguards, of whether the relevant person has reached age 18.	**4.23–4.24**
Approved mental health professional	A social worker or other professional approved by a local social services authority to act on behalf of a local social services authority in carrying out a variety of functions.	4.52, 4.53, 4.60
Assessor	A person who carries out a deprivation of liberty safeguards assessment.	**Chapter 4 (all)** 1.16–1.17, 3.21, 5.22, 9.10 Best interests, and appointing a relevant person's representative: 7.10–7.23
Best interests assessment	An assessment, for the purpose of the deprivation of liberty safeguards, of whether deprivation of liberty is in a detained person's best interests, is necessary to prevent harm to the person and is a proportionate response to the likelihood and seriousness of that harm.	**4.58–4.76** Best interests, and appointing a relevant person's representative: 7.10–7.23
Bournewood judgment	The commonly used term for the October 2004 judgment by the European Court of Human Rights in the case of *HL v the United Kingdom* that led to the introduction of the deprivation of liberty safeguards.	**Introduction to chapter 1** 1.19, 2.2, 2.22
Capacity	Short for mental capacity. The ability to make a decision about a particular matter at the time the decision needs to be made. A legal definition is contained in section 2 of the Mental Capacity Act 2005.	Throughout

Care home	A care facility registered under the Care Standards Act 2000.	Throughout
Care Quality Commission	The new integrated regulator for health and adult social care that, subject to the passage of legislation, will take over regulation of health and adult social care from 1 April 2009.	Chapter 11
Carer	Someone who provides unpaid care by looking after a friend or neighbour who needs support because of sickness, age or disability. In this document, the term carer does not mean a paid care worker.	Throughout
Children Act 1989	A law relating to children and those with parental responsibility for children.	1.12, 5.22
Conditions	Requirements that a supervisory body may impose when giving a standard deprivation of liberty authorisation, after taking account of any recommendations made by the best interests assessor.	4.74–4.75 5.5 Review of: 8.14, 8.16
Consent	Agreeing to a course of action – specifically in this document, to a care plan or treatment regime. For consent to be legally valid, the person giving it must have the capacity to take the decision, have been given sufficient information to make the decision, and not have been under any duress or inappropriate pressure.	Throughout
Court of Protection	The specialist court for all issues relating to people who lack capacity to make specific decisions.	**Chapter 10**
Deprivation of liberty	Deprivation of liberty is a term used in the European Convention on Human Rights about circumstances when a person's freedom is taken away. Its meaning in practice is being defined through case law.	**Chapter 2** Throughout
Deprivation of liberty safeguards	The framework of safeguards under the Mental Capacity Act 2005 for people who need to be deprived of their liberty in a hospital or care home in their best interests for care or treatment and who lack the capacity to consent to the arrangements made for their care or treatment.	Throughout
Deprivation of liberty safeguards assessment	Any one of the six assessments that need to be undertaken as part of the standard deprivation of liberty authorisation process.	**Chapter 4**

Deputy	Someone appointed by the Court of Protection with ongoing legal authority, as prescribed by the Court, to make decisions on behalf of a person who lacks capacity to make particular decisions.	4.26, 4.65, 5.11, 5.22, 7.7, 7.13–7.15, 7.18, 7.23, 7.29, 10.3, 10.8
Donee	Someone appointed under a Lasting Power of Attorney who has the legal right to make decisions within the scope of their authority on behalf of the person (the donor) who made the Lasting Power of Attorney.	3.9, 4.26, 4.65, 5.11, 5.22, 7.7, 7.13–7.15, 7.18, 7.23, 7.29, 10.3, 10.8
Eligibility assessment	An assessment, for the purpose of the deprivation of liberty safeguards, of whether or not a person is rendered ineligible for a standard deprivation of liberty authorisation because the authorisation would conflict with requirements that are, or could be, placed on the person under the Mental Health Act 1983.	**4.40–4.57**
European Convention on Human Rights	A convention drawn up within the Council of Europe setting out a number of civil and political rights and freedoms, and setting up a mechanism for the enforcement of the obligations entered into by contracting states.	Chapter 1, Chapter 2
European Court of Human Rights	The court to which any contracting state or individual can apply when they believe that there has been a violation of the European Convention on Human Rights.	Introduction to Chapter 1, 2.1–2.2
Guardianship under the Mental Health Act 1983	The appointment of a guardian to help and supervise patients in the community for their own welfare or to protect other people. The guardian may be either a local authority or a private individual approved by the local authority.	4.43, 4.44
Independent Mental Capacity Advocate (IMCA)	Someone who provides support and representation for a person who lacks capacity to make specific decisions, where the person has no-one else to support them. The IMCA service was established by the Mental Capacity Act 2005 and is not the same as an ordinary advocacy service.	**3.22–3.28, 7.34–7.41** 3.16, 4.7, 5.7–5.8, 5.18, 6.8, 6.19, 6.27–6.28, 7.4, 7.23, 7.26, 8.18, 8.28, 9.6, 9.9
Lasting Power of Attorney	A Power of Attorney created under the Mental Capacity Act 2005 appointing an attorney (donee), or attorneys, to make decisions about the donor's personal welfare, including health care, and/or deal with the donor's property and affairs.	10.8

Life-sustaining treatment	Treatment that, in the view of the person providing health care, is necessary to keep a person alive.	5.13
Local authority	In the deprivation of liberty safeguards context, the local council responsible for social services in any particular area of the country.	1.4, 2.18, 2.21, 3.3, 3.11, 3.21, 4.77
Local health board (LHB)	Local health boards cover the same geographic areas as local authorities in Wales. They work alongside their respective local authorities in planning long-term strategies for dealing with issues of health and wellbeing in their areas.	1.4, 3.3
Main Code	The Code of Practice for the Mental Capacity Act 2005.	Throughout
Managing authority	The person or body with management responsibility for the hospital or care home in which a person is, or may become, deprived of their liberty.	**1.4–1.5, 3.1** Throughout
Maximum authorisation period	The maximum period for which a supervisory body may give a standard deprivation of liberty authorisation, which must not exceed the period recommended by the best interests assessor, and which cannot be for more than 12 months.	4.71
Mental Capacity Act 2005	Legislation that governs decision-making for people who lack capacity to make decisions for themselves or who have capacity and want to make preparations for a time when they may lack capacity in the future. It sets out who can take decisions, in which situations, and how they should go about this.	Throughout
Mental capacity assessment	An assessment, for the purpose of the deprivation of liberty safeguards, of whether a person lacks capacity in relation to the question of whether or not they should be accommodated in the relevant hospital or care home for the purpose of being given care or treatment.	4.29–4.32
Mental disorder	Any disorder or disability of the mind, apart from dependence on alcohol or drugs. This includes all learning disabilities.	1.4, 1.7, 1.9, 3.9, 4.33–4.35, 4.45, 4.50, 5.9, 5.22, 6.3
Mental Health Act 1983	Legislation mainly about the compulsory care and treatment of patients with mental health problems. It covers detention in hospital for mental health treatment, supervised community treatment and guardianship.	**4.33–4.57** 1.1, 1.11–1.12, 2.13, 4.5, 5.19, 5.22, 7.8, 8.3, 8.19–8.21

Mental health assessment	An assessment, for the purpose of the deprivation of liberty safeguards, of whether a person has a mental disorder.	4.33–4.39
No refusals assessment	An assessment, for the purpose of the deprivation of liberty safeguards, of whether there is any other existing authority for decision-making for the relevant person that would prevent the giving of a standard deprivation of liberty authorisation. This might include any valid advance decision, or valid decision by a deputy or donee appointed under a Lasting Power of Attorney.	4.25–4.28
Qualifying requirement	Any one of the six qualifying requirements (age, mental health, mental capacity, best interests, eligibility and no refusals) that need to be assessed and met in order for a standard deprivation of liberty authorisation to be given.	4.1
Relevant hospital or care home	The hospital or care home in which the person is, or may become, deprived of their liberty.	Throughout
Relevant person	A person who is, or may become, deprived of their liberty in a hospital or care home.	Throughout
Relevant person's representative	A person, independent of the relevant hospital or care home, appointed to maintain contact with the relevant person, and to represent and support the relevant person in all matters relating to the operation of the deprivation of liberty safeguards.	**Chapter 7**
Restraint	The use or threat of force to help carry out an act that the person resists. Restraint may only be used where it is necessary to protect the person from harm and is proportionate to the risk of harm.	2.8–2.15
Restriction of liberty	An act imposed on a person that is not of such a degree or intensity as to amount to a deprivation of liberty.	Chapter 2
Review	A formal, fresh look at a relevant person's situation when there has been, or may have been, a change of circumstances that may necessitate an amendment to, or termination of, a standard deprivation of liberty authorisation.	**Chapter 8**
Standard authorisation	An authorisation given by a supervisory body, after completion of the statutory assessment process, giving lawful authority to deprive a relevant person of their liberty in the relevant hospital or care home.	**Chapter 4** Throughout

Supervised community treatment	Arrangements under which people can be discharged from detention in hospital under the Mental Health Act 1983, but remain subject to the Act in the community rather than in hospital. Patients on supervised community treatment can be recalled to hospital if treatment in hospital is necessary again.	4.41, 4.50, 4.51
Supervisory body	A primary care trust, local authority, Welsh Ministers or a local health board that is responsible for considering a deprivation of liberty request received from a managing authority, commissioning the statutory assessments and, where all the assessments agree, authorising deprivation of liberty.	**1.4, 3.3** Throughout
Unauthorised deprivation of liberty	A situation in which a person is deprived of their liberty in a hospital or care home without the deprivation being authorised by either a standard or urgent deprivation of liberty authorisation.	Chapter 9
Urgent authorisation	An authorisation given by a managing authority for a maximum of seven days, which may subsequently be extended by a maximum of a further seven days by a supervisory body, that gives the managing authority lawful authority to deprive a person of their liberty in a hospital or care home while the standard deprivation of liberty authorisation process is undertaken.	**Chapter 6** Throughout

Supervised community treatment	Arrangements under which people can be discharged from detention in hospital under the Mental Health Act 1983, but remain subject to the Act in the community rather than in hospital. Patients on supervised community treatment can be recalled to hospital if treatment in hospital is necessary.	1.51, 4.30, 4.57
Supervisory body	A primary care trust, local authority, Welsh Minister, or a head health board that is responsible for considering a deprivation of liberty request received from a managing authority, commissioning its statutory assessments and, where all the assessments agree, authorising deprivation of liberty.	1.1.3.2, Throughout
Unauthorised deprivation of liberty	A situation in which a person is deprived of their liberty in a hospital or care home without the deprivation being authorised by either a standard or urgent deprivation of liberty authorisation.	Chapter 9
Urgent authorisation	An authorisation given by a managing authority for a maximum of seven days, which may subsequently be extended by a maximum of a further seven days by a supervisory body, that gives the managing authority lawful authority to deprive a person of their liberty in a hospital or care home while the standard deprivation of liberty authorisation process is undertaken.	Chapter 6, Throughout

PART VII

Forms

PART VII: Forms

Contents

Court of Protection Forms	1853
Form COP1 – Application	1854
COP1A – Annex A: Supporting information for property and financial affairs applications	1865
COP1B – Annex B: Supporting information for personal welfare applications	1877
Form COP1C – Annex C: Supporting information for statutory will, codicil, gift(s), deed of variation or settlement of property	1884
Form COP1D – Annex D: Supporting information for applications to appoint or discharge a trustee	1889
Form COP1E – Annex E: Supporting information for an application by existing deputy or attorney	1894
Form COP1F – Annex F: Supporting information relating to validity or operation of enduring power of attorney (EPA) or lasting power of attorney (LPA)	1898
Form COP3 – Assessment of capacity	1902
Form COP4 – Deputy's declaration	1914
Form COP5 – Acknowledgment of service/notification	1921
Form COP5A – Guidance notes on completing form COP5 Acknowledgment of service/notification	1925
Form COP7 – Application to object to the registration of a Lasting Power of Attorney	1927
Form COP8 – Application relating to the registration of an Enduring Power of Attorney	1933
Form COP9 – Application notice	1939
Form COP10 – Application notice for applications to be joined as a party	1944
Form COP12 – Special undertaking by trustees	1949
Form COP14 – Proceedings about you in the Court of Protection	1953
Form COP14A – Guidance notes on completing form COP14	1955
Form COP15 – Notice that an application form has been issued	1957
Form COP15A – Guidance notes for completing form COP15	1959
Form COP20A – Certificate of notification/non-notification of the person to whom proceedings relate	1960
COP 21A – Guidance notes on completing form COP20A	1964
Form COP20B – Certificate of service/non-service notification/non-notification	1966
COP 21B – Guidance notes on completing form COP20B	1970
Form COP22 – Certificate of suitability of litigation friend	1972
Form COP23 – Certificate of failure or refusal of witness to attend before an examiner	1976
Form COP24 – Witness statement	1980
Form COP25 – Affidavit	1984

Form COP28 – Notice of hearing	1988
Form COP29 – Notice of hearing for committal order	1989
Form COP30 – Notice of change of solicitor	1990
Form COP31 – Notice of intention to file evidence by deposition	1993
Form COP35 – Appellant's notice	1995
Form COP36 – Respondent's notice	2006
Form COP37 – Skeleton argument	2016
COP GN1 – Applications for the appointment of a deputy for property and financial affairs	2019
COP GN2 – Guidance on the sale of jointly owned property	2021
COP GN3 – Guidance Note – Applications by existing deputies	2025
COP GN4 – Making a personal welfare application to the Court of Protection	2027
COP GN5 – Coming for a Hearing at the Court of Protection in London or at one of our regional courts	2034
COP GN8 – Applications for Statutory Wills, Gifts, Settlements and other dealings with P's property	2037
EX343 – Unhappy with our service – what can you do?	2038
Form EX343A – Complaint	2041
Applications to the Court of Protection in relation to tenancy agreements	2042
Lasting Powers of Attorney Forms	**2045**
Form LP1F and LP1H – Lasting Power of Attorney	2046
Form LP2 – Register your lasting power of attorney	2092
Form LP3 – Form to notify people	2100
Form LPA003A – Notice to attorney: application to register a lasting power of attorney	2106
Form LPA003B – Notice to donor: application to register a lasting power of attorney	2108
Form LPA005 – Disclaimer by a proposed or acting attorney under a Lasting Power of Attorney	2109
Form LPA006 – Objection by the donor to the registration of a lasting power of attorney	2112
Form LPA007 – Objection to the Office of the Public Guardian of a proposed registration of a Lasting Power of Attorney on factual grounds	2113
Form LPA008 – Notice to the Office of the Public Guardian of an application to object to registration of a lasting power of attorney made to the Court of Protection	2114
LP12 – Make and register your lasting power of attorney: a guide	2116
LPA120 – LPA and EPA fees plus Application for exemption or remission of LPA/EPA application fees	2117
Form LPC – Continuation sheets	2121
Enduring Power of Attorney Forms	**2129**
Form EP1 PG – Notice of intention to apply for registration of an Enduring Power of Attorney	2129
Form EP2 PG – Application to register an Enduring Power of Attorney	2131

Form EP3 PG – Notice to the Office of the Public Guardian of an
    objection to registration of an Enduring Power of Attorney   2143
Deprivation of Liberty Forms   2145
  DLA – Deprivation of Liberty Application form for urgent
    consideration   2145
  DLB – Deprivation of liberty declaration of exceptional urgency   2154
  DLD – Deprivation of liberty Certificate of Service/Non-service;
    Certificate of Notification/Non-notification   2156
  DLE – Deprivation of Liberty acknowledgment of
    service/notification   2158
  DOL10 – Application to authorise a deprivation of liberty   2160

COURT OF PROTECTION FORMS

The Court of Protection can be contacted at:

Court of Protection
PO Box 70185
First Avenue House
42–49 High Holborn
London
WC1A 9JA
DX: 160013 Kingsway 7
Tel: 0300 456 4600 (9am to 5pm)
Court building open: 8.30am to 4.30pm
Court counter open: 9.30am to 4.30pm
Email: courtofprotectionenquiries@hmcts.gsi.gov.uk

Form COP1 – Application

Court of Protection
Application form

Full name of person to whom the application relates
(this is the name of the person who lacks, or is alleged to lack, capacity)

For office use only
Case no.
Application no.
Date received
Date issued

Your application will not be complete unless all the relevant forms and annexes, including where appropriate COP3 (and COP4), are submitted together with a fee or remission request (Please see COP1 guidance). Please submit the COP1 application form in duplicate.

This form is **not to be used** in respect of applications concerning deprivation of liberty (DoL) under section 21A of the Mental Capacity Act 2005 (the Act) relating to a standard or urgent authorisation under Schedule A1 or the streamlined application under section 4A(3) and 16(2)(a) of the Act. For those applications please visit our website at www.gov.uk/court-of-protection

Section 1 – Type of application

1.1 What type of application do you intend to make?

Deputy, proposed deputy or other:	Tick	Enclose Annex/Form:
Appointment of deputy for property and affairs	☐	COP1A
Property and affairs (where deputy not required)	☐	COP1A
Appointment of deputy for personal welfare	☐	COP1B
Personal welfare order (where deputy not required)	☐	COP1B
Application relating to a statutory will, codicil, gift(s), deed of variation or other settlement of property	☐	COP1C
Application relating to the appointment or discharge of a trustee	☐	COP1D and COP12
Application by existing deputy	☐	COP1E
Other applications	☐	COP24
Enduring Powers of Attorney (EPA) or Lasting Powers of Attorney (LPA):	**Tick**	**Enclose Annex/Form:**
Question of validity or operation of an EPA/LPA	☐	COP1F
Application relating to a statutory will, codicil, gift(s), deed of variation or other settlement of property	☐	COP1C
Application relating to the appointment or discharge of a trustee	☐	COP1D and COP12
Application by existing attorney	☐	COP1E
Other applications	☐	COP24

© Crown Copyright 2015

Form COP1 – Application

1.2 Do you require permission to make the application? ☐ Yes, **you must complete section 6**
☐ No

1.3 Do you require **urgent** interim order/directions? ☐ Yes, complete the box below
☐ No

Please state the order/directions sought and reasons for the urgency – You can attach draft interim order/directions

Section 2 – Your details (the applicant(s))

2.1 First applicant ☐ Mr. ☐ Mrs. ☐ Miss ☐ Ms. ☐ Other _____

Full name

Address

Phone

Email

Your relationship to the person to whom this application relates (eg Mother, Father, Brother)

Second applicant ☐ Mr. ☐ Mrs. ☐ Miss ☐ Ms. ☐ Other _____

Full name

Address

Phone

Email

Your relationship to the person to whom this application relates (eg Mother, Father, Brother)

(If more than 2 applicants, please continue on a separate sheet)

PART VII

COURT OF PROTECTION PRACTICE 2016

2.2 In what capacity are you making the application?

☐ Proposed deputy/deputy ☐ I am the person to whom this application relates

☐ Attorney ☐ Other (give details) [ ]

2.3 Please state **one** address that official documentation should be sent to at this stage (please note unless stated below the documentation will be sent to Applicant 1's address)

☐ Applicant 1's address ☐ Applicant 2's address

☐ Solicitors address (if a solicitor is representing you, please give details below)

☐ Other address (if you do not have a solicitor but have an alternative address you would like documentation to be sent to, please give details below)

Contact or Solicitors name	
Address	
Phone	
Email	
DX no.	

Section 3 – The person to whom this application relates

3.1 ☐ Mr. ☐ Mrs. ☐ Miss ☐ Ms. ☐ Other _____

First name(s)	
Last name	
Address	
Phone	
Date of birth	☐ Male ☐ Female

Form COP1 – Application

3.2 What type of accommodation is the person to whom the application relates living in?

(eg. Own home, rented, care home)

Date moved [ ] Temporary [ ] Permanent

3.3 Is the person to whom the application relates:

[ ] Married or in a civil partnership   Date of marriage/civil partnership

[ ] Divorced or their civil partnership has dissolved   Date of divorce/dissolution

[ ] Widowed or a surviving civil partner   Date of death of spouse/civil partner

[ ] In a relationship with a person who is not a spouse or civil partner, but living together as if they were   [ ] Single   [ ] Separated

3.4 Please identify any previous Court of Protection proceedings in respect of the person to whom the application relates

Ref no.   Date of proceedings

Section 4 – Your application

4.1 What order are you asking the court to make?

PART VII

PART VII COURT OF PROTECTION PRACTICE 2016

Section 5 – People to be served with/notified of this application

5.1 Please give details of all respondents who are to be served with this application

Full name including title	Relationship	Full address including postcode

5.2 Please give details of all persons who are to be notified of this application

Full name including title	Relationship	Full address including postcode

Section 6 - Permission

If you do not require permission, go to section 7

6.1 What are you seeking permission for?

☐ to make an application to start proceedings?

6.2 What are your reasons for making the application?

6.3 How would the order you have set out in Section 8.1 of the COP1B (Supporting information for personal welfare applications) benefit the person to whom the application relates? Is there any other way this benefit could be achieved?

Section 7 – Attending court hearings

7.1 If the court requires you to attend a hearing do you need any special assistance or facilities?   ☐ Yes   ☐ No

If Yes, please say what your requirements are. If necessary, court staff may contact you about your requirements.

PART VII

Section 8 – Statement of truth

The statement of truth is to be signed by you, your solicitor or your litigation friend.

*(I believe) (The applicant(s) believe(s)) that the facts stated in this form and its annexes are true.

	First applicant	Second applicant
Signed		
	*Applicant('s litigation friend)('s solicitor)	*Applicant('s litigation friend)('s solicitor)
Name		
Date		
Name of firm		
Position or office held		

* Please delete the options in brackets that do not apply.

If there are more than two applicants, please continue on a separate sheet.

Court of Protection

COP1 Notes
Guidance notes on completing form COP1 Application Form

Please read the following notes before completing form COP1

If you wish to start proceedings in the Court of Protection, you must complete form COP1 and the relevant annex and file it with the court. Refer to Section 1 of the form and the table at the end of these notes to decide what forms you need to complete.

If your application relates to: deprivation of liberty under sections 4A(3) or 21A of the Mental Capacity Act 2005; an objection to the registration of a lasting power of attorney; or the registration of an enduring power of attorney, you need to complete a different application form. Refer to the website www.gov.uk/court-of-protection for more information.

If your application is made in the course of existing proceedings, i.e. you have already made an application; you need to complete a different form: COP9 Application notice for applications within proceedings.

If you are appealing a Court of Protection decision, you need to complete form COP35 Appellant's notice.

You must pay a fee when you make an application. Refer to the leaflet COP44 Court of Protection – Fees for details.

You may need to pay for any legal costs or expenses you incur in connection with your application. In some situations you may be allowed to be reimbursed from the funds of the person to whom the application relates. If the court considers that you have acted unreasonably, it can order you to pay the costs of other parties.

Completing form COP1

Type of application (Section 1)

Please indicate what type of application you intend to make by ticking the relevant box. If you need to make more than one application, for example to appoint a deputy, and appoint or discharge a trustee; you must submit separate applications.

The court cannot accept your application unless you send all the relevant forms with your application. Refer to the table at the end of these notes to decide what other forms you need to complete.

Your application (Section 4)

You need to state what order or declaration you are asking the court to make. In each case the court needs to decide whether the person to whom the application relates is capable of making a decision in relation to the matter to which your application relates.

Please provide specific details about what you want the court to do. For example, you may be asking the court to appoint a deputy, or you may want the court to order that the person to whom the application relates moves to a particular residence, or that a particular investment is made. In each of the examples you would need to explain why the appointment of a deputy is required, or provide the particular details of the residence or investment.

You should also explain to the court why the order or declaration you are seeking will benefit the person to whom the application relates. If you are asking the court to appoint a deputy, please explain why you think this is necessary and why the court should not make the decision on behalf of the person to whom the application relates.

Respondents (Section 5.1)

You must provide the details of any person who you reasonably believe has an interest which means they ought to be heard by the court in relation to the application. Respondents have the opportunity to be joined as parties to the proceedings if they wish to participate in the hearing.

Once the court has issued your application form, you must serve respondents with copies of all documents relating to your application, in order to allow them the opportunity to support or oppose your application.

Other people to be notified (section 5.2)

You must provide the details of other people who are likely to have an interest in being notified of your application. You must notify these people when the court has issued your application form. They have the opportunity to apply to the court to be joined as parties to the proceedings if they wish to participate.

You should seek to identify at least three people to be notified of your application. If you have not already named the following close family members as respondents, they should be notified in descending order as appropriate to the circumstances of the person to whom the application relates:

a) spouse or civil partner
b) person who is not a spouse or a civil partner but who has been living with the person to whom the application relates as if they were
c) parent or guardian
d) child
e) brother or sister
f) grandparent or grandchild
g) aunt or uncle
h) niece or nephew
i) step-parent
j) half-brother or half-sister

Where you think that a person listed in one of the categories ought to be notified, and there are other people in that category (e.g. the person has four siblings) you should provide the details of all of the people falling within that category – unless there is good reason not to do so

You do not need to provide the details for a close family member who has little or no involvement with the person to whom the application relates, or if there is another good reason why they should not be notified.

In some cases, the person to whom the application relates may be closer to people who are not relatives and if so, it will be appropriate to provide their details instead of close family members.

For further guidance on who is to be notified of an application, see practice direction 9B.

Permission (Section 6)

In some cases you will need the court's permission to make an application. You must complete section 6 of this form if you need the court's permission.

a) You do not need the court's permission if the application:
- is made by a person who lacks or is alleged to lack capacity (or, if the person is under 18 years, by anyone with parental responsibility);
- is made by the Official Solicitor, the Public Guardian, or a court appointed deputy;
- concerns the property and affairs of the person to whom the application relates;
- concerns a lasting power of attorney or an enduring power of attorney;
- relates to an application concerning deprivation of liberty under sections 4A(3) or 21A of the Mental Capacity Act 2005; or
- is about an existing court order and is made by a person named in that order.

b) You do need the court's permission for all other applications.

Where part of the application concerns a matter that requires permission, and part of it does not, you need the court's permission only for that part of it which requires permission.

Attending court hearings (Section 7)

If you need special assistance or special facilities for a disability or impairment, please set out your requirements in full. It is important that you make the court aware of your needs to avoid causing any delays.

The court staff will need to know, for example, whether you want documents to be supplied in an alternative format, such as Braille or large print. They will also need to know about any specific requirements should there be a hearing, such as wheelchair access, a hearing loop or a sign language interpreter.

If the person to whom the application relates is a child, you must provide the details of the any person with parental responsibility for the child, so they can be served with your application. If there is no person with parental responsibility, you should name an adult who lives with or cares for the child.

What you need to do next

When you have completed this form, you will need to consider what other forms you need to complete.

The forms to be completed will be different depending on the type of application. Refer to the table at the end of these notes to help you decide what forms to complete.

Forms to be completed

Type of application	Forms to be completed	Where to obtain further guidance
Your application relates to property and affairs	• COP3 Assessment of capacity • COP1A Annex A: Supporting information for property and affairs applications If you are applying to be appointed as a deputy for property and afairs then you must also complete: • COP4 Deputy's declaration	• Practice direction 9A the application form • COP42 Making an application to the Court of Protection • COP GN1 Applications for the appointment of a deputy for property and affairs
Your application relates to personal welfare	• COP3 Assessment of capacity • COP1B Annex B: Supporting information for personal welfare applications If you are applying to be appointed as a deputy for personal welfare then you must also complete: • COP4 Deputy's declaration	• Practice direction 8A Permission • Practice direction 9A the application form • COP42 Making an application to the Court of Protection • COP GN4 Making a personal welfare application to the Court of Protection
Your application relates to a statutory will, codicil, gift(s), deed of variation or settlement of property	• COP3 Assessment of capacity • COP1C Annex C: Supporting information for applications relating to a statutory will, codicil, gift(s), deed of variation or settlement of property	• Practice direction 9A the application form • Practice direction 9F Applications relating to statutory wills, codicils, settlements and other dealings with P's property • COP42 Making an application to the Court of Protection • COP GN8 Applications for statutory wills, codicils, settlements and other dealings with P's property
Your application relates to the appointment or discharge of trustees	• COP1D Annex D: Supporting information for applications to appoint or discharge a trustee • COP12 Special undertaking by trustees	• Practice direction 9A the application form • Practice direction 9G Applications to appoint or discharge a trustee • COP42 Making an application to the Court of Protection • COP GN2 Guidance on the sale of jointly owned property
Your application relates to an existing deputy order or a registered enduring or lasting power of attorney	• COP1E Annex E: Supporting information for an application by an existing deputy or attorney • COP24 Witness statement (if required)	• Practice direction 9D Applications by currently appointed deputies, attorneys and donees in relation to P's property and affairs • COP GN3 Applications by existing deputies
Your application relates to the operation and validity of an enduring power of attorney or a lasting power of attorney	• COP1F Annex F: Supporting information for applications relating to the operation and validity of an enduring power of attorney or a lasting power of attorney • COP24 Witness statement (if required)	• Practice direction 9A the application form • COP42 Making an application to the Court of Protection

Other documents to be filed

You may need to file other documents with your application. The annex to the application form, or practice direction may set out additional information or material required, but you should also file the following documents, if applicable:

- the order appointing a deputy, where the application relates to or is made by a deputy;
- a copy of any lasting or enduring power of attorney;
- the order appointing a litigation friend, where the application is made by, or where the application relates to the appointment of a litigation friend;
- the order of the Court of Protection, where the application relates to the order;
- the order of another court, where the application relates to the order;
- any written evidence on which you intend to rely (in accordance with the relevant practice direction) using the COP24 witness statement form; and
- any other documents you refer to in the application form.

The court requires 2 copies of this form, COP1 Application form and one copy of every other form or document. You should keep copies of each form and document for your own records.

When you have completed all the forms you should take, or send them to the Court of Protection, along with any fee. For details on where to send your application check the website: www.gov.uk/court-of-protection.

What happens next

If you need permission to apply

If your application relates to personal welfare and you need permission to apply, the court will consider your application for permission as soon as practicable after your application form has been issued, and will notify you whether permission is granted, refused, or whether a date has been fixed to consider permission separately.

If permission is granted and the court has received the correct completed forms, you will need to serve a copy on each respondent and notify the person to whom the application relates and the other people you have named in section 5 of this form.

If you do not need permission to apply

If the court has received the correct completed forms, the court will issue your application form and legal proceedings will start. The court will notify you when your application form has been issued and will return a sealed copy of the application form. You will need to serve a copy on each respondent and notify the person to whom the application relates and the other people you have named in section 5 of this form

Disclaimer

Court of Protection staff cannot give legal advice. If you need legal advice please contact a solicitor or your local Citizens Advice Bureau. Information in this guidance is believed to be correct at the time of publication; however we do not accept any liability for any error it may contain.

If you need further help with your application, please check the website: www.gov.uk/court-of-protection.

COP1A – Annex A: Supporting information for property and financial affairs applications

Court of Protection
Annex A: Supporting information for property and financial affairs applications

For office use only
Case no. (if known)
Date received

Full name of person to whom the application relates (this is the name of the person who lacks, or is alleged to lack, capacity)

Please refer to COP1A guidance before completing this form. It is important that this annex form is fully completed. If you do not have enough information you should consider asking for an interim order authorising you to obtain information from banks and other financial institutions.

Please note: This annex must be submitted with COP1.

Section 1 - Your details (the applicant) and details of any proposed deputies

1.1 **(a) Applicant 1**

Proposed deputy? ☐ Yes ☐ No

☐ Mr. ☐ Mrs. ☐ Miss ☐ Ms. ☐ Other _____

First name(s)

Last name

(b) Applicant 2

Proposed deputy? ☐ Yes ☐ No

☐ Mr. ☐ Mrs. ☐ Miss ☐ Ms. ☐ Other _____

First name(s)

Last name

© Crown Copyright 2015

PART VII

If applicable, additional proposed deputies

(c) Proposed deputy

☐ Mr. ☐ Mrs. ☐ Miss ☐ Ms. ☐ Other _____

First name(s) [   ]

Last name [   ]

(d) Proposed deputy

☐ Mr. ☐ Mrs. ☐ Miss ☐ Ms. ☐ Other _____

First name(s) [   ]

Last name [   ]

1.2 ☐ Sole deputyship ☐ Joint deputyship ☐ Joint and several deputyship

Section 2 - Enduring power of attorney or lasting power of attorney

2.1 Has the person to whom the application relates granted a power of attorney, enduring power of attorney or lasting power of attorney? ☐ Yes ☐ No ☐ Don't know

If Yes, please state which type(s) the date granted and the date registered (if known).

	Date made	Date registered
☐ Enduring power of attorney		
☐ Lasting power of attorney property and financial affairs		
☐ Lasting power of attorney health and welfare		

COP1A – Annex A: Supporting information for property and financial affairs applications

2.2 Please state the name(s) and address(es) of the attorney(s) named in the power of attorney

Attorney 1
Name
Address

Attorney 2
Name
Address

Attorney 3
Name
Address

2.3 Has the power of attorney been registered? ☐ Yes ☐ No
☐ Don't know

If Yes, please explain why the appointment of a deputy is sought

If No, please explain why an application to register the power of attorney has not been made

PART VII

Section 3 - Will

3.1 Has the person to whom the application relates made a will? ☐ Yes ☐ No

If Yes, please attched a copy if possible. ☐ Not known

3.2 If you cannot obtain a copy of the will but you know who holds a copy, please give their name and contact details.

[   ]

3.3 Do you seek authority to obtain a copy of the will? ☐ Yes ☐ No

3.4 If known, please provide the names of the executor(s) of the will

[   ]

Section 4 - Income and assets

4.1 What is the national insurance number of the person to whom the application relates?

letters [ ] numbers [   ] letter [ ]

4.2 Is the person to whom the application relates entitled to any benefits? ☐ Yes ☐ No

If Yes, are the benefits received by the person to whom the application relates? ☐ Yes ☐ No

If No, please give details of who receives the benefits:

[   ]

4.3 Please give details below of all income including social security benefits that the person to whom the application relates is entitled.

Income	Annual amount	Social security benefits	Annual amount
Earnings	£	State retirement pension	£
Occupational pension	£	Pension credit	£
Other pensions	£	Attendance allowance	£
Annuities	£	Severe disablement allowance	£
Other income	£	Disability living allowance	£
Trust	£	Incapacity benefit	£
Interest	£	Income support	£
Investment income	£	Council tax benefit	£
	£	Child benefit	£
	£	Other benefits	£
Total	£	Total	£

Interest in a deceased's estate

4.4 Does the person to whom the application relates have any interest in the estate of someone who has died? ☐ Yes ☐ No

If No, go to Section 4.5

Name of deceased

Name of executor/administrator

Approximate value of interest in estate

Is an order required to allow the proposed deputy to obtain a grant in order to deal with the estate of the deceased? ☐ Yes ☐ No

Damages and criminal injuries compensation

4.5 Has a claim been made for an award for damages or, for compensation from the Criminal Injuries Compensation Authority or is such a claim likely to be made? ☐ Yes ☐ No

If No, go to Section 4.8

If Yes, please give details, including the name and address of solicitors involved, the present position regarding the litigation, the likely value of the claim and details of any interim payments that have been, or are going to be, made.

4.6 If a final award has been made please provide details ☐ Copy of final order enclosed

4.7 If the award is in excess of £500,000 please annex a brief statement providing the following details:

(1) Any proposed major capital expenditure (e.g. property)

(2) A budget setting out annual income and the projected annual costs of care

(3) Investment proposal in outline if known

PART VII

PART VII
COURT OF PROTECTION PRACTICE 2016

4.8 Does the person to whom the application relates have any money held in bank or building society accounts (or similar)? ☐ Yes ☐ No

(You must include any money held at the Court Funds Office) If No, go to Section 4.9

Bank/Building Society (or similar accounts)	Account Number	Type of account	Names on the account	Balance
				Total

Continue on separate sheet if necessary

4.9 Does any other person or organisation (other than those already mentioned) hold money for, or owe money to, the person to whom the application relates? ☐ Yes ☐ No

If Yes, please give full details including the name and address of those involved the amount held and the reason for holding the money, or the amount owed and reason for loan.

Investments

4.10 Does the person to whom the application relates own any investments such as stocks and shares, unit trusts, bonds etc? ☐ Yes ☐ No

If Yes, please provide an approximate value of the investments held and the name of the fund manager (if applicable)

Total

COP1A – Annex A: Supporting information for property and financial affairs applications

Land and property

4.11 Does the person to whom the application relates own any land or property? ☐ Yes ☐ No

If Yes, please enter details below If No, go to Section 4.13

Property 1 - address

Market value

Balance of any outstanding mortgage or other legal charge (e.g. equity release)

If the property is not owned solely by the person to whom the application relates please provide the following information:

How is the property held? ☐ Joint tenants

Name and address of the co-owner(s): ☐ Tenants in common

1 Name
  Address

2 Name
  Address

3 Name
  Address

What is the percentage share to which the person to whom the application relates is entitled? ___ %

PART VII

PART VII
COURT OF PROTECTION PRACTICE 2016

Property 2 - address

Market value

Balance of any outstanding mortgage or other legal charge (e.g. equity release)

If the property is not owned solely by the person to whom the application relates please provide the following information:

How is the property held?

☐ Joint tenants

☐ Tenants in common

Name and address of the co-owner(s):

1 Name
  Address

2 Name
  Address

3 Name
  Address

What is the percentage share to which the person to whom the application relates is entitled?

%

If more than 2 properties, please continue on a separate sheet

COP1A – Annex A: Supporting information for property and financial affairs applications

4.12 Is authority sought to sell the property (properties)? ☐ Yes ☐ No

If Yes and there is more than one property, please specify which property is to be sold ☐ 1 ☐ 2 ☐ 3

If No, please set out proposals for dealing with the property (properties) below:

Important
If a property is held in joint names, the deputy, when appointed, will not have the legal authority to deal with its sale. This also applies when a property is held as tenants in common and the co-owner is deceased. Please refer to guidance notes for further information.

Personal possessions

4.13 Please provide details of any possessions with an approximate overall value in excess of £10,000 (e.g. paintings, antiques, collections)

Total value

PART VII

Business

4.14 Does the person to whom the application relates own or have any interest in a business? ☐ Yes ☐ No

If Yes, please provide the following:

a) the name and nature of the business and its legal status, e.g. partnership, sole trader etc.

b) the approximate value of the business

c) the value of the share owned by the person to whom the application relates and their role in the business

d) a draft of any directions or order sought in relation to the business

Expenditure

4.15 Please provide details of the **annual costs** of care (maintenance)

Where the person to whom the application relates lives in a nursing/care home, are they liable to contribute towards the cost? ☐ Yes ☐ No

If Yes, what is the **weekly amount**?

Debts and money owed

4.16 Does the person to whom the application relates have any outstanding debts in excess of £1,000? ☐ Yes ☐ No

If Yes, please give details of any debts of the person to whom the application relates including the name(s) of any creditors and the amount of the debt.

Creditor	Amount
Total	

COP1A – Annex A: Supporting information for property and financial affairs applications

Section 5 - Visits

Please provide details of who visits the person to whom the application relates and how often.

Section 6 - Other information

Please provide any background or additional information which you think might be relevant, or of assistance to the court, when making its decision, including consideration of section 4(6) of the Mental Capacity Act 2005.

Section 7 - Statement of truth

The statement of truth is to be signed by you, your solicitor or your litigation friend.

*(I believe) (The applicant(s) believe(s)) that the facts stated in this annex are true.

	Applicant (1)		Applicant (2)
Signed		Signed	
	*Applicant('s litigation friend)('s solicitor)		*Applicant('s litigation friend)('s solicitor)
Name		Name	
Date		Date	
Name of firm		Name of firm	
Position or office held		Position or office held	

* Please delete the options in brackets that do not apply.

If there are more than 2 applicants, please continue on a separate sheet.

PART VII

1875

Court of Protection

COP1A Notes

Guidance notes on completing form COP1A Annex A: Supporting information for property and financial affairs applications

Please read the following notes before completing Annex A

You must complete and file this annex to form COP1 if your application relates to property and affairs matters. This includes applications to appoint a deputy for property and affairs.

If your application relates to another matter then you may need to complete a different annex. Refer to Section 1 of form COP1 and the notes to form COP1 for information on what forms to complete.

Disclaimer

Court of Protection staff cannot give legal advice. If you need legal advice please contact a solicitor or your local Citizens Advice Bureau. Information in this guidance is believed to be correct at the time of publication; however we do not accept any liability for any error it may contain.

If you need further help with your application, please check the website www.gov.uk/court-of-protection

Completing form Annex A

Please ensure that you provide all relevant information to support your application. If you do not have full details of bank/building society accounts and investments you may need to apply to the court for an interim order to obtain these details.

Please continue on a separate sheet of paper if you need more space to answer a question. Write your name, the name and date of birth of the person to whom the application relates, and the number of the question you are answering.

What you need to do next

When you have completed this form, you will need to consider what other forms and documents you need to complete. Refer to the guidance notes on form COP1 for information on what forms to complete and what you need to do next.

When you have completed all the forms you should take, or send them to the Court of Protection, along with any fee. For details on where to send your application check the website:
www.gov.uk/court-of-protection

12

COP1B – Annex B: Supporting information for personal welfare applications

Court of Protection

Annex B: Supporting information for personal welfare applications

For office use only
Case no.
Date received

Full name of person to whom the application relates (this is the name of the person who lacks, or is alleged to lack, capacity)

Please note: COP1 and this annex are **not** to be used in respect of applications concerning deprivation of liberty (DoL) under section 21A of the Mental Capacity Act 2005 (the Act) relating to a standard or urgent authorisation under Schedule A1 or the streamlined application under section 4A(3) and 16(2)(a) of the Act. For those applications please visit our website at www.gov.uk/court-of-protection

Please note: This form must be submitted with COP1

Section 1 - Type of application - A fee is payable per application (see COP44)

1.1 This application relates to:

- ☐ Serious medical treatment — Enclose COP3 or alternative evidence of capacity and all evidence referred to in Practice Direction 9(E)

- ☐ Healthcare or medical treatment
- ☐ Residence
- ☐ Contact — Enclose COP3 or alternative evidence of capacity
- ☐ Prohibited contact order
- ☐ Other (see below)

- ☐ Appointment of deputy for personal welfare — Enclose COP3 or alternative evidence of capacity and form COP4 deputy's declaration

- ☐ Other (please give details below)

1.2 Are you seeking a declaration of **exceptional urgency**?
☐ Yes, **you must complete section 6**
☐ No

1.3 Do you require **urgent interim order/directions**?
☐ Yes, **you must complete section 7**
☐ No

© Crown Copyright 2015

PART VII
COURT OF PROTECTION PRACTICE 2016

Section 2 - Your details (the applicant)

2.1 **(a) Applicant 1**

☐ Mr. ☐ Mrs. ☐ Miss ☐ Ms. ☐ Other _____

First name(s) [   ]

Last name [   ]

(b) Applicant 2

☐ Mr. ☐ Mrs. ☐ Miss ☐ Ms. ☐ Other _____

First name(s) [   ]

Last name [   ]

Section 3 - Information about the person to whom the application relates

3.1 Do you personally visit the person to whom the application relates? ☐ Yes ☐ No

If Yes, how frequently? [   ]

3.2 Does anyone else visit the person to whom the application relates? ☐ Yes ☐ No

If Yes, please provide details of the most frequent visitors

Name	Connection to the person to whom the application relates	Frequency of visits

3.3 **Doctor's details**

Full name [   ]

Address [   ]

1878

COP1B – Annex B: Supporting information for personal welfare applications

3.4 **Local Authority Social Services details**

Name of local authority

Full name

Address

3.5 **Details of NHS body with responsibility for treatment for the person to whom the application relates**

Full name

Address

Section 4 - Advance decisions and Lasting Powers of Attorney

4.1 Has the person to whom this application relates made an advance decision? ☐ Yes ☐ No ☐ Unknown

If Yes, please give details

4.2 Has the person to whom this application relates granted a Lasting Power of Attorney for health and welfare? ☐ Yes ☐ No

If Yes, please give details

Date made   Date registered

Please provide a certified copy of the registered instrument

4.3 **Attorney (1)**

Full name

Address

Phone no.

3

PART VII

1879

Attorney (2)

Full name	
Address	
Phone no.	

Section 5 - Guardianship

5.1 Have powers of guardianship under the Mental Health Act 1983 been conferred on the Social Services Department of the Local Authority or some other approved person in relation to the welfare of the person to whom the application relates?   ☐ Yes ☐ No

If Yes, please give details

Name of guardian or Local Authority	
Address (including postcode)	
Phone no.	

Section 6 - Declaration of exceptional urgency (only complete if you ticked 'Yes' at 1.2 on page 1)

6.1 Please give your reasons for the urgency:

6.2 By proposed timetable

Please tick the boxes that apply

☐ The application for interim order or directions should be considered within ____ hours/days

☐ Request for permission (if applicable) should be considered within ____ hours/days

☐ Abridgement of time is sought for the lodging of acknowledgments of service ____ hours/days

☐ If permission granted, a substantive hearing is sought by ____ date

COP1B – Annex B: Supporting information for personal welfare applications

Section 7 - Urgent interim orders/directions (only complete if you ticked 'Yes' at 1.3)

7.1 Please state the order/directions sought and the reasons for the urgency?

You may wish to attach draft interim order/directions.

Section 8 - Order sought

8.1 The order I seek is as follows:

8.2 I enclose COP24 Witness Statement setting out evidence in support of my application ☐

Section 9 - Attending court hearings

9.1 If the court requires you to attend a hearing do you need any special assistance or facilities? ☐ Yes ☐ No

If Yes, please say what your requirements are. If necessary, court staff may contact you about your requirements.

PART VII

PART VII												COURT OF PROTECTION PRACTICE 2016

Section 10 - Statement of truth

The statement of truth is to be signed by you, your solicitor or your litigation friend.

*(I believe) The applicant(s) believe(s) that the facts stated in this annex are true.

	Applicant (1)	Applicant (2)
Signed		
	*Applicant('s litigation friend)('s solicitor)	*Applicant('s litigation friend)('s solicitor)
Name		
Date		
Name of firm		
Position or office held		

* Please delete the options in brackets that do not apply.

If there are more than two applicants, please continue on a separate sheet.

Court of Protection

COP1B Notes

Guidance notes on completing form COP1B Annex B: Supporting information for personal welfare applications

Please read the following notes before completing form COP1B

You must complete and file this form if your application relates to personal welfare matters. This includes applications relating to health matters and applications to appoint a deputy for personal welfare.

You must also complete this form if your application relates to both property and affairs and personal welfare, for example if you are applying for appointment as deputy for property and affairs and personal welfare.

If your application relates to property and affairs only (which includes financial matters), or is about a lasting or enduring power of attorney, you do not need to complete this form. The guidance notes to form COP1 explain what forms you need to complete for the different types of application.

Completing form COP1B

Type of application (Section 1)

Please state what type of application you are seeking to make by ticking one of the boxes in section 1.1.

Please note: Form COP1B must not be used for applications concerning applications under section 21A of the Mental Capacity Act 2005 relating to the deprivation of liberty safeguards (DoLS) or for applications for a court-authorised deprivation of liberty under the streamlined procedure. If you do need to make a deprivation of liberty application, refer to practice direction 10AA, which you can download from the website.

You may need the court's permission to make a personal welfare application. The guidance notes to form COP1 Application form explain when you will need the court's permission to make an application.

Advance decisions and lasting powers of attorney (Section 4)

If the person the application is about has made an advance decision or lasting power of attorney for health and welfare, provide details. Please provide a copy or if you are unable to do so, explain why. If the lasting power of attorney has not been registered, explain why.

There is no need to provide details of an enduring power of attorney or lasting powers of attorney for property and financial affairs.

Declaration of exceptional urgency (Section 6)

Complete this section if your application is extremely urgent and you require the court to consider it immediately. You must state the reasons for the urgency, including the time by which the court should consider the application; and what order you are asking it to make. Where possible you should provide a draft order with the application.

Please note: You should only seek a declaration of exceptional urgency in cases of emergency. If the judge has concerns that the procedure has been abused, he may ask you or your representative to attend the court to explain your reasons in person.

Urgent interim orders/directions (Section 7)

Complete this section if you are asking the court to make a temporary order, or if there is a matter that requires the courts immediate attention.

Order sought (Section 8)

You need to state what order or declaration you are asking the court to make. In each case, the court needs to decide whether the person to whom the application relates is capable of making a decision in the matter to which your application relates.

Please provide specific detail of the type of matter that you have indicated in section 1.1; and what you are asking the court to do. For example if your application relates to residence you may require the court to decide whether person to whom the application relates is capable of deciding where they should live, and to make an order that they move to a particular residence.

Form COP1C – Annex C: Supporting information for statutory will, codicil, gift(s), deed of variation or settlement of property

Court of Protection

Annex C: Supporting information for statutory will, codicil, gift(s), deed of variation or settlement of property

For office use only
Case no. (if known)
Date received

Full name of person to whom the application relates (this is the name of the person who lacks, or is alleged to lack, capacity)

Please note: This annex must be submitted with COP1

Section 1 - Your details (the applicant)

1.1 **(a) Applicant 1**

☐ Mr. ☐ Mrs. ☐ Miss ☐ Ms. ☐ Other _____

First name(s)

Last name

(b) Applicant 2

☐ Mr. ☐ Mrs. ☐ Miss ☐ Ms. ☐ Other _____

First name(s)

Last name

1.2 I attach

☐ a copy of the order appointing a deputy

☐ an office copy or certified copy of the registered enduring power of attorney or lasting power of attorney for property and financial affairs

☐ written consent of my co-deputy or co-attorney

☐ details confirming I have notified my co-deputy or co-attorney about this application

© Crown Copyright 2015

Form COP1C – Annex C: Supporting information for statutory will, codicil, gift(s), deed of variation or settlement of property

Section 2 - Your application

2.1   Please state the order you are asking the court to make:

Section 3 - Statutory Wills or Codicils

3.1   You must provide the following information to support your application:

☐ A medical report on the current testamentary capacity of the person to whom this application relates

☐ COP24 Witness statement setting out evidence in support of your application and confirmation that the person to whom the application relates is domiciled in England and Wales

☐ COP1A or a summary schedule of assets and their value, annual income and expenditure of the person to whom this application relates

☐ Copy of all previous and existing wills and codicils

☐ Draft proposed will or codicil

☐ Consent to act by proposed Executor(s)

☐ Details of the family of the person to whom this application relates with full names and dates of birth, where known (preferably in the style of a family tree)

PART VII COURT OF PROTECTION PRACTICE 2016

Section 4 - Gift(s), deeds of variation or settlements of property

4.1   You must provide the following information to support your application:

- [ ] A COP3 report or other relevant statement upon capacity

- [ ] Up-to-date report of medical condition of the person to whom this application relates, life expectancy, likelihood of required increased expenditure in the foreseeable future

- [ ] COP24 Witness statement setting out evidence in support of your application, including where appropriate
    - (a) the needs of the person to whom this application relates both current and future estimates and general circumstances
    - (b) details of any capital gains tax, inheritance tax or income tax which may be chargeable in respect of the subject matter of the application
    - (c) an explanation of the effect, if any, that the proposed changes will have on the circumstance of the person to whom the application relates; preferably in the form of a 'before and after' schedule of assets and income.
    - (d) A statement of whether any land would be affected by the proposed settlement and if so, details of its location and title number, if applicable.

- [ ] COP1A or a summary schedule of assets and their value, annual income and expenditure of the person to whom this application relates

- [ ] Copy of current will and any codicil

- [ ] Copy of existing settlement of property if any

- [ ] Draft of proposed deed, deed of variation or trust (if applicable)

- [ ] Details of the family of the person to whom this application relates with full names and dates of birth, where known (preferably in the style of a family tree)

Form COP1C – Annex C: Supporting information for statutory will, codicil, gift(s), deed of variation or settlement of property

Section 5 - Statement of truth

The statement of truth is to be signed by you, your solicitor or your litigation friend.

*(I believe) The applicant(s) believe(s) that the facts stated in this annex are true.

	Applicant (1)	Applicant (2)
Signed		
	*Applicant('s litigation friend)('s solicitor)	*Applicant('s litigation friend)('s solicitor)
Name		
Date		
Name of firm		
Position or office held		

* Please delete the options in brackets that do not apply.

If there are more than two applicants, please continue on a separate sheet.

Court of Protection

COP1C Notes

Guidance notes on completing form COP1C Annex C: Supporting information for statutory will, codicil, gift(s), deed of variation or settlement of property

Please read the following notes before completing form COP1C

You must complete and file this form if your application relates to a statutory will, codicil, gift, deed of variation, or other settlement of property.

The following must be named in your COP1 as respondents to be served with your application as set out in paragraph 9 of practice direction 9F:

- Any beneficiary under an existing will or codicil who is likely to be materially or adversely affected by the application
- Any beneficiary under a proposed will or codicil who is likely to be materially or adversely affected by the application
- Any prospective beneficiary under any intestacy of the person to whom this application relates

Completing form COP1C

Please ensure that you provide all relevant information to support your application. Refer to practice direction 9F for further guidance.

Please continue on a separate sheet of paper if you need more space to answer a question. Write your name, the name and date of birth of the person to whom the application relates, and the number of the question you are answering.

What you need to do next

When you have completed this form, you will need to consider what other forms and documents you need to complete. Refer to the guidance notes on form COP1 for information on what forms to complete and what you need to do next.

When you have completed all the forms you should take, or send them to the Court of Protection, along with any fee. For details on where to send your application check the website: www.gov.uk/court-of-protection.

Disclaimer

Court of Protection staff cannot give legal advice. If you need legal advice please contact a solicitor or your local Citizens Advice Bureau. Information in this guidance is believed to be correct at the time of publication; however we do not accept any liability for any error it may contain.

If you need further help with your application, please check the website www.gov.uk/court-of-protection

Form COP1D – Annex D: Supporting information for applications to appoint or discharge a trustee

Form COP1D – Annex D: Supporting information for applications to appoint or discharge a trustee

Court of Protection

Annex D: Supporting information for applications to appoint or discharge a trustee

For office use only
Case no. (if known)
Date received

Full name of person to whom the application relates (this is the name of the person who lacks, or is alleged to lack, capacity)

Please note: This annex must be submitted with COP1

Section 1 - Your details (the applicant(s))

1.1 **(a) Applicant 1**

☐ Mr. ☐ Mrs. ☐ Miss ☐ Ms. ☐ Other _____

First name(s)

Last name

(b) Applicant 2

☐ Mr. ☐ Mrs. ☐ Miss ☐ Ms. ☐ Other _____

First name(s)

Last name

1.2 I attach

☐ a copy of the order appointing you deputy for the property and affairs of the peson who lacks capacity

☐ an office copy or certified copy of the registered enduring power of attorney or lasting power of attorney for property and financial affairs made by the person who lacks capacity (where the application does not relate to a trust of land)

☐ written consent of your co-deputy or co-attorney

☐ details confirming you have notified your co-deputy or co-attorney about this application

© Crown Copyright 2015

PART VII   COURT OF PROTECTION PRACTICE 2016

Section 2 - Your application

2.1   Please state the order you are asking the court to make?

      [   ]
      [   ]
      [   ]
      [   ]
      [   ]

2.2   I am providing the following information to support my application:

      ☐ COP3 Evidence of capacity or if previously filed in support of an earlier application

            date of report [D][D][M][M][Y][Y][Y][Y]

            and date filed [D][D][M][M][Y][Y][Y][Y]

      ☐ COP24 Witness statement setting out evidence in support of my application incorporating:
            (i) All necessary information specified in Practice Direction 9G
            (ii) Confirmation that any continuing trustee is still capable of carrying out his/her duties (where continuing trustee has executed an enduring power of attorney or a lasting power of attorney for property and financial affairs)

      ☐ COP12 Special undertaking by trustees

      ☐ A witness statement in form COP24 confirming the proposed new trustee's fitness to act (not applicable where the proposed new trustee is a solicitor, trust corporation or deputy)

      ☐ Supporting documents including:

            (a) In respect of all trusts of property: A copy of the entries at the Land Registry or, if the land is unregistered, a copy of the original conveyance or other trust instrument

            (b) In respect of applications under s.54 (where the co-owner is deceased and there is no capable continuing trustee)
                  (i) A copy of the will of the deceased and the grant of representation
                  (ii) A copy of any notice of severance

            (c) In respect of other trusts:
                  (i) A copy of the trust instrument and of any subsequent deeds of appointment and retirement
                  (ii) If a vesting order is required, a schedule of the investments

            (d) A copy of the registered power of attorney in respect of any co-trustee

Form COP1D – Annex D: Supporting information for applications to appoint or discharge a trustee

2.3 I also provide the following additional information in relation to real property:

Address of the property (including postcode)

2.4 Details of proposed new trustees:

Name of proposed trustee (1)

Relationship to the person to whom the application relates

Date of birth D D M M Y Y Y Y   ☐ Male ☐ Female

Address (including postcode)

Name of proposed trustee (2)

Relationship to the person to whom the application relates

Date of birth D D M M Y Y Y Y   ☐ Male ☐ Female

Address (including postcode)

PART VII

PART VII   COURT OF PROTECTION PRACTICE 2016

Section 3 - Statement of truth

The statement of truth is to be signed by you, your solicitor or your litigation friend.

*(I believe) (The applicant(s) believe(s)) that the facts stated in this annex are true.

	Applicant (1)	**Applicant (2)**
Signed		
	*Applicant('s litigation friend)('s solicitor)	*Applicant('s litigation friend)('s solicitor)
Name		
Date		
Name of firm		
Position or office held		

* Please delete the options in brackets that do not apply.

Form COP1D – Annex D: Supporting information for applications to appoint or discharge a trustee

Court of Protection

COP1D Notes

Guidance notes on completing form COP1D Annex D: Supporting information for applications to appoint or discharge trustee

Please read the following notes before completing form COP1D

You must complete and file this form if your application relates to the appointment or discharge of trustees.

Completing form COP1D

Please ensure that you provide all relevant information to support your application. Refer to practice direction 9G for further guidance.

Please continue on a separate sheet of paper if you need more space to answer a question. Write your name, the name and date of birth of the person to whom the application relates, and the number of the question you are answering.

What you need to do next

When you have completed this form, you will need to consider what other forms and documents you need to complete. Refer to the guidance notes on form COP1 for information on what forms to complete and what you need to do next.

When you have completed all the forms you should take, or send them to the Court of Protection, along with any fee. For details on where to send your application check the website: www.gov.uk/court-of-protection

Disclaimer

Court of Protection staff cannot give legal advice. If you need legal advice please contact a solicitor or your local Citizens Advice Bureau. Information in this guidance is believed to be correct at the time of publication; however we do not accept any liability for any error it may contain.

If you need further help with your application, please check the website www.gov.uk/court-of-protection

PART VII   COURT OF PROTECTION PRACTICE 2016

Form COP1E – Annex E: Supporting information for an application by existing deputy or attorney

Court of Protection

Annex E: Supporting information for an application by existing deputy or attorney

For office use only
Case no. (if known)
Date received

Full name of person to whom the application relates
(this is the name of the person who is the subject of the application)

SEAL

Please note: This annex must be submitted with COP1

Section 1 - Your details (the applicant(s))

1.1 **(a) Applicant 1**

☐ Mr.   ☐ Mrs.   ☐ Miss   ☐ Ms.   ☐ Other _____

First name(s)

Last name

(b) Applicant 2

☐ Mr.   ☐ Mrs.   ☐ Miss   ☐ Ms.   ☐ Other _____

First name(s)

Last name

1.2 Please attach if applicable

☐ a copy of the order appointing you deputy

☐ an office copy or certified copy of the registered enduring power of attorney or lasting power of attorney for property and financial affairs

© Crown Copyright 2015

Form COP1E – Annex E: Supporting information for an application by existing deputy or attorney

Section 2 - Your application

2.1 In what capacity are you making the application?

☐ Deputy

☐ Attorney/donee

☐ Other
(please give details)

2.2 ☐ If joint deputy for property and affairs, attorney or donee, I attach the consent of my joint deputy, joint attorney or joint donee

☐ If joint and several deputy, attorney or donee, I have notified my joint deputy, joint attorney or joint donee about this application

2.3 Please state the order you are asking the court to make having regard to the guidance in Practice Direction 9D

2.4 You must file a COP24 witness statement in support of your application and relevant exhibits if necessary

☐ Evidence attached

Section 3 - Statement of truth

The statement of truth is to be signed by you, your solicitor or your litigation friend.

*(I believe) (The applicant believes) that the facts stated in this annex are true.

	Applicant (1)	Applicant (2)
Signed		
	*Applicant('s litigation friend)('s solicitor)	*Applicant('s litigation friend)('s solicitor)
Name		
Date		
Name of firm		
Position or office held		

* Please delete the options in brackets that do not apply.

If there are more than two applicants, please continue on a separate sheet.

Form COP1E – Annex E: Supporting information for an application by existing deputy or attorney

Court of Protection

COP1E Notes

Guidance notes on completing form COP1E (Supporting information for an application by existing deputy or attorney)

Please read the following notes before completing form COP1E

This form should only be used where:

- You are currently appointed deputy for property and affairs for the person to whom the application relates; or you are an attorney under a registered enduring power of attorney, or lasting power of attorney for property and financial affairs; and
- **for a deputy:** your application relates to the powers and duties set out in the order appointing you as deputy, and you are asking the court to vary those powers;
- **for an attorney:** you need to make a decision concerning the property and affairs of the person to whom the application relates, and the enduring power of attorney or lasting power of attorney instrument does not provide you with the authority to make the decision in question.

This form should not be used for applications to appoint a deputy, applications relating to the appointment and discharge of trustees, applications relating to the registration of enduring or lasting powers of attorney; nor should it be used for any other applications for which there is a specific annex to the COP1 Application form. Please refer to the guidance notes to form COP1.

Completing form COP1E

Please ensure that you provide all relevant information to support your application. Refer to practice direction 9D and guidance note COP GN3 Applications by existing deputies for further guidance.

Please continue on a separate sheet of paper if you need more space to answer a question. Write your name, the name and date of birth of the person to whom the application relates, and the number of the question you are answering.

The court will require the following information on form COP24 Witness statement in support of your application:

- A summary of all capital assets belonging to the person to whom the application relates. Please include money held at the Court Funds Office, savings, investments and any funds held by you as deputy.

- Details, including occupation and the current value, of any property belonging to the person to whom the application relates, and whether you intend to sell the property. Please note that if the property is held jointly then a deputy cannot deal with the sale and you will need to make a separate application to appoint a trustee (see Guidance Note 1 for details)
- The approximate annual income including pensions, social security benefits, dividends from investments and interest from savings.
- The current level of security set by the court and confirmation that all premiums have been paid to date.

You must also enclose with your application either:

- A copy of the current order appointing you as deputy; or
- the registered enduring or lasting power of attorney for property and financial affairs.

What you need to do next

When you have completed this form, you will need to consider what other forms and documents you need to complete. Refer to the guidance notes on form COP1 for information on what forms to complete and what you need to do next.

When you have completed all the forms you should take, or send them to the Court of Protection, along with any fee. For details on where to send your application check the website:
www.gov.uk/court-of-protection.

Disclaimer

Court of Protection staff cannot give legal advice. If you need legal advice please contact a solicitor or your local Citizens Advice Bureau. Information in this guidance is believed to be correct at the time of publication; however we do not accept any liability for any error it may contain.

If you need further help with your application, please check the website www.gov.uk/court-of-protection.

PART VII   COURT OF PROTECTION PRACTICE 2016

Form COP1F – Annex F: Supporting information relating to validity or operation of enduring power of attorney (EPA) or lasting power of attorney (LPA)

Court of Protection

Annex F: Supporting information relating to validity or operation of enduring power of attorney (EPA) or lasting power of attorney (LPA)

For office use only
Case no. (if known)
Date received

SEAL

Name of the donor of the EPA/LPA
(this is the person who made the EPA/LPA)

If you are objecting to the registration of an EPA or LPA **do not complete this form**
Please note: This annex must be submitted with COP1

Section 1 - Your application

1.1 Your name

1.2 Your description
- [ ] Donor
- [ ] Attorney/Donee   [ ] Sole   [ ] Joint   [ ] Joint and several
- [ ] Other
(please give details)

Section 2 - Details of EPA/LPA

2.1 Full name of attorney(s)/donee(s)

[ ] Mr.   [ ] Mrs.   [ ] Miss   [ ] Ms.   [ ] Other _____

First name(s)

Last name

[ ] Mr.   [ ] Mrs.   [ ] Miss   [ ] Ms.   [ ] Other _____

First name(s)

Last name

[ ] Mr.   [ ] Mrs.   [ ] Miss   [ ] Ms.   [ ] Other _____

First name(s)

Last name

© Crown Copyright 2015

Form COP1F – Annex F: Supporting information relating to validity or operation of enduring power of attorney (EPA) or lasting power of attorney (LPA)

2.2 Date donor signed the EPA/LPA

2.3 Date of registration (if applicable)

2.4 ☐ I enclose a copy of the EPA/LPA

(For LPAs only)
☐ It is a property and financial affairs LPA
☐ It is health and welfare LPA

2.5 Please state the order you are asking the court to make?

2.6 You must file a COP24 witness statement in support of your application and relevant exhibits if necessary

☐ Evidence attached

PART VII

Section 3 - Statement of truth

The statement of truth is to be signed by you, your solicitor or your litigation friend.

*(I believe) (The applicant believes) that the facts stated in this annex are true.

Signed

*Applicant('s litigation friend)('s solicitor)

Name

Date

Name of firm

Position or office held

* Please delete the options in brackets that do not apply.

Form COP1F – Annex F: Supporting information relating to validity or operation of enduring power of attorney (EPA) or lasting power of attorney (LPA)

Court of Protection

COP1F Notes

Guidance notes on completing form COP1F Annex F: Supporting information relating to validity or operation of enduring power of attorney (EPA) or lasting power of attorney (LPA)

Please read the following notes before completing form COP1F

You must complete and file this form if your application relates to the validity or operation of an LPA or EPA.

Completing form COP1F

Please ensure that you provide all relevant information to support your application. Refer to practice direction 9G for further guidance.

Please continue on a separate sheet of paper if you need more space to answer a question. Write your name, the name and date of birth of the person to whom the application relates, and the number of the question you are answering.

What you need to do next

When you have completed this form, you will need to consider what other forms and documents you need to complete. Refer to the guidance notes on form COP1 for information on what forms to complete and what you need to do next.

When you have completed all the forms you should take, or send them to the Court of Protection, along with any fee. For details on where to send your application check the website: www.gov.uk/court-of-protection.

Disclaimer

Court of Protection staff cannot give legal advice. If you need legal advice please contact a solicitor or your local Citizens Advice Bureau. Information in this guidance is believed to be correct at the time of publication; however we do not accept any liability for any error it may contain.

If you need further help with your application, please check the website www.gov.uk/court-of-protection

Form COP3 – Assessment of capacity

Court of Protection
Assessment of capacity

For office use only
Date received
Case no.

Full name of person to whom the application relates
(this is the name of the person who lacks, or is alleged to lack, capacity)

Please read first

- If you are applying to start proceedings with the court you must file this form with your COP1 application form. The assessment must contain current information.

- You must complete Part A of this form.

- You then need to provide the form with Part A completed to the practitioner who will complete Part B. The practitioner will return the form to you or your solicitor for filing with the court.

- The practitioner may be a registered:

    – medical practitioner, for example the GP of the person to whom the application relates;

    – psychiatrist

    – approved mental health professional

    – social worker

    – psychologist

    – nurse, or

    – occupational therapist

    who has examined and assessed the capacity of the person to whom the application relates. In some circumstances it might be appropriate for a registered therapist, such as a speech therapist or occupational therapist, to complete the form.

- When the form has been completed, its contents will be confidential to the court and those authorised by the court to see it, such as parties to the proceedings.

- Please continue on a separate sheet of paper if you need more space to answer a question. Write your name, the name and date of birth of the person to whom the application relates, and number of the question you are answering on each separate sheet.

- There are additional guidance notes at the end of this form.

- If you need help completing this form please check the website, www.gov.uk/court-of-protection, for further guidance or information, or contact Court Enquiry Service on 0300 456 4600 or courtofprotectionenquiries@hmcts.gsi.gov.uk

- Court of Protection staff cannot give legal advice. If you need legal advice please contact a solicitor.

- This form has been prepared in consultation with the British Medical Association, the Royal College of Physicians, Royal College of Psychiatrists and the Department of Health.

© Crown Copyright 2013

Form COP3 – Assessment of capacity

Part A - To be completed by the applicant

Section 1 - Your details (the applicant)

1.1 Your details ☐ Mr. ☐ Mrs. ☐ Miss ☐ Ms. ☐ Other _____

   First name

   Middle name(s)

   Last name

1.2 Address (including postcode)

   Telephone no. | Daytime
                 | Evening
                 | Mobile

   E-mail address

1.3 Is a solicitor representing you? ☐ Yes ☐ No

   If Yes, please give the solicitor's details.

   Name

   Address (including postcode)

   Telephone no. | | Fax no. |
   DX no.
   E-mail address

1.4 To which address should the practitioner return the form when they have completed Section 2?

   ☐ Your address

   ☐ Solicitor's address

   ☐ Other address (please provide details)

Section 2 - The person to whom the application relates (the person to be assessed by the practitioner)

2.1 ☐ Mr. ☐ Mrs. ☐ Miss ☐ Ms. ☐ Other _____

First name

Middle name(s)

Last name

Address (including postcode)

Telephone no.

Date of birth ☐☐|☐☐|☐☐☐☐ ☐ Male ☐ Female

Section 3 - About the application

3.1 Please state the matter you are asking the court to decide. (see note 1)

3.2 What order are you asking the court to make?

3.3 How would the order benefit the person to whom the application relates?

3.4 What is your relationship or connection to the person to whom the application relates?

Form COP3 – Assessment of capacity

Section 4 - Further information

Please provide any further information about the circumstances of the person to whom the application relates that would be useful to the practitioner in assessing his or her capacity to make any decision(s) that is the subject of your application. **(see note 2)**

PART VII

Now read note 3 about what you need to do next.

Part B - To be completed by the practitioner

Section 5 - Your details (the practitioner)

5.1 ☐ Mr.   ☐ Mrs.   ☐ Miss   ☐ Ms.   ☐ Dr.   ☐ Other _____

First name

Middle name(s)

Last name

Address (including postcode)

Telephone no.

E-mail address

5.2 Nature of your professional relationship with the person to whom the application relates
(For example, social worker or general practitioner (GP))

5.3 Please state your professional qualifications and practial experience with particular reference to making assessments of capacity in accordance with the Mental Capacity Act 2005 and associated Code of Practice.

Form COP3 – Assessment of capacity

If there is information that you do not wish to provide in this form because of its sensitive nature you can provide the information directly to the court.

6.1 Are you providing any sensitive information separately to the court? ☐ Yes ☐ No

Please provide it in writing to:
　Court of Protection
　PO Box 70185
　First Avenue House
　42-49 High Holborn
　London WC1A 9JA

　DX 160013
　Kingsway 7

Please include your name and contact details, and the name, address and date of birth of the person to whom the application relates on any information you provide separately to the court.

Section 7 - Assessment of capacity

7.1 The person to whom the application relates has the following impairment of, or disturbance in the functioning of, the mind or brain. Where this impairment or disturbance arises out of a specific diagnosis, please set out the diagnosis or diagnoses here: **(see note 4)**

This has lasted since:

As a result, the person is unable to make a decision for themselves in relation to the following matter(s) in question:

PART VII

PART VII   COURT OF PROTECTION PRACTICE 2016

7.2   The person to whom the application relates is unable to make a decision in relation to the relevant matter because: **(see note 5)**

☐ he or she is unable to understand the following relevant information (please give details);

[ ]

and/or

☐ he or she is unable to retain the following relevant information (please give details);

[ ]

and/or

☐ he or she is unable to use or weigh the following relevant information as part of the process of making the decision(s) (please give details);

[ ]

and/or

☐ is unable to communicate his or her decision(s) by any means at all (please give details).

[ ]

Form COP3 – Assessment of capacity

7.3 My opinion is based on the following evidence of a lack of capacity:

7.4 Please answer either (a) **or** (b).

(a) I have acted as a practitioner for the person to whom the application relates since ☐☐/☐☐/☐☐☐☐ and last assessed him or her on ☐☐/☐☐/☐☐☐☐

(b) I assessed the person to whom the application relates on ☐☐/☐☐/☐☐☐☐

following a referral from:

PART VII

PART VII

7.5 Has the person to whom this application relates made you aware of any views they have in relation to the relevant matter? ☐ Yes ☐ No

If Yes, please give details.

7.6 Do you consider there is a prospect that the person to whom the application relates might regain or acquire capacity in the future in respect of the decision to which the application relates? **(see note 6)**

☐ Yes – please state why and give an indication of when this might happen.

☐ No – please state why.

7.7 Are you aware of anyone who holds a different view regarding the capacity of the person to whom the application relates? ☐ Yes ☐ No

If Yes, please give details.

Form COP3 – Assessment of capacity

7.8 Do you, your family or friends have any interest (financial or otherwise) in any matter concerning the person to whom the application relates? ☐ Yes ☐ No

If Yes, please give details.

7.9 Do you have any general comments or any other recommendations for future care? **(see note 7)**

Signed

Name   Date

Now read note 8 about what you need to do next.

PART VII

Guidance notes

About the application

These questions are repeated on the COP1 application form. Please copy your answers from the COP1 form so that the information on both forms is the same.

Further information

Please provide any further information about the circumstances of the person to whom the application relates that would be relevant in assessing their capacity. For example, if your application relates to property and financial affairs, it would be useful for the practitioner to know the general financial circumstances of the person concerned. This information will help the practitioner evaluate the decision-making responsibility of the person to whom the application relates and may help to inform the practitioner's view on whether that person can make the decision(s) in question.

What you need to do next

Please provide this form to the practitioner who will complete Part B.

The practitioner will return the form to you or your solicitor when they have completed Part B. You will then need to file the form with the court together with the COP1 application form and any other information the court requires. See note 8 on the COP1 form for further information.

Assessing capacity

For the purpose of the Mental Capacity Act 2005 a person lacks capacity if, at the time a decision needs to be made, he or she is unable to make or communicate the decision because of an impairment of, or a disturbance in the functioning of, the mind or brain.

The Act contains a two-stage test of capacity:

1. Is there an impairment of, or disturbance in the functioning of, the person's mind or brain?
2. If so, is the impairment or disturbance sufficient that the person lacks the capacity to make a decision in relation to the matter in question?

Please refer to Part A of this form where the applicant has set out details of the application and relevant information about the circumstances of the person to whom the application relates. In particular, section 3.1 sets out the matter the applicant is asking the court to decide.

The assessment of capacity must be based on the person's ability to make a decision in relation to the relevant matter, and not their ability to make decisions in general. It does not matter therefore if the lack of capacity is temporary, if the person retains the capacity to make other decisions, or if the person's capacity fluctuates.

Under the Act, a person is regarded as being unable to make a decision if they cannot:

- understand information about the decision to be made;
- retain that information;
- use or weigh the information as part of the decision-making process; or
- communicate the decision (by any means).

A lack of capacity cannot be established merely by reference to a person's age or appearance or to a particular condition or an aspect of behaviour. A person is not to be treated as being unable to make a decision merely because they have made an unwise decision.

The test of capacity is not the same as the test for detention and treatment under the Mental Health Act 1983. Many people covered by the Mental Health Act have the capacity to make decisions for themselves. On the other hand, most people who lack capacity to make decisions will never be affected by the Mental Health Act.

Practitioners are required to have regard to the Mental Capacity Act 2005 Code of Practice. The Code of Practice is available online at www.gov.uk/court-of-protection Hard copies are available from The Stationery Office (TSO), for a fee, by:

- phoning 0870 600 5522;
- emailing customerservices@tso.co.uk; or
- ordering online at www.tsoshop.co.uk.

For further advice please see (for example):

- Making Decisions: A guide for people who work in health and social care (2nd edition), Mental Capacity Implementation Programme, 2007.
- Assessment of Mental Capacity: Guidance for Doctors and Lawyers (2nd edition), British Medical Association and Law Society (London: BMJ Books, 2004)

Form COP3 – Assessment of capacity

Note 5

Capacity to make the decision in question

Please give your opinion of the nature of the lack of capacity and the grounds on which this is based. This requires a diagnosis and a statement giving clear evidence that the person to whom the application relates lacks capacity to make the decision(s) relevant to the application. It is important that the evidence of lack of capacity shows how this prevents the person concerned from being able to take decision(s).

Note 6

Prospect of regaining or acquiring capacity

When reaching any decision the court must apply the principles set out in the Act and in particular must make a determination that is in the best interests of the person to whom the application relates. It would therefore assist the court if you could indicate whether the person to whom the application relates is likely to regain or acquire capacity sufficiently to be able to make decisions in relation to the relevant matter.

Note 7

General comments

The court may make any order it considers appropriate even if that order is not specified in the application form. Where possible, the court will make a one-off decision rather than appointing a deputy with on-going decision making power. If you think that an order other than the one being sought by the applicant would be in the best interests of the person to whom the application relates, please give details including your reasons.

Note 8

What you need to do next

Please return the completed form to the applicant or their solicitor, as specified in section 1.4. You are advised to keep a copy for your records.

PART VII   COURT OF PROTECTION PRACTICE 2016

Form COP4 – Deputy's declaration

Court of Protection
Deputy's declaration

For office use only
Case no. (if known)
Date received

Full name of person to whom the application relates
(this is the name of the person who lacks, or is alleged to lack, capacity)

Section 1 - Your details (the person applying to be appointed as a deputy)

1.1 Your title ☐ Mr. ☐ Mrs. ☐ Miss ☐ Ms. ☐ Other _____

First name

Middle name(s)

Last name

1.2 Address (including postcode)

Telephone no.
Daytime	
Evening	
Mobile	

E-mail address

1.3 Date of birth D D / M M / Y Y Y Y

1.4 What is your connection to the person to whom the application relates?

© Crown Copyright 2015

1914

Form COP4 – Deputy's declaration

Details of the person to whom the application relates

1.5 Full name

Address (including postcode)

Date of birth: D D M M Y Y Y Y

Section 2 - Your personal circumstances

2.1 What is your current occupation?
If you are not in paid employment, please give details of your current circumstances or previous occupation if retired.

2.2 How long have you worked in your current occupation?

[ ] Years [ ] Months

2.3 Have you ever been appointed to act as a deputy or attorney for anyone else? ☐ Yes ☐ No

If Yes, please give the name(s) of the person(s) and (if known) the court reference(s).

2.4 Have you ever been convicted of a criminal offence? ☐ Yes ☐ No
(Do not include convictions spent under the Rehabilitation of Offenders Act 1974).

If Yes, please provide details of the offence, including the date of conviction.

2.5 Are there any circumstances (personal or otherwise) which would interfere with your ability to carry out the duties of a deputy effectively? (e.g. ill health or business/family commitments). ☐ Yes ☐ No

If Yes, please provide details.

PART VII

PART VII   COURT OF PROTECTION PRACTICE 2016

2.6 If you are not appointed as a deputy or become unable to take up an appointment, ☐ Yes ☐ No
     are you aware of any other person (or officer holder) who might wish to be
     considered as a deputy?

     If Yes, please provide details.

     ┌───┐
     │   │
     │   │
     └───┘

Section 3 - Your financial circumstances

Please complete this section if you are applying to be appointed as a property and affairs deputy.

3.1 Do you have a personal bank or building society current/deposit account?   ☐ Yes ☐ No

3.2 Have you ever been refused credit? (e.g. having a personal loan application refused) ☐ Yes ☐ No

     If Yes, please provide details.

     ┌───┐
     │   │
     │   │
     └───┘

3.3 Do you have any outstanding judgment debts?   ☐ Yes ☐ No

     If Yes, please provide details.

     ┌───┐
     │   │
     │   │
     └───┘

3.4 Have you personally ever been declared bankrupt or the debtor under an   ☐ Yes ☐ No
     Individual Voluntary Arrangement under Part VIII of the Insolvency Act 1986 or
     subject to a debt relief order?

     If Yes, please provide details.

     ┌───┐
     │   │
     │   │
     └───┘

3.5 Are you currently an undischarged bankrupt or the debtor under an Individual ☐ Yes ☐ No
     Voluntary Arrangement or subject to a Debt Relief Order?

     If Yes, please give provide details.

     ┌───┐
     │   │
     │   │
     └───┘

3

Form COP4 – Deputy's declaration

3.6 Has any business that you have been involved with (whether a company, partnership or otherwise) been subject to a recognised insolvency regime (e.g. voluntary arrangement, winding-up, administration, receivership, administrative receivership)? ☐ Yes ☐ No

If Yes, please provide details.

3.7 Have you been the subject of a declaration under section 213 (fraudulent trading) or section 214 (wrongful trading) of the Insolvency Act 1986? ☐ Yes ☐ No

If Yes, please provide details.

3.8 Have you been the subject of a bankruptcy restrictions order under section 281A or Schedule 4A of the Insolvency Act 1986, or a disqualification order under section 1 of the Company Directors (Disqualification) Act 1986? ☐ Yes ☐ No

If Yes, please provide details.

3.9 Are you aware of any matter in which your financial interests may conflict with those of the person to whom the application relates? (e.g. occupation of a property which the person owns, any interest under the terms of their will) ☐ Yes ☐ No

If Yes, please provide details.

PART VII

Section 4 - Your personal undertakings to the person to whom the application relates

Becoming a deputy means that you have to take on a number of duties and responsibilities and have to act in accordance with certain standards. If you are appointed as a deputy, the court order will set out the exact powers conferred on you.

The main duties and responsibilities you may have to take on are set out below. Please review each one and tick 'Yes' if you give your undertaking to act in accordance with the duty or responsibility. You can use the 'Comments' section to support your undertakings. Please mention if you have a particular professional skill, life experience, public duty or role that you think is relevant.

If you do not give your undertaking and tick 'No', please use the 'Comments' section to explain your reasons. It may be because you do not yet have experience in the particular duty, or think you might not have the skills needed. It will not necessarily prevent your appointment as deputy.

Not all of the undertakings set out below will be relevant to every deputy. If you think this is the case, tick 'No' and explain in the 'Comments' section that the undertaking would be irrelevant to your appointment.

	Undertaking	Yes or No	Comments
1	I will have regard to the Mental Capacity Act 2005 Code of Practice and I will apply the principles of the Act when making a decision. In particular I will act in the best interests of the person to whom the application relates and I will only make those decisions that the person cannot make themselves.	☐ Yes ☐ No	
2	I will act within the scope of the powers conferred on me by the court as set out in the order of appointment and will apply to the court if I feel additional powers are needed.	☐ Yes ☐ No	
3	I will act with due care, skill and diligence, as I would do in making my own decisions and conducting my own affairs. Where I undertake my duties as a deputy in the course of my professional work (if relevant), I will abide by professional rules and standards.	☐ Yes ☐ No	
4	I will make decisions on behalf of the person to whom the application relates as required under the court order appointing me. I will not delegate any of my powers as a deputy unless this is expressly permitted in the court order appointing me.	☐ Yes ☐ No	
5	I will ensure that my personal interests do not conflict with my duties as a deputy, and I will not use my position for any personal benefit.	☐ Yes ☐ No	
6	I will act with honesty and integrity, and will take any decisions made by the person to whom the application relates while they still had capacity, into account when determing their best interests.	☐ Yes ☐ No	
7	I will keep the person's financial and personal information confidential (unless there is a good reason that requires me to disclose it).	☐ Yes ☐ No	

Form COP4 – Deputy's declaration

8	I will comply with any directions of the court or reasonable requests made by the Public Guardian, including requests for reports to be submitted.	☐ Yes ☐ No
9	I will visit the person to whom the application relates as regularly as is appropriate and take an interest in their welfare.	☐ Yes ☐ No
10	I will work with the person to whom the application relates and any carer(s) to achieve the best quality of life for him or her within the funds available.	☐ Yes ☐ No
11	I will co-operate with any representative of the court or the Public Guardian who might wish to meet me or the person to whom the application relates to check that the deputyship arrangements are working.	☐ Yes ☐ No
12	I will immediately inform the court and the Public Guardian if I have any reason to believe that the person to whom the application relates no longer lacks capacity and may be able to manage his or her own affairs.	☐ Yes ☐ No

	Further undertakings if you are applying to be appointed as a property and affairs deputy	Yes or No	Comments
13	I understand that I may be required to provide security for my actions as deputy. If I am required to purchase insurance, such as a guarantee bond, I undertake to pay premiums promptly from the funds of the person to whom the application relates.	☐ Yes ☐ No	
14	I will keep accounts of dealings and transactions taken on behalf of the person to whom the application relates.	☐ Yes ☐ No	
15	I will keep the money and property of the person to whom the application relates separate from my own.	☐ Yes ☐ No	
16	I will ensure so far as is reasonable that the person to whom the application relates receives all benefits and other income to which they are entitled, that their bills are paid and that a tax return for them is completed annually.	☐ Yes ☐ No	
17	I will take reasonable steps to maintain the property of the person to whom the application relates (if applicable), for example arranging for insurance, repairs or improvements. If necessary I will arrange and oversee a sale or letting of property with appropriate legal advice.	☐ Yes ☐ No	

PART VII

PART VII   COURT OF PROTECTION PRACTICE 2016

Section 5 - Personal statement to the court

Please state why you wish to be the deputy of the person to whom the application relates.

[blank box]

Section 6 - Statement of truth

The statement of truth is to be signed by the person applying to be appointed as a deputy.

I believe that the facts stated in this declaration are true.

Signed

Name   **Date**

//
Form COP5 – Acknowledgment of service/notification

Court of Protection

Acknowledgment of service/notification

If you do not wish to take part in the court proceedings, you do not need to complete this form.

For office use only
Case no.

Full name of person to whom the application relates
(this is the name of the person who lacks, or is alleged to lack, capacity)

Failure to answer any of the relevant sections may result in you not being joined as a party or having your views taken into account.

Section 1 – Your details (the person served/notified)

1.1 Your details ☐ Mr.   ☐ Mrs.   ☐ Miss   ☐ Ms.   ☐ Other _____

   First name

   Middle name(s)

   Last name

1.2 Address (including postcode)

   Telephone no.   Daytime
                   Evening
                   Mobile

   E-mail address

PART VII

© Crown Copyright 2015

1.3 Is a solicitor representing you? ☐ Yes ☐ No

If Yes, please give the solicitor's details.

Name	
Address (including postcode)	

Telephone no.		Fax no.	
DX no.			
E-mail address			

1.4 Which address should official documentation be sent to?

☐ Your address

☐ Your solicitor's address

☐ Other address (please provide details)

1.5 What is your role in these proceedings?

☐ Person to whom the application relates

☐ Respondent*

☐ Person notified that the application form has been issued

*You are a respondent if you have been served with a copy of the COP1 application form.

Form COP5 – Acknowledgment of service/notification

Section 2 – Application to be joined as a party

if you are the person to whom the application relates or a person notified that the application form has been issued and you wish to apply to be joined as a party, you must complete this section.

2.1 Do you wish to be joined as a party to proceedings? ☐ Yes ☐ No

2.2 If Yes, Please state your interest in the proceedings.

2.3 You must file evidence of your interest in the proceedings either now, or you can send it later. If you are sending it later it must reach the court within 28 days of the date on which you were given notice. Use form COP24 witness statement to provide your evidence.

☐ Evidence attached

Section 3 – Acknowledgment of service/notification

3.1 I,

☐ consent to the application

☐ oppose the application

☐ seek a different order

☐ seek a different direction

3.2 Please provide brief reasons including the order or directions you are seeking, or if you consent, provide any relevant information you would like the court to consider.

PART VII

3

PART VII COURT OF PROTECTION PRACTICE 2016

3.3 If you oppose the application or seek a different order, you must file any evidence on which you intend to rely now, or you can send it later. If you are sending it later it must reach the court 28 days of the date on which you were served or given notice. Use form COP24 witness statement to provide your evidence.

☐ Evidence attached

Section 4 – Attending court hearings

4.1 If the court requires you to attend a hearing do you need any special assistance or facilities?

☐ Yes ☐ No

If Yes, please say what your requirements are. If necessary, court staff may contact you about your requirements.

Section 5 – Signature

Signed

*Person served/notified('s solicitor)('s litigation friend)

Name

Date

Name of firm

Position or office held

* Please delete the options in brackets that do not apply.

Form COP5A – Guidance notes on completing form COP5 Acknowledgment of service/notification

 Court of Protection

Guidance notes on completing form COP5 Acknowledgment of service/notification

Please read the following notes before completing form COP5

You have been served with or notified of proceedings in the Court of Protection as you may have an interest in this application.

You should only complete the form if you oppose the application; wish to seek a different order or direction; or wish to make representations for the court to consider before it makes a decision.

You do not need to do anything if you consent to the application and do not wish to participate in the court proceedings.

Please note: You may need to pay for any costs you incur during proceedings. If the court considers that you have acted unreasonably it may order you to pay the costs incurred by other parties.

People who have an interest:

A. If you are **the person to whom this application/ appeal relates** the application is about your finances and/or personal welfare. You should have been given a form COP14 explaining the decision the court has been asked to make. This form should have been given to you in person. If you wish to participate, you must complete form COP5 and request that you are joined as a party to the proceedings. The court may decide to appoint a person to act on your behalf as your 'litigation friend'. You must complete all sections in COP5.

B. If you are a **respondent**, you will have been served with a copy of the application and any relevant papers in support. By completing and filing COP5 with the court, you will be made a party to the proceedings. You must complete Sections 1, 3, 4 and 5 of COP5.

C. If you have been notified as a **person with an interest in the application**, and wish to participate, you must complete COP5 and request that you are joined as a party to the proceedings. The court will then consider this and make a decision. The applicant should have given you a COP15 notice, which explains the order the court has been asked to make. You must complete all sections in COP5.

Action required to participate:
You have **14 days** from the day you were given notice or served to complete form COP5 and file it with the court.

Completing form COP5
Failure to answer any of the relevant sections on form COP5 may result in you not being joined as a party. Refer to practice direction 9C for further guidance.

Your details (Section 1)
If you are legally represented, please provide your solicitors full contact details at section 1.3

Please indicate at section 1.4 to which address official documentation should be sent.

Please indicate at section 1.5 your role in these proceedings.

Application to be joined as a party (Section 2)
If you wish to participate in the proceedings and apply to be joined as a party answer sections 2.1 and 2.2.

You will need to explain your interest in the proceedings and why you wish to be joined as a party. This should include your connection to the person to whom the application relates, how long you have known them and any information that explains why you have an interest in the proceedings.

You will also need to provide written evidence of your interest in the proceedings on the COP24 Witness statement form available from the website www.gov.uk/court-of-protection. You can send your evidence with your acknowledgment, or if you intend to send it separately you must send it to the court within 28 days of the date you were given notice on form COP14 or COP15.

Responding to the application or seeking a different order/direction (Section 3)

Consenting to the application:
You can use this form to let the court know about anything you consider relevant to the application, even if you do not oppose the application.

Opposing the application:
If you oppose the application you must explain your reasons for doing so at section 3.2. The evidence on which you intend to rely must be provided on COP24 Witness statement form, available from www.gov.uk/court-of-protection. You can send your evidence with your acknowledgment, or if you intend to send it separately you must send it to the court within 28 days of the date you were served with a copy of the application.

PART VII   COURT OF PROTECTION PRACTICE 2016

Seeking a different order:
If you propose that a different order should be made you must explain your reasons for doing so at section 3.2. You should also explain how this different order would benefit the person to whom the application relates. The evidence on which you intend to rely must be filed with your COP5 form, by completing COP24 Witness statement form, available from www.gov.uk/court-of-protection. You can send your evidence with your acknowledgment, or if you intend to send it separately you must send it to the court within 28 days of the date you were served with a copy of the application.

Seeking directions:
If you are seeking guidance/instructions from the court as to the case management of the application, including the filing of evidence, please explain what directions you seek at section 3.2.

Attending court hearings (Section 4)
If you need special assistance or special facilities for a disability or impairment, please set out your requirements in full. It is important that you make the court aware of your needs to to avoid causing any delays.

The court staff will need to know for example whether you want documents to be supplied in any alternative format such as Braille or large print. They will also need to know about any specific requirements should there be a hearing, such as wheelchair access, a hearing loop or a sign language interpreter.

Signature (Section 5)
The certificate provided to the court must be signed and dated by the applicant or their appointed agents.

What you need to do next
When you have completed the form you should take, or send it to the Court of Protection. For details on where to send the form check the website: www.gov.uk/court-of-protection

Disclaimer
Court of Protection staff cannot give legal advice. If you need legal advice please contact a solicitor or your local Citizens Advice. Information in this guidance is believed to be correct at the time of publication; however we do not accept any liability for any error it may contain.

If you need further help completing form COP5, please check the website www.gov.uk/court-of-protection

© Crown Copyright 2015

Form COP7 – Application to object to the registration of a Lasting Power of Attorney

Form COP7 – Application to object to the registration of a Lasting Power of Attorney

 Court of Protection

Application to object to the registration of a lasting power of attorney (LPA)

For office use only
Date received
Case no.
Date issued

Name of the donor of the LPA (this is the person who made the LPA)

SEAL

Please read first

- You can only object using this form if you are an intended attorney or a named person who received an LPA001 notice of intention to apply for registration of a lasting power of attorney.

- You may have to pay a fee when you make an application. Refer to the leaflet COP44 Court of Protection – Fees for details.

- An application to object must be made within three weeks from the day on which you received the LPA001 notice.

- If you are not one of the people who received the LPA001 notice but you wish to object, you can still do so but you need to file a COP1 application form and pay the specified fee.
  You need to notify the Public Guardian of your application. See note 1 at the end of this form for information on notifying the Public Guardian.

- An objection should be made to the Public Guardian (instead of the court) in the following circumstances:

  – if you are the donor, by using the form LPA006 objection by the donor to the registration of a lasting power of attorney;

  or

  – if you object on certain specified factual grounds, by using the form LPA007 objection to the Office of the Public Guardian of a proposed registration of a lasting power of attorney on factual grounds.

- You may need to pay for any costs you incur during the proceedings. If the court considers that you have acted unreasonably you can be ordered to pay the costs incurred by other parties.

- Please continue on a separate sheet of paper if you need more space to answer a question. Write your name, the name and date of birth of the person to whom the application relates, and the number of the question you are answering on each separate sheet.

- For assistance in completing the form please see guidance notes and website:
  www.gov.uk/court-of-protection

- Court of Protection staff cannot give legal advice. If you need legal advice please contact a solicitor.

PART VII

1

© Crown Copyright 2015

1927

PART VII

COURT OF PROTECTION PRACTICE 2016

Section 1 - Your details (the applicant)

1.1 Your details ☐ Mr. ☐ Mrs. ☐ Miss ☐ Ms. ☐ Other _____

   First name

   Middle name(s)

   Last name

1.2 Address (including postcode)

   Telephone no.
Daytime	
Evening	
Mobile	

   E-mail address

1.3 Is a solicitor representing you? ☐ Yes ☐ No

   If Yes, please give the solicitor's details.

   Name

   Address (including postcode)

   Telephone no. _____ Fax no. _____

   DX no.

   E-mail address

Form COP7 – Application to object to the registration of a Lasting Power of Attorney

1.4 To which address should all official documentation be sent?

☐ Your address

☐ Solicitor's address

☐ Other address (please provide details)

1.5 Your description

☐ Attorney

☐ Other person entitled to be notified of the application to register the LPA

Section 2 - Objection to the registration of an LPA

2.1 Full name of the donor

☐ Mr. ☐ Mrs. ☐ Miss ☐ Ms. ☐ Other _____

First name:

Middle name(s):

Last name:

2.2 Full name of intended attorney(s)

☐ Mr. ☐ Mrs. ☐ Ms. ☐ Miss ☐ Other _____

First name:

Last name:

☐ Mr. ☐ Mrs. ☐ Ms. ☐ Miss ☐ Other _____

First name:

Last name:

PART VII

2.3 Date donor signed the LPA

    | D | D | M | M | Y | Y | Y | Y |

2.4 Date you were given notice of the application to register the LPA

    | D | D | M | M | Y | Y | Y | Y |

2.5 You can only object to the court against the registration of the LPA on grounds which are prescribed in regulations under the Mental Capacity Act 2005.

Please indicate your grounds for objecting to the proposed registration:

- [ ] The power purported to be created by the instrument* is not valid as a LPA.
  (e.g. the donor did not have capacity to make an LPA).
- [ ] The power created by the instrument no longer exists
  (e.g. the donor revoked it at a time when he or she had capacity to do so)
- [ ] Fraud or undue pressure was used to induce the donor to make the power.
- [ ] The attorney proposes to behave in a way that would contravene his authority or would not be in the donor's best interests.

*The instrument means the LPA made by the donor.

2.6 Any evidence in support of your application must be filed with this application form. If you are attaching any written evidence please use the COP24 witness statement form.   [ ] Evidence attached

2.7 You must have notified the Public Guardian of your intention to apply to the court to object to the registration of the LPA. **(See note 1)**   [ ] I confirm that I have notified the Public Guardian

Section 3 - Attending court hearings

3.1 If the court requires you to attend a hearing do you need any special assistance or facilities? **(See note 2)**   [ ] Yes   [ ] No

If Yes, please say what your requirements are. If necessary, court staff may contact you about your requirements.

Form COP7 – Application to object to the registration of a Lasting Power of Attorney

Section 4 – Statement of truth

The statement of truth is to be signed by you, your solicitor or your litigation friend.

*(I believe) (The applicant believes) that the facts stated in this application form are true.

Signed

*Applicant('s litigation friend)('s solicitor)

Name

Date

Name of firm

Position or office held

* Please delete the option in brackets that do not apply.

Now read note 3 about what you need to do next.

PART VII

1931

Guidance notes

Notifying the Public Guardian

You need to notify the Public Guardian, using the LPA008 form, without delay of your application to object. Upon notification the Office of the Public Guardian will suspend the registration until the court provides further directions. If the Public Guardian is not notified there is a risk that the LPA will be registered.

You can get copies of Office of the Public Guardian forms by calling 0300 456 0300, by downloading them at www.justice.gov.uk/forms/opg or by writing to:

    Office of the Public Guardian
    PO BOX 16185
    Birmingham B2 2WH

Attending court hearings

If you need special assistance or special facilities for a disability or impairment, please set out your requirements in full. It is important that you make the court aware of your needs to avoid causing any delays.

The court staff will need to know, for example, whether you want documents to be supplied in an alternative format, such as Braille or large print. They will also need to know about any specific requirements should there be a hearing, such as wheelchair access, a hearing loop or a sign language interpreter.

What you need to do next

The court requires two copies (i.e. the original plus one copy) of each form and document you file.

Please return the original completed form and copies to the Court of Protection, along with any fee. For details on where to send your application check the website: www.gov.uk/court-of-protection

What happens next?

The court will notify you when your application form has been issued and will return a sealed copy of the application form. You will need to serve a copy on the donor and each attorney of the LPA.

Form COP8 – Application relating to the registration of an Enduring Power of Attorney

Court of Protection
Application relating to the registration of an enduring power of attorney (EPA)

For office use only
Date received
Case no.
Date issued

Name of the donor of the EPA (this is the person who made the EPA)

SEAL

Please read first

- You need to complete and file this application form if you are the donor, an intended attorney or a relative of the donor entitled by Schedule 4 of the Mental Capacity Act 2005 (the Act) to be notified of the application to register the EPA and:
  - you wish to object to the registration of the EPA; or
  - you wish to seek the registration of the EPA where you have been notified that the registration has been suspended.
- If you are entitled to be notified then either you will have received an EP1PG notice of intention to apply for registration, or the Public Guardian will have notified you that the registration has been suspended.
- You may have to pay a fee when you make an application. Refer to the leaflet COP44 Court of Protection – Fees for details.
- Schedule 4 of the Act provides for the court to dispense with the requirement to give notice. If you are one of the people entitled by the Act to be notified then you can object to the court using this form even if you have not received an EP1PG notice but you find out about the application through other means.
- If you wish to apply to object to the registration of the EPA then you should do so as soon as reasonably possible after receiving the EP1PG notice. You should notify the Public Guardian of your application. If you do not make an application, the Public Guardian will ask for the court's directions on registration. See note 1 at the end of this form for information on notifying the Public Guardian.

- You may need to pay for any costs you incur during the proceedings. If the court considers that you have acted unreasonably you can be ordered to pay the costs incurred by other parties.
- If you are not one of the people entitled by the Act to be notified of the application to register the EPA but you wish to object you can still do so but you need to file a COP1 application form and pay the specified fee. You should notify the Public Guardian of your application. See note 1 in the separate guidance for information on notifying the Public Guardian.
- Please continue on a separate sheet of paper if you need more space to answer a question. Write your name, the name and date of birth of the donor, and the number of the question you are answering on each separate sheet.
- For assistance in completing the form please see guidance notes and website: www.gov.uk/court-of-protection
- Court of Protection staff cannot give legal advice. If you need legal advice please contact a solicitor.

PART VII

© Crown Copyright 2015

PART VII COURT OF PROTECTION PRACTICE 2016

Section 1 - Your details (the applicant)

1.1 Your details ☐ Mr. ☐ Mrs. ☐ Miss ☐ Ms. ☐ Other _____

　　First name　　　[　　　　　　　　　　　]

　　Middle name(s)　[　　　　　　　　　　　]

　　Last name　　　[　　　　　　　　　　　]

1.2 Address (including postcode)
[　　　　　　　　　　　　　　　　　　　　　]

　　Telephone no.
Daytime	
Evening	
Mobile	

　　E-mail address [　　　　　　　　　　　　　]

1.3 Is a solicitor representing you?　　☐ Yes　☐ No

　　If Yes, please give the solicitor's details.

　　Name　　　　[　　　　　　　　　　　　　]

　　Address (including postcode)
[　　　　　　　　　　　　　　　　　　　　　]

Telephone no.		Fax no.	
DX no.			
E-mail address			

1.4 Which address should official documentation be sent to?

　　☐ Your address

　　☐ Solicitor's address

　　☐ Other address (please provide details)
[　　　　　　　　　　　　　　]

2

1934

Form COP8 – Application relating to the registration of an Enduring Power of Attorney

1.5 Your description
- [ ] Donor (person making the EPA)
- [ ] Attorney
- [ ] Other person entitled to be notified of the application to register the EPA

Section 2 - Details of the EPA

2.1 Full name of the donor (if you are not the donor)

- [ ] Mr. [ ] Mrs. [ ] Miss [ ] Ms. [ ] Other _____

First name:

Middle name(s):

Last name:

2.2 Donor's address and telephone number (if you are not the donor)

Address (including postcode):

Telephone no.
- Daytime:
- Evening:
- Mobile:

E-mail address:

2.3 Donor's date of birth: D D M M Y Y Y Y

PART VII COURT OF PROTECTION PRACTICE 2016

2.4 Full name of intended attorney(s)

☐ Mr.   ☐ Mrs.   ☐ Ms.   ☐ Miss   ☐ Other _____

First name [   ]

Last name [   ]

☐ Mr.   ☐ Mrs.   ☐ Ms.   ☐ Miss   ☐ Other _____

First name [   ]

Last name [   ]

☐ Mr.   ☐ Mrs.   ☐ Ms.   ☐ Miss   ☐ Other _____

First name [   ]

Last name [   ]

2.5 Date donor signed the EPA

| D | D | M | M | Y | Y | Y | Y |

2.6 Date you were given notice of the application to register the EPA

| D | D | M | M | Y | Y | Y | Y |

Section 3 - Your application

3.1 Please state the directions you are seeking.

[   ]

Form COP8 – Application relating to the registration of an Enduring Power of Attorney

3.2 If you object to the registration of the EPA you can only do so on grounds which are prescribed in the Mental Capacity Act 2005.

Please indicate your grounds for objecting to the proposed registration:

☐ The power purported to be created by the instrument* is not valid as an enduring power of attorney

☐ The power created by the instrument no longer subsists

☐ The application is premature because the donor is not yet becoming mentally incapable

☐ Fraud or undue pressure was used to induce the donor to make the power

☐ The attorney is unsuitable to be the donor's attorney (having regard to all the circumstances and in particular the attorney's relationship to or connection with the donor).

The instrument means the EPA made by the donor.

Please tick to confirm

3.3 I have notified the Public Guardian of my intention to apply to the court in relation to the registration of the EPA. **(See note 1)** ☐ I confirm I have notified the Public Guardian

3.4 If you seek registration please state your reasons for doing so.

[ ]

3.5 Any evidence in support of your application must be filed with this application form. If you are attaching any written evidence please use the COP24 witness statement form.   ☐ Evidence attached

Section 4 - Attending court hearings

4.1 If the court requires you to attend a hearing do you need any special assistance or facilities? **(See note 2)**   ☐ Yes   ☐ No

If Yes, please say what your requirements are. If necessary, court staff may contact you about your requirements

[ ]

Section 5 – Statement of truth

The statement of truth is to be signed by you, your solicitor or your litigation friend.

*(I believe) (The applicant believes) that the facts stated in this application form are true.

Signed

*Applicant('s solicitor)('s litigation friend)

Name

Date

Name of firm

Position or office held

* Please delete the option in brackets that do not apply.

Now read note 3 about what you need to do next.

Guidance notes

Notifying the Public Guardian

If you have not already done so, you should notify the Public Guardian of your objection within five weeks of receiving the EP1PG notice. Upon notification the Office of the Public Guardian will suspend the registration until the court provides further directions. If the Public Guardian is not notified there is a risk that the EPA will be registered.

You should also notify the Public Guardian of your application to the court.

You can notify the Public Guardian by writing to:
PO BOX 15118
Birmingham B16 6GX
or
DX744240
Birmingham 79

Note 2

Attending court hearings

If you need special assistance or special facilities for a disability or impairment, please set out your requirements in full. It is important that you make the court aware of your needs to avoid causing any delays.

The court staff will need to know, for example, whether you want documents to be supplied in an alternative format, such as Braille or large print.

They will also need to know about any specific requirements should there be a hearing, such as wheelchair access, a hearing loop or a sign language interpreter.

What you need to do next

The court requires two copies (i.e. the original plus one copy) of the each form and document you file.

Please return the original completed form and copies to the Court of Protection, along with any fee. For details on where to send your application check the website: www.gov.uk/court-of-protection

What happens next?

The court will notify you when your application form has been issued and the court will return a sealed copy of the application form. You will need to serve a copy on the donor and each attorney of the EPA.

Form COP9 – Application notice

Form COP9 – Application notice

Court of Protection
Application notice

For office use only
Date received
Date issued

SEAL

Case no.

Full name of person to whom the application relates
(this is the person who lacks, or is alleged, to lack capacity)

Please read first

- This form can be used in a variety of circumstances and must be used for applications within proceedings. For further guidance on when this form is to be used please see the Court of Protection Rules 2007 and the Practice Directions accompanying the Rules or contact Customer Services at the number below.
- If you wish to apply to start proceedings please complete the COP1 application form.
- If you wish to apply to be joined as a party to the proceedings please complete the COP10 application notice for applications to be joined as a party.
- You may have to pay a fee when you make an application. Refer to the leaflet COP44 Court of Protection – Fees for details.
- You may need to pay for any costs you incur during the proceedings. If the court considers that you have acted unreasonably you can be ordered to pay the costs incurred by other parties.

- Please continue on a separate sheet of paper if you need more space to answer a question. Write the case number, your name, the name of the person to whom the application relates, and number of the question you are answering on each separate sheet.
- For assistance in completing this form please see guidance notes and website: www.gov.uk/court-of-protection
- Court of Protection staff cannot give legal advice. If you need legal advice please contact a solicitor.

PART VII

© Crown Copyright 2015

PART VII   COURT OF PROTECTION PRACTICE 2016

Section 1 - Your details

1.1 Your details ☐ Mr.   ☐ Mrs.   ☐ Miss   ☐ Ms.   ☐ Other _____

 First name

 Middle name(s)

 Last name

1.2 Address (including postcode)

 Telephone no. Daytime
                Evening
                Mobile

 E-mail address

1.3 Is a solicitor representing you?   ☐ Yes   ☐ No

 If Yes, please give the solicitor's details.

 Name

 Address (including postcode)

 Telephone no.   Fax no.
 DX no.
 E-mail address

1.4 Which address should official documentation be sent to?

  ☐ Your address

  ☐ Solicitor's address

  ☐ Other address (please provide details)

Form COP9 – Application notice

1.5 What is your role in the proceedings?

☐ Applicant (the person who filed the COP1 application form)

☐ Person to whom the application relates

☐ Other party to the proceedings

☐ Other (please give details)

Section 2 - Your application

2.1 What order or direction are you seeking from the court?

2.2 Please set out the grounds on which you are seeking the order or direction?

2.3 Any evidence in support of your application must be filed with this application notice. If you are attaching any written evidence please use the COP24 witness statement form.

☐ Evidence attached

If the court requires that evidence be given by affidavit then you need to use the COP25 affidavit form.

PART VII

2.4 Please provide the details of any person who you reasonably believe has an interest which means they ought to be heard by the court in relation to this application notice and who is not already a party to the proceedings.

Full name including title	Full address including postcode	Connection to the person to whom the proceedings relate

Section 3 – Statement of truth

The statement of truth is to be signed by you, your solicitor or your litigation friend.

*(I believe) (The applicant believes) that the facts stated in this application notice are true.

Signed

*Applicant('s litigation friend)('s solicitor)

Name

Date

Name of firm

Position or office held

* Please delete the options in brackets that do not apply.

Now read note 1 about what you need to do next.

Form COP9 – Application notice

Guidance notes

What you need to do next
The court requires two copies (i.e. the original plus one copy) of each form and document you file.

Please return the original completed form and copies to the Court of Protection, along with any fee. For details on where to send your application check the website: www.gov.uk/court-of-protection

What happens next?
The court will notify you when your application notice has been issued. The court will return a sealed copy of the application notice. You may need to serve copies on:

- every other party to the proceedings;
- anyone who is named as a respondent in the application notice; and
- any other person as the court may direct.

PART VII   COURT OF PROTECTION PRACTICE 2016

Form COP10 – Application notice for applications to be joined as a party

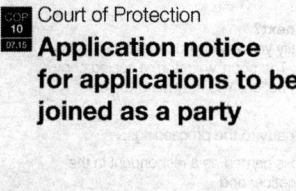

Court of Protection
Application notice for applications to be joined as a party

For office use only
Date received
Date issued

Case no.

Full name of person to whom the application relates
(this is the name of the person who lacks, or is alleged to lack, capacity)

SEAL

Please read first

- If you wish to apply to be joined as a party to the proceedings then you need to complete this application notice. You must be joined as a party to oppose an application or seek a different order.

- Do not complete this form if you have been served with a copy of COP1 application form or have received a COP15 notice that an application form has been issued. Instead you need to complete and file a COP5 acknowledgment of service/notification in order to be joined as a party.

- If your application relates to another matter and is made in the course of existing proceedings then you need to complete the COP9 application notice.

- You may have to pay a fee when you make an application. Refer to the leaflet COP44 Court of Protection – Fees for details.

- You may need to pay for any costs you incur during the proceedings. If the court considers that you have acted unreasonably you can be ordered to pay the costs incurred by other parties.

- Please continue on a separate sheet of paper if you need more space to answer a question. Write the case number, your name and the name of the person to whom the application relates, and the number of the question you are answering on each separate sheet.

- For assistance in completing this form please see guidance notes and website www.gov.uk/court-of-protection

- Court of Protection staff cannot give legal advice. If you need legal advice please contact a solicitor.

© Crown Copyright 2015

Form COP10 – Application notice for applications to be joined as a party

Section 1 - Your details (the person applying to be joined as a party)

1.1 Your details ☐ Mr. ☐ Mrs. ☐ Miss ☐ Ms. ☐ Other _____

First name

Middle name(s)

Last name

1.2 Address (including postcode)

Telephone no.
Daytime	
Evening	
Mobile	

E-mail address

1.3 Is a solicitor representing you? ☐ Yes ☐ No

If Yes, please give the solicitor's details.

Name

Address (including postcode)

Telephone no.   Fax no.

DX no.

E-mail address

1.4 Which address should official documentation be sent to?

☐ Your address

☐ Solicitor's address

☐ Other address (please provide details)

Section 2 - Your application

2.1 What is your connection to the person to whom the application relates?

2.2 What is your interest in the proceedings?

2.3 Do you consent to the application? ☐ Yes ☐ No

2.4 Do you oppose the application? ☐ Yes ☐ No

If Yes, please set out your grounds for doing so.

2.5 Do you propose that a different order should be made? ☐ Yes ☐ No
If Yes, please set out what the order is.

Form COP10 – Application notice for applications to be joined as a party

2.6 Any evidence in support of your application must be filed with this application notice. If you are attaching any written evidence please use the COP24 witness statement form ☐ Evidence attached

Section 3 – Attending court hearings

3.1 If the court requires you to attend a hearing do you need any special assistance or facilities? **(see note 1)** ☐ Yes ☐ No

If Yes, please say what your requirements are. If necessary, court staff may contact you about your requirements.

Section 4 - Statement of truth

The statement of truth is to be signed by you, or your solicitor or your litigation friend.

*(I believe) (The applicant believes) the facts stated in this application notice are true.

Signed

*Applicant('s litigation friend)('s solicitor)

Name

Date

Name of firm

Position or office held

* Please delete the options in brackets that do not apply.

Now read note 2 about what you need to do next.

Guidance notes

Attending court hearings

If you need special assistance or special facilities for a disability or impairment, please set out your requirements in full. It is important that you make the court aware of your needs to avoid causing any delays.

The court staff will need to know, for example, whether you want documents to be supplied in an alternative format, such as Braille or large print. They will also need to know about any specific requirements should there be a hearing, such as wheelchair access, a hearing loop or a sign language interpreter.

What you need to do next

The court requires a sufficient number of copies of this form to provide a copy to every party to the proceedings. Please contact Court Enquiry Service on 0300 456 4600 to find out how many copies you need to provide.

Please return the original completed form and copies to the Court of Protection, along with any fee. For details on where to send your application check the website: www.gov.uk/court-of-protection

What happens next?

The court will serve the application notice and any accompanying documents on every party to the proceedings.

The court will consider your application to be joined and if it decides to do so, will make an order to that effect.

Form COP12 – Special undertaking by trustees

Form COP12 – Special undertaking by trustees

Court of Protection
Special undertaking by trustees

For office use only
Date received
Case no.

Full name of person to whom the application relates
(this is the name of the person who lacks, or is alleged to lack, capacity)

Please read first

- If your application relates to the appointment of a trustee then you need to complete this undertaking and file it with the court together with a COP1 application form and any other required forms and documents. All new and continuing trustees must sign the undertaking (not just the person making the application).

- For further information on applications relating to trustees please see Practice Direction G that supplements Part 9 of the Court of Protection Rules 2007.

- Please continue on a separate sheet of paper if you need more space to answer a question. Write your name, the name and date of birth of the person to whom the application relates, and the number of the question you are answering on each separate sheet.

- If you need help completing this form please check the website, www.justice.gov.uk or www.direct.gov.uk, for further guidance or information, or contact Court Enquiry Service on 0300 456 4600 or email courtofprotectionenquiries@hmcts.gsi.gov.uk

- Court of Protection staff cannot give legal advice. If you need legal advice please contact a solicitor.

PART VII

© Crown Copyright 2012

PART VII

COURT OF PROTECTION PRACTICE 2016

Section 1 - Details of the person to whom the application relates

1.1 Full name

Address (including postcode)

Date of birth D D M M Y Y Y Y

Section 2 - Special undertaking by trustees

2.1 Name of continuing trustee

Address (including postcode)

Name of second continuing trustee (if applicable)

Address (including postcode)

Name of new trustee (if applicable)

Address (including postcode)

2

1950

Name of second new trustee (if applicable)

Address (including postcode)

2.2 Name of property, will, settlement, etc.

2.3 I/WE HEREBY UNDERTAKE that in the event of such appointment being approved and made, where the above named person lacks capacity in relation to the trust, to sell any land or property to the whole of any part of which the person is absolutely entitled in equity at such fair and reasonable price as can be obtained through a sale on the open market.

AND THAT in the event of the sale being effected where the above named person lacks capacity in relation to the trust we will deal with the proceeds of sale or with the person's undivided share thereof, as the case may be, in such manner as the court may direct but so that where the person is a joint tenant we will deal with the proceeds in such manner as the court (on behalf of the person) and the other joint tenant shall jointly direct and on severance of the joint tenancy we will deal with the person's share of the proceeds in such manner as the court may direct.

PART VII   COURT OF PROTECTION PRACTICE 2016

Section 5 – Signature

Signed

Name

Date

Signed

Name

Date

Signed

Name

Date

Signed

Name

Date

Now read note 8 of the COP1 application form about what you need to do next.

Form COP14 – Proceedings about you in the Court of Protection

Court of Protection

Proceedings about you in the Court of Protection

For office use only

To (enter name and address of person to whom the application relates)

Name

Address

The court has powers to make decisions about the property and affairs and personal welfare of people who lack capacity to make such decisions.

If you have any questions or need further information about this notice you can:
- ring Court Enquiry Service on 0300 456 4600;
- write to the Court of Protection, PO Box 70185, First Avenue House, 42-49 High Holborn, London WC1A 9JA, DX 160013 Kingsway 7; or
- check the website, www.justice.gov.uk or www.direct.gov.uk.

The Court of Protection staff cannot give legal advice. If you need legal advice please contact a solicitor.

Details of the proceedings

Case number

Date the *(application)(appeal) was issued

D D M M Y Y Y Y

Name of the *(applicant)(appellant)

The *(application)(appeal) relates to your:
- [ ] property and affairs
- [ ] personal welfare
- [ ] property and affairs and personal welfare.

* Please delete the options in brackets that do not apply.

© Crown Copyright 2013

PART VII

PART VII COURT OF PROTECTION PRACTICE 2016

This notice is to tell you that

Signed

Name

Date

Name of firm

Position or office held

Form COP14A – Guidance notes on completing form COP14

Court of Protection
Guidance notes on completing form COP14

The person to whom the application/appeal relates must be notified personally of certain matters.

You must also provide the person to whom the application/appeal relates with a COP14 notice which explains the matter for which notification is being provided.

The box that begins "This notice is to tell you that…" should be completed using simple, clear language as follows:

Nature of notification	Information to be included in the notice
The court has made a decision about how the person being notified is to participate in the proceedings (including the appointment of a litigation friend or representative to act on their behalf)	Complete the sentence that starts "This notice is to tell you that…" with the following words – **The court has made a decision about how you should take part in the proceedings.** Please add the following information: • Whether the court has directed that the person being notified should be a party to the proceedings; • Whether the court has appointed a litigation friend or representative to act on their behalf in relation to the proceedings, and details of who that person is; • If the court has directed that the person being notified should be a party to the proceedings, but no litigation friend, accredited legal representative was appointed the reasons why no appointment was made; and • Whether the person being notified has been given the opportunity to address the judge directly, or indirectly.
Application has been issued by the court	Complete the sentence that starts "This notice is to tell you that…" with the following words – **an application about you will be considered by the Court of Protection.** Please add the following information: • the application raises the question of whether the person being notified lacks capacity in relation to a matter or matters and what that means; • what will happen if the court makes the order or direction that has been applied for; and • where the application contains a proposal for the appointment of a person to make decisions on behalf of the person to whom the application relates, details of who that person is. You must also provide the person being notified with a COP5 Acknowledgment of notification.
The date when a hearing in relation to the application is to be held	Complete the sentence that starts "This notice is to tell you that…" with the following words – **a hearing of an application about you will be held at the Court of Protection on [insert the date and time] at [insert address].**
Application has been withdrawn	Complete the sentence that starts "This notice is to tell you that…" with the following words – **an application about you has been withdrawn from the Court of Protection.** Please add information about the consequence of the withdrawal.

© Crown Copyright 2015

Appellant's notice has been issued by the court	Complete the sentence that starts "This notice is to tell you that…" with the following words – **an appeal regarding a court decision about you will be considered by the Court of Protection**. Please add the following information: • the issues raised by the appeal; and • what will happen if the court makes the order or direction that has been applied for. You must also provide the person being notified with a COP5 Acknowledgment of notification.	
The date when a hearing in relation to the appeal is to be held	Complete the sentence that starts "This notice is to tell you that…" with the following words – **a hearing of an appeal regarding a court decision about you will be held at the Court of Protection on [insert the date and time] at [insert address]**.	
Appellant's notice has been withdrawn	Complete the sentence that starts "This notice is to tell you that…" with the following words – **an appeal regarding a court decision about you has been withdrawn from the Court of Protection**. Please add information about the consequence of the withdrawal.	
A decision has been made by the court	Complete the sentence that starts "This notice is to tell you that…" with the following words – **a decision about you has been made by the Court of Protection**. Please add information about the effect of the order or decision. You must also provide P with a copy of the order.	
Any other matter as directed by the court	Complete the sentence that starts "This notice is to tell you that…" with information to briefly summarise the matter. Please add information about the matter as directed by the court.	

Where the person is notified that an application form or appellant's notice has been issued then you must provide them with a COP5 acknowledgment of notification form.

You must complete a COP20A certificate of notification/non-notification and return it to the court within seven days of notification being provided, unless otherwise directed by a court order.

Form COP15 – Notice that an application form has been issued

Court of Protection
Notice that an application form has been issued

For office use only

(enter name and address of person to be notified)

Name

Address

This notice is to tell you that an application form has been issued by the Court of Protection.

The court has powers to make decisions regarding the property and affairs and personal welfare of people who lack capacity to make such decisions.

If you wish to be involved in the proceedings, then you need to complete and file the COP5 acknowledgment of notification with the court and apply to be joined as a party.

If you have any questions or need further information about the application you can:
- ring Court Enquiry Service on 0300 456 4600;
- write to the Court of Protection, PO Box 70185, First Avenue House, 42-49 High Holborn, London WC1A 9JA, DX 160013 Kingsway 7; or
- check the website, www.justice.gov.uk or www.direct.gov.uk

Court of Protection staff cannot give legal advice. If you need legal advice please contact a solicitor.

Details of the application

Case number

Date the application was issued
D D M M Y Y Y Y

Name of the applicant

Name of the person to whom the application relates (this is the person who lacks, or is alleged to lack, capacity)

Applicant's connection to the person to whom the application relates

The application relates to the exercise of the court's jurisdiction in relation to the person's:
- [ ] property and affairs
- [ ] personal welfare
- [ ] property and affairs and personal welfare.

© Crown Copyright 2013

PART VII

PART VII
COURT OF PROTECTION PRACTICE 2016

The matter the court has been asked to decide:

Order(s) the court has been asked to make:

Name

Date

Form COP15A – Guidance notes for completing form COP15

Court of Protection

Guidance notes for completing form COP15

- You must notify the people who are likely to have an interest in being notified of your application within 14 days of the date on which your application form was issued by the court.
- These are the people whose details you provided in section 5.2 of the COP1 application form.
- You must also notify any other people that the court may direct.
- To notify people that your application has been issued by the court you provide each person to be notified with:
    - a COP15 notice that an application has been issued; and
    - a COP5 acknowledgment of notification.
- You must complete and sign the COP15 notice. Some of the questions are the same as those on the COP1 application form. Where the questions are the same you should copy the answers you provided on the application form.
- You can provide this information by:
    - delivering it to the person to be notified personally;
    - delivering it to their home address; or
    - posting it to their home address by first class post.
- You must complete a COP20B certificate of notification/non-notification and return it to the court within 7 days of notification being provided.

© Crown Copyright 2015

Form COP20A – Certificate of notification/non-notification of the person to whom proceedings relate

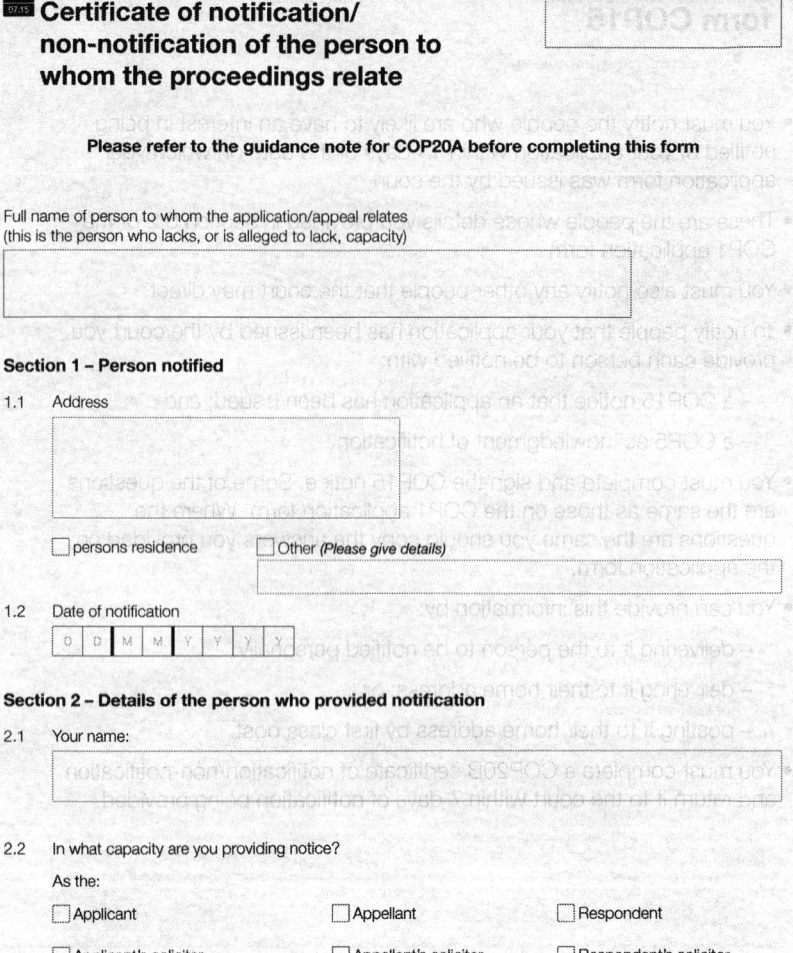

Form COP20A – Certificate of notification/non-notification of the person to whom proceedings relate

Section 3 – Nature of the notification (For non-notification please go to section 4)

Please tick one of the following statements:

If you were unable to notify the person to whom the application relates, all of the items in the relevant statement below, you must explain in section 4 why you could not carry out a full notification.

3.1 ☐ **Participation in the proceedings**

I have notified the person to whom the application relates that the court has made a decision about how the person the application is about is to participate in the proceedings (including the appointment of a litigation friend or representative to act on their behalf)

- Whether the court has directed that the person being notified should be a party to the proceedings;
- Whether the court has appointed a litigation friend or other representative to act on their behalf and details of who that person is;
- If the court has directed that the person being notified should be a party to the proceedings, but no litigation friend, accredited legal representative was appointed the reasons why no appointment was made; and
- Whether the person being notified has been given the opportunity to address the judge directly, or indirectly;

3.2 ☐ **Application form has been issued**

I have notified the person to whom the application relates that an application form has been issued and I explained to the person:

- Who the applicant is;
- That the application raises the question of whether they lack capacity in relation to a matter or matters, and what that means;
- What will happen if the court makes the order or direction that has been applied for;
- Where the application contains a proposal for the appointment of a person to make decisions on their behalf in relation to the matter to which the application relates, details of who that person is; and
- That they may seek advice and assistance in relation to the application.
- I have provided form COP5 Acknowledgment of notifcation.

3.3 ☐ **Application has been withdrawn**

I have notified the person to whom the application relates that an application has been withdrawn and I explained to the person:

- That the application has been withdrawn;
- The consequence of the withdrawal; and
- That they may seek advice and assistance in relation to the application.

PART VII

PART VII

3.4 ☐ **Appellant's notice has been issued**

I have notified the person to whom the application relates that an appellant's notice has been issued and I explained to the person:
- Who the appellant is;
- The issues raised by the appeal;
- What will happen if the court makes the order or direction applied for; and
- That they may seek advice and assistance in relation to the appeal;
- I have provided with form COP5 Acknowledgment of notification.

3.5 ☐ **Appellant's notice has been withdrawn**

I have notified the person to whom the application relates that an appellant's notice has been withdrawn and I explained to the person:
- That the notice has been withdrawn;
- The consequence of the withdrawal; and
- That they may seek advice and assistance in relation to the appeal.

3.6 ☐ **A decision has been made by the court**

I have notified the person to whom the application relates that a decision except for a case management decision has been made by the court and I explained to the person:
- The effect of the decision or order; and
- That they may seek advice and assistance in relation to the decision or order;
- I have provided a copy of the order made by the court to the person.

3.7 ☐ **Another matter as directed by the court**

I have notified the person to whom the application relates of another matter as directed by the court and I explained to the person:
- The matters directed by the court; and
- That they may seek advice and assistance in relation to the matter.

3.8 ☐ **Manner of notification**

Describe the steps you took to explain the matter or matters to the person to whom the application relates and the extent to which they understood or appeared to understand the information given. Please also describe what, if anything the person to whom the application relates said or did in response to that notification.

Form COP20A – Certificate of notification/non-notification of the person to whom proceedings relate

Section 4 – Non-notification

If you could not provide notification, please describe your attempt to do so, and explain the reasons why notification was not provided.

Section 5 – Statement of truth

The statement of truth must be signed by the person who provided notification.

I believe that the facts stated in this certificate are true.

Signed		Date	D D M M Y Y Y Y

Name

Name of firm   Position or office held

Please return the completed certificate to the Court of Protection

Note:
No other forms need to be attached with this form. However, it may assist the court if your completed **COP20A** and **COP20B** could be returned at the same time.

PART VII

COP 21A – Guidance notes on completing form COP20A

 Court of Protection: Guidance notes on completing form COP20A Certificate of notification/non-notification of the person to whom the proceedings relate

Please read the following notes before completing form COP20A

The person to whom the application/appeal relates must be notified **personally** of the commencement/withdrawal of any proceedings, a decision of the court; a decision about how the person is to participate in the proceedings; or any other matter as directed by the court.

You must provide the person to whom the application/appeal relates with a COP14 notice which includes details of why the notification is being given to him/her. **Please read this note in conjunction with guidance note COP14A.**

Where the person is notified that an application form or appellant's notice has been issued, you must provide them with a COP5 acknowledgement of notification form.

When you have notified or attempted to notify the person to whom the application/appeal relates, you need to complete and file form COP20A with the court. You must complete and return the COP20A to the court **within seven days of notification taking place.**

In the case of non-notification, the COP20A **must be returned to the court within seven days of the latest date on which notification should have been made.**

Only the court can dispense with the requirement for notification. The requirement for notification cannot be dispensed with just because the person does not or appears not to understand. You must attempt to notify the person in a way that is appropriate to their circumstances for example using simple language or visual aids.

You do not need to notify the person to whom the application/appeal relates if they are a child under the age of 18. You will need to serve a copy of your application on the child's parents or the person with parental responsibility for the child. Refer to the guidance notes to form COP20B for details of how to do this.

An application to dispense with notification may be made using a COP9 application form, with evidence in support on form COP24 Witness Statement. Such an application would be appropriate where, for example, the person concerned is in a permanent vegetative state or a minimally conscious state; or where notification by the applicant is likely to cause significant and disproportionate distress to that person.

Failure to answer any of the sections on form COP20A may result in consideration of the application/appeal being delayed.

Definitions:

- **Accredited legal representative** – a person appointed by the court from a panel of legally qualified representatives to represent the person to whom the application/appeal relates in the proceedings when it is not possible or necessary to appoint a litigation friend.
- **Agent** – a person carrying out the notification on another's behalf, e.g. nursing home proprietor
- **Applicant** – the person applying to the court for a court order.
- **Appellant** – the person who is appealing against a decision made in court.
- **A decision of the court** – any order or decision of the court that relates to property and financial affairs, or personal welfare of the person to whom the application/appeal relates, e.g. an order appointing a deputy. You do not need to provide notification where the decision of the court relates purely to case management, e.g. an order setting out the time limits for sending evidence or documents to the court.
- **Litigation friend** – a person acting in legal proceedings on behalf of a person who lacks capacity (or on behalf of a child).
- **Other** – a person not covered by any of the above categories, e.g. a neighbour.
- **Representative** – a (usually non-legally qualified) person appointed to represent the person to whom the application/appeal relates in the proceedings when it is not possible or necessary to appoint a litigation friend.

Completing form COP20A

Person notified (Section 1)

You must include the full name and address of the person notified and the date of notification. The address should be the address at which the notification was given.

Details of the person who provided notification (Section 2)

Provide your name and the capacity in which you are providing notification.

Nature of the notification (Section 3)

The certificate provided to the court must have the **relevant** tick-box answered, e.g. if you are notifying the person that an application has been issued, you tick the box in section 3.2: if you are notifying the person that an application has been withdrawn, you tick the box in section 3.3. If you are notifiying the person about more than one matter, tick all the relevant boxes.

You must describe to the court at section 3.8, the steps you took to explain the matter or matters to the person, and the extent to which they understood or appeared to understand the information given. If the person expressed any views about the application or said anything or did anything in response to the notification, you must describe it to the court here.

Non-notification (Section 4)

If for any reason you unable to provide notification, you must explain as fully as possible why notification was not provided.

Statement of truth (Section 5)

The certificate provided to the court must include a signed and dated statement by the applicant/appellant or his/her appointed agents.

What you need to do next

When you have completed the COP20A form you should take, or send it to the Court of Protection. For details on where to send the form check the website: www.gov.uk/court-of-protection.

Disclaimer

Court of Protection staff cannot give legal advice. If you need legal advice please contact a solicitor or your local Citizens Advice. Information in this guidance is believed to be correct at the time of publication; however we do not accept any liability for any error it may contain.

If you need further help completing the form, please check the website www.gov.uk/court-of-protection

Form COP20B – Certificate of service/non-service notification/non-notification

Court of Protection
Certificate of service/non-service notification/non-notification

Case no.

Please refer to the guidance notes for COP20B before completing this form

Full name of person to whom the application relates
(this is the person who lacks, or is alleged to lack, capacity)

Section 1 – Details of the person who provided service/notification

1.1 Full name:

1.2 In what capacity are you serving/providing notice? (Please see guidance)

As the:

☐ Applicant ☐ Appellant ☐ Respondent

☐ Applicant's solicitor ☐ Appellant's solicitor ☐ Respondent's solicitor

☐ Applicant's litigation friend ☐ Appellant's litigation friend ☐ Respondent's litigation friend

☐ Agent

☐ Other (Please give details)

Section 2 – People served (See Section 3 for people notified)

2.1 Title or description of the document (tick only one box)

☐ Application form (plus supporting evidence)
☐ Appellant's notice
☐ Respondent's notice
☐ Certificate of suitability of litigation friend
☐ Other (Please give details)

© Crown Copyright 2015

Form COP20B – Certificate of service/non-service notification/non-notification

Please photocopy this sheet before use if additional people need to be served

2.2   In respect of all served

1. Name of person served

Date of service

| D | D | M | M | Y | Y | Y | Y |

Address of service

Method of service
- [ ] 1st class post
- [ ] fax
- [ ] in person
- [ ] other electronic means
- [ ] DX
- [ ] permitted address
- [ ] alternative method as directed by court order

2. Name of person served

Date of service

| D | D | M | M | Y | Y | Y | Y |

Address of service

Method of service
- [ ] 1st class post
- [ ] fax
- [ ] in person
- [ ] other electronic means
- [ ] DX
- [ ] permitted address
- [ ] alternative method as directed by court order

3. Name of person served

Date of service

| D | D | M | M | Y | Y | Y | Y |

Address of service

Method of service
- [ ] 1st class post
- [ ] fax
- [ ] in person
- [ ] other electronic means
- [ ] DX
- [ ] permitted address
- [ ] alternative method as directed by court order

4. Name of person served

Date of service

| D | D | M | M | Y | Y | Y | Y |

Address of service

Method of service
- [ ] 1st class post
- [ ] fax
- [ ] in person
- [ ] other electronic means
- [ ] DX
- [ ] permitted address
- [ ] alternative method as directed by court order

PART VII

Section 3 – People notified Please photocopy this sheet before use if additional people need to be notified

I have given notice of issue of application form (COP15) to the following:

1. **Name of person notified**

   [   ]

   Address of notification

   [   ]

   Date of notification

   [D | D | M | M | Y | Y | Y | Y]

   Method of notification

   ☐ 1st class post   ☐ fax
   ☐ in person   ☐ other electronic means
   ☐ DX   ☐ permitted address
   ☐ alternative method as directed by court order

2. **Name of person notified**

   [   ]

   Address of notification

   [   ]

   Date of notification

   [D | D | M | M | Y | Y | Y | Y]

   Method of notification

   ☐ 1st class post   ☐ fax
   ☐ in person   ☐ other electronic means
   ☐ DX   ☐ permitted address
   ☐ alternative method as directed by court order

3. **Name of person notified**

   [   ]

   Address of notification

   [   ]

   Date of notification

   [D | D | M | M | Y | Y | Y | Y]

   Method of notification

   ☐ 1st class post   ☐ fax
   ☐ in person   ☐ other electronic means
   ☐ DX   ☐ permitted address
   ☐ alternative method as directed by court order

4. **Name of person notified**

   [   ]

   Address of notification

   [   ]

   Date of notification

   [D | D | M | M | Y | Y | Y | Y]

   Method of notification

   ☐ 1st class post   ☐ fax
   ☐ in person   ☐ other electronic means
   ☐ DX   ☐ permitted address
   ☐ alternative method as directed by court order

Form COP20B – Certificate of service/non-service notification/non-notification

Section 4 – Non-service/Non-notification

I could not serve/give notice to:

1. Name

   Reason:

2. Name

   Reason:

3. Name

   Reason:

Section 5 – Statement of truth

The statement of truth must be signed by the person who served/provided notification.

I believe that the facts stated in this certificate are true.

Signed

Date: D D M M Y Y Y Y

Name

Name of firm

Position or office held

Please return the completed certificate to the Court of Protection

Note:
No other forms need to be attached with this form. However, it may assist the court if your completed **COP20A** and **COP20B** could be returned at the same time.

PART VII

COP 21B – Guidance notes on completing form COP20B

 Court of Protection: Guidance notes on completing form COP20B Certificate of service non-service notification/non-notification

Please read the following notes before completing form COP20B

You must complete form COP20B to tell the court when you:

- serve a copy of an application form;
- serve a copy of an appellant's notice;
- serve a copy of a respondent's notice
- serve a copy of a certificate of suitability of a litigation friend;
- provide notice that you have issued an application or;
- serve a copy of any other document, as directed by the court.

The court requires that anyone who has an interest in the application/appeal must either be either be **served** by giving them a copy of the issued application/appeal and supporting evidence; or **notified** by serving form COP15 Notice that an application form has been issued.

Where the person is served or notified that an application form or appellant's notice has been issued, you **must** provide them with a COP5 Acknowledgement of Service notification form at the same time as you serve or notify.

You **must** complete and return the COP20B to the court **within seven days of service or notification taking place.**

In the case of non-service or non-notification, the COP20B **must** be returned to the court within **seven days of the latest date on which notification or service should have been made.**

Failure to answer any of the sections on form COP20B may result in consideration of the application/appeal being delayed.

Completing form COP20B

Details of the person who provided service/notification (Section 1)

Definitions:
- **Agent** – a person carrying out the notification on another's behalf, e.g. nursing home proprietor.
- **Applicant** – the person applying to the court for a court order.
- **Appellant** – the person who is appealing against a decision made in court.
- **Litigation friend** – a person acting in legal proceedings on behalf of a person who lacks capacity (or on behalf of a child).

- **Respondent** – a party to the proceedings (other than the Applicant or Appellant).
- **Other** – a person not covered by any of the above categories, e.g. a neighbour.

2. Persons served or notified (Sections 2 and 3)

You must serve or notify the following:

- anyone named as a respondent to be served with your application in section 5.1 of the COP1 Application form;
- anyone named to be notified in section 5.2 of the COP1 Application form;
- anyone named in section 2.5 of the COP35 Appellant's notice;
- the appellant if you are issuing a COP36 Respondent's notice
- the person who is to be served on behalf of the child or protected party and every other person who is a party to the proceedings if you are serving a COP22 Certificate of suitability of litigation friend; or
- any other person or persons as the court may direct.

The date of service/notification depends on the method of delivery used:
- First class post (or other service for next-day delivery): date of posting.
- Personal: date of personal service
- Document exchange: Date when the document was left at the document exchange.
- Delivery of document to permitted address: Date when document was delivered to the permitted address.
- Fax: Date of transmission.
- Other electronic means: Date of transmission and the means used.
- Alternative method permitted by the court: If the court has permitted an alternative method of delivery it will specify the date or other details to be stated on the Certificate of service.

You must confirm the method of service/notification by completing the relevant tick box.

Non-service/Non-notification (Section 4)

Where the applicant/appellant or his/her agent is unable to serve a document or to provide notification, he/she must provide details of the person(s) not served or notified and state the reason(s) why service/notification could not be made.

Statement of truth (Section 5)

The certificate provided to the court must include a signed and dated statement by the applicant/appellant or his/her appointed agents.

What you need to do next

When you have completed the COP20B form you should take, or send it to the Court of Protection. For details on where to send the form check the website: www.gov.uk/court-of-protection

Disclaimer

Court of Protection staff cannot give legal advice. If you need legal advice please contact a solicitor or your local Citizens Advice. Information in this guidance is believed to be correct at the time of publication; however we do not accept any liability for any error it may contain.

If you need further help completing form COP20B, please check the www.gov.uk/court-of-protection

PART VII   COURT OF PROTECTION PRACTICE 2016

Form COP22 – Certificate of suitability of litigation friend

 Court of Protection
Certificate of suitability of litigation friend

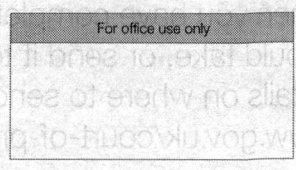
For office use only

Case no.

Full name of person to whom the application relates
(this is the person who lacks, or is alleged to lack, capacity)

Please read first

- If you wish to act as a litigation friend for a party to the proceedings then you must complete this certificate and file it with the court.

- This does not apply if you wish to act as a litigation friend for the person to whom the application relates. You can apply for an order to be appointed as the litigation friend for the person to whom the application relates (where they are party to the proceedings) by filing a COP9 application notice.

- Please continue on a separate sheet of paper if you need more space to answer a question. Write the case number, your name, the name of the person to whom the application relates, and the number of the question you are answering on each separate sheet.

- If you need help completing this form please check the website, www.justice.gov.uk or www.direct.gov.uk, for further guidance or information, or contact Court Enquiry Service on 0300 456 4600 or email courtofprotectionenquiries@hmcts.gsi.gov.uk

- Court of Protection staff cannot give legal advice. If you need legal advice please contact a solicitor.

© Crown Copyright 2013

Form COP22 – *Certificate of suitability of litigation friend*

Section 1 - Your details (the litigation friend)

1.1 Your full name ☐ Mr. ☐ Mrs. ☐ Miss ☐ Ms. ☐ Other _____

First name

Middle name(s)

Last name

1.2 Address (including postcode)

Telephone no.
Daytime	
Evening	
Mobile	

1.3 What is your relationship or connection to the person on whose behalf you wish to act as a litigation friend?

Section 2 - Details of the person on whose behalf you wish to act as a litigation friend

2.1 I consent to act as a litigation friend for:

Name

Address (including postcode)

Telephone no.

PART VII

2

2.2 Please tick to confirm:

☐ I know or believe that the person named in section 2.1 lacks capacity to conduct the proceedings on his or her own behalf.

The grounds for my belief are as follows:

[ ]

If your belief is based upon medical opinion, please attach any relevant document and file it with the court. You are not required to serve the document on every other party to the proceedings (unless the court directs otherwise).   ☐ Document(s) attached

Section 3 - Suitability to be a litigation friend

3.1 Please tick to confirm:

☐ I am able to conduct proceedings on behalf of the person named in section 2.1 competently and fairly;

☐ I have no interests adverse to those of the person; and

☐ I have served a copy of this certificate on the relevant person specified in the table below and on every other person who is a party to the proceedings.

Nature of party	Person to be served
Child	• A person who has parental responsibility for the child within the meaning of the Children Act 1989; or • if there is no such person, a person with whom the child lives with or in whose care the child is.
Protected party (a person who lacks capacity to conduct proceedings, other than a child or the person to whom the application relates)	• The person who is authorised to conduct the proceedings in the protected party's name or on his or her behalf; • a person who is a duly appointed attorney or deputy of the protected party; or • if there is no such person, a person with whom the protected party lives or in whose care the latter is.

You must complete and file a COP20 certificate of service/non-service for every person served with a copy of this certificate.

Form COP22 – Certificate of suitability of litigation friend

Section 4 – Statement of truth

This statement of truth is to be signed by the person who wishes to become the litigation friend or their solicitor.

*(I believe)(The litigation friend believes) that the facts stated in this certificate are true.

Signed

*Litigation friend('s solicitor)

Name

Date

Name of firm

Position or office held

* Please delete the options in brackets that do not apply.

Please return the completed certificate to:
Court of Protection, PO Box 70185, First Avenue House, 42-49 High Holborn, London WC1A 9JA
DX 160013 Kingsway 7

PART VII

Form COP23 – Certificate of failure or refusal of witness to attend before an examiner

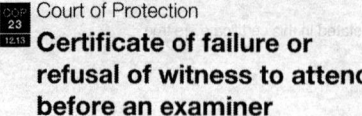

Court of Protection

Certificate of failure or refusal of witness to attend before an examiner

For office use only

Case no.

Full name of person to whom the application relates
(this is the person who lacks, or is alleged to lack, capacity)

Please read first

- If you required a deposition and the person ordered to attend before the examiner failed to attend or refused to be sworn, answer a question or produce a document, then you need to complete this certificate and file it with the court.

- You need to arrange for the examiner to complete and sign section 1 of this certificate.

- You may apply to the court for a further order in respect of the witness after this certificate has been filed.

- Please continue on a separate sheet of paper if you need more space to answer a question. Write the case number, your name, the name of the person to whom the application relates, and the number of the question you are answering on each separate sheet.

- If you need help completing this form please check the website, www.justice.gov.uk or www.direct.gov.uk, for further guidance or information, or contact Court Enquiry Service on 0300 456 4600 or email courtofprotectionenquiries@hmcts.gsi.gov.uk

- Court of Protection staff cannot give legal advice. If you need legal advice please contact a solicitor.

© Crown Copyright 2013

Form COP23 – Certificate of failure or refusal of witness to attend before an examiner

Section 1 - Failure or refusal of witness to attend before an examiner

This section is to be completed and signed by the examiner

1.1 What is the name of the witness?

1.2 What was the date of the order directing the examination?

| D | D | M | M | Y | Y | Y | Y |

1.3 On what day and at what time was the examination due to take place?

| D | D | M | M | Y | Y | Y | Y |

Time

1.4 Where was the examination due to take place?

1.5 The above named witness:

☐ failed to attend the examination

☐ refused to be sworn for the purpose of the examination

☐ refused to answer the following lawful question(s) at the examination (please specify)

☐ refused to produce the following document(s) at the examination (please specify)

PART VII

PART VII   COURT OF PROTECTION PRACTICE 2016

1.6   Please provide any comments as to the conduct of the deponent or of any person attending the examination.

Signed   **Position or office held**

Name   **Date**

Form COP23 – Certificate of failure or refusal of witness to attend before an examiner

Section 2 - Your details (party requiring the deposition)

This section is to be completed and signed by the party requiring the deposition

2.1 ☐ Mr. ☐ Mrs. ☐ Miss ☐ Ms. ☐ Other _____

First name

Middle name(s)

Last name

2.2 Address (including postcode)

Telephone no.

2.3 What is your role in these proceedings?

☐ Applicant (the person who filed the COP1 application form)

☐ Respondent

☐ Other (please provide details)

Section 3 - Signature

Signed

*(Applicant)(Respondent)('s litigation friend)('s solicitor)

Name

Date

Name of firm

Position or office held

* Please delete the options in brackets that do not apply.

Please return the completed certificate to:
Court of Protection,
PO Box 70185, First Avenue House, 42-49 High Holborn,
London WC1A 9JA

DX 160013 Kingsway 7

PART VII   COURT OF PROTECTION PRACTICE 2016

Form COP24 – Witness statement

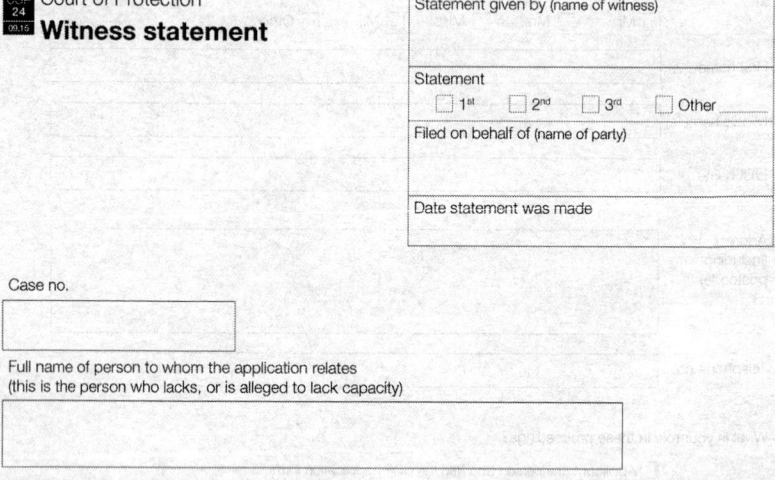

Please read first

- If you are filing written evidence with the court then it should be included in or attached to this form.
- If the court requires that evidence be given by affidavit then you need to use the COP25 affidavit form.
- You must initial any alterations to the witness statement.
- A document referred to in a witness statement and provided to the court is known as an exhibit. Each exhibit must be identified in some way (e.g. 'Exhibit A'). The first page of the exhibit must contain all of the information provided in the box in the top-right corner of this page.
- Practice Direction A accompanying Part 14 of the Court of Protection Rules 2007 sets out more detailed requirements in relation to witness statements.

- Please continue on a separate sheet of paper if you need more space to provide your witness statement. Please mark each separate sheet with all of the information provided in the box in the top-right corner of this page.
- For assistance in completing the form please see guidance notes and website: www.gov.uk/court-of-protection
- Court of Protection staff cannot give legal advice. If you need legal advice please contact a solicitor.

© Crown Copyright 2015

Form COP24 – *Witness statement*

Witness statement

1 Enter your full name

I,

2 Enter your occupation or description

3 Enter your full address including postcode or, if making the statement in your professional, business or other occupational capacity, the position you hold, the name of your firm or employer and the address at which you work

of

☐ am a party to the proceedings

☐ am employed by a party to the proceedings

and state that:

4 Set out in numbered paragraphs indicating:
- which of the statements are from your own knowledge and which are matters of information or belief, and
- the source for any matters of information or belief.

Where you refer to an exhibit, you should state the identifier you have used. For example, 'I refer to the (description of document) marked Exhibit A...'

continued over

PART VII

PART VII

COURT OF PROTECTION PRACTICE 2016

continued over

Form COP24 – Witness statement

4

Statement of truth

The statement of truth is to be signed by the witness.

I believe that the facts stated in this witness statement are true.

Signed

Name   **Date**

Please return the completed witness statement to the Court of Protection

PART VII   COURT OF PROTECTION PRACTICE 2016

Form COP25 – Affidavit

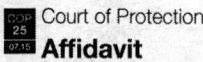 **Court of Protection**
Affidavit

Sworn by (name of deponent)
Affidavit
☐ 1st   ☐ 2nd   ☐ 3rd   ☐ Other ___
Filed on behalf of (name of party)
Date sworn

Case no.

Full name of person to whom the application relates
(this is the person who lacks, or is alleged to lack, capacity)

Please read first

- If the court requires that evidence be given by affidavit then it must be included in or attached to this form.
- Only the following may administer oaths:
    - Commissioners for Oaths;
    - practising solicitors;
    - other persons specified by statute;
    - certain officials of the Senior Courts;
    - a circuit judge or district judge;
    - any justice of the peace;
    - certain officials of the county court appointed for the purpose.
- Practice Direction A accompanying Part 14 of the Court of Protection Rules 2007 sets out more detailed requirements in relation to affidavits.

- Please continue on a separate sheet of paper if you need more space to provide the affidavit. Please mark each separate sheet with all of the information provided in the box in the top-right corner of this page.
- For assistance in completing the form please see guidance notes and website: www.gov.uk/court-of-protection
- Court of Protection staff cannot give legal advice. If you need legal advice please contact a solicitor.

© Crown Copyright 2015

Form COP25 – Affidavit

Affidavit

1 Enter full name of deponent

I, **1**

2 Enter occupation or description

2

3 Enter your full address including postcode or, if making the affidavit in your professional, business or other occupational capacity, the position you hold, the name of your firm or employer and the address at which you work

of **3**

☐ am a party to the proceedings

☐ am employed by a party to the proceedings

and ☐ state on oath **or** ☐ do solemnly and sincerely affirm

4 Set out in numbered paragraphs indicating:
- which of the statements are from your own knowledge and which are matters of information or belief, and
- the source for any matters of information or belief.

Where you refer to an exhibit, you should state the identifier you have used. For example, 'I refer to the (description of document) marked Exhibit A...'

4

continued over

PART VII

PART VII — COURT OF PROTECTION PRACTICE 2016

Form COP25 – Affidavit

4

Sworn/affirmed by (signature)

before me (signature)

Full name

Qualifications

at (address)

On (date)

Please return the completed affidavit to the Court of Protection

PART VII

PART VII   COURT OF PROTECTION PRACTICE 2016

Form COP28 – Notice of hearing

Court of Protection
Notice of hearing

For office use only

To (enter name and address of person to be notified)

Name

Address

This notice is to tell you that the hearing date for the following case has been fixed.

Details of the case

Case no.

Applicant

Person to whom the application relates

Details of the hearing

Date

Time

Location

The hearing is for:

☐ directions

☐ disposing of the matter

☐ other

If you have any questions or need further information please check the website, www.justice.gov.uk or www.direct.gov.uk or contact Court Enquiry Service on 0300 456 4600.

If you are attending the hearing and you need any special assistance or facilities please contact Court Enquiry Service on the above number immediately so that arrangements can be made (if you have not done so already).

© Crown Copyright 2012

Form COP29 – Notice of hearing for committal order

Court of Protection
Notice of hearing for committal order

For office use only

To (enter name and address of person to be notified)

Name

Address

This notice is to tell you that the hearing date for the following case has been fixed.

Details of the case

Case no.

Applicant

Details of the hearing

Date

Time

Location

Important notice

The court has the power to send you to prison and to fine you if it finds that any of the allegations made against you are true and amount to a contempt of court.

You must attend court on the date shown on this form. It is in your own interest to do so. You should bring with you any witnesses and documents which you think will help you put your side of the case.

If you consider the allegations are not true you must tell the court why. If it is established that they are true, you must tell the court of any good reason why they do not amount to a contempt of court, or, if they do, why you should not be punished.

If you have any questions or need further information about the hearing please check the website, www.justice.gov.uk or www.direct.gov.uk or contact Court Enquiry Service on 0300 456 4600.
Court of Protection staff cannot give legal advice. If you need legal advice please contact a solicitor.

If you need any special assistance or facilities to attend the hearing please contact Court Enquiry Service on the number above immediately so that arrangements can be made (if you have not done so already).

© Crown Copyright 2012

PART VII   COURT OF PROTECTION PRACTICE 2016

Form COP30 – Notice of change of solicitor

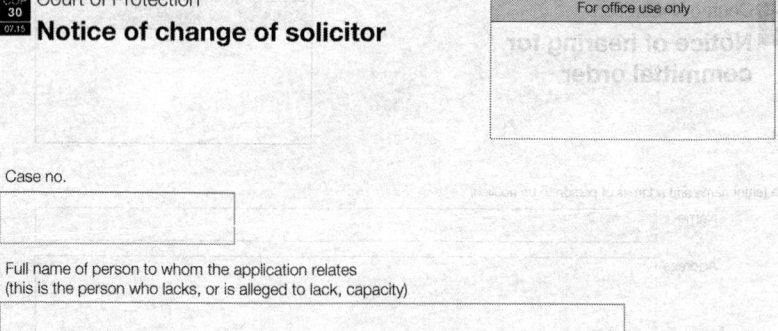

Court of Protection
Notice of change of solicitor

For office use only

Case no.

Full name of person to whom the application relates
(this is the person who lacks, or is alleged to lack, capacity)

Please read first

- You must complete this notice and file it with the court if you:
  - are changing the solicitor who is acting for you;
  - have been conducting the proceedings in person and are now appointing a solicitor to act on your behalf; or
  - have had a solicitor acting on your behalf and now intend to act in person.
- You may have to pay a fee when you make an application. Refer to the leaflet COP44 Court of Protection – Fees for details
- If you are applying for an order declaring that the solicitor acting for another party has ceased to act, then you need to use the COP9 application notice.
- You must provide a copy of this notice to every other party to the proceedings. If applicable, you must also provide a copy to the solicitor who is ceasing to act for you.

- The court will not consider that a change has occurred until you have filed this notice.
- Please continue on a separate sheet of paper if you need more space to answer a question. Write the case number, your name, the name of the person to whom the application relates, and the number of the question you are answering on each separate sheet.
- For assistance in completing the form please see guidance notes and website:
www.gov.uk/court-of-protection
- Court of Protection staff cannot give legal advice. If you need legal advice please contact a solicitor.

© Crown Copyright 2015

Form COP30 – Notice of change of solicitor

Section 1 - Your details (party changing solicitor)

1.1 ☐ Mr. ☐ Mrs. ☐ Miss ☐ Ms. ☐ Other _____

First name

Middle name(s)

Last name

Address (including postcode)

Telephone no.

1.2 What is your role in these proceedings?

☐ Applicant (the person who filed the COP1 application form)

☐ Respondent

☐ Other (please provide details)

Section 2 - Change of solicitor

2.1 I give notice that:

☐ I am changing the solicitor who is acting for me.

☐ I have been conducting the proceedings in person but am now appointing a solicitor to act on my behalf.

☐ I have had a solicitor acting on my behalf but now intend to act in person.

PART VII

1991

2.2 Details of solicitor being appointed (if applicable)

Name of solicitor

Name of firm

Address
(including postcode)

Telephone no.

Fax no.

DX no.

E-mail address

2.3 Details of solicitor who will cease to act (if applicable)

2.4 Which address should official documentation be sent to?

☐ Your address

☐ Solicitor's address

☐ Other address (please provide details)

2.5 Please tick to confirm:

☐ I have provided a copy of this notice to every other party to the proceedings and to my former solicitor (if applicable).

Section 3 – Signature

Signed

Name of firm

Name

Position or office held

Date

Please return the completed certificate to the Court of Protection

Form COP31 – Notice of intention to file evidence by deposition

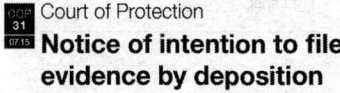
Court of Protection
Notice of intention to file evidence by deposition

For office use only

Case no.

Full name of person to whom the application relates
(this is the person who lacks, or is alleged to lack, capacity)

Please read first

- If you intend to use a deposition as evidence at a hearing then you must complete this notice to inform the court.
- You must file this notice at least 14 days before the date fixed for the hearing.
- You must provide a copy of this notice to every other party to the proceedings.
- The court may require the deponent (the person who was examined) to attend the hearing and give evidence in person.
- Please continue on a separate sheet of paper if you need more space to answer a question. Write the case number, your name, the name of the person to whom the application relates, and the number of the question you are answering on each separate sheet.

- For assistance in completing the form please see guidance notes and website:
www.gov.uk/court-of-protection
- Court of Protection staff cannot give legal advice. If you need legal advice please contact a solicitor.

© Crown Copyright 2015

Section 1 – Your details (party intending to file evidence by deposition)

1.1 ☐ Mr. ☐ Mrs. ☐ Miss ☐ Ms. ☐ Other _____

Full name

1.2 Address (including postcode)

Telephone no.

1.3 What is your role in these proceedings?

☐ Applicant (the person who filed the COP1 application form)

☐ Respondent

☐ Other (please provide details)

Section 2 – Evidence by deposition

2.1 I intend to put a deposition in evidence at the hearing fixed to take place on | D | D | M | M | Y | Y | Y | Y |

2.2 Full name of deponent (person who gave evidence by deposition)

Section 3 – Signature

Signed

Name of firm

Name

Position or office held

Date

Please return the completed certificate to the Court of Protection

Form COP35 – Appellant's notice

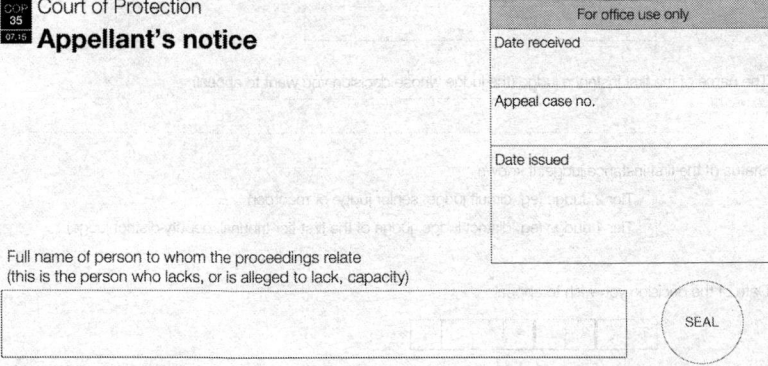

Court of Protection
Appellant's notice

For office use only
Date received
Appeal case no.
Date issued

Full name of person to whom the proceedings relate
(this is the person who lacks, or is alleged to lack, capacity)

SEAL

Please read first

- If you wish to appeal against a decision of the Court of Protection then you must complete this form and file it with the court.
- Do not use this form if you are appealing to the Court of Appeal. You need to follow the Court of Appeal procedures.
- The first person to appeal against any decision of the court is called the appellant. Any other party to the appeal is called a respondent.
- Respondents can apply for permission if they wish to make an additional, different appeal, or can apply to have the order of the first instance judge upheld on different or additional grounds by filing a COP36 respondent's notice.
- You have limited time to file your appellant's notice with the court. You must file it:
  – within the time limit set by the first instance judge; or
  – where the first instance judge did not set a time limit, within 21 days of the date of the decision you wish to appeal against.
- You must pay a fee when you file an appellant's notice. Please refer to the fees leaflet for details.

- You may need to pay for any costs you incur during proceedings. If the court considers that you have acted unreasonably you can be ordered to pay the costs incurred by other parties.
- Please continue on a separate sheet of paper if you need more space to answer a question. Write your name, the name and date of birth of the person to whom the application relates, and the number of the question you are answering on each separate sheet.
- There are additional guidance notes at the end of this form.
- For assistance in completing the form please see guidance notes and website: www.gov.uk/court-of-protection
- Court of Protection staff cannot give legal advice. If you need legal advice please contact a solicitor.

© Crown Copyright 2015

PART VII   COURT OF PROTECTION PRACTICE 2016

Section 1 – Details of the decision you are appealing against

1.1   Case number

      [   ]

1.2   The name of the first instance judge (the judge whose decision you want to appeal)

      [   ]

1.3   Status of the first instance judge, if known

              ☐ Tier 2 Judge (eg. circuit judge, senior judge or recorder)
              ☐ Tier 1 Judge (eg. district judge, judge of the first tier tribunal, deputy district judge)

1.4   Date of the decision you wish to appeal

      [D][D][M][M][Y][Y][Y][Y]

1.5   Address of the person to whom the proceedings relate

      [   ]

1.6   Date of birth of the person to whom the proceedings relate

      [D][D][M][M][Y][Y][Y][Y]

Form COP35 – Appellant's notice

Section 2 – Details of appellant and respondent(s)

Your details (the appellant)

2.1 Your details ☐ Mr. ☐ Mrs. ☐ Miss ☐ Ms. ☐ Other _____

First name

Middle name(s)

Last name

2.2 Address (including postcode)

Telephone no.
Daytime	
Evening	
Mobile	

E-mail address

2.3 Is a solicitor representing you? ☐ Yes ☐ No

If Yes, please give the solicitor's details.

Name

Address (including postcode)

Telephone no. _____ Fax no. _____

DX no.

E-mail address

PART VII

PART VII   COURT OF PROTECTION PRACTICE 2016

2.4 Which address should official documentation be sent to?

         ☐ Your address

         ☐ Solicitor's address

         ☐ Other address (please provide details)

Details of respondent(s) to the appeal (see note 1)

2.5

Full name including title	Full address including postcode

Section 3 – Application for permission to appeal

3.1 Do you need permission from the court to appeal? **(see note 2)**

         ☐ Yes

         ☐ No, I am appealing against an order for committal to prison

3.2 If Yes, has permission to appeal been granted?

         ☐ Yes

         ☐ No, I now seek permission to appeal

Form COP35 – Appellant's notice

Section 4 – Details of appeal

4.1 Nature of decision you wish to appeal **(see note 3)**
- [ ] Case management decision
- [ ] Grant or refusal of an interim application
- [ ] Final decision
- [ ] Other (please give details)

4.2 What are you asking the appeal judge to do? **(see note 4)**

4.3 If you are asking the appeal judge to affirm, set aside or vary part of the order please specify which part

PART VII

1999

Section 5 – Grounds for appeal and skeleton argument

5.1 Please set out your grounds for appeal. **(see note 5)**

5.2 Please use the COP37 skeleton argument form for your arguments in support of your grounds for appeal.

A skeleton argument: (tick only one box)

☐ is filed with this notice; or

☐ will follow within 21 days of filing this notice.

Form COP35 – Appellant's notice

Section 6 – Other applications

Please complete this section if you are asking for orders in addition to the order asked for in section 4.2. If you make other applications with your appellant's notice the court can either deal with these at any hearing which deals with your application for permission to appeal, or at another separate hearing before the hearing of your appeal.

6.1 Are you applying for a stay of execution of any order against you? ☐ Yes ☐ No

If Yes, please state why you are applying for a stay of execution.

6.2 Are you applying for an extension of time for filing the appellant's notice? **(see note 6)** ☐ Yes ☐ No

If Yes, please state the reasons for the delay.

6.3 Are you making any other applications to the court? **(see note 7)** ☐ Yes ☐ No

If Yes, please state what order you are asking the court to make and state the reasons for your application.

Evidence in support

6.4 Any evidence in support of other applications must be filed with this appellant's notice. If you are attaching any written evidence please use the COP24 witness statement form.   ☐ Evidence attached

PART VII

PART VII

COURT OF PROTECTION PRACTICE 2016

Section 7 – Supporting documents

7.1 To support your appeal you should file all relevant documents listed below with this notice. To show which documents you are filing, please tick the appropriate boxes.

- ☐ Two copies of your appellant's notice for the court (i.e. the original plus one copy);
- ☐ One copy of your skeleton argument;
- ☐ A sealed (stamped by the court) copy of the order being appealed;
- ☐ A suitable record of the judgment of the first instance judge;
- ☐ A copy of any order giving or refusing permission to appeal, together with a copy of the judge's reasons for allowing or refusing permission to appeal;
- ☐ Any witness statements or affidavits in support of any other applications included in your appellant's notice;
- ☐ The application form and any application notice or response (where relevant to the subject of the appeal);
- ☐ In cases where the decision itself was made on appeal, the order of the first instance judge, the reasons given and the appellant's notice used to appeal from that order;
- ☐ Any other documents which you reasonably consider necessary to enable the court to reach its decision on the hearing of the application or appeal; and
- ☐ Such other documents as the court may direct.

7.2 If you have not been able to obtain any of the documents listed in 7.1 within the time allowed to file the appellant's notice please list the documents in the table and explain why you cannot provide them. You will still need to file the documents with the court – please give the date you expect to be able to do so.

Title of document	Reason not supplied	Date when it will be supplied

Form COP35 – Appellant's notice

Section 8 – Statement of truth

The statement of truth is to be signed by you, your solicitor or your litigation friend.

*(I believe) (The appellant believes) that the facts stated in this appellant's notice are true.

Signed

*Appellant('s solicitor)('s litigation friend)

Name

Date

Name of firm

Position or office held

* Please delete the options in brackets that do not apply.

Now read note 8 about what you need to do next.

Guidance notes

Details of respondent(s) to the appeal

You must provide the details of the parties to the proceedings before the first instance judge who are affected by the appeal. You must serve respondents with copies of all documents relating to your appeal when the court has issued your appellant's notice in order to allow them the opportunity to respond.

Application for permission to appeal

You do not need permission from the court to appeal if the order you are appealing against is an order for committal to prison.

You do need permission to appeal against any other order. Permission to appeal will be granted only where:

- the court considers that the appeal would have a real prospect of success; or
- there is some other compelling reason why the appeal should be heard.

Details of appeal

Case management decisions include orders relating to:

- the timetable for hearing;
- the filing and exchange of information (of witnesses and experts);
- disclosure of documents; or
- adding a party to proceedings.

A grant or refusal of an interim application might include an injunction to prevent you from doing something or a declaration confirming an action is lawful.

What are you asking the appeal judge to do?

You need to explain in section 4.3 what order you are asking the court to make. Please be specific about what you are asking the appeal judge to do. The appeal judge has the power to:

- affirm, set aside or vary any order made by the first instance judge;
- refer any claim or issue to that judge for determination;
- order a new hearing; or
- make a costs order.

Grounds for appeal and arguments in support

An appeal must be based on relevant grounds (i.e. reasons for appealing). An appeal judge will only allow an appeal against a decision that is either wrong or unjust because of a serious procedural or other irregularity in the proceedings before the first instance judge.

Please set out briefly why you are appealing the judge's decision. Remember that you must not include any grounds for appeal that rely on new evidence (that is evidence that has become available since the order was made). You may not produce new evidence in your appeal unless the court allows you to do so (see section 6).

Extension of time for filing the appellant's notice

If the time for filing your appellant's notice has expired then you need to file this notice and include an application for an extension of time. You need to state the reason(s) for the delay and the steps you have taken in attempting to avoid the delay.

Other applications

If you wish to produce new evidence in your appeal you need to apply to the court to do so. You need to tell the court why the evidence was not available to the first instance judge and explain why you think it is necessary for the appeal.

What you need to do next

When you have completed your appellant's notice and supporting documents, you should take, or send them to the Court of Protection, along with any fee. For details on where to send your notice check the website: www.gov.uk/court-of-protection.

If your skeleton argument will follow your appellant's notice, it must be filed within 21 days of the appellant's notice.

Any supporting documents that you cannot obtain in time to file with your appellant's notice must be filed with the court in such time as the court may direct, and in any case as soon as possible.

What happens next?

If you need permission to appeal

The court will tell you if permission is granted, refused or if a date has been fixed for a hearing of the application for permission.

If permission is granted the court will issue your appellant's notice and will return a sealed copy. You will need to serve a copy on each respondent and notify the person to whom the proceedings relate.

If you already have permission, or do not need permission to appeal

The court will issue your appellant's notice and will return a sealed copy. You will need to serve a copy on each respondent and notify the person to whom the proceedings relate.

Form COP36 – Respondent's notice

Court of Protection
Respondent's notice

For office use only
Date received
Date issued

Appeal case no.

Full name of person to whom the proceedings relate
(this is the person who lacks, or is alleged to lack, capacity)

SEAL

Please read first

- You must file this respondent's notice if you are served with a COP35 appellant's notice and you wish to:
  - appeal on different grounds against the same order; or
  - ask the court to uphold the order of the first instance judge for reasons different from, or additional to, those given by the first instance judge.
- You do not need to file a respondent's notice if you:
  - agree with the original order and reasons given by the first instance judge; or
  - agree with the appellant and support the appeal.
- The first person to appeal against any decision of the court is called the appellant. Any other party to the appeal is a respondent.
- You must file your respondent's notice:
  - within the time limit set by the first instance judge; or
  - where the first instance judge has set no time limit, within 21 days beginning with the date you were served with:
    - the appellant's notice, where permission to appeal has been given or is not required; or
    - notification that permission has been granted; or
    - notification that the application for permission and the appeal are to be heard together.

- You may need to pay for any costs you incur during proceedings. If the court considers that you have acted unreasonably you can be ordered to pay the costs incurred by other parties.
- Please continue on a separate sheet of paper if you need more space to answer a question. Write the appeal case number, your name, the name of the person to whom the application relates, and the number of the question you are answering on each separate sheet.
- There are additional guidance notes at the end of this form.
- If you need help completing this form please check the website, www.justice.gov.uk or www.direct.gov.uk, for further guidance or information, or contact Court Enquiry Service on 0300 456 4600 or email courtofprotectionenquiries@hmcts.gsi.gov.uk
- Court of Protection staff cannot give legal advice. If you need legal advice please contact a solicitor.

© Crown Copyright 2013

Form COP36 – Respondent's notice

Section 1 – Details of the case being appealed

1.1 Case number

Section 2 – Your details (the respondent)

2.1 ☐ Mr. ☐ Mrs. ☐ Miss ☐ Ms. ☐ Other _____

First name

Middle name

Last name

2.2 Address (including postcode)

Telephone no.
- Daytime
- Evening
- Mobile

E-mail address

2.3 Is a solicitor representing you? ☐ Yes ☐ No

If Yes, please give the solicitor's details.

Name

Address (including postcode)

Telephone no.   Fax no.

DX no.

E-mail address

PART VII

PART VII   COURT OF PROTECTION PRACTICE 2016

2.4   To which address should all official documentation be sent?

        ☐ Your address

        ☐ Solicitor's address

        ☐ Other address (please provide details)

Section 3 – Application for permission to make a different appeal

If you wish only to ask that the appeal judge upholds the judgment or order of the first instance judge you do not require permission - please go to section 4.

3.1   Do you need permission from the court to appeal? **(see note 1)**

        ☐ Yes

        ☐ No, I am appealing an order for committal to prison

3.2   If Yes, has permission to appeal been granted?

        ☐ Yes

        ☐ No, I now seek permission to appeal

Section 4 – Details of response to appeal

4.1   Nature of decision you wish to appeal **(see note 2)**

        ☐ Case management decision

        ☐ Grant or refusal of an interim application

        ☐ Final decision

        ☐ Other (please give details)

Form COP36 – Respondent's notice

4.2 What are you asking the appeal judge to do? **(see note 3)**

4.3 If you are asking the appeal judge to affirm, set aside or vary part of the order please specify which part.

4.4 If you are asking the appeal judge to uphold an order on different or additional grounds please specify those grounds.

PART VII

PART VII   COURT OF PROTECTION PRACTICE 2016

Section 5 – Grounds for response to an appeal and skeleton argument

5.1   Please set out your grounds for appeal. **(see note 4)**

[ ]

5.2   Please use the COP37 skeleton argument form for your arguments in support of your grounds for appeal.

A skeleton argument: (tick only one box)

         ☐ is filed with this notice; or
         ☐ will follow within 21 days of filing this notice.

Form COP36 – Respondent's notice

Section 6 – Other applications

Please complete this section if you are asking for orders in addition to the order asked for in section 4.2. If you make other applications with your respondent's notice the court can either deal with these at any hearing which deals with your application for permission to appeal, or at another separate hearing before the hearing of your appeal.

6.1 Are you applying for a stay of execution of any order against you? ☐ Yes ☐ No

If Yes, please state why you are applying for a stay of execution.

6.2 Are you applying for an extension of time for filing the respondent's notice? **(see note 5)** ☐ Yes ☐ No

If Yes, please state the reasons for the delay.

6.3 Are you making any other applications to the court? **(see note 6)** ☐ Yes ☐ No

If Yes, please state what order you are asking the court to make and state the reasons for your application.

Evidence in support

6.4 Any evidence in support of other applications must be filed with this respondent's notice. If you are attaching any written evidence please use the COP24 witness statement form. ☐ Evidence attached

PART VII

Section 7 – Supporting documents

7.1 To support your appeal you should file all relevant documents listed below with this notice. To show which documents you are filing, please tick the appropriate boxes.

- [ ] Two copies of your respondent's notice for the court (i.e. the original and one copy);
- [ ] One copy of your skeleton argument;
- [ ] A sealed copy of the order being appealed;
- [ ] A copy of any order giving or refusing permission to appeal, together with a copy of the judge's reasons for allowing or refusing permission to appeal;
- [ ] Any witness statements or affidavits in support of any other applications included in your respondent's notice;
- [ ] Any other documents which you reasonably consider necessary to enable the court to reach its decision on the hearing of your application or appeal; and
- [ ] Such other documents as the court may direct.

7.2 If you have not been able to obtain any of the documents listed in 7.1 within the time allowed to file the respondent's notice please list the documents in the table and explain why you cannot provide them. You will still need to file the documents with the court. Please give the date you expect to be able to do so.

Title of document	Reason not supplied	Date when it will be supplied

Form COP36 – Respondent's notice

Section 8 – Statement of truth

The statement of truth is to be signed by you, your solicitor or your litigation friend.

*(I believe) (The respondent believes) that the facts stated in this respondent's notice are true.

Signed

*Respondent('s solicitor)('s litigation friend)

Name

Date

Name of firm

Position or office held

* Please delete the options in brackets that do not apply.

Now read note 7 about what you need to do next.

Guidance notes

Application for permission to make a different appeal

You do not need permission from the court to appeal if the order you are appealing against is an order for committal to prison.

You do need permission to appeal against any other order. Permission to appeal will be granted only where:

- the court considers that the appeal would have a real prospect of success: or
- there is some other compelling reason why the appeal should be heard.

Nature of the decision you want to appeal

Case management decisions include orders relating to:

- the timetable for hearing;
- the filing and exchange of information (of witnesses and experts);
- disclosure of documents; or
- adding a party to proceedings.

A grant or refusal of an interim application might include an injunction to prevent you from doing something or a declaration confirming an action is lawful.

What are you asking the appeal judge to do?

You need to explain in section 4.2 what order you are asking the court to make. Please be specific about what you are asking the appeal judge to do. The appeal judge has the power to:

- affirm, set aside or vary any order made by the first instance judge;
- refer any claim or issue to that judge for determination;
- order a new hearing; or
- make a costs order.

Grounds for response to appeal

Your response to an appeal must be based on relevant grounds. This applies if you wish to appeal the order, or if you wish the appeal judge to uphold the order on different or additional grounds. An appeal judge will only allow an appeal against a decision that is either wrong or unjust because of a serious procedural or other irregularity in the proceedings before the first instance judge.

Please set out briefly your grounds for appeal or for seeking to uphold the order. Remember that you must not include any grounds for appeal or for upholding the order that rely on new evidence (that is evidence that has become available since the order was made). You may not produce new evidence in your appeal unless the court allows you to do so (see section 6).

Extension of time for filing the respondent's notice

Where the time for filing your respondent's notice has expired, you need to file this notice and include an application for an extension of time. You need to state the reason(s) for the delay and the steps you have taken in attempting to avoid the delay.

Note 6

Other applications

If you wish to produce new evidence in your appeal you need to apply to the court to do so. You need to tell the court why the evidence was not available to the first instance judge and explain why you think it is necessary for the appeal.

Note 7

What you need to do next

Please return the respondent's notice and supporting documents to:
>   Court of Protection
>   PO Box 70185
>   First Avenue House
>   42-49 High Holborn
>   London WC1A 9JA
>
>   DX 160013 Kingsway 7

If your skeleton argument will follow your respondent's notice, it must be filed within 21 days of the respondent's notice.

Any supporting documents that you cannot obtain in time to file with your respondent's notice must be filed with the court in such time as the court may direct, and in any case as soon as possible.

Note 8

What happens next?

If you need permission to appeal

The court will tell you if permission is granted, refused or if a date has been fixed for a hearing of the application for permission.

If permission is granted, the court will issue your respondent's notice and will return a sealed copy. You will need to serve a copy on the appellant and any other respondents.

If you already have permission, or do not need permission to appeal

The court will issue your respondent's notice and will return a sealed copy. You will need to serve a copy on the appellant and any other respondents.

PART VII — COURT OF PROTECTION PRACTICE 2016

Form COP37 – Skeleton argument

Court of Protection
Skeleton argument

For office use only
Date received
Date issued

Section 1 – Details of the case being appealed

Appeal case no. (if known)

Case no.

Full name of person to whom the proceedings relate
(this is the person who lacked, or was alleged to lack, capacity)

Section 2 – Your details

In the appeal, are you the:

☐ Appellant

☐ Respondent

☐ Mr.   ☐ Mrs.   ☐ Miss   ☐ Ms.   ☐ Other _____

First name

Last name

Address (including postcode)

Telephone no.   Daytime
                Mobile

© Crown Copyright 2015

2016

Form COP37 – Skeleton argument

Section 3 – Skeleton argument

I *(the appellant) (the respondent) will rely on the following arguments at the hearing of the appeal:
(See note 1)

*delete as appropriate

continued over

PART VII

Section 3 – Skeleton argument (continued)

Section 3 – Signature

Signed

Name of firm

Name

Position or office held

Date

Now read note 2 about what you need to do next.

COP GN1 – Applications for the appointment of a deputy for property and financial affairs

 Court of Protection

Applications for the appointment of a deputy for property and financial affairs

What is a deputy?
A deputy is someone appointed by the court to deal with the property and financial affairs of a person who lacks the mental capacity to do so themselves.

They must use the assets under their control for the benefit of the person who lacks capacity and always act in the best interests of that person.

The powers of a deputy can include:

- Taking control of any cash accounts and investments
- Receiving any income (such as a private or occupational pension to which the person is entitled)
- Entering into, or terminating, tenancy agreements
- Obtaining a grant to an estate to which the person may be entitled (when there is no one able or willing to be appointed)
- Selling or letting a house or land.

A deputy may not deal with any jointly owned property or land. Please see the guidance note on selling jointly owned property for further information (Guidance Note COP GN2).

When should I apply to be a deputy for property and affairs?
If the person lacks capacity to make decisions about their property and financial affairs and has not made a valid enduring or lasting power of attorney.

If the person who lacks capacity has no savings and the only income is social security benefits, it will not usually be necessary to appoint a deputy. The Department of Work and Pensions can appoint someone called an 'appointee' to receive benefits on their behalf. For more information about appointees visit www.gov.uk and search 'becoming an appointee'.

Can more than one person be appointed as deputy?
Yes. The court can appoint one or more deputies to act either jointly (they must act together at all times) or jointly and severally (they can act together or independently of each other).

Will I have to appear in court?
In the vast majority of cases, the court will make a decision based on the papers submitted without the need for a hearing.

Security
The court requires all deputies for property and financial affairs to arrange a security bond with an insurer. Security is a type of insurance policy that protects the person who lacks mental capacity in the unlikely event that the deputy was to misuse their funds. The arrangement is a standard business practice and does not reflect on the deputy's personal integrity.

The court will calculate the level of security according to the value of the assets that will be under the control of the deputy.

The deputy must pay the premium on the bond before the court sends out the order appointing a deputy, and the deputy is responsible for paying the annual premiums.

How to apply
The following forms must be completed and signed:

- COP1 Application form
- COP1A Annex A: Supporting information for property and affairs applications
- COP3 Assessment of capacity
- COP4 Deputy's declaration

You can download the forms from the website: www.gov.uk/court-of-protection

It is important that you complete all the relevant sections of the form and provide all the information requested. If you do not provide all the information, the court may not be able to deal with your application straight away.

You should send **two copies of the COP1 but only one copy of the other forms**, together with the appropriate fee or an application for fee remission

Supporting documents to accompany the application

Where possible you should also provide:

- Copies of all previous orders made by the court;

- A copy of the will of the person to whom the application relates;

- A copy of any lasting or enduring power of attorney made by the person to whom the application relates;

- If there is an existing attorney who no longer wishes to act, a signed deed of disclaimer;

- If the application is to replace an existing deputy, and the deputy is not the applicant, a statement from the current deputy consenting to the application.

Urgent matters

If you need to do something straight away, before the appointment of a deputy, you can ask the court to make an interim order. For example, you may need to pay outstanding care home fees, or if you cannot obtain all the information, you need to complete Annex A: Supporting information for property and affairs (form COP1A), you may need to ask for an 'investigate and report' order to obtain the information from banks and building societies.

You can ask the court for an interim order at the same time as you apply for appointment as deputy by completing section 1.2 of form COP1A; or if you need to do something after applying, by completing an Application notice (form COP9).

You should only apply for an interim order in cases of genuine urgency, and you must explain to the court why the situation is urgent.

Court Fees

An application fee is payable when you make an application. Cheques should be made payable to HM Courts & Tribunals Service (HMCTS). For applications concerning property and financial affairs, you can recover the fee from the assets of the person who lacks capacity after a deputy is appointed.

There are circumstances in which the court can waive all or part payment of the application fee depending on financial circumstances.

For further details, please see booklet COP44 - Court of Protection fees available from the website: www.gov.uk/court-of-protection.

Disclaimer

Court of Protection staff cannot give legal advice. If you need legal advice, please contact a solicitor or your local Citizens Advice. Information in this guidance is believed to be correct at the time of publication; however, we do not accept any liability for any error it may contain.

If you need further help with your application, please check the website: www.gov.uk/court-of-protection.

COP GN2 – Guidance on the sale of jointly owned property

 Court of Protection
Guidance on the sale of jointly owned property

(You should also read Practice Direction 9G available from the website www.gov.uk/court-of-protection)

Introduction

1. When two or more people own real property, i.e. land and houses, together they are referred to as the trustees of that property. If one or more of those trustees becomes incapable of managing their property and affairs they will not be able to sign any legally binding documents dealing with the property. If such a property is to be sold an application will need to be made for an order appointing someone to replace the incapable trustee, or trustees.

2. Section 20(3)(c) of the Mental Capacity Act 2005 restricts deputies from carrying out trustee functions. This does not mean that a person appointed as a deputy cannot also be appointed as a trustee. However, they are distinct and separate roles and require separate applications because the appointments are made under different statutes.

3. Applications for the appointment of a new trustee for real property can be divided into two main categories. Those where there is an existing and capable co-owner ('the continuing trustee'), and those where the incapable person is the only surviving trustee.

4. Where there is a continuing trustee, or trustees, an application needs to be made to the court under Section 36(9) of the Trustee Act 1925 for the court's permission for the continuing trustee to appoint a new trustee in place of the incapable person.

Where the incapable person is the only remaining trustee, an application needs to be made to the court under Section 54 of the Trustee Act 1925 for an order appointing at least two trustees in their place. (A minimum of two trustees need to be appointed in order to sell a property.) This situation most commonly arises when the property is held as tenants in common and the co-owner is deceased. It is important to note that unless the executors of the deceased's estate have been put on the title to the property they cannot legally deal with its transfer or sale as they are not trustees of the property.

How to apply

Section 36(9) applications

- COP1 Application form

- COP1D Annex D: Supporting information for applications to appoint or discharge a trustee

- COP24 Witness statement. This is to provide the court with the necessary information as set out in paragraph 5 of Practice Direction 9G

- COP12 Special undertaking by trustees. With the details of the continuing and proposed new trustees, and the property in question. The form must be signed by all parties.

- COP24 Witness statement. A certificate of fitness. This is only required when the proposed new trustee is not the deputy, proposed deputy or a solicitor. The certificate of fitness must be completed by someone who has known the proposed new trustee for at least two years and can attest to their suitability to act.

Section 54 applications

- These applications consist of the same forms listed above.

- In cases where a co-trustee is deceased the application must be supported by a copy of the will and grant of representation to the estate of the deceased.

- If the joint tenancy of the property has been severed a copy of the notice of severance must also be filed.

Supporting documents

- If the land is registered the application must be supported by an official copy of the entries at HM Land Registry. If the land is not registered a copy of the conveyance or other trust instrument showing who has legal title must be filed.

- Where a trustee has made an enduring, or lasting power of attorney a copy should be filed.

Attorneys appointed under Enduring and Lasting Powers of Attorney

In cases where an attorney is acting under a registered power of attorney they have acquired trustee functions in respect of trusts of land under the Trustee Delegation Act 1999. This means that an attorney can exercise the Donor's trustee powers provided that

I. the donor has a beneficial interest in the trust property at the time that the function is exercised

II. there is no indication that the donor did not want the attorney to exercise his/her trustee functions.

Practically this means that an attorney acting under a registered power can

I. act with any continuing trustees in the sale of a property

II. where the attorney is the continuing trustee, or the donor is the sole surviving trustee, appoint a new trustee to act with him/her.

Please note that if you are making an application to appoint new trustees where there is no deputy or attorney already acting for the incapacitated person, you must consider whether a further application to the court is required. For example if the incapacitated person will receive funds from the sale of the property or land then you need to consider whether somebody needs to be appointed by the court to manage these funds on their behalf.

Please note that if trustees intend to sell any land or property (in which the incapacitated person has an interest) to a friend or relative this must be disclosed to the court within the application and suitable valuations supplied from reputable local valuers.

Court Fees

An application fee is payable when you make an application. Cheques should be made payable to HM Courts & Tribunals Service (HMCTS). For applications concerning property and financial affairs, you can recover the fee from the assets of the person who lacks capacity after a deputy is appointed.

There are circumstances in which the court can waive all or part payment of the application fee depending on financial circumstances.

For further details, please see booklet COP44 - Court of Protection fees available from the website: www.gov.uk/court-of-protection

Disclaimer

Court of Protection staff cannot give legal advice. If you need legal advice, please contact a solicitor or your local Citizens Advice. Information in this guidance is believed to be correct at the time of publication; however, we do not accept any liability for any error it may contain.

If you need further help with your application, please check the website: www.gov.uk/court-of-protection

PRACTICE DIRECTION – HOW TO START PROCEEDINGS

This practice direction supplements Part 9 of the Court of Protection Rules 2007

Practice Direction G – Applications to appoint or discharge a trustee

General

1. Rule 71 enables a practice direction to make additional or different provision in relation to specified applications.

Applications to which this practice direction applies

2. This practice direction makes provision for applications:
   (a) for the exercise of any power (including a power to consent) vested in P whether as a trustee or otherwise (section 18(1)(j) of the Act);
   (b) under section 36(9) of the Trustee Act 1925 for leave to appoint a new trustee in place of P;
   (c) under section 54 of the Trustee Act 1925 as to the court's jurisdiction;
   (d) under section 20 of the Trusts of Land and Appointment of Trustees Act 1996; or
   (e) for the court's approval of the appointment of a trustee in accordance with the terms of a trust.

3. A deputy may not be appointed to exercise any power vested in P, whether as a trustee or otherwise[1]. Hence, an application must be made to the court for the court to make such a decision.

Permission to make applications to the court

4. Section 50(1) of, paragraph 20(2) to Schedule 3 to, the Act and rules 51 and 52 set out the circumstances in which permission is or is not required to make an application to the court for the exercise of any of its powers under the Act.

Information to be provided with the application form

5. In addition to the application form COP1 (and its annexes) and any information or documents required to be provided by the Rules or another practice direction, the following information must be provided (in the form of a witness statement, attaching documents as exhibits where necessary) for any application to which this practice direction applies:
   (a) a copy of the existing trust document;
   (b) where relevant, a copy of any original conveyance, transfer, lease, assignment, settlement trust or will trust;
   (c) the names and addresses of any present trustees and details of any beneficial interest they have in the trust property. If the present trustees are not the original trustees, an explanation should be provided as to how they became trustees and copies of any deeds of appointment and retirement should be provided;
   (d) the full name, address and date of birth of any person proposed to replace P as a trustee, and details of his relationship to P;
   (e) confirmation that the trust is not under an order for administration in the Chancery Division;
   (f) if there is only one continuing trustee, the applicant must confirm that both the trustee and the proposed new trustee have not made an enduring power of attorney or a lasting power of attorney in favour of the other party;
   (g) if an enduring power of attorney or a lasting power of attorney has been executed by a continuing trustee, a certified copy of that document must be provided. If the power has not been registered, the applicant must confirm that the trustee is still capable of carrying out his duties as a trustee;

---

1. Section 20(3) of the Act prevents a deputy being given power to exercise such powers on behalf of P.

(h) the full name and address of any person who has an interest in any trust property as the beneficiary of a will, and whether any of them are children or persons who lack capacity;

(i) if the proposed new trustee is not a solicitor or a trust corporation (for example, a bank) and has not been appointed as a deputy for the trustee lacking capacity, the applicant must provide a witness statement from a person independent of the applicant, who has no interest in the trust property, attesting to the applicant's fitness to be appointed as trustee;

(j) if the application relates to a transfer of assets in a will trust or similar settlement into the names of new trustees, accurate details of the trust assets must be provided (including full details of any stocks and shares held);

(k) a copy of any notice of severance and evidence of service;

(l) a copy of the will and grant of probate to the deceased's estate (where relevant);

(m) confirmation of all relevant consents; and

(n) a copy of a signed trustee's special undertaking.

6. The court may direct that other material is to be filed by the applicant, and if it does, the information will be set out in the form of a witness statement.

7. If any of the information mentioned above has been provided already (e.g. by way of inclusion in an annex to the application form) it need not be provided again.

Additional information to be provided where the application relates to real property

8. In addition to the information specified in paragraph 5 above, where the application relates to real property, the information specified in paragraph 9 below must be provided. The information will be set out in the form of a witness statement.

9. The information which must be provided is:

(a) the address of the property concerned, and whether it is freehold or leasehold;

(b) the title number of the property and a copy of its entry in the Land Registry (if registered land). If the land is unregistered, the applicant should inform the court accordingly; and

(c) if the property is leasehold the applicant should advise the court as to whether he has a licence or consent to the assignment, and provide a copy of the same (or advise if a licence or consent is not necessary and the reason why it is not needed).

10. If any of the information mentioned above has been provided already (e.g. by way of inclusion in an annex to the application form) it need not be provided again.

COP GN3 – Guidance Note – Applications by existing deputies

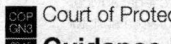
Court of Protection
Guidance Note
Applications by existing deputies

Who should read this guidance?
This leaflet explains how deputies for property and affairs may apply to the Court of Protection to change their deputyship powers to make decisions that are not covered in the original order.

When to apply?
The order appointing you as deputy will set out what decisions you can make on behalf of the person who lacks capacity. The order may also list some decisions that you cannot make. For example, the order might say you cannot sell any property, or it may set a limit on how much money you can withdraw from the bank.

If your order does not allow you to make a decision, you can apply to court to change your deputyship, or to ask for a separate order allowing you to make a one-off decision.

Examples of when you should use the procedure set out in this guidance include applications to:

- sell property except where the property is owned jointly;
- purchase property on behalf of the person who lacks capacity;
- renew the deputyship, where the appointment is time-limited; and
- change the amount of the deputy's security.

The procedure set out in this guidance is not suitable for applications to:

- sell jointly owned property (see GN2 Guidance on the sale of jointly owned property);
- make a will or codicil on behalf of the person who lacks capacity (see GN8 Applications for statutory wills, codicils, gifts and other dealings with P's property or refer to the website www.gov.uk/court-of-protection);

- make gifts on behalf of the person who lacks capacity (see GN8 Applications for statutory wills, codicils, gifts and other dealings with P's property or refer to the website www.gov.uk/court-of-protection); and
- remove or replace you as deputy.

How to apply

The following forms must be completed and signed:

- COP1 Application form
- COP1E Annex E: Supporting information for an application by an existing deputy or attorney
- COP24 Witness statement

The COP24 Witness statement should include:

- a summary of the assets of the person who lacks capacity e.g. bank accounts and money held at the Court Funds Office
- details, including the value, of any real property (house or land) they own;
- their total annual income and expenditure;
- the value of the security bond set by the court; and
- copies of any previous orders made by the court, which should be attached to your statement.

To download the forms, visit the website:
www.gov.uk/court-of-protection

You should send two copies of the COP1 but only one copy of the other forms, together with the appropriate fee or an application for fee remission

PART VII — COURT OF PROTECTION PRACTICE 2016

Court Fees
An application fee is payable when you make an application. Cheques should be made payable to HM Courts & Tribunals Service (HMCTS). For applications concerning property and financial affairs, you can recover the fee from the assets of the person who lacks capacity.

There are circumstances in which the court can waive all or part payment of the application fee depending on financial circumstances.

For further details, please see booklet COP44 - Court of Protection fees available from the website: www.gov.uk/court-of-protection.

What happens after I make the application?
For most applications made by an existing deputy, you do not need to tell anyone about your application. Sometimes the court will decide that you should tell other people about your application, and it will write to tell you how to do this.

The court will contact you after you send your application, and will either send you an order, or tell you what additional information it needs.

Disclaimer
Court of Protection staff cannot give legal advice. If you need legal advice, please contact a solicitor or your local Citizens Advice Bureau. Information in this guidance is believed to be correct at the time of publication; however, we do not accept any liability for any error it may contain.

If you need further help with your application, please check the website: www.gov.uk/court-of-protection

COP GN4 – Making a personal welfare application to the Court of Protection

 Court of Protection

Making a personal welfare application to the Court of Protection

About this guidance leaflet
This leaflet will provide you with help about making a personal welfare application to the Court of Protection (the 'court'). It also explains what the Court does, what decisions it can make, the powers it holds and how it appoints a deputy to make personal welfare decisions on behalf of someone who lacks capacity.

This guidance is designed for people who have no legal knowledge who may wish to make an application to the court in person, or who are making an application with the help of solicitors and wish to understand the process better.

The Mental Capacity Act
The Mental Capacity Act 2005 applies to England and Wales and provides a framework to empower and protect people who may lack capacity to make certain decisions for themselves.

The Mental Capacity Act is supported by a code of practice which provides guidance to all those who care for and/or make decisions on behalf of those who lack capacity. The Code includes case studies and explains in more detail the key features of the Act.

You can down load the code from www.gov.uk - search 'Mental Capacity Act Code of Practice'.

The Court of Protection
The Court of Protection is the specialist court for all issues relating to people who lack capacity to make specific decisions. The court can make decisions and appoint deputies to make decisions about someone's property and financial affairs or their healthcare and personal welfare.

Under the Mental Capacity Act, the court has the power to:

- make decisions about the personal welfare or property and financial affairs of people who lack the capacity to make such decisions themselves;

- make declarations about a person's capacity to make a decision;

- make decisions in relation to serious medical treatment cases, which relate to providing, withdrawing or withholding treatment to a person who lacks capacity;

- authorise deprivation of liberty in relation to a person's care and residence arrangements;

- appoint a deputy to make ongoing decisions on behalf of a person who lacks capacity, in relation to either the person's personal welfare or property and financial affairs; and

- make decisions about a Lasting Power of Attorney or Enduring Power of Attorney, including whether the power is valid, objections to registration, the scope of the attorney's powers and the removal of attorney's powers.

When to apply to the Court of Protection
The Mental Capacity Act sets out five 'statutory principles' that support the legal requirements in the Act. The five principles are

1. A person must be assumed to have capacity unless it is established that he lacks capacity.

2. A person is not to be treated as unable to make a decision unless all practical steps to help him do so have been taken without success.

3. A person is not to be treated as unable to make a decision merely because he makes an unwise decision.

4. An act done, or decision made, under the Act for or on behalf of a person who lacks capacity must be done, or made, in his best interests. Section 4 of the Act consists of a checklist to help the court or decision-maker determine whether something is in the person's best interests.

5. Before the act is done, or the decision is made, regard must be had to whether the purpose for which it is needed can be as effectively achieved in a way that is less restrictive of the person's rights and freedom of action.

Personal welfare matters generally – do you need to make an application to the court?

If the decision concerns the person's health and welfare, then applying the five principles above will usually be enough to make a decision about their care or treatment. Section 5 of the Act provides protection for carers, health care and social care staff to carry out certain tasks without fear of liability. This may include personal care or treatment of people who lack capacity to consent. The aim is to give legal backing for acts that need to be carried out in the best interests of the person who lacks capacity to consent to the doing of those acts.

In most matters concerning personal welfare, those principles will enable you to:

- take action or make a decision in the best interests of someone who lacks capacity; and
- find ways of settling disagreements about actions or decisions.

There are however important limitations on acts that can be carried out with protection from liability. Key areas include where there is inappropriate use of restraint or where a person who lacks capacity is deprived of their liberty.

It may be necessary to apply to court where:

- The decision concerns treatment to which the person cannot consent.
- The decision is difficult or complex.
- Someone disputes or disagrees with a course of action.
- The person needs ongoing help with decisions relating to personal health and welfare.

The Mental Capacity Act is supported by a Code of Practice which gives more guidance on when to make an application about someone's personal welfare:

- the proposed withholding or withdrawal of artificial nutrition and hydration (ANH) from a patient in a permanent vegetative state (PVS)
- cases where it is proposed that a person who lacks capacity to consent should donate an organ or bone marrow to another person
- the proposed non-therapeutic sterilisation of a person who lacks capacity to consent (for example, for contraceptive purposes)
- cases where there is a dispute about whether a particular treatment will be in a person's best interests.

Practice direction 9E gives further guidance on the types of serious medical decisions that must be made by the court. You can download practice directions from the website:
www.gov.uk/court-of-protection.

The Code also gives some more general guidance on when the Court of Protection ought to be accessed to make a decision about someone's personal welfare, including:

- There is a major disagreement regarding a serious decision, which cannot be settled in any other way; this includes where a person should live (6.12 and 8.28).
- It is unclear whether proposed serious and/or invasive medical treatment is likely to be in the best interests of the person who lacks capacity to consent (8.24).
- There is genuine doubt or disagreement about the existence, validity or applicability of an advance decision to refuse treatment (8.28).
- A family carer or a solicitor asks for personal information about someone who lacks capacity to consent to that information being revealed (8.28).
- Stopping or limiting contact with a named individual because of a risk of harm or abuse to a person lacking capacity to decide on the contact (8.28)

When to apply for the appointment of a deputy for personal welfare

Important note: If you are considering making a personal welfare application, you must take particular care to establish whether the Court of Protection must make the decision, or whether you can make the decision without applying to the court. If the court decides that the application was not necessary, you may be liable to pay the costs and court fees.

If the person lacks mental capacity to make decisions about their personal welfare, an application to be a welfare deputy will not usually be necessary. Most care and treatment decisions can be made by those involved in providing care, so long as they are acting in the person's best interests. The court will only appoint a personal welfare deputy in the most difficult cases. Examples might include where there is a history of disputes within the family, or where the person is at high risk of abuse or when there is a need for someone to make a series of linked welfare decisions over time.

For more guidance please refer to Chapter 8 of the Code of Practice.

Welfare decision

Permission to apply
In most personal welfare applications, the court's permission to apply is needed in order to make an application. The following will usually need permission:

- local authorities;
- NHS trusts;
- family members or friends;
- professionals;
- advocates, including Independent Mental Capacity Advocates (IMCAs).

The following do not need permission to apply:

- the person alleged to lack capacity;
- the person's litigation friend;
- attorneys appointed under a Lasting Power of Attorney to which the decision relates;
- deputies appointed by the court (including a deputy for property and affairs);
- relevant person's representatives (for applications under DoLS (the Deprivation of Liberty Safeguards));
- anyone applying for a court-authorised deprivation of liberty;
- the Public Guardian;
- the Official Solicitor;

- a person named in an existing order if the application relates to that order.

The guidance notes on the COP1 form and practice direction 8A explain all the circumstances when you need permission to apply.

If you need permission, your application cannot go ahead until the court grants you permission to apply.

Which application forms must I complete?
To make an application to the court, you will need to complete the following forms:

- COP1 - Application form
- COP1B - Supporting information for personal welfare applications
- COP3 - Assessment of capacity form

If you need permission to apply, you will need to complete section 6 of form COP1 and explain why you are making the application and how the application will benefit the person who lacks capacity.

If you are making an application as a person's litigation friend, the forms should be filled out in the person's name and signed by the litigation friend. The litigation friend will then take on the role of 'applicant'.

If a solicitor is helping you, then the solicitor can complete the forms and sign them on your behalf.

You can download the forms from the website: www.gov.uk/court-of-protection

Court fees
An application fee is payable when you make an application. Cheques should be made payable to HM Courts & Tribunals Service (HMCTS).

There are circumstances in which the court can waive all or part payment of the application fee depending on financial circumstances.

For further details, please see booklet COP44 - Court of Protection fees available from the website: www.gov.uk/court-of-protection

If you qualify for legal aid, then the fee must be paid even if you would otherwise qualify for fee remission or exemption. In such circumstances the fee will be included as part of the legal aid costs.

PART VII   COURT OF PROTECTION PRACTICE 2016

Emergency applications
If there is a clear risk that someone may suffer serious loss or harm, then you can apply to the court using the emergency procedure. This is only for when you need an immediate decision, where the court needs to consider the application within 24 hours or on the same day. Examples include:

- applications about urgent medical treatment;

- applications to prevent someone being removed from the place where they live;

- applications relating to deprivation of liberty where it is alleged that a person who lacks capacity is being unlawfully deprived of their liberty.

To make your emergency application, you should contact the court and ask to speak to the 'Urgent Business Officer'. They will discuss the case with you and arrange to receive your application and present it to a judge. Urgent Business Officers are available between 10:00 am – 4:00 pm.

Making an emergency application outside of office hours
If you need to make an emergency application outside of normal office hours (for example, at the weekend, or before 9.00 am or after 4.30 pm on a weekday) you should telephone the Royal Courts of Justice switchboard on 020 7947 6000.

More information on urgent applications can be found in Court practice direction 10B available from the website: www.gov.uk/court-of-protection.

Submitting your application
You should send two copies of your application form (COP1) and one copy of the other forms.

You should also keep a copy of every document you send for your own reference.

What happens after I submit my application?

Permission
If you need permission, the court will consider this first. In deciding whether to grant permission, it will consider:

- the reason the application is being made

- the benefits to the person of the application

- whether the benefits can be achieved any other way.

After considering whether to grant permission, the court will send you an order telling you either:

- permission has been granted

- permission has been refused, or

- a date has been fixed for a hearing of the application for permission.

Issuing the application
If permission is granted, or permission is not required and the application is complete, you will receive a copy of the application form stamped as issued by the court.

You will now need to tell others about your application using the following forms:

- COP5 Acknowledgement of service / notification of an application to the court

- COP14 Proceedings about you in the Court of Protection (not applicable if P – the incapacitated person - is the applicant or has been joined as a party); (and guidance notes for completing this);

- COP15 Notice (for others) that an application has been issued (and guidance notes for completing this)

- COP20A Certificate of service for form COP14

- COP20B Certificate of service for all other forms.

Who to tell about your application
Under the Court of Protection Rules you need to tell certain people about your application. You must do this within 14 days of the court issuing your application.

The person to whom the application relates (if not making the application themselves) should be given:

- a completed COP14 form

- a blank copy of the COP5 form.

Anyone named as a respondent should be given:

- a copy of the application and any supporting documents

- a blank copy of the COP5 form.

Relatives, IMCAs and anyone else named in section 5.2 of the application form as likely to have an interest, should be given:

- a completed and signed COP15 form. Some of the questions are the same as those on the application form, and here the answers should be copied from the original form
- a blank copy of the COP5 form.

How do I notify the person to whom the application relates?

You must notify the person to whom the application relates personally within 14 days of the court issuing the application form.

You or your representative must provide the information in a way that is appropriate to the person's circumstances, for example using simple language, visual aids or any other means. You must explain:

- who the applicant is;
- that the application raises the question of whether they lack capacity and what that means;
- what effect the outcome of the application would have;
- details of any person who would be appointed to make decisions on their behalf; and
- that they may seek advice and assistance in relation to the application.

You must also leave with the person to whom the application relates with the following forms:

- COP5 - Acknowledgement of service/notification; and
- COP14 - Proceedings about you in the Court of Protection.

How to serve or notify others

A document is served, or a person is notified by:

- delivering it to the person personally;
- delivering it to their home address; or
- sending it to that address, by first-class post or by an alternative method of service that provides for delivery on the next working day.

What do I do after service/notification?

After you have served or notified people about your application you must complete and return to the court:

- Form COP20A in relation to the person the application is about
- Form COP20B listing on the form other people you have served or notified.

You should send these within 7 days of the date of service/notification.

Where possible please send in form COP20A and COP20B together so that your application is not delayed.

If you cannot achieve the 14-day timeframe for service and notification, you must explain this to the court on the forms COP20A/COP20B.

What if I cannot serve or notify someone?

If for any reason you are unable to serve a document, for example you do not know a person's address and are unable to contact them within the 14 day time limit, you must explain the circumstances on the COP20A or COP20B form. This must be sent to the court within seven days of the latest date on which the documents should have been served.

What should a person do once they are served or notified?

A respondent who is served with a copy of the application form, COP5 must then decide whether they want to take part in the proceedings and put forward their views about the case. If so, they will need to complete and send form COP5 form to the court within 14 days of service.

When a respondent files a COP5 they will automatically become a party to the proceedings.

If someone is notified on form COP15 that an application has been issued, they too must decide whether they want to participate in the proceedings and put forward their views about the case. If so they will need to complete and send form COP5 form to the court within 14 days of notification.

When someone who is notified files a COP5, they will only become a party if the court joins them to the proceedings. In effect, the COP5 form is an application to be joined to the proceedings.

If the person filing a COP5 form opposes the application or wants the court to make a different decision, they should provide supporting evidence on form COP24 either at the same time as they file the COP5, or within 28 days of the date upon which they were served or notified.

What if a person has not been served or notified, but thinks they should be involved?

If a person has not been served or notified but wishes to participate in the case, they must make an application to the court to be joined as a party to the proceedings using form COP10 Application notice for applications to be joined as a party, which should include:

- their name and address
- their interest in the proceedings
- whether they agree or disagree with what is being proposed, or propose an alternative
- if they disagree, the reasons why.

The signed and dated application notice should be sent to the court along with:

- a witness statement using a COP24 form containing evidence of their interest in the proceedings and, if proposing an alternative to what is set out in the application, evidence that they will be relying on should the case progress to a hearing
- enough copies of the application notice for the court to serve on other parties to the proceedings.

The court will consider the application and if it agrees, make an order to join the person as a party to the case.

What will the court do with my application?

The court will not usually take any action until after the 14 days for responding to the court is over.

The next steps will depend on what has been asked for in the application, and whether those notified have objected, or suggested doing something different.

The court will then:

Give directions about the application and next steps to be taken.

The court may not be able to make a decision on the information that it has at this stage. It may give directions on what needs to be done in order that it can make a decision. Examples of directions are:

- provide additional evidence
- obtain the opinion of an outside agency, for example social services or a Court of Protection Visitor
- decide whether anyone else needs to be involved in the case

In these circumstances, all parties must follow the instructions given and provide any information that they are asked for. The court will then use this information either to make a decision or set a date for a hearing.

Or fix a date for the application to be heard by the court.

The court may decide straight away to set a date for a hearing. If this is the case, all parties will receive a letter from the court or a COP28 Notice of hearing form which will give details of when and where the hearing will take place.

What happens when the court makes a decision?

Once the court has made a decision, every other party will receive a copy of this. The court's decision is referred to as an 'order'.

What if I do not agree with the court's decision?

If the decision was made without a hearing, or without notice to any person affected by the order

You or any person affected by the decision may apply to the court for the decision to be reconsidered. You have 21 days to do this from the date the order is served and the application should be made using a COP9 form.

If the decision was made at a hearing

In this situation, you or any other party, or any person affected by the decision, may ask for permission to appeal against the decision. You have 21 days to do this from the date you receive the decision and the application should be made using a COP35 form.

Who pays for the costs of the application?

For proceedings in the Court of Protection that concern personal welfare decisions, there is usually no order made about costs. This means that each party will not be liable to pay anything except their own costs. If the court thinks that a party has acted unreasonably, the court may order one of the parties to pay another party's costs.

If the court thinks that a party has acted unreasonably, the court may order one of the parties to pay another party's costs.

COP GN4 – Making a personal welfare application to the Court of Protection

Disclaimer
Court of Protection staff cannot give legal advice.
If you need legal advice, please contact a solicitor or
your local Citizens Advice. Information in this guidance
is believed to be correct at the time of publication;
however, we do not accept any liability for any error it
may contain.

If you need further help with your application, please
check the website: www.gov.uk/court-of-protection

COP GN5 – Coming for a Hearing at the Court of Protection in London or at one of our regional courts

 Court of Protection
Coming for a Hearing at the Court of Protection in London or at one of our regional courts

The Court of Protection is a specialist Court established by the Mental Capacity Act 2005 and is governed by the Court of Protection Rules 2007. The court has a Listing Policy which sets out the way in which the court aims to list cases for hearings.

Court of Protection hearings can be in London or at one of our regional courts in England and Wales. When considering an application the judge will decide whether the hearing will be transferred out of London to a regional court, if this is more convenient for all the parties. The court will write to you to let you know if the hearing has been transferred to a regional court. If the hearing is to be at a regional court please ensure that you send all your evidence directly to the regional court and not to the Court of Protection in London. Similarly if you have queries about a hearing at a regional court please make your enquiries directly with the listing officer at the regional court, not the Court of Protection in London.

As a rule, all Court of Protection hearings are held in private unless stated otherwise. However persons other than invited parties, who wish to attend a hearing, can make an application to the judge hearing the matter. You can do this on form COP9 giving your reasons within form COP24.

The Court's procedures are set down in a number of Practice Directions and both lay and professional applicants are encouraged to familiarise themselves with these. Practice Directions for the Court can be found on www.gov.uk/court-of-protection. The Practice Direction relating to attended hearings is Practice Direction 13A.

Please note that all decisions are made by the court on the basis of a formal application using the appropriate forms. For reasons of impartiality judges are not able to engage in correspondence.

Please contact us should you require any assistance or have any general procedural queries in relation to an attended hearing (also known as an 'oral hearing'). This can be done by telephone (**0300 456 4600**), in writing (other than where formal application is required, for example, to ask for a hearing date to be changed), or e-mail. Our e-mail address is **courtofprotectionhearings@hmcts.gsi.gov.uk**

Staff in the court's Listing & Appeals section provide administrative support to the Court of Protection but cannot provide any legal advice. If you need legal advice please contact a solicitor.

When contacting us please always quote the full reference given in our covering letter e.g. L&A/FTG/11234567-02, the name of the person to which the case relates and the date of the hearing. This will help us deal promptly with your query.

If you are unrepresented (e.g. you do not have a solicitor to help you) and are concerned about going to Court on your own, we can supply a leaflet from the **PSU – Personal Support Unit** who may be able to help you. The PSU can be contacted on **020 7421 8533**. You can also seek general guidance from the Citizens Advice Bureau on **03444 111 444**.

Coming for a hearing – frequently asked questions

Q1. What is 'Service'?

A1. If you made the original application to the court you are the 'Applicant'. To comply with the Mental Capacity Act and Court Rules, you must inform the person (to whom the application refers) of the hearing within 14 days of receiving notice of the hearing, and where practicable, no later than 14 days before the hearing. These are the usual timescales for service. If you receive a court order (see Q3 below) this may specify different methods or timescales for service and you should comply with the directions in that Order.

You should use form COP14 'Proceedings about you in the Court' to inform the person about the hearing and then complete and return to Listing & Appeals form COP20A 'Certificate of Service/Non Service' (enclosed). These forms and guidance are available on our website www.gov.uk/court-of-protection

COP GN5 – Coming for a Hearing at the Court of Protection in London or at one of our regional courts

Q2. What if I can't serve the person in time?

A2. We recognise that there are circumstances where it may not be possible to serve the person (that the application is about) in time. If this happens, please ensure you note any service/notification forms clearly of the date that service/notification was achieved.

Q3. What is a Directions Order?

A3. Before any hearing, the Judge may issue a directions order which might ask you to provide certain information, for example in the form of a statement. You may be asked to 'file' certain documents with the Court – this means that you have to send them to the Court within the specified time or as quickly as possible. (See notes above on contacting us)

Q4. What will happen at the hearing?

A4. The hearing will take place in a court room. The room will have equipment to record the evidence being given. The judge will conduct the hearing and generally will hear the views of all parties or their representatives. Parties are reminded that the Court of Protection is part of the High Court and attendees are expected to act respectfully to staff, judges and each other.

Q5. I can't come on the date that has been set for the hearing - Can the hearing be adjourned/vacated?

A5. If there is no alternative but to request an adjournment/re-listing or to vacate a hearing, a formal application must be made to the Court on form COP9 which can be obtained from the Court's website www.gov.uk/court-of-protection. You should clearly set out the reasons and either obtain the consent of all parties or notify them of your request. Your request will be conveyed to a judge to consider.

Judicial time is very limited and ONLY the judge can agree to adjourn/re-list/vacate a hearing.

If the judge has agreed to the vacation of the hearing (e.g. to have the hearing on a different date), you will be notified by a member of the Listing & Appeals staff.

Q6 Are there any fees or costs for Hearings?

A6 Yes - there is a hearing fee, currently £500 the court will write to you when this needs to be paid.

Please refer to our Fees booklet COP44. Our booklet EX160A tells you what to do if you are unable to afford to pay part or all of the fee.

Q7. Who is the Official Solicitor?

A7. The Official Solicitor acts for people who, because they lack mental capacity and cannot properly manage their own affairs, are unable to represent themselves and no other suitable person or agency is able and willing to act. He usually becomes formally involved when appointed by the Court, and he may act as his own solicitor, or instruct a private firm of solicitors to act for him.

If the person to whom the application refers is to be represented by the Official Solicitor, the Applicant must serve the Official Solicitor immediately with copies of the application and supporting evidence, and let him have copies of any further evidence filed in due course. His address is Victory House, 30-34 Kingsway, London WC2B 6EX (DX 141423 Bloomsbury 7). Telephone 020 3681 2751

Q8. What is a 'Bundle'?

A8. Unless otherwise directed by the Court a bundle is prepared by the Applicant. It is an indexed, paginated list of documents relevant to the hearing. Papers should be set out in chronological order from the front of the bundle and divided into separate sections (each section being separately paginated). If possible the contents shall be agreed by ALL parties. The bundle shall be contained in one or more A4 size ring binders or lever arch files. Practice Direction 13B provides guidance about bundles. The completed bundle shall be lodged with the Court not less than 3 working days before the hearing, or at such other time as may be specified by the judge. Please mark any bundle for the urgent attention of Listing & Appeals Section. Bundles cannot be accepted by fax or email. Staff are unable to alter Bundles once received.

PART VII

Please note that paragraph 9.1 of Practice Direction 13B provides that following completion of the hearing the party responsible for the bundle must retrieve it from the court immediately or, if that is not practicable, must arrange to collect it from the court within five working days. Bundles which are not collected within the stipulated time may be destroyed. If you do not collect your bundle, HMCTS may make a charge for the cost of disposal.

Q.9 How do I arrange a Telephone Conference Hearing?

A9. If the Court directs that a hearing be conducted by telephone it is the responsibility of the Applicant or the Objector (person objecting to an application) to arrange and book the telephone hearing with either BT or Legal Connect conferencing services.

Please contact either BT Conferencing Services on 0800 0284194 or Legal Connect on 0800 953 0405

You will need the direct telephone number of ALL the parties.

You will need the telephone number of the Court – this will be our Public Counter Number 020 7421 8718.

You will need to send us confirmation of the booking at least 2 days prior to the hearing.

Q10. How do I get to the Court?

A10. Our address is The Court of Protection, First Avenue House, 42-49 High Holborn, London, WC1V 6NP

National Rail
The nearest train stations are City Thameslink (Holborn Viaduct exit) Farringdon, Charing Cross, Kings Cross and Euston.

Underground
The nearest tube stations are Chancery Lane on the Central Line and Holborn on the Piccadilly line.

Bus
Bus numbers 8, 25, 242 and 521 stop outside First Avenue House. Go to www.tfl.gov.uk for more detailed updated travel information.

Car
Unfortunately there is no parking available at First Avenue House.

There is parking available in Lincolns Inn Fields and Maltravers St. The nearest car park is in New Court, Carey Street, with additional ones at Drury Lane, Holborn and Shoe Lane.

Should you have any disability requirements please contact our Public Counter Reception on 020 7421 8718. All our courtrooms at First Avenue House in London are wheelchair accessible.

COP GN8 – Applications for Statutory Wills, Gifts, Settlements and other dealings with P's property

 Court of Protection

Applications for Statutory Wills, Gifts, Settlements and other dealings with P's property

Who should read this guidance?
This leaflet explains how to make an application for a statutory will, codicil, gift, or other settlement of property.

For further detailed guidance about making an application, refer to Court of Protection practice direction 9F available from the website www.gov.uk/court-of-protection

The Office of the Public Guardian (OPG) also publishes a helpful guide for deputies about making gifts. You can obtain this guide from the OPG on 0300 456 0300

How to apply
The following forms must be completed and signed:

- COP1 Application form

- COP1C Annex C: Supporting information for applications relating to a statutory will, codicil, gift, or other settlement of property

- COP3 Assessment of capacity

You must also provide all the additional information specified in form COP1C and practice direction 9F.

Please note the following:
Any application for a statutory will, gift, settlement, etc must be free standing and separate from, say, an application for the appointment of a deputy.

Evidence of capacity must relate to the decision in question (e.g. capacity to make a will, or make a gift). It will not usually be acceptable to rely on evidence submitted with an earlier application to the court

In most cases, the Court will join the person who lacks capacity as a party to the proceedings and will invite the Official Solicitor to act as the litigation friend.

The general rule is that costs in proceedings for applications relating to property and affairs (such as applications for statutory wills, gifts and settlements) are paid out of the estate the person who lacks capacity. This is only a general rule and the court may make an order that someone else should pay. Costs will include the costs of the Official Solicitor and he is happy to provide details of his charges once he has accepted appointment as litigation friend.

The Official Solicitor recommends making early contact with his office to discuss the application and you can find his details on his website: www.gov.uk/government/organisations/official-solicitor-and-public-trustee

Court fees
An application fee is payable when you make an application. Cheques should be made payable to HM Courts & Tribunals Service (HMCTS).

For further details, please see booklet COP44 - Court of Protection fees available from the website: www.gov.uk/court-of-protection.

Disclaimer
Court of Protection staff cannot give legal advice. If you need legal advice, please contact a solicitor or your local Citizens Advice Bureau. Information in this guidance is believed to be correct at the time of publication; however, we do not accept any liability for any error it may contain.

If you need further help with your application, please check the website: www.gov.uk/court-of-protection

EX343 – Unhappy with our service – what can you do?

HM Courts &
Tribunals Service

EX343

Unhappy with our service – what can you do?

A guide for all our users

We understand that if something goes wrong, you want us to look into it and answer you quickly and accurately. We want to know when we don't deliver the service you expect so that we can learn from your experience and put things right.

This leaflet tells you how you can complain about the administrative service we provided. Complaints are helpful as they make us aware of how we can improve. It is also good to hear from you when you have experienced an excellent service from us.

Complaints procedure

Who do I contact?

You can tell us what went wrong by phone or in writing. Because we want to sort things out quickly for you, please contact the office where you had the problem as staff there are best placed to investigate your complaint and will try to do so promptly. If your complaint needs looking into further, we will aim to reply to you within 10 working days. We try to answer all complaints at this first step but will tell you what to do next if you are not happy with our reply.

Review

If you are not happy with the reply to your complaint or the way it was handled, you can ask the senior manager at the office to carry out a review. You should explain why you are not satisfied. The manager will aim to reply to you within 10 working days.

Appeal

If you are not satisfied with the senior manager's reply, you can appeal to the Customer Service Team. The senior manager responsible for the review will give you their contact details.

The Customer Service Team will take a fresh look at the way the court or tribunal handled your complaint and aim to reply to you within 15 working days.

Page 1

Parliamentary and Health Service Ombudsman (PHSO)

If you are still not happy with the reply from the Customer Service Team, you can ask the PHSO to look again at your complaint. The PHSO is an independent organisation which investigates complaints where a customer thinks they have been treated unfairly or received poor service from a government department.

If your complaint is about a court or tribunal in England and Wales or a tribunal in Scotland which is part of HM Courts & Tribunals Service, you need to ask an MP to refer your complaint to the PHSO. To find the contact details of your local MP, go to www.parliament.uk/mps-lords-and-offices/mps or contact the House of Commons Information Office on 020 7219 4272.

We follow the PHSO's principles when considering complaints. These principles are on their website.

If you would like more information about the work of the PHSO, you can call their office on 0345 015 4033, email phso.enquiries@ombudsman.org.uk or visit the website at www.ombudsman.org.uk

Scotland

If your complaint is about any court in Scotland, or a tribunal in Scotland which is not part of HM Courts & Tribunals Service, contact the Scottish Public Services Ombudsman. Information on how to do this is on their website at www.spso.org.uk and their helpline number is 0800 377 7330.

Victims and witnesses of crime

We welcome feedback, including complaints, from all our customers and users. If you are a victim or a witness in a criminal case, you are entitled to information and support under the Victims' Code and the Witness Charter. You can find more information at www.gov.uk

When we cannot help

Judicial decisions

If you feel that the judiciary have made a wrong decision, you need to consider the appeal process. We can't help you to decide this or investigate it through our administrative complaints process so we suggest you get legal advice.

Judicial behaviour

If you want to complain about the way a tribunal judge or panel member, a court judge or magistrate behaved towards you, you must make your complaint to the relevant office within three months from when this happened.

i) For district judges in magistrates' courts or judges in other courts contact:

> Judicial Conduct Investigations Office
>
> Room 81-82
>
> Queen's Building
>
> Royal Courts of Justice
>
> Strand
>
> London
>
> WC2A 2LL
>
> Email: inbox@jcio.gsi.gov.uk
>
> Website: judicialconduct.judiciary.gov.uk

ii) For magistrates, contact the court and they will give you details of the local advisory committee.

iii) For tribunal judges and members, contact the office where the problem arose and they will tell you whether your complaint should be sent to the regional judge, Tribunal President or the Judicial Conduct Investigations Office (see above).

EX343 Unhappy with our service – what can you do? (10.15) ©Crown copyright 2015

Page 3

Form EX343A – Complaint

Form EX343A – Complaint

Complaint

- HM Courts & Tribunals Service **cannot consider complaints about** a decision a judge or magistrate has made, or the conduct of a judge or magistrate.
- For more information on our complaints process, and how to make a judicial complaint, see leaflet EX343 available from hmctsformfinder.justice.gov.uk
- Please use black ink as the form may be copied. Please return the completed form to the office where the problem occurred. This will help us to sort things out quickly for you.

For official use

Date received

Reference number

Please give the name and address of the venue you are making your complaint about.

About you
Name
Address
Daytime telephone number
Email (if any)

Your case
Case/claim number (if you have one)
Names of parties in the case   v

Your complaint
Please:
- explain clearly what your complaint is about;
- include any facts and events relating to it;
- say why you think a mistake has been made; and
- what loss if any, you have incurred as a result

Please continue on a separate sheet if necessary.

Your signature   Date

Do you have any suggestions to improve the service you have received?

EX343A Complaint form (10.15)   © Crown copyright 2015

PART VII

Applications to the Court of Protection in relation to tenancy agreements

Applications to the Court of Protection in relation to tenancy agreements

Introduction

The Association of Public Authority Deputies (APAD), and other court users have asked the court to issue guidance about applications in relation to signing or terminating tenancy agreements on behalf of adults who lack the mental capacity to understand or sign the agreement themselves. Often this is where adults with learning disabilities are moved from hospital or care home settings into supported living arrangements in the community, that allow greater autonomy and independent decision making. Many of the adults will have the capacity to make certain decisions, such as dealing with social security benefit payments, but will lack the capacity deal with the tenancy arrangement.

This guidance has been drawn up with the approval of the senior judge of the Court of Protection, and sets out the circumstances when it may be necessary to make an application, and puts in place streamlined procedures for receiving applications relating to more than one person, thereby simplifying some parts of the court procedure.

When is it necessary to apply to the Court of Protection?

If a person lacks the mental capacity to make his or her own informed decision about whether or not to accept a tenancy offer, then an appropriate person can make the decision through the best interest process outlined in the Mental Capacity Act 2005.

Alternatively, if there is a registered enduring or lasting power of attorney in place; or a deputy for property and affairs has already been appointed, then the attorney or deputy would usually make that decision (see below).

Although the Mental Capacity Act 2005 enables the making of certain decisions without the need to obtain any formal authority to act, it does not extend to **signing** legal documents, such as tenancy agreements. Someone can only sign a tenancy agreement on the person's behalf if they are:

- An attorney under a registered lasting power of attorney (LPA) or enduring power of attorney (EPA);
- A deputy appointed by the Court of Protection; or
- Someone else authorised to sign by the Court of Protection.

In some circumstances, landlords may be willing to accept unsigned tenancies, but this guidance applies to the situation where the landlord wants the tenancy to be signed. Even if the landlord will accept an unsigned agreement, it would also be appropriate to make an application where there is a dispute or if it is not clear whether the tenancy offer is in the person's best interests.

Applications to the Court of Protection in relation to tenancy agreements

Can a deputy or attorney sign or terminate the tenancy agreement?

If the person has a registered attorney under an EPA or LPA, or has a deputy appointed to make decisions on their behalf, then the deputy or attorney can terminate or enter into a tenancy agreement without further authorisation from the court. Please note, however that deputies acting under an old style short order or receivership order made before the Mental Capacity Act came into force, may not have sufficient authority to sign the agreement, and it may be necessary to apply for 'reappointment' with the full powers of a deputy.

Does a deputy need to be appointed in all cases?

No, if the sole purpose of the application is to sign or terminate the tenancy, then the application should be for an order that specifically deals with the tenancy matter (see how to make an application, below). If, however, the adult lacks capacity to manage other aspects of their property and affairs and they have assets and income other than social security benefits then it will usually be necessary to appoint a deputy to deal with all these decisions.

What if the person lacking capacity is under 18 years of age?

Section 18(3) Mental Capacity Act enables the court to make decisions about a child's property or finances (or appoint a deputy to make these decisions) if the child lacks capacity to make such decisions and is likely to still lack capacity to make financial decisions when they reach the age of 18.

These provisions do not extend to tenancies because a person under 18 cannot legally enter into a contract, because in law, a child is deemed to lack capacity because of their age. In addition, a tenancy is a legal estate and a child cannot hold a legal estate.

As the tenant is under 18 and cannot legally sign a contract, the Court of Protection cannot appoint a deputy or authorise someone else to sign the agreement on behalf of the child. This is because the court could not authorise a transaction that would not be legal, even if the person had mental capacity. The only option here would be for someone with parental responsibility to sign, although this would have the effect of making the parent the tenant.

How to make an application

The court is prepared to deal with all of the adults required to sign the tenancy agreement(s) in a single application. This is on the understanding that the only order required from the court relates to the tenancy agreement and no further directions, for example the appointment of a deputy, are necessary.

The court will require:

- A single COP1 Application form setting out the order or declaration required with a list of all the adults required to sign the agreement annexed;
- A COP3 Assessment of capacity for **each** adult. The assessment should deal specifically with the adult's capacity to sign or terminate the agreement;
- A COP24 Witness statement for **each** person setting out the circumstances behind the moves and confirming that a best interests assessment has been carried out, including consultation with close family members, or people in close contact with the person, where applicable.
- An application fee.
- A covering letter clearly stating that the applications relates to tenancy agreements in respect of more than one person

The application form should request the court to make a single order or declaration that it is in all the adult service users' best interests for the tenancy arrangement to be signed or terminated on their behalf.

The procedure above can also be adapted for applications relating to individuals.

How will the court deal with the application?

When the court issues the application, the applicant will notify each adult personally using form COP14 and provide evidence that they have done on form COP20A. Once notified, the person will have 21days to object or respond to the application.

If the court receives an objection to the application it will deal with it as a discrete issue, in accordance with the usual procedure.

Once the 21 day time limit expires, the court will issue a single order that deals with the tenancy matter for all the service users.

Will the court remit the fee?

No. The court is only charging a single fee for an application that relates to more than one person and will not remit fees in relation to bulk applications. The applicant is responsible for paying the fee, which must accompany the application.

If the application relates to a single individual only, then the usual policy on fee remissions and exemption will apply.

Further help and information

If you need any further help or information about making an application, please contact:

- **courtofprotectionenquiries@hmcts.gsi.gov.uk**
- **0300 456 4600**

Please note that while court staff can provide guidance about making an application, they cannot give legal advice. We recommend that you seek independent legal advice where appropriate.

LASTING POWERS OF ATTORNEY FORMS

These forms are taken from the Lasting Powers of Attorney, Enduring Powers of Attorney and Public Guardian Regulations 2007 (SI 2007/1253), as amended by the Lasting Powers of Attorney, Enduring Powers of Attorney and Public Guardian (Amendment) Regulations 2009 (SI 2009/1884).

PART VII   COURT OF PROTECTION PRACTICE 2016

Form LP1F and LP1H – Lasting Power of Attorney
Lasting power of attorney – Financial decisions

Office of the
Public Guardian

Form
LP1F

Lasting power of attorney

Financial decisions

Registering
an LPA costs

£110

This fee is means-tested:
see the application
Guide part B

Use this for:

- running your bank and savings accounts
- making or selling investments
- paying your bills
- buying or selling your house

How to complete this form

| PLEASE WRITE IN CAPITAL LETTERS USING A BLACK PEN |

☒ Mark your choice with an X

■ If you make a mistake, fill in the box and then mark the correct
choice with an X

Making an LPA online is simpler, clearer and faster ←
Our smart online form gives you just the right amount of help
exactly when you need it: **www.gov.uk/power-of-attorney**

— Before
you start...

This form is also available in Welsh. Call the helpline on 0300 456 0300.

This page is not part of the form   **LP1F** Property and financial
affairs (08.15)

The people involved in your LPA

Helpline
0300 456 0300

You'll find it easier to make an LPA if you first choose the people you want to help you. **Note their names here now** so you can refer back later.

People you must have to make an LPA

Donor

If you are filling this form in for yourself, you are the donor. If you are filling this in for a friend or relative, they are the donor.

Attorneys

Attorneys are the people you pick to make decisions for you. They don't need legal training.

They should be people you trust and know well; for example, your husband, wife, partner, adult children or good friends.

Choose one attorney or more. If you have a lot, they might find it hard to make decisions together.

Certificate provider

You need someone to confirm that no one is forcing you to make an LPA and you understand what you are doing. This is your 'certificate provider'. They must either:

- have relevant professional skills, such as a doctor or lawyer
- have known you well for at least two years, such as a friend or colleague

Some people can't be a certificate provider. See the list in the Guide, part A10.

Witnesses

You can't witness your attorneys' signatures and they can't witness yours. Anyone else over 18 years old can be a witness.

People you might want to include in your LPA

Replacement attorneys

You don't have to appoint replacement attorneys but they help protect your LPA. Without them, your LPA might not work if one of your original attorneys stops acting for you.

People to notify

'People to notify' add security. They can raise concerns about your LPA before it's registered – for example, if they think you are under pressure to make the LPA.

This page is not part of the form

LP1F Property and financial affairs (08.15)

PART VII

Office of the Public Guardian

Helpline
0300 456 0300

Lasting power of attorney for property and financial affairs

Section 1
The donor

You are appointing other people to make decisions on your behalf. You are 'the donor'.

Restrictions – you must be at least 18 years old and be able to understand and make decisions for yourself (called 'mental capacity').

Help?
For help with this section, see the Guide, part A1.

Title   First names

Last name

Any other names you're known by (optional – eg your married name)

Date of birth

Day Month Year

Address

Postcode

Email address (optional)

If you are filling this in for a friend or relative and they can no longer make decisions independently, they can't make an LPA. See the Guide 'Before you start' for more information.

For OPG office use only

LPA registration date

OPG reference number

Day Month Year

Only valid with the official stamp here.

LP1F Property and financial affairs (07.15)

1

Section 2
The attorneys

Helpline
0300 456 0300

The people you choose to make decisions for you are called your 'attorneys'. Your attorneys don't need special legal knowledge or training. They should be people you trust and know well. Common choices include your husband, wife or partner, son or daughter, or your best friend.

You need at least one attorney, but you can have more.

You'll also be able to choose 'replacement attorneys' in section 4. They can step in if one of the attorneys you appoint here can no longer act for you.

To appoint a trust corporation, fill in the first attorney space and tick the box in that section. They must sign Continuation sheet 4. For more about trust corporations, see the Guide, part A2.

Restrictions – Attorneys must be at least 18 years old and must have mental capacity to make decisions. They must not be bankrupt or subject to a debt relief order.

Help?

For help with this section, see the Guide, part A2.

Title   First names

Last name   (or trust corporation name)

Date of birth
Day   Month   Year

Address

Postcode

Email address (optional)

☐ This attorney is a trust corporation.

Title   First names

Last name

Date of birth
Day   Month   Year

Address

Postcode

Email address (optional)

Only valid with the official stamp here.

LP1F Property and financial affairs (07.15)

PART VII

Section 2 – continued

Helpline
0300 456 0300

Title First names

Last name

Date of birth
Day Month Year

Address

Postcode

Email address (optional)

Title First names

Last name

Date of birth
Day Month Year

Address

Postcode

Email address (optional)

☐ **More attorneys** – I want to appoint more than 4 attorneys. Use Continuation sheet 1.

Only valid with the official stamp here.

LP1F Property and financial affairs (07.15)

Form LP1F and LP1H – Lasting Power of Attorney

Section 3
How should your attorneys make decisions?

Helpline
0300 456 0300

You need to choose whether your attorneys can make decisions on their own or must agree some or all decisions unanimously.

Whatever you choose, they must always act in your best interests.

☐ **I only appointed one attorney** (turn to section 4)

How do you want your attorneys to work together? (tick one only)

☐ **Jointly and severally**
Attorneys can make decisions on their own or together. Most people choose this option because it's the most practical. Attorneys can get together to make important decisions if they wish, but can make simple or urgent decisions on their own. It's up to the attorneys to choose when they act together or alone. It also means that if one of the attorneys dies or can no longer act, your LPA will still work.

If one attorney makes a decision, it has the same effect as if all the attorneys made that decision.

☐ **Jointly**
Attorneys must agree unanimously on every decision, however big or small. Remember, some simple decisions could be delayed because it takes time to get the attorneys together. If your attorneys can't agree a decision, then they can only make that decision by going to court.

Be careful – if one attorney dies or can no longer act, all your attorneys become unable to act. This is because the law says a group appointed 'jointly' is a single unit. Your LPA will stop working unless you appoint at least one replacement attorney (in section 4).

☐ **Jointly for some decisions, jointly and severally for other decisions**
Attorneys must agree unanimously on some decisions, but can make others on their own. If you choose this option, you must list the decisions your attorneys should make jointly and agree unanimously on Continuation sheet 2. The wording you use is important. There are examples in the Guide, part A3.

Be careful – if one attorney dies or can no longer act, none of your attorneys will be able to make any of the decisions you've said should be made jointly. Your LPA will stop working for those decisions unless you appoint at least one replacement attorney (in section 4). Your original attorneys will still be able to make any of the other decisions alongside your replacement attorneys.

Help?
For help with this section, see the Guide, part A3.

 If you choose 'jointly for some decisions...', you may want to take legal advice, particularly if the examples in part A3 of the the Guide, don't match your needs.

PART VII

Only valid with the official stamp here.

LP1F Property and financial affairs (07.15)

4

Section 4
Replacement attorneys

Helpline
0300 456 0300

This section is optional, but we recommend you consider it

Replacement attorneys are a backup in case one of your original attorneys can't make decisions for you any more.

To appoint a trust corporation, fill in the first attorney space below and tick the box in that section. They must sign Continuation sheet 4.

Reasons replacement attorneys step in — If one of your original attorneys dies, loses capacity, no longer wants to be your attorney, becomes bankrupt or subject to a debt relief order or is no longer legally your husband, wife or civil partner.

Restrictions — replacement attorneys must be at least 18 years old and have mental capacity to make decisions. They must not be bankrupt or subject to a debt relief order.

Help?

For help with this section, see the Guide, part A4.

Title First names

Last name (or trust corporation name)

Date of birth
Day Month Year

Address

Postcode

☐ This attorney is a trust corporation.

Title First names

Last name

Date of birth
Day Month Year

Address

Postcode

☐ **More replacements** — I want to appoint more than two replacements. Use Continuation sheet 1.

When and how your replacement attorneys can act

Replacement attorneys usually step in when one of your **original** attorneys stops acting for you. If there's more than one **replacement** attorney, they will all step in at once. If they **fully** replace your original attorney(s) at once, they will usually act jointly. You can change some aspects of this, but most people don't. See the Guide, part A4.

You should consider taking legal advice if you want to change when or how your replacement attorneys act.

☐ I want to change when or how my attorneys can act (optional). Use Continuation sheet 2.

Only valid with the official stamp here.

LP1F Property and financial affairs (07.15)

5

Section 5
When can your attorneys make decisions?

**Helpline
0300 456 0300**

You can allow your attorneys to make decisions:
- as soon as the LPA has been registered by the Office of the Public Guardian
- only when you don't have mental capacity

While you have mental capacity you will be in control of all decisions affecting you. If you choose the first option, your attorneys can only make decisions on your behalf if you allow them to. They are responsible to you for any decisions you let them make.

Your attorneys must always act in your best interests.

Help?
For help with this section, see the Guide, part A5.

When do you want your attorneys to be able to make decisions?
(mark one only)

☐ **As soon as my LPA has been registered
(and also when I don't have mental capacity)**

Most people choose this option because it is the most practical.

While you still have mental capacity, your attorneys can only act **with your consent**. If you later lose capacity, they can continue to act on your behalf for all decisions covered by this LPA.

This option is useful if you are able to make your own decisions but there's another reason you want your attorneys to help you – for example, if you're away on holiday, or if you have a physical condition that makes it difficult to visit the bank, talk on the phone or sign documents.

☐ **Only when I don't have mental capacity**

Be careful – this can make your LPA a lot less useful. Your attorneys might be asked to prove you do not have mental capacity each time they try to use this LPA.

Only valid with the official stamp here.

LP1F Property and financial affairs (07.15)

6

Section 6
People to notify when the LPA is registered

Helpline
0300 456 0300

This section is optional

You can let people know that you're going to register your LPA. They can raise any concerns they have about the LPA - for example, if there was any pressure or fraud in making it.

When the LPA is registered, the person applying to register (you or one of your attorneys) must send a notice to each 'person to notify'.

You can't put your attorneys or replacement attorneys here.

People to notify can object to the LPA, but only for certain reasons (listed in the notification form LP3). After that, they are no longer involved in the LPA. Choose people who care about your best interests and who would be willing to speak up if they were concerned.

Help?

For help with this section, see the Guide, part A6.

Title	First names
Last name	
Address	
Postcode	

Title	First names
Last name	
Address	
Postcode	

Title	First names
Last name	
Address	
Postcode	

Title	First names
Last name	
Address	
Postcode	

☐ I want to appoint another person to notify (maximum is 5) - use Continuation sheet 1.

Only valid with the official stamp here.

LP1F Property and financial affairs (07.15)

7

Form LP1F and LP1H – Lasting Power of Attorney

Section 7
Preferences and instructions

Helpline
0300 456 0300

This section is optional

You can tell your attorneys how you'd **prefer** them to make decisions, or give them specific **instructions** which they must follow when making decisions.

Most people leave this page blank – you can just talk to your attorneys so they understand how you want them to make decisions for you.

 **Help?**
For help with this section, see the Guide, part A7.

Preferences

Your attorneys don't have to follow your preferences but they should keep them in mind. For examples of preferences, see the Guide, part A7.

Preferences – use words like 'prefer' and 'would like'

☐ I need more space – use Continuation sheet 2.

Instructions

Your attorneys will have to follow your instructions exactly. For examples of instructions, see the Guide, part A7.

Be careful – if you give instructions that are not legally correct they would have to be removed before your LPA could be registered.

If you want to give instructions, you may want to take legal advice.

Instructions – use words like 'must' and 'have to'

☐ I need more space – use Continuation sheet 2.

Only valid with the official stamp here.

LP1F Property and financial affairs (07.15)

8

Section 8
Your legal rights and responsibilities

Helpline
0300 456 0300

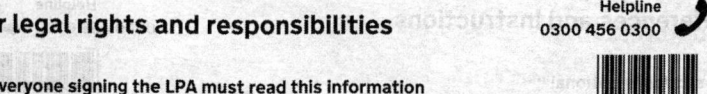

❗ Everyone signing the LPA must read this information

In sections 9 to 11, you, the certificate provider, all your attorneys and your replacement attorneys must sign this lasting power of attorney to form a legal agreement between you (a deed).

By signing this lasting power of attorney, you (the donor) are appointing people (attorneys) to make decisions for you.

LPAs are governed by the Mental Capacity Act 2005 (MCA), regulations made under it and the MCA Code of Practice. Attorneys must have regard to these documents. The Code of Practice is available from www.gov.uk/opg/mca-code or from The Stationery Office.

Help?
For help with this section, see the Guide, part A8.

Your attorneys must follow the principles of the Mental Capacity Act:
1. Your attorneys must assume that you can make your own decisions unless it is established that you cannot do so.
2. Your attorneys must help you to make as many of your own decisions as you can. They must take all practical steps to help you to make a decision. They can only treat you as unable to make a decision if they have not succeeded in helping you make a decision through those steps.
3. Your attorneys must not treat you as unable to make a decision simply because you make an unwise decision.
4. Your attorneys must act and make decisions in your best interests when you are unable to make a decision.
5. Before your attorneys make a decision or act for you, they must consider whether they can make the decision or act in a way that is less restrictive of your rights and freedom but still achieves the purpose.

Your attorneys must always act in your best interests. This is explained in the Application guide, part A8, and defined in the MCA Code of Practice.

Before this LPA can be used:
- it must be registered by the Office of the Public Guardian (OPG)
- it may be limited to when you don't have mental capacity, according to your choice in section 5

Cancelling your LPA: You can cancel this LPA at any time, as long as you have mental capacity to do so. It doesn't matter if the LPA has been registered or not. For more information, see the Guide, part D.

Your will and your LPA: Your attorneys cannot use this LPA to change your will. This LPA will expire when you die. Your attorneys must then send the registered LPA, any certified copies and a copy of your death certificate to the Office of the Public Guardian.

Data protection: For information about how OPG uses your personal data, see the Guide, part D.

Only valid with the official stamp here.

LP1F Property and financial affairs (07.15)

9

Form LP1F and LP1H – Lasting Power of Attorney

Section 9
Signature: donor

By signing on this page I confirm all of the following:

- I have read this lasting power of attorney (LPA) including section 8 'Your legal rights and responsibilities', or I have had it read to me
- I appoint and give my attorneys authority to make decisions about my property and financial affairs, including when I cannot act for myself because I lack mental capacity, subject to the terms of this LPA and to the provisions of the Mental Capacity Act 2005
- I have either appointed people to notify (in section 6) or I have chosen not to notify anyone when the LPA is registered
- I agree to the information I've provided being used by the Office of the Public Guardian in carrying out its duties

Helpline
0300 456 0300

Be careful

Sign this page (and any continuation sheets) before anyone signs sections 10 and 11.

Donor
Signed (or marked) by the person giving this lasting power of attorney and delivered as a deed.

Signature or mark

Date signed or marked
Day Month Year

If you have used Continuation sheets 1 or 2 you must sign and date each continuation sheet at the same time as you sign this page.

If you can't sign this LPA you can make a mark instead. If you can't sign or make a mark you can instruct someone else to sign for you, using Continuation sheet 3.

Witness
The witness must not be an attorney or replacement attorney appointed under this LPA, and must be aged 18 or over.

Signature or mark

Full name of witness

Address

Postcode

Help? For help with this section, see the Guide, part A9.

Only valid with the official stamp here.

LP1F Property and financial affairs (07.15)

10

PART VII

Section 10
Signature: certificate provider

Helpline
0300 456 0300

! Only sign this section after the donor has signed section 9

The 'certificate provider' signs to confirm they've discussed the lasting power of attorney (LPA) with the donor, that the donor understands what they're doing and that nobody is forcing them to do it. The 'certificate provider' should be either:

- someone who has known the donor personally for at least 2 years, such as a friend, neighbour, colleague or former colleague
- someone with relevant professional skills, such as the donor's GP, a healthcare professional or a solicitor

A certificate provider **can't** be one of the attorneys.

Help?

For help with this section, see the Guide, part A10.

Certificate provider's statement

I certify that, as far as I'm aware, at the time of signing section 9:
- the donor understood the purpose of this LPA and the scope of the authority conferred under it
- no fraud or undue pressure is being used to induce the donor to create this LPA
- there is nothing else which would prevent this LPA from being created by the completion of this instrument

By signing this section I confirm that:
- I am aged 18 or over
- I have read this LPA, including section 8 'Your legal rights and responsibilities'
- there is no restriction on my acting as a certificate provider
- the donor has chosen me as someone who has known them personally for at least 2 years **OR**
- the donor has chosen me as a person with relevant professional skills and expertise

Restrictions – the certificate provider must not be:
- an attorney or replacement attorney named in this LPA or any other LPA or enduring power of attorney for the donor
- a member of the donor's family or of one of the attorneys' families, including husbands, wives, civil partners, in-laws and step-relatives
- an unmarried partner, boyfriend or girlfriend of either the donor or one of the attorneys (whether or not they live at the same address)
- the donor's or an attorney's business partner
- the donor's or an attorney's employee
- an owner, manager, director or employee of a care home where the donor lives

Certificate provider

Title First names

Last name

Address

Postcode

Signature or mark

Date signed or marked

Day Month Year

Only valid with the official stamp here.

LP1F Property and financial affairs (07.15)

Form LP1F and LP1H – Lasting Power of Attorney

Section 11
Signature: attorney or replacement

Helpline
0300 456 0300

 Only sign this section after the certificate provider has signed section 10

All the attorneys and replacement attorneys need to sign.
There are 4 copies of this page – make more copies if you need to.

By signing this section I understand and confirm all of the following:

- I am aged 18 or over
- I have read this lasting power of attorney (LPA) including section 8 'Your legal rights and responsibilities', or I have had it read to me
- I have a duty to act based on the principles of the Mental Capacity Act 2005 and to have regard to the Mental Capacity Act Code of Practice
- I must make decisions and act in the best interests of the donor
- I must take into account any instructions or preferences set out in this LPA
- I can make decisions and act only when this LPA has been registered and at the time indicated in section 5 of this LPA

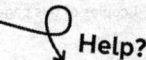 **Help?**
For help with this section, see the Guide, part A11.

Further statement by a replacement attorney: I understand that I have the authority to act under this LPA only after an original attorney's appointment is terminated. I must notify the Public Guardian if this happens.

Attorney or replacement attorney	Witness
Signed (or marked) by the attorney or replacement attorney and delivered as a deed.	The witness must not be the donor of this LPA, and must be aged 18 or over.
Signature or mark	Signature or mark
Date signed or marked Day Month Year	Full names of witness
Title First names	Address
Last name	
	Postcode

PART VII

Only valid with the official stamp here.

LP1F Property and financial affairs (07.15)

12

Section 11
Signature: attorney or replacement

Helpline
0300 456 0300

 Only sign this section after the certificate provider has signed section 10

All the attorneys and replacement attorneys need to sign.
There are 4 copies of this page – make more copies if you need to.

By signing this section I understand and confirm all of the following:

- I am aged 18 or over
- I have read this lasting power of attorney (LPA) including section 8 'Your legal rights and responsibilities', or I have had it read to me
- I have a duty to act based on the principles of the Mental Capacity Act 2005 and to have regard to the Mental Capacity Act Code of Practice
- I must make decisions and act in the best interests of the donor
- I must take into account any instructions or preferences set out in this LPA
- I can make decisions and act only when this LPA has been registered and at the time indicated in section 5 of this LPA

Help?
For help with this section, see the Guide, part A11.

Further statement by a replacement attorney: I understand that I have the authority to act under this LPA only after an original attorney's appointment is terminated. I must notify the Public Guardian if this happens.

Attorney or replacement attorney	Witness
Signed (or marked) by the attorney or replacement attorney and delivered as a deed.	The witness must not be the donor of this LPA, and must be aged 18 or over.
Signature or mark	Signature or mark
Date signed or marked Day Month Year	Full names of witness
Title First names	Address
Last name	
	Postcode

Only valid with the official stamp here.

LP1F Property and financial affairs (07.15)

Form LP1F and LP1H – Lasting Power of Attorney

Section 11
Signature: attorney or replacement

Helpline
0300 456 0300

 Only sign this section after the certificate provider has signed section 10

All the attorneys and replacement attorneys need to sign.
There are 4 copies of this page – make more copies if you need to.

By signing this section I understand and confirm all of the following:

- I am aged 18 or over
- I have read this lasting power of attorney (LPA) including section 8 'Your legal rights and responsibilities', or I have had it read to me
- I have a duty to act based on the principles of the Mental Capacity Act 2005 and to have regard to the Mental Capacity Act Code of Practice
- I must make decisions and act in the best interests of the donor
- I must take into account any instructions or preferences set out in this LPA
- I can make decisions and act only when this LPA has been registered and at the time indicated in section 5 of this LPA

Help?
For help with this section, see the Guide, part A11.

Further statement by a replacement attorney: I understand that I have the authority to act under this LPA only after an original attorney's appointment is terminated. I must notify the Public Guardian if this happens.

Attorney or replacement attorney	Witness
Signed (or marked) by the attorney or replacement attorney and delivered as a deed.	The witness must not be the donor of this LPA, and must be aged 18 or over.
Signature or mark	Signature or mark
Date signed or marked Day Month Year	Full names of witness
Title First names	Address
Last name	Postcode

Only valid with the official stamp here.

LP1F Property and financial affairs (07.15)

14

PART VII

Section 11
Signature: attorney or replacement

Helpline
0300 456 0300

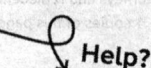

! Only sign this section after the certificate provider has signed section 10

All the attorneys and replacement attorneys need to sign.
There are 4 copies of this page – make more copies if you need to.

By signing this section I understand and confirm all of the following:

- I am aged 18 or over
- I have read this lasting power of attorney (LPA) including section 8 'Your legal rights and responsibilities', or I have had it read to me
- I have a duty to act based on the principles of the Mental Capacity Act 2005 and to have regard to the Mental Capacity Act Code of Practice
- I must make decisions and act in the best interests of the donor
- I must take into account any instructions or preferences set out in this LPA
- I can make decisions and act only when this LPA has been registered and at the time indicated in section 5 of this LPA

Help?
For help with this section, see the Guide, part A11.

Further statement by a replacement attorney: I understand that I have the authority to act under this LPA only after an original attorney's appointment is terminated. I must notify the Public Guardian if this happens.

Attorney or replacement attorney	Witness
Signed (or marked) by the attorney or replacement attorney and delivered as a deed.	The witness must not be the donor of this LPA, and must be aged 18 or over.
Signature or mark	Signature or mark
Date signed or marked Day Month Year	Full names of witness
Title First names	Address
Last name	Postcode

Only valid with the official stamp here.

LP1F Property and financial affairs (07.15)

15

**Helpline
0300 456 0300**

Now register your LPA

Before the LPA can be used, it **must** be registered by the Office of the Public Guardian (OPG). Continue filling in this form to register the LPA. See part B of the Guide.

People to notify

If there are any 'people to notify' listed in section 6, you must notify them that you are registering the LPA now. See part C of the Guide.

Fill in and send each of them a copy of the form to notify people – LP3.

When you sign section 15 of this form, you are confirming that you've sent forms to the 'people to notify'.

Register now

You do not have to register immediately, but it's a good idea in case you've made any mistakes. If you delay until after the donor loses mental capacity, it will be impossible to fix any errors. This could make the whole LPA invalid and it will not be possible to register or use it.

PART VII

Register your lasting power of attorney

Helpline
0300 456 0300

Section 12
The applicant

You can only apply to register if you are either the donor or attorney(s) for this LPA. The donor and attorney(s) should not apply together.

Who is applying to register the LPA? (tick one only)

☐ **Donor** – the donor needs to sign section 15

☐ **Attorney(s)** – If the attorneys were appointed jointly (in section 3) then they **all** need to sign section 15. Otherwise, only one of the attorneys needs to sign

Help?

For help with this section, see the Guide, part B2.

Write the name and date of birth for each attorney that is applying to register the LPA. Don't include any attorneys who are not applying.

Title First names

Last name

Date of birth
Day Month Year

Title First names

Last name

Date of birth
Day Month Year

Title First names

Last name

Date of birth
Day Month Year

Title First names

Last name

Date of birth
Day Month Year

LP1F Register your LPA (07.15)

Form LP1F and LP1H – Lasting Power of Attorney

Section 13
Who do you want to receive the LPA?

Helpline
0300 456 0300

We need to know who to send the LPA to once it is registered. We might also need to contact someone with questions about the application.

We already have the addresses of the donor and attorneys, so you don't have to repeat any of those here, unless they have changed.

Who would you like to receive the LPA and any correspondence?
- [ ] The donor
- [ ] **An attorney** (write name below)
- [ ] **Other** (write name and address below)

Title   First names

Last name

Company (optional)

Address

Postcode

Help?

For help with this section, see the Guide, part B3.

How would the person above prefer to be contacted?
You can choose more than one.

- [ ] Post
- [ ] Phone
- [ ] Email
- [ ] **Welsh** (we will write to the person in Welsh)

LP1F Register your LPA (07.15)
18

Section 14
Application fee

Helpline
0300 456 0300

There's a fee for registering a lasting power of attorney – the amount is shown on the cover sheet of this form or on form LPA120.

The fee changes from time to time. You can check you are paying the correct amount at www.gov.uk/power-of-attorney/how-much-it-costs or call 0300 456 0300. The Office of the Public Guardian can't register your LPA until you have paid the fee.

How would you like to pay?

☐ **Card** For security, **don't** write your credit or debit card details here. We'll contact you to process the payment.

Your phone number

Help?
For help with this section, see the Guide, part B4.

☐ **Cheque** Enclose a cheque with your application.

Reduced application fee

If the donor has a low income, you may not have to pay the full amount. See the Guide, part B4 for details.

☐ **I want to apply to pay a reduced fee**

You'll need to fill in form LPA120 and include it with your application. You'll also **need to send proof** that the donor is eligible to pay a reduced fee.

Are you making a repeat application?

If you've already applied to register an LPA and the Office of the Public Guardian said that it was not possible to register it, you can apply again within 3 months and pay a reduced fee.

☐ **I'm making a repeat application**

Case number

For OPG office use only

Payment reference

Payment date

Day Month Year

Amount

LP1F Register your LPA (07.15)

Section 15
Signature

 Do not sign this section until after sections 9, 10 and 11 have been signed.

Helpline
0300 456 0300

The person applying to register the LPA (see section 12) must sign and date this section. This is either the donor or attorney(s) but not both together.

If the **attorneys** are applying to register the LPA and they were appointed to act **jointly** (in section 3), they must all sign.

By signing this section I confirm the following:
- I apply to register the LPA that accompanies this application
- I have informed 'people to notify' named in section 6 of the LPA (if any) of my intention to register the LPA
- I certify that the information in this form is correct to the best of my knowledge and belief

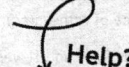 **Help?**

For help with this section, see the Guide, part B5.

Signature or mark	Signature or mark
Date signed	Date signed
Day / Month / Year	Day / Month / Year
Signature or mark	Signature or mark
Date signed	Date signed
Day / Month / Year	Day / Month / Year

If more than 4 attorneys need to sign, make copies of this page.

Check your lasting power of attorney

You don't have to use this checklist, but it'll help you make sure you've completed your LPA correctly.

☐ The donor filled in sections 1 to 7.

☐ The donor signed section 9 in the presence of a witness. The donor also signed any copies of continuation sheets 1 and 2 that were used, on the same date as signing section 9.

☐ The certificate provider signed section 10.

☐ All the attorneys and replacement attorneys signed section 11, in the presence of witness(es).

☐ Sections 9, 10 and 11 were signed in order. Section 9 must have been signed first, then section 10, then section 11. They can be dated the same day or different days.

☐ The donor or an attorney completed sections 12 to 15. If the attorneys are applying and were appointed 'jointly' (section 3), they have all signed section 15 of this form.

☐ I've paid the application fee or applied for a reduced fee. If I've applied for a reduced fee, I've included the required evidence and completed form LPA120A.

☐ If there were any people to notify in section 6, I've notified them using form LP3.

☐ I've not left out any of the pages of the LPA, even the ones where I didn't write anything or there were no boxes to fill in.

Helpline
0300 456 0300

Send to:

**Office of the Public Guardian
PO Box 16185
Birmingham B2 2WH**

This page is not part of the form

LP1F Property and financial affairs (08.15)

Form LP1F and LP1H – Lasting Power of Attorney

Lasting power of attorney – Health and care decisions

Office of the
Public Guardian

Form
LP1H

Lasting power of attorney

Health and care decisions

Registering an LPA costs

£110

This fee is means-tested: see the application Guide part B

PART VII

Use this for:
- the type of health care and medical treatment you receive, including life-sustaining treatment
- where you live
- day-to-day matters such as your diet and daily routine

How to complete this form

PLEASE WRITE IN CAPITAL LETTERS USING A BLACK PEN

☒ Mark your choice with an X

■ If you make a mistake, fill in the box and then mark the correct choice with an X

Making an LPA online is simpler, clearer and faster
Our smart online form gives you just the right amount of help exactly when you need it: **www.gov.uk/power-of-attorney**

Before you start...

This form is also available in Welsh. Call the helpline on 0300 456 0300.

This page is not part of the form

LP1H Health and welfare (08.15)

The people involved in your LPA

Helpline
0300 456 0300

You'll find it easier to make an LPA if you first choose the people you want to help you. **Note their names here now** so you can refer back later.

People you must have to make an LPA

Donor

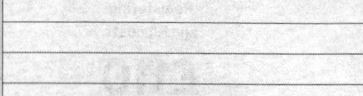

If you are filling this form in for yourself, you are the donor. If you are filling this in for a friend or relative, they are the donor.

Attorneys

Attorneys are the people you pick to make decisions for you. They don't need legal training.

They should be people you trust and know well; for example, your husband, wife, partner, adult children or good friends.

Choose one attorney or more. If you have a lot, they might find it hard to make decisions together.

Certificate provider

You need someone to confirm that no one is forcing you to make an LPA and you understand what you are doing. This is your 'certificate provider'. They must either:

- have relevant professional skills, such as a doctor or lawyer
- have known you well for at least two years, such as a friend or colleague

Some people can't be a certificate provider. See the list in the Guide, part A10.

Witnesses

You can't witness your attorneys' signatures and they can't witness yours. Anyone else over 18 years old can be a witness.

People you might want to include in your LPA

Replacement attorneys

You don't have to appoint replacement attorneys but they help protect your LPA. Without them, your LPA might not work if one of your original attorneys stops acting for you.

People to notify

'People to notify' add security. They can raise concerns about your LPA before it's registered – for example, if they think you are under pressure to make the LPA.

This page is not part of the form

LP1H Health and welfare (08.15)

Office of the Public Guardian

Helpline
0300 456 0300

Lasting power of attorney for health and welfare

Section 1
The donor

You are appointing other people to make decisions on your behalf.
You are 'the donor'.

Restrictions – you must be at least 18 years old and be able to understand and make decisions for yourself (called 'mental capacity').

Help?

For help with this section, see the Guide, part A1.

If you are filling this in for a friend or relative and they can no longer make decisions independently, they can't make an LPA. See the Guide 'Before you start' for more information.

Title First names

Last name

Any other names you're known by (optional – eg your married name)

Date of birth
Day Month Year

Address

Postcode

Email address (optional)

For OPG office use only

LPA registration date   OPG reference number
Day Month Year

Only valid with the official stamp here.

LP1H Health and welfare (07.15)

PART VII

Section 2
The attorneys

The people you choose to make decisions for you are called your 'attorneys'. Your attorneys don't need special legal knowledge or training. They should be people you trust and know well. Common choices include your husband, wife or partner, son or daughter, or your best friend.

You need at least one attorney, but you can have more.

You'll also be able to choose 'replacement attorneys' in section 4. They can step in if one of the attorneys you appoint here can no longer act for you.

Restrictions – Attorneys must be at least 18 years old and must have mental capacity to make decisions.

Helpline
0300 456 0300

Help?

For help with this section, see the Guide, part A2.

Title First names

Last name

Date of birth
Day Month Year

Address

Postcode

Email address (optional)

Title First names

Last name

Date of birth
Day Month Year

Address

Postcode

Email address (optional)

Only valid with the official stamp here.

LP1H Health and welfare (07.15)

Form LP1F and LP1H – Lasting Power of Attorney

Section 2 - continued

**Helpline
0300 456 0300**

Title First names	Title First names
Last name	Last name
Date of birth Day Month Year	Date of birth Day Month Year
Address	Address
Postcode	Postcode
Email address (optional)	Email address (optional)

☐ **More attorneys** – I want to appoint more than 4 attorneys. Use Continuation sheet 1.

Only valid with the official stamp here.

LP1H Health and welfare (07.15)

3

PART VII

Section 3
How should your attorneys make decisions?

Helpline
0300 456 0300

You need to choose whether your attorneys can make decisions on their own or must agree some or all decisions unanimously.

Whatever you choose, they must always act in your best interests.

☐ **I only appointed one attorney** (turn to section 4)

How do you want your attorneys to work together? (tick one only)

☐ **Jointly and severally**
Attorneys can make decisions on their own or together. Most people choose this option because it's the most practical. Attorneys can get together to make important decisions if they wish, but can make simple or urgent decisions on their own. It's up to the attorneys to choose when they act together or alone. It also means that if one of the attorneys dies or can no longer act, your LPA will still work.

If one attorney makes a decision, it has the same effect as if all the attorneys made that decision.

☐ **Jointly**
Attorneys must agree unanimously on every decision, however big or small. Remember, some simple decisions could be delayed because it takes time to get the attorneys together. If your attorneys can't agree a decision, then they can only make that decision by going to court.

Be careful – if one attorney dies or can no longer act, all your attorneys become unable to act. This is because the law says a group appointed 'jointly' is a single unit. Your LPA will stop working unless you appoint at least one replacement attorney (in section 4).

☐ **Jointly for some decisions, jointly and severally for other decisions**
Attorneys must agree unanimously on some decisions, but can make others on their own. If you choose this option, you must list the decisions your attorneys should make jointly and agree unanimously on Continuation sheet 2. The wording you use is important. There are examples in the Guide, part A3.

Be careful – if one of your attorneys dies or can no longer act, none of your attorneys will be able to make any of the decisions you've said should be made jointly. Your LPA will stop working for those decisions unless you appoint at least one replacement attorney (in section 4). Your original attorneys will still be able to make any of the other decisions alongside your replacement attorneys.

Help?
For help with this section, see the Guide, part A3.

If you choose 'jointly for some decisions...', you may want to take legal advice, particularly if the examples in part A3 of the Guide don't match your needs.

Only valid with the official stamp here.

LP1H Health and welfare (07.15)

Form LP1F and LP1H – Lasting Power of Attorney

Section 4
Replacement attorneys

Helpline
0300 456 0300

This section is optional, but we recommend you consider it

Replacement attorneys are a backup in case one of your original attorneys can't make decisions for you any more.

Reasons replacement attorneys step in – if one of your original attorneys dies, loses capacity, no longer wants to be your attorney or is no longer legally your husband, wife or civil partner.

Restrictions – replacement attorneys must be at least 18 years old and have mental capacity to make decisions.

Help?

For help with this section, see the Guide, part A4.

Title	First names

Last name

Date of birth

Day Month Year

Address

Postcode

Title	First names

Last name

Date of birth

Day Month Year

Address

Postcode

☐ **More replacements** – I want to appoint more than two replacements. Use Continuation sheet 1.

When and how your replacement attorneys can act

Replacement attorneys usually step in when one of your **original** attorneys stops acting for you. If there's more than one **replacement** attorney, they will all step in at once. If they **fully** replace your original attorney(s) at once, they will usually act jointly. You can change some aspects of this, but most people don't. See the Guide, part A4.

You should consider taking legal advice if you want to change how your replacement attorneys act.

☐ I want to change when or how my attorneys can act (optional). Use Continuation sheet 2.

Only valid with the official stamp here.

LP1H Health and welfare (07.15)

PART VII

Section 5
Life-sustaining treatment

Helpline
0300 456 0300

! **This is an important part of your LPA.**

You must choose whether your attorneys can give or refuse consent to life-sustaining treatment on your behalf.

Life-sustaining treatment means care, surgery, medicine or other help from doctors that's needed to keep you alive, for example:
- a serious operation, such as a heart bypass or organ transplant
- cancer treatment
- artificial nutrition or hydration (food or water given other than by mouth)

Whether some treatments are life-sustaining depends on the situation. If you had pneumonia, a simple course of antibiotics could be life-sustaining.

Decisions about life-sustaining treatment can be needed in unexpected circumstances, such as a routine operation that didn't go as planned.

You can use section 7 of this LPA to let your attorneys know more about your preferences in particular circumstances (this is optional).

Help?
For help with this section, including how your LPA relates to an 'advance decision', see the Guide, part A5.

Who do you want to make decisions about life-sustaining treatment? (sign only one option)

Option A – I give my attorneys authority to give or refuse consent to life-sustaining treatment on my behalf.

If you choose this option, your attorneys can speak to doctors on your behalf as if they were you.

Signature or mark

Date signed or marked
Day Month Year

Option B – I do not give my attorneys authority to give or refuse consent to life-sustaining treatment on my behalf.

If you choose this option, your doctors will take into account the views of the attorneys and of people who are interested in your welfare as well as any written statement you may have made, where it is practical and appropriate.

Signature or mark

Date signed or marked
Day Month Year

Witness
The witness must not be an attorney or replacement attorney appointed under this LPA, and must be aged 18 or over.

Signature or mark

Full name of witness

Address

Postcode

Only valid with the official stamp here.

LP1H Health and welfare (07.15)

6

Section 6
People to notify when the LPA is registered

Helpline
0300 456 0300

This section is optional

You can let people know that you're going to register your LPA. They can raise any concerns they have about the LPA – for example, if there was any pressure or fraud in making it.

When the LPA is registered, the person applying to register (you or one of your attorneys) must send a notice to each 'person to notify'.

You can't put your attorneys or replacement attorneys here.

People to notify can object to the LPA, but only for certain reasons (listed in the notification form LP3). After that, they are no longer involved in the LPA. Choose people who care about your best interests and who would be willing to speak up if they were concerned.

For help with this section, see the Guide, part A6.

Title	First names
Last name	
Address	
Postcode	

Title	First names
Last name	
Address	
Postcode	

Title	First names
Last name	
Address	
Postcode	

Title	First names
Last name	
Address	
Postcode	

☐ I want to appoint another person to notify (maximum is 5) – use Continuation sheet 1.

Only valid with the official stamp here.

LP1H Health and welfare (07.15)

Section 7
Preferences and instructions

Helpline
0300 456 0300

This section is optional

You can tell your attorneys how you'd **prefer** them to make decisions, or give them specific **instructions** which they must follow when making decisions.

Most people leave this page blank – you can just talk to your attorneys so they understand how you want them to make decisions for you.

Preferences

Your attorneys don't have to follow your preferences but they should keep them in mind. For examples of preferences, see the Guide, part A7.

 **Help?**
For help with this section, see the Guide, part A7.

Preferences – use words like 'prefer' and 'would like'

☐ I need more space – use Continuation sheet 2.

Instructions

Your attorneys will have to follow your instructions exactly. For examples of instructions, see the Guide, part A7.

Be careful – if you give instructions that are not legally correct they would have to be removed before your LPA could be registered.

If you want to give instructions, you may want to take legal advice.

Instructions – use words like 'must' and 'have to'

☐ I need more space – use Continuation sheet 2.

Only valid with the official stamp here.

LP1H Health and welfare (07.15)

8

Form LP1F and LP1H – Lasting Power of Attorney

Section 8
Your legal rights and responsibilities

Helpline
0300 456 0300

 Everyone signing the LPA must read this information

In sections 9 to 11, you, the certificate provider, all your attorneys and your replacement attorneys must sign this lasting power of attorney to form a legal agreement between you (a deed).

By signing this lasting power of attorney, you (the donor) are appointing people (attorneys) to make decisions for you.

LPAs are governed by the Mental Capacity Act 2005 (MCA), regulations made under it and the MCA Code of Practice. Attorneys must have regard to these documents. The Code of Practice is available from www.gov.uk/opg/mca-code or from The Stationery Office.

Help?

For help with this section, see the Guide, part A8.

Your attorneys must follow the principles of the Mental Capacity Act:
1. Your attorneys must assume that you can make your own decisions unless it is established that you cannot do so.
2. Your attorneys must help you to make as many of your own decisions as you can. They must take all practical steps to help you to make a decision. They can only treat you as unable to make a decision if they have not succeeded in helping you make a decision through those steps.
3. Your attorneys must not treat you as unable to make a decision simply because you make an unwise decision.
4. Your attorneys must act and make decisions in your best interests when you are unable to make a decision.
5. Before your attorneys make a decision or act for you, they must consider whether they can make the decision or act in a way that is less restrictive of your rights and freedom but still achieves the purpose.

Your attorneys must always act in your best interests. This is explained in the Application guide, part A8, and defined in the MCA Code of Practice.

Before this LPA can be used it must be registered by the Office of the Public Guardian (OPG). Your attorneys can only use this LPA if you don't have mental capacity.

Cancelling your LPA: You can cancel this LPA at any time, as long as you have mental capacity to do so. It doesn't matter if the LPA has been registered or not. For more information, see the Guide, part D.

Your will and your LPA: Your attorneys cannot use this LPA to change your will. This LPA will expire when you die. Your attorneys must then send the registered LPA, any certified copies and a copy of your death certificate to the Office of the Public Guardian.

Data protection: For information about how OPG uses your personal data, see the Guide, Part D.

Only valid with the official stamp here.

LP1H Health and welfare (07.15)

PART VII

Section 9
Signature: donor

Helpline
0300 456 0300

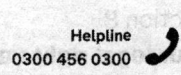

By signing on this page I confirm all of the following:

- I have read this lasting power of attorney (LPA) including section 8 'Your legal rights and responsibilities', or I have had it read to me

- I appoint and give my attorneys authority to make decisions about my health and welfare, when I cannot act for myself because I lack mental capacity, subject to the terms of this LPA and to the provisions of the Mental Capacity Act 2005

- I confirm I have chosen either Option A or Option B about life sustaining treatment in section 5 of this LPA

- I have either appointed people to notify (in section 6) or I have chosen not to notify anyone when the LPA is registered

- I agree to the information I've provided being used by the Office of the Public Guardian in carrying out its duties

Be careful

Sign this page and section 5 (and any continuation sheets) before anyone signs sections 10 and 11.

Donor

Signed (or marked) by the person giving this lasting power of attorney and delivered as a deed.

Signature or mark

Date signed or marked

Day Month Year

You must also sign Section 5 (page 6) at the same time as you sign this page.

If you have used Continuation sheets 1 or 2 you must sign and date each continuation sheet at the same time as you sign this page.

If you can't sign this LPA you can make a mark instead. If you can't sign or make a mark you can instruct someone else to sign for you, using Continuation sheet 3.

Witness

The witness must not be an attorney or replacement attorney appointed under this LPA, and must be aged 18 or over.

Signature or mark

Full name of witness

Address

Postcode

Help? For help with this section, see the Guide, part A9.

Only valid with the official stamp here.

LP1H Health and welfare (07.15)

10

Form LP1F and LP1H – Lasting Power of Attorney

Section 10
Signature: certificate provider

Helpline
0300 456 0300

 Only sign this section after the donor has signed section 9

The 'certificate provider' signs to confirm they've discussed the lasting power of attorney (LPA) with the donor, that the donor understands what they're doing and that nobody is forcing them to do it. The 'certificate provider' should be either:

- someone who has known the donor personally for at least 2 years, such as a friend, neighbour, colleague or former colleague
- someone with relevant professional skills, such as the donor's GP, a healthcare professional or a solicitor

A certificate provider **can't** be one of the attorneys.

Help?
For help with this section, see the Guide, part A10.

Certificate provider's statement

I certify that, as far as I'm aware, at the time of signing section 9:
- the donor understood the purpose of this LPA and the scope of the authority conferred under it
- no fraud or undue pressure is being used to induce the donor to create this LPA
- there is nothing else which would prevent this LPA from being created by the completion of this instrument

By signing this section I confirm that:
- I am aged 18 or over
- I have read this LPA, including section 8 'Your legal rights and responsibilities'
- there is no restriction on my acting as a certificate provider
- the donor has chosen me as someone who has known them personally for at least 2 years **OR**
- the donor has chosen me as a person with relevant professional skills and expertise

Restrictions – the certificate provider must not be:
- an attorney or replacement attorney named in this LPA or any other LPA or enduring power of attorney for the donor
- a member of the donor's family or of one of the attorneys' families, including husbands, wives, civil partners, in-laws and step-relatives
- an unmarried partner, boyfriend or girlfriend of either the donor or one of the attorneys (whether or not they live at the same address)
- the donor's or an attorney's business partner
- the donor's or an attorney's employee
- an owner, manager, director or employee of a care home where the donor lives

Certificate provider

Title   First names

Last name

Address

Postcode

Signature or mark

Date signed or marked

Day   Month   Year

Only valid with the official stamp here.

LP1H Health and welfare (07.15)

PART VII

Section 11
Signature: attorney or replacement

Helpline
0300 456 0300

 Only sign this section after the certificate provider has signed section 10

All the attorneys and replacement attorneys need to sign.
There are 4 copies of this page – make more copies if you need to.

By signing this section I understand and confirm all of the following:

- I am aged 18 or over
- I have read this lasting power of attorney (LPA) including section 8 'Your legal rights and responsibilities', or I have had it read to me
- I have a duty to act based on the principles of the Mental Capacity Act 2005 and to have regard to the Mental Capacity Act Code of Practice
- I must make decisions and act in the best interests of the donor
- I must take into account any instructions or preferences set out in this LPA
- I can make decisions and act only when this LPA has been registered
- I can make decisions and act only when the donor lacks mental capacity

Help?
For help with this section, see the Guide, part A11.

Further statement by a replacement attorney: I understand that I have the authority to act under this LPA only after an original attorney's appointment is terminated. I must notify the Public Guardian if this happens.

Attorney or replacement attorney	Witness
Signed (or marked) by the attorney or replacement attorney and delivered as a deed.	The witness must not be the donor of this LPA, and must be aged 18 or over.
Signature or mark	Signature or mark
Date signed or marked Day Month Year	Full names of witness
Title First names	Address
Last name	Postcode

Only valid with the official stamp here.

LP1H Health and welfare (07.15)
12

Form LP1F and LP1H – Lasting Power of Attorney

Section 11
Signature: attorney or replacement

Helpline
0300 456 0300

> **!** Only sign this section after the certificate provider has signed section 10
>
> All the attorneys and replacement attorneys need to sign.
> There are 4 copies of this page – make more copies if you need to.

By signing this section I understand and confirm all of the following:

- I am aged 18 or over
- I have read this lasting power of attorney (LPA) including section 8 'Your legal rights and responsibilities', or I have had it read to me
- I have a duty to act based on the principles of the Mental Capacity Act 2005 and to have regard to the Mental Capacity Act Code of Practice
- I must make decisions and act in the best interests of the donor
- I must take into account any instructions or preferences set out in this LPA
- I can make decisions and act only when this LPA has been registered
- I can make decisions and act only when the donor lacks mental capacity

Help?
For help with this section, see the Guide, part A11.

Further statement by a replacement attorney: I understand that I have the authority to act under this LPA only after an original attorney's appointment is terminated. I must notify the Public Guardian if this happens.

Attorney or replacement attorney	Witness
Signed (or marked) by the attorney or replacement attorney and delivered as a deed.	The witness must not be the donor of this LPA, and must be aged 18 or over.
Signature or mark	Signature or mark
Date signed or marked Day Month Year	Full names of witness
Title First names	Address
Last name	Postcode

PART VII

Only valid with the official stamp here.

LP1H Health and welfare (07.15)
13

Section 11
Signature: attorney or replacement

Helpline
0300 456 0300

! Only sign this section after the certificate provider has signed section 10

All the attorneys and replacement attorneys need to sign.
There are 4 copies of this page – make more copies if you need to.

By signing this section I understand and confirm all of the following:

- I am aged 18 or over
- I have read this lasting power of attorney (LPA) including section 8 'Your legal rights and responsibilities', or I have had it read to me
- I have a duty to act based on the principles of the Mental Capacity Act 2005 and to have regard to the Mental Capacity Act Code of Practice
- I must make decisions and act in the best interests of the donor
- I must take into account any instructions or preferences set out in this LPA
- I can make decisions and act only when this LPA has been registered
- I can make decisions and act only when the donor lacks mental capacity

Help?
For help with this section, see the Guide, part A11.

Further statement by a replacement attorney: I understand that I have the authority to act under this LPA only after an original attorney's appointment is terminated. I must notify the Public Guardian if this happens.

Attorney or replacement attorney	Witness
Signed (or marked) by the attorney or replacement attorney and delivered as a deed.	The witness must not be the donor of this LPA, and must be aged 18 or over.
Signature or mark	Signature or mark
Date signed or marked Day Month Year	Full names of witness
Title First names	Address
Last name	
	Postcode

Only valid with the official stamp here.

LP1H Health and welfare (07.15)

14

Form LP1F and LP1H – Lasting Power of Attorney

Section 11
Signature: attorney or replacement

Helpline
0300 456 0300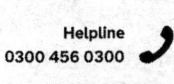

 Only sign this section after the certificate provider has signed section 10

All the attorneys and replacement attorneys need to sign.
There are 4 copies of this page – make more copies if you need to.

By signing this section I understand and confirm all of the following:

- I am aged 18 or over
- I have read this lasting power of attorney (LPA) including section 8 'Your legal rights and responsibilities', or I have had it read to me
- I have a duty to act based on the principles of the Mental Capacity Act 2005 and to have regard to the Mental Capacity Act Code of Practice
- I must make decisions and act in the best interests of the donor
- I must take into account any instructions or preferences set out in this LPA
- I can make decisions and act only when this LPA has been registered
- I can make decisions and act only when the donor lacks mental capacity

 **Help?**
For help with this section, see the Guide, part A11.

Further statement by a replacement attorney: I understand that I have the authority to act under this LPA only after an original attorney's appointment is terminated. I must notify the Public Guardian if this happens.

Attorney or replacement attorney	Witness
Signed (or marked) by the attorney or replacement attorney and delivered as a deed.	The witness must not be the donor of this LPA, and must be aged 18 or over.
Signature or mark	Signature or mark
Date signed or marked Day Month Year	Full names of witness
Title First names	Address
Last name	Postcode

PART VII

Only valid with the official stamp here.

LP1H Health and welfare (07.15)
15

Helpline
0300 456 0300

Now register your LPA

Before the LPA can be used, it **must** be registered by the Office of the Public Guardian (OPG). Continue filling in this form to register the LPA. See part B of the Guide.

People to notify

If there are any 'people to notify' listed in section 6, you must notify them that you are registering the LPA now. See Part C of the Guide.

Fill in and send each of them a copy of the form to notify people – LP3.

When you sign section 15 of this form, you are confirming that you've sent forms to the 'people to notify'.

Register now

You do not have to register immediately, but it's a good idea in case you've made any mistakes. If you delay until after the donor loses mental capacity, it will be impossible to fix any errors. This could make the whole LPA invalid and it will not be possible to register or use it.

Register your lasting power of attorney

Helpline
0300 456 0300

Section 12
The applicant

You can only apply to register if you are the donor or attorney(s) for this LPA. The donor and attorney(s) should not apply together.

Who is applying to register the LPA? (tick one only)

☐ **Donor** – the donor needs to sign section 15

☐ **Attorney(s)** – If the attorneys were appointed jointly (in section 3) then they **all** need to sign in section 15. Otherwise, only one of the attorneys needs to sign

Help?

For help with this section, see the Guide, part B2.

Write the name and date of birth for each attorney that is applying to register the LPA. Don't include any attorneys who are not applying.

Title	First names

Last name

Date of birth

Day / Month / Year

Title	First names

Last name

Date of birth

Day / Month / Year

Title	First names

Last name

Date of birth

Day / Month / Year

Title	First names

Last name

Date of birth

Day / Month / Year

LP1H Register your LPA (07.15)

Section 13
Who do you want to receive the LPA?

We need to know who to send the LPA to once it is registered. We might also need to contact someone with questions about the application.

We already have the addresses of the donor and attorneys, so you don't have to repeat any of those here, unless they have changed.

Helpline
0300 456 0300

Who would you like to receive the LPA and any correspondence?
- [ ] The donor
- [ ] An attorney (write name below)
- [ ] Other (write name and address below)

Title   First names

Last name

Company (optional)

Address

Postcode

Help?

For help with this section, see the Guide, part B3.

How would the person above prefer to be contacted?
You can choose more than one.

- [ ] Post
- [ ] Phone
- [ ] Email
- [ ] Welsh (We will write to the person in Welsh)

Section 14
Application fee

There's a fee for registering a lasting power of attorney – the amount is shown on the cover sheet of this form or on form LPA120.

The fee changes from time to time. You can check you are paying the correct amount at www.gov.uk/power-of-attorney/how-much-it-costs or call 0300 456 0300. The Office of the Public Guardian can't register your LPA until you have paid the fee.

Helpline
0300 456 0300

How would you like to pay?

☐ **Card** For security, **don't** write your credit or debit card details here. We'll contact you to process the payment.

Your phone number
[ ][ ][ ][ ][ ][ ][ ][ ][ ][ ][ ][ ][ ][ ][ ]

☐ **Cheque** Enclose a cheque with your application.

Reduced application fee

If the donor has a low income, you may not have to pay the full amount. See the Guide, part B4 for details.

☐ **I want to apply to pay a reduced fee**

You'll need to fill in form LPA120 and include it with your application. You'll also **need to send proof** that the donor is eligible to pay a reduced fee.

Are you making a repeat application?

If you've already applied to register an LPA and the Office of the Public Guardian said that it was not possible to register it, you can apply again within 3 months and pay a reduced fee.

☐ **I'm making a repeat application**

Case number
[ ][ ][ ][ ][ ][ ][ ][ ][ ][ ][ ][ ]

Help?

For help with this section, see the Guide, part B4.

For OPG office use only

Payment reference
[   ]

Payment date
[ ][ ] [ ][ ] [ ][ ][ ][ ]
Day Month Year

Amount
[   ]

PART VII

LP1H Register your LPA (07.15)

Section 15
Signature

Helpline
0300 456 0300

 Do not sign this section until after sections 9, 10 and 11 have been signed.

The person applying to register the LPA (see section 12) must sign and date this section. This is either the donor or attorney(s) but not both together.

If the **attorneys** are applying to register the LPA and they were appointed to act **jointly** (in section 3), they must all sign.

By signing this section I confirm the following:

- I apply to register the LPA that accompanies this application
- I have informed 'people to notify' named in section 6 of the LPA (if any) of my intention to register the LPA
- I certify that the information in this form is correct to the best of my knowledge and belief

Help?

For help with this section, see the Guide, part B5.

Signature or mark	Signature or mark
Date signed	Date signed
Day / Month / Year	Day / Month / Year
Signature or mark	Signature or mark
Date signed	Date signed
Day / Month / Year	Day / Month / Year

If more than 4 attorneys need to sign, make copies of this page.

LP1H Register your LPA (07.15)

Form LP1F and LP1H – Lasting Power of Attorney

Check your lasting power of attorney

You don't have to use this checklist, but it'll help you make sure you've completed your LPA correctly.

Helpline
0300 456 0300

- [ ] The donor filled in sections 1 to 7.
- [ ] The donor signed both section 5 and section 9 in the presence of a witness. The donor also signed any copies of continuation sheets 1 and 2 that were used, on the same date as signing section 9.
- [ ] The certificate provider signed section 10.
- [ ] All the attorneys and replacement attorneys signed section 11, in the presence of witness(es).
- [ ] Sections 9, 10 and 11 were signed in order. Section 9 must have been signed first, then section 10, then section 11. They can be dated the same day or different days.
- [ ] The donor or an attorney completed sections 12 to 15. If the attorneys are applying and were appointed 'jointly' (section 3), they have all signed section 15 of this form.
- [ ] I've paid the application fee or applied for a reduced fee. If I've applied for a reduced fee, I've included the required evidence and completed form LPA120A.
- [ ] If there were any people to notify in section 6, I've notified them using form LP3.
- [ ] I've not left out any of the pages of the LPA, even the ones where I didn't write anything or there were no boxes to fill in.

Send to:

Office of the Public Guardian
PO Box 16185
Birmingham B2 2WH

PART VII

This page is not part of the form

LP1H Health and welfare (08.15)

PART VII   COURT OF PROTECTION PRACTICE 2016

Form LP2 – Register your lasting power of attorney

Office of the
Public Guardian

Form
LP2

Register your lasting power of attorney

Registering an LPA costs

£110

This fee is means-tested:
see the application
Guide part B

Use this form if the LPA you want to register
was made and signed before 1 July 2015.

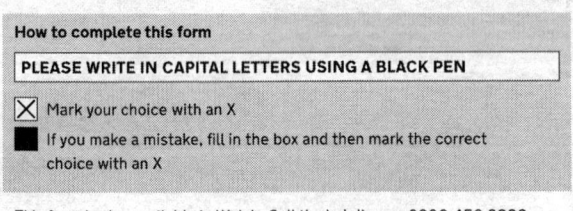

How to complete this form

| PLEASE WRITE IN CAPITAL LETTERS USING A BLACK PEN |

☒   Mark your choice with an X

■   If you make a mistake, fill in the box and then mark the correct
choice with an X

This form is also available in Welsh. Call the helpline on 0300 456 0300.

This page is not part of the form   **LP2** Register LPA (07.15)

Form LP2 – Register your lasting power of attorney

Before you start

Before the lasting power of attorney (LPA) can be used, it **must** be registered by the Office of the Public Guardian (OPG). Fill in this form to register the LPA. See the Registration guide, part B.

Helpline
0300 456 0300

People to notify

If there are any 'people to notify' (also called 'people to be told' or 'named people') listed in the LPA, you must notify them that you are registering the LPA now. See the Registration guide, part C.

Fill in and send each of them a copy of the form to notify people – form LP3.

When you sign section 5 of this form, you confirm that you've sent them the forms to the 'people to notify'.

Two lasting powers of attorney

If you are applying to register two LPAs, you must complete a copy of this form for each LPA.

Check your registration

When you've filled in this form you can use this checklist to help you make sure you have completed it correctly.

- [ ] I am either the donor or an attorney on the enclosed LPA form.
- [ ] I've completed sections 1 to 5 of this form.
- [ ] I used form LP3 to notify the 'people to notify' (also called 'people to be told' or 'named people'), if any were named on the LPA form.
- [ ] If the attorneys are applying to register the LPA and were appointed 'jointly' in the attached LPA, they have all signed section 5 of this form.
- [ ] (Optional) I've paid the application fee or applied for a reduced fee. If I've applied for a reduced fee, I've included form LPA120A and the required evidence.
- [ ] I've included all the pages of the LPA form in the envelope, even the ones where I didn't write anything or there were no boxes to fill in.

When completed send to:

Office of the Public Guardian
PO Box 16185
Birmingham B2 2WH

This page is not part of the form

LP2 Register LPA (07.15)

Register your lasting power of attorney

Section 1
About the lasting power of attorney

Donor

Title   First names

Last name

What type of lasting power of attorney (LPA) is being registered?
(tick one only)

If you are registering 2 LPAs, you must fill in one form for each LPA.

☐ Property and financial affairs

☐ Health and welfare

Help?

For help with this section, see the Guide, part B1.

LP2 Register LPA (07.15)

Form LP2 – Register your lasting power of attorney

Section 2
The applicant

Helpline
0300 456 0300

You can only apply to register if you are either the donor or attorney(s) for this lasting power of attorney (LPA). The donor and attorneys should not apply together.

Who is applying to register the LPA? (tick one only)

☐ **Donor** – the donor needs to sign section 5 of this form.

☐ **Attorney(s)** – If the attorneys were appointed jointly in the LPA then they **all** need to sign section 5 of this form. Otherwise, only one of the attorneys needs to sign.

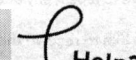 **Help?**

For help with this section, see the Guide, part B2.

Write the name and date of birth for each attorney that is applying to register the LPA. Don't include any attorneys who are not applying.

| Title | First names |
| Last name |
| Date of birth | Day | Month | Year |

| Title | First names |
| Last name |
| Date of birth | Day | Month | Year |

| Title | First names |
| Last name |
| Date of birth | Day | Month | Year |

| Title | First names |
| Last name |
| Date of birth | Day | Month | Year |

PART VII

LP2 Register LPA (07.15)

2

Section 3
Who do you want to receive the LPA?

We need to know who to send the LPA to once it is registered. We might also need to contact someone with questions about the application.

We already have the addresses of the donor and attorneys on the LPA form, so you don't have to repeat any of these here unless they have changed.

Helpline
0300 456 0300

Who would you like to receive the LPA and any correspondence?
- [ ] The donor
- [ ] An attorney (write name below)
- [ ] Other (write name and address below)

Title   First names

Last name

Company (optional)

Address

Postcode

Help?

For help with this section, see the Guide, part B3.

How would the person above prefer to be contacted?
You can choose more than one.
- [ ] Post
- [ ] Phone
- [ ] Email
- [ ] Welsh (We will write to the person in Welsh)

If you need to update anyone else's address, use section 6.

LP2 Register LPA (07.15)

Form LP2 – Register your lasting power of attorney

Section 4
Application fee

Helpline
0300 456 0300

There's a fee for registering a lasting power of attorney – the amount is shown on the cover sheet of this form and on form LPA120.

The fee changes from time to time. You can check you are paying the correct amount at www.gov.uk/power-of-attorney/how-much-it-costs or call 0300 456 0300. The Office of the Public Guardian can't register your LPA until you have paid the fee.

How would you like to pay?

☐ **Card** For security, don't write your credit or debit card details here. We'll contact you to process the payment.

Your phone number

☐ **Cheque** Enclose a cheque with your application.

Help?

For help with this section, see the Guide, part B4.

Reduced application fee

If the donor has a low income, you may not have to pay the full amount. See the Guide, Part B4 for details.

☐ **I want to apply to pay a reduced fee**

You'll need to fill in form LPA120 and include it with your application. You'll also need to send proof that the donor is eligible to pay a reduced fee.

PART VII

For OPG office use only

Payment reference

Payment date
Day Month Year

Amount

LP2 Register LPA (07.15)

Section 5
Signature

Helpline
0300 456 0300

The person applying to register the lasting power of attorney (LPA) (see section 2) must sign and date this section. This is either the donor or attorney(s) but not both together.

If the **attorneys** are applying to register the LPA and they were appointed to act **jointly** they must all sign.

By signing this section I confirm the following:

- I apply to register the LPA that accompanies this application
- I have informed 'people to notify' named in the LPA (if any) of my intention to register the LPA
- I certify that the information in this form is correct to the best of my knowledge and belief

Help?

For help with this section, see the Guide, part B5.

Signature or mark	Signature or mark
Date signed Day / Month / Year	Date signed Day / Month / Year
Signature or mark	Signature or mark
Date signed Day / Month / Year	Date signed Day / Month / Year

If more than 4 attorneys need to sign, make copies of this page.

LP2 Register LPA (07.15)

Form LP2 – Register your lasting power of attorney

Section 6
Addresses

Helpline
0300 456 0300

Use this page:
- if the LPA was made before 1 October 2009, to tell us **all** the attorneys' addresses
- if the LPA was made since 1 October 2009 and the donor or any attorney has changed address

Title First names

Last name

Address

Postcode

Email address

Title First names

Last name

Address

Postcode

Email address

Title First names

Last name

Address

Postcode

Email address

Title First names

Last name

Address

Postcode

Email address

LP2 Register LPA (07.15)

PART VII COURT OF PROTECTION PRACTICE 2016

Form LP3 – Form to notify people

Office of the
Public Guardian

Form
LP3

Form to notify people

You only need to fill in this form if there are 'people to notify' (also called 'people to be told' or 'named people') listed in the lasting power of attorney.

> **How to complete this form**
>
> **PLEASE WRITE IN CAPITAL LETTERS USING A BLACK PEN**
>
> Mark your choice with an X
>
> ■ If you make a mistake, fill in the box and then mark the correct choice with an X

This page is not part of the form   LP3 People to notify (07.15)

Before you start

You only need to fill in this form if there are 'people to notify' (also called 'people to be told' or 'named people') listed in the lasting power of attorney (LPA). See the Guide, part C.

**Helpline
0300 456 0300**

A 'person to notify' is someone a person who makes an LPA (the 'donor') chooses to inform about the registration of their LPA. They don't have to choose anyone to notify, so if that section of the LPA is blank, you don't need to fill in this form.

When you apply to register the LPA you must tell the people to notify that the LPA will be registered.

You must send a copy of this form to each of the people to notify, before you send the LPA to be registered. You can send them this form or hand it to them in person.

You can save time by filling in pages 2 and 3 and making a photocopy to send to each person.

The donor's relatives are not entitled to be notified unless they have been named in the LPA.

Detach this cover sheet before sending the form to them.

Notice of intention to register a lasting power of attorney

Person to notify

Title   First names

Last name

Address

Postcode

Date

Day   Month   Year

You have received this notice because the person named on page 2 has made a lasting power of attorney.

A lasting power of attorney (LPA) is a legal document that lets someone (known as a 'donor') appoint people (known as 'attorneys') to make decisions on their behalf. It can apply to financial decisions or health and care decisions. An LPA can be used if the donor is unable to make their own decisions.

In other words, the person on page 2 is appointing the people on page 3 to make decisions on their behalf.

When they made the LPA, the donor decided you should be told about it before it's registered. This is so you can raise any concerns you may have. If you do have concerns, you can only object to the registration of the LPA for the reasons listed on page 4 of this form.

If you want to object, you must do so within 3 weeks of the date of this notice.

If you don't want to object you don't have to do anything.

LP3 People to notify (07.15)

Form LP3 – Form to notify people

Details of the lasting power of attorney

Helpline
0300 456 0300

About the donor – the person who made the LPA

Title

First names

Last name

Address

Postcode

About the lasting power of attorney

Who is applying to register the LPA?
- [ ] Donor
- [ ] Attorney(s)

What type of LPA is being registered?
- [ ] Property and financial affairs
- [ ] Health and welfare

When did the donor sign the LPA?

Day Month Year

PART VII

LP3 People to notify (07.15)

About the attorneys

Helpline
0300 456 0300

How are the attorneys appointed?

☐ There's only 1 attorney
☐ Jointly and severally
☐ Jointly
☐ Jointly for some decisions, jointly and severally for other decisions

Title	First names

Last name

Address

Postcode

Title	First names

Last name

Address

Postcode

Title	First names

Last name

Address

Postcode

Title	First names

Last name

Address

Postcode

If there are more than 4 attorneys, please make a copy of this page.
You don't need to list replacement attorneys appointed in the LPA (if any).

LP3 People to notify (07.15)

How to object

If you wish to object, you must do so within 3 weeks of being given this notice.

Helpline
0300 456 0300

You can only object to an LPA for one of the reasons below.

Factual objections:

- the donor or an attorney has died
- the donor and an attorney were married or had a civil partnership but have divorced or ended the civil partnership (unless the LPA says the attorney can still act if that happens)
- an attorney doesn't have the mental capacity to be an attorney (they must be able to understand and make decisions for themselves)
- an attorney has chosen to stop acting (known as 'disclaiming their appointment')
- the donor or an attorney is bankrupt, interim bankrupt or subject to a debt relief order (LPA for financial decisions only)
- the attorney is a trust corporation and is wound up or dissolved (LPA for financial decisions only)

To make a factual objection, complete form LPA007 and send it to the Office of the Public Guardian. Get the form from www.gov.uk/power-of-attorney/object-registration or by calling 0300 456 0300.

Prescribed objections:

- the LPA isn't legally valid – for example, you don't believe the donor had mental capacity to make an LPA
- the donor cancelled their LPA when they had mental capacity to do so
- there was fraud or the donor was pressured to make the LPA
- an attorney is acting above their authority or against the donor's best interests (or you know that they intend to do this)

To make a prescribed objection:

- complete form COP7 and send it to the Court of Protection. Get the form from www.gov.uk/object-registration or by calling 0300 456 4000 **AND**
- complete form LPA008 and send it to the Office of the Public Guardian. Get the form from www.gov.uk/object-registration or by calling 0300 456 0300

If you are objecting to a specific attorney, it may not prevent registration if other attorneys or a replacement attorney have been appointed.

You can find out more about lasting powers of attorney at www.gov.uk/power-of-attorney or by calling 0300 456 0300.

LP3 People to notify (07.15)

PART VII

Form LPA003A – Notice to attorney: application to register a lasting power of attorney

Office of the
Public Guardian

Office of the Public Guardian
PO Box 16185
Birmingham B2 2WH

Tel: 0300 456 0300
Fax: 0870 739 5780

customerservices@publicguardian.gsi.gov.uk
www.gov.uk/opg

Notice to attorney: application to register a lasting power of attorney (LPA003A)

Date:

Case number:

To:

You have received this notice because:

- _____ (the 'donor') made a lasting power of attorney (LPA) for _____

- they named you as attorney in that LPA
- the person(s) named below has applied to register the LPA

Person(s) who applied to register the LPA
The following person(s) applied to register the LPA:

Your right to object
You can object to the proposed registration of the LPA.

You have 3 weeks from _____ to object. Page 2 of this notice tells you how to object.

LPA003A (04.15)

How to object
If you wish to object, you must do so within 3 weeks of being given this notice.
You can only object to an LPA for one of the reasons below.

Factual objections:
- the donor or an attorney has died
- the donor and an attorney were married or had a civil partnership but have divorced or ended the civil partnership (unless the LPA says the attorney can still act if that happens)
- an attorney doesn't have the mental capacity to be an attorney (they must be able to understand and make decisions for themselves)
- an attorney has chosen to stop acting (known as 'disclaiming their appointment')
- the donor or an attorney is bankrupt, interim bankrupt or subject to a debt relief order (financial decisions LPA)
- the attorney is a trust corporation and is wound up or dissolved (financial decisions LPA)

To make a factual objection, complete form LPA007 and send it to the Office of the Public Guardian. Get the form from www.gov.uk/power-of-attorney/object-registration or by calling 0300 456 0300.

Prescribed objections:
- the LPA isn't legally valid – for example, you don't believe the donor had mental capacity to make an LPA
- the donor cancelled their LPA when they had mental capacity to do so
- there was fraud or the donor was pressured to make the LPA
- an attorney is acting above their authority or against the donor's best interests (or you know that they intend to do this)

To make a prescribed objection:
- complete form COP7 and send it to the Court of Protection. Get the form from www.gov.uk/object-registration or by calling 0300 456 4000 **AND**
- complete form LPA008 and send it to the Office of the Public Guardian. Get the form from www.gov.uk/object-registration or by calling 0300 456 0300

If you are objecting to a specific attorney, it may not prevent registration if other attorneys or a replacement attorney have been appointed.

You can find out more about lasting powers of attorney at www.gov.uk/power-of-attorney or by calling 0300 456 0300.

LPA003A (04.15)

Form LPA003B – Notice to donor: application to register a lasting power of attorney

Office of the
Public Guardian

Office of the Public Guardian
PO Box 16185
Birmingham B2 2WH

Tel: 0300 456 0300
Fax: 0870 739 5780

customerservices@publicguardian.gsi.gov.uk
www.gov.uk/opg

Notice to donor: application to register a lasting power of attorney (LPA003B)

Date:

Case number:

To:

You have received this notice because:

- You made a lasting power of attorney (LPA) for
- the person(s) named below has applied to register the LPA

Person(s) who applied to register the LPA
The following attorney(s) applied to register the LPA:

Your right to object
You can object to the proposed registration of the LPA.

You have 3 weeks from   to object.

How to object
Complete form LPA006 and send it to the Office of the Public Guardian – get the form from www.gov.uk/object-registration or by calling 0300 456 0300.

LPA003B (04.15)

Form LPA005 – Disclaimer by a proposed or acting attorney under a Lasting Power of Attorney

Office of the
Public Guardian

Form
LPA005

Disclaimer by a proposed or acting attorney under a lasting power of attorney

1. Donor details (the person who made the lasting power of attorney)

Title   First names

Last name

Address

Postcode

To the donor

You have received this notice because:
- you made a lasting power of attorney (LPA)
- you chose the person named on page 2 (the 'disclaiming attorney') as an attorney for that LPA
- that person now wishes to give up their role as an attorney (this is called 'disclaiming their appointment').

2. About the lasting power of attorney (LPA)

What type of LPA is it?

☐ Property and financial affairs

☐ Health and welfare

When did the donor sign the LPA?
(To find out, look at Part A of the LPA if it was made before 1 July 2015 or section 9 if it was made on or after that date)

Date

Day	Month	Year

Was the LPA registered by the Office of the Public Guardian?
(see page 1 of the LPA – the section marked 'OPG office use only')

☐ Yes

☐ No

When was the LPA registered?

Date

Day	Month	Year

What is the 'OPG reference number'? (see page 1 of the LPA)

3. Disclaiming attorney details (the person sending this notice)

Title   First names

Last name

Address

Postcode

Phone number

LPA005 (07.15)

Form LPA005 – Disclaimer by a proposed or acting attorney under a Lasting Power of Attorney

4. Signature and date

I disclaim my appointment as attorney under the lasting power of attorney made by the donor named on this form. I will send copies of this form to any other attorneys named on the lasting power of attorney and to the Office of the Public Guardian:

Signature or mark

Date signed

Day Month Year

Notes for the person completing this form

When you have completed and signed this form:
- send the original form to the donor
- send a copy of this form to any other attorneys that were named in the LPA
- if you are the only attorney, send a copy of the form to any replacement attorneys named in the LPA

If the Office of the Public Guardian (OPG) has registered the LPA, you should also:
- send a copy of this form to OPG
- send any copies of the LPA that you have to OPG

Address: Office of the Public Guardian, PO BOX 16185, Birmingham, B2 2WH

If you have any queries call the OPG contact centre on 0300 456 0300.

LPA005 (07.15)

Form LPA006 – Objection by the donor to the registration of a lasting power of attorney

LPA 006 09.13

Objection by the donor to the registration of a lasting power of attorney

If you **do not want** your LPA to be registered then you need to complete and sign this form and return it to the Office of the Public Guardian. It would help if you tell us why you do not want your LPA registered by using the space below your signature but you do not have to give a reason.

Your full name

Date of birth D D M M Y Y Y Y

Case no. (if known)

Please sign to confirm your objection

Signed

Dated D D M M Y Y Y Y

Note: The registration of your LPA will be suspended by the Office of the Public Guardian upon receipt of this form. This means your attorney(s) will not be able to use the LPA, unless the attorney applies to the Court of Protection and the Court directs registration.

The reason(s) for your objection

Send your completed form to:
Office of the Public Guardian, PO Box 16185, Birmingham, B2 2WH

© Crown copyright 2013

Form LPA007 – Objection to the Office of the Public Guardian of a proposed registration of a Lasting Power of Attorney on factual grounds

LPA 007 | 09.13

Objection to the Office of the Public Guardian of a proposed registration of a Lasting Power of Attorney on factual grounds

This form can only be used by the attorneys or people to be told

Donor's full name

Date of birth (if known) [D D M M Y Y Y Y]

Case no. (if known)

On what grounds are you objecting to the registration?

You must place an '**X**' in **at least one box** and provide evidence or proof of each ground to accompany this notice.

- [ ] The donor is bankrupt or interim bankrupt (Property and Financial Affairs LPA only)
- [ ] The attorney is bankrupt or interim bankrupt (Property and Financial Affairs LPA only)
- [ ] The attorney is a trust corporation that has been wound up or dissolved
- [ ] The donor is dead
- [ ] The attorney is dead
- [ ] There has been dissolution or annulment of a marriage or civil partnership between the donor and attorney (and the LPA does not provide for this event)
- [ ] The attorney lacks capacity to act
- [ ] The attorney has disclaimed appointment

Please list opposite the evidence on which your objection is based and attach a copy to this form.

Signed

- [ ] attorney
- [ ] person to be told

Full name

Dated [D D M M Y Y Y Y]

Send your completed form and evidence to:
Office of the Public Guardian, PO Box 16185, Birmingham, B2 2WH

© Crown copyright 2013

PART VII

PART VII   COURT OF PROTECTION PRACTICE 2016

Form LPA008 – Notice to the Office of the Public Guardian of an application to object to registration of a lasting power of attorney made to the Court of Protection

LPA 008 09.13

Notice to the Office of the Public Guardian of an application to object to registration of a lasting power of attorney made to the Court of Protection

This notice is confirmation that I have applied to the Court of Protection to object to the registration of the lasting power of attorney, detailed below.

Note: You should notify the Office of the Public Guardian of an objection to the Court of Protection or the LPA may be registered.

Case no.
(if known)

Details of the donor

Your name

Address

Telephone no.

Postcode

Details of the person making the objection

Your name

Address

Telephone no.

Postcode

continued over

© Crown copyright 2013

2114

Form LPA008 – Notice to the Office of the Public Guardian of an application to object to registration of a lasting power of attorney made to the Court of Protection

Reasons for making the objection

Tell us here about the prescribed grounds on which you have objected to the Court of Protection about the registration of the LPA.

When did you send your objection to the Court of Protection? D D M M Y Y Y Y

Signature and date

Signed

Dated D D M M Y Y Y Y

Send your completed form to:
Office of the Public Guardian, PO Box 16185, Birmingham, B2 2WH

PART VII

2115

LP12 – Make and register your lasting power of attorney: a guide

Guide LP12 can be downloaded at *www.gov.uk/government/publications/make-a-lasting-power-of-attorney*

LPA120 – LPA and EPA fees plus Application for exemption or remission of LPA/EPA application fees

Office of the Public Guardian

LPA120

LPA and EPA fees
with effect from 1 October 2013

	Full fee	Exemption or remission available
Lasting power of attorney (LPA) application fee	£110	If the donor qualifies, exemption or remission may be available (see details below)
Enduring power of attorney (EPA) application fee	£110	
Repeat LPA application fee	£55	
Office copy/certified copy of an LPA	£35	No exemption or remission available
Office copy/certified copy of an EPA	£25	

Exemption – when a donor doesn't have to pay because they get certain means-tested benefits

Remission – a 50% fee reduction based on a donor's financial circumstances or a reduction based on the donor receiving Universal Credit

Office copy/certified copy – official copies that are only supplied in exceptional cases

- You must pay an application fee when you apply to register a power of attorney. Fees are non-refundable, even if the power of attorney isn't registered.
- Application fees are paid by or on behalf of the donor – the person making the power of attorney. If they make both types of LPA they need to pay 2 fees.
- Office copy fees are paid by the person requesting the document.

Make a payment

Online payment – if you make your LPA using the digital LPA tool, you can make a secure online payment by credit or debit card.

On the phone by credit or debit card – if you want to pay this way, please say so in your application form (LPA002) or covering letter and we will contact you.

Cheque payment – please make your cheque payable to 'Office of the Public Guardian' and write the donor's full name on the back.

Make your LPA online
If you haven't already made your LPA you could **use the digital LPA tool**. It will:
- help you make your LPA
- guide you through to registration
- let you pay online or by cheque

www.gov.uk/lasting-power-of-attorney

Exemption and remission of application fees

A donor may be entitled to an exemption or remission of application fees based on their financial circumstances. It's only the donor whose benefits and income matter.

To apply you must:

- fill in form LPA120A (which follows this information sheet) and sign the declaration
- gather supporting evidence – **without evidence we can't consider a claim** so make sure you read the sections on page 2 about acceptable supporting evidence
- send us form LPA120A and your evidence along with your LPA or EPA forms when you apply to register.

If you're registering 2 powers of attorney at the same time you only need to fill in 1 form LPA120A.

PART VII

Exemption

If the donor receives any of the following **means-tested benefits** when an application to register is made, they can apply for an exemption, or their attorney or solicitor can do so on their behalf:

- Income Support
- Income-based Employment and Support Allowance
- Income-based Jobseeker's Allowance
- **Guarantee Credit element** of State Pension Credit
- Housing Benefit
- Council Tax Reduction/Support – also known by other names (not the 25% single person discount or the Class U exemption)
- Local Housing Allowance
- A combination of Working Tax Credit **and at least one of**:
  - Child Tax Credit
  - Disability Element of Working Tax Credit
  - Severe Disability Element of Working Tax Credit

Not included: Disability Living Allowance, Invalidity Benefit, Personal Independence Payment

Exception

If the donor has been awarded **personal injury damages of more than £16,000** which were ignored when they were assessed for one of the above benefits, they won't qualify for exemption.

Supporting evidence for exemption

You need to **send copies of letters from a benefit provider** showing the donor received at least 1 of the listed benefits at the time you applied to register. Letters must confirm that the benefit was being paid to the donor and include their printed details (title, full name, address and postcode).

Contact OPG

Office of the Public Guardian
PO Box 16185
Birmingham B2 2WH

DX: 744240 Birmingham 79

Telephone: 0300 456 0300
(+44 300 456 0300 outside the UK)
Textphone: 0115 934 2778
Fax: 0870 739 5780
Phone line open - Monday to Friday 9am to 5pm
(Wednesday 10am to 5pm)

Email: customerservices@publicguardian.gsi.gov.uk
Online: www.gov.uk/power-of-attorney

Remission based on income

If the donor's gross annual income is less than £12,000, they may be eligible for a 50% reduction of the fee. Gross annual income is income **before** tax. It may come from employment, non-means-tested benefits (such as Attendance Allowance, Disability Living Allowance or Personal Independence Payment), pensions, Pensions Savings Credit, interest from savings and investments, or the rent of property.

Supporting evidence for remission

You need to **send proof of the donor's gross annual income**. Evidence must relate to the time you sent the application to register. We can't accept bank statements. Evidence can be:

Paid employment – A P60 or 3 months' consecutive wage slips from current employment.

Non-means-tested benefits and pensions – an official letter or notice from the payer.

Interest from capital, stocks, shares or bonds – statements or vouchers showing gross income.

Self-employment – most recent self-assessment tax return and HMRC tax calculation, or audited account certified by a qualified accountant.

If the donor receives no income, they must send a signed statement explaining how they support themselves. If they don't have mental capacity their attorney or solicitor can supply and sign this statement.

Remission based on Universal Credit

A donor may qualify for remission if they receive Universal Credit.

Supporting evidence of Universal Credit

You need to send copies of letters showing the donor received Universal Credit at the time you applied to register. Letters must confirm that the benefit was being paid to the donor and include their printed details (title, full name, address and postcode).

Review

If an application for exemption or remission is unsuccessful, you can appeal within 4 weeks of the decision by writing to the Head of Corporate Services. If the original decision is upheld, it will be referred to the Public Guardian for confirmation.

Hardship

If the donor doesn't qualify for remission or exemption, but paying fees would cause hardship – for example, paying would mean they couldn't meet normal living costs – you can apply to have fees waived. To claim write to OPG explaining why payment would cause hardship, enclosing bank statements and other documents showing all savings, income and outgoings.

LPA120 – LPA and EPA fees plus Application for exemption or remission of LPA/EPA application fees

Application for exemption or remission of LPA/EPA application fees

LPA120A

Section 1 – About the case

Donor's full name

Donor's address

Case number/ref. (if known)
You will find this on our letters

Which fee does this application relate to?
- [ ] LPA application fee
- [ ] EPA application fee
- [ ] Repeat LPA application fee

Which powers of attorney have you enclosed for registration?
- [ ] LPA for health and welfare
- [ ] LPA for property and financial affairs
- [ ] EPA

Section 2 – About you

What is your relationship to the case?
- [ ] Donor
- [ ] Attorney
- [ ] Other (Please specify)

Title
- [ ] Mr
- [ ] Ms
- [ ] Miss
- [ ] Mrs
- [ ] Other

First name

Last name

Address (including postcode)

Telephone number — Daytime / Mobile

Email address

If you have already paid the fee, who do you want the money paid to if your application for exemption/remission is successful?

continued overleaf →

LPA120A Application for exemption or remission of LPA/EPA application fees (10.13)   © Crown copyright 2013

Section 3 – Fee exemption based on permitted benefits

3a Does the donor receive any of the benefits listed?

- Income Support
- Income-based Employment and Support Allowance
- Income-based Jobseeker's Allowance
- **Guarantee Credit element** of State Pension Credit
- Housing Benefit
- Council Tax Reduction/Support – also known by other names (not the 25% single person discount or the Class U exemption)
- Local Housing Allowance
- A combination of Working Tax Credit and **at least one of**:
  – Child Tax Credit
  – Disability Element of Working Tax Credit
  – Severe Disability Element of Working Tax Credit

Not included: Disability Living Allowance, Invalidity Benefit, Personal Independence Payment

☐ Yes → **Go to question 3b**

☐ No → **Go to Section 4**

3b Has the donor been awarded personal injury damages of more than £16,000 which were ignored when the donor was assessed for the benefit listed at question 3a?

☐ Yes → **Go to Section 4**

☐ No. The donor is eligible for exemption.

Section 4 – Fee remission based on gross annual income or Universal Credit

Is the donor's gross annual income less than £12,000?

☐ Yes, I want to apply for a remission of 50% of the fee based on the donor's gross annual income. → **Evidence must be enclosed.**

☐ No

Does the donor receive Universal Credit?

☐ Yes, I want to apply for a remission based on the donor receiving Universal Credit. → **Evidence must be enclosed.**

☐ No

Section 5 – Declaration

I declare that the information I have given is true to the best of my knowledge, and I enclose the required evidence to support the claim for a fee exemption or remission.

I understand that this application will be refused if I fail to provide evidence.

Signature

Date

Send your completed application to:
Office of the Public Guardian, PO Box 16185, Birmingham B2 2WH
or
DX 744240 Birmingham 79

Form LPC – Continuation sheets

Office of the
Public Guardian

Form
LPC

Continuation sheets

Only use these continuation sheets if you are told to in the lasting power of attorney (LPA) form. Many people make an LPA without needing to use a continuation sheet.

If you make two LPAs and you need to use continuation sheets for both of them, use separate sheets for each LPA.

PART VII — COURT OF PROTECTION PRACTICE 2016

Continuation sheets

Only use these continuation sheets if you are told to in the lasting power of attorney (LPA) form. Many people make an LPA without needing to use a continuation sheet.

If you make two LPAs and you need to use continuation sheets for both of them, use separate sheets for each LPA.

Continuation sheet 1 – Additional people

- Use this sheet if you need space to write more names for sections 2, 4 or 6 of the LPA form.
- Sign and date the sheet on the same day as you sign the LPA form.

Continuation sheet 2 – Additional information

- Use this sheet if you need more space to write information for sections 3, 4 or 7 of the LPA form.
- If you have to write extra information for more than one of those sections, use a fresh copy of the sheet for each one.
- Sign and date the sheet on the same day as you sign the LPA form.

Continuation sheet 3 – If the donor cannot sign or make a mark

- Use this sheet if you can't sign or make a mark yourself.
- You will need someone else to sign on your behalf and two people must witness their signature.
- If you're making an LPA for health and care decisions, the person signing for you must also sign section 5 of the LPA on the same day as they sign this sheet.

Continuation sheet 4 – Trust corporation appointed as an attorney

- Use this sheet if you appointed a trust corporation as an attorney or replacement attorney.
- Someone from the trust corporation must sign this sheet instead of signing section 11 of the LPA form.
- They must sign this sheet after your 'certificate provider' has signed section 10 of the LPA form.

This page is not part of the form

Continuation sheet 1
Additional people

Helpline
0300 456 0300

Use this page if told to in section 2, 4 or 6 of the lasting power of attorney form.

If you use this page, you must sign it.

Help?

For help with this section, see the Guide, parts A2, A4 and A6.

☐ **Attorney** LPA section 2
☐ **Replacement attorney** LPA section 4
☐ **Person to notify** LPA section 6

Title   First names

Last name

Date of birth (not required for 'person to notify')
Day   Month   Year

Address

Postcode

Email address (optional)

☐ **Attorney** LPA section 2
☐ **Replacement attorney** LPA section 4
☐ **Person to notify** LPA section 6

Title   First names

Last name

Date of birth (not required for 'person to notify')
Day   Month   Year

Address

Postcode

Email address (optional)

Donor
You must sign here before you sign section 9 of the LPA, or on the same day.

Full name

Signature or mark

Date signed or marked
Day   Month   Year

Only valid with the official stamp here.

LPC Continuation sheet 1 (07.15)

PART VII

Continuation sheet 1
Additional people

Use this page if told to in section 2, 4 or 6 of the lasting power of attorney form.

If you use this page, you must sign it.

Helpline
0300 456 0300

Help? For help with this section, see the Guide, parts A2, A4 and A6.

☐ **Attorney** LPA section 2
☐ **Replacement attorney** LPA section 4
☐ **Person to notify** LPA section 6

Title First names

Last name

Date of birth (not required for 'person to notify')
Day Month Year

Address

Postcode

Email address (optional)

☐ **Attorney** LPA section 2
☐ **Replacement attorney** LPA section 4
☐ **Person to notify** LPA section 6

Title First names

Last name

Date of birth (not required for 'person to notify')
Day Month Year

Address

Postcode

Email address (optional)

Donor

You must sign here before you sign section 9 of the LPA, or on the same day.

Full name

Signature or mark

Date signed or marked
Day Month Year

Only valid with the official stamp here.

Continuation sheet 1 (07.15)

Form LPC – Continuation sheets

Continuation sheet 2
Additional information

Use this page if told to in section 3, 4 or 7 of the lasting power of attorney form.

If you use this page, you must sign it.

Helpline
0300 456 0300

What additional information are you providing?

Use a fresh copy of this page for each type of additional information

☐ **Decisions attorneys should make jointly** LPA section 3
☐ **How replacement attorneys step in and act** LPA section 4
☐ **Preferences** LPA section 7
☐ **Instructions** LPA section 7

Help?

For help with this section, see the Guide, parts A3, A4 and A7.

Donor

You must sign here before you sign section 9 of the LPA, or on the same day.

Full name

Signature or mark

Date signed or marked

Day Month Year

Only valid with the official stamp here.

LPC Continuation sheet 2 (07.15)

PART VII

Continuation sheet 2
Additional information

Helpline
0300 456 0300

Use this page if told to in section 3, 4 or 7 of the lasting power of attorney form.

If you use this page, you must sign it.

What additional information are you providing?

Use a fresh copy of this page for each type of additional information

- [ ] Decisions attorneys should make jointly LPA section 3
- [ ] How replacement attorneys step in and act LPA section 4
- [ ] Preferences LPA section 7
- [ ] Instructions LPA section 7

Help?

For help with this section, see the Guide, parts A3, A4 and A7.

Donor

You must sign here before you sign section 9 of the LPA, or on the same day.

Full name

Signature or mark

Date signed or marked

Day Month Year

Only valid with the official stamp here.

Continuation sheet 2 (07.15)

Form LPC – Continuation sheets

Continuation sheet 3
If the donor cannot sign or mark

Helpline
0300 456 0300

Only fill in this page if the donor cannot sign or make a mark in section 9 of the lasting power of attorney form

Donor
Full name

Signatory
You must:
- sign in the donor's presence and in the presence of 2 witnesses
- sign in your own name
- not also be a witness to this LPA
- sign any copies of Continuation Sheet 1 and 2 used in this LPA at the same time

If the LPA is for health and care decisions:
- you must also sign and date either Option A or Option B of Section 5, as directed by the donor
- your signature in Section 5 must be witnessed

Signed as a deed and delivered in the presence of and at the direction of the person giving this lasting power of attorney and in the presence of two witnesses.

Signature or mark

Full name of person signing

Date signed or marked

Day Month Year

Witnesses
Witnesses must **not** be attorneys or replacement attorneys appointed under this LPA and must be aged 18 or over.

Signature or mark of first witness

Full name of first witness

Address of first witness

Postcode

Signature or mark of second witness

Full name of second witness

Address of second witness

Postcode

Help? For help with this section, see the Guide, part A9.

Only valid with the official stamp here.

LPC Continuation sheet 3 (07.15)

PART VII

Continuation sheet 4
Trust corporation appointed as an attorney

Helpline
0300 456 0300

Only use this page if the donor has appointed a trust corporation as an attorney or replacement attorney

By execution of this deed the trust corporation understands and confirms all of the following:

- It has read this lasting power of attorney (LPA), including section 8 'Your legal rights and responsibilities'.
- It has a duty to act based on the principles of the Mental Capacity Act 2005 and to have regard to the Mental Capacity Act Code of Practice.
- It can make decisions and act only when this LPA has been registered.
- It must make decisions and act in the best interests of the person giving this LPA.
- It is not going through winding-up proceedings.
- It can spend money to make gifts but only to charities or on customary occasions such as birthdays, and for reasonable amounts, with regard to size of the donor's estate.
- It has a duty to keep accounts and financial records and produce them to the Office of the Public Guardian or to the Court of Protection on request.
- It can make decisions and act regarding the donor's property and financial affairs only at the time indicated in section 5 of this LPA.

Further statement by a trust corporation acting as a replacement attorney: It has the authority to act under this LPA only after an original attorney's appointment is terminated. It must notify the Public Guardian if that happens.

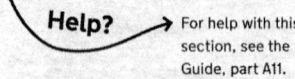

Help? For help with this section, see the Guide, part A11.

Company registration number

I/We are authorised to sign on behalf of the trust corporation acting as attorney whose details are given in this continuation sheet to this lasting power of attorney.

Signed as a deed and delivered by:

Signature of first authorised person

Full name of first authorised person

Date signed or marked

Day Month Year

Signature of second authorised person (if required)

Full name of second authorised person (if required)

Date signed or marked (if required)

Day Month Year

Only valid with the official stamp here.

LPC Continuation sheet 4 (07.15)

ENDURING POWER OF ATTORNEY FORMS

Form EP1 PG – Notice of intention to apply for registration of an Enduring Power of Attorney

Form EP1PG

Mental Capacity Act 2005
Enduring Power of Attorney

Notice of intention to apply for registration of an Enduring Power of Attorney

To..

Of..

TAKE NOTICE THAT

> *This form may be adapted for use by three or more attorneys*

I ....

of ....

> *Give the name and address of the donor*

and I ....

of ....

The attorney(s) of ....

....

of ....

....

intend to apply to the Public Guardian for registration of the enduring power of attorney appointing me (us) attorney(s) and made by the donor on the ....

1. You have the right to object to the proposed registration on one or more of the grounds set out below. You must notify the Office of the Public Guardian of your objection within five weeks from the day this notice was given to you. You may make an application to the Court of Protection under rule 68 of the Court of Protection Rules 2007 for a decision on the matter. No fee is payable for such an application. If you do not make such an application, the Public Guardian may ask for the court's directions about registration.

> *The grounds upon which you can object are limited and are shown at 2 overleaf*

PART VII

Note: The instrument means the document used to make the enduring power of attorney made by the donor, which it is sought to register	2. The grounds on which you may object to the proposed registration are: • That the power purported to be created by the instrument is not valid as an enduring power of attorney • That the power created by the instrument no longer subsists • That the application is premature because the donor is not yet becoming mentally incapable • That fraud or undue pressure was used to induce the donor to make the power • That the attorney is unsuitable to be the donor's attorney (having regard to all the circumstances and in particular the attorney's relationship to or connection with the donor).
The attorney(s) does not have to be a relative. Relatives are not entitled to know of the existence of the enduring power of attorney prior to being given this notice	
Our staff will be able to assist with any questions you have regarding the objection(s). However, they cannot provide advice about your particular objection.	3. If you object, you must notify the Office of the Public Guardian and state which of the grounds you are relying on within five weeks from the day this notice was given to you. You can obtain the necessary court forms to object by. • Calling the court on 0300 456 4600 • Downloading the forms from www.justice.gov.uk/global/forms/hmcts/index.htm
Note: Part 4 is addressed only to the donor	4. You are informed that while the enduring power of attorney remains registered, you will not be able to revoke it until the Court of Protection confirms the revocation.
Note: This notice should be signed by every one of the attorneys who are applying to register the enduring power of attorney	Signed: .... Dated: .... Signed: .... Dated: ....
Note: The attorney(s) must keep a record of the date on which notice was given to the donor and to relatives. This information will be required from the attorney(s) when an application to register the EPA is made	**Please write to:** **Office of the Public Guardian** **PO Box 16185** **Birmingham** **B2 2WH** www.gov.uk/power-of-attorney

Form EP2 PG – Application to register an Enduring Power of Attorney

Office of the Public Guardian
Mental Capacity Act 2005
Form EP2PG
Application for Registration of an Enduring Power of Attorney

IMPORTANT: Please complete the form in BLOCK CAPITALS using a black ball-point pen. Place a clear cross 'X' mark inside square option boxes ☒ - do not circle the option.

Part One - The Donor

Please state the full name and present address of the donor. State the donor's first name in 'Forename 1' and the donor's other forenames in full in 'Other Forenames'. Company Name should be completed with the name of the nursing/care home or hospital where applicable.

Mr Mrs Ms Miss Other
☐   ☐   ☐   ☐   ☐
Place a cross against one option ☒   If Other, please specify here: ☐☐☐☐☐☐☐☐☐☐☐☐☐☐☐

Last Name:
Forename 1:
Other Forenames:
Company Name:
Address 1:
Address 2:
Address 3:
Town/City:
County:
Postcode:
Donor Date of Birth: D D M M Y Y Y Y   *If the exact date is unknown please state the year of birth*

Please do not write below this line - For Office Use Only

Produced in association with the Office of the Public Guardian   © Crown Copyright 2007   Provider details

Page 1 of 7

PART VII

Part Two - Attorney One

Please state the full name and present address of the attorney. Professionals e.g. Solicitors or Accountants, should complete the Company Name field.

Mr ☐ Mrs ☐ Ms ☐ Miss ☐ Other ☐
Place a cross against one option ☒

If Other, please specify here: [ ]

Last Name: [ ]

Forename 1: [ ]

Other Forenames: [ ]

Company Name: [ ]

Address 1: [ ]

Address 2: [ ]

Address 3: [ ]

Town/City: [ ]

County: [ ]

Postcode: [ ]   DX No. (solicitors only): [ ]

DX Exchange (solicitors only): [ ]

Attorney Date of Birth: [D D M M Y Y Y Y]   Daytime Tel No.: [ ] (STD Code): [ ]

Email Address: [ ]

Occupation: [ ]

Relationship to donor:

Civil Partner / Spouse ☐   Child ☐   Other Relation ☐   No Relation ☐   Solicitor ☐   Other Professional ☐

If 'Other Relation' or 'Other Professional', specify relationship: [ ]

Place a cross against one option ☒

Part B of the Enduring Power of Attorney states whether the attorney is to act jointly, jointly and severally, or alone.

Appointment (*Place a cross against one option* ☒):

Jointly ☐

Jointly and Severally ☐

Alone ☐

Form EP2 PG – Application to register an Enduring Power of Attorney

Part Three - Attorney Two

Please state the full name and present address of the attorney. Professionals e.g. Solicitors or Accountants, should complete the Company Name field.

Mr ☐ Mrs ☐ Ms ☐ Miss ☐ Other ☐
Place a cross against one option ☒

If Other, please specify here:

Last Name:

Forename 1:

Other Forenames:

Company Name:

Address 1:

Address 2:

Address 3:

Town/City:

County:

Postcode: DX No. (solicitors only):

DX Exchange (solicitors only):

Attorney Date of Birth: D D M M Y Y Y Y

Daytime Tel No.:   (STD Code):

Email Address:

Occupation:

Relationship to donor:

Civil Partner / Spouse ☐   Child ☐   Other Relation ☐   No Relation ☐   Other Solicitor ☐   Professional ☐

If 'Other Relation' or 'Other Professional', specify relationship:

Place a cross against one option ☒

Part Four - Attorney Three

Please state the full name and present address of the attorney. Professionals e.g. Solicitors or Accountants, should complete the Company Name field.

Mr ☐ Mrs ☐ Ms ☐ Miss ☐ Other ☐
Place a cross against one option ☒

If Other, please specify here:

Last Name:

Forename 1:

Part Four Continued Overleaf

PART VII   COURT OF PROTECTION PRACTICE 2016

Part Four - Attorney Three cont'd

Other Forenames:

Company Name:

Address 1:

Address 2:

Address 3:

Town/City:

County:

Postcode:

DX No. (solicitors only):

DX Exchange (solicitors only):

Attorney Date of Birth: D D M M Y Y Y Y

Daytime Tel No.: (STD Code)

Email Address:

Occupation:

Relationship to donor:

☐ Civil Partner / Spouse   ☐ Child   ☐ Other Relation   ☐ No Relation   ☐ Solicitor   ☐ Other Professional

If 'Other Relation' or 'Other Professional', specify relationship:

Place a cross against one option ☒

If there are additional attorneys, please complete the above details in the 'Additional Information' section (at the end of this form).

Part Five - The Enduring Power of Attorney

I (We) the attorney(s) apply to register the Enduring Power of Attorney made by the donor under the Enduring Powers of Attorney Act 1985, the original, or if the original is lost or destroyed, a certified copy of which accompanies this application.

I (We) have reason to believe that the donor is or is becoming mentally incapable.

Date that the **Donor** signed the Enduring Power of Attorney. *You can find this in Part B of the Enduring Power of Attorney.*

D D M M Y Y Y Y

To your knowledge, has the Donor made any other Enduring Powers of Attorney?:

☐ Yes   ☐ No

Place a cross against one option ☒

If 'Yes', please give details below including registration date if applicable:

....
....

Form EP2 PG – Application to register an Enduring Power of Attorney

---

Part Six - Notice of Application to Donor

Notice must be given personally to the donor. It should be made clear if someone other than the attorney(s) gives the notice. The date on which the notice was given MUST be completed.

I (We) have given notice of the application to register in the prescribed form (EP1PG) to the donor personally,

on this date: ☐☐ ☐☐ ☐☐☐☐
              D D M M Y Y Y Y

If someone other than the attorney gives notice to the donor please complete the name and address details below. Please also complete the date above:

Full Name:
Address 1:
Address 2:
Address 3:
Town/City:
County: Postcode:

Part Seven - Notice of Application to Relatives

Please complete details of all relatives entitled to notice.

Please place a cross in the box ☒ if no relatives are entitled to notice: ☐

I (We) have given notice to register in the prescribed form (EP1PG) to the following relatives of the donor:

Full Name: Relationship to Donor:
Address: Date notice given:
                                                            D D M M Y Y Y Y

Full Name: Relationship to Donor:
Address: Date notice given:
                                                            D D M M Y Y Y Y

Full Name: Relationship to Donor:
Address: Date notice given:
                                                            D D M M Y Y Y Y

Full Name: Relationship to Donor:
Address: Date notice given:
                                                            D D M M Y Y Y Y

Full Name: Relationship to Donor:
Address: Date notice given:
                                                            D D M M Y Y Y Y

If there are additional relatives please complete the Relative Name, Relationship, Address and Date details in the 'Additional Information' section (at the end of this form).

PART VII

PART VII COURT OF PROTECTION PRACTICE 2016

Part Eight - Notice of Application to Co-Attorney(s)

Do not complete this section if it does not apply. If there are additional co-attorneys please complete the Attorney Name, Relationship, Address and Date details in the 'Additional Information' section (at the end of this form).

Are all the attorneys applying to register? Yes ☐ No ☐   *Place a cross against one option* ☒

If no, I (We) have given notice to my (our) co-attorney(s) as follows:

Full Name:		Relationship to Donor:	
Address:		Date notice given: D D M M Y Y Y Y	

Full Name:		Relationship to Donor:	
Address:		Date notice given: D D M M Y Y Y Y	

Part Nine - Fees

Guidelines on remission and postponement of fees can be obtained from the Office of the Public Guardian.

Have you enclosed a cheque for the registration fee for this application? Yes ☐ No ☐ *Place a cross against one option* ☒

Do you wish to apply for postponement, exemption or remission of the fee? Yes ☐ No ☐ *Place a cross against one option* ☒

If yes, please complete the application for exemption or remission form.

Part Ten - Declaration

Note: The application should be signed by all attorneys who are making the application. This must not pre-date the date(s) when the notices were given.

I (We) certify that the above information is correct and that to the best of my (our) knowledge and belief I (We) have complied with the provisions of the Mental Capacity Act 2005.

Signed: _____ Dated: D D M M Y Y Y Y

Signed: _____ Dated: D D M M Y Y Y Y

Signed: _____ Dated: D D M M Y Y Y Y

Form EP2 PG – Application to register an Enduring Power of Attorney

Part Eleven - Correspondence Address

Solicitors please note: The address to which the correspondence should be sent **MUST** be entered here if this is different to the address of Attorney One. State the full name and present address. Insert the name of the Solicitor's Firm in the Company Name field, if appropriate, and the correspondence reference in the Company Reference field.

Mr ☐   Mrs ☐   Ms ☐   Miss ☐   Other ☐

Place a cross against one option ☒

If Other, please specify here: _____

- Last Name:
- Forename 1:
- Other Forenames:
- Company Name:
- Company Reference:
- Address 1:
- Address 2:
- Address 3:
- Town/City:
- County:
- Postcode:
- DX No. (solicitors only):
- DX Exchange (solicitors only):
- Daytime Tel No.: (STD Code)
- Email Address:

Part Twelve - Additional Information

Please write down any additional information to support this application in the space below. If necessary attach additional paper to the end of this form.

_____
_____
_____
_____
_____
_____
_____
_____
_____
_____

PART VII

Guidance notes for completing form EP2PG: Application to register an Enduring Power of Attorney

Please complete every section of the form clearly in BLOCK CAPITALS using BLACK ink.

Part One – The Donor

- This section of the form covers the information we need to know about the Donor of the Enduring Power of Attorney (EPA). The Donor is the person who appointed the Attorney or Attorneys when the EPA was set up.
- Place a cross in the box that relates to the Donor's title or write it in the space provided.
- Last Name: The Donor's last name is their surname.
- Forename 1 and Other Forenames: Put the Donor's first name next to Forename 1, and put their second name and any other middle names next to Other Forenames.
- Company Name: If the Donor is living in, for example, a hospital or care home, write the name of that place in this section. If not, write 'not applicable'.
- Address 1- Address 3: When filling in the Donor's address, ensure that you don't write the town/city, county or postcode in this section.
- Town/City, County, Postcode: Ensure you only write the relevant information on each line.
- If the Donor's address on the EPA is different to the one you wrote on the EP2PG form, explain why this is the case under Part Twelve – Additional Information – the final section of the form.
- Donor Date of Birth: Complete the boxes requesting the Donor's date of birth, including the day, month and year. If you do not know this, you can find it in the EPA itself, under the Donor's name and address. If the date of birth you enter here is different from that on the EPA itself, explain the reason for the difference in Part Twelve – Additional Information and provide a copy of the birth certificate as evidence.

Form EP2 PG – Application to register an Enduring Power of Attorney

Part Two – Attorney One

This section covers the information required about the first Attorney. This is someone who has accepted responsibility for financial management or personal welfare given to them in the 'power' under the EPA.

The reader of this guidance may be an Attorney or someone advising an Attorney – however you should note that only an Attorney or somebody acting on their behalf can actually register an EPA and sign this form.

- As the Attorney, write your title, Last Name, Forename 1 and Other Forenames in the relevant boxes of the form.
- If you are a professionally appointed Attorney, put the name of your firm next to Company Name, and insert your company address details.
- The boxes entitled DX Exchange are for those wishing to use this as an alternative to the postal service.
- Attorney One's Date of Birth should be entered in the boxes provided, including the day, month and year.
- Attorney One's Daytime Tel No, Email Address and Occupation, if applicable, must be entered on the form.
- It is important to explain Attorney One's Relationship to the donor by putting a cross in the appropriate square, or entering other details if applicable in the space provided.
- Part B of the Enduring Power of Attorney states whether the attorney is to act jointly, jointly and severally, or alone.
- Attorneys appointed 'jointly' must always act together. They must all agree before taking any action.
- Attorneys appointed 'jointly and severally' can act independently and can act together. This means that any one Attorney can decide on a particular issue independently of the others.

You should place a cross in the box next to the option that is applicable to Attorney One.

Part Three – Attorney Two

- Part Three of the form is for inputting details about the second Attorney, if one has been appointed.
- Refer to Part Two for guidance on completing this section.

Part Four – Attorney Three

- Part Four of the form is for inputting details about the third Attorney, if one has been appointed.
- Refer to Part Two for guidance on completing this section.
- If there are more than three Attorneys you should enter their details at Part 12 – Additional Information, or attach additional sheets of paper to the form.

Part Five – The Enduring Power of Attorney

- Part Five is to record the date the Donor signed the original EPA. Please enter the day, month and year in the relevant boxes.
- If you know that the Donor has made other EPAs, put a cross in the relevant square.

Part Six – Notice of Application to Donor

- Part Six of the form covers the requirement to personally notify the Donor that you are registering the EPA. It asks you to record the details of when this happened, using the notice in form EP1PG.
- If someone other than the Attorney personally notifies the Donor, enter that person's full name and address. Input the actual date (using the day, month and year boxes) that the Donor was given the notice in person.
- Please note that in certain circumstances the Court of Protection (the 'Court') may consider dispensing with the requirement to notify the Donor. This will normally only happen if a doctor certifies that it will cause the Donor harm or distress. You would then need to contact the Court to make an application to dispense with notice and pay the Court application fee.
- Part Six of the form must be completed unless the Court has agreed that you are not required to notify the Donor. If this is the case you must explain this in Part 12 – Additional Information.

Part Seven – Notice of Application to Relatives

- Part Seven of the form covers the details of the relatives that you must notify that you intend to register the EPA.
- Input their Full Names, Relationship to Donor and their Addresses in the spaces provided.
- Next to each person's contact details, input the actual date that notice was given to that person, including the day, month and year.
- If more relatives need to be notified than you can fit in this section, attach additional sheets of papers to the form with their details.
- In certain circumstances the Court may consider dispensing with the requirement to notify relatives. You would need to contact the Court to make an application and pay the Court application fee.

Part Eight – Notice of Application to Co-Attorney(s)

- Part Eight of the form is to be used only if there is more than one Attorney and the other Attorney(s) are not making this application with you. The details of those Attorney(s) are to be entered in this section.

- This section does not apply if the Attorneys are appointed jointly – as this would mean that they would both (or all) have had to make the application with you because the Donor appointed you to act together.

Part Nine – Fees

- This section of the form covers fee information. There is separate guidance available from the Office of the Public Guardian (OPG) on fees, exemptions and remissions. If you wish to apply for an exemption or remission of the fee, you should fill in the appropriate box. You will also need to complete the relevant application form.

- If the OPG provided you with the EP2PG registration application form, you should have received our fees guidance at the same time. You can also download it from our website.

Part Ten – Declaration

- Part Ten is the Attorney(s) declaration. This is where you and any other Attorney making the application certify that you have complied with the provisions of the Mental Capacity Act 2005 and all the relevant statutory instruments made under it. Please note that false declarations may make the signatory liable to criminal prosecution.

- Input the date that you signed the application, including day, month and year.

Part Eleven – Correspondence Address

- Part Eleven of the form requests the address for all correspondence. This information is vital to your application and care should be taken to ensure accuracy.

- The address must be that of an Attorney or a solicitor acting on behalf of an Attorney.

- The registered EPA will be returned to this address. If this section is left blank, all correspondence will be sent to Attorney One.

- The boxes entitled DX Exchange are for those wishing to use Document Exchange as an alternative to the postal service.

- The telephone number and email address should be completed if applicable.

Part Twelve – Additional Information

- Part Twelve is for any additional information. For instance if there are more than three Attorneys, the details of the additional Attorney(s) should be entered here.

Further Assistance

- The OPG publishes guidance about EPAs, Lasting Powers of Attorney (LPA) and the role of the Attorney. These are available to download from our website or you can call us for a hard copy.

- If you need further help in completing the EP2PG form please contact us.

Contact Us

Office of the Public Guardian
PO Box 16185
Birmingham B2 2WH

Phone Number: 0300 456 0300

Fax Number: 0870 739 5780

Email: customerservices@publicguardian.gsi.gov.uk

Website: www.gov.uk/power-of-attorney

DX: 744240 Birmingham 79

Textphone: 0115 934 2778 (If you have speech or hearing difficulties and have access to a textphone, you can call the OPG textphone for assistance.)

International Calls: +44 300 456 0300

Disclaimer

OPG and Court staff can provide advice about OPG and Court processes only and cannot provide legal advice or services. We recommend that you seek independent legal advice where appropriate. Information in this publication is believed to be correct at the time of printing, however we do not accept liability for any error it may contain.

Form EP3 PG – Notice to the Office of the Public Guardian of an objection to registration of an Enduring Power of Attorney

EP3PG 02.14

Notice to the Office of the Public Guardian of an objection to registration of an Enduring Power of Attorney

You should tell the OPG of an objection within 35 days of the date the form **EP1PG** was given to you. If you do not the EPA may be registered. If the form EP1PG was posted to you, it is treated as given on the date of posting.

This is my notification to the OPG that I am objecting to the registration of the enduring power of attorney, detailed below.

Case no. (if known)

Details of the donor
Name

Address

Telephone no.

Postcode

Details of 1st Attorney (if known)
Name

Address

Telephone no.

Postcode

Details of 2nd Attorney (if known)
Name

Address

Telephone no.

Postcode

Details of 3rd Attorney (if known)
Name

Address

Telephone no.

Postcode

© Crown copyright 2014

PART VII

PART VII   COURT OF PROTECTION PRACTICE 2016

Details of the person making the objection

Name

Address

Telephone no.

Postcode

Please tick which of the prescribed ground(s) is the basis of your objection to the registration of the EPA.
It is not possible to object on a ground not listed here e.g. *"I know that the Donor would have wanted/ always intended that I would be appointed as an Attorney along with my brother/sister/father etc."* This is an unacceptable ground and registration will NOT be suspended.

☐ That the power claimed to be created by the instrument is not valid as an enduring power of attorney

☐ That the power created by the instrument no longer subsists (exists)

☐ That the application is premature because the donor is not yet becoming mentally incapable

☐ That fraud or undue pressure was used to induce the donor to make the power

☐ That the attorney is unsuitable to be the donor's attorney (having regard to all the circumstances and in particular the attorney's relationship to or connection with the donor).
If you select this ground, and the Donor has appointed more than one attorney, please provide the OPG with the name(s) of the unsuitable attorney(s) in the box below.

Have you sent your objection (Form COP8) to the Court of Protection? ☐ Yes ☐ No

If Yes, when did you send it? D D M M Y Y Y Y

Signature and date

Signed

Dated   D D M M Y Y Y Y

Send your completed form to: Office of the Public Guardian, PO Box 16185, Birmingham, B2 2WH and send your form COP8 to the Court of Protection, PO Box 70185, First Avenue House, 42-49 High Holborn, London, WC1A 9JA – DX 160013 Kingsway 7 or Telephone 0300 456 4600 –
Email courtofprotectionenquiries@hmcourts-service.gsi.gov.uk – www.gov.uk/power-of-attorney

DEPRIVATION OF LIBERTY FORMS

DLA – Deprivation of Liberty Application form for urgent consideration

COP DLA 07.15 Court of Protection
Deprivation of liberty
Application form
For urgent consideration

Case no.	
Date of application	
Date of issue	

This form should only be used for applications to vary or terminate a standard or urgent authorisation made by a supervisory body under Schedule A1 of the Mental Capacity Act 2005.

Full name of person to whom the application relates including their date of birth
(this is the name of the person who lacks, or is alleged to lack, capacity)

Date of birth / /

Date of urgent/standard authorisation / /   Date of effective detention / /

Section 1 – Contact details

Applicant

Name
Address
Telephone no.
Mobile no.
Postcode
Email

What is the applicant's relationship to the relevant person? (This is the person that the application is about)

Applicant's solicitor or representatives

Name
Address
Telephone no.
Mobile no.
Fax no.
Postcode
Email

PART VII

© Crown copyright 2015

PART VII   COURT OF PROTECTION PRACTICE 2016

Relevant person's details if not applicant

Name

Address   Telephone no.

Mobile no.

Fax no.

Postcode

Email

Supervisory body PCT/LA

Name

Address   Telephone no.

Mobile no.

Fax no.

Postcode

Email

Managing Authority/Hospital/Care Home

Name

Address   Telephone no.

Mobile no.

Fax no.

Postcode

Email

DLA – Deprivation of Liberty Application form for urgent consideration

IMCA

Name

Address

Telephone no.

Mobile no.

Fax no.

Postcode

Email

Relevant person's representative

Name

Address

Telephone no.

Mobile no.

Fax no.

Postcode

Email

PART VII

PART VII COURT OF PROTECTION PRACTICE 2016

Section 2 – Details of other interested parties

Name

Address

Telephone no.

Fax no.

DX no.

Postcode

Email

Name

Address

Telephone no.

Fax no.

DX no.

Postcode

Email

Section 3 – Details of issue to be challenged

3.1 Date of decision ☐☐/☐☐/☐☐☐☐

3.2 Where an **urgent** authorisation has been given, the court may determine any question relating to any of the following matters:

☐ whether the urgent authorisation should have been given

☐ the period during which the urgent authorisation is to be in force

☐ the purpose for which the urgent authorisation is given

☐ other

DLA – Deprivation of Liberty Application form for urgent consideration

3.3 Where a **standard** authorisation has been given, the court may determine any question relating to any of the following matters:

- [ ] whether the relevant person meets one or more of the qualifying requirements
- [ ] the period during which the standard authorisation is to be in force
- [ ] the purpose for which the standard authorisation is given
- [ ] the conditions subject to which the standard authorisation is given
- [ ] other

3.4 Other issues that may arise

	Yes	No
Are you making an interim application?	☐	☐
Do you intend to bring other applications if this application succeds in whole or in part?	☐	☐
Do you intend to bring other applications if this application fails?	☐	☐

Section 4 – Detailed statement of grounds

- [ ] Set out below   - [ ] Attached

PART VII

PART VII COURT OF PROTECTION PRACTICE 2016

Section 5 – Other issues of the case

5.1 Are there other issues that will arise for determination in respect of the relevant person and any applications that you have made or intend to make in respect of them? ☐ Yes ☐ No

If Yes, please give details below

Section 6 – Other applications

6.1 Are you aware of any previous application(s) to the Court of Protection regarding the person to whom this application relates? ☐ Yes ☐ No

If Yes, please give as much of the following information as you can. If there has been more than one previous application please attach the information about other previous applications on a separate sheet of paper.

The name of the applicant

The date of the order
☐☐ / ☐☐ / ☐☐☐☐

Case number

Please attach a copy of the order(s), if available.

☐ Copy attached ☐ Not available

Section 7 - Attending court hearings

7.1 If the court requires you to attend a hearing do you need any special assistance or facilities? ☐ Yes ☐ No

If Yes, please say what your requirements are. If necessary, court staff may contact you about your requirements.

PART VII

PART VII　　　　　　　　　　　　　　COURT OF PROTECTION PRACTICE 2016

Section 8 – Statement of facts relied on

Section 9 - Statement of truth

The statement of truth is to be signed by you, your solicitor or your litigation friend.

*(I believe) (The applicant believes) that the facts stated in this application form and its annex(es) are true.

Signed		Date	□□/□□/□□□□
Name			
Name of firm		Position or office held	

8

2152

Section 10 - Supporting documents

10.1 Which of the following documents are you filing with this application and any you will be filing later?

- ☐ Standard authorisation
- ☐ Urgent authorisation
- ☐ Age assessment
- ☐ No refusals assessment
- ☐ Mental capacity assessment
- ☐ Mental health assessment
- ☐ Eligibility assessment
- ☐ Best interests assessment
- ☐ Form COP DLB Declaration of exceptional urgency
- ☐ Form COP 24 Witness Statement
- ☐ A copy of the Legal Aid or CSLF certificate (if legally represented)
- ☐ Copies of any relevant statutory material
- ☐ Draft Order or Directions

10.2 The following documents not being in my possession. I request the Supervisory Body/Managing Authority, to file copies of the following documents with their acknowledgment of service

- ☐ Standard authorisation
- ☐ Urgent authorisation
- ☐ Age assessment
- ☐ No refusals assessment
- ☐ Mental capacity assessment
- ☐ Mental health assessment
- ☐ Eligibility assessment
- ☐ Best interests assessment
- ☐ Care plan

10.3 Please explain why you have not supplied a document and a date when you expect it to be available:

Signed _____ Applicant's Solicitor _____

PART VII

DLB – Deprivation of liberty declaration of exceptional urgency

Court of Protection
Deprivation of liberty
Declaration of exceptional urgency

Case no.
Date of application
Date of issue

This form should only be used for applications to vary or terminate a standard or urgent authorisation made by a supervisory body under Schedule A1 of the Mental Capacity Act 2005.

Full name of person to whom the application relates
(this is the name of the person who is deprived/will be deprived of their liberty)

Date of urgent/standard authorisation [ ]/[ ]/[   ]   Date of effective detention [ ]/[ ]/[   ]

Section 1 – Reasons for urgency

1.1 Please give reasons for the urgency

1.2 Please state what interim relief is sought and why?

Signed _____   Dated [ ]/[ ]/[   ]

Section 2 – Proposed timetable

2.1 Please tick the boxes that apply

☐ The application for interim relief should be considered within [   ] ☐ hours ☐ days

☐ Abridgement of time is sought for the lodging of acknowledgments of service

© Crown Copyright 2015

DLB – Deprivation of liberty declaration of exceptional urgency

Section 3 – Service

3.1 On whom have you served a copy of this form?

☐ **Relevant person**

Date served
☐☐/☐☐/☐☐☐☐

☐ by fax machine
Fax no.
Time sent

☐ by handing it to or leaving it with
Name

☐ by e-mail (please give address below)

☐ **Managing Authority**

Date served
☐☐/☐☐/☐☐☐☐

☐ by fax machine
Fax no.
Time sent

☐ by handing it to or leaving it with
Name

☐ by e-mail (please give address below)

☐ **Supervisory Body**

Date served
☐☐/☐☐/☐☐☐☐

☐ by fax machine
Fax no.
Time sent

☐ by handing it to or leaving it with
Name

☐ by e-mail (please give address below)

☐ **IMCA**

Date served
☐☐/☐☐/☐☐☐☐

☐ by fax machine
Fax no.
Time sent

☐ by handing it to or leaving it with
Name

☐ by e-mail (please give address below)

☐ **Relevant persons representative**

Date served
☐☐/☐☐/☐☐☐☐

☐ by fax machine
Fax no.
Time sent

☐ by handing it to or leaving it with
Name

☐ by e-mail (please give address below)

☐ **Interested parties**

Date served
☐☐/☐☐/☐☐☐☐

☐ by fax machine
Fax no.
Time sent

☐ by handing it to or leaving it with
Name

☐ by e-mail (please give address below)

PART VII

DLD – Deprivation of liberty Certificate of Service/Non-service; Certificate of Notification/Non-notification

Court of Protection
Deprivation of liberty
Certificate of service/ non-service
Certificate of notification/ non-notification

Case no.	
Name of applicant	
Name of respondent	
Filed by	
Date	

This form should only be used for applications to vary or terminate a standard or urgent authorisation made by a supervisory body under Schedule A1 of the Mental Capacity Act 2005.

Full name of person to whom the application relates
(this is the person who is deprived/will be deprived of their liberty)

Section 1 – Details of the person served/notified

1.1 Name of the person(s) served/notified:

Name	Date served/notified
Name	Date served/notified
Name	Date served/notified
Name	Date served/notified

Section 2 – Document served

2.1 Title or description of the document (tick only **one** box)

☐ application form

☐ other (please give details)

© Crown Copyright 2015

DLD – Deprivation of liberty Certificate of Service/Non-service; Certificate of Notification/Non-notification

Section 3 – Person(s) not served or notified

3.1 Name of the person(s) who have not been served/notified:

Name

Reason

Name

Reason

Name

Reason

Name

Reason

Section 4 – Statement of truth

The statement of truth must be signed by the person who served/provided notification.

I believe that the facts stated in this certificate are true.

Signed		Date	/ /
Name			
Name of firm		Position or office held	

PART VII

PART VII COURT OF PROTECTION PRACTICE 2016

DLE – Deprivation of Liberty acknowledgment of service/notification

Court of Protection
Deprivation of liberty
Acknowledgment of service/notification

Case no.	
Name of applicant	
Name of respondent	
Name of party acknowledging	
Date	

This form should only be used for applications to vary or terminate a standard or urgent authorisation made by a supervisory body under Schedule A1 of the Mental Capacity Act 2005.

Full name of person to whom the application relates
(this is the name of the person who is deprived/will be deprived of their liberty)

Section 1 - The person served/notified

1.1 Your details ☐ Mr. ☐ Mrs. ☐ Miss ☐ Ms. ☐ Other _____

   First name

   Last name

1.2 Address (including postcode)

   Telephone no.

   E-mail address

1.3 Is a solicitor representing you? ☐ Yes ☐ No

   If Yes, please give the solicitor's details.

   Name

   Address (including postcode)

   Telephone no.

   Fax no.

   DX no.

   E-mail address

© Crown Copyright 2015

DLE – Deprivation of Liberty acknowledgment of service/notification

1.4 Which address should official documentation be sent to?

☐ Your address

☐ Solicitor's address

☐ Other address (please provide details)

Section 2 – Attending court hearings

2.1 If the court requires you to attend a hearing do you need any special assistance or facilities? ☐ Yes ☐ No

If Yes, please say what your requirements are. If necessary, court staff may contact you about your requirements.

Section 3 – Signature

Signed

Date served/notified [ ]/[ ]/[ ]

Person served/notified ('s solicitor) ('s litigation friend)

Name

Name of firm

Position or office held

Section 4 – Supervisory Body or Managing Authority only

4.1 I am serving and filing the following documents:

1.
2.
3.
4.

Signed

Date [ ]/[ ]/[ ]

PART VII

DOL10 – Application to authorise a deprivation of liberty

Court of Protection

Application to authorise a deprivation of liberty

(section 4A(3) and 16(2)(a) of the Mental Capacity Act 2005)

A streamlined procedure pursuant to Re X and Ors (Deprivation of Liberty) [2014] EWCOP 25 and Re X and Ors (Deprivation of Liberty)(Number 2) Re [2014] EWCOP 37

For office use only
Date received
Case no.
Date issued

SEAL

Before completing this form please read the guidance leaflet attached. You can download forms and leaflets at hmctsformfinder.justice.gov.uk. Search for form type: 'Court of Protection'.

Please give the full name of the person to whom the application is about

1. Statement of reasons for urgency

Any factors that ought to be brought specifically to the court's attention (the applicant being under a specific duty to make full and frank disclosure to the court of all facts and matters that might have an impact upon the court's decision).

DOL10 – Application to authorise a deprivation of liberty

2. Order sought

Please specify the nature of the order you seek and attach a draft.

[   ]

Duration of the Order sought [   ]

If granted the deprivation of liberty will be reviewed by the court at least annually. Do you consider that the authorisation will require a shorter review period? ☐ Yes ☐ No

If Yes, please provide details

[   ]

3. Your details (the applicant)

☐ Mr. ☐ Mrs. ☐ Miss ☐ Ms. ☐ Other _____

Full name [   ]

Post held/Job title [   ]

Name of organisation [   ]

Address [   ]

DX number [   ]

Telephone [   ]

Email [   ]

PART VII

PART VII — COURT OF PROTECTION PRACTICE 2016

4. Permission
Are you applying for permission to make this application? ☐ Yes

5. The person the application is about
(a) Personal details

☐ Mr.   ☐ Mrs.   ☐ Miss   ☐ Ms.   ☐ Other _____

First name

Middle name(s)

Last name

Maiden name (if applicable)

Date of birth [D D M M Y Y Y Y]

Is the person:
☐ Married or in a civil partnership
☐ In a relationship with a person who is not a spouse or civil partner
☐ Separated
☐ Divorced (give date)
☐ Widowed (give date of death of spouse or civil partner)
☐ Single

Full address including postcode

What type of accommodation is this?
eg. supported living arrangement, shared lives, own home, other

Name of local authority or NHS body responsible for the care placement

Is the person the application about subject to

☐ Detention under the Mental Health Act 1983
☐ A Community Treatment Order
☐ Guardianship

Will the proposed deprivation of liberty conflict with any such treatment or measure?   ☐ Yes   ☐ No

If Yes, please give details

[ ]

(b) Decisions already made

Has the person the application is about made a relevant advance decision?   ☐ Yes   ☐ No

If Yes, please provide details and set out whether the decision made conflicts with the order sought in this application.

[ ]

Has the person the application is about made a lasting power of attorney?   ☐ Yes   ☐ No

If Yes, please provide details and set out whether any relevant decision(s) made by the attorney(s) conflicts with the order sought in this application.

[ ]

PART VII

Has the court made an order appointing a deputy? ☐ Yes ☐ No

If Yes, please provide details of the deputy(s) and set out whether any relevant decision(s) made by the deputy(s) conflict with the order sought in this application

Are you aware of any previous application to the court regarding the person the application is about? ☐ Yes ☐ No

If Yes, please provide details.

I enclose a copy of the
☐ advance decision
☐ LPA
☐ relevant court order

6. Statement of truth

I believe the facts stated in this application form are true.

Signed

*Applicant ('s solicitor)

* Please delete the options in brackets that do not apply.

Name

Date

Name of organisation

Position or office held

DOL10 – Application to authorise a deprivation of liberty

Annex A: Evidence in support of an application to authorise a deprivation of liberty
(Section 4A(3) and 16(2)(a) of the Mental Capacity Act 2005)

Please give the full name of the person the application is about

[   ]

1. Assessment of capacity

☐ I confirm that the person the application is about has been assessed as having an impairment or disturbance in the functioning of the mind or brain and lacks capacity to consent to the measures proposed and the deprivation of liberty which is identified within the application.

☐ I attach form COP3 or other evidence of capacity

2. Mental Health Assessment - Unsoundness of mind

☐ I confirm that the person has been medically diagnosed as being of "unsound mind" and I attach written evidence from a medical practitioner

If your assessment of capacity on form COP3 has not been completed by a registered medical practitioner, you must also attach written evidence from a registered medical practitioner containing a diagnosis that the person this application is about suffers from a diagnosis of 'unsoundness of mind'.

☐ I am submitting the mental health assessment and assessment of capacity as a single document

☐ COP3 completed by a medical practitioner

PART VII

3. Deprivation of liberty

Describe the factual circumstances relating to the deprivation of liberty with particular reference to whether the person the application is about is free to leave their residence and what type of supervision arrangements are in place.

(a) Is the person free to leave? ☐ Yes ☐ No

If No, please give details

[ ]

(b) Is the person under constant supervision and control? ☐ Yes ☐ No

If Yes, please give details

[ ]

(c) Is the person under physical restraint? ☐ Yes ☐ No
(d) Is sedation being used? ☐ Yes ☐ No

If you have answered Yes to either question above, please give details

[ ]

DOL10 – Application to authorise a deprivation of liberty

(e) Is the person prevented from having contact with others? ☐ Yes ☐ No
If Yes, please give details

(f) What restrictions if any are imposed or measures used which affect the person's access to the community?
Please give details

(g) Are there any other relevant factors that relate to the deprivation of liberty? ☐ Yes ☐ No
If Yes, please give details

PART VII

(h) Please explain why the proposed deprivation of liberty is thought to be imputable to the state

In the light of the responses to the questions under this heading, do you consider that the arrangements represent a deprivation of liberty?   ☐ Yes   ☐ No

4. Statement of best interests

State why the arrangements for which the authorisation as a deprivation of liberty is sought are necessary in the best interests of the person the application is about.

State what harm may occur or what the risks would be if the person were not deprived of their liberty. Provide detail of what the harm would be, how serious it would be and how likely it is to arise.

DOL10 – Application to authorise a deprivation of liberty

State why the deprivation of liberty is proportionate
Explain why it is considered that the risk of harm and the seriousness of harm justifies the restrictions amounting to a deprivation of liberty.

What less restrictive options have been tried or considered?
Explain why the option you propose is the least restrictive option and is in the best interests of the person.

☐ I attach the care plan

☐ I attach a copy of the best interests assessment relating to the placement

PART VII

PART VII
COURT OF PROTECTION PRACTICE 2016

5. Other information

Provide any other information you think may be relevant in helping the court reach a decision

6. Statement of truth

I believe the facts stated in this annex are true.

Signed

Name

Date

Name of organisation

Position or office held

DOL10 – Application to authorise a deprivation of liberty

Annex B: Consultation with people with an interest in an application to authorise a deprivation of liberty

(Section 4A(3) and 16(2)(a) of the Mental Capacity Act 2005)

Please give the full name of the person the application is about

[   ]

Section 4(7) of the Mental Capacity Act places a duty on a decision maker to take into account the views of other people who have an interest in the person's personal welfare.

You should consult with:
  (a) any donee of a lasting power of attorney granted by the person;
  (b) any deputy appointed for the person by the court;

and, if possible, with at least three people from the following categories:
  (c) anyone named by the person to whom the application is about as someone to be consulted on the matters raised by the application; and
  (d) anyone engaged in caring for the person or interested in their welfare

You must inform the people consulted with of the information contained in section 40 of the Practice Direction 10AA and provide details, including attaching statements.

PART VII

1. People who have been consulted and who fall within the categories (a) - (d) above

Name	Address	Connection to the person	Date consulted	Please state whether they support or object to the proposed arrangements and provide details of any views expressed. If none, insert 'none'.

2. People who have not been consulted within the categories (a) - (d) above

Name	Address	Reason why they were not consulted	Connection to the person

DOL10 – *Application to authorise a deprivation of liberty*

3. Litigation friend

If required, please list who would be prepared to act as Litigation Friend

Name	Address

4. Statement of truth

I believe the facts stated in this annex are true.

Signed

Name

Date

Name of organisation

Position or office held

Annex C: Consultation with the person the application is about in support of an application to authorise a deprivation of liberty

(Section 4A(3) and 16(2)(a) of the Mental Capacity Act 2005)

Please give the full name of the person the application is about

[ ]

Notes:
The person this application is about must be consulted about the application and the person undertaking this consultation must take all reasonable steps to assist the person to make a decision. If the person the application is about does not have capacity to consent to being deprived of their liberty, they must be given the opportunity to be involved in the proceedings, and to express their wishes and views, to help the court reach a decision about whether the proposed deprivation of liberty would be in their best interests.

Chapter 3 of the Mental Capacity Act Code of Practice contains practical guidance about consulting and encouraging participation.

The person undertaking the consultation should be someone who knows the person the application is about, and who is best placed to express their wishes and views. It could be a relative or close friend, or someone who the person has previously chosen to act on their behalf (for example an attorney). If no suitable person is available, then an IMCA (Independent Mental Capacity Advocate) or another similar or independent advocate should be appointed to perform the role.

1. Details of the person undertaking the consultation

☐ Mr.   ☐ Mrs.   ☐ Miss   ☐ Ms.   ☐ Other _____

First name [ ]

Middle name(s) [ ]

Last name [ ]

DOL10 – Application to authorise a deprivation of liberty

2. Statement by the person undertaking the consultation

Describe your relationship to the person

How long have you known them?

Date of consultation | D | D | M | M | Y | Y | Y | Y |

(a) Confirm that you explained to the person the application is about:
   (i) that the applicant is making an application to court;
   (ii) that the application is to consider whether the person lacks capacity to make decisions in relation to their residence and care, and whether to authorise a deprivation of their liberty in connection with the arrangements set out in the care plan;
   (iii) what the proposed arrangements under the order sought are;
   (iv) that the person is entitled to express their views, wishes and feelings in relation to the proposed arrangements and the application, and that the person undertaking the consultation will ensure that these are communicated to the court;
   (v) that the person is entitled to seek to take part in the proceedings by being joined as a party or otherwise, what that means, and that the person undertaking the consultation will ensure that any such request is communicated to the court;
   (vi) that the person undertaking the consultation can help them to obtain advice and assistance if they do not agree with the proposed arrangements in the application.

Please give details

PART VII

(b) Did the person this application is about express any views, wishes or feelings in relation to the application and the proposed/actual deprivation of liberty? ☐ Yes ☐ No

If Yes, please give details and the manner of expressing those views if appropriate

(c) Does the person wish to take part in the proceedings? ☐ Yes ☐ No

If Yes, please explain how

(d) Are you aware of any present or past wishes, feelings or beliefs (including religious, cultural and moral beliefs of the person this application is about) and values that must be taken into account before the court authorises a deprivation of liberty? ☐ Yes ☐ No

If Yes, please give details; include in particular any relevant oral or written statements made or views expressed when they had capacity. Set out any beliefs and values which might influence the decision if they had capacity and any other factors that they would be likely to consider were they able to do so.

DOL10 – Application to authorise a deprivation of liberty

(e) Provide any other information that you consider to be relevant to the court

3. **Statement of truth**

I believe the facts stated in this annex are true.

Signed

Name

Date

Name of organisation

Position or office held

PART VII

Checklist for completing form
COPDL10 for a Court authorised deprivation of liberty.

Every question on the forms should be completed, or stated that information is not available. Failure to provide the information required by the court could lead to unnecessary delays to proceedings.

A separate application must be made for each individual for whom an authorisation of a deprivation of liberty is sought.

Please ensure that the following forms have been completed:

- [ ] **COPDL10** Application under section 4A(3) and 16(2)(a) of the Mental Capacity Act 2005 to authorise a deprivation of liberty

- [ ] **Annex A** Evidence in support of an application under section 4A(3) and 16(2)(a) of the Mental Capacity Act 2005 to authorise a deprivation of liberty

- [ ] **Annex B** Consultation with people with an interest in an application under section 4A(3) and 16(2)(a) of the Mental Capacity Act 2005 to authorise a deprivation of liberty

- [ ] **Annex C** Consultation with the person the application is about for an application under section 4A(3) and 16(2)(a) of the Mental Capacity Act 2005 to authorise a deprivation of liberty.

You must also supply:
- [ ] COP3 Evidence of capacity
- [ ] Mental Health Assessment
- [ ] a copy of any Advance Decision
- [ ] a copy of any Lasting Power of Attorney (LPA)
- [ ] any relevant Court orders
- [ ] Care Plan
- [ ] Best Interest Assessment
- [ ] the application fee

DOL10 – *Application to authorise a deprivation of liberty*

General information for completing form
COPDL10 for a Court authorised deprivation of liberty.

These forms should be used to make applications to the Court of Protection for the court to authorise a deprivation of liberty for people who are receiving care in domestic settings such as shared lives and supported living. The forms should not be used for applications to vary or terminate a standard or urgent authorisation made by a supervisory body under Schedule A1 of the Mental Capacity Act.

1. COPDL10 — The Application Form

- Order sought – you must specify in the box the nature of the order you seek, i.e a declaration that the person the application is about lacks capacity to make decisions relating to their care and residence or an order that it is in the best interests of the person the application is about to deprive that person of their liberty.
- Explain why the proposed deprivation of liberty is thought to be imputable to the state. Are the care arrangements which give rise to the deprivation of liberty being made either by a local authority or the NHS?
- Permission. These applications fall under the personal welfare jurisdiction of the Court therefore permission is required in all cases.
- Date of Birth – Proof that the person the application is about is 16 years old or over.

2. Annex A — Evidence in Support of Application

In most cases the allocated social worker with the relevant skill and knowledge, involved with the care arrangements may complete the form. However, if one or more of the trigger factors apply, someone independent (who may still be employed by the applicant public authority) to the allocated social worker should provide the evidence.

- The purpose of the mental health assessment is to establish that the person the application is about has been diagnosed as being of 'unsound mind', and therefore comes within the scope of article 5 of the European Convention on Human Rights.
- The evidence may be provided by a registered medical practitioner or psychiatrist, evidence from a social worker or other non-medical practitioner listed in the notes to form COP3 will not be accepted.
- The mental health assessment may take the form of a letter setting out the diagnosis, the name of the practitioner and their qualifications. If it is not possible to provide the original letter, a copy certified by the applicant as a true copy of the original will be acceptable. The evidence should not be more than 12 months old and should also make reference to the person's eligibility to be deprived of their liberty.
- In cases where suitable mental health evidence is not readily available, then it would be acceptable to provide the assessment of capacity and mental health assessment as a single document using form COP3, but the combined evidence must be provided by a registered medical practitioner or psychiatrist.
- Is the person the application is about free to leave? This does not relate to the ability of the person to express a desire to leave but on what those with control over their care arrangements would do if they attempted to leave.
- Is the person the application is about under constant supervision and control? Provide details of the number of hours of supervision and under what situations. Provide details of the type of control exercised by staff/carers other than physical restraint.
- Is the person the application is about under physical restraint/is sedation being used? You should describe the situations when physical restraint is used. The type of restraint the frequency and duration. If sedation is used please describe the type of sedation administered.

- Is the person the application is about prevented from having contact with others? Authorisations for deprivation of liberty cannot be used to regulate or restrict contact between the person for whom the authorisation is sought and others –this includes family members or others who share living arrangements with the person the application is about.
- Statement of Best Interests You may find it helpful to refer to paragraph 5.13 in the Mental Capacity Act Code of Practice.

3. Annex B — Consultation with People with an interest in an application to authorise a deprivation of liberty.

Section 4(7) of the Mental Capacity Act places a duty on a decision maker to consult with other people who have an interest in the person's personal welfare.

You should consult with:

(a) any donee of a lasting power of attorney granted by the person;

(b any deputy appointed for the person by the court;

together with, if possible, at least three people in the following categories:

(c) anyone named by the person the application is about as someone to be consulted on the matters raised by the application; and

(d) anyone engaged in caring for the person or interested in their welfare

You must tell the people you consult with that

(a) that the applicant is making an application to court;

(b) that the application is to consider whether the person the application is about lacks capacity to make decisions in relation to his or her residence and care and whether they should be deprived of their liberty in connection with the arrangements set out in the care plan;

(c) what the proposed arrangements under the order sought are.

and that you are under an obligation to tell the person the application is about:

(d) that they are entitled to express their views, wishes and feelings in relation to the proposed arrangements and the application and that the person undertaking the consultation with them will ensure that these are communicated to the court;

(e) that they are entitled to seek to take part in the proceedings by being joined as a party or otherwise, what that means, and that the person consulting with them will ensure that any such request is communicated to the court;

(f) that the person consulting them can help them to obtain advice and assistance if they do not agree with the proposed arrangements in the application.

If the people you consult with express any views about the application or the proposed deprivation of liberty you should provide details, including attaching statements.

4. Annex C

Annex C Consultation with the person the application is about is used to inform the court that the person the application is about has been consulted about the application.

The person undertaking the consultation should be someone who knows the person the application is about, and who is best placed to express their wishes and views. It could be a relative or close friend, or someone who the person has previously chosen to act on their behalf (for example an attorney).

If no one is available, then the allocated social worker may undertake the consultation and complete the form, but where appropriate, an IMCA (Independent Mental Capacity Advocate) or another independent advocate should be appointed to assist.

The person the application is about must be consulted regarding the application and the person undertaking the consultation must take all reasonable steps to assist the person to make a decision. If the person the application is about does not have capacity to consent to being deprived of their liberty, they must be given the opportunity to be involved in the proceedings, and to express their wishes and views, to help the court reach a decision about whether the detention would be in their best interests.

Chapter 3 of the Mental Capacity Act Code of Practice contains practical guidance about consulting and encouraging participation.

Application to authorise a deprivation of liberty
(section 4A(3) and 16(2)(a) of the Mental Capacity Act 2005)

Your application must answer the following matters, either in the body of the application form or in attached documents.

Failure to provide the information required may result in the case not being suitable for the application to be dealt with under the streamlined process for an authorisation to deprive a person of their liberty under existing or continuing care arrangements.

Information required:

1.	Are there any reasons for particular **urgency** in determining the application?	☐ Yes	☐ No
2.	Have you confirmed that 'P' (the person the application is about) is 16 years old or more and is not ineligible to be deprived of liberty under the 2005 Act?	☐ Yes	☐ No
3.	Have you attached the relevant medical evidence stating the basis upon which it is said that 'P' suffers from unsoundness of mind?	☐ Yes	☐ No
4.	Have you attached the relevant medical evidence stating the basis upon which it is said that 'P' lacks the capacity to consent to the care arrangements?	☐ Yes	☐ No
5.	Have you attached a copy of 'P's' care plan?	☐ Yes	☐ No
6.	Does the care plan state the nature of 'P's' care arrangements and why it is said that they do or may amount to a deprivation of liberty?	☐ Yes	☐ No
7.	Have you stated the basis upon which it is said that the arrangements are or may be imputable to the state?	☐ Yes	☐ No
8.	Have you attached a best interests assessment?	☐ Yes	☐ No
9.	Have steps been taken to consult 'P' and all other relevant people in 'P's' life (who should be identified) of the application and to canvass their wishes, feelings and views?	☐ Yes	☐ No
10.	Have you recorded in Annex B any relevant wishes and feelings expressed by 'P' and any views expressed by any relevant person?	☐ Yes	☐ No
11.	Have you provided details of any relevant advance decision by 'P' and any relevant decisions under a lasting power of attorney or by 'P's' deputy (who should be identified)?	☐ Yes	☐ No
12.	Have you identified anyone who might act as a litigation friend for the person to whom the application relates?	☐ Yes	☐ No
13.	Have you listed any factors that ought to be brought specifically to the court's attention (the applicant being under a specific duty to make full and frank disclosure to the court of all facts and matters that might impact upon the court's decision), being factors: a) needing particular judicial scrutiny; or b) suggesting that the arrangements may not in fact be in 'P's' best interests or be the least restrictive option; or c) otherwise indicating that the order sought should not be made.	☐ Yes	☐ No
14.	Have you enclosed the fee?	☐ Yes	☐ No

The following triggers may indicate that your application is not suitable to be made under the streamlined process and that an oral hearing may be required in the first instance:

1. Any contest by the person the application is about or by anyone else to any of the matters listed at 2 – 8 above
2. Any failure to comply with any of the requirements referred in 9 above.
3. Any concerns arising out of information supplied in accordance with 10, 12 and 13 above.
4. Any objection by the person this application is about.
5. Any potential conflict with any decision of the kind referred to in 11 above.
6. If for any other reason the court thinks that an oral hearing is necessary or appropriate

PART VIII

Precedents

PART VIII: Precedents

Contents

Section A: Deputy Orders	2189
A 1 – GENERAL TITLE	2189
A 2 – ORDER appointing a deputy for property and affairs	2189
A 3 – ORDER appointing local authority as deputy for property and affairs	2193
A 4 – ORDER appointing a new deputy for property and affairs	2194
A 5 – ORDER revoking an EPA and appointing a deputy for property and affairs	2195
A 6 – ORDER appointing an interim deputy for property and affairs	2196
A 7 – ORDER discharging a property and affairs deputy where capacity is regained	2197
A 8 – ORDER refusing permission to be appointed as deputy for personal welfare	2198
A 9 – ORDER appointing a deputy for personal welfare	2199
A 9 – Additional Clauses in Deputy Orders	2201
Section B: Interim Orders	2205
B 1 – MULTI-PURPOSE INTERIM ORDER	2205
B 2 – INTERIM ORDER with penal notice attached	2209
B 3 – INTERNATIONAL ORDER	2210
B 4 – INTERNATIONAL ORDER: ABDUCTION	2213
Section C: EPA and LPA Orders	2216
C 1 – GENERAL TITLE	2216
C 2 – DIRECTIONS on objections to EPA	2217
C 3 – ORDER on objections to EPA	2218
C 4 – ORDER on severance of provisions in EPA	2219
C 5 – DIRECTIONS on objections to LPA	2220
C 6 – ORDER on objections to LPA	2221
C 7 – ORDER on severance of provisions in LPA	2222
C 8 – DIRECTIONS on transfer to a regional court	2223
C 9 – DIRECTION to encourage Mediation	2223

Section D: Case Management Directions Orders 2225

D 1 – CASE MANAGEMENT CHECKLIST 2225

D 2 – MULTI-PURPOSE DIRECTIONS ORDER 2227

D 3 – DIRECTIONS on contested application 2233

D 4 – DIRECTIONS on gift or statutory will application 2234

D 5 – DIRECTIONS on transfer to regional court of personal welfare application 2235

D 6 – FIRST DIRECTIONS ORDER family dispute as to residence and contact 2237

D 7 – DIRECTIONS ORDER 'adult care' case 2240

D 8 – DIRECTIONS ORDER local authority personal welfare application 2243

D 9 – DIRECTIONS on DOLs application 2248

D 10 – Sundry clauses in Orders 2249

D 11 – Orders in Family-type Personal Welfare Cases 2252

D 12 – Official Solicitor 2253

D 13 – Contact plans 2254

D 14 – ORDER Transparency 2257

Section E: Final Orders 2262

E 1 – ORDER Capacity: financial affairs 2262

E 2 – ORDER EPA or Deputy 2263

E 3 – ORDER Discharge from the jurisdiction 2264

E 4 – ORDER Change of financial Deputy 2266

E 5 – ORDER Cancellation of EPA and appointment of financial Deputy 2268

E 6 – ORDER Appointment of financial Deputy in respect of large brain injury award 2270

E 7a – ORDER for repairs to property 2273

E 7b – ORDER for repairs to property (continued) 2276

E 7c – ORDER for repairs to property (continued) 2277

Section F: Statutory wills 2280

F 1 – ORDER authorising statutory will 2280

F 2 – PRECEDENT for statutory will 2280

Section G: Deprivation of Liberty 2282

G 1 – Re X [Order 1] Model Re X Order 2282

G 2 – Re X [Order 2] 2284

G 3 – Re X [Order 3] 2285

Section A: Deputy Orders

A selection of the most frequently used orders of the Court of Protection is reproduced below. These orders are generally made 'on paper' at the Central Office and Registry (since December 2013 at First Avenue House, 42–49 High Holborn, London WC1A 9JA but previously at Thomas More Building, RCJ and until January 2012 at Archway) following uncontested applications and the content should be varied as appropriate to suit the circumstances of the particular case.

A 1
GENERAL TITLE

(Used for uncontested Orders)

THIS ORDER IS NOT VALID UNLESS IT BEARS THE IMPRESSED SEAL OF THE COURT OF PROTECTION ON ALL PAGES

COURT OF PROTECTION

MENTAL CAPACITY ACT 2005

Case No: 00000000

In the Matter of
[*A B*]

ORDER

[*state nature of Order as in headings below*]

MADE by District Judge [*name*] – *or authorised officer*

AT First Avenue House, 42–49 High Holborn, London WC1A 9JA [*or regional court address*]

ON [*date*]

* * * * * * *

A 2
ORDER appointing a deputy for property and affairs[1]

[*GENERAL TITLE*][2]

UPON the court being satisfied that *A B* lacks capacity to make various decisions for himself/herself in relation to a matter or matters concerning

---

[1] This order contemplates *A B* being either male or female and should be suitably amended. Joint deputies may be appointed and this order should then be amended throughout accordingly.

[2] Insert A1 above.

his/her property and affairs, and that the purpose for which this order is needed cannot be as effectively achieved in a way that is less restrictive of his/her rights and freedom of action.

IT IS ORDERED THAT

1. Appointment of deputy

(a) [*Name of deputy*] of [*address*] is appointed as deputy ('the deputy') to make decisions on behalf of *A B* that he/she is unable to make for himself/herself in relation to his/her property and affairs subject to any conditions or restrictions set out in this order

Or where joint or joint and several deputies are appointed:

[(a) [*Name of first deputy*] of [*address of first deputy*] and [*name of second deputy*] of [*address of second deputy*] are appointed [jointly] *or* [jointly and severally] as deputies ('the deputies') to make decisions on behalf of *A B* that he/she is unable to make for himself/herself in relation to his/her property and affairs subject to any conditions or restrictions set out in this order]

(b) The appointment will last until [further order] *or where there are significant assets eg. brain injury damages award* [three years from the date of the order]

(c) The deputy must apply the principles set out in Section 1 of the Mental Capacity Act 2005 and have regard to the guidance in the Code of Practice to the Act

2. Authority of deputy

(a) The court confers general authority on the deputy to take possession or control of the property and affairs of *A B* and to exercise the same powers of management and investment [including selling and letting property][3] as he/she has as beneficial owner, subject to the terms and conditions set out in this order

(b) The deputy cannot purchase any freehold or leasehold property on *A B*'s behalf without obtaining further authority from the court.

(c) [The deputy must not sell, lease or charge any freehold or leasehold property in which *A B* has a beneficial interest without obtaining further authority from the court][4]

(d) [The deputy is authorised to sell the property of *A B* known as [*name of property and address*] on the best possible terms and after payment of legal fees and other professional charges to invest the net proceeds for his/her benefit][5]

---

[3] Delete if para (c) below is included.
[4] Optional clause for use if the next clause is not appropriate.
[5] This clause will be included where a home is to be sold.

Section A: Deputy Orders

(e) If the deputy considers it in *A B*'s best interests to do so the deputy may appoint an investment manager, who is regulated and authorised to undertake investment business, to manage his/her assets on a discretionary basis under the standard terms and conditions applicable to such service from time-to-time, and to permit the investments to be held in the name of the investment manager nominee company

(f) The deputy may make provision for the needs of anyone who is related or connected with *A B*, if he/she provided for or might be expected to provide for that person's needs, by doing whatever he/she did or might reasonably be expected to do to meet those needs

(g) The deputy may (without obtaining any further authority from the court) dispose of *A B*'s money or property by way of gift to any charity to which he/she made or might have been expected to make gifts and on customary occasions to persons who are related to or connected with him/her, provided that the value of each such gift is not unreasonable having regard to all the circumstances and, in particular, the size of his/her estate

(h) [The deputy may withdraw a sum not exceeding £... .a year from the funds belonging to *A B* without needing to obtain the prior approval of the Court of Protection][6]

(i) [On *A B*'s behalf the deputy may take such steps as may be necessary to obtain (either alone or with a co-administrator) a grant of representation to the estate of [*name of deceased*] and to use the share to which *A B* is entitled for his/her benefit][7]

(j) For the purpose of giving effect to any decision the deputy may execute or sign any necessary deeds or documents[8]

3. Investments[9]

(a) The deputy must exercise such care and skill as is reasonable in the circumstances when investing the assets of *A B*

(b) The deputy may make any kind of investment that the person absolutely entitled to those assets could make

(c) This general power of investment includes investment in land and investment in assets outside England and Wales

(d) In exercising the power of investment, the deputy must have regard to the standard investment criteria namely the suitability of the investments and the need for diversification in so far as is appropriate to the circumstances of *A B*

---

[6] This clause may be included where there are very significant assets.
[7] Optional clause.
[8] This provision will be included in most orders that appoint or empower a deputy for property and affairs.
[9] This clause is not required unless there are significant assets

(e) The deputy must from time to time review the investments, and consider whether, having regard to the standard investment criteria, they should be varied

(f) Unless the deputy reasonably concludes that in all the circumstances it is unnecessary or inappropriate to do so, before exercising any power of investment, the deputy must obtain and consider proper advice about the way in which, having regard to the standard investment criteria, the power should be exercised

'Proper advice' is the advice of a person who the deputy reasonably believes to be qualified to give it by his ability in and practical experience of financial and other matters relating to the proposed investment

4. Reports

(a) The deputy is required to keep statements, vouchers, receipts and other financial records

(b) The deputy must submit a report to the Public Guardian as and when required

5. Costs and expenses

(a) The deputy is entitled to be reimbursed for reasonable expenses incurred provided they are in proportion to the size of *A B*'s estate and the functions performed by the deputy[10]

(b) The deputy is authorised to pay [*name of solicitors*] fixed costs for this application and if the amount sought exceeds the fixed costs allowed the deputy is authorised to agree their costs and pay them from the funds belonging to *A B*

In default of agreement, or if the deputy or solicitors would prefer the costs to be assessed, this order is to be treated as authority to the Senior Court Costs Office to carry out a detailed assessment on the standard basis[11]

(c) The deputy is entitled to receive fixed costs in relation to this application and to receive fixed costs for the general management of *A B*'s affairs

If the deputy would prefer the costs to be assessed, this order is to be treated as authority to the Senior Court Costs Office to carry out a detailed assessment on the standard basis[12]

---

[10] This clause relates to lay deputies only.
[11] This clause relates to lay deputies where a solicitor has submitted the application.
[12] This clause relates to professional deputies only.

6. Security

(a) The deputy is required forthwith to obtain and maintain security in the sum of £[*amount*] in accordance with the standard requirements as to the giving of security

(b) The deputy must ensure that the level of security ordered by the court is in place before discharging any of the functions conferred by this order

7. Right to apply for reconsideration of order[13]

Any person who is affected by this order may apply to the court within 21 days of the order being served for reconsideration

* * * * * * *

A 3
ORDER appointing local authority as deputy for property and affairs[14]

[GENERAL TITLE]

Whereas

UPON the court being satisfied that A B lacks capacity to make various decisions for himself in relation to a matter or matters concerning his property and affairs, and that the purpose for which this order is needed cannot be as effectively achieved in a way that is less restrictive of his rights and freedom of action

IT IS ORDERED THAT

1. Appointment of deputy

(a) The authorised officer for property and affairs deputyships of [*name of council and address*] is appointed as deputy ('the deputy') to make decisions on behalf of *A B* that he is unable to make for himself in relation to his property and affairs subject to any conditions or restrictions set out in this order

(b) The appointment will last until further order

(c) The deputy must apply the principles set out in Section 1 of the Mental Capacity Act 2005 and have regard to the guidance in the Code of Practice to the Act

2. Authority of deputy

Adopt clauses from A2 above, as appropriate.

---

[13] This provision (or the different version in A8 below) is always appropriate when the order has been made following perusal of the papers (ie. without a hearing).
[14] Where *A B* is female this order should be appropriately amended as in A2 above.

4. Reports

Adopt clauses from A2 above.

5. Costs and expenses

The deputy is entitled to receive fixed costs in relation to this application and to receive fixed costs for the general management of A B's affairs

6. Right to apply for reconsideration of order

Adopt clauses from A2 above.

* * * * * * *

A 4

ORDER appointing a new deputy for property and affairs

[GENERAL TITLE]

Whereas

(1) By an order dated *[date]* *[name of former deputy]* was appointed as deputy for property and affairs for *A B*

(2) It appears that the said *[name of former deputy]* (died on *[date of death]*) (is unable to continue as deputy) (desires to retire from the deputyship) and an application has been made for an order under the Mental Capacity Act 2005 ('the Act')

(3) The court is satisfied that *A B* continues to lack capacity to make various decisions for himself in relation to a matter or matters concerning his property and affairs and that the purpose for which the order is needed cannot be as effectively achieved in a way that is less restrictive of his rights and freedom of action

IT IS ORDERED THAT

1. Discharge of deputy

If the former deputy is still alive

(a) The said *[name of former deputy]* is discharged from the deputyship and his powers are terminated

(b) The said *[name of former deputy]* is to provide the deputy hereinafter appointed with a final account to the date of this order by *[date]*

(c) The said *[name of former deputy]* shall disclose to the deputy hereinafter appointed copies of all documents, correspondence or records that he holds or has access to that relate to *A B*'s property and affairs

(d) The said [*name of former deputy*] is to transfer all property belonging to *A B* which remains under his control to the deputy hereinafter appointed

Or, if the former deputy is deceased

(a) The personal representatives of the late [*name of former deputy*] are to provide the deputy hereinafter appointed with a final account to the date of this order by [*date*]

(b) The personal representatives of the late [*name of former deputy*] shall disclose to the deputy hereinafter appointed copies of all documents, correspondence or records held by the late [*name of former deputy*] that relate to *A B*'s property and affairs

(c) The personal representatives of the late [*name of former deputy*] are to transfer all property belonging to *A B* which remains under the control of the late [*name of former deputy*] to the deputy hereinafter appointed

2. **Appointment of new deputy**

Continue as in A2 or A3 above, as appropriate.

* * * * * * * *

A 5
ORDER revoking an EPA and appointing a deputy for property and affairs
[*GENERAL TITLE*]

Whereas

(1) On [*date*] *A B* executed an Enduring Power of Attorney ('EPA') in favour of [*name of attorney*] ('the Attorney') for the purpose of the Enduring Powers of Attorney Act 1985 and the Court of Protection registered the power on [*date*]

(2) An application has been made by [*name*] ('the Applicant') for an order under the Mental Capacity Act 2005

(3) The court is satisfied that *A B* lacks capacity to make various decisions for himself in relation to a matter or matters concerning his property and affairs and that the purpose for which the order is needed cannot be as effectively achieved in a way that is less restrictive of his rights and freedom of action

(4) The attorney has disclaimed the Enduring Power of Attorney

IT IS ORDERED THAT

1. **Revocation of EPA**

The said EPA executed by A B on [date] is hereby revoked and cancelled.

2. Appointment of deputy

Continue as in A2 or A3 above, as appropriate.

* * * * * * *

A 6
ORDER appointing an interim deputy for property and affairs

[*GENERAL TITLE*]

Whereas

(1) An application has been made under the Mental Capacity Act 2005

Either:

(2) The court is satisfied that *A B* is unable to make various decisions for himself in relation to a matter or matters concerning his property and affairs because of an impairment of or a disturbance in the functioning of his mind or brain

(3) The court is satisfied that the purpose for which the order is needed cannot be as effectively achieved in a way that is less restrictive of his rights and freedom of action

Or, where there is insufficient evidence to make a finding

(4) The court has reason to believe that *A B* may lack capacity in relation to matters concerning his property and affairs and considers that pending the determination of the application it is in his best interests to make this order without delay

IT IS ORDERED THAT

1. Appointment of interim deputy

(a) [*Name of interim deputy*] of [*address*] is appointed as interim deputy ('the interim deputy') forthwith to make decisions on behalf of *A B* that he is unable to make for himself in relation to his property and affairs subject to any conditions or restrictions set out in this order

(b) The appointment will last until [*date*] *or* [further order]

(c) The interim deputy must apply the principles set out in section 1 of the Mental Capacity Act 2005 and have regard to the guidance in the Code of Practice to the Act

2. Authority of interim deputy

(a) The court confers general authority on the interim deputy to take possession or control of the property and affairs of *A B* and to exercise the same powers of management and investment as he has as beneficial owner subject to the terms and conditions set out in this order

(b) The interim deputy may make provision for the needs of anyone who is related to or connected with *A B* if he provided for or might be expected to provide for that person's needs by doing whatever he did or might reasonably be expected to do to meet those needs

(c) The interim deputy may (without obtaining any further authority from the court) dispose of money or property of *A B* by way of gift to any charity to which he made or might have been expected to make gifts and on customary occasions to persons who are related to or connected with him, provided that the value of each such gift is not unreasonable having regard to all the circumstances and, in particular, the size of his estate

(d) For the purpose of giving effect to any decision the interim deputy may execute or sign any necessary deeds or documents

Continue with provisions as to Reports, Costs and expenses, Security and reconsideration as in A2 above. This order would be followed with further directions.

* * * * * * *

A 7
ORDER discharging a property and affairs deputy where capacity is regained

[GENERAL TITLE]

Whereas

Either

(1) By order dated [*date*] X Y was appointed as receiver under section 99 of the Mental Health Act 1983

(2) On [*date*] the receiver ('the deputy') became a deputy for property and affairs by virtue of paragraph 1(2)(a) of Schedule 5 to the Mental Capacity Act 2005

Or

(1) By order dated [*date*] [*name*] was appointed deputy for property and affairs ('the deputy')

Continue

(2/3) [*Name of applicant*] has applied for an order under Rule 202 of the Court of Protection Rules 2007 (supplemented by Practice Direction B to Part 23), which applies where a person ceases to lack capacity

(3/4) From evidence that accompanied the application the Court is satisfied that *A B* is able to make decisions in relation to his property and affairs

(4/5) Notice of the application has been given to the deputy

IT IS ORDERED THAT

1. The deputy is discharged and his powers are terminated
2. A final account by the deputy is dispensed with
3. The deputy's security is to be discharged
4. All property belonging to *A B* which remains under the control of the deputy is to be transferred forthwith to *A B* or as he directs
5. The funds in court are to be transferred to *A B* as directed in the payment schedule which is attached to and forms part of the order
6. The deputy's costs relating to this application and any outstanding costs of general management are to be assessed on the standard basis and when certified paid by *A B*

Payment Schedule

(Insert details of any funds held in court to be transferred to A B)

* * * * * * *

A 8
ORDER refusing permission to be appointed as deputy for personal welfare

[GENERAL TITLE]

Whereas

1. *[Name of the applicant]* ('the Applicant') has sought permission to apply to the Court to be appointed as a deputy to make personal welfare decisions for *A B*
2. Section 5 of the Mental Capacity Act 2005 confers a general authority to act without the need for any formal authorisation by the court if a person does an act in connection with the care or treatment of a person who lacks capacity and acts in that person's best interests
3. Section 16(4) of the Mental Capacity Act 2005 provides that when deciding whether it is in a person's best interests to appoint a deputy the Court must have regard to the principles that

    (a) a decision of the Court is to be preferred to the appointment of a deputy and

    (b) the powers conferred on a deputy should be as limited in scope and duration as is reasonably practicable in the circumstances

4. In the permission form the Applicant failed to identify with sufficient particularity the reasons why it is necessary in this case to appoint a deputy to make personal welfare decisions and what specific personal welfare powers the Applicant was seeking

Section A: Deputy Orders

IT IS ORDERED THAT

1. The application for such permission is refused pursuant to Section 50(3)(b) and (c) of the Mental Capacity Act 2005

2. For the avoidance of doubt if an issue arises upon which a personal welfare decision or direction of the Court is sought this decision does not preclude the Applicant from re-applying at the material time [nor does it prejudice the Applicant's application to be appointed deputy to make decisions regarding *A B*'s property and financial affairs (which application is continuing)] – *as appropriate*

3. This order was made of the Court's own initiative without a hearing and without notice pursuant to rule 27 of the Court of Protection Rules 2007. Any person affected by it may apply, pursuant to Rule 89 of the Court of Protection Rules 2007 within 21 days of the date on which the order was served to have it set aside

* * * * * * *

A 9
ORDER appointing a deputy for personal welfare

[GENERAL TITLE]

Whereas

1. An application has been made for an order under the Mental Capacity Act 2005

2. The Court is satisfied that:
   (a) *A B* is unable to make various decisions for himself in relation to a matter or matters concerning his personal welfare because of an impairment of or a disturbance in the functioning of his mind or brain
   (b) the purpose for which the order is needed cannot be as effectively achieved in a way that is less restrictive of his rights and freedom of action

IT IS ORDERED THAT

1. **Appointment of deputy**

(a) *[Deputy's forename and surname]* of *[address]* is appointed as deputy ('the deputy') to make personal welfare decisions on behalf of *A B* that he is unable to make for himself subject to the conditions and restrictions set out in the Mental Capacity Act 2005 and in this order

(b) The appointment will last until [three years from the date of the order] *or where appropriate* [further order]

(c) The deputy must apply the principles set out in Section 1 of the Mental Capacity Act 2005 and have regard to the guidance in the Code of Practice to the Mental Capacity Act 2005

2. **Authority of deputy**

(a) The Court authorises the deputy to make the following decisions on behalf of *A B* that he is unable to make for himself when the decision needs to be made in relation to

    (i) where he should live

    (ii) with whom he should live

    (iii) decisions on day-to-day care including diet and dress

    (iv) consenting to medical or dental examination and treatment on his behalf

    (v) making arrangements for the provision of care services

    (vi) whether he should take part in particular leisure or social activities and

    (vii) complaints about his care or treatment

(b) For the purpose of giving effect to any of these decisions the deputy may execute or sign any necessary deeds or documents

(c) The deputy does not have authority to make a decision on behalf of *A B* in relation to a matter if the deputy knows or has reasonable grounds for believing that he has capacity in relation to the matter

(d) The deputy does not have the authority to make the following decisions or do the following things in relation to *A B*:

    (i) to prohibit any person from having contact with him

    (ii) to direct a person responsible for his health care to allow a different person to take over that responsibility

    (iii) to make a decision that is inconsistent with a decision made, within the scope of his authority and in accordance with the Mental Capacity Act 2005 by the donee of a lasting power of attorney granted by him (or if there is more than one donee by any of them)

    (iv) to consent to specific treatment if he has made a valid and applicable advance decision to refuse that specific treatment

    (v) to refuse consent to the carrying out or continuation of life sustaining treatment in relation to him

    (vi) to do an act that is intended to restrain him otherwise than in accordance with the conditions specified in the Mental Capacity Act 2005

Section A: Deputy Orders

3. **Reports**

 (a) The deputy is required to keep a record of any decisions made or acts done pursuant to this order and the reasons for making or doing them

 (b) The deputy must submit an annual report to the Public Guardian

4. **Right to apply for reconsideration of order**[15]

Any person who is affected by this order may apply to the court within 21 days of the order being served for reconsideration

* * * * * * *

A 9
Additional Clauses in Deputy Orders

A selection of the most frequently used provisions is reproduced below. Some of the provisions set out at B1 below for Interim Orders may also be appropriate for final Orders

Litigation friend

1. The deputy is hereby authorised to conduct proceedings in the action in the name and on behalf of *A B* and to act therein as litigation friend

2. The deputy is hereby authorised to act as litigation friend for *A B* in the divorce and financial remedies proceedings and to approve any financial settlement

3. The deputy is authorised to conduct proceedings as litigation friend in the name and on behalf of *A B* under the Inheritance (Provision for Family and Dependants) Act 1975 in relation to the estate of [*name*] deceased

Withdrawal of funds

4.

 (a) The Applicant is authorised to withdraw the sum of £2,000 being part of the amount held on behalf of A B on account no. [*number*] at the Court Funds Office and to use that sum for the general benefit of A B until a substantive deputy is appointed

 (b) The Applicant must retain all receipts and invoices and presented these to the Public Guardian if required to do so

 (c) For the purpose of giving effect to this order the Applicant may execute or sign any necessary documents

---

[15] This provision (or the different version in A8 below) is always appropriate when the order has been made following perusal of the papers (ie. without a contested hearing).

Purchase unspecified property

5.

(a) The deputy is authorised to purchase such property in the name of A B to a maximum of £[amount] and to ensure good title to the same

(b) Upon completion of the purchase the deputy shall cause a restriction to be lodged at HM Land Registry against dealings without order of the Court of Protection

(c) The deputy is authorised to draw down capital to enable purchase of the property and to pay legal costs of the purchase including stamp duty and disbursements

(d) For the purpose of giving effect to this order the deputy may execute or sign any necessary deeds or documents

Sale & purchase of property

6.

(a) The deputy is authorised to sell the property of A B known as [address] on the best possible terms and after payment of any legal fees and other professional charges the net proceeds shall be applied for the purchase of the property known as [address] for the sole benefit of A B at the lowest possible price and the deputy shall ensure good legal and beneficial title to the property is obtained

(b) If it is preferred that the solicitors' costs be assessed and this order is to be treated as authority to the Senior Court Costs Office to carry out a detailed assessment on the standard basis

Sale & purchase with co-trustee

7.

(a) The deputy is authorised to sell the property of A B known as [address] on the best possible terms and after payment of any legal fees and other professional charges to invest the net proceeds in the purchase of a property with a co-trustee and the deputy shall ensure good legal and beneficial title to the property is obtained

(b) The deputy must ensure that a declaration of trust is filed at court setting out the respective contributions of those who have a beneficial interest in the newly purchased property and an appropriate restriction must be entered at HM Land Registry

Equity release authority

8.

(a) The deputy is authorised to realise £[amount] by entering into an equity release scheme over the property known as [address] and preparing a trust deed to protect A B's beneficial share in the said property

(b) For the purpose of giving effect to this order the deputy may execute or sign any necessary deeds or documents

Section 49 Report from Public Guardian

9. A report is required by the court under section 49 of the Mental Capacity Act 2005 in relation to A B

(a) The report is to be prepared by Office of the Public Guardian in writing and produced as soon as is reasonably practicable before [date]

(b) Subject to any directions given under the next paragraph, the report must contain all the material required by the relevant practice direction and be prepared in the form therein specified

(c) The report is to be confined to the management and administration of the property and affairs of A B by her Attorney and need not address issues relating to her personal welfare

(d) The court will send a copy of the report to the parties and to such persons as the court may direct

Appointment of new trustees (section 36(9) applications

10. Permission is granted to [*names of continuing trustees*] to appoint [*name of new trustee*] as new trustee in place of A B in relation to the trusts affecting the trust property

Appointment of new trustees (section 54 applications

11.

(a) [*name of new trustee*] is appointed to be the new trustee in place of A B in relation to the trusts affecting the trust property

(b) The property subject to the trusts does now vest in the new trustees upon the subsisting trusts

Interest in company

12. The Applicant is authorised in the name and on behalf of A B to take such steps and to execute such transfer to himself of [number] shares of £x each belonging to A B in [name of company] in order that he may qualify as a Director of the said Company upon his undertaking to credit A B's bank account with the dividends on such shares and to retransfer such shares to A B and resign from the office of Director if and when directed to do so by the Court

13. The Applicant is to procure the appointment of himself as such Director and authorised in the name and on behalf of A B at any Annual or General Meeting of the company to exercise in the best interests of A B the powers of voting in respect of the remaining shares held by him in the Company and for that purpose to execute such form of Proxy or other documents as may

be necessary but so far as regards the following matters such voting powers are only to be exercised subject to the prior approval of the Court:

a   Borrowing by the Company

b   Increase or reduction of authorised or issued capital

c   Alterations and amendments of or additions to the Memorandum or Articles of Association of the Company

d   Fixing from time to time the amount of the Directors' fees

e   Winding up of the Company

f   Sale of the assets goodwill and business of the Company

g   The appointment and removal of Directors

h   Entering into partnership with any person or company

Discharge (following death of *A B*)

14.

(a) The deputy is discharged and his powers are terminated

(b) The deputy is to render a final account which is to be filed by [date]

(c) Any outstanding costs of the deputy are to be assessed on the standard basis by the Supreme Court Costs Office and paid from the estate of A B

Removal of deputy

15. The deputy having failed to comply with the order dated [date] the order made on [date] appointing [name] as deputy for A B's property and affairs is revoked forthwith.

* * * * * * *

Section B: Interim Orders

A selection of the most frequently used provisions in Interim Orders is reproduced below. Interim Orders are generally made before sufficient evidence is available to make a final order or even a finding as to lack of capacity. Many of these provisions may also be used in a final order.

B 1
MULTI-PURPOSE INTERIM ORDER

THIS ORDER IS NOT VALID UNLESS IT BEARS THE IMPRESSED SEAL OF THE COURT OF PROTECTION ON ALL PAGES

COURT OF PROTECTION

MENTAL CAPACITY ACT 2005

Case No: 00000000

In the Matter of

[*A B*]

INTERIM ORDER

MADE by District Judge [*name*] – *or authorised officer*

AT First Avenue House, 42–49 High Holborn, London WC1A 9JA [*or regional court address*]

ON [*date*]

Whereas

(1) [*Name of applicant*] ('the Applicant') has applied for an order under the Mental Capacity Act 2005

(2) The Court has reason to believe that *A B* lacks capacity in relation to matters concerning his property and affairs because of an impairment of or a disturbance in the functioning of his mind or brain and considers it in his best interests to make this interim order without delay[16]

OR

(2) From evidence that accompanied the application the Court is satisfied that:[17]

---

[16] The court has power to make interim orders before making a finding of lack of capacity when there is 'reason to believe' that there is a lack of capacity in relation to the matter – MCA 2005 s 48.

[17] The court may choose to make an interim order prior to a final determination even though it is possible to make a finding of lack of capacity.

2205

(a) *A B* is unable to make various decisions for himself in relation to a matter or matters concerning his property and affairs because of an impairment of or a disturbance in the functioning of his mind or brain

(b) the purpose for which the order is needed cannot be as effectively achieved in a way that is less restrictive of his rights and freedom of action

IT IS ORDERED THAT

[Include the following provisions as appropriate]

Access to health records

1. The Applicant is authorised in the name and on behalf of *A B* to apply under the Data Protection Act to any holder of a persons records relating to *A B* (including health records, social services records) for access to such records or any part thereof

Letting property

2. The Applicant is authorised to manage and let the property known as [*address*] belonging to *A B* on an assured shorthold tenancy for a period of not less than six months but not exceeding twelve months with authority to extend any tenancy of less than twelve months up to a total of twelve months and to pay all proper outgoings in respect thereof

Selling property

3. The Applicant is authorised to sell the property known as [*address*] on the best possible terms and after payment of legal fees and other professional charges the net proceeds will be held and invested by Messrs [*name*] solicitors pending the appointment of a deputy for property and affairs

Dealing with debts

4. The Applicant is authorised in the name and on behalf of *A B* to negotiate with the creditors of *A B* over his debts and liabilities and to report back to the Court

Freezing account

5. The Applicant is authorised in the name and on behalf of *A B* to take such steps as may be necessary to freeze all withdrawals from his account at [*name*] Bank plc or other bank or building society accounts held in the name of *A B* and for that purpose to execute or sign any necessary documents

Investigation

6. The Applicant is authorised to investigate and report to the Court as to the assets, liabilities and property of *A B* and any dealings therewith and to report to the court by [date]

Mortgage

7. The Applicant is authorised in the name and on behalf of *A B* jointly with [*name of other owner*] to enter into a mortgage of the jointly owned property known as [*property*] with [*lender*] and to execute any necessary documents

Transfer of file

8. The Applicant is authorised in the name and on behalf of *A B* to execute any documents necessary to instruct Messrs [*name*] to transfer the papers relating to his personal injury claim and to receive those papers

Leases

9. The Applicant is authorised in the name and on behalf of *A B* to instruct solicitors for and in the name of *A B* to enter into and grant leases for the property belonging to him known as [*property*] with [*name of lessee*]

Closing bank account

10. (The Applicant is) *or* (Messrs [*name*] solicitors of [*address*] are) authorised to receive and give a discharge for the sum of £XX part of the sum of £YY or other the amount standing to the credit of *A B* in account no. [*number*] at [*name*] Bank plc of [*address*]

Agreement with employer

11. The Applicant is authorised in the name and on behalf of *A B* to sign any necessary documents to enter into an agreement regarding his previous employment with [*employer*] and to apply to the Court for directions as to dealing with any funds emanating from any agreement

Maintaining 'P'

12. The Applicant is directed to apply the sum of £XX or so much as may be necessary in or towards the maintenance or other necessary requirements of *A B*

Obtaining Grant for 'P'

13. The Applicant is authorised to take such steps as may be necessary to obtain (either alone or with a co-administrator) a grant of representation to the estate of [*name*] deceased for the use and benefit of *A B* during his incapacity

Withdrawal from Court Funds Office

14. The Applicant is authorised to withdraw the sum of £XX being part of the sum of £YY standing to the credit of account no. [*number*] in respect of the action against [*name*] held at the Court Funds Office such sum to be used for the general benefit of *A B* until a deputy is appointed

Insurance claim

15. The Applicant may submit an insurance claim in the name and on behalf of *A B* for the fire damage to the property known as [*name*] and the contents therein. Any insurance payout (unless earmarked for repairs) is to be held by the Applicant in an interest bearing account until further order

Notice at Land Registry

16. The Applicant is authorised in the name and on behalf of *A B* to apply to the Land Registry to issue a unilateral notice to be entered in respect of the titles [*title numbers*] in respect of the property and land at [*property*]

Abuse by Attorney

17. The authority of [*name*] as attorney under an enduring power of attorney, which was registered by the court on [*date*] is suspended forthwith until further order

18. [*name*] of [*address*] is appointed interim deputy with general authority to take possession or control of all of the property and financial affairs of *A B*

19. The interim deputy is required to investigate:

    a   the current assets and liabilities, income and expenditure of *A B*

    b   the conduct of [*name*] as his attorney or otherwise; and

    c   whether anyone has in his possession or under his control or has any knowledge of any testamentary document executed by A B

General provisions (where appropriate)

20. The Applicant is to keep a record of how such sums have been utilised for the general benefit of *A B*, retain all receipts and invoices and account to the Public Guardian if so required

21. For the purpose of giving effect to this order [any decision] the Applicant may execute or sign any necessary deeds or documents

22. This order was made on the court's own initiative without hearing the parties or giving them the opportunity to make representations. Any person affected by it may apply to the court within 21 days of the order being served for reconsideration of its terms[18]

[NOTE: in some instances the Court may wish to provide that 'Messrs [name] solicitors of [address] are ...' instead of 'The Applicant is ...']

* * * * * * *

---

[18] It will be appropriate to include This clause in any interim order.

B 2

INTERIM ORDER with penal notice attached

[GENERAL TITLE]

Whereas

(1) [*Name of applicant*] ('the Applicant') has applied for an order under the Mental Capacity Act 2005

(2) The First Respondent is *A B* and the Second Respondent is [*name*]

(3) The Court has reason to believe that *A B* lacks capacity to litigate and to make decisions as to his residence contact and care because of an impairment of or a disturbance in the functioning of his mind or brain and considers it in his best interests to make this interim order without delay

(4) The Court has read the Applicant's urgent application and supporting information in the absence of the parties

(5) The Court grants permission to the Applicant to make this application

IT IS DECLARED THAT

1. It is lawful and in the First Respondent's best interest to reside at [*place*]

2. It is in the First Respondent's best interests to remain within the jurisdiction until further order

IT IS ORDERED THAT

3. The Second Respondent [*name*] be forbidden, whether by himself or by instructing or encouraging others from removing *A B* from the jurisdiction of England and Wales or attempting to remove him by encouraging or persuading him to leave the jurisdiction

4. The application together with the evidence in support and this order be served on all parties by the Applicant forthwith

5. The matter be listed before a District Judge on [*date and time*] at First Avenue House, 42–49 High Holborn, London WC1A 9JA [*or regional court address*]

6. The continuation of this order shall be considered at the hearing listed above

7. These proceedings shall be in private and nothing shall be published which identifies any party to these proceedings

8. The costs of this application are reserved to the listed hearing

4. Any person who is affected by this order may apply to the court within 21 days of the order being served for reconsideration

PENAL NOTICE[19]

If you the Second Respondent [*name*] disobey clause 3 of this order you may be held in Contempt of Court and may be imprisoned, fined or have your assets seized

Any other person who knows of this order and does anything which helps or permits the Second Respondent [*name*] to breach clause 3 of this order may also be held in Contempt of Court and may be imprisoned, fined or have their assets seized

To:

1. Applicant (or solicitors)
2. First Respondent
3. Second Respondent

* * * * * * * *

B 3
INTERNATIONAL ORDER

THIS ORDER IS NOT VALID UNLESS IS BEARS THE IMPRESSED SEAL OF THE COURT OF PROTECTION ON ALL PAGES

COURT OF PROTECTION

MENTAL CAPACITY ACT 2005

Case No: 00000000

IN THE MATTER OF [*A B*]

BETWEEN:

X LOCAL AUTHORITY
(England)

Applicant

and

A B [*full name*]
by her litigation friend The Official Solicitor

The person to whom the application relates

C D [*full name – father*]

First Respondent

and

E F [*full name – mother*]

Second Respondent

---

[19] Personal service of this order on the Second Respondent will be required.

and

Y LOCAL AUTHORITY
(Scotland)

Third Respondent

DIRECTIONS ORDER

BEFORE the Honourable Mr/Mrs Justice [name] sitting at the Royal Courts of Justice, Strand, London WC2A 2LL [or regional court address] on [*date*]

UPON hearing counsel for the Applicant, counsel for A B and counsel for the Third Respondent and the first and second Respondents attending in person and not being represented [or as appropriate].

AND UPON reading all documents filed and in particular [list relevant documents]

AND UPON the Court noting that:

(a) A B is habitually resident in Scotland and her current placement at [enter English address] is arranged and funded by the Third Respondent;

(b) The Scottish courts have primary jurisdiction to determine matters concerning A B's welfare;

(c) This Court has jurisdiction to hear this matter under paragraph 7(1)(d) of Schedule 3 to the Mental Capacity Act 2005 as A B is present in England and this order is a protective measure which is temporary and limited in its effect to England and Wales;

(d) The Third Respondent intends to lodge a Guardianship application with the [enter Scottish court] in respect of A B's welfare.

IT IS DECLARED, PURSUANT TO SECTION 48 OF THE MENTAL CAPACITY ACT 2005 ON AN INTERIM BASIS AND THE COURT EXCERCISING ITS FUNCTIONS UNDER THAT ACT PURSUANT TO PARAGRAPH 7(1)(d) OF PART 2 OF SCHEDULE 3 TO THAT ACT AND UNTIL SUBSTANTIVE ORDERS OF THE APPROPRIATE SCOTTISH COURT AS CONTEMPLATED BY PARAGRAPHS 6 AND 7 BELOW:

1. There is reason to believe A B lacks capacity to make decisions with regards to her (a) residence; (b) treatment and care; and (c) contact with others.

2. It is in the First Respondent's best interests to continue to reside at *[enter English address]*;

3. Staff providing care to A B may take reasonable and proportionate measures to prevent her from leaving *[enter English address]* and to return her there if she absconds.

4. Any deprivation of liberty to which A B is subject at [enter English address] is authorised under sections 16(2)(a) and 4A(3) of the Mental Capacity Act 2005.

NOTICE TO THE FIRST AND SECOND RESPONDENTS: BREACH OF PARAGRAPH 5 OF THIS ORDER WILL BE CONTEMPT OF COURT AND WILL BE PUNISHABLE BY IMPRISONMENT, FINE OR SEIZURE OF ASSETS – IT IS FURTHER ORDERED that:

1. Until further order the First and Second Respondents are forbidden, whether by themselves or by instructing or encouraging others, from:

    (a) Removing or attempting to remove A B from *[enter English address]*.

    (b) Encouraging or attempting to encourage A B to leave [enter English address].

2. Paragraphs 1-5 of this Order shall continue until such time as they are recognised by the Scottish court of competent authority with primary jurisdiction to determine matters concerning A B's welfare or further order.

3. The Third Respondent is requested to lodge an application in respect of A B's residence and contact by *[enter date and time]* to the Scottish court of competent authority with primary jurisdiction to determine matters concerning A B's welfare. A copy of such application, if made, is to be filed with this Court and served on all parties to these proceedings by *[enter date and time]*.

4. In the event that the Third Respondent considers that it is not in a position to make an application in accordance with paragraph 7 of this order, it shall apply to this Court without delay setting out the reasons for this in a position statement on no less than 48 hours' notice to the parties whereupon the matter shall be listed for further urgent consideration by a Judge of the Court of Protection.

5. The matter is listed for a review hearing to consider any further directions on [enter date] before *[enter name of Judge]* sitting at *[enter court]* with a time estimate of *[enter time estimate]*. In preparation for this hearing the following directions shall apply:

    (a) The Applicant shall file and serve an up to date bundle and preliminary documents five working days before the hearing;

    (b) The parties to each file and serve a position statement by 4pm three working days before the hearing;

    (c) In the event that by then the appropriate Scottish court is seised of this matter and any further orders (if any) required of this Court are subsidiary to, or reflective of, orders of that court such that an oral review hearing in this Court is unnecessary or disproportionate, the said review shall be vacated and the

Applicant may submit any required further order for consideration by [enter name of Judge] on paper.

6. This Order may be disclosed to staff caring for A B, the police and the Scottish court of competent authority with primary jurisdiction to determine matters concerning A B's welfare.

7. Leave to the parties and anyone affected by this Order to apply to the Court on at least 48hours' notice to the parties to vary or revoke this Order.

8. No order as to the costs.

* * * * * * * *

B 4
INTERNATIONAL ORDER: ABDUCTION

THIS ORDER IS NOT VALID UNLESS IS BEARS THE IMPRESSED SEAL OF THE COURT OF PROTECTION ON ALL PAGES

IN THE COURT OF PROTECTION

MENTAL CAPACITY ACT 2005

Case Number: 0000000

IN THE MATTER OF [A B]

BETWEEN:

ORDER

BEFORE the Honourable Mr/Mrs Justice [name] sitting at the Royal Courts of Justice, Strand, London WC2A 2LL [or regional court address] on [date]

PENAL NOTICE

TO [C D]. TAKE NOTICE that if you disobey paragraph 1 of this order you may be held to be in contempt of court and may be imprisoned, fined or have your assets seized.

UPON HEARING Counsel for the Applicant and Counsel for the First and Second Respondents

AND WHEREAS

(1) A B is a British citizen and currently believed to be travelling outside England and Wales with a passport issued by [name of State] and on the basis that (1) A B was born on [date] (2) his place of birth was [town and country], his parents are [name] and [name] and his passport number is [insert details].

(2) In consequence of the fact that A B has been found to lack mental capacity to decide where to live, this Court is empowered and required to exercise its protective jurisdiction over him and to ascertain his best interests and to facilitate and protect those best interests.

(3) It appears that A B was habitually resident in England and Wales on [date], the date he was removed from the jurisdiction and [date], the date of the application for his return.

(4) This Honourable Court is anxious to protect and secure his well-being and best interests and to ensure that he may freely express his wishes concerning his country and place of residence.

(5) This Honourable Court is satisfied that all interested parties are before the Court including the Official Solicitor, A B's litigation friend.

(6) This Honourable Court has in the interests of A B determined that he should be returned to England and Wales.

AND NOW THEREFORE THIS COURT RESPECTFULLY REQUESTS any person not within the jurisdiction of this Court who is in a position to do so to co-operate in assisting and securing the immediate return to England and Wales of A B.

AND THIS COURT RESPECTFULLY INVITES all judicial and administrative bodies in the [name of State] to render assistance in establishing the whereabouts of A B and in arranging for him to be placed in contact with and facilitating his travel to the British Consulate/Embassy in [place], with a view to his immediate return to England & Wales.

AND NOW THEREFORE THIS COURT RESPECTFULLY REQUESTS all judicial, administrative and law enforcement authorities of the [name of State] to use their best endeavours to assist in taking any steps which may to them appear necessary and appropriate in locating, safeguarding and facilitating the return to England and Wales of A B pursuant to the laws of [name of State].

AND UPON the court making the orders below under the Mental Capacity Act 2005

IT IS HEREBY DECLARED PURSUANT TO SECTION 48 OF THE MENTAL CAPACITY ACT 2005 that it is A B's best interests to return to England and Wales and in the interim to live in his own home at [address] supported by a package of specialist care arranged by X Local Authority as set out in the interim care plan appended hereto as a Schedule to this Order.

IT IS ORDERED THAT

1. C D shall cause A B to return to England and Wales by [date and time].

2. If it becomes apparent to X Local Authority that the said property will not be available for occupation by [date and time] it shall make an urgent application on 48 hours' notice to the other parties to vary the terms of paragraph 1 of this order.

Section B: Interim Orders

3. Upon his return to the jurisdiction it shall be lawful and in A B's best interests that he resides in the interim in his own home as aforesaid supported by a package of care provided by X Local Authority.

4. Upon his return to the jurisdiction A B's passport(s) shall be held by the Tipstaff to the order of the court.

5. Every person within the jurisdiction of this Court who is in a position to do so shall co-operate in assisting and securing the immediate return to England and Wales of A B.

6. These proceedings shall be heard restored for a hearing on [date] with a time estimate of one hour.

7. There is permission to serve this order upon C D:

    a. By personal service out of the jurisdiction; and/or

    b. By email to the address [insert] and/or

    c. By notification to her of its contents personally over the telephone.

8. There is permission to the applicant to disclose the case papers to XY Solicitors for their use in any proceedings taken in [name of State] to enforce compliance with this order.

9. XY Solicitors, represented by [name] is authorised to undertake all actions and take all steps as shall be appropriate and/or required in order to record and register and enforce before all relevant authorities and bodies in the [name of State] the order made before this Court on [date] for the return without delay to the Jurisdiction of the Courts of England and Wales of A B at the cost to X Local Authority and whom is authorised to liaise with and deal and act before the authorities in [name of State] and includes but is not limited to the Public Prosecutors Office, Public Police or National Guard Police, Judicial Police, Local Authority and/or any Commission for the protection of the vulnerable and/or shall be appropriate.

10. Liberty to any party to apply on notice to the court for further directions or to vary or discharge any of the terms of this order.

11. Costs reserved.

* * * * * * *

PART VIII   COURT OF PROTECTION PRACTICE 2016

Section C: EPA and LPA Orders

A selection of the most frequently used directions and disposal orders relating to EPAs and LPAs is reproduced below. These orders are generally made 'on paper' at the Central Office and Registry (since December 2013 at First Avenue House, 42–49 High Holborn, London WC1A 9JA but previously at Thomas More Building, RCJ and until January 2012 at Archway) following applications to object to registration and the content should be varied as appropriate to suit the circumstances of the particular case.

C 1
GENERAL TITLE

(Used for uncontested Orders)

THIS ORDER IS NOT VALID UNLESS IT BEARS THE IMPRESSED SEAL OF THE COURT OF PROTECTION ON ALL PAGES

COURT OF PROTECTION

MENTAL CAPACITY ACT 2005

Case No: 00000000

In the Matter of

[*A B*]

ORDER

[state nature of Order as in headings below]

MADE by District Judge *[name]* – *or authorised officer*

AT First Avenue House, 42–49 High Holborn, London WC1A 9JA [*or regional court address*]

ON [*date*]

* * * * * * *

C 2
DIRECTIONS on objections to EPA[20]
[GENERAL TITLE][21]

Whereas

(1) On [date] A B ('the donor') executed an instrument in which he appointed [names of attorney(s)] to be his (sole attorney) or (joint/joint and several attorneys) ('the attorney/attorneys') under an Enduring Power of Attorney ('the EPA')

(2) On [date] an application was made to the Public Guardian by [names] to register the EPA

(3) On [date] [name(s) of objectors] ('the objector/objectors') applied to the court to object to the registration of the EPA

(4) The objector has/objectors have filed evidence with his/her/their application

(5) Capacity to make/revoke the EPA is/is not in issue

IT IS ORDERED THAT

1. If they have not yet done so by 4.00 p.m. on [insert 14 days from date of order] the objector/objectors shall file with the court and serve on the attorney/attorneys

    (a) all witness evidence in form COP24 (attaching all documentary evidence relied on) and

    (b) if applicable all medical evidence relied on in respect of the donor's capacity to make and revoke the EPA

2. By 4.00 p.m. on the [insert 42 days from date of order] the attorney/attorneys shall file with the court and serve on the objector/objectors

    (a) all witness evidence in form COP24 (attaching all documentary evidence relied on); and

    (b) if applicable all medical evidence relied on in respect of the donor's capacity to make and revoke the EPA

3. The application will be referred to a judge on the first available date after [insert 63 days from date of order] who will decide without a hearing

    (a) whether to uphold or dismiss the objection(s) or

    (b) whether to list the matter for hearing with further directions

---

[20] Amend for male or female and singular or plural.
[21] Insert C1 above.

4. Any person who is affected by this order may apply to the court within 21 days of the order being served for reconsideration

To:

1. Objector(s) (or solicitors)
2. Attorney(s) (or solicitors)

* * * * * * *

C 3
ORDER on objections to EPA
[GENERAL TITLE]

Whereas

The court having considered the letter/application notice dated [date] received from the objector/objectors stating that he/she/they withdraw his/her/their application objecting to the registration of the Enduring Power of Attorney ('the EPA')

or

(1) On [date] A B ('the donor') executed an instrument in which he appointed [names of attorney(s)] to be his (sole attorney) or (joint/joint and several attorneys) ('the attorney/attorneys') under an Enduring Power of Attorney ('the EPA')

(2) On [date] an application was made to the Public Guardian by [names] to register the EPA

(3) On [date] [name(s) of objectors] ('the objector/objectors') applied to the court to object to the registration of the EPA

(4) The court has considered the evidence filed

(5) The burden of proof is on the objector/objectors

(6) Further to the written evidence filed the court considers that [recite reasons of the court]

IT IS ORDERED THAT

1. The proceedings are concluded

or

1. The application dated [date] to object to the registration is dismissed for the reason that none of the grounds of objection to the registration of the EPA has been established to the satisfaction of the court

2. The Public Guardian is directed to proceed with the registration of the EPA

3. Any person who is affected by this order may apply to the court within 21 days of the order being served for reconsideration

To:

1. Objector(s) (or solicitors)
2. Attorney(s) (or solicitors)
3. The Public Guardian, P.O. Box No. 16185, Birmingham, B2 2WH

* * * * * * *

C 4
ORDER on severance of provisions in EPA
[GENERAL TITLE]

Whereas

(1) On [date] A B executed an Enduring Power of Attorney ('the EPA') in which he appointed [names of attorney(s)] to be his (sole attorney) or (joint/joint and several attorneys) ('the attorney/attorneys')

(2) The EPA contains the provision that [text of provisions to be severed]

(3) Pursuant to paragraph 4(5) of Schedule 4 to the Mental Capacity Act 2005 the attorney(s) have referred to the court for its determination of the question as to the validity of the EPA

IT IS ORDERED THAT

1. The court determines that the provision would be ineffective as part of the EPA
2. The court hereby severs the provision
3. The court hereby gives notice to the Public Guardian that it has severed the provision and that when the attorney(s) apply to register the EPA the Public Guardian must register the instrument with a note to that effect attached to it
4. Any person who is affected by this order may apply to the court within 21 days of the order being served for reconsideration

To:

1. Applicant(s) (or solicitors)
2. The Public Guardian, P.O. Box No. 16185, Birmingham, B2 2WH

* * * * * * *

C 5
DIRECTIONS on objections to LPA[22]

[GENERAL TITLE][23]

Whereas

(1) On *[date]* A B ('the donor') executed an instrument in which he appointed *[names of attorney(s)]* to be his (sole attorney) or (joint/joint and several attorneys) ('the attorney/attorneys') under a Lasting Power of Attorney for [property and affairs] or [personal welfare] ('the LPA')[24]

(2) On *[date]* an application was made to the Public Guardian by *[names]* to register the LPA

(3) On *[date]* *[name(s) of objectors]* ('the objector/objectors') applied to the court to object to the registration of the LPA

(4) The objector has/objectors have filed evidence with his/her/their application

(5) Capacity to make/revoke the LPA is/is not in issue

IT IS ORDERED THAT

1. If they have not yet done so, by 4.00 p.m. on the *[insert 14 days from date of order]* the objector/objectors shall file with the court and serve on the attorney/attorneys

    (a) all witness evidence in form COP24 (attaching all documentary evidence relied on) and

    (b) if applicable, all medical evidence relied on in respect of the donor's capacity to make and revoke the EPA

2. By 4.00 p.m. on the *[insert 42 days from date of order]* the attorney/attorneys shall file with the court and serve on the objector/objectors

    (a) all witness evidence in form COP24 (attaching all documentary evidence relied on); and

    (b) if applicable, all medical evidence relied on in respect of the donor's capacity to make and revoke the EPA

3. The application will be referred to a judge on the first available date after *[insert 63 days from date of order]* who will decide without a hearing

    (a) whether to uphold or dismiss the objection(s) or

    (b) whether to list the matter for hearing with further directions

---

[22] Amend for male or female and singular or plural.
[23] Insert C1 above.
[24] In some instances both types of LPA will be dealt with together.

4. Any person who is affected by this order may apply to the court within 21 days of the order being served for reconsideration

To:

1. Objector(s) (or solicitors)
2. Attorney(s) (or solicitors)

* * * * * * * *

C 6
ORDER on objections to LPA
[GENERAL TITLE]

Whereas

The court having considered the letter/application notice dated [*date*] received from the objector/objectors stating that he/she/they withdraw his/her/their application objecting to the registration of the Lasting Power of Attorney for [*property and affairs*] or [*personal welfare*] ('the LPA')

or

(1) On [*date*] A B ('the donor') executed an instrument in which he appointed [*names of attorney(s)*] to be his (sole attorney) *or* (joint/joint and several attorneys) ('the attorney/attorneys') under a Lasting Power of Attorney for [property and affairs] *or* [personal welfare] ('the LPA')

(2) On [*date*] an application was made to the Public Guardian by [*names*] to register the LPA

(3) On [*date*] [*name(s) of objectors*] ('the objector/objectors') applied to the court to object to the registration of the LPA

(4) The court has considered the evidence filed

(5) The burden of proof is on the objector/objectors

(6) Further to the written evidence filed the court considers that [*recite reasons of the court*]

IT IS ORDERED THAT

1. The proceedings are concluded

or

1. The application dated [*date*] to object to the registration is dismissed for the reason that none of the grounds of objection to the registration of the LPA has been established to the satisfaction of the court

2. The Public Guardian is directed to proceed with the registration of the LPA for [property and affairs] or [personal welfare]

3. Any person who is affected by this order may apply to the court within 21 days of the order being served for reconsideration

To:

1. Objector(s) (or solicitors)
2. Attorney(s) (or solicitors)
3. The Public Guardian, P.O. Box No. 16185, Birmingham, B2 2WH

* * * * * * *

C 7
ORDER on severance of provisions in LPA
[GENERAL TITLE]

Whereas

(1) On [date] A B executed a Lasting Power of Attorney for [property and affairs] or [personal welfare] ('the LPA') in which he appointed [names of attorney(s)] to be his [sole attorney] or [joint/joint and several attorneys] ('the attorney/attorneys')

(2) The LPA contains the provision that [text of provisions to be severed]

(3) Pursuant to section 23(1) of the Mental Capacity Act 2005 the attorney(s) have referred to the court for its determination of the question as to the validity of the LPA

IT IS ORDERED THAT

1. The court determines that the provision would be ineffective as part of the LPA
2. The court hereby severs the provision
3. The court hereby gives notice to the Public Guardian that it has severed the provision and that when the attorney(s) apply to register the LPA the Public Guardian must register the instrument with a note to that effect attached to it
4. Any person who is affected by this order may apply to the court within 21 days of the order being served for reconsideration

To:

1. Applicant(s) (or solicitors)
2. The Public Guardian, P.O. Box No. 16185, Birmingham, B2 2WH

* * * * * * *

Section C: EPA and LPA Orders

C 8
DIRECTIONS on transfer to a regional court
[GENERAL TITLE]

Whereas

(1) On [date] A B executed a Lasting/Enduring Power of Attorney [for [property and affairs] or [personal welfare]] ('the LPA/EPA') in which he appointed [names of attorney(s)] to be his [sole attorney] or [joint/joint and several attorneys] ('the attorney/attorneys')

(2) Evidence has been filed and served by the donor/objector/objectors and the attorney/attorneys pursuant to the directions order of [date]

(3) It is appropriate for the matter to be listed for oral hearing

IT IS ORDERED THAT

1. The matter be transferred to the regional court sitting at [regional court]

2. The matter be listed on the first open date after [21 days] on the direction of the regional judge (suggested time estimate [2] hours)

3. The evidence filed and served pursuant to the directions order of [date] shall stand as evidence in chief and no further evidence shall be filed and served without the permission of the court

4. An agreed and fully paginated bundle of documents be lodged with the court by the objector(s) not less than five days before the hearing, and skeleton arguments shall be filed and exchanged by all parties no less than three working days before the hearing

4. Any person who is affected by this order may apply to the court within 21 days of the order being served for reconsideration

To:

1. Objector(s) (or solicitors)

2. Applicant(s) (or solicitors)

* * * * * * *

C 9
DIRECTION to encourage Mediation

In the interim the Objector is directed to meet with the Attorney (or a solicitor instructed by him) for the purpose of discussions with a view to resolving any misunderstandings between them and reaching agreement whereby the Attorney may continue to handle the affairs of the Donor pursuant to the enduring power of attorney. To this intent

(a) the Attorney is released from any duty of confidentiality to the Donor in regard to his financial affairs

(b) both parties are to write to District Judge [*name*] no later than [date] stating whether such meeting has taken place and whether a solution may be possible

* * * * * * *

Section D: Case Management Directions Orders

There is a perception that one of the weaknesses of the new Court of Protection is that there are no precedents for case management orders. In consequence the nominated district judges constantly find themselves needing to 're-invent the wheel' leading to a lack of consistency. Also practitioners are denied the opportunity to submit a draft order in advance of a directions hearing based on their knowledge of the case thereby assisting the judges with their work.

In this Part a few suggested pro-forma orders are set out, based on the orders that some judges have been making, in the hope that this may promote the development of more useful precedents.

* * * * * * *

D 1
CASE MANAGEMENT CHECKLIST

This checklist is reproduced first to help with the content and structure of any case management order.

PRELIMINARY

JURISDICTION

Does the Court have jurisdiction based on

☐	Residence	See Hague Conference
☐	Domicile	Chapter 9
☐	Property	CoPR, r 87

PERMISSION

Does the applicant need permission to apply

☐	property and affairs	CoPR, Pt 8
☐	personal welfare	CoPR, Pt 8

LACK OF CAPACITY

Does 'P' lack capacity in regard to

☐	property and affairs	MCA, s 2
☐	personal welfare	MCA, s 2
☐	conduct of proceedings	MCA, s 2 & CoPR, Pt 17

APPLICATION

Is the application:

☐	a new application	CoPR, Pt 9
☐	within existing proceedings	CoPR, Pt 10
☐	in proper form	CoPR, Pt 4 and Pt 9 or Pt 10

TRANSFER
Should the application be transferred to:
- ☐ a Regional Hearing Centre — CoPR, Pt 2
- ☐ a particular Nominated Judge — CoPR, Pt 2

PERSONS INVOLVED

NOTICE
Has notice been given to:
- ☐ 'P' — CoPR, Pt 7
- ☐ Y — CoPR, Pt 9
- ☐ anyone else who should be given an opportunity to participate

PARTIES
Have the following been identified:
- ☐ the Applicant(s) — CoPR, rr 73 and 85
- ☐ the Respondents — CoPR, rr 73 and 85

Should:
- ☐ 'P' be a party — CoPR, r 73
- ☐ any other persons be invited to become parties — CoPR, rr 73 and 85

LITIGATION FRIENDS
Does:
- ☐ 'P' need a litigation friend — CoPR, Pt 17
- ☐ any other party need a litigation friend — CoPR, Pt 17

DIRECTIONS

DISCLOSURE
Are directions needed for: — CoPR Pt 16
- ☐ disclosure of documents
- ☐ inspection of documents

EVIDENCE
Are directions needed for: — CoPR Pt 14
- ☐ exchange of witness statements
- ☐ examination of witness

EXPERTS
Is there a need for expert evidence: — CoPR Pt 15
- ☐ what discipline
- ☐ produced by party
- ☐ jointly instructed

REPORTS
Will the Court be assisted by a report from: — CoPR Pt 14 – PD14E
- ☐ a General Visitor
- ☐ a Special Visitor
- ☐ the Public Guardian

☐ social services
☐ a health authority

HEARING

REQUIREMENT

At this stage: CoPR, Pt 13
☐ can a final order be made
☐ can a provisional order be made
☐ should a telephone directions hearing be listed
☐ should an attended directions hearing be listed
☐ can a final hearing be listed

ADMINISTRATIVE

FILING OF DOCUMENTS

Should these be sent:
☐ to the RCJ
☐ to a Regional Hearing Centre
☐ to a nominated Judge by email

* * * * * * *

D 2
MULTI-PURPOSE DIRECTIONS ORDER

This pro-forma Order contains many provisions that may be adopted when initial Directions are given by a nominated District Judge. It should be modified to meet the particular circumstances.

THIS ORDER IS NOT VALID UNLESS IT BEARS THE IMPRESSED SEAL OF THE COURT OF PROTECTION ON ALL PAGES

COURT OF PROTECTION

MENTAL CAPACITY ACT 2005

Case No: 00000000

IN THE MATTER OF [*FULL NAME*]

(referred to in this Order as '*A B*')

DIRECTIONS ORDER

MADE by District Judge [*name*]

AT First Avenue House, 42–49 High Holborn, London WC1A 9JA [*or regional court address*]

ON [*date*]

UPON THE APPLICATION OF [*name*]

AND UPON READING the papers *and/or*

AND UPON HEARING counsel/solicitors for [*name*] and – *complete as appropriate*

WHEREAS

1. An application has been made by [*name and any relationship to A B*] for an order under the Mental Capacity Act 2005 in relation to *A B*

2. The application concerns *A B*'s personal welfare *and/or* property and affairs

3. [The Court has granted permission for the application to be brought] – *where required*

4. [The application has been referred to a nominated District Judge at this regional Court]

5. Acknowledgments have been received from [*names and relationship to A B (if any)*]

[*Personal welfare application*]

6. The personal welfare decisions that may need to be considered by the Court appear to be: – *complete as appropriate*

    (a) where and with whom *A B* is to live

    (b) with whom *A B* is to have contact

    (c) whether [*name*] is to be prohibited from having contact with to *A B*

    (d) whether *A B* should *give/refuse* consent to the carrying out or continuation of treatment by a person providing health care for *A B*

    (e) whether *A B* should take part in particular leisure or social activities

    (f) [*identify any other decision*]

7. It appears that there is a dispute *and/or* uncertainty as to the decisions that should be made

8. The application was accompanied by evidence that *A B* is personally unable to make these decisions because of an impairment of, or a disturbance in the functioning of, the mind or brain

[*Property and affairs application*]

9. The application was accompanied by evidence that *A B* is personally unable to make various decisions regarding the management of property and financial affairs because of an impairment of, or a disturbance in the functioning of, the mind or brain

Section D: Case Management Directions Orders

10. The application was also accompanied by an inventory of the assets and liabilities and the income and expenditure of *A B*

[*All applications*]

11. The Court is satisfied on the evidence already presented that *A B* does not have capacity to make a decision on these matter *or*

    There is a **preliminary issue** as to whether *A B* has capacity to make decisions on these matters

12. Notice of the application has been given to A B and to relatives and other persons to be notified in accordance with the Court of Protection Rules 2007

THE COURT NOW ORDERS THAT

The parties

1. The parties to these proceedings are

    1.1. the Applicant(s), being [*names*]

    1.2. [*name any other person identified at this stage*]

    1.3. *A B* – *if appropriate at this stage*

    [The Official Solicitor is to be served by the Court with a copy of the application and this Order and to notify the Court within 8 weeks of service as to whether he consents to being appointed as litigation friend of *A B*]

2. Any other person (whether or not served with notice of the application) who wishes to be joined as a party must apply to the Court at the earliest opportunity

3. *A B* need not be joined as a party to these proceedings *or*

    A copy of this Order is to be served by the Court on *A B* and any request that *he/she* be joined as a party (which may be made by *A B* or someone on *his/her* behalf) is to be made in writing to the Court within 14 days of service *or*

Involvement of person to whom application relates - *if not a party*

4. *A B* even though not a party should be involved in these proceedings to the extent that *he/she* is able to contribute and wishes to do so

    4.1 a party who does not serve statements or documents on *A B* must be in a position to justify this at the hearing

    4.2 *A B* is to be enabled to attend any hearing if such attendance would not be too distressing or detrimental to health

Preliminary issue - *if appropriate*

5. The proceedings are stayed pending the determination of the preliminary issue and the following directions relate to that issue only

   or

   At the commencement of the [directions] hearing the Court will address the preliminary issue

6. The parties are to send to the Court and copy to each other no later than [*date*] any evidence that is to be relied upon as to the capacity of *A B*:

   6.1. medical evidence shall preferably be in the form of a report

   6.2. other evidence shall preferably be in the form of a statement exhibiting any documents relied upon

7. The Public Guardian is to arrange for one of the Court of Protection Special Visitors to attend upon and assess the capacity of *A B* at the present time in regard to decisions of the nature identified in this Order

   7.1. A report is to be produced to the Court before [*date*]

   7.2. The Court will send a copy of the report to the parties and such other persons as the Court may direct

Statements

8. All statements to be relied upon in these proceedings shall BE IN Form COP24

   8.1. be headed with the title to these proceedings as set out in this Order

   8.2. be in legible form (preferably typed) and with numbered paragraphs

   8.3. commence with the name and address of the person making the statement

   8.4. have attached any documents referred to

   8.5. be dated and signed at the end

   8.6. be copied with any attached documents to all other parties (or their solicitors) at the same time as they are sent to the Court

9. The Applicant(s) shall no later than [*date*] send to the Court a statement (or separate statements) in support of their application which shall

   9.1. identify the declarations or orders that the Court is requested to make

   9.2. concisely set out the facts and evidence to be relied upon

10. The other parties shall no later than [*date*] send to the Court their statements in response to the statement(s) received from the Applicant(s)

Section D: Case Management Directions Orders

Documentary and other evidence

11. Each party shall send to the Court and the other parties no later than [*date*] a copy of any other documents to be relied upon

12. The evidence of any other person that is to be relied upon is to be submitted in the form of a statement or a signed and dated letter to the Court [by *date*] or [at least 14 days before the hearing] and copied to the other parties

Reports – *when required*

13. The Public Guardian is requested to arrange or produce the following report no later than [*date*]

    13.1. a report as to the contents of any file maintained by the Office of the Public Guardian [or the former Public Guardianship Office]

    13.2. a report by the [*name*] social services department or [*name*] health authority as to [*identify the nature of the report*]

    13.3. a report by one of the Court of Protection General/Special Visitors as to [*identify the nature of the report*]

14. The Court will send a copy of the report to the parties and such other persons as the Court may direct or The Court will decide the extent to which this report is to be disclosed

Directions hearing – *when required*

15. There will be a directions hearing before District Judge [*name*] at [*name and address of court*] on [*date*] at [*time*] with a time estimate of [*duration of hearing*]

    15.1. the parties should attend either personally or by their legal representatives

    15.2. this hearing may be by telephone and the solicitors for the [*party*] shall arrange the telephone conference in the manner provided for in the Civil Procedure Rules 1998 (PD 23 para 6)

Hearing – *if required at this stage*

16. There will be a full hearing before District Judge [*name*] at [*name and address of court*] on [*date*] at [*time*] with a time estimate of [*duration of hearing*]

    16.1. the parties are encouraged to attend (with or without their legal representatives)

    16.2. the hearing may continue in the absence of a party who does not attend or is not represented

    16.3. the Court has a discretion to decide who may be present for the whole or a part of the hearing

17. The Court may refuse to consider any statements or documents that have not been disclosed to the other parties prior to the hearing

18. The parties should be prepared to produce any financial records that are available (or a summary of the financial position of the *A B*) when they attend the hearing – *financial cases only*

19. If the hearing cannot be concluded further directions may be given to ensure that outstanding matters are properly dealt with at an adjourned hearing

Costs

20. A party who seeks to recover costs or expenses shall bring a summary or estimate of those costs to the hearing on the basis that

    20.1. the Court may wish to consider a summary assessment or payment of a specified contribution

    20.2. where justified costs may be ordered to be paid out of *A B's* estate

    20.3. a party who has acted unreasonably may be refused costs and ordered to pay the costs of another party in whole or in part

Further directions – *where Order made without a hearing*

21. This Order was made of the Court's own initiative without a hearing and without notice pursuant to Rule 27 of the Court of Protection Rules 2007 and any person affected by it may apply pursuant to Rule 89 within 21 days of the date on which the Order was served to have it varied or set aside

22. Any request to postpone the hearing or for further or other directions should be made with reasons to the Court in writing within 21 days of service of this Order

23. All communications with the Court in response to this order shall state the above Case Number and be sent to

    Court of Protection, First Avenue House, 42–49 High Holborn, London WC1A 9JA *or state address of regional court*

    [and if urgent or otherwise appropriate may be copied to District Judge [*name*] by email at the following address: [*email address of judge*]] – *not all judges are willing to communicate in this way*

* * * * * * *

D 3
DIRECTIONS on contested application[25]

[GENERAL TITLE][26]

Whereas

(1) Upon considering an application by [*name*] ('the Applicant(s)') for *describe application*

(2) And upon considering objections by [*name*] and [*name*] ('the Objector(s)')

IT IS ORDERED THAT

1. If they have not yet done so, by 4.00 p.m. on the [*insert 14 days from date of order*] the Objector(s) shall file with the court and serve on the Applicant(s)

   (a) A single A4 sheet identifying specifically the grounds of objection pursuant to the Mental Capacity Act 2005

   (b) A statement in Form COP24 upon which they intend to rely in objection

   (c) Medical evidence (if any) upon which they wish to rely as to capacity

2. By 4.00 p.m. on the [*insert 42 days from date of order*] the Applicant(s) shall file with the court and serve on the objector/objectors

   (a) A statement in Form COP24 upon which they intend to rely in objection

   (b) Medical evidence (if any) upon which they wish to rely as to capacity

3. The application will be referred to a judge on the first available date after [*insert 63 days from date of order*] who will decide without a hearing

   (a) whether to uphold or dismiss the objection(s) or

   (b) whether to list the matter for oral hearing if necessary with further directions

or

3. The final hearing is listed on [date] (time estimate 1 hour) at Court of Protection, First Avenue House, 42–49 High Holborn, London WC1A 9JA or **state address of regional court** parties shall attend at least 30 minutes before the hearing for final consultation

---

[25] Amend for male or female and singular or plural.
[26] Insert C1 above.

(a) No hearing may be vacated save with the prior consent of a Judge of the Court of Protection

(b) Permission for any party to request further directions

(c) The party requesting the directions to fax the application to the court and to the parties and to be responsible for the organisation of the telephone conference hearing

4. Any person who is affected by this order may apply to the court within 21 days of the order being served for reconsideration

To:

1. Objector(s) (or solicitors)

2. Applicant(s) (or solicitors)

* * * * * * *

D 4

DIRECTIONS on gift or statutory will application

[GENERAL TITLE]

Whereas

An application has been made by [*name*] ('the Applicant') [as attorney appointed by A B by a registered Lasting/Enduring Power of Attorney] or [the deputy for property and affairs of A B] for an order to execute a statutory will/deed of variation/gift under the Mental Capacity Act 2005.

IT IS ORDERED THAT

1. A B is joined as a party, and subject to his consent, the Official Solicitor is appointed to act on behalf of A B as Litigation Friend

2. The Applicant shall serve notice of this application upon [*name other people to be joined*] who shall be joined as parties to the proceedings

3. The Applicant shall no later than [*date*] serve on each party a copy of

   (a) the application

   (b) the statement of evidence in support

   (c) the Exhibits and documents required pursuant to the Court of Protection Rules 2007 Part 9 Practice Direction F.6

4. The statements of evidence that any party seeks to rely upon at the final hearing shall be filed and served by [*date*] and in the event that oral evidence is to be given those statements shall stand as evidence in chief

5. The parties shall agree not less than 5 working days before the final hearing the contents of the final hearing bundle and the bundle shall be filed with the Appeals and Listing section of the Court of Protection by

the Applicant not less than 3 working days before the final hearing together with any skeleton arguments and authorities

6. The final hearing is listed on [*date and time*] (time estimate 2 hours) at Court of Protection, First Avenue House, 42–49 High Holborn, London WC1A 9JA *or state address of regional court*

    (a) The parties shall attend at least 30 minutes before the hearing for final consultation

    (b) No hearing may be vacated save with the prior consent of a Judge of the Court of Protection

    (c) Permission for any party to request further directions

    (d) The party requesting the directions to fax the application to the court and to the parties and to be responsible for the organisation of the telephone conference hearing

7. Any person who is affected by this order may apply to the court within 21 days of the order being served for reconsideration

* * * * * * * *

D 5
DIRECTIONS on transfer to regional court of personal welfare application

[*GENERAL TITLE*]

Whereas

An application has been made for a Declaration Order under the Mental Capacity Act 2005 by [name of council] ('the Applicant') to determine the issues of A B's residence/care and/or contact/where he/she should live, his/her care and supervision, with whom he/she should have contact and under what supervision and whether this constitutes a deprivation of his/her liberty

IT IS ORDERED THAT

1. Permission is granted pursuant to section 50(2) of the Mental Capacity Act 2005 to the Applicant to make this application

2. A B is joined as a party, and subject to his consent, the Official Solicitor is appointed to act on his/her behalf as Litigation Friend

3. The Applicant shall forthwith serve notice of this application upon [*name other people to be joined*] who shall be joined as parties to the proceedings, only if they acknowledge and contest the proceedings

4. The Applicant shall forthwith serve on each party

    (a) a copy of this order

(b) the application (forms COP1, COP1B and COP2 and witness statement of [*name*])

In addition the Applicant shall serve on the Official Solicitor

    (a) such reports from social services, National Health organisations and independent advocates as may be in the possession of the Applicant

    (b) any proposed care plan

    (c) copies of all relevant medical evidence and supporting exhibits and report

5. The case shall be listed for a directions and interim hearing at the Regional Court in [address] on a date to be fixed not later than [date] with a time estimate of 2 hours

    (a) The parties must attend at least 30 minutes before the hearing for final consultation

    (b) Not less than 2 working days before the hearing the Applicant shall file with the Regional Court an indexed paginated case management bundle for the use of the judge containing so far as the same has been obtained to date

        (i) applications and appendices

        (ii) orders

        (iii) witness evidence

        (iv) medical evidence

        (v) other expert evidence

        (vi) care plans

    (c) Not less than 3 working days before the directions hearing each party shall file with the Regional Court and serve on the other parties

        (i) a position statement, setting out on a single page the issues and the party's stance on the issue

        (ii) a draft of any orders or directions sought

        (iii) details of any expert the party will be proposing to instruct

        (iv) copies of any authorities relied upon

6. For the purpose of funding his legal costs of this application the Official Solicitor is authorized to

    (a) make all investigations into the property and financial means of the protected party

(b) require that his costs are paid from such property or charged thereon

(c) apply for public funding if appropriate and to sign all or any documentation required to exercise the authority given by this order

4. Any person who is affected by this order may apply to the court within 21 days of the order being served for reconsideration

* * * * * * *

D 6
FIRST DIRECTIONS ORDER
family dispute as to residence and contact

This is an example of a first Directions Order made by a Regional District Judge in a case where there is a dispute between family members as to where an elderly parent should live and whether contact to certain members should be restricted. It is not considered proportionate for the parent to be made a party because the issue is between the family members and sufficient evidence of the care choices will be provided.

THIS ORDER IS NOT VALID UNLESS IT BEARS THE IMPRESSED SEAL OF THE COURT OF PROTECTION IN THE BOTTOM RIGHT HAND CORNER ON ALL PAGES

COURT OF PROTECTION

MENTAL CAPACITY ACT 2005

Case No: 000000

IN THE MATTER OF [*FULL NAME*]

(referred to in this Order as 'Mrs B')

DIRECTIONS ORDER

MADE by District Judge [*name*]

AT [*name*] Court of [*address*]

ON [*date*]

UPON THE APPLICATION OF [*name*]

WHEREAS

1. An application has been made by [*name*] through solicitors for an order under the Mental Capacity Act 2005 in relation to her mother Mrs B

2. The application concerns the personal welfare of Mrs B

3. The decisions that may need to be considered by the Court appear to be:

(a) whether a personal welfare Deputy should be appointed for Mrs B

(b) whether Mrs B is to live and be cared for in the vicinity of [*town 1*] or [*town 2*]

(c) whether any person is to be prohibited from having contact with Mrs B

4. There is a dispute and/or uncertainty as to the decisions that should be made

5. The application was accompanied by evidence that Mrs B is personally unable to make these decisions because of an impairment of, or a disturbance in the functioning of, the mind or brain

6. The Court is satisfied on the evidence already presented that Mrs B does not have capacity to make a decision on these matter

7. Notice of the application has been given to Mrs B and to relatives and other persons to be notified in accordance with the Court of Protection Rules 2007

8. The Court has power to record the wishes of Mrs B and any decisions that she would make but not to direct that any specific care provision be provided for her

THE COURT NOW ORDERS THAT:

1. Permission is granted for this application to be brought

2. The appointment of a personal welfare Deputy is refused on the basis that it is sufficient for the Court to make decisions on the matters in issue

The parties

3. The parties to these proceedings are:

   3.1. the Applicant, being [*name*] of [*address*].

   3.2. [*name*] (son) of [*address*]

   3.3. [*name*] (daughter) of [*address*]

4. Any other person including a local authority (whether or not served with notice of the application) who wishes to be joined as a party must apply to the Court at the earliest opportunity

5. Mrs B need not be joined as a party to these proceedings

Involvement of the local authorities

6. The Applicant shall send a copy of this Order to the social services authorities for [*town 1*] and [*town 2*] having present or prospective responsibility for the care of Mrs B

7. If those authorities do not wish to become parties they may nevertheless send to the Court a statement addressing the best interests of Mrs B and exhibiting any relevant documents by [*date*]

8. Any such statements shall be copied by the Court to the parties

Statements

9. All statements to be relied upon in these proceedings shall: [set out as in B2 Multi-Purpose Directions Order]

10. The Applicant's statement dated [*date*] is admitted in support of her application but she shall no later than [*date*] send to the Court an updated statement which shall:

    10.1. identify the declarations or orders that the Court is requested to make, and in particular specifying any care home to which Mrs B could be moved (including whether there is a vacancy and funding can be available)

    10.2. concisely set out any further facts and evidence to be relied upon

11. The other parties shall no later than [*date*] send to the Court their statements in response to the statements received from the Applicant

Documentary and other evidence

12. Each party shall send to the Court and the other parties no later than [*date*] a copy of any other documents to be relied upon

13. The evidence of any other person that is to be relied upon is to be submitted in the form of a statement or a signed and dated letter to the Court at least 14 days before the hearing and copied to the other parties

Hearing

14. There will be a hearing before District Judge [*name*] at [*court address*] on [*date*] at [*time*] with a time estimate of [*duration*]

    14.1. the parties are encouraged to attend (with or without their legal representatives)

    14.2. the hearing may continue in the absence of a party who does not attend or is not represented

    14.3. the Court has a discretion to decide who may be present for the whole or a part of the hearing

15. The Court may refuse to consider any statements or documents that have not been disclosed to the other parties prior to the hearing

16. The parties should be prepared to produce any financial records that are available (or a summary of the financial position of Mrs B) when they attend the hearing

17. If the hearing cannot be concluded further directions may be given to ensure that outstanding matters are properly dealt with at an adjourned hearing

Further directions

18. Any party may apply within 14 days of receipt of this Order for its terms to be varied or reconsidered

19. All communications with the Court in response to this order shall state the above Case Number and be sent to: [*as in D2 Multi-Purpose Directions Order*]

* * * * * * * *

D 7
DIRECTIONS ORDER
'adult care' case

This is an example of a first Directions Order made in a case where there had been previous care proceedings relating to an abused child with severe learning disabilities. The child has now attained, or is shortly to attain, legal majority whereupon the care order under the Children Act 1989 is no longer effective but the parents seek to intervene.

THIS ORDER IS NOT VALID UNLESS IT BEARS THE IMPRESSED SEAL OF THE COURT OF PROTECTION ON ALL PAGES

COURT OF PROTECTION
MENTAL CAPACITY ACT 2005

Case No: 00000000

IN THE MATTER OF [*FULL NAME*]

(referred to in this Order as '*R M*')

BETWEEN:

X COUNTY COUNCIL

Applicant

and

R M [*full name*]
by her litigation friend The
Official Solicitor

The person to whom
the application relates

M M [*full name – father*]

First Respondent

and

D M [*full name*]

Second Respondent

DIRECTIONS ORDER

BEFORE District Judge [*name*] sitting at First Avenue House, 42–49 High Holborn, London WC1A 9JA [*or regional court address*]

On [*date*]

UPON reading all documents filed and in particular [*list relevant documents*]

AND UPON HEARING by way of a telephone conference the solicitor for the Applicant local authority, counsel for *R M* and the solicitor for the First and Second Respondents [*or as appropriate*]

BY CONSENT IT IS ORDERED THAT:

Parties

1. D M (step-mother of *R M*) be named as Second Respondent in these proceedings

2. Having consented the Official Solicitor is appointed to act as *R M*'s litigation friend

3. In the interests of fairness [*name*] is given 14 days from the date of this order to apply to be made a party to these proceedings

4. The Applicant is to use its best endeavours to locate [*name*] (*R M*'s natural mother) on the basis that:

    (a) the Respondents have agreed to provide such contact details as they possess

    (b) if the Applicant locates her it is to serve her with all papers from these proceedings and the Official Solicitor is to be informed of her address

5. *R M*'s current address is not to be disclosed to the Respondents or any other person without the permission of the Official Solicitor or further order of the Court

Statements

6. The Applicant by [*date*] file and serve on all parties and instructed experts a statement setting out the history of its involvement with *R M*, details of her current care arrangements and its view on future arrangements

7. The Respondents by [*date*] file and serve on all parties and instructed experts their statements in response to the Applicant's statement and containing all further information upon which they wish to rely

Expert reports

8. The Applicant, the Official Solicitor and the Respondents shall instruct an independent consultant psychiatrist in learning disabilities with particular expertise in the area of Autistic Spectrum Disorder, to investigate and report as to

    (a) *R M*'s capacity and best interests regarding future contact arrangements with the Respondents and others, including her sibling/half-siblings

    (b) where *R M* should reside and the care she should receive

9. The Applicant, the Official Solicitor and the Respondent shall instruct an independent social worker with a specialism in working with young adults and autistic spectrum disorders and learning difficulties, to investigate and report as to

    (a) *R M*'s best interests regarding future contact arrangements with the Respondents and others, including her sibling/half siblings

    (b) where *R M* should reside and the care she should receive

10. The identities of the consultant psychiatrist and independent social worker are to be notified to the Court by [*date*]

    (a) These experts are to be instructed by way of joint letters of instruction to be drafted by the Official Solicitor by [*date*]

    (b) The cost of instructing these experts be shared equally between the parties and be deemed a reasonable cost for the purposes of any public funding certificates

    (c) To the extent that they consider it necessary these experts have permission to interview *R M* and any other person they consider to be necessary

11. These experts have permission to read *R M*'s social services' files and medical records, including any general practitioner records which are to be produced by her G.P. on the written request of the Official Solicitor who shall make such request within 14 days from the date of this order

Disclosure

12. The Official Solicitor and his representative have permission to read R. M's social services files and to draw any material they consider relevant to the attention of the Court and the parties

13. The Applicant do disclose to the Official Solicitor all papers from the judicial review proceedings brought against it by the Second Respondent, under claim number [*number*] within 7 days from the date of this order

14. The Chief Constable of [*place*] is directed to disclose to the Official Solicitor by [*date*] all information held relating to the investigation into *R M*'s allegation made on [*date*] of assault against the First Respondent

(a) such information shall on receipt be disclosed by the Official Solicitor to the other parties and any experts instructed within these proceedings

(b) there be permission to apply as to the need for and implementation of this order

15. The Applicant is to seek permission of [*name*] County Court to disclose papers from the care proceedings brought by the Applicant pursuant to section 31 of the Children Act 1989, under case number [*number*], relating to *R M* The papers are to then be disclosed to the other parties and any experts instructed within these proceedings

Interim Orders

16. In the interim it will not be unlawful for *R M* to continue to reside in her current accommodation or for the Applicant to restrict her contact with her family at its discretion

Hearing

17. The matter be listed for a further directions hearing before District Judge [*name*] at [*name*] Court [*address*] with a time estimate of [*time*] on the first available date after [*date*] to consider

    (a) the reports of the independent experts

    (b) any further directions

    (c) timetabling of a final hearing

18. Costs reserved save for detailed assessment of any publicly funded parties' costs

* * * * * * *

D 8
DIRECTIONS ORDER
local authority personal welfare application

This is an example of an Order made when there was a threat by a mother to remove an incapacitated adult child from health authority care. It contains many provisions that may be requested by the Official Solicitor when acting as litigation friend of the person to whom the application relates. Not all clauses will be required and it should be modified to meet the particular circumstances.

THIS ORDER IS NOT VALID UNLESS IT BEARS THE IMPRESSED SEAL OF THE COURT OF PROTECTION ON ALL PAGES

COURT OF PROTECTION

MENTAL CAPACITY ACT 2005

Case No: 00000000

IN THE MATTER OF [*FULL NAME*]

(referred to in this Order as '*AM*')

BETWEEN

[NAME] COUNTY COUNCIL ('The Council')

Applicant

-and-

[NAME] ('AM')
by his litigation friend, the Official Solicitor

First Respondent

and the person to whom the application relates

[NAME] ('PM')

Second Respondent

[NAME] NHS FOUNDATION TRUST ('The Trust')

Third Respondent

-and-

[NAME] PRIMARY CARE TRUST ('The PCT')

Fourth Respondent

BEFORE District Judge [*name*] sitting at First Avenue House, 42–49 High Holborn, London WC1A 9JA [*or regional court address*]

On [*date*]

UPON HEARING the solicitor for the Applicant, counsel for the First Respondent and the Second Respondent in person [and the social worker involved in care provision] (there being no attendance on behalf of Third and Fourth Respondents) [*or as appropriate*]

AND UPON reading the bundle of documents lodged by the Applicant *or* all documents filed and in particular [*list relevant documents*]

AND UPON it being recorded that the Fourth Respondent is the supervisory authority in respect of the relevant DoLS authorisation and the Third Respondent is the relevant managing authority.

AND UPON the bases that

(a) the parties are those recorded in the Heading to this Order

(b) the parties shall henceforth be referred in all orders and documents in these proceedings by the abbreviations appearing in brackets after their names (which shall for clarity be included in future Headings)

Section D: Case Management Directions Orders

(c) the mother of AM shall be referred to as 'NJ'

(d) the responsible treating medical practitioners, social workers and any witness (other than an expert witness who gives evidence in these proceedings whether by statement or otherwise in writing or orally) shall be referred to by their initials

IN THE INTERIM and until further order IT IS ORDERED AND DECLARED that:

1. AM lacks capacity to litigate in these proceedings and to make decisions

    (a) as to his residence

    (b) as to the contact he should have with others

    (c) as to the care package that he should receive

    (d) about treatment in relation to both his general health and his medical needs

2. It is lawful and in AM's best interests that he continues to

    (a) reside at the [name] Home ('the nursing home') in the care of The PCT

    (b) have contact with his family by agreement between individual members and the Council

    (c) receive a care package provided by The PCT in accordance with his assessed needs

IT IS FURTHER ORDERED AND DIRECTED that:

Parties

3. The Official Solicitor having accepted the invitation of the Court to act as litigation friend of AM

    (a) is appointed as litigation friend

    (b) is authorised in the name and on behalf of AM to apply for and accept any offer of public funding made to him by the Legal Services Commission and to sign the offer of public funding on AM's behalf

4. The Trust and The PCT are made parties to these proceedings

5. PM (the father of AM) is also made a party at his request

6. Although NJ (the mother of AM) has not engaged with the Court and is not presently a party she is to receive from the Council a copy of this Order and may be shown and (at her request) given copies of all documents in the proceedings subject to the requirements of confidentiality recorded at the end of this Order

Disclosure

7. The Council file and serve on all parties no later than [*date*] a copy of the Order dated [*date*] appointing its nominee to be a receiver for AM (becoming a deputy for financial affairs from [*date*])

8. Any third party is hereby directed and authorised to release to the Official Solicitor such information and documents as he may require on behalf of AM in the course of his investigations

Documents

9. The Council, the Trust and the PCT prepare and serve upon the Official Solicitor no later than [*date*] a paginated bundle of any medical, social work or other care records (including those relating to safeguarding adults meetings and deprivation of liberty issues) held by them in relation to AM

    (a) from [*date*] to [*date*]

    (b) pre-dating [*date*] if relevant

Experts

10. The parties instruct on a joint basis

    (a) a consultant psychiatrist or psychologist to prepare a report on AM's capacity to make decisions of the nature specified in paragraph 1 of this Order and if AM lacks capacity, what is in his best interests in respect of residence, care and contact

    (b) an independent social worker to prepare a report as to AM's best interests in respect of residence, care and contact

11. The identity of such experts be agreed between the instructing parties by [*date*]

12. The Official Solicitor draft letters of instruction to the experts, to be circulated to the instructing parties for comment by 4pm on [*date*] and sent to the experts no later than 4pm on [*date*]. In the event of any disagreement, the parties may send side letters to the experts

13. These experts have permission to interview AM and read all and any records in respect of AM

14. The experts file and serve their reports by [*date*]

15. The costs of the instruction of the experts and their attendance at court to give evidence be met in the following shares and the same be a reasonable expense for the purposes of any party's LSC public funding certificate:

    (a) The Council – one third

    (b) The Official Solicitor – one third

(c) The Trust and The PCT – one third (to be shared between them in such proportions as they may agree)

Further Evidence

16. The statement of [*name*] (social worker) dated [*date*] and the Minutes of the multi-disciplinary meeting on [*date*] be admitted in evidence and copies made available to the parties

17. By 4pm on [*date*] The Council (and The PCT and The Trust if so advised) file and serve all statements upon which they intend to rely as to AM's best interests and his eligibility for detention under Schedule 1A of the Mental Capacity Act 2005

18. By 4pm on [*date*] The Official Solicitor file and serve any statements upon which he intends to rely as to AM's best interests

Procedure

19. The Council by 4pm on [*date*] produce an index for a bundle of all documents to be used at the next hearing, and serve it on the other parties

    (a) The bundle be prepared in accordance with the President's Direction in respect of the format of bundles in the Family Division

    (b) The index be updated and circulated as appropriate when further documents are filed in these proceedings

20. This directions hearing is adjourned to [*time*] on [*date*] before District Judge [*name*] at [*name*] Court [*address*] with a time estimate of [*duration*]

21. The Council provide a copy of this Order (unsealed if a sealed copy is not then available) to The PCT and The Trust by 4pm on [*date*]:

    (a) The PCT and/or The Trust may apply to set aside or vary this Order on 72 hours' notice to the other parties

    (b) Any such application is to be made by 4pm on [*date*] and referred to District Judge [*name*] who will consider further directions

22. Any party has permission to apply to District Judge [*name*] for further directions or orders before the adjourned hearing

23. All communications with the Court in response to this order shall state the above Case Number and be sent to: [*as in D2 Multi-Purpose Directions Order*]

Costs

24. The costs of this hearing are reserved to the final hearing save that there be detailed assessment of any publicly funded parties' costs at the conclusion of the proceedings

* * * * * * *

D 9

DIRECTIONS on DOLs application

[GENERAL TITLE]

Whereas

(1) An application has been by [*name*] ('the Applicant') for an order under section 21A of the Mental Capacity Act 2005

(2) On [*date*] [*name of council*] ('the Council') gave a standard authorisation for *A B* to be deprived of his liberty

IT IS ORDERED THAT

Permission

1. The applicant has applied for permission to make this application and permission is granted pursuant to section 50(2) of the Mental Capacity Act 2005

Service and parties to these proceedings

2. *A B* is joined as a party to these proceedings and subject to his consent, the Official Solicitor is appointed to act on his behalf as litigation friend

3. The Applicant shall forthwith serve this order, notice of application and a copy of all papers filed with this application dated [*date*] upon the Official Solicitor

4. The Applicant shall by 4:00pm on [*date*] serve a copy of this application upon

    (a) [*name*]

    (b) [*name*]

5. The Respondents are to file forms DLE Acknowledgements of service within 72 hours of service

Evidence

6. The Applicant shall by 4:00pm on [*date*] file at court and serve on all parties the COP24 in support

Section D: Case Management Directions Orders

7. Any statements of evidence that any party wishes to rely on at a hearing shall be filed and served not later than 48 hours before the directions hearing and if oral evidence is to be given, the statements so served shall stand as evidence in chief

8. The Council is to file the following documents with form DLE and serve copies on the Applicant and the Official Solicitor only by 4:00pm on [*date*]:

    (a)   draft interim care plan

    (b)   age assessment

    (c)   no refusals assessment

    (d)   mental capacity assessment

    (e)   mental health assessment

    (f)   eligibility assessment and

    (g)   best interests assessment.

9. The parties shall agree not less than [7] working days before the first hearing, the contents of the hearing bundle which shall be filed with the Clerk of the Rules Office in the Royal Court of Justice

Case management directions and allocations of the case

10. The application is to be transferred to the Royal Courts of Justice for hearing by a puisne Judge of the High Court

11. The first directions hearing will take place at the Royal Courts of Justice on a date to be advised within the next [*number*] days.

12. The final hearing of this matter shall take place on a date to be advised.

Miscellaneous

12. Any person who is affected by this order may apply to the court within 21 days of the order being served for reconsideration.

* * * * * * *

D 10
Sundry clauses in Orders

Headings

A. For the purposes of these proceedings, the Applicant shall be referred to as 'A', the First Respondent shall be referred to as 'B', the Second Respondent as 'C', and the Third Respondent as 'D'.

B. These proceedings are in private, and the parties shall be identified as follows:

    (a)   Kellow Borough Council: 'the Applicant'

(b) John Brown: 'JB'

(c) William Brown: 'WB'.

C. For the purposes of these proceedings, the Applicant shall be referred to as Surrey, the First Respondent as Gary, the Third Respondent as Mr Briggs and the Fourth Respondent as Mrs Briggs.

Identifying issues

A. The following issues have been identified as requiring determination at the final hearing:

(a) Whether it is in A's best interests to return to live with his parents in the family home full or part time; and if not,

(b) Whether it is in A's best interests to remain where he is, living at The Grange Centre; or

(c) Whether it is in A's best interest to reside elsewhere on the basis of other options that are available.

Declarations

A. It is declared in the interim that it is in P's best interests to be cared for at [ ] and to be cared for there by [local authority], its servants or agents, in accordance with the current care plan maintained by [the local authority].

B. The First Respondent lacks the capacity

(a) to litigate;

(b) to make decisions about where she should live;

(c) to make decisions as to her care requirements;

(d) to make decisions about with whom she should have contact.

C. It shall be lawful and in the First Respondent's best interests for him:

(a) to continue to reside at [ ] and

(b) to have contact with the Second Respondent in accordance with the Contact Schedule dated [date] annexed hereto.

D. It is declared that pursuant to s 48 of the Mental Capacity Act 2005, John Smith lacks capacity to give instructions to his solicitors and to decide what medical treatment he should have.

Expert and other reports

E.

1. NHS Keltshire is directed under the provisions of s 49 Mental Capacity Act 2005 ('MCA 2005') to obtain a report from the

Second Respondent's GP, [*name*] [*address*], addressing his capacity to engage in this litigation and give instructions to solicitors.

2. The Official Solicitor on behalf of X shall circulate a letter of instruction to the Applicant for comments by 4pm on [*date*].

3. The Applicant shall send the letter of instruction by 4pm on [*date*].

4. The report is to be provided to the Applicant by 4pm on [*date*].

5. The report is to be filed and served by 4 pm on [*date*].

F. Pursuant to s 49 of the Mental Capacity Act 2005, a Court of Protection Medical Visitor shall prepare a report on P's mental capacity and in particular his ability to decide where to live. The report shall be filed at court by 4pm on [8 weeks] when it will be referred to a judge for further directions.

G. The Applicant shall as soon as reasonably practicable and in any event by 4pm on [*date*] provide a statement from the Second Respondent's allocated social worker addressing:

(a) whether the First Respondent's sister-in-law, AB, will consent to any invitation to act as the Second Respondent's litigation friend;

(b) whether the Applicant is aware of any other individual who could properly act as (and would be willing to act as) the Second Respondent's litigation friend;

(c) the Second Respondent's financial circumstances, including his eligibility for any state benefits.

H.

1. There be permission to the parties jointly to instruct an independent social work expert ('the expert') to report upon P's best interests as regards his residence and care arrangements, and as to how contact with B could be facilitated. For the avoidance of doubt, the expert is to consider whether Happy Care Home is an appropriate placement for A or whether the Applicant should consider alternative placements and whether P could live at home.

2. The parties shall seek to agree the identity of the expert by 4 pm on [*date*]. In default of agreement, the court will select the expert in accordance with r 130 of the Court of Protection Rules 2007.

3. The Applicant shall prepare and circulate a draft letter of instruction by 4 pm on [*date*].

4. The parties shall agree the letter of instruction and serve the same on the expert by [*date*].

5. There be permission to the expert to interview P and to review all records relating to him for the purpose of conducting his/her assessment.

6. The expert shall either see P in person or speak to such legal representatives as are instructed to act on his behalf to ascertain his views. There be permission to such legal representatives as are instructed to act on B's behalf to provide relevant information to the expert.

7. The expert shall provide his report to P's solicitors by 4 pm on [*date*] and P's solicitors shall forthwith serve the report on the other parties.

8. The cost of instructing the expert shall be divided equally between the instructing parties [and shall be a necessary disbursement for the purposes of any party's public funding certificate as the instruction of the expert is needed to assist the court determine the issues in this case].

* * * * * * *

D 11

Orders in Family-type Personal Welfare Cases

A. No person with notice of this Order shall, whether by themselves or by instructing or encouraging any other person, remove or attempt to remove P from her current placement at [ ] save for the purposes of contact in accordance with the Contact Schedule annexed to this order.

B. The parties shall jointly prepare a schedule of P's needs and support and the schedule shall itemise each specific need and the support P requires, how the support will be provided, how it will be funded and the position of each party in relation to each item. The schedule shall be filed and served by 4pm on [*date*].

C. It is in the [First Respondent's] [P's] best interests that reasonable and proportionate steps be taken to return him to Sunny Care Home in the event that he seeks to leave the premises other than with the permission of the staff there.

D. The Second Respondent is hereby prohibited from threatening or abusing or intimidating any member of staff or servant or agent of the Applicant whether in writing or verbally in person or on the telephone or otherwise.

E. The Second Respondent is hereby prohibited from threatening or abusing or intimidating any member of staff or servant or agent of Happy Days Nursing Home including all members of P's multidisciplinary care team whether in writing or verbally in person or on the telephone or otherwise.

F. The Second Respondent shall not orally discuss any aspect of P's care or treatment with staff, servants or agents of Happy Days Care Home save (1) in the event of a medical or other emergency or (2) with the Nurse in Charge or the Matron each Monday between the times of [ ] and [ ].

G. The Second Respondent is prohibited from taking any photographic image or video recording of P without the prior agreement of the manager of Happy Days Care Home.

H. Nothing in this order shall prevent the Second Respondent from making use of the NHS complaints procedure by making a written complaint by a letter sent by post.

I. The Applicant shall have permission to serve a copy of this order and annexed Contact Schedule dated [date] upon the independent contact supervisor [the Constabulary] and [any hospital or hospice to which the First Respondent may be admitted in the future].

* * * * * * *

D 12

Official Solicitor

A. By 4pm on [date], the Applicant shall disclose to the Official Solicitor's representatives:

1. P's social services records from [date] to date and ongoing; and
2. Records held by [ ] in respect of P.

B. The Applicant shall by 4 pm on [date] provide to the solicitors instructed by the Official Solicitor on behalf of P two copies of all medical, care and social records relating to P within their control created since [date] and any other relevant records.

C. A copy of P's social services file and any medical records, if requested by the Official Solicitor, shall be provided within 7 working days of receipt of any such request with permission to any Primary Care Trust and/or NHS Trust to apply to vary or discharge this requirement upon 48 hours' notice.

D. (* *These directions should form a separate single order to the main directions order as it is intended to be served on third parties who should not be informed of other aspects of the proceedings*).

1. The Official Solicitor to the Senior Courts [and (*insert name of local authority if appropriate*) are] is authorised to investigate the property and financial affairs of [*insert P's full name and address*] for the purposes of ensuring that the costs of his/her legal representation are provided to the Official Solicitor in these proceedings.

2. Any third party, including HM Revenue & Customs, is hereby directed and authorised to release to the Official Solicitor to the Senior Courts [and (*insert name of local authority if appropriate*)] such information and documents as he [they] may require on behalf of [*insert P's full name*] in the course of his [their] investigations within 7 days of any request.

3. In the event that [*insert P's full name*] is eligible for public funding (legal aid) the Official Solicitor is authorised in his/her name and on his/her behalf:

    (a) to accept any offer of public funding made to [*insert P's full name*] by the Legal Aid Agency Commission;

    (b) to sign the offer on [*insert P's full name*] behalf;

    (c) to give any necessary notices of withdrawal (including establishing a standing order) to pay any public funding contributions from any amount standing to the credit of [*insert P's full name*] P with any bank or building society;

* * * * * * * *

D 13
Contact plans

1. The local authority shall circulate a draft contact plan to the other parties by 4pm on [*insert date*]

2. The First and Second Respondents shall inform the local authority by 4pm on [*insert date*] if they agree the contact plan and, if not, they shall set out the areas in dispute and the amendments they wish to include on the contact plan.

3. Following comments/agreed amendments from the other parties, the local authority shall file a copy of the contact plan with the court by 4pm on [*insert date*]. In the event that there are any disagreements about the content of the contact plan, those areas of disagreement shall be set out by the parties in a joint note, to be filed at court by 4pm on [*insert date which should ideally be the same date as for the filing of the plan*].

4. The court file shall be placed before [*HHJ/District Judge...*] when the court [will consider what further directions are required] [approve the contact plan in the event of agreement].

5. There shall be a case management conference on the first available date after [*insert date*] before [*HHJ/District Judge...*] at [*time*] [*venue*] with a time estimate of 1 hour when the court will consider the contact plan and give further directions or make such orders as are appropriate.

Section D: Case Management Directions Orders

6. X may have regular weekly supervised face-to-face contact with P at Happy Days Home subject to the provisions of this [schedule] [order]and otherwise no other contact shall take place.

7.
    A. Contact between X and P shall take place as follows:

        (i) Week 1: on Sunday, Tuesday and Thursday between 10am and 12pm

        (ii) Week 2: on Monday, Wednesday and Friday between 10am and 12pm

        (iii) Week 3: as week 1

        (iv) Week 4: as week 2.

    B. Week 1 shall commence on [insert date].

    C. On the first Saturday of each month commencing [insert date], in addition to the contact set out at A above, there shall be contact between 10 and 4pm.

    D. Contact at paragraph A shall take place at [Happy Days Home] [X's home] and contact at C shall take place outside of Happy Days Home at a venue to be decided by X [and approved by Happy Days Home].

8. Visits between X and P shall be once a week initially for up to one hour save that the manager of Happy Days Home may inform X at the outset of the contact that given P's health or general presentation that day, the length of the session shall be varied.

9. The time and frequency of contact shall be reviewed after one month and thereafter on a monthly basis. The conditions in this [schedule] [order] may also be varied by agreement between the local authority, Happy Days Home and X.

10. All contact between X and P shall be subject to P's wishes. Face-to-face contact shall end earlier than the allotted time should P indicate that he wishes it to end. Should P not wish contact to take place on the specified day for X's visit, it shall not proceed, and X shall be informed and the contact rescheduled on a day agreed with X.

11. Staff may cancel a visit between X and P should they consider that he is not well enough for it to proceed. The visit shall be rescheduled for another day which shall be agreed with P if possible.

12. The local authority shall arrange and fund transport for X to and from his home to Happy Days Home for each supervised visit.

13. Contact visits shall not disrupt P's timetable for activities at Happy Days Home if possible.

14. Contact between X and P shall take place in the [*insert the room or specific venue*] at Happy Days Home and X shall both enter and leave by the main reception area.

15. The local authority shall arrange the presence of and funding for a social worker [*from a different local authority who has not previously been involved in the case*] to supervise each weekly visit between X and P. The local authority shall notify the parties of the identity of the supervisor not later than 7 days before the first contact [*visit*] [*session*] on [*insert date*]. The supervisor shall document each contact session [*and copies of the contact records shall be provided to the local authority within three days of each contact session*]. The local authority shall provide copies of the contact notes to [*the parties*] every month.

16. The contact supervisor shall do his/her best to ensure that supervision is as least intrusive as possible.

17. The supervisor shall meet P at Happy Days Home prior to his first contact session with X to ensure that P understands his/her role in contact sessions.

18. Any contact session shall be terminated by the supervisor, and/or contact may be suspended by Happy Days Home in P's best interests, pending an urgent review,

    (a) should P at any time appear distressed by X's behaviour during his visit; and/or

    (b) should X:

        (i) interfere or attempt to interfere with P's care;

        (ii) approach any resident other than P, or interfere or attempt to interfere with their care;

        (iii) behave in a threatening or intimidating manner towards any person;

        (iv) force P to take any medication whether prescribed or otherwise.

19. Should suspension or termination of contact visits be considered necessary in P's best interests, an urgent contact review meeting shall be organised by the local authority within 7 days, which the manager of Happy Days Home shall attend. X and the Official Solicitor's representative shall also be invited. If agreement cannot be reached at the meeting, the local authority can return the matter to Court urgently.

* * * * * * *

D 14
ORDER
Transparency

Guidance for completing a draft Pilot Order and the Record of Information Sheet

1. The individuals who should not be identified should be anonymised with 2 random letters. This will often only be P and P's family members but may include others. See the site below for a letter sequence generator:

http://www.dave-reed.com/Nifty/randSeq.html

2. The default position is that the names of public bodies shall be named unless the judge directs otherwise. On occasions where this is necessary, they should be anonymized, as follows:

    a. Local Authorities are to be anonymised as '**A Local Authority**'

    b. NHS trusts are to be anonymised as '**A NHS Trust**'

    c. Clinical commissioning groups are to be anonymised as '**A Clinical Commissioning Group**'

3. The names of care homes shall not be used; they are to be anonymised as 'a care home'.

4. Where the pilot order refers to other people who are not party to the proceedings they should be anonymised in the same way as outlined at 1 above.

5. All addresses are to be anonymised as '**Address 1**', '**Address 2**', '**Address 3**' and added to the information sheet.

PILOT ORDER TEMPLATE WITH NOTES

IN THE COURT OF PROTECTION

CASE NO: [*CASE NUMBER*]

IN THE MATTER OF THE MENTAL CAPACITY ACT 2005

IN THE MATTER OF [*INITIALS OF P NOT FULL NAME*][1]

BEFORE [*JUDGE*] **on** [*DATE OF ORDER*]

BETWEEN:

[*APPLICANT*][2]

Applicant

- and -

[*FIRST_RESPONDENT*]

First Respondent

- and -

[SECOND_RESPONDENT]

Second Respondent

[PARTIES IN APPROPRIATELY ANONYMISED FORM]

IMPORTANT

If any person disobeys the order in paragraph (5) they may be found guilty of contempt of court and may be sent to prison, fined or have their assets seized. They have the right to ask the court to vary or discharge the order.

UPON READING the Court file

AND UPON HEARING [PARTIES WHO ATTENDED HEARING][3]

AND UPON IT APPEARING TO THE COURT that there should be an attended hearing to which the pilot provided for by *Practice Direction – Transparency Pilot* should apply

IT IS HEREBY ORDERED that:

(1) This application be set down for an attended hearing on [HEARING DATE] with a time estimate of [HEARING TIME] at which the Court will consider the following issues:[4]

    (a) [ISSUE 1],

    (b) [ISSUE 2]

[DEFINE THE ISSUES]

(2) Subject to further order of the Court that attended hearing and any further attended hearing of this application is to be in public PROVIDED ALWAYS THAT the court may exclude from the attended hearing any person (other than a party) who refuses a request to sign a document recording their attendance and that they are aware of the terms of this order

(3) The attended hearing is to be listed as follows:[5]

[DESCRIPTION] [SET OUT A DESCRIPTION BY REFERENCE TO THE GENERAL DESCRIPTION LIST]

(4) Part 3 of Practice Direction 13A to the Court of Protection Rules 2007 (which relates to proceedings held in private) shall continue to apply to these proceedings.

(5) (A) The following persons (the Persons Bound by the Injunctive Order) are bound by this injunctive order:

    (i) the parties and their representatives

    (ii) the witnesses,

(iii) all persons who attend all or any part of an attended hearing,

(iv) all persons who by any means obtain or are given an account or record of all or any part of an attended hearing or of any order or judgment made or given as a result of an attended hearing, and

(v) any body, authority or organisation (and their officers, employees, servants and agents) for whom any such person works or is giving evidence.

(B) The material and information (the Information) covered by this injunctive order is:

(i) any material or information that identifies or is likely to identify that[6]

(a) [*INITIALS OF P NOT FULL NAME*] and members of [*INITIALS OF P NOT FULL NAME*]'s family are respectively the subject (and so a P as defined in the Court of Protection Rules 2007) or members of the family of a subject of these proceedings, or that

(b) [*ANONYMYSED PERSON*] [*ANONYMISED REFERENCE TO ANY OTHER PARTY*] is a party to these proceedings, or that

(c) [*ANONYMYSED PERSON*] [*ANONYMISED PERSON WHOSE IDENTITY SHOULD NOT BE PUBLISHED*] (who the Court has so identified to the parties in private) [has taken a part in / or been referred to in] these proceedings; and

(ii) any material or information that identifies or is likely to identify where any person listed above lives, or is being cared for, or their contact details.

(C) Subject to further order of the Court and save as provided by sub-paragraph (D) the Persons Bound by this Injunctive Order shall not by any means directly or indirectly:

(i) publish the Information or any part or parts of it, or

(ii) cause, enable, assist in or encourage the publication of the Information or any part or parts of it.

(D) Subject to further order of the Court this injunctive order does not prevent the Persons Bound by this Injunctive Order from communicating information relating to these proceedings on the basis that Part 3 of Practice Direction 13A to the Court of Protection Rules 2007 (which relates to proceedings held in private) applies to these proceedings.

(6) Subject to further order of the Court any transcript of a hearing of and any judgment or order given in these proceedings shall be anonymised so that it shall contain no reference by name or address to the persons or bodies referred to in paragraph (5)(B) and shall refer to them by their descriptions therein.[7]

(7) Subject to further order of the Court all position statements, statements of issues, chronologies and skeleton arguments prepared when the injunctive order in paragraph (5) is in force shall refer to the persons or bodies referred to in paragraph (5)(B) by their descriptions therein.

(8) Subject to further order or direction of the Court (including directions relating to payment, use, copying, return and the means by which a copy of a document may be provided):

 (A) the documents prepared in accordance with paragraph (5) will if requested by them be provided to duly accredited representatives of news gathering and reporting organisations who attend the hearing referred to in paragraph (1) (and any later hearing), and

 (B) at those attended hearings the Court shall give such further directions as it thinks fit concerning the provision of copies of documents put before the Court and the terms on which they are to be provided to any person who attends the hearing (and is not a person to whom the document can be provided under Part 3 of Practice Direction 13A to the Court of Protection Rules 2007).

(9) A record (the Record) of the Information shall be kept by the Court. The Record shall contain a list of the names separately from the other parts of the Information. The Record or some of it may on request be made available to anyone who attends or has attended a hearing on such terms as the Court thinks fit.[8]

(10) Application may be made to the Court by any person who has not been present at an attended hearing (and so become aware of or been able to request the Information) for a direction that they be provided with the Information or some of it on such terms as the Court thinks fit. Any such application must be accompanied by evidence setting out why such a direction is sought.

(11) The parties and any person affected by this order may apply to the Court for an order (and the Court may of its own motion make an order) that:

 (i) varies or discharges this order or any part or parts of it, or which

 (ii) permits the publication of any of the Information on the basis that it is lawfully in the public domain or for such other reason as the Court thinks fit.

(12) Subject to further order of the Court, any person who would have been entitled under the Legal Services Act 2007 to exercise rights of audience at the attended hearing if this order had not been made and it

Section D: Case Management Directions Orders

was held in private (and is not otherwise entitled to exercise such rights), shall be entitled to exercise equivalent rights of audience at that attended hearing and any further attended hearing of this application.

(13) Costs reserved.

Dated: [DATE OF ORDER]

Address for notifying the Court:[9]

[NAME OF COURT]

[COURT ADDRESS 1]

[COURT ADDRESS 2]

[COURT ADDRESS 3]

[COURT ADDRESS 4]

[COURT ADDRESS 5]

1 To be anonymised as outlined at 1 above.
2 The applicant will not always be P. If the applicant or respondent is a public body, they should be named in full unless the judge directs otherwise. The relevant public bodies should be inserted as follows, eg:
'**The London Borough of Barnet A Local Authority**'
'**South London, Maudsley NHS Trust/A NHS Trust**'
'**Reading Clinical Commissioning Group/A Clinical Commissioning Group.**'
The Judge will determine which is to be used.
3 If the application is being looked at on papers only remove this sentence.
4 The details for this section will be completed by the Judge.
5 Refer to the general list of descriptions and type in the one that fits the case as detailed in the COP 1.
6 (a)–(c) Complete this in line with the record of information sheet. Often this will only be P and any other anonymisation should only be as directed by the judge.
7 If you are drafting any other order along with the pilot order ensure that this is also anonymised.
8 Ensure that the Record of Information sheet is also completed and attached to the file for the Judge to see.
9 Type in the name and address of the Court that made the order.

CASE NUMBER:

FULL DETAILS OF PERSON/ADDRESS TO BE ANONYMISED	ANONYMISED REFERENCE

* * * * * * *

Section E: Final Orders

As the Court of Protection develops precedents for final Orders will become accepted and available. A few are set out here, based on the orders that some judges have been making, in the hope that this may promote the development of more useful precedents.

* * * * * * *

E 1
ORDER
Capacity: financial affairs

This is an example of an Order made at a Regional hearing following a dispute as to whether the person to whom the application relates has capacity in regard to his financial affairs.

THIS ORDER IS NOT VALID UNLESS IT BEARS THE IMPRESSED SEAL OF THE COURT OF PROTECTION ON ALL PAGES

COURT OF PROTECTION

MENTAL CAPACITY ACT 2005

Case No: 00000000

IN THE MATTER OF [*FULL NAME*]

(referred to in this Order as '*J T*')

FINAL ORDER

BEFORE District Judge [*name*] sitting at [*regional court address*] on [*date*]

UPON HEARING the solicitors for *J T* in his presence (there being no attendance by the Applicant)

WHEREAS

1. An application has been made by [*name and any relationship to J T*] for an order under the Mental Capacity Act 2005 in relation to *J T*

2. Notice of the application has been given to *J T* and to relatives and other persons to be notified in accordance with the Court of Protection Rules 2007

3. The application concerns *J T's* property and affairs

4. The Court has considered medical and other evidence as to whether *J T* is personally unable to make various decisions regarding the management of property and financial affairs because of an impairment of, or a disturbance in the functioning of, the mind or brain

5. The Court has been assisted by a Report of the Medical Visitor [*name*] dated [*date*] following perusal of all previous medical evidence

THE COURT NOW ORDERS THAT:

1. It be declared that *J T* has capacity to manage his property and financial affairs
2. The costs of the solicitors who represented *J T* in this application shall be paid by *J T* and assessed on the standard basis if not agreed by him

* * * * * * *

E 2
ORDER
EPA or Deputy

This Order was made at a Regional hearing following a dispute as to whether an enduring powers of attorney should be registered or a deputy be appointed for financial affairs.

THIS ORDER IS NOT VALID UNLESS IT BEARS THE IMPRESSED SEAL OF THE COURT OF PROTECTION ON ALL PAGES

COURT OF PROTECTION

MENTAL CAPACITY ACT 2005

Case No: 00000000

IN THE MATTER OF [*FULL NAME*]

(referred to in this Order as '*M M*')

FINAL ORDER

BEFORE District Judge [*name*] sitting at [*regional court address*] on [*date*]

UPON considering the application of [*name*] County Council for appointment as a financial deputy and the further application for registration of an enduring power of attorney

AND UPON noting the consent of all parties involved to a compromise whereby *E J* (a solicitor and one of the proposed attorneys) be appointed as a finance deputy

AND UPON the Court being satisfied that

(a) *MM* is personally unable to make various decisions regarding the management of property and financial affairs because of an impairment of, or a disturbance in the functioning of, the mind or brain

(b) the compromise is in the best interests of *M M*

THE COURT NOW ORDERS THAT:

1. The application for registration of the document purporting to be an enduring power of attorney dated [*date*] be refused and that document be revoked

2. E J of [*name of firm*], solicitors, [*address*] be appointed as a financial deputy for *M M* with comprehensive powers in the terms of an Order to be settled by a resident District Judge sitting at First Avenue House, 42–49 High Holborn, London WC1A 9JA – *for the terms of an Order see A 2 above*

3. The deputy is to agree and pay from the funds of *M M* the reasonable costs of [*name*] County Council in respect of the Council's application with permission to apply to District Judge [*name*] in the event of agreement not being reached

4. The costs of [*name*], solicitors are also to be paid from the funds of M M after approval by District Judge [*name*]. For the purpose of such approval a summary of the costs is to be submitted to District Judge [*name*] [by email *or* at [*name*] Court]

5. Any party may apply within 7 days of receipt of this Order for its terms to be varied or reconsidered

6. All written communications with the Court in response to this order shall be sent to First Avenue House, 42–49 High Holborn, London WC1A 9JA *or address of regional court*

* * * * * * *

E 3
ORDER
Discharge from the jurisdiction

This 'imaginative' Order was made following a decision that the Applicant was capable of handling her financial affairs which included substantial damages recovered in a personal injury claim. Capacity depended upon taking professional advice and there were fears that due to her brain injury the Applicant may act without advice despite her assurances to the contrary.

THIS ORDER IS NOT VALID UNLESS IT BEARS THE IMPRESSED SEAL OF THE COURT OF PROTECTION ON ALL PAGES

COURT OF PROTECTION

MENTAL CAPACITY ACT 2005

Case No: 00000000

IN THE MATTER OF [*FULL NAME*]

(referred to in this Order as '*J B*')

Section E: Final Orders

FINAL ORDER

BEFORE District Judge [*name*] sitting at [*regional court address*] on [*date*]

UPON the application of *J B* for an Order discharging her from the jurisdiction of the Court of Protection on the ground that she ceases to lack capacity to make decisions in relation to the matters to which these proceedings relate

AND UPON reading

1. the said application and accompanying Report of Dr [*name*], consultant clinical neuropsychologist dated [*date*]
2. the statement of the Deputy, [*name*], dated [*name*]
3. the Report of the Special Visitor, [*name*], consultant in adult psychiatry dated [*date*]
4. the further documents submitted by *J B* pursuant to the directions Order dated [*name*]

AND UPON hearing *J B* and her financial deputy [*name*] and her daughter [*name*]

AND WHEREAS it appears to the Court that

(a) by an Order dated [*date*], [*name*] was appointed as receiver under section 99 of the Mental Health Act 1983

(b) on [*date*] the receiver became a deputy by virtue of paragraph 1(2)(a) of Schedule 5 to the Mental Capacity Act 2005

(c) *J B* is now able to make decisions for herself in relation to her property and affairs

(d) this is dependent upon her continuing to seek and rely upon advice and guidance of the nature and quality that has hitherto been available to her

(e) without such advice she may not understand the implications of any significant decisions and be vulnerable to abuse if she failed to avail herself of such support

THE COURT NOW ORDERS THAT:

1. *J B* be discharged from the jurisdiction of this Court and the appointment of [*name*] as Deputy do cease with effect from [*date*] unless before that date an application is made pursuant to the following paragraph of this Order

2. Either the said [*name*] or the daughter [*name*] may apply at any time for this decision to be reconsidered or for the Court again to assume jurisdiction based upon evidence of a deterioration in the health or serious inappropriate conduct on the part of *J B* arising after the date of this Order

3. An application may be made to the Court for the purpose of implementing this Order and in particular for

   3.1. a final account to be delivered or dispensed with

   3.2. the discharge of any security

   3.3. funds and property to be released to *J B*

4. Following or immediately prior to the termination of her appointment the reasonable costs of [*name*] as Deputy and in connection with this application be paid by *J B* or from her estate, such costs to be assessed if not agreed

* * * * * * *

E 4
ORDER
Change of financial Deputy

The following two Orders were made in response to persistent applications to be discharged from the jurisdiction and, failing this, to change the professional deputy. The Applicant had sustained brain injuries in an accident and proved irresponsible when given some discretion in regard to the management of the damages award. He was given permission to instruct his own solicitor to pursue the application.

THIS ORDER IS NOT VALID UNLESS IT BEARS THE IMPRESSED SEAL OF THE COURT OF PROTECTION ON ALL PAGES

COURT OF PROTECTION

MENTAL CAPACITY ACT 2005

Case No: 00000000

IN THE MATTER OF [*FULL NAME*]

(referred to in this Order as '*J M*')

ORDER 1

UPON READING the Court file

AND UPON considering a Report dated [*date*] by [*name*], consultant psychiatrist which was submitted by the solicitors acting for *J M*

IT IS ORDERED THAT:

1. The application by *J M* to be discharged from the jurisdiction of this Court is dismissed

2. The appointment of the Deputy is to continue on the existing terms pending further order

Section E: Final Orders

3. *J M* (through his solicitor) is to send to the Court at First Avenue House, 42–49 High Holborn, London WC1A 9JA and copy to the Deputy no later than [*date*] a statement explaining why he wishes to have a change of deputy and indicating who he wishes to be appointed

4. In default the application to change the deputy is dismissed

5. The Deputy is to send to the Court at First Avenue House, 42–49 High Holborn, London WC1A 9JA and copy to *J M* (through his solicitor) a statement in response and updating the Court as to the present position within 28 days of receiving the statement from *J M*

6. Any further reference to the Court is to be reserved to District Judge [*name*] or in his absence the Senior Judge

7. The Deputy is to agree and pay the costs of *J M*'s solicitors in connection with this application (with reference to District Judge [*name*] if not agreed)

ORDER 2

UPON READING the Court file

AND UPON considering:

(a) the Directions Order made on [*date*]

(b) a statement by *J M* dated [*date*]

(c) a statement by the Deputy, [*name*] dated [*date*] (a copy of which will have been made available to *J M*

IT IS ORDERED THAT:

1. The application by *J M* to change the Deputy is dismissed and the appointment of [*name*] is to continue on the existing terms until further order

2. The Deputy is to pay the costs of [*name*] solicitors in connection with this application in the sum of £[*amount*] plus VAT

3. If *J M* is dissatisfied with this decision he may within 21 days of receipt request that it be reviewed at a hearing before District Judge [*name*] sitting at [*Court*]

4. Any further reference to the Court is to be reserved to District Judge [*name*] or in his absence the Senior Judge

* * * * * * * *

E 5
ORDER
Cancellation of EPA and appointment of financial Deputy

This is an example of an Order made when, following a reserved Judgment, registration of an EPA was refused and a financial Deputy was appointed.

THIS ORDER IS NOT VALID UNLESS IT BEARS THE IMPRESSED SEAL OF THE COURT OF PROTECTION ON ALL PAGES

COURT OF PROTECTION

MENTAL CAPACITY ACT 2005

Case No: 00000000

IN THE MATTER OF [*FULL NAME*]

(referred to in this Order as '*M S*')

FINAL ORDER

BEFORE District Judge [*name*] sitting at [*regional court address*] on [*date*] pursuant to a reserved Judgment dated [*date*]

WHEREAS

1. An application has been made for an order under the Mental Capacity Act 2005

2. The court is satisfied that *M S* is unable to make various decisions for herself in relation to a matter or matters concerning her property and affairs because of an impairment of, or a disturbance in the functioning of, her mind or brain

3. The court is satisfied that the purpose for which the order is needed cannot be as effectively achieved in a way that is less restrictive of her rights and freedom of action

IT IS ORDERED THAT:

Cancellation of enduring power of attorney

1. In relation to the enduring power of attorney dated [*date*] of *M S*

    1.1. registration be cancelled

    1.2. the document be revoked as a power of attorney

Appointment of deputy

2. [*name*] of [*address*] is appointed as deputy ('the deputy') to make decisions on behalf of *M S* that she is unable to make for herself in relation to her property and affairs subject to any conditions or restrictions set out in this order

3. The appointment will last until further order

4. The deputy must apply the principles set out in section 1 of the Mental Capacity Act 2005 and have regard to the guidance in the Code of Practice to the Act

Authority of deputy

5. The court confers general authority on the deputy to take possession or control of the property and affairs of *M S* and to exercise the same powers of management and investment as she has as beneficial owner, subject to the terms and conditions set out in this order

6. The deputy may make provision for the needs of anyone who is related to or connected with *M S*, if she provided for or might be expected to provide for that person's needs, by doing whatever she did or might reasonably be expected to do to meet those needs

7. The deputy may (without obtaining any further authority from the court) dispose of money and property of *M S* by way of gift to any charity to which she made or might have been expected to make gifts and on customary occasions to persons who are related to or connected with her, provided that the value of each such gift is not unreasonable having regard to all the circumstances and, in particular, the size of her estate

8. The deputy is authorised to sell the property of *M S* known as [*address*] on the best possible terms and after payment of legal fees and other professional charges to invest the net proceeds for her benefit

9. For the purpose of giving effect to any decision the deputy may execute or sign any necessary deeds or documents

Reports

10. The deputy is required to keep statements, vouchers, receipts and other financial records

11. The deputy must submit an annual report to the Public Guardian

12. The deputy must submit a financial summary to the three children of *M S* on 1 June and 1 December each year commencing 1 December 2009

Costs and expenses

13. The deputy is entitled to be reimbursed for reasonable expenses incurred provided they are in proportion to the size of the estate of *M S* and the functions performed by the deputy

14. The deputy is authorised to pay a contribution of £[*amount*] to the costs of [*name*], solicitors for this application, from the funds belonging to *M S*

Security

15. The deputy is required forthwith to obtain and maintain security in the sum of £[*amount*] in accordance with the standard requirements as to the giving of security

16. To enable the deputy to give security, this order becomes effective one calendar month from the date it was made

17. The deputy must not discharge any functions until the security is in place

* * * * * * * * *

E 6
ORDER
Appointment of financial Deputy in respect of large brain injury award

This is an example of a purpose made Order following a fund management hearing where a parent was appointed as a financial Deputy in respect of a high value damages award for a young son. Additional supervision and safeguards were considered necessary as the parent although a dedicated carer was inexperienced in financial matters.

THIS ORDER IS NOT VALID UNLESS IT BEARS THE IMPRESSED SEAL OF THE COURT OF PROTECTION ON ALL PAGES

COURT OF PROTECTION

MENTAL CAPACITY ACT 2005

Case No: 00000000

IN THE MATTER OF JOHN XX

(referred to in this Order as '*John*')

FINAL ORDER

BEFORE District Judge [*name*] sitting at [*regional court address*] on [*date*]

WHEREAS

1. An application has been made for an order under the Mental Capacity Act 2005

2. The Court is satisfied that:

   (I) John is unable to make various decisions for himself in relation to a matter or matters concerning his property and affairs because of an impairment of or a disturbance in the functioning of his mind or brain

(II) the purpose for which the order is needed cannot be as effectively achieved in a way that is less restrictive of his rights and freedom of action

IT IS ORDERED THAT:

1. **Appointment of deputy**

(a) XY of ADDRESS is appointed as deputy ('the deputy') to make decisions on behalf of John that he is unable to make for himself in relation to his property and affairs subject to any conditions or restrictions set out in this order

(b) The appointment will last until DATE

(c) The deputy must apply the principles set out in Section 1 of the Mental Capacity Act 2005 and have regard to the guidance in the Code of Practice to the Act

2. **Authority of deputy**

(a) The Court confers general authority on the deputy to take possession or control of the property and affairs of John and to exercise the same powers of management and investment as he has as beneficial owner, subject to the terms and conditions set out in this order

(b) The deputy may make provision for the needs of anyone who is related or connected with John, if he might be expected to provide for that person's needs, by doing whatever he might reasonably be expected to do to meet those needs

(c) The deputy may expend the income of John for his benefit without needing to obtain the prior approval of the Court

(d) The deputy may now withdraw a sum not exceeding £100,000 from the funds belonging to John for the purpose of funding modifications to the home at ADDRESS, a suitable motor vehicle and (if desired) a residential caravan (this sum being in addition to the sum already released)

(e) The deputy may withdraw a sum not exceeding £30,000 a year from the funds belonging to John without needing to obtain the prior approval of the Court

(f) The deputy may withdraw further sums from the funds belonging to John without needing to obtain the prior approval of the Court for the purpose of investment as authorized by this order

(g) For the purpose of giving effect to any decision the deputy may execute or sign any necessary deeds or documents

3. **Restrictions on deputy**

The following restrictions are imposed upon the powers of the deputy.

(a) The initial investment scheme shall be approved by the Court before it is implemented, provided that the recommendations made by NAME of ADDRESS in their letter dated DATE are approved for this purpose.

(b) Save as provided by this order the investment adviser must not release capital for any purpose other than for investment and capital from investments cannot be remitted to the deputy without the prior approval of the Court

(c) Unspent income (including payments under the structured settlement) exceeding £2,500 in any year shall be accumulated and treated as capital

(d) The deputy shall obtain the permission of the Court for expenditure of capital exceeding £30,000 in any 12 month period or for any single investment outside the United Kingdom exceeding £25,000 in value

4. **Investments**

(a) The deputy must exercise such care and skill as is reasonable in the circumstances when investing the assets of John

(b) The deputy may make any kind of investment that the person absolutely entitled to those assets could make, subject to the terms and conditions set out in this order

(c) This general power of investment includes investment in land and investment in assets outside England and Wales

(d) In exercising the power of investment, the deputy must have regard to the standard investment criteria namely the suitability of the investments and the need for diversification in so far as is appropriate to the circumstances of John

(e) The deputy must from time to time review the investments, and consider whether, having regard to the standard investment criteria, they should be varied

(f) Unless the deputy reasonably concludes that in all the circumstances it is unnecessary or inappropriate to do so, before exercising any power of investment, the deputy must obtain and consider proper advice about the way in which, having regard to the standard investment criteria, the power should be exercised. 'Proper advice' is the advice of an Independent Financial Adviser who the deputy reasonably believes to be appropriately qualified and experienced

5. **Reports**

(a) The deputy is required to keep statements, vouchers, receipts and other financial records

(b) The deputy must submit an annual report to the Public Guardian

6. Costs and expenses

(a) The deputy is entitled to be reimbursed for reasonable expenses incurred provided they are in proportion to the size of the estate and to the actual functions performed by the deputy

(b) The deputy is authorised to pay YY, solicitors fixed costs for this application and if the amount sought exceeds the fixed costs allowed the deputy is authorised to agree their costs and pay them from the funds belonging to John. In default of agreement, or if the deputy or solicitors would prefer the costs to be assessed, this order is to be treated as authority to the Senior Court Costs Office to carry out a detailed assessment on the standard basis.

7. Security

(a) The deputy is required forthwith to obtain and maintain security in the sum of £700,000 in accordance with the standard requirements as to the giving of security

(b) To enable the deputy to give security, this order will come into force one calendar month after the date on which it was made

(c) The deputy must not discharge any functions until the security is in place and if the deputy acts without security the court may revoke this order and the deputy may be personally liable for any loss to the estate

6. Further applications

(a) This hearing is adjourned generally on terms that the deputy may within 12 months of the date of this Order request by letter addressed to First Avenue House, 42–49 High Holborn, London WC1A 9JA without a further court fee that:

    (i) further capital sums be released or

    (ii) the hearing be restored

(b) Any such request shall be referred to District Judge NAME for further directions or (if he is not available) to a resident district judge at First Avenue House, 42–49 High Holborn, London WC1A 9JA

* * * * * * *

E 7a
ORDER for repairs to property

This is an example of an imaginative approach being adopted to resolve an issue which would otherwise have presented the court with some difficulty.

THIS ORDER IS NOT VALID UNLESS IT BEARS THE IMPRESSED SEAL OF THE COURT OF PROTECTION ON ALL PAGES

COURT OF PROTECTION

MENTAL CAPACITY ACT 2005

Case No: 00000000

IN THE MATTER OF [*FULL NAME*]

(referred to in this Order as '*M U*')

DIRECTIONS ORDER

BEFORE District Judge [*name*] sitting at [*regional court address*] on [*date*]

UPON THE APPLICATION of [*local authority*] ('the Applicant')

UPON HEARING the Applicant's solicitor in the presence of [*name*] (social worker to M U)

AND UPON READING a letter dated [*date*] from *M U* to the effect that she cannot attend due to health problems.

WHEREAS

(1) The application concerns the property and financial affairs of *M U* and in particular decisions as to the expenditure of significant sums on the maintenance and repair of her home ('the relevant decisions')

(2) Notice of the application has been given to *M U* but

    (a) no relatives or other persons have been identified who should be notified in accordance with the Court of Protection Rules 2007 and

    (b) no person has been named as a Respondent to the application

(3) The application was accompanied by

    (a) an inventory of the assets and liabilities of *M U* and

    (b) evidence in Form COP3 that *M U* is personally unable to make the relevant decisions because of an impairment of, or a disturbance in the functioning of, the mind or brain

(4) There is a preliminary issue, because *M U* disputes the medical evidence presented, as to whether she has capacity to

    (a) make the relevant decisions and/or

    (b) conduct these proceedings

(5) The Court is satisfied on the evidence already presented that:

    (a) there is reason to believe that M U does not have capacity to make the relevant decisions and

    (b) it is in her best interests to make this interim order pursuant to Mental Capacity Act 2005 section 48

Section E: Final Orders

(6) The social worker [*name*] is requested to hand a copy of this Order to *M U* and give her any explanations that she reasonably requests

THE COURT NOW ORDERS THAT

The parties

1. Only the Applicant is a party to the proceedings at this stage
2. A copy of this Order is to be served by the Court on *M U* and any request that she be joined as a party (which may be made by her or someone on her behalf) is to be made in writing to the Court within 14 days of service
3. Any other person (whether or not served with notice of the application) who wishes to be joined as a party must apply to the Court at the earliest opportunity
4. *M U* should be involved in these proceedings to the extent that she is able to contribute and wishes to do so

    a   party who does not serve statements or documents on *M U* must be in a position to justify this at the hearing

    b   *M U* is to be enabled to attend any hearing if such attendance would not be too distressing or detrimental to health

Preliminary issue

5. Save as provided in this Order the proceedings are stayed pending the determination of the preliminary issue and the following directions relate to that issue.
6. Service of Form COP3 on *M U* is excused at this stage
7. The Public Guardian is to arrange for a medical Visitor to attend upon and assess the capacity of *M U* at the present time in regard to decisions of the nature identified in recital 4 to this Order and to produce a Report no later than [*date*]
8. The medical Visitor is to

    (a) have access (so far as may be required) to all medical records and social services records of *M U*

    (b) be provided by the Applicant's solicitors with copies of the application and accompanying documents together with any statement or report lodged in the Court

    (c) communicate with the social worker [*name*] in regard to an attendance upon *M U*

Reports

9. The Applicant is to arrange at the reasonable expense of *M U* a Report by a reputable local surveyor following an inspection of her home and to lodge this Report in the Court no later than [*date*]

10. The Report shall identify

    (a) any work that urgently needs to be carried out to make this home safe and fit for occupation by *M U*

    (b) the reasonable cost of such work

11. In preparing this Report the surveyor shall take into account the wishes and preferences of *M U* so far as ascertainable

Directions hearing

12. Copies of the Reports by the medical Visitor and the surveyor are to be made available to *M U* when available

13. Prior to the adjourned directions hearing the social worker [*name*] is to prepare a statement as to the response of *M U* to these Reports and the extent to which she will co-operate in allowing the work recommended by the surveyor to be carried out in her home by independent local contractors

14. There will be an adjourned directions hearing before District Judge [*name*] at [*regional court address*] on a date to be fixed after [*date*]

    (a) the attendance of *M U* is desirable

    (b) any request made by *M U* by letter for the hearing to be at her home or another nearby venue will be considered by the District Judge

    (c) if *M U* wishes she may attend the hearing, or part of the hearing, by telephone

    (d) any written communication sent to the Court by *M U* prior to the adjourned hearing will be taken into consideration

Further directions

15. All communications with the Court in response to this Order shall be sent to [*regional court address*]

* * * * * * *

E 7b

ORDER for repairs to property (continued)

BEFORE District Judge [*name*] sitting at [*regional court address*] on [*date*]

UPON READING further to the Directions Order dated 3 May 2011

(a) a Report dated [*date*] from Dr [*name*], special visitor to the Court of Protection as to the capacity of *M U* to make decisions as to the expenditure of significant sums on the maintenance and repair of her home at [*address*]

(b) a Report dated [*date*] from [*name*] Surveyors as to work that urgently needs to be carried out to make her home safe and fit for occupation and the reasonable cost of such work

(c) an undated letter from *M U* recording the work that she believes should be carried out

THE COURT NOW ORDERS THAT

1. [*name*] Council are to make copies of the two Reports available to *M U* either by post or personal delivery no later than [*date*]

2. [*name*] Council have permission to disclose the Report by the special Visitor to the treating general practitioner and psychiatrist of *M U*

3. There will be an inspection of *MU*'s home at [*address*] by District Judge [*name*] on [*date and time*]

    (a) in the presence of the representatives of [*name*] Council

    (b) *M U* is to be present and will have the opportunity to discuss with the Judge the work to be carried out and the manner in which this may be arranged

All communications with the Court in response to this Order shall be sent to [*regional court address*]

* * * * * * *

E 7c
ORDER for repairs to property (continued)

BEFORE District Judge [*name*] sitting at [*regional court address*] on [*date*]

UPON THE BASES THAT

(a) this Order is supplemental to a Directions Order dated [*date*]

(b) an accompanied inspection of the home of *M U* at [*address*] took place on [*date*] in the presence of *M U*, representatives of [*name*] Council ([*name*] social worker and [*name*] solicitor) and District Judge [*name*]

(c) there was a discussion involving those present at this inspection when certain understandings were reached

(d) the court proceeds on the basis that *M U* is capable of managing her day to day finances and is at present also capable of coping with the court proceedings because of the manner in which they are being conducted

(e) the court finds that *M U* is incapable within the meaning of the Mental Capacity Act 2005 of making and implementing on her own decisions to render her property fit for occupation but will co-operate with procedures set up by the court

(f) the purpose for which the order is needed cannot be as effectively achieved in a way that is less restrictive of her rights and freedom of action

THE COURT NOW ORDERS THAT

1. The authorised officer for property and affairs deputyships of [name] Council is appointed as deputy ('the deputy') to make decisions on behalf of M U that she is unable to make for herself in relation to her property and affairs, subject to the conditions or restrictions set out in this order

2. The appointment will last until 30 April 2012 but shall be reviewed on or before that date

Authority of deputy

3. The court confers authority on the deputy to arrange for necessary work to be carried out to the home of *M U* at [*address*] and to take possession or control of her savings and capital to the extent only that may be necessary to fund such work

   (a) The necessary work comprises the work described in the Report dated [*date*] of Messrs [*name*] Surveyors but shall not include a new bathroom suite without the consent of *M U*

   (b) The nature and extent of the work may be varied by agreement between the deputy and *M U* or otherwise with the approval of the court

   (c) The deputy may engage the services of a suitable building surveyor to commission and supervise the work and approve any invoices

   (d) The deputy and persons instructed by the deputy shall seek to co-operate at all times with *M U* and a further reference may be made to the court (by communication direct with District Judge [*name*]) in the event of deadlock

4. For the purpose of giving effect to any decision the deputy may execute or sign any necessary deeds or documents

Reports

5. The deputy is required to keep statements, vouchers, receipts and other financial records and to produce these to the court if required

6. The deputy shall report on progress by email to District Judge [*name*] at monthly intervals

Section E: Final Orders

Costs and expenses

7. The deputy is not without the permission of the court entitled to receive any costs for the implementation of this order

General

8. This order having been made without a hearing, M U may request by letter within 14 days of receipt of the order for it to be varied or reconsidered if she does not accept its terms

9. If such request is made a hearing will be arranged at [*address of regional court*] before District Judge [*name*] which M U will be expected to attend

10. All communications with the Court in response to this order shall quote the above reference number and be sent to [*address of regional court*]

Section F: Statutory wills

F 1
ORDER authorising statutory will

THIS ORDER IS NOT VALID UNLESS IT BEARS THE IMPRESSED SEAL OF THE COURT OF PROTECTION ON ALL PAGES

COURT OF PROTECTION

MENTAL CAPACITY ACT 2005

Case No: 00000000

In the Matter of
[A B]

MADE by District Judge [*name*] – *or authorised officer*

AT First Avenue House, 42–49 High Holborn, London WC1A 9JA [*or regional court address*]

ON [*date*]

UPON HEARING Counsel for the Applicant and Second Respondent, Counsel for the Official Solicitor (as litigation friend for *AB*) and counsel for the Third to Seventh Respondents

IT IS ORDERED that:

1. The Applicant be authorised in the name and on behalf of A B to execute a statutory will in the form annexed hereto (and initialed by the judge for the purpose of identification).

2. Upon execution, the said will is to be delivered to and held in the safe custody of [name of solicitors] in the name of A B during his lifetime or pending further order of the Court of Protection

3. The parties' costs shall be subject to detailed assessment on the standard basis and raised and paid out of the estate of A B.

* * * * * * * *

F 2
PRECEDENT for statutory will
LAST WILL AND TESTAMENT

THIS IS THE LAST WILL AND TESTAMENT of me A B the person who lacks capacity of [insert address] acting by C D of [insert address] the person authorised in that behalf by an order dated the   day of   20   made under the Mental Capacity Act 2005.

1. **I REVOKE** all former testamentary dispositions made by me and declare this to be my last will.

Section F: Statutory wills

2. **I APPOINT** *E F* and *G H* to be executors and trustees of this my will
3. **I GIVE**
4. The standard provisions of the Society of Trust and Estate Practitioners (2nd Edition) shall apply

IN WITNESS of which this will is signed by me *A B* acting by *C D* under the order mentioned above on   day of   20   .

SIGNED by the said *A B* acting by the said *C D* with his own name pursuant to the said order in our presence and attested by us in the presence of the said *C D*

WITNESS 1	WITNESS 2
Signature:	Signature:
Full Name:	Full Name:
Address:	Address:
Occupation:	Occupation:

Sealed with the official seal of the Court of Protection on the   day of   2013

* * * * * * *

Section G: Deprivation of Liberty

G 1
Re X [Order 1]
Model Re X Order

This is a final order made by the judge after reading the papers.

UPON the Court having read the application dated [*insert date*] and accompanying evidence as listed in the schedule attached hereto and including in particular the care plan dated [*insert date*] ('the Care Plan'), which has been signed and dated by the judge and kept on the Court file

AND UPON the Court being satisfied on the basis of the evidence filed by the Applicant (which is the only evidence before it) that:

1   [P] has been consulted about this application and given the support necessary to express views about the application, including whether or not s/he wishes to participate in proceedings by being joined as a party or otherwise;

2   [P] has not expressed a wish to be joined as a party and his/her joinder is not necessary or appropriate because [*insert reasons*];

3   Appropriate steps have been taken to consult [*insert names of those consulted*], being other relevant people in [P's] life, of this application and to canvass their wishes, feelings and views as to what is in [P's] best interests;

4   [*Recite any other matter which is relevant to the decision*] ;

5   The purpose for which this order is needed cannot be as effectively achieved in a way that is less restrictive of the rights and freedoms of [P];

6   It is appropriate for the application to be determined on the papers pursuant to the streamlined procedure described in *Re X and Others (Deprivation of Liberty) Number 1 [2014] EWCOP 25 and Number 2 [2014] EWCOP 37.*

IT IS ORDERED THAT:

7   Permission: The Applicant is granted permission to bring these proceedings.

8   Confidentiality: Until further order, these proceedings shall be heard in private and no person shall publish or disclose any information which enables the identification of [P] or any other party to these proceedings, save for the purpose of caring for [P] or for the purpose of communicating with a person exercising a relevant function authorised by statute or for the purpose of complying with an order of any court of competent jurisdiction.

9   Any requirement to comply with Rules 54 (filing of a permission form), 42, 69 and 70 (notification) of the Court of Protection Rules 2007 is dispensed with.

IT IS DECLARED THAT:

10 [P] lacks capacity to decide where s/he should live and what care and treatment s/he needs.

FURTHER, PURSUANT TO SECTIONS 4 AND 16 OF THE MENTAL CAPACITY ACT 2005 IT IS ORDERED THAT:

Placement and authorisation of deprivation of liberty

11 For the review period as defined below, [P] is to reside and receive care at [insert address] ('the placement') pursuant to arrangements made by [the Applicant] and set out in the Care Plan; and to the extent that the restrictions in place pursuant to the Care Plan are a deprivation of [P]'s liberty, such deprivation of [P's] liberty is hereby authorised.

Review

12 If a change or changes to the Care Plan that render it more restrictive have as a matter of urgent necessity been implemented [the Applicant] must apply to the Court for an urgent review of this order on the first available date after the implementation of any such changes.

13 If a change or changes to the Care Plan that render it more restrictive are proposed (but are not required as a matter of urgent necessity) [the Applicant] must apply to the Court for review of this order before any such changes are made.

14 In any event, [the Applicant] must make an application to the Court no less than one month before the expiry of the review period as defined below for a review of this order if at that time the Care Plan still applies to [P]. Such application shall be made in accordance with any Rules and Practice Directions in effect at the date of the application being filed or, if not otherwise specified, on form COPDOL10.

15 Any review hearing shall be conducted as a consideration of the papers unless any party requests an oral hearing or the Court decides that an oral hearing is required.

16 'The review period' shall mean [insert – usually 12 months; may be less, not more] from the date on which this order was made or, if an application for review has been filed at Court before that date, until determination of such review application.

17 This order shall cease to have effect on the death of [P].

Costs

18 No order as to costs.

Reconsideration

19 [P], any party to the proceedings, any person who is affected by this order and any person who is properly interested in [P's] welfare may apply to the Court at any time for its reconsideration, variation or discharge by any judge of the court including the judge who made this order.

20 Such application should be made without notice by filing an application in form COP9 and the court will make such order or give such directions as it thinks fit, including, where appropriate, who should be consulted about or notified of that application.

* * * * * * *

G 2
Re X [Order 2]

This is the order that will be used where the application has been considered and the judge does not feel that it is appropriate to use the Re X procedure.

IN THE COURT OF PROTECTION

IN THE MATTER OF THE MENTAL CAPACITY ACT 2005

Case No:

IN THE MATTER OF [INSERT P's FULL NAME]

ORDER

MADE BY [*add title and name*], a nominated Judge of the Court of Protection

ON [*date*]

ISSUED from the Court of Protection, First Avenue House, 42–49 High Holborn, London WC1A 9JA [*or insert alternative address as appropriate*]

UPON the Court having read the application dated [*insert date*] and accompanying evidence

AND UPON the Court considering that it is not appropriate to determine this matter on the papers pursuant to the streamlined procedure described in *Re X and Others (Deprivation of Liberty) Number 1* [2014] EWCOP 25 and *Number 2* [2014] EWCOP 37 because:

1 [*insert reasons*]

Section G: Deprivation of Liberty

IT IS ORDERED that

2 The application shall be considered further on the papers by a nominated judge of the Court of Protection who will make such orders or directions as may be appropriate. [*If practicable, such consideration should be by a judge sitting in the area of (insert geographical location of P)*].

Reconsideration

3 [P], any party to the proceedings, any person who is affected by this order and any person who is properly interested in [P's] welfare may apply to the Court at any time for its reconsideration, variation or discharge by any judge of the court including the judge who made this order.

* * * * * * *

G 3
Re X [Order 3]

This is the order that will be used where the judge requires further information before being able to proceed further to determine if a final order can be made or not.

IN THE COURT OF PROTECTION

IN THE MATTER OF THE MENTAL CAPACITY ACT 2005

Case No:

IN THE MATTER OF [INSERT P's FULL NAME]

ORDER

MADE BY [*add title and name*], a nominated Judge of the Court of Protection

ON [*date*]

ISSUED from the Court of Protection, First Avenue House, 42–49 High Holborn, London WC1A 9JA [*or insert alternative address as appropriate*]

UPON the Court having read the application dated [*insert date*] and accompanying evidence

AND UPON the Court requiring further information.

IT IS ORDERED that:

1 The Applicant shall by 4pm on [*insert time period – x days*] file at [*insert address*] the following information/documents:

2 [P], any party to the proceedings, any person who is affected by this order and any person who is properly interested in [P's] welfare may apply to the Court at any time for its reconsideration, variation or discharge by any judge of the court including the judge who made this order.

* * * * * * *

PART IX

Case Summaries

PART IX

Case Summaries

PART IX: Case Summaries

Contents

CAPACITY: PROCEDURE	2299
Assessment of capacity without medical evidence	2299
Baker Tilly (A Firm) v Makar [2013] EWHC 759 (QB), [2013] COPLR 245	2299
Discretion whether to make a declaration as to capacity	2300
YLA v PM and Another [2013] EWHC 4020 (COP), [2014] COPLR 114	2300
Expertise and conduct of experts conducting assessments of capacity	2300
SC v BS and A Local Authority [2012] COPLR 567	2300
Proper approach to assessing capacity	2300
PC and NC v City of York Council [2013] EWCA Civ 478, [2013] COPLR 409	2300
RT v LT and A Local Authority [2010] EWHC 1910 (Fam), [2010] COPLR Con Vol 1061	2300
PH v A Local Authority and Others [2011] EWHC 1704 (Fam), [2012] COPLR 128	2301
CC v KK and STCC [2012] EWHC 2136 (COP), [2012] COPLR 627	2301
Relevance of unwise nature of the decision	2301
Re S, D v R and S [2010] EWHC 2405 (COP), [2010] COPLR Con Vol 1112	2301
CAPACITY: THE SUBSTANTIVE LAW	2301
Test for capacity to agree to use of contraception	2301
A Local Authority v Mrs A and Mr A [2010] EWHC 1549 (Fam), [2010] COPLR Con Vol 138	2301
Test for capacity to consent to sexual relations	2302
IM v (1) LM (By Her Litigation Friend the Official Solicitor) (2) AB (3) Liverpool City Council [2014] EWCA Civ 37, [2014] COPLR 246	2302
A Local Authority v TZ (By his Litigation Friend, the Official Solicitor) [2013] EWHC 2322 (COP), [2013] COPLR 477	2302

London Borough of Tower Hamlets v TB (By Her Litigation Friend the Official Solicitor) [2014] EWCOP 53, [2015] COPLR 87   2302

Test for capacity to litigate   2303

Re S, D v R and S [2010] EWHC 2405 (COP), [2010] COPLR Con Vol 1112   2303

Test for capacity to marry, to make a will, execute a power of attorney, manage affairs and to litigate   2303

A, B and C v X and Z [2012] EWHC 2400 (COP), [2013] COPLR 1   2303

Test for capacity to marry   2303

A Local Authority v AK and Others (Capacity to Marry) [2012] EWHC B29 (COP), [2013] COPLR 163   2303

DEPRIVATION OF LIBERTY: SUBSTANTIVE LAW   2304

Applicability of Code of Practice accompanying DOLS regime   2304

R (C) v A Local Authority [2011] EWHC 1539 (Admin), [2011] COPLR Con Vol 972   2304

Inherent jurisdiction may be used to authorise deprivation of liberty of incapacitated adult in appropriate circumstances   2304

NHS Trust v Dr A [2013] EWHC 2442 (COP), [2013] COPLR 605   2304

MCA 2005 imposes no duty to accommodate person subject to provisions of Sch A1 to the 2005 Act   2304

DM v Doncaster Metropolitan Borough Council [2011] EWHC 3652 (Admin), [2012] COPLR 362   2304

Positive duties under Article 5 ECHR   2305

Re A and C (Equality and Human Rights Commission Intervening) [2010] EWHC 978 (Fam), [2010] COPLR Con Vol 10   2305

Universal test for determining whether objective element made out   2305

P (By His Litigation Friend the Official Solicitor) v Cheshire West and Chester Council and Another; P and Q (By Their Litigation Friend the Official Solicitor) v Surrey County Council [2014] UKSC 19, [2014] COPLR 313   2305

Deprivation of liberty at home   2305

W City Council v Mrs L (By Her Litigation Friend PC) (Deprivation of Liberty: Own Home) [2015] EWCOP 20, [2015] COPLR 337   2305

Deprivation of liberty in children's home or residential special school   2306

Barnsley Metropolitan Borough Council v GS and Others [2014] EWCOP 46, [2015] COPLR 51   2306

DEPRIVATION OF LIBERTY: OVERLAP BETWEEN MCA 2005 AND MHA 1983   2306

Court of Protection has no jurisdiction to determine P's place of residence when P subject to guardianship   2306

C (By his Litigation Friend the Official Solicitor v Blackburn with Darwen BC & Ors [2011] EWHC 3321 (COP), [2012] COPLR 350   2306

The MHA has primacy where it applies   2306

GJ v (1) The Foundation Trust (2) The PCT and (3) The Secretary of State for Health [2009] EWHC 2972 (Fam), [2009] COPLR Con Vol 567   2306

Test to determine whether detention should be under DOLS regime or under MHA 1983   2307

AM v South London and Maudsley NHS Foundation Trust and Another [2013] UKUT 365 (AAC), [2013] COPLR 510   2307

(1) Northamptonshire Healthcare NHS Foundation Trust and (2) Northampton and Nene CCG v ML (By His Litigation Friend the Official Solicitor), EL and BL [2014] EWCOP 2, [2014] COPLR 439   2307

KD v A Borough Council, the Department of Health and Others [2015] UKUT 251 (AAC), [2015] COPLR 486   2307

DEPRIVATION OF LIBERTY: PRACTICE AND PROCEDURE   2308

Approach to challenging DOLS   2308

AJ (By Her Litigation Friend the Official Solicitor) v A Local Authority [2015] EWCOP 5, [2015] COPLR 167   2308

Appropriate steps to be taken in borderline DOLS cases   2308

A Local Authority v PB and P (By his Litigation Friend the Official Solicitor) [2011] EWHC 2675 (COP), [2012] COPLR 1   2308

Court of Protection may not act as a rubber stamp in applications under s.21A MCA 2005   2308

A v A Local Authority, A Care Home Manager and S [2011] EWHC 727 (COP), [2011] COPLR Con Vol 190   2308

Deprivation of liberty under the MCA compatible with Article 5 ECHR   2308

G v E [2010] EWCA Civ 822, [2010] COPLR Con Vol 431   2308

Proper approach for avoiding lapses in authorisations under Schedule A1   2309

A County Council v MB, JB and A Residential Home [2010] EWHC 2508 (COP), [2011] 1 FLR 790, [2010] COPLR Con Vol 65   2309

Streamlined procedure   2309

Re NRA and Others [2015] EWCOP 59, [2015] COPLR 690   2309

Termination of standard authorisation and public funding   2309

Re UF [2013] EWHC 4289 (COP) [2014] COPLR 93   2309

DEPUTIES   2310

Appointment   2310

Re P (Vulnerable Adults: Deputies) [2010] EWHC 1592 (Fam), [2010] 2 FLR 1712, [2010] COPLR Con Vol 922   2310
G v E (Deputyship and Litigation Friend) [2010] EWHC 2512 (COP), [2011] 1 FLR 1652, [2010] COPLR Con Vol 470   2310
London Borough of Havering v LD and KD [2010] EWHC 3876 (COP), [2010] COPLR Con Vol 809   2310
SBC v and PBA and Others [2011] EWHC 2580 (Fam), [2011] COPLR Con Vol 1095   2310
Re AS [2013] COPLR 29   2311
Re M; N v O and P [2013] COPLR 91   2311

Failed application by a professional to be appointed as deputy may sound in costs.   2311

EG v RS, JS and BEN PCT [2010] EWHC 3073 (COP), [2010] COPLR Con Vol 350   2311

Gift giving by deputies   2311

Re GM [2013] COPLR 290   2311
Re Joan Treadwell, Deceased; Public Guardian v Lutz [2013] EWHC 2409 (COP), [2013] COPLR 587   2311

Test for removal of deputy   2312

Re Rodman; Long v Rodman and Others [2012] EWHC 347 (Ch), [2012] COPLR 433   2312

Test for setting the level of security that deputy required to post   2312

Re H; Baker v H & Anor [2009] COPLR Con Vol 606   2312

Whether and in what circumstances it is appropriate for the
Court of Protection to authorise the creation of a personal
injury trust of P's assets rather than appointing a deputy for
him 2312

SM v HM [2012] COPLR 187 2312

INHERENT JURISDICTION 2313

Extent of jurisdiction 2313

LBL v RYJ and VJ [2010] EWHC 2665 (COP), [2011] 1 FLR 1279,
[2010] COPLR Con Vol 795 2313
DL v A Local Authority and Others [2012] EWCA Civ 253, [2012]
COPLR 504 2313
NHS Trust v Dr A [2013] EWHC 2442 (COP), [2013] COPLR 605 2313

Relevant considerations in exercise of inherent jurisdiction 2314

XCC v AA and Others [2012] EWHC 2183 (COP), [2012] COPLR
730 2314
NCC v PB and TB [2014] EWCOP 14, [2015] COPLR 118 2314

INTERNATIONAL 2314

Exercise of jurisdiction dependent on habitual residence 2314

Re MN [2010] EWHC 1926 (Fam), [2010] COPLR Con Vol 893 2314

Meaning of habitual residence for purposes of MCA 2005, Sch 3 2314

JO v GO (Re PO) [2013] EWHC 3932 (COP), [2014] COPLR 62 2314
An English Local Authority v SW and Others [2014] EWCOP 43,
[2015] COPLR 29 2315

Recognition and enforcement of foreign protective measure governed by the terms of MCA 2005, Sch 3 2315

Re M [2011] EWHC 3590 (COP), [2012] COPLR 430 2315
Health Service Executive of Ireland v PA and Others [2015]
EWCOP 38, [2015] COPLR 447 2315
Re PD; *Health Service Executive of Ireland v CNWL* [2015]
EWCOP 48, [2015] COPLR 544 2316

MEDICAL TREATMENT 2316

Advance decisions to refuse medical treatment 2316

A Local Authority v E and Others [2012] EWHC 1639 (COP),
[2012] COPLR 441 2316
X Primary Care Trust v XB [2012] EWHC 1390 (Fam), [2012]
COPLR 577 2316

Nottinghamshire Healthcare NHS Trust v RC [2014] EWCOP 137,
  [2015] COPLR 468   2316

Approach to be adopted by court   2317

*W (By her Litigation Friend B) v (1) M (By her Litigation Friend the
  Official Solicitor) (2) S and (3) A NHS Primary Care Trust*
  [2011] EWHC 2443 (Fam), [2012] COPLR 222   2317
Aintree University Hospitals NHS Foundation Trust v James [2013]
  UKSC 67, [2013] COPLR 492   2317

Practice and procedure   2317

A Local Authority v K and Others [2013] EWHC 242 (COP), [2013]
  COPLR 194   2317

PRACTICE AND PROCEDURE   2318

Contempt proceedings   2318

*MASM v MMAM (By Her Litigation Friend the Official Solicitor)
  and Others* [2015] EWCOP 3, [2015] COPLR 239   2318

**Correct approach to withholding of documentary material from
a party to proceedings before Court of Protection**   2318

RC v CC and X Local Authority [2013] EWHC 1424 (COP), [2013]
  COPLR 431   2318

**Hearsay evidence is admissible from person not competent to
give evidence**   2318

London Borough of Enfield v SA [2010] EWHC 196 (Admin),
  [2010] COPLR Con Vol 362   2318

Privacy and media reporting   2318

Independent News Media v A [2010] EWCA Civ 343, [2010]
  COPLR Con Vol 686   2318
Hillingdon London Borough Council v Neary [2011] EWHC 413
  (COP), [2011] COPLR Con Vol 677   2319
P v Independent Print Ltd & Ors [2011] EWCA Civ 756, [2012]
  COPLR 110   2319
W v M and S (Reporting Restriction Order) [2011] EWHC 1197
  (COP), [2011] COPLR Con Vol 1205   2319
Re Gladys Meek; Jones v Parkin and Others [2014] EWCOP 1,
  [2014] COPLR 535   2320
*The Press Association v Newcastle upon Tyne Hospitals Foundation
  Trust* [2014] EWCOP 6, [2014] COPLR 502   2320
Re G (Adult); London Borough of Redbridge v G, C and F [2014]
  EWCOP 1361, [2014] COPLR 416   2320
*A Healthcare NHS Trust v P (By His Litigation Friend the Official
  Solicitor) and Q* [2015] EWCOP 15, [2015] COPLR 147   2320

Test to apply when considering whether to grant permission to bring application   2321

NK v (1) VW (By her Litigation Friend the Official Solicitor) (2) LCC (3) JW and (4) WW [2012] COPLR 105   2321

Test for joinder as a party   2321

Re SK (By His Litigation Friend, the Official Solicitor) [2012] EWHC 1990 (COP), [2012] COPLR 712   2321

TEST FOR DISPENSING WITH SERVICE UPON A RESPONDENT   2321

Re AB [2014] COPLR 381   2321

Threshold for engaging the jurisdiction of the Court   2321

Re F [2009] EWHC B30 (Fam), [2009] COPLR Con Vol 390   2321
SMBC v WMP and Others [2011] COPLR Con Vol 1177   2322

When fact-finding necessary and approach to be taken   2322

A Local Authority v M (By His Litigation Friend the Official Solicitor), E and A [2014] EWCOP 33, [2015] COPLR 6   2322
LBB v JM, BK and CM [2010] COPLR Con Vol 779 (Hedley J)   2322

When to identify matters and facts in issue and how such identification to be done   2322

A Local Authority v PB and P (No 1) [2011] EWHC 502 (COP), [2011] COPLR Con Vol 166   2322

PRACTICE AND PROCEDURE: COSTS   2323

Delay and expense in the Court of Protection   2323

A and B (Court of Protection: Delay and Costs) [2014] EWCOP 48, [2015] COPLR 1   2323

Relevant principles for costs decisions in the Court of Protection   2323

Re RC (Deceased) [2010] COPLR Con Vol 1022   2323
Manchester City Council v G, E (by his Litigation Friend the Official Solicitor) and F [2011] EWCA Civ 939, [2012] COPLR 95   2323
Re AH (Costs); AH and Others v Hertfordshire Partnership NHS Foundation Trust [2011] EWHC 3524 (COP), [2012] COPLR 327   2323
Re G (Adult) (Costs) [2014] EWCOP 5, [2014] COPLR 432   2324
Re G (An Adult) (By Her Litigation Friend The Official Solicitor) (Costs) [2015] EWCA Civ 446, [2015] COPLR 438   2324

Medical treatment cases 2324

Re D (Costs) [2012] EWHC 886 (COP), [2012] COPLR 499 2324

Power to consider likely outcome of the case for purposes of determining costs where settlement reached 2324

JS v KB and MP (Property and Affairs Deputy for DB) [2014] EWHC 483 (COP), [2014] COPLR 275 2324

Wasted costs procedure in the Court of Protection is the same as in the High Court 2325

Sharma and Judkins v Hunters [2011] EWHC 2546 (COP), [2012] COPLR 166 2325

PROPERTY AND AFFAIRS 2325

Court of Protection has power to approve altruistic payments in P's best interests 2325

Re X, Y and Z [2014] EWHC 87 (COP), [2014] COPLR 364 2325

Duties upon attorney in the management of P's monies 2325

Re Buckley [2013] COPLR 39 2325

Proper approach to making statutory will 2326

NT v FS and Others [2013] EWHC 684 (COP), [2013] COPLR 313 2326

When appropriate to order a statutory will to be made 2326

VAC v JAD & Others [2010] EWHC 2159 (Ch), [2010] COPLR Con Vol 302 2326

Replacement for replacement attorney cannot be appointed 2326

Public Guardian v Boff [2013] COPLR 653 2326

Attorneys can be appointed to act jointly with survivorship 2326

Miles v The Public Guardian; Beattie v The Public Guardian [2015] EWHC 2960 (Ch), [2015] COPLR 676 2326

Public Guardian's powers in relation to registration of powers of attorney 2327

Re XZ; XZ v The Public Guardian [2015] EWCOP 35, [2015] COPLR 630 2327

Revocation of power of attorney 2327

Re J [2011] COPLR Con Vol 716 2327
Re Harcourt [2013] COPLR 69 2327

Re DP (Revocation of Lasting Power of Attorney) [2014] COPLR
188   2327

BEST INTERESTS   2328

Construction and application of statutory defence under Mental Capacity Act 2005, s 5   2328

The Commissioner of Police of the Metropolis v ZH [2013] EWCA
Civ 69, [2013] COPLR 332   2328

Factors relevant to consideration of best interests as regards ending of marriage   2328

Sandwell Metropolitan Borough Council v RG & Ors [2013] EWHC
2373 (COP), [2013] COPLR 643   2328

The importance of country and culture of origin in best interests analysis   2328

An NHS Trust and B PCT v DU and Others [2009] EWHC
3504 (Fam), [2009] COPLR Con Vol 210   2328

No presumption in favour of family life in best interests analysis   2329

K v LBX and Others [2012] EWCA Civ 79, [2012] COPLR 411   2329

The purpose of MCA 2005   2329

Re P (Abortion) [2013] EWHC 50 (COP), [2013] COPLR 405   2329
*RB (By His Litigation Friend the Official Solicitor) v Brighton and
Hove City Council* [2014] EWCA Civ 561, [2014] COPLR 629   2329

Relevance of adult's own views   2329

Re S and S (Protected Persons); C v V [2008] COPLR Con Vol 1074   2329
Re M, ITW v Z and Others [2009] EWHC 2525 (Fam), [2009]
COPLR Con Vol 828   2329
Re P [2009] EWHC 163 (Ch), [2009] COPLR Con Vol 906   2330
The PCT v P, AH and A Local Authority [2009] COPLR Con
Vol 956   2330
Re G (TJ) [2010] EWHC 3005 (COP), [2010] COPLR Con Vol 403   2330
RGB v Cwm Taf Health Board and Others [2013] EWHC B23
(COP), [2014] COPLR 83   2331
Re M (Best Interests: Deprivation of Liberty) [2013] EWHC 3456
(COP), [2014] COPLR 35   2331
Aintree University Hospitals NHS Foundation Trust v James [2013]
UKSC 67, [2013] COPLR 492   2331

When duty to consult regarding P's welfare arises   2331

Re A; D v B [2009] COPLR Con Vol 1   2331

THE COURT OF PROTECTION AND THE HRA 2331
When interference in private and family life is justified 2331
Re GC and Anor [2008] EWHC 3402 (Fam), [2008] COPLR Con Vol 422 2331

No presumption in favour of family life in best interests analysis 2332
K v LBX and Others [2012] EWCA Civ 79, [2012] COPLR 411 2332

Need to justify interference in private life so as to comply with Article 8 ECHR 2332
J Council v GU, J Partnership NHS Foundation Trust, Care Quality Commission, X Limited [2012] EWHC 3531 (COP), [2013] COPLR 83 2332

Jurisdiction of the Court of Protection 2332
YA (F) v A Local Authority [2010] EWHC 2770 (COP), [2010] COPLR Con Vol 1226 2332
Re MN (Adult) [2015] EWCA Civ 411, [2015] COPLR 505 2332

Case Summaries[1]

Although the Court of Appeal has warned both against adding glosses to the plain words of MCA 2005[2] and slavish attempts to translate the decisions reached on the facts of one case to the facts of another,[3] it nonetheless remains the case that certain aspects of the substantive law have been fleshed out by decisions of the courts. Further, there is now an increasingly substantial body of case law relating to the practice and procedure of the Court of Protection.

To this end, this Part seeks to provide a quick reference guide to the key cases decided by the Court of Protection since October 2007,[4] and to stand as a complementary service to the authoritative Court of Protection Law Reports series. The part contains cases reported before October 2014; a few cases decided (or in respect of which transcripts became available) subsequently have been referred to in the body of this work. All the cases are judgments handed down by judges of the Court of Protection, unless otherwise stated.

Note also that from April 2014 there has been a dedicated case reference to all reported Court of Protection cases in the following style: [2015] EWCOP 50. This has been applied retrospectively by Bailii although the old citation will still find the case in the database and has been retained in this part and this volume generally.

Capacity: procedure

Assessment of capacity without medical evidence

Baker Tilly (A Firm) v Makar [2013] EWHC 759 (QB), [2013] COPLR 245 (Sir Raymond Jack, QBD)

Medical evidence is ordinarily required before the court will make a finding of lack of capacity on the ground of an impairment of the mind or brain, but the

---

[1] This chapter remains a work in progress, and comments and/or suggestions for inclusions of cases are very much welcomed. They can be made to the publishers or directly to annabel.lee@39essex.com. The assistance of Nicola Kohn of Thirty Nine Essex Street Chambers in compiling this edition of the case summaries chapter is gratefully acknowledged.
[2] *PC and NC v City of York Council* [2013] EWCA Civ 478, [2013] COPLR 409, at [37], per McFarlane LJ.
[3] *IM v (1) LM (By Her Litigation Friend the Official Solicitor) (2) AB (3) Liverpool City Council* [2014] EWCA Civ 37 [2014] COPLR 246.
[4] Some authorities decided before the enactment of MCA 2005 will in certain cases continue to have relevance, a good example being the decision in *Martin Masterman-Lister v Brutton & Co and Jewell & Home Counties Dairies* [2002] EWCA Civ 1889 which, along with *Sheffield CC v E & S* [2004] EWHC 2808 (Fam), continues regularly to be cited in the context of assessing litigation capacity. The 'balance sheet' approach to determining what lies in P's best interests, endorsed by Thorpe LJ in *Re A* [2000] 1 FLR 549 and *Re S* [2000] 2 FLR 389, also continues to be cited before the Court. Where relevant, case-law pre-dating October 2007 is dealt with in the main body of this work.

absence of medical evidence is not a bar to making such a finding. However, where medical evidence cannot be obtained, the court should be most cautious before making such a finding.

Discretion whether to make a declaration as to capacity

YLA v PM and Another [2013] EWHC 4020 (COP), [2014] COPLR 114 (Parker J)

While MCA 2005, s 15 gives the court a discretionary power to make a declaration, there is no true 'discretion' or choice as to whether to make a declaration as to capacity, as the determination of capacity is a necessary precursor of any consideration of best interests and the question whether a declaration of incapacity is in P's best interests is not relevant in deciding whether to make that declaration. It is not an invasion of private or family life to declare that a person lacks capacity in any particular respect.

Expertise and conduct of experts conducting assessments of capacity

SC v BS and A Local Authority [2012] COPLR 567 (Baker J)

Professional experience of capacity under MCA 2005 does not necessarily equate to sufficient experience in applying the capacity test in the context of Court of Protection litigation. No expert should give a patient a provisional view of their capacity without reading the patient's history.

Proper approach to assessing capacity

PC and NC v City of York Council [2013] EWCA Civ 478, [2013] COPLR 409 (McFarlane, Richards, Lewison LJJ, CA)

The determination of capacity under MCA 2005 is decision-specific: while some decisions, set down in MCA 2005, s 27, are status- or act-specific (such as agreeing to marry or consenting to divorce), others are person-specific (such as decisions upon contact), and removing the factual context from such decisions would leave nothing for the evaluation of capacity to bite upon. There has to be a clear causative link between any mental impairment ('the diagnostic element', set down in MCA 2005, s 2) and the inability of the person to take the relevant decision ('the functional element', set down in MCA 2005, s 3).

RT v LT and A Local Authority [2010] EWHC 1910 (Fam), [2010] COPLR Con Vol 1061 (Sir Nicholas Wall P)

Wherever possible, when assessing capacity, the court should apply the plain words of MCA 2005 directly to the facts of the particular case, avoiding complicating factors such as case-law pre-dating the statute. The individual capacities in MCA 2005, s 3(1) are not cumulative – if one of sections (a)–(d) applies then P lacks capacity.

Case Summaries

***PH v A Local Authority and Others* [2011] EWHC 1704 (Fam), [2012] COPLR 128 (Baker J)**

In assessing the question of capacity, the court must consider all the relevant evidence. The opinion of an independently instructed expert will be likely to be of very considerable importance, but in many cases the evidence of other clinicians and professionals who have experience of treating and working with P will be just as important and in some cases more important. The court must be aware of the risk that professionals involved with treating and helping that person may feel drawn towards an outcome that is more protective of the adult and thus, in certain circumstances, fail to carry out an assessment of capacity that is detached and objective.

***CC v KK and STCC* [2012] EWHC 2136 (COP), [2012] COPLR 627 (Baker J)**

In evaluating capacity, the court must recognise that different individuals may give different weight to different factors. It is wrong to conflate a capacity assessment with a best interests assessment and conclude that the person under review should attach greater weight to her physical safety and less weight to the emotional security and comfort of being in her own home. In assessing capacity, the person under review should be presented with detailed options so that their capacity to weigh up those options can be assessed. It is not necessary for a person to demonstrate a capacity to understand and weigh up every detail of the respective options so long as they understand the salient features.

Relevance of unwise nature of the decision

***Re S, D v R and S* [2010] EWHC 2405 (COP), [2010] COPLR Con Vol 1112 (Henderson J)**

That a decision is unwise or foolish may not, without more, be treated as conclusive, but it remains a relevant consideration for the court to take into account in considering whether the criteria of inability to make a decision for oneself in MCA 2005, s 3(1) are satisfied. This will particularly be the case where there is a marked contrast between the unwise nature of the impugned decision and the person's former attitude to the conduct of his affairs at a time when his capacity was not in question.

Capacity: the substantive law

Test for capacity to agree to use of contraception

***A Local Authority v Mrs A and Mr A* [2010] EWHC 1549 (Fam), [2010] COPLR Con Vol 138 (Bodey J)**

The test for capacity to decide whether to agree to the use of contraception should be applied so as to ascertain the woman's ability to understand and weigh up the immediate medical issues surrounding contraceptive treatment. It does not extend to consideration of the woman's understanding of what bringing up a child would be like in practice; nor should any opinion be attempted as to how she would be likely to get on or whether any child would be likely to be removed from her care.

Test for capacity to consent to sexual relations

IM v (1) LM (By Her Litigation Friend the Official Solicitor) (2) AB (3) Liverpool City Council [2014] EWCA Civ 37, [2014] COPLR 246 (Sir Brian Leveson, President of the QBD, Tomlinson and McFarlane LJJ, CA)

Every issue of capacity which falls to be determined under MCA 2005 must be evaluated by applying s 3(1) in full. In the context of capacity to consent to sexual relations, the ability to use and weigh information is unlikely to loom large: the notional process of using and weighing information attributed to the protected person should not involve a refined analysis of the sort which does not typically inform the decision to consent to sexual relations made by a person of full capacity. Decisions about capacity within the Court of Protection have a necessary forward looking focus, in contrast to the criminal law which focuses on the specific occasion when capacity is actually deployed and consent is either given or withheld. The test for capacity to consent to sexual relationships under the MCA 2005 is general and issue specific, rather than person or event specific.

A Local Authority v TZ (By his Litigation Friend, the Official Solicitor) [2013] EWHC 2322 (COP), [2013] COPLR 477 (Baker J)

The test for capacity to consent to sexual relations is act – rather than person – specific. In the case of someone gay or lesbian, it is ordinarily unnecessary to establish that the person has an understanding or awareness that sexual activity between a man and a woman might result in pregnancy. However, where an individual has been attracted to both men and women, it would be necessary to establish an understanding and awareness of the fact that sex between a man and a woman may result in pregnancy as part of the assessment of capacity to consent to sexual relations.

In assessing the capacity to consent to sexual relations, the real issue in the case before the court is whether P is able to use and weigh the relevant information. This is a relatively straightforward decision balancing the risks of ill health (and possible pregnancy if the relations are heterosexual) with pleasure, sexual and emotional, brought about by intimacy.

London Borough of Tower Hamlets v TB (By Her Litigation Friend the Official Solicitor) [2014] EWCOP 53, [2015] COPLR 87 (Mostyn J)

When determining the question of sexual capacity under MCA 2005, the relevant information comprises an awareness of the following elements on the part of P: (i) the mechanics of the act; (ii) that there were health risks involved; and (iii) that he or she has a choice and can refuse.

Case Summaries

Test for capacity to litigate

Re S, D v R and S [2010] EWHC 2405 (COP), [2010] COPLR Con Vol 1112 (Henderson J)

Capacity to litigate requires a basic understanding of the nature of the claim, of the legal issues involved and of the circumstances that have given rise to the claim. The need for an understanding of the claim is particularly pronounced where the claim is founded on a rebuttable presumption of undue influence, and where the relationship that arguably gave rise to the claim is still in existence.

Test for capacity to marry, to make a will, execute a power of attorney, manage affairs and to litigate

A, B and C v X and Z [2012] EWHC 2400 (COP), [2013] COPLR 1 (Hedley J)

The test for capacity to consent to marry set down in *Sheffield City Council v E & Anr* [2004] EWHC 2808 (Fam), [2005] 1 FLR 965 remains the appropriate test to apply. Where an individual's capacity to make a will or to execute a lasting power of attorney fluctuates, a 'qualified' declaration of capacity may be appropriate, to the effect that any will made or LPA executed unaccompanied by contemporaneous medical evidence asserting capacity would give rise to a serious risk of challenge. By contrast, the general concept of managing affairs is an ongoing act and therefore quite unlike the specific act of making a will or granting power of attorney. The management of affairs relates to a continuous state of affairs whose demands may be unpredictable and may occasionally be urgent. The question of whether a person has capacity to litigate inevitably follows closely on the question of management of one's own affairs, but requires separate consideration because it operates in a separate and more restricted time frame, but a time frame quite different to the decision to make a will or to grant a power of attorney.

Test for capacity to marry

A Local Authority v AK and Others (Capacity to Marry) [2012] EWHC B29 (COP), [2013] COPLR 163 (Bodey J)

The test for capacity to marry remains that set by pre-MCA 2005 case-law, in particular *Sheffield City Council v E & Anr* [2004] EWHC 2808 (Fam), [2005] 1 FLR 965, together with the additional requirement set down in *X City Council v MB, NB and MAB (By his litigation friend the Official Solicitor)* [2006] EWHC 168 (Fam), [2006] 2 FLR 968 that the person must have the capacity to consent to sexual relations, because a sexual relationship is generally implicit in marriage.

Deprivation of liberty: substantive law

Applicability of Code of Practice accompanying DOLS regime

R (C) v A Local Authority [2011] EWHC 1539 (Admin), [2011] COPLR Con Vol 972 (Ryder J)

Sch A1 of the MCA 2005 does not apply where P is placed in a children's home. However, the Court of Protection will of necessity have regard to the same material as contained in the DOLS Code of Practice when making determinations of best interests in such a case. The Mental Health Act 1983 Code of Practice should apply as a matter of good practice in cases of the seclusion and restraint of children and young persons in schools that have the status of children's homes. This should be the case even where their learning disability does not fall within the definition of mental disorder for purposes of MCA 2005.

Inherent jurisdiction may be used to authorise deprivation of liberty of incapacitated adult in appropriate circumstances

NHS Trust v Dr A [2013] EWHC 2442 (COP), [2013] COPLR 605 (Baker J)

The prohibition in MCA 2005, s 16A(1) against authorising the deprivation of liberty of patients subject to detention under the MHA 1983 is expressly restricted to the Court of Protection and does not extend to the High Court exercising its inherent jurisdiction. Parliament did not intend to prevent the High Court exercising its jurisdiction in the best interests of and so as to uphold the Art 2 ECHR rights of a person or to remove the safety net of the inherent jurisdiction in order to prevent his death. The High Court has the power to authorise a deprivation of liberty of an incapacitated adult for purposes of bringing about forcible feeding where such could not be authorised under MCA 2005 and where such treatment could not be administered under MHA 1983, s 63, so long as such order complies with the provisions of Art 5 ECHR, in particular the provision for adequate review at reasonable intervals.

MCA 2005 imposes no duty to accommodate person subject to provisions of Sch A1 to the 2005 Act

DM v Doncaster Metropolitan Borough Council [2011] EWHC 3652 (Admin), [2012] COPLR 362 (Langstaff J, Admin Court)

MCA 2005 imposes no obligation upon a local authority to accommodate a person subject to the provisions of Sch A1, whether by way of necessary implication or otherwise, nor does it require the local authority to pay for such accommodation.

Case Summaries

Positive duties under Article 5 ECHR

Re A and C (Equality and Human Rights Commission Intervening) [2010] EWHC 978 (Fam), [2010] COPLR Con Vol 10 (Munby LJ)

A local authority's positive obligations under Art 5 ECHR do not clothe them with any power to regulate, control, restrain or coerce – there must be specific statutory authority for such actions or they must be authorised by the court. To engage Art 5, a deprivation of liberty must be attributable to the State. However, where the State knows or ought to know that a vulnerable child or adult is subject to restrictions on their liberty by a private individual, this arguably gives rise to positive obligations to investigate and take steps to bring that deprivation to an end. Where, upon investigation, the State is satisfied that the objective element is not made out, then its duty will have been discharged, subject to any continuing duty to monitor the situation. Where there is a deprivation of liberty, the State has a positive duty to take reasonable and proportionate measures to bring that state of affairs to an end.

Universal test for determining whether objective element made out

P (By His Litigation Friend the Official Solicitor) v Cheshire West and Chester Council and Another; P and Q (By Their Litigation Friend the Official Solicitor) v Surrey County Council [2014] UKSC 19, [2014] COPLR 313 (Lord Neuberger of Abbotsbury, President, Baroness Hale of Richmond, Deputy President, Lord Kerr of Tonaghmore, Lord Clarke of Stone-cum-Ebony, Lord Sumption, Lord Carnwath of Notting Hill and Lord Hodge, Supreme Court)

The 'acid test' for determining whether there has been a deprivation of liberty is: that the person concerned is under continuous supervision and control and is not free to leave. In applying the acid test, the person's compliance or lack of objection is not relevant; the relative normality of the placement (whatever the comparison made) is not relevant; and the reason or purpose behind a particular placement is also not relevant.

Deprivation of liberty at home

W City Council v Mrs L (By Her Litigation Friend PC) (Deprivation of Liberty: Own Home) [2015] EWCOP 20, [2015] COPLR 337 (Bodey J)

The 'own home' consideration must be a relevant factor in the mix in determining whether there is a deprivation of liberty. There are also references in the authorities suggesting that it had been relevant that the individual concerned, or someone acting on his behalf was the complainant. Situations involving a person's own home are different to those involving institutional accommodation with arrangements designed to confine the person for his or her safety, and where that person, or someone on his or her behalf, is challenging the need for such confinement; (obiter) the role of the family in care arrangements is also relevant to determining whether any deprivation of liberty is imputable to the state.

Deprivation of liberty in children's home or residential special school

Barnsley Metropolitan Borough Council v GS and Others [2014] EWCOP 46, [2015] COPLR 51 (Holman J)

There could be circumstances in which the Court of Protection may authorise a children's home or residential special school to impose restraint that amounts to a deprivation of liberty. Whether or not it would be lawful, necessary, proportionate and in any given individual's best interests for the Court of Protection to authorise a deprivation of liberty will require thorough investigation and assessment.

Deprivation of liberty: overlap between MCA 2005 and MHA 1983

Court of Protection has no jurisdiction to determine P's place of residence when P subject to guardianship

C (By his Litigation Friend the Official Solicitor v Blackburn with Darwen BC & Ors [2011] EWHC 3321 (COP), [2012] COPLR 350 (Peter Jackson J)

The Court of Protection has no jurisdiction to determine the place of residence of a person subject to the guardianship regime. Even if the Court of Protection did have jurisdiction, it could only make an order that conflicted with the guardianship scheme in exceptional circumstances of a breach of ECHR, Arts 5 or 8. Where there were genuinely contested issues about the place of residence, the Court of Protection should make such a decision pursuant to its powers under MCA 2005, s 16. Substantial decisions of that kind ought properly to be made by the Court of Protection, using its power to make welfare decisions under MCA 2005, s 16.

The MHA has primacy where it applies

GJ v (1) The Foundation Trust (2) The PCT and (3) The Secretary of State for Health [2009] EWHC 2972 (Fam), [2009] COPLR Con Vol 567 (Charles J)

The Mental Health Act 1983 ('MHA') has primacy in that the decision-makers under both the MHA and MCA 2005 should approach the questions they have to answer relating to the application of the MHA on the basis of an assumption that an alternative solution is not available under MCA 2005. The decision-maker should approach the status test concerning eligibility in MCA 2005, Sch A1, para 12(1)(a), (b) by asking himself whether in his view the criteria set by ss 2 or 3 of the MHA are met, and if an application was made under them a hospital would detain P. In applying para 5(3) of Sch 1A, the decision-maker should focus on the reason P should be deprived of his liberty by applying a 'but for' approach – is the only effective reason why P should be detained in hospital the need for physical treatment unconnected to the treatment for his mental disorder? The decision-maker should approach the test in para 5(4) of Sch 1A without taking any fine distinctions between the potential reasons for P's objection to treatment of different types or to simply being in hospital.

Note: this decision must now be read subject to the decision of the same judge in *AM v South London and Maudsley NHS Foundation Trust and Another* [2013] UKUT 365 (AAC), [2013] COPLR 510.

Test to determine whether detention should be under DOLS regime or under MHA 1983

AM v South London and Maudsley NHS Foundation Trust and Another [2013] UKUT 365 (AAC), [2013] COPLR 510 (Charles J)

Decision-makers under the Mental Health Act 1983 (MHA) are required to consider three questions in respect of patients who they are considering detaining under the compulsory provisions of that Act: (1) does the person have capacity to consent to admission as an informal patient? (2) Might the hospital be able to rely on the provisions of MCA 2005 to lawfully assess or treat the patient? (3) If there is a choice between reliance on the MHA and MCA 2005, which is the least restrictive way of best achieving the proposed assessment or treatment? This evaluation must be undertaken in respect of each patient by reference to the specific facts of their case.

(1) Northamptonshire Healthcare NHS Foundation Trust and (2) Northampton and Nene CCG v ML (By His Litigation Friend the Official Solicitor), EL and BL [2014] EWCOP 2, [2014] COPLR 439 (Hayden J)

Where P falls within Case E of Sch 1A, para 2(a) of the MCA 2005, such that he is ineligible to be deprived of his liberty under the MCA 2005, the MHA 1983 will apply. The MHA 1983 has primacy where it applies and is the magnetic north when contemplating the deprivation of liberty of those who fall within Case E.

KD v A Borough Council, the Department of Health and Others [2015] UKUT 251 (AAC), [2015] COPLR 486 (Charles J, UT (ACC))

The First-tier Tribunal (FTT) could consider whether to discharge a guardianship order where the alternative placement entails a lawful deprivation of liberty. The FTT should consider whether there is an alternative actually in place and whether, if that alternative entails a deprivation of liberty, it is authorised either under MCA 2005, Sch A1 or by an order of the Court of Protection.

Deprivation of liberty: practice and procedure

Approach to challenging DOLS

AJ (By Her Litigation Friend the Official Solicitor) v A Local Authority [2015] EWCOP 5, [2015] COPLR 167 (Baker J)

There is an obligation on the state to ensure that a person deprived of liberty is not only entitled but enabled to have the lawfulness of his detention reviewed speedily by a court. The ultimate responsibility for guaranteeing the effective protection of the Art 5 rights of those subject to DOLS lies with the relevant local authority. A relevant person's representative (RPR) should be selected or confirmed for appointment unless it is clear that they will support the detained person to exercise their rights under Sch A1.

Appropriate steps to be taken in borderline DOLS cases

A Local Authority v PB and P (By his Litigation Friend the Official Solicitor) [2011] EWHC 2675 (COP), [2012] COPLR 1 (Charles J)

Where questions of deprivation of liberty arise, the most important issue is whether the care regime is in the person's best interests, not whether the person is being deprived of his liberty. In borderline cases and cases where there will be deprivation of liberty if identified, contingency planning is implemented, care providers should ensure that there is no breach of Art 5 ECHR and review the regime to check that it remains in P's best interests. This may involve applying the DOLS regime, or, at the very least, considering the qualifying requirements identified in Sch A1 to the MCA 2005. Where the DOLS regime under Sch A1 applies, it should be used in preference to authorisation and review by the court.

Court of Protection may not act as a rubber stamp in applications under s.21A MCA 2005

A v A Local Authority, A Care Home Manager and S [2011] EWHC 727 (COP), [2011] COPLR Con Vol 190 (Sir Nicholas Wall P)

The terms of the MCA 2005 establishes stringent conditions for the deprivation of liberty. However beneficial the arrangements authorised pursuant to a standard authorisation might appear for the individual concerned, the court could not act as a rubber stamp and in an appropriate case a Visitor should be appointed to report under the terms of s 49 of MCA 2005.

Deprivation of liberty under the MCA compatible with Article 5 ECHR

G v E [2010] EWCA Civ 822, [2010] COPLR Con Vol 431 (President of the Family Division, Thorpe LJ and Hedley J, Court of Appeal)

MCA 2005 generally, and Schedule A1 thereto specifically, plug the 'Bournewood gap' and are compliant with Art 5 ECHR. The justification of detention under MCA 2005 is not a medical decision for which psychiatric evidence is required, but a decision for the court to be made in the best interests of the person whom it is sought to detain.

Proper approach for avoiding lapses in authorisations under Schedule A1

A County Council v MB, JB and A Residential Home [2010] EWHC 2508 (COP), [2011] 1 FLR 790, [2010] COPLR Con Vol 65 (Charles J)

Once an urgent authorisation has been given under Sch A1 to MCA 2005 (and, if appropriate extended), detention can only lawfully be extended by a standard authorisation or by court order. Where a further authorisation cannot be given under DOLS then it will not be correct to issue an application under MCA 2005, s 21A (challenge to an authorisation) as the relief that can be granted by the court will not be adequate. 'Standard' Court of Protection proceedings will be required. If necessary, pending application to the court, it may be possible to rely on MCA 2005, s 4B but only if a decision is made with express reference to s 4 and recorded with full reasons in writing.

Streamlined procedure

Re NRA and Others [2015] EWCOP 59, [2015] COPLR 690 (Charles J)

P does not have to be a party to all applications for welfare orders sought to authorise, and which when they are made will authorise, a deprivation of P's liberty caused by the implementation of the care package on which the welfare order is based. Where there is a family member or friend who can act in a balanced way to promote P's interests, they can and should, without making P a party, effectively provide an independent check and the equivalent safeguards provided by an IMCA or an RPR. In most cases it would be appropriate to make such a family member or friend a r 3A representative with a direction to keep the care package under review. Where there is no such family member or friend, the Court of Protection may exercise its investigatory jurisdiction to obtain information through s 49 reports or the issue of witness summonses.

Termination of standard authorisation and public funding

Re UF [2013] EWHC 4289 (COP) [2014] COPLR 93 (Charles J)

In circumstances where the termination of a standard authorisation results in a termination of non-means tested public funding, the appropriate way forward in respect of non-means tested public funding is for the local authority to consider imposing a new standard authorisation under Sch A1 to MCA 2005, which the court may then extend, exercising its powers under ss 21A, 47, 48 and para 61(2) of Sch A1 to MCA 2005, the Ministry of Justice and the LAA having confirmed that this would not be viewed as a contrivance. The approach adopted in Re HA, whereby the court granted interim declarations in place of the standard authorisation, would no longer be appropriate, but nor would it be appropriate for the court to leave the continuing authorisation of deprivation of liberty to the statutory bodies.

Deputies

Appointment

Re P (Vulnerable Adults: Deputies) [2010] EWHC 1592 (Fam), [2010] 2 FLR 1712, [2010] COPLR Con Vol 922 (Hedley J)

Although s 16(4) of the MCA 2005 might at first glance suggest that the appointment of deputies is a rarity, this would be inconsistent with the aim of MCA 2005. Insofar as applications by family members to be appointed deputies are concerned, the courts should be sympathetic to their requests provided the family members are not embroiled in disputes with one another and appear able to carry out the functions of a deputy appropriately.

G v E (Deputyship and Litigation Friend) [2010] EWHC 2512 (COP), [2011] 1 FLR 1652, [2010] COPLR Con Vol 470 (Baker J)

The scheme of MCA 2005 is that decisions should ordinarily be taken by those looking after and responsible for incapacitated adults, with particularly grave decisions or issues that are the subject of dispute being resolved by the courts. The appointment of a deputy, which entails giving one person a protected position regarding decision-making, is not appropriate except in limited circumstances, notably those identified in the MCA Code of Practice. These include cases where P is at risk of harm from family members or there is a long history of disputes, or where P has substantial financial assets that require regular management.

Hedley J had not in *Re P* [2010] EWHC 1592 (Fam), [2010] COPLR Con Vol 922 been intending to give general guidance as to the meaning of s 16(4) of the MCA 2005 because, on the facts of that former case, the question was not whether deputies should be appointed, but as to the identity of those deputies.

London Borough of Havering v LD and KD [2010] EWHC 3876 (COP), [2010] COPLR Con Vol 809 (HHJ Turner QC sitting as a nominated judge of the Court of Protection)

Welfare deputies should be appointed rarely; there is a preference for specific decisions of the court. Where appointed, a deputy's role should be of the narrowest scope and for the shortest time reasonably practicable in the circumstances.

SBC v and PBA and Others [2011] EWHC 2580 (Fam), [2011] COPLR Con Vol 1095 (Roderic Wood J)

The test to be applied when determining whether to appoint a deputy (whether to manage a person's property and affairs or to take decision regarding their health and welfare) is to be derived from the unvarnished words of the MCA 2005. There is no additional requirement from the Code of Practice that in order for a deputy to be appointed it is necessary that the case before the Court be one of the 'most difficult' categories of case.

Re AS [2013] COPLR 29 (Senior Judge Lush)

Generally speaking, the order of preference for the appointment of a deputy is: P's spouse or partner; any other relative who takes a personal interest in P's affairs; a close friend; a professional adviser, such as the family's solicitor or accountant; a local authority's Social Services Department; and finally a panel deputy, as deputy of last resort.

Re M; N v O and P [2013] COPLR 91 (Senior Judge Lush)

Pre-MCA 2005 authorities on the appointment of a committee or receiver are still relevant to the appointment of deputies. They reinforce the order of preference set out in Re AS [2013] COPLR 29. The court will not, however, automatically appoint a spouse even though they are usually at the top of the order of preference.

Failed application by a professional to be appointed as deputy may sound in costs

EG v RS, JS and BEN PCT [2010] EWHC 3073 (COP), [2010] COPLR Con Vol 350 (HHJ Cardinal sitting as a nominated judge of the Court of Protection)

While applications by professionals seeking appointment as deputies should not be discouraged, it was not appropriate for such applications to be made where the would-be deputy would not be viewed by all parties as a neutral arbitrator. A failed application could sound in costs.

Gift giving by deputies

Re GM [2013] COPLR 290 (Senior Judge Lush)

It is important that deputies and attorneys should realise that they have only a very limited authority to make gifts. They should understand why their authority is limited and be aware that, in an appropriate case, they may apply to the Court of Protection for more extensive gift-making powers. Subject to a de minimis exception, deputies and attorneys must apply to the Court for authority to make a gift that exceeds the scope of their authority.

Re Joan Treadwell, Deceased; Public Guardian v Lutz [2013] EWHC 2409 (COP), [2013] COPLR 587 (Senior Judge Lush)

In cases involving allegations of unlawful gift-giving by deputies, the Office of the Public Guardian was correct in its general approach to quantifying loss to the estate by identifying, first, the gifts that the deputy was authorised to make and, secondly, any additional gifts that, having regard to all the circumstances, might reasonably have been ratified by the court. Gifts made at a christening, housewarming and graduation may be regarded as gifts that are made on customary occasions, along with birthday and Christmas presents, but subject to the proviso that they are not unreasonable having regard to all the circumstances and, in particular, the size of the donor's estate.

In the context of testate succession, at least, the principle that deputies should interfere with succession rights as little as possible is compatible with the principle set out in MCA 2005, s 1(5). Further, by MCA 2005, s 4(6), one of the factors that any substitute decision-maker is required to take into account is any relevant written statement made by the individual when they had capacity. In the context of someone's property and financial affairs, it is not possible to think of a written statement that is more relevant or more important than a will, and when testators make a will, they have a reasonable expectation that their wishes will be respected by deputies.

Test for removal of deputy

Re Rodman; Long v Rodman and Others [2012] EWHC 347 (Ch), [2012] COPLR 433 (Newey J, ChD)

A decision whether to vary or discharge an order appointing a deputy for P must be made in the best interests of P. In determining that, all the relevant circumstances must be considered and the Court must in particular take into account the views of 'anyone engaged in caring for the person or interested in P's welfare'.

Test for setting the level of security that deputy required to post

Re H; Baker v H & Anor [2009] COPLR Con Vol 606 (HHJ Marshall QC sitting as a nominated judge of the Court of Protection)

The court outlined the factors for setting the level of security that a property and affairs deputy is required to post. Where there are doubts as to whether or not the deputy should be trusted, the court must consider not appointing him as a deputy or limiting the funds in his control.

Whether and in what circumstances it is appropriate for the Court of Protection to authorise the creation of a personal injury trust of P's assets rather than appointing a deputy for him

SM v HM [2012] COPLR 187 (HHJ Marshall QC sitting as a nominated judge of the Court of Protection)

The authorisation of a settlement for P can only be justified if it is in P's best interests to do so. Since the statutory scheme of deputyship has been provided with the very objective of being in P's best interests in the usual case, departing from this needs to be justified on the basis that such departure is in P's best interest in the particular case. This requires demonstration that the proposed settlement and its terms provide a sufficiently clear and significant overall state of advantage to P over that which is capable of being created by an appropriate deputyship order that it justifies such a departure. The burden of establishing this to the court's satisfaction is on the applicant seeking authorisation of the settlement.

Inherent jurisdiction

Extent of jurisdiction

LBL v RYJ and VJ [2010] EWHC 2665 (COP), [2011] 1 FLR 1279, [2010] COPLR Con Vol 795 (Macur J)

The inherent jurisdiction survives the enactment of MCA 2005 to supplement its protection for those who, while 'capacitous' for the purposes of the Act, are incapacitated by external forces – whatever they may be – outside their control from reaching a decision. However, it cannot be used in the case of a capacitous adult to impose a decision upon him/her whether as to welfare or finance. Rather, the inherent jurisdiction exists to facilitate the process of unencumbered decision-making by those who they have determined have capacity free of external pressure or physical restraint in making those decisions. If a person is unable to withstand external pressure of 'normal/everyday' degree, whether emotional or physical, then this is likely to be a pointer that, on a proper analysis, they lack the relevant capacity for purposes of MCA 2005.

DL v A Local Authority and Others [2012] EWCA Civ 253, [2012] COPLR 504 (Maurice Kay, McFarlane and Davis LJJ, CA)

The High Court's inherent jurisdiction remains available to make declarations in relation to vulnerable adults who do not fall within the MCA 2005, but who are for some other reason incapacitated or disabled from making a relevant decision or free choice or from expressing real and genuine consent. The decision of *Re SA (Vulnerable Adult with Capacity: Marriage)* [2005] EWHC 2942 (Fam) was not a 'one off'; it is clear that by virtue of the lack of express provision within MCA 2005 that, where there are matters outside the statutory scheme to which the inherent jurisdiction applies, then that jurisdiction continues to be available as a great safety net. The jurisdiction of the High Court in this regard is not limited solely to the creation of a temporary 'safe space'.

NHS Trust v Dr A [2013] EWHC 2442 (COP), [2013] COPLR 605 (Baker J)

The prohibition in MCA 2005, s 16A(1) against authorising the deprivation of liberty of patients subject to detention under the MHA 1983 is expressly restricted to the Court of Protection and does not extend to the High Court exercising its inherent jurisdiction. Parliament did not intend to prevent the High Court exercising its jurisdiction in the best interests of and so as to uphold the Art 2 ECHR rights of a person or to remove the safety net of the inherent jurisdiction in order to prevent his death. The High Court has the power to authorise a deprivation of liberty of an incapacitated adult for purposes of bringing about forcible feeding where such could not be authorised under MCA 2005 and where such treatment could not be administered under MHA 1983, s 63, so long as such order complies with the provisions of Art 5 ECHR, in particular the provision for adequate review at reasonable intervals.

Relevant considerations in exercise of inherent jurisdiction

XCC v AA and Others [2012] EWHC 2183 (COP), [2012] COPLR 730 (Parker J)

The inherent jurisdiction of the High Court can be used to provide relief that is not provided for in the MCA 2005. Because the MCA 2005 provides no power of itself to grant a non-recognition declaration, the making of such a declaration falls to be considered by reference to the inherent jurisdiction of the High Court. When making such a decision, the High Court is not confined to a consideration of best interests or welfare considerations, and may take into account public policy considerations.

NCC v PB and TB [2014] EWCOP 14, [2015] COPLR 118 (Parker J)

In determining whether the causative nexus between the individual's mental impairment and an inability to make a decision was satisfied, the question was whether the impairment/disturbance of mind was an effective, material or operative cause of the incapacity, even if other factors came into play; (obiter) if a person has capacity, the High Court could still exercise its inherent jurisdiction to require their placement in the care home, even if that entailed a deprivation of her liberty, if the requirements of Art 5(1)(e) are satisfied.

International

Exercise of jurisdiction dependent on habitual residence

Re MN [2010] EWHC 1926 (Fam), [2010] COPLR Con Vol 893 (Hedley J)

Whether the Court of Protection can exercise its full original jurisdiction depends on whether the person is habitually resident in England and Wales. It is a question of fact to be determined in the individual circumstances of the case. Wrongful removal of an incapacitated adult from the jurisdiction in which they were originally habitually resident should generally mean that the habitual residence of the person does not change. When determining whether to recognise and enforce a foreign protective measure under the provisions of Sch 3 to MCA 2005, the Court is not required to undertake a full best interests assessment, although a limited assessment will be required to determine whether the specific method of implementation of the measure accords with MCA 2005, s 1(5).

Meaning of habitual residence for purposes of MCA 2005, Sch 3

JO v GO (Re PO) [2013] EWHC 3932 (COP), [2014] COPLR 62 (Sir James Munby P)

Schedule 3 to MCA 2005 is not entirely in force in England and Wales, because the Convention is not yet in force in England and Wales 'in accordance with Article 57' of the Convention.

Habitual residence is a question of fact to be determined having regard to all the circumstances of the particular case. Habitual residence can in principle be lost and another habitual residence acquired on the same day. In the case of an adult who lacks the capacity to decide where to live, habitual residence can in principle be lost and another habitual residence acquired without the need for any court order or other formal process, such as the appointment of an attorney or deputy. In deciding whether the actions taken by relatives or carers have led to a change in the habitual residence of P, the doctrine of necessity is relevant to determining whether the move is wrongful. There will be no change in the habitual residence of the person if the removal from the jurisdiction has been wrongful. The doctrine of perpetuatio fori does not apply when it comes to determining changes in habitual residence such that the position falls to be considered as at the point of the hearing, not at the point of issue of the relevant application.

The doctrine of forum non conveniens applies in the context of incapacitated adults as between England/Scotland in the same way as it would with children. It would also apply subject to the provisions of the 2000 Hague Convention as and when ratified. A decision to refuse to exercise jurisdiction on the basis of forum non conveniens is not a decision falling within the scope of MCA 2005, s 1(5).

An English Local Authority v SW and Others [2014] EWCOP 43, [2015] COPLR 29 (Moylan J)

The definition of 'habitual residence' under MCA 2005 should be the same as that applied in other family law instruments.

Recognition and enforcement of foreign protective measure governed by the terms of MCA 2005, Sch 3

Re M [2011] EWHC 3590 (COP), [2012] COPLR 430 (Mostyn J)

The Court of Protection is not barred by operation of the provisions of MCA 2005, Sch 1A from recognising a foreign order placing an incapacitated adult in a psychiatric institution in circumstances amounting to a deprivation of their liberty because such an order is not a welfare order under MCA 2005, s 16(2)(a).

Health Service Executive of Ireland v PA and Others [2015] EWCOP 38, [2015] COPLR 447 (Baker J)

It was only where the court concludes that recognition of the foreign measure would be manifestly contrary to public policy that the discretionary ground to refuse recognition would arise. A finding of a foreign court that the individual was habitually resident in that country could not be challenged in any process to recognise or enforce a measure in this country, although the process by which the measure was ordered may be challenged and the measure itself may be challenged. Recognition and enforcement is likely to require close co-operation, not only between the medical and social care authorities of the two countries, but also between the courts and legal systems.

Re PD; Health Service Executive of Ireland v CNWL [2015] EWCOP 48, [2015] COPLR 544 (Baker J)

Where an adult has been a party and represented in the proceedings before the foreign court, it is not 'indispensable' for that adult also to be a party before the court on an application for recognition and enforcement of the foreign order, given the limited scope of the inquiry required of the court. In some cases, joinder of the adult as a party would be considered necessary but in the majority of cases it would not. The flexibility provided by the new r 3A was well-suited to applications under Sch 3.

Medical treatment

Advance decisions to refuse medical treatment

A Local Authority v E and Others [2012] EWHC 1639 (COP), [2012] COPLR 441 (Peter Jackson J)

For an advance decision relating to life-sustaining treatment to be valid and applicable, there should be clear evidence establishing on the balance of probability that the maker had capacity at the relevant time. Where the evidence of capacity is doubtful or equivocal it is not appropriate to uphold the decision. Where there is a genuine doubt or disagreement about the validity of an advance decision, the Court of Protection can make a decision, and applications to the court for such decisions should be made in a timely fashion.

X Primary Care Trust v XB [2012] EWHC 1390 (Fam), [2012] COPLR 577 (Theis J)

In the event that there is an issue raised about the validity of an advance decision, it is important that this is investigated by the relevant bodies as a matter of urgency. There is no set form for advance decisions, but the MCA 2005 Code of Practice provides guidance as to what should be included in an advance decision. Caution should be exercised when using pro forma advance decision forms that include a 'valid until' date.

Nottinghamshire Healthcare NHS Trust v RC [2014] EWCOP 137, [2015] COPLR 468 (Mostyn J)

Where a patient's approved clinician makes a decision not to impose treatment under MHA 1983, s 63 and where the consequences of that decision may prove to be life-threatening, the NHS Trust in question is well advised to apply to the High Court for declaratory relief. In such an application, the expressed wishes of the patient are highly relevant; any advance decision complying with the MCA 2005 will weigh most heavily in the scales, beyond this, considerations such as whether the treatment would be futile will no doubt be relevant. The ability to weigh information as part of an assessment of capacity to refuse medical treatment must be applied very cautiously and carefully when religious beliefs are in play. It would be an extreme example of the application of the law of unintended consequences were an iron tenet of an accepted religion to give rise to questions of capacity under the MCA 2005.

Approach to be adopted by court

W (By her Litigation Friend B) v (1) M (By her Litigation Friend the Official Solicitor) (2) S and (3) A NHS Primary Care Trust [2011] EWHC 2443 (Fam), [2012] COPLR 222 (Baker J)

The Court of Protection has power to consider an application to withdraw life-sustaining treatment from a patient in a minimally conscious state. In considering such application, the Court will apply the same balancing exercise as in other cases in which it is called to consider P's best interests. The importance of securing the right to life will dictate that only limited weight can be placed upon wishes and feelings expressed by P while she had capacity where those wishes and feelings were not recorded in an advance directive. General guidance also given as to the practice to be adopted (and the evidence required) in such cases.

Aintree University Hospitals NHS Foundation Trust v James [2013] UKSC 67, [2013] COPLR 492 (Lord Neuberger, Lady Hale, Lord Clarke, Lord Carnwath and Lord Hughes, Supreme Court)

The right question to ask in the context of the withdrawal of life-sustaining treatment is whether it is in the patient's best interests for the treatment to be given, nor whether it is in his best interests to withdraw it. In considering the best interests of a particular patient at a particular time, decision-makers must look at his welfare in the widest sense, not just medical but social and psychological; they must consider the nature of the medical treatment in question, what it involves and its prospects of success; they must consider what the outcome of that treatment for the patient is likely to be; they must try to put themselves in the place of the individual patient and ask what his attitude to the treatment is or would be likely to be; and they must consult others who are looking after him or interested in his welfare, in particular for their view of what his attitude would be. In the context of medical treatment, 'futile' means 'ineffective or of no benefit to the patient'; 'No prospect of recovery' means 'no prospect of resuming a quality of life which the patient would regard as worthwhile'.

Practice and procedure

A Local Authority v K and Others [2013] EWHC 242 (COP), [2013] COPLR 194 (Cobb J)

In a case of non-therapeutic sterilisation, a referral to the Court of Protection needs to be made as quickly as possible, having particular regard to the steps in Practice Direction 9E, paras 6.18 and 8.18–29 of the Code of Practice to MCA 2005 and r 92 of the Court of Protection Rules 2007.

Practice and procedure

Contempt proceedings

***MASM v MMAM (By Her Litigation Friend the Official Solicitor) and Others* [2015] EWCOP 3, [2015] COPLR 239 (Hayden J)**

A declaration of best interests connotes the superlative or extreme quality of welfare options. An order drafted in declaratory terms could not trigger contempt proceedings.

Correct approach to withholding of documentary material from a party to proceedings before Court of Protection

***RC v CC and X Local Authority* [2013] EWHC 1424 (COP), [2013] COPLR 431 (Sir James Munby P)**

The same principles apply to issues of disclosure in the Court of Protection as in the Family Division, although the application of those principles may differ. The correct test is whether non-disclosure is strictly necessary. The correct question is not whether it is necessary for documents to be disclosed; rather it is whether it is necessary in P's interests that documents are not disclosed.

Hearsay evidence is admissible from person not competent to give evidence

***London Borough of Enfield v SA* [2010] EWHC 196 (Admin), [2010] COPLR Con Vol 362 (McFarlane J)**

Rule 95(d) of the Court of Protection Rules gives the Court of Protection power to admit hearsay evidence that originates from a person who is not competent as a witness and that would otherwise be inadmissible under the Civil Evidence Act 1995. The weight to be attached to any particular piece of hearsay evidence will be a matter for specific evaluation in each individual case. Within that evaluation, the fact that the individual from whom the evidence originates is not a competent witness will no doubt be an important factor, just as it is, in a different context, when the family court has to evaluate what has been said by a very young child. The rule before the Court of Protection should be that parties are required to give full and frank disclosure of all relevant material.

Privacy and media reporting

***Independent News Media v A* [2010] EWCA Civ 343, [2010] COPLR Con Vol 686 (Lord Judge CJ, Lord Neuberger of Abbotsbury MR, Sir Mark Potter P, CA)**

The new statutory scheme established by MCA 2005 starts with the assumption that the conduct of the affairs of those adults who were incapacitated was private business. Before the court allows anyone to be present at the hearing or to authorise publication of information relating to the proceedings, a two-stage process is required: the first stage involves deciding whether there was 'good reason' to make an order under r 90(2), 91(1) or 92; if there is, the second stage is to decide whether the requisite balancing exercise justifies the making of the order, because, even when good reason appears, better reasons might lead the court to refuse the necessary authorisation. The words 'good reason' meant what, taken together, they said. Arguments about whether the general rule that the hearing should be in private amounted either to a presumption or to a starting point were in practice unlikely to be anything other than semantic; if in the judgment of the court there was good reason to grant the authorisation, the order could be made; otherwise not. No doubt more compelling reasons would be likely to be required in support of a full public hearing, rather than in support of a suitably anonymised publication of the court's judgment. When undertaking the balancing exercise, the court should weigh the Art 8 rights of any person whose private life was intended to be protected by r 90(1).

Hillingdon London Borough Council v Neary [2011] EWHC 413 (COP), [2011] COPLR Con Vol 677 (Peter Jackson J)

Hearings before the Court of Protection should be held in private unless there was a good reason why they should not be. The court must first decide whether there is a good reason and, if so, go on to determine whether the requisite human rights balancing exercise justifies the order being made. In determining whether there was a good reason to allow the media to attend a hearing, the question is not whether the individual is exceptional but whether the issue is one of general public interest.

P v Independent Print Ltd & Ors [2011] EWCA Civ 756, [2012] COPLR 110 (Ward, Carnwarth and Tomlinson LJJ, CA)

Permitting the press to attend or report a judgment is not an act done on behalf of P, and there is no requirement to consider P's best interests, although these remain a material factor. It is not for the Court of Appeal to lay down rules for applications for press attendance in the Court of Protection; this guidance should be established by the President and the judges of the Family Division.

W v M and S (Reporting Restriction Order) [2011] EWHC 1197 (COP), [2011] COPLR Con Vol 1205 (Baker J)

When considering whether to make a reporting restriction in the Court of Protection, neither Arts 8 nor 10 of the ECHR has precedence over the other – the court is to carry out a balancing exercise between the two. The balancing exercise will usually be confined to Arts 8 and 10 but Art 6 may also be in issue, where it is argued that attempts by the media to contact the litigant would affect the capacity or willingness of a party to participate in the litigation. Decisions on the balancing exercise between Arts 8 and 10 outside of the Court of Protection context are unlikely to be helpful because Court of Protection cases are usually not conducted in the public domain.

Re Gladys Meek; Jones v Parkin and Others [2014] EWCOP 1, [2014] COPLR 535 (HHJ Hodge QC)

P's death does not automatically render it appropriate to authorise the publication of a Court of Protection judgment in unanonymised form. However, where P no longer has any need for the special protection afforded by anonymity and the court has jurisdiction under r 91(2)(b) of the Court of Protection Rules 2007 to authorise the reporting of an unanonymised judgment even after the protected person's death, if there are good reasons for making such an order, the judgment should be published.

The Press Association v Newcastle upon Tyne Hospitals Foundation Trust [2014] EWCOP 6, [2014] COPLR 502 (Peter Jackson J)

The court has power to preserve the anonymity of a protected party after death. This power does not depend upon whether a case is heard in public or in private, nor does a person's death automatically lead to all protection being lost. Where a court has restricted the publication of information during proceedings that were in existence during a person's lifetime, it has a duty to consider when requested to do so whether that information should continue to be protected following the person's death and to balance the factors that arise in the particular case. There is a proper interest in the name of a person who dies being a matter of public record whether or not there is to be an inquest. The right to privacy is only likely to outweigh this consideration in very special circumstances.

Re G (Adult); London Borough of Redbridge v G, C and F [2014] EWCOP 1361, [2014] COPLR 416 (Sir James Munby P)

The identification by the Court of Protection of a source's capacity or best interests as regards contact with a journalist does not give rise to any justiciable issue between the source and the journalist under Art 10 of the European Convention. Before the journalist's right to receive information from the source arises, the source must wish or be willing to impart that information. If there is a conflict between the source's best interests as determined by the court and the journalist's rights under Art 10, the court will undertake a balancing exercise under its ordinary jurisdiction under the European Convention between the relevant competing interests.

A Healthcare NHS Trust v P (By His Litigation Friend the Official Solicitor) and Q [2015] EWCOP 15, [2015] COPLR 147 (Newton J)

The media are prevented from revealing the parties' names on receipt of an application for reporting restrictions.

Test to apply when considering whether to grant permission to bring application

NK v (1) VW (By her Litigation Friend the Official Solicitor) (2) LCC (3) JW and (4) WW [2012] COPLR 105 (Macur J)

When deciding to grant permission to bring an application in relation to P pursuant to MCA 2005, s 50 and r 50 of Court of Protection Rules, the Court of Protection must have regard to: (a) the applicant's connection to P; (b) the reasons for the application; (c) the benefit to P; and (d) whether the benefit can be achieved in any other way. The Court is required to prevent applications with no realistic prospect of success or that represent a disproportionate response to perceived problems by the applicant as well as to frivolous and abusive applications.

Test for joinder as a party

Re SK (By His Litigation Friend, the Official Solicitor) [2012] EWHC 1990 (COP), [2012] COPLR 712 (Bodey J)

The Court of Protection Rules 2007 as to joinder (rr 73 and 75) should be read together, as they together govern decisions about joinder. Read in that light, r 75 requires that 'sufficient interest' be interpreted to mean 'sufficient interest in the proceedings' as distinct from a commercial interest of the applicant's own. An applicant for joinder who or which does not have an interest in the ascertainment of the incapacitated person's best interests is unlikely to be a person with 'sufficient interest' for the purpose of r 75. The import of r 73 is that the joinder of an applicant should enable the court better to deal with the substantive application.

Test for dispensing with service upon a respondent

Re AB [2014] COPLR 381 (District Judge Batten)

The court's decision whether to direct that a party should not be served with an application is one made in the exercise of powers given by the Court of Protection Rules 2007 and is not an act done or a decision made on behalf of P. The principles of the MCA 2005 cannot be strictly applied to such a decision. However, service should only be dispensed with in exceptional circumstance where there are compelling reasons for doing so. Otherwise the interests of justice will not be served and the court will not be seen to be acting fairly towards all parties.

Threshold for engaging the jurisdiction of the Court

Re F [2009] EWHC B30 (Fam), [2009] COPLR Con Vol 390 (HHJ Marshall QC sitting as a nominated judge of the Court of Protection)

The proper test for the engagement of MCA 2005, s 48 in the first instance is whether there is sufficient evidence to justify a reasonable belief that P may lack capacity in some relevant regard. Once that is raised as a serious possibility, the court then moves on to the second stage to decide what action, if any, it is in P's best interests to take before a final determination of his capacity can be made. Such action can include not only taking immediate safeguarding steps (which may be positive or negative) with regard to P's affairs or life decisions, but it can also include giving directions to enable evidence to resolve the issue of capacity to be obtained quickly.

SMBC v WMP and Others [2011] COPLR Con Vol 1177 (HHJ Cardinal sitting as a nominated judge of the Court of Protection)

In taking into account all of the evidence available to determine whether the threshold in MCA 2005, s 48 has been crossed, the court can take into account evidence obtained in a manner open to criticism.

When fact-finding necessary and approach to be taken

A Local Authority v M (By His Litigation Friend the Official Solicitor), E and A [2014] EWCOP 33, [2015] COPLR 6 (Baker J)

The legal principles to be applied at a fact-finding hearing in the Court of Protection should be broadly the same as in children's proceedings.

LBB v JM, BK and CM [2010] COPLR Con Vol 779 (Hedley J)

Where there is a contested factual basis for the justification under Art 8(2) of the ECHR for an intervention into private and family life, it may often be that the court must investigate and make findings of fact. It is contrary to the philosophy of best interests under MCA 2005, s 4 to require an incapacitous person to have contact with someone she does not want to see unless to accede to her views is itself at variance with her best interests because, for example, her expression of views are not in fact a reflection of her genuine thoughts.

When to identify matters and facts in issue and how such identification to be done

A Local Authority v PB and P (No 1) [2011] EWHC 502 (COP), [2011] COPLR Con Vol 166 (Charles J)

As a matter of general practice, parties to welfare proceedings should be required to identify at an early stage facts in issue, and judicial consideration be given to (for instance) whether a specific fact-finding hearing is required. Where questions arise as to whether a public authority is prepared to put an option on the table for consideration by the Court, it is likely that challenges to any decision not to put such an option on the table must be by way of judicial review; again, it is important to identify at an early stage whether such a challenge will arise and for directions to be set as to its resolution.

Practice and Procedure: Costs

Delay and expense in the Court of Protection

A and B (Court of Protection: Delay and Costs) [2014] EWCOP 48, [2015] COPLR 1 (Peter Jackson J)

A common driver of delay and expense is the search for the ideal solution, leading to decent but imperfect outcomes being rejected. The role of a litigation friend in representing P's interests is not merely a passive one, discharged by critiquing other peoples' efforts. Where he considers it is in his client's best interests, a litigation friend is entitled to research and present any realistic alternatives. The time has come to introduce the same disciplines in the Court of Protection as now apply in the Family Court.

Relevant principles for costs decisions in the Court of Protection

Re RC (Deceased) [2010] COPLR Con Vol 1022 (Senior Judge Lush)

The Court of Protection retains a residual jurisdiction after the death of the person to whom the proceedings relate in respect of the payment of costs and fees. The court will be slow to depart from the general order as to costs in welfare proceedings under r 157 of the Court of Protection Rules 2007 (no order as to costs). Circumstances where such a departure would be merited include conduct where the person against whom it is proposed to award costs is clearly acting in bad faith. Even then, there should be a carefully worded warning that costs could be awarded against them, and a consideration of their ability to pay. If one were to depart from r 157 in all the cases involving litigants who were 'extreme product champions', the court would be overwhelmed by satellite litigation on costs, enforcement orders, and committal proceedings.

Manchester City Council v G, E (by his Litigation Friend the Official Solicitor) and F [2011] EWCA Civ 939, [2012] COPLR 95 (Mummery and Hooper LJJ and McFarlane J, CA)

Appeals from costs decisions made in the Court of Protection fell to be considered by reference to the same principles as costs decisions in other civil proceedings, such that the trial judge must have gone seriously wrong if the Court of Appeal was to interfere. Local authorities and other public bodies could not be excluded from liability to pay costs. Only local authorities who broke the law or who were guilty of misconduct within r 159 of the Court of Protection Rules 2007 had reason to fear a costs order. A costs order would not be awarded in cases where, with hindsight, it was demonstrated that the local authority had made a misjudgment.

Re AH (Costs); AH and Others v Hertfordshire Partnership NHS Foundation Trust [2011] EWHC 3524 (COP), [2012] COPLR 327 (Peter Jackson J)

Had there been a need to give general guidance over and above their wording as to the application of the costs rules, the Court of Appeal would have considered it in *Manchester City Council v G, E (by his Litigation Friend the Official*

Solicitor) and F [2012] COPLR 95. While there is a general rule from which the court can depart where the circumstances justify, it adds nothing to say that a case must be exceptional or atypical for costs to be ordered. Each application for costs must be considered on its own merit or lack of merit with the clear appreciation that there must be a good reason before the court will contemplate departure from the general rule. The same principles apply equally to proceedings that have been compromised.

Re G (Adult) (Costs) [2014] EWCOP 5, [2014] COPLR 432
(Sir James Munby P)

The overall scheme of rr 156–157 of the Court of Protection Rules 2007 is, first, the drawing of a distinction between proceedings which 'concern P's property and affairs' and those which 'concern P's personal welfare' and, secondly, the principle that, where the proceedings concern both, the costs should be apportioned between 'that part of the proceedings that concerns' the one and 'that part of the proceedings that concerns' the other. Where the proceedings themselves concern P's personal welfare, the fact that a specific application within those proceedings does not, itself, concern P's personal welfare does not mean that different considerations should be applied to that specific application.

Re G (An Adult) (By Her Litigation Friend The Official Solicitor) (Costs) [2015] EWCA Civ 446, [2015] COPLR 438 (Sullivan, Ryder LJJ and Dame Janet Smith, CA)

The Civil Procedure Rules (CPR 1998) are not engaged in the Court of Protection as regards the determination of costs and the court has a broad discretion as to costs.

Medical treatment cases

Re D (Costs) [2012] EWHC 886 (COP), [2012] COPLR 499 (Peter Jackson J)

The 2007 Rules have not changed the approach to costs in medical treatment cases and the approach of Sir Mark Potter in *A Hospital v SW and A PCT* [2007] EWHC 425 (Fam) (in which the health authority was to pay half the Official Solicitor's costs) should continue to be followed. Any change to the 'rules of the game' would be for Parliament to make.

Power to consider likely outcome of the case for purposes of determining costs where settlement reached

JS v KB and MP (Property and Affairs Deputy for DB) [2014] EWHC 483 (COP), [2014] COPLR 275 (Cobb J)

The court has the power to make a costs order when the substantive proceedings have been resolved without a trial, but when the parties have not agreed about costs. At each end of the spectrum there will be cases where it is obvious which side would have won had the substantive issues been fought to a conclusion. In between, the position will, in differing degrees, be less clear. How far the court will be prepared to look into the previously unresolved substantive issues will depend on the circumstances of the particular case, not least the amount of costs at stake and the conduct of the parties.

Wasted costs procedure in the Court of Protection is the same as in the High Court

Sharma and Judkins v Hunters [2011] EWHC 2546 (COP), [2012] COPLR 166 (Henderson J)

The procedure for determining whether to make a wasted costs order is in practice the same in the Court of Protection as it is in the High Court, subject to such modifications as may be appropriate, following from r 160(1) of the Court of Protection Rules 2007.

Property and affairs

Court of Protection has power to approve altruistic payments in P's best interests

Re X, Y and Z [2014] EWHC 87 (COP), [2014] COPLR 364 (Baker J)

The court has power under the Mental Capacity Act 2005 to approve altruistic payments for the maintenance or other benefit of members of P's family, notwithstanding the absence of an express provision to that effect in the Act, provided such payments are in P's best interests. Where a parent has lost mental capacity at a time when still responsible for his or her children, those responsibilities are part of his or her 'interests'; payments to meet the reasonable needs of those children are manifestly capable of being described as in her 'best interests'.

Duties upon attorney in the management of P's monies

Re Buckley [2013] COPLR 39 (Senior Judge Lush)

An attorney acting under an LPA is constrained in their decision-making by (1) the fiduciary relationship between attorney and donor; and (2) the obligation of the attorney to act in the best interests of donor upon the donor's incapacity. The court gave guidance as to the investment strategies that are appropriate for an attorney to follow in the management of monies belonging to an individual with a life expectancy of 5 years or less, and emphasised the obligation upon all attorneys: (1) to keep the donor's money and property separate from their own; (2) (subject to a sensible de minimis exception) to make an application to the Court of Protection for an order under MCA 2005, s 23 in respect of (a) gifts that exceed the limited scope of the authority conferred on attorneys by MCA 2005, s 12; (b) loans to the attorney or to members of the attorney's family; (c) any investment in the attorney's own business; (d) sales or purchases at an undervalue; and (e) any other transactions in which there is a conflict between the interests of the donor and the interests of the attorney; and (3) to be aware of the law regarding their role and responsibilities.

Proper approach to making statutory will

**NT v FS and Others [2013] EWHC 684 (COP), [2013] COPLR 313
(HHJ Behrens sitting as a nominated judge of the Court of Protection)**

The approach to making a statutory will is as follows: (a) the overarching principle is that any decision made on behalf of P must be in P's best interests. This is not the same as inquiring what P would have decided if he or she had capacity. It is not a test of substituted judgment but requires the court to apply an objective test of what would be in P's best interests. (b) The court must follow the structured decision-making process laid down by MCA 2005. Thus, the court must consider all relevant circumstances and in particular must consider and take into account the matters set out in ss 4(6) and 4(7) of the 2005 Act. (c) The court must make a value judgment giving effect to the paramount statutory instruction that the decision must be made in P's best interests. (d) The 2005 Act contains no hierarchy between the various factors that have to be borne in mind. The weight to be attached to different factors will inevitably differ depending on the individual circumstances of the particular case. There may, however, in a particular case be one or more features that, in a particular case, are of 'magnetic importance' in influencing or even determining the outcome.

When appropriate to order a statutory will to be made

**VAC v JAD & Others [2010] EWHC 2159 (Ch), [2010] COPLR Con Vol 302
(HHJ Hodge QC sitting as a nominated judge of the Court of Protection)**

The court may direct the execution of a statutory will even where the validity of an earlier will is in dispute. In an appropriate case, the court may decide that it was in P's best interests to order a statutory will than to leave P to be remembered for having bequeathed a contentious probate dispute.

Replacement for replacement attorney cannot be appointed

Public Guardian v Boff [2013] COPLR 653 (Senior Judge Lush)

On a proper construction of MCA 2005, s 10(8), a donor of a Lasting Power of Attorney cannot appoint a replacement attorney to succeed another replacement attorney.

Attorneys can be appointed to act jointly with survivorship

Miles v The Public Guardian; Beattie v The Public Guardian [2015] EWHC 2960 (Ch), [2015] COPLR 676 (Nugee J)

It is possible to appoint attorneys under an LPA to act jointly with survivorship. The wording that should be used would be 'I appoint the named individuals A and B to act jointly and in the event of one of them ceasing to be capable or willing to act, I appoint the surviving one, A or B as the case may be, to act alone'.

Public Guardian's powers in relation to registration of powers of attorney

Re XZ; XZ v The Public Guardian [2015] EWCOP 35, [2015] COPLR 630

The Public Guardian's functions under para 11 of Sch 1 to the Act are limited to considering whether the conditions and restrictions in an LPA (a) are ineffective as part of an LPA or (b) would prevent the instrument from operating as a valid LPA. If he concludes that they cannot be given legal effect, then he is under a duty to apply to the court for a determination of the point under s 23(1). Otherwise, he has a duty to register the power. Neither the court nor the Public Guardian is concerned with whether a restriction that does not contravene the terms of MCA 2005 might pose practical difficulties in its operation.

Revocation of power of attorney

Re J [2011] COPLR Con Vol 716 (HHJ Marshall QC sitting as a nominated judge of the Court of Protection)

In deciding whether to revoke a lasting power of attorney under MCA 2005, s 22(3)(b), the court can consider any past behaviour or apparent prospective power by the attorney. Depending on the circumstances and the gravity of the offending behaviour, the court can take whatever steps it regards as appropriate in P's best interests to deal with the situation.

Re Harcourt [2013] COPLR 69 (Senior Judge Lush)

The lasting powers of attorney scheme is based on trust and envisages minimal intervention by public authorities. Even where a donor lacks the capacity to ask the attorney to provide accounts and records, the court would not normally exercise its supervisory powers under MCA 2005, s 23, unless it had reason to do so, possibly because of concerns raised by the Office of the Public Guardian. The court's powers in this respect simply duplicate those of a capable donor. Upon an application for an order to revoke an LPA under MCA 2005, s 22(4)(b), the court will consider the question by reference to whether revocation is in P's best interests. The factor of magnetic importance upon such an application is likely to be that it is in P's best interests for their affairs to be managed competently, honestly and for their benefit. Revocation where it is in P's best interests represents a necessary and proportionate interference with P's rights under Art 8 ECHR.

Re DP (Revocation of Lasting Power of Attorney) [2014] COPLR 188 (Senior Judge Lush)

To be able to revoke an LPA on the basis of the attorney's past performance, the court needs to be satisfied that: (i) the attorney has contravened his authority; or (ii) the attorney has not acted in the donor's best interests; and (iii) the donor lacks capacity to revoke the LPA.

Best interests

Construction and application of statutory defence under Mental Capacity Act 2005, s 5

The Commissioner of Police of the Metropolis v ZH [2013] EWCA Civ 69, [2013] COPLR 332 (Lord Dyson MR, Richards and Black LJJ, CA)

The statutory defence contained in MCA 2005, s 5 is pervaded by the concepts of reasonableness, practicability and appropriateness. What is reasonable, practicable and appropriate where there is time to reflect and take measured action may be quite different to that which is so in an emergency or what is reasonably believed to be an emergency.

Factors relevant to consideration of best interests as regards ending of marriage

Sandwell Metropolitan Borough Council v RG & Ors [2013] EWHC 2373 (COP), [2013] COPLR 643 (Holman J)

By operation of the provisions of the Matrimonial Causes Act 1973, a marriage contracted with a person who lacked the capacity to consent thereto was voidable rather than void. Parties to the marriage have discretion as to whether to bring the marriage to an end. Where a person lacked capacity to make that decision, it fell to the Court of Protection to make that decision in his best interests, pursuant to MCA 2005, s 1(5). In making that decision, the Court of Protection could not take into account policy considerations such as the reinforcing of a message that arranged marriages where one party is incapacitated will not be tolerated.

The importance of country and culture of origin in best interests analysis

An NHS Trust and B PCT v DU and Others [2009] EWHC 3504 (Fam), [2009] COPLR Con Vol 210 (Hedley J)

The importance of country and culture of origin and the location of family members is implicit in the concept of best interests and would often take precedence over such facts as risk avoidance and the quality of care available in different places. It is further an integral part of the concept of best interests when dealing with an elderly individual that the court recognises the imminent possibility of death and the importance of making arrangements so as to secure that the experience of death may be in a context that is the most congenial and peaceful that can be devised.

No presumption in favour of family life in best interests analysis

K v LBX and Others [2012] EWCA Civ 79, [2012] COPLR 411 (Thorpe, Black and Davis LJJ, CA)

The approach in cases under MCA 2005 is to ascertain the best interests of P on the application of the s 4 checklist. Only then should the judge ask whether that conclusion amounts to a violation of Art 8 rights and, if so, if this is necessary and proportionate. No additional starting point should be added to the exercise. In practice, there may well be a conflict between P's family life and P's right to private life, but family life will not always trump private life.

The purpose of MCA 2005

Re P (Abortion) [2013] EWHC 50 (COP), [2013] COPLR 405 (Hedley J)

The intention of MCA 2005 is not to dress an incapacitous person in forensic cotton wool but to allow them as far as possible to make the same mistakes that all other human beings are at liberty to make and not infrequently do.

RB (By His Litigation Friend the Official Solicitor) v Brighton and Hove City Council [2014] EWCA Civ 561, [2014] COPLR 629 (Arden, Jackson and Fulford LJJ, CA)

The court's task is to apply the statutory provisions playing close heed to the language of the MCA 2005. Other decisions are not models to be followed but merely examples of its application. It would be unacceptable to say that the best interests of a person always 'positively require' that he/she should be prevented from making unwise decisions.

Relevance of adult's own views

Re S and S (Protected Persons); C v V [2008] COPLR Con Vol 1074 (HHJ Marshall QC sitting as a nominated judge of the Court of Protection)

Where P can and does express a wish or view that is not irrational is not impracticable as far as its physical implementation is concerned, and is not irresponsible having regard to the extent of P's resources, then that situation carries great weight and effectively gives rise to a presumption in favour of implementing those wishes, unless there is some potential sufficiently detrimental effect for P of doing so which outweighs this.

Re M, ITW v Z and Others [2009] EWHC 2525 (Fam), [2009] COPLR Con Vol 828 (Munby J)

MCA 2005 provides a structured decision-making process that requires the decision-maker to take a number of steps before reaching a decision, including encouraging P to participate in the decision, considering P's past and present wishes, her beliefs and values, and taking into account the views of third parties as to what would be in P's best interests. Having gone through those steps, the decision-maker must come to a value judgment of his own as to what is in P's best interests.

There is no hierarchy between the various factors that must be borne in mind. P's wishes and feelings will always be a significant factor to which the court must pay close regard. The weight to be attached to these wishes and feelings will vary from case to case, and the court set out five considerations for assessing the weight and importance to be attached to wishes and feelings. Material that does not fall inside ss 4(6) and (7) of MCA 2005 may still be a 'relevant consideration' within s 4(2). P's best interests also include how P will be remembered after P's death.

Re P [2009] EWHC 163 (Ch), [2009] COPLR Con Vol 906 (Lewison J)

Re S and S [2008] COPLR Con Vol 1074 went too far. P's wishes are to be given great weight, but there is no presumption. Testing a decision by reference to what P would have done runs the risk of amounting to substituted judgment. The decision-maker must consider the beliefs and values that would be likely to influence P's decision if he had capacity and also the other factors that P would be likely to consider if he were able to do so. This does not necessarily require those to be given effect.

The guidance given under the Mental Health Acts 1959 and 1983 about the making of settlements or wills can no longer be directly applied to a decision being made under MCA 2005. The goal of the enquiry is not what P might have been expected to have done, but what is in his best interests, and the enquiry is to follow the structured approach provided for under the Act.

The PCT v P, AH and A Local Authority [2009] COPLR Con Vol 956 (Hedley J)

Following *Re M* [2009] COPLR Con Vol 828, the nearer a person is to capacity, the greater the weight that must be given to their views. Regard must be had to both the strength and consistency of their views as well as the impact on the individual of knowing that his wishes are not being given effect. Consideration should also be given to the extent to which the individual's wishes are rational, sensible, responsible and practical.

Re G (TJ) [2010] EWHC 3005 (COP), [2010] COPLR Con Vol 403 (Morgan J)

The balance sheet of factors that P would draw up, if he had capacity to make the decision, is a relevant factor for the court's decision. Further, in most cases the court will be able to determine what decision it is likely that P would have made, if he had capacity. This can be taken into account by the court, any element of substituted judgment arising thereby being subsumed into the best interests tests provided for by MCA 2005, s 4. Absent any countervailing factors, respect for what the Court can identify to have been P's wishes can define what would be in P's best interests.

***RGB v Cwm Taf Health Board and Others* [2013] EWHC B23 (COP), [2014] COPLR 83 (Moor J)**

While the Court of Protection does have jurisdiction theoretically to make a different determination from the wishes expressed in an advance statement based upon P's best interests, there would have to be some extremely compelling reason to make a different determination. The wishes and feelings articulated in an advance statement are absolutely central in deciding what is in P's best interests.

***Re M (Best Interests: Deprivation of Liberty)* [2013] EWHC 3456 (COP), [2014] COPLR 35 (Peter Jackson J)**

In assessing the risks of a return home by the detained resident of a care home clearly expressing a desire to do so, the court has to have regard to P's own assessment of her quality of life. There is little to be said for a solution that attempts, without any guarantee of success, to preserve for P a daily life without meaning or happiness and which she regards as insupportable.

***Aintree University Hospitals NHS Foundation Trust v James* [2013] UKSC 67, [2013] COPLR 492 (Lord Neuberger, Lady Hale, Lord Clarke, Lord Carnwath and Lord Hughes, Supreme Court)**

The test of the patient's wishes and feelings is not what the reasonable patient would think; the purpose of the 'best interests' test is to consider matters from the patient's point of view.

When duty to consult regarding P's welfare arises

***Re A; D v B* [2009] COPLR Con Vol 1 (Senior Judge Lush)**

Where any attempt at consultation required by MCA 2005, s 4 will inevitably be unduly onerous, futile, or serve no useful purpose, it cannot be in P's best interests and it would be neither practicable nor appropriate to embark on that process in the first place.

The Court of Protection and the HRA

When interference in private and family life is justified

***Re GC and Anor* [2008] EWHC 3402 (Fam), [2008] COPLR Con Vol 422 (Hedley J)**

The state does not intervene in the private family life of an individual unless the continuance of that private family life is clearly inconsistent with the welfare of the person whose best interests the court is required to determine. That is the same principle that governs State intervention under the Children Act 1989 and, while the Children Act and MCA 2005 deal with quite different problems and must be treated quite separately, the fundamental principle governing the welfare agencies of the State's interventions in private life should be the same.

No presumption in favour of family life in best interests analysis

K v LBX and Others [2012] EWCA Civ 79, [2012] COPLR 411 (Thorpe, Black and Davis LJJ, CA)

The approach in cases under MCA 2005 is to ascertain the best interests of P on the application of the s 4 checklist. Only then should the judge ask whether that conclusion amounts to a violation of Art 8 rights and, if so, if this is necessary and proportionate. No additional starting point should be added to the exercise. In practice, there may well be a conflict between P's family life and P's right to private life, but family life will not always trump private life.

Need to justify interference in private life so as to comply with Article 8 ECHR

J Council v GU, J Partnership NHS Foundation Trust, Care Quality Commission, X Limited [2012] EWHC 3531 (COP), [2013] COPLR 83 (Mostyn J)

Where a private body such as a care home wields coercive powers, it is exercising functions of a public nature for purposes of the application of Art 8 ECHR. Where there is going to be a long-term restrictive regime accompanied by invasive monitoring in a private institution, policies validated and overseen by a public body (and, where relevant, the Care Quality Commission) are likely to be necessary if serious doubts as to compliance with Art 8 are to be avoided.

Jurisdiction of the Court of Protection

YA (F) v A Local Authority [2010] EWHC 2770 (COP), [2010] COPLR Con Vol 1226 (Charles J)

The Court of Protection has jurisdiction to hear argument that acts done in relation to P constitute breaches of her European Convention rights, and to make declarations as to the lawfulness of those acts and in respect of breaches of her European Convention rights as a result of those acts. The Court of Protection also has jurisdiction and power to award damages under the Human Rights Act 1998.

Re MN (Adult) [2015] EWCA Civ 411, [2015] COPLR 505 (Sir James Munby, Treacy and Gloster LJJ)

The function of the Court of Protection is to take, on behalf of adults who lack capacity, the decisions which, if they had capacity, they would take themselves. The Court of Protection has no more power to obtain resources or facilities from a third party, whether a private individual or a public authority, than the adult if he had capacity would be able to obtain himself. The Court of Protection is thus confined to choosing between available options, including those which there is good reason to believe would be forthcoming in the foreseeable future, and should not embark on a factual inquiry in relation to abstract possibilities. The Court of Protection could explore the care plan being put forward by a public authority and, where appropriate, require the authority to reconsider its position.

Rigorous probing, searching questions and persuasion is permissible; pressure is not. The Court of Protection could not compel a public authority to agree to a care plan which the authority was unwilling to implement.

PART X

Scottish Legislation and Guidance

PART X

Scottish Legislation and Guidance

PART X: Scottish Legislation and Guidance

Contents

Statutes 2339
Adults with Incapacity (Scotland) Act 2000 2339

Statutory Instruments 2427
Act of Sederunt (Summary Applications, Statutory Applications and
    Appeals etc Rules) 1999 2427

Guidance 2434
Guidance on Continuing and Welfare Powers of Attorney 2434
Vulnerable Clients Guidance 2438

PART X: Scottish Legislation and Guidance

Contents

Statutes
Adults with Incapacity (Scotland) Act 2000

Statutory Instruments
Act of Sederunt (Summary Applications, Statutory Applications and Appeals etc. Rules) 1999

Guidance
Guidance on Continuing and Welfare Powers of Attorney
Vulnerable Clients Guidance

Statutes

Adults with Incapacity (Scotland) Act 2000

PART 1
GENERAL

General

1 General principles and fundamental definitions

(1) The principles set out in subsections (2) to (4) shall be given effect to in relation to any intervention in the affairs of an adult under or in pursuance of this Act, including any order made in or for the purpose of any proceedings under this Act for or in connection with an adult.

(2) There shall be no intervention in the affairs of an adult unless the person responsible for authorising or effecting the intervention is satisfied that the intervention will benefit the adult and that such benefit cannot reasonably be achieved without the intervention.

(3) Where it is determined that an intervention as mentioned in subsection (1) is to be made, such intervention shall be the least restrictive option in relation to the freedom of the adult, consistent with the purpose of the intervention.

(4) In determining if an intervention is to be made and, if so, what intervention is to be made, account shall be taken of –

(a) the present and past wishes and feelings of the adult so far as they can be ascertained by any means of communication, whether human or by mechanical aid (whether of an interpretative nature or otherwise) appropriate to the adult;
(b) the views of the nearest relative, named person and the primary carer of the adult, in so far as it is reasonable and practicable to do so;
(c) the views of –
  (i) any guardian, continuing attorney or welfare attorney of the adult who has powers relating to the proposed intervention; and
  (ii) any person whom the sheriff has directed to be consulted,
  in so far as it is reasonable and practicable to do so; and
(d) the views of any other person appearing to the person responsible for authorising or effecting the intervention to have an interest in the welfare of the adult or in the proposed intervention, where these views have been made known to the person responsible, in so far as it is reasonable and practicable to do so.

(5) Any guardian, continuing attorney, welfare attorney or manager of an establishment exercising functions under this Act or under any order of the sheriff in relation to an adult shall, in so far as it is reasonable and practicable to do so, encourage the adult to exercise whatever skills he has concerning his property, financial affairs or personal welfare, as the case may be, and to develop new such skills.

(6) For the purposes of this Act, and unless the context otherwise requires –

'adult' means a person who has attained the age of 16 years;
'incapable' means incapable of –
  (a) acting; or
  (b) making decisions; or
  (c) communicating decisions; or
  (d) understanding decisions; or
  (e) retaining the memory of decisions,
as mentioned in any provision of this Act, by reason of mental disorder or of inability to communicate because of physical disability; but a person shall not fall within this definition by reason only of a lack or deficiency in a faculty of communication if that lack or deficiency can be made good by human or mechanical aid (whether of an interpretative nature or otherwise); and
'incapacity' shall be construed accordingly.

(7) In subsection (4)(c)(i) any reference to –
  (a) a guardian shall include a reference to a guardian (however called) appointed under the law of any country to, or entitled under the law of any country to act for, an adult during his incapacity, if the guardianship is recognised by the law of Scotland;
  (b) a continuing attorney shall include a reference to a person granted, under a contract, grant or appointment governed by the law of any country, powers (however expressed), relating to the granter's property or financial affairs and having continuing effect notwithstanding the granter's incapacity;
  (c) a welfare attorney shall include a reference to a person granted, under a contract, grant or appointment governed by the law of any country, powers (however expressed) relating to the granter's personal welfare and having effect during the granter's incapacity.

Amendments—SSI 2001/81.

Judicial proceedings

2 Applications and other proceedings and appeals

(1) This section shall apply for the purposes of any application which may be made to and any other proceedings before the sheriff under this Act.

(2) An application to the sheriff under this Act shall be made by summary application.

(3) Unless otherwise expressly provided for, any decision of the sheriff at first instance in any application to, or in any other proceedings before, him under this Act may be appealed to the sheriff principal, and the decision upon such appeal of the sheriff principal may be appealed, with the leave of the sheriff principal, to the Court of Session.

(4) Rules made under section 32 of the Sheriff Courts (Scotland) Act 1971 may make provision as to the evidence which the sheriff shall take into account when deciding whether to give a direction under section 11(1).

3 Powers of sheriff

(1) In an application or any other proceedings under this Act, the sheriff may make such consequential or ancillary order, provision or direction as he considers appropriate.

(2) Without prejudice to the generality of subsection (1) or to any other powers conferred by this Act, the sheriff may –

- (a) make any order granted by him subject to such conditions and restrictions as appear to him to be appropriate;
- (b) order that any reports relating to the person who is the subject of the application or proceedings be lodged with the court or that the person be assessed or interviewed and that a report of such assessment or interview be lodged;
- (c) make such further inquiry or call for such further information as appears to him to be appropriate;
- (d) make such interim order as appears to him to be appropriate pending the disposal of the application or proceedings.

(3) On an application by any person (including the adult himself) claiming an interest in the property, financial affairs or personal welfare of an adult, the sheriff may give such directions to any person exercising –

- (a) functions conferred by this Act; or
- (b) functions of a like nature conferred by the law of any country,

as to the exercise of those functions and the taking of decisions or action in relation to the adult as appear to him to be appropriate.

(4) In an application or any other proceedings under this Act, the sheriff –

- (a) shall consider whether it is necessary to appoint a person for the purpose of safeguarding the interests of the person who is the subject of the application or proceedings; and
- (b) without prejudice to any existing power to appoint a person to represent the interests of the person who is the subject of the application or proceedings may, if he thinks fit, appoint a person to act for the purpose specified in paragraph (a).

(5) Safeguarding the interests of a person shall, for the purposes of subsection (4), include conveying his views so far as they are ascertainable to the sheriff; but if the sheriff considers that it is inappropriate that a person appointed to safeguard the interests of another under this section should also convey that other's views to the sheriff, the sheriff may appoint another person for that latter purpose only.

(5A) In determining an application or any other proceedings under this Act, the sheriff shall, without prejudice to the generality of section 1(4)(a), take account of the wishes and feelings of the adult who is the subject of the application or proceedings so far as they are expressed by a person providing independent advocacy services.

(5B) In subsection (5A), 'independent advocacy services' has the same meaning as it has in section 259(1) of the Mental Health (Care and Treatment) (Scotland) Act 2003.

(6) The sheriff may, on an application by –

- (a) the person authorised under the order;
- (b) the adult; or
- (c) any person entitled to apply for the order,

make an order varying the terms of an order granted under subsection (2)(a).

Amendments—Adult Support and Protection (Scotland) Act 2007, s 55.

4 Power of Court of Session or sheriff with regard to nearest relative

(1) The court may, having regard to section 1 and being satisfied that to do so will benefit an adult with incapacity, make an order that –

   (a) certain information shall not be disclosed, or intimation of certain applications shall not be given, to the nearest relative of the adult;
   (b) the functions of the nearest relative of the adult shall, during the continuance in force of the order, be exercised by a person, specified in the order, who is not the nearest relative of the adult but who –
      (i) is a person who would otherwise be entitled to be the nearest relative in terms of this Act;
      (ii) in the opinion of the court is a proper person to act as the nearest relative; and
      (iii) is willing to so act; or
   (c) no person shall, during the continuance in force of the order, exercise the functions of the nearest relative.

(2) An order made under subsection (1) shall apply only to the exercise of the functions under this Act of the nearest relative.

(3) The court may make an order varying the terms of an order granted under subsection (1).

(3A) The court may make an order under subsection (1) or (3) only on the application of –

   (a) the adult to whom the application relates; or
   (b) any person claiming an interest in that adult's property, financial affairs or personal welfare.

(3B) The court may dispose of an application for an order under subsection (1) or (3) by making –

   (a) the order applied for; or
   (b) such other order under this section as it thinks fit.

(4) (*repealed*)

Amendments—Adult Support and Protection (Scotland) Act 2007, s 56.

5 Safeguarding of interests in Court of Session appeals or proceedings

(1) In determining any appeal or in any other proceedings under this Act the Court of Session –

   (a) shall consider whether it is necessary to appoint a person for the purpose of safeguarding the interests of the person who is the subject of the appeal or other proceedings; and
   (b) without prejudice to any existing power to appoint a person to represent the interests of the second mentioned person, may if it thinks fit appoint a person to act for the purpose specified in paragraph (a).

(2) Safeguarding the interests of a person shall, for the purposes of subsection (1), include conveying his views so far as they are ascertainable to the court; but if the

court considers that it is inappropriate that a person appointed to safeguard the interests of another under this section should also convey that other's views to the court, the court may appoint another person for that latter purpose only.

The Public Guardian

6 The Public Guardian and his functions

(1) The Accountant of Court shall be the Public Guardian.

(2) The Public Guardian shall have the following general functions under this Act –

 (a) to supervise any guardian or any person who is authorised under an intervention order in the exercise of his functions relating to the property or financial affairs of the adult;
 (b) to establish, maintain and make available during normal office hours for inspection by members of the public on payment of the prescribed fee, separate registers of –
  (i) all documents relating to continuing powers of attorney governed by the law of Scotland;
  (ii) all documents relating to welfare powers of attorney governed by the law of Scotland;
  (iii) all authorisations relating to intromission with funds under Part 3;
  (iv) all documents relating to guardianship orders under Part 6;
  (v) all documents relating to intervention orders under Part 6,

in which he shall enter any matter which he is required to enter under this Act and any other matter of which he becomes aware relating to the existence or scope of the power, authorisation or order as the case may be;

 (c) to receive and investigate any complaints regarding the exercise of functions relating to the property or financial affairs of an adult made –
  (i) in relation to continuing attorneys;
  (ii) concerning intromissions with funds under Part 3;
  (iii) in relation to guardians or persons authorised under intervention orders;
 (d) to investigate any circumstances made known to him in which the property or financial affairs of an adult seem to him to be at risk;
 (da) to take part as a party in any proceedings before a court or to initiate such proceedings where he considers it necessary to do so to safeguard the property or financial affairs of an adult who is incapable for the purposes of this Act;
 (e) to provide, when requested to do so, a guardian, a continuing attorney, a withdrawer or a person authorised under an intervention order with information and advice about the performance of functions relating to property or financial affairs under this Act;
 (f) to consult the Mental Welfare Commission and any local authority on cases or matters relating to the exercise of functions under this Act in which there is, or appears to be, a common interest.

(3) In subsection (2)(c) any reference to –

 (a) a guardian shall include a reference to a guardian (however called) appointed under the law of any country to, or entitled under the law of any country to act for, an adult during his incapacity, if the guardianship is recognised by the law of Scotland;

(b) a continuing attorney shall include a reference to a person granted, under a contract, grant or appointment governed by the law of any country, powers (however expressed), relating to the granter's property or financial affairs and having continuing effect notwithstanding the granter's incapacity.

(4) In subsection 2(f), where a function under this Act is delegated by a local authority to a person in pursuance of an integration scheme prepared under section 1 or 2 of the Public Bodies (Joint Working) (Scotland) Act 2014, the reference to a local authority includes a reference to that person

Amendments—Adult Support and Protection (Scotland) Act 2007, ss 67, 77(1), Sch 1, para 5(a); SI 2015/157.

7 The Public Guardian: further provision

(1) The Scottish Ministers may prescribe –
   (a) the form and content of the registers to be established and maintained under section 6(2)(b) and the manner and medium in which they are to be established and maintained;
   (b) the form and content of any certificate which the Public Guardian is empowered to issue under this Act;
   (c) the forms and procedure for the purposes of any application required or permitted to be made under this Act to the Public Guardian in relation to any matter;
   (d) the evidence which the Public Guardian shall take into account when deciding under section 11(2) whether to dispense with intimation or notification to the adult.

(2) The Public Guardian may charge the prescribed fee for anything done by him in connection with any of his functions under this Act and he shall not be obliged to act until such fee is paid.

(3) Any certificate which the Public Guardian issues under this Act shall, for the purposes of any proceedings, be conclusive evidence of the matters contained in it.

Expenses in court proceedings

8 Expenses in court proceedings

(1) Where in any court proceedings (other than, in the case of a local authority, an application under section 68(3)) the Public Guardian, Mental Welfare Commission or local authority is a party for the purpose of protecting the interests of an adult, the court may make an award of expenses against the adult or against any person whose actings have resulted in the proceedings.

(2) Where in any court proceedings (other than, in the case of a local authority, an application under section 68(3)) the Public Guardian, Mental Welfare Commission or local authority is a party for the purpose of representing the public interest, the court may make an award of expenses against any person whose actings have resulted in the proceedings or on whose part there has been unreasonable conduct in relation to the proceedings.

The Mental Welfare Commission

9 Functions of the Mental Welfare Commission

(1) The Mental Welfare Commission shall have the following general functions under this Act in relation to any adult to whom this Act applies by reason of, or by reasons which include, mental disorder –

  (a), (b) (*repealed*)
  (c) to consult the Public Guardian and any local authority on cases or matters relating to the exercise of functions under this Act in which there is, or appears to be, a common interest;
  (d) where they are not satisfied with any investigation made by a local authority into a complaint made under section 10(1)(c), or where the local authority have failed to investigate the complaint, to receive and investigate any complaints relating to the exercise of functions relating to the personal welfare of the adult made –
    (i) in relation to welfare attorneys;
    (ii) in relation to guardians or persons authorised under intervention orders;
  (e), (f) (*repealed*)
  (g) to provide a guardian, welfare attorney or person authorised under an intervention order, when requested to do so, with information and advice in connection with the performance of his functions in relation to personal welfare under this Act.

(2) A guardian or welfare attorney of such an adult or a person authorised under an intervention order in relation to such an adult or the local authority shall afford the Mental Welfare Commission all facilities necessary to enable them to carry out their functions in respect of the adult.

(3) In subsection (1)(d) any reference to –

  (a) a guardian shall include a reference to a guardian (however called) appointed under the law of any country to, or entitled under the law of any country to act for, an adult during his incapacity, if the guardianship is recognised by the law of Scotland;
  (b) a welfare attorney shall include a reference to a person granted, under a contract, grant or appointment governed by the law of any country, powers (however expressed) relating to the granter's personal welfare and having effect during the granter's incapacity.

(4) In subsection (1)(c), where a function under this Act is delegated by a local authority to a person in pursuance of an integration scheme prepared under section 1 or 2 of the Public Bodies (Joint Working) (Scotland) Act 2014, the reference to a local authority includes a reference to that person.

(5) In subsection (1)(d), where a function under section 10(1)(c) is delegated by a local authority in pursuance of an integration scheme prepared under section 1 or 2 of the Public Bodies (Joint Working) (Scotland) Act 2014, the references to a local authority are to be read as if they were references to the person to whom the function is delegated.

Amendments—Mental Health (Care and Treatment) (Scotland) Act 2003, s 331(2), Sch 5, Pt 1; SI 2015/157.

Local authorities

10 Functions of local authorities

(1) A local authority shall have the following general functions under this Act –

  (a) to supervise a guardian appointed with functions relating to the personal welfare of an adult in the exercise of those functions;
  (b) to consult the Public Guardian and the Mental Welfare Commission on cases or matters relating to the exercise of functions under this Act in which there is, or appears to be, a common interest;
  (c) to receive and investigate any complaints relating to the exercise of functions relating to the personal welfare of an adult made –
    (i) in relation to welfare attorneys;
    (ii) in relation to guardians or persons authorised under intervention orders;
  (d) to investigate any circumstances made known to them in which the personal welfare of an adult seems to them to be at risk;
  (e) to provide a guardian, welfare attorney or person authorised under an intervention order, when requested to do so, with information and advice in connection with the performance of his functions in relation to personal welfare under this Act.

(2) For the purposes of subsection (1)(d), 'local authority' includes a local authority for an area in which the adult is present.

(3) The Scottish Ministers may make provision by regulations as regards the supervision by local authorities of the performance of their functions –

  (a) by guardians, in relation to the personal welfare of adults under this Act;
  (b) where the supervision has been ordered by the sheriff –
    (i) by persons authorised under intervention orders;
    (ii) by welfare attorneys.

(4) In subsection (1)(c) any reference to –

  (a) a guardian shall include a reference to a guardian (however called) appointed under the law of any country to, or entitled under the law of any country to act for, an adult during his incapacity, if the guardianship is recognised by the law of Scotland;
  (b) a welfare attorney shall include a reference to a person granted, under a contract, grant or appointment governed by the law of any country, powers (however expressed) relating to the granter's personal welfare and having effect during the granter's incapacity.

Intimation

11 Intimation not required in certain circumstances

(1) Where, apart from this subsection, intimation of any application or other proceedings under this Act, or notification of any interlocutor relating to such application or other proceedings, would be given to an adult and the court considers that the intimation or notification would be likely to pose a serious risk to the health of the adult the court may direct that such intimation or notification shall not be given.

(2) Where, apart from this subsection and subsection (1), any intimation or notification to him under this Act would be given by the Public Guardian to an adult

and the Public Guardian considers that the intimation or notification would be likely to pose a serious risk to the health of the adult the Public Guardian shall not give the intimation or notification.

Investigations

12 Investigations

(1) In consequence of any investigation carried out under –

   (a) section 6(2)(c) or (d) by the Public Guardian;
   (b) section 9(1)(d) by the Mental Welfare Commission; or
   (c) section 10(1)(c) or (d) by a local authority,

the Public Guardian, Mental Welfare Commission or local authority, as the case may be, may take such steps, including the making of an application to the sheriff, as seem to him or them to be necessary to safeguard the property, financial affairs or personal welfare, as the case may be, of the adult.

(2) For the purposes of any investigation mentioned in subsection (1), the Public Guardian, Mental Welfare Commission and local authority shall provide each other with such information and assistance as may be necessary to facilitate the investigation.

Amendments—Mental Health (Care and Treatment) (Scotland) Act 2003, s 331(2), Sch 5, Pt 1.

Codes of practice

13 Codes of practice

(1) The Scottish Ministers shall prepare, or cause to be prepared for their approval, and from time to time revise, or cause to be revised for their approval, codes of practice containing guidance as to the exercise by –

   (a) local authorities and their chief social work officers and mental health officers;
   (b) continuing and welfare attorneys;
   (c) persons authorised under intervention orders;
   (d) guardians;
   (e) withdrawers;
   (f) managers of authorised establishments;
   (g) supervisory bodies;
   (h) persons authorised to carry out medical treatment or research under Part 5,

of their functions under this Act and as to such other matters arising out of or connected with this Act as the Scottish Ministers consider appropriate.

(2) Before preparing or approving any code of practice under this Act or making or approving any alteration in it the Scottish Ministers shall consult such bodies as appear to them to be concerned.

(3) The Scottish Ministers shall lay copies of any such code and of any alteration in it before the Parliament.

(4) The Scottish Ministers shall publish every code of practice made under this Act as for the time being in force.

Appeal against decision as to incapacity

14 Appeal against decision as to incapacity

A decision taken for the purposes of this Act, other than by the sheriff, as to the incapacity of an adult may be appealed by –

(a) the adult; or
(b) any person claiming an interest in the adult's property, financial affairs or personal welfare relating to the purpose for which the decision was taken,

to the sheriff or, where the decision was taken by the sheriff, to the sheriff principal and thence, with the leave of the sheriff principal, to the Court of Session.

PART 2
CONTINUING POWERS OF ATTORNEY AND WELFARE POWERS OF ATTORNEY

15 Creation of continuing power of attorney

(1) Where an individual grants a power of attorney relating to his property or financial affairs in accordance with the following provisions of this section that power of attorney shall, notwithstanding any rule of law, continue to have effect in the event of the granter's becoming incapable in relation to decisions about the matter to which the power of attorney relates.

(2) In this Act a power of attorney granted under subsection (1) is referred to as a 'continuing power of attorney' and a person on whom such power is conferred is referred to as a 'continuing attorney'.

(3) A continuing power of attorney shall be valid only if it is expressed in a written document which –

(a) is subscribed by the granter;
(b) incorporates a statement which clearly expresses the granter's intention that the power be a continuing power;
(ba) where the continuing power of attorney is exercisable only if the granter is determined to be incapable in relation to decisions about the matter to which the power relates, states that the granter has considered how such a determination may be made;
(c) incorporates a certificate in the prescribed form by a practising solicitor or by a member of another prescribed class that –
  (i) he has interviewed the granter immediately before the granter subscribed the document;
  (ii) he is satisfied, either because of his own knowledge of the granter or because he has consulted another person (whom he names in the certificate) who has knowledge of the granter, that at the time the continuing power of attorney is granted the granter understands its nature and extent;
  (iii) he has no reason to believe that the granter is acting under undue influence or that any other factor vitiates the granting of the power.

(4) A practising solicitor or member of another prescribed class may not grant a certificate under subsection (3)(c) if he is the person to whom the power of attorney has been granted.

(5) It is declared that the rule of law which provides that an agent's authority ends in the event of the bankruptcy of the principal or the agent applies, and has applied since subsection (1) came into force, in relation to continuing powers of attorney.

Amendments—Adult Support and Protection (Scotland) Act 2007, s 57(1).

16 Creation and exercise of welfare power of attorney

(1) An individual may grant a power of attorney relating to his personal welfare in accordance with the following provisions of this section.

(2) In this Act a power of attorney granted under this section is referred to as a 'welfare power of attorney' and an individual on whom such power is conferred is referred to as a 'welfare attorney'.

(3) A welfare power of attorney shall be valid only if it is expressed in a written document which –

- (a) is subscribed by the granter;
- (b) incorporates a statement which clearly expresses the granter's intention that the power be a welfare power to which this section applies;
- (ba) states that the granter has considered how a determination as to whether he is incapable in relation to decisions about the matter to which the welfare power of attorney relates may be made for the purposes of subsection (5)(b);
- (c) incorporates a certificate in the prescribed form by a practising solicitor or by a member of another prescribed class that –
  - (i) he has interviewed the granter immediately before the granter subscribed the document;
  - (ii) he is satisfied, either because of his own knowledge of the granter or because he has consulted another person (whom he names in the certificate) who has knowledge of the granter, that at the time the welfare power of attorney is granted the granter understands its nature and extent;
  - (iii) he has no reason to believe that the granter is acting under undue influence or that any other factor vitiates the granting of the power.

(4) A practising solicitor or member of another prescribed class may not grant a certificate under subsection (3)(c) if he is the person to whom the power of attorney has been granted.

(5) A welfare power of attorney –

- (a) may be granted only to an individual (which does not include a person acting in his capacity as an officer of a local authority or other body established by or under an enactment); and
- (b) shall not be exercisable unless –
  - (i) the granter is incapable in relation to decisions about the matter to which the welfare power of attorney relates; or
  - (ii) the welfare attorney reasonably believes that sub-paragraph (i) applies.

(6) A welfare attorney may not –

- (a) place the granter in a hospital for the treatment of mental disorder against his will;
- (b) consent on behalf of the granter to any form of treatment in relation to

which the authority conferred by section 47(2) does not apply by virtue of regulations made under section 48(2);
(c) make, on behalf of the granter, a request under section 4(1) of the Anatomy Act 1984;
(d) give, on behalf of the granter, an authorisation under, or by virtue of, section 6(1), 17, 29(1) or 42(1) of the Human Tissue (Scotland) Act 2006; or
(e) make, on behalf of the granter, a nomination under section 30(1) of that Act.

(7) A welfare power of attorney shall not come to an end in the event of the bankruptcy of the granter or the welfare attorney.

(8) Any reference to a welfare attorney –
(a) in relation to subsection (5)(b) in a case where the granter is habitually resident in Scotland; and
(b) in subsection (6),

shall include a reference to a person granted, under a contract, grant or appointment governed by the law of any country, powers (however expressed) relating to the granter's personal welfare and having effect during the granter's incapacity.

Amendments—Human Tissue (Scotland) Act 2006, s 57(2); Adult Support and Protection (Scotland) Act 2007, s 57(2).

16A Continuing and welfare power of attorney: accompanying certificate

Where a document confers both –
(a) a continuing power of attorney; and
(b) a welfare power of attorney,

the validity requirements imposed by sections 15(3)(c) and 16(3)(c) may be satisfied by incorporating a single certificate which certifies the matters set out in those provisions.

17 Attorney not obliged to act in certain circumstances

A continuing or welfare attorney shall not be obliged to do anything which would otherwise be within the powers of the attorney if doing it would, in relation to its value or utility, be unduly burdensome or expensive.

18 Power of attorney not granted in accordance with this Act

A power of attorney granted after the commencement of this Act which is not granted in accordance with section 15 or 16 shall have no effect during any period when the granter is incapable in relation to decisions about the matter to which the power of attorney relates.

19 Registration of continuing or welfare power of attorney

(1) A continuing or welfare attorney shall have no authority to act until the document conferring the power of attorney has been registered under this section.

(2) For the purposes of registration, the document conferring the power of attorney shall be sent to the Public Guardian who, if he is satisfied that a person appointed to act is prepared to act, shall –

   (a) enter prescribed particulars of it in the register maintained by him under section 6(2)(b)(i) or (ii) as the case may be;
   (b) send a copy of it with a certificate of registration to the sender;
   (c) if it confers a welfare power of attorney, give notice of the registration of the document to both the local authority and the Mental Welfare Commission.

(3) The document conferring a continuing or welfare power of attorney may contain a condition that the Public Guardian shall not register it under this section until the occurrence of a specified event and in that case the Public Guardian shall not register it until he is satisfied that the specified event has occurred.

(4) A copy of a document conferring a continuing or welfare power of attorney authenticated by the Public Guardian shall be accepted for all purposes as sufficient evidence of the contents of the original and of any matter relating thereto appearing in the copy.

(5) The Public Guardian shall –

   (a) on the registration of a document conferring a continuing or welfare power of attorney, send a copy of it to the granter;
   (b) where the document conferring the continuing or welfare power of attorney so requires, send a copy of it to not more than two specified individuals or holders of specified offices or positions;
   (c) where the document confers a welfare power of attorney and the local authority requests a copy of it, send such a copy to the local authority; and
   (d) where the document confers a welfare power of attorney and the Mental Welfare Commission requests a copy of it, send such a copy to the Mental Welfare Commission.

(6) A decision of the Public Guardian under subsection (2) as to whether or not a person is prepared to act or under subsection (3) as to whether or not the specified event has occurred may be appealed to the sheriff, whose decision shall be final.

Amendments—Adult Support and Protection (Scotland) Act 2007, s 57(4)(b).

19A Electronic copies

(1) The Public Guardian may, for the purposes of section 19 –

   (a) accept a copy of a document conferring a power of attorney sent electronically, instead of the original, to the Public Guardian's email address, and
   (b) register the copy document accordingly.

(2) The Public Guardian may refuse to accept a copy document unless it is –

   (a) sent by such person or type of person, and
   (b) received in such format,

as the Public Guardian may from time to time direct.

This subsection does not limit the Public Guardian's general discretion to accept a copy document in pursuance of subsection (1).

(3) References in this Part to documents registered (or sent for registration) under section 19 include references to copy documents registered (or sent) in pursuance of subsection (1).

Amendments—Inserted by SSI 2008/380.

20 Powers of sheriff

(1) An application for an order under subsection (2) may be made to the sheriff by any person claiming an interest in the property, financial affairs or personal welfare of the granter of a continuing or welfare power of attorney.

(2) Where, on an application being made under subsection (1), the sheriff is satisfied that the granter is incapable in relation to decisions about, or of acting to safeguard or promote his interests in, his property, financial affairs or personal welfare insofar as the power of attorney relates to them, and that it is necessary to safeguard or promote these interests, he may make an order –

  (a) ordaining that the continuing attorney shall be subject to the supervision of the Public Guardian to such extent as may be specified in the order;
  (b) ordaining the continuing attorney to submit accounts in respect of any period specified in the order for audit to the Public Guardian;
  (c) ordaining that the welfare attorney shall be subject to the supervision of the local authority to such extent as may be specified in the order;
  (d) ordaining the welfare attorney to give a report to him as to the manner in which the welfare attorney has exercised his powers during any period specified in the order;
  (e) revoking –
    (i) any of the powers granted by the continuing or welfare power of attorney; or
    (ii) the appointment of an attorney.

(3) Where the sheriff makes an order under this section the sheriff clerk shall send a copy of the interlocutor containing the order to the Public Guardian who shall –

  (a) enter prescribed particulars in the register maintained by him under section 6(2)(b)(i) or (ii) as the case may be;
  (b) notify –
    (i) the granter;
    (ii) the continuing or welfare attorney;
    (iii) where it is the welfare attorney who is notified, the local authority and the Mental Welfare Commission;
    (iv) where the sheriff makes an order under subsection (2)(c), the local authority.

(4) A decision of the sheriff under subsection (2)(a) to (d) shall be final.

(5) In this section any reference to –

  (a) a continuing power of attorney shall include a reference to a power (however expressed) under a contract, grant or appointment governed by the law of any country, relating to the granter's property or financial affairs and having continuing effect notwithstanding the granter's incapacity;
  (b) a welfare power of attorney shall include a reference to a power (however expressed) under a contract, grant or appointment governed by the law of any country, relating to the granter's personal welfare and having effect during the granter's incapacity,

and 'continuing attorney' and 'welfare attorney' shall be construed accordingly.

Amendments—Adult Support and Protection (Scotland) Act 2007, s 57(5).

21 Records: attorneys
A continuing or welfare attorney shall keep records of the exercise of his powers.

22 Notification to Public Guardian
(1) After a document conferring a continuing or welfare power of attorney has been registered under section 19, the attorney shall notify the Public Guardian –

    (a) of any change in his address;
    (b) of any change in the address of the granter of the power of attorney;
    (c) of the death of the granter of the power of attorney; or
    (d) of any other event which results in the termination of the power of attorney,

and the Public Guardian shall enter prescribed particulars in the register maintained by him under section 6(2)(b)(i) or (ii) as the case may be and shall notify the granter (in the case of an event mentioned in paragraph (a) or (d)) and, where the power of attorney relates to the personal welfare of the adult, both the local authority and the Mental Welfare Commission.

(2) If, after a document conferring a continuing or welfare power of attorney has been registered under section 19, the attorney dies, his personal representatives shall, if aware of the existence of the power of attorney, notify the Public Guardian who shall enter prescribed particulars in the register maintained by him under section 6(2)(b)(i) or (ii) as the case may be, and shall notify the granter and, where the power of attorney relates to the personal welfare of the adult, both the local authority and the Mental Welfare Commission.

Amendments—Adult Support and Protection (Scotland) Act 2007, s 57(6).

22A Revocation of continuing or welfare power of attorney
(1) The granter of a continuing or welfare power of attorney may revoke the power of attorney (or any of the powers granted by it) after the document conferring the power of attorney has been registered under section 19 by giving a revocation notice to the Public Guardian.

(2) A revocation notice shall be valid only if it is expressed in a written document which –

    (a) is subscribed by the granter; and
    (b) incorporates a certificate in the prescribed form by a practising solicitor or by a member of another prescribed class that –
        (i) he has interviewed the granter immediately before the granter subscribed the document;
        (ii) he is satisfied, either because of his own knowledge of the granter or because he has consulted another person (whom he names in the certificate) who has knowledge of the granter, that at the time the revocation is made the granter understands its effect;
        (iii) he has no reason to believe that the granter is acting under undue influence or that any other factor vitiates the revocation of the power.

(3) The Public Guardian, on receiving a revocation notice, shall –

  (a) enter the prescribed particulars of it in the register maintained by him under section 6(2)(b)(i) or (ii) as the case may be; and
  (b) notify –
    (i) the continuing or welfare attorney; and
    (ii) where it is the welfare attorney who is notified, the local authority and the Mental Welfare Commission.

(4) A revocation has effect when the revocation notice is registered under this section.

(5) No liability shall be incurred by any person who acts in good faith in ignorance of the revocation of a power of attorney under this section. Nor shall any title to heritable property acquired by such a person be challengeable on that ground alone.

Amendments—Inserted by Adult Support and Protection (Scotland) Act 2007, s 57(7).

23 Resignation of continuing or welfare attorney

(1) A continuing or welfare attorney who wishes to resign after the document conferring the power of attorney has been registered under section 19 shall give notice in writing of his intention to do so to –

  (a) the granter of the power of attorney;
  (b) the Public Guardian;
  (c) any guardian or, where there is no guardian, the granter's primary carer;
  (d) the local authority, where they are supervising the welfare attorney.

(2) Subject to subsection (4), the resignation shall not have effect until the expiry of a period of 28 days commencing with the date of receipt by the Public Guardian of the notice given under subsection (1); and on its becoming effective the Public Guardian shall enter prescribed particulars in the register maintained by him under section 6(2)(b)(i) or (ii) as the case may be.

(3) Where the resignation is of a welfare attorney, the Public Guardian shall notify the local authority and the Mental Welfare Commission.

(4) The resignation of a joint attorney, or an attorney in respect of whom the granter has appointed a substitute attorney, shall take effect on the receipt by the Public Guardian of notice under subsection (1)(b) if evidence that –

  (a) the remaining joint attorney is willing to continue to act; or
  (b) the substitute attorney is willing to act,

accompanies the notice.

Amendments—Inserted by Adult Support and Protection (Scotland) Act 2007, s 57(8).

24 Termination of continuing or welfare power of attorney

(1) If the granter and the continuing or welfare attorney are married to each other the power of attorney shall, unless the document conferring it provides otherwise, come to an end upon the granting of –

  (a) a decree of separation to either party;
  (b) a decree of divorce to either party;
  (c) declarator of nullity of the marriage.

(1A) If the granter and the continuing or welfare attorney are in civil partnership with each other the power of attorney shall, unless the document conferring it provides otherwise, come to an end on the granting of –

    (a) a decree of separation of the partners in the civil partnership;
    (b) a decree of dissolution of the civil partnership;
    (c) a declarator of nullity of the civil partnership.

(2) The authority of a continuing or welfare attorney in relation to any matter shall come to an end on the appointment of a guardian with powers relating to that matter.

(3) In subsection (2) any reference to –

    (a) a continuing attorney shall include a reference to a person granted, under a contract, grant or appointment governed by the law of any country, powers (however expressed), relating to the granter's property or financial affairs and having continuing effect notwithstanding the granter's incapacity;
    (b) a welfare attorney shall include a reference to a person granted, under a contract, grant or appointment governed by the law of any country, powers (however expressed) relating to the granter's personal welfare and having effect during the granter's incapacity.

(4) No liability shall be incurred by any person who acts in good faith in ignorance of –

    (a) the coming to an end of a power of attorney under subsection (1) or subsection (1A); or
    (b) the appointment of a guardian as mentioned in subsection (2),

nor shall any title to heritable property acquired by such a person be challengeable on those grounds alone.

Amendments—Family Law (Scotland) Act 2006, s 36.

PART 3
ACCOUNTS AND FUNDS

Amendments—Part substituted by Adult Support and Protection (Scotland) Act 2007, s 57(8).

24A Intromissions with funds

(1) This Part makes provision for the authorisation of persons by the Public Guardian to intromit with the funds of an adult for the purposes mentioned in subsection (2).

(2) Those purposes are –

    (a) the payment of central and local government taxes for which the adult is responsible;
    (b) the provisions of sustenance, accommodation, fuel, clothing and related goods and services for the adult;
    (c) the provision of other services provided for the purposes of looking after or caring for the adult;
    (d) the settlement of debts owed by or incurred in respect of the adult, including any prescribed fees charged by the Public Guardian in connection with an application under this Part;

(e) the payment for the provision of items other than those mentioned in paragraphs (a) to (d) such as the Public Guardian may, in any case, authorise.

Amendments—Substituted by Adult Support and Protection (Scotland) Act 2007, s 57(8).

24B Adults in respect of whom applications may be made

(1) An application to the Public Guardian under this Part may be made only in relation to an adult who is incapable in relation to decisions about, or of safeguarding the adult's interests in, the funds to which the application relates.

(2) But an application may not be made in the case of an adult in relation to whom –

  (a) there is a guardian of the type mentioned in section 33(1)(a) with powers relating to the funds in question;
  (b) there is a continuing attorney with powers relating to the funds in question; or
  (c) an intervention order relating to the funds in question has been granted.

Amendments—Substituted by Adult Support and Protection (Scotland) Act 2007, s 57(8).

Authority to take preliminary steps

24C Authority to provide information about funds

(1) This section applies where a person –

  (a) believes than an adult holds funds in an account in the adult's sole name; but
  (b) cannot make an application under section 25 or section 26G because the person does not know –
      (i) where the account is held;
      (ii) the account details;
      (iii) how much is held in the account; or
      (iv) any other information needed to complete the application.

(2) Where this section applies, the person may apply to the Public Guardian for a certificate authorising any fundholder to provide the person with such information as the person may reasonably require in order to make an application under section 25 or 26G.

(3) Where the Public Guardian grants an application under subsection (2), the Public Guardian must issue the certificate to the applicant.

(4) A fundholder presented with a certificate issued under subsection (3) is not prevented by –

  (a) any obligation as to secrecy; or
  (b) any other restriction on disclosure of information,

from providing the person who presents the certificate to it with such information as the person may reasonably require in order to make an application under section 25 or 26G about funds held by it on behalf of the adult.

Amendments—Substituted by Adult Support and Protection (Scotland) Act 2007, s 57(8).

24D Authority to open account in adult's name

(1) This section applies where –
- (a) a person believes that –
    - (i) an adult holds funds;
    - (ii) an adult is entitled to income or other payments or is likely to become so entitled; or
    - (iii) a fundholder holds funds on behalf of an adult; but
- (b) the adult does not have a suitable account in the adult's sole name in which the funds, income or other payments can be placed for the purposes of intromitting with the adult's funds under this Part.

(2) Where this section applies, the person may apply to the Public Guardian for a certificate authorising the opening of an account in the adult's name for the purpose of intromitting with the adult's funds.

(3) Where the Public Guardian grants an application under subsection (2), the Public Guardian must issue the certificate to the applicant.

(4) The certificate issued under subsection (3) may specify the kind of account which may be opened by a fundholder.

(5) A fundholder presented with a certificate issued under subsection (3) may open an account in the adult's name.

(6) But, if the certificate specifies a kind of account, the fundholder may open only an account of the type specified.

(7) On an account being opened in pursuance of subsection (5), the applicant must notify prescribed particulars of the account to the Public Guardian.

Amendments—Substituted by Adult Support and Protection (Scotland) Act 2007, s 57(8).

Authority to intromit

25 Authority to intromit

(1) A person mentioned in subsection (2) may apply to the Public Guardian for a certificate authorising the person to intromit with an adult's funds.

(2) Those persons are –
- (a) an individual (other than an individual acting in his capacity as an officer of a local authority or other body established by or under an enactment);
- (b) two or more individuals who wish to act jointly; or
- (c) a body (other than a manager of an authorised establishment within the meaning of section 35(2)).

(3) An application under subsection (1) which is accompanied by an application under section 24D may only be granted if –
- (a) an account is opened in pursuance of section 24D(5); and
- (b) prescribed particulars of that account are notified to the Public Guardian in pursuance of section 24D(7).

(4) Where the Public Guardian grants an application under subsection (1), the Public Guardian must –
- (a) enter prescribed particulars in the register maintained by the Public Guardian under section 6(2)(b)(iii); and

(b) issue a certificate of authority (a 'withdrawal certificate') to the applicant.

(5) No application may be made under subsection (1) if a person is already authorised to intromit with the funds of the adult to whom the application relates (unless the application is made by that person).

(6) In this Act, an individual or a body who holds a valid withdrawal certificate issued under this Part is referred to as a 'withdrawer'.

Amendments—Substituted by Adult Support and Protection (Scotland) Act 2007, s 57(8).

26 Authority to intromit: application

(1) An application under section 25(1) must –
   (a) state the purposes of the proposed intromission with the adult's funds, setting out the specific sums relating to each purpose;
   (b) specify an account held by a fundholder in the adult's sole name which the applicant wishes to use for the purpose of intromitting with the adult's funds (or be accompanied by an application under section 24D to open an account for that purpose);
   (c) contain an undertaking that the applicant will open an account (the 'designated account') solely for the purposes of –
      (i) receiving funds transferred under the authority of any certificate granted; and
      (ii) intromitting with those funds;

(2) The application may also specify another account held by a fundholder in the adult's sole name which the applicant also wishes to use for the purpose of intromitting with the adult's funds (or be accompanied by an application under section 24D to open an account for that purpose).

(3) In this Part –
   (a) the account specified or, as the case may be, opened for the purposes of subsection (1)(b) is referred to as the adult's current account.
   (b) the account specified or, as the case may be, opened for the purposes of subsection (2) is referred to as the adult's second account.

Amendments—Substituted by Adult Support and Protection (Scotland) Act 2007, s 57(8).

Withdrawal certificates

26A Withdrawal certificates

(1) A withdrawal certificate may –
   (a) authorise the transfer of funds –
      (i) from the adult's current account to the designated account;
      (ii) from the adult's current account to the adult's second account;
      (iii) from the designated account to the adult's second account;
   (b) authorise the continuance or making of arrangements for the regular or occasional payment of funds from the adult's current account for specified purposes (for example: by standing order or direct debit);
   (c) authorise the withdrawal of funds from the designated account for specified purposes;

(d) place limits on the amount of funds that may be so transferred, paid or withdrawn.

(2) But such a certificate does not authorise a transfer of funds or payment that would cause –

    (a) the adult's current account;
    (b) the adult's second account; or
    (c) the designated account,

to become overdrawn.

(3) If any of the accounts mentioned in paragraphs (a) to (c) of subsection (2) is overdrawn, the fundholder of that account has a right of relief against the withdrawer.

(4) In subsection (1)(b), 'specified' means specified in the certificate of appointment.

Amendments—Substituted by Adult Support and Protection (Scotland) Act 2007, s 57(8).

Joint and reserve withdrawers

26B Addition of joint withdrawer

(1) This section applies where an individual has or individuals have been appointed as a withdrawer in relation to an adult.

(2) Where this sections applies, another individual may apply to the Public Guardian for appointment as a joint withdrawer.

(3) An application under subsection (1) must be signed by the existing withdrawer.

(4) Where the Public Guardian grants an application under subsection (1), the Public Guardian must –

    (a) enter prescribed particulars in the register maintained by the Public Guardian under section 6(2)(b)(iii); and
    (b) issue a certificate of authority (a 'withdrawal certificate') to the existing withdrawer and the applicant.

(5) Subject to sections 31(2) and 31A, a certificate issued under subsection (4)(b) is valid until the date on which the withdrawal certificate held by the existing withdrawer would cease to be valid under section 31(1) or 31E(6), as the case may be (regardless of any subsequent extension, reduction, termination or suspension of the existing withdrawer's authority).

(6) In this section, 'the existing withdrawer' means the individual or individuals mentioned in subsection (1).

(7) In this Part, where two or more individuals are appointed as withdrawers, each individual is referred to as a 'joint withdrawer'.

Amendments—Substituted by Adult Support and Protection (Scotland) Act 2007, s 57(8).

26C Joint withdrawers: supplementary

(1) Joint withdrawers may, subject to subsection (2), exercise their functions individually, and each joint withdrawer is liable for any loss incurred by the adult arising out of –

(a) the joint withdrawer's own acts or omissions; or
(b) the joint withdrawer's failure to take reasonable steps to ensure that another joint withdrawer does not breach any duty of care or fiduciary duty owed to the adult.

(2) Where more than one joint withdrawer is liable under subsection (1), they are liable jointly and severally.

(3) A joint withdrawer must, before exercising any function conferred on the joint withdrawer, consult the other joint withdrawers, unless –

(a) consultation would be impracticable in the circumstances; or
(b) the joint withdrawers agree that consultation is not necessary.

(4) Where joint withdrawers disagree as to the exercise of their functions, one or more of them may apply to the Public Guardian for directions.

(5) Directions given by the Public Guardian in pursuance of subsection (4) may be appealed to the sheriff, whose decision is final.

(6) Where there are joint withdrawers –

(a) a third party in good faith is entitled to rely on the authority to act of any one or more of them; and
(b) section 31A(5) (interim authority) only applies where the Public Guardian terminates the authority of all of the joint withdrawers.

Amendments—Substituted by Adult Support and Protection (Scotland) Act 2007, s 57(8).

26D Reserve withdrawers: applications

(1) In any case where an individual is issued with a withdrawal certificate ('a main withdrawer'), the Public Guardian may, on an application by the main withdrawer, appoint another individual ('a reserve withdrawer') to act as a withdrawer in the event of the main withdrawer temporarily becoming unable to act.

(2) An application for appointment of a reserve withdrawer may be made at the time of the application under section 25 for a withdrawal certificate or at any later time.

(3) The application for appointment as a reserve withdrawer must be signed by the proposed reserve withdrawer.

(4) Where the Public Guardian grants the application, the Public Guardian must enter prescribed particulars in the register maintained by the Public Guardian under section 6(2)(b)(iii).

Amendments—Substituted by Adult Support and Protection (Scotland) Act 2007, s 57(8).

26E Reserve withdrawers: authority to act

(1) Where –

(a) a reserve withdrawer has been appointed under section 26D; and
(b) the main withdrawer considers that the main withdrawer is or will be unable to carry out some or all of the main withdrawer's functions under this Part,

the main withdrawer may notify the Public Guardian that the main withdrawer wishes the Public Guardian to authorise the reserve withdrawer to intromit with the adult's funds for a specified period.

(2) Where a reserve withdrawer becomes aware that the main withdrawer is unable –

   (a) to carry out some or all of the main withdrawer's functions in relation to intromitting with the funds concerned; and
   (b) to notify the Public Guardian under subsection (1),

the reserve withdrawer may apply to the Public Guardian for a certificate authorising the reserve withdrawer to intromit with the adult's funds for a specified period.

(3) The Public Guardian, on being notified under subsection (1), must or, on an application under subsection (2), may –

   (a) enter prescribed particulars in the register maintained by him under section 6(2)(b)(iii);
   (b) issue a certificate of authority (a 'withdrawal certificate') to the reserve withdrawer; and
   (c) notify the adult and the main withdrawer.

(4) The certificate issued under subsection (3)(b) is –

   (a) valid for the specified period, or such shorter period as the Public Guardian thinks fit, but does not extend beyond the date on which the validity of the withdrawal certificate issued to the main withdrawer would cease under section 31(1) or 31E(6), as the case may be;
   (b) suspended during any period when the authority of the main withdrawer is suspended;
   (c) terminated if the authority of the main withdrawer is terminated.

(5) The main withdrawer and the reserve withdrawer are liable (jointly and severally) for any loss incurred by the adult arising out of the reserve withdrawer's acts or omissions.

(6) In this section, 'specified' means specified in the notice or, as the case may be, application.

Amendments—Substituted by Adult Support and Protection (Scotland) Act 2007, s 57(8).

Variation of withdrawer's authority

26F Variation of withdrawal certificate

(1) The Public Guardian may –

   (a) on the application of a withdrawer, or
   (b) if notified under section 30A,

vary the withdrawal certificate (the 'existing certificate') issued to the withdrawer.

(2) But a withdrawal certificate may not be varied under this section so as to alter the period of validity of the certificate.

(3) Where the Public Guardian decides to vary the withdrawal certificate under subsection (1), the Public Guardian must –

   (a) enter prescribed particulars in the register maintained by the Public Guardian under section 6(2)(b)(iii); and

(b) issue a varied withdrawal certificate to the withdrawer.

(4) The existing certificate ceases to be valid on the date the varied certificate is issued under subsection (3)(b).

Amendments—Substituted by Adult Support and Protection (Scotland) Act 2007, s 57(8).

Authority to transfer funds

26G Authority to transfer specified sums

(1) A person mentioned in subsection (2) may apply to the Public Guardian for a certificate authorising the transfer of a specified sum from a specified account ('the original account') in an adult's sole name to –

    (a) the designated account;
    (b) the adult's current account;
    (c) the adult's second account; or
    (d) such other account as may be specified.

(2) Those persons are –

    (a) a withdrawer;
    (b) a person who has applied for a withdrawal certificate under section 25;

(3) An application under subsection (1) may also seek authority –

    (a) to close the original account;
    (b) to terminate an arrangement for the payment of funds from the original account to another account (for example: a standing order or direct debit).

(4) Where the Public Guardian grants an application under subsection (1), the Public Guardian must –

    (a) enter prescribed particulars in the register maintained by the Public Guardian under section 6(2)(b)(iii); and
    (b) issue the certificate to the applicant.

(5) In this section, 'specified' means specified in the application under subsection (1) or, as the case may be, in the certificate granted under subsection (4).

Amendments—Substituted by Adult Support and Protection (Scotland) Act 2007, s 57(8).

Applications: general

27 Applications: general requirements]

An application under section 24C, 24D, 25, 26B, 26D, 26F or 26G must –

    (a) be signed by the applicant;
    (b) contain the name and addresses of the nearest relative, named person and primary carer of the adult, if known;
    (c) be submitted to the Public Guardian no later than 14 days after –
        (i) where it is required to be countersigned under section 27A, the day the application is so countersigned, or
        (ii) in any other case, the day the application is signed by the applicant as mentioned in paragraph (a).

Amendments—Substituted by Adult Support and Protection (Scotland) Act 2007, s 57(8).

27A Countersigning of applications

(1) An application under section 24C, 24D, 25, or 26B must be countersigned by a person who must declare in the application that –
- (a) the person knows the applicant and has known the applicant for at least one year prior to the date of the application;
- (b) the person is not any of the following –
    - (i) a relative of or person residing with the applicant or the adult;
    - (ii) a director or employee of the fundholder;
    - (iii) a solicitor acting on behalf of the adult or any other person mentioned in this paragraph in relation to any matter under this Act;
    - (iv) the medical practitioner who has issued the certificate under section 27B in connection with the application;
    - (v) a guardian of the adult;
    - (vi) a welfare or continuing attorney of the adult;
    - (vii) a person who is authorised under an intervention order in relation to the adult;
- (c) the person believes the information contained in the application to be true; and
- (d) the person believes the applicant to be a fit and proper person to intromit with the adult's funds.

(2) An application under section 26D (reserve withdrawers) must be countersigned by a person who must declare in the application the matters set out in paragraphs (a) to (d) of subsection (1) but with references in those paragraphs to 'applicant' read as references to the proposed reserve withdrawer.

(3) This section does not apply to an application made by a body.

Amendments—Substituted by Adult Support and Protection (Scotland) Act 2007, s 57(8).

27B Medical certificates

An application under section 24C, 24D, or 25 must be accompanied by a certificate in prescribed form from a medical practitioner that the adult is –
- (a) incapable in relation to decisions about; or
- (b) incapable of acting to safeguard or promote the adult's interests in,

the adult's funds.

Amendments—Substituted by Adult Support and Protection (Scotland) Act 2007, s 57(8).

27C Intimation of applications

(1) On receipt of a competent application under section 24C, 24D, 25, 26B, 26D, 26F or 26G, the Public Guardian must intimate the application to –
- (a) the adult;
- (b) the adult's nearest relative;
- (c) the adult's primary carer;
- (d) the adult's named person;
- (e) where the applicant is –
    - (i) the individual mentioned in both paragraph (b) and (c); or
    - (ii) a body other than a local authority,
    the chief social work officer of the local authority; and

(f) any other person who the Public Guardian considers has an interest in the application.

(2) A competent application is an application which complies with section 27 and, where appropriate, sections 27A and 27B.

Amendments—Substituted by Adult Support and Protection (Scotland) Act 2007, s 57(8).

27D Determination of applications: applicant to be fit and proper

(1) The Public Guardian may grant an application made under section 24C, 24D, 25, 26B or 26D only if satisfied that –

(a) the applicant in an application under section 24C, 24D, 25 or 26B, or
(b) the proposed reserve withdrawer in an application under section 26D,

is a fit and proper person to intromit with the funds of the adult.

(2) In deciding whether a person is fit and proper, the Public Guardian must have regard to any guidance issued in relation to that matter by the Scottish Ministers.

Amendments—Substituted by Adult Support and Protection (Scotland) Act 2007, s 57(8).

27E Determination of applications: opportunity to make representations

(1) The Public Guardian must not grant an application under section 24C, 24D, 25, 26B, 26D, 26F or 26G without affording to any person who receives intimation of the application under section 27C or any other person who wishes to object an opportunity to make representations.

(2) Where the Public Guardian proposes to refuse the application the Public Guardian must intimate the proposed decision to the applicant and advise the applicant of the prescribed period within which the applicant may object to the proposed refusal.

(3) The Public Guardian must not refuse an application without affording to the applicant, if the applicant objects, an opportunity to make representations.

Amendments—Substituted by Adult Support and Protection (Scotland) Act 2007, s 57(8).

27F Referral of application to sheriff

(1) The Public Guardian may remit an application under section 24C, 24D, 25, 26B, 26D, 26F or 26G for determination by the sheriff at the instance of –

(a) the Public Guardian;
(b) the applicant; or
(c) any person who objects to the granting of the application.

(2) The sheriff's decision on an application remitted under subsection (1) is final.

Amendments—Substituted by Adult Support and Protection (Scotland) Act 2007, s 57(8).

27G Multiple applications etc

(1) Where a person who has made an application under section 24C, 24D or 25 in respect of an adult makes another application under any of those sections in respect of the same adult, the Public Guardian may disapply any of the provisions in sections 27 to 27B to that application.

(2) Where the Public Guardian is to issue more than one certificate under this Part to the same person, the Public Guardian may instead issue a combined certificate to the person.

(3) References in this Part to a withdrawal certificate or other certificate issued under this Part include references to any combined certificate issued by the Public Guardian instead of the withdrawal or other certificate.

Amendments—Substituted by Adult Support and Protection (Scotland) Act 2007, s 57(8).

Fundholders

28 Fundholders of adult's current account and adult's second account

(1) The fundholder of an adult's current account may act on the instructions of a withdrawer to the extent authorised by the withdrawal certificate issued to the withdrawer.

(2) The fundholder of an adult's current account presented with a withdrawal certificate must not allow any operations to be carried out on that account other than those carried out in accordance with the certificate by the withdrawer.

(3) The fundholder of an adult's current account or an adult's second account presented with a withdrawal certificate may provide the withdrawer with a copy of any statement or other correspondence issued by the fundholder to the adult during the period when the withdrawal certificate is valid.

Amendments—Substituted by Adult Support and Protection (Scotland) Act 2007, s 57(8).

28A Fundholder of original account

The fundholder of an original account may act on the instructions of a withdrawer to the extent authorised by the certificate issued to the withdrawer under section 26G(4).

Amendments—Substituted by Adult Support and Protection (Scotland) Act 2007, s 57(8).

29 Fundholder's liability

The fundholder of an account mentioned in section 28 or 28A is liable to the adult for any funds removed from the account under that section at any time when it was aware that the withdrawer's authority had been terminated or suspended by the Public Guardian under section 31A but, on meeting such liability, the fundholder of the account has a right of relief against the withdrawer.

Amendments—Substituted by Adult Support and Protection (Scotland) Act 2007, s 57(8).

Withdrawers

30 Use of funds by withdrawer

(1) Any funds used by the withdrawer must be applied only for the benefit of the adult.

(2) Despite subsection (1), where the withdrawer lives with the adult, the withdrawer may, to the extent authorised by the certificate, apply any funds withdrawn towards household expenses.

Amendments—Substituted by Adult Support and Protection (Scotland) Act 2007, s 57(8).

30A Notification of change of address

(1) A withdrawer must notify the Public Guardian –

(a) of any change in the withdrawer's address; and
(b) of any change in the address of the adult.

(2) A notice under subsection (1) must be given within 7 days of the date of the change to which it relates.

Amendments—Substituted by Adult Support and Protection (Scotland) Act 2007, s 57(8).

30B Records and inquiries

(1) A withdrawer must keep records of the exercise of the withdrawer's powers.

(2) The Public Guardian may make inquiries from time to time as to the manner in which a withdrawer has exercised the withdrawer's functions under this Part.

Amendments—Substituted by Adult Support and Protection (Scotland) Act 2007, s 57(8).

Duration etc of authority

31 Duration of withdrawal certificate

(1) Unless this Part provides otherwise, a withdrawal certificate issued under section 25 is valid for a period of 3 years commencing with the date of issue of the certificate.

(2) The Public Guardian may reduce or extend the period of validity of a withdrawal certificate; and an extension may be without limit of time.

(3) Subsections (1) and (2) are without prejudice to the right of the withdrawer to make subsequent applications under section 25 after the withdrawal certificate ceases to be valid or, as the case may be, a suspension or termination of the withdrawer's authority.

(4) The validity of a withdrawal certificate ceases –

(a) on the appointment of a guardian with powers relating to the funds or account in question;
(b) on the granting of an intervention order relating to the funds or account in question; or
(c) on a continuing attorney's acquiring authority to act in relation to the funds or account in question,

but no liability is incurred by any person who acts in good faith under this Part in ignorance of the withdrawal certificate ceasing to be valid under this subsection.

Amendments—Substituted by Adult Support and Protection (Scotland) Act 2007, s 57(8).

31A Suspension and termination of authority

(1) The Public Guardian may suspend or terminate the authority of a withdrawer under a withdrawal certificate.

(2) The Public Guardian must without delay intimate the suspension or termination to –

    (a)   the withdrawer whose authority is suspended or terminated;
    (b)   any other joint withdrawer;
    (c)   any reserve withdrawer; and
    (d)   the fundholder of the designated account; and
    (e)   such other persons as the Public Guardian thinks fit.

(3) A suspension or termination under subsection (1) suspends or, as the case may be, terminates all operations on the designated account by the withdrawer whose authority is suspended or terminated.

(4) The Public Guardian must on suspending or terminating the authority of the withdrawer enter prescribed particulars in the register maintained by the Public Guardian under section 6(2)(b)(iii).

(5) The Public Guardian may on terminating the authority of the withdrawer issue to the withdrawer an interim withdrawal certificate to continue to intromit with the adult's funds for a period not exceeding 4 weeks from the date of the termination.

Amendments—Substituted by Adult Support and Protection (Scotland) Act 2007, s 57(8).

31B Renewal of authority to intromit

(1) This section applies to an application under section 25 if condition A or B is satisfied.

(2) Condition A is that the application is made by a person holding an existing withdrawal certificate.

(3) Condition B is that –

    (a)   the main withdrawer has died or become incapable or the main withdrawer's authority under this Part has been terminated; and
    (b)   the application is made, without undue delay, by an individual who was the reserve withdrawer at the time of the death, incapacity, or termination, as the case may be.

(4) Where this section applies, the Public Guardian may disapply any of the provisions in sections 26(1), 27A and 27B to an application to which this section applies (but may require the applicant to provide such other information as the Public Guardian requires to determine the application).

(5) Where condition A is satisfied in relation to an application under section 25, the existing withdrawal certificate will continue to be valid until the application is determined.

(6) Where an application to which this section applies is granted, the existing withdrawal certificate ceases to be valid.

Amendments—Substituted by Adult Support and Protection (Scotland) Act 2007, s 57(8).

31C Duration of certificates issued under section 24C, 24D, and 26G etc

(1) A certificate issued under section 24C, 24D or 26G is valid for such period as it may specify.

(2) But the Public Guardian may cancel the certificate at any time before the end of any period so specified.

(3) The Public Guardian must without delay intimate such a cancellation to –

 (a) the person to whom the certificate was issued,
 (b) where the certificate was issued under section 26G, the fundholder of the original account, and
 (c) such other persons as the Public Guardian thinks fit.

Amendments—Substituted by Adult Support and Protection (Scotland) Act 2007, s 57(8).

Appeals

31D Appeals

(1) A decision of the Public Guardian –

 (a) to grant or refuse an application under section 24C, 24D, 25, 26B, 26D, 26E, 26F or 26G;
 (b) to refuse to remit an application to the sheriff under section 27F;
 (c) to reduce or extend the period of validity of a withdrawal certificate under section 31(2); or
 (d) to suspend or terminate the authority of a withdrawer under section 31A,

may be appealed to the sheriff.

(2) The sheriff's decision on an appeal under subsection (1) is final.

Amendments—Substituted by Adult Support and Protection (Scotland) Act 2007, s 57(8).

Transition from guardianship

31E Transition from guardianship

(1) This section applies where –

 (a) there is a guardian with powers relating to the property or financial affairs of an adult; and
 (b) an application is made under section 25 in relation to the adult's funds.

(2) Section 27A does not apply to the application if it is made by the adult's guardian.

(3) The Public Guardian may disapply section 27B to the application.

(4) Where –

(a) it appears to the Public Guardian that, if the application were granted, the adult's interests in the adult's property and affairs can be satisfactorily safeguarded or promoted otherwise than by the existing guardianship; and
(b) the Public Guardian proposes to grant the application,

the Public Guardian must initiate the recall of the guardianship under section 73.

(5) The Public Guardian may not grant the application unless the guardianship is recalled.

(6) Where the Public Guardian grants the application, the withdrawal certificate issued to the withdrawer is valid for such period as the Public Guardian specifies at the time the Public Guardian grants the application.

(7) This section does not apply, and no application under this Part may be made, in the case of an adult if there is a person who is –

(a) appointed or otherwise entitled under the law of any country other than Scotland to act as a guardian (however called) in relation to the adult's property and financial affairs during the adult's incapacity; and
(b) recognised by the law of Scotland as the adult's guardian.

(8) Despite subsection (7), no liability is incurred by any person who acts in good faith under this Part in ignorance of any guardian of the type mentioned in that subsection.

Amendments—Substituted by Adult Support and Protection (Scotland) Act 2007, s 57(8).

Miscellaneous

32 Joint accounts

Where an individual who along with one or more others is the holder of a joint account with a fundholder becomes incapable in relation to decisions about, or of safeguarding the individual's interests in, the funds in the account, any other joint account holder may continue to operate the account unless –

(a) the terms of the account provide otherwise; or
(b) the joint account holder is barred by an order of any court from so doing.

Amendments—Substituted by Adult Support and Protection (Scotland) Act 2007, s 57(8).

Interpretation

33 Interpretation of Part

(1) In section 24B, 27A and 31 any reference to –

(a) a guardian includes a reference to a guardian (however called) appointed under the law of any country to, or entitled under the law of any country to act for, an adult during his incapacity, if the guardianship is recognised by the law of Scotland;
(b) a continuing attorney includes a reference to a person granted, under a contract, grant or appointment governed by the law of any country, powers (however expressed) relating to the granter's property or financial affairs and having continuing effect notwithstanding the granter's incapacity.
(c) a welfare attorney includes a reference to a person granted, under a contract, grant or appointment governed by the law of any country, powers

(however expressed) relating to the granter's personal welfare and having effect during the granter's incapacity.

(2) In this Part –

'fundholder' means a bank, building society or other similar body which holds funds on behalf of another person;

'withdrawal certificate' means a certificate issued under section 25, 26B, 26E, 26F or 31A.

Amendments—Substituted by Adult Support and Protection (Scotland) Act 2007, s 57(8).

34 (*repealed*)

PART 4
MANAGEMENT OF RESIDENTS' FINANCES

35 Application of Part 4

(1) Subject to subsection (3), this Part applies to the management of the matters set out in section 39 relating to any resident of any of the following establishments –

(a) a health service hospital;
(b) an independent hospital or private psychiatric hospital;
(c) a State hospital;
(d) a care home service; and
(e) a limited registration service.

(2) In this Part establishments mentioned in paragraph (b), (d) or (e) of subsection (1) are referred to as 'registered establishments', all other establishments mentioned in subsection (1) are referred to as 'unregistered establishments', and registered and unregistered establishments together are referred to as 'authorised establishments'.

(3) This Part shall not apply to a registered establishment where notice in writing is given to the supervisory body by –

(a) the managers of the registered establishment; or
(b) an applicant, under section 59(1) of the Public Services Reform (Scotland) Act 2010 or section 10P(1) of the National Health Service (Scotland) Act 1978, as the case may be, for registration of the service which comprises that establishment,

that it shall not apply.

(4) The Scottish Ministers may by regulations amend the list of authorised establishments set out in subsection (1).

(5) In this Part, 'the managers' has the meaning set out in schedule 1; and 'resident' in relation to an authorised establishment means an adult whose main residence for the time being is the authorised establishment or whose detention there is authorised by virtue of the Criminal Procedure (Scotland) Act 1995 or the 2003 Act.

(6) Expressions used in subsection (1) and in –

(a) the Public Services Reform (Scotland) Act 2010 have the same meanings in that subsection as in that Act;
(b) the National Health Service (Scotland) Act 1978 have the same meanings in that subsection as in that Act.

Amendments—Regulation of Care (Scotland) Act 2001, s 79, Sch 3, para 23; Mental Health (Care and Treatment) (Scotland) Act 2003, s 331, Sch 4, para 9, Sch 5, Pt 1; SSI 2005/610; SSI 2011/211.

36 (*repealed*)

37 Residents whose affairs may be managed

(1) The managers of an authorised establishment shall be entitled to manage on behalf of any resident in the establishment in relation to whom a certificate has been issued under subsection (2) any of the matters set out in section 39.

(2) Where the managers of an authorised establishment, having considered all other appropriate courses of action, have decided that management on behalf of the resident of the matters set out in section 39 by them is the most appropriate course of action, they shall cause to be examined by a medical practitioner any resident in the establishment who they believe may be incapable in relation to decisions as to, or of safeguarding his interest in, any of the resident's affairs referred to in section 39; and if the medical practitioner finds that the resident is so incapable he shall issue a certificate in prescribed form to that effect.

(3) Subject to subsection (8), the managers of the authorised establishment shall intimate their intention of requiring an examination under subsection (2) to the resident and to the resident's nearest relative and named person.

(4) Subject to subsection (8), the managers of the authorised establishment shall –

    (a) send a copy of the certificate to the resident and to the supervisory body, who shall notify the resident's nearest relative and named person;

    (b) notify the resident and the supervisory body that they intend to manage the resident's affairs.

(5) Notification under subsection (4)(b) shall include a statement as to what other courses of action had been considered and why they were not considered appropriate.

(6) The medical practitioner who certifies under this section shall not –

    (a) be related to the resident or to any of the managers of the authorised establishment;

    (b) have any direct or indirect financial interest in the authorised establishment.

(7) A certificate –

    (a) shall be reviewed where it appears to the managers of the authorised establishment, the medical practitioner who certifies under this section or any person having an interest in any of the resident's affairs mentioned in section 39 that there has been any change in the condition or circumstances of the resident bearing on the resident's incapacity; and

    (b) shall expire 3 years after it was issued.

(8) If the managers of the authorised establishment consider that intimation to the resident under subsection (3) or any action under subsection (4) would be likely to pose a serious risk to the health of the resident they may apply to the supervisory body for a direction that they need not make the intimation or take the action.

(9) The Scottish Ministers may prescribe the evidence which the supervisory body shall take into account in reaching a decision under subsection (8).

Amendments—SSI 2005/465.

38 (*repealed*)

39 Matters which may be managed

(1) The matters which may be managed under this Part by the managers of an authorised establishment are –

    (a) claiming, receiving, holding and spending any pension, benefit, allowance or other payment other than under the Social Security Contributions and Benefits Act 1992, the State Pensions Credit Act 2002, Part 1 of the Welfare Reform Act 2007 , Part 1 of the Welfare Reform Act 2007 or Part 1 or 4 of the Welfare Reform Act 2012;

    (b) claiming, receiving, holding and spending any money to which a resident is entitled;

    (c) holding any other moveable property to which the resident is entitled;

    (d) disposing of such moveable property,

and in this Part these matters, or any of them, are referred to as residents' affairs; and cognate expressions shall be construed accordingly.

(2) In managing these matters, the managers of an authorised establishment shall –

    (a) act only for the benefit of the resident; and

    (b) have regard to the sentimental value that any item might have for the resident, or would have but for the resident's incapacity.

(3) The managers of an authorised establishment shall not, without the consent of the supervisory body, manage any matter if that matter has a value greater than that which is prescribed for the purposes of this subsection.

(4) The supervisory body may in relation to an individual resident permit the managers of the authorised establishment to manage any matter which has a value greater than that which is prescribed in relation to it under subsection (3).

(5) For the purpose of this section, 'manage' denotes no greater responsibility than complying with the duties set out in this section.

Amendments—Adult Support and Protection (Scotland) Act 2007, s 77(1), Sch 5, para 5(b); SSI 2013/137.

40 Supervisory bodies

(1) The supervisory body for the purposes of this Part is, in relation to –

    (a) a registered establishment which is –

        (i) registered under the Public Services Reform (Scotland) Act 2010, Social Care and Social Work Improvement Scotland;

        (ii) registered under the National Health Service (Scotland) Act 1978, Healthcare Improvement Scotland; and

    (b) an unregistered establishment, the Health Board for the area in which the establishment is situated;

and any reference in this Part to an authorised establishment in relation to a supervisory body is a reference to an authorised establishment for which the supervisory body is responsible.

(2) The supervisory body shall from time to time make inquiry as to the manner in which the managers of an authorised establishment are carrying out the management of residents' affairs and in particular the manner in which they are carrying out their functions under section 41.

(3) The supervisory body shall investigate any complaint received as to the manner in which the managers of an authorised establishment are managing residents' affairs.

(4) The Scottish Ministers may, as respects any authorised establishment, amend subsection (1) by substituting for the supervisory body allotted to that establishment a different supervisory body.

Amendments—Regulation of Care (Scotland) Act 2001, s 79, Sch 3, para 23(3); SSI 2011/211.

41 Duties and functions of managers of authorised establishment

The managers of an authorised establishment shall, in relation to residents whose affairs they are managing under section 39 –

(a) claim, receive and hold any pension, benefit, allowance or other payment to which the resident is entitled other than under the Social Security Contributions and Benefits Act 1992, the State Pensions Credit Act 2002, Part 1 of the Welfare Reform Act 2007 or Part 1 or 4 of the Welfare Reform Act 2012;

(b) keep the funds of residents separate from the funds of the establishment;

(c) comply with any requirements of the supervisory body as respects keeping the funds of residents separate or distinguishable from each other;

(d) ensure that where, at any time, the total amount of funds held on behalf of any resident exceeds such sum as may from time to time be prescribed they shall be placed so as to earn interest;

(e) keep records of all transactions made in relation to the funds held by them in respect of each resident for whose benefit the funds are held and managed and, in particular, ensure that details of the balance and any interest due to each resident can be ascertained at any time;

(f) produce such records when requested to do so by the resident, his nearest relative, his named person, or the supervisory body;

(g) spend money only on items or services which are of benefit to the resident on whose behalf the funds are held;

(h) not spend money on items or services which are provided by the establishment to or for such resident as part of its normal service;

(i) make proper provision for indemnifying residents against any loss attributable to –

(i) any act or omission on the part of the managers of the establishment in exercising the powers conferred by this Part or of others for whom the managers are responsible or attributable to any expenditure in breach of paragraph (g);

(ii) any breach of duty, misuse of funds or failure to act reasonably and in good faith on the part of the managers.

Amendments—SSI 2005/465; Adult Support and Protection (Scotland) Act 2007, s 77(1), Sch 5, para 5(c); SSI 2013/137.

42 Authorisation of named manager to withdraw from resident's account

(1) On an application in writing by the managers of an authorised establishment the supervisory body may issue a certificate of authority under this section in relation to any resident named in the application.

(2) An application under subsection (1) shall specify one or more persons (being managers, officers or members of staff of the establishment) who shall exercise the authority conferred by this section.

(3) A certificate of authority shall be signed by the officer of the supervisory body authorised by the body to do so and shall –

 (a) specify accounts or other funds of the resident;
 (b) name the persons specified in the application (the 'authorised persons');
 (c) specify the period of validity of the certificate of authority, being a period not exceeding the period of validity of the certificate issued under section 37(2).

(4) The authorised persons may make withdrawals from such account or source of funds of the named resident as is specified in the certificate of authority and the fundholder may make payments accordingly.

(5) The supervisory body may at any time after it has issued a certificate of authority, revoke it and if it does so it shall notify the fundholder of the revocation.

43 Statement of resident's affairs

(1) In this section, 'resident' means a resident of an authorised establishment whose affairs are being managed in accordance with the provisions of this Part and 'statement' means a statement of the affairs of the resident.

(2) Where a resident ceases to be incapable of managing his affairs, the managers of the establishment shall prepare a statement as at the date on which he ceases to be incapable and shall give a copy to him.

(3) Where a resident moves from an authorised establishment to another authorised establishment, the managers of the establishment from which he moves shall, except where he has ceased to be incapable, prepare a statement as at the date on which he moves and shall send a copy of the statement to the managers of the other establishment.

(4) Where a resident leaves an authorised establishment, other than to move to another authorised establishment and except where he has ceased to be incapable, the managers of the establishment shall prepare a statement as at the date on which he leaves and shall give a copy of the statement to any person who appears to them to be the person who will manage his affairs.

44 Resident ceasing to be resident of authorised establishment

(1) Where a resident ceases to be a resident of an authorised establishment, or ceases to be incapable, the managers of the establishment shall continue, for a period not exceeding 3 months from the date on which he ceases to be a resident or, as the case may be, to be incapable, to manage his affairs while such other arrangements as are necessary for managing his affairs are being made.

(2) At the end of the period referred to in subsection (1) during which the managers of the establishment have continued to manage the resident's affairs, they shall prepare a statement and shall give a copy of it to –

(a) the resident, if he has ceased to be incapable; or
(b) any person who appears to them to be the person who will manage his affairs.

(3) Where a resident ceases to be a resident of an authorised establishment and his affairs are to be managed by another establishment, authority or person (including himself) the managers of the establishment shall take such steps as are necessary to transfer his affairs to that establishment, authority or person, as the case may be.

(4) Where a resident ceases to be a resident of an authorised establishment the managers of the establishment shall within 14 days of that event inform –

(a) the supervisory body; and
(b) where the resident has not ceased to be incapable and has moved neither –
   (i) to another authorised establishment; nor
   (ii) into the care of a local authority,

the local authority of the area in which they expect him to reside.

45 Appeal, revocation etc

(1) Where it appears to the supervisory body that the managers of an authorised establishment are no longer operating as such or have failed to comply with any requirement of this Part or that, for any other reason, it is no longer appropriate that they should continue to manage residents' affairs it may revoke that power to manage.

(2) (*repealed*)

(3) Where a power to manage has been revoked under this section, the supervisory body shall within a period of 14 days from such revocation take over management of the residents' affairs and, where they do so, comply with the requirements imposed by and under this Part upon the managers of an authorised establishment.

(4) The supervisory body shall, within the period of 3 months after taking over management of residents' affairs under subsection (3), cause that management to be transferred to such other establishment, authority or person (who may be the resident) as they consider appropriate.

(5) Where the supervisory body is satisfied that the circumstances mentioned in subsection (1) no longer apply in relation to an establishment whose power to manage it has revoked, it may annul the revocation of the power and, where necessary, of the registration.

(6) Any decision of the supervisory body may be appealed to the sheriff, whose decision shall be final.

Amendments—Regulation of Care (Scotland) Act 2001, s 79, Sch 3, para 23(4).

46 Disapplication of Part 4

(1) This Part shall not apply to any of the matters which may be managed under section 39 if –

(a) there is a guardian, continuing attorney, or other person with powers relating to that matter; or
(b) an intervention order has been granted relating to that matter,

but no liability shall be incurred by any person who acts in good faith under this Part in ignorance of any guardian, continuing attorney, other person or intervention order.

(2) In this section any reference to –
(a) a guardian shall include a reference to a guardian (however called) appointed under the law of any country to, or entitled under the law of any country to act for, an adult during his incapacity, if the guardianship is recognised by the law of Scotland;
(b) a continuing attorney shall include a reference to a person granted, under a contract, grant or appointment governed by the law of any country, powers (however expressed), relating to the granter's property or financial affairs and having continuing effect notwithstanding the granter's incapacity.

PART 5
MEDICAL TREATMENT AND RESEARCH

47 Authority of persons responsible for medical treatment

(1) This section applies where any of the persons mentioned in subsection (1A) –
(a) is of the opinion that an adult is incapable in relation to a decision about the medical treatment in question; and
(b) has certified in accordance with subsection (5) that he is of this opinion.

(1A) The persons are –
(a) the medical practitioner primarily responsible for the medical treatment of the adult;
(b) a person who is –
   (i) a dental practitioner;
   (ii) an ophthalmic optician;
   (iii) a registered nurse; or
   (iv) an individual who falls within such description of persons as may be prescribed by the Scottish Ministers,

who satisfies such requirements as may be so prescribed and who is primarily responsible for medical treatment of the kind in question.

(2) The person who by virtue of subsection (1) has issued a certificate for the purposes of that subsection shall have, during the period specified in the certificate, authority to do what is reasonable in the circumstances, in relation to medical treatment in question, to safeguard or promote the physical or mental health of the adult.

(2A) Subsection (2) –
(a) does not affect any authority conferred by any other enactment or rule of law; and
(b) is subject to –
   (i) the following provisions of this section;
   (ii) sections 49 and 50; and
   (iii) sections 234, 237, 240, 242, 243 and 244 of the 2003 Act.

(3) The authority conferred by subsection (2) shall be exercisable also by any other person who is authorised by the person on whom that authority is conferred to carry out the medical treatment in question and who is acting –

  (a) on his behalf under his instructions; or
  (b) with his approval or agreement.

(4) In this Part 'medical treatment' includes any procedure or treatment designed to safeguard or promote physical or mental health.

(5) A certificate for the purposes of subsection (1) shall be in the prescribed form and shall specify the period during which the authority conferred by subsection (2) shall subsist, being a period which –

  (a) the person who issues the certificate considers appropriate to the condition or circumstances of the adult; but
  (b) does not exceed –
     (i) one year; or
     (ii) if, in the opinion of the person issuing the certificate any of the conditions or circumstances prescribed by the Scottish Ministers applies as respects the adult, 3 years,

from the date of the examination on which the certificate is based.

(6) If after issuing a certificate, the person who issued it is of the opinion that the condition or circumstances of the adult have changed he may –

  (a) revoke the certificate;
  (b) issue a new certificate specifying such period not exceeding –
     (i) one year; or
     (ii) if, in the opinion of that person any of the conditions or circumstances prescribed by the Scottish Ministers apply as respects the adult, 3 years,

from the date of revocation of the old certificate as he considers appropriate to the new condition or circumstances of the adult.

(7) The authority conferred by subsection (2) shall not authorise –

  (a) the use of force or detention, unless it is immediately necessary and only for so long as is necessary in the circumstances;
  (b) action which would be inconsistent with any decision by a competent court;
  (c) placing an adult in a hospital for the treatment of mental disorder against his will.

(8) (*repealed*)

(9) Subject to subsection (10), where any question as to the authority of any person to provide medical treatment in pursuance of subsection (2) –

  (a) is the subject of proceedings in any court (other than for the purposes of any application to the court made under regulations made under section 48); and
  (b) has not been determined,

medical treatment authorised by subsection (2) shall not be given unless it is authorised by any other enactment or rule of law for the preservation of the life of the adult or the prevention of serious deterioration in his medical condition.

(10) Nothing in subsection (9) shall authorise the provision of any medical treatment where an interdict has been granted and continues to have effect prohibiting the provision of such medical treatment.

(11) In subsection (1A) –

'dental practitioner' has the same meaning as in section 108(1) of the National Health Service (Scotland) Act 1978;

'ophthalmic optician' means a person registered in either of the registers kept under section 7 of the Opticians Act 1989 of ophthalmic opticians.

Amendments—Smoking, Health and Social Care (Scotland) Act 2005, s 35(2)(a)(i); Adult Support and Protection (Scotland) Act 2007, s 77(2), Sch 2.

48 Exceptions to authority to treat

(1) (*repealed*)

(2) The Scottish Ministers may by regulations specify medical treatment, or a class or classes of medical treatment, in relation to which the authority conferred by section 47(2) shall not apply and make provision about the medical treatment, or a class or classes of medical treatment, in relation to which that authority does apply.

(3) Regulations made under subsection (2) may provide for the circumstances in which the specified medical treatment or specified class or classes of medical treatment may be carried out.

Amendments—Mental Health (Care and Treatment) (Scotland) Act 2003, s 331(2), Sch 5, Pt 1.

49 Medical treatment where there is an application for intervention or guardianship order

(1) Subsection (2) of section 47 shall not apply if, to the knowledge of the person on whom authority is conferred by that subsection, an application for an intervention order or a guardianship order with power in relation to any medical treatment referred to in that subsection has been made to the sheriff and has not been determined.

(2) Until the application has been finally determined, medical treatment authorised by section 47(2) shall not be given unless it is authorised by any other enactment or rule of law for the preservation of the life of the adult or the prevention of serious deterioration in his medical condition.

(3) Nothing in subsection (2) shall authorise the provision of any medical treatment where an interdict has been granted and continues to have effect prohibiting the provision of such medical treatment.

Amendments—Smoking, Health and Social Care (Scotland) Act 2005, s 35(3).

50 Medical treatment where guardian etc has been appointed

(1) This section applies where a guardian or a welfare attorney has been appointed or a person has been authorised under an intervention order with power in relation to any medical treatment referred to in section 47.

(2) The authority conferred by section 47(2) shall not apply where –

(a) subsection (1) applies;
(b) the person who issued the certificate for the purposes of section 47(1) is aware of the appointment or, as the case may be, authorisation; and
(c) it would be reasonable and practicable for that person to obtain the consent of the guardian, welfare attorney or person authorised under the intervention order, as the case may be, to any proposed medical treatment but he has failed to do so.

(3) Where the person who issued the certificate for the purposes of section 47(1) has consulted the guardian, welfare attorney or person authorised under the intervention order and there is no disagreement as to the medical treatment of the adult, the medical practitioner primarily responsible for the medical treatment of the adult (in a case where the person who so issued the certificate was someone other than that practitioner) or any person having an interest in the personal welfare of the adult may appeal the decision as to the medical treatment to the Court of Session.

(4) Where the person who issued the certificate for the purposes of section 47(1) has consulted the guardian, welfare attorney or person authorised under the intervention order and there is a disagreement as to the medical treatment of the adult, the person who issued the certificate shall request the Mental Welfare Commission to nominate a practitioner who the Commission consider has professional knowledge or expertise relevant to medical treatment of the kind in question (the 'nominated practitioner') from the list established and maintained by them under subsection (9) to give an opinion as to the medical treatment proposed.

(5) Where the nominated practitioner certifies that, in his opinion, having regard to all the circumstances and having consulted the guardian, welfare attorney or person authorised under the intervention order as the case may be and, if it is reasonable and practicable to do so, a person nominated by such guardian, welfare attorney or person authorised under the intervention order as the case may be, the proposed medical treatment should be given, the person who issued the certificate for the purposes of section 47(1) may give the treatment or may authorise any other person to give the treatment notwithstanding the disagreement with the guardian, welfare attorney, or person authorised under the intervention order, as the case may be.

(6) Where the nominated practitioner certifies that, in his opinion, having regard to all the circumstances and having consulted the guardian, welfare attorney or person authorised under the intervention order as the case may be and, if it is reasonable and practicable to do so, a person nominated by such guardian, welfare attorney or person authorised under the intervention order as the case may be, the proposed medical treatment should or, as the case may be, should not be given, the medical practitioner primarily responsible for the medical treatment of the adult, or any person having an interest in the personal welfare of the adult (including, where the certificate issued for the purposes of section 47(1) was issued by another person, that person), may apply to the Court of Session for a determination as to whether the proposed treatment should be given or not.

(7) Subject to subsection (8), where an appeal has been made to the Court of Session under subsection (3) or an application has been made under subsection (6), and has not been determined, medical treatment authorised by section 47(2) shall not be given unless it is authorised by any other enactment or rule of law for the preservation of the life of the adult or the prevention of serious deterioration in his medical condition.

(8) Nothing in subsection (7) shall authorise the provision of any medical treatment where an interdict has been granted and continues to have effect prohibiting the giving of such medical treatment.

(9) The Mental Welfare Commission shall establish and maintain a list of practitioners from whom they shall nominate the practitioner who is to give the opinion under subsection (4).

(10) In this section any reference to –

    (a) a guardian shall include a reference to a guardian (however called) appointed under the law of any country to, or entitled under the law of any country to act for, an adult during his incapacity, if the guardianship is recognised by the law of Scotland;

    (b) a welfare attorney shall include a reference to a person granted, under a contract, grant or appointment governed by the law of any country, powers (however expressed) relating to the granter's personal welfare and having effect during the granter's incapacity.

Amendments—Smoking, Health and Social Care (Scotland) Act 2005, s 35(4).

51 Authority for research

(1) No surgical, medical, nursing, dental or psychological research shall be carried out on any adult who is incapable in relation to a decision about participation in the research unless –

    (a) research of a similar nature cannot be carried out on an adult who is capable in relation to such a decision; and

    (b) the circumstances mentioned in subsection (2) are satisfied.

(2) The circumstances referred to in subsection (1) are that –

    (a) the purpose of the research is to obtain knowledge of –

        (i) the causes, diagnosis, treatment or care of the adult's incapacity; or

        (ii) the effect of any treatment or care given during his incapacity to the adult which relates to that incapacity; and

    (b) subject to subsection (3A), the conditions mentioned in subsection (3) are fulfilled.

(3) The conditions are –

    (a) the research is likely to produce real and direct benefit to the adult;

    (b) the adult does not indicate unwillingness to participate in the research;

    (c) the research has been approved by the Ethics Committee;

    (d) the research entails no foreseeable risk, or only a minimal foreseeable risk, to the adult;

    (e) the research imposes no discomfort, or only minimal discomfort, on the adult; and

    (f) consent has been obtained from any guardian or welfare attorney who has power to consent to the adult's participation in research or, where there is no such guardian or welfare attorney, from the adult's nearest relative.

(3A) Where the research consists of a clinical trial of a medicinal product, the research may be carried out –

    (a) without being approved by the Ethics Committee, if a favourable opinion on the trial has been given by an ethics committee, other than the Ethics Committee, in accordance with regulation 15 of the Medicines for Human Use (Clinical Trials) Regulations 2004;

    (b) without the consent of any guardian or welfare attorney, or the adult's nearest relative, if –

(i) it has not been practicable to contact any such person before the decision to enter the adult as a subject of the clinical trial is made, and
(ii) consent has been obtained from a person, other than a person connected with the conduct of the clinical trial, who is –
(a) the doctor primarily responsible for the medical treatment provided to that adult, or
(b) a person nominated by the relevant health care provider;
(c) without the consent of any guardian or welfare attorney, or the adult's nearest relative, if –
   (i) treatment is being, or is about to be, provided for an adult who is incapable in relation to a decision about participation in the research as a matter of urgency;
   (ii) having regard to the nature of the clinical trial and of the particular circumstances of the case it is necessary to take action for the purposes of the clinical trial as a matter of urgency;
   (iii) it has not been reasonably practicable to obtain the consent of any such person;
   (iv) it has not been reasonably practicable to obtain the consent of any of the persons mentioned in paragraph (b)(ii)(A) or (B); and
   (v) the action to be taken is carried out in accordance with a procedure approved by the Ethics Committee or any other ethics committee or by an appeal panel appointed under Schedule 4 of the Medicines for Human Use (Clinical Trials) Regulations 2004 (SI 2004/1031) at the time it gave its favourable opinion in relation to the clinical trial.

(4) Where the research is not likely to produce real and direct benefit to the adult, it may nevertheless be carried out if it will contribute through significant improvement in the scientific understanding of the adult's incapacity to the attainment of real and direct benefit to the adult or to other persons having the same incapacity, provided the other circumstances or conditions mentioned in subsections (1) to (3) are fulfilled.

(5) In granting approval under subsection (3)(c), the Ethics Committee may impose such conditions as it sees fit.

(6) The Ethics Committee shall be constituted by regulations made by the Scottish Ministers and such regulations may make provision as to the composition of, appointments to and procedures of the Ethics Committee and may make such provision for the payment of such remuneration, expenses and superannuation as the Scottish Ministers may determine.

(7) Regulations made by the Scottish Ministers under subsection (6) may prescribe particular matters which the Ethics Committee shall take into account when deciding whether to approve any research under this Part.

(8) In this section any reference to –
   (a) a guardian shall include a reference to a guardian (however called) appointed under the law of any country to, or entitled under the law of any country to act for, an adult during his incapacity, if the guardianship is recognised by the law of Scotland;
   (b) a welfare attorney shall include a reference to a person granted, under a contract, grant or appointment governed by the law of any country, powers (however expressed) relating to the granter's personal welfare and having effect during the granter's incapacity.

(9) In this section –

'clinical trial on a medicinal product' means a clinical trial as defined by regulation 2(1) of the Medicines for Human Use (Clinical Trials) Regulations 2004;

'an ethics committee' has the meaning given by that regulation;

'person connected with the conduct of the trial' and 'relevant health care provider' have the meanings given by Schedule 1 to those regulations.

Amendments—SI 2004/1031; SI 2006/2984.

52 Appeal against decision as to medical treatment

Any decision taken for the purposes of this Part, other than a decision by a medical practitioner under section 50, as to the medical treatment of the adult may be appealed by any person having an interest in the personal welfare of the adult to the sheriff and thence, with the leave of the sheriff, to the Court of Session.

PART 6
INTERVENTION ORDERS AND GUARDIANSHIP ORDERS

Intervention orders

53 Intervention orders

(1) The sheriff may, on an application by any person (including the adult himself) claiming an interest in the property, financial affairs or personal welfare of an adult, if he is satisfied that the adult is incapable of taking the action, or is incapable in relation to the decision about his property, financial affairs or personal welfare to which the application relates, make an order (in this Act referred to as an 'intervention order').

(2) In considering an application under subsection (1), the sheriff shall have regard to any intervention order or guardianship order which may have been previously made in relation to the adult, and to any order varying, or ancillary to, such an order.

(3) Where it appears to the local authority that –

    (a) the adult is incapable as mentioned in subsection (1); and

    (b) no application has been made or is likely to be made for an order under this section in relation to the decision to which the application under this subsection relates; and

    (c) an intervention order is necessary for the protection of the property, financial affairs or personal welfare of the adult,

they shall apply under this section for an order.

(4) Subsections (3), (3A), (3B) and (4) of section 57 shall apply to an application under this section and, for this purpose, for the reference to the individual or office holder nominated for appointment as guardian there shall be substituted a reference to a person nominated in such application.

(5) An intervention order may –

    (a) direct the taking of any action specified in the order;

    (b) authorise the person nominated in the application to take such action or make such decision in relation to the property, financial affairs or personal welfare of the adult as is specified in the order.

(6) Where an intervention order directs the acquisition of accommodation for, or the disposal of any accommodation used for the time being as a dwelling house by, the adult, the consent of the Public Guardian as respects the consideration shall be required before the accommodation is acquired or, as the case may be, disposed of.

(7) In making or varying an intervention order the sheriff may, in the case of an intervention order relating to property or financial affairs require the person authorised under the order to find caution or to give such other security as the sheriff thinks fit.

(8) The sheriff may, on an application by –

 (a) the person authorised under the intervention order; or
 (b) the adult; or
 (c) any person claiming an interest in the property, financial affairs or personal welfare of the adult,

make an order varying the terms of, or recalling, the intervention order or any other order made for the purposes of the intervention order.

(9) Anything done under an intervention order shall have the same effect as if done by the adult if he had the capacity to do so.

(10) Where an intervention order is made, the sheriff clerk shall forthwith send a copy of the interlocutor containing the order to the Public Guardian who shall –

 (a) enter in the register maintained by him under section 6(2)(b)(v) such particulars of the order as may be prescribed;
 (aa) when satisfied that the person authorised under the order has found caution or given other security if so required, issue a certificate of appointment to the person; and
 (b) notify the adult, the local authority and (in a case where the adult's incapacity is by reason of, or reasons which include, mental disorder and the intervention order relates to the adult's personal welfare or factors which include it) the Mental Welfare Commission of the terms of the interlocutor.

(11) A transaction for value between a person authorised under an intervention order, purporting to act as such, and a third party acting in good faith shall not be invalid on the ground only that –

 (a) the person acted outwith the scope of his authority;
 (b) the person failed to observe any requirement, whether substantive or procedural, imposed by or under this Act or by the sheriff or by the Public Guardian; or
 (c) there was any irregularity whether substantive or procedural in the authorisation of the person.

(12) A person authorised under an intervention order may recover from the estate of the adult the amount of such reasonable outlays as he incurs in doing anything directed or authorised under the order.

(13) Where a third party has acquired, in good faith and for value, title to any interest in heritable property from a person authorised under an intervention order that title shall not be challengeable on the ground only –

 (a) of any irregularity of procedure in the making of the intervention order; or
 (b) that the person authorised under the intervention order has acted outwith the scope of the authority.

(14) Sections 64(2) and 67(3) and (4) shall apply to an intervention order as they apply to a guardianship order and, for this purpose, for any reference to a guardian there shall be substituted a reference to the person authorised under the order.

Amendments—Adult Support and Protection (Scotland) Act 2007, s 59(1).

54 Records: intervention orders

A person authorised under an intervention order shall keep records of the exercise of his powers.

55 Notification of change of address

After particulars relating to an intervention order are entered in the register under section 53 the person authorised under the intervention order shall, not later than 7 days after any change of the person's or the adult's address, notify the Public Guardian of the change who shall enter prescribed particulars in the register maintained by him under section 6(2)(b)(v) and notify the local authority and (in a case where the adult's incapacity is by reason of, or reasons which include, mental disorder and the intervention order relates to the adult's personal welfare or factors which include it) the Mental Welfare Commission.

Amendments—Adult Support and Protection (Scotland) Act 2007, s 59(2).

56 Registration of intervention order relating to heritable property

(1) This section applies where the sheriff makes an intervention order which vests in the person authorised under the order any right to deal with, convey or manage any interest in heritable property which is recorded or is capable of being recorded in the General Register of Sasines or is registered or is capable of being registered in the Land Register of Scotland.

(2) In making such an order the sheriff shall specify each property affected by the order, in such terms as enable it to be identified in the Register of Sasines or, as the case may be, the Land Register of Scotland.

(3) The person authorised under the order shall forthwith apply to the Keeper of the Registers of Scotland for recording of the interlocutor containing the order in the General Register of Sasines or, as the case may be, for registering of it in the Land Register of Scotland.

(4) An application under subsection (3) shall contain –

    (a) the name and address of the person authorised under the order;
    (b) a statement that the person authorised under the order has powers relating to each property specified in the order;
    (c) a copy of the interlocutor.

(5) Where the interlocutor is to be recorded in the General Register of Sasines, the Keeper shall –

    (a) record the interlocutor in the Register; and
    (b) endorse the interlocutor to the effect that it has been so recorded.

(6) Where the interlocutor is to be registered in the Land Register of Scotland, the Keeper shall update the title sheet of the property to show it.

(7) The person authorised under the order shall send the endorsed interlocutor or, as the case may be, an extract of the updated title sheet to the Public Guardian who shall enter prescribed particulars of it in the register maintained by him under section 6(2)(b)(v).

Amendments—Land Registration etc (Scotland) Act 2012, s 119, Sch 5, para 38(2).

56A Death of person authorised to intervene

Where a person authorised under an intervention order dies, the person's personal representatives shall, if aware of the existence of the authority, notify the Public Guardian who shall –

(a) notify –
 (i) the adult;
 (ii) the local authority; and
 (iii) in a case where the adult's incapacity is by reason of, or reasons which include, mental disorder and the intervention order relates to the adult's personal welfare or factors including it, the Mental Welfare Commission; and
(b) enter prescribed particulars in the register maintained under section 6(2)(b)(v).

Amendments—Inserted by Adult Support and Protection (Scotland) Act 2007, s 59(3).

Guardianship orders

57 Application for guardianship order

(1) An application may be made under this section by any person (including the adult himself) claiming an interest in the property, financial affairs or personal welfare of an adult to the sheriff for an order appointing an individual or office holder as guardian in relation to the adult's property, financial affairs or personal welfare.

(2) Where it appears to the local authority that –
 (a) the conditions mentioned in section 58(1)(a) and (b) apply to the adult; and
 (b) no application has been made or is likely to be made for an order under this section; and
 (c) a guardianship order is necessary for the protection of the property, financial affairs or personal welfare of the adult,

they shall apply under this section for an order.

(3) There shall be lodged in court along with an application under this section –
 (a) reports, in prescribed form, of an examination and assessment of the adult carried out not more than 30 days before the lodging of the application by at least two medical practitioners one of whom, in a case where the incapacity is by reason of mental disorder, must be a relevant medical practitioner;
 (b) where the application relates to the personal welfare of the adult, a report, in prescribed form, from the mental health officer, (but where it is in jeopardy only because of the inability of the adult to communicate, from the chief social work officer), containing his opinion as to –
  (i) the general appropriateness of the order sought, based on an interview

and assessment of the adult carried out not more than 30 days before the lodging of the application; and

 (ii) the suitability of the individual nominated in the application to be appointed guardian; and

(c) where the application relates only to the property or financial affairs of the adult, a report, in prescribed form, based on an interview and assessment of the adult carried out not more than 30 days before the lodging of the application, by a person who has sufficient knowledge to make such a report as to the matters referred to in paragraph (b)(i) and (ii).

(3A) Subsection (3B) applies where a report lodged under subsection (3)(a) relates to an examination and assessment carried out more than 30 days before the lodging of the application.

(3B) Where this subsection applies, the sheriff may, despite subsection (3)(a), continue to consider the application if satisfied that there has been no change in circumstances since the examination and assessment was carried out which may be relevant to matters set out in the report.

(4) Where an applicant claims an interest in the personal welfare of the adult and is not the local authority, he shall give notice to the chief social work officer of his intention to make an application under this section and the report referred to in subsection (3)(b) shall be prepared by the chief social work officer or, as the case may be, the mental health officer, within 21 days of the date of the notice.

(5) The sheriff may, on an application being made to him, at any time before the disposal of the application made under this section, make an order for the appointment of an interim guardian.

(6) The appointment of an interim guardian in pursuance of this section shall, unless recalled earlier, cease to have effect –

 (a) on the appointment of a guardian under section 58; or
 (b) at the end of the effective period,

whichever is the earlier.

(6A) The 'effective period', for the purposes of subsection (6), means –

 (a) the period of 3 months beginning with the date of appointment; or
 (b) such longer period (not exceeding 6 months) beginning with that date as the sheriff may specify in the order.

(6B) In subsection (3)(a), 'relevant medical practitioner' means –

 (a) an approved medical practitioner;
 (b) where the adult concerned is not present in Scotland, a person who –
  (i) holds qualifications recognised in the place where the adult is present and has special experience in relation to the diagnosis and treatment of mental disorder which correspond to the qualifications and experience needed to be an approved medical practitioner; and
  (ii) has consulted the Mental Welfare Commission for Scotland about the report concerned; or
 (c) any other type of individual described (by reference to skills, qualifications, experience or otherwise) by regulations made by the Scottish Ministers.

(6C) The Scottish Ministers shall consult the Mental Welfare Commission before making regulations under subsection (6B)(c).

(7) In subsection (6B), 'approved medical practitioner' has the meaning given by section 22 of the 2003 Act.

Amendments—Mental Health (Care and Treatment) (Scotland) Act 2003, s 331, Sch 4, para 9(4), Sch 5, Pt 1; Adult Support and Protection (Scotland) Act 2007, s 60(1).

58 Disposal of application

(1) Where the sheriff is satisfied in considering an application under section 57 that –

  (a) the adult is incapable in relation to decisions about, or of acting to safeguard or promote his interests in, his property, financial affairs or personal welfare, and is likely to continue to be so incapable; and
  (b) no other means provided by or under this Act would be sufficient to enable the adult's interests in his property, financial affairs or personal welfare to be safeguarded or promoted,

he may grant the application.

(2) In considering an application under section 57, the sheriff shall have regard to any intervention order or guardianship order which may have been previously made in relation to the adult, and to any order varying, or ancillary to, such an order.

(3) Where the sheriff is satisfied that an intervention order would be sufficient as mentioned in subsection (1), he may treat the application under this section as an application for an intervention order under section 53 and may make such order as appears to him to be appropriate.

(4) Where the sheriff grants the application under section 57 he shall make an order (in this Act referred to as a 'guardianship order') appointing the individual or office holder nominated in the application to be the guardian of the adult for a period of 3 years or such other period (including an indefinite period) as, on cause shown, he may determine.

(5) Where more than one individual or office holder is nominated in the application, a guardianship order may, without prejudice to the power under section 62(1) to appoint joint guardians, appoint two or more guardians to exercise different powers in relation to the adult.

(6) In making a guardianship order relating to the property or financial affairs of the adult the sheriff may

require an individual appointed as guardian to find caution or to give such other security as the sheriff thinks fit.

(7) Where the sheriff makes a guardianship order the sheriff clerk shall forthwith send a copy of the interlocutor containing the order to the Public Guardian who shall –

  (a) enter prescribed particulars of the appointment in the register maintained by him under section 6(2)(b)(iv);
  (b) when satisfied that the guardian has found caution or given other security if so required, issue a certificate of appointment to the guardian;
  (c) notify the adult of the appointment of the guardian; and
  (d) notify the local authority and (in a case where the incapacity of the adult is by reason of, or reasons which include, mental disorder and the guardianship order relates to the adult's personal welfare or factors which include it) the Mental Welfare Commission of the terms of the interlocutor.

Amendments—Adult Support and Protection (Scotland) Act 2007, s 60(2).

59 Who may be appointed as guardian

(1) The sheriff may appoint as guardian –

(a) any individual whom he considers to be suitable for appointment and who has consented to being appointed;
(b) where the guardianship order is to relate only to the personal welfare of the adult, the chief social work officer of the local authority.

(2) Where the guardianship order is to relate to the property and financial affairs and to the personal welfare of the adult and joint guardians are to be appointed, the chief social work officer of the local authority may be appointed guardian in relation only to the personal welfare of the adult.

(3) The sheriff shall not appoint an individual as guardian to an adult unless he is satisfied that the individual is aware of –

(a) the adult's circumstances and condition and of the needs arising from such circumstances and condition; and
(b) the functions of a guardian.

(4) In determining if an individual is suitable for appointment as guardian, the sheriff shall have regard to –

(a) the accessibility of the individual to the adult and to his primary carer;
(b) the ability of the individual to carry out the functions of guardian;
(c) any likely conflict of interest between the adult and the individual;
(d) any undue concentration of power which is likely to arise in the individual over the adult;
(e) any adverse effects which the appointment of the individual would have on the interests of the adult;
(f) such other matters as appear to him to be appropriate.

(5) Paragraphs (c) and (d) of subsection (4) shall not be regarded as applying to an individual by reason only of his being a close relative of, or person residing with, the adult.

60 Renewal of guardianship order by sheriff

(1) At any time before the end of a period in respect of which a guardianship order has been made or renewed, an application may be made to the sheriff under this section by the guardian for the renewal of such order, and where such an application is so made, the order shall continue to have effect until the application is determined.

(2) Where it appears to the local authority that an application for renewal of a guardianship order under subsection (1) is necessary but that no such application has been made or is likely to be made, they shall apply under subsection (1) for the renewal of such an order and, where such an application is so made, the order shall continue to have effect until the application is determined.

(3) There must be lodged in court along with an application under this section –

(a) at least one report, in the prescribed form, of an examination and assessment of the adult carried out by a medical practitioner not more than 30 days before the lodging of the application;
(b) where the application relates to the adult's personal welfare, a report, in the

prescribed form, from the mental health officer (but where it is in jeopardy only because of the adult's inability to communicate, from the chief social work officer), containing the officer's opinion as to –
  (i) the general appropriateness of continuing the guardianship, based on an interview and assessment of the adult carried out not more than 30 days before the lodging of the application; and
  (ii) the suitability of the applicant to continue to be the adult's guardian; and
(c) where the application relates to the adult's property or financial affairs, a report from the Public Guardian, in the prescribed form, containing the Public Guardian's opinion as to –
  (i) the applicant's conduct as the adult's guardian; and
  (ii) the suitability of the applicant to continue to be the adult's guardian.

(3A) In a case where the incapacity is by reason of mental disorder –
  (a) where a single report is lodged under subsection (3)(a), the related examination and assessment must be carried out by a relevant medical practitioner;
  (b) where 2 or more reports are so lodged, at least one of the related examinations and assessments must be carried out by a relevant medical practitioner.
'Relevant medical practitioner' has the same meaning in this subsection as it has in section 57(3)(a) (see definition in section 57(6B)).

(4) Section 58 shall apply to an application under this section as it applies to an application under section 57; and for the purposes of so applying that section –
  (a) references to the making of a guardianship order and the appointment of a guardian (however expressed) shall be construed as references to, respectively, the renewal of the order and the continuation of appointment;
  (b) for subsection (4) there shall be substituted –
    '(4) Where the sheriff grants an application under section 60, he may continue the guardianship order for a period of 5 years or for such other period (including an indefinite period) as, on cause shown, he may determine.'.

(4A) A sheriff may determine an application made under this section without hearing the parties.

(5) Where the sheriff refuses an application under this section, the sheriff clerk shall forthwith send a copy of the interlocutor containing the refusal to the Public Guardian who shall –
  (a) enter prescribed particulars in the register maintained by him under section 6(2)(b)(iv); and
  (b) notify the adult and the local authority and (in a case where the adult's incapacity is by reason of, or reasons which include, mental disorder and the guardianship order relates to the adult's personal welfare or factors which include it) the Mental Welfare Commission.

Amendments—Adult Support and Protection (Scotland) Act 2007, s 60(3).

61 Registration of guardianship order relating to heritable property

(1) This section applies where the sheriff makes a guardianship order which vests in the guardian any right of the adult to deal with, convey or manage any interest in

heritable property which is recorded or is capable of being recorded in the General Register of Sasines or is registered or is capable of being registered in the Land Register of Scotland.

(2) In making such an order the sheriff shall specify each property affected by the order, in such terms as enable it to be identified in the Register of Sasines or, as the case may be, the Land Register of Scotland.

(3) The guardian shall, after finding caution or giving other security if so required, forthwith apply to the Keeper of the Registers of Scotland for recording of the interlocutor containing the order in the General Register of Sasines or, as the case may be, registering of it in the Land Register of Scotland.

(4) An application under subsection (3) shall contain –

(a) the name and address of the guardian;
(b) a statement that the guardian has powers relating to each property specified in the order;
(c) a copy of the interlocutor.

(5) Where the interlocutor is to be recorded in the General Register of Sasines, the Keeper shall –

(a) record the interlocutor in the Register; and
(b) endorse the interlocutor to the effect that it has been so recorded.

(6) Where the interlocutor is to be registered in the Land Register of Scotland, the Keeper shall update the title sheet of the property to show the interlocutor.

(7) The guardian shall send the endorsed interlocutor or, as the case may be, an extract of the updated title sheet to the Public Guardian who shall enter prescribed particulars of it in the register maintained by him under section 6(2)(b)(iv).

Amendments—Adult Support and Protection (Scotland) Act 2007, s 60(4); Land Registration etc (Scotland) Act 2012, s 119, Sch 5, para 38(3).

Joint and substitute guardians

62 Joint guardians

(1) An application may be made to the sheriff –

(a) by two or more individuals seeking appointment, for their appointment as joint guardians to an adult; or
(b) by an individual seeking appointment, for his appointment as an additional guardian to an adult jointly with one or more existing guardians.

(2) Joint guardians shall not be appointed to an adult unless –

(a) the individuals so appointed are parents, siblings or children of the adult; or
(b) the sheriff is satisfied that, in the circumstances, it is appropriate to appoint as joint guardians individuals who are not related to the adult as mentioned in paragraph (a).

(3) Where an application is made under subsection (1)(a), sections 58 and 59 shall apply for the purposes of the disposal of that application as they apply for the disposal of an application under section 57.

(4) In deciding if an individual is suitable for appointment as additional guardian under subsection (1)(b), the sheriff shall have regard to the matters set out in section 59(3) to (5).

(5) Where the sheriff appoints an additional guardian under this section, the sheriff clerk shall send a copy of the order appointing him to the Public Guardian who shall –

    (a) enter prescribed particulars in the register maintained by him under section 6(2)(b)(iv) of this Act;

    (b) when satisfied that the additional guardian has found caution or given other security if so required, issue a certificate of appointment to the additional guardian and a new certificate of appointment to the existing guardian;

    (c) notify the adult and the local authority and (in a case where the adult's incapacity is by reason of, or reasons which include, mental disorder and the guardianship order relates to the adult's personal welfare or factors which include it) the Mental Welfare Commission.

(6) Joint guardians may, subject to subsection (7), exercise their functions individually, and each guardian shall be liable for any loss or injury caused to the adult arising out of –

    (a) his own acts or omissions; or

    (b) his failure to take reasonable steps to ensure that a joint guardian does not breach any duty of care or fiduciary duty owed to the adult,

and where more than one such guardian is so liable they shall be liable jointly and severally.

(7) A joint guardian shall, before exercising any functions conferred on him, consult the other joint guardians, unless –

    (a) consultation would be impracticable in the circumstances; or

    (b) the joint guardians agree that consultation is not necessary.

(8) Where joint guardians disagree as to the exercise of their functions, either or both of them may apply to the sheriff for directions under section 3.

(9) Where there are joint guardians, a third party in good faith is entitled to rely on the authority to act of any one or more of them.

Amendments—Adult Support and Protection (Scotland) Act 2007, s 60(5).

63 Substitute guardian

(1) In any case where an individual is appointed as guardian under section 58 the sheriff may, on an application, appoint to act as guardian in the event of the guardian so appointed becoming unable to act any individual or office holder who could competently be appointed by virtue of section 59.

(2) In this Act an individual appointed under section 58 and an individual or office holder appointed under this section are referred to respectively as an 'original guardian' and a 'substitute guardian'.

(3) The appointment of a substitute guardian shall be for the same period as the appointment of the original guardian under section 58(4).

(4) An application for appointment as a substitute guardian may be made at the time of the application for the appointment of the original guardian or at any time thereafter.

(5) In making an order appointing an individual as substitute guardian with powers relating to the property or financial affairs of the adult the sheriff may require an individual appointed as substitute guardian to find caution or to give such other security as the sheriff thinks fit.

(6) Subsection (1) shall apply to an individual who, having been appointed as a substitute guardian subsequently, by virtue of this section, becomes the guardian as it applies to an individual appointed under section 58 and, for this purpose, any reference in this section to the 'original guardian' shall be construed accordingly.

(7) Where the sheriff appoints a substitute guardian (other than a substitute guardian appointed in the same order as an original guardian) under subsection (1), the sheriff clerk shall send a copy of the interlocutor containing the order appointing the substitute guardian to the Public Guardian who shall –

 (a) enter prescribed particulars in the register maintained by him under section 6(2)(b)(iv); and
 (b) notify the adult, the original guardian and the local authority and (in a case where the adult's incapacity is by reason of, or by reasons which include, mental disorder and the guardianship order relates to the adult's personal welfare or factors which include it) the Mental Welfare Commission.

(8) On the death or incapacity of the original guardian, the substitute guardian shall, without undue delay, notify the Public Guardian –

 (a) of the death or incapacity (and where the original guardian has died, provide the Public Guardian with documentary evidence of the death); and
 (b) whether or not he is prepared to act as guardian.

(9) The Public Guardian on being notified under subsection (8) shall, if the substitute guardian is prepared to act –

 (a) enter prescribed particulars in the register maintained by him under section 6(2)(b)(iv);
 (b) when satisfied that the substitute guardian has found caution or given other security if so required, issue the substitute guardian with a certificate of appointment;
 (c) notify the adult, the original guardian, the local authority and (in a case where the adult's incapacity is by reason of, or by reasons which include, mental disorder and the guardianship order relates to the adult's personal welfare or factors which include it) the Mental Welfare Commission that the substitute guardian is acting.

(10) Unless otherwise specified in the order appointing him, the substitute guardian shall have the same functions and powers as those exercisable by the original guardian immediately before the event mentioned in subsection (1).

Amendments—SSI 2001/81; Adult Support and Protection (Scotland) Act 2007, s 60(6).

Functions etc of guardian

64 Functions and duties of guardian

(1) Subject to the provisions of this section, an order appointing a guardian may confer on him –

(a) power to deal with such particular matters in relation to the property, financial affairs or personal welfare of the adult as may be specified in the order;
(b) power to deal with all aspects of the personal welfare of the adult, or with such aspects as may be specified in the order;
(c) power to pursue or defend an action of declarator of nullity of marriage, or of divorce or separation in the name of the adult;
(d) power to manage the property or financial affairs of the adult, or such parts of them as may be specified in the order;
(e) power to authorise the adult to carry out such transactions or categories of transactions as the guardian may specify.

(2) A guardian may not –
  (a) place the adult in a hospital for the treatment of mental disorder against his will;
  (b) consent on behalf of the adult to any form of treatment in relation to which the authority conferred by section 47(2) does not apply by virtue of regulations made under section 48(2);
  (c) make, on behalf of the adult, a request under section 4(1) of the Anatomy Act 1984;
  (d) give, on behalf of the adult, an authorisation under, or by virtue of, section 6(1), 17, 29(1) or 42(1) of the Human Tissue (Scotland) Act 2006; or
  (e) make, on behalf of the adult, a nomination under section 30(1) of that Act.

(3) A guardian shall (unless prohibited by an order of the sheriff and subject to any conditions or restrictions specified in such an order) have power by virtue of his appointment to act as the adult's legal representative in relation to any matter within the scope of the power conferred by the guardianship order.

(4) The guardian shall not later than 7 days after any change of his own or the adult's address notify the Public Guardian who shall –
  (a) notify the adult (in a case where it is the guardian's address which has changed), the local authority and (in a case where the adult's incapacity is by reason of, or reasons which include, mental disorder and the guardianship order relates to the adult's personal welfare or factors which include it) the Mental Welfare Commission of the change; and
  (b) enter prescribed particulars in the register maintained by him under section 6(2)(b)(iv).

(5) A guardian having powers relating to the property or financial affairs of the adult shall, subject to –
  (a) such restrictions as may be imposed by the court;
  (b) any management plan prepared under paragraph 1 of schedule 2; or
  (c) paragraph 6 of that schedule,

be entitled to use the capital and income of the adult's estate for the purpose of purchasing assets, services or accommodation so as to enhance the adult's quality of life.

(6) The guardian may arrange for some or all of his functions to be exercised by one or more persons acting on his behalf but shall not be entitled to surrender or transfer any part of them to another person.

(7) The guardian shall comply with any order or demand made by the Public Guardian in relation to the property or financial affairs of the adult in so far as so

complying would be within the scope of his authority; and where the guardian fails to do so the sheriff may, on the application of the Public Guardian, make an order to the like effect as the order or demand made by the Public Guardian, and the sheriff's decision shall be final.

(8) An interim guardian appointed under section 57(5) having powers relating to –

(a) the property or financial affairs of an adult shall report to the Public Guardian;
(b) the personal welfare of an adult shall report to the chief social work officer of the local authority,

every month as to his exercise of those powers.

(9) Where the chief social work officer of the local authority has been appointed guardian he shall, not later than 7 working days after his appointment, notify any person who received notification under section 58(7) of the appointment of the name of the officer responsible at any time for carrying out the functions and duties of guardian.

(10) If, in relation to the appointment of the chief social work officer as guardian, the sheriff has directed that that intimation or notification of any application or other proceedings should not be given to the adult, the chief social work officer shall not notify the adult under subsection (9).

(11) The Scottish Ministers may by regulations define the scope of the powers which may be conferred on a guardian under subsection (1) and the conditions under which they shall be exercised.

(12) Schedule 2 (which makes provision as to the guardian's management of the estate of an adult) has effect.

Amendments—Human Tissue (Scotland) Act 2006, s 57(3); Adult Support and Protection (Scotland) Act 2007, s 60(7).

65 Records: guardians

A guardian shall keep records of the exercise of his powers.

66 Gifts

(1) A guardian having powers relating to the property or financial affairs of an adult may make a gift out of the adult's estate only if authorised to do so by the Public Guardian.

(2) Authorisation by the Public Guardian under subsection (1) may be given generally, or in respect of a particular gift.

(3) On receipt of an application in the prescribed form for an authorisation to make a gift, the Public Guardian shall, subject to subsection (4), intimate the application to the adult, his nearest relative, his named person, his primary carer and any other person who the Public Guardian considers has an interest in the application and advise them of the prescribed period within which they may object to the granting of the application; and he shall not grant the application without affording to any objector an opportunity of being heard.

(4) Where the Public Guardian is of the opinion that the value of the gift is such that intimation is not necessary, he may dispense with intimation.

(5) Having heard any objections as mentioned in subsection (3), the Public Guardian may grant the application.

(6) Where the Public Guardian proposes to refuse the application he shall intimate his decision to the guardian and advise him of the prescribed period within which he may object to the refusal; and he shall not refuse the application without affording to the guardian, if he objects, an opportunity of being heard.

(7) The Public Guardian may at his own instance or at the instance of the guardian or of any person who objects to the granting of the application remit the application for determination by the sheriff, whose decision shall be final.

(8) A decision of the Public Guardian –

    (a) to grant an application under subsection (5) or to refuse an application; or
    (b) to refuse to remit an application to the sheriff under subsection (7),

may be appealed to the sheriff, whose decision shall be final.

Amendments—SSI 2005/465.

67 Effect of appointment and transactions of guardian

(1) The adult shall have no capacity to enter into any transaction in relation to any matter which is within the scope of the authority conferred on the guardian except in a case where he has been authorised by the guardian under section 64(1)(e); but nothing in this subsection shall be taken to affect the capacity of the adult in relation to any other matter.

(2) Where the guardian has powers relating to the property or financial affairs of the adult, the certificate of appointment issued to him by the Public Guardian shall, subject to the terms of the order appointing him, have the effect of –

    (a) authorising the guardian to take possession of, manage and deal with any moveable or immoveable estate (wherever situated) of the adult;
    (b) requiring any payment due to the adult to be made to the guardian,

in so far as the estate, payment or matter falls within the scope of the guardian's authority.

(3) A guardian having powers relating to the personal welfare of an adult may exercise these powers in relation to the adult whether or not the adult is in Scotland at the time of the exercise of the powers.

(4) The guardian shall be personally liable under any transaction entered into by him –

    (a) without disclosing that he is acting as guardian of the adult; or
    (b) which falls outwith the scope of his authority,

but where a guardian has acted as mentioned in paragraph (a) and is not otherwise in breach of any requirement of this Act relating to such guardians, he shall be entitled to be reimbursed from the estate of the adult in respect of any loss suffered by him in consequence of a claim made upon him personally by virtue of this subsection.

(5) Where a third party with whom the adult entered into a transaction was aware at the date of entering into the transaction that authority had been granted by the guardian under section 64(1)(e), the transaction shall not be void only on the ground that the adult lacked capacity.

(6) A transaction for value between the guardian purporting to act as such and a third party acting in good faith shall not be invalid on the ground only that –

(a) the guardian acted outwith the scope of his authority; or
(b) the guardian failed to observe any requirement, whether substantive or procedural, imposed by or under this Act, or by the sheriff or by the Public Guardian; or
(c) there was any irregularity whether substantive or procedural in the appointment of the guardian.

(7) In subsections (3) and (4) any reference to a guardian shall include a reference to a guardian (however called) appointed under the law of any country to, or entitled under the law of any country to act for, an adult during his incapacity, if the guardianship is recognised by the law of Scotland.

68 Reimbursement and remuneration of guardian

(1) A guardian shall be entitled to be reimbursed out of the estate of the adult for any outlays reasonably incurred by him in the exercise of his functions.

(2) In subsection (1), 'outlays', in relation to a guardian –

(a) who is someone other than the chief social work officer of a local authority, includes payment for items and services other than those items and services which the guardian is expected to provide as part of his functions;
(b) who is the chief social work officer of a local authority, includes payment for items and services only if they would not normally be provided free of charge by the local authority to a person who is in similar circumstances but who does not have a guardian.

(3) The local authority shall, in relation to the cost of any application by them for appointment of their chief social work officer as guardian or of any subsequent application by that officer while acting as guardian –

(a) where the application relates to the personal welfare of the adult, meet such cost;
(b) where the application relates to the property or financial affairs of the adult, be entitled to recover such cost from the estate of the adult,

and where the application relates to the personal welfare and to the property or financial affairs of the adult the sheriff shall, in determining the application, apportion the cost as he thinks fit.

(4) Remuneration shall be payable out of the adult's estate –

(a) in respect of the exercise of functions relating to the personal welfare of the adult, only in a case where special cause is shown;
(b) in respect of the exercise of functions relating to the property or financial affairs of the adult, unless the sheriff directs otherwise in the order appointing the guardian,

but shall not be payable to a local authority in respect of the exercise by their chief social work officer of functions relating to the personal welfare of the adult.

(5) In determining whether or not to make a direction under subsection (4)(b), the sheriff shall take into account the value of the estate and the likely difficulty of managing it.

(6) Any remuneration payable to the guardian and the amount of outlays to be allowed under subsection (1) shall be fixed by the Public Guardian –

(a) in a case where the guardian is required to submit accounts, when the guardian's accounts for that period are audited;
(b) in any other case, on an application by the guardian,

and in fixing the remuneration to be paid to the guardian the Public Guardian shall take into account the value of the estate.

(7) The Public Guardian may allow payments to account to be made by way of remuneration during the accounting period if it would be unreasonable to expect the guardian to wait for payment until the end of an accounting period.

(8) A decision by the Public Guardian –
(a) under subsection (6) as to the remuneration payable and the outlays allowable to the guardian;
(b) under subsection (7) as to payments to account to the guardian

may be appealed to the sheriff, whose decision shall be final.

69 Forfeiture of guardian's remuneration

Where a guardian is in breach of any duty of care, fiduciary duty or obligation imposed by this Act the sheriff may, on an application being made to him by any person claiming an interest in the property, financial affairs or personal welfare of the adult, order the forfeiture (in whole or in part) of any remuneration due to the guardian.

70 Non-compliance with decisions of guardian with welfare powers

(1) Where any decision of a guardian with powers relating to the personal welfare of the adult is not complied with by the adult, and the adult might reasonably be expected to comply with the decision, the sheriff may, on an application by the guardian –
(a) make an order ordaining the adult to implement the decision of the guardian;
(b) where the non-compliance relates to a decision of the guardian as to the place of residence of the adult, grant a warrant authorising a constable –
(i) to enter any premises where the adult is, or is reasonably supposed to be;
(ii) to apprehend the adult and to remove him to such place as the guardian may direct.

(2) Where any decision of a guardian with powers relating to the personal welfare of the adult is not complied with by any person other than the adult, and that person might reasonably be expected to comply with the decision, the sheriff may, on an application by the guardian make an order ordaining the person named in the order to implement the decision of the guardian.

(3) On receipt of an application in the prescribed form for an order or warrant under subsection (1) or for an order under subsection (2), the court shall intimate the application to the adult or, as the case may be, to the person named in the application as a person against whom the order or warrant is sought and shall advise them of the prescribed period within which they may object to the granting of the application; and the sheriff shall not grant the order or warrant without affording to any objector an opportunity of being heard.

(4) Having heard any objections as mentioned in subsection (3), the sheriff may grant the application.

(4A) The sheriff may, on cause shown, disapply or modify the application of –
  (a) subsection (3); and
  (b) subsection (4) in so far as it requires the sheriff to hear objections.

(5) A constable executing a warrant under subsection (1)(b) may use such force as is reasonable in the circumstances and shall be accompanied by the guardian or such person as the guardian may authorise in writing.

(6) In this section any reference to a guardian shall include a reference to a guardian (however called) appointed under the law of any country to, or entitled under the law of any country to act for, an adult during his incapacity, if the guardianship is recognised by the law of Scotland.

Amendments—Adult Support and Protection (Scotland) Act 2007, s 60(8).

Termination and variation of guardianship and replacement, removal or resignation of guardian

71 Replacement or removal of guardian or recall of guardianship by sheriff

(1) The sheriff, on an application made to him by an adult subject to guardianship or by any other person claiming an interest in the adult's property, financial affairs or personal welfare, may –
  (a) replace a guardian by an individual or office holder nominated in the application if he is satisfied, in relation to an individual, that he is suitable for appointment having regard to the matters set out in section 59(3) to (5);
  (b) remove a guardian from office if he is satisfied –
    (i) that there is a substitute guardian who is prepared to act as guardian; or
    (ii) in a case where there are joint guardians, that the remaining guardian is or remaining guardians are prepared to continue to act; or
  (c) recall a guardianship order or otherwise terminate a guardianship if he is satisfied –
    (i) that the grounds for appointment of a guardian are no longer fulfilled; or
    (ii) that the interests of the adult in his property, financial affairs or personal welfare can be satisfactorily safeguarded or promoted otherwise than by guardianship,

and where an application under this subsection is granted, the sheriff clerk shall send a copy of the interlocutor to the Public Guardian.

(2) In making an order replacing a guardian by an individual with powers relating to the property or financial affairs of the adult or removing a guardian from office where there is a substitute guardian with such powers prepared to act as guardian, the sheriff may require an individual appointed as guardian or the substitute guardian to find caution or to give such other security as the sheriff thinks fit.

(3) The Public Guardian on receiving a copy of the interlocutor under subsection (1) shall –

(a) enter prescribed particulars in the register maintained by him under section 6(2)(b)(iv);
(b) where the sheriff –
  (i) replaces the guardian by the individual or office holder nominated in the application, when satisfied that, in the case of an individual, the individual has found caution or given other security if so required, issue him with a certificate of appointment;
  (ii) removes a guardian from office and a substitute guardian is prepared to act, when satisfied that the substitute guardian has found caution or given other security if so required, issue the substitute guardian with a certificate of appointment;
  (iii) removes a joint guardian from office and there is a joint guardian who is prepared to continue to act, issue a remaining joint guardian with a new certificate of appointment;
(c) notify the adult and the local authority and (in a case where the incapacity of the adult is by reason of, or reasons which include, mental disorder and the guardianship order relates to the adult's personal welfare or factors including it) the Mental Welfare Commission.

(4) Where the sheriff recalls the guardianship order he may at the same time make an intervention order.

(5) In this section any reference to a guardian shall include a reference to a guardian (however called) appointed under the law of any country to, or entitled under the law of any country to act for, an adult during his incapacity, if the guardianship is recognised by the law of Scotland; and 'guardianship order' shall be construed accordingly.

Amendments—Adult Support and Protection (Scotland) Act 2007, s 60(9).

72 Discharge of guardian with financial powers

(1) At any time after –
  (a) the recall of a guardianship order appointing a guardian with powers relating to the property or financial affairs of an adult;
  (aa) the expiry of such a guardianship order;
  (b) the resignation, removal or replacement of such a guardian; or
  (c) the death of the adult,

the Public Guardian may, on an application by the former guardian or, if the former guardian has died, his representative, grant a discharge in respect of the former guardian's actings and intromissions with the estate of the adult.

(2) On receipt of an application in the prescribed form, the Public Guardian shall intimate the application to the adult, his nearest relative, his primary carer, his named person and any other person who the Public Guardian considers has an interest in the application and advise them of the prescribed period within which they may object to the granting of the application; and he shall not grant the application without affording to any objector an opportunity of being heard.

(3) Having heard any objections as mentioned in subsection (2) the Public Guardian may grant the application.

(4) Where the Public Guardian proposes to refuse the application he shall intimate his decision to the applicant and advise him of the prescribed period within which he

may object to the refusal; and he shall not refuse the application without affording to the applicant, if he objects, an opportunity of being heard.

(5) The Public Guardian may at his own instance or at the instance of the applicant or of any person who objects to the granting of the application remit the application for determination by the sheriff, whose decision shall be final.

(6) A decision of the Public Guardian –

   (a) to grant a discharge under subsection (1) or to refuse a discharge;
   (b) to grant an application under subsection (3) or to refuse an application;
   (c) to refuse to remit an application to the sheriff under subsection (5)

may be appealed to the sheriff, whose decision shall be final.

Amendments—Adult Support and Protection (Scotland) Act 2007, s 60(10);SSI 2005/465.

73 Recall of powers of guardian

(1) The Public Guardian, at his own instance or on an application by any person (including the adult himself) claiming an interest in the property and financial affairs of an adult in respect of whom a guardian has been appointed, may recall the powers of a guardian relating to the property or financial affairs of the adult if it appears to him that –

   (a) the grounds for appointment of a guardian with such powers are no longer fulfilled; or
   (b) the interests of the adult in his property and financial affairs can be satisfactorily safeguarded or promoted otherwise than by guardianship.

(2) Where the Public Guardian recalls the powers of a guardian under subsection (1) he shall –

   (a) enter prescribed particulars in the register maintained by him under section 6(2)(b)(iv);
   (b) notify the adult, the guardian and the local authority.

(3) The Mental Welfare Commission or the local authority in whose area an adult in respect of whom a guardian has been appointed habitually resides, at their own instance or on an application by any person (including the adult himself) claiming an interest in the personal welfare of the adult, may recall the powers of a guardian relating to the personal welfare of the adult if it appears to them that –

   (a) the grounds for appointment of a guardian with such powers are no longer fulfilled; or
   (b) the interests of the adult in his personal welfare can be satisfactorily safeguarded or promoted otherwise than by guardianship.

(3A) The Mental Welfare Commission may recall the powers of a guardian under subsection (3) only if those powers were granted in a case where the adult's incapacity is by reason of, or reasons which include, mental disorder.

(4) Where the Mental Welfare Commission or the local authority recall the powers of a guardian under subsection (3) they shall notify the other and the Public Guardian who shall –

   (a) enter prescribed particulars in the register maintained by him under section 6(2)(b)(iv);
   (b) notify the adult and the guardian.

(5) The Public Guardian, Mental Welfare Commission or local authority, as the case may be, shall –

    (a) where acting on an application, on receipt of the application in the prescribed form intimate it;
    (b) where acting at his or their own instance, intimate the intention to recall the powers of a guardian,

to the adult, his nearest relative, his primary carer, his named person and any person who he or they consider has an interest in the recall of the powers and advise them of the prescribed period within which they may object to such recall; and he or they shall not recall the powers without affording to any objector an opportunity of being heard.

(6) Having heard any objections as mentioned in subsection (5) the Public Guardian, Mental Welfare Commission or local authority may recall the powers of a guardian.

(7) Where the Public Guardian, Mental Welfare Commission or local authority proposes or propose to refuse the application he or they shall intimate the decision to the applicant and the adult and advise them of the prescribed period within which they may object to the refusal; and he or they shall not refuse the application without affording to the applicant or the adult, if he objects, an opportunity of being heard.

(8) The Public Guardian, Mental Welfare Commission or local authority may at his or their own instance or at the instance of an applicant or of any person who objects to the recall of the powers of the guardian remit the matter for determination by the sheriff whose decision shall be final.

(9) A decision of –

    (a) the Public Guardian, Mental Welfare Commission or local authority to recall the powers of a guardian under subsection (6);
    (b) the Public Guardian, Mental Welfare Commission or local authority to remit or not to remit the matter to the sheriff under subsection (8),

may be appealed to the sheriff, whose decision shall be final, and the decision of the Public Guardian, Mental Welfare Commission or local authority as to the recall of the powers of a guardian shall remain in force pending the final determination of the appeal.

(10) The Scottish Ministers may prescribe the forms and procedure for the purposes of any recall of guardianship powers by the Mental Welfare Commission or the local authority.

(11) Section 73A modifies the application of this section in relation to the recall by a local authority of guardianship powers held by their chief social work officer.

Amendments—Adult Support and Protection (Scotland) Act 2007, s 60(11);SSI 2005/465.

73A Recall of chief social work officer's guardianship powers

(1) This section applies where –

    (a) a local authority's chief social work officer is appointed as a guardian; and
    (b) either –
        (i) the local authority wish to recall their chief social work officer's guardianship powers at their own instance; or

(ii) another person (including the adult himself) applies to the local authority for such a recall.

(2) Where this section applies –

(a) the local authority shall, for the purposes of section 73(5), treat the Public Guardian and the Mental Welfare Commission as persons whom they consider to have an interest in the recall of the guardian's powers; and
(b) if the Public Guardian, the Mental Welfare Commission or any other person to whom intimation is given under section 73(5) objects to the recall of the guardian's powers, the local authority –
    (i) shall not recall the guardian's powers; but
    (ii) shall instead remit the matter for determination by the sheriff under section 73(8).

Amendments—Inserted by Adult Support and Protection (Scotland) Act 2007, s 60(12).

74 Variation of guardianship order

(1) The sheriff, on an application by any person (including the adult himself) claiming an interest in the property, financial affairs or personal welfare of the adult, may vary the powers conferred by the guardianship order and may vary any existing ancillary order.

(2) In varying powers relating to the property or financial affairs of the adult conferred by the guardianship order or in varying any ancillary order in relation to such powers the sheriff may require the guardian to find caution or to give such other security as the sheriff thinks fit.

(3) In considering an application under subsection (1), the sheriff shall have regard to any intervention order or guardianship order which may have been previously made in relation to the adult or any other order varying such an order, and to any order ancillary to such an order.

(4) Notwithstanding subsection (1), an application which seeks to vary the powers conferred by a guardianship order or to vary an ancillary order so that –

(a) a guardian, appointed only in relation to the personal welfare of an adult, shall be appointed also or instead in relation to the property or financial affairs of the adult; or
(b) a guardian, appointed only in relation to the property or financial affairs of an adult, shall be appointed also or instead in relation to the personal welfare of the adult;

shall be made under section 57.

(5) Where the sheriff varies the powers conferred by a guardianship order or varies an ancillary order under this section, the sheriff clerk shall send a copy of the interlocutor containing the order to the Public Guardian who shall –

(a) enter prescribed particulars in the register maintained by him under section 6(2)(b)(iv);
(b) notify the adult and the local authority and (in a case where the incapacity of the adult is by reason of, or reasons which include, mental disorder and the guardianship order relates to the adult's personal welfare or factors including it) the Mental Welfare Commission; and

(c) if he is satisfied that the guardian has caution or other security, if so required, which covers the varied order, issue a new certificate of appointment where necessary.

Amendments—Adult Support and Protection (Scotland) Act 2007, s 60(13).

75 Resignation of guardian

(1) A joint guardian, or a guardian in respect of whom a substitute guardian has been appointed, may resign by giving notice in writing of his intention to do so to the Public Guardian and the local authority and (in a case where the incapacity of the adult is by reason of, or reasons which include, mental disorder and the guardianship order relates to the adult's personal welfare or factors including it) the Mental Welfare Commission.

(2) The resignation of a guardian as mentioned in subsection (1) –
  (a) shall not take effect unless –
    (i) the remaining joint guardian is willing to continue to act; or
    (ii) the substitute guardian is willing to act;
  (b) shall take effect on the receipt by the Public Guardian of notice in writing under subsection (1) together with evidence as to the matters contained in paragraph (a)(i) or (ii).

(3) On receiving notice in writing and evidence as mentioned in subsection (2)(b), the Public Guardian shall –
  (a) enter prescribed particulars in the register maintained by him under section 6(2)(b)(iv);
  (b) if satisfied that the substitute guardian has found caution or given other security if so required, issue him with a new certificate of appointment;
  (c) issue a remaining joint guardian with a new certificate of appointment;
  (d) notify the adult.

(4) A substitute guardian who has not subsequently become guardian by virtue of section 63 may resign by giving notice in writing to the Public Guardian and the local authority and (in the case mentioned in subsection (1)) the Mental Welfare Commission and the resignation shall take effect on the date of receipt of the notice by the Public Guardian; and on its becoming effective, the Public Guardian shall –
  (a) notify the guardian and the adult; and
  (b) enter prescribed particulars in the register maintained by him under section 6(2)(b)(iv).

(5) A guardian –
  (a) who has no joint guardian; or
  (b) in respect of whom no substitute guardian has been appointed; or
  (c) being a joint guardian or guardian in respect of whom a substitute has been appointed who cannot effectively resign by reason of subsection (2)(a)(i) or (ii),

shall not resign until a replacement guardian has been appointed under section 71.

Amendments—Adult Support and Protection (Scotland) Act 2007, s 60(14).

75A Death of guardian

The personal representatives of a guardian who dies shall, if aware of the existence of the guardianship, notify the Public Guardian who shall –

   (a) notify –
       (i) the adult;
       (ii) the local authority; and
       (iii) in a case where the adult's incapacity is by reason of, or reasons which include, mental disorder and the guardianship order relates to the adult's personal welfare or factors including it, the Mental Welfare Commission;
   (b) enter prescribed particulars in the register maintained under section 6(2)(b)(iv); and
   (c) issue a new certificate of appointment –
       (i) to any surviving joint guardian;
       (ii) where the Public Guardian is satisfied that any substitute guardian appointed in respect of the dead guardian is willing to act and has found caution or given other security if so required, to the substitute guardian.

Amendments—Inserted by Adult Support and Protection (Scotland) Act 2007, s 60(15).

76 Change of habitual residence

(1) Where the guardian is the chief social work officer of the local authority and the adult changes his place of habitual residence to the area of another local authority, the chief social work officer of the first mentioned local authority shall notify the chief social work officer of the second mentioned local authority (the 'receiving authority') who shall become guardian on receipt of the notification and shall within 7 days of that receipt notify the Public Guardian and (in a case where the incapacity of the adult is by reason of, or reasons which include, mental disorder and the guardianship order relates to the adult's personal welfare or factors which include it) the Mental Welfare Commission.

(2) The Public Guardian shall –
   (a) enter prescribed particulars in the register maintained by him under section 6(2)(b)(iv) and issue a certificate of appointment to the new guardian; and
   (b) subject to subsection (4), notify the adult within 7 days of receipt of the notification from the receiving authority.

(3) Subject to subsection (4), the chief social work officer of the receiving authority shall, within 7 working days of receipt of the notification, notify any person who received notification under section 58(7) of the appointment of the name of the officer responsible at any time for carrying out the functions and duties of guardian.

(4) If, in relation to the original application for a guardianship order, the sheriff has directed that intimation or notification of any application or other proceedings should not be given to the adult, the Public Guardian and the chief social work officer shall not notify the adult under subsection (2)(b) or (3) as the case may be.

Termination of authority to intervene and guardianship on death of adult

77 Termination of authority to intervene and guardianship on death of adult

(1) An intervention order or a guardianship order in respect of an adult under this Part shall cease to have effect on his death.

(2) A person authorised under an intervention order or a guardian having powers relating to the property or financial affairs of the adult shall, until he becomes aware of the death of the adult or of any other event which has the effect of terminating his authority, be entitled to act under those powers if he acts in good faith.

(3) Where the authority of a person authorised under an intervention order or of a guardian (including a joint guardian) is terminated or otherwise comes to an end, a third party in good faith is entitled to rely on the authority of the person or guardian if he is unaware of the termination or ending of that authority.

(4) No title to any interest in heritable property acquired by a third party in good faith and for value from a person authorised under an intervention order or from a guardian having powers relating to the property or financial affairs of the adult shall be challengeable on the grounds only of the termination or coming to an end of the authority of the person or of the guardian.

(5) In this section any reference to a guardian shall include a reference to a guardian (however called) appointed under the law of any country to, or entitled under the law of any country to act for, an adult during his incapacity, if the guardianship is recognised by the law of Scotland.

78 Amendment of registration under section 61 on events affecting guardianship or death of adult

(1) The Public Guardian shall –
   (a) where under section 71(3)(a), 73(2)(a), 74(5)(a) or 75(3)(a) he enters in the register maintained by him under section 6(2)(b)(iv) prescribed particulars relating to a guardianship order in respect of which the appointment of the guardian was recorded or registered under section 61; or
   (b) where an adult in respect of whom there was such a guardianship order has died,

apply forthwith to the Keeper of the Registers of Scotland for the recording of the interlocutor or other document vouching the event giving rise to the entry or, as the case may be, the certificate of the death or, as the case may be, the registering of the event or the death in the Land Register of Scotland.

(2) On an application under subsection (1), the Keeper shall, as appropriate –
   (a) record the interlocutor or other document or certificate in the Register of Sasines and endorse it that it has been so recorded;
   (b) update the title sheet of the heritable property accordingly.

79 Protection of third parties: guardianship

Where a third party has acquired, in good faith and for value, title to any interest in heritable property from a guardian that title shall not be challengeable on the ground only –

(a) of any irregularity of procedure in making the guardianship order; or
(b) that the guardian has acted outwith the scope of his authority.

Guardianship orders: children

79A Guardianship orders: children

Sections 57 to 79 apply in relation to a child who will become an adult within 3 months as they apply in relation to an adult; but no guardianship order made in relation to a child shall have effect until the child becomes an adult.

Amendments—Inserted by Adult Support and Protection (Scotland) Act 2007, s 60(16).

PART 7
MISCELLANEOUS

80 Future appointment of curator bonis etc incompetent

In any proceedings begun after the commencement of this Act it shall not be competent to appoint a curator bonis, tutor-dative or tutor-at-law to a person who has attained the age of 16 years.

81 Repayment of funds

(1) Where –

(a) a continuing attorney;
(b) a welfare attorney;
(c) a withdrawer;
(d) a guardian;
(e) a person authorised under an intervention order; or
(f) the managers of an authorised establishment within the meaning of Part 4,

uses or use any funds of an adult in breach of their fiduciary duty or outwith their authority or power to intervene in the affairs of the adult or after having received intimation of the termination or suspension of their authority or power to intervene, they shall be liable to repay the funds so used, with interest thereon at the rate fixed by Act of Sederunt as applicable to a decree of the sheriff, to the account of the adult.

(2) Subsection (1) shall be without prejudice to sections 69 and 82.

81A Public Guardian's power to obtain records

(1) The Public Guardian may, when carrying out an investigation under section 6(2)(c) or (d) or inquiries under section 30(2)(a) –

(a) require any person falling within subsection (2) to provide the Public Guardian with –
   (i) the person's records of the exercise of the person's powers in relation to the adult to whom the investigation relates; and
   (ii) such other information relating to the exercise of those powers as the Public Guardian may reasonably require,

(b) require any person who holds (or who has held) funds on behalf of the adult to whom the investigation relates to provide the Public Guardian with –
   (i) its records of the account; and
   (ii) such other information relating to those accounts as the Public Guardian may reasonably require.

(2) A person falls within this subsection if the person is or has been –
   (a) a continuing attorney appointed by the adult to whom the investigation relates;
   (b) a withdrawer with authority to intromit with that adult's funds;
   (c) a person authorised under an intervention order to act in relation to that adult; or
   (d) that adult's guardian.

(3) A fundholder may charge a reasonable fee for complying with a requirement under subsection (1)(b) and may recover that fee from the account concerned.

Amendments—Inserted by Adult Support and Protection (Scotland) Act 2007, s 61. Amended by SSI 2007/334.

82 Limitation of liability

(1) No liability shall be incurred by a guardian, a continuing attorney, a welfare attorney, a person authorised under an intervention order, a withdrawer or the managers of an establishment for any breach of any duty of care or fiduciary duty owed to the adult if he has or they have –
   (a) acted reasonably and in good faith and in accordance with the general principles set out in section 1; or
   (b) failed to act and the failure was reasonable and in good faith and in accordance with the said general principles.

(2) In this section any reference to –
   (a) a guardian shall include a reference to a guardian (however called) appointed under the law of any country to, or entitled under the law of any country to act for, an adult during his incapacity, if the guardianship is recognised by the law of Scotland;
   (b) a continuing attorney shall include a reference to a person granted, under a contract, grant or appointment governed by the law of any country, powers (however expressed), relating to the granter's property or financial affairs and having continued effect notwithstanding the granter's incapacity; and
   (c) a welfare attorney shall include a reference to a person granted, under a contract, grant or appointment governed by the law of any country, powers (however expressed) relating to the granter's personal welfare and having effect during the granter's incapacity.

83 Offence of ill-treatment and wilful neglect

(1) It shall be an offence for any person exercising powers under this Act relating to the personal welfare of an adult to ill-treat or wilfully neglect that adult.

(2) A person guilty of an offence under subsection (1) shall be liable –

(a) on summary conviction, to imprisonment for a term not exceeding 6 months or to a fine not exceeding the statutory maximum or both;
(b) on conviction on indictment, to imprisonment for a term not exceeding 2 years or to a fine, or both.

84 Application to guardians appointed under Criminal Procedure (Scotland) Act 1995

(1) Parts 1, 5, 6 and 7 shall apply to a guardian appointed under section 57(2)(c) or section 58(1) of the Criminal Procedure (Scotland) Act 1995 ('the 1995 Act') as they apply to a guardian with powers relating to the personal welfare of an adult appointed under Part 6; and accordingly the 1995 Act shall be amended as follows.

(2) After section 58 there shall be inserted –

'58A Application of Adults with Incapacity (Scotland) Act 2000

(1) Subject to the provisions of this section, the provisions of Parts 1, 5, 6 and 7 of the Adults with Incapacity (Scotland) Act 2000 ('the 2000 Act') apply –

(a) to a guardian appointed by an order of the court under section 57(2)(c), 58(1) or 58(1A) of this Act (in this section referred to as a 'guardianship order') whether appointed before or after the coming into force of these provisions, as they apply to a guardian with powers relating to the personal welfare of an adult appointed under section 58 of that Act;
(b) to a person authorised under an intervention order under section 60B of this Act as they apply to a person so authorised under section 53 of that Act.

(2) In making a guardianship order the court shall have regard to any regulations made by the Scottish Ministers under section 64(11) of the 2000 Act and –

(a) shall confer powers, which it shall specify in the order, relating only to the personal welfare of the person;
(b) may appoint a joint guardian;
(c) may appoint a substitute guardian;
(d) may make such consequential or ancillary order, provision or direction as it considers appropriate.

(3) Without prejudice to the generality of subsection (2), or to any other powers conferred by this Act, the court may –

(a) make any order granted by it subject to such conditions and restrictions as appear to it to be appropriate;
(b) order that any reports relating to the person who will be the subject of the order be lodged with the court or that the person be assessed or interviewed and that a report of such assessment or interview be lodged;
(c) make such further inquiry or call for such further information as appears to it to be appropriate;
(d) make such interim order as appears to it to be appropriate pending the disposal of the proceedings.

(4) Where the court makes a guardianship order it shall forthwith send a copy of the interlocutor containing the order to the Public Guardian who shall –

(a) enter prescribed particulars of the appointment in the register maintained by him under section 6(2)(b)(iv) of the 2000 Act;
(b) unless he considers that the notification would be likely to pose a serious risk to the person's health notify the person of the appointment of the guardian; and
(c) notify the local authority and the Mental Welfare Commission of the terms of the interlocutor.

(5) A guardianship order shall continue in force for a period of 3 years or such other period (including an indefinite period) as, on cause shown, the court may determine.

(6) Where any proceedings for the appointment of a guardian under section 57(2)(c) or 58(1) of this Act have been commenced and not determined before the date of coming into force of section 84 of, and paragraph 26 of schedule 5 to, the Adults with Incapacity (Scotland) Act 2000 they shall be determined in accordance with this Act as it was immediately in force before that date.'.

Amendments—Regulation of Care (Scotland) Act 2001, s 79, Sch 3, para 23(5).

84A Application to storage of gametes without adult's consent where adult is incapable

(1) The storage of gametes under paragraph 10 of Schedule 3 to the Human Fertilisation and Embryology Act 1990 (storage of gametes without patient's consent where patient is incapable) is to be treated as an intervention in the affairs of an adult under this Act.

(2) Sections 2 to 5, 8, 11, 14 and 85 of this Act apply to a registered medical practitioner's decision under that paragraph as they apply to decisions taken for the purposes of this Act.

(3) Section 52 of this Act applies to a practitioner's decision under that paragraph as it applies to decisions taken for the purposes of section 47 of this Act.

(4) Part 5 of this Act (other than section 52) does not apply to the storage of gametes under that paragraph.

(5) Section 83 of this Act applies to a practitioner's decision under that paragraph as if the practitioner were exercising powers under this Act.

(6) Nothing in this section authorises any person, other than the person whose gametes are to be stored, to consent to the storage of the gametes.

Amendments—Inserted by Human Fertilisation and Embryology Act 2008, s 65, Sch 7, para 18.

84B Application to use of human cells to create an embryo in vitro without adult's consent

(1) The use of an adult's human cells to bring about the creation in vitro of an embryo or human admixed embryo for use for the purposes of a project of research –

(a) without the adult's consent, and
(b) where the adult is incapable,

is to be treated as an intervention in the affairs of an adult under this Act.

(2) Sections 2 to 5, 8, 11, 14 and 85 of this Act apply to decisions made under paragraphs 16 and 18 of Schedule 3 to the Human Fertilisation and Embryology Act 1990 (when consent to the use of human cells is not required due to adult being incapable of consenting) as they apply to decisions taken for the purposes of this Act.

(3) Section 51 of this Act does not apply to the use of an adult's human cells to bring about the creation in vitro of an embryo or human admixed embryo for use for the purposes of a project of research.

(4) Section 83 of this Act applies to a decision made under paragraphs 16 and 18 of Schedule 3 to the Human Fertilisation and Embryology Act 1990 as if the person making the decision were exercising powers under this Act.

(5) Expressions used in this section and in Schedule 3 to the Human Fertilisation and Embryology Act 1990 have the same meaning in this section as in that Schedule.

Amendments—Inserted by Human Fertilisation and Embryology Act 2008, s 65, Sch 7, para 18.

85 Jurisdiction and private international law

Schedule 3 shall have effect for the purposes of defining the jurisdiction, in respect of adults who are incapable within the meaning of this Act, of the Scottish judicial and administrative authorities and for making provision as to the private international law of Scotland in that respect.

86 Regulations

(1) Any power of the Scottish Ministers to make regulations under this Act shall be exercisable by statutory instrument subject to annulment in pursuance of a resolution of the Scottish Parliament.

(2) Any such power may be exercised to make different provision for different cases or classes of case and includes power to make such incidental, supplemental, consequential or transitional provision or savings as appear to the Scottish Ministers to be appropriate.

87 Interpretation

(1) In this Act, unless the context otherwise requires –

  'adult' shall be construed in accordance with section 1;
  'continuing attorney' shall be construed in accordance with section 15;
  'guardianship order' shall be construed in accordance with section 58;
  'incapable' and 'incapacity' shall be construed in accordance with section 1;
  'intervention order' shall be construed in accordance with section 53;
  'local authority' means a council constituted under section 2 of the Local Government etc (Scotland) Act 1994, and references to a local authority shall be construed as references to the local authority for the area in which the adult resides;
  'managers of an establishment' shall be construed in accordance with schedule 1;
  'mental disorder' has the meaning given by section 328 of the 2003 Act;

'mental health officer' has the meaning given by section 329 of the 2003 Act;
'Mental Welfare Commission' means the Mental Welfare Commission for Scotland continued in being by section 4 of the 2003 Act;
'named person' has the meaning given by section 329 of the 2003 Act;
'nearest relative' has the meaning given by section 254 of the 2003 Act;
'office holder', in relation to a guardian, means the chief social work officer of the local authority;
'person claiming an interest' includes the local authority, the Mental Welfare Commission and the Public Guardian;
'power of attorney' includes a factory and commission;
'practising solicitor' means a solicitor holding a practising certificate issued in accordance with Part 2 of the Solicitors (Scotland) Act 1980;
'prescribe', except for the purposes of anything which may be or is to be prescribed by the Public Guardian, means prescribe by regulations; and 'prescribed' shall be construed accordingly;
'primary carer' in relation to an adult, means the person or organisation primarily engaged in caring for him;
'Public Guardian' shall be construed in accordance with section 6;
'State hospital' shall be construed in accordance with section 102 of the National Health Service (Scotland) Act 1978;
'substitute guardian' shall be construed in accordance with section 63;
'welfare attorney' shall be construed in accordance with section 16;
'withdrawer' shall be construed in accordance with section 26;
'the 1984 Act' means the Mental Health (Scotland) Act 1984;
'the 2003 Act' means the Mental Health (Care and Treatment) (Scotland) Act 2003.

(1A) Any power under this Act to prescribe anything by regulations is exercisable by the Scottish Ministers.

(2), (3) *(repealed)*

(4) For the purposes of this Act, a person is bankrupt if his estate has been sequestrated for insolvency or he has granted a trust deed which has become a protected trust deed under Schedule 5 to the Bankruptcy (Scotland) Act 1985, or he has been adjudged bankrupt in England and Wales, or he has become bankrupt (however expressed) under the law of any other country.

Amendments—Mental Health (Care and Treatment) (Scotland) Act 2003, s 331, Sch 4, para 9(5), Sch 5, Pt 1; SSI 2005/465; Adult Support and Protection (Scotland) Act 2007, ss 57(9), 77(1), Sch 1, para 5(e).

88 Continuation of existing powers, minor and consequential amendments and repeals

(1) Schedule 4, which contains provisions relating to the continuation of existing powers, shall have effect.

(2) Schedule 5, which contains minor amendments and amendments consequential on the provisions of this Act, shall have effect.

(3) The enactments mentioned in Schedule 6 are hereby repealed to the extent specified in the third column of that schedule.

89 Citation and commencement

(1) This Act may be cited as the Adults with Incapacity (Scotland) Act 2000.

(2) This Act shall come into force on such day as the Scottish Ministers may by order made by statutory instrument appoint and different days may be appointed for different purposes.

(3) Without prejudice to the provisions of schedule 4, an order under subsection (2) may make such transitional provisions and savings as appear to the Scottish Ministers necessary or expedient in connection with any provision brought into force by the order; and where it does so, the statutory instrument under which it is made shall be subject to annulment in pursuance of a resolution of the Scottish Parliament.

SCHEDULE 1
MANAGERS OF AN ESTABLISHMENT

1 For the purposes of Part 4 'the managers' of an establishment means –

  (a) in relation to a hospital vested in the Scottish Ministers under the National Health Service (Scotland) Act 1978, the Health Board responsible for the administration of that hospital;

  (b) in relation to a hospital managed by a National Health Service trust established under section 12A of the said Act of 1978, the directors of the trust;

  (c) in relation to a State hospital –

      (i) the Scottish Ministers;

      (ii) *(repealed)*

      (iii) if the management of that hospital has been delegated to a Health Board, to a Special Health Board, to a National Health Service trust or to the Common Services Agency for the Scottish Health Service, that Board, trust or Agency, as the case may be, or any person appointed by the Board, trust or agency, as the case may be, to manage the hospital;

  (d) in relation to a care service or limited registration service –

      (i) the person identified under section 59(2)(b) of the Public Services Reform (Scotland) Act 2010 in the application for registration of the service;

      (ii) if the application is made under section 83(1) of that Act, the local authority or any person appointed by the local authority to manage the service; or

      (iii) if another person has been identified in pursuance of regulations under section 78(2) of that Act, the other person so identified,

      and in paragraph (d) above 'care service' and 'limited registration service' have the same meanings as in Part 5 of the Public Services Reform (Scotland) Act 2010;

  (e) in relation to an independent hospital or private psychiatric hospital (as defined in section 10F(2) of the National Health Service (Scotland) Act 1978), the person identified under section 10P(2)(b) of that Act in the application for registration of the service.

2 The Scottish Ministers may by regulations amend the list of managers in paragraph 1.

Amendments—Regulation of Care (Scotland) Act 2001, s 79, Sch 3, para 23(6); Mental Health (Care and Treatment) (Scotland) Act 2003, s 331(2), Sch 5, Pt 1; SSI 2011/211.

SCHEDULE 2
MANAGEMENT OF ESTATE OF ADULT

1 Management plan

(1) A guardian with powers relating to the property and financial affairs of the adult shall, unless the sheriff otherwise directs, prepare a plan (a 'management plan'), taking account of any directions given by the sheriff in the order appointing him, for the management, investment and realisation of the adult's estate and for the application of the estate to the adult's needs, so far as the estate falls within the guardian's authority.

(2) The management plan shall be submitted in draft by the guardian to the Public Guardian for his approval, along with the inventory of the adult's estate prepared under paragraph 3, not more than one month, or such other period as the Public Guardian may allow, after the submission of the inventory.

(3) The Public Guardian may approve the management plan submitted to him under sub-paragraph (2) or he may approve it with amendments and the plan as so approved or as so amended shall be taken account of by the guardian in the exercise of his functions in relation to the adult.

(4) Before the management plan is approved, the guardian shall, unless the sheriff on appointing him has conferred wider powers, have power only to –

(a) ingather and take control of the assets of the adult's estate so as to enable him, when the management plan has been approved, to intromit with them;

(b) make such payments as are necessary to provide for the adult's day to day needs.

(5) The Public Guardian may authorise the guardian to exercise any function within the scope of his authority before the management plan is approved, if it would be unreasonable to delay him exercising that function until the plan had been approved.

(6) The guardian shall keep the management plan under review and shall put forward to the Public Guardian proposals for variation of it whenever it appears to him to be appropriate.

(7) The Public Guardian –

(a) may at any time propose any variation to the management plan; and

(b) shall review the plan whenever the guardian submits his accounts for audit.

(8) The Public Guardian shall notify the guardian of any variation which he proposes to make to the management plan and shall not make any such variation without affording the guardian an opportunity to object.

(9) Having heard any objections by the guardian as mentioned in sub-paragraph (8) the Public Guardian may make the variation with or without amendment.

2 Directions from sheriff

Where the guardian disagrees with any decision made by the Public Guardian in relation to a management plan prepared under paragraph 1, he may apply to the sheriff for a determination in relation to the matter and the sheriff's decision shall be final.

3 Inventory of estate

(1) A guardian with powers relating to the property or financial affairs of the adult shall, as soon after his appointment as possible and in any event within 3 months of the date of registration of his appointment or such other period as the Public Guardian may allow, submit to the Public Guardian for examination and approval a full inventory of the adult's estate in so far as it falls within the scope of the guardian's authority, along with such supporting documents and additional information as the Public Guardian may require.

(2) The inventory shall be in a form, and contain information, prescribed by the Public Guardian.

(3) Errors in and omissions from the inventory which are discovered by the guardian after the inventory has been approved by the Public Guardian shall be notified by him to the Public Guardian within 6 months of the date of discovery or when submitting his next accounts to the Public Guardian, whichever occurs sooner.

(4) The Public Guardian may dispense with the need for the guardian to submit an inventory under sub-paragraph (1) or may require the guardian to take such other action as he thinks appropriate in lieu of submitting an inventory.

4 Money

The guardian shall deposit all money received by him as guardian in a bank or a building society in an account in the name of the adult and shall ensure that all sums in excess of £500 (or such other sum as may be prescribed) so deposited shall earn interest.

5 Powers relating to investment and carrying on of business by guardian

(1) Subject to the following provisions of this paragraph, a guardian with powers relating to the property or financial affairs of the adult shall be entitled –

(a) after obtaining and considering proper advice, to retain any existing investment of the adult;
(b) to use the adult's estate to make new investments in accordance with the management plan prepared under paragraph 1 or with the consent of the Public Guardian.

(2) For the purpose of sub-paragraph (1) –

(a) proper advice is the advice of a person who has permission for the purposes of the Financial Services and Markets Act 2000 to advise on investments who is not the guardian or any person who is an employer, employee or business partner of the guardian; and
(b) the advice must be given or subsequently confirmed in writing.

(2A) Sub-paragraph (2) must be read with –

  (a) section 22 of the Financial Services and Markets Act 2000;
  (b) any relevant order under that section; and
  (c) Schedule 2 to that Act.

(3) The guardian shall keep every investment under review and in doing so shall have regard to the following principles –

  (a) that the investment must be prudent;
  (b) that there must be diversification of investments; and
  (c) that the investment must be suitable for the adult's estate.

(4) The Public Guardian may at any time direct the guardian to realise any investment.

(5) The guardian may, subject to any direction given by the Public Guardian, carry on any business of the adult.

(6) Any decision by the Public Guardian –

  (a) under sub-paragraph (4) as to directing the guardian to realise investments;
  (b) under sub-paragraph (5) as to giving directions to the guardian in carrying on the business of the adult,

may be appealed to the sheriff, whose decision shall be final.

6 Purchase or disposal of accommodation

(1) The guardian shall not, without the consent of the Public Guardian –

  (a) in principle; and
  (b) to the purchase or selling price,

purchase accommodation for, or dispose of any accommodation used for the time being as a dwelling house by, the adult.

(2) On receipt of an application for consent in principle under sub-paragraph (1)(a) in the prescribed form, the Public Guardian shall intimate the application to the adult, his nearest relative, his primary carer, his named person and any person who the Public Guardian considers has an interest in the application and advise them of the prescribed period within which they may object to the granting of the application.

(3) The Public Guardian shall remit any objection under sub-paragraph (2) for determination by the sheriff (whose decision shall be final) and –

  (a) if the sheriff upholds the objection, shall refuse the application;
  (b) if the sheriff dismisses the objection, shall grant the application.

(4) Where the Public Guardian proposes to refuse the application other than under sub-paragraph (3)(a) he shall intimate his decision to the applicant and advise him of the prescribed period within which he may object to the refusal; and he shall not refuse the application without affording the applicant, if he objects, an opportunity of being heard.

(5) Having heard any objections as mentioned in sub-paragraph (4) or where there is no objection as mentioned in sub-paragraph (2), the Public Guardian may grant the application.

(6) The Public Guardian may at his own instance or at the instance of any person who objects to the granting or refusal (other than a refusal under

sub-paragraph (3)(a)) of the application remit the application to the sheriff for determination by the sheriff, whose decision shall be final.

(7) If consent in principle to the purchase or disposal of the accommodation is given, the guardian shall apply to the Public Guardian for consent under sub-paragraph (1)(b) to the purchase or selling price.

(8) A decision of the Public Guardian –

    (a) to grant or to refuse (other than under sub-paragraph (3)(a)) an application; or

    (b) to refuse to remit an application to the sheriff under sub-paragraph (6),

may be appealed to the sheriff, whose decision shall be final.

(9) A decision of the Public Guardian to give or to refuse consent under sub-paragraph (1)(b) shall be final.

7 Accounting and auditing

(1) A guardian with powers relating to the property or financial affairs of the adult shall submit accounts in respect of each accounting period to the Public Guardian within one month from the end of the accounting period or such longer period as the Public Guardian may allow.

(2) There shall be submitted with the accounts under sub-paragraph (1) such supporting documents as the Public Guardian may require, and the Public Guardian may require the guardian to furnish him with such information in connection with the accounts as the Public Guardian may determine.

(3) For the purposes of this paragraph, the first accounting period shall commence with the date of appointment of the guardian and end at such date not later than 18 months after the date of registration of the guardian's appointment as the Public Guardian may determine; and thereafter each accounting period shall be a year commencing with the date on which the immediately previous accounting period ended.

(4) Notwithstanding the foregoing provisions of this paragraph, the Public Guardian may at any time –

    (a) give directions as to the frequency of accounting periods;
    (b) dispense with the need for the submission of accounts by the guardian; or
    (c) require the guardian to do anything which the Public Guardian thinks appropriate in lieu of submitting accounts.

(5) The accounts shall be in such form as is prescribed by the Public Guardian and different forms may be prescribed for different cases or descriptions of case.

(6) Where the estate of the adult includes a business or an interest in a business that part of the accounts which relates to the business or to the interest in the business shall be accompanied by a certificate from such person and in such form as may be prescribed by the Public Guardian, certifying the accuracy of that part of the accounts.

(7) The accounts submitted to the Public Guardian under sub-paragraph (1) (other than any part to which a certificate as mentioned in sub-paragraph (6) relates) shall be audited by the Public Guardian or by an accountant appointed by, and responsible to, the Public Guardian for that purpose.

8 Approval of accounts

(1) After the accounts of the guardian have been audited, the Public Guardian shall, if the accounts appear to him –

(a) to be a true and fair view of the guardian's management of the adult's estate, approve them and fix the remuneration (if any) due to the guardian;

(b) not to be a true and fair view of the guardian's management of the adult's estate, prepare a report as to the extent to which they do not represent such a true and fair view and adjusting the accounts accordingly.

(2) The Public Guardian may approve the accounts, notwithstanding any minor inconsistencies or absence of full documentation in the accounts, if he is satisfied that the guardian acted reasonably and in good faith.

(3) The Public Guardian shall send any report prepared by him under sub-paragraph (1)(b) to the guardian, who may object to anything contained in the report within 28 days of it being sent to him.

(4) If no objection is taken to the report, the accounts as adjusted by the Public Guardian shall be regarded as approved by him.

(5) Where any objection taken to the report cannot be resolved between the guardian and the Public Guardian, the matter may be determined by the sheriff on an application by the guardian, and the sheriff's decision shall be final.

(6) Without prejudice to sub-paragraph (7), the guardian shall be liable to make good any deficiency revealed by the accounts as approved by the Public Guardian under sub-paragraph (1)(a).

(7) Where a deficiency is revealed as mentioned in sub-paragraph (6), the Public Guardian may require the guardian to pay interest to the adult's estate on the amount of the deficiency at the rate fixed by Act of Sederunt as applicable to a decree of the sheriff in respect of the period for which it appears that the deficiency has existed.

Amendments—SI 2001/3649; Adult Support and Protection (Scotland) Act 2007, s 77(1), Sch 1, para 5(f).

SCHEDULE 3
JURISDICTION AND PRIVATE INTERNATIONAL LAW

1 General

(1) The Scottish judicial and administrative authorities shall have jurisdiction to dispose of an application or other proceedings and otherwise carry out functions under this Act in relation to an adult if –

(a) the adult is habitually resident in Scotland; or

(b) property which is the subject of the application or proceedings or in respect of which functions are carried out under this Act is in Scotland; or

(c) the adult, although not habitually resident in Scotland is there or property belonging to the adult is there and, in either case, it is a matter of urgency that the application is or the proceedings are dealt with; or

(d) the adult is present in Scotland and the intervention sought in the application or proceedings is of a temporary nature and its effect limited to Scotland.

(2) As from the ratification date, the Scottish judicial and administrative authorities shall, in addition to the jurisdiction mentioned in sub-paragraph (1) in the circumstances set out therein, have the jurisdiction mentioned in that sub-paragraph in the following circumstances –

(a) the adult –
  (i) is a British citizen; and
  (ii) has a closer connection with Scotland than with any other part of the United Kingdom; and
(b) Article 7 of the Convention has been complied with,

or if the Scottish Central Authority, having received a request under Article 8 of the Convention from an authority of the State in which the adult is habitually resident and consulted such authorities in Scotland as would, under this Act, have functions in relation to the adult, have agreed to the request.

(3) As from the ratification date, the provisions of the Convention shall apply to the exercise of jurisdiction under this schedule where the adult –

(a) is habitually resident in a Contracting State other than the United Kingdom; or
(b) not being habitually resident in Scotland, is or has been the subject of protective proceedings in such a Contracting State.

(4) As from the ratification date, any application made to a Scottish judicial or administrative authority under this Act which –

(a) relates to an adult who is not habitually resident in Scotland; and
(b) does not require to be determined as a matter of urgency,

shall be accompanied by information as to which State the adult habitually resides in and as to any other application relating to the adult which has been dealt with or is being made, or proceedings so relating which have been or are being brought, in any Contracting State other than the United Kingdom.

(5) For the purposes of this paragraph, an adult –

(a) whose habitual residence cannot be ascertained; or
(b) who is a refugee or has been internationally displaced by disturbance in the country of his habitual residence,

shall be taken to be habitually resident in the State which he is in.

2 Appropriate sheriff

(1) The sheriff having jurisdiction under this schedule to take measures is the sheriff in whose sheriffdom –

(a) in relation to a case falling within paragraph 1(1)(a), the adult is habitually resident;
(b) in relation to a case falling within paragraph 1(1)(b), the property is located;
(c) in relation to a case falling within paragraph 1(1)(c), the adult or property belonging to the adult is present;
(d) in relation to a case falling within paragraph 1(1)(d), the adult is present.

(2) The sheriff shall also have jurisdiction to vary or recall any intervention order or guardianship order made by him under this Act if no Contracting State other than the United Kingdom has, by way of its judicial or administrative authorities, jurisdiction; and –

(a) no other court or authority has jurisdiction; or
(b) another court or authority has jurisdiction but –
  (i) it would be unreasonable to expect an applicant to invoke it; or
  (ii) that court or authority has declined to exercise it.

(3) Notwithstanding that any other judicial or administrative authority has jurisdiction under sub-paragraph (1)(a) to take measures, a sheriff shall have jurisdiction to take measures if –

(a) the adult is present in the sheriffdom; and
(b) the sheriff considers that it is necessary, in the interests of the adult, to take the measures immediately.

(4) Where, by operation of paragraph 1, jurisdiction falls to be exercised by a sheriff but the case is one appearing to fall outside sub-paragraphs (1) and (2), the sheriff having jurisdiction is the Sheriff of the Lothians and Borders at Edinburgh.

3 Applicable law

(1) The law applicable to anything done under this Act by a Scottish judicial or administrative authority in relation to an adult is the law of Scotland.

(2) Sub-paragraph (1) does not prevent a Scottish judicial or administrative authority from applying the law of a country other than Scotland if, in circumstances which demonstrate a substantial connection with that other country and having regard to the interests of the adult, it appears appropriate to do so.

(3) Such an authority shall, however, in the exercise of the powers conferred by section 20 of this Act, take into consideration to the extent possible the law which, as provided in paragraph 4, governs the power of attorney.

(4) Where a measure for the protection of an adult has been taken in one State and is implemented in another, the conditions of its implementation are governed by the law of that other State.

(5) Any question whether a person has authority by virtue of any enactment or rule of law to represent an adult shall be governed –

(a) where such representation is for the purposes of the immediate personal welfare of the adult and the adult is in Scotland, by the law of Scotland; and
(b) in any other case, by the law of the country in which the adult is habitually resident.

4 (1) The law governing the existence, extent, modification and extinction of continuing or welfare powers of attorney (including like powers, however described) shall be that of the State in which the granter habitually resided at the time of the grant of these powers.

(2) Where, however, the granter of such a power of attorney so provides in writing, the law so applicable shall instead be the law of a State –

(a) of which the granter is a national;
(b) in which the granter was habitually resident before the grant; or
(c) in which the property of the granter is located.

(3) The manner of exercise of such a power shall be governed by the law of the State in which its exercise takes place.

(4) The law of a State may be applied under sub-paragraph (2)(c) above only in respect of the property referred to in that provision.

(5) Nothing in sub-paragraphs (1) and (2) prevents the sheriff from exercising powers under section 20 of this Act if a power of attorney is not being exercised so as to safeguard the welfare or property of the granter.

(6) It is not an objection to the validity of any contract or other transaction between a person acting or purporting to act as the representative of an adult and any other person that the person so acting or purporting to act was not entitled so to act under the law of a country other than the country where the contract or other transaction was concluded.

(7) Sub-paragraph (6) does not, however apply where the other person knew or ought to have known that the entitlement so to act of the person acting or purporting to act as representative was governed by the law of that other country.

(8) Sub-paragraph (6) applies only if the persons entering into the contract or other transaction were, when they did so, both (or all) in the same country.

5 Nothing in this schedule displaces any enactment or rule of law which has mandatory effect for the protection of an adult with incapacity in Scotland whatever law would otherwise be applicable.

6 Nothing in this schedule requires or enables the application in Scotland of any provision of the law of a country other than Scotland so as to produce a result which would be manifestly contrary to public policy.

7 Recognition and enforcement

(1) Any measure taken under the law of a country other than Scotland for the personal welfare or the protection of property of an adult with incapacity shall, if one of the conditions specified in sub-paragraph (2) is met, be recognised by the law of Scotland.

(2) These conditions are –
- (a) that the jurisdiction of the authority of the other country was based on the adult's habitual residence there;
- (b) that the United Kingdom and the other country were, when the measure was taken, parties to the Convention and the jurisdiction of the authority of the other country was based on a ground of jurisdiction provided for in the Convention.

(3) Recognition of a measure may, however, be refused –
- (a) if, except in a case of urgency –
  - (i) the authority which took it did so without the adult to whom it related being given an opportunity to be heard; and
  - (ii) these circumstances constituted a breach of natural justice;
- (b) if it would be manifestly contrary to public policy to recognise the measure;
- (c) if the measure conflicts with any enactment or rule of law of Scotland which is mandatory whatever law would otherwise be applicable;
- (d) if the measure is incompatible with a later measure taken in Scotland or recognised by the law of Scotland;

(e) if the measure would have the effect of placing the adult in an establishment in Scotland and –
   (i) the Scottish Central Authority has not previously been provided with a report on the adult and a statement of the reasons for the proposed placement and has not been consulted on the proposed placement; or
   (ii) where the Authority has been provided with such a report and statement and so consulted, it has, within a reasonable time thereafter, declared that it disapproves of the proposed placement.

8 (1) A measure which is enforceable in the country of origin and which is recognised under paragraph 7 by the law of Scotland may, in accordance with rules of court, be registered.

(2) A measure so registered shall be as enforceable as a measure having the like effect granted by a court in Scotland.

9 (1) For the purposes of recognition or enforcement of a measure taken outside Scotland in relation to an adult, findings of fact going to jurisdiction made by the authority taking the measure are conclusive of the facts found.

(2) The validity or merits of a measure falling to be recognised by the law of Scotland by virtue of this schedule shall not be questioned in any proceedings except for the purposes of ascertaining its compliance with any provision of this schedule.

10 (1) The Scottish Ministers may, by order, provide for the recognition and enforcement of orders made and other measures taken by authorities in any part of the United Kingdom other than Scotland.

(2) The provision so made shall accord no less recognition and secure that these orders and measures are no less enforceable than if they were measures which are recognised by the law of Scotland under paragraph 7.

11 Co-operation, avoidance of conflict of jurisdiction and compliance with the Convention

(1) Her Majesty may by Order in Council confer on the Scottish Central Authority, and the Scottish judicial and administrative authorities such powers, and impose on them such duties additional, in each case, to those which they have under this Act, as are necessary or expedient to enable them to give effect in Scotland to the Convention on and after the ratification date.

(2) An Order in Council under sub-paragraph (1) shall be subject to annulment in pursuance of a resolution of the Scottish Parliament.

(3) A certificate delivered in pursuance of Article 38 of the Convention by a designated authority of a Contracting State other than Scotland shall be proof of the matters stated in it unless the contrary is proved.

12 General

No provision of this schedule deriving from or giving effect to the Convention extends to any matter to which the Convention, by Article 4 thereof, does not apply.

13 Orders or regulations under this schedule shall be made by statutory instrument subject to annulment in pursuance of a resolution of the Scottish Parliament.

14 In this schedule –

'the Convention' means the Hague Convention of 13 January 2000 on the International Protection of Adults;

a 'measure for the personal welfare or protection of the property' of an adult with incapacity includes any order, direction or decision effecting or relating to –

   (a) the determination of the incapacity and the institution of appropriate measures of protection;

   (b) the placing of the adult under the protection of a judicial or administrative authority;

   (c) guardianship, curatorship or analogous institutions;

   (d) the appointment and functions of any person or body having charge of the adult's person or property or otherwise representing the adult;

   (e) the placement of the adult in an establishment or other place where the personal welfare of the adult is safeguarded;

   (f) the administration, conservation or disposal of the adult's property; or

   (g) the authorisation of a specific intervention for the personal welfare or protection of the property of the adult;

the 'ratification date' means the date when the Convention is ratified as respects Scotland;

the 'Scottish Central Authority' means –

   (a) an authority designated under Article 28 of the Convention for the purposes of acting as such; or

   (b) if no authority has been so designated any authority appointed by the Scottish Ministers for the purposes of carrying out the functions to be carried out under this schedule by the Scottish Central Authority;

the 'Scottish judicial and administrative authorities' means the courts having functions under this Act and the Public Guardian, the Mental Welfare Commission, local authorities and supervisory bodies.

Amendments—Adult Support and Protection (Scotland) Act 2007, s 77(1), Sch 1, para 5(g).

SCHEDULE 4
CONTINUATION OF EXISTING CURATORS, TUTORS, GUARDIANS AND ATTORNEYS UNDER THIS ACT

1 Curators and tutors

(1) On the relevant date, any person holding office as curator bonis to an adult shall become guardian of that adult with power to manage the property or financial affairs of the adult.

(2) Where a person –

   (a) before the relevant date, holds office as curator bonis to a person who has not attained the age of 16 years and does not hold such office for the sole reason that the person has not attained the age of 16 years; or

   (b) after the relevant date, is appointed as curator bonis to such a person, he shall become guardian of that person when that person attains the age of 16 years, with power to manage his property or financial affairs.

(3) Where any proceedings for the appointment of a curator bonis to an adult have been commenced and not determined before the relevant date, they shall be determined in accordance with the law as it was immediately before that date; and any person appointed curator bonis shall become guardian of that adult with power to manage the property or financial affairs of the adult.

(4) On the relevant date, any person holding office as tutor-dative to an adult shall become guardian of that adult and shall continue to have the powers conferred by the court on his appointment as tutor-dative.

(5) Where any proceedings for the appointment of a tutor-dative to an adult have been commenced and not determined before the relevant date, they shall be determined in accordance with the law as it was immediately before that date; and any person appointed tutor-dative shall become guardian of that adult with such power to manage the property, financial affairs or personal welfare of the adult as the court may determine.

(6) On the relevant date, any person holding office as tutor-at-law to an adult shall become guardian of that adult with power to manage the property, financial affairs or personal welfare of the adult.

(7) Where any proceedings for the appointment of a tutor-at-law to an adult have been commenced and not determined before the relevant date, they shall be determined in accordance with the law as it was immediately before that date; and any person appointed tutor-at-law shall become guardian of that adult with power to manage the property, financial affairs or personal welfare of the adult.

2 Guardians

(1) On the relevant date, any person holding office as guardian of an adult under the 1984 Act shall become guardian of that adult under this Act and shall continue to have the powers set out in paragraphs (a) to (c) of section 41(2) of that Act notwithstanding the repeal of that section by this Act.

(2) Where any proceedings for the appointment of such a guardian of an adult have been commenced and not determined before the relevant date, they shall be determined in accordance with the 1984 Act as it was in force immediately before that date; and any person appointed guardian shall become guardian of that adult under this Act with the powers set out in the said paragraphs (a) to (c) of section 41(2) of the 1984 Act.

3 Proceedings relating to existing appointments

Where any proceedings in relation to the functions of an existing curator bonis, tutor-dative, tutor-at-law or guardian have been commenced and not determined before the relevant date, they shall be determined in accordance with the law as it was immediately before that date.

4 Attorneys

(1) On the relevant date, any person holding office as –

(a) an attorney under a contract of mandate or agency with powers relating solely to the property or financial affairs of an adult shall become a continuing attorney under this Act;
(b) an attorney under a contract of mandate or agency with powers relating solely to the personal welfare of an adult shall become a welfare attorney under this Act;
(c) an attorney under a contract of mandate or agency with powers relating both to the property and financial affairs and to the personal welfare of an adult shall become a continuing attorney and a welfare attorney under this Act.

(2) Where, under the provisions of a contract of mandate or agency executed before the relevant date, a person is appointed as an attorney after that date he shall be a continuing attorney, a welfare attorney or a continuing and welfare attorney, as provided for in sub-paragraph (1), under this Act.

(3) Sections 6(2)(c)(i), 15, 19, 20(3)(a), 21, 22, and 23 shall not apply to persons who have become continuing attorneys by virtue of sub-paragraph (1)(a) or (c).

(4) Sections 16(1) to (4) and (7), 19, 20(3)(a), 21, 22, and 23 shall not apply to persons who have become welfare attorneys by virtue of sub-paragraph (1)(b) or (c).

5 Managers

(1) Any managers of a hospital who have received and hold money and valuables on behalf of any person under section 94 of the 1984 Act may continue to do so under this Act for a period not exceeding 3 years from the relevant date.

(2) This Act applies to managers as mentioned in sub-paragraph (1) notwithstanding that no certificate has been issued under section 37 in respect of the owner of the money or valuables.

(3) Sections 35 and 38 shall not apply in the case of managers who continue to hold money by virtue of sub-paragraph (1).

(4) Where the managers have authority from the Mental Welfare Commission to hold and manage money and other property in excess of the aggregate value mentioned in section 41 they may do so in relation to the money and valuables of any person which they continue to hold under sub-paragraph (1).

6 Application of Act to persons who become guardians by virtue of this schedule

(1) For the purposes of their application to persons who have become guardians by virtue of this schedule, the following provisions shall have effect as modified or disapplied by this paragraph.

(2) In section 67(2) the reference to the certificate of appointment issued under section 58 shall be construed as a reference to the order of the court appointing the person as curator bonis, tutor-dative, tutor-at-law or guardian under the 1984 Act, as the case may be.

(3) Section 60 shall apply to a person who has become a guardian to an adult by virtue of this schedule and who was a curator bonis, tutor dative or tutor-at-law to that adult; and, for the purpose of that application, for the reference in section 60(1) to a period in respect of which a guardianship order has been made or renewed there shall be substituted a reference –

(a) in the case of a curator bonis who, under paragraph 1(2), became guardian to a person on the person attaining the age of 16 years, to the period of 2 years from the later of the following dates –
   (i) the date on which section 60(17) (which amends this paragraph) of the Adult Support and Protection (Scotland) Act 2007 came into force;
   (ii) the date on which the person attained the age of 16 years,
(b) in any other case, to the period of 2 years from the date on which section 60(17) (which amends this paragraph) of the Adult Support and Protection (Scotland) Act 2007 came into force.

(3A) A person who has become a guardian to an adult by virtue of this schedule and who was a curator bonis, tutor dative or tutor-in-law to that adult shall cease to be authorised to act as that adult's guardian –

(a) where the person does not apply for renewal of guardianship within the 2 year period set by sub-paragraph (3), on the expiry of that period;
(b) where –
   (i) the person applies for such a renewal within that period; and
   (ii) the sheriff refuses the application,

on the date of refusal;

(c) where –
   (i) the person applies for such a renewal within that period; and
   (ii) the sheriff grants the application,

in accordance with the provisions of this Act.

(3B) Sub-paragraph (3A) does not prevent the authority of a guardian of the type mentioned in that sub-paragraph from being terminated (by virtue of the terms on which the guardian is authorised to act or sections 71, 73, 75 or 79A) earlier than the date on which it would otherwise terminate by operation of that sub-paragraph.

(3C) Where –

(a) a person ('G') who was a curator bonis, tutor dative or tutor-at-law to an adult becomes the adult's guardian by virtue of this schedule; and
(b) another person is appointed under section 62 as an additional guardian to the adult before G's appointment as guardian has been renewed in accordance with the provisions of this Act,

subsection (3A) applies in relation to the additional guardian as it applies in relation to G.

(3D) The Public Guardian must take reasonable steps to give notice of the effect of sub-paragraph (3A) to any person who –

(a) is a guardian to an adult by virtue of this schedule;
(b) was a curator bonis to that adult; and
(c) has not applied for renewal of guardianship.

(3E) A local authority must take reasonable steps to give notice of the effect of sub-paragraph (3A) to any person who –

(a) is a guardian to an adult residing within the local authority's area by virtue of this schedule;
(b) was a tutor dative or tutor-in-law to that adult; and
(c) has not applied for renewal of guardianship,

(4) Section 60 shall not apply to a person who has become a guardian to an adult by virtue of this schedule and who was a guardian of that adult under the 1984 Act, in which case the powers shall continue until such time as they would have continued had he not become a guardian by virtue of this schedule to this Act.

(5) In sections 68(2) and (3) and 76 the references to the chief social work officer of the local authority shall be construed as including references to the local authority.

(6) Schedule 2 shall apply only –
   (a) in a case where; and
   (b) to the extent that,

the Public Guardian has determined that it should apply.

(7) Any determination by the Public Guardian under sub-paragraph (6), or a decision by him not to make such a determination, may be appealed to the sheriff, whose decision shall be final.

(8) No reference in this Act to registration shall have effect in relation to any person who becomes a guardian by virtue of this schedule.

7 Transitional Provisions

Until Part 6 comes into force –
   (a) the references in section 23(1)(c) to a guardian shall be omitted;
   (b) in section 31(7), the reference in paragraph (a) to the appointment of a guardian shall be construed as a reference to the appointment of a curator bonis or tutor-dative or tutor-at-law with powers relating to the funds or accounts in question and paragraph (b) shall be omitted;
   (c) in section 34(1), the reference in paragraph (a) to a guardian shall be construed as a reference to a curator bonis or tutor-dative or tutor-at-law with powers relating to the funds or account in question and paragraph (b) shall be omitted;
   (d) in section 46(1), the reference in paragraph (a) to a guardian shall be construed as a reference to a curator bonis or tutor-dative or tutor-at-law with powers relating to the matter and paragraph (b) shall be omitted.

8 Interpretation

In this schedule the 'relevant date' in relation to any paragraph in which it appears means the date of coming into force of that paragraph.

Amendments—Adult Support and Protection (Scotland) Act 2007, ss 60(17), 77(1), Sch 1, para 5(h).

****

Note—Schedule 5 (Minor and consequential amendments) and Schedule 6 (Repeals) are not reproduced here.

Statutory Instruments

Act of Sederunt (Summary Applications, Statutory Applications and Appeals etc Rules) 1999, SI 1999/929

****

CHAPTER 3
RULES ON APPLICATIONS UNDER SPECIFIC STATUTES
****

Part XVI

Adults with Incapacity (Scotland) Act 2000

3.16.1 Interpretation

In this Part –

'the 2000 Act' means the Adults with Incapacity (Scotland) Act 2000;
'the 2003 Act' means the Mental Health (Care and Treatment) (Scotland) Act 2003;
'adult' means a person who is the subject of an application under the 2000 Act and –
  (a) has attained the age of 16 years; or
  (b) in relation to an application for a guardianship order, will attain the age of 16 years within 3 months of the date of the application;
'authorised establishment' has the meaning ascribed to it in section 35(2) of the 2000 Act;
'continuing attorney' means a person on whom there has been conferred a power of attorney granted under section 15(1) of the 2000 Act;
'guardianship order' means an order made under –
  (a) section 57(2)(c) or section 58(1A) of the Criminal Procedure (Scotland) Act 1995; or
  (b) section 58(4) of the 2000 Act;'incapable' has the meaning ascribed to it at section 1(6) of the 2000 Act, and 'incapacity' shall be construed accordingly;
'intervention order' means an order made under section 53(1) of the 2000 Act;
'local authority' has the meaning ascribed to it by section 87(1) of the 2000 Act;
'managers' has the meaning ascribed to it in paragraph 1 of Schedule 1 to the 2000 Act;
'Mental Welfare Commission' has the meaning ascribed to it by section 87(1) of the 2000 Act;
'named person' has the meaning ascribed to it by section 329 of the Mental Health (Care and Treatment) (Scotland) Act 2003;
'nearest relative' means, subject to section 87(2) of the 2000 Act, the person who would be, or would be exercising the functions of, the adult's nearest relative under sections 53 to 57 of the 1984 Act if the adult were a patient within the

meaning of that Act and notwithstanding that the person neither is or was caring for the adult for the purposes of section 53(3) of that Act;
'power of attorney' includes a factory and commission;
'primary carer' means the person or organisation primarily engaged in caring for an adult;
'Public Guardian' shall be construed in accordance with section 6 of the 2000 Act; and
'welfare attorney' means a person on whom there has been conferred a power of attorney granted under section 16(1) of the 2000 Act.

Amendments—Inserted by SSI 2001/142. Amended by SSI 2002/146; SSI 2005/445; SSI 2008/111.

3.16.2 Appointment of hearing

On an application or other proceedings being submitted under or in pursuance of the 2000 Act the sheriff shall –

(a) fix a hearing;
(b) order answers to be lodged (where he considers it appropriate to do so) within a period that he shall specify; and
(c) appoint service and intimation of the application or other proceedings.

Amendments—Inserted by SSI 2001/142.

3.16.3 Place, and privacy, of any hearing

The sheriff may, where he considers it appropriate in all the circumstances, appoint that the hearing of an application or other proceedings shall take place –

(a) in a hospital, or any other place than the court building;
(b) in private.

Amendments—Inserted by SSI 2001/142. Substituted by SSI 2004/197.

3.16.4 Service of application and renewal proceedings

(1) Service of the application or other proceedings and subsequent proceedings, including proceedings for renewal of guardianship orders, shall be made in Form 20 on –

(a) the adult;
(b) the nearest relative of the adult;
(c) the primary carer of the adult (if any);
(d) the named person of the adult (if any);
(e) any guardian, continuing attorney or welfare attorney of the adult who has any power relating to the application or proceedings;
(f) the Public Guardian;
(g) where appropriate, the Mental Welfare Commission;
(h) where appropriate, the local authority;
(i) where a guardianship order has been made under section 57(2)(c) or section 58(1A) of the Criminal Procedure (Scotland) Act 1995, to the Lord Advocate and, where the order was made by –
   (i) the High Court of Justiciary, to the Clerk of Justiciary; or

(ii) a sheriff, to the sheriff clerk of the Sheriff Court in which the order was made; and

(j) any other person directed by the sheriff.

(2) Where the applicant is an individual person without legal representation service shall be effected by the sheriff clerk.

(3) Where the adult is in an authorised establishment the person effecting service shall not serve Form 20 on the adult under paragraph (1)(a) but shall instead serve Forms 20 and 21, together with Form 22, on the managers of that authorised establishment by –

(a) first class recorded delivery post; or
(b) personal service by a sheriff officer.

(4) On receipt of Forms 20 and 21 in terms of paragraph (3) the managers of the authorised establishment shall, subject to rule 3.16.5 –

(a) immediately deliver the notice in Form 20 to the adult; and
(b) as soon as practicable thereafter, and in any event before the date of the hearing specified in Form 20, complete and return to the sheriff clerk a certificate of such delivery in Form 22.

(5) Where the application or other proceeding follows on a remit under rule 3.16.9 the order for service of the application shall include an order for service on the Public Guardian or other party concerned.

(6) Where the application is for an intervention order or a guardianship order, copies of the reports lodged in accordance with section 57(3) of the 2000 Act (reports to be lodged in court along with application) shall be served along with Form 20, or Forms 20, 21 and 22 as the case may be.

Amendments—Inserted by SSI 2001/142. Amended by SSI 2002/146; SSI 2008/111; SSI 2013/171.

3.16.5 Dispensing with service on adult

(1) Where, in relation to any application or proceeding under or in pursuance of the 2000 Act, two medical certificates are produced stating that intimation of the application or other proceeding, or notification of any interlocutor relating to such application or other proceeding, would be likely to pose a serious risk to the health of the adult the sheriff may dispense with such intimation or notification.

(2) Any medical certificates produced under paragraph (1) shall be prepared by medical practitioners independent of each other.

(3) In any case where the incapacity of the adult is by reason of mental disorder, one of the two medical practitioners must be a medical practitioner approved for the purposes of section 22(4) of the 2003 Act as having special experience in the diagnosis or treatment of mental disorder.

Amendments—Inserted by SSI 2001/142. Amended by SSI 2005/445.

3.16.6 Hearing

(1) A hearing to determine any application or other proceeding shall take place within 28 days of the interlocutor fixing the hearing under rule 3.16.2 unless any person upon whom the application is to be served is outside Europe.

(2) At the hearing referred to in paragraph (1) the sheriff may determine the application or other proceeding or may order such further procedure as he thinks fit.

Amendments—Inserted by SSI 2001/142. Amended by SSI 2002/146;

3.16.7 Prescribed forms of application

(1) An application submitted to the sheriff under or in pursuance of the 2000 Act, other than an appeal or remitted matter, shall be in Form 23.

(2) An appeal to the sheriff under or in pursuance of the 2000 Act shall be in Form 24.

Amendments—Inserted by SSI 2001/142.

3.16.8 Subsequent applications

(1) Unless otherwise prescribed in this Part or under the 2000 Act, any application or proceedings subsequent to an initial application or proceeding considered by the sheriff, including an application to renew an existing order, shall take the form of a minute lodged in the process.

(1ZA) Where a guardianship order has been made under section 57(2)(c) or section 58(1A) of the Criminal Procedure (Scotland) Act 1995, an application to renew it shall be made –

    (a) on the first such application, in Form 23;
    (b) on any subsequent application, in the form of a minute lodged in the process.

(1A) Except where the sheriff otherwise directs, any minute lodged under this rule shall be lodged in accordance with, and regulated by, Chapter 14 of the Ordinary Cause Rules.

(2) Where any subsequent application or proceedings under paragraph (1) above are made to a court in another sheriffdom the sheriff clerk shall transmit the court process to the court dealing with the current application or proceeding.

(3) Transmission of the process in terms of paragraph (2) shall be made within 4 days of it being requested by the sheriff clerk of the court in which the current application or proceedings have been raised.

(4) Where the application is for renewal of a guardianship order, a copy of any report lodged under section 60 of the 2000 Act shall be served along with the minute.

Amendments—Inserted by SSI 2001/142. Amended by SSI 2002/146; SSI 2008/111; SSI 2013/171.

3.16.9 Remit of applications by the Public Guardian etc.

Where an application is remitted to the sheriff by the Public Guardian or by any other party authorised to do so under the 2000 Act the party remitting the application shall, within 4 days of the decision to remit, transmit the papers relating to the application to the sheriff clerk of the court where the application is to be considered.

Amendments—Inserted by SSI 2001/142.

3.16.10 Caution and Other Security

(1) Where the sheriff requires a person authorised under an intervention order or any variation of an intervention order, or appointed as a guardian, to find caution he shall specify the amount and period within which caution is to be found in the interlocutor authorising or appointing the person or varying the order (as the case may be).

(1A) The amount of caution specified by the sheriff in paragraph (1) may be calculated and expressed as a percentage of the value of the adult's estate.

(2) The sheriff may, on application made by motion before the expiry of the period for finding caution and on cause shown, allow further time for finding caution in accordance with paragraph (1).

(3) Caution shall be lodged with the Public Guardian.

(4) Where caution has been lodged to the satisfaction of the Public Guardian he shall notify the sheriff clerk.

(5) The sheriff may at any time while a requirement to find caution is in force –

    (a) increase the amount of, or require the person to find new, caution; or
    (b) authorise the amount of caution to be decreased.

(6) Where the sheriff requires the person referred to in paragraph (1) to give security other than caution, the rules of Chapter 27 of the Ordinary Cause Rules shall apply with the necessary modifications.

Amendments—Inserted by SSI 2002/146. Amended by SSI 2008/111.

3.16.11 Appointment of interim guardian

An application under section 57(5) of the 2000 Act (appointment of interim guardian) may be made in the crave of the application for a guardianship order to which it relates or, if made after the submission of the application for a guardianship order, by motion in the process of that application.

Amendments—Inserted by SSI 2002/146.

3.16.12 Registration of intervention order or guardianship order relating to heritable property

Where an application for an intervention order or a guardianship order seeks to vest in the person authorised under the order, or the guardian, as the case may be, any right to deal with, convey or manage any interest in heritable property which is recorded or capable of being recorded in the General Register of Sasines or is registered or capable of being registered in the Land Register of Scotland, the applicant must specify the necessary details of the property in the application to enable it to be identified in the Register of Sasines or the Land Register of Scotland, as the case may be.

Amendments—Inserted by SSI 2002/146.

3.16.13 Non-compliance with decisions of guardians with welfare powers

(1) Where the court is required under section 70(3) of the 2000 Act to intimate an application for an order or warrant in relation to non-compliance with the decision of a guardian with welfare powers, the sheriff clerk shall effect intimation in Form 20 in accordance with paragraphs (2) and (3).

(2) Intimation shall be effected –

    (a) where the person is within Scotland, by first class recorded delivery post, or, in the event that intimation by first class recorded delivery post is unsuccessful, by personal service by a sheriff officer; or

    (b) where the person is furth of Scotland, in accordance with rule 2.12 (service on persons furth of Scotland).

(3) Such intimation shall include notice of the period within which any objection to the application shall be lodged.

Amendments—Inserted by SSI 2002/146.

****

Part XXIV
International Protection of Adults

3.24.1 Interpretation

In this Part –

    'the Act' means the Adults with Incapacity (Scotland) Act 2000;

    'the Convention' means the Hague Convention of 13 January 2000 on the International Protection of Adults;

    'international measure' means any measure taken under the law of a country other than Scotland for the personal welfare, or the protection of property, of an adult with incapacity, where –

        (a) jurisdiction in the other country was based on the adult's habitual residence there; or

        (b) the other country and the United Kingdom were when that measure was taken parties to the Convention, and jurisdiction in that other country was based on a ground of jurisdiction in the Convention; and

    'Public Guardian' shall be construed in accordance with section 6 (the public guardian and his functions) of the Act.

Amendments—Inserted by SI 2003/556.

3.24.2 Application

(1) An application to register an international measure under paragraph 8(1) of schedule 3 to the Act shall be by summary application made under this Part.

(2) The original document making the international measure, or a copy of that document duly certified as such by an officer of the issuing or a requesting body, shall be lodged with an application under paragraph (1), together with (as necessary) an English translation of that document and that certificate.

(3) Any translation under paragraph (2) must be certified as a correct translation by the person making it, and the certificate must contain the full name, address and qualifications of the translator.

Amendments—Inserted by SI 2003/556.

3.24.3 Intimation of application

(1) The sheriff shall order intimation of an application to register an international measure –

    (a) except where the sheriff is satisfied that the person to whom the international measure relates had an opportunity to be heard in the country where that measure was taken, to that person;
    (b) which if registered would have the effect of placing the adult to whom the international measure relates in an establishment in Scotland, to the –
        (i) Scottish Central Authority; and
        (ii) Mental Welfare Commission;
    (c) to the Public Guardian; and
    (d) to any other person whom the sheriff considers appropriate.

(2) In this rule –

    (a) 'Scottish Central Authority' means an authority –
        (i) designated under Article 28 of the Convention for the purposes of acting as such; or
        (ii) appointed by the Scottish Ministers for the purposes of carrying out the functions to be carried out under schedule 3 of the Act by the Scottish Central Authority, where no authority is designated for the purposes of sub paragraph (i); and
    (b) 'Mental Welfare Commission' means the Mental Welfare Commission for Scotland continued in being by section 4 of the Mental Health (Care and Treatment) (Scotland) Act 2003.

Amendments—Inserted by SI 2003/556. Amended by SSI 2005/445.

3.24.4 Notice to the Public Guardian

The sheriff clerk shall within 7 days after the date of an order registering an international measure, provide the Public Guardian with –

    (a) a copy of that order; and
    (b) a copy of the international measure, and of any translation.

Amendments—Inserted by SI 2003/556.

3.24.5 Register of recognised foreign measures

(1) There shall be a register of international measures ('the register') registered by order under this Part.

(2) The register shall include –

    (a) the nature of the international measure;
    (b) the date of the international measure;

(c) the date of the order under this Part granting recognition of the international measure;
(d) the name and address of –
  (i) the person who applied for recognition of the international measure under this Part;
  (ii) the person in respect of whom the international measure was taken; and
  (iii) if applicable, the person on whom any power is conferred by the international measure; and
(e) a copy of the international measure, and of any translation.

(3) The Public Guardian shall maintain the register, and make it available during normal office hours for inspection by members of the public.

(4) The Public Guardian shall if requested by any person certify that an international measure registered under this Part has been entered in the register.

Amendments—Inserted by SI 2003/556.

****

Guidance

Guidance on Continuing and Welfare Powers of Attorney

Introduction

1 This guidance applies whenever a solicitor is consulted or instructed with a view to preparing and/or certifying a continuing or welfare Power of Attorney under the Adults with Incapacity (Scotland) Act 2000 ('2000 Act'). 'POA' refers to such a Power of Attorney. 'Rule' and 'Rules' refer to the Law Society of Scotland Practice Rules 2011. 'Must' refers to a binding obligation under statute, regulations, Rules or the like. 'Should' refers to good practice: failure to comply may be taken into account in disciplinary or other proceedings. Where a solicitor considers that particular circumstances justify departure from this guidance, a written record of those circumstances and the reasons for the departure should be kept. 'Client' includes a prospective client.

2 This guidance should be read in conjunction with, and subject to, the Society's vulnerable clients guidance. Both this guidance and the vulnerable clients guidance have been issued following publication of a report by the Mental Welfare Commission for Scotland ('MWC') on 'An investigation into the response by statutory services and professionals to concerns raised in respect of Mr and Mrs D' (published 13 February 2012) ('the D Report').

Solicitors to whom this guidance applies should read at least the Summary to the D Report. The D Report includes a recommendation that the Law Society of Scotland should:

'Update existing guidance for solicitors in respect of Powers of Attorney to take account of the changes in the AWI Act. Such guidance should address situations where the process of granting a Power of Attorney is initiated by a party other than the granter, as well as situations where there may be some question as to the granter's capacity, the presence of undue influence, or other vitiating factors. Guidance should also emphasise the different ethical considerations involved for the granter in delegating welfare as opposed to financial powers.'

The Society accepted that recommendation and is grateful to MWC for assisting in the preparation of this guidance, which relates specifically to continuing and welfare POA's granted under the 2000 Act.

Note—The Vulnerable Clients Guidance is set out below. The D Report is available at www.mwcscot.org.uk/media/56140/powers_of_attorney_and_their_safeguards.pdf

3 This guidance supersedes the Law Society guidelines on Powers of Attorney [July 1998]; apart from which it should be read subject to the terms of relevant Rules and guidance published by the Society thereon. It is not the purpose of guidance to state or interpret the law, and it should not be read as seeking to do so.

Taking instructions

4 It may be appropriate to defer accepting engagement, or taking anyone's instructions, until capacity to grant the POA has been established, and in the event of incapacity it may be appropriate to accept instructions from the initiator to apply for guardianship or to initiate other measures, provided that there is no conflict of interest in doing so.

5 Solicitors should discuss with the client and assess whether a POA is appropriate in the particular case, compared with other available techniques. Both the benefits of POA's and also the risks, including the risk that the attorney could misuse the power, should be explained. The lesser official supervision of attorneys, compared with guardians, should be explained. The distinction between property and financial powers, on the one hand, and welfare powers, on the other, should be explained, and express instructions taken as to whether the granter wishes to confer both categories of powers. It should be explained that a POA, particularly if it includes welfare powers, can be a very powerful document. Within both categories of powers, the solicitor should ascertain whether the granter wishes to confer plenary powers, and further specific powers without prejudice to the plenary powers, or alternatively specific powers only.

6 Where relevant, the solicitor should explain powers which by law are excluded, require to be express, or are conferred by statute; and that it may be best to state expressly any powers which the granter wishes to exclude.

7 The solicitor should take express instructions as to any powers of compulsion or restraint, and should explain both the possible need and the particular risks of conferring such powers. Where the granter proposes to confer powers which could result in a deprivation of liberty in terms of Article 5 of the European Convention on Human Rights, the solicitor should explain the current position and any legal developments.

8 Matters on which the solicitor should normally advise and take instructions include:

- Continuing or welfare powers, or both?
- Single or joint attorneys?
- Substitute or substitutes? The relative merits of larger joint appointments,

or substitution arrangements, should be explained, and clear instructions should be taken as to when and in what order substitutions should take place.
- In the case of continuing powers, should they come into force immediately, or upon request, and/or upon reasonable belief or certification?
- In the case of welfare powers, should they come into force upon reasonable belief or certification?
- Should there be different trigger provisions for first attorneys and substitute attorneys (for example, reasonable belief in the case of a spouse who is first attorney but certification in the case of a child or children as substitute(s))?
- Powers? See paragraphs 6–7above.
- Are the proposed attorney(s) and any proposed substitute(s) willing to act?
- Should there be a requirement to consult specified persons in the exercise of some or all powers?
- Should a record of wishes and feelings be included in the document, or in a separate document?
- Should the POA be linked to an Advance Directive?
- Where the attorney is a spouse or civil partner, should section 24 of the 2000 Act be excluded?
- Should provisions regarding choice of applicable law be included (see 2000 Act, Schedule 3, para 4)?
- Should the effects of bankruptcy be taken into account (see 2000 Act, sections 15(5) and 16(7))?
- Should registration be deferred (see 2000 Act, section 19(3)), and if so what should be the trigger for registration?
- To whom should copies of the POA document be sent by the Office of the Public Guardian following registration (see 2000 Act, section 19(5)(b))?
- Should anyone else be notified?

Certification

9 Continuing and welfare POA's cannot be operated unless registered, and cannot be registered unless certified. Practising solicitors may act as certifiers. They should consult as to capacity and name the person whom they have consulted, in accordance with the relevant provisions of statute and of the prescribed form of certificate, unless confident from their own knowledge of the granter that the granter has relevant capacity. Where the solicitor as certifier has significant cause for doubt as to capacity, it is recommended that paragraph 9 of the vulnerable clients guidance be followed, and that guidance would normally be sought from a medical practitioner or clinical psychologist. Where the solicitor as certifier has formed a clear view as to capacity or incapacity, and seeks corroboration of that view, it may be appropriate to seek the views of another professional, such as a nurse or social worker. Exceptionally, the views of a lay person may be sought. However it is not good practice to consult a proposed attorney for purposes of certification, and in the D Report MWC recommended that consideration be given to amending the 2000 Act to exclude reference to a proposed attorney for this purpose.

10 Solicitors as prospective certifiers should satisfy themselves as to capacity before taking instructions and preparing the document, though should be alert to the possibility that capacity may have altered between taking instructions and time of execution.

11 Solicitors should take particular care if asked to act as certifier when they themselves have not taken instructions and prepared the document. In that situation

they may require to proceed in the same manner as if they were taking instructions to prepare the document. Likewise, they should not without good reason ask someone else to certify execution of a document which they have prepared. If the proposed certifier is not a practising solicitor, they may require to ensure that the certifier understands the requirements for capacity and the meaning in law of undue influence and of other vitiating factors. As noted in paragraph 10 above, the certifier must not simply rely upon any presumption of capacity.

12 Neither the 2000 Act nor the prescribed form of certificate provides for consultation as to undue influence or other vitiating factors. The solicitor as certifier shall nevertheless consider whether it is appropriate or necessary to make enquiries or consult upon those elements. The prescribed wording 'I have no reason to believe …' should be applied by reference to the standards of a solicitor competent to act in relation to continuing and welfare POA's (see paragraph 11 of the vulnerable clients guidance) acting as a careful and conscientious professional.

13 Notwithstanding any consultation in the matter of capacity or otherwise, the solicitor as certifier retains responsibility for the certificate issued by that solicitor.

Who is my client?

14 The granter of a Power of Attorney, is the solicitor's client. All relevant Rules should be complied with in relation to that client – including Rule B 4.2 (providing written intimation in accordance with that Rule 'when tendering for business or at the earliest practicable opportunity upon receiving instructions'); Rule B 6.23.1 (compliance with Money Laundering Regulations); Rule B 1.4.1 (acting in the best interests of your client); Rule B 1.9.1 (communicating effectively with your clients and others); Rule B 1.10 (only acting in those matters where you are competent to do so); and Rule B 1.15.1 (not unlawfully discriminating in your professional dealings with other lawyers, clients, employees and others). Of particular importance in the context of vulnerable clients are Rule B 1.5.1: 'You are the agent of your client and must have the authority of your client for your actings…'; Rule B 1.7.1, under which solicitors must not act where there is a conflict of interest; and Rule B 1.7.2, under which solicitors must exercise caution where there is a potential conflict of interest and, if the potential for conflict is significant, not act for both parties without the full knowledge and express consent of the clients. If there is doubt as to the capacity to instruct, that should be resolved before accepting engagement of a new client, or before accepting instructions from an existing client.

15 Where a solicitor issues any document for signature to a party or prospective party 'to a transaction of any kind' the solicitor should consider Rule B 2.1.7. 'Issue' means issuing in any way, including giving the document to the client or other third party to take to the proposed signatory. In the case of continuing and/or welfare Powers of Attorney, these should only be prepared by a solicitor acting for the granter.

16 Proposed appointees under the Adults with Incapacity (Scotland) Act 2000 should be referred to relevant Codes of Practice and other material available on the Public Guardian's website, as may be appropriate.

Revocation

17 The foregoing guidance on taking instructions in relation to continuing and welfare POA's should so far as relevant be followed when taking instructions to

revoke such a POA. Particular care should be taken to identify vulnerability which may have arisen or developed since time of granting. The same guidance in relation to certification should be followed.

18 Solicitors instructed in relation to the Revocation of a POA must also consider upon whom intimation of any Revocation is made. This should include intimation upon any attorney who has accepted appointment and is acting as such. An attorney is party to a contract of mandate and therfore, the granter (and by extension, any solicitor instructed by the granter), seeking to revoke a POA, would require to give notice of termination of the contract to the attorney. A Revocation Notice must also be certified and sent to the Public Guardian. It is questionable whether a Revocation Notice can be properly certified if the contract of mandate has not been first terminated by notice to the attorney. Good practice would suggest that where an attorney has been appointed, and appropriate instructions to revoke appointment are implemented, the attorney should be given notice of the termination prior to certification of a Revocation Notice and transmission of the same to the Public Guardian.

Vulnerable Clients Guidance

Introduction

1 This guidance applies whenever a client or prospective client of whatever age may lack full capacity, whether having attained the legal age of capacity or not, to instruct a solicitor, or to instruct and validly carry through the contemplated act or transaction, or may be subject to undue influence or other factors which might vitiate that act or transaction. Such a client or prospective client is termed a 'vulnerable client'. 'Vulnerable' is used as a convenient comprehensive term, not limited to any definition of that term for any other purpose. 'Vulnerability' is used accordingly. 'Client' includes a prospective client. 'Other vitiating factors' include facility and circumvention; force, fear or fraud; and misrepresentation. 'Initiator' refers to a person other than the client who initiates any proposed engagement, instructions or process to which it is contemplated that the client will be a party. 'Appointee' means someone to be appointed in a fiduciary role, such as an attorney, executor or trustee. 'Donee' means someone likely to benefit personally.

2 'Rule' and 'Rules' refer to the Law Society of Scotland Practice Rules 2011. 'Must' refers to a binding obligation under statute, regulations, Rules or the like. 'Should' refers to good practice: failure to comply may be taken into account in disciplinary or other proceedings. Where a solicitor considers that particular circumstances justify departure from this guidance, a written record of those circumstances and the reasons for the departure should be kept.

Note—The Law Society of Scotland Practice Rules 2011 are available at www.lawscot.org.uk/rules-and-guidance/table-of-contents.

3 Both this guidance and the 'Guidance on Continuing and Welfare Powers of Attorney' ('the POA guidance') were issued following publication of reports from other stakeholders and consultations that raised issues regarding vulnerability. Vulnerability may be relevant to any contemplated act or transaction about which a solicitor may be consulted or instructed. This guidance seeks to address vulnerability generally.

Note—The Guidance on Continuing and Welfare Powers of Attorney is set out above.

4 This guidance should be read subject to the terms of relevant Rules and guidance published by the Society thereon. It is not the purpose of guidance to state or interpret the law, and it should not be read as seeking to do so: this guidance assumes compliance with Rule B 1.10 – see paragraph 11 below.

Capacity and incapacity

5 Solicitors should balance the positive obligation to facilitate valid and competent acts and transactions against the negative obligation to avoid purported acts or transactions which are incompetent, void or voidable.

6 Solicitors should as far as reasonably practicable assist vulnerable clients to express their wishes, understand relevant advice, give valid instructions, and carry through valid acts and transactions. Where appropriate, solicitors should take advice as to optimum place, time and other arrangements for advising and taking instructions. A person confused by a lengthy or complex document, or unable to sustain the concentration necessary to understand it, may nevertheless be able to understand (and if so desired, validly execute) a simple and straightforward document which is nevertheless adequate for its intended purpose. Under Rule B 1.9.1 solicitors must communicate effectively with their clients; therefore if a client is capable of understanding, a solicitor must communicate by whatever means is necessary to enable the client to understand. Assistance with communication is addressed in paragraph 15 below.

7 The definition of incapacity in the Adults with Incapacity (Scotland) Act 2000 ('2000 Act') applies for the purposes of that Act, but it may reasonably be referred to for guidance in determining capacity for other purposes. Note that the definition includes 'incapable of acting', which may include acting to resist undue influence or other vitiating factors, or acting so as to adhere to and implement otherwise valid decisions, or to maintain consistency.

8 A solicitor may, and in some circumstances should, seek and carefully consider expert guidance. However the solicitor retains responsibility for compliance with all relevant Rules and should not abdicate responsibility to the expert. Solicitors should not simply rely upon the legal presumption of capacity. On the contrary, they 'must … be satisfied when taking instructions, that his or her client has the capacity to give instructions in relation to that matter' (guidance related to Rule B 1.5).

9 In cases of doubt as to the extent to which, and circumstances in which, capacity can be exercised, or conversely as to the extent to which incapacity prevents a contemplated act or transaction, the advice of a medical practitioner or clinical psychologist should be sought. It may be necessary to approach someone with particular specialist expertise. The solicitor should not seek a generalised and simplistic verdict of 'capable' or 'incapable'. The solicitor should explain the act or transaction contemplated and the legal requirements for it to be valid. The solicitor should explain any indications of relevant capacity or incapacity of which the solicitor is aware, and any steps which the solicitor proposes in order to facilitate exercise of capacity.

Vulnerability generally

10 The possibility of vulnerability should be considered whenever a solicitor is consulted or instructed in any matter. Often the solicitor will be able to decide quickly and confidently that there is no question of vulnerability; but solicitors should always be alert to any indications of possible vulnerability.

11 A solicitor 'must only act in those matters where you are competent to do so' (Rule B 1.10). However solicitors must not discriminate contrary to Rule B 1.15.1. They may accordingly require to refer to another solicitor whose particular skills are required in determining capacity, identifying vulnerability, or in advising and acting for a particular client (including the requirement to communicate effectively – see paragraph 6 above).

12 Indications of possible vulnerability may arise from the normal process of ascertaining a client's wishes and intentions, exploring circumstances, and advising as to merits, risks, advantages and disadvantages of a proposed act or transaction, or of alternatives. However, on the one hand an apparently unwise act or transaction may represent a client's valid and competent choice; while conversely an apparently wise act or transaction could be invalid through lack of relevant capacity, or undue influence, or other vitiating factors.

Influence and undue influence

13 Influence, even powerful influence, is not necessarily undue influence. A client may attend to make a Will or grant a Power of Attorney only because someone has strongly influenced them that they ought to do so. Influence may be powerful but benign. Or it may be subtle, but undue. Influence to make a Will, but not as to who should benefit or who should be appointed executor, or to grant a Power of Attorney, but not as to whom to appoint, is unlikely to be undue. If however (in those examples) influence seeks to affect choice of beneficiaries, executor(s) or attorney(s), it is likely to be undue, particularly where the influencer or someone connected to the influencer so benefits, though the extent of realistic (or sensible) choice in the matter may also be relevant. The solicitor should use reasonable endeavours to ascertain such matters from the client.

14 While a solicitor must not act in accordance with purported instructions which the client does not have capacity to give validly, there is no equivalent direct prohibition where the solicitor detects undue influence or other vitiating factors. Where a solicitor believes that a purported act or transaction will be voidable on grounds of undue influence or other vitiating factors, the solicitor may decline to act in accordance with such instructions, but is not bound to do so unless the solicitor reasonably considers that to facilitate the act or transaction would put the solicitor in breach of the requirement of Rule B 1.4.1 to act in the best interests of the client. If the solicitor declines, the solicitor should explain the reasons. If the solicitor acts, the solicitor should warn the client that the purported act or transaction may be voidable and (if such be the case) may prove to be contrary to the client's interests. The solicitor should also obtain the client's authorisation to disclose such advice and the reasons for it, should the validity of the act or transaction be put in issue following impairment of capacity or death of the client.

15 A dominated client may deny or conceal undue influence. Where there is a possibility of vulnerability, the client should be seen alone except where the client reasonably prefers someone to give support, or to assist communication, in which case such third party should if at all possible be neutral in relation to the matter in hand. Undue influence can be exercised regardless of presence, though the effect may be greater if the influencer is present, or present elsewhere in the building, or is the initiator, or brings the client and then leaves.

16 A client who is subject to two different spheres of influence may express different, or even contradictory, wishes or make contradictory purported decisions when the client perceives himself (or herself) to be within each of those spheres of influence. This is a clear indication of incapacity to resist influence. However, while

inability to resist influence may indicate incapacity, the concepts of undue influence and other vitiating factors are of course not dependent upon incapacity and may apply in cases where capacity is not impaired.

Who is my client?

17 The granter of a Power of Attorney, Will, guarantee, a document (including a Deed of Trust) incorporating a gift, or other document is the solicitor's client. All relevant Rules should be complied with in relation to that client – including Rule B 4.2 (providing written intimation in accordance with that Rule 'when tendering for business or at the earliest practicable opportunity upon receiving instructions'); Rule B 6.23.1 (compliance with Money Laundering Regulations); and Rules B 1.4.1, 1.9.1, 1.10 and 1.15.1 (all referred to above). Of particular importance in the context of vulnerable clients are Rule B 1.5.1: 'You are the agent of your client and must have the authority of your client for your actings ...'; Rule B 1.7.1, under which solicitors must not act where there is a conflict of interest; and Rule B 1.7.2, under which solicitors must exercise caution where there is a potential conflict of interest and, if the potential for conflict is significant, not act for both parties without the full knowledge and express consent of the clients. If there is doubt as to capacity to instruct, that should be resolved before accepting engagement if a new client, or before accepting instructions from an existing client.

18 Where a solicitor issues any document for signature to a party or prospective party 'to a transaction of any kind' the solicitor should consider Rule B 2.1.7. 'Issue' means issuing in any way, including giving the document to the client or other third party to take to the proposed signatory. In the case of continuing and/or welfare Powers of Attorney, Wills and gratuitous documents, these should only be prepared by a solicitor acting for the granter or donor. A solicitor may occasionally prepare a Power of Attorney for commercial purposes, which is not a continuing or welfare Power of Attorney, or include such power in a longer document, when not acting for the proposed granter. Even in that situation, the solicitor should carefully consider whether he or she can properly proceed if the proposed granter is not separately represented. In any event, the solicitor should consider Rule B 2.1.7. Similar considerations may apply in relation to other documents, such as guarantees.

19 Proposed appointees under the Adults with Incapacity (Scotland) Act 2000 should be referred to relevant Codes of Practice and other material available on the Public Guardian's website, as may be appropriate.

Indicators

20 The following possible situations and indicators are offered as examples, not as a comprehensive list.

Some categories of situations

The situations are described simplistically in that they are stated as applying with certainty, whereas in practice they will present with varying degrees of probability.

Type A: Capable client making own independent decisions, has justified faith in competence and trustworthiness of proposed appointee. (Capacity and no undue influence)

Type B: Client dominated by proposed appointee, nevertheless capable and proposed appointee competent and motivated to act properly. (Capacity and influence, influence not undue or malign)

Type C: Client capable and not subject to undue influence, but instructions seem unwise. (The solicitor's role is to advise, perhaps in strong terms, but in this situation there are no grounds for refusing to act. It is wise to record concerns, advice given, and reasons for acting. See also paragraph 12 above)

Type D: Client of limited but sufficient capacity, vulnerable to undue influence but not in fact unduly influenced. (The solicitor must respect and if necessary support the client's capacity, without discrimination on grounds of the client's disability)

Type E: Client subject to influence which is undue and malign, not benign, and unable to resist it through incapacity or facility or the dominance of the influencer(s). (Regardless of level of capacity to consult and instruct, the solicitor will not be able to implement instructions)

Type F: Presents as any of types A–D, but there is in fact undue and malign influence which may be covert or deliberately concealed (including by the person influenced)

Type G: Client aged 15 years wishes separate legal advice about a matter that concerns them; client dominated by parents, nevertheless capable and parents competent and motivated to act properly. (Capacity and influence, influence not undue or malign)

Type H: Client aged 13 years wishes to appeal detention to the Mental Health Tribunal for Scotland; supported by independent advocacy worker to contact solicitor, which worker is present during the meeting with the client and speaks regularly for the client. Client of limited but sufficient capacity, vulnerable to undue influence but not unduly influenced. (The solicitor must respect and if necessary support the client's capacity, without discrimination on grounds of the client's mental disorder. Care needed to ensure the instructions are clear)

Difficulty: Strong influence is not necessarily undue influence (see paragraph 13 above). It may be necessary to try to assess the motives and intentions of an influencer (or influencers) whom the solicitor may not even have met.

Who has approached the solicitor ('initiator')?

- Client who is well known? Be alert to possible changes in capacity, vulnerability
- A new client? Be alert to possible incapacity or vulnerability
- Neutral person on behalf of the client? Be careful – see below if there is possible significant influence
- Proposed appointee or donee on behalf of the client? Be very careful – (but this could still be a type A or B, or even D, situation)
- Initiator reluctant to 'stay completely out of the way' when instructions are taken? Be very careful
- Initiator resistant to possibility of joint appointment or additional donees? Be very careful

Other possible indicators

- Any references to family disunity? Be very careful
- Initiator a dominant personality? Be very careful
- Client appears to be very influenced by initiator? Be very careful, and if initiator is proposed appointee or donee – danger sign!
- Client 'doesn't want to upset' proposed appointee or donee? Danger sign!
- Client 'doesn't want to upset' family or others? Be very careful

– Proposed appointee or donee seems largely motivated by need to mitigate tax, avoid means-testing? Danger sign!

Possibility of some form of 'mental disorder' (broadly defined)? Investigate

Diagnosis or information that there is some degree of 'mental disorder'? Enquire, take great care, but the solicitor has a duty to help clients exercise such capacity and autonomy as they can. Consider simple form of document.

Illiteracy, communication difficulties, sensory impairments, other physical issues, frailty? The solicitor's approach needs to be supportive, facilitative, well-informed and careful.

PART XI

International Conventions and Recommendations

PART XI

International Conventions and Recommendations

PART XI: International Conventions and Recommendations

Contents

Hague Convention on the International Protection of Adults	2449
UN Convention on the Rights of Persons with Disabilities	2463
Council of Europe Committee of Ministers Recommendation No R (99) 4 of the Committee of Ministers to Member States on Principles Concerning the Legal Protection of Incapable Adults – Explanatory memorandum	2486
Council of Europe Committee of Ministers Recommendation No R (99) 4[1] of the Committee of Ministers to Member States on Principles Concerning the Legal Protection of Incapable Adults	2507
Recommendation CM/REC(2009)11 of the Committee of Ministers to Member States on Principles Concerning Continuing Powers of Attorney and Advance Directives for Incapacity and its Explanatory Memorandum	2515

Hague Convention on the International Protection of Adults

(Concluded 13 January 2000)

The States signatory to the present Convention,

Considering the need to provide for the protection in international situations of adults who, by reason of an impairment or insufficiency of their personal faculties, are not in a position to protect their interests,

Wishing to avoid conflicts between their legal systems in respect of jurisdiction, applicable law, recognition and enforcement of measures for the protection of adults,

Recalling the importance of international co-operation for the protection of adults,

Affirming that the interests of the adult and respect for his or her dignity and autonomy are to be primary considerations,

Have agreed on the following provisions –

CHAPTER I – SCOPE OF THE CONVENTION

Article 1

(1) This Convention applies to the protection in international situations of adults who, by reason of an impairment or insufficiency of their personal faculties, are not in a position to protect their interests.

(2) Its objects are –

    (a) to determine the State whose authorities have jurisdiction to take measures directed to the protection of the person or property of the adult;
    (b) to determine which law is to be applied by such authorities in exercising their jurisdiction;
    (c) to determine the law applicable to representation of the adult;
    (d) to provide for the recognition and enforcement of such measures of protection in all Contracting States;
    (e) to establish such co-operation between the authorities of the Contracting States as may be necessary in order to achieve the purposes of this Convention.

Article 2

(1) For the purposes of this Convention, an adult is a person who has reached the age of 18 years.

(2) The Convention applies also to measures in respect of an adult who had not reached the age of 18 years at the time the measures were taken.

Article 3

The measures referred to in Article 1 may deal in particular with –

    (a) the determination of incapacity and the institution of a protective regime;
    (b) the placing of the adult under the protection of a judicial or administrative authority;

(c) guardianship, curatorship and analogous institutions;
(d) the designation and functions of any person or body having charge of the adult's person or property, representing or assisting the adult;
(e) the placement of the adult in an establishment or other place where protection can be provided;
(f) the administration, conservation or disposal of the adult's property;
(g) the authorisation of a specific intervention for the protection of the person or property of the adult.

Article 4

(1) The Convention does not apply to –

(a) maintenance obligations;
(b) the formation, annulment and dissolution of marriage or any similar relationship, as well as legal separation;
(c) property regimes in respect of marriage or any similar relationship;
(d) trusts or succession;
(e) social security;
(f) public measures of a general nature in matters of health;
(g) measures taken in respect of a person as a result of penal offences committed by that person;
(h) decisions on the right of asylum and on immigration;
(i) measures directed solely to public safety.

(2) Paragraph 1 does not affect, in respect of the matters referred to therein, the entitlement of a person to act as the representative of the adult.

CHAPTER II – JURISDICTION

Article 5

(1) The judicial or administrative authorities of the Contracting State of the habitual residence of the adult have jurisdiction to take measures directed to the protection of the adult's person or property.

(2) In case of a change of the adult's habitual residence to another Contracting State, the authorities of the State of the new habitual residence have jurisdiction.

Article 6

(1) For adults who are refugees and those who, due to disturbances occurring in their country, are internationally displaced, the authorities of the Contracting State on the territory of which these adults are present as a result of their displacement have the jurisdiction provided for in Article 5, paragraph 1.

(2) The provisions of the preceding paragraph also apply to adults whose habitual residence cannot be established.

Article 7

(1) Except for adults who are refugees or who, due to disturbances occurring in their State of nationality, are internationally displaced, the authorities of a Contracting State of which the adult is a national have jurisdiction to take measures

for the protection of the person or property of the adult if they consider that they are in a better position to assess the interests of the adult, and after advising the authorities having jurisdiction under Article 5 or Article 6, paragraph 2.

(2) This jurisdiction shall not be exercised if the authorities having jurisdiction under Article 5, Article 6, paragraph 2, or Article 8 have informed the authorities of the State of which the adult is a national that they have taken the measures required by the situation or have decided that no measures should be taken or that proceedings are pending before them.

(3) The measures taken under paragraph 1 shall lapse as soon as the authorities having jurisdiction under Article 5, Article 6, paragraph 2, or Article 8 have taken measures required by the situation or have decided that no measures are to be taken. These authorities shall inform accordingly the authorities which have taken measures in accordance with paragraph 1.

Article 8

(1) The authorities of a Contracting State having jurisdiction under Article 5 or Article 6, if they consider that such is in the interests of the adult, may, on their own motion or on an application by the authority of another Contracting State, request the authorities of one of the States mentioned in paragraph 2 to take measures for the protection of the person or property of the adult. The request may relate to all or some aspects of such protection.

(2) The Contracting States whose authorities may be addressed as provided in the preceding paragraph are –

    (a) a State of which the adult is a national;
    (b) the State of the preceding habitual residence of the adult;
    (c) a State in which property of the adult is located;
    (d) the State whose authorities have been chosen in writing by the adult to take measures directed to his or her protection;
    (e) the State of the habitual residence of a person close to the adult prepared to undertake his or her protection;
    (f) the State in whose territory the adult is present, with regard to the protection of the person of the adult.

(3) In case the authority designated pursuant to the preceding paragraphs does not accept its jurisdiction, the authorities of the Contracting State having jurisdiction under Article 5 or Article 6 retain jurisdiction.

Article 9

The authorities of a Contracting State where property of the adult is situated have jurisdiction to take measures of protection concerning that property, to the extent that such measures are compatible with those taken by the authorities having jurisdiction under Articles 5 to 8.

Article 10

(1) In all cases of urgency, the authorities of any Contracting State in whose territory the adult or property belonging to the adult is present have jurisdiction to take any necessary measures of protection.

(2) The measures taken under the preceding paragraph with regard to an adult habitually resident in a Contracting State shall lapse as soon as the authorities which have jurisdiction under Articles 5 to 9 have taken the measures required by the situation.

(3) The measures taken under paragraph 1 with regard to an adult who is habitually resident in a non-Contracting State shall lapse in each Contracting State as soon as measures required by the situation and taken by the authorities of another State are recognised in the Contracting State in question.

(4) The authorities which have taken measures under paragraph 1 shall, if possible, inform the authorities of the Contracting State of the habitual residence of the adult of the measures taken.

Article 11

(1) By way of exception, the authorities of a Contracting State in whose territory the adult is present have jurisdiction to take measures of a temporary character for the protection of the person of the adult which have a territorial effect limited to the State in question, in so far as such measures are compatible with those already taken by the authorities which have jurisdiction under Articles 5 to 8, and after advising the authorities having jurisdiction under Article 5.

(2) The measures taken under the preceding paragraph with regard to an adult habitually resident in a Contracting State shall lapse as soon as the authorities which have jurisdiction under Articles 5 to 8 have taken a decision in respect of the measures of protection which may be required by the situation.

Article 12

Subject to Article 7, paragraph 3, the measures taken in application of Articles 5 to 9 remain in force according to their terms, even if a change of circumstances has eliminated the basis upon which jurisdiction was founded, so long as the authorities which have jurisdiction under the Convention have not modified, replaced or terminated such measures.

CHAPTER III – APPLICABLE LAW

Article 13

(1) In exercising their jurisdiction under the provisions of Chapter II, the authorities of the Contracting States shall apply their own law.

(2) However, in so far as the protection of the person or the property of the adult requires, they may exceptionally apply or take into consideration the law of another State with which the situation has a substantial connection.

Article 14

Where a measure taken in one Contracting State is implemented in another Contracting State, the conditions of its implementation are governed by the law of that other State.

Article 15

(1) The existence, extent, modification and extinction of powers of representation granted by an adult, either under an agreement or by a unilateral act, to be exercised when such adult is not in a position to protect his or her interests, are governed by the law of the State of the adult's habitual residence at the time of the agreement or act, unless one of the laws mentioned in paragraph 2 has been designated expressly in writing.

(2) The States whose laws may be designated are –
   (a) a State of which the adult is a national;
   (b) the State of a former habitual residence of the adult;
   (c) a State in which property of the adult is located, with respect to that property.

(3) The manner of exercise of such powers of representation is governed by the law of the State in which they are exercised.

Article 16

Where powers of representation referred to in Article 15 are not exercised in a manner sufficient to guarantee the protection of the person or property of the adult, they may be withdrawn or modified by measures taken by an authority having jurisdiction under the Convention. Where such powers of representation are withdrawn or modified, the law referred to in Article 15 should be taken into consideration to the extent possible.

Article 17

(1) The validity of a transaction entered into between a third party and another person who would be entitled to act as the adult's representative under the law of the State where the transaction was concluded cannot be contested, and the third party cannot be held liable, on the sole ground that the other person was not entitled to act as the adult's representative under the law designated by the provisions of this Chapter, unless the third party knew or should have known that such capacity was governed by the latter law.

(2) The preceding paragraph applies only if the transaction was entered into between persons present on the territory of the same State.

Article 18

The provisions of this Chapter apply even if the law designated by them is the law of a non-Contracting State.

Article 19

In this Chapter the term 'law' means the law in force in a State other than its choice of law rules.

Article 20

This Chapter does not prevent the application of those provisions of the law of the State in which the adult is to be protected where the application of such provisions is mandatory whatever law would otherwise be applicable.

Article 21

The application of the law designated by the provisions of this Chapter can be refused only if this application would be manifestly contrary to public policy.

CHAPTER IV – RECOGNITION AND ENFORCEMENT

Article 22

(1) The measures taken by the authorities of a Contracting State shall be recognised by operation of law in all other Contracting States.

(2) Recognition may however be refused –

   (a) if the measure was taken by an authority whose jurisdiction was not based on, or was not in accordance with, one of the grounds provided for by the provisions of Chapter II;
   (b) if the measure was taken, except in a case of urgency, in the context of a judicial or administrative proceeding, without the adult having been provided the opportunity to be heard, in violation of fundamental principles of procedure of the requested State;
   (c) if such recognition is manifestly contrary to public policy of the requested State, or conflicts with a provision of the law of that State which is mandatory whatever law would otherwise be applicable;
   (d) if the measure is incompatible with a later measure taken in a non-Contracting State which would have had jurisdiction under Articles 5 to 9, where this later measure fulfils the requirements for recognition in the requested State;
   (e) if the procedure provided in Article 33 has not been complied with.

Article 23

Without prejudice to Article 22, paragraph 1, any interested person may request from the competent authorities of a Contracting State that they decide on the recognition or non-recognition of a measure taken in another Contracting State. The procedure is governed by the law of the requested State.

Article 24

The authority of the requested State is bound by the findings of fact on which the authority of the State where the measure was taken based its jurisdiction.

Article 25

(1) If measures taken in one Contracting State and enforceable there require enforcement in another Contracting State, they shall, upon request by an interested

party, be declared enforceable or registered for the purpose of enforcement in that other State according to the procedure provided in the law of the latter State.

(2) Each Contracting State shall apply to the declaration of enforceability or registration a simple and rapid procedure.

(3) The declaration of enforceability or registration may be refused only for one of the reasons set out in Article 22, paragraph 2.

Article 26

Without prejudice to such review as is necessary in the application of the preceding Articles, there shall be no review of the merits of the measure taken.

Article 27

Measures taken in one Contracting State and declared enforceable, or registered for the purpose of enforcement, in another Contracting State shall be enforced in the latter State as if they had been taken by the authorities of that State. Enforcement takes place in accordance with the law of the requested State to the extent provided by such law.

CHAPTER V – CO-OPERATION

Article 28

(1) A Contracting State shall designate a Central Authority to discharge the duties which are imposed by the Convention on such authorities.

(2) Federal States, States with more than one system of law or States having autonomous territorial units shall be free to appoint more than one Central Authority and to specify the territorial or personal extent of their functions. Where a State has appointed more than one Central Authority, it shall designate the Central Authority to which any communication may be addressed for transmission to the appropriate Central Authority within that State.

Article 29

(1) Central Authorities shall co-operate with each other and promote co-operation amongst the competent authorities in their States to achieve the purposes of the Convention.

(2) They shall, in connection with the application of the Convention, take appropriate steps to provide information as to the laws of, and services available in, their States relating to the protection of adults.

Article 30

The Central Authority of a Contracting State, either directly or through public authorities or other bodies, shall take all appropriate steps to –

(a) facilitate communications, by every means, between the competent authorities in situations to which the Convention applies;
(b) provide, on the request of a competent authority of another Contracting

State, assistance in discovering the whereabouts of an adult where it appears that the adult may be present and in need of protection within the territory of the requested State.

Article 31

The competent authorities of a Contracting State may encourage, either directly or through other bodies, the use of mediation, conciliation or similar means to achieve agreed solutions for the protection of the person or property of the adult in situations to which the Convention applies.

Article 32

(1) Where a measure of protection is contemplated, the competent authorities under the Convention, if the situation of the adult so requires, may request any authority of another Contracting State which has information relevant to the protection of the adult to communicate such information.

(2) A Contracting State may declare that requests under paragraph 1 shall be communicated to its authorities only through its Central Authority.

(3) The competent authorities of a Contracting State may request the authorities of another Contracting State to assist in the implementation of measures of protection taken under this Convention.

Article 33

(1) If an authority having jurisdiction under Articles 5 to 8 contemplates the placement of the adult in an establishment or other place where protection can be provided, and if such placement is to take place in another Contracting State, it shall first consult with the Central Authority or other competent authority of the latter State. To that effect it shall transmit a report on the adult together with the reasons for the proposed placement.

(2) The decision on the placement may not be made in the requesting State if the Central Authority or other competent authority of the requested State indicates its opposition within a reasonable time.

Article 34

In any case where the adult is exposed to a serious danger, the competent authorities of the Contracting State where measures for the protection of the adult have been taken or are under consideration, if they are informed that the adult's residence has changed to, or that the adult is present in, another State, shall inform the authorities of that other State about the danger involved and the measures taken or under consideration.

Article 35

An authority shall not request or transmit any information under this Chapter if to do so would, in its opinion, be likely to place the adult's person or property in danger, or constitute a serious threat to the liberty or life of a member of the adult's family.

Article 36

(1) Without prejudice to the possibility of imposing reasonable charges for the provision of services, Central Authorities and other public authorities of Contracting States shall bear their own costs in applying the provisions of this Chapter.

(2) Any Contracting State may enter into agreements with one or more other Contracting States concerning the allocation of charges.

Article 37

Any Contracting State may enter into agreements with one or more other Contracting States with a view to improving the application of this Chapter in their mutual relations. The States which have concluded such an agreement shall transmit a copy to the depositary of the Convention.

CHAPTER VI – GENERAL PROVISIONS

Article 38

(1) The authorities of the Contracting State where a measure of protection has been taken or a power of representation confirmed may deliver to the person entrusted with protection of the adult's person or property, on request, a certificate indicating the capacity in which that person is entitled to act and the powers conferred.

(2) The capacity and powers indicated in the certificate are presumed to be vested in that person as of the date of the certificate, in the absence of proof to the contrary.

(3) Each Contracting State shall designate the authorities competent to draw up the certificate.

Article 39

Personal data gathered or transmitted under the Convention shall be used only for the purposes for which they were gathered or transmitted.

Article 40

The authorities to whom information is transmitted shall ensure its confidentiality, in accordance with the law of their State.

Article 41

All documents forwarded or delivered under this Convention shall be exempt from legalisation or any analogous formality.

Article 42

Each Contracting State may designate the authorities to which requests under Article 8 and Article 33 are to be addressed.

Article 43

(1) The designations referred to in Article 28 and Article 42 shall be communicated to the Permanent Bureau of the Hague Conference on Private International Law not later than the date of the deposit of the instrument of ratification, acceptance or approval of the Convention or of accession thereto. Any modifications thereof shall also be communicated to the Permanent Bureau.

(2) The declaration referred to in Article 32, paragraph 2, shall be made to the depositary of the Convention.

Article 44

A Contracting State in which different systems of law or sets of rules of law apply to the protection of the person or property of the adult shall not be bound to apply the rules of the Convention to conflicts solely between such different systems or sets of rules of law.

Article 45

In relation to a State in which two or more systems of law or sets of rules of law with regard to any matter dealt with in this Convention apply in different territorial units –

- (a) any reference to habitual residence in that State shall be construed as referring to habitual residence in a territorial unit;
- (b) any reference to the presence of the adult in that State shall be construed as referring to presence in a territorial unit;
- (c) any reference to the location of property of the adult in that State shall be construed as referring to location of property of the adult in a territorial unit;
- (d) any reference to the State of which the adult is a national shall be construed as referring to the territorial unit designated by the law of that State or, in the absence of relevant rules, to the territorial unit with which the adult has the closest connection;
- (e) any reference to the State whose authorities have been chosen by the adult shall be construed
    - as referring to the territorial unit if the adult has chosen the authorities of this territorial unit;
    - as referring to the territorial unit with which the adult has the closest connection if the adult has chosen the authorities of the State without specifying a particular territorial unit within the State;
- (f) any reference to the law of a State with which the situation has a substantial connection shall be construed as referring to the law of a territorial unit with which the situation has a substantial connection;
- (g) any reference to the law or procedure or authority of the State in which a measure has been taken shall be construed as referring to the law or procedure in force in such territorial unit or authority of the territorial unit in which such measure was taken;
- (h) any reference to the law or procedure or authority of the requested State shall be construed as referring to the law or procedure in force in such territorial unit or authority of the territorial unit in which recognition or enforcement is sought;

(i) any reference to the State where a measure of protection is to be implemented shall be construed as referring to the territorial unit where the measure is to be implemented;
(j) any reference to bodies or authorities of that State, other than Central Authorities, shall be construed as referring to those authorised to act in the relevant territorial unit.

Article 46

For the purpose of identifying the applicable law under Chapter III, in relation to a State which comprises two or more territorial units each of which has its own system of law or set of rules of law in respect of matters covered by this Convention, the following rules apply –

(a) if there are rules in force in such a State identifying which territorial unit's law is applicable, the law of that unit applies;
(b) in the absence of such rules, the law of the relevant territorial unit as defined in Article 45 applies.

Article 47

For the purpose of identifying the applicable law under Chapter III, in relation to a State which has two or more systems of law or sets of rules of law applicable to different categories of persons in respect of matters covered by this Convention, the following rules apply –

(a) if there are rules in force in such a State identifying which among such laws applies, that law applies;
(b) in the absence of such rules, the law of the system or the set of rules of law with which the adult has the closest connection applies.

Article 48

In relations between the Contracting States this Convention replaces the Convention concernant l'interdiction et les mesures de protection analogues, signed at The Hague 17 July 1905.

Article 49

(1) The Convention does not affect any other international instrument to which Contracting States are Parties and which contains provisions on matters governed by this Convention, unless a contrary declaration is made by the States Parties to such instrument.

(2) This Convention does not affect the possibility for one or more Contracting States to conclude agreements which contain, in respect of adults habitually resident in any of the States Parties to such agreements, provisions on matters governed by this Convention.

(3) Agreements to be concluded by one or more Contracting States on matters within the scope of this Convention do not affect, in the relationship of such States with other Contracting States, the application of the provisions of this Convention.

(4) The preceding paragraphs also apply to uniform laws based on special ties of a regional or other nature between the States concerned.

Article 50

(1) The Convention shall apply to measures only if they are taken in a State after the Convention has entered into force for that State.

(2) The Convention shall apply to the recognition and enforcement of measures taken after its entry into force as between the State where the measures have been taken and the requested State.

(3) The Convention shall apply from the time of its entry into force in a Contracting State to powers of representation previously granted under conditions corresponding to those set out in Article 15.

Article 51

(1) Any communication sent to the Central Authority or to another authority of a Contracting State shall be in the original language, and shall be accompanied by a translation into the official language or one of the official languages of the other State or, where that is not feasible, a translation into French or English.

(2) However, a Contracting State may, by making a reservation in accordance with Article 56, object to the use of either French or English, but not both.

Article 52

The Secretary General of the Hague Conference on Private International Law shall at regular intervals convoke a Special Commission in order to review the practical operation of the Convention.

CHAPTER VII – FINAL CLAUSES

Article 53

(1) The Convention shall be open for signature by the States which were Members of the Hague Conference on Private International Law on 2 October 1999.

(2) It shall be ratified, accepted or approved and the instruments of ratification, acceptance or approval shall be deposited with the Ministry of Foreign Affairs of the Kingdom of the Netherlands, depositary of the Convention.

Article 54

(1) Any other State may accede to the Convention after it has entered into force in accordance with Article 57, paragraph 1.

(2) The instrument of accession shall be deposited with the depositary.

(3) Such accession shall have effect only as regards the relations between the acceding State and those Contracting States which have not raised an objection to its accession in the six months after the receipt of the notification referred to in sub-paragraph (b) of Article 59. Such an objection may also be raised by States at

the time when they ratify, accept or approve the Convention after an accession. Any such objection shall be notified to the depositary.

Article 55

(1) If a State has two or more territorial units in which different systems of law are applicable in relation to matters dealt with in this Convention, it may at the time of signature, ratification, acceptance, approval or accession declare that the Convention shall extend to all its territorial units or only to one or more of them and may modify this declaration by submitting another declaration at any time.

(2) Any such declaration shall be notified to the depositary and shall state expressly the territorial units to which the Convention applies.

(3) If a State makes no declaration under this Article, the Convention is to extend to all territorial units of that State.

Article 56

(1) Any State may, not later than the time of ratification, acceptance, approval or accession, or at the time of making a declaration in terms of Article 55, make the reservation provided for in Article 51, paragraph 2. No other reservation shall be permitted.

(2) Any State may at any time withdraw the reservation it has made. The withdrawal shall be notified to the depositary.

(3) The reservation shall cease to have effect on the first day of the third calendar month after the notification referred to in the preceding paragraph.

Article 57

(1) The Convention shall enter into force on the first day of the month following the expiration of three months after the deposit of the third instrument of ratification, acceptance or approval referred to in Article 53.

(2) Thereafter the Convention shall enter into force –

   (a) for each State ratifying, accepting or approving it subsequently, on the first day of the month following the expiration of three months after the deposit of its instrument of ratification, acceptance, approval or accession;
   (b) for each State acceding, on the first day of the month following the expiration of three months after the expiration of the period of six months provided in Article 54, paragraph 3;
   (c) for a territorial unit to which the Convention has been extended in conformity with Article 55, on the first day of the month following the expiration of three months after the notification referred to in that Article.

Article 58

(1) A State Party to the Convention may denounce it by a notification in writing addressed to the depositary. The denunciation may be limited to certain territorial units to which the Convention applies.

(2) The denunciation takes effect on the first day of the month following the expiration of twelve months after the notification is received by the depositary. Where a longer period for the denunciation to take effect is specified in the notification, the denunciation takes effect upon the expiration of such longer period.

Article 59

The depositary shall notify the States Members of the Hague Conference on Private International Law and the States which have acceded in accordance with Article 54 of the following –

(a) the signatures, ratifications, acceptances and approvals referred to in Article 53;
(b) the accessions and objections raised to accessions referred to in Article 54;
(c) the date on which the Convention enters into force in accordance with Article 57;
(d) the declarations referred to in Article 32, paragraph 2, and Article 55;
(e) the agreements referred to in Article 37;
(f) the reservation referred to in Article 51, paragraph 2, and the withdrawal referred to in Article 56, paragraph 2;
(g) the denunciations referred to in Article 58.

In witness whereof the undersigned, being duly authorised thereto, have signed this Convention.

Done at The Hague, on the 13th day of January, 2000, in the English and French languages, both texts being equally authentic, in a single copy which shall be deposited in the archives of the Government of the Kingdom of the Netherlands, and of which a certified copy shall be sent, through diplomatic channels, to each of the States Members of the Hague Conference on Private International Law.

UN Convention on the Rights of Persons with Disabilities

PREAMBLE

The States Parties to the present Convention,

a. Recalling the principles proclaimed in the Charter of the United Nations which recognize the inherent dignity and worth and the equal and inalienable rights of all members of the human family as the foundation of freedom, justice and peace in the world,

b. Recognizing that the United Nations, in the Universal Declaration of Human Rights and in the International Covenants on Human Rights, has proclaimed and agreed that everyone is entitled to all the rights and freedoms set forth therein, without distinction of any kind,

c. Reaffirming the universality, indivisibility, interdependence and interrelatedness of all human rights and fundamental freedoms and the need for persons with disabilities to be guaranteed their full enjoyment without discrimination,

d. Recalling the International Covenant on Economic, Social and Cultural Rights, the International Covenant on Civil and Political Rights, the International Convention on the Elimination of All Forms of Racial Discrimination, the Convention on the Elimination of All Forms of Discrimination against Women, the Convention against Torture and Other Cruel, Inhuman or Degrading Treatment or Punishment, the Convention on the Rights of the Child, and the International Convention on the Protection of the Rights of All Migrant Workers and Members of Their Families,

e. Recognizing that disability is an evolving concept and that disability results from the interaction between persons with impairments and attitudinal and environmental barriers that hinders their full and effective participation in society on an equal basis with others,

f. Recognizing the importance of the principles and policy guidelines contained in the World Programme of Action concerning Disabled Persons and in the Standard Rules on the Equalization of Opportunities for Persons with Disabilities in influencing the promotion, formulation and evaluation of the policies, plans, programmes and actions at the national, regional and international levels to further equalize opportunities for persons with disabilities,

g. Emphasizing the importance of mainstreaming disability issues as an integral part of relevant strategies of sustainable development,

h. Recognizing also that discrimination against any person on the basis of disability is a violation of the inherent dignity and worth of the human person,

i. Recognizing further the diversity of persons with disabilities,

j. Recognizing the need to promote and protect the human rights of all persons with disabilities, including those who require more intensive support,

k. Concerned that, despite these various instruments and undertakings, persons with disabilities continue to face barriers in their participation as equal members of society and violations of their human rights in all parts of the world,

l. Recognizing the importance of international cooperation for improving the living conditions of persons with disabilities in every country, particularly in developing countries,

m. Recognizing the valued existing and potential contributions made by persons with disabilities to the overall well-being and diversity of their communities, and that the promotion of the full enjoyment by persons with disabilities of their human rights and fundamental freedoms and of full participation by persons with disabilities will result in their enhanced sense of belonging and in significant advances in the human, social and economic development of society and the eradication of poverty,

n. Recognizing the importance for persons with disabilities of their individual autonomy and independence, including the freedom to make their own choices,

o. Considering that persons with disabilities should have the opportunity to be actively involved in decision-making processes about policies and programmes, including those directly concerning them,

p. Concerned about the difficult conditions faced by persons with disabilities who are subject to multiple or aggravated forms of discrimination on the basis of race, colour, sex, language, religion, political or other opinion, national, ethnic, indigenous or social origin, property, birth, age or other status,

q. Recognizing that women and girls with disabilities are often at greater risk, both within and outside the home of violence, injury or abuse, neglect or negligent treatment, maltreatment or exploitation,

r. Recognizing that children with disabilities should have full enjoyment of all human rights and fundamental freedoms on an equal basis with other children, and recalling obligations to that end undertaken by States Parties to the Convention on the Rights of the Child,

s. Emphasizing the need to incorporate a gender perspective in all efforts to promote the full enjoyment of human rights and fundamental freedoms by persons with disabilities,

t. Highlighting the fact that the majority of persons with disabilities live in conditions of poverty, and in this regard recognizing the critical need to address the negative impact of poverty on persons with disabilities,

u. Bearing in mind that conditions of peace and security based on full respect for the purposes and principles contained in the Charter of the United Nations and observance of applicable human rights instruments are indispensable for the full protection of persons with disabilities, in particular during armed conflicts and foreign occupation,

v. Recognizing the importance of accessibility to the physical, social, economic and cultural environment, to health and education and to information and communication, in enabling persons with disabilities to fully enjoy all human rights and fundamental freedoms,

w. Realizing that the individual, having duties to other individuals and to the community to which he or she belongs, is under a responsibility to strive for the promotion and observance of the rights recognized in the International Bill of Human Rights,

x. Convinced that the family is the natural and fundamental group unit of society and is entitled to protection by society and the State, and that persons with disabilities and their family members should receive the necessary protection and assistance to enable families to contribute towards the full and equal enjoyment of the rights of persons with disabilities,

y. Convinced that a comprehensive and integral international convention to promote and protect the rights and dignity of persons with disabilities will make a significant contribution to redressing the profound social disadvantage of persons with disabilities and promote their participation in the civil, political, economic, social and cultural spheres with equal opportunities, in both developing and developed countries,

Have agreed as follows:

Article 1: Purpose

The purpose of the present Convention is to promote, protect and ensure the full and equal enjoyment of all human rights and fundamental freedoms by all persons with disabilities, and to promote respect for their inherent dignity.

Persons with disabilities include those who have long-term physical, mental, intellectual or sensory impairments which in interaction with various barriers may hinder their full and effective participation in society on an equal basis with others.

Article 2: Definitions

For the purposes of the present Convention:

- 'Communication' includes languages, display of text, Braille, tactile communication, large print, accessible multimedia as well as written, audio, plain-language, human-reader and augmentative and alternative modes, means and formats of communication, including accessible information and communication technology;
- 'Language' includes spoken and signed languages and other forms of non spoken languages;
- 'Discrimination on the basis of disability' means any distinction, exclusion or restriction on the basis of disability which has the purpose or effect of impairing or nullifying the recognition, enjoyment or exercise, on an equal basis with others, of all human rights and fundamental freedoms in the political, economic, social, cultural, civil or any other field. It includes all forms of discrimination, including denial of reasonable accommodation;
- 'Reasonable accommodation' means necessary and appropriate modification and adjustments not imposing a disproportionate or undue burden, where needed in a particular case, to ensure to persons with disabilities the enjoyment or exercise on an equal basis with others of all human rights and fundamental freedoms;
- 'Universal design' means the design of products, environments, programmes and services to be usable by all people, to the greatest extent possible, without the need for adaptation or specialized design. 'Universal design' shall not exclude assistive devices for particular groups of persons with disabilities where this is needed.

Article 3: General principles

The principles of the present Convention shall be:

- a Respect for inherent dignity, individual autonomy including the freedom to make one's own choices, and independence of persons;
- b Non-discrimination;
- c Full and effective participation and inclusion in society;
- d Respect for difference and acceptance of persons with disabilities as part of human diversity and humanity;
- e Equality of opportunity;
- f Accessibility;
- g Equality between men and women;
- h Respect for the evolving capacities of children with disabilities and respect for the right of children with disabilities to preserve their identities.

Article 4: General obligations

1 States Parties undertake to ensure and promote the full realization of all human rights and fundamental freedoms for all persons with disabilities without discrimination of any kind on the basis of disability. To this end, States Parties undertake:

- a To adopt all appropriate legislative, administrative and other measures for the implementation of the rights recognized in the present Convention;
- b To take all appropriate measures, including legislation, to modify or abolish existing laws, regulations, customs and practices that constitute discrimination against persons with disabilities;
- c To take into account the protection and promotion of the human rights of persons with disabilities in all policies and programmes;
- d To refrain from engaging in any act or practice that is inconsistent with the present Convention and to ensure that public authorities and institutions act in conformity with the present Convention;
- e To take all appropriate measures to eliminate discrimination on the basis of disability by any person, organization or private enterprise;
- f To undertake or promote research and development of universally designed goods, services, equipment and facilities, as defined in article 2 of the present Convention, which should require the minimum possible adaptation and the least cost to meet the specific needs of a person with disabilities, to promote their availability and use, and to promote universal design in the development of standards and guidelines;
- g To undertake or promote research and development of, and to promote the availability and use of new technologies, including information and communications technologies, mobility aids, devices and assistive technologies, suitable for persons with disabilities, giving priority to technologies at an affordable cost;
- h To provide accessible information to persons with disabilities about mobility aids, devices and assistive technologies, including new technologies, as well as other forms of assistance, support services and facilities;
- i To promote the training of professionals and staff working with persons with disabilities in the rights recognized in this Convention so as to better provide the assistance and services guaranteed by those rights.

2 With regard to economic, social and cultural rights, each State Party undertakes to take measures to the maximum of its available resources and, where needed, within the framework of international cooperation, with a view to achieving progressively the full realization of these rights, without prejudice to those obligations contained in the present Convention that are immediately applicable according to international law.

3 In the development and implementation of legislation and policies to implement the present Convention, and in other decision-making processes concerning issues relating to persons with disabilities, States Parties shall closely consult with and actively involve persons with disabilities, including children with disabilities, through their representative organizations.

4 Nothing in the present Convention shall affect any provisions which are more conducive to the realization of the rights of persons with disabilities and which may be contained in the law of a State Party or international law in force for that State. There shall be no restriction upon or derogation from any of the human rights and fundamental freedoms recognized or existing in any State Party to the present Convention pursuant to law, conventions, regulation or custom on the pretext that the present Convention does not recognize such rights or freedoms or that it recognizes them to a lesser extent.

5 The provisions of the present Convention shall extend to all parts of federal states without any limitations or exceptions.

Article 5: Equality and non-discrimination

1 States Parties recognize that all persons are equal before and under the law and are entitled without any discrimination to the equal protection and equal benefit of the law.

2 States Parties shall prohibit all discrimination on the basis of disability and guarantee to persons with disabilities equal and effective legal protection against discrimination on all grounds.

3 In order to promote equality and eliminate discrimination, States Parties shall take all appropriate steps to ensure that reasonable accommodation is provided.

4 Specific measures which are necessary to accelerate or achieve de facto equality of persons with disabilities shall not be considered discrimination under the terms of the present Convention.

Article 6: Women with disabilities

1 States Parties recognize that women and girls with disabilities are subject to multiple discrimination, and in this regard shall take measures to ensure the full and equal enjoyment by them of all human rights and fundamental freedoms.

2 States Parties shall take all appropriate measures to ensure the full development, advancement and empowerment of women, for the purpose of guaranteeing them the exercise and enjoyment of the human rights and fundamental freedoms set out in the present Convention.

Article 7: Children with disabilities

1 States Parties shall take all necessary measures to ensure the full enjoyment by children with disabilities of all human rights and fundamental freedoms on an equal basis with other children.

2 In all actions concerning children with disabilities, the best interests of the child shall be a primary consideration.

3 States Parties shall ensure that children with disabilities have the right to express their views freely on all matters affecting them, their views being given due weight in accordance with their age and maturity, on an equal basis with other children, and to be provided with disability and age-appropriate assistance to realize that right.

Article 8: Awareness-raising

1 States Parties undertake to adopt immediate, effective and appropriate measures:

- a To raise awareness throughout society, including at the family level, regarding persons with disabilities, and to foster respect for the rights and dignity of persons with disabilities;
- b To combat stereotypes, prejudices and harmful practices relating to persons with disabilities, including those based on sex and age, in all areas of life;
- c To promote awareness of the capabilities and contributions of persons with disabilities.

Measures to this end include:

- a Initiating and maintaining effective public awareness campaigns designed:
  - i To nurture receptiveness to the rights of persons with disabilities;
  - ii To promote positive perceptions and greater social awareness towards persons with disabilities;
  - iii To promote recognition of the skills, merits and abilities of persons with disabilities, and of their contributions to the workplace and the labour market;
- b Fostering at all levels of the education system, including in all children from an early age, an attitude of respect for the rights of persons with disabilities;
- c Encouraging all organs of the media to portray persons with disabilities in a manner consistent with the purpose of the present Convention;
- d Promoting awareness-training programmes regarding persons with disabilities and the rights of persons with disabilities.

Article 9: Accessibility

1 To enable persons with disabilities to live independently and participate fully in all aspects of life, States Parties shall take appropriate measures to ensure to persons with disabilities access, on an equal basis with others, to the physical environment, to transportation, to information and communications, including information and communications technologies and systems, and to other facilities and services open or provided to the public, both in urban and in rural areas. These measures, which shall include the identification and elimination of obstacles and barriers to accessibility, shall apply to, inter alia:

- a Buildings, roads, transportation and other indoor and outdoor facilities, including schools, housing, medical facilities and workplaces;

b   Information, communications and other services, including electronic services and emergency services.

2 States Parties shall also take appropriate measures to:

a   Develop, promulgate and monitor the implementation of minimum standards and guidelines for the accessibility of facilities and services open or provided to the public;
b   Ensure that private entities that offer facilities and services which are open or provided to the public take into account all aspects of accessibility for persons with disabilities;
c   Provide training for stakeholders on accessibility issues facing persons with disabilities;
d   Provide in buildings and other facilities open to the public signage in Braille and in easy to read and understand forms;
e   Provide forms of live assistance and intermediaries, including guides, readers and professional sign language interpreters, to facilitate accessibility to buildings and other facilities open to the public;
f   Promote other appropriate forms of assistance and support to persons with disabilities to ensure their access to information;
g   Promote access for persons with disabilities to new information and communications technologies and systems, including the Internet;
h   Promote the design, development, production and distribution of accessible information and communications technologies and systems at an early stage, so that these technologies and systems become accessible at minimum cost.

Article 10: Right to life

States Parties reaffirm that every human being has the inherent right to life and shall take all necessary measures to ensure its effective enjoyment by persons with disabilities on an equal basis with others.

Article 11: Situations of risk and humanitarian emergencies

States Parties shall take, in accordance with their obligations under international law, including international humanitarian law and international human rights law, all necessary measures to ensure the protection and safety of persons with disabilities in situations of risk, including situations of armed conflict, humanitarian emergencies and the occurrence of natural disasters.

Article 12: Equal recognition before the law

1 States Parties reaffirm that persons with disabilities have the right to recognition everywhere as persons before the law.

2 States Parties shall recognize that persons with disabilities enjoy legal capacity on an equal basis with others in all aspects of life.

3 States Parties shall take appropriate measures to provide access by persons with disabilities to the support they may require in exercising their legal capacity.

4 States Parties shall ensure that all measures that relate to the exercise of legal capacity provide for appropriate and effective safeguards to prevent abuse in accordance with international human rights law. Such safeguards shall ensure that

measures relating to the exercise of legal capacity respect the rights, will and preferences of the person, are free of conflict of interest and undue influence, are proportional and tailored to the person's circumstances, apply for the shortest time possible and are subject to regular review by a competent, independent and impartial authority or judicial body. The safeguards shall be proportional to the degree to which such measures affect the person's rights and interests.

5 Subject to the provisions of this article, States Parties shall take all appropriate and effective measures to ensure the equal right of persons with disabilities to own or inherit property, to control their own financial affairs and to have equal access to bank loans, mortgages and other forms of financial credit, and shall ensure that persons with disabilities are not arbitrarily deprived of their property.

Article 13: Access to justice

1 States Parties shall ensure effective access to justice for persons with disabilities on an equal basis with others, including through the provision of procedural and age-appropriate accommodations, in order to facilitate their effective role as direct and indirect participants, including as witnesses, in all legal proceedings, including at investigative and other preliminary stages.

2 In order to help to ensure effective access to justice for persons with disabilities, States Parties shall promote appropriate training for those working in the field of administration of justice, including police and prison staff.

Article 14: Liberty and security of the person

1 States Parties shall ensure that persons with disabilities, on an equal basis with others:

a   Enjoy the right to liberty and security of person;
b   Are not deprived of their liberty unlawfully or arbitrarily, and that any deprivation of liberty is in conformity with the law, and that the existence of a disability shall in no case justify a deprivation of liberty.

2 States Parties shall ensure that if persons with disabilities are deprived of their liberty through any process, they are, on an equal basis with others, entitled to guarantees in accordance with international human rights law and shall be treated in compliance with the objectives and principles of this Convention, including by provision of reasonable accommodation.

Article 15: Freedom from torture or cruel, inhuman or degrading treatment or punishment

1 No one shall be subjected to torture or to cruel, inhuman or degrading treatment or punishment. In particular, no one shall be subjected without his or her free consent to medical or scientific experimentation.

2 States Parties shall take all effective legislative, administrative, judicial or other measures to prevent persons with disabilities, on an equal basis with others, from being subjected to torture or cruel, inhuman or degrading treatment or punishment.

Article 16: Freedom from exploitation, violence and abuse

1 States Parties shall take all appropriate legislative, administrative, social, educational and other measures to protect persons with disabilities, both within and outside the home, from all forms of exploitation, violence and abuse, including their gender-based aspects.

2 States Parties shall also take all appropriate measures to prevent all forms of exploitation, violence and abuse by ensuring, inter alia, appropriate forms of gender- and age-sensitive assistance and support for persons with disabilities and their families and caregivers, including through the provision of information and education on how to avoid, recognize and report instances of exploitation, violence and abuse. States Parties shall ensure that protection services are age-, gender- and disability-sensitive.

3 In order to prevent the occurrence of all forms of exploitation, violence and abuse, States Parties shall ensure that all facilities and programmes designed to serve persons with disabilities are effectively monitored by independent authorities.

4 States Parties shall take all appropriate measures to promote the physical, cognitive and psychological recovery, rehabilitation and social reintegration of persons with disabilities who become victims of any form of exploitation, violence or abuse, including through the provision of protection services. Such recovery and reintegration shall take place in an environment that fosters the health, welfare, self-respect, dignity and autonomy of the person and takes into account gender- and age-specific needs.

5 States Parties shall put in place effective legislation and policies, including women- and child-focused legislation and policies, to ensure that instances of exploitation, violence and abuse against persons with disabilities are identified, investigated and, where appropriate, prosecuted.

Article 17: Protecting the integrity of the person

Every person with disabilities has a right to respect for his or her physical and mental integrity on an equal basis with others.

Article 18: Liberty of movement and nationality

1 States Parties shall recognize the rights of persons with disabilities to liberty of movement, to freedom to choose their residence and to a nationality, on an equal basis with others, including by ensuring that persons with disabilities:

    a   Have the right to acquire and change a nationality and are not deprived of their nationality arbitrarily or on the basis of disability;

    b   Are not deprived, on the basis of disability, of their ability to obtain, possess and utilize documentation of their nationality or other documentation of identification, or to utilize relevant processes such as immigration proceedings, that may be needed to facilitate exercise of the right to liberty of movement;

    c   Are free to leave any country, including their own;

    d   Are not deprived, arbitrarily or on the basis of disability, of the right to enter their own country.

2 Children with disabilities shall be registered immediately after birth and shall have the right from birth to a name, the right to acquire a nationality and, as far as possible, the right to know and be cared for by their parents.

Article 19: Living independently and being included in the community

States Parties to this Convention recognize the equal right of all persons with disabilities to live in the community, with choices equal to others, and shall take effective and appropriate measures to facilitate full enjoyment by persons with disabilities of this right and their full inclusion and participation in the community, including by ensuring that:

a   Persons with disabilities have the opportunity to choose their place of residence and where and with whom they live on an equal basis with others and are not obliged to live in a particular living arrangement;
b   Persons with disabilities have access to a range of in-home, residential and other community support services, including personal assistance necessary to support living and inclusion in the community, and to prevent isolation or segregation from the community;
c   Community services and facilities for the general population are available on an equal basis to persons with disabilities and are responsive to their needs.

Article 20: Personal mobility

States Parties shall take effective measures to ensure personal mobility with the greatest possible independence for persons with disabilities, including by:

a   Facilitating the personal mobility of persons with disabilities in the manner and at the time of their choice, and at affordable cost;
b   Facilitating access by persons with disabilities to quality mobility aids, devices, assistive technologies and forms of live assistance and intermediaries, including by making them available at affordable cost;
c   Providing training in mobility skills to persons with disabilities and to specialist staff working with persons with disabilities;
d   Encouraging entities that produce mobility aids, devices and assistive technologies to take into account all aspects of mobility for persons with disabilities.

Article 21: Freedom of expression and opinion, and access to information

States Parties shall take all appropriate measures to ensure that persons with disabilities can exercise the right to freedom of expression and opinion, including the freedom to seek, receive and impart information and ideas on an equal basis with others and through all forms of communication of their choice, as defined in article 2 of the present Convention, including by:

a   Providing information intended for the general public to persons with disabilities in accessible formats and technologies appropriate to different kinds of disabilities in a timely manner and without additional cost;
b   Accepting and facilitating the use of sign languages, Braille, augmentative

and alternative communication, and all other accessible means, modes and formats of communication of their choice by persons with disabilities in official interactions;

c   Urging private entities that provide services to the general public, including through the Internet, to provide information and services in accessible and usable formats for persons with disabilities;

d   Encouraging the mass media, including providers of information through the Internet, to make their services accessible to persons with disabilities;

e   Recognizing and promoting the use of sign languages.

Article 22: Respect for privacy

1 No person with disabilities, regardless of place of residence or living arrangements, shall be subjected to arbitrary or unlawful interference with his or her privacy, family, home or correspondence or other types of communication or to unlawful attacks on his or her honour and reputation. Persons with disabilities have the right to the protection of the law against such interference or attacks.

2 States Parties shall protect the privacy of personal, health and rehabilitation information of persons with disabilities on an equal basis with others.

Article 23: Respect for home and the family

1 States Parties shall take effective and appropriate measures to eliminate discrimination against persons with disabilities in all matters relating to marriage, family, parenthood and relationships, on an equal basis with others, so as to ensure that:

a   The right of all persons with disabilities who are of marriageable age to marry and to found a family on the basis of free and full consent of the intending spouses is recognized;

b   The rights of persons with disabilities to decide freely and responsibly on the number and spacing of their children and to have access to age-appropriate information, reproductive and family planning education are recognized, and the means necessary to enable them to exercise these rights are provided;

c   Persons with disabilities, including children, retain their fertility on an equal basis with others.

2 States Parties shall ensure the rights and responsibilities of persons with disabilities, with regard to guardianship, wardship, trusteeship, adoption of children or similar institutions, where these concepts exist in national legislation; in all cases the best interests of the child shall be paramount. States Parties shall render appropriate assistance to persons with disabilities in the performance of their child-rearing responsibilities.

3 States Parties shall ensure that children with disabilities have equal rights with respect to family life. With a view to realizing these rights, and to prevent concealment, abandonment, neglect and segregation of children with disabilities, States Parties shall undertake to provide early and comprehensive information, services and support to children with disabilities and their families.

4 States Parties shall ensure that a child shall not be separated from his or her parents against their will, except when competent authorities subject to judicial review determine, in accordance with applicable law and procedures, that such

separation is necessary for the best interests of the child. In no case shall a child be separated from parents on the basis of a disability of either the child or one or both of the parents.

5 States Parties shall, where the immediate family is unable to care for a child with disabilities, undertake every effort to provide alternative care within the wider family, and failing that, within the community in a family setting.

Article 24: Education

1 States Parties recognize the right of persons with disabilities to education. With a view to realizing this right without discrimination and on the basis of equal opportunity, States Parties shall ensure an inclusive education system at all levels and life long learning directed to:

- a The full development of human potential and sense of dignity and self-worth, and the strengthening of respect for human rights, fundamental freedoms and human diversity;
- b The development by persons with disabilities of their personality, talents and creativity, as well as their mental and physical abilities, to their fullest potential;
- c Enabling persons with disabilities to participate effectively in a free society.

2 In realizing this right, States Parties shall ensure that:

- a Persons with disabilities are not excluded from the general education system on the basis of disability, and that children with disabilities are not excluded from free and compulsory primary education, or from secondary education, on the basis of disability;
- b Persons with disabilities can access an inclusive, quality and free primary education and secondary education on an equal basis with others in the communities in which they live;
- c Reasonable accommodation of the individual's requirements is provided;
- d Persons with disabilities receive the support required, within the general education system, to facilitate their effective education;
- e Effective individualized support measures are provided in environments that maximize academic and social development, consistent with the goal of full inclusion.

3 States Parties shall enable persons with disabilities to learn life and social development skills to facilitate their full and equal participation in education and as members of the community. To this end, States Parties shall take appropriate measures, including:

- a Facilitating the learning of Braille, alternative script, augmentative and alternative modes, means and formats of communication and orientation and mobility skills, and facilitating peer support and mentoring;
- b Facilitating the learning of sign language and the promotion of the linguistic identity of the deaf community;
- c Ensuring that the education of persons, and in particular children, who are blind, deaf or deafblind, is delivered in the most appropriate languages and modes and means of communication for the individual, and in environments which maximize academic and social development.

4 In order to help ensure the realization of this right, States Parties shall take appropriate measures to employ teachers, including teachers with disabilities, who

are qualified in sign language and/or Braille, and to train professionals and staff who work at all levels of education. Such training shall incorporate disability awareness and the use of appropriate augmentative and alternative modes, means and formats of communication, educational techniques and materials to support persons with disabilities.

5 States Parties shall ensure that persons with disabilities are able to access general tertiary education, vocational training, adult education and lifelong learning without discrimination and on an equal basis with others. To this end, States Parties shall ensure that reasonable accommodation is provided to persons with disabilities.

Article 25: Health

States Parties recognize that persons with disabilities have the right to the enjoyment of the highest attainable standard of health without discrimination on the basis of disability. States Parties shall take all appropriate measures to ensure access for persons with disabilities to health services that are gender-sensitive, including health-related rehabilitation. In particular, States Parties shall:

- a Provide persons with disabilities with the same range, quality and standard of free or affordable health care and programmes as provided to other persons, including in the area of sexual and reproductive health and population-based public health programmes;
- b Provide those health services needed by persons with disabilities specifically because of their disabilities, including early identification and intervention as appropriate, and services designed to minimize and prevent further disabilities, including among children and older persons;
- c Provide these health services as close as possible to people's own communities, including in rural areas;
- d Require health professionals to provide care of the same quality to persons with disabilities as to others, including on the basis of free and informed consent by, inter alia, raising awareness of the human rights, dignity, autonomy and needs of persons with disabilities through training and the promulgation of ethical standards for public and private health care;
- e Prohibit discrimination against persons with disabilities in the provision of health insurance, and life insurance where such insurance is permitted by national law, which shall be provided in a fair and reasonable manner;
- f Prevent discriminatory denial of health care or health services or food and fluids on the basis of disability.

Article 26: Habilitation and rehabilitation

1 States Parties shall take effective and appropriate measures, including through peer support, to enable persons with disabilities to attain and maintain maximum independence, full physical, mental, social and vocational ability, and full inclusion and participation in all aspects of life. To that end, States Parties shall organize, strengthen and extend comprehensive habilitation and rehabilitation services and programmes, particularly in the areas of health, employment, education and social services, in such a way that these services and programmes:

- a Begin at the earliest possible stage, and are based on the multidisciplinary assessment of individual needs and strengths;
- b Support participation and inclusion in the community and all aspects of

society, are voluntary, and are available to persons with disabilities as close as possible to their own communities, including in rural areas.

2 States Parties shall promote the development of initial and continuing training for professionals and staff working in habilitation and rehabilitation services.

3 States Parties shall promote the availability, knowledge and use of assistive devices and technologies, designed for persons with disabilities, as they relate to habilitation and rehabilitation.

Article 27: Work and employment

1 States Parties recognize the right of persons with disabilities to work, on an equal basis with others; this includes the right to the opportunity to gain a living by work freely chosen or accepted in a labour market and work environment that is open, inclusive and accessible to persons with disabilities. States Parties shall safeguard and promote the realization of the right to work, including for those who acquire a disability during the course of employment, by taking appropriate steps, including through legislation, to, inter alia:

a   Prohibit discrimination on the basis of disability with regard to all matters concerning all forms of employment, including conditions of recruitment, hiring and employment, continuance of employment, career advancement and safe and healthy working conditions;
b   Protect the rights of persons with disabilities, on an equal basis with others, to just and favourable conditions of work, including equal opportunities and equal remuneration for work of equal value, safe and healthy working conditions, including protection from harassment, and the redress of grievances;
c   Ensure that persons with disabilities are able to exercise their labour and trade union rights on an equal basis with others;
d   Enable persons with disabilities to have effective access to general technical and vocational guidance programmes, placement services and vocational and continuing training;
e   Promote employment opportunities and career advancement for persons with disabilities in the labour market, as well as assistance in finding, obtaining, maintaining and returning to employment;
f   Promote opportunities for self-employment, entrepreneurship, the development of cooperatives and starting one's own business;
g   Employ persons with disabilities in the public sector;
h   Promote the employment of persons with disabilities in the private sector through appropriate policies and measures, which may include affirmative action programmes, incentives and other measures;
I   Ensure that reasonable accommodation is provided to persons with disabilities in the workplace;
j   Promote the acquisition by persons with disabilities of work experience in the open labour market;
k   Promote vocational and professional rehabilitation, job retention and return-to-work programmes for persons with disabilities.

2 States Parties shall ensure that persons with disabilities are not held in slavery or in servitude, and are protected, on an equal basis with others, from forced or compulsory labour.

Article 28: Adequate standard of living and social protection

1 States Parties recognize the right of persons with disabilities to an adequate standard of living for themselves and their families, including adequate food, clothing and housing, and to the continuous improvement of living conditions, and shall take appropriate steps to safeguard and promote the realization of this right without discrimination on the basis of disability.

2 States Parties recognize the right of persons with disabilities to social protection and to the enjoyment of that right without discrimination on the basis of disability, and shall take appropriate steps to safeguard and promote the realization of this right, including measures:

- a   To ensure equal access by persons with disabilities to clean water services, and to ensure access to appropriate and affordable services, devices and other assistance for disability-related needs;
- b   To ensure access by persons with disabilities, in particular women and girls with disabilities and older persons with disabilities, to social protection programmes and poverty reduction programmes;
- c   To ensure access by persons with disabilities and their families living in situations of poverty to assistance from the State with disability-related expenses, including adequate training, counselling, financial assistance and respite care;
- d   To ensure access by persons with disabilities to public housing programmes;
- e   To ensure equal access by persons with disabilities to retirement benefits and programmes.

Article 29: Participation in political and public life

States Parties shall guarantee to persons with disabilities political rights and the opportunity to enjoy them on an equal basis with others, and shall undertake to:

- a   Ensure that persons with disabilities can effectively and fully participate in political and public life on an equal basis with others, directly or through freely chosen representatives, including the right and opportunity for persons with disabilities to vote and be elected, inter alia, by:
  - i   Ensuring that voting procedures, facilities and materials are appropriate, accessible and easy to understand and use;
  - ii Protecting the right of persons with disabilities to vote by secret ballot in elections and public referendums without intimidation, and to stand for elections, to effectively hold office and perform all public functions at all levels of government, facilitating the use of assistive and new technologies where appropriate;
  - iii Guaranteeing the free expression of the will of persons with disabilities as electors and to this end, where necessary, at their request, allowing assistance in voting by a person of their own choice;
- b   Promote actively an environment in which persons with disabilities can effectively and fully participate in the conduct of public affairs, without discrimination and on an equal basis with others, and encourage their participation in public affairs, including:
  - i   Participation in non-governmental organizations and associations concerned with the public and political life of the country, and in the activities and administration of political parties;

ii Forming and joining organizations of persons with disabilities to represent persons with disabilities at international, national, regional and local levels.

Article 30: Participation in cultural life, recreation, leisure and sport

1 States Parties recognize the right of persons with disabilities to take part on an equal basis with others in cultural life, and shall take all appropriate measures to ensure that persons with disabilities:

a   Enjoy access to cultural materials in accessible formats;
b   Enjoy access to television programmes, films, theatre and other cultural activities, in accessible formats;
c   Enjoy access to places for cultural performances or services, such as theatres, museums, cinemas, libraries and tourism services, and, as far as possible, enjoy access to monuments and sites of national cultural importance.

2 States Parties shall take appropriate measures to enable persons with disabilities to have the opportunity to develop and utilize their creative, artistic and intellectual potential, not only for their own benefit, but also for the enrichment of society.

3 States Parties shall take all appropriate steps, in accordance with international law, to ensure that laws protecting intellectual property rights do not constitute an unreasonable or discriminatory barrier to access by persons with disabilities to cultural materials.

4 Persons with disabilities shall be entitled, on an equal basis with others, to recognition and support of their specific cultural and linguistic identity, including sign languages and deaf culture.

5 With a view to enabling persons with disabilities to participate on an equal basis with others in recreational, leisure and sporting activities, States Parties shall take appropriate measures:

a   To encourage and promote the participation, to the fullest extent possible, of persons with disabilities in mainstream sporting activities at all levels;
b   To ensure that persons with disabilities have an opportunity to organize, develop and participate in disability-specific sporting and recreational activities and, to this end, encourage the provision, on an equal basis with others, of appropriate instruction, training and resources;
c   To ensure that persons with disabilities have access to sporting, recreational and tourism venues;
d   To ensure that children with disabilities have equal access with other children to participation in play, recreation and leisure and sporting activities, including those activities in the school system;
e   To ensure that persons with disabilities have access to services from those involved in the organization of recreational, tourism, leisure and sporting activities.

Article 31: Statistics and data collection

1 States Parties undertake to collect appropriate information, including statistical and research data, to enable them to formulate and implement policies to give effect to the present Convention. The process of collecting and maintaining this information shall:

a Comply with legally established safeguards, including legislation on data protection, to ensure confidentiality and respect for the privacy of persons with disabilities;
b Comply with internationally accepted norms to protect human rights and fundamental freedoms and ethical principles in the collection and use of statistics.

2 The information collected in accordance with this article shall be disaggregated, as appropriate, and used to help assess the implementation of States Parties' obligations under the present Convention and to identify and address the barriers faced by persons with disabilities in exercising their rights.

3 States Parties shall assume responsibility for the dissemination of these statistics and ensure their accessibility to persons with disabilities and others.

Article 32: International cooperation

1 States Parties recognize the importance of international cooperation and its promotion, in support of national efforts for the realization of the purpose and objectives of the present Convention, and will undertake appropriate and effective measures in this regard, between and among States and, as appropriate, in partnership with relevant international and regional organizations and civil society, in particular organizations of persons with disabilities. Such measures could include, inter alia:

a Ensuring that international cooperation, including international development programmes, is inclusive of and accessible to persons with disabilities;
b Facilitating and supporting capacity-building, including through the exchange and sharing of information, experiences, training programmes and best practices;
c Facilitating cooperation in research and access to scientific and technical knowledge;
d Providing, as appropriate, technical and economic assistance, including by facilitating access to and sharing of accessible and assistive technologies, and through the transfer of technologies.

2 The provisions of this article are without prejudice to the obligations of each State Party to fulfil its obligations under the present Convention.

Article 33: National implementation and monitoring

1 States Parties, in accordance with their system of organization, shall designate one or more focal points within government for matters relating to the implementation of the present Convention, and shall give due consideration to the establishment or designation of a coordination mechanism within government to facilitate related action in different sectors and at different levels.

2 States Parties shall, in accordance with their legal and administrative systems, maintain, strengthen, designate or establish within the State Party, a framework, including one or more independent mechanisms, as appropriate, to promote, protect and monitor implementation of the present Convention. When designating or establishing such a mechanism, States Parties shall take into account the principles relating to the status and functioning of national institutions for protection and promotion of human rights.

3 Civil society, in particular persons with disabilities and their representative organizations, shall be involved and participate fully in the monitoring process.

Article 34: Committee on the Rights of Persons with Disabilities

1 There shall be established a Committee on the Rights of Persons with Disabilities (hereafter referred to as 'the Committee'), which shall carry out the functions hereinafter provided.

2 The Committee shall consist, at the time of entry into force of the present Convention, of twelve experts. After an additional sixty ratifications or accessions to the Convention, the membership of the Committee shall increase by six members, attaining a maximum number of eighteen members.

3 The members of the Committee shall serve in their personal capacity and shall be of high moral standing and recognized competence and experience in the field covered by the present Convention. When nominating their candidates, States Parties are invited to give due consideration to the provision set out in article 4.3 of the present Convention.

4 The members of the Committee shall be elected by States Parties, consideration being given to equitable geographical distribution, representation of the different forms of civilization and of the principal legal systems, balanced gender representation and participation of experts with disabilities.

5 The members of the Committee shall be elected by secret ballot from a list of persons nominated by the States Parties from among their nationals at meetings of the Conference of States Parties. At those meetings, for which two thirds of States Parties shall constitute a quorum, the persons elected to the Committee shall be those who obtain the largest number of votes and an absolute majority of the votes of the representatives of States Parties present and voting.

6 The initial election shall be held no later than six months after the date of entry into force of the present Convention. At least four months before the date of each election, the Secretary-General of the United Nations shall address a letter to the States Parties inviting them to submit the nominations within two months. The Secretary-General shall subsequently prepare a list in alphabetical order of all persons thus nominated, indicating the State Parties which have nominated them, and shall submit it to the States Parties to the present Convention.

7 The members of the Committee shall be elected for a term of four years. They shall be eligible for re-election once. However, the term of six of the members elected at the first election shall expire at the end of two years; immediately after the first election, the names of these six members shall be chosen by lot by the chairperson of the meeting referred to in paragraph 5 of this article.

8 The election of the six additional members of the Committee shall be held on the occasion of regular elections, in accordance with the relevant provisions of this article.

9 If a member of the Committee dies or resigns or declares that for any other cause she or he can no longer perform her or his duties, the State Party which nominated the member shall appoint another expert possessing the qualifications and meeting the requirements set out in the relevant provisions of this article, to serve for the remainder of the term.

10 The Committee shall establish its own rules of procedure.

11 The Secretary-General of the United Nations shall provide the necessary staff and facilities for the effective performance of the functions of the Committee under the present Convention, and shall convene its initial meeting.

12 With the approval of the General Assembly, the members of the Committee established under the present Convention shall receive emoluments from United Nations resources on such terms and conditions as the Assembly may decide, having regard to the importance of the Committee's responsibilities.

13 The members of the Committee shall be entitled to the facilities, privileges and immunities of experts on mission for the United Nations as laid down in the relevant sections of the Convention on the Privileges and Immunities of the United Nations.

Article 35: Reports by States Parties

1 Each State Party shall submit to the Committee, through the Secretary-General of the United Nations, a comprehensive report on measures taken to give effect to its obligations under the present Convention and on the progress made in that regard, within two years after the entry into force of the present Convention for the State Party concerned.

2 Thereafter, States Parties shall submit subsequent reports at least every four years and further whenever the Committee so requests.

3 The Committee shall decide any guidelines applicable to the content of the reports.

4 A State Party which has submitted a comprehensive initial report to the Committee need not, in its subsequent reports, repeat information previously provided. When preparing reports to the Committee, States Parties are invited to consider doing so in an open and transparent process and to give due consideration to the provision set out in article 4.3 of the present Convention.

5 Reports may indicate factors and difficulties affecting the degree of fulfilment of obligations under the present Convention.

Article 36: Consideration of reports

1 Each report shall be considered by the Committee, which shall make such suggestions and general recommendations on the report as it may consider appropriate and shall forward these to the State Party concerned. The State Party may respond with any information it chooses to the Committee. The Committee may request further information from States Parties relevant to the implementation of the present Convention.

2 If a State Party is significantly overdue in the submission of a report, the Committee may notify the State Party concerned of the need to examine the implementation of the present Convention in that State Party, on the basis of reliable information available to the Committee, if the relevant report is not submitted within three months following the notification. The Committee shall invite the State Party concerned to participate in such examination. Should the State Party respond by submitting the relevant report, the provisions of paragraph 1 of this article will apply.

3 The Secretary-General of the United Nations shall make available the reports to all States Parties.

4 States Parties shall make their reports widely available to the public in their own countries and facilitate access to the suggestions and general recommendations relating to these reports.

5 The Committee shall transmit, as it may consider appropriate, to the specialized agencies, funds and programmes of the United Nations, and other competent bodies, reports from States Parties in order to address a request or indication of a need for technical advice or assistance contained therein, along with the Committee's observations and recommendations, if any, on these requests or indications.

Article 37: Cooperation between States Parties and the Committee

1 Each State Party shall cooperate with the Committee and assist its members in the fulfilment of their mandate.

2 In its relationship with States Parties, the Committee shall give due consideration to ways and means of enhancing national capacities for the implementation of the present Convention, including through international cooperation.

Article 38: Relationship of the Committee with other bodies

In order to foster the effective implementation of the present Convention and to encourage international cooperation in the field covered by the present Convention:

a   The specialized agencies and other United Nations organs shall be entitled to be represented at the consideration of the implementation of such provisions of the present Convention as fall within the scope of their mandate. The Committee may invite the specialized agencies and other competent bodies as it may consider appropriate to provide expert advice on the implementation of the Convention in areas falling within the scope of their respective mandates. The Committee may invite specialized agencies and other United Nations organs to submit reports on the implementation of the Convention in areas falling within the scope of their activities;

b   The Committee, as it discharges its mandate, shall consult, as appropriate, other relevant bodies instituted by international human rights treaties, with a view to ensuring the consistency of their respective reporting guidelines, suggestions and general recommendations, and avoiding duplication and overlap in the performance of their functions.

Article 39: Report of the Committee

The Committee shall report every two years to the General Assembly and to the Economic and Social Council on its activities, and may make suggestions and general recommendations based on the examination of reports and information received from the States Parties. Such suggestions and general recommendations shall be included in the report of the Committee together with comments, if any, from States Parties.

Article 40: Conference of States Parties

1 The States Parties shall meet regularly in a Conference of States Parties in order to consider any matter with regard to the implementation of the present Convention.

2 No later than six months after the entry into force of the present Convention, the Conference of the States Parties shall be convened by the Secretary-General of the United Nations. The subsequent meetings shall be convened by the Secretary-General of the United Nations biennially or upon the decision of the Conference of States Parties.

Article 41: Depositary

The Secretary-General of the United Nations shall be the depositary of the present Convention.

Article 42: Signature

The present Convention shall be open for signature by all States and by regional integration organizations at United Nations Headquarters in New York as of 30 March 2007.

Article 43: Consent to be bound

The present Convention shall be subject to ratification by signatory States and to formal confirmation by signatory regional integration organizations. It shall be open for accession by any State or regional integration organization which has not signed the Convention.

Article 44: Regional integration organizations

1 'Regional integration organization' shall mean an organization constituted by sovereign States of a given region, to which its member States have transferred competence in respect of matters governed by this Convention. Such organizations shall declare, in their instruments of formal confirmation or accession, the extent of their competence with respect to matters governed by this Convention. Subsequently, they shall inform the depositary of any substantial modification in the extent of their competence.

2 References to 'States Parties' in the present Convention shall apply to such organizations within the limits of their competence.

3 For the purposes of article 45, paragraph 1, and article 47, paragraphs 2 and 3, any instrument deposited by a regional integration organization shall not be counted.

4 Regional integration organizations, in matters within their competence, may exercise their right to vote in the Conference of States Parties, with a number of votes equal to the number of their member States that are Parties to this Convention. Such an organization shall not exercise its right to vote if any of its member States exercises its right, and vice versa.

Article 45: Entry into force

1 The present Convention shall enter into force on the thirtieth day after the deposit of the twentieth instrument of ratification or accession.

2 For each State or regional integration organization ratifying, formally confirming or acceding to the Convention after the deposit of the twentieth such instrument, the Convention shall enter into force on the thirtieth day after the deposit of its own such instrument.

Article 46: Reservations

1 Reservations incompatible with the object and purpose of the present Convention shall not be permitted.

2 Reservations may be withdrawn at any time.

Article 47: Amendments

1 Any State Party may propose an amendment to the present Convention and submit it to the Secretary-General of the United Nations. The Secretary-General shall communicate any proposed amendments to States Parties, with a request to be notified whether they favour a conference of States Parties for the purpose of considering and deciding upon the proposals. In the event that, within four months from the date of such communication, at least one third of the States Parties favour such a conference, the Secretary-General shall convene the conference under the auspices of the United Nations. Any amendment adopted by a majority of two thirds of the States Parties present and voting shall be submitted by the Secretary-General to the General Assembly for approval and thereafter to all States Parties for acceptance.

2 An amendment adopted and approved in accordance with paragraph 1 of this article shall enter into force on the thirtieth day after the number of instruments of acceptance deposited reaches two thirds of the number of States Parties at the date of adoption of the amendment. Thereafter, the amendment shall enter into force for any State Party on the thirtieth day following the deposit of its own instrument of acceptance. An amendment shall be binding only on those States Parties which have accepted it.

3 If so decided by the Conference of States Parties by consensus, an amendment adopted and approved in accordance with paragraph 1 of this article which relates exclusively to articles 34, 38, 39 and 40 shall enter into force for all States Parties on the thirtieth day after the number of instruments of acceptance deposited reaches two thirds of the number of States Parties at the date of adoption of the amendment.

Article 48: Denunciation

A State Party may denounce the present Convention by written notification to the Secretary-General of the United Nations. The denunciation shall become effective one year after the date of receipt of the notification by the Secretary-General.

Article 49: Accessible format

The text of the present Convention shall be made available in accessible formats.

Article 50: Authentic texts

The Arabic, Chinese, English, French, Russian and Spanish texts of the present Convention shall be equally authentic.

In witness thereof the undersigned plenipotentiaries, being duly authorized thereto by their respective Governments, have signed the present Convention.

Council of Europe Committee of Ministers Recommendation No R (99) 4 of the Committee of Ministers to Member States on Principles Concerning the Legal Protection of Incapable Adults – Explanatory memorandum

(Adopted by the Committee of Ministers on 23 February 1999 at the 660th meeting of the Ministers' Deputies)

EXPLANATORY MEMORANDUM

I. General considerations

1 The 3rd European Conference on Family Law on the subject 'Family law in the future' (Cadiz, Spain, 20–22 April 1995) addressed, in particular, he question of the protection of incapable adults. The conference requested the Council of Europe to invite a group of specialists on this matter to examine the desirability of drafting a European instrument to protect incapable adults, guaranteeing their integrity and rights and, wherever possible, their independence. Following this proposal the Committee of Ministers of the Council of Europe set up, in 1995, the Group of Specialists on Incapable and Other Vulnerable Adults (CJ-S-MI), later re-named the Group of Specialists on Incapable Adults.

2 The Group of Specialists on Incapable Adults (CJ-S-MI), under the authority of the European Committee on Legal Co-operation (CDCJ), was instructed 'to study and prepare draft principles concerning the legal aspects of acts of incapable adults; td study and prepare draft principles concerning the role and duties of representatives, carers, judicial and administrative authorities to assist and protect such persons; and to make proposals toe CDCJ with a view to the drafting of an international instrument (convention or recommendation) in these matters.' The CDCJ, at its 67th meeting, authorised the CJ-S-MI to prepare a draft recommendation on principles concerning the legal protection of incapable adults.

3 The Group of Specialists on Incapable Adults, under authority of the CDCJ, held six meetings under the chairmanship of Mr Jacques Jansen (Netherlands). At its first meeting, the CJ-S-MI prepared a questionnaire on issues concerning incapable adults to be sent to states, in order to prepare a comparative study on the existing measures of protection in the member states of the Council of Europe and to ascertain the number of persons concerned during recent years. Mr Eric Clive, law commissioner of the Scottish Law Commission and Vice-Chair of the CJ-S- MI, prepared a study concerning incapable adults on the basis of the replies to the questionnaire.

4 The Group of Specialists prepared a draft recommendation on principles concerning the legal protection on incapable adults at its fourth meeting on the basis of the first draft of principles concerning incapable adults which was prepared by the CJ-S-MI at its second and third meetings. The CJ-S-MI finalised the draft recommendation in two joint meetings with the Steering Committee on Bioethics (CDBI) and with the Committee of Experts on Family Law (CJ-FA), in order to adopt a multi-disciplinary approach affording more effective overall protection for incapable adults. For the same reasons, the CDCJ decided, at its sixty-eighth meeting, to transmit, for information and comments, the text of the draft

recommendation to the European Health Committee (CDSP), the Steering Committee on Social Policy (CDPS) and the Steering Committee for Human Rights (CDDH).

5 The Group of Specialists on Incapable Adults completed its work on the draft recommendation on principles concerning the legal protection of incapable adults during its sixth meeting. The draft recommendation was subsequently revised by the CDCJ and adopted by the Committee of Ministers on 23 February 1999 as Recommendation No. R (99) 4.

II. Comments on the recommendation

6 The reports and following discussions at the 3rd European Conference on Family Law showed clearly that the issue of incapable adults was likely to be arguably the most topical issue in the years to come. The reasons for this increased interest in this group of adults are manifold: demographic changes, medical developments, social changes and increased overall interest in the protection of human rights.

7 The number of elderly people is rising steadily in European populations, due to improving living conditions and medical advances. These persons' mental faculties often decline with age and the number of persons suffering from senile dementia is increasing markedly in European countries. Nevertheless, concerning this question of demographic changes, it is necessary to underline that the current life expectation in certain countries of central and eastern Europe is, at this moment, lower than in the western European countries, even if a tendency to increase appears. Despite this difference in the life expectation, it can be said that the general trend in Europe is towards an increase in the number of elderly people. In this respect Recommendation 1035 (1986) of the Parliamentary Assembly of the Council of Europe on ageing of populations in Europe: economic and social consequences, noted that during the period from 1990 to 2020 'increases of 20% and more are expected in the 45–60 age-group and of 15–20% in the 65 and over and there will be a disproportionate growth in the number of very old people, aged 80 and over, which would be one-third of the size of this group'; while Parliamentary Assembly Resolution 1008 (1993) on social policies for elderly persons and their self-reliance, noted that 'in the Council of Europe member states, over 60 million people out of a total population of 480 million are in the elderly category, and the proportion is growing constantly.'

8 As has been said, medical developments are one of the reasons for this increase in the number of elderly people. In effect, medical developments have meant that some people who would formerly have died of a disease, condition or injury can now be kept alive, sometimes, however, with a reduced mental capacity. Medical developments in the treatment of mental illness have also meant that a large number of patients who would formerly have required institutional care can now live in the community. Some such people may be vulnerable and in need of measures of protection.

9 Changing lifestyles separate many people from their families, who are not always able to care for relatives whose mental faculties are impaired. On the other hand, there is, at least in some countries, a more widespread distribution of resources. Many incapable adults will have a right to some state benefits or pensions and many older people suffering from dementia will have had an opportunity to accumulate some property during their working lives. Laws, which may have been designed at one time to deal with the problems of a small property owning minority now have to be applied much more widely.

10 The second half of the twentieth century has seen a greatly increased emphasis on human rights. This affects attitudes to the care and protection of incapable people. There is a recognition that existing freedoms and capacities should be preserved as much as possible and those measures which needlessly take away people's rights are indefensible. There is also a much greater emphasis on personal welfare as opposed to the preservation of property.

11 The Group of Specialists, when preparing the recommendation, took into account the international legal background to this matter. Particular attention was paid, as is reflected in the Preamble, to the international instruments prepared in the framework of the Council of Europe. In this respect, the Group examined the Convention for the Protection of Human Rights and Fundamental Freedoms of 4 November 1950 and its additional protocols (in particular Articles 5, 6 and 8 of the Convention, and Article I of the First Protocol to the Convention), as well as the case law of the European Commission and Court of Human Rights relating to this matter. Moreover, especial attention was paid to the provisions of the recent Convention for the Protection of Human Rights and Dignity of the Human Being with regard to the Application of Biology and Medicine: Convention on Human Rights and Biomedicine (henceforth referred to in this text as the Convention on Human Rights and Biomedicine) of 4 April1997 concerning interventions in the health field on persons not able to consent. Finally, the group examined the different resolutions and recommendation adopted by the Committee of Ministers and the Parliamentary Assembly of the Council of Europe relating to the protection and welfare of people suffering from disabilities and vulnerabilities of various types in order to avoid any duplication.

12 The Group of Specialists also paid attention to the international instruments prepared in the framework of the United Nations relating to this subject: the Universal Declaration of Human Rights proclaimed by the General Assembly of the United Nations on 10 December 1948; the International Covenant on Civil and Political Rights and the International Covenant on Economic, Social and Cultural Rights of 16 December 1966; the Declaration on the rights of mentally retarded persons proclaimed by the General Assembly of the United Nations on 20 December 1971; the Declaration on the rights of disabled persons proclaimed by the General Assembly of the United Nations on 9 December 1975; the General Assembly Resolution on implementation of the international plan of action on ageing and related activities of 16 December 1991 and the General Assembly Resolution on the protection of persons with mental illness and the improvement of mental health care of 17 December 1991.

13 Finally, the Group of Specialists took into account tile preparatory work of the Hague Conference on Private International Law concerning the protection of adults. In this respect, the Group of Specialists underlined that the present recommendation, which deals with substantive law matters, and the preliminary draft convention on jurisdiction, applicable law, recognition, enforcement and co-operation in respect of the protection of adults prepared by the Hague Conference, would deal with the international private law aspects of the protection of incapable adults and would be complementary.

14 A comparative survey, based on the responses to the questionnaire on issues concerning incapable adults, has shown that legislative reforms on the protection, by representation or assistance, of incapable adults have been introduced or are under consideration in a number of member states of the Council of Europe and that, even if these reforms have common features, wide disparities in the legislation of member states in this area still exist. Despite these disparities, it is possible to discern a certain pattern in the European laws covered by the responses. In effect, according to

Mr Clive's report, there are three types of systems in national laws relating to the protection of incapable adults. First, there is what might be called the traditional type of system, where the typical legal response is deprivation or restriction of legal capacity, usually coupled with the appointment of a tutor who represents the adult in almost all matters. Secondly, there is what might be called the functionally modified traditional type of system, where perceived social needs have been met by additions to the legal framework and where there is a wider range of measures available and more flexibility in response. Thirdly, there is what might be called the radically recast type of system, where the emphasis is firmly and consistently on protection and assistance rather than deprivation of legal capacity.

III. Introductory provisions on scope

15 Part I of the recommendation deals with scope of application and contains the definition of certain concepts, as understood in the context of the recommendation. First of all it focuses on the crucial question of the definition of the term 'incapable adult'; secondly it refers to the causes of incapacity; thirdly it deals with the type of measures to which the principles apply; fourthly it deals with the meaning of the term 'adult' and finally it deals with the meaning of the term 'intervention in the health field' which appears in Part V.

16 The first paragraph of Part I deals with the crucial question of who are considered 'incapable adults' in the context of this recommendation. According to the definition, an adult may be incapable due to an impairment or insufficiency of his or her personal faculties. For the purpose of the principles, incapacity is a functional concept relating to decision-making. Incapacity may be, and often will be, only partial or temporary. The incapacity might be temporary in its effect depending on, for example, the particular stage of an illness or the effects of treatment. In other words, the primary focus of the definition is on decision-making capacity.

17 However, to define incapable adults in terms only of decision-making would be too narrow and would result in indefensible anomalies. There may be people – sometimes called 'vulnerable adults' – who can make decisions but who are unable, because of some mental or physical disorder, to understand or to express them or act upon them. For such people decision-making is possible but effective decision-making is not. One example of a person who may be able to make decisions, but who may be as vulnerable and as in need of protection by representation or assistance as a person who cannot, would be a person who is totally unable to communicate or to express decisions. A second example would be an adult who is able to make decisions but who, because of some non-cognitive mental disorder, makes wildly irrational decisions, which could not reasonably be regarded as a proper basis for the management of his or her personal or economic interests. A third example would be a person who can make decisions but who, because of a mental disorder, cannot remember them for more than a minute or two and who is accordingly unable properly to manage his or her affairs. A fourth example, would be a person who can make and remember decisions but who, because of a mental disorder, is wholly incapable of acting on them or on some of them. Yet another example would be a person who can make decisions but who, because of extreme suggestibility, is in need of protection by representation or assistance. The definition therefore covets not only those who are unable to make decisions but also those who are unable to understand, express or act upon decisions.

18 Some legal systems expressly include people who abuse alcohol or other substances or even prodigals, who dissipate their assets to the prejudice of their

families, within the category of those for whom measures of protection may be provided. Others expressly exclude them from this category. Others may not mention them one way or the other. Substance abuse or prodigality should not by themselves be regarded as bringing a person) into the category of 'incapable'. However, a person who was in fact incapable as a result such abuses would be within the scope of the principles.

19 The concept of autonomy is an important element in the first paragraph. It is used in a wide sense – based on the idea of the authenticity of decisions in the light of a person's character, values and life history. An autonomous decision must be free from external coercion and internal compulsion due, for example to such factors as schizophrenic delusions or severe depressive episodes. It should also be based on a sufficient understanding of the importance and consequences of the decision. Another important concept – namely rationality – is not used in this context. There is a danger that a reference to rationality could be misinterpreted and that merely eccentric behaviour, or behaviour deviating from prevailing norms, might be regarded as irrational. In this respect, the European Court of Human Rights stated in the *Winterwerp* case: 'the Convention does not permit the confinement of1an individual simply because his views or behaviour deviate from norms prevailing in a particular society' (European Court of Human Rights, *Winterwerp v the Netherlands*, judgment of 24 October 1979, Series A, No. 33).

20 Paragraph 2 of the first part of the recommendation states that an adult may be considered incapable, as established in Article 6, paragraph 3, of the recent Convention on Human Rights and Biomedicine, due to 'mental disability, a disease or similar reasons'. Following the explanatory report of this Convention the term 'similar reasons' refers to such situations as accidents or states of coma, for example, where the patient is unable to formulate his or her wishes or to communicate them (see paragraph 43 of the Explanatory Report of the Convention on Human Rights and Biomedicine). Although the important point, from the point of view of the taking of legal measures of protection, is the nature of incapacity rather than its underlying cause, it may be helpful to give some examples of ways which incapacity may arise. However, one danger in referring to particular causes is that scientific and medical knowledge in this area is constantly changing. Fashions in terminology also change, partly because certain terms, which are initially intended to be purely descriptive, gradually seem to become derogatory. There is therefore a risk that any list of particular conditions or causes might soon become out of date. It is not easy to devise a suitable list. Nevertheless, the following mental and behavioural disorders among others may lead, in certain cases, to incapacity within the definition: mental retardation; senile dementia, in particular Alzheimer's disease in its later stages; certain forms of manic depressive illness and schizophrenia. Severe physical disabilities, such as total inability to communicate, may also bring a person under the scope of paragraph 1.

21 As the title of the recommendation shows, it is important to underline the rather juridical nature of the protection with which the instrument is concerned. This instrument is not concerned with the whole range of social security or social service measures, and not with different treatments for mental illness, but essentially with legal protection by representation or assistance. The terms 'representation' and 'assistance' are used here in a functional sense. Representation means primarily taking decisions for or on behalf of the adult. Assistance means primarily providing help or advice to the adult in relation to decisions or consenting to decisions taken by the adult. Both may include management functions. The third paragraph of Part I of the recommendation refers to 'measures of protection' stricto sensu and 'other arrangements', both in a legal sense. The difference between 'measure' and

'arrangement' turns mainly on the person or body who has taken the decision: a 'measure' is adopted by a judicial or administrative authority and an 'arrangement' is made by the individual himself or by others not acting in a judicial or administrative capacity.

22 Paragraph 4 of Part I of the recommendation deals with the meaning of the term 'adult' as understood in these principles. The ages at which people cease to be legally incapable on the ground that they are still regarded as children vary from country to country. Eighteen is now a very common age for the attainment of majority but in some countries legal capacity in many or most civil law matters is attained at the age of 16. There would be a gap in protection in such countries if a person ceased to have a legal representative as a child at the age of 16 but could not yet be provided with a legal representative as an adult. Therefore, the principles refer to persons who are treated as being of full age under the applicable law on capacity in civil law matters. This formula ('treated as') has the additional advantage of covering emancipated minors.

23 Paragraph 5 of Part I of the recommendation deals with the meaning of the term 'intervention in the health field' as understood in the context of the recommendation (Part V). In this respect, it is necessary to underline that the Convention on Human Rights and Biomedicine uses the expression 'intervention in the health field' but does not define it in the text. However, the explanatory report gives some indications. It is a useful expression because it covers not only medical, surgical or dental treatment but also acts carried out for the purposes of preventive care, diagnosis, rehabilitation or research. In the context of the Convention on Human Rights and Biomedicine it may be that a definition is not necessary because the convention is aimed at experts in a particular field. In the context of a new instrument, which is aimed at legislators and policy advisers generally, rather than at health care experts in particular, a definition is useful. In this respect an 'intervention in the health field' means any act performed professionally on a person for reasons of health. It includes, in particular, interventions for the purposes of preventive care, diagnosis, treatment, rehabilitation or research.

IV. Comments on the principles

Part II – Governing principles

Principle 1 – Respect for human rights

24 Principle 1 inaugurates Part II of the recommendation entitled 'Governing principles'. This heading underlines that when taking a measure of protections for an incapable adult or operating another legal arrangement it is necessary to take into account these essential and basic principles.

25 Incapable adults are in a weak position due to their incapacity, and they can easily be the object of abuse. Therefore, in the Preamble, and in particular in Principle I, it is stressed that respect for the dignity of each person as a human being is • principle which underlies all the other principles. Principle I also states that laws, procedures and practices relating to the protection of incapable adults shall be based on respect of their human rights and fundamental freedoms. The reference to human rights is a general one, In order to avoid any duplication with the provisions of other international instruments concerning human rights (some of them appearing in the Preamble).

26 There are certain cases where in the interests of the person concerned there may have to be an infringement of, for example, the right to liberty or the tight to the

enjoyment of possessions. There may also be cases where, for example, the right to liberty has to be restricted in the interests of others. The recommendation expressly leaves the regulation of these matters to other international legal instruments mentioned in the Preamble, in particular to the Convention for the Protection of Human Rights and Fundamental Freedoms and the Convention on Human Rights and Biomedicine.

Principle 2 – Flexibility in legal response

27 The first essential, when a country's laws on this subject are being reconsidered, is that there should be an adequate legislative framework providing for sufficient flexibility in legal response. There is no point, for example, in having a principle of adopting the least restrictive alternative, or a principle of having a response tailor-made to the needs of the situation, if the legal framework does not provide an adequate range of responses. The range may be provided either by making different types of measure or arrangement available, or by making available a type of measure which can be varied in content to suit the needs of each case, or by a combination of these methods. The choice of technique is left to national laws.

28 Effective emergency measures should always be available. In this context it is necessary to take into account the principles of Recommendation No. R (91) 9 of the Committee of Ministers to member states on emergency measures in family matters.

29 This flexibility principle implies also that the legal framework should provide for simple and inexpensive measures or other legal arrangements. Examples of such measures or arrangements might be the administration of sums within certain limits by hospital or other authorities, or the appointment by administrative authorities, under a simple and inexpensive procedure, of representatives with strictly limited powers.

30 The range of measures available should include measures which do not necessarily restrict the legal capacity of the person concerned. This is a corollary of the general policy in favour of maximum preservation of capacity set out in Principle 3. In many cases the persons to whom measures of protection are applied are in a passive state and in a condition where there is no risk that they will enter into legal agreements. Accordingly there is no reason to remove their legal capacity. A need for such a step may, however, arise if the person concerned, regardless or rather because of the handicap, is active and it is felt necessary to protect him or her against making decisions which entail risks. It may also be necessary to prevent exploitation by others.

31 The range of measures should also provide for measures limited to one specific act or intervention. There are many situations where the appointment of a representative with continuing powers is unnecessary. Indeed, the appointment of any type of representative may be unnecessary. It may be sufficient for the court or other body itself to authorise the intervention. Examples might be the authorisation of the sale of a house, or the authorisation of a particular medical intervention.

32 Paragraph 6 deals with arrangements whereby an appointed person acts jointly with the adult concerned, who might well not be wholly incapable. Another form of joint representation might also be worth mentioning – namely that where there are two or more joint representatives. The advantage of such an arrangement is that the representatives can make different skills available. Another advantage in some situations is increased protection. There might, for example, be one representative who could provide valuable personal support but who might be unreliable financially. Joint guardianship could provide supervision and protection. Another

technique involving two representatives is that of appointing a representative and an alternate representative who would take over if the principal representative died or became incapable of acting.

33 Paragraph 7 states the advantages of giving legal recognition to arrangements made in advance by the person himself or herself while still fully capable. Some may require no legal regulation. For example, a person may be able to enter into a contractual arrangement with his or her bank or similar institution whereby payments may be made to a nominated person if certain evidence of later incapacity is produced. It may be possible to establish joint accounts to achieve similar results. Some such advance arrangements may require rather more in the way of legal regulation. Examples of such arrangements might be continuing powers of attorney or advance directives in the health field. There has been an increasing use of specially adapted powers of attorney in some legal systems. A power of attorney is simply a power or authority granted by one person (the granter, or donor, or mandant, or principal) to another (the attorney, or donee, or mandatory, or agent) authorising the attorney to act on behalf of the granter. The scope of the power or authority depends on the terms of the grant or mandate which confers it. The basic concept of a power or authority to act, granted voluntarily by a mandate or commission, is a familiar one in European legal systems. A typical example might be the authority of a factor or estate manager to act on behalf of an absent landowner. However, the particular application of this concept in relation to incapable adults raises some special difficulties. Much depends, first, on whether the applicable law has a rule that the power ceases to have effect if the granter subsequently becomes incapable or a rule that it continues to have effect notwithstanding the onset of incapacity. If the general rule is cessation then the need is for the legal system to provide for an exception so that in specified circumstances, and subject to appropriate safeguards, the power can continue after the onset of incapacity. If the general rule is continuance then the need is for the legal system to consider what safeguards are needed for the situation which arises after the onset of incapacity.

34 Paragraph 8 refers to the advantages of providing some legal recognition for the functions commonly exercised de facto by family members and those involved in the affairs of the incapable adult, for instance a partner cohabiting with the incapable adult, or close friends. Two of the governing principles on the establishment of measures of protection are the principles of necessity and subsidiarity (see Principle 5 below). If the necessary protection and assistance can be provided in an appropriate way by family members or other persons involved in the affairs of the incapable adult then there may be no need for formal/measures. At present it seems probable that in many legal systems family members and those involved in the affairs of the incapable adult are operating in a legal vacuum or at least in an unclear legal situation. Doctrines such as negotiorum gestio[1] may not provide a complete answer,[2] even in those systems where they are well developed. Of course, if legal recognition is given to decision-making by family members and those involved in the affairs of the incapable adult any powers conferred or recognised will have to be carefully limited, controlled and supervised.

1   This is the doctrine of 'management of affairs' whereby a person may lawfully intervene to manage or protect the affairs of someone else who is not available to do so, either because of absence or, at least in some systems, because of incapacity. The manager can recover his or her expenses for doing so. The manager has no authorisation from the person whose affairs are managed: the authority to intervene is derived from the law itself.
2   It may not be clear, for example, whether they have any application in relation to decisions on personal welfare.

Principle 3 – Maximum preservation of capacity

35 The legislative framework should recognise that different degrees of incapacity may exist and that incapacity may vary from time to time. Therefore the legislative framework should be such that extreme consequences are not attached automatically to measures of protection. In particular a measure of protection should not result in an automatic complete removal of legal capacity. However, a restriction of legal capacity should be available if necessary for the protection of the person concerned. There will never, it is submitted, be any need to restrict the capacity to vote or make a will or to consent or refuse consent to any medical treatment or other intervention in the health field or make other decisions of a personal nature such as the decision to marry. Such acts should depend on the presence or absence of actual capacity at the relevant time. Any rules on the assessment of capacity should make it clear that the assessment should be directed to capacity to take particular decisions or types of decision, or to undertake specific acts or acts in a specific area.

36 The representative of an incapable adult should promote, where possible, action by the adult on his or her own. The general principle here is that, so far as is possible and appropriate, the adult concerned should be involved in the establishment and implementation of any measures of protection. A particular application of this principle might be an arrangement whereby a representative could permit the adult to undertake certain specific acts or acts in a specific area, even in areas within the general competence of the represtIntative. This principle is also applicable in the health care field (in this respect see Article 6 paragraph 3 of the Convention on Human Rights and Biomedicine).

Principle 4 – Publicity

37 The question of the publicity to be given to measures of protection is a difficult one. On the one hand this publicity can undoubtedly be stigmatising for the person concerned. On the other hand in some cases publicity may serve to protect not only third parties but also the adult concerned. Perhaps the only safe conclusion is that the need for publicity in relation to particular types of measures should be carefully assessed, as also should the particular type of publicity used. An entry in a register which is open to inspection by those who may be affected by a measure, but which in practice might only rarely be inspected, would be less stigmatising, for example, than a public notice or an annotation of a birth certificate. It seems to be preferable to leave some discretion to national laws in this matter so far as actual techniques are concerned. However the importance of avoiding unnecessarily stigmatising publicity seems clear.

Principle 5 – Necessity and subsidiarity

38 Two of the key principles in recent reforms of this branch of the law are the principles of necessity and subsidiarity. They are also known as the principle of minimum necessary intervention. They imply, first of all, that no measure of protection should be established unless it is necessary, taking into account the circumstances of the particular case. Secondly, in deciding whether a measure is necessary, account should be taken of any less formal arrangements which might be made or used, and of any assistance which might be provided by family members, public authorities or other means. The latter is the principle known as 'subsidiarity': a response by means of legal measures should be subsidiary to a response by means of the use of informal arrangements or the provision of assistance. Any legislation addressing the problem of incapable adults should give a prominent place to these

principles. The necessity principle would not, however, prevent a measure which is not strictly necessary from being taken with the adult's consent if it is ascertained that he or she has sufficient capacity to give such consent. For instance, it is possible that a measure of protection is established in order to provide for any subsequent incapacity (for example, a person suffering from Alzheimer's disease in its preliminary stages).

39 The reference to 'necessity' raises a question about the criterion to be applied. Necessary for what? It is implicit that the measure must be necessary for the protection of the adult or his or her interests or welfare. Protection in turn implies protection against some danger or disadvantage, including the disadvantage of losing a benefit or opportunity which would otherwise be available.

Principle 6 – Proportionality

40 Another principle, which has also been regarded as important in all recent reforms, is the principle that where a measure of protection is necessary it should be proportional to the degree of capacity of the person concerned and tailored to the individual circumstances of the case. This is also known as the principle of the least restrictive alternative. The measure should restrict the legal capacity, rights and freedoms of the person concerned by the minimum which is consistent with achieving the purpose of the intervention. Laws of the more traditional type which provide that the taking of a certain measure of protection automatically deprives the person concerned of legal capacity or involves a very substantial restriction in legal capacity without regard to the needs of the particular situation would clearly not conform to this principle.

Principle 7 – Procedural fairness and efficiency

41 This Principle establishes that fair and efficient procedures for the taking of measures of protection should be provided. The 'fairness' of the procedures should be understood as a principle applicable during the development of the proceedings. This implies, in particular, that there are adequate procedures for investigation and assessment (see Principle 12 below). The efficiency of the procedures is connected with Principle 11 below concerning the rules on competence to initiate proceedings.

42 There should be adequate procedural safeguards to protect the human rights of the adult concerned and to prevent possible abuses. It is necessary to be on guard against the danger that a change to welfare terminology will conceal the essential nature of what is being done. A measure which is called a measure of protection or assistance may in reality be an infringement of rights and freedoms from the point of view of the adult concerned.

Principle 8 – Paramountcy of interests and welfare of person concerned

43 It is important to stress that the interests and welfare[3] 10fthe adult concerned should be the paramount consideration in the establishment or implementation of a measure of protection. They are not necessarily the only consideration. Other people, such as those looking after the person concerned and, in some cases, neighbours and members of the public might also have interests which have to be taken into consideration. However, the emphasis should be firmly on the interests and welfare of the adult concerned.

3   There are various ways of expressing this principle. Terms like 'best interests', 'welfare' or

'benefit' have been considered. The formula 'interests and welfare' is the same as that used in the Convention on Human Rights and Biomedicine

44 This principle implies among other things that the choice of any person to represent or assist an incapable adult should be governed by the suitability of that person to safeguard and promote the adult's interests and welfare. In some family situations there are quite acute conflicts of interest and, while the invaluable and irreplaceable role of family members must be fully recognised and valued, the law must also be aware of the dangers which exist in certain situations of family conflict.

45 The safeguard and promotion of the adult's interests and welfare appear as cumulative conditions on the choice of the representative. It is necessary to take into account the close links between paragraph 2 of this Principle and paragraph 2 of Principle 9. The wishes of the adult as to the choice of any person to represent or assist him or he should be taken into account and given due respect provided that the person chosen by the adult is suitable for safeguarding and promoting the adult's interests and welfare (see paragraph 7 below).

46 The principle of the paramountcy of the interests and welfare of the adult concerned also implies that the property of the adult should not be preserved for the benefit of heirs or others if it can usefully and appropriately be managed and used for the benefit and for an improvement in the quality of life of the adult concerned.

Principle 9 – Respect for wishes and feelings of person concerned

47 One of the theoretical debates in relation to incapable adults is whether the principle governing intervention should be a 'best interests' principle or a 'substituted judgement' principle. When the choice is between the interests of the adult and the interests of other people, and when the adult has no known wishes on the matter, then it seems reasonable, as suggested above, to regard the interests of the adult as the paramount consideration. The question in some cases, however, may be between the interests of the adult and the wishes or supposed wishes of the adult. There can be no rigid answer to this question. In some cases it would be unreasonable and probably unacceptable to give full and automatic effect to what may be supposed to be the wishes of the adult. Incapacity can affect all kinds of people. To regard previously expressed wishes as absolutely binding on any representative in all circumstances would not always be a good idea. It seems clear, however, that one of the governing principles should be that in establishing or implementing a measure of protection the past and present wishes and feelings of the person concerned should be ascertained so far as possible, and should be taken into account and given due respect. The formula 'due respect' allows some room for discretion.

48 The principle of respect for the wishes and feelings of the person concerned implies in particular that the wishes of the person as to the choice of any representative or assistant should be taken into account and, as far as possible, given due respect. It also implies that the representative should inform the adult concerned with regard to any decisions in major matters affecting him or her so that he or she can express a view. Respect for the wishes of the adult may, for example, justify the making of small gifts in accordance with the adult's wishes.

49 The principle also has implications in relation to directions that certain types of medical treatment should not be given. In this context it is useful to recall Article 9 of the Council of Europe's Convention on Human Rights and Biomedicine of 1997 which provides that: 'The previously expressed wishes relating to a medical

intervention by a patient who is not, at the time of the intervention, in a state to express his or her wishes shall be taken into account.'

Principle 10 – Consultation

50 The principle of minimum necessary intervention means that there will very often be situations where either family members (or other persons involved informally in the affairs of the incapable adult) and appointed representatives have a role in protecting and assisting the adult concerned. There may also be situations where there are two or more representatives, and situations where a court or other body or person is called on to authorise or approve a particular intervention in a case where a representative is already in place. It seems clear that where people are involved in protecting and promoting the welfare of the adult it should be a fundamental principle that they should be consulted, so far is reasonable and practicable, by any person establishing or implementing a measure of protection. The way in which the consultation should be conducted, and the effects of the consultation or its absence are left to national law. It is also left to national law to decide which persons should be consulted.

Part III – Procedural principles

Principle 11 – Institution of proceedings

51 The list of those persons who have competence to initiate proceedings for the taking of measures of protection of incapable adults should be sufficiently wide to ensure that measures of protection can be considered in all cases where they are necessary. The list should include the adult concerned. It is no longer possible to assume, particularly in the case of old people, that there will always be responsible and interested members of the adult's family who are prepared to initiate proceedings. As has been said above, this principle shapes one of the aspects of the efficiency of the procedures (see Principle 7).

52 When instituting these proceedings it is necessary to give full effect to one particular procedural safeguard, namely the giving to the person concerned of information about the institution of proceedings which could affect his or her legal capacity, unless it would be manifestly meaningless to the person concerned or would present a severe danger to his or her health. In this respect, it is necessary to recall the requirements of Article 6 (especially paragraphs 1 and 3, a) of the Convention for the Protection of Human Rights and Fundamental Freedoms.

Principle 12 – Investigation and assessment

53 There should be adequate procedures for the investigation and assessment of the adult's personal faculties. This forms part of the fairness of the procedures as established in Principle 7.

54 A judge or other person taking any measure of protection which restricts the legal capacity of an adult should see personally the adult concerned before taking the measure or be personally satisfied as to the adult's condition. There should always be a requirement of expert reports in the case of more formal measures which interfere with capacity. These reports could be in written form or recorded in writing in those cases where the experts present their reports in an oral form, for instance during the decision-making process of the measure of protection. Even

where the adult has been seen by the decision-maker, an expert report could also be a useful safeguard. In this respect, it is necessary to underline the requirement of an evaluation of social capability by qualified experts in the United Nations Declaration on the rights of mentally retarded persons (RES 2856 (XXVI) of the General Assembly, 20 December 1971).

Principle 13 – Right to be heard in person

55 Another particular procedural safeguard is the person's right to be heard, in person, in any proceedings which could affect his or her legal capacity. The person who has the right to be heard may, however, not be able to exercise this right in a particular case, for example if he or she is unable to intervene and to express an opinion or is too unwell to take part in the proceedings. The exercise of the right may also have to be controlled if, for example, the person proves to be disruptive. In these cases a right of representation of the adult concerned should be assured. Concerning this right to be heard, it is necessary to take into account the provisions of the Convention for the Protection of Human Rights and Fundamental Freedoms, in particular its Article 6, paragraph 1, as well as the case-law of the European Commission and Court of Human Rights concerning the right to be heard.

Principle 14 – Duration, review and appeal

56 Measures of protection should not be established for an indefinite duration unless this is necessary or appropriate in the interests of the adult concerned, for instance when the adult who needs the appointment of a representative suffers from senile dementia from which there is no possibility of recovery. Consideration should be given to the institution of periodical reviews of any measure of protection taken, unless the measure of protection is of fixed, and short, duration. The periodicity of such a review could be fixed, for example, by the authority establishing the measure of protection. The national law should determine the persons entitled to demand a review of measures of protection. In this respect, the adult concerned should be entitled to demand such a review.

57 Taking into account the present recommendation's approach – which recognises that there may be different degrees of incapacity, that incapacity may vary from time to time, and that therefore any measure of protection should be governed by the idea of the maximum preservation of capacity of the adult concerned – any change of circumstances and, above all, a change in the condition of the adult should lead to a review of measures of protection. Relevant changes of circumstances other than changes in the adult's condition might include, for example, the inheritance of property by the adult or changes in the adult's place of residence. Furthermore, if the conditions which determined the establishment of a measure of protection are no longer fulfilled, that measure should be terminated.

58 There should also be adequate provision for appeals, as required by the United Nations Declaration on the rights of mentally retarded persons (RES 2856 (XXVI) of the General Assembly, 20 December 1971).

Principle 15 – Provisional measures in case of emergency

59 In cases of emergency there should, as far as possible, be simple and expeditious procedures for taking provisional measures of protection. In these cases, the principles concerning the institution of proceedings (Principle 11), the investigation

and assessment (Principle 12), the right to be heard in person (Principle 13) and duration, review and appeal (Principle 14) should also be applicable as far as possible according to the circumstances.

Principle 16 – Adequate control

60 Adequate control of the operation of measures of protection and of the acts and decisions of representatives should be provided. However, there is a balancing exercise to be done. Too much control, particularly of less formal measures, may be counterproductive and indeed may make the measures totally impracticable. The control may take into account that excessive costs and burdens may prevent or discourage the use of measures which could be advantageous to the persons concerned.

Principle 17 – Qualified persons

61 Steps should be taken with a view to providing an adequate number of suitably qualified persons for the representation and assistance of incapable adults. What constitute suitable qualifications will differ widely according to the role and functions of the person who provides representation or assistance. In some countries, notably Austria and France, it has been found extremely useful to establish and support associations will the functions of providing and training people who can represent or assist incapable adults.

Part IV – The role of representatives

Principle 18 – Control of powers arising by operation of law

62 Principle 18 is the first principle of Part IV of the recommendation, which deals with the role of representatives.

63 In some countries certain people may have fairly wide powers by operation of law in some circumstances. For example, the parents of a person who is incapable while in minority may continue to have the powers of legal representatives after the attainment of majority by the person. Other countries, however, do not recognise that any person has wide powers by operation of law in relation to the affairs of an incapable adult. In particular they do not recognise that parental responsibility can continue after the child has become an adult. There may be a general policy in such countries against 'infantilisation' of incapable adults. However, even in these countries, it is probable that there will be limited powers which arise by operation of law. For example, the law on negotiorum gestio (or 'management of affairs') may allow acts of administration or acts for the protection of property to be one on behalf of an adult who is incapable of authorising them to be done. It would be inappropriate to declare all such powers unacceptable. Indeed, the conferment or recognition of some limited powers might be very useful if the role of family members and carers, and medical professionals, is to be sufficiently emphasised and valued and if a technical legal vacuum is Ito be avoided.

64 What does seem clear is the need to limit and control the exercise of any powers conferred on any person by operation of law to act or take decision on behalf of an incapable adult. There are obvious human rights implications here and obvious dangers of contravening the principles of necessity and proportionality. Therefore, it is necessary to underline that the conferment of any powers by operation of law

should never deprive the adult concerned of legal capacity. Any such powers should be seen as supplementary. They shod be capable of being modified or terminated at any time by a measure of protection taken by a judicial or administrative authority. The need to control the exercise of such power does not mean that a burdensome system of supervision must be established. It would be sufficient to ensure that the exercise of the powers could be subjected to control where necessary.

65 The principles concerning the paramountcy of the interests and welfare of the person concerned (Principle 8), respect for the wishes and feelings of the adult (Principle 9) and consultation (Principle 10) should apply to the exercise of such powers conferred on any person by operation of law.

Principle 19 – Limitation of powers of representatives

66 Some legal systems expressly provide that there are certain matters of a highly personal nature which a representative cannot undertake on behalf of the incapable adult. It seems fairly clear that there are certain matters which almost everyone would agree were so personal that a representative should never undertake them on behalf of the adult concerned. Examples would be voting, marrying, recognising and adopting a child. There is a range of other measures where different views would be taken and where the appropriate course might well be to leave decisions to national laws, taking into account the relevant other principles.

For example, there are arguments both ways on such questions as making, varying or revoking a will on behalf of the incapable adult, the making of donations, or the bringing or defending of divorce proceedings.

67 Another technique which is often used is to require a court or other body to give specific approval to certain decisions of a serious nature, such as consent to certain serious or controversial interventions in the health field, the disposal of capital in certain ways, or the incurring of certain types of obligation. National laws may require such approval in specified cases.

Principle 20 – Liability

68 The general principle is that representatives are liable, in accordance with national law, for any loss or damage caused by them to incapable adults while exercising their functions. In particular, the laws on liability for wrongful acts, negligence or maltreatment should apply to representatives and others involved in the affairs of incapable adults.

69 However, the normal laws on responsibility may have to be adjusted in the light of some of the principles. For example, should a representative be liable for a diminution in the estate of the adult concerned if the diminution is the direct result of compliance with the principle requiring the past wishes of the adult to be taken into account and given due respect? Again, should a representative be liable for loss to the estate of the adult if it results from compliance with the principle of allowing the adult to become involved in his or her own affairs? In such cases, if the representative has acted reasonably and in good faith in accordance with the principles he or she should not be liable. On the other hand, it would be necessary, or at least advisable to establish an obligatory insurance in order to enable any eventual responsibility to be met.

Principle 21 – Remuneration and expenses

70 The question of the remuneration of representatives or other assistants is clearly a very important one in practice. Reimbursement of expenses is also important. A great deal has to be left to national laws. Where the estate of the incapable adult is substantial, there would seem to be no reason of principle why the costs of representation should not be met out of the estate. The problem becomes more acute when the means of the adult are modest, and in such cases some public assistance may well be necessary or desirable. Another distinction, which is made in some national laws, is between those who are acting in a professional capacity and those who are acting as family members. There may also be cases where a distinction between the management of personal matters and the management of economic matters would be justifiable. However, the point of the principle is that national laws should have provisions on this important matter.

Part V – Interventions in the health field

71 Part V deals with the question of interventions in the health field. In this respect, it is necessary to underline that the Group of Specialists who prepared the present recommendation examined the relationship between this recommendation concerning the legal protection of incapable adults and the Convention on Human Rights and Biomedicine in a joint meeting with the Steering Committee on Bioethics (CDBI). The conclusions reached in this first binding international legal instrument in these matters are followed in so far as they cover questions within the scope of this recommendation. However, it has been decided that the recommendation on principles concerning the legal protection of incapable !adults should contain some principles on interventions in the health field. First of all, there are some points which are left unresolved by the Convention on Human Rights and Biomedicine. F9r example, this convention left aside the important question whether, as a general rule, capacity to consent to a medical intervention should be based on actual capacity at the time of the proposed intervention or on legal incapacity. Secondly, even where the matter in question has been dealt with in the Convention on Human Rights and Biomedicine, there could be value in repeating the most relevant conclusions in the present recommendation. There may be countries which do not ratify the Convention on Human Rights and Biomedicine for reasons unconnected with the rules on incapable adults. In relation to such countries principles in a recommendation could be influential. There is, however, a problem in this area. Certain interventions (or non-interventions) in relation to incapable adults in the health field – such as terminating or withholding life support treatment, or undertaking non-therapeutic research – give rise to such acute differences of opinion that concern about them could dominate discussions of the whole instrument and prevent fair consideration of the proposals on measures of protection generally. Therefore, it was decided not to include detailed recommendations on these topics.

72 For the reasons mentioned in the above paragraphs, Part V of the draft recommendation reproduces, slightly amended, some of the provisions of the Convention on Human Rights and Biomedicine. It is necessary to note the specificity of this part in the context of the recommendation. Part V does not provide for the representation and assistance of the adult, as the rest of the provisions of the recommendation do, but for the protection of the adult in cases where an intervention in the health field is envisaged.

Principle 22 – Consent

73 Paragraph I of this principle underlines that where an adult, even if subject to a measure of protection, is in fact capable at the relevant time of giving free and informed consent to an intervention in the health field, the intervention may only be carried out with his or her consent. This principle is a direct consequence of the recommendation's approach of favouring actual capacity wherever possible. It also takes account of the fact that an adult may be subject only to a limited measure of protection – for example one relating only to property. The principle does not prevent the possibility, for an adult subject to a measure of protection, of consultation with his or her representative. The second sentence of this principle deals with the active role that the health care professionals and representatives should play in order to seek the consent of the adult concerned. In some cases it may be necessary for the adult's consent to be communicated through a person he or she trusts.

74 If a disagreement concerning the adult's actual capacity exists between, for instance, a doctor and the representative of the adult, and the disagreement cannot otherwise be resolved, the competent authority might have to be asked to decide.

75 Concerning the protection of adults not able to give consent (paragraph 2), it is appropriate to adopt the solutions in Article 6 of the Convention on Human Rights and Biomedicine with appropriate alterations in the wording.[4] It is necessary to remember that, save in exceptional circumstances (see comment on Principle 24), Article 6 requires the intervention to be for the direct benefit of the adult concerned and also requires the authorisation of his or her representative or of 'an authority or a person or body provided for by law'. It should be noted that Principles 8 to 10 apply to interventions in the health field (see Principle 27). Accordingly, even if the adult is not able to consent to a particular intervention, his or her wishes should still be ascertained, so far as possible, taken into account and given due respect. This principle should not be interpreted as limiting or otherwise affecting the possibility for national law to grant a wider protection to the individual with regard to healthcare interventions.

[4] It does not seem to be necessary to repeat the rules about the giving of information as they are of general application and are not concerned specifically with incapable adults.

76 The question of which authorities, persons or bodies should be provided for by law as having decision-making powers in relation to incapable adults is particularly important in relation to medical treatment (Paragraph 3). At any one time in any country there will be many potential patients who are in fact incapable of giving free and informed consent to medical treatment but who have no formally appointed legal representative. The rules on treatment in emergencies provide a partial answer to the practical problems which arise,[5] but not a complete answer.

[5] The rules are not confined to life-saving interventions. See the explanatory report to the Convention on Human Rights and Biomedicine, paragraphs 56–59.

77 It is probable that there are many minor and routine treatments or interventions, which may not arise in situations of emergency, which may be slightly invasive, but which would not justify the formal appointment of a legal representative or even the seeking of authorisation from a court or similar body. Consider, for example, the freezing-off of a wart, which causes irritation or discomfort, or the stitching of a small cut which would heal, but less well, without stitching. In practice there is little doubt that many such treatments will simply be provided. But unless the law actually gives some authority to act in such cases the intervention will technically be of doubtful legality. Doctors who are doing their best for their patients, and who are trying to act in accordance with internationally accepted standards and codes of

professional ethics, deserve better of the law than being left to intervene in a legal vacuum. And it is in no-one's interests that legal proceedings should have to be taken in such cases for the appointment of a representative or the formal giving of authority.

78 It is suggested that states reviewing their laws on incapable adults should consider what authorities, persons or bodies should be allowed by law to authorise medical treatment which, in the opinion of the medical professionals in charge of the c se, is clearly for the benefit of an incapable adult. There is a strong argument for enabling medical professionals themselves to authorise certain minor interventions. Certain particularly serious interventions might require authorisation from an appointed representative with appropriate powers or, in some cases, from some special body or court. The details and scope of authorisation systems are for national laws to determine. The important point is that the principles draw attention to the need for such matters to be given careful consideration. The new emphasis on subsidiarity and proportionality means that it will be quite normal for an incapable adult not to have a representative with extensive powers. That is something to be welcomed rather than deplored but it does mean that care will have to be taken not to leave any unnecessary legal gaps.

79 A particularly sensitive question appears in those cases where there exists a disagreement between persons or bodies authorised to consent or refuse consent to interventions in the health field in relation to adults who are incapable of giving consent (Paragraph 4). Internal law should establish mechanisms for the resolution of such conflicts. A typical case might concern two representatives of the incapable adult: one representative with general powers and the other representative with powers in the health field. In these cases it is possible that the representative with the general powers might oppose or veto a medical treatment for the adult which is available and which the doctors or others in charge of medical care, including the representative with power in the health field, consider is necessary in the Interests of the adult. One approach, which seems suspect on human rights grounds, is to say that a representative with general powers can refuse the treatment on behalf of the adult in precisely the same way as the adult could refuse treatment if fully capable. Another approach is to provide that that representative can refuse the treatment on behalf of the adult but will thereby expose himself or herself to a claim for damages for acting contrary to the adult's best interests. This approach is also suspect. It would seem to be preferable to deal with the problem before, rather than after irreparable damage has been done to the person concerned. Another approach is to provide that, while the representative with general powers may have a right to be consulted, he or she never has right of veto or a right to impose any delay or reconsideration. Due to the different possible approaches and the sensitive nature of this matter, the present principle provides only for the need to establish mechanisms for the resolution of the conflict without suggesting the way to solve it. However, the solution adopted should always be in agreement with the other principles of his recommendation, in particular those concerning respect for human rights and the paramountcy of the interests and welfare of the person concerned.

Principle 23 – Consent (alternative rules)

80 As mentioned above, the Convention on Human Rights and Biomedicine left aside the important question of whether, as a general rule, capacity to consent to an intervention in the health field should be based on actual capacity at the time of the proposed intervention or on legal incapacity. The present recommendation deals with this question and considers that in this matter the main rule should be based on

actual capacity at the time of the proposed intervention (see comments above on Principle 22). However, the recommendation also includes Principle 23 in order to take into account the fact that in the legal systems of some member states of the Council of Europe the notion of factual capacity is unknown and a declaration of incapacity by a judicial authority is required. Countries with such systems will be able to use the alternative approach set out in Principle 23.

81 Paragraph 1 deals with those cases where an adult is subject to a measure of protection and accordingly an intervention in the health field can be carried out only with the authorisation of a person or a body provided for by law. However, the adult's consent should be sought if it is ascertained that the adult has sufficient capacity to give such consent.

82 Paragraph 2 deals with those cases where an adult is not in a position to give free and informed consent to an intervention in the health field according to the law. In these cases it is appropriate to adopt the solutions in Article 6 of the Convention on Human Rights and Biomedicine which requires the intervention to be for the direct benefit of the adult concerned and also requires the authorisation of his or her representative or of 'an authority or a person or body provided for by law' (see comments in paragraph 75 above).

83 Paragraph 3 deals with the need to establish appropriate remedies in national law in order to allow the adult to be heard by an independent official body (for example, a court) before any important medical intervention is carried out. This rule is applicable to both situations described in the previous paragraphs. The idea is that in those cases where the adult opposes an important medical intervention, national law should provide appropriate remedies to enable a fair hearing of the person concerned by an independent official body in the course of which the adult may voice his or her views. The medical intervention should not be carried out until then.

Principle 24: Exceptional cases

84 This principle deals with interventions of a special nature which require special rules and where, sometimes, the normal principle that an intervention must be for the direct benefit of the person concerned may have to be slightly modified. The concept of 'benefit' is notoriously difficult to apply in a case where a person is, for example, reliably diagnosed as being in a persistent vegetative state – permanently unconscious and perhaps only kept alive by artificial measures. The concept of 'benefit' is also difficult to apply in cases where any intervention would at most prolong artificially for a few minutes or hours the natural process of dying. However any modification of the concept of 'direct benefit' in such areas would have to be balanced by extra protection for the person concerned so as to guard against the possibility of abuse or irregularity. In this respect, it is necessary to take into account that the Convention on Human Rights and Biomedicine permits an intervention which is not of direct benefit to the individual in exceptional circumstances (see Article 17, paragraph 2 of the Convention).

85 The issues surrounding research on incapable adults have been very thoroughly investigated and discussed in relation to the Convention on Human Rights and Biomedicine. They also raise difficult questions of a slightly different nature from those dealt with in this recommendation and also involve some diminution in the concept of direct benefit coupled with additional protection. Furthermore, other international legal instruments have dealt with these questions of medical research.[6] For these reasons, the present recommendation does not deal specifically with the question of medical research.

6 There are many international instruments, apart from the Convention on Human Rights and Biomedicine, with a bearing on these questions. See in particular recommendation No. R (90) 3 of the Committee of Ministers of the Council of Europe concerning medical research on human beings. For a review of the international and national positions in relation to medical research see the report by Professor Roscam Abbing prepared in connection with the work of the Council of Europe's Steering Committee on Bioethics in 1994 (DIR/JUR (94) 9).

86 This principle says that special rules may be provided by national laws, in accordance with relevant international instruments, in relation to interventions, which, because of their special nature, require the provision of additional protection for the person concerned. Such rules may involve a limited derogation from the criterion of direct benefit, provided that the additional protection is such as to minimise the possibility of any abuse or irregularity.

Principle 25 – Protection of adults with a mental disorder

87 Article 7 of the Convention on Human Rights and Biomedicine deals with interventions aimed at treating the mental disorder of a person who has a mental disorder or a serious nature. Such persons form a particular sub-category of vulnerable persons. They may actually be capable of making a decision but may still require compulsory treatment. It seems to be appropriate to adopt the solution of Article 7 of the Convention on Human Rights and Biomedicine.

88 During the preparation of the present recommendation, the Group of Specialists also took into account the work carried out by the Working Party on Psychiatry and Human Rights (CDBI- PH), which was dealing with the revision of Recommendation No. R (83) 2 of the Committee of Ministers to member states concerning the legal protection of persons suffering from mental disorder placed as involuntary patients.

Principle 26 – Permissibility of intervention in emergency situation

89 It is clearly essential to allow interventions without consent in cases of emergency. This is dealt with in Article 8 of the Convention on Human Rights and Biomedicine, which can again usefully be adopted for the purposes of the recommendation. The explanatory report on the Convention on Human Rights and Biomedicine explains that 'emergency' is not to be construed too narrowly: it is not limited to life-saving situations, but also it applies to medically necessary interventions which cannot be delayed.

Principle 27 – Applicability of certain principles applying to measures of protection

90 It is necessary to underline that due to the specificity of Part V of the recommendation (it provides not for representation but for interventions in their health field), there are only a few of the preceding principles which will be applicable to interventions in the health field. It is obvious that Principle I (on respect for human rights) will always be applicable. Furthermore, the principles of the paramountcy of the interests and welfare of the person concerned, of respect for the past and present wishes and feelings of the person concerned, and of consultation, apply to interventions in the health field as they apply to measures of protection. In particular, and in accordance with Principle 9, the previously expressed wishes relating to a medical intervention by a patient who is not, at the

time of the intervention, in a state to express his or her wishes should be taken into account. This may be particularly important in those cases where the adult has, while capable, executed a valid refusal of consent to a particular type of intervention. The principle relating to consultation is also relevant here because, for example, a person or body specifically empowered by law to authorise an intervention should consult with close relatives in so far as this is practicable and reasonable. All of this is entirely consistent with the approach of the Convention on Human Rights and Biomedicine.

Principle 28: Permissibility of special rules on certain matters

91 Principle 28 makes it possible for the states to introduce special rules containing derogations from the principles of Part V. Such rules may be provided under the condition that they are in accordance with relevant international instruments, and are necessary in a democratic society in the interests of public safety, for the prevention of crime, for the protection of public health or for the protection of the rights and freedoms of others. The principle reiterates paragraph 1 of Article 26 of the Convention of Human Rights and Biomedicine. Special rules may be necessary, for instance, in cases where a treatment is needed in order to prevent the adult from infecting other people or, where the adult is a risk to public safety and must, therefore, be kept in a hospital for treatment.

Council of Europe Committee of Ministers Recommendation No R (99) 4[1] of the Committee of Ministers to Member States on Principles Concerning the Legal Protection of Incapable Adults

(Adopted by the Committee of Ministers on 23 February 1999 at the 660th meeting of the Ministers' Deputies)

The Committee of Ministers, under the terms of Article 15.b of the Statute of the Council of Europe,

Hearing in mind the Universal Declaration of Human Rights proclaimed by the General Assembly of the United Nations on 10 December 1948;

Bearing in mind the International Covenant on Civil and Political Rights and the International Covenant on Economic, Social and Cultural Rights of 16 December 1966;

Bearing in mind the Convention for the Protection of Human Rights and Fundamental Freedoms of 4 November 1950;

Bearing in mind the Convention for the Protection of Human Rights and Dignity of the Human Being with regard to the Application of Biology and Medicine: Convention on Human Rights and Biomedicine of 4 April 1997;

Considering that the aim of the Council of Europe is to achieve a greater unity between its members, in particular by promoting the adoption of common rules in legal matters;

Noting that demographic and medical changes have resulted in an increased number of people who, although of full age, are incapable of protecting their interests by reason of an impairment or insufficiency of their personal faculties;

Noting also that social changes have resulted in an increased need for adequate legislation to ensure the protection of such people;

Noting that legislative reforms on the protection, by representation or assistance, of incapable adults have been introduced or are under consideration in a number of member states and that these reforms have common features;

[1] When adopting this decision, the Representative of Ireland indicated that, in accordance with Article 10.2c of the Rules of Procedure for the meetings of the Ministers' Deputies, he reserved the right of his Government to comply or not with principles 5 and 6 of the Recommendation. When adopting this decision, the Representative of France indicated that, in accordance with Article 10.2c of the Rules of Procedure for the meetings of the Ministers' Deputies, the following reservation should be made: France considers that the application of principle 23, para. 3 should be subject to a request by the person concerned.

Recognising, however, that wide disparities in the legislation of member states in this area still exist;

Convinced of the importance in this context of respect for human rights and tor the dignity of each person as a human being,

Recommends the governments of member states to take or reinforce, in their legislation and practice, all measures they consider necessary with a view to the implementation of the following principles:

PRINCIPLES

Part I – Scope of application

1 The following principles apply to the protection of adults who, by reason of an impairment or insufficiency of their personal faculties, are incapable of making, in an autonomous way, decisions concerning any or all of their personal or economic affairs, or understanding, expressing or acting upon such decisions, and who consequently cannot protect their interests.

2 The incapacity may be due to a mental disability, a disease or a similar reason.

3 The principles apply to measures of protection or other legal arrangements enabling such adults to benefit from representation or assistance in relation to those affairs.

4 In these principles 'adult' means a person who is treated as being of full age under the applicable law on capacity in civil matters.

5 In these principles 'intervention in the health field' means any act performed professionally on a person tor reasons of health. It includes, in particular, interventions tor the purposes of preventive care, diagnosis, treatment, rehabilitation or research.

Part II – Governing principles

Principle 1 – Respect for human rights

In relation to the protection of incapable adults the fundamental principle, underlying all the other principles, is respect for the dignity of each person as a human being. The laws, procedures and practices relating to the protection of incapable adults shall be based on respect for their human rights and fundamental freedoms, taking into account any qualifications on those rights contained in the relevant international legal instruments.

Principle 2 – Flexibility in legal response

1 The measures of protection and other legal arrangements available for the protection of the personal and economic interests of incapable adults should be sufficient, in scope or flexibility, to enable a suitable legal response to be made to different degrees of incapacity and various situations.

2 Appropriate measures of protection or other legal arrangements should be available in cases of emergency.

3 The law should provide for simple and inexpensive measures of protection or other legal arrangements.

4 The range of measures of protection should include, in appropriate cases, those which do not restrict the legal capacity of the person concerned.

5 The range of measures of protection should include those which are limited to one specific act without requiring the appointment of a representative or a representative with continuing powers.

6 Consideration should be given to the inclusion of measures under which the appointed person acts jointly with the adult concerned, and of measures involving the appointment of more than one representative.

7 Consideration should be given to the need to provide for, and regulate, legal arrangements which a person who is still capable can take to provide for any subsequent incapacity.

8 Consideration should be given to the need to provide expressly that certain decisions, particularly those of a minor or routine nature relating to health or personal welfare, may be taken for an incapable adult by those deriving their powers !Tom the law rather than from a judicial or administrative measure.

Principle 3 – Maximum preservation of capacity

1 The legislative framework should, so far as possible, recognise that different degrees of incapacity may exist and that incapacity may vary from time to time. Accordingly, a measure of protection should not result automatically in a complete removal of legal capacity. However, a restriction of legal capacity should be possible where it is shown to be necessary for the protection of the person concerned.

2 In particular, a measure of protection should not automatically deprive the person concerned of the right to vote, or to make a will, or to consent or refuse consent to any intervention in the health field, or to make other decisions of a personal character at any time when his or her capacity permits him or her to do so.

3 Consideration should be given to legal arrangements whereby, even when representation in a particular area is necessary, the adult may be permitted, with the representative's consent, to undertake specific acts or acts in a specific area.

4 Whenever possible the adult should be enabled to enter into legally effective transactions of an everyday nature.

Principle 4 – Publicity

The disadvantage of automatically giving publicity to measures of protection or similar legal arrangements should be weighed in the balance against any protection which might be afforded to the adult concerned or to third parties.

Principle 5 – Necessity and subsidiarity

1 No measure of protection should be established for an incapable adult unless the measure is necessary, taking into account the individual circumstances and the needs of the person concerned. A measure of protection may be established, however, with the full and free consent of the person concerned.

2 In deciding whether a measure of protection is necessary, account should be taken of any less formal arrangements which might be made, and of any assistance which might be provided by family members or by others.

Principle 6 – Proportionality

1 Where a measure of protection is necessary it should be proportional to the degree of capacity of the person concerned and tailored to the individual circumstances and needs of the person concerned.

2 The measure of protection should interfere with the legal capacity, rights and freedoms of the person concerned to the minimum extent which is consistent with achieving the purpose of the intervention.

Principle 7 – Procedural fairness and efficiency

1 There should be fair and efficient procedures for the taking of measures for the protection of incapable adults.

2 There should be adequate procedural safeguards to protect the human rights of the persons concerned and to prevent possible abuses.

Principle 8 – Paramountcy of interests and welfare of the person concerned

1 In establishing or implementing a measure of protection for an incapable adult the interests and welfare of that person should be the paramount consideration.

2 This principle implies, in particular, that the choice of any person to represent or assist an incapable adult should be governed primarily by the suitability of that person to safeguard and promote the adult's interests and welfare.

3 This principle also implies that the property of the incapable adult should be managed and used for the benefit of the person concerned and to secure his or her welfare.

Principle 9 – Respect for wishes and feelings of the person concerned

1 In establishing or implementing a measure of protection for an incapable adult the past and present wishes and feelings of the adult should be ascertained so far as possible, and should be taken into account and given due respect.

2 This principle implies, in particular, that the wishes of the adult as to the choice of any person to represent or assist him or her should be taken into account and, as far as possible, given due respect.

3 It also implies that a person representing or assisting an incapable adult should give him or her adequate information, whenever this is possible and appropriate, in particular concerning any major decision affecting him or her, so that he or she may express a view.

Principle 10 – Consultation

In the establishment and implementation of a measure of protection there should be consultation, so far as reasonable and practicable, with those having a close interest in the welfare of the adult concerned, whether as representative, close family member or otherwise. It is for national law to determine which persons should be consulted and the effects of consultation or its absence.

Part III – Procedural principles

Principle 11 – Institution of proceedings

1 The list of those entitled to institute proceedings for the taking of measures for the protection of incapable adults should be sufficiently wide to ensure that measures of protection can be considered in all cases where they are necessary. It may, in particular, be necessary to provide for proceedings to be initiated by a public official or body, or by the court or other competent authority on its own motion.

2 The person concerned should be informed promptly in a language, or by other means, which he or she understands of the institution of proceedings which could affect his or her legal capacity, the exercise of his or her rights or his or her interests unless such information would be manifestly without meaning to the person concerned or would present a severe danger to the health of the person concerned.

Principle 12 – Investigation and assessment

1 There should be adequate procedures for the investigation and assessment of the adult's personal faculties.

2 No measure of protection which restricts the legal capacity of an incapable adult should be taken unless the person taking the measure has seen the adult or is personally satisfied as to the adult's condition and an up-to-date report from at least one suitably qualified expert has been submitted. The report should be in writing or recorded in writing.

Principle 13 – Right to be heard in person

The person concerned should have the right to be heard in person in any proceedings which could affect his or her legal capacity.

Principle 14 – Duration, review and appeal

1 Measures of protection should, whenever possible and appropriate, be of limited duration. Consideration should be given to the institution of periodical reviews.

2 Measures of protection should be reviewed on a change of circumstances and, in particular, on a change in the adult's condition. They should be terminated if the conditions for them are no longer fulfilled.

3 There should be adequate rights of appeal.

Principle 15 – Provisional measures in case of emergency

If a provisional measure is needed in a case of emergency, principles 11 to 14 should be applicable as far as possible according to the circumstances.

Principle 16 – Adequate control

There should be adequate control of the operation of measures of protection and of the acts and decisions of representatives.

Principle 17 – Qualified persons

1 Steps should be taken with a view to providing an adequate number of suitably qualified persons for the representation and assistance of incapable adults.

2 Consideration should be given, in particular, to the establishment or support of associations or other bodies with the function of providing and training such people.

Part IV – The role of representatives

Principle 18 – Control of powers arising by operation of law

1 Consideration should be given to the need to ensure that any powers conferred on any person by operation of law, without the intervention of a judicial or administrative authority, to act or take decisions on behalf of an incapable adult are limited and their exercise controlled.

2 The conferment of any such powers should not deprive the adult of legal capacity.

3 Any such powers should be capable of being modified or terminated at any time by a measure of protection taken by a judicial or administrative authority.

4 Principles 8 to 10 apply to the exercise of such powers as they apply to the implementation of measures of protection.

Principle 19 – Limitation of powers of representatives

1 It is for national law to determine which juridical acts are of such a highly personal nature that they cannot be done by a representative.

2 It is also for national law to determine whether decisions by a representative on certain serious matters should require the specific approval of a court or other body.

Principle 20 – Liability

1 Representatives should be liable, in accordance with national law, for any loss or damage caused by them to incapable adults while exercising their functions.

2 In particular, the laws on liability for wrongful acts, negligence or maltreatment should apply to representatives and others involved in the affairs of incapable adults.

Principle 21 – Remuneration and expenses

1 National law should address the questions of the remuneration and the reimbursement of expenses of those appointed to represent or assist incapable adults.

2 Distinctions may be made between those acting in a professional capacity and those acting in other capacities, and between the management of personal matters of the incapable adult and the management of his or her economic matters.

Part V – Interventions in the health field

Principle 22 – Consent

1 Where an adult, even if subject to a measure of protection, is in fact capable of giving free and informed consent to a given intervention in the health field, the intervention may only be carried out with his or her consent. The consent should be solicited by the person empowered to intervene.

2 Where an adult is not in fact capable of giving free and informed consent to a given intervention, the intervention may, nonetheless, be carried out provided that:
– it is for his or her direct benefit, and
– authorisation has been given by his or her representative or by an authority or a person or body provided tor by law.

3 Consideration should be given to the designation by the law of appropriate authorities, persons or bodies for the purpose of authorising interventions of different types, when adults who are incapable of giving free and informed consent do not have a representative with appropriate powers. Consideration should also be given to the need to provide for the authorisation of a court or other competent body in the case of certain serious types of intervention.

4 Consideration should be given to the establishment of mechanisms for the resolution of any conflicts between persons or bodies authorised to consent or refuse consent to interventions in the health field in relation to adults who are incapable of giving consent.

Principle 23 – Consent (alternative rules)

If the government of a member state does not apply the rules contained in paragraphs 1 and 2 of Principle 22, the following rules should be applicable:

1 Where an adult is subject to a measure of protection under which a given intervention in the health field can be carried out only with the authorisation of a body or a person provided for by law, the consent of the adult should nonetheless be sought if he or she has the capacity to give it.

2 Where, according to the law, an adult is not in a position to give free and informed consent to an intervention in the health field, the intervention may nonetheless be carried out if:
– it is for his or her direct benefit, and
– authorisation has been given by his or her representative or by an authority or a person or body provided tor by law.

3 The law should provide for remedies allowing the person concerned to be heard by an independent official body before any important medical intervention is carried out.

Principle 24 – Exceptional cases

1 Special rules may be provided by national law. in accordance with relevant international instruments, in relation to interventions which, because of their special nature, require the provision of additional protection for the person concerned.

2 Such rules may involve a limited derogation from the criterion of direct benefit provided that the additional protection is such as to minimise the possibility of any abuse or irregularity.

Principle 25 – Protection of adults with a mental disorder

Subject to protective conditions prescribed by law, including supervisory, control and appeal procedures, an adult who has a mental disorder of a serious nature may be subjected, without his or her consent, to an intervention aimed at treating his or her mental disorder only where, without such treatment, serious harm is likely to result to his or her health.

Principle 26 – Permissibility of intervention in emergency situation

When, because of an emergency situation, the appropriate consent or authorisation cannot be obtained, any medically necessary intervention may be carried out immediately for the benefit of the health of the person concerned.

Principle 27 – Applicability of certain principles applying to measures of protection

1 Principles 8 to 10 apply to any intervention in the health field concerning an incapable adult as they apply to measures of protection.

2 In particular, and in accordance with principle 9, the previously expressed wishes relating to a medical intervention by a patient who is not, at the time of the intervention, in a state to express his or her wishes should be taken into account.

Principle 28 – Permissibility of special rules on certain matters

Special rules may be provided by national law, in accordance with relevant international instruments, in relation to interventions which are necessary in a democratic society in the interest of public safety, for the prevention of crime, for the protection of public health or for the protection of the rights and freedom of others.

Recommendation CM/REC(2009)11 of the Committee of Ministers to Member States on Principles Concerning Continuing Powers of Attorney and Advance Directives for Incapacity and its Explanatory Memorandum

(As Adopted by the Committee of Ministers 9 December 2009 at the 1073rd meeting of the Ministers' Deputies)

The Committee of Ministers, under the terms of Article 15.b of the Statute of the Council of Europe,

Considering that the aim of the Council of Europe is to achieve a greater unity between its member states, in particular by promoting adoption of common rules in legal matters;

Noting that demographic changes have resulted in an increasing number of elderly people who have become incapable of protecting their interests by reason of an impairment or insufficiency of their personal faculties;

Noting that there continue to be other circumstances in which adults become incapacitated;

Having regard to relevant instruments of the Council of Europe, including the Convention for the Protection of Human Rights and Fundamental Freedoms (ETS No. 5, 1950), the Convention on Human Rights and Biomedicine (Oviedo Convention, ETS No. 164, 1997) and Recommendation Rec(2006)5 of the Committee of Ministers to member states on the Council of Europe Action Plan to promote the rights and full participation of people with disabilities in society: improving the quality of life of people with disabilities in Europe 2006–2015;

Having regard to the Hague Convention on the International Protection of Adults (2000) and the United Nations Convention on the Rights of Persons with Disabilities (2006);

Bearing in mind the relevant case law of the European Court of Human Rights;

Agreeing that Recommendation No. R (99) 4 of the Committee of Ministers to member states on principles concerning the legal protection of incapable adults is a valuable and up-to-date international instrument containing detailed guidance and general advice on legal rules dealing with measures of protection of such adults;

Noting that the above recommendation and the legislation of the member states concerning adults with incapacity strongly promotes self-determination and autonomy;

Considering that self-determination is essential in respecting the human rights and dignity of each human being;

Noting that in some member states continuing powers of attorney are a preferred alternative to court decisions on representation;

Noting that legislation on continuing powers of attorney and advance directives has recently been passed or proposed in some member states;

Noting that in legal systems where continuing powers of attorney and advance directives are available, adults of all ages increasingly make use of them;

Recognising that there are considerable disparities between the legislation of member states as regards these issues;

Building upon the principles of subsidiarity and necessity contained in Recommendation No. R (99) 4 and supplementing it with principles on self-determination,

Recommends that governments of member states promote self-determination for capable adults by introducing legislation on continuing powers of attorney and advance directives or by amending existing legislation with a view to implementing the principles contained in the appendix to this recommendation.

Part I – Scope of application

Principle 1 – Promotion of self-determination

1 States should promote self-determination for capable adults in the event of their future incapacity, by means of continuing powers of attorney and advance directives.

2 In accordance with the principles of self-determination and subsidiarity, states should consider giving those methods priority over other measures of protection.

Principle 2 – Definition of terms used in the present recommendation

1 A 'continuing power of attorney' is a mandate given by a capable adult with the purpose that it shall remain in force, or enter into force, in the event of the granter's incapacity.

2 The 'granter' is the person giving the continuing power of attorney. The person mandated to act on behalf of the granter is referred to as the 'attorney'.

3 'Advance directives' are instructions given or wishes made by a capable adult concerning issues that may arise in the event of his or her incapacity.

Part II – Continuing powers of attorney

Principle 3 – Content

States should consider whether it should be possible for a continuing power of attorney to cover economic and financial matters, as well as health, welfare and other personal matters, and whether some particular matters should be excluded.

Principle 4 – Appointment of attorney

1 The granter may appoint as attorney any person whom he or she considers to be appropriate.

2 The granter may appoint more than one attorney and may appoint them to act jointly, concurrently, separately, or as substitutes.

3 States may consider such restrictions as are deemed necessary for the protection of the granter.

Principle 5 – Form

1 A continuing power of attorney shall be in writing.

2 Except in states where such is the general rule, the document shall explicitly state that it shall enter into force or remain in force in the event of the granter's incapacity.

2 States should consider what other provisions and mechanisms may be required to ensure the validity of the document.

Principle 6 – Revocation

A capable granter shall have the possibility to revoke the continuing power of attorney at any time. Principle 5, paragraph 3, is applicable.

Principle 7 – Entry into force

1 States should regulate the manner of entry into force of the continuing power of attorney in the event of the granter's incapacity.

2 States should consider how incapacity should be determined and what evidence should be required.

Principle 8 – Certification, registration and notification

States should consider introducing systems of certification, registration and/or notification when the continuing power of attorney is granted, revoked, enters into force or terminates.

Principle 9 – Preservation of capacity

The entry into force of a continuing power of attorney shall not as such affect the legal capacity of the granter.

Principle 10 – Role of the attorney

1 The attorney acts in accordance with the continuing power of attorney and in the interests of the granter.

2 The attorney, as far as possible, informs and consults the granter on an ongoing basis. The attorney, as far as possible, ascertains and takes account of the past and present wishes and feelings of the granter and gives them due respect.

3 The granter's economic and financial matters are, as far as possible, kept separate from the attorney's own.

4 The attorney keeps sufficient records in order to demonstrate the proper exercise of his or her mandate.

Principle 11 – Conflict of interest

States should consider regulating conflicts of the granter's and the attorney's interests.

Principle 12 – Supervision

1 The granter may appoint a third party to supervise the attorney.

2 States should consider introducing a system of supervision under which a competent authority is empowered to investigate. When an attorney is not acting in accordance with the continuing power of attorney or in the interests of the granter, the competent authority should have the power to intervene. Such intervention might include terminating the continuing power of attorney in part or in whole. The competent authority should be able to act on request or on its own motion.

Principle 13 – Termination

1 States should consider under which circumstances a continuing power of attorney ceases to have effect.

1 When a continuing power of attorney ceases to have effect in part or in whole, the competent authority should consider which measures of protection might be taken.

Part III – Advance directives

Principle 14 – Content

Advance directives may apply to health, welfare and other personal matters, to economic and financial matters, and to the choice of a guardian, should one be appointed.

Principle 15 – Effect

1 States should decide to what extent advance directives should have binding effect. Advance directives which do not have binding effect should be treated as statements of wishes to be given due respect.

2. States should address the issue of situations that arise in the event of a substantial change in circumstances.

Principle 16 – Form

1 States should consider whether advance directives or certain types of advance directives should be made or recorded in writing if intended to have binding effect.

2 States should consider what other provisions and mechanisms may be required to ensure the validity and effectiveness of those advance directives.

Principle 17 – Revocation

An advance directive shall be revocable at any time and without any formalities.

EXPLANATORY MEMORANDUM

1 General comments

1.1 Moving forward from Recommendation No R (99) 4

1 The Council of Europe commenced addressing the issue of protection of incapable adults when the Third European Conference on Family Law, held in Cadiz, Spain, in April 1995, entitled 'Family Law in the Future', discussed this question. The Conference requested the Council of Europe to invite a group of specialists in this field to examine the desirability of drafting a European legal instrument. The aim was to guarantee the integrity and rights of incapable adults and, wherever possible, their independence. Following this proposal, the Committee of Ministers of the Council of Europe set up the Group of Specialists on Incapable and Other Vulnerable Adults (CJ-S-MI) in 1995, later re-named the Group of Specialists on Incapable Adults.

2 The result of the Group's work was Recommendation No. R (99) 4 on Principles concerning the legal protection of incapable adults. It contains quite detailed principles and is accompanied by an extensive explanatory memorandum. According to the recommendation's scope of application, its principles 'apply to the protection of adults who, by reason of an impairment or insufficiency of their personal faculties, are incapable of making, in an autonomous way, decisions concerning any or all of their personal or economic affairs, or understanding, expressing or acting upon such decisions, and who consequently cannot protect their own interests. The incapacity may be due to a mental disability, a disease or a similar reason'. The principles address measures of protection or other legal arrangements enabling such adults to benefit from representation or assistance in relation to those affairs. The recommendation contains governing principles as well as parts on 'procedural principles' and on 'the role of representatives'.

3 Principle 2, entitled 'Flexibility in legal response', stipulates that the measures of protection and other legal arrangements 'should be sufficient, in scope or flexibility, to enable a suitable legal response to be made to different degrees of incapacity and various situations'. Principle 5, 'Necessity and subsidiarity', indicates that 'no measure of protection should be established for an incapable adult unless the measure is necessary, taking into account the individual circumstances and the needs of the person concerned. In deciding whether a measure of protection is necessary, account should be taken of any less formal arrangements which might be made and of any assistance which might be provided by family members or by others'. Principle 6 on 'Proportionality' underlines that a measure of protection 'should be proportional to the degree of capacity of the person concerned and tailored to the individual circumstances and needs of the person concerned'. Principle 3 concerns 'maximum preservation of capacity'. It provides that 'the legislative framework should, as far as possible, recognise that different degrees of incapacity may exist and that incapacity may vary from time to time. Accordingly, a measure of protection should not result automatically in a complete removal of legal capacity. However, a restriction of legal capacity should be possible where it is shown to be necessary for the protection of the person concerned'. It is supplemented by Principle 2, paragraph 4 according to which, 'the range of measures of protection should include, in appropriate cases, those which do not restrict the legal capacity of the person concerned'. The recommendation strongly promotes self-determination and autonomy, which are essential in respecting the human rights and dignity of each person. Principle 2, paragraph 7 states that 'consideration should be given to the need to provide for, and regulate, legal arrangements which a person who is still capable can take to provide for any subsequent incapacity'. Such a possibility

clearly facilitates flexibility and proportionality of the legal response, as mentioned in Principles 2 and 6, as well as respecting the principles of necessity and subsidiarity in accordance with Principle 5. Finally, Principle 9, paragraph 1 states that 'in establishing or implementing a measure of protection for an incapable adult, the past and present wishes and feelings of the adult should be ascertained so far as possible, and should be taken into account and given due respect'.

4 Since incapacitated persons are amongst the most vulnerable in society, the Committee of Experts on Family Law (CJ-FA), at its 36th meeting on 15–17 November 2006, decided, in the light of the increased number of elderly people in Europe, to set up a Working Party on Incapable Adults (CJ-FA-GT2) to examine the usefulness of upgrading the Recommendation No. R (99) 4 on principles concerning the legal protection of incapable adults to a convention.

5 During the first meeting of the Working Party on 17–19 September 2007, it was assessed that little value would be added by preparing new binding rules, as they would have almost the same content as the existing recommendation. The Working Party considered that the Recommendation No. R (99) 4 continues to be of great relevance, and that it remains entirely up-to-date. Its strength is that it is addressed to all member states and provides detailed guidance on how to reform national legislation. Indeed, it has guided several member states in the preparation of recent legislative reforms. Further reference to this recommendation has been made in three judgments of the European Court of Human Rights, namely H.F. v. Slovakia of 8 November 2005 (Application No. 54797/00), *Shtukaturov v Russia* of 27 March 2008 (Application No. 44009/05) and X v. Croatia of 17 July 2008 (Application No. 11223/04). In the Shtukaturov case, the Court concluded in paragraph 95: 'Although these principles [of the Recommendation No. R (99) 4] have no force of law for this Court, they may define a common European standard in this area'. The Working Party proposed therefore to build on that recommendation and to elaborate new principles focusing upon self-determination, in particular upon continuing powers of attorney and advance directives.

6 On the basis of the conclusions of the Working Party, which were supported by the CJ-FA at its 37th meeting held on 28–30 November 2007, and by the Bureau of the European Committee on Legal Co-operation (CDCJ) at its 80th meeting on 13–14 December 2007, the Committee of Ministers of the Council of Europe adopted new terms of reference for the CJ-FA for the period January 2008–June 2009, which included, inter alia, the task of drawing up a new recommendation dealing with planning for future incapacity, by means of continuing powers of attorney and advance directives.

7 Because of the revised mandate of the Working Party, its composition was changed and new members selected, in consultation with the Chair of the CJ-FA. It met four times in 2008, under the chairmanship of Mr Kees BLANKMAN (the Netherlands) and with Mr Svend DANIELSEN (Denmark) as consultant.

8 After its second meeting on 14–16 May 2008, the Working Party sent its preliminary draft recommendation and a preliminary explanatory memorandum to the members of the CJ-FA for information and possible comments. Other relevant bodies and institutions were also invited to comment. The replies received were discussed and taken into account at the third meeting of the Working Party on 3–5 September 2008.

9 The draft recommendation and its explanatory memorandum, as prepared by the Working Party, were examined by the CJ-FA at its 38th plenary meeting on 17–20 March 2009 and submitted to the CDCJ for approval at its 84th plenary

meeting on 6–9 October 2009 before their transmission to the Committee of Ministers for adoption on 19 November 2009.

1.2 The need for a new recommendation

10 Experience on both a national and international level during the last decades shows that the issue of adults with incapacity is arguably the most topical issue of family law at present; this may also prove to be true in years to come. Despite the overall improvement in the protection of human rights, this area of law was underdeveloped or even completely neglected in a number of member states.

11 It should be borne in mind that the numbers of elderly people are rising steadily in Europe, due to an overall improvement of living conditions, demographic and social changes and medical advances. However, the mental faculties of the elderly often decline with age and the number of persons suffering from diseases such as senile dementia or Alzheimer's disease is increasing throughout Europe. In addition, groups other than the elderly may also experience impairments of capacity.

12 Measures to address incapacity may be put into two broad categories, responsive and anticipatory. Responsive measures are initiated after impairment of capacity, responding to that incapacity, and generally require judicial or other public intervention. Anticipatory measures, on the other hand, are put in place by a capable person, prior to any impairment of capacity.

13 In several member states, attention has recently been focussed on persons' self-determination as opposed to judicial or other public intervention. However, at present there is no instrument at the European level which provides guidance for member states to reform laws to allow planning for future incapacity. A new international instrument might therefore be relevant and timely. It could benefit the lives of many citizens who might wish to plan for their own possible future incapacity with the help of an instrument of legal nature, which might provide added value.

14 Continuing powers of attorney and advance directives constitute two methods of self-determination for capable adults for periods when they are not capable of making decisions. They are both anticipatory measures, which subsequently have a direct impact on granters' lives during periods when their capacity to make decisions is impaired. They are both defined in Principle 2 of the new recommendation. The terminology of the recommendation is explained in section 1.5 'Terminology'.

15 Where continuing powers of attorney have been available for some years, they are increasingly viewed as something which everyone should consider having, in the same manner that it is generally recommended to make a will. Increasingly, continuing powers of attorney are granted by people of all ages on the basis that incapacity can arise suddenly. Further, medical trends towards early diagnosis of progressive conditions likely to result in incapacity, and the availability of treatments which slow the progress of such conditions, mean that there are many people who are aware that they are in the early stages of a progressive deterioration of capacity, but who still have sufficient capacity to appoint someone to represent them. Therefore, certain people with some degree of incapacity, including those with lifelong incapacities, may be able to grant a valid continuing power of attorney to appoint someone of their choice to deal with matters which they themselves would find very difficult, if not beyond their capacity. Some legislation recognises that people may have adequate legal capacity to select an attorney and grant a continuing power of attorney even though they might not have adequate capacity to do themselves everything which the attorney is appointed to do on their behalf.

1.3 Other international instruments

16 Many recent international instruments deal with persons with disabilities, other vulnerable persons, incapacity issues and methods of self-determination. The following are particularly relevant.

17 The United Nations' Convention of 13 December 2006 on the Rights of Persons with Disabilities stipulates in its preamble and in Article 4 that states who are parties to the convention reaffirm the universality, indivisibility, interdependence and interrelatedness of all human rights and fundamental freedoms, and also reaffirm the need for persons with disabilities to be guaranteed full enjoyment of such rights without discrimination. This convention entered into force on 3 May 2008 after being ratified by the required number of 20 states. By that time, over 100 other states had signed the convention. The convention recognises the capacity of persons with disabilities to make their own decisions, and its Optional Protocol further allows those persons to petition an international expert body. Lastly, the convention foresees national mechanisms of implementation and monitoring (Article 33).

18 This United Nations' Convention addresses all disabilities, including physical, sensory and intellectual disabilities. Article 12.1 re-affirms the right of all persons with disabilities to recognition everywhere as persons before the law. On the one hand, across the great range of intellectual disabilities, human rights can be put at risk on the one hand by ascribing incapacity to those who have capacity, but may still require support in exercising their legal capacity. On the other hand, they can be put at risk by suggesting that only support – rather than enforceable legal safeguards – is required by those lacking capacity, and whose apparent compliance with the guidance and decisions of others is not a valid exercise of legal capacity.

19 The first situation is addressed in Article 12.3, which gives new authoritative force to existing best practice principles that, where there is capacity but difficulty in exercising it, all necessary support should be given to facilitate, encourage and develop the exercise of capacity. Therefore, where needed, such support should be given to enable a continuing power of attorney to be granted. Article 12.4 briefly restates the main guiding principles applicable where there is impairment of capacity and 'measures that relate to the exercise of legal capacity' are required. This article, however, does not contain principles explicitly addressing such incapacity. Recommendation No. R (99) 4 therefore remains an important starting-point for the continued development of legislation in Europe to ensure the protection of the human rights and fundamental freedoms of those with impaired capacity to make valid decisions, and effectively to exercise and assert their rights. The present recommendation includes principles necessary to provide such protection for granters who no longer have capacity when the attorney is acting.

20 Furthermore, the Hague Convention of 13 January 2000 on the International Protection of Adults regulates jurisdiction, applicable law, recognition, enforcement and co-operation. The convention entered into force on 1 January 2009 upon ratification by the required number of three states. Of special interest is the fact that Articles 15, 16 and 38 of the convention deal with international private law issues as regards continuing powers of attorney. As the new recommendation does not deal with those issues, those articles are of relevance as a supplement. Article 15, paragraph 2, regulates which law is applicable, and prescribes that 'the existence, extent, modification and extinction of powers of representation granted by an adult, either under an agreement or by a unilateral act, to be exercised when such an adult is not in a position to protect his or her interests, are governed by the law of the State of the adult's habitual residence at the time of the agreement or act, unless one of the laws mentioned in paragraph 2 has been designated expressly in writing'. According

to paragraph 3, 'the manner of exercise of powers of representation is governed by the law of the State in which they are exercised'. Article 16 deals with withdrawal and modification of continuing powers of attorney if they 'are not exercised in a manner sufficient to guarantee the protection of the person or property of the adult'. A decision to that effect may be 'taken by an authority having jurisdiction under the convention. Where such powers of representation are withdrawn or modified, the law referred to in Article 15 should be taken into consideration to the extent possible.' Article 38 deals with an international certificate: 'the authorities of the contracting State where a power of representation [has been] confirmed may deliver to the person entrusted with protection of the adult's person or property, on request, a certificate indicating the capacity in which that person is entitled to act and the powers conferred'.

21 On a European level, mention should first be made to the Convention for the Protection of Human Rights and Fundamental Freedoms. Another important instrument is the 1997 Convention for the Protection of Human Rights and Dignity of the Human Being with regard to the Application of Biology and Medicine: Convention on Human Rights and Biomedicine (Oviedo Convention). Its various provisions are relevant in this context, but particular attention should be paid to Article 9 which stipulates: 'the previously expressed wishes relating to a medical intervention by a patient who is not, at the time of the intervention, in a state to express his or her wishes shall be taken into account.' The explanatory report indicates on this point: 'nevertheless, taking previously expressed wishes into account does not mean that they should necessarily be followed. For example, when the wishes were expressed a long time before the intervention and science has since progressed, there may be grounds for not heeding the patient's opinion.'

22 Finally, Recommendation Rec(2006)5 of the Committee of Ministers to member states on the 'Council of Europe Action Plan to promote the rights and full participation of people with disabilities in society: improving the quality of life of people with disabilities in Europe 2006-2015', deserves also to be mentioned.

1.4 Relevant developments in certain member states

23 The legal concept 'continuing powers of attorney' was first introduced in English-speaking countries, and it is found throughout Australia, Canada and the United States of America. The first legislation based upon Recommendation No. R (99) 4 was the Adults with Incapacity (Scotland) Act 2000 which has been improved in light of experience by an Act of 2007. It is a code with unifying principles and provisions, which includes continuing powers of attorney. In England and Wales, the 1985 legislation was replaced by the Mental Capacity Act 2005 supplemented by Statutory Instrument 2007 No. 253 on lasting powers of attorney, enduring powers of attorney and public guardian regulations. In Ireland, a bill to change the 1996 Power of Attorney Act was presented to Parliament at the beginning of 2007 (Mental Capacity and Guardianship Bill 2007, No. 12).

24 In states such as Belgium, Denmark, Finland, Germany and the Netherlands, powers of attorney have for some years been in use after the granter's incapacity without specific regulations other than the general legislation on powers of attorney. In Germany, the situation changed when the 2nd Guardianship Modification Act of 21 April 2005 (Law Gazette 2005, part I, 1073) entered into force in July 2005 with the purpose of strengthening self-determination for persons unable to take care of their interests. Continuing powers of attorney, called Vorsorgevollmacht, constitute its main tool.

25 Legislation on continuing powers of attorney has recently been introduced in other states as well. In Spain, Ley 41/2003 de 18 de noviembre de protección patrimonial de las personas con discapacidad introduced a new provision in Article 1732 whereby the mandate terminates upon supervening incapacity of the granter, unless the mandate provides that it should continue in that event or unless the mandate has been given for the purpose of exercise in the event of the granter's incapacity as assessed according to the granter's instructions. In Austria, the Guardianship Act of 1984 was revised by Sachwalterrechts – Änderungsgesetz 2006 which came into force on 1 July 2007 (Law Gazette 2006, part I No. 92, Art. 284 f, 284 g and 284 h of the Civil Code). The new law introduces continuing powers of attorney, called Vorsorgevollmacht. In Finland, in April 2007 the Parliament passed Lag om interessevakningsfullmakt (Law No. 648/2007) concerning representation powers of attorney, which entered into force on 1 November 2007. In France, Law No. 2007-308 of 5 March 2007 (JORF No. 56) on the reform of the legal protection of adults entitled Mandat de protection future and Articles 477 – 494 of the Civil Code introduced a new form of legal protection for adults, including continuing powers of attorney. It entered into force on 1 January 2009. In Switzerland, the modification of 19 December 2008 of the Swiss Civil Code (Protection de l'adulte, droit des personnes et droit de la filiation) foresees new legal instruments aimed at self-determination in case of incapacity. Firstly, this would allow a natural or legal person to be responsible for providing the granter with personal assistance or for representing him or her in the event that he or she becomes incapable of proper judgment. Secondly, this law regulates the ways of deciding, in advance directives, which medical treatment the granter would consent to in the event that he or she becomes incapable of proper judgment.

26 Work is in progress in some other states. In Norway, a Law Reform Committee published its report 'Guardianship' (Vergemål) in 2004 (NOU 2004:16). In accordance with this report, the Government proposed a bill to the Parliament in September 2009 (Ot.prp.nr. 110 (2008-2009) Om lov om vergemål (vergemålsloven). Chapter 10 (Fremtidsfuldmagter mv) deals with future powers of attorney. That same year, in Sweden, a Law Reform Committee published a report on the 'Questions concerning guardians and substitutes for adults" (Frågor om Förmyndare och ställföreträdare för vuxna, SOU 2004:112) containing a proposal for the Law on future powers of attorney (Lag om Fremtidsfuldmagter mv).

27 The experience of states where continuing powers of attorney have been in place for some time indicates that adults of all ages increasingly make use of them.

28 In England and Wales, under the old system the registration of enduring powers of attorney took place at the onset of the granter's incapacity. The registration of the new lasting powers of attorney must take place before the attorney can use them, irrespectively of whether or not the granter has lost capacity. Once registered, the attorney may use the power and many powers come into force immediately after signing. In the first 13 months after the new system came into force (1 October 2007), the number of registrations of enduring and lasting powers of attorney was 69,377.

29 In Scotland, the present regime of continuing powers of attorney was introduced in 2001. Since then, the registrations have continued to grow. Documents are most commonly registered at the time of granting, rather than later at the time of loss of capacity. 5,592 powers of attorney were registered in the year to 31 March 2002. The number rose to 18,113 in the year to 31 March 2005, and to 32,066 in the year to 31 March 2008. The figure for 2007/2008 could usefully be compared with the number of guardianships in that year (only 876). In 2007/2008, 791 of the registered powers conferred only personal welfare powers, 1,850 only financial powers, and

14,451 both welfare and financial powers. In 2001/2002, 29% of powers of attorney registered concerned personal matters, in 2003/2004 the number had risen to 48%, and now it is 82%. 80% of granters were 60 years old or more.

30 In Germany, it was estimated that more than 1.5 million continuing powers of attorney had been set up by autumn 2008, and the proportion of adults whose affairs were not managed by a publicly appointed legal representative, but instead by an attorney, was constantly increasing. According to a recent study, the proportion of the total number of residents in German care homes for the elderly who were represented by an attorney amounted to 30%.

31 Furthermore, in Austria, 5,155 registrations were made from the entry into force of the new legislation on 1 July 2007 to October 2008.

32 Advance directives are recognised in a number of member states. They are found either in legislation concerning measures of protection of incapacitated adults, or in legislation on continuing powers of attorney, or in health legislation. All these rules permit capable persons to make statements about certain aspects of their lives in the event of incapacity. Some may be legally binding, others may be wishes which must be taken into consideration and given due respect. As they may deal with health issues, they are often called 'living wills' or Patientenverfügung.

33 In Austria, instructions may be given to a medical doctor orally or in writing (Beachtliche Patientenverfügung), about objections to future medical treatment. They are not legally binding, but should be used as guidelines. The Verbindliche Patientenverfügung is a binding instruction made in writing with a lawyer or a public notary following the receipt of detailed and extensive information from the person concerned. Such instructions have effect for a five-year period and can be renewed. If requested, such a binding instruction may be registered in a centralised register, Patientenverfügungsregister, of the Austrian Chamber of Notaries.

34 In Denmark, where the Health Law, Sundhedslov nr 546 of 24 June 2005, provides for 'living wills' (livstestamenter), the patient may express wishes as regards treatment in case he or she is no longer able to make decisions him/herself.

35 The same holds true in Finland, where the Act on the Status and Rights of Patients No. 785 of 1992 imposes an obligation on the health care professionals and the patient's representatives to respect the previously expressed will of the patient.

36 In the Mental Capacity Act 2005 of England and Wales, there are also some principles on advance decisions limited to decisions to refuse treatment.

37 In Belgium, France and the Netherlands, it exists the possibility to state wishes regarding care, and eventual refusal of a treatment in the event of incapacity.

38 Another possibility relates to statements by the person concerned about who should be guardian, if a decision of guardianship is to be made (Betreuungsverfügung or Sachwalterverfügung in German-speaking countries). This is the case in Austrian, Belgian, French, German and Italian law.

1.5 Terminology

39 The present recommendation, and this explanatory memorandum distinguish between 'capacity' and 'legal capacity'. Here the terms 'capacity' and 'capable' are the counterparts of 'incapacity' and 'incapable'. 'Incapacity' is limited to what might be termed 'factual incapacity', or in some states 'mental incapacity', although the latter term is outdated and unpopular. Such incapacity may impair the ability of an adult to make decisions, assert and exercise rights, and so forth. An extreme form

is the incapacity of a person in a coma or in persistent vegetative state. Although severe dementia or a profound learning disability (formerly 'mental handicap') can cause substantial incapacity, many other conditions can cause various lesser degrees of incapacity. It is, however, fundamental that such factual or mental incapacity, here termed 'incapacity', never detracts from the adult's rights and status in law.

40 While in the past 'capacity' and 'legal capacity' have often been used synonymously, a trend has emerged of sometimes using 'legal capacity' to encompass the adult's rights and status themselves, rather than the ability to exercise and assert them. Under that usage, 'legal incapacity' refers to the diminution by law of an adult's rights and status, similar to that which might be imposed upon some criminal offenders, or upon bankrupted persons. Persons with disabilities should never have such legal incapacity imposed upon them by reason of their disabilities. This point is stressed by Recommendation No. R (99) 4, Principle 3 'maximum preservation of capacity' and by the 2006 United Nations Convention on the Rights of Persons with Disabilities, which uses 'legal capacity' in that sense. Article 12.2 of that convention provides: 'States Parties shall recognize that persons with disabilities enjoy legal capacity on an equal basis with others in all aspects of life.' The present recommendation uses 'legal incapacity' in that same sense, but requires to do so only once, in Principle 9, to emphasise in accordance with Article 12.2 that the granter of a continuing power of attorney loses no legal capacity when the power continues in force, or enters into force, upon the granter's incapacity.

41 This recommendation uses 'enter into force' in relation to a continuing power of attorney which is not operable before the granter's incapacity. The term refers to the point in time when the continuing power of attorney becomes operable and the attorney becomes entitled to act.

1.6 Characteristics and perspective of the new recommendation

42 The new recommendation differs from Recommendation No. R (99) 4, which deals with public measures of protection, procedural rules and the role of the representative appointed by a competent authority. The present complementary instrument primarily deals with decisions made privately by the persons concerned. Self-determination implies that the granters, to a large extent, are free to make decisions on their future life. National legislation may contain specific limitations on this freedom.

43 There might be a unilateral document describing who shall be the attorney, what he or she has the power to do, and under what conditions, though this model requires the acceptance of the appointee before it becomes effective, and will often be treated as a species of contract following such acceptance. The acceptance, and the establishment of the contract, may be delayed until after loss of capacity. Where there is a substitute appointment, there may be a later acceptance, and subsequent contract, if and when the substitution is triggered. Another possibility is a contract from the outset between the granter and the appointed attorney.

44 The drafting of the new recommendation was influenced by the fact that only a minority of member states already have legislation or draft proposals on continuing powers of attorney and advance directives. The intention has been to draw the attention of member states that are in the process of adopting, or that are considering drafting, legislation concerning persons with incapacity, to the possibility of introducing or refining these methods of self-determination, and to a number of issues and principles which may be addressed in this respect. Member states are recommended to consider most of them. However, some principles regarding

continuing power of attorney contain more specific advice. This explanatory memorandum describes the issues in more detail, with examples illustrating how the problems have been addressed in states that have already introduced new legislation.

45 The recommendation also deals with advance directives as defined in Principle 2, paragraph 3. The principles in Part III are broadly formulated and address general questions to be taken into account. In the future, they might be built upon in the light of developing experience on a national and international level. Advance directives, in practice, vary considerably in the matters which they cover. The more detailed the regulations are, the more they may depend on specific national legislation, especially in the health field.

46 In accordance with the revised terms of reference of the Committee of Experts on Family Law (CJ-FA) from January 2008 to June 2009, the recommendation does not deal with methods of facilitating selfdetermination other than continuing powers of attorney and advance directives, such as supported decision-making. This recommendation concerns anticipatory measures which address possible future loss of capacity, as opposed to the very different situation of people who are capable, but require support to exercise that capacity. These areas overlap where a person requires support in order to grant a valid continuing power of attorney or issue a valid advance directive. Therefore, the recommendation's perspective differs from that of the 2006 United Nations Convention on the Rights of Persons with Disabilities, although the two instruments shall be considered as complementary.

1.7 Continuing powers of attorney

1.7.1 General remarks

47 There is a clear need to introduce the possibility of establishing continuing powers of attorney as an alternative to public representation, as that possibility is less restrictive of the person's rights. It permits adults, and even encourages them, to prepare for what shall happen if and when they are no longer able to take care of their own interests. Such powers of attorney may also be created by younger people as a precaution against unexpected illnesses or accidents. This step might be considered at the same time as making a will or buying property.

48 It might be reassuring for the granters to be able to decide who, in the event of their incapacity, shall make decisions on their behalf and take care of their interests; this is often going to be someone they know and trust. They may appoint one or more persons from among their family members or friends, or a professional such as a lawyer, notary or accountant. This might be felt as preferable to a competent authority deciding who should be the person appointed and what powers should be conferred. A valid continuing power of attorney may prevent the courts or other public authorities from intervening and interfering in the granter's affairs. To a large extent, public supervision can be avoided to a large extent and the sometimes strict rules on administration and investing capital do not have to be followed. The granters will thus be able to maintain confidentiality in respect of their economic and financial affairs. They may decide when the document may be used and what decisions it shall cover. Where a power of attorney has been designed to remain in force during incapacity, the mandate continues without interruption after the granter loses capacity.

49 In using one of these options, the granter can be more certain that he or she will not be dragged into time-consuming and sometimes costly, sensitive and burdensome judicial or administrative proceedings to establish public

representation. The relatives would not have to take the potentially unpleasant initiative of instituting such proceedings, a task they are often reluctant to undertake.

50 Another important aspect might be a need to reduce the demands on public resources in this area. The growing number of people who cannot make decisions themselves, and therefore need to be represented, has put pressure on judicial and administrative authorities which are facing an increasing number of cases in which an application for a public measure of protection has to be dealt with and measures of control have to be applied to the publicly-appointed representatives.

51 Public resources thus have to be taken into consideration. Where continuing powers of attorney to become a real alternative to public representation, there can well be considerable savings for public authorities. Some states that have recently introduced the system have identified a further benefit in reducing the workload of the judicial and administrative authorities concerning measures of protection, having regard to the time required, the rising public costs and the risk that the public representation might be ineffective. Therefore, in some states continuing powers of attorney have been given priority over public measures of representation, which should be used as a last resort, restricted to serious and contested cases, when they are necessary and unavoidable in order to protect the adult concerned. The goal is to minimise the administrative and financial obstacles to making a continuing power of attorney whilst retaining appropriate protection of rights. A balance has to be found when considering rules on involvement of public authorities as regards the creation, certification, registration, notification and control of continuing powers of attorney. It is generally considered an advantage of continuing powers of attorney that they are relatively simple, flexible and effective compared to public representation.

52 There can of course be disadvantages and risks with continuing powers of attorney. One is that the granter, when the document is created, already lacks sufficient capacity or is weak and/or under undue pressure, or misled, e.g. by the person who wishes to be appointed as attorney. The satisfactory use of powers of attorney depends to a large extent on the attorney's integrity and honesty. In most states, it is felt necessary to regulate the creation of the document, although requirements should not be too formalistic or burdensome. It is important that the granter is informed, so that he or she is able fully to understand the nature and scope of the document and the effects of the power. It is equally important that the attorney accepts the appointment. He or she must be aware that they differ from a publicly-established representation, as, depending on the national legislation, the same rules of protection may not be applicable: there might not be the same public supervision, no requirement to have important decisions approved, and few or no formalities for record-keeping. An important safeguard against misuse is the liability of the attorney. The granter therefore has to be warned in advance about possible conflicts of interests and risks of misuse. Circumstances may change in ways not foreseen at the time of signing, while at the same time the granter may have become unable to guide the attorney or to change or withdraw the document.

53 As provisions regarding the granting of powers of attorney are intended to replace public representation, the use of the power of attorney is thereafter regulated only to a limited extent, and public authorities are rarely involved in monitoring and supervision to protect the interests of the incapacitated adult. The attorney may act contrary to the intention and the interests of the granter and operate in a way which the latter, if capable, would not have accepted. Relatives may consider that if the granter were capable, he or she would have preferred their assistance. Financial abuse can occur where attorneys act in ignorance of their obligations or otherwise negligently. Unfortunately, a liability case against the attorney may be of no value if there is nobody to take the initiative or if the attorney has already spent the granter's

funds. On the other hand, a person who wishes to abuse the granter's trust might find an easier way than having a power created. By way of example, the weaker person may be persuaded to transfer funds. Similarly, his or her signature may be faked.

54 Any measures addressing incapacity, whether anticipatory or responsive, face particular challenges where there is a history of family conflict and/or mistrust. Such measures require recognising such issues, but are unlikely to resolve the underlying causes. Depending upon the granter and the circumstances, a continuing power of attorney may be the best way of addressing such issues; or it may be fraught with difficulties, or even unworkable. Legislation on continuing powers of attorney should provide a relatively straightforward and uncomplicated framework for the principal target-group of well-functioning, cooperative families. However, it should also allow for the more sophisticated provisions and controls which may be required by a granter aware of such difficult issues and seeking realistically to establish arrangements which will be workable despite them. In some such cases, granters may be unwilling or unable to address likely problems in advance, and may be better advised not to attempt anticipatory measures, leaving incapacity – should it arise – to be addressed under responsive measures. For cases where powers of attorney have been granted but are misused, or have encountered serious conflict, or have become unworkable, it is necessary for legislators to provide for resolution of such situations, if necessary by public intervention.

55 Before making a continuing power of attorney, the granter and the attorney must, with reasonable certainty, be convinced that the document will have the intended effect after the granter has become incapacitated. They must find it to be the right solution. The situation of the granter and his or her relationship with his or her family must be taken into account. In individual cases, there might be reasons to consider the likely reaction of relatives to deterioration in the granter's health. Furthermore, the most suitable attorney has to be identified.

56 To sum up, the wish to have an informal, simple, flexible, effective and inexpensive arrangement should be weighed against the necessity to protect persons with impairment of capacity against abuse and the consequences of unresolved family conflicts.

1.7.2 Types: in force before or upon incapacity?

57 According to the definition in Principle 2, paragraph 1, a continuing power of attorney is a mandate given by a capable adult with the purpose that it shall remain in force, or enter into force, in the event of the granter's incapacity. This is the case, as stated in Principle 5, paragraph 2, regardless of whether it is according to a legal rule or to an individual decision by the granter. This wording of Principle 2 reflects the fact that there are different types of continuing powers of attorney concerning economic and financial matters. A continuing power of attorney concerning issues of health, welfare and other personal matters should not enter into force and be used before the granter has become incapable of making decisions in this regard.

58 The first type is a power of attorney that the attorney may use immediately after the signing and may continue to use after the granter has become incapacitated. In a number of states, the general rules on powers of attorney state or imply that the document remains in force after the granter's incapacity. Legislation may contain an explicit rule whereby a power of attorney remains in force unless the granter expressly provides that it is terminated by his incapacity. Another possibility is a rule indicating whether the specific legislation on continuing powers of attorney covers this type of power of attorney, or not.

59 The second type is a power of attorney which enters into force only if and when the granter has become incapacitated. The phrase 'enter into force' refers to the point in time when the continuing power of attorney becomes operable and the attorney becomes entitled to act. In some states, this is the only type possible, covered by the special legislation on continuing powers of attorney.

60 A third possibility the granter may choose is a power of attorney that enters into force at a later, fixed date, or when the granter informs the attorney that he or she wishes the document to be used.

61 A power of attorney concerning economic and financial matters that remain in force after the granter's incapacity is governed by the general legislation on powers of attorney as long as the granter is able to make his or her own decisions. After that, the principles of the recommendation apply fully unless otherwise indicated. As mentioned in the commentary to this principle, the need to consider Principle 5, paragraph 3, as regards 'provisions and mechanisms ... required to ensure the validity of the document' is less necessary when the legislation of powers of attorney implies that they remain in force after the granter's incapacity. Principle 7 deals mainly with powers of attorney that enter 'into force ... in the event of the granter's incapacity'. It is important that Principle 10 on 'Role of the attorney', Principle 12 on 'Oversight' and Principle 13 on 'Termination' are also applicable after the granter's incapacity as regards powers that have been in force before that time.

62 There might be certain advantages with continuing powers of attorney that remain in force after the granter's incapacity. They require more contact between the granter and the attorney as they have to agree whether, and, if so, when the document should be used while the granter is still capable of deciding relevant matters. If the attorney acts while the granter is still capable, the latter can monitor whether the power of attorney is being used as intended. A further important advantage is that it is not necessary to follow the procedures described under Principle 7 when the granter has become incapacitated. This may also make it easier for third parties to accept the attorney's decisions.

1.8 Advance directives

63 Advance directives enable a capable adult to give instructions or make wishes about issues that may arise in the event of the author's incapacity. According to Principle 9 of Recommendation No. R (99) 4, legal representatives shall have 'respect for wishes and feelings of the person concerned'. Principle 10, paragraph 2 of the present recommendation similarly states that 'the attorney, as far as possible, ascertains and takes account of the past and present wishes and feelings of the granter and gives them due respect'.

64 National law may contain rules enabling a capable adult to anticipate and address in a more formalised way problems and issues which may arise after he or she has become incapacitated. The directives are addressed to the persons who may be required to make decisions on behalf of or affecting the incapacitated author. Such a person may be a publicly-appointed representative if a measure of protection is established, or an attorney acting under a continuing power of attorney. It may also be medical staff who may operate or who may make decisions concerning life-saving, life-maintaining or life-prolonging treatment, social workers or any other person who may make decisions affecting the author.

65 The most important type of legally-regulated advance directives concerns health issues. Most rules in this regard are found in special health legislation, and often in the same laws as measures of protection. The term 'living will' is often used, even if

the directions are meant to be taken into consideration before the adult has died and therefore are not, stricto sensu, wills. They might concern life-saving, maintaining or prolonging treatment. The author may not wish to be subjected to relentless pursuit of treatment where there is no hope of improvement, recovery or cure. In the same context, the author may wish to refuse any harsh and painful treatment, or treatment which would merely serve to prolong the process of dying and suffering. The directive may deal with a wish to receive palliative care to ease suffering, a wish to receive sufficient medication to keep the adult free from pain even if this entails a risk of shortening life, and a wish to be given the possibility to die with dignity and in peace. A further possibility is a wish not to be resuscitated in a state of unconsciousness. On the contrary, the directive may be to keep the author alive for as long as possible, using whatever forms of medical treatment available.

66 The legislation in some states gives further examples of the subject matter of advance directives. For instance, the directives may contain a wish to be placed into residential care, if the author can no longer live independently at home, to be allowed to stay at home for as long as possible, or to go to an appropriate day-care centre, should circumstances necessitate and permit this. In the above cases, the advance directive may be addressed to close relatives.

67 A third type of directive concerns the choice of a representative if a court order about legal representation should be proposed.

68 In general, some advance directives are incorporated within, or linked to, continuing powers of attorney.

2 Comments on the principles

Part I – Scope of application

Principle 1 – Promotion of self-determination

69 Principle 1 introduces promotion of self-determination. It encourages states to enable capable adults to make decisions about their lives for periods when they are not capable of making decisions. The requirement that the decision has to be taken by an adult implicitly excludes persons who have not reached the age of majority.

70 In paragraph 2, there is a reference to the notion of subsidiarity, which is also the topic of Principle 5 of Recommendation No. R (99) 4 ('Necessity and subsidiarity'). It reflects the trend in legislation towards giving priority to the establishment of private continuing powers of attorney and binding advance directives over public measures of protection.

71 These anticipatory measures, put in place by the adult, will accordingly have priority over all responsive measures. For example, it will not usually be appropriate to appoint a guardian with powers which are contained in a continuing power of attorney which is in operation and working well or can be brought into operation. Such appointment would be unnecessary, because of the existing appointment of an attorney. It would thus contravene Principle 5 of Recommendation No(99)4, which includes the provision that 'no measure of protection should be established for an incapable adult unless the measure is necessary'. It would also contravene Principle 9 of the same recommendation, because the fact that the granter has appointed an attorney is a clear expression of the granter's wishes and feelings. Principle 9, paragraph 1 requires that, in relation to the establishment of any measure of protection, the adult's wishes and feelings should be ascertained as far as possible, taken into account, and given due respect. Principle 9, paragraph 2 requires

that the wishes of the adult as to the choice of any person to represent or assist him or her should particularly be taken into account and, as far as possible, and given due respect.

72 Even in relation to a proposed measure of protection to address some issue not covered by a continuing power of attorney or advance directive, the fact that the adult has granted a continuing power of attorney or issued an advance directive, and the terms of such documents, represent a clear statement of the adult's wishes and feelings which should be taken into account and given due respect.

73 In accordance with Principle 13 of this recommendation, measures of protection might become necessary upon termination of a continuing power of attorney, including termination by a competent authority under Principle 12. These are the only situations in which a measure of protection might replace a continuing power of attorney.

Principle 2 – Definitions of terms used in this recommendation

74 In paragraphs 1 and 2 the term 'continuing powers of attorney' is defined as a mandate given by a capable person with the purpose that it shall enter into force, or remain in force, in the event of the granter's incapacity.

75 The terminology varies from one state to another. In England and Wales, the term 'enduring power of attorney' has been replaced by 'lasting power of attorney'. In Scotland, the term 'continuing powers of attorney' is used to cover economic and financial matters. In Austria and Germany, the term is 'Vorsorgevollmacht', in Switzerland, 'Vorsorgeauftrag', in France, it is 'mandat de protection future'. The terminology in the Norwegian and Swedish proposals may be translated by 'future powers of attorney', and in the Finnish law by 'representation powers of attorney'.

76 It is unusual to have a special name for powers of attorney as regards health, welfare and other personal matters, but in England and Wales, and Scotland, such powers are called 'welfare powers of attorney'. It is equally unusual to have special terminology for powers that enter into force only in the event of the granter's incapacity, although the terms 'springing powers of attorney' and 'trigger mechanism' are sometimes used.

77 The person issuing the power of attorney may be called the granter, the principal, the donor or the appointer. The person who is appointed to act on behalf of the granter may be called the attorney, the agent, the donee, or the appointee. As stated in paragraph 2, the words 'granter' and 'attorney' are used for the purpose of this recommendation. The word 'attorney' reflects the use of the term 'continuing power of attorney', and it therefore does not imply that an attorney needs to be a lawyer.

78 Paragraph 1 uses 'enter into force' in relation to a continuing power of attorney which is not operable before the granter's incapacity. The phrase refers to the point in time when the continuing power of attorney becomes operable and the attorney becomes entitled to act.

79 Paragraph 3 contains a definition of 'advance directives', the second form of self-determination covered by the recommendation. Like continuing powers of attorney, advance directives are issued by a capable adult with the purpose of giving instructions, or making wishes concerning issues that may arise in the event of the author's incapacity. The term 'living wills' is commonly used in national legislation, even if it covers two different types of decisions, the binding instructions, as well as wishes to be given due consideration (and therefore often called 'advance statements'). Paragraph 3 uses only the term 'advance directives' but, as described in

the definition and expanded in Principle 15, paragraph 1, the term covers both instructions with binding effects and wishes. Advance directives are addressed to persons who may take decisions during the granter's incapacity. They might in particular be addressed to medical staff, social workers, legal representatives, or attorneys appointed under continuing powers of attorney. If the directive takes the form of a wish, it shall, as mentioned in Principle 15, paragraph 1, be given due respect.

80 In the definitions contained in paragraphs 1 and 3, the term 'capable' is used without defining it. It is necessary that the granter has capacity relevant for this particular document. English case law has established that the granter must know who the attorney will be, what his or her task will be when the granter has become unable to act, and that the document can be withdrawn without the intervention of a court. If the power is of a general nature, the granter must have understood that the attorney may make decisions in all areas and dispose of all of his or her assets.

81 The title of the Recommendation No. R (99) 4 is 'Principles concerning the legal protection of incapable adults'. The term 'incapable adults' is not used in the present recommendation, as it is replaced by the more modern 'adults with incapacity', but the terms cover the same reality. It was not felt necessary to define it, as reference can be made to Part I of Recommendation No. R (99) 4 and the definition provided there.

82 Further explanations are found in the explanatory memorandum to the Recommendation No. R (99) 4 (paragraphs 15–20). The incapacity may only be temporary as the granter may recover. It may also be partial, in which case it is necessary to decide if it is of such nature that it prevents the person from making decisions about issues covered by the continuing power of attorney. Indeed, there is no place in modern incapacity law for the outmoded and factually inaccurate concept that people are either completely capable or completely incapable. All of the recommendation's references to capacity, incapacity and impairment of capacity should be taken as meaning 'relevant capacity'. This is particularly important in relation to powers about health, welfare and other personal matters, where legislative practice is to permit the attorney to make only decisions of which the granter is incapable so that in some cases the attorney may exercise only some of the powers conferred by the document. As already indicated, relevant incapacity is obviously independent of an adult's age.

Part II – Continuing powers of attorney

Principle 3 – Content

83 Principle 3 deals with the content of the power of attorney and requires states to consider whether it should be possible to cover economic and financial matters, as well as health, welfare and other personal matters.

84 The main rule is that the granter is free to decide on the content of the document. It is important that such content is clearly described. Because of its special nature and due to the fact that it will be used when the granter may no longer be able to influence it, certain legal requirements about its content may be needed. In most states, a continuing power of attorney is unilateral at the time of granting and becomes a contract upon subsequent acceptance by the attorney. In others, it takes the form of a contract between the granter and the attorney from the outset.

85 As stated in Principle 5, paragraph 2, the document, except in states where such is the general rule, shall explicitly state that it shall enter into force or remain in force in the event of the granter's incapacity. These two types of powers of attorney are described above in Part I, 1.7.2.

86 Traditionally, powers of attorney refer to 'economic and financial matters' or use the terminology 'property and financial matters'. This has also been the case with continuing powers of attorney. Economic and financial matters may, inter alia, include:

- buying or selling property,
- dealing with the granter's mortgages, rent and household expenses,
- insuring, maintaining and repairing the granter's property,
- repaying interest or capital on any loan taken out by the granter,
- opening, closing or operating bank accounts,
- obtaining and giving access to the granter's financial information,
- claiming, receiving and using all benefits, pensions, allowances and rebates,
- receiving any income and other entitlements on behalf of the granter,
- accepting or renouncing an inheritance or legacy,
- investing the granter's savings,
- making and accepting gifts,
- paying for medical care and residential care or nursing home fees,
- applying for any entitlements to funding for care and social care,
- representing the granter in certain court proceedings.

87 In recent years, it has become more common to widen continuing powers to health, welfare and other personal matters. In accordance with the principle of self-determination, the person concerned makes decisions in such matters when he or she is still capable of doing so. When he or she becomes incapacitated, and if the power of attorney so provides, the attorney can make decisions for him or her. The powers might include a whole range of primarily non-economic decisions, for instance:

- where the person lives and with whom, for example the place of provisional or permanent residence,
- assessments for and provision of community services,
- whether the granter works and, if so, the kind and place of work and the employer,
- education and training,
- in which social or leisure activities the granter should take part,
- right of access to personal information about the granter,
- arrangements needed for the granter to be given medical, including dental or ophthalmologic, treatment,
- consenting to or refusing medical examination and treatment,
- consenting to social care,
- complaints about the granter's care and treatment.

88 There are differences between economic powers on the one hand and personal powers on the other. The latter should not be used as long as the granter is capable of making such decisions him/herself. Therefore, a power of attorney about personal matters should be operable only during the granter's incapacity. The competent authority which, according to Principle 12, paragraph 2, may intervene, may be different from the one dealing with economic matters. Furthermore, as mentioned in Principle 3, some particular matters may be excluded. Finally, in most jurisdictions, the bankruptcy of the granter or a sole attorney will end economic powers, but not welfare powers.

89 The power of attorney is often of a general nature, covering all economic and financial, as well as health, welfare and other personal matters. However, it might be preferable to provide in the document or in legislation examples of more important decisions the attorney is authorised to make, as it reinforces the awareness of the granter as to the step he or she is taking in signing the document.

90 There may be reasons for creating two continuing powers of attorney, one about economic and financial matters, and another about health, welfare and other personal matters, as the granter may not wish his or her business associates to learn, through the document, about the latter matters.

91 It is possible to limit the power of attorney to certain specific areas, either by listing the areas covered, or by excluding some of them. The power may also be limited in time. The risk with such limitations is that a need for decisions may arise concerning matters which the attorney is not authorised and the granter is unable to deal with. It might then be necessary to obtain a court order of legal representation covering such decisions.

92 The granter may insert binding conditions, restrictions and instructions to the attorney in advance directives, for example, for a house to be bought or sold, or funds invested. Due to the importance of such decisions, they have to be considered carefully, and sometimes it is recommended to grant the continuing power of attorney unconditionally. It is preferable to issue a special document about such directives, as it might not be advisable that a third party – who wishes to consult the power of attorney document – comes aware of such conditions. Such advance directives should comply with Principle 16.

93 It is essential to the principles of self-determination that legislation should be widely framed, enabling individual granters each to select what is best for them in relation to the matters discussed above, to confer wider or narrower powers as they may choose and to decide what limitations or conditions should be imposed.

94 As mentioned in Principle 3, states should consider whether some particular matters should be excluded. Any such exclusions should be kept to a minimum. Certain legislation contains a rule that some questions are of such a character that the attorney is not permitted to deal with them and that they are therefore excluded. Examples are agreeing to marriage or a registered partnership, adoption, acknowledgement of paternity or maternity, or making or revoking a will. Some health issues may also be excluded, as they may pose various problems, such as may be the case as regards the representative appointed by a competent authority. If there is a possibility to exclude or include health and social welfare issues, this might necessitate a change of the relevant health and social welfare legislation.

Principle 4 – Appointment of attorney

95 Principle 4 deals with the appointment of the person who has a mandate to act after the granter's incapacity. The word 'attorney' is, as mentioned under Principle 2, paragraph 2, closely linked to the term 'continuing power of attorney', and this does not mean that the attorney must be a legal professional or a person with other formal qualifications.

96 The granter's choice of attorney is crucial to the success of the power of attorney. It is important that the granter considers the person or persons whom he or she wishes to appoint as appropriate, as stated in paragraph 1. The granter should have confidence in the appointed person(s), as he or she will be unable to control the attorney's decisions, to appoint a new attorney, or to revoke the power of attorney

when he or she becomes incapacitated. The appointed person(s) must be relied upon to take care of the interests of the granter. An attorney must have the necessary integrity and ability to resist a wish from family members to use money outside the limits of the power. If these conditions are not fulfilled, there is a risk that the power of attorney will not function properly. A family member may often be preferred by the granter, but he or she may also wish to appoint his or her lawyer, notary, accountant, or simply a friend.

97 According to paragraph 2, the granter may appoint more than one attorney and may appoint them to act jointly, concurrently or separately, or as substitutes. Clearly, if the granter makes such a choice, it must be specified in the document.

98 Two or more attorneys acting jointly may be the solution in cases where there are several children involved, as a reasonable assurance against misuse or undue concentration of power, or to reduce the risk of family dispute. If one of the attorneys cannot or will not take on the task, or if one subsequently resigns or dies, it should be made clear either in the document or in the law whether the other(s) may continue to act. It might be prescribed, either in the document or by law, that if three or more attorneys are appointed to act jointly, a decision by the majority might be deemed to be a decision of all.

99 The appointment may be concurrent, as there may be different attorneys each dealing with some matters, for example one acting as regards the economic and financial matters, and another dealing with health, welfare and other personal matters. The reason might be a wish to ensure that someone who has a special competence in the relevant field makes adequate decisions.

100 If the attorneys may act separately, any risk of conflict should be addressed in the continuing power of attorney document. Otherwise, a solution may exist in the law relating to all powers of attorney, or it may be considered necessary to provide a solution.

101 Obviously, a variety of combinations is possible. It may be prescribed that a decision by one of the attorneys is sufficient in most cases, but that two or three attorneys have to agree on major decisions, for example, the sale of a house. Legislation may also prescribe that if the granter has not decided otherwise, each attorney may exercise his or her authority individually, but in consultation with the others.

102 A final possibility is to appoint one or more substitute attorneys to act in case the first-mentioned attorney is not able or willing to take on the task, has resigned or has died. If more attorneys are appointed, it may be prescribed that they shall act successively in the order in which they are named.

103 According to paragraph 3, states may consider such restrictions as are deemed necessary for the protection of the granter. In some legislation, there are requirements as regards the choice of the attorney. Usually the attorney has to be an individual, natural person, but it might also be a legal person, for example an organisation or an association, sometimes even in cases where the mandate concerns health, welfare and other personal matters. The appointed natural person must be an adult and capable. If the power of attorney covers economic and financial matters, the attorney must not be a bankrupt. One jurisdiction prescribes that the attorney may not be employed by, or closely associated with, a hospital or another institution where the granter is living. Other requirements may be included in a certification or registration procedure as described under principle 8.

104 The formal arrangements between the granter and the attorney may vary. The continuing power of attorney may take the form of an agreement between them, but

it may also be unilateral. It is preferable that the attorney is informed about the creation of the power, and has at the time of creation accepted the role or prospective role. The two persons are thereby able to discuss what shall happen if and when the power is used. It may be advisable that the attorney signs the document, as is sometimes prescribed. Some granters may not wish to disclose their intentions to the attorney and therefore may instruct a third person to hand over the power once they have become incapacitated. In this case, it is up to the attorney to accept or refuse the mandate. Even when the power of attorney is granted unilaterally, there should be a requirement for acceptance by the attorney (and by each successive substitute attorney where substitutes are appointed) before the attorney may commence to act. A contract is concluded by such acceptance.

105 A further question is whether the attorney must act personally or may delegate powers to a third person without a legal basis in the document. This question is not addressed in this recommendation.

Principle 5 – Form

106 The form of the continuing power of attorney is dealt with in Principle 5. It is supplemented by Principle 8, which concerns certification, registration and notification.

107 Paragraph 1 requires a written document. It shall be signed or confirmed by the granter. It is preferable that the document is dated, as required by some legislation.

108 Paragraph 2 deals with the requirement for the granter to state in the document when the continuing power may be used, if this is not regulated by the legislation. As described above in Part I, 1.7.2, in some legislation powers of attorney normally remain in force after the granter's incapacity. If under such a rule the granter wishes for the power of attorney to be brought to an end in the event of his or her incapacity, this must be stated explicitly in the document. In other legislation, it is the general rule, that a continuing power of attorney enters into force only in the event of the granter's incapacity, and then it is not necessary for the granter to state that fact. In states where powers of attorney are presumed to terminate in the event of the granter's incapacity, and the legislation about continuing powers of attorney covers both possibilities, it is necessary for the granter to state explicitly in the document if it is the intention that the power of attorney shall remain in force or that the power should enter into force only in the event of the granter's incapacity.

109 A further question not addressed in the recommendation is whether a type of form should be offered. It might be a form issued by an official body. In states where forms are found, they offer a number of choices as regards particular questions. Various forms might be accessible via the internet. It may be an advantage that it is simple and cheap to produce the document, perhaps seeking advice on the internet or by using a 'do it yourself kit'. The risk is that the granter might not consider carefully enough the steps to be taken, which may facilitate abuse. The option of an individualised document prepared with professional advice should always be available. The purpose of using a more detailed form is to ensure that the granter understands all of the powers which are granted, and can delete any specific powers which he or she does not wish to confer.

110 It should be considered whether professional assistance should be recommended or even made compulsory. In some legislation, there is a requirement that a professional, such as a lawyer, a notary, or a court official assists, at least if the decision covers more important matters, for example major medical treatment, a change of the place of the granter's habitual residence, and important economic and

financial matters. This implies that the granter has been duly informed about the consequences of the document and the possibility of revocation.

111 Since continuing powers of attorney will be effective at a time when the granter is no longer able to intervene or to revoke the power, it is important, as stated in paragraph 3, that states consider what provisions and mechanisms may be required to ensure the validity of the document. Safeguards and procedures may be considered necessary at the time when the document is signed or confirmed. They are probably more necessary when there is specific legislation covering both types of continuing powers of attorney, those that remain in force and those that enter into force in the event of the granter's incapacity, and less necessary if the use after incapacity is a consequence of general rules on powers of attorney. The purpose of regulation is to confirm that the granter, when the document is created, is capable of doing so and not subject to undue influence, and perhaps also that he or she knows the content of the document and that he or she is informed about or confirms that he or she is aware of its consequences. The reason for such considerations is that the granter, at the time of the signing, may be frail and somebody may have an interest in obtaining a mandate to act when the granter is no longer able to do so. A parallel can be drawn with procedures for making wills, and in some legislation they are followed as models. The requirements must be weighed against the consideration that it should not be too difficult and bureaucratic to create the document.

112 In some legislation, it is possible to handwrite the document from beginning to end and if this is not the case, the granters have to sign or confirm their signatures in the presence of one or more witnesses. In other legislation, the use of witnesses is the only possibility. These witnesses are required to be independent and unbiased and, for this reason, neither the attorney nor persons connected to the granter or the attorney may act as witnesses. There might be a requirement that the witnesses must have known the granter for a specified time.

113 Other alternatives require professional involvement. It may be required that the document be established or certified by a notary, a court official or a person with other specific qualifications.

114 Depending on the national system, the primary purpose of a certifier or witnesses is to confirm, if necessary by taking professional advice, that the granter has capacity to grant the continuing power of attorney, as implied by the document. They may be asked to certify that the granter signed voluntarily, that there are no reasons to believe that the granter acted under undue influence, that there is no fraud, and that the document is not, for other reasons, invalid. In some legislation, the certifier or witnesses are required to confirm that they are convinced that the granter, at the time of signature, has knowledge of the character and the effects of the document or to confirm that the granter has an awareness of them. The certifier or witnesses may be required to read the document aloud if the granter has not confirmed his or her knowledge of the document.

115 The role of the appointed attorney at the time of signature is generally not described. In some legislation, a continuing power may take the form of a contract, in which case the attorney is a party. In other legislation, where the power is granted unilaterally, the attorney may be obliged to sign the document, thus confirming his or her willingness to take on the task, or to provide signed acceptance separately, for example in a registration application. The attorney may have to confirm a readiness to take the necessary steps to have the document certified and registered when the time comes. If the signature of the attorney is not required, the granter runs the risk that, when it is time to act, the appointed person may not become aware of the document, or may not be willing to act as attorney.

Principle 6 – Revocation

116 Principle 6 deals with the granter's ability to revoke a continuing power of attorney while he or she is still capable of doing so. A continuing power of attorney, because of its nature, and particularly since it will have effect after the incapacity of the granter, should not be irrevocable. It is also one way of rectifying undue pressure at the time of the signing. This principle applies when the continuing power of attorney is made in the form of a contract, as well as when it is granted unilaterally. The principle does not prevent states from regulating the possibility of changing or amending the mandate.

117 The reference to Principle 5, paragraph 3, indicates that states should consider what provisions and mechanisms should be in place to ensure the validity of the revocation, for example to establish that the granter has the necessary capacity to make the decision to revoke. Revoking the power potentially raises the same issues and concerns as the granting of the power.

118 An attorney who has knowledge of the power of attorney must be informed about a revocation, as must third parties appointed to monitor the attorney. If the document is already entered into a register, it is necessary to register the revocation.

119 Termination of the continuing power of attorney during the granter's incapacity is dealt with in Principle 13.

Principle 7 – Entry into force

120 As mentioned above under 1.5 Terminology, this recommendation uses 'enter into force' in relation to a continuing power of attorney which is not operable before the granter's incapacity. The term refers to the point in time when the continuing power of attorney becomes operable and the attorney becomes entitled to act.

121 According to Principle 7, paragraph 1, states should regulate the manner of entry into force of the continuing power of attorney in the event of the granter's incapacity. Where, according to legislation or the terms of the document, a power of attorney already in force remains in force in the event of incapacity, there is no need for special provisions about the continued use, unless some form of registration or notification is required to trigger enhanced monitoring.

122 In situations covered by this principle, it is necessary to establish the incapacity of the granter.

123 Other considerations have to be taken into account. It is important that the granter, if he or she is able to understand the information, is made aware that the attorney intends to use the document. Close family members may also have an interest in being informed that a continuing power has been granted as well as of its content, and that it is now going to be used by the attorney. Furthermore, the attorney may need certification to act as regards third parties, for example banks, which may require proof from an independent source of the existence and validity of the mandate, and that it has entered into force.

124 Various procedures are used to establish the existence of the requirements for the entry into force of the document. As stated in paragraph 2, states should consider what evidence should be required to determine the granter's incapacity. Those procedures must protect the confidentiality of the detailed medical information upon which incapacity is certified, if such certification is required.

125 The decision about the entering into force of the power may be made in different ways and Principles 7 and 8 do not give examples or express preferences, although Principle 8 lists some possible mechanisms.

126 Application of the principle of self-determination might allow the granter to decide him/herself what kind of evidence about his or her health situation shall be produced, whether or not it is the intent of the legislator that there should be any public involvement. The granter might choose to make it the duty of the attorney to take action and decide to use the power. In those countries where it exists, a medical certificate about the condition of the granter normally will be necessary and sufficient. There might be a provision, in the legislation or in the document, that the attorney has a right to obtain such a certificate regardless of the rules on professional confidentiality. The attorney may, as described below under Principle 8, be required to notify close relatives, as specified in legislation or by the granter. According to the general rules on powers of attorney, the attorney may be held responsible to third parties for ensuring that the power is valid. The attorney has perhaps not been informed in advance of the existence of the document, but that is a risk taken by the granter.

127 Another possibility is that the granter establishes a procedure in the document whereby a third person has to make a written declaration that the granter has become incapacitated, perhaps requiring that a medical certificate about the incapacity be attached or referred to. In some states, such arrangements are imposed by law. A third party holding the document, while the appointed attorney has no knowledge of it, will have the same duty to decide that it is time to use the power and to hand over the document to the attorney. Such a procedure reduces the risk of the power being used before intended.

128 Legislation may require that a court or the appropriate administrative authority be involved to certify that the document is effective. This often implies a registration procedure. Both procedures are mentioned in Principle 8 and described below.

129 The choice between the possibilities described depends on the extent to which legislators wish public authorities to be involved. Public involvement usually means a delay in the use of the power of attorney and more work for public authorities. It is important that the power of attorney is accepted by third parties, who might be less inclined to do so if the attorney makes the decision him/herself, rather than if the attorney is able to produce a public certificate. Where evidence of medical certification of medical incapacity is requested by third parties, the certificate produced should contain only certification of the fact of incapacity, and not any detailed medical information on which that conclusion is based.

Principle 8 – Certification, registration and notification

130 Principle 8 lists three different systems which states should consider introducing: certification, registration and notification. They apply in different situations as they may refer to the time of the creation of the power or to the time when it enters into force. Their purposes may vary. They may constitute alternative solutions, or may supplement each other. Once again, it is necessary to find the right balance between the self-determination of the granter and the need for some degree of public involvement.

131 Certification may be required or available at any time and may serve various purposes.

132 Certification may be carried out by a public authority for various purposes. Such a certificate may be issued as part of a registration procedure connected with the creation as described below, and it is then considered to be a certificate of registration, but it might also be independent of such procedure.

133 As already indicated above under 1.3, states which have ratified the Hague Convention of 2000 may, according to Article 38, deliver, on request, a certificate to the person entrusted with protection of the adult's person and property, indicating the capacity in which the person is entitled to act and the powers conferred. A model form is recommended for use. According to the form, the validity of the power of representation is confirmed.

134 Another possibility is certification when a continuing power of attorney enters into force, to confirm that the granter has now become incapacitated, and that other possible procedures, mentioned under Principle 7, paragraph 1, have been duly followed. The purpose may then be to supply the attorney with a certificate stating that he or she has authority to act.

135 As regards continuing powers of attorney that remain in force as well as those that enter into force, the certificate may be sent to the attorney or, where combined with a registration procedure, to whoever initiated the registration. Such a certificate, perhaps annexed to an authenticated copy of the document, may be required for submission to third parties (for instance banks where the granter has accounts or deposits) in order to prove the appointment of the attorney and that he or she has authority to carry out certain transactions on behalf of the granter.

136 In countries where a notarial system exists, a notary could be given the task of issuing a certificate to the effect that the power of attorney is to enter into force. This may follow submission of the power of attorney and, where it is required, a medical certificate about the granter's incapacity to the notary. The notary would confirm the powers conferred upon the attorney in a certificate and issue it to the attorney. Any third person may rely on such a certificate.

137 Rules about registration of continuing powers of attorney exist in a number of states and registration may be voluntary or compulsory. Rules vary as regards the time of the registration and the procedure followed by the registration authorities. The purpose of the registration may vary and is to a large extent dependent on whether there is a certification procedure attached to the registration as well on the rules about access to the register. The registration may be carried out with the competent authority, in a central register of notaries, or in a central data bank.

138 Registration most often takes place following upon creation of a continuing power of attorney and may be a part of the mechanism to ensure the validity of the document, mentioned in Principle 5, paragraph 3. If registration is compulsory, the power may not be used by the attorney before it is registered. This may be the case both as regards powers of attorney that remain in force after the incapacity of the granter and powers that only enter into force in the event of impairment of capacity. If a lawyer or a notary has taken part in the creation of the document, the application for registration may be one of the lawyer's tasks. Another possibility may be that the application may be lodged by the granter as long as he or she is still capable, or by the attorney on an application form which includes acceptance of appointment by the attorney and provides other relevant information.

139 The registration authority may have different tasks to perform. It may check the validity of the document as described above under Principle 5, paragraph 3, for instance whether witnesses were present, and confirm that the required statements form part of the document. There may be a duty to notify the granter and the attorney about the application for registration, and possibly close relatives, as

described below. This may result in an intervention from the granter and perhaps another person having the right to do so. The authority may then be required to investigate. It may be helpful to include registration of the attorney's acceptance of the mandate, of any resignation or revocation, of any event causing a substitute attorney to take over, or any other event relevant to the effectiveness or continuation of the power of attorney.

140 Registration may also take place when a power of attorney is to enter into force in the event of the granter's incapacity. The granter may also want registration to be postponed until a specific event has occurred. Then, the application may form part of the procedure and manner described above under Principle 7, paragraph 1. Usually, the attorney applies to the authority for registration if he or she finds that there are good reasons to believe that the granter has become incapacitated. The attorney, before applying, often has to provide a medical certificate and occasionally, as described below, documentation attesting that the granter (and sometimes others, such as family members) have been notified accordingly. If the authority receives protests from interested persons on the grounds that there is a real and actual risk of misuse of the power, or that there are good reasons to believe that the person appointed is not suitable for the task, this has to be taken into consideration by the authority.

141 In other legislation, registration is dependent on the wishes of the granter and therefore is voluntary. It requires that the document be created with the assistance of a lawyer or a notary, who attends to registration. The granter may be informed about the registration.

142 If registration of a continuing power of attorney is a possibility, the question arises concerning who may have access to the information contained in the register. In some legislation, courts and other authorities may obtain information from the register, in particular if the registration is carried out by a notary. The relevant court may wish to ascertain whether the adult concerned has granted a continuing power of attorney. Health and social welfare authorities may also wish to learn about the existence of a document, its content and who the decision-maker is. In other legislation, the register may be consulted by the granter, relatives and third parties should the need arise, but also by courts or other authorities, such as social welfare authorities. When the register is accessible to the public, then banks and other third parties, when approached by the attorney, may wish to verify whether a power of attorney is registered. Access to the register may depend on legislation, in particular concerning data protection.

143 In Principle 8, notification is also mentioned. It is particularly important that the granter be notified of events such as certification, registration, revocation, entry into force, or termination, whether or not the granter is believed to have become incapable, except where there is compelling reason not to do so. It may be a requirement that the attorney notify, or it may be part of a registration procedure. It is important that a granter should be made aware that the continuing power of attorney is about to enter into force and that the attorney intends to begin to act. The granter may then intervene on the grounds that he or she is still capable of revoking the power of attorney.

144 There may be other persons or bodies who should be notified, under the terms of the power of attorney, for example the granter's spouse, partner and/or close relatives. Such persons may also have an interest in being informed that a continuing power has been granted, as well as of its content, either when the document is created or once it enters into force. Notification gives the persons informed a possibility, within a fixed period of time, to intervene or protest by contacting the competent authority. They may be of the opinion that the granter is still capable of

making decisions; they may claim that the document is invalid because the signing procedure has not been followed, that the granter was under undue pressure at the time of signing, or that the mandate has been revoked. Furthermore, they may find that the appointed attorney is unsuitable for the task, perhaps because of conflicts of interest or because of a risk of misuse.

Principle 9 – Preservation of capacity

145 As stated in Principle 9, the entry into force of a continuing power of attorney shall not as such affect the legal capacity of the granter. The legal situation then accords with Recommendation No. R (99) 4 under which appointment of a legal representative does not decrease or completely remove the adult's legal capacity. The granting or entry into force of a continuing power of attorney can never disqualify or prevent the granter from doing or deciding anything of which he or she is capable.

146 A continuing power of attorney that can only be exercised in the event of the granter's incapacity may not be operated during periods when the granter has regained capacity.

Principle 10 – Role of the attorney

147 Principle 10 deals with the role of the attorney when the mandate is exercised during the granter's incapacity.

148 As a general rule, the attorney is bound by the scope, content and limitations of the powers conferred upon him or her. As stated in paragraph 1, the attorney shall act in accordance with the power of attorney and in the interests of the granter. Decisions should be in accordance with what the granter, if capable, would have decided, in so far as this can reasonably be ascertained. Possible supervision of whether the attorney is doing so is described below under Principle 12.

149 Circumstances may arise in which the attorney becomes aware of a need to do something not authorised by the continuing power of attorney. Some states have procedures under which the attorney may seek specific authority, but not an amendment to the continuing power of attorney.

150 According to paragraph 2, the attorney, as far as possible, informs and consults the granter on an ongoing basis to the extent that this will be meaningful, which depends upon the granter's condition. It is essential that there is a good relationship between the attorney and the granter. Informing and consulting the granter about decisions which the attorney intends to make and about the state of the granter's economic and financial matters is necessary, so that the granter has the opportunity to express an opinion or, to the extent capable, give instructions. Paragraph 2 has a parallel in the Recommendation No. R (99) 4, Principle 9, about 'respect for the wishes and feelings of the person concerned' when implementing a measure of protection, in that it provides that the attorney shall take the granter's past and present wishes and feelings into account and give them due respect. Such past wishes are especially mentioned because advance directives, as mentioned above under Principle 3, may be addressed to an attorney to whom a continuing power of attorney is granted.

151 Paragraph 3 states, that the granter's economic and financial matters, as far as possible, should be kept separate from the attorney's own. The two persons' assets

and incomes should, in principle, not be intermingled. The attorney shall therefore ensure that share certificates, bank accounts and other documents are kept separately and in the name of the granter.

152 In paragraph 4, it is stated that the attorney keeps sufficient records about dealings and transactions made under the power. The extent of the duty to keep a file of the paperwork depends on the nature of the mandate, and must be proportionate. If there is significant capital, it is necessary to keep records on major decisions and transactions. It might normally be expected to preserve bank records, receipts of larger payments, as well as documentation about major decisions. In the case of a power of attorney about health, welfare and other personal matters, major decisions must be recorded. It may be useful to make notes on a regular basis.

153 One reason for the requirement to keep records is – as mentioned in Principle 10 – that the attorney must be able to demonstrate the proper exercise of his or her mandate. Such records shall be presented when the mandate comes to an end, for example if the granter recovers and becomes capable again, in the event of the granter's death, or when a public measure of representation has been decided. Furthermore, the attorney must, as mentioned in the present principle, be able to produce at least on request documentation or accounts to a third person mentioned in the continuing power, for example a person appointed to supervise the attorney, as stated in Principle 12, paragraph 1. This may be the granter's lawyer or accountant. A competent authority may, as an important element of the supervision mentioned in Principle 12, paragraph 2, in individual cases require the attorney to present accounts, and it may be necessary that they cover the whole period of the mandate.

154 As regards the role of the attorney, it is questionable if and to what extent, the general rules of national legislation about powers of attorney shall apply as a supplement to or a modification of these special powers. Such legislation may regulate the protection of third parties, the attorney's liability and the extent of his or her obligations, and the conditions under which the document can be deemed invalid. Certain legislation on continuing powers of attorney refers to these rules. In other legislation, some or many of the general rules on powers of attorney are repeated in the special legislation.

Principle 11 – Conflict of interest

155 States should, as stated in Principle 11, consider regulating conflicts of the granter's and the

attorney's interests. It could be presumed that a conflict of interest arises in the case of any transactions between the attorney, acting for him/herself, and the attorney, acting on behalf of the granter. Rules may be required to specify or regulate situations in which such transactions may be permitted.

156 A very important and – for continuing powers of attorney – a particularly relevant issue is the requirement that the attorney acts impartially. The attorney may be a member of the family of a granter, who previously has made donations to the attorney, as well as to relatives, and the attorney may feel that such practice should continue. In other situations, the attorney may consider it appropriate to buy the granter's house for him/herself. The attorney may also request an exceptional remuneration.

157 Other typical examples of conflicts of interest are when attorneys wish to give gifts to themselves, their spouses or children, or other persons. In legislation there may be very detailed rules to prevent conflicts of interest, often inspired by what is

prescribed as regards representatives appointed by competent authority. One example is that the attorney has no right to represent the granter if there is a possibility of a contract between the granter on the one hand, and the attorney, his or her spouse or partner or somebody else being represented by the attorney, on the other. Another, even more specific rule, is that the attorney's child, grandchild, siblings, parents or grandparents or such person's spouse or partner may not be such contracting parties.

158 On this topic, as with others, a balance between protection and self-determination can be achieved by having clear rules as to conflict of interest, but allowing the granter to permit – by express provision in the power of attorney – what would otherwise be a prohibited conflict. It can be particularly relevant in this situation to have a system of certification that the granter fully understands the meaning and effect of the document, has capacity, and is not subject to undue influence (cf. commentary above on Principles 5 and 8). The granter should thus be free to specify in the document that the attorney may make individual decisions that he or she otherwise could not have made. There may be detailed instructions about who may receive gifts, the maximum value of gifts, the continuation of previous practices, or measures taken for tax-planning purposes. To a certain extent, legislative rules have been designed to overcome some specific conflicts of interest. The attorney may be allowed to make usual gifts on customary occasions to persons, including him/herself, who are related to or connected with the granter, or gifts to a charity to which the granter may have made or might have wished to make gifts.

159 The granter is free to decide that the attorney may be reimbursed for expenses incurred in connection with the task. The granter may decide that the attorney should be entitled to specified remuneration if the assistance is substantial, or when a professional, for example the granter's lawyer, notary or accountant, is appointed as attorney (except in states where a professional attorney is automatically entitled to remuneration). If nothing is prescribed in the document, the attorney may expect to have his or her out-of-pocket expenses in connection with the task reimbursed.

Principle 12 – Supervision

160 A basic concern is that continuing powers of attorney be used in accordance with the granter's intention and in his or her interests, as mentioned in Principle 10, paragraph 1. The starting point is that the decision to appoint a trusted attorney and to confer upon him or her power to act is a calculated risk taken by a capable granter, with the result that the attorney is allowed, as a rule, to do whatever he or she decides within the scope of the powers conferred with the granter's capital, income and property once the latter becomes incapacitated. The granter should, at time of signing, be informed and aware of the fact that the attorney will act without automatic supervision. He or she might well see it as an advantage that public authorities are not involved. On the other hand, it can be pointed out that the risk of misuse may be overestimated, and that the same risk might exist without a document. An essential feature of a continuing power of attorney is therefore that public authorities are not automatically and routinely involved in supervising all actions of the attorneys.

161 According to Principle 12, paragraph 1, the granter may establish a private supervision system. A third person may be appointed in the document to supervise the attorney during the granter's incapacity. He or she may be called a supervising attorney. The attorney may be required to produce annual accounts with documentation or regular reports to the appointed third person, who may be given power to veto certain specified decisions, such as larger gifts or sale of the granter's

house. The granter may have prescribed that any request for remuneration from the attorney should require authorisation by this third person. The legislation may impose an obligation that, if no supervising attorney is appointed, an annual accounting shall be provided to the closest relative (other than the attorney him/herself) of the granter. The purpose of privately-organised supervision is to ensure that the attorney takes proper care of the interests of the granter, that he or she does not act in situations where there is a potential conflict of interest, and that there is no misuse.

162 Paragraph 2 deals with involvement of public authorities if a person with an interest in the economic and financial matters or the health, welfare or other personal matters of the granter requests it, or if the authority in the individual case finds that there are reasons to investigate the attorney's exercise of the mandate. One example is that requests for supervision may be made by the granter, the attorney, the closest relative of the granter and a recipient of an accounting, the granter's spouse, partner, parents, siblings or descendants.

163 The point at which a need for public supervision arises depends on the nature of the problem. Supervision is probably necessary in case of risk of misuse of the power, for example if the attorney wishes to use the money for his or her own benefit or to give relatives large gifts. The attorney may also have shown him/herself to be unable to perform the task. A particular problem is whether the power should be terminated in case of conflicts between the attorney and close family members about what is in the granter's interest. It is probably not sufficient that the relatives are simply dissatisfied with the attorney or his or her performance, as long as he or she takes care of the interests of the granter, according to the provisions of the document.

164 If the competent authority has reason to believe that the interests or the welfare of the granter may be at risk, such an authority should have appropriate powers and duties to investigate. These may include requiring the attorney to produce accounts and documentation concerning the use of capital and income as well as reporting about decisions and failures to do something. Furthermore, the authority might examine the living conditions of the granter to find out if his or her interests are being taken care of satisfactorily by the attorney.

165 If the competent authority finds that there are clear and specific reasons for intervention, the available forms of intervention vary greatly between different jurisdictions. The attorney may be required to file accounts yearly or for a certain period, to report on decisions as regards personal matters and to produce documentation. He or she may be given instructions as to the exercise of the functions, for example concerning gifts. In some legislation, the scope of the power may be reduced. It should not be possible to extend the powers contained within the continuing power of attorney (cf. commentary on Principle 10). The attorney may be replaced by another one, and the power may be declared invalid or terminated. In some legislation, the only decision available is to establish a representation whereby the continuing power of attorney becomes null and void. The only method of intervention singled out in Principle 12, paragraph 2, is the termination of the continuing power of the attorney in part or in whole.

166 Occasionally, there is deviation from the above pattern. In such cases, when the power enters into force, the attorney has always to make a statement to the relevant public authority about the economic and financial matters of the granter, the assets and income, as well as the debts and expenses. The granter may have prescribed in the document that the attorney must file accounts and other information with the

authority and that the attorney cannot make certain important decisions without permission, for example under the same conditions which apply to a representative appointed by a competent authority.

167 Further possibilities for supervision, not addressed in the principles, may exist in general law relating to all powers of attorney, or may be considered necessary. While the principle of self-determination would normally minimize the provision for judicial or other intervention in the operation of continuing powers of attorney, circumstances can arise where it may be better that there be such intervention in relation to a particular issue, rather than that the continuing power of attorney should become unworkable, or the attorney should resign because of unresolved difficulties. In some states, there are procedures under which a court or other competent authority may give authorisation or directions to an attorney.

168 A wide range of possible circumstances could be addressed in this way. In some states, when an attorney is unsure about whether a particular matter is within his or her competence, or about how he or she should decide a difficult and important matter, a decision in the matter by a court or other competent authority may provide clarity to all concerned, and reassurance to the attorney. In other states, certain specified matters must be referred to a court or other competent authority for authorisation.

169 Joint attorneys may disagree with each other, a close family member may disagree with an attorney, or a third party – because of genuine doubt or for no good reason – may be reluctant to accept an instruction or decision from the attorney. There may be questions about whether, in a particular case, formalities for creation, certification or registration have been properly followed.

Principle 13 – Termination

170 Paragraph 1 deals with termination of a continuing power of attorney when the granter is no longer capable. When the granter is still capable, he or she, according to Principle 6, is free to revoke the power of attorney.

171 It is left to states to determine the circumstances under which the power of attorney should be terminated. One example of termination in part or in whole is mentioned in Principle 12, paragraph 2. An intervention by a public authority where the attorney is not acting in accordance with the continuing power of attorney may take the form of a termination.

172 The death of the granter may be another reason for termination, but in certain legislation there is a possibility for the attorney, after the granter's death, to continue to act temporarily or as regards certain decisions. This needs to be carefully co-ordinated with the role of the executors or other personal representatives.

173 The power of attorney also terminates if a sole attorney dies, resigns, or becomes incapacitated, and no alternative or substitute attorney is mentioned in the document. In some states, there is a rule stating that, if the attorney is the spouse or partner of the granter, the power is terminated if the couple gets separated or divorced, or the partnership is dissolved. A continuing power of attorney as regards economic and financial matters is terminated in the event of bankruptcy of the granter or a sole attorney. States may wish to specify what should happen in the event of the bankruptcy of one joint attorney, and following discharge from bankruptcy.

174 The attorney is free to resign at any time, including after the incapacity of the granter. If the attorney has not accepted the task in advance, he or she may also

refuse to take it on. It goes without saying that the granter has to be dully informed of the intended refusal or resignation, if this is meaningful, and that the attorney should be required to give advance notice. In one state, the competent authority has to consent. If only one attorney is appointed in the continuing power of attorney and he or she resigns, then the power is terminated.

175 The consequence of the termination is that the competent authority, as stated in paragraph 2, should consider whether appropriate measures of protection are required. Appointment of a legal representative would in many cases constitute such a measure. Where there is a system for registering the termination of a continuing power of attorney, notification to the competent authority can be part of the registration procedure.

Part III – Advance directives

Principle 14 – Content

176 This principle contains examples of areas where advance directives may be of use. Health issues are mentioned first. In general, there is a need for careful regulation in this area. Directives may address welfare and other personal matters, such as the place of care and residence of the author. They may also address economic and financial matters. Another example concerns who should be guardian, if a decision about legal representation is to be made.

177 Such directives may or may not be addressed to particular persons such as representatives appointed by a competent authority, attorneys, medical staff or other persons who make decisions on behalf of or affecting the author during incapacity. They are always unilateral documents which do not establish a contract with any such person.

Principle 15 – Effect

178 As described in the definition in Principle 2, paragraph 3, there are two types of advance directives. Some are binding instructions. In others, wishes for the future are made. The question of the nature of the advance directives should, as mentioned in Principle 15, paragraph 1, be addressed in legislation as regards each individual type.

179 Issues may arise as to whether the advance directive was intended to address the situation which has in fact occurred. That is a question of interpretation of the document.

180 As described in paragraph 2, it is also important to regulate through legislation situations that arise in the event of a substantial change in circumstances. Examples might include cases where, since the advance directive was issued, a medical procedure prohibited by the advance directive has been much improved so that it is less hazardous, or less intrusive, or there has been a substantial change in family circumstances. This is especially necessary if the advance directive is binding. In this context, reference could usefully be made to the 1997 Oviedo Convention (cf. paragraph 21 above).

181 An advance directive may not be applicable in certain instances. There may be reasonable grounds for believing that circumstances have arisen which the author did not anticipate at the time when the advance directive was issued, and which would have affected the directive had they been anticipated.

Principle 16 – Form

182 As described above, advance directives may be made in writing or may be expressed orally to family members, medical staff or others. States should consider whether all or certain types of advance directives shall be made or recorded in writing if intended to have binding effect. In some national legislation, a written document is required in relation to more serious health issues.

183 It is important that the principle of self-determination is not impaired by doubts about validity of an advance directive. States should therefore, as stated in paragraph 2, consider what other provisions and mechanisms may be required to ensure the validity and effectiveness of those advance directives, mentioned in paragraph 1. If a directive is about health issues, in some states it is deemed advisable that the adult receives guidance from a lawyer, a notary or a medical doctor in order to ensure that the directive is clear and that the adult is aware of the consequences of the choice.

184 An advance directive is of no value if it is not known by or accessible to persons who need to make decisions on behalf of or in relation to the incapacitated adult. A general consideration is whether there should be an obligation to enter some, or all, advance directives into a public register, or whether this should be done on a voluntary basis. It might consequently be necessary to establish who should have access to such a register, especially bearing in mind data protection legislation.

Principle 17 – Revocation

185 It is well established that when persons express views, including strong ones, about a possible future situation, their views may change when they actually find themselves in that situation.

186 This principle states that it should be possible to revoke an advance directive at any time and without any formalities, even if the directive is binding. This can be done as long as the adult is still capable of making the decision on revocation. A capable person with severe physical disability may be able to revoke orally or by an unequivocal gesture only.

PART XII

Directories

PART XII

Directories

PART XII: Directories

Organisations 2555

Websites 2570

Useful publications 2579

Organisations

CARERS AND NURSING SERVICES

Name of organisation	Address
British Nursing Association	Group House 92–96 Lind Road Sutton SM1 4PL Tel: 0871 873 3324 Email: info@bna.org
Carers Trust	32–36 Loman Street London SE1 0EH Tel: 0844 800 4361 Email: info@carers.org
Carers UK	20 Great Dover Street London SE1 4LX Tel: 020 7378 4999 Email: info@carersuk.org
National Care Association	Suite 4 Beaufort House Beaufort Court Sir Thomas Langley Road Rochester ME2 4FB Tel: 01634 716615 Email: info@nationalcareassociation.org.uk
National Council for Palliative Care	34–44 Britannia St London WC1X 9JG Tel: 020 7697 1520 Email: enquiries@ncpc.org.uk
The Relatives & Residents Association	1 The Ivories 6–18 Northampton Street London N1 2HY Tel: 020 7359 8148 Email: info@relres.org

ELDERLY

Name of organisation	Address
Action on Elder Abuse	PO Box 60001
	Streatham SW16 9BY
	Tel: 020 8835 9280
	Email: enquiries@elderabuse.org.uk
Age Cymru	Tŷ John Pathy
	13/14 Neptune Court
	Vanguard Way
	Cardiff CF24 5PJ
	Tel: 029 2043 1555
	Email: enquiries@agecymru.org.uk
Age NI	3 Lower Crescent
	Belfast BT7 1NR
	Tel: 0808 808 7575
	Email: info@ageni.org
Age Scotland	Causewayside House
	160 Causewayside
	Edinburgh EH9 1PR
	Tel: 0333 3232 400
	Email: enquiries@ageconcernandscotland.org.uk
Age UK	Tavis House
	1–6 Tavistock Square
	London WC1H 9NA
	Tel: 0800 169 2081
	Email: contact@ageuk.org.uk
Aid for the Aged in Distress	9 Bonhill Street
	London EC2A 4PE
	Tel: 0870 803 1950
	Email: info@aftaid.org.uk

Name of organisation	Address
Alzheimer's Disease Society	Devon House
	58 St Katharine's Way
	London E1W 1LB
	Tel: 020 20 7423 3500
	Email: enquiries@alzheimers.org.uk
Charities Aid Foundation	25 Kings Hill Avenue
	Kings Hill
	West Malling
	Kent ME19 4TA
	Tel: 03000 123 000
	Email: enquiries@caf.org
Charity Search	25 Portview Road
	Avonmouth
	Bristol BS11 9LD
	Tel: 0117 982 4060
	Email: info@charitysearch.org.uk
Contact the Elderly	2 Grosvenor Gardens
	London
	SW1W 0DH
	Tel: 020 7240 0630
	Email: info@contact-the-elderly.org.uk
Dementia UK	Second Floor, Resource for London
	356 Holoway Road
	London N7 6PA
	Tel: 020 7697 4160
	Email: info@dementiauk.org
Independent Age	18 Avonmore Road
	London W14 8RR
	Tel: 020 7605 4200
	Email: charity@independentage.org

FINANCIAL

Name of organisation	Address
Pensions Advisory Service	11 Belgrave Road London SW1V 1RB Tel: 0300 123 1047 Email: enquiries@opas.org.uk
Pensions and Lifetime Savings Association	Cheapside House 138 Cheapside London EC2V 6AE Tel: 020 7601 1700
Society for the Assistance of Ladies in Reduced Circumstances	Lancaster House 25 Hornyold Road Malvern WR14 1QQ Tel: 0300 365 1886 Email: info@salrc.org.uk
Society of Pension Professionals	2nd Floor St Bartholomew House 92 Fleet Street London EC4Y 1DG Tel: 020 7353 1688 Email: info@the-spp.co.uk

GENERAL

Name of organisation	Address
Citizens Advice	3rd Floor North 200 Aldersgate London EC1A 4HD Tel: 03444 111 444

Directories

Name of organisation	Address
The Grandparents Association	Moot House
	The Stow
	Harlow CM20 3AG
	Tel: 01279 428040
	Email: info@grandparents-association.org.uk
National Council of Voluntary Organisations	Society Building
	8 All Saints Street
	London N1 9RL
	Tel: 020 7713 6161
	Email: ncvo@ncvo-vol.org.uk
Salvation Army	101 Newington Causeway
	London SE1 6BN
	Tel: 020 7367 4500
	Email: info@salvationarmy.org.uk
The Samaritans	The Upper Mill
	Kingston Road
	Ewell KT17 2AF
	Tel: 020 8394 8300
	Email: admin@samaritans.org

HEALTH AND DISABILITY

Name of organisation	Address
Action against Medical Accidents (AvMA)	Freedman House
	Christopher Wren Yard
	117 High Street
	Croyden CR0 1QG
	Tel: 0845 123 2352
Action on Hearing Loss	19–23 Featherstone Street
	London EC1Y 8SL
	Tel: 0808 808 0123
	Email: informationline@hearingloss.org.uk

PART XII

Name of organisation	Address
Arthritis Care	Floor 4
	Linen Court
	10 East Road
	London N1 6AD
	Tel: 020 7380 6500
	Email: info@arthritiscare.org.uk
Arthritis Research UK	Copeman House
	St Mary's Gate
	Chesterfield S41 7TD
	Tel: 0300 790 0400
	Email: enquiries@arthritisresearchuk.org
British Heart Foundation	Greater London House,
	180 Hampstead Road
	London NW1 7AW
	Email: supporterservices@bhf.org.uk
	Tel: 020 7554 0000
British Red Cross	44 Moorfields
	London EC2Y 9AL
	Tel: 020 7562 2050
	Email: information@redcross.org.uk
Cancer Research UK	Angel Building
	407 St John Street
	London EC1V 4AD
	Tel: 0300 123 1022
	Email: info@cancerresearchuk.org
Diabetes Research and Wellness Foundation	010–012 Northney Marina
	Hayling Island PO11 0NH
	Tel: 02392 637 808

Name of organisation	Address
Diabetes UK	Macleod House
	10 Parkway
	London NW1 7AA
	Tel: 0345 123 2399
	Email: info@diabetes.org.uk
Disability Rights UK	Ground Floor
	CAN Mezzanine
	49–51 East Rd
	London N1 6AH
	Tel: 020 7250 8181
	Email: enquiries@disabilityrightsuk.org
Disabled Living Foundation	4th Floor
	Jessica House
	Red Lion Square
	191 Wandsworth High Street
	London SW18 4LS
	Tel: 020 7289 6111
	Email: info@dlf.org.uk
Macmillan Cancer Support	89 Albert Embankment
	London SE1 7UQ
	Tel: 0808 808 0000
Marie Curie Cancer Care	89 Albert Embankment
	London SE1 7TP
	Tel: 0800 090 2309
	Email: info@mariecurie.org.uk
MIND	15–19 Broadway
	Stratford
	London E15 4BQ
	Tel: 020 8519 2122
	Email: contact@mind.org.uk

Name of organisation	Address
Motability	City Gate House
	22 Southwark Bridge Road
	London SE1 9HB
	Tel: 0300 456 4566
Multiple Sclerosis Society	MS National Centre
	372 Edgware Road
	London NW2 6ND
	Tel: 020 8438 0700
	Email: helpline@mssociety.org.uk
MS Trust	Spirella Building
	Bridge Road
	Letchworth SG6 4ET
	Tel: 01462 476700
	Email: info@mstrust.org.uk
Parkinson's UK	215 Vauxhall Bridge Road
	London SW1V 1EJ
	Tel: 020 7931 8080
	Email: hello@parkinsons.org.uk
Patients Association	PO Box 935
	Harrow HA1 3YJ
	Tel: 0845 608 4455
	Email: helpline@patients-association.com
The Royal College of Surgeons	35–43 Lincoln's Inn Fields
	London WC2A 3PE
	Tel: 020 7405 3474
Royal National Institute of the Blind	105 Judd Street
	London WC1H 9NE
	Tel: 0303 123 9999
	Email: helpline@rnib.org.uk

Directories

Name of organisation	Address
Scope	6 Market Road
	London N7 9PW
	Tel: 020 7619 7100
	Email: helpline@scope.org.uk
Stroke Association	Stroke House
	240 City Road
	London EC1V 2PR
	Tel: 020 7566 0300
	Email: info@stroke.org.uk

HOUSING AND CARE HOMES

Name of organisation	Address
The Abbeyfield Society	St Peter's House
	2 Bricket Road
	St Albans AL1 3UW
	Tel: 01727 857536
	Email: post@abbeyfield.com
Elderly Accommodation Counsel	3rd Floor
	89 Albert Embankment
	London SE1 7TP
	Tel: 0800 377 7070
	Email: info@firststopadvice.org.uk
Homes and Communities Agency	Fry Building
	2 Marsham Street
	London SW1P 4DF
	Tel: 0300 1234 500
	Email: mail@homesandcommunities.co.uk
Hospice UK	34–44 Britannia Street
	London WC1X 9JG
	Tel: 020 7520 8200
	Email: info@hospiceuk.org

Registered Nursing Home Association	Derek Whittaker House
	Tunnel Lane
	Off Lifford Lane
	Kings Norton
	Birmingham B30 3JN
	Tel: 0121 451 1088
	Email: frankursell@rnha.co.uk
Shelter	88 Old Street
	London EC1V 9HU
	0808 800 4444
	Email: info@shelter.org.uk

HUMAN RIGHTS

Name of organisation	Address
Amnesty International UK	Human Rights Action Centre
	17–25 New Inn Yard
	London EC2A 3EA
	Tel: 020 7033 1500
	Email: sct@amnesty.org.uk
JUSTICE	59 Carter Lane
	London EC4V 5AQ
	Tel: 020 7329 5100
	Email: admin@justice.org.uk
Liberty	Liberty House
	26–30 Strutton Ground
	London SW1P 2HR
	Tel: 020 7403 3888

LEGAL

Name of organisation	Address
Association of Personal Injury Lawyers	3 Alder Court Rennie Hogg Road Nottingham NG2 1RX Tel: 0115 958 0585 Email: mail@apil.org.uk
Bar Council	289-293 High Holborn London WC1V 7HZ Tel: 020 7242 0082 Email: ContactUs@BarCouncil.org.uk
The Law Society	113 Chancery Lane London WC2A 1PL Tel: 020 7242 1222 Email: findasolicitor@lawsociety.org.uk
Legal Aid Practitioners' Group	3rd Floor Universal House 88–94 Wentworth Street London E1 7SA Tel: 020 7833 7431
Society of Trust and Estate Practitioners	Artillery House (South) 11–19 Artillery Row London SW1P 1RT Tel: 020 3752 3700 Email: step@step.org
Solicitors for the Elderly	Studio 209 Mill Studio Business Centre Crane Mead Ware SG12 9PY Tel: 0844 567 6173 Email: admin@sfe.legal

Name of organisation	Address
Solicitors Regulation Authority	The Cube 199 Wharfside Street Birmingham B1 1RN Tel: 0370 606 2555

OFFICIAL ADDRESSES

Name of organisation	Address
Care Quality Commission	Citygate Gallowgate Newcastle upon Tyne NE1 4PA Tel: 03000 616161 Email: enquiries@cqc.org.uk
Charity Commission	PO Box 211 Bootle L20 7YX
Court Funds Office	Glasgow G58 1AB Tel: 0300 0200 199 Email:enquiries@cfo.gsi.gov.uk
Court of Protection	PO Box 70185 First Avenue House 42–49 High Holborn London WC1A 9JA Tel: 0300 456 4600 Email: courtofprotectionenquiries@hmcts.gsi.gov.uk
Department of Health	Richmond House 79 Whitehall London SW1A 2NS Tel: 020 7210 4850
Department for Works and Pensions	Caxton House Tothill Street London SW1H 9NA Email: ministers@dwp.gsi.gov.uk

Directories

Name of organisation	Address
Equality and Human Rights Commission	Arndale House The Arndale Centre Manchester M4 3AQ Tel: 0161 829 8100
Government Legal Department	One Kemble Street London WC2B 4TS Tel: 020 7210 3000 Email: thetreasurysolicitor@governmentlegal.gov.uk
HM Courts and Tribunals Service	102 Petty France London SW1H 9AJ
Judicial Office for England and Wales	11th floor, Thomas More Building Royal Courts of Justice Strand London WC2A 2LL
Law Commission	1st Floor Tower 52 Queen Anne's Gate London SW1H 9AG Tel: 020 3334 0200 Email: enquries@lawcommission.gsi.gov.uk
Legal Aid Agency	Unit B8, Berkley Way Viking Business Park Jarrow NE31 1SF Tel: 0300 200 2020 Email: contactcivil@legalaid.gsi.gov.uk
Ministry of Justice	102 Petty France London SW1H 9AJ

PART XII

2567

Name of organisation	Address
Office of the Public Guardian	PO Box 16185
	Birmingham B2 2WH
	Tel: 0300 456 0300
	Email: customerservices@publicguardian.gsi.gov.uk
Official Solicitor and Public Trustee	Victory House
	30–34 Kingsway
	London WC2B 6EX
	Tel: 020 3681 2750 (Civil Litigation)
	Tel: 020 3681 2751 (Healthcare & Welfare)
	Tel: 020 3681 2758 (Property & Affairs)
	Tel: 020 3681 2759 (Trust and Deputy Services)
	Email: enquiries@offsol.gsi.gov.uk
Royal Courts of Justice	The Strand
	London WC2A 2LL

OMBUDSMEN

Name of organisation	Address
Financial Ombudsman Service	Exchange Tower
	London E14 9SR
	Tel: 020 7964 1000
	Email: complaint.info@financial-ombudsman.org.uk
Housing Ombudsman Service	81 Aldwych
	London WC2B 4HN
	Tel: 0300 111 3000
	Email: info@housing-ombudsman.org.uk
Legal Ombudsman	PO Box 6806
	Wolverhampton WV1 9WJ
	Tel: 0300 555 0333
	Email: enquiries@legalombudsman.org.uk

Directories

Name of organisation	Address
Local Government Ombudsman	PO Box 4771
	Coventry CV4 0EH
	Tel: 0300 061 0614
Parliamentary and Health Service Ombudsman	Millbank Tower
	30 Millbank
	London SW1P 4QP
	Tel: 0345 015 4033
Pensions Ombudsman	11 Belgrave Road
	London SW1V 1RB
	Tel: 020 7630 2200
	Email: enquiries@pensions-ombudsman.org.uk

PUBLISHERS

Name of organisation	Address
Bloomsbury Professional	41-43 Boltro Road
	Haywards Heath RH16 1BJ
	Tel: 01444 416119
	Email: customerservices@bloomsburyprofessional.com
Child Poverty Action Group	30 Micawber Street
	London N1 7TB
	Tel: 020 7837 7979
	Email: info@cpag.org.uk
Jessica Kingsley Publishers	73 Collier Street
	London N1 9BE
	Tel: 020 7833 2307
	Email: hello@jkp.com

PART XII

Name of organisation	Address
Jordan Publishing	Regus Castlemead, Terrace Floor
	Lower Castle Street
	Bristol BS1 3AG
	Tel: 0117 917 5085
	Email: Jordans-customerservice@lexisnexis.co.uk
LexisNexis	Lexis House
	30 Farringdon Street
	London EC4A 4HH
	Tel: 0845 370 1234
	Email: customer.services@lexisnexis.co.uk
Oxford University Press	Great Clarendon Street
	Oxford OX2 6DP
	Tel: 01865 556767
	Email: WebEnquiry.UK@oup.com
Sweet & Maxwell	Cheriton House
	PO Box 1000
	Andover SP10 9AH
	Tel: 0845 600 9355
	Email: TRLUKI.CS@thomsonreuters.com

Websites

FINANCIAL

Name	Website
Equity Release Council	www.equityreleasecouncil.com
Financial Times (electronic share information)	www.ft.com
HM Revenue & Customs (tax rates and allowances)	www.gov.uk/government/organisations/hm-revenue-customs

Directories

Name	Website
Land Registry	www.gov.uk/government/organisations/land-registry
Occupational Pensions Regulatory Authority	www.opra.co.uk
Office for National Statistics	www.ons.gov.uk
Pensions Advisory Service	www.pensionsadvisoryservice.org.uk
Pensions and Lifetime Savings Association	www.plsa.co.uk
The Pensions Regulator	www.thepensionsregulator.gov.uk

GOVERNMENT

Name	Website
Cabinet Office	www.gov.uk/government/organisations/cabinet-office
Charity Commission	www.gov.uk/government/organisations/charity-commission
Department for Communities and Local Government	www.gov.uk/government/organisations/department-for-communities-and-local-government
Department of Health	www.gov.uk/government/organisations/department-of-health
Department for Transport	www.gov.uk/government/organisations/department-for-transport
Department for Work and Pensions	www.gov.uk/government/organisations/department-for-work-pensions
Government Equalities Office	www.gov.uk/government/organisations/government-equalities-office
HM Revenue & Customs	www.gov.uk/government/organisations/hm-revenue-customs
HM Treasury	www.gov.uk/government/organisations/hm-treasury
Home Office	www.gov.uk/government/organisations/home-office
Houses of Parliament	www.parliament.uk

Name	Website
Ministry of Justice	www.gov.uk/government/organisations/ministry-of-justice
The National Archives	www.nationalarchives.gov.uk
No 10 Downing Street	www.gov.uk/government/organisations/prime-ministers-office-10-downing-street
Social Security and Child Support Tribunal	www.gov.uk/courts-tribunals/first-tier-tribunal-social-security-and-child-support
UK Government	www.gov.uk

HOUSING

Name	Website
Homes and Communities Agency	www.gov.uk/government/organisations/homes-and-communities-agency
National House Building Council	www.nhbc.co.uk

HUMAN RIGHTS

Name	Website
Amnesty International	www.amnesty.org.uk
British Institute of Human Rights	www.bihr.org.uk
Equality and Human Rights Commission	www.equalityhumanrights.com
European Court of Human Rights	www.coe.int/t/democracy/migration/bodies/echr_en.asp
Human Rights Watch	www.hrw.org
Justice	www.justice.org.uk
Liberty	www.liberty-human-rights.org.uk

Directories

LEGAL

Name	Website
Civil Justice Council	www.judiciary.gov.uk/related-offices-and-bodies/advisory-bodies/cjc/
Court Funds Office	www.gov.uk/contact-court-funds-office
HM Courts Service	www.gov.uk/government/organisations/hm-courts-and-tribunals-service
Judiciary of England &Wales	www.judiciary.gov.uk
The Law Commission	www.lawcom.gov.uk
Legal Aid Agency	www.gov.uk/government/organisations/legal-aid-agency
Legislation	www.legislation.gov.uk/
Office of the Public Guardian	www.gov.uk/government/organisations/office-of-the-public-guardian
Official Solicitor and Public Trustee	www.gov.uk/government/organisations/official-solicitor-and-public-trustee

LEGAL INFORMATION RESOURCES

Name	Website
British and Irish Legal Information Institute	www.bailii.org
Casetrack (full-text judgments)	www.casetrack.com
Incorporated Council of Law Reporting	www.iclr.co.uk
infolaw	www.infolaw.co.uk
Justis (full text legal database)	www.justis.com
Law on the Web	www.lawontheweb.co.uk
Law Society Gazette	www.lawgazette.co.uk
Lawtel	www.lawtel.co.uk
Legal Hub	www.legalhub.co.uk
rightsnet (welfare law resource)	www.rightsnet.org.uk

Name	Website
Solicitors Practices (directory of solicitors)	www.lawdirect.co.uk
Venables (legal resources)	www.venables.co.uk

LEGAL PROFESSIONAL

Name	Website
Association of Pensions Lawyers	www.apl.org.uk
Association of Personal Injury Lawyers	www.apil.org.uk
The Bar Council	www.barcouncil.org.uk
The Law Society	www.lawsociety.org.uk
Law Society Directory of Solicitors	http://solicitors.lawsociety.org.uk
Legal Aid Practitioners Group	www.lapg.co.uk
Society for Computers and Law	www.scl.org
Society of Trust and Estate Practitioners	www.step.org
Sole Practitioners Group	www.spg.uk.com
Solicitors for the Elderly	www.sfe.legal
Solicitors for Older People Scotland	www.solicitorsforolderpeoplescotland.co.uk
Solicitors Regulation Authority	www.sra.org.uk

LEGAL PUBLISHERS

Name	Website
Ark Group Publishing	www.ark-group.com
Bloomsbury Professional	www.bloomsburyprofessional.com
Child Poverty Action Group	www.cpag.org.uk
Family Law	www.familylaw.co.uk
Financial Times	www.ft.com

Directories

Name	Website
Hammicks Legal Information Services	www.hammickslegal.co.uk
Informa Group Publishers	www.informa.com
Jessica Kingsley Publishers	www.jkp.com
Jordan Publishing	www.jordanpublishing.co.uk
The Lawyer	www.thelawyer.com
Legal Action Group	www.lag.org.uk
LexisNexis	www.lexisnexis.co.uk
Oxford University Press	http://global.oup.com
Routledge	www.routledge.com
The Stationery Office	www.tso.co.uk
Sweet & Maxwell	www.sweetandmaxwell.co.uk
The Times	www.thetimes.co.uk
Wildy and Sons Ltd	www.wildy.com
UK legislation	www.legislation.gov.uk

OMBUDSMEN

Name	Website
Financial Ombudsman Service	www.financial-ombudsman.org.uk/
Housing Ombudsman Service	www.housing-ombudsman.org.uk
The Legal Ombudsman	www.legalombudsman.org.uk
Local Government Ombudsman	www.lgo.org.uk
Parliamentary and Health Service Ombudsman	www.ombudsman.org.uk
Pensions Ombudsman	www.pensions-ombudsman.org.uk

ORGANISATIONS – CARERS

Name	Website
Association of Independent Care Advisors	www.aica.org.uk
Bettercaring	www.bettercaring.com
The Care Directory	www.nursing-home-directory.co.uk
Care Quality Commission	www.cqc.org.uk
Carers Trust	www.carers.org
Carers UK	www.carersuk.org
Hospice UK	www.hospiceuk.org
National Association of Hospice Fundraisers Directory	www.nahf.org.uk/hospice-directory.html

ORGANISATIONS – ELDERLY

Name	Website
Abbeyfield	www.abbeyfield.com
Action on Elder Abuse	www.elderabuse.org.uk
Age UK	www.ageuk.org.uk
Aid for the Aged in Distress	www.aftaid.org.uk
Alzheimer's Society	www.alzheimers.org.uk
Charity Search for Older People	www.charitysearch.org.uk
Community Care	www.communitycare.co.uk
Contact the Elderly	www.contact-the-elderly.org.uk
Dementia UK	www.dementiauk.org
Elderly Accommodation Counsel	www.eac.org.uk
Independent Age	www.independentage.org.uk

ORGANISATIONS – GENERAL

Name	Website
Action against Medical Accidents (AvMA)	www.avma.co.uk
Citizen's Advice	www.citizensadvice.org.uk
The Grandparents' Association	www.grandparents-association.org.uk
National Council for Voluntary Organisations	www.ncvo.org.uk
The Salvation Army	www.salvationarmy.org.uk
The Samaritans	www.samaritans.org
Shelter	www.shelter.org.uk

ORGANISATIONS – HEALTH AND DISABILITY

Name	Website
Action on Hearing Loss	www.actiononhearingloss.org.uk
Arthritis Care	www.arthritiscare.org.uk
The Arthritis Research Campaign	www.arthritisresearchuk.org
British Heart Foundation	www.bhf.org.uk
British Red Cross	www.redcross.org.uk
CancerLinks	www.cancerlinks.org
Cancer Research UK	www.cancerresearchuk.org
Diabetes UK	www.diabetes.org.uk
Disability Rights UK	www.disabilityrightsuk.org
Disabled Living Foundation	www.dlf.org.uk
Hospice Directory	www.hospicedirectory.org
International Glaucoma Association	www.glaucoma-association.com
London City Mission	www.lcm.org.uk
Macmillan Cancer Support	www.macmillan.org.uk
Marie Curie Cancer	www.mariecurie.org.uk

Name	Website
Mencap	www.mencap.org.uk
Mind	www.mind.org.uk
Motability	www.motability.co.uk
Multiple Sclerosis Society	www.mssociety.org.uk
Multiple Sclerosis Trust	www.mstrust.org.uk
National Health Service	www.nhs.uk
National Institute for Health and Clinical Excellence	www.nice.org.uk
Pancreatic Cancer UK	www.pancreaticcancer.org.uk
Parkinson's UK	www.parkinsons.org.uk
Public Health England	www.gov.uk/government/organisations/public-health-england
Royal National Institute for the Blind	www.rnib.org.uk
Scope	www.scope.org.uk
The Stroke Association	www.stroke.org.uk

ORGANISATIONS – PROFESSIONALS

Name	Website
Association of Directors of Social Services	www.adass.org.uk
British Medical Association	www.bma.org.uk
British Nursing Association	www.bna.co.uk
Chartered Institute of Taxation	www.tax.org.uk
National Society of Allied and Independent Funeral Directors	www.saif.org.uk
Society of Pension Professionals	http://the-spp.co.uk

Useful publications

CORONERS

Blackstone's Guide to the Coroners and Justice Act 2009 (2010) Glassom & Knowles, OUP
Coroners: A Guide to the New Law (2010) Urpeth, Law Society
Coroners' Courts: A Guide to Law & Practice (2014) Dorries, OUP
Inquests: A Practitioner's Guide (2014) Thomas et al, LAG
Jervis on Coroners (2014) Matthews, Sweet & Maxwell

COURTS AND PROCEDURE

A Practitioner's Guide to the Court of Protection (2009) Terrell, Tottel Publishing
Blackstone's Magistrates' Court Handbook 2016 (2015) Edwards, OUP
Civil Court Service 2016 (2016) Laws & Smith, Jordan Publishing
Court of Protection Handbook: a user's guide (2015) Ruck Keene et al, LAG
Court of Protection Law Reports, Jordan Publishing
Court of Protection Practice (2016) Ashton, Jordan Publishing
Heywood & Massey: Court of Protection Practice (looseleaf) Rees, Sweet & Maxwell
Legal Aid Handbook 2015/16 (2015) Ling, Pugh & Edwards, LAG
Solicitors' Duties and Liabilities (2009) Billins, Law Society
The Solicitor's Handbook 2015 (2015) Hopper & Treverton-Jones, Law Society
Todd's Relationship Agreements (2013) Todd & Todd, Sweet & Maxwell
Urgent Applications in the Court of Protection (2014) Pearce and Jackson, Jordan Publishing

DISCRIMINATION

Age Discrimination (2007) Davies, Tottel Publishing
Age Discrimination Handbook (2006) O'Dempsey et al, LAG
Blackstone's Guide to the Equality Act 2010 (2012) Wadham et al, OUP
Disability Rights Handbook 2015–16 (2015) Disability Right UK
Discrimination in Employment: A Claims Handbook (2013) O'Dempsey et al, LAG
Discrimination Law (looseleaf), Hughes, Bloomsbury Professional
Equality Act 2010: A Guide to the New Law (2010) Duggan, Law Society
Equality and Discrimination (2010) Doyle, Jordan Publishing

ELDERLY CLIENTS

Elder Law Journal, Griffiths, Jordan Publishing
Elderly Client Handbook (2010) Bielanska, Terrell & Ashton, Law Society

Elderly Clients – A Precedent Manual (2013) Lush & Bielanska, Jordan Publishing

Elderly People and the Law (2014) Ashton & Bielanska, Jordan Publishing

ESTATE AND FINANCIAL MANAGEMENT

Cretney & Lush on Lasting and Enduring Powers of Attorney (2013) Lush, Jordan Publishing

Drafting Trusts and Will Trusts (2014) Kessler, Sweet & Maxwell

Finance and Law for the Older Client (looseleaf), Abrey, Bielanska & Whitehouse, LexisNexis

Lasting Powers of Attorney: A Practical Guide (2011) Ward, Law Society

Underhill and Hayton Law of Trusts and Trustees (2010) Hayton, Matthews, Mitchell, LexisNexis

The Law of Trusts (2014) Penner, OUP

A Modern Approach to Lifetime Tax Planning for Private Clients (with Precedents) (2015) Whitehouse & King, Jordan Publishing

Pensions Law Handbook (2015) Bell & Jones, Bloomsbury Professional

Pensions Law and Practice with Precedents (looseleaf), Ellison, Sweet & Maxwell

Powers of Attorney (2007) Aldridge, Sweet & Maxwell

Practical Trust Precedents (looseleaf), Withers LLP, Sweet & Maxwell

A Practitioner's Guide to Executorship and Administration (2009) Thurston, Bloomsbury Professional

A Practitioner's Guide to Powers of Attorney (2015) Thurston, Bloomsbury Professional

A Practitioner's Guide to Trusts (2013) Thurston, Bloomsbury Professional

Ray and McLaughlin's Practical Inheritance Tax Planning (2016) McLaughlin et al, Bloomsbury Professional

Tolley's Pensions Administration and Trustees Service (looseleaf), Tolley, LexisNexis

Trust Drafting and Precedents (looseleaf), Harris, Bloomsbury Professional

Trust Practitioner's Handbook (2012) Steel, Law Society

Trust Taxation and Estate Planning (2014) Chamberlain & Whitehouse, Sweet & Maxwell

HEALTH AND MEDICAL CARE

Health Care Law (2014) Montgomery, OUP

Mason and McCall Smith's Law and Medical Ethics (2013) Mason & Laurie, OUP

Medical Law (2011) Herring, OUP

Medical Law and Ethics (2014) Herring, OUP

Medical Law and Ethics (2014) Pattinson, Sweet & Maxwell

Medical Treatment and the Law: Issues of Consent (2014) Harper, Jordan Publishing

Medical Treatment Decisions and the Law (2009) Johnston, Bloomsbury Professional

HUMAN RIGHTS

Blackstone's Guide to the Human Rights Act 1998 (2015) Wadham et al, OUP
Human Rights Alerter (journal), Harby & Patel, Sweet & Maxwell
Human Rights Law & Practice (2009) Lester and Pannick, LexisNexis
Human Rights Practice (looseleaf), Simor, Sweet & Maxwell

MENTAL HEALTH

Assessment of Mental Capacity: A Practical Guide for Doctors and Lawyers (2015) Ruck Keene, BMA & The Law Society
Blackstone's Guide to the Mental Capacity Act 2005 (2008) Bartlett, OUP
Blackstone's Guide to the Mental Health Act 2007 (2008) Bowen, OUP
Dementia and the Law (2014) Harrop-Griffiths et al, Jordan Publishing
Mental Capacity Act Manual (2014) Jones, Sweet & Maxwell
Mental Capacity – A Guide to the New Law (2008) Greaney, Morris & Taylor, Law Society
Mental Capacity – Law and Practice (2015) Ashton, Jordan Publishing
Mental Health Act Manual (2015) Jones, Sweet & Maxwell
Mental Health Law (2010) Hale, Sweet & Maxwell
Mental Health Law & Practice (2011) Fennell, Jordan Publishing
Mental Health Tribunals (2013) Butler, Jordan Publishing

WELFARE

Care Standards: A Practical Guide (2010) Ridout, Jordan Publishing
Care Standards Legislation Handbook (2009) Pearl, Jordan Publishing
Coldrick on Care Home Fees (2012) Coldrick, Bradley & Thornton, Ark Group
Community Care Law and Local Authority Handbook (2015) Butler, Jordan Publishing
Community Care Law Reports, LAG
Community Care Practice and the Law (2008) Mandelstam, Jessica Kingsley Publishers
Council Tax Handbook (2015) CPAG
Debt Advice Handbook (2015) CPAG
Disability Rights Handbook 2015–16 (2015) Disability Rights UK
Fuel Rights Handbook (2014) CPAG
Guide to Housing Benefit (2014–2017), Lister, Shelter
Personal Independence Payment – what you need to know (2013) CPAG
Safeguarding Adults and the Law (2013) Mandelstam, Jessica Kingsley Publishers
Universal Credit: what you need to know (2015) CPAG
Welfare Benefits and Tax Credits Handbook 2015/2016 (2015) CPAG

WILLS AND PROBATE

Butterworths Wills, Probate and Administration Service (looseleaf), LexisNexis

Inheritance Act Claims Law Practice and Procedure (looseleaf) Francis and Lord Walker, Jordan Publishing

Inheritance Act Claims: Law and Practice (2011) Ross, Sweet & Maxwell

Inheritance Tax Planning (2008) Chamberlain & Whitehouse, Sweet & Maxwell

A Modern Approach to Wills, Administration and Estate Planning (with Precedents) (2015) King & Whitehouse, Jordan Publishing

Parker's Will Precedents (2014) Dew & Shannon, Bloomsbury Professional

Practical Will Precedents (looseleaf), Hallam et al, Sweet & Maxwell

A Practitioner's Guide to Wills (2010) King et al, Wildy

Probate Disputes and Remedies (2014) Goodman, Hewitt & Mason, Jordan Publishing

Probate Practice Manual (looseleaf), Butcher, Sweet & Maxwell

Probate Practitioner's Handbook (2010) King, Law Society

Theobald on Wills (2016) Martin et al, Sweet & Maxwell

Tristram and Coote's Probate Practice (2015) D'Costa, Teverson & Synak, LexisNexis

Will Draftsman's Handbook (2012) Gausden, King & Riddett, Law Society

Williams, Mortimer & Sunnucks – Executors, Administrators and Probate (2015) Martyn & Caddick, Sweet & Maxwell

Williams on Wills (2014) Barlow et al, LexisNexis

Wills, Administration and Taxation Law and Practice (2014) Barlow, King & King, Sweet & Maxwell

Index

References are to page numbers.

Abortion
   capacity   102
   decisions that should be brought to Court   319
Absence of incapacitated party   820
Abuse see also Ill-treatment or neglect
   Disabilities Convention   2471
   Investigations Unit   426
Access to justice see also Participation in proceedings   58
   Disabilities Convention   2470
Accommodation see Care homes; Hospital or care homes, detention in; Residential accommodation
Accountant General
   funds in court   446
   investments   447
      framework   447
Acknowledgment of service
   change of address   914
   filing   807
   forms   1921
   service   807
   signing   914
   time limits   401
Acts in connection with care or treatment see Medical treatment; Permitted acts
Administration
   HM Courts and Tribunals Service   387
   Public Guardian, by   387
Administrative Court
   judicial review   464
Admissions
   notice   407, 827
Adoption
   excluded decisions   175, 594
Adult autonomy, principle of   332
'Adult care'
   directions orders   2240
Adult contact disputes   279
Advance decisions see also Advance statements
   absence of, decisions made in   339
   alteration   592
   applicability   335
   applications to Court   336
   care arrangements   334
   case illustrating dangers   337
   circumstances where invalid   335
   Code of Practice   1637
   Code of Practice guidance   337
   common law, position at   332
   effect   336, 593

Advance decisions —*continued*
   lasting powers of attorney compared   213, 339
   life sustaining treatment   593
   life-sustaining treatment   334, 335, 340
   meaning   592
   refusal of treatment   334
      deprivation of liberty safeguards   369
   requests for treatment   333, 334
   statutory recognition   334
   treatment pending decisions on   336
   validity   593
      assessment by health care professionals   340
      doubts over   336
   withdrawal   592
Advance directives
   Principles (Council of Europe)   2515
Advance statements
   transitional provisions (made before 1 Oct 2007)   1304
   wishes and feelings of person   150
Advice
   Official Solicitor, from   436
Advocacy see also Independent mental capacity advocates   449
Advocates
   litigation friend, appointment as   1491
      agreement to act   1494
      checklist   1504
   proceedings brought by   1493
      checklist   1503
Affidavit evidence
   alterations   967
   form   967
   forms   1984
   inability to read or sign   967
   outside jurisdiction, made   830
   Rules of Court   966
   witness statements   829
Affirmations
   wording   969
Age see also Children; Young persons
   deprivation of liberty, requirement for   365
   discrimination   47, 50
   elderly persons lacking capacity   277
   electro-convulsive therapy   176
   majority, of   115
Agency
   powers of attorney and   185
Agent see Principal and agent

2583

Index

Alcohol or drug misuse
   mental impairment from   114
Allocation
   costs order, effect on   1141, 1147
Allocation of cases   389
   judges   404, 819
   jurisdiction   819
   serious medical treatment cases   320
Alternative dispute resolution
   encouragement   395
Alzheimer's disease *see also* Dementia
ANH *see* Artificial nutrition and hydration, withdrawal of
Anorexia
   capacity   123
   decision-making   123
Appeal
   detailed assessment of costs, against   1175
Appeals
   Court of Appeal   620
   definitions   863
   fees   1266
   forms   1995
   hearings, court decision on   863
   judges
      powers of   867
   Mental Capacity Act 2005   414
   Mental Health Act patients   348, 1022
   nominated officers, decisions of   875
   notice   795
      forms   1995
   permission *see* Permission to appeal
   reviews or re-hearings   868
   rules   620
   Rules of Court   862
   skeleton arguments   1008, 1011
   transcripts   1009
Applicants
   party, as   808
Application
   within proceedings
      application without notice   813
Applications
   amendment   779
      endorsement   779
   dealing with applications   817
   deprivation of liberty safeguards
      Practice Direction   816
   disposal without hearings   817
   fees   1266
   filing   802
   form   1854
   forms
      contents   801
      court authentication   773
      documents to be filed with   802
      notice of issue   912, 1957
      statement of truth   774
   gifts, approval of   289

Applications—*continued*
   hearings   817
      considerations for holding   404
   interim   933
   interim remedies   815
   lasting powers of attorney   275
   notice   773, 774
      amendment   779
      forms   1939
   notification   805
      incapacitated persons   400
   Official Solicitor, brought by   438
   permission *see* Permission applications
   procedure   618
   responding to   401
   responding to (Practice Direction)   914
   serious medical treatment   318
   service   803
      lasting powers of attorney   804
   settlements, approval of   307
   specified applications   806
   statement of truth   908
   statutory wills   297
   urgency   304
   urgency (Practice Direction)   933
   within proceedings   403, 811
      application notice   403
      application without notice   403
      interim remedies   403
      notice   811
      Practice Direction   930, 933
Appointees
   ill-treatment or neglect by   179
Appointing or discharging a trustee, decisions on
   applications
      information in support   1889
Appropriate adult   39
Arrest
   committal   873
   warrants   873
Artificial nutrition and hydration, withdrawal of   319, 320, 323
Asian communities   37
Assessment of capacity *see also* Doctors: assessment of capacity
   absence of guidance in MCA 2005   129
   carers, by   130, 139
   Code of Practice   101, 1539
   confidentiality   29, 136
   decisions   113
   diagnostic threshold   86, 113
   evidence   131, 550
   experts   123, 133
   false impressions   24
   formal   131, 132, 139
   golden rule   133
   guidance   129
   highest level of functioning, when person is at   135

Assessment of capacity—*continued*
how capacity is assessed 135
human rights issues 129
legal and professional requirements 133
mental health legislation, under 139
personal injuries 141, 467
records 139
 formal reports or certificates 140
refusal to be assessed 138
short-term memory problems 121
solicitors, by
 pitfalls 140
testamentary capacity 294
threshold test 102
time for 130
use or weigh information, ability to 123
who assesses 130
Assessments
assessors
 selection 1335
best interests assessors 1334
best interests test 1789
completion 1797
deprivation of liberty safeguards 371, 375, 1333, 1780
deprivation of liberty standards 638
information for standard authorisation 1337
mental health 1334
time limits 1336
Assisted decision-making 29
Association of Independent Visitors 432
Associations
discrimination by 51
Attorney *see* Enduring powers of attorney; Lasting powers of attorney; Power of attorney
Authorised court officers
Practice Direction 881
work devolved to 393
Autonomy 332

Bankruptcy
warrants of control 1240
Best interests test
advance requests for treatment 334
assessments 1789
assessors 1328, 1334, 1336
checklist 142, 143
Code of Practice 1559
compliance with CRPD 86
concept 27, 142
 statutory enshrinement 92
consultation 155, 568
 'practicable or appropriate', where not 155
 right to confidentiality and requirement for 156
Court's powers 262
declarations 260

Best interests test—*continued*
deprivation of liberty safeguards 366, 639
 assessments 371, 376
 challenge to decisions 371
deputies, appointment of 266
detention, authorisation of 1334
determination, of 568
determining best interests 142
duty to apply principle 157
emotional dimension 151
equal consideration principle, and 145
fiduciary duties, breach of 254
future capacity to make decision 146
intervention by Court 255
Joint Committee, views of 108
lasting powers of attorney 200, 209, 254
Law
 Commission's recommendations 107
life-sustaining treatment 148, 322
medical treatment 311
participation of person lacking capacity 147
parties to proceedings 402
personal injuries 470
principle 108, 142
reasonable belief that person lacks capacity 157
relevant circumstances, consideration of all 145
religion or beliefs 150, 151
residential accommodation 465
statutory will *see* Wills: best interests test
'substituted judgment' element 151
threshold for engagement of powers 391
wills 264
wishes and feelings of person 150, 151
young persons 128
Bournewood gap 169
MCA solution 352
Brain injuries
financial deputies, appointment of 2270
lack of capacity 278
settlements 265, 270
Bundles
contents 958
format 960
Practice Direction 971
preparation 958
timetable 961
Burden of proof
European Convention on Human Rights 476

Capacity *see also* Mental Capacity Act 2005
abortion 102
anorexia 123
assessments
 form and guidance notes 1902
brain injuries 278

2585

Capacity—*continued*
- burden of proof 100
- causation 111
- certificates *see* Lasting powers of attorney: certificates
- cessation of lack of capacity
  - discharge of property and affairs deputies 2197
- common law tests 125, 311
  - interaction with MCA 2005 125
- decision-specific, as 111
- definition 24, 110, 111, 565, 769
- diagnostic hurdles 114
- doubts, procedure for resolving 547
- elderly persons 277
- evidence of 24
- financial affairs, final orders as to 2262
- fluctuating 313
- groups lacking capacity 25
- health care decisions 312
- identity, protection of 824
- impending incapacity of donor, action on 709
- incapacitated person, definition of 769
- incapacity, imprecision of term 33
- jurisdiction 262
- justification for denial of personal capacity 21
- lack of
  - concept 92
  - definition of 'a person who lacks capacity' 180
  - for reason outside MCA 2005 460
- learning disabilities 277
- legal competence 23
- litigation, for 207
- mental disabilities or disorders, persons with 277
- Mental Health Act 1983, consent to treatment under 349
- notification requirement 793
- partial 21, 25
- parties 786
- power of attorney, to create *see also* Lasting powers of attorney: capacity 242
- presumption *see also* Lasting powers of attorney: capacity: presumption 23, 100
  - principle of 101
  - rebuttal 101
  - statutory enshrinement of 92
- reasonable belief that person lacks capacity 126
  - best interests test 157
  - reasonable steps 126
- regaining 146
- scope of mental impairment 114
- sexual relations, consent to 315
- temporary lack of capacity 22

Capacity—*continued*
- test for lack of 24
  - appearance 115
  - threshold test 102
  - two-stage procedure 112
- threshold for engagement of powers 101
- time-specific, as 111
- undue influence 29
- welfare decisions 312

Care arrangements
- advance statements 334

Care homes *see also* Hospital or care homes, detention in; Residential accommodation
- ill-treatment or neglect by 179, 180
- independent mental capacity advocates, instructions of 603
- managing authorities 674
- supervisory bodies 675

Care or treatment, acts in connection with *see* Medical treatment; Permitted acts

Care plans 140

Care Quality Commission
- monitoring deprivation of liberty 379

Care services *see* Social care

Carers
- assessment of capacity by 130, 139
- Code of Practice 96, 97
- consultation 155
- ill-treatment or neglect by 179
- negligence by 165
- payment for goods and services 173
- permitted acts 158, 164
  - protection from liability 160

Case management
- active 395
- active case management 763
- checklist 2225
- court officers 882
- general powers 779
- overriding objective 395, 763
- Rules of Court 396
- serious medical treatment cases 322

Causation
- capacity 111
- gross-negligence manslaughter 182

Certificates of capacity *see* Lasting powers of attorney: certificates

Cessation of lack of capacity or death
- learning disabilities 147
- personal representatives and administrators 1027
- Practice Direction 1026

Child or protected party
- costs where money payable by or to 1136, 1143
- costs, summary assessment of 1132

Children *see also* Young persons
- age 116
- Code of Practice 1682
- definition 1085

Children—*continued*
Disabilities Convention 2468
excluded decisions 175, 594
Gillick competence 127
investments 1111
litigation friend
 conducting
  proceedings without 1091
litigation friend, requirement for *see also*
 Litigation friend 1091
money, control of 1102, 1111
parties, as 1091
property and affairs, decisions on 264
service 785
settlements 1109
 approval 1100
transfer of proceedings 263, 390
transfer of proceedings, provision
 for 588
Civil partnerships
excluded decisions 175, 594
incapacity issues 57
legislation 56
social attitudes 56
status of civil partner 57
Civil Procedure Rules
application 772
children 1085
doubt over capacity 549
Clinical negligence
pre-commencement funding
 arrangements 1179
Clinical trials *see also* Medical
 research 341
Code of Practice
acts in connection with care or treatment
 examples of acts 161
 serious acts 162
advance decisions 337, 1637
application 94
approval procedure 98
assessment of capacity 101, 1539
best interests test 1559
 consultation 156
 emotional dimension 152
children 1682
compliance with
 monitoring compliance 97
 sanctions for non-compliance 97
consultation 98
criminal or civil proceedings, relevance
 to 97
deprivation of liberty safeguards 1753
deputies, appointment of 96, 266
dispute resolution 1714
dissemination 94
future capacity to make decision 147
independent mental capacity
 advocates 1653
informal carers, position of 96, 97

Code of Practice—*continued*
information provision 1724
issue 93
key words and phrases 1840
lasting powers of attorney 1600
legal status 95, 1519
medical research 1671
Mental Capacity Act 2005 93, 610
Mental Health Act 1983, relationship
 with 1690
Mental Health Act patients
 Mental Capacity Act 2005,
  relationship with 1690
persons with duty to 'have regard to' 96
practicable steps to enable
 decision-making 104
preparation 98
procedure 612
protection of persons lacking
 capacity 1581, 1704
publication 98
revision 94, 98
statutory principles 1524
supplement 94
text 1515
young persons 1682
Commencement of proceedings
initial steps 801
permission applications 801
time for commencement 801
Committal
contempt of court 1015
discharge 873
hearings 872
notice of hearings 1988, 1989
Rules of Court 870
suspension of orders 873
Communication
aids 62
impairment of 23
inability to communicate 118, 124
interpreters 23, 62
sign language 23
Community care
assessments 42
background 41
legislation 42
 guidance and
  circulars supplementing 44
 list of 43
 policy initiatives 42
  legislation 43
reviews 42
Community treatment orders *see*
 Compulsory community treatment
 orders
Community treatment orders (CTOs) 347
criteria for 348
Compromise *see* Settlements

2587

Conduct
costs 413
Confidentiality
disclosure of lack of capacity 136
duty owed 28
duty to consult and requirement for 156
publicity restrictions 406
Conflict of laws *see* Hague Convention on the Protection of Adults
Consent
clinical trials, to 342
medical treatment, to *see* Medical treatment: consent
Consent order
agreement over costs 1131
Consultation
best interests test 155
'practicable or appropriate', where not 155
right to confidentiality and requirement for 156
Contact
local authorities' restricting contact 279
resolution of adult contact disputes 279
Contempt of court
committal 871
committal order
open court (PD) 1418, 1505, 1508
penal notices 873
Practice Guidance 394
Rules of Court 870
Continuing powers of attorney
Principles (Council of Europe) 2515
Contract
goods or services
enforcement 170
Controlled goods, claims on 1252
Conveyancing
costs 1000
Costs
allocation, on 1140, 1147
amount of costs, deciding
factors to be taken into account 1118
where costs payable under contract 1118, 1129
apportionment 858
basis of assessment 1117, 1129
bill of costs
form of 1161
budgets 1126
charges on estate 622
child or protected party, for 1136, 1143
Civil Procedure Rules, application of 859
claims on controlled goods and executed goods 1261
conduct 413
convenyancing 1000
court discretion 1115, 1127
damages-based agreements, effect of 1123

Costs—*continued*
death of incapacitated party, charge on estate on 861
deputies or attorrneys, remuneration of 862
detailed assessment 413, 860, 861
appeal 1175
assisted person 1156, 1172
authorised court officer, powers of 1148, 1159
basis of assessment 1139, 1145
commencement deadline 1150, 1165
commencement notice 1149, 1160
costs are agreed, procedure where 1152, 1165
costs of, liability for 1157
costs of, offer to settle 1174
default costs certificate 1151, 1152, 1166, 1167
discontinuance 1166
final costs certificate 1155, 1171
funds, costs payable out of 1156, 1173
hearing 1153, 1167
interim certificate 1155, 1171
Legal Services Commission, costs payable by 1173
Lord Chancellor, costs payable by 1173
model forms 1123
points of dispute 1151, 1153, 1165, 1167
procedure 1140, 1145
provisional assessment 1154, 1170
stay pending appeal 1148, 1159
time for 1148, 1158
venue 1149, 1159
disclosure 1134
documents, signature of 1123
estimates 780
fast track trial costs 1140, 1146
fees of counsel 1128
fixed 413
default costs certificate, on issue of 1166
fixed costs
Practice Direction 997, 1002
general rule 412
general rule, departure from 413, 858
group litigation orders 1137
interpretation 1114
lasting powers of attorney 862
litigants in person 1126, 1136, 1143
misconduct 1120, 1133
mortgage, relating to a 1129, 1131
non-parties, for or against 413, 861
Official Solicitor 442, 861
order
cases where order deemed to be made 1119

Costs—*continued*
　order—*continued*
　　notification duty　　　　1119, 1133
　　time for complying with　　　1119
　　order silent as to costs　　　　1120
　　Parts 44 to 47, scope of application
　　　of　　　　　　　　　　　　1115
　　payments on account　　　　　997
　　personal welfare decisions　　413, 858
　　practice direction　　　　862, 995
　　pro bono representation　　1138, 1143
　　procedure for assessing　　　　1118
　　procedure for assessment　　　861
　　property and affairs, decisions on　412, 857
　　re-allocation, on　　　　1140, 1147
　　remuneration of deputy or attorney　413, 862
　　Rules of Court　　　　　　412, 856
　　security for costs　　　　　　　397
　　separate representation, of　　　860
　　set-off　　　　　　　　　　　1121
　　small claim　　　　　　1140, 1146
　　statutory wills　　　　　　　　305
　　summary assessment　　　413, 861
　　　assisted person　　　　　　1132
　　　child or protected party　　1132
　　　consent orders　　　　　　1131
　　　costs officer, by　　　　　　1132
　　　court power　　　　　　　1131
　　　disproportionate or unreasonable
　　　　costs　　　　　　　　　1133
　　　duty of parties and legal
　　　　representatives　　　　　1131
　　　model form　　　　　　　1123
　　　mortgagee's costs, of　　　1131
　　　timing of　　　　　　　　1131
　　trustee, in favour of　　　1135, 1142
　　VAT on　　　　　　　　　　1124
　　wasted costs　　　　　　　412, 621
　　wasted costs order　　　　1139, 1144
Costs-only proceedings
　procedure　　　　　　　　1141, 1147
Council of Europe
　Principles Concerning Continuing
　　Powers of Attorney and Advance
　　Directives for Incapacity　　2515
　Principles Concerning the Legal
　　Protection of Incapable Adults
　　　explanatory memorandum　　2486
　　　text　　　　　　　　　　2507
Counsel
　fees　　　　　　　　　　　　1128
Court Funds Office　　　　446, 1376
　address　　　　　　　　　　　448
　administrative responsibility　　446
　investments
　　annual review of cases　　　　448
　　appointment of deputies　　　448
　　framework　　　　　　　　　448

Court Funds Office—*continued*
　protected parties　　　　　　　546
　rules　　　　　　　　　　　　447
Court of Protection
　administration of　　　　　　　428
　application to *see* Applications
　creation by MCA 2005　　　　　387
　exercise of powers, case on　　　259
　former Court *see* Historical background
　judges *see also* Judges　　　　770
　name　　　　　　　　　　　　387
　powers *see* Jurisdiction
　procedural rules *see* Rules of Court
　public authority, as　　　　　　55
　Public Guardian, relationship with　427
　volume of cases　　　　　　　　416
Court officer
　detailed assessment of costs　1148, 1159
Court officers *see* Authorised court officers
　authorised court officers　　　　881
　case management　　　　　　　882
　role　　　　　　　　　　　　770
　work devolved to　　　　　　　393
Courts
　discrimination by　　　　　　　51
　public authorities, as　　　　　　54
Creation of Court of Protection
　Mental Capacity Act 2005　　93, 614
Criminal offences *see also* Fraud
　ill-treatment or neglect　　　　　178
Cross-border issues *see* Hague Convention
　on the Protection of Adults;
　International protection of adults;
　Scotland
CRPD *see* United Nations Convention on
　the Rights of Persons with
　Disabilities
CTOs *see* Community treatment orders
Cultural context *see also* Religion
　or beliefs
**Cultural life, recreation, sport and leisure,
　participation in**　　　　　　2478
Damages
　double recovery　　　　　　　473
　European Convention on Human Rights,
　　for breaches of　　　　　455, 476
　management　　　　　　　　　471
　personal injuries　　　　　　　471
　trusts　　　　　　　　　　　　472
Damages-based agreements
　effect on costs　　　　　　　　1123
***De minimis* exception**
　lasting powers of attorney　　　206
Decision-makers
　advance choice of　　　　　　　27
　conflicts between decision-makers　268
　consultation by　　　　　　　　156
　disputed decisions　　　　　　　22
　motivation in life-sustaining treatment
　　decisions　　　　　　　　　148

2589

Decision-makers—*continued*
  roles 26
  scope of decisions 22
Decision-making
  anorexia 123
  assisted 29
  Court's approach 269
  delegated 26
  inherent jurisdiction, under 456
  MCA 2005's approach 88
  participation of person lacking capacity 147
  substituted 87
Decisions *see also* Advance decisions; Financial decisions; Health care decisions; Personal welfare decisions; Property and affairs, decisions on
  appointment of deputy to make 262, 263
  assessment of capacity 113
  benefit of another person, made for 283
  Court order 583
  definition 21
  deputies, by 266
    conflicts with other decision-makers 170, 268
    excluded 174
  excluded decisions 594
  inability to communicate 124
  inability to make 21, 111
    specific decisions 117, 120
  interrelated or sequential 106
  Mental Capacity Act 2005 112
    framework under 91
  order, made by 262
  practicable steps to help decision-making 146
    Code of Practice 104
    principle 102
  procedure, introduction of 27
  specific decisions 112
  test for decision-making 567
  test of inability to make 113
    inability to communicate 124
    reasonably foreseeable consequences 119, 120
    retention of information 121
    understanding the relevant information 118
    using and weighing the information 122
  types 22, 26
  unwise
    principle 105
Declarations
  best interests, as to 260
  capacity 552
  contingent 313
  Court's powers 582

Declarations—*continued*
  deputies
    forms 1914
  European Convention on Human Rights, for breaches of 455, 476
  High Court 31, 260
    vulnerable adults 32
  inherent jurisdiction 260
  interim 815
  medical treatment, as to 163, 260, 310
  Royal prerogative 31
  welfare decisions 260, 310
Declarations of incompatibility 320
Definition of Court of Protection 1826
Delegated decision-making 26
Dementia
  lack of capacity 277
Dental treatment *see also* Medical treatment
  young persons 128
Department for Work and Pensions
  support services 38
Depositions 408
  conduct of examination 831
  examiner's fees and expenses 832
  hearings, use at 833
  oaths 831
  Practice Direction 976
  travelling expenses and compensation for loss of time 977
Deprivation of liberty *see* Liberty and security, right to
Deprivation of liberty safeguards
  age requirement 365
  applications
    statistics 380
    streamlined process 359
  assessments 371, 375, 1780
  authorisation 347, 362, 1771, 1816
    lack of 1823
    procedure 365
    standard 352, 370, 375, 635
    urgent 352, 374
  authorisation of deprivation 630
  best interests 366
    assessments 371, 376
    challenge to decisions 371
  Bournewood gap 169
    MCA solution 352
  care homes 606
  checklists 1830
  Code of Practice 1753
  Court's powers 362
  definitions 631
  eligibility requirement 366
  force feeding 368
  hospital and care homes, detention in 606, 631

Index

Deprivation of liberty safeguards—*continued*
  hospital or care homes, detention in   162, 363, 607
    representatives   1327
    standard procedure   1333
  independent mental capacity advocate   606
  independent mental capacity advocates   1778
  inherent jurisdiction, interaction with   457
  interim orders   589
  lawful circumstances   352
  liability   631
  life sustaining treatment   572
  life-sustaining treatment, deprivation pending order for   362
  litigation friends, duty of   1500, 1502
  meaning and identification of deprivation   352
    Cheshire West case   353
    comparator, role of a   356
    degree and intensity of restrictions   353
    irrelevant factors   355
    lack of objection, relevance of   355, 357
    relative normality, concept of   355, 356
    Rochdale MBC v KW case   357
    twin ingredients   355
  medical treatment, deprivation pending order for   362
  Mental Capacity Act 2005   607, 687
  mental capacity requirement   365
  Mental Health Act patients   584
  mental health requirement   365
  monitoring   379, 1829
  negligent acts   631
  no refusals requirement   369
  permitted acts   168, 210
  post-legislative scrutiny   381
  Practice Direction   816
  representatives   374, 377
  restrictions   571
  reviews   374, 378, 589, 630
  standard authorisation
    assessments   662
    reviews   655
  supervisory body, role of   373
  suspension of standard authorisation   653
  urgency   1802
  urgent authorisations   649

Deputies
  application by (Practice Direction)   916
    list of suitable applications   916
  appointment   262, 263, 266, 583
    application procedure   533
    best interests test   266

Deputies—*continued*
  appointment—*continued*
    cancellation of enduring powers of attorney, after   2268
    change of   2266
    enduring powers of attorney registration as alternative, final orders on   2263
    local authorities (property and affairs)   2193, 2194, 2195, 2196, 2209, 2217, 2219, 2220, 2221, 2222, 2223, 2233, 2234, 2235, 2248
    orders
      precedents (property and affairs)   2189
    refusal of permission   2198
    register of orders   422
    revocation   269
    threshold test   96
    two or more   267
    who may be appointed   267
  appointment of   586
    local authority (property and affairs)   2218
  capacity, doubts over   268
  complaints
    Public Guardian powers   426, 1295
  Court's powers   266
  decisions of   266
    conflicts with other decision-maker   574
    conflicts with other decision-makers   170, 268
  declarations
    forms   1914
  directions   266
  discharge where capacity is regained   2197
  expenses   267
  financial appointment
    brain injuries, large awards for   2270
    appointment after cancellation of enduring powers of attorney   2268
    change of   2266
  gifts, authority to make   285
  investment powers   267
  investments   448
  joint   267
  life sustaining treatment, restrictions on powers relating to   268
  litigation friend   990
  maintenance, authority to provide   286, 288
  panel   424
  personal welfare decisions
    refusal of permission   2198

Index

Deputies—*continued*
powers 267
  exclusions 268
  restrictions on 267
powers, restriction of 587
property and affairs, decisions on 267, 469
public authorities, remuneration of 1004
receivers, replacement of 270, 452
remuneration of 267, 413, 862
reports 267
  content 1294
  extension of time 1293
  final report 1294
representations and complaints 422
restraints, powers as to 268
restrictions on powers 266
security for discharge of functions 267, 875
solicitors, remuneration of 1003
supervision fees 423
Detention *see* Deprivation of liberty safeguards; Hospital or care homes, detention in; Liberty and security, right to
Diagnostic threshold 86
Directions 404
checklist 2226
interim 391
power of attorney
  objection to registering
    Practice Direction 1024
pro-forma orders 2227
  'adult care' cases 2240
first directions orders (family dispute as to residence and contact) 2237
local authority personal welfare applications 2243
multi-purpose orders 2227
Rules of Court 818
Disabilities Convention
access to justice 2470
accessibility 2468
awareness raising 2468
children 2468
Committee on the Rights of Persons with Disabilities 2480
cultural life, recreation, sport and leisure, participation in 2478
education 2474
employment and work 2476
equal recognition before the law 2469
exploitation, violence and abuse, freedom from 2471
freedom of expression 2472
freedom of movement 2471
health standards 2475
home and family, respect for 2473
humanitarian emergencies 2469

Disabilities Convention—*continued*
independent living 2472
information provision 2472
integrity 2471
international cooperation 2479
liberty and security, right to 2470
life, right to 2469
national implementation and monitoring 2479
nationality 2471
participation in political and public life 2477
personal mobility 2472
privacy 2473
rehabilitation and habilitation 2475
reports by state parties 2481
risky situations 2469
standard of living and social protection 2477
statistics and data collection 2478
text of 2463
women 2467
Disability *see also* Disability discrimination; United Nations Convention on the Rights of Persons with Disabilities
attitudes, changes in 35
facilities at hearings 61
judicial training 58
terminology, use of appropriate 36
Disability discrimination
discrimination arising from disability 48
harassment 50
protected characteristics 47
reasonable adjustments, duty to make 49
victimisation 50
Disclosure
costs payable 1134
definition 410, 842
failure, consequences of 845
general 410, 843, 844
inspection, right of 410, 844, 845
  withholding claim 845
list of documents 410
Mental Capacity Act 2005 671
non-parties 777
ongoing duty 844
privacy 410
Rules of Court 410, 842
specific 410, 843, 844
Discrimination *see also* European Convention on Human Rights
associations, by 51
courts, by 51
diagnostic threshold 86
direct 48
disability *see* Disability discrimination
disposal and management of premises 51
forms of 34
harmonisation 47, 50

2592

Index

Discrimination—*continued*
   indirect 49
   legal services 59
   legislative framework 46
   prohibited conduct 48, 50
   protected characteristics 47
Dispute resolution *see also* Alternative dispute resolution
   alternatives to the Court of Protection 1503
   Code of Practice 1714
   Public Guardian's role 425
District judges
   adult contact disputes 279
   allocation of cases 390
   nomination 389
Divorce
   excluded decisions 175, 594
Doctors
   assessment of capacity 131, 132
     records 139
     witnesses to wills 133
   certificate providers for LPAs 236
   defence to medical treatment without authority 213
   Special Visitor, as 430
Document
   signature
     costs assessment proceedings 1123
Documents
   authorised court officers 886
   copies 399, 776
   deputies, supervision of 778
   editing information 778
   electronic signature 774, 886
   exhibits 968
   fees 1267
   filing *see* Filing
   inspection 399, 776
   list of documents 773
   non-parties 777
   personal details, omission of 398
   Public Guardian, copies to 778
   qualifying documents, definition of 778
   Rules of Court 398
   service *see* Service
   statement of truth 398, 773
   subsequent use 778
   types 398
   verification 398, 774
DOLS *see* Deprivation of liberty safeguards
Double recovery
   personal injuries 473
Dual jurisdiction 419
Duress *see* Undue influence

Ecclesiastical property
   writs relating to 1234
Education
   Disabilities Convention 2474

Elderly persons
   client practices, development of 41
   lack of capacity 277
   mental health legislation, relevance of 350
Electro-convulsive therapy (ECT) 176
   young persons 176
Electronic service
   Rules of Court 891
Electronic signature 774
   authorised court officers 886
Eligibility assessments 641
Emergencies *see* Urgency
Employment and work 2476
Empowerment
   definition 39
   protection, balancing with 39
Enduring power of attorney *see also* Power of attorney
Enduring power of attorney or lasting power of attorney, validity or operation of, decisions on
   applications
     information in support 1898
Enduring powers of attorney
   abolition 194
   applications 916
   cancellation and appointment of financial deputy 2268
   cancellation of registration 715
   capacity to create 242
   creation 188
   deputies appointment as alternative, final orders on 2263
   Enduring Powers of Attorney Act 1985 repeal of 722
   existing EPAs 194, 256, 451
   gifts 284
   invalid/revoked power, protection provisions concerning 716
   joint and joint and several attorneys 717
   lasting power of attorney and EPA, choice between 256
   Law Commission 33
   Law Commission report 188
   level of protection 189
   maintenance of others 288
   Mental Capacity Act 2005 706
   notification prior to registration 710
   number of registrations 190
   popularity 190
   Practice Direction 416
   problems with 191
   Public Guardian 33
   registration 189, 451, 1288
     application procedure 531
     fees 424
     forms 1933
     objection procedure 877
     objection to 928

Index

Enduring powers of attorney—*continued*
registration—*continued*
    Public Guardian, role of   276
registration of instrument creating
    power   712
Regulations   1287
safeguards   189
service   804
transitional provisions   451, 453
visit to donor, historical   73

Enforcement
Court's powers   415
methods   415
penal notices   415
Practice Direction   1015
Rules of Court   868
taking control of goods, by   1245

Enquiries, duty to make   462
EPA *see* Enduring powers of attorney
Equal consideration principle   114, 145
Equality *see also* Discrimination
legislative framework   46

Error
orders   779
procedural errors, waiver of   783

Ethnic communities
attitudes in   37
judicial training   58

European Convention on Human Rights
see also Liberty and security, right to;
Life, right to; Private and family life,
right to respect for
burden of proof   476
conflict between rights of those
    involved   55, 79
Convention rights, list of   52
damages, Court's jurisdiction to
    award   455, 476
declarations of incompatibility   53
declarations, Court's jurisdiction to
    grant   455, 476
discrimination   46
duty to have regard to rights   475
individual petition, right of   52
interpretation   56
legality, principle of   55
litigation friend, position of   1499
margin of appreciation   54
Mental Capacity Act 2005   79
obligations of States   53
participation in proceedings   79
proportionality   54
public authorities,
    proceedings against   54, 55
remedies   54

European Union
evidence   978

Evidence
assessment of capacity   131, 550
court control   407

Evidence—*continued*
depositions   831
    conduct of examination   831
    examiner of the court   832
    examiner's fees and expenses   832
    hearings, use at   833
    notice of intention to file   1993
European Union member states,
    between   978
expert *see* Experts
hearsay
    admissibility   407
    historical background   64
Information provision   831
medical *see* Assessment of capacity
mental disorder, of a   365
notarial acts or instruments   830
office copies of orders   390
outside the jurisdiction   833
powers of Court   827
Practice Direction   966
Rules of Court   407
Taking of Evidence Regulation   833
transcripts   1009
video link
    guidance (PD)   972
witness *see* Witnesses

Examiner of the court
fees and expenses   832, 981

Excluded decisions   174
examples   594

Executed goods, claims on   1252

Execution
statutory will   303

Exhibits
Rules of Court   968

Existing deputy or attorney, decisions on
applications
    information in support   1894

Expenditure
necessary goods and services, on   173, 575

Expert
directions
    right to ask for   841

Experts *see also* Doctors
assessment of capacity   123, 132, 133
definition   836
discussions between xperts   841
form of evidence   839
golden rule   133
Official Solicitor, instruction by   440
overriding duty to court   838
Practice Direction   988
property and affairs, decisions on   468
questions to experts   989
reports   837, 839
    contents   840
    disclosure, use after   841
    form and content   988

Index

Experts —*continued*
- restrict evidence, duty to — 837
- restrict evidence, power to — 838
- Rules of Court — 409
- single joint experts
  - Court power as to — 841
  - instructions — 842
  - written questions to — 839

Exploitation, violence and abuse, freedom from — 2471

Family Division
- Court of Protection work — 389
- health care decisions — 278
- President, appointment of — 388

Family life, respect for *see* Private and family life, right to respect for

Family member(s)
- carer, as *see* Carers

Family relationships
- decision on — 594
- excluded decisions — 175, 210

Fast track
- trial
- costs — 1140, 1146

Feelings of person *see* Wishes and feelings of person

Fees
- charges on estate — 622
- counsel — 1128
- Court of Protection — 1265
- exemptions — 414
- list — 1268
- Lord Chancellor's order — 414
- orders — 621
- Public Guardian — 423, 427, 1321
- reductions — 414
- Rules of Court — 412
- schedule of fees — 1265
- subsidies — 413
- transitional provisions — 1325

Fiduciary duties
- best interests test — 254
- power of attorney — 186, 201
- breach of duty — 253

Filing
- checklist — 2227
- date — 886
- fax, by — 886

Final orders
- precedents — 2262

Financial decisions *see also* Property and affairs, decisions on
- deputies, change of — 2266
- final orders as to capacity in regard to — 2262
- Mental Capacity Act 2005 — 91

Force feeding — 368

Foreign currency
- funds in court: — 1381

Former Court of Protection *see* Historical background

Forms
- commencement of proceedings — 401
- costs assessment — 1123
- lasting powers of attorney — 214

Fraud
- lasting powers of attorney — 253, 272

Freedom of expression — 2472

Funding of litigation *see also* Legal aid — 442

Funds in court
- account types — 1379
- Court Funds Office — 446, 546, 1376
- death of entitled person
  - inheritance tax — 1385
  - payment to PR — 1384
- deposit of funds, documentation on — 1376
- foreign currency — 1381
- information request — 1389
- interest accrual — 1380
- interest on payments — 1384
- investment
  - authority for — 1381
- investment of
  - limitations — 1380
  - securities (pre-3 Oct 2011) — 1381
- payment out — 1383
  - interest — 1384
  - method — 1387
  - Part 36 offers, in respect of — 1385
  - public funding of claimant — 1386
  - refusal — 1387
  - regular payments — 1386
  - timing — 1386
- rules for — 1375
- statement of accounts for children or persons lacking capacity — 1389
- transfer of — 1389
- unclaimed — 1388

General Visitors *see* Visitors: General

Gifts
- deputy's authority to make — 285
- enduring powers of attorney — 284
- lasting powers of attorney — 285, 579
  - Court authority — 275
  - not requiring Court's authority — 284
  - permitted decisions — 283
  - requiring Court's approval — 289
  - short procedure — 290
  - unreasonable — 286

***Gillick* competence** — 127

Golden rule
- assessment of capacity — 133

Goods
- claims on controlled goods and executed goods — 1252
- delivery, order for
  - enforcement — 1237

2595

Goods—*continued*
   enforcement by taking control of   1245
Goods and services *see* Payment
   for goods and services
Gross negligence manslaughter   182
Group litigation order
   costs   1137
Guardianship   348

Hague Convention on the Protection of Adults
   applicable law   700
   certificates   704
   cross-border co-operation   704
   Mental Capacity Act 2005   626, 697
   mutual recognition and enforcement   702
   protective measures   698
   text   2449
Harassment
   types   50
Health care
   Disabilities Convention   2475
Health care decisions *see also* Medical treatment
   applications   327
      forms   1854
      information in support   1877
   capacity, issue-specific nature of   312
   decisions that should be brought to Court   326
   jurisdiction, scope of   278, 311
   lasting powers of attorney   208
   Mental Capacity Act 2005   91
   permitted acts   161
Hearings
   absence of incapacitated party   820
   applications   817
   arrangements for disabled persons   61
   checklist   2227
   considerations for holding   404
   fees   1266
   participation   820
   permission to take part   820
   private   327
      attendance   405
   private hearings   822
      waiver   824
   public hearings
      orders for   824
   publicity   823
   statutory wills   301
   supplementary provisions   825
   time estimates   962
High Court *see also* Family Division
   allocation of cases   390
   Court of Protection work   389
   declarations   260
   health and welfare cases
      inherent jurisdiction   455

High Court—*continued*
   inherent jurisdiction *see* Inherent jurisdiction
   medical treatment decisions   309
   transitional provisions (proceedings commenced before 1 Oct 2007)   1303
Historical background   62
   cessation of former Court   387
   contested hearings   68
   evaluation   67
   evidence   64
   regional hearings   67
   rules and procedure   63
   venue   66
   visitors   71
HM Courts and Tribunals Service
   administration   387
Home and family, respect for
   Disabilities Convention   2473
Hospital or care home, detention in
   assessments   638
Hospital or care homes
   detention in
      representatives   1327
Hospital or care homes detention in
   authorisation
      powers of   589
   ineligible persons   687
Hospital or care homes, detention in *see also* Deprivation of liberty safeguards
   authorisation   363, 630, 631
      precautionary   364
      purpose   364
      standard procedure   1333
   detained resident, definition of   631
   Mental Capacity Act 2005   638
   negligence   631
   qualifying requirements   632
   residence disputes   1338
   restraints   1766
   standard procedure   1333
   urgent procedure   649
Hospital, admission to
   long-stay accommodation
      independent mental capacity advocates, instructions of   603
   mental disorder, treatment of   347
   grounds for admission   348
Hospitals
   managing authorities   673
Human rights *see* European Convention on Human Rights; Human Rights Act 1998; Liberty and security, right to; Life, right to; Private and family life, right to respect for
Human Rights Act 1998 *see also* European Convention on Human Rights
   declarations of incompatibility   320
   Practice Direction   945

Human Rights Act 1998—*continued*
   Rules of Court   816
Humanitarian emergencies   2469

Identity
   restrictions on publication   824
Ill-treatment or neglect *see also* Abuse
   criminal offences   178, 612
      creation of   179
      scope   179
   definition of 'a person who
      lacks capacity'   180
   gross negligence
      manslaughter distinguished   182
   separate offences   181
   single acts   181
   wilful neglect   181
IMCAs *see* Independent mental capacity advocates
Inability to make decision *see* Decisions: inability to make
Incapacitated adults
   inherent jurisdiction   455, 458
Incapacity *see* Capacity
Independent living   2472
Independent mental capacity advocates
   accommodation, provision by NHS body
      of   603
   appointment   600, 606, 607, 608
      circumstances for   163
      eligibility   329
      exceptions   609
      limitations on duties   609
   certificate providers for LPAs   236
   challenges to decisions   450
   Code of Practice   1653
   deprivation of liberty safeguards: 1778
   establishment   328, 449
   functions   329, 602, 670
      restrictions   670
   House of Lords Select Committee report,
      recommendations in   332
   instruct, duty to   330, 610
   litigation friend, appointment as   1491
      agreement to act   1494
      instruction of lawyers   1496
      instructions to give   1501
   Mental Capacity Act 2005   669
   powers   331
   residential accommodation   604
   role   331
   serious medical treatment   602
   service users   449
      who can be   450
Information provision
   Code of Practice   1724
   directions   831
   Disabilities Convention   2472
Inherent jurisdiction
   declarations   260

Inherent jurisdiction—*continued*
   deprivation of liberty, interaction
      with   457
   facilitating decision-making   456
   force feeding   368
   incapacitated adults   455, 458
   medical treatment   310
   preventing removal from
      jurisdiction   457
   statutory jurisdiction, interaction with   32, 455
   test for   456
   transfer of proceedings   327
   vulnerable adults   455, 456
Injunctions
   interim   403, 815
   medical treatment   311, 934
   third parties   457
Insolvency-related proceedings
   pre-commencement funding
      arrangements   1179
Inspection
   court records   777
   disclosure   410, 844, 845
Interested persons
   list of persons   677
Interests, preservation of   266
Interim orders and directions
   applications within proceedings   403
   Mental Capacity Act 2005   391, 616
Interim remedies
   orders   815
International protection of adults *see also*
   Hague Convention on the Protection
   of Adults
Interpreters   23
   arrangements, making   62
Intervention
   best interests test   255
   lasting powers of attorney   253, 270
   Mental Capacity Act 2005, consistency
      with   255
   personal injuries   470
Investigations and reports
   interim orders   2205
Investigations Unit of Public Guardian   426
Investments
   Court Funds Office   447
Ireland
   General Solicitor for Minors and
      Wards of Court   441
   wardship jurisdiction   71

Jewish community   37
Joinder
   parties   810
   personal injuries   467
Joint attorneys   221
Judges *see also* Lord Chief Justice
   allocation of cases   389, 404, 819

Judges —*continued*
  appointments 386
  district 279, 389
  dual jurisdiction 313
  High Court 389
  jurisdiction of particular judges 946
  nomination 388, 614
  part time 388
  Practice Direction 946
  regional 389
  Senior Judge 770
  training through Judicial
      Studies Board 58
  training, guidance and deployment 386
Judgment or order
  enforcement 1208
Judgments *see also* Orders
  Practice Guidance on reporting 394
  publication
    serious medical treatment cases 322
Judgments and orders
  note of judgment 1008
  records 1008
  unrepresented parties 1009
  writing, in 1008
Judicial review
  Administrative Court 464
  overlap of jurisdiction 455, 462
  parallel proceedings 463
Judicial support 418
Jurisdiction *see also* Transfer of
    proceedings
  capacity, person ceasing to lack 262, 947
  discharge from the jurisdiction 2264
  disputing 405
    Practice Direction 947
  disputing jurisdiction, procedure for 819
  dual 419
  Hague Convention on Protection of the
    Adults, competent
    authorities under 699
  health care decisions 278, 311
  increase in number of cases 416
  inherent *see* Inherent jurisdiction
  judges 946
  judicial review, overlap with 462
  need for special jurisdiction 27
  no jurisdiction, declarations that court
    has 819
  origins 62
  personal care decisions 279
  personal injuries, overlapping with 466
  personal welfare decisions 311
  property and affairs, decisions on 278
  removal of vulnerable adults from 457
  Rules of Court 755
  scope 390
  serious medical treatment 313

Lack of capacity *see* Capacity: lack of

Land
  enforcement of judgment
      or order for possession of 1236
Lasting power of attorney
  costs 862
  welfare decisions
    limitations 579
Lasting powers of attorney *see also*
    Power of attorney
  absence of, decisions made in 339
  accounts, rendering of 274
  advance decisions compared 339
  applications 275
    permission 276
    Practice Direction 916
    service 804
  appointment
    replacement attorney, of 224
  appointment of donee 220, 577
  attorney's statement 239
  authority
    scope and restrictions 198, 209, 579
  best interests test 200, 209, 254
  capacity 242
    Court's powers 272
    delay in registering 196
    execution, at time of 238
    presumption 195, 197
    relevance to registration 244
  certificates 226
    assessment of
      donor's understanding 273
    lay or professional providers 236
    persons excluded from being
      providers 237
    persons who may be providers 235
    professional skills of provider 236
  Code of Practice 1600
  complaints about conduct of donee 276,
      277, 422, 426
  conduct of attorney 273
  content 219
  Court's powers 271, 590, 591
    exercise of own volition 276
    intervention 253, 270
  creation 194
    forms 1298
  definition 195, 576
  deputies, conflicts with 268
  directions to donee 274, 591
  disclaimer 1286
  donor's declaration 220
  drafting and execution 212
  duties of attorney 240
  enduring power of attorney and LPA,
    choice between 256
  fees 1321
  fiduciary duties 201
    breach of 253

Lasting powers of attorney—*continued*
  forms 214, 680
    attorney's statement 239
    completion and execution 241
    defects 215
    donor's declaration 220
    failure to comply 215
    parts 219
    personal welfare matters 214
    prescribed 1298
    property and affairs 214
  fraud 253, 272
  gifts 285, 579
    applications to Court 275
    Court authority for 275
  health care decisions 208
  joint attorneys 221
    professional attorney, where one is 222
  legal proceedings, capacity to conduct 207
  life-sustaining treatment 210, 211
  losses caused by attorney 253
  maintenance of others 288
  meaning and effect determination 274
  medical treatment, consent to 210
  Mental Capacity Act 2005 199
  more than one attorney 221
    separate forms 215
  notification of named persons 226, 247
  operation, different levels of 196
  personal welfare decisions *see also* 'life-sustaining treatment' *above* 196, 208
    alternatives 213
    capacity of donor 196
    limitations 209
    prescribed form 214
    use and applicability 211
  practical difficulties 197
  property and affairs, decisions on 196
    prescribed form 214
    scope of authority 199
  protection of donees 581
  protection of donors 197
    levels of protection 226
  Public Guardian, role of 276
  records, production of 274
  registration
    application 1282
    application procedure 532
    attorney's status prior to 247
    cancellation 252, 686
    capacity, relevance of 244
    Court's powers 272
    Court's powers where objection to 251
    defective forms 215
    delay in registering 196, 197
    early registration, problems with 245

Lasting powers of attorney—*continued*
  registration—*continued*
    evidence 685
    fees 424, 1322
    notices 247
    objection procedure 249, 255, 684, 1283
    objection procedure forms 1927
    procedure 246, 682, 1281
    refusal 272
    register 421
    requirement 244
    status of unregistered form 241, 242
    withdrawal of objection 274
  Regulations 1279
  relief of attorney from liability 275
  replacement of attorney 218
    form 240
    procedure 224
  restraints 209
  restrictions 578
  revocation 252, 580
    Court's powers 271, 272
  safeguards *see* 'protection of donee' *and* 'protection of donor' *above*
  signatures, witnesses to 226, 235
  stages of completion 240
  trustee, donor as 207
  undue influence 238, 253, 272
  unsuitability ground 254
  validity 252, 590
    applications to Court on 275
  welfare decisions *see* 'personal welfare decisions' *above*
  who may grant 214
Law Commission
  acts in connection with care or treatment, recommendations on 158
  best interests test, recommendations on 107
  capacity presumption and proof, recommendations on 101
  less restrictive alternative, recommendations on 109
  powers of attorney, reports concerning 188, 194
  practicable steps to help decision-making, recommendations on 102
  unwise decisions, recommendations on 105
Lawyers *see also* **Solicitors**
  certificate providers for LPAs 236
  conflict of interests 40
  elderly client practices, development of 41
  expertise in law on elderly and disabled people 40
  identifying wishes of client 40
  instructions from third parties 40
  role of 40

Learning disabilities
  assessment of capacity 136
  capacity 277
  cessation of lack of capacity
    or death 147
  mental health legislation, relevance
    of 349
Legal aid *see* Public funding
Legal competence *see* Capacity
Legal publishing initiatives 41
Legal services
  discrimination 59
Legal Services Commission
  costs payable by 1173
  funding certificate, revocation
    or discharge of 855
Legislation
  amendments (minor and
    consequential) 453, 454, 1305
  background 33
  compatibility with Convention rights 53
  Mental Capacity Act 2005 *see also*
    Mental Capacity Act 2005
  repeals 454
  Scotland 70, 77
    comparison 98
  terminology 32
Less restrictive alternative principle 109
Letters of request 834
  draft 979
Liability
  permitted acts 160, 165, 572
Liberty and security, right to
  deprivation of liberty safeguards *see also*
    Deprivation of liberty
    safeguards 352
    Mental Health Act 1983 352
  Disabilities Convention 2470
  Mental Capacity Act 2005 475
  restraint *see* Restraints
Life sustaining treatment *see also* Medical
  treatment
  advance decisions 334, 335, 340, 593
  best interests 148, 322
  definition 148, 569
  deprivation of liberty pending order 362
  deprivation of liberty safeguards 572
  deputies, powers of 268
  lasting powers of attorney 210, 211
  wishes of person 324
Life, right to 2469
  force feeding 368
Litigants in person
  costs 1126, 1136, 1143
  disadvantages 60
  lay representatives 61
  McKenzie friend 60
  reasons for self-representation 59
Litigation capacity 207
Litigation friend
  agreement to act 1493

Litigation friend—*continued*
  alternative options for resolving
    disputes 1503
  appointment 1495
    cessation 852
    court orders 1091, 1096, 1098, 1107,
      1495
    service 851
  appointment, orders for 849
  bringing a case to the Court 1502
  capacity, where person regains 852
  certificates of suitability 550, 1496,
      1972
  cessation of appointment 852, 1099
  change in 850
  change of litigation friend 1097
  choice of 208
  deprivation of liberty cases 1500, 1502
  deputies 990
  duties 1498
  expenses 1104, 1113
  Guidance Note 1490
  human rights issues 1499
  Independent Mental Capacity
    Advocates (IMCAs) 1491, 1494
    instructions to give 1501
  instruction of lawyers 1496
  instructions to give 1501
  Official Solicitor 438, 552
    criteria for appointment 435, 1490
  personal injuries 471
  practice direction 854, 990, 1107
  prevention from acting as 850
  procedure without court orders 1095
  protected party, for 548
  Relevant
    Person's Representatives (RPRs)491
  requirement for 1091
  Rules of Court 410, 847
  service 786
  stage of proceedings 1093
  suitability criteria 1491
  where person is later found to lack
    capacity 549
  who may act 551, 846, 1490
  without court order 848
Litigation misconduct 1120, 1133
Local authorities
  accommodation
    independent mental capacity
      advocates, instructions of 604
  appointment as deputies (property and
    affairs) 2219
  deprivation of liberty safeguards
    supervisory body, role as 373
  deputies (property and affairs) 2193,
    2194, 2195, 2196, 2209, 2217,
    2220, 2221, 2222, 2223, 2233,
    2234, 2235, 2248
  enquiries, duty to make 462

Index

Local authorities—*continued*
  independent mental capacity advocates,
    duty to instruct 331
  personal welfare application,
    directions order 2243
  reports 391
  residence, disputes over 364, 1338
  residential care, guidance on removal
    to 162
  social services departments 38
Local authority
  deputies (property and affairs) 2218
Lord Chancellor
  capacity jurisdiction 385
  Codes of Practice *see* Code of Practice
  costs payable by 1173
  Lord Chief Justice, concordat with 385
  Public Guardian
    functions, conferring of 422
    officers and staff, provision of 421
  role 385
Lord Chief Justice
  responsibilities in relation to
    judiciary 386
LPA *see* Lasting powers of attorney

Maintenance
  authority to provide 286, 288
Manslaughter *see* Gross negligence
  manslaughter
Marriage
  excluded decisions 175, 594
McKenzie friend 60
Medical evidence *see* Assessment of
  capacity 550
Medical practitioners *see* Doctors;
  Psychiatrists
Medical research
  approval 597
  carers, consultation of 598
  clinical trials 341, 596
  consent 342
  Code of Practice 1671
  common law position 340
  intrusive research 596
  loss of capacity 600
  Mental Capacity Act 2005 596
  Mental Capacity Act 2005,
    provisions in 342
  pre-conditions and
    safeguards for adults 343, 596,
      597, 598, 599
Medical treatment *see also* Dental
  treatment; Health care decisions; Life
  sustaining treatment
  acts in connection with, authority
    for 160, 572
    examples of acts 161
  advance decisions
    refusal of treatment 166, 213, 332,
      334, 340, 592, 593

Medical treatment—*continued*
  advance decisions—*continued*
    requests for treatment 333, 334
  artificial nutrition and hydration,
    withdrawal of 319, 320, 323
  authorisation by High Court 309
  best interests test 311
  capacity
    common law test 311
    fluctuating 313
  consent 595
  consent to
    assessment of capacity 131, 139
    common law 309
    lasting powers of attorney 208, 210
  declarations as to 163, 260, 310
  deprivation of liberty pending order 362
  deputies, powers of 268
  force feeding 368
  inherent jurisdiction 310
  injunctive relief 311
  liability protection 160, 572
  necessity, principle of 158
  Official Solicitor 920
  serious medical treatment
    allocation of cases 320
    applications to court 318, 919
    best interests 322
    case management 322
    decisions that should be brought to
      Court 318
    declarations as to 260
    declarations of incompatibility 320
    definition 318
    independent mental capacity
      advocates, instructions of 602
    jurisdiction 278, 313
    Official Solicitor, appointment
      of 440
    parties 318
    permitted acts 162, 163
    Practice Direction 318, 919
    publication of judgments 322
    urgent cases 321
  statutory framework 312
  types of decision 309
  young persons 128
Memory *see also* Dementia
  assessment of capacity 121
Mental capacity *see* Capacity
Mental Capacity Act 2005 78
  ad hoc Rules Committees 82, 84, 393
  Code of Practice 1515
  conflict with CRPD 88
  decisions 112
  draft bill 78
  essential provisions 92
  establishment of lack of capacity 565

2601

Mental Capacity Act 2005—*continued*
House of Lords Select Committee
    report 83
    Government response 84
human rights compatibility 79
initial assessment 79
interpretation 626
intervention of Court and 255
lack of capacity for reason outside 460
lasting powers of attorney 199
liberty and security, right to 475
Mental Health Act 1983 compared 349
Mental Health Act 1983, interrelationship
    with 349, 366
Mental Health Act patients
    Code of Practice 1690
orders 583
principles 98, 564
    statement of 99
private and family life, right to respect
    for 475
review of implementation 95
scope 91, 626
transitional provisions 452, 719

Mental disabilities or disorders,
    persons with *see also* **Psychiatric**
    conditions
compulsory detention
    medical treatment excluded
        under MCA 2005 350
definition of 'mental disorder' 26
excluded decisions 176, 210
hospital, admission to
    reviews and appeal 348
lack of capacity 277
mental disorder, definition of 347
treatment
    excluded decisions 176

Mental Health Act patients
appeals 348, 1022
capacity to consent to treatment 349
Code of Practice
    Mental Capacity Act 2005,
        relationship with 1690
community treatment orders 347
    criteria for 348
eligibility under deprivation of liberty
    safeguards 366
evidence of mental disorder 365
hospital, admission to 347
    grounds for 348
Mental Capacity Act, application of 349, 366
reviews 348

Mental health treatment
decisions 595

Mesothelioma claim
pre-commencement funding
    arrangements 1178

Minimally Conscious State, persons in *see*
    Artificial nutrition and hydration,
    withdrawal of
Minors *see* **Children**
Misconduct, litigation 1120, 1133
Monies, management of
personal injuries 471
Mortgage
costs relating to a 1129, 1131

National Health Service (NHS)
independent mental capacity advocates,
    duty to instruct 330
reports 391
support services 38
Nationality
Disabilities Convention 2471
Nearest relative
same sex partners 58
Necessity
principle of 158
Neglect *see* **Gross negligence manslaughter;**
    Ill-treatment or neglect
Negligence
carers, by 165
hospital and care homes, detention
    in 631
Non-instructed advocacy 449
Non-parties
costs orders 861
documents, inspection and copies of 777
Non-party
costs orders in favour of or against 1135
Northern Ireland
High Court jurisdiction 70
Office of Care and Protection 71
Official Solicitor 441
Notarial acts or instruments
evidence, as 830
Notification
acknowledgment 797, 807
applications 805
    forms, issue of 912
capacity 793
    circumstances when notice
        is required 794
certificates 798
checklist 2226
forms 1921
incapacitated persons 400, 401
issue of forms 805
Practice Direction 905

Oaths
persons who may administer oaths 967
Office of the Public Guardian *see* **Public**
    Guardian
Office of the Public Guardian Board 424
Official Solicitor
address 433
advice from 436

Official Solicitor—*continued*
  applications brought by 438
  appointment for incapacitated
    persons 431, 436
  assistance to courts, provision of 438
    assistance to Court of Protection 438
  costs 442, 861
  experts, instruction of 440
  function 433
  investigations 440
  litigation friend, appointment as 438, 552
    criteria for 435, 1490
  medical treatment 920
  other jurisdictions 441
  permission applications 799
  Practice Notes issued by 434
  present encumbent 433, 434
  representation by 436
  serious medical treatment case,
    appointment in 440
  status and office 433
Official Solicitor and Public Trustee, joint office of 433
OPG *see* Public Guardian
Orders
  clerical error, correction of 779
  court authentication 773
  Court's powers 780
  decisions made by 262
  definition 769
  final 2262
    capacity in regard to financial
      affairs 2262
    discharge from the jurisdiction 2264
    enduring powers of attorney
      or deputies,
        decisions as to 2263
    financial deputies, change of 2266
  inspection and copies 777
  interim 391, 815
    investigations and reports 2205
  office copies, admissibility of 390
  own initiative powers 782
  precedent standard orders 2189, 2205, 2216
  reconsideration 405
  reconsideration, reasons for 821
  service
    Public Guardian 779
  standard orders, precedents for 2189
  variation or discharge 262
OSPT *see* Official Solicitor and Public
    Trustee, joint office of
Overriding objective 395
  active case management 395, 763
  Mental Capacity Act 2005 395
  parties, duties of 762
  Rules of Court 756

Panel deputies 424
Parallel proceedings 463
Parens patriae jurisdiction 31, 310
Part 36 offer
  cost consequences 1174
Part time judges 388
Participation in proceedings *see also*
    Access to justice; Best interests test:
    participation of person lacking
    capacity 79
Parties 808
  best interests test 402
  bound as if parties, persons who are 809
  capacity 786
  identification
    checklist 2226
  joinder 810
    forms 1944
  removal applications 810
  serious medical treatment 318
Payment for goods and services
  capacity 170, 171
  expenditure, methods of 173, 575
  legal responsibility 172
  Mental Capacity Act 2004 575
  Mental Capacity Act 2005 575
  'necessary', definition of 171
  necessary, definition of 575
  settlement of bills by carers 173
Penal notices 415
  contempt of court 873
Permission
  forms
    statement of truth 774
Permission applications
  appeals 800
  circumstances for 798
  commencement of proceedings 801
  exceptions 799
  factors for grant 110
  forms 800
  inconvenience and expense,
    avoiding 400
  lasting powers of attorney 276
  notification 912
  Official Solicitor 799
  persons not requiring permission 798, 799
  Practice Direction 907
  property and affairs, decisions on 799
  Public Guardian 799
  service 800
  statutory wills 296
  time limits 803
  when permission required 907
Permission to appeal
  appellant's notice 866
  factors for grant 415, 865
  respondent's notice 866
  Rules of Court 414, 864

2603

Permission to appeal—*continued*
  time-limits, variation of   867
Permitted acts
  advance decision to refuse treatment,
    where   166
  decisions of donees/deputies,
    conflicts with   170
  exclusions   174
  limitations   166, 573
  position prior to MCA 2005   158
  protection from liability   160
    no protection in cases of
      negligence   165
  reasonableness, concept of   165
  serious acts   161
  who can act   164
Persistent Vegetative State, persons in *see*
  Artificial nutrition and hydration,
  withdrawal of
Personal care decisions
  jurisdiction, scope of   279
  permitted acts   161
Personal injuries
  assessment of capacity   141, 467
  best interests test   470
  damages
    management   471
  double recovery   473
  intervention   470
  joinder   467
  jurisdiction, overlap of   466
  litigation friend   471
  monies, management of   471
  property and affairs, decisions on   468
  settlements
    Court's powers   265
    jurisdiction   270
  transfer of proceedings   467
  trusts   472
Personal representative
  costs in favour of   1135, 1142
**Personal representatives and
  administrators**
  cessation of lack of capacity
    or death   1027
Personal welfare decisions   91
  applications   327
    forms   1854
    information in support   1877
    procedural guide   535
  capacity, issue-specific nature of   312
  costs   413, 858
  Court's powers   262, 263
  decisions that should be brought to
    Court   326
  declarations   260, 310
  deputies
    appointment   2199
    refusal of permission
      for appointment   2198
  jurisdiction, scope of   91, 311, 584

Personal welfare decisions—*continued*
  lasting powers of attorney   196, 208
    alternatives   213
    capacity of donor   196
    limitations   209
    prescribed form   214
  local authority application,
    directions order   2243
  Official Solicitor, assistance from   439
  power to make   584, 589, 630
  statutory framework   312
  types   309
**Political and public life, participation
  in**   2477
Possession claim
  enforcement of judgment or order   1236
Power of attorney
  application by (Practice Direction)   916
  applications (Practice Direction)
    list of suitable applications   917
  assessment of capacity   131
  best interests test   157
  conflict of interests, disclosure of   186
  decisions made by, precedence of   574
  definition   185
  enduring *see* Enduring powers of
    attorney
  fees   1321
  fiduciary duties   186
  lasting *see* Lasting powers of attorney
  law relating to   185
  limitations   186
  precedence of decisions made by   170
  Principles (Council of Europe)   2515
  revocation by supervening incapacity of
    donor   185, 187
  rights of audience   61
  two jurisdictions co-existing, complexity
    of   452
Powers of Court of Protection
  Mental Capacity Act 2005   616
Practice Directions
  bodies responsible for   386
  enduring powers of attorney   416
  judges   946
  permission applications   908
  President's power to issue   394
  scope   620
Practice Guidance
  contempt of court   394
  issue   394
  judgments, reporting of   394
  transparency   394
Premises
  discrimination
    disposal and management   51
    reasonable adjustments, duty to
      make   49
President   388
Presumption *see* Capacity: presumption

Index

Principles
  Mental Capacity Act 2005   98
    1st principle   101
    2nd principle   102
    3rd principle   105
    4th principle   108
    5th principle   109
    statement of principles   99
Principles Concerning Continuing Powers of Attorney and Advance Directives for Incapacity   2515
Principles Concerning the Legal Protection of Incapable Adults
  explanatory memorandum   2486
  text   2507
Privacy
  Disabilities Convention   2473
Privacy proceedings
  pre-commencement funding arrangements   1179
Private and family life, right to respect for
  Mental Capacity Act 2005   475
Private hearings   327
  attendance   405
Private international law *see* Hague Convention on the Protection of Adults
Pro bono representation
  costs   1138, 1143
Proceedings *see also* Applications
  participation in *see also* Access to justice   79
Professionals *see also* Experts
  assessment of capacity records   139
Property and affairs, decisions on
  applications
    forms   1854
    information in support   1865
  capacity
    cessation of lack of   878
  costs   412, 857
  Court's powers   262, 264, 585
  deputies, appointment of   469, 533
  experts   468
  jurisdiction, scope of   278
  lasting powers of attorney   196
    prescribed form   214
    scope of authority   199
  personal injuries   468
  supplementary provisions   693
Proportionality
  principle of   54
Protected beneficiaries
  definition   208, 446, 548
  investments   447
Protected parties
  definition   208, 769
  investments   1112

Protected parties—*continued*
  litigation friend, requirement for *see also* Litigation friend   548, 1091, 1092
  effect of no litigation friend   549
  meaning   1085
  money, control of   1102, 1111
  procedural guide   536
  service   785
  settlements   1109
    approval   1100
Protective measures
  Hague Convention on the Protection of Adults: 698
Psychiatric conditions *see also* Mental disabilities or disorders, persons with
Psychiatrists
  Special Visitor, appointment as   431
Public bodies
  contravention of ECHR   55
  equality duty   48
Public funding *see also* Legal Services Commission
  adequacy   39
  costs
    detailed assessment   1156, 1172
    summary assessment   1132
  cuts   416
Public Guardian *see also* Office of the Public Guardian Board
  address   423
  administration of Court, former   387
  Annual Report   424, 624
  consultation paper   428
  Court of Protection, relationship with   427
  creation   421, 622
  digital service   426, 428
  dispute resolution   425
  documents, copies of   778
  enduring powers of attorney register   1289
  fees   423, 427, 1321
  former office compared   425
  functions   421, 428, 623
    applications to Court in connection with   423
    categories of   422
    Regulations   1289
    regulatory power of Lord Chancellor   422
  funding   427
  historical background   69
  Investigations Unit   426
  lasting powers of attorney
    complaints about conduct of donee   276, 277, 422, 426
    notification   247
    objections, notification of   250
    registration of   249, 1289
    role   276

Public Guardian—*continued*
office of
  creation 93
  officers and staff, provision of 421
  partnerships with
    other organisations 427
  permission applications 799
  powers 423
  public authority, as 55
  publication of information 422
  recognition and funding 421
  records, examination and copies of 423
  registers
    duties 1289
  reports 391
    Practice Direction 984
  role 276, 425
  service 779
  Visitors, relationship with 432
Public hearings 824
Public Trustee
  present encumbent 433, 434
Publication of judgments
  serious medical treatment cases 322
Publication proceedings
  pre-commencement funding
    arrangements 1179
Publicity
  authorisation 823
  restrictions 405
Publishing initiatives 41

Qualified one-way costs shifting
  effect of 1121
  exceptions to (where permission not
    required) 1122
  exceptions to (where permission
    required) 1122
  interpretation 1121
  Practice Direction 1133
  scope of application 1121
  transitional provision 1123

Reasonableness
  permitted acts 165
Receivers
  appointment 187
  deputies, replacement by 452
  old regime 270
  transitional provisions 452, 719, 874
    Practice Direction 1017
Reconsideration of order
  time limits 405
Records
  assessment of capacity 139
    formal reports or certificates 140
  examination and copy for preparation of
    report 391
  judgments and orders 1008
  lasting powers of attorney 274
  Public Guardian, examination by 423

Records—*continued*
  transitional provisions 452
  Visitors, examination by 432
Reform
  Lord Chancellor, abolition of office
    of 385
Refusal to be assessed 138
Regional hearings 67
Regional judges 389
Registration
  enduring power of attorney *see* Enduring
    powers of attorney: registration
  lasting power of attorney *see* Lasting
    powers of attorney: registration
Rehabilitation 2475
Relative, nearest *see* Nearest relative
Relevant Person's Representatives (RPRs)
  litigation friend, appointment as 1491
Relevant written statement *see* Written
  statements
Religion or beliefs
  best interests test 150, 151
Removal from jurisdiction
  vulnerable adults 457
Reporting restrictions *see also* Publicity
Reports
  Court orders 987
  Court power to require 391, 429, 835
    Practice Direction 984
  expert
    disclosure, use after 841
  experts 837, 839, 840
  power to require 617
  Public Guardian 617
  records, examination and copy
    for preparation of 391
  Visitors, by 431
  written questions 836
  written questions to maker of report 408
Representation
  adequacy 39
  Official Solicitor, by 436
  pro bono
    costs 1138, 1143
Representatives
  appointment by supervisory bodies 666
  hospital or care homes, detention
    in 1327
  role 1809
Research, medical *see* Medical research
Residence
  change of
    safeguards 162, 163
  disputes 1338
Residential accommodation
  best interests test 465
  long stay
    independent mental capacity
      advocates, instructions of 604
Residential home *see* Care homes

2606

Index

Respect for private and family life *see*
Private and family life, right to
respect for
Respondents
party, as   808
Respondent's notice
forms   2006
Responding to applications   807
Practice Direction   914
Restraints
decisions which should be brought to
Court   319
deputies, powers of   268
hospital or care homes, detention
in   1766
lasting powers of attorney   209
permitted acts   166, 574
Reviews
deprivation of liberty safeguards   374, 378
implementation of MCA 2005   95
Mental Health Act patients   348
Rights, human *see* European Convention on
Human Rights; Human Rights Act
1998; Liberty and security, right to;
Life, right to; Private and family life,
right to respect for
RPRs *see* Relevant
Person's Representatives
Rules of Court   259
ad hoc Rules Committees   82, 84, 393
bodies responsible for   386
definitions   768
dispensing with Rules, power to   782
first rules made   393, 755
former Court rules, uncertainties of   392
interpretation   396
jurisdiction   755
Lord Chancellor's power to make   392
overriding objective   756
policy aims   756
scope   619
transitional provisions   874

Safeguarding   462
Sale of property
Court's powers   264
Same sex partners *see also* Civil
partnerships
nearest relative   57
Scotland
best interests test   108
enquiries, duty to make   462
incapacitated persons moving to
Scotland   441
legislation   70, 77
comparison   98
'no intervention' and 'least restrictive
option' provisions   110
Official Solicitor, no position of   441

Searches of register
Public Guardian   1290
Security
costs, for   397
Deputies   875
discharge of functions, for   875
Public Guardian   1291
Public Guardian, receipt by   422
Security, right to *see* Liberty and security,
right to
Senior Judge   388
Sequestration, writ of
permission   1229
Serious medical treatment *see* Medical
treatment: serious medical treatment
Service
acknowledgement of service *see also*
Acknowledgement of service
acknowledgment of service   807
certificate of non-service   788
certificates of service   787
children or protected parties, on   785
court, by   892
deemed service   787
dispensing with service   788
document exchange, by   891, 892
electronic service   891
litigation friend   786
methods   399, 784
partners   892
Practice Direction   891
provisions for   399
scope   783
substituted service   786
who serves   399
who to serve   783
Set-off   1121
Settlements   466
applications for approval   306
applications for approval of   307
children   1109
Court's powers   264, 265
permitted decisions   283
personal injuries   265
Practice Direction   923
when necessary   306
Sex offences
cohabitation with persons convicted
of   107
Sexual relations
capacity to consent to   315
excluded decisions   175, 594
Sign language   23
Skeleton arguments
appeals   1008, 1011
forms   2016
Small claim
costs   1140, 1146
Social care
acts in connection with, authority
for   160, 572

Index

Social care—*continued*
   consent to provision of services   131
Social protection   2477
Social services departments
   support services   38
Social workers
   certificate providers for LPAs   236
Solicitor
   assessment of bill to client
     basis of assessment   1139, 1145
     procedure   1140, 1145
   costs order notification duty   1119, 1133
Solicitors *see also* Lawyers
   assessment of capacity   131
     pitfalls   140
     records   140
   change of
     notice of   411, 1990
     Practice Direction   994
     public funding certificates on
       revocation or discharge   855
   change of solicitors   854
   Court of Protection work, move into   416
   deputies, remuneration of   1003
   fixed costs   1002
   practice direction   856
   removal
     ceased to act, where solicitor has   855
     parties, application to remove by
       other   856
     reasons   856
   service on   784
Special Visitors *see* Visitors: Special
Standard of living   2477
Standard orders
   precedent   2216
   precedents   2205
Statement of truth
   definition   398
   form of   888
   list of documents   774
   signing   888
   witness statements   970
Statutory will, codicil, gift(s), deed of variation or settlement of property, decisions on
   applications
     information in support   1884
Statutory wills   291
   applications   297
   costs   305
   evidence of incapacity   294
   execution   303
   hearing   301
   Official Solicitor, assistance from   439
   permission to make application   296
   respondents and persons notified   299
   substituted judgment   151
   testator, criteria for   293
   urgent applications   304

Sterilisation
   non-therapeutic, Court reference for   319
Stop notices   1225
Stop orders   1223
Substituted decision-making   87
Substituted judgment   151
Suitability
   lasting powers of attorney   254
   litigation friend   1491
Supervised community treatment *see* Community treatment orders
Supervisory responsibility
   change in   655
Support services
   compliance with CRPD   86, 87
   passing of buck between   39
   sources   38

Taking control of goods, enforcement by   1245
Telephone hearings
   urgency   934
Terminations *see* Abortion
Testamentary capacity   294
   test of   131
Third parties
   injunctions   457
   instructions from   40
Time estimates
   hearings   962
Time-limits
   computation rules   772
   permission to appeal   867
   variation   779
Transcripts
   appeals   1009
Transfer of proceedings *see also* Inherent jurisdiction: transfer of proceedings
   dual jurisdiction   420
   family courts, to and from   116, 390, 1300
   personal injuries   467
   persons under age of 18   263
Transitional provisions
   enduring powers of attorney   451, 453
   fees   1325
   Mental Capacity Act 2005   415, 452
   Practice Direction   1017
   regulations   1303
Transparency
   Practice Guidance   394
Travelling expenses and compensation for loss of time   977, 983
Trust corporations
   lasting powers of attorney, donees of   220, 577
Trustees
   application to appoint or discharge (Practice Direction)   926
   costs in favour of   1135, 1142
   lasting powers of attorney   207

Trustees—*continued*
   special undertakings   1949
Trusts
   damages   472
   personal injury damages   472

UN Convention on the Rights of Persons with Disabilities *see* Disabilities Convention

Undertakings
   trustees   1949

Undue influence   29
   inherent jurisdiction   456
   lasting powers of attorney   238, 253, 272
   presumption   30

United Nations Convention on the Rights of Persons with Disabilities   84

Unrepresented parties
   judgments and orders   1009

Unrepresented party *see* Litigants in person

Unsuitability *see* Suitability

Urgency
   applications   304, 933
   deprivation of liberty safeguards   374, 1802
   draft on disk required   767
   humanitarian emergencies   2469
   injunctions   934
   medical treatment   934
   Mental Capacity Act 2005   649
   permitted acts   165
   serious medical treatment cases   321
   telephone applications   934
   telephone hearings   934
   without notice applications   933

VAT
   on costs   1124

Venue   387
   historical background   66
   regional hearings   67

Verification *see also* Statement of truth
   documents   774

Vice-President   388

Victimisation   50

Video link evidence
   guidance (PD)   972
   Rules of Court   828

Visitors *see also* Association of Independent Visitors
   accountability   430, 432
   appointment   429
   definition   625
   General   429, 625
   historical background   71
      confidentiality of Visitor's reports   74
      General Visitor   71
      Medical Visitor   72
      visits   72

Visitors—*continued*
   powers   432
   protection   432
   Public Guardian
      directions from   422
      relationship with   432
   records, examination of   432
   Regulations   1296
   reports   391, 431
   risk-based approach   430
   self-employed   430
   Special   429, 430, 625
      examination of patients   392

Voting
   decisions on   178, 211, 596

Vulnerable adults
   declarations
      High Court power to make   32
   definition   456, 460
   inherent jurisdiction   455, 456
   Investigations Unit of Public Guardian   426
   lack of powers to protect   80
   removal from environment   457
   safeguarding   462
   sources of protection   39

Wales
   directions by National Assembly   671
   enquiries, duty to make   462

Warrant of delivery   1226
Warrant of possession   1226

Wasted costs
   definition   412, 621

Welfare decisions *see* Personal welfare decisions

Wilful neglect   181

Wills
   assessment of capacity   131
      golden rule   133
   best interests test   264
   capacity   294
   Court's powers   264
      best interests test   264
   execution, orders for   264
   permitted decisions   283
   Practice Direction   923
   statutory *see* Statutory wills

Wishes and feelings of person
   best interests test   150, 151
   medical treatment
      life-sustaining treatment   324
      written statements   339
   written statement *see* Advance statements

Witness statements
   affidavit evidence   829
   body of statement   970
   definition   407
   evidence-in-chief   827
   form   828

Witness statements—*continued*
  format 970
  forms 1980
  Practice Direction 969
  service 829
  statement of truth 828, 970
  summaries 829
  verification 774
Witnesses *see also* Witness statements
  attendance, enforcing 832
  certificate of failure/refusal to attend
    before examiner 1976
  depositions 831
    conduct of examination 831
    examiner of the court 832
    examiner's fees and expenses 832
    use at hearings 833
  Rules of Court 827
  summonses 408, 830
    Practice Direction 983

Witnesses —*continued*
  travelling expenses and compensation
    for loss of time 983
  video link evidence 828
Writ of execution 1226
Writ or warrant of control 1226
Written evidence
  Rules of Court 828
Written statements *see also* Advance
  decisions 213, 339

Young persons
  aged 16 or 17 115
  Code of Practice 1682
  competence and capacity 128
    presumption of capacity 128
  electro-convulsive therapy 176
  medical and dental treatment 128
    best interests test 128
  transfer of proceedings 263

FIXED COSTS IN THE COURT OF PROTECTION
Date in effect: 1 May 2009

Category I	Amount £825 (plus VAT)
Category II	Amount £370 (plus VAT)
Category III	Annual management fee where the court appoints a professional deputy for property and affairs, payable on the anniversary of the court order For the first year: Amount £1,440 (plus VAT) For the second and subsequent years: Amount £1,140 (plus VAT) Provided that, where the net assets of P are below £16,000, the professional deputy for property and affairs may take an annual management fee not exceeding 4.5% of P's net assets on the anniversary of the court order appointing the professional as deputy.
Category IV	Where the court appoints a professional deputy for health and welfare, the deputy may take an annual management fee not exceeding 2.5% of P's net assets on the anniversary of the court order appointing the professional as deputy for health and welfare up to a maximum of £500.
Category V	Amount £225 (plus VAT)
Category VI	Preparation of an HMRC income tax return on behalf of P. Amount £225 (plus VAT)

Remuneration of public authority deputies

Category I	Amount £645 (plus VAT)
Category II	For the first year: Amount £670 (plus VAT) For the second and subsequent years: Amount £565 (plus VAT) Provided that, where the net assets of P are below £16,000, the local authority deputy for property and affairs may take an annual management fee not exceeding 3% of P's net assets on the anniversary of the court order appointing the local authority as deputy Where the court appoints a local authority deputy for health and welfare, the local authority may take an annual management fee not exceeding 2.5% of P's net assets on the anniversary of the court order appointing the local authority as deputy for health and welfare up to a maximum of £500.
Category III	Amount £260 (plus VAT)
Category IV	Amount £185 (plus VAT)

FIXED COSTS IN THE COURT OF PROTECTION
Date in effect: 1 February 2011

	An amount not exceeding
Category I	£850 (plus VAT)
Category II	£385 (plus VAT)

Remuneration of solicitors appointed as deputy for P

	An amount not exceeding
Category III	For the first year: £1,500 (plus VAT) For the second and subsequent years: £1,185 (plus VAT) Where the net assets. of P are below £16,000, the professional deputy for property and affairs may take an annual management fee not exceeding 4.5% of P's net assets. on the anniversary of the court order appointing the professional as deputy.
Category IV	Where the court appoints a professional deputy for personal welfare, the deputy may take an annual management fee not exceeding 2.5% of P's net assets. on the anniversary of the court order appointing the professional as deputy for personal up to a maximum of £500.
Category V	£235 (plus VAT)
Category VI	£235 (plus VAT)

Conveyancing costs

Category VII	A value element of 0.15% of the consideration with a minimum sum of £350 and a maximum sum of £1,500, plus disbursements.

Remuneration of public authority deputies

	An amount not exceeding
Category I	£670
Category II	For the first year: £700 For the second and subsequent years: £585 Where the net assets* of P are below £16,000, the local authority deputy for property and affairs may take an annual management fee not exceeding 3% of P's net assets on the anniversary of the court order appointing the local authority as deputy Where the court appoints a local authority deputy for personal welfare, the local authority may take an annual management fee not exceeding 2.5% of P's net assets* on the anniversary of the court order appointing the local authority as deputy for personal welfare up to a maximum of £500.
Category III	£270
Category IV	£195